UNDER THE GENERAL EDITORSHIP OF

Perry Miller
Harvard University

THE EDITORS

NEWTON ARVIN
Smith College, Retired

IRVING HOWE
Stanford University

ERIC BENTLEY
Columbia University

ALFRED KAZIN

MARIUS BEWLEY
Fordham University

J. C. LEVENSON
University of Minnesota

R. P. BLACKMUR
Princeton University

R. W. B. LEWIS
Yale University

LOUISE BOGAN

KENNETH S. LYNN
Harvard University

WILLIAM CHARVAT
Ohio State University

PERRY MILLER
Harvard University

RICHARD CHASE
Columbia University

SAMUEL ELIOT MORISON
Harvard University, Emeritus

EDWARD H. DAVIDSON
University of Illinois

ERNEST SAMUELS
Northwestern University

F. W. DUPEE
Columbia University

MARK SCHORER
University of California, Berkeley

NORTHROP FRYE
Victoria College, University of Toronto

HENRY NASH SMITH
University of California, Berkeley

WILLIAM L. HEDGES
Goucher College

AUSTIN WARREN
University of Michigan

RICHARD WILBUR
Wesleyan University

UNDER THE GENERAL EDITORSHIP OF

Perry Miller
Harvard University

THE EDITORS

NEWTON ARVIN
Smith College, Retired

ERIC BENTLEY
Columbia University

MARIUS BEWLEY
Fordham University

R. P. BLACKMUR
Princeton University

LOUISE BOGAN

WILLIAM CHARVAT
Ohio State University

RICHARD CHASE
Columbia University

EDWARD H. DAVIDSON
University of Illinois

F. W. DUPEE
Columbia University

NORTHROP FRYE
Victoria College, University of Toronto

WILLIAM L. HEDGES
Goucher College

IRVING HOWE
Stanford University

ALFRED KAZIN

J. C. LEVENSON
University of Minnesota

R. W. B. LEWIS
Yale University

KENNETH S. LYNN
Harvard University

PERRY MILLER
Harvard University

SAMUEL ELIOT MORISON
Harvard University, Emeritus

ERNEST SAMUELS
Northwestern University

MARK SCHORER
University of California, Berkeley

HENRY NASH SMITH
University of California, Berkeley

AUSTIN WARREN
University of Michigan

RICHARD WILBUR
Wesleyan University

MAJOR WRITERS OF
AMERICA

II

Dickinson · Mark Twain

James · Adams · Crane

Dreiser · O'Neill · Frost

Anderson · Fitzgerald · Hemingway

Eliot · Faulkner

NEW YORK  BURLINGAME

HARCOURT, BRACE & WORLD, INC.

COPYRIGHTS AND ACKNOWLEDGMENTS

EPIGRAPH. From *The Collected Poems of Wallace Stevens.* Copyright 1942, 1954 by Wallace Stevens. Used by permission of Alfred A. Knopf, Inc.

EMILY DICKINSON. Selections from *The Poems of Emily Dickinson,* Thomas H. Johnson, Editor, and *The Letters of Emily Dickinson,* Thomas H. Johnson and Theodora W. Ward, Editors, Cambridge, Mass., The Belknap Press of Harvard University Press, copyright 1951, 1955, 1958, by The President and Fellows of Harvard College. Reprinted by permission of Harvard University Press and Houghton Mifflin Company. Selections from *Emily Dickinson Face to Face,* by Martha D. Bianchi, 1932. Reprinted by permission of Houghton Mifflin Company. Selections from *The Complete Poems of Emily Dickinson.* Copyright 1914, 1918, 1919, 1929, 1930, 1935, 1937, 1942 by Martha Dickinson Bianchi. Copyright, ©, 1957 by Mary L. Hampson. Reprinted by permission of Little, Brown & Company.

MARK TWAIN. "The Quarles Farm" from *Mark Twain's Autobiography.* Copyright 1924 by Clara Gabrilowitsch. Reprinted by permission of Harper & Brothers. "Platform Readings, October 10, 1907" from *Mark Twain in Eruption,* edited by Bernard DeVoto. Copyright 1922 by Harper & Brothers. Reprinted by permission. "The War Prayer" from *Europe and Elsewhere* by Mark Twain. Copyright 1923 by The Mark Twain Company. Reprinted by permission of Harper & Brothers. "Fenimore Cooper's Further Literary Offenses" by Mark Twain. Copyright 1946 by The Mark Twain Company. Reprinted by permission of Harper & Brothers. "William Dean Howells" from *What Is Man? and Other Stories* by Mark Twain. Copyright 1906 by Harper & Brothers. Reprinted by permission. "Whittier Birthday Dinner Speech," *Harvard Library Bulletin,* Spring, 1955. Reprinted by permission of the President and fellows of Harvard College.

HENRY JAMES. "The Pupil" from *The Lesson of the Master,* Macmillan & Co., 1891; "The Real Thing" from *The Real Thing and Other Tales,* Macmillan & Co., 1892; "Europe" from *The Soft Side,* Macmillan & Co., 1900. Reprinted by permission of John Farquharson, Ltd. Selections from *The Notebooks of Henry James,* edited by F. O. Matthiessen and Kenneth B. Murdock, copyright 1947 by Oxford University Press, Inc. Reprinted by permission of the publisher. "Five Letters" from *The Letters of Henry James,* Volume I, pp. 24–25, 28–29, 30–31, 100–102, and Volume II, pp. 350–361, edited by Percy Lubbock, are used by permission of Charles Scribner's Sons. Copyright 1920 Charles Scribner's Sons; renewal copyright 1948 William James, Margaret James Porter. "The Beast in the Jungle" reprinted with the permission of Charles Scribner's Sons from *The Better Sort* by Henry James (1903).

HENRY ADAMS. Selections from *Letters of Henry Adams,* W. C. Ford editor, copyright 1920, 1930; *Henry Adams and His Friends,* by H. D. Cater, copyright 1947; *A Cycle of Adams Letters,* W. C. Ford editor, copyright 1920; *The Education of Henry Adams* by Henry Adams, copyright 1918; and *Letters to a Niece* by Mabel LaFarge, copyright 1920 are reprinted by permission of and arrangement with Houghton Mifflin Company, the authorized publishers.

STEPHEN CRANE. "Tell me not in joyous numbers" by Stephen Crane from *The Poetry of Stephen Crane* by Daniel G. Hoffman, Columbia University Press, 1957. Reprinted by permission of the Columbia University Press and the Columbia University Libraries. "A Man Adrift on a Slim Spar" by Stephen Crane. Reprinted from *The Collected Poems of Stephen Crane,* edited by Wilson Follett, by permission of Alfred A. Knopf, Inc. Copyright 1930 by Alfred A. Knopf, Inc.

THEODORE DREISER. "Sanctuary" from *Chains.* Copyright 1927 by Theodore Dreiser; copyright 1955 by Helen Dreiser. "Nigger Jeff" and "The Lost Phoebe" from *Free and Other Stories.* Copyright 1918 by Boni & Liveright, Inc.; copyright 1945 by Theodore Dreiser. "My Brother Paul" from *Twelve Men.* Copyright 1919 by Boni & Liveright; copyright 1946 by Helen Dreiser. Chapters 38–47 from Book II of *An American Tragedy.* Copyright 1925 by Horace Liveright, Inc.; copyright 1926 by Theodore Dreiser; copyright 1953 by Helen Dreiser. Reprinted by permission of The World Publishing Company.

EUGENE O'NEILL. *The Iceman Cometh,* by Eugene O'Neill. Copyright, as an unpublished work, 1940, by Eugene O'Neill. Copyright 1946, by Eugene O'Neill. Reprinted by permission of Random House, Inc. Caution: Professionals and amateurs are hereby warned that *The Iceman Cometh,* being fully protected under the copyright laws of the United States of America, the British Empire, including the Dominion of Canada, and all other countries of the copyright union, is subject to a royalty. All rights, including professional, amateur, motion pictures, recitation, public reading, radio broadcasting, and the rights of translation into foreign languages are strictly reserved. All inquiries regarding this play should be addressed to Richard J. Madden at 52 Vanderbilt Ave., New York 27, N.Y.

ROBERT FROST. Introduction by Robert Frost from *The Arts Anthology: Dartmouth Verse 1925.* Reprinted by permission of the Trustees of Dartmouth College, Robert Frost, and Holt, Rinehart and Winston, Inc. Selections from *Complete Poems of Robert Frost.* Copyright 1916, 1921, 1923, 1928, 1930, 1935, 1939, 1947 by Holt, Rinehart and Winston, Inc. Copyright 1936, 1942 by Robert Frost. Copyright renewed 1944, 1951, © 1956, by Robert Frost. Reprinted by permission of Holt, Rinehart and Winston, Inc. Introduction by Robert Frost from *King Jasper: A Poem* by Edwin Arlington Robinson. Copyright 1935 by the Macmillan Company. Reprinted by permission of the Macmillan Company, Robert Frost, and Holt, Rinehart and Winston, Inc.

SHERWOOD ANDERSON, F. SCOTT FITZGERALD, ERNEST HEMINGWAY. "Could Man Be Drunk for Ever" from *Complete Poems* of A. E. Housman. Copyright 1922, Holt, Rinehart and Winston, Inc. Copyright renewed 1950 by Barclays Bank, Ltd. Reprinted by permission of Holt, Rinehart and Winston, Inc., The Society of Authors as the literary representative of the Estate of the late A. E. Housman, and Messrs. Jonathan Cape, Ltd., publishers of A. E. Housman's *Collected Poems.* Selections from *Letters of Sherwood Anderson,* edited by H. M. Jones and Walter Rideout. Copyright 1953, by Eleanor Anderson. Reprinted by permission of Little, Brown & Company. "Echoes of the Jazz Age," "Ring," and "The Crack-Up" from *The Crack-Up* by F. Scott Fitzgerald, edited by Edmund Wilson. Copyright 1945 by New Directions. Reprinted by permission of New Directions. "The Egg" and "I Want to Know Why" from *The Triumph of the Egg* by Sherwood Anderson. "The Egg" copyright, 1920, by Eleanor Anderson. Copyright renewed. "I Want to Know Why" copyright, 1919, by Eleanor Anderson. Copyright renewed. Selections from *A Story Teller's Story* by Sherwood Anderson. *A Story Teller's Story* copyright, 1924 by B. W. Huebsch, Inc. Copyright renewed, 1951, by Eleanor Anderson. Reprinted by permission of Harold Ober Associates Incorporated. "Four American Impressions" by Sherwood Anderson. Copyright 1919, by Sherwood Anderson. Copyright renewed, 1947, by Eleanor Copenhaver Anderson. Reprinted by permission of Harold Ober Associates Incorporated. "The Rich Boy" by F. Scott Fitzgerald. Copyright 1925, 1926 Consolidated Magazines Corporation; renewal copyright 1953, 1954 Frances Scott Fitzgerald Lanahan. Reprinted with the permission of Charles Scribner's Sons from *All the Sad Young Men* by F. Scott Fitzgerald. "Big Two-Hearted River" by Ernest Hemingway. Reprinted with the permission of Charles Scribner's Sons from *In Our Time* by Ernest Hemingway. Copyright 1925 Charles Scribner's Sons; renewal copyright 1953 Ernest Hemingway. The selections from *Green Hills of Africa,* pp. 2–9, 18–28, by Ernest Hemingway are used by permission of Charles Scribner's Sons. Copyright 1935 Charles Scribner's Sons. "The Book of the Grotesque" from *Winesburg, Ohio,* by Sherwood Anderson. Copyright 1919 by B. W. Huebsch, 1947 by Eleanor Copenhaver Anderson. Reprinted by permission of The Viking Press, Inc.

T. S. ELIOT. "Milton I" and "Milton II" from *On Poetry and Poets* by T. S. Eliot. Reprinted by permission of Faber and Faber, Ltd., and Farrar, Straus & Cudahy, Inc. Copyright © 1957 by T. S. Eliot. "The Love Song of J. Alfred Prufrock," "The *Boston Evening Transcript,*" "Cousin Nancy," "La Figlia Che Piange," "Whispers of Immortality," "The Waste Land," "Journey of the Magi," and "Lines for an Old Man" from *Collected Poems: 1909–1935* by T. S. Eliot, copyright, 1936, by Harcourt, Brace & World, Inc. Reprinted by permission of Harcourt, Brace & World, Inc., and Faber and Faber, Inc. "Dry Salvages" from *Four Quartets,* copyright, 1943, by T. S. Eliot. Reprinted by permission of Harcourt, Brace & World, Inc., and Faber and Faber, Ltd. From *The Family Reunion,* copyright, 1939, by T. S. Eliot. Reprinted by permission of Harcourt, Brace & World, Inc., and Faber and Faber, Ltd. "Tradition and the Individual Talent," "Hamlet and His Problems," "William Blake," "Ben Jonson," "Thomas Middleton," and "Religion and Literature" from *Selected Essays:* New Edition by T. S. Eliot, copyright, 1932, 1936, 1950, by Harcourt, Brace & World, Inc.; copyright, 1960, by T. S. Eliot. Reprinted by permission of Harcourt, Brace & World, Inc., and Faber and Faber, Ltd. From *Murder in the Cathedral* by T. S. Eliot, copyright, 1935, by Harcourt, Brace & World, Inc. Reprinted by permission of Harcourt, Brace & World, Inc. and Faber and Faber, Ltd. Material reprinted by permission of the publishers from The Loeb Classical Library, Ovid, *Metamorphoses,* Vol. I, translated by Frank J. Miller, Cambridge, Mass.: Harvard University Press, 1916.

WILLIAM FAULKNER. "The Bear" by William Faulkner. Copyright 1942 by The Curtis Publishing Co. Copyright 1942 by William Faulkner. Reprinted from *Go Down Moses and Other Stories,* by William Faulkner, by permission of Random House, Inc. "Spotted Horses" by William Faulkner. Copyright 1931, 1940 and renewed 1958 by William Faulkner. Reprinted from *The Hamlet,* by William Faulkner, by permission of Random House, Inc.

A NOTE ON THE COVER: The eagle incorporated in the cover design is copyrighted by America House and is used by kind permission.

© 1962 BY HARCOURT, BRACE & WORLD, INC.

All rights reserved. No part of this book may be reproduced in any form or by any mechanical means, including mimeograph and tape recorder, without permission in writing from the publisher.

Library of Congress Catalog Card Number: 62–12181

[a·2·62] PRINTED IN THE UNITED STATES OF AMERICA

*T*HE *lean cats of the arches of the churches,*
That's the old world. In the new, all men are priests.

They preach and they are preaching in a land
To be described. They are preaching in a time
To be described. Evangelists of what?
If they could gather their theses into one,
Collect their thoughts together into one,
Into a single thought . . .

. . . .

Panjandrum and central heart and mind of minds—
If they could! Or is it the multitude of thoughts,
Like insects in the depths of the mind, that kill
The single thought? The multitudes of men
That kill the single man, starvation's head,
One man, their bread and their remembered wine?

WALLACE STEVENS

from
"Extracts from Addresses to the Academy of Fine Ideas"
(1942)

Contents

Preface by the General Editor   xv

EMILY DICKINSON

EDITED BY
Northrop Frye

Introduction   3
Reading Suggestions   16

POEMS

9. Through lane it lay – thro' bramble –   17
24. There is a morn by men unseen –   17
30. Adrift! A little boat adrift!   17
49. I never lost as much but twice   18
55. By Chivalries as tiny   18
67. Success is counted sweetest   18
80. Our lives are Swiss –   18
81. We should not mind so small a flower –   18
94. Angels, in the early morning   18
119. Talk with prudence to a Beggar   18
128. Bring me the sunset in a cup   18
141. Some, too fragile for winter winds   19
160. Just lost, when I was saved!   19
187. How many times these low feet staggered –   19
214. I taste a liquor never brewed –   19
216. Safe in their Alabaster Chambers –   19
241. I like a look of Agony   20

249. Wild Nights – Wild Nights!   20
258. There's a certain Slant of light   20
266. This – is the land – the Sunset washes –   20
272. I breathed enough to take the Trick –   20
274. The only Ghost I ever saw   20
280. I felt a Funeral, in my Brain   21
281. 'Tis so appalling – it exhilirates –   21
287. A Clock stopped –   21
292. If your Nerve, deny you –   21
303. The Soul selects her own Society –   22
305. The difference between Despair   22
306. The Soul's Superior instants   22
311. It sifts from Leaden Sieves –   22
322. There came a Day at Summer's full   22
341. After great pain, a formal feeling comes –   23
346. Not probable – The barest Chance –   23
358. If any sink, assure that this, now standing –   23
378. I saw no Way – The Heavens were stitched –   23
384. No Rack can torture me –   23
398. I had not minded – Walls –   23
410. The first Day's Night had come –   24
441. This is my letter to the World   24
448. This was a Poet – It is That   24
457. Sweet – safe – Houses   24
465. I heard a Fly buzz – when I died –   24
483. A Solemn thing within the Soul   24
505. I would not paint – a picture –   25

507. She sights a Bird – she chuckles – 25

531. We dream – it is good we are dreaming – 25

537. Me prove it now – Whoever doubt 25

540. I took my Power in my Hand – 25

578. The Body grows without – 26

585. I like to see it lap the Miles – 26

590. Did you ever stand in a Cavern's Mouth – 26

619. Glee – The great storm is over – 26

652. A Prison gets to be a friend – 26

664. Of all the Souls that stand create – 27

683. The Soul unto itself 27

712. Because I could not stop for Death – 27

756. One Blessing had I than the rest 27

777. The Loneliness One dare not sound – 28

793. Grief is a Mouse – 28

809. Unable are the Loved to die 28

817. Given in Marriage unto Thee 28

822. This Consciousness that is aware 28

835. Nature and God – I neither knew 28

842. Good to hide, and hear'em hunt! 28

861. Split the Lark – and you'll find the Music – 29

870. Finding is the first Act 29

871. The Sun and Moon must make their haste – 29

872. As the Starved Maelstrom laps the Navies 29

889. Crisis is a Hair 29

945. This is a Blossom of the Brain – 29

956. What shall I do when the Summer troubles – 30

959. A loss of something ever felt I – 30

970. Color – Caste – Denomination – 30

983. Ideals are the Fairy Oil 30

986. A narrow Fellow in the Grass 30

1000. The Fingers of the Light 31

1014. Did We abolish Frost 31

1017. To die – without the Dying 31

1021. Far from Love the Heavenly Father 31

1039. I heard as if I had no Ear 31

1046. I've dropped my Brain – My Soul is Numb – 31

1052. I never saw a Moor – 31

1067. Except the smaller size 32

1068. Further in Summer than the Birds 32

1082. Revolution is the Pod 32

1084. At Half past Three, a single Bird 32

1090. I am afraid to own a Body – 32

1126. Shall I take thee, the Poet said 32

1129. Tell all the Truth but tell it slant – 32

1142. The Props assist the House 33

1181. When I hoped I feared – 33

1197. I should not dare to be so sad 33

1200. Because my Brook is fluent 33

1226. The Popular Heart is a Cannon first – 33

1232. The Clover's simple Fame 33

1247. To pile like Thunder to it's close 33

1286. I thought that nature was enough 33

1298. The Mushroom is the Elf of Plants – 34

1317. Abraham to kill him 34

1339. A Bee his burnished Carriage 34

1377. Forbidden Fruit a flavor has 34

1393. Lay this Laurel on the One 34

1400. What mystery pervades a well! 34

1405. Bees are Black, with Gilt Surcingles – 35

1428. Water makes many Beds 35

1432. Spurn the temerity – 35

1434. Go not too near a House of Rose – 35

1450. The Road was lit with Moon and star –   35

1462. We knew not that we were to live –   35

1463. A Route of Evanescence   35

1474. Estranged from Beauty – none can be –   35

1475. Fame is the one that does not stay –   35

1483. The Robin is a Gabriel   35

1487. The Savior must have been   36

1510. How happy is the little Stone   36

1553. Bliss is the plaything of the child –   36

1557. Lives he in any other world   36

1599. Though the great Waters sleep   36

1625. Back from the cordial Grave I drag thee   36

1628. A Drunkard cannot meet a Cork   36

1631. Oh Future! thou secreted peace   36

1645. The Ditch is dear to the Drunken Man   36

1651. A Word made Flesh is seldom   36

1679. Rather arid delight   37

1695. There is a solitude of space   37

1697. They talk as slow as Legends grow   37

1712. A Pit – but Heaven over it –   37

1717. Did life's penurious length   37

1731. Love can do all but raise the Dead   37

1732. My life closed twice before its close   37

1736. Proud of my broken heart, since thou didst break it   37

1741. That it will never come again   38

1745. The mob within the heart   38

1749. The waters chased him as he fled   38

1764. The saddest noise, the sweetest noise   38

LETTERS

193. To Samuel Bowles   38

260. To T. W. Higginson   39

261. To T. W. Higginson   39

265. To T. W. Higginson   40

268. To T. W. Higginson   40

269. To Dr. and Mrs. J. G. Holland   41

271. To T. W. Higginson   41

318. To Mrs. J. G. Holland   41

330. To T. W. Higginson   42

339. To Louise and Frances Norcross   42

353. To T. W. Higginson   43

354. To Mrs. J. G. Holland   43

368. To T. W. Higginson   44

415. To Samuel Bowles   44

432. To Mrs. J. G. Holland   44

459A. To T. W. Higginson   45

580. To Susan Gilbert Dickinson   45

605. To Edward (Ned) Dickinson   45

609. To Mrs. Samuel Bowles   45

787. To Martha Dickinson   45

864. To Samuel Bowles the younger   45

868. To Susan Gilbert Dickinson   45

1024. To Susan Gilbert Dickinson   46

MARK TWAIN

EDITED BY
Henry Nash Smith

Introduction   47

Reading Suggestions   58

PART I: THE RIVER AND THE WEST   59

  The Quarles Farm: From *Mark Twain's Autobiography* [1924]   59

  The Boys' Ambition: From *Life on the Mississippi* [1883]   62

Rank and Dignity of Piloting: From
Life on the Mississippi [1883]   63

Captain Montgomery   66

Lost in a Snowstorm: From *Roughing
It* [1872]   67

The Case of Hyde vs. Morgan: From
Roughing It [1872]   70

The Story of the Old Ram: From
Roughing It [1872]   72

Colonel Sellers: From *The Gilded Age*
[1873]   74

PART II: SOME ANIMALS   79

Cruelty to Animals: The Histrionic Pig   79

The Celebrated Jumping Frog of
Calaveras County   80

The Pilgrim Bird: From *The Innocents
Abroad* [1869]   83

The Cayote: From *Roughing It* [1872]   83

Tom Quartz, the Cat: From *Roughing
It* [1872]   84

Jim Baker's Bluejay Yarn: From *A
Tramp Abroad* [1880]   86

The Indian Crow: From *Following the
Equator* [1897]   88

PART III: DRAMATIC & LITERARY CRITI-
CISM   89

Over the Mountains   89

Gladiatorial Spectacles in the Coliseum: From *The Innocents
Abroad* [1869]   92

Whittier Birthday Dinner Speech   94

How to Tell a Story   96

Fenimore Cooper's Further Literary
Offenses   99

William Dean Howells   102

Platform Readings   106

PART IV: SOCIAL CRITICISM   111

A True Story Repeated Word for
Word As I Heard It   111

The Man That Corrupted Hadleyburg   113

The War Prayer   134

HENRY JAMES

EDITED BY
F. W. Dupee

Introduction   137

Reading Suggestions   148

DAISY MILLER: A Study   149

THE PUPIL   174

THE REAL THING   194

'EUROPE'   206

THE BEAST IN THE JUNGLE   214

from HAWTHORNE   234

    The Scarlet Letter   234

GUY DE MAUPASSANT   239

THE ART OF FICTION   252

from THE NOTEBOOKS   262

    The Real Thing   262

    The Cambridge Cemetery   264

FIVE LETTERS   264

    To William James   265

    To Henry James, Sr.   265

    To Charles Eliot Norton   266

    To Miss Grace Norton   267

    To Henry Adams   267

HENRY ADAMS

EDITED BY
Ernest Samuels

Introduction   269

Reading Suggestions   282

from DEMOCRACY: An American Novel   283

    Chapter 1   283

    Chapter 4   285

from ESTHER   289

    Chapter 7   289

from THE HISTORY OF THE UNITED STATES DURING THE ADMINISTRATIONS OF JEFFERSON AND MADISON   297

    from VOLUME I

    Chapter 6. American Ideals [1800]   298

    from VOLUME IX

    CHAPTER 10. American Character [1817]   306

from MONT-SAINT-MICHEL AND CHARTRES   313

    Preface   313

    CHAPTER 1. Saint Michiel de la Mer del Peril   314

    CHAPTER 6. The Virgin of Chartres   319

    from CHAPTER 7. Roses and Apses   326

    from CHAPTER 11. The Three Queens   327

    CHAPTER 14. Abélard   328

PRAYER TO THE VIRGIN OF CHARTRES   342

from THE EDUCATION OF HENRY ADAMS   345

    Editor's Preface   345

    Preface   345

    CHAPTER 1. Quincy (1838–1848)   346

    CHAPTER 22. Chicago (1893)   354

    CHAPTER 25. The Dynamo and the Virgin (1900)   360

    CHAPTER 33. A Dynamic Theory of History (1904)   365

LETTERS OF HENRY ADAMS   371

    To Charles Francis Adams, Jr.   372

    To Charles Francis Adams, Jr.   374

    To William James   375

    To His Wife, Marian Hooper Adams   376

    To Elizabeth Cameron   377

    To John Hay   379

    To Charles Milnes Gaskell   381

    To Henry James   381

STEPHEN CRANE

EDITED BY
J. C. Levenson

Introduction   383

Reading Suggestions   397

REPORTAGE   397

    On the New Jersey Coast   397

    Dark Side of War   398

STORIES   399

    An Experiment in Misery   399

    A Mystery of Heroism   404

    The Open Boat   408

    The Monster   419

    The Bride Comes to Yellow Sky   444

    Death and the Child   449

POEMS   458

    Tell me not in joyous numbers   458

    Once there came a man   458

    The ocean said to me once   459

    A man feared that he might find an assassin   459

    Do not weep, maiden, for war is kind   459

    I have heard the sunset song of the birches   459

    In the night   459

    A man adrift on a slim spar   460

    Unwind my riddle   460

THEODORE DREISER

EDITED BY
Alfred Kazin

Introduction	461
Reading Suggestions	472
NIGGER JEFF	472
THE LOST PHOEBE	484
MY BROTHER PAUL	491
SANCTUARY	503
from AN AMERICAN TRAGEDY	516

from BOOK II

Chapter 38	516
Chapter 39	522
Chapter 40	525
Chapter 41	526
Chapter 42	528
Chapter 43	532
Chapter 44	537
Chapter 45	542
Chapter 46	546
Chapter 47	549

EUGENE O'NEILL

EDITED BY
Eric Bentley

Introduction	557
Reading Suggestions	575
THE ICEMAN COMETH	576

ROBERT FROST

EDITED BY
Louise Bogan

Introduction	643
Reading Suggestions	653
THE PASTURE	654
from A BOY'S WILL [1913]	654
In Hardwood Groves	654
October	654
from NORTH OF BOSTON [1914]	654
The Black Cottage	654
After Apple-Picking	656
from MOUNTAIN INTERVAL [1916]	656
An Old Man's Winter Night	656
The Gum-Gatherer	656
The Sound of Trees	657
from NEW HAMPSHIRE [1923]	657
Two Witches II: The Pauper Witch of Grafton	657
Stopping by Woods on a Snowy Evening	658
To Earthward	658
On a Tree Fallen Across the Road	659
from WEST-RUNNING BROOK [1928]	659
The Cocoon	659
Acquainted with the Night	659
The Egg and the Machine	659
from A FURTHER RANGE [1936]	
Desert Places	660
Leaves Compared with Flowers	660
Neither Out Far Nor in Deep	660
Provide, Provide	661

from A WITNESS TREE [1942]

The Silken Tent   661
The Wind and the Rain   661
The Subverted Flower   662
The Gift Outright   662

from STEEPLE BUSH [1947]

One Step Backward Taken   663
Directive   663
The Ingenuities of Debt   663

PROSE

The Waterspout   664
Introduction to *King Jasper*   664
The Figure a Poem Makes   667

SHERWOOD ANDERSON
F. SCOTT FITZGERALD
ERNEST HEMINGWAY

EDITED BY
Mark Schorer

Introduction   671
Reading Suggestions   683

Sherwood Anderson

from A STORY TELLER'S STORY   684
THE BOOK OF THE GROTESQUE   689
THE EGG   691
I WANT TO KNOW WHY   695
FOUR AMERICAN IMPRESSIONS: Gertrude
  Stein, Paul Rosenfeld, Ring Lardner,
  Sinclair Lewis   700
from LETTERS, 1918–1938   702

29: To Van Wyck Brooks   702
45: To Van Wyck Brooks   703
63: To Paul Rosenfeld   704
65: To Mr. Lewis Galantière   706
67: To Miss Gertrude Stein   706
84: To Alfred Stieglitz   706
147: To Roger Sergel   707
162: To Robert Anderson   708
215: To the Dramatic Publishing Com-
     pany, Chicago, Illinois   709
260: To Roy Jansen   710
284: To Ralph Church   710
342: To George Freitag   711

F. Scott Fitzgerald

THE RICH BOY   713
ECHOES OF THE JAZZ AGE   729
RING   734
THE CRACK-UP   737

Ernest Hemingway

BIG TWO-HEARTED RIVER   744
from THE GREEN HILLS OF AFRICA   752

T. S. ELIOT

EDITED BY
R. P. Blackmur

Introduction   759
Reading Suggestions   770

THE LOVE SONG OF J. ALFRED PRUFROCK
  [1915]   770

The Boston Evening Transcript [1915]   772

Cousin Nancy [1915]   773

La Figlia Che Piange [1917]   773

Whispers of Immortality [1918]   773

The Waste Land [1922]   774

Journey of the Magi [1927]   781

Lines for an Old Man [1935]   782

Two Choruses: From *The Family Reunion* [1939]   783

The Dry Salvages [1941]   784

Tradition and the Individual Talent [1919]   787

Hamlet and His Problems [1919]: [A Review of J. M. Robertson's *The Problem of Hamlet* (1919)]   791

A Sceptical Patrician: A Review of *The Education of Henry Adams* [1919]   793

William Blake [1920]   796

Ben Jonson [1919]   798

Thomas Middleton [1927]   803

Religion and Literature [1935]   807

Milton I and II [1936, 1947]   812

WILLIAM FAULKNER

EDITED BY

Irving Howe

Introduction   825

Reading Suggestions   840

Spotted Horses   841

The Bear   866

A Preface

BY THE GENERAL EDITOR

MAJOR WRITERS OF AMERICA is made possible at this point in time not so much because the energies of its editors have been prodigious but because the study of American literature—inside and outside the universities—is now systematic and mature. This happy state of affairs is relatively recent. In fact, like the professional study of English literature, it is only about seventy-five years old. Of the two literatures, however, the American remained largely terra incognita for several decades after its discovery. History repeated itself: the Old World was settled first. Yet the New did not lack for those who could rise to the challenge of its promise. The essential landmarks were discerned. The terrain was mapped. In the perspective of these seventy-five years of discovery and exploration then, the present work acknowledges many profound debts: to the pioneer adventurers, such as Moses Coit Tyler, William Peterfield Trent, and Barrett Wendell; to subsequent masters who are represented herein by entries in the bibliographies as well as by their students; and, further, to a host of scholars contemporary with the editors, often younger than they, who attest the vitality of the vocation.

It was altogether natural that in the initial stages of this American "Great Instauration" claimants to academic dignity should strive to impress their colleagues in departments devoted to the magnificent literatures of England or of the Continent or of antiquity by heaping up as mountainous a bulk of American expression as research could excavate. While it was indisputably evident that American literary history was of painfully short duration—commencing with the seventeenth century and even then for a hundred years or more offering only "colonial" documents—still there were unearthed such permanently significant minorities as Philip Freneau, Joel Barlow, Charles Brockden Brown, and the authors of *The Contrast* and *Modern Chivalry*.

These beginnings made, the advance continued into the wilderness. New recruits expended tremendous energy in "rediscovering" forgotten authors—

or sometimes in actually discovering those who had never been known at all. Among the former the pre-eminent names are Herman Melville and Emily Dickinson; among the latter, Edward Taylor. The great object in view was to establish the canon of American literature on as broad a basis as possible. Nothing canonizes literature more quickly than print. It followed that anthologies of constantly increasing poundage were compiled, and with an ever lengthening array of persons deserving inclusion, if only because they had written in America or about American things. The tacit assumption of almost all these productions was that they had to silence professional rivals who would constantly inquire, with eyebrows raised in elaborately simulated ignorance, "American literature? Oh, is there any?"

Today, after seven or eight decades of skirmishing, the battle for American literature is won. It is established as a reputable and incontestable subdivision of the English department. Courses in it proliferate. Outside the academies it has triumphed even more conclusively: hundreds of "popular" surveys, biographies, interpretations—most of them eschewing the stigmata of scholarship—are sold annually. In fact, among conscientious practitioners a dreadful anxiety now arises for fear the victory has been too overwhelming. No doubt, Philip Freneau—to take him as a test case—is a fascinating figure; but is it really a healthy curriculum which requires that he be read by a student who is utterly ignorant of Racine?

The premise of *Major Writers of America* is by no means intended as a hostile comment on those compilations which exhibit the now vast accumulation of American writings. A serious student of American civilization must come to terms with Philip Freneau, as with a multitude of his stature. Yet, while the canon is at long last becoming established, a realization gradually forces itself upon us that, as the age of discovery and of elementary mapping closes, the era of evaluation opens. Not that any piece of terrain, however minute, should be forgotten once more; nor should any possible open territory be foreclosed. Yet it is incumbent upon us to make clear which are the few peaks and which the many low-lying hills. We must, if we can, suppress an undiscriminating pedantry by distinguishing just wherein the great are truly great. We must set apart those who belong to world literature rather than merely to local (or, to what is worse, regional) patriotism. We must vindicate the study of American literature because primarily the matter is literature, and only secondarily because it is American. For this end *Major Writers of America* has been designed.

The first requirement of the design, therefore, was inevitably that the authors so nominated be represented fully enough to testify to their superiority. This meant that exclusions had to be perpetrated with surgical ruthlessness. There can be no question that Edwards, Emerson, Hawthorne, Melville, Henry James, and Mark Twain belong. When the problem arises of, say Longfellow or Whittier, decision necessarily becomes arbitrary. And, as the list extends into the twentieth century, determinations are bound to appear, even to those who make them, not much more than arbitrary or even capricious indulgences of taste. However, the editors stake their credibility upon the choices they have made; moreover they have endeavored in lengthy Introductions to make plain their particular sense of the writers from whose works they have made coherent selections.

An immediately apparent corollary of this policy was a recognition that for most writers of fiction no portions of long novels could be included. Spacious as these pages be, they are not copious enough to include all of *The Scarlet Letter, Moby-Dick, The Adventures of Huckleberry Finn, The Ambassadors*. Certain set-pieces, separable from the narrative in Cooper's romances, or the chapters reproduced from the novels of Adams and Dreiser that have an independence vigorous enough to sustain the separation, may legitimately be taken out of context. But no segments of more closely knit works of art can be so excised. The editors feel consoled for these omissions because by now inexpensive paperback reprints of all the formidable titles are available. Wherever possible we have exhibited the techniques of master storytellers in long short stories, with what Henry James liked to call the "blest *nouvelle*."

An anthology designed to give a generous sample of the record in all its representative particulars is obliged to include too many writers. The result inevitably distorts the literary stature of the more important writers. For the purposes of a historical survey such even-handed continuity is necessary. When, however, attention is turned from the record itself to the delicate task of evaluation, no one editor, nor partnership of editors, is capable of supplying the essential discrimination. There still remains, of course, the need for respecting continuity, of remembering the historical forces, and above all for reverencing chronology. Also there persists an obligation to relate, in some degree, the works to the authors' biographies, especially when, as with Franklin and Henry Adams, the historical biography is parallel to but far from identical with the literary rendition. Still, fully granting these considerations, the second requirement of our design demanded that each major author, or each grouping of major figures—where two or three writers obviously belong together—be dealt with by an editor solely responsible for the selection, the criticism, the annotations, and the bibliographies. Not only has there been no "party line" to which individual editors were obliged to cleave, there has been no substantive line whatsoever. Certain minor editorial uniformities have been maintained—e.g., minimum standards for what in the texts required footnoting and what did not—but these were kept to a reasonable minimum. There was also an implicit rule that each contributor should be dedicated to the highest standards of excellence and clarity he could conceive, but it never had to be explicitly promulgated.

In matters of spelling, punctuation, and capitalization editors have exercised their discretion. After the early decades of the nineteenth century, the standard printed texts have generally been followed. A date at the end of the selection, when on the right, is that of composition; on the left, that of publication. Omissions within texts, when they constitute more than a paragraph, are indicated by the insertion of ellipses at the end of one paragraph and at the beginning of the next. A note has been appended to the introductory essays whenever there are variations from this practice. Unless otherwise indicated, footnotes are those of the editor of the section. Bibliographies have been kept to an essential minimum for obvious reasons of spatial economy. The reader who wishes to pursue a writer further should turn to the third volume (*Bibliography*) of the Robert E. Spiller *et al. Literary History of the United States* (1948) and to the *Bibliographical Supplement* (1959) of the same work, edited by Richard M. Ludwig.

The General Editor thinks it fair to say that while these volumes have been composed with the student chiefly in mind, yet the editors have striven to make *Major Writers of America* something more than a textbook. The concerted aim of the enterprise has been to construct a book with which anyone might sit down and in which he might read with pleasure. We have thought of students as those who help to constitute the noble company of "general readers," not merely as undergraduates earning course credits. We have, in short, endeavored to pay both the student and the general reader the compliment of treating them as interchangeable designations.

The Publisher and the General Editor take pleasure in thanking the several editors for their patience, their readiness to heed suggestions, to conform their presentations to spatial formats dictated by practical necessities. In one sense, this thanks should also mention their cooperation, for cooperate in myriad ways they did. In a more basic sense, however, the thanks must recognize their healthy lack of cooperation. The finished achievement is in no strict sense a collaboration, the report of a committee of certified experts. Beyond agreement among contributors to cultivate their own gardens intensely and to raid the plots and seedbeds of others solely under the decorous excuse of enriching comparative judgments, no demands were made by Publisher or General Editor. But this is not to say that the American *writers* represented in the pages which follow left their editors alone. Quite the contrary. In fact, *Major Writers of America* may best be taken as a varied testimony to the force that the literature continues to exert over and against time. Such attraction at such a distance is what signalizes a major writer.

PERRY MILLER

Cambridge, Massachusetts
December 15, 1961

MAJOR WRITERS OF
AMERICA

NORTHROP FRYE
Editor

Emily Dickinson

1830–1886

EMILY DICKINSON was born in Amherst, Massachusetts, in the Connecticut River Valley, in 1830. She died in the house she was born in, and her travels out of the region consisted of one trip to Washington and Philadelphia and two or three to Boston and Cambridge. Amherst had recently acquired, largely through the energy of her grandfather, an academy, which she attended, and a college. Her father, Edwin Dickinson, was a leading citizen of the town, a lawyer, active and successful in state politics, and treasurer of the college. Such a town illustrated, more effectively than any Oneida or Brook Farm, the Utopian pattern in nineteenth-century American society. It was a little world in itself, so well balanced economically as to be nearly self-sufficient, with a provincial but intense religious and intellectual culture, the latter growing as the college grew. Throughout her life Emily Dickinson was able to say what she had said at sixteen: "I dont know anything more about affairs in the world, than if I was in a trance," and her ability to shut all distractions out of her life owed much to the social coherence of her surroundings.

There was a strong family feeling among the Dickinsons, and neither Emily nor her younger sister Lavinia married or left home. The older brother, Austin, went to Harvard Law School, where Emily pelted him with affec-tionate letters telling him how much he was missed, then returned to Amherst to practice law. Gossip said that the father's possessiveness kept his daughters beside him ministering to his domestic comforts, but this may not be true. The image of awful integrity he inspired, which made his daughter say at his death: "His Heart was pure and terrible, and I think no other like it exists," may have grown on her gradually, as her youthful remarks in letters to Austin sound normally bratty. Thus: "Father and mother sit in state in the sitting room perusing such papers only, as they are well assured have nothing carnal in them." Her mother she was never close to until later years. Austin's wife, Susan Gilbert, was another person whom Emily Dickinson seems always to have loved passionately, in spite of a good deal of tension and occasional open ruptures. To Sue, across the fence, Emily sent nearly three hundred poems, besides messages, epigrams, gifts, and other symbols of affection.

At seventeen, Emily left the Amherst Academy and went to Mount Holyoke College, or Seminary, as it was then called, a few miles away in South Hadley. The discipline there was strict but humane, and she seems to have enjoyed herself in spite of the religious instruction, but her father withdrew her after a year. Emily thus had, for a poet, relatively little formal education. It is unlikely that she read any language except her own. She knew the Bible (involuntarily), she knew Shakespeare, she knew the classical myths, and she took a good deal of interest in contemporary women writers, especially Elizabeth Browning, George Eliot, and the Brontës. The Brontë references in earlier letters are to Charlotte, but "gigantic Emily Brontë" haunts the later ones. Dickens and Robert Browning appear in her rare literary allusions; there are one or two echoes of Tennyson; and, of the more serious American writers, she knew Emerson and something of Thoreau and Hawthorne. Her main literary instructors, however, were her dictionary and her hymnbook. She has a large vocabulary for a poet so limited in subject matter, and most of her stanzas, as has often been pointed out, are the ordinary hymn stanzas, the eight-six-eight-six "common meter" and the six-six-eight-six "short meter" being especially frequent.

Creative people often seem to need certain types of love or friendship that make manifest for them the human relations or conflicts with which their work is concerned. A poet of Shakespeare's day could hardly set up in business without a "mistress" to whom he vowed eternal devotion, though this mistress might have little if any part to play in his actual life, and very seldom had anything to do with his marriage. Emily Dickinson seemed to need in her life an older man to act as her "preceptor" or "master," to use her own terms, who could keep her in touch with qualities she did not profess to have: intellectual consistency, sociability, knowledge of the world, firm and settled convictions. Benjamin F. Newton, a lawyer who had articled with her father, was apparently her first "preceptor." Her letters to him have not been preserved, but he seems to have awakened her literary tastes, expanded her cultural horizons, and perhaps given her a more liberal idea of her religion—at any rate she refers to him as "a friend, who taught me Immortality." He died in 1853, before Emily had started to write poetry in earnest.

Then came Charles Wadsworth, a Presbyterian clergyman whom Emily may have heard on her trip to Philadelphia, and who, for all his married and middle-aged respectability, seems to have been the one great love of the poet's life. It is unlikely that the kind of love she offered him would have interfered with his marriage or social position, but some pathetic drafts of letters addressed to a "Master," if they were intended for Wadsworth, indicate something of the tumult of her feelings. In 1862 Wadsworth accepted a call to a church in San Francisco, a removal which seems to have been a profound shock to the poet, for reasons we can only guess at—again the correspondence has not survived. The name of the church he went to—Calvary—became the center of a drama of loss and renunciation in which the poet becomes "Empress of Calvary," and the bride of an invisible marriage followed immediately by separation instead of union.

But Wadsworth, whatever her feeling for him, could hardly have had more than a perfunctory interest in the poetry that was now becoming the central activity of her life. In her early years she seems to have written little except letters and the occasional valentine, of which two most elaborate and ingenious efforts have been preserved. In the later 1850's she began writing poetry consistently, binding her completed poems up into packets, and sometimes sending copies to Sue or enclosing them in letters to other correspondents. In addition to her fair copies, there are many worksheet drafts scribbled on anything within reach —once on the back of an invitation to a "candy pulling" sent her twenty-six years earlier. Her impetus to write seems to have come on her in a flood, as the poems written or copied out in the year 1862 alone average one a day. With Wadsworth gone, another "preceptor" was urgently needed, this time a literary critic. Having liked an article by Thomas Wentworth Higginson she had read in the *Atlantic Monthly*, Emily sent the author a letter (No. 260, see p. 39), enclosing her card and four poems, and asking if in his opinion her poetry was "alive" and "breathed." Higginson had been a Unitarian clergyman but had resigned his pastorate to devote himself to writing, and was then on the point of organizing a Negro regiment to fight in the Civil War (hence his later title of Colonel Higginson).

Higginson was an influential critic, and as such a natural target for amateur poets pretending that they wanted his frank opinion of their work when what they really wanted was advice on how to get published. He saw at once that Emily Dickinson was more serious business than this. She said explicitly that she wanted her work criticized by the literary standards that he knew about, and he was bound to be misled by that. But he realized, perhaps more quickly than she did, that she did not want specific criticisms of her poems, which she had no intention of altering for anyone's views. Nor was she interested in publication, as she made clear. All she wanted was contact with a sympathetic reader of informed taste and knowledge of the world of thought and action. Higginson had the sense to be flattered by her confidence, and seems to have responded with unfailing courtesy to her gentle but persistent nudgings to write her. She may have been exaggerating when she told him that he had saved her life, but she was not underestimating the service he did her, nor should we. At the same time, she was never in love with Higginson, and her attitude toward him was one of devotion tempered by an ironic detachment.

After 1862, the poet became increasingly a recluse, dressing in white, apparently with reference to her inner "Calvary" drama of renunciation. For the last decade of her life she did not leave her house and refused to see any strangers, her experience bounded by her house and garden, her social life completely absorbed in the brief letters she constantly sent to friends and neighbors, which sometimes contained poems and often accompanied small gifts of flowers or fruit. She expected her friends to be cultivated and tolerant people, and most of them were, prizing her enigmatic notes and respecting her privacy. There was no mistaking the good will and affection in her letters, however oblique in expression. One feels something Oriental in her manner of existence: the seclusion, the need for a "preceptor," the use of brief poems as a form of social communication, would have seemed normal enough in the high cultures of the Far East, however unusual in her own. And even her culture was one in which the telephone had not yet destroyed the traditional balance between the spoken and the written word.

Of her friends, some were well-known writers in their day, apart from Higginson. She was much attached to Samuel Bowles, editor of the Springfield *Republican,* one of the liveliest of the New England local papers, and representing a type of highly articulate journalism now practically extinct. Helen Hunt Jackson, born in Amherst in the same year as Emily Dickinson and a childhood playmate, came back into her life in later years. Mrs. Jackson was also a disciple of Higginson, and was the author of the Indian romance *Ramona* and the Saxe Holm stories. Whatever this may mean to the contemporary reader, it meant in her day that she was at the top of the literary tree. Another novel, *Mercy Philbrick's Choice,* and a short story, seem to have made some use of Emily Dickinson's smothered love affair for copy. She told Emily that she was a great poet and was defrauding her public by not publishing, and finally, after strenuous efforts, got one poem, "Success is counted sweetest," into a collection of anonymous verse called *A Masque of Poets,* many readers taking it to be Emerson's.

In the last decade of Emily Dickinson's life her father's friend Judge Otis P. Lord became a widower, and his friendship with the poet quickly ripened into love. Though, as usual, the letters themselves have disappeared, we do have a few drafts of letters to him among her papers which put the fact beyond doubt. After living as she had, the adjustment needed for marriage would have been formidable, probably impossible. But she was deeply in love, which indicates that her retired life was the choice of her temperament, not a dedication. She was not a nun *manquée,* even if she does call herself a "Wayward Nun." Conscious human perception is, we are told, highly selective, and very efficient about excluding whatever threatens its balance. "Strong" people and men of action are those for whom such perception functions predictably: they are made strong by habit, by continually meeting the expected response. Creative abilities normally go with more delicate and mysterious nuances of awareness, hence they are often accompanied by some kind of physical or psychic weakness. Emily Dickinson's perceptions were so immediate that they absorbed her whole energy, or as she says, "The mere sense of living is joy enough":

> To be alive – is Power –
> Existence – in itself –
> Without a further function –

But she realized that there was danger as well as ecstasy in so sensitive a response. "Had we the first intimation of the Definition of Life," she says, "the calmest of us would be Lunatics!" To reverse a well-known phrase from Lewis Carroll, it took all the staying in the same place she could do to keep running. The intensity of her ordinary consciousness left her with few reserves to spend on a social life.

In a life so retired it was inevitable that the main events should be the deaths of friends, and Emily Dickinson became a prolific writer of notes of condolence. Her father, her mother, Sue's little boy Gilbert (struck down by typhoid fever at the age of eight), Bowles, Wadsworth, Lord, Helen Jackson, all died in the last few years of her life. As early as 1883 she had a nervous collapse, and observed: "The Crisis of the sorrow of so many years is all that tires me." Two years later a more serious illness began. In the second week of May, 1886, she wrote to her cousins Louisa and Fanny Norcross:

> Little Cousins,
> Called back.
> Emily.

A few days later she was dead.

A life in which such things as the death of her dog or an unexpected call by Wadsworth are prominent incidents is not simply a quiet life but a carefully obliterated one. There are poets—and they include Shakespeare—who seem to have pursued a policy of keeping their lives away from their readers. Human nature being what it is, it is precisely such poets who are most eagerly read for biographical allusions. We shall find Emily Dickinson most rewarding if we look in her poems for what her imagination has created, not for what event may have suggested it. When, under the spell of Ik Marvel's *Reveries of a Bachelor* (1850), a favorite book of hers, she writes:

> Many cross the Rhine
> In this cup of mine.
> Sip old Frankfort air
> From my brown Cigar

it would be a literal-minded reader who would infer that she had actually taken up cigar-smoking, yet this would be no more farfetched than many other biographical inferences. A poet is entitled to speak in many voices, male, female, or childlike, to express many different moods and to develop an experience in reading or life into an imaginative form that has no resemblance whatever to the original experience. Just as she made the whole of her conception of nature out of the bees and bobolinks and roses of her garden, so she constructed her drama of life, death and immortality, of love and renunciation, ecstasy and suffering, out of tiny incidents in her life. But to read biographical allegory where we ought to be reading poetry is precisely the kind of vulgarity that made her dread publication and describe it as a foul thing. Higginson's comment on her "Wild Nights!", that "the malignant" might "read into it more than that virgin recluse ever dreamed of putting there," indicates that glib speculations about the sexual feelings of virgins are much older than the popularizing of Freud. But whenever they are made they are incompetent as literary criticism.

It would be hard to name another poet in the history of the English language with so little interest in social or political events. The Civil War seemed to her "oblique," outside her orbit, and her only really peevish letter describes her reaction to a woman who told her that she ought to use her gifts for the good of humanity. There are one or two patriotic poems, but they show no freshness of insight. "My business is Circumference," she told Higginson. She concerned herself only with what she felt she could surround. It is characteristic of lyrical poetry to turn its back on the reader: the lyrical poet regularly pretends to be addressing his mistress or friend or God, or else he is soliloquizing or apostrophizing something in nature. But lyrical poetry also tends to create its own highly selected and intimate audience, like the sonnets and love poems of Shakespeare's day that circulated in manuscript among friends long before they reached print. For Emily Dickinson poetry was a form of private correspondence: "This is my letter to the World," is what she says of her poetry, and she describes the Gospel as "The Savior's

. . . Letter he wrote to all mankind." Such a correspondence forms what, for Emily Dickinson, was the only genuine kind of human community, the small body of friends united in love and understanding. "Please to need me," as she wrote to Bowles.

> By a flower – By a letter –
> By a nimble love –
> If I weld the Rivet faster –
> Final fast – above –
>
> Never mind my breathless Anvil!
> Never mind Repose!
> Never mind the sooty faces
> Tugging at the Forge!

II

AT HER death Emily Dickinson was the author of seven published poems, all anonymous, some issued without her authorization, six of them at least in what she would have considered garbled versions, altered by editors to make them more conventional. Her friends knew that she wrote poetry, but nobody, not even her sister Lavinia who had lived with her all her life, had any notion that she had written close to eighteen-hundred poems. She left instructions to Lavinia that her "papers" were to be destroyed, as was customary at that time, but no instructions were given about the piled-up packets of verse that Lavinia, to her astonishment, discovered in her sister's room. Lavinia took the packets to Sue, with a demand that they be transcribed and published immediately, meeting all complaints about the length and difficulty of the task with: "But they are Emily's poems!" Sue proved to be indolent, and perhaps jealous, and after a long wait Lavinia took them to Mrs. Mabel Loomis Todd, wife of an Amherst professor of astronomy, an attractive and highly accomplished young woman, who knew Emily, so to speak, by ear, having played the piano in the Dickinson house while the poet sat invisibly in the dark hall outside and commented on the music.

Higginson's help was enlisted. At first he felt that it would be a mistake to publish Emily Dickinson, perhaps thinking of an appeal she had made to him to talk Helen Jackson out of publishing "Success." But he gradually became, first interested, then fascinated, by what he found, and helped publicize her by writing articles about her. The two editors, Mrs. Todd and Higginson, produced *Poems by Emily Dickinson* in 1890, where a selection of her poems was distributed in various categories labeled "Life," "Love," "Nature" and the like, with titles for individual poems supplied by Higginson. A second and a third selection appeared in 1891 and 1896, respectively. Although Mrs. Todd's original transcripts were accurate, the poems were systematically smoothed out in punctuation, meter, grammar, and rhymes. Higginson took the lead in this at first, but as he went on he began to realize that the poet's liberties were not those of carelessness or incompetence. When the second selection was being prepared, he wrote to Mrs. Todd: "Let us alter as little as possible, now that the public ear is opened," including his own ear; but by that time Mrs. Todd had caught the improving fever. Mrs. Todd also went through the laborious task of collecting and publishing two volumes of Emily Dickinson's letters, where she had to engage in a long tactful struggle with the owners, and prevented a good many of them from being irreparably lost. Through no fault of hers, some of them, notably those to the Norcross sisters, survive only in mutilated versions.

Some highly unedifying family squabbles stopped further publication. Sue had been alienated by the giving of the manuscripts to Mrs. Todd; then Lavinia, for reasons too complicated to go into here, turned against Mrs. Todd after Austin Dickinson's death and brought suit to recover a strip of land willed to Mrs. Todd by Austin. Nothing further was done until the next generation grew up, in the form of Sue's daughter, Martha Dickinson Bianchi, and Mrs. Todd's daughter, Millicent Todd Bingham, who produced a series of editions of both poems and letters between 1914 and 1950. Finally, the bulk of the manuscripts came into the possession of Harvard. With Thomas H. Johnson's definitive edition of the poems (1955) and letters (1958), Emily Dickinson achieved publication on her own uncompromising terms.

When Mrs. Todd's volumes appeared, there were, despite her editorial efforts, some hostile reviews and some complaints about the poet's lack of "technique," by which was meant smooth rhymes and meters. The complaints came mainly from such minor poets as Andrew Lang in England and Thomas Bailey Aldrich in America, who naturally ascribed the greatest importance and difficulty to the only poetic quality they themselves had. Against this, we may set the fact that the first volume alone went through sixteen editions in eight years, and was constantly reprinted thereafter. Mrs. Todd gave dozens of lectures on the poet, and could have given far more. It is inconceivable that the first volume of an unknown poet to-day could achieve such a success, unless fortified by pornography. *Somebody* wanted Emily Dickinson's poetry, and we cannot avoid the inference that in the 1890's she was a genuinely popular poet who found her own public in spite of what the highbrows said. When she reappeared in the 1920's, her reputation was curiously reversed. Then the highbrows took her up, hailed her as a precursor of whatever happened to be fashionable at the time, such as imagism or free verse or metaphysical poetry, and emphasized everything in her work that was unconventional, difficult, or quaint. Both conceptions have some truth in them.

The good popular poet is usually one who does well what a great many have tried to do with less success. For the thousands of people, most of them women, who make verse out of a limited range of imaginative experience in life, love, nature, and religion, who live without fame and without much knowledge of literature beyond their schoolbooks, Emily Dickinson is the literary spokesman. She is popular too in her conceptual use of language, for popular expression tends to the proverbial, and the unsophisticated poet is usually one who tries to put prose statements into verse. The Sibyl of Amherst is no Lorelei: she has no Keatsian faery lands forlorn or Tennysonian low-lying Claribels; she does not charm and she seldom sings. Mrs. Todd often spoke of encountering poems in Emily Dickinson that took her breath away, but what surprises in her work is almost always some kind of direct statement, sharpened into wit or epigram. When she describes a hummingbird as "A route of evanescence," or says of the bluebird:

Her conscientious Voice will soar unmoved
Above ostensible Vicissitude.

she is using what medieval poets called "aureate diction," big soft bumbling abstract words that absorb images into categories and ideas. She does not—like, for example, D. H. Lawrence—try to get inside the bird's skin and identify herself with it; she identifies the bird with the human consciousness in herself. Many of her poems start out by making some kind of definition of an abstract noun:

Presentiment – is that long Shadow –
on the Lawn –

Renunciation – is a piercing Virtue –

Publication – is the Auction
Of the Mind of Man –

and most of her best-loved poems are in one of the oldest and most primitive forms of poetry, the riddle or oblique description of some object. In "A route of evanescence" there is no explicit mention of a hummingbird, because the poem tries to catch the essence of the feeling of the bird without mentioning it. Similarly with the snow in "It sifts from leaden sieves," and with the railway train in "I like to see it lap the miles."

Such popular features in her work have their own difficulties, and there are others inherent in her peculiar style. She has for the most part no punctuation, except a point represented in the Johnson edition by a dash, which, as the editor points out, is really a rhythmical beat, and is of little use in unraveling the syntax. She also shows a curious preference for an indirect subjunctive form of expression that appears in such phrases as "Beauty be not caused," and she has what seems a most unreasonable dislike of adding the *s* to the third person singular of verbs. The effect of such sidelong grammar is twofold: it increases the sense of epigrammatic wit, and it makes her poetry sound oracular, as though the explicit statements of which her poetry is so largely made up were coming to us shrouded in mystery. As she says:

Tell all the Truth but tell it slant –
Success in Circuit lies

The result is not invariably success: sometimes we may agree with enthusiasm:

> How powerful the Stimulus
> Of an Hermetic Mind –

at other times we can only say, with the captain in *Pinafore* confronted with a similar type of gnomic utterance: "I don't see at what you're driving, mystic lady":

> Endanger it, and the Demand
> Of tickets for a sigh
> Amazes the Humility
> Of Credibility –
>
> Recover it to Nature
> And that dejected Fleet
> Find Consternation's Carnival
> Divested of it's Meat

Every age has its conventional notions of what poetry ought to be like, and the conventional notions of Emily Dickinson's day were that poetry should be close to prose in its grammar and syntax, and that its vocabulary should be more refined than that of ordinary speech. Thus Robert Louis Stevenson was outraged by the word "hatter" in a poem of Whitman's, and asserted that using such a word was not "literary tact." Emily Dickinson deliberately flouts both conventions. Her beat punctuation and offbeat syntax go with an abrupt and colloquial diction. The tang of her local speech comes out in such spellings as "Febuary" and "boquet," in such locutions as "it don't" and "it is him," and in such words as "heft" for "weight." Speaking of heaven, she writes:

> Yet certain am I of the spot
> As if the Checks were given –

meaning railway checks, the guarantee the conductor gives that one is proceeding to the right destination. Her editors altered this to "chart," which was a more conventionally poetic word, being slightly antique. Emily Dickinson could easily have provided such a word herself, but preferred to form her diction at a humorously twisted angle to the conventional expectations of the reader.

There is little in Emily Dickinson, then, of the feeling that a writer must come to terms with conventional language at all costs. When she meets an inadequacy in the English language she simply walks through it, as a child might do. If the dictionary does not provide an abstract noun for "giant," the poet will coin "gianture"; if the ordinary "diminution" does not give her enough sense of movement, she will substitute "diminuet." Similarly the fact that there is no singular form for "grass" or "hay" does not stop her from speaking of "every Grass," or from writing, to Higginson's horror:

> The Grass so little has to do
> I wish I were a Hay –

A similar teasing of the conventional reader's ear comes out in her slanting rhymes, which often have the effect of disappointing or letting down one's sense of an expected sound. At the same time even a conventional reader can see that her commonplace stanza forms could hardly achieve any variety of nuance without some irregularities. This is particularly true of the sinewy rhythm that syncopates against her rigid hymnbook meters and keeps them so far out of reach of monotony or doggerel:

> Those not live yet
> Who doubt to live again –
> "Again" is of a twice
> But this – is one –
> The Ship beneath the Draw
> Aground – is he?
> Death – so – the Hyphen of the Sea –
> Deep is the Schedule
> Of the Disk to be –
> Costumeless Consciousness –
> That is he –

In sophisticated poetry close attention is paid to the sounds of words: vowels and consonants are carefully balanced for assonance and variety, and we feel, when such poetry is successful, that we have the inevitably right words in their inevitably right order. In popular poetry there is a clearly marked rhythm and the words chosen to fill it up give approximately the intended meaning, but there is no sense of any *mot juste* or uniquely appropriate word. In the ballad, for example, we may have a great number of verbal variants of the same poem. Here again Emily Dickinson's practice is the popular, not the sophisticated one. For a great many of her poems she has provided alternative words, phrases, even whole lines, as though the rhythm, like a figured bass in music, allowed the editor or reader to establish his own text. Thus in the last line of one poem, "To meet so enabled a Man," we have "religious," "accomplished," "discerning," "accoutred," "established," and "conclusive" all suggested as alternates for "enabled." Another poem ends:

> And Kinsmen as divulgeless
> As throngs of Down –

with "Kindred as responsive," "Clans of Down," "And Pageants as impassive As Porcelain"—or, presumably, any combination of these—as possible variants. It is rather more disconcerting to find "New" suggested as an alternate for "Old" in a poem ending with a reference to "Our Old Neighbor–God."

What we find in Emily Dickinson's poetry, then, is a diffused vitality in rhythm and the free play of a lively and exhilarating mind, crackling with wit and sharp perception. These were clearly the qualities that she herself knew were there and especially prized. She asked Higginson simply whether her verse was "alive." As a poet, she is popular in the sense of being able, like Burns or Kipling or the early Wordsworth, to introduce poetry to readers who have had no previous experience of it. She has, on the other hand, a withdrawn consciousness and an intense intellectual energy that makes her almost esoteric, certainly often difficult.

In any case she seems, after her early valentines, to have reached her mature style almost in a single bound. It is otherwise with her prose, no doubt because we have so much more of it from her early years. Her schoolgirl letters, with their engaging mixture of child's prattle and adolescent's self-consciousness, show a Lamb-like gift for fantasy and a detached and humorous shrewdness. She speaks of other girls who "are perfect models of propriety," and remarks: "There 'most always are a few, whom the teachers look up to and regard as their satellites"—which is sharp observation for a fourteen-year-old. After her writing of poetry begins, her prose rhythm moves very close to verse. The first letter to Higginson is really a free verse poem; some of her

earlier poems were originally written as prose, and she often falls into her favorite metrical rhythms, as in the opening of a letter to Bowles: "I am so far from Land–To offer *you* the cup–it might some Sabbath come *my* turn–Of wine how solemn–full!", which is a short meter stanza. Her later letters show a remarkable command of the techniques of discontinuous prose: they were most carefully composed, and the appearance of random jottings is highly deceptive. Continuous or expository prose assumes an equality between writer and reader: the writer is putting all he has in front of us. Discontinuous prose, with gaps in the sense that only intuition can cross, assumes an aloofness on the writer's part, a sense of reserves of connection that we must make special efforts to reach. The aphoristic style of her later letters is, if slightly more frequent in Continental literatures, extremely rare in England or America, yet she seems to have developed it without models or influences.

> Her Grace is all she has –
> And that, so least displays –
> One Art to recognize, must be,
> Another Art, to praise.

III

THE MOST cursory glance at Emily Dickinson will reveal that she is a deeply religious poet, preoccupied, to the verge of obsession, with the themes of death and of immortality—the latter being, as she called it, the "Flood subject." Even in her use of the Bible, her most frequent references are to the passages in Corinthians and Revelation usually read at funeral services; and Paul's remark, that we now see in a riddle, translated as "through a glass darkly," is echoed in her recurrent use of the words "Riddle" and "Disc":

> Further than Guess can gallop
> Further than Riddle ride –
> Oh for a Disc to the Distance
> Between Ourselves and the Dead!

Yet another glance at her letters will also show that in her evangelical surroundings she steadily resisted all revivals, all spiritual exhortations, all the solicitous and charitable heat that, at home, at school and at church, was steadily turned on the uncommitted. Like Huckleberry Finn, whom she resembles in more ways than one, Emily Dickinson had a great respect for orthodox religion and morality, did not question the sincerity of those who practiced it, and even turned to it for help. But she never felt that the path of social conformity and assent to doctrine was her path. Her resistance gave her no feeling of superiority: even her schoolgirl letters are full of a wistful regret that she could not feel what her friends all asserted that they felt. As she recalled later: "When a Child and fleeing from Sacrament I could hear the Clergyman saying 'All who loved the Lord Jesus Christ–were asked to remain–.' My flight kept time to the Words." She belonged in the congregation but not in the Church.

Her elders referred her to the Bible: she read the Bible and took an immediate dislike to the deity that she calls "Burglar! Banker–Father!" —that is, the legal providential God who seems to ratify everything that is meaningless and cruel in life. She remarked to Higginson that her family were all religious except her, "and address an Eclipse, every morning–whom they call their 'Father'." She read with distaste the stories of Elisha and the bears ("I believe the love of God may be taught not to seem like bears"), of the sacrifice of Isaac, of the drowning of the world in a divine tantrum and the corresponding threat to burn it later:

> No vacillating God
> Created this Abode
> To put it out.

of Adam who was asserted to be alone responsible for his fall:

> Of Heaven above the firmest proof
> We fundamental know
> Except for it's marauding Hand
> It had been Heaven below.

The whole "punishing" aspect of religious doctrine struck her as "a doubtful solace finding tart response in the lower Mind," and she asks: "Why should we censure Othello, when the Criterion Lover says, 'Thou shalt have no other Gods before Me'?" That is, why blame Othello for being jealous when God tells us that he is himself? She concluded that "I do not respect 'doctrines,'" and added, with a touch of snobbery: "I wish the 'faith of the fathers' didn't wear brogans, and carry blue um-

brellas." In short, she took no care to distinguish the Father of Christianity from the cloud-whiskered scarecrow that Blake called Nobodaddy and Bernard Shaw an old man in the sky looking like the headmaster of an inferior public school.

The Son of God for her was also caught in this Father's legal machinery. "When Jesus tells us about his Father, we distrust him." She has a poem in which she compares the doctrine of the revelation of the Father in the Son to the courtship of Miles Standish, and another in which she speaks with contempt of the "some day we'll understand" rationalizings of suffering:

> I shall know why – when Time is over –
> And I have ceased to wonder why –
> Christ will explain each separate anguish
> In the fair schoolroom of the sky –

At other times, she seems to accept Jesus as everything that Christianity says he is. Thus: "That the Divine has been human is at first an unheeded solace, but it shelters without our consent." It seems clear that her relation to the Nonconformist faith in which she was brought up was itself nonconformist, and that it would have violated her conscience ever to have made either a final acceptance or a final rejection of that faith. Her method, the reverse of Tennyson's in *In Memoriam,* was to prove where she could not believe. She did not want to repudiate her faith but to struggle with it. She was fascinated by the story of the "bewildered Gymnast" Jacob, wrestling with and finally defeating an angel who—according to a literal reading of the text which the poet promptly adopted—turned out to be God, and to this story she reverts more than once in her letters. When she compares the Bible unfavorably with Orpheus, whose sermon captivated and did not condemn; when she speaks of Cupid as an authentic deity and asks if God is Love's adversary, she is saying that there is another kind of religious experience that counterbalances, but does not necessarily contradict, the legal and doctrinal Christianity which she had been taught. As she says with a calculated ambivalence: " 'We thank thee Oh Father' for these strange Minds, that enamor us against thee."

This other kind of religious experience is a state of heightened consciousness often called "Transport" and associated with the word "Circumference," when the poet feels directly in communion with nature and in a state of "identity"—another frequent term—with it. Nature is then surrounded by the circumference of human consciousness, and such a world is Paradise, the Biblical Eden, a nature with a human shape and meaning, a garden for man. "Home is the definition of God," and home is what is inside the circumference of one's being. In this state the mind feels immortal: "To include, is to be touchless, for Ourself cannot cease." It also enters into a condition of unity or oneness which is partly what the word identity means. "*One* is a dainty sum! One bird, one cage, one flight; one song in those far woods, as yet suspected by faith only!" Similarly the poet can speak, without any violation of grammar, of a "Myriad Daisy" (compare Wordsworth's "tree, of many, one"[1]), and, with Emerson, of the single Man who is all men:

> What News will do when every **Man**
> Shall comprehend as one
> And not in all the Universe
> A thing to tell remain?

Such an experience is based, not on the compelling argument, but on the infinitely suggestive image, or "emblem" as she calls it. "Emblem is immeasurable," she says, and speaks of human beings as the "trembling Emblems" of love. The language of emblems is as rational as the language of doctrine, but its logic is the poetic logic of metaphor, not the abstract logic of syllogism.

Circumference in its turn is the "Bride of Awe," and "Awe" is her most frequent name for the God that is reached by this experience. The human circumference is surrounded by a greater consciousness, to which the poet is related as bride to bridegroom, as sea to moon, as daisy to sun, as brook to ocean—all recurring images. Sometimes the poet uses the word "peninsula" to describe an individual consciousness projecting into experience and attached to an invisible mainland. Invisible, because "No

---

[1] See Wordsworth, "Ode: Intimations of Immortality from Recollections of Early Childhood," l. 52.

man saw awe," any more than we can see our own backbones. Awe is a lover, incarnate in the bee who loves the rose and the harebell, and a divine lover for whom a feminine poet may make the response of a bacchante or of a vestal virgin with equal appropriateness. Thus Emily Dickinson may say both:

> Circumference thou Bride of Awe
> Possessing thou shalt be
> Possessed by every hallowed Knight
> That dares to covet thee

and (where "their" means the world of her bodily impulses):

> To their apartment deep
> No ribaldry may creep
> Untumbled this abode
> By any man but God —

Awe is not a dogmatic God, and is tolerant enough to satisfy not only the poet's Christian longings but the paganism that makes her feel that there ought to be a god for every mood of the soul and every department of nature:

> If "All is possible with" him
> As he besides concedes
> He will refund us finally
> Our confiscated Gods —

In fact he may even be female, a sheltering mother. "I always ran Home to Awe when a child . . . He was an awful Mother, but I liked him better than none."

In Christian terms, this divine Awe, as she well understood, is the third person of the Trinity, the Holy Spirit, symbolized in the Bible by two of her favorite images, the bird and the wind, the giver of life to nature and of inspiration to humanity, the creative force that makes the poet's verses "breathe," and the "Conscious Ear" that imagination hears with. The conventional Biblical image for the Holy Spirit is the dove, and the poet, picturing herself as Noah sailing the flood of experience, associates the dove who brought him news of land with the fact that the name of another well-known navigator, Christopher Columbus, also means dove:

> Thrice to the floating casement
> The Patriarch's bird returned,
> Courage! My brave Columba!
> There may yet be *Land!*

To this person of God, Emily Dickinson continually turned when other things in Christianity puzzled her imagination or were rejected by her reason. She seems to associate him with the power which "stands in the Bible between the Kingdom and the Glory, because it is wilder than either of them." In the detached comment on the Atonement which she superimposes on the famous proverb, "God tempers the wind to the shorn lamb," the "Wind" is the power that escapes from the breakdown of doctrinal machinery:

> How ruthless are the gentle –
> How cruel are the kind –
> God broke his contract to his Lamb
> To qualify the Wind –

In a congratulatory message on the occasion of a wedding, the divine power of making one flesh out of two bodies is associated, not with the Father or the Son, but with the wind that bloweth where it listeth:

> The Clock strikes one that just struck two –
> Some schism in the Sum –
> A Vagabond from Genesis
> Has wrecked the Pendulum –

The confusion with a female principle, as when she says that "the Little Boy in the Trinity had no Grandmama, only a Holy Ghost," is at least as old as the apocryphal Gospels, where Jesus speaks of the Holy Spirit as his mother. When she says, "The Bible dealt with the Centre, not with the Circumference," she means apparently that the Bible considers man in his ordinary state of isolation, separated from God by a gulf that only God can cross. Such a God is thought of as coming from the outside; but while God is known "By his intrusion," his movement in the human soul is to be compared rather to the tides moving in the sea. "They say that God is everywhere, and yet we always think of Him as somewhat of a recluse." If so, it takes a recluse to find him, and to discover him as the inmost secret of consciousness.

The first fact of Emily Dickinson's experience, then, was that whatever the Bible may mean by Paradise or Eden, the world of lost innocence and happiness symbolized by the unfallen Adam and Eve, it is something that is already given in experience. It is attainable;

the poet has attained it; it is not, therefore, a "superhuman site," nor could it survive the extinction of the human mind. Earth is heaven, whether heaven is heaven or not: the supernatural is only the natural disclosed: the charms of the heaven in the bush are superseded by the heaven in the hand—to paraphrase almost at random. To her the essence of the Gospel was the proclamation of the Paradisal vision in such passages as "consider the lilies." But the Bible also speaks of regaining this Paradise and living in it eternally after death. If so, then the experience of Paradise in life is identical with the experience of eternity.

The people we ordinarily call mystics are the people for whom this is true. Eternity to them is not endless time, but a real present, a "now" which absorbs all possible hereafters. Emily Dickinson also often speaks with the mystics of death as a rejoining of heaven, of "Forever" as "composed of Nows," of an eternal state of consciousness symbolized by a continuous summer and noon, of a coming "Aurora," a dawn that will have no night. But in her background there were two powerful antimystical tendencies at work. One was the rationalism of her generation; the other was the Puritanism in which she had been reared, with its insistence that the divine will was inscrutable, that it made sense only to itself, not to man, and that no human experience could transcend the limits of fallen humanity. For Emily Dickinson, therefore, the identity between the experience of circumference she had had and the postmortal eternity taught in the Bible remained a matter of "inference." It could be held by faith or hope but not by direct knowledge. This "inference" became the central issue in her struggle with her faith, a fact which she expresses most poignantly when she says: "Consciousness is the only home of which we *now* know. That sunny adverb had been enough, were it not foreclosed."

Paradoxically, the experience of unity with God and nature also produces a sense of division, or "bisection" as the poet often calls it, in the mind. Part of oneself is certainly mortal; part may not be, though even it must also go through death. In a poem beginning "Conscious am I in my Chamber" she speaks of the indwelling Spirit as the immortal part of herself; sometimes the distinction is between the poet herself and her soul; sometimes, and more commonly, it is between the soul and the mind or consciousness. "We know that the mind of the Heart must live," she says, and a letter to her seems like immortality because "it is the mind alone without corporeal friend." She also speaks of the body as a "trinket" which is worn but not owned, and in one striking poem the soul is attended by a "single Hound" which is its own identity. But she never seemed to accept the Platonic view that the soul is immortal by nature. If the first fact of her experience is a vision of earth as heaven, the second fact is that this vision is "evanescent," comes and goes unpredictably, and, so far as experience itself goes, ceases entirely at death. It is significant, therefore, that Emily Dickinson should so often symbolize her vision as a temporary and abnormal state of drunkenness:

> Inebriate of Air – am I –
> And Debauchee of Dew –
> Reeling – thro endless summer days –
> From inns of Molten Blue –

The liquor responsible for this state is usually called rum, or some synonym like "Domingo," "Manzanilla," or "Jamaica." When it is the more traditional wine, the word "sacrament," as in the poem "Exhiliration – is within," is seldom far away, for such imaginative drunkenness is a genuine communion. Still, it can lead to hangovers, "With a to-morrow knocking," and, whatever it is or means, it goes and is replaced by ordinary experience.

Ordinary experience is the sacramental or ecstatic experience turned inside-out. Here the mind is not a circumference at all, but a center, and the only circumference is an indifferent and unresponsive Nature – "Nature – in Her monstrous House." We may still realize that such "Vastness – is but the Shadow of the Brain which casts it," but in this state the brain cannot cast any other shadow. Where the mind is a center and nature the circumference, there is no place for any divinity: that has vanished somewhere beyond the sky or beyond life. This is the state of "Those Evenings of the Brain," in which the body, so far from being a circumference incorporating its ex-

perience, is a "magic Prison," sealed against all intimations of immortality:

> The Rumor's Gate was shut so tight
> Before my Mind was sown,
> Not even a Prognostic's Push
> Could make a Dent thereon –

Like Blake, with whom she has been compared ever since Higginson's preface to the 1890 volume, Emily Dickinson shows us two contrary states of the human soul, a vision of innocence and a vision of "experience," or ordinary life. One is a vision of "Presence," the other of "Place"; in one the primary fact of life is partnership, in the other it is parting. Thus she may say, depending on the context, both "Were Departure Separation, there would be neither Nature nor Art, for there would be no World" and

> Parting is all we know of heaven,
> And all we need of hell.

But she has nothing of Blake's social vision, and the state that he associates with child labor, Negro slavery, prostitution, and war she associates only with loneliness.

Her two states are often associated with summer and winter, or, less frequently, with day and night. Often, especially in poems addressed to Sue, she speaks of a "Summer – Sister – Seraph!" who inhabits the paradisal world, in contrast to herself as a "dark sister," a "Druid" spirit of winter, frost and the north, waiting for the birds to come back, like Noah's dove, to tell her of a sunnier world beyond. Hence the times of year that have the greatest significance for her are the equinoxes, the March when the birds return and the white dress of winter breaks into color, and the moment in late summer when the invisible presence of autumn enters the year and makes "a Druidic Difference" in nature. The association of this latter period with the moment at which human life faces death makes it particularly the point at which the two lines of her imagination converge:

> God made a little Gentian –
> It tried – to be a Rose –
> And failed – and all the Summer laughed –
> But just before the Snows

There rose a Purple Creature –
That ravished all the Hill –
And Summer hid her Forehead –
And Mockery – was still –

The Frosts were her condition –
The Tyrian would not come
Until the North – invoke it –
Creator – Shall I – bloom?

Emily Dickinson is an impressionist in the sense that she tends to organize her visual experience by color rather than outline, and purple, the color of mourning and of triumph, is the central symbol for her of the junction between life and death. Various synonyms of it such as "Iodine," "Amethyst" and the "Tyrian" above run through her writings.

At times the poet speaks of the paradisal vision as being, not only a "stimulant" given in cases of despair or stupor, but a light by which all the rest of life can be lived, as providing a final answer to the question raised by its passing:

Why Bliss so scantily disburse –
Why Paradise defer –
Why Floods be served to Us – in Bowls –
I speculate no more –

At other times, in such poems as those beginning "Why – do they shut Me out of Heaven?" and "If I'm lost – now," she laments over a lost vision that hints at a still greater loss. Such sudden changes of mood would be inconsistent if she were arguing a thesis, but, being a poet, what she is doing is expressing a variety of possible imaginative reactions to a central unsolved riddle. The fact that her vision is transient sharpens the intensity of her relation to it, for

In Insecurity to lie
Is Joy's insuring quality.

Two recurring words in her poems are "suspense" and "expanse." The former refers to the shadow that falls between an experience and the realization that it has happened, the shadow that adumbrates death; the latter to the possession of the spiritual body which, for us, brings vision but not peace. "These sudden intimacies with Immortality, are expanse – not Peace – as Lightning at our feet, instills a foreign Landscape." She deals mainly with the

virtues of faith, hope, and love, but her life had shown her that love, which normally tends to union, may incorporate a great deal of its opposite, which is renunciation. Similarly with faith and hope: "Faith is *Doubt*," she says, and hope is the thinnest crust of ice over despair:

Could Hope inspect her Basis
Her Craft were done –
Has a fictitious Charter
Or it has none –

Like the Puritans before her, who refused to believe that their own righteousness would necessarily impress God into recognizing them, Emily Dickinson refused to believe that her own vision of Paradise guaranteed the existence of Paradise, even though she had nothing else to go on. And—Puritan to the last—she even faced the possibility that the Spirit of life within her might turn out to be Death, hence the ambiguous tone of such poems as "Doubt Me! My Dim Companion!" and "Struck, was I, nor yet by Lightning." She told Sue that if Jesus did not recognize her at the last day, "there is a darker spirit will not disown it's child." She means death, not the devil, though her pose recalls the demonic figures in Hawthorne. There are many poems about the physical experience of dying, some tranquil, some agonizing, some dealing with death by execution, by warfare, by drowning—in at least two poems the poet is an Andromeda swallowed by a sea monster. The region of death to be entered, or traversed, is usually a sea, sometimes a forest, or a "Maelstrom – in the Sky," or simply "a wild Night and a new Road," and in "I never told the buried gold," it is an underworld guarded by a dragon.

The world of death is not one that we have to die to explore: it is there all the time, the end and final cause of the vision of the center, just as Awe is the end and final cause of the vision of circumference. "I suppose there are depths in every Consciousness," she says, "from which we cannot rescue ourselves – to which none can go with us – which represent to us Mortally – the Adventure of Death." Some of her psychological poems take us into this buried jungle of the mind. There are a few about ghosts, where the two aspects of the self are treated in the vein of Henry James's *The Jolly*

Corner. But Emily Dickinson's sharp inquiring mind has little in common with the ectoplasmic, and these poems impress us as made rather than born. A more genuine fear comes out at the end of this:

> Remembrance has a Rear and Front –
> 'Tis something like a House –
> It has a Garret also
> For Refuse and the Mouse.
>
> Besides the deepest Cellar
> That ever Mason laid –
> Look to it by it's Fathoms
> Ourselves be not pursued –

This is as near to hell as she ever brings us, as the original version of the last two lines indicates:

> Leave me not ever there alone
> Oh thou Almighty God!

Yet even such a hell as this has a place and a function. Its presence is in an odd way the basis of vision itself, for "the unknown is the largest need of the intellect," and "could we see all we hope – there would be madness near." Emily Dickinson has a poem about Enoch and Elijah, the two Biblical prophets who were taken directly to heaven, but the figure she identifies herself with is Moses, standing on the mountain top with the wilderness of death on one side and the Promised Land on the other, able to see his Paradise if not to enter it:

> Such are the inlets of the mind –
> His outlets – would you see
> Ascend with me the Table Land
> Of immortality –

Many, perhaps most, of Emily Dickinson's readers will simply take their favorite poems from her and leave the rest, with little curiosity about the larger structure of her imagination. For many, too, the whole bent of her mind will seem irresponsible or morbid. It is perhaps as well that this should be so. "It is essential to the sanity of mankind," the poet remarks, "that each one should think the other crazy." There are more serious reasons: a certain perversity, an instinct for looking in the opposite direction from the rest of society, is frequent among creative minds. When the United States was beginning to develop an entrepreneur capitalism on a scale unprecedented in history, Thoreau retired to Walden to discover the meaning of the word "property," and found that it meant only what was proper or essential to unfettered human life. When the Civil War was beginning to force on America the troubled vision of its revolutionary destiny, Emily Dickinson retired to her garden to remain, like Wordsworth's skylark, within the kindred points of heaven and home. She will always have readers who will know what she means when she says: "Each of us gives or takes heaven in corporeal person, for each of us has the skill of life." More restless minds will not relax from taking thought for the morrow to spend much time with her. But even some of them may still admire the energy and humor with which she fought her angel until she had forced out of him the crippling blessing of genius.

NOTE

The texts of the poems and letters that follow are taken from the Johnson edition, and the poems bear the numbers assigned to them in that edition, where they are arranged in chronological order. Poems in this selection range in date from No. 9, written about 1858, to No. 1645, written about 1885, the dates of those from No. 1651 to the end being unknown.

As explained in the Introduction, Emily Dickinson provided alternative words, phrases, or even whole lines, on the margins of her manuscripts of some of the poems, thus enabling the reader in a sense to construct his own text. In the following selection all the poems are printed in their original forms, ignoring all the suggested alternatives except in one or two cases. For full information about variant readings, as well as for the dates of the individual poems, the student is referred to the Johnson edition.

READING SUGGESTIONS

The definitive edition of Emily Dickinson consists of *The Poems of Emily Dickinson* (1955), in three volumes, edited by Thomas H. Johnson, and *The Letters of Emily Dickinson* (1958), in three volumes, edited by Thomas H. Johnson and Theodora W.

Ward, and published by the Belknap Press of Harvard University Press.

The best biographical and critical studies are:
GEORGE F. WHICHER, *This Was a Poet: A Critical Biography of Emily Dickinson* (1938).
RICHARD CHASE, *Emily Dickinson* (1951), in the American Men of Letters series.
THOMAS H. JOHNSON, *Emily Dickinson: An Interpretative Biography* (1955).
CHARLES B. ANDERSON, *Emily Dickinson's Poetry: Stairway of Surprise* (1960).

JAY LEYDA, *The Years and Hours of Emily Dickinson* (1960).

Owing to the piecemeal way in which Emily Dickinson's writings were given to the world, the earlier editions and critical studies are now somewhat dated, though Genevieve Taggard's *The Life and Mind of Emily Dickinson* (1930) is written with genuine feeling. The story of the disputes surrounding the publication of the early editions is told in Millicent Todd Bingham's *Ancestors' Brocades* (1945).

POEMS

9

Through lane it lay – thro' bramble –
Through clearing and thro' wood –
Banditti often passed us
Upon the lonely road.

The wolf came peering curious –
The owl looked puzzled down –
The serpent's satin figure
Glid stealthily along –

The tempests touched our garments –
The lightning's poinards gleamed –   10
Fierce from the Crag above us
The hungry Vulture screamed –

The satyrs fingers beckoned –
The valley murmured "Come" –
These were the mates –
This was the road
These children fluttered home.

24

There is a morn by men unseen –
Whose maids upon remoter green
Keep their Seraphic May –
And all day long, with dance and game,
And gambol I may never name –
Employ their holiday.

Here to light measure, move the feet
Which walk no more the village street –
Nor by the wood are found –
Here are the birds that sought the sun   10
When last year's distaff idle hung
And summer's brows were bound.

Ne'er saw I such a wondrous scene –
Ne'er such a ring on such a green –
Nor so serene array –
As if the stars some summer night
Should swing their cups of Chrysolite –
And revel till the day –

Like thee to dance – like thee to sing –
People upon that mystic green –   20
I ask, each new May Morn.
I wait thy far, fantastic bells –
Announcing me in other dells –
Unto the different dawn!

30

Adrift! A little boat adrift!
And night is coming down!
Will *no* one guide a little boat
Unto the nearest town?

So Sailors say – on yesterday –
Just as the dusk was brown
One little boat gave up it's strife
And gurgled down and down.

So angels say – on yesterday –
Just as the dawn was red   10
One little boat – o'erspent with gales –
Retrimmed it's masts – redecked it's sails –
And shot – exultant on!

49

I never lost as much but twice,
And that was in the sod.
Twice have I stood a beggar
Before the door of God!

Angels – twice descending
Reimbursed my store –
Burglar! Banker – Father!
I am poor once more!

55

By Chivalries as tiny,
A Blossom, or a Book,
The seeds of smiles are planted –
Which blossom in the dark.

67

Success is counted sweetest
By those who ne'er succeed.
To comprehend a nectar
Requires sorest need.

Not one of all the purple Host
Who took the Flag today
Can tell the definition
So clear of Victory

As he defeated – dying –
On whose forbidden ear   10
The distant strains of triumph
Burst agonized and clear!

80

Our lives are Swiss –
So still – so Cool –
Till some odd afternoon
The Alps neglect their Curtains
And we look farther on!

Italy stands the other side!
While like a guard between –
The solemn Alps –
The siren Alps
Forever intervene!   10

81

We should not mind so small a flower –
Except it quiet bring

Our little garden that we lost
Back to the Lawn again.

So spicy her Carnations nod –
So drunken, reel her Bees –
So silver steal a hundred flutes
From out a hundred trees –

That whoso sees this little flower
By faith may clear behold   10
The Bobolinks around the throne
And Dandelions gold.

94

Angels, in the early morning
May be seen the Dews among,
Stooping – plucking – smiling – flying –
Do the Buds to them belong?

Angels, when the sun is hottest
May be seen the sands among,
Stooping – plucking – sighing – flying –
Parched the flowers they bear along.

119

Talk with prudence to a Beggar
Of "Potosi," and the mines!
Reverently, to the Hungry
Of your viands, and your wines!

Cautious, hint to any Captive
You have passed enfranchized feet!
Anecdotes of air in Dungeons
Have sometimes proved deadly sweet!

128

Bring me the sunset in a cup,
Reckon the morning's flagon's up
And say how many Dew,
Tell me how far the morning leaps –
Tell me what time the weaver sleeps
Who spun the breadths of blue!

Write me how many notes there be
In the new Robin's extasy
Among astonished boughs –
How many trips the Tortoise makes –   10
How many cups the Bee partakes,
The Debauchee of Dews!

POEMS.   **67.** Published anonymously, with several alterations, in *A Masque of Poets* (1878), ed. by Thomas Niles (see Introduction).

119. 2. "Potosi": a town in Bolivia famous for its silver mines.

Also, who laid the Rainbow's piers,
Also, who leads the docile spheres
By withes of supple blue?
Whose fingers string the stalactite –
Who counts the wampum of the night
To see that none is due?

Who built this little Alban House
And shut the windows down so close   20
My spirit cannot see?
Who'll let me out some gala day
With implements to fly away,
Passing Pomposity?

141

Some, too fragile for winter winds
The thoughtful grave encloses –
Tenderly tucking them in from frost
Before their feet are cold.

Never the treasures in her nest
The cautious grave exposes,
Building where schoolboy dare not look,
And sportsman is not bold.

This covert have all the children
Early aged, and often cold,   10
Sparrows, unnoticed by the Father –
Lambs for whom time had not a fold.

160

Just lost, when I was saved!
Just felt the world go by!
Just girt me for the onset with Eternity,
When breath blew back,
And on the other side
I heard recede the disappointed tide!

Therefore, as One returned, I feel,
Odd secrets of the line to tell!
Some Sailor, skirting foreign shores –
Some pale Reporter, from the awful doors   10
Before the Seal!

Next time, to stay!
Next time, the things to see
By Ear unheard,
Unscrutinized by Eye –

Next time, to tarry,
While the Ages steal –
Slow tramp the Centuries,
And the Cycles wheel!

187

How many times these low feet staggered –
Only the soldered mouth can tell –
Try – can you stir the awful rivet –
Try – can you lift the hasps of steel!

Stroke the cool forehead – hot so often –
Lift – if you care – the listless hair –
Handle the adamantine fingers
Never a thimble – more – shall wear –

Buzz the dull flies – on the chamber window –   9
Brave – shines the sun through the freckled pane –
Fearless – the cobweb swings from the ceiling –
Indolent Housewife – in Daisies – lain!

214

I taste a liquor never brewed –
From Tankards scooped in Pearl –
Not all the Frankfort Berries
Yield such an Alcohol!

Inebriate of Air – am I –
And Debauchee of Dew –
Reeling – thro endless summer days –
From inns of Molten Blue –

When "Landlords" turn the drunken Bee
Out of the Foxglove's door –   10
When Butterflies – renounce their "drams" –
I shall but drink the more!

Till Seraphs swing their snowy Hats –
And Saints – to windows run –
To see the little Tippler
From Manzanilla come!

216

Safe in their Alabaster Chambers –
Untouched by Morning
And untouched by Noon –

214. 3. **Frankfort Berries:** explained by the alternative reading, "Vats upon the Rhine." 16. **Manzanilla:** Manzanillo, a city in Cuba, clearly associated here with rum. Most readers would prefer the alternative reading, "Leaning against the – Sun –." 216. The revision of this poem appears to have been the result of criticism by Sue. The earlier version was published anonymously in the Springfield *Daily Republican* in 1862.

128. 19. **Alban House:** a house built of Alban stone, much used in ancient Rome. 141. 11. **Sparrows:** Cf. Luke 12:6. 160. 11. **Seal:** Cf. Matt. 27:66; cf. No. 322. 13–15. Next . . . **Eye:** Cf. I Cor. 2:9; II Cor. 12:3–4.

Sleep the meek members of the Resurrection –
Rafter of satin,
And Roof of stone.

Light laughs the breeze
In her Castle above them –
Babbles the Bee in a stolid Ear,
Pipe the Sweet Birds in ignorant cadence –   10
Ah, what sagacity perished here!

version of 1859

Safe in their Alabaster Chambers –
Untouched by Morning –
And untouched by Noon –
Lie the meek members of the Resurrection –
Rafter of Satin – and Roof of Stone!

Grand go the Years – in the Crescent – above
    them –
Worlds scoop their Arcs –
And Firmaments – row –
Diadems – drop – and Doges – surrender –
Soundless as dots – on a Disc of Snow –   10

version of 1861

241

I like a look of Agony,
Because I know it's true –
Men do not sham Convulsion,
Nor simulate, a Throe –

The Eyes glaze once – and that is Death –
Impossible to feign
The Beads upon the Forehead
By homely Anguish strung.

249

Wild Nights – Wild Nights!
Were I with thee
Wild Nights should be
Our luxury!

Futile – the Winds –
To a Heart in port –
Done with the Compass –
Done with the Chart!

Rowing in Eden –
Ah, the Sea!   10
Might I but moor – Tonight –
In Thee!

258

There's a certain Slant of light,
Winter Afternoons –
That oppresses, like the Heft
Of Cathedral Tunes –

Heavenly Hurt, it gives us –
We can find no scar,
But internal difference,
Where the Meanings, are –

None may teach it – Any –
'Tis the Seal Despair –   10
An imperial affliction
Sent us of the Air –

When it comes, the Landscape listens –
Shadows – hold their breath –
When it goes, 'tis like the Distance
On the look of Death –

266

This – is the land – the Sunset washes –
These – are the Banks of the Yellow Sea –
Where it rose – or whither it rushes –
These – are the Western Mystery!

Night after Night
Her purple traffic
Strews the landing with Opal Bales –
Merchantmen – poise upon Horizons –
Dip – and vanish like Orioles!

272

I breathed enough to take the Trick –
And now, removed from Air –
I simulate the Breath, so well –
That One, to be quite sure –

The Lungs are stirless – must descend
Among the Cunning Cells –
And touch the Pantomime – Himself,
How numb, the Bellows feels!

274

The only Ghost I ever saw
Was dressed in Mechlin – so –
He had no sandal on his foot –
And stepped like flakes of snow –

266. 6. **purple traffic:** Cf. Tennyson, "Locksley Hall," 121–22.
274. 2. **Mechlin:** the English name for the town of Malines in
France, famous for fine lace.

His Mien, was soundless, like the Bird –
But rapid – like the Roe –
His fashions, quaint, Mosaic –
Or haply, Mistletoe –

His conversation – seldom –
His laughter, like the Breeze   10
That dies away in Dimples
Among the pensive Trees –

Our interview – was transient –
Of me, himself was shy –
And God forbid I look behind –
Since that appalling Day!

280

I felt a Funeral, in my Brain,
And Mourners to and fro
Kept treading – treading – till it seemed
That Sense was breaking through –

And when they all were seated,
A Service, like a Drum –
Kept beating – beating – till I thought
My Mind was going numb –

And then I heard them lift a Box
And creak across my Soul   10
With those same Boots of Lead, again,
Then Space – began to toll,

As all the Heavens were a Bell,
And Being, but an Ear,
And I, and Silence, some strange Race
Wrecked, solitary, here –

And then a Plank in Reason, broke,
And I dropped down, and down –
And hit a World, at every plunge,
And Finished knowing – then –   20

281

'Tis so appalling – it exhilirates –
So over Horror, it half Captivates –
The Soul stares after it, secure –
To know the worst, leaves no dread more –

To scan a Ghost, is faint –
But grappling, conquers it –
How easy, Torment, now –
Suspense kept sawing so –

The Truth, is Bald, and Cold –
But that will hold –   10
If any are not sure –
We show them – prayer –
But we, who know,
Stop hoping, now –

Looking at Death, is Dying –
Just let go the Breath –
And not the pillow at your Cheek
So Slumbereth –

Others, Can wrestle –
Your's, is done –   20
And so of Wo, bleak dreaded – come,
It sets the Fright at liberty –
And Terror's free –
Gay, Ghastly, Holiday!

287

A Clock stopped –
Not the Mantel's –
Geneva's farthest skill
Cant put the puppet bowing –
That just now dangled still –

An awe came on the Trinket!
The Figures hunched, with pain –
Then quivered out of Decimals –
Into Degreeless Noon –

It will not stir for Doctor's –   10
This Pendulum of snow –
The Shopman importunes it –
While cool – concernless No –

Nods from the Gilded pointers –
Nods from the Seconds slim –
Decades of Arrogance between
The Dial life –
And Him –

292

If your Nerve, deny you –
Go above your Nerve –
He can lean against the Grave,
If he fear to swerve –

That's a steady posture –
Never any bend
Held of those Brass arms –
Best Giant made –

7–8. His . . . Mistletoe: He reminded one of the quaint, stylized figures in Byzantine mosaics, or, perhaps, of the rites of the Druids, connected with the mistletoe. Cf. No. 1068.

287. 3. Geneva's: Geneva, Switzerland, famous for clocks and watches.

If your Soul seesaw –
Lift the Flesh door –   10
The Poltroon wants Oxygen –
Nothing more –

303

The Soul selects her own Society –
Then – shuts the Door –
To her divine Majority –
Present no more –

Unmoved – she notes the Chariots – pausing –
At her low Gate –
Unmoved – an Emperor be kneeling
Upon her Mat –

I've known her – from an ample nation –
Choose One –   10
Then – close the Valves of her attention –
Like Stone –

305

The difference between Despair
And Fear – is like the One
Between the instant of a Wreck –
And when the Wreck has been –

The Mind is smooth – no Motion –
Contented as the Eye
Upon the Forehead of a Bust –
That knows – it cannot see –

306

The Soul's Superior instants
Occur to Her – alone –
When friend – and Earth's occasion
Have infinite withdrawn –

Or She – Herself – ascended
To too remote a Hight
For lower Recognition
Than Her Omnipotent –

This Mortal Abolition
Is seldom – but as fair   10
As Apparition – subject
To Autocratic Air –

Eternity's disclosure
To favorites – a few –
Of the Colossal substance
Of Immortality

311

It sifts from Leaden Sieves –
It powders all the Wood.
It fills with Alabaster Wool
The Wrinkles of the Road –

It makes an Even Face
Of Mountain, and of Plain –
Unbroken Forehead from the East
Unto the East again –

It reaches to the Fence –
It wraps it Rail by Rail   10
Till it is lost in Fleeces –
It deals Celestial Vail

To Stump, and Stack – and Stem –
A Summer's empty Room –
Acres of Joints, where Harvests were,
Recordless, but for them –

It Ruffles Wrists of Posts
As Ankles of a Queen –
Then stills it's Artisans – like Ghosts –
Denying they have been –   20

322

There came a Day at Summer's full,
Entirely for me –
I thought that such were for the Saints,
Where Resurrections – be –

The Sun, as common, went abroad,
The flowers, accustomed, blew,
As if no soul the solstice passed
That maketh all things new –

The time was scarce profaned, by speech –
The symbol of a word   10
Was needless, as at Sacrament,
The Wardrobe – of our Lord –

Each was to each The Sealed Church,
Permitted to commune this – time –
Lest we too awkward show
At Supper of the Lamb.

The Hours slid fast – as Hours will,
Clutched tight, by greedy hands –
So faces on two Decks, look back,
Bound to opposing lands –   20

322. 8. new: Cf. Rev. 21:5.   **11. needless:** i.e., at Sacrament, where the Word becomes Flesh, no conception of clothing is needed; cf. John 20:5–7.   **13. Sealed Church:** Cf. Rev. 7:3.

And so when all the time had leaked,
Without external sound
Each bound the Other's Crucifix –
We gave no other Bond –

Sufficient troth, that we shall rise –
Deposed – at length, the Grave –
To that new Marriage,
Justified – through Calvaries of Love –

341

After great pain, a formal feeling comes –
The Nerves sit ceremonious, like Tombs –
The stiff Heart questions was it He, that bore,
And Yesterday, or Centuries before?

The Feet, mechanical, go round –
Of Ground, or Air, or Ought –
A Wooden way
Regardless grown,
A Quartz contentment, like a stone –

This is the Hour of Lead –   10
Remembered, if outlived,
As Freezing persons, recollect the Snow –
First – Chill – then Stupor – then the letting go –

346

Not probable – The barest Chance –
A smile too few – a word too much
And far from Heaven as the Rest –
The Soul so close on Paradise –

What if the Bird from journey far –
Confused by Sweets – as Mortals – are –
Forget the secret of His wing
And perish – but a Bough between –
Oh, Groping feet –
Oh Phantom Queen!   10

358

If any sink, assure that this, now standing –
Failed like Themselves – and conscious that it rose –
Grew by the Fact, and not the Understanding
How Weakness passed – or Force – arose –

Tell that the Worst, is easy in a Moment –
Dread, but the Whizzing, before the Ball –
When the Ball enters, enters Silence –
Dying – annuls the power to kill.

378

I saw no Way – The Heavens were stitched –
I felt the Columns close –
The Earth reversed her Hemispheres –
I touched the Universe –

And back it slid – and I alone –
A Speck upon a Ball –
Went out upon Circumference –
Beyond the Dip of Bell –

384

No Rack can torture me –
My Soul – at Liberty –
Behind this mortal Bone
There knits a bolder One –

You Cannot prick with saw –
Nor pierce with Cimitar –
Two Bodies – therefore be –
Bind One – The Other fly –

The Eagle of his Nest
No easier divest –   10
And gain the Sky
Than mayest Thou –

Except Thyself may be
Thine Enemy –
Captivity is Consciousness –
So's Liberty.

398

I had not minded – Walls –
Were Universe – one Rock –
And far I heard his silver Call
The other side the Block –

I'd tunnel – till my Groove
Pushed sudden thro' to his –
Then my face take her Recompense –
The looking in his Eyes –

But 'tis a single Hair –
A filament – a law –   10
A Cobweb – wove in Adamant –
A Battlement – of Straw –

A limit like the Vail
Unto the Lady's face –
But every Mesh – a Citadel –
And Dragons – in the Crease –

384. 8. Bind . . . fly: Cf. Lev. 14:49–53.

410

The first Day's Night had come –
And grateful that a thing
So terrible – had been endured –
I told my Soul to sing –

She said her Strings were snapt –
Her Bow – to Atoms blown –
And so to mend her – gave me work
Until another Morn –

And then – a Day as huge
As Yesterdays in pairs,   10
Unrolled it's horror in my face –
Until it blocked my eyes –

My Brain – begun to laugh –
I mumbled – like a fool –
And tho' 'tis Years ago – that Day –
My Brain keeps giggling – still.

And Something's odd – within –
That person that I was –
And this One – do not feel the same –
Could it be Madness – this?   20

441

This is my letter to the World
That never wrote to Me –
The simple News that Nature told –
With tender Majesty

Her Message is committed
To Hands I cannot see –
For love of Her – Sweet – countrymen –
Judge tenderly – of Me

448

This was a Poet – It is That
Distills amazing sense
From ordinary Meanings –
And Attar so immense

From the familiar species
That perished by the Door –
We wonder it was not Ourselves
Arrested it – before –

Of Pictures, the Discloser –
The Poet – it is He –   10
Entitles Us – by Contrast –
To ceaseless Poverty –

Of Portion – so unconscious –
The Robbing – could not harm –
Himself – to Him – a Fortune –
Exterior – to Time –

457

Sweet – safe – Houses –
Glad – gay – Houses –
Sealed so stately tight –
Lids of Steel – on Lids of Marble –
Locking Bare feet out –

Brooks of Plush – in Banks of Satin
Not so softly fall
As the laughter – and the whisper –
From their People Pearl –

No Bald Death – affront their Parlors –   10
No Bold Sickness come
To deface their Stately Treasures –
Anguish – and the Tomb –

Hum by – in Muffled Coaches –
Lest they – wonder Why –
Any – for the Press of Smiling –
Interrupt – to die –

465

I heard a Fly buzz – when I died –
The Stillness in the Room
Was like the Stillness in the Air –
Between the Heaves of Storm –

The Eyes around – had wrung them dry –
And Breaths were gathering firm
For that last Onset – when the King
Be witnessed – in the Room –

I willed my Keepsakes – Signed away
What portion of me be   10
Assignable – and then it was
There interposed a Fly –

With Blue – uncertain stumbling Buzz –
Between the light – and me –
And then the Windows failed – and then
I could not see to see –

483

A Solemn thing within the Soul
To feel itself get ripe –
And golden hang – while farther up –
The Maker's Ladders stop –

And in the Orchard far below –
You hear a Being – drop –

A Wonderful – to feel the Sun
Still toiling at the Cheek
You thought was finished –
Cool of eye, and critical of Work –   10
He shifts the stem – a little –
To give your Core – a look –

But solemnest – to know
Your chance in Harvest moves
A little nearer – Every Sun
The Single – to some lives.

505

I would not paint – a picture –
I'd rather be the One
It's bright impossibility
To dwell – delicious – on –
And wonder how the fingers feel
Whose rare – celestial – stir –
Evokes so sweet a Torment –
Such sumptuous – Despair –

I would not talk, like Cornets –
I'd rather be the One   10
Raised softly to the Ceilings –
And out, and easy on –
Through Villages of Ether –
Myself endued Balloon
By but a lip of Metal –
The pier to my Pontoon –

Nor would I be a Poet –
It's finer – own the Ear –
Enamored – impotent – content –
The License to revere,   20
A privilege so awful
What would the Dower be,
Had I the Art to stun myself
With Bolts of Melody!

507

She sights a Bird – she chuckles –
She flattens – then she crawls –
She runs without the look of feet –
Her eyes increase to Balls –

Her Jaws stir – twitching – hungry –
Her Teeth can hardly stand –
She leaps, but Robin leaped the first –
Ah, Pussy, of the Sand,

The Hopes so juicy ripening –
You almost bathed your Tongue –   10
When Bliss disclosed a hundred Toes –
And fled with every one –

531

We dream – it is good we are dreaming –
It would hurt us – were we awake –
But since it is playing – kill us,
And we are playing – shriek –

What harm? Men die – externally –
It is a truth – of Blood –
But we – are dying in Drama –
And Drama – is never dead –

Cautious – We jar each other –
And either – open the eyes –   10
Lest the Phantasm – prove the Mistake –
And the livid Surprise

Cool us to Shafts of Granite –
With just an Age – and Name –
And perhaps a phrase in Egyptian –
It's prudenter – to dream –

537

Me prove it now – Whoever doubt
Me stop to prove it – now –
Make haste – the Scruple! Death be scant
For Opportunity –

The River reaches to my feet –
As yet – My Heart be dry –
Oh Lover – Life could not convince –
Might Death – enable Thee –

The River reaches to My Breast –
Still – still – My Hands above   10
Proclaim with their remaining Might –
Dost recognize the Love?

The River reaches to my Mouth –
Remember – when the Sea
Swept by my searching eyes – the last –
Themselves were quick – with Thee!

540

I took my Power in my Hand –
And went against the World –

537. 5. **River:** The image of the river of death may come from
the conclusion of the second part of *Pilgrim's Progress.*

'Twas not so much as David – had –
But I – was twice as bold –

I aimed my Pebble – but Myself
Was all the one that fell –
Was it Goliah – was too large –
Or was myself – too small?

578

The Body grows without –
The more convenient way –
That if the Spirit – like to hide
It's Temple stands, alway,

Ajar – secure – inviting –
It never did betray
The Soul that asked it's shelter
In solemn honesty

585

I like to see it lap the Miles –
And lick the Valleys up –
And stop to feed itself at Tanks –
And then – prodigious step

Around a Pile of Mountains –
And supercilious peer
In Shanties – by the sides of Roads –
And then a Quarry pare

To fit it's sides
And crawl between   10
Complaining all the while
In horrid – hooting stanza –
Then chase itself down Hill –

And neigh like Boanerges –
Then – prompter than a Star
Stop – docile and omnipotent
At it's own stable door –

590

Did you ever stand in a Cavern's Mouth –
Widths out of the Sun –
And look – and shudder, and block your breath –
And deem to be alone

In such a place, what horror,
How Goblin it would be –
And fly, as 'twere pursuing you?
Then Loneliness – looks so –

540. 3. **David**: For the story of David and Goliath, see I Sam. 17.
585. 14. **Boanerges**: "sons of thunder"; cf. Mark 3-17.

Did you ever look in a Cannon's face –
Between whose Yellow eye –   10
And your's – the Judgment intervened –
The Question of "To die" –

Extemporizing in your ear
As cool as Satyr's Drums –
If you remember, and were saved –
It's liker so – it seems –

619

Glee – The great storm is over –
Four – have recovered the Land –
Forty – gone down together –
Into the boiling Sand –

Ring – for the Scant Salvation –
Toll – for the bonnie Souls –
Neighbor – and friend – and Bridegroom –
Spinning upon the Shoals –

How they will tell the Story –
When Winter shake the Door –   10
Till the Children urge –
But the Forty –
Did they – come back no more?

Then a softness – suffuse the Story –
And a silence – the Teller's eye –
And the Children – no further question –
And only the Sea – reply –

652

A Prison gets to be a friend –
Between it's Ponderous face
And Our's – a Kinsmanship express –
And in it's narrow Eyes –

We come to look with gratitude
For the appointed Beam
It deal us – stated as our food –
And hungered for – the same –

We learn to know the Planks –
That answer to Our feet –   10
So miserable a sound – at first –
Nor even now – so sweet –

As plashing in the Pools –
When Memory was a Boy –
But a Demurer Circuit –
A Geometric Joy –

The Posture of the Key
That interrupt the Day
To Our Endeavor – Not so real
The Cheek of Liberty –   20

As this Phantasm Steel –
Whose features – Day and Night –
Are present to us – as Our Own –
And as escapeless – quite –

The narrow Round – the Stint –
The slow exchange of Hope –
For something passiver – Content
Too steep for looking up –

The Liberty we knew
Avoided – like a Dream –   30
Too wide for any Night but Heaven –
If That – indeed – redeem –

664

Of all the Souls that stand create –
I have elected – One –
When Sense from Spirit – files away –
And Subterfuge – is done –
When that which is – and that which was –
Apart – intrinsic – stand –
And this brief Tragedy of Flesh –
Is shifted – like a Sand –
When Figures show their royal Front –
And Mists – are carved away,   10
Behold the Atom – I preferred –
To all the lists of Clay!

683

The Soul unto itself
Is an imperial friend –
Or the most agonizing Spy –
An Enemy – could send –

Secure against it's own –
No treason it can fear –
Itself – it's Sovereign – of itself
The Soul should stand in Awe –

712

Because I could not stop for Death –
He kindly stopped for me –
The Carriage held but just Ourselves –
And Immortality.

We slowly drove – He knew no haste
And I had put away
My labor and my leisure too,
For His Civility –

We passed the School, where Children strove
At Recess – in the Ring –   10
We passed the Fields of Gazing Grain –
We passed the Setting Sun –

Or rather – He passed Us –
The Dews drew quivering and chill –
For only Gossamer, my Gown –
My Tippet – only Tulle –

We paused before a House that seemed
A Swelling of the Ground –
The Roof was scarcely visible –
The Cornice – in the Ground –   20

Since then – 'tis Centuries – and yet
Feels shorter than the Day
I first surmised the Horses Heads
Were toward Eternity –

756

One Blessing had I than the rest
So larger to my Eyes
That I stopped guaging – satisfied –
For this enchanted size –

It was the limit of my Dream –
The focus of my Prayer –
A perfect – paralyzing Bliss –
Contented as Despair –

I knew no more of Want – or Cold –
Phantasms both become   10
For this new Value in the Soul –
Supremest Earthly Sum –

The Heaven below the Heaven above –
Obscured with ruddier Blue –
Life's Latitudes leant over – full –
The Judgment perished – too –

Why Bliss so scantily disburse –
Why Paradise defer –
Why Floods be served to Us – in Bowls –
I speculate no more –   20

777

The Loneliness One dare not sound –
And would as soon surmise
As in it's Grave go plumbing
To ascertain the size –

The Loneliness whose worst alarm
Is lest itself should see –
And perish from before itself
For just a scrutiny –

The Horror not to be surveyed –
But skirted in the Dark – 10
With Consciousness suspended –
And Being under Lock –

I fear me this – is Loneliness –
The Maker of the soul
It's Caverns and it's Corridors
Illuminate – or seal –

793

Grief is a Mouse –
And chooses Wainscot in the Breast
For His Shy House –
And baffles quest –

Grief is a Thief – quick startled –
Pricks His Ear – report to hear
Of that Vast Dark –
That swept His Being – back –

Grief is a Juggler – boldest at the Play –
Lest if He flinch – the eye that way 10
Pounce on His Bruises – One – say – or Three –
Grief is a Gourmand – spare His luxury –

Best Grief is Tongueless – before He'll tell –
Burn Him in the Public Square –
His Ashes – will
Possibly – if they refuse – How then know –
Since a Rack could'nt coax a syllable – now

809

Unable are the Loved to die
For Love is Immortality,
Nay, it is Deity –

Unable they that love – to die
For Love reforms Vitality
Into Divinity.

817

Given in Marriage unto Thee
Oh thou Celestial Host –
Bride of the Father and the Son
Bride of the Holy Ghost.

Other Betrothal shall dissolve –
Wedlock of Will, decay –
Only the Keeper of this Ring
Conquer Mortality –

822

This Consciousness that is aware
Of Neighbors and the Sun
Will be the one aware of Death
And that itself alone

Is traversing the interval
Experience between
And most profound experiment
Appointed unto Men –

How adequate unto itself
It's properties shall be 10
Itself unto itself and none
Shall make discovery.

Adventure most unto itself
The Soul condemned to be –
Attended by a single Hound
It's own identity.

835

Nature and God – I neither knew
Yet Both so well knew me
They startled, like Executors
Of My identity.

Yet Neither told – that I could learn –
My Secret as secure
As Herschel's private interest
Or Mercury's affair –

842

Good to hide, and hear 'em hunt!
Better, to be found,
If one care to, that is,
The Fox fits the Hound –

817. 3. **Bride:** Cf. Rev. 21:2.   835. 7. **Herschel's:** i.e., the planet Uranus, discovered by Sir William Herschel in the eighteenth century and for a time called Herschel after him.

Good to know, and not tell,
Best, to know and tell,
Can one find the rare Ear
Not too dull –

861

Split the Lark – and you'll find the Music –
Bulb after Bulb, in Silver rolled –
Scantily dealt to the Summer Morning
Saved for your Ear when Lutes be old.

Loose the Flood – you shall find it patent –
Gush after Gush, reserved for you –
Scarlet Experiment! Sceptic Thomas!
Now, do you doubt that your Bird was true?

870

Finding is the first Act
The second, loss,
Third, Expedition for
the "Golden Fleece"

Fourth, no Discovery –
Fifth, no Crew –
Finally, no Golden Fleece –
Jason – sham – too.

871

The Sun and Moon must make their haste –
The Stars express around
For in the Zones of Paradise
The Lord alone is burned –

His Eye, it is the East and West –
The North and South when He
Do concentrate His Countenance
Like Glow Worms, flee away –

Oh Poor and Far –
Oh Hindered Eye   10
That hunted for the Day –
The Lord a Candle entertains
Entirely for Thee –

872

As the Starved Maelstrom laps the Navies
As the Vulture teazed
Forces the Broods in lonely Valleys
As the Tiger eased

861. 7. Thomas: Cf. John 20:24–25.   870. 3. Expedition: the
quest of the Argonauts, under the command of Jason, to obtain
the Golden Fleece on the east coast of the Black Sea.
871. 4. burned: Cf. Rev. 22:5.   12. Candle: Cf. Ps. 18:28.

By but a Crumb of Blood, fasts Scarlet
Till he meet a Man
Dainty adorned with Veins and Tissues
And partakes – his Tongue

Cooled by the Morsel for a moment
Grows a fiercer thing   10
Till he esteem his Dates and Cocoa
A Nutrition mean

I, of a finer Famine
Deem my Supper dry
For but a Berry of Domingo
And a Torrid Eye.

889

Crisis is a Hair
Toward which forces creep
Past which forces retrograde
If it come in sleep

To suspend the Breath
Is the most we can
Ignorant is it Life or Death
Nicely balancing.

Let an instant push
Or an Atom press   10
Or a Circle hesitate
In Circumference

It – may jolt the Hand
That adjusts the Hair
That secures Eternity
From presenting – Here –

945

This is a Blossom of the Brain –
A small – italic Seed
Lodged by Design or Happening
The Spirit fructified –

Shy as the Wind of his Chambers
Swift as a Freshet's Tongue
So of the Flower of the Soul
It's process is unknown.

When it is found, a few rejoice
The Wise convey it Home   10
Carefully cherishing the spot
If other Flower become.

When it is lost, that Day shall be
The Funeral of God,

Upon his Breast, a closing Soul
The Flower of our Lord.

956

What shall I do when the Summer troubles –
What, when the Rose is ripe –
What when the Eggs fly off in Music
From the Maple Keep?

What shall I do when the Skies a'chirrup
Drop a Tune on me –
When the Bee hangs all Noon in the Buttercup
What will become of me?

Oh, when the Squirrel fills His Pockets
And the Berries stare   10
How can I bear their jocund Faces
Thou from Here, so far?

'Twould'nt afflict a Robin –
All His Goods have Wings –
I – do not fly, so wherefore
My Perennial Things?

959

A loss of something ever felt I –
The first that I could recollect
Bereft I was – of what I knew not
Too young that any should suspect

A Mourner walked among the children
I notwithstanding went about
As one bemoaning a Dominion
Itself the only Prince cast out –

Elder, Today, a session wiser
And fainter, too, as Wiseness is –   10
I find myself still softly searching
For my Delinquent Palaces –

And a Suspicion, like a Finger
Touches my Forehead now and then
That I am looking oppositely
For the site of the Kingdom of Heaven –

970

Color – Caste – Denomination –
These – are Times's Affair –
Death's diviner Classifying
Does not know they are –

As in sleep – All Hue forgotten –
Tenets – put behind –

Death's large – Democratic fingers
Rub away the Brand –

If Circassian – He is careless –
If He put away   10
Chrysalis of Blonde – or Umber –
Equal Butterfly –

They emerge from His Obscuring –
What Death – knows so well –
Our minuter intuitions –
Deem unplausible

983

Ideals are the Fairy Oil
With which we help the Wheel
But when the Vital Axle turns
The Eye rejects the Oil.

986

A narrow Fellow in the Grass
Occasionally rides –
You may have met Him – did you not
His notice sudden is –

The Gass divides as with a Comb –
A spotted shaft is seen –
And then it closes at your feet
And opens further on –

He likes a Boggy Acre
A Floor too cool for Corn –   10
Yet when a Boy, and Barefoot –
I more than once at Noon
Have passed, I thought, a Whip lash
Unbraiding in the Sun
When stooping to secure it
It wrinkled, and was gone –

Several of Nature's People
I know, and they know me –
I feel for them a transport
Of cordiality –   20

But never met this Fellow
Attended, or alone
Without a tighter breathing
And Zero at the Bone –

970. 9. **Circassian:** i.e., white. **986. 10. A . . . Corn:**
Samuel Bowles, editor of the Springfield *Daily Republican*, where
this poem was published anonymously in 1866, is said to have
commented on this line: "How did that girl ever know that a
boggy field wasn't good for corn?"

1000

The Fingers of the Light
Tapped soft upon the Town
With "I am great and cannot wait
So therefore let me in."

"You're soon," the Town replied,
"My Faces are asleep –
But swear, and I will let you by
You will not wake them up."

The easy Guest complied
But once within the Town   10
The transport of His Countenance
Awakened Maid and Man

The Neighbor in the Pool
Upon His Hip elate
Made loud obeisance and the Gnat
Held up His Cup for Light.

1014

Did We abolish Frost
The Summer would not cease –
If Seasons perish or prevail
Is optional with Us –

1017

To die – without the Dying
And live – without the Life
This is the hardest Miracle
Propounded to Belief.

1021

Far from Love the Heavenly Father
Leads the Chosen Child,
Oftener through Realm of Briar
Than the Meadow mild.

Oftener by the Claw of Dragon
Than the Hand of Friend
Guides the Little One predestined
To the Native Land.

1039

I heard, as if I had no Ear
Until a Vital Word
Came all the way from Life to me
And then I knew I heard.

I saw, as if my Eye were on
Another, till a Thing
And now I know 'twas Light, because
It fitted them, came in.

I dwelt, as if Myself were out,
My Body but within   10
Until a Might detected me
And set my kernel in.

And Spirit turned unto the Dust
"Old Friend, thou knowest me,"
And Time went out to tell the News
And met Eternity

1046

I've dropped my Brain – My Soul is numb –
The Veins that used to run
Stop palsied – 'tis Paralysis
Done perfecter on stone.

Vitality is Carved and cool.
My nerve in Marble lies –
A Breathing Woman
Yesterday – Endowed with Paradise.

Not dumb – I had a sort that moved –
A Sense that smote and stirred –   10
Instincts for Dance – a caper part –
An Aptitude for Bird –

Who wrought Carrara in me
And chiselled all my tune
Were it a Witchcraft – were it Death –
I've still a chance to strain

To Being, somewhere – Motion – Breath –
Though Centuries beyond,
And every limit a Decade –
I'll shiver, satisfied.   20

1052

I never saw a Moor –
I never saw the Sea –
Yet know I how the Heather looks
And what a Billow be.

I never spoke with God
Nor visited in Heaven –
Yet certain am I of the spot
As if the Checks were given –

1021. Cf. Blake's poem, "A Little Girl Lost."

1046. 13. Carrara: i.e., marble, for which Carrara in Italy is a
source.

1067

Except the smaller size
No lives are round –
These – hurry to a sphere
And show and end –
The larger – slower grow
And later hang –
The Summers of Hesperides
Are long.

1068

Further in Summer than the Birds
Pathetic from the Grass
A minor Nation celebrates
It's unobtrusive Mass.

No Ordinance be seen
So gradual the Grace
A pensive Custom it becomes
Enlarging Loneliness.

Antiquest felt at Noon
When August burning low   10
Arise this spectral Canticle
Repose to typify

Remit as yet no Grace
No Furrow on the Glow
Yet a Druidic Difference
Enhances Nature now

1082

Revolution is the Pod
Systems rattle from
When the Winds of Will are stirred
Excellent is Bloom

But except it's Russet Base
Every Summer be
The Entomber of itself,
So of Liberty –

Left inactive on the Stalk
All it's Purple fled   10
Revolution shakes it for
Test if it be dead.

1084

At Half past Three, a single Bird
Unto a silent Sky
Propounded but a single term
Of cautious melody.

At Half past Four, Experiment
Had subjugated test
And lo, Her silver Principle
Supplanted all the rest.

At Half past Seven, Element
Nor Implement, be seen –   10
And Place was where the Presence was
Circumference between.

1090

I am afraid to own a Body –
I am afraid to own a Soul –
Profound – precarious Property –
Possession, not optional –

Double Estate – entailed at pleasure
Upon an unsuspecting Heir –
Duke in a moment of Deathlessness
And God, for a Frontier.

1126

Shall I take thee, the Poet said
To the propounded word?
Be stationed with the Candidates
Till I have finer tried –

The Poet searched Philology
And was about to ring
for the suspended Candidate
There came unsummoned in –

That portion of the Vision
The Word applied to fill   10
Not unto nomination
The Cherubim reveal –

1129

Tell all the Truth but tell it slant –
Success in Circuit lies
Too bright for our infirm Delight
The Truth's superb surprise

1067. 7. Hesperides: according to Greek mythology, a fabulous garden on an island in the western ocean where golden apples grew that were guarded by a dragon.   **1068. 15. Druidic:** This word associates the song of the crickets with a mysterious ritual (cf. "Mass," above) connected with the dying of the year into winter.

1126. 12. Cherubim: Cf. Ezek. 10:5; I Pet. 1:12. This is one of several poems in which Emily Dickinson associates the Christian conception of a divine Word with poetry.

As Lightning to the Children eased
With explanation kind
The Truth must dazzle gradually
Or every man be blind –

1142

The Props assist the House
Until the House is built
And then the Props withdraw
And adequate, erect,
The House support itself
And cease to recollect
The Augur and the Carpenter –
Just such a retrospect
Hath the perfected Life –
A past of Plank and Nail   10
And slowness – then the Scaffolds drop
Affirming it a Soul.

1181

When I hoped I feared –
Since I hoped I dared
Everywhere alone
As a Church remain –
Spectre cannot harm –
Serpent cannot charm –
He deposes Doom
Who hath suffered him –

1197

I should not dare to be so sad
So many Years again –
A Load is first impossible
When we have put it down –

The Superhuman then withdraws
And we who never saw
The Giant at the other side
Begin to perish now.

1200

Because my Brook is fluent
I know 'tis dry –
Because my Brook is silent
It is the Sea –

And startled at it's swelling
I try to flee
To where the Strong assure me
Is "no more Sea" –

1226

The Popular Heart is a Cannon first –
Subsequent a Drum –
Bells for an Auxiliary
And an Afterward of Rum –

Not a Tomorrow to know it's name
Nor a Past to stare –
Ditches for Realms and a Trip to Jail
For a Souvenir

1232

The Clover's simple Fame
Remembered of the Cow –
Is better than enameled Realms
Of notability.
Renown perceives itself
And that degrades the Flower –
The Daisy that has looked behind
Has compromised it's power –

1247

To pile like Thunder to it's close
Then crumble grand away
While Everything created hid
This – would be Poetry –

Or Love – the two coeval come –
We both and neither prove –
Experience either and consume –
For None see God and live –

1286

I thought that nature was enough
Till Human nature came
But that the other did absorb
As Parallax a Flame –

Of Human nature just aware
There added the Divine
Brief struggle for capacity
The power to contain

Is always as the contents
But give a Giant room   10
And you will lodge a Giant
And not a smaller man

1200. 8. Sea: Cf. Rev. 21:1.

1247. 8. For . . . live: Cf. Exod. 33:20.

1298

The Mushroom is the Elf of Plants –
At Evening, it is not –
At Morning, in a Truffled Hut
It stop upon a Spot

As if it tarried always
And yet it's whole Career
Is shorter than a Snake's Delay
And fleeter than a Tare –

'Tis Vegetation's Juggler –
The Germ of Alibi –   10
Doth like a Bubble antedate
And like a Bubble, hie –

I feel as if the Grass was pleased
To have it intermit –
This surreptitious scion
Of Summer's circumspect.

Had Nature any supple Face
Or could she one contemn –
Had Nature an Apostate –
That Mushroom – it is Him!   20

1317

Abraham to kill him
Was distinctly told –
Isaac was an Urchin –
Abraham was old –

Not a hesitation –
Abraham complied –
Flattered by Obeisance
Tyranny demurred –

Isaac – to his children
Lived to tell the tale –   10
Moral – with a Mastiff
Manners may prevail.

1339

A Bee his burnished Carriage
Drove boldly to a Rose –
Combinedly alighting –
Himself – his Carriage was –
The Rose received his visit
With frank tranquility
Witholding not a Crescent
To his Cupidity –

Their Moment consummated –
Remained for him – to flee –
Remained for her – of rapture   10
But the humility.

1377

Forbidden Fruit a flavor has
That lawful Orchards mocks –
How luscious lies within the Pod
The Pea that Duty locks –

1393

Lay this Laurel on the One
Too intrinsic for Renown –
Laurel – vail your deathless tree –
Him you chasten, that is He!

1400

What mystery pervades a well!
The water lives so far –
A neighbor from another world
Residing in a jar

Whose limit none have ever seen,
But just his lid of glass –
Like looking every time you please
In an abyss's face!

The grass does not appear afraid,
I often wonder he   10
Can stand so close and look so bold
At what is awe to me.

Related somehow they may be,
The sedge stands next the sea –
Where he is floorless
And does no timidity betray

But nature is a stranger yet;
The ones that cite her most
Have never passed her haunted house,
Nor simplified her ghost.   20

To pity those that know her not
Is helped by the regret
That those who know her, know her less
The nearer her they get.

1393. This quatrain was sent to Higginson in a letter and was inspired by his poem "Decoration" (reprinted in the Johnson edition, III, 961). Higginson admitted that it was the "condensed essence" of his twenty-eight line poem. The subject of Emily Dickinson's poem is probably her father.

1317. 1–2. Abraham . . . told: The story alluded to is told in Gen. 22.

1405

Bees are Black, with Gilt Surcingles –
Bucaneers of Buzz.
Ride abroad in ostentation
And subsist on Fuzz.

Fuzz ordained – not Fuzz contingent –
Marrows of the Hill.
Jugs – a Universe's fracture
Could not jar or spill.

1428

Water makes many Beds
For those averse to sleep –
It's awful chamber open stands –
It's Curtains blandly sweep –
Abhorrent is the Rest
In undulating Rooms
Whose Amplitude no end invades –
Whose Axis never comes.

1432

Spurn the temerity –
Rashness of Calvary –
Gay were Gethsemane
Knew we of Thee –

1434

Go not too near a House of Rose –
The depredation of a Breeze
Or inundation of a Dew
Alarm it's walls away –
Nor try to tie the Butterfly,
Nor climb the Bars of Ecstasy,
In insecurity to lie
Is Joy's insuring quality.

1450

The Road was lit with Moon and star –
The Trees were bright and still –
Descried I – by the distant Light
A Traveller on a Hill –
To magic Perpendiculars
Ascending, though Terrene –
Unknown his shimmering ultimate –
But he indorsed the sheen –

1462

We knew not that we were to live –
Nor when – we are to die –
Our ignorance – our cuirass is –
We wear Mortality
As lightly as an Option Gown
Till asked to take it off –
By his intrusion, God is known –
It is the same with Life –

1463

A Route of Evanescence
With a revolving Wheel –
A Resonance of Emerald –
A Rush of Cochineal –
And every Blossom on the Bush
Adjusts it's tumbled Head –
The mail from Tunis, probably,
An easy Morning's Ride –

1474

Estranged from Beauty – none can be –
For Beauty is Infinity –
And power to be finite ceased
Before Identity was creased.

1475

Fame is the one that does not stay –
It's occupant must die
Or out of sight of estimate
Ascend incessantly –
Or be that most insolvent thing
A Lightning in the Germ –
Electrical the embryo
But we demand the Flame

1483

The Robin is a Gabriel
In humble circumstances –
His Dress denotes him socially,
Of Transport's Working Classes –
He has the punctuality
Of the New England Farmer –
The same oblique integrity,
A Vista vastly warmer –

1432. Probably sent in a letter to Helen Hunt Jackson, who endorsed the autograph with the note—"Wonderful twelve words!"

1463. 7. Tunis: perhaps derived from Shakespeare's *Tempest*, II.i.241.   **1475. 3. Or:** either.   **1483. 1. Gabriel:** the angel of the Annunciation; cf. Luke 1:26.

A small but sturdy Residence,
A self denying Household, 10
The Guests of Perspicacity
Are all that cross his Threshold –
As covert as a Fugitive,
Cajoling Consternation
By Ditties to the Enemy
And Sylvan Punctuation –

1487

The Savior must have been
A docile Gentleman –
To come so far so cold a Day
For little Fellowmen –

The Road to Bethlehem
Since He and I were Boys
Was leveled, but for that twould be
A rugged billion Miles –

1510

How happy is the little Stone
That rambles in the Road alone,
And does'nt care about Careers
And Exigencies never fears –
Whose Coat of elemental Brown
A passing Universe put on,
And independent as the Sun
Associates or glows alone,
Fulfilling absolute Decree
In casual simplicity – 10

1553

Bliss is the plaything of the child –
The secret of the man
The sacred stealth of Boy and Girl
Rebuke it if we can

1557

Lives he in any other world
My faith cannot reply
Before it was imperative
Twas all distinct to me –

1599

Though the great Waters sleep,
That they are still the Deep,
We cannot doubt –
No vacillating God
Ignited this Abode
To put it out –

1625

Back from the cordial Grave I drag thee
He shall not take thy Hand
Nor put his spacious arm around thee
That none can understand

1628

A Drunkard cannot meet a Cork
Without a Revery –
And so encountering a Fly
This January Day
Jamaicas of Remembrance stir
That send me reeling in –
The moderate drinker of Delight
Does not deserve the spring –
Of juleps, part are in the Jug
And more are in the joy – 10
Your connoisseur in Liquors
Consults the Bumble Bee –

1631

Oh Future! thou secreted peace
Or subterranean wo –
Is there no wandering route of grace
That leads away from thee –
No circuit sage of all the course
Descried by cunning Men
To balk thee of thy sacred Prey –
Advancing to thy Den –

1645

The Ditch is dear to the Drunken man
for is it not his Bed –
his Advocate – his Edifice –
How safe his fallen Head
In her disheveled Sanctity –
Above him is the sky –
Oblivion bending over him
And Honor leagues away

1651

A Word made Flesh is seldom
And tremblingly partook
Nor then perhaps reported
But have I not mistook
Each one of us has tasted
With ecstasies of stealth
The very food debated
To our specific strength –

1651. 7. **food debated:** The reference is to the sacrament of the

A Word that breathes distinctly
Has not the power to die   10
Cohesive as the Spirit
It may expire if He –
"Made Flesh and dwelt among us"
Could condescension be
Like this consent of Language
This loved Philology

1679

Rather arid delight
If Contentment accrue
Make an abstemious Ecstasy
Not so good as joy –

But Rapture's Expense
Must not be incurred
With a to-morrow knocking
And the Rent unpaid –

1695

There is a solitude of space
A solitude of sea
A solitude of death, but these
Society shall be
Compared with that profounder site
That polar privacy
A soul admitted to itself –
Finite Infinity.

1697

They talk as slow as Legends grow
No mushroom is their mind
But foliage of sterility
Too stolid for the wind –

They laugh as wise as Plots of Wit
Predestined to unfold
The point with bland prevision
Portentously untold

1712

A Pit – but Heaven over it –
And Heaven beside, and Heaven abroad;
And yet a Pit –
With Heaven over it.

To stir would be to slip –
To look would be to drop –
To dream – to sap the Prop
That holds my chances up.
Ah! Pit! With Heaven over it!

The depth is all my thought –   10
I dare not ask my feet –
'Twould start us where we sit
So straight you'd scarce suspect
It was a Pit – with fathoms under it
Its Circuit just the same
Seed – summer – tomb –
Whose Doom to whom

1717

Did life's penurious length
Italicize its sweetness,
The men that daily live
Would stand so deep in joy
That it would clog the cogs
Of that revolving reason
Whose esoteric belt
Protects our sanity.

1731

Love can do all but raise the Dead
I doubt if even that
From such a giant were withheld
Were flesh equivalent

But love is tired and must sleep,
And hungry and must graze
And so abets the shining Fleet
Till it is out of gaze.

1732

My life closed twice before its close;
It yet remains to see
If Immortality unveil
A third event to me,

So huge, so hopeless to conceive
As these that twice befel.
Parting is all we know of heaven,
And all we need of hell.

1736

Proud of my broken heart, since thou didst break
    it,
Proud of the pain I did not feel till thee,

Eucharist, but the meaning of "debated" is obscure, as the context seems to demand some such word as "allotted." The text is derived only from Sue's transcript.   **13. "Made . . . us":** Cf. John 1:14. Apparently, the meaning is that if the analogy holds between the Christian and the poetic meanings of "word" ("consent of Language"), then the poetic word is also immortal, or can die only in the way in which Christ did, to rise again.

Proud of my night, since thou with moons dost
    slake it,
Not to partake thy passion, *my* humility.

Thou can'st not boast, like Jesus, drunken without
    companion
Was the strong cup of anguish brewed for the
    Nazarene

Thou can'st not pierce tradition with the peerless
    puncture,
See! I usurped *thy* crucifix to honor mine!

1741

    That it will never come again
    Is what makes life so sweet.
    Believing what we don't believe
    Does not exhilarate.

    That if it be, it be at best
    An ablative estate –
    This instigates an appetite
    Precisely opposite.

1745

    The mob within the heart
    Police cannot suppress
    The riot given at the first
    Is authorized as peace

    Uncertified of scene
    Or signified of sound
    But growing like a hurricane
    In a congenial ground.

1749

    The waters chased him as he fled,
    Not daring look behind;
    A billow whispered in his Ear,
    "Come home with me, my friend;
    My parlor is of shriven glass,
    My pantry has a fish
    For every palate in the Year," –
    To this revolting bliss
    The object floating at his side
    Made no distinct reply.   10

1764

    The saddest noise, the sweetest noise,
    The maddest noise that grows, –

1736. 6. cup: Cf. Matt. 26:42.   **1741. 6. ablative estate:**
condition of removal or deprivation.

    The birds, they make it in the spring,
    At night's delicious close.

    Between the March and April line –
    That magical frontier
    Beyond which summer hesitates,
    Almost too heavenly near.

    It makes us think of all the dead
    That sauntered with us here,   10
    By separation's sorcery
    Made cruelly more dear.

    It makes us think of what we had,
    And what we now deplore.
    We almost wish those siren throats
    Would go and sing no more.

    An ear can break a human heart
    As quickly as a spear,
    We wish the ear had not a heart
    So dangerously near.

LETTERS

193: TO SAMUEL BOWLES

late August 1858?

Dear Mr Bowles.

I got the little pamphlet. I think you sent it to
me, though unfamiliar with your hand – I may
mistake.

Thank you if I am right. Thank you, if not,
since here I find bright pretext to ask you how you
are tonight, and for the health of four more,
Elder and Minor "Mary," Sallie and Sam, tenderly to inquire. I hope your cups are full. I hope
your vintage is untouched. In such a porcelain
life, one likes to be *sure* that all is well, lest one
stumble upon one's hopes in a pile of broken
crockery.

My friends are my "estate." Forgive me then
the avarice to hoard them! They tell me those
were poor early, have different views of gold. I
dont know how that is. God is not so wary as we,
else he would give us no friends, lest we forget
him! The Charms of the Heaven in the bush are
superceded I fear, by the Heaven in the hand, occasionally. Summer stopped since you were here.
Nobody noticed her – that is, no men and women.

Doubtless, the fields are rent by petite anguish, and "mourners go about" [1] the Woods. But this is not for us. Business enough indeed, our stately Resurrection! A special Courtesy, I judge, from what the Clergy say! To the "natural man," Bumblebees would seem an improvement, and a spicing of Birds, but far be it from me, to impugn such majestic tastes. Our Pastor says we are a "Worm." How is that reconciled? "Vain – sinful Worm" is possibly of another species.

Do you think we shall "see God"? Think of "Abraham" strolling with him in genial promenade! [2]

The men are mowing the second Hay. The cocks are smaller than the first, and spicier.

I would distill a cup, and bear to all my friends, drinking to her no more astir, by beck, or burn, or moor!

Good night, Mr Bowles! This is what they say who come back in the morning, also the closing paragraph on repealed lips. Confidence in Daybreak modifies Dusk.

Blessings for Mrs Bowles, and kisses for the bairns' lips. We want to see you, Mr Bowles, but spare you the rehearsal of "familiar truths."

Good Night,
Emily.

260: TO T. W. HIGGINSON

15 April 1862

Mr Higginson,

Are you too deeply occupied to say if my Verse is alive?

The Mind is so near itself – it cannot see, distinctly – and I have none to ask –

Should you think it breathed – and had you the leisure to tell me, I should feel quick gratitude –

If I make the mistake – that you dared to tell me – would give me sincerer honor – toward you –

I enclose my name – asking you, if you please – Sir – to tell me what is true?

That you will not betray me – it is needless to ask – since Honor is it's own pawn –

261: TO T. W. HIGGINSON

25 April 1862

Mr. Higginson,

Your kindness claimed earlier gratitude – but I was ill – and write today from my pillow.

Thank you for the surgery [1] – it was not so painful as I supposed. I bring you others – as you ask – though they might not differ –

While my thought is undressed – I can make the distinction, but when I put them in the Gown – they look alike, and numb.

You asked how old I was? I made no verse – but one or two – until this winter – Sir –

I had a terror – since September – I could tell to none – and so I sing, as the Boy does by the Burying Ground – because I am afraid – You inquire my Books – For Poets – I have Keats – and Mr and Mrs Browning. For prose – Mr Ruskin – Sir Thomas Browne – and the Revelations. I went to school – but in your manner of the phrase – had no education. When a little Girl, I had a friend,[2] who taught me Immortality – but venturing too near, himself – he never returned – Soon after, my Tutor, died – and for several years, my Lexicon – was my only companion – Then I found one more [3] – but he was not contented I be his scholar – so he left the Land.

You ask of my Companions Hills – Sir – and the Sundown – and a Dog – large as myself, that my Father bought me – They are better than Beings – because they know – but do not tell – and the noise in the Pool, at Noon – excels my Piano. I have a Brother and Sister – My Mother does not care for thought – and Father, too busy with his Briefs – to notice what we do – He buys me many Books – but begs me not to read them – because he fears they joggle the Mind. They are religious – except me – and address an Eclipse, every morning – whom they call their "Father." But I fear my story fatigues you – I would like to learn – Could you tell me how to grow – or is it unconveyed – like Melody – or Witchcraft?

You speak of Mr Whitman – I never read his Book – but was told that he was disgraceful –

I read Miss Prescott's "Circumstance," [4] but it followed me, in the Dark – so I avoided her –

Two Editors of Journals [5] came to my Father's House, this winter – and asked me for my Mind – and when I asked them "Why," they said I was penurious – and they, would use it for the World –

I could not weigh myself – Myself –

My size felt small – to me – I read your Chapters in the Atlantic – and experienced honor for

261. **1.** The allusion is to the criticisms Higginson had made on the poems enclosed in the previous letter.   **2.** Usually identified with Benjamin F. Newton.   **3.** Probably Charles Wadsworth.   **4.** "Circumstance": a story recently (May, 1860) published in the *Atlantic Monthly*.   **5.** Perhaps Samuel Bowles and J. G. Holland.

LETTERS.   **193. 1.** Cf. Eccles. 12:5.   **2.** "Abraham" . . . promenade: The allusion appears to be to Gen. 18.

you – I was sure you would not reject a confiding question –

Is this – Sir – what you asked me to tell you?

Your friend,

E – Dickinson

265: TO T. W. HIGGINSON

7 June 1862

Dear friend.

Your letter gave no Drunkenness, because I tasted Rum before – Domingo comes but once – yet I have had few pleasures so deep as your opinion, and if I tried to thank you, my tears would block my tongue –

My dying Tutor told me that he would like to live till I had been a poet, but Death was much of Mob as I could master – then – And when far afterward – a sudden light on Orchards, or a new fashion in the wind troubled my attention – I felt a palsy, here – the Verses just relieve –

Your second letter surprised me, and for a moment, swung – I had not supposed it. Your first – gave no dishonor, because the True – are not ashamed – I thanked you for your justice – but could not drop the Bells whose jingling cooled my Tramp – Perhaps the Balm, seemed better, because you bled me, first.

I smile when you suggest that I delay "to publish" – that being foreign to my thought, as Firmament to Fin –

If fame belonged to me, I could not escape her – if she did not, the longest day would pass me on the chase – and the approbation of my Dog, would forsake me – then – My Barefoot-Rank is better –

You think my gait "spasmodic" – I am in danger – Sir –

You think me "uncontrolled" – I have no Tribunal.

Would you have time to be the "friend" you should think I need? I have a little shape – it would not crowd your Desk – nor make much Racket as the Mouse, that dents your Galleries –

If I might bring you what I do – not so frequent to trouble you – and ask you if I told it clear – 'twould be control, to me –

The Sailor cannot see the North – but knows the Needle can –

The "hand you stretch me in the Dark," I put mine in, and turn away – I have no Saxon, now –

> As if I asked a common Alms,
> And in my wondering hand
> A Stranger pressed a Kingdom,
> And I, bewildered, stand –

> As if I asked the Orient
> Had it for me a Morn –
> And it should lift it's purple Dikes,
> And shatter me with Dawn!

But, will you be my Preceptor, Mr Higginson?

Your friend

E Dickinson –

268: TO T. W. HIGGINSON

July 1862

Could you believe me – without? I had no portrait, now, but am small, like the Wren, and my Hair is bold, like the Chestnut Bur – and my eyes, like the Sherry in the Glass, that the Guest leaves – Would this do just as well?

It often alarms Father – He says Death might occur, and he has Molds [1] of all the rest – but has no Mold of me, but I noticed the Quick wore off those things, in a few days, and forestall the dishonor – You will think no caprice of me –

You said "Dark." I know the Butterfly – and the Lizard – and the Orchis –

Are not those *your* Countrymen?

I am happy to be your scholar, and will deserve the kindness, I cannot repay.

If you truly consent, I recite, now –

Will you tell me my fault, frankly as to yourself, for I had rather wince, than die. Men do not call the surgeon, to commend – the Bone, but to set it, Sir, and fracture within, is more critical. And for this, Preceptor, I shall bring you – Obedience – the Blossom from my Garden, and every gratitude I know. Perhaps you smile at me. I could not stop for that – My Business is Circumference – An ignorance, not of Customs, but if caught with the Dawn – or the Sunset see me – Myself the only Kangaroo among the Beauty, Sir, if you please, it afflicts me, and I thought that instruction would take it away.

Because you have much business, beside the growth of me – you will appoint, yourself, how often I shall come – without your inconvenience. And if at any time – you regret you received me, or I prove a different fabric to that you supposed – you must banish me –

When I state myself, as the Representative of the Verse – it does not mean – me – but a supposed person. You are true, about the "perfection."

Today, makes Yesterday mean.

You spoke of Pippa Passes [2] – I never heard anybody speak of Pippa Passes – before.

268. **1. Molds:** here meaning "pictures." **2. Pippa Passes:** a dramatic poem by Robert Browning, published in 1841.

You see my posture is benighted.

To thank you, baffles me. Are you perfectly powerful? Had I a pleasure you had not, I could delight to bring it.

Your Scholar

269: TO DR. AND MRS. J. G. HOLLAND

summer 1862?

Dear Friends,

I write to you. I receive no letter.

I say "they dignify my trust." I do not disbelieve. I go again. *Cardinals*[1] wouldn't do it. Cockneys wouldn't do it, but I can't *stop* to strut, in a world where bells toll. I hear through visitor in town, that "Mrs. Holland is not strong." The little peacock in me, tells me not to inquire again. Then I remember my tiny friend – how brief she is – how dear she is, and the peacock quite dies away. Now, you need not speak, for perhaps you are weary, and "Herod"[2] requires all your thought, but if you are *well* – let Annie draw me a little picture of an erect flower; if you are *ill,* she can hang the flower a little on one side!

Then, I shall understand, and you need not stop to write me a letter. Perhaps you laugh at me! Perhaps the whole United States are laughing at me too! *I* can't stop for that! *My* business is to love. I found a bird, this morning, down – down – on a little bush at the foot of the garden, and wherefore sing, I said, since nobody *hears?*

One sob in the throat, one flutter of bosom – *"My* business is to *sing"* – and away she rose! How do I know but cherubim, once, themselves, as patient, listened, and applauded her unnoticed hymn?

Emily.

271: TO T. W. HIGGINSON

August 1862

Dear friend –

Are these more orderly? I thank you for the Truth –

I had no Monarch in my life, and cannot rule myself, and when I try to organize – my little Force explodes – and leaves me bare and charred –

I think you called me "Wayward." Will you help me improve?

I suppose the pride that stops the Breath, in the Core of Woods, is not of Ourself –

You say I confess the little mistake,[1] and omit the large – Because I can see Orthography – but the Ignorance out of sight – is my Preceptor's charge –

Of "shunning Men and Women" – they talk of Hallowed things, aloud – and embarrass my Dog – He and I dont object to them, if they'll exist their side. I think Carl[o] would please you – He is dumb, and brave – I think you would like the Chestnut Tree, I met in my walk. It hit my notice suddenly – and I thought the Skies were in Blossom –

Then there's a noiseless noise in the Orchard – that I let persons hear – You told me in one letter, you could not come to see me, "now," and I made no answer, not because I had none, but did not think myself the price that you should come so far –

I do not ask so large a pleasure, lest you might deny me –

You say "Beyond your knowledge." You would not jest with me, because I believe you – but Preceptor – you cannot mean it? All men say "What" to me, but I thought it a fashion –

When much in the Woods as a little Girl, I was told that the Snake would bite me, that I might pick a poisonous flower, or Goblins kidnap me, but I went along and met no one but Angels, who were far shyer of me, than I could be of them, so I hav'nt that confidence in fraud which many exercise.

I shall observe your precept – though I dont understand it, always.

I marked a line in One Verse – because I met it after I made it – and never consciously touch a paint, mixed by another person –

I do not let go it, because it is mine.

Have you the portrait of Mrs Browning? Persons sent me three – If you had none, will you have mine?

Your Scholar –

318: TO MRS. J. G. HOLLAND

early May 1866

Dear Sister,

After you went, a low wind warbled through the house like a spacious bird, making it high but lonely. When you had gone the love came. I supposed it would. The supper of the heart is when the guest has gone.

Shame is so intrinsic in a strong affection we

269. 1. **Cardinals:** perhaps a reference to the ruthless hero of Bulwer-Lytton's melodrama *Richelieu* (1839). 2. **"Herod":** here apparently a symbol of illness, perhaps of children.

271. 1. Emily Dickinson was always ready to correct spellings, but refused to alter the irregular syntax and meter which Higginson regarded as mistakes.

must all experience Adam's reticence.[1] I suppose the street that the lover travels is thenceforth divine, incapable of turnpike aims.

That you be with me annuls fear and I await Commencement with merry resignation. Smaller than David you clothe me with extreme Goliath.

Friday I tasted life. It was a vast morsel. A circus passed the house – still I feel the red in my mind though the drums are out.

The book you mention, I have not met. Thank you for tenderness.

The lawn is full of south and the odors tangle, and I hear today for the first the river in the tree.

You mentioned spring's delaying – I blamed her for the opposite. I would eat evanescence slowly.

Vinnie[2] is deeply afflicted in the death of her dappled cat, though I convince her it is immortal which assists her some. Mother resumes lettuce, involving my transgression – suggestive of yourself, however, which endears disgrace.

"House" is being "cleaned." I prefer pestilence. That is more classic and less fell.

Yours was my first arbutus. It was a rosy boast.

I will send you the first witch hazel.

A woman died last week, young and in hope but a little while – at the end of our garden. I thought since of the power of death, not upon affection, but its mortal signal. It is to us the Nile.[3]

You refer to the unpermitted delight to be with those we love. I suppose that to be the license not granted of God.

> Count not that far that can be had,
> Though sunset lie between –
> Nor that adjacent, that beside,
> Is further than the sun.

Love for your embodiment of it.

Emily.

330: TO T. W. HIGGINSON

June 1869

Dear friend

A Letter always feels to me like immortality because it is the mind alone without corporeal friend. Indebted in our talk to attitude and accent, there seems a spectral power in thought that walks alone – I would like to thank you for your great kindness but never try to lift the words which I cannot hold.

Should you come to Amherst, I might then

succeed, though Gratitude is the timid wealth of those who have nothing. I am sure that you speak the truth, because the noble do, but your letters always surprise me. My life has been too simple and stern to embarrass any.

"Seen of Angels"[1] scarcely my responsibility

It is difficult not to be fictitious in so fair a place, but test's severe repairs are permitted all.

When a little Girl I remember hearing that remarkable passage and preferring the "Power," not knowing at the time that "Kingdom" and "Glory" were included.

You noticed my dwelling alone – To an Emigrant, Country is idle except it be his own. You speak kindly of seeing me. Could it please your convenience to come so far as Amherst I should be very glad, but I do not cross my Father's ground to any House or town.

Of our greatest acts we are ignorant –

You were not aware that you saved my Life. To thank you in person has been since then one of my few requests. The child that asks my flower "Will you," he says – "Will you" – and so to ask for what I want I know no other way.

You will excuse each that I say, because no other taught me?

Dickinson

339: TO LOUISE AND FRANCES NORCROSS

early spring 1870

Dear Children,

I think the bluebirds do their work exactly like me. They dart around just so, with little dodging feet, and look so agitated. I really feel for them, they seem to be so tried.

The mud is very deep – up to the wagons' stomachs – arbutus making pink clothes, and everything alive.

Even the hens are touched with the things of Bourbon,[1] and make republicans like me feel strangely out of scene.

Mother went rambling, and came in with a burdock on her shawl, so we know that the snow has perished from the earth. Noah[2] would have liked mother.

I am glad you are with Eliza. It is next to shade to know that those we love are cool on a parched day.

Bring my love to —— and Mr. ——. You will not need a hod. C[lara] writes often, full of joy and liberty. I guess it is a case of peace. . . .

Pussy has a daughter in the shavings barrel.

318. 1. Cf. Gen. 3:7. 2. **Vinnie:** her sister, Lavinia. 3. Perhaps an allusion to the fact that the rising of the Nile, on which the life of Egypt depended, was heralded by the rising of the Dog Star, its "signal."

330. 1. Cf. I Tim. 3:16. 339. 1. **Bourbon:** i.e., with plumage like royalty. 2. Cf. Gen. 8:11.

Father steps like Cromwell when he gets the kindlings.

Mrs. S[weetser] gets bigger, and rolls down the lane to church like a reverend marble. Did you know little Mrs. Holland was in Berlin for her eyes? . . .

Did you know about Mrs. J——? She fledged her antique wings. 'Tis said that "nothing in her life became her like the leaving it." [3]

Great Streets of Silence led away
To Neighborhoods of Pause –
Here was no Notice – no Dissent,
No Universe – no Laws –

By Clocks – 'twas Morning, and for Night
The Bells at Distance called –
But Epoch had no basis here,
For Period exhaled.

Emily.

353: TO T. W. HIGGINSON

about October 1870

The Riddle that we guess
We speedily despise –
Not anything is stale so long
As Yesterday's Surprise –

The Risks of Immortality are perhaps its' charm – A secure Delight suffers in enchantment –

The larger Haunted House it seems, of maturer Childhood – distant, an alarm – entered intimate at last as a neighbor's Cottage –

The Spirit said unto the Dust
Old Friend, thou knewest me
And Time went out to tell the news
Unto Eternity –

Those of that renown personally precious, harrow like a Sunset, proved but not obtained –

Tennyson knew this, "Ah Christ – if it be possible" [1] and even in Our Lord's ["] that they be with me where I am," [2] I taste interrogation.

Experiment escorts us last –
His pungent company
Will not allow an Axiom
An Opportunity –

You speak of "tameless tastes" – A Beggar came last week – I gave him Food and Fire and as he went, "Where do you go,"

"In all the directions" –

That was what you meant
Too happy Time dissolves itself
And leaves no remnant by –

'Tis Anguish not a Feather hath
Or too much weight to fly –

I was much refreshed by your strong Letter –

Thank you for Greatness – I will have deserved it in a longer time!

I thought I spoke to you of the shadow –

It affects me –

This was still another –

I saw it's notice in the Papers just before you came – Is there a magazinine called the "Woman's Journal"? I think it was said to be in that – a Gate, or Door, or Latch –

Someone called me suddenly, and I never found it –

You told me Mrs Lowell was Mr Lowell's "inspiration" What is inspiration?

You place the truth in opposite – because the fear is mine, dear friend, and the power your's –

'Tis Glory's far sufficiency   far sufficiency] overtake-lessness

that make's our trying poor –   trying] running

With the Kingdom of Heaven on his knee, could Mr. Emerson hesitate?

"Suffer little Children" –

Could you not come without the Lecture, if the project failed?

354: TO MRS. J. G. HOLLAND

early October 1870

I guess I wont send that note now, for the mind is such a new place, last night feels obsolete.

Perhaps you thought dear Sister, I wanted to elope with you and feared a vicious Father.

It was not quite that.

The Papers thought the Doctor was mostly in New York. Who then would read for you? Mr. Chapman, doubtless, or Mr. Buckingham! The Doctor's sweet reply makes me infamous.

Life is the finest secret.

So long as that remains, we must all whisper.

With that sublime exception I had no clandestineness.

It was lovely to see you and I hope it may happen again. These beloved accidents must become more frequent.

We are by September and yet my flowers are bold as June. Amherst has gone to Eden.

To shut our eyes is Travel.

The Seasons understand this.

How lonesome to be an Article! I mean – to have no soul.

An Apple fell in the night and a Wagon stopped.

I suppose the Wagon ate the Apple and resumed it's way.

3. "nothing . . . it": See *Macbeth*, I.iv.7–8.   353. 1. "Ah . . . possible": from Tennyson's *Maud*, II.iv.3.   2. "that . . . am": Cf. John 17:24.

How fine it is to talk.
What Miracles the News is!
Not Bismark [1] but ourselves.

> The Life we have is very great.
> The Life that we shall see
> Surpasses it, we know, because
> It is Infinity.
> But when all Space has been beheld
> And all Dominion shown
> The smallest Human Heart's extent
> Reduces it to none.

Love for the Doctor, and the Girls.
Ted might not acknowledge me.

Emily.

368: TO T. W. HIGGINSON

November 1871

I did not read Mr Miller [1] because I could not care about him –

Transport is not urged –

Mrs Hunt's Poems are stronger than any written by Women since Mrs – Browning, with the exception of Mrs Lewes [2] – but truth like Ancestor's Brocades can stand alone – You speak of "Men and Women." That is a broad Book – "Bells and Pomegranates" [3] I never saw but have Mrs Browning's endorsement. While Shakespeare remains Literature is firm –

An Insect cannot run away with Achilles' Head. [4] Thank you for having written the "Atlantic Essays." They are a fine Joy – though to possess the ingredient for Congratulation renders congratulation superfluous.

Dear friend, I trust you as you ask – If I exceed permission, excuse the bleak simplicity that knew no tutor but the North. Would you but guide

Dickinson

415: TO SAMUEL BOWLES

late June 1874

I should think you would have few Letters for your own are so noble that they make men afraid – and sweet as your Approbation is – it is had in fear – lest your depth convict us.

You compel us each to remember that when Water ceases to rise – it has commenced falling. That is the law of Flood. The last Day that I saw you was the newest and oldest of my life.

Resurrection can come but once – first – to the same House. Thank you for leading us by it.

Come always, dear friend, but refrain from going. You spoke of not liking to be forgotten. Could you, tho' you would? Treason never knew you.

Emily.

432: TO MRS. J. G. HOLLAND

late January 1875

Sister.

This austere Afternoon is more becoming to a Patriot than to one whose Friend is it's sole Land.

No event of Wind or Bird breaks the Spell of Steel.

Nature squanders Rigor – now – where she squandered Love.

Chastening – it may be – the Lass that she receiveth.

My House is a House of Snow – true – sadly – of few.

Mother is asleep in the Library – Vinnie – in the Dining Room – Father – in the Masked Bed – in the Marl House.

> How soft his Prison is –
> How sweet those sullen Bars –
> No Despot – but the King of Down
> Invented that Repose!

When I think of his firm Light – quenched so causelessly, it fritters the worth of much that shines. "Dust unto the Dust" indeed – but the final clause of that marvelous sentence – who has rendered it?

"I say unto you," Father would read at Prayers, with a militant Accent that would startle one.

Forgive me if I linger on the first Mystery of the House.

It's specific Mystery – each Heart had before – but within this World. Father's was the first Act distinctly of the Spirit.

Austin's Family went to Geneva, and Austin lived with us four weeks. It seemed peculiar – pathetic – and Antediluvian. We missed him while he was with us and missed him when he was gone.

All is so very curious.

Thank you for that "New Year" – the first with a fracture. I trust it is whole and hale – to you.

"Kingsley" rejoins "Argemone" [1] –

354. 1. Bismarck was at the time Chancellor of Prussia, and as the Franco-Prussian War had just begun he was the chief name in the news. 368. 1. Mr Miller: Joaquin Miller (1841–1913), author of *Songs of the Sierras*, and a stentorian urger of transport. 2. Mrs Lewes: better known as George Eliot, from whose *Mill on the Floss*, Chap. 12, the allusion to ancestors' brocades comes. 3. "Bells and Pomegranates": Under this title, for which see Exod. 28:33, Robert Browning published a series of volumes of verse and verse drama, including *Pippa Passes* (see Letter 268), between 1841 and 1846. 4. There may be an allusion to the old philosophical puzzle known as "Achilles and the Tortoise."

432. 1. "Argemone": the heroine of Charles Kingsley's first novel, *Yeast*.

Thank you for the Affection. It helps me up the Stairs at Night, where as I passed my Father's Door – I used to think was safety. The Hand that plucked the Clover – I seek, and am

Emily.

459A: TO T. W. HIGGINSON

1876

Nature is a Haunted House – but Art – a House that tries to be haunted.

580: TO SUSAN GILBERT DICKINSON

about 1878

The Solaces of Theft are first – Theft – second – Superiority to Detection –

Emily.

605: TO EDWARD (NED) DICKINSON [1]

about 1879

Dear Ned—

Dennis [2] was happy yesterday, and it made him graceful – I saw him waltzing with the Cow – and suspected his status, but he afterward started for your House in a frame that was unmistakable –

You told me he had'nt tasted Liquor since his Wife's decease – then she must have been living at six o'clock last Evening –

I fear for the rectitude of the Barn –

Love for the Police –

609: TO MRS. SAMUEL BOWLES

1879?

How lovely to remember! How tenderly they told of you! Sweet toil for smitten hands to console the smitten!

Labors as endeared may engross our lost. Buds of other days quivered in remembrance. Hearts of other days lent their solemn charm.

Life of flowers lain in flowers – what a home of dew! And the bough of ivy; was it as you said? Shall I plant it softly?

There were little feet, white as alabaster.

Dare I chill them with the soil?

Nature is our eldest mother, she will do no harm.

Let the phantom love that enrolls the sparrow shield you softer than a child.

787: TO MARTHA DICKINSON

late 1882

That's the Little Girl I always meant to be, but was'nt – The very Hat I always meant to wear, but did'nt and the attitude toward the Universe, so precisely my own, that I feel very much, as if I were returning Elisha's Horses, or the Vision of John at Patmos – [1]

Emily –

864: TO SAMUEL BOWLES THE YOUNGER

early autumn 1883

Dear friend,

There is more than one "Deluge," though but one is recorded, and the duplicate of the "Dove," hallows your own Heart. I had feared that the Angel with the Sword would dissuade you from Eden, but rejoice that it only ushered you. "Every several Gate is of one Pearl." [1]

Morning is due to all –
To some – the Night –
To an imperial few –
The Auroral Light.

Reverently,
E. Dickinson.

868: TO SUSAN GILBERT DICKINSON

early October 1883

Dear Sue –

The Vision of Immortal Life has been fulfilled –

How simply at the last the Fathom comes! The Passenger and not the Sea, we find surprises us –

Gilbert rejoiced in Secrets –

His Life was panting with them – With what menace of Light he cried "Dont tell, Aunt Emily"! Now my ascended Playmate must instruct *me*. Show us, prattling Preceptor, but the way to thee!

He knew no niggard moment – His Life was full of Boon – The Playthings of the Dervish were not so wild as his –

No crescent was this Creature – He traveled from the Full –

Such soar, but never set –

I see him in the Star, and meet his sweet velocity in everything that flies – His Life was

605. 1. Edward (Ned) Dickinson: Emily's nephew, the oldest son of Austin and Sue. 2. Dennis: Dennis Scannell, a handyman who worked for the Dickinsons and whose wife had recently died.

787. 1. Elisha's . . . Patmos: The references are to II Kings 2:12 and to the Book of Revelation, the latter always her favorite part of the Bible. 864. 1. The references are to Gen. 8:9,

like the Bugle, which winds itself away, his Elegy
an echo – his Requiem ecstasy –

Dawn and Meridian in one.

Wherefore would he wait, wronged only of
Night, which he left for us –

Without a speculation, our little Ajax [1] spans the
whole –

> Pass to thy Rendezvous of Light,
> Pangless except for us –
> Who slowly ford the Mystery
> Which thou hast leaped across!

Emily.

Gen. 3:24, and Rev. 21:21.   **868. 1. Ajax:** The name is used
here as a symbol of defiant heroism.

1024: TO SUSAN GILBERT DICKINSON

late 1885

The World hath not known her, but *I* have
known her, was the sweet Boast of Jesus – [1]

The small Heart cannot break – The Ecstasy of
it's penalty solaces the large –

Emerging from an Abyss, and reentering it –
that is Life, is it not, Dear?

The tie between us is very fine, but a Hair never
dissolves.

Lovingly –
Emily –

1024. 1. The . . . Jesus: See John 17:25.

HENRY NASH SMITH
Editor

Mark Twain

1835–1910

THE LIFE of Mark Twain is a part of our culture—even of our folklore, for it is clothed in an aura of legend that he himself created. His best books are all autobiographical: at first glance his imagination seems almost childishly self-centered. But the appearance is deceptive because he viewed his experience with detachment. He had the remarkable gift of seeing his own life as if it were a work of fiction composed by someone else.

This state of affairs poses a special problem for Mark Twain's biographers: they know at once too much and too little about their subject. He has exhibited himself at length in volume after volume, but he wore many different disguises. What was the man himself like behind the masks? The question is even more difficult than it might seem because the role of the "Mark Twain" who assumed the character of a boy to tell his greatest story, and signed it "Yours truly, Huck Finn," is itself a persona, a kind of mask that partially conceals the features of the actual Samuel L. Clemens. Yet only partially; for Clemens often thought of himself as Mark Twain, and signed himself "Mark" in letters to such friends as William Dean Howells and the Rev. Joseph H. Twichell, and to his manager James Redpath. On the other hand, in writing to members of his family he was more often "Sam" or "Saml." It is not surprising that he was preoccupied with the problem

of identity, and that his books are filled with characters who, like Huck Finn, assume a variety of names and roles.

Samuel Langhorne Clemens was born on November 30, 1835 in the backwoods settlement of Florida, in northeastern Missouri, some thirty miles inland from the Mississippi. His parents had arrived from Tennessee only six months earlier, in response to the urging of relatives who had come west the previous year. John Marshall Clemens, Sam's father, was a Virginian—"a stern, unsmiling man," as the son remembered him, "of perfect probity and high principle." He was ambitious to practice law and held office as justice of the peace and county judge, but was condemned to farming and storekeeping in a never quite successful effort to support his family. Sam's mother, Jane Lampton of Adair County, Kentucky, was described by her granddaughter as "a great beauty, a fine dancer, and very witty." She came of a family of Indian fighters; Sam inherited from her his red hair and also, no doubt, his fiery temper. He was the sixth of seven children, of whom three died in childhood and a fourth, Henry, the youngest, was killed in a steamboat explosion in 1858 at the age of twenty.

When Sam was four years old his father, having failed as a storekeeper in Florida, moved to Hannibal, a town on the river, in yet another effort to improve his fortunes. Although he was a prominent man in the community and served on various committees dedicated to civic projects, he continued on the edge of bankruptcy until his death in 1847, when Sam was eleven years old. During this last phase of the father's frustrating life, Sam Clemens was passing through the archetypal boyhood of America, storing up memories that were to become the basic vocabulary of the artist for the expression of his thought about the human condition.

It was only a brief period—six or seven years. Sam's real boyhood came to an end when he was eleven; for soon after his father's death he was apprenticed to a printer. He had no further formal education. In 1850, when his elder brother Orion started a weekly newspaper in Hannibal, Sam went to work for him as printer and editorial assistant. Together they undertook to support their mother and sister. But Sam grew more and more exasperated with Orion, who had his father's gift for high-minded failure, and in 1853 he struck out on his own. It took him more than fifteen years to decide on a vocation. In the course of that time he was a printer in St. Louis, New York, Philadelphia, Washington, Cincinnati, and a couple of towns in Iowa; a steamboat pilot on the Mississippi between St. Louis and New Orleans; a soldier, of sorts, for a couple of weeks in a vaguely Confederate militia company;[1] a prospector in various parts of Nevada; a local reporter for the *Territorial Enterprise* in Virginia City; a free-lance journalist in San Francisco; a traveling newspaper correspondent in Hawaii, Europe, and the Near East; a newspaper editor in Buffalo; and a humorous lecturer.

The crucial period in his development began in June, 1867, when he persuaded the San Francisco *Alta California* to send him as a correspondent with a company of tourists bound from New York to Europe and the Holy Land on board the steamer *Quaker City*. During the next three years both Mark Twain's conception of himself and the image he presented to the world underwent an extraordinary change. When he booked passage on the *Quaker City*, he was an irresponsible, Bohemian newspaper-

man, rejoicing in the sobriquet of "The Wild Humorist of the Pacific Slope." A New York publisher he called on to discuss publication of a volume of his sketches thought he looked too disreputable to bother with. The pose he affected—for it was a pose, closely related to the "moral paradox" Bret Harte was just beginning to make into a literary formula—is indicated in a letter to his mother written a few days before he sailed describing Dan Slote, with whom he was to share a cabin: "I have got a splendid, immoral, tobacco-smoking, wine-drinking, godless roommate who is as good and true and right-minded a man as ever lived. . . ."

This was in the spring of 1867. By the spring of 1870 Clemens was married to the delicate and fastidious Olivia Langdon of Elmira, New York, who would presently inherit a quarter of a million dollars from her father; the young couple were living in a handsome house in Buffalo, given them by the bride's parents as a wedding present; Mark Twain was editing the Buffalo *Express*, in which his father-in-law had helped him to buy an interest; and he had acquired many of the attitudes appropriate to Livy's social environment.

Neither the Bohemianism of 1867 nor the respectability of 1870 means quite what it seems to on the surface, because each image shows the histrionic exaggeration that was a part of Clemens' personal style. He was not so raffish as he made himself out to be before he met Livy nor so conventional, by far, as he seemed to be after they were married. Just here, perhaps, is where Van Wyck Brooks went astray in his famous contention that Mark Twain destroyed himself as an artist by surrendering to the philistinism of Elmira and Hartford. A sounder interpretation would recognize that he was expressing some part of his true self all along by means of the successive poses and disguises with which he experimented. Augustin Daly told him he could have been a great actor: to assume by turns a variety of roles was a part of his essential nature. But there was something solid underneath. In the end, when the marriage had attained its durable harmony, Livy had given up more of her habits and attitudes than he had of his.

The power of imagination that enabled Mark Twain to conceive of many different ways of

---

[1] Mark Twain describes this experience with comic exaggeration in "The Private History of a Campaign That Failed," *Century* (December, 1885).

life made it difficult for him to settle upon one. The arrangement for him to buy an interest in the Buffalo *Express* had rested on the assumption that his true vocation was journalism. But he could not endure for very long the relentless routine of getting a daily paper to press. Fortunately, an alternative vocation now came into view. *The Innocents Abroad*, published in August, 1869 on almost the very day he reported for work in the *Express* office, quickly became a best-seller: twelve thousand copies were sold within a month and sixty-seven thousand during the first year. Elisha Bliss, president of the American Publishing Company of Hartford, was eager for a second book. When Mark Twain was convinced he could make a good income by writing books, he sold out his interest in the *Express* (at a loss of ten thousand dollars), and in October, 1871 he moved his family to Hartford.

The success of *Roughing It*, published the following spring, and the acclaim with which Mark Twain was received when he lectured in England later that year, confirmed his decision to give up journalism. The Clemenses acquired an ample lot in the Nook Farm community on the western edge of Hartford, and in the spring of 1873 began building a house, which they moved into something more than a year later. It was three stories high and contained a score of rooms. On the outside were a half-dozen balconies, two towers, a porte-cochere, and a broad veranda. With the furnishings, it cost more than $120,000 at a time when the dollar had perhaps three times its present purchasing power. The house symbolized Clemens' new status; it was also the realization of the kind of dream he had ascribed to himself and Calvin Higbie in *Roughing It*, when for ten days they thought they had struck it rich in the mines. At an even deeper level the house gave expression to what he called the "circus side" of his nature—the Tom Sawyer strain in him which reveled in theatrical display and believed with Hank Morgan, the Connecticut Yankee, that "you can't throw too much style into a miracle."

The Hartford house was also a monument to domesticity, to the idea of the family. It was built for Livy, for the eldest daughter (Susy) who had been born in 1872, and for the two

other daughters (Clara and Jean) who would be born during the next ten years. Even by nineteenth-century standards, the Clemenses were a close-knit group. Although Mark Twain might disappear into his study for several hours a day, parents and children all gathered at meals, where he talked with unfailing energy and brilliance about whatever was on his mind; and the habitual evening program consisted of reading aloud in the family circle—often from the pages he had written during the day. The girls were taught at home by tutors. When Susy reached eighteen and it seemed inevitable she should receive some education outside the household, she entered Bryn Mawr. Both parents went down with her when she enrolled, stayed at a near-by hotel for two or three weeks, and returned for frequent visits. In February of her freshman year Clemens wrote to Howells:

Mrs. Clemens has been in Philadelphia a week at the Continental Hotel with Susy (who, to my private regret is beginning to love Bryn Mawr) & I've had to stay here alone. But this is the last time this brace of old fools, old indispensables-to-each-other, are going to separate themselves in this foolish fashion.

His regret was unfounded: Susy was so homesick she was ill much of the time, and she withdrew from college in April. This was the only effort the Clemenses made to send any of the daughters away from home to be educated. Later, when Clara was studying music in Europe, they often took up residence in the cities where her teachers were situated.

The other side of the coin was Mark Twain's gregariousness and love of excitement. There was much visiting back and forth in the Nook Farm community, and the Clemenses had frequent house guests. As one of the leading citizens of Hartford, Mark Twain was elected to the Monday Evening Club which met every two weeks to discuss papers read by members. He was invited to lecture for the benefit of various charities and to speak at Republican rallies —until he scandalized his friends by supporting Cleveland in 1884. By the middle of the 1870's he was finding he could count on uninterrupted time for writing only during the summers, which the family usually spent at

Quarry Farm, the home of Livy's foster sister, Susan Crane, near Elmira. The program of entertaining, added to the routine expense of maintaining the great house with its staff of six servants, became so burdensome that in 1878–79, and again in the early 1890's, the Clemenses made long visits to Europe in order to cut down their household expenses.

The most important literary influence on Mark Twain during his Hartford period was his friendship with Howells, novelist, editor of the *Atlantic Monthly* (until 1881), and the leading critic in the United States. From the time when Howells singled out *The Innocents Abroad* for review in 1869, until Mark Twain's death, and after, he acclaimed his friend's extraordinary gifts as an artist. He urged him to contribute to the *Atlantic*, defended him in Brahmin circles that were inclined to look down on the unconventional Westerner, helped him to distinguish good work from bad in his own writing, and on occasion cheerfully read proof or performed any function, however menial, that would help Clemens get his books into print. In return, Clemens declared that Howells was his "only author." He often sent enthusiastic praise of Howells' novels as they came out serially in the magazines, and toward the end of his life published the expert analysis of Howells' style which is reproduced here.

Except for Livy's semi-invalidism, the later 1870's and early 1880's were a period of golden prosperity and happiness for Clemens. He adored his wife and daughters; his fame and his income were constantly increasing. Yet his prickly disposition caused him to be continually dissatisfied with his publishers. Upon the death of Elisha Bliss in 1880, he turned from the American Publishing Company to James R. Osgood of Boston and then to his own publishing firm, which he established in New York in 1884 under the management of his nephew, Charles L. Webster. The company throve. Its first book, *Adventures of Huckleberry Finn*, sold fifty-one thousand copies within fourteen months, and its handling of the *Personal Memoirs of Ulysses S. Grant* was a landmark in mass publishing. But Clemens was involved in other business enterprises that were less profitable, especially the promotion of the Paige typesetter. This machine was ingenious and,

within its limitations, successful, but it was too complicated for general service. In the later 1880's the construction of a pilot model in the Pratt & Whitney machine shops in Hartford was costing him two or three thousand dollars a month. During these same years the Webster company needed capital to sustain a pioneer plan for selling the Stedman and Hutchinson ten-volume *Library of American Literature* on the instalment plan. By 1894 the shortage of credit resulting from the panic of 1893 brought matters to a crisis. The Webster company faced bankruptcy. Clemens was forced to abandon his efforts to put the Paige machine into production, after he had sunk about two-hundred thousand dollars in it. His finances would have been hopeless had it not been for the intervention of Henry H. Rogers, Standard Oil executive and one of the powers of Wall Street, who generously took over direction of Clemens' business affairs, compounded with the creditors, and eventually made an arrangement whereby Harper & Brothers became publishers of all his works and guaranteed him a substantial income. Although Mark Twain was not legally liable for the debts remaining after the Webster company was liquidated, he insisted, like Walter Scott before him, on paying all legitimate claims in full. Largely by means of a lecture tour around the world in 1895–96, he achieved this goal in 1898.

Bankruptcy was but one of the disasters in store for Clemens. Psychological disturbances in his daughter Jean were diagnosed in 1896 as symptoms of epilepsy. (She was never entirely well again, and in 1909 she died as the result of an epileptic seizure.) While he was still in England on his way home from his lecture tour, Susy died in Hartford of spinal meningitis. It was a shattering blow for both parents. Livy, never very strong, suffered in 1902 a violent attack of asthma. It left her in such a state of nervous exhaustion that for months on end her husband was allowed to see her only a few minutes each day. On the recommendation of the doctors, he established the family in a villa near Florence for the sake of the milder climate, but Livy did not really gain strength, and she died in 1904.

Mark Twain was growing old. He was inconsolably lonely, and some of his basic attitudes and beliefs had undergone a change that weakened his power of imagination. But his trip through the southern hemisphere had broadened his political horizon, and in the years before and after the turn of the century he published scathing attacks on the imperialistic ventures of Britain and Belgium in Africa, and of the United States in Asia. Howells shared his old friend's views; both men were heatedly denounced in the press as subversives for their protests against American occupation of the Philippines. Clemens also took a vigorous part in the New York municipal elections of 1901 which led to the defeat of Boss Richard Croker. As time went on, however, his disillusionment with the promises of democracy led him to a gloomy acquiescence in the trend toward what he called "monarchy."

In 1907 he made a triumphal trip to Oxford to receive the degree of Litt.D. This was his fourth honorary degree. The others had been an M.A. (1888) and Litt.D. (1901) from Yale, and an LL.D. (1902) from the University of Missouri. He was an international celebrity whose comings and goings and opinions on the affairs of the world were reported constantly in the press.

After the death of Livy, Clemens lived for a time in rented houses in New York, spending his summers in the White Mountains or the Adirondacks. He was much in demand as an after-dinner speaker at banquets, and the emptiness of his life led him to accept many invitations. As his energies slowly declined, however, he left New York to live in a handsome villa designed by Howells' son, John Mead Howells, which he built in 1906–07 near Redding, Connecticut. He called it "Stormfield" after one of his favorite characters, the hero of "Captain Stormfield's Visit to Heaven." Here he was delighted to be able to preside over the wedding of his daughter Clara to Ossip Gabrilowitsch, a brilliant pianist and conductor, and to welcome the guests who never ceased coming—Howells, the publisher George Harvey, Joe Twichell, Helen Keller, the actress Billie Burke. He dictated further chapters of his rambling memoirs, or struggled to revise and to complete the unfinished stories and novels into whose confused symbolism he poured the bitterness of his last years. He was heavily dependent psychologically on Albert Bigelow Paine, the young editor and free-lance writer who had been given permission in 1906 to write his biography, and who became an almost constant companion. It was Paine who went to Bermuda to bring Clemens back home when the angina pectoris that had been threatening him for some time grew suddenly worse. He died at Stormfield on April 21, 1910.

II

JUST AS the man Samuel L. Clemens wore now one mask, now another, his writings also have had widely different meanings for different audiences. Most readers in his own day considered him simply a funny man, a literary comedian like Artemus Ward, Bill Arp, or Josh Billings; and amid the solemnities of twentieth-century criticism it is worth remembering that even after we discard much joking which no longer comes off, Mark Twain's work is often very funny indeed. It was his humor that made him a best-selling writer and a popular favorite on the lecture platform. This mass appeal brought him a handsome income and freed him from the necessity of turning out copy month in and month out, whether he felt like it or not, as Howells was compelled to do for half a century. But as both Mark Twain and Howells recognized, there was something ambiguous about his relation to his public. Howells observed that "no book of literary quality was made to go by subscription except Mr. Clemens's books, and I think these went because the subscription public never knew what good literature they were." After Mark Twain's death Howells returned to this point, remarking that the "average practical American public . . . was his first tribunal, and must always be his court of final appeal." The word "practical" here means something like "lowbrow"; it alludes to the fact that, except for Howells and one or two other friends, no literary critic took Mark Twain seriously enough during his lifetime to analyze and discuss his work as literature. This was the great disadvantage of his status as a writer for the mass audience: he was deprived of the benefit of discriminating criticism. It was not that he might have learned something about his craft from the critics—although Howells certainly helped him in this regard—but rather that serious critical attention might have spared him his lifelong struggle to justify to himself what he was doing, and might have helped him not to take himself at too low a valuation.

From the very first Howells called attention to the "pure human nature" in Mark Twain's work and its evocation of whole areas of American experience. He also noted with approval Mark Twain's function as a critic of society who attacked tyranny and superstition in the name of democracy and enlightenment. These emphases determined the prevalent view of Mark Twain until quite recently. But the cult of realism has given way to the cults of symbolism and of form in literature. For twenty years and more a new Mark Twain has been coming into view, a Mark Twain who is an artist rather than a chronicler, a creator of symbols as well as an observer of society. And it has become clear that he was not an illiterate backwoodsman but a man of considerable if unsystematic reading. Walter Blair, for example, has called attention to echoes of a dozen writers—from Shakespeare and Cervantes to Saint-Simon, Taine, Carlyle, and Lecky—in *Huckleberry Finn* alone.

The student will get the most out of Mark Twain who does not commit himself exclusively to any one of these critical perspectives but tries to find what is valid in each of them; for Mark Twain is too rich a writer to be exhausted by any formula. Nevertheless, the inspired humorist and the incomparable chronicler in him still seem more accessible than the artist engaged in advanced technical experiments that laid the foundation for a native American literary prose.

The equipment with which he began, the tradition of native American humor and the insouciance of Nevada and California journalism, gave him what may be called for convenience a vernacular perspective, and also a feeling for the poetic vividness of colloquial language. But these are matters involving primarily the texture of prose; they have little bearing on the problem of structure. When he undertook to be a writer of books rather than a journalist, and therefore faced the task of constructing a long narrative, he was at a frontier of literary experiment. This was his situation when he sat down in San Francisco in April, 1868, to make over his dispatches from the *Quaker City* excursion into *The Innocents Abroad*. He could not follow the example of Bayard Taylor and produce a travel book by merely stringing his newspaper pieces together because he was not just describing what he had seen, but writing what was in effect a work of fiction. Yet he could hardly use as a model the only large fictional form that lay to hand, that of the novel, because a novel was axiomatically a love story. He would have to contrive a new imaginative pattern to provide a structure for his book.

He adopted the only logical course: he undertook to expand the fictional elements in the newspaper dispatches into a larger narrative pattern. These fictional elements were implicit in the tradition of backwoods humor, which often involved a contrast or conflict between a "straight" and a vernacular character. Mark Twain had experimented with many variations on this pattern. In "The Celebrated Jumping Frog of Calaveras County," for example, which brought Mark Twain his first national recognition when it was published in the New York *Saturday Press* in 1865, the tall tale about filling a frog with shot is merely a pretext for bringing the straight narrator into contact with Simon Wheeler, whose simplicity and candor the writer finds admirable. It is a form of the pastoral pattern which European poets had used through the centuries.

The polarity of the two roles suggested the device of heightening the gentility of the straight character and the vulgarity of his vernacular companion or adversary. In the letters sent to the Sacramento *Union* from Hawaii in 1866, Mark Twain cast himself as straight man and for contrast created the violently antigenteel Mr. Brown. He continued using Mr. Brown in the *Quaker City* dispatches: Brown, for example, was confused by what he took to be the names of the railway stations in France because they were all the same: "Côte des hommes." But the device was actually in conflict with the meanings Mark Twain had discovered in his materials during the journey. In proportion as he grew irritated with the representatives of the official culture who dominated the group of passengers, he realized that his basic sympathies lay with the subversives, the outsiders. The antagonism between Mark Twain and the cronies whom he calls "Sinners," on the one hand, and, on the other, the austere "Pilgrims," is depicted in the description of the Pilgrim Bird in the Marseilles zoo—a passage, incidentally, that was added in revision.

In this situation Mark Twain found himself gravitating toward the role of Mr. Brown rather than that of the straight character. When he revised the *Quaker City* dispatches, therefore, he abolished Brown and parceled out Brown's impertinencies among the Sinners. The transformation was not complete—Mark Twain was in a hurry, and he was always bored with the job of revision; he was so far from realizing the implications of his decision that he actually added a number of passages, such as the rhapsody about the Sphinx, exhibiting the narrator in the role of genteel tourist. But he had at least glimpsed the possibility of using the vernacular character as narrator, and this maneuver, developed in successive episodes, gives a rudimentary coherence to the narrative.

In *Roughing It*, at least in the first half of the book, Mark Twain uses the narrator more effectively. He is a tenderfoot being initiated into the community of men who have "seen the elephant" by undergoing the hardships of prospecting in Nevada. The pronoun "I" as used by the narrator refers simultaneously to this tenderfoot and to the seasoned Old Timer looking back on his own callowness as he tells the story. The subject matter of the narrative— the initiation of the tenderfoot—is thus assimilated into the narrative point of view. The crisis in the narrator's initiation comes in the snowstorm episode; the account of the Buncombe trial reveals him as an accepted member of the community. These chapters show how humorous anecdotes of the sort that had traditionally stood alone could take on new meaning when they were incorporated into a larger narrative pattern. The anecdote of the cayote illustrates the same phenomenon. Here the "town-bred" tenderfoot dog is exposed to the firmer and more durable values of the Far West. At the hands of the Old Timer cayote of unpretentious appearance but hidden power, the tenderfoot gains a fresh (and in this environment, indispensable) humility—although the educational process is painful and the ten-

derfoot must be humiliated before he can learn his lesson.

Mark Twain's next book after *Roughing It*, written in collaboration with his new neighbor, Charles Dudley Warner, was *The Gilded Age* (1873), a satire on the political corruption involved in Congressional pork-barrel appropriations. Although the authors set out to undercut the sentimental clichés of the contemporary popular novel, they ended up using many novelistic stereotypes themselves, including a melodramatic subplot about a beautiful heroine who shoots her betrayer. Neither a skillful example of the conventional novel nor a successful burlesque of the genre, the book contributed nothing to the solution of Mark Twain's problem of narrative structure. It does, however, contain one unforgettable character, Colonel Sellers; and his creation marks a significant step toward Mark Twain's discovery of his prime literary resource in what may be called the Matter of Hannibal—the store of boyhood memories that was to provide the substance of his best work for the next thirty years. This material is used even more extensively in "Old Times on the Mississippi," the series of articles he wrote at the instance of Howells for the *Atlantic Monthly* (January– August, 1875). These sketches resemble *Roughing It* in being the story of an initiation, and in exploiting the contrast between the callowness of the narrator as a cub pilot and the sophistication with which he looks back on his experiences. The chapters added later to make the book published as *Life on the Mississippi* (1883) resemble the section on Hawaii in *Roughing It*; they fail to sustain the imaginative power achieved in the "Old Times" series by skillful management of point of view.

In the Preface to *The Adventures of Tom Sawyer* (1876) Mark Twain declares: "Most of the adventures recorded in this book really occurred; one or two were experiences of my own, the rest those of boys who were schoolmates of mine." But the story is told in the third person. It was perhaps a necessary choice for a narrative centering about Tom; his basic conformity makes him an unlikely spokesman for satire directed against the society of Hannibal, and his chronic viewing of experience through the lens of his reading in historical romances would have made it difficult to present either incidents or characters in Tom's words without distortion. But whatever may have been the cause, the management of the narrative is a good deal more awkward than it is in "Old Times on the Mississippi."

Nevertheless, the subject matter almost redeems the uncertainties of technique; the book is truly, as Mark Twain called it later, a prose hymn—to boyhood and to pre-industrial America. And the writing of the story brought a priceless stroke of good fortune in the discovery of Huckleberry Finn. Even before *The Adventures of Tom Sawyer* was published, Mark Twain plunged into the writing of the story of "Tom Sawyer's Comrade." In his customary fashion, he put the manuscript aside more than once; it was seven years before he finished it. In the meantime he had written *A Tramp Abroad* (1880), a travel book about Europe in which he unfortunately cast himself again in the straight role of genteel traveler, and a carefully constructed children's story, *The Prince and the Pauper* (1882), which has a few echoes of the Matter of Hannibal—the pauper, Tom Canty, has been described as "an amalgam of the characteristics of Huck Finn and Tom Sawyer." But these books are much thinner in substance than *Tom Sawyer,* and neither represents an advance in narrative technique.

For that, we must turn to the momentous decision to tell Huck's story not only from his point of view but in his own words. The difference between this method of narration and the one used in *Tom Sawyer* can best be seen in a comparison of passages. Here is the description (in *Tom Sawyer*) of Tom's reaction to being unjustly scolded by Aunt Polly for a misdemeanor committed by his half-brother Sid:

He pictured himself lying sick unto death and his aunt bending over him beseeching one little forgiving word, but he would turn his face to the wall, and die with that word unsaid. . . . And he pictured himself brought home from the river, dead, with his curls all wet, and his sore heart at rest. How she would throw herself upon him, and how her tears would fall like rain . . . But he would lie there cold and white and make no sign—a poor little sufferer, whose griefs were at an end. He so

worked upon his feelings with the pathos of these dreams, that he had to keep swallowing, he was so like to choke . . .

Mark Twain has in mind here a standard comic device, a form of burlesque that consists in using elevated diction for trivial subjects. He intends to exploit the discrepancy between the slight injury Tom has received and his false dramatization of it. But Mark Twain is not capable of managing the third-person point of view so as to achieve his effect consistently; the exalted language is not located firmly in either Tom's consciousness or the writer's, and the ironic contrast is therefore unstable. A further sign of confusion is the conspicuous colloquialism "he was . . . like to choke," which must be ascribed to the author.

The use of Huck as narrator for *Adventures of Huckleberry Finn* helps keep things under control. In the following passage, Huck suffers a real injury and is threatened with worse. His Pap has taken him to a cabin on the Illinois shore:

But by-and-by Pap got too handy with his hick'ry, and I couldn't stand it. I was all over welts. He got to going away so much, too, and locking me in. Once he locked me in and was gone three days. It was dreadful lonesome. I judged he had got drowned and I wasn't ever going to get out any more. I was scared. I made up my mind I would fix up some way to leave there.

The elimination of the omniscient author has removed the temptation to comment directly on the action. This not only makes for economy, it prevents confusion about whose language is being used; the reader is not forced to concern himself with the sensibility of an unidentified observer who both is and is not in the story.

Other passages in *Huckleberry Finn* show even more remarkable consequences of the new method. The contrast between Huck's vernacular speech and the high-flown diction of false pathos leads to a discovery of new meanings in the material. When Huck is about to commit himself irrevocably to the awe-inspiring sin of helping Jim escape from slavery, he reports an inner debate in which he tries to defend himself against the accusations of his conscience. His conscience employs the inflated diction of the pulpit, tinged to be sure with Huck's colloquial grammar, but clearly a mode of speech not his own:

> . . . it hit me all of a sudden that here was the plain hand of Providence slapping me in the face and letting me know my wickedness was being watched all the time from up there in heaven, whilst I was stealing a poor old woman's nigger that hadn't ever done me no harm, and now was showing me there's One that's always on the lookout, and ain't agoing to allow no such miserable doings to go on only just so fur and no further . . .

The contrast between elevated and vernacular diction becomes here a means of representing the conflict between what Mark Twain later called Huck's sound heart and his depraved conscience. Without resorting to an abstract technical vocabulary, Mark Twain shows how the mores of a corrupt society have been internalized as Huck's categorical imperatives, and thus come into conflict with his naturally humane impulses.

Unfortunately, the technical discoveries that Mark Twain made in writing *Huckleberry Finn* did not enable him to repeat his triumph. The power of that book depends on more than the use of his memories of the River and the choice of Huck as narrator; it depends also on the theme of freedom versus bondage, which is important in itself and of deep concern to the writer. The overt plot dealing with Jim's effort to escape is reinforced by the indirect statement of the theme of freedom in the contrast between the happiness and peace of Huck and Jim on the raft, and the degraded society of the towns along the shore, where actual slavery is only one aspect of the pervasive fraud, greed, meanness, and gullibility. Mark Twain tried several times to write a sequel to *Huckleberry Finn*, using Huck as narrator. These efforts are mediocre or worse, evidently because they are built around inconsequential themes. The Phelps plantation sequence at the end of *Huckleberry Finn* had already shown the disastrous consequences of substituting a trivial theme for a serious one. When Tom reappears in Chapter 33, the author has decided to abandon the story of how Huck helped his friend in spite of danger and inner suffering. In its place we have a farcical treatment of Jim's escape. Since Tom knows that Jim has been freed in Miss

Watson's will, the elaborate ceremonies and paraphernalia that follow are but a prolonged boyish prank. Huck is pushed to the periphery of the narrative as a mere observer; Jim is transformed from a human being into a character from a blackface minstrel show; and in place of the significant action of the middle section of the book, we are given a burlesque of Tom's favorite cloak-and-sword fiction.

The real fable of *Huckleberry Finn* ends up in the air as Huck approaches the Phelps plantation in Chapter 32, helplessly seeking some way to release Jim from the cabin where he is locked up until he can be delivered to his owner. The boyhood Eden of St. Petersburg has been destroyed by Huck's discovery of the truth about the river towns; and although the decadence of these towns might be considered peculiar to the prewar South because it is the result of slavery, there has been a strong hint that Bricksville and its people are but a metaphor for the human condition in general. Colonel Sherburn of Bricksville is all too directly speaking for the author when he says to the mob in front of his house: "I know you clear through. I was born and raised in the South, and I've lived in the North, so I know the average all around. The average man's a coward."

Mark Twain's next book was an effort to test this dark generalization, to determine whether human society could be changed so that the possibility of happiness would not be confined to the dream-like isolation of a raft. To state the problem more abstractly, Mark Twain now confronted the contradiction between his growing disillusionment concerning human nature and human society, and his deeply rooted faith in the idea of progress. *A Connecticut Yankee in King Arthur's Court*, like *Huckleberry Finn*, passed through several stages in the course of its gestation, and the final result was perhaps not at all what the author had intended when he first began playing with the idea of a burlesque of Malory's *Morte d'Arthur*. As the book was finally published, sixth-century Britain is a magnified Bricksville, and Hank Morgan is a vernacular hero, an "ignoramus" devoid of culture but equipped with the whole arsenal of modern technical skills, who is launched upon the magnificent adventure of transforming a sty of filth and poverty and superstition and tyranny into its polar opposite—an enlightened republic where industrialization will provide the material basis for comfort and general happiness.

In the end Hank fails because he is unable to educate "the superstition out of those people." His proclamation of a republic has no effect because the Established Church is able to coerce the populace by an Interdict into supporting the "righteous cause" of monarchy. He is surprised by this outcome, and we must imagine that the author was to some extent surprised also. Mark Twain's career had been sustained by a basic confidence in the sanity, health, and sturdiness of the mass of mankind. He had also assumed that technology was the peculiar possession of the common people as contrasted with the upper classes. Thus democracy and progress—especially the general enlightenment of mankind as a result of industrialization—had seemed to him so closely related that one could not be imagined without the other. But in the course of writing *A Connecticut Yankee* he had become aware that his assumptions might not be valid. Whether we are to seek the cause in outer events of the 1880's, or in his penetration to a deeper level of intuitive awareness within himself when he tried to imagine in detail a Utopia of progressive democracy, his loss of faith both in the soundness of the common people and in the benign effects of technology is unmistakable.

This disillusionment deprived Mark Twain's fictive universe of meaning and threatened to paralyze him as a writer. During the last twenty years of his life he produced thousands of pages of manuscript in the form of incomplete stories and novels, some of them running to book length. Recurrent, even obsessive images and situations in this material indicate that he felt enclosed with his family and a few other companions in a hermetically sealed universe. He had the sensation of being bound on an endless voyage to an unknown destination; he was haunted by the idea that he was experiencing a nightmare from which he might at any moment awaken. Most of this late fiction is so baldly symbolic that it fails to create the illusion of reality. But even during the years of financial strain in the early 1890's, Mark Twain was able, by prolonged labor, to bring one major novel to completion. *Pudd'nhead Wilson* (1894) is marred by vestiges of a pair of Siamese twins who originally figured in it and had to be almost surgically removed. Except for this blemish, however, it is an impressive work.

Once again, the setting is a town on the shore of the Mississippi. Pudd'nhead Wilson, isolated from the townspeople by his superior intelligence, belongs to a series of transcendent figures who appear with increasing frequency in Mark Twain's later works. In their developed form—represented by Satan in *The Mysterious Stranger*—these creatures of fantasy enjoy immunity from the constraints of determinism, the sense of guilt, and the limited intellectual horizons that are the bane of all merely human beings. Wilson's transcendence is only rudimentary, but it is perceptible. Through his independent discovery of the principle of identification by means of fingerprints, he solves a murder mystery and establishes the identity of two characters exchanged years before in the cradle. His extraordinary gift of analysis, that is, confers on him the power to intervene decisively in the affairs of the village. The fact that his secret is revealed dramatically in a courtroom scene gives him the air of a grown-up Tom Sawyer. A more serious link between Wilson and the author is the bitter maxims from "Pudd'nhead Wilson's Calendar" placed at the chapter headings: they seem to say that both author and hero have attained a superhuman perspective on mortal affairs. Although Mark Twain does not tell the story in the first person, the general point of view is Wilson's: the author no longer finds congenial the vernacular persona he had adopted in *Huckleberry Finn* and *A Connecticut Yankee*, but is identifying himself with a quite different character. For the transcendent figure has nothing in common with the vernacular hero.

The sardonic negations of "Puddn'head Wilson's Calendar" are belied by the immense vitality of Roxie, fair of complexion, beautiful of face, noble and stately of carriage, but "a slave, and saleable as such" because she is one-sixteenth Negro. Her intelligence and force of character are the mainspring of the action. But these human qualities are of no avail against the organized injustice of the slave system.

Pudd'nhead Wilson's revelation of the true state of affairs beneath the deceptive surface of appearances benefits no one: Roxie's son, reared as the "white" heir to a leading citizen, but eventually revealed as a Negro, is sold down the River; the "white" boy who has been reared as a Negro has received the stamp of caste beyond the possibility of change even after his identity is revealed: "He could neither read nor write, and his speech was the basest dialect of the negro quarter. His gait, his attitudes, his gestures, his bearing, his laugh—all were vulgar and uncouth; his manners were the manners of a slave." As for Roxie herself: ". . . the spirit in her eye was quenched, her martial bearing departed with it, and the voice of her laughter ceased in the land." The story seems to say that the penetration of the surface of society by analytical intelligence is as useless as was Hank Morgan's effort to transform it by means of technology. Since the author has closely identified himself with his principal character, we can hardly avoid finding one of the meanings of the book to be the futility of the artist's revelation of the hidden truth about man and the human condition.

The other important work of fiction published during the last twenty years of Mark Twain's life is the sardonic fable called "The Man That Corrupted Hadleyburg" (1898). Hadleyburg is Hannibal, it is everybody's home town. The characters are chosen for their commonplaceness, and nothing seems remarkable about the community except its self-righteous claim to be honest. The mysterious stranger who proves the townspeople to be dishonest merely by dropping a sum of money into their midst is another transcendent figure. His motive is said to be revenge, but the offense offered him by the town is never specified, and since his plan to corrupt all the leaders of the community merely provides an occasion for latent dishonesty to show itself, his function resembles Pudd'nhead Wilson's. The emphasis falls on the universality of guilt: the whole human race is tainted and damned.

The other writings of the 1890's now seem of minor importance, although Mark Twain and many of his contemporaries thought highly of the *Personal Recollections of Joan of Arc* (serialized, at first anonymously to make sure

no one would take it for a joke, in *Harper's Magazine* in 1895). Later readers, while recognizing the pathos of the author's fixation upon this story of doomed innocence, have found the characterization of Joan too idolatrous to be convincing. And the presence of a character of such absolute purity imposes on the story the pattern of melodrama: Joan's adversaries are necessarily villains of the deepest dye. *Following the Equator* (1897) is a travel diary produced by force of will in order to pay the author's debts. The short pieces of fiction published during these later years—such as the intensely sentimental "A Horse's Tale" and "A Dog's Tale"—are negligible, or worse.

The Mysterious Stranger, left unfinished at Mark Twain's death and somewhat arbitrarily constructed by Albert B. Paine through the addition of a last chapter found separately among the author's papers, is of more consequence. It carries to their logical extremity the principal themes of the last period: the inexorable determinism of man's actions; the burdensomeness of life; man's inferiority in consequence of his being endowed with the "moral sense"—i.e., the capacity to feel guilt, which makes him cruel. The angel Satan, nephew of His Satanic Majesty, is the supreme transcendent figure. Like Tom Sawyer arranging Jim's "evasion" from the Phelps plantation, or Hank Morgan industrializing Arthur's Britain, or the stranger who corrupts Hadleyburg, or Pudd'nhead Wilson with his fingerprints, Satan comes from without to intervene in the lives of earth-bound mortals, but it makes no real difference because, as he eventually informs the narrator, "Life itself is only a vision, a dream. . . . Nothing exists save empty space—and you!" It is the only consolation Mark Twain can find for having to continue life as a member of "the damned human race" in a universe apparently presided over by the God preached from all the pulpits:

. . . a God who could make good children as easily as bad, yet preferred to make bad ones; who could have made every one of them happy, yet never made a single happy one; who made them prize their bitter life, yet stingily cut it short; who mouths justice and invented hell—mouths mercy and invented hell—mouths Golden Rules, and forgiveness multiplied by seventy times seven, and invented hell; who created man without invitation, then tries to shuffle the responsibility for man's acts upon man, instead of honorably placing it where it belongs, upon himself; and finally, with altogether divine obtuseness, invites this poor, abused slave to worship him!

The distance from *Huckleberry Finn* to this bleak epilogue is not so great as it might seem: the senseless violence of the Shepherdson-Grangerford feud made Huck sick, and he was ashamed of the human race when he watched the King and the Duke gulling the fellow townsmen of Peter Wilks. But the Mark Twain who is cherished all over the world in our day is the writer who could affirm life in spite of his recognition of the dark abysses in human nature. He continues to be read by many people who are quite indifferent to sophisticated critical opinion. They value him for his humor, which at its best provides some of the world's great comic moments, and for his unmatched depiction of American character and American society in the years of the nation's turbulent, expansive, formless youth. In recent decades he has also come to be recognized as a pioneer technician. The often-quoted, over-dogmatic assertion in Hemingway's *Green Hills of Africa* (1935) that "all modern American literature comes from one book by Mark Twain called *Huckleberry Finn*" has been echoed by Faulkner, who declared that "all of us . . . are his heirs," and by Eliot, who said that he "discovered a new way of writing" by creating "a literary language based on American colloquial speech." Although some critics have rightly pointed out the existence of a different American literary tradition represented by Melville, Hawthorne, and Henry James, Mark Twain's unique and continuing appeal to highbrows and lowbrows alike goes far toward justifying H. L. Mencken's claim that he is "the true father of our national literature."

READING SUGGESTIONS

EDITIONS

No complete edition of Mark Twain's writings has ever been published. The least inadequate edition—inac-

curately called "Definitive" on its title pages—is that in thirty-seven volumes issued by Gabriel Wells (1923–25). It is a scandal that the work of none of the major American writers has been properly edited on the scale, for example, of the Columbia edition of John Milton. Several projects now under way have begun the prodigious work required to remedy this condition. Harper & Brothers, designated in Mark Twain's will as his official publishers, control the copyright of the books not yet in the public domain, but only a few volumes are kept in print. For a summary of the complex bibliographical problems connected with Mark Twain's work, see pp. 264–69 of the E. Hudson Long *Handbook* (listed below). Several recent reprints of books by Mark Twain contain useful introductions, especially the editions of *Adventures of Huckleberry Finn* by Lionel Trilling (1948), T. S. Eliot (1950), and Henry Nash Smith (1958); of *The Adventures of Tom Sawyer* by Bernard DeVoto (1939); of *Life on the Mississippi* by Willis Wager and Edward Wagenknecht (1944), and Dixon Wecter (1950); of *Roughing It* by Henry Nash Smith (1959); and of *A Connecticut Yankee in King Arthur's Court* by William M. Gibson (1960).

WILLIAM M. GIBSON AND HENRY NASH SMITH, editors, *Mark Twain-Howells Letters: The Correspondence of Samuel L. Clemens and William Dean Howells, 1872–1910*, 2 vols., (1960). The record of a friendship between the leading critic and the most famous American writer of their day, covering virtually the entire literary career of Mark Twain.

BIOGRAPHY AND CRITICISM

KENNETH R. ANDREWS, *Nook Farm: Mark Twain's Hartford Years* (1950). A careful and richly detailed account of the New England community in which the Clemens family lived for almost twenty years.

WALTER BLAIR, *Mark Twain and Huck Finn* (1960). The "biography of a book," setting forth the entire history of *Adventures of Huckleberry Finn*, from its long gestation to its publication and critical reception. A major work of historical criticism which throws new light on the central themes of Mark Twain's work down to 1885.

WALTER BLAIR, *Native American Humor* (1937). An anthology of the Down East humor, the humor of the Old Southwest, the work of the literary comedians, and the local-color writing that made up the tradition within which Mark Twain began his development as a writer. Blair's two hundred pages of introduction and bibliography contain the best all-around account of Mark Twain's relation to this background.

VAN WYCK BROOKS, *The Ordeal of Mark Twain* (1920; revised edition 1933). This pioneer study is devoted to the thesis that Mark Twain's development as an artist was thwarted by the repressive influence of his mother and his wife, and by the general philistinism of the Gilded Age. The book has been enormously influential, but it presents a distorted view of Mark Twain because Brooks's primary object was to criticize American society in the twentieth century. The book also suffers from the fact that Brooks shows no appreciation for humor.

BERNARD DEVOTO, *Mark Twain's America* (1932). An energetic reply to Van Wyck Brooks which maintains that Mark Twain fulfilled himself as "a humorist, realist, and satirist of the frontier." The book is vividly written, and contains much valuable information about the American West, but it exaggerates both the creative impulse Mark Twain derived from his Western experiences and the supposed decadence of the East.

BERNARD DEVOTO, *Mark Twain at Work* (1942). Brilliant criticism of Mark Twain's work based on long study of the unpublished materials in the Mark Twain Papers. In recognizing that Mark Twain's later work embodies many "Symbols of Despair," DeVoto moves toward the Brooks thesis he had rejected ten years earlier.

DELANCEY FERGUSON, *Mark Twain: Man and Legend* (1943). The best single book about Mark Twain's life and work: clear, balanced, thorough, and interesting.

E. HUDSON LONG, *Mark Twain Handbook* (1957). A convenient summary of all important information about Mark Twain as a man and as a writer, including scholarship and criticism devoted to him.

KENNETH S. LYNN, *Mark Twain and Southwestern Humor* (1960). Presents an original analysis of the tradition in which Mark Twain worked. The chapters on the writer himself contain the most recent study of his entire literary career, and illustrate the use of psychological ideas as instruments of critical analysis.

ALBERT B. PAINE, *Mark Twain: A Biography*, 3 vols. (1912). Paine was Mark Twain's official biographer and literary executor, and this book is an indispensable source of information. But it is flawed by Paine's uncritical admiration for his subject; by the fact that he sometimes tampered with texts in quoting them; and by his acceptance of genteel canons of literary taste.

ARTHUR L. SCOTT, editor, *Mark Twain: Selected Criticism* (1955). Thirty-four items chosen from the vast bibliography of discussion devoted to Mark Twain's work, from the one-page "Advertisement" inserted by the publisher, Charles H. Webb, in *The Celebrated Jumping Frog of Calaveras County, and Other Sketches* (1867) to a selection from Henry Seidel Canby's *Turn West, Turn East* (1951).

DIXON WECTER, *Sam Clemens of Hannibal* (1952). A thorough study of Sam Clemens' life down to the age of eighteen, when he left Hannibal, and therefore a presentation of the facts concerning the boyhood experiences that provide the material for all Mark Twain's major books.

PART I:
THE RIVER AND THE WEST

◊

❨ MARK TWAIN's autobiographical reminiscences consist of fact transformed by the refracting medium of his imagination—even when, as in his *Autobiography*, his conscious intention was to set down events just as they occurred. ". . . I am grown old and my memory is not as active as it used to be," he said on the day when he dictated his description of the Quarles farm. "When I was younger I could remember anything, whether it happened or not; but my faculties are decaying now, and soon I shall be so I cannot remember any but the things that never happened." Nevertheless, the reader who does not confuse imaginative truth with literal fact can find in Mark Twain's work an unmatched record of American experience in the nearer and farther Wests of the mid-nineteenth century.

◊

THE QUARLES FARM
FROM *Mark Twain's Autobiography* [1924]

❨ THIS passage was dictated in 1897 or 1898. John Adams Quarles, a genial, open-hearted native of Virginia, married Jane Lampton Clemens' younger sister Martha Ann (nicknamed "Patsy") in Kentucky in 1825. After living for a time in Tennessee, the Quarleses moved westward again in 1834 with Jane Clemens' father, Benjamin Lampton, and settled near the three-year-old village of Florida in Monroe County, Missouri. John Marshall Clemens was Quarles's partner in a general store for a couple of years after he arrived in Missouri, but Mark Twain's recollections of the Quarles farm refer to a period after 1839, when the Clemens family moved from Florida to Hannibal.

MY UNCLE, John A. Quarles, was a farmer, and his place was in the country four miles from Florida. He had eight children and fifteen or twenty negroes, and was also fortunate in other ways, particularly in his character. I have not come across a better man than he was. I was his guest for two or three months every year, from the fourth year after we removed to Hannibal till I was eleven or twelve years old. I have never consciously used him or his wife in a book, but his farm has come very handy to me in literature once or twice. In *Huck Finn* and in *Tom Sawyer, Detective* I moved it down to Arkansas. It was all of six hundred miles, but it was no trouble; it was not a very large farm—five hundred acres, perhaps—but I could have done it if it had been twice as large. And as for the morality of it, I cared nothing for that; I would move a state if the exigencies of literature required it.

It was a heavenly place for a boy, that farm of my uncle John's. The house was a double log one, with a spacious floor (roofed in) connecting it with the kitchen. In the summer the table was set in the middle of that shady and breezy floor, and the sumptuous meals—well, it makes me cry to think of them. Fried chicken, roast pig; wild and tame turkeys, ducks, and geese; venison just killed; squirrels, rabbits, pheasants, partridges, prairie-chickens; biscuits, hot batter cakes, hot buckwheat cakes, hot "wheat bread," hot rolls, hot corn pone; fresh corn boiled on the ear, succotash, butter-beans, string-beans, tomatoes, peas, Irish potatoes, sweet potatoes; buttermilk, sweet milk, "clabber"; watermelons, muskmelons, cantaloupes—all fresh from the garden; apple pie, peach pie, pumpkin pie, apple dumplings, peach cobbler—I can't remember the rest. The way that the things were cooked was perhaps the main splendor—particularly a certain few of the dishes. For instance, the corn bread, the hot biscuits and wheat bread, and the fried chicken. These things have never been properly cooked in the North—in fact, no one there is able to learn the art, so far as my experience goes. The North thinks it knows how to make corn bread, but this is mere superstition. Perhaps no bread in the world is quite so good as Southern corn bread, and perhaps no bread in the world is quite so bad as the Northern imitation of it. The North seldom tries to fry chicken, and this is well; the art cannot be learned north of the line of Mason and Dixon, nor anywhere in Europe. This is not hearsay; it is experience that is speaking. In Europe it is imagined that the custom of serving various kinds of bread blazing hot is "American," but that is too broad a spread; it is custom in the South, but is much less than that in the North. In the North and in Europe hot bread is considered unhealthy. This is probably another fussy superstition, like the European superstition that ice-water is unhealthy. Europe does not need ice-water and does not drink it; and yet, notwithstanding this, its word for it is better than ours, because it describes it,

whereas ours doesn't. Europe calls it "iced" water. Our word describes water made from melted ice—a drink which has a characterless taste and which we have but little acquaintance with.

It seems a pity that the world should throw away so many good things merely because they are unwholesome. I doubt if God has given us any refreshment which, taken in moderation, is unwholesome, except microbes. Yet there are people who strictly deprive themselves of each and every eatable, drinkable, and smokable which has in any way acquired a shady reputation. They pay this price for health. And health is all they get for it. How strange it is! It is like paying out your whole fortune for a cow that has gone dry.

The farmhouse stood in the middle of a very large yard, and the yard was fenced on three sides with rails and on the rear side with high palings; against these stood the smoke-house; beyond the palings was the orchard; beyond the orchard were the negro quarters and the tobacco fields. The front yard was entered over a stile made of sawed-off logs of graduated heights; I do not remember any gate. In a corner of the front yard were a dozen lofty hickory trees and a dozen black walnuts, and in the nutting season riches were to be gathered there.

Down a piece, abreast the house, stood a little log cabin against the rail fence; and there the woody hill fell sharply away, past the barns, the corn-crib, the stables, and the tobacco-curing house, to a limpid brook which sang along over its gravelly bed and curved and frisked in and out and here and there and yonder in the deep shade of overhanging foliage and vines—a divine place for wading, and it had swimming pools, too, which were forbidden to us and therefore much frequented by us. For we were little Christian children and had early been taught the value of forbidden fruit.

In the little log cabin lived a bedridden white-headed slave woman whom we visited daily and looked upon with awe, for we believed she was upward of a thousand years old and had talked with Moses. The younger negroes credited these statistics and had furnished them to us in good faith. We accommodated all the details which came to us about her; and so we believed that she had lost her health in the long desert trip coming out of Egypt, and had never been able to get it back again. She had a round bald place on the crown of her head, and we used to creep around and gaze at it in reverent silence, and reflect that it was caused by fright through seeing Pharaoh drowned. We called her "Aunt" Hannah, Southern fashion. She was superstitious, like the other negroes; also, like them, she was deeply religious. Like them, she had great faith in prayer and employed it in all ordinary exigencies, but not in cases where a dead certainty of result was urgent. Whenever witches were around she tied up the remnant of her wool in little tufts, with white thread, and this promptly made the witches impotent.

All the negroes were friends of ours, and with those of our own age we were in effect comrades. I say in effect, using the phrase as a modification. We were comrades, and yet not comrades; color and condition interposed a subtle line which both parties were conscious of and which rendered complete fusion impossible. We had a faithful and affectionate good friend, ally, and adviser in "Uncle Dan'l," a middle-aged slave whose head was the best one in the negro quarter, whose sympathies were wide and warm, and whose heart was honest and simple and knew no guile. He has served me well these many, many years. I have not seen him for more than half a century, and yet spiritually I have had his welcome company a good part of that time, and have staged him in books under his own name and as "Jim," and carted him all around—to Hannibal, down the Mississippi on a raft, and even across the Desert of Sahara in a balloon [1]—and he has endured it all with the patience and friendliness and loyalty which were his birthright. It was on the farm that I got my strong liking for his race and my appreciation of certain of its fine qualities. This feeling and this estimate have stood the test of sixty years and more, and have suffered no impairment. The black face is as welcome to me now as it was then.

In my schoolboy days I had no aversion to slavery. I was not aware that there was anything wrong about it. No one arraigned it in my hearing; the local papers said nothing against it; the local pulpit taught us that God approved it, that it was a holy thing, and that the doubter need only look in the Bible if he wished to settle his mind—and then the texts were read aloud to us to make the matter sure; if the slaves themselves had an aversion to slavery, they were wise and said nothing. In Hannibal we seldom saw a slave misused; on the farm, never.

There was, however, one small incident of my boyhood days which touched this matter, and it must have meant a good deal to me or it would not have stayed in my memory, clear and sharp, vivid and shadowless, all these slow-drifting years. We had a little slave boy whom we had hired from some one, there in Hannibal. He was from the eastern shore of Maryland, and had been brought away from his family and his friends, halfway across the American continent, and sold. He was a cheery spirit, innocent and gentle, and the noisiest creature that ever was, perhaps. All day long he was singing, whistling, yelling, whooping, laughing—it was maddening, devastating, unendurable. At last, one day, I lost all my temper, and went raging to my mother and said Sandy had been singing for an hour without a single break, and I couldn't stand it, and *wouldn't* she please shut him up. The tears came into her eyes and her lip trembled, and she said something like this:

"Poor thing, when he sings it shows that he is not remembering, and that comforts me; but when he is still I am afraid he is thinking, and I cannot bear it. He will never see his mother again; if he can sing, I must not hinder it, but be thankful for it. If you were older, you would understand me; then that friendless child's noise would make you glad."

It was a simple speech and made up of small words, but it went home, and Sandy's noise was not a trouble to me any more. She never used large words, but she had a natural gift for making small ones do effective work. She lived to reach the neighborhood of ninety years and was capable with her tongue to the last—especially when a meanness or an injustice roused her spirit. She has come handy to me several times in my books, where she figures as Tom Sawyer's Aunt Polly. I fitted her out with a dialect and tried to think up other improvements for her, but did not find any. I used Sandy once, also; it was in *Tom Sawyer*. I tried to get him to whitewash the fence, but it did not work. I do not remember what name I called him by in the book.[2]

I can see the farm yet, with perfect clearness. I can see all its belongings, all its details; the family room of the house, with a "trundle" bed in one corner and a spinning-wheel in another—a wheel whose rising and falling wail, heard from a distance, was the mournfulest of all sounds to me, and made me homesick and low spirited, and filled my atmosphere with the wandering spirits of the dead; the vast fireplace, piled high, on winter nights, with flaming hickory logs from whose ends a sugary sap bubbled out, but did not go to waste, for we scraped it off and ate it; the lazy cat spread out on the rough hearthstones; the drowsy dogs braced against the jambs and blinking; my aunt in one chimney corner, knitting; my uncle in the other, smoking his corn-cob pipe; the slick and carpetless oak floor faintly mirroring the dancing flame tongues and freckled with black indentations where fire coals had popped out and died a

THE QUARLES FARM.   **1. across . . . balloon:** in *Tom Sawyer Abroad.*

2. what . . . book: He was also called Jim.

leisurely death; half a dozen children romping in the background twilight; "split"-bottomed chairs here and there, some with rockers; a cradle—out of service, but waiting, with confidence; in the early cold mornings a snuggle of children, in shirts and chemises, occupying the hearthstone and procrastinating—they could not bear to leave that comfortable place and go out on the wind-swept floor space between the house and kitchen where the general tin basin stood, and wash.

THE BOYS' AMBITION

FROM *Life on the Mississippi* [1883]

❨ THIS was first published in the *Atlantic Monthly*, (January, 1875).

WHEN I was a boy, there was but one permanent ambition among my comrades in our village [1] on the west bank of the Mississippi River. That was, to be a steamboatman. We had transient ambitions of other sorts, but they were only transient. When a circus came and went, it left us all burning to become clowns; the first negro minstrel show that came to our section left us all suffering to try that kind of life; now and then we had a hope that if we lived and were good, God would permit us to be pirates. These ambitions faded out, each in its turn; but the ambition to be a steamboatman always remained.

Once a day a cheap, gaudy packet arrived upward from St. Louis, and another downward from Keokuk. Before these events, the day was glorious with expectancy; after them, the day was a dead and empty thing. Not only the boys, but the whole village, felt this. After all these years I can picture that old time to myself now, just as it was then: the white town drowsing in the sunshine of a summer's morning; the streets empty, or pretty nearly so; one or two clerks sitting in front of the Water Street stores, with their splint-bottomed chairs tilted back against the wall, chins on breasts, hats slouched over their faces, asleep—with shingle-shavings enough around to show what broke them down; a sow and a litter of pigs loafing along the sidewalk, doing a good business in watermelon rinds and seeds; two or three lonely little freight piles scattered about the "levee;" a pile of "skids" on the slope of the stone-paved wharf, and the fragrant town drunkard asleep in the shadow of them; two or three wood flats at the head of the wharf, but nobody to listen to the peaceful lapping

THE BOYS' AMBITION.   1. our village: "Hannibal, Missouri" [Mark Twain's note].

of the wavelets against them; the great Mississippi, the majestic, the magnificent Mississippi, rolling its mile-wide tide along, shining in the sun; the dense forest away on the other side; the "point" above the town, and the "point" below, bounding the river-glimpse and turning it into a sort of sea, and withal a very still and brilliant and lonely one. Presently a film of dark smoke appears above one of those remote "points;" instantly a negro drayman, famous for his quick eye and prodigious voice, lifts up the cry, "S-t-e-a-m-boat a-comin'!" and the scene changes! The town drunkard stirs, the clerks wake up, a furious clatter of drays follows, every house and store pours out a human contribution, and all in a twinkling the dead town is alive and moving. Drays, carts, men, boys, all go hurrying from many quarters to a common centre, the wharf. Assembled there, the people fasten their eyes upon the coming boat as upon a wonder they are seeing for the first time. And the boat *is* rather a handsome sight, too. She is long and sharp and trim and pretty; she has two tall, fancy-topped chimneys, with a gilded device of some kind swung between them; a fanciful pilot-house, all glass and "gingerbread," perched on top of the "texas" deck behind them; the paddle-boxes are gorgeous with a picture or with gilded rays above the boat's name; the boiler deck, the hurricane deck, and the texas deck are fenced and ornamented with clean white railings; there is a flag gallantly flying from the jack-staff; the furnace doors are open and the fires glaring bravely; the upper decks are black with passengers; the captain stands by the big bell, calm, imposing, the envy of all; great volumes of the blackest smoke are rolling and tumbling out of the chimneys—a husbanded grandeur created with a bit of pitch pine just before arriving at a town; and the crew are grouped on the forecastle; the broad stage is run far out over the port bow, and an envied deck-hand stands picturesquely on the end of it with a coil of rope in his hand; the pent steam is screaming through the gauge-cocks; the captain lifts his hand, a bell rings, the wheels stop; then they turn back, churning the water to foam, and the steamer is at rest. Then such a scramble as there is to get aboard, and to get ashore, and to take in freight and to discharge freight, all at one and the same time; and such a yelling and cursing as the mates facilitate it all with! Ten minutes later the steamer is under way again, with no flag on the jack-staff and no black smoke issuing from the chimneys. After ten more minutes the town is dead again, and the town drunkard asleep by the skids once more.

My father was a justice of the peace, and I supposed he possessed the power of life and death over all men and could hang anybody that offended him. This was distinction enough for me as a general thing; but the desire to be a steamboatman kept intruding, nevertheless. I first wanted to be a cabin-boy, so that I could come out with a white apron on and shake a table-cloth over the side, where all my old comrades could see me; later I thought I would rather be the deckhand who stood on the end of the stage-plank with the coil of rope in his hand, because he was particularly conspicuous. But these were only day-dreams,—they were too heavenly to be contemplated as real possibilities. By and by one of our boys went away. He was not heard of for a long time. At last he turned up as apprentice engineer or "striker" on a steamboat. This thing shook the bottom out of all my Sunday-school teachings. That boy had been notoriously worldly, and I just the reverse; yet he was exalted to this eminence, and I left in obscurity and misery. There was nothing generous about this fellow in his greatness. He would always manage to have a rusty bolt to scrub while his boat tarried at our town, and he would sit on the inside guard and scrub it, where we could all see him and envy him and loathe him. And whenever his boat was laid up he would come home and swell around the town in his blackest and greasiest clothes, so that nobody could help remembering that he was a steamboatman; and he used all sorts of steamboat technicalities in his talk, as if he were so used to them that he forgot common people could not understand them. He would speak of the "labboard" side of a horse in an easy, natural way that would make one wish he was dead. And he was always talking about "St. Looy" like an old citizen; he would refer casually to occasions when he "was coming down Fourth Street," or when he was "passing by the Planter's House," or when there was a fire and he took a turn on the brakes [2] of "the old Big Missouri;" and then he would go on and lie about how many towns the size of ours were burned down there that day. Two or three of the boys had long been persons of consideration among us because they had been to St. Louis once and had a vague general knowledge of its wonders, but the day of their glory was over now. They lapsed into a humble silence, and learned to disappear when the ruthless "cub"-engineer approached. This fellow had money, too, and hair oil. Also an ignorant silver watch and a showy brass watch chain. He wore a leather belt and used no suspenders. If ever a youth was cordially admired and hated by his comrades, this one was.

2. brakes: handles of a pump.

No girl could withstand his charms. He "cut out" every boy in the village. When his boat blew up at last, it diffused a tranquil contentment among us such as we had not known for months. But when he came home the next week, alive, renowned, and appeared in church all battered up and bandaged, a shining hero, stared at and wondered over by everybody, it seemed to us that the partiality of Providence for an undeserving reptile had reached a point where it was open to criticism.

This creature's career could produce but one result, and it speedily followed. Boy after boy managed to get on the river. The minister's son became an engineer. The doctor's and the postmaster's sons became "mud clerks;" the wholesale liquor dealer's son became a bar-keeper on a boat; four sons of the chief merchant, and two sons of the county judge, became pilots. Pilot was the grandest position of all. The pilot, even in those days of trivial wages, had a princely salary —from a hundred and fifty to two hundred and fifty dollars a month, and no board to pay. Two months of his wages would pay a preacher's salary for a year. Now some of us were left disconsolate. We could not get on the river—at least our parents would not let us.

So by and by I ran away. I said I never would come home again till I was a pilot and could come in glory. But somehow I could not manage it. I went meekly aboard a few of the boats that lay packed together like sardines at the long St. Louis wharf, and very humbly inquired for the pilots, but got only a cold shoulder and short words from mates and clerks. I had to make the best of this sort of treatment for the time being, but I had comforting day-dreams of a future when I should be a great and honored pilot, with plenty of money, and could kill some of these mates and clerks and pay for them.

RANK AND DIGNITY OF PILOTING

FROM *Life on the Mississippi* [1883]

⟨ THE story was first published in the *Atlantic Monthly* (June, 1875).

IN MY preceding chapters I have tried, by going into the minutiæ of the science of piloting, to carry the reader step by step to a comprehension of what the science consists of; and at the same time I have tried to show him that it is a very curious and wonderful science, too, and very worthy of his attention. If I have seemed to love my subject, it is no surprising thing, for I loved the profession far better than any I have followed since, and I took a measureless pride in it. The reason is plain: a pilot, in those days, was the only unfettered and entirely independent human being that lived in the earth. Kings are but the hampered servants of parliament and people; parliaments sit in chains forged by their constituency; the editor of a newspaper cannot be independent, but must work with one hand tied behind him by party and patrons, and be content to utter only half or two thirds of his mind; no clergyman is a free man and may speak the whole truth, regardless of his parish's opinions; writers of all kinds are manacled servants of the public. We write frankly and fearlessly, but then we "modify" before we print. In truth, every man and woman and child has a master, and worries and frets in servitude; but in the day I write of, the Mississippi pilot had *none*. The captain could stand upon the hurricane deck, in the pomp of a very brief authority, and give him five or six orders while the vessel backed into the stream, and then that skipper's reign was over. The moment that the boat was under way in the river, she was under the sole and unquestioned control of the pilot. He could do with her exactly as he pleased, run her when and whither he chose, and tie her up to the bank whenever his judgment said that that course was best. His movements were entirely free; he consulted no one, he received commands from nobody, he promptly resented even the merest suggestions. Indeed, the law of the United States forbade him to listen to commands or suggestions, rightly considering that the pilot necessarily knew better how to handle the boat than anybody could tell him. So here was the novelty of a king without a keeper, an absolute monarch who was absolute in sober truth and not by a fiction of words. I have seen a boy of eighteen taking a great steamer serenely into what seemed almost certain destruction, and the aged captain standing mutely by, filled with apprehension but powerless to interfere. His interference, in that particular instance, might have been an excellent thing, but to permit it would have been to establish a most pernicious precedent. It will easily be guessed, considering the pilot's boundless authority, that he was a great personage in the old steamboating days. He was treated with marked courtesy by the captain and with marked deference by all the officers and servants; and this deferential spirit was quickly communicated to the passengers, too. I think pilots were about the only people I ever knew who failed to show, in some degree, embarrassment in the presence of travelling foreign princes. But then, people in one's own grade of life are not usually embarrassing objects.

By long habit, pilots came to put all their wishes in the form of commands. It "gravels" me, to this day, to put my will in the weak shape of a request, instead of launching it in the crisp language of an order.

In those old days, to load a steamboat at St. Louis, take her to New Orleans and back, and discharge cargo, consumed about twenty-five days, on an average. Seven or eight of these days the boat spent at the wharves of St. Louis and New Orleans, and every soul on board was hard at work, except the two pilots; *they* did nothing but play gentleman up town, and receive the same wages for it as if they had been on duty. The moment the boat touched the wharf at either city, they were ashore; and they were not likely to be seen again till the last bell was ringing and everything in readiness for another voyage.

When a captain got hold of a pilot of particularly high reputation, he took pains to keep him. When wages were four hundred dollars a month on the Upper Mississippi, I have known a captain to keep such a pilot in idleness, under full pay, three months at a time, while the river was frozen up. And one must remember that in those cheap times four hundred dollars was a salary of almost inconceivable splendor. Few men on shore got such pay as that, and when they did they were mightily looked up to. When pilots from either end of the river wandered into our small Missouri village, they were sought by the best and the fairest, and treated with exalted respect. Lying in port under wages was a thing which many pilots greatly enjoyed and appreciated; especially if they belonged in the Missouri River in the heyday of that trade (Kansas times),[1] and got nine hundred dollars a trip, which was equivalent to about eighteen hundred dollars a month. Here is a conversation of that day. A chap out of the Illinois River, with a little stern-wheel tub, accosts a couple of ornate and gilded Missouri River pilots:—

"Gentlemen, I've got a pretty good trip for the up-country, and shall want you about a month. How much will it be?"

"Eighteen hundred dollars apiece."

"Heavens and earth! You take my boat, let me have your wages, and I'll divide!"

I will remark, in passing, that Mississippi steamboatmen were important in landsmen's eyes (and in their own, too, in a degree) according to the dignity of the boat they were on. For instance, it was a proud thing to be of the crew of such stately craft as the "Aleck Scott" or the "Grand Turk." Negro firemen, deck hands, and barbers belonging to those boats were distinguished personages

RANK AND DIGNITY OF PILOTING.   1. **Kansas times:** the period of heavy migration to Kansas in the late 1850's.

in their grade of life, and they were well aware of that fact, too. A stalwart darkey once gave offence at a negro ball in New Orleans by putting on a good many airs. Finally one of the managers bustled up to him and said,—

"Who *is* you, any way? Who *is* you? dat's what *I* wants to know!"

The offender was not disconcerted in the least, but swelled himself up and threw that into his voice which showed that he knew he was not putting on all those airs on a stinted capital.

"Who *is* I? Who *is* I? I let you know mighty quick who I is! I want you niggers to understan' dat I fires de middle do'[2] on de 'Aleck Scott!'"

That was sufficient.

The barber of the "Grand Turk" was a spruce young negro, who aired his importance with balmy complacency, and was greatly courted by the circle in which he moved. The young colored population of New Orleans were much given to flirting, at twilight, on the banquettes of the back streets. Somebody saw and heard something like the following, one evening, in one of those localities. A middle-aged negro woman projected her head through a broken pane and shouted (very willing that the neighbors should hear and envy), "You Mary Ann, come in de house dis minute! Stannin' out dah foolin' 'long wid dat low trash, an' heah's de barber off'n de 'Gran' Turk' wants to conwerse wid you!"

My reference, a moment ago, to the fact that a pilot's peculiar official position placed him out of the reach of criticism or command, brings Stephen W—— naturally to my mind. He was a gifted pilot, a good fellow, a tireless talker, and had both wit and humor in him. He had a most irreverent independence, too, and was deliciously easy-going and comfortable in the presence of age, official dignity, and even the most august wealth. He always had work, he never saved a penny, he was a most persuasive borrower, he was in debt to every pilot on the river, and to the majority of the captains. He could throw a sort of splendor around a bit of harum-scarum, devil-may-care piloting, that made it almost fascinating—but not to everybody. He made a trip with good old Captain Y—— once, and was "relieved" from duty when the boat got to New Orleans. Somebody expressed surprise at the discharge. Captain Y—— shuddered at the mere mention of Stephen. Then his poor, thin old voice piped out something like this:—

"Why, bless me! I would n't have such a wild creature on my boat for the world—not for the whole world! He swears, he sings, he whistles, he

yells—I never saw such an Injun to yell. All times of the night—it never made any difference to him. He would just yell that way, not for anything in particular, but merely on account of a kind of devilish comfort he got out of it. I never could get into a sound sleep but he would fetch me out of bed, all in a cold sweat, with one of those dreadful war-whoops. A queer being,—very queer being; no respect for anything or anybody. Sometimes he called me 'Johnny.' And he kept a fiddle, and a cat. He played execrably. This seemed to distress the cat, and so the cat would howl. Nobody could sleep where that man—and his family—was. And reckless? There never was anything like it. Now you may believe it or not, but as sure as I am sitting here, he brought my boat a-tilting down through those awful snags at Chicot under a rattling head of steam, and the wind a-blowing like the very nation, at that! My officers will tell you so. They saw it. And, sir, while he was a-tearing right down through those snags, and I a-shaking in my shoes and praying, I wish I may never speak again if he did n't pucker up his mouth and go to *whistling!* Yes, sir; whistling 'Buffalo gals, can't you come out to-night, can't you come out to-night, can't you come out to-night;' and doing it as calmly as if we were attending a funeral and were n't related to the corpse. And when I remonstrated with him about it, he smiled down on me as if I was his child, and told me to run in the house and try to be good, and not be meddling with my superiors!"[3]

Once a pretty mean captain caught Stephen in New Orleans out of work and as usual out of money. He laid steady siege to Stephen, who was in a very "close place," and finally persuaded him to hire with him at one hundred and twenty-five dollars per month, just half wages, the captain agreeing not to divulge the secret and so bring down the contempt of all the guild upon the poor fellow. But the boat was not more than a day out of New Orleans before Stephen discovered that the captain was boasting of his exploit, and that all the officers had been told. Stephen winced, but said nothing. About the middle of the afternoon the captain stepped out on the hurricane deck, cast his eye around, and looked a good deal surprised. He glanced inquiringly aloft at Stephen, but Stephen was whistling placidly, and attending to business. The captain stood around a while in evident discomfort, and once or twice seemed about to make a suggestion; but the etiquette of the river taught him to avoid that sort of rash-

2. do': "Door" [M T].

3. superiors: "Considering a captain's ostentatious but hollow chieftainship, and a pilot's real authority, there was something impudently apt and happy about that way of phrasing it" [M T].

ness, and so he managed to hold his peace. He chafed and puzzled a few minutes longer, then retired to his apartments. But soon he was out again, and apparently more perplexed than ever. Presently he ventured to remark, with deference,—

"Pretty good stage of the river now, ain't it, sir?"

"Well, I should say so! Bank-full *is* a pretty liberal stage."

"Seems to be a good deal of current here."

"Good deal don't describe it! It's worse than a mill-race."

"Is n't it easier in toward shore than it is out here in the middle?"

"Yes, I reckon it is; but a body can't be too careful with a steamboat. It's pretty safe out here; can't strike any bottom here, you can depend on that."

The captain departed, looking rueful enough. At this rate, he would probably die of old age before his boat got to St. Louis. Next day he appeared on deck and again found Stephen faithfully standing up the middle of the river, fighting the whole vast force of the Mississippi, and whistling the same placid tune. This thing was becoming serious. In by the shore was a slower boat clipping along in the easy water and gaining steadily; she began to make for an island chute; Stephen stuck to the middle of the river. Speech was *wrung* from the captain. He said,—

"Mr. W——, don't that chute cut off a good deal of distance?"

"I think it does, but I don't know."

"Don't know! Well, is n't there water enough in it now to go through?"

"I expect there is, but I am not certain."

"Upon my word this is odd! Why, those pilots on that boat yonder are going to try it. Do you mean to say that you don't know as much as they do?"

"*They!* Why, *they* are two-hundred-and-fifty-dollar pilots! But don't you be uneasy; I know as much as any man can afford to know for a hundred and twenty-five!"

The captain surrendered.

Five minutes later Stephen was bowling through the chute and showing the rival boat a two-hundred-and-fifty-dollar pair of heels.

CAPTAIN MONTGOMERY

[FIRST published in the San Francisco *Golden Era* (January 28, 1866), "Captain Montgomery" is one of the earliest bits of Mark Twain's writing based on memories of his steamboating days. Captain Montgomery has some traits later developed in Captain Stormfield. The selection is from *The Washoe Giant in San Francisco,* ed. by G. Ezra Dane (1938).

WHENEVER he commenced helping anybody, Captain Ed. Montgomery never relaxed his good offices as long as help was needed.

As soon as he found that no steamboat ever stopped to wood with old Mother Utterback in the bend below Grand Gulf, Mississippi, and that she was poor and needed assistance, he began to stop there every trip and take her little pile of wood and smile grimly, when the engineers protested that it wouldn't burn any more than so many icicles—and stop there again the very next trip. He used to go ashore and talk to the old woman, and it flattered her to the last degree to be on such sociable terms with the high chief officer of a splendid passenger steamer. She would welcome him to her shabby little floorless log cabin with a royal flourish, and make her six gawky "gals" fly around and make him comfortable. He used to bring his lady passengers ashore to be entertained with Mother Utterback's quaint conversation.

I do not know that this incident is worth recording, but still, as it may let in the light of instruction to some darkened mind, I will just set down the circumstances of one of Captain Montgomery's visits to Mother Utterback and her daughters. He brought some fine ladies with him to enjoy the old woman's talk.

"Good morning, Captain Montgomery!" said she with many a bustling bow and flourish; "Good morning, Captain Montgomery; good morning, ladies all; how de do, Captain Montgomery—how de do—how de do? Sakes alive, it 'pears to me it's ben years sense I seed you. Fly around, gals, fly around! You Bets, you slut, highst yoself off'n that candle-box and give it to the lady. How *have* you ben, Captain Montgomery?—make yoself at home, ladies all—you 'Liza Jane, stan' out of the way—move yoself! Thar's the jug, help yoself, Captain Montgomery; take that cob out and make yoself free, Captain Montgomery—and ladies all. You Sal, you hussy, git up f'm thar this minit, and take some exercise! for the land's sake, ain't you got no sense at all?— settin' thar on that cold rock and you jes' ben married last night, and your pores all open!"

The ladies wanted to go aboard the boat, they bade the kind, hospitable old woman good by, and went away. But Captain Montgomery staid behind, because he knew how badly the old lady wanted to talk, and he was a good soul and loved to please her.

Ah, that was a good man was Captain Ed. Montgomery, and the moment I saw that paragraph about him the other day I remembered how kind it was of him to always stop and buy that old Arkansas woman's green wood and pay her the highest market price for it when he could no more burn it than he could burn an iceberg. It was so soggy, too, and wet, and heavy. I remember how, whenever he blew the whistle to land there, the mate used to sing out hoarsely and in bitterness of spirit, "Larboard watch—turn out! Stand by, men, to take in some ballast!" But you can rest assured I am not sorry old Captain Ed. Montgomery is alive and well yet.

LOST IN A SNOWSTORM
FROM *Roughing It* [1872]

[THE narrator is returning with his two companions from Unionville, in the Humboldt mining region, to Carson City, Nevada Territory. Clemens made such a trip in January, 1862, with an elderly blacksmith named Tillou and a German named Pfersdorff, but the account in *Roughing It* has evidently been elaborated in the author's imagination.

THE NEXT morning it was still snowing furiously when we got away with our new stock of saddles and accoutrements. We mounted and started. The snow lay so deep on the ground that there was no sign of a road perceptible, and the snow-fall was so thick that we could not see more than a hundred yards ahead, else we could have guided our course by the mountain ranges. The case looked dubious, but Ollendorff said his instinct was as sensitive as any compass, and that he could "strike a bee-line" for Carson city and never diverge from it. He said that if he were to straggle a single point out of the true line his instinct would assail him like an outraged conscience. Consequently we dropped into his wake happy and content. For half an hour we poked along warily enough, but at the end of that time we came upon a fresh trail, and Ollendorff shouted proudly:

"I knew I was as dead certain as a compass, boys! Here we are, right in somebody's tracks that will hunt the way for us without any trouble. Let's hurry up and join company with the party."

So we put the horses into as much of a trot as the deep snow would allow, and before long it was evident that we were gaining on our predecessors, for the tracks grew more distinct. We hurried along, and at the end of an hour the tracks looked still newer and fresher—but what surprised us was, that the *number* of travelers in advance of us seemed to steadily increase. We wondered how so large a party came to be traveling at such a time and in such a solitude. Somebody suggested that it must be a company of soldiers from the fort, and so we accepted that solution and jogged along a little faster still, for they could not be far off now. But the tracks still multiplied, and we began to think the platoon of soldiers was miraculously expanding into a regiment—Ballou said they had already increased to five hundred! Presently he stopped his horse and said:

"Boys, these are our own tracks, and we've actually been circussing round and round in a circle for more than two hours, out here in this blind desert! By George this is perfectly hydraulic!"

Then the old man waxed wroth and abusive. He called Ollendorff all manner of hard names—said he never saw such a lurid fool as he was, and ended with the peculiarly venomous opinion that he "did not know as much as a logarythm!"

We certainly had been following our own tracks. Ollendorff and his "mental compass" were in disgrace from that moment. After all our hard travel, here we were on the bank of the stream again, with the inn beyond dimly outlined through the driving snow-fall. While we were considering what to do, the young Swede landed from the canoe and took his pedestrian way Carson-wards, singing his same tiresome song about his "sister and his brother" and "the child in the grave with its mother," and in a short minute faded and disappeared in the white oblivion. He was never heard of again. He no doubt got bewildered and lost, and Fatigue delivered him over to Sleep and Sleep betrayed him to Death. Possibly he followed our treacherous tracks till he became exhausted and dropped.

Presently the Overland stage forded the now fast receding stream and started toward Carson on its first trip since the flood came. We hesitated no longer, now, but took up our march in its wake, and trotted merrily along, for we had good confidence in the driver's bump of locality. But our horses were no match for the fresh stage team. We were soon left out of sight; but it was no matter, for we had the deep ruts the wheels made for a guide. By this time it was three in the afternoon, and consequently it was not very long before night came—and not with a lingering twilight, but with a sudden shutting down like a cellar door, as is its habit in that country. The snow-fall was still as thick as ever, and of course we could not see fifteen steps before us; but all about us the white glare of the snow-bed enabled us to discern the smooth sugar-loaf mounds made by the covered sage-bushes, and just in front of us the two faint grooves which we knew were the steadily filling and slowly disappearing wheel-tracks.

Now those sage-bushes were all about the same height—three or four feet; they stood just about seven feet apart, all over the vast desert; each of them was a mere snow-mound, now; in *any* direction that you proceeded (the same as in a well laid out orchard) you would find yourself moving down a distinctly defined avenue, with a row of these snow-mounds on either side of it—an avenue the customary width of a road, nice and level in its breadth, and rising at the sides in the most natural way, by reason of the mounds. But we had not thought of this. Then imagine the chilly thrill that shot through us when it finally occurred to us, far in the night, that since the last faint trace of the wheel-tracks had long ago been buried from sight, we might now be wandering down a mere sage-brush avenue, miles away from the road and diverging further and further away from it all the time. Having a cake of ice slipped down one's back is placid comfort compared to it. There was a sudden leap and stir of blood that had been asleep for an hour, and as sudden a rousing of all the drowsing activities in our minds and bodies. We were alive and awake at once—and shaking and quaking with consternation, too. There was an instant halting and dismounting, a bending low and an anxious scanning of the road-bed. Useless, of course; for if a faint depression could not be discerned from an altitude of four or five feet above it, it certainly could not with one's nose nearly against it.

We seemed to be in a road, but that was no proof. We tested this by walking off in various directions—the regular snow-mounds and the regular avenues between them convinced each man that *he* had found the true road, and that the others had found only false ones. Plainly the situation was desperate. We were cold and stiff and the horses were tired. We decided to build a sage-brush fire and camp out till morning. This was wise, because if we were wandering from the right road and the snow-storm continued another day our case would be the next thing to hopeless if we kept on.

All agreed that a camp fire was what would come nearest to saving us, now, and so we set about building it. We could find no matches, and so we tried to make shift with the pistols. Not a man in the party had ever tried to do such a thing before, but not a man in the party doubted that it *could* be done, and without any trouble—because every man in the party had read about it in books many a time and had naturally come to believe it, with trusting simplicity, just as he had long ago accepted and believed *that other* common book-fraud about Indians and lost hunters making a fire by rubbing two dry sticks together.

We huddled together on our knees in the deep snow, and the horses put their noses together and bowed their patient heads over us; and while the feathery flakes eddied down and turned us into a group of white statuary, we proceeded with the momentous experiment. We broke twigs from a sage bush and piled them on a little cleared place in the shelter of our bodies. In the course of ten or fifteen minutes all was ready, and then, while conversation ceased and our pulses beat low with anxious suspense, Ollendorff applied his revolver, pulled the trigger and blew the pile clear out of the county! It was the flattest failure that ever was.

This was distressing, but it paled before a greater horror—the horses were gone! I had been appointed to hold the bridles, but in my absorbing anxiety over the pistol experiment I had unconsciously dropped them and the released animals had walked off in the storm. It was useless to try to follow them, for their footfalls could make no sound, and one could pass within two yards of the creatures and never see them. We gave them up without an effort at recovering them, and cursed the lying books that said horses would stay by their masters for protection and companionship in a distressful time like ours.

We were miserable enough, before; we felt still more forlorn, now. Patiently, but with blighted hope, we broke more sticks and piled them, and once more the Prussian shot them into annihilation. Plainly, to light a fire with a pistol was an art requiring practice and experience, and the middle of a desert at midnight in a snow-storm was not a good place or time for the acquiring of the accomplishment. We gave it up and tried the other. Each man took a couple of sticks and fell to chafing them together. At the end of half an hour we were thoroughly chilled, and so were the sticks. We bitterly execrated the Indians, the hunters and the books that had betrayed us with the silly device, and wondered dismally what was next to be done. At this critical moment Mr. Ballou fished out four matches from the rubbish of an overlooked pocket. To have found four gold bars would have seemed poor and cheap good luck compared to this. One cannot think how good a match looks under such circumstances—or how lovable and precious, and sacredly beautiful to the eye. This time we gathered sticks with high hopes;

and when Mr. Ballou prepared to light the first match, there was an amount of interest centred upon him that pages of writing could not describe. The match burned hopefully a moment, and then went out. It could not have carried more regret with it if it had been a human life. The next match simply flashed and died. The wind puffed the third one out just as it was on the imminent verge of success. We gathered together closer than ever, and developed a solicitude that was rapt and painful, as Mr. Ballou scratched our last hope on his leg. It lit, burned blue and sickly, and then budded into a robust flame. Shading it with his hands, the old gentleman bent gradually down and every heart went with him—everybody, too, for that matter—and blood and breath stood still. The flame touched the sticks at last, took gradual hold upon them—hesitated—took a stronger hold—hesitated again—held its breath five heart-breaking seconds, then gave a sort of human gasp and went out.

Nobody said a word for several minutes. It was a solemn sort of silence; even the wind put on a stealthy, sinister quiet, and made no more noise than the falling flakes of snow. Finally a sad-voiced conversation began, and it was soon apparent that in each of our hearts lay the conviction that this was our last night with the living. I had so hoped that I was the only one who felt so. When the others calmly acknowledged their conviction, it sounded like the summons itself. Ollendorff said:

"Brothers, let us die together. And let us go without one hard feeling towards each other. Let us forget and forgive bygones. I know that you have felt hard towards me for turning over the canoe, and for knowing too much and leading you round and round in the snow—but I meant well; forgive me. I acknowledge freely that I have had hard feelings against Mr. Ballou for abusing me and calling me a logarythm, which is a thing I do not know what, but no doubt a thing considered disgraceful and unbecoming in America, and it has scarcely been out of my mind and has hurt me a great deal—but let it go; I forgive Mr. Ballou with all my heart, and—"

Poor Ollendorff broke down and the tears came. He was not alone, for I was crying too, and so was Mr. Ballou. Ollendorff got his voice again and forgave me for things I had done and said. Then he got out his bottle of whisky and said that whether he lived or died he would never touch another drop. He said he had given up all hope of life, and although ill-prepared, was ready to submit humbly to his fate; that he wished he could be spared a little longer, not for any selfish reason, but to make a thorough reform in his character, and by devoting himself to helping the poor, nursing the sick, and pleading with the people to guard themselves against the evils of intemperance, make his life a beneficent example to the young, and lay it down at last with the precious reflection that it had not been lived in vain. He ended by saying that his reform should begin at this moment, even here in the presence of death, since no longer time was to be vouchsafed wherein to prosecute it to men's help and benefit—and with that he threw away the bottle of whisky.

Mr. Ballou made remarks of similar purport, and began the reform he could not live to continue, by throwing away the ancient pack of cards that had solaced our captivity during the flood and made it bearable. He said he never gambled, but still was satisfied that the meddling with cards in any way was immoral and injurious, and no man could be wholly pure and blemishless without eschewing them. "And therefore," continued he, "in doing this act I already feel more in sympathy with that spiritual saturnalia necessary to entire and obsolete reform." These rolling syllables touched him as no intelligible eloquence could have done, and the old man sobbed with a mournfulness not unmingled with satisfaction.

My own remarks were of the same tenor as those of my comrades, and I know that the feelings that prompted them were heartfelt and sincere. We were all sincere, and all deeply moved and earnest, for we were in the presence of death and without hope. I threw away my pipe, and in doing it felt that at last I was free of a hated vice and one that had ridden me like a tyrant all my days. While I yet talked, the thought of the good I might have done in the world and the still greater good I might *now* do, with these new incentives and higher and better aims to guide me if I could only be spared a few years longer, overcame me and the tears came again. We put our arms about each other's necks and awaited the warning drowsiness that precedes death by freezing.

It came stealing over us presently, and then we bade each other a last farewell. A delicious dreaminess wrought its web about my yielding senses, while the snow-flakes wove a winding sheet about my conquered body. Oblivion came. The battle of life was done.

I do not know how long I was in a state of forgetfulness, but it seemed an age. A vague consciousness grew upon me by degrees, and then came a gathering anguish of pain in my limbs and through all my body. I shuddered. The thought flitted through my brain, "this is death—this is the hereafter."

Then came a white upheaval at my side, and a voice said, with bitterness:

"Will some gentleman be so good as to kick me behind?"

It was Ballou—at least it was a towzled snow image in a sitting posture, with Ballou's voice.

I rose up, and there in the gray dawn, not fifteen steps from us, were the frame buildings of a stage station, and under a shed stood our still saddled and bridled horses!

An arched snow-drift broke up, now, and Ollendorff emerged from it, and the three of us sat and stared at the houses without speaking a word. We really had nothing to say. We were like the profane man who could not "do the subject justice," the whole situation was so painfully ridiculous and humiliating that words were tame and we did not know where to commence anyhow.

The joy in our hearts at our deliverance was poisoned; well-nigh dissipated, indeed. We presently began to grow pettish by degrees, and sullen; and then, angry at each other, angry at ourselves, angry at everything in general, we moodily dusted the snow from our clothing and in unsociable single file plowed our way to the horses, unsaddled them, and sought shelter in the station.

I have scarcely exaggerated a detail of this curious and absurd adventure. It occurred almost exactly as I have stated it. We actually went into camp in a snow-drift in a desert, at midnight in a storm, forlorn and hopeless, within fifteen steps of a comfortable inn.

For two hours we sat apart in the station and ruminated in disgust. The mystery was gone, now, and it was plain enough why the horses had deserted us. Without a doubt they were under that shed a quarter of a minute after they had left us, and they must have overheard and enjoyed all our confessions and lamentations.

After breakfast we felt better, and the zest of life soon came back. The world looked bright again, and existence was as dear to us as ever. Presently an uneasiness came over me—grew upon me—assailed me without ceasing. Alas, my regeneration was not complete—I wanted to smoke! I resisted with all my strength, but the flesh was weak. I wandered away alone and wrestled with myself an hour. I recalled my promises of reform and preached to myself persuasively, upbraidingly, exhaustively. But it was all vain, I shortly found myself sneaking among the snow-drifts hunting for my pipe. I discovered it after a considerable search, and crept away to hide myself and enjoy it. I remained behind the barn a good while, asking myself how I would feel if my braver, stronger, truer comrades should

catch me in my degradation. At last I lit the pipe, and no human being can feel meaner and baser than I did then. I was ashamed of being in my own pitiful company. Still dreading discovery, I felt that perhaps the further side of the barn would be somewhat safer, and so I turned the corner. As I turned the one corner, smoking, Ollendorff turned the other with his bottle to his lips, and between us sat unconscious Ballou deep in a game of "solitaire" with the old greasy cards!

Absurdity could go no farther. We shook hands and agreed to say no more about "reform" and "examples to the rising generation."

THE CASE OF HYDE VS. MORGAN
FROM *Roughing It* [1872]

⟪ THERE actually was an Isaac N. Roop who had been first provisional governor of Nevada Territory, and other characters in the sketch bear names suggesting those of actual residents of Nevada: Attorney General Benjamin B. Bunker, for example, and Hal Clayton, a noted Confederate sympathizer.

THE MOUNTAINS are very high and steep about Carson, Eagle and Washoe Valleys—very high and very steep, and so when the snow gets to melting off fast in the Spring and the warm surface-earth begins to moisten and soften, the disastrous landslides commence. The reader cannot know what a land-slide is, unless he has lived in that country and seen the whole side of a mountain taken off some fine morning and deposited down in the valley, leaving a vast, treeless, unsightly scar upon the mountain's front to keep the circumstance fresh in his memory all the years that he may go on living within seventy miles of that place.

General Buncombe was shipped out to Nevada in the invoice of Territorial officers, to be United States Attorney. He considered himself a lawyer of parts, and he very much wanted an opportunity to manifest it—partly for the pure gratification of it and partly because his salary was Territorially meagre (which is a strong expression). Now the older citizens of a new territory look down upon the rest of the world with a calm, benevolent compassion, as long as it keeps out of the way—when it gets in the way they snub it. Sometimes this latter takes the shape of a practical joke.

One morning Dick Hyde rode furiously up to General Buncombe's door in Carson city and rushed into his presence without stopping to tie his horse. He seemed much excited. He told the General that he wanted him to conduct a suit for him and would pay him five hundred dollars if he achieved a victory. And then, with violent gestures and a world of profanity, he poured out his griefs. He said it was pretty well known that for some years he had been farming (or ranching as the more customary term is) in Washoe District, and making a successful thing of it, and furthermore it was known that his ranch was situated just in the edge of the valley, and that Tom Morgan owned a ranch immediately above it on the mountain side. And now the trouble was, that one of those hated and dreaded land-slides had come and slid Morgan's ranch, fences, cabins, cattle, barns and everything down on top of *his* ranch and exactly covered up every single vestige of his property, to a depth of about thirty-eight feet. Morgan was in possession and refused to vacate the premises—said he was occupying his own cabin and not interfering with anybody else's—and said the cabin was standing on the same dirt and same ranch it had always stood on, and he would like to see anybody make him vacate.

"And when I reminded him," said Hyde, weeping, "that it was on top of my ranch and that he was trespassing, he had the infernal meanness to ask me why didn't I *stay* on my ranch and hold possession when I see him a-coming! Why didn't I *stay* on it, the blathering lunatic—by George, when I heard that racket and looked up that hill it was just like the whole world was a-ripping and a-tearing down that mountain side—splinters, and cord-wood, thunder and lightning, hail and snow, odds and ends of hay stacks, and awful clouds of dust!—trees going end over end in the air, rocks as big as a house jumping 'bout a thousand feet high and busting into ten million pieces, cattle turned inside out and a-coming head on with their tails hanging out between their teeth!—and in the midst of all that wrack and destruction sot that cussed Morgan on his gate-post, a-wondering why I didn't *stay and hold possession!* Laws bless me, I just took one glimpse, General, and lit out'n the county in three jumps exactly.

"But what grinds me is that that Morgan hangs on there and won't move off'n that ranch—says it's his'n and he's going to keep it—likes it better'n he did when it was higher up the hill. Mad! Well, I've been so mad for two days I couldn't find my way to town—been wandering around in the brush in a starving condition—got anything here to drink, General? But I'm here *now,* and I'm a-going to law. You hear *me!"*

Never in all the world, perhaps, were a man's feelings so outraged as were the General's. He said he had never heard of such high-handed con-

duct in all his life as this Morgan's. And he said there was no use in going to law—Morgan had no shadow of right to remain where he was—nobody in the wide world would uphold him in it, and no lawyer would take his case and no judge listen to it. Hyde said that right there was where he was mistaken—everybody in town sustained Morgan; Hal Brayton, a very smart lawyer, had taken his case; the courts being in vacation, it was to be tried before a referee, and ex-Governor Roop had already been appointed to that office and would open his court in a large public hall near the hotel at two that afternoon.

The General was amazed. He said he had suspected before that the people of that Territory were fools, and now he knew it. But he said rest easy, rest easy and collect the witnesses, for the victory was just as certain as if the conflict were already over. Hyde wiped away his tears and left.

At two in the afternoon referee Roop's Court opened, and Roop appeared throned among his sheriffs, the witnesses, and spectators, and wearing upon his face a solemnity so awe-inspiring that some of his fellow-conspirators had misgivings that maybe he had not comprehended, after all, that this was merely a joke. An unearthly stillness prevailed, for at the slightest noise the judge uttered sternly the command:

"Order in the Court!"

And the sheriffs promptly echoed it. Presently the General elbowed his way through the crowd of spectators, with his arms full of law-books, and on his ears fell an order from the judge which was the first respectful recognition of his high official dignity that had ever saluted them, and it trickled pleasantly through his whole system:

"Way for the United States Attorney!"

The witnesses were called—legislators, high government officers, ranchmen, miners, Indians, Chinamen, negroes. Three fourths of them were called by the defendant Morgan, but no matter, their testimony invariably went in favor of the plaintiff Hyde. Each new witness only added new testimony to the absurdity of a man's claiming to own another man's property because his farm had slid down on top of it. Then the Morgan lawyers made their speeches, and seemed to make singularly weak ones—they did really nothing to help the Morgan cause. And now the General, with exultation in his face, got up and made an impassioned effort; he pounded the table, he banged the law-books, he shouted, and roared, and howled, he quoted from everything and everybody, poetry, sarcasm, statistics, history, pathos, bathos, blasphemy, and wound up with a grand war-whoop for free speech, freedom of the press, free schools, the Glorious Bird of America and the principles of eternal justice! [Applause.]

When the General sat down, he did it with the conviction that if there was anything in good strong testimony, a great speech and believing and admiring countenances all around, Mr. Morgan's case was killed. Ex-Governor Roop leant his head upon his hand for some minutes, thinking, and the still audience waited for his decision. Then he got up and stood erect, with bended head, and thought again. Then he walked the floor with long, deliberate strides, his chin in his hand, and still the audience waited. At last he returned to his throne, seated himself, and began, impressively:

"Gentlemen, I feel the great responsibility that rests upon me this day. This is no ordinary case. On the contrary it is plain that it is the most solemn and awful that ever man was called upon to decide. Gentlemen, I have listened attentively to the evidence, and have perceived that the weight of it, the overwhelming weight of it, is in favor of the plaintiff Hyde. I have listened also to the remarks of counsel, with high interest—and especially will I commend the masterly and irrefutable logic of the distinguished gentleman who represents the plaintiff. But gentlemen, let us beware how we allow mere human testimony, human ingenuity in argument and human ideas of equity, to influence us at a moment so solemn as this. Gentlemen, it ill becomes us, worms as we are, to meddle with the decrees of Heaven. It is plain to me that Heaven, in its inscrutable wisdom, has seen fit to move this defendant's ranch for a purpose. We are but creatures, and we must submit. If Heaven has chosen to favor the defendant Morgan in this marked and wonderful manner; and if Heaven, dissatisfied with the position of the Morgan ranch upon the mountain side, has chosen to remove it to a position more eligible and more advantageous for its owner, it ill becomes us, insects as we are, to question the legality of the act or inquire into the reasons that prompted it. No —Heaven created the ranches and it is Heaven's prerogative to rearrange them, to experiment with them, to shift them around at its pleasure. It is for us to submit, without repining. I warn you that this thing which has happened is a thing with which the sacrilegious hands and brains and tongues of men must not meddle. Gentlemen, it is the verdict of this court that the plaintiff, Richard Hyde, has been deprived of his ranch by the visitation of God! And from this decision there is no appeal."

Buncombe seized his cargo of law-books and plunged out of the court-room frantic with indignation. He pronounced Roop to be a miraculous fool, an inspired idiot. In all good faith he returned at night and remonstrated with Roop upon his extravagant decision, and implored him to walk the floor and think for half an hour, and see if he could not figure out some sort of modification of the verdict. Roop yielded at last and got up to walk. He walked two hours and a half, and at last his face lit up happily and he told Buncombe it had occurred to him that the ranch underneath the new Morgan ranch still belonged to Hyde, that his title to the ground was just as good as it had ever been, and therefore he was of opinion that Hyde had a right to dig it out from under there and—

The General never waited to hear the end of it. He was always an impatient and irascible man, that way. At the end of two months the fact that he had been played upon with a joke had managed to bore itself, like another Hoosac Tunnel, through the solid adamant of his understanding.

THE STORY OF THE OLD RAM

FROM *Roughing It* [1872]

❨ THE setting is Virginia City. This version of the story should be compared with the version revised for oral delivery contained in "Platform Readings" (see pp. 108– 09).

EVERY now and then, in these days, the boys used to tell me I ought to get one Jim Blaine to tell me the stirring story of his grandfather's old ram—but they always added that I must not mention the matter unless Jim was drunk at the time—just comfortably and sociably drunk. They kept this up until my curiosity was on the rack to hear the story. I got to haunting Blaine; but it was of no use, the boys always found fault with his condition; he was often moderately but never satisfactorily drunk. I never watched a man's condition with such absorbing interest, such anxious solicitude; I never so pined to see a man uncompromisingly drunk before. At last, one evening I hurried to his cabin, for I learned that this time his situation was such that even the most fastidious could find no fault with it —he was tranquilly, serenely, symmetrically drunk —not a hiccup to mar his voice, not a cloud upon his brain thick enough to obscure his memory. As I entered, he was sitting upon an empty powderkeg, with a clay pipe in one hand and the other raised to command silence. His face was round, red, and very serious; his throat was bare and his hair tumbled; in general appearance and costume he was a stalwart miner of the period. On the pine table stood a candle, and its dim light revealed "the boys" sitting here and there on bunks, candle-boxes, powder-kegs, etc. They said:

"Sh—! Don't speak—he's going to commence."

THE STORY OF THE OLD RAM

I found a seat at once, and Blaine said:

"I don't reckon them times will ever come again. There never was a more bullier old ram than what he was. Grand-father fetched him from Illinois—got him of a man by the name of Yates —Bill Yates—maybe you might have heard of him; his father was a deacon—Baptist—and he was a rustler, too; a man had to get up ruther early to get the start of old Thankful Yates; it was him that put the Greens up to jining teams with my grand-father when he moved west. Seth Green was prob'ly the pick of the flock; he married a Wilkerson—Sarah Wilkerson—good cretur, she was—one of the likeliest heifers that was ever raised in old Stoddard, everybody said that knowed her. She could heft a bar'l of flour as easy as I can flirt a flapjack. And spin? Don't mention it! Independent? Humph! When Sile Hawkins come a browsing around her, she let him know that for all his tin he couldn't trot in harness alongside of *her*. You see, Sile Hawkins was— no, it warn't Sile Hawkins, after all—it was a galoot by the name of Filkins—I disremember his first name; but he *was* a stump—come into pra'r meeting drunk, one night, hooraying for Nixon, becuz he thought it was a primary; and old deacon Ferguson up and scooted him through the window and he lit on old Miss Jefferson's head, poor old filly. She was a good soul—had a glass eye and used to lend it to old Miss Wagner, that hadn't any, to receive company in; it warn't big enough, and when Miss Wagner warn't noticing, it would get twisted around in the socket, and look up, maybe, or out to one side, and every which way, while t' other one was looking as straight ahead as a spy-glass. Grown people didn't mind it, but it most always made the children cry, it was so sort of scary. She tried packing it in raw cotton, but it wouldn't work, somehow—the cotton would get loose and stick out and look so kind of awful that the children couldn't stand it no way. She was always dropping it out, and turning up her old dead-light on the company empty, and making them on-comfortable, becuz *she* never could tell when it hopped out, being blind on that side, you see. So somebody would have to hunch her and say, "Your game eye has fetched loose, Miss Wagner dear"—and then all of them would have to sit and wait till she jammed it in again—wrong side be-fore, as a general thing, and green as a bird's egg, being a bashful cretur and easy sot back before company. But being wrong side before warn't much difference, anyway, becuz her own eye was sky-blue and the glass one was yaller on the front side, so whichever way she turned it it didn't match nohow. Old Miss Wagner was considerable on the borrow, she was. When she had a quilting, or Dorcas S'iety at her house she gen'ally bor-rowed Miss Higgins's wooden leg to stump around on; it was considerable shorter than her other pin, but much *she* minded that. She said she couldn't abide crutches when she had company, becuz they were so slow; said when she had company and things had to be done, she wanted to get up and hump herself. She was as bald as a jug, and so she used to borrow Miss Jacops's wig—Miss Jacops was the coffin-peddler's wife—a ratty old buz-zard, he was, that used to go roosting around where people was sick, waiting for 'em; and there that old rip would sit all day, in the shade, on a coffin that he judged would fit the can'idate; and if it was a slow customer and kind of uncertain, he'd fetch his rations and a blanket along and sleep in the coffin nights. He was anchored out that way, in frosty weather, for about three weeks, once, before old Robbins's place, waiting for him; and after that, for as much as two years, Jacops was not on speaking terms with the old man, on account of his disapp'inting him. He got one of his feet froze, and lost money, too, becuz old Rob-bins took a favorable turn and got well. The next time Robbins got sick, Jacops tried to make up with him, and varnished up the same old coffin and fetched it along; but old Robbins was too many for him; he had him in, and 'peared to be powerful weak; he bought the coffin for ten dol-lars and Jacops was to pay it back and twenty-five more besides if Robbins didn't like the coffin after he'd tried it. And then Robbins died, and at the funeral he bursted off the lid and riz up in his shroud and told the parson to let up on the per-formances, becuz he could *not* stand such a coffin as that. You see he had been in a trance once be-fore, when he was young, and he took the chances on another, cal'lating that if he made the trip it was money in his pocket, and if he missed fire he couldn't lose a cent. And by George he sued Jacops for the rhino and got jedgment; and he set up the coffin in his back parlor and said he 'lowed to take his time, now. It was always an aggrava-tion to Jacops, the way that miserable old thing acted. He moved back to Indiany pretty soon— went to Wellsville—Wellsville was the place the Hogadorns was from. Mighty fine family. Old Maryland stock. Old Squire Hogadorn could carry around more mixed licker, and cuss better than most any man I ever see. His second wife was the widder Billings—she that was Becky Martin; her dam was deacon Dunlap's first wife. Her oldest child, Maria, married a missionary and died in grace—et up by the savages. They et *him,* too, poor feller—biled him. It warn't the custom, so they say, but they explained to friends of his'n that went down there to bring away his things, that they'd tried missionaries every other way and never could get any good out of 'em—and so it annoyed all his relations to find out that that man's life was fooled away just out of a dern'd experiment, so to speak. But mind you, there ain't anything ever reely lost; everything that people can't understand and don't see the reason of does good if you only hold on and give it a fair shake; Prov'dence don't fire no blank ca'tridges, boys. That there missionary's substance, unbeknowns to himself, actu'ly converted every last one of them heathens that took a chance at the barbacue. Nothing ever fetched them but that. Don't tell *me* it was an accident that he was biled. There ain't no such a thing as an accident. When my uncle Lem was leaning up agin a scaffolding once, sick, or drunk, or suthin, an Irishman with a hod full of bricks fell on him out of the third story and broke the old man's back in two places. People said it was an accident. Much accident there was about that. He didn't know what he was there for, but he was there for a good object. If he hadn't been there the Irishman would have been killed. Nobody can ever make me believe anything different from that. Uncle Lem's dog was there. Why didn't the Irishman fall on the dog? Becuz the dog would a seen him a coming and stood from under. That's the reason the dog warn't appinted. A dog can't be depended on to carry out a special providence. Mark my words it was a put-up thing. Accidents don't happen, boys. Uncle Lem's dog—I wish you could a seen that dog. He was a reglar shepherd—or ruther he was part bull and part shepherd—splendid animal; belonged to parson Hagar before Uncle Lem got him. Parson Hagar belonged to the Western Reserve Hagars; prime family; his mother was a Watson; one of his sisters married a Wheeler; they settled in Morgan county, and he got nipped by the machinery in a carpet factory and went through in less than a quarter of a minute; his widder bought the piece of carpet that had his remains wove in, and people came a hundred mile to 'tend the funeral. There was fourteen yards in the piece. She wouldn't let them roll him up, but planted him just so—full length. The church was middling small where they preached the funeral, and they had to let one end of the coffin stick out of the window. They didn't bury him—they planted one end, and let him stand up, same as a monument. And they nailed a sign on it and put—put on—put on it—sacred to—the m-e-m-o-r-y—of fourteen y-a-r-d-s—of three-ply—car - - - pet—containing all that was—m-o-r-t-a-l—of—of—W-i-l-l-i-a-m—W-h-e—"

Jim Blaine had been growing gradually drowsy and drowsier—his head nodded, once, twice, three times—dropped peacefully upon his breast, and he fell tranquilly asleep. The tears were running down the boys' cheeks—they were suffocating with suppressed laughter—and had been from the start, though I had never noticed it. I perceived that I was "sold." I learned then that Jim Blaine's peculiarity was that whenever he reached a certain stage of intoxication, no human power could keep him from setting out, with impressive unction, to tell about a wonderful adventure which he had once had with his grandfather's old ram—and the mention of the ram in the first sentence was as far as any man had ever heard him get, concerning it. He always maundered off, interminably, from one thing to another, till his whisky got the best of him and he fell asleep. What the thing was that happened to him and his grandfather's old ram is a dark mystery to this day, for nobody has ever yet found out.

COLONEL SELLERS

FROM *The Gilded Age* [1873]

⟨ Washington Hawkins, in his early twenties, arrives at Hawkeye, Missouri, from the even more remote village where his family have lived for ten years since they emigrated from Tennessee. Financial distress has compelled Squire Hawkins to send his son out into the world to seek his fortune under the guidance of Colonel Sellers, an old friend and former business associate of the Squire. Mark Twain declared later that Colonel Sellers was an exact portrait of his mother's cousin, James Lampton. Biographers have seen in Squire Hawkins certain traits of John Marshall Clemens and in Washington Hawkins certain traits of Orion Clemens.

Toward evening, the stage-coach came thundering into Hawkeye with a perfectly triumphant ostentation—which was natural and proper, for Hawkeye was a pretty large town for interior Missouri. Washington, very stiff and tired and hungry, climbed out, and wondered how he was to proceed now. But his difficulty was quickly solved. Col. Sellers came down the street on a run and arrived panting for breath. He said:

"Lord bless you—I'm glad to see you, Washington—perfectly delighted to see you, my boy! I got your message. Been on the look-out for you. Heard the stage horn, but had a party I couldn't shake off—man that's got an enormous thing on hand—wants me to put some capital into it—and I tell you, my boy, I could do worse, I could do a deal worse. No, now, let that luggage alone; I'll fix that. Here, Jerry, got anything to do? All right —shoulder this plunder and follow me. Come along, Washington. Lord I'm glad to see you! Wife and the children are just perishing to look at you. Bless you, they won't know you, you've grown so. Folks all well, I suppose? That's good— glad to hear that. We're always going to run down and see them, but I'm into so many operations, and they're not things a man feels like trusting to other people, and so somehow we keep putting it off. Fortunes in them! Good gracious, it's the country to pile up wealth in! Here we are—here's where the Sellers dynasty hangs out. Dump it on the door-step, Jerry—the blackest niggro in the State, Washington, but got a good heart—mighty likely boy, is Jerry. And now I suppose you've got to have ten cents, Jerry. That's all right—when a man works for me—when a man—in the other pocket, I reckon—when a man—why, where the mischief *is* that portmonnaie!—when a—well now that's odd—Oh, now I remember, must have left it at the bank; and b'George I've left my check-book, too—Polly says I ought to have a nurse—well, no matter. Let me have a dime, Washington, if you've got—ah, thanks. Now clear out, Jerry, your complexion has brought on the twilight half an hour ahead of time. Pretty fair joke—pretty fair. Here he is, Polly! Washington's come, children!—come now, don't eat him up— finish him in the house. Welcome, my boy, to a mansion that is proud to shelter the son of the best man that walks on the ground. Si Hawkins has been a good friend to me, and I believe I can say that whenever I've had a chance to put him into a good thing I've done it, and done it pretty cheerfully, too. I put him into that sugar speculation—what a grand thing that was, if we hadn't held on too long!"

True enough; but holding on too long had utterly ruined both of them; and the saddest part of it was, that they never had had so much money to lose before, for Sellers's sale of their mule crop that year in New Orleans had been a great financial success. If he had kept out of sugar and gone back home content to stick to mules it would have been a happy wisdom. As it was, he managed to kill two birds with one stone—that is to say, he killed the sugar speculation by holding for high rates till he had to sell at the bottom figure, and that calamity killed the mule that laid the golden egg—which is but a figurative expression and will be so understood. Sellers had returned home cheerful but empty-handed, and the mule business lapsed into other hands. The sale of the Hawkins property by the Sheriff had followed, and the Hawkins' hearts been torn to see Uncle Dan'l and his wife pass from the auction-block into the hands of a negro trader and depart for the remote South to be seen no more by the family. It had seemed like seeing their own flesh and blood sold into banishment.

Washington was greatly pleased with the Sellers mansion. It was a two-story-and-a-half brick, and much more stylish than any of its neighbors. He was borne to the family sitting room in triumph by the swarm of little Sellerses, the parents following with their arms about each other's waists.

The whole family were poorly and cheaply dressed; and the clothing, although neat and clean, showed many evidences of having seen long service. The Colonel's "stovepipe" hat was napless and shiny with much polishing, but nevertheless it had an almost convincing expression about it of having been just purchased new. The rest of his clothing was napless and shiny, too, but it had the air of being entirely satisfied with itself and blandly sorry for other people's clothes. It was growing rather dark in the house, and the evening air was chilly, too. Sellers said:

"Lay off your overcoat, Washington, and draw up to the stove and make yourself at home—just consider yourself under your own shingles my boy—I'll have a fire going, in a jiffy. Light the lamp, Polly, dear, and let's have things cheerful —just as glad to see you, Washington, as if you'd been lost a century and we'd found you again!"

By this time the Colonel was conveying a lighted match into a poor little stove. Then he propped the stove door to its place by leaning the poker against it, for the hinges had retired from business. This door framed a small square of isinglass, which now warmed up with a faint glow. Mrs. Sellers lit a cheap, showy lamp, which dissipated a good deal of the gloom, and then everybody gathered into the light and took the stove into close companionship.

The children climbed all over Sellers, fondled him, petted him, and were lavishly petted in return. Out from this tugging, laughing, chattering disguise of legs and arms and little faces, the Colonel's voice worked its way and his tireless tongue ran blithely on without interruption; and the purring little wife, diligent with her knitting, sat near at hand and looked happy and proud and grateful; and she listened as one who listens to oracles and gospels and whose grateful soul is being refreshed with the bread of life. Bye and bye the children quieted down to listen; clustered about their father, and resting their elbows on his legs, they hung upon his words as if he were uttering the music of the spheres.

A dreary old hair-cloth sofa against the wall; a few damaged chairs; the small table the lamp stood on; the crippled stove—these things constituted the furniture of the room. There was no carpet on the floor; on the wall were occasional square-shaped interruptions of the general tint of the plaster which betrayed that there used to be pictures in the house—but there were none now. There were no mantel ornaments, unless one might bring himself to regard as an ornament a clock which never came within fifteen strokes of striking the right time, and whose hands always hitched together at twenty-two minutes past anything and traveled in company the rest of the way home.

"Remarkable clock!" said Sellers, and got up and wound it. "I've been offered—well, I wouldn't expect you to believe what I've been offered for that clock. Old Gov. Hager never sees me but he says, 'Come, now, Colonel, name your price—I *must* have that clock!' But my goodness I'd as soon think of selling my wife. As I was saying to ————silence in the court, now, she's begun to strike! You can't talk against her—you have to just be patient and hold up till she's said her say. Ah—well, as I was saying, when—she's beginning again! Nineteen, twenty, twenty-one, twenty-two, twen————ah, that's all.—Yes, as I was saying to old Judge————go it, old girl, don't mind me.—Now how is that?—isn't that a good, spirited tone? She can wake the dead! Sleep? Why you might as well try to sleep in a thunder-factory. Now just listen at that. She'll strike a hundred and fifty, now, without stopping,—you'll see. There ain't another clock like that in Christendom."

Washington hoped that this might be true, for the din was distracting—though the family, one and all, seemed filled with joy; and the more the clock "buckled down to her work" as the Colonel expressed it, and the more insupportable the clatter became, the more enchanted they all appeared to be. When there was silence, Mrs. Sellers lifted upon Washington a face that beamed with a child-like pride, and said:

"It belonged to his grandmother."

The look and the tone were a plain call for admiring surprise, and therefore Washington said—

(it was the only thing that offered itself at the moment:)

"Indeed!"

"Yes, it did, didn't it father!" exclaimed one of the twins. "She was my great-grandmother—and George's too; wasn't she, father! *You* never saw her, but Sis has seen her, when Sis was a baby—didn't you, Sis! Sis has seen her most a hundred times. She was awful deef—she's dead, now. Ain't she, father!"

All the children chimed in, now, with one general Babel of information about deceased—nobody offering to read the riot act or seeming to discountenance the insurrection or disapprove of it in any way—but the head twin drowned all the turmoil and held his own against the field:

"It's our clock, now—and it's got wheels inside of it, and a thing that flutters every time she strikes—don't it, father! Great-grandmother died before hardly any of us was born—she was an Old-School Baptist and had warts all over her—you ask father if she didn't. She had an uncle once that was bald-headed and used to have fits; he wasn't *our* uncle, I don't know what he was to us—some kin or another I reckon—father's seen him a thousand times—hain't you, father! We used to have a calf that et apples and just chawed up dishrags like nothing, and if you stay here you'll see lots of funerals—won't he, Sis! Did you ever see a house afire? *I* have! Once me and Jim Terry————"

But Sellers began to speak now, and the storm ceased. He began to tell about an enormous speculation he was thinking of embarking some capital in—a speculation which some London bankers had been over to consult with him about—and soon he was building glittering pyramids of coin, and Washington was presently growing opulent under the magic of his eloquence. But at the same time Washington was not able to ignore the cold entirely. He was nearly as close to the stove as he could get, and yet he could not persuade himself that he felt the slightest heat, notwithstanding the isinglass door was still gently and serenely glowing. He tried to get a trifle closer to the stove, and the consequence was, he tripped the supporting poker and the stove-door tumbled to the floor. And then there was a revelation—there was nothing in the stove but a lighted tallow-candle!

The poor youth blushed and felt as if he must die with shame. But the Colonel was only disconcerted for a moment—he straightway found his voice again:

"A little idea of my own, Washington—one of the greatest things in the world! You must write and tell your father about it—don't forget that, now. I have been reading up some European Scientific reports—friend of mine, Count Fugier, sent them to me—sends me all sorts of things from Paris—he thinks the world of me, Fugier does. Well, I saw that the Academy of France had been testing the properties of heat, and they came to the conclusion that it was a non-conductor or something like that, and of course its influence must necessarily be deadly in nervous organizations with excitable temperaments, especially where there is any tendency toward rheumatic affections. Bless you I saw in a moment what was the matter with us, and says I, out goes your fires!—no more slow torture and certain death for me, sir. What you want is the *appearance* of heat, not the heat itself—that's the idea. Well how to do it was the next thing. I just put my head to work, pegged away a couple of days, and here you are! Rheumatism? Why a man can't any more start a case of rheumatism in this house than he can shake an opinion out of a mummy! Stove with a candle in it and a transparent door—that's it—it has been the salvation of this family. Don't you fail to write your father about it, Washington. And tell him the idea is mine—I'm no more conceited than most people, I reckon, but you know it is human nature for a man to want credit for a thing like that."

Washington said with his blue lips that he would, but he said in his secret heart that he would promote no such iniquity. He tried to believe in the healthfulness of the invention, and succeeded tolerably well; but after all he could not feel that good health in a frozen body was any real improvement on the rheumatism.

[*Two months later*].

The Sellers family were just starting to dinner when Washington burst upon them. . . . For an instant the Colonel looked nonplussed, and just a bit uncomfortable; and Mrs. Sellers looked actually distressed; but the next moment the head of the house was himself again, and exclaimed:

"All right, my boy, all right—always glad to see you—always glad to hear your voice and take you by the hand. Don't wait for special invitations—that's all nonsense among friends. Just come whenever you can, and come as often as you can—the oftener the better. You can't please us any better than that, Washington; the little woman will tell you so herself. We don't pretend to style. Plain folks, you know—plain folks. Just a plain family dinner, but such as it is, our friends are *always* welcome, I reckon you know that yourself Washington. Run along, children, run

along; Lafayette,[1] stand off the cat's tail, child, can't you see what you're doing?—Come, come, come, Roderick Dhu, it isn't nice for little boys to hang onto young gentlemen's coat tails—but never mind him, Washington, he's full of spirits and don't mean any harm. Children will be children, you know. Take the chair next to Mrs. Sellers, Washington—tut, tut, Marie Antoinette, let your brother have the fork if he wants it, you are bigger than he is."

Washington contemplated the banquet, and wondered if he were in his right mind. Was this the plain family dinner? And was it all present? It was soon apparent that this was indeed the dinner: it was all on the table: it consisted of abundance of clear, fresh water, and a basin of raw turnips—nothing more.

Washington stole a glance at Mrs. Sellers's face, and would have given the world, the next moment, if he could have spared her that. The poor woman's face was crimson, and the tears stood in her eyes. Washington did not know what to do. He wished he had never come there and spied out this cruel poverty and brought pain to that poor little lady's heart and shame to her cheek; but he was there, and there was no escape. Col. Sellers hitched back his coat sleeves airily from his wrists as who should say *"Now* for solid enjoyment!"* seized a fork, flourished it and began to harpoon turnips and deposit them in the plates before him:

"Let me help you, Washington—Lafayette pass this plate to Washington—ah, well, well, my boy, things are looking pretty bright, now, *I* tell you. Speculation—my! the whole atmosphere's full of money. I wouldn't take three fortunes for one little operation I've got on hand now—have anything from the casters? No? Well, you're right, you're right. Some people like mustard with turnips, but—now there was Baron Poniatowski—Lord, but that man did know how to live!—true Russian you know, Russian to the back bone; I say to my wife, give me a Russian every time, for a table comrade. The Baron used to say, 'Take mustard, Sellers, try the mustard,—a man *can't* know what turnips are in perfection without mustard,' but I always said, 'No, Baron, I'm a plain

COLONEL SELLERS.   1. **Lafayette:** "In those old days the average man called his children after his most revered literary and historical idols; consequently there was hardly a family, at least in the West, but had a Washington in it—and also a Lafayette, a Franklin, and six or eight sounding names from Byron, Scott, and the Bible, if the offspring held out. To visit such a family, was to find one's self confronted by a congress made up of representatives of the imperial myths and the majestic dead of all the ages. There was something thrilling about it, to a stranger, not to say awe inspiring" [M T].

man, and I want my food plain—none of your embellishments for Eschol Sellers—no made dishes for me! And it's the best way—high living kills more than it cures in this world, you can rest assured of that.—Yes indeed, Washington, I've got one little operation on hand that—take some more water—help yourself, won't you?—help yourself, there's plenty of it.—You'll find it pretty good, I guess. How does that fruit strike you?"

Washington said he did not know that he had ever tasted better. He did not add that he detested turnips even when they were cooked—loathed them in their natural state. No, he kept this to himself, and praised the turnips to the peril of his soul.

"I thought you'd like them. Examine them—examine them—they'll bear it. See how perfectly firm and juicy they are—they can't start any like them in this part of the country, I can tell you. These are from New Jersey—I imported them myself. They cost like sin, too; but lord bless me, I go in for having the best of a thing, even if it does cost a little more—it's the best economy, in the long run. These are the Early Malcolm—it's a turnip that can't be produced except in just one orchard, and the supply never is up to the demand. Take some more water, Washington—you can't drink too much water with fruit—all the doctors say that. The plague can't come where this article is, my boy!"

"Plague? What plague?"

"What plague, indeed? Why the Asiatic plague that nearly depopulated London a couple of centuries ago."

"But how does that concern us? There is no plague here, I reckon."

"Sh! I've let it out! Well, never mind—just keep it to yourself. Perhaps I oughtn't said anything, but it's *bound* to come out sooner or later, so what is the odds? Old McDowells wouldn't like me to—to—bother it all, I'll just tell the whole thing and let it go. You see, I've been down to St. Louis, and I happened to run across old Dr. McDowells—thinks the world of me, does the doctor. He's a man that keeps himself to himself, and well he may, for he knows that he's got a reputation that covers the whole earth—he won't condescend to open himself out to many people, but lord bless you, he and I are just like brothers; he won't let me go to a hotel when I'm in the city—says I'm the only man that's company to him, and I don't know but there's some truth in it, too, because although I never like to glorify myself and make a great to-do over what I am or what I can do or what I know, I don't mind saying here among friends that I *am* better read up in most

sciences, maybe, than the general run of professional men in these days. Well, the other day he let me into a little secret, strictly on the quiet, about this matter of the plague.

"You see it's booming right along in our direction—follows the Gulf Stream, you know, just as all those epidemics do,—and within three months it will be just waltzing through this land like a whirlwind! And whoever it touches can make his will and contract for the funeral. Well you can't *cure* it, you know, but you can prevent it. How? Turnips! that's it! Turnips and water! Nothing like it in the world, old McDowells says, just fill yourself up two or three times a day, and you can snap your fingers at the plague. Sh!—keep mum, but just you confine yourself to that diet and you're all right. I wouldn't have old McDowells know that I told about it for anything—he never would speak to me again. Take some more water, Washington—the more water you drink, the better. Here, let me give you some more of the turnips. No, no, no, now, I insist. There, now. Absorb those. They're mighty sustaining—brim full of nutriment—all the medical books say so. Just eat from four to seven good-sized turnips at a meal, and drink from a pint and a half to a quart of water, and then just sit around a couple of hours and let them ferment. You'll feel like a fighting cock next day."

Fifteen or twenty minutes later the Colonel's tongue was still chattering away—he had piled up several future fortunes out of several incipient "operations" which he had blundered into within the past week, and was now soaring along through some brilliant expectations born of late promising experiments upon the lacking ingredient of the eye-water.[2] And at such a time Washington ought to have been a rapt and enthusiastic listener, but he was not, for two matters disturbed his mind and distracted his attention. One was, that he discovered, to his confusion and shame, that in allowing himself to be helped a second time to the turnips, he had robbed those hungry children. He had not needed the dreadful "fruit," and had not wanted it; and when he saw the pathetic sorrow in their faces when they asked for more and there was no more to give them, he hated himself for his stupidity and pitied the famishing young things with all his heart. The other matter that disturbed him was the dire inflation that had begun in his stomach. It grew and grew, it became more and more insupportable. Evidently

2. **eye-water:** "Sellers's Infallible Imperial Oriental Optic Liniment and Salvation for Sore Eyes," which the Colonel is trying to perfect by discovering the one essential ingredient not yet identified.

the turnips were "fermenting." He forced himself to sit still as long as he could, but his anguish conquered him at last.

He rose in the midst of the Colonel's talk and excused himself on the plea of a previous engagement. The Colonel followed him to the door, promising over and over again that he would use his influence to get some of the Early Malcolms for him, and insisting that he should not be such a stranger but come and take pot-luck with him every chance he got. Washington was glad enough to get away and feel free again. He immediately bent his steps toward home.

In bed he passed an hour that threatened to turn his hair gray, and then a blessed calm settled down upon him that filled his heart with gratitude. Weak and languid, he made shift to turn himself about and seek rest and sleep; and as his soul hovered upon the brink of unconsciousness, he heaved a long, deep sigh, and said to himself that in his heart he had cursed the Colonel's preventive of rheumatism, before, and now *let* the plague come if it must—he was done with preventives; if ever any man beguiled him with turnips and water again, let him die the death.

PART II:
SOME ANIMALS

◇

❨ MARK TWAIN's interest in animals is conspicuous from beginning to end of his career. It appears, for example, in the sympathetic attention to the "fiery untamed steed" in the production of *Mazeppa* (see p. 91, below), and in the observation that the horses of the travelers lost in the Nevada snowstorm "were under that shed a quarter of a minute after they had left us, and . . . must have overheard and enjoyed all our confessions and lamentations" (above, p. 70). The passages about animals reprinted in this section, covering a span of thirty years, are among the most amusing things Mark Twain ever wrote; limitation of space has made it necessary to omit others equally good, such as the description of the horse Oahu in his dispatches from the Sandwich Islands. Like the cayote and the Indian crow in the selections brought together here, Mark Twain's animals usually have a vernacular point of view, but not always: the camel who eats the narrator's overcoat in Chapter 3 of *Roughing It* is definitely one of the genteel, or would-be genteel, and so is the Pilgrim Bird described below.

◇

CRUELTY TO ANIMALS:
THE HISTRIONIC PIG

❨ FIRST published in the San Francisco *Alta California* under the date line New York, April 30, 1867, this text is from *Mark Twain's Travels with Mr. Brown*, ed. by Franklin Walker and G. Ezra Dane (1940).

ONE OF the most praiseworthy institutions in New York, and one which must plead eloquently for it when its wickedness shall call down the anger of the gods, is the Society for the Prevention of Cruelty to Animals. Its office is located on the corner of Twelfth street and Broadway, and its affairs are conducted by humane men who take a genuine interest in their work, and who have got worldly wealth enough to make it unnecessary for them to busy themselves about anything else. They have already put a potent check upon the brutality of draymen and others to their horses, and in future will draw a still tighter reign upon such abuses, a late law of the Legislature having quadrupled their powers, and distinctly marked and specified them. You seldom see a horse beaten or otherwise cruelly used in New York now, so much has the society made itself feared and respected. Its members promptly secure the arrest of guilty parties and relentlessly prosecute them.

The new law gives the Society power to designate an adequate number of agents in every county, and these are appointed by the Sheriff, but work independently of all other branches of the civil organization. They can make arrests of guilty persons on the spot, without calling upon the regular police, and what is better, they can compel a man to stop abusing his horse, his dog, or any other animal, at a moment's warning. The object of the Society, as its name implies, is to prevent cruelty to animals, rather than punish men for being guilty of it.

They are going to put up hydrants and water tanks at convenient distances all over the city, for drinking places for men, horses and dogs.

Mr. Bergh,[1] the President of the Society, is a sort of enthusiast on the subject of cruelty to animals—or perhaps it would do him better justice to say he is full of honest earnestness upon the subject. Nothing that concerns the happiness of a brute is a trifling matter with him—no brute of whatever position or standing, however plebeian or insignificant, is beneath the range of his merciful interest. I have in my mind an example of his kindly solicitude for his dumb and helpless friends.

CRUELTY TO ANIMALS: THE HISTRIONIC PIG. **1. Mr. Bergh:** Henry Bergh (1811–88), who had obtained the first charter for the American S.P.C.A. in 1866.

He went to see the dramatic version of "Griffith Gaunt" [2] at Wallack's Theatre.[3] The next morning he entered the manager's office and the following conversation took place:

Mr. Bergh—"Are you the manager of this theatre?"

Manager—"I am, sir. What can I do for you?"

Mr. B.—"I am President of the Society for the Prevention of Cruelty to Animals, and I have come to remonstrate against your treatment of that pig in the last act of the play last night. It is cruel and wrong, and I beg that you will leave the pig out in future."

"That is impossible! The pig is necessary to the play."

"But it is cruel, and you could alter the play in some way so as to leave the pig out."

"It cannot possibly be done, and besides I do not see anything wrong about it at all. What is it you complain of?"

"Why, it is plain enough. They punch the pig with sticks, and chase him and harass him, and contrive all manner of means to make him unhappy. The poor thing runs about in its distress, and tries to escape, but is met at every turn by its tormentors and its hopes blighted. The pig does not understand it. If the pig understood it, it might be well enough, but the pig does not know it is a play, but takes it all as reality, and is frightened and bewildered by the crowd of people and the glare of the lights, and yet no time is given it for reflection—no time is given it to arrive at a just appreciation of its circumstances—but its persecutors constantly assail it and keep its mind in such a chaotic state that it can form no opinion upon any point in the case. And besides, the pig is cast in the play without its consent, is forced to conduct itself in a manner which cannot but be humiliating to it, and leaves that stage every night with a conviction that it would rather die than take a character in a theatrical performance again. Pigs are not fitted for the stage; they have no dramatic talent; all their inclinations are toward a retired and unostentatious career in the humblest walks of life, and——"

Manager—"Say no more, sir. The pig is yours. I meant to have educated him for tragedy and made him a blessing to mankind and an ornament to his species, but I am convinced, now, that I ought not to do this in the face of his marked opposition to the stage, and so I present him to you, who will treat him well, I am amply satisfied. I am the more willing to part with him, since the play he performs in was taken off the stage last night, and I could not conveniently arrange a part for him in the one we shall run for the next three weeks, which is Richard III."

THE CELEBRATED JUMPING FROG OF CALAVERAS COUNTY

❲ THIS is from *The Celebrated Jumping Frog of Calaveras County, and Other Sketches* (1867). It was first published in the New York *Saturday Press* (November 18, 1865). Mark Twain's notebook for the period he spent at Jackass Hill and Angel's Camp in Calaveras County, California, from December, 1864 to February, 1865, contains the following entry: "Coleman with his jumping frog—bet stranger $50.—Stranger had no frog and C. got him one:—in the meantime stranger filled C's frog full of shot and he couldn't jump. The stranger's frog won." Over this penciled entry Mark Twain later wrote in ink: "Wrote this story for Artemus—his idiot publisher [G. W.] Carleton gave it to [Henry] Clapp's Saturday Press." Mark Twain heard the story from Ben Coon, a pocket-miner who had once been a pilot on the Illinois River. But in its main outlines the story was well known in the mining camps: Walter Blair (*Native American Humor*, 1937, p. 156) mentions three earlier versions of it. Artemus Ward had invited Clemens to contribute a sketch to an anthology he was compiling, but Clemens was delayed in receiving the letter and the manuscript of "The Celebrated Jumping Frog" arrived in New York too late for inclusion in the anthology. It was widely reprinted from the *Saturday Press* and gave Mark Twain his first national reputation.

IN COMPLIANCE with the request of a friend of mine, who wrote me from the East, I called on good-natured, garrulous old Simon Wheeler, and inquired after my friend's friend, *Leonidas W.* Smiley, as requested to do, and I hereunto append the result. I have a lurking suspicion that *Leonidas W.* Smiley is a myth; that my friend never knew such a personage; and that he only conjectured that, if I asked old Wheeler about him, it would remind him of his infamous *Jim* Smiley, and he would go to work and bore me nearly to death with some infernal reminiscence of him as long and tedious as it should be useless to me. If that was the design, it certainly succeeded.

I found Simon Wheeler dozing comfortably by the bar-room stove of the old, dilapidated tavern in the ancient mining camp of Angel's, and I noticed that he was fat and bald-headed, and had an expression of winning gentleness and simplicity upon his tranquil countenance. He roused up and gave me good-day. I told him a friend of mine had commissioned me to make some inquiries about

---

2. "**Griffith Gaunt**": Augustin Daly's dramatization of Charles Reade's novel, first produced on November 7, 1866.   3. **Wallack's Theatre:** on Broadway at 13th Street.

a cherished companion of his boyhood named *Leonidas W.* Smiley—*Rev. Leonidas W.* Smiley—a young minister of the Gospel, who he had heard was at one time a resident of Angel's Camp. I added that, if Mr. Wheeler could tell me any thing about this Rev. Leonidas W. Smiley, I would feel under many obligations to him.

Simon Wheeler backed me into a corner and blockaded me there with his chair, and then sat me down and reeled off the monotonous narrative which follows this paragraph. He never smiled, he never frowned, he never changed his voice from the gentle-flowing key to which he tuned the initial sentence, he never betrayed the slightest suspicion of enthusiasm; but all through the interminable narrative there ran a vein of impressive earnestness and sincerity, which showed me plainly that, so far from his imagining that there was any thing ridiculous or funny about his story, he regarded it as a really important matter, and admired its two heroes as men of transcendent genius in *finesse*. To me, the spectacle of a man drifting serenely along through such a queer yarn without ever smiling, was exquisitely absurd. As I said before, I asked him to tell me what he knew of Rev. Leonidas W. Smiley, and he replied as follows. I let him go on in his own way, and never interrupted him once:

There was a feller here once by the name of *Jim* Smiley, in the winter of '49—or may be it was the spring of '50—I don't recollect exactly, somehow, though what makes me think it was one or the other is because I remember the big flume wasn't finished when he first came to the camp; but any way, he was the curiosest man about always betting on any thing that turned up you ever see, if he could get any body to bet on the other side; and if he couldn't, he'd change sides. Any way that suited the other man would suit him—any way just so's he got a bet, *he* was satisfied. But still he was lucky, uncommon lucky; he most always come out winner. He was always ready and laying for a chance; there couldn't be no solitry thing mentioned but that feller'd offer to bet on it, and take any side you please, as I was just telling you. If there was a horse-race, you'd find him flush, or you'd find him busted at the end of it; if there was a dog-fight, he'd bet on it; if there was a cat-fight, he'd bet on it; if there was a chicken-fight, he'd bet on it; why, if there was two birds setting on a fence, he would bet you which one would fly first; or if there was a camp-meeting, he would be there reg'lar, to bet on Parson Walker, which he judged to be the best exhorter about here, and so he was, too, and

a good man. If he even seen a straddle-bug start to go anywheres, he would bet you how long it would take him to get wherever he was going to, and if you took him up, he would foller that straddle-bug to Mexico but what he would find out where he was bound for and how long he was on the road. Lots of the boys here has seen that Smiley, and can tell you about him. Why, it never made no difference to *him*—he would bet on *any* thing—the dangdest feller. Parson Walker's wife laid very sick once, for a good while, and it seemed as if they warn't going to save her; but one morning he come in, and Smiley asked how she was, and he said she was considerable better—thank the Lord for his inf'nit mercy—and coming on so smart that, with the blessing of Prov'dence, she'd get well yet; and Smiley, before he thought, says, "Well, I'll risk two-and-a-half that she don't, any way."

Thish-yer Smiley had a mare—the boys called her the fifteen-minute nag, but that was only in fun, you know, because, of course, she was faster than that—and he used to win money on that horse, for all she was so slow and always had the asthma, or the distemper, or the consumption, or something of that kind. They used to give her two or three hundred yards start, and then pass her under way; but always at the fag-end of the race she'd get excited and desperate-like, and come cavorting and straddling up, and scattering her legs around limber, sometimes in the air, and sometimes out to one side amongst the fences, and kicking up m-o-r-e dust, and raising m-o-r-e racket with her coughing and sneezing and blowing her nose—and always fetch up at the stand just about a neck ahead, as near as you could cipher it down.

And he had a little small bull pup, that to look at him you'd think he wan't worth a cent, but to set around and look ornery, and lay for a chance to steal something. But as soon as money was up on him, he was a different dog; his under-jaw'd begin to stick out like the fo'castle of a steamboat, and his teeth would uncover, and shine savage like the furnaces. And a dog might tackle him, and bully-rag him, and bite him, and throw him over his shoulder two or three times, and Andrew Jackson—which was the name of the pup—Andrew Jackson would never let on but what *he* was satisfied, and hadn't expected nothing else—and the bets being doubled and doubled on the other side all the time, till the money was all up; and then all of a sudden he would grab that other dog jest by the j'int of his hind leg and freeze to it—not chaw, you understand, but only jest grip and hang on till they throwed up the sponge, if it was a year. Smiley always come out winner on that pup, till he harnessed a dog once that didn't have no hind legs, because they'd been sawed off by a circular saw, and when the thing had gone along far enough, and the money was all up, and he come to make a snatch for his pet holt, he saw in a minute how he'd been imposed on, and how the other dog had him in the door, so to speak, and he 'peared surprised, and then he looked sorter discouraged-like, and didn't try no more to win the fight, and so he got shucked out bad. He give Smiley a look, as much as to say his heart was broke, and it was *his* fault, for putting up a dog that hadn't no hind legs for him to take holt of, which was his main dependence in a fight, and then he limped off a piece and laid down and died. It was a good pup, was that Andrew Jackson, and would have made a name for hisself if he'd lived, for the stuff was in him, and he had genius —I know it, because he hadn't had no opportunities to speak of, and it don't stand to reason that a dog could make such a fight as he could under them circumstances, if he hadn't no talent. It always makes me feel sorry when I think of that last fight of his'n, and the way it turned out.

Well, thish-yer Smiley had rat-terriers, and chicken cocks, and tom-cats, and all them kind of things, till you couldn't rest, and you couldn't fetch nothing for him to bet on but he'd match you. He ketched a frog one day, and took him home, and said he cal'klated to edercate him; and so he never done nothing for three months but set in his back yard and learn that frog to jump. And you bet you he *did* learn him, too. He'd give him a little punch behind, and the next minute you'd see that frog whirling in the air like a dough-nut—see him turn one summerset, or may be a couple, if he got a good start, and come down flat-footed and all right, like a cat. He got him up so in the matter of catching flies, and kept him in practice so constant, that he'd nail a fly every time as far as he could see him. Smiley said all a frog wanted was education, and he could do most any thing—and I believe him. Why, I've seen him set Dan'l Webster down here on this floor—Dan'l Webster was the name of the frog—and sing out, "Flies, Dan'l, flies!" and quicker'n you could wink, he'd spring straight up, and snake a fly off'n the counter there, and flop down on the floor again as solid as a gob of mud, and fall to scratching the side of his head with his hind foot as indifferent as if he hadn't no idea he'd been doin' any more'n any frog might do. You never see a frog so modest and straightfor'ard as he was, for all he was so gifted. And when it come to fair and square jumping on a dead level, he could get over more ground at one straddle than any animal of his breed you ever see. Jumping on a dead level was his strong suit, you understand; and when it come to that, Smiley would ante up money on him as long as he had a red. Smiley was monstrous proud of his frog, and well he might be, for fellers that had traveled and been everywheres, all said he laid over any frog that ever *they* see.

Well, Smiley kept the beast in a little lattice box, and he used to fetch him down town sometimes and lay for a bet. One day a feller—a stranger in the camp, he was—come across him with his box, and says:

"What might it be that you've got in the box?"

And Smiley says, sorter indifferent like, "It might be a parrot, or it might be a canary, may be, but it an't—it's only just a frog."

And the feller took it, and looked at it careful, and turned it round this way and that, and says, "H'm—so 'tis. Well, what's *he* good for?"

"Well," Smiley says, easy and careless, "He's good enough for *one* thing, I should judge—he can outjump ary frog in Calaveras county."

The feller took the box again, and took another long, particular look, and give it back to Smiley, and says, very deliberate, "Well, I don't see no p'ints about that frog that's any better'n any other frog."

"May be you don't," Smiley says. "May be you understand frogs, and may be you don't understand 'em; may be you've had experience, and may be you an't only a amature, as it were. Anyways, I've got *my* opinion, and I'll risk forty dollars that he can outjump any frog in Calaveras county."

And the feller studied a minute, and then says, kinder sad like, "Well, I'm only a stranger here, and I an't got no frog; but if I had a frog, I'd bet you."

And then Smiley says, "That's all right—that's all right—if you'll hold my box a minute, I'll go and get you a frog." And so the feller took the box, and put up his forty dollars along with Smiley's, and set down to wait.

So he set there a good while thinking and thinking to hisself, and then he got the frog out and prized his mouth open and took a teaspoon and filled him full of quail shot—filled him pretty near up to his chin—and set him on the floor. Smiley he went to the swamp and slopped around in the mud for a long time, and finally he ketched a frog, and fetched him in, and give him to this feller, and says:

"Now, if you're ready, set him alongside of Dan'l, with his fore-paws just even with Dan'l, and I'll give the word." Then he says, "One—

two—three—jump!" and him and the feller touched up the frogs from behind, and the new frog hopped off, but Dan'l give a heave, and hysted up his shoulders—so—like a Frenchman, but it wan't no use—he couldn't budge; he was planted as solid as an anvil, and he couldn't no more stir than if he was anchored out. Smiley was a good deal surprised, and he was disgusted too, but he didn't have no idea what the matter was, of course.

The feller took the money and started away; and when he was going out at the door, he sorter jerked his thumb over his shoulders—this way— at Dan'l, and says again, very deliberate, "Well, *I* don't see no p'ints about that frog that's any better'n any other frog."

Smiley he stood scratching his head and look- ing down at Dan'l a long time, and at last he says, "I do wonder what in the nation that frog throw'd off for—I wonder if there an't something the matter with him—he 'pears to look mighty baggy, somehow." And he ketched Dan'l by the nap of the neck, and lifted him up and says, "Why, blame my cats, if he don't weigh five pound!" and turned him upside down, and he belched out a double handful of shot. And then he see how it was, and he was the maddest man—he set the frog down and took out after that feller, but he never ketched him. And——

[Here Simon Wheeler heard his name called from the front yard, and got up to see what was wanted.] And turning to me as he moved away, he said: "Jest set where you are, stranger, and rest easy—I an't going to be gone a second."

But, by your leave, I did not think that a con- tinuation of the history of the enterprising vaga- bond *Jim* Smiley would be likely to afford me much information concerning the Rev. *Leoni- das W.* Smiley, and so I started away.

At the door I met the sociable Wheeler return- ing, and he buttonholed me and recommenced:

"Well, thish-yer Smiley had a yaller one-eyed cow that didn't have no tail, only jest a short stump like a bannanner, and——"

"Oh! hang Smiley and his afflicted cow!" I mut- tered, good-naturedly, and bidding the old gentle- man good-day, I departed.

THE PILGRIM BIRD

FROM *The Innocents Abroad* [1869]

❮ THE Zoölogical Gardens were in Marseilles. Mark Twain and several of his companions had just landed from the *Quaker City* and would soon take a train for Paris.

IN THE great Zoölogical Gardens, we found specimens of all the animals the world produces, I think, including a dromedary, a monkey orna- mented with tufts of brilliant blue and carmine hair—a very gorgeous monkey he was—a hippo- potamus from the Nile, and a sort of tall, long- legged bird with a beak like a powder-horn, and close-fitting wings like the tails of a dress coat. This fellow stood up with his eyes shut and his shoulders stooped forward a little, and looked as if he had his hands under his coat tails. Such tran- quil stupidity, such supernatural gravity, such self- righteousness, and such ineffable self-complacency as were in the countenance and attitude of that gray-bodied, dark-winged, bald-headed, and pre- posterously uncomely bird! He was so ungainly, so pimply about the head, so scaly about the legs; yet so serene, so unspeakably satisfied! He was the most comical looking creature that can be imagined. It was good to hear Dan [1] and the doctor [2] laugh—such natural and such enjoyable laughter had not been heard among our excur- sionists since our ship sailed away from America. This bird was a god-send to us, and I should be an ingrate if I forgot to make honorable mention of him in these pages. Ours was a pleasure excur- sion; therefore we stayed with that bird an hour, and made the most of him. We stirred him up oc- casionally, but he only unclosed an eye and slowly closed it again, abating no jot of his stately piety of demeanor or his tremendous seriousness. He only seemed to say, "Defile not Heaven's anointed with unsanctified hands." We did not know his name, and so we called him "The Pilgrim." Dan said:

"All he wants now is a Plymouth Collec- tion." [3]

THE CAYOTE

FROM *Roughing It* [1872]

THE CAYOTE is a long, slim, sick and sorry- looking skeleton, with a gray wolf-skin stretched over it, a tolerably bushy tail that forever sags

THE PILGRIM BIRD.   **1. Dan:** Dan Slote, of New York, a stationer. He later manufactured and marketed Mark Twain's patented scrapbook containing dots of dry mucilage that could be moistened for sticking in clippings, etc.   **2. the doctor:** A. Reeve Jackson, the ship's surgeon of the *Quaker City.* **3. Plymouth Collection:** a hymn book published for the use of Henry Ward Beecher's Plymouth Church in Brooklyn, of which many *Quaker City* tourists were members.

down with a despairing expression of forsaken-ness and misery, a furtive and evil eye, and a long, sharp face, with slightly lifted lip and exposed teeth. He has a general slinking expression all over. The cayote is a living, breathing allegory of Want. He is *always* hungry. He is always poor, out of luck and friendless. The meanest creatures despise him, and even the fleas would desert him for a velocipede. He is so spiritless and cowardly that even while his exposed teeth are pretending a threat, the rest of his face is apologizing for it. And he is *so* homely!—so scrawny, and ribby, and coarse-haired, and pitiful. When he sees you he lifts his lip and lets a flash of his teeth out, and then turns a little out of the course he was pursuing, depresses his head a bit, and strikes a long, soft-footed trot through the sage-brush, glancing over his shoulder at you, from time to time, till he is about out of easy pistol range, and then he stops and takes a deliberate survey of you; he will trot fifty yards and stop again—another fifty and stop again; and finally the gray of his gliding body blends with the gray of the sage-brush, and he disappears. All this is when you make no demonstration against him; but if you do, he develops a livelier interest in his journey, and instantly electrifies his heels and puts such a deal of real estate between himself and your weapon, that by the time you have raised the hammer you see that you need a minie rifle, and by the time you have got him in line you need a rifled cannon, and by the time you have "drawn a bead" on him you see well enough that nothing but an unusually long-winded streak of lightning could reach him where he is now. But if you start a swift-footed dog after him, you will enjoy it ever so much—especially if it is a dog that has a good opinion of himself, and has been brought up to think he knows something about speed. The cayote will go swinging gently off on that deceitful trot of his, and every little while he will smile a fraudful smile over his shoulder that will fill that dog entirely full of encouragement and worldly ambition, and make him lay his head still lower to the ground, and stretch his neck further to the front, and pant more fiercely, and stick his tail out straighter behind, and move his furious legs with a yet wilder frenzy, and leave a broader and broader, and higher and denser cloud of desert sand smoking behind, and marking his long wake across the level plain! And all this time the dog is only a short twenty feet behind the cayote, and to save the soul of him he cannot understand why it is that he cannot get perceptibly closer; and he begins to get aggravated, and it makes him madder and madder to see how gently the cayote glides along and never pants or sweats or ceases to smile; and he grows still more and more incensed to see how shamefully he has been taken in by an entire stranger, and what an ignoble swindle that long, calm, soft-footed trot is; and next he notices that he is getting fagged, and that the cayote actually has to slacken speed a little to keep from running away from him—and *then* that town-dog is mad in earnest, and he begins to strain and weep and swear, and paw the sand higher than ever, and reach for the cayote with concentrated and desperate energy. This "spurt" finds him six feet behind the gliding enemy, and two miles from his friends. And then, in the instant that a wild new hope is lighting up his face, the cayote turns and smiles blandly upon him once more, and with a something about it which seems to say: "Well, I shall have to tear myself away from you, bub—business is business, and it will not do for me to be fooling along this way all day"—and forthwith there is a rushing sound, and the sudden splitting of a long crack through the atmosphere, and behold that dog is solitary and alone in the midst of a vast solitude!

It makes his head swim. He stops, and looks all around; climbs the nearest sand-mound, and gazes into the distance; shakes his head reflectively, and then, without a word, he turns and jogs along back to his train, and takes up a humble position under the hindmost wagon, and feels unspeakably mean, and looks ashamed, and hangs his tail at half-mast for a week. And for as much as a year after that, whenever there is a great hue and cry after a cayote, that dog will merely glance in that direction without emotion, and apparently observe to himself, "I believe I do not wish any of the pie."

TOM QUARTZ, THE CAT
FROM *Roughing It* [1872]

❨ DICK BAKER is a fictional name for Jim Gillis, the pocket-miner whom Mark Twain visited on Jackass Hill in the winter of 1864–65.

ONE OF my comrades there—another of those victims of eighteen years of unrequited toil and blighted hopes—was one of the gentlest spirits that ever bore its patient cross in a weary exile: grave and simple Dick Baker, pocket-miner of Dead-House Gulch.—He was forty-six, gray as a rat, earnest, thoughtful, slenderly educated, slouchily dressed and clay-soiled, but his heart was finer metal than any gold his shovel ever brought to light—than any, indeed, that ever was mined or minted.

Whenever he was out of luck and a little down-hearted, he would fall to mourning over the loss of a wonderful cat he used to own (for where women and children are not, men of kindly impulses take up with pets, for they must love something). And he always spoke of the strange sagacity of that cat with the air of a man who believed in his secret heart that there was something human about it—maybe even supernatural.

I heard him talking about this animal once. He said:

"Gentlemen, I used to have a cat here, by the name of Tom Quartz, which you'd a took an interest in I reckon—most any body would. I had him here eight year—and he was the remarkablest cat *I* ever see. He was a large gray one of the Tom specie, an' he had more hard, natchral sense than any man in this camp—'n' a *power* of dignity—he wouldn't let the Gov'ner of Californy be familiar with him. He never ketched a rat in his life—'peared to be above it. He never cared for nothing but mining. He knowed more about mining, that cat did, than any man *I* ever, ever see. You couldn't tell *him* noth'n' 'bout placer diggin's—'n' as for pocket mining, why he was just born for it. He would dig out after me an' Jim when we went over the hills prospect'n', and he would trot along behind us for as much as five mile, if we went so fur. An' he had the best judgment about mining ground—why you never see anything like it. When we went to work, he'd scatter a glance around, 'n' if he didn't think much of the indications, he would give a look as much as to say, 'Well, I'll have to get you to excuse *me*,' 'n' without another word he'd hyste his nose into the air 'n' shove for home. But if the ground suited him, he would lay low 'n' keep dark till the first pan was washed, 'n' then he would sidle up 'n' take a look, an' if there was about six or seven grains of gold *he* was satisfied—he didn't want no better prospect 'n' that—'n' then he would lay down on our coats and snore like a steamboat till we'd struck the pocket, an' then get up 'n' superintend. He was nearly lightnin' on superintending.

"Well, bye an' bye, up comes this yer quartz excitement. Every body was into it—every body was pick'n' 'n' blast'n' instead of shovelin' dirt on the hill side—every body was put'n' down a shaft instead of scrapin' the surface. Noth'n' would do Jim, but *we* must tackle the ledges, too, 'n' so we did. We commenced put'n' down a shaft, 'n' Tom Quartz he begin to wonder what in the Dickens it was all about. *He* hadn't ever seen any mining like that before, 'n' he was all upset, as you

may say—he couldn't come to a right understanding of it no way—it was too many for *him*. He was down on it, too, you bet you—he was down on it powerful—'n' always appeared to consider it the cussedest foolishness out. But that cat, you know, was *always* agin new fangled arrangements—somehow he never could abide 'em. *You* know how it is with old habits. But by an' by Tom Quartz begin to git sort of reconciled a little, though he never *could* altogether understand that eternal sinkin' of a shaft an' never pannin' out any thing. At last he got to comin' down in the shaft, hisself, to try to cipher it out. An' when he'd git the blues, 'n' feel kind o' scruffy, 'n' aggravated 'n' disgusted—knowin' as he did, that the bills was runnin' up all the time an' we warn't makin' a cent—he would curl up on a gunny sack in the corner an' go to sleep. Well, one day when the shaft was down about eight foot, the rock got so hard that we had to put in a blast—the first blast'n' we'd ever done since Tom Quartz was born. An' then we lit the fuse 'n' clumb out 'n' got off 'bout fifty yards—'n' forgot 'n' left Tom Quartz sound asleep on the gunny sack. In 'bout a minute we seen a puff of smoke bust up out of the hole, 'n' then everything let go with an awful crash, 'n' about four million ton of rocks 'n' dirt 'n' smoke 'n' splinters shot up 'bout a mile an' a half into the air, an' by George, right in the dead centre of it was old Tom Quartz a goin' end over end, an' a snortin' an' a sneez'n', an' a clawin' an' a reachin' for things like all possessed. But it warn't no use, you know, it warn't no use. An' that was the last we see of *him* for about two minutes 'n' a half, an' then all of a sudden it begin to rain rocks and rubbage, an' directly he come down ker-whop about ten foot off f'm where we stood. Well, I reckon he was p'raps the orneriest lookin' beast you ever see. One ear was sot back on his neck, 'n' his tail was stove up, 'n' his eye-winkers was swinged off, 'n' he was all blacked up with powder an' smoke, an' all sloppy with mud 'n' slush f'm one end to the other. Well sir, it warn't no use to try to apologize—we couldn't say a word. He took a sort of a disgusted look at hisself, 'n' then he looked at us—an' it was just exactly the same as if he had said—'Gents, may be *you* think it's smart to take advantage of a cat that 'ain't had no experience of quartz minin', but *I* think *different*'—an' then he turned on his heel 'n' marched off home without ever saying another word.

"That was jest his style. An' may be you won't believe it, but after that you never see a cat so prejudiced agin quartz mining as what he was. An' by an' bye when he *did* get to goin' down in the shaft agin, you'd 'a been astonished at his sagacity. The minute we'd tetch off a blast 'n' the fuse'd begin to sizzle, he'd give a look as much as to say: 'Well, I'll have to git you to excuse *me*,' an' it was surpris'n' the way he'd shin out of that hole 'n' go f'r a tree. Sagacity? It ain't no name for it. 'Twas *inspiration!*"

I said, "Well, Mr. Baker, his prejudice against quartz-mining *was* remarkable, considering how he came by it. Couldn't you ever cure him of it?"

"*Cure him!* No! When Tom Quartz was sot once, he was *always* sot—and you might a blowed him up as much as three million times 'n' you'd never a broken him of his cussed prejudice agin quartz mining."

The affection and the pride that lit up Baker's face when he delivered this tribute to the firmness of his humble friend of other days, will always be a vivid memory with me.

JIM BAKER'S BLUEJAY YARN
FROM *A Tramp Abroad* [1880]

⟮ Jim Baker is another pseudonym for Jim Gillis.

ANIMALS talk to each other, of course. There can be no question about that; but I suppose there are very few people who can understand them. I never knew but one man who could. I knew he could, however, because he told me so himself. He was a middle-aged, simple-hearted miner who had lived in a lonely corner of California, among the woods and mountains, a good many years, and had studied the ways of his only neighbors, the beasts and the birds, until he believed he could accurately translate any remark which they made. This was Jim Baker. According to Jim Baker, some animals have only a limited education, and use only very simple words, and scarcely ever a comparison or a flowery figure; whereas, certain other animals have a large vocabulary, a fine command of language and a ready and fluent delivery; consequently these latter talk a great deal; they like it; they are conscious of their talent, and they enjoy "showing off." Baker said, that after long and careful observation, he had come to the conclusion that the blue-jays were the best talkers he had found among birds and beasts. Said he:—

"There's more *to* a blue-jay than any other creature. He has got more moods, and more different kinds of feelings than other creature; and mind you, whatever a blue-jay feels, he can put into language. And no mere commonplace lan-guage, either, but rattling, out-and-out book-talk—and bristling with metaphor, too—just bristling! And as for command of language—why *you* never see a blue-jay get stuck for a word. No man ever did. They just boil out of him! And another thing: I've noticed a good deal, and there's no bird, or cow, or anything that uses as good gram-mar as a blue-jay. You may say a cat uses good grammar. Well, a cat does—but you let a cat get excited, once; you let a cat get to pulling fur with another cat on a shed, nights, and you'll hear grammar that will give you the lockjaw. Ignorant people think it's the *noise* which fighting cats make that is so aggravating, but it ain't so; it's the sick-ening grammar they use. Now I've never heard a jay use bad grammar but very seldom; and when they do, they are as ashamed as a human; they shut right down and leave.

"You may call a jay a bird. Well, so he is, in a measure—because he's got feathers on him, and don't belong to no church, perhaps; but otherwise he is just as much a human as you be. And I'll tell you for why. A jay's gifts, and instincts, and feel-ings, and interests, cover the whole ground. A jay hasn't got any more principle than a Congress-man. A jay will lie, a jay will steal, a jay will de-ceive, a jay will betray; and four times out of five, a jay will go back on his solemnest promise. The sacredness of an obligation is a thing which you can't cram into no blue-jay's head. Now on top of all this, there's another thing: a jay can out-swear any gentleman in the mines. You think a cat can swear. Well, a cat can; but you give a blue-jay a subject that calls for his reserve-powers, and where is your cat? Don't talk to *me*—I know too much about this thing. And there's yet another thing: in the one little particular of scolding—just good, clean, out-and-out scolding—a blue-jay can lay over anything, human or divine. Yes, sir, a jay is everything that a man is. A jay can cry, a jay can laugh, a jay can feel shame, a jay can reason and plan and discuss, a jay likes gossip and scan-dal, a jay has got a sense of humor, a jay knows when he is an ass just as well as you do—maybe better. If a jay ain't human, he better take in his sign, that's all. Now I'm going to tell you a per-fectly true fact about some blue-jays.

"When I first begun to understand jay language correctly, there was a little incident happened here. Seven years ago, the last man in this region but me, moved away. There stands his house,—been empty ever since; a log house, with a plank roof—just one big room, and no more; no ceiling —nothing between the rafters and the floor. Well, one Sunday morning I was sitting out here in front of my cabin, with my cat, taking the sun, and looking at the blue hills, and listening to the leaves rustling so lonely in the trees, and thinking of the home away yonder in the States, that I hadn't heard from in thirteen years, when a blue-jay lit on that house, with an acorn in his mouth, and says, 'Hello, I reckon I've struck something.' When he spoke, the acorn dropped out of his mouth and rolled down the roof, of course, but he didn't care; his mind was all on the thing he had struck. It was a knot-hole in the roof. He cocked his head to one side, shut one eye and put the other one to the hole, like a 'possum looking down a jug; then he glanced up with his bright eyes, gave a wink or two with his wings—which signifies gratification, you understand,—and says, 'It looks like a hole, it's located like a hole,—blamed if I don't believe it *is* a hole!'

"Then he cocked his head down and took another look; he glances up perfectly joyful, this time; winks his wings and his tail both, and says, 'O, no, this ain't no fat thing, I reckon! If I ain't in luck!—why it's a perfectly elegant hole!' So he flew down and got that acorn, and fetched it up and dropped it in, and was just tilting his head back, with the heavenliest smile on his face, when all of a sudden he was paralyzed into a listening attitude and that smile faded gradually out of his countenance like breath off'n a razor, and the queerest look of surprise took its place. Then he says, 'Why I didn't hear it fall!' He cocked his eye at the hole again, and took a long look; raised up and shook his head; stepped around to the other side of the hole and took another look from that side; shook his head again. He studied a while, then he just went into the *de*tails—walked round and round the hole and spied into it from every point of the compass. No use. Now he took a thinking attitude on the comb of the roof and scratched the back of his head with his right foot a minute, and finally says, 'Well, it's too many for *me,* that's certain; must be a mighty long hole; however, I ain't got no time to fool around here, I got to 'tend to business; I reckon it's all right—chance it, anyway.'

"So he flew off and fetched another acorn and dropped it in, and tried to flirt his eye to the hole quick enough to see what become of it, but he was too late. He held his eye there as much as a minute; then he raised up and sighed, and says, 'Consound it, I don't seem to understand this thing, no way; however, I'll tackle her again.' He fetched another acorn, and done his level best to see what become of it, but he couldn't. He says, 'Well, *I* never struck no such a hole as this, before; I'm of

the opinion it's a totally new kind of a hole.' Then he begun to get mad. He held in for a spell, walking up and down the comb of the roof and shaking his head and muttering to himself; but his feelings got the upper hand of him, presently, and he broke loose and cussed himself black in the face. I never see a bird take on so about a little thing. When he got through he walks to the hole and looks in again for half a minute; then he says, 'Well, you're a long hole, and a deep hole, and a mighty singular hole altogether—but I've started in to fill you, and I'm d—d if I *don't* fill you, if it takes a hundred years!'

"And with that, away he went. You never see a bird work so since you was born. He laid into his work like a nigger, and the way he hove acorns into that hole for about two hours and a half was one of the most exciting and astonishing spectacles I ever struck. He never stopped to take a look any more—he just hove 'em in and went for more. Well at last he could hardly flop his wings, he was so tuckered out. He comes a-drooping down, once more, sweating like an ice-pitcher, drops his acorn in and says, '*Now* I guess I've got the bulge on you by this time!' So he bent down for a look. If you'll believe me, when his head come up again he was just pale with rage. He says, 'I've shoveled acorns enough in there to keep the family thirty years, and if I can see a sign of one of 'em I wish I may land in a museum with a belly full of sawdust in two minutes!'

"He just had strength enough to crawl up on to the comb and lean his back agin the chimbly, and then he collected his impressions and begun to free his mind. I see in a second that what I had mistook for profanity in the mines was only just the rudiments, as you may say.

"Another jay was going by, and heard him doing his devotions, and stops to inquire what was up. The sufferer told him the whole circumstance, and says, 'Now yonder's the hole, and if you don't believe me, go and look for yourself.' So this fellow went and looked, and comes back and says, 'How many did you say you put in there?' 'Not any less than two tons,' says the sufferer. The other jay went and looked again. He couldn't seem to make it out, so he raised a yell, and three more jays come. They all examined the hole, they all made the sufferer tell it over again, then they all discussed it, and got off as many leather-headed opinions about it as an average crowd of humans could have done.

"They called in more jays; then more and more, till pretty soon this whole region 'peared to have a blue flush about it. There must have been five thousand of them; and such another jawing and disputing and ripping and cussing, you never heard. Every jay in the whole lot put his eye to the hole and delivered a more chuckle-headed opinion about the mystery than the jay that went there before him. They examined the house all over, too. The door was standing half open, and at last one old jay happened to go and light on it and look in. Of course that knocked the mystery galley west in a second. There lay the acorns, scattered all over the floor. He flopped his wings and raised a whoop. 'Come here!' he says, 'Come here, everybody; hang'd if this fool hasn't been trying to fill up a house with acorns!' They all came a-swooping down like a blue cloud, and as each fellow lit on the door and took a glance, the whole absurdity of the contract that that first jay had tackled hit him home and he fell over backwards suffocating with laughter, and the next jay took his place and done the same.

"Well, sir, they roosted around here on the house-top and the trees for an hour, and guffawed over that thing like human beings. It ain't any use to tell me a blue-jay hasn't got a sense of humor, because I know better. And memory, too. They brought jays here from all over the United States to look down that hole, every summer for three years. Other birds too. And they could all see the point, except an owl that come from Nova Scotia to visit the Yo Semite, and he took this thing in on his way back. He said he couldn't see anything funny in it. But then he was a good deal disappointed about Yo Semite, too."

THE INDIAN CROW

FROM *Following the Equator* [1897]

❰ THIS passage forms part of a journal entry dated Bombay, January 20, 1896, when Mark Twain was on a lecture tour.

SOME natives—I don't remember how many—went into my bedroom, now, and put things to rights and arranged the mosquito-bar, and I went to bed to nurse my cough. It was about nine in the evening. What a state of things! For three hours the yelling and shouting of natives in the hall continued, along with the velvety patter of their swift bare feet—what a racket it was! They were yelling orders and messages down three flights. Why, in the matter of noise it amounted to a riot, an insurrection, a revolution. And then there were other noises mixed up with these and at intervals tremendously accenting them—roofs falling in, I judged, windows smashing, persons being murdered, crows squawking, and deriding, and cursing, canaries screeching, monkeys jabbering, macaws blaspheming, and every now and then fiendish bursts of laughter and explosions of dynamite. By midnight I had suffered all the different kinds of shocks there are, and knew that I could never more be disturbed by them, either isolated or in combination. Then came peace—stillness deep and solemn—and lasted till five.

Then it all broke loose again. And who re-started it? The Bird of Birds—the Indian crow. I came to know him well, by and by, and be infatuated with him. I suppose he is the hardest lot that wears feathers. Yes, and the cheerfulest, and the best satisfied with himself. He never arrived at what he is by any careless process, or any sudden one; he is a work of art, and "art is long"; he is the product of immemorial ages, and of deep calculation; one can't make a bird like that in a day. He has been re-incarnated more times than Shiva; and he has kept a sample of each incarnation, and fused it into his constitution. In the course of his evolutionary promotions, his sublime march toward ultimate perfection, he has been a gambler, a low comedian, a dissolute priest, a fussy woman, a blackguard, a scoffer, a liar, a thief, a spy, an informer, a trading politician, a swindler, a professional hypocrite, a patriot for cash, a reformer, a lecturer, a lawyer, a conspirator, a rebel, a royalist, a democrat, a practicer and propagator of irreverence, a meddler, an intruder, a busybody, an infidel, and a wallower in sin for the mere love of it. The strange result, the incredible result, of this patient accumulation of all damnable traits is, that he does not know what care is, he does not know what sorrow is, he does not know what remorse is, his life is one long thundering ecstasy of happiness, and he will go to his death untroubled, knowing that he will soon turn up again as an author or something, and be even more intolerably capable and comfortable than ever he was before.

In his straddling wide forward-step, and his springy side-wise series of hops, and his impudent air, and his cunning way of canting his head to one side upon occasion, he reminds one of the American blackbird. But the sharp resemblances stop there. He is much bigger than the blackbird; and he lacks the blackbird's trim and slender and beautiful build and shapely beak; and of course his sober garb of gray and rusty black is a poor and humble thing compared with the splendid lustre of the blackbird's metallic sables and shifting and flashing bronze glories. The blackbird is a perfect gentleman, in deportment and attire, and is not noisy, I believe, except when holding religious services and political conventions in a tree; but this Indian sham Quaker is just a rowdy, and is always noisy when awake—always chaffing, scolding, scoffing, laughing, ripping, and cursing, and carrying on about something or other. I never saw such a bird for delivering opinions. Nothing escapes him; he notices everything that happens, and brings out his opinion about it, particularly if it is a matter that is none of his business. And it is never a mild opinion, but always violent—violent and profane—the presence of ladies does not affect him. His opinions are not the outcome of reflection, for he never thinks about anything, but heaves out the opinion that is on top in his mind, and which is often an opinion about some quite different thing and does not fit the case. But that is his way; his main idea is to get out an opinion, and if he stopped to think he would lose chances.

I suppose he has no enemies among men. The whites and Mohammedans never seemed to molest him; and the Hindoos, because of their religion, never take the life of any creature, but spare even the snakes and tigers and fleas and rats. If I sat on one end of the balcony, the crows would gather on the railing at the other end and talk about me; and edge closer, little by little, till I could almost reach them; and they would sit there, in the most unabashed way, and talk about my clothes, and my hair, and my complexion, and probable character and vocation and politics, and how I came to be in India, and what I had been doing, and how many days I had got for it, and how I had happened to go unhanged so long, and when would it probably come off, and might there be more of my sort where I came from, and when would *they* be hanged,—and so on, and so on, until I could not longer endure the embarrassment of it; then I would shoo them away, and they would circle around in the air a little while, laughing and deriding and mocking, and presently settle on the rail and do it all over again.

They were very sociable when there was anything to eat—oppressively so. With a little encouragement they would come in and light on the table and help me eat my breakfast; and once when I was in the other room and they found themselves alone, they carried off everything they could lift; and they were particular to choose things which they could make no use of after they got them. In India their number is beyond estimate, and their noise is in proportion. I suppose they cost the country more than the government does; yet that is not a light matter. Still, they pay; their company pays; it would sadden the land to take their cheerful voice out of it.

PART III: DRAMATIC & LITERARY CRITICISM

❖

❲ MARK TWAIN seldom dealt in general principles or the systematic analysis of works of art. Yet the small amount of criticism he published is nearer the taste of our own day than is the work of such professional critics as James Russell Lowell or even Howells. Whereas they tended to be vague and moralistic, Mark Twain was usually specific and technical. Both in his rejection of ornate rhetoric—as in the essay on Cooper—and in his preference for direct, colloquial language—as in the essays on Howells' prose and on the art of oral storytelling—he anticipates the revolution in taste that would occur during the two decades following his death.

❖

OVER THE MOUNTAINS

❲ THE selection that follows is taken from *Mark Twain of the "Enterprise,"* edited by Henry Nash Smith (1957). It was first published in the Virginia City *Territorial Enterprise* under the dateline San Francisco, September 13, 1863. The miscellaneous contents of this dispatch are characteristic of the newspaper correspondence Clemens had begun earlier that year to sign with his pseudonym "Mark Twain." On this occasion he is in San Francisco on vacation but is sending back an occasional column to his paper. It is classified as dramatic criticism because the longest item is the review of Adah Isaacs Menken's performance in *Mazeppa*—the play by H. M. Milner based on Byron's poem, first performed in London in 1831. Miss Menken (1835–68) played this role for sixty nights at five hundred dollars a night in San Francisco. When she brought her company to Virginia City in February, 1864, Mark Twain met her. She had literary ambitions and wrote quantities of rhapsodic free verse. According to Albert B. Paine, he "became briefly fascinated by her charms."

EDITORS ENTERPRISE: The trip from Virginia to Carson by Messrs. Carpenter & Hoog's stage is a pleasant one, and from thence over the mountains by the Pioneer would be another, if there were less of it. But you naturally want an outside seat in the day time, and you feel a good deal like riding inside when the cold night winds begin to blow; yet if you commence your journey on the outside, you will find that you will be allowed to enjoy the desire I speak of unmolested from twilight to sunrise. An outside seat is preferable, though, day or night. All you want to do is to prepare for it thoroughly. You should sleep forty-eight hours in succession before starting so that you may not have to do anything of that kind on the box. You should also take a heavy overcoat with you. I did neither. I left Carson feeling very miserable for want of sleep, and the voyage from there to Sacramento did not refresh me perceptibly. I took no overcoat and I almost shivered the shirt off myself during that long night ride from Strawberry Valley to Folsom. Our driver was a very companionable man, though, and this was a happy circumstance for me, because, being drowsy and worn out, I would have gone to sleep and fallen overboard if he had not enlivened the dreary hours with his conversation. Whenever I stopped coughing, and went to nodding, he always watched me out of the corner of his eye until I got to pitching in his direction, and then he would stir me up and inquire if I were asleep. If I said "No" (and I was apt to do that), he always said "it was a bully good thing for me that I warn't, you know," and then went on to relate cheerful anecdotes of people who had got to nodding by his side when he wasn't noticing, and had fallen off and broken their necks. He said he could see those fellows before him now, all jammed and bloody and quivering in death's agony—"G'lang! d——n that horse, he knows there's a parson and an old maid inside, and that's what makes him cut up so; I've saw him act jes' so more'n a thousand times!" The driver always lent an additional charm to his conversation by mixing his horrors and his general information together in this way. "Now," said he, after urging his team at a furious speed down the grade for a while, plunging into deep bends in the road brimming with a thick darkness almost palpable to the touch, and darting out again and again on the verge of what instinct told me was a precipice, "Now, I seen a poor cuss—but you're asleep again, you know, and you've rammed your head agin' my side-pocket and busted a bottle of nasty rotten medicine that I'm taking to the folks at the Thirty-five Mile House; do you notice that flavor? ain't it a ghastly old stench? The man that takes it down there don't live on anything else—it's vittles and drink to him; anybody that ain't used to him can't go a-near him; he'd stun 'em—he'd suffocate 'em; his breath smells like a graveyard after an earthquake—you Bob! I allow to skelp that ornery horse, yet, if he keeps on this way; you see he's been on the overland till about two weeks ago, and every stump he sees he cal'-lates it's an Injun." I was awake by this time, holding on with both hands bouncing up and down just as I do when I ride a horseback. The driver took up the thread of his discourse and proceeded to soothe me again: "As I was a saying, I see a poor cuss tumble off along here one night—

he was monstrous drowsy, and went to sleep when I'd took my eye off of him for a moment—and he fetched up agin a boulder, and in a second there wasn't anything left of him but a promiscus pile of hash! It was moonlight, and when I got down and looked at him he was quivering like jelly, and sorter moaning to himself, like, and the bones of his legs was sticking out through his pantaloons every which way, like that." (Here the driver mixed his fingers up after the manner of a stack of muskets, and illuminated them with the ghostly light of his cigar.) "He warn't in misery long though. In a minute and a half he was deader'n a smelt—Bob! I say I'll cut that horse's throat if he stays on this route another week." In this way the genial driver caused the long hours to pass sleeplessly away, and if he drew upon his imagination for his fearful histories, I shall be the last to blame him for it, because if they had taken a milder form I might have yielded to the dullness that oppressed me, and got my own bones smashed out of my hide in such a way as to render me useless forever after—unless, perhaps, some one chose to turn me to account as an uncommon sort of hat-rack.

MR. BILLET IS COMPLIMENTED BY A STRANGER

Not a face in either stage was washed from the time we left Carson until we arrived in Sacramento; this will give you an idea of how deep the dust lay on those faces when we entered the latter town at eight o'clock on Monday morning. Mr. Billet, of Virginia, came in our coach, and brought his family with him—Mr. R. W. Billet of the great Washoe Stock and Exchange Board of Highwaymen—and instead of turning his complexion to a dirty cream color, as it generally serves white folks, the dust changed it to the meanest possible shade of black: however, Billet isn't particularly white, anyhow, even under the most favorable circumstances. He stepped into an office near the railroad depot, to write a note, and while he was at it, several lank, gawky, indolent immigrants, fresh from the plains, gathered around him. Missourians—Pikes—I can tell my brethren as far as I can see them. They seemed to admire Billet very much, and the faster he wrote the higher their admiration rose in their faces, until it finally boiled over in words, and one of my countrymen ejaculated in his neighbor's ear,—"Dang it, but he writes mighty well for a nigger!"

THE MENKEN—WRITTEN ESPECIALLY FOR GENTLEMEN

When I arrived in San Francisco, I found there was no one in town—at least there was no body in town but "the Menken"—or rather, that no one was being talked about except that manly young female. I went to see her play "Mazeppa," of course. They said she was dressed from head to foot in flesh-colored "tights," but I had no opera-glass, and I couldn't see it, to use the language of the inelegant rabble. She appeared to me to have but one garment on—a thin tight white linen one, of unimportant dimensions; I forget the name of the article, but it is indispensable to infants of tender age—I suppose any young mother can tell you what it is, if you have the moral courage to ask the question. With the exception of this superfluous rag, the Menken dresses like the Greek Slave; [1] but some of her postures are not so modest as the suggestive attitude of the latter. She is a finely formed woman down to her knees; if she could be herself that far, and Mrs. H. A. Perry [2] the rest of the way, she would pass for an unexceptionable Venus. Here every tongue sings the praises of her matchless grace, her supple gestures, her charming attitudes. Well, possibly, these tongues are right. In the first act, she rushes on the stage, and goes cavorting around after "Olinska"; [3] she bends herself back like a bow; she pitches head-foremost at the atmosphere like a battering-ram; she works her arms, and her legs, and her whole body like a dancing-jack: her every movement is as quick as thought; in a word, without any apparent reason for it, she carries on like a lunatic from the beginning of the act to the end of it. At other times she "whallops" herself down on the stage, and rolls over as does the sportive pack-mule after his burden is removed. If this be grace then the Menken is eminently graceful. After a while they proceed to strip her, and the high chief Pole calls for the "fiery untamed steed"; a sub-ordinate Pole brings in the fierce brute, stirring him up occasionally to make him run away, and then hanging to him like death to keep him from doing it; the monster looks round pensively upon the brilliant audience in the theatre, and seems very willing to stand still—but a lot of those Poles grab him and hold on to him, so as to be prepared for him in case he changes his mind. They are posted as to his fiery untamed nature, you know, and they give him no chance to get loose and eat up the orchestra. They strap Mazeppa on his back, fore and aft, and face upper-most, and the horse goes cantering up-stairs over the painted mountains, through tinted clouds of theatrical mist, in a brisk exciting way, with the wretched victim he bears unconsciously digging her heels into his hams, in the agony of her sufferings, to make him go faster. Then a tempest of applause bursts forth, and the curtain falls. The fierce old circus horse carries his prisoner around through the back part of the theatre, behind the scenery, and although assailed at every step by the savage wolves of the desert, he makes his way at last to his dear old home in Tartary down by the footlights, and beholds once more, O, gods! the familiar faces of the fiddlers in the orchestra. The noble old steed is happy, then, but poor Mazeppa is insensible—"ginned out" by his trip, as it were. Before the act closes, however, he is restored to consciousness and his doting old father, the king of Tartary; and the next day, without taking time to dress—without even borrowing a shirt, or stealing a fresh horse—he starts off on the fiery untamed, at the head of the Tartar nation, to exterminate the Poles, and carry off his own sweet Olinska from the Polish court. He succeeds, and the curtain falls upon a bloody combat, in which the Tartars are victorious. "Mazeppa" proved a great card for Maguire [4] here; he put it on the boards in first-class style, and crowded houses went crazy over it every night it was played. But Virginians will soon have an opportunity of seeing it themselves, as "the Menken" will go direct from our town there without stopping on the way. The "French Spy" [5] was played last night and the night before, and as this spy is a frisky Frenchman, and as dumb as an oyster, Miss Menken's extravagant gesticulations do not seem so overdone in it as they do in "Mazeppa." She don't talk well, and as she goes on her shape and her acting, the character of a fidgety "dummy" is peculiarly suited to her line of business. She plays the Spy, without words, with more feeling than she does Mazeppa with them.

I am tired writing, now, so you will get no news in this letter. I have got a note-book full of interesting hieroglyphics, but I am afraid that by the time I am ready to write them out, I shall have forgotten what they mean. The lady who asked me to furnish her with the Lick House [6] fashions, shall have them shortly—or if I ever get time, I will dish up those displayed at the great Pioneer ball, at Union Hall, last Wednesday night.

MARK TWAIN

OVER THE MOUNTAINS. **1.** the Greek Slave: a celebrated nude statue by Hiram Powers (1805–73). **2.** Mrs. H. A. Perry: an actress in the Menken troupe. **3.** "Olinska": the Polish maiden beloved by the Tartar Mazeppa. Miss Menken had the leading male role in the play.

4. Maguire: Tom Maguire, manager of Maguire's Opera House and the dominant impresario of the West Coast. **5.** The "French Spy": a popular melodrama of uncertain authorship, first performed in this country in 1832. **6.** Lick House: a fashionable San Francisco hotel.

GLADIATORIAL SPECTACLES IN THE COLISEUM

FROM *The Innocents Abroad* [1869]

⟨ WHILE Mark Twain worked as a local reporter on the *Enterprise* and later on the San Francisco *Morning Call*, his duties included writing notices of current plays. He also probably wrote criticism for the San Francisco *Dramatic Chronicle*. Thus, he was familiar with the world of the theater and with the practice of dramatic criticism, which he is burlesquing here. At the same time—and this is as characteristic of him as is the burlesque—he is making a serious indictment of Roman brutality.

SEVENTEEN or eighteen centuries ago this Coliseum was *the* theatre of Rome, and Rome was mistress of the world. Splendid pageants were exhibited here, in presence of the Emperor, the great ministers of State, the nobles, and vast audiences of citizens of smaller consequence. Gladiators fought with gladiators and at times with warrior prisoners from many a distant land. It was *the* theatre of Rome—of the world—and the man of fashion who could not let fall in a casual and unintentional manner something about "my private box at the Coliseum" could not move in the first circles. When the clothing-store merchant wished to consume the corner grocery man with envy, he bought secured seats in the front row and let the thing be known. When the irresistible dry goods clerk wished to blight and destroy, according to his native instinct, he got himself up regardless of expense and took some other fellow's young lady to the Coliseum, and then accented the affront by cramming her with ice cream between the acts, or by approaching the cage and stirring up the martyrs with his whalebone cane for her edification. The Roman swell was in his true element only when he stood up against a pillar and fingered his moustache, unconscious of the ladies; when he viewed the bloody combats through an opera-glass two inches long; when he excited the envy of provincials by criticisms which showed that he had been to the Coliseum many and many a time and was long ago over the novelty of it; when he turned away with a yawn at last and said, *"He a star! handles his sword like an apprentice brigand! he'll do for the country, may be, but he don't answer for the metropolis!"*

Glad was the contraband that had a seat in the pit at the Saturday matinee, and happy the Roman street-boy who ate his peanuts and guyed the gladiators from the dizzy gallery.

For me was reserved the high honor of discovering among the rubbish of the ruined Coliseum the only playbill of that establishment now extant. There was a suggestive smell of mint-drops about it still, a corner of it had evidently been chewed, and on the margin, in choice Latin, these words were written in a delicate female hand:

"Meet me on the Tarpeian Rock to-morrow evening, dear, at sharp seven. Mother will be absent on a visit to her friends in the Sabine Hills.

CLAUDIA."

Ah, where is that lucky youth to-day, and where the little hand that wrote those dainty lines? Dust and ashes these seventeen hundred years!

Thus reads the bill:

ROMAN COLISEUM.

UNPARALLELED ATTRACTION!

NEW PROPERTIES! NEW LIONS! NEW GLADIATORS!

Engagement of the renowned

MARCUS MARCELLUS VALERIAN!

FOR SIX NIGHTS ONLY!

The management beg leave to offer to the public an entertainment surpassing in magnificence any thing that has heretofore been attempted on any stage. No expense has been spared to make the opening season one which shall be worthy the generous patronage which the management feel sure will crown their efforts. The management beg leave to state that they have succeeded in securing the services of a

GALAXY OF TALENT!

such as has not been beheld in Rome before.

The performance will commence this evening with a

GRAND BROADSWORD COMBAT!

between two young and promising amateurs and a celebrated Parthian gladiator who has just arrived a prisoner from the Camp of Verus.

This will be followed by a grand moral

BATTLE-AX ENGAGEMENT!

between the renowned Valerian (with one hand tied behind him,) and two gigantic savages from Britain.

After which the renowned Valerian (if he survive,) will fight with the broadsword,

LEFT HANDED!

against six Sophomores and a Freshman from the Gladiatorial College!

A long series of brilliant engagements will follow, in which the finest talent of the Empire will take part.

After which the celebrated Infant Prodigy known as

"THE YOUNG ACHILLES,"

will engage four tiger whelps in combat, armed with no other weapon than his little spear!

The whole to conclude with a chaste and elegant

GENERAL SLAUGHTER!

In which thirteen African Lions and twenty-two Barbarian Prisoners will war with each other until all are exterminated.

BOX OFFICE NOW OPEN.

Dress Circle One Dollar; Children and Servants half price.

An efficient police force will be on hand to preserve order and keep the wild beasts from leaping the railings and discommoding the audience.

Doors open at 7; performance begins at 8.

POSITIVELY NO FREE LIST.

Diodorus Job Press.

It was as singular as it was gratifying that I was also so fortunate as to find among the rubbish of the arena, a stained and mutilated copy of the *Roman Daily Battle-Ax,* containing a critique upon this very performance. It comes to hand too late by many centuries to rank as news, and therefore I translate and publish it simply to show how very little the general style and phraseology of dramatic criticism has altered in the ages that have dragged their slow length along since the carriers laid this one damp and fresh before their Roman patrons:

"THE OPENING SEASON.—COLISEUM.—Notwithstanding the inclemency of the weather, quite a respectable number of the rank and fashion of the city assembled last night to witness the debut upon metropolitan boards of the young tragedian who has of late been winning such golden opinions in the amphitheatres of the provinces. Some sixty thousand persons were present, and but for the fact that the streets were almost impassable, it is fair to presume that the house would have been full. His august Majesty, the Emperor Aurelius, occupied the imperial box, and was the cynosure of all eyes. Many illustrious nobles and generals of the Empire graced the occasion with their presence, and not the least among them was the young patrician lieutenant whose laurels, won in the ranks of the "Thundering Legion," are still so green upon his brow. The cheer which greeted his entrance was heard beyond the Tiber!

"The late repairs and decorations add both to the comeliness and the comfort of the Coliseum. The new cushions are a great improvement upon the hard marble seats we have been so long accustomed to. The present management deserve well of the public. They have restored to the Coliseum the gilding, the rich upholstery and the uniform magnificence which old Coliseum frequenters tell us Rome was so proud of fifty years ago.

"The opening scene last night—the broadsword combat between two young amateurs and a famous Parthian gladiator who was sent here a prisoner—was very fine. The elder of the two young gentlemen handled his weapon with a grace that marked the possession of extraordinary talent. His feint of thrusting, followed instantly by a happily delivered blow which unhelmeted the Parthian, was received with hearty applause. He was not thoroughly up in the backhanded stroke, but it was very gratifying to his numerous friends to know that, in time, practice would have overcome this defect. However, he was killed. His sisters, who were present, expressed considerable regret. His mother left the Coliseum. The other youth maintained the contest with such spirit as to call forth enthusiastic bursts of applause. When at last he fell a corpse, his aged mother ran screaming, with hair disheveled and tears streaming from her eyes, and swooned away just as her hands were clutching at the railings of the arena. She was promptly removed by the police. Under the circumstances the woman's conduct was pardonable, perhaps, but we suggest that such exhibitions interfere with the decorum which should be preserved during the performances, and are highly improper in the presence of the Emperor. The Parthian prisoner fought bravely and well; and well he might, for he was fighting for both life and liberty. His wife and children were there to nerve his arm with their love, and to remind him of the old home he should see again if he conquered. When his second assailant fell, the woman clasped her children to her breast and wept for joy. But it was only a transient happiness. The captive staggered toward her and she saw that the liberty he had earned was earned too late. He was wounded unto death. Thus the first act closed in a manner which was entirely satisfactory. The manager was called before the curtain and returned his thanks for the honor done him, in a speech which was replete with wit and humor, and closed by hoping that his humble efforts to afford cheerful and instructive entertainment would continue to meet with the approbation of the Roman public.

"The star now appeared, and was received with vociferous applause and the simultaneous waving of sixty thousand handkerchiefs. Marcus Marcellus Valerian (stage name—his real name is Smith,) is a splendid specimen of physical development, and an artist of rare merit. His management of the battle-ax is wonderful. His gayety and his playfulness are irresistible, in his comic parts, and yet they are inferior to his sublime conceptions in the grave realm of tragedy. When his ax was describing fiery circles about the heads of the bewildered barbarians, in exact time with his springing body and his prancing legs, the audience gave way to uncontrollable bursts of laughter; but when the back of his weapon broke the skull of one and almost in the same instant its edge clove the other's body in twain, the howl of enthusiastic applause that shook the building, was the acknowledgement of a critical assemblage that he was a master of the noblest department of his profession. If he has a fault, (and we are sorry to even intimate that he has,) it is that of glancing at the audience, in the midst of the most exciting moments of the performance, as if seeking admiration. The pausing in a fight to bow when bouquets are thrown to him is also in bad taste. In the great left-handed combat he appeared to be looking at the audience half the time, instead of carving his adversaries; and when he had slain all the sophomores and was dallying with the freshman, he stooped and snatched a bouquet as it fell, and offered it to his adversary at a time when a blow was descending which promised favorably to be his death-warrant. Such levity is proper enough in the provinces, we make no doubt, but it ill suits the dignity of the metropolis. We trust our young friend will take these remarks in good part, for we mean them solely for his benefit. All who know us are aware that although we are at times justly severe upon tigers and martyrs, we never intentionally offend gladiators.

"The Infant Prodigy performed wonders. He overcame his four tiger whelps with ease, and with no other hurt than the loss of a portion of his scalp. The General Slaughter was rendered with a faithfulness to details which reflects the highest credit upon the late participants in it.

"Upon the whole, last night's performances shed honor not only upon the management but upon the city that encourages and sustains such wholesome and instructive entertainments. We would simply suggest that the practice of vulgar young boys in the gallery of shying peanuts and paper pellets at the tigers, and saying "Hi-yi!" and manifesting approbation or dissatisfaction by such observations as "Bully for the lion!" "Go it, Gladdy!" "Boots!" "Speech!" "Take a walk round the block!" and so on, are extremely reprehensible, when the Emperor is present, and ought to be stopped by the police. Several times last night, when the supernumeraries entered the arena to drag out the bodies, the young ruffians in the gallery shouted, "Supe! supe!" and also, "Oh, what a coat!" and "Why don't you pad them shanks?" and made use of various other remarks expressive of derision. These things are very annoying to the audience.

"A matinee for the little folks is promised for this afternoon, on which occasion several martyrs will be eaten by the tigers. The regular performance will continue every night till further notice. Material change of programme every evening. Benefit of Valerian, Tuesday, 29th, if he lives."

I have been a dramatic critic myself, in my time, and I was often surprised to notice how much more I knew about Hamlet than Forrest [1] did; and it gratifies me to observe, now, how much better my brethren of ancient times knew how a broad-sword battle ought to be fought than the gladiators.

GLADIATORIAL SPECTACLES IN THE COLISEUM. **1. Forrest:** Edwin Forrest (1806–72) was the most famous American actor of his period.

WHITTIER BIRTHDAY DINNER SPEECH

⟨ THIS speech (which was delivered on December 17, 1877) is reprinted here from the text of the original manuscript reproduced in the *Harvard Library Bulletin* (Spring, 1955). Mark Twain wrote the speech out and memorized it for the program of a dinner given by H. O. Houghton & Co., publishers of the *Atlantic Monthly*, in honor of John G. Whittier's seventieth birthday. After a number of conventional laudatory addresses and poems had been read, Mark Twain was introduced to provide comic relief. Some of his auditors, however, felt that his little burlesque was in bad taste, and both Clemens and Howells, who was presiding, came away suffering under the conviction that the speech had been a serious affront to Longfellow, Emerson, and Holmes, all of whom were present. Mark Twain wrote an abject letter of apology to these men and received polite reassurances in return, but he continued to brood over the incident for many years, unable to make up his mind whether or not he had been at fault. The sources of the verse quotations, in the order of their appearance in the text, are as follows:

1. Holmes, "The Chambered Nautilus"
2. Emerson, "Mithridates"
3. Longfellow, "Hiawatha"
4. Holmes, "Mare Rebrum 1858"
5. Longfellow, "Evangeline"
6. Emerson, "Concord Hymn"
7. Emerson, "Brahma"
8. Emerson, "Song of Nature"
9. Longfellow, "The Village Blacksmith"
10. Holmes, "A Voice of the Loyal North 1861 (January Third)"
11. Longfellow, "A Psalm of Life"

MR. CHAIRMAN—This is an occasion peculiarly meet for the digging up of pleasant reminiscences concerning literary folk; therefore I will drop lightly into history myself. Standing here on the shore of the Atlantic & contemplating certain of its biggest literary billows, I am reminded of a thing which happened to me fifteen years ago, when I had just succeeded in stirring up a little Nevadian literary ocean-puddle myself, whose spume-flakes were beginning to blow thinly California-wards. I started on an inspection-tramp through the Southern mines of California. I was callow & conceited, & I resolved to try the virtue of my nom de plume. I very soon had an opportunity. I knocked at a miner's lonely log cabin in the foot-hills of the Sierras just at nightfall. It was snowing at the time. A jaded, melancholy man of fifty, barefooted, opened to me. When he heard my nom de plume, he looked more dejected than before. He let me in—pretty reluctantly, I thought —& after the customary bacon & beans, black coffee & a hot whisky, I took a pipe. This sorrowful man had not said three words up to this time. Now he spoke up & said in the voice of one who is secretly suffering, "You're the fourth—I'm a-going to move." "The fourth what?" said I. "The fourth littery man that's been here in twenty-four hours—I'm a-going to move." "You don't tell me!" said I; "Who were the others?" "Mr. Longfellow, Mr. Emerson, & Mr. Oliver Wendell Holmes—dad fetch the lot!"

THE MINER'S STORY

You can easily believe I was interested.—I supplicated—three hot whiskies did the rest—& finally the melancholy miner began. Said he—

They came here just at dark yesterday evening, & I let them in, of course. Said they were going to Yo Semite. They were a rough lot—but that's nothing—everybody looks rough that travels afoot. Mr. Emerson was a seedy little bit of a chap —red headed. Mr. Holmes was as fat as a balloon —he weighed as much as three hundred, & had double chins all the way down to his stomach. Mr. Longfellow was built like a prize fighter. His head was cropped & bristly—like as if he had a wig made of hair-brushes. His nose lay straight down his face, like a finger, with the end-joint tilted up. They had been drinking—I could see that. And what queer talk they used! Mr. Holmes inspected this cabin, then he took me by the button-hole, & says he—

"Through the deep caves of thought
   I hear a voice that sings:
Build thee more stately mansions,
   O my Soul!"

Says I, "I can't afford it, Mr. Holmes, & moreover I don't want to." Blamed if I liked it pretty well, either, coming from a stranger, that way! However, I started to get out my bacon & beans, when Mr. Emerson came & looked on a while, & then *he* takes me aside by the button-hole & says—

"Give me agates for my meat;
   Give me cantharids to eat;
From air & ocean bring me foods,
   From all zones & altitudes."

Says I, "Mr. Emerson, if you'll excuse me, this ain't no hotel." You see it sort of riled me—I warn't used to the ways of littery swells. But I went on a-sweating over my work, & next comes Mr. Longfellow & button-holes me, & interrupts me. Says he—

"Honor be to Mudjekeewis!
   You shall hear how Pau-Puk-Kee-wis—"

But I broke in, & says I, "Begging your pardon, Mr. Longfellow, if you'll be so kind as to hold your yawp for about five minutes, & let me get this grub ready, you'll do me proud." Well, sir, after they'd filled up, I set out the jug. Mr. Holmes looks at it, & then he fires up all of a sudden & yells—

"Flash out a stream of blood-red wine!—
   For I would drink to other days."

By George, I was getting kind of worked up. I don't deny it, I was getting kind of worked up. I turns to Mr. Holmes, & says I, "Looky-here, my fat friend, I'm a-running this shanty, & if the court knows herself, you'll take whisky-straight or you'll go dry!" Them's the very words I said to him. Now I didn't want to sass such famous littery people, but you see they kind of forced me. There ain't nothing onreasonable 'bout me; I don't mind a passel of guests a-tread'n on my tail three or four times, but when it comes to *standing* on it, it's different, & if the court knows herself, you'll take whisky-straight or you'll go dry!" Well, between drinks they'd swell around the cabin & strike attitudes & spout. Says Mr. Longfellow—

"This is the forest primeval."

Says Mr. Emerson—

"Here once the embattled farmers stood,
   And fired the shot heard round the world."

Says I, "O, blackguard the premises as much as you want to—it don't cost you a cent." Well, they went on drinking, & pretty soon they got out a greasy old deck & went to playing cut-throat euchre at ten cents a corner—on trust. I begun to notice some pretty suspicious things. Mr. Emerson dealt, looked at his hand, shook his head, says—

"I am the doubter & the doubt—"

—& calmly bunched the hands & went to shuffling for a new lay-out. Says he—

"They reckon ill who leave me out;
   They know not well the subtle ways
   I keep. [*pause*] I pass, & deal *again!*"

Hang'd if he didn't go ahead & do it, too! O, he was a cool one! Well, in about a minute, things were running pretty tight, but all of a sudden I see by Mr. Emerson's eye that he judged he had 'em. He had already coralled two tricks, & each of the others one. So now he kinds of lifts a little, in his chair, & says—

"I tire of globes & aces!—
Too long the game is played!"

—and down he fetches a right bower. Mr. Longfellow smiles as sweet as pie, & says—:

"Thanks, thanks to thee, my worthy friend,
For the lesson thou hast taught!"

—and dog my cats if he didn't down with *another* right bower! Well, sir, up jumps Holmes, a-war-whooping, as usual, & says—

"God help them if the tempest swings
The pine against the palm!"

—and I wish I may go to grass if he didn't swoop down with *another* right bower! Emerson claps his hand on his bowie, Longfellow claps his on his revolver, & I went under a bunk. There was going to be trouble; but that monstrous Holmes rose up, wobbling his double chins, & says he, "Order, gentlemen; the first man that draws, I'll lay down on him & smother him!" All quiet on the Potomac, you bet you! They were pretty how-come-you-so, now, & they begun to blow. Emerson says, "The bulliest thing I ever wrote, was Barbara Frietchie." Says Longfellow, "It don't begin with my Biglow Papers." Says Holmes, "My Thanatopsis lays over 'em both." They mighty near ended in a fight. Then they wished they had some more company—& Mr. Emerson pointed at me & says—

"Is yonder squalid peasant all
That this proud nursery could breed?"

He was a-whetting his bowie on his boot—so I let it pass. Well, sir, next they took it into their heads that they would like some music; so they made me stand up & sing "When Johnny Comes Marching Home" till I dropped—at thirteen minutes past four this morning. That's what I've been through, my friend. When I woke at seven, they were leaving, thank goodness, & Mr. Longfellow had my only boots on, & his own under his arm. Says I, "Hold on, there, Evangeline, what you going to do with *them?*"—He says: "Going to make tracks with 'em; because—

"Lives of great men all remind us
We can make our lives sublime;
And departing, leave behind us
Footprints on the sands of Time."

[As I said, Mr. Twain, you are the fourth in twenty-four hours—and I'm going to move; I ain't suited to a'] littery atmosphere." [1]

WHITTIER BIRTHDAY DINNER SPEECH.   **1.** Mark Twain's manuscript has been mutilated here. The omitted words are supplied from the version of the speech he inclosed in his **Auto**biographical Dictation.

I said to the miner, "Why my dear sir, *these* were not the gracious singers to whom we & the world pay loving reverence & homage: these were impostors." The miner investigated me with a calm eye for a while, then said he, "Ah—impostors, were they? are *you?*" I did not pursue the subject; and since then I haven't traveled on my nom de plume enough to hurt. Such is the reminiscence I was moved to contribute, Mr. Chairman. In my enthusiasm I may have exaggerated the details a little, but you will easily forgive me that fault since I believe it is the first time I have ever deflected from perpendicular fact on an occasion like this.

HOW TO TELL A STORY

⟨ REPRINTED here from Definitive Edition, Vol. XXIV, "How to Tell a Story" was first published in *Youth's Companion* (1895). This discussion of the technique of oral storytelling should be compared with the discussion in "Platform Readings" (see pp. 106–07). The simulated laughter which James Whitcomb Riley used in his role of "a dull-witted old farmer" might be described as a reverse dead-pan: it seems to violate Mark Twain's prescription that the teller of a humorous story "does his best to conceal the fact that he even dimly suspects there is anything funny about it," but is actually an illustration of the same underlying principle of the use of a mask or persona by the artist.

I DO NOT claim that I can tell a story as it ought to be told. I only claim to know how a story ought to be told, for I have been almost daily in the company of the most expert story-tellers for many years.

There are several kinds of stories, but only one difficult kind—the humorous. I will talk mainly about that one. The humorous story is American, the comic story is English, the witty story is French. The humorous story depends for its effect upon the *manner* of the telling; the comic story and the witty story upon the *matter*.

The humorous story may be spun out to great length, and may wander around as much as it pleases, and arrive nowhere in particular; but the comic and witty stories must be brief and end with a point. The humorous story bubbles gently along, the others burst.

The humorous story is strictly a work of art—high and delicate art—and only an artist can tell it; but no art is necessary in telling the comic and the witty story; anybody can do it. The art of telling a humorous story—understand, I mean by word of mouth, not print—was created in America, and has remained at home.

The humorous story is told gravely; the teller does his best to conceal the fact that he even dimly suspects that there is anything funny about it; but the teller of the comic story tells you beforehand that it is one of the funniest things he has ever heard, then tells it with eager delight, and is the first person to laugh when he gets through. And sometimes, if he has had good success, he is so glad and happy that he will repeat the "nub" of it and glance around from face to face, collecting applause, and then repeat it again. It is a pathetic thing to see.

Very often, of course, the rambling and disjointed humorous story finishes with a nub, point, snapper, or whatever you like to call it. Then the listener must be alert, for in many cases the teller will divert attention from that nub by dropping it in a carefully casual and indifferent way, with the pretense that he does not know it is a nub.

Artemus Ward [1] used that trick a good deal; then when the belated audience presently caught the joke he would look up with innocent surprise, as if wondering what they had found to laugh at. Dan Setchell [2] used it before him, Nye [3] and Riley [4] and others use it to-day.

But the teller of the comic story does not slur the nub; he shouts it at you—every time. And when he prints it, in England, France, Germany, and Italy, he italicizes it, puts some whooping exclamation-points after it, and sometimes explains it in a parenthesis. All of which is very depressing, and makes one want to renounce joking and lead a better life.

Let me set down an instance of the comic method, using an anecdote which has been popular all over the world for twelve or fifteen hundred years. The teller tells it in this way:

THE WOUNDED SOLDIER

In the course of a certain battle a soldier whose leg had been shot off appealed to another soldier who was hurrying by to carry him to the rear, informing him at the same time of the loss which he had sustained; whereupon the generous son of Mars, shouldering the unfortunate, proceeded to carry out his desire. The bullets and cannon-balls were flying in all directions, and presently one of the latter took the wounded man's head off—without, however, his deliverer being aware of it. In no long time he was hailed by an officer, who said:

"Where are you going with that carcass?"

"To the rear, sir—he's lost his leg!"

"His leg, forsooth?" responded the astonished officer; "you mean his head, you booby."

Whereupon the soldier dispossessed himself of his burden, and stood looking down upon it in great perplexity. At length he said:

"It is true, sir, just as you have said." Then after a pause he added, *"But he* TOLD *me* IT WAS HIS LEG! ! ! ! !"

Here the narrator bursts into explosion after explosion of thunderous horse-laughter, repeating that nub from time to time through his gaspings and shriekings and suffocatings.

It takes only a minute and a half to tell that in its comic-story form; and isn't worth the telling, after all. Put into the humorous-story form it takes ten minutes, and is about the funniest thing I have ever listened to—as James Whitcomb Riley tells it.

He tells it in the character of a dull-witted old farmer who has just heard it for the first time, thinks it is unspeakably funny, and is trying to repeat it to a neighbor. But he can't remember it; so he gets all mixed up and wanders helplessly round and round, putting in tedious details that don't belong in the tale and only retard it; taking them out conscientiously and putting in others that are just as useless; making minor mistakes now and then and stopping to correct them and explain how he came to make them; remembering things which he forgot to put in in their proper place and going back to put them in there; stopping his narrative a good while in order to try to recall the name of the soldier that was hurt, and finally remembering that the soldier's name was not mentioned, and remarking placidly that the name is of no real importance, anyway—better, of course, if one knew it, but not essential, after all—and so on, and so on, and so on.

The teller is innocent and happy and pleased with himself, and has to stop every little while to hold himself in and keep from laughing outright; and does hold in, but his body quakes in a jelly-like way with interior chuckles; and at the end of the ten minutes the audience have laughed until they are exhausted, and the tears are running down their faces.

The simplicity and innocence and sincerity and unconsciousness of the old farmer are perfectly simulated, and the result is a performance which is thoroughly charming and delicious. This is art—

HOW TO TELL A STORY. **1. Artemus Ward:** pseudonym of Charles Farrar Browne (1834–67), newspaper humorist and lecturer. **2. Dan Setchell:** a famous comic actor on the New York and Boston stages in the 1850's and 1860's. **3. Nye:** Edgar W. Nye (1850–96), a popular literary comedian in the tradition of Artemus Ward. **4. Riley:** James Whitcomb Riley (1849–1916), best known for his dialect poems about Indiana, such as "The Old Swimmin' Hole," but also a gifted platform artist with whom Mark Twain once contemplated making a tour in a joint program of readings.

and fine and beautiful, and only a master can compass it; but a machine could tell the other story.

To string incongruities and absurdities together in a wandering and sometimes purposeless way, and seem innocently unaware that they are absurdities, is the basis of the American art, if my position is correct. Another feature is the slurring of the point. A third is the dropping of a studied remark apparently without knowing it, as if one were thinking aloud. The fourth and last is the pause.

Artemus Ward dealt in numbers three and four a good deal. He would begin to tell with great animation something which he seemed to think was wonderful; then lose confidence, and after an apparently absent-minded pause add an incongruous remark in a soliloquizing way; and that was the remark intended to explode the mine—and it did.

For instance, he would say eagerly, excitedly, "I once knew a man in New Zealand who hadn't a tooth in his head"—here his animation would die out; a silent, reflective pause would follow, then he would say dreamily, and as if to himself, "and yet that man could beat a drum better than any man I ever saw."

The pause is an exceedingly important feature in any kind of story, and a frequently recurring feature, too. It is a dainty thing, and delicate, and also uncertain and treacherous; for it must be exactly the right length—no more and no less—or it fails of its purpose and makes trouble. If the pause is too short [long?] the impressive point is passed, and the audience have had time to divine that a surprise is intended—and then you can't surprise them, of course.

On the platform I used to tell a negro ghost story that had a pause in front of the snapper on the end, and that pause was the most important thing in the whole story. If I got it the right length precisely, I could spring the finishing ejaculation with effect enough to make some impressible girl deliver a startled little yelp and jump out of her seat—and that was what I was after. This story was called "The Golden Arm," [5] and was told in this fashion. You can practise with it yourself—and mind you look out for the pause and get it right.

THE GOLDEN ARM

Once 'pon a time dey wuz a monsus mean man, en he live 'way out in de prairie all 'lone by hisself, 'cep'n he had a wife. En bimeby she died, en he

5. **"The Golden Arm"**: Mark Twain had learned this story from his father's slave, Uncle Ned, when he was a child in Florida, Mo. The story is mentioned again in "Platform Readings" (see p. 110).

tuck en toted her way out dah in de prairie en buried her. Well, she had a golden arm—all solid gold, fum de shoulder down. He wuz pow'ful mean—pow'ful; en dat night he couldn't sleep, caze he want dat golden arm so bad.

When it come midnight he couldn't stan' it no mo'; so he git up, he did, en tuck his lantern en shoved out thoo de storm en dug her up en got de golden arm; en he bent his head down 'gin de win', en plowed en plowed en plowed thoo de snow. Den all on a sudden he stop (make a considerable pause here, and look startled, and take a listening attitude) en say: "My lan', what's dat?"

En he listen—en listen—en de win' say (set your teeth together and imitate the wailing and wheezing singsong of the wind), "Bzzz-z-zzz"—en den, way back yonder whah de grave is, he hear a *voice!*—he hear a voice all mix' up in de win'—can't hardly tell 'em 'part—"Bzzz—zzz—W-h-o—g-o-t—m-y—g-o-l-d-e-n *arm?*" (You must begin to shiver violently now.)

En he begin to shiver en shake, en say, "Oh, my! *Oh,* my lan'!" en de win' blow de lantern out, en de snow en sleet blow in his face en mos' choke him, en he start a-plowin' knee-deep towards home mos' dead, he so sk'yerd—en pooty soon he hear de voice agin, en (pause) it 'us comin' *aft-er* him! "Bzzz—zzz—zzz—W-h-o—g-o-t—m-y—g-o-l-d-e-n—*arm?*"

When he git to de pasture he hear it agin—closter now, en a-*comin'!*—a-comin' back dah in de dark en de storm—(repeat the wind and the voice). When he git to de house he rush up-stairs en jump in de bed en kiver up, head and years, en lay dah shiverin' en shakin'—en den way out dah he hear it *agin!*—en a-*comin'!* En bimeby he hear (pause—awed, listening attitude)—pat—pat—pat—*hit's a-comin' up-stairs!* Den he hear de latch, en he *know* it's in de room!

Den pooty soon he know it's a-*stannin' by de bed!* (Pause.) Den—he know it's a-*bendin' down over him*—en he cain't skasely git his breath! Den—den—he seem to feel somethin' *c-o-l-d,* right down 'most agin his head! (Pause.)

Den de voice say, *right at his year*—"W-h-o—g-o-t—m-y—g-o-l-d-e-n *arm?*" (You must wail it out very plaintively and accusingly; then you stare steadily and impressively into the face of the farthest-gone auditor—a girl, preferably—and let that awe-inspiring pause begin to build itself in the deep hush. When it has reached exactly the right length, jump suddenly at that girl and yell, *"You've* got it!")

If you've got the *pause* right, she'll fetch a dear little yelp and spring right out of her shoes. But you *must* get the pause right; and you will find it the most troublesome and aggravating and uncertain thing you ever undertook.

FENIMORE COOPER'S FURTHER LITERARY OFFENSES

⟨ WRITTEN in 1894 or 1895, this essay is the second of two which purport to be lectures by "Mark Twain, M.A., Professor of Belles Lettres in the Veterinary College of Arizona." The first was published in the *North American Review* in July, 1895. At the head of it Mark Twain placed quotations from Thomas R. Lounsbury, Brander Matthews, and Wilkie Collins praising Cooper as a literary artist. He then listed nineteen "rules governing literary art in the domain of romantic fiction" and demonstrated that in *The Deerslayer* and *The Pathfinder* Cooper violated almost all of them. The second lecture was not published until 1946, when Bernard DeVoto edited it with a commentary. The following text is from the *New England Quarterly* (September, 1946).

YOUNG GENTLEMEN: In studying Cooper you will find it profitable to study him in detail—word by word, sentence by sentence. For every sentence of his is interesting. Interesting because of its make-up; its peculiar make-up, its original make-up. Let us examine a sentence or two, and see. Here is a passage from Chapter XI of *The Last of the Mohicans*, one of the most famous and most admired of Cooper's books:

Notwithstanding the swiftness of their flight, one of the Indians had found an opportunity to strike a straggling fawn with an arrow, and had borne the more preferable fragments of the victim, patiently on his shoulders, to the stopping-place. Without any aid from the science of cookery, he was immediately employed, in common with his fellows, in gorging himself with this digestible sustenance. Magua alone sat apart, without participating in the revolting meal, and apparently buried in the deepest thought.

This little paragraph is full of matter for reflection and inquiry. The remark about the swiftness of the flight was unnecessary, as it was merely put in to forestall the possible objection of some overparticular reader that the Indian couldn't have found the needed "opportunity" while fleeing swiftly. The reader would not have made that objection. He would care nothing about having that small matter explained and justified. But that is Cooper's way; frequently he will explain and justify little things that do not need it and then make up for this by as frequently failing to explain important ones that do need it. For instance he allowed that astute and cautious person, Deerslayer-Hawkeye, to throw his rifle heedlessly down and

leave it lying on the ground where some hostile Indians would presently be sure to find it—a rifle prized by that person above all things else in the earth—and the reader gets no word of explanation of that strange act. There was a reason, but it wouldn't bear exposure. Cooper meant to get a fine dramatic effect out of the finding of the rifle by the Indians, and he accomplished this at the happy time; but all the same, Hawkeye could have hidden the rifle in a quarter of a minute where the Indians could not have found it. Cooper couldn't think of any way to explain why Hawkeye didn't do that, so he just shirked the difficulty and did not explain at all. In another place Cooper allowed Heyward to shoot at an Indian with a pistol that wasn't loaded—and grants us not a word of explanation as to how the man did it.

No, the remark about the swiftness of their flight was not necessary; neither was the one which said that the Indian found an opportunity; neither was the one which said he *struck* the fawn; neither was the one which explained that it was a "straggling" fawn; neither was the one which said the striking was done with an arrow; neither was the one which said the Indian bore the "fragments;" nor the remark that they were preferable fragments; nor the remark that they were *more* preferable fragments; nor the explanation that they were fragments of the "victim;" nor the over-particular explanation that specifies the Indian's "shoulders" as the part of him that supported the fragments; nor the statement that the Indian bore the fragments patiently. None of those details has any value. We don't care what the Indian struck the fawn with; we don't care whether it was a straggling fawn or an unstraggling one; we don't care which fragments the Indian saved; we don't care why he saved the "more" preferable ones when the merely preferable ones would have amounted to just the same thing and couldn't have been told from the more preferable ones by anybody, dead or alive; we don't care whether the Indian carried them on his shoulders or in his handkerchief; and finally, we don't care whether he carried them patiently or struck for higher pay and shorter hours. We are indifferent to that Indian and all his affairs.

There was only one fact in that long sentence that was worth stating, and it could have been squeezed into these few words—and with advantage to the narrative, too:

"During the flight one of the Indians had killed a fawn, and he brought it into camp." You will notice that "During the flight one of the Indians had killed a fawn and he brought it into camp," is more straightforward and businesslike, and less mincing and smirky, than it is to say "Notwithstanding the swiftness of their flight, one of the Indians had found an opportunity to strike a straggling fawn with an arrow, and had borne the more preferable fragments of the victim, patiently on his shoulders, to the stopping-place." You will notice that the form "During the flight one of the Indians had killed a fawn and he brought it into camp" holds up its chin and moves to the front with the steady stride of a grenadier, whereas the form "Notwithstanding the swiftness of their flight, one of the Indians had found an opportunity to strike a straggling fawn with an arrow, and had borne the more preferable fragments of the victim, patiently on his shoulders, to the stopping-place," simpers along with an airy, complacent, monkey-with-a-parasol gait which is not suited to the transportation of raw meat.

I beg to remind you that an author's way of setting forth a matter is called his Style, and that an author's style is a main part of his equipment for business. The style of some authors has variety in it, but Cooper's style is remarkable for the absence of this feature. Cooper's style is always grand and stately and noble. Style may be likened to an army, the author to its general, the book to the campaign. Some authors proportion an attacking force to the strength or weakness, the importance or unimportance, of the object to be attacked; but Cooper doesn't. It doesn't make any difference to Cooper whether the object of attack is a hundred thousand men or a cow; he hurls his entire force against it. He comes thundering down with all his battalions at his back, cavalry in the van, artillery on the flanks, infantry massed in the middle, forty bands braying, a thousand banners streaming in the wind; and whether the object be an army or a cow you will see him come marching sublimely in, at the end of the engagement, bearing the more preferable fragments of the victim patiently on his shoulders, to the stopping-place. Cooper's style is grand, awful, beautiful; but it is sacred to Cooper, it is his very own, and no student of the Veterinary College of Arizona will be allowed to filch it from him.

In one of his chapters Cooper throws an ungentle slur at one Gamut because he is not exact enough in his choice of words. But Cooper has that failing himself, as was remarked in our first Lecture. If the Indian had "struck" the fawn with a brick, or with a club, or with his fist, no one could find fault with the word used. And one cannot find much fault when he strikes it with an arrow; still it sounds affected, and it might have been a little better to lean to simplicity and say he shot it with an arrow.

"Fragments" is well enough, perhaps, when one is speaking of the parts of a dismembered deer, yet it hasn't just exactly the right sound—and sound is something; in fact sound is a good deal. It makes the difference between good music and poor music, and it can sometimes make the difference between good literature and indifferent literature. "Fragments" sounds all right when we are talking about the wreckage of a breakable thing that has been smashed; it also sounds all right when applied to cat's-meat; but when we use it to describe large hunks and chunks like the fore- and hind-quarters of a fawn, it grates upon the fastidious ear.

"Without any aid from the science of cookery, he was immediately employed, in common with his fellows, in gorging himself with this digestible sustenance."

This was a mere statistic; just a mere cold, colorless statistic; yet you see Cooper has made a chromo out of it. To use another figure, he has clothed a humble statistic in flowing, voluminous and costly raiment, whereas both good taste and economy suggest that he ought to have saved these splendors for a king, and dressed the humble statistic in a simple breech-clout. Cooper spent twenty-four words here on a thing not really worth more than eight. We will reduce the statistic to its proper proportions and state it in this way:

"He and the others ate the meat raw."

"Digestible sustenance" is a handsome phrase, but it was out of place there, because we do not know these Indians or care for them; and so it cannot interest us to know whether the meat was going to agree with them or not. Details which do not assist a story are better left out.

"Magua alone sat apart, without participating in the revolting meal," is a statement which we understand, but that is our merit, not Cooper's. Cooper is not clear. He does not say who it is that is revolted by the meal. It is really Cooper himself, but there is nothing in the statement to indicate that it isn't Magua. Magua is an Indian and likes raw meat.

The word "alone" could have been left out and space saved. It has no value where it is.

I must come back with some frequency, in the course of these Lectures, to the matter of Cooper's inaccuracy as an Observer. In this way I shall hope to persuade you that it is well to look at a thing carefully before you try to describe it; but I shall rest you between times with other matters and thus try to avoid over-fatiguing you with that detail of our theme. In *The Last of the Mohicans* Cooper gets up a stirring "situation" on an island flanked by great cataracts—a lofty island with steep sides—a sort of tongue which projects downstream from the midst of the divided waterfall. There are caverns in this mass of rock, and a party of Cooper people hide themselves in one of these to get away from some hostile Indians. There is a small exit at each end of this cavern. These exits are closed with blankets and the light excluded. The exploring hostiles back themselves up against the blankets and rave and rage in a blood-curdling way, but they are Cooper Indians and of course fail to discover the blankets; so they presently go away baffled and disappointed. Alice, in her gratitude for this deliverance, flings herself on her knees to return thanks. The darkness in there must have been pretty solid; yet if we may believe Cooper, it was a darkness which could not have been told from daylight; for here are some nice details which were visible in it:

"Both Heyward and the more tempered Cora witnessed the act of involuntary emotion with powerful sympathy, the former secretly believing that piety had never worn a form so lovely as it had now assumed in the youthful person of Alice. Her eyes were radiant with the glow of grateful feelings; the flush of her beauty was again seated on her cheeks, and her whole soul seemed ready and anxious to pour out its thanksgivings, through the medium of her eloquent features. But when her lips moved, the words they should have uttered appeared frozen by some new and sudden chill. Her bloom gave place to the paleness of death; her soft and melting eyes grew hard, and seemed contracting with horror; while those hands which she had raised, clasped in each other, towards heaven, dropped in horizontal lines before her, the fingers pointed forward in convulsed motion."

It is a case of strikingly inexact observation. Heyward and the more tempered Cora could not have seen the half of it in the dark that way.

I must call your attention to certain details of this work of art which invite particular examination. "Involuntary" is surplusage, and violates Rule 14.[1] All emotion is involuntary when genuine, and then the qualifying term is not needed; a qualifying term is needed only when the emotion is pumped-up and ungenuine. "Secretly" is surplusage, too; because Heyward was not believing out loud, but all to himself; and a person cannot believe a thing all to himself without doing it privately. I do not approve of the word "seated," to describe the process of locating a flush. No one can seat a flush. A flush is not a deposit on an exterior surface, it is a something which squashes out from within.

I cannot approve of the word "new." If Alice had had an old chill, formerly, it would be all right to distinguish this one from that one by calling this one the new chill; but she had not had any old chill, this one was the only chill she had had, up till now, and so the tacit reference to an old anterior chill is unwarranted and misleading. And I do not altogether like the phrase "while those hands which she had raised." It seems to imply that she had some other hands—some other ones which she had put on the shelf a minute so as to give her a better chance to raise those ones; but it is not true; she had only the one pair. The phrase is in the last degree misleading. But I like to see her extend these ones in front of her and work the fingers. I think that that is a very good effect. And it would have almost doubled the effect if the more tempered Cora had done it some, too.

A Cooper Indian who has been washed is a poor thing, and commonplace; it is the Cooper Indian in his paint that thrills. Cooper's extra words are Cooper's paint—his paint, his feathers, his tomahawk, his warwhoop.

In the two-thirds of a page elsewhere referred to, wherein Cooper scored 114 literary transgressions out of a possible 115, he appears before us with all his things on. As follows, the italics are mine—they indicate violations of Rule 14:

In a minute he was once more fastened to the tree, *a helpless object of any insult or wrong that might be offered. So eagerly did every one now act, that nothing was said.* The fire was immediately lighted *in the pile, and the end of all was anxiously expected.*

It was not the intention of the Hurons *absolutely* to destroy *the life of* their victim by *means of* fire. They designed merely to put his *physical fortitude* to the severest proofs it could endure, short of that extremity. In the end, they fully intended to carry his scalp into their village, but it was their wish first to break down his resolution, and to reduce him to *the level of* a complaining sufferer. With this view, the pile of brush *and branches* had been placed at a *proper* distance, *or one* at which it was thought the heat would soon become intolerable, though *it might* not *be* immediately dangerous. *As often happened, however, on these occasions,* this distance had been miscalculated, and the flames *began to wave their forked tongues in a proximity to the face of the victim that* would have proved fatal in another instant had not Hetty rushed through the crowd, armed with a stick, and scattered the blazing pile *in a dozen directions.* More than one hand was raised to strike the *presumptuous* intruder *to* the earth; but the chiefs prevented the blows by reminding their *irritated* followers of the state of her mind. Hetty, herself, was insensible to the risk she ran; but, *as soon as she had performed this bold act,*

FENIMORE COOPER'S FURTHER LITERARY OFFENSES. 1. Rule 14: "Eschew surplusage."

she stood looking about her in frowning resentment, as if to rebuke the *crowd of attentive* savages *for their cruelty.*

'God bless you, dear*est sister,* for that brave and ready act,' murmured Judith, *herself unnerved so much as to be incapable of exertion;* 'Heaven itself has sent you on its holy errand.'

Number of words, 320; necessary ones, 220; words wasted by the generous spendthrift, 100.

In our day those 100 unnecessary words would have to come out. We will take them out presently and make the episode approximate the modern requirement in the matter of compression.

If we may consider each unnecessary word in Cooper's report of that barbecue a separate and individual violation of Rule 14, then that rule is violated 100 times in that report. Other rules are violated in it. Rule 12,[2] two instances; Rule 13,[3] three instances; Rule 15,[4] one instance; Rule 16,[5] two instances; Rule 17,[6] one or two little instances; the Report in its entirety is an offense against Rule 18 [7]—also against Rule 16. Total score, about 114 violations of the laws of literary art out of a possible 115.

Let us now bring forward the Report again, with the most of the unnecessary words knocked out. By departing from Cooper's style and manner, all the facts could be put into 150 words, and the effects heightened at the same time—this is manifest, of course—but that would not be desirable. We must stick to Cooper's language as closely as we can:

In a minute he was once more fastened to the tree. The fire was immediately lighted. It was not the intention of the Hurons to destroy Deerslayer's life by fire; they designed merely to put his fortitude to the severest proofs it could endure short of that extremity. In the end, they fully intended to take his life, but it was their wish first to break down his resolution and reduce him to a complaining sufferer. With this view the pile of brush had been placed at a distance at which it was thought the heat would soon become intolerable, without being immediately dangerous. But this distance had been miscalculated; the fire was so close to the victim that he would have been fatally burned in another instant if Hetty had not rushed through the crowd and scattered the brands with a stick. More than one Indian raised his hand to strike her down but the chiefs saved her by reminding them of the state of her mind. Hetty herself was insensible to the risk she ran; she stood looking about her in frowning resentment, as if to rebuke the savages for their cruelty.

2. Rule 12: "*Say* what he is proposing to say, not merely come near it."   3. Rule 13: "Use the right word, not its second cousin."   4. Rule 15: "Not omit necessary details."   5. Rule 16: "Avoid slovenliness of form."   6. Rule 17: "Use good grammar."   7. Rule 18: "Employ a simple and straightforward style."

'God bless you, dear!' cried Judith, 'for that brave and ready act. Heaven itself has sent you on its holy errand, and you shall have a chromo.'

Number of words, 220—and the facts are all in.

WILLIAM DEAN HOWELLS

[FIRST published in *Harper's Magazine* (July, 1906), the essay was signed "S. L. Clemens" rather than "Mark Twain," as if the author wished to emphasize the fact that he spoke in his own person, without even the hint of indirection conveyed by his pseudonym. Howells wrote to his sister concerning the article: "I thought nothing could be more affectionate; and he is really a great literary critic, so that his praise is better worth having now than any other man's." The text that follows is from the Definitive Edition, Vol. XXVI.

IS IT TRUE that the sun of a man's mentality touches noon at forty and then begins to wane toward setting? Doctor Osler is charged with saying so. Maybe he said it, maybe he didn't; I don't know which it is. But if he said it, I can point him to a case which proves his rule. Proves it by being an exception to it. To this place I nominate Mr. Howells.

I read his *Venetian Days* [1] about forty years ago. I compare it with his paper on Machiavelli in a late number of *Harper,*[2] and I cannot find that his English has suffered any impairment. For forty years his English has been to me a continual delight and astonishment. In the sustained exhibition of certain great qualities—clearness, compression, verbal exactness, and unforced and seemingly unconscious felicity of phrasing—he is, in my belief, without his peer in the English-writing world. *Sustained.* I intrench myself behind that protecting word. There are others who exhibit those great qualities as greatly as does he, but only by intervaled distributions of rich moonlight, with stretches of veiled and dimmer landscape between; whereas Howells's moon sails cloudless skies all night and all the nights.

In the matter of verbal exactness Mr. Howells has no superior, I suppose. He seems to be almost always able to find that elusive and shifty grain of gold, the *right word.* Others have to put up with approximations, more or less frequently; he has better luck. To me, the others are miners working with the gold-pan—of necessity some of the gold

WILLIAM DEAN HOWELLS.   1. *Venetian Days:* The correct title is *Venetian Life* (1866), as Howells reminded Mark Twain in his letter of thanks for the article.   2. *Harper:* A short notice of Louis Dyer, *Machiavelli and the Modern State,* in the "Editor's Easy Chair" of *Harper's Magazine* for April, 1906.

washes over and escapes; whereas, in my fancy, he is quicksilver raiding down a riffle—no grain of the metal stands much chance of eluding him. A powerful agent is the right word: it lights the reader's way and makes it plain; a close approximation to it will answer, and much traveling is done in a well-enough fashion by its help, but we do not welcome it and applaud it and rejoice in it as we do when *the* right one blazes out on us. Whenever we come upon one of those intensely right words in a book or a newspaper the resulting effect is physical as well as spiritual, and electrically prompt: it tingles exquisitely around through the walls of the mouth and tastes as tart and crisp and good as the autumn-butter that creams the sumac-berry. One has no time to examine the word and vote upon its rank and standing, the automatic recognition of its supremacy is so immediate. There is a plenty of acceptable literature which deals largely in approximations, but it may be likened to a fine landscape seen through the rain; the right word would dismiss the rain, then you would see it better. It doesn't rain when Howells is at work.

And where does he get the easy and effortless flow of his speech? and its cadenced and undulating rhythm? and its architectural felicities of construction, its graces of expression, its pemmican quality of compression, and all that? Born to him, no doubt. All in shining good order in the beginning, all extraordinary; and all just as shining, just as extraordinary to-day, after forty years of diligent wear and tear and use. He passed his fortieth year long and long ago; but I think his English of to-day—his perfect English, I wish to say—can throw down the glove before his English of that antique time and not be afraid.

I will go back to the paper on Machiavelli now, and ask the reader to examine this passage from it which I append. I do not mean examine it in a bird's-eye way; I mean search it, study it. And, of course, read it aloud. I may be wrong, still it is my conviction that one cannot get out of finely wrought literature all that is in it by reading it mutely:

Mr. Dyer is rather of the opinion, first luminously suggested by Macaulay, that Machiavelli was in earnest, but must not be judged as a political moralist of our time and race would be judged. He thinks that Machiavelli was in earnest, as none but an idealist can be, and he is the first to imagine him an idealist immersed in realities, who involuntarily transmutes the events under his eye into something like the visionary issues of reverie. The Machiavelli whom he depicts does not cease to be politically a republican and socially a just man because he holds up an atrocious despot like Cæsar Borgia as a mirror for rulers. What

Machiavelli beheld round him in Italy was a civic disorder in which there was oppression without statecraft, and revolt without patriotism. When a miscreant like Borgia appeared upon the scene and reduced both tyrants and rebels to an apparent quiescence, he might very well seem to such a dreamer the savior of society whom a certain sort of dreamers are always looking for. Machiavelli was no less honest when he honored the diabolical force of Cæsar Borgia than Carlyle was when at different times he extolled the strong man who destroys liberty in creating order. But Carlyle has only just ceased to be mistaken for a reformer, while it is still Machiavelli's hard fate to be so trammeled in his material that his name stands for whatever is most malevolent and perfidious in human nature.

You see how easy and flowing it is; how unvexed by ruggednesses, clumsinesses, broken meters; how simple and—so far as you or I can make out—unstudied; how clear, how limpid, how understandable, how unconfused by cross-currents, eddies, under-tows; how seemingly unadorned, yet is all adornment, like the lily-of-the-valley; and how compressed, how compact, without a complacency-signal hung out anywhere to call attention to it.

There are twenty-three lines in the quoted passage. After reading it several times aloud, one perceives that a good deal of matter is crowded into that small space. I think it is a model of compactness. When I take its materials apart and work them over and put them together in my way, I find I cannot crowd the result back into the same hole, there not being room enough. I find it a case of a woman packing a man's trunk: he can get the things out, but he can't ever get them back again.

The proffered paragraph is a just and fair sample; the rest of the article is as compact as it is; there are no waste words. The sample is just in other ways: limpid, fluent, graceful, and rhythmical as it is, it holds no superiority in these respects over the rest of the essay. Also, the choice phrasing noticeable in the sample is not lonely; there is a plenty of its kin distributed through the other paragraphs. This is claiming much when that kin must face the challenge of a phrase like the one in the middle sentence: "an idealist immersed in realities who involuntarily transmutes the events under his eye into something like the visionary issues of reverie." With a hundred words to do it with, the literary artisan could catch that airy thought and tie it down and reduce it to a concrete condition, visible, substantial, understandable and all right, like a cabbage; but the artist does it with twenty, and the result is a flower.

The quoted phrase, like a thousand others that have come from the same source, has the quality of certain scraps of verse which take hold of us and stay in our memories, we do not understand why, at first: all the words being the right words, none of them is conspicuous, and so they all seem inconspicuous, therefore we wonder what it is about them that makes their message take hold.

> The mossy marbles rest
> On the lips that he has prest
> In their bloom,
> And the names he loved to hear
> Have been carved for many a year
> On the tomb.[3]

It is like a dreamy strain of moving music, with no sharp notes in it. The words are all "right" words, and all the same size. We do not notice it at first. We get the effect, it goes straight home to us, but we do not know why. It is when the right words are conspicuous that they thunder:

The glory that was Greece and the grandeur that was Rome! [4]

When I go back from Howells old to Howells young I find him arranging and clustering English words well, but not any better than now. He is not more felicitous in concreting abstractions now than he was in translating, then, the visions of the eyes of flesh into words that reproduced their forms and colors:

In Venetian streets they give the fallen snow no rest. It is at once shoveled into the canals by hundreds of half-naked *facchini;* and now in St. Mark's Place the music of innumerable shovels smote upon my ear; and I saw the shivering legion of poverty as it engaged the elements in a struggle for the possession of the Piazza. But the snow continued to fall, and through the twilight of the descending flakes all this toil and encounter looked like that weary kind of effort in dreams, when the most determined industry seems only to renew the task. The lofty crest of the bell-tower was hidden in the folds of falling snow, and I could no longer see the golden angel upon its summit. But looked at across the Piazza, the beautiful outline of St. Mark's Church was perfectly penciled in the air, and the shifting threads of the snowfall were woven into a spell of novel enchantment around the structure that always seemed to me too exquisite in its fantastic loveliness to be anything but the creation of magic. The tender snow had compassionated the beautiful edifice for all the wrongs of time, and so hid the stains and ugliness of decay that it looked as if just from the hand of the builder—or, better said, just from the brain of the architect. There was marvelous freshness in the colors of the mosaics in the great arches of the façade, and all that gracious harmony into which the temple rises, of marble scrolls and leafy exuberance airily supporting the statues of the saints, was a hundred times etherealized by the purity and whiteness of the drifting flakes. The snow lay lightly on the golden globes that tremble like peacock-crests above the vast domes, and plumed them with softest white; it robed the saints in ermine; and it danced over all its work, as if exulting in its beauty—beauty which filled me with subtle, selfish yearning to keep such evanescent loveliness for the little-while-longer of my whole life, and with despair to think that even the poor lifeless shadow of it could never be fairly reflected in picture or poem.

Through the wavering snowfall, the Saint Theodore upon one of the granite pillars of the Piazzetta did not show so grim as his wont is, and the winged lion on the other might have been a winged lamb, so gentle and mild he looked by the tender light of the storm. The towers of the island churches loomed faint and far away in the dimness; the sailors in the rigging of the ships that lay in the Basin wrought like phantoms among the shrouds; the gondolas stole in and out of the opaque distance more noiselessly and dreamily than ever; and a silence, almost palpable, lay upon the mutest city in the world.

The spirit of Venice is there: of a city where Age and Decay, fagged with distributing damage and repulsiveness among the other cities of the planet in accordance with the policy and business of their profession, come for rest and play between seasons, and treat themselves to the luxury and relaxation of sinking the shop and inventing and squandering charms all about, instead of abolishing such as they find, as is their habit when not on vacation.

In the working season they do business in Boston sometimes, and a character in *The Undiscovered Country* [5] takes accurate note of pathetic effects wrought by them upon the aspects of a street of once dignified and elegant homes whose occupants have moved away and left them a prey to neglect and gradual ruin and progressive degradation; a descent which reaches bottom at last, when the street becomes a roost for humble professionals of the faith-cure and fortune-telling sort.

What a queer, melancholy house, what a queer, melancholy street! I don't think I was ever in a street before where quite so many professional ladies, with English surnames, preferred Madam to Mrs. on their door-plates. And the poor old place has such a desperately conscious air of going to the deuce. Every house seems to wince as you go by, and button itself up to the chin for fear you should find out it had no shirt on—so to speak. I don't know what's the reason, but these material tokens of a social decay afflict me terribly: a tipsy woman isn't dreadfuler than a haggard old house, that's once been a home, in a street like this.

Mr. Howells's pictures are not mere stiff, hard, accurate photographs; they are photographs with

---

3. The . . . tomb: a stanza from Holmes's "The Last Leaf."
4. The . . . Rome!: From Poe's "To Helen."

5. *The Undiscovered Country:* a novel published in 1880.

feeling in them, and sentiment, photographs taken in a dream, one might say.

As concerns his humor, I will not try to say anything, yet I would try, if I had the words that might approximately reach up to its high place. I do not think any one else can play with humorous fancies so gracefully and delicately and deliciously as he does, nor has so many to play with, nor can come so near making them look as if they were doing the playing themselves and he was not aware that they were at it. For they are unobtrusive, and quiet in their ways, and well conducted. His is a humor which flows softly all around about and over and through the mesh of the page, pervasive, refreshing, health-giving, and makes no more show and no more noise than does the circulation of the blood.

There is another thing which is contentingly noticeable in Mr. Howells's books. That is his "stage directions"—those artifices which authors employ to throw a kind of human naturalness around a scene and a conversation, and help the reader to see the one and get at meanings in the other which might not be perceived if intrusted unexplained to the bare words of the talk. Some authors overdo the stage directions, they elaborate them quite beyond necessity; they spend so much time and take up so much room in telling us how a person said a thing and how he looked and acted when he said it that we get tired and vexed and wish he hadn't said it at all. Other authors' directions are brief enough, but it is seldom that the brevity contains either wit or information. Writers of this school go in rags, in the matter of stage directions; the majority of them have nothing in stock but a cigar, a laugh, a blush, and a bursting into tears. In their poverty they work these sorry things to the bone. They say:

". . . replied Alfred, flipping the ash from his cigar." (This explains nothing; it only wastes space.)

". . . responded Richard, with a laugh." (There was nothing to laugh about; there never is. The writer puts it in from habit—automatically; he is paying no attention to his work, or he would see that there is nothing to laugh at; often, when a remark is unusually and poignantly flat and silly, he tries to deceive the reader by enlarging the stage direction and making Richard break into "frenzies of uncontrollable laughter." This makes the reader sad.)

". . . murmured Gladys, blushing." (This poor old shop-worn blush is a tiresome thing. We get so we would rather Gladys would fall out of the book and break her neck than do it again. She is always doing it, and usually irrelevantly.

Whenever it is her turn to murmur she hangs out her blush; it is the only thing she's got. In a little while we hate her, just as we do Richard.)

". . . repeated Evelyn, bursting into tears." (This kind keep a book damp all the time. They can't say a thing without crying. They cry so much about nothing that by and by when they have something to cry *about* they have gone dry; they sob, and fetch nothing; we are not moved. We are only glad.)

They gravel me, these stale and overworked stage directions, these carbon films [filaments?] that got burnt out long ago and cannot now carry any faintest thread of light. It would be well if they could be relieved from duty and flung out in the literary back yard to rot and disappear along with the discarded and forgotten "steeds" and "halidomes" and similar stage-properties once so dear to our grandfathers. But I am friendly to Mr. Howells's stage directions; more friendly to them than to any one else's, I think. They are done with a competent and discriminating art, and are faithful to the requirements of a stage direction's proper and lawful office, which is to inform. Sometimes they convey a scene and its conditions so well that I believe I could see the scene and get the spirit and meaning of the accompanying dialogue if some one would read merely the stage directions to me and leave out the talk. For instance, a scene like this, from *The Undiscovered Country:*

". . . and she laid her arms with a beseeching gesture on her father's shoulder."

". . . she answered, following his gesture with a glance."

". . . she said, laughing nervously."

". . . she asked, turning swiftly upon him that strange, searching glance."

". . . she answered, vaguely."

". . . she reluctantly admitted."

". . . but her voice died wearily away, and she stood looking into his face with puzzled entreaty."

Mr. Howells does not repeat his forms, and does not need to; he can invent fresh ones without limit. It is mainly the repetition over and over again, by the third-rates, of worn and commonplace and juiceless forms that makes their novels such a weariness and vexation to us, I think. We do not mind one or two deliveries of their wares, but as we turn the pages over and keep on meeting them we presently get tired of them and wish they would do other things for a change:

". . . replied Alfred, flipping the ash from his cigar."

". . . responded Richard, with a laugh."

". . . murmured Gladys, blushing."

". . . repeated Evelyn, bursting into tears."

". . . replied the Earl, flipping the ash from his cigar."

". . . responded the undertaker, with a laugh."

". . . murmured the chambermaid, blushing."

". . . repeated the burglar, bursting into tears." tears."

". . . replied the conductor, flipping the ash from his cigar."

". . . responded Arkwright, with a laugh."

". . . murmured the chief of police, blushing."

". . . repeated the house-cat, bursting into tears."

And so on and so on; till at last it ceases to excite. I always notice stage directions, because they fret me and keep me trying to get out of their way, just as the automobiles do. At first; then by and by they become monotonous and I get run over.

Mr. Howells has done much work, and the spirit of it is as beautiful as the make of it. I have held him in admiration and affection so many years that I know by the number of those years that he is old now; but his heart isn't, nor his pen; and years do not count. Let him have plenty of them: there is profit in them for us.

PLATFORM READINGS

⟨ FROM the Autobiographical Dictation of October 10, 1907, first published in *Mark Twain in Eruption*, edited by Bernard DeVoto (1940), these comments on "reading" in public are the observations of one of the great masters of the art. They have a direct bearing on Mark Twain's writing; for he created a written style cunningly designed to simulate oral speech. And this style has been one of the major influences on American prose in the twentieth century.

WHAT is called a "reading," as a public platform entertainment, was first essayed by Charles Dickens, I think. He brought the idea with him from England in 1867. He had made it very popular at home and he made it so acceptable and so popular in America that his houses were crowded everywhere, and in a single season he earned two hundred thousand dollars. I heard him once during that season; it was in Steinway Hall, in December,[1] and it made the fortune of my life—not in dollars, I am not thinking of dollars; it made the real fortune of my life in that it made the happiness of my life; on that day I called at the St. Nicholas Hotel to see my *Quaker City* Excursion shipmate,

Charley Langdon, and was introduced to a sweet and timid and lovely young girl, his sister. The family went to the Dickens reading, and I accompanied them. It was forty years ago; from that day to this the sister has never been out of my mind nor heart.

Mr. Dickens read scenes from his printed books. From my distance, he was a small and slender figure, rather fancifully dressed, and striking and picturesque in appearance. He wore a black velvet coat with a large and glaring red flower in the button-hole. He stood under a red upholstered shed behind whose slant was a row of strong lights—just such an arrangement as artists use to concentrate a strong light upon a great picture. Dickens's audience sat in a pleasant twilight, while he performed in the powerful light cast upon him from the concealed lamps. He read with great force and animation, in the lively passages, and with stirring effect. It will be understood that he did not merely read but also acted. His reading of the storm scene in which Steerforth lost his life was so vivid, and so full of energetic action, that his house was carried off its feet, so to speak.

Dickens had set a fashion which others tried to follow, but I do not remember that anyone was any more than temporarily successful in it. The public reading was discarded after a time and was not resumed until something more than twenty years after Dickens had introduced it; then it rose and struggled along for a while in that curious and artless industry called Authors' Readings. When Providence had had enough of that kind of crime the Authors' Readings ceased from troubling and left the world at peace.

Lecturing and reading were quite different things; the lecturer didn't use notes or manuscript or book, but got his lecture by heart and delivered it night after night in the same words during the whole lecture season of four winter months. The lecture field had been a popular one all over the country for many years when I entered it in 1868;[2] it was then at the top of its popularity; in every town there was an organization of citizens who occupied themselves in the off season, every year, in arranging for a course of lectures for the coming winter; they chose their platform people from the Boston Lecture Agency list and they chose according to the town's size and ability to

PLATFORM READINGS.   1. **in December:** actually, January 2 or 3, 1868. Clemens had first met Olivia Langdon on December 27, 1867.

2. **in 1868:** Mark Twain means that he first set out on a lecture tour in 1868 under the management of James Redpath's Boston Lyceum Bureau (not "Lecture Agency"). He had first appeared on a public platform for pay in San Francisco in 1866 with a lecture on the Sandwich Islands and then had toured the Mother Lode country and Nevada with it.

pay the prices. The course usually consisted of eight or ten lectures. All that was wanted was that it should pay expenses; that it should come out with a money balance at the end of the season was not required. Very small towns had to put up with fifty-dollar men and women, with one or two second-class stars at a hundred dollars each as an attraction; big towns employed hundred-dollar men and women altogether, and added John B. Gough, or Henry Ward Beecher, or Anna Dickinson, or Wendell Phillips, as a compelling attraction; [3] large cities employed this whole battery of stars. Anna Dickinson's price was four hundred dollars a night; so was Henry Ward Beecher's; so was Gough's, when he didn't charge five or six hundred. I don't remember Wendell Phillips's price but it was high.

I remained in the lecture field three seasons— long enough to learn the trade; then domesticated myself in my new married estate after a weary life of wandering, and remained under shelter at home for fourteen or fifteen years. Meantime, speculators and money-makers had taken up the business of hiring lecturers, with the idea of getting rich at it. In about five years they killed that industry dead and when I returned to the platform for a season, in 1884, there had been a happy and holy silence for ten years, and a generation had come to the front who knew nothing about lectures and readings and didn't know how to take them nor what to make of them. They were difficult audiences, those untrained squads, and Cable [4] and I had a hard time with them sometimes.

Cable had been scouting the country alone for three years with readings from his novels, and he had been a good reader in the beginning for he had been born with a natural talent for it, but unhappily he prepared himself for his public work by taking lessons from a teacher of elocution, and so by the time he was ready to begin his platform work he was so well and thoroughly educated that he was merely theatrical and artificial and not half as pleasing and entertaining to a house as he had been in the splendid days of his ignorance. I had

never tried reading as a trade and I wanted to try it. I hired Major Pond [5] on a percentage to conduct me over the country, and I hired Cable as a helper at six hundred dollars a week and expenses, and we started out on our venture.

It was ghastly! At least in the beginning. I had selected my readings well enough, but had not studied them. I supposed it would only be necessary to do like Dickens—get out on the platform and read from the book. I did that and made a botch of it. Written things are not for speech; their form is literary; they are stiff, inflexible, and will not lend themselves to happy and effective delivery with the tongue—where their purpose is to merely entertain, not instruct; they have to be limbered up, broken up, colloquialized, and turned into the common forms of unpremeditated talk— otherwise they will bore the house, not entertain it. After a week's experience with the book I laid it aside and never carried it to the platform again; but meantime I had memorized those pieces, and in delivering them from the platform they soon transformed themselves into flexible talk, with all their obstructing precisenesses and formalities gone out of them for good.

One of the readings which I used was a part of an extravagant chapter in dialect from *Roughing It* which I entitled "His Grandfather's Old Ram." After I had memorized it it began to undergo changes on the platform and it continued to edit and revise itself, night after night, until by and by, from dreading to begin on it before an audience I came to like it and enjoy it. I never knew how considerable the changes had been when I finished the season's work; I never knew until ten or eleven years later, when I took up that book in a parlor in New York one night to read that chapter to a dozen friends of the two sexes who had asked for it. It *wouldn't read*—that is, it wouldn't read aloud. I struggled along with it for five minutes and then gave it up and said I should have to tell the tale as best I might from memory. It turned out that my memory was equal to the emergency; it reproduced the platform form of the story pretty faithfully, after that interval of years. I still remember that form of it, I think, and I wish to recite it here, so that the reader may compare it with the story as told in *Roughing It,* [6] if he pleases, and note how different the spoken version is from the written and printed version.

The idea of the tale is to exhibit certain bad ef-

3. **John B. Gough . . . attraction:** Gough (1817–86) was a famous temperance lecturer. Beecher (1813–87) had made his reputation by antislavery discourses in this country and in England. Later he spoke often on evolution and religion, and on many other topics. Miss Dickinson (1842–1932) specialized in slavery and women's rights. Phillips (1811–84), also a noted antislavery orator before the Civil War, subsequently lectured on historical, literary, and humanitarian subjects.   4. **Cable:** George Washington Cable (1844–1925), a native of New Orleans and a Confederate veteran, aroused such hostility in the South with articles and speeches on the rights of the Negro that he was forced to move with his family to Massachusetts. The tour he made with Mark Twain lasted four months in the winter of 1884–85.

5. **Major Pond:** James B. Pond (1838–1903) had bought out Redpath's interest in the Boston Lyceum Bureau in 1875 and had opened his own lecture agency in New York in 1879. 6. **as told in *Roughing It*:** The version from *Roughing It* is reprinted above, pp. 73–74.

fects of a good memory: the sort of memory which is too good, which remembers everything and forgets nothing, which has no sense of proportion and can't tell an important event from an unimportant one but preserves them all, states them all, and thus retards the progress of a narrative, at the same time making a tangled, inextricable confusion of it and intolerably wearisome to the listener. The historian of "His Grandfather's Old Ram" had that kind of a memory. He often tried to communicate that history to his comrades, the other surface miners, but he could never complete it because his memory defeated his every attempt to march a straight course; it persistently threw remembered details in his way that had nothing to do with the tale; these unrelated details would interest him and sidetrack him; if he came across a name or a family or any other thing that had nothing to do with his tale, he would diverge from his course to tell about the person who owned that name or explain all about that family —with the result that as he plodded on he always got further and further from his grandfather's memorable adventure with the ram, and finally went to sleep before he got to the end of the story, and so did his comrades. Once he did manage to approach so nearly to the end, apparently, that the boys were filled with an eager hope; they believed that at last they were going to find out all about the grandfather's adventure and what it was that had happened. After the usual preliminaries, the historian said:

"Well, as I was a-sayin', he bought that old ram from a feller up in Siskiyou County and fetched him home and turned him loose in the medder, and next morning he went down to have a look at him, and accident'ly dropped a ten-cent piece in the grass and stooped down—so—and was a-fumblin' around in the grass to git it, and the ram he was a-standin' up the slope taking notice; but my grandfather wasn't taking notice, because he had his back to the ram and was int'rested about the dime. Well, there he was, as I was a-sayin', down at the foot of the slope a-bendin' over—so—fumblin' in the grass, and the ram he was up there at the top of the slope, and Smith—Smith was a-standin' there—no, not jest there, a little further away—fifteen foot perhaps—well, my grandfather was a-stoopin' way down—so—and the ram was up there observing, you know, and Smith he . . . (musing) . . . the ram he bent his head down, so . . . Smith of Calaveras . . . no, no it couldn't ben Smith of Calaveras—I remember now that he—b'George it was Smith of Tulare County—course it was, I remember it now perfectly plain.

"Well, Smith he stood just there, and my grandfather he stood just here, you know, and he was a-bendin' down just so, fumblin' in the grass, and when the old ram see him in that attitude he took it fur an invitation—and here he come! down the slope thirty mile an hour and his eye full of business. You see my grandfather's back being to him, and him stooping down like that, of course he—why sho! it *warn't* Smith of Tulare at all, it was Smith of Sacramento—my goodness, how did I ever come to get them Smiths mixed like that—why, Smith of Tulare was jest a nobody, but Smith of Sacramento—why the Smiths of Sacramento come of the best Southern blood in the United States; there warn't ever any better blood south of the line than the Sacramento Smiths. Why look here, one of them married a Whitaker! I reckon that gives you an idea of the kind of society the Sacramento Smiths could 'sociate around in; there ain't no better blood than that Whitaker blood; I reckon anybody'll tell you that.

"Look at Mariar Whitaker—there was a girl for you! Little? Why yes, she was little, but what of that? Look at the heart of her—had a heart like a bullock—just as good and sweet and lovely and generous as the day is long; if she had a thing and you wanted it, you could have it—have it and welcome; why Mariar Whitaker couldn't have a thing and another person need it and not get it—get it and welcome. She had a glass eye, and she used to lend it to Flora Ann Baxter that hadn't any, to receive company with; well, she was pretty large, and it didn't fit; it was a number seven, and she was excavated for a fourteen, and so that eye wouldn't lay still; every time she winked it would turn over. It was a beautiful eye and set her off admirable, because it was a lovely pale blue on the front side—the side you look out of—and it was gilded on the back side; didn't match the other eye, which was one of them browny-yellery eyes and tranquil and quiet, you know, the way that kind of eyes are; but that warn't any matter—they worked together all right and plenty picturesque. When Flora Ann winked, that blue and gilt eye would whirl over, and the other one stand still, and as soon as she begun to get excited that handmade eye would give a whirl and then go on a-whirlin' and a-whirlin' faster and faster, and a-flashin' first blue and then yaller and then blue and then yaller, and when it got to whizzing and flashing like that, the oldest man in the world couldn't keep up with the expression on that side of her face. Flora Ann Baxter married a Hogadorn. I reckon that lets you understand what kind of blood she was—old Maryland Eastern Shore blood; not a better family in the United States than the Hogadorns.

"Sally—that's Sally Hogadorn—Sally married a missionary, and they went off carrying the good news to the cannibals out in one of them way-off islands round the world in the middle of the ocean somers, and they et her; et him too, which was irregular; it warn't the custom to eat the missionary, but only the family, and when they see what they had done they was dreadful sorry about it, and when the relations sent down there to fetch away the things they said so—said so right out—said they was sorry, and 'pologized, and said it shouldn't happen again; said 'twas an accident.

"Accident! now that's foolishness; there ain't no such thing as an accident; there ain't nothing happens in the world but what's ordered just so by a wiser Power than us, and it's always fur a good purpose; we don't know what the good purpose was, sometimes—and it was the same with the families that was short a missionary and his wife. But that ain't no matter, and it ain't any of our business; all that concerns us is that it was a special providence and it had a good intention. No, sir, there ain't no such thing as an accident. Whenever a thing happens that you think is an accident you make up your mind it ain't no accident at all—it's a special providence.

"You look at my Uncle Lem—what do you say to that? That's all I ask you—you just look at my Uncle Lem and talk to me about accidents! It is like this: one day my Uncle Lem and his dog was downtown, and he was a-leanin' up against a scaffolding—sick, or drunk, or somethin'—and there was an Irishman with a hod of bricks up the ladder along about the third story, and his foot slipped and down he come, bricks and all, and hit a stranger fair and square and knocked the everlasting aspirations out of him; he was ready for the coroner in two minutes. Now then people said it was an accident.

"Accident! there warn't no accident about it; 'twas a special providence, and had a mysterious, noble intention back of it. The idea was to save that Irishman. If the stranger hadn't been there that Irishman would have been killed. The people said 'special providence—sho! the dog was there—why didn't the Irishman fall on the dog? Why warn't the dog app'inted?' Fer a mighty good reason—the dog would 'a' seen him a-coming; you can't depend on no dog to carry out a special providence. You couldn't hit a dog with an Irishman because—lemme see, what was that dog's name . . . (musing) . . . oh, yes, Jasper—and a mighty good dog too; he wa'n't no common dog, he wa'n't no mongrel; he was a composite. A composite dog is a dog that's made up of all the valuable qualities that's in the dog breed—kind of a syndicate; and a mongrel is made up of the riff-raff that's left over. That Jasper was one of the most wonderful dogs you ever see. Uncle Lem got him of the Wheelers. I reckon you've heard of the Wheelers; ain't no better blood south of the line than the Wheelers.

"Well, one day Wheeler was a-meditating and dreaming around in the carpet factory and the machinery made a snatch at him and first you know he was a-meandering all over that factory, from the garret to the cellar, and everywhere, at such another gait as—why, you couldn't even see him; you could only hear him whiz when he went by. Well, you know a person can't go through an experience like that and arrive back home the way he was when he went. No, Wheeler got wove up into thirty-nine yards of best three-ply carpeting. The widder was sorry, she was uncommon sorry, and loved him and done the best she could fur him in the circumstances, which was unusual. She took the whole piece—thirty-nine yards—and she wanted to give him proper and honorable burial, but she couldn't bear to roll him up; she took and spread him out full length, and said she wouldn't have it any other way. She wanted a buy a tunnel for him but there wasn't any tunnel for sale, so she boxed him in a beautiful box and stood it on the hill on a pedestal twenty-one foot high, and so it was monument and grave together, and economical—sixty foot high—you could see it from everywhere—and she painted on it 'To the loving memory of thirty-nine yards best three-ply carpeting containing the mortal remainders of Millington G. Wheeler go thou and do likewise.' "

At this point the historian's voice began to wobble and his eyelids to droop with weariness, and he fell asleep; and so from that day to this we are still in ignorance; we don't know whether the old grandfather ever got the ten-cent piece out of the grass; we haven't any idea what it was that happened, or whether anything happened at all.

Upon comparing the above with the original in *Roughing It,* I find myself unable to clearly and definitely explain why the one can be effectively *recited* before an audience and the other can't; there is a reason but it is too subtle for adequate conveyance by the lumbering vehicle of words; I sense it but cannot express it; it is as elusive as an odor, pungent, pervasive, but defying analysis. I give it up. I merely know that the one version will recite, and the other won't.

By reciting I mean, of course, delivery from memory; neither version can be read effectively from the book. There are plenty of good reasons why this should be so, but there is one reason which is sufficient by itself, perhaps; in reading from the book you are telling another person's tale at secondhand; you are a mimic, and not the person involved; you are an artificiality, not a reality; whereas in telling the tale without the book you absorb the character and presently become the man himself, just as is the case with the actor.

The greatest actor would not be able to carry his audience by storm with a book in his hand; reading from the book renders the nicest shadings of delivery impossible. I mean those studied fictions which seem to be the impulse of the moment and which are so effective: such as, for instance, fictitious hesitancies for the right word, fictitious unconscious pauses, fictitious unconscious side remarks, fictitious unconscious embarrassments, fictitious unconscious emphases placed upon the wrong word with a deep intention back of it— these and all the other artful fictive shades which give to a recited tale the captivating naturalness of an impromptu narration can be attempted by a book reader and are attempted, but they are easily detectable as artifice, and although the audience may admire their cleverness and their ingenuity as artifice, they only get at the intellect of the house, they don't get at its heart; and so the reader's success lacks a good deal of being complete.

When a man is reading from a book on the platform, he soon realizes that there is one powerful gun in his battery of artifice that he can't work with an effect proportionate to its caliber: that is the *pause*—that impressive silence, that eloquent silence, that geometrically progressive silence which often achieves a desired effect where no combination of words howsoever felicitous could accomplish it. The pause is not of much use to the man who is reading from a book because he cannot know what the exact length of it ought to be; he is not the one to determine the measurement— the audience must do that for him. He must perceive by their faces when the pause has reached the proper length, but his eyes are not on the faces, they are on the book; therefore he must determine the proper length of the pause by guess; he cannot guess with exactness and nothing but exactness, absolute exactness, will answer.

The man who recites without the book has all the advantage; when he comes to an old familiar remark in his tale which he has uttered nightly for a hundred nights—a remark preceded or followed by a pause—the faces of the audience tell him when to end the pause. For one audience the pause will be short, for another a little longer, for another a shade longer still; the performer must vary the length of the pause to suit the shades of

difference between audiences. These variations of measurement are so slight, so delicate, that they may almost be compared with the shadings achieved by Pratt and Whitney's ingenious machine which measures the five-millionth part of an inch. An audience is that machine's twin; it can measure a pause down to that vanishing fraction.

I used to play with the pause as other children play with a toy. In my recitals, when I went reading around the world for the benefit of Mr. Webster's creditors,[7] I had three or four pieces in which the pauses performed an important part, and I used to lengthen them or shorten them according to the requirements of the case, and I got much pleasure out of the pause when it was accurately measured, and a certain discomfort when it wasn't. In the negro ghost story of "The Golden Arm"[8] one of these pauses occurs just in front of the closing remark. Whenever I got the pause the right length, the remark that followed it was sure of a satisfactorily startling effect, but if the length of the pause was wrong by the five-millionth of an inch, the audience had had time in that infinitesimal fraction of a moment to wake up from its deep concentration in the grisly tale and foresee the climax, and be prepared for it before it burst upon them—and so it fell flat.

In Susy's little biography of me she tells about my proceeding to tell this ghost tale to the multitude of young lady students at Vassar College[9]— a tale which poor Susy always dreaded—and she tells how this time she gathered her fortitude together and was resolved that she wouldn't be startled, and how all her preparations were of no avail, and how when the climax fell that multitude of girls "jumped as one man"—which is an indication that I had the pause rightly measured that time.

In "His Grandfather's Old Ram" a pause has place; it follows a certain remark, and Mrs. Clemens and Clara, when we were on our way around the world, would afflict themselves with my whole performance every night when there was no sort of necessity for it, in order that they might watch the house when that pause came; they believed that by the effect they could accurately measure the high or low intelligence of the audience. I

7. **Mr. Webster's creditors:** It was a fixed idea of Clemens in his last years that his financial disaster in 1894 had been caused by Charles L. Webster's mismanagement of the publishing company that bore his name. This notion was erroneous, as is evident from the correspondence published by Webster's son, Samuel C. Webster, in *Mark Twain, Business Man* (1946). When Charles L. Webster retired from the company on account of ill health in 1888, its affairs were in a sound condition.
8. **"The Golden Arm":** The story is reprinted above, p. 98.
9. **at Vassar College:** on May 15, 1885.

knew better but it was not in my interest to say so. When the pause was right, the effect was sure; when the pause was wrong in length, by the five-millionth of an inch, the laughter was only mild, never a crash. That passage occurs in "His Grand-father's Old Ram" where the question under dis-cussion is whether the falling of the Irishman on the stranger was an accident, or was a special providence. If it was a special providence, and if the sole purpose of it was to save the Irishman, why was it necessary to sacrifice the stranger? "The dog was there. Why didn't he fall on the dog? Why wa'n't the dog app'inted? Becuz *the dog would 'a' seen him a-comin'*." That last remark was the one the family waited for. A pause *after* the remark was absolutely necessary with any and all audiences because no man, howsoever intelligent he may be, can instantly adjust his mind to a new and unfamiliar, and yet for a moment or two apparently plausible, logic which recog-nizes in a dog an instrument too indifferent to pious restraints and too alert in looking out for his own personal interest to be safely depended upon in an emergency requiring self-sacrifice for the benefit of another, even when the command comes from on high.

PART IV:
SOCIAL CRITICISM

◊

⟨ IN San Francisco in the 1860's, Mark Twain was some-times called "The Moralist of the Main" in joking ac-knowledgment of his concern with social abuses. He criticized speculators in mining stocks, volunteer fire de-partments, undertakers, and especially the police force, which he accused of brutality to Chinese and to all prisoners without money or influential friends. Many passages in *The Innocents Abroad* are devoted to the poverty, filth, and disease which Mark Twain considered the result of corrupt or despotic government in Italy and the Near East. *The Gilded Age* satirizes graft in the Fed-eral Congress; *Huckleberry Finn* is, among other things, a powerful attack on Negro slavery; and *The Prince and the Pauper* and *A Connecticut Yankee in King Arthur's Court* make frontal assaults on various forms of tyranny and inhumane punishments for crime. But his most pow-erful satire belongs to the last fifteen years of his life, when he had become convinced that accumulating wealth had caused a "moral rot" in American life and broadened the scope of his invective to denounce what

he believed to be the universal and ineradicable coward-ice, cruelty, and hypocrisy of mankind. The unfinished moral fable *The Mysterious Stranger* is the major work of this period. Its indictment of the human race was anticipated, however, in *Pudd'nhead Wilson* (1894) and *The Man That Corrupted Hadleyburg* (1899). *The Man That Corrupted Hadleyburg* is also re-markable for the hard symmetry of its plot and its severe economy of means.

◊

A TRUE STORY REPEATED
WORD FOR WORD AS
I HEARD IT

⟨ FIRST published in the *Atlantic Monthly* (November, 1874), this was Mark Twain's first contribution to the *Atlantic*. Publication in that magazine, recognized as the highest-ranking literary journal in the United States, conferred a status on the author that no amount of popular success could have earned for him. The setting of the sketch is the porch of the Cranes's house on Quarry Farm, and "Aunt Rachel" is Auntie Cord, the Cranes's cook. Many years later Howells recalled "A True Story" as "one of those noble pieces of humanity with which the South has atoned chiefly, if not solely, through him for all its despite to the Negro." The text is taken from the Definitive Edition, Vol. VII.

IT WAS summer-time, and twilight. We were sit-ting on the porch of the farmhouse, on the summit of the hill, and "Aunt Rachel" was sitting respect-fully below our level, on the steps—for she was our servant, and colored. She was of mighty frame and stature; she was sixty years old, but her eye was undimmed and her strength unabated. She was a cheerful, hearty soul, and it was no more trouble for her to laugh than it is for a bird to sing. She was under fire now, as usual when the day was done. That is to say, she was being chaffed without mercy, and was enjoying it. She would let off peal after peal of laughter, and then sit with her face in her hands and shake with throes of enjoyment which she could no longer get breath enough to express. At such a moment as this a thought oc-curred to me, and I said:

"Aunt Rachel, how is it that you've lived sixty years and never had any trouble?"

She stopped quaking. She paused, and there was a moment of silence. She turned her face over her shoulder toward me, and said, without even a smile in her voice:

"Misto C——, is you in 'arnest?"

It surprised me a good deal; and it sobered my manner and my speech, too. I said:

"Why, I thought—that is, I meant—why, you *can't* have had any trouble. I've never heard you sigh, and never seen your eye when there wasn't a laugh in it."

She faced fairly around now, and was full of earnestness.

"Has I had any trouble? Misto C——, I's gwyne to tell you, den I leave it to you. I was bawn down 'mongst de slaves; I knows all 'bout slavery, 'case I ben one of 'em my own se'f. Well, sah, my ole man—dat's my husban'—he was lovin' an' kind to me, jist as kind as you is to yo' own wife. An' we had chil'en—seven chil'en—an' we loved dem chil'en jist de same as you loves yo' chil'en. Dey was black, but de Lord can't make no chil'en so black but what dey mother loves 'em an' wouldn't give 'em up, no, not for anything dat's in dis whole world.

"Well, sah, I was raised in ole Fo'ginny, but my mother she was raised in Maryland; an' my *souls!* she was turrible when she'd git started! My *lan'!* but she'd make de fur fly! When she'd git into dem tantrums, she always had one word dat she said. She'd straighten herse'f up an' put her fists in her hips an' say, 'I want you to understan' dat I wa'n't bawn in de mash to be fool' by trash! I's one o' de ole Blue Hen's Chickens, *I* is!' 'Ca'se, you see, dat's what folks dat's bawn in Maryland calls deyselves, an' dey's proud of it. Well, dat was her word. I don't ever forgit it, beca'se she said it so much, an' beca'se she said it one day when my little Henry tore his wris' awful, and most busted his head, right up at de top of his forehead, an' de niggers didn't fly aroun' fas' enough to 'tend to him. An' when dey talk' back at her, she up an' she says, 'Look-a-heah!' she says, 'I want you niggers to understan' dat I wa'n't bawn in de mash to be fool' by trash! I's one o' de ole Blue Hen's Chickens, *I* is!' an' den she clar' dat kitchen an' bandage' up de chile herse'f. So I says dat word, too, when I's riled.

"Well, bymeby my ole mistis say she's broke, an' she got to sell all de niggers on de place. An' when I heah dat dey gwyne to sell us all off at oc-tion in Richmon', oh, de good gracious! I know what dat mean!"

Aunt Rachel had gradually risen, while she warmed to her subject, and now she towered above us, black against the stars.

"Dey put chains on us an' put us on a stan' as high as dis po'ch—twenty foot high—an' all de people stood aroun', crowds an' crowds. An' dey'd come up dah an' look at us all roun', an' squeeze our arm, an' make us git up an' walk, an' den say, 'Dis one too ole,' or 'Dis one lame,' or 'Dis one don't 'mount to much.' An' dey sole my ole man, an' took him away, an' dey begin to sell my chil'en an' take *dem* away, an' I begin to cry; an' de

man say, 'Shet up yo' damn blubberin',' an' hit me on de mouf wid his han'. An' when de las' one was gone but my little Henry, I grab *him* clost up to my breas' so, an' I ris up an' says, 'You sha'n't take him away,' I says; 'I'll kill de man dat tetches him!' I says. But my little Henry whisper an' say, 'I gwyne to run away, an' den I work an' buy yo' freedom.' Oh, bless de chile, he always so good! But dey got him—dey got him, de men did; but I took and tear de clo'es mos' off of 'em an' beat 'em over de head wid my chain; an' *dey* give it to *me*, too, but I didn't mine dat.

"Well, dah was my ole man gone, an' all my chil'en, all my seven chil'en—an' six of 'em I hain't set eyes on ag'in to dis day, an' dat's twenty-two year ago las' Easter. De man dat bought me b'long' in Newbern, an' he took me dah. Well, bymeby de years roll on an' de waw come. My marster he was a Confedrit colonel, an' I was his family's cook. So when de Unions took dat town, dey all run away an' lef' me all by myse'f wid de other niggers in dat mons'us big house. So de big Union officers move in dah, an' dey ask me would I cook for *dem*. 'Lord bless you,' says I, 'dat's what I's *for*.'

"Dey wa'n't no small-fry officers, mine you, dey was de biggest dey *is;* an' de way dey made dem sojers mosey roun'! De Gen'l he tole me to boss dat kitchen; an' he say, 'If anybody come meddlin' wid you, you jist make 'em walk chalk; don't you be afeared,' he say; 'you's 'mong frens now.'

"Well, I thinks to myse'f, if my little Henry ever got a chance to run away, he'd make to de Norf, o' course. So one day I comes in dah whar de big officers was, in de parlor, an' I drops a kurtchy, so, an' I up an' tole 'em 'bout my Henry, dey a-listenin' to my troubles jist de same as if I was white folks; an' I says, 'What I come for is beca'se if he got away and got up Norf whar you gemmen comes from, you might 'a' seen him, maybe, an' could tell me so as I could fine him ag'in; he was very little, an' he had a sk-yar on his lef' wris' an' at de top of his forehead.' Den dey look mournful, an' de Gen'l says, 'How long since you los' him?' an' I say, 'Thirteen year.' Den de Gen'l say, 'He wouldn't be little no mo' now—he's a man!'

"I never thought o' dat befo'! He was only dat little feller to *me* yit. I never thought 'bout him growin' up an' being' big. But I see it den. None o' de gemmen had run acrost him, so dey couldn't do nothin' for me. But all dat time, do' *I* didn't know it, my Henry *was* run off to de Norf, years an' years, an' he was a barber, too, an' worked for hisse'f. An' bymeby, when de waw come he ups an' he says: 'I's done barberin',' he says, 'I's gwyne to fine my ole mammy, less'n she's dead.' So he sole out an' went to whar dey was recruitin', an' hired hisse'f out to de colonel for his servant; an' den he went all froo de battles everywhah, huntin' for his ole mammy; yes, indeedy, he'd hire to fust one officer an' den another, tell he'd ransacked de whole Souf; but you see *I* didn't know nuffin 'bout *dis.* How was *I* gwyne to know it?

"Well, one night we had a big sojer ball; de sojers dah at Newbern was always havin' balls an' carryin' on. Dey had 'em in my kitchen, heaps o' times, 'ca'se it was so big. Mine you, I was *down* on sich doin's; beca'se my place was wid de officers, an' it rasp me to have dem common sojers cavortin' roun' my kitchen like dat. But I alway' stood aroun' an' kep' things straight, I did; an' sometimes dey'd git my dander up, an' den I'd make 'em clar dat kitchen, mine I *tell* you!

"Well, one night—it was a Friday night—dey comes a whole platoon f'm a *nigger* ridgment dat was on guard at de house—de house was headquarters, you know—an' den I was jist a-*bilin'!* Mad? I was jist a-*boomin'!* I swelled aroun', an' swelled aroun'; I jist was a-itchin' for 'em to do somefin for to start me. *An'* dey was a-waltzin' an' a-dancin'! *my!* but dey was havin' a time! an' I jist a-swellin' an' a-swellin' up! Pooty soon, 'long comes *sich* a spruce young nigger a-sailin' down de room wid a yaller wench roun' de wais'; an' roun' an' roun' an' roun' dey went, enough to make a body drunk to look at 'em; an' when dey got abreas' o' me, dey went to kin' o' balacin' aroun' fust on one leg an' den on t'other, an' smilin' at my big red turban, an' makin' fun, an' I ups an' says '*Git* along wid you!—rubbage!' De young man's face kin' o' changed, all of a sudden, for 'bout a second, but den he went to smilin' ag'in, same as he was befo'. Well, 'bout dis time, in comes some niggers dat played music and b'long' to de ban', an' dey *never* could git along widout puttin' on airs. An' de very fust air dey put on dat night, I lit into 'em! Dey laughed, an' dat made me wuss. De res' o' de niggers got to laughin', an' den my soul *alive* but I was hot! My eye was jist a-blazin'! I jist straightened myself up so—jist as I is now, plum to de ceilin', mos'—an' I digs my fists into my hips, an' I says, 'Look-a-heah!' I says, 'I want you niggers to understan' dat I wa'n't bawn in de mash to be fool' by trash! I's one o' de ole Blue Hen's Chickens, *I* is!' an' den I see dat young man stan' a-starin' an' stiff, lookin' kin' o' up at de ceilin' like he fo'got somefin, an' couldn't 'member it no mo'. Well, I jist march' on dem niggers—so, lookin' like a gen'l—

an' dey jist cave' away befo' me an' out at de do'. An' as dis young man was a-goin' out, I heah him say to another nigger, 'Jim,' he says, 'you go 'long an' tell de cap'n I be on han' 'bout eight o'clock in de mawnin'; dey's somefin on my mine,' he says; 'I don't sleep no mo' dis night. You go 'long,' he says, 'an' leave me by my own se'f.'

"Dis was 'bout one o'clock in de mawnin'. Well, 'bout seven, I was up an' on han', gittin' de officers' breakfast. I was a-stoopin' down by de stove—jist so, same as if yo' foot was de stove—an' I'd opened de stove do' wid my right han'—so, pushin' it back, jist as I pushes yo' foot—an' I'd jist got de pan o' hot biscuits in my han' an' was 'bout to raise up, when I see a black face come aroun' under mine, an' de eyes a-lookin' up into mine, jist as I's a-lookin' up clost under yo' face now; an' I jist stopped *right dah,* an' never budged! jist gazed an' gazed so; an' de pan begin to tremble, an' all of a sudden I *knowed!* De pan drop' on de flo' an' I grab his lef' han' an' shove back his sleeve—jist so, as I's doin' to you—an' den I goes for his forehead an' push de hair back so, an' 'Boy!' I says, 'if you an't my Henry, what is you doin' wid dis welt on yo' wris' an' dat sk-yar on yo' forehead? De Lord God ob heaven be praise', I got my own ag'in!'

"Oh no, Misto C——, *I* hain't had no trouble. An' no *joy!*"

THE MAN THAT CORRUPTED HADLEYBURG

《 FIRST published in *Harper's Magazine* (December, 1899), this tale was written at a time when Mark Twain was also working on *The Mysterious Stranger.* The outsider who decides to corrupt Hadleyburg belongs to the series of transcendent figures of which Satan in *The Mysterious Stranger* is the fully developed example; indeed, Richards in his delirium says that the checks given to him by the stranger "came from Satan." The story is an apologue on Mark Twain's favorite theme in this period, "the damned human race." The text that follows is from the Definitive Edition, Vol. XXIII.

I

IT WAS many years ago. Hadleyburg was the most honest and upright town in all the region around about. It had kept that reputation unsmirched during three generations, and was prouder of it than of any other of its possessions. It was so proud of it, and so anxious to insure its perpetuation, that it began to teach the principles of honest dealing to its babies in the cradle, and made the like teachings the staple of their culture thenceforward through all the years devoted to their education. Also, throughout the formative years temptations were kept out of the way of the young people, so that their honesty could have every chance to harden and solidify, and become a part of their very bone. The neighboring towns were jealous of this honorable supremacy, and affected to sneer at Hadleyburg's pride in it and call it vanity; but all the same they were obliged to acknowledge that Hadleyburg was in reality an incorruptible town; and if pressed they would also acknowledge that the mere fact that a young man hailed from Hadleyburg was all the recommendation he needed when he went forth from his natal town to seek for responsible employment.

But at last, in the drift of time, Hadleyburg had the ill luck to offend a passing stranger—possibly without knowing it, certainly without caring, for Hadleyburg was sufficient unto itself, and cared not a rap for strangers or their opinions. Still, it would have been well to make an exception in this one's case, for he was a bitter man and revengeful. All through his wanderings during a whole year he kept his injury in mind, and gave all his leisure moments to trying to invent a compensating satisfaction for it. He contrived many plans, and all of them were good, but none of them was quite sweeping enough; the poorest of them would hurt a great many individuals, but what he wanted was a plan which would comprehend the entire town, and not let so much as one person escape unhurt. At last he had a fortunate idea, and when it fell into his brain it lit up his whole head with an evil joy. He began to form a plan at once, saying to himself, "That is the thing to do—I will corrupt the town."

Six months later he went to Hadleyburg, and arrived in a buggy at the house of the old cashier of the bank about ten at night. He got a sack out of the buggy, shouldered it, and staggered with it through the cottage yard, and knocked at the door. A woman's voice said "Come in," and he entered, and set his sack behind the stove in the parlor, saying politely to the old lady who sat reading the *Missionary Herald* by the lamp:

"Pray keep your seat, madam, I will not disturb you. There—now it is pretty well concealed; one would hardly know it was there. Can I see your husband a moment, madam?"

No, he was gone to Brixton, and might not return before morning.

"Very well, madam, it is no matter. I merely wanted to leave that sack in his care, to be delivered to the rightful owner when he shall be found. I am a stranger; he does not know me; I am merely passing through the town to-night to discharge a matter which has been long in my mind. My errand is now completed, and I go pleased and a little proud, and you will never see me again. There is a paper attached to the sack which will explain everything. Good night, madam."

The old lady was afraid of the mysterious big stranger, and was glad to see him go. But her curiosity was roused, and she went straight to the sack and brought away the paper. It began as follows:

TO BE PUBLISHED; or, the right man sought out by private inquiry—either will answer. This sack contains gold coin weighing a hundred and sixty pounds four ounces—

"Mercy on us, and the door not locked!"

Mrs. Richards flew to it all in a tremble and locked it, then pulled down the window-shades and stood frightened, worried, and wondering if there was anything else she could do toward making herself and the money more safe. She listened awhile for burglars, then surrendered to curiosity and went back to the lamp and finished reading the paper:

I am a foreigner, and am presently going back to my own country, to remain there permanently. I am grateful to America for what I have received at her hands during my long stay under her flag; and to one of her citizens—a citizen of Hadleyburg—I am especially grateful for a great kindness done me a year or two ago. Two great kindnesses, in fact. I will explain. I was a gambler. I say I WAS. I was a ruined gambler. I arrived in this village at night, hungry and without a penny. I asked for help—in the dark; I was ashamed to beg in the light. I begged of the right man. He gave me twenty dollars—that is to say, he gave me life, as I considered it. He also gave me fortune; for out of that money I have made myself rich at the gaming-table. And finally, a remark which he made to me has remained with me to this day, and has at last conquered me; and in conquering has saved the remnant of my morals; I shall gamble no more. Now I have no idea who that man was, but I want him found, and I want him to have this money, to give away, throw away, or keep, as he pleases. It is merely my way of testifying my gratitude to him. If I could stay, I would find him myself; but no matter, he will be found. This is an honest town, an incorruptible town, and I know I can trust it without fear. This man can be identified by the remark which he made to me; I feel persuaded that he will remember it.

And now my plan is this: If you prefer to conduct the inquiry privately, do so. Tell the contents of this present writing to any one who is likely to be the right man. If he shall answer, 'I am the man; the remark I made was so-and-so,' apply the test—to wit: open the sack, and in it you will find a sealed envelope containing that remark. If the remark mentioned by the candidate tallies with it, give him the money, and ask no further questions, for he is certainly the right man.

But if you shall prefer a public inquiry, then publish this present writing in the local paper—with these instructions added, to wit: Thirty days from now, let the candidate appear at the town-hall at eight in the evening (Friday), and hand his remark, in a sealed envelope, to the Rev. Mr. Burgess (if he will be kind enough to act); and let Mr. Burgess there and then destroy the seals of the sack, open it, and see if the remark is correct; if correct, let the money be delivered, with my sincere gratitude, to my benefactor thus identified.

Mrs. Richards sat down, gently quivering with excitement, and was soon lost in thinkings—after this pattern: "What a strange thing it is! . . . And what a fortune for that kind man who set his bread afloat upon the waters! . . . If it had only been my husband that did it!—for we are so poor, so old and poor! . . ." Then, with a sigh—"But it was not my Edward; no, it was not he that gave a stranger twenty dollars. It is a pity, too; I see it now. . . ." Then, with a shudder—"But it is *gambler's* money! the wages of sin: we couldn't take it; we couldn't touch it. I don't like to be near it; it seems a defilement." She moved to a farther chair. . . . "I wish Edward would come and take it to the bank; a burglar might come at any moment; it is dreadful to be here all alone with it."

At eleven Mr. Richards arrived, and while his wife was saying, "I am *so* glad you've come!" he was saying, "I'm so tired—tired clear out; it is dreadful to be poor, and have to make these dismal journeys at my time of life. Always at the grind, grind, grind, on a salary—another man's slave, and he sitting at home in his slippers, rich and comfortable."

"I am so sorry for you, Edward, you know that; but be comforted: we have our livelihood; we have our good name—"

"Yes, Mary, and that is everything. Don't mind my talk—it's just a moment's irritation and doesn't mean anything. Kiss me—there, it's all gone now, and I am not complaining any more. What have you been getting? What's in the sack?"

Then his wife told him the great secret. It dazed him for a moment; then he said:

"It weighs a hundred and sixty pounds? Why, Mary, it's for-ty thou-sand dollars—think of it—a whole fortune! Not ten men in this village are worth that much. Give me the paper."

He skimmed through it and said:

"Isn't it an adventure! Why, it's a romance; it's like the impossible things one reads about in books, and never sees in life." He was well stirred up now; cheerful, even gleeful. He tapped his old wife on the cheek, and said, humorously, "Why,

we're rich, Mary, rich; all we've got to do is to bury the money and burn the papers. If the gambler ever comes to inquire, we'll merely look coldly upon him and say: 'What is this nonsense you are talking? We have never heard of you and your sack of gold before'; and then he would look foolish, and—"

"And in the mean time, while you are running on with your jokes, the money is still here, and it is fast getting along toward burglar-time."

"True. Very well, what shall we do—make the inquiry private? No, not that: it would spoil the romance. The public method is better. Think what a noise it will make! And it will make all the other towns jealous; for no stranger would trust such a thing to any town but Hadleyburg, and they know it. It's a great card for us. I must get to the printing-office now, or I shall be too late."

"But stop—stop—don't leave me here alone with it, Edward!"

But he was gone. For only a little while, however. Not far from his own house he met the editor-proprietor of the paper, and gave him the document, and said, "Here is a good thing for you, Cox—put it in."

"It may be too late, Mr. Richards, but I'll see."

At home again he and his wife sat down to talk the charming mystery over; they were in no condition for sleep. The first question was, Who could the citizen have been who gave the stranger the twenty dollars? It seemed a simple one; both answered it in the same breath:

"Barclay Goodson."

"Yes," said Richards, "he could have done it, and it would have been like him, but there's not another in the town."

"Everybody will grant that, Edward—grant it privately, anyway. For six months, now, the village has been its own proper self once more—honest, narrow, self-righteous, and stingy."

"It is what he always called it, to the day of his death—said it right out publicly, too."

"Yes, and he was hated for it."

"Oh, of course; but he didn't care. I reckon he was the best-hated man among us, except the Reverend Burgess."

"Well, Burgess deserves it—he will never get another congregation here. Mean as the town is, it knows how to estimate *him*. Edward, doesn't it seem odd that the stranger should appoint Burgess to deliver the money?"

"Well, yes—it does. That is—that is—"

"Why so much that-*is*-ing? Would *you* select him?"

"Mary, maybe the stranger knows him better than this village does."

"Much *that* would help Burgess!"

The husband seemed perplexed for an answer; the wife kept a steady eye upon him, and waited. Finally Richards said, with the hesitancy of one who is making a statement which is likely to encounter doubt:

"Mary, Burgess is not a bad man."

His wife was certainly surprised.

"Nonsense!" she exclaimed.

"He is not a bad man. I know. The whole of his unpopularity had its foundation in that one thing —the thing that made so much noise."

"That 'one thing,' indeed! As if that 'one thing' wasn't enough, all by itself."

"Plenty. Plenty. Only he wasn't guilty of it."

"How you talk! Not guilty of it! Everybody knows he *was* guilty."

"Mary, I give you my word—he was innocent."

"I can't believe it, and I don't. How do you know?"

"It is a confession. I am ashamed, but I will make it. I was the only man who knew he was innocent. I could have saved him, and—and—well, you know how the town was wrought up—I hadn't the pluck to do it. It would have turned everybody against me. I felt mean, ever so mean; but I didn't dare; I hadn't the manliness to face that."

Mary looked troubled, and for a while was silent. Then she said, stammeringly:

"I—I don't think it would have done for you to—to— One mustn't—er—public opinion—one has to be so careful—so—" It was a difficult road, and she got mired; but after a little she got started again. "It was a great pity, but— Why, we couldn't afford it, Edward—we couldn't indeed. Oh, I wouldn't have had you do it for anything!"

"It would have lost us the good will of so many people, Mary; and then—and then—"

"What troubles me now is, what *he* thinks of us, Edward."

"He? *He* doesn't suspect that I could have saved him."

"Oh," exclaimed the wife, in a tone of relief, "I am glad of that! As long as he doesn't know that you could have saved him, he—he—well, that makes it a great deal better. Why, I might have known he didn't know, because he is always trying to be friendly with us, as little encouragement as we give him. More than once people have twitted me with it. There's the Wilsons, and the Wilcoxes, and the Harknesses, they take a mean pleasure in saying, '*Your friend* Burgess,' because they know it pesters me. I wish he wouldn't persist in liking us so; I can't think why he keeps it up."

"I can explain it. It's another confession. When the thing was new and hot, and the town made a plan to ride him on a rail, my conscience hurt me so that I couldn't stand it, and I went privately and gave him notice, and he got out of the town and staid out till it was safe to come back."

"Edward! If the town had found it out—"

"*Don't!* It scares me yet, to think of it. I repented of it the minute it was done; and I was even afraid to tell you, lest your face might betray it to somebody. I didn't sleep any that night, for worrying. But after a few days I saw that no one was going to suspect me, and after that I got to feeling glad I did it. And I feel glad yet, Mary— glad through and through."

"So do I, now, for it would have been a dreadful way to treat him. Yes, I'm glad; for really you did owe him that, you know. But, Edward, suppose it should come out yet, some day!"

"It won't."

"Why?"

"Because everybody thinks it was Goodson."

"Of course they would!"

"Certainly. And of course *he* didn't care. They persuaded poor old Sawlsberry to go and charge it on him, and he went blustering over there and did it. Goodson looked him over, like as if he was hunting for a place on him that he could despise the most, then he says, 'So you are the Committee of Inquiry, are you?' Sawlsberry said that was about what he was. 'Hm. Do they require particulars, or do you reckon a kind of a *general* answer will do?' 'If they require particulars, I will come back, Mr. Goodson; I will take the general answer first.' 'Very well, then, tell them to go to hell—I reckon that's general enough. And I'll give you some advice, Sawlsberry; when you come back for the particulars, fetch a basket to carry the relics of yourself home in.' "

"Just like Goodson; it's got all the marks. He had only one vanity: he thought he could give advice better than any other person."

"It settled the business, and saved us, Mary. The subject was dropped."

"Bless you, I'm not doubting *that*."

Then they took up the gold-sack mystery again, with strong interest. Soon the conversation began to suffer breaks—interruptions caused by absorbed thinkings. The breaks grew more and more frequent. At last Richards lost himself wholly in thought. He sat long, gazing vacantly at the floor, and by and by he began to punctuate his thoughts with little nervous movements of his hands that seemed to indicate vexation. Meantime his wife too had relapsed into a thoughtful silence, and her movements were beginning to show a troubled discomfort. Finally Richards got up and strode aimlessly about the room, plowing his hands through his hair, much as a somnambulist might do who was having a bad dream. Then he seemed to arrive at a definite purpose; and without a word he put on his hat and passed quickly out of the house. His wife sat brooding, with a drawn face, and did not seem to be aware that she was alone. Now and then she murmured, "Lead us not into t— . . . but—but—we are so poor, so poor! . . . Lead us not into . . . Ah, who would be hurt by it?—and no one would ever know. . . . Lead us . . ." The voice died out in mumblings. After a little she glanced up and muttered in a half-frightened, half-glad way:

"He is gone! But, oh dear, he may be too late —too late. . . . Maybe not—maybe there is still time." She rose and stood thinking, nervously clasping and unclasping her hands. A slight shudder shook her frame, and she said, out of a dry throat, "God forgive me—it's awful to think such things—but . . . Lord, how we are made—how strangely we are made!"

She turned the light low, and slipped stealthily over and kneeled down by the sack and felt of its ridgy sides with her hands, and fondled them lovingly; and there was a gloating light in her poor old eyes. She fell into fits of absence; and came half out of them at times to mutter, "If we had only waited!—oh, if we had only waited a little, and not been in such a hurry!"

Meantime Cox had gone home from his office and told his wife all about the strange thing that had happened, and they had talked it over eagerly, and guessed that the late Goodson was the only man in the town who could have helped a suffering stranger with so noble a sum as twenty dollars. Then there was a pause, and the two became thoughtful and silent. And by and by nervous and fidgety. At last the wife said, as if to herself:

"Nobody knows this secret but the Richardses . . . and us . . . nobody."

The husband came out of his thinkings with a slight start, and gazed wistfully at his wife, whose face was become very pale; then he hesitatingly rose, and glanced furtively at his hat, then at his wife—a sort of mute inquiry. Mrs. Cox swallowed once or twice, with her hand at her throat, then in place of speech she nodded her head. In a moment she was alone, and mumbling to herself.

And now Richards and Cox were hurrying through the deserted streets, from opposite directions. They met, panting, at the foot of the printing-office stairs; by the night light there they read each other's face. Cox whispered:

"Nobody knows about this but us?"

The whispered answer was,

"Not a soul—on honor, not a soul!"

"If it isn't too late to—"

The men were starting up-stairs; at this moment they were overtaken by a boy, and Cox asked:

"Is that you, Johnny?"

"Yes, sir."

"You needn't ship the early mail—nor *any* mail; wait till I tell you."

"It's already gone, sir."

"*Gone?*" It had the sound of an unspeakable disappointment in it.

"Yes, sir. Time-table for Bixton and all the towns beyond changed to-day, sir—had to get the papers in twenty minutes earlier than common. I had to rush; if I had been two minutes later—"

The men turned and walked slowly away, not waiting to hear the rest. Neither of them spoke during ten minutes; then Cox said, in a vexed tone:

"What possessed you to be in such a hurry, *I* can't make out."

The answer was humble enough:

"I see it now, but somehow I never thought, you know, until it was too late. But the next time—"

"Next time be hanged! It won't come in a thousand years."

Then the friends separated without a good night, and dragged themselves home with the gait of mortally stricken men. At their homes their wives sprang up with an eager "Well?"—then saw the answer with their eyes and sank down sorrowing, without waiting for it to come in words. In both houses a discussion followed of a heated sort—a new thing; there had been discussions before, but not heated ones, not ungentle ones. The discussions to-night were a sort of seeming plagiarisms of each other. Mrs. Richards said,

"If you had only waited, Edward—if you had only stopped to think; but no, you must run straight to the printing-office and spread it all over the world."

"It *said* publish it."

"That is nothing; it also said do it privately, if you liked. There, now—is that true, or not?"

"Why, yes—yes, it is true; but when I thought what a stir it would make, and what a compliment it was to Hadleyburg that a stranger should trust it so—"

"Oh, certainly, I know all that; but if you had only stopped to think, you would have seen that you *couldn't* find the right man, because he is in his grave, and hasn't left chick nor child nor relation behind him; and as long as the money went to somebody that awfully needed it, and nobody would be hurt by it, and—and—"

She broke down, crying. Her husband tried to think of some comforting thing to say, and presently came out with this:

"But after all, Mary, it must be for the best—it *must* be; we know that. And we must remember that it was so ordered—"

"Ordered! Oh, everything's *ordered,* when a person has to find some way out when he has been stupid. Just the same, it was *ordered* that the money should come to us in this special way, and it was you that must take it on yourself to go meddling with the designs of Providence—and who gave you the right? It was wicked, that is what it was—just blasphemous presumption, and no more becoming to a meek and humble professor of—"

"But, Mary, you know how we have been trained all our lives long, like the whole village, till it is absolutely second nature to us to stop not a single moment to think when there's an honest thing to be done—"

"Oh, I know it, I know it—it's been one everlasting training and training and training in honesty—honesty shielded, from the very cradle, against every possible temptation, and so it's *artificial* honesty, and weak as water when temptation comes, as we have seen this night. God knows I never had shade nor shadow of a doubt of my petrified and indestructible honesty until now—and now, under the very first big and real temptation, I—Edward, it is my belief that this town's honesty is as rotten as mine is; as rotten as yours is. It is a mean town, a hard, stingy town, and hasn't a virtue in the world but this honesty it is so celebrated for and so conceited about; and so help me, I do believe that if ever the day comes that its honesty falls under great temptation, its grand reputation will go to ruin like a house of cards. There, now, I've made confession, and I feel better; I am a humbug, and I've been one all my life, without knowing it. Let no man call me honest again—I will not have it."

"I—well, Mary, I feel a good deal as you do; I certainly do. It seems strange, too, so strange. I never could have believed it—never."

A long silence followed; both were sunk in thought. At last the wife looked up and said:

"I know what you are thinking, Edward."

Richards had the embarrassed look of a person who is caught.

"I am ashamed to confess it, Mary, but—"

"It's no matter, Edward, I was thinking the same question myself."

"I hope so. State it."

"You were thinking, if a body could only guess out *what the remark was* that Goodson made to the stranger."

"It's perfectly true. I feel guilty and ashamed. And you?"

"I'm past it. Let us make a pallet here; we've got to stand watch till the bank vault opens in the morning and admits the sack. . . . Oh dear, oh dear—if we hadn't made the mistake!"

The pallet was made, and Mary said:

"The open sesame—what could it have been? I do wonder what that remark could have been? But come; we will get to bed now."

"And sleep?"

"No: think."

"Yes, think."

By this time the Coxes too had completed their spat and their reconciliation, and were turning in—to think, to think, and toss, and fret, and worry over what the remark could possibly have been which Goodson made to the stranded derelict; that golden remark; that remark worth forty thousand dollars, cash.

The reason that the village telegraph-office was open later than usual that night was this: The foreman of Cox's paper was the local representative of the Associated Press. One might say its honorary representative, for it wasn't four times a year that he could furnish thirty words that would be accepted. But this time it was different. His despatch stating what he had caught got an instant answer:

Send the whole thing—all the details—twelve hundred words.

A colossal order! The foreman filled the bill; and he was the proudest man in the State. By breakfast-time the next morning the name of Hadleyburg the Incorruptible was on every lip in America, from Montreal to the Gulf, from the glaciers of Alaska to the orange-groves of Florida; and millions and millions of people were discussing the stranger and his money-sack, and wondering if the right man would be found, and hoping some more news about the matter would come soon—right away.

II

HADLEYBURG village woke up world-celebrated—astonished—happy—vain. Vain beyond imagination. Its nineteen principal citizens and their wives went about shaking hands with each other, and beaming, and smiling, and congratulating, and saying *this* thing adds a new word to the dictionary—*Hadleyburg,* synonym for *incorruptible*—destined to live in dictionaries forever! And the minor and unimportant citizens and their wives went around acting in much the same way. Everybody ran to the bank to see the gold-sack; and before noon grieved and envious crowds began to flock in from Brixton and all neighboring towns; and that afternoon and next day reporters began to arrive from everywhere to verify the sack and its history and write the whole thing up anew, and make dashing free-hand pictures of the sack, and of Richards's house, and the bank, and the Presbyterian church, and the Baptist church, and the public square, and the town-hall where the test would be applied and the money delivered; and damnable portraits of the Richardses, and Pinkerton the banker, and Cox, and the foreman, and Reverend Burgess, and the postmaster—and even of Jack Halliday, who was the loafing, good-natured, no-account, irreverent fisherman, hunter, boys' friend, stray-dogs' friend, typical "Sam Lawson" [1] of the town. The little mean, smirking, oily Pinkerton showed the sack to all comers, and rubbed his sleek palms together pleasantly, and enlarged upon the town's fine old reputation for honesty and upon this wonderful indorsement of it, and hoped and believed that the example would now spread far and wide over the American world, and be epoch-making in the matter of moral regeneration. And so on, and so on.

By the end of a week things had quieted down again; the wild intoxication of pride and joy had sobered to a soft, sweet, silent delight—a sort of deep, nameless, unutterable content. All faces bore a look of peaceful, holy happiness.

Then a change came. It was a gradual change: so gradual that its beginnings were hardly noticed; maybe were not noticed at all, except by Jack Halliday, who always noticed everything; and always made fun of it, too, no matter what it was. He began to throw out chaffing remarks about people not looking quite so happy as they did a day or two ago; and next he claimed that the new aspect was deepening to positive sadness; next, that it was taking on a sick look; and finally he said that everybody was become so moody, thoughtful, and absentminded that he could rob the meanest man in town of a cent out of the bottom of his breeches pocket and not disturb his revery.

At this stage—or at about this stage—a saying like this was dropped at bedtime—with a sigh, usually—by the head of each of the nineteen principal households: "Ah, what *could* have been the remark that Goodson made?"

THE MAN THAT CORRUPTED HADLEYBURG. 1. "Sam Lawson": The homely philosopher who is used as narrator in Harriet Beecher Stowe's *Sam Lawson's Oldtown Fireside Stories* (1872).

And straightway—with a shudder—came this, from the man's wife:

"Oh, *don't!* What horrible thing are you mulling in your mind? Put it away from you, for God's sake!"

But that question was wrung from those men again the next night—and got the same retort. But weaker.

And the third night the men uttered the question yet again—with anguish, and absently. This time—and the following night—the wives fidgeted feebly, and tried to say something. But didn't.

And the night after that they found their tongues and responded—longingly:

"Oh, if we *could* only guess!"

Halliday's comments grew daily more and more sparklingly disagreeable and disparaging. He went diligently about, laughing at the town, individually and in mass. But his laugh was the only one left in the village: it fell upon a hollow and mournful vacancy and emptiness. Not even a smile was findable anywhere. Halliday carried a cigar-box around on a tripod, playing that it was a camera, and halted all passers and aimed the thing and said, "Ready!—now look pleasant, please," but not even this capital joke could surprise the dreary faces into any softening.

So three weeks passed—one week was left. It was Saturday evening—after supper. Instead of the aforetime Saturday-evening flutter and bustle and shopping and larking, the streets were empty and desolate. Richards and his old wife sat apart in their little parlor—miserable and thinking. This was become their evening habit now: the lifelong habit which had preceded it, of reading, knitting, and contented chat, or receiving or paying neighborly calls, was dead and gone and forgotten, ages ago—two or three weeks ago; nobody talked now, nobody read, nobody visited—the whole village sat at home, sighing, worrying, silent. Trying to guess out that remark.

The postman left a letter. Richards glanced listlessly at the superscription and the postmark—unfamiliar, both—and tossed the letter on the table and resumed his might-have-beens and his hopeless dull miseries where he had left them off. Two or three hours later his wife got wearily up and was going away to bed without a good night—custom now—but she stopped near the letter and eyed it awhile with a dead interest, then broke it open, and began to skim it over. Richards, sitting there with his chair tilted back against the wall and his chin between his knees, heard something fall. It was his wife. He sprang to her side, but she cried out:

"Leave me alone, I am too happy. Read the letter—read it!"

He did. He devoured it, his brain reeling. The letter was from a distant state, and it said:

I am a stranger to you, but no matter: I have something to tell. I have just arrived home from Mexico, and learned about that episode. Of course you do not know who made that remark, but I know, and I am the only person living who does know. It was GOODSON. I knew him well, many years ago. I passed through your village that very night, and was his guest till the midnight train came along. I overheard him make that remark to the stranger in the dark—it was in Hale Alley. He and I talked of it the rest of the way home, and while smoking in his house. He mentioned many of your villagers in the course of his talk—most of them in a very uncomplimentary way, but two or three favorably; among these latter yourself. I say "favorably"—nothing stronger. I remember his saying he did not actually LIKE any person in the town—not one; but that you—I THINK he said you—am almost sure—had done him a very great service once, possibly without knowing the full value of it, and he wished he had a fortune, he would leave it to you when he died, and a curse apiece for the rest of the citizens. Now, then, if it was you that did him that service, you are his legitimate heir, and entitled to the sack of gold. I know that I can trust to your honor and honesty, for in a citizen of Hadleyburg these virtues are an unfailing inheritance, and so I am going to reveal to you the remark, well satisfied that if you are not the right man you will seek and find the right one and see that poor Goodson's debt of gratitude for the service referred to is paid. This is the remark: "YOU ARE FAR FROM BEING A BAD MAN: GO, AND REFORM."

HOWARD L. STEPHENSON.

"Oh, Edward, the money is ours, and I am so grateful, *oh,* so grateful—kiss me, dear, it's forever since we kissed—and we needed it so—the money—and now you are free of Pinkerton and his bank, and nobody's slave any more; it seems to me I could fly for joy."

It was a happy half-hour that the couple spent there on the settee caressing each other; it was the old days come again—days that had begun with their courtship and lasted without a break till the stranger brought the deadly money. By and by the wife said:

"Oh, Edward, how lucky it was you did him that grand service, poor Goodson! I never liked him, but I love him now. And it was fine and beautiful of you never to mention it or brag about it." Then, with a touch of reproach, "But you ought to have told *me,* Edward, you ought to have told your wife, you know."

"Well, I—er—well, Mary, you see—"

"Now stop hemming and hawing, and tell me about it, Edward. I always loved you, and now I'm proud of you. Everybody believes there was only one good generous soul in this village, and now it turns out that you—Edward, why don't you tell me?"

"Well—er—er—Why, Mary, I can't!"

"You *can't? Why* can't you?"

"You see, he—well, he—he made me promise I wouldn't."

The wife looked him over, and said, very slowly:

"Made—you—promise? Edward, what do you tell me that for?"

"Mary, do you think I would lie?"

She was troubled and silent for a moment, then she laid her hand within his and said:

"No . . . no. We have wandered far enough from our bearings—God spare us that! In all your life you have never uttered a lie. But now—now that the foundations of things seem to be crumbling from under us, we—we—" She lost her voice for a moment, then said, brokenly, "Lead us not into temptation. . . . I think you made the promise, Edward. Let it rest so. Let us keep away from that ground. Now—that is all gone by; let us be happy again; it is no time for clouds."

Edward found it something of an effort to comply, for his mind kept wandering—trying to remember what the service was that he had done Goodson.

The couple lay awake the most of the night, Mary happy and busy, Edward busy but not so happy. Mary was planning what she would do with the money. Edward was trying to recall that service. At first his conscience was sore on account of the lie he had told Mary—if it was a lie. After much reflection—suppose it *was* a lie? What then? Was it such a great matter? Aren't we always *acting* lies? Then why not *tell* them? Look at Mary—look what she had done. While he was hurrying off on his honest errand, what was she doing? Lamenting because the papers hadn't been destroyed and the money kept! Is theft better than lying?

That point lost its sting—the lie dropped into the background and left comfort behind it. The next point came to the front: *Had* he rendered that service? Well, here was Goodson's own evidence as reported in Stephenson's letter; there could be no better evidence than that—it was even *proof* that he had rendered it. Of course. So that point was settled. . . . No, not quite. He recalled with a wince that this unknown Mr. Stephenson was just a trifle unsure as to whether the performer of it was Richards or some other—and, oh dear, he had put Richards on his honor! He must himself decide whither that money must go—and Mr. Stephenson was not doubting that if he was the wrong man he would go honorably and find the right one. Oh, it was odious to put a man in such a situation—ah, why couldn't Stephenson have left out that doubt! What did he want to intrude that for?

Further reflection. How did it happen that *Richards's* name remained in Stephenson's mind as indicating the right man, and not some other man's name? That looked good. Yes, that looked very good. In fact, it went on looking better and better, straight along—until by and by it grew into positive *proof*. And then Richards put the matter at once out of his mind, for he had a private instinct that a proof once established is better left so.

He was feeling reasonably comfortable now, but there was still one other detail that kept pushing itself on his notice: of course he had done that service—that was settled; but what *was* that service? He must recall it—he would not go to sleep till he had recalled it; it would make his peace of mind perfect. And so he thought and thought. He thought of a dozen things—possible services, even probable services—but none of them seemed adequate, none of them seemed large enough, none of them seemed worth the money—worth the fortune Goodson had wished he could leave in his will. And besides, he couldn't remember having done them, anyway. Now, then —now, then—what *kind* of a service would it be that would make a man so inordinately grateful? Ah—the saving of his soul! That must be it. Yes, he could remember, now, how he once set himself the task of converting Goodson, and labored at it as much as—he was going to say three months; but upon closer examination it shrunk to a month, then to a week, then to a day, then to nothing. Yes, he remembered now, and with unwelcome vividness, that Goodson had told him to go to thunder and mind his own business—*he* wasn't hankering to follow Hadleyburg to heaven!

So that solution was a failure—he hadn't saved Goodson's soul. Richards was discouraged. Then after a little came another idea: had he saved Goodson's property? No, that wouldn't do—he hadn't any. His life? That is it! Of course. Why, he might have thought of it before. This time he was on the right track, sure. His imagination-mill was hard at work in a minute, now.

Thereafter during a stretch of two exhausting hours he was busy saving Goodson's life. He saved it in all kinds of difficult and perilous ways. In every case he got it saved satisfactorily up to a certain point; then, just as he was beginning to get well persuaded that it had really happened, a troublesome detail would turn up which made the whole thing impossible. As in the matter of drowning, for instance. In that case he had swum out and tugged Goodson ashore in an unconscious state with a great crowd looking on and applauding, but when he had got it all thought out and was just beginning to remember all about it, a whole swarm of disqualifying details arrived on the ground: the town would have known of the circumstance, Mary would have known of it, it would glare like a limelight in his own memory instead of being an inconspicuous service which he had possibly rendered "without knowing its full value." And at this point he remembered that he couldn't swim, anyway.

Ah—*there* was a point which he had been overlooking from the start: it had to be a service which he had rendered "possibly without knowing the full value of it." Why, really, that ought to be an easy hunt—much easier than those others. And sure enough, by and by he found it. Goodson, years and years ago, came near marrying a very sweet and pretty girl, named Nancy Hewitt, but in some way or other the match had been broken off; the girl died, Goodson remained a bachelor, and by and by became a soured one and a frank despiser of the human species. Soon after the girl's death the village found out, or thought it had found out, that she carried a spoonful of negro blood in her veins. Richards worked at these details a good while, and in the end he thought he remembered things concerning them which must have gotten mislaid in his memory through long neglect. He seemed to dimly remember that it was *he* that found out about the negro blood; that it was he that told the village; that the village told Goodson where they got it; that he thus saved Goodson from marrying the tainted girl; that he had done him this great service "without knowing the full value of it," in fact without knowing that he *was* doing it; but that Goodson knew the value of it, and what a narrow escape he had had, and so went to his grave grateful to his benefactor and wishing he had a fortune to leave him. It was all clear and simple now, and the more he went over it the more luminous and certain it grew; and at last, when he nestled to sleep satisfied and happy, he remembered the whole thing just as if it had been yesterday. In fact, he dimly remembered Goodson's *telling* him his gratitude once. Meantime Mary had spent six thousand dollars on a new house for herself and a pair of slippers for her pastor, and then had fallen peacefully to rest.

That same Saturday evening the postman had delivered a letter to each of the other principal citizens—nineteen letters in all. No two of the envelopes were alike, and no two of the superscriptions were in the same hand, but the letters inside were just like each other in every detail but one. They were exact copies of the letter received by Richards—handwriting and all—and were all signed by Stephenson, but in place of Richards's name each receiver's own name appeared.

All night long eighteen principal citizens did what their caste-brother Richards was doing at the same time—they put in their energies trying to remember what notable service it was that they had unconsciously done Barclay Goodson. In no case was it a holiday job; still they succeeded.

And while they were at this work, which was difficult, their wives put in the night spending the money, which was easy. During that one night the nineteen wives spent an average of seven thousand dollars each out of the forty thousand in the sack—a hundred and thirty-three thousand altogether.

Next day there was a surprise for Jack Halliday. He noticed that the faces of the nineteen chief citizens and their wives bore that expression of peaceful and holy happiness again. He could not understand it, neither was he able to invent any remarks about it that could damage it or disturb it. And so it was his turn to be dissatisfied with life. His private guesses at the reasons for the happiness failed in all instances, upon examination. When he met Mrs. Wilcox and noticed the placid ecstasy in her face, he said to himself, "Her cat has had kittens"—and went and asked the cook: it was not so; the cook had detected the happiness, but did not know the cause. When Halliday found the duplicate ecstasy in the face of "Shadbelly" Billson (village nickname), he was sure some neighbor of Billson's had broken his leg, but inquiry showed that this had not happened. The subdued ecstasy in Gregory Yates's face could mean but one thing—he was a mother-in-law short: it was another mistake. "And Pinkerton—Pinkerton—he has collected ten cents that he thought he was going to lose." And so on, and so on. In some cases the guesses had to remain in doubt, in the others they proved distinct errors. In the end Halliday said to himself, "Anyway it foots up that there's nineteen Hadleyburg families temporarily in heaven: I don't know how it happened; I only know Providence is off duty today."

An architect and builder from the next state had lately ventured to set up a small business in this unpromising village, and his sign had now been hanging out a week. Not a customer yet; he was a discouraged man, and sorry he had come. But his weather changed suddenly now. First one and then another chief citizen's wife said to him privately:

"Come to my house Monday week—but say nothing about it for the present. We think of building."

He got eleven invitations that day. That night he wrote his daughter and broke off her match with her student. He said she could marry a mile higher than that.

Pinkerton the banker and two or three other well-to-do men planned country-seats—but waited. That kind don't count their chickens until they are hatched.

The Wilsons devised a grand new thing—a fancy-dress ball. They made no actual promises, but told all their acquaintanceship in confidence that they were thinking the matter over and thought they should give it—"and if we do, you will be invited, of course." People were surprised, and said, one to another, "Why, they are crazy, those poor Wilsons, they can't afford it." Several among the nineteen said privately to their husbands, "It is a good idea: we will keep still till their cheap thing is over, then *we* will give one that will make it sick."

The days drifted along, and the bill of future squanderings rose higher and higher, wilder and wilder, more and more foolish and reckless. It began to look as if every member of the nineteen would not only spend his whole forty thousand dollars before receiving-day, but be actually in debt by the time he got the money. In some cases light-headed people did not stop with planning to spend, they really spent—on credit. They bought land, mortgages, farms, speculative stocks, fine clothes, horses, and various other things, paid down the bonus, and made themselves liable for the rest—at ten days. Presently the sober second thought came, and Halliday noticed that a ghastly anxiety was beginning to show up in a good many faces. Again he was puzzled, and didn't know what to make of it. "The Wilcox kittens aren't dead, for they weren't born; nobody's broken a leg; there's no shrinkage in mother-in-laws; *nothing* has happened—it is an unsolvable mystery."

There was another puzzled man, too—the Rev. Mr. Burgess. For days, wherever he went, people seemed to follow him or to be watching out for him; and if he ever found himself in a retired spot, a member of the nineteen would be sure to appear, thrust an envelope privately into his hand, whisper "To be opened at the town-hall Friday evening," then vanish away like a guilty thing. He was expecting that there might be one claimant for the sack—doubtful, however, Goodson being dead—but it never occurred to him that all this crowd might be claimants. When the great Friday came at last, he found that he had nineteen envelopes.

III

THE TOWN hall had never looked finer. The platform at the end of it was backed by a showy draping of flags; at intervals along the walls were festoons of flags; the gallery fronts were clothed in flags; the supporting columns were swathed in flags; all this was to impress the stranger, for he would be there in considerable force, and in a large degree he would be connected with the press. The house was full. The 412 fixed seats were occupied; also the 68 extra chairs which had been packed into the aisles; the steps of the platform were occupied; some distinguished strangers were given seats on the platform; at the horseshoe of tables which fenced the front and sides of the platform sat a strong force of special correspondents who had come from everywhere. It was the best-dressed house the town had ever produced. There were some tolerably expensive toilets there, and in several cases the ladies who wore them had the look of being unfamiliar with that kind of clothes. At least the town thought they had that look, but the notion could have arisen from the town's knowledge of the fact that these ladies had never inhabited such clothes before.

The gold-sack stood on a little table at the front of the platform where all the house could see it. The bulk of the house gazed at it with a burning interest, a mouth-watering interest, a wistful and pathetic interest; a minority of nineteen couples gazed at it tenderly, lovingly, proprietarily, and the male half of this minority kept saying over to themselves the moving little impromptu speeches of thankfulness for the audience's applause and congratulations which they were presently going to get up and deliver. Every now and then one of these got a piece of paper out of his vest pocket and privately glanced at it to refresh his memory.

Of course there was a buzz of conversation going on—there always is; but at last when the Rev. Mr. Burgess rose and laid his hand on the sack he could hear his microbes gnaw, the place was so still. He related the curious history of the sack, then went on to speak in warm terms of Hadleyburg's old and well-earned reputation for spotless honesty, and of the town's just pride in this reputation. He said that this reputation was a treasure of priceless value; that under Providence its value had now become inestimably enhanced, for the recent episode had spread this fame far and wide, and thus had focused the eyes of the American world upon this village, and made its name for all time, as he hoped and believed, a synonym for

commercial incorruptibility. [*Applause.*] "And who is to be the guardian of this noble treasure—the community as a whole? No! The responsibility is individual, not communal. From this day forth each and every one of you is in his own person its special guardian, and individually responsible that no harm shall come to it. Do you—does each of you—accept this great trust? [*Tumultuous assent.*] Then all is well. Transmit it to your children and to your children's children. To-day your purity is beyond reproach—see to it that it shall remain so. To-day there is not a person in your community who could be beguiled to touch a penny not his own—see to it that you abide in this grace. [*"We will! we will!"*] This is not the place to make comparisons between ourselves and other communities—some of them ungracious toward us; they have their ways, we have ours; let us be content. [*Applause.*] I am done. Under my hand, my friends, rests a stranger's eloquent recognition of what we are; through him the world will always henceforth know what we are. We do not know who he is, but in your name I utter your gratitude, and ask you to raise your voices in indorsement."

The house rose in a body and made the walls quake with the thunders of its thankfulness for the space of a long minute. Then it sat down, and Mr. Burgess took an envelope out of his pocket. The house held its breath while he slit the envelope open and took from it a slip of paper. He read its contents—slowly and impressively—the audience listening with tranced attention to this magic document, each of whose words stood for an ingot of gold:

" '*The remark which I made to the distressed stranger was this: "You are very far from being a bad man: go, and reform.'* " Then he continued:

"We shall know in a moment now whether the remark here quoted corresponds with the one concealed in the sack; and if that shall prove to be so—and it undoubtedly will—this sack of gold belongs to a fellow-citizen who will henceforth stand before the nation as the symbol of the special virtue which has made our town famous throughout the land—Mr. Billson!"

The house had gotten itself all ready to burst into the proper tornado of applause; but instead of doing it, it seemed stricken with a paralysis; there was a deep hush for a moment or two, then a wave of whispered murmurs swept the place—of about this tenor: "*Billson!* oh, come, this is *too* thin! Twenty dollars to a stranger—or *anybody*—*Billson!* tell it to the marines!" And now at this point the house caught its breath all of a sudden in a new access of astonishment, for it discovered that whereas in one part of the hall Deacon Billson was standing up with his head meekly bowed, in another part of it Lawyer Wilson was doing the same. There was a wondering silence now for a while.

Everybody was puzzled, and nineteen couples were surprised and indignant.

Billson and Wilson turned and stared at each other. Billson asked, bitingly:

"Why do *you* rise, Mr. Wilson?"

"Because I have a right to. Perhaps you will be good enough to explain to the house why *you* rise?"

"With great pleasure. Because I wrote that paper."

"It is an impudent falsity! I wrote it myself."

It was Burgess's turn to be paralyzed. He stood looking vacantly at first one of the men and then the other, and did not seem to know what to do. The house was stupefied. Lawyer Wilson spoke up, now, and said,

"I ask the Chair to read the name signed to that paper."

That brought the Chair to itself, and it read out the name:

" 'John Wharton *Billson*.' "

"There!" shouted Billson, "what have you got to say for yourself, now? And what kind of apology are you going to make to me and to this insulted house for the imposture which you have attempted to play here?"

"No apologies are due, sir; and as for the rest of it, I publicly charge you with pilfering my note from Mr. Burgess and substituting a copy of it signed with your own name. There is no other way by which you could have gotten hold of the test-remark; I alone, of living men, possessed the secret of its wording."

There was likely to be a scandalous state of things if this went on; everybody noticed with distress that the short-hand scribes were scribbling like mad; many people were crying "Chair, Chair! Order! order!" Burgess rapped with his gavel, and said:

"Let us not forget the proprieties due. There has evidently been a mistake somewhere, but surely that is all. If Mr. Wilson gave me an envelope—and I remember now that he did—I still have it."

He took one out of his pocket, opened it, glanced at it, looked surprised and worried, and stood silent a few moments. Then he waved his hand in a wandering and mechanical way, and made an effort or two to say something, then gave it up, despondently. Several voices cried out:

"Read it! read it! What is it?"

So he began in a dazed and sleep-walker fashion:

" *'The remark which I made to the unhappy stranger was this: "You are far from being a bad man. [The house gazed at him, marveling.] Go, and reform.' "* [*Murmurs:* "Amazing! what can this mean?"] This one," said the Chair, "is signed Thurlow G. Wilson."

"There!" cried Wilson. "I reckon that settles it! I know perfectly well my note was purloined."

"Purloined!" retorted Billson. "I'll let you know that neither you nor any man of your kidney must venture to—"

The Chair. "Order, gentlemen, order! Take your seats, both of you, please."

They obeyed, shaking their heads and grumbling angrily. The house was profoundly puzzled; it did not know what to do with this curious emergency. Presently Thompson got up. Thompson was the hatter. He would have liked to be a Nineteener; but such was not for him: his stock of hats was not considerable enough for the position. He said:

"Mr. Chairman, if I may be permitted to make a suggestion, can both of these gentlemen be right? I put it to you, sir, can both have happened to say the very same words to the stranger? It seems to me—"

The tanner got up and interrupted him. The tanner was a disgruntled man; he believed himself entitled to be a Nineteener, but he couldn't get recognition. It made him a little unpleasant in his ways and speech. Said he:

"Sho, *that's* not the point! *That* could happen—twice in a hundred years—but not the other thing. *Neither* of them gave the twenty dollars!"

[*A ripple of applause.*]

Billson. "*I* did!"

Wilson. "*I* did!"

Then each accused the other of pilfering.

The Chair. "Order! Sit down, if you please—both of you. Neither of the notes has been out of my possession at any moment."

A Voice. "Good—that settles *that!*"

The Tanner. "Mr. Chairman, one thing is now plain: one of these men has been eavesdropping under the other one's bed, and filching family secrets. If it is not unparliamentary to suggest it, I will remark that both are equal to it. [*The Chair.* "Order! order!"] I withdraw the remark, sir, and will confine myself to suggesting that if one of them has overheard the other reveal the test-remark to his wife, we shall catch him now."

A Voice. "How?"

The Tanner. "Easily. The two have not quoted the remark in exactly the same words. You would have noticed that, if there hadn't been a considerable stretch of time and an exciting quarrel inserted between the two readings."

A Voice. "Name the difference."

The Tanner. "The word *very* is in Billson's note, and not in the other."

Many Voices. "That's so—he's right!"

The Tanner. "And so, if the Chair will examine the test-remark in the sack, we shall know which of these two frauds—[*The Chair.* "Order!"] —which of these two adventurers—[*The Chair.* "Order! order!"]—which of these two gentlemen—[*laughter and applause*]—is entitled to wear the belt as being the first dishonest blatherskite ever bred in this town—which he has dishonored, and which will be a sultry place for him from now out!" [*Vigorous applause.*]

Many Voices. "Open it!—open the sack!"

Mr. Burgess made a slit in the sack, slid his hand in and brought out an envelope. In it were a couple of folded notes. He said:

"One of these is marked, 'Not to be examined until all written communications which have been addressed to the Chair—if any—shall have been read.' The other is marked 'The Test.' Allow me. It is worded—to wit:

" 'I do not require that the first half of the remark which was made to me by my benefactor shall be quoted with exactness, for it was not striking, and could be forgotten; but its closing fifteen words are quite striking, and I think easily rememberable; unless *these* shall be accurately reproduced, let the applicant be regarded as an impostor. My benefactor began by saying he seldom gave advice to any one, but that it always bore the hall-mark of high value when he did give it. Then he said this—and it has never faded from my memory: *"You are far from being a bad man—"* ' "

Fifty Voices. "That settles it—the money's Wilson's! Wilson! Wilson! Speech! Speech!"

People jumped up and crowded around Wilson, wringing his hand and congratulating fervently—meantime the Chair was hammering with the gavel and shouting:

"Order, gentlemen! Order! Order! Let me finish reading, please." When quiet was restored, the reading was resumed—as follows:

" ' *"Go, and reform—or, mark my words— some day, for your sins, you will die and go to hell or Hadleyburg—*TRY AND MAKE IT THE FORMER.*" '* "

A ghastly silence followed. First an angry cloud began to settle darkly upon the faces of the citizenship; after a pause the cloud began to rise, and a tickled expression tried to take its place; tried so hard that it was only kept under with great and painful difficulty; the reporters, the Brixtonites, and other strangers bent their heads down and shielded their faces with their hands, and managed to hold in by main strength and heroic courtesy. At this most inopportune time burst upon the stillness the roar of a solitary voice—Jack Halliday's:

"That's got the hall-mark on it!"

Then the house let go, strangers and all. Even Mr. Burgess's gravity broke down presently, then the audience considered itself officially absolved from all restraint, and it made the most of its privilege. It was a good long laugh, and a tempestuously whole-hearted one, but it ceased at last—long enough for Mr. Burgess to try to resume, and for the people to get their eyes partially wiped; then it broke out again; and afterward yet again; then at last Burgess was able to get out these serious words:

"It is useless to try to disguise the fact—we find ourselves in the presence of a matter of grave import. It involves the honor of your town, it strikes at the town's good name. The difference of a single word between the test-remarks offered by Mr. Wilson and Mr. Billson was itself a serious thing, since it indicated that one or the other of these gentlemen had committed a theft—"

The two men were sitting limp, nerveless, crushed; but at these words both were electrified into movement, and started to get up—

"Sit down!" said the Chair, sharply, and they obeyed. "That, as I have said, was a serious thing. And it was—but for only one of them. But the matter has become graver; for the honor of *both* is now in formidable peril. Shall I go even further, and say in inextricable peril? *Both* left out the crucial fifteen words." He paused. During several moments he allowed the pervading stillness to gather and deepen its impressive effects, then added: "There would seem to be but one way whereby this could happen. I ask these gentlemen —Was there *collusion?—agreement?*"

A low murmur sifted through the house; its import was, "He's got them both."

Billson was not used to emergencies; he sat in a helpless collapse. But Wilson was a lawyer. He struggled to his feet, pale and worried, and said:

"I ask the indulgence of the house while I explain this most painful matter. I am sorry to say what I am about to say, since it must inflict irreparable injury upon Mr. Billson, whom I have always esteemed and respected until now, and in whose invulnerability to temptation I entirely believed—as did you all. But for the preservation of my own honor I must speak—and with frankness.

I confess with shame—and I now beseech your pardon for it—that I said to the ruined stranger all of the words contained in the test-remark, including the disparaging fifteen. [*Sensation.*] When the late publication was made I recalled them, and I resolved to claim the sack of coin, for by every right I was entitled to it. Now I will ask you to consider this point, and weigh it well: that stranger's gratitude to me that night knew no bounds; he said himself that he could find no words for it that were adequate, and that if he should ever be able he would repay me a thousandfold. Now, then, I ask you this: Could I expect—could I believe—could I even remotely imagine—that, feeling as he did, he would do so ungrateful a thing as to add those quite unnecessary fifteen words to his test?—set a trap for me? —expose me as a slanderer of my own town before my own people assembled in a public hall? It was preposterous; it was impossible. His test would contain only the kindly opening clause of my remark. Of that I had no shadow of doubt. You would have thought as I did. You would not have expected a base betrayal from one whom you had befriended and against whom you had committed no offense. And so, with perfect confidence, perfect trust, I wrote on a piece of paper the opening words—ending with 'Go, and reform,'— and signed it. When I was about to put it in an envelope I was called into my back office, and without thinking I left the paper lying open on my desk." He stopped, turned his head slowly toward Billson, waited a moment, then added: "I ask you to note this: when I returned, a little later, Mr. Billson was retiring by my street door." [*Sensation.*]

In a moment Billson was on his feet and shouting:

"It's a lie! It's an infamous lie!"

The Chair. "Be seated, sir! Mr. Wilson has the floor."

Billson's friends pulled him into his seat and quieted him, and Wilson went on:

"Those are the simple facts. My note was now lying in a different place on the table from where I had left it. I noticed that, but attached no importance to it, thinking a draught had blown it there. That Mr. Billson would read a private paper was a thing which could not occur to me; he was an honorable man, and he would be above it. If you will allow me to say it, I think his extra word '*very*' stands explained; it is attributable to a defect of memory. I was the only man in the world who could furnish here any detail of the test-remark—by *honorable* means. I have finished."

There is nothing in the world like a persuasive speech to fuddle the mental apparatus and upset the convictions and debauch the emotions of an audience not practised in the tricks and delusions of oratory. Wilson sat down victorious. The house submerged him in tides of approving applause; friends swarmed to him and shook him by the hand and congratulated him, and Billson was shouted down and not allowed to say a word. The Chair hammered and hammered with its gavel, and kept shouting:

"But let us proceed, gentlemen, let us proceed!"

At last there was a measurable degree of quiet, and the hatter said:

"But what is there to proceed with, sir, but to deliver the money?"

Voices. "That's it! That's it! Come forward, Wilson!"

The Hatter. "I move three cheers for Mr. Wilson, Symbol of the special virtue which—"

The cheers burst forth before he could finish; and in the midst of them—and in the midst of the clamor of the gavel also—some enthusiasts mounted Wilson on a big friend's shoulder and were going to fetch him in triumph to the platform. The Chair's voice now rose above the noise—

"Order! To your places! You forget that there is still a document to be read." When quiet had been restored he took up a document, and was going to read it, but laid it down again, saying, "I forgot; this is not to be read until all written communications received by me have first been read." He took an envelope out of his pocket, removed its inclosure, glanced at it—seemed astonished—held it out and gazed at it—stared at it.

Twenty or thirty voices cried out:

"What is it? Read it! read it!"

And he did—slowly, and wondering:

"'The remark which I made to the stranger— [*Voices.* "Hello! how's this?"]—was this: "You are far from being a bad man. [*Voices.* "Great Scott!"] Go, and reform.'" [*Voice.* "Oh, saw my leg off!"] Signed by Mr. Pinkerton, the banker."

The pandemonium of delight which turned itself loose now was of a sort to make the judicious weep. Those whose withers were unwrung laughed till the tears ran down; the reporters, in throes of laughter, set down disordered pot-hooks, which would never in the world be decipherable; and a sleeping dog jumped up, scared out of its wits, and barked itself crazy at the turmoil. All manner of cries were scattered through the din: "We're getting rich—*two* Symbols of Incorruptibility!—without counting Billson!" "*Three!*—count Shadbelly in—we can't have too many!" "All right—

Billson's elected!" "Alas, poor Wilson—victim of *two* thieves!"

A Powerful Voice. "Silence! The Chair's fished up something more out of its pocket."

Voices. "Hurrah! Is it something fresh? Read it! read! read!"

The Chair [*reading*]. " 'The remark which I made,' etc.: ' "You are far from being a bad man. Go," ' etc. Signed, 'Gregory Yates.' "

Tornado of Voices. "Four Symbols!" " 'Rah for Yates!" "Fish again!"

The house was in a roaring humor now, and ready to get all the fun out of the occasion that might be in it. Several Nineteeners, looking pale and distressed, got up and began to work their way toward the aisles, but a score of shouts went up:

"The doors, the doors—close the doors; no Incorruptible shall leave this place! Sit down, everybody!"

The mandate was obeyed.

"Fish again! Read! read!"

The Chair fished again, and once more the familiar words began to fall from its lips—" 'You are far from being a bad man.' "

"Name! name! What's his name?"

" 'L. Ingoldsby Sargent.' "

"Five elected! Pile up the Symbols! Go on, go on!"

" 'You are far from being a bad—' "

"Name! name!"

" 'Nicholas Whitworth.' "

"Hooray! hooray! it's a symbolical day!"

Somebody wailed in, and began to sing this rhyme (leaving out "it's") to the lovely "Mikado" tune of "When a man's afraid, a beautiful maid—"; the audience joined in, with joy; then, just in time, somebody contributed another line—

And don't you this forget—

The house roared it out. A third line was at once furnished—

Corruptibles far from Hadleyburg are—

The house roared that one too. As the last note died, Jack Halliday's voice rose high and clear, freighted with a fine line—

But the Symbols are here, you bet!

That was sung, with booming enthusiasm. Then the happy house started in at the beginning and sang the four lines through twice, with immense swing and dash, and finished up with a crashing three-times-three and a tiger for "Hadleyburg the Incorruptible and all Symbols of it which we shall find worthy to receive the hall-mark to-night."

Then the shoutings at the Chair began again, all over the place:

"Go on! go on! Read! read some more! Read all you've got!"

"That's it—go on! We are winning eternal celebrity!"

A dozen men got up now and began to protest. They said that this farce was the work of some abandoned joker, and was an insult to the whole community. Without a doubt these signatures were all forgeries—

"Sit down! sit down! Shut up! You are confessing. We'll find *your* names in the lot."

"Mr. Chairman, how many of those envelopes have you got?"

The Chair counted.

"Together with those that have been already examined, there are nineteen."

A storm of derisive applause broke out.

"Perhaps they all contain the secret. I move that you open them all and read every signature that is attached to a note of that sort—and read also the first eight words of the note."

"Second the motion!"

It was put and carried—uproariously. Then poor old Richards got up, and his wife rose and stood at his side. Her head was bent down, so that none might see that she was crying. Her husband gave her his arm, and so supporting her, he began to speak in a quavering voice:

"My friends, you have known us two—Mary and me—all our lives, and I think you have liked us and respected us—"

The Chair interrupted him:

"Allow me. It is quite true—that which you are saying, Mr. Richards: this town *does* know you two; it *does* like you; it *does* respect you; more—it honors you and *loves* you—"

Halliday's voice rang out:

"That's the hall-marked truth, too! If the Chair is right, let the house speak up and say it. Rise! Now, then—hip! hip! hip!—all together!"

The house rose in mass, faced toward the old couple eagerly, filled the air with a snow-storm of waving handkerchiefs, and delivered the cheers with all its affectionate heart.

The Chair then continued:

"What I was going to say is this: We know your good heart, Mr. Richards, but this is not a time for the exercise of charity toward offenders. [*Shouts of "Right! right!"*] I see your generous purpose in your face, but I cannot allow you to plead for these men—"

"But I was going to—"

"Please take your seat, Mr. Richards. We must examine the rest of these notes—simple fairness

to the men who have already been exposed requires this. As soon as that has been done—I give
you my word for this—you shall be heard."

Many Voices. "Right!—the Chair is right—no
interruption can be permitted at this stage! Go
on!—the names! the names!—according to the
terms of the motion!"

The old couple sat reluctantly down, and the
husband whispered to the wife, "It is pitifully hard
to have to wait; the shame will be greater than
ever when they find we were only going to plead
for *ourselves.*"

Straightway the jollity broke loose again with
the reading of the names.

" 'You are far from being a bad man—'
Signature, 'Robert J. Titmarsh.'

" 'You are far from being a bad man—' Signature, 'Eliphalet Weeks.'

" 'You are far from being a bad man—' Signature, 'Oscar B. Wilder.' "

At this point the house lit upon the idea of taking the eight words out of the Chairman's hands.
He was not unthankful for that. Thenceforward
he held up each note in its turn, and waited. The
house droned out the eight words in a massed and
measured and musical deep volume of sound
(with a daringly close resemblance to a well
known church chant)—" 'You are f-a-r from being a b-a-a-a-d man.' " Then the Chair said, "Signature, 'Archibald Wilcox.' " And so on, and so
on, name after name, and everybody had an increasingly and gloriously good time except the
wretched Nineteen. Now and then, when a particularly shining name was called, the house made
the Chair wait while it chanted the whole of the
test-remark from the beginning to the closing
words, "And go to hell or Hadleyburg—try and
make it the for-or-m-e-r!" and in these special
cases they added a grand and agonized and imposing "A-a-a-a-*men!*"

The list dwindled, dwindled, dwindled, poor old
Richards keeping tally of the count, wincing when
a name resembling his own was pronounced, and
waiting in miserable suspense for the time to come
when it would be his humiliating privilege to rise
with Mary and finish his plea, which he was intending to word thus: ". . . for until now we
have never done any wrong thing, but have gone
our humble way unreproached. We are very poor,
we are old, and have no chick nor child to help
us; we were sorely tempted, and we fell. It was
my purpose when I got up before to make confession and beg that my name might not be read out
in this public place, for it seemed to us that we
could not bear it; but I was prevented. It was just;
it was our place to suffer with the rest. It has been

hard for us. It is the first time we have ever
heard our name fall from any one's lips—sullied.
Be merciful—for the sake of the better days;
make our shame as light to bear as in your charity
you can." At this point in his revery Mary nudged
him, perceiving that his mind was absent. The
house was chanting, "You are f-a-r," etc.

"Be ready," Mary whispered. "Your name
comes now; he has read eighteen."

The chant ended.

"Next! next! next!" came volleying from all over
the house.

Burgess put his hand into his pocket. The old
couple, trembling, began to rise. Burgess fumbled
a moment, then said,

"I find I have read them all."

Faint with joy and surprise, the couple sank into
their seats, and Mary whispered:

"Oh, bless God, we are saved!—he has lost ours
—I wouldn't give this for a hundred of those
sacks!"

The house burst out with its "Mikado" travesty,
and sang it three times with ever-increasing enthusiasm, rising to its feet when it reached for the
third time the closing line—

But the Symbols are here, you bet!

and finishing up with cheers and a tiger for "Hadleyburg purity and our eighteen immortal representatives of it."

Then Wingate, the saddler, got up and proposed
cheers "for the cleanest man in town, the one solitary important citizen in it who didn't try to steal
that money—Edward Richards."

They were given with great and moving heartiness; then somebody proposed that Richards be
elected sole guardian and Symbol of the now Sacred Hadleyburg Tradition, with power and right
to stand up and look the whole sarcastic world in
the face.

Passed, by acclamation; then they sang the
"Mikado" again, and ended it with:

And there's *one* Symbol left, you bet!

There was a pause; then—

A Voice. "Now, then, who's to get the sack?"

The Tanner [*with bitter sarcasm*]. "That's
easy. The money has to be divided among the
eighteen Incorruptibles. They gave the suffering
stranger twenty dollars apiece—and that remark
—each in his turn—it took twenty-two minutes for the procession to move past. Staked the
stranger—total contribution, $360. All they want
is just the loan back—and interest—forty thousand dollars altogether."

Many Voices [*derisively*]. "That's it! Divvy! divvy! Be kind to the poor—don't keep them waiting!"

The Chair. "Order! I now offer the stranger's remaining document. It says: 'If no claimant shall appear [*grand chorus of groans*] I desire that you open the sack and count out the money to the principal citizens of your town, they to take it in trust [*cries of "Oh! Oh! Oh!"*], and use it in such ways as to them shall seem best for the propagation and preservation of your community's noble reputation for incorruptible honesty [*more cries*]—a reputation to which their names and their efforts will add a new and far-reaching luster.' [*Enthusiastic outburst of sarcastic applause.*] That seems to be all. No—here is a postscript:

"'P. S.—CITIZENS OF HADLEYBURG: There *is* no test-remark—nobody made one. [*Great sensation.*] There wasn't any pauper stranger, nor any twenty-dollar contribution, nor any accompanying benediction and compliment—these are all inventions. [*General buzz and hum of astonishment and delight.*] Allow me to tell my story—it will take but a word or two. I passed through your town at a certain time, and received a deep offense which I had not earned. Any other man would have been content to kill one or two of you and call it square, but to me that would have been a trivial revenge, and inadequate; for the dead do not *suffer*. Besides, I could not kill you all—and, anyway, made as I am, even that would not have satisfied me. I wanted to damage every man in the place, and every woman—and not in their bodies or in their estate, but in their vanity—the place where feeble and foolish people are most vulnerable. So I disguised myself and came back and studied you. You were easy game. You had an old and lofty reputation for honesty, and naturally you were proud of it—it was your treasure of treasures, the very apple of your eye. As soon as I found out that you carefully and vigilantly kept yourselves and your children *out of temptation,* I knew how to proceed. Why, you simple creatures, the weakest of all weak things is a virtue which has not been tested in the fire. I laid a plan, and gathered a list of names. My project was to corrupt Hadleyburg the Incorruptible. My idea was to make liars and thieves of nearly half a hundred smirchless men and women who had never in their lives uttered a lie or stolen a penny. I was afraid of Goodson. He was neither born nor reared in Hadleyburg. I was afraid that if I started to operate my scheme by getting my letter laid before you, you would say to yourselves, "Goodson is the only man among us who would give away twenty dollars to a poor devil"—and then you might not bite at my bait. But Heaven took Goodson; then I knew I was safe, and I set my trap and baited it. It may be that I shall not catch all the men to whom I mailed the pretended test secret, but I shall catch the most of them, if I know Hadleyburg nature. [*Voices.* "Right—he got every last one of them."] I believe they will even steal ostensible *gamble*-money, rather than miss, poor, tempted, and mistrained fellows. I am hoping to eternally and everlastingly squelch your vanity and give Hadleyburg a new renown—one that will *stick*—and spread far. If I have succeeded, open the sack and summon the Committee on Propagation and Preservation of the Hadleyburg Reputation.' "

A Cyclone of Voices. "Open it! Open it! The Eighteen to the front! Committee on Propagation of the Tradition! Forward—the Incorruptibles!"

The Chair ripped the sack wide, and gathered up a handful of bright, broad, yellow coins, shook them together, then examined them—

"Friends, they are only gilded disks of lead!"

There was a crashing outbreak of delight over this news, and when the noise had subsided, the tanner called out:

"By right of apparent seniority in this business, Mr. Wilson is Chairman of the Committee on Propagation of the Tradition. I suggest that he step forward on behalf of his pals, and receive in trust the money."

A Hundred Voices. "Wilson! Wilson! Wilson! Speech! Speech!"

Wilson [*in a voice trembling with anger*]. "You will allow me to say, and without apologies for my language, *damn* the money!"

A Voice. "Oh, and him a Baptist!"

A Voice. "Seventeen Symbols left! Step up, gentlemen, and assume your trust!"

There was a pause—no response.

The Saddler. "Mr. Chairman, we've got *one* clean man left, anyway, out of the late aristocracy; and he needs money, and deserves it. I move that you appoint Jack Halliday to get up there and auction off that sack of gilt twenty-dollar pieces, and give the result to the right man—the man whom Hadleyburg delights to honor—Edward Richards."

This was received with great enthusiasm, the dog taking a hand again; the saddler started the bids at a dollar, the Brixton folk and Barnum's representative fought hard for it, the people cheered every jump that the bids made, the excitement climbed moment by moment higher and higher, the bidders got on their mettle and grew steadily more and more daring, more and more determined, the jumps went from a dollar up to five, then to ten, then to twenty, then fifty, then to a hundred, then—

At the beginning of the auction Richards whispered in distress to his wife: "O Mary, can we allow it? It—it—you see, it is an honor-reward, a testimonial to purity of character, and—and—can we allow it? Hadn't I better get up and—O Mary, what ought we to do?—what do you think we—" [*Halliday's voice. "Fifteen I'm bid!—fifteen for the sack!—twenty!—ah, thanks!—thirty—thanks again! Thirty, thirty, thirty!—do I hear forty?— forty it is! Keep the ball rolling, gentlemen, keep it rolling!—fifty! thanks, noble Roman! going at fifty, fifty, fifty!—seventy!—ninety!—splendid!— a hundred!—pile it up, pile it up!—hundred and twenty—forty!—just in time!—hundred and fifty! —TWO hundred!—superb! Do I hear two h— thanks!—two hundred and fifty!—"*]

"It is another temptation, Edward—I'm all in a tremble—but, oh, we've escaped *one* temptation, and that ought to warn us to—[*"Six did I hear? —thanks!—six-fifty, six-f—*SEVEN *hundred!"*] And yet, Edward, when you think—nobody susp— [*"Eight hundred dollars!—hurrah!— make it nine!—Mr. Parsons, did I hear you say— thanks—nine!—this noble sack of virgin lead going at only nine hundred dollars, gilding and all— come! do I hear—a thousand!—gratefully yours! —did some one say eleven?—a sack which is going to be the most celebrated in the whole Uni—"*] O Edward" (beginning to sob), "we are *so* poor!—but—but—do as you think best—do as you think best."

Edward fell—that is, he sat still; sat with a conscience which was not satisfied, but which was overpowered by circumstances.

Meantime a stranger, who looked like an amateur detective gotten up as an impossible English earl, had been watching the evening's proceedings with manifest interest, and with a contented expression in his face; and he had been privately commenting to himself. He was now soliloquizing somewhat like this: "None of the Eighteen are bidding; that is not satisfactory; I must change that—the dramatic unities require it; they must buy the sack they tried to steal; they must pay a heavy price, too—some of them are rich. And another thing, when I make a mistake in Hadleyburg nature the man that puts that error upon me is entitled to a high honorarium, and some one must pay it. This poor old Richards has brought my judgment to shame; he is an honest man:—I don't understand it, but I acknowledge it. Yes, he saw my deuces *and* with a straight flush, and by rights the pot is his. And it shall be a jack-pot, too, if I can manage it. He disappointed me, but let that pass."

He was watching the bidding. At a thousand, the market broke; the prices tumbled swiftly. He waited—and still watched. One competitor dropped out; then another, and another. He put in a bid or two, now. When the bids had sunk to ten dollars, he added a five; some one raised him a three; he waited a moment, then flung in a fifty-dollar jump, and the sack was his—at $1,282. The house broke out in cheers—then stopped; for he was on his feet, and had lifted his hand. He began to speak.

"I desire to say a word, and ask a favor. I am a speculator in rarities, and I have dealings with persons interested in numismatics all over the world. I can make a profit on this purchase, just as it stands; but there is a way, if I can get your approval, whereby I can make every one of these leaden twenty-dollar pieces worth its face in gold, and perhaps more. Grant me that approval, and I will give part of my gains to your Mr. Richards, whose invulnerable probity you have so justly and so cordially recognized to-night; his share shall be ten thousand dollars, and I will hand him the money to-morrow. [*Great applause from the house. But the "invulnerable probity" made the Richardses blush prettily; however, it went for modesty, and did no harm.*] If you will pass my proposition by a good majority—I would like a two-thirds vote—I will regard that as the town's consent, and that is all I ask. Rarities are always helped by any device which will rouse curiosity and compel remark. Now if I may have your permission to stamp upon the faces of each of these ostensible coins the names of the eighteen gentlemen who—"

Nine-tenths of the audience were on their feet in a moment—dog and all—and the proposition was carried with a whirlwind of approving applause and laughter.

They sat down, and all the Symbols except "Dr." Clay Harkness got up, violently protesting against the proposed outrage, and threatening to—

"I beg you not to threaten me," said the stranger, calmly. "I know my legal rights, and am not accustomed to being frightened at bluster." [*Applause.*] He sat down. "Dr." Harkness saw an opportunity here. He was one of the two very rich men of the place, and Pinkerton was the other. Harkness was proprietor of a mint; that is to say, a popular patent medicine. He was running for the legislature on one ticket, and Pinkerton on the other. It was a close race and a hot one, and getting hotter every day. Both had strong appetites for money; each had bought a great tract of land, with a purpose; there was going to be a new railway, and each wanted to be in the legislature and help locate the route to his own advantage; a single vote might make the decision, and with it two or three fortunes. The stake was large, and Harkness was a daring speculator. He was sitting close to the stranger. He leaned over while one or another of the other Symbols was entertaining the house with protests and appeals, and asked, in a whisper.

"What is your price for the sack?"

"Forty thousand dollars."

"I'll give you twenty."

"No."

"Twenty-five."

"No."

"Say thirty."

"The price is forty thousand dollars; not a penny less."

"All right, I'll give it. I will come to the hotel at ten in the morning. I don't want it known: will see you privately."

"Very good." Then the stranger got up and said to the house:

"I find it late. The speeches of these gentlemen are not without merit, not without interest, not without grace; yet if I may be excused I will take my leave. I thank you for the great favor which you have shown me in granting my petition. I ask the Chair to keep the sack for me until to-morrow, and to hand these three five-hundred-dollar notes to Mr. Richards." They were passed up to the Chair. "At nine I will call for the sack, and at eleven will deliver the rest of the ten thousand to Mr. Richards in person, at his home. Good night."

Then he slipped out, and left the audience making a vast noise, which was composed of a mixture of cheers, the "Mikado" song, dog-disapproval, and the chant, "You are f-a-r from being a b-a-a-d man—a-a-a-a-men!"

IV

AT HOME the Richardses had to endure congratulations and compliments until midnight. Then they were left to themselves. They looked a little sad, and they sat silent and thinking. Finally Mary sighed and said,

"Do you think we are to blame, Edward— *much* to blame?" and her eyes wandered to the accusing triplet of big bank-notes lying on the table, where the congratulators had been gloating over them and reverently fingering them. Edward did not answer at once; then he brought out a sigh and said, hesitatingly:

"We—we couldn't help it, Mary. It—well, it was ordered. *All* things are."

Mary glanced up and looked at him steadily, but he didn't return the look. Presently she said:

"I thought congratulations and praises always tasted good. But—it seems to me, now—Edward?"

"Well?"

"Are you going to stay in the bank?"

"N-no."

"Resign?"

"In the morning—by note."

"It does seem best."

Richards bowed his head in his hands and muttered:

"Before, I was not afraid to let oceans of people's money pour through my hands, but—Mary, I am so tired, so tired—"

"We will go to bed."

At nine in the morning the stranger called for the sack and took it to the hotel in a cab. At ten Harkness had a talk with him privately. The stranger asked for and got five checks on a metropolitan bank—drawn to "Bearer"—four for $1,500 each, and one for $34,000. He put one of the former in his pocketbook, and the remainder, representing $38,500, he put in an envelope, and with these he added a note, which he wrote after Harkness was gone. At eleven he called at the Richards house and knocked. Mrs. Richards peeped through the shutters, then went and received the envelope, and the stranger disappeared without a word. She came back flushed and a little unsteady on her legs, and gasped out:

"I am sure I recognized him! Last night it seemed to me that maybe I had seen him somewhere before."

"He is the man that brought the sack here?"

"I am almost sure of it."

"Then he is the ostensible Stephenson, too, and sold every important citizen in this town with his bogus secret. Now if he has sent checks instead of money, we are sold, too, after we thought we had escaped. I was beginning to feel fairly comfortable once more, after my night's rest, but the look of that envelope makes me sick. It isn't fat enough; $8,500 in even the largest bank-notes makes more bulk than that."

"Edward, why do you object to checks?"

"Checks signed by Stephenson! I am resigned to take the $8,500 if it could come in bank-notes —for it does seem that it was so ordered, Mary— but I have never had much courage, and I have not the pluck to try to market a check signed with that disastrous name. It would be a trap. That man tried to catch me; we escaped somehow or other;

and now he is trying a new way. If it is checks—"

"Oh, Edward, it is *too* bad!" and she held up the checks and began to cry.

"Put them in the fire! quick! we mustn't be tempted. It is a trick to make the world laugh at *us,* along with the rest, and— Give them to *me,* since you can't do it!" He snatched them and tried to hold his grip till he could get to the stove; but he was human, he was a cashier, and he stopped a moment to make sure of the signature. Then he came near to fainting.

"Fan me, Mary, fan me! They are the same as gold!"

"Oh, how lovely, Edward! Why?"

"Signed by Harkness. What can the mystery of that be, Mary?"

"Edward, do you think—"

"Look here—look at this! Fifteen—fifteen—fifteen—thirty-four. Thirty-eight thousand five hundred! Mary, the sack isn't worth twelve dollars, and Harkness—apparently—has paid about par for it."

"And does it all come to us, do you think—instead of the ten thousand?"

"Why, it looks like it. And the checks are made to 'Bearer,' too."

"Is that good, Edward? What is it for?"

"A hint to collect them at some distant bank, I reckon. Perhaps Harkness doesn't want the matter known. What is that—a note?"

"Yes. It was with the checks."

It was in the "Stephenson" handwriting, but there was no signature. It said:

"I am a disappointed man. Your honesty is beyond the reach of temptation. I had a different idea about it, but I wronged you in that, and I beg pardon, and do it sincerely. I honor you—and that is sincere too. This town is not worthy to kiss the hem of your garment. Dear sir, I made a square bet with myself that there were nineteen debauchable men in your self-righteous community. I have lost. Take the whole pot, you are entitled to it."

Richards drew a deep sigh, and said:

"It seems written with fire—it burns so. Mary—I am miserable again."

"I, too. Ah, dear, I wish—"

"To think, Mary—he *believes* in me."

"Oh, don't, Edward—I can't bear it."

"If those beautiful words were deserved, Mary—and God knows I believed I deserved them once—I think I could give the forty thousand dollars for them. And I would put that paper away, as representing more than gold and jewels, and keep it always. But now— We could not live in the shadow of its accusing presence, Mary."

He put it in the fire.

A messenger arrived and delivered an envelope. Richards took from it a note and read it; it was from Burgess.

"You saved me, in a difficult time. I saved you last night. It was at cost of a lie, but I made the sacrifice freely, and out of a grateful heart. None in this village knows so well as I know how brave and good and noble you are. At bottom you cannot respect me, knowing as you do of that matter of which I am accused, and by the general voice condemned; but I beg that you will at least believe that I am a grateful man; it will help me to bear my burden.
                    *[Signed]   "*BURGESS."

"Saved, once more. And on such terms!" He put the note in the fire. "I—I wish I were dead, Mary, I wish I were out of it all."

"Oh, these are bitter, bitter days, Edward. The stabs, through their very generosity, are so deep—and they come so fast!"

Three days before the election each of two thousand voters suddenly found himself in possession of a prized memento—one of the renowned bogus double-eagles. Around one of its faces was stamped these words: "THE REMARK I MADE TO THE POOR STRANGER WAS—" Around the other face was stamped these: "GO, AND REFORM. [SIGNED] PINKERTON." Thus the entire remaining refuse of the renowned joke was emptied upon a single head, and with calamitous effect. It revived the recent vast laugh and concentrated it upon Pinkerton; and Harkness's election was a walkover.

Within twenty-four hours after the Richardses had received their checks their consciences were quieting down, discouraged; the old couple were learning to reconcile themselves to the sin which they had committed. But they were to learn, now, that a sin takes on new and real terrors when there seems a chance that it is going to be found out. This gives it a fresh and most substantial and important aspect. At church the morning sermon was of the usual pattern; it was the same old things said in the same old way; they had heard them a thousand times and found them innocuous, next to meaningless, and easy to sleep under; but now it was different: the sermon seemed to bristle with accusations; it seemed aimed straight and specially at people who were concealing deadly sins. After church they got away from the mob of congratulators as soon as they could, and hurried homeward, chilled to the bone at they did not know what—vague, shadowy, indefinite fears. And by chance they caught a glimpse of Mr. Burgess as he turned a corner. He paid no attention to their nod of recognition! He hadn't seen it; but they did not know that. What could his conduct mean? It might mean—it might mean—oh, a dozen dreadful things. Was it possible that he knew that Richards could have cleared him of guilt in that bygone time, and had been silently waiting for a chance to even up accounts? At home, in their distress they got to imagining that their servant might have been in the next room listening when Richards revealed the secret to his wife that he knew of Burgess's innocence; next, Richards began to imagine that he had heard the swish of a gown in there at that time; next, he was sure he *had* heard it. They would call Sarah in, on a pretext, and watch her face: if she had been betraying them to Mr. Burgess, it would show in her manner. They asked her some questions—questions which were so random and incoherent and seemingly purposeless that the girl felt sure that the old people's minds had been affected by their sudden good fortune; the sharp and watchful gaze which they bent upon her frightened her, and that completed the business. She blushed, she became nervous and confused, and to the old people these were plain signs of guilt—guilt of some fearful sort or other—without doubt she was a spy and a traitor. When they were alone again they began to piece many unrelated things together and get horrible results out of the combination. When things had got about to the worst, Richards was delivered of a sudden gasp, and his wife asked:

"Oh, what is it?—what is it?"

"The note—Burgess's note! Its language was sarcastic, I see it now." He quoted: " 'At bottom you cannot respect me, *knowing*, as you do, of *that matter* of which I am accused'—oh, it is perfectly plain, now, God help me! He knows that I know! You see the ingenuity of the phrasing. It was a trap—and like a fool, I walked into it. And Mary—?"

"Oh, it is dreadful—I know what you are going to say—he didn't return your transcript of the pretended test-remark."

"No—kept it to destroy us with. Mary, he has exposed us to some already. I know it—I know it well. I saw it in a dozen faces after church. Ah, he wouldn't answer our nod of recognition—*he knew* what he had been doing!"

In the night the doctor was called. The news went around in the morning that the old couple were rather seriously ill—prostrated by the exhausting excitement growing out of their great windfall, the congratulations, and the late hours, the doctor said. The town was sincerely distressed; for these old people were about all it had left to be proud of, now.

Two days later the news was worse. The old couple were delirious, and were doing strange things. By witness of the nurses, Richards had exhibited checks—for $8,500? No—for an amazing sum—$38,500! What could be the explanation of this gigantic piece of luck?

The following day the nurses had more news—and wonderful. They had concluded to hide the checks, lest harm come to them; but when they searched they were gone from under the patient's pillow—vanished away. The patient said:

"Let the pillow alone; what do you want?"

"We thought it best that the checks—"

"You will never see them again—they are destroyed. They came from Satan. I saw the hell-brand on them, and I knew they were sent to betray me to sin." Then he fell to gabbling strange and dreadful things which were not clearly understandable, and which the doctor admonished them to keep to themselves.

Richards was right; the checks were never seen again.

A nurse must have talked in her sleep, for within two days the forbidden gabblings were the property of the town; and they were of a surprising sort. They seemed to indicate that Richards had been a claimant for the sack himself, and that Burgess had concealed that fact and then maliciously betrayed it.

Burgess was taxed with this and stoutly denied it. And he said it was not fair to attach weight to the chatter of a sick old man who was out of his mind. Still, suspicion was in the air, and there was much talk.

After a day or two it was reported that Mrs. Richards's delirious deliveries were getting to be duplicates of her husband's. Suspicion flamed up into conviction, now, and the town's pride in the purity of its one undiscredited important citizen began to dim down and flicker toward extinction.

Six days passed, then came more news. The old couple were dying. Richards's mind cleared in his latest hour, and he sent for Burgess. Burgess said:

"Let the room be cleared. I think he wishes to say something in privacy."

"No!" said Richards: "I want witnesses. I want you all to hear my confession, so that I may die a man, and not a dog. I was clean—artificially—like the rest; and like the rest I fell when temptation came. I signed a lie, and claimed the miserable sack. Mr. Burgess remembered that I had done him a service, and in gratitude (and ignorance) he suppressed my claim and saved me. You know the thing that was charged against Burgess years ago. My testimony, and mine alone, could have cleared him, and I was a coward, and left him to suffer disgrace—"

"No—no—Mr. Richards, you—"

"My servant betrayed my secret to him—"

"No one has betrayed anything to me—"

—"and then he did a natural and justifiable thing, he repented of the saving kindness which he had done me, and he *exposed* me—as I deserved—"

"Never!—I make oath—"

"Out of my heart I forgive him."

Burgess's impassioned protestations fell upon deaf ears; the dying man passed away without knowing that once more he had done poor Burgess a wrong. The old wife died that night.

The last of the sacred Nineteen had fallen a prey to the fiendish sack; the town was stripped of the last rag of its ancient glory. Its mourning was not showy, but it was deep.

By act of the Legislature—upon prayer and petition—Hadleyburg was allowed to change its name to (never mind what—I will not give it away), and leave one word out of the motto that for many generations had graced the town's official seal.

It is an honest town once more, and the man will have to rise early that catches it napping again.

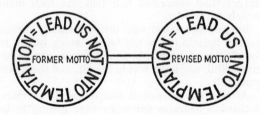

THE WAR PRAYER

[DICTATED in 1904 or 1905 but first published posthumously in 1923, "The War Prayer" is reprinted from the Definitive Edition, Vol. XXIX. Mark Twain had followed with rapt attention the various wars, declared and undeclared, of the years just before and after the turn of the twentieth century: the Spanish-American War and its aftermath—the campaign against Aguinaldo in the Philippines; the Boer War; the European invasion of China during the Boxer uprising of 1900; and the Russo-Japanese War. This prayer concentrates in brief space his repudiation of the nationalist and imperialist enthusiasms of his day.

IT WAS a time of great and exalting excitement. The country was up in arms, the war was on, in every breast burned the holy fire of patriotism; the drums were beating, the bands playing, the toy pistols popping, the bunched firecrackers hissing and spluttering; on every hand and far down the receding and fading spread of roofs and balconies a fluttering wilderness of flags flashed in the sun; daily the young volunteers marched down the wide avenue gay and fine in their new uniforms, the proud fathers and mothers and sisters and sweethearts cheering them with voices choked with happy emotion as they swung by; nightly the packed mass meetings listened, panting, to patriot oratory which stirred the deepest deeps of their hearts, and which they interrupted at briefest intervals with cyclones of applause, the tears running down their cheeks the while; in the churches the pastors preached devotion to flag and country, and invoked the God of Battles, beseeching His aid in our good cause in outpouring of fervid eloquence which moved every listener. It was indeed a glad and gracious time, and the half dozen rash spirits that ventured to disapprove of the war and cast a doubt upon its righteousness straightway got such a stern and angry warning that for their personal safety's sake they quickly shrank out of sight and offended no more in that way.

Sunday morning came—next day the battalions would leave for the front; the church was filled; the volunteers were there, their young faces alight with martial dreams—visions of the stern advance, the gathering momentum, the rushing charge, the flashing sabers, the flight of the foe, the tumult, the enveloping smoke, the fierce pursuit, the surrender!—them home from the war, bronzed heroes, welcomed, adored, submerged in golden seas of glory! With the volunteers sat their dear ones, proud, happy, and envied by the neighbors and friends who had no sons and brothers to send forth to the field of honor, there to win for the flag, or, failing, die the noblest of noble deaths. The service proceeded; a war chapter from the Old Testament was read; the first prayer was said; it was followed by an organ burst that shook the building, and with one impulse the house rose, with glowing eyes and beating hearts, and poured out that tremendous invocation—

"God the all-terrible! Thou who ordainest,
Thunder thy clarion and lightning thy sword!"

Then came the "long" prayer. None could remember the like of it for passionate pleading and moving and beautiful language. The burden of its supplication was, that an ever-merciful and benignant Father of us all would watch over our noble young soldiers, and aid, comfort, and encourage them in their patriotic work; bless them, shield them in the day of battle and the hour of peril, bear them in His mighty hand, make them strong and confident, invincible in the bloody onset; help them to crush the foe, grant to them and to their flag and country imperishable honor and glory—

An aged stranger entered and moved with slow and noiseless step up the main aisle, his eyes fixed upon the minister, his long body clothed in a robe that reached to his feet, his head bare, his white hair descending in a frothy cataract to his shoulders, his seamy face unnaturally pale, pale even to ghastliness. With all eyes following him and wondering, he made his silent way; without pausing, he ascended to the preacher's side and stood there, waiting. With shut lids the preacher, unconscious of his presence, continued his moving prayer, and at last finished it with the words, uttered in fervent appeal, "Bless our arms, grant us the victory, O Lord our God, Father and Protector of our land and flag!"

The stranger touched his arm, motioned him to step aside—which the startled minister did—and took his place. During some moments he surveyed the spellbound audience with solemn eyes, in which burned an uncanny light; then in a deep voice he said:

"I come from the Throne—bearing a message from Almighty God!" The words smote the house with a shock; if the stranger perceived it he gave no attention. "He has heard the prayer of His servant your shepherd, and will grant it if such shall be your desire after I, His messenger, shall have explained to you its import—that is to say, its full import. For it is like unto many of the prayers of men, in that it asks for more than he who utters it is aware of—except he pause and think.

"God's servant and yours has prayed his prayer. Has he paused and taken thought? Is it one prayer? No, it is two—one uttered, the other not. Both have reached the ear of Him Who heareth all supplications, the spoken and the unspoken. Ponder this—keep it in mind. If you would beseech a blessing upon yourself, beware! lest without intent you invoke a curse upon a neighbor at the same time. If you pray for the blessing of rain upon your crop which needs it, by that act you are possibly praying for a curse upon some neighbor's crop which may not need rain and can be injured by it.

"You have heard your servant's prayer—the uttered part of it. I am commissioned of God to put into words the other part of it—that part which the pastor—and also you in your hearts—fervently prayed silently. And ignorantly and unthinkingly? God grant that it was so! You heard these words: 'Grant us the victory, O Lord our God!' That is sufficient. The *whole* of the uttered prayer is compact into those pregnant words Elaborations were not necessary. When you have prayed for victory you have prayed for many unmentioned results which follow victory—*must* follow it, cannot help but follow it. Upon the listening spirit of God the Father fell also the unspoken part of the prayer. He commandeth me to put it into words. Listen!

"O Lord our Father, our young patriots, idols of our hearts, go forth to battle—be Thou near them! With them—in spirit—we also go forth from the sweet peace of our beloved firesides to smite the foe. O Lord our God, help us to tear their soldiers to bloody shreds with our shells; help us to cover their smiling fields with the pale forms of their patriot dead; help us to drown the thunder of the guns with the shrieks of their wounded, writhing in pain; help us to lay waste their humble homes with a hurricane of fire; help us to wring the hearts of their unoffending widows with unavailing grief; help us to turn them out roofless with their little children to wander unfriended the wastes of their desolated land in rags and hunger and thirst, sports of the sun flames of summer and the icy winds of winter, broken in spirit, worn with travail, imploring Thee for the refuge of the grave and denied it—for our sakes who adore Thee, Lord, blast their hopes, blight their lives, protract their bitter pilgrimage, make heavy their steps, water their way with their tears, stain the white snow with the blood of their wounded feet! We ask it, in the spirit of love, of Him Who is the Source of Love, and Who is the ever-faithful refuge and friend of all that are sore beset and seek His aid with humble and contrite hearts. Amen."

(*After a pause.*) "Ye have prayed it; if ye still desire it, speak! The messenger of the Most High waits."

It was believed afterward that the man was a lunatic, because there was no sense in what he said.

F. W. DUPEE

Editor

Henry James

1843–1916

H ENRY JAMES tried as hard as any writer ever has to make his stories and novels self-contained and self-explanatory. Ideally, they require no special knowledge of his life and times, no research into his literary sources, no analysis of his ideas as such. One need ask questions of them as little as one does of some good play in lively progress before one's eyes in a theater.

But James's ideal was not always realized in his fiction. And when it was, which was more often than not, the very means he employed to realize it can prove puzzling to some readers on their first encounter with his work. His scenes are highly allusive and concentrated. His style is exceptionally rich in implication. His judgment as to what materials are relevant, and what irrelevant, to a given story is strict. Inevitably, such judgments are more than matters of literary technique; they suggest what to James was more important and less important in life itself. And inevitably, some readers are less impressed by what he puts into his work than they are *de*pressed by what he leaves out.

Doesn't he appear to make life center in the drawing room and other settings of polite intercourse among human beings: the formal garden, the terrace, the museum, the restaurant, the public square? Where in his work are the bedroom, the factory, the business office,

the farm, the forest, the sea, and those other backgrounds against which men and women experience the elemental hardships, animal pleasures, and sheer accidents of life? If such experiences are implied in his work, as in fact they often are, why are they *merely* implied rather than being dealt with openly and fully? Why are they not at the heart of things, as they are apt to be in the fiction of Cooper, Melville, Mark Twain, Dreiser, Hemingway, and Faulkner, to name only novelists of America? What is Henry James doing in such company?

Self-contained though they are, James's stories and novels have always given rise to questions of this kind. They still do today, although he was long ago recognized as a major writer and given a high place in American literature. He remains a very exceptional writer by the standards of our literature. Indeed, certain modern British critics claim him for British literature. And we should probably not try to situate him too firmly in *any* national tradition. Yet he is too great a writer to be described as a mere "sport." If he belongs exclusively to no single national tradition, he belongs very definitely to the modern literature of what we now call the West, that is, Western Europe and America. No writer has ever cultivated more passionately his intellectual and emotional ties (his "relations," as he called them) to family and friends, to other writers, to cities and countries, and to the cultural manifestations of the various modern nations—in particular the United States, England, France, and Italy. It was out of his intimate responses to the forms of literature and life in these countries that he shaped his special variety of "humanism," his idea of what was highest in human culture and character. His very conception of the art of the novel was a blend of influences stemming from the American Hawthorne, the English George Eliot, the French Balzac and Flaubert, the Russian Turgenev. The essays he wrote on these and other novelists are not merely examples of good literary criticism; they are also implied testimonials to his relations, literary and sometimes personal, with these and other novelists. Similarly with his travel essays (*Italian Hours*, 1909; *A Little Tour of France*, 1885; *The American Scene*, 1907; etc.); his biographies (*Hawthorne*, 1879; *William Wetmore Story*, 1903); and his autobiographical writings (*A Small Boy and Others*, 1913; *Notes of a Son and Brother*, 1914; and the posthumously published fragment *The Middle Years*, 1917). All these writings are made lively and often profound by his peculiar genius for relating himself to the most far-flung persons, places, and things. He was himself, what he believed Americans generally were by reason of the newness and greatness of their country, "the heir of all the ages."

In a sense, therefore, no great writer was ever more thoroughly involved in tradition or committed to a profession and a way of life than James was. The old belief that he was a "rootless cosmopolitan" is no longer widely held. On the other hand, his idea of tradition was so complex, his way of life so unusual, and his work so selective in its values and methods, that he is not easily defined and classified. It is a part of the interest he has for us that he *is* exceptional and that every reader has to come to his own terms with him.

II

JAMES was born in New York City on April 15, 1843. His parents, Henry and Mary Walsh James, were descended from prosperous Hudson Valley families of largely Irish ancestry. His paternal grandfather was the prime mover in the extremely animated history of the James family. A youth from County Cavan in Ireland, the first American James, William, settled in Albany in 1793, bore numerous children by three successive wives, and accumulated an enormous fortune. Improbably enough, this successful Irishman was also a doctrinaire Calvinist; and when he died, his son Henry, father of the novelist, fell heir not only to a good deal of money but to recollections of grim Sundays, hell-fire sermons, and other strictly imposed disciplines as well.

Similar memories did not prevent many of his brothers and sisters from frankly enjoying their legacies. In most cases they left their native Albany and austere childhood background far behind. Marrying into other rich families, settling in New York City or Rome or Paris, many of them joined that small band of newly rich Americans who, in the mid-nineteenth century, traveled extensively, cultivated their minds a little and their pleasures a lot, and sometimes thought of themselves as composing a new American aristocracy. Gay, talkative, affectionate, impulsive, they suffered in some instances from the very excess of these qualities and led troubled or empty lives which made a mild mockery of their aristocratic claims. As a child, the future novelist was surrounded by the members of this populous "cousinage," as he was to call it; and he later drew from its members much of his knowledge of American society—its individual types, its problems and promises. One cousin, Mary ("Minny") Temple, was to become an especially engaging and tragic figure in the family annals. Pretty, intelligent, spirited, she was exceptionally attractive to Henry and other young men of his circle. But, expectant of life though she was, she died young. Minny Temple lived on, however, in Henry's affections and literary work, representing for him a type of the American girl to which he was to return again and again throughout his long career.

As it happened, young Henry James knew the "cousinage" not only from the inside, so to speak, but also from the outside. His own branch of the James family was always a little apart from the rest of it, more serious and purposive. His father, Henry James, Sr., combined the family gaiety with unusual gifts of mind and character. Having lost a leg in an accident during his Albany boyhood, he experienced a long and painful convalescence in the course of which he acquired the habit of reflection and a passion for ideas and literature. Eventually, his share in the family fortune made a life of leisure possible for him and he resolved to devote it to two main pursuits. One of these was the effort to replace his father's Calvinism with a religious faith which would be more "spiritual" (a favorite word of his) and would allow the individual believer a greater freedom to develop his peculiar mind and talents. Such a faith Henry James, Sr., finally found, partly through his own mystical experiences, partly through his readings in Emmanuel Swedenborg, the Swedish philosopher. The second pursuit to which he gave himself was the raising of a family whose members would be allowed to develop their individualities with a minimum of imposed discipline. He married Mary Walsh and their devotion to one another became legendary; it was equaled only by their devotion to their five children: Henry, the future novelist; an older son, William, the future philosopher and psychologist; a younger daughter, and two younger sons.

"Father's Ideas," as the James children came to call them, were many; and he expounded them in books and articles which were little read then and are little read now. But neither his ideas, his writing habits, nor his cork leg kept Henry James, Sr., from being an energetic, genial, and witty man. He was a great force in the James family, and a considerable force in American intellectual life of the time. If his books were not much read, his letters and conversation were widely attended to by Carlyle in England, by Emerson, Thoreau, Ripley, Dana, and others in America. His mysticism provided him with a vantage point from which he could criticize, often sharply, the "flagrant moralism" of certain contemporaries, the too optimistic humanism and patriotism of others. These, like other intellectual tendencies of the time, seemed to him to be weak substitutes for a true religious faith—substitutes that enfeebled the personal and intellectual powers of their advocates. He could call Emerson "a virgin" and "a man without a handle," Bronson Alcott a man in whom "the moral sense

was wholly dead, and the aesthetic sense had never been born." Inclined though he himself was to take an enthusiastically hopeful view of man's future, and especially America's future, the elder James insisted that "life is no farce; that it is not even genteel comedy; that it flowers and fructifies on the contrary out of the profoundest tragic depths . . ." Man was a part, however noble, of the natural creation and hence subject to evil and death.

On their tragic side his views resembled Hawthorne's rather than those of the Transcendentalist school, with which, in other respects, the elder James was to some extent associated. He admired Hawthorne's work; one of Henry, Jr.'s, earliest memories was of a new novel lying on the library table with the somewhat scary title of *The Scarlet Letter*. But the elder James was Emerson's friend and longtime correspondent, despite all their differences. Emerson sometimes visited the Jameses in their New York house; young Henry was always to recall his kindly but somewhat dim presence by the fireside. He had memories of visitors from other lands as well, including Thackeray, who stayed with the family in the course of a tour of America; and in his early manhood Henry was to be presented to Dickens, whose novels he had devoured as they came out during his childhood and youth.

From these and other such experiences the young Jameses learned more than they ever learned by the usual routines of the classroom. Their father wanted it that way, giving them a peculiar kind of education which greatly affected their minds and future lives. He distrusted education of the formal variety. The average schoolroom of the time seemed to him a place where children were made to conform to rules and conventions rather than encouraged to develop their own natures. So the young Jameses received their principal education in the family circle. Reading, games and travel, and, above all, conversation made up their "routines." Their father urged them to talk, dispute, examine everything, declare their minds, articulate their least feelings. All this was done informally, amid shouts and laughter, with Henry James, Sr., playing his part in the proceedings as a near equal. To be sure, the children had some training of the formal kind, although this tended to be chaotic. They went from institution to institution, tutor to tutor, governess to governess, while their father vainly sought the ideal school or teacher. Meanwhile, they attended no church as other children did. Their father's Christian mysticism was passionately superior to Christian institutions and rituals. Nor did he have any recognized profession or job which could give the family a point of reference in society. It was his profession to be, in the broadest sense, simply a man.

This way of life was stimulating and in the long run rewarding for some of the James children. But it put a severe strain on their minds and nerves, throwing the family as a whole very much on its own, and each small member of the family very much on his or her own. At first, young Henry seems to have been more the victim than the beneficiary of his father's liberality. By his own account, in *A Small Boy and Others*, he was on his own to the point of feeling somewhat helpless. His childhood years were largely spent in the Washington Square neighborhood of New York, a quiet and distinguished quarter of what was already a large and busy metropolis. His central experience in those years was of the "otherness" of things and people. The world seemed to be oddly estranged from him. The James family was very unlike other families and he was not only very unlike other children, he was very unlike his own brothers and boy cousins, especially his energetic, brilliant, probably rather bossy, older brother William. By contrast with these "others," Henry tended to think himself uncommonly passive, incompetent, dreamy, and slow of speech—something of a silent partner in the enterprise of education by conversation. But if this was his fate, he did not rebel against it in any of the usual ways. Then, as later on, he was devoted to most members of his immediate family, solicitous of their welfare, solicitous of their good opinion of himself.

When Henry James, Sr., died, in 1881, a few months after his wife's death, William saluted him as "sacred old Father." To Henry, Jr., he was scarcely less sacred. Father and son were, however, quite different in temperament and Henry, Jr., in his memoirs, was to gently criti-

cize his father's radical mysticism and experimental mode of life. Towards his mother he cherished emotions, as he said simply, "too deep for any words." He seems to have had a great deal in common with her. Like him, she was quiet, gentle, moderate in her opinions. Amid the excitement of their lives she seems to have embodied stability, order, and a capacity for self-sacrifice when it was necessary. Her affectionate presence evidently fortified young Henry in his possession of similar qualities. She probably helped to give him confidence in himself, however different he was from "others."

Confidence is the title of one of his early novels; confidence in the self is a recurring theme in all his work; and the search for confidence in his own self seems to have occupied him deeply during his youth. He quietly cultivated his peculiar attitudes and powers; if he "accepted his fate," he *made* it acceptable by converting it into something good and promising. How this came about is told with modesty and humor, though with much complication of language, in *A Small Boy and Others* and its sequels, *Notes of a Son and Brother* and *The Middle Years*. He read endlessly and wrote quantities of juvenile stories and plays. He observed the sights of New York with rare intentness: the people, the streets, the houses, above all the stage plays, to which he was frequently taken by his parents, and the paintings that were sometimes on exhibit in commercial galleries (there was no Metropolitan Museum of Art, or anything like it, in those days). Thus he made the "otherness" of things more familiar and understandable, and thus he developed fantastic powers of memory and observation.

Such powers are part of the standard equipment of major novelists; and James's youthful habit of "gaping," as he called it, and of brooding on what he gaped at, became the basis of his literary vocation, indeed of his very methods as a storyteller. For "observation" was to have a more specialized meaning for him than for many of the literary realists and naturalists of the nineteenth century. His idea of it tended to be less scientific, more visionary, than theirs. To "observe" was to accumulate, not facts and appearances but images, or in the more technical term often employed by James, "impressions." A fully developed Jamesian impression of a phenomenon combines a glimpse of its external appearance with a hint as to its moral significance. Thus he writes of one of his characters, a New York hostess, that her home was a "wedge of brownstone violently driven into 53rd Street." From this, we get a peculiarly vivid picture of a New York brownstone house, narrow, solid, fiercely holding its own against the narrow, solid houses on both sides. We also get a possible suggestion that the occupant of the house is a socially ambitious woman, intent on thrusting her way into Society.

Thus, in the course of time, James's childish sense of "otherness" was converted into a working quality of his imagination and art. Two major strains of experience contributed to this development. One, more or less negative, was his rather consistent feeling of powerlessness, a feeling that received concentrated expression when, during his adolescent years, he suffered a spinal injury while fighting a fire. A severe illness followed. He was unable to take part in the Civil War as his younger brothers did, and he continued to feel the effects of the injury at intervals throughout his life.

Meanwhile the other and more positive strain of experience had begun to play its part in his growth as an artist. Between his twelfth and seventeenth years he lived for the most part in Europe with his family. Leaving New York, the Jameses settled by turns in London, Paris, and Boulogne; and Henry continued to receive schooling, partly in the family circle, partly at institutions in Switzerland and elsewhere. Europe seemed very far away from America in those days. Ocean travel in primitive steamships was still a prolonged and hazardous affair. Europe was still the "Old World," the very antithesis of the "New World" of America. Indeed, Europe, with England at its head, then ruled the earth; whereas the United States was as yet only the land of promise—young, isolated, relatively unformed in its institutions, manners, and art. To the eye of the young American visitor, Europe's greatness was fully and richly formed. It was embodied in the splendid cities; in the wealth of magnificent buildings, museums, theaters, paintings; in the long-established social customs which gave definition and color to the daily life of people of all classes. All this fed young Henry's habitual fascination with whatever was "other"; it also gratified his desire for stability, order, and beauty. Later on, when he visited Europe on his own, and even more when he made Europe his residence, he came to view its civilization in a highly critical spirit. His mature novels mirror sharply the corrupting effects of excessive power and outworn institutions. What was fully "formed" could also be oppressive. Yet the Old World continued to haunt James's imagination, much as memories of the sea haunted Melville's, though with quite different implications. If he became a realistic social critic, he remained primarily an artist, that is, a man of imagination; and to the artist in him Europe remained, as he remarked himself, "vast, vague, and dazzling—an irradiation of light from objects undefined."

Henry James became one of the most thoroughly reasonable and self-controlled figures in all of literature. He nevertheless continued to consult his dreams and desires, however wayward, intangible and contradictory. The "inward romantic principle," as he called it, was never to be denied. He obeyed his artist's instinct to remain open to the solicitations of experience, whether rational or irrational, conscious or unconscious. His mind, beneath its composed and purposeful surface, seethed with powerful associations. At this depth "Europe" (he himself eventually put the word in quotation marks) ceased to be a place and became a symbol. It was associated not only with historic cities and beautiful works of art but with the human values he felt to be embodied in those spectacles. As he makes clear in *Notes of a Son and Brother*, "Europe" at its best symbolized "the general sense of glory."

Yet it was in the United States, more particularly in New England, that he came of age as a man and embarked on his career as a writer. Returning from Europe in 1860, the James family settled eventually in Cambridge, Massachusetts. New England had been the dominant force in American literature throughout James's childhood and youth. He had first felt its impact through his father's connections and he now came to know it at first hand. Harvard College was across the street from the family residence; Boston was a short ride by horsecar or carriage; Concord was only some seven miles distant. Many of the writers associated with these places were his father's acquaintances; several of their sons and daughters were youthful companions of Henry and William. William Dean Howells, another young emigrant to New England, became Henry's closest literary friend. William James entered Harvard as a student of science, finished his studies there, and, after travel and study abroad, stayed on till the end of his life as a famous lecturer in psychology and philosophy. Henry himself was briefly enrolled in the Harvard Law School. When he turned to literature, it was the *Atlantic Monthly* and the *North American Review* (then edited in New England) that printed many of his early stories and articles and thus helped to give him an audience.

But Henry James could not become an adoptive son of New England to the extent that William James was to do or that Howells did for many years. After all, he had been born in New York City, a fact which he always recalled with pride, and he had spent several formative years in Europe. He was cosmopolitan, almost by nature. He admired large, complex, pleasure-loving societies—societies in which good and evil, and the freedom to choose between them, existed in abundance. On the whole, the New England society was the opposite of cosmopolitan. It was proudly pastoral, self-contained, exclusive. Could not the whole meaning of the universe be read in the annals of its history and the character of its people? Were not the very hills, fields, woods, ponds, and coasts of the region images of eternity? As it happened, the New England culture was not timeless and universal, much as its original greatness depended on the heroic fiction that it was. In time the genius of the region declined, and with its decline the New England pride gave way to a sort of self-protective complacency. Boston claimed to be "the hub of the universe" in proportion as Boston became a city of the past.

It was James's partial awareness of these historical considerations, together with his New York background, that made him a diffident

citizen of literary New England. He came of age there during the years of the Civil War, when the literary consciousness of Americans was becoming more and more national, less and less regional and local. This development contributed to the decline of the New England culture, making it seem what James in his youth liked to call "provincial." But if the New England order was passing, a new intellectual and literary order was coming into existence in America. It is a fact of some historical interest that James published his first story in 1864, the same year during which Hawthorne died after a protracted and fruitless struggle to recover his creative powers.

Thus, in relation to New England, James was in an advantageous position. He could profit from the energies originally set flowing by that culture and at the same time escape the worst effects of their dwindling. He could become, as T. S. Eliot has said, "positively a continuator of the New England genius." In this much-quoted remark the word "positively" should be stressed. Whatever James perpetuated of the New England genius, he transformed thoroughly, often beyond easy recognition.

III

AMONG New England writers, Hawthorne was James's chief inspiration, in fact his only important one. For Hawthorne had been an artist of fiction, as James hoped to be. Moreover his art was based on a deep awareness of the human past, a feeling for human continuity, a recognition of human fallibility, all of which were congenial to James. In an essay on Emerson published in 1888, he was to declare (with some exaggeration) that Hawthorne's "vision was all for the evil and sin of the world; a side of life as to which Emerson's eyes were thickly bandaged." James had meanwhile acknowledged his relation to Hawthorne by frankly imitating him in certain youthful stories. And he was to publish in his thirty-sixth year, during the first flush of his international fame as a novelist, a searching and delightful biography of Hawthorne. The small book, published in 1879, was a sort of affectionate hail and farewell to the author of *The Scarlet Letter*. On the subject of Emerson, as we have seen, James's writings amounted to a respectful farewell with a very muted hail. He could not forgive Emerson his hyperbolic confidence in the universe. He could feel little literary sympathy for a man who confessed to seeing nothing in *Don Quixote* or the novels of Dickens and Jane Austen—or, for that matter, in Hawthorne's novels. (Emerson said that his Concord neighbor's books were "not worthy of him.") If we consider what the writing and reading of novels imply about the importance of worldly adventure, realistic social experience, and the here and now in the scheme of things; and if we compare Emerson's dismissal of the novel with James's devotion to it, we shall have a succinct idea of the differences between the two men and—Hawthorne excepted—their two generations.

James stated the differences clearly in the Hawthorne biography. The meaning of Hawthorne's career, with its fine achievements and partial failures, was that "the flower of art blooms only where the soil is deep, that it takes a great deal of history to produce a little literature, that it needs a complex social machinery to set a writer in motion." Much history had been made in the course of the Civil War and a new "era in the history of the American mind" had arrived. Americans would find the world "a more complicated place than it had hitherto seemed, the future more treacherous, success more difficult . . . The good American, in days to come, will be a more critical person than his complacent and confident grandfather. He has eaten of the tree of knowledge." As James presents them here, the advantages afforded him by the "new era" look somewhat grim. Whereas Thoreau, following Emerson, had confidently cried, "Simplify, simplify!", James now talks about "complication" and "difficulty" and a general failure of confidence. Americans are left in the position of Adam and Eve when the apple has been eaten and the newly acquired knowledge of good and evil hangs over them like a curse. What then? In *The American Scene*, a book published late in his life (1907), James could answer, with all confidence, the "what then?" The post-Civil War years had seen America embarked on the "great adventure" of "reaching out into the apparent void for the amenities, the consummations, after having earnestly gathered in so many of the preparations and necessities." In other words, the practical work of settling the continent and securing the political unity of the nation was complete enough to allow Americans to reach out for the relatively refined pleasures of conversation, travel, and art.

Conversation, travel, and art were pursuits of the cultivated life, as James conceived it. The "great adventure" thus consisted in the search for a broader American culture. In this, as in any genuine adventure, however, there were possibilities not only of pleasure and instruction but also of danger and frustration. By exchanging one's own poor culture for another, a person could lose his own rich necessary identity. It thus became James's affair as a novelist to record the adventure of culture in its double aspect; so, he compounded the pleasures he saw in it and added the frustrations and dangers he perceived to the sum. And he tried to see the whole adventure as it affected men and women engaged in the common routines of loving, marrying, and making their way in the world. What literary form was better suited to these purposes than the novel? For the novel, considered as a fully developed instrument of realistic social representation, was as new to American literature as the adventure of culture was.

Such were some of the literary opportunities present to James in post-Civil War America. But peculiarities of temperament and social position made it hard for him and others of his generation to take full and immediate advantage of them. James was an exceptionally reticent youth; marked feelings of powerlessness still mingled in him with strong feelings of pride and ambition. By belonging to a rich and cultivated family he belonged in some degree to a social class and literary generation which included—to take a notable example—Henry Adams. Many members of this class and generation tended to believe that they were in some important ways excluded from American life in the years following the Civil War. Their patrician birthright seemed to be threatened by the growing corruption of American politics, the rise of industrialism, the intrusion into the social picture of families newly rich and immigrants newly arrived in masses. In this situation, how could they exercise the duties and responsibilities, as well as enjoy the privileges, of their patrician heritage? James often speaks of "possessing oneself" of something, making something "one's own." Such phrases are a clue to his whole performance as an artist and moralist; they also make clear his affinity with this half-disinherited class and generation.

In time he did create a world of experience which was supremely his own. And thus he overcame in himself the worst distortions of character experienced by certain of the others: the nostalgia for Europe and the past, the snobbishness, the feeling of uselessness. He sank his roots into the firm ground of a profession, that of novelist, and made the ground still firmer by taking his profession with immense seriousness. Partly for professional, partly for temperamental reasons, he eventually took up residence in Europe. This step was grave but it was better than hovering between worlds and feeling a perpetual conflict between duty and nostalgia. In England, his eventual residence, he could attach himself to a society in which the aristocratic standard was still stoutly planted. There, too, he could find the "complex social machinery" to set him in motion as a writer.

Whether or not that machinery could have been found in America is probably an academic question, so far as James is concerned. For him, with his temperament and his youthful experience of Europe, the machinery was over there; and he had, as we have noted, the artist's instinct to trust to his experience and temperament rather than to socially imposed duties and hypothetical alternatives. The result was not, of course, an unqualified triumph. James's work is not the wholly self-contained and self-sufficient creation of a supreme free spirit. His work has a negative, or at least a problematical, aspect and has been rejected by certain generations and types of readers and critics. In their minds James is connected with the "genteel tradition" which Adams, Mark Twain, and Howells had also to cope with in their various ways, even when they did not belong to the patriciate. And it is probably true that there is a strain of unresolved personal gentility in James and his work. He makes, at times, an excessive evaluation of refinement, consciousness, and polite manners for their own sake. He tends generally to view the sexual life of man as a lurid mystery. Even his profound dedication to art can look negative when, as in certain of his Prefaces and his tales of writers and painters, he associates art too exclusively with difficulty, complexity, obliquity, sickness, and death. Yet he once wrote to Henry Adams that the practice of art is "an act of life," and this belief is strongly impressed on all the greater aspects of his work. For the body of his work is vast and various; it changes in mode and matter from period to period throughout his long career; and in the scale of the whole work the "genteel" or sentimental part of it looks increasingly small. It is the temerity and originality of James, rather than his refinements and inhibitions, which more and more command the interest of readers.

He published his first story, "A Tragedy of Error," in the *Continental Monthly* in February, 1864. This was followed by many other stories and by numerous book reviews and travel essays. His early critical writings are still readable; they show a rather self-consciously classical intelligence working to absorb, besides Hawthorne, the gentle realism of George Eliot, the fierce realism of Balzac, Flaubert, and other Europeans whose work was still new to America, still touched with scandal. His early stories were a little dim and derivative. Certain of them have the biographical interest, however, of reflecting some of his own youthful problems and of anticipating his later themes. The heroes of several of them are young men suffering from wounds, illnesses, or simply lack of animal spirits; they have a difficult time living, loving, and becoming mature men. The theme of the young or otherwise inexperienced person's initiation into "maturity"—the word means many things in James—is to be a persistent theme in his major work. But the drama of self-discovery was not treated memorably until it was combined with his other great source of drama, the discovery of Europe. This fusion was first fully accomplished in "A Passionate Pilgrim" (1871), a story about a young American who inherits a magnificent old property in England.

IV

AS A YOUNG man James had made two trips to Europe on his own, and in 1876, aged thirty-three, he came to his momentous decision to try living abroad permanently. The decision cost him much anxious thought at the time and was to have incalculable consequences for his mind, work and reputation. As he became more famous through his books, he also became more notorious: he was that queer monster of perversity, frivolity, or near-treason, an "expatriate." His notoriety had its peculiar disadvantages: people tended to read and review his books with the queer monster, rather than the books' actual contents, in mind. On the other hand his embattled state probably strengthened his character, fortified his resolve to be a great writer, and clarified his general point of view. On the whole he acquitted himself magnificently as the accused in the long expatriation trial which was his life. Throughout the ordeal he kept his American sympathies very much alive, his sense of humor intact. But it is hard to judge, pro or con, the deeper effects of his self-exile, for the evidence is intricately strewn through a long complex life and work. Speculation on the subject used to be rife among his critics but has now generally been abandoned as idle.

After a year spent in Paris, where he met Flaubert, Turgenev, and other novelists of the realist school, he removed to England; and there he remained, except for frequent journeys to the Continent and very occasional visits to America. His English life was centered in London until, in his fifty-fifth year, he acquired a small estate in the country town of Rye and went into semiretirement. In general, his life was devoid of dramatic incident or variety. He remained unmarried and, so far as we positively know, otherwise unattached except by way of friendship, a form of communion for which he had a genius and to which we owe his large legacy of extraordinary letters. Solitary work and social intercourse, both pursued on a grand scale, were the stable poles of his existence. They also helped to determine the character of his novels, in which conversation alternates with intimate private reflection, and the advantages and evils of life in society are paralleled by the advantages and dangers of the private life. If the dangers of society involve a loss of individual integrity, those of the private life consist in loneliness, egotism, and a tendency towards self-delusion. James's twin existences nourished him as long as his work went well and he got reasonable recognition from a discerning public. This he did get during his early London years, when he enjoyed considerable fame as the inventor of that charming novelty, the "international" subject, as he was the first to call it.

This subject consisted of the bringing together, in intimate situations, of persons of various nationalities. There were recent precedents for the subject in such writers as Stendhal, Mérimée, and Dickens. But James made more of the element of conflicting manners, less of the element of physical adventure, than others before him had done; and his ability to depict national traits in the form of individual characters was, and has remained, unsurpassed. Besides, his characters belong to one or the other of two "worlds," the American and the European, the new and the old, the democratic and the aristocratic, which then figured as intense opposites and rivals, not only in the casual journalism of the day but in the serious social studies of, for example, Tocqueville, Mrs. Trollope, and Dickens. As James treated the subject, say in *Daisy Miller*, contrasting systems of manners imply contrasting systems of morality, and the contrasts can prove by turns comic and fatal. Moreover, James's American characters are themselves far from being all of a piece. The general drama of differences is intensified by his eye for the differences observable among persons of American nationality. He gives us Yankee Puritans, newly rich New Yorkers, Southerners, cosmopolitan types long habituated to Europe. He gives us people for whom "culture" implies the lighter pleasures, and people for whom it is synonymous with the perfection of the self. He gives us people who claim a certain innocence as part of their American birthright, and people whose innocence is more intrinsic, complex, and durable.

The international subject proved moderately popular and James treated it in a variety of moods, bringing all aspects of the subject to a high state of development in *The Portrait of a Lady* (1881). In the later eighties he devoted his major efforts to the writing of three lengthy novels (*The Bostonians*, 1886; *The Princess Cassamassima*, 1886; *The Tragic Muse*, 1890), all of which deal with the more general problems of humanity. The action of these novels takes place not in the fairly enchanted world of the tourist but in a thoroughly disenchanted Boston or New York, Paris or London. These books failed with the public, however, and James, hoping to recover his audience and market, attempted a career in the theater (1890–95). (Despite his family's onetime wealth, he was a self-supporting writer.) This theatrical venture failed too, but for altogether different reasons. The three long novels were too rich and strange for the public taste of the time. The plays were dull from any point of view. In writing them James emptied himself of everything except his skill in mechanical contrivance. They suggest large ornate houses from which the owners have decamped with all their belongings. After he was booed from the stage while taking a curtain call at the first-night performance of *Guy Domville* in 1895, he retired from playwriting considered as a career in itself.

This half-tragic, half-ridiculous period in James's career was to have extraordinary consequences. He recovered his mastery of himself and his art—recovered it all the more firmly perhaps for having briefly, and in part, lost it. Instead of expecting a large popular audience, such as Dickens and Balzac had enjoyed, he began to write for a small advanced audience, and gradually he acquired one. Meanwhile, out of his experience of loss and isolation came a series of tales based on relatively new situations and human types. Obsessed men and women, forlorn children, even ghosts fill his shorter narratives, from *The Pupil* (1890) to *The Turn of the Screw* (1898) to *The Beast in the Jungle* (1903) and beyond. Meanwhile, returning to the full-length novel, he went through two quite distinct phases of fiction writing. The first, extending from 1897 to 1900, gave rise to *What Maisie Knew* (1897), *The Spoils of Poynton* (1897), and *The Awkward Age* (1899). In these novels, "the moral sense" is austerely affirmed by the principal charac-

ters, living as they do in a social milieu corrupt beyond any James had yet imagined.

In *The Awkward Age*, however, the comic sense wins at least a partial victory over the moral sense. In *The Ambassadors*, which ushered in his last great period, the comic sense is omnipresent, and James's powers of plot making, scene writing and character creating reach a supreme height. *The Ambassadors* (completed 1901, published 1903), *The Wings of the Dove* (1902), and *The Golden Bowl* (1904) are the principal achievements of his final phase as a novelist. The three novels have in common the fact that they return to the international subject of James's earlier days. Again American characters of relative inexperience travel to Europe, form intimacies there, and are conspired against by their more experienced intimates. But there are striking differences between the new uses and the old uses of the international subject, differences which obviously reflect James's own long habituation to Europe. The two "worlds," the American and the European, now seem less incompatible than formerly. The comedy and tragedy of comparative manners are somewhat in abeyance; there are no villains. The American characters are more positively "innocent," the Europeans less secure in their possession of "experience." The former win victories only through an intricate process of collaboration with the latter. It follows that the moral question, so prominent in the novels of the nineties, is, in these last novels, merged with the question of culture considered in a broad historical light. There is a growing recognition of what culture costs, almost necessarily, in terms of unregenerate passion, intrigue, and violence. With all their "sins," Mme. de Vionnet of *The Ambassadors* and Prince Amerigo of *The Golden Bowl* remain magnificent embodiments of their respective civilizations, the French and the Italian, as opposed to the thinner civilization of the Americans, which is still in the making. In these last novels, especially *The Golden Bowl*, the sometimes conflicting claims of morality and culture give rise to ambiguities which are the delight of some readers, the torment of others. And the settings of the novels loom prodigiously with symbolic import. When the guilt-stricken hero of *The*

Wings of the Dove wanders disconsolately around Venice in an autumn storm he sees his own state of soul reflected in the appearance of the storm-bound Piazza San Marco: that famous public square is "more than ever like a great drawing-room, the drawing-room of Europe, profaned and bewildered by some reverse of fortune." The drawing room, once the scene of more or less polite intercourse in James's novels, has here become the setting of a great international tragedy.

V

THE LAST novels bring several aspects of James's art of fiction to their fullest development. What are the most important of these aspects and how do they unite to form that peculiar phenomenon which we call Henry James's "world"? His world is peculiar in that it rests on an ideal abundance of money, beauty, intelligence, and informed good will. By contrast, the world of *Huckleberry Finn*—and those of other representative American novels—rests on something more like an ideal destitution: life is happiest and most "real" for Huck when he and Jim are together on the raft with a minimum of worldly goods, a maximum of instinctive daring, endurance, know-how, and fellowship. Where Mark Twain and so many others seek the authentic America by reconstituting in an idealized form the conditions of the frontier, even of the wilderness, Henry James seeks it in the contrary impulse towards a high civilization. His America is, quite literally, what the old slogan says it is: "the land of plenty." Its great problem is what to do with this plenty, this wealth of space, energy, good will, and money. For the abundance that prevails in James's world can itself be a cause of weakness and failure. In theory, it promises freedom of moral choice to all and makes it at least possible that all will choose the good. In fact, it often promotes egotism, greed, and other negative distortions of character. These impair or subvert the good in some characters, while others can retain their hold on the good only by strenuous moral exertions and practical sacrifices.

Indeed, the failure of good will in James's world is the more appalling because the conditions for its success seem so favorable. This contrast between the possible and the actual, appearance and reality, makes for the Jamesian irony. Implicit in all his major work, the irony is greatly magnified in his late novels. With it, there is a further development of his characteristic forms and methods of storytelling. His style grows ever denser in images, implications, and subtle humor. The style suggests not the aloof impersonal speech of an omniscient author but the living voice of one deeply committed to his creations, thoroughly intent on suffusing them with mind and sensibility. More particularly, the story has always been told in such a way that the narrator seems to be an intimate observer of the action, usually a direct participant in it. Moreover, in order to enhance the appearance of free will and personal power on the part of his characters, James has always made them reveal themselves as much as possible through pointed dialogue and small but decisive actions. "Dramatize, dramatize!" was his slogan, and his narratives consequently tend to fall into long, highly developed "scenes" like those in stage plays. All such Jamesian elements—the style, the irony, the role of the observer-narrator, the scenic arrangement—undergo intensive development in his later work. They help to account for its triumphs as well as its occasional excesses of subtlety and complication.

With the publication of *The Golden Bowl* his work as a novelist was substantially complete. In his remaining years he wrote some excellent shorter narratives (for example, "The Jolly Corner" and "The Bench of Desolation") and worked at two long novels (*The Sense of the Past* and *The Ivory Tower*) which were published as fragments after his death. He visited the United States in 1904–05 and wrote *The American Scene* on the basis of his impressions. Between 1907 and 1909 there appeared the twenty-four volumes of the New York Edition of *The Novels and Tales of Henry James*, a monumental project for which he selected about two-thirds of his published fiction, revised it thoroughly, and provided prefaces formulating his practices as a novelist. This invaluable edition was not widely appreciated at the time. In 1910 James fell seriously ill from the combined effects of fatigue and disappointment. Following his brother William's death in that year, he recovered sufficiently to undertake the writing of the autobiographical volumes we have referred to above. He was able to respond intensely to the tragedy of the First World War, to take an active part in war work, and in 1915, the year before his death, to make his bold gesture of sympathy towards England in her historic crisis —he became a British subject.

Meanwhile, amid all his sufferings and disappointments, James had availed himself of the traditionally English privilege of becoming a "character." The character he assumed was that of a gentleman fallen among roaring democrats, a master craftsman of literature fallen among slipshod performers. He played the dual role with a dignity which nevertheless permitted him displays of delicate humor and pathos at his own expense. A portly figure, formal in dress, exquisite in manners, he had a head which one observer described as "majestic" and large eyes which were capable, another observer said, of an "intolerable scrutiny." Adored by some, scorned by others, constantly quoted and misquoted in the press, formally painted in oils by Sargent and other famous portraitists, caricatured by Max Beerbohm, subjected to the dubious flattery of having his literary style and personal conversation parodied again and again, he was perhaps the most conspicuously unread author in the Anglo-American world of the time. Only the widely read Mark Twain, among American writers, surpassed him as an international figure.

He died on February 28, 1916, after a series of strokes. In her recollections of James, Edith Wharton, a friend of his old age, reports a rumor which, whether true or apocryphal, is entirely "in character." "He is said to have told his old friend Lady Prothero, when she saw him after his first stroke, that in the very act of falling, he heard in the room a voice which was distinctly, it seemed, not his own, saying: 'So here it is at last, the distinguished thing!' " This gentlemanly salute to death was the end

for Henry James of his great life and work, and of the great adventure of culture they exemplified.

READING SUGGESTIONS

Morton Dauwen Zabel, editor, *The Portable Henry James* (1951). The most useful single volume for the student of James, this book includes a large sampling of his fiction, essays, travel writings, and autobiographic writings, as well as extensive bibliographies and an excellent general introduction.

Percy Lubbock, editor, *The Letters of Henry James*, 2 vols. (1920). The largest collection to date of James's spirited and informative letters.

Leon Edel, editor, *The Selected Letters of Henry James* (1955). An inexpensive volume containing many letters not in Lubbock's collection.

F. W. Dupee, editor, *The Autobiography of Henry James* (1956). James's three autobiographic volumes, *A Small Boy and Others* (1913), *Notes of a Son and Brother* (1914), and *The Middle Years* (1917) are here collected in a single volume. An essential and beautiful work, although a difficult one for the reader who is untried in the ways of James's later style.

R. P. Blackmur, editor, *The Art of the Novel* (1935). A reprinting of the prefaces James wrote for the New York Edition of his fiction. Highly important.

F. O. Matthiessen and Kenneth B. Murdock, editors, *The Notebooks of Henry James* (1947). An important work for those interested in the sources and processes of James's art.

F. O. Matthiessen, *The James Family* (1947). An encyclopedic study of the Jameses considered as "a family of minds." Selections from the writings of James's father, brothers, and sister are included, together with passages from his own writings.

Leon Edel, *Henry James: The Untried Years* (1953). The first volume in a projected three-volume "life" by the most authoritative of James's biographers.

F. W. Dupee, *Henry James* (1951; reissued with revisions in 1956). A brief survey of his life and writings.

F. W. Dupee, editor, *The Question of Henry James* (1945). An anthology of representative essays written before 1945. Those by William Dean Howells, T. S. Eliot, Van Wyck Brooks, Constance Rourke, and Edmund Wilson are of special interest to American readers.

Lionel Trilling, Introduction to *The Princess Cassamassima* (1948). A comprehensive appreciation.

NOTE

A reissue of the New York Edition of James's work is now in progress.

DAISY MILLER:
A Study

❖

❲ James gave the subtitle of "A Study" to *Daisy Miller* because he feared that his picture of the heroine was more of a sketch than a full-fledged portrait. Nevertheless, the work came as close to being a popular success as any other book he wrote. First published in England in the *Cornhill Magazine* (1878), it was reprinted in the United States later in the same year and has since reappeared in numerous collections and anthologies, including the New York Edition. Two "pirated," or unauthorized, publications of the book in 1878 testified to its contemporary fame, a part of which arose from a mild scandal provoked by the heroine's unconventional behavior. One reviewer asked if the portrait of Daisy were not an "outrage on American girlhood."

Through the years *Daisy Miller* has been read with ever increasing pleasure in its mastery of the *nouvelle* form, the precision and wit of its characterizations, the meaningful use made of its Swiss and Roman settings, the subtlety with which a comedy of manners is joined to something bordering on a tragedy, the delicacy with which the claims of Roman manners are balanced against the claims of American manners (or the lack of them). Indeed *Daisy Miller* is now generally called the small masterpiece, as *The Portrait of a Lady* is called the large masterpiece, of James's early concern with the "international subject."

❖

I

At the little town of Vevey, in Switzerland, there is a particularly comfortable hotel. There are, indeed, many hotels; for the entertainment of tourists is the business of the place, which, as many travellers will remember, is seated upon the edge of a remarkably blue lake—a lake that it behooves every tourist to visit. The shore of the lake presents an unbroken array of establishments of this order, of every category, from the "grand hotel" of the newest fashion, with a chalk-white front, a hundred balconies, and a dozen flags flying from its roof, to the little Swiss *pension* of an elder day, with its name inscribed in German-looking lettering upon a pink or yellow wall, and an awkward summer-house in the angle of the garden. One of the hotels at Vevey, however, is famous, even classical, being distinguished from many of its upstart neighbors by an air both of luxury and of maturity. In this region, in the month of June, American travellers are extremely numerous; it may be said, indeed, that Vevey assumes at this period some of the characteristics of an American watering-place. There are sights and sounds which evoke a vision, an echo, of Newport and Saratoga. There is a flitting hither and thither of "stylish" young girls, a rustling of muslin flounces, a rattle of dance-music in the morning hours, a sound of high-pitched voices at all times. You receive an impression of these things at the excellent inn of the "Trois Couronnes," and are transported in fancy to the Ocean House or to Congress Hall. But at the "Trois Couronnes," it must be added, there are other features that are much at variance with these suggestions: neat German waiters, who look like secretaries of legation; Russian princesses sitting in the garden; little Polish boys walking about, held by the hand, with their governors; a view of the sunny crest of the Dent du Midi and the picturesque towers of the Castle of Chillon.

I hardly know whether it was the analogies or the differences that were uppermost in the mind of a young American, who, two or three years ago, sat in the garden of the "Trois Couronnes," looking about him, rather idly, at some of the graceful objects I have mentioned. It was a beautiful summer morning, and in whatever fashion the young American looked at things, they must have seemed to him charming. He had come from Geneva the day before, by the little steamer, to see his aunt, who was staying at the hotel—Geneva having been for a long time his place of residence. But his aunt had a headache—his aunt had almost always a headache—and now she was shut up in her room, smelling camphor, so that he was at liberty to wander about. He was some seven-and-twenty years of age; when his friends spoke of him, they usually said that he was at Geneva, "studying." When his enemies spoke of him, they said—but, after all, he had no enemies; he was an extremely amiable fellow, and universally liked. What I should say is, simply, that when certain persons spoke of him they affirmed that the reason of his spending so much time at Geneva was that he was extremely devoted to a lady who lived there—a foreign lady—a person older than himself. Very few Americans—indeed I think none—had ever seen this lady, about whom there were some singular stories. But Winterbourne had an old attachment for the little metropolis of Calvinism; he had been put to school there as a boy, and he had afterwards gone to college there—circumstances which had led to his forming a great many youthful friendships. Many of these he had kept, and they were a source of great satisfaction to him.

After knocking at his aunt's door and learning that she was indisposed, he had taken a walk about the town, and then he had come in to his breakfast. He had now finished his breakfast; but he was drinking a small cup of coffee, which had been served to him on a little table in the garden by one of the waiters who looked like an *attaché*. At last he finished his coffee and lit a cigarette. Presently a small boy came walking along the path—an urchin of nine or ten. The child, who was diminutive for his years, had an aged expression of countenance, a pale complexion, and sharp little features. He was dressed in knickerbockers, with red stockings, which displayed his poor little spindleshanks; he also wore a brilliant red cravat. He carried in his hand a long alpenstock, the sharp point of which he thrust into everything that he approached—the flower-beds, the garden-benches, the trains of the ladies' dresses. In front of Winterbourne he paused, looking at him with a pair of bright, penetrating little eyes.

"Will you give me a lump of sugar?" he asked, in a sharp, hard little voice—a voice immature, and yet, somehow, not young.

Winterbourne glanced at the small table near him, on which his coffee-service rested, and saw that several morsels of sugar remained. "Yes, you may take one," he answered; "but I don't think sugar is good for little boys."

This little boy stepped forward and carefully selected three of the coveted fragments, two of which he buried in the pocket of his knickerbockers, depositing the other as promptly in another place. He poked his alpenstock, lance-fashion, into Winterbourne's bench, and tried to crack the lump of sugar with his teeth.

"Oh, blazes; it's har-r-d!" he exclaimed, pronouncing the adjective in a peculiar manner.

Winterbourne had immediately perceived that he might have the honour of claiming him as a fellow-countryman. "Take care you don't hurt your teeth," he said, paternally.

"I haven't got any teeth to hurt. They have all come out. I have only got seven teeth. My mother counted them last night, and one came out right afterwards. She said she'd slap me if any more came out. I can't help it. It's this old Europe. It's the climate that makes them come out. In America they didn't come out. It's these hotels."

Winterbourne was much amused. "If you eat three lumps of sugar, your mother will certainly slap you," he said.

"She's got to give me some candy, then," rejoined his young interlocutor. "I can't get any candy here—any American candy. American candy's the best candy."

"And are American little boys the best little boys?" asked Winterbourne.

"I don't know. I'm an American boy," said the child.

"I see you are one of the best!" laughed Winterbourne.

"Are you an American man?" pursued this vivacious infant. And then, on Winterbourne's affirmative reply—"American men are the best," he declared.

His companion thanked him for the compliment; and the child, who had now got astride of his alpenstock, stood looking about him, while he attacked a second lump of sugar. Winterbourne wondered if he himself had been like this in his infancy, for he had been brought to Europe at about this age.

"Here comes my sister!" cried the child, in a moment. "She's an American girl."

Winterbourne looked along the path and saw a beautiful young lady advancing. "American girls are the best girls," he said, cheerfully, to his young companion.

"My sister ain't the best!" the child declared. "She's always blowing at me."

"I imagine that is your fault, not hers," said Winterbourne. The young lady meanwhile had drawn near. She was dressed in white muslin, with a hundred frills and flounces, and knots of pale-colored ribbon. She was bare-headed; but she balanced in her hand a large parasol, with a deep border of embroidery; and she was strikingly, admirably pretty. "How pretty they are!" thought Winterbourne, straightening himself in his seat, as if he were prepared to rise.

The young lady paused in front of his bench, near the parapet of the garden, which overlooked the lake. The little boy had now converted his alpenstock into a vaulting-pole, by the aid of which he was springing about in the gravel, and kicking it up not a little.

"Randolph," said the young lady, "what *are* you doing?"

"I'm going up the Alps," replied Randolph. "This is the way!" And he gave another little jump, scattering the pebbles about Winterbourne's ears.

"That's the way they come down," said Winterbourne.

"He's an American man!" cried Randolph, in his little hard voice.

The young lady gave no heed to this announcement, but looked straight at her brother. "Well, I guess you had better be quiet," she simply observed.

It seemed to Winterbourne that he had been in a manner presented. He got up and stepped slowly towards the young girl, throwing away his cigarette. "This little boy and I have made acquaintance," he said, with great civility. In Geneva, as he had been perfectly aware, a young man was not at liberty to speak to a young unmarried lady except under certain rarely-occurring conditions; but here at Vevey, what conditions could be better than these?—a pretty American girl coming and standing in front of you in a garden. This pretty American girl, however, on hearing Winterbourne's observation, simply glanced at him; she then turned her head and looked over the parapet, at the lake and the opposite mountains. He wondered whether he had gone too far; but he decided that he must advance farther, rather than retreat. While he was thinking of something else to say, the young lady turned to the little boy again.

"I should like to know where you got that pole," she said.

"I bought it!" responded Randolph.

"You don't mean to say you're going to take it to Italy."

"Yes, I am going to take it to Italy!" the child declared.

The young girl glanced over the front of her dress, and smoothed out a knot or two of ribbon. Then she rested her eyes upon the prospect again. "Well, I guess you had better leave it somewhere," she said, after a moment.

"Are you going to Italy?" Winterbourne inquired, in a tone of great respect.

The young lady glanced at him again. "Yes, sir," she replied. And she said nothing more.

"Are you—a—going over the Simplon?"[1] Winterbourne pursued, a little embarrassed.

"I don't know," she said. "I suppose it's some mountain. Randolph, what mountain are we going over?"

"Going where?" the child demanded.

"To Italy," Winterbourne explained.

"I don't know," said Randolph. "I don't want to go to Italy. I want to go to America."

"Oh, Italy is a beautiful place!" rejoined the young man.

"Can you get candy there?" Randolph loudly inquired.

"I hope not," said his sister. "I guess you have had enough candy, and mother thinks so too."

"I haven't had any for ever so long—for a hundred weeks!" cried the boy, still jumping about.

The young lady inspected her flounces and smoothed her ribbons again; and Winterbourne presently risked an observation upon the beauty of the view. He was ceasing to be embarrassed, for he had begun to perceive that she was not in the least embarrassed herself. There had not been the slightest alteration in her charming complexion; she was evidently neither offended nor fluttered. If she looked another way when he spoke to her, and seemed not particularly to hear him, this was simply her habit, her manner. Yet, as he talked a little more, and pointed out some of the objects of interest in the view, with which she appeared quite unacquainted, she gradually gave him more of the benefit of her glance; and then he saw that this glance was perfectly direct and unshrinking. It was not, however, what would have been called an immodest glance, for the young girl's eyes were singularly honest and fresh. They were wonderfully pretty eyes; and, indeed, Winterbourne had not seen for a long time anything prettier than his fair countrywoman's various features—her complexion, her nose, her ears, her teeth. He had a great relish for feminine beauty; he was addicted to observing and analyzing it; and as regards this young lady's face he made several observations. It was not at all insipid, but it was not exactly expressive; and though it was eminently delicate Winterbourne mentally accused it—very forgivingly—of a want of finish. He thought it very possible that Master Randolph's sister was a coquette; he was sure she had a spirit of her own; but in her bright, sweet, superficial little visage there was no mockery, no irony. Before long it became obvious that she was much disposed towards conversation. She told him that they were going to Rome for the winter—she and her mother and Randolph. She asked him if he was a "real American"; she shouldn't have taken him for one; he seemed more like a German—this was said after a little hesitation, especially when he spoke. Winterbourne, laughing, answered that he had met Germans who spoke like Americans; but that he had not, so far as he remembered, met an American who spoke like a German. Then he asked her if she should not be more comfortable in sitting upon the bench which he had just quitted. She answered that she liked standing up and walking about; but she presently sat down. She told him she was from New York State—"if you know where that is." Winterbourne learned more about her by catching hold of her small, slippery brother and making him stand a few minutes by his side.

"Tell me your name, my boy," he said.

"Randolph C. Miller," said the boy, sharply. "And I'll tell you her name;" and he levelled his alpenstock at his sister.

DAISY MILLER.   1. **Simplon:** One of the two passes through the Alps from Switzerland into Italy.

"You had better wait till you are asked!" said this young lady, calmly.

"I should like very much to know your name," said Winterbourne.

"Her name is Daisy Miller!" cried the child. "But that isn't her real name; that isn't her name on her cards."

"It's a pity you haven't got one of my cards!" said Miss Miller.

"Her real name is Annie P. Miller," the boy went on.

"Ask him *his* name," said his sister, indicating Winterbourne.

But on this point Randolph seemed perfectly indifferent; he continued to supply information in regard to his own family. "My father's name is Ezra B. Miller," he announced. "My father ain't in Europe; my father's in a better place than Europe."

Winterbourne imagined for a moment that this was the manner in which the child had been taught to intimate that Mr. Miller had been removed to the sphere of celestial rewards. But Randolph immediately added, "My father's in Schenectady. He's got a big business. My father's rich, you bet."

"Well!" ejaculated Miss Miller, lowering her parasol and looking at the embroidered border. Winterbourne presently released the child, who departed, dragging his alpenstock along the path. "He doesn't like Europe," said the young girl. "He wants to go back."

"To Schenectady, you mean?"

"Yes; he wants to go right home. He hasn't got any boys here. There is one boy here, but he always goes round with a teacher; they won't let him play."

"And your brother hasn't any teacher?" Winterbourne inquired.

"Mother thought of getting him one to travel round with us. There was a lady told her of a very good teacher; an American lady—perhaps you know her—Mrs. Sanders. I think she came from Boston. She told her of this teacher, and we thought of getting him to travel round with us. But Randolph said he didn't want a teacher travelling round with us. He said he wouldn't have lessons when he was in the cars. And we *are* in the cars about half the time. There was an English lady we met in the cars—I think her name was Miss Featherstone; perhaps you know her. She wanted to know why I didn't give Randolph lessons—give him 'instructions,' she called it. I guess he could give me more instruction than I could give him. He's very smart."

"Yes," said Winterbourne; "he seems very smart."

"Mother's going to get a teacher for him as soon as we get to Italy. Can you get good teachers in Italy?"

"Very good, I should think," said Winterbourne.

"Or else she's going to find some school. He ought to learn some more. He's only nine. He's going to college." And in this way Miss Miller continued to converse upon the affairs of her family, and upon other topics. She sat there with her extremely pretty hands, ornamented with very brilliant rings, folded in her lap, and with her pretty eyes now resting upon those of Winterbourne, now wandering over the garden, the people who passed by, and the beautiful view. She talked to Winterbourne as if she had known him a long time. He found it very pleasant. It was many years since he had heard a young girl talk so much. It might have been said of this unknown young lady, who had come and sat down beside him upon a bench, that she chattered. She was very quiet; she sat in a charming tranquil attitude, but her lips and her eyes were constantly moving. She had a soft, slender, agreeable voice, and her tone was decidedly sociable. She gave Winterbourne a history of her movements and intentions, and those of her mother and brother, in Europe, and enumerated, in particular, the various hotels at which they had stopped. "That English lady, in the cars," she said—"Miss Featherstone—asked me if we didn't all live in hotels in America. I told her I had never been in so many hotels in my life as since I came to Europe. I have never seen so many—it's nothing but hotels." But Miss Miller did not make this remark with a querulous accent; she appeared to be in the best humor with everything. She declared that the hotels were very good, when once you got used to their ways, and that Europe was perfectly sweet. She was not disappointed—not a bit. Perhaps it was because she had heard so much about it before. She had ever so many intimate friends that had been there ever so many times. And then she had had ever so many dresses and things from Paris. Whenever she put on a Paris dress she felt as if she were in Europe.

"It was a kind of a wishing-cap," said Winterbourne.

"Yes," said Miss Miller, without examining this analogy; "it always made me wish I was here. But I needn't have done that for dresses. I am sure they send all the pretty ones to America; you see the most frightful things here. The only thing I don't like," she proceeded, "is the society. There isn't any society; or, if there is, I don't know where it keeps itself. Do you? I suppose there is some society somewhere, but I haven't seen anything of it. I'm very fond of society, and I have always had a great deal of it. I don't mean only in Schenectady, but in New York. I used to go to New York every winter. In New York I had lots of society. Last winter I had seventeen dinners given me; and three of them were by gentlemen," added Daisy Miller. "I have more friends in New York than in Schenectady—more gentlemen friends; and more young lady friends too," she resumed in a moment. She paused again for an instant; she was looking at Winterbourne with all her prettiness in her lively eyes and in her light, slightly monotonous smile. "I have always had," she said, "a great deal of gentlemen's society."

Poor Winterbourne was amused, perplexed, and decidedly charmed. He had never yet heard a young girl express herself in just this fashion; never, at least, save in cases where to say such things seemed a kind of demonstrative evidence of a certain laxity of deportment. And yet was he to accuse Miss Daisy Miller of actual or potential *inconduite*,[2] as they said at Geneva? He felt that he had lived at Geneva so long that he had lost a good deal; he had become dishabituated to the American tone. Never, indeed, since he had grown old enough to appreciate things, had he encountered a young American girl of so pronounced a type as this. Certainly she was very charming, but how deucedly sociable! Was she simply a pretty girl from New York State—were they all like that, the pretty girls who had a good deal of gentlemen's society? Or was she also a designing, an audacious, an unscrupulous young person? Winterbourne had lost his instinct in this matter, and his reason could not help him. Miss Daisy Miller looked extremely innocent. Some people had told him that, after all, American girls were exceedingly innocent; and others had told him that, after all, they were not. He was inclined to think Miss Daisy Miller was a flirt—a pretty American flirt. He had never, as yet, had any relations with young ladies of this category. He had known, here in Europe, two or three women—persons older than Miss Daisy Miller, and provided, for respectability's sake, with husbands—who were great coquettes—dangerous, terrible women, with whom one's relations were liable to take a serious turn. But this young girl was not a coquette in that sense; she was very unsophisticated; she was only a pretty American flirt. Winterbourne was almost grateful for having found the formula that applied to Miss Daisy Miller. He leaned back in his seat; he remarked to himself that she had the most charming nose he had ever seen; he wondered what were the regular conditions and limitations of one's intercourse with a pretty American flirt. It presently became apparent that he was on the way to learn.

"Have you been to that old castle?" asked the young girl, pointing with her parasol to the far-gleaming walls of the Château de Chillon.[3]

"Yes, formerly, more than once," said Winterbourne. "You too, I suppose, have seen it?"

"No; we haven't been there. I want to go there dreadfully. Of course I mean to go there. I wouldn't go away from here without having seen that old castle."

"It's a very pretty excursion," said Winterbourne, "and very easy to make. You can drive, you know, or you can go by the little steamer."

"You can go in the cars," said Miss Miller.

"Yes; you can go in the cars," Winterbourne assented.

"Our courier says they take you right up to the castle," the young girl continued. "We were going last week; but my mother gave out. She suffers dreadfully from dyspepsia. She said she couldn't go. Randolph wouldn't go either; he says he doesn't think much of old castles. But I guess we'll go this week, if we can get Randolph."

"Your brother is not interested in ancient monuments?" Winterbourne inquired, smiling.

"He says he don't care much about old castles. He's only nine. He wants to stay at the hotel. Mother's afraid to leave him alone, and the courier won't stay with him; so we haven't been to many places. But it will be too bad if we don't go up there." And Miss Miller pointed again at the Château de Chillon.

"I should think it might be arranged," said Winterbourne. "Couldn't you get some one to stay—for the afternoon—with Randolph?"

Miss Miller looked at him a moment; and then, very placidly, "I wish *you* would stay with him!" she said.

Winterbourne hesitated a moment. "I should much rather go to Chillon with you."

"With me?" asked the young girl, with the same placidity.

She didn't rise, blushing, as a young girl at Geneva would have done; and yet Winterbourne, conscious that he had been very bold, thought it possible she was offended. "With your mother," he answered, very respectfully.

But it seemed that both his audacity and his respect were lost upon Miss Daisy Miller. "I guess

---

2. *inconduite:* indiscretion. Unless otherwise noted, foreign expressions are French throughout the selections from James.

3. **Château de Chillon:** See Byron's poem "The Prisoner of Chillon."

my mother won't go after all," she said. "She don't like to ride round in the afternoon. But did you really mean what you said just now; that you would like to go up there?"

"Most earnestly," Winterbourne declared.

"Then we may arrange it. If mother will stay with Randolph, I guess Eugenio will."

"Eugenio?" the young man inquired.

"Eugenio's our courier. He doesn't like to stay with Randolph; he's the most fastidious man I ever saw. But he's a splendid courier. I guess he'll stay at home with Randolph if mother does, and then we can go to the castle."

Winterbourne reflected for an instant as lucidly as possible—"we" could only mean Miss Daisy Miller and himself. This programme seemed almost too agreeable for credence; he felt as if he ought to kiss the young lady's hand. Possibly he would have done so—and quite spoiled the project; but at this moment another person—presumably Eugenio—appeared. A tall, handsome man, with superb whiskers, wearing a velvet morning-coat and a brilliant watch-chain, approached Miss Miller, looking sharply at her companion. "Oh, Eugenio!" said Miss Miller, with the friendliest accent.

Eugenio had looked at Winterbourne from head to foot; he now bowed gravely to the young lady. "I have the honour to inform mademoiselle that luncheon is upon the table."

Miss Miller slowly rose. "See here, Eugenio," she said. "I'm going to that old castle, anyway."

"To the Château de Chillon, mademoiselle?" the courier inquired. "Mademoiselle has made arrangements?" he added, in a tone which struck Winterbourne as very impertinent.

Eugenio's tone apparently threw, even to Miss Miller's own apprehension, a slightly ironical light upon the young girl's situation. She turned to Winterbourne, blushing a little—a very little. "You won't back out?" she said.

"I shall not be happy till we go!" he protested.

"And you are staying in this hotel?" she went on. "And you are really an American?"

The courier stood looking at Winterbourne, offensively. The young man, at least, thought his manner of looking an offence to Miss Miller; it conveyed an imputation that she "picked up" acquaintances. "I shall have the honour of presenting to you a person who will tell you all about me," he said, smiling, and referring to his aunt.

"Oh, well, we'll go some day," said Miss Miller. And she gave him a smile and turned away. She put up her parasol and walked back to the inn beside Eugenio. Winterbourne stood looking after her; and as she moved away, drawing her muslin furbelows over the gravel, said to himself that she had the *tournure* [4] of a princess.

He had, however, engaged to do more than proved feasible, in promising to present his aunt, Mrs. Costello, to Miss Daisy Miller. As soon as the former lady had got better of her headache he waited upon her in her apartment; and, after the proper inquiries in regard to her health, he asked her if she had observed, in the hotel, an American family—a mamma, a daughter, and a little boy.

"And a courier?" said Mrs. Costello. "Oh, yes, I have observed them. Seen them—heard them—and kept out of their way." Mrs. Costello was a widow with a fortune; a person of much distinction, who frequently intimated that, if she were not so dreadfully liable to sick-headaches, she would probably have left a deeper impress upon her time. She had a long pale face, a high nose, and a great deal of very striking white hair, which she wore in large puffs and *rouleaux* [5] over the top of her head. She had two sons married in New York, and another who was now in Europe. This young man was amusing himself at Hombourg, [6] and, though he was on his travels, was rarely perceived to visit any particular city at the moment selected by his mother for her own appearance there. Her nephew, who had come up to Vevey expressly to see her, was therefore more attentive than those who, as she said, were nearer to her. He had imbibed at Geneva the idea that one must always be attentive to one's aunt. Mrs. Costello had not seen him for many years, and she was greatly pleased with him, manifesting her approbation by initiating him into many of the secrets of that social sway which, as she gave him to understand, she exerted in the American capital. She admitted that she was very exclusive; but, if he were acquainted with New York, he would see that one had to be. And her picture of the minutely hierarchical constitution of the society of that city, which she presented to him in many different lights, was, to Winterbourne's imagination, almost oppressively striking.

He immediately perceived, from her tone, that Miss Daisy Miller's place in the social scale was low. "I am afraid you don't approve of them," he said.

"They are very common," Mrs. Costello declared. "They are the sort of Americans that one does one's duty by not—not accepting."

"Ah, you don't accept them?" said the young man.

4. *tournure:* carriage.　5. *rouleaux:* rolls or coils.　6. Hombourg: a health resort, not to be confused with the northwest-German metropolis, Hamburg.

"I can't, my dear Frederick. I would if I could, but I can't."

"The young girl is very pretty," said Winterbourne, in a moment.

"Of course she's pretty. But she is very common."

"I see what you mean, of course," said Winterbourne, after another pause.

"She has that charming look that they all have," his aunt resumed. "I can't think where they pick it up; and she dresses in perfection—no, you don't know how well she dresses. I can't think where they get their taste."

"But, my dear aunt, she is not, after all, a Comanche savage."

"She is a young lady," said Mrs. Costello, "who has an intimacy with her mamma's courier."

"An intimacy with the courier?" the young man demanded.

"Oh, the mother is just as bad! They treat the courier like a familiar friend—like a gentleman. I shouldn't wonder if he dines with them. Very likely they have never seen a man with such good manners, such fine clothes, so like a gentleman. He probably corresponds to the young lady's idea of a count. He sits with them in the garden, in the evening. I think he smokes."

Winterbourne listened with interest to these disclosures; they helped him to make up his mind about Miss Daisy. Evidently she was rather wild.

"Well," he said, "I am not a courier, and yet she was very charming to me."

"You had better have said at first," said Mrs. Costello with dignity, "that you had made her acquaintance."

"We simply met in the garden, and we talked a bit."

"*Tout bonnement!* [7] And pray what did you say?"

"I said I should take the liberty of introducing her to my admirable aunt."

"I am much obliged to you."

"It was to guarantee my respectability," said Winterbourne.

"And pray who is to guarantee hers?"

"Ah, you are cruel!" said the young man. "She's a very nice young girl."

"You don't say that as if you believed it," Mrs. Costello observed.

"She is completely uncultivated," Winterbourne went on. "But she is wonderfully pretty, and, in short, she is very nice. To prove that I believe it, I am going to take her to the Château de Chillon."

7. *"Tout bonnement!":* "Oh, really!", spoken with an ironic edge, would approximate it in American English.

"You two are going off there together? I should say it proved just the contrary. How long had you known her, may I ask, when this interesting project was formed? You haven't been twenty-four hours in the house."

"I had known her half an hour!" said Winterbourne, smiling.

"Dear me!" cried Mrs. Costello. "What a dreadful girl!"

Her nephew was silent for some moments. "You really think, then," he began, earnestly, and with a desire for trustworthy information—"you really think that—" But he paused again.

"Think what, sir?" said his aunt.

"That she is the sort of young lady who expects a man—sooner or later—to carry her off?"

"I haven't the least idea what such young ladies expect a man to do. But I really think that you had better not meddle with little American girls that are uncultivated, as you call them. You have lived too long out of the country. You will be sure to make some great mistake. You are too innocent."

"My dear aunt, I am not so innocent," said Winterbourne, smiling and curling his moustache.

"You are too guilty, then!"

Winterbourne continued to curl his moustache, meditatively. "You won't let the poor girl know you, then?" he asked at last.

"Is it literally true that she is going to the Château de Chillon with you?"

"I think that she fully intends it."

"Then, my dear Frederick," said Mrs. Costello, "I must decline the honour of her acquaintance. I am an old woman, but I am not too old—thank Heaven—to be shocked!"

"But don't they all do these things—the young girls in America?" Winterbourne inquired.

Mrs. Costello stared a moment. "I should like to see my granddaughters do them!" she declared, grimly.

This seemed to throw some light upon the matter, for Winterbourne remembered to have heard that his pretty cousins in New York were "tremendous flirts." If, therefore, Miss Daisy Miller exceeded the liberal margin allowed to these young ladies, it was probable that anything might be expected of her. Winterbourne was impatient to see her again, and he was vexed with himself that, by instinct, he should not appreciate her justly.

Though he was impatient to see her, he hardly knew what he should say to her about his aunt's refusal to become acquainted with her; but he discovered, promptly enough, that with Miss Daisy Miller there was no great need of walking on tiptoe. He found her that evening in the garden, wandering about in the warm starlight, like an indolent sylph, and swinging to and fro the largest fan he had ever beheld. It was ten o'clock. He had dined with his aunt, had been sitting with her since dinner, and had just taken leave of her till the morrow. Miss Daisy Miller seemed very glad to see him; she declared it was the longest evening she had ever passed.

"Have you been all alone?" he asked.

"I have been walking round with mother. But mother gets tired walking round," she answered.

"Has she gone to bed?"

"No; she doesn't like to go to bed," said the young girl. "She doesn't sleep—not three hours. She says she doesn't know how she lives. She's dreadfully nervous. I guess she sleeps more than she thinks. She's gone somewhere after Randolph; she wants to try to get him to go to bed. He doesn't like to go to bed."

"Let us hope she will persuade him," observed Winterbourne.

"She will talk to him all she can; but he doesn't like her to talk to him," said Miss Daisy, opening her fan. "She's going to try to get Eugenio to talk to him. But he isn't afraid of Eugenio. Eugenio's a splendid courier, but he can't make much impression on Randolph! I don't believe he'll go to bed before eleven." It appeared that Randolph's vigil was in fact triumphantly prolonged, for Winterbourne strolled about with the young girl for some time without meeting her mother. "I have been looking round for that lady you want to introduce me to," his companion resumed. "She's your aunt." Then, on Winterbourne's admitting the fact, and expressing some curiosity as to how she had learned it, she said she had heard all about Mrs. Costello from the chambermaid. She was very quiet, and very *comme il faut;* [8] she wore white puffs; she spoke to no one, and she never dined at the *table d'hôte*. Every two days she had a headache. "I think that's a lovely description, headache and all!" said Miss Daisy, chattering along in her thin, gay voice. "I want to know her ever so much. I know just what *your* aunt would be; I know I should like her. She would be very exclusive. I like a lady to be exclusive; I'm dying to be exclusive myself. Well, we *are* exclusive, mother and I. We don't speak to every one—or they don't speak to us. I suppose it's about the same thing. Anyway, I shall be ever so glad to know your aunt."

Winterbourne was embarrassed. "She would be most happy," he said; "but I am afraid those headaches will interfere."

8. *comme il faut:* mannerly.

The young girl looked at him through the dusk. "But I suppose she doesn't have a headache every day," she said, sympathetically.

Winterbourne was silent a moment. "She tells me she does," he answered at last—not knowing what to say.

Miss Daisy Miller stopped, and stood looking at him. Her prettiness was still visible in the darkness; she was opening and closing her enormous fan. "She doesn't want to know me!" she said, suddenly. "Why don't you say so? You needn't be afraid. I'm not afraid!" And she gave a little laugh.

Winterbourne fancied there was a tremor in her voice; he was touched, shocked, mortified by it. "My dear young lady," he protested, "she knows no one. It's her wretched health."

The young girl walked on a few steps, laughing still. "You needn't be afraid," she repeated. "Why should she want to know me?" Then she paused again; she was close to the parapet of the garden, and in front of her was the starlit lake. There was a vague sheen upon its surface, and in the distance were dimly-seen mountain forms. Daisy Miller looked out upon the mysterious prospect, and then she gave another little laugh. "Gracious! she *is* exclusive!" she said. Winterbourne wondered whether she was seriously wounded, and for a moment almost wished that her sense of injury might be such as to make it becoming in him to attempt to reassure and comfort her. He had a pleasant sense that she would be very approachable for consolatory purposes. He felt then, for the instant, quite ready to sacrifice his aunt, conversationally; to admit that she was a proud, rude woman, and to declare that they needn't mind her. But before he had time to commit himself to this perilous mixture of gallantry and impiety, the young lady, resuming her walk, gave an exclamation in quite another tone. "Well; here's mother! I guess she hasn't got Randolph to go to bed." The figure of a lady appeared, at a distance, very indistinct in the darkness, and advancing with a slow and wavering movement. Suddenly it seemed to pause.

"Are you sure it is your mother? Can you distinguish her in this thick dusk?" Winterbourne asked.

"Well!" cried Miss Daisy Miller, with a laugh, "I guess I know my own mother. And then she has got on my shawl, too! She is always wearing my things."

The lady in question, ceasing to advance, hovered vaguely about the spot at which she had checked her steps.

"I am afraid your mother doesn't see you,"

said Winterbourne. "Or perhaps," he added—thinking, with Miss Miller, the joke permissible—"perhaps she feels guilty about your shawl."

"Oh, it's a fearful old thing!" the young girl replied, serenely. "I told her she could wear it. She won't come here, because she sees you."

"Ah, then," said Winterbourne, "I had better leave you."

"Oh, no; come on!" urged Miss Daisy Miller.

"I'm afraid your mother doesn't approve of my walking with you."

Miss Miller gave him a serious glance. "It isn't for me; it's for you—that is, it's for *her*. Well, I don't know who it's for! But mother doesn't like any of my gentlemen friends. She's right down timid. She always makes a fuss if I introduce a gentleman. But I *do* introduce them—almost always. If I didn't introduce my gentlemen friends to mother," the young girl added, in her little soft, flat monotone, "I shouldn't think I was natural."

"To introduce me," said Winterbourne, "you must know my name." And he proceeded to pronounce it.

"Oh, dear, I can't say all that!" said his companion, with a laugh. But by this time they had come up to Mrs. Miller, who, as they drew near, walked to the parapet of the garden and leaned upon it, looking intently at the lake, and turning her back to them. "Mother!" said the young girl, in a tone of decision. Upon this the elder lady turned round. "Mr. Winterbourne," said Miss Daisy Miller, introducing the young man very frankly and prettily. "Common" she was, as Mrs. Costello had pronounced her; yet it was a wonder to Winterbourne that, with her commonness, she had a singularly delicate grace.

Her mother was a small, spare, light person, with a wandering eye, a very exiguous nose, and a large forehead, decorated with a certain amount of thin, much-frizzled hair. Like her daughter, Mrs. Miller was dressed with extreme elegance; she had enormous diamonds in her ears. So far as Winterbourne could observe, she gave him no greeting—she certainly was not looking at him. Daisy was near her, pulling her shawl straight. "What are you doing, poking round here?" this young lady inquired; but by no means with that harshness of accent which her choice of words may imply.

"I don't know," said her mother, turning towards the lake again.

"I shouldn't think you'd want that shawl!" Daisy exclaimed.

"Well—I do!" her mother answered, with a little laugh.

"Did you get Randolph to go to bed?" asked the young girl.

"No; I couldn't induce him," said Mrs. Miller, very gently. "He wants to talk to the waiter. He likes to talk to that waiter."

"I was telling Mr. Winterbourne," the young girl went on; and to the young man's ear her tone might have indicated that she had been uttering his name all her life.

"Oh, yes!" said Winterbourne; "I have the pleasure of knowing your son."

Randolph's mamma was silent; she turned her attention to the lake. But at last she spoke. "Well, I don't see how he lives!"

"Anyhow, it isn't so bad as it was at Dover," said Daisy Miller.

"And what occurred at Dover?" Winterbourne asked.

"He wouldn't go to bed at all. I guess he sat up all night—in the public parlour. He wasn't in bed at twelve o'clock; I know that."

"It was half-past twelve," declared Mrs. Miller, with mild emphasis.

"Does he sleep much during the day?" Winterbourne demanded.

"I guess he doesn't sleep much," Daisy rejoined.

"I wish he would!" said her mother. "It seems as if he couldn't."

"I think he's real tiresome," Daisy pursued.

Then, for some moments, there was silence. "Well, Daisy Miller," said the elder lady, presently, "I shouldn't think you'd want to talk against your own brother!"

"Well, he *is* tiresome, mother," said Daisy, quite without the asperity of a retort.

"He's only nine," urged Mrs. Miller.

"Well, he wouldn't go to that castle," said the young girl. "I'm going there with Mr. Winterbourne."

To this announcement, very placidly made, Daisy's mamma offered no response. Winterbourne took for granted that she deeply disapproved of the projected excursion; but he said to himself that she was a simple, easily-managed person, and that a few deferential protestations would take the edge from her displeasure. "Yes," he began; "your daughter has kindly allowed me the honour of being her guide."

Mrs. Miller's wandering eyes attached themselves, with a sort of appealing air, to Daisy, who, however, strolled a few steps farther, gently humming to herself. "I presume you will go in the cars," said her mother.

"Yes; or in the boat," said Winterbourne.

"Well, of course, I don't know," Mrs. Miller rejoined. "I have never been to that castle."

"It is a pity you shouldn't go," said Winterbourne, beginning to feel reassured as to her opposition. And yet he was quite prepared to find that, as a matter of course, she meant to accompany her daughter.

"We've been thinking ever so much about going," she pursued; "but it seems as if we couldn't. Of course Daisy—she wants to go round. But there's a lady here—I don't know her name—she says she shouldn't think we'd want to go to see castles *here;* she should think we'd want to wait till we got to Italy. It seems as if there would be so many there," continued Mrs. Miller, with an air of increasing confidence. "Of course, we only want to see the principal ones. We visited several in England," she presently added.

"Ah, yes! in England there are beautiful castles," said Winterbourne. "But Chillon, here, is very well worth seeing."

"Well, if Daisy feels up to it—," said Mrs. Miller, in a tone impregnated with a sense of the magnitude of the enterprise. "It seems as if there was nothing she wouldn't undertake."

"Oh, I think she'll enjoy it!" Winterbourne declared. And he desired more and more to make it a certainty that he was to have the privilege of a *tête-à-tête* with the young lady, who was still strolling along in front of them, softly vocalizing. "You are not disposed, madam," he inquired, "to undertake it yourself?"

Daisy's mother looked at him, an instant, askance, and then walked forward in silence. Then —"I guess she had better go alone," she said, simply. Winterbourne observed to himself that this was a very different type of maternity from that of the vigilant matrons who massed themselves in the forefront of social intercourse in the dark old city at the other end of the lake. But his meditations were interrupted by hearing his name very distinctly pronounced by Mrs. Miller's unprotected daughter.

"Mr. Winterbourne!" murmured Daisy.

"Mademoiselle!" said the young man.

"Don't you want to take me out in a boat?"

"At present?" he asked.

"Of course!" said Daisy.

"Well, Annie Miller!" exclaimed her mother.

"I beg you, madam, to let her go," said Winterbourne, ardently; for he had never yet enjoyed the sensation of guiding through the summer starlight a skiff freighted with a fresh and beautiful young girl.

"I shouldn't think she'd want to," said her mother. "I should think she'd rather go indoors."

"I'm sure Mr. Winterbourne wants to take me," Daisy declared. "He's so awfully devoted!"

"I will row you over to Chillon, in the starlight."

"I don't believe it!" said Daisy.

"Well!" ejaculated the elder lady again.

"You haven't spoken to me for half an hour," her daughter went on.

"I have been having some very pleasant conversation with your mother," said Winterbourne.

"Well, I want you to take me out in a boat!" Daisy repeated. They had all stopped, and she had turned round and was looking at Winterbourne. Her face wore a charming smile, her pretty eyes were gleaming, she was swinging her great fan about. No; it's impossible to be prettier than that, thought Winterbourne.

"There are half a dozen boats moored at that landing-place," he said, pointing to certain steps which descended from the garden to the lake. "If you will do me the honour to accept my arm, we will go and select one of them."

Daisy stood there smiling; she threw back her head and gave a little, light laugh. "I like a gentleman to be formal!" she declared.

"I assure you it's a formal offer."

"I was bound I would make you say something," Daisy went on.

"You see it's not very difficult," said Winterbourne. "But I am afraid you are chaffing me."

"I think not, sir," remarked Mrs. Miller, very gently.

"Do, then, let me give you a row," he said to the young girl.

"It's quite lovely, the way you say that!" cried Daisy.

"It will be still more lovely to do it."

"Yes, it would be lovely!" said Daisy. But she made no movement to accompany him; she only stood there laughing.

"I should think you had better find out what time it is," interposed her mother.

"It is eleven o'clock, madam," said a voice, with a foreign accent, out of the neighbouring darkness; and Winterbourne, turning, perceived the florid personage who was in attendance upon the two ladies. He had apparently just approached.

"Oh, Eugenio," said Daisy, "I am going out in a boat!"

Eugenio bowed. "At eleven o'clock, mademoiselle?"

"I am going with Mr. Winterbourne. This very minute."

"Do tell her she can't," said Mrs. Miller to the courier.

"I think you had better not go out in a boat, mademoiselle," Eugenio declared.

Winterbourne wished to Heaven this pretty girl

were not so familiar with her courier; but he said nothing.

"I suppose you don't think it's proper!" Daisy exclaimed. "Eugenio doesn't think anything's proper."

"I am at your service," said Winterbourne.

"Does mademoiselle propose to go alone?" asked Eugenio of Mrs. Miller.

"Oh, no; with this gentleman!" answered Daisy's mamma.

The courier looked for a moment at Winterbourne—the latter thought he was smiling—and then, solemnly, with a bow, "As mademoiselle pleases!" he said.

"Oh, I hoped you would make a fuss!" said Daisy. "I don't care to go now."

"I myself shall make a fuss if you don't go," said Winterbourne.

"That's all I want—a little fuss!" And the young girl began to laugh again.

"Mr. Randolph has gone to bed!" the courier announced, frigidly.

"Oh, Daisy; now we can go!" said Mrs. Miller.

Daisy turned away from Winterbourne, looking at him, smiling, and fanning herself. "Good-night," she said; "I hope you are disappointed, or disgusted, or something!"

He looked at her, taking the hand she offered him. "I am puzzled," he answered.

"Well, I hope it won't keep you awake!" she said, very smartly; and, under the escort of the privileged Eugenio, the two ladies passed towards the house.

Winterbourne stood looking after them; he was indeed puzzled. He lingered beside the lake for a quarter of an hour, turning over the mystery of the young girl's sudden familiarities and caprices. But the only very definite conclusion he came to was that he should enjoy deucedly "going off" with her somewhere.

Two days afterwards he went off with her to the Castle of Chillon. He waited for her in the large hall of the hotel, where the couriers, the servants, the foreign tourists were lounging about and staring. It was not the place he should have chosen, but she had appointed it. She came tripping downstairs, buttoning her long gloves, squeezing her folded parasol against her pretty figure, dressed in the perfection of a soberly elegant travelling-costume. Winterbourne was a man of imagination and, as our ancestors used to say, sensibility; as he looked at her dress and, on the great staircase, her little rapid, confiding step, he felt as if there were something romantic going forward. He could have believed he was going to elope with her. He passed out with her among all the idle people that were assembled there; they were all looking at her very hard; she had begun to chatter as soon as she joined him. Winterbourne's preference had been that they should be conveyed to Chillon in a carriage; but she expressed a lively wish to go in the little steamer; she declared that she had a passion for steamboats. There was always such a lovely breeze upon the water, and you saw such lots of people. The sail was not long, but Winterbourne's companion found time to say a great many things. To the young man himself their little excursion was so much of an escapade—an adventure—that, even allowing for her habitual sense of freedom, he had some expectation of seeing her regard it in the same way. But it must be confessed that, in this particular, he was disappointed. Daisy Miller was extremely animated, she was in charming spirits; but she was apparently not at all excited; she was not fluttered; she avoided neither his eyes nor those of any one else; she blushed neither when she looked at him nor when she felt that people were looking at her. People continued to look at her a great deal, and Winterbourne took much satisfaction in his pretty companion's distinguished air. He had been a little afraid that she would talk loud, laugh overmuch, and even, perhaps, desire to move about the boat a good deal. But he quite forgot his fears; he sat smiling, with his eyes upon her face, while, without moving from her place, she delivered herself of a great number of original reflections. It was the most charming garrulity he had ever heard. He had assented to the idea that she was "common"; but was she so, after all, or was he simply getting used to her commonness? Her conversation was chiefly of what metaphysicians term the objective cast; but every now and then it took a subjective turn.

"What on *earth* are you so grave about?" she suddenly demanded, fixing her agreeable eyes upon Winterbourne's.

"Am I grave?" he asked. "I had an idea I was grinning from ear to ear."

"You look as if you were taking me to a funeral. If that's a grin, your ears are very near together."

"Should you like me to dance a hornpipe on the deck?"

"Pray do, and I'll carry round your hat. It will pay the expenses of our journey."

"I never was better pleased in my life," murmured Winterbourne.

She looked at him a moment, and then burst into a little laugh. "I like to make you say those things! You're a queer mixture!"

In the castle, after they had landed, the subjective element decidedly prevailed. Daisy tripped about the vaulted chambers, rustled her skirts in the corkscrew staircases, flirted back with a pretty little cry and a shudder from the edge of the *oubliettes,* and turned a singularly well-shaped ear to everything that Winterbourne told her about the place. But he saw that she cared very little for feudal antiquities, and that the dusky traditions of Chillon made but a slight impression upon her. They had the good fortune to have been able to walk without other companionship than that of the custodian; and Winterbourne arranged with this functionary that they should not be hurried—that they should linger and pause wherever they chose. The custodian interpreted the bargain generously—Winterbourne, on his side, had been generous—and ended by leaving them quite to themselves. Miss Miller's observations were not remarkable for logical consistency; for anything she wanted to say she was sure to find a pretext. She found a great many pretexts in the rugged embrasures of Chillon for asking Winterbourne sudden questions about himself—his family, his previous history, his tastes, his habits, his intentions—and for supplying information upon corresponding points in her own personality. Of her own tastes, habits, and intentions Miss Miller was prepared to give the most definite, and, indeed, the most favourable, account.

"Well, I hope you know enough!" she said to her companion, after he had told her the history of the unhappy Bonnivard.[9] "I never saw a man that knew so much!" The history of Bonnivard had evidently, as they say, gone into one ear and out of the other. But Daisy went on to say that she wished Winterbourne would travel with them, and "go round" with them; they might know something, in that case. "Don't you want to come and teach Randolph?" she asked. Winterbourne said that nothing could possibly please him so much; but that he had unfortunately other occupations. "Other occupations? I don't believe it!" said Miss Daisy. "What do you mean? You are not in business." The young man admitted that he was not in business; but he had engagements which, even within a day or two, would force him to go back to Geneva. "Oh, bother!" she said; "I don't believe it!" and she began to talk about something else. But a few moments later, when he was pointing out to her the pretty design of an antique fireplace, she broke out irrelevantly,

"You don't mean to say you are going back to Geneva?"

"It is a melancholy fact that I shall have to return to-morrow."

"Well, Mr. Winterbourne," said Daisy, "I think you're horrid!"

"Oh, don't say such dreadful things!" said Winterbourne—"just at the last!"

"The last!" cried the young girl; "I call it the first. I have half a mind to leave you here and go straight back to the hotel alone." And for the next ten minutes she did nothing but call him horrid. Poor Winterbourne was fairly bewildered; no young lady had as yet done him the honour to be so agitated by the announcement of his movements. His companion, after this, ceased to pay any attention to the curiosities of Chillon or the beauties of the lake; she opened fire upon the mysterious charmer in Geneva, whom she appeared to have instantly taken for granted that he was hurrying back to see. How did Miss Daisy Miller know that there was a charmer in Geneva? Winterbourne, who denied the existence of such a person, was quite unable to discover; and he was divided between amazement at the rapidity of her induction and amusement at the frankness of her *persiflage*. She seemed to him, in all this, an extraordinary mixture of innocence and crudity. "Does she never allow you more than three days at a time?" asked Daisy, ironically. "Doesn't she give you a vacation in summer? There is no one so hard worked but they can get leave to go off somewhere at this season. I suppose, if you stay another day, she'll come after you in the boat. Do wait over till Friday, and I will go down to the landing to see her arrive!" Winterbourne began to think he had been wrong to feel disappointed in the temper in which the young lady had embarked. If he had missed the personal accent, the personal accent was now making its appearance. It sounded very distinctly, at last, in her telling him she would stop "teasing" him if he would promise her solemnly to come down to Rome in the winter.

"That's not a difficult promise to make," said Winterbourne. "My aunt has taken an apartment in Rome for the winter, and has already asked me to come and see her."

"I don't want you to come for your aunt," said Daisy; "I want you to come for me." And this was the only allusion that the young man was ever to hear her make to his invidious kinswoman. He declared that, at any rate, he would certainly come. After this Daisy stopped teasing. Winterbourne took a carriage, and they drove back to Vevey in the dusk; the young girl was very quiet.

9. **Bonnivard:** François Bonivard (or Bonnivard) (1496–1570), Swiss patriot, religious and political martyr, who was confined for seven years by the Duke of Savoy in the Castle of Chillon. See Byron's poem "The Prisoner of Chillon."

In the evening Winterbourne mentioned to Mrs. Costello that he had spent the afternoon at Chillon with Miss Daisy Miller.

"The Americans—of the courier?" asked this lady.

"Ah, happily," said Winterbourne, "the courier stayed at home."

"She went with you all alone?"

"All alone."

Mrs. Costello sniffed a little at her smelling-bottle. "And that," she exclaimed, "is the young person whom you wanted me to know!"

II

WINTERBOURNE, who had returned to Geneva the day after his excursion to Chillon, went to Rome towards the end of January. His aunt had been established there for several weeks, and he had received a couple of letters from her. "Those people you were so devoted to last summer at Vevey have turned up here, courier and all," she wrote. "They seem to have made several acquaintances, but the courier continues to be the most *intime*. The young lady, however, is also very intimate with some third-rate Italians, with whom she rackets about in a way that makes much talk. Bring me that pretty novel of Cherbuliez's [10]— 'Paule Méré'—and don't come later than the 23rd."

In the natural course of events, Winterbourne, on arriving in Rome, would presently have ascertained Mrs. Miller's address at the American banker's, and have gone to pay his compliments to Miss Daisy. "After what happened at Vevey I think I may certainly call upon them," he said to Mrs. Costello.

"If, after what happens—at Vevey and everywhere—you desire to keep up the acquaintance, you are very welcome. Of course a man may know every one. Men are welcome to the privilege!"

"Pray what is it that happens—here, for instance?" Winterbourne demanded.

"The girl goes about alone with her foreigners. As to what happens further, you must apply elsewhere for information. She has picked up half-a-dozen of the regular Roman fortune-hunters, and she takes them about to people's houses. When she comes to a party she brings with her a gentleman with a good deal of manner and a wonderful moustache."

"And where is the mother?"

"I haven't the least idea. They are very dreadful people."

10. **Cherbuliez's:** Victor Cherbuliez (1829–99), minor French novelist of Swiss origin.

Winterbourne meditated a moment. "They are very ignorant—very innocent only. Depend upon it they are not bad."

"They are hopelessly vulgar," said Mrs. Costello. "Whether or no being hopelessly vulgar is being 'bad' is a question for the metaphysicians. They are bad enough to dislike, at any rate; and for this short life that is quite enough."

The news that Daisy Miller was surrounded by half-a-dozen wonderful moustaches checked Winterbourne's impulse to go straightway to see her. He had perhaps not definitely flattered himself that he had made an ineffaceable impression upon her heart, but he was annoyed at hearing of a state of affairs so little in harmony with an image that had lately flitted in and out of his own meditations; the image of a very pretty girl looking out of an old Roman window and asking herself urgently when Mr. Winterbourne would arrive. If, however, he determined to wait a little before reminding Miss Miller of his claims to her consideration, he went very soon to call upon two or three other friends. One of these friends was an American lady who had spent several winters at Geneva, where she had placed her children at school. She was a very accomplished woman, and she lived in the Via Gregoriana. Winterbourne found her in a little crimson drawing-room, on a third floor; the room was filled with southern sunshine. He had not been there ten minutes when the servant came in, announcing "Madame Mila!" This announcement was presently followed by the entrance of little Randolph Miller, who stopped in the middle of the room and stood staring at Winterbourne. An instant later his pretty sister crossed the threshold; and then, after a considerable interval, Mrs. Miller slowly advanced.

"I know you!" said Randolph.

"I'm sure you know a great many things," exclaimed Winterbourne, taking him by the hand. "How is your education coming on?"

Daisy was exchanging greetings very prettily with her hostess; but when she heard Winterbourne's voice she quickly turned her head. "Well, I declare!" she said.

"I told you I should come, you know," Winterbourne rejoined, smiling.

"Well—I didn't believe it," said Miss Daisy.

"I am much obliged to you," laughed the young man.

"You might have come to see me!" said Daisy.

"I arrived only yesterday."

"I don't believe that!" the young girl declared.

Winterbourne turned with a protesting smile to her mother; but this lady evaded his glance, and, seating herself, fixed her eyes upon her son. "We've got a bigger place than this," said Randolph. "It's all gold on the walls."

Mrs. Miller turned uneasily in her chair. "I told you if I were going to bring you, you would say something!" she murmured.

"I told *you!*" Randolph exclaimed. "I tell *you,* sir!" he added, jocosely, giving Winterbourne a thump on the knee. "It *is* bigger, too!"

Daisy had entered upon a lively conversation with her hostess; and Winterbourne judged it becoming to address a few words to her mother. "I hope you have been well since we parted at Vevey," he said.

Mrs. Miller now certainly looked at him—at his chin. "Not very well, sir," she answered.

"She's got the dyspepsia," said Randolph. "I've got it, too. Father's got it. I've got it most!"

This announcement, instead of embarrassing Mrs. Miller, seemed to relieve her. "I suffer from the liver," she said. "I think it's this climate; it's less bracing than Schenectady, especially in the winter season. I don't know whether you know we reside at Schenectady. I was saying to Daisy that I certainly hadn't found any one like Dr. Davis, and I didn't believe I should. Oh, at Schenectady he stands first; they think everything of him. He has so much to do, and yet there was nothing he wouldn't do for me. He said he never saw anything like my dyspepsia, but he was bound to cure it. I'm sure there was nothing he wouldn't try. He was just going to try something new when we came off. Mr. Miller wanted Daisy to see Europe for herself. But I wrote to Mr. Miller that it seems as if I couldn't get on without Dr. Davis. At Schenectady he stands at the very top; and there's a great deal of sickness there, too. It affects my sleep."

Winterbourne had a good deal of pathological gossip with Dr. Davis's patient, during which Daisy chattered unremittingly to her own companion. The young man asked Mrs. Miller how she was pleased with Rome. "Well, I must say I am disappointed," she answered. "We had heard so much about it; I suppose we had heard too much. But we couldn't help that. We had been led to expect something different."

"Ah, wait a little, and you will become very fond of it," said Winterbourne.

"I hate it worse and worse every day!" cried Randolph.

"You are like the infant Hannibal," [11] said Winterbourne.

11. infant Hannibal: Carthaginian general (247–183 B.C.), sworn by his father, Hamilcar Barca, to an eternal hatred of Rome.

"No, I ain't!" Randolph declared, at a venture.

"You are not much like an infant," said his mother. "But we have seen places," she resumed, "that I should put a long way before Rome." And in reply to Winterbourne's interrogation, "There's Zürich," she concluded; "I think Zürich is lovely; and we hadn't heard half so much about it."

"The best place we've seen is the City of Richmond!" said Randolph.

"He means the ship," his mother explained. "We crossed in that ship. Randolph had a good time on the *City of Richmond.*"

"It's the best place I've seen," the child repeated. "Only it was turned the wrong way."

"Well, we've got to turn the right way some time," said Mrs. Miller, with a little laugh. Winterbourne expressed the hope that her daughter at least found some gratification in Rome, and she declared that Daisy was quite carried away. "It's on account of the society—the society's splendid. She goes round everywhere; she has made a great number of acquaintances. Of course she goes round more than I do. I must say they have been very sociable; they have taken her right in. And then she knows a great many gentlemen. Oh, she thinks there's nothing like Rome. Of course, it's a great deal pleasanter for a young lady if she knows plenty of gentlemen."

By this time Daisy had turned her attention again to Winterbourne. "I've been telling Mrs. Walker how mean you were!" the young girl announced.

"And what is the evidence you have offered?" asked Winterbourne, rather annoyed at Miss Miller's want of appreciation of the zeal of an admirer who on his way down to Rome had stopped neither at Bologna nor at Florence, simply because of a certain sentimental impatience. He remembered that a cynical compatriot had once told him that American women—the pretty ones, and this gave a largeness to the axiom— were at once the most exacting in the world and the least endowed with a sense of indebtedness.

"Why, you were awfully mean at Vevey," said Daisy. "You wouldn't do anything. You wouldn't stay there when I asked you."

"My dearest young lady," cried Winterbourne, with eloquence, "have I come all the way to Rome to encounter your reproaches?"

"Just hear him say that!" said Daisy to her hostess, giving a twist to a bow on this lady's dress. "Did you ever hear anything so quaint?"

"So quaint, my dear?" murmured Mrs. Walker, in a tone of a partisan of Winterbourne.

"Well, I don't know," said Daisy, fingering Mrs.

Walker's ribbons. "Mrs. Walker, I want to tell you something."

"Mother-r," interposed Randolph, with his rough ends to his words, "I tell you you've got to go. Eugenio'll raise—something!"

"I'm not afraid of Eugenio," said Daisy, with a toss of her head. "Look here, Mrs. Walker," she went on, "you know I'm coming to your party."

"I am delighted to hear it."

"I've got a lovely dress!"

"I am very sure of that."

"But I want to ask a favour—permission to bring a friend."

"I shall be happy to see any of your friends," said Mrs. Walker, turning with a smile to Mrs. Miller.

"Oh, they are not my friends," answered Daisy's mamma, smiling shyly, in her own fashion. "I never spoke to them."

"It's an intimate friend of mine—Mr. Giovanelli," said Daisy, without a tremor in her clear little voice, or a shadow on her brilliant little face.

Mrs. Walker was silent a moment; she gave a rapid glance at Winterbourne. "I shall be glad to see Mr. Giovanelli," she then said.

"He's an Italian," Daisy pursued, with the prettiest serenity. "He's a great friend of mine—he's the handsomest man in the world—except Mr. Winterbourne! He knows plenty of Italians, but he wants to know some Americans. He thinks ever so much of Americans. He's tremendously clever. He's perfectly lovely!"

It was settled that this brilliant personage should be brought to Mrs. Walker's party, and then Mrs. Miller prepared to take her leave. "I guess we'll go back to the hotel," she said.

"You may go back to the hotel, mother, but I'm going to take a walk," said Daisy.

"She's going to walk with Mr. Giovanelli," Randolph proclaimed.

"I am going to the Pincio," said Daisy, smiling.

"Alone, my dear—at this hour?" Mrs. Walker asked. The afternoon was drawing to a close— it was the hour for the throng of carriages and of contemplative pedestrians. "I don't think it's safe, my dear," said Mrs. Walker.

"Neither do I," subjoined Mrs. Miller. "You'll get the fever, as sure as you live. Remember what Dr. Davis told you!"

"Give her some medicine before she goes," said Randolph.

The company had risen to its feet; Daisy, still showing her pretty teeth, bent over and kissed her hostess. "Mrs. Walker, you are too perfect," she said. "I'm not going alone; I am going to meet a friend."

"Your friend won't keep you from getting the fever," Mrs. Miller observed.

"Is it Mr. Giovanelli?" asked the hostess.

Winterbourne was watching the young girl; at this question his attention quickened. She stood there smiling and smoothing her bonnet ribbons; she glanced at Winterbourne. Then, while she glanced and smiled, she answered, without a shade of hesitation, "Mr. Giovanelli—the beautiful Giovanelli."

"My dear young friend," said Mrs. Walker, taking her hand, pleadingly, "don't walk off to the Pincio at this hour to meet a beautiful Italian."

"Well, he speaks English," said Mrs. Miller.

"Gracious me!" Daisy exclaimed, "I don't want to do anything improper. There's an easy way to settle it." She continued to glance at Winterbourne. "The Pincio is only a hundred yards distant, and if Mr. Winterbourne were as polite as he pretends, he would offer to walk with me!"

Winterbourne's politeness hastened to affirm itself, and the young girl gave him gracious leave to accompany her. They passed down stairs before her mother, and at the door Winterbourne perceived Mrs. Miller's carriage drawn up, with the ornamental courier whose acquaintance he had made at Vevey seated within. "Good-bye, Eugenio!" cried Daisy, "I'm going to take a walk." The distance from the Via Gregoriana to the beautiful garden at the other end of the Pincian Hill is, in fact, rapidly traversed. As the day was splendid, however, and the concourse of vehicles, walkers, and loungers numerous, the young Americans found their progress much delayed. This fact was highly agreeable to Winterbourne, in spite of his consciousness of his singular situation. The slow-moving, idly-gazing Roman crowd bestowed much attention upon the extremely pretty young foreign lady who was passing through it upon his arm; and he wondered what on earth had been in Daisy's mind when she proposed to expose herself, unattended, to its appreciation. His own mission, to her sense, apparently, was to consign her to the hands of Mr. Giovanelli; but Winterbourne, at once annoyed and gratified, resolved that he would do no such thing.

"Why haven't you been to see me?" asked Daisy. "You can't get out of that."

"I have had the honour of telling you that I have only just stepped out of the train."

"You must have stayed in the train a good while after it stopped!" cried the young girl, with her little laugh. "I suppose you were asleep. You have had time to go to see Mrs. Walker."

"I knew Mrs. Walker—" Winterbourne began to explain.

"I know where you knew her. You knew her at Geneva. She told me so. Well, you knew me at Vevey. That's just as good. So you ought to have come." She asked him no other question than this; she began to prattle about her own affairs. "We've got splendid rooms at the hotel; Eugenio says they're the best rooms in Rome. We are going to stay all winter, if we don't die of the fever; and I guess we'll stay then. It's a great deal nicer than I thought; I thought it would be fearfully quiet; I was sure it would be awfully poky. I was sure we should be going round all the time with one of those dreadful old men that explain about the pictures and things. But we only had about a week of that, and now I'm enjoying myself. I know ever so many people, and they are all so charming. The society's extremely select. There are all kinds—English, and Germans, and Italians. I think I like the English best. I like their style of conversation. But there are some lovely Americans. I never saw anything so hospitable. There's something or other every day. There's not much dancing; but I must say I never thought dancing was everything. I was always fond of conversation. I guess I shall have plenty at Mrs. Walker's—her rooms are so small." When they had passed the gate of the Pincian Gardens, Miss Miller began to wonder where Mr. Giovanelli might be. "We had better go straight to that place in front," she said, "where you look at the view."

"I certainly shall not help you to find him," Winterbourne declared.

"Then I shall find him without you," said Miss Daisy.

"You certainly won't leave me!" cried Winterbourne.

She burst into her little laugh. "Are you afraid you'll get lost—or run over? But there's Giovanelli, leaning against that tree. He's staring at the women in the carriages; did you ever see anything so cool?"

Winterbourne perceived at some distance a little man standing with folded arms, nursing his cane. He had a handsome face, an artfully poised hat, a glass in one eye, and a nosegay in his button-hole. Winterbourne looked at him a moment, and then said, "Do you mean to speak to that man?"

"Do I mean to speak to him? Why, you don't suppose I mean to communicate by signs?"

"Pray understand, then," said Winterbourne, "that I intend to remain with you."

Daisy stopped and looked at him, without a sign of troubled consciousness in her face; with nothing but the presence of her charming eyes and her happy dimples. "Well, she's a cool one!" thought the young man.

"I don't like the way you say that," said Daisy. "It's too imperious."

"I beg your pardon if I say it wrong. The main point is to give you an idea of my meaning."

The young girl looked at him more gravely, but with eyes that were prettier than ever. "I have never allowed a gentleman to dictate to me, or to interfere with anything I do."

"I think you have made a mistake," said Winterbourne. "You should sometimes listen to a gentleman—the right one."

Daisy began to laugh again. "I do nothing but listen to gentlemen!" she exclaimed. "Tell me if Mr. Giovanelli is the right one."

The gentleman with the nosegay in his bosom had now perceived our two friends, and was approaching the young girl with obsequious rapidity. He bowed to Winterbourne as well as to the latter's companion; he had a brilliant smile, an intelligent eye; Winterbourne thought him not a bad-looking fellow. But he nevertheless said to Daisy, "No, he's not the right one."

Daisy evidently had a natural talent for performing introductions; she mentioned the name of each of her companions to the other. She strolled along with one of them on each side of her; Mr. Giovanelli, who spoke English very cleverly—Winterbourne afterwards learned that he had practised the idiom upon a great many American heiresses—addressed to her a great deal of very polite nonsense; he was extremely urbane, and the young American, who said nothing, reflected upon that profundity of Italian cleverness which enables people to appear more gracious in proportion as they are more acutely disappointed. Giovanelli, of course, had counted upon something more intimate; he had not bargained for a party of three. But he kept his temper in a manner which suggested far-stretching intentions. Winterbourne flattered himself that he had taken his measure. "He is not a gentleman," said the young American; "he is only a clever imitation of one. He is a music-master, or a penny-a-liner, or a third-rate artist. Damn his good looks!" Mr. Giovanelli had certainly a very pretty face; but Winterbourne felt a superior indignation at his own lovely fellow-country woman's not knowing the difference between a spurious gentleman and a real one. Giovanelli chattered and jested, and made himself wonderfully agreeable. It was true that, if he was an imitation, the imitation was brilliant. "Nevertheless," Winterbourne said to himself, "a nice girl ought to know!" And then he came back to the question whether this was, in fact, a nice girl. Would a nice girl—even allowing for her being a little American flirt— make a rendezvous with a presumably low-lived foreigner? The rendezvous in this case, indeed, had been in broad daylight, and in the most crowded corner of Rome; but was it not impossible to regard the choice of these circumstances as a proof of extreme cynicism? Singular though it may seem, Winterbourne was vexed that the young girl, in joining her *amoroso*,[12] should not appear more impatient of his own company, and he was vexed because of his inclination. It was impossible to regard her as a perfectly well-conducted young lady; she was wanting in a certain indispensable delicacy. It would therefore simplify matters greatly to be able to treat her as the object of one of those sentiments which are called by romancers "lawless passions." That she should seem to wish to get rid of him would help him to think more lightly of her, and to be able to think more lightly of her would make her much less perplexing. But Daisy, on this occasion, continued to present herself as an inscrutable combination of audacity and innocence.

She had been walking some quarter of an hour, attended by her two cavaliers, and responding in a tone of very childish gaiety, as it seemed to Winterbourne, to the pretty speeches of Mr. Giovanelli, when a carriage that had detached itself from the revolving train drew up beside the path. At the same moment Winterbourne perceived that his friend Mrs. Walker—the lady whose house he had lately left—was seated in the vehicle, and was beckoning to him. Leaving Miss Miller's side, he hastened to obey her summons. Mrs. Walker was flushed; she wore an excited air. "It is really too dreadful," she said. "That girl must not do this sort of thing. She must not walk here with you two men. Fifty people have noticed her."

Winterbourne raised his eyebrows. "I think it's a pity to make too much fuss about it."

"It's a pity to let the girl ruin herself!"

"She is very innocent," said Winterbourne.

"She's very crazy!" cried Mrs. Walker. "Did you ever see anything so imbecile as her mother? After you had all left me, just now, I could not sit still for thinking of it. It seemed too pitiful not even to attempt to save her. I ordered the carriage and put on my bonnet, and came here

as quickly as possible. Thank Heaven I have found you!"

"What do you propose to do with us?" asked Winterbourne, smiling.

"To ask her to get in, to drive her about here for half-an-hour, so that the world may see that she is not running absolutely wild, and then to take her safely home."

"I don't think it's a very happy thought," said Winterbourne; "but you can try."

Mrs. Walker tried. The young man went in pursuit of Miss Miller, who had simply nodded and smiled at his interlocutor in the carriage, and had gone her way with her companion. Daisy, on learning that Mrs. Walker wished to speak to her, retraced her steps with a perfect good grace and with Mr. Giovanelli at her side. She declared that she was delighted to have a chance to present this gentleman to Mrs. Walker. She immediately achieved the introduction, and declared that she had never in her life seen anything so lovely as Mrs. Walker's carriage-rug.

"I am glad you admire it," said this lady, smiling sweetly. "Will you get in and let me put it over you?"

"Oh no, thank you," said Daisy. "I shall admire it much more as I see you driving round with it."

"Do get in and drive with me!" said Mrs. Walker.

"That would be charming, but it's so enchanting just as I am!" and Daisy gave a brilliant glance at the gentlemen on either side of her.

"It may be enchanting, dear child, but it is not the custom here," urged Mrs. Walker, leaning forward in her victoria, with her hands devoutly clasped.

"Well, it ought to be, then!" said Daisy. "If I didn't walk I should expire."

"You should walk with your mother, dear," cried the lady from Geneva, losing patience.

"With my mother, dear!" exclaimed the young girl. Winterbourne saw that she scented interference. "My mother never walked ten steps in her life. And then, you know," she added, with a laugh, "I am more than five years old."

"You are old enough to be more reasonable. You are old enough, dear Miss Miller, to be talked about."

Daisy looked at Mrs. Walker, smiling intensely. "Talked about? What do you mean?"

"Come into my carriage, and I will tell you."

Daisy turned her quickened glance again from one of the gentlemen beside her to the other. Mr. Giovanelli was bowing to and fro, rubbing down his gloves and laughing very agreeably; Winterbourne thought it a most unpleasant scene.

12. *amoroso:* Italian for lover.

"I don't think I want to know what you mean," said Daisy, presently. "I don't think I should like it."

Winterbourne wished that Mrs. Walker would tuck in her carriage-rug and drive away; but this lady did not enjoy being defied, as she afterwards told him. "Should you prefer being thought a very reckless girl?" she demanded.

"Gracious!" exclaimed Daisy. She looked again at Mr. Giovanelli, then she turned to Winterbourne. There was a little pink flush in her cheek; she was tremendously pretty. "Does Mr. Winterbourne think," she asked slowly, smiling, throwing back her head and glancing at him from head to foot, "that—to save my reputation—I ought to get into the carriage?"

Winterbourne coloured; for an instant he hesitated greatly. It seemed so strange to hear her speak that way of her "reputation." But he himself, in fact, must speak in accordance with gallantry. The finest gallantry here was simply to tell her the truth; and the truth for Winterbourne—as the few indications I have been able to give have made him known to the reader—was that Daisy Miller should take Mrs. Walker's advice. He looked at her exquisite prettiness; and then said, very gently, "I think you should get into the carriage."

Daisy gave a violent laugh. "I never heard anything so stiff! If this is improper, Mrs. Walker," she pursued, "then I am all improper, and you must give me up. Good-bye; I hope you'll have a lovely ride!" and, with Mr. Giovanelli, who made a triumphantly obsequious salute, she turned away.

Mrs. Walker sat looking after her, and there were tears in Mrs. Walker's eyes. "Get in here, sir," she said to Winterbourne, indicating the place beside her. The young man answered that he felt bound to accompany Miss Miller; whereupon Mrs. Walker declared that if he refused her this favour she would never speak to him again. She was evidently in earnest. Winterbourne overtook Daisy and her companion, and, offering the young girl his hand, told her that Mrs. Walker had made an imperious claim upon his society. He expected that in answer she would say something rather free, something to commit herself still further to that "recklessness" from which Mrs. Walker had so charitably endeavoured to dissuade her. But she only shook his hand, hardly looking at him; while Mr. Giovanelli bade him farewell with a too emphatic flourish of the hat.

Winterbourne was not in the best possible humour as he took his seat in Mrs. Walker's victoria. "That was not clever of you," he said, candidly, while the vehicle mingled again with the throng of carriages.

"In such a case," his companion answered, "I don't wish to be clever; I wish to be *earnest!*"

"Well, you earnestness has only offended her and put her off."

"It has happened very well," said Mrs. Walker. "If she is so perfectly determined to compromise herself, the sooner one knows it the better; one can act accordingly."

"I suspect she meant no harm," Winterbourne rejoined.

"So I thought a month ago. But she has been going too far."

"What has she been doing?"

"Everything that is not done here. Flirting with any man she could pick up; sitting in corners with mysterious Italians; dancing all the evening with the same partners; receiving visits at eleven o'clock at night. Her mother goes away when visitors come."

"But her brother," said Winterbourne, laughing, "sits up till midnight."

"He must be edified by what he sees. I'm told that at their hotel every one is talking about her, and that a smile goes round among all the servants when a gentleman comes and asks for Miss Miller."

"The servants be hanged!" said Winterbourne, angrily. "The poor girl's only fault," he presently added, "is that she is very uncultivated."

"She is naturally indelicate," Mrs. Walker declared. "Take that example this morning. How long had you known her at Vevey?"

"A couple of days."

"Fancy, then, her making it a personal matter that you should have left the place!"

Winterbourne was silent for some moments; then he said, "I suspect, Mrs. Walker, that you and I have lived too long at Geneva!" And he added a request that she should inform him with what particular design she had made him enter her carriage.

"I wished to beg you to cease your relations with Miss Miller—not to flirt with her—to give her no further opportunity to expose herself—to let her alone, in short."

"I'm afraid I can't do that," said Winterbourne. "I like her extremely."

"All the more reason that you shouldn't help her to make a scandal."

"There shall be nothing scandalous in my attentions to her."

"There certainly will be in the way she takes them. But I have said what I had on my conscience," Mrs. Walker pursued. "If you wish to rejoin the young lady I will put you down. Here, by-the-way, you have a chance."

The carriage was traversing that part of the Pincian Garden that overhangs the wall of Rome and overlooks the beautiful Villa Borghese. It is bordered by a large parapet, near which there are several seats. One of the seats, at a distance, was occupied by a gentleman and a lady, towards whom Mrs. Walker gave a toss of her head. At the same moment these persons rose and walked towards the parapet. Winterbourne had asked the coachman to stop; he now descended from the carriage. His companion looked at him a moment in silence; then, while he raised his hat, she drove majestically away. Winterbourne stood there: he had turned his eyes towards Daisy and her cavalier. They evidently saw no one; they were too deeply occupied with each other. When they reached the low garden-wall they stood a moment looking off at the great flat-topped pine-clusters of the Villa Borghese; then Giovanelli seated himself familiarly upon the broad ledge of the wall. The western sun in the opposite sky sent out a brilliant shaft through a couple of cloud-bars, whereupon Daisy's companion took her parasol out of her hands and opened it. She came a little nearer, and he held the parasol over her; then, still holding it, he let it rest upon her shoulder, so that both of their heads were hidden from Winterbourne. This young man lingered a moment, then he began to walk. But he walked—not towards the couple with the parasol—towards the residence of his aunt, Mrs. Costello.

He flattered himself on the following day that there was no smiling among the servants when he, at least, asked for Mrs. Miller at her hotel. This lady and her daughter, however, were not at home; and on the next day after, repeating his visit, Winterbourne again had the misfortune not to find them. Mrs. Walker's party took place on the evening of the third day, and, in spite of the frigidity of his last interview with the hostess, Winterbourne was among the guests. Mrs. Walker was one of those American ladies who, while residing abroad, make a point, in their own phrase, of studying European society; and she had on this occasion collected several specimens of her diversely-born fellow-mortals to serve, as it were, as text-books. When Winterbourne arrived, Daisy Miller was not there, but in a few moments he saw her mother come in alone, very shyly and ruefully. Mrs. Miller's hair above her exposed-looking temples was more frizzled than ever. As she approached Mrs. Walker, Winterbourne also drew near.

"You see I've come all alone," said poor Mrs. Miller. "I'm so frightened I don't know what to do. It's the first time I've ever been to a party alone, especially in this country. I wanted to bring Randolph, or Eugenio, or some one, but Daisy just pushed me off by myself. I ain't used to going round alone."

"And does not your daughter intend to favour us with her society?" demanded Mrs. Walker, impressively.

"Well, Daisy's all dressed," said Mrs. Miller, with that accent of the dispassionate, if not of the philosophic, historian with which she always recorded the current incidents of her daughter's career. "She got dressed on purpose before dinner. But she's got a friend of hers there; that gentleman—the Italian—that she wanted to bring. They've got going at the piano; it seems as if they couldn't leave off. Mr. Giovanelli sings splendidly. But I guess they'll come before very long," concluded Mrs. Miller, hopefully.

"I'm sorry she should come—in that way," said Mrs. Walker.

"Well, I told her that there was no use in her getting dressed before dinner if she was going to wait three hours," responded Daisy's mamma. "I didn't see the use of her putting on such a dress as that to sit round with Mr. Giovanelli."

"This is most horrible!" said Mrs. Walker, turning away and addressing herself to Winterbourne. *Elle s'affiche.*[13] It's her revenge for my having ventured to remonstrate with her. When she comes I shall not speak to her."

Daisy came after eleven o'clock; but she was not, on such an occasion, a young lady to wait to be spoken to. She rustled forward in radiant loveliness, smiling and chattering, carrying a large bouquet, and attended by Mr. Giovanelli. Every one stopped talking, and turned and looked at her. She came straight to Mrs. Walker. "I'm afraid you thought I never was coming, so I sent mother off to tell you. I wanted to make Mr. Giovanelli practise some things before he came; you know he sings beautifully, and I want you to ask him to sing. This is Mr. Giovanelli; you know I introduced him to you; he's got the most lovely voice, and he knows the most charming set of songs. I made him go over them this evening on purpose; we had the greatest time at the hotel." Of all this Daisy delivered herself with the sweetest, brightest audibleness, looking now at her hostess and now round the room, while she gave a series of little pats round her shoulders to the edges of her dress. "Is there any one I know?" she asked.

"I think every one knows you!" said Mrs.

13. *Elle s'affiche:* "She's making a public spectacle of herself."

Walker, pregnantly, and she gave a very cursory greeting to Mr. Giovanelli. This gentleman bore himself gallantly. He smiled and bowed, and showed his white teeth; he curled his moustaches and rolled his eyes, and performed all the proper functions of a handsome Italian at an evening party. He sang very prettily half-a-dozen songs, though Mrs. Walker afterwards declared that she had been quite unable to find out who asked him. It was apparently not Daisy who had given him his orders. Daisy sat at a distance from the piano; and though she had publicly, as it were, professed a high admiration for his singing, talked, not inaudibly, while it was going on.

"It's a pity these rooms are so small; we can't dance," she said to Winterbourne, as if she had seen him five minutes before.

"I am not sorry we can't dance," Winterbourne answered; "I don't dance."

"Of course you don't dance; you're too stiff," said Miss Daisy. "I hope you enjoyed your drive with Mrs. Walker!"

"No, I didn't enjoy it; I preferred walking with you."

"We paired off; that was much better," said Daisy. "But did you ever hear anything so cool as Mrs. Walker's wanting me to get into her carriage and drop poor Mr. Giovanelli, and under the pretext that it was proper? People have different ideas! It would have been most unkind; he had been talking about that walk for ten days."

"He should not have talked about it at all," said Winterbourne; "he would never have proposed to a young lady of this country to walk about the streets with him."

"About the streets?" cried Daisy, with her pretty stare. "Where, then, would he have proposed to her to walk? The Pincio is not the streets, either; and I, thank goodness, am not a young lady of this country. The young ladies of this country have a dreadfully poky time of it, so far as I can learn; I don't see why I should change my habits for *them.*"

"I am afraid your habits are those of a flirt," said Winterbourne, gravely.

"Of course they are," she cried, giving him her little smiling stare again. "I'm a fearful, frightful flirt! Did you ever hear of a nice girl that was not? But I suppose you will tell me now that I am not a nice girl."

"You're a very nice girl; but I wish you would flirt with me, and me only," said Winterbourne.

"Ah! thank you—thank you very much; you are the last man I should think of flirting with. As I have had the pleasure of informing you, you are too stiff."

"You say that too often," said Winterbourne.

Daisy gave a delighted laugh. "If I could have the sweet hope of making you angry, I should say it again."

"Don't do that; when I am angry I'm stiffer than ever. But if you won't flirt with me, do cease, at least, to flirt with your friend at the piano; they don't understand that sort of thing here."

"I thought they understood nothing else!" exclaimed Daisy.

"Not in young unmarried women."

"It seems to me much more proper in young unmarried women than in old married ones," Daisy declared.

"Well," said Winterbourne, "when you deal with natives you must go by the custom of the place. Flirting is a purely American custom; it doesn't exist here. So when you show yourself in public with Mr. Giovanelli, and without your mother—"

"Gracious! poor mother!" interposed Daisy.

"Though you may be flirting, Mr. Giovanelli is not; he means something else."

"He isn't preaching, at any rate," said Daisy with vivacity. "And if you want very much to know, we are neither of us flirting; we are too good friends for that; we are very intimate friends."

"Ah!" rejoined Winterbourne, "if you are in love with each other it is another affair."

She had allowed him up to this point to talk so frankly that he had no expectation of shocking her by this ejaculation; but she immediately got up, blushing visibly, and leaving him to exclaim mentally that little American flirts were the queerest creatures in the world. "Mr. Giovanelli, at least," she said, giving her interlocutor a single glance, "never says such very disagreeable things to me."

Winterbourne was bewildered; he stood staring. Mr. Giovanelli had finished singing; he left the piano and came over to Daisy. "Won't you come into the other room and have some tea?" he asked, bending before her with his ornamental smile.

Daisy turned to Winterbourne, beginning to smile again. He was still more perplexed, for this inconsequent smile made nothing clear, though it seemed to prove, indeed, that she had a sweetness and softness that reverted instinctively to the pardon of offences. "It has never occurred to Mr. Winterbourne to offer me any tea," she said, with her little tormenting manner.

"I have offered you advice," Winterbourne rejoined.

"I prefer weak tea!" cried Daisy, and she went

off with the brilliant Giovanelli. She sat with him in the adjoining room, in the embrasure of the window, for the rest of the evening. There was an interesting performance at the piano, but neither of these young people gave heed to it. When Daisy came to take leave of Mrs. Walker, this lady conscientiously repaired the weakness of which she had been guilty at the moment of the young girl's arrival. She turned her back straight upon Miss Miller and left her to depart with what grace she might. Winterbourne was standing near the door; he saw it all. Daisy turned very pale and looked at her mother, but Mrs. Miller was humbly unconscious of any violation of the usual social forms. She appeared, indeed, to have felt an incongruous impulse to draw attention to her own striking observance of them. "Good-night, Mrs. Walker," she said; "we've had a beautiful evening. You see, if I let Daisy come to parties without me, I don't want her to go away without me." Daisy turned away, looking with a pale, grave face at the circle near the door; Winterbourne saw that, for the first moment, she was too much shocked and puzzled even for indignation. He on his side was greatly touched.

"That was very cruel," he said to Mrs. Walker.

"She never enters my drawing-room again!" replied his hostess.

Since Winterbourne was not to meet her in Mrs. Walker's drawing-room, he went as often as possible to Mrs. Miller's hotel. The ladies were rarely at home; but when he found them the devoted Giovanelli was always present. Very often the brilliant little Roman was in the drawing-room with Daisy alone, Mrs. Miller being apparently constantly of the opinion that discretion is the better part of surveillance. Winterbourne noted, at first with surprise, that Daisy on these occasions was never embarrassed or annoyed by his own entrance; but he very presently began to feel that she had no more surprises for him; the unexpected in her behaviour was the only thing to expect. She showed no displeasure at her *tête-à-tête* with Giovanelli being interrupted; she could chatter as freshly and freely with two gentlemen as with one; there was always, in her conversation, the same odd mixture of audacity and puerility. Winterbourne remarked to himself that if she was seriously interested in Giovanelli, it was very singular that she should not take more trouble to preserve the sanctity of their interviews; and he liked her the more for her innocent-looking indifference and her apparently inexhaustible good humour. He could hardly have said why, but she seemed to him a girl who would

never be jealous. At the risk of exciting a somewhat derisive smile on the reader's part, I may affirm that with regard to the women who had hitherto interested him, it very often seemed to Winterbourne among the possibilities that, given certain contingencies, he should be afraid—literally afraid—of these ladies; he had a pleasant sense that he should never be afraid of Daisy Miller. It must be added that this sentiment was not altogether flattering to Daisy; it was part of his conviction, or rather of his apprehension, that she would prove a very light young person.

But she was evidently very much interested in Giovanelli. She looked at him whenever he spoke; she was perpetually telling him to do this and to do that; she was constantly "chaffing" and abusing him. She appeared completely to have forgotten that Winterbourne had said anything to displease her at Mrs. Walker's little party. One Sunday afternoon, having gone to St. Peter's with his aunt, Winterbourne perceived Daisy strolling about the great church in company with the inevitable Giovanelli. Presently he pointed out the young girl and her cavalier to Mrs. Costello. This lady looked at them a moment through her eyeglass, and then she said,

"That's what makes you so pensive in these days, eh?"

"I had not the least idea I was pensive," said the young man.

"You are very much pre-occupied; you are thinking of something."

"And what is it," he asked, "that you accuse me of thinking of?"

"Of that young lady's—Miss Baker's, Miss Chandler's—what's her name?—Miss Miller's intrigue with that little barber's block."

"Do you call it an intrigue," Winterbourne asked—"an affair that goes on with such peculiar publicity?"

"That's their folly," said Mrs. Costello, "it's not their merit."

"No," rejoined Winterbourne, with something of that pensiveness to which his aunt had alluded. "I don't believe that there is anything to be called an intrigue."

"I have heard a dozen people speak of it; they say she is quite carried away by him."

"They are certainly very intimate," said Winterbourne.

Mrs. Costello inspected the young couple again with her optical instrument. "He is very handsome. One easily sees how it is. She thinks him the most elegant man in the world, the finest gentleman. She has never seen anything like him; he is better even than the courier. It was the courier, probably, who introduced him; and if he succeeds in marrying the young lady, the courier will come in for a magnificent commission."

"I don't believe she thinks of marrying him," said Winterbourne, "and I don't believe he hopes to marry her."

"You may be very sure she thinks of nothing. She goes on from day to day, from hour to hour, as they did in the Golden Age. I can imagine nothing more vulgar. And at the same time," added Mrs. Costello, "depend upon it that she may tell you any moment that she is 'engaged.' "

"I think that is more than Giovanelli expects," said Winterbourne.

"Who is Giovanelli?"

"The little Italian. I have asked questions about him and learned something. He is apparently a perfectly respectable little man. I believe he is, in a small way, a *cavaliere avvocato*.[14] But he doesn't move in what are called the first circles. I think it is really not absolutely impossible that the courier introduced him. He is evidently immensely charmed with Miss Miller. If she thinks him the finest gentleman in the world, he, on his side, has never found himself in personal contact with such splendour, such opulence, such expensiveness, as this young lady's. And then she must seem to him wonderfully pretty and interesting. I rather doubt that he dreams of marrying her. That must appear to him too impossible a piece of luck. He has nothing but his handsome face to offer, and there is a substantial Mr. Miller in that mysterious land of dollars. Giovanelli knows that he hasn't a title to offer. If he were only a count or a *marchese*! He must wonder at his luck, at the way they have taken him up."

"He accounts for it by his handsome face, and thinks Miss Miller a young lady *qui se passe ses fantaisies!*"[15] said Mrs. Costello.

"It is very true," Winterbourne pursued, "that Daisy and her mamma have not yet risen to that stage of—what shall I call it?—of culture, at which the idea of catching a count or a *marchese* begins. I believe that they are intellectually incapable of that conception."

"Ah! but the *avvocato* can't believe it," said Mrs. Costello.

Of the observation excited by Daisy's "intrigue," Winterbourne gathered that day at St. Peter's sufficient evidence. A dozen of the American colonists in Rome came to talk with Mrs. Costello, who sat on a little portable stool at the base of one of the great pilasters. The vesper service was going forward in splendid chants and organ-tones in the adjacent choir, and meanwhile, between Mrs. Costello and her friends, there was a great deal said about poor little Miss Miller's going really "too far." Winterbourne was not pleased with what he heard; but when, coming out upon the great steps of the church, he saw Daisy, who had emerged before him, get into an open cab with her accomplice and roll away through the cynical streets of Rome, he could not deny to himself that she was going very far indeed. He felt very sorry for her—not exactly that he believed that she had completely lost her head, but because it was painful to hear so much that was pretty, and undefended, and natural, assigned to a vulgar place among the categories of disorder. He made an attempt after this to give a hint to Mrs. Miller. He met one day in the Corso[16] a friend—a tourist like himself, who had just come out of the Doria Palace, where he had been walking through the beautiful gallery. His friend talked for a moment about the superb portrait of Innocent X., by Velasquez[17] which hangs in one of the cabinets of the palace, and then said, "And in the same cabinet, by-the-way, I had the pleasure of contemplating a picture of a different kind—that pretty American girl whom you pointed out to me last week." In answer to Winterbourne's inquiries, his friend narrated that the pretty American girl—prettier than ever—was seated with a companion in the secluded nook in which the great papal portrait was enshrined.

"Who was her companion?" asked Winterbourne.

"A little Italian with a bouquet in his buttonhole. The girl is delightfully pretty; but I thought I understood from you the other day that she was a young lady *du meilleur monde*."[18]

"So she is!" answered Winterbourne; and having assured himself that his informant had seen Daisy and her companion but five minutes before, he jumped into a cab and went to call on Mrs. Miller. She was at home; but she apologized to him for receiving him in Daisy's absence.

"She's gone out somewhere with Mr. Giovanelli," said Mrs. Miller. "She's always going round with Mr. Giovanelli."

"I have noticed that they are very intimate," Winterbourne observed.

"Oh, it seems as if they couldn't live without

---

14. *cavaliere avvocato:* Italian for lawyer; *cavaliere* is is an honorific designation.   15. *qui . . . fantaisies:* "who is indulging her whims."

16. **Corso:** principal Roman avenue.   17. **Velasquez:** Diego Rodríguez de Silva y Velázquez (1599–1660), Spanish painter.
18. *du meilleur monde:* "of the best society."

each other!" said Mrs. Miller. "Well, he's a real gentleman, anyhow. I keep telling Daisy she's engaged!"

"And what does Daisy say?"

"Oh, she says she isn't engaged. But she might as well be!" this impartial parent resumed. "She goes on as if she was. But I've made Mr. Giovanelli promise to tell me, if *she* doesn't. I should want to write to Mr. Miller about it—shouldn't you?"

Winterbourne replied that he certainly should; and the state of mind of Daisy's mamma struck him as so unprecedented in the annals of parental vigilance that he gave up as utterly irrelevant the attempt to place her upon her guard.

After this Daisy was never at home, and Winterbourne ceased to meet her at the houses of their common acquaintances because, as he perceived, these shrewd people had quite made up their minds that she was going too far. They ceased to invite her, and they intimated that they desired to express to observant Europeans the great truth that, though Miss Daisy Miller was a young American lady, her behaviour was not representative—was regarded by her compatriots as abnormal. Winterbourne wondered how she felt about all the cold shoulders that were turned towards her, and sometimes it annoyed him to suspect that she did not feel at all. He said to himself that she was too light and childish, too uncultivated and unreasoning, too provincial, to have reflected upon her ostracism, or even to have perceived it. Then at other moments he believed that she carried about in her elegant and irresponsible little organism a defiant, passionate, perfectly observant consciousness of the impression she produced. He asked himself whether Daisy's defiance came from the consciousness of innocence, or from her being, essentially, a young person of the reckless class. It must be admitted that holding one's self to a belief in Daisy's "innocence" came to seem to Winterbourne more and more a matter of fine-spun gallantry. As I have already had occasion to relate, he was angry at finding himself reduced to chopping logic about this young lady; he was vexed at his want of instinctive certitude as to how far her eccentricities were generic, national, and how far they were personal. From either view of them he had somehow missed her, and now it was too late. She was "carried away" by Mr. Giovanelli.

A few days after his brief interview with her mother, he encountered her in that beautiful abode of flowering desolation known as the Palace of the Caesars. The early Roman spring had filled the air with bloom and perfume, and the rugged surface of the Palatine was muffled with tender verdure. Daisy was strolling along the top of one of those great mounds of ruin that are embanked with mossy marble and paved with monumental inscriptions. It seemed to him that Rome had never been so lovely as just then. He stood looking off at the enchanting harmony of line and colour that remotely encircles the city, inhaling the softly humid odours, and feeling the freshness of the year and the antiquity of the place reaffirm themselves in mysterious interfusion. It seemed to him, also, that Daisy had never looked so pretty; but this had been an observation of his whenever he met her. Giovanelli was at her side, and Giovanelli, too, wore an aspect of even unwonted brilliancy.

"Well," said Daisy, "I should think you would be lonesome!"

"Lonesome?" asked Winterbourne.

"You are always going round by yourself. Can't you get any one to walk with you?"

"I am not so fortunate," said Winterbourne, "as your companion."

Giovanelli, from the first, had treated Winterbourne with distinguished politeness; he listened with a deferential air to his remarks; he laughed, punctiliously, at his pleasantries; he seemed disposed to testify to his belief that Winterbourne was a superior young man. He carried himself in no degree like a jealous wooer; he had obviously a great deal of tact; he had no objection to your expecting a little humility of him. It even seemed to Winterbourne at times that Giovanelli would find a certain mental relief in being able to have a private understanding with him—to say to him, as an intelligent man, that, bless you, *he* knew how extraordinary was this young lady, and didn't flatter himself with delusive—or, at least, *too* delusive—hopes of matrimony and dollars. On this occasion he strolled away from his companion to pluck a sprig of almond-blossom, which he carefully arranged in his button-hole.

"I know why you say that," said Daisy, watching Giovanelli. "Because you think I go round too much with *him*." And she nodded at her attendant.

"Every one thinks so—if you care to know," said Winterbourne.

"Of course I care to know!" Daisy exclaimed, seriously. "But I don't believe it. They are only pretending to be shocked. They don't really care a straw what I do. Besides, I don't go round so much."

"I think you will find they do care. They will show it—disagreeably."

Daisy looked at him a moment. "How—disagreeably?"

"Haven't you noticed anything?" Winterbourne asked.

"I have noticed you. But I noticed you were as stiff as an umbrella the first time I saw you."

"You will find I am not so stiff as several others," said Winterbourne, smiling.

"How shall I find it?"

"By going to see the others."

"What will they do to me?"

"They will give you the cold shoulder. Do you know what that means?"

Daisy was looking at him intently; she began to colour.

"Do you mean as Mrs. Walker did the other night?"

"Exactly!" said Winterbourne.

She looked away at Giovanelli, who was decorating himself with his almond-blossom. Then, looking back at Winterbourne, "I shouldn't think you would let people be so unkind!" she said.

"How can I help it?" he asked.

"I should think you would say something."

"I did say something;" and he paused a moment. "I say that your mother tells me that she believes you are engaged."

"Well, she does," said Daisy very simply.

Winterbourne began to laugh. "And does Randolph believe it?" he asked.

"I guess Randolph doesn't believe anything," said Daisy. Randolph's scepticism excited Winterbourne to further hilarity, and he observed that Giovanelli was coming back to them. Daisy, observing it too, addressed herself again to her countryman. "Since you have mentioned it," she said, "I *am* engaged.". . . Winterbourne looked at her; he had stopped laughing. "You don't believe it!" she added.

He was silent a moment; and then, "Yes, I believe it," he said.

"Oh, no, you don't!" she answered. "Well, then—I am not!"

The young girl and her cicerone were on their way to the gate of the enclosure, so that Winterbourne, who had but lately entered, presently took leave of them. A week afterwards he went to dine at a beautiful villa on the Caelian Hill, and, on arriving, dismissed his hired vehicle. The evening was charming, and he promised himself the satisfaction of walking home beneath the Arch of Constantine and past the vaguely-lighted monuments of the Forum. There was a waning moon in the sky, and her radiance was not brilliant, but she was veiled in a thin cloud-curtain which seemed to diffuse and equalize it. When, on his return from the villa (it was eleven o'clock), Winterbourne approached the dusky circle of the Colosseum, it occurred to him, as a lover of the picturesque, that the interior, in the pale moonshine, would be well worth a glance. He turned aside and walked to one of the empty arches, near which, as he observed, an open carriage—one of the little Roman street-cabs—was stationed. Then he passed in, among the cavernous shadows of the great structure, and emerged upon the clear and silent arena. The place had never seemed to him more impressive. One-half of the gigantic circus was in deep shade; the other was sleeping in the luminous dusk. As he stood there he began to murmur Byron's famous lines, out of "Manfred" [19]; but before he had finished his quotation he remembered that if nocturnal meditations in the Colosseum are recommended by the poets, they are deprecated by the doctors. The historic atmosphere was there, certainly; but the historic atmosphere, scientifically considered, was no better than a villainous miasma. Winterbourne walked to the middle of the arena, to take a more general glance, intending thereafter to make a hasty retreat. The great cross in the centre was covered with shadow; it was only as he drew near it that he made it out distinctly. Then he saw that two persons were stationed upon the low steps which formed its base. One of these was a woman, seated; her companion was standing in front of her.

Presently the sound of the woman's voice came to him distinctly in the warm night-air. "Well, he looks at us as one of the old lions or tigers may have looked at the Christian martyrs!" These were the words he heard, in the familiar accent of Miss Daisy Miller.

"Let us hope he is not very hungry," responded the ingenious Giovanelli. "He will have to take me first; you will serve for dessert!"

Winterbourne stopped, with a sort of horror; and, it must be added, with a sort of relief. It was as if a sudden illumination had been flashed upon the ambiguity of Daisy's behaviour, and the riddle had become easy to read. She was a young lady whom a gentleman need no longer be at pains to respect. He stood there looking at her —looking at her companion, and not reflecting that though he saw them vaguely, he himself must have been more brightly visible. He felt angry with himself that he had bothered so much

19. **"Manfred"**: The lines are from Manfred's soliloquy in Act III, sc. iv, and begin: "The stars are forth, the moon above the tops . . ."

about the right way of regarding Miss Daisy Miller. Then, as he was going to advance again, he checked himself; not from the fear that he was doing her injustice, but from the sense of the danger of appearing unbecomingly exhilarated by this sudden revulsion from cautious criticism. He turned away towards the entrance of the place; but, as he did so, he heard Daisy speak again.

"Why, it was Mr. Winterbourne! He saw me—and he cuts me!"

What a clever little reprobate she was, and how smartly she played at injured innocence! But he wouldn't cut her. Winterbourne came forward again, and went towards the great cross. Daisy had got up; Giovanelli lifted his hat. Winterbourne had now begun to think simply of the craziness, from a sanitary point of view, of a delicate young girl lounging away the evening in this nest of malaria. What if she *were* a clever little reprobate? that was no reason for her dying of the *perniciosa*.[20] "How long have you been here?" he asked, almost brutally.

Daisy, lovely in the flattering moonlight, looked at him a moment. Then—"All the evening," she answered, gently. . . . "I never saw anything so pretty."

"I am afraid," said Winterbourne, "that you will not think Roman fever very pretty. This is the way people catch it. I wonder," he added, turning to Giovanelli, "that you, a native Roman, should countenance such a terrible indiscretion."

"Ah," said the handsome native, "for myself I am not afraid."

"Neither am I—for you! I am speaking for this young lady."

Giovanelli lifted his well-shaped eyebrows and showed his brilliant teeth. But he took Winterbourne's rebuke with docility. "I told the signorina it was a grave indiscretion; but when was the signorina ever prudent?"

"I never was sick, and I don't mean to be!" the signorina declared. "I don't look like much, but I'm healthy! I was bound to see the Colosseum by moonlight; I shouldn't have wanted to go home without that; and we have had the most beautiful time, haven't we, Mr. Giovanelli? If there has been any danger, Eugenio can give me some pills. He has got some splendid pills."

"I should advise you," said Winterbourne, "to drive home as fast as possible and take one!"

"What you say is very wise," Giovanelli rejoined. "I will go and make sure the carriage is at hand." And he went forward rapidly.

Daisy followed with Winterbourne. He kept looking at her; she seemed not in the least embar-

20. *perniciosa:* Italian for malaria.

rassed. Winterbourne said nothing; Daisy chattered about the beauty of the place. "Well, I *have* seen the Colosseum by moonlight!" she exclaimed. "That's one good thing." Then, noticing Winterbourne's silence, she asked him why he didn't speak. He made no answer; he only began to laugh. They passed under one of the dark archways; Giovanelli was in front with the carriage. Here Daisy stopped a moment, looking at the young American. "*Did* you believe I was engaged the other day?" she asked.

"It doesn't matter what I believed the other day," said Winterbourne, still laughing.

"Well, what do you believe now?"

"I believe that it makes very little difference whether you are engaged or not!"

He felt the young girl's pretty eyes fixed upon him through the thick gloom of the archway; she was apparently going to answer. But Giovanelli hurried her forward. "Quick! quick!" he said; "if we get in by midnight we are quite safe."

Daisy took her seat in the carriage, and the fortunate Italian placed himself beside her. "Don't forget Eugenio's pills!" said Winterbourne, as he lifted his hat.

"I don't care," said Daisy, in a little strange tone, "whether I have Roman fever or not!" Upon this the cab-driver cracked his whip, and they rolled away over the desultory patches of the antique pavement.

Winterbourne—to do him justice, as it were —mentioned to no one that he had encountered Miss Miller, at midnight, in the Colosseum with a gentleman; but, nevertheless, a couple of days later, the fact of her having been there under these circumstances was known to every member of the little American circle, and commented accordingly. Winterbourne reflected that they had of course known it at the hotel, and that, after Daisy's return, there had been an exchange of remarks between the porter and the cab-driver. But the young man was conscious, at the same moment, that it had ceased to be a matter of serious regret to him that the little American flirt should be "talked about" by low-minded menials. These people, a day or two later, had serious information to give: the little American flirt was alarmingly ill. Winterbourne, when the rumour came to him, immediately went to the hotel for more news. He found that two or three charitable friends had preceded him, and that they were being entertained in Mrs. Miller's salon by Randolph.

"It's going round at night," said Randolph—"that's what made her sick. She's always going round at night. I shouldn't think she'd want to—

it's so plaguy dark. You can't see anything here at night, except when there's a moon! In America there's always a moon!" Mrs. Miller was invisible; she was now, at least, giving her daughter the advantage of her society. It was evident that Daisy was dangerously ill.

Winterbourne went often to ask for news of her, and once he saw Mrs. Miller, who, though deeply alarmed, was—rather to his surprise—perfectly composed, and, as it appeared, a most efficient and judicious nurse. She talked a good deal about Dr. Davis, but Winterbourne paid her the compliment of saying to himself that she was not, after all, such a monstrous goose. "Daisy spoke of you the other day," she said to him. "Half the time she doesn't know what she's saying, but that time I think she did. She gave me a message; she told me to tell you—she told me to tell you that she never was engaged to that handsome Italian. I am sure I am very glad; Mr. Giovanelli hasn't been near us since she was taken ill. I thought he was so much of a gentleman; but I don't call that very polite! A lady told me that he was afraid I was angry with him for taking Daisy round at night. Well, so I am; but I suppose he knows I'm a lady. I would scorn to scold him. Anyway, she says she's not engaged. I don't know why she wanted you to know; but she said to me three times, 'Mind you tell Mr. Winterbourne.' And then she told me to ask if you remembered the time you went to that castle in Switzerland. But I said I wouldn't give any such messages as that. Only, if she is not engaged, I'm sure I'm glad to know it."

But, as Winterbourne had said, it mattered very little. A week after this the poor girl died; it had been a terrible case of the fever. Daisy's grave was in the little Protestant cemetery, in an angle of the wall of imperial Rome, beneath the cypresses and the thick spring-flowers. Winterbourne stood there beside it, with a number of other mourners—a number larger than the scandal excited by the young lady's career would have led you to expect. Near him stood Giovanelli, who came nearer still before Winterbourne turned away. Giovanelli was very pale; on this occasion he had no flower in his buttonhole; he seemed to wish to say something. At last he said, "She was the most beautiful young lady I ever saw, and the most amiable." And then he added in a moment, "and she was the most innocent."

Winterbourne looked at him, and presently repeated his words, "And the most innocent?"

"The most innocent!"

Winterbourne felt sore and angry. "Why the devil," he asked, "did you take her to that fatal place?"

Mr. Giovanelli's urbanity was apparently imperturbable. He looked on the gound a moment, and then he said, "For myself, I had no fear; and she wanted to go."

"That was no reason!" Winterbourne declared.

The subtle Roman again dropped his eyes. "If she had lived, I should have got nothing. She would never have married me, I am sure."

"She would never have married you?"

"For a moment I hoped so. But no, I am sure."

Winterbourne listened to him; he stood staring at the raw protuberance among the April daisies. When he turned away again, Mr. Giovanelli with his light, slow step, had retired.

Winterbourne almost immediately left Rome; but the following summer he again met his aunt, Mrs. Costello, at Vevey. Mrs. Costello was fond of Vevey. In the interval Winterbourne had often thought of Daisy Miller and her mystifying manners. One day he spoke of her to his aunt—said it was on his conscience that he had done her injustice.

"I am sure I don't know," said Mrs. Costello. "How did your injustice affect her?"

"She sent me a message before her death which I didn't understand at the time. But I have understood it since. She would have appreciated one's esteem."

"Is that a modest way," asked Mrs. Costello, "of saying that she would have reciprocated one's affection?"

Winterbourne offered no answer to this question; but he presently said, "You were right in that remark that you made last summer. I was booked to make a mistake. I have lived too long in foreign parts."

Nevertheless, he went back to live at Geneva, whence there continue to come the most contradictory accounts of his motives of sojourn: a report that he is "studying" hard—an intimation that he is much interested in a very clever foreign lady.

THE PUPIL

❖

⟨ *The Pupil* belongs to that class of story which James called "the blest nouvelle" and which includes *Daisy Miller, The Aspern Papers, The Turn of the Screw, The*

Beast in the Jungle, and other of his best-known writings. The *nouvelle* seemed "blest" to James because of its peculiar length, somewhat greater than that of the "tale" and very much less than that of the "novel," permitted him to develop situations and characters in considerable detail while imposing a helpful economy. He did some of his most perfect and most easily readable work, as distinguished from his most searching work, in the *nouvelle* form. Congenial as it was to James, this form was not so acceptable to magazine editors as was the tale, which could be printed in a single issue, or the full-length novel, which could enlist the continuing interest of readers by being serialized in several issues. It was probably from fear of distressing his American readers, however, that the then editor of the *Atlantic Monthly,* to which James first submitted the manuscript, rejected it. It was published in the English *Longmans* (March–April, 1891), reprinted in the collection *The Lesson of the Master* (1892), and reprinted again in the New York Edition of *The Novels and Tales of Henry James.*

◊

I

THE POOR young man hesitated and procrastinated: it cost him such an effort to broach the sub-subject of terms, to speak of money to a person who spoke only of feelings and, as it were, of the aristocracy. Yet he was unwilling to take leave, treating his engagement as settled, without some more conventional glance in that direction than he could find an opening for in the manner of the large, affable lady who sat there drawing a pair of soiled *gants de Suède*[1] through a fat, jewelled hand and, at once pressing and gliding, repeated over and over everything but the thing he would have liked to hear. He would have liked to hear the figure of his salary; but just as he was nervously about to sound that note the little boy came back—the little boy Mrs. Moreen had sent out of the room to fetch her fan. He came back without the fan, only with the casual observation that he couldn't find it. As he dropped this cynical confession he looked straight and hard at the candidate for the honour of taking his education in hand. This personage reflected, somewhat grimly, that the first thing he should have to teach his little charge would be to appear to address himself to his mother when he spoke to her—especially not to make her such an improper answer as that.

When Mrs. Moreen bethought herself of this pretext for getting rid of their companion, Pemberton supposed it was precisely to approach the delicate subject of his remuneration. But it had been only to say some things about her son which it was better that a boy of eleven shouldn't

THE PUPIL.   1. *gants de Suède:* suede gloves.

catch. They were extravagantly to his advantage, save when she lowered her voice to sigh, tapping her left side familiarly: "And all overclouded by *this,* you know—all at the mercy of a weakness—!" Pemberton gathered that the weakness was in the region of the heart. He had known the poor child was not robust: this was the basis on which he had been invited to treat, through an English lady, an Oxford acquaintance, then at Nice, who happened to know both his needs and those of the amiable American family looking out for something really superior in the way of a resident tutor.

The young man's impression of his prospective pupil, who had first come into the room, as if to see for himself, as soon as Pemberton was admitted, was not quite the soft solicitation the visitor had taken for granted. Morgan Moreen was, somehow, sickly without being delicate, and that he looked intelligent (it is true Pemberton wouldn't have enjoyed his being stupid), only added to the suggestion that, as with his big mouth and big ears he really couldn't be called pretty, he might be unpleasant. Pemberton was modest—he was even timid; and the chance that his small scholar might prove cleverer than himself had quite figured, to his nervousness, among the dangers of an untried experiment. He reflected, however, that these were risks one had to run when one accepted a position, as it was called, in a private family; when as yet one's University honours had, pecuniarily speaking, remained barren. At any rate, when Mrs. Moreen got up as if to intimate that, since it was understood he would enter upon his duties within the week she would let him off now, he succeeded, in spite of the presence of the child, in squeezing out a phrase about the rate of payment. It was not the fault of the conscious smile which seemed a reference to the lady's expensive identity, if the allusion did not sound rather vulgar. This was exactly because she became still more gracious to reply: "Oh! I can assure you that all that will be quite regular."

Pemberton only wondered, while he took up his hat, what "all that" was to amount to—people had such different ideas. Mrs. Moreen's words, however, seemed to commit the family to a pledge definite enough to elicit from the child a strange little comment, in the shape of the mocking, foreign ejaculation, "Oh, là-là!"

Pemberton, in some confusion, glanced at him as he walked slowly to the window with his back turned, his hands in his pockets and the air in his elderly shoulders of a boy who didn't play. The young man wondered if he could teach him to play, though his mother had said it would never do and that this was why school was impossible. Mrs. Moreen exhibited no discomfiture; she only continued blandly: "Mr. Moreen will be delighted to meet your wishes. As I told you, he has been called to London for a week. As soon as he comes back you shall have it out with him."

This was so frank and friendly that the young man could only reply, laughing as his hostess laughed: "Oh! I don't imagine we shall have much of a battle."

"They'll give you anything you like," the boy remarked unexpectedly, returning from the window. "We don't mind what anything costs—we live awfully well."

"My darling, you're too quaint!" his mother exclaimed, putting out to caress him a practiced but ineffectual hand. He slipped out of it, but looked with intelligent, innocent eyes at Pemberton, who had already had time to notice that from one moment to the other his small satiric face seemed to change its time of life. At this moment it was infantine; yet it appeared also to be under the influence of curious intuitions and knowledges. Pemberton rather disliked precocity, and he was disappointed to find gleams of it in a disciple not yet in his teens. Nevertheless he divined on the spot that Morgan wouldn't prove a bore. He would prove on the contrary a kind of excitement. This idea held the young man, in spite of a certain repulsion.

"You pompous little person! We're not extravagant!" Mrs. Moreen gayly protested, making another unsuccessful attempt to draw the boy to her side. "You must know what to expect," she went on to Pemberton.

"The less you expect the better!" her companion interposed. "But we *are* people of fashion."

"Only so far as *you* make us so!" Mrs. Moreen mocked, tenderly. "Well, then, on Friday—don't tell me you're superstitious—and mind you don't fail us. Then you'll see us all. I'm so sorry the girls are out. I guess you'll like the girls. And, you know, I've another son, quite different from this one."

"He tries to imitate me," said Morgan to Pemberton.

"He tries? Why, he's twenty years old!" cried Mrs. Moreen.

"You're very witty," Pemberton remarked to the child—a proposition that his mother echoed with enthusiasm, declaring that Morgan's sallies were the delight of the house. The boy paid no heed to this; he only inquired abruptly of the visitor, who was surprised afterwards that he hadn't struck him as offensively forward: "Do you *want* very much to come?"

"Can you doubt it, after such a description of what I shall hear?" Pemberton replied. Yet he didn't want to come at all; he was coming because he had to go somewhere, thanks to the collapse of his fortune at the end of a year abroad, spent on the system of putting his tiny patrimony into a single full wave of experience. He had had his full wave, but he couldn't pay his hotel bill. Moreover, he had caught in the boy's eyes the glimpse of a far-off appeal.

"Well, I'll do the best I can for you," said Morgan; with which he turned away again. He passed out of one of the long windows; Pemberton saw him go and lean on the parapet of the terrace. He remained there while the young man took leave of his mother, who, on Pemberton's looking as if he expected a farewell from him, interposed with: "Leave him, leave him; he's so strange!" Pemberton suspected she was afraid of something he might say. "He's a genius—you'll love him," she added. "He's much the most interesting person in the family." And before he could invent some civility to oppose to this, she wound up with: "But we're all good, you know!"

"He's a genius—you'll love him!" were words that recurred to Pemberton before the Friday, suggesting, among other things that geniuses were not invariably lovable. However, it was all the better if there was an element that would make tutoring absorbing: he had perhaps taken too much for granted that it would be dreary. As he left the villa after his interview, he looked up at the balcony and saw the child leaning over it. "We shall have great larks!" he called up.

Morgan hesitated a moment; then he answered, laughing: "By the time you come back I shall have thought of something witty!"

This made Pemberton say to himself: "After all he's rather nice."

II

ON THE Friday he saw them all, as Mrs. Moreen had promised, for her husband had come back and the girls and the other son were at home. Mr. Moreen had a white moustache, a confiding manner and, in his buttonhole, the ribbon of a foreign order—bestowed, as Pemberton eventually learned, for services. For what services he never clearly ascertained: this was a point—one of a large number—that Mr. Moreen's manner never confided. What it emphatically did confide was that he was a man of the world. Ulick, the firstborn, was in visible training for the same profession—under the disadvantage as yet, however, of a buttonhole only feebly floral and a moustache with no pretensions to type. The girls had hair and figures and manners and small fat feet, but had never been out alone. As for Mrs. Moreen, Pemberton saw on a nearer view that her elegance was intermittent and her parts didn't always match. Her husband, as she had promised, met with enthusiasm Pemberton's ideas in regard to a salary. The young man had endeavoured to make them modest, and Mr. Moreen confided to him that *he* found them positively meagre. He further assured him that he aspired to be intimate with his children, to be their best friend, and that he was always looking out for them. That was what he went off for, to London and other places—to look out; and this vigilance was the theory of life, as well as the real occupation, of the whole family. They all looked out, for they were very frank on the subject of its being necessary. They desired it to be understood that they were earnest people, and also that their fortune, though quite adequate for earnest people, required the most careful administration. Mr. Moreen, as the parent bird, sought sustenance for the nest. Ulick found sustenance mainly at the club, where Pemberton guessed that it was usually served on green cloth. The girls used to do up their hair and their frocks themselves, and our young man felt appealed to to be glad, in regard to Morgan's education, that, though it must naturally be of the best, it didn't cost too much. After a little he *was* glad, forgetting at times his own needs in the interest inspired by the child's nature and education and the pleasure of making easy terms for him.

During the first weeks of their acquaintance Morgan had been as puzzling as a page in an unknown language—altogether different from the obvious little Anglo-Saxons who had misrepresented childhood to Pemberton. Indeed the whole mystic volume in which the boy had been bound demanded some practice in translation. To-day, after a considerable interval, there is something phantasmagoric, like a prismatic reflection or a serial novel, in Pemberton's memory of the queerness of the Moreens. If it were not for a few tangible tokens—a lock of Morgan's hair, cut by his own hand, and the half-dozen letters he got from him when they were separated—the whole episode and the figures peopling it would seem too inconsequent for anything but dreamland. The queerest thing about them was their success (as it appeared to him for a while at the time), for he had never seen a family so brilliantly equipped for failure. Wasn't it success to have kept him so hatefully long? Wasn't it success to have drawn him in that first morning at *déjeuner*,[2] the Friday

he came—it was enough to *make* one superstitious—so that he utterly committed himself, and this not by calculation or a *mot d'ordre*,[3] but by a happy instinct which made them, like a band of gipsies, work so neatly together? They amused him as much as if they had really been a band of gipsies. He was still young and had not seen much of the world—his English years had been intensely usual; therefore the reversed conventions of the Moreens (for they had their standards), struck him as topsyturvy. He had encountered nothing like them at Oxford; still less had any such note been struck to his younger American ear during the four years at Yale in which he had richly supposed himself to be reacting against Puritanism. The reaction of the Moreens, at any rate, went ever so much further. He had thought himself very clever that first day in hitting them all off in his mind with the term "cosmopolite." Later, it seemed feeble and colourless enough—confessedly, helplessly provisional.

However, when he first applied it to them he had a degree of joy—for an instructor he was still empirical—as if from the apprehension that to live with them would really be to see life. Their sociable strangeness was an intimation of that—their chatter of tongues, their gaiety and good humour, their infinite dawdling (they were always getting themselves up, but it took forever, and Pemberton had once found Mr. Moreen shaving in the drawing-room), their French, their Italian and, in the spiced fluency, their cold, tough slices of American. They lived on macaroni and coffee (they had these articles prepared in perfection); but they knew recipes for a hundred other dishes. They overflowed with music and song, were always humming and catching each other up, and had a kind of professional acquaintance with continental cities. They talked of "good places" as if they had been strolling players. They had at Nice a villa, a carriage, a piano and a banjo, and they went to official parties. They were a perfect calendar of the "days" of their friends, which Pemberton knew them, when they were indisposed, to get out of bed to go to, and which made the week larger than life when Mrs. Moreen talked of them with Paula and Amy. Their romantic initiations gave their new inmate at first an almost dazzling sense of culture. Mrs. Moreen had translated something, at some former period—an author whom it made Pemberton fell *borné*[4] never to have heard of. They could imitate Venetian and sing Neapolitan, and when they wanted to say something very particular they communicated

---

2. *déjeuner:* a late breakfast, or lunch.   3. *mot d'ordre:* password.   4. *borné:* limited, inexperienced.

with each other in an ingenious dialect of their own—a sort of spoken cipher, which Pemberton at first took for Volapuk, but which he learned to understand as he would not have understood Volapuk.

"It's the family language—Ultramoreen," Morgan explained to him drolly enough; but the boy rarely condescended to use it himself, though he attempted colloquial Latin as if he had been a little prelate.

Among all the "days" with which Mrs. Moreen's memory was taxed she managed to squeeze in one of her own, which her friends sometimes forgot. But the house derived a frequented air from the number of fine people who were freely named there and from several mysterious men with foreign titles and English clothes whom Morgan called the princes and who, on sofas with the girls, talked French very loud, as if to show they were saying nothing improper. Pemberton wondered how the princes could ever propose in that tone and so publicly: he took for granted cynically that this was what was desired of them. Then he acknowledged that even for the chance of such an advantage Mrs. Moreen would never allow Paula and Amy to receive alone. These young ladies were not at all timid, but it was just the safeguards that made them so graceful. It was a houseful of Bohemians who wanted tremendously to be Philistines.

In one respect, however, certainly, they achieved no rigour—they were wonderfully amiable and ecstatic about Morgan. It was a genuine tenderness, an artless admiration, equally strong in each. They even praised his beauty, which was small, and were rather afraid of him, as if they recognised that he was of a finer clay. They called him a little angel and a little prodigy and pitied his want of health effusively. Pemberton feared at first that their extravagance would make him hate the boy, but before this happened he had become extravagant himself. Later, when he had grown rather to hate the others, it was a bribe to patience for him that they were at any rate nice about Morgan, going on tiptoe if they fancied he was showing symptoms, and even giving up somebody's "day" to procure him a pleasure. But mixed with this was the oddest wish to make him independent, as if they felt that they were not good enough for him. They passed him over to Pemberton very much as if they wished to force a constructive adoption on the obliging bachelor and shirk altogether a responsibility. They were delighted when they perceived that Morgan liked his preceptor, and could think of no higher praise for the young man. It was strange how they contrived to reconcile the

appearance, and indeed the essential fact, of adoring the child with their eagerness to wash their hands of him. Did they want to get rid of him before he should find them out? Pemberton was finding them out month by month. At any rate, the boy's relations turned their backs with exaggerated delicacy, as if to escape the charge of interfering. Seeing in time how little he had in common with them (it was by *them* he first observed it —they proclaimed it with complete humility), his preceptor was moved to speculate on the mysteries of transmission, the far jumps of heredity. Where his detachment from most of the things they represented had come from was more than an observer could say—it certainly had burrowed under two or three generations.

As for Pemberton's own estimate of his pupil, it was a good while before he got the point of view, so little had he been prepared for it by the smug young barbarians to whom the tradition of tutorship, as hitherto revealed to him, had been adjusted. Morgan was scrappy and surprising, deficient in many properties supposed commom to the *genus* and abounding in others that were the portion only of the supernaturally clever. One day Pemberton made a great stride: it cleared up the question to perceive that Morgan *was* supernaturally clever and that, though the formula was temporarily meagre, this would be the only assumption on which one could successfully deal with him. He had the general quality of a child for whom life had not been simplified by school, a kind of homebred sensibility which might have been bad for himself but was charming for others, and a whole range of refinement and perception —little musical vibrations as taking as picked-up airs—begotten by wandering about Europe at the tail of his migratory tribe. This might not have been an education to recommend in advance, but its results with Morgan were as palpable as a fine texture. At the same time he had in his composition a sharp spice of stoicism, doubtless the fruit of having had to begin early to bear pain, which produced the impression of pluck and made it of less consequence that he might have been thought at school rather a polyglot little beast. Pemberton indeed quickly found himself rejoicing that school was out of the question: in any million of boys it was probably good for all but one, and Morgan was that millionth. It would have made him comparative and superior—it might have made him priggish. Pemberton would try to be school himself—a bigger seminary than five hundred grazing donkeys; so that, winning no prizes, the boy would remain unconscious and irresponsible and amusing—amusing, because, though life was already intense in his childish nature, freshness still made there a strong draught for jokes. It turned out that even in the still air of Morgan's various disabilities jokes flourished greatly. He was a pale, lean, acute, undeveloped little cosmopolite, who liked intellectual gymnastics and who, also, as regards the behaviour of mankind, had noticed more things than you might suppose, but who nevertheless had his proper playroom of superstitions, where he smashed a dozen toys a day.

III

AT NICE once, towards evening, as the pair sat resting in the open air after a walk, looking over the sea at the pink western lights, Morgan said suddenly to his companion: "Do you like it—you know, being with us all in this intimate way?"

"My dear fellow, why should I stay if I didn't?"

"How do I know you will stay? I'm almost sure you won't, very long."

"I hope you don't mean to dismiss me," said Pemberton.

Morgan considered a moment, looking at the sunset. "I think if I did right I ought to."

"Well, I know I'm supposed to instruct you in virtue; but in that case don't do right."

"You're very young—fortunately," Morgan went on, turning to him again.

"Oh yes, compared with you!"

"Therefore, it won't matter so much if you do lose a lot of time."

"That's the way to look at it," said Pemberton accommodatingly.

They were silent a minute; after which the boy asked: "Do you like my father and mother very much?"

"Dear me, yes. They're charming people."

Morgan received this with another silence; then, unexpectedly, familiarly, but at the same time affectionately, he remarked: "You're a jolly old humbug!"

For a particular reason the words made Pemberton change colour. The boy noticed in an instant that he had turned red, whereupon he turned red himself and the pupil and the master exchanged a longish glance in which there was a consciousness of many more things than are usually touched upon, even tacitly, in such a relation. It produced for Pemberton an embarrassment; it raised, in a shadowy form, a question (this was the first glimpse of it), which was destined to play as singular and, as he imagined, owing to the altogether peculiar conditions, an unprecedented part in his intercourse with his little companion. Later, when he found himself talking with this small boy in a way in which few small boys could ever have

been talked with, he thought of that clumsy moment on the bench at Nice as the dawn of an understanding that had broadened. What had added to the clumsiness then was that he thought it his duty to declare to Morgan that he might abuse him (Pemberton) as much as he liked, but must never abuse his parents. To this Morgan had the easy reply that he hadn't dreamed of abusing them; which appeared to be true: it put Pemberton in the wrong.

"Then why am I a humbug for saying *I* think them charming?" the young man asked, conscious of a certain rashness.

"Well—they're not *your* parents."

"They love you better than anything in the world—never forget that," said Pemberton.

"Is that why you like them so much?"

"They're very kind to me," Pemberton replied, evasively.

"You *are* a humbug!" laughed Morgan, passing an arm into his tutor's. He leaned against him, looking off at the sea again and swinging his long, thin legs.

"Don't kick my shins," said Pemberton, while he reflected: "Hang it, I can't complain of them to the child!"

"There's another reason, too," Morgan went on, keeping his legs still.

"Another reason for what?"

"Besides their not being your parents."

"I don't understand you," said Pemberton.

"Well, you will before long. All right!"

Pemberton did understand, fully, before long; but he made a fight even with himself before he confessed it. He thought it the oddest thing to have a struggle with the child about. He wondered he didn't detest the child for launching him in such a struggle. But by the time it began the resource of detesting the child was closed to him. Morgan was a special case, but to know him was to accept him on his own odd terms. Pemberton had spent his aversion to special cases before arriving at knowledge. When at last he did arrive he felt that he was in an extreme predicament. Against every interest he had attached himself. They would have to meet things together. Before they went home that evening, at Nice, the boy had said, clinging to his arm:

"Well, at any rate you'll hang on to the last."

"To the last?"

"Till you're fairly beaten."

"*You* ought to be fairly beaten!" cried the young man, drawing him closer.

IV

A YEAR after Pemberton had come to live with them Mr. and Mrs. Moreen suddenly gave up the villa at Nice. Pemberton had got used to suddenness, having seen it practiced on a considerable scale during two jerky little tours—one in Switzerland the first summer, and the other late in the winter, when they all ran down to Florence and then, at the end of ten days, liking it much less than they had intended, straggled back in mysterious depression. They had returned to Nice "for ever," as they said; but this didn't prevent them from squeezing, one rainy, muggy May night, into a second-class railway-carriage—you could never tell by which class they would travel— where Pemberton helped them to stow away a wonderful collection of bundles and bags. The explanation of this manœuvre was that they had determined to spend the summer "in some bracing place;" but in Paris they dropped into a small furnished apartment—a fourth floor in a third-rate avenue, where there was a smell on the staircase and the *portier* [5] was hateful—and passed the next four months in blank indigence.

The better part of this baffled sojourn was for the preceptor and his pupil, who, visiting the Invalides and Notre Dame, the Conciergerie and all the museums, took a hundred remunerative rambles. They learned to know their Paris, which was useful, for they came back another year for a longer stay, the general character of which in Pemberton's memory to-day mixes pitiably and confusedly with that of the first. He sees Morgan's shabby knickerbockers—the everlasting pair that didn't match his blouse and that as he grew longer could only grow faded. He remembers the particular holes in his three or four pair of coloured stockings.

Morgan was dear to his mother, but he never was better dressed than was absolutely necessary —partly, no doubt, by his own fault, for he was as indifferent to his appearance as a German philosopher. "My dear fellow, you *are* coming to pieces," Pemberton would say to him in sceptical remonstrance; to which the child would reply, looking at him serenely up and down: "My dear fellow, so are you! I don't want to cast you in the shade." Pemberton could have no rejoinder for this—the assertion so closely represented the fact. If however the deficiencies of his own wardrobe were a chapter by themselves he didn't like his little charge to look too poor. Later he used to say: "Well, if we are poor, why, after all, shouldn't we look it?" and he consoled himself with thinking there was something rather elderly and gentlemanly in Morgan's seediness—it differed from the untidiness of the urchin who plays and spoils his

things. He could trace perfectly the degrees by which, in proportion as her little son confined himself to his tutor for society, Mrs. Moreen shrewdly forbore to renew his garments. She did nothing that didn't show, neglected him because he escaped notice, and then, as he illustrated this clever policy, discouraged at home his public appearances. Her position was logical enough—those members of her family who did show had to be showy.

During this period and several others Pemberton was quite aware of how he and his comrade might strike people; wandering languidly through the Jardin des Plantes as if they had nowhere to go, sitting, on the winter days, in the galleries of the Louvre, so splendidly ironical to the homeless, as if for the advantage of the *calorifère*.[6] They joked about it sometimes: it was the sort of joke that was perfectly within the boy's compass. They figured themselves as part of the vast, vague, hand-to-mouth multitude of the enormous city and pretended they were proud of their position in it— it showed them such a lot of life and made them conscious of a sort of democratic brotherhood. If Pemberton could not feel a sympathy in destitution with his small companion (for after all Morgan's fond parents would never have let him really suffer), the boy would at least feel it with him, so it came to the same thing. He used sometimes to wonder what people would think they were— fancy they were looked askance at, as if it might be a suspected case of kidnapping. Morgan wouldn't be taken for a young patrician with a preceptor—he wasn't smart enough; though he might pass for his companion's sickly little brother. Now and then he had a five-franc piece, and except once, when they bought a couple of lovely neckties, one of which he made Pemberton accept, they laid it out scientifically in old books. It was a great day, always spent on the quays, rummaging among the dusty boxes that garnish the parapets. These were occasions that helped them to live, for their books ran low very soon after the beginning of their acquaintance. Pemberton had a good many in England, but he was obliged to write to a friend and ask him kindly to get some fellow to give him something for them.

If the bracing climate was untasted that summer the young man had an idea that at the moment they were about to make a push the cup had been dashed from their lips by a movement of his own. It had been his first blow-out, as he called it, with his patrons; his first successful attempt (though there was little other success about it), to bring them to a consideration of his impossible position. As the ostensible eve of a costly journey the moment struck him as a good one to put in a signal protest—to present an ultimatum. Ridiculous as it sounded he had never yet been able to compass an uninterrupted private interview with the elder pair or with either of them singly. They were always flanked by their elder children, and poor Pemberton usually had his own little charge at his side. He was conscious of its being a house in which the surface of one's delicacy got rather smudged; nevertheless he had kept the bloom of his scruple against announcing to Mr. and Mrs. Moreen with publicity that he couldn't go on longer without a little money. He was still simple enough to suppose Ulick and Paula and Amy might not know that since his arrival he had only had a hundred and forty francs; and he was magnanimous enough to wish not to compromise their parents in their eyes. Mr. Moreen now listened to him, as he listened to every one and to everything, like a man of the world, and seemed to appeal to him—though not of course too grossly—to try and be a little more of one himself. Pemberton recognised the importance of the character from the advantage it gave Mr. Moreen. He was not even confused, whereas poor Pemberton was more so than there was any reason for. Neither was he surprised—at least any more than a gentleman had to be who freely confessed himself a little shocked, though not, strictly, at Pemberton.

"We must go into this, mustn't we, dear?" he said to his wife. He assured his young friend that the matter should have his very best attention; and he melted into space as elusively as if, at the door, he were taking an inevitable but deprecatory precedence. When, the next moment, Pemberton found himself alone with Mrs. Moreen it was to hear her say: "I see, I see," stroking the roundness of her chin and looking as if she were only hesitating between a dozen easy remedies. If they didn't make their push Mr. Moreen could at least disappear for several days. During his absence his wife took up the subject again spontaneously, but her contribution to it was merely that she had thought all the while they were getting on so beautifully. Pemberton's reply to this revelation was that unless they immediately handed him a substantial sum he would leave them for ever. He knew she would wonder how he would get away, and for a moment expected her to inquire. She didn't, for which he was almost grateful to her, so little was he in a position to tell.

"You won't, you know you won't—you're too interested," she said. "You *are* interested, you know you are, you dear, kind man!" She laughed, with almost condemnatory archness, as if it were a reproach (but she wouldn't insist), while she flirted a soiled pocket-handkerchief at him.

Pemberton's mind was fully made up to quit the house the following week. This would give him time to get an answer to a letter he had despatched to England. If he did nothing of the sort—that is, if he stayed another year and then went away only for three months—it was not merely because before the answer to his letter came (most unsatisfactory when it did arrive), Mr. Moreen generously presented him—again with all the precautions of a man of the world—three hundred francs. He was exasperated to find that Mrs. Moreen was right, that he couldn't bear to leave the child. This stood out clearer for the very reason that, the night of his desperate appeal to his patrons, he had seen fully for the first time where he was. Wasn't it another proof of the success with which those patrons practiced their arts that they had managed to avert for so long the illuminating flash? It descended upon Pemberton with a luridness which perhaps would have struck a spectator as comically excessive, after he had returned to his little servile room, which looked into a close court where a bare, dirty opposite wall took, with the sound of shrill clatter, the reflection of lighted back-windows. He had simply given himself away to a band of adventurers. The idea, the word itself, had a sort of romantic horror for him—he had always lived on such safe lines. Later it assumed a more interesting, almost a soothing, sense: it pointed a moral, and Pemberton could enjoy a moral. The Moreens were adventurers not merely because they didn't pay their debts, because they lived on society, but because their whole view of life, dim and confused and instinctive, like that of clever colour-blind animals, was speculative and rapacious and mean. Oh! they were "respectable," and that only made them more *immondes*.[7] The young man's analysis of them put it at last very simply—they were adventurers because they were abject snobs. That was the completest account of them—it was the law of their being. Even when this truth became vivid to their ingenious inmate he remained unconscious of how much his mind had been prepared for it by the extraordinary little boy who had now become such a complication in his life. Much less could he then calculate on the information he was still to owe to the extraordinary little boy.

V

BUT it was during the ensuing time that the real problem came up—the problem of how far it was

7. *immondes:* unclean.

excusable to discuss the turpitude of parents with a child of twelve, of thirteen, of fourteen. Absolutely inexcusable and quite impossible it of course at first appeared; and indeed the question didn't press for a while after Pemberton had received his three hundred francs. They produced a sort of lull, a relief from the sharpest pressure. Pemberton frugally amended his wardrobe and even had a few francs in his pocket. He thought the Moreens looked at him as if he were almost too smart, as if they ought to take care not to spoil him. If Mr. Moreen hadn't been such a man of the world he would perhaps have said something to him about his neckties. But Mr. Moreen was always enough a man of the world to let things pass—he had certainly shown that. It was singular how Pemberton guessed that Morgan, though saying nothing about it, knew something had happened. But three hundred francs, especially when one owed money, couldn't last for ever; and when they were gone —the boy knew when they were gone—Morgan did say something. The party had returned to Nice at the beginning of the winter, but not to the charming villa. They went to an hotel, where they stayed three months, and then they went to another hotel, explaining that they had left the first because they had waited and waited and couldn't get the rooms they wanted. These apartments, the rooms they wanted, were generally very splendid; but fortunately they never *could* get them—fortunately, I mean, for Pemberton, who reflected always that if they had got them there would have been still less for educational expenses. What Morgan said at last was said suddenly, irrelevantly, when the moment came, in the middle of a lesson, and consisted of the apparently unfeeling words: "You ought to *filer,*[8] you know—you really ought."

Pemberton stared. He had learnt enough French slang from Morgan to know that to *filer* meant to go away. "Ah, my dear fellow, don't turn me off!"

Morgan pulled a Greek lexicon toward him (he used a Greek-German), to look out a word, instead of asking it of Pemberton. "You can't go on like this, you know."

"Like what, my boy?"

"You know they don't pay you up," said Morgan, blushing and turning his leaves.

"Don't pay me?" Pemberton stared again and feigned amazement. "What on earth put that into your head?"

"It has been there a long time," the boy replied, continuing his search.

8. *filer:* to sneak off.

Pemberton was silent, then he went on: "I say, what are you hunting for? They pay me beautifully."

"I'm hunting for the Greek for transparent fiction," Morgan dropped.

"Find that rather for gross impertinence, and disabuse your mind. What do I want of money?"

"Oh, that's another question!"

Pemberton hesitated—he was drawn in different ways. The severely correct thing would have been to tell the boy that such a matter was none of his business and bid him go on with his lines. But they were really too intimate for that; it was not the way he was in the habit of treating him; there had been no reason it should be. On the other hand Morgan had quite lighted on the truth—he really shouldn't be able to keep it up much longer; therefore why not let him know one's real motive for forsaking him? At the same time it wasn't decent to abuse to one's pupil the family of one's pupil; it was better to misrepresent than to do that. So in reply to Morgan's last exclamation he just declared, to dismiss the subject, that he had received several payments.

"I say—I say!" the boy ejaculated, laughing.

"That's all right," Pemberton insisted. "Give me your written rendering."

Morgan pushed a copybook across the table, and his companion began to read the page, but with something running in his head that made it no sense. Looking up after a minute or two he found the child's eyes fixed on him, and he saw something strange in them. Then Morgan said: "I'm not afraid of the reality."

"I haven't yet seen the thing that you *are* afraid of—I'll do you that justice!"

This came out with a jump (it was perfectly true), and evidently gave Morgan a pleasure. "I've thought of it a long time," he presently resumed.

"Well, don't think of it any more."

The child appeared to comply, and they had a comfortable and even an amusing hour. They had a theory that they were very thorough, and yet they seemed always to be in the amusing part of lessons, the intervals between the tunnels, where there were waysides and views. Yet the morning was brought to a violent end by Morgan's suddenly leaning his arms on the table, burying his head in them and bursting into tears. Pemberton would have been startled at any rate; but he was doubly startled because, as it then occurred to him, it was the first time he had ever seen the boy cry. It was rather awful.

The next day, after much thought, he took a decision and, believing it to be just, immediately acted upon it. He cornered Mr. and Mrs. Moreen again and informed them that if, on the spot, they didn't pay him all they owed him, he would not only leave their house, but would tell Morgan exactly what had brought him to it.

"Oh, you *haven't* told him?" cried Mrs. Moreen, with a pacifying hand on her well-dressed bosom.

"Without warning you? For what do you take me?"

Mr. and Mrs. Moreen looked at each other, and Pemberton could see both that they were relieved and that there was a certain alarm in their relief. "My dear fellow," Mr. Moreen demanded, "what use *can* you have, leading the quiet life we all do, for such a lot of money?"—an inquiry to which Pemberton made no answer, occupied as he was in perceiving that what passed in the mind of his patrons was something like: "Oh, then, if we've felt that the child, dear little angel, has judged us and how he regards us, and we haven't been betrayed, he must have guessed—and, in short, it's *general!*" an idea that rather stirred up Mr. and Mrs. Moreen, as Pemberton had desired that it should. At the same time, if he had thought that his threat would do something towards bringing them round, he was disappointed to find they had taken for granted (how little they appreciated his delicacy!) that he had already given them away to his pupil. There was a mystic uneasiness in their parental breasts, and that was the way they had accounted for it. None the less his threat did touch them; for if they had escaped it was only to meet a new danger. Mr. Moreen appealed to Pemberton, as usual, as a man of the world; but his wife had recourse, for the first time since the arrival of their inmate, to a fine *hauteur*, reminding him that a devoted mother, with her child, had arts that protected her against gross misrepresentation.

"I should misrepresent you grossly if I accused you of common honesty!" the young man replied; but as he closed the door behind him sharply, thinking he had not done himself much good, while Mr. Moreen lighted another cigarette, he heard Mrs. Moreen shout after him, more touchingly:

"Oh, you do, you *do,* put the knife to one's throat!"

The next morning, very early, she came to his room. He recognised her knock, but he had no hope that she brought him money; as to which he was wrong, for she had fifty francs in her hand. She squeezed forward in her dressing-gown, and he received her in his own, between his bath-tub and his bed. He had been tolerably schooled by this time to the "foreign ways" of his hosts. Mrs. Moreen was zealous, and when she was zealous she didn't care what she did; so she now sat down on his bed, his clothes being on the chairs, and, in her preoccupation, forgot, as she glanced round, to be ashamed of giving him such a nasty room. What Mrs. Moreen was zealous about on this occasion was to persuade him that in the first place she was very good-natured to bring him fifty francs, and, in the second, if he would only see it, he was really too absurd to expect to be *paid*. Wasn't he paid enough, without perpetual money —wasn't he paid by the comfortable, luxurious home that he enjoyed with them all, without a care, an anxiety, a solitary want? Wasn't he sure of his position, and wasn't that everything to a young man like him, quite unknown, with singularly little to show, the ground of whose exorbitant pretensions it was not easy to discover? Wasn't he paid, above all, by the delightful relation he had established with Morgan—quite ideal, as from master to pupil—and by the simple privilege of knowing and living with so amazingly gifted a child, than whom really—she meant literally what she said—there was no better company in Europe? Mrs. Moreen herself took to appealing to him as a man of the world; she said "Voyons, mon cher," and "My dear sir, look here now;" and urged him to be reasonable, putting it before him that it was really a chance for him. She spoke as if, according as he *should* be reasonable, he would prove himself worthy to be her son's tutor and of the extraordinary confidence they had placed in him.

After all, Pemberton reflected, it was only a difference of theory, and the theory didn't matter much. They had hitherto gone on that of remunerated, as now they would go on that of gratuitous, service; but why should they have so many words about it? Mrs. Moreen, however, continued to be convincing; sitting there with her fifty francs she talked and repeated, as women repeat, and bored and irritated him, while he leaned against the wall with his hands in the pockets of his wrapper, drawing it together round his legs and looking over the head of his visitor at the grey negations of his window. She wound up with saying: "You see I bring you a definite proposal."

"A definite proposal?"

"To make our relations regular, as it were—to put them on a comfortable footing."

"I see—it's a system," said Pemberton. "A kind of blackmail."

Mrs. Moreen bounded up, which was what the young man wanted.

"What do you mean by that?"

"You practice on one's fears—one's fears about the child if one should go away."

"And, pray, what would happen to him in that event?" demanded Mrs. Moreen, with majesty.

"Why, he'd be alone with *you*."

"And pray, with whom *should* a child be but with those whom he loves most?"

"If you think that, why don't you dismiss me?"

"Do you pretend that he loves you more than he loves *us?*" cried Mrs. Moreen.

"I think he ought to. I make sacrifices for him. Though I've heard of those *you* make, I don't see them."

Mrs. Moreen stared a moment; then, with emotion, she grasped Pemberton's hand. "*Will* you make it—the sacrifice?"

Pemberton burst out laughing. "I'll see—I'll do what I can—I'll stay a little longer. Your calculation is just—I *do* hate intensely to give him up; I'm fond of him and he interests me deeply, in spite of the inconvenience I suffer. You know my situation perfectly; I haven't a penny in the world, and, occupied as I am with Morgan, I'm unable to earn money."

Mrs. Moreen tapped her undressed arm with her folded bank-note. "Can't you write articles? Can't you translate, as *I* do?"

"I don't know about translating; it's wretchedly paid."

"I am glad to earn what I can," said Mrs. Moreen virtuously, with her head high.

"You ought to tell me who you do it for." Pemberton paused a moment, and she said nothing; so he added: "I've tried to turn off some little sketches, but the magazines won't have them—they're declined with thanks."

"You see then you're not such a phœnix—to have such pretensions," smiled his interlocutress.

"I haven't time to do things properly," Pemberton went on. Then as it came over him that he was almost abjectly good-natured to give these explanations he added: "If I stay on longer it must be on one condition—that Morgan shall know distinctly on what footing I am."

Mrs. Moreen hesitated. "Surely you don't want to show off to a child?"

"To show *you* off, do you mean?"

Again Mrs. Moreen hesitated, but this time it was to produce a still finer flower. "And *you* talk of blackmail!"

"You can easily prevent it," said Pemberton.

"And *you* talk of practicing on fears," Mrs. Moreen continued.

"Yes, there's no doubt I'm a great scoundrel."

His visitor looked at him a moment—it was evident that she was sorely bothered. Then she thrust out her money at him. "Mr. Moreen desired me to give you this on account."

"I'm much obliged to Mr. Moreen; but we have no account."

"You won't take it?"

"That leaves me more free," said Pemberton.

"To poison my darling's mind?" groaned Mrs. Moreen.

"Oh, your darling's mind!" laughed the young man.

She fixed him a moment, and he thought she was going to break out tormentedly, pleadingly: "For God's sake, tell me what *is* in it!" But she checked this impulse—another was stronger. She pocketed the money—the crudity of the alternative was comical—and swept out of the room with the desperate concession: "You may tell him any horror you like!"

VI

A COUPLE of days after this, during which Pemberton had delayed to profit by Mrs. Moreen's permission to tell her son any horror, the two had been for a quarter of an hour walking together in silence when the boy became sociable again with the remark: "I'll tell you how I know it; I know it through Zénobie."

"Zénobie? Who in the world is *she?*"

"A nurse I used to have—ever so many years ago. A charming woman. I liked her awfully, and she liked me."

"There's no accounting for tastes. What is it you know through her?"

"Why, what their idea is. She went away because they didn't pay her. She did like me awfully, and she stayed two years. She told me all about it—that at last she could never get her wages. As soon as they saw how much she liked me they stopped giving her anything. They thought she'd stay for nothing, out of devotion. And she did stay ever so long—as long as she could. She was only a poor girl. She used to send money to her mother. At last she couldn't afford it any longer, and she went away in a fearful rage one night—I mean of course in a rage against *them*. She cried over me tremendously, she hugged me nearly to death. She told me all about it," Morgan repeated. "She told me it was their idea. So I guessed, ever so long ago, that they have had the same idea with you."

"Zénobie was very shrewd," said Pemberton. "And she made you so."

"Oh, that wasn't Zénobie; that was nature. And experience!" Morgan laughed.

"Well, Zénobie was a part of your experience."

"Certainly I was a part of hers, poor dear!"

the boy exclaimed. "And I'm a part of yours."

"A very important part. But I don't see how you know that I've been treated like Zénobie."

"Do you take me for an idiot?" Morgan asked. "Haven't I been conscious of what we've been through together?"

"What we've been through?"

"Our privations—our dark days."

"Oh, our days have been bright enough."

Morgan went on in silence for a moment. Then he said: "My dear fellow, you're a hero!"

"Well, you're another!" Pemberton retorted.

"No, I'm not; but I'm not a baby. I won't stand it any longer. You must get some occupation that pays. I'm ashamed, I'm ashamed!" quavered the boy in a little passionate voice that was very touching to Pemberton.

"We ought to go off and live somewhere together," said the young man.

"I'll go like a shot if you'll take me."

"I'd get some work that would keep us both afloat," Pemberton continued.

"So would I. Why shouldn't *I* work? I ain't such a *crétin!*" [9]

"The difficulty is that your parents wouldn't hear of it," said Pemberton. "They would never part with you; they worship the ground you tread on. Don't you see the proof of it? They don't dislike me; they wish me no harm; they're very amiable people; but they're perfectly ready to treat me badly for your sake."

The silence in which Morgan received this graceful sophistry struck Pemberton somehow as expressive. After a moment Morgan repeated: "You *are* a hero!" Then he added: "They leave me with you altogether. You've all the responsibility. They put me off on you from morning till night. Why, then, should they object to my taking up with you completely? I'd help you."

"They're not particularly keen about my being helped, and they delight in thinking of you as *theirs*. They're tremendously proud of you."

"I'm not proud of them. But you know *that*," Morgan returned.

"Except for the little matter we speak of they're charming people," said Pemberton, not taking up the imputation of lucidity, but wondering greatly at the child's own, and especially at this fresh reminder of something he had been conscious of from the first—the strangest thing in the boy's large little composition, a temper, a sensibility, even a sort of ideal, which made him privately resent the general quality of his kinsfolk. Morgan had in secret a small loftiness which begot an ele-

ment of reflection, a domestic scorn not imperceptible to his companion (though they never had any talk about it), and absolutely anomalous in a juvenile nature, especially when one noted that it had not made this nature "old-fashioned," as the word is of children—quaint or wizened or offensive. It was as if he had been a little gentleman and had paid the penalty by discovering that he was the only such person in the family. This comparison didn't make him vain; but it could make him melancholy and a trifle austere. When Pemberton guessed at these young dimnesses he saw him serious and gallant, and was partly drawn on and partly checked, as if with a scruple, by the charm of attempting to sound the little cool shallows which were quickly growing deeper. When he tried to figure to himself the morning twilight of childhood, so as to deal with it safely, he perceived that it was never fixed, never arrested, that ignorance, at the instant one touched it, was already flushing faintly into knowledge, that there was nothing that at a given moment you could say a clever child didn't know. It seemed to him that *he* both knew too much to imagine Morgan's simplicity and too little to disembroil his tangle.

The boy paid no heed to his last remark; he only went on: "I should have spoken to them about their idea, as I call it, long ago, if I hadn't been sure what they would say."

"And what would they say?"

"Just what they said about what poor Zénobie told me—that it was a horrid, dreadful story, that they had paid her every penny they owed her."

"Well, perhaps they had," said Pemberton.

"Perhaps they've paid you!"

"Let us pretend they have, and *n'en parlons plus.*" [10]

"They accused her of lying and cheating," Morgan insisted perversely. "That's why *I* don't want to speak to them."

"Lest they should accuse me, too?"

To this Morgan made no answer, and his companion, looking down at him (the boy turned his eyes, which had filled, away), saw that he couldn't have trusted himself to utter.

"You're right. Don't squeeze them," Pemberton pursued. "Except for that, they *are* charming people."

"Except for *their* lying and *their* cheating?"

"I say—I say!" cried Pemberton, imitating a little tone of the lad's which was itself an imitation.

"We must be frank, at the last; we *must* come to an understanding," said Morgan, with the im-

---

9. *crétin:* dunce.

10. *n'en parlons plus:* "let us talk of it no more."

portance of the small boy who lets himself think he is arranging great affairs—almost playing at shipwreck or at Indians. "I know all about everything," he added.

"I daresay your father has his reasons," Pemberton observed, too vaguely, as he was aware.

"For lying and cheating?"

"For saving and managing and turning his means to the best account. He has plenty to do with his money. You're an expensive family."

"Yes, I'm very expensive," Morgan rejoined, in a manner which made his preceptor burst out laughing.

"He's saving for *you*," said Pemberton. "They think of you in everything they do."

"He might save a little——" The boy paused. Pemberton waited to hear what. Then Morgan brought out oddly: "A little reputation."

"Oh, there's plenty of that. That's all right!"

"Enough of it for the people they know, no doubt. The people they know are awful."

"Do you mean the princes? We mustn't abuse the princes."

"Why not? They haven't married Paula—they haven't married Amy. They only clean out Ulick."

"You *do* know everything!" Pemberton exclaimed.

"No, I don't, after all. I don't know what they live on, or how they live, or *why* they live! What have they got and how did they get it? Are they rich, are they poor, or have they a *modeste aisance?* [11] Why are they always chiveying about—living one year like ambassadors and the next like paupers? Who are they, any way, and what are they? I've thought of all that—I've thought of a lot of things. They're so beastly worldly. That's what I hate most—oh, I've *seen* it! All they care about is to make an appearance and to pass for something or other. What do they want to pass for? What *do* they, Mr. Pemberton?"

"You pause for a reply," said Pemberton, treating the inquiry as a joke, yet wondering too, and greatly struck with the boy's intense, if imperfect, vision. "I haven't the least idea."

"And what good does it do? Haven't I seen the way people treat them—the "nice" people, the ones they want to know? They'll take anything from them—they'll lie down and be trampled on. The nice ones hate that—they just sicken them. You're the only really nice person we know."

"Are you sure? They don't lie down for me!"

"Well, you shan't lie down for them. You've got to go—that's what you've got to do," said Morgan.

"And what will become of you?"

"Oh, I'm growing up. I shall get off before long. I'll see you later."

"You had better let me finish you," Pemberton urged, lending himself to the child's extraordinarily competent attitude.

Morgan stopped in their walk, looking up at him. He had to look up much less than a couple of years before—he had grown, in his loose leanness, so long and high. "Finish me?" he echoed.

"There are such a lot of jolly things we can do together yet. I want to turn you out—I want you to do me credit."

Morgan continued to look at him. "To give you credit—do you mean?"

"My dear fellow, you're too clever to live."

"That's just what I'm afraid you think. No, no; it isn't fair—I can't endure it. We'll part next week. The sooner it's over the sooner to sleep."

"If I hear of anything—any other chance, I promise to go," said Pemberton.

Morgan consented to consider this. "But you'll be honest," he demanded; "you won't pretend you haven't heard?"

"I'm much more likely to pretend I have."

"But what can you hear of, this way, stuck in a hole with us? You ought to be on the spot, to go to England—you ought to go to America."

"One would think you were *my* tutor!" said Pemberton.

Morgan walked on, and after a moment he began again: "Well, now that you know that I know and that we look at the facts and keep nothing back—it's much more comfortable, isn't it?"

"My dear boy, it's so amusing, so interesting, that it surely will be quite impossible for me to forego such hours as these."

This made Morgan stop once more. "You *do* keep something back. Oh, you're not straight—*I* am!"

"Why am I not straight?"

"Oh, you've got your idea!"

"My idea?"

"Why, that I probably sha'n't live, and that you can stick it out till I'm removed."

"You *are* too clever to live!" Pemberton repeated.

"I call it a mean idea," Morgan pursued. "But I shall punish you by the way I hang on."

"Look out or I'll poison you!" Pemberton laughed.

"I'm stronger and better every year. Haven't you noticed that there hasn't been a doctor near me since you came?"

"*I'm* your doctor," said the young man, taking his arm and drawing him on again.

---

11. *modeste aisance:* modest affluence.

Morgan proceeded, and after a few steps he gave a sigh of mingled weariness and relief. "Ah, now that we look at the facts, it's all right!"

VII

THEY looked at the facts a good deal after this; and one of the first consequences of their doing so was that Pemberton stuck it out, as it were, for the purpose. Morgan made the facts so vivid and so droll, and at the same time so bald and so ugly, that there was fascination in talking them over with him, just as there would have been heartlessness in leaving him alone with them. Now that they had such a number of perceptions in common it was useless for the pair to pretend that they didn't judge such people; but the very judgment, and the exchange of perceptions, created another tie. Morgan had never been so interesting as now that he himself was made plainer by the sidelight of these confidences. What came out in it most was the soreness of his characteristic pride. He had plenty of that, Pemberton felt—so much that it was perhaps well it should have had to take some early bruises. He would have liked his people to be gallant, and he had waked up too soon to the sense that they were perpetually swallowing humble-pie. His mother would consume any amount, and his father would consume even more than his mother. He had a theory that Ulick had wriggled out of an "affair" at Nice: there had once been a flurry at home, a regular panic, after which they all went to bed and took medicine, not to be accounted for on any other supposition. Morgan had a romantic imagination, fed by poetry and history, and he would have liked those who "bore his name" (as he used to say to Pemberton with the humour that made his sensitiveness manly), to have a proper spirit. But their one idea was to get in with people who didn't want them and to take snubs as if they were honourable scars. Why people didn't want them more he didn't know— that was people's own affair; after all they were not superficially repulsive—they were a hundred times cleverer than most of the dreary grandees, the "poor swells" they rushed about Europe to catch up with. "After all, they *are* amusing— they are!" Morgan used to say, with the wisdom of the ages. To which Pemberton always replied: "Amusing—the great Moreen troupe? Why, they're altogether delightful; and if it were not for the hitch that you and I (feeble performers!) make in the *ensemble,* they would carry everything before them."

What the boy couldn't get over was that this particular blight seemed, in a tradition of self-respect, so undeserved and so arbitrary. No doubt people had a right to take the line they liked; but why should *his* people have liked the line of pushing and toadying and lying and cheating? What had their forefathers—all decent folk, so far as he knew—done to them, or what had *he* done to them? Who had poisoned their blood with the fifth-rate social ideal, the fixed idea of making smart acquaintances and getting into the *monde chic,*[12] especially when it was foredoomed to failure and exposure? They showed so what they were after; that was what made the people they wanted not want *them.* And never a movement of dignity, never a throb of shame at looking each other in the face, never any independence or resentment or disgust. If his father or his brother would only knock some one down once or twice a year! Clever as they were they never guessed how they appeared. They were good-natured, yes —as good-natured as Jews at the doors of clothing-shops! But was that the model one wanted one's family to follow? Morgan had dim memories of an old grandfather, the maternal, in New York, whom he had been taken across the ocean to see, at the age of five: a gentleman with a high neck-cloth and a good deal of pronunciation, who wore a dress-coat in the morning, which made one wonder what he wore in the evening, and had, or was supposed to have, "property" and something to do with the Bible Society. It couldn't have been but that *he* was a good type. Pemberton himself remembered Mrs. Clancy, a widowed sister of Mr. Moreen's, who was as irritating as a moral tale and had paid a fortnight's visit to the family at Nice shortly after he came to live with them. She was "pure and refined," as Amy said, over the banjo, and had the air of not knowing what they meant and of keeping something back. Pemberton judged that what she kept back was an approval of many of their ways; therefore it was to be supposed that she too was of a good type, and that Mr. and Mrs. Moreen and Ulick and Paula and Amy might easily have been better if they would.

But that they wouldn't was more and more perceptible from day to day. They continued to "chivey," as Morgan called it, and in due time became aware of a variety of reasons for proceeding to Venice. They mentioned a great many of them —they were always strikingly frank, and had the brightest friendly chatter, at the late foreign breakfast in especial, before the ladies had made up their faces, when they leaned their arms on the table, had something to follow the *demi-tasse,* and, in the heat of familiar discussion as to what they

12. *monde chic:* fashionable society.

"really ought" to do, fell inevitably into the languages in which they could *tutoyer*.[13] Even Pemberton liked them, then; he could endure even Ulick when he heard him give his little flat voice for the "sweet sea-city." That was what made him have a sneaking kindness for them—that they were so out of the workaday world and kept him so out of it. The summer had waned when, with cries of ecstasy, they all passed out on the balcony that overhung the Grand Canal; the sunsets were splendid—the Dorringtons had arrived. The Dorringtons were the only reason they had not talked of at breakfast; but the reasons that they didn't talk of at breakfast always came out in the end. The Dorringtons, on the other hand, came out very little; or else, when they did, they stayed— as was natural—for hours, during which periods Mrs. Moreen and the girls sometimes called at their hotel (to see if they had returned) as many as three times running. The gondola was for the ladies; for in Venice too there were "days," which Mrs. Moreen knew in their order an hour after she arrived. She immediately took one herself, to which the Dorringtons never came, though on a certain occasion when Pemberton and his pupil were together at St. Mark's—where, taking the best walks they had ever had and haunting a hundred churches, they spent a great deal of time —they saw the old lord turn up with Mr. Moreen and Ulick, who showed him the dim basilica as if it belonged to them. Pemberton noted how much less, among its curiosities, Lord Dorrington carried himself as a man of the world; wondering too whether, for such services, his companions took a fee from him. The autumn, at any rate, waned, the Dorringtons departed, and Lord Verschoyle, the eldest son, had proposed neither for Amy nor for Paula.

One sad November day, while the wind roared round the old palace and the rain lashed the lagoon, Pemberton, for exercise and even somewhat for warmth (the Moreens were horribly frugal about fires—it was a cause of suffering to their inmate), walked up and down the big bare *sala* with his pupil. The scagliola floor was cold, the high battered casements shook in the storm, and the stately decay of the place was unrelieved by a particle of furniture. Pemberton's spirits were low, and it came over him that the fortune of the Moreens was now even lower. A blast of desolation, a prophecy of disaster and disgrace, seemed to draw through the comfortless hall. Mr. Moreen and Ulick were in the Piazza, looking out

for something, strolling drearily, in mackintoshes, under the arcades; but still, in spite of mackintoshes, unmistakable men of the world. Paula and Amy were in bed—it might have been thought they were staying there to keep warm. Pemberton looked askance at the boy at his side, to see to what extent he was conscious of these portents. But Morgan, luckily for him, was now mainly conscious of growing taller and stronger and indeed of being in his fifteenth year. This fact was intensely interesting to him—it was the basis of a private theory (which, however, he had imparted to his tutor) that in a little while he should stand on his own feet. He considered that the situation would change—that, in short, he should be "finished," grown up, producible in the world of affairs and ready to prove himself of sterling ability. Sharply as he was capable, at times, of questioning his circumstances, there were happy hours when he was as superficial as a child; the proof of which was his fundamental assumption that he should presently go to Oxford, to Pemberton's college, and, aided and abetted by Pemberton, do the most wonderful things. It vexed Pemberton to see how little, in such a project, he took account of ways and means: on other matters he was so sceptical about them. Pemberton tried to imagine the Moreens at Oxford, and fortunately failed; yet unless they were to remove there as a family there would be no *modus vivendi* for Morgan. How could he live without an allowance, and where was the allowance to come from? He (Pemberton) might live on Morgan; but how could Morgan live on him? What was to become of him anyhow? Somehow, the fact that he was a big boy now, with better prospects of health, made the question of his future more difficult. So long as he was frail the consideration that he inspired seemed enough of an answer to it. But at the bottom of Pemberton's heart was the recognition of his probably being strong enough to live and not strong enough to thrive. He himself, at any rate, was in a period of natural, boyish rosiness about all this, so that the beating of the tempest seemed to him only the voice of life and the challenge of fate. He had on his shabby little overcoat, with the collar up, but he was enjoying his walk.

It was interrupted at last by the appearance of his mother at the end of the *sala*.[14] She beckoned to Morgan to come to her, and while Pemberton saw him, complacent, pass down the long vista, over the damp false marble, he wondered what was in the air. Mrs. Moreen said a word to the boy and made him go into the room she had quitted.

---

13. *tutoyer:* to use the second person singular, which in French and certain other languages means to be on terms of intimacy.

14. *sala:* Italian for drawing room.

Then, having closed the door after him, she directed her steps swiftly to Pemberton. There *was* something in the air, but his wildest flight of fancy wouldn't have suggested what it proved to be. She signified that she had made a pretext to get Morgan out of the way, and then she inquired—without hesitation—if the young man could lend her sixty francs. While, before bursting into a laugh, he stared at her with surprise, she declared that she was awfully pressed for the money; she was desperate for it—it would save her life.

"Dear lady, *c'est trop fort!*" [15] Pemberton laughed. "Where in the world do you suppose I should get sixty francs, *du train dont vous allez?*" [16]

"I thought you worked—wrote things; don't they pay you?"

"Not a penny."

"Are you such a fool as to work for nothing?"

"You ought surely to know that."

Mrs. Moreen stared an instant, then she coloured a little. Pemberton saw she had quite forgotten the terms—if "terms" they could be called —that he had ended by accepting from herself; they had burdened her memory as little as her conscience. "Oh, yes, I see what you mean—you have been very nice about that; but why go back to it so often?" She had been perfectly urbane with him ever since the rough scene of explanation in his room, the morning he made her accept *his* "terms"—the necessity of his making his case known to Morgan. She had felt no resentment, after seeing that there was no danger of Morgan's taking the matter up with her. Indeed, attributing this immunity to the good taste of his influence with the boy, she had once said to Pemberton: "My dear fellow; it's an immense comfort you're a gentleman." She repeated this, in substance, now. "Of course you're a gentleman—that's a bother the less!" Pemberton reminded her that he had not "gone back" to anything; and she also repeated her prayer that, somewhere and somehow, he would find her sixty francs. He took the liberty of declaring that if he could find them it wouldn't be to lend them to *her*—as to which he consciously did himself injustice, knowing that if he had them he would certainly place them in her hand. He accused himself, at bottom and with some truth, of a fantastic, demoralised sympathy with her. If misery made strange bedfellows it also made strange sentiments. It was moreover a part of the demoralisation and of the general bad effect of living with such people that one had to make rough retorts, quite out of the tradition of

good manners. "Morgan, Morgan, to what pass have I come for you?" he privately exclaimed, while Mrs. Moreen floated voluminously down the *sala* again, to liberate the boy; groaning, as she went, that everything was too odious.

Before the boy was liberated there came a thump at the door communicating with the staircase, followed by the apparition of a dripping youth who poked in his head. Pemberton recognised him as the bearer of a telegram and recognised the telegram as addressed to himself. Morgan came back as, after glancing at the signature (that of a friend in London), he was reading the words: "Found jolly job for you—engagement to coach opulent youth on own terms. Come immediately." The answer, happily, was paid, and the messenger waited. Morgan, who had drawn near, waited too, and looked hard at Pemberton; and Pemberton, after a moment, having met his look, handed him the telegram. It was really by wise looks (they knew each other so well), that, while the telegraph-boy, in his waterproof cape, made a great puddle on the floor, the thing was settled between them. Pemberton wrote the answer with a pencil against the frescoed wall, and the messenger departed. When he had gone Pemberton said to Morgan:

"I'll make a tremendous charge; I'll earn a lot of money in a short time, and we'll live on it."

"Well, I hope the opulent youth will be stupid —he probably will—" Morgan parenthesised, "and keep you a long time."

"Of course, the longer he keeps me the more we shall have for our old age."

"But suppose *they* don't pay you!" Morgan awfully suggested.

"Oh, there are not two such—!" Pemberton paused, he was on the point of using an invidious term. Instead of this he said "two such chances."

Morgan flushed—the tears came to his eyes. "*Dites toujours,* [17] two such rascally crews!" Then, in a different tone, he added: "Happy opulent youth!"

"Not if he's stupid!"

"Oh, they're happier then. But you can't have everything, can you?" the boy smiled.

Pemberton held him, his hands on his shoulders. "What will become of *you,* what will you do?" He thought of Mrs. Moreen, desperate for sixty francs.

"I shall turn into a man." And then, as if he recognised all the bearings of Pemberton's allusion: "I shall get on with them better when you're not here."

---

15. *c'est trop fort!:* "This is going too far!"   16. *du train dont vous allez:* "considering the way you are behaving."

17. *Dites toujours:* "say frankly."

"Ah, don't say that—it sounds as if I set you against them!"

"You do—the sight of you. It's all right; you know what I mean. I shall be beautiful. I'll take their affairs in hand; I'll marry my sisters."

"You'll marry yourself!" joked Pemberton; as high, rather tense pleasantry would evidently be the right, or the safest, tone for their separation.

It was, however, not purely in this strain that Morgan suddenly asked: "But I say—how will you get to your jolly job? You'll have to telegraph to the opulent youth for money to come on."

Pemberton bethought himself. "They won't like that, will they?"

"Oh, look out for them!"

Then Pemberton brought out his remedy. "I'll go to the American Consul; I'll borrow some money of him—just for the few days, on the strength of the telegram."

Morgan was hilarious. "Show him the telegram—then stay and keep the money!"

Pemberton entered into the joke enough to reply that, for Morgan, he was really capable of that; but the boy, growing more serious, and to prove that he hadn't meant what he said, not only hurried him off to the Consulate (since he was to start that evening, as he had wired to his friend), but insisted on going with him. They splashed through the tortuous perforations and over the humpbacked bridges, and they passed through the Piazza, where they saw Mr. Moreen and Ulick go into a jeweller's shop. The Consul proved accommodating (Pemberton said it wasn't the letter, but Morgan's grand air), and on their way back they went into St. Mark's for a hushed ten minutes. Later they took up and kept up the fun of it to the very end; and it seemed to Pemberton a part of that fun that Mrs. Moreen, who was very angry when he had announced to her his intention, should charge him, grotesquely and vulgarly, and in reference to the loan she had vainly endeavoured to effect, with bolting lest they should "get something out" of him. On the other hand he had to do Mr. Moreen and Ulick the justice to recognise that when, on coming in, *they* heard the cruel news, they took it like perfect men of the world.

VIII

WHEN Pemberton got at work with the opulent youth, who was to be taken in hand for Balliol,[18] he found himself unable to say whether he was really an idiot or it was only, on his own part, the long association with an intensely living little mind that made him seem so. From Morgan he heard half-a-dozen times: the boy wrote charming young letters, a patchwork of tongues, with indulgent postscripts in the family Volapuk and, in little squares and rounds and crannies of the text, the drollest illustrations—letters that he was divided between the impulse to show his present disciple, as a kind of wasted incentive, and the sense of something in them that was profanable by publicity. The opulent youth went up, in due course, and failed to pass; but it seemed to add to the presumption that brilliancy was not expected of him all at once that his parents, condoning the lapse, which they good-naturedly treated as little as possible as if were Pemberton's, should have sounded the rally again, begged the young coach to keep his pupil in hand another year.

The young coach was now in a position to lend Mrs. Moreen sixty francs, and he sent her a post-office order for the amount. In return for this favour he received a frantic, scribbled line from her: "Implore you to come back instantly—Morgan dreadfully ill." They were on the rebound, once more in Paris—often as Pemberton had seen them depressed he had never seen them crushed—and communication was therefore rapid. He wrote to the boy to ascertain the state of his health, but he received no answer to his letter. Accordingly he took an abrupt leave of the opulent youth and, crossing the Channel, alighted at the small hotel, in the quarter of the Champs Elysées, of which Mrs. Moreen had given him the address. A deep if dumb dissatisfaction with this lady and her companions bore him company: they couldn't be vulgarly honest, but they could live at hotels, in velvety *entresols*,[19] amid a smell of burnt pastilles, in the most expensive city in Europe. When he had left them, in Venice, it was with an irrepressible suspicion that something was going to happen; but the only thing that had happened was that they succeeded in getting away. "How is he? where is he?" he asked of Mrs. Moreen; but before she could speak, these questions were answered by the pressure round his neck of a pair of arms, in shrunken sleeves, which were perfectly capable of an effusive young foreign squeeze.

"Dreadfully ill—I don't see it!" the young man cried. And then, to Morgan: "Why on earth didn't you relieve me? Why didn't you answer my letter?"

Mrs. Moreen declared that when she wrote he was very bad, and Pemberton learned at the same time from the boy that he had answered every letter he had received. This led to the demonstra-

---

18. **Balliol:** one of the Oxford colleges.

19. *entresols:* mezzanines.

tion that Pemberton's note had been intercepted. Mrs. Moreen was prepared to see the fact exposed, as Pemberton perceived, the moment he faced her, that she was prepared for a good many other things. She was prepared above all to maintain that she had acted from a sense of duty, that she was enchanted she had got him over, whatever they might say; and that it was useless of him to pretend that he didn't *know,* in all his bones, that his place at such a time was with Morgan. He had taken the boy away from them, and now he had no right to abandon him. He had created for himself the gravest responsibilities; he must at least abide by what he had done.

"Taken him away from you?" Pemberton exclaimed indignantly.

"Do it—do it, for pity's sake; that's just what I want. I can't stand *this*—and such scenes. They're treacherous!" These words broke from Morgan, who had intermitted his embrace, in a key which made Pemberton turn quickly to him, to see that he had suddenly seated himself, was breathing with evident difficulty and was very pale.

"*Now* do you say he's not ill—my precious pet?" shouted his mother, dropping on her knees before him with clasped hands, but touching him no more than if he had been a gilded idol. "It will pass—it's only for an instant; but don't say such dreadful things!"

"I'm all right—all right," Morgan panted to Pemberton, whom he sat looking up at with a strange smile, his hands resting on either side on the sofa.

"Now do you pretend I've been treacherous—that I've deceived?" Mrs. Moreen flashed at Pemberton as she got up.

"It isn't *he* says it, it's I!" the boy returned, apparently easier, but sinking back against the wall; while Pemberton, who had sat down beside him, taking his hand, bent over him.

"Darling child, one does what one can; there are so many things to consider," urged Mrs. Moreen. "It's his *place*—his only place. You see *you* think it is now."

"Take me away—take me away," Morgan went on, smiling to Pemberton from his white face.

"Where shall I take you, and how—oh, *how,* my boy?" the young man stammered, thinking of the rude way in which his friends in London held that, for his convenience, and without a pledge of instantaneous return, he had thrown them over; of the just resentment with which they would already have called in a successor, and of the little help as regarded finding fresh employment that resided for him in the flatness of his having failed to pass his pupil.

"Oh, we'll settle that. You used to talk about it," said Morgan. "If we can only go, all the rest's a detail."

"Talk about it as much as you like, but don't think you can attempt it. Mr. Moreen would never consent—it would be so precarious," Pemberton's hostess explained to him. Then to Morgan she explained: "It would destroy our peace, it would break our hearts. Now that he's back it will be all the same again. You'll have your life, your work and your freedom, and we'll all be happy as we used to be. You'll bloom and grow perfectly well, and we won't have any more silly experiments, will we? They're too absurd. It's Mr. Pemberton's place—every one in his place. You in yours, your papa in his, me in mine—*n'est-ce pas, chéri?* [20] We'll all forget how foolish we've been, and we'll have lovely times."

She continued to talk and to surge vaguely about the little draped, stuffy *salon,* while Pemberton sat with the boy, whose colour gradually came back; and she mixed up her reasons, dropping that there were going to be changes, that the other children might scatter (who knew?—Paula had her ideas), and that then it might be fancied how much the poor old parent-birds would want the little nestling. Morgan looked at Pemberton, who wouldn't let him move; and Pemberton knew exactly how he felt at hearing himself called a little nestling. He admitted that he had had one or two bad days, but he protested afresh against the iniquity of his mother's having made them the ground of an appeal to poor Pemberton. Poor Pemberton could laugh now, apart from the comicality of Mrs. Moreen's producing so much philosophy for her defence (she seemed to shake it out of her agitated petticoats, which knocked over the light gilt chairs), so little did the sick boy strike him as qualified to repudiate any advantage.

He himself was in for it, at any rate. He should have Morgan on his hands again indefinitely; though indeed he saw the lad had a private theory to produce which would be intended to smooth this down. He was obliged to him for it in advance; but the suggested amendment didn't keep his heart from sinking a little, any more than it prevented him from accepting the prospect on the spot, with some confidence moreover that he would do so even better if he could have a little supper. Mrs. Moreen threw out more hints about the changes that were to be looked for, but she was such a mixture of smiles and shudders (she confessed she was very nervous), that he couldn't tell whether she were in high feather or only in hyster-

20. *n'est-ce pas, chéri?:* "isn't it so, dear?"

ics. If the family were really at last going to pieces why shouldn't she recognise the necessity of pitching Morgan into some sort of lifeboat? This presumption was fostered by the fact that they were established in luxurious quarters in the capital of pleasure; that was exactly where they naturally *would* be established in view of going to pieces. Moreover didn't she mention that Mr. Moreen and the others were enjoying themselves at the opera with Mr. Granger, and wasn't *that* also precisely where one would look for them on the eve of a smash? Pemberton gathered that Mr. Granger was a rich, vacant American—a big bill with a flourishy heading and no items; so that one of Paula's "ideas" was probably that this time she had really done it, which was indeed an unprecedented blow to the general cohesion. And if the cohesion was to terminate what was to become of poor Pemberton? He felt quite enough bound up with them to figure, to his alarm, as a floating spar in case of a wreck.

It was Morgan who eventually asked if no supper had been ordered for him; sitting with him below, later, at the dim, delayed meal, in the presence of a great deal of corded green plush, a plate of ornamental biscuit and a languor marked on the part of the waiter. Mrs. Moreen had explained that they had been obliged to secure a room for the visitor out of the house; and Morgan's consolation (he offered it while Pemberton reflected on the nastiness of lukewarm sauces), proved to be, largely, that this circumstance would facilitate their escape. He talked of their escape (recurring to it often afterwards), as if they were making up a "boy's book" together. But he likewise expressed his sense that there was something in the air, that the Moreens couldn't keep it up much longer. In point of fact, as Pemberton was to see, they kept it up for five or six months. All the while, however, Morgan's contention was designed to cheer him. Mr. Moreen and Ulick, whom he had met the day after his return, accepted that return like perfect men of the world. If Paula and Amy treated it even with less formality an allowance was to be made for them, inasmuch as Mr. Granger had not come to the opera after all. He had only placed his box at their service, with a bouquet for each of the party; there was even one apiece, embittering the thought of his profusion, for Mr. Moreen and Ulick. "They're all like that," was Morgan's comment; "at the very last, just when we think we've got them fast, we're chucked!"

Morgan's comments, in these days, were more and more free; they even included a large recognition of the extraordinary tenderness with which he had been treated while Pemberton was away. Oh, yes, they couldn't do enough to be nice to him, to show him they had him on their mind and make up for his loss. That was just what made the whole thing so sad, and him so glad, after all, of Pemberton's return—he had to keep thinking of their affection less, had less sense of obligation. Pemberton laughed out at this last reason, and Morgan blushed and said: "You know what I mean." Pemberton knew perfectly what he meant; but there were a good many things it didn't make any clearer. This episode of his second sojourn in Paris stretched itself out wearily, with their resumed readings and wanderings and maunderings, their potterings on the quays, their hauntings of the museums, their occasional lingerings in the Palais Royal, when the first sharp weather came on and there was a comfort in warm emanations, before Chevet's wonderful succulent window. Morgan wanted to hear a great deal about the opulent youth—he took an immense interest in him. Some of the details of his opulence—Pemberton could spare him none of them—evidently intensified the boy's appreciation of all his friend had given up to come back to him; but in addition to the greater reciprocity established by such a renunciation he had always his little brooding theory, in which there was a frivolous gaiety too, that their long probation was drawing to a close. Morgan's conviction that the Moreens couldn't go on much longer kept pace with the unexpended impetus with which, from month to month, they did go on. Three weeks after Pemberton had rejoined them they went on to another hotel, a dingier one than the first; but Morgan rejoiced that his tutor had at least still not sacrificed the advantage of a room outside. He clung to the romantic utility of this when the day, or rather the night, should arrive for their escape.

For the first time, in this complicated connection, Pemberton felt sore and exasperated. It was, as he had said to Mrs. Moreen in Venice, *trop fort* —everything was *trop fort*. He could neither really throw off his blighting burden nor find in it the benefit of a pacified conscience or of a rewarded affection. He had spent all the money that he had earned in England, and he felt that his youth was going and that he was getting nothing back for it. It was all very well for Morgan to seem to consider that he would make up to him for all inconveniences by settling himself upon him permanently—there was an irritating flaw in such a view. He saw what the boy had in his mind; the conception that as his friend had had the generosity to come back to him he must show his gratitude by giving him his life. But the poor friend didn't desire the gift—what could he do with Morgan's life? Of course at the same time that Pemberton was irritated he remembered the reason, which was very honourable to Morgan and which consisted simply of the fact that he was perpetually making one forget that he was after all only a child. If one dealt with him on a different basis one's misadventures were one's own fault. So Pemberton waited in a queer confusion of yearning and alarm for the catastrophe which was held to hang over the house of Moreen, of which he certainly at moments felt the symptoms brush his cheek and as to which he wondered much in what form it would come.

Perhaps it would take the form of dispersal—a frightened *sauve qui peut*,[21] a scuttling into selfish corners. Certainly they were less elastic than of yore; they were evidently looking for something they didn't find. The Dorringtons hadn't reappeared, the princes had scattered; wasn't that the beginning of the end? Mrs. Moreen had lost her reckoning of the famous "days;" her social calendar was blurred—it had turned its face to the wall. Pemberton suspected that the great, the cruel, discomfiture had been the extraordinary behaviour of Mr. Granger, who seemed not to know what he wanted, or, what was much worse, what *they* wanted. He kept sending flowers, as if to bestrew the path of his retreat, which was never the path of return. Flowers were all very well, but —Pemberton could complete the proposition. It was now positively conspicuous that in the long run the Moreens were a failure; so that the young man was almost grateful the run had not been short. Mr. Moreen, indeed, was still occasionally able to get away on business, and, what was more surprising, he was also able to get back. Ulick had no club, but you could not have discovered it from his appearance, which was as much as ever that of a person looking at life from the window of such an institution; therefore Pemberton was doubly astonished at an answer he once heard him make to his mother, in the desperate tone of a man familiar with the worst privations. Her question Pemberton had not quite caught; it appeared to be an appeal for a suggestion as to whom they could get to take Amy. "Let the devil take her!" Ulick snapped; so that Pemberton could see that not only they had lost their amiability, but had ceased to believe in themselves. He could also see that if Mrs. Moreen was trying to get people to take her children she might be regarded as closing the hatches for the storm. But Morgan would be the last she would part with.

One winter afternoon—it was a Sunday—he and the boy walked far together in the Bois de Boulogne. The evening was so splendid, the cold lemon-coloured sunset so clear, the stream of carriages and pedestrians so amusing and the fascination of Paris so great, that they stayed out later than usual and became aware that they would have to hurry home to arrive in time for dinner. They hurried accordingly, arm-in-arm, good-humoured and hungry, agreeing that there was nothing like Paris after all and that after all, too, that had come and gone they were not yet sated with innocent pleasures. When they reached the hotel they found that, though scandalously late, they were in time for all the dinner they were likely to sit down to. Confusion reigned in the apartments of the Moreens (very shabby ones this time, but the best in the house), and before the interrupted service of the table (with objects displaced almost as if there had been a scuffle, and a great wine stain from an overturned bottle), Pemberton could not blink the fact that there had been a scene of proprietary mutiny. The storm had come —they were all seeking refuge. The hatches were down—Paula and Amy were invisible (they had never tried the most casual art upon Pemberton, but he felt that they had enough of an eye to him not to wish to meet him as young ladies whose frocks had been confiscated), and Ulick appeared to have jumped overboard. In a word, the host and his staff had ceased to "go on" at the pace of their guests, and the air of embarrassed detention, thanks to a pile of gaping trunks in the passage, was strangely commingled with the air of indignant withdrawal.

When Morgan took in all this—and he took it in very quickly—he blushed to the roots of his hair. He had walked, from his infancy, among difficulties and dangers, but he had never seen a public exposure. Pemberton noticed, in a second glance at him, that the tears had rushed into his eyes and that they were tears of bitter shame. He wondered for an instant, for the boy's sake, whether he might successfully pretend not to understand. Not successfully, he felt, as Mr. and Mrs. Moreen, dinnerless by their extinguished hearth, rose before him in their little dishonoured *salon,* considering apparently with much intensity what lively capital would be next on their list. They were not prostrate, but they were very pale, and Mrs. Moreen had evidently been crying. Pemberton quickly learned however that her grief was not for the loss of her dinner, much as she usually enjoyed it, but on account of a necessity much more tragic. She lost no time in laying this necessity bare, in telling him how the change

21. *sauve qui peut:* "every man for himself."

had come, the bolt had fallen, and how they would all have to turn themselves about. Therefore cruel as it was to them to part with their darling she must look to him to carry a little further the influence he had so fortunately acquired with the boy—to induce his young charge to follow him into some modest retreat. They depended upon him, in a word, to take their delightful child temporarily under his protection—it would leave Mr. Moreen and herself so much more free to give the proper attention (too little, alas! had been given), to the readjustment of their affairs.

"We trust you—we feel that we can," said Mrs. Moreen, slowly rubbing her plump white hands and looking, with compunction, hard at Morgan, whose chin, not to take liberties, her husband stroked with a tentative paternal forefinger.

"Oh, yes; we feel that we can. We trust Mr. Pemberton fully, Morgan," Mr. Moreen conceded.

Pemberton wondered again if he might pretend not to understand; but the idea was painfully complicated by the immediate perception that Morgan had understood.

"Do you mean that he may take me to live with him—for ever and ever?" cried the boy. "Away, away, anywhere he likes?"

"For ever and ever? *Comme vous-y-allez!*" [22] Mr. Moreen laughed indulgently. "For as long as Mr. Pemberton may be so good."

"We've struggled, we've suffered," his wife went on; "but you've made him so your own that we've already been through the worst of the sacrifice."

Morgan had turned away from his father—he stood looking at Pemberton with a light in his face. His blush had died out, but something had come that was brighter and more vivid. He had a moment of boyish joy, scarcely mitigated by the reflection that, with this unexpected consecration of his hope—too sudden and too violent; the thing was a good deal less like a boy's book—the "escape" was left on their hands. The boyish joy was there for an instant, and Pemberton was almost frightened at the revelation of gratitude and affection that shone through his humiliation. When Morgan stammered "My dear fellow, what do you say to *that?*" he felt that he should say something enthusiastic. But he was still more frightened at something else that immediately followed and that made the lad sit down quickly on the nearest chair. He had turned very white and had raised his hand to his left side. They were all three looking at him, but Mrs. Moreen was the

first to bound forward. "Ah, his darling little heart!" she broke out; and this time, on her knees before him and without respect for the idol, she caught him ardently in her arms. "You walked him too far, you hurried him too fast!" she tossed over her shoulder at Pemberton. The boy made no protest, and the next instant his mother, still holding him, sprang up with her face convulsed and with the terrified cry "Help, help! he's going, he's gone!" Pemberton saw, with equal horror, by Morgan's own stricken face, that he *was* gone. He pulled him half out of his mother's hands, and for a moment, while they held him together, they looked, in their dismay, into each other's eyes. "He couldn't stand it, with his infirmity," said Pemberton—"the shock, the whole scene, the violent emotion."

"But I thought he *wanted* to go to you!" wailed Mrs. Moreen.

"I *told* you he didn't, my dear," argued Mr. Moreen. He was trembling all over, and he was, in his way, as deeply affected as his wife. But, after the first, he took his bereavement like a man of the world.

THE REAL THING

◇

("The Real Thing" is one of James's many tales about the conflicts between illusion and reality, art and life, as they affect the lives and works of artists and writers (and here of models). The setting, as in most of his artist tales, is contemporary London. In a general way the theme was familiar in the contemporary London of Oscar Wilde and his fellow Aesthetes. But the theme acquired special meanings and intensities for James in the nineties by reason of the concurrent crisis in his own creative life. "The Real Thing" was first published in the English periodical *Black and White* (April, 1892), republished in the collection *The Real Thing and Other Tales* (1893), and again in the New York Edition. For James's account of the genesis and development of "The Real Thing" see the passage from his notebooks (pp. 262–64).

◇

I

WHEN the porter's wife (she used to answer the house-bell), announced "A gentleman—with a lady, sir," I had, as I often had in those days, for the wish was father to the thought, an immediate

22. *Comme vous-y-allez!:* "How you do go on!"

vision of sitters. Sitters my visitors in this case proved to be; but not in the sense I should have preferred. However, there was nothing at first to indicate that they might not have come for a portrait. The gentleman, a man of fifty, very high and very straight, with a moustache slightly grizzled and a dark grey walking-coat admirably fitted, both of which I noted professionally—I don't mean as a barber or yet as a tailor—would have struck me as a celebrity if celebrities often were striking. It was a truth of which I had for some time been conscious that a figure with a good deal of frontage was, as one might say, almost never a public institution. A glance at the lady helped to remind me of this paradoxical law: she also looked too distinguished to be a "personality." Moreover one would scarcely come across two variations together.

Neither of the pair spoke immediately—they only prolonged the preliminary gaze which suggested that each wished to give the other a chance. They were visibly shy; they stood there letting me take them in—which, as I afterwards perceived, was the most practical thing they could have done. In this way their embarrassment served their cause. I had seen people painfully reluctant to mention that they desired anything so gross as to be represented on canvas; but the scruples of my new friends appeared almost insurmountable. Yet the gentleman might have said "I should like a portrait of my wife," and the lady might have said "I should like a portrait of my husband." Perhaps they were not husband and wife—this naturally would make the matter more delicate. Perhaps they wished to be done together—in which case they ought to have brought a third person to break the news.

"We come from Mr. Rivet," the lady said at last, with a dim smile which had the effect of a moist sponge passed over a "sunk" piece of painting, as well as of a vague allusion to vanished beauty. She was as tall and straight, in her degree, as her companion, and with ten years less to carry. She looked as sad as a woman could look whose face was not charged with expression; that is her tinted oval mask showed friction as an exposed surface shows it. The hand of time had played over her freely, but only to simplify. She was slim and stiff, and so well-dressed, in dark blue cloth, with lappets and pockets and buttons, that it was clear she employed the same tailor as her husband. The couple had an indefinable air of prosperous thrift—they evidently got a good deal of luxury for their money. If I was to be one of their luxuries it would behove me to consider my terms.

"Ah, Claude Rivet recommended me?" I inquired; and I added that it was very kind of him, though I could reflect that, as he only painted landscape, this was not a sacrifice.

The lady looked very hard at the gentleman, and the gentleman looked round the room. Then staring at the floor a moment and stroking his moustache, he rested his pleasant eyes on me with the remark: "He said you were the right one."

"I try to be, when people want to sit."

"Yes, we should like to," said the lady anxiously.

"Do you mean together?"

My visitors exchanged a glance. "If you could do anything with *me,* I suppose it would be double," the gentleman stammered.

"Oh yes, there's naturally a higher charge for two figures than for one."

"We should like to make it pay," the husband confessed.

"That's very good of you," I returned, appreciating so unwonted a sympathy—for I supposed he meant pay the artist.

A sense of strangeness seemed to dawn on the lady. "We mean for the illustrations—Mr. Rivet said you might put one in."

"Put one in—an illustration?" I was equally confused.

"Sketch her off, you know," said the gentleman, colouring.

It was only then that I understood the service Claude Rivet had rendered me; he had told them that I worked in black and white, for magazines, for story-books, for sketches of contemporary life, and consequently had frequent employment for models. These things were true, but it was not less true (I may confess it now—whether because the aspiration was to lead to everything or to nothing I leave the reader to guess), that I couldn't get the honours, to say nothing of the emoluments, of a great painter of portraits out of my head. My "illustrations" were my pot-boilers; I looked to a different branch of art (far and away the most interesting it had always seemed to me), to perpetuate my fame. There was no shame in looking to it also to make my fortune; but that that fortune was by so much further from being made from the moment my visitors wished to be "done" for nothing. I was disappointed; for in the pictorial sense I had immediately *seen* them. I had seized their type—I had already settled what I would do with it. Something that wouldn't absolutely have pleased them, I afterwards reflected.

"Ah, you're—you're—a—?" I began, as soon as I had mastered my surprise. I couldn't bring out the dingy word "models"; it seemed to fit the case so little.

"We haven't had much practice," said the lady.

"We've got to *do* something, and we've thought that an artist in your line might perhaps make something of us," her husband threw off. He further mentioned that they didn't know many artists and that they had gone first, on the off-chance (he painted views of course, but sometimes put in figures—perhaps I remembered), to Mr. Rivet, whom they had met a few years before at a place in Norfolk where he was sketching.

"We used to sketch a little ourselves," the lady hinted.

"It's very awkward, but we absolutely *must* do something," her husband went on.

"Of course, we're not so *very* young," she admitted, with a wan smile.

With the remark that I might as well know something more about them, the husband had handed me a card extracted from a neat new pocket-book (their appurtenances were all of the freshest) and inscribed with the words "Major Monarch." Impressive as these words were they didn't carry my knowledge much further; but my visitor presently added: "I've left the army, and we've had the misfortune to lose our money. In fact our means are dreadfully small."

"It's an awful bore," said Mrs. Monarch.

They evidently wished to be discreet—to take care not to swagger because they were gentlefolks. I perceived they would have been willing to recognise this as something of a drawback, at the same time that I guessed at an underlying sense—their consolation in adversity—that they *had* their points. They certainly had; but these advantages struck me as preponderantly social; such for instance as would help to make a drawing-room look well. However, a drawing-room was always, or ought to be, a picture.

In consequence of his wife's allusion to their age Major Monarch observed: "Naturally, it's more for the figure that we thought of going in. We can still hold ourselves up." On the instant I saw that the figure was indeed their strong point. His "naturally" didn't sound vain, but it lighted up the question. *"She* has got the best," he continued, nodding at his wife, with a pleasant after-dinner absence of circumlocution. I could only reply, as if we were in fact sitting over our wine, that this didn't prevent his own from being very good; which led him in turn to rejoin: "We thought that if you ever have to do people like us, we might be something like it. *She,* particularly—for a lady in a book, you know."

I was so amused by them that, to get more of it, I did my best to take their point of view; and though it was an embarrassment to find myself appraising physically, as if they were animals on hire or useful blacks, a pair whom I should have expected to meet only in one of the relations in which criticism is tacit, I looked at Mrs. Monarch judicially enough to be able to exclaim, after a moment, with conivction: "Oh yes, a lady in a book!" She was singularly like a bad illustration.

"We'll stand up, if you like," said the Major; and he raised himself before me with a really grand air.

I could take his measure at a glance—he was six feet two and a perfect gentleman. It would have paid any club in process of formation and in want of a stamp to engage him at a salary to stand in the principle window. What struck me immediately was that in coming to me they had rather missed their vocation; they could surely have been turned to better account for advertising purposes. I couldn't of course see the thing in detail, but I could see them make someone's fortune—I don't mean their own. There was something in them for a waistcoat-maker, an hotel-keeper or a soap-vendor. I could imagine "We always use it" pinned on their bosoms with the greatest effect; I had a vision of the promptitude with which they would launch a table d'hôte.

Mrs. Monarch sat still, not from pride but from shyness, and presently her husband said to her: "Get up my dear and show how smart you are." She obeyed, but she had no need to get up to show it. She walked to the end of the studio, and then she came back blushing, with her fluttered eyes on her husband. I was reminded of an incident I had accidentally had a glimpse of in Paris—being with a friend there, a dramatist about to produce a play—when an actress came to him to ask to be intrusted with a part. She went through her paces before him, walked up and down as Mrs. Monarch was doing. Mrs. Monarch did it quite as well, but I abstained from applauding. It was very odd to see such people apply for such poor pay. She looked as if she had ten thousand a year. Her husband had used the word that described her: she was, in the London current jargon, essentially and typically "smart." Her figure was, in the same order of ideas, conspicuously and irreproachably "good." For a woman of her age her waist was surprisingly small; her elbow moreover had the orthodox crook. She held her head at the conventional angle; but why did she come to *me?* She ought to have tried on jackets at a big shop. I feared my visitors were not only destitute, but "artistic"—which would be a great complication. When she sat down again I thanked her, observing that what a draughtsman most valued in his model was the faculty of keeping quiet.

"Oh, *she* can keep quiet," said Major Monarch. Then he added, jocosely: "I've always kept her quiet."

"I'm not a nasty fidget, am I?" Mrs. Monarch appealed to her husband.

He addressed his answer to me. "Perhaps it isn't out of place to mention—because we ought to be quite business-like, oughtn't we?—that when I married her she was known as the Beautiful Statue."

"Oh dear!" said Mrs. Monarch, ruefully.

"Of course I should want a certain amount of expression," I rejoined.

"Of *course!*" they both exclaimed.

"And then I suppose you know that you'll get awfully tired."

"Oh, we *never* get tired!" they eagerly cried.

"Have you had any kind of practice?"

They hesitated—they looked at each other. "We've been photographed, *immensely,*" said Mrs. Monarch.

"She means the fellows have asked us," added the Major.

"I see—because you're so good-looking."

"I don't know what they thought, but they were always after us."

"We always got our photographs for nothing," smiled Mrs. Monarch.

"We might have brought some, my dear," her husband remarked.

"I'm not sure we have any left. We've given quantities away," she explained to me.

"With our autographs and that sort of thing," said the Major.

"Are they to be got in the shops?" I inquired, as a harmless pleasantry.

"Oh, yes; *hers*—they used to be."

"Not now," said Mrs. Monarch, with her eyes on the floor.

II

I COULD fancy the "sort of thing" they put on the presentation-copies of their photographs, and I was sure they wrote a beautiful hand. It was odd how quickly I was sure of everything that concerned them. If they were now so poor as to have to earn shillings and pence, they never had had much of a margin. Their good looks had been their capital, and they had good-humouredly made the most of the career that this resource marked out for them. It was in their faces, the blankness, the deep intellectual repose of the twenty years of country-house visiting which had given them pleasant intonations. I could see the

sunny drawing-rooms, sprinkled with periodicals she didn't read, in which Mrs. Monarch had continuously sat; I could see the wet shrubberies in which she had walked, equipped to admiration for either exercise. I could see the rich covers the Major had helped to shoot and the wonderful garments in which, late at night, he repaired to the smoking-room to talk about them. I could imagine their leggings and waterproofs, their knowing tweeds and rugs, their rolls of sticks and cases of tackle and neat umbrellas; and I could evoke the exact appearance of their servants and the compact variety of their luggage on the platforms of country stations.

They gave small tips, but they were liked; they didn't do anything themselves, but they were welcome. They looked so well everywhere; they gratified the general relish for stature, complexion and "form." They knew it without fatuity or vulgarity, and they respected themselves in consequence. They were not superficial; they were thorough and kept themselves up—it had been their line. People with such a taste for activity had to have some line. I could feel how, even in a dull house, they could have been counted upon for cheerfulness. At present something had happened —it didn't matter what, their little income had grown less, it had grown least—and they had to do something for pocket-money. Their friends liked them, but didn't like to support them. There was something about them that represented credit —their clothes, their manners, their type; but if credit is a large empty pocket in which an occasional chink reverberates, the chink at least must be audible. What they wanted of me was to help to make it so. Fortunately they had no children— I soon divined that. They would also perhaps wish our relations to be kept secret: this was why it was "for the figure"—the reproduction of the face would betray them.

I liked them—they were so simple; and I had no objection to them if they would suit. But, somehow, with all their perfections I didn't easily believe in them. After all they were amateurs, and the ruling passion of my life was the detestation of the amateur. Combined with this was another perversity—an innate preference for the represented subject over the real one: the defect of the real one was so apt to be a lack of representation. I liked things that appeared; then one was sure. Whether they *were* or not was a subordinate and almost always a profitless question. There were other considerations, the first of which was that I already had two or three people in use, notably a young person with big feet, in alpaca, from Kilburn, who for a couple of years had come to me regularly for my illustrations and with whom I was still—perhaps ignobly—satisfied. I frankly explained to my visitors how the case stood; but they had taken more precautions than I supposed. They had reasoned out their opportunity, for Claude Rivet had told them of the projected *édition de luxe* of one of the writers of our day— the rarest of the novelists—who, long neglected by the multitudinous vulgar and dearly prized by the attentive (need I mention Philip Vincent?) had had the happy fortune of seeing, late in life, the dawn and then the full light of a higher criticism—an estimate in which, on the part of the public, there was something really of expiation. The edition in question, planned by a publisher of taste, was practically an act of high reparation; the wood-cuts with which it was to be enriched were the homage of English art to one of the most independent representatives of English letters. Major and Mrs. Monarch confessed to me that they had hoped I might be able to work *them* into my share of the enterprise. They knew I was to do the first of the books, "Rutland Ramsay," but I had to make clear to them that my participation in the rest of the affair—this first book was to be a test —was to depend on the satisfaction I should give. If this should be limited my employers would drop me without a scruple. It was therefore a crisis for me, and naturally I was making special preparations, looking about for new people, if they should be necessary, and securing the best types. I admitted however that I should like to settle down to two or three good models who would do for everything.

"Should we have often to—a—put on special clothes?" Mrs. Monarch timidly demanded.

"Dear, yes—that's half the business."

"And should we be expected to supply our own costumes?"

"Oh, no; I've got a lot of things. A painter's models put on—or put off—anything he likes."

"And do you mean—a—the same?"

"The same?"

Mrs. Monarch looked at her husband again.

"Oh, she was just wondering," he explained, "if the costumes are in *general* use." I had to confess that they were, and I mentioned further that some of them (I had a lot of genuine, greasy last-century things), had served their time, a hundred years ago, on living, world-stained men and women. "We'll put on anything that *fits*," said the Major.

"Oh, I arrange that—they fit in the pictures."

"I'm afraid I should do better for the modern books. I would come as you like," said Mrs. Monarch.

"She has got a lot of clothes at home: they might do for contemporary life," her husband continued.

"Oh, I can fancy scenes in which you'd be quite natural." And indeed I could see the slip-shod rearrangements of stale properties—the stories I tried to produce pictures for without the exasperation of reading them—whose sandy tracts the good lady might help to people. But I had to return to the fact that for this sort of work—the daily mechanical grind—I was already equipped; the people I was working with were fully adequate.

"We only thought we might be more like *some* characters," said Mrs. Monarch mildly, getting up.

Her husband also rose; he stood looking at me with a dim wistfulness that was touching in so fine a man. "Wouldn't it be rather a pull sometimes to have—a—to have—?" He hung fire; he wanted me to help him by phrasing what he meant. But I couldn't—I didn't know. So he brought it out, awkwardly: "The *real* thing; a gentleman, you know, or a lady." I was quite ready to give a general assent—I admitted that there was a great deal in that. This encouraged Major Monarch to say, following up his appeal with an unacted gulp: "It's awfully hard—we've tried everything." The gulp was communicative; it proved too much for his wife. Before I knew it Mrs. Monarch had dropped again upon a divan and burst into tears. Her husband sat down beside her, holding one of her hands; whereupon she quickly dried her eyes with the other, while I felt embarrassed as she looked up at me. "There isn't a confounded job I haven't applied for—waited for—prayed for. You can fancy we'd be pretty bad first. Secretaryships and that sort of thing? You might as well ask for a peerage. I'd be *anything*—I'm strong; a messenger or a coalheaver. I'd put on a gold-laced cap and open carriage-doors in front of the haberdasher's; I'd hang about a station, to carry portmanteaus; I'd be a postman. But they won't *look* at you; there are thousands, as good as yourself, already on the ground. *Gentlemen*, poor beggars, who have drunk their wine, who have kept their hunters!"

I was as reassuring as I knew how to be, and my visitors were presently on their feet again while, for the experiment, we agreed on an hour. We were discussing it when the door opened and Miss Churm came in with a wet umbrella. Miss Churm had to take the omnibus to Maida Vale [1] and then walk half-a-mile. She looked a trifle

THE REAL THING.   1. **Maida Vale**: unfashionable residential quarter of London.

blowsy and slightly splashed. I scarcely ever saw her come in without thinking afresh how odd it was that, being so little in herself, she should yet be so much in others. She was a meagre little Miss Churm, but she was an ample heroine of romance. She was only a freckled cockney, but she could represent everything, from a fine lady to a shepherdess; she had the faculty, as she might have had a fine voice or long hair. She couldn't spell, and she loved beer, but she had two or three "points," and practice, and a knack, and mother-wit, and a kind of whimsical sensibility, and a love of the theatre, and seven sisters, and not an ounce of respect, especially for the *h*. The first thing my visitors saw was that her umbrella was wet, and in their spotless perfection they visibly winced at it. The rain had come on since their arrival.

"I'm all in a soak; there *was* a mess of people in the 'bus. I wish you lived near a styton," said Miss Churm. I requested her to get ready as quickly as possible, and she passed into the room in which she always changed her dress. But before going out she asked me what she was to get into this time.

"It's the Russian princess, don't you know?" I answered; "the one with the 'golden eyes,' in black velvet, for the long thing in the *Cheapside*." [2]

"Golden eyes? I *say!*" cried Miss Churm, while my companions watched her with intensity as she withdrew. She always arranged herself, when she was late, before I could turn round; and I kept my visitors a little, on purpose, so that they might get an idea, from seeing her, what would be expected of themselves. I mentioned that she was quite my notion of an excellent model —she was really very clever.

"Do you think she looks like a Russian princess?" Major Monarch asked, with lurking alarm.

"When I make her, yes."

"Oh, if you have to *make* her—!" he reasoned, acutely.

"That's the most you can ask. There are so many that are not makeable."

"Well now, *here's* a lady"—and with a persuasive smile he passed his arm into his wife's— "who's already made!"

"Oh, I'm not a Russian princess," Mrs. Monarch protested, a little coldly. I could see that she had known some and didn't like them. There, immediately, was a complication of a kind that I never had to fear with Miss Churm.

This young lady came back in black velvet— the gown was rather rusty and very low on her

lean shoulders—and with a Japanese fan in her red hands. I reminded her that in the scene I was doing she had to look over someone's head. "I forget whose it is; but it doesn't matter. Just look over a head."

"I'd rather look over a stove," said Miss Churm; and she took her station near the fire. She fell into position, settled herself into a tall attitude, gave a certain backward inclination to her head and a certain forward droop to her fan, and looked, at least to my prejudiced sense, distinguished and charming, foreign and dangerous. We left her looking so, while I went down-stairs with Major and Mrs. Monarch.

"I think I could come about as near it as that," said Mrs. Monarch.

"Oh, you think she's shabby, but you must allow for the alchemy of art."

However, they went off with an evident increase of comfort, founded on their demonstrable advantage in being the real thing. I could fancy them shuddering over Miss Churm. She was very droll about them when I went back, for I told her what they wanted.

"Well, if *she* can sit I'll tyke to bookkeeping," said my model.

"She's very lady-like," I replied, as an innocent form of aggravation.

"So much the worse for *you*. That means she can't turn round."

"She'll do for the fashionable novels."

"Oh yes, she'll *do* for them!" my model humorously declared. "Ain't they bad enough without her?" I had often sociably denounced them to Miss Churm.

III

IT WAS for the elucidation of a mystery in one of these works that I first tried Mrs. Monarch. Her husband came with her, to be useful if necessary —it was sufficiently clear that as a general thing he would prefer to come with her. At first I wondered if this were for "propriety's" sake—if he were going to be jealous and meddling. The idea was too tiresome, and if it had been confirmed it would speedily have brought our acquaintance to a close. But I soon saw there was nothing in it and that if he accompanied Mrs. Monarch it was (in addition to the chance of being wanted), simply because he had nothing else to do. When she was away from him his occupation was gone—she never *had* been away from him. I judged, rightly, that in their awkward situation their close union was their main comfort and that this union had no weak spot. It was a real marriage, an encouragement to the hesitating, a nut for pessimists to

2. *Cheapside:* imaginary magazine named after London's famous commercial thoroughfare.

crack. Their address was humble (I remember afterwards thinking it had been the only thing about them that was really professional), and I could fancy the lamentable lodgings in which the Major would have been left alone. He could bear them with his wife—he couldn't bear them without her.

He had too much tact to try and make himself agreeable when he couldn't be useful; so he simply sat and waited, when I was too absorbed in my work to talk. But I liked to make him talk—it made my work, when it didn't interrupt it, less sordid, less special. To listen to him was to combine the excitement of going out with the economy of staying at home. There was only one hindrance: that I seemed not to know any of the people he and his wife had known. I think I wondered extremely, during the term of our intercourse, whom the deuce I *did* know. He hadn't a stray sixpence of an idea to fumble for; so we didn't spin it very fine—we confined ourselves to questions of leather and even of liquor (saddlers and breeches-makers and how to get good claret cheap), and matters like "good trains" and the habits of small game. His lore on these last subjects was astonishing, he managed to interweave the station-master with the ornithologist. When he couldn't talk about greater things he could talk cheerfully about smaller, and since I couldn't accompany him into reminiscences of the fashionable world he could lower the conversation without a visible effort to my level.

So earnest a desire to please was touching in a man who could so easily have knocked one down. He looked after the fire and had an opinion on the draught of the stove, without my asking him, and I could see that he thought many of my arrangements not half clever enough. I remember telling him that if I were only rich I would offer him a salary to come and teach me how to live. Sometimes he gave a random sigh, of which the essence was: "Give me even such a bare old barrack as *this,* and I'd do something with it!" When I wanted to use him he came alone; which was an illustration of the superior courage of women. His wife could bear her solitary second floor, and she was in general more discreet; showing by various small reserves that she was alive to the propriety of keeping our relations markedly professional—not letting them slide into sociability. She wished it to remain clear that she and the Major were employed, not cultivated, and if she approved of me as a superior, who could be kept in his place, she never thought me quite good enough for an equal.

She sat with great intensity, giving the whole of her mind to it, and was capable of remaining for an hour almost as motionless as if she were before a photographer's lens. I could see she had been photographed often, but somehow the very habit that made her good for that purpose unfitted her for mine. At first I was extremely pleased with her lady-like air, and it was a satisfaction, on coming to follow her lines, to see how good they were and how far they could lead the pencil. But after a few times I began to find her too insurmountably stiff; do what I would with it my drawing looked like a photograph or a copy of a photograph. Her figure had no variety of expression—she herself had no sense of variety. You may say that this was my business, was only a question of placing her. I placed her in every conceivable position, but she managed to obliterate their differences. She was always a lady certainly, and into the bargain was always the same lady. She was the real thing, but always the same thing. There were moments when I was oppressed by the serenity of her confidence that she *was* the real thing. All her dealings with me and all her husband's were an implication that this was lucky for *me.* Meanwhile I found myself trying to invent types that approached her own, instead of making her own transform itself—in the clever way that was not impossible, for instance, to poor Miss Churm. Arrange as I would and take the precautions I would, she always, in my pictures, came out too tall—landing me in the dilemma of having represented a fascinating woman as seven feet high, which, out of respect perhaps to my own very much scantier inches, was far from my idea of such a personage.

The case was worse with the Major—nothing I could do would keep *him* down, so that he became useful only for the representation of brawny giants. I adored variety and range, I cherished human accidents, the illustrative note; I wanted to characterise closely, and the thing in the world I most hated was the danger of being ridden by a type. I had quarrelled with some of my friends about it—I had parted company with them for maintaining that one *had* to be, and that if the type was beautiful (witness Raphael and Leonardo), the servitude was only a gain. I was neither Leonardo nor Raphael; I might only be a presumptuous young modern searcher, but I held that everything was to be sacrificed sooner than character. When they averred that the haunting type in question could easily *be* character, I retorted, perhaps superficially: "Whose?" It couldn't be everybody's—it might end in being nobody's.

After I had drawn Mrs. Monarch a dozen times I perceived more clearly than before that the value of such a model as Miss Churm resided precisely in the fact that she had no positive stamp, combined of course with the other fact that what she did have was a curious and inexplicable talent for imitation. Her usual appearance was like a curtain which she could draw up at request for a capital performance. This performance was simply suggestive; but it was a word to the wise—it was vivid and pretty. Sometimes, even, I thought it, though she was plain herself, too insipidly pretty; I made it a reproach to her that the figures drawn from her were monotonously (*bête-ment*,[3] as we used to say) graceful. Nothing made her more angry: it was so much her pride to feel that she could sit for characters that had nothing in common with each other. She would accuse me at such moments of taking away her "reputytion."

It suffered a certain shrinkage, this queer quantity, from the repeated visits of my new friends. Miss Churm was greatly in demand, never in want of employment, so I had no scruple in putting her off occasionally, to try them more at my ease. It was certainly amusing at first to do the real thing—it was amusing to do Major Monarch's trousers. They *were* the real thing, even if he did come out colossal. It was amusing to do his wife's back hair (it was so mathematically neat,) and the particular "smart" tension of her tight stays. She lent herself especially to positions in which the face was somewhat averted or blurred; she abounded in lady-like back views and *profils perdus*.[4] When she stood erect she took naturally one of the attitudes in which court-painters represent queens and princesses; so that I found myself wondering whether, to draw out this accomplishment, I couldn't get the editor of the *Cheapside* to publish a really royal romance, "A Tale of Buckingham Palace." Sometimes, however, the real thing and the make-believe came into contact; by which I mean that Miss Churm, keeping an appointment or coming to make one on days when I had much work in hand, encountered her invidious rivals. The encounter was not on their part, for they noticed her no more than if she had been the housemaid; not from intentional loftiness, but simply because, as yet, professionally, they didn't know how to fraternise, as I could guess that they would have liked—or at least that the Major would. They couldn't talk about the omnibus—they always walked; and they didn't know what else to try—she wasn't interested in good trains or cheap claret. Besides, they must have felt—in the air—that she was amused at them, secretly derisive of their ever knowing how.

She was not a person to conceal her scepticism if she had had a chance to show it. On the other hand Mrs. Monarch didn't think her tidy; for why else did she take pains to say to me (it was going out of the way, for Mrs. Monarch), that she didn't like dirty women?

One day when my young lady happened to be present with my other sitters (she even dropped in, when it was convenient, for a chat), I asked her to be so good as to lend a hand in getting tea—a service with which she was familiar and which was one of a class that, living as I did in a small way, with slender domestic resources, I often appealed to my models to render. They liked to lay hands on my property, to break the sitting, and sometimes the china—I made them feel Bohemian. The next time I saw Miss Churm after this incident she surprised me greatly by making a scene about it—she accused me of having wished to humiliate her. She had not resented the outrage at the time, but had seemed obliging and amused, enjoying the comedy of asking Mrs. Monarch, who sat vague and silent, whether she would have cream and sugar, and putting an exaggerated simper into the question. She had tried intonations—as if she too wished to pass for the real thing; till I was afraid my other visitors would take offence.

Oh, *they* were determined not to do this; and their touching patience was the measure of their great need. They would sit by the hour, uncomplaining, till I was ready to use them; they would come back on the chance of being wanted and would walk away cheerfully if they were not. I used to go to the door with them to see in what magnificent order they retreated. I tried to find other employment for them—I introduced them to several artists. But they didn't "take," for reasons I could appreciate, and I became conscious, rather anxiously, that after such disappointments they fell back upon me with a heavier weight. They did me the honour to think that it was I who was most *their* form. They were not picturesque enough for the painters, and in those days there were not so many serious workers in black and white. Besides, they had an eye to the great job I had mentioned to them—they had secretly set their hearts on supplying the right essence for my pictorial vindication of our fine novelist. They knew that for this undertaking I should want no costume-effects, none of the frippery of past ages —that it was a case in which everything would be contemporary and satirical and, presumably, genteel. If I could work them into it their future would be assured, for the labour would of course be long and the occupation steady.

3. *bêtement*: beastly.　　4. *profils perdus*: averted glances.

One day Mrs. Monarch came without her husband—she explained his absence by his having had to go to the City.[5] While she sat there in her usual anxious stiffness there came, at the door, a knock which I immediately recognised as the subdued appeal of a model out of work. It was followed by the entrance of a young man whom I easily perceived to be a foreigner and who proved in fact an Italian acquainted with no English word but my name, which he uttered in a way that made it seem to include all others. I had not then visited his country, nor was I proficient in his tongue; but as he was not so meanly constituted—what Italian is?—as to depend only on that member for expression he conveyed to me, in familiar but graceful mimicry, that he was in search of exactly the employment in which the lady before me was engaged. I was not struck with him at first, and while I continued to draw I emitted rough sounds of discouragement and dismissal. He stood his ground, however, not importunately, but with a dumb, dog-like fidelity in his eyes which amounted to innocent impudence—the manner of a devoted servant (he might have been in the house for years), unjustly suspected. Suddenly I saw that this very attitude and expression made a picture, whereupon I told him to sit down and wait till I should be free. There was another picture in the way he obeyed me, and I observed as I worked that there were others still in the way he looked wonderingly, with his head thrown back, about the high studio. He might have been crossing himself in St. Peter's. Before I finished I said to myself: "The fellow's a bankrupt orange-monger, but he's a treasure."

When Mrs. Monarch withdrew he passed across the room like a flash to open the door for her, standing there with the rapt, pure gaze of the young Dante spellbound by the young Beatrice.[6] As I never insisted, in such situations, on the blankness of the British domestic, I reflected that he had the making of a servant (and I needed one, but couldn't pay him to be only that), as well as of a model; in short I made up my mind to adopt my bright adventurer if he would agree to officiate in the double capacity. He jumped at my offer, and in the event my rashness (for I had known nothing about him), was not brought home to me. He proved a sympathetic though a desultory ministrant, and had in a wonderful degree the *sentiment de la pose*.[7] It was uncultivated, instinctive; a part of the happy instinct which

had guided him to my door and helped him to spell out my name on the card nailed to it. He had had no other introduction to me than a guess, from the shape of my high north window, seen outside, that my place was a studio and that as a studio it would contain an artist. He had wandered to England in search of fortune, like other itinerants, and had embarked, with a partner and a small green hand-cart, on the sale of penny ices. The ices had melted away and the partner had dissolved in their train. My young man wore tight yellow trousers with reddish stripes and his name was Oronte. He was sallow but fair, and when I put him into some old clothes of my own he looked like an Englishman. He was as good as Miss Churm, who could look, when required, like an Italian.

IV

I THOUGHT Mrs. Monarch's face slightly convulsed when, on her coming back with her husband, she found Oronte installed. It was strange to have to recognise in a scrap of a *lazzarone*[8] a competitor to her magnificent Major. It was she who scented danger first, for the Major was anecdotically unconscious. But Oronte gave us tea, with a hundred eager confusions (he had never seen such a queer process), and I think she thought better of me for having at last an "establishment." They saw a couple of drawings that I had made of the establishment, and Mrs. Monarch hinted that it never would have struck her that he had sat for them. "Now the drawings you make from *us,* they look exactly like us," she reminded me, smiling in triumph; and I recognised that this was indeed just their defect. When I drew the Monarchs I couldn't, somehow, get away from them—get into the character I wanted to represent; and I had not the least desire my model should be discoverable in my picture. Miss Churm never was, and Mrs. Monarch thought I hid her, very properly, because she was vulgar; whereas if she was lost it was only as the dead who go to heaven are lost—in the gain of an angel the more.

By this time I had got a certain start with "Rutland Ramsay," the first novel in the great projected series; that is I had produced a dozen drawings, several with the help of the Major and his wife, and I had sent them in for approval. My understanding with the publishers, as I have already hinted, had been that I was to be left to do my work, in this particular case, as I liked, with the whole book committed to me; but my connection with the rest of the series was only contingent.

5. the City: London's banking and commercial center.
6. Beatrice: Dante's youthful love for Beatrice Portinari is told in his *La Vita Nuova*.   7. *sentiment de la pose:* "the instinct for striking poses."

8. *lazzarone:* Italian for beggar.

There were moments when, frankly, it *was* a comfort to have the real thing under one's hand; for there were characters in "Rutland Ramsay" that were very much like it. There were people presumably as straight as the Major and women of as good a fashion as Mrs. Monarch. There was a great deal of country-house life—treated, it is true, in a fine, fanciful, ironical, generalised way—and there was a considerable implication of knickerbockers and kilts. There were certain things I had to settle at the outset; such things for instance as the exact appearance of the hero, the particular bloom of the heroine. The author of course gave me a lead, but there was a margin for interpretation. I took the Monarchs into my confidence, I told them frankly what I was about, I mentioned my embarrassments and alternatives. "Oh, take *him!*" Mrs. Monarch murmured sweetly, looking at her husband; and "What could you want better than my wife?" the Major inquired, with the comfortable candour that now prevailed between us.

I was not obliged to answer these remarks—I was only obliged to place my sitters. I was not easy in mind, and I postponed, a little timidly perhaps, the solution of the question. The book was a large canvas, the other figures were numerous, and I worked off at first some of the episodes in which the hero and the heroine were not concerned. When once I had set *them* up I should have to stick to them—I couldn't make my young man seven feet high in one place and five feet nine in another. I inclined on the whole to the latter measurement, though the Major more than once reminded me that *he* looked about as young as anyone. It was indeed quite possible to arrange him, for the figure, so that it would have been difficult to detect his age. After the spontaneous Oronte had been with me a month, and after I had given him to understand several different times that his native exuberance would presently constitute an insurmountable barrier to our further intercourse, I waked to a sense of his heroic capacity. He was only five feet seven, but the remaining inches were latent. I tried him almost secretly at first, for I was really rather afraid of the judgment my other models would pass on such a choice. If they regarded Miss Churm as little better than a snare, what would they think of the representation by a person so little the real thing as an Italian street-vendor of a protagonist formed by a public school?

If I went a little in fear of them it was not because they bullied me, because they had got an oppressive foothold, but because in their really pathetic decorum and mysteriously permanent new-ness they counted on me so intensely. I was therefore very glad when Jack Hawley came home: he was always of such good counsel. He painted badly himself, but there was no one like him for putting his finger on the place. He had been absent from England for a year; he had been somewhere—I don't remember where—to get a fresh eye. I was in a good deal of dread of any such organ, but we were old friends; he had been away for months and a sense of emptiness was creeping into my life. I hadn't dodged a missile for a year.

He came back with a fresh eye, but with the same old black velvet blouse, and the first evening he spent in my studio we smoked cigarettes till the small hours. He had done no work himself, he had only got the eye; so the field was clear for the production of my little things. He wanted to see what I had done for the *Cheapside,* but he was disappointed in the exhibition. That at least seemed the meaning of two or three comprehensive groans which, as he lounged on my big divan, on a folded leg, looking at my latest drawings, issued from his lips with the smoke of the cigarette.

"What's the matter with you?" I asked.

"What's the matter with *you?*"

"Nothing save that I'm mystified."

"You are indeed. You're quite off the hinge. What's the meaning of this new fad?" And he tossed me, with visible irreverence, a drawing in which I happened to have depicted both my majestic models. I asked if he didn't think it good, and he replied that it struck him as execrable, given the sort of thing I had always represented myself to him as wishing to arrive at; but I let that pass, I was so anxious to see exactly what he meant. The two figures in the picture looked colossal, but I supposed this was *not* what he meant, inasmuch as, for aught he knew to the contrary, I might have been trying for that. I maintained that I was working exactly in the same way as when he last had done me the honour to commend me. "Well, there's a big hole somewhere," he answered; "wait a bit and I'll discover it." I depended upon him to do so: where else was the fresh eye? But he produced at last nothing more luminous than "I don't know—I don't like your types." This was lame, for a critic who had never consented to discuss with me anything but the question of execution, the direction of strokes and the mystery of values.

"In the drawings you've been looking at I think my types are very handsome."

"Oh, they won't do!"

"I've had a couple of new models."

"I see you have. *They* won't do."

"Are you very sure of that?"

"Absolutely—they're stupid."

"You mean *I* am—for I ought to get round that."

"You *can't*—with such people. Who are they?"

I told him, as far as was necessary, and he declared, heartlessly: *"Ce sont des gens qu'il faut mettre à la porte."* [9]

"You've never seen them; they're awfully good," I compassionately objected.

"Not seen them? Why, all this recent work of yours drops to pieces with them. It's all I want to see of them."

"No one else has said anything against it—the *Cheapside* people are pleased."

"Everyone else is an ass, and the *Cheapside* people the biggest asses of all. Come, don't pretend, at this time of day, to have pretty illusions about the public, especially about publishers and editors. It's not for *such* animals you work—it's for those who know, *coloro che sanno;* [10] so keep straight for *me* if you can't keep straight for yourself. There's a certain sort of thing you tried for from the first—and a very good thing it is. But this twaddle isn't *in* it." When I talked with Hawley later about "Rutland Ramsay" and its possible successors he declared that I must get back into my boat again or I would go to the bottom. His voice in short was the voice of warning.

I noted the warning, but I didn't turn my friends out of doors. They bored me a good deal; but the very fact that they bored me admonished me not to sacrifice them—if there was anything to be done with them—simply to irritation. As I look back at this phase they seem to me to have pervaded my life not a little. I have a vision of them as most of the time in my studio, seated, against the wall, on an old velvet bench to be out of the way, and looking like a pair of patient courtiers in a royal ante-chamber. I am convinced that during the coldest weeks of the winter they held their ground because it saved them fire. Their newness was losing its gloss, and it was impossible not to feel that they were objects of charity. Whenever Miss Churm arrived they went away, and after I was fairly launched in "Rutland Ramsay" Miss Churm arrived pretty often. They managed to express to me tacitly that they supposed I wanted her for the low life of the book, and I let them suppose it, since they had attempted to study the work—it was lying about the studio—without discovering that it dealt only with the highest circles. They had dipped into the most brilliant of our

novelists without deciphering many passages. I still took an hour from them, now and again, in spite of Jack Hawley's warning: it would be time enough to dismiss them, if dismissal should be necessary, when the rigour of the season was over. Hawley had made their acquaintance—he had met them at my fireside—and thought them a ridiculous pair. Learning that he was a painter they tried to approach him, to show him too that they were the real thing; but he looked at them, across the big room, as if they were miles away: they were a compendium of everything that he most objected to in the social system of his country. Such people as that, all convention and patent-leather, with ejaculations that stopped conversation, had no business in a studio. A studio was a place to learn to see, and how could you see through a pair of feather beds?

The main inconvenience I suffered at their hands was that, at first, I was shy of letting them discover how my artful little servant had begun to sit to me for "Rutland Ramsay." They knew that I had been odd enough (they were prepared by this time to allow oddity to artists,) to pick a foreign vagabond out of the streets, when I might have had a person with whiskers and credentials; but it was some time before they learned how high I rated his accomplishments. They found him in an attitude more than once, but they never doubted I was doing him as an organ-grinder. There were several things they never guessed, and one of them was that for a striking scene in the novel, in which a footman briefly figured, it occurred to me to make use of Major Monarch as the menial. I kept putting this off, I didn't like to ask him to don the livery—besides the difficulty of finding a livery to fit him. At last, one day late in the winter, when I was at work on the despised Oronte (he caught one's idea in an instant), and was in the glow of feeling that I was going very straight, they came in, the Major and his wife, with their society laugh about nothing (there was less and less to laugh at), like country-callers—they always reminded me of that—who have walked across the park after church and are presently persuaded to stay to luncheon. Luncheon was over, but they could stay to tea—I knew they wanted it. The fit was on me, however, and I couldn't let my ardour cool and my work wait, with the fading daylight, while my model prepared it. So I asked Mrs. Monarch if she would mind laying it out—a request which, for an instant, brought all the blood to her face. Her eyes were on her husband's for a second, and some mute telegraphy passed between them. Their folly was over the next instant; his cheerful shrewdness put an end to it. So far from pitying their wounded pride, I must add, I was moved to give it as complete a lesson as I could. They bustled about together and got out the cups and saucers and made the kettle boil. I know they felt as if they were waiting on my servant, and when the tea was prepared I said: "He'll have a cup, please—he's tired." Mrs. Monarch brought him one where he stood, and he took it from her as if he had been a gentleman at a party, squeezing a crush-hat with an elbow.

Then it came over me that she had made a great effort for me—made it with a kind of nobleness —and that I owed her a compensation. Each time I saw her after this I wondered what the compensation could be. I couldn't go on doing the wrong thing to oblige them. Oh, it *was* the wrong thing, the stamp of the work for which they sat—Hawley was not the only person to say it now. I sent in a large number of the drawings I had made for "Rutland Ramsay," and I received a warning that was more to the point that Hawley's. The artistic adviser of the house for which I was working was of opinion that many of my illustrations were not what had been looked for. Most of these illustrations were the subjects in which the Monarchs had figured. Without going into the question of what *had* been looked for, I saw at this rate I shouldn't get the other books to do. I hurled myself in despair upon Miss Churm, I put her through all her paces. I not only adopted Oronte publicly as my hero, but one morning when the Major looked in to see if I didn't require him to finish a figure for the *Cheapside,* for which he had begun to sit the week before, I told him that I had changed my mind—I would do the drawing from my man. At this my visitor turned pale and stood looking at me. "Is *he* your idea of an English gentleman?" he asked.

I was disappointed, I was nervous, I wanted to get on with my work; so I replied with irritation: "Oh, my dear Major—I can't be ruined for *you!*"

He stood another moment; then, without a word, he quitted the studio. I drew a long breath when he was gone, for I said to myself that I shouldn't see him again. I had not told him definitely that I was in danger of having my work rejected, but I was vexed at his not having felt the catastrophe in the air, read with me the moral of our fruitless collaboration, the lesson that, in the deceptive atmosphere of art, even the highest respectability may fail of being plastic.

I didn't owe my friends money, but I did see them again. They re-appeared together, three days later, and under the circumstances there was something tragic in the fact. It was a proof to me

that they could find nothing else in life to do. They had threshed the matter out in a dismal conference—they had digested the bad news that they were not in for the series. If they were not useful to me even for the *Cheapside* their function seemed difficult to determine, and I could only judge at first that they had come, forgivingly, decorously, to take a last leave. This made me rejoice in secret that I had little leisure for a scene; for I had placed both my other models in position together and I was pegging away at a drawing from which I hoped to derive glory. It had been suggested by the passage in which Rutland Ramsay, drawing up a chair to Artemisia's piano-stool, says extraordinary things to her while she ostensibly fingers out a difficult piece of music. I had done Miss Churm at the piano before—it was an attitude in which she knew how to take on an absolutely poetic grace. I wished the two figures to "compose" together, intensely, and my little Italian had entered perfectly into my conception. The pair were vividly before me, the piano had been pulled out; it was a charming picture of blended youth and murmured love, which I had only to catch and keep. My visitors stood and looked at it, and I was friendly to them over my shoulder.

They made no response, but I was used to silent company and went on with my work, only a little disconcerted (even though exhilarated by the sense that *this* was at least the ideal thing), at not having got rid of them after all. Presently I heard Mrs. Monarch's sweet voice beside, or rather above me: "I wish her hair were a little better done." I looked up and she was staring with a strange fixedness at Miss Churm, whose back was turned to her. "Do you mind my just touching it?" she went on—a question which made me spring up for an instant, as with the instinctive fear that she might do the young lady a harm. But she quieted me with a glance I shall never forget— I confess I should like to have been able to paint *that*—and went for a moment to my model. She spoke to her softly, laying a hand upon her shoulder and bending over her; and as the girl, understanding, gratefully assented, she disposed her rough curls, with a few quick passes, in such a way as to make Miss Churm's head twice as charming. It was one of the most heroic personal services I have ever seen rendered. Then Mrs. Monarch turned away with a low sigh and, looking about her as if for something to do, stooped to the floor with a noble humility and picked up a dirty rag that had dropped out of my paint-box.

The Major meanwhile had also been looking for something to do and, wandering to the other end of the studio, saw before him my breakfast things, neglected, unremoved. "I say, can't I be useful *here?*" he called out to me with an irrepressible quaver. I assented with a laugh that I fear was awkward and for the next ten minutes, while I worked, I heard the light clatter of china and the tinkle of spoons and glass. Mrs. Monarch assisted her husband—they washed up my crockery, they put it away. They wandered off into my little scullery, and I afterwards found that they had cleaned my knives and that my slender stock of plate had an unprecedented surface. When it came over me, the latent eloquence of what they were doing, I confess that my drawing was blurred for a moment—the picture swam. They had accepted their failure, but they couldn't accept their fate. They had bowed their heads in bewilderment to the perverse and cruel law in virtue of which the real thing could be so much less precious than the unreal; but they didn't want to starve. If my servants were my models, my models might be my servants. They would reverse the parts—the others would sit for the ladies and gentlemen, and *they* would do the work. They would still be in the studio—it was an intense dumb appeal to me not to turn them out. "Take us on," they wanted to say—"we'll do *anything.*"

When all this hung before me the *afflatus* vanished—my pencil dropped from my hand. My sitting was spoiled and I got rid of my sitters, who were also evidently rather mystified and awestruck. Then, alone with the Major and his wife, I had a most uncomfortable moment. He put their prayer into a single sentence: "I say, you know—just let *us* do for you, can't you?" I couldn't—it was dreadful to see them emptying my slops; but I pretended I could, to oblige them, for about a week. Then I gave them a sum of money to go away; and I never saw them again. I obtained the remaining books, but my friend Hawley repeats that Major and Mrs. Monarch did me a permanent harm, got me into a second-rate trick. If it be true I am content to have paid the price—for the memory.

'EUROPE'

◇

❲ " 'Europe' " recalls certain of James's early stories about the frustration, in an American setting, of the desire for experience, especially the desire for travel in the Old World. But it reflects the later James in its more concentrated form and more severely ironic spirit. 'Europe,' in quotation marks, has become a kind of cliché. First published in *Scribner's Monthly* (June, 1899), the story was reprinted in the collection *The Soft Side* (1900) and reprinted again in the New York Edition.

◇

I

'OUR feeling is, you know, that Becky *should* go.' That earnest little remark comes back to me, even after long years, as the first note of something that began, for my observation, the day I went with my sister-in-law to take leave of her good friends. It is a memory of the American time, which revives so at present—under some touch that doesn't signify—that it rounds itself off as an anecdote. That walk to say good-bye was the beginning; and the end, so far as I was concerned with it, was not till long after; yet even the end also appears to me now as of the old days. I went, in those days, on occasion, to see my sister-in-law, in whose affairs, on my brother's death, I had had to take a helpful hand. I continued to go, indeed, after these little matters were straightened out, for the pleasure, periodically, of the impression—the change to the almost pastoral sweetness of the good Boston suburb from the loud, longitudinal New York. It was another world, with other manners, a different tone, a different taste; a savour nowhere so mild, yet so distinct, as in the square white house—with a pair of elms, like gigantic wheat-sheaves in front, the rustic orchard not far behind, the old-fashioned door-lights, the big blue and white jars in the porch, the straight, bricked walk from the high gate—that enshrined the extraordinary merit of Mrs. Rimmle and her three daughters.

These ladies were so much of the place and the place so much of themselves that, from the first of their being revealed to me, I felt that nothing else at Brookbridge much mattered. They were what, for me, at any rate, Brookbridge had most to give: I mean in the way of what it was naturally strongest in, the thing that we called in New York the New England expression, the air of Puritanism reclaimed and refined. The Rimmles had brought it down to a wonderful delicacy. They struck me even then—all four almost equally—as very ancient and very earnest, and I think theirs must have been the house, in all the world, in which 'culture' first came to the aid of morning calls. The head of the family was the widow of a great public character—as public characters were understood at Brookbridge—whose speeches on anniversaries formed a part of the body of national eloquence spouted in the New England schools by little boys covetous of the most marked, though perhaps the easiest, distinction. He was reported to have been celebrated, and in such fine declamatory connections that he seemed to gesticulate even from the tomb. He was understood to have made, in his wife's company, the tour of Europe at a date not immensely removed from that of the battle of Waterloo. What was the age, then, of the bland, firm, antique Mrs. Rimmle at the period of her being first revealed to me? That is a point I am not in a position to determine—I remember mainly that I was young enough to regard her as having reached the limit. And yet the limit for Mrs. Rimmle must have been prodigiously extended; the scale of its extension is, in fact, the very moral of this reminiscence. She was old, and her daughters were old, but I was destined to know them all as older. It was only by comparison and habit that—however much I recede—Rebecca, Maria, and Jane were the 'young ladies.'

I think it was felt that, though their mother's life, after thirty years of widowhood, had had a grand backward stretch, her blandness and firmness—and this in spite of her extreme physical frailty—would be proof against any surrender not overwhelmingly justified by time. It had appeared, years before, at a crisis of which the waves had not even yet quite subsided, a surrender not justified by anything, that she should go, with her daughters, to Europe for her health. Her health was supposed to require constant support; but when it had at that period tried conclusions with the idea of Europe, it was not the idea of Europe that had been insidious enough to prevail. She had not gone, and Becky, Maria, and Jane had not gone, and this was long ago. They still merely floated in the air of the visit achieved, with such introductions and such acclamations, in the early part of the century; they still, with fond glances at the sunny parlour-walls, only referred, in conversation, to divers pictorial and other reminders of it. The Miss Rimmles had quite been brought up on it, but Becky, as the most literary, had most mastered the subject. There were framed letters—tributes to their eminent father—suspended among the mementos, and of two or three of these, the most foreign and complimentary, Becky had executed translations that figured beside the text. She knew already, through this and other illumination, so much about Europe that it was hard to believe, for her, in that limit of adventure which consisted only of her having been twice to Philadelphia. The others had not been to Philadelphia, but there was a legend that Jane had been to Saratoga. Becky was a short, stout, fair person with round, serious eyes, a high forehead, the sweetest, neatest enunciation, and a miniature of her father—'done in Rome'—worn as a breastpin. She had written the life, she had edited the speeches, of the original of this ornament, and now at last, beyond the seas, she was really to tread in his footsteps.

Fine old Mrs. Rimmle, in the sunny parlour and with a certain austerity of cap and chair—though with a gay new 'front' that looked like rusty brown plush—had had so unusually good a winter that the question of her sparing two members of her family for an absence had been threshed as fine, I could feel, as even under that Puritan roof any case of conscience had ever been threshed. They were to make their dash while the coast, as it were, was clear, and each of the daughters had tried—heroically, angelically, and for the sake of each of her sisters—not to be one of the two. What I encountered that first time was an opportunity to concur with enthusiasm in the general idea that Becky's wonderful preparation would be wasted if she were the one to stay with their mother. They talked of Becky's preparation —they had a sly, old-maidish humour that was as mild as milk—as if it were some mixture, for application somewhere, that she kept in a precious bottle. It had been settled, at all events, that, armed with this concoction and borne aloft by their introductions, she and Jane were to start. They were wonderful on their introductions, which proceeded naturally from their mother and were addressed to the charming families that, in vague generations, had so admired vague Mr. Rimmle. Jane, I found at Brookbridge, had to be described, for want of other description, as the pretty one, but it would not have served to identify her unless you had seen the others. *Her* preparation was only this figment of her prettiness—only, that is, unless one took into account something that, on the spot, I silently divined: the lifelong, secret, passionate ache of her little rebellious desire. They were all growing old in the yearning to go, but Jane's yearning was the sharpest. She struggled with it as people at Brookbridge mostly struggled with what they liked, but fate, by threatening to prevent what she *dis*liked, and what was therefore duty—which was to stay at home instead of Maria—had bewildered her, I judged, not a little. It was she who, in the words I have quoted, mentioned to me Becky's case and Becky's affinity as the clearest of all. Her mother, moreover, on the general subject, had still more to say.

'I positively desire, I really quite insist that they shall go,' the old lady explained to us from her stiff chair. 'We've talked about it so often, and they've had from me so clear an account—I've amused them again and again with it—of what is to be seen and enjoyed. If they've had hitherto too many duties to leave, the time seems to have come to recognise that there are also many duties to *seek*. Wherever we go we find them—I always remind the girls of that. There's a duty that calls them to those wonderful countries, just as it called, at the right time, their father and myself—if it be only that of laying up for the years to come the same store of remarkable impressions, the same wealth of knowledge and food for conversation as, since my return, I have found myself so happy to possess.' Mrs. Rimmle spoke of her return as of something of the year before last, but the future of her daughters was, somehow, by a different law, to be on the scale of great vistas, of endless aftertastes. I think that, without my being quite ready to say it, even this first impression of her was somewhat upsetting; there was a large, placid perversity, a grim secrecy of intention, in her estimate of the ages.

'Well, I'm so glad you don't delay it longer,' I said to Miss Becky before we withdrew. 'And whoever should go,' I continued in the spirit of the sympathy with which the good sisters had already inspired me, 'I quite feel, with your family, you know, that *you* should. But of course I hold that every one should.' I suppose I wished to attenuate my solemnity; there was something in it, however, that I couldn't help. It must have been a faint foreknowledge.

'Have you been a great deal yourself?' Miss Jane, I remember, inquired.

'Not so much but that I hope to go a good deal more. So perhaps we shall meet,' I encouragingly suggested.

I recall something—something in the nature of susceptibility to encouragement—that this brought into the more expressive brown eyes to which Miss Jane mainly owed it that she was the pretty one. 'Where, do you think?'

I tried to think. 'Well, on the Italian lakes—Como, Bellagio, Lugano.' I liked to say the names to them.

' "Sublime, but neither bleak nor bare—nor misty are the mountains there!" ' Miss Jane softly breathed, while her sister looked at her as if her familiarity with the poetry of the subject made her the most interesting feature of the scene she evoked.

But Miss Becky presently turned to me. 'Do you know everything——?'

'Everything?'

'In Europe.'

'Oh, yes,' I laughed, 'and one or two things even in America.'

The sisters seemed to me furtively to look at each other. 'Well, you'll have to be quick—to meet *us*,' Miss Jane resumed.

'But surely when you're once there you'll stay on.'

'Stay on?'—they murmured it simultaneously and with the oddest vibration of dread as well as of desire. It was as if they had been in the presence of a danger and yet wished me, who 'knew everything,' to torment them with still more of it.

Well, I did my best. 'I mean it will never do to cut it short.'

'No, that's just what I keep saying,' said brilliant Jane. 'It would be better, in that case, not to go.'

'Oh, don't talk about not going—at this time!' It was none of my business, but I felt shocked and impatient.

'No, not at *this* time!' broke in Miss Maria, who, very red in the face, had joined us. Poor Miss Maria was known as the flushed one; but she was not flushed—she only had an unfortunate surface. The third day after this was to see them embark.

Miss Becky, however, desired as little as any one to be in any way extravagant. 'It's only the thought of our mother,' she explained.

I looked a moment at the old lady, with whom my sister-in-law was engaged. 'Well—your mother's magnificent.'

'*Isn't* she magnificent?'—they eagerly took it up.

She *was*—I could reiterate it with sincerity, though I perhaps mentally drew the line when Miss Maria again risked, as a fresh ejaculation: 'I think she's better than Europe!'

'Maria!' they both, at this, exclaimed with a strange emphasis; it was as if they feared she had suddenly turned cynical over the deep domestic drama of their casting of lots. The innocent laugh with which she answered them gave the measure of her cynicism.

We separated at last, and my eyes met Mrs. Rimmle's as I held for an instant her aged hand. It was doubtless only my fancy that her calm, cold look quietly accused me of something. Of what *could* it accuse me? Only, I thought, of thinking.

II

I LEFT Brookbridge the next day, and for some time after that had no occasion to hear from my kinswoman; but when she finally wrote there was a passage in her letter that affected me more than all the rest. 'Do you know the poor Rimmles never, after all, "went"? The old lady, at the eleventh hour, broke down; everything broke down, and all of *them* on top of it, so that the dear things are with us still. Mrs. Rimmle, the night after our call, had, in the most unexpected manner, a turn for the worse—something in the nature (though they're rather mysterious about it) of a seizure; Becky and Jane felt it—dear, devoted, stupid angels that they are—heartless to leave her at such a moment, and Europe's indefinitely postponed. However, they think they're still going—or *think* they think it—when she's better. They also think—or think they think—that she *will* be better. I certainly pray she may.' So did I—quite fervently. I was conscious of a real pang—I didn't know how much they had made me care.

Late that winter my sister-in-law spent a week in New York; when almost my first inquiry on meeting her was about the health of Mrs. Rimmle.

'Oh, she's rather bad—she really is, you know. It's not surprising that at her age she should be infirm.'

'Then what the deuce *is* her age?'

'I can't tell you to a year—but she's immensely old.'

'That of course I saw,' I replied—'unless you literally mean so old that the records have been lost.'

My sister-in-law thought. 'Well, I believe she wasn't positively young when she married. She lost three or four children before these women were born.'

We surveyed together a little, on this, the 'dark backward.' 'And they were born, I gather, *after* the famous tour? Well, then, as the famous tour was in a manner to celebrate—wasn't it?—the restoration of the Bourbons [1]—' I considered, I gasped. 'My dear child, what on earth do you make her out?'

My relative, with her Brookbridge habit, transferred her share of the question to the moral plane—turned it forth to wander, by implication at least, in the sandy desert of responsibility. 'Well, you know, we all immensely admire her.'

'You can't admire her more than I do. She's awful.'

My interlocutress looked at me with a certain fear. 'She's *really* ill.'

'Too ill to get better?'

'Oh, no—we hope not. Because then they'll be able to go.'

'And *will* they go, if she should?'

'Oh, the moment they should be quite satisfied. I mean *really,*' she added.

I'm afraid I laughed at her—the Brookbridge 'really' was a thing so by itself. 'But if she shouldn't get better?' I went on.

'Oh, don't speak of it! They want so to go.'

'It's a pity they're so infernally good,' I mused.

'No—don't say that. It's what keeps them up.'

'Yes, but isn't it what keeps *her* up too?'

My visitor looked grave. 'Would you like them to kill her?'

I don't know that I was then prepared to say I should—though I believe I came very near it. But later on I burst all bounds, for the subject grew and grew. I went again before the good sisters ever did—I mean I went to Europe. I think I went twice, with a brief interval, before my fate again brought round for me a couple of days at Brookbridge. I had been there repeatedly, in the previous time, without making the acquaintance of the Rimmles; but now that I had had the revelation I couldn't have it too much, and the first request I preferred was to be taken again to see them. I remember well indeed the scruple I felt—the real delicacy—about betraying that *I* had, in the pride of my power, since our other meeting, stood, as their phrase went, among romantic scenes; but they were themselves the first to speak of it, and what, moreover, came home to me was that the coming and going of their friends in general—Brookbridge itself having even at that period one foot in Europe—was such as to place constantly before them the pleasure that was only postponed. They were thrown back, after all, on what the situation, under a final analysis, had most to give—the sense that, as every one kindly said to them and they kindly said to every one, Europe would keep. Every one felt for them so deeply that their own kindness in alleviating every one's feeling was really what came out most. Mrs. Rimmle was still in her stiff chair and in the sunny parlour, but if *she* made no scruple of introducing the Italian lakes my heart sank to observe that she dealt with them, as a topic, not in the least in the leave-taking manner in which Falstaff babbled of green fields.

I am not sure that, after this, my pretexts for a day or two with my sister-in-law were not apt to be a mere cover for another glimpse of these particulars: I at any rate never went to Brookbridge without an irrepressible eagerness for our customary call. A long time seems to me thus to have passed, with glimpses and lapses, considerable impatience and still more pity. Our visits indeed grew shorter, for, as my companion said, they

'EUROPE.'   1. the . . . Bourbons: The return of the Bourbon dynasty to the French throne after the Revolution occurred in 1814.

were more and more of a strain. It finally struck me that the good sisters even shrank from me a little, as from one who penetrated their consciousness in spite of himself. It was as if they knew where I thought they ought to be, and were moved to deprecate at last, by a systematic silence on the subject of that hemisphere, the criminality I fain would fix on them. They were full instead—as with the instinct of throwing dust in my eyes—of little pathetic hypocrisies about Brookbridge interests and delights. I dare say that as time went on my deeper sense of their situation came practically to rest on my companion's report of it. I think I recollect, at all events, every word we ever exchanged about them, even if I have lost the thread of the special occasions. The impression they made on me after each interval always broke out with extravagance as I walked away with her.

'*She* may be as old as she likes—I don't care. It's the fearful age the "girls" are reaching that constitutes the scandal. One shouldn't pry into such matters, I know; but the years and the chances are really going. They're all growing old together—it will presently be too late; and their mother meanwhile perches over them like a vulture—what shall I call it?—calculating. Is she waiting for them successively to drop off? She'll survive them each and all. There's something too remorseless in it.'

'Yes; but what do you want her to do? If the poor thing *can't* die, she can't. Do you want her to take poison or to open a blood-vessel? I dare say she would prefer to go.'

'I beg your pardon,' I must have replied; 'you daren't say anything of the sort. If she would prefer to go she *would* go. She would feel the propriety, the decency, the necessity of going. She just prefers *not* to go. She prefers to stay and keep up the tension, and her calling them "girls" and talking of the good time they'll still have is the mere conscious mischief of a subtle old witch. They won't have *any* time—there isn't any time to have! I mean there's, on her own part, no real loss of measure or of perspective in it. She *knows* she's a hundred and ten, and takes a cruel pride in it.'

My sister-in-law differed with me about this; she held that the old woman's attitude was an honest one and that her magnificent vitality, so great in spite of her infirmities, made it inevitable that she should attribute youth to persons who had come into the world so much later. 'Then suppose she should die?'—so my fellow-student of the case always put it to me.

'Do you mean while her daughters are away? There's not the least fear of that—not even if at the very moment of their departure she should be

in extremis. They would find her all right on their return.'

'But think how they would feel not to have been with her!'

'That's only, I repeat, on the unsound assumption. If they would only go to-morrow—literally make a good rush for it—they'll be with her when they come back. That will give them plenty of time.' I'm afraid I even heartlessly added that if she *should,* against every probability, pass away in their absence, they wouldn't have to come back at all—which would be just the compensation proper to their long privation. And then Maria would come out to join the two others, and they would be—though but for the too scanty remnant of their career—as merry as the day is long.

I remained ready, somehow, pending the fulfilment of that vision, to sacrifice Maria; it was only over the urgency of the case for the others respectively that I found myself balancing. Sometimes it was for Becky I thought the tragedy deepest—sometimes, and in quite a different manner, I thought it most dire for Jane. It was Jane, after all, who had most sense of life. I seemed in fact dimly to descry in Jane a sense—as yet undescried by herself or by any one—of all sorts of queer things. Why didn't *she* go? I used desperately to ask; why didn't she make a bold personal dash for it, strike up a partnership with some one or other of the travelling spinsters in whom Brookbridge more and more abounded? Well, there came a flash for me at a particular point of the grey middle desert: my correspondent was able to let me know that poor Jane at last *had* sailed. She had gone of a sudden—I liked my sister-in-law's view of suddenness—with the kind Hathaways, who had made an irresistible grab at her and lifted her off her feet. They were going for the summer and for Mr. Hathaway's health, so that the opportunity was perfect, and it was impossible not to be glad that something very like physical force had finally prevailed. This was the general feeling at Brookbridge, and I might imagine what Brookbridge had been brought to from the fact that, at the very moment she was hustled off, the doctor, called to her mother at the peep of dawn, had considered that *he* at least must stay. There had been real alarm—greater than ever before; it actually did seem as if this time the end had come. But it was Becky, strange to say, who, though fully recognising the nature of the crisis, had kept the situation in hand and insisted upon action. This, I remember, brought back to me a discomfort with which I had been familiar from the first. One of the two had sailed, and I was sorry it was not the other.

But if it had been the other I should have been equally sorry.

I saw with my eyes, that very autumn, what a fool Jane would have been if she had again backed out. Her mother had of course survived the peril of which I had heard, profiting by it indeed as she had profited by every other; she was sufficiently better again to have come down stairs. It was there that, as usual, I found her, but with a difference of effect produced somehow by the absence of one of the girls. It was as if, for the others, though they had not gone to Europe, Europe had come to them: Jane's letters had been so frequent and so beyond even what could have been hoped. It was the first time, however, that I perceived on the old woman's part a certain failure of lucidity. Jane's flight was, clearly, the great fact with her, but she spoke of it as if the fruit had now been plucked and the parenthesis closed. I don't know what sinking sense of still further physical duration I gathered, as a menace, from this first hint of her confusion of mind.

'My daughter has been; my daughter has been ——' She kept saying it, but didn't say where; that seemed unnecessary, and she only repeated the words to her visitors with a face that was all puckers and yet now, save in so far as it expressed an ineffaceable complacency, all blankness. I think she wanted us a little to know that she had not stood in the way. It added to something—I scarce knew what—that I found myself desiring to extract privately from Becky. As our visit was to be of the shortest my opportunity—for one of the young ladies always came to the door with us—was at hand. Mrs. Rimmle, as we took leave, again sounded her phrase, but she added this time: 'I'm so glad she's going to have always——'

I knew so well what she meant that, as she again dropped, looking at me queerly and becoming momentarily dim, I could help her out. 'Going to have what *you* have?'

'Yes, yes—my privilege. Wonderful experience,' she mumbled. She bowed to me a little as if I would understand. 'She has things to tell.'

I turned, slightly at a loss, to Becky. 'She has then already arrived?'

Becky was at that moment looking a little strangely at her mother, who answered my question. 'She reached New York this morning—she comes on to-day.'

'Oh, then——!' But I let the matter pass as I met Becky's eye—I saw there was a hitch somewhere. It was not she but Maria who came out with us; on which I cleared up the question of their sister's reappearance.

'Oh, no, not to-night,' Maria smiled; 'that's only the way mother puts it. We shall see her about the end of November—the Hathaways are so indulgent. They kindly extend their tour.'

'For *her* sake? How sweet of them!' my sister-in-law exclaimed.

I can see our friend's plain, mild old face take on a deeper mildness, even though a higher colour, in the light of the open door. 'Yes, it's for Jane they prolong it. And do you know what they write?' She gave us time, but it was too great a responsibility to guess. 'Why, that it has brought her out.'

'Oh, I knew it *would!*' my companion sympathetically sighed.

Maria put it more strongly still. 'They say we wouldn't know her.'

This sounded a little awful, but it was, after all, what I had expected.

III

MY correspondent in Brookbridge came to me that Christmas, with my niece, to spend a week; and the arrangement had of course been prefaced by an exchange of letters, the first of which from my sister-in-law scarce took space for acceptance of my invitation before going on to say: 'The Hathaways are back—but without Miss Jane!' She presented in a few words the situation thus created at Brookbridge, but was not yet, I gathered, fully in possession of the other one—the situation created in 'Europe' by the presence there of that lady. The two together, at any rate, demanded, I quickly felt, all my attention, and perhaps my impatience to receive my relative was a little sharpened by my desire for the whole story. I had it at last, by the Christmas fire, and I may say without reserve that it gave me all I could have hoped for. I listened eagerly, after which I produced the comment: 'Then she simply refused——'

'To budge from Florence? Simply. She had it out there with the poor Hathaways, who felt responsible for her safety, pledged to restore her to her mother's, to her sisters' hands, and showed herself in a light, they mention under their breath, that made their dear old hair stand on end. Do you know what, when they first got back, they said of her—at least it was *his* phrase—to two or three people?'

I thought a moment. 'That she had "tasted blood"?'

My visitor fairly admired me. 'How clever of you to guess! It's exactly what he did say. She appeared—she continues to appear, it seems—in a new character.'

I wondered a little. 'But that's exactly—don't

you remember?—what Miss Maria reported to us from them; that we "wouldn't know her." '

My sister-in-law perfectly remembered. 'Oh, yes —she broke out from the first. But when they left her she was worse.'

'Worse?'

'Well, different—different from anything she ever *had* been, or—for that matter—had had a chance to be.' My interlocutress hung fire a moment, but presently faced me. 'Rather strange and free and obstreperous.'

'Obstreperous?' I wondered again.

'Peculiarly so, I inferred, on the question of not coming away. She wouldn't hear of it, and, when they spoke of her mother, said she had given her mother up. She had thought she should like Europe, but didn't know she should like it so much. They had been fools to bring her if they expected to take her away. She was going to see what she could—she hadn't yet seen half. The end of it was, at any rate, that they had to leave her alone.'

I seemed to see it all—to see even the scared Hathaways. 'So she *is* alone?'

'She told them, poor thing, it appears, and in a tone they'll never forget, that she was, at all events, quite old enough to be. She cried—she quite went on—over not having come sooner. That's why the only way for her,' my companion mused, '*is,* I suppose, to stay. They wanted to put her with some people or other—to find some American family. But she says she's on her own feet.'

'And she's still in Florence?'

'No—I believe she was to travel. She's bent on the East.'

I burst out laughing. 'Magnificent Jane! It's most interesting. Only I feel that I distinctly *should* "know" her. To my sense, always, I must tell you, she had it in her.'

My relative was silent a little. 'So it now appears Becky always felt.'

'And yet pushed her off? Magnificent Becky!'

My companion met my eyes a moment. 'You don't know the queerest part. I mean the way it has *most* brought her out.'

I turned it over; I felt I should like to know— to that degree indeed that, oddly enough, I jocosely disguised my eagerness. 'You don't mean she has taken to drink?'

My visitor hesitated. 'She has taken to flirting.'

I expressed disappointment. 'Oh, she took to *that* long ago. Yes,' I declared at my kinswoman's stare, 'she positively flirted—with *me!*'

The stare perhaps sharpened. 'Then you flirted with *her?*'

'How else could I have been as sure as I wanted to be? But has she means?'

'Means to flirt?'—my friend looked an instant as if she spoke literally. 'I don't understand about the means—though of course they have something. But I have my impression,' she went on. 'I think that Becky——' It seemed almost too grave to say.

But *I* had no doubts. 'That Becky's backing her?'

She brought it out. 'Financing her.'

'Stupendous Becky! So that morally then——'

'Becky's quite in sympathy. But isn't it too odd?' my sister-in-law asked.

'Not in the least. Didn't we know, as regards Jane, that Europe was to bring her out? Well, it has also brought out Rebecca.'

'It has indeed!' my companion indulgently sighed. 'So what would it do if she were there?'

'I should like immensely to see. And we *shall* see.'

'Why, do you believe she'll still go?'

'Certainly. She *must.*'

But my friend shook it off. 'She won't.'

'She shall!' I retorted with a laugh. But the next moment I said: 'And what does the old woman say?'

'To Jane's behaviour? Not a word—never speaks of it. She talks now much less than she used—only seems to wait. But it's my belief she thinks.'

'And—do you mean—knows?'

'Yes, knows that she's abandoned. In her silence there she takes it in.'

'It's her way of making Jane pay?' At this, somehow, I felt more serious. 'Oh, dear, dear— she'll disinherit her!'

When, in the following June, I went on to return my sister-in-law's visit the first object that met my eyes in her little white parlour was a figure that, to my stupefaction, presented itself for the moment as that of Mrs. Rimmle. I had gone to my room after arriving, and, on dressing, had come down: the apparition I speak of had arisen in the interval. Its ambiguous character lasted, however, but a second or two—I had taken Becky for her mother because I knew no one but her mother of that extreme age. Becky's age was quite startling; it had made a great stride, though, strangely enough, irrecoverably seated as she now was in it, she had a wizened brightness that I had scarcely yet seen in her. I remember indulging on this occasion in two silent observations: one to the effect that I had not hitherto been conscious of her full resemblance to the old lady, and the other to the effect that, as I had said to my sister-in-law at

Christmas, 'Europe,' even as reaching her only through Jane's sensibilities, had really at last brought her out. She was in fact 'out' in a manner of which this encounter offered to my eyes a unique example: it was the single hour, often as I had been at Brookbridge, of my meeting her elsewhere than in her mother's drawing-room. I surmise that, besides being adjusted to her more marked time of life, the garments she wore abroad, and in particular her little plain bonnet, presented points of resemblance to the close sable sheath and the quaint old headgear that, in the white house behind the elms, I had from far back associated with the eternal image in the stiff chair. Of course I immediately spoke of Jane, showing an interest and asking for news; on which she answered me with a smile, but not at all as I had expected.

'*Those* are not really the things you want to know—where she is, whom she's with, how she manages and where she's going next—oh, no!' And the admirable woman gave a laugh that was somehow both light and sad—sad, in particular, with a strange, long weariness. 'What you do want to know is when she's coming back.'

I shook my head very kindly, but out of a wealth of experience that, I flattered myself, was equal to Miss Becky's. 'I do know it. Never.'

Miss Becky, at this, exchanged with me a long, deep look. 'Never.'

We had, in silence, a little luminous talk about it, in the course of which she seemed to tell me the most interesting things. 'And how's your mother?' I then inquired.

She hesitated, but finally spoke with the same serenity. 'My mother's all right. You see, she's not alive.'

'Oh, Becky!' my sister-in-law pleadingly interjected.

But Becky only addressed herself to me. 'Come and see if she is. *I* think she isn't—but Maria perhaps isn't so clear. Come, at all events, and judge and tell me.'

It was a new note, and I was a little bewildered. 'Ah, but I'm not a doctor!'

'No, thank God—you're not. That's why I ask you.' And now she said good-bye.

I kept her hand a moment. '*You're* more alive than ever!'

'I'm very tired.' She took it with the same smile, but for Becky it was much to say.

IV

'NOT alive,' the next day, was certainly what Mrs. Rimmle looked when, coming in according to my promise, I found her, with Miss Maria, in her usual place. Though shrunken and diminished she still occupied her high-backed chair with a visible theory of erectness, and her intensely aged face—combined with something dauntless that belonged to her very presence and that was effective even in this extremity—might have been that of some centenarian sovereign, of indistinguishable sex, brought forth to be shown to the people as a disproof of the rumour of extinction. Mummified and open-eyed she looked at me, but I had no impression that she made me out. I had come this time without my sister-in-law, who had frankly pleaded to me—which also, for a daughter of Brookbridge, was saying much—that the house had grown too painful. Poor Miss Maria excused Miss Becky on the score of her not being well—and that, it struck me, was saying most of all. The absence of the others gave the occasion a different note; but I talked with Miss Maria for five minutes and perceived that—save for her saying, of her own movement, anything about Jane—she now spoke as if her mother had lost hearing or sense, or both, alluding freely and distinctly, though indeed favourably, to her condition. 'She has expected your visit and she much enjoys it,' my interlocutress said, while the old woman, soundless and motionless, simply fixed me without expression. Of course there was little to keep me; but I became aware, as I rose to go, that there was more than I had supposed. On my approaching her to take leave Mrs. Rimmle gave signs of consciousness.

'Have you heard about Jane?'

I hesitated, feeling a responsibility, and appealed for direction to Maria's face. But Maria's face was troubled, was turned altogether to her mother's. 'About her life in Europe?' I then rather helplessly asked.

The old woman fronted me, on this, in a manner that made me feel silly. 'Her life?'—and her voice, with this second effort, came out stronger. 'Her death, if you please.'

'Her death?' I echoed, before I could stop myself, with the accent of deprecation.

Miss Maria uttered a vague sound of pain, and I felt her turn away, but the marvel of her mother's little unquenched spark still held me. 'Jane's dead. We've heard,' said Mrs. Rimmle. 'We've heard from—where is it we've heard from?' She had quite revived—she appealed to her daughter.

The poor old girl, crimson, rallied to her duty. 'From Europe.'

Mrs. Rimmle made at us both a little grim inclination of the head. 'From Europe.' I responded, in silence, with a deflection from every rigour, and, still holding me, she went on: 'And now Rebecca's going.'

She had gathered by this time such emphasis to say it that again, before I could help myself, I vibrated in reply. 'To Europe—now?' It was as if for an instant she had made me believe it.

She only stared at me, however, from her wizened mask; then her eyes followed my companion. 'Has she gone?'

'Not yet, mother.' Maria tried to treat it as a joke, but her smile was embarrassed and dim.

'Then where is she?'

'She's lying down.'

The old woman kept up her hard, queer gaze, but directing it, after a minute, to me. 'She's going.'

'Oh, some day!' I foolishly laughed; and on this I got to the door, where I separated from my younger hostess, who came no further. Only, as I held the door open, she said to me under cover of it and very quietly:

'It's poor mother's idea.'

I saw—it was her idea. Mine was—for some time after this, even after I had returned to New York and to my usual occupations—that I should never again see Becky. I had seen her for the last time, I believed, under my sister-in-law's roof, and in the autumn it was given to me to hear from that fellow-admirer that she had succumbed at last to the situation. The day of the call I have just described had been a date in the process of her slow shrinkage—it was literally the first time she had, as they said at Brookbridge, given up. She had been ill for years, but the other state of health in the contemplation of which she had spent so much of her life had left her, till too late, no margin for meeting it. The encounter, at last, came simply in the form of the discovery that it *was* too late; on which, naturally, she had given up more and more. I had heard indeed, all summer, by letter, how Brookbridge had watched her do so; whereby the end found me in a manner prepared. Yet in spite of my preparation there remained with me a soreness, and when I was next —it was some six months later—on the scene of her martyrdom I replied, I fear, with an almost rabid negative to the question put to me in due course by my kinswoman. 'Call on them? Never again!'

I went, none the less, the very next day. Everything was the same in the sunny parlour—everything that most mattered, I mean: the immemorial mummy in the high chair and the tributes, in the little frames on the walls, to the celebrity of its late husband. Only Maria Rimmle was different: if Becky, on my last seeing her, had looked as old as her mother, Maria—save that she moved about—looked older. I remember that she moved about, but I scarce remember what she said; and indeed what was there to say? When I risked a question, however, she had a reply.

'But *now* at least——?' I tried to put it to her suggestively.

At first she was vague. ' "Now?" '

'Won't Miss Jane come back?'

Oh, the headshake she gave me! 'Never.' It positively pictured to me, for the instant, a well-preserved woman, a sort of rich, ripe *seconde jeunesse* [2] by the Arno.

'Then that's only to make more sure of your finally joining her.'

Maria Rimmle repeated her headshake. 'Never.'

We stood so, a moment, bleakly face to face; I could think of no attenuation that would be particularly happy. But while I tried I heard a hoarse gasp that, fortunately, relieved me—a signal strange and at first formless from the occupant of the high-backed chair. 'Mother wants to speak to you,' Maria then said.

So it appeared from the drop of the old woman's jaw, the expression of her mouth opened as if for the emission of sound. It was difficult to me, somehow, to seem to sympathise without hypocrisy, but, so far as a step nearer could do so, I invited communication. 'Have you heard where Becky's gone?' the wonderful witch's white lips then extraordinarily asked.

It drew from Maria, as on my previous visit, an uncontrollable groan, and this, in turn, made me take time to consider. As I considered, however, I had an inspiration. 'To Europe?'

I must have adorned it with a strange grimace, but my inspiration had been right. 'To Europe,' said Mrs. Rimmle.

THE BEAST IN THE JUNGLE

◇

⟦ WRITTEN as early as 1901, *The Beast in the Jungle* proved unacceptable to magazine editors and was first published in the collection *The Better Sort* (1903). It was republished in a volume of the New York Edition devoted to stories of the supernatural and near-supernatural. It is now the most celebrated of James's efforts

2. *seconde jeunesse:* second youth.

in a vein of realistic fantasy which has the historical interest of looking back to the Hawthorne of "Ethan Brand" (see Vol. I, pp. 757–64) and forward to the work of such twentieth-century writers as T. S. Eliot and Franz Kafka.

◊

I

WHAT determined the speech that startled him in the course of their encounter scarcely matters, being probably but some words spoken by himself quite without intention—spoken as they lingered and slowly moved together after their renewal of acquaintance. He had been conveyed by friends, an hour or two before, to the house at which she was staying; the party of visitors at the other house, of whom he was one, and thanks to whom it was his theory, as always, that he was lost in the crowd, had been invited over to luncheon. There had been after luncheon much dispersal, all in the interest of the original motive, a view of Weatherend itself and the fine things, intrinsic features, pictures, heirlooms, treasures of all the arts, that made the place almost famous; and the great rooms were so numerous that guests could wander at their will, hang back from the principal group, and, in cases where they took such matters with the last seriousness, give themselves up to mysterious appreciations and measurements. There were persons to be observed, singly or in couples, bending toward objects in out-of-the-way corners with their hands on their knees and their heads nodding quite as with the emphasis of an excited sense of smell. When they were two they either mingled their sounds of ecstasy or melted into silences of even deeper import, so that there were aspects of the occasion that gave it for Marcher much the air of the "look round," previous to a sale highly advertised, that excites or quenches, as may be, the dream of acquisition. The dream of acquisition at Weatherend would have had to be wild indeed, and John Marcher found himself, among such suggestions, disconcerted almost equally by the presence of those who knew too much and by that of those who knew nothing. The great rooms caused so much poetry and history to press upon him that he needed to wander apart to feel in a proper relation with them, though his doing so was not, as happened, like the gloating of some of his companions, to be compared to the movements of a dog sniffing a cupboard. It had an issue promptly enough in a direction that was not to have been calculated.

It led, in short, in the course of the October afternoon, to his closer meeting with May Bar-tram, whose face, a reminder, yet not quite a remembrance, as they sat, much separated, at a very long table, had begun merely by troubling him rather pleasantly. It affected him as the sequel of something of which he had lost the beginning. He knew it, and for the time quite welcomed it, as a continuation, but didn't know what it continued, which was an interest, or an amusement, the greater as he was also somehow aware—yet without a direct sign from her—that the young woman herself had not lost the thread. She had not lost it, but she wouldn't give it back to him, he saw, without some putting forth of his hand for it; and he not only saw that, but saw several things more, things odd enough in the light of the fact that at the moment some accident of grouping brought them face to face he was still merely fumbling with the idea that any contact between them in the past would have had no importance. If it had had no importance he scarcely knew why his actual impression of her should so seem to have so much; the answer to which, however, was that in such a life as they all appeared to be leading for the moment one could but take things as they came. He was satisfied, without in the least being able to say why, that this young lady might roughly have ranked in the house as a poor relation; satisfied also that she was not there on a brief visit, but was more or less a part of the establishment—almost a working, a remunerated part. Didn't she enjoy at periods a protection that she paid for by helping, among other services, to show the place and explain it, deal with the tiresome people, answer questions about the dates of the buildings, the styles of the furniture, the authorship of the pictures, the favourite haunts of the ghost? It wasn't that she looked as if you could have given her shillings—it was impossible to look less so. Yet when she finally drifted toward him, distinctly handsome, though ever so much older—older than when he had seen her before—it might have been as an effect of her guessing that he had, within the couple of hours, devoted more imagination to her than to all the others put together, and had thereby penetrated to a kind of truth that the others were too stupid for. She *was* there on harder terms than anyone; she was there as a consequence of things suffered, in one way and another, in the interval of years; and she remembered him very much as she was remembered—only a good deal better.

By the time they at last thus came to speech they were alone in one of the rooms—remarkable for a fine portrait over the chimney-place—out of which their friends had passed, and the charm of it was that even before they had spoken they had practically arranged with each other to stay behind for talk. The charm, happily, was in other things too; it was partly in there being scarce a spot at Weatherend without something to stay behind for. It was in the way the autumn day looked into the high windows as it waned; in the way the red light, breaking at the close from under a low, sombre sky, reached out in a long shaft and played over old wainscots, old tapestry, old gold, old colour. It was most of all perhaps in the way she came to him as if, since she had been turned on to deal with the simpler sort, he might, should he choose to keep the whole thing down, just take her mild attention for a part of her general business. As soon as he heard her voice, however, the gap was filled up and the missing link supplied; the slight irony he divined in her attitude lost its advantage. He almost jumped at it to get there before her. "I met you years and years ago in Rome. I remember all about it." She confessed to disappointment— she had been so sure he didn't; and to prove how well he did he began to pour forth the particular recollections that popped up as he called for them. Her face and her voice, all at his service now, worked the miracle—the impression operating like the torch of a lamplighter who touches into flame, one by one, a long row of gas jets. Marcher flattered himself that the illumination was brilliant, yet he was really still more pleased on her showing him, with amusement, that in his haste to make everything right he had got most things rather wrong. It hadn't been at Rome—it had been at Naples; and it hadn't been seven years before—it had been more nearly ten. She hadn't been either with her uncle and aunt, but with her mother and her brother; in addition to which it was not with the Pembles that *he* had been, but with the Boyers, coming down in their company from Rome—a point on which she insisted, a little to his confusion, and as to which she had her evidence in hand. The Boyers she had known, but she didn't know the Pembles, though she had heard of them, and it was the people he was with who had made them acquainted. The incident of the thunderstorm that had raged round them with such violence as to drive them for refuge into an excavation—this incident had not occurred at the Palace of the Cæsars, but at Pompeii, on an occasion when they had been present there at an important find.

He accepted her amendments, he enjoyed her corrections, though the moral of them was, she pointed out, that he *really* didn't remember the least thing about her; and he only felt it as a drawback that when all was made conformable to the truth there didn't appear much of anything left. They lingered together still, she neglecting her of-

fice—for from the moment he was so clever she had no proper right to him—and both neglecting the house, just waiting as to see if a memory or two more wouldn't again breathe upon them. It had not taken them many minutes, after all, to put down on the table, like the cards of a pack, those that constituted their respective hands; only what came out was that the pack was unfortunately not perfect—that the past, invoked, invited, encouraged, could give them, naturally, no more than it had. It had made them meet—her at twenty, him at twenty-five; but nothing was so strange, they seemed to say to each other, as that, while so occupied, it hadn't done a little more for them. They looked at each other as with the feeling of an occasion missed; the present one would have been so much better if the other, in the far distance, in the foreign land, hadn't been so stupidly meagre. There weren't, apparently, all counted, more than a dozen little old things that had succeeded in coming to pass between them; trivialities of youth, simplicities of freshness, stupidities of ignorance, small possible germs, but too deeply buried—too deeply (didn't it seem?) to sprout after so many years. Marcher said to himself that he ought to have rendered her some service—saved her from a capsized boat in the Bay, or at least recovered her dressing-bag, filched from her cab, in the streets of Naples, by a lazzarone with a stiletto. Or it would have been nice if he could have been taken with fever, alone, at his hotel, and she could have come to look after him, to write to his people, to drive him out in convalescence. *Then* they would be in possession of the something or other that their actual show seemed to lack. It yet somehow presented itself, this show, as too good to be spoiled; so that they were reduced for a few minutes more to wondering a little helplessly why—since they seemed to know a certain number of the same people—their reunion had been so long averted. They didn't use that name for it, but their delay from minute to minute to join the others was a kind of confession that they didn't quite want it to be a failure. Their attempted supposition of reasons for their not having met but showed how little they knew of each other. There came in fact a moment when Marcher felt a positive pang. It was vain to pretend she was an old friend, for all the communities were wanting, in spite of which it was as an old friend that he saw she would have suited him. He had new ones enough—was surrounded with them, for instance, at that hour at the other house; as a new one he probably wouldn't have so much as noticed her. He would have liked to invent something, get her to make-believe with him that some passage of a romantic or critical kind *had* originally occurred. He was really almost reaching out in imagination—as against time—for something that would do, and saying to himself that if it didn't come this new incident would simply and rather awkwardly close. They would separate, and now for no second or for no third chance. They would have tried and not succeeded. Then it was, just at the turn, as he afterwards made it out to himself, that, everything else failing, she herself decided to take up the case and, as it were, save the situation. He felt as soon as she spoke that she had been consciously keeping back what she said and hoping to get on without it; a scruple in her that immensely touched him when, by the end of three or four minutes more, he was able to measure it. What she brought out, at any rate, quite cleared the air and supplied the link—the link it was such a mystery he should frivolously have managed to lose.

"You know you told me something that I've never forgotten and that again and again has made me think of you since; it was that tremendously hot day when we went to Sorrento, across the bay, for the breeze. What I allude to was what you said to me, on the way back, as we sat, under the awning of the boat, enjoying the cool. Have you forgotten?"

He had forgotten, and he was even more surprised than ashamed. But the great thing was that he saw it was no vulgar reminder of any "sweet" speech. The vanity of women had long memories, but she was making no claim on him of a compliment or a mistake. With another woman, a totally different one, he might have feared the recall possibly even some imbecile "offer." So, in having to say that he had indeed forgotten, he was conscious rather of a loss than of a gain; he already saw an interest in the matter of her reference. "I try to think—but I give it up. Yet I remember the Sorrento day."

"I'm not very sure you do," May Bartram after a moment said; "and I'm not very sure I ought to want you to. It's dreadful to bring a person back, at any time, to what he was ten years before. If you've lived away from it," she smiled, "so much the better."

"Ah, if *you* haven't why should I?" he asked.

"Lived away, you mean, from what I myself was?"

"From what *I* was. I was of course an ass," Marcher went on; "but I would rather know from you just the sort of ass I was than—from the moment you have something in your mind—not know anything."

Still, however, she hesitated. "But if you've completely ceased to be that sort——?"

"Why, I can then just so all the more bear to know. Besides, perhaps I haven't."

"Perhaps. Yet if you haven't," she added, "I should suppose you would remember. Not indeed that *I* in the least connect with my impression the invidious name you use. If I had only thought you foolish," she explained, "the thing I speak of wouldn't so have remained with me. It was about yourself." She waited, as if it might come to him; but as, only meeting her eyes in wonder, he gave no sign, she burnt her ships. "Has it ever happened?"

Then it was that, while he continued to stare, a light broke for him and the blood slowly came to his face, which began to burn with recognition. "Do you mean I told you——?" But he faltered, lest what came to him shouldn't be right, lest he should only give himself away.

"It was something about yourself that was natural one shouldn't forget—that is if one remembered you at all. That's why I ask you," she smiled, "if the thing you then spoke of has ever come to pass?"

Oh, then he saw, but he was lost in wonder and found himself embarrassed. This, he also saw, made her sorry for him, as if her allusion had been a mistake. It took him but a moment, however, to feel that it had not been, much as it had been a surprise. After the first little shock of it her knowledge on the contrary began, even if rather strangely, to taste sweet to him. She was the only other person in the world then who would have it, and she had had it all these years, while the fact of his having so breathed his secret had unaccountably faded from him. No wonder they couldn't have met as if nothing had happened. "I judge," he finally said, "that I know what you mean. Only I had strangely enough lost the consciousness of having taken you so far into my confidence."

"Is it because you've taken so many others as well?"

"I've taken nobody. Not a creature since then."

"So that I'm the only person who knows?"

"The only person in the world."

"Well," she quickly replied, "I myself have never spoken. I've never, never repeated of you what you told me." She looked at him so that he perfectly believed her. Their eyes met over it in such a way that he was without a doubt. "And I never will."

She spoke with an earnestness that, as if almost excessive, put him at ease about her possible derision. Somehow the whole question was a new luxury to him—that is, from the moment she was in possession. If she didn't take the ironic view she clearly took the sympathetic, and that was what he

had had, in all the long time, from no one whom-
soever. What he felt was that he couldn't at present have begun to tell her and yet could profit perhaps exquisitely by the accident of having done so
of old. "Please don't then. We're just right as
it is."

"Oh, I am," she laughed, "if you are!" To
which she added: "Then you do still feel in the
same way?"

It was impossible to him not to take to himself
that she was really interested, and it all kept coming as a sort of revelation. he had thought of himself so long as abominably alone, and, lo, he wasn't
alone a bit. He hadn't been, it appeared, for an
hour—since those moments on the Sorrento boat.
It was *she* who had been, he seemed to see as he
looked at her—she who had been made so by the
graceless fact of his lapse of fidelity. To tell her
what he had told her—what had it been but to ask
something of her? something that she had given, in
her charity, without his having, by a remembrance,
by a return of the spirit, failing another encounter,
so much as thanked her. What he had asked of her
had been simply at first not to laugh at him. She
had beautifully not done so for ten years, and she
was not doing so now. So he had endless gratitude
to make up. Only for that he must see just how he
had figured to her. "What, exactly, was the account I gave——?"

"Of the way you did feel? Well, it was very simple. You said you had had from your earliest time,
as the deepest thing within you, the sense of being kept for something rare and strange, possibly
prodigious and terrible, that was sooner or later to
happen to you, that you had in your bones the
foreboding and the conviction of, and that would
perhaps overwhelm you."

"Do you call that very simple?" John Marcher
asked.

She thought a moment. "It was perhaps because I seemed, as you spoke, to understand it."

"You do understand it?" he eagerly asked.

Again she kept her kind eyes on him. "You still
have the belief?"

"Oh!" he exclaimed helplessly. There was too
much to say.

"Whatever it is to be," she clearly made out, "it
hasn't yet come."

He shook his head in complete surrender now.
"It hasn't yet come. Only, you know, it isn't anything I'm to *do*, to achieve in the world, to be distinguished or admired for. I'm not such an ass as
that. It would be much better, no doubt, if I were."

"It's to be something you're merely to suffer?"

"Well, say to wait for—to have to meet, to face,
to see suddenly break out in my life; possibly de-

stroying all further consciousness, possibly annihilating me; possibly, on the other hand, only altering everything, striking at the root of all my world
and leaving me to the consequences, however they
shape themselves."

She took this in, but the light in her eyes continued for him not to be that of mockery. "Isn't
what you describe perhaps but the expectation—
or, at any rate, the sense of danger, familiar to so
many people—of falling in love?"

John Marcher thought. "Did you ask me that
before?"

"No—I wasn't so free-and-easy then. But it's
what strikes me now."

"Of course," he said after a moment, "it
strikes you. Of course it strikes *me*. Of course
what's in store for me may be no more than that.
The only thing is," he went on, "that I think that
if it had been that, I should by this time know."

"Do you mean because you've *been* in love?"
And then as he but looked at her in silence:
"You've been in love, and it hasn't meant such a
cataclysm, hasn't proved the great affair?"

"Here I am, you see. It hasn't been overwhelming."

"Then it hasn't been love," said May Bartram.

"Well, I at least thought it was. I took it for that
—I've taken it till now. It was agreeable, it was delightful, it was miserable," he explained. "But it
wasn't strange. It wasn't what *my* affair's to be."

"You want something all to yourself—something that nobody else knows or *has* known?"

"It isn't a question of what I 'want'—God
knows I don't want anything. It's only a question
of the apprehension that haunts me—that I live
with day by day."

He said this so lucidly and consistently that, visibly, it further imposed itself. If she had not been
interested before she would have been interested
now. "Is it a sense of coming violence?"

Evidently now too, again, he liked to talk of it.
"I don't think of it as—when it does come—necessarily violent. I only think of it as natural and as of
course, above all, unmistakable. I think of it simply as *the* thing. *The* thing will of itself appear
natural."

"Then how will it appear strange?"

Marcher bethought himself. "It won't—to *me*."

"To whom then?"

"Well," he replied, smiling at last, "say to you."

"Oh then, I'm to be present?"

"Why, you *are* present—since you know."

"I see." She turned it over. "But I mean at the
catastrophe."

At this, for a minute, their lightness gave way to
their gravity; it was as if the long look they ex-

changed held them together. "It will only depend on yourself—if you'll watch with me."

"Are you afraid?" she asked.

"Don't leave me *now*," he went on.

"Are you afraid?" she repeated.

"Do you think me simply out of my mind?" he pursued instead of answering. "Do I merely strike you as a harmless lunatic?"

"No," said May Bartram. "I understand you. I believe you."

"You mean you feel how my obsession—poor old thing!—may correspond to some possible reality?"

"To some possible reality."

"Then you *will* watch with me?"

She hesitated, then for the third time put her question. "Are you afraid?"

"Did I tell you I was—at Naples?"

"No, you said nothing about it."

"Then I don't know. And I should *like* to know," said John Marcher. "You'll tell me yourself whether you think so. If you'll watch with me you'll see."

"Very good then." They had been moving by this time across the room, and at the door, before passing out, they paused as if for the full wind-up of their understanding. "I'll watch with you," said May Bartram.

II

THE fact that she "knew"—knew and yet neither chaffed him nor betrayed him—had in a short time begun to constitute between them a sensible bond, which became more marked when, within the year that followed their afternoon at Weatherend, the opportunities for meeting multiplied. The event that thus promoted these occasions was the death of the ancient lady, her great-aunt, under whose wing, since losing her mother, she had to such an extent found shelter, and who, though but the widowed mother of the new successor to the property, had succeeded—thanks to a high tone and a high temper—in not forfeiting the supreme position at the great house. The deposition of this personage arrived but with her death, which, followed by many changes, made in particular a difference for the young woman in whom Marcher's expert attention had recognised from the first a dependent with a pride that might ache though it didn't bristle. Nothing for a long time had made him easier than the thought that the aching must have been much soothed by Miss Bartram's now finding herself able to set up a small home in London. She had acquired property, to an amount that made that luxury just possible, under her aunt's extremely complicated will, and when the whole matter be-

gan to be straightened out, which indeed took time, she let him know that the happy issue was at last in view. He had seen her again before that day, both because she had more than once accompanied the ancient lady to town and because he had paid another visit to the friends who so conveniently made of Weatherend one of the charms of their own hospitality. These friends had taken him back there; he had achieved there again with Miss Bartram some quiet detachment; and he had in London succeeded in persuading her to more than one brief absence from her aunt. They went together, on these latter occasions, to the National Gallery and the South Kensington Museum, where, among vivid reminders, they talked of Italy at large—not now attempting to recover, as at first, the taste of their youth and their ignorance. That recovery, the first day at Weatherend, had served its purpose well, had given them quite enough; so that they were, to Marcher's sense, no longer hovering about the head-waters of their stream, but had felt their boat pushed sharply off and down the current.

They were literally afloat together; for our gentleman this was marked, quite as marked as that the fortunate cause of it was just the buried treasure of her knowledge. He had with his own hands dug up this little hoard, brought to light—that is to within reach of the dim day constituted by their discretions and privacies—the object of value the hiding-place of which he had, after putting it into the ground himself, so strangely, so long forgotten. The exquisite luck of having again just stumbled on the spot made him indifferent to any other question; he would doubtless have devoted more time to the odd accident of his lapse of memory if he had not been moved to devote so much to the sweetness, the comfort, as he felt, for the future, that this accident itself had helped to keep fresh. It had never entered into his plan that anyone should "know," and mainly for the reason that it was not in him to tell anyone. That would have been impossible, since nothing but the amusement of a cold world would have waited on it. Since, however, a mysterious fate had opened his mouth in youth, in spite of him, he would count that a compensation and profit by it to the utmost. That the right person *should* know tempered the asperity of his secret more even than his shyness had permitted him to imagine; and May Bartram was clearly right, because—well, because there she was. Her knowledge simply settled it; he would have been sure enough by this time had she been wrong. There was that in his situation, no doubt, that disposed him too much to see her as a mere confidant, taking all her light for him from the fact

—the fact only—of her interest in his predicament, from her mercy, sympathy, seriousness, her consent not to regard him as the funniest of the funny. Aware, in fine, that her price for him was just in her giving him this constant sense of his being admirably spared, he was careful to remember that she had, after all, also a life of her own, with things that might happen to *her,* things that in friendship one should likewise take account of. Something fairly remarkable came to pass with him, for that matter, in this connection—something represented by a certain passage of his consciousness, in the suddenest way, from one extreme to the other.

He had thought himself, so long as nobody knew, the most disinterested person in the world, carrying his concentrated burden, his perpetual suspense, ever so quietly, holding his tongue about it, giving others no glimpse of it nor of its effect upon his life, asking of them no allowance and only making on his side all those that were asked. He had disturbed nobody with the queerness of having to know a haunted man, though he had had moments of rather special temptation on hearing people say that they were "unsettled." If they were as unsettled as he was—he who had never been settled for an hour in his life—they would know what it meant. Yet it wasn't, all the same, for him to make them, and he listened to them civilly enough. This was why he had such good—though possibly such rather colourless—manners; this was why, above all, he could regard himself, in a greedy world, as decently—as, in fact, perhaps even a little sublimely—unselfish. Our point is accordingly that he valued this character quite sufficiently to measure his present danger of letting it lapse, against which he promised himself to be much on his guard. He was quite ready, none the less, to be selfish just a little, since, surely, no more charming occasion for it had come to him. "Just a little," in a word, was just as much as Miss Bartram, taking one day with another, would let him. He never would be in the least coercive, and he would keep well before him the lines on which consideration for her—the very highest—ought to proceed. He would thoroughly establish the heads under which her affairs, her requirements, her peculiarities—he went so far as to give them the latitude of that name—would come into their intercourse. All this naturally was a sign of how much he took the intercourse itself for granted. There was nothing more to be done about *that.* It simply existed; had sprung into being with her first penetrating question to him in the autumn light there at Weatherend. The real form it should have taken on the basis that stood out large was the form of

their marrying. But the devil in this was that the very basis itself put marrying out of the question. His conviction, his apprehension, his obsession, in short, was not a condition he could invite a woman to share; and that consequence of it was precisely what was the matter with him. Something or other lay in wait for him, amid the twists and the turns of the months and the years, like a crouching beast in the jungle. It signified little whether the crouching beast were destined to slay him or to be slain. The definite point was the inevitable spring of the creature; and the definite lesson from that was that a man of feeling didn't cause himself to be accompanied by a lady on a tiger-hunt. Such was the image under which he had ended by figuring his life.

They had at first, none the less, in the scattered hours spent together, made no allusion to that view of it; which was a sign he was handsomely ready to give that he didn't expect, that he in fact didn't care always to be talking about it. Such a feature in one's outlook was really like a hump on one's back. The difference it made every minute of the day existed quite independently of discussion. One discussed, of course, *like* a hunchback, for there was always, if nothing else, the hunchback face. That remained, and she was watching him; but people watched best, as a general thing, in silence, so that such would be predominantly the manner of their vigil. Yet he didn't want, at the same time, to be solemn; solemn was what he imagined he too much tended to be with other people. The thing to be, with the one person who knew, was easy and natural—to make the reference rather than be seeming to avoid it, to avoid it rather than be seeming to make it, and to keep it, in any case, familiar, facetious even, rather than pedantic and portentous. Some such consideration as the latter was doubtless in his mind, for instance, when he wrote pleasantly to Miss Bartram that perhaps the great thing he had so long felt as in the lap of the gods was no more than this circumstance, which touched him so nearly, of her acquiring a house in London. It was the first allusion they had yet again made, needing any other hitherto so little; but when she replied, after having given him the news, that she was by no means satisfied with such a trifle, as the climax to so special a suspense, she almost set him wondering if she hadn't even a larger conception of singularity for him than he had for himself. He was at all events destined to become aware little by little, as time when by, that she was all the while looking at his life, judging it, measuring it, in the light of the thing she knew, which grew to be at last, with the consecration of the years, never mentioned between them save as "the real truth" about him. That had always been his own current form of reference to it, but she adopted the form so quietly that, looking back at the end of a period, he knew there was no moment at which it was traceable that she had, as he might say, got inside his condition, or exchanged the attitude of beautifully indulging for that of still more beautifully believing him.

It was always open to him to accuse her of seeing him but as the most harmless of maniacs, and this, in the long run—since it covered so much ground—was his easiest description of their friendship. He had a screw loose for her, but she liked him in spite of it, and was practically, against the rest of the world, his kind, wise keeper, unremunerated, but fairly amused and, in the absence of other near ties, not disreputably occupied. The rest of the world of course thought him queer, but she, she only, knew how, and above all why, queer; which was precisely what enabled her to dispose the concealing veil in the right folds. She took his gaiety from him—since it had to pass with them for gaiety—as she took everything else; but she certainly so far justified by her unerring touch his finer sense of the degree to which he had ended by convincing her. *She* at least never spoke of the secret of his life except as "the real truth about you," and she had in fact a wonderful way of making it seem, as such, the secret of her own life too. That was in fine how he so constantly felt her as allowing for him; he couldn't on the whole call it anything else. He allowed for himself, but she, exactly, allowed still more; partly because, better placed for a sight of the matter, she traced his unhappy perversion through portions of its course into which he could scarce follow it. He knew how he felt, but, besides knowing that, she knew how he *looked* as well; he knew each of the things of importance he was insidiously kept from doing, but she could add up the amount they made, understand how much, with a lighter weight on his spirit, he might have done, and thereby establish how, clever as he was, he fell short. Above all she was in the secret of the difference between the forms he went through—those of his little office under Government, those of caring for his modest patrimony, for his library, for his garden in the country, for the people in London whose invitations he accepted and repaid—and the detachment that reigned beneath them and that made of all behaviour, all that could in the least be called behaviour, a long act of dissimulation. What it had come to was that he wore a mask painted with the social simper, out of the eye-holes of which there looked eyes of an expression not in the least matching the other features. This the stupid world, even after

years, had never more than half discovered. It was only May Bartram who had, and she achieved, by an art indescribable, the feat of at once—or perhaps it was only alternately—meeting the eyes from in front and mingling her own vision, as from over his shoulder, with their peep through the apertures.

So, while they grew older together, she did watch with him, and so she let this association give shape and colour to her own existence. Beneath *her* forms as well detachment had learned to sit, and behaviour had become for her, in the social sense, a false account of herself. There was but one account of her that would have been true all the while, and that she could give, directly, to nobody, least of all to John Marcher. Her whole attitude was a virtual statement, but the perception of that only seemed destined to take its place for him as one of the many things necessarily crowded out of his consciousness. If she had, moreover, like himself, to make sacrifices to their real truth, it was to be granted that her compensation might have affected her as more prompt and more natural. They had long periods, in this London time, during which, when they were together, a stranger might have listened to them without in the least pricking up his ears; on the other hand, the real truth was equally liable at any moment to rise to the surface, and the auditor would then have wondered indeed what they were talking about. They had from an early time made up their mind that society was, luckily, unintelligent, and the margin that this gave them had fairly become one of their commonplaces. Yet there were still moments when the situation turned almost fresh—usually under the effect of some expression drawn from herself. Her expressions doubtless repeated themselves, but her intervals were generous. "What saves us, you know, is that we answer so completely to so usual an appearance: that of the man and woman whose friendship has become such a daily habit, or almost, as to be at last indispensable." That, for instance, was a remark she had frequently enough had occasion to make, though she had given it at different times different developments. What we are especially concerned with is the turn it happened to take from her one afternoon when he had come to see her in honour of her birthday. This anniversary had fallen on a Sunday, at a season of thick fog and general outward gloom; but he had brought her his customary offering, having known her now long enough to have established a hundred little customs. It was one of his proofs to himself, the present he made her on her birthday, that he had not sunk into real selfishness. It was mostly nothing more than a small trinket, but it was always fine of its kind, and he was regularly careful to pay for it more than he thought he could afford. "Our habit saves you, at least, don't you see? because it makes you, after all, for the vulgar, indistinguishable from other men. What's the most inveterate mark of men in general? Why, the capacity to spend endless time with dull women—to spend it, I won't say without being bored, but without minding that they are, without being driven off at a tangent by it; which comes to the same thing. I'm your dull woman, a part of the daily bread for which you pray at church. That covers your tracks more than anything."

"And what covers yours?" asked Marcher, whom his dull woman could mostly to this extent amuse. "I see of course what you mean by your saving me, in one way and another, so far as other people are concerned—I've seen it all along. Only, what is it that saves *you?* I often think, you know, of that."

She looked as if she sometimes thought of that too, but in rather a different way. "Where other people, you mean, are concerned?"

"Well, you're really so in with me, you know— as a sort of result of my being so in with yourself. I mean of my having such an immense regard for you, being so tremendously grateful for all you've done for me. I sometimes ask myself if it's quite fair. Fair I mean to have so involved and—since one may say it—interested you. I almost feel as if you hadn't really had time to do anything else."

"Anything else but be interested?" she asked. "Ah, what else does one ever want to be? If I've been 'watching' with you, as we long ago agreed that I was to do, watching is always in itself an absorption."

"Oh, certainly," John Marcher said, "if you hadn't had your curiosity——! Only, doesn't it sometimes come to you, as time goes on, that your curiosity is not being particularly repaid?"

May Bartram had a pause. "Do you ask that, by any chance, because you feel at all that yours isn't? I mean because you have to wait so long."

Oh, he understood what she meant. "For the thing to happen that never does happen? For the beast to jump out? No, I'm just where I was about it. It isn't a matter as to which I can *choose,* I can decide for a change. It isn't one as to which there *can* be a change. It's in the lap of the gods. One's in the hands of one's law—there one is. As to the form the law will take, the way it will operate, that's its own affair."

"Yes," Miss Bartram replied; "of course one's fate is coming, of course it *has* come, in its own form and its own way, all the while. Only, you know, the form and the way in your case were to have been—well, something so exceptional and, as one may say, so particularly *your* own."

Something in this made him look at her with suspicion. "You say 'were to *have* been,' as if in your heart you had begun to doubt."

"Oh!" she vaguely protested.

"As if you believed," he went on, "that nothing will now take place."

She shook her head slowly, but rather inscrutably. "You're far from my thought."

He continued to look at her. "What then is the matter with you?"

"Well," she said after another wait, "the matter with me is simply that I'm more sure than ever my curiosity, as you call it, will be but too well repaid."

They were frankly grave now; he had got up from his seat, had turned once more about the little drawing-room to which, year after year, he brought his inevitable topic; in which he had, as he might have said, tasted their intimate community with every sauce, where every object was as familiar to him as the things of his own house and the very carpets were worn with his fitful walk very much as the desks in old countinghouses are worn by the elbows of generations of clerks. The generations of his nervous moods had been at work there, and the place was the written history of his whole middle life. Under the impression of what his friend had just said he knew himself, for some reason, more aware of these things, which made him, after a moment, stop again before her. "Is it, possibly, that you've grown afraid?"

"Afraid?" He thought, as she repeated the word, that his question had made her, a little, change colour; so that, lest he should have touched on a truth, he explained very kindly. "You remember that that was what you asked *me* long ago—that first day at Weatherend."

"Oh yes, and you told me you didn't know— that I was to see for myself. We've said little about it since, even in so long a time."

"Precisely," Marcher interposed—"quite as if it were too delicate a matter for us to make free with. Quite as if we might find, on pressure, that I *am* afraid. For then," he said, "we shouldn't, should we? quite know what to do."

She had for the time no answer to this question. "There have been days when I thought you were. Only, of course," she added, "there have been days when we have thought almost anything."

"Everything. Oh!" Marcher softly groaned as with a gasp, half spent, at the face, more uncovered just then than it had been for a long while, of the imagination always with them. It had always had its incalculable moments of glaring out, quite as with the very eyes of the very Beast, and, used as he was to them, they could still draw from him the tribute of a sigh that rose from the depths of his being. All that they had thought, first and last, rolled over him; the past seemed to have been reduced to mere barren speculation. This in fact was what the place had just struck him as so full of— the simplification of everything but the state of suspense. That remained only by seeming to hang in the void surrounding it. Even his original fear, if fear it had been, had lost itself in the desert. "I judge, however," he continued, "that you see I'm not afraid now."

"What I see is, as I make it out, that you've achieved something almost unprecedented in the way of getting used to danger. Living with it so long and so closely, you've lost your sense of it; you know it's there, but you're indifferent, and you cease even, as of old, to have to whistle in the dark. Considering what the danger is," May Bartram wound up, "I'm bound to say that I don't think your attitude could well be surpassed."

John Marcher faintly smiled. "It's heroic?"

"Certainly—call it that."

He considered. "I *am,* then, a man of courage?"

"That's what you were to show me."

He still, however, wondered. "But doesn't the man of courage know what he's afraid of—or *not* afraid of? I don't know *that,* you see. I don't focus it. I can't name it. I only know I'm exposed."

"Yes, but exposed—how shall I say?—so directly. So intimately. That's surely enough."

"Enough to make you feel, then—as what we may call the end of our watch—that I'm not afraid?"

"You're not afraid. But it isn't," she said, "the end of our watch. That is it isn't the end of yours. You've everything still to see."

"Then why haven't *you?*" he asked. He had had, all along, to-day, the sense of her keeping something back, and he still had it. As this was his first impression of that, it made a kind of date. The case was the more marked as she didn't at first answer; which in turn made him go on. "You know something I don't." Then his voice, for that of a man of courage, trembled a little. "You know what's to happen." Her silence, with the face she showed, was almost a confession—it made him sure. "You know, and you're afraid to tell me. It's so bad that you're afraid I'll find out."

All this might be true, for she did look as if, unexpectedly to her, he had crossed some mystic line that she had secretly drawn round her. Yet she might, after all, not have worried; and the real upshot was that he himself, at all events, needn't. "You'll never find out."

III

IT WAS all to have made, none the less, as I have said, a date; as came out in the fact that again and again, even after long intervals, other things that passed between them were, in relation to this hour, but the character of recalls and results. Its immediate effect had been indeed rather to lighten insistence—almost to provoke a reaction; as if their topic had dropped by its own weight and as if moreover, for that matter, Marcher had been visited by one of his occasional warnings against egotism. He had kept up, he felt, and very decently on the whole, his consciousness of the importance of not being selfish, and it was true that he had never sinned in that direction without promptly enough trying to press the scales the other way. He often repaired his fault, the season permitting, by inviting his friend to accompany him to the opera; and it not infrequently thus happened that, to show he didn't wish her to have but one sort of food for her mind, he was the cause of her appearing there with him a dozen nights in the month. It even happened that, seeing her home at such times, he occasionally went in with her to finish, as he called it, the evening, and, the better to make his point, sat down to the frugal but always careful little supper that awaited his pleasure. His point was made, he thought, by his not eternally insisting with her on himself; made for instance, at such hours, when it befell that, her piano at hand and each of them familiar with it, they went over passages of the opera together. It chanced to be on one of these occasions, however, that he reminded her of her not having answered a certain question he had put to her during the talk that had taken place between them on her last birthday. "What is it that saves *you?*"—saved her, he meant, from that appearance of variation from the usual human type. If he had practically escaped remark, as she pretended, by doing, in the most important particular, what most men do—find the answer to life in patching up an alliance of a sort with a woman no better than himself—how had she escaped it, and how could the alliance, such as it was, since they must suppose it had been more or less noticed, have failed to make her rather positively talked about?

"I never said," May Bartram replied, "that it hadn't made me talked about."

"Ah well then, you're not 'saved.' "

"It has not been a question for me. If you've had your woman, I've had," she said, "my man."

"And you mean that makes you all right?"

She hesitated. "I dont know why it shouldn't

make me—humanly, which is what we're speaking of—as right as it makes you."

"I see," Marcher returned. "'Humanly,' no doubt, as showing that you're living for something. Not, that is, just for me and my secret."

May Bartram smiled. "I don't pretend it exactly shows that I'm not living for you. It's my intimacy with you that's in question."

He laughed as he saw what she meant. "Yes, but since, as you say, I'm only, so far as people make out, ordinary, you're—aren't you?—no more than ordinary either. You help me to pass for a man like another. So if I *am,* as I understand you, you're not compromised. Is that it?"

She had another hesitation, but she spoke clearly enough. "That's it. It's all that concerns me—to help you to pass for a man like another."

He was careful to acknowledge the remark handsomely. "How kind, how beautiful, you are to me! How shall I ever repay you?"

She had her last grave pause, as if there might be a choice of ways. But she chose. "By going on as you are."

It was into this going on as he was that they relapsed, and really for so long a time that the day inevitably came for a further sounding of their depths. It was as if these depths, constantly bridged over by a structure that was firm enough in spite of its lightness and of its occasional oscillation in the somewhat vertiginous air, invited on occasion, in the interest of their nerves, a dropping of the plummet and a measurement of the abyss. A difference had been made moreover, once for all, by the fact that she had, all the while, not appeared to feel the need of rebutting his charge of an idea within her that she didn't dare to express, uttered just before one of the fullest of their later discussions ended. It had come up for him then that she "knew" something and that what she knew was bad—too bad to tell him. When he had spoken of it as visibly so bad that she was afraid he might find it out, her reply had left the matter too equivocal to be let alone and yet, for Marcher's special sensibility, almost too formidable again to touch. He circled about it at a distance that alternately narrowed and widened and that yet was not much affected by the consciousness in him that there was nothing she could "know," after all, any better than he did. She had no source of knowledge that he hadn't equally—except of course that she might have finer nerves. That was what women had where they were interested; they made out things, where people were concerned, that the people often couldn't have made out for themselves. Their nerves, their sensibility, their imagination, were conductors and revealers, and the beauty of

May Bartram was in particular that she had given herself so to his case. He felt in these days what, oddly enough, he had never felt before, the growth of a dread of losing her by some catastrophe—some catastrophe that yet wouldn't at all be *the* catastrophe: partly because she had, almost of a sudden, begun to strike him as useful to him as never yet, and partly by reason of an appearance of uncertainty in her health, coincident and equally new. It was characteristic of the inner detachment he had hitherto so successfully cultivated and to which our whole account of him is a reference, it was characteristic that his complications, such as they were, had never yet seemed so as at this crisis to thicken about him, even to the point of making him ask himself if he were, by any chance, of a truth, within sight or sound, within touch or reach, within the immediate jurisdiction of the thing that waited.

When the day came, as come it had to, that his friend confessed to him her fear of a deep disorder in her blood, he felt somehow the shadow of a change and the chill of a shock. He immediately began to imagine aggravations and disasters, and above all to think of her peril as the direct menace for himself of personal privation. This indeed gave him one of those partial recoveries of equanimity that were agreeable to him—it showed him that what was still first in his mind was the loss she herself might suffer. "What if she should have to die before knowing, before seeing——?" It would have been brutal, in the early stages of her trouble, to put that question to her; but it had immediately sounded for him to his own concern, and the possibility was what most made him sorry for her. If she did "know," moreover, in the sense of her having had some—what should he think?—mystical, irresistible light, this would make the matter not better, but worse, inasmuch as her original adoption of his own curiosity had quite become the basis of her life. She had been living to see what would *be* to be seen, and it would be cruel to her to have to give up before the accomplishment of the vision. These reflections, as I say, refreshed his generosity; yet, make them as he might, he saw himself, with the lapse of the period, more and more disconcerted. It lapsed for him with a strange, steady sweep, and the oddest oddity was that it gave him, independently of the threat of much inconvenience, almost the only positive surprise his career, if career it could be called, had yet offered him. She kept the house as she had never done, he had to go to her to see her—she could meet him nowhere now, though there was scarce a corner of their loved old London in which she had not in the past, at one time or another, done so;

and he found her always seated by her fire in the deep, old-fashioned chair she was less and less able to leave. He had been struck one day, after an absence exceeding his usual measure, with her suddenly looking much older to him than he had ever thought of her being; then he recognised that the suddenness was all on his side—he had just been suddenly struck. She looked older because inevitably, after so many years, she *was* old, or almost; which was of course true in still greater measure of her companion. If she was old, or almost, John Marcher assuredly was, and yet it was her showing of the lesson, not his own, that brought the truth home to him. His surprises began here; when once they had begun they multiplied; they came rather with a rush: it was as if, in the oddest way in the world, they had all been kept back, sown in a thick cluster, for the late afternoon of life, the time at which, for people in general, the unexpected has died out.

One of them was that he should have caught himself—for he *had* so done—*really* wondering if the great accident would take form now as nothing more than his being condemned to see this charming woman, this admirable friend, pass away from him. He had never so unreservedly qualified her as while confronted in thought with such a possibility; in spite of which there was small doubt for him that as an answer to his long riddle the mere effacement of even so fine a feature of his situation would be an abject anticlimax. It would represent, as connected with his past attitude, a drop of dignity under the shadow of which his existence could only become the most grotesque of failures. He had been far from holding it a failure—long as he had waited for the appearance that was to make it a success. He had waited for a quite other thing, not for such a one as that. The breath of his good faith came short, however, as he recognised how long he had waited, or how long, at least, his companion had. That she, at all events, might be recorded as having waited in vain—this affected him sharply, and all the more because of his at first having done little more than amuse himself with the idea. It grew more grave as the gravity of her condition grew, and the state of mind it produced in him, which he ended by watching, himself, as if it had been some definite disfigurement of his outer person, may pass for another of his surprises. This conjoined itself still with another, the really stupefying consciousness of a question that he would have allowed to shape itself had he dared. What did everything mean—what, that is, did *she* mean, she and her vain waiting and her probable death and the soundless admonition of it all—unless that, at this time of day, it was simply, it was over-

whelmingly too late? He had never, at any stage of his queer consciousness, admitted the whisper of such a correction; he had never, till within these last few months, been so false to his conviction as not to hold that what was to come to him had time, whether *he* struck himself as having it or not. That at last, at last, he certainly hadn't it, to speak of, or had it but in the scantiest measure—such, soon enough, as things went with him, became the inference with which his old obsession had to reckon: and this it was not helped to do by the more and more confirmed appearance that the great vagueness casting the long shadow in which he had lived had, to attest itself, almost no margin left. Since it was in Time that he was to have met his fate, so it was in Time that his fate was to have acted; and as he waked up to the sense of no longer being young, which was exactly the sense of being stale, just as that, in turn, was the sense of being weak, he waked up to another matter beside. It all hung together; they were subject, he and the great vagueness, to an equal and indivisible law. When the possibilities themselves had, accordingly, turned stale, when the secret of the gods had grown faint, had perhaps even quite evaporated, that, and that only, was failure. It wouldn't have been failure to be bankrupt, dishonoured, pilloried, hanged; it was failure not to be anything. And so, in the dark valley into which his path had taken its unlooked-for twist, he wondered not a little as he groped. He didn't care what awful crash might overtake him, with what ignominy or what monstrosity he might yet be associated—since he wasn't, after all, too utterly old to suffer—if it would only be decently proportionate to the posture he had kept, all his life, in the promised presence of it. He had but one desire left—that he shouldn't have been "sold."

IV

THEN it was that one afternoon, while the spring of the year was young and new, she met, all in her own way, his frankest betrayal of these alarms. He had gone in late to see her, but evening had not settled, and she was presented to him in that long, fresh light of waning April days which affects us often with a sadness sharper than the greyest hours of autumn. The week had been warm, the spring was supposed to have begun early, and May Bartram sat, for the first time in the year, without a fire, a fact that, to Marcher's sense, gave the scene of which she formed part a smooth and ultimate look, an air of knowing, in its immaculate order and its cold, meaningless cheer, that it would never see a fire again. Her own aspect—he could scarce have said why—intensified this note. Almost as white as wax, with the marks and signs in her face as numerous and as fine as if they had been etched by a needle, with soft white draperies relieved by a faded green scarf, the delicate tone of which had been consecrated by the years, she was the picture of a serene, exquisite, but impenetrable sphinx, whose head, or indeed all whose person, might have been powdered with silver. She was a sphinx, yet with her white petals and green fronds she might have been a lily too—only an artificial lily, wonderfully imitated and constantly kept, without dust or stain, though not exempt from a slight droop and a complexity of faint creases, under some clear glass bell. The perfection of household care, of high polish and finish, always reigned in her rooms, but they especially looked to Marcher at present as if everything had been wound up, tucked in, put away, so that she might sit with folded hands and with nothing more to do. She was "out of it," to his vision; her work was over; she communicated with him as across some gulf, or from some island of rest that she had already reached, and it made him feel strangely abandoned. Was it—or, rather, wasn't it—that if for so long she had been watching with him the answer to their question had swum into her ken and taken on its name, so that her occupation was verily gone? He had as much as charged her with this in saying to her, many months before, that she even then knew something she was keeping from him. It was a point he had never since ventured to press, vaguely fearing, as he did, that it might become a difference, perhaps a disagreement, between them. He had in short, in this later time, turned nervous, which was what, in all the other years, he had never been; and the oddity was that his nervousness should have waited till he had begun to doubt, should have held off so long as he was sure. There was something, it seemed to him, that the wrong word would bring down on his head, something that would so at least put an end to his suspense. But he wanted not to speak the wrong word; that would make everything ugly. He wanted the knowledge he lacked to drop on him, if drop it could, by its own august weight. If she was to forsake him it was surely for her to take leave. This was why he didn't ask her again, directly, what she knew; but it was also why, approaching the matter from another side, he said to her in the course of his visit: "What do you regard as the very worst that, at this time of day, *can* happen to me?"

He had asked her that in the past often enough; they had, with the odd, irregular rhythm of their intensities and avoidances, exchanged ideas about it and then had seen the ideas washed away by cool intervals, washed like figures traced in sea-sand. It had ever been the mark of their talk that the oldest allusions in it required but a little dismissal and reaction to come out again, sounding for the hour as new. She could thus at present meet his inquiry quite freshly and patiently. "Oh yes, I've repeatedly thought, only it always seemed to me of old that I couldn't quite make up my mind. I thought of dreadful things, between which it was difficult to choose; and so must you have done."

"Rather! I feel now as if I had scarce done anything else. I appear to myself to have spent my life in thinking of nothing *but* dreadful things. A great many of them I've at different times named to you, but there were others I couldn't name."

"They were too, too dreadful?"

"Too, too dreadful—some of them."

She looked at him a minute, and there came to him as he met it an inconsequent sense that her eyes, when one got their full clearness, were still as beautiful as they had been in youth, only beautiful with a strange, cold light—a light that somehow was a part of the effect, if it wasn't rather a part of the cause, of the pale, hard sweetness of the season and the hour. "And yet," she said at last, "there are horrors we have mentioned."

It deepened the strangeness to see her, as such a figure in such a picture, talk of "horrors," but she was to do, in a few minutes, something stranger yet—though even of this he was to take the full measure but afterwards—and the note of it was already in the air. It was, for the matter of that, one of the signs that her eyes were having again such a high flicker of their prime. He had to admit, however, what she said. "Oh yes, there were times when we did go far." He caught himself in the act, speaking as if it all were over. Well, he wished it were; and the consummation depended, for him, clearly, more and more on his companion.

But she had now a soft smile. "Oh, far——!"

It was oddly ironic. "Do you mean you're prepared to go further?"

She was frail and ancient and charming as she continued to look at him, yet it was rather as if she had lost the thread. "Do you consider that we went so far?"

"Why, I thought it the point you were just making—that we *had* looked most things in the face."

"Including each other?" She still smiled. "But you're quite right. We've had together great imaginations, often great fears; but some of them have been unspoken."

"Then the worst—we haven't faced that. I *could* face it, I believe, if I knew what you think it. I feel," he explained, "as if I had lost my power to conceive such things." And he wondered if he looked as blank as he sounded. "It's spent."

"Then why do you assume," she asked, "that mine isn't?"

"Because you've given me signs to the contrary. It isn't a question for you of conceiving, imagining, comparing. It isn't a question now of choosing." At last he came out with it. "You know something that I don't. You've showed me that before."

These last words affected her, he could see in a moment, remarkably, and she spoke with firmness. "I've shown you, my dear, nothing."

He shook his head. "You can't hide it."

"Oh, oh!" May Bartram murmured over what she couldn't hide. It was almost a smothered groan.

"You admitted it months ago, when I spoke of it to you as of something you were afraid I would find out. Your answer was that I couldn't, that I wouldn't, and I don't pretend I have. But you had something therefore in mind, and I see now that it must have been, that it still is, the possibility that, of all possibilities, has settled itself for you as the worst. This," he went on, "is why I appeal to you. I'm only afraid of ignorance now— I'm not afraid of knowledge." And then as for a while she said nothing: "What makes me sure is that I see in your face and feel here, in this air and amid these appearances, that you're out of it. You've done. You've had your experience. You leave me to my fate."

Well, she listened, motionless and white in her chair, as if she had in fact a decision to make, so that her whole manner was a virtual confession, though still with a small, fine, inner stiffness, an imperfect surrender. "It *would* be the worst," she finally let herself say. "I mean the thing that I've never said."

It hushed him a moment. "More monstrous than all the monstrosities we've named?"

"More monstrous. Isn't that what you sufficiently express," she asked, "in calling it the worst?"

Marcher thought. "Assuredly—if you mean, as I do, something that includes all the loss and all the shame that are thinkable."

"It would if it *should* happen," said May Bartram. "What we're speaking of, remember, is only my idea."

"It's your belief," Marcher returned. "That's enough for me. I feel your beliefs are right. Therefore if, having this one, you give me no more light on it, you abandon me."

"No, no!" she repeated. "I'm with you—don't you see?—still." And as if to make it more vivid to him she rose from her chair—a movement she seldom made in these days—and showed herself, all

draped and all soft, in her fairness and slimness. "I haven't forsaken you."

It was really, in its effort against weakness, a generous assurance, and had the success of the impulse not, happily, been great, it would have touched him to pain more than to pleasure. But the cold charm in her eyes had spread, as she hovered before him, to all the rest of her person, so that it was, for the minute, almost like a recovery of youth. He couldn't pity her for that; he could only take her as she showed—as capable still of helping him. It was as if, at the same time, her light might at any instant go out; wherefore he must make the most of it. There passed before him with intensity the three or four things he wanted most to know; but the question that came of itself to his lips really covered the others. "Then tell me if I shall consciously suffer."

She promptly shook her head. "Never!"

It confirmed the authority he imputed to her, an what's better than that? Do you call that the worst?"

"You think nothing is better?" she asked.

She seemed to mean something so special that he again sharply wondered, though still with the dawn of a prospect of relief. "Why not, if one doesn't *know?*" After which, as their eyes, over his question, met in a silence, the dawn deepened and something to his purpose came, prodigiously, out of her very face. His own, as he took it in, suddenly flushed to the forehead, and he gasped with the force of a perception to which, on the instant, everything fitted. The sound of his gasp filled the air; then he became articulate. "I see—if I don't suffer!"

In her own look, however, was doubt. "You see what?"

"Why, what you mean—what you've always meant."

She again shook her head. "What I mean isn't what I've always meant. It's different."

"It's something new?"

She hesitated. "Something new. It's not what you think. I see what you think."

His divination drew breath then; only her correction might be wrong. "It isn't that I *am* a donkey?" he asked between faintness and grimness. "It isn't that it's all a mistake?"

"A mistake?" she pityingly echoed. *That* possibility, for her, he saw, would be monstrous; and if she guaranteed him the immunity from pain it would accordingly not be what she had in mind. "Oh, no," she declared; "it's nothing of that sort. You've been right."

Yet he couldn't help asking himself if she weren't, thus pressed, speaking but to save him. It seemed to him he should be most lost if his history should prove all a platitude. "Are you telling me the truth, so that I sha'n't have been a bigger idiot than I can bear to know? I *haven't* lived with a vain imagination, in the most besotted illusion? I haven't waited but to see the door shut in my face?"

She shook her head again. "However the case stands *that* isn't the truth. Whatever the reality, it *is* a reality. The door isn't shut. The door's open," said May Bartram.

"Then something's to come?"

She waited once again, always with her cold, sweet eyes on him. "It's never too late." She had, with her gliding step, diminished the distance between them, and she stood nearer to him, close to him, a minute, as if still full of the unspoken. Her movement might have been for some finer emphasis of what she was at once hesitating and deciding to say. He had been standing by the chimney-piece, fireless and sparely adorned, a small, perfect old French clock and two morsels of rosy Dresden constituting all its furniture; and her hand grasped the shelf while she kept him waiting, grasped it a little as for support and encouragement. She only kept him waiting, however; that is he only waited. It had become suddenly, from her movement and attitude, beautiful and vivid to him that she had something more to give him; her wasted face delicately shone with it, and it glittered, almost as with the white lustre of silver, in her expression. She was right, incontestably, for what he saw in her face was the truth, and strangely, without consequence, while their talk of it as dreadful was still in the air, she appeared to present it as inordinately soft. This, prompting bewilderment, made him but gape the more gratefully for her revelation, so that they continued for some minutes silent, her face shining at him, her contact imponderably pressing, and his stare all kind, but all expectant. The end, none the less, was that what he had expected failed to sound. Something else took place instead, which seemed to consist at first in the mere closing of her eyes. She gave way at the same instant to a slow, fine shudder, and though he remained staring—though he stared, in fact, but the harder—she turned off and regained her chair. It was the end of what she had been intending, but it left him thinking only of that.

"Well, you don't say——?"

She had touched in her passage a bell near the chimney and had sunk back, strangely pale. "I'm afraid I'm too ill."

"Too ill to tell me?" It sprang up sharp to him, and almost to his lips, the fear that she would die without giving him light. He checked himself in

time from so expressing his question, but she answered as if she had heard the words.

"Don't you know—now?"

" 'Now——?" She had spoken as if something that had made a difference had come up within the moment. But her maid, quickly obedient to her bell, was already with them. "I know nothing." And he was afterwards to say to himself that he must have spoken with odious impatience, such an impatience as to show that, supremely disconcerted, he washed his hands of the whole question.

"Oh!" said May Bartram.

"Are you in pain?" he asked, as the woman went to her.

"No," said May Bartram.

Her maid, who had put an arm round her as if to take her to her room, fixed on him eyes that appealingly contradicted her; in spite of which, however, he showed once more his mystification. "What then has happened?"

She was once more, with her companion's help, on her feet, and, feeling withdrawal imposed on him, he had found, blankly, his hat and gloves and had reached the door. Yet he waited for her answer. "What *was* to," she said.

V

HE CAME back the next day, but she was then unable to see him, and as it was literally the first time this had occurred in the long stretch of their acquaintance he turned away, defeated and sore, almost angry—or feeling at least that such a break in their custom was really the beginning of the end—and wandered alone with his thoughts, especially with one of them that he was unable to keep down. She was dying, and he would lose her; she was dying, and his life would end. He stopped in the park, into which he had passed, and stared before him at his recurrent doubt. Away from her the doubt pressed again; in her presence he had believed her, but as he felt his forlornness he threw himself into the explanation that, nearest at hand, had most of a miserable warmth for him and least of a cold torment. She had deceived him to save him—to put him off with something in which he should be able to rest. What could the thing that was to happen to him be, after all, but just this thing that had begun to happen? Her dying, her death, his consequent solitude—*that* was what he had figured as the beast in the jungle, that was what had been in the lap of the gods. He had had her word for it as he left her; for what else, on earth, could she have meant? It wasn't a thing of a monstrous order; not a fate rare and distinguished; not a stroke of fortune that overwhelmed and immortalised; it had only the stamp of the common doom. But poor Marcher, at this hour, judged the common doom sufficient. It would serve his turn, and even as the consummation of infinite waiting he would bend his pride to accept it. He sat down on a bench in the twilight. He hadn't been a fool. Something had *been,* as she had said, to come. Before he rose indeed it had quite struck him that the final fact really matched with the long avenue through which he had had to reach it. As sharing his suspense, and as giving herself all, giving her life, to bring it to an end, she had come with him every step of the way. He had lived by her aid, and to leave her behind would be cruelly, damnably to miss her. What could be more overwhelming than that?

Well, he was to know within the week, for though she kept him a while at bay, left him restless and wretched during a series of days on each of which he asked about her only again to have to turn away, she ended his trial by receiving him where she had always received him. Yet she had been brought out at some hazard into the presence of so many of the things that were, consciously, vainly, half their past, and there was scant service left in the gentleness of her mere desire, all too visible, to check his obsession and wind up his long trouble. That was clearly what she wanted; the one thing more, for her own peace, while she could still put out her hand. He was so affected by her state that, once seated by her chair, he was moved to let everything go; it was she herself therefore who brought him back, took up again, before she dismissed him, her last word of the other time. She showed how she wished to leave their affair in order. "I'm not sure you understood. You've nothing to wait for more. It *has* come."

Oh, how he looked at her! "Really?"

"Really."

"The thing that, as you said, *was* to?"

"The thing that we began in our youth to watch for."

Face to face with her once more he believed her; it was a claim to which he had so abjectly little to oppose. "You mean that it has come as a positive, definite occurrence, with a name and a date?"

"Positive. Definite. I don't know about the 'name,' but, oh, with a date!"

He found himself again too helplessly at sea. "But come in the night—come and passed me by?"

May Bartram had her strange, faint smile. "Oh no, it hasn't passed you by!"

"But if I haven't been aware of it, and it hasn't touched me——?"

"Ah, your not being aware of it," and she seemed to hesitate an instant to deal with this—"your not being aware of it is the strangeness *in* the strangeness. It's the wonder *of* the wonder." She spoke as with the softness almost of a sick child, yet now at last, at the end of all, with the perfect straightness of a sybil. She visibly knew that she knew, and the effect on him was of something co-ordinate, in its high character, with the law that had ruled him. It was the true voice of the law; so on her lips would the law itself have sounded. "It *has* touched you," she went on. "It has done its office. It has made you all its own."

"So utterly without my knowing it?"

"So utterly without your knowing it." His hand, as he leaned to her, was on the arm of her chair, and, dimly smiling always now, she placed her own on it. "It's enough if *I* know it."

"Oh!" he confusedly sounded, as she herself of late so often had done.

"What I long ago said is true. You'll never know now, and I think you ought to be content. You've *had* it," said May Bartram.

"But had what?"

"Why, what was to have marked you out. The proof of your law. It has acted. I'm too glad," she then bravely added, "to have been able to see what it's *not.*"

He continued to attach his eyes to her, and with the sense that it was all beyond him, and that *she* was too, he would still have sharply challenged her, had he not felt it an abuse of her weakness to do more than take devoutly what she gave him, take it as hushed as to a revelation. If he did speak, it was out of the foreknowledge of his loneliness to come. "If you're glad of what it's 'not,' it might then have been worse?"

She turned her eyes away, she looked straight before her with which, after a moment: "Well, you know our fears."

He wondered. "It's something then we never feared?"

On this, slowly, she turned to him. "Did we ever dream, with all our dreams, that we should sit and talk of it thus?"

He tried for a little to make out if they had; but it was as if their dreams, numberless enough, were in solution in some thick, cold mist, in which thought lost itself. "It might have been that we couldn't talk?"

"Well"—she did her best for him—"not from this side. This, you see," she said, "is the *other* side."

"I think," poor Marcher returned, "that all sides are the same to me." Then, however, as she softly shook her head in correction: "We mightn't, as it were, have got across——?"

"To where we are—no. We're *here*"—she made her weak emphasis.

"And much good does it do us!" was her friend's frank comment.

"It does us the good it can. It does us the good that *it* isn't here. It's past. It's behind," said May Bartram. "Before――" but her voice dropped.

He had got up, not to tire her, but it was hard to combat his yearning. She after all told him nothing but that his light had failed—which he knew well enough without her. "Before――?" he blankly echoed.

"Before, you see, it was always to *come*. That kept it present."

"Oh, I don't care what comes now! Besides," Marcher added, "it seems to me I liked it better present, as you say, than I can like it absent with *your* absence."

"Oh, mine!"—and her pale hands made light of it.

"With the absence of everything." He had a dreadful sense of standing there before her for—so far as anything but this proved, this bottomless drop was concerned—the last time of their life. It rested on him with a weight he felt he could scarce bear, and this weight it apparently was that still pressed out what remained in him of speakable protest. "I believe you; but I can't begin to pretend I understand. *Nothing,* for me, is past; nothing *will* pass until I pass myself, which I pray my stars may be as soon as possible. Say, however," he added, "that I've eaten my cake, as you contend, to the last crumb—how can the thing I've never felt at all be the thing I was marked out to feel?"

She met him, perhaps, less directly, but she met him unperturbed. "You take your 'feelings' for granted. You were to suffer your fate. That was not necessarily to know it."

"How in the world—when what is such knowledge but suffering?"

She looked up at him a while, in silence. "No—you don't understand."

"I suffer," said John Marcher.

"Don't, don't!"

"How can I help at least *that?*"

"*Don't!*" May Bartram repeated.

She spoke it in a tone so special, in spite of her weakness, that he stared an instant—stared as if some light, hitherto hidden, had shimmered across his vision. Darkness again closed over it, but the gleam had already become for him an idea. "Because I haven't the right――?"

"Don't *know*—when you needn't," she mercifully urged. "You needn't—for we shouldn't."

"Shouldn't?" If he could but know what she meant!

"No—it's too much."

"Too much?" he still asked—but with a mystification that was the next moment, of a sudden, to give way. Her words, if they meant something, affected him in this light—the light also of her wasted face—as meaning *all,* and the sense of what knowledge had been for herself came over him with a rush which broke through into a question. "Is it of that, then, you're dying?"

She but watched him, gravely at first, as if to see, with this, where he was, and she might have seen something, or feared something, that moved her sympathy. "I would live for you still—if I could." Her eyes closed for a little, as if, withdrawn into herself, she were, for a last time, trying. "But I can't!" she said as she raised them again to take leave of him.

She couldn't indeed, as but too promptly and sharply appeared, and he had no vision of her after this that was anything but darkness and doom. They had parted forever in that strange talk; access to her chamber of pain, rigidly guarded, was almost wholly forbidden him; he was feeling now moreover, in the face of doctors, nurses, the two or three relatives attracted doubtless by the presumption of what she had to "leave," how few were the rights, as they were called in such cases, that he had to put forward, and how odd it might even seem that their intimacy shouldn't have given him more of them. The stupidest fourth cousin had more, even though she had been nothing in such a person's life. She had been a feature of features in *his,* for what else was it to have been so indispensable? Strange beyond saying were the ways of existence, baffling for him the anomaly of his lack, as he felt it to be, of producible claim. A woman might have been, as it were, everything to him, and it might yet present him in no connection that anyone appeared obliged to recognise. If this was the case in these closing weeks it was the case more sharply on the occasion of the last offices rendered, in the great grey London cemetery, to what had been mortal, to what had been precious, in his friend. The concourse at her grave was not numerous, but he saw himself treated as scarce more nearly concerned with it than if there had been a thousand others. He was in short from this moment face to face with the fact that he was to profit extraordinarily little by the interest May Bartram had taken in him. He couldn't quite have said what he expected, but he had somehow not expected this approach to a double privation. Not only had her interest failed him, but he seemed to feel himself unattended—and for a reason he couldn't sound—by the distinction, the dignity, the propriety, if nothing else, of the man markedly bereaved. It was as if, in the view of society, he had not *been* markedly bereaved, as if there still failed some sign or proof of it, and as if, none the less, his character could never be affirmed, nor the deficiency ever made up. There were moments, as the weeks went by, when he would have liked, by some almost aggressive act, to take his stand on the intimacy of his loss, in order that it *might* be questioned and his retort, to the relief of his spirit, so recorded; but the moments of an irritation more helpless followed fast on these, the moments during which, turning things over with a good conscience but with a bare horizon, he found himself wondering if he oughtn't to have begun, so to speak, further back.

He found himself wondering indeed at many things, and this last speculation had others to keep it company. What could he have done, after all, in her lifetime, without giving them both, as it were, away? He couldn't have made it known she was watching him, for that would have published the superstition of the Beast. This was what closed his mouth now—now that the Jungle had been threshed to vacancy and that the Beast had stolen away. It sounded too foolish and too flat; the difference for him in this particular, the extinction in his life of the element of suspense, was such in fact as to surprise him. He could scarce have said what the effect resembled; the abrupt cessation, the positive prohibition, of music perhaps, more than anything else, in some place all adjusted and all accustomed to sonoriety and to attention. If he could at any rate have conceived lifting the veil from his image at some moment of the past (what had he done, after all, if not lift it to *her?*) so to do this to-day, to talk to people at large of the jungle cleared and confide to them that he now felt it as safe, would have been not only to see them listen as to a goodwife's tale, but really to hear himself tell one. What it presently came to in truth was that poor Marcher waded through his beaten grass, where no life stirred, where no breath sounded, where no evil eye seemed to gleam from a possible lair, very much as if vaguely looking for the Beast, and still more as if missing it. He walked about in an existence that had grown strangely more spacious, and, stopping fitfully in places where the undergrowth of life struck him as closer, asked himself yearningly, wondered secretly and sorely, if it would have lurked here or there. It would have at all events *sprung;* what was at least complete was his belief in the truth itself of the assurance given him. The change from his old sense to his new was absolute and final: what was to happen *had* so absolutely and finally happened that he was as little able to know a fear

for his future as to know a hope; so absent in short was any question of anything still to come. He was to live entirely with the other question, that of his unidentified past, that of his having to see his fortune impenetrably muffled and masked.

The torment of this vision became then his occupation; he couldn't perhaps have consented to live but for the possibility of guessing. She had told him, his friend, not to guess; she had forbidden him, so far as he might, to know, and she had even in a sort denied the power in him to learn: which were so many things, precisely, to deprive him of rest. It wasn't that he wanted, he argued for fairness, that anything that had happened to him should happen over again; it was only that he shouldn't, as an anticlimax, have been taken sleeping so sound as not to be able to win back by an effort of thought the lost stuff of consciousness. He declared to himself at moments that he would either win it back or have done with consciousness for ever; he made this idea his one motive, in fine, made it so much his passion that none other, to compare with it, seemed ever to have touched him. The lost stuff of consciousness became thus for him as a strayed or stolen child to an unappeasable father; he hunted it up and down very much as if he were knocking at doors and inquiring of the police. This was the spirit in which, inevitably, he set himself to travel; he started on a journey that was to be as long as he could make it; it danced before him that, as the other side of the globe couldn't possibly have less to say to him, it might, by a possibility of suggestion, have more. Before he quitted London, however, he made a pilgrimage to May Bartram's grave, took his way to it through the endless avenues of the grim suburban necropolis, sought it out in the wilderness of tombs, and, though he had come but for the renewal of the act of farewell, found himself, when he had at last stood by it, beguiled into long intensities. He stood for an hour, powerless to turn away and yet powerless to penetrate the darkness of death; fixing with his eyes her inscribed name and date, beating his forehead against the fact of the secret they kept, drawing his breath, while he waited as if, in pity of him, some sense would rise from the stones. He kneeled on the stones, however, in vain; they kept what they concealed; and if the face of the tomb did become a face for him it was because her two names were like a pair of eyes that didn't know him. He gave them a last long look, but no palest light broke.

VI

HE STAYED away, after this, for a year; he visited the depths of Asia, spending himself on scenes of romantic interest, of superlative sanctity; but what was present to him everywhere was that for a man who had known what *he* had known the world was vulgar and vain. The state of mind in which he had lived for so many years shone out to him, in reflection, as a light that coloured and refined, a light beside which the glow of the East was garish, cheap and thin. The terrible truth was that he had lost—with everything else—a distinction as well; the things he saw couldn't help being common when he had become common to look at them. He was simply now one of them himself—he was in the dust, without a peg for the sense of difference; and there were hours when, before the temples of gods and the sepulchres of kings, his spirit turned, for nobleness of association, to the barely discriminated slab in the London suburb. That had become for him, and more intensely with time and distance, his one witness of a past glory. It was all that was left to him for proof or pride, yet the past glories of Pharaohs were nothing to him as he thought of it. Small wonder then that he came back to it on the morrow of his return. He was drawn there this time as irresistibly as the other, yet with a confidence, almost, that was doubtless the effect of the many months that had elapsed. He had lived, in spite of himself, into his change of feeling, and in wandering over the earth had wandered, as might be said, from the circumference to the centre of his desert. He had settled to his safety and accepted perforce his extinction; figuring to himself, with some colour, in the likeness of certain little old men he remembered to have seen, of whom, all meagre and wizened as they might look, it was related that they had in their time fought twenty duels or been loved by ten princesses. They indeed had been wondrous for others, while he was but wondrous for himself; which, however, was exactly the cause of his haste to renew the wonder by getting back, as he might put it, into his own presence. That had quickened his steps and checked his delay. If his visit was prompt it was because he had been separated so long from the part of himself that alone he now valued.

It is accordingly not false to say that he reached his goal with a certain elation, and stood there again with a certain assurance. The creature beneath the sod *knew* of his rare experience, so that, strangely now, the place had lost for him its mere blankness of expression. It met him in mildness—not, as before, in mockery; it wore for him the air of conscious greeting that we find, after absence, in things that have closely belonged to us and which seem to confess of themselves to the connection. The plot of ground, the graven tablet, the tended flowers affected him so as belonging to him that he quite felt for the hour like a contented landlord reviewing a piece of property. Whatever had happened—well, had happened. He had not come back this time with the vanity of that question, his former worrying, "What, *what?*" now practically so spent. Yet he would, none the less, never again so cut himself off from the spot; he would come back to it every month, for if he did nothing else by its aid he at least held up his head. It thus grew for him, in the oddest way, a positive resource; he carried out his idea of periodical returns, which took their place at last among the most inveterate of his habits. What it all amounted to, oddly enough, was that, in his now so simplified world, this garden of death gave him the few square feet of earth on which he could still most live. It was as if, being nothing anywhere else for anyone, nothing even for himself, he were just everything here, and if not for a crowd of witnesses, or indeed for any witness but John Marcher, then by clear right of the register that he could scan like an open page. The open page was the tomb of his friend, and *there* were the facts of the past, there the truth of his life, there the backward reaches in which he could lose himself. He did this, from time to time, with such effect that he seemed to wander through the old years with his hand in the arm of a companion who was, in the most extraordinary manner, his other, his younger self; and to wander, which was more extraordinary yet, round and round a third presence—not wandering she, but stationary, still, whose eyes, turning with his revolution, never ceased to follow him, and whose seat was his point, so to speak, of orientation. Thus in short he settled to live—feeding only on the sense that he once *had* lived, and dependent on it not only for a support but for an identity.

It sufficed him, in its way, for months, and the year elapsed; it would doubtless even have carried him further but for an accident, superficially slight, which moved him, in a quite other direction, with a force beyond any of his impressions of Egypt or of India. It was a thing of the merest chance—the turn, as he afterwards felt, of a hair, though he was indeed to live to believe that if light hadn't come to him in this particular fashion it would still have come in another. He was to live to believe this, I say, though he was not to live, I may not less definitely mention, to do much else. We allow him at any rate the benefit of the conviction, struggling up for him at the end, that, whatever might have happened or not happened, he would have come round of himself to the light. The incident of an autumn day had put the match to the train laid from of old by his misery. With the light before him he knew that even of late his ache had only been smothered. It was strangely drugged, but it throbbed; at the touch it began to bleed. And the touch, in the event, was the face of a fellow-mortal. This face, one grey afternoon when the leaves were thick in the alleys, looked into Marcher's own, at the cemetery, with an expression like the cut of a blade. He felt it, that is, so deep down that he winced at the steady thrust. The person who so mutely assaulted him was a figure he had noticed, on reaching his own goal, absorbed by a grave a short distance away, a grave apparently fresh, so that the emotion of the visitor would probably match it for frankness. This fact alone forbade further attention, though during the time he stayed he remained vaguely conscious of his neighbour, a middle-aged man apparently, in mourning, whose bowed back, among the clustered monuments and mortuary yews, was constantly presented. Marcher's theory that these were elements in contact with which he himself revived, had suffered, on this occasion, it may be granted, a sensible though inscrutable check. The autumn day was dire for him as none had recently been, and he rested with a heaviness he had not yet known on the low stone table that bore May Bartram's name. He rested without power to move, as if some spring in him, some spell vouchsafed, had suddenly been broken forever. If he could have done that moment as he wanted he would simply have stretched himself on the slab that was ready to take him, treating it as a place prepared to receive his last sleep. What in all the wide world had he now to keep awake for? He stared before him with the question, and it was then that, as one of the cemetery walks passed near him, he caught the shock of the face.

His neighbour at the other grave had withdrawn, as he himself, with force in him to move, would have done by now, and was advancing along the path on his way to one of the gates. This brought him near, and his pace was slow, so that—and all the more as there was a kind of hunger in his look—the two men were for a minute directly confronted. Marcher felt him on the spot as one of the deeply stricken—a perception so sharp that nothing else in the picture lived for it, neither his dress, his age, nor his presumable character and class; nothing lived but the deep ravage of the features that he showed. He *showed* them—that was the point; he was moved, as he passed, by some impulse that was either a signal for sympathy or, more possibly, a challenge to another sorrow. He might already have been aware of our friend, might, at some previous hour, have noticed in him the smooth habit of the scene, with which the state of his own senses so scantly consorted, and might thereby have been stirred as by a kind of overt discord. What Marcher was at all events conscious of was, in the first place, that the image of scarred passion presented to him was conscious too—of something that profaned the air; and, in the second, that, roused, startled, shocked, he was yet the next moment looking after it, as it went, with envy. The most extraordinary thing that had happened to him—though he had given that name to other matters as well—took place, after his immediate vague stare, as a consequence of this impression. The stranger passed, but the raw glare of his grief remained, making our friend wonder in pity what wrong, what wound it expressed, what injury not to be healed. What had the man *had* to make him, by the loss of it, so bleed and yet live?

Something—and this reached him with a pang —that *he,* John Marcher, hadn't; the proof of which was precisely John Marcher's arid end. No passion had ever touched him, for this was what passion meant; he had survived and maundered and pined, but where had been *his* deep ravage? The extraordinary thing we speak of was the sudden rush of the result of this question. The sight that had just met his eyes named to him, as in letters of quick flame, something he had utterly, insanely missed, and what he had missed; made these things a train of fire, made them mark themselves in an anguish of inward throbs. He had seen *outside* of his life, not learned it within, the way a woman was mourned when she had been loved for herself; such was the force of his conviction of the meaning of the stranger's face, which still flared for him like a smoky torch. It had not come to him, the knowledge, on the wings of experience; it had brushed him, jostled him, upset him, with the disrespect of chance, the insolence of an accident. Now that the illumination had begun, however, it blazed to the zenith, and what he presently stood there gazing at was the sounded void of his life. He gazed, he drew breath, in pain; he turned in his dismay, and, turning, he had before him in sharper incision than ever the open page of his story. The name on the table smote him as the passage of his neighbour had done, and what it said to him, full in the face, was that *she* was what he had missed. This was the awful thought, the answer to all the past, the vision at the dread clearness of which he turned as cold as the stone beneath him. Everything fell together, confessed, explained, overwhelmed; leaving him most of all stupefied at the blindness he had cherished. The fate he had been marked for he had met with a vengeance—he had emptied the cup to the lees; he had been the man of his time, *the* man, to whom nothing on earth was to have happened. That was the rare stroke—that was his visitation. So he saw it, as we say, in pale horror, while the pieces fitted and fitted. So *she* had seen it, while he didn't, and so she served at this hour to drive the truth home. It was the truth, vivid and monstrous, that all the while he had waited the wait was itself his portion. This the companion of his vigil had at a given moment perceived, and she had then offered him the chance to baffle his doom. One's doom, however, was never baffled, and on the day she had told him that his own had come down she had seen him but stupidly stare at the escape she offered him.

The escape would have been to love her; then, *then* he would have lived. *She* had lived—who could say now with what passion?—since she had loved him for himself; whereas he had never thought of her (ah, how it hugely glared at him!) but in the chill of his egotism and the light of her use. Her spoken words came back to him, and the chain stretched and stretched. The beast had lurked indeed, and the beast, at its hour, had sprung; it had sprung in that twilight of the cold April when, pale, ill, wasted, but all beautiful, and perhaps even then recoverable, she had risen from her chair to stand before him and let him imaginably guess. It had sprung as he didn't guess; it had sprung as she hopelessly turned from him, and the mark, by the time he left her, had fallen where it *was* to fall. He had justified his fear and achieved his fate; he had failed, with the last exactitude, of all he was to fail of; and a moan now rose to his lips as he remembered she had prayed he mightn't know. This horror of waking—*this* was knowledge, knowledge under the breath of which the very tears in his eyes seemed to freeze. Through them, none the less, he tried to fix it and hold it; he kept it there before him so that he might feel the pain. That at least, belated and bitter, had something of the taste of life. But the bitterness suddenly sickened him, and it was as if, horribly, he saw, in the truth, in the cruelty of his image, what had been appointed and done. He saw the Jungle of his life and saw the lurking Beast; then, while he looked, perceived it, as by a stir of the air, rise, huge and hideous, for the leap that was to settle him. His eyes darkened—it was close; and, instinctively turning, in his hallucination, to avoid it, he flung himself, on his face, on the tomb.

FROM
HAWTHORNE

◇

《 IN 1879 James published *Hawthorne*, a brief critical biography of the author whose work had meant so much to him in his youth and to which he was to return in a centenary essay in 1904. Appearing in England in the English Men of Letters series, edited by John Morley, the book was also issued in America, where James's strictures on "provincial" American conditions provoked some angry replies. To Howells, who mildly objected to some of the book's conclusions, James replied that it had been a "tolerably deliberate and meditated performance, and I should be prepared to do battle for most of the convictions expressed." For further comment on *Hawthorne*, see the Introduction.

◇

THE SCARLET LETTER

HIS PUBLISHER, Mr. Fields,[1] in a volume entitled *Yesterdays with Authors*, has related the circumstances in which Hawthorne's masterpiece came into the world. "In the winter of 1849, after he had been ejected from the Custom-house, I went down to Salem to see him and inquire after his health, for we heard he had been suffering from illness. He was then living in a modest wooden house. . . . I found him alone in a chamber over the sitting-room of the dwelling, and as the day was cold he was hovering near a stove. We fell into talk about his future prospects, and he was, as I feared I should find him, in a very desponding mood." His visitor urged him to bethink himself of publishing something, and Hawthorne replied by calling his attention to the small popularity his published productions had yet acquired, and declaring he had done nothing and had no spirit for doing anything. The narrator of the incident urged upon him the necessity of a more hopeful view of his situation, and proceeded to take leave. He had not reached the street, however, when Hawthorne hurried to overtake him, and, placing a roll of MS. in his hand, bade him take it to Boston, read it, and pronounce upon it. "It is either very good or very bad," said the author; "I don't know which." "On my way back to Boston," says Mr. Fields, "I read the germ of *The Scarlet Letter;* before I slept that night I wrote him a note all

HAWTHORNE.   1. **Mr. Fields:** James Thomas Fields (1817–81), a leading American publisher of the mid-nineteenth century, author of *Yesterdays with Authors* (1872).

aglow with admiration of the marvellous story he had put into my hands, and told him that I would come again to Salem the next day and arrange for its publication. I went on in such an amazing state of excitement, when we met again in the little house, that he would not believe I was really in earnest. He seemed to think I was beside myself, and laughed sadly at my enthusiasm." Hawthorne, however, went on with the book and finished it, but it appeared only a year later. His biographer quotes a passage from a letter which he wrote in February, 1850, to his friend Horatio Bridge. "I finished my book only yesterday; one end being in the press at Boston, while the other was in my head here at Salem, so that, as you see, my story is at least fourteen miles long. . . . My book, the publisher tells me, will not be out before April. He speaks of it in tremendous terms of approbation; so does Mrs. Hawthorne, to whom I read the conclusion last night. It broke her heart, and sent her to bed with a grievous headache—which I look upon as a triumphant success. Judging from the effect upon her and the publisher, I may calculate on what bowlers call a ten-strike. But I don't make any such calculation." And Mr. Lathrop [2] calls attention, in regard to this passage, to an allusion in the *English Note-Books* (September 14, 1855). "Speaking of Thackeray, I cannot but wonder at his coolness in respect to his own pathos, and compare it to my emotions when I read the last scene of *The Scarlet Letter* to my wife, just after writing it—tried to read it rather, for my voice swelled and heaved as if I were tossed up and down on an ocean as it subsides after a storm. But I was in a very nervous state then, having gone through a great diversity of emotion while writing it, for many months."

The work has the tone of the circumstances in which it was produced. If Hawthorne was in a sombre mood, and if his future was painfully vague, *The Scarlet Letter* contains little enough of gaiety or of hopefulness. It is densely dark, with a single spot of vivid colour in it; and it will probably long remain the most consistently gloomy of English novels of the first order. But I just now called it the author's masterpiece, and I imagine it will continue to be, for other generations than ours, his most substantial title to fame. The subject had probably lain a long time in his mind, as his subjects were apt to do; so that he appears completely to possess it, to know it and feel it. It is simpler and more complete than his other novels; it achieves more prefectly what it attempts,

and it has about it that charm, very hard to express, which we find in an artist's work the first time he has touched his highest mark—a sort of straightness and naturalness of execution, an unconsciousness of his public, and freshness of interest in his theme. It was a great success, and he immediately found himself famous. The writer of these lines, who was a child at the time, remembers dimly the sensation the book produced, and the little shudder with which people alluded to it, as if a peculiar horror were mixed with its attractions. He was too young to read it himself, but its title, upon which he fixed his eyes as the book lay upon the table, had a mysterious charm. He had a vague belief, indeed, that the "letter" in question was one of the documents that come by the post, and it was a source of perpetual wonderment to him that it should be of such an unaccustomed hue. Of course it was difficult to explain to a child the significance of poor Hester Prynne's blood-coloured *A*. But the mystery was at last partly dispelled by his being taken to see a collection of pictures (the annual exhibition of the National Academy), where he encountered a representation of a pale, handsome woman, in a quaint black dress and a white coif, holding between her knees an elfish-looking little girl, fantastically dressed, and crowned with flowers. Embroidered on the woman's breast was a great crimson *A,* over which the child's fingers, as she glanced strangely out of the picture, were maliciously playing. I was told that this was Hester Prynne and little Pearl, and that when I grew older I might read their interesting history. But the picture remained vividly imprinted on my mind; I had been vaguely frightened and made uneasy by it; and when, years afterwards, I first read the novel, I seemed to myself to have read it before, and to be familiar with its two strange heroines. I mention this incident simply as an indication of the degree to which the success of *The Scarlet Letter* had made the book what is called an actuality. Hawthorne himself was very modest about it; he wrote to his publisher, when there was a question of his undertaking another novel, that what had given the history of Hester Prynne its "vogue" was simply the introductory chapter. In fact, the publication of *The Scarlet Letter* was in the United States a literary event of the first importance. The book was the finest piece of imaginative writing yet put forth in the country. There was a consciousness of this in the welcome that was given it—a satisfaction in the idea of America having produced a novel that belonged to literature, and to the forefront of it. Something might at last be sent to Europe as exquisite in quality as

---

2. **Mr. Lathrop:** George Parsons Lathrop (1851–98), Hawthorne's son-in-law, author of *A Study of Hawthorne* (1876).

anything that had been received, and the best of it was that the thing was absolutely American; it belonged to the soil, to the air; it came out of the very heart of New England.

It is beautiful, admirable, extraordinary; it has in the highest degree that merit which I have spoken of as the mark of Hawthorne's best things—an indefinable purity and lightness of conception, a quality which in a work of art affects one in the same way as the absence of grossness does in a human being. His fancy, as I just now said, had evidently brooded over the subject for a long time; the situation to be represented had disclosed itself to him in all its phases. When I say in all its phases, the sentence demands modification; for it is to be remembered that if Hawthorne laid his hand upon the well-worn theme, upon the familiar combination of the wife, the lover, and the husband, it was after all but to one period of the history of these three persons that he attached himself. The situation is the situation after the woman's fault has been committed, and the current of expiation and repentance has set in. In spite of the relation between Hester Prynne and Arthur Dimmesdale, no story of love was surely ever less of a "love story." To Hawthorne's imagination the fact that these two persons had loved each other too well was of an interest comparatively vulgar; what appealed to him was the idea of their moral situation in the long years that were to follow. The story, indeed, is in a secondary degree that of Hester Prynne; she becomes, really, after the first scene, an accessory figure; it is not upon her the *dénoûment* depends. It is upon her guilty lover that the author projects most frequently the cold, thin rays of his fitfully-moving lantern, which makes here and there a little luminous circle, on the edge of which hovers the livid and sinister figure of the injured and retributive husband. The story goes on, for the most part, between the lover and the husband—the tormented young Puritan minister, who carries the secret of his own lapse from pastoral purity locked up beneath an exterior that commends itself to the reverence of his flock, while he sees the softer partner of his guilt standing in the full glare of exposure and humbling herself to the misery of atonement—between this more wretched and pitiable culprit, to whom dishonour would come as a comfort and the pillory as a relief, and the older, keener, wiser man, who, to obtain satisfaction for the wrong he has suffered, devises the infernally ingenious plan of conjoining himself with his wronger, living with him, living upon him, and while he pretends to minister to his hidden ailment and to sympathise with his pain, revels in his unsuspected knowledge of these things and stimulates them by malignant arts. The attitude of Roger Chillingworth, and the means he takes to compensate himself—these are the highly original elements in the situation that Hawthorne so ingeniously treats. None of his works are so impregnated with that after-sense of the old Puritan consciousness of life to which allusion has so often been made. If, as M. Montégut [3] says, the qualities of his ancestors *filtered* down through generations into his composition, *The Scarlet Letter* was, as it were, the vessel that gathered up the last of the precious drops. And I say this not because the story happens to be of so-called historical cast, to be told of the early days of Massachusetts and of people in steeple-crowned hats and sad-coloured garments. The historical colouring is rather weak than otherwise; there is little elaboration of detail, of the modern realism of research; and the author has made no great point of causing his figures to speak the English of their period. Nevertheless, the book is full of the moral presence of the race that invented Hester's penance—diluted and complicated with other things, but still perfectly recognisable. Puritanism, in a word, is there, not only objectively, as Hawthorne tried to place it there, but subjectively as well. Not, I mean, in his judgment of his characters, in any harshness of prejudice, or in the obtrusion of a moral lesson; but in the very quality of his own vision, in the tone of the picture, in a certain coldness and exclusiveness of treatment.

The faults of the book are, to my sense, a want of reality and an abuse of the fanciful element—of a certain superficial symbolism. The people strike me not as characters, but as representatives, very picturesquely arranged, of a single state of mind; and the interest of the story lies, not in them, but in the situation, which is insistently kept before us, with little progression, though with a great deal, as I have said, of a certain stable variation; and to which they, out of their reality, contribute little that helps it to live and move. I was made to feel this want of reality, this over-ingenuity, of *The Scarlet Letter,* by chancing not long since upon a novel which was read fifty years ago much more than to-day, but which is still worth reading—the story of *Adam Blair,* by John Gibson Lockhart.[4] This interesting and powerful little tale has a great deal of analogy with Hawthorne's novel—quite enough, at least, to suggest

3. **M. Montégut:** Émile Montégut (1825–95), French critic, author of *Un Romancier Pessimiste* (*Revue des Deux Mondes*, 1860) and other studies of American writers. 4. **John Gibson Lockhart:** Scottish writer and editor (1794–1854), son-in-law and biographer of Sir Walter Scott, author of *Adam Blair* (1822).

a comparison between them; and the comparison is a very interesting one to make, for it speedily leads us to larger considerations than simple resemblances and divergences of plot.

Adam Blair, like Arthur Dimmesdale, is a Calvinistic minister who becomes the lover of a married woman, is overwhelmed with remorse at his misdeed, and makes a public confession of it; then expiates it by resigning his pastoral office and becoming the humble tiller of the soil, as his father had been. The two stories are of about the same length, and each is the masterpiece (putting aside of course, as far as Lockhart is concerned, the *Life of Scott*) of the author. They deal alike with the manners of a rigidly theological society, and even in certain details they correspond. In each of them, between the guilty pair, there is a charming little girl; though I hasten to say that Sarah Blair (who is not the daughter of the heroine, but the legitimate offspring of the hero, a widower) is far from being as brilliant and graceful an apparition as the admirable little Pearl of *The Scarlet Letter.* The main difference between the two tales is the fact that in the American story the husband plays an all-important part, and in the Scottish plays almost none at all. *Adam Blair* is the history of the passion, and *The Scarlet Letter* the history of its sequel; but nevertheless, if one has read the two books at a short interval, it is impossible to avoid confronting them. I confess that a large portion of the interest of *Adam Blair,* to my mind, when once I had perceived that it would repeat in a great measure the situation of *The Scarlet Letter,* lay in noting its difference of tone. It threw into relief the passionless quality of Hawthorne's novel, its element of cold and ingenious fantasy, its elaborate imaginative delicacy. These things do not precisely constitute a weakness in *The Scarlet Letter;* indeed, in a certain way they constitute a great strength; but the absence of a certain something warm and straightforward, a trifle more grossly human and vulgarly natural, which one finds in *Adam Blair,* will always make Hawthorne's tale less touching to a large number of even very intelligent readers, than a love-story told with the robust, synthetic pathos which served Lockhart so well. His novel is not of the first rank (I should call it an excellent second-rate one), but it borrows a charm from the fact that his vigorous, but not strongly imaginative, mind was impregnated with the reality of his subject. He did not always succeed in rendering this reality; the expression is sometimes awkward and poor. But the reader feels that his vision was clear, and his feeling about the matter very strong and rich. Hawthorne's imagination, on the other hand, plays with his theme so

incessantly, leads it such a dance through the moon-lighted air of his intellect, that the thing cools off, as it were, hardens and stiffens, and, producing effects much more exquisite, leaves the reader with a sense of having handled a splendid piece of silversmith's work. Lockhart, by means much more vulgar, produces at moments a greater illusion, and satifies our inevitable desire for something, in the people in whom it is sought to interest us, that should be of the same pitch and the same continuity with ourselves. Above all, it is interesting to see how the same subject appears to two men of a thoroughly different cast of mind and of a different race. Lockhart was struck with the warmth of the subject that offered itself to him, and Hawthorne with its coldness; the one with its glow, its sentimental interest—the other with its shadow, its moral interest. Lockhart's story is as decent, as severely draped, as *The Scarlet Letter;* but the author has a more vivid sense than appears to have imposed itself upon Hawthorne, of some of the incidents of the situation he describes; his tempted man and tempting woman are more actual and personal; his heroine in especial, though not in the least a delicate or a subtle conception, has a sort of credible, visible, palpable property, a vulgar roundness and relief, which are lacking to the dim and chastened image of Hester Prynne. But I am going too far; I am comparing simplicity with subtlety, the usual with the refined. Each man wrote as his turn of mind impelled him, but each expressed something more than himself. Lockhart was a dense, substantial Briton, with a taste for the concrete, and Hawthorne was a thin New Englander, with a miasmatic conscience.

In *The Scarlet Letter* there is a great deal of symbolism; there is, I think, too much. It is overdone at times, and becomes mechanical; it ceases to be impressive, and grazes triviality. The idea of the mystic *A* which the young minister finds imprinted upon his breast and eating into his flesh, in sympathy with the embroidered badge that Hester is condemned to wear, appears to me to be a case in point. This suggestion should, I think, have been just made and dropped; to insist upon it and return to it, is to exaggerate the weak side of the subject. Hawthorne returns to it constantly, plays with it, and seems charmed by it; until at last the reader feels tempted to declare that his enjoyment of it is puerile. In the admirable scene, so superbly conceived and beautifully executed, in which Mr. Dimmesdale, in the stillness of the night, in the middle of the sleeping town, feels impelled to go and stand upon the scaffold where his mistress had formerly enacted her dreadful penance, and then, seeing Hester pass along the street, from watching at a sick-bed, with little Pearl at her side, calls them both to come and stand there beside him—in this masterly episode the effect is almost spoiled by the introduction of one of these superficial conceits. What leads up to it is very fine—so fine that I cannot do better than quote it as a specimen of one of the striking pages of the book.

But before Mr. Dimmesdale had done speaking, a light gleamed far and wide over all the muffled sky. It was doubtless caused by one of those meteors which the night-watcher may so often observe burning out to waste in the vacant regions of the atmosphere. So powerful was its radiance that it thoroughly illuminated the dense medium of cloud, betwixt the sky and earth. The great vault brightened, like the dome of an immense lamp. It showed the familiar scene of the street with the distinctness of mid-day, but also with the awfulness that is always imparted to familiar objects by an unaccustomed light. The wooden houses, with their jutting stories and quaint gable-peaks; the door-steps and thresholds, with the early grass springing up about them; the garden-plots, black with freshly-turned earth; the wheel-track, little worn, and, even in the market-place, margined with green on either side;—all were visible, but with a singularity of aspect that seemed to give another moral interpretation to the things of this world than they had ever borne before. And there stood the minister, with his hand over his heart; and Hester Prynne, with the embroidered letter glimmering on her bosom; and little Pearl, herself a symbol, and the connecting-link between these two. They stood in the noon of that strange and solemn splendour, as if it were the light that is to reveal all secrets, and the daybreak that shall unite all that belong to one another.

That is imaginative, impressive, poetic; but when, almost immediately afterwards, the author goes on to say that "the minister looking upward to the zenith, beheld there the appearance of an immense letter—the letter *A*—marked out in lines of dull red light," we feel that he goes too far and is in danger of crossing the line that separates the sublime from its intimate neighbour. We are tempted to say that this is not moral tragedy, but physical comedy. In the same way, too much is made of the intimation that Hester's badge had a scorching property, and that if one touched it one would immediately withdraw one's hand. Hawthorne is perpetually looking for images which shall place themselves in picturesque correspondence with the spiritual facts with which he is concerned, and of course the search is of the very essence of poetry. But in such a process discretion is everything, and when the image becomes importunate it is in danger of seeming to stand for nothing more serious than itself. When Hester meets the minister by appointment in the forest, and sits talking with him while little Pearl wanders away and plays by the edge of the brook, the child is represented as at last making her way over to the other side of the woodland stream, and disporting herself there in a manner which makes her mother feel herself "in some indistinct and tantalising manner, estranged from Pearl; as if the child, in her lonely ramble through the forest, had strayed out of the sphere in which she and her mother dwelt together, and was now vainly seeking to return to it." And Hawthorne devotes a chapter to this idea of the child's having, by putting the brook between Hester and herself, established a kind of spiritual gulf, on the verge of which her little fantastic person innocently mocks at her mother's sense of bereavement. This conception belongs, one would say, quite to the lighter order of a story-teller's devices, and the reader hardly goes with Hawthorne in the large development he gives to it. He hardly goes with him either, I think, in his extreme predilection for a small number of vague ideas which are represented by such terms as "sphere" and "sympathies." Hawthorne makes too liberal a use of these two substantives; it is the solitary defect of his style; and it counts as a defect partly because the words in question are a sort of specialty with certain writers immeasurably inferior to himself.

I had not meant, however, to expatiate upon his defects, which are of the slenderest and most venial kind. *The Scarlet Letter* has the beauty and harmony of all original and complete conceptions, and its weaker spots, whatever they are, are not of its essence; they are mere light flaws and inequalities of surface. One can often return to it; it supports familiarity and has the inexhaustible charm and mystery of great works of art. It is admirably written. Hawthorne afterwards polished his style to a still higher degree, but in his later productions—it is almost always the case in a writer's later productions—there is a touch of mannerism. In *The Scarlet Letter* there is a high degree of polish, and at the same time a charming freshness; his phrase is less conscious of itself. His biographer very justly calls attention to the fact that his style was excellent from the beginning; that he appeared to have passed through no phase of learning how to write, but was in possession of his means from the first of his handling a pen. His early tales, perhaps, were not of a character to subject his faculty of expression to a very severe test, but a man who had not Hawthorne's natural sense of language would certainly have contrived to write them less well. This natural sense of language—this turn for saying things lightly and yet touchingly, picturesquely yet simply, and for infusing a gently colloquial tone into matter of the most unfamiliar import, he had evidently cultivated with great assiduity. I have spoken of the anomalous character of his Note-Books—of his going to such pains often to make a record of incidents which either were not worth remembering or could be easily remembered without its aid. But it helps us to understand the Note-Books if we regard them as a literary exercise. They were compositions, as school-boys say, in which the subject was only the pretext, and the main point was to write a certain amount of excellent English. Hawthorne must at least have written a great many of these things for practice, and he must often have said to himself that it was better practice to write about trifles, because it was a greater tax upon one's skill to make them interesting. And his theory was just, for he has almost always made his trifles interesting. In his novels his art of saying things well is very positively tested, for here he treats of those matters among which it is very easy for a blundering writer to go wrong—the subtleties and mysteries of life, the moral and spiritual maze. In such a passage as one I have marked for quotation from *The Scarlet Letter,* there is the stamp of the genius of style.

Hester Prynne, gazing steadfastly at the clergyman, felt a dreary influence come over her, but wherefore or whence she knew not, unless that he seemed so remote from her own sphere and utterly beyond her reach. One glance of recognition she had imagined must needs pass between them. She thought of the dim forest with its little dell of solitude, and love, and anguish, and the mossy tree-trunk, where, sitting hand in hand, they had mingled their sad and passionate talk with the melancholy murmur of the brook. How deeply had they known each other then! And was this the man? She hardly knew him now! He, moving proudly past, enveloped as it were in the rich music, with the procession of majestic and venerable fathers; he, so unattainable in his worldly position, and still more so in that far vista in his unsympathising thoughts, through which she now beheld him! Her spirit sank with the idea that all must have been a delusion, and that vividly as she had dreamed it, there could be no real bond betwixt the clergyman and herself. And thus much of woman there was in Hester, that she could scarcely forgive him—least of all now, when the heavy footstep of their approaching fate might be heard, nearer, nearer, nearer!—for being able to withdraw himself so completely from their mutual world, while she groped darkly, and stretched forth her cold hands, and found him not!

GUY DE MAUPASSANT

◆

❬ FIRST published in the *Fortnightly Review*, a conservative English magazine, in March, 1888, the following essay was reprinted in the same year in *Partial Portraits*, a volume of James's literary essays. The immediate occasion of the essay was, as James makes clear, the publication in Paris earlier in the same year of *Pierre et Jean*, a novel of Maupassant's to which that French writer and master of the short story had contributed an Introduction setting forth his theories of fiction. The deeper reason for the essay was James's long immersion in the French fiction of the Realist and Naturalist schools, including the work of Maupassant himself, with whom he was personally acquainted.

No important American or English writer of his time knew France, its people, its language and its literature, better than James did, and from his early youth he had written essays praising the fine art and tough honesty of such novelists as Balzac, Stendhal, and Flaubert—novelists who were then generally dismissed as "indecent" and "pessimistic" in England and the United States—that is, when they were read at all. Guy de Maupassant (1850–93) was Flaubert's disciple and successor and won great fame in France with his successive volumes of short stories, beginning with *La Maison Tellier* (1881). In time his work was translated into English and just about all other languages, eventually exerting a considerable influence on American writing, including that of Ernest Hemingway. (Note in this connection what James says below about Maupassant's "hardness" and his preference for the "epic" over the "analytic" approach.)

But Maupassant's fame in the "Anglo-Saxon" (James's term) countries had to wait until H. G. Wells and Arnold Bennett in England, Stephen Crane and Theodore Dreiser in America, had overcome some of our puritan scruples against the frank representation of what James calls "the sexual impulse." Through the efforts of these and other similar writers, the French sensuality, together with the French art of storytelling, has of course become thoroughly naturalized in the English-writing countries, even influencing the early poetry of T. S. Eliot (e.g., "The Fire Sermon" in *The Waste Land*).

Meanwhile, in the Maupassant essay, James strove to deal courageously and intelligently with the moral and aesthetic issues presented by such fiction as Maupassant's. And if James's liberality is undermined by his occasional prudishness, his prudishness is more than matched by his sometimes devastating remarks about the Anglo-Saxon literary mind, its needless reticences, its "optimism of ignorance." For James is also indirectly engaged in analyzing and defending his own morality as an artist. "M. de Maupassant has simply skipped the whole reflective part of his men and women—that reflective part which governs conduct and produces character," James writes, perhaps unfairly to Maupassant, but with a firm sense of what is important in men and women from his own viewpoint. Indeed, in 1899, he published a story, "Paste," which he acknowledged to be an attempt to reverse the blind fate ruling the characters in Maupassant's famous tale "The Necklace" (*Le Collier*).

◊

I

THE FIRST artists, in any line, are doubtless not those whose general ideas about their art are most often on their lips—those who most abound in precept, apology, and formula and can best tell us the reasons and the philosophy of things. We know the first usually by their energetic practice, the constancy with which they apply their principles, and the serenity with which they leave us to hunt for their secret in the illustration, the concrete example. None the less it often happens that a valid artist utters his mystery, flashes upon us for a moment the light by which he works, shows us the rule by which he holds it just that he should be measured. This accident is happiest, I think, when it is soonest over; the shortest explanations of the products of genius are the best, and there is many a creator of living figures whose friends, however full of faith in his inspiration, will do well to pray for him when he sallies forth into the dim wilderness of theory. The doctrine is apt to be so much less inspired than the work, the work is often so much more intelligent than the doctrine. M. Guy de Maupassant has lately traversed with a firm and rapid step a literary crisis of this kind; he has clambered safely up the bank at the further end of the morass. If he has relieved himself in the preface to *Pierre et Jean*, the last-published of his tales, he has also rendered a service to his friends; he has not only come home in a recognisable plight, escaping gross disaster with a success which even his extreme good sense was far from making in advance a matter of course, but he has expressed in intelligible terms (that by itself is a ground of felicitation) his most general idea, his own sense of his direction. He has arranged, as it were, the light in which he wishes to sit. If it is a question of attempting, under however many disadvantages, a sketch of him, the critic's business therefore is simplified: there will be no difficulty in placing him, for he himself has chosen the spot, he has made the chalk-mark on the floor.

I may as well say at once that in dissertation M. de Maupassant does not write with his best pen; the philosopher in his composition is perceptibly inferior to the story-teller. I would rather have written half a page of *Boule de Suif* [1] than the whole of the introduction to Flaubert's *Letters to Madame Sand;* [2] and his little disquisition on the novel in general, attached to that particular example of it which he has just put forth, is considerably less to the point than the masterpiece which it ushers in. In short, as a commentator M. de Maupassant is slightly common, while as an artist he is wonderfully rare. Of course we must, in judging a writer, take one thing with another, and if I could make up my mind that M. de Maupassant is weak in theory, it would almost make me like him better, render him more approachable, give him the touch of softness that he lacks, and show us a human flaw. The most general quality of the author of *La Maison Tellier* [3] and *Bel-Ami*, [4] the impression that remains last, after the others have been accounted for, is an essential hardness— hardness of form, hardness of nature; and it would put us more at ease to find that if the fact with him (the fact of execution) is so extraordinarily definite and adequate, his explanations, after it, were a little vague and sentimental. But I am not sure that he must even be held foolish to have noticed the race of critics: he is at any rate so much less foolish than several of that fraternity. He has said his say concisely and as if he were saying it once for all. In fine, his readers must be grateful to him for such a passage as that in which he remarks that whereas the public at large very legitimately says to a writer, "Console me, amuse me, terrify me, make me cry, make me dream, or make me think," what the sincere critic says is, "Make me something fine in the form that shall suit you best, according to your temperament." This seems to me to put into a nutshell the whole question of the different classes of fiction, concerning which there has recently been so much discourse. There are simply as many different kinds as there are persons practising the art, for if a picture, a tale, or a novel be a direct

MAUPASSANT.   **1.** *Boule de Suif*: literally "ball of fat," but called by its French title in *The Collected Novels and Stories of Guy de Maupassant*, trans. and ed. by Ernest Boyd, 18 vols., New York (1922–26), Vol. I. In the footnotes that follow, other stories referred to by James will be given the English titles they bear in Boyd's standard edition, together with the numbers of the volumes in which they appear. Some of James's lengthy lists of titles have, however, been omitted from the text of the essay. The excisions are indicated by three dots.   **2.** *Letters to Madame Sand*: A volume of Flaubert's letters to the French novelist George Sand (1804–76), with an Introduction by Maupassant, was published at Paris in 1884.   **3.** *La Maison Tellier*: *Madame Tellier's Establishment*, Vol. I.   **4.** *Bel-Ami*: *Bel-Ami*, Vol. VII.

impression of life (and that surely constitutes its interest and value), the impression will vary according to the plate that takes it, the particular structure and mixture of the recipient.

I am not sure that I know what M. de Maupassant means when he says, "The critic shall appreciate the result only according to the nature of the effort; he has no right to concern himself with tendencies." The second clause of that observation strikes me as rather in the air, thanks to the vagueness of the last word. But our author adds to the definiteness of his contention when he goes on to say that any form of the novel is simply a vision of the world from the standpoint of a person constituted after a certain fashion, and that it is therefore absurd to say that there is, for the novelist's use, only one reality of things. This seems to me commendable, not as a flight of metaphysics, hovering over bottomless gulfs of controversy, but, on the contrary, as a just indication of the vanity of certain dogmatisms. The particular way we see the world is our particular illusion about it, says M. de Maupassant, and this illusion fits itself to our organs and senses; our receptive vessel becomes the furniture of *our* little plot of the universal consciousness.

"How childish, moreover, to believe in reality, since we each carry our own in our thought and in our organs. Our eyes, our ears, our sense of smell, of taste, differing from one person to another, create as many truths as there are men upon earth. And our minds, taking instruction from these organs, so diversely impressed, understand, analyse, judge, as if each of us belonged to a different race. Each one of us, therefore, forms for himself an illusion of the world, which is the illusion poetic, or sentimental, or joyous, or melancholy, or unclean, or dismal, according to his nature. And the writer has no other mission than to reproduce faithfully this illusion, with all the contrivances of art that he has learned and has at his command. The illusion of beauty, which is a human convention! The illusion of ugliness, which is a changing opinion! The illusion of truth, which is never immutable! The illusion of the ignoble, which attracts so many! The great artists are those who make humanity accept their particular illusion. Let us, therefore, not get angry with any one theory, since every theory is the generalised expression of a temperament asking itself questions."

What is interesting in this is not that M. de Maupassant happens to hold that we have no universal measure of the truth, but that it is the last word on a question of art from a writer who is rich in experience and has had success in a very rare degree. It is of secondary importance that our impression should be called, or not called, an illusion; what is excellent is that our author has

stated more neatly than we have lately seen it done that the value of the artist resides in the clearness with which he gives forth that impression. His particular organism constitutes a *case,* and the critic is intelligent in proportion as he apprehends and enters into that case. To quarrel with it because it is not another, which it could not possibly have been without a wholly different outfit, appears to M. de Maupassant a deplorable waste of time. If this appeal to our disinterestedness may strike some readers as chilling (through their inability to conceive of any other form than the one they like—a limitation excellent for a reader but poor for a judge), the occasion happens to be none of the best for saying so, for M. de Maupassant himself precisely presents all the symptoms of a "case" in the most striking way, and shows us how far the consideration of them may take us. Embracing such an opportunity as this, and giving ourselves to it freely, seems to me indeed to be a course more fruitful in valid conclusions, as well as in entertainment by the way, than the more common method of establishing one's own premises. To make clear to ourselves those of the author of *Pierre et Jean*—those to which he is committed by the very nature of his mind—is an attempt that will both stimulate and repay curiosity. There is no way of looking at his work less dry, less academic, for as we proceed from one of his peculiarities to another, the whole horizon widens, yet without our leaving firm ground, and we see ourselves landed, step by step, in the most general questions—those explanations of things which reside in the race, in the society. Of course there are cases and cases, and it is the salient ones that the disinterested critic is delighted to meet.

What makes M. de Maupassant salient is two facts: the first of which is that his gifts are remarkably strong and definite, and the second that he writes directly *from* them, as it were: holds the fullest, the most uninterrupted—I scarcely know what to call it—the boldest communication with them. A case is poor when the cluster of the artist's sensibilities is small, or they themselves are wanting in keenness, or else when the personage fails to admit them—either through ignorance, or diffidence, or stupidity, or the error of a false ideal —to what may be called a legitimate share in his attempt. It is, I think, among English and American writers that this latter accident is most liable to occur; more than the French we are apt to be misled by some convention or other as to the sort of feeler we *ought* to put forth, forgetting that the best one will be the one that nature happens to have given us. We have doubtless often enough the courage of our opinions (when it befalls that we have opinions), but we have not so constantly that of our perceptions. There is a whole side of our perceptive apparatus that we in fact neglect, and there are probably many among us who would erect this tendency into a duty. M. de Maupassant neglects nothing that he possesses; he cultivates his garden with admirable energy; and if there is a flower you miss from the rich parterre, you may be sure that it could not possibly have been raised, his mind not containing the soil for it. He is plainly of the opinion that the first duty of the artist, and the thing that makes him most useful to his fellow-men, is to master his instrument, whatever it may happen to be.

His own is that of the senses, and it is through them alone, or almost alone, that life appeals to him; it is almost alone by their help that he describes it, that he produces brilliant works. They render him this great assistance because they are evidently, in his constitution, extraordinarily alive; there is scarcely a page in all his twenty volumes that does not testify to their vivacity. Nothing could be further from his thought than to disavow them and to minimise their importance. He accepts them frankly, gratefully, works them, rejoices in them. If he were told that there are many English writers who would be sorry to go with him in this, he would, I imagine, staring, say that that is about what was to have been expected of the Anglo-Saxon race, or even that many of them probably could not go with him if they would. Then he would ask how our authors can be so foolish as to sacrifice such a *moyen*,[5] how they can afford to, and exclaim, "They must be pretty works, those they produce, and give a fine, true, complete account of life, with such omissions, such lacunæ!" M. de Maupassant's productions teach us, for instance, that his sense of smell is exceptionally acute—as acute as that of those animals of the field and forest whose subsistence and security depend upon it. It might be thought that he would, as a student of the human race, have found an abnormal development of this faculty embarrassing, scarcely knowing what to do with it, where to place it. But such an apprehension betrays an imperfect conception of his directness and resolution, as well as of his constant economy of means. Nothing whatever prevents him from representing the relations of men and women as largely governed by the scent of the parties. Human life in his pages (would this not be the most general description he would give of it?) appears for the most part as a

sort of concert of odours, and his people are perpetually engaged, or he is engaged on their behalf, in sniffing up and distinguishing them, in some pleasant or painful exercise of the nostril. "If everything in life speaks to the nostril, why on earth shouldn't we say so?" I suppose him to inquire; "and what a proof of the empire of poor conventions and hypocrisies, *chez vous autres*,[6] that you should pretend to describe and characterise, and yet take no note (or so little that it comes to the same thing) of that essential sign!"

Not less powerful is his visual sense, the quick, direct discrimination of his eye, which explains the singularly vivid concision of his descriptions. These are never prolonged nor analytic, have nothing of enumeration, of the quality of the observer, who counts the items to be sure he has made up the sum. His eye *selects* unerringly, unscrupulously, almost impudently—catches the particular thing in which the character of the object or the scene resides, and, by expressing it with the artful brevity of a master, leaves a convincing, original picture. If he is inveterately synthetic, he is never more so than in the way he brings this hard, short, intelligent gaze to bear. His vision of the world is for the most part a vision of ugliness, and even when it is not, there is in his easy power to generalise a certain absence of love, a sort of bird's-eye-view contempt. He has none of the superstitions of observation, none of our English indulgences, our tender and often imaginative superficialities. If he glances into a railway carriage bearing its freight into the Parisian suburbs of a summer Sunday, a dozen dreary lives map themselves out in a flash.

"There were stout ladies in farcical clothes, those middle-class goodwives of the *banlieue* who replace the distinction they don't possess by an irrelevant dignity; gentlemen weary of the office, with sallow faces and twisted bodies, and one of their shoulders a little forced up by perpetual bending at work over a table. Their anxious, joyless faces spoke moreover of domestic worries, incessant needs for money, old hopes finally shattered; for they all belonged to the army of poor threadbare devils who vegetate frugally in a mean little plaster house, with a flower-bed for a garden.". . .

Even in a brighter picture, such as the admirable vignette of the drive of Madame Tellier and her companions, the whole thing is an impression, as painters say nowadays, in which the figures are cheap. The six women at the station clamber into a country cart and go jolting through the Norman landscape to the village.

---

5. *moyen:* talent.

6. *chez vous autres:* "among you others" (i.e., Anglo-Saxons).

"But presently the jerky trot of the nag shook the vehicle so terribly that the chairs began to dance, tossing up the travellers to right, to left, with movements like puppets, scared grimaces, cries of dismay suddenly interrupted by a more violent bump. They clutched the sides of the trap, their bonnets turned over on to their backs, or upon the nose or the shoulder; and the white horse continued to go, thrusting out his head and straightening the little tail, hairless like that of a rat, with which from time to time he whisked his buttocks. Joseph Rivet, with one foot stretched upon the shaft, the other leg bent under him, and his elbows very high, held the reins and emitted from his throat every moment a kind of cluck which caused the animal to prick up his ears and quicken his pace. On either side of the road the green country stretched away. The colza, in flower, produced in spots a great carpet of undulating yellow, from which there rose a strong, wholesome smell, a smell penetrating and pleasant, carried very far by the breeze. In the tall rye the cornflowers held up their little azure heads, which the women wished to pluck; but M. Rivet refused to stop. Then, in some place, a whole field looked as if it were sprinkled with blood, it was so crowded with poppies. And in the midst of the great level, taking colour in this fashion from the flowers of the soil, the trap passed on with the jog of the white horse, seeming itself to carry a nosegay of richer hues; it disappeared behind the big trees of a farm, to come out again where the foliage stopped and parade afresh through the green and yellow crops, pricked with red or blue, its blazing cartload of women, which receded in the sunshine."

As regards the other sense, the sense *par excellence*, the sense which we scarcely mention in English fiction, and which I am not very sure I shall be allowed to mention in an English periodical, M. de Maupassant speaks for that, and of it, with extraordinary distinctness and authority. To say that it occupies the first place in his picture is to say too little; it covers in truth the whole canvas, and his work is little else but a report of its innumerable manifestations. These manifestations are not, for him, so many incidents of life; they are life itself, they represent the standing answer to any question that we may ask about it. He describes them in detail, with a familiarity and a frankness which leave nothing to be added; I should say with singular truth, if I did not consider that in regard to this article he may be taxed with a certain exaggeration. M. de Maupassant would doubtless affirm that where the empire of the sexual sense is concerned, no exaggeration is possible: nevertheless it may be said that whatever depths may be discovered by those who dig for them, the impression of the human spectacle for him who takes it as it comes has less analogy with that of the monkeys' cage than this admirable writer's account of it. I speak of the human

spectacle as we Anglo-Saxons see it—as we Anglo-Saxons pretend we see it, M. de Maupassant would possibly say.

At any rate, I have perhaps touched upon this peculiarity sufficiently to explain my remark that his point of view is almost solely that of the senses. If he is a very interesting case, this makes him also an embarrassing one, embarrassing and mystifying for the moralist. I may as well admit that no writer of the day strikes me as equally so. To find M. de Maupassant a lion in the path—that may seem to some people a singular proof of want of courage; but I think the obstacle will not be made light of by those who have really taken the measure of the animal. We are accustomed to think, we of the English faith, that a cynic is a living advertisement of his errors, especially in proportion as he is a thorough-going one; and M. de Maupassant's cynicism, unrelieved as it is, will not be disposed of off-hand by a critic of a competent literary sense. Such a critic is not slow to perceive, to his no small confusion, that though, judging from usual premises, the author of *Bel-Ami* ought to be a warning, he somehow is not. His baseness, as it pervades him, ought to be written all over him; yet somehow there are there certain aspects—and those commanding, as the house-agents say—in which it is not in the least to be perceived. It is easy to exclaim that if he judges life only from the point of view of the senses, many are the noble and exquisite things that he must leave out. What he leaves out has no claim to get itself considered till after we have done justice to what he takes in. It is this positive side of M. de Maupassant that is most remarkable—the fact that his literary character is so complete and edifying. *"Auteur à peu près irréprochable dans un genre qui ne l'est pas,"* as that excellent critic M. Jules Lemaître [7] says of him, he disturbs us by associating a conscience and a high standard with a temper long synonymous, in our eyes, with an absence of scruples. The situation would be simpler certainly if he were a bad writer; but none the less it is possible, I think, on the whole, to circumvent him, even without attempting to prove that after all he is one.

The latter part of his introduction to *Pierre et Jean* is less felicitous than the beginning, but we learn from it—and this is interesting—that he regards the analytic fashion of telling a story, which has lately begotten in his own country some such remarkable experiments (few votaries as it has attracted among ourselves), as very much less profit-

7. *Auteur . . .* **Lemaître:** "An almost irreproachable author in a field that is *not* irreproachable." Jules Lemaître (1853–1914), French critic.

able than the simple epic manner which "avoids with care all complicated explanations, all dissertations upon motives, and confines itself to making persons and events pass before our eyes." M. de Maupassant adds that in his view "psychology should be hidden in a book, as it is hidden in reality under the facts of existence. The novel conceived in this manner gains interest, movement, colour, the bustle of life." When it is a question of an artistic process, we must always mistrust very sharp distinctions, for there is surely in every method a little of every other method. It is as difficult to describe an action without glancing at its motive, its moral history, as it is to describe a motive without glancing at its practical consequence. Our history and our fiction are what we do; but it surely is not more easy to determine where what we do begins than to determine where it ends—notoriously a hopeless task. Therefore it would take a very subtle sense to draw a hard and fast line on the borderland of explanation and illustration. If psychology be hidden in life, as, according to M. de Maupassant, it should be in a book, the question immediately comes up, "From whom is it hidden?" From some people, no doubt, but very much less from others; and all depends upon the observer, the nature of one's observation, and one's curiosity. For some people motives, reasons, relations, explanations, are a part of the very surface of the drama, with the footlights beating full upon them. For me an act, an incident, an attitude, may be a sharp, detached, isolated thing, of which I give a full account in saying that in such and such a way it came off. For you it may be hung about with implications, with relations, and conditions as necessary to help you to recognise it as the clothes of your friends are to help you know them in the street. You feel that they would seem strange to you without petticoats and trousers.

M. de Maupassant would probably urge that the right thing is to know, or to guess, how events come to pass, but to say as little about it as possible. There are matters in regard to which he feels the importance of being explicit, but that is not one of them. The contention to which I allude strikes me as rather arbitrary, so difficult is it to put one's finger upon the reason why, for instance, there should be so little mystery about what happened to Christiane Andermatt, in *Mont-Oriol,*[8] when she went to walk on the hills with Paul Brétigny, and so much, say, about the forces that formed her for that gentleman's convenience, or those lying behind any other odd collapse that

8. *Mont-Oriol: Mont-Oriol*, Vol. XI.

our author may have related. The rule misleads, and the best rule certainly is the tact of the individual writer, which will adapt itself to the material as the material comes to him. The cause we plead is ever pretty sure to be the cause of our idiosyncrasies, and if M. de Maupassant thinks meanly of "explanations," it is, I suspect, that they come to him in no great affluence. His view of the conduct of man is so simple as scarcely to require them; and indeed so far as they are needed he *is,* virtually, explanatory. He deprecates reference to motives, but there is one, covering an immense ground in his horizon, as I have already hinted, to which he perpetually refers. If the sexual impulse be not a moral antecedent, it is none the less the wire that moves almost all M. de Maupassant's puppets, and as he has not hidden it, I cannot see that he has eliminated analysis or made a sacrifice to discretion. His pages are studded with that particular analysis; he is constantly peeping behind the curtain, telling us what he discovers there. The truth is that the admirable system of simplification which makes his tales so rapid and so concise (especially his shorter ones, for his novels in some degree, I think, suffer from it), strikes us as not in the least a conscious intellectual effort, a selective, comparative process. He tells us all he knows, all he suspects, and if these things take no account of the moral nature of man, it is because he has no window looking in that direction, and not because artistic scruples have compelled him to close it up. The very compact mansion in which he dwells presents on that side a perfectly dead wall.

This is why, if his axiom that you produce the effect of truth better by painting people from the outside than from the inside has a large utility, his example is convincing in a much higher degree. A writer is fortunate when his theory and his limitations so exactly correspond, when his curiosities may be appeased with such precision and promptitude. M. de Maupassant contends that the most that the analytic novelist can do is to put himself—his own peculiarities—into the costume of the figure analysed. This may be true, but if it applies to one manner of representing people who are not ourselves, it applies also to any other manner. It is the limitation, the difficulty of the novelist, to whatever clan or camp he may belong. M. de Maupassant is remarkably objective and impersonal, but he would go too far if he were to entertain the belief that he has kept himself out of his books. They speak of him eloquently, even if it only be to tell us how easy—how easy, given his talent of course—he has found this impersonality. Let us hasten to add that in the case of describing a character it is doubtless more difficult to convey the impression of something that is not one's self (the constant effort, however delusive at bottom, of the novelist), than in the case of describing some object more immediately visible. The operation is more delicate, but that circumstance only increases the beauty of the problem.

On the question of style our author has some excellent remarks; we may be grateful indeed for every one of them, save an odd reflection about the way to "become original" if we happen not to be so. The recipe for this transformation, it would appear, is to sit down in front of a blazing fire, or a tree in a plain, or any object we encounter in the regular way of business, and remain there until the tree, or the fire, or the object, whatever it be, become different for us from all other specimens of the same class. I doubt whether this system would always answer, for surely the resemblance is what we wish to discover, quite as much as the difference, and the best way to preserve it is not to look for something opposed to it. Is not this indication of the road to take to become, as a writer, original touched with the same fallacy as the recommendation about eschewing analysis? It is the only *naïveté* I have encountered in M. de Maupassant's many volumes. The best originality is the most unconscious, and the best way to describe a tree is the way in which it has struck us. "Ah, but we don't always know how it has struck us," the answer to that may be, "and it takes some time and ingenuity—much fasting and prayer—to find out." If we do not know, it probably has not struck us very much: so little indeed that our inquiry had better be relegated to that closed chamber of an artist's meditations, that sacred back kitchen, which no *a priori* rule can light up. The best thing the artist's adviser can do in such a case is to trust him and turn away, to let him fight the matter out with his conscience. And be this said with a full appreciation of the degree in which M. de Maupassant's observations on the whole question of a writer's style, at the point we have come to to-day, bear the stamp of intelligence and experience. His own style is of so excellent a tradition that the presumption is altogether in favour of what he may have to say.

He feels oppressively, discouragingly, as many another of his countrymen must have felt—for the French have worked their language as no other people have done—the penalty of coming at the end of three centuries of literature, the difficulty of dealing with an instrument of expression so worn by friction, of drawing new sounds from the old familiar pipe. "When we read, so saturated with French writing as we are that our whole body gives us the impression of being a paste made of words, do we ever find a line, a thought, which is not familiar to us, and of which we have not had at least a confused presentiment?" And he adds that the matter is simple enough for the writer who only seeks to amuse the public by means already known; he attempts little, and he produces "with confidence, in the candour of his mediocrity," works which answer no question and leave no trace. It is he who wants to do more than this that has less and less an easy time of it. Everything seems to him to have been done, every effect produced, every combination already made. If he be a man of genius, his trouble is lightened, for mysterious ways are revealed to him, and new combinations spring up for him even after novelty is dead. It is to the simple man of taste and talent, who has only a conscience and a will, that the situation may sometimes well appear desperate; he judges himself as he goes, and he can only go step by step over ground where every step is already a footprint.

If it be a miracle whenever there is a fresh tone, the miracle has been wrought for M. de Maupassant. Or is he simply a man of genius to whom short cuts have been disclosed in the watches of the night? At any rate he has had faith—religion has come to his aid; I mean the religion of his mother tongue, which he has loved well enough to be patient for her sake. He has arrived at the peace which passeth understanding, at a kind of conservative piety. He has taken his stand on simplicity, on a studied sobriety, being persuaded that the deepest science lies in that direction rather than in the multiplication of new terms, and on this subject he delivers himself with superlative wisdom. "There is no need of the queer, complicated, numerous, and Chinese vocabulary which is imposed on us to-day under the name of artistic writing, to fix all the shades of thought; the right way is to distinguish with an extreme clearness all those modifications of the value of a word which come from the place it occupies. Let us have fewer nouns, verbs and adjectives of an almost imperceptible sense, and more different phrases variously constructed, ingeniously cast, full of the science of sound and rhythm. Let us have an excellent general form rather than be collectors of rare terms." M. de Maupassant's practice does not fall below his exhortation (though I must confess that in the foregoing passage he makes use of the detestable expression "stylist," which I have not reproduced). Nothing can exceed the masculine firmness, the quiet force of his own style, in which every phrase is a close sequence, every epithet a paying piece, and the ground is completely cleared of the vague, the ready-made and the second-best. Less than any one to-day does he beat the air; more than any one does he hit out from the shoulder.

II

HE HAS produced a hundred short tales and only four regular novels; but if the tales deserve the first place in any candid appreciation of his talent it is not simply because they are so much the more numerous: they are also more characteristic; they represent him best in his originality, and their brevity, extreme in some cases, does not prevent them from being a collection of masterpieces. (They are very unequal, and I speak of the best.) The little story is but scantily relished in England, where readers take their fiction rather by the volume than by the page, and the novelist's idea is apt to resemble one of those old-fashioned carriages which require a wide court to turn round. In America, where it is associated pre-eminently with Hawthorne's name, with Edgar Poe's, and with that of Mr. Bret Harte,[9] the short tale has had a better fortune. France, however, has been the land of its great prosperity, and M. de Maupassant had from the first the advantage of addressing a public accustomed to catch on, as the modern phrase is, quickly. In some respects, it may be said, he encountered prejudices too friendly, for he found a tradition of indecency ready made to his hand. I say indecency with plainness, though my indication would perhaps please better with another word, for we suffer in English from a lack of roundabout names for the *conte leste* [10]—that element for which the French, with their *grivois,* their *gaillard,* their *égrillard,* their *gaudriole,* have so many convenient synonyms. It is an honoured tradition in France that the little story, in verse or in prose, should be liable to be more or less obscene (I can think only of that alternative epithet), though I hasten to add that among literary forms it does not monopolise the privilege. Our uncleanness is less producible—at any rate it is less produced.

For the last ten years our author has brought forth with regularity these condensed composi-

tions, of which, probably, to an English reader, at a first glance, the most universal sign will be their licentiousness. They really partake of this quality, however, in a very differing degree, and a second glance shows that they may be divided into numerous groups. It is not fair, I think, even to say that what they have most in common is their being extremely *lestes.* What they have most in common is their being extremely strong, and after that their being extremely brutal. A story may be obscene without being brutal, and *vice versâ,* and M. de Maupassant's contempt for those interdictions which are supposed to be made in the interest of good morals is but an incident—a very large one indeed—of his general contempt. A pessimism so great that its alliance with the love of good work, or even with the calculation of the sort of work that pays best in a country of style, is, as I have intimated, the most puzzling of anomalies (for it would seem in the light of such sentiments that nothing is worth anything), this cynical strain is the sign of such gems of narration as *La Maison Tellier* . . . The author fixes a hard eye on some small spot of human life, usually some ugly, dreary, shabby, sordid one, takes up the particle, and squeezes it either till it grimaces or till it bleeds. Sometimes the grimace is very droll, sometimes the wound is very horrible; but in either case the whole thing is real, observed, noted, and represented, not an invention or a castle in the air. M. de Maupassant sees human life as a terribly ugly business relieved by the comical, but even the comedy is for the most part the comedy of misery, of avidity, of ignorance, helplessness, and grossness. When his laugh is not for these things, it is for the little *saletés* [11] (to use one of his own favourite words) of luxurious life, which are intended to be prettier, but which can scarcely be said to brighten the picture. I like . . . many others of this category much better than his anecdotes of the mutual confidences of his little *marquises* and *baronnes.*

Not counting his novels for the moment, his tales may be divided into the three groups of those which deal with the Norman peasantry, those which deal with the *petit employé* and small shopkeeper, usually in Paris, and the miscellaneous, in which the upper walks of life are represented, and the fantastic, the whimsical, the weird, and even the supernatural, figure as well as the unexpurgated. . . . To these might almost be added as a special category the various forms in which M. de Maupassant relates adventures in railway carriages. Numerous, to his imagination, are the

---

9. **Mr. Bret Harte:** [Francis] Bret[t] Harte (1836–1902), sentimental American local-color realist and dialect poet, the popularity of whose best subject—the life of the Sierra gold camps in the 1850's and 1860's—cruelly outlasted his interest in it.
10. *conte leste:* mildly improper, or risqué, tale. The French words that follow are traditional designations of different kinds or degrees of the *conte leste.* They have no exact equivalents in English, and the shades of meaning attached to them in French are not precise in that language either.

11. *saletés:* nastinesses.

pretexts for enlivening fiction afforded by first, second, and third class compartments; the accidents (which have nothing to do with the conduct of the train) that occur there constitute no inconsiderable part of our earthly transit.

It is surely by his Norman peasant that his tales will live; he knows this worthy as if he had made him, understands him down to the ground, puts him on his feet with a few of the freest, most plastic touches. M. de Maupassant does not admire him, and he is such a master of the subject that it would ill become an outsider to suggest a revision of judgment. He is a part of the contemptible furniture of the world, but on the whole, it would appear, the most grotesque part of it. His caution, his canniness, his natural astuteness, his stinginess, his general grinding sordidness, are as unmistakable as that quaint and brutish dialect in which he expresses himself, and on which our author plays like a virtuoso. It would be impossible to demonstrate with a finer sense of the humour of the thing the fatuities and densities of his ignorance, the bewilderments of his opposed appetites, the overreachings of his caution. His existence has a gay side, but it is apt to be the barbarous gaiety commemorated in *Farce Normande,*[12] an anecdote which, like many of M. de Maupassant's anecdotes, it is easier to refer the reader to than to repeat. If it is most convenient to place *La Maison Tellier* among the tales of the pesantry, there is no doubt that it stands at the head of the list. It is absolutely unadapted to the perusal of ladies and young persons, but it shares this peculiarity with most of its fellows, so that to ignore it on that account would be to imply that we must forswear M. de Maupassant altogether, which is an incongruous and insupportable conclusion. Every good story is of course both a picture and an idea, and the more they are interfused the better the problem is solved. In *La Maison Tellier* they fit each other to perfection; the capacity for sudden innocent delights latent in natures which have lost their innocence is vividly illustrated by the singular scenes to which our acquaintance with Madame and her staff (little as it may be a thing to boast of), successively introduces us. The breadth, the freedom, and brightness of all this give the measure of the author's talent, and of that large, keen way of looking at life which sees the pathetic and the droll, the stuff of which the whole piece is made, in the queerest and humblest patterns. The tone of *La Maison Tellier* and the few compositions which closely resemble it, expresses M. de Maupassant's nearest

approach to geniality. Even here, however, it is the geniality of the showman exhilarated by the success with which he feels that he makes his mannikins (and especially his womankins) caper and squeak, and who after the performance tosses them into their box with the irreverence of a practised hand. If the pages of the author of *Bel-Ami* may be searched almost in vain for a manifestation of the sentiment of respect, it is naturally not by Mme. Tellier and her charges that we must look most to see it called forth; but they are among the things that please him most.

Sometimes there is a sorrow, a misery, or even a little heroism, that he handles with a certain tenderness (*Une Vie* [13] is the capital example of this), without insisting on the poor, the ridiculous, or, as he is fond of saying, the bestial side of it. Such an attempt, admirable in its sobriety and delicacy, is the sketch, in *L'Abandonné,*[14] of the old lady and gentleman, Mme. de Cadour and M. d'Apreval, who, staying with the husband of the former at a little watering-place on the Normandy coast, take a long, hot walk on a summer's day, on a straight, white road, into the interior, to catch a clandestine glimpse of a young farmer, their illegitimate son. He has been pensioned, he is ignorant of his origin, and is a commonplace and unconciliatory rustic. They look at him, in his dirty farmyard, and no sign passes between them; then they turn away and crawl back, in melancholy silence, along the dull French road. The manner in which this dreary little occurrence is related makes it as large as a chapter of history. There is tenderness in *Miss Harriet,*[15] which sets forth how an English old maid, fantastic, hideous, sentimental, and tract-distributing, with a smell of india-rubber, fell in love with an irresistible French painter, and drowned herself in the well because she saw him kissing the maid-servant; but the figure of the lady grazes the farcical. Is it because we know Miss Harriet (if we are not mistaken in the type the author has had in his eye) that we suspect the good spinster was not so weird and desperate, addicted though her class may be, as he says, to "haunting all the *tables d'hôte* in Europe, to spoiling Italy, poisoning Switzerland, making the charming towns of the Mediterranean uninhabitable, carrying everywhere their queer little manias, their *mœurs de vestales pétrifiées,*[16] their indescribable garments, and that odour of india-rubber which makes one think that at night they

---

12. *Farce Normande: A Normandy Joke,* Vol. II.

13. *Une Vie: A Woman's Life,* Vol. IV.   14. *L'Abandonné: The Castaway,* Vol. VIII.   15. *Miss Harriet: Miss Harriet,* Vol. VI.   16. *mœurs . . . pétrifiées:* "manners of petrified vestal virgins."

must be slipped into a case"? What would Miss Harriet have said to M. de Maupassant's friend, the hero of the *Découverte*,[17] who, having married a little Anglaise because he thought she was charming when she spoke broken French, finds she is very flat as she becomes more fluent, and has nothing more urgent than to denounce her to a gentleman he meets on the steamboat, and to relieve his wrath in ejaculations of "Sales Anglais"?

M. de Maupassant evidently knows a great deal about the army of clerks who work under government, but it is a terrible tale that he has to tell of them and of the *petit bourgeois* in general. It is true that he has treated the *petit bourgeois* in *Pierre et Jean* [18] without holding him up to our derision, and the effort has been so fruitful, that we owe it the work for which, on the whole, in the long list of his successes, we are most thankful. But of *Pierre et Jean,* a production neither comic nor cynical (in the degree, that is, of its predecessors), but serious and fresh, I will speak anon. In . . . many other pitiless little pieces, the author opens the window wide to his perception of everything mean, narrow, and sordid. The subject is ever the struggle for existence in hard conditions, lighted up simply by more or less *polissonnerie*.[19] Nothing is more striking to an Anglo-Saxon reader than the omission of all the other lights, those with which our imagination, and I think it ought to be said our observation, is familiar, and which our own works of fiction at any rate do not permit us to forget: those of which the most general description is that they spring from a certain mixture of good-humour and piety—piety, I mean, in the civil and domestic sense quite as much as in the religious. The love of sport, the sense of decorum, the necessity for action, the habit of respect, the absence of irony, the pervasiveness of childhood, the expansive tendency of the race, are a few of the qualities (the analysis might, I think, be pushed much further) which ease us off, mitigate our tension and irritation, rescue us from the nervous exasperation which is almost the commonest element of life as depicted by M. de Maupassant. No doubt there is in our literature an immense amount of conventional blinking, and it may be questioned whether pessimistic representation in M. de Maupassant's manner do not follow his particular original more closely than our perpetual quest of pleasantness (does not Mr. Rider Haggard [20] make even his African carnage

pleasant?) adheres to the lines of the world we ourselves know.

Fierce indeed is the struggle for existence among even our pious and good-humoured millions, and it is attended with incidents as to which after all little testimony is to be extracted from our literature of fiction. It must never be forgotten that the optimism of that literature is partly the optimism of women and of spinsters; in other words the optimism of ignorance as well as of delicacy. It might be supposed that the French, with their mastery of the *arts d'agrément*, would have more consolations than we, but such is not the account of the matter given by the new generation of painters. To the French we seem superficial, and we are certainly open to the reproach; but none the less even to the infinite majority of readers of good faith there will be a wonderful want of correspondence between the general picture of *Bel-Ami*, of *Mont-Oriol*, of *Une Vie, Yvette* [21] and *En Famille*,[22] and our own vision of reality. It is an old impression of course that the satire of the French has a very different tone from ours; but few English readers will admit that the feeling of life is less in ours than in theirs. The feeling of life is evidently, *de part et d'autre*,[23] a very different thing. If in ours, as the novel illustrates it, there are superficialities, there are also qualities which are far from being negatives and omissions: a large imagination and (is it fatuous to say?) a large experience of the positive kind. Even those of our novelists whose manner is most ironic pity life more and hate it less than M. de Maupassant and his great initiator Flaubert. It comes back I suppose to our good-humour (which may apparently also be an artistic force); at any rate, we have reserves about our shames and our sorrows, indulgences and tolerances about our Philistinism, forbearances about our blows, and a general friendliness of conception about our possibilities, which take the cruelty from our self-derision and operate in the last resort as a sort of tribute to our freedom. There is a horrible, admirable scene in *Monsieur Parent*, [24] which is a capital example of triumphant ugliness. The harmless gentleman who gives his name to the tale has an abominable wife, one of whose offensive attributes is a lover (unsuspected by her husband), only less impudent than herself. M. Parent comes in from a walk with his little boy, at dinner-time, to encounter suddenly in his

English author of *King Solomon's Mines* (1885) and other adventure stories situated in Africa.   21. *Yvette: Yvette*, Vol. VIII.   22. *En Famille:* A *Family Affair*, Vol. I.   23. *de . . . autre:* "in either case."   24. *Monsieur Parent: Monsieur Parent*, Vol. X.

17. *Découverte: Unmasked*, Vol. X.   18. *Pierre et Jean: Pierre and Jean*, Vol. XIII.   19. *polissonnerie:* indecent talk. 20. **Haggard:** Sir Henry Rider Haggard (1856–1925), popular

abused, dishonoured, deserted home, convincing proof of her misbehaviour. He waits and waits dinner for her, giving her the benefit of every doubt; but when at last she enters, late in the evening, accompanied by the partner of her guilt, there is a tremendous domestic concussion. It is to the peculiar vividness of this scene that I allude, the way we hear it and see it, and its most repulsive details are evoked for us: the sordid confusion, the vulgar noise, the disordered table and ruined dinner, the shrill insolence of the wife, her brazen mendacity, the scared inferiority of the lover, the mere momentary heroics of the weak husband, the scuffle and somersault, the eminently unpoetic justice with which it all ends.

When Thackeray [25] relates how Arthur Pendennis goes home to take pot-luck with the insolvent Newcomes at Boulogne, and how the dreadful Mrs. Mackenzie receives him, and how she makes a scene, when the frugal repast is served, over the diminished mutton-bone, we feel that the notation of that order of misery goes about as far as we can bear it. But this is child's play to the history of M. and Mme. Caravan and their attempt, after the death (or supposed death) of the husband's mother, to transfer to their apartment before the arrival of the other heirs certain miserable little articles of furniture belonging to the deceased, together with the frustration of the manœuvre not only by the grim resurrection of the old woman (which is a sufficiently fantastic item), but by the shock of battle when a married daughter and her husband appear. No one gives us like M. de Maupassant the odious words exchanged on such an occasion as that: no one depicts with so just a hand the feelings of small people about small things. These feelings are very apt to be "fury"; that word is of strikingly frequent occurrence in his pages. *L'Héritage* [26] is a drama of private life in the little world of the Ministère de la Marine—a world, according to M. de Maupassant, of dreadful little jealousies and ineptitudes. Readers of a robust complexion should learn how the wretched M. Lesable was handled by his wife and her father on his failing to satisfy their just expectations, and how he comported himself in the singular situation thus prepared for him. The story is a model of narration, but it leaves our poor average humanity dangling like a beaten rag.

Where does M. de Maupassant find the great multitude of his detestable women? or where at least does he find the courage to represent them in such colours? Jeanne de Lamare, in *Une Vie*, receives the outrages of fate with a passive fortitude; and there is something touching in Mme. Roland's *âme tendre de caissière*,[27] as exhibited in *Pierre et Jean*. But for the most part M. de Maupassant's heroines are a mixture of extreme sensuality and extreme mendacity. They are a large element in that general disfigurement, that *illusion de l'ignoble, qui attire tant d'êtres*,[28] which makes the perverse or the stupid side of things the one which strikes him first, which leads him, if he glances at a group of nurses and children sunning themselves in a Parisian square, to notice primarily the *yeux de brute* [29] of the nurses; or if he speaks of the longing for a taste of the country which haunts the shopkeeper fenced in behind his counter, to identify it as the *amour bête de la nature;* [30] or if he has occasion to put the boulevards before us on a summer's evening, to seek his effect in these terms: "The city, as hot as a stew, seemed to sweat in the suffocating night. The drains puffed their pestilential breath from their mouths of granite, and the underground kitchens poured into the streets, through their low windows, the infamous miasmas of their dishwater and old sauces." I do not contest the truth of such indications, I only note the particular selection and their seeming to the writer the most *apropos*.

Is it because of the inadequacy of these indications when applied to the long stretch that M. de Maupassant's novels strike us as less complete, in proportion to the talent expended upon them, than his *contes* and *nouvelles?* [31] I make this invidious distinction in spite of the fact that *Une Vie* (the first of the novels in the order of time) is a remarkably interesting experiment, and that *Pierre et Jean* is, so far as my judgment goes, a faultless production. *Bel-Ami* is full of the bustle and the crudity of life (its energy and expressiveness almost bribe one to like it), but it has the great defect that the physiological explanation of things here too visibly contracts the problem in order to meet it. The world represented is too special, too little inevitable, too much to take or to leave as we like—a world in which every man is a cad and every woman a harlot. M. de Maupassant traces the career of a finished blackguard who succeeds in life through women, and he represents him primarily as succeeding in the profession of journalism. His colleagues and his

25. **Thackeray**: William Makepeace Thackeray (1811–63), English novelist, author of *The Newcomes* (1854) and other famous novels. 26. *L'Héritage*: The Legacy, Vol. V.

27. *âme . . . caissière:* "tender soul of a cashier." 28. *illusion . . . d'êtres:* "illusion of ignobleness that tempts so many people." 29. *yeux de brute:* "eyes like wild animals." 30. *amour . . . nature:* "animal passion of nature." 31. *contes:* tales; *nouvelles:* short novels.

mistresses are as depraved as himself, greatly to the injury of the ironic idea, for the real force of satire would have come from seeing him engaged and victorious with natures better than his own. It may be remarked that this was the case with the nature of Mme. Walter; but the reply to that is—hardly! Moreover the author's whole treatment of the episode of Mme. Walter is the thing on which his admirers have least to congratulate him. The taste of it is so atrocious, that it is difficult to do justice to the way it is made to stand out. Such an instance as this pleads with irresistible eloquence, as it seems to me, the cause of that salutary diffidence or practical generosity which I mentioned on a preceding page. I know not the English or American novelist who could have written this portion of the history of *Bel-Ami* if he would. But I also find it impossible to conceive of a member of that fraternity who would have written it if he could. The subject of *Mont-Oriol* is full of queerness to the English mind. Here again the picture has much more importance than the idea, which is simply that a gentleman, if he happen to be a low animal, is liable to love a lady very much less if she presents him with a pledge of their affection. It need scarcely be said that the lady and gentleman who in M. de Maupassant's pages exemplify this interesting truth are not united in wedlock—that is with each other.

M. de Maupassant tells us that he has imbibed many of his principles from Gustave Flaubert, from the study of his works as well as, formerly, the enjoyment of his words. It is in *Une Vie* that Flaubert's influence is most directly traceable, for the thing has a marked analogy with *L'Education Sentimentale*.[32] That is, it is the presentation of a simple piece of a life (in this case a long piece), a series of observations upon an episode *quelconque*,[33] as the French say, with the minimum of arrangement of the given objects. It is an excellent example of the way the impression of truth may be conveyed by that form, but it would have been a still better one if in his search for the effect of dreariness (the effect of dreariness may be said to be the subject of *Une Vie,* so far as the subject is reducible) the author had not eliminated excessively. He has arranged, as I say, as little as possible; the necessity of a "plot" has in no degree imposed itself upon him, and his effort has been to give the uncomposed, unrounded look of life, with its accidents, its broken rhythm, its queer resemblance to the fa-

mous description of "Bradshaw"—a compound of trains that start but don't arrive, and trains that arrive but don't start. It is almost an arrangement of the history of poor Mme. de Lamare to have left so many things out of it, for after all she is described in very few of the relations of life. The principal ones are there certainly; we see her as a daughter, a wife, and a mother, but there is a certain accumulation of secondary experience that marks any passage from youth to old age which is a wholly absent element in M. de Maupassant's narrative, and the suppression of which gives the thing a tinge of the arbitrary. It is in the power of this secondary experience to make a great difference, but nothing makes any difference for Jeanne de Lamare as M. de Maupassant puts her before us. Had she no other points of contact than those he describes?—no friends, no phases, no episodes, no chances, none of the miscellaneous *remplissage*[34] of life? No doubt M. de Maupassant would say that he has had to select, that the most comprehensive enumeration is only a condensation, and that, in accordance with the very just principles enunciated in that preface to which I have perhaps too repeatedly referred, he has sacrificed what is uncharacteristic to what is characteristic. It characterises the career of this French country lady of fifty years ago that its long gray expanse should be seen as peopled with but five or six figures. The essence of the matter is that she was deceived in almost every affection, and that essence is given if the persons who deceived her are given.

The reply is doubtless adequate, and I have only intended my criticism to suggest the degree of my interest. What it really amounts to is that if the subject of this artistic experiment had been the existence of an English lady, even a very dull one, the air of verisimilitude would have demanded that she should have been placed in a denser medium. *Une Vie* may after all be only a testimony to the fact of the melancholy void of the coast of Normandy, even within a moderate drive of a great seaport, under the Restoration and Louis Philippe.[35] It is especially to be recommended to those who are interested in the question of what constitutes a "story," offering as it does the most definite sequences at the same time that it has nothing that corresponds to the usual idea of a plot, and closing with an implication that finds us prepared. The picture again in this case is much more dominant than the idea, unless it be an idea that loneliness and grief are terrible.

32. *L'Education Sentimentale:* Gustave Flaubert's novel, *The Sentimental Education*, was published at Paris in 1869. 33. *quelconque:* however unimportant.

34. *remplissage:* rubbish.   35. *Louis Philippe:* between the restoration of the Bourbon monarchy in 1814 and the fall of King Louis Philippe in 1848.

The picture, at any rate, is full of truthful touches, and the work has the merit and the charm that it is the most delicate of the author's productions and the least hard. In none other has he occupied himself so continuously with so innocent a figure as his soft, bruised heroine; in none other has he paid our poor blind human history the compliment (and this is remarkable, considering the flatness of so much of the particular subject) of finding it so little *bête*.[36] He may think it, here, but comparatively he does not say it. He almost betrays a sense of moral things. Jeanne is absolutely passive, she has no moral spring, no active moral life, none of the edifying attributes of character (it costs her apparently as little as may be in the way of a shock, a complication of feeling, to discover, by letters, after her mother's death, that this lady has not been the virtuous woman she has supposed); but her chronicler has had to handle the immaterial forces of patience and renunciation, and this has given the book a certain purity, in spite of two or three "physiological" passages that come in with violence—a violence the greater as we feel it to be a result of selection. It is very much a mark of M. de Maupassant that on the most striking occasion, with a single exception, on which his picture is not a picture of libertinage it is a picture of unmitigated suffering. Would he suggest that these are the only alternatives?

The exception that I here allude to is for *Pierre et Jean*, which I have left myself small space to speak of. Is it because in this masterly little novel there is a show of those immaterial forces which I just mentioned, and because Pierre Roland is one of the few instances of operative character that can be recalled from so many volumes, that many readers will place M. de Maupassant's latest production altogether at the head of his longer ones? I am not sure, inasmuch as after all the character in question is not extraordinarily distinguished, and the moral problem not presented in much complexity. The case is only relative. Perhaps it is not of importance to fix the reasons of preference in respect to a piece of writing so essentially a work of art and of talent. *Pierre et Jean* is the best of M. de Maupassant's novels mainly because M. de Maupassant has never before been so clever. It is a pleasure to see a mature talent able to renew itself, strike another note, and appear still young. This story suggests the growth of a perception that everything has not been said about the actors on the world's stage when they are represented either as helpless victims or as mere bundles of appetites. There is an

air of responsibility about Pierre Roland, the person on whose behalf the tale is mainly told, which almost constitutes a pledge. An inquisitive critic may ask why in this particular case M. de Maupassant should have stuck to the *petit bourgeois,* the circumstances not being such as to typify that class more than another. There are reasons indeed which on reflection are perceptible; it was necessary that his people should be poor, and necessary even that to attenuate Madame Roland's misbehaviour she should have had the excuse of the contracted life of a shopwoman in the Rue Montmartre. Were the inquisitive critic slightly malicious as well, he might suspect the author of a fear that he should seem to give way to the *illusion du beau* [37] if in addition to representing the little group in *Pierre et Jean* as persons of about the normal conscience he had also represented them as of the cultivated class. If they belong to the humble life this belittles and—I am still quoting the supposedly malicious critic—M. de Maupassant *must,* in one way or the other, belittle. To the English reader it will appear, I think, that Pierre and Jean are rather more of the cultivated class than two young Englishmen in the same social position. It belongs to the drama that the struggle of the elder brother—educated, proud, and acute—should be partly with the pettiness of his opportunities. The author's choice of a *milieu,* moreover, will serve to English readers as an example of how much more democratic contemporary French fiction is than that of his own country. The greater part of it—almost all the work of Zola and of Daudet, the best of Flaubert's novels, and the best of those of the brothers De Goncourt [38]—treat of that vast, dim section of society which, lying between those luxurious walks on whose behalf there are easy presuppositions and that darkness of misery which, in addition to being picturesque, brings philanthropy also to the writer's aid, constitutes really, in extent and expressiveness, the substance of any nation. In England, where the fashion of fiction still sets mainly to the country house and the hunting-field, and yet more novels are published than anywhere else in the world, that thick twilight of mediocrity of condition has been little explored. May it yield triumphs in the years to come!

It may seem that I have claimed little for M. de Maupassant, so far as English readers are con-

36. *bête:* beastly.

37. *illusion du beau:* "illusion of the beautiful." 38. Zola . . . De Goncourt: Émile Zola (1840–1902), Alphonse Daudet (1840–97), Edmond de Goncourt (1822–96), and Jules de Goncourt (1830–70) were all French novelists who belonged in some degree to the naturalist school.

cerned with him, in saying that after publishing twenty improper volumes he has at last published a twenty-first, which is neither indecent nor cynical. It is not this circumstance that has led me to dedicate so many pages to him, but the circumstance that in producing all the others he yet remained, for those who are interested in these matters, a writer with whom it was impossible not to reckon. This is why I called him, to begin with, so many ineffectual names: a rarity, a "case," an embarrassment, a lion in the path. He is still in the path as I conclude these observations, but I think that in making them we have discovered a legitimate way round. If he is a master of his art and it is discouraging to find what low views are compatible with mastery, there is satisfaction, on the other hand, in learning on what particular condition he holds his strange success. This condition, it seems to me, is that of having totally omitted one of the items of the problem, an omission which has made the problem so much easier that it may almost be described as a short cut to a solution. The question is whether it be a fair cut. M. de Maupassant has simply skipped the whole reflective part of his men and women—that reflective part which governs conduct and produces character. He may say that he does not see it, does not know it; to which the answer is, "So much the better for you, if you wish to describe life without it. The strings you pull are by so much the less numerous, and you can therefore pull those that remain with greater promptitude, consequently with greater firmness, with a greater air of knowledge." Pierre Roland, I repeat, shows a capacity for reflection, but I cannot think who else does, among the thousand figures who compete with him—I mean for reflection addressed to anything higher than the gratification of an instinct. We have an impression that M. d'Apreval and Madame de Cadour reflect, as they trudge back from their mournful excursion, but that indication is not pushed very far. An aptitude for this exercise is a part of disciplined manhood, and disciplined manhood M. de Maupassant has simply not attempted to represent. I can remember no instance in which he sketches any considerable capacity for conduct, and his women betray that capacity as little as his men. I am much mistaken if he has once painted a gentleman, in the English sense of the term. His gentlemen, like Paul Brétigny and Gontran de Ravenel, are guilty of the most extraordinary deflections. For those who are conscious of this element in life, look for it and like it, the gap will appear to be immense. It will lead them to say, "No wonder you have a contempt if that is the way you limit the field. No

wonder you judge people roughly if that is the way you see them. Your work, on your premises, remains the admirable thing it is, but is your 'case' not adequately explained?"

The erotic element in M. de Maupassant, about which much more might have been said, seems to me to be explained by the same limitation, and explicable in a similar way wherever else its literature occurs in excess. The carnal side of man appears the most characteristic if you look at it a great deal; and you look at it a great deal if you do not look at the other, at the side by which he reacts against his weaknesses, his defeats. The more you look at the other, the less the whole business to which French novelists have ever appeared to English readers to give a disproportionate place—the business, as I may say, of the senses—will strike you as the only typical one. Is not this the most useful reflection to make in regard to the famous question of the morality, the decency, of the novel? It is the only one, it seems to me, that will meet the case as we find the case to-day. Hard and fast rules, *a priori* restrictions, mere interdictions (you shall not speak of this, you shall not look at that), have surely served their time, and will in the nature of the case never strike an energetic talent as anything but arbitrary. A healthy, living and growing art, full of curiosity and fond of exercise, has an indefeasible mistrust of rigid prohibitions. Let us then leave this magnificent art of the novelist to itself and to its perfect freedom, in the faith that one example is as good as another, and that our fiction will always be decent enough if it be sufficiently general. Let us not be alarmed at this prodigy (though prodigies are alarming) of M. de Maupassant, who is at once so licentious and so impeccable, but gird ourselves up with the conviction that another point of view will yield another perfection.

THE ART OF FICTION

◊

〖 PUBLISHED in *Longman's Magazine* (September, 1884) and reprinted in *Partial Portraits* (1888), "The Art of Fiction" was James's answer to a lecture on the art and morality of the novel delivered before the Royal Institution of London by Walter Besant (1826–1901), an English novelist and man of letters. Robert Louis Stevenson disagreed with both James and Besant in an essay, "A Humble Remonstrance," published in *Longman's* (December, 1884).

◇

I SHOULD not have affixed so comprehensive a title to these few remarks, necessarily wanting in any completeness upon a subject the full consideration of which would carry us far, did I not seem to discover a pretext for my temerity in the interesting pamphlet lately published under this name by Mr. Walter Besant. Mr. Besant's lecture at the Royal Institution—the original form of his pamphlet—appears to indicate that many persons are interested in the art of fiction, and are not indifferent to such remarks, as those who practise it may attempt to make about it. I am therefore anxious not to lose the benefit of this favourable association, and to edge in a few words under cover of the attention which Mr. Besant is sure to have excited. There is something very encouraging in his having put into form certain of his ideas on the mystery of story-telling.

It is a proof of life and curiosity—curiosity on the part of the brotherhood of novelists as well as on the part of their readers. Only a short time ago it might have been supposed that the English novel was not what the French call *discutable*.[1] It had no air of having a theory, a conviction, a consciousness of itself behind it—of being the expression of an artistic faith, the result of choice and comparison. I do not say it was necessarily the worse for that: it would take much more courage than I possess to intimate that the form of the novel as Dickens and Thackeray (for instance) saw it had any taint of incompleteness. It was, however, *naïf* (if I may help myself out with another French word); and evidently if it be destined to suffer in any way for having lost its *naïveté* it has now an idea of making sure of the corresponding advantages. During the period I have alluded to there was a comfortable, good-humoured feeling abroad that a novel is a novel, as a pudding is a pudding, and that our only business with it could be to swallow it. But within a year or two, for some reason or other, there have been signs of returning animation—the era of discussion would appear to have been to a certain extent opened. Art lives upon discussion, upon experiment, upon curiosity, upon variety of attempt, upon the exchange of views and the comparison of standpoints; and there is a presumption that those times when no one has anything particular to say about it, and has no reason to give for practice or

THE ART OF FICTION.   1. *discutable:* discussable.

preference, though they may be times of honour, are not times of development—are times, possibly even, a little of dulness. The successful application of any art is a delightful spectacle, but the theory too is interesting; and though there is a great deal of the latter without the former I suspect there has never been a genuine success that has not had a latent core of conviction. Discussion, suggestion, formulation, these things are fertilizing when they are frank and sincere. Mr. Besant has set an excellent example in saying what he thinks, for his part, about the way in which fiction should be written, as well as about the way in which it should be published; for his view of the "art," carried on into an appendix, covers that too. Other labourers in the same field will doubtless take up the argument, they will give it the light of their experience, and the effect will surely be to make our interest in the novel a little more what it had for some time threatened to fail to be—a serious, active, inquiring interest, under protection of which this delightful study may, in moments of confidence, venture to say a little more what it thinks of itself.

It must take itself seriously for the public to take it so. The old superstition about fiction being "wicked" has doubtless died out in England; but the spirit of it lingers in a certain oblique regard directed toward any story which does not more or less admit that it is only a joke. Even the most jocular novel feels in some degree the weight of the proscription that was formerly directed against literary levity: the jocularity does not always succeed in passing for orthodoxy. It is still expected, though perhaps people are ashamed to say it, that a production which is after all only a "make-believe" (for what else is a "story"?) shall be in some degree apologetic—shall renounce the pretension of attempting really to represent life. This, of course, any sensible, wide-awake story declines to do, for it quickly perceives that the tolerance granted to it on such a condition is only an attempt to stifle it disguised in the form of generosity. The old evangelical hostility to the novel, which was as explicit as it was narrow, and which regarded it as little less favourable to our immortal part than a stage-play, was in reality far less insulting. The only reason for the existence of a novel is that it does attempt to represent life. When it relinquishes this attempt, the same attempt that we see on the canvas of the painter, it will have arrived at a very strange pass. It is not expected of the picture that it will make itself humble in order to be forgiven; and the analogy between the art of the painter and the art of the novelist is, so far as I am able to see, complete. Their inspiration is the same, their process (allowing for the different quality of the vehicle) is the same, their success is the same. They may learn from each other, they may explain and sustain each other. Their cause is the same, and the honour of one is the honour of another. The Mahometans think a picture an unholy thing, but it is a long time since any Christian did, and it is therefore the more odd that in the Christian mind the traces (dissimulated though they may be) of a suspicion of the sister art should linger to this day. The only effectual way to lay it to rest is to emphasize the analogy to which I just alluded—to insist on the fact that as the picture is reality, so the novel is history. That is the only general description (which does it justice) that we may give of the novel. But history also is allowed to represent life; it is not, any more than painting, expected to apologize. The subject-matter of fiction is stored up likewise in documents and records, and if it will not give itself away, as they say in California, it must speak with assurance, with the tone of the historian. Certain accomplished novelists have a habit of giving themselves away which must often bring tears to the eyes of people who take their fiction seriously. I was lately struck, in reading over many pages of Anthony Trollope, with his want of discretion in this particular. In a digression, a parenthesis or an aside, he concedes to the reader that he and this trusting friend are only "making believe." He admits that the events he narrates have not really happened, and that he can give his narrative any turn the reader may like best. Such a betrayal of a sacred office seems to me, I confess, a terrible crime; it is what I mean by the attitude of apology, and it shocks me every whit as much in Trollope as it would have shocked me in Gibbon or Macaulay. It implies that the novelist is less occupied in looking for the truth (the truth, of course I mean, that he assumes, the premises that we must grant him, whatever they may be) than the historian, and in doing so it deprives him at a stroke of all his standing-room. To represent and illustrate the past, the actions of men, is the task of either writer, and the only difference that I can see is, in proportion as he succeeds, to the honour of the novelist, consisting as it does in his having more difficult in collecting his evidence, which is so far from being purely literary. It seems to me to give him a great character, the fact that he has at once so much in common with the philosopher and the painter; this double analogy is a magnificent heritage.

It is of all this evidently that Mr. Besant is full when he insists upon the fact that fiction is one of the *fine* arts, deserving in its turn of all the honours and emoluments that have hitherto been reserved for the successful profession of music, poetry, painting, architecture. It is impossible to insist too much on so important a truth, and the place that Mr. Besant demands for the work of the novelist may be represented, a trifle less abstractly, by saying that he demands not only that it shall be reputed artistic, but that it shall be reputed very artistic indeed. It is excellent that he should have struck this note, for his doing so indicates that there was need of it, that his proposition may be to many people a novelty. One rubs one's eyes at the thought; but the rest of Mr. Besant's essay confirms the revelation. I suspect in truth that it would be possible to confirm it still further, and that one would not be far wrong in saying that in addition to the people to whom it has never occurred that a novel ought to be artistic, there are a great many others who, if this principle were urged upon them, would be filled with an indefinable mistrust. They would find it difficult to explain their repugnance, but it would operate strongly to put them on their guard. "Art," in our Protestant communities, where so many things have got so strangely twisted about, is supposed in certain circles to have some vaguely injurious effect upon those who make it an important consideration, who let it weigh in the balance. It is assumed to be opposed in some mysterious manner to morality, to amusement, to instruction. When it is embodied in the work of the painter (the sculptor is another affair!) you know what it is: it stands there before you, in the honesty of pink and green and a gilt frame; you can see the worst of it at a glance, and you can be on your guard. But when it is introduced into literature it becomes more insidious—there is danger of its hurting you before you know it. Literature should be either instructive or amusing, and there is in many minds an impression that these artistic preoccupations, the search for form, contribute to neither end, interfere indeed with both. They are too frivolous to be edifying, and too serious to be diverting; and they are moreover priggish and paradoxical and superfluous. That, I think, represents the manner in which the latent thought of many people who read novels as an exercise in skipping would explain itself if it were to become articulate. They would argue, of course, that a novel ought to be "good," but they would interpret this term in a fashion of their own, which indeed would vary considerably from one critic to another. One would say that being good means representing virtuous and aspiring characters, placed in prominent positions; another would say that it depends on a "happy ending," on a distribution at the last of prizes, pensions, husbands, wives, babies, millions, appended paragraphs, and cheerful remarks. Another still would say that it means being full of incident and movement, so that we shall wish to jump ahead, to see who was the mysterious stranger, and if the stolen will was ever found, and shall not be distracted from this pleasure by any tiresome analysis or "description." But they would all agree that the "artistic" idea would spoil some of their fun. One would hold it accountable for all the description, another would see it revealed in the absence of sympathy. Its hostility to a happy ending would be evident, and it might even in some cases render any ending at all impossible. The "ending" of a novel is, for many persons, like that of a good dinner, a course of dessert and ices, and the artist in fiction is regarded as a sort of meddlesome doctor who forbids agreeable aftertastes. It is therefore true that this conception of Mr. Besant's of the novel as a superior form encounters not only a negative but a positive indifference. It matters little that as a work of art it should really be as little or as much of its essence to supply happy endings, sympathetic characters, and an objective tone, as if it were a work of mechanics: the association of ideas, however incongruous, might easily be too much for it if an eloquent voice were not sometimes raised to call attention to the fact that it is at once as free and as serious a branch of literature as any other.

Certainly this might sometimes be doubted in presence of the enormous number of works of fiction that appeal to the credulity of our generation, for it might easily seem that there could be no great character in a commodity so quickly and easily produced. It must be admitted that good novels are much compromised by bad ones, and that the field at large suffers discredit from overcrowding. I think, however, that this injury is only superficial, and that the superabundance of written fiction proves nothing against the principle itself. It has been vulgarized, like all other kinds of literature, like everything else to-day, and it has proved more than some kinds accessible to vulgarization. But there is as much difference as there ever was between a good novel and a bad one: the bad is swept with all the daubed canvases and spoiled marble into some unvisited limbo, or infinite rubbish-yard beneath the back-windows of the world, and the good subsists and emits its light and stimulates our desire for perfection. As I shall take the liberty of making but a single criticism of Mr. Besant, whose tone is so full of the love of his art, I may as well have done with it at once. He seems to me to mistake in attempting to say so definitely beforehand what sort of an affair the good novel will be. To indicate the danger of such an error as that has been the purpose of these few pages; to suggest that certain traditions on the subject, applied *a priori,* have already had much to answer for, and that the good health of an art which undertakes so immediately to reproduce life must demand that it be perfectly free. It lives upon exercise, and the very meaning of exercise is freedom. The only obligation to which in advance we may hold a novel, without incurring the accusation of being arbitrary, is that it be interesting. That general responsibility rests upon it, but it is the only one I can think of. The ways in which it is at liberty to accomplish this result (of interesting us) strike me as innumerable, and such as can only suffer from being marked out or fenced in by prescription. They are as various as the temperament of man, and they are successful in proportion as they reveal a particular mind, different from others. A novel is in its broadest definition a personal, a direct impression of life: that, to begin with, constitutes its value, which is greater or less according to the intensity of the impression. But there will be no intensity at all, and therefore no value, unless there is freedom to feel and say. The tracing of a line to be followed, of a tone to be taken, of a form to be filled out, is a limitation of that freedom and a suppression of the very thing that we are most curious about. The form, it seems to me, is to be appreciated after the fact: then the author's choice has been made, his standard has been indicated; then we can follow lines and directions and compare tones and resemblances. Then in a word we can enjoy one of the most charming of pleasures, we can estimate quality, we can apply the test of execution. The execution belongs to the author alone; it is what is most personal to him, and we measure him by that. The advantage, the luxury, as well as the torment and responsibility of the novelist, is that there is no limit to what he may attempt as an executant—no limit to his possible experiments, efforts, discoveries, successes. Here it is especially that he works, step by step, like his brother of the brush, of whom we may always say that he has painted his picture in a manner best known to himself. His manner is his secret, not necessarily a jealous one. He cannot disclose it as a general thing if he would; he would be at a loss to teach it to others. I say this with a due recollection of having insisted on the community of method of the artist who paints a picture and the artist who writes a novel. The painter *is* able to teach the rudiments of his practice, and it is possible, from the study of good work (granted the aptitude), both to learn how to paint and to learn how to write. Yet it remains true, without injury to the *rapprochement,* that the literary artist would be obliged to say to his pupil much more than the other, "Ah, well, you must do it as you can!" It is a question of degree, a matter of delicacy. If there are exact sciences, there are also exact arts, and the grammar of painting is so much more definite that it makes the difference.

I ought to add, however, that if Mr. Besant says at the beginning of his essay that the "laws of fiction may be laid down and taught with as much precision and exactness as the laws of harmony, perspective, and proportion," he mitigates what might appear to be an extravagance by applying his remark to "general" laws, and by expressing most of these rules in a manner with which it would certainly be unaccommodating to disagree. That the novelist must write from his experience, that his "characters must be real and such as might be met with in actual life"; that "a young lady brought up in a quiet country village should avoid descriptions of garrison life," and "a writer whose friends and personal experiences belong to the lower middle-class should carefully avoid introducing his characters into society"; that one should enter one's notes in a common-place book; that one's figures should be clear in outline; that making them clear by some trick of speech or of carriage is a bad method, and "describing them at length" is a worse one; that English Fiction should have a "conscious moral purpose"; that "it is almost impossible to estimate too highly the value of careful workmanship—that is, of style"; that "the most important point of all is the story," that "the story is everything": these are principles with most of which it is surely impossible not to sympathize. That remark about the lower middle-class writer and his knowing his place is perhaps rather chilling; but for the rest I should find it difficult to dissent from any one of these recommendations. At the same time, I should find it difficult positively to assent to them, with the exception, perhaps, of the injunction as to entering one's notes in a common-place book. They scarcely seem to me to have the quality that Mr. Besant attributes to the rules of the novelist—the "precision and exactness" of "the laws of harmony, perspective, and proportion." They are suggestive, they are even inspiring, but they are not exact, though they are doubtless as much so as the case admits of: which is a proof of that liberty of interpretation for which I just contended. For the value of these different injunctions—so beautiful and so vague—is wholly in the meaning one attaches to them. The characters, the situation, which strike one as real will be those that touch and interest one most, but the measure of reality is very difficult to fix. The reality of Don Quixote or of Mr. Micawber is a very delicate shade; it is a reality so coloured by the author's vision that, vivid as it may

be, one would hesitate to propose it as a model: one would expose one's self to some very embarrassing questions on the part of a pupil. It goes without saying that you will not write a good novel unless you possess the sense of reality; but it will be difficult to give you a recipe for calling that sense into being. Humanity is immense, and reality has a myriad forms; the most one can affirm is that some of the flowers of fiction have the odour of it, and others have not; as for telling you in advance how your nosegay should be composed, that is another affair. It is equally excellent and inconclusive to say that one must write from experience; to our supposititious aspirant such a declaration might savour of mockery. What kind of experience is intended, and where does it begin and end? Experience is never limited, and it is never complete; it is an immense sensibility, a kind of huge spider-web of the finest silken threads suspended in the chamber of consciousness, and catching every air-borne particle in its tissue. It is the very atmosphere of the mind; and when the mind is imaginative—much more when it happens to be that of a man of genius—it takes to itself the faintest hints of life, it converts the very pulses of the air into revelations. The young lady living in a village has only to be a damsel upon whom nothing is lost to make it quite unfair (as it seems to me) to declare to her that she shall have nothing to say about the military. Greater miracles have been seen than that, imagination assisting, she should speak the truth about some of these gentlemen. I remember an English novelist, a woman of genius, telling me that she was much commended for the impression she had managed to give in one of her tales of the nature and way of life of the French Protestant youth. She had been asked where she learned so much about this recondite being, she had been congratulated on her peculiar opportunities. These opportunities consisted in her having once, in Paris, as she ascended a staircase, passed an open door where, in the household of a *pasteur*,[2] some of the young Protestants were seated at table round a finished meal. The glimpse made a picture; it lasted only a moment, but that moment was experience. She had got her direct personal impression, and she turned out her type. She knew what youth was, and what Protestantism; she also had the advantage of having seen what it was to be French, so that she converted these ideas into a concrete image and produced a reality. Above all, however, she was blessed with the faculty which when you give it an inch takes an ell, and which for the artist is a much greater

2. *pasteur:* pastor, clergyman.

source of strength than any accident of residence or of place in the social scale. The power to guess the unseen from the seen, to trace the implication of things, to judge the whole piece by the pattern, the condition of feeling life in general so completely that you are well on your way to knowing any particular corner of it—this cluster of gifts may almost be said to constitute experience, and they occur in country and in town, and in the most differing stages of education. If experience consists of impressions, it may be said that impressions *are* experience, just as (have we not seen it?) they are the very air we breathe. Therefore, if I should certainly say to a novice, "Write from experience and experience only," I should feel that this was rather a tantalizing monition if I were not careful immediately to add, "Try to be one of the people on whom nothing is lost!"

I am far from intending by this to minimize the importance of exactness—of truth of detail. One can speak best from one's own taste, and I may therefore venture to say that the air of reality (solidity of specification) seems to me to be the supreme virtue of a novel—the merit on which all its other merits (including that conscious moral purpose of which Mr. Besant speaks) helplessly and submissively depend. If it be not there they are all as nothing, and if these be there, they owe their effect to the success with which the author has produced the illusion of life. The cultivation of this success, the study of this exquisite process, form, to my taste, the beginning and the end of the art of the novelist. They are his inspiration, his despair, his reward, his torment, his delight. It is here in very truth that he competes with life; it is here that he competes with his brother the painter in *his* attempt to render the look of things, the look that conveys their meaning, to catch the colour, the relief, the expression, the surface, the substance of the human spectacle. It is in regard to this that Mr. Besant is well inspired when he bids him take notes. He cannot possibly take too many, he cannot possibly take enough. All life solicits him, and to "render" the simplest surface, to produce the most momentary illusion, is a very complicated business. His case would be easier, and the rule would be more exact, if Mr. Besant had been able to tell him what notes to take. But this, I fear, he can never learn in any manual; it is the business of his life. He has to take a great many in order to select a few, he has to work them up as he can, and even the guides and philosophers who might have most to say to him must leave him alone when it comes to the application of precepts, as we leave the painter in communion with his palette. That his characters "must be clear in outline," as

Mr. Besant says—he feels that down to his boots; but how he shall make them so is a secret between his good angel and himself. It would be absurdly simple if he could be taught that a great deal of "description" would make them so, or that on the contrary the absence of description and the cultivation of dialogue, or the absence of dialogue and the multiplication of "incident," would rescue him from his difficulties. Nothing, for instance, is more possible than that he be of a turn of mind for which this odd, literal opposition of description and dialogue, incident and description, has little meaning and light. People often talk of these things as if they had a kind of internecine distinctness, instead of melting into each other at every breath, and being intimately associated parts of one general effort of expression. I cannot imagine composition existing in a series of blocks, nor conceive, in any novel worth discussing at all, of a passage of description that is not in its intention narrative, a passage of dialogue that is not in its intention descriptive, a touch of truth of any sort that does not partake of the nature of incident, or an incident that derives its interest from any other source than the general and only source of the success of a work of art—that of being illustrative. A novel is a living thing, all one and continuous, like any other organism, and in proportion as it lives will it be found, I think, that in each of the parts there is something of each of the other parts. The critic who over the close texture of a finished work shall pretend to trace a geography of items will mark some frontiers as artificial, I fear, as any that have been known to history. There is an old-fashioned distinction between the novel of character and the novel of incident which must have cost many a smile to the intending fabulist who was keen about his work. It appears to me as little to the point as the equally celebrated distinction between the novel and the romance—to answer as little to any reality. There are bad novels and good novels, as there are bad pictures and good pictures; but that is the only distinction in which I see any meaning, and I can as little imagine speaking of a novel of character as I can imagine speaking of a picture of character. When one says picture one says of character, when one says novel one says of incident, and the terms may be transposed at will. What is character but the determination of incident? What is incident but the illustration of character? What is either a picture or a novel that is *not* of character? What else do we seek in it and find in it? It is an incident for a woman to stand up with her hand resting on a table and look out at you in a certain way; or if it be not an incident I think it will be hard to say what it is. At the same time it is an expression of character. If you say you don't see it (character in *that—allons donc!* [3]), this is exactly what the artist who has reasons of his own for thinking he *does* see it undertakes to show you. When a young man makes up his mind that he has not faith enough after all to enter the church as he intended, that is an incident, though you may not hurry to the end of the chapter to see whether perhaps he doesn't change once more. I do not say that these are extraordinary or startling incidents. I do not pretend to estimate the degree of interest proceeding from them, for this will depend upon the skill of the painter. It sounds almost puerile to say that some incidents are intrinsically much more important than others, and I need not take this precaution after having professed my sympathy for the major ones in remarking that the only classification of the novel that I can understand is into that which has life and that which has it not.

The novel and the romance, the novel of incident and that of character—these clumsy separations appear to me to have been made by critics and readers for their own convenience, and to help them out of some of their occasional queer predicaments, but to have little reality or interest for the producer, from whose point of view it is of course that we are attempting to consider the art of fiction. The case is the same with another shadowy category which Mr. Besant apparently is disposed to set up—that of the "modern English novel"; unless indeed it be that in this matter he has fallen into an accidental confusion of standpoints. It is not quite clear whether he intends the remarks in which he alludes to it to be didactic or historical. It is as difficult to suppose a person intending to write a modern English as to suppose him writing an ancient English novel: that is a label which begs the question. One writes the novel, one paints the picture, of one's language and of one's time, and calling it modern English will not, alas! make the difficult task any easier. No more, unfortunately, will calling this or that work of one's fellow-artist a romance—unless it be, of course, simply for the pleasantness of the thing, as for instance when Hawthorne gave this heading to his story of *Blithedale.* The French, who have brought the theory of fiction to remarkable completeness, have but one name for the novel, and have not attempted smaller things in it, that I can see, for that. I can think of no obligation to which the "romancer" would not be held equally with the novelist; the standard of execution is equally high for each. Of course it is of execution that we are talking—that

being the only point of a novel that is open to contention. This is perhaps too often lost sight of, only to produce interminable confusions and cross-purposes. We must grant the artist his subject, his idea, his *donnée:* [4] our criticism is applied only to what he makes of it. Naturally I do not mean that we are bound to like it or find it interesting: in case we do not our course is perfectly simple— to let it alone. We may believe that of a certain idea even the most sincere novelist can make nothing at all, and the event may perfectly justify our belief; but the failure will have been a failure to execute, and it is in the execution that the fatal weakness is recorded. If we pretend to respect the artist at all, we must allow him his freedom of choice, in the face, in particular cases, of innumerable presumptions that the choice will not fructify. Art derives a considerable part of its beneficial exercise from flying in the face of presumptions, and some of the most interesting experiments of which it is capable are hidden in the bosom of common things. Gustave Flaubert [5] has written a story about the devotion of a servant-girl to a parrot, and the production, highly-finished as it is, cannot on the whole be called a success. We are perfectly free to find it flat, but I think it might have been interesting; and I, for my part, am extremely glad he should have written it; it is a contribution to our knowledge of what can be done—or what cannot. Ivan Turgénieff [6] has written a tale about a deaf and dumb serf and a lap-dog, and the thing is touching, loving, a little masterpiece. He struck the note of life where Gustave Flaubert missed it—he flew in the face of a presumption and achieved a victory.

Nothing, of course, will ever take the place of the good old fashion of "liking" a work of art or not liking it: the most improved criticism will not abolish that primitive, that ultimate test. I mention this to guard myself from the accusation of intimating that the idea, the subject, of a novel or a picture, does not matter. It matters, to my sense, in the highest degree, and if I might put up a prayer it would be that artists should select none but the richest. Some, as I have already hastened to admit, are much more remunerative than others, and it would be a world happily arranged in which persons intending to treat them should be exempt from confusions and mistakes. This fortunate con-

---

3. *allons donc!:* "go on!"

4. *donnée:* what is given, the subject as distinguished from the final or entire treatment of a novel or story. A standard term in James's criticism. 5. **Gustave Flaubert:** French novelist (1821–80). His *Un Coeur Simple* (*A Simple Heart*) (1877), one of his *Trois Contes,* is "about" something much less simple than James's account here suggests. 6. **Turgénieff:** The story by Ivan Turgenev (1818–83), as the Russian novelist's name is now commonly spelled, is "Mumu" (1854).

dition will arrive only, I fear, on the same day that critics become purged from error. Meanwhile, I repeat, we do not judge the artist with fairness unless we say to him, "Oh, I grant you your starting-point, because if I did not I should seem to prescribe to you, and heaven forbid I should take that responsibility. If I pretend to tell you what you must not take, you will call upon me to tell you then what you must take; in which case I shall be prettily caught. Moreover, it isn't till I have accepted your data that I can begin to measure you. I have the standard, the pitch; I have no right to tamper with your flute and then criticize your music. Of course I may not care for your idea at all; I may think it silly, or stale, or unclean; in which case I wash my hands of you altogether. I may content myself with believing that you will not have succeeded in being interesting, but I shall, of course, not attempt to demonstrate it, and you will be as indifferent to me as I am to you. I needn't remind you that there are all sorts of tastes: who can know it better? Some people, for excellent reasons, don't like to read about carpenters; others, for reasons even better, don't like to read about courtesans. Many object to Americans. Others (I believe they are mainly editors and publishers) won't look at Italians. Some readers don't like quiet subjects; others don't like bustling ones. Some enjoy a complete illusion, others the consciousness of large concessions. They choose their novels accordingly, and if they don't care about your idea they won't, *a fortiori,* care about your treatment."

So that it comes back very quickly, as I have said, to the liking: in spite of M. Zola, who reasons less powerfully than he represents, and who will not reconcile himself to this absoluteness of taste, thinking that there are certain things that people ought to like, and that they can be made to like. I am quite at a loss to imagine anything (at any rate in this matter of fiction) that people *ought* to like or to dislike. Selection will be sure to take care of itself, for it has a constant motive behind it. That motive is simply experience. As people feel life, so they will feel the art that is most closely related to it. This closeness of relation is what we should never forget in talking of the effort of the novel. Many people speak of it as a factitious, artificial form, a product of ingenuity, the business of which is to alter and arrange the things that surround us, to translate them into conventional, traditional moulds. This, however, is a view of the matter which carries us but a very short way, condemns the art to an eternal repetition of a few familiar *clichés,* cuts short its development, and leads us straight up to a dead wall. Catching the very note and trick, the strange irregular rhythm of life, that

is the attempt whose strenuous force keeps Fiction upon her feet. In proportion as in what she offers us we see life *without* rearrangement do we feel that we are touching the truth; in proportion as we see it *with* rearrangement do we feel that we are being put off with a substitute, a compromise and convention. It is not uncommon to hear an extraordinary assurance of remark in regard to this matter of rearranging, which is often spoken of as if it were the last word of art. Mr. Besant seems to me in danger of falling into the great error with his rather unguarded talk about "selection." Art is essentially selection, but it is a selection whose main care is to be typical, to be inclusive. For many people art means rose-coloured window-panes, and selection means picking a bouquet for Mrs. Grundy. They will tell you glibly that artistic considerations have nothing to do with the disagreeable, with the ugly; they will rattle off shallow commonplaces about the province of art and the limits of art till you are moved to some wonder in return as to the province and the limits of ignorance. It appears to me that no one can ever have made a seriously artistic attempt without becoming conscious of an immense increase—a kind of revelation—of freedom. One perceives in that case—by the light of a heavenly ray—that the province of art is all life, all feeling, all observation, all vision. As Mr. Besant so justly intimates, it is all experience. That is a sufficient answer to those who maintain that it must not touch the sad things of life, who stick into its divine unconscious bosom little prohibitory inscriptions on the end of sticks, such as we see in public gardens—"It is forbidden to walk on the grass; it is forbidden to touch the flowers; it is not allowed to introduce dogs or to remain after dark; it is requested to keep to the right." The young aspirant in the line of fiction whom we continue to imagine will do nothing without taste, for in that case his freedom would be of little use to him; but the first advantage of his taste will be to reveal to him the absurdity of the little sticks and tickets. If he have taste, I must add, of course he will have ingenuity, and my disrespectful reference to that quality just now was not meant to imply that it is useless in fiction. But it is only a secondary aid; the first is a capacity for receiving straight impressions.

Mr. Besant has some remarks on the question of "the story" which I shall not attempt to criticize, though they seem to me to contain a singular ambiguity, because I do not think I understand them. I cannot see what is meant by talking as if there were a part of a novel which is the story and part of it which for mystical reasons is not—unless indeed the distinction be made in a sense in which it is difficult to suppose that any one should attempt to convey anything. "The story," if it represents anything, represents the subject, the idea, the *don-née* of the novel; and there is surely no "school"—Mr. Besant speaks of a school—which urges that a novel should be all treatment and no subject. There must assuredly be something to treat; every school is intimately conscious of that. This sense of the story being the idea, the starting-point, of the novel, is the only one that I see in which it can be spoken of as something different from its organic whole; and since in proportion as the work is successful the idea permeates and penetrates it, informs and animates it, so that every word and every punctuation-point contribute directly to the expression, in that proportion do we lose our sense of the story being a blade which may be drawn more or less out of its sheath. The story and the novel, the idea and the form, are the needle and thread, and I never heard of a guild of tailors who recommended the use of the thread without the needle, or the needle without the thread. Mr. Besant is not the only critic who may be observed to have spoken as if there were certain things in life which constitute stories, and certain others which do not. I find the same odd implication in an entertaining article in the *Pall Mall Gazette*, devoted, as it happens, to Mr. Besant's lecture. "The story is the thing!" says this graceful writer, as if with a tone of opposition to some other idea. I should think it was, as every painter who, as the time for "sending in" his picture looms in the distance, finds himself still in quest of a subject—as every belated artist not fixed about his theme will heartily agree. There are some subjects which speak to us and others which do not, but he would be a clever man who should undertake to give a rule—an *index expurgatorius*—by which the story and the no-story should be known apart. It is impossible (to me at least) to imagine any such rule which shall not be altogether arbitrary. The writer in the *Pall Mall* opposes the delightful (as I suppose) novel of *Margot la Balafrée* to certain tales in which "Bostonian nymphs" appear to have "rejected English dukes for psychological reasons."[7] I am not acquainted with the romance just designated, and can scarcely forgive the *Pall Mall* critic for not mentioning the name of the author, but the title appears to refer to a lady who may have received a scar in some heroic adventure. I am inconsolable at not being acquainted with this episode, but am utterly at a loss to see why it is a story when the rejection (or acceptance) of a duke

7. **psychological reasons:** In Henry James's story "An International Episode" (1878) a girl of Boston origins refuses an English duke for various reasons.

is not, and why a reason, psychological or other, is not a subject when a cicatrix is. They are all particles of the multitudinous life with which the novel deals, and surely no dogma which pretends to make it lawful to touch the one and unlawful to touch the other will stand for a moment on its feet. It is the special picture that must stand or fall, according as it seem to possess truth or to lack it. Mr. Besant does not, to my sense, light up the subject by intimating that a story must, under penalty of not being a story, consist of "adventures." Why of adventures more than of green spectacles? He mentions a category of impossible things, and among them he places "fiction without adventure." Why without adventure, more than without matrimony, or celibacy, or parturition, or cholera, or hydropathy, or Jansenism? This seems to me to bring the novel back to the hapless little *rôle* of being an artificial, ingenious thing—bring it down from its large, free character of an immense and exquisite correspondence with life. And what *is* adventure, when it comes to that, and by what sign is the listening pupil to recognize it? It is an adventure—an immense one—for me to write this little article; and for a Bostonian nymph to reject an English duke is an adventure only less stirring, I should say, than for an English duke to be rejected by a Bostonian nymph. I see dramas within dramas in that, and innumerable points of view. A psychological reason is, to my imagination, an object adorably pictorial; to catch the tint of its complexion—I feel as if that idea might inspire one to Titianesque efforts. There are few things more exciting to me, in short, than a psychological reason, and yet, I protest, the novel seems to me the most magnificent form of art. I have just been reading, at the same time, the delightful story of *Treasure Island*, by Mr. Robert Louis Stevenson and, in a manner less consecutive, the last tale from M. Edmond de Goncourt, which is entitled *Chérie*. One of these works treats of murders, mysteries, islands of dreadful renown, hair-breadth escapes, miraculous coincidences and buried doubloons. The other treats of a little French girl who lived in a fine house in Paris, and died of wounded sensibility because no one would marry her. I call *Treasure Island* delightful, because it appears to me to have succeeded wonderfully in what it attempts; and I venture to bestow no epithet upon *Chérie*, which strikes me as having failed deplorably in what it attempts—that is in tracing the development of the moral consciousness of a child. But one of these productions strikes me as exactly as much of a novel as the other, and as having a "story" quite as much. The moral consciousness of a child is as much a part of life as the islands of the Spanish Main, and the one sort of geography seems to me to have those "surprises" of which Mr. Besant speaks quite as much as the other. For myself (since it comes back in the last resort, as I say, to the preference of the individual), the picture of the child's experience has the advantage that I can at successive steps (an immense luxury, near to the "sensual pleasure" of which Mr. Besant's critic in the *Pall Mall* speaks) say Yes or No, as it may be, to what the artist puts before me. I have been a child in fact, but I have been on a quest for a buried treasure only in supposition, and it is a simple accident that with M. de Goncourt I should have for the most part to say No. With George Eliot, when she painted that country with a far other intelligence, I always said Yes.

The most interesting part of Mr. Besant's lecture is unfortunately the briefest passage—his very cursory allusion to the "conscious moral purpose" of the novel. Here again it is not very clear whether he be recording a fact or laying down a principle; it is a great pity that in the latter case he should not have developed his idea. This branch of the subject is of immense importance, and Mr. Besant's few words point to considerations of the widest reach, not to be lightly disposed of. He will have treated the art of fiction but superficially who is not prepared to go every inch of the way that these considerations will carry him. It is for this reason that at the beginning of these remarks I was careful to notify the reader that my reflections on so large a theme have no pretension to be exhaustive. Like Mr. Besant, I have left the question of the morality of the novel till the last, and at the last I find I have used up my space. It is a question surrounded with difficulties, as witness the very first that meets us, in the form of a definite question, on the threshold. Vagueness, in such a discussion, is fatal, and what is the meaning of your morality and your conscious moral purpose? Will you not define your terms and explain how (a novel being a picture) a picture can be either moral or immoral? You wish to paint a moral picture or carve a moral statue: will you not tell us how you would set about it? We are discussing the Art of Fiction; questions of art are questions (in the widest sense) of execution; questions of morality are quite another affair, and will you not let us see how it is that you find it so easy to mix them up? These things are so clear to Mr. Besant that he has deduced from them a law which he sees embodied in English Fiction, and which is "a truly admirable thing and a great cause for congratulation." It is a great cause for congratulation indeed when such thorny problems become as smooth as silk. I may add that in so far as Mr. Besant perceives that in point of fact English Fiction has addressed itself preponderantly to these delicate questions he will appear to many people to have made a vain discovery. They will have been positively struck, on the contrary, with the moral timidity of the usual English novelist; with his (or with her) aversion to face the difficulties with which on every side the treatment of reality bristles. He is apt to be extremely shy (whereas the picture that Mr. Besant draws is a picture of boldness), and the sign of his work, for the most part, is a cautious silence on certain subjects. In the English novel (by which of course I mean the American as well), more than in any other, there is a traditional difference between that which people know and that which they agree to admit that they know, that which they see and that which they speak of, that which they feel to be a part of life and that which they allow to enter into literature. There is the great difference, in short, between what they talk of in conversation and what they talk of in print. The essence of moral energy is to survey the whole field, and I should directly reverse Mr. Besant's remark and say not that the English novel has a purpose, but that it has a diffidence. To what degree a purpose in a work of art is a source of corruption I shall not attempt to inquire; the one that seems to me least dangerous is the purpose of making a perfect work. As for our novel, I may say lastly on this score that as we find it in England to-day it strikes me as addressed in a large degree to "young people," and that this in itself constitutes a presumption that it will be rather shy. There are certain things which it is generally agreed not to discuss, not even to mention, before young people. That is very well, but the absence of discussion is not a symptom of the moral passion. The purpose of the English novel—"a truly admirable thing, and a great cause for congratulation"—strikes me therefore as rather negative.

There is one point at which the moral sense and the artistic sense lie very near together; that is in the light of the very obvious truth that the deepest quality of a work of art will always be the quality of the mind of the producer. In proportion as that intelligence is fine will the novel, the picture, the statue partake of the substance of beauty and truth. To be constituted of such elements is, to my vision, to have purpose enough. No good novel will ever proceed from a superficial mind; that seems to me an axiom which, for the artist in fiction, will cover all needful moral ground: if the youthful aspirant take it to heart it will illuminate for him many of the mysteries of "purpose." There are many other useful things that might be said to him, but I have come to the end of my article, and can only touch them as I pass. The critic in the *Pall Mall Gazette,* whom I have already quoted, draws attention to the danger, in speaking of the art of fiction, of generalizing. The danger that he has in mind is rather, I imagine, that of particularizing, for there are some comprehensive remarks which, in addition to those embodied in Mr. Besant's suggestive lecture, might without fear of misleading him be addressed to the ingenuous student. I should remind him first of the magnificence of the form that is open to him, which offers to sight so few restrictions and such innumerable opportunities. The other arts, in comparison, appear confined and hampered; the various conditions under which they are exercised are so rigid and definite. But the only condition that I can think of attaching to the composition of the novel is, as I have already said, that it be sincere. This freedom is a splendid privilege, and the first lesson of the young novelist is to learn to be worthy of it.

"Enjoy it as it deserves [I should say to him]; take possession of it, explore it to its utmost extent, publish it, rejoice in it. All life belongs to you, and do not listen either to those who would shut you up into corners of it and tell you that it is only here and there that art inhabits, or to those who would persuade you that this heavenly messenger wings her way outside of life altogether, breathing a superfine air, and turning away her head from the truth of things. There is no impression of life, no manner of seeing it and feeling it, to which the plan of the novelist may not offer a place; you have only to remember that talents so dissimilar as those of Alexandre Dumas and Jane Austen, Charles Dickens and Gustave Flaubert have worked in this field with equal glory. Do not think too much about optimism and pessimism; try and catch the colour of life itself. In France to-day we see a prodigious effort (that of Émile Zola, to whose solid and serious work no explorer of the capacity of the novel can allude without respect), we see an extraordinary effort vitiated by a spirit of pessimism on a narrow basis. M. Zola is magnificent, but he strikes an English reader as ignorant; he has an air of working in the dark; if he had as much light as energy, his results would be of the highest value. As for the aberrations of a shallow optimism, the ground (of English fiction especially) is strewn with their brittle particles as with broken glass. If you must indulge in conclusions, let them have the taste of a wide knowledge. Remember that your first duty is to be as complete as possible—to make as perfect a work. Be generous and delicate and pursue the prize."

◊

FROM
THE NOTEBOOKS

◊

⟨ JAMES kept a series of notebooks, of which those dating from 1878 to 1910 have survived. They were collected by F. O. Matthiessen and Kenneth B. Murdock in *The Notebooks of Henry James* (1947). For the most part he used them to record ideas for stories and novels, often to outline their development, to list possible names for his characters, and, in a few important instances, to meditate on his personal experiences and his general problems as an artist. The two selections that follow illustrate, respectively, the two main types of entry, professional and confessional. The notebooks were not intended for publication.

◊

THE REAL THING
Paris, Hotel Westminster, February 22d, 1891.

IN PURSUANCE of my plan of writing some very short tales—things of from 7000 to 10,000 words, the easiest length to 'place,' I began yesterday the little story that was suggested to me some time ago by an incident related to me by George du Maurier [1]—the lady and gentleman who called upon him with a word from Frith, an oldish, faded, ruined pair—he an officer in the army—who unable to turn a penny in any other way, were trying to find employment as models. I was struck with the pathos, the oddity and typicalness of the situation—the little tragedy of good-looking gentlefolk, who had been all their life stupid and well-dressed, living, on a fixed income, at country-houses, watering places and clubs, like so many others of their class in England, and were now utterly unable to *do* anything, had no cleverness, no art nor craft to make use of as a *gagne-pain* [2]—could only *show* themselves, clumsily, for the fine, clean, well-groomed animals that they were, only hope to make a little money by—in this manner—just simply *being.* I thought I saw a subject for very brief treatment in this *donnée* [3]—and I think I do still; but to do anything worth while with it I must (as always, great Heavens!) be very clear as to what is in it and what I wish to get out of it. I tried a beginning yesterday, but I instantly became conscious that I must straighten out the little idea. It

NOTEBOOKS. **1. George du Maurier:** English artist and writer of French birth (1834–96), illustrator of certain of James's works. **2.** *gagne-pain:* means of livelihood. **3.** *donnée:* See note above, page 258.

must be an idea—it can't be a 'story' in the vulgar sense of the word. It must be a picture; it must illustrate something. God knows that's enough—if the thing *does* illustrate. To make little anecdotes of this kind real *morceaux de vie* [4] is a plan quite inspiring enough. *Voyons un peu,* therefore, what one can put into this one—I mean how much of life. One must put a little action—not a stupid, mechanical, arbitrary action, but something that is of the real essence of the subject. I thought of representing the husband as jealous of the wife—that is, jealous of the artist employing her, from the moment that, in point of fact, she begins to sit. But this is vulgar and obvious—worth nothing. What I wish to represent is the baffled, ineffectual, incompetent character of their attempt, and how it illustrates once again the everlasting English amateurishness—the way superficial, untrained, unprofessional effort goes to the wall when confronted with trained, competitive, intelligent, *qualified* art—in whatever line it may be a question of. It is out of *that* element that my little action and movement must come; and now I begin to see just how—as one always *does*—Glory be to the Highest—when one begins to look at a thing hard and straight and seriously—to fix it—as I am so sadly lax and desultory about doing. What subjects I should find—for *everything*—if I could only achieve this more as a habit! Let my contrast and complication here come from the opposition —to my melancholy Major and his wife—of a couple of little vulgar professional people *who know,* with the consequent bewilderment, vagueness, depression of the former—their failure to understand how such people can be better than *they* —their failure, disappointment, disappearance—going forth into the vague again. *Il y a bien quelque chose à tirer de ça.* [5] They have no pictorial sense. They are only clean and stiff and stupid. The others are dirty, even—the melancholy Major and his wife remark on it, wondering. The artist is beginning a big illustrated book, a new edition of a famous novel—say *Tom Jones:* and he is willing to try to work them in—for he takes an interest in their predicament, and feels—sceptically, but, with his flexible artistic sympathy—the appeal of their type. He is willing to give them a trial. Make it out that *he* himself is on trial—he is young and 'rising,' but he has still his golden spurs to win. He can't afford, *en somme,* to make many mistakes. He has regular work in drawing every week for a serial novel in an illustrated paper; but the great project—that of a big house—of issuing an illustrated Fielding promises him a big lift. He has been intrusted with (say) *Joseph Andrews,* [6] experimentally; he will have to do this brilliantly in order to have the engagement for the rest confirmed. He has already 2 models in his service—the 'complication' must come from *them.* One is a common, clever, London girl, of the smallest origin and without conventional beauty, but of aptitude, of perceptions—knowing thoroughly *how.* She says 'lydy' and 'plice,' but she has the pictorial sense; and can look like anything he wants her to look like. She poses, in short, in perfection. So does her colleague, a professional Italian, a little fellow—ill dressed, smelling of garlic, but admirably serviceable, quite universal. They must be contrasted, confronted, *juxtaposed* with the others; whom they take for people who *pay,* themselves, till they learn the truth when they are overwhelmed with derisive amazement. The denouement simply that the melancholy Major and his wife won't do—they're not 'in it.' Their surprise—their helpless, proud assent—without other prospects: yet at the same time *their* degree of more silent amazement at the success of the two inferior people—who are so much less nice-looking than themselves. Frankly, however, is this contrast enough of a *story,* by itself? It seems to me Yes—for it's an IDEA—and how the deuce should I get *more* into 7000 words? It must be simply 50 pp. of my manuscript. The little tale of *The Servant* (*Brooksmith*) [7] which I did the other day for *Black and White* and which I thought of at the same time as this, proved a very tight squeeze into the same tiny number of words, and I probably shall find that there is much more to be done with this than the compass will admit of. Make it tremendously succinct—with a very short pulse or rhythm —and the closest selection of detail—in other words *summarize* intensely and keep down the lateral development. It *should* be a little gem of bright, quick, vivid form. I shall get every grain of 'action' that the space admits of if I make something, for the artist, hang in the balance—depend on the way he does this particular work. It's when he finds that he shall lose his great opportunity if he keeps on with them, that he has to tell the gentlemanly couple, that, frankly, they won't serve his turn—and make them wander forth into the cold world again. I must keep them the age I've made them—50 and 40—because it's more touching; but I must bring up the age of the 2 real models to almost the same thing. That increases the incomprehensibility (to the amateurs)

4. *morceaux de vie:* morsels of life.   5. *Il y a . . . ça:* "there's certainly something to be got out of that."

6. *Joseph Andrews:* novel (1742) by Henry Fielding (1707-54), author also of *Tom Jones* (1749).   7. *Brooksmith:* "Brooksmith" was published in *Black and White* (May, 1891).

of their usefulness. Picture the immanence, in the latter, of the idle, provided-for, country-house habit—the blankness of their *manière d'être.*[8] But in how tremendously few words I must do it. This is a lesson—a *magnificent* lesson—if I'm to do a good many. Something as admirably compact and *selected* as a Maupassant.

THE CAMBRIDGE CEMETERY
Coronado Beach, Wednesday, March 29th, 1905.

BUT THESE are wanton lapses [9] and impossible excursions; irrelevant strayings of the pen, in defiance of every economy. My subject awaits me, all too charged and too bristling with the most artful economy possible. What I seem to feel is that the Cambridge *tendresse* stands in the path like a waiting lion—or, more congruously, like a cooing dove that I shrink from scaring away. I want a little of the *tendresse,* but it trembles away over the whole field—or would if it could. Yet to present these accidents is what it is to be a *master:* that and that only. Isn't the highest deepest note of the whole thing the never-to-be-lost memory of that evening hour at Mount Auburn—at the Cambridge Cemetery when I took my way alone—after much waiting for the favouring hour—to that unspeakable group of graves.[10] It was late, in November; the trees all bare, the dusk to fall early, the air all still (at Cambridge, in general, *so* still), with the western sky more and more turning to that terrible, deadly, pure polar pink that shows behind American winter woods. But I can't go over this—I can only, oh, so gently, so tenderly, brush it and breathe upon it—breathe upon it and brush it. It was the moment; it was the hour; it was the blessed flood of emotion that broke out at the touch of one's sudden *vision* and carried me away. I seemed then to know why I had done this; I seemed then to know why I had *come*—and to feel how not to have come would have been miserably, horribly to miss it. It made everything right—it made everything priceless. The moon was there, early, white and young, and seemed reflected in the white face of the great empty Stadium, forming one of the boundaries of Soldiers' Field,

that looked over at me, stared over at me, through the clear twilight, from across the Charles. Everything was there, everything *came;* the recognition, stillness, the strangeness, the pity and the sanctity and the terror, the breath-catching passion and the divine relief of tears. William's inspired transcript, on the exquisite little Florentine urn of Alice's ashes, William's divine gift to us, and to *her,* of the Dantean lines—

> *Dopo lungo exilio e martiro*
> *Viene a questa pace—* [11]

took me so at the throat by its penetrating *rightness,* that it was as if one sank down on one's knees in a kind of anguish of gratitude before something for which one had waited with a long, deep *ache.* But why do I write of the all unutterable and the all abysmal? Why does my pen not drop from my hand on approaching the infinite pity and tragedy of all the past? It does, poor helpless pen, with what it meets of the ineffable, what it meets of the cold Medusa-face of life, of all the life *lived,* on every side. *Basta,*[12] *basta!*

FIVE LETTERS

◇

[FEW American writers have left as full and vivid a chronicle of their personal lives and literary careers as Henry James left in his numerous letters to members of his family, friends, fellow writers, and publishers in America, England, France, and elsewhere. The following sampling begins with two letters, addressed respectively to his brother William and his father, which record his excited impressions of Europe during his first adult trans-Atlantic journey, in 1869–70. The third letter, written shortly after his return to Cambridge, is addressed to Charles Eliot Norton (1827–1908), editor, critic, and later professor of the history of art at Harvard, who was making a long stay in England at the time. The Norton letter suggests some of the reasons for James's decision, finally reached four years later, to live and write in Europe. In the fourth letter, offering condolence to Miss Grace Norton (1834–1926), Professor Norton's sister, James opens his mind, as he rarely does, to its philosophical foundations. The fifth

---

8. *manière d'être:* way of life.   9. *wanton lapses:* memories evoked by a visit to Cambridge, Massachusetts, which he made during a tour of the United States (his first in more than twenty years) in 1904–05. At the California resort of Coronado Beach he wrote this and other passages in his notebooks. "My subject" is his impressions of America, published in *The American Scene* (1907).   10. *graves:* In the James family plot of the Cambridge Cemetery, across the Charles River from the Harvard football stadium, were buried his mother (d. 1882), his father (d. 1882), and his sister Alice (d. 1892). His own ashes were interred in the same plot following his funeral and cremation in London in 1916.

11. *Dopo . . . pace:* James mis-remembered the lines. They read, *ed essa da martiro / e da esilio venne a questa pace,* "and itself from martyrdom and exile came into this peace." (*Paradiso* X.128).   12. *Basta:* Italian for enough.

letter, addressed to Henry Adams, whom he had known since they were young men in the Boston-Cambridge world, is often quoted for its eloquent defense of his life as an artist.

◇

TO WILLIAM JAMES

Hôtel d'Angleterre, Rome, Oct. 30th [1869].
MY DEAREST WM.

. . . The afternoon after I had posted those two letters I took a walk out of Florence to an enchanting old Chartreuse [1]—an ancient monastery, perched up on top of a hill and turreted with little cells like a feudal castle. I attacked it and carried it by storm—i.e. obtained admission and went over it. On coming out I swore to myself that while I had life in my body I wouldn't leave a country where adventures of that complexion are the common incidents of your daily constitutional: but that I would hurl myself upon Rome and fight it out on this line at the peril of my existence. Here I am then in the Eternal City. It was easy to leave Florence; the cold had become intolerable and the rain perpetual. I started last night, and at 10½ o'clock and after a bleak and fatiguing journey of 12 hours found myself here with the morning light. There are several places on the route I should have been glad to see; but the weather and my own condition made a direct journey imperative. I rushed to this hotel (a very slow and obstructed rush it was, I confess, thanks to the longueurs and lenteurs [2] of the Papal dispensation) and after a wash and a breakfast let myself loose on the city. From midday to dusk I have been roaming the streets. Que vous en dirai-je? [3] At last—for the first time—I live! It beats everything: it leaves the Rome of your fancy—your education—nowhere. It makes Venice—Florence—Oxford—London—seem like little cities of pasteboard. I went reeling and moaning thro' the streets, in a fever of enjoyment. In the course of four or five hours I traversed almost the whole of Rome and got a glimpse of everything—the Forum, the Coliseum (stupendissimo!), the Pantheon, the Capitol, St. Peter's, the Column of Trajan, the Castle of St. Angelo—all the Piazzas and ruins and monuments. The effect is something indescribable. For the first time I know what the picturesque is. In St. Peter's I stayed some time. It's even beyond its reputation. It was filled with foreign ecclesiastics —great armies encamped in prayer on the marble plains of its pavement—an inexhaustible physiognomical study. To crown my day, on my way home, I met his Holiness in person—driving in prodigious purple state—sitting dim within the shadows of his coach with two uplifted benedictory fingers—like some dusky Hindoo idol in the depths of its shrine. Even if I should leave Rome tonight I should feel that I have caught the keynote of its operation on the senses. I have looked along the grassy vista of the Appian Way and seen the topmost stone-work of the Coliseum sitting shrouded in the light of heaven, like the edge of an Alpine chain. I've trod the Forum and I have scaled the Capitol. I've seen the Tiber hurrying along, as swift and dirty as history! From the high tribune of a great chapel of St. Peter's I have heard in the papal choir a strange old man sing in a shrill unpleasant soprano. I've seen troops of little tonsured neophytes clad in scarlet, marching and countermarching and ducking and flopping, like poor little raw recruits for the heavenly host. In fine I've seen Rome, and I shall go to bed a wiser man than I last rose—yesterday morning. . . .

A toi,
H. J. jr.

TO HENRY JAMES, SR.

Great Malvern,[4] March 19th, '70.
DEAR FATHER,

. . . The other afternoon I trudged over to Worcester—through a region so thick-sown with good old English 'effects'—with elm-scattered meadows and sheep-cropped commons and the ivy-smothered dwellings of small gentility, and high-gabled, heavy-timbered, broken-plastered farmhouses, and stiles leading to delicious meadow footpaths and lodge-gates leading to far-off manors—with all things suggestive of the opening chapters of half-remembered novels, devoured in infancy—that I felt as if I were pressing all England to my soul. As I neared the good old town I saw the great Cathedral tower, high and square, rise far into the cloud-dappled blue. And as I came nearer still I stopped on the bridge and viewed the great ecclesiastical pile cast downward into the yellow Severn. And going further yet I entered the town and lounged about the close and gazed my fill at that most soul-sustaining sight—the waning afternoon, far aloft on the broad perpendicular field of the Cathedral spire—tasted too, as deeply, of the peculiar stillness and repose of the close—

LETTERS.   1. **Chartreuse:** the Certosa del Galluzzo, fourteenth-century Carthusian monastery some four miles south of Florence.   2. **longueurs and lenteurs:** tedium and slowness.   3. **Que . . . je?:** "What shall I say?"

4. **Great Malvern:** health resort in Worcestershire.

saw a ruddy English lad come out and lock the door of the old foundation school which marries its heavy gothic walls to the basement of the church, and carry the vast big key into one of the still canonical houses—and stood wondering as to the effect on a man's mind of having in one's boyhood haunted the Cathedral shade as a King's scholar and yet kept ruddy with much cricket in misty meadows by the Severn. This is a sample of the meditations suggested in my daily walks. Envy me—if you can without hating! I wish I could describe them all—Colwell Green especially, where, weather favouring, I expect to drag myself this afternoon—where each square yard of ground lies verdantly brimming with the deepest British picturesque, and half begging, half deprecating a sketch. You should see how a certain stile-broken footpath here winds through the meadows to a little grey rook-haunted church. Another region fertile in walks is the great line of hills. Half an hour's climb will bring you to the top of the Beacon—the highest of the range—and here is a breezy world of bounding turf with twenty counties at your feet—and when the mist is thick something immensely English in the situation (as if you were wandering on some mighty seaward cliffs or downs, haunted by vague traditions of an early battle). You may wander for hours—delighting in the great green landscape as it responds forever to the cloudy movements of heaven—scaring the sheep—wishing horribly that your mother and sister were—I can't say *mounted*—on a couple of little white-aproned donkeys, climbing comfortably at your side. But at this rate I shall tire you out with my walks as effectually as I sometimes tire myself. . . . Kiss mother for her letter—and for that villainous cold. I enfold you all in an immense embrace.

Your faithful son,

H.

TO CHARLES ELIOT NORTON

Cambridge, (Mass.), Jan. 16, '71.

MY DEAR CHARLES,

If I had needed any reminder and quickener of a very old-time intention to take some morning and put into most indifferent words my frequent thoughts of you, I should have found one very much to the purpose in a letter from Grace,[5] received some ten days ago. But really I needed no deeper consciousness of my great desire to punch a hole in the massive silence which has grown up between us. . . .

5. Grace: Grace Norton.

Cambridge and Boston society still rejoices in that imposing fixedness of outline which is ever so inspiring to contemplate. In Cambridge I see Arthur Sedgwick [6] and Howells; but little of any one else. Arthur seems not perhaps an enthusiastic, but a well-occupied man, and talks much in a wholesome way of meaning to go abroad. Howells edits, and observes and produces—the latter in his own particular line with more and more perfection. His recent sketches in the *Atlantic,* collected into a volume, belong, I think, by the wondrous cunning of their manner, to very good literature. He seems to have resolved himself, however, [into] one who can write solely of what his fleshly eyes have seen; and for this reason I wish he were "located" where they would rest upon richer and fairer things than this immediate landscape. Looking about for myself, I conclude that the face of nature and civilization in this our country is to a certain point a very sufficient literary field. But it will yield its secrets only to a really *grasping* imagination. This I think Howells lacks. (Of course *I* don't!) To write well and worthily of American things one need even more than elsewhere to be a *master.* But unfortunately one is less! . . . I myself have been scribbling some little tales which in the course of time you will have a chance to read. To write a series of good little tales I deem ample work for a life-time. I dream that my life-time shall have done it. It's at least a relief to have arranged one's life-time. . . .

There is an immensity of stupid feeling and brutal writing prevalent here about recent English conduct and attitude [7]—innocuous to some extent, I think, from its very stupidity; but I confess there are now, to my mind, few things of more appealing interest than the various problems with which England finds herself confronted: and this owing to the fact that, on the whole, the country is so deeply—so tragically—charged with a consciousness of her responsibilities, dangers and duties. She presents in this respect a wondrous contrast to ourselves. We, retarding our healthy progress by all the gross weight of our maniac contempt of the refined idea: England striving vainly to compel her lumbersome carcase by the straining wings of conscience and desire. Of course I speak of the better spirits there and the worst here. . . . We have over here the high natural light of chance and space and prosperity; but at moments dark things seem to be almost more blessed by the dim-

6. **Arthur Sedgwick**: Norton's brother-in-law. 7. **attitude**: James refers to the "*Alabama* affair," the bitter controversy with England arising out of her support of the Confederate Navy during the Civil War.

mer radiance shed by impassioned thought. . . .
But I must stay my gossiping hand. . . .

TO MISS GRACE NORTON

131 Mount Vernon St., Boston, July 28th [1883].
MY DEAR GRACE,

Before the sufferings of others I am always utterly powerless, and your letter reveals such depths of suffering that I hardly know what to say to you. This indeed is not my last word—but it must be my first. You are not isolated, verily, in such states of feeling as this—that is, in the sense that you appear to make all the misery of all mankind your own; only I have a terrible sense that you give all and receive nothing—that there is no reciprocity in your sympathy—that you have all the affliction of it and none of the returns. However—I am determined not to speak to you except with the voice of stoicism. I don't know *why* we live—the gift of life comes to us from I don't know what source or for what purpose; but I believe we can go on living for the reason that (always of course up to a certain point) life is the most valuable thing we know anything about, and it is therefore presumptively a great mistake to surrender it while there is any yet left in the cup. In other words consciousness is an illimitable power, and though at times it may seem to be all consciousness of misery, yet in the way it propagates itself from wave to wave, so that we never cease to feel, and though at moments we appear to, try to, pray to, there is something that holds one in one's place, makes it a standpoint in the universe which it is probably good not to forsake. You are right in your consciousness that we are all echoes and reverberations of the *same,* and you are noble when your interest and pity as to everything that surrounds you, appears to have a sustaining and harmonizing power. Only don't, I beseech you, *generalize* too much in these sympathies and tendernesses—remember that every life is a special problem which is not yours but another's, and content yourself with the terrible algebra of your own. Don't melt too much into the universe, but be as solid and dense and fixed as you can. We all live together, and those of us who love and know, live so most. We help each other—even unconsciously, each in our own effort, we lighten the effort of others, we contribute to the sum of success, make it possible for others to live. Sorrow comes in great waves—no one can know that better than you—but it rolls over us, and though it may almost smother us it leaves us on the spot, and we know that if it is strong we are stronger, inasmuch as it passes and we remain. It wears us, uses us, but we wear it and use it in return; and it is blind, whereas we after a manner see. My dear Grace, you are passing through a darkness in which I myself in my ignorance see nothing but that you have been made wretchedly ill by it; but it is only a darkness, it is not an end, or *the* end. Don't think, don't feel, any more than you can help, don't conclude or decide—don't do anything but *wait.* Everything will pass, and serenity and *accepted* mysteries and disillusionments, and the tenderness of a few good people, and new opportunities and ever so much of life, in a word, will remain. You will do all sorts of things yet, and I will help you. The only thing is not to *melt* in the meanwhile. I insist upon the necessity of a sort of mechanical condensation—so that however fast the horse may run away there will, when he pulls up, be a somewhat agitated but perfectly identical G. N. left in the saddle. Try not to be ill—that is all; for in that there is a failure. You are marked out for success, and you must not fail. You have my tenderest affection and all my confidence. Ever your faithful friend—

HENRY JAMES.

TO HENRY ADAMS

21 Carlyle Mansions,
Cheyne Walk, S.W. [London], March 21, 1914.
MY DEAR HENRY,

I have your melancholy outpouring of the 7th, and I know not how better to acknowledge it than by the full recognition of its unmitigated blackness. *Of course* we are lone survivors, of course the past that was our lives is at the bottom of an abyss—if the abyss *has* any bottom; of course, too, there's no use talking unless one particularly *wants* to. But the purpose, almost, of my printed divagations [8] was to show you that one *can,* strange to say, still want to—or at least can behave as if one did. Behold me therefore so behaving—and apparently capable of continuing to do so. I still find my consciousness interesting—under *cultivation* of the interest. Cultivate it *with* me, dear Henry—that's what I hoped to make you do—to cultivate yours for all that it has in common with mine. *Why* mine yields an interest I don't know that I can tell you, but I don't challenge or quarrel with it—I encourage it with a ghastly grin. You see I still, in presence of life (or of what you deny to be such,) have reactions—as many as possible—and the book I sent you is a proof of them. It's, I suppose, because I am that queer monster, the artist, an obstinate finality, an inexhaustible sensibility. Hence

8. **divagations:** *Notes of a Son and Brother,* James's second autobiographical volume, of which he had sent Adams a copy.

the reactions—appearances, memories, many things, go on playing upon it with consequences that I note and "enjoy" (grim word!) noting. It all takes doing—and I *do*. I believe I shall do yet again—it is still an act of life. But you perform them still yourself—and I don't know what keeps me from calling your letter a charming one! There we are, and it's a blessing that you understand—I admit indeed alone—your all-faithful

HENRY JAMES.

ERNEST SAMUELS
Editor

Henry Adams

1838–1918

As a result of the revolution of taste that reduced the reputations of Longfellow, Dr. Holmes, and Lowell from Brahmin high priests to Saturday Club sentimentalists, it is now evident that much of the old authority passed into the hands of Henry Adams and Henry James, though they both abandoned Boston to escape such a destiny. Brought up to revere the keepers of the genteel tradition, each in turn rebelled against its narrow provinciality. Yet, ironically, it was to be a common bond of their lifelong intimacy that they carried with them into exile the quintessence of that tradition. The rebellion of Henry Adams against the Brahmin failure of nerve was all the deeper for his having been Boston born and bred, anchored by ancestral ties to its historic ground. A patrician to the marrow, Adams was fated to quarrel with his class, aware all the while that though he was a brand plucked from the burning he had been deeply scorched. From the time he left Boston in 1877, he wore his nativity like a hairshirt through all his wanderings, clinging with a certain guilty pride to the finicking tastes he owed to it. In one of his incomparable letters to Henry James he held up the mirror to their class: "God knows that we knew our want of knowledge! the self-distrust became introspection—nervous self-consciousness—irritable dislike of America, and antipathy to Boston."

Adams found no repose in the frictionless complacencies of Beacon Hill. His moral idealism vaulted a long half-century to draw its strength from the older and more austere Puritan ethos. His father's motto was "Work and Pray." It served as well for the restless son, though he learned to pray to strange gods— and goddesses. His brother Brooks once wrote a book to celebrate the emancipation of Massachusetts from the Puritan priests. Henry dissented from the harsh estimate. The Puritans may have been intolerant but they had the courage of their moral vision. As practical Calvinists they did not overrate the possibilities of average human nature.

Henry Adams was not a literary figure in the traditional sense. His closest friendships were not with novelists or poets. Socially he was on friendly terms with many writers, including Browning, Arnold, Kipling, Stevenson, James, Howells, S. Weir Mitchell, Richard Watson Gilder, Bret Harte, and Charles Warren Stoddard. He belonged to no literary school and generally avoided discussion of his books and his literary problems. He had no overmastering drive toward literary distinction. When his ambitious elder brother, Charles Francis Adams, Jr., prodded him to seek a literary career, he rejected the meanness of an existence devoted to feeding the monthly magazines as a popular literary entertainer. Even when he had begun to make a name for himself as a crusading Washington journalist for the *Nation* and the *North American Review*, he bristled like a porcupine to defend an inner ideal. "I will not go down into the rough-and-tumble," he told his brother,

nor mix with the crowd, nor write anonymously, except for mere literary practice. . . . You like the strife of the world. I detest it and despise it. You work for power. I work for my own satisfaction. You like roughness and strength; I like taste and dexterity. For God's sake, let us go our own ways and not try to be like each other.

His was an Emersonian self-reliance; his heart vibrated to that iron string as he marched alone on "chaos and the dark." If he would not keep pace with his companions it was because, like Thoreau, he heard "a different drummer."

Adams belonged to the generation of Mark Twain and William Dean Howells. He did not begin to figure significantly in literary history until after his death on March 27, 1918, at the age of eighty. In academic circles he had been widely known as a leading historian, the author of the monumental nine-volume *History of the United States During the Administrations of Jefferson and Madison* and of two important political biographies—*Albert Gallatin*, a massively documented study of Jefferson's Secretary of the Treasury, and *John Randolph*, the fiery spokesman of the antebellum South. Elected president of the American Historical Association in 1894, he ended his one-year term with a characteristic gesture, flight from the public eye. He decamped to Mexico, leaving behind him his iconoclastic presidential address, "The Tendency of History." For years he lived in the shadow of his friend and neighbor, Secretary of State John Hay, as a political oracle at the service of high-ranking officials and diplomats. His career as a distinguished, if somewhat eccentric, litterateur came to light only by stages, reluctantly and after many importunities. That the dignified aristocrat, whose famous Romanesque house on Lafayette Square overlooked the White House, was a literary artist of the highest order was known only to a small circle of friends and a court of nieces who "matronized" at his famous twelve o'clock breakfasts. In 1913 the architect Ralph Adams Cram, a leading Gothic enthusiast, per-

suaded him to allow the publication of his *Mont-Saint-Michel and Chartres*. This masterly evocation of the art and thought of the Middle Ages in northern France had been privately printed in 1904 and distributed to friends and a few university libraries. In 1915 his poem "Buddha and Brahma," which had passed about in manuscript for twenty years, appeared in the *Yale Review*. Adams did not really come into his own until late in 1918 when his study of twentieth-century multiplicity, as he described his autobiography, *The Education of Henry Adams*, was posthumously published. It, too, had been privately printed and issued in 1907 to a select circle of readers who broadcast its brilliant paradoxes far and wide. The book excited a profound interest among war-weary intellectuals. Awarded the Pulitzer prize in 1919, it soon established itself as an American classic and one of the half-dozen great autobiographies of the world.

For more than forty years Adams's reputation has been dominated by that "wise and witty book," as Robert Spiller calls it, a dazzling enigma of a book, compounded of poetic feeling and scientific speculation. Its good-humored cynicism and Voltairean mockery captivated the generation of intellectuals who lost their ideals at Versailles. The incantatory symbols of the Virgin and the Dynamo marked the appearance of a Carlylean prophet in the modern wasteland. T. S. Eliot and Ezra Pound would soon echo his themes in their sardonic elegies. Few critics have been able to resist quoting the *Education* for its urbane epigrams, its inexhaustible ironies on things-in-general, and its vignettes of nineteenth-century history. To disillusioned idealists of the right and left, the book seemed the authentic swan song of an amoral acquisitive society. Adams's image of himself as a "weary Titan of Unity," an Ishmael of the spirit lost in the darkening chaos of the modern world, still exerts a hypnotic influence. In the long shadow of the radioactive mushroom cloud, his menacing vision of the future is as meaningful to our time as Melville's desperate thrusting through the mask of fate in *Moby-Dick* and Hawthorne's glimpses into the infernos of the human soul.

Nothing, perhaps, would have astonished

Adams more than the perversity of fate that has placed him among the major American writers. It was hardly what he bargained for. When he sought fame and power, they eluded him. When he contemptuously turned his back on the public, fame hunted him out. It was enough to justify one's lifelong quarrel with the lack of order in human affairs. The question of fame and success haunted him more, perhaps, than it did any other American writer, until its ramifications overwhelmed him in philosophical quicksands. To an important degree the *Education* is a study in the philosophy of success. As a young man Adams had dreamed of "a national set of young men like ourselves or better, to start new influences not only in politics, but in literature, in law, in society, and throughout the whole social organization of the country—a national school of our own generation." In old age he felt himself to be a kind of John the Baptist, seeking a new Redeemer who would save the world from the irresponsible "Atom King."

The vision of the *Education* is romantic and grandiose. In its cosmic glare Adams's own life seems indeed an ordeal of frustration, no matter how much it may have surpassed that of his rivals in interest and achievement. Self-depreciation was his vice, he observed, and in the *Education* he indulged it to the full, though at the expense of his fellow men. The Olympian detachment reflected the doubleness of his nature, the incessant oscillation of his feelings between the life of action and the life of thought, of the participator and the bystander. He was like the heroine of his anonymous novel *Democracy*. He had a scientific curiosity about the workings of his own mind and would take off his "mental clothing" and study it as if "it belonged to some one else." In Ed Howe's salty phrase, he was "the only man in America who could sit on a fence and see himself go by." Political journalism attracted him because he could be at the center of power and yet remain calm on his high stool above the battle. In his diminishing phrase he saw himself as a "stable companion" of statesmen. Justice Oliver Wendell Holmes was one of the first to protest Adams's too exacting standards:

I note in your *Education* you talk very absurdly as if your work has been futile. I for one have owed you more than you in the least suspect. And I have no doubt that there are many others not to be neglected who do the same. Of course you may reply that it is also futile—but that is the dogmatism that often is disguised under pessimism. . . . If a man has counted in the actual striving of his fellows he cannot pronounce it vain.

The debate on the worthwhileness of human exertion goes on with unquenchable liveliness as men continue to ask, Whither mankind? Adams captured in his candid lens the secret doubts of even the most convinced pragmatist—Are all human values in the timeless flux of things merely relative? He brought to light the hidden second thoughts of the philosophical idealists—Is the world in fact only a dream in the mind of man? Adams put the practical dilemma on the point of an aphorism: "Pessimists are social bores. Optimists are intellectual idiots." It all depended where one stood. Outraged by the dehumanizing of man in the new industrial society, Adams felt a prophet's share in the common guilt and despised himself for his complicity. The twentieth century swept in to the rumble of imperialist guns in China, the Philippines, and South Africa. The spectacle of Christian progress upset him as much as it did Mark Twain. "The little good I ever knew of my own century," he told a correspondent,

quite disappears and is lost to my eyes in the dazzle of having, since the first year of my era—according to the Christians, 1838—won all my stakes, triumphed in all my interests, betrayed all my principles, lost all my self-respect, and been mistaken in every opinion I ever held. The consequence is that I am respected, sought, and if I live to be wholly, instead of partially imbecile, shall be admired. Under these favorable circumstances I try not to be impatient of—other people's—cant or hypocrisy or lies.

The "sentimental pessimism"—Paul Elmer More's phrase—has long stood between Henry Adams and a just appreciation of his literary career. In the general eye he has been thought of as a man of one book. The world accepted the image he created. That image was the creature of the transforming power of time and memory. "The actual journey," he said of a boyhood visit to Washington, "may have been quite different, but the actual journey has no interest for education. The memory was all that mattered." The hero of the book was the double behind which an enormously sensitive temperament could hide itself from posterity or at least save a vestige of heroism. Only by careful study of his immense correspondence, by reascending the actual path of his career can we fully appreciate the artistry—and the artfulness—of the persona he created. Ridden by the urgency of his thesis, the need to master the chaotic new forces of science and technology, he obscured his career in a web of understatement. The whole middle section of his life, nearly twenty years of prolific writing and the period of his happy marriage, was consigned to limbo by the tyrannous scheme. One must disengage his career from the power nexus which obsessed his later life, free it from the exaggerated pessimism of the *fin de siècle,* unearth the buried life of his maturity to see the true stature of his achievement.

II

ONE OF Adams's many private jokes was that he had been an average young man. Nothing was farther from the fact. Born with a silver spoon and a steel-nibbed pen, he soon learned that he stood apart from his fellows by birth and by virtue of family tradition. The Boston State House that cast its protective shadow over his boyhood home daily reminded him of his heritage. The history of Massachusetts and of the nation were a familiar part of the family record; genealogy and politics went hand in hand. The first Henry Adams had emigrated from Somersetshire in 1636 to settle in what is now Quincy, Massachusetts. For three generations the family multiplied with Biblical abundance in respectable obscurity. In the middle of the eighteenth century a member of the family suddenly made his entrance on the stage of history. The Boston authorities summoned thirty-year-old John Adams, then a part-time village lawyer and farmer, to argue the invalidity of the Stamp Act. For the next hundred years after that event, he and his descendants helped shape the destiny of the new nation. He became the second President of the United States. His eldest son, John Quincy Adams, followed in his footsteps as a lawyer and inde-

pendent political leader, broke with the pro-British crowd of State Street, and supported Thomas Jefferson's Embargo. Rising to Secretary of State under James Monroe, John Quincy was largely responsible for the issuance of the Monroe Doctrine. In 1825 he became the sixth President of the United States, a storm center of controversy like his father and like him a mixture of passionate ambition and unyielding moral principle. His third son, Charles Francis Adams, the father of Henry Adams, gravitated toward politics, became a congressman and then American minister to England. The family fortunes had been steadily rising but as a result of the marriage in 1829 of Charles Francis Adams to one of the daughters of Peter Chardon Brooks, the leading New England millionaire, for the first time an Adams was a rich man. Henry Adams of the *Education* was the third of four sons who grew to manhood. In spite of notable promise, none was able to win political eminence.

Henry Adams began life at an altitude that gave him a unique perspective of the terrain below where ordinary mortals shouldered their way to success or oblivion. The Quincy chapter of the *Education* wonderfully evokes the half-mythic character of a boyhood drenched in history, dominated by a sense of family mission. The young Henry steeped himself as his father had before him in the self-probing diaries of his forebears, so like the old Puritans' daily accounting of the ordeal of their souls. He took up the hereditary quarrels of the Adamses which eventually fell to his lot to settle at the bar of history: the malice of English statesmen like Canning and Perceval, the calumnies of the Federalists who had disowned them, the slanders of John Randolph, the enmities that had denied re-election to their presidents.

The noblest fighter of them all had been John Quincy Adams. Defeated by Jackson in the fierce campaign of 1828, he had swallowed his pride and gone back to the House of Representatives to carry on the fight against the Slave Power. As "Old Man Eloquent" he won his fight against the "Gag Rule," staying on to die at last in harness. There was Roman stoicism in his advice to his son, Charles: "Fortify your mind against disappointments . . . Keep up your courage, and go ahead." There was also bitterness. Looking back over his astonishing career, he could not "recollect a single instance of success in anything." His son, in like mood, after a distinguished career in diplomacy, wrote to a young friend, "When I was entering into life I was disposed to mount a high horse and challenge the world to disputation for prizes which now I would not cross the room to secure." The pattern of courage and disenchantment descended to the "Fourth Generation" of the line that first emerged with John Adams. In Henry Adams it was to be deepened by personal tragedy.

Adams's early career showed the vitality of the Brahmin ideal. A handsome, almost dapper little fellow, not more than five feet three, with dark wavy hair, he was the center of a coterie of convivial college mates at Harvard in the Class of 1858, a group of ninety young men. He was a serious and bookish student. He had a flair for the classics and carried a pocket Horace with him. His capacious memory became a concordance of literary allusions to Shakespeare, Byron, Voltaire, Carlyle, and scores of others whose apt phrases would leap to his pen. He was most at home in French in which his father had tutored him. He studied the Italian of Dante under Luigi Monti at Harvard. One of his favorite pastimes, many years later, was to translate a canto of the *Divine Comedy* or a sonnet from Petrarch. Thirty years after he left college he could still take pleasure, while resting on the beach at Tahiti, in translating the hexameters of Homer's *Iliad*. German came hard to his Gallic temperament, but in time he was able to worry his way through the most abstruse scientific treatises in that language. To prepare himself for a visit to Spain he taught himself the language by plowing through an array of plays and novels. At another time, anticipating a journey to China he set himself a stint of a thousand characters every two weeks. He even tried his hand at Tahitian in order to translate some of the oral literature.

In philosophy and economics the instruction at Harvard was safely conservative. Only much later did Adams encounter the *Communist Manifesto*. One of his most glaring slips of recollection in the *Education* reproached his teachers for not acquainting him with Karl Marx's *Capital*—the book did not appear until

a dozen years after he left Harvard. The small faculty had uncommon distinction, especially in science. Charles Darwin admired Asa Gray and envied him the extraordinary set of colleagues. The two men who most influenced Adams were Louis Agassiz, one of the greatest geologists of the time, and James Russell Lowell. Within a few years Asa Gray became the defender of *The Origin of Species* and Agassiz its most severe critic. Lowell brought with him the aura of vast literary success. His *Biglow Papers* were on every table. Adams contributed frequently to the *Harvard Magazine*, essays with a rather moralistic slant; he won a literary prize, and achieved glory as Class Day orator. A newspaper editor remembered the oration for its irony and cynicism, overlooking the intense moral idealism on which Adams based his attack on their materialistic society. In all the subsequent turns of his thought he remained faithful to this affirmation of the supremacy of spiritual values.

After Harvard he began his career as a world traveler that ultimately qualified him for the role of geopolitician to the American secretary of state. Unable to follow the lectures in civil law at Berlin, he doggedly studied the language among the youngsters in a German preparatory school. For two years he studied and traveled in Switzerland, Italy, and France. The Boston *Courier* published a series of his travel letters from Italy, his most notable coup being an interview with the victorious Garibaldi in Sicily. His plan to study law and follow the "family go-cart" fell by the wayside when he joined his father in Washington as private secretary during the secession winter of 1860. Henry acted as correspondent for the Boston *Advertiser* and did his youthful best to support his father's work as a leading peacemaker. Lincoln appointed the elder Adams to the Court of St. James's, disposing as well of Henry's fate. From a distance young Adams envied the military exploits of his classmates, but he soon accepted his fate as a private secretary and made the most of his opportunity to study at close range the course of power politics. For a year he contributed a weekly column to the New York *Times*, skillfully taking the pulse of British public opinion. The series ended abruptly when his identity was inadvertently disclosed by the proud editor of the Boston *Courier* as the author of a special report to that paper.

London was much more than a school of diplomacy to him. It gave him a postgraduate course in art appreciation, literature, science, and public affairs. His teachers were the best that England had to offer. He sat at the feet of liberal statesmen like Cobden, Bright, and Forster; argued with John Stuart Mill, the great Utilitarian and popularizer of Auguste Comte, the founder of scientific Positivism; attached himself to Charles Lyell, England's leading geologist and new champion of Darwin. Excited by the tremendous upsurge of discovery, Adams thought for a time of making a career in science. He bowed at Court before Queen Victoria, resplendent in knee breeches and sword. He dined out incessantly, became an inveterate clubman, and learned to be bored by small talk with dukes and duchesses. He liked best the medieval charm of the country house of his friend Charles Milnes Gaskell at Wenlock Abbey in Shropshire; they remained lifelong friends. The successful close of the Civil War made Adams impatient to begin an independent career, for time was running out as he neared thirty. His eldest brother, John Quincy II, plunged hopefully into politics; Charles aimed for the railroads and the scandals of the Erie as a free-lance journalist; Henry made his debut with a slashing article for the *North American Quarterly* debunking the patron saint of Virginia, Captain John Smith. He quickly followed this up with two able historical studies of British finance after the Napoleonic wars to warn Americans against inflationary nostrums during the postwar period. He next turned his versatile pen to a long and penetrating essay-review of Lyell's tenth edition of the *Principles of Geology*, the edition in which Lyell aligned himself with Darwin. To Adams the occasion offered a dramatic confrontation between his Harvard teacher Louis Agassiz and the Darwinians. Torn between two eminent parties, he characteristically suspended judgment on the theories.

Now known as a leading writer for the *North American*, Adams confidently headed for Washington in 1868, sure of an entree into the highest official circles. For two years he was one of the most active members of the press corps, dashing off articles for the recently founded reform weekly, the *Nation*, and the New York *Evening Post*, directing his gadfly attacks upon the spoils system and the mismanagement of government finances. His masterly analysis of Congressional incompetence in his annual "Session" articles and in one on civil service reform showed the birth of a powerful new writer. The most notable of his muckraking efforts was "The New York Gold Conspiracy," a devastating exposé of the efforts of Jim Fisk and Jay Gould to corner the gold market right under the nose of gullible President Grant.

At the height of Adams's success as a crusading journalist, family counsels again prevailed. As it was obvious that Grant would not reward so dangerous a critic, Henry was shunted off to Harvard to become an assistant professor of history and to help Charles William Eliot carry out his ambitious scheme of reforming instruction. The editorship of the *North American* went along with the offer. Determined not to vegetate in Cambridge, Adams made the quarterly a vehicle for the Liberal Republican movement, pooling efforts with his brother Charles and with his younger brother Brooks, who was just beginning his career as a lawyer and publicist. Adams recruited authorities in the most varied fields—politics, science, philosophy, literature, linguistics, history, economics—and himself reviewed more than a score of books, ranging from learned treatises like Sohm's *Lex Salica* to a Howells novel, *Their Wedding Journey*.

In the classroom he was a vigorously Socratic lecturer. His revolutionary premise was that education existed for the student; the professor existed to incite the student to work on his own. He borrowed the intensive research methods of German scholarship and in the seminars, which he initiated at Harvard, he taught the young men to go to the primary documents. Students responded with the greatest enthusiasm to his unconventional approach and embarrassed him by crowding his classes. Assigned first to medieval history, he soon mastered the subject, thanks to his incredible intellectual energy. He then branched off into American history where the full significance of his heritage opened up to him, and he began to dream of a magnum opus on the early years of the republic. His monument to his medieval studies was an enormously learned essay on Anglo-Saxon law, showing his adoption of the institutional approach to history, which he published with essays by his three doctoral students, the first to receive such degrees at Harvard. He had a lasting influence on the teaching of history. Among his scholars who rose to distinction were Edward Channing, Henry Osborn Taylor (the noted Medievalist), and James Lawrence Laughlin (the political economist). His protégé was Henry Cabot Lodge who went on from history into politics, rose to leadership in the United States Senate, and found his place in history as chief adversary of Woodrow Wilson.

Adams married in 1872 a bluestocking Boston heiress, Marian Hooper, an intimate friend of the young Henry James and a witty satirist in her own right. The marriage brought Adams into a wider circle of artists and writers. They spent a wedding year in Europe, renewing a host of acquaintances and establishing fresh intellectual alliances. On their return Cambridge and Boston grew more and more confining to the two rebels. Weary of teaching schoolboys and anxious to begin a new career as a professional historian, Adams decamped from Boston in 1877 for the genial freedom of Washington. His chance came when he accepted a commission to do a biography of Albert Gallatin, whose philosophical statesmanship was for Adams an American model.

The chapter of life that now opened was a brilliant idyl for the two happy expatriated Bostonians. Marian presided over their exclusive salon in Lafayette Square which quickly became the chief intellectual center of society. Cabinet members, ambassadors, senators, congressmen, bureau chiefs, and visiting notables made their rendezvous at the five o'clock tea table. Good talk, fine wines, and an imaginative cuisine delighted the intimate dinners of six and eight. Henry James, returning briefly from his own exile in London, thought his friends a little too severe in their standards of political and social propriety; their salon "left out on the whole, more people than it took in." What it took in was of the best. Here the repartee of Clarence King and John Hay crackled about the hearth; here Carl Schurz improvised

on the piano; here the Congressional leader James A. Garfield planned strategy. William James came down full of the new psychology. Matthew Arnold renewed their London acquaintance. Whenever weather permitted, Henry and Marian rode out to Rock Creek and the Virginia countryside to enjoy the dogwood and the Judas tree. Summers they joined the quiet summer colony at Beverly Farms within sound of the Massachusetts surf.

The *Gallatin* came out in 1879, first fruit of Adams's efficient labors in the archives of the State Department. The biographical narrative was largely carried by quotations from original sources. This method, common to the "Life and Letters" biographies of the time made for a ponderous structure. For Adams it served as a trial run for the *History* in which he would refine the method into high art. The volume showed his assimilation of the grand style of his favorite historians, Gibbon and Macaulay, in many of its key passages. It established his authority as an important historian and was to remain the definitive study of Gallatin for nearly seventy-five years.

For many years Adams had toyed with the notion of writing a novel, for literary practice if for nothing else. The opportunity arrived when he finished the Gallatin manuscript late in 1878. He turned his now well-seasoned pen to a novel of his favorite city, a satire on the Washington which now lay like an open book before him, crying to be anatomized. The surgery was much too ruthless to be publicly acknowledged by a sober—and vulnerable—historian. Issued anonymously as *Democracy: An American Novel*, it made a sensational success in England and then became, by reflex action, a best seller in America. Critics praised the unknown author as the peer of Henry James and William Dean Howells and superior to Disraeli in the mixing of politics and Romance. Friends like Lord Bryce deplored the mischief it might do and Clarence King, who was in on the secret, started an abortive novel on aristocracy to answer it. The easily recognized victims accused various members of the Adams circle. One of them, Senator James G. Blaine, who figured prominently as the egregious Senator Ratcliffe, publicly snubbed King, believing him to be the author. The secret was perfectly kept by the Adams inner circle, "The Five of Hearts," and Adams's authorship remained almost unknown until the 1920's. A minor classic among political novels, it was frequently reprinted during Adams's lifetime, its psychological insight into the motives of politicians undimmed by the passage of time. Its heroine, Mrs. Lightfoot Lee, like her creator, hungered to touch the levers of power but shrank from the price which democracy seemed to exact for the privilege.

Adams went off to Europe again, as a scholar to whom archives magically opened. He mined away for his *History* in Paris, Madrid, and London, setting copyists to work after the lavish example of cousin George Bancroft, the dean of American historians. In the frequent intervals of work he settled down to being lionized a little in London and enjoying the constant companionship of Henry James. Among the new intellectual lights, he made the acquaintance of men like William Lecky (the historian of rationalism), John Richard Green, Herbert Spencer, and Ernest Renan.

Returning to Lafayette Square late in 1880, Adams briefly diverted himself with a popular biography of John Randolph for the American Statesmen series as a kind of outrider for the great work which was slowly taking shape. Unlike the massive *Gallatin*, the *Randolph* moves with a fine novelistic verve, sharply focused on the drama of Randolph's eccentric career. In this book Adams fully settled the family score against another traducer of John Quincy Adams. The tragic figure that stalks half-dementedly through Adams's pages still rankles in the hearts of loyal Virginians. Modern scholarship, however, has not substantially altered the portrait, still less matched the supple and vigorous prose. The success of the *Randolph* inspired Adams to dash off a similar study of Aaron Burr, the "Mephistopheles of politics," now chiefly remembered for having killed Alexander Hamilton in a duel. The publisher shied away from dignifying Burr as a statesman. Adams angrily suppressed the volume though his wife thought it even better than the *Randolph*. Much of the manuscript seems to have been incorporated in the *History*.

By 1884 Adams reached the halfway mark in his long labors and sought respite from historical scholarship in another novel, again choosing a woman for his central figure. *Esther* is an imaginative re-creation of the debates over religion and science and their relation to art and poetry in the world which had been overturned by Darwin, Spencer, and the new psychology, debates that regularly enlivened the Adams salon. What was an enlightened woman's role in such a world? Could the new woman fulfill herself in love and marriage? The book explored controversies that are still unsettled. As a psychological study of a woman's character it surpasses *Democracy*. Its philosophical themes foreshadow those of the *Mont-Saint-Michel and Chartres* and the *Education*. Adams persuaded his publisher, Henry Holt, to issue the book without advertising in order to test the responsiveness of public taste. He also affixed a pseudonym to the title page, "Frances Snow Compton." The critics, almost to a man, ignored the book which paid such little heed to the prevailing formulas of Romantic sentiment. It vanished from sight, confirming Adams's low opinion of the state of American culture.

A mixture of motives—pride, diffidence, an almost morbid sensitivity to criticism—led Adams to guard the secret of authorship even more carefully than that of *Democracy*. Its charming and cultivated heroine was closely modelled on his wife. His natural chivalry turned to a kind of panic dread in the following year. On December 6, 1885, Marian, who had become widely known as an amateur photographer, took her own life, using one of the chemicals of the darkroom. She had been unable to endure the recent loss of her father to whom she had been deeply attached since childhood when the death of her mother had made her entirely dependent on him. The heroine of *Esther* surmounted a similar ordeal; she could not, in spite of all of Adams's devoted care. The tragedy was front page news in Washington, New York, and Boston. The shock to Adams was appalling, as his life tumbled in ruins about him. It was made no easier to bear by the fact that their marriage had been childless. His life broken in half, he felt for a long time that he also had died, and he sometimes startled inquirers by insisting on the grim jest. He was humored in his morbid fancies by the sympathetic young matrons of their circle, especially by the wife of Senator James Donald Cameron whose beauty he had idealized in the character of Catherine Brooks in *Esther*. Henceforth, Adams withdrew as far as possible from public notice. Lonely and embittered, he made Mrs. Cameron his closest confidante and gradually condemned himself to hopeless adoration, a Chateaubriand, as he came to think of himself, to her Madame Recamier.

Life, even "posthumous" life, had to go on and Adams, shutting away his grief, the only outward sign of it being the enigmatic statue in Rock Creek cemetery sculptured by Augustus Saint-Gaudens, bent again to his work with his usual driving energy. The tragedy brought out all his latent restlessness. Marriage had made him quiet. Now his belated romantic attachment for Elizabeth Cameron made him a lovelorn wanderer who complained that he could not be happy in any one place more than three days. He made travel a fine art and his letters grew to be masterpieces of acute observation. The reticent Henry James marveled at his power to bare his soul. The more than thirty years of active existence remaining to him took him all over the globe. In 1886 he voyaged to Japan with the artist John La Farge, feeding his historical imagination on Japanese art and religion. In 1890, the nine volumes of the *History* finally in print, he escaped to the South Seas, again in the company of La Farge, sketching under his companion's tutelage, geologizing, and studying Polynesian folklore and history. He became interested in the fortunes of his Tahitian hosts, leaders of the dethroned Teva family, and wrote a touching historical memoir of the last queen, privately printing the book in 1893.

He finished his tour around the world late in 1891, after savagely sampling the decadence of Paris. He shared the common American opinion of its immorality but recognized it as the most civilized and intellectually alive place in the world. He became a connoisseur of World Fairs measuring the progress of civilization by their display of scientific marvels. The Far West was one of his earliest enthusiasms: first he traversed Wyoming and Colorado by pack train in the summer of 1870; there he first met the fabulous Clarence King, a geologist then with the United States Fortieth Parallel Survey. Later journeyings carried him from Canada to the Rio Grande. The exotic life of Cuba and the West Indies fascinated him. He was drawn in by King as an active partisan in the movement for Cuban independence. In Mexico, nearing sixty, he could still manage twenty miles a day on horseback. But Europe drew him most as the shadow of coming wars and revolutions added a dangerous charm to the sight of jostling cultures. Egypt had long been a familiar story. His interest in geopolitics deepened as he circled the Mediterranean basin in the late nineties, saturating himself in archaeology and art and pouring out his inspired commentary in essay-letters to his friends. Italy drew him again and again, especially Rome where he felt himself another Gibbon meditating on the steps of the church of Aracoeli above the Forum. One long deferred expedition took him in the company of the Lodges to Moscow. He then went on alone to Scandanavia and the North Cape to meditate like a new Teufelsdröckh on the coming struggle for power between Russian inertia and the dynamism of Western Europe.

Wherever Adams traveled he projected his lines back into the past and forward into the future. His most significant travel in time carried him back to the Middle Ages, to the birth of Gothic architecture. John Ruskin and the Pre-Raphaelite poets and artists of the medieval revival of the nineteenth century had already given an idealistic turn to his earlier study of medieval history and architecture. His brother Brooks had also "mapped out the lines and indicated the emotions," as Henry afterwards remembered. The terrible depression of 1893 revealed to him all the ugly tendencies of *laissez-faire* economics and the growing despotism of the "gold bug," the finance capitalist. Never did the remote past seem so winning and fair as he saw it one summer in 1895 in the Gothic cathedrals of Normandy, when he accompanied the Lodges in his favorite role of avuncular schoolmaster. His letters radiated his new intuitions as he worshiped before the great "glass gods" of Chartres whose stained glass is the wonder of Christendom. Suffused with a sense of history, he felt a return to spiritual fountains, experiencing a vaulting back in imagination to his Norman ancestors. "I can almost remember," he wrote John Hay,

the faith that gave me energy and the sacred boldness that made my towers seem to me so daring. . . . Nearly eight hundred years have passed since I made the fatal mistake of going to England, and since then I have never done anything in the world to compare in the perfection of spirit and art with my cathedral of Coutances.

Thereafter, the Gothic renaissance of the twelfth century became his anchor in history and his symbol-haunted mind assimilated to it all the imagined virtues of archaic societies everywhere. To him it was filled with a primal moral vigor, a society whose art and poetry affirmed universal values, whose maternal women inspired their warrior husbands to selfless devotion and heroism. For the remaining twenty years of his life Adams steeped himself obsessively in the art and lore of medieval France, bringing to a focus on that period all his far ranging studies in archaeology, history, and science. He formed the almost invariable habit of spending his summers in France, dashing recklessly down the country roads in his Mercedes, learning the statuary and stained glass by heart. The other half of each year he spent in intense study of modern science, technology, and world politics, trying to predict the future course of human history.

The new drift of his thinking had emerged in his presidential address of 1894. History must become a science in spite of the resistance of such vested interests as the State, the Church, Capital, and Labor. His brother Brook's recent *Law of Civilization and Decay* analyzed the discontents of the time in terms of the centralizing tendencies of capitalist society. The decline of the West was the logical result of the legitimation of usury. Brooks's "Bible of Hell" traced the process from Roman times to the present. For Henry, his favorite twelfth century was a doomed interlude in his brother's panorama of history, a moment of precious respite in the march of universal avarice. At the turn of the century he wrote the *Chartres* to wrest from history the secret of the movement that covered northern France with great cathedrals. His *History of the United States* had established a datum line

in American history for future historians, a mark from which to measure progress—or failure. The *Chartres* did the same thing for the Western world. Against its background the chaos and anarchy of the twentieth century might stand etched in all its horror. Adams aimed at no mere historical analysis. The work was a means of esthetic identification, a lyrical evocation of the spirit of the age. Dubious as history, it triumphed as art.

He returned to the charge in the *Education*, proposing as a model for future historians a "Dynamic Theory of History," in which his emerging theory of all history as an onrushing deterministic system of interchangeable mechanical forces found first expression. He elaborated this conception in "The Rule of Phase Applied to History" (1909), not published until 1919, in the *Degradation of the Democratic Dogma*. The essay is based on a highly impressionistic reading of Willard Gibbs's phase rule formulas in physical chemistry concerning the "coexistence of phases in the equilibrium of heterogeneous substances." What Adams thought he had found was a scientific analogy to illustrate the *succession* of increasingly complex stages in modern civilization. Still tinkering with the impossibly difficult task of absorbing into an all-encompassing philosophy of history the latest developments in social psychology and atomic science, Adams next tried to utilize the second law of thermodynamics, the tendency of energy in a closed system to reach a maximum of equilibrium, to explain the apparent decline of social and psychic energy in modern society. Adams assumed that the cosmos was a vast heat machine that was running down. The resulting essay was *A Letter to American Teachers of History* which he issued privately in 1910 to historians and university librarians throughout the country. It remains a brilliant curiosity of pseudoscientific speculation.

With the death of his most intimate friend, John Hay, in 1905, at the height of his influence as Secretary of State, Adams's role as an unofficial elder statesman virtually came to an end. President Theodore Roosevelt admired his genius and continued to cultivate him but preferred the more aggressive imperialism of Brooks Adams. Henry prepared an edition of

Hay's letters at the request of his widow, excessive diffidence preventing him from doing a biography which would entail the "obtrusion of a third person" between the reader and the subject. It may also be, as Herbert Croly suggests, that his high estimate of Hay's achievement rapidly declined. Knowing Hay as one of the best talkers of his time, Adams selected "everything that resembled conversation;—everything he said to me without literary purpose." His public career he left to history. "The result," he conceded, "was desperately muddled." Unfortunately, Mrs. Hay in bringing out the private edition deleted nearly all the names. Usable only with the "Key" which Adams prepared for his own use, the work remains little known. His lingering protest to Ambassador Whitelaw Reid illuminates his own early literary escapades:

My view is that we, who set up to be educated society, should stand up in our harness and should play our parts without awkward stage-fright of amateurs. . . . God knows, I have no love of notoriety, but I have never shrunk from it, if it seemed to be a proper and becoming part of social work.

Another duty of friendship fell upon him in 1910 after the sudden death, at thirty-six, of the poet George Cabot Lodge, who had been Adams's window on the literary Bohemia of Paris in the late nineties. Adams once again used his favorite device of letting the letters tell most of the story. Adams's scruple worked against the poet. As Edith Wharton said, Lodge was not meant for "an active task in letters" and his intellectual dependence on older men like Adams and Hay kept him in a state of "brilliant immaturity." Published in 1911 by Houghton Mifflin the book received little notice, for Adams had too accurately caught "the spirit of the man and his circle." It was reprinted in 1943 in Edmund Wilson's anthology of neglected classics, *The Shock of Recognition*, but even he felt a certain chill in its Rhadamanthine judgments.

With the declining years Adams became to his dismay a "benevolent sage" to the large circle of acquaintances who won the privilege of paying their court at the twelve o'clock breakfasts in Lafayette Square or in Adams's luxurious "garret" in the Avenue du Bois de Boulogne. Beneath the incorrigibly sardonic witticisms they recognized one of the most extraordinary intelligences of the time, an intellectual bystander who had attained Matthew Arnold's ideal of the highest culture. In his book-lined study surrounded by a favorite Corot or Turner, choice water colors, and rare objects of Oriental art, Adams maintained an impregnable island where the old Brahmin order stood up manfully to the despotisms of the new. Here in his final years, especially after a temporarily paralyzing stroke in 1912, Adams worked on in his Voltairean garden, listening to medieval music and old French chansons, hunting out forgotten chansons in French archives, and sometimes putting his hand to a translation from Old French or Latin, his marvelously precise script now flawed by age.

Despite the formidable authority of his manner, he continued to draw the ablest men to him and to hold their friendship with his superb letters. One of those whose judgment he specially prized was the art critic and connoisseur Bernard Berenson, who was creating at I Tatti in Florence a private refuge of culture like that of Adams in Washington. Adams cultivated still another interest in the work of Henri Hubert, a distinguished French archaeologist, and for a number of years he cheerfully subsidized Hubert's fruitless excavations near Les Eyzies. His political interests steadily changed. For a time in the nineties he backed Bryan against the Wall Street combine, then losing faith in the socialistic tendencies of the reform movement, disgusted by the bourgeois ambitions of the underdog, he proclaimed himself a "Conservative Christian Anarchist" with the right to call down a plague on all political houses.

Believing that the contradictions in modern industrial society must lead to an overwhelming collapse when the financial colossi began to prey upon each other in an economic Twilight of the Gods, Adams professed himself a "goldbug" Republican, justifying himself with the thought that he would thus help bring on the salutary collapse sooner. His anarchistic philosophy thus conspired to ally him with his politically conservative friends. This development was complicated, however, by his hereditary patriotism. Moral philosophy might demand the repudiation of contemporary society, but patriotism required that the United States achieve supremacy in the international jungle. Thus though he sided with the anti-imperialist minority during the Spanish-American War and likened the struggles of the Boers against England to the American War for Independence, he came round to the position that the United States must sustain England in order to block the imperial ambitions of Germany in the Pacific and elsewhere. Theodore Roosevelt's trustbusting seemed to him a mere defiance of inevitable economic processes and he deplored his crude diplomacy in Latin America. A born mugwump, he supported the regular Republican candidates, however reluctantly, chiefly because of his hysterical dread of political disorder. Once Woodrow Wilson was elected he refused to countenance indecent attacks upon him at his table. World War I confirmed all his geopolitical predictions. After forty years of close friendship with British diplomats and statesmen from Joseph Chamberlain to Cecil Spring Rice, his sympathies forbade any course but the rescue of England.

His opinions remained as peppery and picturesquely extravagant as ever. Democracy as an equalitarian shibboleth seemed now irrelevant in the onrushing era of vast social revolution. From the height of philosophic contemplation he looked on with sardonic pessimism at the working out of mysterious forces, insisting he had foretold it all in the final chapters of the *Education*. The cosmic forces which man had summoned out of nature were running away with him while man as a form of energy was steadily undergoing degradation, impoverishment, dissolution. This view led to utter skepticism and stoicism, and yet a close reading of his sulphurous letters leads one to conclude that the sustained hysteria that runs through them is that of an actor who became the captive of his role, who had played Hamlet so long that he became him. His role was to convince his high-placed fellow men that there were more things in heaven and earth than were dreamed of in their shallow philosophies. He expressed himself in a kind of philosophic shriek because most men were deaf to quiet persuasion and needed to be startled into an awareness of the tragic complexities of the human condition. If he spoke wildly of the end of the world, it was the cry of a sensitive soul outraged by the multiplying barbarisms of the world he had survived into.

III

ADAMS was a bundle of contradictions. His lifelong quest for unity was no more than his effort to answer the most overwhelming of personal questions: Who am I? What am I? He felt that Rousseau had disgraced the ego; yet few writers have had such a capacity for baring their souls. He repeatedly warned his correspondents that contradiction was unavoidable. It was the law of life. He could say with Whitman, "Do I contradict myself? / Very well then I contradict myself, / (I am large, I contain multitudes)." As Adams says in the *Education*, "Words are slippery and thought is viscous." Or in a different key, "Did he himself quite know what he meant? Certainly not! If he had known enough to state his problem, his education would have been complete at once." He felt his personality whirl among contending polarities. He loved order and decorum and created in his heretical image of the Virgin Mother the type of all rebellion against the status quo. He was prudish and finicking in his fastidiousness yet affirmed the fact of sex and fecundity as the most vital of social energies. He had a Byronic passion for solitude and would not travel without a companion. He scorned the pageant of a bleeding heart and for his intimates wore his own on his sleeve. He scorned bourgeois taste and the preoccupation with material things and wistfully envied the possessors of great wealth. High society repelled him with its inhibitions and artifice but he would associate only with those entitled to be of it. He complained of nerves and dyspepsia all his life, neurotically feared the loss of his mental powers, and lived "to dance on the graves" of practically all of his contemporaries. He was passionately addicted to scientific discovery and then turned science upside down to show its limitations. He despised business and prided himself on his business acumen.

As a biographer he saw his own contradictions mirrored in the men he analyzed. Reading Morley's *Gladstone*, he remarked, "Of course in him, as in most people, there were two or three or a dozen men; in these emotional, abnormal natures, there are never less than three." He applied this principle to his conception of character in all his writings. The psychological tensions of both of his novels arise from the inner warfare of the psyche. His great portraits in the biographies and the *History*—figures like Jefferson, Canning, Napoleon, Toussaint, Tecumseh—all illustrate it.

In fiction his power of invention was not great; he approached plot and character intellectually. His strength lay in dramatizing ideas, pursuing them to their ambiguous consequences. Men and women were more important—at any rate, more interesting—for what they thought than for what they did. For the serious writer only the ironic posture was possible. To think was to satirize. Satire expressed the ultimate self-awareness of the writer. As a literary stylist Adams worked toward a Swiftian directness of statement yet with a craftsman's knowledge of the infinite variety of English syntax. He had a Flaubertian zeal for adapting the style to the matter of his discourse. In historical exposition he relied mainly on a flexible and fluid prose with muscular nouns and verbs, but he knew also the value of modulation and color for his climaxes and the rolling arrest of balanced sentences. At first imitative of the great stylists of his craft, Gibbon and Macaulay, he adapted their medium to the developing character of American colloquial speech. He had a keen ear for slang and flavored his letters with the going idioms. His literary allusions please the reader with the repeated compliment to his taste. In the great works of Adams's literary maturity, the *Chartres* and the *Education*, he experienced the epiphany of the poet and the artist. He learned to apply to prose the lessons of color harmony taught him by John La Farge, to charge his terms with associations as an artist blends his colors on the palette. His use of image and symbol is thoroughly modern. So, the broken arch of the Gothic church supports a whole domain of aspiration. Like Emerson he saw words as symbols of things and things as symbols of spiritual truths. Philosophy comes to life in the dramatic confrontations of the *Chartres*. Abelard and Bernard argue the subtleties of essence and sub-

stance because life did depend on it, as in a later age men disputed about the atom because it held the secret of the common destiny.

In the *Education* Adams created his richest fabric of symbols. From the initial conception of the Carlylean mannikin upon whom he is to display the dress of education to the image of the comet-meteor for the acceleration of mind, Adams constantly surmounts the limitations of objective statement. The mind may be caught by argument but the image holds it. The image best hints at the polarity of things, the unity and multiplicity which define the limit of thought. Thus the Virgin and the Dynamo incarnate their ages as symbols of infinite power, the one centripetal, drawing the chaos of existence into patterns of order; the other, centrifugal, accelerating the flight toward chaos. The voyage toward multiplicity in which the old man found himself enmeshed rises to a heroic and even tragic quest in which the homunculus hero figures in a variety of guises —Ulysses and Tannhauser, Teufelsdröckh and Faust.

Adams's writings have aroused an enormous amount of interest among intellectuals, touching as they do upon almost every field of serious inquiry. He is abhorred as a cynical snob by those who are put off by his pose and his affectations. He is hailed as a realistic critic of democracy and the rare example of a fully civilized man. The great Jeffersonian partisan, Vernon Louis Parrington, saw him as a wholesome critic of the Hamiltonian tradition as well as a master stylist. To the conservative reaction of the 1950's he seemed a defender of the Burkean tradition in politics and society. He himself hoped to serve no faction. His *History* may have been overrated by Yvor Winters as the greatest work of its kind since Gibbon but it stands in any case as the high-water mark of American historiography. Perhaps the most unstinted praise has gone to the *Chartres*, whatever cavils it may deserve for its romantic distortions of life in the Middle Ages and for its highly unorthodox theology. The Virgin of his creation is undoubtedly one of the remarkable heroines of literature. The *Education* continues to have an almost topical vitality and will continue to have it so long as the age of crisis continues. Undeniably one of the most brilliant commentaries on the shaping forces of American culture since 1865, it stands in need of constant correction of its sardonic parallax, not so much for its facts as for its one-sided evaluations of men and events. The science of it cannot be taken seriously, yet Adams shows in his virtuosity in manipulating the new concepts that a new field of metaphor is available to the literary artist and that scientific reality can add a new idiom to poetry. His writings show the infinite capacity of the mind to feel, to be aware, and to respond to the full reach of experience. From the depths of his despair he affirms the boundless possibilities of the human spirit.

READING SUGGESTIONS

EDITIONS

There is as yet no collected edition of the writings of Henry Adams. A descriptive listing of the separate editions of his works appears in Jacob Blanck, *Bibliography of American Literature*, Vol. I (1955).

BIOGRAPHY

ARTHUR F. BERINGAUSE, *Brooks Adams* (1955). A liberally documented account of the intellectual collaboration of Henry Adams and his brother Brooks.

ERNEST SAMUELS, *The Young Henry Adams* (1948); *Henry Adams: The Middle Years* (1958). The first biography to make substantial use of the large collection of unpublished Henry Adams papers at the Massachusetts Historical Society. His life and writings are presented against the social and intellectual background of his time. The third, and concluding, volume is in preparation.

ELIZABETH STEVENSON, *Henry Adams* (1955). Reassesses the dramatic tensions of Adams's life in an interestingly written synthesis of all the published materials.

LETTERS

WORTHINGTON C. FORD, editor, *A Cycle of Adams Letters, 1861–1865*, 2 vols. (1920). An absorbing interchange of family letters during the Civil War in which the young Henry Adams figures prominently as an apprentice in diplomacy. By the same editor, *Letters of Henry Adams, 1858–1891* (1930), *Letters of Henry Adams, 1892–1918* (1938). Significant aspects of Adams's life are edited out; yet it remains the most brilliant collection of letters in American literature.

HAROLD DEAN CATER, editor, *Henry Adams and His Friends* (1947). Adds several hundred unpublished letters, many of them of first importance. The long biographical introduction is indispensable for many sidelights on Adams's personal life.

WARD THORON, editor, *Letters of Mrs. Henry Adams, 1865–1883* (1936). A gossipy and often witty record of the social side of Adams's married life. It is an eloquent commentary on one of the major silences of *The Education of Henry Adams*.

SPECIAL STUDIES

MAX I. BAYM, *The French Education of Henry Adams* (1951). An exhaustive review of Adams's indebtedness to French writers, based largely on the marginal annotations in the books in his library.

WILLIAM H. JORDY, *Henry Adams: Scientific Historian* (1952). Searchingly analyzes Adams's use—and misuse—of contemporary science in the formulation of his theories of history. Valuable also for its comprehensive annotated bibliography.

J. C. LEVENSON, *The Mind and Art of Henry Adams* (1957). A perceptive study of the developing intellectual and aesthetic patterns of Adams's principal writings.

SOME ARTICLES AND ESSAYS

RICHARD P. BLACKMUR, "The Expense of Greatness," *Virginia Quarterly Review*, XII (1936), 396–415. An inquiry into the philosophical and aesthetic implications of Adams's sense of failure. Reprinted in *The Lion and the Honeycomb* (1955), pp. 79–96.

HENRY STEELE COMMAGER, "Henry Adams," in William T. Hutchinson, editor, *Marcus W. Jernegan Essays in American Historiography* (1937), pp. 191–206. One of the best studies of Adams as a historian.

ROBERT M. LOVETT, "The Betrayal of Henry Adams," *Dial*, LXV (1918), 468–72. An excellent contemporary review of the *Education*.

FERNER NUHN, "Henry Adams and the Hand of the Fathers," in *The Wind Blew from the East* (1942), pp. 164–94. A penetrating study of the European influence.

YVOR WINTERS, "Henry Adams," in *The Anatomy of Nonsense* (1943), pp. 23–87. An analysis of the effect of the Puritan ethos on Adams's later work.

The mass of critical essays and articles on the varied aspects of Adams's achievement as a writer and thinker has grown so large that no adequate selection can be given here. The more important ones are listed in Volume III of the *Literary History of the United States* (1948) and in the *Bibliography Supplement*, ed. by Richard M. Ludwig (1959).

FROM

DEMOCRACY: AN AMERICAN NOVEL

❖

⟨ THE ACTION of the novel takes place in the months following the election of a new President. Mrs. Lee, a widow of thirty, establishes an exclusive salon in Lafayette Square with her beautiful younger sister, Sybil Ross. John Carrington, a high-minded Washington lawyer from Virginia, acts as Mrs. Lee's guide into the inner circles of Washington politics. She meets Senator Silas P. Ratcliffe, the most powerful boss in the President-elect's party, whom Adams modeled on the popular idol, Senator James G. Blaine, with touches drawn from Senator Roscoe Conkling. Both had tried to dictate to the recently elected President Rutherford B. Hayes as they had to Ulysses S. Grant before him. The bitter overtones of the scandal-ridden years of Grant's administration and the "stolen" Hayes-Tilden election of 1876 run through the novel. Ratcliffe becomes an admirer of Mrs. Lee and almost persuades her of his probity, but when Carrington proves him guilty of corruption she throws him over and abandons Washington in disgust. The successive episodes take the characters through the odious intrigues and social climbing of a Washington season that ends with the inauguration of the captive President. The climax of the satire on democratic pretensions is the grand ball for visiting royalty.

Democracy was first published in 1880. By 1908 it had gone through sixteen printings. The seventeenth printing, in 1925, was the first to carry Adams's name as author.

❖

CHAPTER 1

FOR REASONS which many persons thought ridiculous, Mrs. Lightfoot Lee decided to pass the winter in Washington. She was in excellent health, but she said that the climate would do her good. In New York she had troops of friends, but she suddenly became eager to see again the very small number of those who lived on the Potomac. It was only to her closest intimates that she honestly acknowledged herself to be tortured by *ennui*. Since her husband's death, five years before, she had lost her taste for New York society; she had felt no interest in the price of stocks, and very little in the men who dealt in them; she had become serious. What was it all worth, this wilderness of men and women as monotonous as the brown stone houses they lived in? In her despair she had

resorted to desperate measures. She had read philosophy in the original German, and the more she read, the more she was disheartened that so much culture should lead to nothing—nothing. After talking of Herbert Spencer for an entire evening with a very literary transcendental commission-merchant, she could not see that her time had been better employed than when in former days she had passed it in flirting with a very agreeable young stock-broker; indeed, there was an evident proof to the contrary, for the flirtation might lead to something—had, in fact, led to marriage; while the philosophy could lead to nothing, unless it were perhaps to another evening of the same kind, because transcendental philosophers are mostly elderly men, usually married, and, when engaged in business, somewhat apt to be sleepy towards evening. Nevertheless Mrs. Lee did her best to turn her study to practical use. She plunged into philanthrophy, visited prisons, inspected hospitals, read the literature of pauperism and crime, saturated herself with the statistics of vice, until her mind had nearly lost sight of virtue. At last it rose in rebellion against her, and she came to the limit of her strength. This path, too, seemed to lead nowhere. She declared that she had lost the sense of duty, and that, so far as concerned her, all the paupers and criminals in New York might henceforward rise in their majesty and manage every railway on the continent. Why should she care? What was the city to her? She could find nothing in it that seemed to demand salvation. What gave peculiar sanctity to numbers? Why were a million people, who all resembled each other, any way more interesting than one person? What aspiration could she help to put into the mind of this great million-armed monster that would make it worth her love or respect? Religion? A thousand powerful churches were doing their best, and she could see no chance for a new faith of which she was to be the inspired prophet. Ambition? High popular ideals? Passion for whatever is lofty and pure? The very words irritated her. Was she not herself devoured by ambition, and was she not now eating her heart out because she could find no one object worth a sacrifice?

Was it ambition—real ambition—or was it mere restlessness that made Mrs. Lightfoot Lee so bitter against New York and Philadelphia, Baltimore and Boston, American life in general and all life in particular? What did she want? Not social position, for she herself was an eminently respectable Philadelphian by birth; her father a famous clergyman; and her husband had been equally irreproachable, a descendant of one branch of the Virginia Lees, which had drifted to New York in search of fortune, and had found it, or enough of it to keep the young man there. His widow had her own place in society which no one disputed. Though not brighter than her neighbours, the world persisted in classing her among clever women; she had wealth, or at least enough of it to give her all that money can give by way of pleasure to a sensible woman in an American city; she had her house and her carriage; she dressed well; her table was good, and her furniture was never allowed to fall behind the latest standard of decorative art. She had travelled in Europe, and after several visits, covering some years of time, had returned home, carrying in one hand, as it were, a green-grey landscape, a remarkably pleasing specimen of Corot, and in the other some bales of Persian and Syrian rugs and embroideries, Japanese bronzes and porcelain. With this she declared Europe to be exhausted, and she frankly avowed that she was American to the tips of her fingers; she neither knew nor greatly cared whether America or Europe were best to live in; she had no violent love for either, and she had no objection to abusing both; but she meant to get all that American life had to offer, good or bad, and to drink it down to the dregs, fully determined that whatever there was in it she would have, and that whatever could be made out of it she would manufacture. "I know," said she, "that America produces petroleum and pigs; I have seen both on the steamers; and I am told it produces silver and gold. There is choice enough for any woman."

Yet, as has been already said, Mrs. Lee's first experience was not a success. She soon declared that New York might represent the petroleum or the pigs, but the gold of life was not to be discovered there by her eyes. Not but that there was variety enough; a variety of people, occupations, aims, and thoughts; but that all these, after growing to a certain height, stopped short. They found nothing to hold them up. She knew, more or less intimately, a dozen men whose fortunes ranged between one million and forty millions. What did they do with their money? What could they do with it that was different from what other men did? After all, it is absurd to spend more money than is enough to satisfy all one's wants; it is vulgar to live in two houses in the same street, and to drive six horses abreast. Yet, after setting aside a certain income sufficient for all one's wants, what was to be done with the rest? To let it accumulate was to own one's failure; Mrs. Lee's great grievance was that it did accumulate, without changing or improving the quality of its owners. To spend it in charity and public works was doubtless praiseworthy, but was it wise? Mrs. Lee had read enough political economy and pauper reports to be nearly convinced that public work should be public duty, and that great benefactions do harm as well as good. And even supposing it spent on these objects, how could it do more than increase and perpetuate that same kind of human nature which was her great grievance? Her New York friends could not meet this question except by falling back upon their native commonplaces, which she recklessly trampled upon, averring that, much as she admired the genius of the famous traveller, Mr. Gulliver, she never had been able, since she became a widow, to accept the Brobdingnagian doctrine[1] that he who made two blades of grass grow where only one grew before deserved better of mankind than the whole race of politicians. She would not find fault with the philosopher had he required that the grass should be of an improved quality; "but," said she, "I cannot honestly pretend that I should be pleased to see two New York men where I now see one; the idea is too ridiculous; more than one and a half would be fatal to me."

Then came her Boston friends, who suggested that higher education was precisely what she wanted; she should throw herself into a crusade for universities and art-schools. Mrs. Lee turned upon them with a sweet smile; "Do you know," said she, "that we have in New York already the richest university[2] in America, and that its only trouble has always been that it can get no scholars even by paying for them? Do you want me to go out into the streets and waylay boys? If the heathen refuse to be converted, can you give me power over the stake and the sword to compel them to come in? And suppose you can? Suppose I march all the boys in Fifth Avenue down to the university and have them all properly taught Greek and Latin, English literature, ethics, and German philosophy. What then? You do it in Boston. Now tell me honestly what comes of it. I suppose you have there a brilliant society; numbers of poets, scholars, philosophers, statesmen, all up and down Beacon Street.[3] Your evenings must be sparkling. Your press must scintillate. How is it that we New Yorkers never hear of it? We don't go much into your society; but when we do, it doesn't seem so very much better than our own. You are just like the rest of us. You grow six inches high, and then you stop. Why will not

DEMOCRACY.   Chapter **1. 1. Brobdingnagian doctrine:** an opinion expressed by the king of Brobdingnag, the land of the giants, in Jonathan Swift's *Gulliver's Travels* (1726).   **2. richest university:** Columbia University, founded in 1754 as King's College.   **3. Beacon Street:** the most aristocratic and fashionable street in Boston, as Fifth Avenue was in New York.

somebody grow to be a tree and cast a shadow?"

The average member of New York society, although not unused to this contemptuous kind of treatment from his leaders, retaliated in his blind, common-sense way. "What does the woman want?" he said. "Is her head turned with the Tuileries and Marlborough House? [4] Does she think herself made for a throne? Why does she not lecture for women's rights? Why not go on the stage? If she cannot be contented like other people, what need is there for abusing us just because she feels herself no taller than we are? What does she expect to get from her sharp tongue? What does she know, any way?"

Mrs. Lee certainly knew very little. She had read voraciously and promiscuously one subject after another. Ruskin and Taine had danced merrily through her mind, hand in hand with Darwin and Stuart Mill, Gustave Droz and Algernon Swinburne.[5] She had even laboured over the literature of her own country. She was, perhaps, the only woman in New York who knew something of American history. Certainly she could not have repeated the list of Presidents in their order, but she knew that the Constitution divided the government into Executive, Legislative, and Judiciary; she was aware that the President, the Speaker, and the Chief Justice were important personages, and instinctively she wondered whether they might not solve her problem; whether they were the shade trees which she saw in her dreams.

Here, then, was the explanation of her restlessness, discontent, ambition,—call it what you will. It was the feeling of a passenger on an ocean steamer whose mind will not give him rest until he has been in the engine-room and talked with the engineer. She wanted to see with her own eyes the action of primary forces; to touch with her own hand the massive machinery of society; to measure with her own mind the capacity of the motive power. She was bent upon getting to the heart of the great American mystery of democracy and government. She cared little where her pursuit might lead her, for she put no extravagant value upon life, having already, as she said, exhausted at least two lives, and being fairly hardened to insensibility in the process. "To lose a husband and a baby," said she, "and keep one's courage and reason, one must become very hard or very soft. I am now pure steel. You may beat my heart with a trip-hammer and it will beat the trip-hammer back again."

Perhaps after exhausting the political world she might try again elsewhere; she did not pretend to say where she might then go, or what she should do; but at present she meant to see what amusement there might be in politics. Her friends asked what kind of amusement she expected to find among the illiterate swarm of ordinary people who in Washington represented constituencies so dreary that in comparison New York was a New Jerusalem, and Broad Street [6] a grove of Academe.[7] She replied that if Washington society were so bad as this, she should have gained all she wanted, for it would be a pleasure to return,—precisely the feeling she longed for. In her own mind, however, she frowned on the idea of seeking for men. What she wished to see, she thought, was the clash of interests, the interests of forty millions of people and a whole continent, centering at Washington; guided, restrained, controlled, or unrestrained and uncontrollable, by men of ordinary mould; the tremendous forces of government, and the machinery of society, at work. What she wanted, was POWER.

Perhaps the force of the engine was a little confused in her mind with that of the engineer, the power with the men who wielded it. Perhaps the human interest of politics was after all what really attracted her, and, however strongly she might deny it, the passion for exercising power, for its own sake, might dazzle and mislead a woman who had exhausted all the ordinary feminine resources. But why speculate about her motives? The stage was before her, the curtain was rising, the actors were ready to enter; she had only to go quietly on among the supernumeraries and see how the play was acted and the stage effects were produced; how the great tragedians mouthed, and the stage-manager swore.

CHAPTER 4

[THE FOLLOWING chapter epitomizes Adams's hopes and fears for the America that had emerged from the Civil War. The education of Madeleine Lee in American politics was a version of his own, just as her ambition for power was an echo of his own. In the cynical Baron Jacobi there speaks another intimate of the Adams circle, the worldly wise Aristarchi Bey, the Turkish ambassador. Nathan Gore, the retired minister to Spain, recalls the historian John Lothrop Motley to whom Grant had taken a dislike for the way he parted his hair. Gore's stoical creed may be taken as that of Adams at this period.]

SUNDAY evening was stormy, and some enthusi-

4. **Marlborough House:** at that time London residence of the Prince of Wales.   5. **Ruskin . . . Swinburne:** contemporary leaders in art, literature, and science. **Gustave Droz:** (1832–95), a very popular French novelist of the psychological school.

6. **Broad Street:** heart of the financial district of New York.
7. **Academe:** garden near ancient Athens where Plato taught.

asm was required to make one face its perils for the sake of society. Nevertheless, a few intimates made their appearance as usual at Mrs. Lee's. The faithful Popoff was there, and Miss Dare also ran in to pass an hour with her dear Sybil; but as she passed the whole evening in a corner with Popoff, she must have been disappointed in her object. Carrington came, and Baron Jacobi. Schneidekoupon and his sister dined with Mrs. Lee, and remained after dinner, while Sybil and Julia Schneidekoupon compared conclusions about Washington society. The happy idea also occurred to Mr. Gore that, inasmuch as Mrs. Lee's house was but a step from his hotel, he might as well take the chance of amusement there as the certainty of solitude in his rooms. Finally, Senator Ratcliffe duly made his appearance, and, having established himself with a cup of tea by Madeleine's side, was soon left to enjoy a quiet talk with her, the rest of the party by common consent occupying themselves with each other. Under cover of the murmur of conversation in the room, Mr. Ratcliffe quickly became confidential.

"I came to suggest that, if you want to hear an interesting debate, you should come up to the Senate tomorrow. I am told that Garrard, of Louisiana, means to attack my last speech, and I shall probably in that case have to answer him. With you for a critic I shall speak better."

"Am I such an amiable critic?" asked Madeleine.

"I never heard that amiable critics were the best," said he; "justice is the soul of good criticism, and it is only justice that I ask and expect from you."

"What good does this speaking do?" inquired she. "Are you any nearer the end of your difficulties by means of your speeches?"

"I hardly know yet. Just now we are in dead water; but this can't last long. In fact, I am not afraid to tell you, though of course you will not repeat it to any human being, that we have taken measures to force an issue. Certain gentlemen, myself among the rest, have written letters meant for the President's eye, though not addressed directly to him, and intended to draw out an expression of some sort that will show us what to expect."

"Oh!" laughed Madeleine, "I knew about that a week ago."

"About what?"

"About your letter to Sam Grimes, of North Bend."

"What have you heard about my letter to Sam Grimes, of North Bend?" ejaculated Ratcliffe, a little abruptly.

"Oh, you do not know how admirably I have organized my secret service bureau," said she. "Representative Cutter cross-questioned one of the Senate pages, and obliged him to confess that he had received from you a letter to be posted, which letter was addressed to Mr. Grimes, of North Bend."

"And, of course, he told this to French, and French told you," said Ratcliffe; "I see. If I had known this I would not have let French off so gently last night, for I prefer to tell you my own story without his embellishments. But it was my fault. I should not have trusted a page. Nothing is a secret here long. But one thing that Mr. Cutter did not find out was that several other gentlemen wrote letters at the same time, for the same purpose. Your friend, Mr. Clinton, wrote; Krebs wrote; and one or two members."

"I suppose I must not ask what you said?"

"You may. We agreed that it was best to be very mild and conciliatory, and to urge the President only to give us some indication of his intentions, in order that we might not run counter to them. I drew a strong picture of the effect of the present situation on the party, and hinted that I had no personal wishes to gratify."

"And what do you think will be the result?"

"I think we shall somehow manage to straighten things out," said Ratcliffe. "The difficulty is only that the new President has little experience, and is suspicious. He thinks we shall intrigue to tie his hands, and he means to tie ours in advance. I don't know him personally, but those who do, and who are fair judges, say that, though rather narrow and obstinate, he is honest enough, and will come around. I have no doubt I could settle it all with him in an hour's talk, but it is out of the question for me to go to him unless I am asked, and to ask me to come would be itself a settlement."

"What, then, is the danger you fear?"

"That he will offend all the important party leaders in order to conciliate unimportant ones, perhaps sentimental ones, like your friend French; that he will make foolish appointments without taking advice.[1] By the way, have you seen French today?"

"No," replied Madeleine; "I think he must be sore at your treatment of him last evening. You were very rude to him."

"Not a bit," said Ratcliffe; "these reformers need it. His attack on me was meant for a challenge. I saw it in his manner."

Chapter 4. 1. In the sequel of events the inexperienced and bewildered President is obliged to turn to Ratcliffe for help. He appoints him Secretary of the Treasury and surrenders control of the Cabinet and the distribution of patronage to him.

"But is reform really so impossible as you describe it? Is it quite hopeless?"

"Reform such as he wants is utterly hopeless, and not even desirable."

Mrs. Lee, with much earnestness of manner, still pressed her question: "Surely something can be done to check corruption. Are we for ever to be at the mercy of thieves and ruffians? Is a respectable government impossible in a democracy?"

Her warmth attracted Jacobi's attention, and he spoke across the room. "What is that you say, Mrs. Lee? What is it about corruption?"

All the gentlemen began to listen and gather about them.

"I am asking Senator Ratcliffe," said she, "what is to become of us if corruption is allowed to go unchecked."

"And may I venture to ask permission to hear Mr. Ratcliffe's reply?" asked the baron.

"My reply," said Ratcliffe, "is that no representative government can long be much better or much worse than the society it represents. Purify society and you purify the government. But try to purify the government artificially and you only aggravate failure."

"A very statesmanlike reply," said Baron Jacobi, with a formal bow, but his tone had a shade of mockery. Carrington, who had listened with a darkening face, suddenly turned to the baron and asked him what conclusion he drew from the reply.

"Ah!" exclaimed the baron, with his wickedest leer, "what for is my conclusion good? You Americans believe yourselves to be excepted from the operation of general laws. You care not for experience. I have lived seventy-five years, and all that time in the midst of corruption. I am corrupt myself, only I do have courage to proclaim it, and you others have it not. Rome, Paris, Vienna, Petersburg, London, all are corrupt; only Washington is pure! Well, I declare to you that in all my experience I have found no society which has had elements of corruption like the United States. The children in the street are corrupt, and know how to cheat me. The cities are all corrupt, and also the towns and the counties and the States' legislatures and the judges. Everywhere men betray trusts both public and private, steal money, run away with public funds. Only in the Senate men take no money. And you gentlemen in the Senate very well declare that your great United States, which is the head of the civilized world, can never learn anything from the example of corrupt Europe. You are right—quite right! The great United States needs not an example. I do much regret that I have not yet one hundred years to live. If I

could then come back to this city, I should find myself very content—much more than now. I am always content where there is much corruption, and *ma parole d'honneur!* [2] broke out the old man with fire and gesture, "the United States will then be more corrupt than Rome under Caligula; more corrupt than the Church under Leo X.; more corrupt than France under the Regent!"

As the baron closed his little harangue, which he delivered directly at the senator sitting underneath him, he had the satisfaction to see that every one was silent and listening with deep attention. He seemed to enjoy annoying the senator, and he had the satisfaction of seeing that the senator was visibly annoyed. Ratcliffe looked sternly at the baron and said, with some curtness, that he saw no reason to accept such conclusions. Conversation flagged, and all except the baron were relieved when Sybil, at Schneidekoupon's request, sat down at the piano to sing what she called a hymn. So soon as the song was over, Ratcliffe, who seemed to have been curiously thrown off his balance by Jacobi's harangue, pleaded urgent duties at his rooms, and retired. The others soon afterwards went off in a body, leaving only Carrington and Gore, who had seated himself by Madeleine, and was at once dragged by her into a discussion of the subject which perplexed her, and for the moment threw over her mind a net of irresistible fascination.

"The baron discomfited the senator," said Gore, with a certain hesitation. "Why did Ratcliffe let himself be trampled upon in that manner?"

"I wish you would explain why," replied Mrs. Lee; "tell me, Mr. Gore—you who represent cultivation and literary taste hereabouts—please tell me what to think about Baron Jacobi's speech. Who and what is to be believed? Mr. Ratcliffe seems honest and wise. Is he a corruptionist? He believes in the people, or says he does. Is he telling the truth or not?"

Gore was too experienced in politics to be caught in such a trap as this. He evaded the question. "Mr. Ratcliffe has a practical piece of work to do; his business is to make laws and advise the President; he does it extremely well. We have no other equally good practical politician; it is unfair to require him to be a crusader besides."

"No!" interposed Carrington, curtly; "but he need not obstruct crusades. He need not talk virtue and oppose the punishment of vice."

"He is a shrewd practical politician," replied Gore, "and he feels first the weak side of any proposed political tactics."

2. *ma parole d'honneur:* "my word of honor."

With a sigh of despair Madeleine went on: "Who, then, is right? How *can* we all be right? Half of our wise men declare that the world is going straight to perdition; the other half that it is fast becoming perfect. Both cannot be right. There is only one thing in life," she went on, laughing, "that I must and will have before I die. I must know whether America is right or wrong. Just now this question is a very practical one, for I really want to know whether to believe in Mr. Ratcliffe. If I throw him overboard, everything must go, for he is only a specimen."

"Why not believe in Mr. Ratcliffe?" said Gore; "I believe in him myself, and am not afraid to say so."

Carrington, to whom Ratcliffe now began to represent the spirit of evil, interposed here, and observed that he imagined Mr. Gore had other guides besides, and steadier ones than Ratcliffe, to believe in; while Madeleine, with a certain feminine perspicacity, struck at a much weaker point in Mr. Gore's armor, and asked point blank whether he believed also in what Ratcliffe represented: "Do you yourself think democracy the best government, and universal suffrage a success?"

Mr. Gore saw himself pinned to the wall, and he turned at bay with almost the energy of despair:

"These are matters about which I rarely talk in society; they are like the doctrine of a personal God; of a future life; or revealed religion; subjects which one naturally reserves for private reflection. But since you ask for my political creed, you shall have it. I only condition that it shall be for you alone, never to be repeated or quoted as mine. I believe in democracy. I accept it. I will faithfully serve and defend it. I believe in it because it appears to me the inevitable consequence of what has gone before it. Democracy asserts the fact that the masses are now raised to higher intelligence than formerly. All our civilization aims at this mark. We want to do what we can to help it. I myself want to see the result. I grant it is an experiment, but it is the only direction society can take that is worth its taking; the only conception of its duty large enough to satisfy its instincts; the only result that is worth an effort or a risk. Every other possible step is backward, and I do not care to repeat the past. I am glad to see society grapple with issues in which no one can afford to be neutral."

"And supposing your experiment fails," said Mrs. Lee; "suppose society destroys itself with universal suffrage, corruption, and communism."

"I wish, Mrs. Lee, you would visit the Observatory with me some evening, and look at Sirius. Did you ever make the acquaintance of a fixed star? I believe astronomers reckon about twenty millions of them in sight, and an infinite possibility of invisible millions, each one of which is a sun, like ours, and may have satellites like our planet. Suppose you see one of these fixed stars suddenly increase in brightness, and are told that a satellite has fallen into it and is burning up, its career finished, its capacities exhausted? Curious, is it not; but what does it matter? Just as much as the burning up of a moth at your candle."

Madeleine shuddered a little. "I cannot get to the height of your philosophy," said she. "You are wandering among the infinites, and I am finite."

"Not at all! But I have faith; not perhaps in the old dogmas, but in the new ones; faith in human nature; faith in science; faith in the survival of the fittest. Let us be true to our time, Mrs. Lee! If our age is to be beaten, let us die in the ranks. If it is to be victorious, let us be first to lead the column. Anyway, let us not be skulkers or grumblers. There! have I repeated my catechism correctly? You would have it! Now oblige me by forgetting it. I should lose my character at home if it got out. Good night!"

Mrs. Lee duly appeared at the Capitol the next day, as she could not but do after Senator Ratcliffe's pointed request. She went alone, for Sybil had positively refused to go near the Capitol again, and Madeleine thought that on the whole this was not an occasion for enrolling Carrington in her service. But Ratcliffe did not speak. The debate was unexpectedly postponed. He joined Mrs. Lee in the gallery, however, sat with her as long as she would allow, and became still more confidential, telling her that he had received the expected reply from Grimes, of North Bend, and that it had enclosed a letter written by the President-elect to Mr. Grimes in regard to the advances made by Mr. Ratcliffe and his friends.

"It is not a handsome letter," said he; "indeed, a part of it is positively insulting. I would like to read you one extract from it, and hear your opinion as to how it should be treated." Taking the letter from his pocket, he sought out the passage, and read as follows: " 'I cannot lose sight, too, of the consideration that these three Senators' (he means Clinton, Krebs, and me) 'are popularly considered to be the most influential members of that so-called senatorial ring, which has acquired such general notoriety. While I shall always receive their communications with all due respect, I must continue to exercise complete freedom of action in consulting other political advisers as well as these, and I must in all cases make it my first object to follow the wishes of the people, not always most truly represented by their nominal representatives.' What say you to that precious piece of presidential manners?"

"At least I like his courage," said Mrs. Lee.

"Courage is one thing; common sense is another. This letter is a studied insult. He has knocked me off the track once. He means to do it again. It is a declaration of war. What ought I to do?"

"Whatever is most for the public good," said Madeleine gravely.

Ratcliffe looked into her face with such undisguised delight—there was so little possibility of mistaking or ignoring the expression of his eyes, that she shrank back with a certain shock. She was not prepared for so open a demonstration. He hardened his features at once, and went on:

"But what *is* most for the public good?"

"That you know better than I," said Madeleine; "only one thing is clear to me. If you let yourself be ruled by your private feelings, you will make a greater mistake than he. Now I must go, for I have visits to make. The next time I come, Mr. Ratcliffe, you must keep your word better."

When they next met, Ratcliffe read to her a part of his reply to Mr. Grimes, which ran thus: "It is the lot of every party leader to suffer from attacks and to commit errors. It is true, as the President says, that I have been no exception to this law. Believing as I do that great results can only be accomplished by great parties, I have uniformly yielded my own personal opinions where they have failed to obtain general assent. I shall continue to follow this course, and the President may with perfect confidence count upon my disinterested support of all party measures, even though I may not be consulted in originating them."

Mrs. Lee listened attentively, and then said: "Have you never refused to go with your party?"

"Never!" was Ratcliffe's firm reply.

Madeleine still more thoughtfully inquired again: "Is nothing more powerful than party allegiance?"

"Nothing, except national allegiance," replied Ratcliffe, still more firmly.

FROM

ESTHER

◇

❨ THE NOVEL appeared in March, 1884, the author disguised under the pen name, "Frances Snow Compton." The *Publishers' Weekly* printed the following description of the book:

Quite unconventional in plot, characters, and denouement. Esther is a New York girl of good social position, who has been educated in an unusual manner. She has been taught no religious belief, and has been allowed perfect independence in choosing her friends and arranging her life. She is a fine artist, and her studio is the lounging place of several notable men. One of them, an Episcopal clergyman, loves her, and is after a struggle accepted by her. The story shows their mutual unfitness for each other—neither being willing to make any concession of opinion—and the final rupture of their engagement.

Issued without advertising, as required by Adams's quixotic experiment, the novel sold about five hundred copies. Years later Adams bought up the remainder of the original printing of a thousand copies and destroyed them as a kind of mourning gesture to the memory of his dead wife who had inspired the portrait of the heroine.

The Rev. Stephen Hazard has just accepted the pulpit of the new church of St. John on Fifth Avenue. Esther Dudley is persuaded to assist the artist Wharton in completing the murals of the church. Her father dies leaving her to confront her destiny at twenty-six. Hazard, confident that he can overcome Esther's religious skepticism, proposes to her. The following chapter depicts her struggle of conscience.

◇

CHAPTER 7

THE INSTANT Esther felt herself really loved, she met her fate as women will when the shock is once over. Hazard had wanted her to love him, had pursued and caught her. Now when she turned to him and answered his call, she seemed to take possession of him and lift him up. By the time he left her house this Saturday evening, he felt that he had found a soul stronger and warmer than his own, and was already a little afraid of it. Every man who has at last succeeded, after long effort, in calling up the divinity which lies hidden in a woman's heart, is startled to find that he must obey the God he summoned.

Esther herself was more astonished than Hazard at the force of this feeling which swept her away. She suddenly found herself passionately attached to a man, whom, down to the last moment, she had thought she could never marry, and now could no more imagine life without him than she could conceive of loving any one else. For the moment she thought that his profession was nothing to her; she could believe whatever he believed and do whatever he did; and if her love, backed by her will, were not strong enough to make his life her own, she cared little what became of her, and could look with indifference on life itself. So far as she was concerned she thought herself ready to worship Woden or Thor, if he did.

The next morning she could not let him preach without being near him, and she made Catherine go with her to St. John's. They took their seats, not in her own pew but in a corner, where no one should notice them under their veils. The experiment was full of peril, though Esther did not know it. This new excitement, coming so swiftly after a fortnight of exhaustion, threw her back into a state of extreme nervousness. Of course the scene of Saturday evening was followed by a sleepless night, and when Sunday morning came, her very restlessness made her hope that she should find repose and calm within the walls of the church. She went believing that she needed nothing so much as the quieting influence of the service, and she was not disappointed, for her sweetest associations were here, and as she glanced timidly up to the scaffolding where her romance had been acted, she felt at home and happy, in spite of the crowd of people who swarmed about her and separated her from the things she loved. In the background stood the solemn and awful associations of the last few weeks, the mysteries and terrors of death, drawing her from thought of earthly things to visions of another world. Full of these deep feelings, saturated with the elixir of love, Esther succumbed to the first notes of the church music. Tears of peaceful delight stood in her eyes. She glanced up towards her Cecilia [1] on the distant wall, wondering at its childishness. How deep a meaning she could give it now, and how religious a feeling!

She was not conscious of rustling silks or waving feathers; she hardly saw the swarm of fashionable people about her; it seemed to her that her old life had vanished as though she were dead; her soul might have taken shelter in the body of some gray linnet for all that she thought or cared about the vanities of human society. She wanted only to be loved and to love, without being thought of, or noticed; to nestle in her own corner, and let the world go by.

Unluckily the world would not go by. This world which she wanted to keep at arms' length, was at church once for all, and meant to stay there; it felt itself at home, and she, with her exclusive griefs and joys, was the stranger. So long as the music lasted, all was sympathetic enough, but when Mr. Hazard read the service, he seemed far-off and strange. He belonged not to her but to the world; a thousand people had rights of property in him, soul and body, and called their claim religion. What had she to do with it? Parts of the service jarred on her ear. She began to take a bitter pleasure in thinking that she had nothing, not even religious ideas, in common with these people who came between her and her lover. Her fatigue steadily worked on her nerves. By the time the creed was read, she could not honestly feel that she believed a word of it, or could force herself to say that she ever should believe it.

With fading self-confidence she listened to the sermon. It was beautiful, simple, full of feeling and even of passion, but she felt that it was made for her, and she shrank before the thousand people who were thus let into the secret chambers of her heart. It treated of death and its mystery, covering ignorance with a veil of religious hope, and ending with an invocation of infinite love so intense in feeling and expression that, beautiful as it was, Esther forgot its beauties in the fear that the next word would reveal her to the world. This sort of publicity was new to her, and threw her back on herself until religion was forgotten in the alarm. She became more jealous than ever. What business had these strangers with her love? Why should she share it with them? When the service was over, she hurried Catherine away so quickly that they were both at home before the church was fairly empty.

This was the end of her short happiness. She knew that through the church door lay the only road to her duty and peace of mind. To see that the first happy impression had lasted barely half an hour, and instead of bringing peace, had brought irritation, was cause enough to alarm the most courageous young woman who ever rushed into the maelstrom of matrimony.

When they had reached home, she flung herself into a chair and covered her face with her hands.

"Catherine!" said she solemnly; "what am I to do? I don't like church."

ESTHER.   **1. Cecilia:** Esther's mural painting of St. Cecilia, posed for by Catherine Brooke, a lovely young newcomer from the West who was the protégée of Esther's aunt, Mrs. Murray. Wharton, a Pre-Raphaelite enthusiast like his original, Adams's artist friend, John La Farge, had urged that the painting should have suggested Nirvana. "passion subsided and heaven attained," a Buddhist idea then much in vogue in Boston intellectual circles.

"You would like yours amazingly," said Catherine, "if you had ever been to mine."

"Was yours worse?"

"If Mrs. Murray hadn't improved my manners so much, I should smile. Was mine worse? I wish you and Mr. Hazard would try it for a change. Mrs. Dyer would like to see you both undergoing discipline. Never joke about serious matters! You had better hold your tongue and be glad to live in a place where your friends let your soul alone."

"But I can't sit still and hear myself turned into a show! I can't share him with all Fifth Avenue. I want no one else to have him. To see him there devoting himself and me to a stupid crowd of people, who have as much right to him as I have, drives religion out of my head."

Catherine treated this weakness with high contempt.

"I might as well be jealous," said she, "of the people who look at Mr. Wharton's pictures, or read Petrarch's sonnets in my sweet translation.[2] Did you ever hear that Laura found fault with Petrarch, or, if she did, that any one believed she was in earnest?"

"It is not the same thing," said Esther. "He believes in his church more than he does in me. If I can't believe in it, he will have to give me up."

"He, give you up!" said Catherine. "The poor saint! You know he is silly about you."

"He must give me up, if I am jealous of his congregation, and won't believe what he preaches," replied Esther mournfully.

"Why should you care what he preaches?" asked Catherine; "you never heard your aunt troubling her head about what Mr. Murray says when he goes to court."

"She is not forced to go to court with him," said Esther; "nor to be a mother to all the old women in the court-room; nor to say that she believes—believes—believes—when in her heart she doesn't believe a word."

Hazard appeared in the middle of this dispute, and Esther, troubled as she was, could not bear to distress him. She still meant to accept every thing and force herself to follow him in silence; she would go where he led, and never once raise her eyes to look for the horizon. As she said to herself quite seriously, though with a want of reverence that augured ill: "I will go down on my knees and help him, though he turn Bonze and burn incense to Buddha in my very studio!" His presence always soothed her. His gayety and af-

2. The little group of aesthetes had taken to translating Petrarch's sonnets of idealized love, a hint of the symbolic parallel between the dilemma of Petrarch and Laura and that of Hazard and Esther.

fection never failed to revive her spirits and confidence.

"Wasn't it a good sermon?" said he to Catherine as he came in, with his boyish laugh of triumph. "Give me a little praise! I never got a word of encouragement from you in my life."

"I should as soon think of encouraging a whole herd of Texas cattle," answered Catherine. "What good can my praise do you?"

"You child of nature, don't you know that children of nature like you always grow wild and need no cultivation, but that we artificial flowers can't live without it?"

"I don't know how to cultivate," answered Catherine; "it is Esther you are thinking about."

Having announced this self-evident fact, Catherine walked off and left him to quiet Esther's alarms as he could. As she went she heard him turn to Esther and repeat his prayer that she should be gentle with him and give his sermon a word of praise.

"How can I stop to think whether it is good or not," said Esther, "when I hear you telling all our secrets to our whole visiting list? I could think of nothing but myself, and how I could get away."

"And whose secrets can I tell if not our own?" asked Hazard triumphant.

While he was with her Esther was peaceful and happy, but no sooner had he gone than her terrors began again.

"He will find me out, Catherine, and it will break my heart," she said. "I never knew I had a jealous temper. I am horribly narrow-minded. I'm not fit for him, and I knew it when he asked me. He will hate me when he finds what a wife he has got."

Catherine, who positively declined to recognize Mr. Hazard's superiority of mind over Esther, took this with unshaken fortitude. "If you can stand it, I guess he can," she remarked curtly. "Where do you expect the poor man to get a wife, if all of us say we are not fit for him?"

This view of the case amused Esther for a time, but not for long—the matter was too serious for any treatment but a joke, and joking made it more serious still. Try which way she would there was no escape from her anxiety. Hazard, who had foreseen some trouble from her old associations with loose religious opinion, had taken it for granted, with his usual self-confidence, that from the moment she came within the reach of his faith and took a place by his side she would find no difficulties that he could not easily overcome. "Love is the great magnet of life, and Religion," he said, "is Love." Nothing could be simpler than his plan, as he explained to her. She had but to trust herself to him and all was sure to go well. So long as he was with her and could gently thrust aside every idea but that of their own happiness, all went as well as he promised; but unluckily for his plan, Esther had all her life been used to act for herself and to order others rather than take orders of any sort. The more confidently Hazard told her to leave every thing to him, the less it occurred to her to do so. She could no more allow him to come into her life and take charge of her thoughts than to go down into her kitchen and take charge of her cook. He might reason with her by the hour, and quite convince her that nothing was of the least consequence provided it were left entirely in his hands, but the moment he was out of sight she forgot that he was to be the keeper of her conscience, and, without a thought of her dependence, she resumed the charge of her own affairs.

Her first idea was to learn something of theology, in the hope of settling her foolish and ignorant doubts as to her fitness for her new position. No sooner did the thought occur to her than she set to work, like a young divinity student, to fit herself for her new calling. Her father's library contained a number of theological books, but these were of a kind that suited Mr. Dudley's way of thinking rather than that of the early fathers. As Esther knew nothing at all about the subject, except what she had gathered from listening to conversation, one book seemed to her as good as another, provided it dealt with the matter that interested her; but when Hazard came in and found her seated on a sofa, with a pile of these works about her, his hair rose on end, and he was forced gently to take them away under the promise of bringing her others of a more correct kind. These in their turn seemed to her not quite clear, and she asked for others still. He found himself, without warning, on the brink of a theological abyss. Unwilling to worry him; eager to accept whatever he told her he believed, but in despair at each failure to understand what it was, Esther became more and more uncomfortable and terrified.

"What would you do, Catherine, if you were in my place?" she asked.

"Let it alone!" said Catherine. "You didn't ask him to marry you. If he wants you, it's his business to suit himself to you."

"But I must go to his church," said Esther, "and sit at his communion."

"How many people at his church could tell you what they believe?" asked Catherine. "Your religion is just as good as theirs as long as you don't know what it is."

"One learns theology fast when one is engaged to be married," said Esther with a repentant face.

She was already sorry that she had tried to learn any thing about the subject, for she already knew too much, and yet a terrible fascination impelled her to read on about the nature of the trinity and the authority of tradition, until she lost patience with her own stupidity and burned to know what other people had to say on such matters. It occurred to her that she should like to have a quiet talk with George Strong.[3]

Meanwhile Mrs. Murray, panic-stricken at learning the engagement, had sent at once for George. The messenger reached him on Sunday evening, a few hours after Esther told her aunt. Mystified by the urgent tone of Mrs. Murray's note, Strong came up at once, and found his uncle and aunt alone, after dinner, in their parlor, where Mr. Murray was quietly smoking a cigar, while his wife was holding a book in her hand and looking hard into the fire.

"George!" said his aunt solemnly; "do you know the mischief you and your friends have done?"

Strong stared. "You don't mean to tell me that Catherine has run off with Wharton?" said he. "She can't have done it, for I left Wharton not fifteen minutes ago at the club."

"No, not that! thank Heaven! Though if she hadn't more head than ever he had, that French wife of his might have given her more unhappiness than he is worth. No, it's not that! Catherine is the only sensible creature in the family."

Strong glared into the fire for a moment with a troubled air, and then looked at his aunt again. "No!" said he. "Esther hasn't joined the church. It can't be!"

"Yes!" said Mrs. Murray grimly.

"Caramba!" growled Strong, with a profusion of Spanish gutturals. Then after a moment's reflection, he added: "Poor child! Why should I care?"

"You irritate me more than your uncle does," broke out Mrs. Murray, at last losing patience. "Do you think I should be so distressed if Esther had only joined the church? I should like nothing better. What has happened is very different. She is engaged to Mr. Hazard."

Strong broke into a laugh, and Mr. Murray, with a quiet chuckle of humor, took his cigar out of his mouth to say:

"Let me explain this little matter to you, George! What troubles your aunt is not so much

---

3. **Strong:** Esther's cousin, a geologist whose characteristic skepticism is borrowed from Clarence King, Adams's intimate friend, director of the United States Geological Survey.

that Esther has joined the church as that she fears the church has joined Esther."

"The church has struck it rich this time;" remarked Strong without a sign of his first alarm. "Now we'll see what they'll make of her."

"The matter is too serious for joking;" said Mrs. Murray. "Either Esther will be unhappy for life, or Mr. Hazard will leave his church, or they will both be miserable whatever they do. I think you are bound to prevent it, since you are the one most to blame for getting them into it."

"I don't want to prevent it;" replied Strong. "It's a case of survival for the fittest. If Hazard can manage to convert Esther, let him do it. If not, let her take him in charge and convert him if she can. I'll not interfere."

"That is just the remark I had the honor to make to your aunt as you came in," said Mr. Murray. "Yesterday I wanted to stop it. Today I want to leave it alone. They are both of them old enough to manage their own case. It has risen now to the dignity of a great cause, and I will be the devil's advocate."

"You are both of you intolerable," said Mrs. Murray, impatiently. "You talk about the happiness of Esther's life as though it were a game of poker. Tell me, George! what kind of a man is Mr. Hazard at heart?"

"Hazard is a priest at heart," replied Strong. "He has the qualities and faults of his class. I understand how this thing happened. He sees nothing good in the world that he does not instantly covet for the glory of God and the church, and just a bit for his own pleasure. He saw Esther; she struck him as something out of his line, for he is used to young women who work altar-cloths; he found that Wharton and I liked her; he thought that such material was too good for heathen like us; so he fell in love with her himself and means to turn her into a candlestick of the church. I don't mind. Let him try! He has done what he liked with us all his life. I have worked like a dog for him and his church because he was my friend. Now he will see whether he has met his match. I double you up all round on Esther."

"You men are simply brutal!" said his aunt. "Esther will be an unhappy woman all her life, whether she marries him or not, and you sit there and will not raise a finger to help her."

"Let him convert her, I say;" repeated Strong. "What is your objection to that, Aunt Sarah?"

"My objection is that the whole family is only a drove of mules," said Mrs. Murray. "Poor Mr. Hazard does not know what he is undertaking."

"Is Esther very much in love?" asked Strong.

"You know her well enough to know that she would never have accepted him if she were not;" replied Mrs. Murray. "He has hunted her down when she was unhappy, and he is going to make her more unhappy still."

"I guess you're right," said Strong, seriously. "The struggle is going to tear both their poor little hearts out; but what can we do about it? None of us are to blame."

"Ah, George!" exclaimed his aunt. "You are the one most to blame. You should have married Esther yourself, and you had not wit enough to see that while you went dancing round the world, as though such women were plenty as your old fossil toads, the only woman you will ever meet who could have made you happy, was slipping through your fingers, and you hadn't the strength to hold her."

"I own it, Aunt Sarah!" said George, and this time he spoke seriously enough to satisfy her. "If I could have fallen in love with Esther and she with me, I believe it would have been better for both of us than that she should marry a high-church parson and I go on digging bones; but some things are too obvious. You can't get a spark without some break in your conductor. I was ready enough to fall in love with Esther, but one can't do that kind of thing in cold blood."

"Well," said Mrs. Murray with a sigh. "You have lost her now, and Mr. Hazard will lose her too. You and he and all your friends are a sort of clever children. We are always expecting you to do something worth doing, and it never comes. You are a sort of water-color, worsted-work, bric-à-brac, washed-out geniuses, just big enough and strong enough to want to do something and never carry it through. I am heartily tired of the whole lot of you, and now I must set to work and get these two girls out of your hands."

"Do you mean to break up this engagement?" asked Strong, who was used to his aunt's criticisms and never answered them.

"The engagement will break itself up," replied his aunt. "It will have to be kept private for a few weeks on account of her father's death and her mourning, and you will see that it never will be announced. If I can, I shall certainly do all in my power to break it up."

"You will?" said Strong. "Well! I mean to do just the contrary. If Esther wants Hazard she shall have him, if I can help her. Why not? Hazard is a good fellow, and will make her a good husband. I have no fault to find with him except that he poaches outside his preserves. He has poached this time to some purpose, but if the parish can stand it, I can."

"The parish cannot stand it," said Mrs. Murray. "They are saying very ugly things already about Esther."

"Then it will not hurt my feelings to see Hazard snub his congregation," replied Strong angrily.

The family conclave ended here, and all parties henceforward fixed their eyes intently on the drama. Mrs. Murray waited with a woman's instinct for her moment to come. Strong tried to counteract her influence by bungling efforts to make the lovers' path smooth. Catherine was a sort of cushion against which all the billiard balls of the game knocked themselves in succession, leaving her cool and elastic temper undisturbed. Three more days passed without throwing much new light on the disputed question whether the engagement could last, except that Esther seemed clearly more anxious and restless. Mr. Hazard was with her several hours every day and watched over her with extreme vigilance. Mrs. Murray took her to drive every afternoon and not a glance of Esther's eyes escaped scrutiny. Strong stopped once or twice at the house but had no chance to interfere until on Thursday morning, his aunt told him that Esther was rapidly getting into a state of mind that must soon bring on a crisis.

"She cannot possibly make it do," said Mrs. Murray. "She is worrying herself to death already. Mr. Hazard ought to see that she can't marry him."

"She will marry him," answered Strong coolly. "Three women out of four think they can't marry a man at first, but when they come to parting with him, they learn better."

"He is passably selfish, your Mr. Hazard. If he thought a little more of his parish, he would not want to put over them a woman like Esther who has not a quality suited to the place."

"Her qualities are excellent," contradicted Strong. "Once in harness she will be kind and gentle, a little tender-mouthed perhaps, and apt to shy at first, but thorough-bred. He is quite right to take her if he can get her, and what does his parish expect to do about it?"

"The first thing they will do about it will be to make Esther miserable. They have begun to gossip already. A young man, even though he is a clergyman, can't be seen always in company with a pretty woman, without exciting remark. Only yesterday I was asked point-blank whether my niece was engaged to Mr. Hazard."

"What did you say?"

"I told a lie of course, all the meaner because it was an equivocation. I said that Mr. Hazard had not honored me with any communication on the subject. I score up this first falsehood to his account."

"If you lie no better than that, Aunt Sarah, Hazard's conscience won't trouble him much. When is the engagement to be out?"

"Very soon, at this rate. I thought that Esther, in common decency, could not announce it for a week or two, but every one already suspects it, and she will have to make it public within another week if she means to do so at all. Now that she is her own mistress and lives by herself, she can't have men so much about the house as she might if her father were living."

"Do you seriously think she will break it off?" asked Strong incredulously.

"I feel surer than ever," answered his aunt. "The criticism is going to be bitter, and the longer Esther waits, the more sharply people will talk. I should not wonder if it ended by driving Mr. Hazard out of the parish. He is not strong enough to shock them much. Then Esther is growing more and more nervous every day because the more she tries to understand, the less she succeeds. Yesterday, when I took her to drive, she was in tears about the atonement, and to-day I suppose she will have gone to bed with a sick headache on account of the Athanasian creed." [4]

"I must talk with her," said Strong. "I think I can make some of those things easier for her."

"You? I thought you laughed at them all."

"So I do, but not because they can't be understood. The trouble is that I think I do understand them. Mystery for mystery science beats religion hollow.[5] I can't open my mouth in my lecture-room without repeating ten times as many unintelligible formulas as ever Hazard is forced to do in his church. I can quiet her mind on that score."

"You had better leave it alone, George! Why should you meddle? Let Mr. Hazard fight his own battles!"

George refused to take this wise advice. He was a tender-hearted fellow and could not bear to see his friends suffer. If Esther loved Hazard and wanted to marry him, she should do so though every dogma of the church stood in her way, and every old woman in the parish shrieked sacrilege. Strong had no respect for the church and no wish to save it trouble, but he believed that Hazard was going blindly under Esther's influence which would

4. **Athanasian creed:** There had been a great deal of controversy in Anglican circles in the early seventies concerning the use of the creed in the Book of Common Prayer, the debate turning on the true relations of the persons of the Trinity.   5. **Mystery . . . hollow:** an echo of the contemporary idealist criticism of positivistic science. Adams's ambivalent attitude toward science may be seen more fully developed in the *Chartres* and the *Education*.

sooner or later end by drawing him away from his old forms of belief; and as this was entirely Hazard's affair, if he chose to risk the danger, Strong chose to help him.

"Why not?" said Strong to himself. "It is not a question of earning a living. Both of them are well enough off. If he can turn her into a light of his church, let him do it. If she ends in dragging him out of the church, so much the better. She can't get a better husband, and he can't find a better wife. I mean to see this thing through."

So George strolled round to Esther's house after this interview with his aunt, thinking that he might be able to do good. Being at home there, he went up-stairs unannounced, and finding no one in the library he climbed to the studio, where, on opening the door, he saw Catherine sitting before the fire, looking very much bored. Poor Catherine found it hard to keep up with life in New York. Fresh from the prairie, she had been first saturated with art, and was now plunged in a bottomless ocean of theology. She was glad to see Strong who had in her eyes the advantage of being more practical than the rest of her friends.

"Catherine, how are your sheep?"

"I am glad you have come to look after them," answered Catherine. "I won't be watch-dog much longer. They are too troublesome."

"What mischief are they doing now?"

"Every thing they can think of to worry me. Esther won't eat and can't sleep, and Mr. Hazard won't sleep and can't eat. She tries not to worry him, so she comes down on me with questions and books enough to frighten a professor. Do tell me what to say!"

"Where are your questions?" asked Strong.

"This morning she wanted to know what I thought of apostolic succession. She said she was reading some book by a Dr. Newman. What is apostolic succession?" [6]

"A curious disease, quite common among the poorer classes of Sandwich Islanders," replied Strong. "No one has ever found a cure for it."

"Don't laugh at us! We do nothing but cry now, except when Mr. Hazard is here, and then we pretend to be happy. When Esther cries, I cry too. That makes her laugh. It's our only joke, and we used to have so many."

"Don't you think it rather a moist joke?" asked Strong. "I take mine dry."

"I can't tell what she will think a joke," replied Catherine. "She asked me to-day what was my idea of heaven, and I said it was reading novels in church. She seemed to think this a rich bonanza of a joke, and laughed herself into hysterics, but I was as serious as Mr. Wharton's apostles." [7]

"You are never so funny as when you are serious. Never be so any more! Why don't you get her to paint?"

"She won't. I'm rather glad of it, for if she did, I should have to sit for melancholy, or an angel, or something I'm not fitted for by education."

"What shall we do about it?" asked Strong. "Things can't go on in this way."

"I think the engagement had better come out," said Catherine. "The longer it is kept private, the more she will doubt whether she ought to marry a clergyman. What do you think about marrying clergymen? Wouldn't it almost be better to marry a painter, or even a professor?"

"That would be playing it too low down," replied Strong gravely. "I would recommend you to look out for a swell. What has become of your admirer, Mr. Van Dam?"

"Gone!" said Catherine sadly. "Mr. Wharton and he went off together. There is something about me that scares them all off the ranche."

While they were thus improving each other's minds, the door opened and Esther entered. She was pale and her face had no longer the bright look which Wharton had thought so characteristic, but there was no other sign of trouble about her, and she welcomed her cousin as pleasantly as ever, so that he could hardly believe in the stories he had just heard of her distress.

"Good day, Cousin George," she said. "Thank you for coming to cheer up this poor girl. She needs it. Do take her out and amuse her."

"Come out yourself, Esther. You need it more than she does."

"Aunt Sarah is coming at two o'clock to take me to drive," said Esther. "Catherine hates driving unless she drives herself."

"I thought you hated it too."

"Oh, I hate nothing now," replied Esther, with a little of her old laugh. "I am learning to like every thing."

"Is that in the marriage service?" asked Strong. "Do you have to begin so high up? Couldn't you start easy, and like a few things first,—me for instance—and let the rest wait?"

"No," she said, "you are to come last. Honestly, I am more afraid of you than of all the rest of the world. If you knew what a bug-bear you are

6. **Dr. Newman . . . succession:** A noted Anglican convert to Roman Catholicism, Newman became a cardinal in 1879. He was a leading figure in the great religious controversies of the time. One of his most influential tracts as an Anglican exhorted the bishops of the Church to proclaim their descent from the early apostles.

7. **apostles:** painted in the murals of St. John's Church.

to me, you would be afraid of yourself. Don't make fun of me any more! I know I am horribly funny, but you must take me in earnest. Poor papa's last words to me were: 'Laugh and you're safe!'—but if I laugh now, I'm lost."

"This is the first time I ever met any one honest enough to acknowledge that marriage was so sad a thing. Catherine, if I ask you to marry me, will you turn serious?"

"She will turn serious enough if she does it," said Esther. "You would stay with her a week, and then tell her that you were obliged to see a friend in Japan. She would never see you again, but the newspapers would tell her that you had set out to look for bones in the Milky Way."

"What you say sounds to me as though it had a grain of truth," replied Strong. "That reminds me that I got a letter telling me of a lot of new bones only yesterday, but I must leave them underground till the summer; if by that time I can do any thing for you in Oregon, let me know."

"I want you very much to do something for me now," said Esther. "Will you try to be serious a moment for my sake?"

"I don't know," said Strong. "You ask too much all at once. Where are you coming out?"

"Will you answer me a question? Say yes or no!"

"That depends on the question, Mistress Esther! Old birds are not to be caught in old traps. State your question, as we say in the lecture-room."

"Is religion true?"

"I thought so! Cousin Esther, I love you as much as I love any one in this cold world, but I can't answer your question. I can tell you all about the mound-builders or cave-men, so far as known, but I could not tell you the difference between the bones of a saint and those of a heathen. Ask me something easier! Ask me whether science is true!"

"Is science true?"

"No!"

"Then why do you believe in it?"

"I don't believe in it."

"Then why do you belong to it?"

"Because I want to help in making it truer. Now, Esther, just take this matter coolly! You are bothered, I suppose, by the idea that you can't possibly believe in miracles and mysteries, and therefore can't make a good wife for Hazard. You might just as well make yourself unhappy by doubting whether you would make a good wife to me because you can't believe the first axiom in Euclid. There is no science which does not begin by requiring you to believe the incredible."

"Are you telling me the truth?"

"I tell you the solemn truth that the doctrine of the Trinity is not so difficult to accept for a working proposition as any one of the axioms of physics. The wife of my mathematical colleague, to my knowledge, never even stopped to ask whether it was true that a point had neither length, breadth nor thickness."

Esther pondered a few moments, looking into the fire with a grave face. Then she went on:

"You are not talking honestly. Why should I dare tell you that your old fossil bones are a humbug, when I would not for the world talk so to Mr. Hazard? You don't care whether geology is true or not."

"Well, no, not much!" said Strong. "I should care more if you told me that my best Japanese lacquer was modern."

"Besides," said Esther; "you have not answered my question. I want to know what you think, and you won't tell me. Oh! don't let me lose faith in you too! I know your opinions. You think the whole church a piece of superstition. I've heard you say so, and I want you to tell me why. You're my cousin and I've a right to your help, but you won't give it."

"You are a desperate little tyrant," said Strong laughing. "You always were. Do you remember how we fought when we were children because you would have your own way? I used to give in then, but I am old now, and obstinate."

"I know that you always ended by making me go your way," replied Esther; "but that was because I never cared much where I went. Now it is a matter of life and death. I can't move a step, or even let our engagement be announced until I feel sure that I shall not be a load on his neck. Do you think I should hesitate to break it off, even if I broke my heart with it, if I thought it was going to bring trouble on him?"

Against this assault jesting was out of the question. Strong was forced out of this line of defense and found himself in an awkward position. Esther, not outwardly excited, but leaning her chin on her hand, and gazing into the fire with a look of set will, had the calmness of despair. Strong was staggered and hesitated.

"The trouble with you is that you start wrong," said he at length. "You need what is called faith, and are trying to get it by reason. It can't be done. Faith is a state of mind, like love or jealousy. You can never reason yourself into it."

"So Mr. Hazard says," rejoined Esther. "He tells me to wait and it will come, but he wants me to go on just as though I were certain of its coming. I can't wait. If it does not come quickly, I must do something desperate. Now tell me what you would do to get faith if the happiness of your whole life hung on it."

Strong rose uneasily from his seat and stood up before the fire. He began to think himself rash for venturing into this arena. He had always believed his cousin to be stronger than Hazard, because Hazard was a clergyman, but he had not hitherto thought her stronger than himself, and he now looked at her carefully, wondering whether he could have managed her. Never in his life had he felt so nearly in love with her as now, under the temptation to try whether she could be made to give up her will to his. This feeling was the stronger because even in his own eyes his conduct so far seemed a little cowardly and ridiculous. He pulled himself up sharply, and, seeing nothing else to be done, he took up the weapons of the church and asserted the tone of authority.

"Every one who marries," he said, "goes it blind, more or less. If you have faith enough in Hazard to believe in him, you have faith enough to accept his church. Faith means submission. Submit!"

"I want to submit," cried Esther piteously, rising in her turn and speaking in accents of real distress and passion. "Why can't some of you make me? For a few minutes at a time I think it done, and then I suddenly find myself more defiant than ever. I want nothing of the church! Why should it trouble me? Why should I submit to it? Why can't it leave me alone?"

"What you want is the Roman church," continued Strong mercilessly. "They know how to deal with pride of will. Millions of men and women have gone through the same struggle, and the church tells them to fix their eyes on a symbol of faith, and if their eyes wander, scourges them for it." As he talked, he took up the little carved ivory crucifix which stood on the mantel-piece among other bits of studio furniture, and holding it up before her, said: "There! How many people do you think, have come to this Christ of yours that has no meaning to you, and in their struggle with doubt, have pressed it against their hearts till it drew blood? Ask it!"

"Is that all?" said Esther, taking the crucifix from his hand and looking curiously at it. Then she silently put it against her heart and pressed it with more and more force, until Strong caught her hand in alarm and pulled it away.

"Come!" said he coolly, as he forced her to give up the crucifix; "my little bluff has failed. I throw up the hand. You must play it out with Hazard." [8]

8. Esther makes a winter visit to Niagara Falls to think through

FROM

THE HISTORY OF THE UNITED STATES DURING THE ADMINISTRATIONS OF JEFFERSON AND MADISON

❖

⟪ THE NINE volumes of the *History* began coming out in 1889, the final three being issued in 1891 while Adams was still in the South Seas. For a work that successfully challenged comparison with Gibbon and Macaulay, the public reception was disappointing. Only a few thousand sets were sold in spite of very favorable reviews. Adams attempted a radical departure from the literary approach of such older contemporaries as Bancroft, Motley, and Parkman whose narratives leaned heavily upon the dramatic and the picturesque. He followed the course, outlined by such thinkers as Auguste Comte and Herbert Spencer, of analyzing social development as the interaction of forces governed by the laws of mechanics. By this shift of emphasis he produced the first example of "scientific" history.

According to his hypothesis the year 1800 was a moment of the equilibrium of earlier forces. The years 1816–17, the period immediately following the War of 1812, were the next great moment of equilibrium, a resolution of the tensions between the centralizing and decentralizing forces in the young republic. The brilliant opening six chapters establish the datum line from which to measure progress, a cross section of the important physical and psychological components. Chapter 6, the climactic chapter of the introductory section, shows the triumph of Adams's genius as a literary artist over the demands of his scientific hypothesis. Chapter 10 of the ninth volume concludes a parallel cross section, exhibiting the emergence of the centralizing forces.

The body of the history stresses the course of politics and diplomacy, fields in which Adams was most expert. His masterly presentation of the military operations of the war has become a classic. There are many notable portraits of statesmen like Jefferson, Napoleon, Canning, Toussaint, and Tecumseh. Adams's thesis never stands in the way of his realizing the recurrent episodes of comedy and tragedy in the long narrative, nor does it impair the urbane wit and pervasive irony of his style.

❖

her dilemma of love in conflict with intellectual scruples. Confronted by the vast forces of nature, she develops a kind of mystical pantheism. Hazard follows her for a last interview, but she rejects his church—and him—as too concerned with personal salvation, with the self.

FROM VOLUME I

CHAPTER 6

AMERICAN IDEALS [1800]

NEARLY every foreign traveller who visited the United States during these early years, carried away an impression sober if not sad. A thousand miles of desolate and dreary forest, broken here and there by settlements; along the sea-coast a few flourishing towns devoted to commerce; no arts, a provincial literature, a cancerous disease of negro slavery, and differences of political theory fortified within geographical lines,—what could be hoped for such a country except to repeat the story of violence and brutality which the world already knew by heart, until repetition for thousands of years had wearied and sickened mankind? Ages must probably pass before the interior could be thoroughly settled; even Jefferson, usually a sanguine man, talked of a thousand years with acquiescence, and in his first Inaugural Address, at a time when the Mississippi River formed the Western boundary, spoke of the country as having "room enough for our descendants to the hundredth and thousandth generation." No prudent person dared to act on the certainty that when settled, one government could comprehend the whole; and when the day of separation should arrive, and America should have her Prussia, Austria, and Italy, as she already had her England, France, and Spain, what else could follow but a return to the old conditions of local jealousies, wars, and corruption which had made a slaughter-house of Europe?

The mass of Americans were sanguine and self-confident, partly by temperament, but partly also by reason of ignorance; for they knew little of the difficulties which surrounded a complex society. The Duc de Liancourt,[1] like many critics, was struck by this trait. Among other instances, he met with one in the person of a Pennsylvania miller, Thomas Lea, "a sound American patriot, persuading himself that nothing good is done, and that no one has any brains, except in America; that the wit, the imagination, the genius of Europe are already in decrepitude;" and the duke added: "This error is to be found in almost all Americans,—legislators, administrators, as well as millers, and is less innocent there." In the year 1796 the House

of Representatives debated whether to insert in the Reply to the President's Speech a passing remark that the nation was "the freest and most enlightened in the world,"—a nation as yet in swaddling-clothes, which had neither literature, arts, sciences, nor history; nor even enough nationality to be sure that it was a nation. The moment was peculiarly ill-chosen for such a claim, because Europe was on the verge of an outburst of genius. Goethe and Schiller, Mozart and Haydn, Kant and Fichte, Cavendish and Herschel were making way for Walter Scott, Wordsworth, and Shelley, Heine and Balzac, Beethoven and Hegel, Oersted and Cuvier, great physicists, biologists, geologists, chemists, mathematicians, metaphysicians, and historians by the score. Turner was painting his earliest landscapes, and Watt completing his latest steam-engine; Napoleon was taking command of the French armies, and Nelson of the English fleets; investigators, reformers, scholars, and philosophers swarmed, and the influence of enlightenment, even amid universal war, was working with an energy such as the world had never before conceived. The idea that Europe was in her decrepitude proved only ignorance and want of enlightenment, if not of freedom, on the part of Americans who could only excuse their error by pleading that notwithstanding these objections, in matters which for the moment most concerned themselves Europe was a full century behind America. If they were right in thinking that the next necessity of human progress was to lift the average man upon an intellectual and social level with the most favored, they stood at least three generations nearer than Europe to their common goal. The destinies of the United States were certainly staked, without reserve or escape, on the soundness of this doubtful and even improbable principle, ignoring or overthrowing the institutions of church, aristocracy, family, army, and political intervention, which long experience had shown to be needed for the safety of society. Europe might be right in thinking that without such safeguards society must come to an end; but even Europeans must concede that there was a chance, if no greater than one in a thousand, that America might, at least for a time, succeed. If this stake of temporal and eternal welfare stood on the winning card; if man actually should become more virtuous and enlightened, by mere process of growth, without church or paternal authority; if the average human being could accustom himself to reason with the logical processes of Descartes and Newton!—what then?

Then, no one could deny that the United States would win a stake such as defied mathematics.

THE HISTORY.   1. **Duc de Liancourt:** François Alexandre Frédéric de La Rochefoucauld-Liancourt (1747–1827), French royalist statesman and social reformer who spent part of his exile, after the abolition of the monarchy in 1792, in the United States.

With all the advantages of science and capital, Europe must be slower than America to reach the common goal. American society might be both sober and sad, but except for negro slavery it was sound and healthy in every part. Stripped for the hardest work, every muscle firm and elastic, every ounce of brain ready for use, and not a trace of superfluous flesh on his nervous and supple body, the American stood in the world a new order of man. From Maine to Florida, society was in this respect the same, and was so organized as to use its human forces with more economy than could be approached by any society of the world elsewhere. Not only were artificial barriers carefully removed, but every influence that could appeal to ordinary ambition was applied. No brain or appetite active enough to be conscious of stimulants could fail to answer the intense incentive. Few human beings, however sluggish, could long resist the temptation to acquire power; and the elements of power were to be had in America almost for the asking. Reversing the old-world system, the American stimulant increased in energy as it reached the lowest and most ignorant class, dragging and whirling them upward as in the blast of a furnace. The penniless and homeless Scotch or Irish immigrant was caught and consumed by it; for every stroke of the axe and the hoe made him a capitalist, and made gentlemen of his children. Wealth was the strongest agent for moving the mass of mankind; but political power was hardly less tempting to the more intelligent and better-educated swarms of American-born citizens, and the instinct of activity, once created, seemed heritable and permanent in the race.

Compared with this lithe young figure, Europe was actually in decrepitude. Mere class distinctions, the *patois* or dialect of the peasantry, the fixity of residence, the local costumes and habits marking a history that lost itself in the renewal of identical generations, raised from birth barriers which paralyzed half the population. Upon this mass of inert matter rested the Church and the State, holding down activity of thought. Endless wars withdrew many hundred thousand men from production, and changed them into agents of waste; huge debts, the evidence of past wars and bad government, created interests to support the system and fix its burdens on the laboring class; courts, with habits of extravagance that shamed common-sense, helped to consume private economies. All this might have been borne; but behind this stood aristocracies, sucking their nourishment from industry, producing nothing themselves, employing little or no active capital or intelligent labor, but pressing on the energies and ambition of society with the weight of an incubus. Picturesque and entertaining as these social anomalies were, they were better fitted for the theatre or for a museum of historical costumes than for an active workshop preparing to compete with such machinery as America would soon command. From an economical point of view, they were as incongruous as would have been the appearance of a mediæval knight in helmet and armor, with battle-axe and shield, to run the machinery of Arkwright's cotton-mill; but besides their bad economy they also tended to prevent the rest of society from gaining a knowledge of its own capacities. In Europe, the conservative habit of mind was fortified behind power. During nearly a century Voltaire himself—the friend of kings, the wit and poet, historian and philosopher of his age—had carried on, in daily terror, in exile and excommunication, a protest against an intellectual despotism contemptible even to its own supporters. Hardly was Voltaire dead, when Priestley, as great a man if not so great a wit, trying to do for England what Voltaire tried to do for France, was mobbed by the people of Birmingham and driven to America. Where Voltaire and Priestley failed, common men could not struggle; the weight of society stifled their thought. In America the balance between conservative and liberal forces was close; but in Europe conservatism held the physical power of government. In Boston a young Buckminster [2] might be checked for a time by his father's prayers or commands in entering that path that led toward freer thought; but youth beckoned him on, and every reward that society could offer was dangled before his eyes. In London or Paris, Rome, Madrid, or Vienna, he must have sacrificed the worldly prospects of his life.

Granting that the American people were about to risk their future on a new experiment, they naturally wished to throw aside all burdens of which they could rid themselves. Believing that in the long run interest, not violence, would rule the world, and that the United States must depend for safety and success on the interests they could create, they were tempted to look upon war and preparations for war as the worst of blunders; for they were sure that every dollar capitalized in industry was a means of overthrowing their enemies more effective than a thousand dollars spent on frigates or standing armies. The success of the American system was, from this point of view, a question of economy. If they could relieve themselves from debts, taxes, armies, and government

---

2. **Buckminster:** Joseph Stevens Buckminster (1784–1812), descendant of a long line of orthodox New England clergymen, became leader of the liberal Unitarian clergy.

interference with industry, they must succeed in outstripping Europe in economy of production; and Americans were even then partly aware that if their machine were not so weakened by these economies as to break down in the working, it must of necessity break down every rival. If their theory was sound, when the day of competition should arrive, Europe might choose between American and Chinese institutions, but there would be no middle path; she might become a confederated democracy, or a wreck.

Whether these ideas were sound or weak, they seemed self-evident to those Northern democrats who, like Albert Gallatin, were comparatively free from slave-owning theories, and understood the practical forces of society. If Gallatin wished to reduce the interference of government to a minimum, and cut down expenditures to nothing, he aimed not so much at saving money as at using it with the most certain effect. The revolution of 1800 was in his eyes chiefly political, because it was social; but as a revolution of society, he and his friends hoped to make it the most radical that had occurred since the downfall of the Roman empire. Their ideas were not yet cleared by experience, and were confused by many contradictory prejudices, but wanted neither breadth nor shrewdness.

Many apparent inconsistencies grew from this undeveloped form of American thought, and gave rise to great confusion in the different estimates of American character that were made both at home and abroad.

That Americans should not be liked was natural; but that they should not be understood was more significant by far. After the downfall of the French republic they had no right to expect a kind word from Europe, and during the next twenty years they rarely received one. The liberal movement of Europe was cowed, and no one dared express democratic sympathies until the Napoleonic tempest had passed. With this attitude Americans had no right to find fault, for Europe cared less to injure them than to protect herself. Nevertheless, observant readers could not but feel surprised that none of the numerous Europeans who then wrote or spoke about America seemed to study the subject seriously. The ordinary traveller was apt to be little more reflective than a bee or an ant, but some of these critics possessed powers far from ordinary; yet Talleyrand alone showed that had he but seen America a few years later than he did, he might have suggested some sufficient reason for apparent contradictions that perplexed him in the national character. The other travellers—great and small,

from the Duc de Liancourt to Basil Hall,[3] a long and suggestive list—were equally perplexed. They agreed in observing the contradictions, but all, including Talleyrand, saw only sordid motives. Talleyrand expresssed extreme astonishment at the apathy of Americans in the face of religious sectarians; but he explained it by assuming that the American ardor of the moment was absorbed in money-making. The explanation was evidently insufficient, for the Americans were capable of feeling and showing excitement, even to their great pecuniary injury, as they frequently proved; but in the foreigner's range of observation, love of money was the most conspicuous and most common trait of American character. "There is, perhaps, no civilized country in the world," wrote Félix de Beaujour,[4] soon after 1800, "where there is less generosity in the souls, and in the heads fewer of those illusions which make the charm or the consolation of life. Man here weighs everything, calculates everything, and sacrifices everything to his interest." An Englishman named Fearon,[5] in 1818, expressed the same idea with more distinctness: "In going to America, I would say generally, the emigrant must expect to find, not an economical or cleanly people; not a social or generous people; not a people of enlarged ideas; not a people of liberal opinions, or toward whom you can express your thoughts free as air; not a people friendly to the advocates of liberty in Europe; not a people who understand liberty from investigation and principle; not a people who comprehend the meaning of the words 'honor' and 'generosity.' " Such quotations might be multiplied almost without limit. Rapacity was the accepted explanation of American peculiarities; yet every traveller was troubled by inconsistencies that required explanations of a different kind. "It is not in order to hoard that the Americans are rapacious," observed Liancourt as early as 1796. The extravagance, or what economical Europeans thought extravagance, with which American women were allowed and encouraged to spend money, was as notorious in 1790 as a century later; the recklessness with which Americans often risked their money, and the liberality with which they used it, were marked even then, in comparison with the ordinary European habit. Europeans saw such contradictions, but made no attempt to reconcile them. No foreigner of that day—neither poet, painter, nor philosopher—

3. **Basil Hall:** (1788–1844), British naval officer and noted travel writer.   4. **Félix de Beaujour:** Baron Louis Auguste Félix (1765–1836), French consul general to the U.S. in 1804, author of *Sketch of the United States* (1814).   5. **Fearon:** Henry B. Fearon (c. 1770–c. 1835), *Sketches of America* (1818).

could detect in American life anything higher than vulgarity; for it was something beyond the range of their experience, which education and culture had not framed a formula to express. Moore [6] came to Washington, and found there no loftier inspiration than any Federalist rhymester of Dennie's [7] school.

> "Take Christians, Mohawks, democrats and all,
> From the rude wigwam to the Congress hall,—
> From man the savage, whether slaved or free,
> To man the civilized, less tame than he:
> 'T is one dull chaos, one unfertile strife
> Betwixt half-polished and half-barbarous life;
> Where every ill the ancient world can brew
> Is mixed with every grossness of the new;
> Where all corrupts, though little can entice,
> And nothing 's known of luxury but vice."

Moore's two small volumes of *Epistles,* printed in 1807, contained much more so-called poetry of the same tone,—poetry more polished and less respectable than that of Barlow and Dwight; [8] while, as though to prove that the Old World knew what grossness was, he embalmed in his lines the slanders which the Scotch libeller Callender invented against Jefferson:—

> "The weary statesman for repose hath fled
> From halls of council to his negro's shed;
> Where, blest, he woos some black Aspasia's grace,
> And dreams of freedom in his slave's embrace."

To leave no doubt of his meaning, he explained in a footnote that his allusion was to the President of the United States; and yet even Moore, trifler and butterfly as he was, must have seen, if he would, that between the morals of politics and society in America and those then prevailing in Europe, there was no room for comparison,— there was room only for contrast.

Moore was but an echo of fashionable England in his day. He seldom affected moral sublimity; and had he in his wanderings met a race of embodied angels, he would have sung of them or to them in the slightly erotic notes which were so well received in the society he loved to frequent and flatter. His remarks upon American character betrayed more temper than truth; but even in this respect he expressed only the common feeling of Europeans, which was echoed by the Federalist society of the United States. Englishmen especially indulged in unbounded invective against the sordid character of American society, and in shaping their national policy on this contempt they carried their theory into practice with so much energy as to produce its own refutation. To their astonishment and anger, a day came when the Americans, in defiance of self-interest and in contradiction of all the qualities ascribed to them, insisted on declaring war; and readers of this narrative will be surprised at the cry of incredulity, not unmixed with terror, with which Englishmen started to their feet when they woke from their delusion on seeing what they had been taught to call the meteor flag of England, which had burned terrific at Copenhagen and Trafalgar, suddenly waver and fall on the bloody deck of the "Guerrière." [9] Fearon and Beaujour, with a score of other contemporary critics, could see neither generosity, economy, honor, nor ideas of any kind in the American breast; yet the obstinate repetition of these denials itself betrayed a lurking fear of the social forces whose strength they were candid enough to record. What was it that, as they complained, turned the European peasant into a new man within half an hour after landing at New York? Englishmen were never at a loss to understand the poetry of more prosaic emotions. Neither they nor any of their kindred failed in later times to feel the "large excitement" of the country boy, whose "spirit leaped within him to be gone before him," when the lights of London first flared in the distance; yet none seemed ever to feel the larger excitement of the American immigrant. Among the Englishmen who criticised the United States was one greater than Moore,—one who thought himself at home only in the stern beauty of a moral presence. Of all poets, living or dead, Wordsworth felt most keenly what he called the still, sad music of humanity; yet the highest conception he could create of America was not more poetical than that of any Cumberland beggar he might have met in his morning walk:—

> "Long-wished-for sight, the Western World appeared;
> And when the ship was moored, I leaped ashore
> Indignantly,—resolved to be a man,
> Who, having o'er the past no power, would live
> No longer in subjection to the past,
> With abject mind—from a tyrannic lord
> Inviting penance, fruitlessly endured.
> So, like a fugitive whose feet have cleared
> Some boundary which his followers may not cross

6. **Moore**: Thomas Moore (1779–1852), Irish poet, chiefly familiar for *Irish Melodies*. The *Epistles* actually came out in 1806. 7. **Dennie**: Joseph Dennie (1768–1812), conservative Federalist journalist and literary critic. **8. Barlow and Dwight**: Joel Barlow (1754–1812), American poet and diplomat. Timothy Dwight (1752–1817), poet and president of Yale. Both were members of the famous literary group the "Connecticut Wits."

9. **To . . . "Guerrière"**: In 1807 the British bombarded and nearly destroyed the defenseless city of Copenhagen when neutral Denmark refused to surrender its fleet. **Trafalgar**: Nelson's brilliant victory in 1805 over the combined French and Spanish fleets. **"Guerrière"**: defeated by the *Constitution* (Old Ironsides), 1812.

In prosecution of their deadly chase,
Respiring, I looked round. How bright the sun,
The breeze how soft! Can anything produced
In the Old World compare, thought I, for power
And majesty, with this tremendous stream
Sprung from the desert? And behold a city
Fresh, youthful, and aspiring! . . .
               Sooth to say,
On nearer view, a motley spectacle
Appeared, of high pretensions—unreproved
But by the obstreperous voice of higher still;
Big passions strutting on a petty stage,
Which a detached spectator may regard
Not unamused. But ridicule demands
Quick change of objects; and to laugh alone,
. . . in the very centre of the crowd
To keep the secret of a poignant scorn,
                   . . . is least fit
For the gross spirit of mankind." [10]

Thus Wordsworth, although then at his prime, indulging in what sounded like a boast that he alone had felt the sense sublime of something interfused, whose dwelling is the light of setting suns, and the round ocean, and the living air, and the blue sky, and in the mind of man,—even he, to whose moods the heavy and the weary weight of all this unintelligible world was lightened by his deeper sympathies with nature and the soul, could do no better, when he stood in the face of American democracy, than "keep the secret of a poignant scorn." [11]

Possibly the view of Wordsworth and Moore, of Weld, Dennie, and Dickens was right. The American democrat possessed little art of expression, and did not watch his own emotions with a view of uttering them either in prose or verse; he never told more of himself than the world might have assumed without listening to him. Only with diffidence could history attribute to such a class of men a wider range of thought or feeling than they themselves cared to proclaim. Yet the difficulty of denying or even ignoring the wider range was still greater, for no one questioned the force or the scope of an emotion which caused the poorest peasant in Europe to see what was invisible to poet and philosopher,—the dim outline of a mountain-summit across the ocean, rising high above the mist and mud of American democracy. As though to call attention to some such difficulty, European and American critics, while affirming that Americans were a race without illusions or enlarged ideas, declared in the same breath that Jefferson was a visionary whose theories would cause the heavens to fall upon them.

10. "Long . . . mankind": From William Wordsworth's *The Excursion*, III.870 ff.   11. **Thus . . . scorn:** The sentence is a mosaic of verbal echoes from Wordsworth's "Tintern Abbey."

Year after year, with endless iteration, in every accent of contempt, rage, and despair, they repeated this charge against Jefferson. Every foreigner and Federalist agreed that he was a man of illusions, dangerous to society and unbounded in power of evil; but if this view of his character was right, the same visionary qualities seemed also to be a national trait, for every one admitted that Jefferson's opinions, in one form or another, were shared by a majority of the American people.

Illustrations might be carried much further, and might be drawn from every social class and from every period in national history. Of all presidents, Abraham Lincoln has been considered the most typical representative of American society, chiefly because his mind, with all its practical qualities, also inclined, in certain directions, to idealism. Lincoln was born in 1809, the moment when American character stood in lowest esteem. Ralph Waldo Emerson, a more distinct idealist, was born in 1803. William Ellery Channing, another idealist, was born in 1780. Men like John Fitch, Oliver Evans, Robert Fulton, Joel Barlow, John Stevens, and Eli Whitney were all classed among visionaries. The whole society of Quakers belonged in the same category. The records of the popular religious sects abounded in examples of idealism and illusion to such an extent that the masses seemed hardly to find comfort or hope in any authority, however old or well established. In religion as in politics, Americans seemed to require a system which gave play to their imagination and their hopes.

Some misunderstanding must always take place when the observer is at cross-purposes with the society he describes. Wordsworth might have convinced himself by a moment's thought that no country could act on the imagination as America acted upon the instincts of the ignorant and poor, without some quality that deserved better treatment than poignant scorn; but perhaps this was only one among innumerable cases in which the unconscious poet breathed an atmosphere which the self-conscious poet could not penetrate. With equal reason he might have taken the opposite view,—that the hard, practical, money-getting American democrat, who had neither generosity nor honor nor imagination, and who inhabited cold shades where fancy sickened and where genius died, was in truth living in a world of dream, and acting a drama more instinct with poetry than all the avatars of the East, walking in gardens of emerald and rubies, in ambition already ruling the world and guiding Nature with a kinder and wiser hand than had ever yet been felt in human history. From this point his critics never approached him,—they stopped at a stone's throw; and at the moment when they declared that the man's mind had no illusions, they added that he was a knave or a lunatic. Even on his practical and sordid side, the American might easily have been represented as a victim to illusion. If the Englishman had lived as the American speculator did,—in the future,—the hyperbole of enthusiasm would have seemed less monstrous. "Look at my wealth!" cried the American to his foreign visitor. "See these solid mountains of salt and iron, of lead, copper, silver, and gold! See these magnificent cities scattered broadcast to the Pacific! See my cornfields rustling and waving in the summer breeze from ocean to ocean, so far that the sun itself is not high enough to mark where the distant mountains bound my golden seas! Look at this continent of mine, fairest of created worlds, as she lies turning up to the sun's never-failing caress her broad and exuberant breasts, overflowing with milk for her hundred million children! See how she glows with youth, health, and love!" Perhaps it was not altogether unnatural that the foreigner, on being asked to see what needed centuries to produce, should have looked about him with bewilderment and indignation. "Gold! cities! cornfields! continents! Nothing of the sort! I see nothing but tremendous wastes, where sickly men and women are dying of home-sickness or are scalped by savages! mountain-ranges a thousand miles long, with no means of getting to them, and nothing in them when you get there! swamps and forests choked with their own rotten ruins! nor hope of better for a thousand years! Your story is a fraud, and you are a liar and swindler!"

Met in this spirit, the American, half perplexed and half defiant, retaliated by calling his antagonist a fool, and by mimicking his heavy tricks of manner. For himself he cared little, but his dream was his whole existence. The men who denounced him admitted that they left him in his forest-swamp quaking with fever, but clinging in the delirium of death to the illusions of his dazzled brain. No class of men could be required to support their convictions with a steadier faith, or pay more devotedly with their persons for the mistakes of their judgment. Whether imagination or greed led them to describe more than actually existed, they still saw no more than any inventor or discoverer must have seen in order to give him the energy of success. They said to the rich as to the poor, "Come and share our limitless riches! Come and help us bring to light these unimaginable stores of wealth and power!" The poor came, and from them were seldom heard complaints of deception or delusion. Within a moment, by the mere contact of a moral atmosphere, they saw the gold and jewels, the summer cornfields and the glowing continent. The rich for a long time stood aloof,—they were timid and narrow-minded; but this was not all,—between them and the American democrat was a gulf.

The charge that Americans were too fond of money to win the confidence of Europeans was a curious inconsistency; yet this was a common belief. If the American deluded himself and led others to their death by baseless speculations; if he buried those he loved in a gloomy forest where they quaked and died while he persisted in seeing there a splendid, healthy, and well-built city,— no one could deny that he sacrificed wife and child to his greed for gain, that the dollar was his god, and a sordid avarice his demon. Yet had this been the whole truth, no European capitalist would have hesitated to make money out of his grave; for, avarice against avarice, no more sordid or meaner type existed in America than could be shown on every 'Change in Europe. With much more reason Americans might have suspected that in America Englishmen found everywhere a silent influence, which they found nowhere in Europe, and which had nothing to do with avarice or with the dollar, but, on the contrary, seemed likely at any moment to sacrifice the dollar in a cause and for an object so illusory that most Englishmen could not endure to hear it discussed. European travellers who passed through America noticed that everywhere, in the White House at Washington and in log-cabins beyond the Alleghanies, except for a few Federalists, every American, from Jefferson and Gallatin down to the poorest squatter, seemed to nourish an idea that he was doing what he could to overthrow the tyranny which the past had fastened on the human mind. Nothing was easier than to laugh at the ludicrous expressions of this simple-minded conviction, or to cry out against its coarseness, or grow angry with its prejudices; to see its nobler side, to feel the beatings of a heart underneath the sordid surface of a gross humanity, was not so easy. Europeans seemed seldom or never conscious that the sentiment could possess a noble side, but found only matter for complaint in the remark that every American democrat believed himself to be working for the overthrow of tyranny, aristocracy, hereditary privilege, and priesthood, wherever they existed. Even where the American did not openly proclaim this conviction in words, he carried so dense an atmosphere of the sentiment with him in his daily life as to give respectable Europeans an uneasy sense of remoteness.

Of all historical problems, the nature of a national character is the most difficult and the most important. Readers will be troubled, at almost every chapter of the coming narrative, by the want of some formula to explain what share the popular imagination bore in the system pursued by government. The acts of the American people during the administrations of Jefferson and Madison were judged at the time by no other test. According as bystanders believed American character to be hard, sordid, and free from illusion, they were severe and even harsh in judgment. This rule guided the governments of England and France. Federalists in the United States, knowing more of the circumstances, often attributed to the democratic instinct a visionary quality which they regarded as sentimentality, and charged with many bad consequences. If their view was correct, history could occupy itself to no better purpose than in ascertaining the nature and force of the quality which was charged with results so serious; but nothing was more elusive than the spirit of American democracy. Jefferson, the literary representative of the class, spoke chiefly for Virginians, and dreaded so greatly his own reputation as a visionary that he seldom or never uttered his whole thought. Gallatin and Madison were still more cautious. The press in no country could give shape to a mental condition so shadowy. The people themselves, although millions in number, could not have expressed their finer instincts had they tried, and might not have recognized them if expressed by others.

In the early days of colonization, every new settlement represented an idea and proclaimed a mission. Virginia was founded by a great, liberal movement aiming at the spread of English liberty and empire. The Pilgrims of Plymouth, the Puritans of Boston, the Quakers of Pennsylvania, all avowed a moral purpose, and began by making institutions that consciously reflected a moral idea. No such character belonged to the colonization of 1800. From Lake Erie to Florida, in long, unbroken line, pioneers were at work, cutting into the forests with the energy of so many beavers, and with no more express moral purpose than the beavers they drove away. The civilization they carried with them was rarely illumined by an idea; they sought room for no new truth, and aimed neither at creating, like the Puritans, a government of saints, nor, like the Quakers, one of love and peace; they left such experiments behind them, and wrestled only with the hardest problems of frontier life. No wonder that foreign observers, and even the educated, well-to-do Americans of the sea-coast, could seldom see anything to admire in the ignorance and brutality of frontiersmen, and should declare that virtue and wisdom no longer guided the United States! What they saw was not encouraging. To a new society, ignorant and semi-barbarous, a mass of demagogues insisted on applying every stimulant that could inflame its worst appetites, while at the same instant taking away every influence that had hitherto helped to restrain its passions. Greed for wealth, lust for power, yearning for the blank void of savage freedom such as Indians and wolves delighted in,—these were the fires that flamed under the caldron of American society, in which, as conservatives believed, the old, well-proven, conservative crust of religion, government, family, and even common respect for age, education, and experience was rapidly melting away, and was indeed already broken into fragments, swept about by the seething mass of scum ever rising in greater quantities to the surface.

Against this Federalist and conservative view of democratic tendencies, democrats protested in a thousand forms, but never in any mode of expression which satisfied them all, or explained their whole character. Probably Jefferson came nearest to the mark, for he represented the hopes of science as well as the prejudices of Virginia; but Jefferson's writings may be searched from beginning to end without revealing the whole measure of the man, far less of the movement. Here and there in his letters a suggestion was thrown out, as though by chance, revealing larger hopes,—as in 1815, at a moment of despondency, he wrote: "I fear from the experience of the last twenty-five years that morals do not of necessity advance hand in hand with the sciences." In 1800, in the flush of triumph, he believed that his task in the world was to establish a democratic republic, with the sciences for an intellectual field, and physical and moral advancement keeping pace with their advance. Without an excessive introduction of more recent ideas, he might be imagined to define democratic progress, in the somewhat affected precision of his French philosophy: "Progress is either physical or intellectual. If we can bring it about that men are on the average an inch taller in the next generation than in this; if they are an inch larger round the chest; if their brain is an ounce or two heavier, and their life a year or two longer,—that is progress. If fifty years hence the average man shall invariably argue from two ascertained premises where he now jumps to a conclusion from a single supposed revelation,—that is progress! I expect it to be made here, under our democratic stimulants, on a great scale, until every man is potentially an athlete in body and an Aristotle in mind." To this doctrine the New Englander replied, "What will you do for moral progress?" Every possible answer to this question opened a chasm. No doubt Jefferson held the faith that men would improve morally with their physical and intellectual growth; but he had no idea of any moral improvement other than that which came by nature. He could not tolerate a priesthood, a state church, or revealed religion. Conservatives, who could tolerate no society without such pillars of order, were, from their point of view, right in answering, "Give us rather the worst despotism of Europe,—there our souls at least may have a chance of salvation!" To their minds vice and virtue were not relative, but fixed terms. The Church was a divine institution. How could a ship hope to reach port when the crew threw overboard sails, spars, and compass, unshipped their rudder, and all the long day thought only of eating and drinking? Nay, even should the new experiment succeed in a worldly sense, what was a man profited if he gained the whole world, and lost his own soul? The Lord God was a jealous God, and visited the sins of the parents upon the children; but what worse sin could be conceived than for a whole nation to join their chief in chanting the strange hymn with which Jefferson, a new false prophet, was deceiving and betraying his people: "It does me no injury for my neighbor to say there are twenty Gods or no God!"

On this ground conservatism took its stand, as it had hitherto done with success in every similar emergency in the world's history, and fixing its eyes on moral standards of its own, refused to deal with the subject as further open to argument. The two parties stood facing opposite ways, and could see no common ground of contact.

Yet even then one part of the American social system was proving itself to be rich in results. The average American was more intelligent than the average European, and was becoming every year still more active-minded as the new movement of society caught him up and swept him through a life of more varied experiences. On all sides the national mind responded to its stimulants. Deficient as the American was in the machinery of higher instruction; remote, poor; unable by any exertion to acquire the training, the capital, or even the elementary text-books he needed for a fair development of his natural powers,—his native energy and ambition already responded to the spur applied to them. Some of his triumphs were famous throughout the world; for Benjamin Franklin had raised high the reputation of American printers, and the actual President of the United States, who signed with Franklin the

treaty of peace with Great Britain, was the son of a small farmer, and had himself kept a school in his youth. In both these cases social recognition followed success; but the later triumphs of the American mind were becoming more and more popular. John Fitch was not only one of the poorest, but one of the least-educated Yankees who ever made a name; he could never spell with tolerable correctness, and his life ended as it began,— in the lowest social obscurity. Eli Whitney was better educated than Fitch, but had neither wealth, social influence, nor patron to back his ingenuity. In the year 1800 Eli Terry, another Connecticut Yankee of the same class, took into his employ two young men to help him make wooden clocks, and this was the capital on which the greatest clock-manufactory in the world began its operations. In 1797 Asa Whittemore, a Massachusetts Yankee, invented a machine to make cards for carding wool, which "operated as if it had a soul," and became the foundation for a hundred subsequent patents. In 1790 Jacob Perkins, of Newburyport, invented a machine capable of cutting and turning out two hundred thousand nails a day; and then invented a process for transferring engraving from a very small steel cylinder to copper, which revolutionized cotton-printing. The British traveller Weld, passing through Wilmington, stopped, as Liancourt had done before him, to see the great flour-mills on the Brandywine. "The improvements," he said, "which have been made in the machinery of the flour-mills in America are very great. The chief of these consist in a new application of the screw, and the introduction of what are called elevators, the idea of which was evidently borrowed from the chain-pump." This was the invention of Oliver Evans, a native of Delaware, whose parents were in very humble life, but who was himself, in spite of every disadvantage, an inventive genius of the first order. Robert Fulton, who in 1800 was in Paris with Joel Barlow, sprang from the same source in Pennsylvania. John Stevens, a native of New York, belonged to a more favored class, but followed the same impulses. All these men were the outcome of typical American society, and all their inventions transmuted the democratic instinct into a practical and tangible shape. Who would undertake to say that there was a limit to the fecundity of this teeming source? Who that saw only the narrow, practical, money-getting nature of the devices could venture to assert that as they wrought their end and raised the standard of millions, they would not also raise the creative power of those millions to a higher plane? If the priests and barons who set their names to Magna Charta had been told that in a few centuries every swine-herd and cobbler's apprentice would write and read with an ease such as few kings could then command, and reason with better logic than any university could then practise, the priest and baron would have been more incredulous than any man who was told in 1800 that within another five centuries the ploughboy would go a-field whistling a sonata of Beethoven, and figure out in quaternions the relation of his furrows. The American democrat knew so little of art that among his popular illusions he could not then nourish artistic ambition; but leaders like Jefferson, Gallatin, and Barlow might without extravagance count upon a coming time when the diffused ease and education should bring the masses into familiar contact with higher forms of human achievement, and their vast creative power, turned toward a nobler culture, might rise to the level of that democratic genius which found expression in the Parthenon; might revel in the delights of a new Buonarotti and a richer Titian; might create for five hundred million people the America of thought and art which alone could satisfy their omnivorous ambition.

Whether the illusions, so often affirmed and so often denied to the American people, took such forms or not, these were in effect the problems that lay before American society: Could it transmute its social power into the higher forms of thought? Could it provide for the moral and intellectual needs of mankind? Could it take permanent political shape? Could it give new life to religion and art? Could it create and maintain in the mass of mankind those habits of mind which had hitherto belonged to men of science alone? Could it physically develop the convolutions of the human brain? Could it produce, or was it compatible with, the differentiation of a higher variety of the human race? Nothing less than this was necessary for its complete success.

FROM **VOLUME IX**

CHAPTER 10

AMERICAN CHARACTER [1817]

UNTIL 1815 nothing in the future of the American Union was regarded as settled. As late as January, 1815, division into several nationalities was still thought to be possible. Such a destiny, repeating the usual experience of history, was not necessarily more unfortunate than the career of a single nationality wholly American; for if the effects of divided nationality were certain to be unhappy, those of a single society with equal certainty defied experience or sound speculation. One uniform and harmonious system appealed to the imagination as a triumph of human progress, offering prospects of peace and ease, contentment and philanthropy, such as the world had not seen; but it invited dangers, formidable because unusual or altogether unknown. The corruption of such a system might prove to be proportionate with its dimensions, and uniformity might lead to evils as serious as were commonly ascribed to diversity.

The laws of human progress were matter not for dogmatic faith, but for study; and although society instinctively regarded small States, with their clashing interests and incessant wars, as the chief obstacle to improvement, such progress as the world knew had been coupled with those drawbacks. The few examples offered by history of great political societies, relieved from external competition or rivalry, were not commonly thought encouraging. War had been the severest test of political and social character, laying bare whatever was feeble, and calling out whatever was strong; and the effect of removing such a test was an untried problem.

In 1815 for the first time Americans ceased to doubt the path they were to follow. Not only was the unity of their nation established, but its probable divergence from older societies was also well defined. Already in 1817 the difference between Europe and America was decided. In politics the distinction was more evident than in social, religious, literary, or scientific directions; and the result was singular. For a time the aggressions of England and France forced the United States into a path that seemed to lead toward European methods of government; but the popular resistance, or inertia, was so great that the most popular party leaders failed to overcome it, and no sooner did foreign dangers disappear than the system began to revert to American practices; the national government tried to lay aside its assumed powers. When Madison vetoed the bill for internal improvements he could have had no other motive than that of restoring to the government, as far as possible, its original American character.

The result was not easy to understand in theory or to make efficient in practice; but while the drift of public opinion, and still more of practical necessity, drew the government slowly toward the European standard of true political sovereignty, nothing showed that the compromise, which must probably serve the public purpose, was to be European in form or feeling. As far as politics supplied a test, the national character had already diverged from any foreign type. Opinions might differ whether the political movement was progressive or retrograde, but in any case the American, in his political character, was a new variety of man.

The social movement was also decided. The war gave a severe shock to the Anglican sympathies of society, and peace seemed to widen the breach between European and American tastes. Interest in Europe languished after Napoleon's overthrow. France ceased to affect American opinion. England became an object of less alarm. Peace produced in the United States a social and economical revolution which greatly curtailed the influence of New England, and with it the social authority of Great Britain. The invention of the steamboat counterbalanced ocean commerce. The South and West gave to society a character more aggressively American than had been known before. That Europe, within certain limits, might tend toward American ideas was possible, but that America should under any circumstances follow the experiences of European development might thenceforward be reckoned as improbable. American character was formed, if not fixed.

The scientific interest of American history centred in national character, and in the workings of a society destined to become vast, in which individuals were important chiefly as types. Although this kind of interest was different from that of European history, it was at least as important to the world. Should history ever become a true science, it must expect to establish its laws, not from the complicated story of rival European nationalities, but from the methodical evolution of a great democracy. North America was the most favorable field on the globe for the spread of a society so large, uniform, and isolated as to answer the purposes of science. There a single homogeneous society could easily attain proportions of three or four hundred million persons, under conditions of undisturbed growth.

In Europe or Asia, except perhaps in China, undisturbed social evolution had been unknown. Without disturbance, evolution seemed to cease. Wherever disturbance occurred, permanence was impossible. Every people in turn adapted itself to the law of necessity. Such a system as that of the United States could hardly have existed for half a century in Europe except under the protection of another power. In the fierce struggle characteristic of European society, systems were permanent in nothing except in the general law, that, whatever other character they might possess they must always be chiefly military.

The want of permanence was not the only or the most confusing obstacle to the treatment of European history as a science. The intensity of the struggle gave prominence to the individual, until the hero seemed all, society nothing; and what was worse for scientific purposes, the men interested more than the societies. In the dramatic view of history, the hero deserved more to be studied than the community to which he belonged; in truth, he was the society, which existed only to produce him and to perish with him. Against such a view historians were among the last to protest, and protested but faintly when they did so at all. They felt as strongly as their audiences that the highest achievements were alone worth remembering either in history or in art, and that a reiteration of common places was commonplace. With all the advantages of European movement and color, few historians succeeded in enlivening or dignifying the lack of motive, intelligence, and morality, the helplessness characteristic of many long periods in the face of crushing problems, and the futility of human efforts to escape from difficulties religious, political, and social. In a period extending over four or five thousand years, more or less capable of historical treatment, historians were content to illustrate here and there the most dramatic moments of the most striking communities. The hero was their favorite. War was the chief field of heroic action, and even the history of England was chiefly the story of war.

The history of the United States promised to be free from such disturbances. War counted for little, the hero for less; [12] on the people alone the eye could permanently rest. The steady growth of a vast population without the social distinctions that confused other histories,—without kings, nobles, or armies; without church, traditions, and prejudices,—seemed a subject for the man of science rather than for dramatists or poets. To scientific treatment only one great obstacle existed. Americans, like Europeans, were not disposed to make of their history a mechanical evolution. They felt that they even more than other nations needed the heroic element, because they breathed an atmosphere of peace and industry where heroism could seldom be displayed; and in unconscious protest against their own social conditions they adorned with imaginary qualities scores of supposed leaders, whose only merit was their faculty of reflecting a popular trait. Instinctively they clung to ancient history as though conscious that of all misfortunes that could befall the national

12. **War . . . less:** For Adams on hero worship, see his letter to William James, July 27, 1882.

character, the greatest would be the loss of the established ideals which alone ennobled human weakness. Without heroes, the national character of the United States had few charms of imagination even to Americans.

Historians and readers maintained Old-World standards. No historian cared to hasten the coming of an epoch when man should study his own history in the same spirit and by the same methods with which he studied the formation of a crystal. Yet history had its scientific as well as its human side, and in American history the scientific interest was greater than the human. Elsewhere the student could study under better conditions the evolution of the individual, but nowhere could he study so well the evolution of a race. The interest of such a subject exceeded that of any other branch of science, for it brought mankind within sight of its own end.

Travellers in Switzerland who stepped across the Rhine where it flowed from its glacier could follow its course among mediæval towns and feudal ruins, until it became a highway for modern industry, and at last arrived at a permanent equilibrium in the ocean. American history followed the same course. With prehistoric glaciers and mediæval feudalism the story had little to do; but from the moment it came within sight of the ocean it acquired interest almost painful. A child could find his way in a river-valley, and a hoy could float on the waters of Holland; but science alone could sound the depths of the ocean, measure its currents, foretell its storms, or fix its relations to the system of Nature. In a democratic ocean science could see something ultimate. Man could go no further. The atom might move, but the general equilibrium could not change.

Whether the scientific or the heroic view were taken, in either case the starting-point was the same, and the chief object of interest was to define national character. Whether the figures of history were treated as heroes or as types, they must be taken to represent the people. American types were especially worth study if they were to represent the greatest democratic evolution the world could know. Readers might judge for themselves what share the individual possessed in creating or shaping the nation; but whether it was small or great, the nation could be understood only by studying the individual. For that reason, in the story of Jefferson and Madison individuals retained their old interest as types of character, if not as sources of power.

In the American character antipathy to war ranked first among political traits. The majority of Americans regarded war in a peculiar light, the consequence of comparative security. No European nation could have conducted a war, as the people of America conducted the War of 1812. The possibility of doing so without destruction explained the existence of the national trait, and assured its continuance. In politics, the divergence of America from Europe perpetuated itself in the popular instinct for peaceable methods. The Union took shape originally on the general lines that divided the civil from the military elements of the British constitution. The party of Jefferson and Gallatin was founded on dislike of every function of government necessary in a military system. Although Jefferson carried his pacific theories to an extreme, and brought about a military reaction, the reactionary movement was neither universal, violent, nor lasting; and society showed no sign of changing its convictions. With greater strength the country might acquire greater familiarity with warlike methods, but in the same degree was less likely to suffer any general change of habits. Nothing but prolonged intestine contests could convert the population of an entire continent into a race of warriors.

A people whose chief trait was antipathy to war, and to any system organized with military energy, could scarcely develop great results in national administration; yet the Americans prided themselves chiefly on their political capacity. Even the war did not undeceive them, although the incapacity brought into evidence by the war was undisputed, and was most remarkable among the communities which believed themselves to be most gifted with political sagacity. Virginia and Massachusetts by turns admitted failure in dealing with issues so simple that the newest societies, like Tennessee and Ohio, understood them by instinct. That incapacity in national politics should appear as a leading trait in American character was unexpected by Americans, but might naturally result from their conditions. The better test of American character was not political but social, and was to be found not in the government but in the people.

The sixteen years of Jefferson's and Madison's rule furnished international tests of popular intelligence upon which Americans could depend. The ocean was the only open field for competition among nations. Americans enjoyed there no natural or artificial advantages over Englishmen, Frenchmen, or Spaniards; indeed, all these countries possessed navies, resources, and experience greater than were to be found in the United States. Yet the Americans developed, in the course of twenty years, a surprising degree of skill in naval affairs. The evidence of their success was to be found nowhere so complete as in the avowals of Englishmen who knew best the history of naval progress. The American invention of the fast-sailing schooner or clipper was the more remarkable because, of all American inventions, this alone sprang from direct competition with Europe. During ten centuries of struggle the nations of Europe had labored to obtain superiority over each other in ship-construction, yet Americans instantly made improvements which gave them superiority, and which Europeans were unable immediately to imitate even after seeing them. Not only were American vessels better in model, faster in sailing, easier and quicker in handling, and more economical in working than the European, but they were also better equipped. The English complained as a grievance that the Americans adopted new and unwarranted devices in naval warfare; that their vessels were heavier and better constructed, and their missiles of unusual shape and improper use. The Americans resorted to expedients that had not been tried before, and excited a mixture of irritation and respect in the English service, until Yankee smartness became a national misdemeanor.

The English admitted themselves to be slow to change their habits, but the French were both quick and scientific; yet Americans did on the ocean what the French, under stronger inducements, failed to do. The French privateer preyed upon British commerce for twenty years without seriously injuring it; but no sooner did the American privateer sail from French ports, than the rates of insurance doubled in London, and an outcry for protection arose among English shippers which the Admiralty could not calm. The British newspapers were filled with assertions that the American cruiser was the superior of any vessel of its class, and threatened to overthrow England's supremacy on the ocean.

Another test of relative intelligence was furnished by the battles at sea. Instantly after the loss of the "Guerrière" the English discovered and complained that American gunnery was superior to their own. They explained their inferiority by the length of time that had elapsed since their navy had found on the ocean an enemy to fight. Every vestige of hostile fleets had been swept away, until, after the battle of Trafalgar, British frigates ceased practice with their guns. Doubtless the British navy had become somewhat careless in the absence of a dangerous enemy, but Englishmen were themselves aware that some other cause must have affected their losses. Nothing showed that Nelson's line-of-battle ships, frigates, or sloops were as a rule better fought than the "Macedonian" and "Java," the "Avon" and

"Reindeer." Sir Howard Douglas, the chief authority on the subject, attempted in vain to explain British reverses by the deterioration of British gunnery. His analysis showed only that American gunnery was extraordinarily good. Of all vessels, the sloop-of-war,—on account of its smallness, its quick motion, and its more accurate armament of thirty-two-pound carronades,—offered the best test of relative gunnery, and Sir Howard Douglas in commenting upon the destruction of the "Peacock" and "Avon" could only say,—

"In these two actions it is clear that the fire of the British vessels was thrown too high, and that the ordnance of their opponents were expressly and carefully aimed at and took effect chiefly in the hull."

The battle of the "Hornet" and "Penguin" as well as those of the "Reindeer" and "Avon," showed that the excellence of American gunnery continued till the close of the war. Whether at point-blank range or at long-distance practice, the Americans used guns as they had never been used at sea before.

None of the reports of former British victories showed that the British fire had been more destructive at any previous time than in 1812, and no report of any commander since the British navy existed showed so much damage inflicted on an opponent in so short a time as was proved to have been inflicted on themselves by the reports of British commanders in the American war. The strongest proof of American superiority was given by the best British officers, like Broke, who strained every nerve to maintain an equality with American gunnery. So instantaneous and energetic was the effort that, according to the British historian of the war, "a British forty-six-gun frigate of 1813 was half as effective again as a British forty-six-gun frigate of 1812;" and, as he justly said, "the slaughtered crews and the shattered hulks" of the captured British ships proved that no want of their old fighting qualities accounted for their repeated and almost habitual mortifications.[13]

Unwilling as the English were to admit the superior skill of Americans on the ocean, they did not hesitate to admit it, in certain respects, on land. The American rifle in American hands was affirmed to have no equal in the world. This admission could scarcely be withheld after the lists of killed and wounded which followed almost every battle; but the admission served to check a wider inquiry. In truth, the rifle played but a small

13. "James, pp. 525, 528" [Adams's note].

part in the war. Winchester's men at the river Raisin may have owed their over-confidence, as the British Forty-first owed its losses, to that weapon, and at New Orleans five or six hundred of Coffee's men, who were out of range, were armed with the rifle; but the surprising losses of the British were commonly due to artillery and musketry fire. At New Orleans the artillery was chiefly engaged. The artillery battle of January 1, according to British accounts, amply proved the superiority of American gunnery on that occasion, which was probably the fairest test during the war. The battle of January 8 was also chiefly an artillery battle; the main British column never arrived within fair musket range; Pakenham [14] was killed by a grapeshot, and the main column of his troops halted more than one hundred yards from the parapet.

The best test of British and American military qualities, both for men and weapons, was Scott's battle of Chippawa. Nothing intervened to throw a doubt over the fairness of the trial. Two parallel lines of regular soldiers, practically equal in numbers, armed with similar weapons, moved in close order toward each other, across a wide open plain, without cover or advantage of position, stopping at intervals to load and fire, until one line broke and retired. At the same time two three-gun batteries, the British being the heavier, maintained a steady fire from positions opposite each other. According to the reports, the two infantry lines in the centre never came nearer than eighty yards. Major-General Riall reported that then, owing to severe losses, his troops broke and could not be rallied. Comparison of the official reports showed that the British lost in killed and wounded four hundred and sixty-nine men; the Americans, two hundred and ninety-six. Some doubts always affect the returns of wounded, because the severity of the wound cannot be known; but dead men tell their own tale. Riall reported one hundred and forty-eight killed; Scott reported sixty-one. The severity of the losses showed that the battle was sharply contested, and proved the personal bravery of both armies. Marksmanship decided the result, and the returns proved that the American fire was superior to that of the British in the proportion of more than fifty per cent if estimated by the entire loss, and of two hundred and forty-two to one hundred if estimated by the deaths alone.

The conclusion seemed incredible, but it was supported by the results of the naval battles. The Americans showed superiority amounting in some cases to twice the efficiency of their enemies in the use of weapons. The best French critic of the naval war, Jurien de la Gravière said: "An enormous superiority in the rapidity and precision of their fire can alone explain the difference in the losses sustained by the combatants." [15] So far from denying this conclusion the British press constantly alleged it, and the British officers complained of it. The discovery caused great surprise, and in both British services much attention was at once directed to improvement in artillery and musketry. Nothing could exceed the frankness with which Englishmen avowed their inferiority. According to Sir Francis Head, "gunnery was in naval warfare in the extraordinary state of ignorance we have just described, when our lean children, the American people, taught us, rod in hand, our first lesson in the art." The English textbook on Naval Gunnery, written by Major-General Sir Howard Douglas immediately after the peace, devoted more attention to the short American war than to all the battles of Napoleon, and began by admitting that Great Britain had "entered with too great confidence on war with a marine much more expert than that of any of our European enemies." The admission appeared "objectionable" even to the author; [16] but he did not add, what was equally true, that it applied as well to the land as to the sea service.

No one questioned the bravery of the British forces, or the ease with which they often routed larger bodies of militia; but the losses they inflicted were rarely as great as those they suffered. Even at Bladensburg, where they met little resistance, their loss was several times greater than that of the Americans. At Plattsburg, where the intelligence and quickness of Macdonough and his men alone won the victory, his ships were in effect stationary batteries, and enjoyed the same superiority in gunnery. "The 'Saratoga,'" said his official report, "had fifty-five round-shot in her hull; the 'Confiance,' one hundred and five. The enemy's shot passed principally just over our heads, as there were not twenty whole hammocks in the nettings at the close of the action."

The greater skill of the Americans was not due to special training, for the British service was better trained in gunnery, as in everything else, than the motley armies and fleets that fought at New Orleans and on the Lakes. Critics constantly said that every American had learned from his child-

---

14. **Pakenham:** Sir Edward, British commanding general, defeated by Jackson at the Battle of New Orleans, January 8, 1815. Word of the signing of the Treaty of Ghent had not yet reached the combatants.

15. "Guerres Maritime, ii, 286, 287" [A].   16. "Douglas, Naval Gunnery (Second edition), p. 3" [A].

hood the use of the rifle, but he certainly had not learned to use cannon in shooting birds or hunting deer, and he knew less than the Englishman about the handling of artillery and muskets. The same intelligence that selected the rifle and the long pivot-gun for favorite weapons was shown in handling the carronade, and every other instrument however clumsy.

Another significant result of the war was the sudden development of scientific engineering in the United States. This branch of the military service owed its efficiency and almost its existence to the military school at West Point, established in 1802. The school was at first much neglected by government. The number of graduates before the year 1812 was very small; but at the outbreak of the war the corps of engineers was already efficient. Its chief was Colonel Joseph Gardner Swift, of Massachusetts, the first graduate of the academy: Colonel Swift planned the defences of New York harbor. The lieutenant-colonel in 1812 was Walker Keith Armistead, of Virginia,—the third graduate, who planned the defences of Norfolk. Major William McRee, of North Carolina, became chief engineer to General Brown, and constructed the fortifications at Fort Erie, which cost the British General Gordon Drummond the loss of half his army, besides the mortification of defeat. Captain Eleazer Derby Wood, of New York, constructed Fort Meigs, which enabled Harrison to defeat the attack of Proctor in May, 1813. Captain Joseph Gilbert Totten, of New York, was chief engineer to General Izard at Plattsburg, where he directed the fortifications that stopped the advance of Prevost's [17] great army. None of the works constructed by a graduate of West Point was captured by the enemy; and had an engineer been employed at Washington by Armstrong and Winder, the city would have been easily saved.

Perhaps without exaggeration the West Point Academy might be said to have decided, next to the navy, the result of the war. The works at New Orleans were simple in character, and as far as they were due to engineering skill were directed by Major Latour, a Frenchman; but the war was already ended when the battle of New Orleans was fought. During the critical campaign of 1814, the West Point engineers doubled the capacity of the little American army for resistance, and introduced a new and scientific character into American life.

In the application of science the steamboat was the most striking success; but Fulton's invention, however useful, was neither the most original nor

17. **Prevost:** Sir George (1767–1816), governor of Canada and commander in chief of British forces in Canada.

the most ingenious of American efforts, nor did it offer the best example of popular characteristics. Perhaps Fulton's torpedo and Stevens's screw-propeller showed more originality than was proved by the "Clermont." The fast-sailing schooner with its pivot-gun—an invention that grew out of the common stock of nautical intelligence—best illustrated the character of the people.

That the individual should rise to a higher order either of intelligence or morality than had existed in former ages was not to be expected, for the United States offered less field for the development of individuality than had been offered by older and smaller societies. The chief function of the American Union was to raise the average standard of popular intelligence and well-being, and at the close of the War of 1812 the superior average intelligence of Americans was so far admitted that Yankee acuteness, or smartness, became a national reproach; but much doubt remained whether the intelligence belonged to a high order, or proved a high morality. From the earliest ages, shrewdness was associated with unscrupulousness; and Americans were freely charged with wanting honesty. The charge could neither be proved nor disproved. American morality was such as suited a people so endowed, and was high when compared with the morality of many older societies; but, like American intelligence, it discouraged excess. Probably the political morality shown by the government and by public men during the first sixteen years of the century offered a fair gauge of social morality. Like the character of the popular inventions, the character of the morals corresponded to the wants of a growing democratic society; but time alone could decide whether it would result in a high or a low national ideal.

Finer analysis showed other signs of divergence from ordinary standards. If Englishmen took pride in one trait more than in another, it was in the steady uniformity of their progress. The innovating and revolutionary quality of the French mind irritated them. America showed an un-English rapidity in movement. In politics, the American people between 1787 and 1817 accepted greater changes than had been known in England since 1688. In religion, the Unitarian movement of Boston and Harvard College would never have been possible in England, where the defection of Oxford or Cambridge, and the best educated society in the United Kingdom, would have shaken Church and State to their foundations. In literature the American school was chiefly remarkable for the rapidity with which it matured. The first book of Irving [18] was a successful burlesque of his own ancestral history; the first poem of Bryant [19] sang of the earth only as a universal tomb; the first preaching of Channing [20] assumed to overthrow the Trinity; and the first paintings of Allston aspired to recover the ideal perfection of Raphael and Titian. In all these directions the American mind showed tendencies that surprised Englishmen more than they struck Americans. Allston defended himself from the criticism of friends who made complaint of his return to America. He found there, as he maintained, not only a growing taste for art, but "a quicker appreciation" of artistic effort than in any European land. If the highest intelligence of American society were to move with such rapidity, the time could not be far distant when it would pass into regions which England never liked to contemplate.

Another intellectual trait, as has been already noticed, was the disposition to relax severity. Between the theology of Jonathan Edwards and that of William Ellery Channing was an enormous gap, not only in doctrines but also in methods. Whatever might be thought of the conclusions reached by Edwards and Hopkins,[21] the force of their reasoning commanded respect. Not often had a more strenuous effort than theirs been made to ascertain God's will, and to follow it without regard to weaknesses of the flesh. The idea that the nature of God's attributes was to be preached only as subordinate to the improvement of man, agreed little with the spirit of their religion. The Unitarian and Universalist movements marked the beginning of an epoch when ethical and humanitarian ideas took the place of metaphysics, and even New England turned from contemplating the omnipotence of the Deity in order to praise the perfections of his creatures.

The spread of great popular sects like the Universalists and Campbellites, founded on assumptions such as no Orthodox theology could tolerate, showed a growing tendency to relaxation of thought in that direction. The struggle for existence was already mitigated, and the first effect of the change was seen in the increasing cheerfulness of religion. Only when men found their actual world almost a heaven, could they lose overpowering anxiety about the world to come. Life had taken a softer aspect, and as a consequence God

was no longer terrible. Even the wicked became less mischievous in an atmosphere where virtue was easier than vice. Punishments seemed mild in a society where every offender could cast off his past, and create a new career. For the first time in history, great bodies of men turned away from their old religion, giving no better reason than that it required them to believe in a cruel Deity, and rejected necessary conclusions of theology because they were inconsistent with human self-esteem.

The same optimism marked the political movement. Society was weary of strife, and settled gladly into a political system which left every disputed point undetermined. The public seemed obstinate only in believing that all was for the best, as far as the United States were concerned, in the affairs of mankind. The contrast was great between this temper of mind and that in which the Constitution had been framed; but it was no greater than the contrast in the religious opinions of the two periods, while the same reaction against severity marked the new literature. The rapid accumulation of wealth and increase in physical comfort told the same story from the standpoint of economy. On every side society showed that ease was for a time to take the place of severity, and enjoyment was to have its full share in the future national existence.

The traits of intelligence, rapidity, and mildness seemed fixed in the national character as early as 1817, and were likely to become more marked as time should pass. A vast amount of conservatism still lingered among the people; but the future spirit of society could hardly fail to be intelligent, rapid in movement, and mild in method. Only in the distant future could serious change occur, and even then no return to European characteristics seemed likely. The American continent was happier in its conditions and easier in its resources than the regions of Europe and Asia, where Nature revelled in diversity and conflict. If at any time American character should change, it might as probably become sluggish as revert to the violence and extravagances of Old-World development. The inertia of several hundred million people, all formed in a similar social mould, was as likely to stifle energy as to stimulate evolution.

With the establishment of these conclusions, a new episode in American history began in 1815. New subjects demanded new treatment, no longer dramatic but steadily tending to become scientific. The traits of American character were fixed; the rate of physical and economical growth was established; and history, certain that at a given distance of time the Union would contain so many mil-

18. Irving: Washington Irving, Diedrich Knickerbocker's *History of New York* (1809).   19. Bryant: William Cullen Bryant, "Thanatopsis," (1817, 1821).   20. Channing: William Ellery Channing (1780–1842) broke with Trinitarians in 1815. His sermon "Unitarian Christianity" (1819) stated the Unitarian creed. 21. Hopkins: Samuel Hopkins (1721–1803) adopted the orthodox Calvinist doctrines of Jonathan Edwards.

lions of people, with wealth valued at so many millions of dollars, became thenceforward chiefly concerned to know what kind of people these millions were to be. They were intelligent, but what paths would their intelligence select? They were quick, but what solution of insoluble problems would quickness hurry? They were scientific, and what control would their science exercise over their destiny? They were mild, but what corruptions would their relaxations bring? They were peaceful, but by what machinery were their corruptions to be purged? What interests were to vivify a society so vast and uniform? What ideals were to ennoble it? What object, besides physical content, must a democratic continent aspire to attain? For the treatment of such questions, history required another century of experience.

FROM

MONT-SAINT-MICHEL AND CHARTRES

◊

◖[ADAMS's *Chartres*, as the book is commonly called, was privately printed in 1904 to the number of one hundred and fifty copies, then revised and privately reprinted in 1912. In 1913 Adams consented to the publication of the book under the auspices of the American Institute of Architects.

The title links the great abbey that dominates the rocky islet just off the coast of France, where Normandy meets Brittany, with the cathedral of Chartres, the most beautiful of all the French cathedrals. Chartres lies fifty-five miles southwest of Paris, the cathedral crowning the hill above the Eure River. Most impressive of all its artistic treasures are the stained glass windows which diffuse an unforgettable radiance throughout the vast interior. The church is noted for its great festival of the Virgin. Mont-Saint-Michel no longer shelters the Benedictine monks. They were dispersed during the French Revolution. The abbey buildings are now maintained as a national monument.

◊

PREFACE

[December, 1904]

SOME OLD Elizabethan play or poem contains the lines:

. . . Who reads me, when I am ashes,
Is my son in wishes . . . .

The relationship, between reader and writer, of son and father, may have existed in Queen Elizabeth's time, but is much too close to be true for ours. The utmost that any writer could hope of his readers now is that they should consent to regard themselves as nephews, and even then he would expect only a more or less civil refusal from most of them. Indeed, if he had reached a certain age, he would have observed that nephews, as a social class, no longer read at all, and that there is only one familiar instance recorded of a nephew who read his uncle. The exception tends rather to support the rule, since it needed a Macaulay to produce, and two volumes to record it.[1] Finally, the metre does not permit it. One may not say: 'Who reads me, when I am ashes, is my nephew in wishes.'

The same objections do not apply to the word 'niece.' The change restores the verse, and, to a very great degree, the fact. Nieces have been known to read in early youth, and in some cases may have read their uncles. The relationship, too, is convenient and easy, capable of being anything or nothing, at the will of either party, like a Mohammedan or Polynesian or American marriage. No valid objection can be offered to this change in the verse. Niece let it be!

The following pages, then, are written for nieces, or for those who are willing, for the time, to be nieces in wish. For convenience of travel in France, where hotels, in out-of-the-way places, are sometimes wanting in space as well as luxury, the nieces shall count as one only. As many more may come as like, but one niece is enough for the uncle to talk to, and one niece is much more likely than two to listen. One niece is also more likely than two to carry a kodak and take interest in it, since she has nothing else, except her uncle, to interest her, and instances occur when she takes interest neither in the uncle nor in the journey. One cannot assume, even in a niece, too emotional a nature, but one may assume a kodak.

The party, then, with such variations of detail as may suit its tastes, has sailed from New York, let us say, early in June for an entire summer in France. One pleasant June morning it has landed at Cherbourg or Havre and takes the train across Normandy to Pontorson, where, with the evening light, the tourists drive along the *chaussée*,[2] over the sands or through the tide, till they stop at Madame Poulard's famous hotel within the Gate of the Mount.

The uncle talks:

MONT-SAINT-MICHEL AND CHARTRES.   1. Macaulay . . . it: Sir George Otto Trevelyan (1838–1928), historian and long-time friend of Adams, wrote *The Life and Letters of Lord Macaulay*, published in 1876.   2. *chaussée:* highway.

CHAPTER 1

SAINT MICHIEL DE LA MER DEL PERIL [3]

THE ARCHANGEL loved heights. Standing on the summit of the tower that crowned his church, wings upspread, sword uplifted, the devil crawling beneath, and the cock, symbol of eternal vigilance, perched on his mailed foot, Saint Michael held a place of his own in heaven and on earth which seems, in the eleventh century, to leave hardly room for the Virgin of the Crypt at Chartres, still less for the Beau Christ of the thirteenth century at Amiens. The Archangel stands for Church and State, and both militant. He is the conqueror of Satan, the mightiest of all created spirits, the nearest to God. His place was where the danger was greatest; therefore you find him here. For the same reason he was, while the pagan danger lasted, the patron saint of France. So the Normans, when they were converted to Christianity, put themselves under his powerful protection. So he stood for centuries on his Mount in Peril of the Sea, watching across the tremor of the immense ocean—*immensi tremor oceani*—as Louis XI, inspired for once to poetry, inscribed on the collar of the Order of Saint Michael which he created. So soldiers, nobles, and monarchs went on pilgrimage to his shrine; so the common people followed, and still follow, like ourselves.

The church stands high on the summit of this granite rock, and on its west front is the platform, to which the tourist ought first to climb. From the edge of this platform, the eye plunges down, two hundred and thirty-five feet, to the wide sands or the wider ocean, as the tides recede or advance, under an infinite sky, over a restless sea, which even we tourists can understand and feel without books or guides; but when we turn from the western view, and look at the church door, thirty or forty yards from the parapet where we stand, one needs to be eight centuries old to know what this mass of encrusted architecture meant to its builders, and even then one must still learn to feel it. The man who wanders into the twelfth century is lost, unless he can grow prematurely young.

One can do it, as one can play with children. Wordsworth,[4] whose practical sense equalled his intuitive genius, carefully limited us to 'a season of calm weather,' which is certainly best; but granting a fair frame of mind, one can still 'have sight of that immortal sea' which brought us hither from the twelfth century; one can even travel thither and see the children sporting on the shore. Our sense is partially atrophied from disuse, but it is still alive, at least in old people, who alone, as a class, have the time to be young.

One needs only to be old enough in order to be as young as one will. From the top of this Abbey Church one looks across the bay to Avranches, and towards Coutances and the Cotentin—the *Constantinus pagus* [5]—whose shore, facing us, recalls the coast of New England. The relation between the granite of one coast and that of the other may be fanciful, but the relation between the people who live on each is as hard and practical a fact as the granite itself. When one enters the church, one notes first the four great triumphal piers or columns, at the intersection of the nave and transepts, and on looking into M. Corroyer's architectural study which is the chief source of all one's acquaintance with the Mount, one learns that these piers were constructed in 1058. Four out of five American tourists will instantly recall the only date of mediaeval history they ever knew, the date of the Norman Conquest. Eight years after these piers were built, in 1066, Duke William of Normandy raised an army of forty thousand men in these parts, and in northern France, whom he took to England, where they mostly stayed. For a hundred and fifty years, until 1204, Normandy and England were united; the Norman peasant went freely to England with his lord, spiritual or temporal; the Norman woman, a very capable person, followed her husband or her parents; Normans held nearly all the English fiefs; filled the English Church; crowded the English Court; created the English law; and we know that French was still currently spoken in England as late as 1400, or thereabouts, 'After the scole of Stratford atte bowe.' [6] The aristocratic Norman names still survive in part, and if we look up their origin here we shall generally find them in villages so remote and insignificant that their place can hardly be found on any ordinary map; but the common people had no surnames, and cannot be traced, although for every noble whose name or blood survived in England or in Normandy, we must reckon hundreds of peasants. Since the generation which followed William to England in 1066, we can reckon twenty-eight or thirty from father to son, and, if you care to figure up the sum, you will find that you had about two hundred and fifty million arithmetical ancestors living in the middle of the eleventh century. The whole population of Eng-

---

3. "Saint Michael of the Sea of Peril." 4. Wordsworth: "Intimations of Immortality," ix.

5. *Constantinus pagus:* "province of Constantine"; Constantine II (316–40), Roman Emperor of Britain, Gaul, and Spain. 6. 'After . . . bowe': the manner of Chaucer's Prioresse in the Prologue to the *Canterbury Tales*.

land and northern France may then have num-bered five million, but if it were fifty it would not much affect the certainty that, if you have any English blood at all, you have also Norman. If we could go back and live again in all our two hun-dred and fifty million arithmetical ancestors of the eleventh century, we should find ourselves doing many surprising things, but among the rest we should pretty certainly be ploughing most of the fields of the Cotentin and Calvados; going to mass in every parish church in Normandy; rendering military service to every lord, spiritual or tempo-ral, in all this region; and helping to build the Ab-bey Church at Mont-Saint-Michel. From the roof of the Cathedral of Coutances over yonder, one may look away over the hills and woods, the farms and fields of Normandy, and so familiar, so home-like are they, one can almost take oath that in this, or the other, or in all, one knew life once and has never so fully known it since.

Never so fully known it since! For we of the eleventh century, hard-headed, close-fisted, grasp-ing, shrewd, as we were, and as Normans are still said to be, stood more fully in the centre of the world's movement than our English descendants ever did. We were a part, and a great part, of the Church, of France, and of Europe. The Leos and Gregories of the tenth and eleventh centuries leaned on us in their great struggle for reform. Our Duke Richard-Sans-Peur,[7] in 966, turned the old canons out of the Mount in order to bring here the highest influence of the time, the Benedictine monks of Monte Cassino. Richard II, grandfather of William the Conqueror, began this Abbey Church in 1020, and helped Abbot Hildebert to build it. When William the Conqueror in 1066 set out to conquer England, Pope Alexander II stood behind him and blessed his banner. From that moment our Norman Dukes cast the Kings of France into the shade. Our activity was not lim-ited to northern Europe, or even confined by An-jou and Gascony. When we stop at Coutances, we will drive out to Hauteville to see where Tancred came from, whose sons Robert and Roger were conquering Naples and Sicily at the time when the Abbey Church was building on the Mount. Nor-mans were everywhere in 1066, and everywhere in the lead of their age. We were a serious race. If you want other proof of it, besides our record in war and in politics, you have only to look at our art. Religious art is the measure of human depth and sincerity; any triviality, any weakness cries aloud. If this church on the Mount is not proof enough of Norman character, we will stop at Cou-

tances for a wider view. Then we will go to Caen and Bayeux. From there, it would almost be worth our while to leap at once to Palermo. It was in the year 1131 or thereabouts that Roger began the Cathedral at Cefalu and the Chapel Royal at Pa-lermo; it was about the year 1174 that his grand-son William began the Cathedral of Monreale. No art—either Greek or Byzantine, Italian or Arab—has ever created two religious types so beautiful, so serious, so impressive, and yet so dif-ferent, as Mont-Saint-Michel watching over its northern ocean, and Monreale, looking down over its forests of orange and lemon, on Palermo and the Sicilian seas.

Down nearly to the end of the twelfth century the Norman was fairly master of the world in architecture as in arms, although the thirteenth century belonged to France, and we must look for its glories on the Seine and Marne and Loire; but for the present we are in the eleventh century—tenants of the Duke or of the Church or of small feudal lords who take their names from the neigh-bourhood—Beaumont, Carteret, Gréville, Percy, Pierpont—who, at the Duke's bidding, will each call out his tenants, perhaps ten men-at-arms with their attendants, to fight in Brittany, or in the Vex-in toward Paris, or on the great campaign for the conquest of England which is to come within ten years—the greatest military effort that has been made in western Europe since Charlemagne and Roland were defeated at Roncesvalles three hun-dred years ago. For the moment, we are helping to quarry granite for the Abbey Church, and to haul it to the Mount, or load it on our boat. We never fail to make our annual pilgrimage to the Mount on the Archangel's Day, October 16. We expect to be called out for a new campaign which Duke William threatens against Brittany, and we hear stories that Harold the Saxon, the powerful Earl of Wessex in England, is a guest, or, as some say, a prisoner or a hostage, at the Duke's Court, and will go with us on the campaign. The year is 1058.

All this time we have been standing on the *par-vis,*[8] looking out over the sea and sands which are as good eleventh-century landscape as they ever were; or turning at times towards the church door which is the *pons seclorum,* the bridge of ages, be-tween us and our ancestors. Now that we have made an attempt, such as it is, to get our minds into a condition to cross the bridge without break-ing down in the effort, we enter the church and stand face to face with eleventh-century architec-ture; a ground-plan which dates from 1020; a central tower, or its piers, dating from 1058; and

7. **Richard-Sans-Peur:** Richard the Fearless (d. 996).

8. *parvis:* paved open space in front of a church.

a church completed in 1135. France can offer few buildings of this importance equally old, with dates so exact. Perhaps the closest parallel to Mont-Saint-Michel is Saint-Benoît-sur-Loire, above Orléans, which seems to have been a shrine almost as popular as the Mount, at the same time. Chartres was also a famous shrine, but of the Virgin, and the west porch of Chartres, which is to be our peculiar pilgrimage, was a hundred years later than the ground-plan of Mont-Saint-Michel, although Chartres porch is the usual starting-point of northern French art. Queen Matilda's Abbaye-aux-Dames, now the church of the Trinity, at Caen, dates from 1066. Saint Sernin at Toulouse, the porch of the Abbey Church at Moissac, Notre-Dame-du-Port at Clermont, the Abbey Church at Vézelay, are all said to be twelfth-century. Even San Marco at Venice was new in 1020.

Yet in 1020 Norman art was already too ambitious. Certainly nine hundred years leave their traces on granite as well as on other material, but the granite of Abbot Hildebert would have stood securely enough, if the Abbot had not asked too much from it. Perhaps he asked too much from the Archangel, for the thought of the Archangel's superiority was clearly the inspiration of his plan. The apex of the granite rock rose like a sugar-loaf two hundred and forty feet (73.6 metres) above mean sea-level. Instead of cutting the summit away to give his church a secure rock foundation, which would have sacrificed about thirty feet of height, the Abbot took the apex of the rock for his level, and on all sides built out foundations of masonry to support the walls of his church. The apex of the rock is the floor of the *croisée,* the intersection of nave and transept. On this solid foundation the Abbot rested the chief weight of the church, which was the central tower, supported by the four great piers which still stand; but from the croisée in the centre westward to the parapet of the platform, the Abbot filled the whole space with masonry, and his successors built out still farther, until some two hundred feet of stonework ends now in a perpendicular wall of eighty feet or more. In this space are several ranges of chambers, but the structure might perhaps have proved strong enough to support the light Romanesque front which was usual in the eleventh century, had not fashions in architecture changed in the great epoch of building, a hundred and fifty years later, when Abbot Robert de Torigny thought proper to reconstruct the west front, and build out two towers on its flanks. The towers were no doubt beautiful, if one may judge from the towers of Bayeux and Coutances, but their weight broke down the vault-

ing beneath, and one of them fell in 1300. In 1618 the whole façade began to give way, and in 1776 not only the façade but also three of the seven spans of the nave were pulled down. Of Abbot Hildebert's nave, only four arches remain.

Still, the overmastering strength of the eleventh century is stamped on a great scale here, not only in the four spans of the nave, and in the transepts, but chiefly in the triumphal columns of the croisée. No one is likely to forget what Norman architecture was, who takes the trouble to pass once through this fragment of its earliest bloom. The dimensions are not great, though greater than safe construction warranted. Abbot Hildebert's whole church did not exceed two hundred and thirty feet in length in the interior, and the span of the triumphal arch was only about twenty-three feet, if the books can be trusted. The nave of the Abbaye-aux-Dames appears to have about the same width, and probably neither of them was meant to be vaulted. The roof was of timber, and about sixty-three feet high at its apex. Compared with the great churches of the thirteenth century, this building is modest but its size is not what matters to us. Its style is the starting-point of all our future travels. Here is your first eleventh-century church! How does it affect you?

Serious and simple to excess! is it not? Young people rarely enjoy it. They prefer the Gothic, even as you see it here, looking at us from the choir, through the great Norman arch. No doubt they are right, since they are young: but men and women who have lived long and are tired— who want rest—who have done with aspirations and ambition—whose life has been a broken arch —feel this repose and self-restraint as they feel nothing else. The quiet strength of these curved lines, the solid support of these heavy columns, the moderate proportions, even the modified lights, the absence of display, of effort, of self-consciousness, satisfy them as no other art does. They come back to it to rest, after a long circle of pilgrimage—the cradle of rest from which their ancestors started. Even here they find the repose none too deep.

Indeed, when you look longer at it, you begin to doubt whether there is any repose in it at all— whether it is not the most unreposeful thought ever put into architectural form. Perched on the extreme point of this abrupt rock, the Church Militant with its aspirant Archangel stands high above the world, and seems to threaten heaven itself. The idea is the stronger and more restless because the Church of Saint Michael is surrounded and protected by the world and the society over which it rises, as Duke William rested on his barons and their men. Neither the Saint nor the Duke was troubled by doubts about his mission. Church and State, Soul and Body, God and Man, are all one at Mont-Saint-Michel, and the business of all is to fight, each is his own way, or to stand guard for each other. Neither Church nor State is intellectual, or learned, or even strict in dogma. Here we do not feel the Trinity at all; the Virgin but little; Christ hardly more; we feel only the Archangel and the Unity of God. We have little logic here, and simple faith, but we have energy. We cannot do many things which are done in the centre of civilization, at Byzantium, but we can fight, and we can build a church. No doubt we think first of the church, and next of our temporal lord; only in the last instance do we think of our private affairs, and our private affairs sometimes suffer for it; but we reckon the affairs of Church and State to be ours, too, and we carry this idea very far. Our church on the Mount is ambitious, restless, striving for effect; our conquest of England, with which the Duke is infatuated, is more ambitious still; but all this is a trifle to the outburst which is coming in the next generation; and Saint Michael on his Mount expresses it all.

Taking architecture as an expression of energy, we can some day compare Mont-Saint-Michel with Beauvais,[9] and draw from the comparison whatever moral suits our frame of mind; but you should first note that here, in the eleventh century, the Church, however simple-minded or unschooled, was not cheap. Its self-respect is worth noticing, because it was short-lived in its art. Mont-Saint-Michel, throughout, even up to the delicate and intricate stonework of its cloisters, is built of granite. The crypts and substructures are as well constructed as the surfaces most exposed to view. When we get to Chartres, which is largely a twelfth-century work, you will see that the cathedral there, too, is superbly built, of the hardest and heaviest stone within reach, which has nowhere settled or given way; while, beneath, you will find a crypt that rivals the church above. The thirteenth century did not build so. The great cathedrals after 1200 show economy, and sometimes worse. The world grew cheap, as worlds must.

You may like it all the better for being less serious, less heroic, less militant, and more what the French call *bourgeois,* just as you may like the style of Louis XV better than that of Louis XIV—Madame du Barry better than Mad-

ame de Montespan—for taste is free, and all styles are good which amuse; but since we are now beginning with the earliest, in order to step down gracefully to the stage, whatever it is, where you prefer to stop, we must try to understand a little of the kind of energy which Norman art expressed, or would have expressed if it had thought in our modes. The only word which describes the Norman style is the French word *naïf.* Littré says that *naïf* comes from *natif,* as *vulgar* comes from *vulgus,* as though native traits must be simple, and commonness must be vulgar. Both these derivative meanings were strange to the eleventh century. Naïveté was simply natural and vulgarity was merely coarse. Norman naïveté was not different in kind from the naïveté of Burgundy or Gascony or Lombardy, but it was slightly different in expression, as you will see when you travel south. Here at Mont-Saint-Michel we have only a mutilated trunk of an eleventh-century church to judge by. We have not even a façade, and shall have to stop at some Norman village—at Thaon or Ouistreham—to find a west front which might suit the Abbey here, but wherever we find it we shall find something a little more serious, more military, and more practical than you will meet in other Romanesque work, farther south. So, too, the central tower or lantern—the most striking feature of Norman churches—has fallen here at Mont-Saint-Michel, and we shall have to replace it from Cérisy-la-Forêt, and Lessay, and Falaise. We shall find much to say about the value of the lantern on a Norman church, and the singular power it expresses. We shall have still more to say of the towers which flank the west front of Norman churches, but these are mostly twelfth-century, and will lead us far beyond Coutances and Bayeux, from *flèche* [10] to *flèche,* till we come to the flèche of all flèches, at Chartres.

We shall have a whole chapter of study, too, over the eleventh-century apse, but here at Mont-Saint-Michel, Abbot Hildebert's choir went the way of his nave and tower. He built out even more boldly to the east than to the west, and although the choir stood for some four hundred years, which is a sufficient life for most architecture, the foundations gave way at last, and it fell in 1421, in the midst of the English wars, and remained a ruin until 1450. Then it was rebuilt, a monument of the last days of the Gothic, so that now, standing at the western door, you can look down the church, and see the two limits of mediaeval architecture married together—the

9. **Beauvais:** Begun in 1247, this cathedral was the most daring achievement of Gothic architecture, the vaults being designed as the highest in Christendom. The nave was never completed.

10. *flèche:* church spire.

earliest Norman and the latest French. Through the Romanesque arches of 1058, you look into the exuberant choir of latest Gothic, finished in 1521. Although the two structures are some five hundred years apart, they live pleasantly together. The Gothic died gracefully in France. The choir is charming—far more charming than the nave, as the beautiful woman is more charming than the elderly man. One need not quarrel about styles of beauty, as long as the man and woman are evidently satisfied and love and admire each other still, with all the solidity of faith to hold them up; but, at least, one cannot help seeing, as one looks from the older to the younger style, that whatever the woman's sixteenth-century charm may be, it is not the man's eleventh-century trait of naïveté;—far from it! The simple, serious, silent dignity and energy of the eleventh century have gone. Something more complicated stands in their place; graceful, self-conscious, rhetorical, and beautiful as perfect rhetoric, with its clearness, light, and line, and the wealth of tracery that verges on the florid.

The crypt of the same period, beneath, is almost finer still, and even in seriousness stands up boldly by the side of the Romanesque; but we have no time to run off into the sixteenth century: we have still to learn the alphabet of art in France. One must live deep into the eleventh century in order to understand the twelfth, and even after passing years in the twelfth, we shall find the thirteenth in many ways a world of its own, with a beauty not always inherited, and sometimes not bequeathed. At the Mount we can go no farther into the eleventh as far as concerns architecture. We shall have to follow the Romanesque to Caen and so up the Seine to the Ile de France, and across to the Loire and the Rhone, far to the South where its home lay. All the other eleventh-century work has been destroyed here or built over, except at one point, on the level of the splendid crypt we just turned from, called the Gros Piliers, beneath the choir.

There, according to M. Corroyer, in a corner between great constructions of the twelfth century and the vast Merveille [11] of the thirteenth, the old refectory of the eleventh was left as a passage from one group of buildings to the other. Below it is the kitchen of Hildebert. Above, on the level of the church, was the dormitory. These eleventh-century abbatial buildings faced north and west, and are close to the present parvis, opposite the

last arch of the nave. The lower levels of Hildebert's plan served as supports or buttresses to the church above, and must therefore be older than the nave; probably older than the triumphal piers of 1058.

Hildebert planned them in 1020, and died after carrying his plans out so far that they could be completed by Abbot Ralph de Beaumont, who was especially selected by Duke William in 1048, 'more for his high birth than for his merits.' Ralph de Beaumont died in 1060, and was succeeded by Abbot Ranulph, an especial favourite of Dutchess Matilda, and held in high esteem by Duke William. The list of names shows how much social importance was attributed to the place. The Abbot's duties included that of entertainment on a great scale. The Mount was one of the most famous shrines of northern Europe. We are free to take for granted that all the great people of Normandy slept at the Mount and, supposing M. Corroyer to be right, that they dined in this room, between 1050, when the building must have been in use, down to 1122 when the new abbatial quarters were built.

How far the monastic rules restricted social habits is a matter for antiquaries to settle if they can, and how far those rules were observed in the case of great secular princes; but the eleventh century was not very strict, and the rule of the Benedictines was always mild, until the Cistercians and Saint Bernard stiffened its discipline toward 1120. Even then the Church showed strong leanings toward secular poetry and popular tastes. The drama belonged to it almost exclusively, and the Mysteries and Miracle plays which were acted under its patronage often contained nothing of religion except the miracle. The greatest poem of the eleventh century was the *Chanson de Roland,* and of that the Church took a sort of possession. At Chartres we shall find Charlemagne and Roland dear to the Virgin, and at about the same time, as far away as at Assisi in the Perugian country, Saint Francis himself— the nearest approach the Western world ever made to an Oriental incarnation of the divine essence— loved the French *romans,* and typified himself in the *Chanson de Roland.* With Mont-Saint-Michel, the *Chanson de Roland* is almost one. The *Chanson* is in poetry what the Mount is in architecture. Without the *Chanson,* one cannot approach the feeling which the eleventh century built into the Archangel's church. Probably there was never a day, certainly never a week, during several centuries, when portions of the *Chanson* were not sung, or recited, at the Mount, and if there was one room where it was most at home,

11. **Merveille:** the famous pile of superimposed buildings presenting an immense façade about 230 feet wide and one hundred feet high. Chapter 3 of the *Chartres* tells its history and significance.

this one, supposing it to be the old refectory, claims to be the place.

[THE FOUR following chapters complete the account of the Abbey, its legendary association with the *Chanson de Roland,* its military and masculine spirit whose religious focus was Saint Michael and God the Father, and define the artistic and spiritual traits of the twelfth century. The "Uncle" guides the "nieces in wish" along the "architectural highway," through space and time, from the Abbey through Normandy, with its expressions of the Norman genius in the chief cathedrals, and quickly reaches the towers and portals of Chartres. "We have set out," he says, "to go from Mont-Saint-Michel to Chartres in three centuries, trying to get, on the way, not technical knowledge. . . . not anything that can possibly be useful or instructive; but only a sense of what those centuries had to say, and a sympathy with their ways of saying it."

Chapter 6 is the key chapter of the nine devoted to Chartres, to its architecture, stained glass, sculpture, and to the poetry, legends, and history associated with them. As Mont-Saint-Michel was the masculine focus, so Chartres is the triumph of the feminine spirit and of love, sacred and profane.]

CHAPTER 6

THE VIRGIN OF CHARTRES

WE MUST take ten minutes to accustom our eyes to the light, and we had better use them to seek the reason why we come to Chartres rather than to Rheims or Amiens or Bourges, for the cathedral that fills our ideal. The truth is, there are several reasons; there generally are, for doing the things we like; and after you have studied Chartres to the ground, and got your reasons settled, you will never find an antiquarian to agree with you; the architects will probably listen to you with contempt; and even these excellent priests, whose kindness is great, whose patience is heavenly, and whose good opinion you would so gladly gain, will turn from you with pain, if not with horror. The Gothic is singular in this; one seems easily at home in the Renaissance; one is not too strange in the Byzantine; as for the Roman, it is ourselves; and we could walk blindfolded through every chink and cranny of the Greek mind; all these styles seem modern, when we come close to them; but the Gothic gets away. No two men think alike about it, and no woman agrees with either man. The Church itself never agreed about it, and the architects agree even less than the priests. To most minds it casts too many shadows; it wraps itself in mystery; and when people talk of mystery, they commonly mean

fear. To others, the Gothic seems hoary with age and decrepitude, and its shadows mean death. What is curious to watch is the fanatical conviction of the Gothic enthusiast, to whom the twelfth century means exuberant youth, the eternal child of Wordsworth, over whom its immortality broods like the day; it is so simple and yet so complicated; it sees so much and so little; it loves so many toys and cares for so few necessities; its youth is so young, its age so old, and its youthful yearning for old thought is so disconcerting, like the mysterious senility of the baby that

> Deaf and silent, reads the eternal deep
> Haunted forever by the eternal mind.[12]

One need not take it more seriously than one takes the baby itself. Our amusement is to play with it, and to catch its meaning in its smile; and whatever Chartres may be now, when young it was a smile. To the Church, no doubt, its cathedral here has a fixed and administrative meaning, which is the same as that of every other bishop's seat and with which we have nothing whatever to do. To us, it is a child's fancy; a toyhouse to please the Queen of Heaven—to please her so much that she would be happy in it—to charm her till she smiled.

The Queen Mother was as majestic as you like; she was absolute; she could be stern; she was not above being angry; but she was still a woman, who loved grace, beauty, ornament—her toilette, robes, jewels;—who considered the arrangements of her palace with attention, and liked both light and colour; who kept a keen eye on her Court, and exacted prompt and willing obedience from king and archbishops as well as from beggars and drunken priests. She protected her friends and punished her enemies. She required space, beyond what was known in the Courts of kings, because she was liable at all times to have ten thousand people begging her for favours— mostly inconsistent with law—and deaf to refusal. She was extremely sensitive to neglect, to disagreeable impressions, to want of intelligence in her surroundings. She was the greatest artist, as she was the greatest philosopher and musician and theologist, that ever lived on earth, except her Son, Who, at Chartres, is still an Infant under her guardianship. Her taste was infallible; her sentence eternally final. This church was built for her in this spirit of simple-minded, practical, utilitarian faith—in this singleness of thought, exactly as a little girl sets up a doll-house for her favourite

12. **Deaf . . . mind:** Wordsworth, "Intimations of Immortality," viii.

blonde doll. Unless you can go back to your dolls, you are out of place here.[13] If you can go back to them, and get rid for one small hour of the weight of custom, you shall see Chartres in glory.

The palaces of earthly queens were hovels compared with these palaces of the Queen of Heaven at Chartres, Paris, Laon, Noyon, Rheims, Amiens, Rouen, Bayeux, Coutances—a list that might be stretched into a volume. The nearest approach we have made to a palace was the Merveille at Mont-Saint-Michel, but no Queen had a palace equal to that. The Merveille was built, or designed, about the year 1200; toward the year 1500, Louis XI built a great castle at Loches in Touraine, and there Queen Anne de Bretagne had apartments which still exist, and which we will visit. At Blois you shall see the residence which served for Catherine de Medicis till her death in 1589. Anne de Bretagne was trebly queen, and Catherine de Medicis took her standard of comfort from the luxury of Florence. At Versailles you can see the apartments which the queens of the Bourbon line occupied through their century of magnificence. All put together, and then trebled in importance, could not rival the splendour of any single cathedral dedicated to Queen Mary in the thirteenth century; and of them all, Chartres was built to be peculiarly and exceptionally her delight.

One has grown so used to this sort of loose comparison, this reckless waste of words, that one no longer adopts an idea unless it is driven in with hammers of statistics and columns of figures. With the irritating demand for literal exactness and perfectly straight lines which lights up every truly American eye, you will certainly ask when this exaltation of Mary began, and unless you get the dates, you will doubt the facts. It is your own fault if they are tiresome; you might easily read them all in the 'Iconographie de la Sainte Vierge,' by M. Rohault de Fleury, published in 1878. You can start at Byzantium with the Empress Helena in 326, or with the Council of Ephesus in 431. You will find the Virgin acting as the patron saint of Constantinople and of the Imperial residence, under as many names as Artemis or Aphrodite had borne. As Godmother (Θεομητηρ), Deipara (Θεοτοκος),[14] Pathfinder ('Οδηγητρια), she was the chief favourite of the Eastern Empire, and her picture was carried at the head of every procession and hung on the wall of every hut and hovel, as it is still wherever the Greek Church goes. In the

year 610, when Heraclius sailed from Carthage to dethrone Phocas at Constantinople, his ships carried the image of the Virgin at their mastheads. In 1143, just before the flèche on the Chartres clocher was begun, the Basileus John Comnenus died, and so devoted was he to the Virgin that, on a triumphal entry into Constantinople, he put the image of the Mother of God in his chariot, while he himself walked. In the Western Church the Virgin had always been highly honoured, but it was not until the crusades that she began to overshadow the Trinity itself. Then her miracles became more frequent and her shrines more frequented, so that Chartres, soon after 1100, was rich enough to build its western portal with Byzantine splendour. A proof of the new outburst can be read in the story of Citeaux. For us, Citeaux means Saint Bernard, who jointed the Order in 1112, and in 1115 founded his Abbey of Clairvaux in the territory of Troyes. In him, the religious emotion of the half-century between the first and second crusades (1095–1145) centred as in no one else. He was a French precursor of Saint Francis of Assisi who lived a century later. If we were to plunge into the story of Citeaux and Saint Bernard we should never escape, for Saint Bernard incarnates what we are trying to understand, and his mind is further from us than the architecture. You would lose hold of everything actual, if you could comprehend in its contradictions the strange mixture of passion and caution, the austerity, the self-abandonment, the vehemence, the restraint, the love, the hate, the miracles, and the scepticism of Saint Bernard. The Cistercian Order, which was founded in 1098, from the first put all its churches under the special protection of the Virgin, and Saint Bernard in his time was regarded as the apple of the Virgin's eye. Tradition as old as the twelfth century, which long afterwards gave to Murillo the subject of a famous painting, told that once, when he was reciting before her statue the 'Ave Maris Stella,'[15] and came to the words, 'Monstra te esse Matrem,' the image, pressing its breast, dropped on the lips of her servant three drops of the milk which had nourished the Saviour. The same miracle, in various forms, was told of many other persons, both saints and sinners; but it made so much impression on the mind of the age that, in the fourteenth century, Dante, seeking in Paradise for some official introduction to the foot of the Throne, found no intercessor with the Queen of Heaven more potent than Saint Bernard. You can still read Bernard's hymns to the

---

13. **Unless . . . here:** Adams was very fond of children and kept a dollhouse behind a panel of his Washington study for the entertainment of his friends' little girls.   14. **Deipara [Latin], Theotokos [Greek]:** God-bearer or Mother of God.

15. **'Ave Maris Stella':** "Hail Star of the Sea," a traditional chant.

Virgin, and even his sermons, if you like. To him she was the great mediator. In the eyes of a culpable humanity, Christ was too sublime, too terrible, too just, but not even the weakest human frailty could fear to approach his Mother. Her attribute was humility; her love and pity were infinite. 'Let him deny your mercy who can say that he has ever asked it in vain.'

Saint Bernard was emotional and to a certain degree mystical, like Adam de Saint-Victor, whose hymns were equally famous, but the emotional saints and mystical poets were not by any means allowed to establish exclusive rights to the Virgin's favour. Abélard was as devoted as they were, and wrote hymns as well. Philosophy claimed her, and Albert the Great, the head of scholasticism, the teacher of Thomas Aquinas, decided in her favour the question: 'Whether the Blessed Virgin possessed perfectly the seven liberal arts.' The Church at Chartres had decided it a hundred years before by putting the seven liberal arts next her throne, with Aristotle himself to witness; but Albertus gave the reason: 'I hold that she did, for it is written, "Wisdom has built herself a house, and has sculptured seven columns." That house is the blessed Virgin; the seven columns are the seven liberal arts. Mary, therefore, had perfect mastery of science.' Naturally she had also perfect mastery of economics, and most of her great churches were built in economic centres. The guilds were, if possible, more devoted to her than the monks; the bourgeoisie of Paris, Rouen, Amiens, Laon, spent money by millions to gain her favour. Most surprising of all, the great military class was perhaps the most vociferous. Of all inappropriate haunts for the gentle, courteous, pitying Mary, a field of battle seems to be the worst, if not distinctly blasphemous; yet the greatest French warriors insisted on her leading them into battle, and in the actual mêlée when men were killing each other, on every battlefield in Europe, for at least five hundred years, Mary was present, leading both sides. The battle-cry of the famous Constable du Guesclin was 'Notre-Dame-Guesclin'; 'Notre-Dame-Coucy' was the cry of the great Sires de Coucy; 'Notre-Dame-Auxerre'; 'Notre-Dame-Sancerre'; 'Notre-Dame-Hainault'; 'Notre-Dame-Gueldres'; 'Notre-Dame-Bourbon'; 'Notre-Dame-Bearn';—all well-known battle-cries. The King's own battle at one time cried, 'Notre-Dame-Saint-Denis-Montjoie'; the Dukes of Burgundy cried, 'Notre-Dame-Bourgogne'; and even the soldiers of the Pope were said to cry, 'Notre-Dame-Saint-Pierre.'

The measure of this devotion, which proves to any religious American mind, beyond possible cavil, its serious and practical reality, is the money it cost. According to statistics, in the single century between 1170 and 1270, the French built eighty cathedrals and nearly five hundred churches of the cathedral class, which would have cost, according to an estimate made in 1840, more than five thousand millions to replace. Five thousand million francs is a thousand million dollars, and this covered only the great churches of a single century. The same scale of expenditure had been going on since the year 1000, and almost every parish in France had rebuilt its church in stone; to this day France is strewn with the ruins of this architecture, and yet the still preserved churches of the eleventh and twelfth centuries, among churches that belong to the Romanesque and Transition period, are numbered by hundreds until they reach well into the thousands. The share of this capital which was—if one may use a commercial figure—invested in the Virgin cannot be fixed, any more than the total sum given to religious objects between 1000 and 1300; but in a spiritual and artistic sense, it was almost the whole, and expressed an intensity of conviction never again reached by any passion, whether of religion, of loyalty, of patriotism, or of wealth; perhaps never even paralleled by any single economic effort except in war. Nearly every great church of the twelfth and thirteenth centuries belonged to Mary, until in France one asks for the church of Notre Dame as though it meant cathedral; but, not satisfied with this, she contracted the habit of requiring in all churches a chapel of her own, called in English the 'Lady Chapel,' which was apt to be as large as the church but was always meant to be handsomer; and there, behind the high altar, in her own private apartment, Mary sat, receiving her innumerable suppliants, and ready at any moment to step up upon the high altar itself to support the tottering authority of the local saint.

Expenditure like this rests invariably on an economic idea. Just as the French of the nineteenth century invested their surplus capital in a railway system in the belief that they would make money by it in this life, in the thirteenth they trusted their money to the Queen of Heaven because of their belief in her power to repay it with interest in the life to come. The investment was based on the power of Mary as Queen rather than on any orthodox Church conception of the Virgin's legitimate station. Papal Rome never greatly loved Byzantine empresses or French queens. The Virgin of Chartres was never wholly sympathetic to the Roman Curia. To this day the Church writers—like the Abbé Bulteau or M. Rohault de Fleury—are singularly shy of the true Virgin of majesty, whether at Chartres or at Byzantium or wherever she is seen. The fathers Martin and Cahier at Bourges alone felt her true value. Had the Church controlled her, the Virgin would perhaps have remained prostrate at the foot of the Cross. Dragged by a Byzantine Court, backed by popular insistence and impelled by overpowering self-interest, the Church accepted the Virgin throned and crowned, seated by Christ, the Judge throned and crowned; but even this did not wholly satisfy the French of the thirteenth century who seemed bent on absorbing Christ in His Mother, and making the Mother the Church, and Christ the Symbol.

The Church had crowned and enthroned her almost from the beginning, and could not have dethroned her if it would. In all Christian art—sculpture or mosaic, painting or poetry—the Virgin's rank was expressly asserted. Saint Bernard, like John Comnenus, and probably at the same time (1120–40), chanted hymns to the Virgin as Queen:

O salutaris Virgo Stella Maris
Generans prolem, Aequitatis solem,
Lucis auctorem, Retinens pudorem,
    Suscipe laudem!

Celi Regina Per quam medicina
Datur aegrotis, Gratia devotis,
Gaudium moestis, Mundo lux coelestis,
    Spesque salutis;

Aula regalis, Virgo specialis,
Posce medelam Nobis et tutelam,
Suscipe vota, Precibusque cuncta
    Pelle molesta!

O saviour Virgin, Star of Sea,
Who bore for child the Son of Justice,
The source of Light, Virgin always
    Hear our praise!

Queen of Heaven who have given
Medicine to the sick, Grace to the devout,
Joy to the sad, Heaven's light to the world
    And hope of salvation;

Court royal, Virgin typical,
Grant us cure and guard,
Accept our vows, and by prayers
    Drive all griefs away!

As the lyrical poet of the twelfth century, Adam de Saint-Victor seems to have held rank higher if possible than that of Saint Bernard, and his hymns on the Virgin are certainly quite as emphatic an assertion of her majesty:

Imperatix supernorum!
Superatrix infernorum!
Eligenda via coeli,
Retinenda spe fideli,
Separatos a te longe
Revocatos ad te junge
    Tuorum collegio!

Empress of the highest,
Mistress over the lowest,
Chosen path of Heaven,
Held fast by faithful hope,
Those separated from you far,
Recalled to you, unite
    In your fold!

To delight in the childish jingle of the mediaeval Latin is a sign of a futile mind, no doubt, and I beg pardon of you and of the Church for wasting your precious summer day on poetry which was regarded as mystical in its age and which now sounds like a nursery rhyme; but a verse or two of Adam's hymn on the Assumption of the Virgin completes the record of her rank, and goes to complete also the documentary proof of her majesty at Chartres:

Salve, Mater Salvatoris!
Vas electum! Vas honoris!
    Vas coelestis Gratiae!
Ab aeterno Vas provisum!
Vas insigne! Vas excisum
    Manu sapientiae!

Salve, Mater pietatis,
Et totius Trinitatis
    Nobile Triclinium!
Verbi tamen incarnati
Speciale majestati
    Praeparans hospitium!

Mother of our Saviour, hail!
Chosen vessel! Sacred Grail!
    Font of celestial grace!
From eternity forethought!
By the hand of Wisdom wrought!
    Precious, faultless Vase!

Hail, Mother of Divinity!
Hail, Temple of the Trinity!
    Home of the Triune God!
In whom the Incarnate Word had birth,
The King! to whom you gave on earth
    Imperial abode.

O Maria! Stella maris!
Dignitate singularis,
Super omnes ordinaris
    Ordines coelestium!
In supermo sita poli
Nos commenda tuae proli,
Ne terrores sive doli
    Nos supplantent hostium!

Oh, Maria! Constellation!
Inspiration! Elevation!
Rule and Law and Ordination
    Of the angels' host!
Highest height of God's Creation,
Pray your Son's commiseration,
Lest, by fear or fraud, salvation
    For our souls be lost!

Constantly—one might better say at once, officially, she was addressed in these terms of supreme majesty: 'Imperatrix supernorum!' 'Coeli Regina!' 'Aula regalis!' [16] but the twelfth century seemed determined to carry the idea out to its logical conclusion in defiance of dogma. Not only was the Son absorbed in the Mother, or represented as under her guardianship, but the Father fared no better, and the Holy Ghost followed. The poets regarded the Virgin as the 'Templum Trinitatis'; 'totius Trinitatis nobile Triclinium.' [17] She was the refectory of the Trinity—the 'Triclinium' —because the refectory was the largest room and contained the whole of the members, and was divided in three parts by two rows of columns. She was the 'Templum Trinitatis,' the Church itself, with its triple aisle. The Trinity was absorbed in her.

This is a delicate subject in the Church, and you must feel it with delicacy, without brutally insisting on its necessary contradictions. All theology and all philosophy are full of contradictions quite as flagrant and far less sympathetic. This particular variety of religious faith is simply human, and has made its appearance in one form or another in nearly all religions; but though the twelfth century carried it to an extreme, and at Chartres you see it in its most charming expression, we have got always to make allowances for what was going on beneath the surface in men's minds, consciously or unconsciously, and for the latent scepticism which lurks behind all faith. The Church itself never quite accepted the full claims of what was called Mariolatry. One may be sure, too, that the bourgeois capitalist and the student of the schools, each from his own point of view, watched the Virgin with anxious interest. The bourgeois had put an enormous share of his capital into what was in fact an economical speculation, not unlike the South Sea Scheme, or the railway system of our own time; except that in one case the energy was devoted to shortening the road to Heaven; in the other, to shortening the road to Paris; but no serious schoolman could have felt entirely convinced that God would enter into a business partnership with man, to establish a sort of joint-stock society for altering the operation of divine and universal laws. The bourgeois cared little for the philosophical doubt if the economical result proved to be good, but he watched this result with his usual practical sagacity, and required an experience of only about three generations (1200–1300) to satisfy himself that relics were not certain in their effects; that the Saints were not always able or willing to help; that Mary herself could not certainly be bought or bribed; that prayer without money seemed to be quite as efficacious as prayer with money; and that neither the road to Heaven nor Heaven itself had been made surer or brought nearer by an investment of capital which amounted to the best part of the wealth of France. Economically speaking, he became satisfied that his enormous money-investment had proved to be an almost total loss, and the reaction on his mind was as violent as the emotion. For three hundred years it prostrated France. The efforts of the bourgeoisie and the peasantry to recover their property, so far as it was recoverable, have lasted to the present day and we had best take care not to get mixed in those passions.

If you are to get the full enjoyment of Chartres, you must, for the time, believe in Mary as Bernard and Adam did, and feel her presence as the architects did, in every stone they placed, and every touch they chiselled. You must try first to rid your mind of the traditional idea that the Gothic is an intentional expression of religious gloom. The necessity for light was the motive of the Gothic architects. They needed light and always more light, until they sacrificed safety and common sense in trying to get it. They converted their walls into windows, raised their vaults, diminished their piers, until their churches could no longer stand. You will see the limits at Beauvais; at Chartres we have not got so far, but even here, in places where the Virgin wanted it—as above the high altar—the architect has taken all the light there was to take. For the same reason, fenestration became the most important part of the Gothic architect's work, and at Chartres was uncommonly interesting because the architect was obliged to design a new system, which should at the same time satisfy the laws of construction and the taste

16. **Imperatrix . . . regalis:** "Empress of the highest," "Queen of Heaven," "Regal Power."   17. **Templum . . . Triclinium:** "Temple of the Trinity," "Noble refectory of the whole Trinity."

and imagination of Mary. No doubt the first command of the Queen of Heaven was for light, but the second, at least equally imperative, was for colour. Any earthly queen, even though she were not Byzantine in taste, loved colour; and the truest of queens—the only true Queen of Queens—had richer and finer taste in colour than the queens of fifty earthly kingdoms, as you will see when we come to the immense effort to gratify her in the glass of her windows. Illusion for illusion—granting for the moment that Mary was an illusion—the Virgin Mother in this instance repaid to her worshippers a larger return for their money than the capitalist has ever been able to get, at least in this world, from any other illusion of wealth which he has tried to make a source of pleasure and profit.

The next point on which Mary evidently insisted was the arrangement for her private apartments, the apse, as distinguished from her throne-room, the choir; both being quite distinct from the hall, or reception-room of the public, which was the nave with its enlargement in the transepts. This arrangement marks the distinction between churches built as shrines for the deity and churches built as halls of worship for the public. The difference is chiefly in the apse, and the apse of Chartres is the most interesting of all apses from this point of view.

The Virgin required chiefly these three things, or, if you like, these four: space, light, convenience; and colour decoration to unite and harmonize the whole. This concerns the interior; on the exterior she required statuary, and the only complete system of decorative sculpture that existed seems to belong to her churches: Paris, Rheims, Amiens, and Chartres. Mary required all this magnificence at Chartres for herself alone, not for the public. As far as one can see into the spirit of the builders, Chartres was exclusively intended for the Virgin, as the Temple of Abydos was intended for Osiris. The wants of man, beyond a mere roof-cover, and perhaps space to some degree, enter to no very great extent into the problem of Chartres. Man came to render homage or to ask favours. The Queen received him in her palace, where she alone was at home, and alone gave commands.

The artist's second thought was to exclude from his work everything that could displease Mary; and since Mary differed from living queens only in infinitely greater majesty and refinement, the artist could admit only what pleased the actual taste of the great ladies who dictated taste at the Courts of France and England, which surrounded the little Court of the Counts of Chartres. What they were —these women of the twelfth and thirteenth centuries—we shall have to see or seek in other directions; but Chartres is perhaps the most magnificent and permanent monument they left of their taste, and we can begin here with learning certain things which they were not.

In the first place, they were not in the least vague, dreamy, or mystical in a modern sense;— far from it! They seemed anxious only to throw the mysteries into a blaze of light; not so much physical, perhaps—since they, like all women, liked moderate shadow for their toilettes—but luminous in the sense of faith. There is nothing about Chartres that you would think mystical, who know your Lohengrin, Siegfried, and Parsifal. If you care to make a study of the whole literature of the subject, read M. Mâle's 'Art Religieux du XIII° Siècle en France,' and use it for a guide-book. Here you need only note how symbolic and how simple the sculpture is, on the portals and porches. Even what seems a grotesque or an abstract idea is no more than the simplest child's personification. On the walls you may have noticed the *Ane qui vielle*—the ass playing the lyre; and on all the old churches you can see 'bestiaries,' as they were called, of fabulous animals, symbolic or not; but the symbolism is as simple as the realism of the oxen at Laon. It gave play to the artist in his effort for variety of decoration, and it amused the people—probably the Virgin also was not above being amused;—now and then it seems about to suggest what you would call an esoteric meaning, that is to say, a meaning which each one of us can consider private property reserved for our own amusement, and from which the public is excluded; yet, in truth, in the Virgin's churches the public is never excluded, but invited. The Virgin even had the additional charm to the public that she was popularly supposed to have no very marked fancy for priests as such; she was a queen, a woman, and a mother, functions, all, which priests could not perform. Accordingly, she seems to have had little taste for mysteries of any sort, and even the symbols that seem most mysterious were clear to every old peasant-woman in her church. The most pleasing and promising of them all is the woman's figure you saw on the front of the cathedral in Paris; her eyes bandaged; her head bent down; her crown falling; without cloak or royal robe; holding in her hand a guidon or banner with its staff broken in more than one place. On the opposite pier stands another woman, with royal mantle, erect and commanding. The symbol is so graceful that one is quite eager to know its meaning; but every child in the Middle Ages would have instantly told you that the woman with the falling crown meant only the

Jewish Synagogue, as the one with the royal robe meant the Church of Christ.

Another matter for which the female taste seemed not much to care was theology in the metaphysical sense. Mary troubled herself little about theology except when she retired into the south transept with Pierre de Dreux.[18] Even there one finds little said about the Trinity, always the most metaphysical subtlety of the Church. Indeed, you might find much amusement here in searching the cathedral for any distinct expression at all of the Trinity as a dogma recognized by Mary. One cannot take seriously the idea that the three doors, the three portals, and the three aisles express the Trinity, because, in the first place, there was no rule about it; churches might have what portals and aisles they pleased; both Paris and Bourges have five; the doors themselves are not allotted to the three members of the Trinity, nor are the portals; while another more serious objection is that the side doors and aisles are not of equal importance with the central, but mere adjuncts and dependencies, so that the architect who had misled the ignorant public into accepting so black a heresy would have deserved the stake, and would probably have gone to it. Even this suggestion of trinity is wanting in the transepts, which have only one aisle, and in the choir, which has five, as well as five or seven chapels, and, as far as an ignorant mind can penetrate, no triplets whatever. Occasionally, no doubt, you will discover in some sculpture or window, a symbol of the Trinity, but this discovery itself amounts to an admission of its absence as a controlling idea, for the ordinary worshipper must have been at least as blind as we are, and to him, as to us, it would have seemed a wholly subordinate detail. Even if the Trinity, too, is anywhere expressed, you will hardly find here an attempt to explain its metaphysical meaning—not even a mystic triangle.

The church is wholly given up to the Mother and the Son. The Father seldom appears; the Holy Ghost still more rarely. At least, this is the impression made on an ordinary visitor who has no motive to be orthodox; and it must have been the same with the thirteenth-century worshipper who came here with his mind absorbed in the perfections of Mary. Chartres represents, not the Trinity, but the identity of the Mother and Son. The Son represents the Trinity, which is thus absorbed in the Mother. The idea is not orthodox, but this is no affair of ours. The Church watches over its own.

The Virgin's wants and tastes, positive and negative, ought now to be clear enough to enable you to feel the artist's sincerity in trying to satisfy them; but first you have still to convince yourselves of the people's sincerity in employing the artists. This point is the easiest of all, for the evidence is express. In the year 1145 when the old flèche was begun—the year before Saint Bernard preached the second crusade at Vézelay—Abbot Haimon, of Saint-Pierre-sur-Dives in Normandy, wrote to the monks of Tutbury Abbey in England a famous letter to tell of the great work which the Virgin was doing in France and which began at the Church of Chartres. 'Hujus sacrae institutionis ritus apud Carnotensem ecclesiam est inchoatus.' [19] From Chartres it had spread through Normandy, where it produced among other things the beautiful spire which we saw at Saint-Pierre-sur-Dives. 'Postremo per totam fere Normanniam longe lateque convaluit ac loca per singula Matri misericordiae dicata praecipue occupavit.' [20] The movement affected especially the places devoted to Mary, but ran through all Normandy, far and wide. Of all Mary's miracles, the best attested, next to the preservation of her church, is the building of it; not so much because it surprises us as because it surprised even more the people of the time and the men who were its instruments. Such deep popular movements are always surprising, and at Chartres the miracle seems to have occurred three times, coinciding more or less with the dates of the crusades, and taking the organization of a crusade, as Archbishop Hugo of Rouen described it in a letter to Bishop Thierry of Amiens. The most interesting part of this letter is the evident astonishment of the writer, who might be talking to us today, so modern is he:

The inhabitants of Chartres have combined to aid in the construction of their church by transporting the materials; our Lord has rewarded their humble zeal by miracles which have roused the Normans to imitate the piety of their neighbours. . . . Since then the faithful of our diocese and of other neighbouring regions have formed associations for the same object; they admit no one into their company unless he has been to confession, has renounced enmities and revenges, and has reconciled himself with his enemies. That done, they elect a chief, under whose direction they conduct their waggons in silence and with humility.

The quarries at Berchhères-l'Evêque are about

---

18. **Pierre de Dreux:** Duke of Brittany, nicknamed Mauclerc, a bad cleric, leader of Saint Louis' ill-fated crusade. He built the south porch of Chartres, presumably as a memorial of his marriage to Alix in 1212.

19. '**Hujus . . . inchoatus**': The observance of this holy rite as begun at Chartres cathedral. 20. '**Postremo . . . occupavit**': This is freely translated by Adams in the following sentence of the text.

five miles from Chartres. The stone is excessively hard, and was cut in blocks of considerable size, as you can see for yourselves; blocks which required great effort to transport and lay in place. The work was done with feverish rapidity, as it still shows, but it is the solidest building of the age, and without a sign of weakness yet. The Abbot told, with more surprise than pride, of the spirit which was built into the cathedral with the stone:

Who has ever seen!—Who has ever heard tell, in times past, that powerful princes of the world, that men brought up in honour and in wealth, that nobles, men and women, have bent their proud and haughty necks to the harness of carts, and that, like beasts of burden, they have dragged to the abode of Christ these waggons, loaded with wines, grains, oil, stone, wood, and all that is necessary for the wants of life, or for the construction of the church? But while they draw these burdens, there is one thing admirable to observe; it is that often when a thousand persons and more are attached to the chariots—so great is the difficulty— yet they march in such silence that not a murmur is heard, and truly if one did not see the thing with one's eyes, one might believe that among such a multitude there was hardly a person present. When they halt on the road, nothing is heard but the confession of sins, and pure and suppliant prayer to God to obtain pardon. At the voice of the priests who exhort their hearts to peace, and uttering to Him, from the depth of the heart, thrown far aside, debts are remitted, the unity of hearts is established.

But if any one is so far advanced in evil as to be unwilling to pardon an offender, or if he rejects the counsel of the priest who has piously advised him, his offering is instantly thrown from the waggon as impure, and he himself ignominiously and shamefully excluded from the society of the holy. There one sees the priests who preside over each chariot exhort every one to penitence, to confession of faults, to the resolution of better life! There one sees old people, young people, little children, calling on the Lord with a suppliant voice, and uttering to Him, from the depth of the heart, sobs and sighs with words of glory and praise! After the people, warned by the sound of trumpets and the sight of banners, have resumed their road, the march is made with such ease that no obstacle can retard it. . . . When they have reached the church they arrange the waggons about it like a spiritual camp, and during the whole night they celebrate the watch by hymns and canticles. On each waggon they light tapers and lamps; they place there the infirm and sick, and bring them the precious relics of the Saints for their relief. Afterwards the priests and clerics close the ceremony by processions which the people follow with devout heart, imploring the clemency of the Lord and of his Blessed Mother for the recovery of the sick.

Of course, the Virgin was actually and constantly present during all this labour, and gave her assistance to it, but you would get no light on the architecture from listening to an account of her miracles, nor do they heighten the effect of popular faith. Without the conviction of her personal presence, men would not have been inspired; but, to us, it is rather the inspiration of the art which proves the Virgin's presence, and we can better see the conviction of it in the work than in the words. Every day, as the work went on, the Virgin was present, directing the architects, and it is in this direction that we are going to study, if you have now got a realizing sense of what it meant. Without this sense, the church is dead. Most persons of a deeply religious nature would tell you emphatically that nine churches out of ten actually were dead-born, after the thirteenth century, and that church architecture became a pure matter of mechanism and mathematics; but that is a question for you to decide when you come to it; and the pleasure consists not in seeing the death, but in feeling the life.

Now let us look about!

from CHAPTER 7

ROSES AND APSES

LIKE ALL great churches, that are not mere storehouses of theology, Chartres expressed, besides whatever else it meant, an emotion, the deepest man ever felt—the struggle of his own littleness to grasp the infinite. You may, if you like, figure in it a mathematic formula of infinity—the broken arch, our finite idea of space; the spire, pointing, with its converging lines, to unity beyond space; the sleepless, restless thrust of the vaults, telling the unsatisfied, incomplete, overstrained effort of man to rival the energy, intelligence, and purpose of God. Thomas Aquinas and the schoolmen tried to put it in words, but their Church is another chapter. In act, all man's work ends there;— mathematics, physics, chemistry, dynamics, optics, every sort of machinery science may invent— to this favour come at last, as religion and philosophy did before science was born. All that the centuries can do is to express the idea differently: a miracle or a dynamo; a dome or a coalpit; a cathedral or a world's fair; and sometimes to confuse the two expressions together. The world's fair tends more and more vigorously to express the thought of infinite energy; the great cathedrals of the Middle Ages always reflected the industries and interests of a world's fair. . . .

. . . If you want to know what churches were made for, come down here on some great festival of the Virgin, and give yourself up to it; but come alone! That kind of knowledge cannot be taught and can seldom be shared. We are not now seeking religion; indeed, true religion generally comes unsought. We are trying only to feel Gothic art. For us, the world is not a schoolroom or a pulpit, but a stage, and the stage is the highest yet seen on earth. In this church the old Romanesque leaps into the Gothic under our eyes; of a sudden, between the portal and the shrine, the infinite rises into a new expression, always a rare and excellent miracle in thought. The two expressions are nowhere far apart; not further than the Mother from the Son. The new artist drops unwillingly the hand of his father or his grandfather; he looks back, from every corner of his own work, to see whether it goes with the old. He will not part with the western portal or the lancet windows; he holds close to the round columns of the choir; he would have kept the round arch if he could, but the round arch was unable to do the work; it could not rise; so he broke it, lifted the vaulting, threw out flying buttresses, and satisfied the Virgin's wish.

The matter of Gothic vaulting, with its two weak points, the flying buttress and the false, wooden shelter-roof, is the bête noire of the Beaux Arts. The duty of defence does not lie on tourists, who are at best hardly able to understand what it matters whether a wall is buttressed without or within, and whether a roof is single or double. No one objects to the dome of Saint Peter's. No one finds fault with the Pont Neuf. Yet it is true that the Gothic architect showed contempt for facts. Since he could not support a heavy stone vault on his light columns, he built the lightest possible stone vault and protected it with a wooden shelter-roof which constantly burned. The lightened vaults were still too heavy for the walls and columns, so the architect threw out buttress beyond buttress resting on separate foundations, exposed to extreme inequalities of weather, and liable to multiplied chances of accident. The results were certainly disastrous. The roofs burned; the walls yielded.

Flying buttresses were not a necessity. The Merveille had none; the Angevin school rather affected to do without them; Albi had none; Assisi stands up independent; but they did give support wherever the architect wanted it and nowhere else; they were probably cheap; and they were graceful. Whatever expression they gave to a church, at least it was not that of a fortress. Amiens and Albi are different religions. The expression concerns us; the construction concerns the Beaux Arts. The problem of permanent equilibrium which distresses the builder of arches is a technical matter which does not worry, but only

amuses, us who sit in the audience and look with delight at the theatrical stage-decoration of the Gothic vault; the astonishing feat of building up a skeleton of stone ribs and vertebrae, on which every pound of weight is adjusted, divided, and carried down from level to level till it touches ground at a distance as a bird would alight. If any stone in any part, from apex to foundation, weathers or gives way, the whole must yield, and the charge for repairs is probably great, but, on the best building the École des Beaux Arts can build, the charge for repairs is not to be wholly ignored, and at least the Cathedral of Chartres, in spite of terribly hard usage, is as solid today as when it was built, and as plumb, without crack or crevice. Even the towering fragment at Beauvais, poorly built from the first, which has broken down oftener than most Gothic structures, and seems ready to crumble again whenever the wind blows over its windy plains, has managed to survive, after a fashion, six or seven hundred years, which is all that our generation had a right to ask. . . .

from CHAPTER 11
THE THREE QUEENS

AFTER worshipping at the shrines of Saint Michael on his Mount and of the Virgin at Chartres, one may wander far and wide over France, and seldom feel lost; all later Gothic art comes naturally, and no new thought disturbs the perfected form. Yet tourists of English blood and American training are seldom or never quite at home there. Commonly they feel it only as a stage-decoration. The twelfth and thirteenth centuries, studied in the pure light of political economy, are insane. The scientific mind is atrophied, and suffers under inherited cerebral weakness, when it comes in contact with the eternal woman—Astarte, Isis, Demeter, Aphrodite, and the last and greatest deity of all, the Virgin. Very rarely one lingers, with a mild sympathy, such as suits the patient student of human error, willing to be interested in what he cannot understand. Still more rarely, owing to some revival of archaic instincts, he rediscovers the woman. This is perhaps the mark of the artist alone, and his solitary privilege. The rest of us cannot feel; we can only study. The proper study of mankind is woman and, by common agreement since the time of Adam, it is the most complex and arduous. The study of Our Lady, as shown by the art of Chartres, leads directly back to Eve, and lays bare the whole subject of sex.

If it were worth while to argue a paradox, one might maintain that Nature regards the female as the essential, the male as the superfluity of her world. Perhaps the best starting-point for study of the Virgin would be a practical acquaintance with bees, and especially with queen bees. Precisely where the French man may come in, on the genealogical tree of parthenogenesis, one hesitates to say; but certain it is that the French woman, from very early times, has shown qualities peculiar to herself, and that the French woman of the Middle Ages was a masculine character. . . .

. . . The superiority of the woman was not a fancy, but a fact. Man's business was to fight or hunt or feast or make love. The man was also the travelling partner in commerce, commonly absent from home for months together, while the woman carried on the business. The woman ruled the household and the workshop; cared for the economy; supplied the intelligence, and dictated the taste. Her ascendancy was secured by her alliance with the Church, into which she sent her most intelligent children; and a priest or clerk, for the most part, counted socially as a woman. Both physically and mentally the woman was robust, as the men often complained, and she did not greatly resent being treated as a man. Sometimes the husband beat her, dragged her about by the hair, locked her up in the house; but he was quite conscious that she always got even with him in the end. As a matter of fact, probably she got more than even. On this point, history, legend, poetry, romance, and especially the popular fabliaux—invented to amuse the gross tastes of the coarser class—are all agreed, and one could give scores of volumes illustrating it. The greatest men illustrate it best, as one might show almost at hazard. The greatest men of the eleventh, twelfth, and thirteenth centuries were William the Norman; his great-grandson Henry II Plantagenet; Saint Louis of France; and, if a fourth be needed, Richard Coeur-de-Lion. Notoriously all these men had as much difficulty as Louis XIV himself with the women of their family. . . .

. . . For a hundred and fifty years, the Virgin and Queens ruled French taste and thought so successfully that the French man has never yet quite decided whether to be more proud or ashamed of it. Life has ever since seemed a little flat to him, and art a little cheap. . . .

[IN CHAPTER 14 Adams dramatizes the central theological problem of medieval thought, the true nature of the Trinity, a problem bound up with the very nature of reality itself. This is the first of the triad of chapters which make explicit the great parable of these "Travels: France," the original subtitle of the book. They stand apart from the rest of the structure and complete it like one of Adams's favorite Norman towers. He remarked to his friend William James that these theological and philosophical chapters were his "anchor in history," and that they and the concluding three chapters of his *Education* were really one didactic work in disguise. In any case these chapters on Abélard, the Mystics, and Saint Thomas Aquinas present the Church Intellectual of the Middle Ages as the harmonious complement of the Church Architectural. And as the Virgin's authority as the greatest of the mother goddesses could not stand against the disintegrating forces of the bourgeois world, so Aquinas's daring solution of the mysteries of the Trinity succumbed to the pragmatism of science.

It should be noted that Adams is commonly careful to precede or follow each Latin quotation with a translation or a paraphrase.]

CHAPTER 14

ABÉLARD

Super cuncta, subter cuncta,
Extra cuncta, intra cuncta,
Intra cuncta nec inclusus,
Extra cuncta nec exclusus,
Super cuncta nec elatus,
Subter cuncta nec substratus,
Super totus, praesidendo,
Subter totus, sustinendo,
Extra totus, complectendo,
Intra totus est, implendo.[21]

ACCORDING to Hildebert, Bishop of Le Mans and Archbishop of Tours, these verses describe God. Hildebert was the first poet of his time; no small merit, since he was contemporary with the *Chanson de Roland* and the first crusade; he was also a strong man, since he was able, as Bishop of Le Mans, to gain great credit by maintaining himself against William the Norman and Fulk of Anjou; and finally he was a prelate of high authority. He lived between 1055 and 1133. Supposing his verses to have been written in middle life, toward the year 1100, they may be taken to represent the accepted doctrine of the Church at the time of the first crusade. They were little more than a versified form of the Latin of Saint Gregory the Great who wrote five hundred years before: 'Ipse manet intra omnia, ipse extra omnia, ipse supra omnia, ipse infra omnia; et superior est per potentiam et inferior per sustentationem; exterior per magnitudinem et interior per subtilitatem; sursum regens, deorsum continens, extra circumdans, interius penetrans; nec alia parte superior, alia inferior, aut alia ex parte exterior atque ex alia manet interior, sed unus idemque totus ubique.' According to Saint Gregory, in the sixth century, God was 'one and the same and wholly every-

21. Super . . . implendo: The poem is translated in the latter part of the opening paragraph—"God is over all things . . ."

where'; 'immanent within everything, without everything, above everything, below everything, *sursum regens, deorsum continens';* while according to Archbishop Hildebert in the eleventh century: 'God is over all things, under all things; outside all, inside all; within but not enclosed; without but not excluded; above but not raised up; below but not depressed; wholly above, presiding; wholly beneath, sustaining; wholly without, embracing; wholly within, filling.' Finally, according to Benedict Spinoza, another five hundred years later still: 'God is a being, absolutely infinite; that is to say, a substance made up of an infinity of attributes, each one of which expresses an eternal and infinite essence.'

Spinoza was the great pantheist, whose name is still a terror to the orthodox, and whose philosophy is—very properly—a horror to the Church; and yet Spinoza never wrote a line that, to the unguided student, sounds more Spinozist than the words of Saint Gregory and Archbishop Hildebert. If God is everywhere; wholly; presiding, sustaining, embracing and filling, 'sursum regens, deorsum continens,' He is the only possible energy, and leaves no place for human will to act. A force which is 'one and the same and wholly everywhere' is more Spinozist than Spinoza, and is likely to be mistaken for frank pantheism by the large majority of religious minds who must try to understand it without a theological course in a Jesuit college. In the year 1100 Jesuit colleges did not exist, and even the great Dominican and Franciscan schools were far from sight in the future; but the School of Notre Dame at Paris existed, and taught the existence of God much as Archbishop Hildebert described it. The most successful lecturer was William of Champeaux, and to any one who ever heard of William at all, the name instantly calls up the figure of Abélard, in flesh and blood, as he sang to Héloïse the songs which he says resounded through Europe. The twelfth century, with all its sparkle, would be dull without Abélard and Héloïse.

With infinite regret, Héloïse must be left out of the story, because she was not a philosopher or a poet or an artist, but only a Frenchwoman to the last millimetre of her shadow. Even though one may suspect that her famous letters to Abélard are, for the most part, by no means above scepticism, she was, by French standards, worth at least a dozen Abélards, if only because she called Saint Bernard a false apostle. Unfortunately, French standards, by which she must be judged in our ignorance, take for granted that she philosophized only for the sake of Abélard, while Abélard taught philosophy to her not so much because he believed in philosophy or in her as because he believed in himself. To this day, Abélard remains a problem as perplexing as he must have been to Héloïse, and almost as fascinating. As the west portal of Chartres is the door through which one must of necessity enter the Gothic architecture of the thirteenth century, so Abélard is the portal of approach to the Gothic thought and philosophy within. Neither art nor thought has a modern equivalent; only Héloïse, like Isolde, unites the ages.

The first crusade seems, in perspective, to have filled the whole field of vision in France at the time; but, in fact, France seethed with other emotions, and while the crusaders set out to scale heaven by force at Jerusalem, the monks, who remained at home, undertook to scale heaven by prayer and by absorption of body and soul in God; the Cistercian Order was founded in 1098, and was joined in 1112 by young Bernard, born in 1090 at Fontaines-lès-Dijon, drawing with him or after him so many thousands of young men into the self-immolation of the monastery as carried dismay into the hearts of half the women of France. At the same time—that is, about 1098 or 1100—Abélard came up to Paris from Brittany, with as much faith in logic as Bernard had in prayer or Godfrey of Bouillon in arms, and led an equal or even a greater number of combatants to the conquest of heaven by force of pure reason. None showed doubt. Hundreds of thousands of young men wandered from their provinces, mostly to Palestine, largely to cloisters, but also in great numbers to Paris and the schools, while few ever returned.

Abélard had the advantage of being well-born; not so highly descended as Albertus Magnus and Thomas Aquinas who were to complete his work in the thirteenth century, but, like Bernard, a gentleman born and bred. He was the eldest son of Bérenger, Sieur du Pallet, a château in Brittany, south of the Loire, on the edge of Poitou. His name was Pierre du Pallet, although, for some unknown reason, he called himself Pierre Abailard, or Abeillard, or Esbaillart, or Beylard; for the spelling was never fixed. He was born in 1079, and when, in 1096, the young men of his rank were rushing off to the first crusade, Pierre, a boy of seventeen, threw himself with equal zeal into the study of science and, giving up his inheritance or birthright, at last came to Paris to seize a position in the schools. The year is supposed to have been 1100.

The Paris of Abélard's time was astonishingly old; so old that hardly a stone of it can be now pointed out. Even the oldest of the buildings still standing in that quarter—Saint-Julien-le-Pauvre,

Saint-Séverin, and the tower of the Lycée Henri IV —are more modern; only the old Roman Thermae, now part of the Musée de Cluny, within the walls, and the Abbey Tower of Saint-Germain-des-Prés, outside, in the fields, were standing in the year 1100. Politically, Paris was a small provincial town before the reign of Louis-le-Gros (1108–37), who cleared its gates of its nearest enemies; but as a school, Paris was even then easily first. Students crowded into it by thousands, till the town is said to have contained more students than citizens. Modern Paris seems to have begun as a university town before it had a university. Students flocked to it from great distances, encouraged and supported by charity, and stimulated by privileges, until they took entire possession of what is still called the Latin Quarter from the barbarous Latin they chattered; and a town more riotous, drunken, and vicious than it became, in the course of time, hardly existed even in the Middle Ages. In 1100, when enthusiasm was fresh and faith in science was strong, the great mass of students came there to study, and, having no regular university organization or buildings, they thronged the cloister of Notre Dame—not our Notre Dame, which dates only from 1163, but the old Romanesque cathedral which stood on the same spot—and there they listened, and retained what they could remember, for they were not encouraged to take notes even if they were rich enough to buy notebooks, while manuscripts were far beyond their means. One valuable right the students seem to have had—that of asking questions and even of disputing with the lecturer provided they followed the correct form of dialectics. The lecturer himself was licenced by the Bishop.

Five thousand students are supposed to have swarmed about the cloister of Notre Dame, across the Petit Pont, and up the hill of Sainte-Geneviève; three thousand are said to have paid fees to Abélard in the days of his great vogue and they seem to have attached themselves to their favourite master as a champion to be upheld against the world. Jealousies ran high, and neither scholars nor masters shunned dispute. Indeed, the only science they taught or knew was the art of dispute —dialectics. Rhetoric, grammar, and dialectics were the regular branches of science, and bold students, who were not afraid of dabbling in forbidden fields, extended their studies to mathematics— 'exercitium nefarium,' [22] according to Abélard, which he professed to know nothing about but which he studied nevertheless. Abélard, whether pupil or master, never held his tongue if he could

22. 'exercitium nefarium': impious exercise.

help it, for his fortune depended on using it well; but he never used it so well in dialectics or theology as he did, toward the end of his life, in writing a bit of autobiography, so admirably told, so vivid, so vibrating with the curious intensity of his generation, that it needed only to have been written in 'Romieu' to be the chief monument of early French prose, as the western portal of Chartres is the chief monument of early French sculpture, and of about the same date. Unfortunately Abélard was a noble scholar, who necessarily wrote and talked Latin, even with Héloïse, and, although the Latin was mediaeval, it is not much the better on that account, because, in spite of its quaintness, the naïvetés of a young language—the egotism, jealousies, suspicions, boastings, and lamentations of a childlike time—take a false air of outworn Rome and Byzantium, although, underneath, the spirit lives:

I arrived at last in Paris where for a long time dialectics had specially flourished under William of Champeaux, rightly reckoned the first of my masters in that branch of study. I stayed some time in his school, but though well received at first, I soon got to be an annoyance to him because I persisted in refuting certain ideas of his, and because, not being afraid to enter into argument against him, I sometimes got the better. This boldness, too, roused the wrath of those fellow-students who were classed higher, because I was the youngest and the last comer. This was the beginning of my series of misfortunes which still last; my renown every day increasing, envy was kindled against me in every direction.

This picture of the boy of twenty, harassing the professor, day after day, in his own lecture-room before hundreds of older students, paints Abélard to the life; but one may safely add a few touches that heighten the effect; as that William of Champeaux himself was barely thirty, and that Abélard throughout his career, made use of every social and personal advantage to gain a point, with little scruple either in manner or in sophistry. One may easily imagine the scene. Teachers are always much the same. Pupils and students differ only in degrees of docility. In 1100, both classes began by accepting the foundations of society, as they have to do still; only they then accepted laws of the Church and Aristotle, while now they accept laws of the legislature and of energy. In 1100, the students took for granted that, with the help of Aristotle and syllogisms, they could build out the Church intellectually, as the architects, with the help of the pointed arch, were soon to enlarge it architecturally. They never doubted the certainty of their method. To them words had fixed values, like numbers, and syllogisms were hewn stones that needed only to be set in place, in order to reach any height or support any weight. Every sentence was made to take the form of a syllogism. One must have been educated in a Jesuit or Dominican school in order to frame these syllogisms correctly, but merely by way of illustration one may timidly suggest how the phrases sounded in their simplest form. For example, Plato or other equally good authority defined substance as that which stands underneath phenomena; the most universal of universals, the ultimate, the highest in order of generalization. The ultimate essence or substance is indivisible; God is substance; God is indivisible. The divine substance is incapable of alteration or accident; all other substance is liable to alteration or accident; therefore, the divine substance differs from all other substance. A substance is a universal; as for example, Humanity, or the Human, is a universal and indivisible; the Man Socrates, for instance, is not a universal, but an individual; therefore, the substance Humanity, being indivisible, must exist entire and undivided in Socrates.

The form of logic most fascinating to youthful minds, as well as to some minds that are only too acute, is the *reductio ad absurdum;* the forcing an opponent into an absurd alternative or admission; and the syllogism lent itself happily to this use. Socrates abused the weapon and Abélard was the first French master of the art; but neither State nor Church likes to be reduced to an absurdity, and, on the whole, both Socrates and Abélard fared ill in the result. Even now, one had best be civil toward the idols of the forum. Abélard would find most of his old problems sensitive to his touch today. Time has settled few or none of the essential points of dispute. Science hesitates, more visibly than the Church ever did, to decide once for all whether unity or diversity is ultimate law; whether order or chaos is the governing rule of the universe, if universe there is; whether anything, except phenomena, exists. Even in matters more vital to society, one dares not speak too loud. Why, and for what, and to whom, is man a responsible agent? Every jury and judge, every lawyer and doctor, every legislator and clergyman has his own views, and the law constantly varies. Every nation may have a different system. One court may hang and another may acquit for the same crime, on the same day; and science only repeats what the Church said to Abélard, that where we know so little, we had better hold our tongues.

According to the latest authorities, the doctrine of universals which convulsed the schools of the twelfth century has never received an adequate

answer. What is a species? what is a genus or a family or an order? More or less convenient terms of classification, about which the twelfth century cared very little, while it cared deeply about the essence of classes! Science has become too complex to affirm the existence of universal truths, but it strives for nothing else, and disputes the problem, within its own limits, almost as earnestly as in the twelfth century, when the whole field of human and superhuman activity was shut between these barriers of substance, universals, and particulars. Little has changed except the vocabulary and the method. The schools knew that their society hung for life on the demonstration that God, the ultimate universal, was a reality, out of which all other universal truths or realities sprang. Truth was a real thing, outside of human experience. The schools of Paris talked and thought of nothing else. John of Salisbury, who attended Abélard's lectures about 1136, and became Bishop of Chartres in 1176, seems to have been more surprised than we need be at the intensity of the emotion. 'One never gets away from this question,' he said. 'From whatever point a discussion starts, it is always led back and attached to that. It is the madness of Rufus about Naevia; "He thinks of nothing else; talks of nothing else, and if Naevia did not exist, Rufus would be dumb." '

Abélard began it. After his first visit to Paris in 1100, he seems to have passed several years elsewhere, while Guillaume de Champeaux in 1108, retired from the school in the cloister of Notre Dame, and, taking orders, established a class in a chapel near by, afterwards famous as the Abbaye-de-Saint-Victor. The Jardin des Plantes and the Gare d'Orléans now cover the ground where the Abbey stood, on the banks of the Seine outside the Latin Quarter, and not a trace is left of its site; but there William continued his course in dialectics, until suddenly Abélard reappeared among his scholars, and resumed his old attacks. This time Abélard could hardly call himself a student. He was thirty years old, and long since had been himself a teacher; he had attended William's course on dialectics nearly ten years before, and was past master in the art; he had nothing to learn from William in theology, for neither William nor he was yet a theologist by profession. If Abélard went back to school, it was certainly not to learn; but indeed, he himself made little or no pretence of it, and told with childlike candour not only why he went, but also how brilliantly he succeeded in his object:

I returned to study rhetoric in his school. Among other controversial battles, I succeeded, by the most irrefutable argument, in making him change, or rather ruin his doctrine of universals. His doctrine consisted in affirming the perfect identity of the essence in every individual of the same species, so that according to him there was no difference in the essence but only in the infinite variety of accidents. He then came to amend his doctrine so as to affirm, not the identity any longer, but the absence of distinction—the want of difference—in the essence. And as this question of universals had always been one of the most important questions of dialectics—so important that Porphyry, touching on it in his Preliminaries, did not dare to take the responsibility of cutting the knot, but said, 'It is a very grave point,'—Champeaux, who was obliged to modify his idea and then renounce it, saw his course fall into such discredit that they hardly let him make his dialectical lectures, as though dialectics consisted entirely in the question of universals.

Why was this point so 'very grave'? Not because it was mere dialectics! The only part of the story that seems grave today is the part that Abélard left out; the part which Saint Bernard, thirty years later, put in, on behalf of William. We should be more credulous than twelfth-century monks, if we believed, on Abélard's word in 1135, that in 1110 he had driven out of the schools the most accomplished dialectician of the age by an objection so familiar that no other dialectician was ever silenced by it—whatever may have been the case with theologians—and so obvious that it could not have troubled a scholar of fifteen. William stated a settled doctrine as old as Plato; Abélard interposed an objection as old as Aristotle. Probably Plato and Aristotle had received the question and answer from philosophers ten thousand years older than themselves. Certainly the whole of philosophy has always been involved in the dispute.

The subject is as amusing as a comedy; so amusing that ten minutes may be well given to playing the scene between William and Abélard, not as it happened, but in a form nearer our ignorance, with liberty to invent arguments for William, and analogies—which are figures intended to serve as fatal weapons if they succeed, and as innocent toys if they fail—such as he never imagined; while Abélard can respond with his true rejoinder, fatal in a different sense. For the chief analogy, the notes of music would serve, or the colours of the solar spectrum, or an energy, such as gravity;—but the best is geometrical, because Euclid was as scholastic as William of Champeaux himself, and his axioms are even more familiar to the schoolboy of the twentieth, than to the schoolman of the twelfth century.

In these scholastic tournaments the two champions started from opposite points:—one, from the ultimate substance, God—the universal, the ideal, the type;—the other from the individual, Socrates, the concrete, the observed fact of experience, the object of sensual perception. The first champion—William in this instance—assumed that the universal was a real thing; and for that reason he was called a realist. His opponent—Abélard—held that the universal was only nominally real; and on that account he was called a nominalist. Truth, virtue, humanity, exist as units and realities, said William. Truth, replied Abélard, is only the sum of all possible facts that are true, as humanity is the sum of all actual human beings. The ideal bed is a form, made by God, said Plato. The ideal bed is a name, imagined by ourselves, said Aristotle. 'I start from the universe,' said William. 'I start from the atom,' said Abélard; and, once having started, they necessarily came into collision at some point between the two.

William of Champeaux, lecturing on dialectics or logic, comes to the question of universals, which he says, are substances. Starting from the highest substance, God, all being descends through created substances by stages, until it reaches the substance animality, from which it descends to the substance humanity: and humanity being, like other essences or substances, indivisible, passes wholly into each individual, becoming Socrates, Plato, and Aristotle, much as the divine substance exists wholly and undivided in each member of the Trinity.

Here Abélard interrupts. The divine substance, he says, operates by laws of its own, and cannot be used for comparison. In treating of human substance, one is bound by human limitations. If the whole of humanity is in Socrates, it is wholly absorbed by Socrates, and cannot be at the same time in Plato, or elsewhere. Following his favourite *reductio ad absurdum,* Abélard turns the idea round, and infers from it that, since Socrates carries all humanity in him, he carries Plato, too; and both must be in the same place, though Socrates is at Athens and Plato in Rome.

The objection is familiar to William, who replies by another commonplace:

'Mr. Abélard, might I, without offence, ask you a simple matter? Can you give me Euclid's definition of a point?'

'If I remember right it is, "illud cujus nulla pars est"; that which has no parts.'

'Has it existence?'

'Only in our minds.'

'Not, then, in God?'

'All necessary truths exist first in God. If the point is a necessary truth, it exists first there.'

'Then might I ask you for Euclid's definition of the line?'

'The line is that which has only extension; "Linea vocatur illa quae solam longitudinem habet." '

'Can you conceive an infinite straight line?'

'Only as a line which has no end, like the point extended.'

'Supposing we imagine a straight line, like opposite rays of the sun, proceeding in opposite directions to infinity—is it real?'

'It has no reality except in the mind that conceives it.'

'Supposing we divide that line which has no reality into two parts at its origin in the sun or star, shall we get two infinities?—or shall we say, two halves of the infinite?'

'We conceive of each as partaking the quality of infinity.'

'Now, let us cut out the diameter of the sun; or rather—since this is what our successors in the school will do—let us take a line of our earth's longitude which is equally unreal, and measure a degree of this thing which does not exist, and then divide it into equal parts which we will use as a measure or metre. This metre, which is still nothing, as I understand you, is infinitely divisible into points? and the point itself is infinitely small? Therefore we have the finite partaking the nature of the infinite?'

'Undoubtedly!'

'One step more, Mr. Abélard, if I do not weary you! Let me take three of these metres which do not exist, and place them so that the ends of one shall touch the ends of the others. May I ask what is that figure?'

'I presume you mean it to be a triangle.'

'Precisely! and what sort of a triangle?'

'An equilateral triangle, the sides of which measure one metre each.'

'Now let me take three more of these metres which do not exist, and construct another triangle which does not exist;—are these two triangles or one triangle?'

'They are most certainly one—a single concept of the only possible equilateral triangle measuring one metre on each face.'

'You told us a moment ago that a universal could not exist wholly and exclusively in two individuals at once. Does not the universal by definition—*the* equilateral triangle measuring one metre on each face—does it not exist wholly, in its integrity of essence, in each of the two triangles we have conceived?'

'It does—as a conception.'

'I thank you! Now, although I fear wearying you, perhaps you will consent to let me add matter to mind. I have here on my desk an object not uncommon in nature, which I will ask you to describe.'

'It appears to be a crystal.'

'May I ask its shape?'

'I should call it a regular octahedron.'

'That is, two pyramids, set base to base? making eight plane surfaces, each a perfect equilateral triangle?'

'Concedo triangula (I grant the triangles).'

'Do you know, perchance, what is this material which seems to give substantial existence to these eight triangles?'

'I do not.'

'Nor I! nor does it matter, unless you conceive it to be the work of man?'

'I do not claim it as man's work.'

'Whose, then?'

'We believe all actual creation of matter, united in form, to be the work of God.'

'Surely not the substance of God himself? Perhaps you mean that this form—this octahedron—is a divine concept.'

'I understand such to be the doctrine of the Church.'

'Then it seems that God uses this concept habitually to create this very common crystal. One question more, and only one, if you will permit me to come to the point. Does the matter—the material—of which this crystal is made affect in any way the form—the nature, the soul—of the universal equilateral triangle as you see it bounding these eight plane surfaces?'

'That I do not know, and do not think essential to decide. As far as these triangles are individual, they are made so by the will of God, and not by the substance you call triangle. The universal—the abstract right angle, or any other abstract form—is only an idea, a concept, to which reality, individuality, or what we might call energy is wanting. The only true energy, except man's free will, is God.'

'Very good, Mr. Abélard! we can now reach our issue. You affirm that, just as the line does not exist in space, although the eye sees little else in space, so the triangle does not exist in this crystal, although the crystal shows eight of them, each perfect. You are aware that on this line which does not exist, and its combination in this triangle which does not exist, rests the whole fabric of mathematics with all its necessary truths. In other words, you know that in this line, though it does not exist, is bound up the truth of the only branch of human knowledge which claims absolute certainty for human processes. You admit that this line and triangle, which are mere figments of our human imagination, not only exist independent of us in the crystal, but are, as we suppose, habitually and invariably used by God Himself to give form to the matter contained within the planes of the crystal. Yet to this line and triangle you deny reality. To mathematical truth, you deny compulsive force. You hold that an equilateral triangle may, to you and all other human individuals, be a right-angled triangle if you choose to imagine it so. Allow me to say, without assuming any claim to superior knowledge, that to me your logic results in a different conclusion. If you are compelled, at one point or another of the chain of being, to deny existence to a substance, surely it should be to the last and feeblest. I see nothing to hinder you from denying your own existence, which is, in fact, impossible to demonstrate. Certainly you are free, in logic, to argue that Socrates and Plato are mere names—that men and matter are phantoms and dreams. No one ever has proved or ever can prove the contrary. Infallibly, a great philosophical school will some day be founded on that assumption. I venture even to recommend it to your acute and sceptical mind; but I cannot conceive how, by any process of reasoning, sensual or supersensual, you can reach the conclusion that the single form of truth which instantly and inexorably compels our submission to its laws—is nothing.'

Thus far, all was familiar ground; certainly at least as familiar as the Pons Asinorum; [23] and neither of the two champions had need to feel ruffled in temper by the discussion. The real struggle began only at this point; for until this point was reached, both positions were about equally tenable. Abélard had hitherto rested quietly on the defensive, but William's last thrust obliged him to strike in his turn, and he drew himself up for what, five hundred years later, was called the 'Coup de Jarnac': [24]

'I do not deny,' he begins; 'on the contrary, I affirm that the universal, whether we call it humanity, or equilateral triangle, has a sort of reality as a concept; that it is something; even a substance, if you insist upon it. Undoubtedly the sum of all individual men results in the concept of humanity. What I deny is that the concept results in the individual. You have correctly stated the essence of the point and the line as sources of our concept of the infinite; what I deny is that they are divisions of the infinite. Universals cannot be di-

vided; what is capable of division cannot be a universal. I admit the force of your analogy in the case of the crystal; but I am obliged to point out to you that, if you insist on this analogy, you will bring yourself and me into flagrant contradiction with the fixed foundations of the Church. If the energy of the triangle gives form to the crystal, and the energy of the line gives reality to the triangle, and the energy of the infinite gives substance to the line, all energy at last becomes identical with the ultimate substance, God Himself. Socrates becomes God in small; Judas is identical with both; humanity is of the divine essence, and exists, wholly and undivided, in each of us. The equilateral triangle we call humanity exists, therefore, entire, identical, in you and me, as a subdivision of the infinite line, space, energy, or substance, which is God. I need not remind you that this is pantheism, and that if God is the only energy, human free will merges in God's free will; the Church ceases to have a reason for existence; man cannot be held responsible for his own acts, either to the Church or to the State; and finally, though very unwillingly, I must, in regard for my own safety, bring the subject to the attention of the Archbishop, which, as you know better than I, will lead to your seclusion, or worse.'

Whether Abélard used these precise words is nothing to the point. The words he left on record were equivalent to these. As translated by M. de Rémusat from a manuscript entitled: 'Glossulae magistri Petri Baelardi super Porphyrium,' the phrase runs: 'A grave heresy is at the end of this doctrine; for, according to it, the divine substance which is recognized as admitting of no form, is necessarily identical with every substance in particular and with all substance in general.' Even had he not stated the heresy so bluntly, his objection necessarily pushed William in face of it. Realism, when pressed, always led to pantheism. William of Champeaux and Bishop or Archbishop Hildebert were personal friends, and Hildebert's divine substance left no more room for human free will than Abélard saw in the geometric analogy imagined for William. Throughout the history of the Church for fifteen hundred years, whenever this theological point has been pressed against churchmen it has reduced them to evasion or to apology. Admittedly, the weak point of realism was its fatally pantheistic term.

Of course, William consulted his friends in the Church, probably Archbishop Hildebert among the rest, before deciding whether to maintain or to abandon his ground, and the result showed that he was guided by their advice. Realism was the Roman arch—the only possible foundation for any

23. Pons Asinorum: bridge of asses, the familiar epithet for Euclid's geometrical proposition that if a triangle has two of its sides equal, the angles opposite these sides are also equal. The epithet stems from the difficulty that beginners have with this proposition.   **24. 'Coup de Jarnac':** so named from the Elizabethan inventor of an adroit and crippling rapier thrust that could not be parried.

Church; because it assumed unity, and any other scheme was compelled to prove it, for a starting-point. Let us see, for a moment, what became of the dialogue, when pushed into theology, in order to reach some of the reasons which reduced William to tacit abandonment of a doctrine he could never have surrendered unless under compulsion. That he was angry is sure, for Abélard, by thus thrusting theology into dialectics, had struck him a foul blow; and William knew Abélard well:

'Ah!' he would have rejoined; 'you are quick, M. du Pallet, to turn what I offered as an analogy, into an argument of heresy against my person. You are at liberty to take that course if you choose, though I give you fair warning that it will lead you far. But now I must ask you still another question. This concept that you talk about—this image in the mind of man, of God, of matter; for I know not where to seek it—whether is it a reality or not?'

'I hold it as, in a manner, real.'

'I want a categorical answer: Yes or No!'

'Distinguo! (I must qualify.)'

'I will have no qualifications. A substance either is, or not. Choose!'

To this challenge Abélard had the choice of answering Yes, or of answering No, or of refusing to answer at all. He seems to have done the last; but we suppose him to have accepted the wager of battle, and to answer:

'Yes, then!'

'Good!' William rejoins; 'now let us see how your pantheism differs from mine. My triangle exists as a reality, or what science will call an energy, outside my mind, in God, and is impressed on my mind as it is on a mirror, like the triangle on the crystal, its energy giving form. Your triangle you say is also an energy, but an essence of my mind itself; you thrust it into the mind as an integral part of the mirror; identically the same concept, energy, or necessary truth which is inherent in God. Whatever subterfuge you may resort to, sooner or later you have got to agree that your mind is identical with God's nature as far as that concept is concerned. Your pantheism goes further than mine. As a doctrine of the Real Presence peculiar to yourself, I can commend it to the Archbishop together with your delation of me.'

Supposing that Abélard took the opposite course, and answered:

'No! my concept is a mere sign.'

'A sign of what, in God's name!'

'A sound! a word! a symbol! an echo only of my ignorance.'

'Nothing, then! So truth and virtue and charity do not exist at all. You suppose yourself to exist, but you have no means of knowing God; therefore, to you God does not exist except as an echo of your ignorance; and, what concerns you most, the Church does not exist except as your concept of certain individuals, whom you cannot regard as a unity, and who suppose themselves to believe in a Trinity which exists only as a sound, or a symbol. I will not repeat your words, M. du Pallet, outside this cloister, because the consequences to you would certainly be fatal; but it is only too clear that you are a materialist, and as such your fate must be decided by a Church Council, unless you prefer the stake by judgment of a secular court.'

In truth, pure nominalism—if, indeed, any one ever maintained it—afforded no cover whatever. Nor did Abélard's concept help the matter, although for want of a better refuge, the Church was often driven into it. Conceptualism was a device, like the false wooden roof, to cover and conceal an inherent weakness of construction. Unity either is, or is not. If soldiers, no matter in what number, can never make an army, and worshippers, though in millions, do not make a Church, and all humanity united would not necessarily constitute a State, equally little can their concepts, individual or united, constitute the one or the other. Army, Church, and State, each is an organic whole, complex beyond all possible addition of units, and not a concept at all, but rather an animal that thinks, creates, devours, and destroys. The attempt to bridge the chasm between multiplicity and unity is the oldest problem of philosophy, religion, and science, but the flimsiest bridge of all is the human concept, unless somewhere, within or beyond it, an energy not individual is hidden; and in that case the old question instantly reappears: What is that energy?

Abélard would have done well to leave William alone, but Abélard was an adventurer, and William was a churchman. To win a victory over a churchman is not very difficult for an adventurer, and is always a tempting amusement, because the ambition of churchmen to shine in worldly contests is disciplined and checked by the broader interests of the Church: but the victory is usually sterile, and rarely harms the churchman. The Church cares for its own. Probably the bishops advised William not to insist on his doctrine, although every bishop may have held the same view. William allowed himself to be silenced without a judgment, and in that respect stands almost if not quite alone among schoolmen. The students divined that he had sold himself to the Church, and consequently deserted him. Very soon he received his reward in the shape of the highest dignity open to private ambition—a bishopric. As Bishop of Chalons-sur-Marne he made for himself a great reputation, which does not concern us, although it deeply concerned the unfortunate Abélard, for it happened, either by chance or design, that within a year or two after William established himself at Chalons, young Bernard of Citeaux chose a neighbouring diocese in which to establish a branch of the Cistercian Order, and Bishop William took so keen an interest in the success of Bernard as almost to claim equal credit for it. Clairvaux was, in a manner, William's creation, although not in his diocese, and yet, if there was a priest in all France who fervently despised the schools, it was young Bernard. William of Champeaux, the chief of schoolmen, could never have gained Bernard's affections. Bishop William of Chalons must have drifted far from dialectics into mysticism in order to win the support of Clairvaux, and train up a new army of allies who were to mark Abélard for an easy prey.

Meanwhile Abélard pursued his course of triumph in the schools, and in due time turned from dialectics to theology, as every ambitious teacher could hardly fail to do. His affair with Héloïse and their marriage seem to have occupied his time in 1117 or 1118, for they both retired into religious orders in 1119, and he resumed his lectures in 1120. With his passion for rule, he was fatally certain to attempt ruling the Church as he ruled the schools; and, as it was always enough for him that any point should be tender in order that he should press upon it, he instantly and instinctively seized on the most sensitive nerve of the Church system to wrench it into his service. He became a sort of apostle of the Holy Ghost.

That the Trinity is a mystery was a law of theology so absolute as in a degree to hide the law of philosophy that the Trinity was meant as a solution of a greater mystery still. In truth, as a matter of philosophy, the Trinity was intended to explain the eternal and primary problem of the process by which unity could produce diversity. Starting from unity alone, philosophers found themselves unable to stir hand or foot until they could account for duality. To the common, ignorant peasant, no such trouble occurred, for he knew the Trinity in its simpler form as the first condition of life, like time and space and force. No human being was so stupid as not to understand that the father, mother, and child made a trinity, returning into each other, and although every father, every mother, and every child, from the dawn of man's intelligence, had asked why, and had never received an answer more intelligible to them than to philosophers, they never showed

difficulty in accepting that trinity as a fact. They might even, in their beneficent blindness, ask the Church why that trinity, which had satisfied the Egyptians for five or ten thousand years, was not good enough for churchmen. They themselves were doing their utmost, though unconsciously, to identify the Holy Ghost with the Mother, while philosophy insisted on excluding the human symbol precisely because it was human and led back to an infinite series. Philosophy required three units to start from; it posed the equilateral triangle, not the straight line, as the foundation of its *deometry*.[25] The first straight line, infinite in extension, must be assumed, but its reflection engendered the second, but whence came the third? Under protest, philosophy was compelled to accept the symbol of Father and Son as a matter of faith, but, if the relation of Father and Son were accepted for the two units which reflected each other, what relation expressed the Holy Ghost? In philosophy, the product of two units was not a third unit, but diversity, multiplicity, infinity. The subject was, for that reason, better handled by the Arabs, whose reasoning worked back on the Christian theologists and made the point more delicate still. Common people, like women and children and ourselves, could never understand the Trinity; naturally, intelligent people understood it still less, but for them it did not matter; they did not need to understand it provided their neighbours would leave it alone.

The mass of mankind wanted something nearer to them than either the Father or the Son; they wanted the Mother, and the Church tried, in what seems to women and children and ourselves rather a feeble way, to give the Holy Ghost, as far as possible, the Mother's attributes—Love, Charity, Grace; but in spite of conscientious effort and unswerving faith, the Holy Ghost remained to the mass of Frenchmen somewhat apart, feared rather than loved. The sin against the Holy Ghost was a haunting spectre, for no one knew what else it was.

Naturally the Church, and especially its official theologians, took an instinctive attitude of defense whenever a question on this subject was asked, and were thrown into a flutter of irritation whenever an answer was suggested. No man likes to have his intelligence or good faith questioned, especially if he has doubts about it himself. The distinguishing essence of the Holy Ghost, as a theological substance, was its mystery. That this mystery should be touched at all was annoying to every one who knew the dangers that lurked

25. *deometry:* the mathematics of the properties of God.

behind the veil, but that it should be freely handled before audiences of laymen by persons of doubtful character was impossible. Such licence must end in discrediting the whole Trinity under pretence of making it intelligible.

Precisely this licence was what Abélard took, and on it he chose to insist. He said nothing heretical; he treated the Holy Ghost with almost exaggerated respect, as though other churchmen did not quite appreciate its merits; but he would not let it alone, and the Church dreaded every moment lest, with his enormous influence in the schools, he should raise a new storm by his notorious indiscretion. Yet so long as he merely lectured, he was not molested; only when he began to publish his theology did the Church interfere. Then a council held at Soissons in 1121 abruptly condemned his book in block, without reading it, without specifying its errors, and without hearing his defence; obliged him to throw the manuscript into the fire with his own hands, and finally shut him up in a monastery.

He had invited the jurisdiction by taking orders, but even the Church was shocked by the summary nature of the judgment, which seems to have been quite irregular. In fact, the Church has never known what it was that the council condemned. The latest great work on the Trinity, by the Jesuit Father de Régnon, suggests that Abélard's fault was in applying to the Trinity his theory of concepts. 'Yes!' he says; 'the mystery is explained; the key of conceptualism has opened the tabernacle, and Saint Bernard was right in saying that, thanks to Abélard, every one can penetrate it and contemplate it at his ease; "even the graceless, even the uncircumcised." Yes! the Trinity is explained, but after the manner of the Sabellians.[26] For to identify the Persons in the terms of human concepts is, in the same stroke, to destroy their "subsistances propres." '

Although the Saviour seems to have felt no compunctions about identifying the persons of the Trinity in the terms of human concepts, it is clear that tourists and heretics had best leave the Church to deal with its 'subsistances propres,' and with its own members, in its own way. In sum, the Church preferred to stand firm on the Roman arch, and the architects seem now inclined to think it was right; that scholastic science and the pointed arch proved to be failures. In the twelfth century the world may have been rough, but it was not stupid. The Council of Soissons was held

26. **Sabellians:** followers of the third century theologian excommunicated for his unorthodox views on the Trinity. Sabellius taught that God was indivisible, appearing successively as each member of the Trinity.

while the architects and sculptors were building the west porch of Chartres and the Aquilon at Mont-Saint-Michel. Averroës was born at Cordova in 1126; Omar Khayyám died at Nishapur in 1123. Poetry and metaphysics owned the world, and their quarrel with theology was a private, family dispute. Very soon the tide turned decisively in Abélard's favour. Suger, a political prelate, became minister of the King, and in March, 1122, Abbot of Saint-Denis. In both capacities he took the part of Abélard, released him from restraint, and even restored to him liberty of instruction, at least beyond the jurisdiction of the Bishop of Paris. Abélard then took a line of conduct singularly parallel with that of Bernard. Quitting civilized life he turned wholly to religion. 'When the agreement,' he said, 'had been executed by both parties to it, in presence of the King and his ministers, I next retired within the territory of Troyes, upon a desert spot which I knew, and on a piece of ground given me by certain persons, I built, with the consent of the bishop of the diocese, a sort of oratory of reeds and thatch, which I placed under the invocation of the Holy Trinity. . . . Founded at first in the name of the Holy Trinity, then placed under its invocation, it was called "Paraclete" in memory of my having come there as a fugitive and in my despair having found some repose in the consolations of divine grace. This denomination was received by many with great astonishment, and some attacked it with violence under pretext that it was not permitted to consecrate a church specially to the Holy Ghost any more than to God the Father, but that, according to ancient usage, it must be dedicated either to the Son alone or to the Trinity.'

The spot is still called Paraclete, near Nogent-sur-Seine, in the Parish of Quincey about halfway between Fontainebleau and Troyes. The name Paraclete as applied to the Holy Ghost meant the Consoler, the Comforter, the Spirit of Love and Grace; as applied to the oratory of Abélard it meant a renewal of his challenge to theologists, a separation of the Persons in the Trinity, a vulgarization of the mystery; and, as his story frankly says, it was so received by many. The spot was not so remote but that his scholars could follow him, and he invited them to do so. They came in great numbers, and he lectured to them. 'In body I was hidden in this spot; but my renown overran the whole world and filled it with my word.' Undoubtedly Abélard taught theology, and, in defiance of the council that had condemned him, attempted to define the persons of the Trinity. For this purpose he had fallen on a spot only fifty or sixty miles from Clairvaux where Bernard was inspiring a contrary spirit of religion; he placed himself on the direct line between Clairvaux and its source at Citeaux near Dijon; indeed, if he had sought for a spot as central as possible to the active movement of the Church and the time, he could have hit on none more convenient and conspicuous unless it were the city of Troyes itself, the capital of Champagne, some thirty miles away. The proof that he meant to be aggressive is furnished by his own account of the consequences. Two rivals, he says, one of whom seems to have been Bernard of Clairvaux, took the field against him, 'and succeeded in exciting the hostility of certain ecclesiastical and secular authorities, by charging monstrous things, not only against my faith, but also against my manner of life, to such a point as to detach from me some of my principal friends; even those who preserved some affection for me dared no longer display it, for fear. God is my witness that I never heard of the union of an ecclesiastical assembly without thinking that its object was my condemnation.' The Church had good reason, for Abélard's conduct defied discipline; but far from showing harshness, the Church this time showed a true spirit of conciliation most creditable to Bernard. Deeply as the Cistercians disliked and distrusted Abélard, they did not violently suppress him, but tacitly consented to let the authorities buy his silence with Church patronage.

The transaction passed through Suger's hands, and offered an ordinary example of political customs as old as history. An abbey in Brittany became vacant; at a hint from the Duke Conan, which may well be supposed to have been suggested from Paris, the monks chose Abélard as their new abbot, and sent some of their number to Suger to request permission for Abélard, who was a monk of Saint-Denis, to become Abbot of Saint-Gildas-de-Rhuys, near Vannes, in Brittany. Suger probably intimated to Abélard, with a certain degree of authority, that he had better accept. Abélard, 'struck with terror, and as it were under the menace of a thunderbolt,' accepted. Of course the dignity was in effect banishment and worse, and was so understood on all sides. The Abbaye-de-Saint-Gildas-de-Rhuys, though less isolated than Mont-Saint-Michel, was not an agreeable winter residence. Though situated in Abélard's native province of Brittany, only sixty or eighty miles from his birthplace, it was for him a prison with the ocean around it and a singularly wild people to deal with; but he could have endured his lot with contentment, had not discipline or fear or pledge compelled him to hold his tongue. From 1125, when he was sent to Brittany until 1135

when he reappeared in Paris, he never opened his mouth to lecture. 'Never, as God is my witness—never would I have acquiesced in such an offer, had it not been to escape, no matter how, from the vexations with which I was incessantly overwhelmed.'

A greater career in the Church was thus opened for him against his will, and if he did not die an archbishop it was not wholly the fault of the Church. Already he was a great prelate, the equal in rank of the Abbé Suger, himself, of Saint-Denis; of Peter the Venerable of Cluny; of Bernard of Clairvaux. He was in a manner a peer of the realm. Almost immediately he felt the advantages of the change. Barely two years passed when, in 1127, the Abbé Suger, in reforming his subordinate Abbey of Argenteuil, was obliged to disturb Héloïse, then a sister in that congregation. Abélard was warned of the necessity that his wife should be protected, and with the assistance of every one concerned, he was allowed to establish his wife at the Paraclete as head of a religious sisterhood. 'I returned there; I invited Héloïse to come there with the nuns of her community; and when they arrived, I made them the entire donation of the oratory and its dependencies. . . . The bishops cherished her as their daughter; the abbots as their sister; the laymen as their mother.' This was merely the beginning of her favour and of his. For ten years they were both of them petted children of the Church.

The formal establishment of Héloïse at the Paraclete took place in 1129. In February, 1130, on the death of the Pope at Rome, a schism broke out, and the cardinals elected two popes, one of whom took the name of Innocent II, and appealed for support to France. Suger saw a great political opportunity and used it. The heads of the French Church agreed in supporting Innocent, and the King summoned a Church council at Étampes to declare its adhesion. The council met in the late summer; Bernard of Clairvaux took the lead; Peter the Venerable, Suger of Saint-Denis, and the Abbot of Saint-Gildas-de-Rhuys supported him; Innocent himself took refuge at Cluny in October, and on January 20, 1131, he stopped at the Benedictine Abbey of Morigny. The Chronicle of the monastery, recording the abbots present on this occasion—the Abbot of Morigny itself, of Feversham; of Saint-Lucien of Beauvais, and so forth—added especially: 'Bernard of Clairvaux, who was then the most famous pulpit orator in France; and Peter Abélard, Abbot of Saint-Gildas, also a monk and the most eminent master of the schools to which the scholars of almost all the Latin races flowed.'

Innocent needed popular support; Bernard and Abélard were the two leaders of popular opinion in France. To attach them, Innocent could refuse nothing. Probably Abélard remained with Innocent, but in any case Innocent gave him, at Auxerre, in the following November, a diploma, granting to Héloïse, prioress of the Oratory of the Holy Trinity, all rights of property over whatever she might possess, against all assailants; which proves Abélard's favour. At this time he seems to have taken great interest in the new sisterhood. 'I made them more frequent visits,' he said, 'in order to work for their benefit.' He worked so earnestly for their benefit that he scandalized the neighbourhood and had to argue at unnecessary length his innocence of evil. He went so far as to express a wish to take refuge among them and to abandon his abbey in Brittany. He professed to stand in terror of his monks; he excommunicated them; they paid no attention to him; he appealed to the Pope, his friend, and Innocent sent a special legate to enforce their submission 'in presence of the Count and the Bishops.'

Even since that, they would not keep quiet. And quite recently, since the expulsion of those of whom I have spoken, when I returned to the abbey, abandoning myself to the rest of the brothers who inspired me with less distrust, I found them even worse than the others. It was no longer a question of poison; it was the dagger that they now sharpened against my breast. I had great difficulty in escaping from them under the guidance of one of the neighbouring lords. Similar perils menace me still and every day I see the sword raised over my head. Even at table I can hardly breathe. . . . This is the torture that I endure every moment of the day; I, a poor monk, raised to the prelacy, becoming more miserable in becoming more great, that by my example the ambitious may learn to curb their greed.

With this, the 'Story of Calamity' ends. The allusions to Innocent II seem to prove that it was written not earlier than 1132; the confession of constant and abject personal fear suggests that it was written under the shock caused by the atrocious murder of the Prior of Saint-Victor by the nephews of the Archdeacon of Paris, who had also been subjected to reforms. This murder was committed a few miles outside of the walls of Paris, on August 20, 1133. The 'Story of Calamity' is evidently a long plea for release from the restraints imposed on its author by his position in the prelacy and the tacit, or possibly the express, contract he had made, or to which he had submitted, in 1125. This plea was obviously written in order to serve one of two purposes: either to be placed before the authorities whose consent

alone could relieve Abélard from his restraints; or to justify him in throwing off the load of the Church, and resuming the profession of schoolman. Supposing the second explanation, the date of the paper would be more or less closely fixed by John of Salisbury, who coming to Paris as a student, in 1136, found Abélard lecturing on the Mont-Sainte-Geneviève; that is to say, not under the licence of the Bishop of Paris or his Chancellor, but independently, in a private school of his own, outside the walls. 'I attached myself to the Palatine Peripatician who then presided on the hill of Sainte-Geneviève, the doctor illustrious, admired by all. There, at his feet, I received the first elements of the dialectic art, and according to the measure of my poor understanding I received with all the avidity of my soul everything that came from his mouth.'

This explanation is hardly reasonable, for no prelate who was not also a temporal lord would have dared throw off his official duties without permission from his superiors. In Abélard's case the only superior to whom he could apply, as Abbot of Saint-Gildas in Brittany, was probably the Pope himself. In the year 1135 the moment was exceedingly favourable for asking privileges. Innocent, driven from Rome a second time, had summoned a council at Pisa for May 30 to help him. Louis-le-Gros and his minister Suger gave at first no support to this council, and were overruled by Bernard of Clairvaux who in a manner drove them into giving the French clergy permission to attend. The principal archbishops, a number of bishops, and sixteen abbots went to Pisa in May, 1135, and some one of them certainly asked Innocent for favours on behalf of Abélard, which the Pope granted.

The proof is a papal bull, dated in 1136, in favour of Héloïse, giving her the rank and title of Abbess, accompanied by another giving to the Oratory of the Holy Trinity the rank and name of Monastery of the Paraclete, a novelty in Church tradition so extraordinary or so shocking that it still astounds churchmen. With this excessive mark of favour Innocent could have felt little difficulty in giving Abélard the permission to absent himself from his abbey, and with this permission in his hands Abélard might have lectured on dialectics to John of Salisbury in the summer or autumn of 1136. He did not, as far as known, resume lectures on theology.

Such success might have turned heads much better balanced than that of Abélard. With the support of the Pope and at least one of the most prominent cardinals, and with relations at court with the ministers of Louis-le-Gros, Abélard seemed to himself as strong as Bernard of Clair-vaux, and a more popular champion of reform. The year 1137, which has marked a date for so many great points in our travels, marked also the moment of Abélard's greatest vogue. The victory of Aristotle and the pointed arch seemed assured when Suger effected the marriage of the young Prince Louis to the heiress Eleanor of Guienne. The exact moment was stamped on the façade of his exquisite creation, the Abbey Church of Saint-Denis, finished in 1140 and still in part erect. From Saint-Denis to Saint-Sulpice was but a step. Louis-le-Grand seems to stand close in succession to Louis-le-Gros.

Fortunately for tourists, the world, restless though it might be, could not hurry, and Abélard was to know of the pointed arch very little except its restlessness. Just at the apex of his triumph, August 1, 1137, Louis-le-Gros died. Six months afterwards the anti-pope also died, the schism ended, and Innocent II needed Abélard's help no more. Bernard of Clairvaux became Pope and King at once. Both Innocent and Louis-le-Jeune were in a manner his personal creations. The King's brother Henry, next in succession, actually became a monk at Clairvaux not long afterwards. Even the architecture told the same story, for at Saint-Denis, though the arch might simulate a point, the old Romanesque lines still assert as firmly as ever their spiritual control. The flèche that gave the façade a new spirit was not added until 1215, which marks Abélard's error in terms of time.

Once arrived at power, Bernard made short work of all that tried to resist him. During 1139 he seems to have been too busy or too ill to take up the affair of Abélard, but in March, 1140, the attack was opened in a formal letter from William of Saint-Thierry, who was Bernard's closest friend, bringing charges against Abélard before Bernard and the Bishop of Chartres. The charges were simple enough:

Pierre Abélard seized the moment, when all the masters of ecclesiastical doctrine have disappeared from the scene of the world, to conquer a place apart, for himself, in the schools, and to create there an exclusive domination. He treats Holy Scripture as though it were dialectics. It is a matter with him of personal invention and annual novelties. He is the censor and not the disciple of the faith; the corrector and not the imitator of the authorized masters.

In substance, this is all. The need of action was even simpler. Abélard's novelties were becoming a danger; they affected not only the schools, but also even the Curia at Rome. Bernard must act because there was no one else to act: 'This man fears you; he dreads you! if you shut your eyes, whom will he fear? . . . The evil has become too public to allow a correction limited to amicable discipline and secret warning.' In fact, Abélard's works were flying about Europe in every direction, and every year produced a novelty. One can still read them in M. Cousin's collected edition; among others, a volume on ethics: 'Ethica, seu Scito teipsum'; on theology in general, an epitome; a 'Dialogus inter Philosophum, Judaeum et Christianum'; and, what was perhaps the most alarming of all, an abstract of quotations from standard authorities, on the principle of the parallel column, showing the fatal contradictions of the authorized masters, and entitled 'Sic et Non'! Not one of these works but dealt with sacred matters in a spirit implying that the Essence of God was better understood by Pierre du Pallet than by the whole array of bishops and prelates in Europe! Had Bernard been fortunate enough to light upon the 'Story of Calamity,' which must also have been in existence, he would have found there Abélard's own childlike avowal that he taught theology because his scholars 'said that they did not want mere words; that one can believe only what one understands; and that it is ridiculous to preach to others what one understands no better than they do.' Bernard himself never charged Abélard with any presumption equal to this. Bernard said only that 'he sees nothing as an enigma, nothing as in a mirror, but looks on everything face to face.' If this had been all, even Bernard could scarcely have complained. For several thousand years mankind has stared Infinity in the face without pretending to be the wiser; the pretension of Abélard was that, by his dialectic method, he could explain the Infinite, while all other theologists talked mere words; and by way of proving that he had got to the bottom of the matter, he laid down the ultimate law of the universe as his starting-point: 'All that God does,' he said, 'He wills necessarily and does it necessarily; for His goodness is such that it pushes Him necessarily to do all the good He can, and the best He can, and the quickest He can. . . . Therefore it is of necessity that God willed and made the world.' Pure logic admitted no contingency; it was bound to be necessitarian or ceased to be logical; but the result, as Bernard understood it, was that Abélard's world, being the best and only possible, need trouble itself no more about God, or Church, or man.

Strange as the paradox seems, Saint Bernard and Lord Bacon, though looking at the world from opposite standpoints, agreed in this: that the scholastic method was false and mischievous, and that the longer it was followed, the greater was its mischief. Bernard thought that because dialectics led wrong, therefore faith led right. He saw no alternative, and perhaps in fact there was none. If he had lived a century later, he would have said to Thomas Aquinas what he said to a schoolman of his own day: 'if you had once tasted true food'—if you knew what true religion is—'how quick you would leave those Jew makers of books (literatoribus judaeis) to gnaw their crusts by themselves!' Locke or Hume might perhaps still have resented a little the 'literator judaeus,' but Faraday or Clerk-Maxwell would have expressed the same opinion with only the change of a word: 'If the twelfth century had once tasted true science, how quick they would have dropped Avicenna and Averroës!' Science admits that Bernard's disbelief in scholasticism was well founded, whatever it may think of his reasons. The only point that remains is personal: Which is the more sympathetic, Bernard or Abélard?

The Church feels no doubt, but is a bad witness. Bernard is not a character to be taken or rejected in a lump. He was many-sided, and even toward Abélard he showed more than one surface. He wanted no unnecessary scandals in the Church; he had too many that were not of his seeking. He seems to have gone through the forms of friendly negotiation with Abélard although he could have required nothing less than Abélard's submission and return to Brittany, and silence; terms which Abélard thought worse than death. On Abélard's refusal, Bernard began his attack. We know, from the 'Story of Calamity,' what Bernard's party could not have certainly known then—the abject terror into which the very thought of a council had for twenty years thrown Abélard whenever he was threatened with it; and in 1140 he saw it to be inevitable. He preferred to face it with dignity, and requested to be heard at a council to meet at Sens in June. One cannot admit that he felt the shadow of a hope to escape. At the utmost he could have dreamed of nothing more than a hearing. Bernard's friends, who had a lively fear of his dialectics, took care to shut the door on even this hope. The council was carefully packed and overawed. The King was present; archbishops, bishops, abbots, and other prelates by the score; Bernard acted in person as the prosecuting attorney; the public outside were stimulated to threaten violence. Abélard had less chance of a judicial hearing than he had had at Soissons twenty years before. He acted with a proper sense of their dignity and his own by simply appearing and entering an appeal to Rome. The council paid no attention to the appeal, but passed to an immediate con-demnation. His friends said that it was done after dinner; that when the volume of Abélard's 'Theology' was produced and the clerk began to read it aloud, after the first few sentences the bishops ceased attention, talked, joked, laughed, stamped their feet, got angry, and at last went to sleep. They were waked only to growl 'Damnamus—namus,' and so made an end. The story may be true, for all prelates, even in the twelfth century, were not Bernards of Clairvaux or Peters of Cluny; all drank wine, and all were probably sleepy after dinner; while Abélard's writings are, for the most part, exceedingly hard reading. The clergy knew quite well what they were doing; the judgment was certain long in advance, and the council was called only to register it. Political trials were usually mere forms.

The appeal to Rome seems to have been taken seriously by Bernard, which is surprising unless the character of Innocent II inspired his friends with doubts unknown to us. Innocent owed everything to Bernard, while Abélard owed everything to Innocent. The Pope was not in a position to alienate the French Church or the French King. To any one who knows only what is now to be known, Bernard seems to have been sure of the Curia, yet he wrote in a tone of excitement as though he feared Abélard's influence there even more than at home. He became abusive; Abélard was a crawling viper (coluber tortuosus) who had come out of his hole (egressus est de caverna sua), and after the manner of a hydra (in similitudinem hydrae), after having one head cut off at Soissons, had thrown out seven more. He was a monk without rule; a prelate without responsibility; an abbot without discipline; 'disputing with boys; conversing with women.' The charges in themselves seem to be literally true, and would not in some later centuries have been thought very serious; neither faith nor morals were impugned. On the other hand, Abélard never affected or aspired to be a saint, while Bernard always affected to judge the acts and motives of his fellow-creatures from a standpoint of more than worldly charity. Bernard had no right to Abélard's vices; he claimed to be judged by a higher standard; but his temper was none of the best, and his pride was something of the worst; which gave to Peter the Venerable occasion for turning on him sharply with a rebuke that cut to the bone: 'You perform all the difficult religious duties,' wrote Peter to the saint who wrought miracles; 'you fast; you watch; you suffer; but you will not endure the easy ones—you do not love (non vis levia ferre, ut diligas).'

This was the end of Abélard. Of course the

Pope confirmed the judgment, and even hurried to do so in order that he might not be obliged to give Abélard a hearing. The judgment was not severe, as judgments went; indeed, it amounted to little more than an order to keep silence, and, as it happened, was never carried into effect. Abélard, at best a nervous invalid, started for Rome, but stopped at Cluny, perhaps the most agreeable stopping-place in Europe. Personally he seems to have been a favourite of Abbot Peter the Venerable, whose love for Bernard was not much stronger than Abélard's or Suger's. Bernard was an excessively sharp critic, and spared worldliness, or what he thought lack of spirituality, in no prelate whatever; Clairvaux existed for nothing else, politically, than as a rebuke to them all, and Bernard's enmity was their bond of union. Under the protection of Peter the Venerable, the most amiable figure of the twelfth century, and in the most agreeable residence in Europe, Abélard remained unmolested at Cluny, occupied, as is believed, in writing or revising his treatises, in defiance of the council. He died there two years later, April 21, 1142, in full communion, still nominal Abbot of Saint-Gildas, and so distinguished a prelate that Peter the Venerable thought himself obliged to write a charming letter to Héloïse at the Paraclete not far away, condoling with her on the loss of a husband who was the Socrates, the Aristotle, the Plato, of France and the West; who, if among logicians he had rivals, had no master; who was the prince of study, learned, eloquent, subtle, penetrating; who overcame everything by the force of reason, and was never so great as when he passed to true philosophy, that of Christ.

All this was in Latin verses, and seems sufficiently strong, considering that Abélard's philosophy had been so recently and so emphatically condemned by the entire Church, including Peter the Venerable himself. The twelfth century had this singular charm of liberty in practice, just as its architecture knew no mathematical formula of precision; but Peter's letter to Héloïse went further still, and rang with absolute passion:

> Thus, dear and venerable sister in God, he to whom you are united, after your tie in the flesh, by the better and stronger bond of the divine love; he, with whom, and under whom, you have served the Lord, the Lord now takes, in your place, like another you, and warms in His bosom; and, for the day of His coming, when shall sound the voice of the archangel and the trumpet of God descending from heaven, He keeps him to restore him to you by His grace.

PRAYER TO THE VIRGIN OF CHARTRES

◇

⟦ THE POEM was written in 1901, just after Adams had completed the first draft of the *Chartres*. He sent it first to Elizabeth Cameron: "No one but you has seen it. No one but you would care to see it." A copy of it was found in a wallet of papers by his Catholic niece, Mabel LaFarge, who published it in *Letters to a Niece* in 1920 with the imaginative suggestion that in it Adams "makes an act of faith in the Son's divinity." When he sent it to Mrs. Winthrop Chanler, also a Catholic, he said, "Throw it into the fire when done" because "you pray in a different spirit." Mrs. Chanler has perceptively written: "There was never a moment's serious thought that Henry Adams might enter the Church; his interest was all intellectual and aesthetic, literary and historical; his sympathies were engaged, never his actual will to believe."

◇

GRACIOUS LADY:—

Simple as when I asked your aid before;
   Humble as when I prayed for grace in vain
Seven hundred years ago; weak, weary, sore
   In heart and hope, I ask your help again.

You, who remember all, remember me;
   An English scholar of a Norman name,
I was a thousand who then crossed the sea
   To wrangle in the Paris schools for fame.

When your Byzantine portal was still young
   I prayed there with my master Abailard;   10
When Ave Maris Stella was first sung,
   I helped to sing it here with Saint Bernard.

When Blanche set up your gorgeous Rose of France
   I stood among the servants of the Queen;
And when Saint Louis made his penitence,
   I followed barefoot where the King had been.

PRAYER TO THE VIRGIN OF CHARTRES. **6. Norman name:** Adams liked to assume that he was of Norman descent. **8. Paris schools:** See the early part of the *Chartres* chapter on Abelard. **11. Ave Maris Stella:** See the *Chartres*, 15n. **13. Blanche:** Blanche of Castile (1187–1252), Queen of France, mother of Louis IX, masterful regent during her son's absence, one of the many superior women of the Middle Ages. **15. Saint Louis:** Louis IX (1214–1270), King of France, regarded as the ideal king of the Middle Ages. After his return from his disastrous crusade he was noted for his self-denying piety. The

For centuries I brought you all my cares,
  And vexed you with the murmurs of a child;
You heard the tedious burden of my prayers;
  You could not grant them, but at least you
    smiled.   20

If then I left you, it was not my crime,
  Or if a crime, it was not mine alone.
All children wander with the truant Time.
  Pardon me too! You pardoned once your Son!

For He said to you:—"Wist ye not that I
  Must be about my Father's business?" So,
Seeking his Father he pursued his way
  Straight to the Cross towards which we all
    must go.

So I too wandered off among the host
  That racked the earth to find the father's clue.
I did not find the Father, but I lost   31
  What now I value more, the Mother,—You!

I thought the fault was yours that foiled my
    search;
  I turned and broke your image on its throne,
Cast down my idol, and resumed my march
  To claim the father's empire for my own.

Crossing the hostile sea, our greedy band
  Saw rising hills and forests in the blue;
Our father's kingdom in the promised land!
  —We seized it, and dethroned the father
    too.   40

And now we are the Father, with our brood,
  Ruling the Infinite, not Three but One;
We made our world and saw that it was good;
  Ourselves we worship, and we have no Son.

Yet we have Gods, for even our strong nerve
  Falters before the Energy we own.
Which shall be master? Which of us shall serve?
  Which wears the fetters? Which shall bear the
    crown?

Brave though we be, we dread to face the Sphinx,
  Or answer the old riddle she still asks.   50
Strong as we are, our reckless courage shrinks
  To look beyond the piece-work of our tasks.

But when we must, we pray, as in the past
  Before the Cross on which your Son was
    nailed.
Listen, dear lady! You shall hear the last
  Of the strange prayers Humanity has wailed.

PRAYER TO THE DYNAMO

Mysterious Power! Gentle Friend!
  Despotic Master! Tireless Force!
You and We are near the End.
Either You or We must bend   60
  To bear the martyrs' Cross.

We know ourselves, what we can bear
  As men; our strength and weakness too;
Down to the fraction of a hair;
And know that we, with all our care
  And knowledge, know not you.

You come in silence, Primal Force,
  We know not whence, or when, or why;
You stay a moment in your course
To play; and, lo! you leap across   70
  To Alpha Centauri!

We know not whether you are kind,
  Or cruel in your fiercer mood;
But be you Matter, be you Mind,
We think we know that you are blind,
  And we alone are good.

We know that prayer is thrown away,
  For you are only force and light;
A shifting current; night and day;
We know this well, and yet we pray,   80
  For prayer is infinite,

Like you! Within the finite sphere
  That bounds the impotence of thought,
We search an outlet everywhere
But only find that we are here
  And that you are—are not!

Rose of France, a circular stained glass window nearly forty-four feet in diameter, in the north transept of Chartres, was erected under the patronage of his mother. The Byzantine Portal, the magnificent west portal of Chartres, shows in its sculpture the Byzantine influences brought back by the crusaders. **26. my Father's business:** Luke 2:49. **34. your . . . throne:** Adams's thesis that the Catholic Church at the close of the Middle Ages dethroned the Virgin of Majesty who had, in spite of orthodox theology, "eclipsed" the Son. **40. dethroned . . . too:** in New England Unitarianism. See the opening sentence of the *Education*.

60. You . . . bend: Adams's growing belief that man must harness the new forces of science or be destroyed by them. **71. Alpha Centauri:** brightest star in the constellation Centaurus, situated near the Southern Cross, four and a half light years from earth and, after the sun, our nearest star.

What are we then? the lords of space?
  The master-mind whose tasks you do?
Jockey who rides you in the race?
Or are we atoms whirled apace,   90
  Shaped and controlled by you?

Still silence! Still no end in sight!
  No sound in answer to our cry!
Then, by the God we now hold tight,
Though we destroy soul, life and light,
  Answer you shall—or die!

We are no beggars! What care we
  For hopes or terrors, love or hate?
What for the universe? We see
Only our certain destiny   100
  And the last word of Fate.

Seize, then, the Atom! rack his joints!
  Tear out of him his secret spring!
Grind him to nothing!—though he points
To us, and his life-blood anoints
  Me—the dead Atom-King!

A curious prayer, dear lady! is it not?
  Strangely unlike the prayers I prayed to you!
Stranger because you find me at this spot,
  Here, at your feet, asking your help anew.   110

Strangest of all, I have ceased to strive,
  Ceased even care what new coin fate shall
    strike.
In truth it does not matter. Fate will give
  Some answer; and all answers are alike.

So, while we slowly rack and torture death
  And wait for what the final void will show,
Waiting I feel the energy of faith
  Not in the future science, but in you!

The man who solves the Infinite, and needs
  The force of solar systems for his play,   120
Will not need me, nor greatly care what deeds
  Made me illustrious in the dawn of day.

He will send me, dethroned, to claim my rights,
  Fossil survival of an age of stone,
Among the cave-men and the troglodytes
  Who carved the mammoth on the mammoth's
    bone.

He will forget my thought, my acts, my fame,
  As we forget the shadows of the dusk,
Or catalogue the echo of a name
  As we the scratches on the mammoth's tusk.

But when, like me, he too has trod the track   131
  Which leads him up to power above control,
He too will have no choice but wander back
  And sink in helpless hopelessness of soul,

Before your majesty of grace and love,
  The purity, the beauty and the faith;
The depth of tenderness beneath; above,
  The glory of the life and of the death.

When your Byzantine portal still was young,
  I came here with my master Abailard;   140
When Ave Maris Stella was first sung,
  I joined to sing it here with Saint Bernard.

When Blanche set up your glorious Rose of
    France,
  In scholar's robes I waited on the Queen;
When good Saint Louis did his penitence,
  My prayer was deep like his: my faith as keen.

What loftier prize seven hundred years shall
    bring,
  What deadlier struggles for a larger air,
What immortality our strength shall wring
  From Time and Space, we may—or may not—
    care;   150

But years, or ages, or eternity,
  Will find me still in thought before your throne,
Pondering the mystery of Maternity,
  Soul within Soul,—Mother and Child in One!

Help me to see! not with my mimic sight—
  With yours! which carried radiance, like the
    sun,
Giving the rays you saw with—light in light—
  Tying all suns and stars and worlds in one.

Help me to know! not with my mocking art—
  With you, who knew yourself unbound by laws;
Gave God your strength, your life, your sight,
    your heart,   161
  And took from him the Thought that Is—the
    Cause.

Help me to feel! not with my insect sense,—
  With yours that felt all life alive in you;
Infinite heart beating at your expense;
  Infinite passion breathing the breath you drew!

Help me to bear! not my own baby load,
  But yours; who bore the failure of the light,
The strength, the knowledge and the thought of
    God,—
  The futile folly of the Infinite!   170

FROM

THE EDUCATION OF HENRY ADAMS

EDITOR'S PREFACE [1]

THIS volume, written in 1905 as a sequel to the same author's *Mont-Saint-Michel and Chartres,* was privately printed, to the number of one hundred copies, in 1906,[2] and sent to the persons interested, for their assent, correction, or suggestion. The idea of the two books was thus explained at the end of Chapter XXIX:—

"Any schoolboy could see that man as a force must be measured by motion from a fixed point. Psychology helped here by suggesting a unit— the point of history when man held the highest idea of himself as a unit in a unified universe. Eight or ten years of study had led Adams to think he might use the century 1150–1250, expressed in Amiens Cathedral and the Works of Thomas Aquinas, as the unit from which he might measure motion down to his own time, without assuming anything as true or untrue, except relation. The movement might be studied at once in philosophy and mechanics. Setting himself to the task, he began a volume which he mentally knew as *Mont Saint-Michel and Chartres: a Study of Thirteenth-Century Unity.* From that point he proposed to fix a position for himself, which he could label: *The Education of Henry Adams: a Study of Twentieth-Century Multiplicity.* With the help of these two points of relation, he hoped to project his lines forward and backward indefinitely, subject to correction from any one who should know better."

The *Chartres* was finished and privately printed in 1904. The *Education* proved to be more difficult. The point on which the author failed to please himself, and could get no light from readers or friends, was the usual one of literary form. Probably he saw it in advance, for he used to say, half in jest, that his great ambition was to complete

St. Augustine's *Confessions,* but that St. Augustine, like a great artist, had worked from multiplicity to unity, while he, like a small one, had to reverse the method and work back from unity to multiplicity. The scheme became unmanageable as he approached his end.

Probably he was, in fact, trying only to work into it his favorite theory of history, which now fills the last three or four chapters of the *Education,* and he could not satisfy himself with his workmanship. At all events, he was still pondering over the problem in 1910, when he tried to deal with it in another way which might be more intelligible to students. He printed a small volume called *A Letter to American Teachers,* which he sent to his associates in the American Historical Association, hoping to provoke some response. Before he could satisfy himself even on this minor point, a severe illness in the spring of 1912 put an end to his literary activity forever.

The matter soon passed beyond his control. In 1913 the Institute of Architects published the *Mont-Saint-Michel and Chartres.* Already the *Education* had become almost as well known as the *Chartres,* and was freely quoted by every book whose author requested it. The author could no longer withdraw either volume; he could no longer rewrite either, and he could not publish that which he thought unprepared and unfinished, although in his opinion the other was historically purposeless without its sequel. In the end, he preferred to leave the *Education* unpublished, avowedly incomplete, trusting that it might quietly fade from memory. According to his theory of history as explained in Chapters XXXIII and XXXIV, the teacher was at best helpless, and, in the immediate future, silence next to good-temper was the mark of sense. After midsummer, 1914, the rule was made absolute.[3]

The Massachusetts Historical Society now publishes the *Education* as it was printed in 1907, with only such marginal corrections as the author made, and it does this, not in opposition to the author's judgment, but only to put both volumes equally within reach of students who have occasion to consult them.

HENRY CABOT LODGE

September, 1918

PREFACE

JEAN JACQUES ROUSSEAU began his famous *Confessions* by a vehement appeal to the Deity: "I have shown myself as I was; contemptible

THE EDUCATION. **1. Editor's Preface:** The Editor's Preface was written by Henry Adams shortly before his death, with the request that Lodge adopt it as his own. The subtitle, "An Autobiography," affixed to the published edition does not appear in the original printing of 1907. The subtitle Adams had in mind is indicated in the quotation from the *Education:* "A Study of Twentieth Century Multiplicity." **2. in 1906:** 1907. See the last paragraph of "Lodge's" Preface and the date at the end of the second Preface.

3. made absolute: outbreak of World War I in August, 1914.

and vile when I was so; good, generous, sublime when I was so; I have unveiled my interior such as Thou thyself hast seen it, Eternal Father! Collect about me the innumerable swarm of my fellows; let them hear my confessions; let them groan at my unworthiness; let them blush at my meannesses! Let each of them discover his heart in his turn at the foot of thy throne with the same sincerity; and then let any one of them tell thee if he dares: 'I was a better man!' "

Jean Jacques was a very great educator in the manner of the eighteenth century, and has been commonly thought to have had more influence than any other teacher of his time; but his peculiar method of improving human nature has not been universally admired. Most educators of the nineteenth century have declined to show themselves before their scholars as objects more vile or contemptible than necessary, and even the humblest teacher hides, if possible, the faults with which nature has generously embellished us all, as it did Jean Jacques, thinking, as most religious minds are apt to do, that the Eternal Father himself may not feel unmixed pleasure at our thrusting under his eyes chiefly the least agreeable details of his creation.

As an unfortunate result the twentieth century finds few recent guides to avoid, or to follow. American literature offers scarcely one working model for high education. The student must go back, beyond Jean Jacques, to Benjamin Franklin, to find a model even of self-teaching. Except in the abandoned sphere of the dead languages,[4] no one has discussed what part of education has, in his personal experience, turned out to be useful, and what not. This volume attempts to discuss it.

As educator, Jean Jacques was, in one respect, easily first; he erected a monument of warning against the Ego. Since his time, and largely thanks to him, the Ego has steadily tended to efface itself, and, for purposes of model, to become a manikin on which the toilet of education is to be draped in order to show the fit or misfit of the clothes. The object of study is the garment, not the figure. The tailor adapts the manikin as well as the clothes to his patron's wants. The tailor's object, in this volume, is to fit young men, in universities or elsewhere, to be men of the world, equipped for any emergency; and the garment offered to them is meant to show the faults of the patchwork fitted on their fathers.

At the utmost, the active-minded young man

should ask of his teacher only mastery of his tools. The young man himself, the subject of education, is a certain form of energy; the object to be gained is economy of his force; the training is partly the clearing away of obstacles, partly the direct application of effort. Once acquired, the tools and models may be thrown away.

The manikin, therefore, has the same value as any other geometrical figure of three or more dimensions, which is used for the study of relation. For that purpose it cannot be spared; it is the only measure of motion, of proportion, of human condition; it must have the air of reality; must be taken for real; must be treated as though it had life. Who knows? Possibly it had!

February 16, 1907

CHAPTER 1

QUINCY (1838–1848)

UNDER the shadow of Boston State House, turning its back on the house of John Hancock, the little passage called Hancock Avenue runs, or ran, from Beacon Street, skirting the State House grounds, to Mount Vernon Street, on the summit of Beacon Hill; and there, in the third house below Mount Vernon Place, February 16, 1838, a child was born, and christened later by his uncle, the minister of the First Church after the tenets of Boston Unitarianism, as Henry Brooks Adams.[5]

Had he been born in Jerusalem under the shadow of the Temple and circumcised in the Synagogue by his uncle the high priest, under the name of Israel Cohen, he would scarcely have been more distinctly branded, and not much more heavily handicapped in the races of the coming century, in running for such stakes as the century was to offer; but, on the other hand, the ordinary traveller, who does not enter the field of racing, finds advantage in being, so to speak, ticketed through life, with the safeguards of an old, established traffic. Safeguards are often irksome, but sometimes convenient, and if one needs them at all, one is apt to need them badly. A hundred years earlier, such safeguards as his would have secured any young man's success; and although in 1838 their value was not very great compared with what they would have had in 1738, yet the mere accident of starting a twentieth-century career from a nest of associations so colonial —so troglodytic—as the First Church, the Boston State House, Beacon Hill, John Hancock and

4. of . . . languages: allusion to St. Augustine's *Confessions*, which Adams greatly admired.

5. Henry Brooks Adams: He dropped the "Brooks" when he became editor of the *North American* in 1870.

John Adams, Mount Vernon Street and Quincy, all crowding on ten pounds of unconscious babyhood, was so queer as to offer a subject of curious speculation to the baby long after he had witnessed the solution. What could become of such a child of the seventeenth and eighteenth centuries, when he should wake up to find himself required to play the game of the twentieth? Had he been consulted, would he have cared to play the game at all, holding such cards as he held, and suspecting that the game was to be one of which neither he nor any one else was back to the beginning of time knew the rules or the risks or the stakes? He was not consulted and was not responsible, but had he been taken into the confidence of his parents, he would certainly have told them to change nothing as far as concerned him. He would have been astounded by his own luck. Probably no child, born in the year, held better cards than he. Whether life was an honest game of chance, or whether the cards were marked and forced, he could not refuse to play his excellent hand. He could never make the usual plea of irresponsibility. He accepted the situation as though he had been a party to it, and under the same circumstances would do it again, the more readily for knowing the exact values. To his life as a whole he was a consenting, contracting party and partner from the moment he was born to the moment he died. Only with that understanding—as a consciously assenting member in full partnership with the society of his age—had his education an interest to himself or to others.

As it happened, he never got to the point of playing the game at all; he lost himself in the study of it, watching the errors of the players; but this is the only interest in the story, which otherwise has no moral and little incident. A story of education—seventy years of it—the practical value remains to the end in doubt, like other values about which men have disputed since the birth of Cain and Abel; but the practical value of the universe has never been stated in dollars. Although every one cannot be a Gargantua-Napoleon-Bismarck [6] and walk off with the great bells of Notre Dame, every one must bear his own universe, and most persons are moderately interested in learning how their neighbors have managed to carry theirs.

This problem of education, started in 1838, went on for three years, while the baby grew, like other babies, unconsciously, as a vegetable, the outside world working as it never had worked

6. **Gargantua-Napoleon-Bismarck:** one of the exploits of Rabelais' Gargantua in *Gargantua and Pantagruel*, here linked with the prodigious political feats of two strong men of history.

before, to get his new universe ready for him. Often in old age he puzzled over the question whether, on the doctrine of chances, he was at liberty to accept himself or his world as an accident. No such accident had ever happened before in human experience. For him, alone, the old universe was thrown into the ash-heap and a new one created. He and his eighteenth-century, troglodytic Boston were suddenly cut apart—separated forever—in act if not in sentiment, by the opening of the Boston and Albany Railroad; the appearance of the first Cunard steamers in the bay; and the telegraphic messages which carried from Baltimore to Washington the news that Henry Clay and James K. Polk were nominated for the Presidency. This was in May, 1844; he was six years old; his new world was ready for use, and only fragments of the old met his eyes.

Of all this that was being done to complicate his education, he knew only the color of yellow. He first found himself sitting on a yellow kitchen floor in strong sunlight. He was three years old when he took this earliest step in education; a lesson of color. The second followed soon; a lesson of taste. On December 3, 1841, he developed scarlet fever. For several days he was as good as dead, reviving only under the careful nursing of his family. When he began to recover strength, about January 1, 1842, his hunger must have been stronger than any other pleasure or pain, for while in after life he retained not the faintest recollection of his illness, he remembered quite clearly his aunt entering the sick-room bearing in her hand a saucer with a baked apple.

The order of impressions retained by memory might naturally be that of color and taste, although one would rather suppose that the sense of pain would be first to educate. In fact, the third recollection of the child was that of discomfort. The moment he could be removed, he was bundled up in blankets and carried from the little house in Hancock Avenue to a larger one which his parents were to occupy for the rest of their lives in the neighboring Mount Vernon Street. The season was midwinter, January 10, 1842, and he never forgot his acute distress for want of air under his blankets, or the noises of moving furniture.

As a means of variation from a normal type, sickness in childhood ought to have a certain value not to be classed under any fitness or unfitness of natural selection; and especially scarlet fever affected boys seriously, both physically and in character, though they might through life puzzle themselves to decide whether it had fitted or unfitted them for success; but this fever of Henry Adams took greater and greater importance in his eyes, from the point of view of education, the longer he lived. At first, the effect was physical. He fell behind his brothers [7] two or three inches in height, and proportionally in bone and weight. His character and processes of mind seemed to share in this fining-down process of scale. He was not good in a fight, and his nerves were more delicate than boys' nerves ought to be. He exaggerated these weaknesses as he grew older. The habit of doubt; of distrusting his own judgment and of totally rejecting the judgment of the world; the tendency to regard every question as open; the hesitation to act except as a choice of evils; the shirking of responsibility; the love of line, form, quality; the horror of ennui; the passion for companionship and the antipathy to society—all these are well-known qualities of New England character in no way peculiar to individuals but in this instance they seemed to be stimulated by the fever, and Henry Adams could never make up his mind whether, on the whole, the change of character was morbid or healthy, good or bad for his purpose. His brothers were the type; he was the variation.

As far as the boy knew, the sickness did not affect him at all, and he grew up in excellent health, bodily and mental, taking life as it was given; accepting its local standards without a difficulty, and enjoying much of it as keenly as any other boy of his age. He seemed to himself quite normal, and his companions seemed always to think him so. Whatever was peculiar about him was education, not character, and came to him, directly and indirectly, as the result of that eighteenth-century inheritance which he took with his name.

The atmosphere of education in which he lived was colonial, revolutionary, almost Cromwellian,[8] as though he were steeped, from his greatest grandmother's birth, in the odor of political crime. Resistance to something was the law of New England nature; the boy looked out on the world with the instinct of resistance; for numberless generations his predecessors had viewed the world chiefly as a thing to be reformed, filled with evil forces to be abolished, and they saw no reason to suppose that they had wholly succeeded in the abolition; the duty was unchanged. That duty implied not only resistance to evil, but hatred of it. Boys naturally look on all force as an enemy, and generally find it so, but the New Englander, whether boy or man, in his long struggle with a stingy or hostile universe, had learned also to love the pleasure of hating; his joys were few.

Politics, as a practice, whatever its professions, had always been the systematic organization of hatreds, and Massachusetts politics had been as harsh as the climate. The chief charm of New England was harshness of contrasts and extremes of sensibility—a cold that froze the blood, and a heat that boiled it—so that the pleasure of hating—one's self if no better victim offered—was not its rarest amusement; but the charm was a true and natural child of the soil, not a cultivated weed of the ancients. The violence of the contrast was real and made the strongest motive of education. The double exterior nature gave life its relative values. Winter and summer, cold and heat, town and country, force and freedom, marked two modes of life and thought, balanced like lobes of the brain. Town was winter confinement, school, rule, discipline; straight, gloomy streets, piled with six feet of snow in the middle; frosts that made the snow sing under wheels or runners; thaws when the streets became dangerous to cross; society of uncles, aunts, and cousins who expected children to behave themselves, and who were not always gratified; above all else, winter represented the desire to escape and go free. Town was restraint, law, unity. Country, only seven miles away, was liberty, diversity, outlawry, the endless delight of mere sense impressions given by nature for nothing, and breathed by boys without knowing it.

Boys are wild animals, rich in the treasures of sense, but the New England boy had a wider range of emotions than boys of more equable climates. He felt his nature crudely, as it was meant. To the boy Henry Adams, summer was drunken. Among senses, smell was the strongest —smell of hot pine-woods and sweet-fern in the scorching summer noon; of new-mown hay; of ploughed earth; of box hedges; of peaches, lilacs, syringas; of stables, barns, cow-yards; of salt water and low tide on the marshes; nothing came amiss. Next to smell came taste, and the children knew the taste of everything they saw or touched, from pennyroyal and flagroot to the shell of a pignut and the letters of a spelling-book—the taste of A-B, AB, suddenly revived on the boy's tongue sixty years afterwards. Light, line, and color as sensual pleasures, came later and were as crude as the rest. The New England light is glare, and the atmosphere harshens color. The boy was a full man before he ever knew what was meant by atmosphere; his idea of pleasure in light was the blaze of a New England sun. His

---

7. **brothers:** John Quincy Adams II (1833–94), Charles Francis Adams, Jr. (1835–1915).   8. **Cromwellian:** after Oliver Cromwell (1599–1658), lord protector of England during the Puritan Revolution that deposed and beheaded Charles I.

idea of color was a peony, with the dew of early morning on its petals. The intense blue of the sea, as he saw it a mile or two away, from the Quincy hills; the cumuli in a June afternoon sky; the strong reds and greens and purples of colored prints and children's picture-books, as the American colors then ran; these were ideals. The opposites or antipathies, were the cold grays of November evenings, and the thick, muddy thaws of Boston winter. With such standards, the Bostonian could not but develop a double nature. Life was a double thing. After a January blizzard, the boy who could look with pleasure into the violent snow-glare of the cold white sunshine, with its intense light and shade, scarcely knew what was meant by tone. He could reach it only by education.

Winter and summer, then, were two hostile lives, and bred two separate natures. Winter was always the effort to live; summer was tropical license. Whether the children rolled in the grass, or waded in the brook, or swam in the salt ocean, or sailed in the bay, or fished for smelts in the creeks, or netted minnows in the salt-marshes, or took to the pine-woods and the granite quarries, or chased muskrats and hunted snapping-turtles in the swamps, or mushrooms or nuts on the autumn hills, summer and country were always sensual living, while winter was always compulsory learning. Summer was the multiplicity of nature; winter was school.

The bearing of the two seasons on the education of Henry Adams was no fancy; it was the most decisive force he ever knew; it ran through life, and made the division between its perplexing, warring, irreconcilable problems, irreducible opposites, with growing emphasis to the last year of study. From earliest childhood the boy was accustomed to feel that, for him, life was double. Winter and summer, town and country, law and liberty, were hostile, and the man who pretended they were not, was in his eyes a schoolmaster— that is, a man employed to tell lies to little boys. Though Quincy was but two hours' walk from Beacon Hill, it belonged in a different world. For two hundred years, every Adams, from father to son, had lived within sight of State Street,[9] and sometimes had lived in it, yet none had ever taken kindly to the town, or been taken kindly by it. The boy inherited his double nature. He knew as yet nothing about his great-grandfather, who had died a dozen years before his own birth: he took for granted that any great-

9. **State Street:** financial center of Boston, stronghold of the conservative Federalist party during the early years of the century.

grandfather of his must have always been good, and his enemies wicked; but he divined his great-grandfather's character from his own. Never for a moment did he connect the two ideas of Boston and John Adams; they were separate and antagonistic; the idea of John Adams went with Quincy. He knew his grandfather John Quincy Adams only as an old man of seventy-five or eighty who was friendly and gentle with him, but except that he heard his grandfather always called "the President," and his grandmother "the Madam," he had no reason to suppose that his Adams grandfather differed in character from his Brooks grandfather who was equally kind and benevolent. He liked the Adams side best, but for no other reason than that it reminded him of the country, the summer, and the absence of restraint. Yet he felt also that Quincy was in a way inferior to Boston, and that socially Boston looked down on Quincy. The reason was clear enough even to a five-year old child. Quincy had no Boston style. Little enough style had either; a simpler manner of life and thought could hardly exist, short of cave-dwelling. The flint-and-steel with which his grandfather Adams used to light his own fires in the early morning was still on the mantelpiece of his study. The idea of a livery or even a dress for servants, or of an evening toilette, was next to blasphemy. Bathrooms, water-supplies, lighting, heating, and the whole array of domestic comforts, were unknown at Quincy. Boston had already a bathroom, a water-supply, a furnace, and gas. The superiority of Boston was evident, but a child liked it no better for that.

The magnificence of his grandfather Brooks's house in Pearl Street or South Street has long ago disappeared, but perhaps his country house at Medford may still remain to show what impressed the mind of a boy in 1845 with the idea of city splendor. The President's place at Quincy was the larger and older and far the more interesting of the two; but a boy felt at once its inferiority in fashion. It showed plainly enough its want of wealth. It smacked of colonial age, but not of Boston style or plush curtains. To the end of his life he never quite overcame the prejudice thus drawn in with his childish breath. He never could compel himself to care for nineteenth-century style. He was never able to adopt it, any more than his father or grandfather or great-grandfather had done. Not that he felt it as particularly hostile, for he reconciled himself to much that was worse; but because, for some remote reason, he was born an eighteenth-century child. The old house at Quincy was eighteenth century. What style it had was in its Queen Anne mahogany panels and its Louis Seize chairs and sofas. The panels belonged to an old colonial Vassall who built the house; the furniture had been brought back from Paris in 1789 or 1801 or 1817, along with porcelain and books and much else of old diplomatic remnants; and neither of the two eighteenth-century styles—neither English Queen Anne nor French Louis Seize— was comfortable for a boy, or for any one else. The dark mahogany had been painted white to suit daily life in winter gloom. Nothing seemed to favor, for a child's objects, the older forms. On the contrary, most boys, as well as grown-up people, preferred the new, with good reason, and the child felt himself distinctly at a disadvantage for the taste.

Nor had personal preference any share in his bias. The Brooks grandfather [10] was as amiable and as sympathetic as the Adams grandfather. Both were born in 1767, and both died in 1848. Both were kind to children, and both belonged rather to the eighteenth than to the nineteenth centuries. The child knew no difference between them except that one was associated with winter and the other with summer; one with Boston, the other with Quincy. Even with Medford, the association was hardly easier. Once as a very young boy he was taken to pass a few days with his grandfather Brooks under charge of his aunt, but became so violently homesick that within twenty-four hours he was brought back in disgrace. Yet he could not remember ever being seriously homesick again.

The attachment to Quincy was not altogether sentimental or wholly sympathetic. Quincy was not a bed of thornless roses. Even there the curse of Cain [11] set its mark. There as elsewhere a cruel universe combined to crush a child. As though three or four vigorous brothers and sisters, with the best will, were not enough to crush any child, every one else conspired towards an education which he hated. From cradle to grave this problem of running order through chaos, direction through space, discipline through freedom, unity through multiplicity, has always been, and must always be, the task of education, as it is the moral of religion, philosophy, science, art, politics, and economy; but a boy's will is his life, and he dies when it is broken, as the colt dies in harness, taking a new nature in becoming tame. Rarely has the boy felt kindly towards his tamers. Between him and his master has always been war. Henry Adams never knew a boy of his genera-

10. **The Brooks grandfather:** Peter Chardon Brooks died in 1849, reputedly the richest man in Boston. 11. **Cain:** Gen. 4:11.

tion to like a master, and the task of remaining on friendly terms with one's own family, in such a relation, was never easy.

All the more singular it seemed afterwards to him that his first serious contact with the President should have been a struggle of will, in which the old man almost necessarily defeated the boy, but instead of leaving, as usual in such defeats, a life-long sting, left rather an impression of as fair treatment as could be expected from a natural enemy. The boy met seldom with such restraint. He could not have been much more than six years old at the time—seven at the utmost—and his mother had taken him to Quincy for a long stay with the President during the summer. What became of the rest of the family he quite forgot; but he distinctly remembered standing at the house door one summer morning in a passionate outburst of rebellion against going to school. Naturally his mother was the immediate victim of his rage; that is what mothers are for, and boys also; but in this case the boy had his mother at unfair disadvantage, for she was a guest, and had no means of enforcing obedience. Henry showed a certain tactical ability by refusing to start, and he met all efforts at compulsion by successful, though too vehement protest. He was in fair way to win, and was holding his own, with sufficient energy, at the bottom of the long staircase which led up to the door of the President's library, when the door opened, and the old man slowly came down. Putting on his hat, he took the boy's hand without a word, and walked with him, paralyzed by awe, up the road to the town. After the first moments of consternation at this interference in a domestic dispute, the boy reflected that an old gentleman close on eighty would never trouble himself to walk near a mile on a hot summer morning over a shadeless road to take a boy to school, and that it would be strange if a lad imbued with the passion of freedom could not find a corner to dodge around, somewhere before reaching the school door. Then and always, the boy insisted that this reasoning justified his apparent submission; but the old man did not stop, and the boy saw all his strategical points turned, one after another, until he found himself seated inside the school, and obviously the centre of curious if not malevolent criticism. Not till then did the President release his hand and depart.

The point was that this act, contrary to the inalienable rights of boys, and nullifying the social compact, ought to have made him dislike his grandfather for life. He could not recall that it had this effect even for a moment. With a certain maturity of mind, the child must have recognized that the President, though a tool of tyranny, had done his disreputable work with a certain intelligence. He had shown no temper, no irritation, no personal feeling, and had made no display of force. Above all, he had held his tongue. During their long walk he had said nothing; he had uttered no syllable of revolting cant about the duty of obedience and the wickedness of resistance to law; he had shown no concern in the matter; hardly even a consciousness of the boy's existence. Probably his mind at that moment was actually troubling itself little about his grandson's iniquities, and much about the iniquities of President Polk, but the boy could scarcely at that age feel the whole satisfaction of thinking that President Polk was to be the vicarious victim of his own sins, and he gave his grandfather credit for intelligent silence. For this forbearance, he felt instinctive respect. He admitted force as a form of right; he admitted even temper, under protest; but the seeds of a moral education would at that moment have fallen on the stoniest soil in Quincy, which is, as every one knows, the stoniest glacial and tidal drift known in any Puritan land.

Neither party to this momentary disagreement can have felt rancor, for during these three or four summers the old President's relations with the boy were friendly and almost intimate. Whether his older brothers and sisters were still more favored he failed to remember, but he was himself admitted to a sort of familiarity which, when in his turn he had reached old age, rather shocked him, for it must have sometimes tried the President's patience. He hung about the library; handled the books; deranged the papers; ransacked the drawers; searched the old purses and pocket-books for foreign coins; drew the sword-cane; snapped the travelling-pistols; upset everything in the corners, and penetrated the President's dressing-closet where a row of tumblers, inverted on the shelf, covered caterpillars which were supposed to become moths or butterflies, but never did. The Madam bore with fortitude the loss of the tumblers which her husband purloined for these hatcheries; but she made protest when he carried off her best cut-glass bowls to plant with acorns or peachstones that he might see the roots grow, but which, she said, he commonly forgot like the caterpillars.

At that time the President rode the hobby of tree-culture, and some fine old trees should still remain to witness it, unless they have been improved off the ground; but his was a restless mind, and although he took his hobbies seriously and would have been annoyed had his grandchild asked whether he was bored like an English duke,

he probably cared more for the processes than for the results, so that his grandson was saddened by the sight and smell of peaches and pears, the best of their kind, which he brought up from the garden to rot on his shelves for seed. With the inherited virtues of his Puritan ancestors, the little boy Henry conscientiously brought up to him in his study the finest peaches he found in the garden, and ate only the less perfect. Naturally he ate more by way of compensation, but the act showed that he bore no grudge. As for his grandfather, it is even possible that he may have felt a certain self-reproach for his temporary rôle of schoolmaster—seeing that his own career did not offer proof of the worldly advantages of docile obedience—for there still exists somewhere a little volume of critically edited Nursery Rhymes with the boy's name in full written in the President's trembling hand on the fly-leaf. Of course there was also the Bible, given to each child at birth, with the proper inscription in the President's hand on the fly-leaf; while their grandfather Brooks supplied the silver mugs.

So many Bibles and silver mugs had to be supplied, that a new house, or cottage, was built to hold them. It was "on the hill," five minutes' walk above "the old house," with a far view eastward over Quincy Bay, and northward over Boston. Till his twelfth year, the child passed his summers there, and his pleasures of childhood mostly centered in it. Of education he had as yet little to complain. Country schools were not very serious. Nothing stuck to the mind except home impressions, and the sharpest were those of kindred children; but as influences that warped a mind, none compared with the mere effect of the back of the President's bald head, as he sat in his pew on Sundays, in line with that of President Quincy, who, though some ten years younger, seemed to children about the same age. Before railways entered the New England town, every parish church showed half-a-dozen of these leading citizens, with gray hair, who sat on the main aisle in the best pews, and had sat there, or in some equivalent dignity, since the time of St. Augustine, if not since the glacial epoch. It was unusual for boys to sit behind a President grandfather, and to read over his head the tablet in memory of a President great-grandfather, who had "pledged his life, his fortune, and his sacred honor" to secure the independence of his country and so forth; but boys naturally supposed, without much reasoning, that other boys had the equivalent of President grandfathers, and that churches would always go on, with the bald-headed leading citizens on the main aisle, and Presidents or their equivalents on the walls. The Irish gardener once said to the child: "You'll be thinkin' you'll be President too!" The casuality of the remark made so strong an impression on his mind that he never forgot it. He could not remember ever to have thought on the subject; to him, that there should be a doubt of his being President was a new idea. What had been would continue to be. He doubted neither about Presidents nor about Churches, and no one suggested at that time a doubt whether a system of society which had lasted since Adam would outlast one Adams more.

The Madam was a little more remote than the President, but more decorative. She stayed much in her own room with the Dutch tiles, looking out on her garden with the box walks, and seemed a fragile creature to a boy who sometimes brought her a note or a message, and took distinct pleasure in looking at her delicate face under what seemed to him very becoming caps. He liked her refined figure; her gentle voice and manner; her vague effect of not belonging there, but to Washington or to Europe, like her furniture, and writing-desk with little glass doors above and little eighteenth-century volumes in old binding, labelled *Peregrine Pickle* or *Tom Jones* or *Hannah More*. Try as she might, the Madam could never be Bostonian, and it was her cross in life, but to the boy it was her charm. Even at that age, he felt drawn to it. The Madam's life had been in truth far from Boston. She was born in London in 1775, daughter of Joshua Johnson, an American merchant, brother of Governor Thomas Johnson of Maryland; and Catherine Nuth, of an English family in London. Driven from England by the Revolutionary War, Joshua Johnson took his family to Nantes, where they remained till the peace. The girl Louisa Catherine was nearly ten years old when brought back to London, and her sense of nationality must have been confused; but the influence of the Johnsons and the services of Joshua obtained for him from President Washington the appointment of Consul in London on the organization of the Government in 1790. In 1794 President Washington appointed John Quincy Adams Minister to The Hague. He was twenty-seven years old when he returned to London, and found the Consul's house a very agreeable haunt. Louisa was then twenty.

At that time, and long afterwards, the Consul's house, far more than the Minister's, was the centre of contact for travelling Americans, either official or other. The Legation was a shifting point, between 1785 and 1815; but the Consulate, far down in the City, near the Tower, was convenient and inviting; so inviting that it proved fatal to young Adams. Louisa was charming, like a Romney portrait, but among her many charms that of being a New England woman was not one. The defect was serious. Her future mother-in-law, Abigail, a famous New England woman whose authority over her turbulent husband, the second President, was hardly so great as that which she exercised over her son, the sixth to be, was troubled by the fear that Louisa might not be made of stuff stern enough, or brought up in conditions severe enough, to suit a New England climate, or to make an efficient wife for her paragon son, and Abigail was right on that point, as on most others where sound judgment was involved; but sound judgment is sometimes a source of weakness rather than of force, and John Quincy already had reason to think that his mother held sound judgments on the subject of daughters-in-law which human nature, since the fall of Eve, made Adams helpless to realize. Being three thousand miles away from his mother, and equally far in love, he married Louisa in London, July 26, 1797, and took her to Berlin to be the head of the United States Legation. During three or four exciting years, the young bride lived in Berlin; whether she was happy or not, whether she was content or not, whether she was socially successful or not, her descendants did not surely know; but in any case she could by no chance have become educated there for a life in Quincy or Boston. In 1801 the overthrow of the Federalist Party [12] drove her and her husband to America, and she became at last a member of the Quincy household, but by that time her children needed all her attention, and she remained there with occasional winters in Boston and Washington, till 1809. Her husband was made Senator in 1803, and in 1809 was appointed Minister to Russia. She went with him to St. Petersburg, taking her baby, Charles Francis, born in 1807; but broken-hearted at having to leave her two older boys behind. The life at St. Petersburg was hardly gay for her; they were far too poor to shine in that extravagant society; but she survived it, though her little girl baby did not, and in the winter of 1814–15, alone with the boy of seven years old, crossed Europe from St. Petersburg to Paris, in her travelling-carriage, passing through the armies, and reaching Paris in the *Cent Jours* [13] after Napoleon's return from Elba. Her husband next went to England as Minister, and she was for two years at the Court of the Regent. In 1817 her

12. overthrow . . . Party: by Thomas Jefferson and his Republican party, at that time the name for the popular democratic party. John Quincy Adams broke with the Federalists to support Jefferson's embargo, forever alienating State Street. 13. *Cent Jours:* the famous Hundred Days of Napoleon's restoration to power, ending with his defeat at Waterloo.

husband came home to be Secretary of State, and she lived for eight years in F Street,[14] doing her work of entertainer for President Monroe's administration. Next she lived four miserable years in the White House. When that chapter was closed in 1829, she had earned the right to be tired and delicate, but she still had fifteen years to serve as wife of a Member of the House, after her husband went back to Congress in 1833. Then it was that the little Henry, her grandson, first remembered her, from 1843 to 1848, sitting in her panelled room, at breakfast, with her heavy silver teapot and sugar-bowl and cream-jug, which still exist somewhere as an heirloom of the modern safety-vault. By that time she was seventy years old or more, and thoroughly weary of being beaten about a stormy world. To the boy she seemed singularly peaceful, a vision of silver gray, presiding over her old President and her Queen Anne mahogany; an exotic, like her Sèvres china; an object of deference to every one, and of great affection to her son Charles; but hardly more Bostonian than she had been fifty years before, on her wedding-day, in the shadow of the Tower of London.

Such a figure was even less fitted than that of her old husband, the President, to impress on a boy's mind, the standards of the coming century. She was Louis Seize, like the furniture. The boy knew nothing of her interior life, which had been, as the venerable Abigail, long since at peace, foresaw, one of severe stress and little pure satisfaction. He never dreamed that from her might come some of those doubts and self-questionings, those hesitations, those rebellions against law and discipline, which marked more than one of her descendants; but he might even then have felt some vague instinctive suspicion that he was to inherit from her the seeds of the primal sin, the fall from grace, the curse of Abel, that he was not of pure New England stock, but half exotic. As a child of Quincy he was not a true Bostonian, but even as a child of Quincy he inherited a quarter taint of Maryland blood. Charles Francis, half Marylander by birth, had hardly seen Boston till he was ten years old, when his parents left him there at school in 1817, and he never forgot the experience. He was to be nearly as old as his mother had been in 1845, before he quite accepted Boston, or Boston quite accepted him.

A boy who began his education in these surroundings, with physical strength inferior to that of his brothers, and with a certain delicacy of mind and bone, ought rightly to have felt at home in the eighteenth century and should, in proper self-respect, have rebelled against the standards of the nineteenth. The atmosphere of his first ten years must have been very like that of his grandfather at the same age, from 1767 till 1776, barring the battle of Bunker Hill, and even as late as 1846, the battle of Bunker Hill remained actual. The tone of Boston society was colonial. The true Bostonian always knelt in self-abasement before the majesty of English standards; far from concealing it as a weakness, he was proud of it as his strength. The eighteenth century ruled society long after 1850. Perhaps the boy began to shake it off rather earlier than most of his mates.

Indeed this prehistoric stage of education ended rather abruptly with his tenth year. One winter morning he was conscious of a certain confusion in the house in Mount Vernon Street, and gathered, from such words as he could catch, that the President, who happened to be then staying there, on his way to Washington, had fallen and hurt himself. Then he heard the word paralysis. After that day he came to associate the word with the figure of his grandfather, in a tall-backed, invalid armchair, on one side of the spare bedroom fireplace, and one of his old friends, Dr. Parkman or P. P. F. Degrand, on the other side, both dozing.

The end of this first, or ancestral and Revolutionary, chapter came on February 21, 1848—and the month of February brought life and death as a family habit—when the eighteenth century, as an actual and living companion, vanished. If the scene on the floor of the House, when the old President fell, struck the still simple-minded American public with a sensation unusually dramatic, its effect on a ten-year-old boy, whose boy-life was fading away with the life of his grandfather, could not be slight. One had to pay for Revolutionary patriots; grandfathers and grandmothers; Presidents; diplomats; Queen Anne mahogany and Louis Seize chairs, as well as for Stuart portraits. Such things warp young life. Americans commonly believed that they ruined it, and perhaps the practical common-sense of the American mind judged right. Many a boy might be ruined by much less than the emotions of the funeral service in the Quincy church, with its surroundings of national respect and family pride. By another dramatic chance it happened that the clergyman of the parish, Dr. Lunt, was an unusual pulpit orator, the ideal of a somewhat austere intellectual type, such as the school of Buckminster and Channing [15] inherited from the old Congre-

14. **F Street:** In 1850 the boy Henry visited his aged grandmother at the F Street house where she stayed on after the death of John Quincy Adams in 1848.

15. **Buckminster and Channing:** See the notes to the *History of*

gational clergy. His extraordinarily refined appearance, his dignity of manner, his deeply cadenced voice, his remarkable English and his fine appreciation, gave to the funeral service a character that left an overwhelming impression on the boy's mind. He was to see many great functions—funerals and festivals—in after-life, till his only thought was to see no more, but he never again witnessed anything nearly so impressive to him as the last services at Quincy over the body of one President and the ashes of another.

The effect of the Quincy service was deepened by the official ceremony which afterwards took place in Faneuil Hall, when the boy was taken to hear his uncle, Edward Everett, deliver a Eulogy. Like all Mr. Everett's orations, it was an admirable piece of oratory, such as only an admirable orator and scholar could create; too good for a ten-year-old boy to appreciate at its value; but already the boy knew that the dead President could not be in it, and had even learned why he would have been out of place there; for knowledge was beginning to come fast. The shadow of the War of 1812 still hung over State Street; the shadow of the Civil War to come had already begun to darken Faneuil Hall.[16] No rhetoric could have reconciled Mr. Everett's audience to his subject. How could he say there, to an assemblage of Bostonians in the heart of mercantile Boston, that the only distinctive mark of all the Adamses, since old Sam Adams's father a hundred and fifty years before, had been their inherited quarrel with State Street, which had again and again broken out into riot, bloodshed, personal feuds, foreign and civil war, wholesale banishments and confiscations, until the history of Florence was hardly more turbulent than that of Boston? How could he whisper the word Hartford Convention[17] before the men who had made it? What would have been said had he suggested the chance of Secession and Civil War?

Thus already, at ten years old, the boy found himself standing face to face with a dilemma that might have puzzled an early Christian. What was he?—where was he going? Even then he felt that something was wrong, but he concluded that it must be Boston. Quincy had always been right, for Quincy represented a moral principle—the principle of resistance to Boston. His Adams ancestors must have been right, since they were always hostile to State Street. If State Street was wrong,

Quincy must be right! Turn the dilemma as he pleased, he still came back on the eighteenth century and the law of Resistance; of Truth; of Duty, and of Freedom. He was a ten-year-old priest and politician. He could under no circumstances have guessed what the next fifty years had in store, and no one could teach him; but sometimes, in his old age, he wondered—and could never decide— whether the most clear and certain knowledge would have helped him. Supposing he had seen a New York stock-list of 1900, and had studied the statistics of railways, telegraphs, coal, and steel— would he have quitted his eighteenth-century, his ancestral prejudices, his abstract ideals, his semi-clerical training, and the rest, in order to perform an expiatory pilgrimage to State Street, and ask for the fatted calf of his grandfather Brooks and a clerkship in the Suffolk Bank?

Sixty years afterwards he was still unable to make up his mind. Each course had its advantages, but the material advantages, looking back, seemed to lie wholly in State Street.

CHAPTER 22
CHICAGO (1893)

DRIFTING in the dead-water of the *fin-de-siècle*[18]—and during this last decade every one talked, and seemed to feel *fin-de-siècle*—where not a breath stirred the idle air of education or fretted the mental torpor of self-content, one lived alone. Adams had long ceased going into society. For years he had not dined out of his own house, and in public his face was as unknown as that of an extinct statesman. He had often noticed that six months' oblivion amounts to newspaper-death, and that resurrection is rare. Nothing is easier, if a man wants it, than rest, profound as the grave.

His friends sometimes took pity on him, and came to share a meal or pass a night on their passage south or northwards, but existence was, on the whole, exceedingly solitary, or seemed so to him. Of the society favorites who made the life of every dinner-table and of the halls of Congress— Tom Reed,[19] Bourke Cockran, Edward Wolcott— he knew not one. Although Calvin Brice was his next neighbor for six years, entertaining lavishly as no one had ever entertained before in Washington, Adams never entered his house. W. C. Whitney[20] rivalled Senator Brice in hospitality, and

the United States.   **16. Faneuil Hall**: in Boston, the "Cradle of Liberty," the Revolutionary meeting place.   **17. Hartford Convention**: secret Federalist meeting, at the end of 1814, protesting the war with England and proposing resistance to the further war measures of the government.

18. *fin-de-siècle*: end of the century decadence.   **19. Tom Reed**: Thomas B. Reed (1839–1902), Speaker of the House (1889–91, 1895–99).   **20. W. C. Whitney**: William C. Whitney (1841–1904), Secretary of the Navy (1885–89), financier and leading reform politician, also noted for his racing stables.

was besides an old acquaintance of the reforming era, but Adams saw him as little as he saw his chief, President Cleveland, or President Harrison, or Secretary Bayard [21] or Blaine [22] or Olney.[23] One has no choice but to go everywhere or nowhere. No one may pick and choose between houses, or accept hospitality without returning it. He loved solitude as little as others did; but he was unfit for social work, and he sank under the surface.

Luckily for such helpless animals as solitary men, the world is not only good-natured but even friendly and generous; it loves to pardon if pardon is not demanded as a right. Adams's social offences were many, and no one was more sensitive to it than himself; but a few houses always remained which he could enter without being asked, and quit without being noticed. One was John Hay's; [24] another was Cabot Lodge's; [25] a third led to an intimacy which had the singular effect of educating him in knowledge of the very class of American politician who had done most to block his intended path in life. Senator Cameron [26] of Pennsylvania had married in 1880 a young niece of Senator John Sherman of Ohio, thus making an alliance of dynastic importance in politics, and in society a reign of sixteen years, during which Mrs. Cameron and Mrs. Lodge led a career, without precedent and without succession, as the dispensers of sunshine over Washington. Both of them had been kind to Adams, and a dozen years of this intimacy had made him one of their habitual household, as he was of Hay's. In a small society, such ties between houses become political and social force. Without intention or consciousness, they fix one's status in the world. Whatever one's preferences in politics might be, one's house was bound to the Republican interest when sandwiched between Senator Cameron, John Hay, and Cabot Lodge, with Theodore Roosevelt equally at home in them all, and Cecil Spring-Rice [27] to

unite them by impartial variety. The relation was daily, and the alliance undisturbed by power or patronage, since Mr. Harrison, in those respects, showed little more taste than Mr. Cleveland for the society and interests of this particular band of followers, whose relations with the White House were sometimes comic, but never intimate.

In February, 1893, Senator Cameron took his family to South Carolina, where he had bought an old plantation at Coffin's Point on St. Helena Island, and Adams, as one of the family, was taken, with the rest, to open the new experience. From there he went on to Havana, and came back to Coffin's Point to linger till near April. In May the Senator took his family to Chicago to see the Exposition,[28] and Adams went with them. Early in June, all sailed for England together, and at last, in the middle of July, all found themselves in Switzerland, at Prangins, Chamounix, and Zermatt. On July 22 they drove across the Furka Pass and went down by rail to Lucerne.

Months of close contact teach character, if character has interest; and to Adams the Cameron type had keen interest, ever since it had shipwrecked his career in the person of President Grant. Perhaps it owed life to Scotch blood; perhaps to the blood of Adam and Eve, the primitive strain of man; perhaps only to the blood of the cottager working against the blood of the townsman; but whatever it was, one liked it for its simplicity. The Pennsylvania mind, as minds go, was not complex; it reasoned little and never talked; but in practical matters it was the steadiest of all American types; perhaps the most efficient; certainly the safest.

Adams had printed as much as this in his books, but had never been able to find a type to describe, the two great historical Pennsylvanians having been, as every one had so often heard, Benjamin Franklin of Boston and Albert Gallatin of Geneva. Of Albert Gallatin, indeed, he had made a voluminous study and an elaborate picture, only to show that he was, if American at all, a New Yorker, with a Calvinistic strain—rather Connecticut than Pennsylvanian. The true Pennsylvanian was a narrower type; as narrow as the kirk; as shy of other people's narrowness as a Yankee; as self-limited as a Puritan farmer. To him, none but Pennsylvanians were white. Chinaman, Negro, Dago, Italian, Englishman, Yankee—all was one in the depths of Pennsylvanian consciousness. The mental machine could run only on what it took for American lines. This was familiar, ever since one's study of President Grant in 1869; but in 1893, as

21. **Bayard:** Thomas F. Bayard (1828–98), Secretary of State (1885–89), ambassador to Great Britain. 22. **Blaine:** James G. Blaine (1830–93), noted Senator, defeated by Cleveland for the Presidency. See notes to *Democracy.* 23. **Olney:** Richard Olney (1835–1917), U.S. Attorney-General (1893–95), Secretary of State (1895–97). 24. **Hay's:** John Milton Hay (1838–1905), private secretary of Lincoln, ambassador to England, Secretary of State (1898–1905), co-author with John Nicolay of *Abraham Lincoln* in 10 vols., Adams's most intimate friend. 25. **Lodge's:** Henry Cabot Lodge (1850–1924), historian, U.S. Senator from Massachusetts (1893–1924), a conservative Republican with whom Adams often differed, but whose friendship he retained to the end. 26. **Cameron:** James Donald Cameron (1833–1918), U.S. Senator (1877–97), Pennsylvania political boss. He married in 1878, not 1880. 27. **Spring-Rice:** Sir Cecil Spring-Rice (1859–1918), British diplomat, served at various periods in Washington and around the world, ambassador to the U.S. (1913–18), one of Adams's "nephews-in-wish."

28. **Exposition:** World's Columbian Exposition at Chicago, May to October, 1893.

then, the type was admirably strong and useful if one wanted only to run on the same lines. Practically the Pennsylvanian forgot his prejudices when he allied his interests. He then became supple in action and large in motive, whatever he thought of his colleagues. When he happened to be right—which was, of course, whenever one agreed with him—he was the strongest American in America. As an ally he was worth all the rest, because he understood his own class, who were always a majority; and knew how to deal with them as no New Englander could. If one wanted work done in Congress, one did wisely to avoid asking a New Englander to do it. A Pennsylvanian not only could do it, but did it willingly, practically, and intelligently.

Never in the range of human possibilities had a Cameron believed in an Adams—or an Adams in a Cameron—but they had, curiously enough, almost always worked together. the Camerons had what the Adamses thought the political vice of reaching their objects without much regard to their methods. The loftiest virtue of the Pennsylvania machine had never been its scrupulous purity or sparkling professions. The machine worked by coarse means on coarse interests; but its practical success had been the most curious subject of study in American history. When one summed up the results of Pennsylvanian influence, one inclined to think that Pennsylvania set up the Government in 1789; saved it in 1861; created the American system; developed its iron and coal power; and invented its great railways. Following up the same line, in his studies of American character, Adams reached the result—to him altogether paradoxical—that Cameron's qualities and defects united in equal share to make him the most useful member of the Senate.

In the interest of studying, at last, a perfect and favorable specimen of this American type which had so persistently suppressed his own, Adams was slow to notice that Cameron strongly influenced him, but he could not see a trace of any influence which he exercised on Cameron. Not an opinion or a view of his on any subject was ever reflected back on him from Cameron's mind; not even an expression or a fact. Yet the difference in age was trifling, and in education slight. On the other hand, Cameron made deep impression on Adams, and in nothing so much as on the great subject of discussion that year—the question of silver.

Adams had taken no interest in the matter, and knew nothing about it, except as a very tedious hobby of his friend Dana Horton; but inevitably, from the moment he was forced to choose sides, he was sure to choose silver. Every political idea and personal prejudice he ever dallied with held him to the silver standard, and made a barrier between him and gold. He knew well enough all that was to be said for the gold standard as economy, but he had never in his life taken politics for a pursuit of economy. One might have a political or an economical policy; one could not have both at the same time. This was heresy in the English school, but it had always been law in the American. Equally he knew all that was to be said on the moral side of the question, and he admitted that his interests were, as Boston maintained, wholly on the side of gold; but, had they been ten times as great as they were, he could not have helped his bankers or croupiers to load the dice and pack the cards to make sure his winning the stakes. At least he was bound to profess disapproval—or thought he was. From early childhood his moral principles had struggled blindly with his interests, but he was certain of one law that ruled all others—masses of men invariably follow interests in deciding morals. Morality is a private and costly luxury. The morality of the silver or gold standards was to be decided by popular vote, and the popular vote would be decided by interests; but on which side lay the larger interest? To him the interest was political; he thought it probably his last chance of standing up for his eighteenth-century principles, strict construction, limited powers, George Washington, John Adams, and the rest. He had, in a half-hearted way, struggled all his life against State Street, banks, capitalism altogether, as he knew it in old England or new England, and he was fated to make his last resistance behind the silver standard.

For him this result was clear, and if he erred, he erred in company with nine men out of ten in Washington, for there was little difference on the merits. Adams was sure to learn backwards, but the case seemed entirely different with Cameron, a typical Pennsylvanian, a practical politician, whom all the reformers, including all the Adamses, had abused for a lifetime for subservience to moneyed interests and political jobbery. He was sure to go with the banks and corporations which had made and sustained him. On the contrary, he stood out obstinately as the leading champion of silver in the East. The reformers, represented by the *Evening Post* and Godkin,[29] whose personal interests lay with the gold standard, at once assumed that Senator Cameron had a personal interest in silver, and denounced his corruption as hotly as

29. **Godkin:** Edwin L. Godkin (1831–1902), founder of the *Nation*, editor of the *Evening Post*, a leader in civil service reform.

though he had been convicted of taking a bribe.

More than silver and gold, the moral standard interested Adams. His own interests were with gold, but he supported silver; the *Evening Post's* and Godkin's interests were with gold, and they frankly said so, yet they avowedly pursued their interests even into politics; Cameron's interests had always been with the corporations, yet he supported silver. Thus morality required that Adams should be condemned for going against his interests; that Godkin was virtuous in following his interests; and that Cameron was a scoundrel whatever he did.

Granting that one of the three was a moral idiot, which was it:—Adams or Godkin or Cameron? Until a Council or a Pope or a Congress or the newspapers or a popular election has decided a question of doubtful morality, individuals are apt to err, especially when putting money into their own pockets; but in democracies, the majority alone gives law. To any one who knew the relative popularity of Cameron and Godkin, the idea of a popular vote between them seemed excessively humorous; yet the popular vote in the end did decide against Cameron, for Godkin.

The Boston moralist and reformer went on, as always, like Dr. Johnson,[30] impatiently stamping his foot and following his interests, or his antipathies; but the true American, slow to grasp new and complicated ideas, groped in the dark to discover where his greater interest lay. As usual, the banks taught him. In the course of fifty years the banks taught one many wise lessons for which an insect had to be grateful whether it liked them or not; but of all the lessons Adams learned from them, none compared in dramatic effect with that of July 22, 1893, when, after talking silver all the morning with Senator Cameron on the top of their travelling-carriage crossing the Furka Pass, they reached Lucerne in the afternoon, where Adams found letters from his brothers requesting his immediate return to Boston because the community was bankrupt and he was probably a beggar.

If he wanted education, he knew no quicker mode of learning a lesson than that of being struck on the head by it; and yet he was himself surprised at his own slowness to understand what had struck him. For several years a sufferer from insomnia, his first thought was of beggary of nerves, and he made ready to face a sleepless night, but although his mind tried to wrestle with the problem how any man could be ruined who had, months before, paid off every dollar of debt he

knew himself to owe, he gave up that insoluble riddle in order to fall back on the larger principle that beggary could be no more for him than it was for others who were more valuable members of society, and, with that, he went to sleep like a good citizen, and the next day started for Quincy where he arrived August 7.

As a starting-point for a new education at fifty-five years old, the shock of finding one's self suspended, for several months, over the edge of bankruptcy, without knowing how one got there, or how to get away, is to be strongly recommended. By slow degrees the situation dawned on him that the banks had lent him, among others, some money—thousands of millions were—as bankruptcy—the same—for which he, among others, was responsible and of which he knew no more than they. The humor of this situation seemed to him so much more pointed than the terror, as to make him laugh at himself with a sincerity he had been long strange to. As far as he could comprehend, he had nothing to lose that he cared about, but banks stood to lose their existence. Money mattered as little to him as to anybody, but money was their life. For the first time he had the banks in his power; he could afford to laugh; and the whole community was in the same position, though few laughed. All sat down on the banks and asked what the banks were going to do about it. To Adams the situation seemed farcical, but the more he saw of it, the less he understood it. He was quite sure that nobody understood it much better. Blindly some very powerful energy was at work, doing something that nobody wanted done. When Adams went to his bank to draw a hundred dollars of his own money on deposit, the cashier refused to let him have more than fifty, and Adams accepted the fifty without complaint because he was himself refusing to let the banks have some hundreds or thousands that belonged to them. Each wanted to help the other, yet both refused to pay their debts, and he could find no answer to the question which was responsible for getting the other into the situation, since lenders and borrowers were the same interest and socially the same person. Evidently the force was one; its operation was mechanical; its effect must be proportional to its power; but no one knew what it meant, and most people dismissed it as an emotion—a panic—that meant nothing.

Men died like flies under the strain, and Boston grew suddenly old, haggard, and thin. Adams alone waxed fat and was happy, for at last he had got hold of his world and could finish his education, interrupted for twenty years. He cared not whether it were worth finishing, if only it amused;

30. **Dr. Johnson:** Samuel Johnson (1709–84), English author, subject of Boswell's *Johnson*, noted for his pragmatic opinions.

but he seemed, for the first time since 1870, to feel that something new and curious was about to happen to the world. Great changes had taken place since 1870 in the forces at work; the old machine ran far behind its duty; somewhere—somehow—it was bound to break down, and if it happened to break precisely over one's head, it gave the better chance for study.

For the first time in several years he saw much of his brother Brooks [31] in Quincy, and was surprised to find him absorbed in the same perplexities. Brooks was then a man of forty-five years old; a strong writer and a vigorous thinker who irritated too many Boston conventions ever to suit the atmosphere; but the two brothers could talk to each other without atmosphere and were used to audiences of one. Brooks had discovered or developed a law of history that civilization followed the exchanges, and having worked it out for the Mediterranean was working it out for the Atlantic. Everything American, as well as most things European and Asiatic, became unstable by this law, seeking new equilibrium and compelled to find it. Loving paradox, Brooks, with the advantages of ten years' study, had swept away much rubbish in the effort to build up a new line of thought for himself, but he found that no paradox compared with that of daily events. The facts were constantly outrunning his thoughts. The instability was greater than he calculated; the speed of acceleration passed bounds. Among other general rules he laid down the paradox that, in the social disequilibrium between capital and labor, the logical outcome was not collectivism, but anarchism; and Henry made note of it for study.

By the time he got back to Washington on September 19, the storm having partly blown over, life had taken on a new face, and one so interesting that he set off to Chicago to study the Exposition again, and stayed there a fortnight absorbed in it. He found matter of study to fill a hundred years, and his education spread over chaos. Indeed, it seemed to him as though, this year, education went mad. The silver question, thorny as it was, fell into relations as simple as words of one syllable, compared with the problems of credit and exchange that came to complicate it; and when one sought rest at Chicago, educational game started like rabbits from every building, and ran out of sight among thousands of its kind before one could mark its burrow. The Exposition itself defied philosophy. One might find fault till the last gate closed, one could still explain nothing that needed explanation. As a scenic display, Paris had never approached it, but the inconceivable scenic display consisted in its being there at all—more surprising, as it was, than anything else on the continent, Niagara Falls, the Yellowstone Geysers, and the whole railway system thrown in, since these were all natural products in their place; while, since Noah's Ark, no such Babel of loose and ill-joined, such vague and ill-defined and unrelated thoughts and half-thoughts and experimental outcries as the Exposition, had ever ruffled the surface of the Lakes.

The first astonishment became greater every day. That the Exposition should be a natural growth and product of the Northwest offered a step in evolution to startle Darwin; but that it should be anything else seemed an idea more startling still; and even granting it were not—admitting it to be a sort of industrial, speculative growth and product of the Beaux Arts [32] artistically induced to pass the summer on the shore of Lake Michigan—could it be made to seem at home there? Was the American made to seem at home in it? Honestly, he had the air of enjoying it as though it were all his own; he felt it was good; he was proud of it; for the most part, he acted as though he had passed his life in landscape gardening and architectural decoration. If he had not done it himself, he had known how to get it done to suit him, as he knew how to get his wives and daughters dressed at Worth's or Paquin's. Perhaps he could not do it again; the next time he would want to do it himself and would show his own faults; but for the moment he seemed to have leaped directly from Corinth and Syracuse and Venice, over the heads of London and New York, to impose classical standards on plastic Chicago. Critics had no trouble in criticising the classicism, but all trading cities had always shown traders' taste, and, to the stern purist of religious faith, no art was thinner than Venetian Gothic. All traders' taste smelt of bric-à-brac; Chicago tried at least to give her taste a look of unity.

One sat down to ponder on the steps beneath Richard Hunt's [33] dome almost as deeply as on the steps of *Ara Cœli,*[34] and much to the same purpose.

---

31. **Brooks:** Brooks Adams (1848–1927), noted for his *Law of Civilization and Decay* (1895), a destructive critique of finance capitalism; he also edited an important collection of Henry Adams's speculative writings on history, *The Degradation of the Democratic Dogma* (1919), to which he contributed a long analysis of Henry's character, "The Heritage of Henry Adams."

32. **Beaux Arts:** chief art academy of Paris, known for its conservatism.   33. **Hunt's:** Richard Morris Hunt (1827–95), American architect, designer of the great Administration Building of the Chicago Fair of 1893.   34. *Ara Cœli:* Church of St. Mary of the Altar of Heaven in Rome, one of the most ancient in the city, situated on a hill above the Forum. It was a favorite place of meditation for Adams whenever he visited Rome, due to its association with the English historian Gibbon.

Here was a breach of continuity—a rupture in historical sequence! Was it real, or only apparent? One's personal universe hung on the answer, for, if the rupture was real and the new American world could take this sharp and conscious twist towards ideals, one's personal friends would come in, at last, as winners in the great American chariot-race for fame. If the people of the Northwest actually knew what was good when they saw it, they would some day talk about Hunt and Richardson,[35] La Farge[36] and St. Gaudens,[37] Burnham[38] and McKim,[39] and Stanford White[40] when their politicians and millionaires were otherwise forgotten. The artists and architects who had done the work offered little encouragement to hope it; they talked freely enough, but not in terms that one cared to quote; and to them the Northwest refused to look artistic. They talked as though they worked only for themselves; as though art, to the Western people, was a stage decoration; a diamond shirt-stud; a paper collar; but possibly the architects of Pæstum and Girgenti had talked in the same way, and the Greek had said the same thing of Semitic Carthage two thousand years ago.

Jostled by these hopes and doubts, one turned to the exhibits for help, and found it. The industrial schools tried to teach so much and so quickly that the instruction ran to waste. Some millions of other people felt the same helplessness, but few of them were seeking education, and to them helplessness seemed natural and normal, for they had grown up in the habit of thinking a steam-engine or a dynamo as natural as the sun, and expected to understand one as little as the other. For the historian alone the Exposition made a serious effort. Historical exhibits were common, but they never went far enough; none were thoroughly worked out. One of the best was that of the Cunard steamers, but still a student hungry for results found himself obliged to waste a pencil and several sheets of paper trying to calculate exactly when, according to the given increase of power, tonnage, and speed, the growth of the ocean steamer

would reach its limits. His figures brought him, he thought, to the year 1927; another generation to spare before force, space, and time should meet. The ocean steamer ran the surest line of triangulation into the future, beause it was the nearest of man's products to a unity; railroads taught less because they seemed already finished except for mere increase in number; explosives taught most, but needed a tribe of chemists, physicists, and mathematicians to explain; the dynamo taught least because it had barely reached infancy, and, if its progress was to be constant at the rate of the last ten years, it would result in infinite costly energy within a generation. One lingered long among the dynamos, for they were new, and they gave to history a new phase. Men of science could never understand the ignorance and naïveté of the historian, who, when he came suddenly on a new power, asked naturally what it was; did it pull or did it push? Was it a screw or thrust? Did it flow or vibrate? Was it a wire or a mathematical line? And a score of such questions to which he expected answers and was astonished to get none.

Education ran riot at Chicago, at least for retarded minds which had never faced in concrete form so many matters of which they were ignorant. Men who knew nothing whatever—who had never run a steam-engine, the simplest of forces—who had never put their hands on a lever—had never touched an electric battery—never talked through a telephone, and had not the shadow of a notion what amount of force was meant by a *watt* or an *ampère* or an *erg,* or any other term of measurement introduced within a hundred years —had no choice but to sit down on the steps and brood as they had never brooded on the benches of Harvard College, either as student or professor, aghast at what they had said and done in all these years, and still more ashamed of the childlike ignorance and babbling futility of the society that let them say and do it. The historical mind can think only in historical processes, and probably this was the first time since historians existed, that any of them had sat down helpless before a mechanical sequence. Before a metaphysical or a theological or a political sequence, most historians had felt helpless, but the single clue to which they had hitherto trusted was the unity of natural force.

Did he himself quite know what he meant? Certainly not! If he had known enough to state his problem, his education would have been complete at once. Chicago asked in 1893 for the first time the question whether the American people knew where they were driving. Adams answered, for one, that he did not know, but would try to find out. On reflecting sufficiently deeply, under the

35. **Richardson:** Henry Hobson Richardson (1838–86), American architect, famous for his Romanesque structures; a college mate of Adams, he designed Adams's house on Lafayette Square. 36. **La Farge:** John La Farge (1835–1910), artist and worker in stained glass, Adams's mentor in art. 37. **St. Gaudens:** Augustus Saint-Gaudens (1848–1907), sculptor; designed and executed the Adams memorial statue in Rock Creek Cemetery in Washington, beneath which are buried Henry Adams and his wife. 38. **Burnham:** Daniel H. Burnham (1846–1912), a chief architect of the Chicago World's Fair and a leading city planner. 39. **McKim:** Charles F. McKim (1847–1909), one of the architects of the Boston Public Library. 40. **White:** Stanford White (1853–1906), architect, designed the setting of the Adams memorial.

shadow of Richard Hunt's architecture, he decided that the American people probably knew no more than he did; but that they might still be driving or drifting unconsciously to some point in thought, as their solar system was said to be drifting towards some point in space; and that, possibly, if relations enough could be observed, this point might be fixed. Chicago was the first expression of American thought as a unity; one must start there.

Washington was the second. When he got back there, he fell headlong into the extra session of Congress called to repeal the Silver Act. The silver minority made an obstinate attempt to prevent it, and most of the majority had little heart in the creation of a single gold standard. The banks alone, and the dealers in exchange, insisted upon it; the political parties divided according to capitalistic geographical lines, Senator Cameron offering almost the only exception; but they mixed with unusual good-temper, and made liberal allowance for each others' actions and motives. The struggle was rather less irritable than such struggles generally were, and it ended like a comedy. On the evening of the final vote, Senator Cameron came back from the Capitol with Senator Brice, Senator Jones, Senator Lodge, and Moreton Frewen,[41] all in the gayest of humors as though they were rid of a heavy responsibility. Adams, too, in a bystander's spirit, felt light in mind. He had stood up for his eighteenth century, his Constitution of 1789, his George Washington, his Harvard College, his Quincy, and his Plymouth Pilgrims, as long as any one would stand up with him. He had said it was hopeless twenty years before, but he had kept on, in the same old attitude, by habit and taste, until he found himself altogether alone. He had hugged his antiquated dislike of bankers and capitalistic society until he had become little better than a crank. He had known for years that he must accept the régime, but he had known a great many other disagreeable certainties—like age, senility, and death—against which one made what little resistance one could. The matter was settled at last by the people. For a hundred years, between 1793 and 1893, the American people had hesitated, vacillated, swayed forward and back, between two forces, one simply industrial, the other capitalistic, centralizing, and mechanical. In 1893, the issue came on the single gold standard, and the majority at last declared itself, once for all, in favor of the capitalistic system with all its necessary machinery. All one's friends, all one's best citizens, reformers, churches, colleges, educated classes, had joined the banks to force submission to capitalism; a submission long foreseen by the mere law of mass. Of all forms of society or government, this was the one he liked least, but his likes or dislikes were as antiquated as the rebel doctrine of State rights. A capitalistic system had been adopted, and if it were to be run at all, it must be run by capital and by capitalistic methods; for nothing could surpass the nonsensity of trying to run so complex and so concentrated a machine by Southern and Western farmers in grotesque alliance with city day-laborers, as had been tried in 1800 and 1828, and had failed even under simple conditions.

There, education in domestic politics stopped. The rest was question of gear; of running machinery; of economy; and involved no disputed principle. Once admitted that the machine must be efficient, society might dispute in what social interest it should be run, but in any case it must work concentration. Such great revolutions commonly leave some bitterness behind, but nothing in politics ever surprised Henry Adams more than the ease with which he and his silver friends slipped across the chasm, and alighted on the single gold standard and the capitalistic system with its methods; the protective tariff; the corporations and trusts; the trades-unions and socialistic paternalism which necessarily made their complement; the whole mechanical consolidation of force, which ruthlessly stamped out the life of the class into which Adams was born, but created monopolies capable of controlling the new energies that America adored.

Society rested, after sweeping into the ash-heap these cinders of a misdirected education. After this vigorous impulse, nothing remained for a historian but to ask—how long and how far!

CHAPTER 25

THE DYNAMO AND THE VIRGIN (1900)

UNTIL the Great Exposition of 1900[42] closed its doors in November, Adams haunted it, aching to absorb knowledge, and helpless to find it. He would have liked to know how much of it could have been grasped by the best-informed man in the world. While he was thus meditating chaos, Langley came by, and showed it to him. At Langley's [43] behest, the Exhibition dropped its superflu-

---

41. **Frewen:** Morton Frewen (1853–1924), one of Adams's influential English friends.

42. **Great Exposition of 1900:** the Paris Exposition. Adams took rooms as close as possible to the Trocadero exhibition palace.
43. **Langley's:** Samuel Pierpont Langley (1834–1906), astronomer and pioneer in aerodynamical experiments, successfully flew

ous rags and stripped itself to the skin, for Langley knew what to study, and why, and how; while Adams might as well have stood outside in the night, staring at the Milky Way. Yet Langley said nothing new, and taught nothing that one might not have learned from Lord Bacon, three hundred years before; but though one should have known the *Advancement of Science* [44] as well as one knew the *Comedy of Errors,* the literary knowledge counted for nothing until some teacher should show how to apply it. Bacon took a vast deal of trouble in teaching King James I and his subjects, American or other, towards the year 1620, that true science was the development or economy of forces; yet an elderly American in 1900 knew neither the formula nor the forces; or even so much as to say to himself that his historical business in the Exposition concerned only the economies or developments of force since 1893, when he began the study at Chicago.

Nothing in education is so astonishing as the amount of ignorance it accumulates in the form of inert facts. Adams had looked at most of the accumulations of art in the storehouses called Art Museums; yet he did not know how to look at the art exhibits of 1900. He had studied Karl Marx and his doctrines of history with profound attention, yet he could not apply them at Paris. Langley, with the ease of a great master of experiment, threw out of the field every exhibit that did not reveal a new application of force, and naturally threw out, to begin with, almost the whole art exhibit. Equally, he ignored almost the whole industrial exhibit. He led his pupil directly to the forces. His chief interest was in new motors to make his airship feasible, and he taught Adams the astonishing complexities of the new Daimler [45] motor, and of the automobile, which, since 1893, had become a nightmare at a hundred kilometres an hour, almost as destructive as the electric tram which was only ten years older; and threatening to become as terrible as the locomotive steam-engine itself, which was almost exactly Adams's own age.

Then he showed his scholar the great hall of dynamos, and explained how little he knew about electricity or force of any kind, even of his own special sun, which spouted heat in inconceivable volume, but which, as far as he knew, might spout

less or more, at any time, for all the certainty he felt in it. To him, the dynamo itself was but an ingenious channel for conveying somewhere the heat latent in a few tons of poor coal hidden in a dirty engine-house carefully kept out of sight; but to Adams the dynamo became a symbol of infinity. As he grew accustomed to the great gallery of machines, he began to feel the forty-foot dynamos as a moral force, much as the early Christians felt the Cross. The planet itself seemed less impressive, in its old-fashioned, deliberate, annual or daily revolution, than this huge wheel, revolving within arm's-length at some vertiginous speed, and barely murmuring—scarcely humming an audible warning to stand a hair's-breadth further for respect of power—while it would not wake the baby lying close against its frame. Before the end, one began to pray to it; inherited instinct taught the natural expression of man before silent and infinite force. Among the thousand symbols of ultimate energy, the dynamo was not so human as some, but it was the most expressive.

Yet the dynamo, next to the steam-engine, was the most familiar of exhibits. For Adams's objects its value lay chiefly in its occult mechanism. Between the dynamo in the gallery of machines and the engine-house outside, the break of continuity amounted to abysmal fracture for a historian's objects. No more relation could he discover between the steam and the electric current than between the Cross and the cathedral. The forces were interchangeable if not reversible, but he could see only an absolute *fiat* in electricity as in faith. Langley could not help him. Indeed, Langley seemed to be worried by the same trouble, for he constantly repeated that the new forces were anarchical, and specially that he was not responsible for the new rays, that were little short of parricidal in their wicked spirit towards science. His own rays, with which he had doubled the solar spectrum, were altogether harmless and beneficent; but Radium [46] denied its God—or, what was to Langley the same thing, denied the truths of his Science. The force was wholly new.

A historian who asked only to learn enough to be as futile as Langley or Kelvin,[47] made rapid progress under this teaching, and mixed himself

the first model airplane in 1896, inventor of the bolometer for measuring solar heat.   **44.** *Advancement of Science:* Adams probably meant the *Advancement of Learning,* published in English in 1605. The *Novum Organon* was published in Latin in 1620.   **45. Daimler:** Gottlieb Daimler (1834–1900), whose automotive inventions resulted in a successful gasoline engine first built in 1884.

46. Radium: discovered in 1898 by Mme. Curie. Antoine Becquerel (1852–1908) discovered the radioactivity of uranium about the same time, establishing the disintegrating character of the element whose puzzling properties aroused the scientific world.   **47. Kelvin:** William Thompson, Lord Kelvin (1824–1907), leader in thermodynamics, one of the first to formulate the principle of the dissipation of energy or entropy, expressed in the second law of thermodynamics. Adams adopted the principle for his later speculations in *A Letter to American Teachers of History,* privately printed and distributed in 1910.

up in the tangle of ideas until he achieved a sort of Paradise of ignorance vastly consoling to his fatigued senses. He wrapped himself in vibrations and rays which were new, and he would have hugged Marconi and Branly [48] had he met them, as he hugged the dynamo; while he lost his arithmetic in trying to figure out the equation between the discoveries and the economies of force. The economies, like the discoveries, were absolute, supersensual, occult; incapable of expression in horse-power. What mathematical equivalent could he suggest as the value of a Branly coherer? Frozen air, or the electric furnace, had some scale of measurement, no doubt, if somebody could invent a thermometer adequate to the purpose; but X-rays had played no part whatever in man's conciousness, and the atom itself had figured only as a fiction of thought. In these seven years man had translated himself into a new universe which had no common scale of measurement with the old. He had entered a supersensual world, in which he could measure nothing except by chance collisions of movements imperceptible to his senses, perhaps even imperceptible to his instruments, but perceptible to each other, and so to some known ray at the end of the scale. Langley seemed prepared for anything, even for an indeterminable number of universes interfused—physics stark mad in metaphysics.

Historians undertake to arrange sequences,—called stories, or histories—assuming in silence a relation of cause and effect. These assumptions, hidden in the depths of dusty libraries, have been astounding, but commonly unconscious and childlike; so much so, that if any captious critic were to drag them to light, historians would probably reply, with one voice, that they had never supposed themselves required to know what they were talking about. Adams, for one, had toiled in vain to find out what he meant. He had even published a dozen volumes of American history for no other purpose than to satisfy himself whether, by the severest process of stating, with the least possible comment, such facts as seemed sure, in such order as seemed rigorously consequent, he could fix for a familiar moment a necessary sequence of human movement. The result had satisfied him as little as at Harvard College. Where he saw sequence, other men saw something quite different, and no one saw the same unit of measure. He cared little about his experiments and less about his statesmen, who seemed to him quite as ignorant as himself and, as a rule, no more honest; but

he insisted on a relation of sequence, and if he could not reach it by one method, he would try as many methods as science knew. Satisfied that the sequence of men led to nothing and that the sequence of their society could lead no further, while the mere sequence of time was artificial, and the sequence of thought was chaos, he turned at last to the sequence of force; and thus it happened that, after ten years' pursuit, he found himself lying in the Gallery of Machines at the Great Exposition of 1900, his historical neck broken by the sudden irruption of forces totally new.

Since no one else showed much concern, an elderly person without other cares had no need to betray alarm. The year 1900 was not the first to upset schoolmasters. Copernicus and Galileo had broken many professorial necks about 1600; Columbus had stood the world on its head towards 1500; but the nearest approach to the revolution of 1900 was that of 310, when Constantine set up the Cross. [49] The rays that Langley disowned, as well as those which he fathered, were occult, supersensual, irrational; they were a revelation of mysterious energy like that of the Cross; they were what, in terms of mediæval science, were called immediate modes of the divine substance.

The historian was thus reduced to his last resources. Clearly if he was bound to reduce all these forces to a common value, this common value could have no measure but that of their attraction on his own mind. He must treat them as they had been felt; as convertible, reversible, interchangeable attractions on thought. He made up his mind to venture it; he would risk translating rays into faith. Such a reversible process would vastly amuse a chemist, but the chemist could not deny that he, or some of his fellow physicists, could feel the force of both. When Adams was a boy in Boston, the best chemist in the place had probably never heard of Venus except by way of scandal, or of the Virgin except as idolatry; neither had he heard of dynamos or automobiles or radium; yet his mind was ready to feel the force of all, though the rays were unborn and the women were dead.

Here opened another totally new education, which promised to be by far the most hazardous of all. The knife-edge along which he must crawl, like Sir Lancelot [50] in the twelfth century, divided two kingdoms of force which had nothing in common but attraction. They were as different as a magnet

48. **Branly:** Édouard Branly (1846–1940), French scientist whose invention of the Branly coherer for detecting radio waves made Marconi's wireless telegraphy possible.

49. **Constantine . . . Cross:** Constantine I (280?–337) at the Battle of the Milvian Bridge in 312, is reported to have seen the cross in the sky heralding victory.   50. **Lancelot:** as told in the medieval romance of Chrétien de Troyes, one of his exploits in rescuing Guinevere from a castle.

is from gravitation, supposing one knew what a magnet was, or gravitation, or love. The force of the Virgin was still felt at Lourdes, and seemed to be as potent as X-rays; but in America neither Venus nor Virgin ever had value as force—at most as sentiment. No American had ever been truly afraid of either.

This problem in dynamics gravely perplexed an American historian. The Woman had once been supreme; in France she still seemed potent, not merely as a sentiment, but as a force. Why was she unknown in America? For evidently America was ashamed of her, and she was ashamed of herself, otherwise they would not have strewn fig-leaves so profusely all over her. When she was a true force, she was ignorant of fig-leaves, but the monthly-magazine-made American female had not a feature that would have been recognized by Adam. The trait was notorious, and often humorous, but any one brought up among Puritans knew that sex was sin. In any previous age, sex was strength. Neither art nor beauty was needed. Every one, even among Puritans, knew that neither Diana of the Ephesians [51] nor any of the Oriental goddesses was worshipped for her beauty. She was goddess because of her force; she was the animated dynamo; she was reproduction—the greatest and most mysterious of all energies; all she needed was to be fecund. Singularly enough, not one of Adams's many schools of education had ever drawn his attention to the opening lines of Lucretius, though they were perhaps the finest in all Latin literature, where the poet invoked Venus exactly as Dante invoked the Virgin:—

"Quae quoniam rerum naturam *sola* gubernas." [52]

The Venus of Epicurean philosophy survived in the Virgin of the Schools:—

"Donna, sei tanto grande, e tanto vali,
    Che qual vuol grazia, e a te non ricorre,
    Sua disianza vuol volar senz' ali." [53]

All this was to American thought as though it had never existed. The true American knew something of the facts, but nothing of the feelings; he read the letter, but he never felt the law. Before this historical chasm, a mind like that of Adams felt itself helpless; he turned from the Virgin to the Dynamo as though he were a Branly coherer. On one side, at the Louvre and at Chartres, as he knew by the record of work actually done and still before his eyes, was the highest energy ever known to man, the creator of four-fifths of his noblest art, exercising vastly more attraction over the human mind than all the steam-engines and dynamos ever dreamed of; and yet this energy was unknown to the American mind. An American Virgin would never dare command; an American Venus would never dare exist.

The question, which to any plain American of the nineteenth century seemed as remote as it did to Adams, drew him almost violently to study, once it was posed; and on this point Langleys were as useless as though they were Herbert Spencers [54] or dynamos. The idea survived only as art. There one turned as naturally as though the artist were himself a woman. Adams began to ponder, asking himself whether he knew of any American artist who had ever insisted on the power of sex, as every classic had always done; but he could think only of Walt Whitman; Bret Harte, as far as the magazines would let him venture; and one or two painters, for the flesh-tones. All the rest had used sex for sentiment, never for force; to them, Eve was a tender flower, and Herodias an unfeminine horror. American art, like the American language and American education, was as far as possible sexless. Society regarded this victory over sex as its greatest triumph, and the historian readily admitted it, since the moral issue, for the moment, did not concern one who was studying the relations of unmoral force. He cared nothing for the sex of the dynamo until he could measure its energy.

Vaguely seeking a clue, he wandered through the art exhibit, and, in his stroll, stopped almost every day before St. Gaudens's General Sherman,[55] which had been given the central post of honor. St. Gaudens himself was in Paris, putting on the work his usual interminable last touches, and listening to the usual contradictory suggestions of brother sculptors. Of all the American artists who gave to American art whatever life it breathed in the seventies, St. Gaudens was perhaps the most sympathetic, but certainly the most inarticulate. General Grant or Don Cameron had scarcely less instinct of rhetoric than he. All the others—the Hunts, Richardson, John La Farge, Stanford White—were exuberant; only St. Gaudens could never discuss or dilate on an emotion, or suggest artistic arguments for giving to his

51. Diana of the Ephesians: Acts 19:24–41.   **52.** Quae . . . gubernas: From *De Rerum Natura*, "Since [thou Venus] alone govern the things of nature."   **53.** "Donna . . . ali": From Dante, *Divine Comedy*, Paradiso, XXXII, 13–16, "Lady, so great art thou, of such avail, That one who wishes grace and seeks not thee, Lo, his desire essays flight without wings" (Thomas G. Bergin, trans.).

54. Spencers: Herbert Spencer (1820–1903), British philosopher whose materialist theories of dynamic evolution greatly influenced Adams's early thought.   **55.** General Sherman: now in Central Park, New York.

work the forms that he felt. He never laid down the law, or affected the despot, or became brutalized like Whistler by the brutalities of his world. He required no incense; he was no egoist; his simplicity of thought was excessive; he could not imitate, or give any form but his own to the creations of his hand. No one felt more strongly than he the strength of other men, but the idea that they could affect him never stirred an image in his mind.

This summer his health was poor and his spirits were low. For such a temper, Adams was not the best companion, since his own gaiety was not *folle;* [56] but he risked going now and then to the studio on Mont Parnasse to draw him out for a stroll in the Bois de Boulogne, or dinner as pleased his moods, and in return St. Gaudens sometimes let Adams go about in his company.

Once St. Gaudens took him down to Amiens, with a party of Frenchmen, to see the cathedral. Not until they found themselves actually studying the sculpture of the western portal, did it dawn on Adams's mind that, for his purposes, St. Gaudens on that spot had more interest to him than the cathedral itself. Great men before great monuments express great truths, provided they are not taken too solemnly. Adams never tired of quoting the supreme phrase of his idol Gibbon, before the Gothic cathedrals: "I darted a contemptuous look on the stately monuments of superstition." Even in the footnotes of his history, Gibbon had never inserted a bit of humor more human than this, and one would have paid largely for a photograph of the fat little historian, on the background of Notre Dame of Amiens, trying to persuade his readers—perhaps himself—that he was darting a contemptuous look on the stately monument, for which he felt in fact the respect which every man of his vast study and active mind always feels before objects worthy of it; but besides the humor, one felt also the relation. Gibbon ignored the Virgin, because in 1789 religious monuments were out of fashion. In 1900 his remark sounded fresh and simple as the green fields to ears that had heard a hundred years of other remarks, mostly no more fresh and certainly less simple. Without malice, one might find it more instructive than a whole lecture of Ruskin. One sees what one brings, and at that moment Gibbon brought the French Revolution. Ruskin brought reaction against the Revolution. St. Gaudens had passed beyond all. He liked the stately monuments much more than he liked Gibbon or Ruskin; he loved their dignity; their unity; their scale; their lines; their lights and shadows; their decorative

sculpture; but he was even less conscious than they of the force that created it all—the Virgin, the Woman—by whose genius "the stately monuments of superstition" were built, through which she was expressed. He would have seen more meaning in Isis [57] with the cow's horns, at Edfoo, who expressed the same thought. The art remained, but the energy was lost even upon the artist.

Yet in mind and person St. Gaudens was a survival of the 1500; he bore the stamp of the Renaissance, and should have carried an image of the Virgin round his neck, or stuck in his hat, like Louis XI. In mere time he was a lost soul that had strayed by chance into the twentieth century, and forgotten where it came from. He writhed and cursed at his ignorance, much as Adams did at his own, but in the opposite sense. St. Gaudens was a child of Benvenuto Cellini, smothered in an American cradle. Adams was a quintessence of Boston, devoured by curiosity to think like Benvenuto. St. Gaudens's art was starved from birth, and Adams's instinct was blighted from babyhood. Each had but half of a nature, and when they came together before the Virgin of Amiens they ought both to have felt in her the force that made them one; but it was not so. To Adams she became more than ever a channel of force; to St. Gaudens she remained as before a channel of taste.

For a symbol of power, St. Gaudens instinctively preferred the horse, as was plain in his horse and Victory of the Sherman monument. Doubtless Sherman also felt it so. The attitude was so American that, for at least forty years, Adams had never realized that any other could be in sound taste. How many years had he taken to admit a notion of what Michael Angelo and Rubens were driving at? He could not say; but he knew that only since 1895 had he begun to feel the Virgin or Venus as force, and not everywhere even so. At Chartres—perhaps at Lourdes—possibly at Cnidos [58] if one could still find there the divinely naked Aphrodite of Praxiteles—but otherwise one must look for force to the goddesses of Indian mythology. The idea died out long ago in the German and English stock. St. Gaudens at Amiens was hardly less sensitive to the force of the female energy than Matthew Arnold at the Grande Chartreuse.[59] Neither of them felt goddesses as power—only as reflected emotion, hu-

---

56. *folle:* wild.

57. **Isis:** Egyptian mother-goddess of fertility.   58. **Cnidos:** ancient shrine of Aphrodite in Asia Minor.   59. **Grande Chartreuse:** ancient Carthusian monastery in the mountains near Grenoble, France; inspiration for Arnold's poem "Stanzas from

man expression, beauty, purity, taste, scarcely even as sympathy. They felt a railway train as power; yet they, and all other artists, constantly complained that the power embodied in a railway train could never be embodied in art. All the steam in the world could not, like the Virgin, build Chartres.

Yet in mechanics, whatever the mechanicians might think, both energies acted as interchangeable forces on man, and by action on man all known force may be measured. Indeed, few men of science measured force in any other way. After once admitting that a straight line was the shortest distance between two points, no serious mathematician cared to deny anything that suited his convenience, and rejected no symbol, unproved or unproveable, that helped him to accomplish work. The symbol was force, as a compass-needle or a triangle was force, as the mechanist might prove by losing it, and nothing could be gained by ignoring their value. Symbol or energy, the Virgin had acted as the greatest force the Western world ever felt, and had drawn man's activities to herself more strongly than any other power, natural or supernatural, had ever done; the historian's business was to follow the track of the energy; to find where it came from and where it went to; its complex source and shifting channels; its values, equivalents, conversions. It could scarcely be more complex than radium; it could hardly be deflected, diverted, polarized, absorbed more perplexingly than other radiant matter. Adams knew nothing about any of them, but as a mathematical problem of influence on human progress, though all were occult, all reacted on his mind, and he rather inclined to think the Virgin easiest to handle.

The pursuit turned out to be long and tortuous, leading at last into the vast forests of scholastic science. From Zeno to Descartes, hand in hand with Thomas Aquinas, Montaigne, and Pascal, one stumbled as stupidly as though one were still a German student of 1860. Only with the instinct of despair could one force one's self into this old thicket of ignorance after having been repulsed at a score of entrances more promising and more popular. Thus far, no path had led anywhere, unless perhaps to an exceedingly modest living. Forty-five years of study had proved to be quite futile for the pursuit of power; one controlled no more force in 1900 than in 1850, although the amount of force controlled by society had enormously increased. The secret of education still hid itself somewhere behind ignorance, and one fumbled over it as feebly as ever. In such labyrinths, the staff is a force almost more necessary than the legs; the pen becomes a sort of blind-man's dog, to keep him from falling into the gutters. The pen works for itself, and acts like a hand, modelling the plastic material over and over again to the form that suits it best. The form is never arbitrary, but is a sort of growth like crystallization, as any artist knows too well; for often the pencil or pen runs into side-paths and shapelessness, loses its relations, stops or is bogged. Then it has to return on its trail, and recover, if it can, its line of force. The result of a year's work depends more on what is struck out than on what is left in; on the sequence of the main lines of thought, than on their play or variety. Compelled once more to lean heavily on this support, Adams covered more thousands of pages with figures as formal as though they were algebra, laboriously striking out, altering, burning, experimenting, until the year had expired, the Exposition had long been closed, and winter drawing to its end, before he sailed from Cherbourg, on January 19, 1901, for home.

CHAPTER 33

A DYNAMIC THEORY OF HISTORY (1904)

A DYNAMIC theory, like most theories, begins by begging the question: it defines Progress as the development and economy of Forces. Further, it defines force as anything that does, or helps to do work. Man is a force; so is the sun; so is a mathematical point, though without dimensions or known existence.

Man commonly begs the question again by taking for granted that he captures the forces. A dynamic theory, assigning attractive force to opposing bodies in proportion to the law of mass, takes for granted that the forces of nature capture man. The sum of force attracts; the feeble atom or molecule called man is attracted; he suffers education or growth; he is the sum of the forces that attract him; his body and his thought are alike their product; the movement of the forces controls the progress of his mind, since he can know nothing but the motions which impinge on his senses, whose sum makes education.

For convenience as an image, the theory may liken man to a spider in its web, watching for chance prey. Forces of nature dance like flies before the net, and the spider pounces on them when it can; but it makes many fatal mistakes, though its theory of force is sound. The spider-mind acquires a faculty of memory, and, with it, a singular skill of analysis and synthesis, taking apart and

the Grande Chartreuse," one of Adams's favorites, telling as it does of the "Wandering between two worlds, one dead / The other powerless to be born."

366] *Henry Adams*

putting together in different relations the meshes of its trap. Man had in the beginning no power of analysis or synthesis approaching that of the spider, or even of the honey-bee; but he had acute sensibility to the higher forces. Fire taught him secrets that no other animal could learn; running water probably taught him even more, especially in his first lessons of mechanics; the animals helped to educate him, trusting themselves into his hands merely for the sake of their food, and carrying his burdens or supplying his clothing; the grasses and grains were academies of study. With little or no effort on his part, all these forces formed his thought, induced his action, and even shaped his figure.

Long before history began, his education was complete, for the record could not have been started until he had been taught to record. The universe that had formed him took shape in his mind as a reflection of his own unity, containing all forces except himself. Either separately, or in groups, or as a whole, these forces never ceased to act on him, enlarging his mind as they enlarged the surface foliage of a vegetable, and the mind needed only to respond, as the forests did, to these attractions. Susceptibility to the highest forces is the highest genius; selection between them is the highest science; their mass is the highest educator. Man always made, and still makes, grotesque blunders in selecting and measuring forces, taken at random from the heap, but he never made a mistake in the value he set on the whole, which he symbolized as unity and worshipped as God. To this day, his attitude towards it has never changed, though science can no longer give to force a name.

Man's function as a force of nature was to assimilate other forces as he assimilated food. He called it the love of power. He felt his own feebleness, and he sought for an ass or a camel, a bow or a sling, to widen his range of power, as he sought a fetish or a planet in the world beyond. He cared little to know its immediate use, he could afford to throw nothing away which he could conceive to have possible value in this or any other existence. He waited for the object to teach him its use, or want of use, and the process was slow. He may have gone on for hundreds of thousands of years, waiting for Nature to tell him her secrets; and, to his rivals among the monkeys, Nature has taught no more than at their start; but certain lines of force were capable of acting on individual apes, and mechanically selecting types of race or sources of variation. The individual that responded or reacted to lines of new force then was possibly the same individual that reacts on it now, and his conception of the unity seems never to have changed in spite of the increasing diversity of forces; but the theory of variation is an affair of other science than history, and matters nothing to dynamics. The individual or the race would be educated on the same lines of illusion, which, according to Arthur Balfour,[60] had not essentially varied down to the year 1900.

To the highest attractive energy, man gave the name of divine, and for its control he invented the science called Religion, a word which meant, and still means, cultivation of occult force whether in detail or mass. Unable to define Force as a unity, man symbolized it and pursued it, both in himself, and in the infinite, as philosophy and theology; the mind is itself the subtlest of all known forces, and its self-introspection necessarily created a science which had the singular value of lifting his education, at the start, to the finest, subtlest, and broadest training both in analysis and synthesis, so that, if language is a test, he must have reached his highest powers early in his history; while the mere motive remained as simple an appetite for power as the tribal greed which led him to trap an elephant. Hunger, whether for food or for the infinite, sets in motion multiplicity and infinity of thought, and the sure hope of gaining a share of infinite power in eternal life would lift most minds to effort.

He had reached this completeness five thousand years ago, and added nothing to his stock of known forces for a very long time. The mass of nature exercised on him so feeble an attraction that one can scarcely account for his apparent motion. Only a historian of very exceptional knowledge would venture to say at what date between 3000 B.C. and 1000 A.D., the momentum of Europe was greatest; but such progress as the world made consisted in economies of energy rather than in its development; it was proved in mathematics, measured by names like Archimedes, Aristarchus,[61] Ptolemy, and Euclid; or in Civil Law, measured by a number of names which Adams had begun life by failing to learn; or in coinage, which was most beautiful near its beginning, and most barbarous at its close; or it was shown in roads, or the size of ships, or harbors; or by the use of metals, instruments, and writing; all of them economies of force, sometimes more forceful than the forces they helped; but the roads were still travelled by the horse, the ass, the camel,

60. **Arthur Balfour:** (1848–1930), British statesman and philosopher. His presidential address to the British Association, August 17, 1904, "On the Future of Science," confirmed Adams's views of the illusory assumptions of nineteenth-century science.
61. **Aristarchus:** third-century Greek philosopher, advanced the heliocentric theory of the universe.

or the slave; the ships were still propelled by sails or oars; the lever, the spring, and the screw bounded the region of applied mechanics. Even the metals were old.

Much the same thing could be said of religious or supernatural forces. Down to the year 300 of the Christian era they were little changed, and in spite of Plato and the sceptics were more apparently chaotic than ever. The experience of three thousand years had educated society to feel the vastness of Nature, and the infinity of her resources of power, but even this increase of attraction had not yet caused economies in its methods of pursuit.

There the Western world stood till the year A.D. 305, when the Emperor Diocletian abdicated; and there it was that Adams broke down on the steps of Ara Cœli, his path blocked by the scandalous failure of civilization at the moment it had achieved complete success. In the year 305 the empire had solved the problems of Europe more completely than they have ever been solved since. The Pax Romana,[62] the Civil Law, and Free Trade should, in four hundred years, have put Europe far in advance of the point reached by modern society in the four hundred years since 1500, when conditions were less simple.

The efforts to explain, or explain away, this scandal had been incessant, but none suited Adams unless it were the economic theory of adverse exchanges and exhaustion of minerals; but nations are not ruined beyond a certain point by adverse exchanges, and Rome had by no means exhausted her resources. On the contrary, the empire developed resources and energies quite astounding. No other four hundred years of history before A.D. 1800 knew anything like it; and although some of these developments, like the Civil Law, the roads, aqueducts, and harbors, were rather economies than force, yet in northwestern Europe alone the empire had developed three energies—France, England, and Germany—competent to master the world. The trouble seemed rather to be that the empire developed too much energy, and too fast.

A dynamic law requires that two masses—nature and man—must go on, reacting upon each other, without stop, as the sun and a comet react on each other, and that any appearance of stoppage is illusive. The theory seems to exact excess, rather than deficiency, of action and reaction to account for the dissolution of the Roman Empire, which should, as a problem of mechanics, have been torn to pieces by acceleration. If the student means to try the experiment of framing a dynamic law, he must assign values to the forces of attraction that caused the trouble; and in this case he has them in plain evidence. With the relentless logic that stamped Roman thought, the empire, which had established unity on earth, could not help establishing unity in heaven. It was induced by its dynamic necessities to economize the gods.

The Church has never ceased to protest against the charge that Christianity ruined the empire, and, with its usual force, has pointed out that its reforms alone saved the State. Any dynamic theory gladly admits it. All it asks is to find and follow the force that attracts. The Church points out this force in the Cross, and history needs only to follow it. The empire loudly asserted its motive. Good taste forbids saying that Constantine the Great speculated as audaciously as a modern stock-broker on values of which he knew at the utmost only the volume; or that he merged all uncertain forces into a single trust, which he enormously over-capitalized, and forced on the market; but this is the substance of what Constantine himself said in his Edict of Milan in the year 313, which admitted Christianity into the Trust of State Religions. Regarded as an Act of Congress, it runs: "We have resolved to grant to Christians as well as all others the liberty to practise the religion they prefer, in order that whatever exists of divinity or celestial power may help and favor us and all who are under our government." The empire pursued power—not merely spiritual but physical—in the sense in which Constantine issued his army order the year before, at the battle of the Milvian Bridge: *In hoc signo vinces!* [63] using the Cross as a train of artillery, which, to his mind, it was. Society accepted it in the same character. Eighty years afterwards, Theodosius marched against his rival Eugene with the Cross for physical champion; and Eugene raised the image of Hercules to fight for the pagans; while society on both sides looked on, as though it were a boxing-match, to decide a final test of force between the divine powers. The Church was powerless to raise the ideal. What is now known as religion affected the mind of old society but little. The laity, the people, the million, almost to a man, bet on the gods as they bet on a horse.

No doubt the Church did all it could to purify the process, but society was almost wholly pagan in its point of view, and was drawn to the Cross because, in its system of physics, the Cross had absorbed all the old occult or fetish-power. The

62. **Pax Romana:** the peace imposed throughout the Mediterranean world by the Roman Empire during the height of its power.

63. *In hoc signo vinces!:* "In this sign we conquer!"

symbol represented the sum of nature—the Energy of modern science—and society believed it to be as real as X-rays; perhaps it was! The emperors used it like gunpowder in politics; the physicians used it like rays in medicine; the dying clung to it as the quintessence of force, to protect them from the forces of evil on their road to the next life.

Throughout these four centuries the empire knew that religion disturbed economy, for even the cost of heathen incense affected the exchanges; but no one could afford to buy or construct a costly and complicated machine when he could hire an occult force at trifling expense. Fetish-power was cheap and satisfactory, down to a certain point. Turgot and Auguste Comte long ago fixed this stage of economy as a necessary phase of social education, and historians seem now to accept it as the only gain yet made towards scientific history. Great numbers of educated people—perhaps a majority—cling to the method still, and practise it more or less strictly; but, until quite recently, no other was known. The only occult power at man's disposal was fetish. Against it, no mechanical force could compete except within narrow limits.

Outside of occult or fetish-power, the Roman world was incredibly poor. It knew but one productive energy resembling a modern machine—the slave. No artificial force of serious value was applied to production or transportation, and when society developed itself so rapidly in political and social lines, it had no other means of keeping its economy on the same level than to extend its slave-system and its fetish-system to the utmost.

The result might have been stated in a mathematical formula as early as the time of Archimedes, six hundred years before Rome fell. The economic needs of a violently centralizing society forced the empire to enlarge its slave-system until the slave-system consumed itself and the empire too, leaving society no resource but further enlargement of its religious system in order to compensate for the losses and horrors of the failure. For a vicious circle, its mathematical completeness approached perfection. The dynamic law of attraction and reaction needed only a Newton to fix it in algebraic form.

At last, in 410, Alaric sacked Rome, and the slave-ridden, agricultural, uncommercial Western Empire—the poorer and less Christianized half —went to pieces. Society, though terribly shocked by the horrors of Alaric's storm, felt still more deeply the disappointment in its new power, the Cross, which had failed to protect its Church. The outcry against the Cross became so loud among Christians that its literary champion, Bishop Augustine of Hippo [64]—a town between Algiers and Tunis—was led to write a famous treatise in defence of the Cross, familiar still to every scholar, in which he defended feebly the mechanical value of the symbol—arguing only that pagan symbols equally failed—but insisted on its spiritual value in the *Civitas Dei* which had taken the place of the *Civitas Romae* in human interest. "Granted that we have lost all we had! Have we lost faith? Have we lost piety? Have we lost the wealth of the inner man who is rich before God? These are the wealth of Christians!" The *Civitas Dei*, in its turn, became the sum of attraction for the Western world, though it also showed the same weakness in mechanics that had wrecked the *Civitas Romae*. St. Augustine and his people perished at Hippo towards 430, leaving society in appearance dull to new attraction.

Yet the attraction remained constant. The delight of experimenting on occult force of every kind is such as to absorb all the free thought of the human race. The gods did their work; history has no quarrel with them; they led, educated, enlarged the mind; taught knowledge; betrayed ignorance, stimulated effort. So little is known about the mind—whether social, racial, sexual or heritable; whether material or spiritual; whether animal, vegetable or mineral—that history is inclined to avoid it altogether; but nothing forbids one to admit, for convenience, that it may assimilate food like the body, storing new force and growing, like a forest, with the storage. The brain has not yet revealed its mysterious mechanism of gray matter. Never has Nature offered it so violent a stimulant as when she opened to it the possibility of sharing infinite power in eternal life, and it might well need a thousand years of prolonged and intense experiment to prove the value of the motive. During these so-called Middle Ages, the Western mind reacted in many forms on many sides, expressing its motives in modes, such as Romanesque and Gothic architecture, glass windows and mosaic walls, sculpture and poetry, war and love, which still affect some people as the noblest work of man, so that, even to-day, great masses of idle and ignorant tourists travel from far countries to look at Ravenna and San Marco, Palermo and Pisa, Assisi, Cordova, Chartres, with vague notions about the force that created them, but with a certain surprise that a social mind of such singular energy and unity should still lurk in their shadows.

64. **Augustine of Hippo:** St. Augustine (354–430), author of the *Civitas Dei* (*City of God*) and the famous *Confessions*, which provided something of the tone and pattern of Adams's *Education*.

The tourist more rarely visits Constantinople or studies the architecture of Sancta Sofia, but when he does, he is distinctly conscious of forces not quite the same. Justinian has not the simplicity of Charlemagne. The Eastern Empire showed an activity and variety of forces that classical Europe had never possessed. The navy of Nicephoras Phocas [65] in the tenth century would have annihilated in half an hour any navy that Carthage or Athens or Rome ever set afloat. The dynamic scheme began by asserting rather recklessly that between the Pyramids (B.C. 3000), and the Cross (A.D. 300), no new force affected Western progress, and antiquarians may easily dispute the fact; but in any case the motive influence, old or new, which raised both Pyramids and Cross was the same attraction of power in a future life that raised the dome of Sancta Sofia and the Cathedral at Amiens, however much it was altered, enlarged, or removed to distance in space. Therefore, no single event has more puzzled historians than the sudden, unexplained appearance of at least two new natural forces of the highest educational value in mechanics, for the first time within record of history. Literally, these two forces seemed to drop from the sky at the precise moment when the Cross on one side and the Crescent [66] on the other, proclaimed the complete triumph of the *Civitas Dei.* Had the Manichean doctrine of Good and Evil as rival deities been orthodox, it would alone have accounted for this simultaneous victory of hostile powers.

Of the compass, as a step towards demonstration of the dynamic law, one may confidently say that it proved, better than any other force, the widening scope of the mind, since it widened immensely the range of contact between nature and thought. The compass educated. This must prove itself as needing no proof.

Of Greek fire and gunpowder, the same thing cannot certainly be said, for they have the air of accidents due to the attraction of religious motives. They belong to the spiritual world; or to the doubtful ground of Magic which lay between Good and Evil. They were chemical forces, mostly explosive, which acted and still act as the most violent educators ever known to man, but they were justly feared as diabolic, and whatever insolence man may have risked towards the milder teachers of his infancy, he was an abject pupil towards explosives. The Sieur de Joinville left a record of the energy with which the relatively harmless Greek fire educated and enlarged the French

mind in a single night in the year 1249, when the crusaders were trying to advance on Cairo. The good king St. Louis and all his staff dropped on their knees at every fiery flame that flew by, praying—"God have pity on us!" and never had man more reason to call on his gods than they, for the battle of religion between Christian and Saracen was trifling compared with that of education between gunpowder and the Cross.

The fiction that society educated itself, or aimed at a conscious purpose, was upset by the compass and gunpowder which dragged and drove Europe at will through frightful bogs of learning. At first, the apparent lag for want of volume in the new energies lasted one or two centuries, which closed the great epochs of emotion by the Gothic cathedrals and scholastic theology. The moment had Greek beauty and more than Greek unity, but it was brief; and for another century or two, Western society seemed to float in space without apparent motion. Yet the attractive mass of nature's energy continued to attract, and education became more rapid than ever before. Society began to resist, but the individual showed greater and greater insistence, without realizing what he was doing. When the Crescent drove the Cross in ignominy from Constantinople in 1453, Gutenberg and Fust were printing their first Bible at Mainz under the impression that they were helping the Cross. When Columbus discovered the West Indies in 1492, the Church looked on it as a victory of the Cross. When Luther and Calvin upset Europe half a century later, they were trying, like St. Augustine, to substitute the *Civitas Dei* for the *Civitas Romae.* When the Puritans set out for New England in 1620, they too were looking to found a *Civitas Dei* in State Street; [67] and when Bunyan made his Pilgrimage in 1678, [68] he repeated St. Jerome. [69] Even when, after centuries of license, the Church reformed its discipline, and, to prove it, burned Giordano Bruno in 1600, besides condemning Galileo in 1630—as science goes on repeating to us every day—it condemned anarchists, not atheists. None of the astronomers were irreligious men; all of them made a point of magnifying God through his works; a form of science which did their religion no credit. Neither Galileo

65. **Nicephoras Phocas:** (913?–69), Emperor of the Eastern Roman Empire.   66. **Crescent:** symbol of Mohammedanism.

67. **State Street:** another one of the ironies of fate, for the business interests of State Street had long since superseded the influence of the New England clergy on New England government.   68. **Bunyan . . . 1678:** date of publication of *Pilgrim's Progress from this world to that which is to come.* A religious nonconformist, Bunyan was influential in undermining the authority of the established church.   69. **St. Jerome:** (c. 340–420), his great work, the Latin translation of the Scriptures, the Vulgate, made the Bible generally available to the Western world, bringing a whole train of revolutionary consequences.

nor Kepler, neither Spinoza nor Descartes, neither Leibnitz nor Newton, any more than Constantine the Great—if so much—doubted Unity. The utmost range of their heresies reached only its personality.

This persistence of thought-inertia is the leading idea of modern history. Except as reflected in himself, man has no reason for assuming unity in the universe, or an ultimate substance, or a prime-motor. The *a priori* insistence on this unity ended by fatiguing the more active—or reactive—minds; and Lord Bacon tried to stop it. He urged society to lay aside the idea of evolving the universe from a thought, and to try evolving thought from the universe. The mind should observe and register forces—take them apart and put them together—without assuming unity at all. "Nature, to be commanded, must be obeyed." "The imagination must be given not wings but weights." As Galileo reversed the action of earth and sun, Bacon reversed the relation of thought to force. The mind was thenceforth to follow the movement of matter, and unity must be left to shift for itself.

The revolution in attitude seemed voluntary, but in fact was as mechanical as the fall of a feather. Man created nothing. After 1500, the speed of progress so rapidly surpassed man's gait as to alarm every one, as though it were the acceleration of a falling body which the dynamic theory takes it to be. Lord Bacon was as much astonished by it as the Church was, and with reason. Suddenly society felt itself dragged into situations altogether new and anarchic—situations which it could not affect, but which painfully affected it. Instinct taught it that the universe in its thought must be in danger when its reflection lost itself in space. The danger was all the greater because men of science covered it with "larger synthesis," and poets called the undevout astronomer mad. Society knew better. Yet the telescope held it rigidly standing on its head; the microscope revealed a universe that defied the senses; gunpowder killed whole races that lagged behind; the compass coerced the most imbruted mariner to act on the impossible idea that the earth was round; the press drenched Europe with anarchism. Europe saw itself, violently resisting, wrenched into false positions, drawn along new lines as a fish that is caught on a hook; but unable to understand by what force it was controlled. The resistance was often bloody, sometimes humorous, always constant. Its contortions in the eighteenth century are best studied in the wit of Voltaire, but all history and all philosophy from Montaigne and Pascal to Schopenhauer and Nietzsche deal with nothing else; and still, throughout it all, the Baco-

nian law held good; thought did not evolve nature, but nature evolved thought. Not one considerable man of science dared face the stream of thought; and the whole number of those who acted, like Franklin, as electric conductors of the new forces from nature to man, down to the year 1800, did not exceed a few score, confined to a few towns in Western Europe. Asia refused to be touched by the stream, and America, except for Franklin, stood outside.

Very slowly the accretion of these new forces, chemical and mechanical, grew in volume until they acquired sufficient mass to take the place of the old religious science, substituting their attraction for the attractions of the *Civitas Dei*, but the process remained the same. Nature, not mind, did the work that the sun does on the planets. Man depended more and more absolutely on forces other than his own, and on instruments which superseded his senses. Bacon foretold it: "Neither the naked hand nor the understanding, left to itself, can effect much. It is by instruments and helps that the work is done." Once done, the mind resumed its illusion, and society forgot its impotence; but no one better than Bacon knew its tricks, and for his true followers science always meant self-restraint, obedience, sensitiveness to impulse from without. "Non fingendum aut excogitandum sed inveniendum quid Natura faciat aut ferat." [70]

The success of this method staggers belief, and even to-day can be treated by history only as a miracle of growth, like the sports of nature. Evidently a new variety of mind had appeared. Certain men merely held out their hands—like Newton, watched an apple; like Franklin, flew a kite; like Watt, played with a tea-kettle—and great forces of nature stuck to them as though she were playing ball. Governments did almost nothing but resist. Even gunpowder and ordnance, the great weapon of government, showed little development between 1400 and 1800. Society was hostile or indifferent, as Priestley [71] and Jenner, [72] and even Fulton, [73] with reason complained in the most ad-

70. **"Non . . . ferat":** "One must not feign or invent what nature does or produces, but investigate." 71. **Priestley:** Joseph Priestley (1733–1804), English philosopher and scientist, advocated the utilitarian standard of the happiness of the majority, believer in scientific progress, sympathizer with the French Revolution, emigrated to America in 1794 because of the unpopularity of his opinions. 72. **Jenner:** Edward Jenner (1749–1823), discoverer of smallpox vaccine. Popular opposition to inoculation continued for several decades after his death. 73. **Fulton:** Robert Fulton (1765–1815), invented the first submarine torpedo but was unable to interest any of the great powers, including the United States. He fared somewhat better with his invention of the first practical steamboat, though years elapsed before the government adopted it for naval use.

vanced societies in the world, while its resistance became acute wherever the Church held control; until all mankind seemed to draw itself out in a long series of groups, dragged on by an attractive power in advance, which even the leaders obeyed without understanding, as the planets obeyed gravity, or the trees obeyed heat and light.

The influx of new force was nearly spontaneous. The reaction of mind on the mass of nature seemed not greater than that of a comet on the sun; and had the spontaneous influx of force stopped in Europe, society must have stood still, or gone backward, as in Asia or Africa. Then only economies of process would have counted as new force, and society would have been better pleased; for the idea that new force must be in itself a good is only an animal or vegetable instinct. As Nature developed her hidden energies, they tended to become destructive. Thought itself became tortured, suffering reluctantly, impatiently, painfully, the coercion of new method. Easy thought had always been movement of inertia, and mostly mere sentiment; but even the processes of mathematics measured feebly the needs of force.

The stupendous acceleration after 1800 ended in 1900 with the appearance of the new class of supersensual forces, before which the man of science stood at first as bewildered and helpless, as in the fourth century, a priest of Isis before the Cross of Christ.

This, then, or something like this, would be a dynamic formula of history. Any schoolboy knows enough to object at once that it is the oldest and most universal of all theories. Church and State, theology and philosophy, have always preached it, differing only in the allotment of energy between nature and man. Whether the attractive energy has been called God or Nature, the mechanism has been always the same, and history is not obliged to decide whether the Ultimate tends to a purpose or not, or whether ultimate energy is one or many. Every one admits that the will is a free force, habitually decided by motives. No one denies that motives exist adequate to decide the will; even though it may not always be conscious of them. Science has proved that forces, sensible and occult, physical and metaphysical, simple and complex, surround, traverse, vibrate, rotate, repel, attract, without stop; that man's senses are conscious of few, and only in a partial degree; but that, from the beginning of organic existence his consciousness has been induced, expanded, trained in the lines of his sensitiveness; and that the rise of his faculties from a lower power to a higher, or from a narrower to a wider field, may be due

to the function of assimilating and storing outside force or forces. There is nothing unscientific in the idea that, beyond the lines of force felt by the senses, the universe may be—as it has always been—either a supersensuous chaos or a divine unity, which irresistibly attracts, and is either life or death to penetrate. Thus far, religion, philosophy, and science seem to go hand in hand. The schools begin their vital battle only there. In the earlier stages of progress, the forces to be assimilated were simple and easy to absorb, but, as the mind of man enlarged its range, it enlarged the field of complexity, and must continue to do so, even into chaos, until the reservoirs of sensuous or supersensuous energies are exhausted, or cease to affect him, or until he succumbs to their excess.

For past history, this way of grouping its sequences may answer for a chart of relations, although any serious student would need to invent another, to compare or correct its errors; but past history is only a value of relation to the future, and this value is wholly one of convenience, which can be tested only by experiment. Any law of movement must include, to make it a convenience, some mechanical formula of acceleration.

LETTERS OF
HENRY ADAMS

◊

❲ HENRY ADAMS was reared in a household in which letter-writing was a carefully cultivated art. The letters of Horace Walpole held a place of peculiar honor as models of the art. Henry's father declared, "There is no species of exercise, in early life, more productive of results useful to the mind, than that of writing letters." To the son the writing of letters became a chief literary passion. No day was well begun without its budget of letters to his far-flung correspondents. The published collections form a brilliant running commentary on his own career and the events of his time in a style that ran increasingly to irony and paradox. The following selections suggest something of the immense range of Adams's intellectual interests in a record spanning more than sixty years.

◊

TO CHARLES FRANCIS ADAMS, JR.

Berlin, February 9, 1859 [1]

. . . .

You try to put me on the horns of a dilemma. You attribute to me a certain kind of mind, and argue that if I am to be a lawyer, or in other words, follow my own plan which I have followed for several years, then what I learn in Europe is worse than thrown away. Hence, to be a lawyer I must cease to be what I am. If I acknowledge that my mind is not adapted to my plan, I must give my plan up. If on the other hand I assert that my mind *is* adapted to my plan, I must give Europe up. This I take to be the ground of your letter. I disagree with it, and think that you are mistaken not only in your judgement of my mind, but also in your idea of the necessary result of two years in Europe. But I shall not go into this subject now. Perhaps in another letter I may give you some reasons for believing that what I am learning here in Europe is not in opposition to what I propose to do hereafter. Just now I prefer to attack your position rather than to defend my own. It's easier and there's more fun in it.

I don't deny the truth of what you say, that law is not a pleasant study, and that we are not adapted to make great lawyers. But beyond this I think you lose yourself and run aground. You say that I am not made for a lawyer; but hardly hint at what I am made for. The same things that you say of me, you also apply to yourself. Now let me see if I can carry out your idea to any result that will give a fellow a minute's firm footing.

The law is bad, you say. Wohlan! [2] what then? Why then, you continue, take something that suits you better. And what would be likely to suit me better? What is this kind of mind that you give me? I must say that you pay me a very left-handed kind of compliment in your estimation of me. You seem to think that I am adapted to nothing but the sugar-plums of intellect and had better not try to digest anything stronger. You would make me a sort of George Curtis or Ik. Marvel,[3] better or worse, a writer of popular sketches in magazines; a lecturer before Lyceums and College societies;

a dabbler in metaphysics, poetry, and art, than which I would rather die, for if it has come to that, alas! verily, as you say, mediocrity has fallen on the name of Adams.

But, I suppose, you will deny that your letter leads to this and assert that such men as Mr. Everett, Mr. Sumner, the Governor, Mr. Palfrey [4] and the like, are a wholly different class. I would just suggest that all these began either as lawyers or clergymen; and I merely propose to do the same. But now let's go back to generalities, and see whether something can't be fished up.

In the most general terms then; you would say, I take it, that my mind if not adapted to law, at least *is* adapted to literary pursuits, in the most extensive meaning of the term; and to nothing else. I couldn't be a physician or a merchant, or a shop-keeper or anything of that kind, so well as I could a lawyer. Literary pursuits are very extensive, but I *must* make some money to support me, so we must say, "literary pursuits that produce money." Now literary pursuits that produce money and that I am eligible for, are very few.

To begin with, perhaps, if I were a better man, I might feel inclined to become a clergyman. But as I'm very much a worser man, we'll count that out.

Then you once proposed to me to go into the newspaper line and become an editor. The objections to this are as many and as strong as to the law, but if you don't see them, will reserve the subject for further discussion.

Of *Atlantic Monthly* and *Putnam* and *Harper* and the men who write for money in them, my opinion is short. Rather than do nothing but that, or make that an object in life, I'd die here in Europe.

No, mein Liebster,[5] this is one of these propositions which would kill any man's chances in America, even though he had all the training of Gorgias [6] (if that was the beggar's name), and all the philosophy of Frank Bacon; (I refer to the Viscount Verulam and not to the young Bostonian of the same name). Yet after all, your idea is not so very distinct from mine, except that it throws out into the strongest relief the object that I proposed to make dependent on circumstances

LETTERS.   1. Berlin, February 9, 1859: Adams made the "Grand Tour" of Europe in 1858–60, setting out with a group of his classmates, all of whom had just graduated from Harvard. He reached Berlin on October 22, 1858 (not "November" as given in the *Education*). This is one of his many long letters to his elder brother Charles (1835–1915) touching on the prospects for their joint careers.   2. Wohlan!: "very well!"   3. George W. Curtis (1824–92), reformer, active in the antislavery movement and later in civil service reform. Ik. Marvel (1822–1908), pseudonym for Donald Grant Mitchell, American author, best liked for his gently sentimental *Reveries of a Bachelor*.

4. Mr. Everett . . . Mr. Palfrey: Edward Everett (1794–1865), statesman and orator, brother-in-law of Adams's mother; Charles Sumner (1811–74), the great antislavery Senator from Massachusetts, an intimate of the Adams family; the Governor, Henry Adams's father, Charles Francis Adams (1807–86); John Gorham Palfrey (1796–1881), chief historian of New England, another intimate of the Adams household, later encouraged the young Henry to write his first magazine article, "Captain John Smith," for the *North American Review* (January, 1867).   5. Liebster: "my dearest fellow."   6. Gorgias: (c. 485–375 B.C.), celebrated Sophist, figures in Plato's dialogue of that name.

and success in other respects. We are considerably in the same box, brother mine, and what applies to me, applies also, with slight alterations, to yourself. As you say, there are differences between us, and my character isn't yours; in fact, I know many respects in which I wish it were; but still we have grown up in the same school and have, until now, drawn our mental nutriment from the breasts, metaphorically speaking, of the same wet-nurse; indeed we may consider ourselves a case of modern Romulus and Remus, only omitting their murderous propensities. What is still more, we are beautifully adapted to work together; that is, *you* are. I stand in continual need of some one to kick me, and you use cow-hides for that purpose. So much the better. Continue to do so. In other words, I need you. Whether there's any corresponding necessity on your side, is your affair. But it's a case of "versteht sich" [7] that we can work better together than apart. Under these circumstances, let us be very careful how we take a step that will probably knock one of us in the head forever, or so separate us that our objects would become different. I shall hesitate a very long time indeed before I decide to earn my living by writing for magazines and newspapers, for I believe it to be one of the most dangerous beginnings that a man can make. Recollect that threadbare old Arabian Nights magnetic mountain *that drew all the metal out of the ships* and then sunk them.

I say that our ideas are not far different. The real difference is this: Yours begins by assuming as your ground plank and corner stone that I am capable of teaching the people and of becoming a light to the nations. Mine on the contrary begins by leaving that to develop itself in the future or to remain proved on the other side, without suffering a public disgrace from slumping as I infallibly should do under your idea. I said in my last what I wanted of the law; that I considered it the best grounding in the world for anything that we wish or are likely to do; that is the strongest point to fall back upon and the best position to advance from; at once offensive and defensive, it gives one a position as literary as if he did nothing but write for periodicals and a good deal more respectable; as a profession it offers many inducements; as merely an occupation it offers still more, and there is much more chance both for you and me to work *up* from it, than there is doubt in my mind that I at least should drop like a stuck monkey from the perch on which you want me to place myself. Perhaps it is my wish and

hope that we may do something of the sort you propose, but I do not wish for so large a scale of action, because I know my own weakness; I do not wish to go to work in the way you propose, because in the first place I believe it to be a wrong way, tending to fritter away the little power of steady and long-continued exertion I have, and in the second, it seems to me not to offer that firm and lasting ground work that the law does. I do wish to adhere to my original plan because, though even that is more, I am afraid, than my powers are up to, yet it seems to me as feasible as any that has yet come before me, and if I can do nothing in that, why let me go to the devil at once, for there's no use staying here. Gott bewahr [8] mich from funny Lyceum lectures and rainbow articles in *Atlantic Monthlys* with a proof of scholarship as exhibited by a line here and there from "the charming old Epicurean Horace" or "the grand thunderbursts of superhuman strength" from God knows what old Greek trotted out for the occasion. If I was born to be the admiration of girls and Tupperian philosophers, I'll cheat fate and quietly do nothing all my life.

So here I will lay aside this subject and wait for your next. As this letter has been written partly in school,[9] partly here, and is the work of some six or eight different sittings, I'll excuse you for finding fault with it, as with my former one, but you must also excuse the faults. On your theory of my proper plan of life, however, I ought never to say any foolish things, but my lips should drool wisdom and my paths should be by the side of Socrates, and Isocrates; (by the way were these two men related and why have they so similar names?) I hope your next will take a more practical view of life.

Meanwhile this last week I've been exceedingly dissipated; out every night in one way or another, and able to do very little real work. The last two days too, the weather has been charming. Yesterday Jim Higginson [10] and I took Mr. Apthorp [11] out on a spree. He has had us there to dine and gave us some of the best champagne I ever tasted; perhaps the very best; I've dined twice with him and got talking very fast both times. The ladies retired to their room and left us to our wine, and as Mr. A. doesn't stint the supply and I make it a rule never to refuse a good glass when it's offered, the inevitable consequence is very clear. A bottle

7. "versteht sich": "agreed."

8. **Gott bewahr:** "God save me." 9. **partly in school:** Not understanding the lectures on the civil law at the university, Adams promptly gave them up and enrolled in a *gymnasium* (high school) to learn the language. 10. **Jim Higginson:** J. J. Higginson (1836–1911), a Harvard college mate. 11. **Mr. Apthorp:** Robert East Apthorp (d. 1882), a fellow Bostonian.

of wine is the outside of what I can carry, and in both cases I drank devilish close onto the limit. Yesterday we returned the hospitality by taking Mr. A. out for a day of it, to show him the style of our ordinary life. Higginson and I went for him at two o'clock and carried him off to our dirty little restauration, and there dined him and gave him a glass of beer. You know the style of our dinners from my letters, I think. Then we went to a concert till six, and leaving the concert before it was over, we walked down to a little theatre called Wallner's, a devil of a way off, and saw a drama called "Berlin wie es weint und lacht"; [12] a thing very popular in Berlin, and has run 137 nights. It's by far the best drama of the sort that I've seen, too. Thence we walked back and sat till twelve o'clock in a wine-cellar, or Wein-Stube as they call it which was crowded with exceedingly respectable old people, but which, though very clean, yet hasn't the vestige of a table-cloth on ary a table, and was hot as hell and filled with clouds of tobacco smoke. Here we eat and drank and talked and Hig and I smoked, and passed a very jolly evening, drinking two bottles and a half of Rhine wine, really better than I've often tasted at home, for which two bottles and a half we paid something less than an American dollar. This is a dear place for wines too. On the Rhine, I am told, they cost much less. I very often come in here after the theatre and drink a bottle, commonly with Higginson, or if I'm on the heavy cheap, go to a cellar and get a couple of boiled sausages and a mug of beer. The sausages I tell you are good. My supper commonly costs quarter of a dollar or less. My dinner the same. As for cigars, I consider myself extravagant when I smoke really good ones which cost me $15.00 the thousand. They're not proud like yours, but curse me if they don't taste as good as any I used to pay at the rate of $50 and $60 for.

So I will now wind up this letter, which though not so long as yours, has yet the excuse that I've more letters to write than you. I will now proceed immediately, as you say, to put on my paint and feathers (devilish dirty paint in the shape of my old dress suit) for a grand ball in the Opera House, at which I suppose all the Court will be, and which I shall try to tell about in my letter to John.[13] I go from a sense of duty, though it costs me three thalers, and I'd rather stay at home, but one ought to see these things and I presume it will be handsome and stupid as double-distilled dam-

nation. I don't know any one except Americans there and if I did, it wouldn't make any difference. Meanwhile, allerhöchstgeborner Herr,[14] accept the assurances of my deep respect. If I knew enough of this cursed language I'd write you a letter in German, but I don't and never shall, curse it.

Give the tokens of my highest consideration to the family at large. My last letter home was February 5th to mamma; before that, January 29th to the Congressman.[15] No letters as yet received this week. Yrs.

TO CHARLES FRANCIS ADAMS, JR.

London, April 11, 1862 [16]

· · · · · · · · · · · · · · · · · · ·

Modest and unassuming as I am, you know, society is not the place for pleasure to me. Even at the Club [17] I talk distantly with Counts and Barons and numberless untitled but high-placed characters, but have never arrived at intimacy with any of them. I am a little sorry for this because there are several very nice fellows among them, and all are polite and seem sufficiently social. Then, too, my unfortunate notoriety, which, I told you of, in a letter that I trust and pray may not be lost, some three months ago, tells against me, though it certainly has brought me into notice. I have no doubt that if I were to stay here another year, I should become extremely fond of the place and the life. There is, too, a certain grim satisfaction in the idea that this people who have worn and irritated and exasperated us for months, and among whom we have lived nearly a year of what was, till lately, a slow torture, should now be innocently dancing and smiling on the volcano, utterly unconscious of the extent of hatred and the greediness for revenge that they've raised. When the storm does finally burst on them, they will have one of their panics and be as astonished as if they'd never heard of anything but brotherly love and affection between the two nations. Of course it would

---

12. "Berlin . . . lacht": "Berlin, How It Cries and Laughs." 13. John: John Quincy Adams II (1833–94), Henry's eldest brother.

14. allerhöchstgeborner Herr: "most high-born Sir." 15. Congressman: in the preceding November their father had been elected from the Quincy, Mass., district. 16. London, April 11, 1862: From 1861 to 1868 Henry served as private secretary to his father, the American minister to the Court of St. James's. This letter reflects his intense interest in the scientific discoveries of the period and shows his early tendency to geopolitical speculation. 17. Club: presumably the St. James' Club, where he was put up for membership in the following year. He became an inveterate clubman, helping to found the Cosmos Club and the Metropolitan Club in Washington. When in New York he made his headquarters at the Century or the Knickerbocker.

be out of the question for me to hint at the state of things to them. I have only to smile and tell gross lies, for which God forgive me, about my feelings towards this country, and the kindness I have received here, which, between ourselves, so far as the pure English go, has been brilliantly conspicuous for its almost total absence. Only a fortnight ago they discovered that their whole wooden navy was useless;[18] rather a weakness than a strength. Yesterday it was formally announced and acknowledged by Government, people and press, that the Warrior and their other new iron ships, are no better than wood, nor can any shot-proof sea-going vessel be made. In order to prove this, they've proved their Armstrong guns a failure, for he has given up the breech-loading system and been compelled to return to the old smooth-bore, muzzle-loader. So within three weeks, they find their wooden navy, their iron navy, and their costly guns, all utterly antiquated and useless.

To me, they seem to be bewildered by all this. I don't think as yet they have dared to look their position in the face. People begin to talk vaguely about the end of war and eternal peace, just as though human nature was changed by the fact that Great Britain's sea-power is knocked in the head. But for my private part, I think I see a thing or two. And one of these things is that the military power of France is nearly doubled by having the seas free; and that our good country the United States is left to a career that is positively unlimited except by the powers of the imagination. And for England there is still greatness and safety, if she will draw her colonies around her, and turn her hegemony into a Confederation of British nations.

You may think all this nonsense, but I tell you these are great times. Man has mounted science, and is now run away with. I firmly believe that before many centuries more, science will be the master of man. The engines he will have invented will be beyond his strength to control. Some day science may have the existence of mankind in its power and the human race commit suicide by blowing up the world. Not only shall we be able to cruize in space, but I see no reason why some future generation shouldn't walk off like a beetle with the world on its back, or give it another rotary motion so that every zone should receive in turn its due portion of heat and light. . . .

TO WILLIAM JAMES

Beverly Farms, Mass.,[19] 27 July, 1882.

MY DEAR JAMES [20]

I have read your two papers[21] with that attention which, etc., etc., etc., and am partially prepared to discuss them with you. As I understand your Faith, your X, your reaction of the individual on the cosmos, it is the old question of Free Will over again. You *choose* to assume that the will is free. Good! Reason proves that the Will cannot be free. Equally good! Free or not, the mere fact that a doubt can exist, proves that X must be a very microscopic quantity. If the orthodox are grateful to you for such gifts, the world has indeed changed, and we have much to thank God for, if there is a God, that he should have left us unable to decide whether our thoughts, if we have thoughts, are our own or his'n.

Although your gift to the church seems to me a pretty darned mean one, I admire very much your manner of giving it, which magnifies the crumb into at least forty loaves and fishes. My wife is quite converted by it. She enjoyed the paper extremely. Since she read it she has talked of giving five dollars to Russell Sturgis's church for napkins. As the impression fades, she talks less of the napkins.

With hero-worship like Carlyle's, I have little patience. In history heroes have neutralised each other, and the result is no more than would have been reached without them. Indeed in military heroes I suspect that the ultimate result has been retardation. Nevertheless you could doubtless at any time stop the entire progress of human thought by killing a few score of men. So far I am with you. A few hundred men represent the entire intellectual activity of the whole thirteen hundred millions. What then? They drag us up the cork-screw stair of thought, but they can no more get their brains to run out of their especial convolutions than a railway train (with a free will of half an inch on three thousand miles) can run free up Mount Shasta. Not one of them has ever got so far as to tell us a single vital fact worth knowing. We can't prove even that we are.

Meanwhile I enclose your letter to Monod.[22]

---

18. **navy was useless:** the two armored vessels, the *Monitor* and the *Merrimac*, had their famous encounter in Hampton Roads, Va., March 9, 1862.

19. **Beverly Farms, Mass.:** the summer home of Adams and his wife which he ceased to use after her death in 1885. 20. **James:** William James (1842–1910), psychologist and philosopher, founder of pragmatism. 21. **two papers:** "Rationality, Activity, and Faith," *Princeton Review* (July, 1882); "Great Men, Great Thoughts, and the Environment," *Atlantic*, (October, 1880). 22. **Monod:** Gabriel Monod (1844–1912), French historian and one of Adams's scholarly "allies" in Paris.

Pleasant voyage and happy return. Our love to Harry.[23]

Ever truly   HENRY ADAMS

TO HIS WIFE, MARIAN HOOPER ADAMS [24]

1607 H Street [Washington],
Friday, 10 April, [1885] 9 A.M.

DEAR MISTRESS

Yours of Tuesday evening reached me yesterday afternoon. I hope for another before I post this at noon.

I told you that the Endicotts came yesterday morning and went over the house. Miss Endicott is a clean-looking girl, with less air of distinction than I expected, but speaking up for herself. Maggie [25] showed them about, up and down stairs, and, on departing, Mrs. Endicott intimated that she should negotiate with Corcoran. I told her that we would leave her pretty much anything she wanted, and do anything in our power to help her; but I would leave details to you.

After Maynard [26] and breakfast, I went to the Smithsonian and hunted porphyries. With the aid of the young man who has charge of the stones I learned that only one purple porphyry, like the African is ever worked in America, and this comes from a large ledge which extends from Braintree beneath Boston harbor to Lynn, where it is found in quantity and sometimes worked, as a special order, though so hard as to be anything but a favorite with the quarrymen.

I am not wild for it, but in the whole Smithsonian collection I could find nothing else that did not suggest a hotel;—with one exception. This was a small slab of Mexican onyx of a sea-green translucency so exquisite as to make my soul yearn. If you can reconcile yourself to it, please have a sea-green onyx fire-place. Should you see Richardson, ask him about this, and if he approves, as he will, let us have a Mexican onyx fire-place. It cannot cost much more than African marble and ought to cost less than porphyry. Strike for green!

After ransacking the Smithsonian, I came back at three o'clock, and started off for a ride on

Prince. The day was fine though cool (Therm. 44°), and I took my first three-hour spring excursion round by the dog-tooth violets and Riggs's farm. A few maples show a faint flush here and there, but not a sign of leaf is to be seen, and even the blood-root and hepatica hid themselves from my eyes. A few frogs sang in the sun, and birds sang in the trees; but no sign of a peach-blossom yet, and not even the magnolias and *Pyrus Japonica* have started. In 1878 the magnolias were in full flower and killed by frost on March 25, and in 1882 the frost killed them on April 10. I have not even seen the yellow Forsythia in flower, though it should have been out as early as March 15. Last year the *Pyrus Japonica* was reddening on April 2.

So you have not yet lost much spring; and to-day is cloudy and raw. The house does get on, no doubt, but the work done is no longer so easily noted from day to day. Hay's last chimney [27] was finished yesterday, and the rest of his roof is getting astride of his dining-room. So far, so good. To get the roof on at all is a triumph.

My dinner was solitary last night, and I stayed at home all the evening. Joe Quincy [28] came in and sat till eleven. He has been here some time, on law business, but has picked up no news, and has little to tell me of what is going on. I held forth to him after my paternal manner, and when he departed I went to bed and slept, for once, without waking, from twelve till nine o'clock. Evidently solitude is good for slumber.

The mail has come in without a letter from you, and I know not whether to direct to Beacon Street or Cambridge. On the whole, Cambridge will be safest. You will get it on Sunday in any case. I am going to see John Field this afternoon, and shall attend Bayard's [29] first reception tonight. The card "requests the pleasure" on Friday evenings in April, and May 1. Your favorite Naito leaves a p. p. c.[30]

I want to join you tomorrow but dare not without permission. Joe Quincy goes in the limited; the John Grays [31] go by the night train. I can take the one or the other; but unless you send, I shall wait, especially as I think your report indicates that I shall not wait long.

Ever Your   HENRY

23. Harry: William's brother, Henry James (1843–1916), the novelist.   24. Marian Hooper Adams: Mrs. Adams was then in Cambridge helping to nurse her father, who died three days later, inducing in her the depression that finally led to her suicide. The Adamses were planning to move out of 1607 H Street to the handsome Romanesque house at 1601 H Street on Lafayette Square that was being built for them by H. H. Richardson. Shortly after Mrs. Adams's death on December 6, Adams moved into the great new house alone.   25. Maggie: Maggie Wade, the Negro servant who remained in Adams's household until her death in 1909.   26. Maynard: his dentist.

27. last chimney: John Hay's magnificent mansion on the corner adjoining Adams's house was simultaneously going up under H. H. Richardson's direction.   28. Joe Quincy: Josiah Phillips Quincy (1829–1910), lawyer and writer, of the famous Massachusetts family.   29. I . . . Bayard's: Thomas F. Bayard (1828–98), became Secretary of State in Cleveland's cabinet. John Field was a family friend.   30. a p. p. c.: a calling card, *pour prendre congé,* in lieu of a leave-taking.   31. Grays: John Chipman Gray (1839–1915), distinguished Massachusetts lawyer, half-brother of Supreme Court Justice Horace Gray.

TO ELIZABETH CAMERON [32]

Apia, October 9, 1890.

Well we are here, and I am sitting in the early morning on the verandah of a rough cottage, in a grove of cocoa-nut palms, with native huts all about me, and across the grass, fifty yards away, I can see and hear the sea with its distant line of surf on the coral reef beyond. Natives clothed mostly in a waist-cloth, but sometimes their toilet completed by a hybiscus or other flower in their hair, pass every moment or two before my cabin, often handsome as Greek gods. I am the guest of Consul Sewall,[33] whose consulate is within the same grove, near the beach. . . .

Sunday morning at nine o'clock or thereabouts, the "Alameda" turned a corner of Tutuila, and I saw the little schooner knocking about in the open sea beyond. The day was overcast, threatening rain. From the shore, half a dozen large boats, filled with naked savages, were paddling down with the wind, singing a curiously wild chant to their paddles. La Farge [34] and I felt that we were to be captured and probably eaten, but the cruise of sixty miles in a forty-ton schooner, beating to windward in tropical squalls, was worse than being eaten. We dropt into the boat among scores of naked Samoans, half of them swimming, or clambering over our backs, with war clubs to sell, and when we reached our schooner, we stood in the rain and watched the "Alameda" steam away. That was our first joy. Whatever fate was in store, we had escaped from the steamer, and might die before another would come.

The cutter was commanded by Captain Peter, a huge captain, but little skilled in the languages with which I am more or less acquainted. His six sailors were as little fluent in English as though they had studied at Harvard. Captain Peter talked what he supposed to be English with excessive energy, but we could catch only the three words "now and again," repeated with frequency but in no apparent connection. "Now and again" something was to happen; meanwhile he beat up under the shore into quieter water, and presently, in a downpour of rain, we cast anchor in a bay, with mountains above, but a sand-beach within the coral reef, and native huts half hidden among the cocoanut palms. I insisted on going ashore straightway without respect for H. M.'s mail, and Captain Peter seemed not unwilling. A splendid naked savage carried La Farge, in an india-rub-ber water-proof, mildly kicking, from the boat to the shore, and returned for me. I embraced his neck with effusive gratitude, and so landed on the island of Tutuila, which does not resemble the picture on the Oceanic Steamship Company's colored advertisement. I found it densely covered with tropical mountains and vegetation, but glad as I was to set foot on mountains and see vegetation, I was soon more interested in the refined hospitality of the cultured inhabitants. We entered the nearest hut, and put on our best manners, which were none too good, for the natives had manners that made me feel withered prematurely in association with the occupants of pig-sties. Grave, courteous, with quiet voices and a sort of benevolence beyond the utmost expressiveness of Benjamin Franklin, they received us and made us at home. The cabin was charming when one looked about it. Nearly circular, with a diameter of some forty feet, its thatched roof, beautifully built up, came within about five feet of the ground, ending there on posts, and leaving the whole house open to the air. Within, mats covered a floor of white corals, smooth and almost soft like coarse sand. Fire was made in the middle of the hut. Only women and children were there. One was staining a tapa-cloth; another was lying down unwell; others were sitting about, and one or two naked children, wonderfully silent and well-behaved, sat and stared at us. We dropped our umbrellas and water-proofs and sat down on the mats to wait for Captain Peter to sail; but presently a proud young woman entered and seated herself in silence after shaking hands. Captain Peter succeeded in making us understand that this was the chief's daughter. Other young women dropped in, shook hands and sat down. Soon we seemed to have a *matinée*. As no one could say more than a word or two in the other's language, communication was as hard as at a Washington party, but it was more successful. In a very short time we were all intimate. La Farge began to draw the Princess, as we called her, and Wakea—for that was her name—was pleased to drop her dress-skirt, and sit for him in her native undress, with a dignity and gravity quite indescribable. The other girls were less imposing, but very amusing. One, Sivà, a younger sister of the Princess, was fascinating. Of course I soon devoted my attention to talking, and, as I could understand nothing, talk was moderately easy; but through Captain Peter we learned a little, and some of the touches of savagery were perfect. I asked Sivà her name—mine was Hen-li—and her age. She did not know her age; even her father, an old man, could not say how many years old she was. I guessed four-

32. **Elizabeth Cameron:** Mrs. James Donald Cameron (1857–1944), after the death of his wife, Adams's lifelong confidante.
33. **Consul Sewall:** Harold Marsh Sewall (1860–1924).
34. **La Farge:** John La Farge (1835–1910); see Introduction.

teen, equivalent to our eighteen. All her motions were splendid, and she threw a plate on the floor, as Martha Braggiotti would say, like a race-horse. Her lines were all antique, and in face she recalled a little my niece Lulu, Molly's sister. Presently she brought a curious pan-shaped wooden dish, standing on eight legs, all of one block; and sitting down behind it, began to grate a dry root, like flag-root but larger, on a grater, over the dish. This was rather hard work, and took some time. Then another girl brought some cocoa-nuts full of water, and she poured the water on the grated root. Then she took a bundle of clean cocoa-nut fibre, and seemed to wash her hands in the water which was already muddy and dirty with the grated root. We divined that she really strained out the grated particles, which were caught on the fibre, and wrung out by another girl. When all the grains were strained off, the drink was ready, and we realised that we had got to swallow it, for this was the *kawa,* and we were grateful that in our first experience the root was grated, not chewed, as it ought to be, by the girls. Please read Kingsley's account [35] of it in the "Earl and the Doctor," a book you will probably be able to borrow from Herbert, as it was done for or by his brother Pembroke. A cocoa-nut half full of it was handed to us, and as usual La Farge, who had kicked at the idea more than I did, took to it at once, and drank it rather freely. I found it "not nice, papa, but funny"; a queer lingering, varying, aromatic, arumatic, Polynesian, old-gold flavor, that clings to the palate like creosote or coal-oil. I drank the milk of a green cocoa-nut to wash it off, but all the green cocoa-nuts in the ocean could not wash out that little taste. After the *kawa* we became still more intimate. Besides Wakea and her sister Sivà, we made the acquaintance of Tuvale, Amerika, Sitoa, and Faaiuro, which is no other than Fayaway,[36] I imagine. We showed them our writing, and found that they could write very well, as they proved by writing us letters on the spot, in choice Samoan, which we tried to translate, with the usual result. So evening came on; we had some supper; a kerosene lamp was lit; and La Farge and I began to cry out for the *Siva.*

The *Siva,* we had learned to know at Hawaii, is the Samoan dance, and the girl, Sivà, had already been unable to resist giving us snatches of the songs and motions. Sivà was fascinating. She danced all over, and seemed more Greek in every new motion. I could not understand what orders

were given by the elders, but, once they were assured that we were not missionaries, all seemed right. The girls disappeared; and after some delay, while I was rather discouraged, thinking that the *Siva* was not to be, suddenly out of the dark, five girls came into the light, with a dramatic effect that really I never felt before. Naked to the waist, their rich skins glistened with cocoa-nut oil. Around their heads and necks they wore garlands of green leaves in strips, like seaweeds, and these too glistened with oil, as though the girls had come out of the sea. Around their waists, to the knee, they wore leaf-clothes, or *lavalavas,* also of fresh leaves, green and red. Their faces and figures varied in looks, some shading the negro too closely; but Sivà was divine, and you can imagine that we found our attention absorbed in watching her. The mysterious depths of darkness behind, against which the skins and dresses of the dancers mingled rather than contrasted; the sense of remoteness and of genuineness in the stage-management; the conviction that at last the kingdom of old-gold was ours, and that we were as good Polynesiacs as our neighbors—the whole scene and association gave so much freshness to our fancy that no future experience, short of being eaten, will ever make us feel so new again. La Farge's spectacles quivered with emotion and gasped for sheer inability to note everything at once. To me the dominant idea was that the girls, with their dripping grasses and leaves, and their glistening breasts and arms, had actually come out of the sea a few steps away. They entered in file, and sat down opposite us. Then the so-called *Siva* dance began. The girls sat cross-legged, and the dance was as much song as motion, although the motion was incessant. As the song or chant, a rhythmical and rather pleasant, quick movement, began, the dancers swayed about; clapped their hands, shoulders, legs; stretched out their arms in every direction and with every possible action, always in harmony, and seldom repeating the same figure. We had dozens of these different motives until I thought the poor girls would be exhausted, for they made so much muscular effort, feet, thighs, hips and even ribs working as energetically as the arms, that they panted at the close of each figure; but they were evidently enjoying it as much as we, and kept it up with glances at us and laughter among themselves. All through this part of the performance, our Princess did not dance but sat before us on the mats, and beat time with a stick. At last she too got up, and after ten minutes' absence, reappeared, costumed like the rest, but taller and more splendid. La Farge exploded with enthusiasm for her, and expressed boundless

35. **Kingsley's account:** George R. C. Herbert, Earl of Pembroke, and George H. Kingsley, *South Sea Bubbles, by the Earl and the Doctor.*   36. **Fayaway:** character in Herman Melville's *Typee.*

contempt for Carmencita. You can imagine the best female figure you ever saw, on about a six foot scale, neck, breast, back, arms and legs, all absolutely Greek in modelling and action, with such freedom of muscle and motion as the Greeks themselves hardly knew, and you can appreciate La Farge's excitement. When she came in the other dancers rose, and then began what I supposed to be a war or sword dance, the Princess brandishing a stick and evidently destroying her enemies, one of whom was a comic character and expressed abject cowardice. With this performance the dance ended; Sivà got out the *kawa* dish; Wakea and the others went for our tobacco, and soon we were all sprawling over the mats, smoking, laughing, trying to talk, with a sense of shoulders, arms, legs, cocoa-nut oil, and general nudeness most strangely mixed with a sense of propriety. Anyone would naturally suppose such a scene to be an orgy of savage license. I don't pretend to know what it was, but I give you my affidavit that we could see nothing in the songs or dances that suggested impropriety, and that not a word or a sign during our whole stay could have brought a blush to the cheek of Senator H—— himself. Unusual as the experience is of half dressed or undressed women lying about the floor, in all sorts of attitudes, and as likely as not throwing their arms or their shoulders across one as one lies or sits near them, as far as we could see the girls were perfectly good, and except occasionally for hinting that they would like a present of a handkerchief, or for giving us perhaps a ring, there was no approach to familiarity with us. Indeed at last we were extinguished by dropping a big mosquito netting over us, so that we were enclosed in a private room; the girls went off to their houses; our household sank into perfect quiet, and we slept in our clothes on the floor as comfortably as we knew how, while the kerosene lamp burned all night in the centre of the floor.

The next morning we very unwillingly tumbled into our boat, after a surf bath, and then, for the next four or five hours, we were pitching about, in a head wind and sea, trying to round the western point of Tutuila. Nothing could be more lovely than the day, the blue sea, and the green island stretching away in different planes of color, till lost in the distance. At two o'clock that afternoon we rounded our point, and our boat went ashore to fetch off Consul Sewall and Lieut. Parker on their return from Pango Pango, where they had gone to settle on the new naval station. They came instantly on board, and we four Americans then lay on the deck of that cutter from two o'clock Monday afternoon, till two

o'clock Wednesday morning, thirty-six hours, going sixty miles, in a calm, with a vertical sun overhead, and three of the four seasick. You can conceive that we were glad to reach Apia on any terms, and tumbled ashore, in a leaky boat, in the dead of night, only too glad to get shelter about the consulate. Our excitement at sea was a huge shark that looked like a whale. Once ashore, supper and bed were paradise; but my brain and stomach went on turning somersaults, and I was not wholly happy. . . .

TO JOHN HAY

Paris, 7 November, 1900.

Now that the circus is over and the beasts put to bed, I take for granted that congratulations are in order. Accept mine! I have no more to give. My little all is at your service. You have had an excessively complicated job, and have, I imagine, very much contributed to the happiness of the excellent Major.[37] You have shown infinite patience, uncommonly correct judgment, and an amount of ability which no one about knows enough to understand, and no one here is intelligent enough to appreciate. You have made no mistakes that I know of. And you have held your tongue.

To a twelfth-century monk in a nineteenth-century attic, in Paris, the whole menagerie seems a queer struggle for reality, and impossible to judge or censure; so my congratulations have only the value of a Latin epitaph on a marble slab at the base of your bronze equestrian statue in Roman armor and a laurel wreath. Let it pass for that:

Hic jacet J. H.; *vir nobilis,* etc., etc., *insignis,* etc., etc., *præcipue felix,* etc., etc., *amicus Adamus,* etc., etc., etc., d. d. d.[38]

Even to discuss it all must be a bore; yet I find it occupies more of my thoughts than anything else except the color-theory of the Chartres glass and Ming vases. You don't expect to be taken as seriously as a Ming jar, of course, so I won't flatter you. Still the Ming dynasty is in it, much more

37. Major: William McKinley, under whom John Hay was serving, had just been re-elected. He was a veteran of the Civil War. Adams's intimacy with Hay put him at the center of world politics, and Hay freely availed himself of Adams's superior knowledge of political history, often trying out his diplomatic schemes on Adams. This was the period of the Boxer Rebellion in China and the occasion for Hay's formulation of the "Open Door" policy. **38.** *Hic . . . d. d. d.:* a facetious memorial— "Here lies J[ohn] H[ay]; a man celebrated, etc., etc., distinguished for, etc., etc., especially blessed by fortune, etc., etc., friend Adam, etc., etc., etc. (*dat, donat, dedicat*), gives, presents, dedicates."

than the Manchus. From the first, I have been absorbed by the conviction that the worst possible solution in China was that of a joint military occupation, which is the solution now inevitable. Joint military partition was to me much safer and more advantageous, and in my belief easier, as it required for the moment only a division of seaports. England would have got a bigger slice this year than she is likely ever to get again, and we could stand outside supporting her.

The whole question is in that last proposition about England. I own up that England has got on my nerves. Every week I see a big drop in her scale, till I get to think she will drop on my head tomorrow. Hicks Beach seems to me to grow in colossal dimensions of incompetence, and when I see that old rat Goschen [39] scuttling out of the ship, and all the intelligent ones, even up to Salisbury, trying to escape, and a young lot coming in, about of the style of George Curzon, leaving Joe Chamberlain and Hicks Beach, and every sort of difficulty close ahead, I turn greener than ever with terror.

The management of the Treasury and the Bank has been such that at last public confidence is affected. The Continent shows distinct tendencies not to trust England with its balances. The exchanges are set dead against her, on all sides. If Gage can let her have a hundred millions of gold now, he can carry her and Russia over, till the gold mines are reopened. Otherwise I see no chance that England can maintain her credit, and for at least five years she has kept her head above water only by credit. She has been insolvent since 1895. Almost invariably I have found the public catch an idea in five years; first, a few theorists; then the most far-sighted Jews; and at last the crowd of speculators for the settlement. The shock of last November very nearly upset England. This November her situation is very much worse, and the hatred of her is intensified to a degree at which an explosion becomes almost inevitable. Financially and politically the current seems to run even stronger against her than it does economically; and I don't wonder; for to me, who look on her as our only ally and our outpost in our future struggle with Europe, her stupidity, brutality, ignorance and senility, have been unendurable since the bimetallic contest in '93, when she so nearly cut our throats.

So I regard the Anglo-German agreement [40] as in effect a capitulation to draw Germany away from Russia; a scheme I have believed to be hopeless. To me, the only correct card is France; but I am only a theorist, without the smallest knowledge of the hands. If we could draw France into a combination which should secure the Philippines and all southern Asia up to the Hoang-ho, it would be all we could hope. Failing that, we lose the game when England falls.

You too want to scuttle. Everybody wants to scuttle, apparently, who sees the mess before him; except perhaps the Major who has a genius for just such situations. Never impatient and never discouraged, he is sure to win because he has the cards. There is to be a new deal after December, and no one can tell how the next hands will fall, but he seems safe for two years. Anyway, to the diseased mind of a Dominican monk like me, seven hundred years old, the lead is no longer his. In this game, Germany leads trumps.

I would give a sixpence, or a string of pice, to know what trumps Germany holds. I can't believe in Germany. She is not big enough to swing the club. If she could unite herself either to eastern or western Europe, she could do it. As it is, I see nothing but a repetition of my own thirteenth century.

This by way of compliment to your success. [41] Of personal matters I have very little to say. The Exposition is closing. To me it has been an education which I have failed to acquire for want of tutors, but it has been an immense amusement and only needed you to be a constant joy. It has brought me so near the end that I hardly care to wait for the last scenes. There are things in it which run close to the day of judgment. It is a new century, and what we used to call electricity is its God. I can already see that the scientific theories and laws of our generation will, to the next, appear as antiquated as the Ptolemaic system, and that the fellow who gets to 1930 will wish he hadn't. The curious mustiness of decay is already over our youth, and all the period from 1840 to 1870. The period from 1870 to 1900 is closed. I see that much in the machine-gallery of the Champ de Mars. The period from 1900 to 1930 is in full swing, and, gee-whacky! how it is going! It will break its damned neck long before it gets through, if it tries to keep up the speed. You are free to deride my sentimentality if you like, but

39. Goschen: George J. Goschen (1831–1907), resigned from the British Admiralty, October 12, 1900.   40. Anglo-German agreement: The agreement did not take final form and was soon abandoned in what proved to be one of Germany's great diplomatic blunders, paving the way to World War I. It represented one phase of the intensely complicated rivalries of the Great Powers in which England, France, Germany, and Russia were struggling for supremacy in Europe, Africa, and the East. 41. your success: allusion to the part played by the American Peace Commissioners at the recently established Hague Court in informally bringing about the Anglo-German agreement.

I assure you that I,—a monk of St. Dominic, absorbed in the Beatitudes of the Virgin Mother—go down to the Champ de Mars and sit by the hour over the great dynamos, watching them run as noiselessly and as smoothly as the planets, and asking them—with infinite courtesy—where in Hell they are going. They are marvelous. The Gods are not in it. Chiefly the Germans! Steam no longer appears, although still behind the scenes; but one feels no certainty that another ten years may not abolish steam too. The charm of the show, to me, is that no one pretends to understand even in a remote degree, what these weird things are that they call electricity, Roentgen rays, and what not. The exhibitors are dead dumped into infinity on a fork.

So my solitude prepares itself for heaven, with a constant eye to the London exchanges. With an humble and contrite heart, I prostrate myself before the Major and the dynamos, and wait for the day of judgment much as I did in the reign of St. Louis. St. Thomas Aquinas and you are my only friends. . . .

TO CHARLES MILNES GASKELL [42]

Paris [Sunday], 15 November, 1903.

Before I sail,—and it may be in a week or a month,—I feel as though a kind of pious duty required my writing you a letter of sympathy about Morley's murder of Gladstone. Not that the world will ever know the dead! On the contrary, the world will no doubt regard Morley as giving, rather than taking, life; but to you the double view must be serious. Gladstone was a very decisive element in your life, and came near being so in mine.

Morley has made a conscientious effort, only too visible. The result is to me painful. These twelfth-century, *a priori*, heroic characters cannot and ought not to be sympathetic. Gladstone believed himself to be divinely inspired, a direct mouthpiece and agent of God. Every entry in his diary shows it. Look at the weird extract Vol. III, p. 310. He was pure Cromwell. Such a man should not be sympathetic. He draws his power from another source. He is by essence egotist. The effect on me of the *Life* is to paint the man exactly as he seemed to me, forty years ago, but more crude. I had not supposed him to be so essentially commonplace in mind and taste, or so warped in thought. I can hardly recall two remarks or observations made by him in the whole book that re-

main in the memory as original, and as for his taste, he had none, except for second-rate porcelain, that I can discover; for I call Homer education, not in him a taste. In fact, he owned it, and this modesty or self-knowledge is his one sympathetic quality; or would be, if it did not smell of the cloister and the hair-cloth.

Of course in him, as in most people, there were two or three or a dozen men; in these emotional, abnormal natures, there are never less than three. When excited, natures appear, one on top of another, till insanity, or absolute dissolution of unity, comes. Contradictory qualities are the law, not the exception. He was full of them. He played parts like a Roman Catholic Jesuit Pope who is trained to deceive himself and is supremely honest in self-deception. This mediaeval type is unintelligible outside the Church and the training.

As a parallel character, one should study the Life of Renan. Both men were trying to do the same thing,—orient their minds to the mind of their time. Both started from the thirteenth century, and neither got to the twentieth; but, of the two, I very strongly suspect that Morley has much more real sympathy with Renan and his honest failure. He at least saw something besides himself. He saw that he could not see.

In short, my impression is that two men gain greatly in the story. One is old Palmerston; the other, John Bright. Of course, Morley's amusing *coups de griffe* [43] at Chamberlain are calculated to delight all parties. As usual, he succeeds in discrediting the Tories better than in defending his own party. As his optimism is an imposed stage-rôle, he is very right to display it with great moderation. A most difficult task,—if not impossible, —and I hope he will be politically stronger for it.

TO HENRY JAMES

Paris, 18 November, 1903.

Although you, like most men of toil, hate to be bored, I can hardly pass over your last work [44] without boring you to the extent of a letter. We have reached a time of solar antiquity when nothing matters, but still we feel what used to be called the law of gravitation, mass, or attraction, and obey it.

More than ever, after devouring your William

---

42. **Charles Milnes Gaskell:** (1842–1919), Adams's lifelong English friend and one of his oldest correspondents.

43. **One . . . Chamberlain:** *coups de griffe:* "strokes of the claw." John Morley (1838–1923), British statesman and writer. Joseph Chamberlain (1836–1914), British Colonial Secretary at this period and ardent imperialist. Henry John Temple Palmerston (1784–1865), Prime Minister of England during the first five years of Adams's service as private secretary in London.
44. **last work:** *William Wetmore Story and His Friends* (1903).

Story, I feel how difficult a job was imposed on you. It is a *tour de force,* of course, but that you knew from the first. Whether you have succeeded or not, I cannot say, because it all spreads itself out as though I had written it, and I feel where you are walking on firm ground, and where you are on thin ice, as though I were in your place. Verily I believe I wrote it. Except your specialty of style, it is me.

The painful truth is that all of my New England generation, counting the half-century, 1820–1870, were in actual fact only one mind and nature; the individual was a facet of Boston. We knew each other to the last nervous centre, and feared each other's knowledge. We looked through each other like microscopes. There was absolutely nothing in us that we did not understand merely by looking in the eye. There was hardly a difference even in depth, for Harvard College and Unitarianism kept us all shallow. We knew nothing—no! but really nothing! of the world. One cannot exaggerate the profundity of ignorance of Story in becoming a sculptor, or Sumner in becoming a statesman, or Emerson in becoming a philosopher. Story and Sumner, Emerson and Alcott, Lowell and Longfellow, Hillard, Winthrop, Motley, Prescott, and all the rest, were the same mind,—and so, poor worm!—was I!

Type bourgeois-bostonien! A type quite as good as another, but more uniform. What you say of Story is at bottom exactly what you would say of Lowell, Motley, and Sumner, barring degrees of egotism. You cannot help smiling at them, but you smile at us all equally. God knows that we knew our want of knowledge! the self-distrust became introspection—nervous self-consciousness—irritable dislike of America, and antipathy to Boston. *Auch ich war in Arcadien geboren!* [45]

So you have written not Story's life, but your own and mine,—pure autobiography,—the more keen for what is beneath, implied, intelligible only to me, and half a dozen other people still living; like Frank Boott: who knew our Boston, London and Rome in the fifties and sixties. You make me curl up, like a trodden-on worm. Improvised Europeans, we were, and—Lord God!—how thin! No, but it is too cruel! Long ago,—at least thirty years ago,—I discovered it, and have painfully held my tongue about it. You strip us, gently and kindly, like a surgeon, and I feel your knife in my ribs.

No one else will ever know it. You have been extremely tactful. The essential superficiality of Story and all the rest, you have made painfully clear to us, but not, I think, to the family or the public. After all the greatest men are weak. Morley's Gladstone is hardly thicker than your Story. Let us pray!

45. *Auch . . . geboren!:* "I, too, was born in Arcadia!"

Stephen Crane

1871–1900

In THE last three decades of the nineteenth century, it was a wise American who knew his own country: the era was one of rapid, confused, and basic change, when the United States was neither still an agrarian nor yet an industrialized nation, neither the old-fashioned antebellum democracy nor the massive mechanized urban society of the present. And Stephen Crane was peculiarly the child of this age—if only because the brevity of his life kept him from knowing any other. He almost completely lacked the sense of the past that his older contemporaries Henry James and Henry Adams had in uncommon measure. They knew full well that the Civil War had riven them from the America they were brought up to understand; Crane, born in 1871 into the thoroughly disrupted postwar era, had no such memory of order to help him comprehend the disorder around him: *The Red Badge of Courage* and the Civil War represent very nearly the limit of his reach into the past. On the other hand, his chance to accumulate experience was cut off early. He died of tuberculosis in 1900, when Theodore Dreiser—also born in 1871—had not yet published a novel. But the circumstances which made him so much the creature of his time also projected him into the timelessness of a classic American legend. He was a kind of innocent in a fallen world: free from the burdens of the past, he went unarmed by its lessons; confronting strange and perilous situations, he had to rely almost entirely on his own gifts and character and vision; certain that true victory was different from worldly success, he struggled towards a goal he could not name.

Being a legendary figure was a doubtful advantage for Crane. His extraordinary gifts and youthful intensity were enviable assets, of course. Thanks to them, his life and writing moved in a world which, though sometimes thin, was vivid, immediate, and momentous. Though he was hardly aware that he faced historic problems of American and human life, he instinctively knew that he was beset by cosmic issues. But his handicaps should not be understated. While his short life partly accounted for his being a man without a historical shadow, his peculiar innocence must be attributed partly to failure of mind. Too much the legendary innocent, he was slow to learn that culture is man's substitute for experience, and that without it a young man is prey to deceptions that arise as much from his own ignorance as from the falsity of the world. Crane's knowledge from books and men was negligible compared to James's or Adams's, and he could not make up for it with an education like Mark Twain's in the lore and customs of a traditional community. He belonged to the middle class, whose literary situation Yeats defined as having lost the culture of the folk without having yet reached the level of high culture. But when folk and high culture are missing, a third kind fills the vacuum. The conventions of popular literature, with all their sensationalism and sentimentality, dominated Crane's experience, so that even when he consciously rejected them, he might do so without any idea of what next step to take. While his lively eye for contrasts between popular illusion and the way things happen might have freed him from the conventions he scorned, he neglected other ways of overcoming the limitations of his milieu. Having early and rightly concluded that direct observation was much more valuable than a fraudulent literary version of reality, he erroneously decided that books were only for the scholar's idle time. He lived hard and observed much, but read little. Within the circumscribed range of his experience, he was undoubtedly one of James's "people on whom nothing is lost"; but his famous irony was the necessary instrument of an intelligence which had so little material on which to work.

Crane's limitations are evident in his best work as well as his failures, as a passage from his greatest story makes clear. "The Open Boat" (see pp. 408–19) is based on his first-hand experience as a correspondent shipwrecked on a filibustering expedition to the Cuban revolutionaries of 1897. The bare facts of four men in a dinghy fighting the sea for twenty-seven hours and reaching land with three safe, one dead, convey neither the suffering of the men nor the meaning of the experience. But once a writer gets past externals and tries to render an event as it has been felt, he has to fall back on the resources of his personal culture. In this case, Crane presented actual heroism by reference to the banality of a schoolboy's poem:

To chime the notes of his emotion, a verse mysteriously entered the correspondent's head. He had even forgotten that he had forgotten this verse, but it suddenly was in his mind.

A *soldier of the Legion lay dying in Algiers;*
There was lack of woman's nursing, there was dearth of woman's tears;

But a comrade stood beside him, and he took that comrade's hand,
And he said, "I never more shall see my own, my native land."

In his childhood the correspondent had been made acquainted with the fact that a soldier of the Legion lay dying in Algiers, but he had never regarded the fact as important. Myriads of his schoolfellows had informed him of the soldier's plight, but the dinning had naturally ended by making him perfectly indifferent. He had never considered it his affair that a soldier of the Legion lay dying in Algiers, nor had it appeared to him as a matter for sorrow. It was less to him than the breaking of a pencil's point.

Now, however, it quaintly came to him as a human, living thing. It was no longer merely a picture of a few throes in the breast of a poet, meanwhile drinking tea and warming his feet at the grate: it was an actuality—stern, mournful, and fine.

The passage is full of Crane's strongest qualities. The realism has a center of consciousness and a style which can dramatize that consciousness. The argument implies some complicated and interesting ideas on the relation of literature to life, especially when we remember that it occurs in a story for readers who will be warming their feet at the grate. If Crane seems to be tethered to the mawkish poem which he quotes, he manages to suggest that such foolish triteness characterizes the culture which is of, by, and for the comfortable classes. A subversive irony is his most striking means of transcending the historic situation into which he was born.

Crane's attack on popular culture is the most consistent and varied theme in all his work, but not the only one. After all, "The Open Boat" is not only a vivid, wryly presented story, but also a considered expression of Crane's disbeliefs and his residual faith. The same thing may be said of all his best work, that it passes the test of high seriousness as well as technical virtuosity. Despite his limited background, he attained this twofold qualification of the genuine artist. The great social and moral questions which are traditionally the substance of literature enter his work also, even though they come in indirectly and without the usual signs. If he scorned to preach like the moralizing authors of popular fiction, he nevertheless learned to shape the significance of the unsaid. If he lacked the recognizable techniques of the acknowledged masters, he developed literary methods of his own. The list of his surprising achievements could be lengthened, provided we not allow ourselves to suggest that sheer genius is explanation enough of how Crane made up for his cultural deficiencies. We would do better to turn to the sources from which he supplied his imagination: firsthand experience, a religious upbringing, and the American literary situation of the nineties.

II

CONSIDERING Crane's ironic relation to popular culture—both dependent and profoundly antagonistic—there is rather too much poetic justice in the fact that his life tended to the pattern of a bad novel: we are forced to remind ourselves that he actually lived what his average countrymen collectively dreamed. He was the youngest child in a happy parsonage; his father died when he was nine; his mother, with a kind of Louisa May Alcott resolution and resourcefulness, kept the household together by writing for the Methodist papers. The boy, whose frail health had been a leading reason for his family's removal from Newark to upstate New York, grew up to be a baseball star—first at military school and then at college. Indeed he might have become a professional athlete had his older brother not persuaded him at least to try college first. He tried two colleges in fact, but it took him less than a year to decide that "humanity was a more interesting study" than the curriculum. In the spring of 1891, he quit Syracuse University and became a full-time reporter. He had worked for his brother Townley's Asbury Park news agency during his summers and had been a college correspondent for a New York paper. Now he resumed his apprenticeship under his brother, until in August, 1892, he seemed to wreck his career—and did wreck Townley's—by writing too candidly and too well about a workingmen's parade in the New Jersey resort.[1] His ironic coverage of the marchers caused an inch-high political scandal and, though the newspaper's editor later denied any connection, he himself suddenly became a free-lance journalist in New York. Thus began what Crane was to call his "artistic education on the Bowery." There he not only sketched the life of poverty, he endured it. Through these years of hardship he worked at his first novel, then at his second. Publishers would not touch his *Maggie, A Girl of the Streets;* when he printed it himself in 1892, booksellers would not handle it. If it had not been for the encouragement of Hamlin Garland (a young literary prophet whom Crane had met as a newspaperman) and of William Dean Howells, he might have given up. The reversal, when it came at last, was sudden: at twenty-four, the neglected and almost starving writer found himself a best-selling novelist. He was shortly to disparage as "a mere episode" *The Red Badge of Courage* (1895) which made him famous, and to prefer to it the poetry which gave his "ideas of life as a whole." But *The Black Riders,* also published in 1895, went into six printings within a year, despite the critical attacks. On whatever terms he chose, Stephen Crane had won through.

The sequel to the boy's success story was melodramatic too. Celebrity helped him become one of the outstanding newspaper correspondents in the heyday of yellow journalism. Traveling to the West and Mexico, enduring shipwreck off the Florida coast, covering wars in Greece and Cuba, he filed his dispatches to Pulitzer and Hearst and often made news himself. He never knew the public, almost official responsibilities of journalism as they had existed for Franklin and Whitman, Sam Clemens and Henry Adams; nor could he, within the newspaper conventions, entertain the public by his *writing* as Franklin and Mark Twain had done. A Mr. Dooley might still exist, but Crane was never a humorist in that broad sense. In those days before film and television shared the market of mass entertainment, Crane was a star reporter who was indeed a star. Though a reporter rather than an actor, he performed for the public: his sensational vehicle was news of famine and war rather than manufactured drama, but his social function was clear. The age of publicity was at hand, and the customers responded gratefully when Crane underwent dangers which made their image of the reporter seem real. The shy

[1] See "On the New Jersey Coast," pp. 397–98, below.

and modest Crane did not glory in his part as did Richard Harding Davis (1864–1916), the Rudolph Valentino of newspaperdom. But he was the prisoner of his role, economically at least, and to some degree psychologically: his journalistic career abetted in him the fascination of violence—of seeing it and testing his courage in it—that wore him out so young.

Domesticity settled upon Crane at twenty-five—in a luridly appropriate manner. Waiting for the filibuster's ship to sail from Jacksonville, he spent the last weeks of 1896 in regular attendance at a favorite night spot of newspapermen and miscellaneous adventurers, the Hotel de Dream, and struck up an alliance with its proprietress. Cora Taylor was a rare woman, even though it may sound as if a script-writer invented her. She had a shadowed and unhappy past—two failed marriages and only one divorce. Beneath the toughness which could preside over a seaport night club and brothel, she had a warm and mettlesome heart. She was intelligent, charming, patient, and loyal. After Crane's ordeal at sea, she took him in and cared for him. Thereafter, she followed him to Greece as the "first woman war correspondent," and when the Greek-Turkish War ended in May, 1897, she and Crane established themselves in England as man and wife. There, in the interval before the Spanish-American War, Crane wrote some of his most remarkable stories, and there he struck up the literary friendships which put him in touch at last with the main international stream of letters. But his career was virtually over. The exposure to which the war correspondent willfully submitted himself and the unremitting frenzy of trying to write his way out of debt took their toll, and by the end of 1899 his tuberculosis entered the final fatal stage. In the spring, Cora arranged, with the financial help of friends, to take Stephen to a sanitarium in the Black Forest, but the stretcher patient was too far gone. He died at Badenweiler, June 5, 1900, hardly more than a week after their arrival.

III

THE SENSATIONAL and pathetic character of Crane's biography is so glaring that it is a break in the melodrama which best helps us find the quality of his life as it was lived. Such a point is the eve of his celebrity, when late in 1895 *The Red Badge of Courage* and his book of verse had been published and the English reviews which made the success of the novel were just beginning to cross the Atlantic. Crane's public recognition at home was signalized by the literary dinner given in his honor by Elbert Hubbard (the "Sage of East Aurora," as he was called), the vulgarizer of Emerson and William Morris, and the charlatan promoter of fine printing, avant-garde literature, and self-culture. Hubbard, whose arty magazine the *Philistine* published authentic Stephen Crane poems as well as forged John Ruskin essays, convened some thirty literary lights of journalism and advertising at a Buffalo, New York, hotel. On the guest list were editors of magazines with such extraordinary names as *Moods* and *Brains*. Down the table from Crane, the celebrants became more and more raucous, and after dinner, they began interrupting the toasts and ragging the speakers, including the guest of honor. Although an older guest protested the rowdiness as an insult to Crane, he himself only wondered what to make of it. He enjoyed the boisterous party—had "the time of his life," one witness later suggested—and when called upon, spoke briefly and quietly about his aims as a writer. But he afterwards wrote to the one close friend who had attended, the sponsor of his dress suit for the occasion: "I am very anxious to hear whether you are satisfied with the dinner. I did not drink much but the excitement soon turned everything into a grey haze for me and I am not sure that I came off decently." His perplexity stands in sharp contrast to the agony of Mark Twain after another literary event just eighteen years before this one. Addressing the Boston worthies at the Whittier Birthday Dinner (see pp. 94–96), Mark Twain was caught between conflicting sets of conventions and ground to powder. Crane, facing men who were not acting under any known convention and able to rely on no formal resources of his own, behaved according to his native simplicity and honesty; his wide-eyed innocence was taken aback only for a moment.

The incident was like a Crane short story, for its importance did not lie in its leading to a second act: an episode which produced no consequences, it nevertheless could stand for more than itself. Its simple plot put Crane in a situation where all accepted social forms were violently disrupted, and he got through the ordeal with his fundamental decency intact. Amid the rampant vulgarity of Hubbard's banquet, he showed as fine a self-possession in the face of chaos as the comedy of manners could conceivably allow. Moreover, the story was adequate to the theme which Crane formulated a month after the event, when the onslaught of publicity had become general. He then wrote of fame as an ordeal of character: "For the first time I saw the majestic forces which are arrayed against man's true success—not the world—the world is silly, changeable, any of its decisions can be reversed—but man's own colossal impulses more strong than chains, and I perceived that the fight was not going to be with the world but with myself."

The ultimate battle might be inward, but Crane obviously looked for outward, physical tests of character—and even of imagination. Two years after his war novel appeared, when he saw actual combat in Greece, he said with evident relief, *"The Red Badge* is all right." With his imagination thus proved trustworthy, he was confirmed in his method of drawing on personal history for literary material. The method sounds like everyone else's, but Crane practiced it with unusual simplicity. He personally knew hunger, exposure, mortal danger, lonely resistance to convention, and self-doubt worse than all, and he could infer from experience his reactions to imaginary ordeals. Hence his candid reply, when he heard that readers took him for a veteran of the Civil War, had been that he learned the emotions of *The Red Badge* on the football field. The transfer of feelings became the main resource of his storytelling, to the exclusion of other techniques that he might have learned from the masters of fiction. Perhaps his imagination worked this way for psychological as well as intellectual reasons: while he could vividly imagine his own response to almost any crucial situation, he was not strong at imagining other kinds of people. The figures in his tales seem to be individuated mainly by circumstances, and their character to be defined by a few primary emotions like fear and courage. Just as the author stands apart

from traditional culture, they stand apart from traditional characters, for the nineteenth-century novel presented people as the rich compound of personal and social history, ideals and knowledge, as well as circumstances and temperament. Crane's bent for *short* fiction can be inferred from his being interested less in the structure of society than in the rendering of situation, less in the sum of character than in the response to a particular crisis. The archetypal event for him, whether experienced or imagined, is intense and isolated, the undergoing of an ultimate trial.

While circumstance and temperament help explain Crane's affinity for this pattern, the concern for physical tests of character was hardly a peculiarity with him. He had distinguished company in his strenuous reaction against the comfortable life: restiveness under uneventful middle-class prosperity affected some of the most sophisticated minds on both sides of the Atlantic—and affected them in a way which must be distinguished from the popular cult of sensationalism. Leslie Stephen in the Alps, Theodore Roosevelt in the Black Hills, even Henry Adams in the Rockies, and above all, Oliver Wendell Holmes, Jr., whose Civil War experience left him permanently "touched with fire," shared feelings that we recognize as typically Crane's. For them all, the trials which allowed a man to rise above himself conformed in a thoroughly naturalistic way with the psychology of conversion, as if physical ordeals filled the unconscious need of men who could no longer practice the introspective spiritual exercises of Protestantism. Conversely, we may say that their religious heritage, even when it was apparently out of mind, lent form and intensity to their response to natural events. So, in turning from the general view of Crane's life and art to the development of his work in the early Bowery fiction and then the tales of war, we may expect to find that his religious history is at least as important as his individual experience.

IV

SUPERFICIALLY, Crane's religious upbringing as a Methodist had a light hold upon him. He recalled, near the end of his life, "I used to like church and prayer meetings when I was a kid but that cooled off and when I was thirteen or about that, my brother Will told me not to believe in Hell after my uncle had been boring me about the lake of fire and the rest of the sideshows." His reminiscing took rather a Huck Finn turn when he said of his mother that "it hurt her that any of us should be slipping from Grace and giving up eternal damnation or salvation or those things." The comfort of religion seemed unnecessary to the comfortable life of a prosperous society, and the discipline of religion appeared superfluous to a life which proceeded happily and decently without the restraints that more coercive societies imposed. The case was not unusual: like Mark Twain, Henry James, and Henry Adams in the older generation, Crane slipped from religion *before* he had intellectual reasons to offer for his defection. Having already become a naturalist in belief, he was not much disturbed by the metaphysical problems that might have been raised for him by Darwinian biology and modern science. He gathered the new knowledge more or less from the air, and he absorbed it easily: his sardonic poem on social Darwinism is of a piece with his poems on newspaper half-truth, churchgoing, or success, all of them alike rebellious against the prevailing culture. What little he knew of the scientific revolution did not cause his disbelief, it merely confirmed it.

Other kinds of religious problems did come to disturb Crane—for example, the irrelevance of the church's questions to the actual choices most people have to make, and the impossibility of solving the paradoxes of tragic life. The inscription which he wrote in several gift copies of *Maggie* indicates one way in which he faced such questions:

It is inevitable that you will be greatly shocked by this book but continue please with all possible courage to the end. For it tries to show that environment is a tremendous thing in the world and frequently shapes lives regardless. If one proves that theory one makes room in Heaven for all sorts of souls (notably an occasional street girl) who are not confidently expected to be there by many excellent people. . . .

And an inscription written three years later, when *Maggie* was reissued, shows how, by 1896, he had given up trying to fit his argument into orthodox theology and begun to regard Biblical religion as evasive of the urgent questions the book raised:

"And the wealth of the few shall be built upon the
    patience of the poor"
Prophecy not made B.C. 1090

These ironic inscriptions reveal the starting point of his thought as surely as his citing the dying soldier at Algiers reveals his roots in popular culture. He had thrown off religion, but his religious inheritance survived.

What he lacked in intellectual subtlety was made up for by the complexity of his personal involvement with the classic problems of religion. The influences which worked upon him, taken separately, were simple, but their combined effect was not. His father, Jonathan Townley Crane, had left the stern Presbyterianism of his boyhood and committed himself to a gentler piety that emphasized redemption more than sin. Against the doctrine of total depravity, he held to a belief in the enduring innocence of created beings and the accessibility to perfect holiness of all God's children. His mild theology corresponded to an equally mild view of what constituted depravity: from his Methodist pulpit and in his writings, he preached against drink, tobacco, baseball, and novels, recommending total abstinence from them all. The vices he denounced could not seem essential to the son who indulged in every one of them and still did not find that they touched upon ultimate evil. And the gentleness of the man who "never drove a horse faster than two yards an hour even if some Christian was dying elsewhere" seemed ineffectual to the son who early guessed—and saw—the cruelty, violence, and Christian and unchristian dyings which were always just beyond the vision of respectable society.

Crane's mother was an even stronger influence than his father. The daughter and niece of ministers, she came of a Methodist line which expressed its evangelism in brimstone exhortation. A book by her uncle, Bishop Jesse Truesdell Peck, which Stephen kept in his library to the end of his life, calls its readers to "hear the language of despair as it comes up from the place where there is weeping, and wailing, and gnashing of teeth." Mrs. Crane fervidly opposed, as her husband gently did, the evident vices, but she had a strong sense also of the sins which unloving piety might commit. Able to discriminate respectability from goodness, she could, if need be, defy social convention in her own way. Crane had the story on hearsay, but the memory of her defiance was important to him:

My brothers tell me that she got herself into trouble before I was old enough to follow proceedings by taking care of a girl who had an accidental baby. Inopportune babies are not part of the Methodist ritual but mother was always more of a Christian than a Methodist and she kept this girl at our house in Asbury until she found a home somewhere. Mother's friends were mostly women and they had the famous feminine aversion to that kind of baby. It is funny that women's interest in babies trickles clean off the mat if they have never met papa socially. . . .

Once again we may be reminded of Huck Finn as Crane rejects the religion of the letter, which society enjoins, and affirms the religion of the spirit. But life is less orderly than literature, and despite the relaxed tone of his reminiscence, Crane did not give up arguing with the letter when he ceased intellectually to believe in it.

Crane obviously had his mother's friends in the back of his mind when he wrote not only the inscriptions, but also the text of *Maggie.* He began the novel when he was in college, that is, before he knew the Bowery as a reporter: even when he put the book into final form, writing with more accurate knowledge and greater skill, he left signs of its origin in his reaction against the women of Asbury. The book has more in common with nineteenth-century religious tracts on the vices of cities than with reportorial investigations like Jacob Riis's *How the Other Half Lives* (1890) or *The Children of the Poor* (1892). Crane's child of the slums, seeing a local saloon hero as the lover "under the trees in her dream garden," is seduced young and deserted early: instead of returning to the sweatshops from which she was rescued by vice, she becomes a prostitute and thus begins a quick downhill journey which leads to the river and suicide. The shock-effect of the story may be measured against the sentimental convention expressed in Oliver Goldsmith's famous song:

When lovely woman stoops to folly,
   And finds too late that men betray,
What charm can soothe her melancholy,
   What art can wash her guilt away?

The only art her guilt to cover,
   To hide her shame from ev'ry eye,
To give repentance to her lover,
   And wring his bosom—is, to die.[1]

The melancholy which descends on Maggie is caused not by guilt, but by helplessness and physical deterioration. Her lover's heart is not wrung in the least by her death; but her slatternly mother, who had cursed her fall and turned her out, ends the novel with a drunken gush of sentiment, screaming "Oh, yes, I'll forgive her! I'll fergive her!" Whereas Crane in his travesty depended on convention, Theodore Dreiser at the end of the decade was to discard it and let his ruined heroine not die, but rise to a kind of success. But Dreiser's *Sister Carrie* was modeled on his own sister's story and the life outside the conventions which he himself knew; Crane, though experienced in vice, was the creature of his own background.

Crane on religion was more unconventional than Crane on sex. In *Maggie,* there is a brief episode in a city mission where the preacher tells his ragged hearers, "You are damned," and they tacitly reply, "Where's our soup?" But religious ineffectualness became the central theme of his other Bowery novel, *George's Mother,* which he originally called "A Woman Without Weapons." Howells summed up the story well by describing the title figure as "a poor, inadequate woman, of commonplace religiosity, whose son goes to the bad." The narrative focuses on the son who in his mother's eyes "was going to become a white and looming king among men." George Kelcey, like Maggie in having neither coercive institutions nor ideals to guide him, makes his choice between the chapel which huddles between tenements and a "little smiling saloon." He joins what is pictured as a mystic brotherhood of louts and hoodlums who

[1] Eliot was to parody the same eighteenth-century song in *The Waste Land,* a generation later. See p. 777.

longed dimly for a time when they could run through decorous streets with crash and roar of war, an army of revenge for pleasures long possessed by others, a wild sweeping compensation for their years without crystal and gilt, women and wine. This thought slumbered in them, as the image of Rome might have lain small in the hearts of the barbarians.

Insofar as environment accounts for the destiny of Maggie Johnson or George Kelcey, Crane recognized that socialism and the changing of environment provided a solution; but having shaken one ideology, he did not care to take on another. In the same tone he used for religion, he once remarked that he "was a Socialist once for two weeks but when a couple of Socialists assured me I had no right to think differently from any other Socialist and then quarrelled with each other about what Socialism meant, I ran away." Instead, he became a radical without a program who distinguished the spirit from the letter. To those who hastily fixed the damnable responsibility for vice on the Maggies of the world, he declared that environment was a "tremendous thing"; he did not say it was all.

What Crane believed in was not doctrinaire reformism, but heart-conviction based on a converting knowledge of ultimate social reality: the historic terms of evangelical Protestantism define thus the moral economy of his secular world. The weakness of the Bowery novels is relevant here, for the thinness of characterization is a clue to the strength of the books also. Maggie and Mrs. Kelcey would be more poignant if Crane could render the inner consciousness as Dreiser does or people's awareness of each other in the manner of James; but the rendering of character is less important to his novels than the vision of horror. The mission preacher's threat of hell in *Maggie* conveys nothing to hearers already in torment from hunger, and poor Mrs. Kelcey, an "intent little warrior" in her militant religion, succeeds only in filling her son's mind with images of green dragons. The irony in both these cases goes beyond the ineffectualness of religion. For Maggie living could say, "Why, this is hell, nor am I out of it"; and George Kelcey, insignificant oaf though he is, vaguely feels a total diabolical rebelliousness. While hellfire preaching is held up for contempt, the characters play their part in a brimstone fable.

If a brimstone fable is to be effective, the reader should be caught up in it. But apart from Crane's difficulties of sympathy, his ironic technique detaches the reader from the characters of his novels and from the horrifying events. "An Experiment in Misery" (see pp. 399–404) solves the problem of ethical distance by shifting the point of view to a consciousness within the story. The dramatic concentration invites the reader to share the protagonist's experience and to sense that the struggle is not only with the world but with oneself. Indeed, Crane later recalled the story as if this were its main point: "In a story of mine called 'An Experiment in Misery' I tried to make plain that the root of Bowery life is a sort of cowardice. Perhaps I mean a lack of ambition or to willingly be knocked flat and accept the licking." But there is more to "An Experiment" than this, for Crane here discovered the most dramatic form for his theme, the story of initiation into a terrible knowledge. The young man, who sees his night in a flophouse in images of the graveyard or the lower world, comes back from his journey into hell with a new sense of reality. After the event, he wears the guilty look "that comes with certain convictions." Having learned the meaning of despair and felt what it is to be cut off from "social position, comfort, the pleasures of living," he implicitly rejects these "unconquerable kingdoms" because they are founded on human wretchedness. Unlike Maggie Johnson and George Kelcey, who are so easily summed up by circumstance, weakness, and mindlessness, he has the capacity not only to feel but to understand. Whether he can also resist the moral undertow of experienced misery we cannot tell, for vision, like environment, is a tremendous thing: he will never again be as he was.

V

WAR, the second great subject Crane turned to, gave him material he could better mold to his conception of outward *and* inner struggle. In his tales of battle, he could so intensify the event and hold attention to ultimate questions that ordinary problems of character and society were excluded. Given his limitations, war was simpler for him to handle than poverty. The all-important circumstances of battle did not imply an environmental determinism; the weaknesses of soldiers did not blur over into degeneracy; the violence of war could without credulity be taken as the absolutely given condition of an action, since men caught up in that ultimate man-made violence do not have occasion to consider causes. War provided a neatly self-enclosing context within which Crane could work out his narratives of spiritual ordeal. The pattern did not change: storybook illusions of glory are the starting point, and yielding to the pressure of battle is an alternative as false as yielding to the moral numbness of misery, whether it be by giving in to fear and turning coward or by submitting to the frenzy of the kill and turning madman. Popular illusion is the characteristic of the once-born; but Crane, the unconscious heir of Jonathan Edwards on religious affections, also showed the delusive states that might pass as evidence of being twice-born. Henry Fleming, in *The Red Badge of Courage* (1895), proves the need for discrimination: little need be said of his fear and panic, but his moment of physical courage, it should be noted, is a travesty of true virtue, "a temporary but sublime absence of selfishness"; his genuine manhood comes with the unassertive knowledge that "he had been to touch the great death, and found that, after all, it was but the great death."

True heroism for Crane cannot be judged by externals, and as the title of "A Mystery of Heroism" (see pp. 404–08) makes clear, that story gives a definitive illustration of his argument. The circumstantially induced courage which prompts Collins to cross under enemy fire to the well, and the panic with which he speeds back to his platoon with the filled bucket, explain away the apparent heroism of his act, while the spilled and empty bucket at the end makes the objective exploit nugatory. But beneath the ironies of heroism which have been generally noticed lies the mystery. For the young soldier, crazed by the terrors of no man's land, runs past a dying artillery officer who asks him for a drink. "I can't" is his screamed answer, and yet, a moment later, he wheels back as if under a power stronger than his own will. There is no conscious goodness

in the act—nor unconscious tenderness either: "Collins tried to hold the bucket steadily, but his shaking hands caused the water to splash all over the face of the dying man. Then he jerked it away and ran on." Yet every detail of the incident helps the reader to penetrate the mystery of heroism. Writing on premises like those of "experimental religion," Crane first takes his character past book-knowledge to an actual confrontation of doom, has him "walk squarely up to the face of death." As a result, Collins comes to know both objective evil and his own lack of merit. But more important than knowledge, conduct is the sign of a man's heart: inarticulate, awkward, acting on an impulse which transcends the logical course of events, he passes the great test by giving water to a dying man. Though his deed is unrecognized by the world or even by himself, it is the secret glory which no irony can reduce.

The dying artilleryman functions in the plot as the person to whom Collins gives water, but he has a nonfunctional role as well, for the story would come out the same if he did not die. Curiously, there is a death in each of the stories I have mentioned except "An Experiment in Misery" where the hero enters a figurative house of the dead. Maggie and Mrs. Kelcey seem to die in vain, as they lived in vain, but Jim Conklin, the tall soldier of *The Red Badge of Courage*, and the wounded officer in "A Mystery" seem to die as part of the order of things—a sense of fitness keeps the pathos from becoming sentimental. The figure of the victim recurs again and again in Crane's narratives, as if the sacrifice were necessary to the initiation into truth. Here, too, the logic of the naturalistic world which his fiction presents resembles the logic of Crane's inherited religion. The pattern is made clearer by the fact that after writing *The Red Badge*, the storyteller turned to poetry: Crane's verse gives his religious opinions with what seems to be the candor of direct emotional expression.[1] The God of wrath and

[1] Like all poems, Crane's cannot be taken as perfectly reliable biographical documents. But the literary explanation of the language of his verse points just as surely to his religious background: his verse often took the form of parable, a fact which is largely explained by his immersion in the Bible at home and in school; and the succinctness of the form virtually required the shorthand of religious terminology.

the God of sacrificial redemption both appear literally in the poetry rather than by remote suggestion as in the prose. Of the two conceptions of divinity, Crane believes in the latter, in the sense of affirming his loyalty, but he also believes that the former presides over the world and he affirms his moral defiance. Poem LIII of *The Black Riders* discloses both aspects of his belief:

I

Blustering God,
Stamping across the sky
With loud swagger,
I fear You not.
No, though from Your highest heaven
You plunge Your spear at my heart,
I fear You not.
No, not if the blow
Is as the lightning blasting a tree.
I fear you not, puffing braggart.

. . . .

III

Withal, there is One whom I fear;
I fear to see grief upon that face.
Perchance, friend, He is not your God;
If so, spit upon Him.
By it you will do no profanity.
But I—
Ah, sooner would I die
Than see tears in those eyes of my soul.

Speaking out of a personal culture which was impoverished compared to Melville's, Crane offers a middle-class schoolboy's version of rebellious Ahab's "Come in thy lowest form of love, and I will kneel and kiss thee: but at thy highest, come as mere supernal power: and though thou launchest navies of full-freighted worlds, there's that in here that still remains indifferent." But Crane had one resource besides vivid accuracy which could save him from his own rhetoric. Setting forth this same religious paradox in another poem, "The Blue Battalions," he achieved an almost Biblical succinctness:

The clang of swords is Thy wisdom,
The wounded make gestures like Thy Son's. . . .

While the religious acceptance in these lines comes from an almost unique moment in the history of Crane's imagination, the enduring paradox is ingrained in his thought. His fiction,

transposing the paradox into a naturalistic world, thereby attains its tragic dimensions.

VI

EXCEPT for the Bible, Crane's literary background all too quickly came down to his contemporaries and in particular to William Dean Howells. In literature as in life, he was virtually without a knowledge of the past. He did read Emerson early and, with more telling effect, Whitman, Flaubert, and Tolstoy. Whitman's universal sympathy gave direction to the young man's eager observation, confirming the desire to record people and emotions beyond the pale of respectability. Flaubert taught a meticulous care for significant detail. Tolstoy, with what one critic has called his "ironic pacifism," supplied ideas of war as an institution, with its pretended control of actual chaos. But the influence of all these writers remained dormant until Howells' realism helped Crane to find himself. Howells' cause, to which he devoted a career that more than spanned Crane's lifetime, was genuinely the cause of literature, even though he held rather too simply that art achieves truth by transcribing its subject accurately. The essential naïveté of his thesis came out in his so admiring Jane Austen for her truthfulness that he seemed unaware of the conventions of comedy of manners which she—and he himself—employed. But naïve or not, he was sound in his basic judgments. Though there are many kinds of literary truth, as twentieth-century criticism usually argues, there is such a thing as literary untruth also. Conventions may be a literary necessity, but they can also stultify the mind. What Howells saw was that in the name of respectability and fine ideals a hollow literature was falsifying the serious issues of life. To be sure, he wanted— for the sake of honesty—a middle-class literature that would represent the life of prudence, prosperity, and pleasantness; and he is condescendingly remembered for having said that "the more smiling aspects of life . . . are the more American,"—a comparative observation which any global view would still probably confirm. What is commonly overlooked is that that phrase states only an observation, and not a convention by which he encouraged in his readers a blindness to their environment and

their fellow men. Not Howells, but his opponents—then and since—lulled men into
thinking that the poor are no longer with us.

The crisis in the war for realism was still very
recent when Crane and his generation began
to write. For the defenders of ideality, the symbolic battleground was "Boston": in the seventies, Mark Twain had jolted the keepers of the
sacred fire by his innocent miscalculation of the
Whittier fête. But soon the ruling class of
American culture and respectability sustained
the greater shock of apparent betrayal from
within by Howells and James. The gentility of
these novelists now seems so unquestionable
that it is hard to conceive that their work of the
eighties was denounced as scandalous; yet *The
Rise of Silas Lapham* (1885) led to Howells'
being regarded as a vulgarizer of literature, and
The Bostonians (1886) lost James a large
American audience for the rest of his life. Boston, as the holy city of the muses, proved to be
a taboo subject for realism: the novelists knew
how to distinguish between genuine values and
sham ideals, but for the reading public sanctity
was indivisible. These writers, who seem so
little dangerous today, fully recognized the implications of the critical wars. James had already, in "The Art of Fiction" (see pp. 252–
62), declared the artist's absolute freedom in
the choice of subject. Howells, though he was
personally as prudish as his opponents, roundly
declared that "the worst French naturalism"
was better than the best "unnaturalism" and
fought for Zola as well as himself. Once the
issues were thus clarified, writers could break
through conventionality of many sorts—as
Stephen Crane did in reporting that Asbury
Park parade of 1892. Even if the paper he
wrote for had not belonged to the Republican
vice-presidential candidate, Crane broke the
journalistic rule of being inoffensive to the
largest possible public of voters and newspaper-
buyers: he simply saw both marchers and audience unglorified by clichés. Whitelaw Reid's
New York *Tribune* apologized to the public
and discontinued its use of Townley Crane's
news agency: on the other hand, Stephen
Crane's career as an inconsequential sketch-
writer and reporter was transformed in a
major campaign for honesty in journalism and
art.

Howells had other principles of fiction besides truthfulness: since a democratic literature
should be of the people, he called for openness
to subjects generally called common and low;
he believed that literary language ought to copy
the language spoken by the people in the particular locale of a story; he insisted that a narrative could convey its true meaning to the people without the author's intruding his own
rhetoric or analysis on the respresentation of
life. His democratic realism—emphasizing the
moral discovery of new material, the renewal of
written language from living speech, and the
exclusion of comment for the sake of coherent
dramatic construction—served the novel well,
and it accounts for the reasoned taste behind
Howells' welcoming the author of *Maggie* to
the front rank of American fiction. By his principles, the development from Realism to Naturalism was a simple shift from middle-class
subjects to the representation of poverty and
violence. But the crude distinction according
to subject matter does not tell us enough about
literature. What we must further notice is that
Howells' literary doctrine was, as he well knew,
the application of Emerson's ideas to the novel.
The tacit assumption from which he argued
against preaching or teaching in fiction was
this: that the unembellished facts could convey meaning because by themselves they *had*
meaning in an implicit universal order. With
an agnostic like Crane, however, for whom the
vision of chaos was constant and glimpses of
order were rare, the meaning of an event came
less from its fitting a general pattern than from
its not fitting the preconceptions with which
society prepared him. Take metaphysical belief away, change certainty for ambiguity, and
irony becomes the method for finding meaning.

Crane's departures from the Howellsian
theory, which he thought "identical" with his
own, may be understood from the way he first
encountered it. In August, 1891, he covered for
his brother's agency a literary lecture at a
nearby New Jersey resort. Hamlin Garland, a
second-generation Realist, was then publishing
somber stories of Middle Western rural life
which violated the conventions of the American agrarian myth. In his zeal as a lecturer and
prophet, Garland added something to the re-

ceived doctrine of simple truthfulness. "The secret of every lasting success in art and literature lies," he later wrote, "in a powerful, sincere, emotional concept of life first, and, second, in the acquired power to convey that concept to others." His "veritism" differed from his master's Realism in its stress on individuality and on skill, and it was precisely here that he pointed the way to the young reporter who heard him at Avon-by-the-Sea. When Crane covered the workingmen's parade at Asbury Park a year later, he was accurate, but he was being true first of all to himself and his way of seeing the event. Though it was not fully evident at the time, the young author of Bowery tales like "An Experiment in Misery" was a reporter of what he himself was sensitive to rather than a historian of things as they actually were. The same may be said even more forcefully of *The Red Badge of Courage*, the subjectivity of which kept Howells from ever admiring it as much as he did *Maggie*. Crane had taken unconsciously the course which Henry James so thoroughly charted: what he saw depended not only on the objects seen, but on the point of view of the observer. As he put it, ". . . I understand that a man is born into the world with his own pair of eyes, and he is not at all responsible for his vision—he is merely responsible for his personal honesty. To keep close to this personal honesty is my supreme ambition."

Crane's artistic achievement was to fuse his particular vision and personal honesty with a language and method that gave them form. Concerning his language, little more need be said of his fertility of ironic reference, his skillful economy in picking out the significant detail of an episode or a scene, his ability to catch the spoken idiom when he wanted to. Concerning his technique, much that he did may be recognized as the reinvention of Jamesian devices: the foreshortening that compresses Maggie's downward career and death into a couple of pages, for example, or his concentrating and intensifying his drama by using the mind of a character as its register. But the pictorial quality of his work, a matter of both style and method, repays a closer look: it is the signature of Crane's imagination. His earliest work shows the knack for vivid phrase which

he gradually disciplined into a style. The prose which evolved from his apprenticeship is best described by analogy to painting: Hamlin Garland's enthusiasm for Monet and the Impressionists and Crane's own life with artist friends (whose studios he haunted and often camped in during his luckless New York years) both help account for the visual effects in his writing. Impressionism in painting developed from the realistic tradition. As Garland understood it, the new practice avoided a literalist rendering of the parts for the sake of catching a true impression of the whole: though Crane could as easily have learned about unity of effect from Poe, or from literary trial and error, Garland was useful in reconciling that aim with Howells' theories. But Crane's own understanding of the painters went deeper than that: he watched his friends record color and light more truthfully as they freed themselves from realistic conventions of seeing. Once, while with his brother in the country, he is reported to have said: "Will, isn't that cloud green? . . . But they wouldn't believe it if I put it in a book." He tested his readers' belief, nonetheless, with his truths of color—"the rushing yellow of the developing day," "the long gray walls of vapor where lay the battle lines," and "the red sun" give *The Red Badge of Courage* its objective setting. Further, Crane went beyond the paintings he knew and mixed realistic impressionism with expressive color and imagery. The columns of troops "like two serpents crawling out of the cavern of the night," the "crimson roar" of battle, and even the red sun "pasted in the sky like a wafer" are Henry Fleming's personal vision. The expressionist technique seems less bizarre because the subjective coloring is not the only vividness in the objectively brilliant scene. And in the ending, when the young soldier has become a man, emotional vision and objective appearance come together in a final harmony —"Over the river a golden ray of sun came through the hosts of leaden rain clouds."

In his mastery of language Crane left Garland and even Howells far behind. The style of *The Red Badge*—impressionist and objective on the one hand, expressionist and subjective on the other—may have been an almost instinctive discovery, but its adaptation and re-use were a matter of conscious skill. Crane had worked out the proper medium for his irony. Because his characters commonly see more or less than is there to be seen, we depend on the author as well as the character for our picture of events. To use James's terms, the center of consciousness does not have, strictly speaking, a monopoly on our point of view. A remarkable tact preserves the illusion of unity. The author sees more than his characters without ever asserting that he knows more than they do. He lets their feelings and their vision conduct our responses along one line, while his own darting images may be reminding us of ironic perspectives and critical doubts. The man who could do this was no longer merely the precocious writer dependent on slim resources: he was becoming the mature artist who could rely on a supple craftsmanship. What he lacked in theory, he made up for by seasoned practice. He was ready for the literary friendship which appropriately marked the second phase of his career: Joseph Conrad, not much of a theoretician either, knew at first sight that the author of *The Red Badge* shared his own aim, "to render the truth of a phase of life in terms of my own temperament with all the sincerity of which I was capable."

VII

TECHNICAL mastery freed Crane's imagination. For one thing, it freed him from the requirement of unremitting visual intensity which he could not have kept up. "People may just as well discover now," he wrote in his earliest days of success, "that the high dramatic key of *The Red Badge* cannot be sustained." In "The Open Boat," he once more found a theme to evoke the "intensity that a writer can't reach every day," but he no longer depended on having the perfect Crane subject. At twenty-five, he had grown to the point where his imagination could embrace a larger world. His war dispatches from Greece, for example, showed a new recognition that battles are not the only events of war, nor soldiers the only sufferers. And "The Monster" (see pp. 419–44) amply testifies that one need not even leave the apparent security of small-town life to find crucial tests of manhood. Given the theme of trial and

the context of everyday society, Crane's double perspective and double style are somewhat changed in "The Monster," but still essential to the narrative. The story is mainly written in a plain flat prose, both in the establishment of the situation and in the long denouement, as if there were nothing special in the tale of Dr. Trescott, his child Jimmy, his Negro coachman Henry Johnson, and the townspeople of Whilomville. After Henry's rescue of the boy from a fire which leaves the rescuer an imbecile faceless monster, the doctor's refusal to give up the care of his servant and benefactor alienates the squeamish townsmen more and more. In a sense, the story is just a fable satirizing conventional citizens who are enthusiastic for the heroic deed and repelled by the uncomfortable responsibility that follows. But when we look for the convincing source of the doctor's loyalty, for which his social happiness and indeed his economic survival are the apparent cost, the sanction of his conduct is something more than his given character: it is the horrifying ordeal of fear, the trial by violence which creates the brotherhood of men who undergo it. The stunning climactic scene, in which the doctor's chemicals glow beautifully into a surrealist garden of destruction, translates the reader into the experience of hell, and the image so endures that the doctor, alone among the characters, seems to share the apprehension of the frightful truth. The brief incident in high key, set off against the muted color of the other scenes, establishes a moral center for the story. With that center giving form to the plot, the thinness of characterization becomes an advantage instead of a liability. Thus, while Henry Johnson is little more than a stock literary Negro, the use of such a stereotype has its value: the townspeople's blindness to his humanity becomes plausible, and the doctor's conduct is a feat of perception as well as courage. And the stereotype itself, inviting condescension without obligation, has a relevant historical meaning: Henry is a kind of stage-Negro, not a creature of the plantation legend, and the society which sees him thus has no semifeudal tradition which can serve as a guide to loyalty. What was true of Henry as a Negro is all the more true when he becomes a characterless and faceless man, the logical extension of his special case. The story in effect criticizes both the conventions of prejudice and the morality of the cash nexus. Whereas in "An Experiment in Misery" the action has very personal and then very general meaning, the plot of "The Monster," while no less personal or general, is richly embedded in the common experience of American life.

The mature art of Stephen Crane, along with its greater social depth, also has a richer literary context. In "The Bride Comes to Yellow Sky" (see pp. 444–49), the writer works with conventions as well as against them. That Jack Potter the town marshal and Scratchy Wilson the ferocious outlaw should be realistically portrayed within a stale convention is the first surprise. More interesting, however, is their failure to fight it out to the death, for in the denouement Crane has crossed his Wild West story with that anticlimactic Western-humor tradition which also keeps Mark Twain's roaring raftsmen from actual combat. While the ordeal is still central to the plot, we see something more than courage at work: the outlaw cannot face the lonely stoical marshal because the code of melodrama doesn't cover the case of bridegrooms: the stylized villain is helplessly a type, unable to break free, and in the ancient comic manner, he is the ridiculous victim of his own routinized mind. Crane's irony is recognizably his own, but here it exists in the same world with Mark Twain and Ben Jonson.

The other side of the easy mastery of "The Bride" is a new humility—which can submit to the discipline of using a model. Tolstoy had always been the writer he admired most, but the young Crane had boyishly mocked at *War and Peace* with the comment "that he could have done the whole business in one-third the time." Without brashness now, he proceeded to make "Death and the Child" (see pp. 449–58) his own variation on themes by the older master. Crane's Peza, like Pierre Bezuhov at Borodino, wanders through a battle where nothing looks like the official version of what goes on and he can never quite mesh with organized reality. He is like Tolstoy's Prince Andrey, too, in his sense that the overarching natural scene diminishes the human event. If he is Crane's own man in his encounter with death

and panic, the sequel to the ordeal is also his own—and yet closer to *War and Peace* than to *The Red Badge*. When the man has been to touch the great death and desperately needs a way back, neither the blue sky nor the golden sun offers reassurance to his spirit. Nor does he find the abandoned child: the child finds him. At the far end of the century from Wordsworth, nature can no longer renew the soul, but the generations of men provide a great fact outside oneself which may help a man back to life. The lost man and the abandoned child are frightening images of human isolation in a violent world, but together they stand for the irreducible minimum of faith in the continuity of the race.

The year's work at the height of his artistic powers came to a sudden end: at the outbreak of the Spanish-American War, Crane responded as if he were personally summoned. One reason for his flight to adventure must certainly have been his often-expressed sense of not being able to sustain his best performances very long. At a lower level, he was in constant anxiety over money since, even at the peak of creativity, he was getting more and more hopelessly into debt. Leaving England, he left behind the absurd and pressing question, Would his imagination or his credit be the first to crack? But he was running headlong into something grimmer still. When he tried to enlist in the Navy, he learned from the medical examiner that he had tuberculosis. Going on to Cuba as a correspondent, he played his role excessively well: besides fever and exhaustion from the campaign, he had within himself good cause for the lassitude of spirit that settled on him. Perhaps his stoical indifference had its roots in quiet depression as well as in his undoubted courage. Clearly, when the correspondent in the white raincoat stood up before the firing Spaniards as if he were in a dream, he was giving himself to death. And although he failed to die in Cuba, he also failed for months to muster the will to go home. Once he did return to England, he was solicited by life. Cora's love, the warm friendship of Conrad and Henry James, and recognition by the literary community might be said to have offered the perfect situation for a young writer. What he kept to himself as much as he could was the overwork and harassment, the falling off of his talent and the giving out of his body. After so often testing literature by experience, he was learning to measure life by imagined possibilities of grace. He could not always meet the standards he set forth in his writing, but he redeemed a portion of dignity from the enveloping chaos.

READING SUGGESTIONS

EDITIONS AND LETTERS

WILSON FOLLETT, editor, *The Work of Stephen Crane*, 12 vols. (1925–27). This is the standard, but not complete, edition. The separate volumes have Introductions by such figures as Amy Lowell, Willa Cather, H. L. Mencken, and Sherwood Anderson.

R. W. STALLMAN, editor, *Stephen Crane: An Omnibus* (1952). A good selection, this volume contains *The Red Badge of Courage* edited from the manuscripts with the various changes and cuts indicated. It also prints news reports of the "Open Boat" incident, including Crane's own. Mr. Stallman's Introductions are stimulating and controversial.

R. W. STALLMAN AND LILLIAN GILKES, editors, *Stephen Crane: Letters* (1960). Aside from the interest of Crane's letters, the editors have included much information which was not available to Crane's biographers.

BIBLIOGRAPHY

AMES W. WILLIAMS AND VINCENT STARRETT, *Stephen Crane: A Bibliography* (1948). This is the best guide to Crane's work, both collected and uncollected.

BIOGRAPHY AND CRITICISM

H. G. WELLS, "Stephen Crane from an English Standpoint," *North American Review*, CLXXI (1900), 233–42. Reprinted in Edmund Wilson, *The Shock of Recognition*, complete, and in *Letters*, Appendix 9, abridged. The first piece on Crane after his death, this brilliantly examines his originality. Wells finds in the American's work "certain enormous repudiations": "It is as if the racial thought and tradition had been razed from his mind and its site plowed and salted. He is more than himself in this; he is the first expression of the opening mind of a new period. . . ."

THOMAS BEER, *Stephen Crane: A Study in American Letters* (1923). A jaunty memoir of Crane and his times, Beer's book has unique information (the evidence having since been destroyed) and irresponsible misinformation (the evidence having since been recovered). Yet it is lively and suggestive, and the Introduction by Joseph Conrad is independently valuable.

JOHN BERRYMAN, *Stephen Crane* (1950). This is the authoritative biography to date, though corrected in some details by the *Letters*. Mr. Berryman, the distinguished poet, offers many valuable insights into both the fiction and the poetry. His Freudian analysis of Crane, persuasive on its own terms, should not distract the reader from the essential literary value of the book.

MARCUS CUNLIFFE, "Stephen Crane and the American Background of *Maggie*," *American Quarterly*, VII (1955), 31–44. This pioneering study takes Crane away from the French novelists he didn't depend on for ideas and restores him to the social and religious context from which he started. The woodcut "The Street Girl's End" which he reproduces from Charles Loring Brace's *The Dangerous Classes of New York* vividly supports his thesis.

DANIEL G. HOFFMAN, *The Poetry of Stephen Crane* (1957). While making the case for Crane's poetry, this book also subjects his intellectual biography to a clear and helpful analysis.

CORWIN K. LINSON, *My Stephen Crane*, ed. by Edwin H. Cady (1958). These reminiscences are by the artist friend whose studio Crane most frequented. The photographs are unique testimony to the youthfulness of Crane's early years.

REPORTAGE

ON THE NEW JERSEY COAST

❡ THE ARTICLE below is the consummation of Stephen Crane's apprentice work as a reporter. It shows how he could get beyond the ephemeral local interest of routine news by grasping his subject both analytically and visually. As the Jacksonian and Victorian term "mechanics" for skilled workmen implies, the Junior Order of United American Mechanics was an organization of pre-Civil War origin. A fraternal society providing insurance benefits for members, it also carried on the spirit of the Know-Nothing party with its "nonpolitical" patriotism and strongly antiforeign social and economic program. In the age of Gompers and Debs, they did not want to be known as a labor organization. Still less did they want to be written about in ironies that could smart before being understood.

Crane's report was published in the New York *Tribune* on August 21, 1892. The *Tribune* apologized on August 24, and the next day, August 25, Crane was writing a letter for a new job!

ASBURY PARK, N.J., Aug. 20 (Special).—The parade of the Junior Order of United American Mechanics here on Wednesday afternoon was a deeply impressive one to some persons. There were hundreds of the members of the order, and they wound through the streets to the music of enough brass bands to make furious discords. It probably was the most awkward, ungainly, uncut and uncarved procession that ever raised clouds of dust on sun-beaten streets. Nevertheless, the spectacle of an Asbury Park crowd confronting such an aggregation was an interesting sight to a few people.

Asbury Park creates nothing. It does not make; it merely amuses. There is a factory where nightshirts are manufactured, but it is some miles from town. This is a resort of wealth and leisure, of women and considerable wine. The throng along the line of march was composed of summer gowns, lace parasols, tennis trousers, straw hats and indifferent smiles. The procession was composed of men, bronzed, slope-shouldered, uncouth and begrimed with dust. Their clothes fitted them illy, for the most part, and they had no ideas of marching. They merely plodded along, not seeming quite to understand, stolid, unconcerned and, in a certain sense, dignified—a pace and a bearing emblematic of their lives. They smiled occasionally and from time to time greeted friends in the crowd on the sidewalk. Such an assemblage of the spraddle-legged men of the middle class, whose hands were bent and shoulders stooped from delving and constructing, had never appeared to an Asbury Park summer crowd, and the latter was vaguely amused.

The bona fide Asbury Parker is a man to whom a dollar, when held close to his eye, often shuts out any impression he may have had that other people possess rights. He is apt to consider that men and women, especially city men and women, were created to be mulcted by him. Hence the tan-colored, sunbeaten honesty in the faces of the members of the Junior Order of United American Mechanics is expected to have a very staggering effect upon them. The visitors were men who possessed principles. . . .

DARK SIDE OF WAR

⟦ JOURNALISM became Crane's substitute for keeping a journal: though he kept working notebooks for his fiction, his record of experience was in his dispatches, like this one from the Greek-Turkish War. Despite his obviously having had to write this piece hastily in snatched moments between the episodes reported, he still main-

tained the control over selection which Willa Cather admired:

> He simply knew from the beginning how to handle detail. He estimated it at its true worth—made it serve his purpose and felt no further responsibility about it. . . . . If he saw one thing that engaged him in a room, he mentioned it. If he saw one thing in a landscape that thrilled him, he put it on paper, but he never tried to make a faithful report of everything else within his field of vision, as if he were a conscientious salesman making out his expense-account.

This war report appeared in the New York *Journal* (May 23, 1897), under a bold headline announcing that Hearst's star reporters were performing: "STEPHEN CRANE AND JULIAN RALPH TELL OF WAR'S HORRORS AND TURKEY'S BOLD PLAN." Further down the same page, a reader would find the further article: "How Novelist Crane Acts on the Battlefield—Journal's War Correspondent's Sangfroid Under Fire at Velestino Described by a Fellow Worker," by John Bass. Hearst exploited the star-system to the fullest, and Crane was the star.

ATHENS, May 22 (On Board the St. Marina, Which Left Chalkis, Greece, May 18.)—We are carrying the wounded away from Domokos. There are eight hundred bullet-torn men aboard, some of them dead. This steamer was formerly used for transporting sheep, but it was taken by the Government for ambulance purposes. It is not a nice place for a well man, but war takes the finical quality out of its victims, and the soldiers do not complain. The ship is not large enough for its dreadful freight. But the men must be moved, and so 800 bleeding soldiers are jammed together in an insufferably hot hole, the light in which is so faint that we cannot distinguish the living from the dead.

Near the hatch where I can see him is a man shot through the mouth. The bullet passed through both cheeks. He is asleep, with his head pillowed on the bosom of a dead comrade. He had been awake for days, doubtless, marching on bread and water, to be finally wounded at Domokos and taken aboard this steamer. He is too weary to mind either his wound or his awful pillow. There is a breeze on the gulf and the ship is rolling, heaving one wounded man against the other.

Some of the wounded were taken off at Chalkis; the others will be taken to Athens, because there is not room for them in the Chalkis hospitals. Already we have travelled a night and a day under these cheerful circumstances that war brings to some of those that engage in it.

When we with our suffering freight arrived at Piraeus they were selling the newspaper extra, and people were shouting, "Hurrah! Hurrah for war!"

And while they shouted a seemingly endless procession of stretchers proceeded from the ship, the still figures upon them.

There is just enough moaning and wailing to make a distinct chorus above the creaking of the deck timbers over that low hole where the lamps are smoking.

This is Wednesday, I think. We are at Stylidia. All day there have been clouds of dust upon the highroad over which Smolenski's division is retreating toward Thermopylae. The movement completely uncovers this place, and the Turks are advancing from Halmyros.

One long line of dust marked the road across the green plain where Smolenski marched away. And the people stared at this and then at the great mountains in back of the town, whence the Turks were coming. All the household goods of the city were piled on the pier. The town was completely empty, except for two battalions of Smolenski's rear guard, who slept in the streets, worn out, after a twenty hours' march. We loaded the steamer and schooner with women and children, and household goods. The anchor was raised by two man-of-war's men, three fugitives, and one Greek Red Cross nurse.

The refugees seemed dazed. The old women particularly, uprooted from the spot they had lived so long, kept their red eyes turned toward the shore as they sat on their rough bundles of clothes and blankets.

Our deck looked like an emigrant quarter of an Atlantic liner, except for the sick soldiers. The Journal steamer then went to St. Marina and landed the hospital stores.

Lieutenant-Colonel Caracolas came aboard there, much disturbed because some bread had been left at Stylidia. He was at the head of the commissary department of Smolenski's division. He asked us if we would try to get the bread. We agreed and found another schooner. We told the captain we were going to take him to Stylidia and he flatly refused to go. There was no time for argument; our extra bluejackets, seven in number, promptly stormed the schooner and took it by assault. I guess the captain of the schooner is talking of the outrage yet. The bluejackets got us a hawser, raised the anchor, and we towed the protesting schooner back to Stylidia, with the captain on the bow, gesticulating violently throughout the voyage. Incidentally we never found the bread.

We steamed back to St. Marina and found Dr. Belline, chief surgeon of the Greek army. He was worried about the safety of the hospital at St. Marina, but no orders had been issued for its removal. The obvious thing to do was to get orders from Thermopylae headquarters, and we carried the doctor across the gulf. He got the orders promptly and we took him back to St. Marina and took aboard the wounded men and Red Cross nurses of the hospital. The last boat had left the shore when a soldier came and said something to the interpreter, who shook his head negatively. The soldier turned quietly away.

On board the steamer your correspondent idly asked the interpreter what the soldier had said, and he answered that the soldier had asked for transportation to Chalkis on the ground that he was sick. The interpreter thought the man too well to go on a boat containing wounded men.

We sent ashore and after some trouble found the soldier. He was ill with fever, was shot through the calf of the leg and his knees were raw from kneeling in the trenches.

There is more of this sort of thing in war than glory and heroic death, flags, banners, shouting and victory.

STORIES

AN EXPERIMENT IN MISERY

⟨ THIS story is in many ways the best of Crane's Bowery fiction (see Introduction, pp. 388–90). The quality of personal vision is partly defined by the way the character who first appears to the youth "like an assassin" is known thereafter by his epithet, "the assassin." Concentrating on the subjective experience, Crane cut from the book version the beginning and end which the story originally carried in the New York *Press* (April 22, 1894):

Two men stood regarding a tramp.

"I wonder how he feels," said one, reflectively. "I suppose he is homeless, friendless, and has, at the most, only a few cents in his pocket. And if this is so, I wonder how he feels."

The other, being the elder, spoke with an air of authoritative wisdom. "You can tell nothing of it unless you are in that condition yourself. It is idle to speculate about it from this distance."

"I suppose so," said the younger man, and then he added as from an inspiration: "I think I'll try it. Rags and tatters, you know, a couple of dimes, and hungry, too, if possible. Perhaps I could discover his point of view or something near it."

"Well, you might," said the other, and from those words begins this veracious narrative of an experiment in misery.

The youth went to the studio of an artist friend, who, from his store, rigged him out in an aged suit and a brown derby hat that had been made long years before. And then the youth went forth to try to eat as the tramp may eat, and sleep as the wanderers sleep. . . .

"Well," said the friend, "did you discover his point of view?"

"I don't know that I did," replied the young man; "but at any rate I think mine own has undergone a considerable alteration."

IT WAS late at night, and a fine rain was swirling softly down, causing the pavements to glisten with hue of steel and blue and yellow in the rays of the innumerable lights. A youth was trudging slowly, without enthusiasm, with his hands buried deep in his trousers pockets, toward the downtown places where beds can be hired for coppers. He was clothed in an aged and tattered suit, and his derby was a marvel of dust-covered crown and torn rim. He was going forth to eat as the wanderer may eat, and sleep as the homeless sleep. By the time he had reached City Hall Park he was so completely plastered with yells of "bum" and "hobo," and with various unholy epithets that small boys had applied to him at intervals, that he was in a state of the most profound dejection. The sifting rain saturated the old velvet collar of his overcoat, and as the wet cloth pressed against his neck, he felt that there no longer could be pleasure in life. He looked about him searching for an outcast of highest degree that they two might share miseries, but the lights threw a quivering glare over rows and circles of deserted benches that glistened damply, showing patches of wet sod behind them. It seemed that their usual freights had fled on this night to better things. There were only squads of well-dressed Brooklyn people who swarmed toward the bridge.

The young man loitered about for a time and then went shuffling off down Park Row. In the sudden descent in style of the dress of the crowd he felt relief, and as if he were at last in his own country. He began to see tatters that matched his tatters. In Chatham Square there were aimless men strewn in front of saloons and lodging-houses, standing sadly, patiently, reminding one vaguely of the attitudes of chickens in a storm. He aligned himself with these men, and turned slowly to occupy himself with the flowing life of the great street.

Through the mists of the cold and storming night, the cable cars went in silent procession, great affairs shining with red and brass, moving with formidable power, calm and irresistible, dangerful and gloomy, breaking silence only by the loud fierce cry of the gong. Two rivers of people swarmed along the sidewalks, spattered with black mud which made each shoe leave a scarlike impression. Overhead, elevated trains with a shrill grinding of the wheels stopped at the station, which upon its leg-like pillars seemed to resemble some monstrous kind of crab squatting over the street. The quick fat puffings of the engines could be heard. Down an alley there were somber curtains of purple and black, on which street lamps dully glittered like embroidered flowers.

A saloon stood with a voracious air on a corner. A sign leaning against the front of the doorpost announced "Free hot soup to-night!" The swing doors, snapping to and fro like ravenous lips, made gratified smacks as the saloon gorged itself with plump men, eating with astounding and endless appetite, smiling in some indescribable manner as the men came from all directions like sacrifices to a heathenish superstition.

Caught by the delectable sign, the young man allowed himself to be swallowed. A bartender placed a schooner of dark and portentous beer on the bar. Its monumental form upreared until the froth atop was above the crown of the young man's brown derby.

"Soup over there, gents," said the bartender affably. A little yellow man in rags and the youth grasped their schooners and went with speed toward a lunch-counter, where a man with oily but imposing whiskers ladled genially from a kettle until he had furnished his two mendicants with a soup that was steaming hot, and in which there were little floating suggestions of chicken. The young man, sipping his broth, felt the cordiality expressed by the warmth of the mixture, and he beamed at the man with oily but imposing whiskers, who was presiding like a priest behind an altar. "Have some more, gents?" he inquired of the two sorry figures before him. The little yellow man accepted with a swift gesture, but the youth shook his head and went out, following a man whose wondrous seediness promised that he would have a knowledge of cheap lodging-houses.

On the sidewalk he accosted the seedy man. "Say, do you know a cheap place to sleep?"

The other hesitated for a time, gazing sideways. Finally he nodded in the direction of the street. "I sleep up there," he said, "when I've got the price."

"How much?"

"Ten cents."

The young man shook his head dolefully. "That's too rich for me."

At that moment there approached the two a reeling man in strange garments. His head was a fuddle of bushy hair and whiskers, from which his eyes peered with a guilty slant. In a close scrutiny it was possible to distinguish the cruel lines of a mouth which looked as if its lips had just closed with satisfaction over some tender and piteous morsel. He appeared like an assassin steeped in crimes performed awkwardly.

But at this time his voice was tuned to the coaxing key of an affectionate puppy. He looked at the men with wheedling eyes, and began to sing a little melody for charity. "Say, gents, can't yeh give a poor feller a couple of cents t' git a bed? I got five, an' I gits anudder two I gits me a bed. Now, on th' square, gents, can't yeh jest gimme two cents t' git a bed? Now, yeh know how a respecterble gentlem'n feels when he's down on his luck, an' I—"

The seedy man, staring with imperturbable countenance at a train which clattered overhead, interrupted in an expressionless voice: "Ah, go t' hell!"

But the youth spoke to the prayerful assassin in tones of astonishment and inquiry. "Say, you must be crazy! Why don't yeh strike somebody that looks as if they had money?"

The assassin, tottering about on his uncertain legs, and at intervals brushing imaginary obstacles from before his nose, entered into a long explanation of the psychology of the situation. It was so profound that it was unintelligible.

When he had exhausted the subject, the young man said to him: "Let's see th' five cents."

The assassin wore an expression of drunken woe at this sentence, filled with suspicion of him. With a deeply pained air he began to fumble in his clothing, his red hands trembling. Presently he announced in a voice of bitter grief, as if he had been betrayed: "There's on'y four."

"Four," said the young man thoughtfully. "Well, look-a here, I'm a stranger here, an' if ye'll steer me to your cheap joint I'll find the other three."

The assassin's countenance became instantly radiant with joy. His whiskers quivered with the wealth of his alleged emotions. He seized the young man's hand in a transport of delight and friendliness.

"B' Gawd," he cried, "if ye'll do that, b' Gawd, I'd say yeh was a damned good fellow, I would, an' I'd remember yeh all m' life, I would, b' Gawd, an' if I ever got a chance I'd return the compliment"—he spoke with drunken dignity— "b' Gawd, I'd treat yeh white, I would, an' I'd allus remember yeh."

The young man drew back, looking at the assassin coldly. "Oh, that's all right," he said. "You show me th' joint—that's all you've got t' do."

The assassin, gesticulating gratitude, led the young man along a dark street. Finally he stopped before a little dusty door. He raised his hand impressively. "Look-a here," he said, and there was a thrill of deep and ancient wisdom upon his face, "I've brought yeh here, an' that's my part, ain't it? If th' place don't suit yeh, yeh needn't git mad at me, need yeh? There won't be no bad feelin', will there?"

"No," said the young man.

The assassin waved his arm tragically, and led the march up the steep stairway. On the way the young man furnished the assassin with three pennies. At the top a man with benevolent spectacles looked at them through a hole in a board. He collected their money, wrote some names on a register, and speedily was leading the two men along a gloom-shrouded corridor.

Shortly after the beginning of this journey the young man felt his liver turn white, for from the dark and secret places of the building there suddenly came to his nostrils strange and unspeakable odors, that assailed him like malignant diseases with wings. They seemed to be from human bodies closely packed in dens; the exhalations from a hundred pairs of reeking lips; the fumes from a thousand bygone debauches; the expression of a thousand present miseries.

A man, naked save for a little snuff-colored undershirt, was parading sleepily along the corridor. He rubbed his eyes and, giving vent to a prodigious yawn, demanded to be told the time.

"Half-past one."

The man yawned again. He opened a door, and for a moment his form was outlined against a black, opaque interior. To this door came the three men, and as it was again opened the unholy odors rushed out like fiends, so that the young man was obliged to struggle as against an overpowering wind.

It was some time before the youth's eyes were good in the intense gloom within, but the man with benevolent spectacles led him skilfully, pausing but a moment to deposit the limp assassin upon a cot. He took the youth to a cot that lay tranquilly by the window, and showing him a tall locker for clothes that stood near the head with the ominous air of a tombstone, left him.

The youth sat on his cot and peered about him. There was a gas-jet in a distant part of the room, that burned a small flickering orange-hued flame. It caused vast masses of tumbled shadows in all parts of the place; save where, immediately about it, there was a little gray haze. As the young man's eyes became used to the darkness, he could see upon the cots that thickly littered the floor the forms of men sprawled out, lying in death-like silence, or heaving and snoring with tremendous effort, like stabbed fish.

The youth locked his derby and his shoes in the mummy-case near him, and then lay down with an old and familiar coat around his shoulders. A blanket he handled gingerly, drawing it over part of the coat. The cot was covered with leather, and as cold as melting snow. The youth was obliged to shiver for some time on this affair, which was like a slab. Presently, however, his chill gave him peace, and during this period of leisure from it he turned his head to stare at his friend the assassin, whom he could dimly discern where he lay sprawled on a cot in the abandon of a man filled with drink. He was snoring with incredible vigor. His wet hair and beard dimly glistened, and his inflamed nose shone with subdued luster like a red light in a fog.

Within reach of the youth's hand was one who lay with yellow breast and shoulders bare to the cold draughts. One arm hung over the side of the cot, and the fingers lay full length upon the wet cement floor of the room. Beneath the inky brows could be seen the eyes of the man, exposed by the partly opened lids. To the youth it seemed that he and this corpse-like being were exchanging a prolonged stare, and that the other threatened with his eyes. He drew back, watching his neighbor from the shadows of his blanket-edge. The man did not move once through the night, but lay in this stillness as of death like a body stretched out expectant of the surgeon's knife.

And all through the room could be seen the tawny hues of naked flesh, limbs thrust into the darkness, projecting beyond the cots; upreared knees, arms hanging long and thin over the cot-edges. For the most part they were statuesque, carven, dead. With the curious lockers standing all about like tombstones, there was a strange effect of a graveyard where bodies were merely flung.

Yet occasionally could be seen limbs wildly tossing in fantastic nightmare gestures, accompanied by guttural cries, grunts, oaths. And there was one fellow off in a gloomy corner, who in his dreams was oppressed by some frightful calamity, for of a sudden he began to utter long wails that went almost like yells from a hound, echoing wailfully and weird through this chill place of tombstones where men lay like the dead.

The sound, in its high piercing beginnings that dwindled to final melancholy moans, expressed a red and grim tragedy of the unfathomable possibilities of the man's dreams. But to the youth these were not merely the shrieks of a vision-pierced man: they were an utterance of the meaning of the room and its occupants. It was to him the protest of the wretch who feels the touch of the imperturbable granite wheels, and who then cries with an impersonal eloquence, with a strength not from him, giving voice to the wail of a whole section, a class, a people. This, weaving into the young man's brain, and mingling with his views of the vast and somber shadows that, like mighty black fingers, curled around the naked bodies, made the young man so that he did not sleep, but lay carving the biographies for these men from his meager experience. At times the fellow in the corner howled in a writhing agony of his imaginations.

Finally a long lance-point of gray light shot through the dusty panes of the window. Without, the young man could see roofs drearily white in the dawning. The point of light yellowed and grew brighter, until the golden rays of the morning sun came in bravely and strong. They touched with radiant color the form of a small fat man who snored in stuttering fashion. His round and shiny bald head glowed suddenly with the valor of a decoration. He sat up, blinked at the sun, swore fretfully, and pulled his blanket over the ornamental splendors of his head.

The youth contentedly watched this rout of the shadows before the bright spears of the sun, and presently he slumbered. When he awoke he heard the voice of the assassin raised in valiant curses. Putting up his head, he perceived his comrade seated on the side of the cot engaged in scratching his neck with long fingernails that rasped like files.

"Hully Jee, dis is a new breed. They've got can-openers on their feet." He continued in a violent tirade.

The young man hastily unlocked his closet and took out his shoes and hat. As he sat on the side of the cot lacing his shoes, he glanced about and saw that daylight had made the room comparatively commonplace and uninteresting. The men, whose faces seemed stolid, serene, or absent, were engaged in dressing, while a great crackle of bantering conversation arose.

A few were parading in unconcerned nakedness. Here and there were men of brawn, whose skins shone clear and ruddy. They took splendid poses, standing massively like chiefs. When they had dressed in their ungainly garments there was an extraordinary change. They then showed bumps and deficiencies of all kinds.

There were others who exhibited many deformities. Shoulders were slanting, humped, pulled this way and pulled that way. And notable among these latter men was the little fat man who had refused to allow his head to be glorified. His pudgy form, builded like a pear, bustled to and fro, while he swore in fishwife fashion. It appeared that some article of his apparel had vanished.

The young man attired himself speedily, and went to his friend the assassin. At first the latter looked dazed at the sight of the youth. This face seemed to be appealing to him through the cloud-wastes of his memory. He scratched his neck and reflected. At last he grinned, a broad smile gradually spreading until his countenance was a round illumination. "Hello, Willie," he cried cheerily.

"Hello," said the young man. "Are yeh ready t' fly?"

"Sure." The assassin tied his shoe carefully with some twine and came ambling.

When he reached the street the young man experienced no sudden relief from unholy atmospheres. He had forgotten all about them, and had been breathing naturally, and with no sensation of discomfort or distress.

He was thinking of these things as he walked along the street, when he was suddenly startled by feeling the assassin's hand, trembling with excitement, clutching his arm, and when the assassin spoke, his voice went into quavers from a supreme agitation.

"I'll be hully, bloomin' blowed if there wasn't a feller with a nightshirt on up there in that joint."

The youth was bewildered for a moment, but presently he turned to smile indulgently at the assassin's humor. "Oh, you're a damned liar," he merely said.

Whereupon the assassin began to gesture extravagantly and take oath by strange gods. He frantically placed himself at the mercy of remarkable fates if his tale were not true. "Yes, he did! I cross m' heart thousan' times!" he protested, and at the moment his eyes were large with amazement, his mouth wrinkled in unnatural glee. "Yessir! A nightshirt! A hully white nightshirt!"

"You lie!"

"No, sir! I hope ter die b'fore I kin git anudder ball if there wasn't a jay wid a hully, bloomin' white nightshirt!"

His face was filled with the infinite wonder of it. "A hully white nightshirt," he continually repeated.

The young man saw the dark entrance to a basement restaurant. There was a sign which read "No mystery about our hash!" and there were other age-stained and world-battered legends which told him that the place was within his means. He stopped before it and spoke to the assassin. "I guess I'll git somethin' t' eat."

At this the assassin, for some reason, appeared to be quite embarrassed. He gazed at the seductive front of the eating-place for a moment. Then he started slowly up the street. "Well, good-bye, Willie," he said bravely.

For an instant the youth studied the departing figure. Then he called out, "Hol' on a minnet." As they came together he spoke in a certain fierce way, as if he feared that the other would think him to be charitable. "Look-a here, if yeh wanta git some breakfas' I'll lend yeh three cents t' do it with. But say, look-a here, you've gotta git out an' hustle. I ain't goin' t' support yeh, or I'll go broke b'fore night. I ain't no millionaire."

"I take me oath, Willie," said the assassin earnestly, "th' on'y thing I really needs is a ball. Me t'roat feels like a fryin'-pan. But as I can't get a ball, why, th' next bes' thing is breakfast, an' if yeh do that for me, b' Gawd, I say yeh was th' whitest lad I ever see."

They spent a few moments in dexterous exchanges of phrases, in which they each protested that the other was, as the assassin had originally said, "a respecterble gentlem'n." And they concluded with mutual assurances that they were the souls of intelligence and virtue. Then they went into the restaurant.

There was a long counter, dimly lighted from hidden sources. Two or three men in soiled white aprons rushed here and there.

The youth bought a bowl of coffee for two cents and a roll for one cent. The assassin purchased the same. The bowls were webbed with brown seams, and the tin spoons wore an air of having emerged from the first pyramid. Upon them were black moss-like encrustations of age, and they were bent and scarred from the attacks of long-forgotten teeth. But over their repast the wanderers waxed warm and mellow. The assassin grew affable as the hot mixture went soothingly down his parched throat, and the young man felt courage flow in his veins.

Memories began to throng in on the assassin, and he brought forth long tales, intricate, incoherent, delivered with a chattering swiftness as from an old woman. "—great job out 'n Orange. Boss keep yeh hustlin', though, all time. I was there three days, and then I went an' ask 'im t' lend me a dollar. 'G-g-go ter the devil,' he says, an' I lose me job.

"South no good. Damn niggers work for twenty-five an' thirty cents a day. Run white man out. Good grub, though. Easy livin'.

"Yas; useter work little in Toledo, raftin' logs. Make two or three dollars er day in the spring. Lived high. Cold as ice, though, in the winter.

"I was raised in northern N' York. O-o-oh, yeh jest oughto live there. No beer ner whisky, though, 'way off in the woods. But all th' good hot grub yeh can eat. B' Gawd, I hung around there long as I could till th' ol' man fired me. 'Git t' hell outa here, yeh wuthless skunk, git t' hell outa here, an' go die,' he says. 'You're a hell of a father,' I says, 'you are,' an' I quit 'im."

As they were passing from the dim eating-place, they encountered an old man who was trying to steal forth with a tiny package of food, but a tall man with an indomitable moustache stood dragon-fashion, barring the way of escape. They heard the old man raise a plaintive protest. "Ah, you always want to know what I take out, and you never see that I usually bring a package in here from my place of business."

As the wanderers trudged slowly along Park Row, the assassin began to expand and grow blithe. "B' Gawd, we've been livin' like kings," he said, smacking appreciative lips.

"Look out, or we'll have t' pay fer it t'-night," said the youth with gloomy warning.

But the assassin refused to turn his gaze toward the future. He went with a limping step, into which he injected a suggestion of lamb-like gambols. His mouth was wreathed in a red grin.

In City Hall Park the two wanderers sat down in the little circle of benches sanctified by traditions of their class. They huddled in their old garments, slumbrously conscious of the march of the hours which for them had no meaning.

The people of the street hurrying hither and thither made a blend of black figures, changing, yet frieze-like. They walked in their good clothes as upon important missions, giving no gaze to the two wanderers seated upon the benches. They expressed to the young man his infinite distance from all that he valued. Social position, comfort, the pleasures of living were unconquerable kingdoms. He felt a sudden awe.

And in the background a multitude of buildings, of pitiless hues and sternly high, were to him emblematic of a nation forcing its regal head into the clouds, throwing no downward glances; in the sublimity of its aspirations ignoring the wretches who may flounder at its feet. The roar of the city in his ear was to him the confusion of strange tongues, babbling heedlessly; it was the clink of coin, the voice of the city's hopes, which were to him no hopes.

He confessed himself an outcast, and his eyes from under the lowered rim of his hat began to glance guiltily, wearing the criminal expression that comes with certain convictions.

A MYSTERY OF HEROISM

[THIS story is truly a companion-piece to *The Red Badge of Courage*, for it first appeared August 1 and 2, 1895, in the Philadelphia *Press*, the newspaper that had serialized the novel eight months before and then brought Crane down to be personally congratulated by the whole enthusiastic staff. The first object of irony in both tales is the popular attitude he was satirizing in verse at about the same time:

> A youth in apparel that glittered
> Went to walk in a grim forest.
> There he met an assassin
> Attired all in garb of old days;
> He, scowling through the thickets,
> And dagger poised quivering,
> Rushed upon the youth.
> "Sir," said this latter,
> "I am enchanted, believe me,
> To die, thus,
> In this medieval fashion,
> According to the best legends;
> Ah, what joy!"
> Then took he the wound, smiling,
> And died, content.

Some of the things that happen to Crane's heroes when they doff their glittering illusions are suggested in the Introduction, pp. 390–92.

THE DARK uniforms of the men were so coated with dust from the incessant wrestling of the two armies that the regiment almost seemed a part of the clay bank which shielded them from the shells. On the top of the hill a battery was arguing in tremendous roars with some other guns, and to the eye of the infantry the artillerymen, the guns, the caissons, the horses, were distinctly outlined upon the blue sky. When a piece was fired, a red streak as round as a log flashed low in the heavens, like a monstrous bolt of lightning. The men of the battery wore white duck trousers, which somehow emphasized their legs; and when they ran and crowded in little groups at the bidding of the shouting officers, it was more impressive than usual to the infantry.

Fred Collins, of A Company, was saying: "Thunder! I wisht I had a drink. Ain't there any water round here?" Then somebody yelled: "There goes th' bugler!"

As the eyes of half the regiment swept in one machine-like movement, there was an instant's picture of a horse in a great convulsive leap of a death-wound and a rider leaning back with a crooked arm and spread fingers before his face. On the ground was the crimson terror of an exploding shell, with fibers of flame that seemed like lances. A glittering bugle swung clear of the rider's back as fell headlong the horse and the man. In the air was an odor as from a conflagration.

Sometimes they of the infantry looked down at a fair little meadow which spread at their feet. Its long green grass was rippling gently in a breeze. Beyond it was the gray form of a house half torn to pieces by shells and by the busy axes of soldiers who had pursued firewood. The line of an old fence was now dimly marked by long weeds and by an occasional post. A shell had blown the well-house to fragments. Little lines of gray smoke ribboning upward from some embers indicated the place where had stood the barn.

From beyond a curtain of green woods there came the sound of some stupendous scuffle, as if two animals of the size of islands were fighting. At a distance there were occasional appearances of swift-moving men, horses, batteries, flags, and with the crashing of infantry volleys were heard, often, wild and frenzied cheers. In the midst of it all Smith and Ferguson, two privates of A Company, were engaged in a heated discussion which involved the greatest questions of the national existence.

The battery on the hill presently engaged in a frightful duel. The white legs of the gunners scampered this way and that way, and the officers redoubled their shouts. The guns, with their demeanors of stolidity and courage, were typical of something infinitely self-possessed in this clamor of death that swirled around the hill.

One of a "swing" team was suddenly smitten quivering to the ground, and his maddened brethren dragged his torn body in their struggle to escape from this turmoil and danger. A young soldier astride one of the leaders swore and fumed in his saddle and furiously jerked at the bridle. An officer screamed out an order so violently that his voice broke and ended the sentence in a falsetto shriek.

The leading company of infantry regiment was somewhat exposed, and the colonel ordered it moved more fully under the shelter of the hill. There was the clank of steel against steel.

A lieutenant of the battery rode down and passed them, holding his right arm carefully in his left hand. And it was as if this arm was not at all a part of him, but belonged to another man. His sober and reflective charger went slowly. The officer's face was grimy and perspiring, and his uniform was tousled as if he had been in direct grapple with an enemy. He smiled grimly when the men stared at him. He turned his horse toward the meadow.

Collins, of A Company, said: "I wisht I had a drink. I bet there's water in that there ol' well yonder!"

"Yes; but how you goin' to git it?"

For the little meadow which intervened was now suffering a terrible onslaught of shells. Its green and beautiful calm had vanished utterly. Brown earth was being flung in monstrous handfuls. And there was a massacre of the young blades of grass. They were being torn, burned, obliterated. Some curious fortune of the battle had made this gentle little meadow the object of the red hate of the shells, and each one as it exploded seemed like an imprecation in the face of a maiden.

The wounded officer who was riding across this expanse said to himself: "Why, they couldn't shoot any harder if the whole army was massed here!"

A shell struck the gray ruins of the house, and as, after the roar, the shattered wall fell in fragments, there was a noise which resembled the flapping of shutters during a wild gale of winter. Indeed, the infantry paused in the shelter of the bank appeared as men standing upon a shore contemplating a madness of the sea. The angel of calamity had under its glance the battery upon the hill. Fewer white-legged men labored about the guns. A shell had smitten one of the pieces, and after the flare, the smoke, the dust, the wrath of this blow were gone, it was possible to see white legs stretched horizontally upon the ground. And at that interval to the rear where it is the business of battery horses to stand with their noses to the fight, awaiting the command to drag their guns out of the destruction, or into it, or wheresoever these incomprehensible humans demanded with whip and spur—in this line of passive and dumb spectators, whose fluttering hearts yet would not let them forget the iron laws of man's control of them—in this rank of brute-soldiers there had been relentless and hideous carnage. From the ruck of bleeding and prostrate horses, the men of the infantry could see one animal raising its stricken body with its forelegs and turning its nose with mystic and profound eloquence toward the sky.

Some comrades joked Collins about his thirst. "Well, if yeh want a drink so bad, why don't yeh go git it?"

"Well, I will in a minnet, if yeh don't shut up!"

A lieutenant of artillery floundered his horse straight down the hill with as little concern as if it were level ground. As he galloped past the colonel of the infantry, he threw up his hand in swift salute. "We've got to get out of that," he roared angrily. He was a black-bearded officer, and his eyes, which resembled beads, sparkled like those of an insane man. His jumping horse sped along the column of infantry.

The fat major, standing carelessly with his sword held horizontally behind him and with his legs far apart, looked after the receding horseman and laughed. "He wants to get back with orders pretty quick, or there'll be no batt'ry left," he observed.

The wise young captain of the second company hazarded to the lieutenant-colonel that the enemy's infantry would probably soon attack the hill, and the lieutenant-colonel snubbed him.

A private in one of the rear companies looked out over the meadow, and then turned to a companion and said, "Look there, Jim!" It was the wounded officer from the battery, who some time before had started to ride across the meadow, supporting his right arm carefully with his left hand. This man had encountered a shell, apparently, at a time when no one perceived him, and he could now be seen lying face downward with a stirruped foot stretched across the body of his dead horse. A leg of the charger extended slantingly upward, precisely as stiff as a stake. Around this motionless pair the shells still howled.

There was a quarrel in A Company. Collins was shaking his fist in the faces of some laughing comrades. "Dern yeh! I ain't afraid t' go. If yeh say much, I will go!"

"Of course, yeh will! You'll run through that there medder, won't yeh?"

Collins said, in a terrible voice: "You see now!"

At this ominous threat his comrades broke into renewed jeers.

Collins gave them a dark scowl, and went to find his captain. The latter was conversing with the colonel of the regiment.

"Captain," said Collins, saluting and standing at attention—in those days all trousers bagged at the knees—"Captain, I want t' get permission to go git some water from that there well over yonder!"

The colonel and the captain swung about simultaneously and stared across the meadow. The captain laughed. "You must be pretty thirsty, Collins?"

"Yes, sir, I am."

"Well—ah," said the captain. After a moment, he asked, "Can't you wait?"

"No, sir."

The colonel was watching Collins's face. "Look here, my lad," he said, in a pious sort of voice—"Look here, my lad"—Collins was not a lad—"don't you think that's taking pretty big risks for a little drink of water?"

"I dunno," said Collins uncomfortably. Some of the resentment toward his companions, which perhaps had forced him into this affair, was beginning to fade. "I dunno w'ether 'tis."

The colonel and the captain contemplated him for a time.

"Well," said the captain finally.

"Well," said the colonel, "if you want to go, why, go."

Collins saluted. "Much obliged t' yeh."

As he moved away the colonel called after him. "Take some of the other boys' canteens with you, an' hurry back, now."

"Yes, sir, I will."

The colonel and the captain looked at each other then, for it had suddenly occurred that they could not for the life of them tell whether Collins wanted to go or whether he did not.

They turned to regard Collins, and as they perceived him surrounded by gesticulating comrades, the colonel said: "Well, by thunder! I guess he's going."

Collins appeared as a man dreaming. In the midst of the questions, the advice, the warnings, all the excited talk of his company mates, he maintained a curious silence.

They were very busy in preparing him for his ordeal. When they inspected him carefully, it was somewhat like the examination that grooms give a horse before a race; and they were amazed, staggered, by the whole affair. Their astonishment found vent in strange repetitions.

"Are yeh sure a-goin'?" they demanded again and again.

"Certainly I am," cried Collins at last, furiously.

He strode sullenly away from them. He was swinging five or six canteens by their cords. It seemed that his cap would not remain firmly on his head, and often he reached and pulled it down over his brow.

There was a general movement in the compact column. The long animal-like thing moved slightly. Its four hundred eyes were turned upon the figure of Collins.

"Well, sir, if that ain't th' derndest thing! I never thought Fred Collins had the blood in him for that kind of business."

"What's he goin' to do, anyhow?"

"He's goin' to that well there after water."

"We ain't dyin' of thirst, are we? That's foolishness."

"Well, somebody put him up to it, an' he's doin' it."

"Say, he must be a desperate cuss."

When Collins faced the meadow and walked away from the regiment, he was vaguely conscious that a chasm, the deep valley of all prides, was suddenly between him and his comrades. It was provisional, but the provision was that he return as a victor. He had blindly been led by quaint emotions, and laid himself under an obligation to walk squarely up to the face of death.

But he was not sure that he wished to make a retraction, even if he could do so without shame. As a matter of truth, he was sure of very little. He was mainly surprised.

It seemed to him supernaturally strange that he had allowed his mind to manœuvre his body into such a situation. He understood that it might be called dramatically great.

However, he had no full appreciation of anything, excepting that he was actually conscious of being dazed. He could feel his dulled mind groping after the form and color of this incident. He wondered why he did not feel some keen agony of fear cutting his sense like a knife. He wondered at this, because human expression had said loudly for centuries that men should feel afraid of certain things, and that all men who did not feel this fear were phenomena—heroes.

He was, then, a hero. He suffered that disappointment which we would all have if we discovered that we were ourselves capable of those deeds which we most admire in history and legend. This, then, was a hero. After all, heroes were not much.

No, it could not be true. He was not a hero. Heroes had no shames in their lives, and, as for him, he remembered borrowing fifteen dollars from a friend and promising to pay it back the next day, and then avoiding that friend for ten months. When, at home, his mother had aroused him for the early labor of his life on the farm, it had often been his fashion to be irritable, childish, diabolical; and his mother had died since he had come to the war.

He saw that, in this matter of the well, the canteens, the shells, he was an intruder in the land of fine deeds.

He was now about thirty paces from his comrades. The regiment had just turned its many faces toward him.

From the forest of terrific noises there suddenly emerged a little uneven line of men. They fired fiercely and rapidly at distant foliage on which appeared little puffs of white smoke. The spatter of skirmish firing was added to the thunder of the guns on the hill. The little line of men ran forward. A color-sergeant fell flat with his flag as if he had slipped on ice. There was hoarse cheering from this distant field.

Collins suddenly felt that two demon fingers were pressed into his ears. He could see nothing but flying arrows, flaming red. He lurched from the shock of this explosion, but he made a mad rush for the house, which he viewed as a man submerged to the neck in a boiling surf might view the shore. In the air little pieces of shell howled, and the earthquake explosions drove him insane with the menace of their roar. As he ran the canteens knocked together with a rhythmical tinkling.

As he neared the house, each detail of the scene became vivid to him. He was aware of some bricks of the vanished chimney lying on the sod. There was a door which hung by one hinge.

Rifle bullets called forth by the insistent skirmishers came from the far-off bank of foliage. They mingled with the shells and the pieces of shells until the air was torn in all directions by hootings, yells, howls. The sky was full of fiends who directed all their wild rage at his head.

When he came to the well, he flung himself face downward and peered into its darkness. There were furtive silver glintings some feet from the surface. He grabbed one of the canteens and, unfastening its cap, swung it down by the cord. The water flowed slowly in with an indolent gurgle.

And now, as he lay with his face turned away, he was suddenly smitten with the terror. It came upon his heart like the grasp of claws. All the power faded from his muscles. For an instant he was no more than a dead man.

The canteen filled with a maddening slowness, in the manner of all bottles. Presently he recovered his strength and addressed a screaming oath to it. He leaned over until it seemed as if he intended to try to push water into it with his hands. His eyes as he gazed down into the well shone like two pieces of metal, and in their expression was a great appeal and a great curse. The stupid water derided him.

There was the blaring thunder of a shell. Crimson light shone through the swift-boiling smoke and made a pink reflection on part of the wall of the well. Collins jerked out his arm and canteen with the same motion that a man would use in withdrawing his head from a furnace.

He scrambled erect and glared and hesitated. On the ground near him lay the old well bucket, with a length of rusty chain. He lowered it swiftly into the well. The bucket struck the water and then, turning lazily over, sank. When, with hand reaching tremblingly over hand, he hauled it out, it knocked often against the walls of the well and spilled some of its contents.

In running with a filled bucket, a man can adopt but one kind of gait. So, through this terrible field over which screamed practical angels of death, Collins ran in the manner of a farmer chased out of a dairy by a bull.

His face went staring white with anticipation —anticipation of a blow that would whirl him around and down. He would fall as he had seen other men fall, the life knocked out of them so suddenly that their knees were no more quick to touch the ground than their heads. He saw the long blue line of the regiment, but his comrades were standing looking at him from the edge of an impossible star. He was aware of some deep wheel-ruts and hoofprints in the sod beneath his feet.

The artillery officer who had fallen in this meadow had been making groans in the teeth of the tempest of sound. These futile cries, wrenched from him by his agony, were heard only by shells, bullets. When wild-eyed Collins came running, this officer raised himself. His face contorted and blanched from pain, he was about to utter some great beseeching cry. But suddenly his face straightened, and he called: "Say, young man, give me a drink of water, will you?"

Collins had no room amid his emotions for surprise. He was mad from the threats of destruction.

"I can't!" he screamed, and in his reply was a full description of his quaking apprehension. His cap was gone and his hair was riotous. His clothes made it appear that he had been dragged over the ground by the heels. He ran on.

The officer's head sank down, and one elbow crooked. His foot in its brass-bound stirrup still stretched over the body of his horse, and the other leg was under the steed.

But Collins turned. He came dashing back. His face had now turned gray, and in his eyes was all terror. "Here it is! here it is!"

The officer was as a man gone in drink. His arm bent like a twig. His head drooped as if his neck were of willow. He was sinking to the ground, to lie face downward.

Collins grabbed him by the shoulder. "Here it is. Here's your drink. Turn over. Turn over, man, for God's sake!"

With Collins hauling at his shoulder, the officer twisted his body and fell with his face turned toward that region where lived the unspeakable noises of the swirling missiles. There was the faintest shadow of a smile on his lips as he looked at Collins. He gave a sigh, a little primitive breath like that from a child.

Collins tried to hold the bucket steadily, but his shaking hands caused the water to splash all over the face of the dying man. Then he jerked it away and ran on.

The regiment gave him a welcoming roar. The grimed faces were wrinkled in laughter.

His captain waved the bucket away. "Give it to the men!"

The two genial, skylarking young lieutenants were the first to gain possession of it. They played over it in their fashion.

When one tried to drink, the other teasingly knocked his elbow. "Don't Billie! You'll make me spill it," said the one. The other laughed.

Suddenly there was an oath, the thud of wood on the ground, and a swift murmur of astonishment among the ranks. The two lieutenants glared at each other. The bucket lay on the ground, empty.

THE OPEN BOAT

A Tale Intended to be after the Fact: Being the Experience of Four Men from the Sunk Steamer
COMMODORE

❡ ON January 1, 1897, the *Commodore* under Captain Edward Murphy left Jacksonville, Florida, with munitions and men for the Cuban rebels. That night she began to founder—sabotage was suspected—and before dawn she had to be abandoned. Among the last to leave the ship was Crane, who with four others got back to Daytona Beach in the ten-foot dinghy. The change in the number of occupants from five to four is one of the ways by which he simplified the story for the sake of fictional truth. But while he simplified the story, he complicated the telling. The dancing point of view of the style implies a fundamental irony of perspective which Crane had worked out in a poem published nine months *before* the event:

> To the maiden
> The sea was blue meadow,
> Alive with little froth-people
> Singing.
>
> To the sailor, wrecked,
> The sea was dead gray walls
> Superlative in vacancy,
> Upon which nevertheless at fateful time
> Was written
> The grim hatred of nature.

The story first appeared in *Scribner's Magazine* (June, 1897). Newspaper accounts, including Crane's own, are reprinted by R. W. Stallman in *Stephen Crane: An Omnibus*.

I

NONE of them knew the color of the sky. Their eyes glanced level, and were fastened upon the waves that swept toward them. These waves were of the hue of slate, save for the tops, which were of foaming white, and all of the men knew the colors of the sea. The horizon narrowed and widened, and dipped and rose, and at all times its edge was jagged with waves that seemed thrust up in points like rocks.

Many a man ought to have a bathtub larger than the boat which here rode upon the sea. These waves were most wrongfully and barbarously abrupt and tall, and each froth-top was a problem in small-boat navigation.

The cook squatted in the bottom, and looked with both eyes at the six inches of gunwale which separated him from the ocean. His sleeves were rolled over his fat forearms, and the two flaps of his unbuttoned vest dangled as he bent to bail out the boat. Often he said, "Gawd! that was a narrow clip." As he remarked it he invariably gazed eastward over the broken sea.

The oiler, steering with one of the two oars in the boat, sometimes raised himself suddenly to keep clear of water that swirled in over the stern. It was a thin little oar, and it seemed often ready to snap.

The correspondent, pulling at the other oar, watched the waves and wondered why he was there.

The injured captain, lying in the bow, was at this time buried in that profound dejection and indifference which comes, temporarily at least, to even the bravest and most enduring when, willy-nilly, the firm fails, the army loses, the ship goes down. The mind of the master of a vessel is rooted deep in the timbers of her, though he command for a day or a decade; and this captain had on him the stern impression of a scene in the grays of dawn of seven turned faces, and later a stump of a topmast with a white ball on it, that slashed to and fro at the waves, went low and lower, and down. Thereafter there was something strange in his voice. Although steady, it was deep with mourning, and of a quality beyond oration or tears.

"Keep 'er a little more south, Billie," said he.

"A little more south, sir," said the oiler in the stern.

A seat in his boat was not unlike a seat upon a bucking broncho, and by the same token a broncho is not much smaller. The craft pranced and reared and plunged like an animal. As each wave came, and she rose for it, she seemed like a horse making at a fence outrageously high. The manner of her scramble over these walls of water is a mystic thing, and, moreover, at the top of them were ordinarily these problems in white water, the foam racing down from the summit of each wave requiring a new leap, and a leap from the air. Then, after scornfully bumping a crest, she would slide and race and splash down a long incline, and arrive bobbing and nodding in front of the next menace.

A singular disadvantage of the sea lies in the fact that after successfully surmounting one wave you discover that there is another behind it just as important and just as nervously anxious to do something effective in the way of swamping boats. In a ten-foot dinghy one can get an idea of the resources of the sea in the line of waves that is not probable to the average experience which is never at sea in a dinghy. As each slaty wall of water approached, it shut all else from the view of the men in the boat, and it was not difficult to imagine that this particular wave was the final outburst of the ocean, the last effort of the grim water. There was a terrible grace in the move of the waves, and they came in silence, save for the snarling of the crests.

In the wan light the faces of the men must have been gray. Their eyes must have glinted in strange ways as they gazed steadily astern. Viewed from a balcony, the whole thing would doubtless have been weirdly picturesque. But the men in the boat had no time to see it, and if they had had leisure, there were other things to occupy their minds. The sun swung steadily up the sky, and they knew it was broad day because the color of the sea changed from slate to emerald green streaked with amber lights, and the foam was like tumbling snow. The process of the breaking day was unknown to them. They were aware only of this effect upon the color of the waves that rolled toward them.

In disjointed sentences the cook and the correspondent argued as to the difference between a life-saving station and a house of refuge. The cook had said: "There's a house of refuge just north of the Mosquito Inlet Light, and as soon as they see us they'll come off in their boat and pick us up."

"As soon as who see us?" said the correspondent.

"The crew," said the cook.

"Houses of refuge don't have crews," said the correspondent. "As I understand them, they are only places where clothes and grub are stored for the benefit of shipwrecked people. They don't carry crews."

"Oh, yes, they do," said the cook.

"No, they don't," said the correspondent.

"Well, we're not there yet, anyhow," said the oiler, in the stern.

"Well," said the cook, "perhaps it's not a house of refuge that I'm thinking of as being near Mosquito Inlet Light; perhaps it's a life-saving station."

"We're not there yet," said the oiler in the stern.

II

AS THE boat bounced from the top of each wave the wind tore through the hair of the hatless men, and as the craft plopped her stern down again the spray slashed past them. The crest of each of these waves was a hill, from the top of which the men surveyed for a moment a broad tumultuous expanse, shining and wind-riven. It was probably splendid, it was probably glorious, this play of the free sea, wild with lights of emerald and white and amber.

"Bully good thing it's an on-shore wind," said the cook. "If not, where would we be? Wouldn't have a show."

"That's right," said the correspondent.

The busy oiler nodded his assent.

Then the captain, in the bow, chuckled in a way that expressed humor, contempt, tragedy, all in one. "Do you think we've got much of a show now, boys?" said he.

Whereupon the three were silent, save for a trifle of hemming and hawing. To express any particular optimism at this time they felt to be childish and stupid, but they all doubtless possessed this sense of the situation in their minds. A young man thinks doggedly at such times. On the other hand, the ethics of their condition was decidedly against any open suggestion of hopelessness. So they were silent.

"Oh, well," said the captain, soothing his children, "we'll get ashore all right."

But there was that in his tone which made them think; so the oiler quoth, "Yes! if this wind holds."

The cook was bailing. "Yes! if we don't catch hell in the surf."

Canton-flannel gulls flew near and far. Sometimes they sat down on the sea, near patches of brown seaweed that rolled over the waves with a movement like carpets on a line in a gale. The birds sat comfortably in groups, and they were envied by some in the dinghy, for the wrath of the sea was no more to them than it was to a covey of prairie chickens a thousand miles inland. Often they came very close and stared at the men with black bead-like eyes. At these times they were uncanny and sinister in their unblinking scrutiny, and the men hooted angrily at them, telling them to be gone. One came, and evidently decided to alight on the top of the captain's head. The bird flew parallel to the boat and did not circle, but made short sidelong jumps in the air in chicken-fashion. His black eyes were wistfully fixed upon the captain's head. "Ugly brute," said the oiler to the bird. "You look as if you were made with a jackknife." The cook and the correspondent swore darkly at the creature. The captain naturally wished to knock it away with the end of the heavy painter, but he did not dare do it, because anything resembling an emphatic gesture would have capsized this freighted boat; and so, with his open hand, the captain gently and carefully waved the gull away. After it had been discouraged from the pursuit the captain breathed easier on account of his hair, and others breathed easier because the bird struck their minds at this time as being somehow gruesome and ominous.

In the meantime the oiler and the correspondent rowed. And also they rowed. They sat together in the same seat, and each rowed an oar. Then the oiler took both oars; then the correspondent took both oars; then the oiler; then the correspondent. They rowed and they rowed. The very ticklish part of the business was when the time came for the reclining one in the stern to take his turn at the oars. By the very last star of truth, it is easier to steal eggs from under a hen than it was to change seats in the dinghy. First the man in the stern slid his hand along the thwart and moved with care, as if he were of Sèvres. Then the man in the rowing-seat slid his hand along the other thwart. It was all done with the most extraordinary care. As the two sidled past each other, the whole party kept watchful eyes on the coming wave, and the captain cried: "Look out, now! Steady, there!"

The brown mats of seaweed that appeared from time to time were like islands, bits of earth. They were traveling, apparently, neither one way nor the other. They were, to all intents, stationary. They informed the men in the boat that it was making progress slowly toward the land.

The captain, rearing cautiously in the bow after the dinghy soared on a great swell, said that he had seen the lighthouse at Mosquito Inlet. Presently the cook remarked that he had seen it. The correspondent was at the oars then, and for some reason he too wished to look at the lighthouse; but his back was toward the far shore, and the waves were important, and for some time he could not seize an opportunity to turn his head. But at last there came a wave more gentle than the others, and when at the crest of it he swiftly scoured the western horizon.

"See it?" said the captain.

"No," said the correspondent, slowly; "I didn't see anything."

"Look again," said the captain. He pointed. "It's exactly in that direction."

At the top of another wave the correspondent did as he was bid, and this time his eyes chanced on a small, still thing on the edge of the swaying horizon. It was precisely like the point of a pin. It took an anxious eye to find a lighthouse so tiny.

"Think we'll make it, Captain?"

"If this wind holds and the boat don't swamp, we can't do much else," said the captain.

The little boat, lifted by each towering sea and splashed viciously by the crests, made progress that in the absence of seaweed was not apparent to those in her. She semed just a wee thing wallowing, miraculously top up, at the mercy of five oceans. Occasionally a great spread of water, like white flames, swarmed into her.

"Bail her, cook," said the captain, serenely.

"All right, Captain," said the cheerful cook.

III

IT WOULD be difficult to describe the subtle brotherhood of men that was here established on the seas. No one said that it was so. No one mentioned it. But it dwelt in the boat, and each man felt it warm him. They were a captain, an oiler, a cook, and a correspondent, and they were friends— friends in a more curiously iron-bound degree than may be common. The hurt captain, lying against the water-jar in the bow, spoke always in a low voice and calmly; but he could never command a more ready and swiftly obedient crew than the motley three of the dinghy. It was more than a mere recognition of what was best for the common safety. There was surely in it a quality that was personal and heart-felt. And after this devotion to the commander of the boat, there was this comradeship, that the correspondent, for instance, who had been taught to be cynical of men, knew even at the time was the best experience of his life. But no one said that it was so. No one mentioned it.

"I wish we had a sail," remarked the captain. "We might try my overcoat on the end of an oar, and give you two boys a chance to rest." So the cook and the correspondent held the mast and spread wide the overcoat; the oiler steered; and the little boat made good way with her new rig. Sometimes the oiler had to scull sharply to keep a sea from breaking into the boat, but otherwise sailing was a success.

Meanwhile the lighthouse had been growing slowly larger. It had now almost assumed color, and appeared like a little gray shadow on the sky. The man at the oars could not be prevented from turning his head rather often to try for a glimpse of this little gray shadow.

At last, from the top of each wave, the men in the tossing boat could see land. Even as the lighthouse was an upright shadow on the sky, this land seemed but a long black shadow on the sea. It certainly was thinner than paper. "We must be about opposite New Smyrna," said the cook, who had coasted this shore often in schooners. "Captain, by the way, I believe they abandoned that life-saving station there about a year ago."

"Did they?" said the captain.

The wind slowly died away. The cook and the correspondent were not now obliged to slave in order to hold high the oar. But the waves continued their old impetuous swooping at the dinghy, and the little craft, no longer under way, struggled woundily over them. The oiler or the correspondent took the oars again.

Shipwrecks are apropos of nothing. If men could only train for them and have them occur when the men had reached pink condition, there would be less drowning at sea. Of the four in the dinghy none had slept any time worth mentioning for two days and two nights previous to embarking in the dinghy, and in the excitement of clambering about the deck of a foundering ship they had also forgotten to eat heartily.

For these reasons, and for others, neither the oiler nor the correspondent was fond of rowing at this time. The correspondent wondered ingenuously how in the name of all that was sane could there be people who thought it amusing to row a boat. It was not an amusement; it was a diabolical punishment, and even a genius of mental aberrations could never conclude that it was anything but a horror to the muscles and a crime against the back. He mentioned to the boat in general how the amusement of rowing struck him, and the weary-faced oiler smiled in full sympathy. Previously to the foundering, by the way, the oiler had worked a double watch in the engine-room of the ship.

"Take her easy now, boys," said the captain. "Don't spend yourselves. If we have to run a surf you'll need all your strength, because we'll sure have to swim for it. Take your time."

Slowly the land arose from the sea. From a black line it became a line of black and a line of white—trees and sand. Finally the captain said that he could make out a house on the shore. "That's the house of refuge, sure," said the cook. "They'll see us before long, and come out after us."

The distant lighthouse reared high. "The

keeper ought to be able to make us out now, if he's looking through a glass," said the captain. "He'll notify the life-saving people."

"None of those other boats could have got ashore to give word of this wreck," said the oiler, in a low voice, "else the life-boat would be out hunting us."

Slowly and beautifully the land loomed out of the sea. The wind came again. It had veered from the north-east to the south-east. Finally a new sound struck the ears of the men in the boat. It was the low thunder of the surf on the shore. "We'll never be able to make the lighthouse now," said the captain. "Swing her head a little more north, Billie."

"A little more north, sir," said the oiler.

Whereupon the little boat turned her nose once more down the wind, and all but the oarsman watched the shore grow. Under the influence of this expansion doubt and direful apprehension were leaving the minds of the men. The management of the boat was still most absorbing, but it could not prevent a quiet cheerfulness. In an hour, perhaps, they would be ashore.

Their backbones had become thoroughly used to balancing in the boat, and they now rode this wild colt of a dinghy like circus men. The correspondent thought that he had been drenched to the skin, but happening to feel in the top pocket of his coat, he found therein eight cigars. Four of them were soaked with sea-water; four were perfectly scatheless. After a search, somebody produced three dry matches; and thereupon the four waifs rode impudently in their little boat and, with an assurance of an impending rescue shining in their eyes, puffed at the big cigars, and judged well and ill of all men. Everybody took a drink of water.

IV

"COOK," remarked the captain, "there don't seem to be any signs of life about your house of refuge."

"No," replied the cook. "Funny they don't see us!"

A broad stretch of lowly coast lay before the eyes of the men. It was of low dunes topped with dark vegetation. The roar of the surf was plain, and sometimes they could see the white lip of a wave as it spun up the beach. A tiny house was blocked out black upon the sky. Southward, the slim lighthouse lifted its little gray length.

Tide, wind, and waves were swinging the dinghy northward. "Funny they don't see us," said the men.

The surf's roar was here dulled, but its tone was nevertheless thunderous and mighty. As the boat swam over the great rollers the men sat listening to this roar. "We'll swamp sure," said everybody.

It is fair to say here that there was not a life-saving station within twenty miles in either direction; but the men did not know this fact, and in consequence they made dark and opprobrious remarks concerning the eyesight of the nation's lifesavers. Four scowling men sat in the dinghy and surpassed records in the invention of epithets.

"Funny they don't see us."

The light-heartedness of a former time had completely faded. To their sharpened minds it was easy to conjure pictures of all kinds of incompetency and blindness and, indeed, cowardice. There was the shore of the populous land, and it was bitter and bitter to them that from it came no sign.

"Well," said the captain, ultimately, "I suppose we'll have to make a try for ourselves. If we stay out here too long, we'll none of us have strength left to swim after the boat swamps."

And so the oiler, who was at the oars, turned the boat straight for the shore. There was a sudden tightening of muscles. There was some thinking.

"If we don't all get ashore," said the captain— "if we don't all get ashore, I suppose you fellows know where to send news of my finish?"

They then briefly exchanged some addresses and admonitions. As for the reflections of the men, there was a great deal of rage in them. Perchance they might be formulated thus: "If I am going to be drowned—if I am going to be drowned—if I am going to be drowned, why, in the name of the seven mad gods who rule the sea, was I allowed to come thus far and contemplate sand and trees? Was I brought here merely to have my nose dragged away as I was about to nibble the sacred cheese of life? It is preposterous. If this old ninny-woman, Fate, cannot do better than this, she should be deprived of the management of men's fortunes. She is an old hen who knows not her intention. If she has decided to drown me, why did she not do it in the beginning and save me all this trouble? The whole affair is absurd.—But no; she cannot mean to drown me. She dare not drown me. She cannot drown me. Not after all this work." Afterward the man might have had an impulse to shake his fist at the clouds. "Just you drown me, now, and then hear what I call you!"

The billows that came at this time were more formidable. They seemed always just about to break and roll over the little boat in a turmoil of foam. There was a preparatory and long growl in the speech of them. No mind unused to the sea

would have concluded that the dinhgy could ascend these sheer heights in time. The shore was
still afar. The oiler was a wily surfman. "Boys,"
he said swiftly, "she won't live three minutes
more, and we're too far out to swim. Shall I take
her to sea again, Captain?"

"Yes; go ahead!" said the captain.

This oiler, by a series of quick miracles and fast
and steady oarsmanship, turned the boat in the
middle of the surf and took her safely to sea
again.

There was a considerable silence as the boat
bumped over the furrowed sea to deeper water.
Then somebody in gloom spoke: "Well, anyhow, they must have seen us from the shore by
now."

The gulls went in slanting flight up the wind toward the gray, desolate east. A squall, marked by
dingy clouds and clouds brick-red like smoke from
a burning building, appeared from the south-east.

"What do you think of those life-saving people? Ain't they peaches?"

"Funny they haven't seen us."

"Maybe they think we're out here for sport!
Maybe they think we're fishin'. Maybe they think
we're damned fools."

It was a long afternoon. A changed tide tried to
force them southward, but wind and wave said
northward. Far ahead, where coast-line, sea, and
sky formed their mighty angle, there were little
dots which seemed to indicate a city on the shore.

"St. Augustine?"

The captain shook his head. "Too near Mosquito Inlet."

And the oiler rowed, and then the correspondent rowed; then the oiler rowed. It was a weary
business. The human back can become the seat of
more aches and pains than are registered in books
for the composite anatomy of a regiment. It is a
limited area, but it can become the theater of innumerable muscular conflicts, tangles, wrenches,
knots, and other comforts.

"Did you ever like to row, Billie?" asked the
correspondent.

"No," said the oiler; "hang it!"

When one exchanged the rowing-seat for a
place in the bottom of the boat, he suffered a bodily depression that caused him to be careless of
everything save an obligation to wiggle one finger.
There was cold sea-water swashing to and fro in
the boat, and he lay in it. His head, pillowed on a
thwart, was within an inch of the swirl of a wave-
crest, and sometimes a particularly obstreperous
sea came inboard and drenched him once more.
But these matters did not annoy him. It is almost
certain that if the boat had capsized he would

have tumbled comfortably out upon the ocean as
if he felt sure that it was a great soft mattress.

"Look! There's a man on the shore!"

"Where?"

"There! See 'im? See 'im?"

"Yes, sure! He's walking along."

"Now he's stopped. Look! He's facing us!"

"He's waving at us!"

"So he is! By thunder!"

"Ah, now we're all right! Now we're all right!
There'll be a boat out here for us in half an hour."

"He's going on. He's running. He's going up
to that house there."

The remote beach seemed lower than the sea,
and it required a searching glance to discern the
little black figure. The captain saw a floating stick,
and they rowed to it. A bath towel was by some
weird chance in the boat, and, tying this on the
stick, the captain waved it. The oarsman did not
dare turn his head, so he was obliged to ask questions.

"What's he doing now?"

"He's standing still again. He's looking, I think.
—There he goes again—toward the house.—Now
he's stopped again."

"Is he waving at us?"

"No, not now; he was, though."

"Look! There comes another man!"

"He's running."

"Look at him go, would you!"

"Why, he's on a bicycle. Now he's met the
other man. They're both waving at us. Look!"

"There comes something up the beach."

"What the devil is that thing?"

"Why, it looks like a boat."

"Why, certainly, it's a boat."

"No; it's on wheels."

"Yes, so it is. Well, that must be the life-boat.
They drag them along shore on a wagon."

"That's the life-boat, sure."

"No, by God, it's—it's an omnibus."

"I tell you it's a life-boat."

"It is not! It's an omnibus. I can see it plain.
See? One of these big hotel omnibuses."

"By thunder, you're right. It's an omnibus, sure
as fate. What do you suppose they are doing with
an omnibus? Maybe they are going around collecting the life-crew, hey?"

"That's it, likely. Look! There's a fellow waving
a little black flag. He's standing on the steps of the
omnibus. There come those other two fellows.
Now they're all talking together. Look at the fellow with the flag. Maybe he ain't waving it!"

"That ain't a flag, is it? That's his coat. Why,
certainly, that's his coat."

"So it is; it's his coat. He's taken it off and is

waving it around his head. But would you look at him swing it!"

"Oh, say, there isn't any life-saving station there. That's just a winter-resort hotel omnibus that has brought over some of the boarders to see us drown."

"What's that idiot with the coat mean? What's he signalling, anyhow?"

"It looks as if he were trying to tell us to go north. There must be a life-saving station up there."

"No; he thinks we're fishing. Just giving us a merry hand. See? Ah, there, Willie!"

"Well, I wish I could make something out of those signals. What do you suppose he means?"

"He don't mean anything; he's just playing."

"Well, if he'd just signal us to try the surf again, or to go to sea and wait, or go north, or go south, or go to hell, there would be some reason in it. But look at him! He just stands there and keeps his coat revolving like a wheel. The ass!"

"There come more people."

"Now there's quite a mob. Look! Isn't that a boat?"

"Where? Oh, I see where you mean. No, that's no boat."

"That fellow is still waving his coat."

"He must think we like to see him do that. Why don't he quit it? It don't mean anything."

"I don't know. I think he is trying to make us go north. It must be that there's a life-saving station there somewhere."

"Say, he ain't tired yet. Look at 'im wave!"

"Wonder how long he can keep that up. He's been revolving his coat ever since he caught sight of us. He's an idiot. Why aren't they getting men to bring a boat out? A fishing-boat—one of those big yawls—could come out here all right. Why don't he do something?"

"Oh, it's all right now."

"They'll have a boat out here for us in less than no time, now that they've seen us."

A faint yellow tone came into the sky over the low land. The shadows on the sea slowly deepened. The wind bore coldness with it, and the men began to shiver.

"Holy smoke!" said one, allowing his voice to express his impious mood, "if we keep on monkeying out here! If we've got to flounder out here all night!"

"Oh, we'll never have to stay here all night! Don't you worry. They've seen us now, and it won't be long before they'll come chasing out after us."

The shore grew dusky. The man waving a coat blended gradually into this gloom, and it swallowed in the same manner the omnibus and the group of people. The spray, when it dashed uproariously over the side, made the voyagers shrink and swear like men who were being branded.

"I'd like to catch the chump who waved the coat. I feel like socking him one, just for luck."

"Why? What did he do?"

"Oh, nothing, but then he seemed so damned cheerful."

In the meantime the oiler rowed, and then the correspondent rowed, and then the oiler rowed. Gray-faced and bowed forward, they mechanically, turn by turn, plied the leaden oars. The form of the lighthouse had vanished from the southern horizon, but finally a pale star appeared, just lifting from the sea. The streaked saffron in the west passed before the all-merging darkness, and the sea to the east was black. The land had vanished, and was expressed only by the low and drear thunder of the surf.

"If I am going to be drowned—if I am going to be drowned—if I am going to be drowned, why, in the name of the seven mad gods who rule the sea, was I allowed to come thus far and contemplate sand and trees? Was I brought here merely to have my nose dragged away as I was about to nibble the sacred cheese of life?"

The patient captain, drooped over the water-jar, was sometimes obliged to speak to the oarsman.

"Keep her head up! Keep her head up!"

"Keep her head up, sir." The voices were weary and low.

This was surely a quiet evening. All save the oarsman lay heavily and listlessly in the boat's bottom. As for him, his eyes were just capable of noting the tall black waves that swept forward in a most sinister silence, save for an occasional subdued growl of a crest.

The cook's head was on a thwart, and he looked without interest at the water under his nose. He was deep in other scenes. Finally he spoke. "Billie," he murmured dreamfully, "what kind of pie do you like best?"

V

"PIE!" said the oiler and the correspondent, agitatedly. "Don't talk about those things, blast you!"

"Well," said the cook, "I was just thinking about ham sandwiches and—"

A night on the sea in an open boat is a long night. As darkness settled finally, the shine of the light, lifting from the sea in the south, changed to full gold. On the northern horizon a new light appeared, a small bluish gleam on the edge of the waters. These two lights were the furniture of the world. Otherwise there was nothing but waves.

Two men huddled in the stern, and distances were so magnificent in the dinghy that the rower was enabled to keep his feet partly warm by thrusting them under his companions. Their legs indeed extended far under the rowing-seat until they touched the feet of the captain forward. Sometimes, despite the efforts of the tired oarsman, a wave came piling into the boat, an icy wave of the night, and the chilling water soaked them anew. They would twist their bodies for a moment and groan, and sleep the dead sleep once more, while the water in the boat gurgled about them as the craft rocked.

The plan of the oiler and the correspondent was for one to row until he lost the ability, and then arouse the other from his sea-water couch in the bottom of the boat.

The oiler plied the oars until his head drooped forward and the overpowering sleep blinded him; and he rowed yet afterward. Then he touched a man in the bottom of the boat, and called his name. "Will you spell me for a little while?" he said, meekly.

"Sure, Billie," said the correspondent, awaking and dragging himself to a sitting position. They exchanged places carefully, and the oiler, cuddling down in the sea-water at the cook's side, seemed to go to sleep instantly.

The particular violence of the sea had ceased. The waves came without snarling. The obligation of the man at the oars was to keep the boat headed so that the tilt of the rollers would not capsize her, and to preserve her from filling when the crests rushed past. The black waves were silent and hard to be seen in the darkness. Often one was almost upon the boat before the oarsman was aware.

In a low voice the correspondent addressed the captain. He was not sure that the captain was awake, although this iron man seemed to be always awake. "Captain, shall I keep her making for that light north, sir?"

The same steady voice answered him. "Yes. Keep it about two points off the port bow."

The cook had tied a life-belt around himself in order to get even the warmth which this clumsy cork contrivance could donate, and he seemed almost stove-like when a rower, whose teeth invariably chattered wildly as soon as he ceased his labour, dropped down to sleep.

The correspondent, as he rowed, looked down at the two men sleeping underfoot. The cook's arm was around the oiler's shoulders, and, with their fragmentary clothing and haggard faces, they were the babes of the sea—a grotesque rendering of the old babes in the wood.

Later he must have grown stupid at his work, for suddenly there was a growling of water, and a crest came with a roar and a swash into the boat, and it was a wonder that it did not set the cook afloat in his life-belt. The cook continued to sleep, but the oiler sat up, blinking his eyes and shaking with the new cold.

"Oh, I'm awful sorry, Billie," said the correspondent, contritely.

"That's all right, old boy," said the oiler, and lay down again and was asleep.

Presently it seemed that even the captain dozed, and the correspondent thought that he was the one man afloat on all the oceans. The wind had a voice as it came over the waves, and it was sadder than the end.

There was a long, loud swishing astern of the boat, and a gleaming trail of phosphorescence, like blue flame, was furrowed on the black waters. It might have been made by a monstrous knife.

Then there came a stillness, while the correspondent breathed with open mouth and looked at the sea.

Suddenly there was another swish and another long flash of bluish light, and this time it was alongside the boat, and might almost been reached with an oar. The correspondent saw an enormous fin speed like a shadow through the water, hurling the crystalline spray and leaving the long glowing trail.

The correspondent looked over his shoulder at the captain. His face was hidden, and he seemed to be asleep. He looked at the babes of the sea. They certainly were asleep. So, being bereft of sympathy, he leaned a little way to one side and swore softly into the sea.

But the thing did not then leave the vicinity of the boat. Ahead or astern, on one side or the other, at intervals long or short, fled the long sparkling streak, and there was to be heard the *whirroo* of the dark fin. The speed and power of the thing was greatly to be admired. It cut the water like a gigantic and keen projectile.

The presence of this biding thing did not affect the man with the same horror that it would if he had been a picnicker. He simply looked at the sea dully and swore in an undertone.

Nevertheless, it is true that he did not wish to be alone with the thing. He wished one of his companions to awake by chance and keep him company with it. But the captain hung motionless over the water-jar, and the oiler and the cook in the bottom of the boat were plunged in slumber.

VI

"IF I AM going to be drowned—if I am going to be drowned, why, in the name of the seven mad gods who rule the sea, was I allowed to come thus far and contemplate sand and trees?"

During this dismal night, it may be remarked that a man would conclude that it was really the intention of the seven mad gods to drown him, despite the abominable injustice of it. For it was certainly an abominable injustice to drown a man who had worked so hard, so hard. The man felt it would be a crime most unnatural. Other people had drowned at sea since galleys swarmed with painted sails, but still—

When it occurs to a man that nature does not regard him as important, and that she feels she would not maim the universe by disposing of him, he at first wishes to throw bricks at the temple, and he hates deeply the fact that there are no bricks and no temples. Any visible expression of nature would surely be pelleted with his jeers.

Then, if there be no tangible thing to hoot, he feels, perhaps, the desire to confront a personification and indulge in pleas, bowed to one knee, and with hands supplicant, saying, "Yes, but I love myself."

A high cold star on a winter's night is the word he feels that she says to him. Thereafter he knows the pathos of his situation.

The men in the dinghy had not discussed these matters, but each had, no doubt, reflected upon them in silence and according to his mind. There was seldom any expression upon their faces save the general one of complete weariness. Speech was devoted to the business of the boat.

To chime the notes of his emotion, a verse mysteriously entered the correspondent's head. He had even forogtten that he had forgotten this verse, but it suddenly was in his mind.

A soldier of the Legion lay dying in Algiers;
There was lack of woman's nursing, there was dearth
    of woman's tears;
But a comrade stood beside him, and he took that
    comrade's hand,
And he said, "I never more shall see my own, my na-
    tive land."

In his childhood the correspondent had been made acquainted with the fact that a soldier of the Legion lay dying in Algiers, but he had never regarded the fact as important. Myriads of his school-fellows had informed him of the soldier's plight, but the dinning had naturally ended by making him perfectly indifferent. He had never considered it his affair that a soldier of the

Legion lay dying in Algiers, nor had it appeared to him as a matter for sorrow. It was less to him than the breaking of a pencil's point.

Now, however, it quaintly came to him as a human, living thing. It was no longer merely a picture of a few throes in the breast of a poet, meanwhile drinking tea and warming his feet at the grate; it was an actuality—stern, mournful, and fine.

The correspondent plainly saw the soldier. He lay on the sand with his feet out straight and still. While his pale left hand was upon his chest in an attempt to thwart the going of his life, the blood came between his fingers. In the far Algerian distance, a city of low square forms was set against a sky that was faint with the last sunset hues. The correspondent, plying the oars and dreaming of the slow and slower movements of the lips of the soldier, was moved by a profound and perfectly impersonal comprehension. He was sorry for the soldier of the Legion who lay dying in Algiers.

The thing which had followed the boat and waited had evidently grown bored at the delay. There was no longer to be heard the slash of the cutwater, and there was no longer the flame of the long trail. The light in the north still glimmered, but it was apparently no nearer to the boat. Sometimes the boom of the surf rang in the correspondent's ears, and he turned the craft seaward then and rowed harder. Southward, some one had evidently built a watch-fire on the beach. It was too low and too far to be seen, but it made a shimmering, roseate reflection upon the bluff in back of it, and this could be discerned from the boat. The wind came stronger, and sometimes a wave suddenly raged out like a mountain cat, and there was to be seen the sheen and sparkle of a broken crest.

The captain, in the bow, moved on his water-jar and sat erect. "Pretty long night," he observed to the correspondent. He looked at the shore. "Those life-saving people take their time."

"Did you see that shark playing around?"

"Yes, I saw him. He was a big fellow, all right."

"Wish I had known you were awake."

Later the correspondent spoke into the bottom of the boat. "Billie!" There was a slow and gradual disentanglement. "Billie, will you spell me?"

"Sure," said the oiler.

As soon as the correspondent touched the cold, comfortable sea-water in the bottom of the boat and had huddled close to the cook's life-belt he was deep in sleep, despite the fact that his teeth played all the popular airs. This sleep was so good to him that it was but a moment before he heard a voice call his name in a tone that demonstrated the last stages of exhaustion. "Will you spell me?"

"Sure, Billie."

The light in the north had mysteriously vanished, but the correspondent took his course from the wide-awake captain.

Later in the night they took the boat farther out to sea, and the captain directed the cook to take one oar at the stern and keep the boat facing the seas. He was to call out if he should hear the thunder of the surf. This plan enabled the oiler and the correspondent to get respite together. "We'll give those boys a chance to get into shape again," said the captain. They curled down and, after a few preliminary chatterings and trembles, slept once more the dead sleep. Neither knew they had bequeathed to the cook the company of another shark, or perhaps the same shark.

As the boat caroused on the waves, spray occasionally bumped over the side and gave them a fresh soaking, but this had no power to break their repose. The ominous slash of the wind and the water affected them as it would have affected mummies.

"Boys," said the cook, with the notes of every reluctance in his voice, "she's drifted in pretty close. I guess one of you had better take her to sea again." The correspondent, aroused, heard the crash of the toppled crests.

As he was rowing, the captain gave him some whisky-and-water, and this steadied the chills out of him. "If I ever get ashore and anybody shows me even a photograph of an oar—"

At last there was a short conversation.

"—Billie!—Billie, will you spell me?"

"Sure," said the oiler.

VII

WHEN the correspondent again opened his eyes, the sea and the sky were each of the gray hue of the dawning. Later, carmine and gold was painted upon the waters. The morning appeared finally, in its splendor, with a sky of pure blue, and the sunlight flamed on the tips of the waves.

On the distant dunes were set many little black cottages, and a tall white windmill reared above them. No man, nor dog, nor bicycle appeared on the beach. The cottages might have formed a deserted village.

The voyagers scanned the shore. A conference was held in the boat. "Well," said the captain, "if no help is coming, we might better try a run through the surf right away. If we stay out here much longer we will be too weak to do anything for ourselves at all." The others silently acquiesced in this reasoning. The boat was headed for the beach. The correspondent wondered if none ever ascended the tall windtower, and if then they never looked seaward. This tower was a giant, standing with its back to the plight of the ants. It represented in a degree, to the correspondent, the serenity of nature amid the struggles of the individual—nature in the wind, and nature in the vision of men. She did not seem cruel to him then, nor beneficent, nor treacherous, nor wise. But she was indifferent, flatly indifferent. It is, perhaps, plausible that a man in this situation, impressed with the unconcern of the universe, should see the innumerable flaws of his life, and have them taste wickedly in his mind, and wish for another chance. A distinction between right and wrong seems absurdly clear to him, then, in this new ignorance of the grave-edge, and he understands that if he were given another opportunity he would mend his conduct and his words, and be better and brighter during an introduction or at a tea.

"Now, boys," said the captain, "she is going to swamp sure. All we can do is to work her in as far as possible, and then when she swamps, pile out and scramble for the beech. Keep cool now, and don't jump until she swamps sure."

The oiler took the oars. Over his shoulders he scanned the surf. "Captain," he said, "I think I'd better bring her about and keep her head-on to the seas and back her in."

"All right, Billie," said the captain. "Back her in." The oiler swung the boat then, and, seated in the stern, the cook and the correspondent were obliged to look over their shoulders to contemplate the lonely and indifferent shore.

The monstrous inshore rollers heaved the boat high until the men were again enabled to see the white sheets of water scudding up the slanted beach. "We won't get in very close," said the captain. Each time a man could wrest his attention from the rollers, he turned his glance toward the shore, and in the expression of the eyes during this contemplation there was a singular quality. The correspondent, observing the others, knew that they were not afraid, but the full meaning of their glances was shrouded.

As for himself, he was too tired to grapple fundamentally with the fact. He tried to coerce his mind into thinking of it, but the mind was dominated at this time by the muscles, and the muscles said they did not care. It merely occurred to him that if he should drown it would be a shame.

There were no hurried words, no pallor, no plain agitation. The men simply looked at the shore. "Now, remember to get well clear of the boat when you jump," said the captain.

Seaward the crest of a roller suddenly fell with a thunderous crash, and the long white comber came roaring down upon the boat.

"Steady now," said the captain. The men were silent. They turned their eyes from the shore to the comber and waited. The boat slid up the incline, leaped at the furious top, bounced over it, and swung down the long back of the wave. Some water had been shipped, and the cook bailed it out.

But the next crest crashed also. The tumbling, boiling flood of white water caught the boat and whirled it almost perpendicular. Water swarmed in from all sides. The correspondent had his hands on the gunwale at this time, and when the water entered at that place he swiftly withdrew his fingers, as if he objected to wetting them.

The little boat, drunken with this weight of water, reeled and snuggled deeper into the sea.

"Bail her out, cook! Bail her out!" said the captain.

"All right, Captain," said the cook.

"Now, boys, the next one will do for us sure," said the oiler. "Mind to jump clear of the boat."

The third wave moved forward, huge, furious, implacable. It fairly swallowed the dinghy, and almost simultaneously the men tumbled into the sea. A piece of life-belt had lain in the bottom of the boat, and as the correspondent went overboard he held this to his chest with his left hand.

The January water was icy, and he reflected immediately that it was colder than he had expected to find it off the coast of Florida. This appeared to his dazed mind as a fact important enough to be noted at the time. The coldness of the water was sad; it was tragic. This fact was somehow mixed and confused with his opinion of his own situation, so that it seemed almost a proper reason for tears. The water was cold.

When he came to the surface he was conscious of little but the noisy water. Afterward he saw his companions in the sea. The oiler was ahead in the race. He was swimming strongly and rapidly. Off to the correspondent's left, the cook's great white and corked back bulged out of the water; and in the rear the captain was hanging with his one good hand to the keel of the overturned dinghy.

There is a certain immovable quality to a shore, and the correspondent wondered at it amid the confusion of the sea.

It seemed also very attractive; but the correspondent knew that it was a long journey, and he paddled leisurely. The piece of life-preserver lay under him, and sometimes he whirled down the incline of a wave as if he were on a hand-sled.

But finally he arrived at a place in the sea where travel was beset with difficulty. He did not pause swimming to inquire what manner of current had caught him, but there his progress ceased. The shore was set before him like a bit of scenery on a stage, and he looked at it and understood with his eyes each detail of it.

As the cook passed, much farther to the left, the captain was calling to him, "Turn over on your back, cook! Turn over on your back and use the oar."

"All right, sir." The cook turned on his back, and, paddling with an oar, went ahead as if he were a canoe.

Presently the boat also passed to the left of the correspondent, with the captain clinging with one hand to the keel. He would have appeared like a man raising himself to look over a board fence if it were not for the extraordinary gymnastics of the boat. The correspondent marveled that the captain could still hold to it.

They passed on nearer to shore—the oiler, the cook, the captain—and following them went the water-jar, bouncing gaily over the seas.

The correspondent remained in the grip of this strange new enemy—a current. The shore, with its white slope of sand and its green bluff topped with little silent cottages, was spread like a picture before him. It was very near to him then, but he was impressed as one who, in a gallery, looks at a scene from Brittany or Algiers.

He thought: "I am going to drown? Can it be possible? Can it be possible? Can it be possible?" Perhaps an individual must consider his own death to be the final phenomenon of nature.

But later a wave perhaps whirled him out of this small deadly current, for he found suddenly that he could again make progress toward the shore. Later still he was aware that the captain, clinging with one hand to the keel of the dinghy, had his face turned away from the shore and toward him, and was calling his name. "Come to the boat! Come to the boat!"

In his struggle to reach the captain and the boat, he reflected that when one gets properly wearied drowning must really be a comfortable arrangement—a cessation of hostilities accompanied by a large degree of relief; and he was glad of it, for the main thing in his mind for some moments had been horror of the temporary agony. He did not wish to be hurt.

Presently he saw a man running along the shore. He was undressing with most remarkable speed. Coat, trousers, shirt, everything flew magically off him.

"Come to the boat!" called the captain.

"All right, Captain." As the correspondent paddled, he saw the captain let himself down to bottom and leave the boat. Then the correspondent performed his one little marvel of the voyage. A large wave caught him and flung him with ease and supreme speed completely over the boat and far beyond it. It struck him even then as an event in gymnastics and a true miracle of the sea. An overturned boat in the surf is not a plaything to a swimming man.

The correspondent arrived in water that reached only to his waist, but his condition did not enable him to stand for more than a moment. Each wave knocked him into a heap, and the undertow pulled at him.

Then he saw the man who had been running and undressing, and undressing and running, come bounding into the water. He dragged ashore the cook, and then waded toward the captain; but the captain waved him away and sent him to the correspondent. He was naked—naked as a tree in winter; but a halo was about his head, and he shone like a saint. He gave a strong pull, and a long drag, and a bully heave at the correspondent's hand. The correspondent, schooled in the minor formulæ, said, "Thanks, old man." But suddenly the man cried, "What's that?" He pointed a swift finger. The correspondent said, "Go."

In the shallows, face downward, lay the oiler. His forehead touched sand that was periodically, between each wave, clear of the sea.

The correspondent did not know all that transpired afterward. When he achieved safe ground he fell, striking the sand with each particular part of his body. It was as if he had dropped from a roof, but the thud was grateful to him.

It seemed that instantly the beach was populated with men with blankets, clothes, and flasks, and women with coffee-pots and all the remedies sacred to their minds. The welcome of the land to the men from the sea was warm and generous; but a still and dripping shape was carried slowly up the beach, and the land's welcome for it could only be the different and sinister hospitality of the grave.

When it came night, the white waves paced to and fro in the moonlight, and the wind brought the sound of the great sea's voice to the men on the shore, and they felt that they could then be interpreters.

THE MONSTER

⟨ THE Whilomville of Crane's fiction is the memory town of his boyhood in Port Jervis, New York, and his habit in a whole sequence of stories was to break through the gilding of reminiscence with little accuracies on how children think or feel. In "The Monster" he breaks through also with his sardonic glimpses of small-town adults. The type he most hated came into a letter from Port Jervis in 1894:

> There is a feminine mule up here who has roused all the bloodthirst in me and I don't know where it will end. She has no more brain than a pig and all she does is to sit in her kitchen and grunt. But every when she grunts something dies howling. It may be a girl's reputation or a political party or the Baptist Church but it stops in its tracks and dies.

Luckily, the representative of the type in this story is more complicated and interesting than this caricature. On the central plot, see Introduction, pp. 395-96.

"The Monster" dates from Crane's first (1897-98) sojourn in England; actually, it was finished in September, 1897, during a vacation in Ireland. *Harper's Magazine* brought out the story in August, 1898, when Crane was in Cuba as a war correspondent.

I

LITTLE JIM was, for the time, engine Number 36, and he was making the run between Syracuse and Rochester. He was fourteen minutes behind time, and the throttle was wide open. In consequence, when he swung around the curve at the flower-bed, a wheel of his cart destroyed a peony. Number 36 slowed down at once and looked guiltily at his father, who was mowing the lawn. The doctor had his back to this accident, and he continued to pace slowly to and fro, pushing the mower.

Jim dropped the tongue of the cart. He looked at his father and at the broken flower. Finally he went to the peony and tried to stand it on its pins, resuscitated, but the spine of it was hurt, and it would only hang limply from his hand. Jim could do no reparation. He looked again toward his father.

He went on to the lawn, very slowly, and kicking wretchedly at the turf. Presently his father came along with the whirring machine, while the sweet, new grass-blades spun from the knives. In a low voice, Jim said, "Pa!"

The doctor was shaving this lawn as if it were a priest's chin. All during the season he had worked at it in the coolness and peace of the evenings after supper. Even in the shadow of the cherry trees the grass was strong and healthy. Jim raised his voice a trifle. "Pa!"

The doctor paused, and with the howl of the

machine no longer occupying the sense, one could hear the robins in the cherry trees arranging their affairs. Jim's hands were behind his back, and sometimes his fingers clasped and unclasped. Again he said, "Pa!" The child's fresh and rosy lip was lowered.

The doctor stared down at his son, thrusting his head forward and frowning attentively. "What is it, Jimmie?"

"Pa!" repeated the child at length. Then he raised his finger and pointed at the flower-bed. "There!"

"What?" said the doctor, frowning more. "What is it, Jim?"

After a period of silence, during which the child may have undergone a severe mental tumult, he raised his finger and repeated his former word —"There!" The father had respected this silence with perfect courtesy. Afterward his glance carefully followed the direction indicated by the child's finger, but he could see nothing which explained to him. "I don't understand what you mean, Jimmie," he said.

It seemed that the importance of the whole thing had taken away the boy's vocabulary. He could only reiterate, "There!"

The doctor mused upon the situation, but he could make nothing of it. At last he said, "Come, show me."

Together they crossed the lawn toward the flower-bed. At some yards from the broken peony Jimmie began to lag. "There!" The word came almost breathlessly.

"Where?" said the doctor.

Jimmie kicked at the grass. "There!" he replied.

The doctor was obliged to go forward alone. After some trouble he found the subject of the incident, the broken flower. Turning then, he saw the child lurking at the rear and scanning his countenance.

The father reflected. After a time he said, "Jimmie, come here." With an infinite modesty of demeanor the child came forward. "Jimmie, how did this happen?"

The child answered, "Now—I was playin' train —and—now—I runned over it."

"You were doing what?"

"I was playin' train."

The father reflected again. "Well, Jimmie," he said, slowly, "I guess you had better not play train any more to-day. Do you think you had better?"

"No, sir," said Jimmie.

During the delivery of the judgment the child had not faced his father, and afterward he went away, with his head lowered, shuffling his feet.

II

IT WAS apparent from Jimmie's manner that he felt some kind of desire to efface himself. He went down to the stable. Henry Johnson, the negro who cared for the doctor's horses, was sponging the buggy. He grinned fraternally when he saw Jimmie coming. These two were pals. In regard to almost everything in life they seemed to have minds precisely alike. Of course there were points of emphatic divergence. For instance, it was plain from Henry's talk that he was a very handsome negro, and he was known to be a light, a weight, and an eminence in the suburb of the town where lived the larger number of the negroes, and obviously this glory was over Jimmie's horizon; but he vaguely appreciated it and paid deference to Henry for it, mainly because Henry appreciated it and deferred to himself. However, on all points of conduct as related to the doctor, who was the moon, they were in complete but unexpressed understanding. Whenever Jimmie became the victim of an eclipse he went to the stable to solace himself with Henry's crimes. Henry, with the elasticity of his race, could usually provide a sin to place himself on a footing with the disgraced one. Perhaps he would remember that he had forgotten to put the hitching-strap in the back of the buggy on some recent occasion, and had been reprimanded by the doctor. Then these two would commune subtly and without words concerning their moon, holding themselves sympathetically as people who had committed similar treasons. On the other hand, Henry would sometimes choose to absolutely repudiate this idea, and when Jimmy appeared in his shame would bully him most virtuously, preaching with assurance the precepts of the doctor's creed, and pointing out to Jimmie all his abominations. Jimmie did not discover that this was odious in his comrade. He accepted it and lived in its shadow with humility, merely trying to conciliate the saintly Henry with acts of deference. Won by this attitude, Henry would sometimes allow the child to enjoy the felicity of squeezing the sponge over a buggy-wheel, even when Jimmie was still gory from unspeakable deeds.

Whenever Henry dwelt for a time in sackcloth, Jimmie did not patronize him at all. This was a justice of his age, his condition. He did not know. Besides, Henry could drive a horse, and Jimmie had a full sense of this sublimity. Henry personally conducted the moon during the splendid journeys through the country roads, where farms spread on all sides, with sheep, cows, and other marvels abounding.

"Hello, Jim!" said Henry, poising his sponge. Water was dripping from the buggy. Sometimes the horses in the stalls stamped thunderingly on the pine floor. There was an atmosphere of hay and of harness.

For a minute Jimmie refused to take an interest in anything. He was very downcast. He could not even feel the wonders of wagon-washing. Henry, while at work, narrowly observed him.

"Your pop done wallop yer, didn't he?" he said at last.

"No," said Jimmie, defensively; "he didn't."

After this casual remark Henry continued his labor, with a scowl of occupation. Presently he said: "I done tol' yer many's th' time not to go a-foolin' an' a-proj-jeckin' with them flowers. Yer pop don't like it nohow." As a matter of fact, Henry had never mentioned flowers to the boy.

Jimmie preserved a gloomy silence, so Henry began to use seductive wiles in this affair of washing a wagon. But it was not until he began to spin a wheel on the tree, and the sprinkling water flew everywhere, that the boy was visibly moved. He had been seated on the sill of the carriage-house door, but at the beginning of this ceremony he arose and circled toward the buggy, with an interest that slowly consumed the remembrance of a late disgrace.

Johnson could then display all the dignity of a man whose duty it was to protect Jimmie from a splashing. "Look out, boy! look out! You done gwi' spile yer pants. I raikon your mommer don't 'low this foolishness, she know it. I ain't gwi' have you round yere spilin' yer pants, an' have Mis' Trescott light on me pressen'ly. 'Deed I ain't."

He spoke with an air of great irritation, but he was not annoyed at all. This tone was merely a part of his importance. In reality he was always delighted to have the child there to witness the business of the stable. For one thing, Jimmie was invariably overcome with reverence when he was told how beautifully a harness was polished or a horse groomed. Henry explained each detail of this kind with unction, procuring great joy from the child's admiration.

III

AFTER Johnson had taken his supper in the kitchen, he went to his loft in the carriage-house and dressed himself with much care. No belle of a court circle could bestow more mind on a toilet than did Johnson. On second thought, he was more like a priest arraying himself for some parade of the church. As he emerged from his room and sauntered down the carriage-drive, no one would have suspected him of ever having washed a buggy.

It was not altogether a matter of the lavender trousers, nor yet the straw hat with its bright silk band. The change was somewhere far in the interior of Henry. But there was no cake-walk hyperbole in it. He was simply a quiet, well-bred gentleman of position, wealth, and other necessary achievements out for an evening stroll, and he had never washed a wagon in his life.

In the morning, when in his working clothes, he had met a friend—"Hello, Pete!" "Hello, Henry!" Now, in his effulgence, he encountered this same friend. His bow was not at all haughty. If it expressed anything, it expressed consummate generosity—"Good-evenin', Misteh Washington." Pete, who was very dirty, being at work in a potato-patch, responded in a mixture of abasement and appreciation—"Good-evenin', Misteh Johnsing."

The shimmering blue of the electric arc-lamps was strong in the main street of the town. At numerous points it was conquered by the orange glare of the out-numbering gaslights in the windows of shops. Through this radiant lane moved a crowd, which culminated in a throng before the post-office, awaiting the distribution of the evening mails. Occasionally there came into it a shrill electric street-car, the motor singing like a cageful of grasshoppers, and possessing a great gong that clanged forth both warnings and simple noise. At the little theater, which was a varnish and red-plush miniature of one of the famous New York theaters, a company of strollers was to play *East Lynne*. The young men of the town were mainly gathered at the corners, in distinctive groups which expressed various shades and lines of chumship, and had little to do with any social gradations. There they discussed everything with critical insight, passing the whole town in review as it swarmed in the street. When the gongs of the electric cars ceased for a moment to harry the ears, there could be heard the sound of the feet of the leisurely crowd on the bluestone pavement, and it was like the peaceful evening lashing at the shore of a lake. At the foot of the hill, where two lines of maples sentinelled the way, an electric lamp glowed high among the embowering branches and made most wonderful shadow-etchings on the road below it.

When Johnson appeared amid the throng a member of one of the profane groups at a corner instantly telegraphed news of this extraordinary arrival to his companions. They hailed him. "Hello, Henry! Going to walk for a cake tonight?"

"Ain't he smooth?"

"Why, you've got that cake right in your pocket, Henry!"

"Throw out your chest a little more."

Henry was not ruffled in any way by these quiet admonitions and compliments. In reply he laughed a supremely good-natured, chuckling laugh, which nevertheless expressed an underground complacency of superior metal.

Young Griscom, the lawyer, was just emerging from Reifsnyder's barber shop, rubbing his chin contentedly. On the steps he dropped his hand and looked with wide eyes into the crowd. Suddenly he bolted back into the shop. "Wow!" he cried to the parliament; "you ought to see the coon that's coming!"

Reifsnyder and his assistant instantly poised their razors high and turned toward the window. Two belathered heads reared from the chairs. The electric shine in the street caused an effect like water to them who looked through the glass from the yellow glamour of Reifsnyder's shop. In fact, the people without resembled the inhabitants of a great aquarium that here had a square pane in it. Presently into this frame swam the graceful form of Henry Johnson.

"Chee!" said Reifsnyder. He and his assistants with one accord threw their obligations to the winds and, leaving their lathered victims helpless, advanced to the window. "Ain't he a taisy?" said Reifsnyder, marvelling.

But the man in the first chair, with a grievance in his mind, had found a weapon. "Why, that's only Henry Johnson, you blamed idiots! Come on now, Reif, and shave me. What do you think I am—a mummy?"

Reifsnyder turned, in a great excitement. "I bait you any money that vas not Henry Johnson! Henry Johnson! Rats!" The scorn put into this last word made it an explosion. "That man was a Pullman-car porter or someding. How could that be Henry Johnson?" he demanded, turbulently. "You vas crazy."

The man in the first chair faced the barber in a storm of indignation. "Didn't I give him those lavender trousers?" he roared.

And young Griscom, who had remained attentively at the window, said: "Yes, I guess that was Henry. It looked like him."

"Oh, vell," said Reifsnyder, returning to his business, "if you think so! Oh, vell!" He implied that he was submitting for the sake of amiability.

Finally the man in the second chair, mumbling from a mouth made timid by adjacent lather, said: "That was Henry Johnson all right. Why, he always dresses like that when he wants to make a front! He's the biggest dude in town—anybody knows that."

"Chinger!" said Reifsnyder.

Henry was not at all oblivious of the wake of wondering ejaculation that streamed out behind him. On other occasions he had reaped this same joy, and he always had an eye for the demonstration. With a face beaming with happiness he turned away from the scene of his victories into a narrow side street, where the electric light still hung high, but only to exhibit a row of tumbledown houses leaning together like paralytics.

The saffron Miss Bella Farragut, in a calico frock, had been crouched on the front stoop, gossiping at long range, but she espied her approaching caller at a distance. She dashed around the corner of the house, galloping like a horse. Henry saw it all, but he preserved the polite demeanor of a guest when a waiter spills claret down his cuff. In this awkward situation he was simply perfect.

The duty of receiving Mr. Johnson fell upon Mrs. Farragut, because Bella, in another room, was scrambling wildly into her best gown. The fat old woman met him with a great ivory smile, sweeping back with the door, and bowing low. "Walk in, Misteh Johnson, walk in. How is you dis ebenin', Misteh Johnson—how is you?"

Henry's faced glowed like a reflector as he bowed and bowed, bending almost from his head to his ankles. "Good-evenin', Mis' Fa'gut; good-evenin'. How is you dis evenin'? Is all you' folks well, Mis' Fa'gut?"

After a great deal of kotow, they were planted in two chairs opposite each other in the living-room. Here they exchanged the most tremendous civilities, until Miss Bella swept into the room, when there was more kotow on all sides, and a smiling show of teeth that was like an illumination.

The cooking-stove was of course in this drawing-room, and on the fire was some kind of long-winded stew. Mrs. Farragut was obliged to arise and attend to it from time to time. Also young Sim came in and went to bed on his pallet in the corner. But to all these domesticities the three maintained an absolute dumbness. They bowed and smiled and ignored and imitated until a late hour, and if they had been the occupants of the most gorgeous salon in the world they could not have been more like three monkeys.

After Henry had gone, Bella, who encouraged herself in the appropriation of phrases, said, "Oh, ma, isn't he divine?"

IV

A SATURDAY evening was a sign always for a

larger crowd to parade the thoroughfare. In summer the band played until ten o'clock in the little park. Most of the young men of the town affected to be superior to this band, even to despise it; but in the still and fragrant evenings they invariably turned out in force, because the girls were sure to attend this concert, strolling slowly over the grass, linked closely in pairs, or preferably in threes, in the curious public dependence upon one another which was their inheritance. There was no particular social aspect to this gathering, save that group regarded group with interest, but mainly in silence. Perhaps one girl would nudge another girl and suddenly say, "Look! there goes Gertie Hodgson and her sister!" And they would appear to regard this as an event of importance.

On a particular evening a rather large company of young men were gathered on the sidewalk that edged the park. They remained thus beyond the borders of the festivities because of their dignity, which would not exactly allow them to appear in anything which was so much fun for the younger lads. These latter were careering madly through the crowd, precipitating minor accidents from time to time, but usually fleeing like mist swept by the wind before retribution could lay hands upon them.

The band played a waltz which involved a gift of prominence to the bass horn, and one of the young men on the sidewalk said that the music reminded him of the new engines on the hill pumping water into the reservoir. A similarity of this kind was not inconceivable, but the young man did not say it because he disliked the band's playing. He said it because it was fashionable to say that manner of thing concerning the band. However, over in the stand, Billie Harris, who played the snare-drum, was always surrounded by a throng of boys, who adored his every whack.

After the mails from New York and Rochester had been finally distributed, the crowd from the post-office added to the mass already in the park. The wind waved the leaves of the maples, and, high in the air, the blue-burning globes of the arc lamps caused the wonderful traceries of leaf shadows on the ground. When the light fell upon the upturned face of a girl, it caused it to glow with a wonderful pallor. A policeman came suddenly from the darkness and chased a gang of obstreperous little boys. They hooted him from a distance. The leader of the band had some of the mannerisms of the great musicians, and during a period of silence the crowd smiled when they saw him raise his hand to his brow, stroke it sentimentally, and glance upward with a look of poetic anguish. In the shivering light, which gave to the park an effect like a great vaulted hall, the throng swarmed, with a gentle murmur of dresses switching the turf, and with a steady hum of voices.

Suddenly, without preliminary bars, there arose from afar the great hoarse roar of a factory whistle. It raised and swelled to a sinister note, and then it sang on the night wind one long call that held the crowd in the park immovable, speechless. The band-master had been about to vehemently let fall his hand to start the band on a thundering career through a popular march, but, smitten by this giant voice from the night, his hand dropped slowly to his knee, and, his mouth agape, he looked at his men in silence. The cry died away to a wail and then to stillness. It released the muscles of the company of young men on the sidewalk, who had been like statues, posed eagerly, lithely, their ears turned. And then they wheeled upon each other simultaneously, and, in a single explosion, they shouted, "One!"

Again the sound swelled in the night and roared its long ominous cry, and as it died away the crowd of young men wheeled upon each other and, in chorus, yelled, "Two!"

There was a moment of breathless waiting. Then they bawled, "Second district!" In a flash the company of indolent and cynical young men had vanished like a snowball disrupted by dynamite.

V

JAKE ROGERS was the first man to reach the home of Tuscarora Hose Company Number Six. He had wrenched his key from his pocket as he tore down the street, and he jumped at the spring-lock like a demon. As the doors flew back before his hands he leaped and kicked the wedges from a pair of wheels, loosened a tongue from its clasp, and in the glare of the electric light which the town placed before each of its hose-houses the next comers beheld the spectacle of Jake Rogers bent like hickory in the manfulness of his pulling, and the heavy cart was moving slowly toward the doors. Four men joined him at the time, and as they swung with the cart out into the street, dark figures sped toward them from the ponderous shadows in back of the electric lamps. Some set up the inevitable question, "What district?"

"Second," was replied to them in a compact howl. Tuscarora Hose Company Number Six swept on a perilous wheel into Niagara Avenue, and as the men, attached to the cart by the rope which had been paid out from the windlass under the tongue, pulled madly in their fervor and abandon, the gong under the axle clanged incitingly.

And sometimes the same cry was heard, "What district?"

"Second."

On a grade Johnnie Thorpe fell and, exercising a singular muscular ability, rolled out in time from the track of the oncoming wheel, and arose, disheveled and aggrieved, casting a look of mournful disenchantment upon the black crowd that poured after the machine. The cart seemed to be the apex of a dark wave that was whirling as if it had been a broken dam. Behind the lad were stretches of lawn, and in that direction front doors were banged by men who hoarsely shouted out into the clamorous avenue, "What district?"

At one of these houses a woman came to the door bearing a lamp, shielding her face from its rays with her hands. Across the cropped grass the avenue represented to her a kind of black torrent, upon which, nevertheless, fled numerous miraculous figures upon bicycles. She did not know that the towering light at the corner was continuing its nightly whine.

Suddenly a little boy somersaulted around the corner of the house as if he had been projected down a flight of stairs by a catapultian boot. He halted himself in front of the house by dint of a rather extraordinary evolution with his legs. "Oh, ma," he gasped, "can I go? Can I, ma?"

She straightened with the coldness of the exterior mother-judgment, although the hand that held the lamp trembled slightly. "No, Willie; you had better come to bed."

Instantly he began to buck and fume like a mustang. "Oh, ma," he cried, contorting himself—"oh, ma, can't I go? Please, ma, can't I go? Can't I go, ma?"

"It's half-past nine now, Willie."

He ended by wailing out a compromise: "Well, just down to the corner, ma? Just down to the corner?"

From the avenue came the sound of rushing men who wildly shouted. Somebody had grappled the bell-rope in the Methodist church, and now over the town rang this solemn and terrible voice, speaking from the clouds. Moved from its peaceful business, this bell gained a new spirit in the portentous night, and it swung the heart to and fro, up and down, with each peal of it.

"Just down to the corner, ma?"

"Willie, it's half-past nine now."

VI

THE OUTLINES of the house of Dr. Trescott had faded quietly into the evening, hiding a shape such as we call Queen Anne against the pall of the blackened sky. The neighborhood was at this time so quiet, and seemed so devoid of obstructions, that Hannigan's dog thought it a good opportunity to prowl in forbidden precincts, and so came and pawed Trescott's lawn, growling, and considering himself a formidable beast. Later, Peter Washington strolled past the house and whistled, but there was no dim light shining from Henry's loft, and presently Peter went his way. The rays from the street, creeping in silvery waves over the grass, caused the row of shrubs along the drive to throw a clear, bold shade.

A wisp of smoke came from one of the windows at the end of the house and drifted quietly into the branches of a cherry tree. Its companions followed it in slowly increasing numbers, and finally there was a current controlled by invisible banks which poured into the fruit-laden boughs of the cherry tree. It was no more to be noted than if a troop of dim and silent gray monkeys had been climbing a grapevine into the clouds.

After a moment the window brightened as if the four panes of it had been stained with blood, and a quick ear might have been led to imagine the fire-imps calling and calling, clan joining clan, gathering to the colors. From the street, however, the house maintained its dark quiet, insisting to a passer-by that it was the safe dwelling of people who chose to retire early to tranquil dreams. No one could have heard this low droning of the gathering clans.

Suddenly the panes of the red windows tinkled and crashed to the ground, and at other windows there suddenly reared other flames, like bloody specters at the apertures of a haunted house. This outbreak had been well planned, as if by professional revolutionists.

A man's voice suddenly shouted: "Fire! Fire! Fire!" Hannigan had flung his pipe frenziedly from him because his lungs demanded room. He tumbled down from his perch, swung over the fence, and ran shouting toward the front door of the Trescotts'. Then he hammered on the door, using his fists as if they were mallets. Mrs. Trescott instantly came to one of the windows on the second floor. Afterward she knew she had been about to say, "The doctor is not at home, but if you will leave your name, I will let him know as soon as he comes."

Hannigan's bawling was for a minute incoherent, but she understood that it was not about croup.

"What?" she said, raising the window swiftly.

"Your house is on fire! You're all ablaze! Move quick if—" His cries were resounding in the street as if it were a cage of echoes. Many feet pattered swiftly on the stones. There was one man who ran with an almost fabulous speed. He wore lavender trousers. A straw hat with a bright silk band was held half crumpled in his hand.

As Henry reached the front door, Hannigan had just broken the lock with a kick. A thick cloud of smoke poured over them, and Henry, ducking his head, rushed into it. From Hannigan's clamor he knew only one thing, but it turned him blue with horror. In the hall a lick of flame had found the cord that supported "Signing the Declaration." The engraving slumped suddenly down at one end, and then dropped to the floor, where it burst with the sound of a bomb. The fire was already roaring like a winter wind among the pines.

At the head of the stairs Mrs. Trescott was waving her arms as if they were two reeds. "Jimmie! Save Jimmie!" she screamed in Henry's face. He plunged past her and disappeared, taking the long-familiar routes among these upper chambers, where he had once held office as a sort of second assistant house-maid.

Hannigan had followed him up the stairs, and grappled the arm of the maniacal woman there. His face was black with rage. "You must come down," he bellowed.

She would only scream at him in reply: "Jimmie! Jimmie! Save Jimmie!" But he dragged her forth while she babbled at him.

As they swung out into the open air a man ran across the lawn and, seizing a shutter, pulled it from its hinges and flung it far out upon the grass. Then he frantically attacked the other shutters one by one. It was a kind of temporary insanity.

"Here, you," howled Hannigan, "hold Mrs. Trescott—and stop—"

The news had been telegraphed by a twist of the wrist of a neighbor who had gone to the fire-box at the corner, and the time when Hannigan and his charge struggled out of the house was the time when the whistle roared its hoarse night call, smiting the crowd in the park, causing the leader of the band, who was about to order the first triumphal clang of a military march, to let his hand drop slowly to his knees.

VII

HENRY pawed awkwardly through the smoke in the upper halls. He had attempted to guide himself by the walls, but they were too hot. The paper was crimpling, and he expected at any moment to have a flame burst from under his hands.

"Jimmie!"

He did not call very loud, as if in fear that the humming flames below would overhear him.

"Jimmie! Oh, Jimmie!"

Stumbling and panting, he speedily reached the entrance to Jimmie's room and flung open the door. The little chamber had no smoke in it at all. It was faintly illuminated by a beautiful rosy light reflected circuitously from the flames that were consuming the house. The boy had apparently just been aroused by the noise. He sat in his bed, his lips apart, his eyes wide, while upon his little white-robed figure played caressingly the light from the fire. As the door flew open he had before him this apparition of his pal, a terror-stricken negro, all tousled and with wool scorching, who leaped upon him and bore him up in a blanket as if the whole affair were a case of kidnapping by a dreadful robber chief. Without waiting to go through the usual short but complete process of wrinkling up his face, Jimmie let out a gorgeous bawl, which resembled the expression of a calf's deepest terror. As Johnson, bearing him, reeled into the smoke of the hall, he flung his arms about his neck and buried his face in the blanket. He called twice in muffled tones: "Mam-ma! Mam-ma!"

When Johnson came to the top of the stairs with his burden, he took a quick step backward. Through the smoke that rolled to him he could see that the lower hall was all ablaze. He cried out then in a howl that resembled Jimmie's former achievement. His legs gained a frightful faculty of bending sidewise. Swinging about precariously on these reedy legs, he made his way back slowly, back along the upper hall. From the way of him then, he had given up almost all idea of escaping from the burning house, and with it the desire. He was submitting, submitting because of his fathers, bending his mind in a most perfect slavery to this conflagration.

He now clutched Jimmie as unconsciously as when, running toward the house, he had clutched the hat with the bright silk band.

Suddenly he remembered a little private staircase which led from a bedroom to an apartment which the doctor had fitted up as a laboratory and work-house, where he used some of his leisure, and also hours when he might have been sleeping, in devoting himself to experiments which came in the way of his study and interest.

When Johnson recalled this stairway the submission to the blaze departed instantly. He had been perfectly familiar with it, but his confusion had destroyed the memory of it.

In his sudden momentary apathy there had been little that resembled fear, but now, as a way of safety came to him, the old frantic terror caught him. He was no longer creature to the flames, and he was afraid of the battle with them. It was a singular and a swift set of alternations in which he feared twice without submission, and submitted once without fear.

"Jimmie!" he wailed, as he staggered on his way. He wished this little inanimate body at his breast to participate in his tremblings. But the child had lain limp and still during these headlong charges and counter-charges, and no sign came from him.

Johnson passed through two rooms and came to the head of the stairs. As he opened the door great billows of smoke poured out, but, gripping Jimmie closer, he plunged down through them. All manner of odors assailed him during this flight. They seemed to be alive with envy, hatred, and malice. At the entrance to the laboratory he confronted a strange spectacle. The room was like a garden in the region where might be burning flowers. Flames of violet, crimson, green, blue, orange, and purple were blooming everywhere. There was one blaze that was precisely the hue of a delicate coral. In another place was a mass that lay merely in phosphorescent inaction like a pile of emeralds. But all these marvels were to be seen dimly through clouds of heaving, turning, deadly smoke.

Johnson halted for a moment on the threshold. He cried out again in the negro wail that had in it the sadness of the swamps. Then he rushed across the room. An orange-colored flame leaped like a panther at the lavender trousers. This animal bit deeply into Johnson. There was an explosion at one side, and suddenly before him there reared a delicate, trembling sapphire shape like a fairy lady. With a quiet smile she blocked his path and doomed him and Jimmie. Johnson shrieked, and then ducked in the manner of his race in flights. He aimed to pass under the left guard of the sapphire lady. But she was swifter than eagles, and her talons caught in him as he plunged past her. Bowing his head as if his neck had been struck, Johnson lurched forward, twisting this way and that way. He fell on his back. The still form in the blanket flung from his arms, rolled to the edge of the floor and beneath the window.

Johnson had fallen with his head at the base of an old-fashioned desk. There was a row of jars upon the top of this desk. For the most part, they were silent amid this rioting, but there was one which seemed to hold a scintillant and writhing serpent.

Suddenly the glass splintered, and a ruby-red snake-like thing poured its thick length out upon the top of the old desk. It coiled and hesitated, and then began to swim a languorous way down the mahogany slant. At the angle it waved its sizzling molten head to and fro over the closed eyes of the man beneath it. Then, in a moment, with a mystic impulse, it moved again, and the red snake flowed directly down into Johnson's upturned face.

Afterward the trail of this creature seemed to reek, and amid flames and low explosions drops like red-hot jewels pattered softly down it at leisurely intervals.

VIII

SUDDENLY all roads led to Dr. Trescott's. The whole town flowed toward one point. Chippeway Hose Company Number One toiled desperately up Bridge Street Hill even as the Tuscaroras came in an impetuous sweep down Niagara Avenue. Meanwhile the machine of the hook-and-ladder experts from across the creek was spinning on its way. The chief of the fire department had been playing poker in the rear room of Whiteley's cigar store, but at the first breath of the alarm he sprang through the door like a man escaping with the kitty.

In Whilomville, on these occasions, there was always a number of people who instantly turned their attention to the bells in the churches and schoolhouses. The bells not only emphasized the alarm, but it was the habit to send these sounds rolling across the sky in a stirring brazen uproar until the flames were practically vanquished. There was also a kind of rivalry as to which bell should be made to produce the greatest din. Even the Valley Church, four miles away among the farms, had heard the voices of its brethren, and immediately added a quaint little yelp.

Dr. Trescott had been driving homeward, slowly smoking a cigar, and feeling glad that this last case was now in complete obedience to him, like a wild animal that he had subdued, when he heard the long whistle, and chirped to his horse under the unlicensed but perfectly distinct impression that a fire had broken out in Oakhurst, a new and rather high-flying suburb of the town which was at least two miles from his own home. But in the second blast and in the ensuing silence he read the designation of his own district. He was then only a few blocks from his house. He took out the whip and laid it lightly on the mare. Surprised and frightened at this extraordinary action, she leaped forward, and as the reins straightened like steel bands, the doctor leaned backward a trifle. When the mare whirled him up to the closed gate he was wondering whose house could be afire. The man who had rung the signal-box yelled something at him, but he already knew. He left the mare to her will.

In front of his door was a maniacal woman in a wrapper. "Ned!" she screamed at sight of him. "Jimmie! Save Jimmie!"

Trescott had grown hard and chill. "Where?" he said. "Where?"

Mrs. Trescott's voice began to bubble. "Up— up—up—" She pointed at the second-story windows.

Hannigan was already shouting: "Don't go in that way! You can't go in that way!"

Trescott ran around the corner of the house and disappeared from them. He knew from the view he had taken of the main hall that it would be impossible to ascend from there. His hopes were fastened now to the stairway which led from the laboratory. The door which opened from this room out upon the lawn was fastened with a bolt and lock, but he kicked close to the lock and then close to the bolt. The door with a loud crash flew back. The doctor recoiled from the roll of smoke, and then, bending low, he stepped into the garden of burning flowers. On the floor his stinging eyes could make out a form in a smoldering blanket near the window. Then, as he carried his son toward the door, he saw that the whole lawn seemed now alive with men and boys, the leaders in the great charge that the whole town was making. They seized him and his burden, and overpowered him in wet blankets and water.

But Hannigan was howling: "Johnson is in there yet! Henry Johnson is in there yet! He went in after the kid! Johnson is in there yet!"

These cries penetrated to the sleepy senses of Trescott, and he struggled with his captors, swearing, unknown to him and to them, all the deep blasphemies of his medical-student days. He rose to his feet and went again toward the door of the laboratory. They endeavored to restrain him, although they were much affrighted at him.

But a young man who was a brakeman on the railway, and lived in one of the rear streets near the Trescotts, had gone into the laboratory and brought forth a thing which he laid on the grass.

IX

THERE were hoarse commands from in front of the house. "Turn on your water, Five!" "Let 'er go, One!" The gathering crowd swayed this way and that way. The flames, towering high, cast a wild red light on their faces. There came the clangor of a gong from along some adjacent street. The crowd exclaimed at it. "Here comes Number Three!" "That's Three a-comin'!" A panting and irregular mob dashed into view, dragging a hose-cart. A cry of exultation arose from the little boys. "Here's Three!" The lads welcomed Never-Die Hose Company Number Three as if it was composed of a chariot dragged by a band of gods. The perspiring citizens flung themselves into the fray. The boys danced in impish joy at the displays of prowess. They acclaimed the approach of Number Two. They welcomed Number Four with cheers. They were so deeply moved by this whole affair that they bitterly guyed the late appearance of the hook-and-ladder company, whose heavy apparatus had almost stalled them on the Bridge Street hill. The lads hated and feared a fire, of course. They did not particularly want to have anybody's house burn, but still it was fine to see the gathering of the companies, and amid a great noise to watch their heroes perform all manner of prodigies.

They were divided into parties over the worth of different companies, and supported their creeds with no small violence. For instance, in that part of the little city where Number Four had its home it would be most daring for a boy to contend the superiority of any other company. Likewise, in another quarter, when a strange boy was asked which fire company was the best in Whilomville, he was expected to answer "Number One." Feuds, which the boys forgot and remembered according to chance or the importance of some recent event, existed all through the town.

They did not care much for John Shipley, the chief of the department. It was true that he went to a fire with the speed of a falling angel, but when there he invariably lapsed into a certain still mood which was almost a preoccupation, moving leisurely around the burning structure and surveying it, puffing meanwhile at a cigar. This quiet man, who even when life was in danger seldom raised his voice, was not much to their fancy. Now old Sykes Huntington, when he was chief, used to bellow continually like a bull and gesticulate in a sort of delirium. He was much finer as a spectacle than this Shipley, who viewed a fire with the same steadiness that he viewed a raise in a large jack-pot. The greater number of the boys could never understand why the members of these companies persisted in re-electing Shipley, although they often pretended to understand it, because "My father says" was a very formidable phrase in argument, and the fathers seemed almost unanimous in advocating Shipley.

At this time there was considerable discussion as to which company had got the first stream of water on the fire. Most of the boys claimed that Number Five owned that distinction, but there was a determined minority who contended for Number One. Boys who were the blood adherents of other companies were obliged to choose between the two on this occasion, and the talk waxed warm.

But a great rumor went among the crowds. It was told with hushed voices. Afterward a reverent silence fell even upon the boys. Jimmie Trescott and Henry Johnson had been burned to death, and Dr. Trescott himself had been most savagely hurt. The crowd did not even feel the police pushing at them. They raised their eyes, shining now with awe, toward the high flames.

The man who had information was at his best. In low tones he described the whole affair. "That was the kid's room—in the corner there. He had measles or somethin', and this coon—Johnson—was a-settin' up with 'im, and Johnson got sleepy or somethin' and upset the lamp, and the doctor he was down in his office, and he came running up, and they all got burned together till they dragged 'em out."

Another man, always preserved for the deliverance of the final judgment, was saying: "Oh, they'll die sure. Burned to flinders. No chance. Hull lot of 'em. Anybody can see." The crowd concentrated its gaze still more closely upon these flags of fire which waved joyfully against the black sky. The bells of the town were clashing unceasingly.

A little procession moved across the lawn and toward the street. There were three cots, borne by twelve of the firemen. The police moved sternly, but it needed no effort of theirs to open a lane for this slow cortège. The men who bore the cots were well known to the crowd, but in this solemn parade during the ringing of the bells and the shouting, and with the red glare upon the sky, they seemed utterly foreign, and Whilomville paid them a deep respect. Each man in this stretcher party had gained a reflected majesty. They were footmen to death, and the crowd made subtle obeisance to this august dignity derived from three prospective graves. One woman turned away with a shriek at sight of the covered body on the first stretcher, and people faced her suddenly in silent and mournful indignation. Otherwise there was barely a sound as these twelve important men with measured tread carried their burdens through the throng.

The little boys no longer discussed the merits of the different fire companies. For the greater part they had been routed. Only the more courageous viewed closely the three figures veiled in yellow blankets.

X

OLD Judge Denning Hagenthorpe, who lived nearly opposite the Trescotts, had thrown his door wide open to receive the afflicted family. When it was publicly learned that the doctor and his son and the negro were still alive, it required a specially detailed policeman to prevent people from scaling the front porch and interviewing these sorely wounded. One old lady appeared with a miraculous poultice, and she quoted most damning Scripture to the officer when he said that she could not pass him. Throughout the night some lads old enough to be given privileges or to compel them from their mothers remained vigilantly upon the kerb in anticipation of a death or some such event. The reporter of the *Morning Tribune* rode thither on his bicycle every hour until three o'clock.

Six of the ten doctors in Whilomville attended at Judge Hagenthorpe's house.

Almost at once they were able to know that Trescott's burns were not vitally important. The child would possibly by scarred badly, but his life was undoubtedly safe. As for the negro Henry Johnson, he could not live. His body was frightfully seared, but more than that, he now had no face. His face had simply been burned away.

Trescott was always asking news of the two other patients. In the morning he seemed fresh and strong, so they told him that Johnson was doomed. They then saw him stir on the bed, and sprang quickly to see if the bandages needed readjusting. In the sudden glance he threw from one to another he impressed them as being both leonine and impracticable.

The morning paper announced the death of Henry Johnson. It contained a long interview with Edward J. Hannigan, in which the latter described in full the performance of Johnson at the fire. There was also an editorial built from all the best words in the vocabulary of the staff. The town halted in its accustomed road of thought, and turned a reverent attention to the memory of this hostler. In the breasts of many people was the regret that they had not known enough to give him a hand and a lift when he was alive, and they judged themselves stupid and ungenerous for this failure.

The name of Henry Johnson became suddenly the title of a saint to the little boys. The one who thought of it first could, by quoting it in an argument, at once overthrow his antagonist, whether it applied to the subject or whether it did not.

"Nigger, nigger, never die,
Black face and shiny eye."

Boys who had called this odious couplet in the rear of Johnson's march buried the fact at the bottom of their hearts.

Later in the day Miss Bella Farragut, of No. 7 Watermelon Alley, announced that she had been engaged to marry Mr. Henry Johnson.

XI

THE OLD judge had a cane with an ivory head. He could never think at his best until he was leaning slightly on this stick and smoothing the white top with slow movements of his hands. It was also to him a kind of narcotic. If by any chance he mislaid it, he grew at once very irritable, and was likely to speak sharply to his sister, whose mental incapacity he had patiently endured for thirty years in the old mansion on Ontario Street. She was not at all aware of her brother's opinion of her endowments, and so it might be said that the judge had successfully dissembled for more than a quarter of a century, only risking the truth at the times when his cane was lost.

On a particular day the judge sat in his armchair on the porch. The sunshine sprinkled through the lilac bushes and poured great coins on the boards. The sparrows disputed in the trees that lined the pavements. The judge mused deeply, while his hands gently caressed the ivory head of his cane.

Finally he arose and entered the house, his brow still furrowed in a thoughtful frown. His stick thumped solemnly in regular beats. On the second floor he entered a room where Dr. Trescott was working about the bedside of Henry Johnson. The bandages on the negro's head allowed only one thing to appear—an eye, which unwinkingly stared at the judge. The latter spoke to Trescott on the condition of the patient. Afterward he evidently had something further to say, but he seemed to be kept from it by the scrutiny of the unwinking eye, at which he furtively glanced from time to time.

When Jimmie Trescott was sufficiently recovered, his mother had taken him to pay a visit to his grandparents in Connecticut. The doctor had remained to take care of his patients, but as a matter of truth he spent most of his time at Judge Hagenthorpe's house, where lay Henry Johnson. Here he slept and ate almost every meal in the long nights and days of his vigil.

At dinner, and away from the magic of the unwinking eye, the judge said, suddenly, "Trescott, do you think it is—" As Trescott paused expectantly, the judge fingered his knife. He said, thoughtfully, "No one wants to advance such ideas, but somehow I think that that poor fellow ought to die."

There was in Trescott's face at once a look of recognition, as if in this tangent of the judge he saw an old problem. He merely sighed and answered, "Who knows?" The words were spoken in a deep tone that gave them an elusive kind of significance.

The judge retreated to the cold manner of the bench. "Perhaps we may not talk with propriety of this kind of action, but I am induced to say that you are performing a questionable charity in preserving this negro's life. As near as I can understand, he will hereafter be a monster, a perfect monster, and probably with an affected brain. No man can observe you as I have observed you and not know that it was a matter of conscience with you, but I am afraid, my friend, that it is one of the blunders of virtue." The judge had delivered his views with his habitual oratory. The last three words he spoke with a particular emphasis, as if the phrase was his discovery.

The doctor made a weary gesture. "He saved my boy's life."

"Yes," said the judge, swiftly—"yes, I know!"

"And what am I to do?" said Trescott, his eyes suddenly lighting like an outburst from smoldering peat. "What am I to do? He gave himself for —for Jimmie. What am I to do for him?"

The Judge abased himself completely before these words. He lowered his eyes for a moment. He picked at his cucumbers.

Presently he braced himself straightly in his chair. "He will be your creation, you understand. He is purely your creation. Nature has very evidently given him up. He is dead. You are restoring him to life. You are making him, and he will be a monster, and with no mind."

"He will be what you like, judge," cried Trescott, in sudden polite fury. "He will be anything, but, by God! he saved my boy."

The judge interrupted in a voice trembling with emotion: "Trescott! Trescott! Don't I know?"

Trescott had subsided to a sullen mood. "Yes, you know," he answered, acidly; "but you don't know all about your own boy being saved from death." This was a perfectly childish allusion to the judge's bachelorhood. Trescott knew that the remark was infantile, but he seemed to take desperate delight in it.

But it passed the judge completely. It was not his spot.

"I am puzzled," said he, in profound thought. "I don't know what to say."

Trescott had become repentant. "Don't think I don't appreciate what you say, judge. But—"

"Of course!" responded the judge, quickly. "Of course."

"It—" began Trescott.

"Of course," said the judge.

In silence they resumed their dinner.

"Well," said the judge, ultimately, "it is hard for a man to know what to do."

"It is," said the doctor, fervidly.

There was another silence. It was broken by the judge: "Look here, Trescott; I don't want you to think—"

"No, certainly not," answered the doctor, earnestly.

"Well, I don't want you to think I would say anything to— It was only that I thought that I might be able to suggest to you that—perhaps—the affair was a little dubious."

With an appearance of suddenly disclosing his real mental perturbation, the doctor said: "Well, what would you do? Would you kill him?" he asked, abruptly and sternly.

"Trescott, you fool," said the old man, gently.

"Oh, well, I know, judge, but then—" He turned red, and spoke with new violence: "Say, he saved my boy—do you see? He saved my boy."

"You bet he did," cried the judge, with enthusiasm. "You bet he did." And they remained for a time gazing at each other, their faces illuminated with memories of a certain deed.

After another silence, the judge said, "It is hard for a man to know what to do."

XII

LATE ONE evening Trescott, returning from a professional call, paused his buggy at the Hagenthorpe gate. He tied the mare to the old tin-covered post, and entered the house. Ultimately he appeared with a companion—a man who walked slowly and carefully, as if he were learning. He was wrapped to the heels in an old-fashioned ulster. They entered the buggy and drove away.

After a silence only broken by the swift and musical humming of the wheels on the smooth road, Trescott spoke. "Henry," he said, "I've got you a home here with old Alek Williams. You will have everything you want to eat and a good place to sleep, and I hope you will get along there all right. I will pay all your expenses, and come to see you as often as I can. If you don't get along, I want you to let me know as soon as possible, and then we will do what we can to make it better."

The dark figure at the doctor's side answered with a cheerful laugh. "These buggy wheels don' look like I washed 'em yestehday, docteh," he said.

Trescott hesitated for a moment, and then went on insistently, "I am taking you to Alek Williams, Henry, and I—"

The figure chuckled again. "No, 'deed! No, seh! Alek Williams don' know a hoss! 'Deed he don't. He don' know a hoss from a pig." The laugh that followed was like the rattle of pebbles.

Trescott turned and looked sternly and coldly at the dim form in the gloom from the buggy-top. "Henry," he said, "I didn't say anything about horses. I was saying—"

"Hoss? Hoss?" said the quavering voice from these near shadows. "Hoss? 'Deed I don' know all erbout a hoss! 'Deed I don't." There was a satirical chuckle.

At the end of three miles the mare slackened and the doctor leaned forward, peering, while holding tight reins. The wheels of the buggy bumped often over out-cropping boulders. A window shone forth, a simple square of topaz on a great black hillside. Four dogs charged the buggy with ferocity, and when it did not promptly retreat, they circled courageously around the flanks, baying. A door opened near the window in the hillside, and a man came and stood on a beach of yellow light.

"Yah! yah! You Roveh! You Susie! Come yah! Come yah this minnet!"

Trescott called across the dark sea of grass, "Hello, Alek!"

"Hello!"

"Come down here and show me where to drive."

The man plunged from the beach into the surf, and Trescott could then only trace his course by the fervid and polite ejaculations of a host who was somewhere approaching. Presently Williams took the mare by the head and, uttering cries of welcome and scolding the swarming dogs, led the equipage toward the lights. When they halted at the door and Trescott was climbing out, Williams cried, "Will she stand, docteh?"

"She'll stand all right, but you better hold her for a minute. Now, Henry." The doctor turned and held both arms to the dark figure. It crawled to him painfully like a man going down a ladder. Williams took the mare away to be tied to a little tree, and when he returned he found them awaiting him in the gloom beyond the rays from the door.

He burst out then like a siphon pressed by a nervous thumb. "Hennery! Hennery, ma ol' frien'. Well, if I ain' glade. If I ain' glade!"

Trescott had taken the silent shape by the arm and led it forward into the full revelation of the light. "Well, now, Alek, you can take Henry and put him to bed, and in the morning I will—"

Near the end of this sentence old Williams had come front to front with Johnson. He gasped for a second, and then yelled the yell of a man stabbed in the heart.

For a fraction of a moment Trescott seemed to be looking for epithets. Then he roared: "You old black chump! You old black— Shut up! Shut up! Do you hear?"

Williams obeyed instantly in the matter of his screams, but he continued in a lowered voice: "Ma Lode a' massy! Who'd ever think? Ma Lode a' massy!"

Trescott spoke again in the manner of a commander of a battalion. "Alek!"

The old negro again surrendered, but to himself he repeated in a whisper, "Ma Lode!" He was aghast and trembling.

As these three points of widening shadows approached the golden doorway a hale old negress appeared there, bowing. "Good-evenin', docteh! Good-evenin'! Come in! come in!" She had evidently just retired from a tempestuous struggle to place the room in order, but she was now bowing rapidly. She made the effort of a person swimming.

"Don't trouble yourself, Mary," said Trescott, entering. "I've brought Henry for you to take care of, and all you've got to do is to carry out what I tell you." Learning that he was not followed, he faced the door, and said, "Come in, Henry."

Johnson entered. "Whee!" shrieked Mrs. Williams. She almost achieved a back somersault. Six young members of the tribe of Williams made a simultaneous plunge for a position behind the stove, and formed a wailing heap.

XIII

"YOU KNOW very well that you and your family lived usually on less than three dollars a week, and now that Dr. Trescott pays you five dollars a week for Johnson's board, you live like millionaires. You haven't done a stroke of work since Johnson began to board with you—everybody knows that—and so what are you kicking about?"

The judge sat in his chair on the porch, fondling his cane, and gazing down at old Williams, who stood under the lilac bushes. "Yes, I know, jedge," said the negro, wagging his head in a puzzled manner. " 'Tain't like as if I didn't 'preciate what the docteh done, but—but—well, yeh see, jedge," he added, gaining a new impetus, "it's—it's hard wuk. This ol' man nev' did wuk so hard. Lode, no."

"Don't talk such nonsense, Alek," spoke the judge, sharply. "You have never really worked in your life—anyhow, enough to support a family of sparrows—and now when you are in a more pros-perous condition than ever before, you come around talking like an old fool."

The negro began to scratch his head. "Yeh see, jedge," he said at last, "my ol' 'ooman she cain't 'ceive no lady callahs, nohow."

"Hang lady callers!" said the judge, irascibly. "If you have flour in the barrel and meat in the pot, your wife can get along without receiving lady callers, can't she?"

"But they won't come ainyhow, jedge," replied Williams, with an air of still deeper stupefaction. "Noner ma wife's frien's ner noner ma frien's 'ill come near ma res'dence."

"Well, let them stay home if they are such silly people."

The old negro seemed to be seeking a way to elude this argument, but, evidently finding none, he was about to shuffle meekly off. He halted, however. "Jedge," said he, "ma ol' 'ooman's near driv' abstracted."

"Your old woman is an idiot," responded the judge.

Williams came very close and peered solemnly through a branch of lilac. "Jedge," he whispered, "the chillens."

"What about them?"

Dropping his voice to funereal depths, Williams said, "They—they cain't eat."

"Can't eat!" scoffed the judge, loudly. "Can't eat! You must think I am as big an old fool as you are. Can't eat—the little rascals! What's to prevent them from eating?"

In answer, Williams said, with mournful emphasis, "Hennery." Moved with a kind of satisfaction at his tragic use of the name, he remained staring at the judge for a sign of its effect.

The judge made a gesture of irritation. "Come, now, you old scoundrel, don't beat around the bush any more. What are you up to? What do you want? Speak out like a man, and don't give me any more of this tiresome rigamarole."

"I ain't er-beatin' round 'bout nuffin, jedge," replied Williams, indignantly. "No, seh; I say whatter got to say right out. 'Deed I do."

"Well, say it, then."

"Jedge," began the negro, taking off his hat and switching his knee with it, "Lode knows I'd do jes' bout as much fer five dollehs er week as ainy cul'd man, but—but this yere business is awful, jedge. I raikon 'ain't been no sleep in—in my house sence docteh done fetch 'im."

"Well, what do you propose to do about it?"

Williams lifted his eyes from the ground and gazed off through the trees. "Raikon I got good appetite, an' sleep jes' like er dog, but he—he's done broke me all up. 'Tain' no good, nohow. I wake up in the night; I hear 'im, mebbe, er-whimperin' an' er-whimperin', an' I sneak an' I sneak until I try th' do' to see if he locked in. An' he keep me er-puzzlin' an' er-quakin' all night long. Don't know how 'll do in th' winter. Can't let 'im out where th' chillen is. He'll done freeze where he is now." Williams spoke these sentences as if he were talking to himself. After a silence of deep reflection he continued: "Folks go round sayin' he ain't Hennery Johnson at all. They say he's er devil!"

"What?" cried the judge.

"Yesseh," repeated Williams, in tones of injury, as if his veracity had been challenged. "Yesseh. I'm ertellin' it to yeh straight, jedge. Plenty cul'd folks up my way say it is a devil."

"Well, you don't think so yourself, do you?"

"No. 'Tain't no devil. It's Hennery Johnson."

"Well, then, what is the matter with you? You don't care what a lot of foolish people say. Go on 'tending to your business, and pay no attention to such idle nonsense."

" 'Tis nonsense, jedge; but he *looks* like er devil."

"What do you care what he looks like?" demanded the judge.

"Ma rent is two dollehs and er half er month," said Williams, slowly.

"It might just as well be ten thousand dollars a month," responded the judge. "You never pay it, anyhow."

"Then, anoth' thing," continued Williams, in his reflective tone. "If he was all right in his haid I could stan' it; but, jedge, he's crazier 'n er loon. Then when he looks like er devil, an' done skears all ma frien's away, an' ma chillens cain't eat, an ma ole 'ooman jes' raisin' Cain all the time, an' ma rent two dollehs an' er half er month, an' him not right in his haid, it seems like five dollehs er week—"

The judge's stick came down sharply and suddenly upon the floor of the porch. "There," he said, "I thought that was what you were driving at."

Williams began swinging his head from side to side in the strange racial mannerism. "Now hol' on a minnet, jedge," he said, defensively. " 'Tain't like as if I didn't 'preciate what the docteh done. 'Tain't that. Docteh Trescott is er kind man, 'an 'tain't like as if I didn't 'preciate what he done; but—but—"

"But what? You are getting painful, Alek. Now tell me this: did you ever have five dollars a week regularly before in your life?"

Williams at once drew himself up with great dignity, but in the pause after that question he drooped gradually to another attitude. In the end he answered, heroically: "No, jedge, I 'ain't. An' 'tain't like as if I was er-sayin' five dollehs wasn't er lot er money for a man like me. But, jedge, what er man oughter git fer this kinder wuk is er salary. Yesseh, jedge," he repeated, with a great impressive gesture; "fer this kinder wuk er man oughter git er Salary." He laid a terrible emphasis upon the final word.

The judge laughed. "I know Dr. Trescott's mind concerning this affair, Alek; and if you are dissatisfied with your boarder, he is quite ready to move him to some other place; so, if you care to leave word with me that you are tired of the arrangement and wish it changed, he will come and take Johnson away."

Williams scratched his head again in deep perplexity. "Five dollehs is er big price fer bo'd, but 'tain't no big price fer the bo'd of er crazy man," he said, finally.

"What do you think you ought to get?" asked the judge.

"Well," answered Alek, in the manner of one deep in a balancing of the scales, "he looks like er devil, an' done skears e'rybody, an' ma chillens cain't eat, an' I cain't sleep, an' he ain't right in his haid, an'—"

"You told me all those things."

After scratching his wool, and beating his knee with his hat, and gazing off through the trees and down at the ground, Williams said, as he kicked nervously at the gravel, "Well, jedge, I think it is wuth—" He stuttered.

"Worth what?"

"Six dollehs," answered Williams, in a desperate outburst.

The judge lay back in his great arm-chair and went through all the motions of a man laughing heartily, but he made no sound save a slight cough. Williams had been watching him with apprehension.

"Well," said the judge, "do you call six dollars a salary?"

"No, seh," promptly responded Williams. " 'Tain't a salary. No, 'deed! 'Tain't a salary." He looked with some anger upon the man who questioned his intelligence in this way.

"Well, supposing your children can't eat?"

"I—"

"And supposing he looks like a devil? And supposing all those things continue? Would you be satisfied with six dollars a week?"

Recollections seemed to throng in Williams's mind at these interrogations, and he answered dubiously. "Of co'se a man who ain't right in his haid, an' looks like er devil— But six dollehs—"

After these two attempts at a sentence Williams suddenly appeared as an orator, with a great shiny palm waving in the air. "I tell yeh, jedge, six dollehs is six dollehs, but if I git six dollehs fer bo'ding Hennery Johnson, I uhns it! I uhns it!"

"I don't doubt that you earn six dollars for every week's work you do," said the judge.

"Well, if I bo'd Hennery Johnson fer six dollehs er week, I uhns it! I uhns it!" cried Williams, wildly.

XIV

REIFSNYDER'S assistant had gone to his supper, and the owner of the shop was trying to placate four men who wished to be shaved at once. Reifsnyder was very garrulous—a fact which made him rather remarkable among barbers, who, as a class, are austerely speechless, having been taught silence by the hammering reiteration of a tradition. It is the customers who talk in the ordinary event.

As Reifsnyder waved his razor down the cheek of a man in the chair, he turned often to cool the impatience of the others with pleasant talk, which they did not particularly heed.

"Oh, he should have let him die," said Bainbridge, a railway engineer, finally replying to one of the barber's orations. "Shut up, Reif, and go on with your business!"

Instead, Reifsnyder paused shaving entirely, and turned to front the speaker. "Let him die?" he demanded. "How vas that? How can you let a man die?"

"By letting him die, you chump," said the engineer. The others laughed a little, and Reifsnyder turned at once to his work, sullenly, as a man overwhelmed by the derision of numbers.

"How vas that?" he grumbled later. "How can you let a man die when he vas done so much for you?"

" 'When he vas done so much for you'?" repeated Bainbridge. "You better shave some people. How vas that? Maybe this ain't a barber shop?"

A man hitherto silent now said, "If I had been the doctor, I would have done the same thing."

"Of course," said Reifsnyder. "Any man vould do it. Any man that vas not like you, you—old—flint-hearted—fish." He had sought the final words with painful care, and he delivered the collection triumphantly at Bainbridge. The engineer laughed.

The man in the chair now lifted himself higher, while Reifsnyder began an elaborate ceremony of anointing and combing his hair. Now free to join comfortably in the talk, the man said: "They say he is the most terrible thing in the world. Young Johnnie Bernard—that drives the grocery wagon —saw him up at Alek Williams's shanty, and he says he couldn't eat anything for two days."

"Chee!" said Reifsnyder.

"Well, what makes him so terrible?" asked another.

"Because he hasn't got any face," replied the barber and the engineer in duet.

"Hasn't got any face!" repeated the man. "How can he do without any face?"

> "He has no face in the front of his head,
>   In the place where his face ought to grow."

Bainbridge sang these lines pathetically as he arose and hung his hat on a hook. The man in the chair was about to abdicate in his favor. "Get a gait on you now," he said to Reifsnyder. "I go out at 7.31."

As the barber foamed the lather on the cheeks of the engineer he seemed to be thinking heavily. Then suddenly he burst out. "How would you like to be with no face?" he cried to the assemblage.

"Oh, if I had to have a face like yours—" answered one customer.

Bainbridge's voice came from a sea of lather. "You're kicking because, if losing faces became popular, you'd have to go out of business."

"I don't think it will become so much popular," said Reifsnyder.

"Not if it's got to be taken off in the way his was taken off," said another man. "I'd rather keep mine, if you don't mind."

"I guess so!" cried the barber. "Just think!"

The shaving of Bainbridge had arrived at a time of comparative liberty for him. "I wonder what the doctor says to himself?" he observed. "He may be sorry he made him live."

"It was the only thing he could do," replied a man. The others seemed to agree with him.

"Supposing you were in his place," said one, "and Johnson had saved your kid. What would you do?"

"Certainly!"

"Of course! You would do anything on earth for him. You'd take all the trouble in the world for him. And spend your last dollar on him. Well, then?"

"I wonder how it feels to be without any face?" said Reifsnyder, musingly.

The man who had previously spoken, feeling that he had expressed himself well, repeated the whole thing. "You would do anything on earth for him. You'd take all the trouble in the world for him. And spend your last dollar on him. Well, then?"

"No, but look," said Reifsnyder; "supposing you don't got a face!"

XV

AS SOON as Williams was hidden from the view of the old judge he began to gesture and talk to himself. An elation had evidently penetrated to his vitals, and caused him to dilate as if he had been filled with gas. He snapped his fingers in the air, and whistled fragments of triumphal music. At times, in his progress toward his shanty, he indulged in a shuffling movement that was really a dance. It was to be learned from the intermediate monologue that he had emerged from his trials laurelled and proud. He was the unconquerable Alexander Williams. Nothing could exceed the bold self-reliance of his manner. His kingly stride, his heroic song, the derisive flourish of his hands —all betokened a man who had successfully defied the world.

On his way he saw Zeke Paterson coming to town. They hailed each other at a distance of fifty yards.

"How do, Broth' Paterson?"

"How do, Broth' Williams?"

They were both deacons.

"Is you' folks well, Broth' Paterson?"

"Middlin', middlin'. How's you' folks, Broth' Williams?"

Neither of them had slowed his pace in the smallest degree. They had simply begun this talk when a considerable space separated them, continued it as they passed, and added polite questions as they drifted steadily apart. Williams's mind seemed to be a balloon. He had been so inflated that he had not noticed that Paterson had definitely shied into the dry ditch as they came to the point of ordinary contact.

Afterward, as he went a lonely way, he burst out again in song and pantomimic celebration of his estate. His feet moved in prancing steps.

When he came in sight of his cabin, the fields were bathed in a blue dusk, and the light in the window was pale. Cavorting and gesticulating, he gazed joyfully for some moments upon this light. Then suddenly another idea seemed to attack his mind, and he stopped, with an air of being suddenly dampened. In the end he approached his home as if it were the fortress of an enemy.

Some dogs disputed his advance for a loud moment, and then, discovering their lord, slunk away embarrassed. His reproaches were addressed to them in muffled tones.

Arriving at the door, he pushed it open with the timidity of a new thief. He thrust his head cautiously sidewise, and his eyes met the eyes of his wife, who sat by the table, the lamplight defining a half of her face. "Sh!" he said, uselessly. His glance traveled swiftly to the inner door which shielded the one bed-chamber. The pickaninnies, strewn upon the floor of the living-room, were softly snoring. After a hearty meal they had promptly dispersed themselves about the place and gone to sleep. "Sh!" said Williams again to his motionless and silent wife. He had allowed only his head to appear. His wife, with one hand upon the edge of the table and the other at her knee, was regarding him with wide eyes and parted lips as if he were a specter. She looked to be one who was living in terror, and even the familiar face at the door had thrilled her because it had come suddenly.

Williams broke the tense silence. "Is he all right?" he whispered, waving his eyes toward the inner door. Following his glance timorously, his wife nodded, and in a low tone answered: "I raikon he's done gone t' sleep."

Williams then slunk noiselessly across his threshold.

He lifted a chair, and with infinite care placed it so that it faced the dreaded inner door. His wife moved slightly, so as to also squarely face it. A silence came upon them in which they seemed to be waiting for a calamity, pealing and deadly.

Williams finally coughed behind his hand. His wife started, and looked upon him in alarm. " 'Pears like he done gwine keep quiet ter-night," he breathed. They continually pointed their speech and their looks at the inner door, paying it the homage due to a corpse or a phantom. Another long stillness followed this sentence. Their eyes shone white and wide. A wagon rattled down the distant road. From their chairs they looked at the window, and the effect of the light in the cabin was a presentation of an intensely black and solemn night. The old woman adopted the attitude used always in church at funerals. At times she seemed to be upon the point of breaking out in prayer.

"He mighty quiet ter-night," whispered Williams. "Was he good ter-day?" For answer his wife raised her eyes to the ceiling in the supplication of Job. Williams moved restlessly. Finally he tiptoed to the door. He knelt slowly and without a sound, and placed his ear near the keyhole. Hearing a noise behind him, he turned quickly. His wife was staring at him aghast. She stood in front of the stove, and her arms were spread out in the natural movement to protect all her sleeping ducklings.

But Williams arose without having touched the door. "I raikon he er-sleep," he said, fingering his wool. He debated with himself for some time. During this interval his wife remained, a great fat statue of a mother shielding her children.

It was plain that his mind was swept suddenly by a wave of temerity. With a sounding step he moved toward the door. His fingers were almost upon the knob when he swiftly ducked and dodged away, clapping his hands to the back of his head. It was as if the portal had threatened him. There was a little tumult near the stove, where Mrs. Williams's desperate retreat had involved her feet with the prostrate children.

After the panic Williams bore traces of a feeling of shame. He returned to the charge. He firmly grasped the knob with his left hand, and with his other hand turned the key in the lock. He pushed the door, and as it swung portentously open he sprang nimbly to one side like the fearful slave liberating the lion. Near the stove a group had formed, the terror-stricken mother, with her arms stretched, and the aroused children clinging frenziedly to her skirts.

The light streamed after the swinging door, and disclosed a room six feet one way and six feet the other way. It was small enough to enable the radiance to lay it plain. Williams peered warily around the corner made by the doorpost.

Suddenly he advanced, retired, and advanced again with a howl. His palsied family had expected him to spring backward, and at his howl they heaped themselves wondrously. But Williams simply stood in the little room emitting his howls before an open window. "He's gone! He's gone! He's gone!" His eye and his hand had speedily proved the fact. He had even thrown open a little cupboard.

Presently he came flying out. He grabbed his hat and hurled the outer door back upon its hinges. Then he tumbled headlong into the night. He was yelling: "Docteh Trescott! Docteh Trescott!" He ran wildly through the fields and galloped in the direction of town. He continued to call to Trescott, as if the latter was within easy hearing. It was as if Trescott was poised in the contemplative sky over the running negro, and could heed this reaching voice—"Docteh Trescott!"

In the cabin, Mrs. Williams, supported by relays from the battalion of children, stood quaking watch until the truth of daylight came as a reinforcement and made them arrogant, strutting, swashbuckler children and a mother who proclaimed her illimitable courage.

XVI

THERESA PAGE was giving a party. It was the outcome of a long series of arguments addressed to her mother, which had been overheard in part by her father. He had at last said five words, "Oh, let her have it." The mother had then gladly capitulated.

Theresa had written nineteen invitations, and distributed them at recess to her schoolmates. Later her mother had composed five large cakes, and still later a vast amount of lemonade.

So the nine little girls and the ten little boys sat quite primly in the dining-room, while Theresa and her mother plied them with cake and lemonade, and also with ice-cream. This primness sat now quite strangely upon them. It was owing to the presence of Mrs. Page. Previously in the parlor alone with their games they had overturned a chair; the boys had let more or less of their hoodlum spirit shine forth. But when circumstances could be possibly magnified to warrant it, the girls made the boys victims of an insufferable pride, snubbing them mercilessly. So in the dining-room they resembled a class at Sunday-school, if it were not for the subterranean smiles, gestures, rebuffs, and poutings which stamped the affair as a children's party.

Two little girls of this subdued gathering were planted in a settle with their backs to the broad window. They were beaming lovingly upon each other with an effect of scorning the boys.

Hearing a noise behind her at the window, one little girl turned to face it. Instantly she screamed and sprang away, covering her face with her hands. "What was it? What was it?" cried every one in a roar. Some slight movement of the eyes of the weeping and shuddering child informed the company that she had been frightened by an appearance at the window. At once they all faced the imperturbable window, and for a moment there was a silence. An astute lad made an immediate census of the other lads. The prank of slipping out and looming spectrally at a window was too venerable. But the little boys were all present and astonished.

As they recovered their minds they uttered warlike cries, and through a side door sallied rapidly out against the terror. They vied with each other in daring.

None wished particularly to encounter a dragon in the darkness of the garden, but there could be no faltering when the fair ones in the dining-room were present. Calling to each other in stern voices, they went dragooning over the lawn, attacking the shadows with ferocity, but still with the caution of reasonable beings. They found, however, nothing new to the peace of the night. Of course there was a lad who told a great lie. He described a grim figure, bending low and slinking off along the fence.

He gave a number of details, rendering his lie more splendid by a repetition of certain forms which he recalled from romances. For instance, he insisted that he had heard the creature emit a hollow laugh.

Inside the house the little girl who had raised the alarm was still shuddering and weeping. With the utmost difficulty was she brought to a state approximating calmness by Mrs. Page. Then she wanted to go home at once.

Page entered the house at this time. He had exiled himself until he concluded that this children's party was finished and gone. He was obliged to escort the little girl home because she screamed again when they opened the door and she saw the night.

She was not coherent even to her mother. Was it a man? She didn't know. It was simply a thing, a dreadful thing.

XVII

IN Watermelon Alley the Farraguts were spending their evening as usual on the little rickety porch. Sometimes they howled gossip to other people on other rickety porches. The thin wail of a baby arose from a near house. A man had a terrific altercation with his wife, to which the alley paid no attention at all.

There appeared suddenly before the Farraguts a monster making a low and sweeping bow. There was an instant's pause, and then occurred something that resembled the effect of an upheaval of the earth's surface. The old woman hurled herself backward with a dreadful cry. Young Sim had been perched gracefully on a railing. At sight of the monster he simply fell over it to the ground. He made no sound, his eyes stuck out, his nerveless hands tried to grapple the rail to prevent a tumble, and then he vanished. Bella, blubbering, and with her hair suddenly and mysteriously disheveled, was crawling on her hands and knees fearsomely up the steps.

Standing before this wreck of a family gathering, the monster continued to bow. It even raised a deprecatory claw. "Don' make no botheration 'bout me, Miss Fa'gut," it said, politely. "No, 'deed. I jes' drap in ter ax if yer well this evenin', Miss Fa'gut. Don' make no botheration. No, 'deed. I gwine ax you to go to er daince with me, Miss Fa'gut. I ax you if I can have the magnifercent gratitude of you' company on that 'casion, Miss Fa'gut."

The girl cast a miserable glance behind her. She was still crawling away. On the ground beside the porch young Sim raised a strange bleat, which expressed both his fright and his lack of wind.

Presently the monster, with a fashionable amble, ascended the steps after the girl.

She groveled in a corner of the room as the creature took a chair. It seated itself very elegantly on the edge. It held an old cap in both hands. "Don' make no botheration, Miss Fa'gut. Don' make no botheration. No, 'deed. I jes' drap in ter ax you if you won' do me the proud of acceptin' ma humble invitation to er daince, Miss Fa'gut."

She shielded her eyes with her arms and tried to crawl past it, but the genial monster blocked the way. "I jes' drap in ter ax you 'bout er daince, Miss Fa'gut. I ax you if I kin have the magnifercent gratitude of you' company on that 'casion, Miss Fa'gut."

In a last outbreak of despair, the girl, shuddering and wailing, threw herself face downward on the floor, while the monster sat on the edge of the chair gabbling courteous invitations, and holding the old hat daintily to his stomach.

At the back of the house, Mrs. Farragut, who was of enormous weight, and who for eight years had done little more than sit in an arm-chair and describe her various ailments, had with speed and agility scaled a high board fence.

XVIII

THE BLACK mass in the middle of Trescott's property was hardly allowed to cool before the builders were at work on another house. It had sprung upward at a fabulous rate. It was like a magical composition born of the ashes. The doctor's office was the first part to be completed, and he had already moved in his new books and instruments and medicines.

Trescott sat before his desk when the chief of police arrived. "Well, we found him," said the latter.

"Did you?" cried the doctor. "Where?"

"Shambling around the streets at daylight this morning. I'll be blamed if I can figure on where he passed the night."

"Where is he now?"

"Oh, we jugged him. I didn't know what else to do with him. That's what I want you to tell me. Of course we can't keep him. No charge could be made, you know."

"I'll come down and get him."

The official grinned retrospectively. "Must say he had a fine career while he was out. First thing he did was to break up a children's party at Page's. Then he went to Watermelon Alley. Whoo! He stampeded the whole outfit. Men, women, and children running pell-mell, and yelling. They say one old woman broke her leg, or something, shinning over a fence. Then he went right out on the main street, and an Irish girl threw a fit, and there was a sort of a riot. He began to run, and a big crowd chased him, firing rocks. But he gave them the slip somehow down there by the foundry and in the railroad yard. We looked for him all night, but couldn't find him."

"Was he hurt any? Did anybody hit him with a stone?"

"Guess there isn't much of him to hurt any more, is there? Guess he's been hurt up to the limit. No. They never touched him. Of course nobody really wanted to hit him, but you know how a crowd gets. It's like—it's like—"

"Yes, I know."

For a moment the chief of the police looked reflectively at the floor. Then he spoke hesitatingly. "You know Jake Winter's little girl was the one that he scared at the party. She is pretty sick, they say."

"Is she? Why, they didn't call me. I always attend the Winter family."

"No? Didn't they?" asked the chief, slowly. "Well—you know—Winter is—well, Winter has gone clean crazy over this business. He wanted—he wanted to have you arrested."

"Have me arrested? The idiot! What in the name of wonder could he have me arrested for?"

"Of course. He is a fool. I told him to keep his trap shut. But then you know how he'll go all over town yapping about the thing. I thought I'd better tip you."

"Oh, he is of no consequence; but then, of course, I'm obliged to you, Sam."

"That's all right. Well, you'll be down to-night and take him out, eh? You'll get a good welcome from the jailer. He don't like his job for a cent. He says you can have your man whenever you want him. He's got no use for him."

"But what is this business of Winter's about having me arrested?"

"Oh, it's a lot of chin about your having no right to allow this—this—this man to be at large. But I told him to tend to his own business. Only I thought I'd better let you know. And I might as well say right now, doctor, that there is a good deal of talk about this thing. If I were you, I'd come to the jail pretty late at night, because there is likely to be a crowd around the door, and I'd bring a—er—mask, or some kind of a veil, anyhow."

XIX

MARTHA GOODWIN was single, and well along into the thin years. She lived with her married sister in Whilomville. She performed nearly all the house-work in exchange for the privilege of existence. Every one tacitly recognized her labor as a form of penance for the early end of her betrothed, who had died of smallpox, which he had not caught from her.

But despite the strenuous and unceasing workaday of her life, she was a woman of great mind. She had adamantine opinions upon the situation in Armenia, the condition of women in China, the flirtation between Mrs. Minster of Niagara Avenue and young Griscom, the conflict in the Bible class of the Baptist Sunday-school, the duty of the United States toward the Cuban insurgents, and many other colossal matters. Her fullest experience of violence was gained on an occasion when she had seen a hound clubbed, but in the plan which she had made for the reform of the world she advocated drastic measures. For instance, she contended that all the Turks should be pushed into the sea and drowned, and that Mrs. Minster and young Griscom should be hanged side by side on twin gallows. In fact, this woman of peace, who had seen only peace, argued constantly for a creed of illimitable ferocity. She was invulnerable on these questions, because eventually she overrode all opponents with a sniff. This sniff was an active force. It was to her antagonists like a bang over the head, and none was known to recover from this expression of exalted contempt. It left them windless and conquered. They never again came forward as candidates for suppression. And Martha walked her kitchen with a stern brow, an invincible being like Napoleon.

Nevertheless her acquaintances, from the pain of their defeats, had been long in secret revolt. It was in no wise a conspiracy, because they did not care to state their open rebellion, but nevertheless it was understood that any woman who could not coincide with one of Martha's contentions was entitled to the support of others in the small circle. It amounted to an arrangement by which all were required to disbelieve any theory for which Martha fought. This, however, did not prevent them from speaking of her mind with profound respect.

Two people bore the brunt of her ability. Her sister Kate was visibly afraid of her, while Carrie Dungen sailed across from her kitchen to sit respectfully at Martha's feet and learn the business of the world. To be sure, afterward, under another sun, she always laughed at Martha and pretended to deride her ideas, but in the presence of the sovereign she always remained silent or admiring. Kate, her sister, was of no consequence at all. Her principal delusion was that she did all the work in the upstairs rooms of the house, while Martha did it downstairs. The truth was seen only by the husband, who treated Martha with a kindness that was half banter, half deference. Martha herself had no suspicion that she was the only pillar of the domestic edifice. The situation was without definitions. Martha made definitions, but she devoted them entirely to the Armenians and Griscom and the Chinese and other subjects. Her dreams, which in early days had been of love, of meadows and the shade of trees, of the face of a man, were now involved otherwise, and they were companioned in the kitchen curiously, Cuba, the hot-water kettle, Armenia, the washing of the dishes, and the whole thing being jumbled. In regard to social misdemeanors, she who was simply the mausoleum of a dead passion was probably the most savage critic in town. This unknown woman, hidden in a kitchen as in a well, was sure to have a considerable effect of the one kind or the other in the life of the town. Every time it moved a yard, she had personally contributed an inch. She could hammer so stoutly upon the door of a proposition that it would break from its hinges and fall upon her, but at any rate it moved. She was an engine, and the fact that she did not know that she was an engine contributed largely to the effect. One reason that she was formidable was that she did not even imagine that she was formidable. She remained a weak, innocent, and pig-headed creature, who alone would defy the universe if she thought the universe merited this proceeding.

One day Carrie Dungen came across from her kitchen with speed. She had a great deal of grist. "Oh," she cried, "Henry Johnson got away from where they was keeping him, and came to town last night, and scared everybody almost to death." Martha was shining a dish-pan, polishing madly. No reasonable person could see cause for this operation, because the pan already glistened like silver. "Well!" she ejaculated. She imparted to the word a deep meaning. "This, my prophecy, has come to pass." It was a habit.

The overplus of information was choking Carrie. Before she could go on she was obliged to struggle for a moment. "And, oh, little Sadie Winter is awful sick, and they say Jake Winter was around this morning trying to get Doctor Trescott arrested. And poor old Mrs. Farragut sprained her ankle in trying to climb a fence. And there's a crowd around the jail all the time. They put Henry in jail because they didn't know what else to do with him, I guess. They say he is perfectly terrible."

Martha finally released the dish-pan and confronted the headlong speaker. "Well!" she said again, poising a great brown rag. Kate had heard the excited newcomer, and drifted down from the novel in her room. She was a shivery little woman. Her shoulder-blades seemed to be two panes of ice, for she was constantly shrugging and shrugging. "Serves him right if he was to lose all his patients," she said suddenly, in bloodthirsty tones. She snipped her words out as if her lips were scissors.

"Well, he's likely to," shouted Carrie Dungen. "Don't a lot of people say that they won't have him any more? If you're sick and nervous, Doctor Trescott would scare the life out of you, wouldn't he? He would me. I'd keep thinking."

Martha, stalking to and fro, sometimes surveyed the two other women with a contemplative frown.

XX

AFTER the return from Connecticut, little Jimmie was at first much afraid of the monster who lived in the room over the carriage-house. He could not identify it in any way. Gradually, however, his fear dwindled under the influence of a weird fascination. He sidled into closer and closer relations with it.

One time the monster was seated on a box behind the stable basking in the rays of the afternoon sun. A heavy crêpe veil was swathed about its head.

Little Jimmie and many companions came around the corner of the stable. They were all in what was popularly known as the baby class, and consequently escaped from school a half-hour before the other children. They halted abruptly at sight of the figure on the box. Jimmie waved his hand with the air of a proprietor.

"There he is," he said.

"O-o-o!" murmured all the little boys—"o-o-o!" They shrank back and grouped according to courage or experience, as at the sound the monster slowly turned its head. Jimmie had remained in the van alone. "Don't be afraid! I won't let him hurt you," he said, delighted.

"Huh!" they replied, contemptuously. "We ain't afraid."

Jimmie seemed to reap all the joys of the owner and exhibitor of one of the world's marvels, while his audience remained at a distance—awed and entranced, fearful and envious.

One of them addressed Jimmie gloomily. "Bet you dassent walk right up to him." He was an older boy than Jimmie, and habitually oppressed him to a small degree. This new social elevation of the smaller lad probably seemed revolutionary to him.

"Huh!" said Jimmie, with deep scorn. "Dassent I? Dassent I, hey? Dassent I?"

The group was immensely excited. It turned its

eyes upon the boy that Jimmie addressed. "No, you dassent," he said, stolidly, facing a moral defeat. He could see that Jimmie was resolved. "No, you dassent," he repeated, doggedly.

"Ho?" cried Jimmie. "You just watch!—you just watch!"

Amid a silence he turned and marched toward the monster. But possibly the palpable wariness of his companions had an effect upon him that weighed more than his previous experience, for suddenly, when near to the monster, he halted dubiously. But his playmates immediately uttered a derisive shout, and it seemed to force him forward. He went to the monster and laid his hand delicately on its shoulder. "Hello, Henry," he said, in a voice that trembled a trifle. The monster was crooning a weird line of negro melody that was scarcely more than a thread of sound, and it paid no heed to the boy.

Jimmie strutted back to his companions. They acclaimed him and hooted his opponent. Amid this clamor the larger boy with difficulty preserved a dignified attitude.

"I dassent, dassent I?" said Jimmie to him. "Now, you're so smart, let's see you do it!"

This challenge brought forth renewed taunts from the others. The larger boy puffed out his cheeks. "Well, I ain't afraid," he explained, sullenly. He had made a mistake in diplomacy, and now his small enemies were tumbling his prestige all about his ears. They crowed like roosters and bleated like lambs, and made many other noises which were supposed to bury him in ridicule and dishonor. "Well, I ain't afraid," he continued to explain through the din.

Jimmie, the hero of the mob, was pitiless. "You ain't afraid, hey?" he sneered. "If you ain't afraid, go do it, then."

"Well, I would if I wanted to," the other retorted. His eyes wore an expression of profound misery, but he preserved steadily other portions of a pot-valiant air. He suddenly faced one of his persecutors. "If you're so smart, why don't you go do it?" This persecutor sank promptly through the group to the rear. The incident gave the badgered one a breathing-spell, and for a moment even turned the derision in another direction. He took advantage of his interval. "I'll do it if anybody else will," he announced, swaggering to and fro.

Candidates for the adventure did not come forward. To defend themselves from this counter-charge, the other boys again set up their crowing and bleating. For a while they would hear nothing from him. Each time he opened his lips their chorus of noises made oratory impossible. But at last he was able to repeat that he would volunteer to dare as much in the affair as any other boy.

"Well, you go first," they shouted.

But Jimmie intervened to once more lead the populace against the large boy. "You're mighty brave, ain't you?" he said to him. "You dared me to do it, and I did—didn't I? Now who's afraid?" The others cheered this view loudly, and they instantly resumed the baiting of the large boy.

He shamefacedly scratched his left shin with his right foot. "Well, I ain't afraid." He cast an eye at the monster. "Well, I ain't afraid." With a glare of hatred at his squalling tormentors, he finally announced a grim intention. "Well, I'll do it, then, since you're so fresh. Now!"

The mob subsided as with a formidable countenance he turned toward the impassive figure on the box. The advance was also a regular progression from high daring to craven hesitation. At last, when some yards from the monster, the lad came to a full halt, as if he had encountered a stone wall. The observant little boys in the distance promptly hooted. Stung again by these cries, the lad sneaked two yards forward. He was crouched like a young cat ready for a backward spring. The crowd at the rear, beginning to respect this display, uttered some encouraging cries. Suddenly the lad gathered himself together, made a white and desperate rush forward, touched the monster's shoulder with a far-outstretched finger, and sped away, while his laughter rang out wild, shrill, and exultant.

The crowd of boys reverenced him at once, and began to throng into his camp, and look at him, and be his admirers. Jimmie was discomfited for a moment, but he and the larger boy, without agreement or word of any kind, seemed to recognize a truce, and they swiftly combined and began to parade before the others.

"Why, it's just as easy as nothing," puffed the larger boy. "Ain't it, Jim?"

"Course," blew Jimmie. "Why, it's as e-e-easy."

They were people of another class. If they had been decorated for courage on twelve battle-fields, they could not have made the other boys more ashamed of the situation.

Meanwhile they condescended to explain the emotions of the excursion, expressing unqualified contempt for any one who could hang back. "Why, it ain't nothin'. He won't do nothin' to you," they told the others, in tones of exasperation.

One of the very smallest boys in the party showed signs of a wistful desire to distinguish himself, and they turned their attention to him, pushing at his shoulders while he swung away from them, and hesitated dreamily. He was eventually induced to make furtive expedition, but it was only for a few yards. Then he paused, motionless, gazing with open mouth. The vociferous entreaties of Jimmie and the large boy had no power over him.

Mrs. Hannigan had come out on her back porch with a pail of water. From this coign she had a view of the secluded portion of the Trescott grounds that was behind the stable. She perceived the group of boys, and the monster on the box. She shaded her eyes with her hand to benefit her vision. She screeched then as if she was being murdered. "Eddie! Eddie! You come home this minute!"

Her son querulously demanded, "Aw, what for?"

"You come home this minute. Do you hear?"

The other boys seemed to think this visitation upon one of their number required them to preserve for a time the hang-dog air of a collection of culprits, and they remained in guilty silence until the little Hannigan, wrathfully protesting, was pushed through the door of his home. Mrs. Hannigan cast a piercing glance over the group, stared with a bitter face at the Trescott house, as if this new and handsome edifice was insulting her, and then followed her son.

There was wavering in the party. An inroad by one mother always caused them to carefully sweep the horizon to see if there were more coming. "This is my yard," said Jimmie, proudly. "We don't have to go home."

The monster on the box had turned its black crêpe countenance toward the sky, and was waving its arms in time to a religious chant. "Look at him now," cried a little boy. They turned, and were transfixed by the solemnity and mystery of the indefinable gestures. The wail of the melody was mournful and slow. They drew back. It seemed to spellbind them with the power of a funeral. They were so absorbed that they did not hear the doctor's buggy drive up to the stable. Trescott got out, tied his horse, and approached the group. Jimmie saw him first, and at his look of dismay the others wheeled.

"What's all this, Jimmie?" asked Trescott, in surprise.

The lad advanced to the front of his companions, halted, and said nothing. Trescott's face gloomed slightly as he scanned the scene.

"What were you doing, Jimmie?"

"We was playin'," answered Jimmie, huskily.

"Playing at what?"

"Just playin'."

Trescott looked gravely at the other boys, and asked them to please go home. They proceeded to the street much in the manner of frustrated and revealed assassins. The crime of trespass on another boy's place was still a crime when they had only accepted the other boy's cordial invitation, and they were used to being sent out of all manner of gardens upon the sudden appearance of a father or a mother. Jimmie had wretchedly watched the departure of his companions. It involved the loss of his position as a lad who controlled the privileges of his father's grounds, but then he knew that in the beginning he had no right to ask so many boys to be his guests.

Once on the sidewalk, however, they speedily forgot their shame as trespassers, and the large boy launched forth in a description of his success in the late trial of courage. As they went rapidly up the street, the little boy who had made the furtive expedition cried out confidently from the rear, "Yes, and I went almost up to him, didn't I, Willie?"

The large boy crushed him in a few words. "Huh!" he scoffed. "You only went a little way. I went clear up to him."

The pace of the other boys was so manly that the tiny thing had to trot, and he remained at the rear, getting entangled in their legs in his attempts to reach the front rank and become of some importance, dodging this way and that way, and always piping out his little claim to glory.

XXI

"BY THE WAY, Grace," said Trescott, looking into the dining-room from his office door, "I wish you would send Jimmie to me before school-time."

When Jimmie came, he advanced so quietly that Trescott did not at first note him. "Oh," he said, wheeling from a cabinet, "here you are, young man."

"Yes, sir."

Trescott dropped into his chair and tapped the desk with a thoughtful finger. "Jimmie, what were you doing in the back garden yesterday—you and the other boys—to Henry?"

"We weren't doing anything, pa."

Trescott looked sternly into the raised eyes of his son. "Are you sure you were not annoying him in any way? Now what were you doing, exactly?"

"Why, we—why, we—now—Willie Dalzel said I dassent go right up to him, and I did; and then he did; and then—the other boys were 'fraid; and then—you comed."

Trescott groaned deeply. His countenance was so clouded in sorrow that the lad, bewildered by the mystery of it, burst suddenly forth in dismal lamentations. "There, there. Don't cry, Jim," said Trescott, going round the desk. "Only—" He sat in a great leather reading-chair, and took the boy on his knee. "Only I want to explain to you—"

After Jimmie had gone to school, and as Trescott was about to start on his round of morning calls, a message arrived from Doctor Moser. It set forth that the latter's sister was dying in the old homestead, twenty miles away up the valley, and asked Trescott to care for his patients for the day at least. There was also in the envelope a little history of each case and of what had already been done. Trescott replied to the messenger that he would gladly assent to the arrangement.

He noted that the first name on Moser's list was Winter, but this did not seem to strike him as an important fact. When its turn came, he rang the Winter bell. "Good-morning, Mrs. Winter," he said, cheerfully, as the door was opened. "Doctor Moser has been obliged to leave town to-day, and he has asked me to come in his stead. How is the little girl this morning?"

Mrs. Winter had regarded him in stony surprise. At last she said: "Come in! I'll see my husband." She bolted into the house. Trescott entered the hall, and turned to the left into the sitting-room.

Presently Winter shuffled through the door. His eyes flashed toward Trescott. He did not betray any desire to advance far into the room. "What do you want?" he said.

"What do I want? What do I want?" repeated Trescott, lifting his head suddenly. He had heard an utterly new challenge in the night of the jungle.

"Yes, that's what I want to know," snapped Winter. "What do you want?"

Trescott was silent for a moment. He consulted Moser's memoranda. "I see that your little girl's case is a trifle serious," he remarked. "I would advise you to call a physician soon. I will leave you a copy of Dr. Moser's record to give to any one you may call." He paused to transcribe the record on a page of his note-book. Tearing out the leaf, he extended it to Winter as he moved toward the door. The latter shrunk against the wall. His head was hanging as he reached for the paper. This caused him to grasp air, and so Trescott simply let the paper flutter to the feet of the other man.

"Good-morning," said Trescott from the hall. This placid retreat seemed to suddenly arouse Winter to ferocity. It was as if he had then recalled all the truths which he had formulated to hurl at Trescott. So he followed him into the hall, and down the hall to the door, and through the door to the porch, barking in fiery rage from a respectful distance. As Trescott imperturbably turned the mare's head down the road, Winter stood on the porch, still yelping. He was like a little dog.

XXII

"HAVE you heard the news?" cried Carrie Dungen, as she sped toward Martha's kitchen. "Have you heard the news?" Her eyes were shining with delight.

"No," answered Martha's sister Kate, bending forward eagerly. "What was it? What was it?"

Carrie appeared triumphantly in the open door. "Oh, there's been an awful scene between Doctor Trescott and Jake Winter. I never thought that Jake Winter had any pluck at all, but this morning he told the doctor just what he thought of him."

"Well what did he think of him?" asked Martha.

"Oh, he called him everything. Mrs. Howarth heard it through her front blinds. It was terrible, she says. It's all over town now. Everybody knows it."

"Didn't the doctor answer back?"

"No! Mrs. Howarth—she says he never said a word. He just walked down to his buggy and got in, and drove off as co-o-o-l. But Jake gave him jinks, by all accounts."

"But what did he say?" cried Kate, shrill and excited. She was evidently at some kind of feast.

"Oh, he told him that Sadie had never been well since that night Henry Johnson frightened her at Theresa Page's party, and he held him responsible, and how dared he cross his threshold—and—and—and—"

"And what?" said Martha.

"Did he swear at him?" said Kate, in fearsome glee.

"No—not much. He did swear at him a little, but not more than a man does anyhow when he is real mad, Mrs. Howarth says."

"O-oh!" breathed Kate. "And did he call him any names?"

Martha, at her work, had been for a time in deep thought. She now interrupted the others. "It don't seem as if Sadie Winter had been sick since that time Henry Johnson got loose. She's been to school almost the whole time since then, hasn't she?"

They combined upon her in immediate indignation. "School? School? I should say not. Don't think for a moment. School!"

Martha wheeled from the sink. She held an iron spoon, and it seemed as if she was going to attack them. "Sadie Winter has passed here many a morning since then carrying her school bag. Where was she going? To a wedding?"

The others, long accustomed to a mental tyranny, speedily surrendered.

"Did she?" stammered Kate. "I never saw her."

Carrie Dungen made a weak gesture.

"If I had been Doctor Trescott," exclaimed Martha, loudly, "I'd have knocked that miserable Jake Winter's head off."

Kate and Carrie, exchanging glances, made an alliance in the air. "I don't see why you say that, Martha," replied Carrie, with considerable boldness, gaining support and sympathy from Kate's smile. "I don't see how anybody can be blamed for getting angry when their little girl gets almost scared to death and gets sick from it, and all that. Besides, everybody says——"

"Oh, I don't care what everybody says," said Martha.

"Well, you can't go against the whole town," answered Carrie, in sudden sharp defiance.

"No, Martha, you can't go against the whole town," piped Kate, following her leader rapidly.

" 'The whole town,' " cried Martha. "I'd like to know what you call 'the whole town.' Do you call these silly people who are scared of Henry Johnson 'the whole town'?"

"Why, Martha," said Carrie, in a reasoning tone, "you talk as if you wouldn't be scared of him!"

"No more would I," retorted Martha.

"O-oh, Martha, how you talk!" said Kate. "Why, the idea! Everybody's afraid of him."

Carrie was grinning. "You've never seen him, have you?" she asked, seductively.

"No," admitted Martha.

"Well, then, how do you know that you wouldn't be scared?"

Martha confronted her. "Have you ever seen him? No? Well, then, how do you know you *would* be scared?"

The allied forces broke out in chorus: "But, Martha, everybody says so. Everybody says so."

"Everybody says what?"

"Everybody that's seen him say they were frightened almost to death. 'Tisn't only women, but it's men too. It's awful."

Martha wagged her head solemnly. "I'd try not to be afraid of him."

"But supposing you could not help it?" said Kate.

"Yes, and look here," cried Carrie. "I'll tell you another thing. The Hannigans are going to move out of the house next door."

"On account of him?" demanded Martha.

Carrie nodded. "Mrs. Hannigan says so herself."

"Well, of all things!" ejaculated Martha. "Going to move, eh? You don't say so! Where they going to move to?"

"Down on Orchard Avenue."

"Well, of all things! Nice house?"

"I don't know about that. I haven't heard. But there's lots of nice houses on Orchard."

"Yes, but they're all taken," said Kate. "There isn't a vacant house on Orchard Avenue."

"Oh yes, there is," said Martha. "The old Hampstead house is vacant."

"Oh, of course," said Kate. "But then I don't believe Mrs. Hannigan would like it there. I wonder where they can be going to move to?"

"I'm sure I don't know," sighed Martha. "It must be to some place we don't know about."

"Well," said Carrie Dungen, after a general reflective silence, "it's easy enough to find out, anyhow."

"Who knows—around here?" asked Kate.

"Why, Mrs. Smith, and there she is in her garden," said Carrie, jumping to her feet. As she dashed out of the door, Kate and Martha crowded at the window. Carrie's voice rang out from near the steps. "Mrs. Smith! Mrs. Smith! Do you know where the Hannigans are going to move to?"

XXIII

THE AUTUMN smote the leaves, and the trees of Whilomville were panoplied in crimson and yellow. The winds grew stronger, and in the melancholy purple of the nights the home shine of a window became a finer thing. The little boys, watching the sear and sorrowful leaves drifting down from the maples, dreamed of the near time when they could heap bushels in the streets and burn them during the abrupt evenings.

Three men walked down Niagara Avenue. As they approached Judge Hagenthorpe's house he came down his walk to meet them in the manner of one who has been waiting.

"Are you ready, judge?" one said.

"All ready," he answered.

The four then walked to Trescott's house. He received them in his office, where he had been reading. He seemed surprised at this visit of four very active and influential citizens, but he had nothing to say of it.

After they were all seated, Trescott looked expectantly from one face to another. There was a little silence. It was broken by John Twelve, the wholesale grocer, who was worth $400,000, and reported to be worth over a million.

"Well, doctor," he said, with a short laugh, "I suppose we might as well admit at once that we've come to interfere in something which is none of our business."

"Why, what is it?" asked Trescott, again looking from one face to another. He seemed to appeal particularly to Judge Hagenthorpe, but the old man had his chin lowered musingly to his cane, and would not look at him.

"It's about what nobody talks of—much," said Twelve. "It's about Henry Johnson."

Trescott squared himself in his chair. "Yes?" he said.

Having delivered himself of the title, Twelve seemed to become more easy. "Yes," he answered, blandly, "we wanted to talk to you about it."

"Yes?" said Trescott.

Twelve abruptly advanced on the main attack. "Now see here, Trescott, we like you, and we have come to talk right out about this business. It may be none of our affairs and all that, and as for me, I don't mind if you tell me so; but I am not going to keep quiet and see you ruin yourself. And that's how we all feel."

"I am not ruining myself," answered Trescott.

"No, maybe you are not exactly ruining yourself," said Twelve, slowly, "but you are doing yourself a great deal of harm. You have changed from being the leading doctor in town to about the last one. It is mainly because there are always a large number of people who are very thoughtless fools, of course, but then that doesn't change the condition."

A man who had not heretofore spoken said, solemnly, "It's the women."

"Well, what I want to say is this," resumed Twelve: "Even if there are a lot of fools in the world, we can't see any reason why you should ruin yourself by opposing them. You can't teach them anything, you know."

"I am not trying to teach them anything." Trescott smiled wearily. "I—it is a matter of—well—"

"And there are a good many of us that admire you for it immensely," interrupted Twelve; "but that isn't going to change the minds of all those ninnies."

"It's the women," stated the advocate of this view again.

"Well, what I want to say is this," said Twelve. "We want you to get out of this trouble and strike your old gait again. You are simply killing your practice through your infernal pig-headedness. Now this thing is out of the ordinary, but there must be ways to—to beat the game somehow, you see. So we've talked it over—about a dozen of us—and, as I say, if you want to tell us to mind our own business, why, go ahead; but we've talked it over, and we've come to the conclusion that the only way to do is to get Johnson a place somewhere off up the valley, and—"

Trescott wearily gestured. "You don't know,

my friend. Everybody is so afraid of him, they can't even give him good care. Nobody can attend to him as I do myself."

"But I have a little no-good farm up beyond Clarence Mountain that I was going to give to Henry," cried Twelve, aggrieved. "And if you—and if you—if you—through your house burning down, or anything—why, all the boys were prepared to take him right off your hands, and—and—"

Trescott arose and went to the window. He turned his back upon them. They sat waiting in silence. When he returned he kept his face in the shadow. "No, John Twelve," he said, "it can't be done."

There was another stillness. Suddenly a man stirred in his chair.

"Well, then, a public institution—" he began.

"No," said Trescott; "public institutions are all very good, but he is not going to one."

In the background of the group old Judge Hagenthorpe was thoughtfully smoothing the polished ivory head of his cane.

XXIV

TRESCOTT loudly stamped the snow from his feet and shook the flakes from his shoulders. When he entered the house he went at once to the dining-room, and then to the sitting-room. Jimmie was there, reading painfully in a large book concerning giraffes and tigers and crocodiles.

"Where is your mother, Jimmie?" asked Trescott.

"I don't know, pa," answered the boy. "I think she is upstairs."

Trescott went to the foot of the stairs and called, but there came no answer. Seeing that the door of the little drawing-room was open, he entered. The room was bathed in the half-light that came from the four dull panes of mica in the front of the great stove. As his eyes grew used to the shadows he saw his wife curled in an arm-chair. He went to her. "Why, Grace," he said, "didn't you hear me calling you?"

She made no answer, and as he bent over the chair he heard her trying to smother a sob in the cushion.

"Grace!" he cried. "You're crying!"

She raised her face. "I've got a headache, a dreadful headache, Ned."

"A headache?" he repeated, in surprise and incredulity.

He pulled a chair close to hers. Later, as he cast his eye over the zone of light shed by the dull red panes, he saw that a low table had been drawn close to the stove, and that it was burdened with many small cups and plates of uncut tea-cake. He remembered that the day was Wednesday, and that his wife received on Wednesdays.

"Who was here to-day, Gracie?" he asked.

From his shoulder there came a mumble, "Mrs. Twelve."

"Was she—um," he said. "Why—didn't Anna Hagenthorpe come over?"

The mumble from his shoulder continued, "She wasn't well enough."

Glancing down at the cups, Trescott mechanically counted them. There were fifteen of them. "There, there," he said. "Don't cry, Grace. Don't cry."

The wind was whining round the house, and the snow beat aslant upon the windows. Sometimes the coal in the stove settled with a crumbling sound, and the four panes of mica flashed a sudden new crimson. As he sat holding her head on his shoulder, Trescott found himself occasionally trying to count the cups. There were fifteen of them.

THE BRIDE COMES TO YELLOW SKY

([CRANE's easy handling of Wild West melodrama and Western humor (see Introduction, p. 396) stemmed from a knowing detachment. Neither literary tradition possessed him as did evangelical preaching or heroic legend, and writing in England in the autumn of 1897, he was almost three years and nearly five thousand miles from any direct experience of the subject. Though he liked the West heartily, he was immune to the prevalent cultural image of it that he once spoofed in inscribing a copy of *George's Mother*: "To Hamlin Garland of the great honest West, from Stephen Crane of the false East."

I

THE GREAT Pullman was whirling onward with such dignity of motion that a glance from the window seemed simply to prove that the plains of Texas were pouring eastward. Vast flats of green grass, dull-hued spaces of mesquit and cactus, little groups of frame houses, woods of light and tender trees, all were sweeping into the east, sweeping over the horizon, a precipice.

A newly married pair had boarded this coach at San Antonio. The man's face was reddened from many days in the wind and sun, and a direct result of his new black clothes was that his brick-colored hands were constantly performing in a most conscious fashion. From time to time he looked down respectfully at his attire. He sat with a hand on each knee, like a man waiting in a barber's shop. The glances he devoted to other passengers were furtive and shy.

The bride was not pretty, nor was she very young. She wore a dress of blue cashmere, with small reservations of velvet here and there, and with steel buttons abounding. She continually twisted her head to regard her puff sleeves, very stiff, straight, and high. They embarrassed her. It was quite apparent that she had cooked, and that she expected to cook, dutifully. The blushes caused by the careless scrutiny of some passengers as she had entered the car were strange to see upon this plain, under-class countenance, which was drawn in placid, almost emotionless lines.

They were evidently very happy. "Ever been in a parlor-car before?" he asked, smiling with delight.

"No," she answered; "I never was. It's fine, ain't it?"

"Great! And then after a while we'll go forward to the diner, and get a big lay-out. Finest meal in the world. Charge a dollar."

"Oh, do they?" cried the bride. "Charge a dollar? Why, that's too much—for us—ain't it, Jack?"

"Not this trip, anyhow," he answered bravely. "We're going to go the whole thing."

Later he explained to her about the trains. "You see, it's a thousand miles from one end of Texas to the other; and this train runs right across it, and never stops but four times." He had the pride of an owner. He pointed out to her the dazzling fittings of the coach; and in truth her eyes opened wider as she contemplated the sea-green figured velvet, the shining brass, silver, and glass, the wood that gleamed as darkly brilliant as the surface of a pool of oil. At one end a bronze figure sturdily held a support for a separated chamber, and at convenient places on the ceiling were frescoes in olive and silver.

To the minds of the pair, their surroundings reflected the glory of their marriage that morning in San Antonio; this was the environment of their new estate; and the man's face in particular beamed with an elation that made him appear ridiculous to the negro porter. This individual at times surveyed them from afar with an amused and superior grin. On other occasions he bullied them with skill in ways that did not make it exactly plain to them that they were being bullied. He subtly used all the manners of the most unconquerable kind of snobbery. He oppressed them; but of this oppression they had small knowledge, and they speedily forgot that infrequently a number of travelers covered them with stares of derisive enjoyment. Historically there was supposed to be something infinitely humorous in their situation.

"We are due in Yellow Sky at 3:42," he said, looking tenderly into her eyes.

"Oh, are we?" she said, as if she had not been aware of it. To evince surprise at her husband's statement was part of her wifely amiability. She took from a pocket a little silver watch; and as she held it before her, and stared at it with a frown of attention, the new husband's face shone.

"I bought it in San Anton' from a friend of mine," he told her gleefully.

"It's seventeen minutes past twelve," she said, looking up at him with a kind of shy and clumsy coquetry. A passenger, noting this play, grew excessively sardonic, and winked at himself in one of the numerous mirrors.

At last they went to the dining-car. Two rows of negro waiters, in glowing white suits, surveyed their entrance with the interest, and also the equanimity, of men who had been forewarned. The pair fell to the lot of a waiter who happened to feel pleasure in steering them through their meal. He viewed them with the manner of a fatherly pilot, his countenance radiant with benevolence. The patronage, entwined with the ordinary deference, was not plain to them. And yet, as they returned to their coach, they showed in their faces a sense of escape.

To the left, miles down a long purple slope, was a little ribbon of mist where moved the keening Rio Grande. The train was approaching it at an angle, and the apex was Yellow Sky. Presently it was apparent that, as the distance from Yellow Sky grew shorter, the husband became commensurately restless. His brick-red hands were more insistent in their prominence. Occasionally he was even rather absent-minded and far-away when the bride leaned forward and addressed him.

As a matter of truth, Jack Potter was beginning to find the shadow of a deed weigh upon him like a leaden slab. He, the town marshal of Yellow Sky, a man known, liked, and feared in his corner, a prominent person, had gone to San Antonio to meet a girl he believed he loved, and there, after the usual prayers, had actually induced her to marry him, without consulting Yellow Sky for any part of the transaction. He was now bringing his bride before an innocent and unsuspecting community.

Of course people in Yellow Sky married as it pleased them, in accordance with a general custom; but such was Potter's thought of his duty to his friends, or of their idea of his duty, or of an unspoken form which does not control men in these matters, that he felt he was heinous. He had

committed an extraordinary crime. Face to face with this girl in San Antonio, and spurred by his sharp impulse, he had gone headlong over all the social hedges. At San Antonio he was like a man hidden in the dark. A knife to sever any friendly duty, any form, was easy to his hand in that remote city. But the hour of Yellow Sky—the hour of daylight—was approaching.

He knew full well that his marriage was an important thing to his town. It could only be exceeded by the burning of the new hotel. His friends could not forgive him. Frequently he had reflected on the advisability of telling them by telegraph, but a new cowardice had been upon him. He feared to do it. And now the train was hurrying him toward a scene of amazement, glee, and reproach. He glanced out of the window at the line of haze swinging slowly in toward the train.

Yellow Sky had a kind of brass band, which played painfully, to the delight of the populace. He laughed without heart as he thought of it. If the citizens could dream of his prospective arrival with his bride, they would parade the band at the station and escort them, amid cheers and laughing congratulations, to his adobe home.

He resolved that he would use all the devices of speed and plainscraft in making the journey from the station to his house. Once within that safe citadel, he could issue some sort of vocal bulletin, and then not go among the citizens until they had time to wear off a little of their enthusiasm.

The bride looked anxiously at him. "What's worrying you, Jack?"

He laughed again. "I'm not worrying, girl; I'm only thinking of Yellow Sky."

She flushed in comprehension.

A sense of mutual guilt invaded their minds and developed a finer tenderness. They looked at each other with eyes softly aglow. But Potter often laughed the same nervous laugh; the flush upon the bride's face seemed quite permanent.

The traitor to the feelings of Yellow Sky narrowly watched the speeding landscape. "We're nearly there," he said.

Presently the porter came and announced the proximity of Potter's home. He held a brush in his hand, and, with all his airy superiority gone, he brushed Potter's new clothes as the latter slowly turned this way and that way. Potter fumbled out a coin and gave it to the porter, as he had seen others do. It was a heavy and muscle-bound business, as that of a man shoeing his first horse.

The porter took their bag, and as the train began to slow they moved forward to the hooded platform of the car. Presently the two engines and their long string of coaches rushed into the station of Yellow Sky.

"They have to take water here," said Potter, from a constricted throat and in mournful cadence, as one announcing death. Before the train stopped his eye had swept the length of the platform, and he was glad and astonished to see there was none upon it but the station-agent, who, with a slightly hurried and anxious air, was walking toward the water-tanks. When the train had halted, the porter alighted first, and placed in position a little temporary step.

"Come on, girl," said Potter, hoarsely. As he helped her down they each laughed on a false note. He took the bag from the negro, and bade his wife cling to his arm. As they slunk rapidly away, his hang-dog glance perceived that they were unloading the two trunks, and also that the station-agent, far ahead near the baggage-car, had turned and was running toward him, making gestures. He laughed, and groaned as he laughed, when he noted the first effect of his marital bliss upon Yellow Sky. He gripped his wife's arm firmly to his side, and they fled. Behind them the porter stood, chuckling fatuously.

II

THE California express on the Southern Railway was due at Yellow Sky in twenty-one minutes. There were six men at the bar of the Weary Gentleman saloon. One was a drummer who talked a great deal and rapidly; three were Texans who did not care to talk at that time; and two were Mexican sheep-herders, who did not talk as a general practice in the Weary Gentleman saloon. The barkeeper's dog lay on the board walk that crossed in front of the door. His head was on his paws, and he glanced drowsily here and there with the constant vigilance of a dog that is kicked on occasion. Across the sandy street were some vivid green grass-plots, so wonderful in appearance, amid the sands that burned near them in a blazing sun, that they caused a doubt in the mind. They exactly resembled the grass mats used to represent lawns on the stage. At the cooler end of the railway station, a man without a coat sat in a tilted chair and smoked his pipe. The fresh-cut bank of the Rio Grande circled near the town, and there could be seen beyond it a great plum-colored plain of mesquit.

Save for the busy drummer and his companions in the saloon, Yellow Sky was dozing. The newcomer leaned gracefully upon the bar, and recited many tales with the confidence of a bard who has come upon a new field.

"—and at the moment that the old man fell downstairs with the bureau in his arms, the old woman was coming up with two scuttles of coal, and of course—"

The drummer's tale was interrupted by a young man who suddenly appeared in the open door. He cried: "Scratchy Wilson's drunk, and has turned loose with both hands." The two Mexicans at once set down their glasses and faded out of the rear entrance of the saloon.

The drummer, innocent and jocular, answered: "All right, old man. S'pose he has? Come in and have a drink, anyhow."

But the information had made such an obvious cleft in every skull in the room that the drummer was obliged to see its importance. All had become instantly solemn. "Say," said he, mystified, "what is this?" His three companions made the introductory gesture of eloquent speech; but the young man at the door forestalled them.

"It means, my friend," he answered, as he came into the saloon, "that for the next two hours this town won't be a health resort."

The barkeeper went to the door, and locked and barred it; reaching out of the window, he pulled in heavy wooden shutters, and barred them. Immediately a solemn, chapel-like gloom was upon the place. The drummer was looking from one to another.

"But say," he cried, "what is this, anyhow? You don't mean there is going to be a gun-fight?"

"Don't know whether there'll be a fight or not," answered one man, grimly; "but there'll be some shootin'—some good shootin'."

The young man who had warned them waved his hand. "Oh, there'll be a fight fast enough, if any one wants it. Anybody can get a fight out there in the street. There's a fight just waiting."

The drummer seemed to be swayed between the interest of a foreigner and a perception of personal danger.

"What did you say his name was?" he asked.

"Scratchy Wilson," they answered in chorus.

"And will he kill anybody? What are you going to do? Does this happen often? Does he rampage around like this once a week or so? Can he break in that door?"

"No; he can't break down that door," replied the barkeeper. "He's tried it three times. But when he comes you'd better lay down on the floor, stranger. He's dead sure to shoot at it, and a bullet may come through."

Thereafter the drummer kept a strict eye upon the door. The time had not yet been called for him to hug the floor, but, as a minor precaution, he sidled near to the wall. "Will he kill anybody?" he said again.

The men laughed low and scornfully at the question.

"He's out to shoot, and he's out for trouble. Don't see any good in experimentin' with him."

"But what do you do in a case like this? What do you do?"

A man responded: "Why, he and Jack Potter—"

"But," in chorus the other men interrupted, "Jack Potter's in San Anton'."

"Well, who is he? What's he got to do with it?"

"Oh, he's the town marshal. He goes out and fights Scratchy when he gets on one of these tears."

"Wow!" said the drummer, mopping his brow. "Nice job he's got."

The voices had toned away to mere whisperings. The drummer wished to ask further questions, which were born of an increasing anxiety and bewilderment; but when he attempted them, the men merely looked at him in irritation and motioned him to remain silent. A tense waiting hush was upon them. In the deep shadows of the room their eyes shone as they listened for sounds from the street. One man made three gestures at the barkeeper; and the latter, moving like a ghost, handed him a glass and a bottle. The man poured a full glass of whisky, and set down the bottle noiselessly. He gulped the whisky in a swallow, and turned again toward the door in immovable silence. The drummer saw that the barkeeper, without a sound, had taken a Winchester from beneath the bar. Later he saw this individual beckoning to him, so he tiptoed across the room.

"You better come with me back of the bar."

"No, thanks," said the drummer, perspiring; "I'd rather be where I can make a break for the back door."

Whereupon the man of bottles made a kindly but peremptory gesture. The drummer obeyed it, and, finding himself seated on a box with his head below the level of the bar, balm was laid upon his soul at sight of various zinc and copper fittings that bore a resemblance to armor-plate. The barkeeper took a seat comfortably upon an adjacent box.

"You see," he whispered, "this here Scratchy Wilson is a wonder with a gun—a perfect wonder; and when he goes on the war-trail, we hunt our holes—naturally. He's about the last one of the old gang that used to hang out along the river here. He's a terror when he's drunk. When he's sober he's all right—kind of simple—wouldn't hurt a fly—nicest fellow in town. But when he's drunk—whoo!"

There were periods of stillness. "I wish Jack Potter was back from San Anton'," said the barkeeper. "He shot Wilson up once—in the leg—and he would sail in and pull out the kinks in this thing."

Presently they heard from a distance the sound of a shot, followed by three wild yowls. It instantly removed a bond from the men in the darkened saloon. There was a shuffling of feet. They looked at each other. "Here he comes," they said.

III

A MAN in a maroon-colored flannel shirt, which had been purchased for purposes of decoration, and made principally by some Jewish women on the East Side of New York, rounded a corner and walked into the middle of the main street of Yellow Sky. In either hand the man held a long, heavy, blue-black revolver. Often he yelled, and these cries rang through a semblance of a deserted village, shrilly flying over the roofs in a volume that seemed to have no relation to the ordinary vocal strength of a man. It was as if the surrounding stillness formed the arch of a tomb over him. These cries of ferocious challenge rang against walls of silence. And his boots had red tops with gilded imprints, of the kind beloved in winter by little sledding boys on the hillsides of New England.

The man's face flamed in a rage begot of whisky. His eyes, rolling, and yet keen for ambush, hunted the still doorways and windows. He walked with the creeping movement of the midnight cat. As it occurred to him, he roared menacing information. The long revolvers in his hands were as easy as straws; they were moved with an electric swiftness. The little fingers of each hand played sometimes in a musician's way. Plain from the low collar of the shirt, the cords of his neck straightened and sank, straightened and sank, as passion moved him. The only sounds were his terrible invitations. The calm adobes preserved their demeanor at the passing of this small thing in the middle of the street.

There was no offer of fight—no offer of fight. The man called to the sky. There were no attractions. He bellowed and fumed and swayed his revolvers here and everywhere.

The dog of the barkeeper of the Weary Gentleman saloon had not appreciated the advance of events. He yet lay dozing in front of his master's door. At sight of the dog, the man paused and raised his revolver humorously. At sight of the man, the dog sprang up and walked diagonally away, with a sullen head, and growling. The man yelled, and the dog broke into a gallop. As it was about to enter an alley, there was a loud noise, a whistling, and something spat the ground directly before it. The dog screamed, and, wheeling in terror, galloped headlong in a new direction. Again there was a noise, a whistling, and sand was kicked viciously before it. Fear-stricken, the dog turned and flurried like an animal in a pen. The man stood laughing, his weapons at his hips.

Ultimately the man was attracted by the closed door of the Weary Gentleman saloon. He went to it and, hammering with a revolver, demanded drink.

The door remaining imperturbable, he picked a bit of paper from the walk, and nailed it to the framework with a knife. He then turned his back contemptuously upon this popular resort and, walking to the opposite side of the street and spinning there on his heel quickly and lithely, fired at the bit of paper. He missed it by a half-inch. He swore at himself, and went away. Later he comfortably fusilladed the windows of his most intimate friend. The man was playing with this town; it was a toy for him.

But still there was no offer of fight. The name of Jack Potter, his ancient antagonist, entered his mind, and he concluded that it would be a glad thing if he should go to Potter's house, and by bombardment induce him to come out and fight. He moved in the direction of his desire, chanting Apache scalp-music.

When he arrived at it, Potter's house presented the same still front as had the other adobes. Taking up a strategic position, the man howled a challenge. But this house regarded him as might a great stone god. It gave no sign. After a decent wait, the man howled further challenges, mingling with them wonderful epithets.

Presently there came the spectacle of a man churning himself into deepest rage over the immobility of a house. He fumed at it as the winter wind attacks a prairie cabin in the North. To the distance there should have gone the sound of a tumult like the fighting of two hundred Mexicans. As necessity bade him, he paused for breath or to reload his revolvers.

IV

POTTER and his bride walked sheepishly and with speed. Sometimes they laughed together shamefacedly and low.

"Next corner, dear," he said finally.

They put forth the efforts of a pair walking bowed against a strong wind. Potter was about to raise a finger to point the first appearance of the new home when, as they circled the corner, they came face to face with a man in a maroon-colored shirt, who was feverishly pushing cartridges into a large revolver. Upon the instant the man dropped his revolver to the ground and, like lightning, whipped another from its holster. The second weapon was aimed at the bridegroom's chest.

There was a silence. Potter's mouth seemed to be merely a grave for his tongue. He exhibited an instinct to at once loosen his arm from the woman's grip, and he dropped the bag to the sand. As for the bride, her face had gone as yellow as old cloth. She was a slave to hideous rites, gazing at the apparitional snake.

The two men faced each other at a distance of three paces. He of the revolver smiled with a new and quiet ferocity.

"Tried to sneak up on me," he said. "Tried to sneak up on me!" His eyes grew more baleful. As Potter made a slight movement, the man thrust his revolver venomously forward. "No; don't you do it, Jack Potter. Don't you move a finger toward a gun just yet. Don't you move an eyelash. The time has come for me to settle with you, and I'm goin' to do it my own way, and loaf along with no interferin'. So if you don't want a gun bent on you, just mind what I tell you."

Potter looked at his enemy. "I ain't got a gun on me Scratchy," he said. "Honest, I ain't." He was stiffening and steadying, but yet somewhere at the back of his mind a vision of the Pullman floated: the sea-green figured velvet, the shining brass, silver, and grass, the wood that gleamed as darkly brilliant as the surface of a pool of oil—all the glory of the marriage, the environment of the new estate. "You know I fight when it comes to fighting, Scratchy Wilson; but I ain't got a gun on me. You'll have to do all the shootin' yourself."

His enemy's face went livid. He stepped forward, and lashed his weapon to and fro before Potter's chest. "Don't you tell me you ain't got no gun on you, you whelp. Don't tell me no lie like that. There ain't a man in Texas ever seen you without no gun. Don't take me for no kid." His eyes blazed with light, and his throat worked like a pump.

"I ain't takin' you for no kid," answered Potter. His heels had not moved an inch backward. "I'm takin' you for a damn fool. I tell you I ain't got a gun, and I ain't. If you're goin' to shoot me up, you better begin now; you'll never get a chance like this again."

So much enforced reasoning had told on Wilson's rage; he was calmer. "If you ain't got a gun, why ain't you got a gun?" he sneered. "Been to Sunday-school?"

"I ain't got a gun because I've just come from San Anton' with my wife. I'm married," said

Potter. "And if I'd thought there was going to be any galoots like you prowling around when I brought my wife home, I'd had a gun, and don't you forget it."

"Married!" said Scratchy, not at all comprehending.

"Yes, married. I'm married," said Potter, distinctly.

"Married?" said Scratchy. Seemingly for the first time, he saw the drooping, drowning woman at the other man's side. "No!" he said. He was like a creature allowed a glimpse of another world. He moved a pace backward, and his arm, with the revolver, dropped to his side. "Is this the lady?" he asked.

"Yes; this is the lady," answered Potter.

There was another period of silence.

"Well," said Wilson at last, slowly, "I s'pose it's all off now."

"It's all off if you say so, Scratchy. You know I didn't make the trouble." Potter lifted his valise.

"Well, I 'low it's off, Jack," said Wilson. He was looking at the ground. "Married!" He was not a student of chivalry; it was merely that in the presence of this foreign condition he was a simple child of the earlier plains. He picked up his starboard revolver, and, placing both weapons in their holsters, he went away. His feet made funnel-shaped tracks in the heavy sand.

DEATH AND THE CHILD

(INTERVIEWED by a fellow correspondent in Greece, Crane casually lit a cigarette while sitting on an ammunition box and said: "Between two great armies battling against each other, the interesting thing is the mental attitude of the men. The Greeks I can see and understand, but the Turks seem unreal. They are shadows on the plain—vague figures in black, indications of a mysterious force." How Crane handled this force in the story based on his Greek experience has been discussed in the Introduction, p. 396.

Crane wrote while self-invited guests were swarming upon his privacy at Ravensbrook, and at the beginning of December, 1897, he even had to go up to London and take a hotel room in order to have a quiet place to finish the story. *Harper's Weekly* published the story the following March, and with "The Bride" it came out in *The Open Boat and Other Stories* in April, in both New York and London.

I

THE PEASANTS who were streaming down the mountain trail had, in their sharp terror, evidently lost their ability to count. The cattle and the huge round bundles seemed to suffice to the minds of the crowd if there were now two in each case where there had been three. This brown stream poured on with a constant wastage of goods and beasts. A goat fell behind to scout the dried grass, and its owner, howling, flogging his donkeys, passed far ahead. A colt, suddenly frightened, made a stumbling charge up the hillside. The expenditure was always profligate, and always unnamed, unnoted. It was as if fear was a river, and this horde had simply been caught in the torrent, man tumbling over beast, beast over man, as helpless in it as the logs that fall and shoulder grindingly through the gorges of a lumber country. It was a freshet that might sear the face of the tall, quiet mountain; it might draw a livid line across the land, this downpour of fear with a thousand homes adrift in the current—men, women, babes, animals. From it there arose a constant babble of tongues, shrill, broken, and sometimes choking, as from men drowning. Many made gestures, painting their agonies on the air with fingers that twirled swiftly.

The blue bay, with its pointed ships, and the white town lay below them, distant, flat, serene. There was upon this vista a peace that a bird knows when, high in air, it surveys the world, a great, calm thing rolling noiselessly toward the end of the mystery. Here on the height one felt the existence of the universe scornfully defining the pain in ten thousand minds. The sky was an arch of stolid sapphire. Even to the mountains, raising their mighty shapes from the valley, this headlong rush of the fugitives was too minute. The sea, the sky, and the hills combined in their grandeur to term this misery inconsequent. Then, too, it sometimes happened that a face seen as it passed on the flood reflected curiously the spirit of them all, and still more. One saw then a woman of the opinion of the vaults above the clouds. When a child cried, it cried always because of some adjacent misfortune—some discomfort of a pack-saddle or rudeness of an encircling arm. In the dismal melody of this flight there were often sounding chords of apathy. Into these preoccupied countenances one felt that needles could be thrust without purchasing a scream. The trail wound here and there, as the sheep had willed in the making of it.

Although this throng seemed to prove that the whole of humanity was fleeing in one direction—with every tie severed that binds us to the soil—a young man was walking rapidly up the mountain, hastening to a side of the path from time to time to avoid some particularly wide rush of people and cattle. He looked at everything in agitation and pity. Frequently he called admonitions to maniacal fugitives, and at other times he ex-changed strange stares with the imperturbable ones. They seemed to him to wear merely the ex-pressions of so many boulders rolling down the hill. He exhibited wonder and awe with his pity-ing glances.

Turning once toward the rear, he saw a man in the uniform of a lieutenant of infantry march-ing the same way. He waited then, subconscious-ly elated at a prospect of being able to make into words the emotion which heretofore had been ex-pressed only in the flash of eyes and sensitive movements of his flexible mouth. He spoke to the officer in rapid French, waving his arms wildly, and often pointing with a dramatic finger. "Ah, this is too cruel, too cruel, too cruel! is it not? I did not think it would be as bad as this. I did not think—God's mercy!—I did not think at all. And yet, I am a Greek; or, at least, my father was a Greek. I did not come here to fight; I am really a correspondent; you see? I was to write for an Ital-ian paper. I have been educated in Italy; I have spent nearly all my life in Italy—at the schools and universities. I knew nothing of war! I was a student—a student. I came here merely because my father was a Greek, and for his sake I thought of Greece. I loved Greece; but I did not dream—"

He paused, breathing heavily. His eyes glis-tened from that soft overflow which comes on oc-casion to the glance of a young woman. Eager, passionate, profoundly moved, his first words while facing the procession of fugitives had been an active definition of his own dimension, his per-sonal relation to men, geography, life. Throughout he had preserved the fiery dignity of a tragedian.

The officer's manner at once deferred to this outburst. "Yes," he said, polite, but mournful; "these poor people—these poor people! I do not know what is to become of these poor people."

The young man declaimed again: "I had no dream—I had no dream that it would be like this! This is too cruel—too cruel! Now I want to be a soldier. Now I want to fight. Now I want to do battle for the land of my father." He made a sweeping gesture into the north-west.

The officer was also a young man, but he was bronzed and steady. Above his high military collar of crimson cloth with one silver star upon it ap-peared a profile stern, quiet, and confident, re-specting fate, fearing only opinion. His clothes were covered with dust; the only bright spot was the flame of the crimson collar. At the violent cries of his companion he smiled as if to himself, mean-while keeping his eyes fixed in a glance ahead.

From a land toward which their faces were bent came a continuous boom of artillery fire. It was sounding in regular measures, like the beating of a colossal clock—a clock that was counting the sec-onds in the lives of the stars, and men had time to die between the ticks. Solemn, oracular, inexora-ble, the great seconds tolled over the hills as if God fronted this dial rimmed by the horizon. The soldier and the correspondent found them-selves silent. The latter in particular was sunk in a great mournfulness, as if he had resolved willy-nilly to swing to the bottom of the abyss where dwelt secrets of this kind, and had learned before-hand that all to be met there was cruelty and hope-lessness. A strap of his bright new leather leggings came unfastened, and he bowed over it slowly, impressively, as one bending over the grave of a child.

Then, suddenly, the reverberations mingled un-til one could not separate one explosion from an-other, and into the hubbub came the drawling sound of a leisurely musketry fire. Instantly, for some reason of cadence, the noise was irritating, silly, infantile. This uproar was childish. It forced the nerves to object, to protest against this racket, which was as idle as the din of a lad with a drum.

The lieutenant lifted his finger and pointed. He spoke in vexed tones, as if he held the other man personally responsible for the noise. "Well, there!" he said. "If you wish for war, you now have an opportunity magnificent."

The correspondent raised himself upon his toes. He tapped his chest with gloomy pride. "Yes! There is war! There is the war I wish to enter. I fling myself in. I am a Greek—a Greek, you un-derstand. I wish to fight for my country. You know the way. Lead me! I offer myself." Struck with a sudden thought, he brought a case from his pocket, and, extracting a card, handed it to the of-ficer with a bow. "My name is Peza," he said simply.

A strange smile passed over the soldier's face. There was pity and pride—the vanity of experi-ence—and contempt in it. "Very well," he said, returning the bow. "If my company is in the mid-dle of the fight, I shall be glad for the honor of your companionship. If my company is not in the middle of the fight, I will make other arrange-ments for you."

Peza bowed once more, very stiffly, and cor-rectly spoke his thanks. On the edge of what he took to be a great venture toward death, he dis-covered that he was annoyed at something in the lieutenant's tone. Things immediately assumed new and extraordinary proportions. The battle, the great carnival of woe, was sunk at once to an equation with a vexation by a stranger. He wanted to ask the lieutenant what was his meaning. He bowed again majestically. The lieutenant bowed. They flung a shadow of manners, of capering tinsel ceremony, across a land that groaned, and it satisfied something within themselves completely.

In the meantime the river of fleeing villagers was changed to simply a last dropping of belated creatures who fled past stammering and flinging their hands high. The two men had come to the top of the great hill. Before them was a green plain as level as an inland sea. It swept northward, and merged finally into a length of silvery mist. Upon the near part of this plain, and upon two gray, treeless mountains at the sides of it, were little black lines from which floated slanting sheets of smoke. It was not a battle, to the nerves; one could survey it with equanimity, as if it were a tea-table. But upon Peza's mind it struck a loud, clanging blow. It was war. Edified, aghast, triumphant, he paused suddenly, his lips apart. He remembered the pageants of carnage that had marched through the dreams of his childhood. Love he knew; that he had confronted alone, isolated, wondering, an individual, an atom taking the hand of a titanic principle. Like the faintest breeze on his forehead, he felt here the vibration from the hearts of forty thousand men.

The lieutenant's nostrils were moving. "I must go at once," he said. "I must go at once."

"I will go with you, wherever you go," shouted Peza, loudly.

A primitive track wound down the side of the mountain, and in their rush they bounded from here to there, choosing risks which in the ordinary caution of man would surely have seemed of remarkable danger. The ardor of the correspondent surpassed the full energy of the soldier. Several times he turned and shouted: "Come on! Come on!"

At the foot of the path they came to a wide road which extended toward the battle in a yellow and straight line. Some men were trudging wearily to the rear. They were without rifles; their clumsy uniforms were dirty and all awry. They turned eyes dully aglow with fever upon the pair striding toward the battle. Others were bandaged with the triangular kerchief, upon which one could still see, through blood-stains, the little explanatory pictures illustrating the ways to bind various wounds—"Fig. 1," "Fig. 2," "Fig. 7." Mingled with the pacing soldiers were peasants, indifferent, capable of smiling, gibbering about the battle, which was to them an ulterior drama. A man was leading a string of three donkeys to the rear, and at intervals he was accosted by wounded or fevered soldiers, from whom he defended his animals with ape-like cries and mad gesticulations.

After much chattering they usually subsided gloomily, and allowed him to go with his sleek little beasts unburdened. Finally he encountered a soldier who walked slowly, with the assistance of a staff. His head was bound with a wide bandage, grimy from blood and mud. He made application to the peasant, and immediately they were involved in a hideous Levantine discussion. The peasant whined and clamored, sometimes spitting like a kitten. The wounded soldier jawed on thunderously, his great hands stretched in claw-like graspings over the peasant's head. Once he raised his staff and made threat with it. Then suddenly the row was at an end. The other sick men saw their comrade mount the leading donkey, and at once begin to drum with his heels. None attempted to gain the backs of the remaining animals. They gazed after him dully. Finally they saw the caravan outlined for a moment against the sky. The soldier was still waving his arms passionately, having it out with the peasant.

Peza was alive with despair for these men who looked at him with such doleful, quiet eyes. "Ah, my God!" he cried to the lieutenant, "these poor souls!—these poor souls!"

The officer faced about angrily. "If you are coming with me, there is no time for this." Peza obeyed instantly and with a sudden meekness. In the moment some portion of egotism left him, and he modestly wondered if the universe took cognizance of him to an important degree. This theater for slaughter, built by the inscrutable needs of the earth, was an enormous affair, and he reflected that the accidental destruction of an individual, Peza by name, would perhaps be nothing at all.

With the lieutenant, he was soon walking along behind a series of little crescent-shaped trenches, in which were soldiers tranquilly interested, gossiping with the hum of a tea-party. Although these men were not at this time under fire, he concluded that they were fabulously brave, else they would not be so comfortable, so at home, in their sticky brown trenches. They were certain to be heavily attacked before the day was old. The universities had not taught him to understand this attitude. At the passing of the young man in very nice tweed, with his new leggings, his new white helmet, his new field-glass case, his new revolver holster, the soiled soldiers turned with the same curiosity which a being in strange garb meets at the corners of streets. He might as well have been promenading a populous avenue. The soldiers volubly discussed his identity.

To Peza there was something awful in the absolute familiarity of each tone, expression, gesture. These men, menaced with battle, displayed the curiosity of the café. Then, on the verge of his great encounter toward death, he found himself extremely embarrassed, composing his face with difficulty, wondering what to do with his hands, like a gawk at a levee.

He felt ridiculous, and also he felt awed, aghast at these men who could turn their faces from the ominous front and debate his clothes, his business. There was an element which was new-born into his theory of war.

He was not averse to the brisk pace at which the lieutenant moved along the line. The roar of fighting was always in Peza's ears. It came from some short hills ahead and to the left. The road curved suddenly and entered a wood. The trees stretched their luxuriant and graceful branches over grassy slopes. A breeze made all this verdure gently rustle and speak in long silken sighs. Absorbed in listening to the hurricane racket from the front, he still remembered that these trees were growing, the grass-blades were extending, according to their process. He inhaled a deep breath of moisture and fragrance from the grove, a wet odor which expressed the opulent fecundity of unmoved nature, marching on with her million plans for multiple life, multiple death.

Farther on, they came to a place where the Turkish shells were landing. There was a long, hurtling sound in the air, and then one had sight of a shell. To Peza it was of the conical missiles which friendly officers had displayed to him on board warships. Curiously enough, too, this first shell smacked of the foundry—of men with smudged faces, of the blare of furnace fires. It brought machinery immediately into his mind. He thought that if he was killed there at that time, it would be as romantic to the old standards as death by a bit of falling iron in a factory.

II

A CHILD was playing on a mountain, and disregarding a battle that was waging on the plain. Behind him was the little cobbled hut of his fled parents. It was now occupied by a pearl-colored cow, that stared out from the darkness, thoughtful and tender-eyed. The child ran to and fro, fumbling with sticks, and making great machinations with pebbles. By a striking exercise of artistic license, the sticks were ponies, cows, and dogs, and the pebbles were sheep. He was managing large agricultural and herding affairs. He was too intent on them to pay much heed to the fight four miles away, which at that distance resembled in sound the beating of surf upon rocks. However, there were occasions when some louder outbreak of that thunder stirred him from his serious occupa-

tion, and he turned then a questioning eye upon the battle, a small stick poised in his hand, interrupted in the act of sending his dog after his sheep. His tranquillity in regard to the death on the plain was as invincible as that of the mountain on which he stood.

It was evident that fear had swept the parents away from their home in a manner that could make them forget this child, the first-born. Nevertheless, the hut was cleaned bare. The cow had committed no impropriety in billeting herself at the domicile of her masters. This smoke-colored and odorous interior contained nothing as large as a humming-bird. Terror had operated on these runaway people in its sinister fashion—elevating details to enormous heights, causing a man to remember a button while he forgot a coat, overpowering every one with recollections of a broken coffee-cup, deluging them with fears for the safety of an old pipe, and causing them to forget their first-born. Meanwhile the child played soberly with his trinkets.

He was solitary. Engrossed in his own pursuits, it was seldom that he lifted his head to inquire of the world why it made so much noise. The stick in his hand was much larger to him than was an army corps of the distance. It was too childish for the mind of the child. He was dealing with sticks.

The battle-lines writhed at times in the agony of a sea-creature on the sands. These tentacles flung and waved in a supreme excitement of pain, and the struggles of the great outlined body brought it near and nearer to the child. Once he looked at the plain, and saw some men running wildly across a field. He had seen people chasing obdurate beasts in such fashion, and it struck him immediately that it was a manly thing, which he would incorporate in his game. Consequently he raced furiously at his stone sheep, flourishing a cudgel, crying the shepherd calls. He paused frequently to get a cue of manner from the soldiers fighting on the plain. He reproduced, to a degree, any movements which he accounted rational to his theory of sheep-herding, the business of men, the traditional and exalted living of his father.

III

IT WAS as if Peza was a corpse walking on the bottom of the sea, and finding there fields of grain, groves, weeds, the faces of men, voices. War, a strange employment of the race, presented to him a scene crowded with familiar objects which wore the livery of their commonness placidly, undauntedly. He was smitten with keen astonishment; a spread of green grass, lit with the flames of poppies, was too old for the company of this new ogre. If he had been devoting the full lens of his mind to this phase, he would have known that he was amazed that the trees, the flowers, the grass, all tender and peaceful nature, had not taken to heels at once upon the outbreak of battle. He venerated the immovable poppies.

The road seemed to lead into the apex of an angle formed by the two defensive lines of the Greeks. There was a struggle of wounded men, and of gunless and jaded men. These latter did not seem to be frightened. They remained very cool, walking with unhurried steps, and busy in gossip. Peza tried to define them. Perhaps during the fight they had reached the limit of their mental storage, their capacity for excitement, for tragedy, and had then simply come away. Peza remembered his visit to a certain place of pictures, where he had found himself amid heavenly skies and diabolic midnights—the sunshine beating red upon desert sands, nude bodies flung to the shore in the green moonglow, ghastly and starving men clawing at a wall in darkness, a girl at her bath, with screened rays falling upon her pearly shoulders, a dance, a funeral, a review, an execution—all the strength of argus-eyed art; and he had whirled and whirled amid this universe, with cries of woe and joy, sin and beauty, piercing his ears until he had been obliged to simply come away. He remembered that as he had emerged he had lit a cigarette with unction, and advanced promptly to a café. A great hollow quiet seemed to be upon the earth.

This was a different case, but in his thoughts he conceded the same causes to many of these gunless wanderers. They, too, may have dreamed at lightning speed, until the capacity for it was overwhelmed. As he watched them, he again saw himself walking toward the café, puffing upon his cigarette. As if to reinforce his theory, a soldier stopped him with an eager but polite inquiry for a match. He watched the man light his little roll of tobacco and paper and begin to smoke ravenously.

Peza no longer was torn with sorrow at the sight of wounded men. Evidently he found that pity had a numerical limit, and when this was passed the emotion became another thing. Now, as he viewed them, he merely felt himself very lucky, and beseeched the continuance of his superior fortune. At the passing of these slouched and stained figures he now heard a reiteration of warning. A part of himself was appealing through the medium of these grim shapes. It was plucking at his sleeve and pointing, telling him to beware of these soldiers only as he would have cared for the harms of broken dolls. His whole vision was focused upon his own chance.

The lieutenant suddenly halted. "Look," he said; "I find that my duty is in another direction; I must go another way. But if you wish to fight, you have only to go forward, and any officer of the fighting line will give you opportunity." He raised his cap ceremoniously. Peza raised his new white helmet. The stranger to battles uttered thanks to his chaperon, the one who had presented him. They bowed punctiliously, staring at each other with civil eyes.

The lieutenant moved quietly away through a field. In an instant it flashed upon Peza's mind that this desertion was perfidious. He had been subjected to a criminal discourtesy. The officer had fetched him into the middle of the thing, and then left him to wander helplessly toward death. At one time he was upon the point of shouting at the officer.

In the vale there was an effect as if one was then beneath the battle. It was going on above, somewhere. Alone, unguided, Peza felt like a man groping in a cellar. He reflected, too, that one should always see the beginning of a fight. It was too difficult to thus approach it when the affair was in full swing. The trees hid all the movements of troops from him, and he thought he might be walking out to the very spot which chance had provided for the reception of a fool. He asked eager questions of passing soldiers. Some paid no heed to him; others shook their heads mournfully. They knew nothing, save that war was hard work. If they talked at all, it was in testimony of having fought well, savagely. They did not know if the army was going to advance, hold its ground, or retreat. They were weary.

A long, pointed shell flashed through the air, and struck near the base of a tree with a fierce upheaval, compounded of earth and flames. Looking back, Peza could see the shattered tree quivering from head to foot. Its whole being underwent a convulsive tremor which was an exhibition of pain and, furthermore, deep amazement. As he advanced through the vale, the shells continued to hiss and hurtle in long, low flights, and the bullets purred in the air. The missiles were flying into the breast of an astounded nature. The landscape, bewildered, agonized, was suffering a rain of infamous shots, and Peza imagined a million eyes gazing at him with the gaze of startled antelopes.

There was a resolute crashing of musketry from the tall hill on the left, and from directly in front there was a mingled din of artillery and musketry firing. Peza felt that his pride was playing a great trick in forcing him forward in this manner under conditions of strangeness, isolation, and ignorance; but he recalled the manner of the lieutenant, the smile on the hilltop among the flying peasants. Peza blushed, and pulled the peak of his helmet down on his forehead. He strode on firmly. Nevertheless, he hated the lieutenant, and he resolved that on some future occasion he would take much trouble to arrange a stinging social revenge upon that grinning jackanapes. It did not occur to him, until later, that he was now going to battle mainly because at a previous time a certain man had smiled.

IV

THE ROAD moved around the base of a little hill, and on this hill a battery of mountain guns was leisurely shelling something unseen. In the lee of the height, the mules, contented under their heavy saddles, were quietly browsing the long grass. Peza ascended the hill by a slanting path. He felt his heart beat swiftly. Once at the top of the hill, he would be obliged to look this phenomenon in the face. He hurried with a mysterious idea of preventing by this strategy the battle from making his appearance a signal for some tremendous renewal. This vague thought seemed logical at the time. Certainly this living thing had knowledge of his coming. He endowed it with the intelligence of a barbaric deity. And so he hurried. He wished to surprise war, this terrible emperor, when it was only growling on its throne. The ferocious and horrible sovereign was not to be allowed to make the arrival a pretext for some fit of smoky rage and blood. In this half-lull, Peza had distinctly the sense of stealing upon the battle unawares.

The soldiers watching the mules did not seem to be impressed by anything august. Two of them sat side by side and talked comfortably; another lay flat upon his back, staring dreamily at the sky; another cursed a mule for certain refractions. Despite their uniforms, their bandoleers and rifles, they were dwelling in the peace of hostlers. However, the long shells were whooping from time to time over the brow of the hill, and swirling in almost straight lines toward the vale of trees, flowers, and grass. Peza, hearing and seeing the shells, and seeing the pensive guardians of the mules, felt reassured. They were accepting the conditions of war as easily as an old sailor accepts the chair behind the counter of a tobacco-shop. Or it was merely that the farm boy had gone to sea, and he had adjusted himself to the circumstances immediately, and with only the usual first misadventures in conduct. Peza was proud and ashamed that he was not of them—these stupid peasants who, throughout the world, hold potentates on their thrones, make statesmen illustrious, provide generals with lasting victories, all with ignorance, indifference, or half-witted hatred, moving the world with the strength of their arms, and getting their heads knocked together, in the name of God, the king, or the stock exchange—immortal, dreaming, hopeless asses who surrender their reason to the care of a shining puppet, and persuade some toy to carry their lives in his purse. Peza mentally abased himself before them, and wished to stir them with furious kicks.

As his eyes ranged above the rim of the plateau, he saw a group of artillery officers talking busily. They turned at once, and regarded his ascent. A moment later a row of infantry soldiers, in a trench beyond the little guns, all faced him. Peza bowed to the officers. He understood at the time that he had made a good and cool bow, and he wondered at it; for his breath was coming in gasps—he was stifling from sheer excitement. He felt like a tipsy man trying to conceal his muscular uncertainty from the people in the street. But the officers did not display any knowledge. They bowed. Behind them Peza saw the plain, glittering green, with three lines of black marked upon it heavily. The front of the first of these lines was frothy with smoke. To the left of this hill was a craggy mountain, from which came a continual dull rattle of musketry. Its summit was ringed with the white smoke. The black lines on the plain slowly moved. The shells that came from there passed overhead, with the sound of great birds frantically flapping their wings. Peza thought of the first sight of the sea during a storm. He seemed to feel against his face the wind that races over the tops of cold and tumultuous billows.

He heard a voice afar off: "Sir, what would you?" He turned, and saw the dapper captain of the battery standing beside him. Only a moment had elapsed.

"Pardon me, sir," said Peza, bowing again.

The officer was evidently reserving his bows. He scanned the new-comer attentively. "Are you a correspondent?" he asked.

Peza produced a card. "Yes; I came as a correspondent," he replied. "But now, sir, I have other thoughts. I wish to help. You see? I wish to help."

"What do you mean?" said the captain. "Are you a Greek? Do you wish to fight?"

"Yes; I am a Greek; I wish to fight." Peza's voice surprised him by coming from his lips in even and deliberate tones. He thought with gratification that he was behaving rather well. Another shell, traveling from some unknown point on the plain, whirled close and furiously in the air, pursuing an apparently horizontal course, as if it were never going to touch the earth. The dark shape swished across the sky.

"Ah," cried the captain, now smiling, "I am

not sure that we will be able to accommodate you with a fierce affair here just at this time, but—" He walked gaily to and fro behind the guns with Peza, pointing out to him the lines of the Greeks, and describing his opinion of the general plan of defense. He wore the air of an amiable host. Other officers questioned Peza in regard to the politics of the war. The king, the ministry, Germany, England, Russia—all these huge words were continually upon their tongues. "And the people in Athens, were they—?" Amid this vivacious babble, Peza, seated upon an ammunition-box, kept his glance high, watching the appearance of shell after shell. These officers were like men who had been lost for days in the forest. They were thirsty for any scrap of news. Nevertheless, one of them would occasionally dispute their informant courteously. What would Servia have to say to that? No, no; France and Russia could never allow it. Peza was elated. The shells killed no one. War was not so bad! He was simply having coffee in the smoking-room of some embassy where reverberate the names of nations.

A rumor had passed along the motley line of privates in the trench. The new arrival with the clean white helmet was a famous English cavalry officer, come to assist the army with his counsel. They stared at the figure of him, surrounded by officers. Peza, gaining sense of the glances and whispers, felt that his coming was an event.

Later, he resolved that he could, with temerity, do something finer. He contemplated the mountain where the Greek infantry was engaged, and announced leisurely to the captain of the battery that he thought presently of going in that direction and getting into the fight. He reaffirmed the sentiments of a patriot. The captain seemed surprised. "Oh, there will be fighting here at this knoll in a few minutes," he said orientally. "That will be sufficient. You had better stay with us. Besides, I have been ordered to resume fire." The officers all tried to dissuade him from departing. It was really not worth the trouble. The battery would begin again directly; then it would be amusing for him.

Peza felt that he was wandering, with his protestations of high patriotism, through a desert of sensible men. These officers gave no heed to his exalted declarations. They seemed too jaded. They were fighting the men who were fighting them. Palaver of the particular kind had subsided before their intense preoccupation in war as a craft. Moreover, many men had talked in that manner, and only talked.

Peza believed at first that they were treating him delicately; they were considerate of his inexperience. War had turned out to be such a gentle business that Peza concluded that he could scorn this idea. He bade them an heroic farewell, despite their objections.

However, when he reflected upon their ways afterward, he saw dimly that they were actuated principally by some universal childish desire for a spectator of their fine things. They were going into action, and they wished to be seen at war, precise and fearless.

V

CLIMBING slowly to the high infantry position, Peza was amazed to meet a soldier whose jaw had been half shot away, and who was being helped down the steep track by two tearful comrades. The man's breast was drenched with blood, and from a cloth which he held to the wound drops were splashing wildly upon the stones of the path. He gazed at Peza for a moment. It was a mystic gaze, which Peza withstood with difficulty. He was exchanging looks with a specter; all aspect of the man was somehow gone from this victim. As Peza went on, one of the unwounded soldiers loudly shouted to him to return and assist in this tragic march. But even Peza's fingers revolted. He was afraid of the specter; he would not have dared to touch it. He was surely craven in the movement of refusal he made to them. He scrambled hastily on up the path. He was running away!

At the top of the hill he came immediately upon a part of the line that was in action. Another battery of mountain guns was here, firing at the streaks of black on the plain. There were trenches filled with men lining parts of the crest, and near the base were other trenches, all crashing away mightily. The plain stretched as far as the eye could see, and from where silver mist ended this emerald ocean of grass, a great ridge of snow-topped mountains poised against a fleckless blue sky. Two knolls, green and yellow with grain, sat on the prairie, confronting the dark hills of the Greek position. Between them were the lines of the enemy. A row of trees, a village, a stretch of road showed faintly on this great canvas, this tremendous picture; but men, the Turkish battalions, were emphasized startlingly upon it. The ranks of troops between the knolls and the Greek position were as black as ink. The first line, of course, was muffled in smoke; but at the rear of it, battalions crawled up, and to and fro, plainer than beetles on a plate. Peza had never understood that masses of men were so declarative, so unmistakable, as if nature makes every arrangement to give information of the coming and the presence of destruction, the end, oblivion. The firing was full, complete, a roar of cataracts, and this pealing of concerted volleys was adjusted to the grandeur of the far-off range of snowy mountains. Peza, breathless, pale, felt that he had been set upon a pillar, and was surveying mankind, the world. In the meantime dust had got in his eye. He took his handkerchief and mechanically administered to it.

An officer with a double stripe of purple on his trousers paced in the rear of the battery of howitzers. He waved a little cane. Sometimes he paused in his promenade to study the field through his glasses. "A fine scene, sir," he cried airily, upon the approach of Peza. It was like a blow in the chest to the wide-eyed volunteer. It revealed to him a point of view.

"Yes, sir; it is a fine scene," he answered.

They spoke in French. "I am happy to be able to entertain monsieur with a little fine practice," continued the officer. "I am firing upon that mass of troops you see there, a little to the right. They are probably forming for another attack."

Peza smiled. Here again appeared manners— manners erect by the side of death.

The right-flank gun of the battery thundered; there was a belch of fire and smoke; the shell, flung swiftly and afar, was known only to the ear, in which rang a broadening, hooting wake of sound. The howitzer had thrown itself backward convulsively, and lay with its wheels moving in the air as a squad of men rushed toward it; and later, it seemed as if each little gun had made the supreme effort of its being in each particular shot. They roared with voices far too loud, and the thunderous effort caused a gun to bound as in a dying convulsion. And then occasionally one was hurled with wheels in air. These shuddering howitzers presented an appearance of so many cowards, always longing to bolt to the rear, but being implacably held up to their business by this throng of soldiers who ran in squads to drag them up again to their obligation. The guns were herded and cajoled and bullied interminably. One by one, in relentless program, they were dragged forward to contribute a profound vibration of steel and wood, a flash and a roar, to the important happiness of men.

The adjacent infantry celebrated a good shot with smiles and an outburst of gleeful talk.

"Look, sir," cried an officer once to Peza. Thin smoke was drifting lazily before Peza, and, dodging impatiently, he brought his eyes to bear upon that part of the plain indicated by the officer's finger. The enemy's infantry was advancing to attack. From the black lines had come forth an inky mass which was shaped much like a human tongue. It advanced slowly, casually, without apparent spirit, but with an insolent confidence that was like a proclamation of the inevitable.

The impetuous part was all played by the defensive side.

Officers called; men plucked each other by the sleeve. There were shouts—motion. All eyes were turned upon the inky mass which was flowing toward the base of the hills, heavily, languorously, as oily and thick as one of the streams that ooze through a swamp.

Peza was chattering a question at every one. In the way, pushed aside, or in the way again, he continued to repeat it: "Can they take the position? Can they take the position? Can they take the position?" He was apparently addressing an assemblage of deaf men. Every eye was busy watching every hand. The soldiers did not even seem to see the interesting stranger in the white helmet, who was crying out so feverishly.

Finally, however, the hurried captain of the battery espied him, and heeded his question. "No, sir! No, sir! It is impossible!" he shouted angrily. His manner seemed to denote that if he had had sufficient time he would have completely insulted Peza. The latter swallowed the crumb of news without regard to the coating of scorn, and, waving his hand in adieu, he began to run along the crest of the hill toward the part of the Greek line against which the attack was directed.

VI

PEZA, as he ran along the crest of the mountain, believed that his action was receiving the wrathful attention of the hosts of the foe. To him, then, it was incredible foolhardiness thus to call to himself the stares of thousands of hateful eyes. He was like a lad induced by playmates to commit some indiscretion in a cathedral. He was abashed; perhaps he even blushed as he ran. It seemed to him that the whole solemn ceremony of war had paused during this commission. So he scrambled wildly over the rocks in his haste to end the embarrassing ordeal. When he came among the crowning rifle-pits, filled with eager soldiers, he wanted to yell with joy. None noticed him, save a young officer of infantry, who said: "Sir, what do you want?" It was obvious that people had devoted some attention to their own affairs.

Peza asserted, in Greek, that he wished above everything to battle for the fatherland. The officer nodded. With a smile he pointed to some dead men, covered with blankets, from which were thrust upturned dusty shoes.

"Yes; I know, I know," cried Peza. He thought the officer was poetically alluding to the danger.

"No," said the officer, at once. "I mean cartridges—a bandoleer. Take a bandoleer from one of them."

Peza went cautiously toward a body. He moved a hand toward a corner of a blanket. There he hesitated, stuck, as if his arm had turned to plaster. Hearing a rustle behind him, he spun quickly. Three soldiers of the close rank in the trench were regarding him. The officer came again, and tapped him on the shoulder. "Have you any tobacco?" Peza looked at him in bewilderment. His hand was still extended toward the blanket which covered the dead soldier.

"Yes," he said; "I have some tobacco." He gave the officer his pouch. As if in compensation, the other directed a soldier to strip the bandoleer from the corpse. Peza, having crossed the long cartridge-belt on his breast, felt that the dead man had flung his two arms around him.

A soldier, with a polite nod and smile, gave Peza a rifle—a relic of another dead man. Thus he felt, besides the clutch of a corpse about his neck, that the rifle was as unhumanly horrible as a snake that lives in a tomb. He heard at his ear something that was in effect like the voices of those two dead men, their low voices speaking to him of bloody death, mutilation. The bandoleer gripped him tighter; he wished to raise his hands to his throat, like a man who is choking. The rifle was clumsy; upon his palms he felt the movement of the sluggish currents of a serpent's life; it was crawling and frightful.

All about him were these peasants, with their interested countenances, gibbering of the fight. From time to time a soldier cried out in semi-humorous lamentations descriptive of his thirst. One bearded man sat munching a great bit of hard bread. Fat, greasy, squat, he was like an idol made of tallow. Peza felt dimly that there was a distinction between this man and a young student who could write sonnets and play the piano quite well. This old blockhead was coolly gnawing at the bread, while he—Peza—was being throttled by a dead man's arms.

He looked behind him, and saw that a head, by some chance, had been uncovered from its blanket. Two liquid-like eyes were staring into his face. The head was turned a little sideways, as if to get better opportunity for the scrutiny. Peza could feel himself blanch. He was being drawn and drawn by these dead men, slowly, firmly down, as to some mystic chamber under the earth, where they could walk, dreadful figures, swollen and blood-marked. He was bidden; they had commanded him; he was going, going, going.

When the man in the new white helmet bolted for the rear, many of the soldiers in the trench thought that he had been struck. But those who had been nearest to him knew better. Otherwise they would have heard the silken, sliding, tender noise of the bullet, and the thud of its impact. They bawled after him curses, and also outbursts of self-congratulation and vanity. Despite the prominence of the cowardly part, they were enabled to see in this exhibition a fine comment upon their own fortitude. The other soldiers thought that Peza had been wounded somewhere in the neck, because, as he ran, he was tearing madly at the bandoleer—the dead man's arms. The soldier with the bread paused in his eating, and cynically remarked upon the speed of the runaway.

An officer's voice was suddenly heard calling out the calculation of the distance to the enemy, the readjustment of the sights. There was a stirring rattle along the line. The men turned their eyes to the front. Other trenches, beneath them, to the right, were already heavily in action. The smoke was lifting toward the blue sky. The soldier with the bread placed it carefully on a bit of paper beside him as he turned to kneel in the trench.

VII

IN THE late afternoon the child ceased his play on the mountain with his flocks and his dogs. Part of the battle had whirled very near to the base of his hill, and the noise was great. Sometimes he could see fantastic, smoky shapes, which resembled the curious figures in foam which one sees on the slant of a rough sea. The plain, indeed, was etched in white circles and whirligigs, like the slope of a colossal wave. The child took seat on a stone, and contemplated the fight. He was beginning to be astonished. He had never before seen cattle herded with such uproar. Lines of flame flashed out here and there. It was mystery.

Finally, without any preliminary indication, he began to weep. If the men struggling on the plain had had time, and greater vision, they could have seen this strange, tiny figure seated on a boulder, surveying them while the tears streamed. It was as simple as some powerful symbol.

As the magic clear light of day amid the mountains dimmed the distances, and the plain shone as a pallid blue cloth marked by the red threads of the firing, the child arose and moved off to the unwelcoming door of his home. He called softly for his mother, and complained of his hunger in the familiar formulæ. The pearl-colored cow, grinding her jaws thoughtfully, stared at him with her large eyes. The peaceful gloom of evening was slowly draping the hills.

The child heard a rattle of loose stones on the hillside, and, facing the sound, saw, a moment later, a man drag himself up to the crest of the hill and fall panting. Forgetting his mother and his hunger, filled with calm interest, the child walked forward, and stood over the heaving form. His eyes, too, were now large and inscrutably wise and sad, like those of the animal in the house.

After a silence, he spoke inquiringly: "Are you a man?"

Peza rolled over quickly, and gazed up into the fearless and cherubic countenance. He did not attempt to reply. He breathed as if life was about to leave his body. He was covered with dust; his face had been cut in some way, and his cheek was ribboned with blood. All the spick of his former appearance had vanished in a general dishevelment, in which he resembled a creature that had been flung to and fro, up and down, by cliffs and prairies during an earthquake. He rolled his eye glassily at the child.

They remained thus until the child repeated his words: "Are you a man?"

Peza gasped in the manner of a fish. Palsied, windless, and abject, he confronted the primitive courage, the sovereign child, the brother of the mountains, the sky, and the sea, and he knew that the definition of his misery could be written on a wee grass-blade.

POEMS

◊

⟨ CRANE called his poems "lines" and disliked being called a poet. His grudge against conventional verse is perhaps sufficiently explained by his parody of Longfellow's "A Psalm of Life" with its theme of uplift; the quatrain, first printed in 1957 from an undated manuscript, need not be an early piece in order to qualify as a logical starting point of Crane's poetic practice. His impulse to write "lines" apparently dates from the evening in 1893 when Howells read aloud to him from the then newly published poems of Emily Dickinson. He construed her departures from strict rhyme and meter as abandonment of them, and in the epigrammatic statements among her dramatic and lyric lines, he noticed the statement more than the wit. She seemed to reaffirm for his time the precedent of Whitman in breaking from meter and "speaking the truth" unadorned. His own unadorned truths often turned out to be rhetorical gestures and obvious ironies (for examples, see pp. 390, 406, above), but his best parables asked questions instead of giving away answers: is the simplicity of

"Once there came a man," below, the simplicity of death or of order? is the wisdom of "A man feared that he might find an assassin" the fear of death or the fear of killing? Occasionally he used his visual style to fix his argument in a presented image.

Lack of literary training created two problems for Crane. His unsuccessful poems show how hard it was for him to develop a poetic idea without serious lapses of taste. A more positive difficulty, on the other hand, was that of sustaining a poetic idea at all: just as in his fiction he often had to reinvent Jamesian techniques, in his poetry he seemed to reinvent poetic form. He had the terseness of a newspaperman who knows how to summarize the essentials of his story, but not many ideas can be adequately treated in three lines. So Crane got back to the stanza and the refrain and regularity of cadence. The patterned meditative progression of his finest verse results from a self-imposed discipline of thought and form. Moreover, in "War is kind" and "A man adrift on a slim spar," his subtle use of rhyme and rhythm gives the proper answer to the Longfellowism he deplored: he did not give up the sensuous resources of language, he controlled them and made them serve his serious poetic aims.

◊

1

Tell me not in joyous numbers
We can make our lives sublime
By—well, at least, not by
Dabbling much in rhyme.

1957

2

Once there came a man
Who said,
"Range me all men of the world in rows."
And instantly
There was terrific clamor among the people
Against being ranged in rows.
There was a loud quarrel, world-wide.
It endured for ages;
And blood was shed
By those who would not stand in rows,   10
And by those who pined to stand in rows.
Eventually, the man went to death, weeping.
And those who stayed in bloody scuffle
Knew not the great simplicity.

1895

POEMS.   1. Manuscript in Columbia University Library, Stephen Crane Collection; published by Daniel G. Hoffman in *The Poetry of Stephen Crane* (1957), p. 41.   2. This and the two succeeding poems appeared in Crane's first book of lines, *The Black Riders* (1895); poems for that volume were written in 1893 and early 1894.

3

The ocean said to me once,
"Look!
Yonder on the shore
Is a woman, weeping.
I have watched her.
Go you and tell her this—
Her lover I have laid
In cool green hall.
There is wealth of golden sand
And pillars, coral-red;   10
Two white fish stand guard at his bier.

"Tell her this
And more—
That the king of the seas
Weeps too, old, helpless man.
The bustling fates
Heap his hands with corpses
Until he stands like a child
With surplus of toys."

1895

4

A man feared that he might find an assassin;
Another that he might find a victim.
One was more wise than the other.

1895

5

Do not weep, maiden, for war is kind.
Because your lover threw wild hands toward the
      sky
And the affrighted steed ran on alone,
Do not weep.
War is kind.

      Hoarse, booming drums of the regiment,
      Little souls who thirst for fight,
      These men were born to drill and die.
      The unexplained glory flies above them,
      Great is the battle-god, great, and his king-
            dom—   10
      A field where a thousand corpses lie.

Do not weep, babe, for war is kind.
Because your father tumbled in the yellow
      trenches,
Raged at his breast, gulped and died,
Do not weep.
War is kind.

5. This and the two succeeding poems appeared in *War Is Kind*
(1899); the first date given on the left after each poem is that of
magazine publication.

      Swift blazing flag of the regiment,
      Eagle with crest of red and gold,
      These men were born to drill and die.
      Point for them the virtue of slaughter,   20
      Make plain to them the excellence of killing
      And a field where a thousand corpses lie.

Mother whose heart hung humble as a button
On the bright splendid shroud of your son,
Do not weep.
War is kind.

1896, 1899

6

"I have heard the sunset song of the birches,
"A white melody in the silence,
"I have seen a quarrel of the pines.
"At nightfall
"The little grasses have rushed by me
"With the wind men.
"These things have I lived," quoth the maniac,
"Possessing only eyes and ears.
"But you—
"You don green spectacles before you look at
      roses."   10

1895, 1899

7

In the night
Gray heavy clouds muffled the valleys,
And the peaks looked toward God alone.
      "O Master that movest the wind with a fin-
            ger,
      "Humble, idle, futile peaks are we.
      "Grant that we may run swiftly across the
            world
      "To huddle in worship at Thy feet."

In the morning
A noise of men at work came the clear blue miles,
And the little black cities were apparent.   10
      "O Master that knowest the meaning of rain-
            drops,
      "Humble, idle, futile peaks are we.
      "Give voice to us, we pray, O Lord,
      "That we may sing Thy goodness to the sun."

In the evening
The far valleys were sprinkled with tiny lights.
      "O Master,
      "Thou that knowest the value of kings and
            birds,
      "Thou hast made us humble, idle, futile
            peaks.

"Thou only needest eternal patience;
   "We bow to Thy wisdom, O Lord—
   "Humble, idle, futile peaks."   20

In the night
Gray heavy clouds muffled the valleys,
And the peaks looked toward God alone.

1896, 1899

8

A man adrift on a slim spar
A horizon smaller than the rim of a bottle.
Tented waves rearing lashy dark points
The near whine of froth in circles.
       God is cold.

The incessant raise and swing of the sea
And the growl after growl of crest
The sinkings, green, seething, endless
The upheaval half-completed.
       God is cold.   10

The seas are in the hollow of Thy Hand;
Oceans may be turned to a spray
Raining down through the stars
Because of a gesture of pity toward a babe.
Oceans may become gray ashes
Die with a long moan and a roar

Amid the tumult of the fishes
And the cries of the ships,
Because The Hand beckons the mice.
A horizon smaller than a doomed assassin's cap,
Inky, surging tumults   21
A reeling, drunken sky and no sky
A pale hand sliding from a polished spar.
       God is cold.

The puff of a coat imprisoning air:
A face kissing the water-death
A weary slow sway of a lost hand
And the sea, the moving sea, the sea.
       God is cold.

1929, 1930

9

   Unwind my riddle.
   Cruel as hawks the hours fly;
   Wounded men seldom come home to die;
   The hard waves see an arm flung high;
   Scorn hits strong because of a lie;
   Yet there exists a mystic tie.
   Unwind my riddle.

1900

8. This poem, not printed in Crane's lifetime but probably written in 1897 or 1898, is to be found in Wilson Follett, editor, *The Collected Poems of Stephen Crane* (1930).

9. Crane used this poem as the epigraph to his story "The Clan of No-Name" (published posthumously in *Wounds in the Rain,* 1900). He wrote it in late 1899 or early 1900. The "clan of No-Name" is the company of true heroes whose reward has been the obliteration of death.

ALFRED KAZIN
Editor

Theodore Dreiser

1871–1945

THEODORE DREISER was born August 27, 1871, in Sullivan, Indiana.[1] His father, John Paul Dreiser, a German immigrant and a pious Catholic who had immigrated in 1844 to escape conscription, was fifty when his ninth child was born; the familiar difficulties between immigrant parents and their native-born children were sharpened by the father's harsh religiosity and the economic misfortunes of the family. A mill of which the father was superintendent burned to the ground, crippling him and costing him his job. Until Theodore was seven, his father had no steady employment at all, but worked at various times in local mills as a laborer, wool-sorter, and spinner. Dreiser's mother, Sarah, a native of Pennsylvania brought up in the quietist Mennonite church, took in boarders; the contrast between the father's sometimes rasping intolerance and the mother's particular sweetness and good nature was to leave Dreiser with a lasting dislike of the Roman Catholic Church and a strong if not always clear-minded interest in the more "native," mystical American Protestant sects. The contrast between his parents was also to leave him with a particular tenderness for women who seemed hardpressed and long-suffering. Dreiser's feeling for women was to give an unprecedented intensity of sexual feeling to the puritanical American novel; his early experiences gave him ample reason for identifying women with selflessness.

By the time Dreiser was eight, his father had become unable to find work at all, and the family split up in the hope of saving money. Dreiser's biographer Robert Elias reports that "even . . . . at Terre Haute and exposed to relatively few suggestions, he had dreams in which colored marbles floated in the air, and bright money lay everywhere on the ground."[2] This longing for affluence was like Dreiser's sense that women alone could bestow the necessary human warmth in a world that seemed to him generally merciless. Unlike the "realists" of an earlier generation, William Dean Howells, Henry James, even Mark Twain, writers who described a relatively comfortable middle-class world in which they felt at home and of which they were an honored part, Dreiser grew up to think of American society as a cruel and often senseless arrangement which he would have to dominate in order to share in. The sense of being an outsider to all the good things in life was to stamp upon him the equally strong conviction that the good things were obtained by means not quite legitimate. It is easier to understand the special

[1] His birthplace is usually given as Terre Haute, but a member of Dreiser's family has recently discovered it to be Sullivan.

[2] Robert Elias, *Theodore Dreiser: Apostle of Nature* (1949), p. 12.

feeling in Dreiser's work for "immoral" women and for men popularly considered reckless and improvident when one considers that, in 1882, the distressed Dreiser family made a new home in Evansville, Indiana, thanks to Annie Brace, the madame of a local brothel who was the mistress of Theodore's elder brother Paul—a songwriter famous at the turn of the century for writing such sentimental favorites as "Just Tell Them That You Saw Me," "I Believe It, For My Mother Told Me So," and "On the Banks of the Wabash" (words by Theodore Dreiser). Similarly, the misadventure of a sister, who was to become the prototype of Sister Carrie, and the misfortune of another sister, on whom he modeled Jennie Gerhardt, were to reinforce Dreiser's angry resistance to the moral codes and traditional religious teachings which his father had harshly tried to instill in him. The family broke up again, and Dreiser worked at various times as a bus boy, dishwasher, and car tracer. In 1889 his high school teacher Mildred Fielding staked him to a year's study at the University of Indiana, but in 1890 his mother died, and Dreiser, making a temporary home in Chicago with his brother Ed and his sister Tillie, drove a laundry wagon until he was discharged for stealing twenty-five dollars from his collections.

In 1892, however, Dreiser, by pleading hard for it, managed to obtain a minor job on the Chicago *Globe*; it was as a newspaperman that he began his slow and tortuous road to authorship. In the worldly and often self-consciously "intellectual" society of newspapermen in the nineties, a time of rising protest against the shocking new inequalities in American life, Dreiser acquired many of his fundamental ideas—and some valuable associations. Before entering newspaper work, he had understandably felt himself to be a failure, and his hatred of his father's dogmas had made him temperamentally suspicious of any conclusive position. But working in Chicago, St. Louis, and New York, among the independent-minded Bohemian newspapermen and newspaper illustrators of the period, Dreiser began to read the popular philosophers and exponents of nineteenth-century science—Tyndall, Huxley, Spencer. As a reporter, observing the extremes

of wealth in the big cities that had become the most spectacular feature of American life at the turn of the century, Dreiser began to connect his own experience and preconceptions to what was new and most significant about American life in the age of the trusts and the great new American fortunes. The "age of confidence" was dying out in America; the concern with relatively personal problems of conduct that had marked the novel of manners in Howells and James now seemed, to young writers born in the 1870's, like Dreiser and Frank Norris and Stephen Crane, to be less significant than the forces of wealth and power and monopoly that were visibly reshaping American life. Above all, it was a new *class* of people in the cities, the slums, people of "foreign" extraction hitherto disregarded by American novelists, who were beginning to interest even those writers, like Norris and Crane, who came from the old Anglo-Saxon stock, but who were eagerly seizing upon the huddled, teeming lives of the immigrants in the big cities as brilliant new material for their novels. Dreiser, reading Spencer and Tyndall, was as excited as young Frank Norris reading Zola. Stephen Crane, the most precociously gifted of these "naturalistic" novelists, was putting into sketches of New York slums like *Maggie: A Girl of the Streets* (1893) his conviction that against the "forces" in the ascendency, the individual could do little. As opposed to the Realists, whose champion, William Dean Howells, insisted that the task of the novelist was to be concerned with the truth of "ordinary" experience, with reproducing faithfully and in a spirit of humor normal middle-class life, no matter how tame, the new young Naturalists insisted on the "enormous, the formidable, the terrible" (Norris)—the typically romantic attributes of art, which they found in describing the automatism of modern industrial life and the grimly hopeless struggle of the isolated individual against the overwhelming forces of a society grown ever more materialistic and indifferent.

The essence of Naturalism as a literary attitude—that which enlisted Dreiser's intellectual sympathies without necessarily requiring adherence to a deliberate "school"—was the conviction that society must now be seen entirely as a force of nature. The most gifted of the Realists, Henry James, had been concerned with society entirely as a human construction, with the conscious and delightful play of manners on the part of individuals who fulfilled themselves as individuals only in their social role. In this, the traditional meaning of the novel as a form evolved from its origins in the eighteenth-century, the novel was, like the theater, the place where social relationships were heightened and made more dramatic, and that illuminated them as the very stuff of man's daily life. Society, to a writer like Henry James, was what men made of it, and it was in a very real sense what constituted the relationship of men. As in the modern theater, the typical norm of the novel of manners was its sense of comedy, of the "situation" and its many unexpected developments; what was comic was exactly this sense of possibility. Society was men and men were society: it was the sum of their personal relationships and it lived by their sense of possibility within society.

The Naturalists, however, did not see society as a flexible and human network of relationships; they saw it as men in the age of Darwin had learned to see nature—gross, beyond human decision, a growth out of dark animal origins, a force that created men in all their weakness but was never responsive to their wishes. Dreiser, the young newspaperman of the nineties, did not consciously become an adherent of "literary" Naturalism; he had only to correlate his reading in Darwin, Haeckel, Huxley, with his daily observations of life in the big American cities to form the essential equation: society is as impersonal as nature, as primitive as nature, as merciless as nature. As man is only a biological accident in the great and still barely deciphered force of nature, so modern society exerts upon the individual the same crushing force and elicits from him the same helpless submission.

Yet in addition to this "scientific" equation of society with nature, there remained in the thinking of young writers like Dreiser a curious kind of religious questioning, a half-articulated mystical veneration of "life" in all its creative evolution that would have been as strange to earlier novelists like Henry James as the crudity of Dreiser's lower-class characters and their clumsy and inarticulate thought. For Naturalism, though in America never a literary "school" as it had been in France under the leadership of Zola, was certainly a deliberate and even aggressive rejection of all existing theologies—to writers like Dreiser and Crane (both of whom had grown up in religious orthodoxy), these seemed false when they proclaimed God's concern with man. Yet Naturalism, by the very bitterness with which it proclaimed the lack of purpose and of transcendent meaning in man's existence, showed itself to be sensitive to the life force in a way that was foreign to American novelists of manners, who studied the daily round of social relationships, not an abstraction called the "universe."

These fierce partisanships and intellectual prejudices of Naturalism were to be embodied in Dreiser's first novel, *Sister Carrie* (1900), and the shocking intransigence of these consciously agnostic values helps to explain the bitter opposition to the book of Dreiser's first publisher, Frank Doubleday. But perhaps even more important in forming Dreiser as a novelist was his training as a newspaperman. It was an editor of the period, Arthur Henry, who first encouraged Dreiser to write—and publish —his first short pieces of fiction, and it was actually by writing conventionally sentimental feature stories for the Sunday supplements about individual victims of the big city that Dreiser acquired some of his most characteristic habits as a writer of narrative. Dreiser, as a novelist, was always to concentrate on the individual "case" rather than on what Henry James called the "situation"—the dramatic situation that results from the development of a plot. Dreiser emphasizes what the writer of a newspaper or magazine "profile" does, the individual's history; his novels leave us not with complex dramatic situations but with a succession of individuals whose history he is writing: Carrie Meeber, Jennie Gerhardt, Frank Cowperwood, Eugene Witla, Clyde Griffiths. James's novels, which are like plays in their plots and in their handling of suspense, describe a society in which people actively and even richly belong—never more so than in their conflict over things that opposed parties want and that both respect. Dreiser's novels portray people who for one reason or another are outsiders, and it is the sense of *distance* from society and from each other that is so affecting—for it carries a final sense of man's homelessness in the universe itself.

So deep a sense of vulnerability and of pathos oddly belongs to the world of newspapers—to rapidly written stories of human accident, lurid in tone and meant to be read quickly and thrown away. Even the line drawings in newspaper illustrations of the period encouraged a moody sense of the picturesque. Dreiser, remembering the Chicago of this period—in his first volume of autobiography, *Dawn* (1931)—emphasized "The art of the jumbled streets, the rancid alleys. . . . the dirty river, with its dark, inscrutable waters. . . . Most of all, the art of the accidental experiences of individuals appealed to me." [1] The school of "feature stories" in the Sunday supplements so encouraged Dreiser to indulge in hard-luck stories of young provincials in the city that his second novel, *Jennie Gerhardt* (1911), deliberately emphasized the pathetic at a time when he was eager to get on with his history of a successful businessman; it is significant that the usual admiring newspaper feature of the "success"—Howells had opened one of his best novels, *The Rise of Silas Lapham* (1885), by employing this tradition as a humorous device—actually meant a great deal to Dreiser. "Success" reflected for Dreiser an ambition and pseudo-Nietzschean myth of individual "power" that was now as real to him as his early sense of pathos. In Dreiser's life, as in Dreiser's novels, pathos was merely the failure to achieve the towering success over men of which he dreamed. Yet despite the slovenly and pretentious and lurid aspects of style, perhaps even the false sentiment, that Dreiser as a newspaperman was not encouraged to drop, it is obvious that without his journalistic experience, Dreiser would not have become a novelist; journalism put him close to the tremendous issues of his time and showed him the social facts with which to document them. Henry James, looking back upon his long career, was

to confess that it was just his ignorance of these facts that had cheated him of his ambition to become an "American Balzac." In becoming a newspaperman, Dreiser secured the only preparation for authorship that was possible to *him*. Journalism in the nineties gave him his one chance to rise, and in rising he grasped the essential forces moving a society of whose cruelty he already knew so much. His brother Paul, in 1894 showing him New York for the first time, said to Dreiser—"The people out West don't know yet what's going on, but the rich are getting control. . . . A writer like you could make 'em see that." [2]

II

IN THE summer of 1899 Dreiser, who had married the year before, gave up regular newspaper work for a while in order to try his hand at fiction. At the urging of his friend Arthur Henry, he settled in Henry's home in Maumee, Ohio, and there wrote his first stories—"The Shining Slave Makers," "Nigger Jeff" (see pp. 472–84), "Butcher Rogaum's Daughter," "When the Old Century Was New," "The World and the Bubble." Then, under Henry's prodding, he "finally," as he put it years later to H. L. Mencken— ". . . took a piece of yellow paper and to please him [Arthur Henry] wrote down a title at random—*Sister Carrie*—and began. From September to Oct. 15th or thereabouts I wrote steadily to where Carrie met Hurstwood. Then I quit, disgusted. I thought it was rotten." [3] Perhaps Dreiser found the book easy to begin because at this stage, at least, he was writing from his deepest, almost unconscious, personal associations. "My mind was blank except for the name. I had no idea who or what she was to be. I have often thought that there was something mystic about it, as if I were being used, like a medium." Since it was the story of one of his own sisters that he was writing, it may be that he bogged down at the point where Carrie meets Hurstwood because this is where Carrie's own story ceases to be the exclusive interest of the novel; the other major character has come into the story. Yet it is also possible that what

[1] Quoted by David Brion Davis, "Dreiser and Naturalism Revisited," in *The Stature of Theodore Dreiser*, ed. by Alfred Kazin and Charles Shapiro (1955), p. 232.

[2] Quoted in Elias, *op. cit.*, p. 79.
[3] To H. L. Mencken, May 13, 1916. In *Letters of Theodore Dreiser*, ed. by Robert Elias (1959), I, 213.

held him back was not only Dreiser's habitual lack of self-confidence but his ignorance of social usage; Robert Elias reports that for Drouet's technique in intrigue, Dreiser had to borrow from George Ade's "Fable of the Two Mandolin Players and the Willing Performer." And this in its turn would suggest that Dreiser's often dispiriting tendency to report things in the greatest possible detail grew, at least in part, from awareness of his inexperience.

Yet whatever role a writer's hesitations and insecurities may play in the origins of his work or in his habits of composition, finally it is only his positive skills that count. And the astonishing thing about *Sister Carrie* is that despite the naïveté with which Dreiser reflects the vulgar usages and prejudices of the time, his narrative has a steady and tragic rhythm that is necessary to a good novel, and that in its strangely affecting way communicates the cruel social process that he is writing about. Dreiser's greatest ability as a novelist is his power to persuade us that the actions and scenes in his novel are necessary consequences of each other without making us question why this should be so. Things follow from each other as they must: Carrie Meeber gets on a train for Chicago, meets the vulgar little salesman, Drouet, whose mistress she eventually becomes when her helplessness forces her upon his "protection"; she is then taken up by the superior and more attractive Hurstwood, whose unexpected weakness is revealed only after he has fallen in love with her and, stealing from his employer, has abandoned everything to take her to New York. At the end of the novel Hurstwood has committed suicide, Carrie has earned some success on the stage—yet despite their different ends, we can hardly say that anything in their conscious philosophies of life has directed their fates. Unlike the characters of Henry James, who not only think of themselves as the moral agents of their fate but whose reflective awareness is the highest good that life can grant them, Dreiser's characters do not possess a fine consciousness; at best, as we see in the ruminations by Carrie with which the novel ends, Dreiser's characters sense that unaccountable forces have pressed upon them, and that these same forces impersonally make us what we are.

To this extent *Sister Carrie*, like all of Dreiser's best novels, suffers from the fact that although we identify with the experiences of Carrie and Hurstwood, we do not know what they think, or if they think at all—we do not see them in their human freedom as thinking, ordering human beings. In a very real sense, indeed, we do not *know* them as we know Huckleberry Finn or Isabel Archer in Henry James's *The Portrait Of A Lady* (1881)— characters whose minds we can reach, whose *minds* are what we know most about them. Carrie and Hurstwood are strangers to us, as indeed they are strangers to themselves and to each other; the sense of distance between man and his society, between man and the universe at large, operates with an ominous heaviness and disturbing actuality in the relations between Carrie and Hurstwood. Yet Carrie's peculiarly raw exposure to the crudity of Chicago at the turn of the century and to the cruelty of relatives and employers around her, the unmistakable cupidity with which Drouet can buy Carrie with the warm winter clothes she urgently needs after her illness— these present us with the fresh social detail, life in its daily truth, that is the particular contribution of a new novelist coming out of a social class whose vital experiences have been ignored by the polite world.

What made *Sister Carrie* such a shocker in 1900 was Dreiser's refusal to see any providence or morals or comfort in such experiences. The story, as many readers have admiringly conceded, seemed to tell itself and to be sufficient to itself; this was just what bothered the publisher of the book, Frank Doubleday, who returned from a trip to discover that his reader, the novelist Frank Norris, had enthusiastically accepted the book. "I don't like it, it's an immoral book," Doubleday complained, and in his indignation tried to prevent publication. When Doubleday found that he could not get out of the contract already signed with Dreiser, he did his best to limit the circulation of the book. Although Norris, who was enthusiastic about *Sister Carrie*, managed to send out some review copies, the hostility of the book's own publisher and the "shocking" nature of its material kept the book from reaching a wide audience. Although there were several perceptive and even sympathetic reviews, the general tendency was either to ignore the book or single out Dreiser's personal crudities and "solecisms" of language. And since Dreiser wrote as if fornication and adultery had no necessary consequence in unhappiness or misfortune, it was easy for those who disliked the book, as so many did, to minimize Dreiser's actual narrative talent on the grounds that he was simply crude and vulgar and described "a class wholly new to literature."

It is perfectly true that Realism as a method has always introduced rising new social classes and types of experience hitherto cut off from polite literature. This was true of the emerging middle class in the days of Defoe, Richardson, and Fielding, and the English novel in the eighteenth century was often termed "crude" and inartistic by the reigning literary elite exactly as Dreiser's "low" characters shocked the American Victorians who in 1900 reigned over what was still the "genteel tradition." And it is a fact that Dreiser was the first important American writer who represented the "new" stocks in American society. But Dreiser's achievement in *Sister Carrie* was a literary and artistic one; he had demonstrated that a certain kind of experience hitherto kept out of our puritanical and genteel American literature could become the basis for a strong, objective, deeply affecting novel. And since the class lines in America were becoming hard, the "moral" prejudices of the established middle class reacted to Dreiser's unwitting assault by snubbing him. Dreiser not only wrote about crude and unattractive people, he was himself a crude fellow who could not write decent English. So far from being a "true" Realist, he was full of pathetic "genteel" affectations.

This line of attack on Dreiser—which fundamentally has never changed, from the appalled early reviews of *Sister Carrie* in 1900, to Lionel Trilling's contemptuous rejection of Dreiser in *The Liberal Imagination* (1950)—was calamitously persuasive to Dreiser himself. Gifted writers can often be as insecure and hesitant in their personal lives as they are strong and talented in their works, and Dreiser, precisely because he did represent a social element new to American literature and did not feel himself supported by a friendly social tradition, was devastated by the "failure" of *Sister Carrie*. After all the early weakness and suffering which he had seemed to transcend by his unexpected power as a novelist, he was now unable to rise to the challenge of so much antagonism. Dreiser had not only the usual American desire to succeed in a society where success seemed possible on every hand, he had, perhaps more urgently than many, the need to find his identity in "success." The failure of *Sister Carrie* now spelled out to him the failure of Theodore Dreiser, and the result was a personal breakdown. Exactly like Hurstwood in *Sister Carrie*, whose collapse he had just described with an incisiveness and steadiness that made this section—Chapters 33–47—perhaps the most impressive feature of his novel, Dreiser now completely lost his grip on things and hid out in Brooklyn furnished rooms as if his personal failure forced him guiltily to flee from other men. At one point he nearly succeeded in committing suicide, and it was only because of the warmth and irresistible generosity of his brother Paul that Dreiser managed to revive. Paul, the one shining success of the Dreiser family and on hail-fellow terms with all the flashy Broadway crowd of the period, managed to get Dreiser off to a "health farm," and later, after working as a railroad laborer, Dreiser regained his health. Dreiser got back to work and by 1904 became an extremely successful editor for some of the most important magazines of the day.

Between 1904, when he became an editor for the well-known publishing firm of Street & Smith, and 1910, when he resigned as chief editorial director of the Butterick Publishing Company to write *Jennie Gerhardt*, Dreiser attained in material terms more success than he had ever known. There were many unattractive and awkward sides to Dreiser that were to become fully apparent only when he was recognized as an important American novelist. But even in this period the often naïve admiration for power which he was to display in his novels about an important businessman, *The Financier* (1912) and *The Titan* (1914), came out in his career as an editor. The same "pioneer realist" who had outraged the timid taste of the period with *Sister Carrie* now, as editor of *Butterick's*, wrote to a correspondent—"We like sentiment, we like humor, we like realism, but it must be tinged with sufficient idealism to make it all of a truly uplifting character." [1] Dreiser tried surprisingly hard to please all his readers, and despite his occasional restlessness, he might very well have gone on being a successful editor. But as he was to confess in *The 'Genius'* (1915), which is more directly about himself than are his other novels, Dreiser was always intensely occupied with one woman or another, and his actual editorial career seems to have ended when the mother of a young girl with whom he was having an affair made things difficult for him.

Dreiser was all his life to be deeply and even obsessively concerned with finding his happiness in women, and both his candid eroticism and his special sympathy for women who were long-suffering and submissive, like his mother, were to give a special vividness to his portraits of women. Twentieth-century critics of American literature have often complained that even our best novelists are immature and timid about sex, that there are few "real" women in our novels, and that our very best books, like *Huckleberry Finn* and those now classic early short stories by Ernest Hemingway entitled *Men Without Women*, are peculiarly concerned with men and boys. It has been charged that in American novels a woman seems to stand as the guardian of repressive moral standards and gentility, forcing men away from their natural sexuality. By contrast, Dreiser's books would seem to be rich in portraits of women— Carrie, Jennie Gerhardt, the wives and mistresses of Frank Cowperwood in *The Financier* and *The Titan*—in 1929 Dreiser was even to publish a book of short stories called *A Gallery of Women*. But it is also true that Dreiser's favorite women characters tend on the whole to be motherly, submissive, all-patient and loving.

The essence of *Jennie Gerhardt* lies in the fact that Jennie, who has an illegitimate child by Senator Brandler and then becomes the mistress of a wealthy carriage manufacturer, Lester Kane, actually represents the deepest and most primitive virtues. As in many novels of this period, when the collapse of external moral standards reflected the coarsening and even the corruption of a wholly materialistic society, the theme of "backstreet" love is actually a critique of existing society as well as of its main support in conventional marriage. The poor little Gerhardt girl is shown, in the opening pages, pathetically gathering up a little coal belonging to the railroad. Later, in her helplessness and inexperience, she is seduced by Senator Brandler; he dies and she becomes Lester Kane's mistress; eventually he succumbs to family pressure and gives her up to make the usual marriage of his class, and just before his death, when her own child has already died, he confesses how bitterly he regrets having given her up. But although Jennie has lived her life wholly outside "good" society, her devotion to her family, to Lester, and her passionate love of her own child Vesta, all show her to be infinitely more loving and more profound than the anxiously, and often cruelly, "good" people. In the affecting last scene, when Jennie follows Lester's coffin to the train, Dreiser's essential gift for expressing solitary emotion makes us see Jennie's gift for love and her lonely destiny as equal symbols of the blind drift of life.

Even when Lester is dead, Jennie cannot get past the wall that divides the possessors from the pure in heart, yet her lovingness is inconsequent in the accidental scheme of things. Life is simply the great flood carrying us along, and our highest relation to the universe lies in our submissive recognition that our petty human wishes count for nothing in world process that creates and destroys us with the same indifference. At most, Dreiser seems to say, we can feel a particular tenderness for women like Jennie, who at least face life honestly in an age of genteel hypocrisy. But Jennie's essential virtues, too, are muted, for as Dreiser writes in the scene where Lester Kane takes Jennie— "We live in an age in which the impact of materialized forces is well-nigh irresistible; the spiritual nature is overwhelmed by the shock." [2] The strongest impression one carries away from *Jennie Gerhardt* is that Dreiser's constant sense of the distance between man and society has now given his characters a faintly somnambu-

---

[1] Elias, *op. cit.*, p. 140.

[2] *Jennie Gerhardt* (1924), p. 132.

listic quality; the speechlessness of the characters suggests not so much social awkwardness as the conscious submission to man's tragic destiny that reminds us of men at war.

Yet as has been noted, Dreiser confessed that there was a deliberate intrusion of pathos into *Jennie Gerhardt*, and by contrast his next novel, *The Financier* (1912), shows an open admiration for power and the "exceptional individual" that reflects Dreiser's consciousness of his growing capacities and opportunities as much as the first part of *Jennie Gerhardt* reflects the deprivations of his youth. *The Financier* is based on the life story of Charles T. Yerkes, a remarkably intelligent and independent-minded speculator of the period who once went to jail for financial irregularities and whose name is memorialized in the famous astronomical observatory he donated to the University of Chicago. It is typical of both Dreiser's literal mind and of his strength as a storyteller that he was able to make of what is essentially an episodic biography of his hero, Frank A. Cowperwood, so continually interesting a novel. The reason for this is Dreiser's patient ability to build up the economic facts behind Cowperwood's career so that the reader can find them intensely real. But the actual effect of the novel derives from the proud, skeptical, and passionate character of Cowperwood himself, who becomes the very type of the superior individual, the dominating "superman" so much admired in a period when men like Rockefeller and Morgan seemed to be the domineering but also creative titans of American society. Of course Dreiser admires Cowperwood in the way that many writers of the period admired the "big" man who advances to his goal, utterly neutral to the ordinary moral code. There was now emerging in Dreiser, despite the sense of pathos that was his familiar reaction to the world's misery, an unexpected identification with the economic "titan" of the time; it is in fact not the usual attributes of the businessman but Cowperwood's superior intelligence, independent taste, and the eroticism of the artist that stand out in Dreiser's portrait of this "financier."

One of the most significant passages in all of Dreiser's work is the scene in Chapter 1 of *The Financier* in which the young Frank Algernon Cowperwood observes a lobster destroy a squid and concludes from this example of superior strength and cunning that he has solved "that riddle which had been annoying him so much in the past: 'How is life organized?' " Near the end of the novel, Cowperwood in the prison yard studies the stars and is chastened for a moment by the evident pettiness of his own ambitions. "He shook these moods off with ease, however, for the man was possessed of a sense of grandeur, largely in relation to himself and his affairs, and his temperament was essentially material and vital." [1] *The Financier* succeeds by reason of Dreiser's ability to describe the economic buccaneer-as-artist. The detail is sometimes laid on with a trowel, and the crudity of Dreiser's instinct as an artist is shown in the way the story alternates mechanically between Dreiser's business affairs and his involvements with women. Even more serious, perhaps, is the vulgar attribution of Dreiser's own lower-class resentments and hungers to his his hero. It is true that Dreiser had come to think of his own wife as unsympathetic to his "higher" concerns and that he was unable to obtain a divorce. But the reader of *The Financier*, who has already been told so much about Cowperwood's quiet dignity and superior taste, finds it rather a shock to come upon the scene in which Cowperwood tells his first wife that he wants a divorce and is described as thinking to himself—"Socially she was not so much." [2]

The language of this is typical of Dreiser's more subjective writing, and Dreiser is an interesting example of the fact that, in general, a talent for narrative can assimilate and transcend many subjective qualities. Whatever Dreiser's limitations, he certainly knew how to attract the reader's interest, to keep a story going; this sense of movement is in fact his greatest strength and usually persuades the reader who may object to many details en route that Dreiser's "story line" is identical with the way things really happen. In both *The Financier* and its sequel, *The Titan* (1914), Dreiser was able to follow the actual career of Charles T. Yerkes closely enough to make Cowperwood's final move to London a symbol of interna-

[1] *The Financier* (rev. ed. 1927), p. 735.
[2] *Ibid.* p. 737.

tional monopoly. But it is interesting that his identification of himself with Cowperwood could not carry him immediately to the third volume, *The Stoic* (1947), of what had been intended as a "trilogy of desire." Instead, Dreiser went on to *The 'Genius'* (1915), which is the most narrowly autobiographical of his novels, probably the poorest novel he published during his lifetime, but which had the distinction of being attacked by John S. Sumner, head of the Society for the Suppression of Vice, who tried to get the book banned.

In *The 'Genius,'* as in Dreiser's other novels, his concern with sex is patently that of the young man in a still puritan culture. What makes this most universal of themes significant in Dreiser is the way in which his heroes identify their longing for a fuller erotic life with their longings to succeed in the harsh and exciting world of business. It is just the connection that Clyde Griffiths sees between the erotic possibilities of the rich girl and success in the great world that makes *An American Tragedy* at once so faithful a report of the sad pattern of American life and so genuinely tragic as a novel. In *The 'Genius,'* however, the identification is more subjective on Dreiser's part and the novel is dispiriting. Eugene Witla identifies his own sexuality with his ambition to become an "artist," hardly a promising ground for fiction. Moreoever, it is much more difficult to show an artist at work than it is to show a businessman in action like Cowperwood or a lowly provincial like Clyde Griffiths grasping the lower rungs of the social ladder. The history of fiction records any number of examples of otherwise good writers writing bad books about what it is that artists do that makes them artists. Dreiser, as has been noted, was actually weaker at writing about himself directly than he was in creating fictional characters, which is why his travel books and autobiographies— like *A Hoosier Holiday* (1916) and *Dawn* (1931)—have never kept their interest for the general reader. Without lessening this fact, it is also true that when a character in a Dreiser novel becomes confused in Dreiser's own mind with himself, his work goes wrong. *The 'Genius'* is a case in point. Apart from the general difficulty of describing an artist at work, Eugene Witla is so much Dreiser himself, a writer rather than a painter, that Dreiser describes Witla's paintings by giving us stirring but highly "literary" versions of the realistic city scenes that were in fashion among the newspaper illustrators among whom he worked and the realistic painters of the so-called "Ash Can" school, like George Luks, George Bellows, John Sloan, with whom Dreiser naturally identified himself. For the most part, we see Eugene confronting only his own ambition, as it were, having fantasies and speaking soliloquies; we do not see him revealed by his relation to other people. Dramatically speaking, his figure is too nebulous and uncertain to persuade us of that necessity underlying character which is the usual strength of Dreiser's fiction. The book is "personal" in the worst sense —it is purely defensive, yet Dreiser would like to detach himself with ironic quotation marks from the character he calls the "genius"—and on this confused defensiveness it is wrecked.

In 1915, *The 'Genius'* was attacked for reasons that would have seemed ludicrous to the 1920's. It is significant that *An American Tragedy*, Dreiser's best and most famous novel, was published in 1925; by then the revolution in manners and morals that made the 1920's famous for its championship of all the new movements in modern literature and art had also firmly prepared the ground for Dreiser himself. *An American Tragedy*, coming out at just the right time, firmly established Dreiser's reputation. The publication of this novel was the high point of his life, for appearing at a time when the public as well as the critics were prepared for a book which even in its title was intransigent and shocking, Dreiser had good reason to feel that American literature and American taste had at last caught up with him.

The effect of *An American Tragedy* is due to Dreiser's dogged and cumulative sense of fact. He followed closely the court records in the murder trial of Chester Gillette, who in 1906 had drowned his mistress, Grace Brown, in Moose Lake, New York. But long before Dreiser's hero, Clyde Griffiths, comes to trial, we have had to assimilate slowly, and in unrelieved material detail, so much of Clyde's longing for a better life that we understand and in a sense even assent to the line of reasoning that has brought him to trial. In a Naturalistic novel like *An American Tragedy*, it is not the characters who have the fullest possible consciousness but the reader observing them. It is the reader as spectator of other people's lives, of the process of life, who sees all around him and who draws the conclusion that the characters themselves are too overwhelmed to draw. The powerlessness of the characters themselves becomes an occasion for the reader's deeper realization of the larger situation in which the characters struggle. And in order that the reader may finally understand and even share Clyde Griffiths' longings and confusions, the novelist must create such a web of fact to support the young hero's temptations, longings, and confusions that we will finally accept even his decision to murder as understandable within his circumstances.

Dreiser's success in handling social fact is due not merely to his doggedness and repetition but to the fact that his main characters are never shown in the round, are never complex. They have one or two sensitive points of ambition to which Dreiser returns again and again, and the intensity with which these hopes press upon them is what finally makes these "simple" characters so moving to us—and so believable. Without Dreiser's implicit sensitiveness and sympathy, so crushing a story of human weakness and folly would be unsupportable. But Dreiser, working with a story that at every point reminds us of how mean history can be, somehow makes us feel that a young man's ambition is still one of the great stories.

Dreiser can do this in *An American Tragedy* because he understands the boundless hope, the mystical fulfillment that Americans associate with material success. In a novel by Balzac, a young Frenchman is likely to be ambitious for an accepted status, to seek a specific title or fortune; in *An American Tragedy* Clyde Griffiths, after an utterly barren childhood wandering about with his innocent and impoverished parents, street evangelists, suddenly, as a bellhop in a Kansas City hotel, gets an inkling of the confidence and pleasure that money can bring to human existence; by the time he becomes a foreman in his rich uncle's factory and is introduced to the social circle in which he meets and falls in love with Sondra Finchley, we can see that he expects literally everything

of an alliance with riches. Roberta Alden, the poor factory girl whom he took up in his earlier loneliness and who now, pregnant, expects him to marry her, has very real claims on his affections. But Clyde has had a glimpse of the stars, and Roberta will never be able to win him back. Roberta's rival is not just a rich girl; it is, literally, the American dream. And as Dreiser is not the first writer to show us, nothing can equal, in its hold on human affections and ambitions, a sudden hope for the infinite; equally, nothing can betray quite so mercilessly as the naïve hope that the infinite can be found in material possessions. The American Dream, by reason of its terrible innocence, has often turned into the American Tragedy. But surely no one handling this familiar theme in our literature has done so with quite the concentrated power and yet with the felt sympathy that Dreiser does here. The process in which Clyde Griffiths is caught up is ruthless and horrifying; Dreiser himself never suggests that vague sense of pride in demonstrating the futility of hope, that almost tangible professional pride in showing up his own characters as naïve before the overwhelming fact of life, that one finds in so sophisticated a writer as Stephen Crane. Dreiser conveys, equally with his professional and even fascinated detachment in telling the story, his own sympathetic helplessness before the story he *must* tell.

What stands out in *An American Tragedy*—along with Dreiser's usual awkward tendency to describe internal states of feeling in language more suitable to documentary social history—is the fact that working with so many minute facts, he can permit himself enough space for establishing firmly such themes as Clyde Griffiths' youthful deprivations and Clyde's realization of the splendor of life seen from a Kansas City hotel. Dreiser's method is seen at its best in Chapters 38–47 of Book II (see pp. 516–56), which, starting from the doctor's refusal to perform an illegal operation on Roberta, takes us with such culmination of effect to Roberta's accidental death in the lake and Clyde's panicky flight back to the city. The rhythm of the narrative itself wins the reader over despite all the objections he is likely to feel toward the unpalatable nature of the material, for the unbearable conflict in Clyde's heart, coming into full consciousness with his decision to kill Roberta, now mounts to its final agonizing tension when he gets her into the boat, decides not to go through with his murder plan, but then withholds help after he accidentally strikes her and she falls overboard and drowns. In this masterly succession of chapters, Dreiser's devices are obvious and his psychology elementary; Clyde doesn't want to kill Roberta, but he certainly wants to be free of her and to marry Sondra. But Dreiser succeeds patiently in making one detail the consequence of another, in making us acknowledge the abysses present in the situation. By the end of this section, we suffer all his confused and guilty strivings; we, too, stand helplessly by while Roberta drowns; and with the sinister screechings of the birds in our ears, it is we who run from the lake that has become the landscape of our own guilt.

No one can respond to *An American Tragedy* without implicitly condemning the society behind it. It is a fact, moreover, that as the twenties drew on to the economic collapse of 1929 and many people began to feel the increasing shakiness of capitalist society, Dreiser for the first time consciously began to think of himself as a radical. In 1927 he visited the Soviet Union, and later he published *Dreiser Looks at Russia* (1928). By 1930, when so many American writers had gone left, Dreiser was increasingly identified with prolabor causes. In 1932, he went down with a committee of writers to investigate conditions among the hard-pressed miners of Harlan County, Kentucky, where local police officials, incensed by his intervention, had him indicted on charges of criminal syndicalism and adultery— charges which were later dropped.

Dreiser had of course always been mordantly critical of a society in which he had so long felt himself to be a victim, but when he first became famous and was often asked for his social and political views, his opinions had often tended to resemble the vaguely cynical and pseudo-aristocratic views of his good friend, H. L. Mencken, who had always been a powerful influence on him. More significant, Dreiser's general view of human existence had continued, in the spirit of his novels, to refuse any solace to mankind. In 1928, contributing

to a symposium on "What I Believe," he had affirmed his well-known disbelief in all explanations and interpretations of life: "In short I catch no meaning from all I have seen, and pass quite as I came, confused and dismayed." [1] But the economic collapse of the 1930's coincided with the time when Dreiser, though at the peak of his fame, was no longer able to muster his old capacity as a novelist. It was just at this time, too, despite the vogue of Realism in the 1930's, that Dreiser as a novelist came to seem particularly crude and old-fashioned when compared with writers like Hemingway and Faulkner. Inevitably, then, Dreiser rather tended to sound off on all social and political questions of the day in default of steady artistic production. During his own lifetime he never published a novel after *An American Tragedy*, and the two novels that he struggled with so long and so confusedly in his last years, *The Bulwark* (1946) and *The Stoic* (1947), show how depleted his energies were as a creative writer. And in regard to these many political and social statements and books, the most famous of which is *Tragic America* (1932), it has to be said, too, that despite Dreiser's characteristically emotional reaction to suffering and oppression, his social and political pronouncements often betrayed crude personal prejudices. Dreiser had never quite gotten over the hysterical distrust of people of German descent during the First World War, and during the Second, he shocked and offended many liberals among his admirers by his truculent remarks about the English and the Jews, made while on a lecture tour in Canada.

In these last years of his life, Dreiser was much taken up by the Communists, and since the newer generation of writers and readers did not have much sympathy for his work, it was perhaps natural for him to seek sympathy and encouragement from a political group which was also unpopular and excluded. Despite his world fame, Dreiser, by the end of his life, had in fact gone back to something like the isolation he had suffered as a young man. Yet it is typical of his essential seriousness and of his fundamental intellectual difference from the Communists that in these very last years, when

[1] The *Bookman* (September, 1928).

he was living in Hollywood and had become increasingly identified with left-wing causes, he also became increasingly more interested in the mystical and quietist tradition of American thought. He edited *The Living Thoughts of Thoreau* in 1939, and in his posthumously published novel, *The Bulwark* (1946), wrote about a religious personality with the affection and admiration that had always been latent in his thought. In *The Stoic* (1947), Frank Cowperwood and his last mistress seemed to be concerned with religious questions and philosophical issues in a way that was bewildering to those who remembered the early Cowperwood as a proud, passionate, and erotic "titan" of American business. Yet like many serious and honest writers who have temporarily or partially given their allegiance to the Communist party, Dreiser *was* moved by a desire for justice and philosophical orientation rather than by mechanical loyalty to a cause.[1] In these last years of his life, essentially isolated from the developing stream of American literature and involved with nonliterary figures and professional left-wingers who had taken him up, he was still—predominantly—concerned with working out the possible meaning to the riddle of human existence. This had been his lifelong concern. In these difficult and lonely years, he found great happiness in taking communion in an Episcopalian church. He died on December 28,

1945. Leaving his entire estate to his wife, Helen Richardson, "he requested that upon her death she should bequeath whatever did not go to designated relatives to some home for Negro orphans."[2]

READING SUGGESTIONS

DOROTHY DUDLEY, *Forgotten Frontiers and the Land of the Free* (1932; republished in 1946 as *Dreiser and the Land of the Free*). A relatively early and passionate defense of Dreiser that is still worth reading for its reflection of the intense critical partisanship surrounding Dreiser's career, but which has been supplanted as a critical guide by later and more objective works.

ROBERT H. ELIAS, *Theodore Dreiser: Apostle of Nature* (1949). The only existing biography of Dreiser. A comprehensive, invaluably detailed record.

F. O. MATTHIESSEN, *Theodore Dreiser* (1951). A most useful critical biography that is perhaps more significant for its intention than for its execution. Matthiessen, a remarkably keen and scholarly critic of American literature, felt rather more sympathy for the tendency of Dreiser's political views than for Dreiser's novels. But as one might expect of a critic of Matthiessen's abilities, even his relative lack of *final* sympathy with Dreiser's work could not keep this book from being penetrating.

ALFRED KAZIN AND CHARLES SHAPIRO, editors, *The Stature of Theodore Dreiser*, with an Introduction by Alfred Kazin (1955). The only collection of Dreiser criticism, from the earliest reviews of *Sister Carrie* up to the many distinguished essays on Dreiser published in recent years by Lionel Trilling, Saul Bellow, John Berryman, David Brion Davis, Eliseo Vivas, and others.

[1] On Dreiser's relation to the Communists, see Daniel Aaron, *Writers on the Left: Episodes in American Literary Communism* (1961).

[2] Elias, *op. cit.*, p. 308.

NIGGER JEFF

◊

❲ DREISER published four books of stories—*Free and Other Stories* (1918), *Twelve Men* (1919), *Chains—Lesser Novels and Stories* (1927), and *A Gallery of Women* (2 vols., 1929). As one might expect from a writer who usually needed so much space and so many factual details in order to write a novel, Dreiser's stories are not distinguished by that lean, deft, ironic touch

which distinguishes the stories of a writer born to this form, like Ernest Hemingway. Dreiser's manner was always too heavy, his style too rambling and imprecise; some of his best-known stories, like "My Brother Paul," are reminiscences rather than the highly artful miniatures that we have come to think of as identical with the short story as a form.

Not only are Dreiser's stories more usually chronicles than dramatically worked out stories leading to an unexpected climax, but they significantly center on a single individual's emotions rather than on any subtle and shifting relationship between characters. In "Nigger Jeff," this old-fashioned emphasis is on the worldly-wise reporter's change of heart after a lynching; in "Sanctuary," it is on a frightened girl's despair of the great world and her return to the convent; in "The Lost Phoebe," it is on the old farmer's loneliness and the unbearable longing for his dead wife that finally drives him, wild with distraction, to unconscious suicide.

Yet in all these stories, and perhaps most unforgettably in the rich and warm tones of "My Brother Paul," what stands out most is Dreiser's ability to bring home to us the profound and yet incommunicable feelings that human beings experience in solitude. No one else in our recent literature has known so well how to dramatize what the individual feels when he is alone entirely with himself.

"Nigger Jeff" is from *Free and Other Stories*.

❖

THE CITY EDITOR was waiting for one of his best reporters, Elmer Davies by name, a vain and rather self-sufficient youth who was inclined to be of that turn of mind which sees in life only a fixed and ordered process of rewards and punishments. If one did not do exactly right, one did not get along well. On the contrary, if one did, one did. Only the so-called evil were really punished, only the good truly rewarded—or Mr. Davies had heard this so long in his youth that he had come nearly to believe it. Presently he appeared. He was dressed in a new spring suit, a new hat and new shoes. In the lapel of his coat was a small bunch of violets. It was one o'clock of a sunny spring afternoon, and he was feeling exceedingly well and good-natured—quite fit, indeed. The world was going unusually well with him. It seemed worth singing about.

"Read that, Davies," said the city editor, handing him the clipping. "I'll tell you afterward what I want you to do."

The reporter stood by the editorial chair and read:

Pleasant Valley, Ko., April 16.
"A most dastardly crime has just been reported here. Jeff Ingalls, a negro, this morning assaulted Ada Whitaker, the nineteen-year-old daughter of Morgan Whitaker, a well-to-do farmer, whose home is four miles south of this place. A posse, headed by Sheriff Mathews, has started in pursuit. If he is caught, it is thought he will be lynched."

The reporter raised his eyes as he finished. What a terrible crime! What evil people there were in the world! No doubt such a creature ought to be lynched, and that quickly.

"You had better go out there, Davies," said the city editor. "It looks as if something might come of that. A lynching up here would be a big thing. There's never been one in this state."

Davies smiled. He was always pleased to be sent out of town. It was a mark of appreciation. The city editor rarely sent any of the other men on these big stories. What a nice ride he would have!

As he went along, however, a few minutes later he began to meditate on this. Perhaps, as the city editor had suggested, he might be compelled to witness an actual lynching. That was by no means so pleasant in itself. In his fixed code of rewards and punishments he had no particular place for lynchings, even for crimes of the nature described, especially if he had to witness the lynching. It was too horrible a kind of reward or punishment. Once, in line of duty, he had been compelled to witness a hanging, and that had made him sick—deathly so—even though carried out as a part of the due process of law of his day and place. Now, as he looked at this fine day and his excellent clothes, he was not so sure that this was a worthwhile assignment. Why should he always be selected for such things—just because he could write? There were others—lots of men on the staff. He began to hope as he went along that nothing really serious would come of it, that they would catch the man before he got there and put him in jail—or, if the worst had to be—painful thought! that it would be all over by the time he got there. Let's see—the telegram had been filed at nine A.M. It was now one-thirty and would be three by the time he got out there, all of that. That would give them time enough, and then, if all were well, or ill, as it were, he could just gather the details of the crime and the—aftermath—and return. The mere thought of an approaching lynching troubled him greatly, and the farther he went the less he liked it.

He found the village of Pleasant Valley a very small affair indeed, just a few dozen houses nestling between green slopes of low hills, with one small business corner and a rambling array of lanes. One or two merchants of K——, the city from which he had just arrived, lived out here, but otherwise it was very rural. He took notes of the whiteness of the little houses, the shimmering beauty of the small stream one had to cross in going from the depot. At the one main corner a few men were gathered about a typical village barroom. Davies headed for this as being the most likely source of information.

In mingling with this company at first he said nothing about his being a newspaper man, being very doubtful as to its effect upon them, their freedom of speech and manner.

The whole company was apparently tense with interest in the crime which still remained unpunished, seemingly craving excitement and desirous of seeing something done about it. No such opportunity to work up wrath and vent their stored-up animal propensities had probably occurred here in years. He took this occasion to inquire into the exact details of the attack, where it had occurred, where the Whitakers lived. Then, seeing that mere talk prevailed here, he went away thinking that he had best find out for himself how the victim was. As yet she had not been described, and it was necessary to know a little something about her. Accordingly, he sought an old man who kept a stable in the village, and procured a horse. No carriage was to be had. Davies was not an excellent rider, but he made a shift of it. The Whitaker home was not so very far away—about four miles out—and before long he was knocking at its front door, set back a hundred feet from the rough country road.

"I'm from the *Times*," he said to the tall, raw-boned woman who opened the door, with an attempt at being impressive. His position as reporter in this matter was a little dubious; he might be welcome, and he might not. Then he asked if this were Mrs. Whitaker, and how Miss Whitaker was by now.

"She's doing very well," answered the woman, who seemed decidedly stern, if repressed and nervous, a Spartan type. "Won't you come in? She's rather feverish, but the doctor says she'll probably be all right later on." She said no more.

Davies acknowledged the invitation by entering. He was very anxious to see the girl, but she was sleeping under the influence of an opiate, and he did not care to press the matter at once.

"When did this happen?" he asked.

"About eight o'clock this morning," said the woman. "She started to go over to our next door neighbor here, Mr. Edmonds, and this negro met her. We didn't know anything about it until she came crying through the gate and dropped down in here."

"Were you the first one to meet her?" asked Davies.

"Yes, I was the only one," said Mrs. Whitaker. "The men had all gone to the fields."

Davies listened to more of the details, the type and history of the man, and then rose to go. Before doing so he was allowed to have a look at the girl, who was still sleeping. She was young and rather pretty. In the yard he met a country man who was just coming to get home news. The latter imparted more information.

"They're lookin' all around south of here," he said, speaking of a crowd which was supposed to be searching. "I expect they'll make short work of him if they get him. He can't get away very well, for he's on foot, wherever he is. The sheriff's after him too, with a deputy or two, I believe. He'll be tryin' to save him an' take him over to Clayton, but I don't believe he'll be able to do it, not if the crowd catches him first."

So, thought Davies, he would probably have to witness a lynching after all. The prospect was most unhappy.

"Does any one know where this negro lived?" he asked heavily, a growing sense of his duty weighing upon him.

"Oh, right down here a little way," replied the farmer. "Jeff Ingalls was his name. We all know him around here. He worked for one and another of the farmers hereabouts, and don't appear to have had such a bad record, either, except for drinkin' a little now and then. Miss Ada recognized him, all right. You follow this road to the next crossing and turn to the right. It's a little log house that sets back off the road—something like that one you see down the lane there, only it's got lots o' chips scattered about."

Davies decided to go there first, but changed his mind. It was growing late, and he thought he had better return to the village. Perhaps by now developments in connection with the sheriff or the posse were to be learned.

Accordingly, he rode back and put the horse in the hands of its owner, hoping that all had been concluded and that he might learn of it here. At the principal corner much the same company was still present, arguing, fomenting, gesticulating. They seemed parts of different companies that earlier in the day had been out searching. He wondered what they had been doing since, and then decided to ingratiate himself by telling them he had just come from the Whitakers and what he had learned there of the present condition of the girl and the movements of the sheriff.

Just then a young farmer came galloping up. He was coatless, hatless, breathless.

"They've got him!" he shouted excitedly. "They've got him!"

A chorus of "whos," "wheres" and "whens" greeted this information as the crowd gathered about the rider.

"Why, Mathews caught him up here at his own house!" exclaimed the latter, pulling out a handkerchief and wiping his face. "He must 'a' gone back there for something. Mathews's takin' him over to Clayton, so they think, but they don't project he'll ever get there. They're after him now, but Mathews says he'll shoot the first man that tries to take him away."

"Which way'd he go?" exclaimed the men in chorus, stirring as if to make an attack.

" 'Cross Sellers' Lane," said the rider. "The boys think he's goin' by way of Baldwin."

"Whoopee!" yelled one of the listeners. "We'll get him away from him, all right! Are you goin', Sam?"

"You bet!" said the latter. "Wait'll I get my horse!"

"Lord!" thought Davies. "To think of being (perforce) one of a lynching party—a hired spectator!"

He delayed no longer, however, but hastened to secure his horse again. He saw that the crowd would be off in a minute to catch up with the sheriff. There would be information in that quarter, drama very likely.

"What's doin'?" inquired the liveryman as he noted Davies' excited appearance.

"They're after him," replied the latter nervously. "The sheriff's caught him. They're going now to try to take him away from him, or that's what they say. The sheriff is taking him over to Clayton, by way of Baldwin. I want to get over there if I can. Give me the horse again, and I'll give you a couple of dollars more."

The liveryman led the horse out, but not without many provisionary cautions as to the care which was to be taken of him, the damages which would ensue if it were not. He was not to be ridden beyond midnight. If one were wanted for longer than that Davies must get him elsewhere or come and get another, to all of which Davies promptly agreed. He then mounted and rode away.

When he reached the corner again several of the men who had gone for their horses were already there, ready to start. The young man who had brought the news had long since dashed off to other parts.

Davies waited to see which road this new company would take. Then through as pleasant a country as one would wish to see, up hill and down dale, with charming vistas breaking upon the gaze at every turn, he did the riding of his life. So disturbed was the reporter by the grim turn things had taken that he scarcely noted the beauty that was stretched before him, save to note that it was so. Death! Death! The proximity of involuntary and enforced death was what weighed upon him now.

In about an hour the company had come in sight of the sheriff, who, with two other men, was driving a wagon he had borrowed along a lone country road. The latter was sitting at the back, a revolver in each hand, his face toward the group, which at sight of him trailed after at a respectful distance. Excited as every one was, there was no disposition, for the time being at least, to halt the progress of the law.

"He's in that wagon," Davies heard one man

say. "Don't you see they've got him in there tied and laid down?"

Davies looked.

"That's right," said another. "I see him now."

"What we ought to do," said a third, who was riding near the front, "is to take him away and hang him. That's just what he deserves, and that's what he'll get before we're through to-day."

"Yes!" called the sheriff, who seemed to have heard this. "You're not goin' to do any hangin' this day, so you just might as well go on back." He did not appear to be much troubled by the appearance of the crowd.

"Where's old man Whitaker?" asked one of the men who seemed to feel that they needed a leader. "He'd get him quick enough!"

"He's with the other crowd, down below Olney," was the reply.

"Somebody ought to go an' tell him."

"Clark's gone," assured another, who hoped for the worst.

Davies rode among the company a prey to mingled and singular feelings. He was very much excited and yet depressed by the character of the crowd which, in so far as he could see, was largely impelled to its jaunt by curiosity and yet also able under sufficient motivation on the part of some one—any one, really—to kill too. There was not so much daring as a desire to gain daring from others, an unconscious wish or impulse to organize the total strength or will of those present into one strength or one will, sufficient to overcome the sheriff and inflict death upon his charge. It was strange—almost intellectually incomprehensible—and yet so it was. The men were plainly afraid of the determined sheriff. They thought something ought to be done, but they did not feel like getting into trouble.

Mathews, a large solemn, sage, brown man in worn clothes and a faded brown hat, contemplated the recent addition to his trailers with apparent indifference. Seemingly he was determined to protect his man and avoid mob justice, come what may. A mob should not have him if he had to shoot, and if he shot it would be to kill. Finally, since the company thus added to did not dash upon him, he seemingly decided to scare them off. Apparently he thought he could do this, since they trailed like calves.

"Stop a minute!" he called to his driver.

The latter pulled up. So did the crowd behind. Then the sheriff stood over the prostrate body of the negro, who lay in the jolting wagon beneath him, and called back:

"Go 'way from here, you people! Go on, now! I won't have you follerin' after me!"

"Give us the nigger!" yelled one in a half-bantering, half-derisive tone of voice.

"I'll give ye just two minutes to go on back out o' this road," returned the sheriff grimly, pulling out his watch and looking at it. They were about a hundred feet apart. "If you don't, I'll clear you out!"

"Give us the nigger!"

"I know you, Scott," answered Mathews, recognizing the voice. "I'll arrest every last one of ye tomorrow. Mark my word!"

The company listened in silence, the horses champing and twisting.

"We've got a right to foller," answered one of the men.

"I give ye fair warning," said the sheriff, jumping from his wagon and leveling his pistols as he approached. "When I count five I'll begin to shoot!"

He was a serious and stalwart figure as he approached, and the crowd fell back a little.

"Git out o' this now!" he yelled. "One— Two——"

The company turned completely and retreated, Davies among them.

"We'll foller him when he gits further on," said one of the men in explanation.

"He's got to do it," said another. "Let him git a little ways ahead."

The sheriff returned to his wagon and drove on. He seemed, however, to realize that he would not be obeyed and that safety lay in haste alone. His wagon was traveling fast. If only he could lose them or get a good start he might possibly get to Clayton and the strong county jail by morning. His followers, however, trailed him swiftly as might be, determined not to be left behind.

"He's goin' to Baldwin," said one of the company of which Davies was a member.

"Where's that?" asked Davies.

"Over west o' here, about four miles."

"Why is he going there?"

"That's where he lives. I guess he thinks if he kin git 'im over there he kin purtect 'im till he kin git more help from Clayton. I cal'late he'll try an' take 'im over yet to-night, or early in the mornin' shore."

Davies smiled at the man's English. This country-side lingo always fascinated him.

Yet the men lagged, hesitating as to what to do. They did not want to lose sight of Mathews, and yet cowardice controlled them. They did not want to get into direct altercation with the law. It wasn't their place to hang the man, although plainly they felt that he ought to be hanged, and that it would be a stirring and exciting thing if he were. Consequently they desired to watch and be on hand— to get old Whitaker and his son Jake, if they could, who were out looking elsewhere. They wanted to see what the father and brother would do.

The quandary was solved by one of the men, who suggested that they could get to Baldwin by going back to Pleasant Valley and taking the Sand River pike, and that in the meantime they might come upon Whitaker and his son en route, or leave word at his house. It was a shorter cut than this the sheriff was taking, although he would get there first now. Possibly they could beat him at least to Clayton, if he attempted to go on. The Clayton road was back via Pleasant Valley, or near it, and easily intercepted. Therefore, while one or two remained to trail the sheriff and give the alarm in case he did attempt to go on to Clayton, the rest, followed by Davies, set off at a gallop to Pleasant Valley. It was nearly dusk now when they arrived and stopped at the corner store— supper time. The fires of evening meals were marked by upcurling smoke from chimneys. Here, somehow, the zest to follow seemed to depart. Evidently the sheriff had worsted them for the night. Morg Whitaker, the father, had not been found; neither had Jake. Perhaps they had better eat. Two or three had already secretly fallen away.

They were telling the news of what had occurred so far to one of the two storekeepers who kept the place, when suddenly Jake Whitaker, the girl's brother, and several companions came riding up. They had been scouring the territory to the north of the town, and were hot and tired. Plainly they were unaware of the developments of which the crowd had been a part.

"The sheriff's got 'im!" exclaimed one of the company, with that blatance which always accompanies the telling of great news in small rural companies. "He taken him over to Baldwin in a wagon a coupla hours ago."

"Which way did he go?" asked the son, whose hardy figure, worn, hand-me-down clothes and rakish hat showed up picturesquely as he turned here and there on his horse.

" 'Cross Sellers' Lane. You won't git 'em that-a-way, though, Jake. He's already over there by now. Better take the short cut."

A babble of voices now made the scene more interesting. One told how the negro had been caught, another that the sheriff was defiant, a third that men were still tracking him or over there watching, until all the chief points of the drama had been spoken if not heard.

Instantly suppers were forgotten. The whole customary order of the evening was overturned once more. The company started off on another excited jaunt, up hill and down dale, through the lovely country that lay between Baldwin and Pleasant Valley.

By now Davies was very weary of this procedure and of his saddle. He wondered when, if ever, this story was to culminate, let alone he write it. Tragic as it might prove, he could not nevertheless spend an indefinite period trailing a possibility, and yet, so great was the potentiality of the present situation, he dared not leave. By contrast with the horror impending, as he now noted, the night was so beautiful that it was all but poignant. Stars were already beginning to shine. Distant lamps twinkled like yellow eyes from the cottages in the valleys and on the hillsides. The air was fresh and tender. Some peafowls were crying afar off, and the east promised a golden moon.

Silently the assembled company trotted on— no more than a score in all. In the dusk, and with Jake ahead, it seemed too grim a pilgrimage for joking. Young Jake, riding silently toward the front, looked as if tragedy were all he craved. His friends seemed considerately to withdraw from him, seeing that he was the aggrieved.

After an hour's riding Baldwin came into view, lying in a sheltering cup of low hills. Already its lights were twinkling softly and there was still an air of honest firesides and cheery suppers about it which appealed to Davies in his hungry state. Still, he had no thought now of anything save this pursuit.

Once in the village, the company was greeted by calls of recognition. Everybody seemed to know what they had come for. The sheriff and his charge were still there, so a dozen citizens volunteered. The local storekeepers and loungers followed the cavalcade up the street to the sheriff's house, for the riders had now fallen into a solemn walk.

"You won't get him though, boys," said one whom Davies later learned was Seavey, the village postmaster and telegraph operator, a rather youthful person of between twenty-five and thirty, as they passed his door. "He's got two deputies in there with him, or did have, and they say he's going to take him over to Clayton."

At the first street corner they were joined by the several men who had followed the sheriff.

"He tried to give us the slip," they volunteered excitedly, "but he's got the nigger in the house, there, down in the cellar. The deputies ain't with him. They've gone somewhere for help—Clayton, maybe."

"How do you know?"

"We saw 'em go out that back way. We think we did, anyhow."

A hundred feet from the sheriff's little white cottage, which backed up against a sloping field, the men parleyed. Then Jake announced that he proposed to go boldly up to the sheriff's door and demand the negro.

"If he don't turn him out I'll break in the door an' take him!" he said.

"That's right! We'll stand by you, Whitaker," commented several.

By now the throng of unmounted natives had gathered. The whole village was up and about, its one street alive and running with people. Heads appeared at doors and windows. Riders pranced up and down, hallooing. A few revolver shots were heard. Presently the mob gathered even closer to the sheriff's gate, and Jake stepped forward as leader. Instead, however, of going boldly up to the door as at first it appeared he would, he stopped at the gate, calling to the sheriff.

"Hello, Mathews!"

"Eh, eh, eh!" bellowed the crowd.

The call was repeated. Still no answer. Apparently to the sheriff delay appeared to be his one best weapon.

Their coming, however, was not as unexpected as some might have thought. The figure of the sheriff was plainly to be seen close to one of the front windows. He appeared to be holding a double-barreled shotgun. The negro, as it developed later, was cowering and chattering in the darkest corner of the cellar, hearkening no doubt to the voices and firing of the revolvers outside.

Suddenly, and just as Jake was about to go forward, the front door of the house flew open, and in the glow of a single lamp inside appeared first the double-barreled end of the gun, followed immediately by the form of Mathews, who held the weapon poised ready for a quick throw to the shoulder. All except Jake fell back.

"Mr. Mathews," he called deliberately, "we want that nigger!"

"Well, you can't git 'im!" replied the sheriff. "He's not here."

"Then what you got that gun fer?" yelled a voice.

Mathews made no answer.

"Better give him up, Mathews," called another, who was safe in the crowd, "or we'll come in an' take him!"

"No you won't," said the sheriff defiantly. "I said the man wasn't here. I say it ag'in. You couldn't have him if he was, an' you can't come in my house! Now if you people don't want trouble you'd better go on away."

"He's down in the cellar!" yelled another.

"Why don't you let us see?" asked another.

Mathews waved his gun slightly.

"You'd better go away from here now," cautioned the sheriff. "I'm tellin' ye! I'll have warrants out for the lot o' ye, if ye don't mind!"

The crowd continued to simmer and stew, while Jake stood as before. He was very pale and tense, but lacked initiative.

"He won't shoot," called some one at the back of the crowd. "Why don't you go in, Jake, an' git him?"

"Sure! Rush in. That's it!" observed a second.

"He won't, eh?" replied the sheriff softly. Then he added in a lower tone, "The first man that comes inside that gate takes the consequences."

No one ventured inside the gate; many even fell back. It seemed as if the planned assault had come to nothing.

"Why not go around the back way?" called some one else.

"Try it!" replied the sheriff. "See what you find on that side! I told you you couldn't come inside. You'd better go away from here now before ye git into trouble," he repeated. "You can't come in, an' it'll only mean bloodshed."

There was more chattering and jesting while the sheriff stood on guard. He, however, said no more. Nor did he allow the banter, turmoil and lust for tragedy to disturb him. Only, he kept his eye on Jake, on whose movements the crowd seemed to hang.

Time passed, and still nothing was done. The truth was that young Jake, put to the test, was not sufficiently courageous himself, for all his daring, and felt the weakness of the crowd behind him. To all intents and purposes he was alone, for he did not inspire confidence. He finally fell back a little, observing, "I'll git 'im before mornin', all right," and now the crowd itself began to disperse, returning to its stores and homes or standing about the postoffice and the one village drugstore. Finally, Davies smiled and came away. He was sure he had the story of a defeated mob. The sheriff was to be his great hero. He proposed to interview him later. For the present, he meant to seek out Seavey, the telegraph operator, and arrange to file a message, then see if something to eat was not to be had somewhere.

After a time he found the operator and told him what he wanted—to write and file a story as he wrote it. The latter indicated a table in the little postoffice and telegraph station which he could use. He became very much interested in the reporter when he learned he was from the *Times*, and when Davies asked where he could get something to eat said he would run across the street and tell the proprietor of the only boarding house to fix him something which he could consume as he wrote. He appeared to be interested in how a newspaper man would go about telling a story of this kind over a wire.

"You start your story," he said, "and I'll come back and see if I can get the *Times* on the wire."

Davies sat down and began his account. He was intent on describing things to date, the uncertainty and turmoil, the apparent victory of the sheriff. Plainly the courage of the latter had won, and it was all so picturesque. "A foiled lynching," he began, and as he wrote the obliging postmaster, who had by now returned, picked up the pages and carefully deciphered them for himself.

"That's all right. I'll see if I can get the *Times* now," he commented.

"Very obliging postmaster," thought Davies as he wrote, but he had so often encountered pleasant and obliging people on his rounds that he soon dropped that thought.

The food was brought, and still Davies wrote on, munching as he did so. In a little while the *Times* answered an often-repeated call.

"Davies at Baldwin," ticked the postmaster, "get ready for quite a story!"

"Let 'er go!" answered the operator at the *Times*, who had been expecting this dispatch.

As the events of the day formulated themselves in his mind, Davies wrote and turned over page after page. Between whiles he looked out through the small window before him where afar off he could see a lonely light twinkling against a hillside. Not infrequently he stopped his work to see if anything new was happening, whether the situation was in any danger of changing, but apparently it was not. He then proposed to remain until all possibility of a tragedy, this night anyhow, was eliminated. The operator also wandered about, waiting for an accumulation of pages upon which he could work but making sure to keep up with the writer. The two became quite friendly.

Finally, his dispatch nearly finished, he asked the postmaster to caution the night editor at K—— to the effect, that if anything more happened before one in the morning he would file it, but not to expect anything more as nothing might happen. The reply came that he was to remain and await developments. Then he and the postmaster sat down to talk.

About eleven o'clock, when both had about convinced themselves that all was over for this night anyhow, and the lights in the village had all but vanished, a stillness of the purest, summery-est, country-est quality having settled down, a faint beating of hoofs, which seemed to suggest the approach of a large cavalcade, could be heard out on the Sand River pike as Davies by now had come to learn it was, back or northwest of the post-office. At the sound the postmaster got up, as did Davies, both stepping outside and listening. On it came, and as the volume increased, the former said, "Might be help for the sheriff, but I doubt it. I telegraphed Clayton six times to-day. They wouldn't come that way, though. It's the wrong road." Now, thought Davies nervously, after all there might be something to add to his story, and he had so wished that it was all over! Lynchings, as he now felt, were horrible things. He wished people wouldn't do such things—take the law, which now more than ever he respected, into their own hands. It was too brutal, cruel. That negro cowering there in the dark probably, and the sheriff all taut and tense, worrying over his charge and his duty, were not happy things to contemplate in the face of such a thing as this. It was true that the crime which had been committed was dreadful, but still why couldn't people allow the law to take its course? It was so much better. The law was powerful enough to deal with cases of this kind.

"They're comin' back, all right," said the post-master solemnly, as he and Davies stared in the direction of the sound which grew louder from moment to moment.

"It's not any help from Clayton, I'm afraid."

"By George, I think you're right!" answered the reporter, something telling him that more trouble was at hand. "Here they come!"

As he spoke there was a clattering of hoofs and crunching of saddle girths as a large company of men dashed up the road and turned into the narrow street of the village, the figure of Jake Whitaker and an older bearded man in a wide black hat riding side by side in front.

"There's Jake," said the postmaster, "and that's his father riding beside him there. The old man's a terror when he gets his dander up. Sompin's sure to happen now."

Davies realized that in his absence writing a new turn had been given to things. Evidently the son had returned to Pleasant Valley and organized a new posse or gone out to meet his father.

Instantly the place was astir again. Lights appeared in doorways and windows, and both were thrown open. People were leaning or gazing out to see what new movement was afoot. Davies noted at once that there was none of the brash enthusiasm about this company such as had characterized the previous descent. There was grimness every-where, and he now began to feel that this was the beginning of the end. After the cavalcade had passed down the street toward the sheriff's house,

which was quite dark now, he ran after it, arriving a few moments after the former which was already in part dismounted. The townspeople followed. The sheriff, as it now developed, had not relaxed any of his vigilance, however; he was not sleeping, and as the crowd reappeared the light inside reappeared.

By the light of the moon, which was almost overhead, Davies was able to make out several of his companions of the afternoon, and Jake, the son. There were many more, though, now, whom he did not know, and foremost among them this old man.

The latter was strong, iron-gray, and wore a full beard. He looked very much like a blacksmith.

"Keep your eye on the old man," advised the postmaster, who had by now come up and was standing by.

While they were still looking, the old man went boldly forward to the little front porch of the house and knocked at the door. Some one lifted a curtain at the window and peeped out.

"Hello, in there!" cried the old man, knocking again.

"What do you want?" asked a voice.

"I want that nigger!"

"Well, you can't have him! I've told you people that once."

"Bring him out or I'll break down the door!" said the old man.

"If you do it's at your own risk. I know you, Whitaker, an' you know me. I'll give ye two minutes to get off that porch!"

"I want that nigger, I tell ye!"

"If ye don't git off that porch I'll fire through the door," said the voice solemnly. "One—Two——"

The old man backed cautiously away.

"Come out, Mathews!" yelled the crowd. "You've got to give him up this time. We ain't goin' back without him."

Slowly the door opened, as if the individual within were very well satisfied as to his power to handle the mob. He had done it once before this night, why not again? It revealed his tall form, armed with his shotgun. He looked around very stolidly, and then addressed the old man as one would a friend.

"Ye can't have him, Morgan," he said. "It's ag'in' the law. You know that as well as I do."

"Law or no law," said the old man, "I want that nigger!"

"I tell you I can't let you have him, Morgan. It's ag'in' the law. You know you oughtn't to be comin' around here at this time o' night actin' so."

"Well, I'll take him then," said the old man, making a move.

"Stand back!" shouted the sheriff, leveling his gun on the instant. "I'll blow ye into kingdom come, sure as hell!"

A noticeable movement on the part of the crowd ceased. The sheriff lowered his weapon as if he thought the danger were once more over.

"You-all ought to be ashamed of yerselves," he went on, his voice sinking to a gentle neighborly reproof, "tryin' to upset the law this way."

"The nigger didn't upset no law, did he?" asked one derisively.

"Well, the law's goin' to take care of the nigger now," Mathews made answer.

"Give us that scoundrel, Mathews; you'd better do it," said the old man. "It'll save a heap o' trouble."

"I'll not argue with ye, Morgan. I said ye couldn't have him, an' ye can't. If ye want bloodshed, all right. But don't blame me. I'll kill the first man that tries to make a move this way."

He shifted his gun handily and waited. The crowd stood outside his little fence murmuring.

Presently the old man retired and spoke to several others. There was more murmuring, and then he came back to the dead line.

"We don't want to cause trouble, Mathews," he began explanatively, moving his hand oratorically, "but we think you ought to see that it won't do any good to stand out. We think that——"

Davies and the postmaster were watching young Jake, whose peculiar attitude attracted their attention. The latter was standing poised at the edge of the crowd, evidently seeking to remain unobserved. His eyes were on the sheriff, who was hearkening to the old man. Suddenly, as the father talked and when the sheriff seemed for a moment mollified and unsuspecting, he made a quick run for the porch. There was an intense movement all along the line as the life and death of the deed became apparent. Quickly the sheriff drew his gun to his shoulder. Both triggers were pressed at the same time, and the gun spoke, but not before Jake was in and under him. The latter had been in sufficient time to knock the gun barrel upward and fall upon his man. Both shots blazed harmlessly over the heads of the crowd in red puffs, and then followed a general onslaught. Men leaped the fence by tens and crowded upon the little cottage. They swarmed about every side of the house and crowded upon the porch, where four men were scuffling with the sheriff. The latter soon gave up, vowing vengeance and the law. Torches were brought, and a rope. A wagon drove up and was backed into the yard. Then began the calls for the negro.

As Davies contemplated all this he could not help thinking of the negro who during all this turmoil must have been crouching in his corner in the cellar, trembling for his fate. Now indeed he must realize that his end was near. He could not have dozed or lost consciousness during the intervening hours, but must have been cowering there, wondering and praying. All the while he must have been terrified lest the sheriff might not get him away in time. Now, at the sound of horses' feet and the new murmurs of contention, how must his body quake and his teeth chatter!

"I'd hate to be that nigger," commented the postmaster grimly, "but you can't do anything with 'em. The county oughta sent help."

"It's horrible, horrible!" was all Davies could say.

He moved closer to the house, with the crowd, eager to observe every detail of the procedure. Now it was that a number of the men, as eager in their search as bloodhounds, appeared at a low cellar entryway at the side of the house carrying a rope. Others followed with torches. Headed by father and son they began to descend into the dark hole. With impressive daring, Davies, who was by no means sure that he would be allowed but who was also determined if possible to see, followed.

Suddenly, in the farthest corner, he espied Ingalls. The latter in his fear and agony had worked himself into a crouching position, as if he were about to spring. His nails were apparently forced into the earth. His eyes were rolling, his mouth foaming.

"Oh, my Lawd, boss," he moaned, gazing almost as one blind, at the lights, "oh, my Lawd, boss, don't kill me! I won't do it no mo'. I didn't go to do it. I didn't mean to dis time. I was just drunk, boss. Oh, my Lawd! My Lawd!" His teeth chattered the while his mouth seemed to gape open. He was no longer sane really, but kept repeating monotonously, "Oh, my Lawd!"

"Here he is, boys! Pull him out," cried the father.

The negro now gave one yell of terror and collapsed, falling prone. He quite bounded as he did so, coming down with a dead chug on the earthen floor. Reason had forsaken him. He was by now a groveling, foaming brute. The last gleam of intelligence was that which notified him of the set eyes of his pursuers.

Davies, who by now had retreated to the grass outside before this sight, was standing but ten feet back when they began to reappear after seizing and binding him. Although shaken to the roots of his being, he still had all the cool observing powers of the trained and relentless reporter. Even now he noted the color values of the scene, the red, smoky heads of the torches, the disheveled appearance of the men, the scuffling and pulling. Then all at once he clapped his hands over his mouth, almost unconscious of what he was doing.

"Oh, my God!" he whispered, his voice losing power.

The sickening sight was that of the negro, foaming at the mouth, bloodshot as to his eyes, his hands working convulsively, being dragged up the cellar steps feet foremost. They had tied a rope about his waist and feet, and so had hauled him out, leaving his head to hang and drag. The black face was distorted beyond all human semblance.

"Oh, my God!" said Davies again, biting his fingers unconsciously.

The crowd gathered about now more closely than ever, more horror-stricken than gleeful at their own work. None apparently had either the courage or the charity to gainsay what was being done. With a kind of mechanical deftness now the negro was rudely lifted and like a sack of wheat thrown into the wagon. Father and son now mounted in front to drive and the crowd took to their horses, content to clatter, a silent cavalcade, behind. As Davies afterwards concluded, they were not so much hardened lynchers perhaps as curious spectators, the majority of them, eager for any variation—any excuse for one—to the dreary commonplaces of their existences. The task to most—all indeed—was entirely new. Wide-eyed and nerve-racked, Davies ran for his own horse and mounting followed. He was so excited he scarcely knew what he was doing.

Slowly the silent company now took its way up the Sand River pike whence it had come. The moon was still high, pouring down a wash of silvery light. As Davies rode he wondered how he was to complete his telegram, but decided that he could not. When this was over there would be no time. How long would it be before they would really hang him? And would they? The whole procedure seemed so unreal, so barbaric that he could scarcely believe it—that he was a part of it. Still they rode on.

"Are they really going to hang him?" he asked of one who rode beside him, a total stranger who seemed however not to resent his presence.

"That's what they got 'im fer," answered the stranger.

And think, he thought to himself, to-morrow night he would be resting in his own good bed back in K——!

Davies dropped behind again and into silence and tried to recover his nerves. He could scarcely realize that he, ordinarily accustomed to the rou-

tine of the city, its humdrum and at least outward social regularity, was a part of this. The night was so soft, the air so refreshing. The shadowy trees were stirring with a cool night wind. Why should any one have to die this way? Why couldn't the people of Baldwin or elsewhere have bestirred themselves on the side of the law before this, just let it take its course? Both father and son now seemed brutal, the injury to the daughter and sister not so vital as all this. Still, also, custom seemed to require death in this way for this. It was like some axiomatic, mathematic law—hard, but custom. The silent company, an articulated, mechanical and therefore terrible thing, moved on. It also was axiomatic, mathematic. After a time he drew near to the wagon and looked at the negro again.

The latter, as Davies was glad to note, seemed still out of his sense. He was breathing heavily and groaning, but probably not with any conscious pain. His eyes were fixed and staring, his face and hands bleeding as if they had been scratched or trampled upon. He was crumpled limply.

But Davies could stand it no longer now. He fell back, sick at heart, content to see no more. It seemed a ghastly, murderous thing to do. Still the company moved on and he followed, past fields lit white by the moon, under dark, silent groups of trees, through which the moonlight fell in patches, up low hills and down into valleys, until at last a little stream came into view, the same little stream, as it proved, which he had seen earlier to-day and for a bridge over which they were heading. Here it ran now, sparkling like electricity in the night. After a time the road drew closer to the water and then crossed directly over the bridge, which could be seen a little way ahead.

Up to this the company now rode and then halted. The wagon was driven up on the bridge, and father and son got out. All the riders, including Davies, dismounted, and a full score of them gathered about the wagon from which the negro was lifted, quite as one might a bag. Fortunately, as Davies now told himself, he was still unconscious, an accidental mercy. Nevertheless he decided now that he could not witness the end, and went down by the waterside slightly above the bridge. He was not, after all, the utterly relentless reporter. From where he stood, however, he could see long beams of iron projecting out over the water, where the bridge was braced, and some of the men fastening a rope to a beam, and then he could see that they were fixing the other end around the negro's neck.

Finally the curious company stood back, and he turned his face away.

"Have you anything to say?" a voice demanded.

There was no answer. The negro was probably lolling and groaning, quite as unconscious as he was before.

Then came the concerted action of a dozen men, the lifting of the black mass into the air, and then Davies saw the limp form plunge down and pull up with a creaking sound of rope. In the weak moonlight it seemed as if the body were struggling, but he could not tell. He watched, wide-mouthed and silent, and then the body ceased moving. Then after a time he heard the company making ready to depart, and finally it did so, leaving him quite indifferently to himself and his thoughts. Only the black mass swaying in the pale light over the glimmering water seemed human and alive, his sole companion.

He sat down upon the bank and gazed in silence. Now the horror was gone. The suffering was ended. He was no longer afraid. Everything was summery and beautiful. The whole cavalcade had disappeared; the moon finally sank. His horse, tethered to a sapling beyond the bridge, waited patiently. Still he sat. He might now have hurried back to the small postoffice in Baldwin and attempted to file additional details of this story, providing he could find Seavey, but it would have done no good. It was quite too late, and anyhow what did it matter? No other reporter had been present, and he could write a fuller, sadder, more colorful story on the morrow. He wondered idly what had become of Seavey? Why had he not followed? Life seemed so sad, so strange, so mysterious, so inexplicable.

As he still sat there the light of morning broke, a tender lavender and gray in the east. Then came the roseate hues of dawn, all the wondrous coloring of celestial halls, to which the waters of the stream responded. The white pebbles shone pinkily at the bottom, the grass and sedges first black now gleamed a translucent green. Still the body hung there black and limp against the sky, and now a light breeze sprang up and stirred it visibly. At last he arose, mounted his horse and made his way back to Pleasant Valley, too full of the late tragedy to be much interested in anything else. Rousing his liveryman, he adjusted his difficulties with him by telling him the whole story, assuring him of his horse's care and handing him a five-dollar bill. Then he left, to walk and think again.

Since there was no train before noon and his duty plainly called him to a portion of another day's work here, he decided to make a day of it, idling about and getting additional details as to what further might be done. Who would cut the body down? What about arresting the lynchers—the father and son, for instance? What about the sheriff now? Would he act as he threatened? If he telegraphed the main fact of the lynching his city editor would not mind, he knew, his coming late, and the day here was so beautiful. He proceeded to talk with citizens and officials, rode out to the injured girl's home, rode to Baldwin to see the sheriff. There was a singular silence and placidity in that corner. The latter assured him that he knew nearly all of those who had taken part, and proposed to swear out warrants for them, but just the same Davies noted that he took his defeat as he did his danger, philosophically. There was no real activity in that corner later. He wished to remain a popular sheriff, no doubt.

It was sundown again before he remembered that he had not discovered whether the body had been removed. Nor had he heard why the negro came back, nor exactly how he was caught. A nine o'clock evening train to the city giving him a little more time for investigation, he decided to avail himself of it. The negro's cabin was two miles out along a pine-shaded road, but so pleasant was the evening that he decided to walk. En route, the last rays of the sinking sun stretched long shadows of budding trees across his path. It was not long before he came upon the cabin, a one-story affair set well back from the road and surrounded with a few scattered trees. By now it was quite dark. The ground between the cabin and the road was open, and strewn with the chips of a woodpile. The roof was sagged, and the windows patched in places, but for all that it had the glow of a home. Through the front door, which stood open, the blaze of a wood-fire might be seen, its yellow light filling the interior with a golden glow.

Hesitating before the door, Davies finally knocked. Receiving no answer he looked in on the battered cane chairs and aged furniture with considerable interest. It was a typical negro cabin, poor beyond the need of description. After a time a door in the rear of the room opened and a little negro girl entered carrying a battered tin lamp without any chimney. She had not heard his knock and started perceptibly at the sight of his figure in the doorway. Then she raised her smoking lamp above her head in order to see better, and approached.

There was something ridiculous about her unformed figure and loose gingham dress, as he noted. Her feet and hands were so large. Her black head was strongly emphasized by little pigtails of hair done up in white twine, which stood out all over her head. Her dark skin was made apparently more so by contrast with her white teeth and the whites of her eyes.

Davies looked at her for a moment but little moved now by the oddity which ordinarily would have amused him, and asked, "Is this where Ingalls lived?"

The girl nodded her head. She was exceedingly subdued, and looked as if she might have been crying.

"Has the body been brought here?"

"Yes, suh," she answered, with a soft negro accent.

"When did they bring it?"

"Dis moanin'."

"Are you his sister?"

"Yes, suh."

"Well, can you tell me how they caught him? When did he come back, and what for?" He was feeling slightly ashamed to intrude thus.

"In de afternoon, about two."

"And what for?" repeated Davies.

"To see us," answered the girl. "To see my motha'."

"Well, did he want anything? He didn't come just to see her, did he?"

"Yes, suh," said the girl, "he come to say good-by. We doan know when dey caught him." Her voice wavered.

"Well, didn't he know he might get caught?" asked Davies sympathetically, seeing that the girl was so moved.

"Yes, suh, I think he did."

She still stood very quietly holding the poor battered lamp up, and looking down.

"Well, what did he have to say?" asked Davies.

"He didn' have nothin' much to say, suh. He said he wanted to see motha'. He was a-goin' away."

The girl seemed to regard Davies as an official of some sort, and he knew it.

"Can I have a look at the body?" he asked.

The girl did not answer, but started as if to lead the way.

"When is the funeral?" he asked.

"Tomorra'."

The girl then led him through several bare sheds of rooms strung in a row to the furthermost one of the line. This last seemed a sort of storage shed for odds and ends. It had several windows, but they were quite bare of glass and open to the moonlight save for a few wooden boards nailed across from the outside. Davies had been wondering all the while where the body was and at the lonely and forsaken air of the place. No one but this little pig-tailed girl seemed about. If they had any colored neighbors they were probably afraid to be seen here.

Now, as he stepped into this cool, dark, exposed outer room, the desolation seemed quite complete. It was very bare, a mere shed or wash-room. There was the body in the middle of the room, stretched upon an ironing board which rested on a box and a chair, and covered with a white sheet. All the corners of the room were quite dark. Only its middle was brightened by splotches of silvery light.

Davies came forward, the while the girl left him, still carrying her lamp. Evidently she thought the moon lighted up the room sufficiently, and she did not feel equal to remaining. He lifted the sheet quite boldly, for he could see well enough, and looked at the still, black form. The face was extremely distorted, even in death, and he could see where the rope had tightened. A bar of cool moonlight lay just across the face and breast. He was still looking, thinking soon to restore the covering, when a sound, half sigh, half groan, reached his ears.

At it he started as if a ghost had made it. It was so eerie and unexpected in this dark place. His muscles tightened. Instantly his heart went hammering like mad. His first impression was that it must have come from the dead.

"Oo-o-ohh!" came the sound again, this time whimpering, as if some one were crying.

Instantly he turned, for now it seemed to come from a corner of the room, the extreme corner to his right, back of him. Greatly disturbed, he approached, and then as his eyes strained he seemed to catch the shadow of something, the figure of a woman, perhaps, crouching against the walls, huddled up, dark, almost indistinguishable.

"Oh, oh, oh!" the sound now repeated itself, even more plaintively than before.

Davies began to understand. He approached slowly, then more swiftly desired to withdraw, for he was in the presence of an old black mammy, doubled up and weeping. She was in the very niche of the two walls, her head sunk on her knees, her body quite still. "Oh, oh, oh!" she repeated, as he stood there near her.

Davies drew silently back. Before such grief his intrusion seemed cold and unwarranted. The guiltlessness of the mother—her love—how could one balance that against the other? The sensation of tears came to his eyes. He instantly covered the dead and withdrew.

Out in the moonlight he struck a brisk pace, but soon stopped and looked back. The whole dreary cabin, with its one golden eye, the door, seemed such a pitiful thing. The weeping mammy, alone in her corner—and he had come back to say "Good-by!" Davies swelled with feeling.

The night, the tragedy, the grief, he saw it all. But also with the cruel instinct of the budding artist that he already was, he was beginning to meditate on the character of story it would make—the color, the pathos. The knowledge now that it was not always exact justice that was meted out to all and that it was not so much the business of the writer to indict as to interpret was borne in on him with distinctness by the cruel sorrow of the mother, whose blame, if any, was infinitesimal.

"I'll get it all in!" he exclaimed feelingly, if triumphantly at last. "I'll get it all in!"

THE LOST PHOEBE

◇

❨ FROM *Free and Other Stories* (1918).

◇

THEY lived together in a part of the country which was not so prosperous as it had once been, about three miles from one of those small towns that, instead of increasing in population, is steadily decreasing. The territory was not very thickly settled; perhaps a house every other mile or so, with large areas of corn- and wheat-land and fallow fields that at odd seasons had been sown to timothy and clover. Their particular house was part log and part frame, the log portion being the old original home of Henry's grandfather. The new portion, of now rain-beaten, time-worn slabs, through which the wind squeaked in the chinks at times, and which several overshadowing elms and a butternut-tree made picturesque and reminiscently pathetic, but a little damp, was erected by Henry when he was twenty-one and just married.

That was forty-eight years before. The furniture inside, like the house outside, was old and mildewy and reminiscent of an earlier day. You have seen the what-not of cherry wood, perhaps, with spiral legs and fluted top. It was there. The old-fashioned four poster bed, with its ball-like protuberances and deep curving incisions, was there also, a sadly alienated descendant of an early Jacobean ancestor. The bureau of cherry was also high and wide and solidly built, but faded-looking, and with a musty odor. The rag carpet that underlay all these sturdy examples of enduring furniture was a weak, faded, lead-and-pink-colored affair woven by Phœbe Ann's own hands, when she was fifteen years younger than she was when she died. The creaky wooden loom on which it had been done now stood like a dusty, bony skeleton, along with a broken rocking-chair, a worm-eaten clothespress—Heaven knows how old—a lime-stained bench that had once been used to keep flowers on outside the door, and other decrepit factors of household utility, in an east room that was a lean-to against this so-called main portion. All sorts of other broken-down furniture were about this place; an antiquated clothes-horse, cracked in two of its ribs; a broken mirror in an old cherry frame, which had fallen from a nail and cracked itself three days before their youngest son, Jerry, died; an extension hat-rack, which once had had porcelain knobs on the ends of its pegs; and a sewing-machine, long since outdone in its clumsy mechanism by rivals of a newer generation.

The orchard to the east of the house was full of gnarled old apple-trees, worm-eaten as to trunks and branches, and fully ornamented with green and white lichens, so that it had a sad, greenish-white, silvery effect in moonlight. The low out-houses, which had once housed chickens, a horse or two, a cow, and several pigs, were covered with patches of moss as to their roof, and the sides had been free of paint for so long that they were blackish gray as to color, and a little spongy. The picket-fence in front, with its gate squeaky and askew, and the side fences of the stake-and-rider type were in an equally run-down condition. As a matter of fact, they had aged synchronously with the persons who lived here, old Henry Reifsneider and his wife Phœbe Ann.

They had lived here, these two, ever since their marriage, forty-eight years before, and Henry had lived here before that from his childhood up. His father and mother, well along in years when he was a boy, had invited him to bring his wife here when he had first fallen in love and decided to marry; and he had done so. His father and mother were the companions of himself and his wife for ten years after they were married, when both died; and then Henry and Phœbe were left with their five children growing lustily apace. But all sorts of things had happened since then. Of the seven children, all told, that had been born to them, three had died; one girl had gone to Kansas; one boy had gone to Sioux Falls, never even to be heard of after; another boy had gone to Washington; and the last girl lived five counties away in the same State, but was so burdened with cares of her own that she rarely gave them a thought. Time and a commonplace home life that had never been attractive had weaned them thoroughly, so that, wherever they were, they gave little thought as to how it might be with their father and mother.

Old Henry Reifsneider and his wife Phœbe were a loving couple. You perhaps know how it is with simple natures that fasten themselves like lichens on the stones of circumstance and weather their days to a crumbling conclusion. The great world sounds widely, but it has no call for them. They have no soaring intellect. The orchard, the meadow, the corn-field, the pig-pen, and the chicken-lot measure the range of their human activities. When the wheat is headed it is reaped and threshed; when the corn is browned and frosted it is cut and shocked; when the timothy is in full head it is cut, and the hay-cock erected. After that comes winter, with the hauling of grain to market, the sawing and splitting of wood, the simple chores of fire-building, meal-getting, occasional repairing, and visiting. Beyond these and the changes of weather—the snows, the rains, and the fair days—there are no immediate, significant things. All the rest of life is a far-off, clamorous phantasmagoria, flickering like Northern lights in the night, and sounding as faintly as cow-bells tinkling in the distance.

Old Henry and his wife Phœbe were as fond of each other as it is possible for two old people to be who have nothing else in this life to be fond of. He was a thin old man, seventy when she died, a queer, crotchety person with coarse gray-black hair and beard, quite straggly and unkempt. He looked at you out of dull, fishy, watery eyes that had deep-brown crow's-feet at the sides. His clothes, like the clothes of many farmers, were aged and angular and baggy, standing out at the pockets, not fitting about the neck, protuberant and worn at elbow and knee. Phœbe Ann was thin and shapeless, a very umbrella of a woman, clad in shabby black, and with a black bonnet for her best wear. As time had passed, and they had only themselves to look after, their movements had become slower and slower, their activities fewer and fewer. The annual keep of pigs had been reduced from five to one grunting porker, and the single horse which Henry now retained was a sleepy animal, not over-nourished and not very clean. The chickens, of which formerly there was a large flock, had almost disappeared, owing to ferrets, foxes, and the lack of proper care, which produces disease. The former healthy garden was now a straggling memory of itself, and the vines and flower-beds that formerly ornamented the windows and dooryard had now become choking thickets. A will had been made which divided

the small tax-eaten property equally among the remaining four, so that it was really of no interest to any of them. Yet these two lived together in peace and sympathy, only that now and then old Henry would become unduly cranky, complaining almost invariably that something had been neglected or mislaid which was of no importance at all.

"Phœbe, where's my corn-knife? You ain't never minded to let my things alone no more."

"Now you hush, Henry," his wife would caution him in a cracked and squeaky voice. "If you don't, I'll leave yuh. I'll git up and walk out of here some day, and then where would y' be? Y' ain't got anybody but me to look after yuh, so yuh just behave yourself. Your corn knife's on the mantel where it's allus been unless you've gone an' put it summers else."

Old Henry, who knew his wife would never leave him in any circumstances, used to speculate at times as to what he would do if she were to die. That was the one leaving that he really feared. As he climbed on the chair at night to wind the old, long-pendulumed, double-weighted clock, or went finally to the front and the back door to see that they were safely shut in, it was a comfort to know that Phœbe was there, properly ensconced on her side of the bed, and that if he stirred restlessly in the night, she would be there to ask what he wanted.

"Now, Henry, do lie still! You're as restless as a chicken."

"Well, I can't sleep, Phœbe."

"Well, yuh needn't roll so, anyhow. Yuh kin let me sleep."

This usually reduced him to a state of somnolent ease. If she wanted a pail of water, it was a grumbling pleasure for him to get it; and if she did rise first to build the fires, he saw that the wood was cut and placed within easy reach. They divided this simple world nicely between them.

As the years had gone on, however, fewer and fewer people had called. They were well-known for a distance of as much as ten square miles as old Mr. and Mrs. Reifsneider, honest, moderately Christian, but too old to be really interesting any longer. The writing of letters had become an almost impossible burden too difficult to continue or even negotiate via others, although an occasional letter still did arrive from the daughter in Pemberton County. Now and then some old friend stopped with a pie or cake or a roasted chicken or duck, or merely to see that they were well; but even these kindly minded visits were no longer frequent.

One day in the early spring of her sixty-fourth

year Mrs. Reifsneider took sick, and from a low fever passed into some indefinable ailment which, because of her age, was no longer curable. Old Henry drove to Swinnerton, the neighboring town, and procured a doctor. Some friends called, and the immediate care of her was taken off his hands. Then one chill spring night she died, and old Henry, in a fog of sorrow and uncertainty, followed her body to the nearest graveyard, an unattractive space with a few pines growing in it. Although he might have gone to the daughter in Pemberton or sent for her, it was really too much trouble and he was too weary and fixed. It was suggested to him at once by one friend and another that he come to stay with them awhile, but he did not see fit. He was so old and so fixed in his notions and so accustomed to the exact surroundings he had known all his days, that he could not think of leaving. He wanted to remain near where they had put his Phœbe; and the fact that he would have to live alone did not trouble him in the least. The living children were notified and the care of him offered if he would leave, but he would not.

"I kin make a shift for myself," he continually announced to old Dr. Morrow, who had attended his wife in this case. "I kin cook a little, and, besides, it don't take much more'n coffee an' bread in the mornin's to satisfy me. I'll get along now well enough. Yuh just let me be." And after many pleadings and proffers of advice, with supplies of coffee and bacon and baked bread duly offered and accepted, he was left to himself. For a while he sat idly outside his door brooding in the spring sun. He tried to revive his interest in farming, and to keep himself busy and free from thought by looking after the fields, which of late had been much neglected. It was a gloomy thing to come in of an evening, however, or in the afternoon and find no shadow of Phœbe where everything suggested her. By degrees he put a few of her things away. At night he sat beside his lamp and read in the papers that were left him occasionally or in a Bible that he had neglected for years, but he could get little solace from these things. Mostly he held his hand over his mouth and looked at the floor as he sat and thought of what had become of her, and how soon he himself would die. He made a great business of making his coffee in the morning and frying himself a little bacon at night; but his appetite was gone. The shell in which he had been housed so long seemed vacant, and its shadows were suggestive of immedicable griefs. So he lived quite dolefully for five long months, and then a change began.

It was one night, after he had looked after the front and the back door, wound the clock, blown out the light, and gone through all the selfsame motions that he had indulged in for years, that he went to bed not so much to sleep as to think. It was a moonlight night. The green-lichen-covered orchard just outside and to be seen from his bed where he now lay was a silvery affair, sweetly spectral. The moon shone through the east windows, throwing the pattern of the panes on the wooden floor, and making the old furniture, to which he was accustomed, stand out dimly in the room. As usual he had been thinking of Phœbe and the years when they had been young together, and of the children who had gone, and the poor shift he was making of his present days. The house was coming to be in a very bad state indeed. The bedclothes were in disorder and not clean, for he made a wretched shift of washing. It was a terror to him. The roof leaked, causing things, some of them, to remain damp for weeks at a time, but he was getting into that brooding state where he would accept anything rather than exert himself. He preferred to pace slowly to and fro or to sit and think.

By twelve o'clock of this particular night he was asleep, however, and by two had waked again. The moon by this time had shifted to a position on the western side of the house, and it now shone in through the windows of the living-room and those of the kitchen beyond. A certain combination of furniture—a chair near a table, with his coat on it, the half-open kitchen door casting a shadow, and the position of a lamp near a paper—gave him an exact representation of Phœbe leaning over the table as he had often seen her do in life. It gave him a great start. Could it be she—or her ghost? He had scarcely ever believed in spirits; and still—— He looked at her fixedly in the feeble half-light, his old hair tingling oddly at the roots, and then sat up. The figure did not move. He put his thin legs out of the bed and sat looking at her, wondering if this could really be Phœbe. They had talked of ghosts often in their lifetime, of apparitions and omens; but they had never agreed that such things could be. It had never been a part of his wife's creed that she could have a spirit that could return to walk the earth. Her after-world was quite a different affair, a vague heaven, no less, from which the righteous did not trouble to return. Yet here she was now, bending over the table in her black skirt and gray shawl, her pale profile outlined against the moonlight.

"Phœbe," he called, thrilling from head to toe and putting out one bony hand, "have yuh come back?"

The figure did not stir, and he arose and walked

uncertainly to the door, looking at it fixedly the while. As he drew near, however, the apparition resolved itself into its primal content—his old coat over the high-backed chair, the lamp by the paper, the half-open door.

"Well," he said to himself, his mouth open, "I thought shore I saw her." And he ran his hand strangely and vaguely through his hair, the while his nervous tension relaxed. Vanished as it had, it gave him the idea that she might return.

Another night, because of this first illusion, and because his mind was now constantly on her and he was old, he looked out of the window that was nearest his bed and commanded a hen-coop and pig-pen and a part of the wagon-shed, and there, a faint mist exuding from the damp of the ground, he thought he saw her again. It was one of those little wisps of mist, one of those faint exhalations of the earth that rise in a cool night after a warm day, and flicker like small white cypresses of fog before they disappear. In life it had been a custom of hers to cross this lot from her kitchen door to the pig-pen to throw in any scrap that was left from her cooking, and here she was again. He sat up and watched it strangely, doubtfully, because of his previous experience, but inclined, because of the nervous titillation that passed over his body, to believe that spirits really were, and that Phœbe, who would be concerned because of his lonely state, must be thinking about him, and hence returning. What other way would she have? How otherwise could she express herself? It would be within the province of her charity so to do, and like her loving interest in him. He quivered and watched it eagerly; but, a faint breath of air stirring, it wound away toward the fence and disappeared.

A third night, as he was actually dreaming, some ten days later, she came to his bedside and put her hand on his head.

"Poor Henry!" she said. "It's too bad."

He roused out of his sleep, actually to see her, he thought, moving from his bed-room into the one living-room, her figure a shadowy mass of black. The weak straining of his eyes caused little points of light to flicker about the outlines of her form. He arose, greatly astonished, walked the floor in the cool room, convinced that Phœbe was coming back to him. If he only thought sufficiently, if he made it perfectly clear by his feeling that he needed her greatly, she would come back, this kindly wife, and tell him what to do. She would perhaps be with him much of the time, in the night, anyhow; and that would make him less lonely, this state more endurable.

In age and with the feeble it is not such a far cry from the subtleties of illusion to actual hallucination, and in due time this transition was made for Henry. Night after night he waited, expecting her return. Once in his weird mood he thought he saw a pale light moving about the room, and another time he thought he saw her walking in the orchard after dark. It was one morning when the details of his lonely state were virtually unendurable that he woke with the thought that she was not dead. How he had arrived at this conclusion it is hard to say. His mind had gone. In its place was a fixed illusion. He and Phœbe had had a senseless quarrel. He had reproached her for not leaving his pipe where he was accustomed to find it, and she had left. It was an aberrated fulfillment of her old jesting threat that if he did not behave himself she would leave him.

"I guess I could find yuh ag'in," he had always said. But her cackling threat had always been:

"Yuh'll not find me if I ever leave yuh. I guess I kin git some place where yuh can't find me."

This morning when he arose he did not think to build the fire in the customary way or to grind his coffee and cut his bread, as was his wont, but solely to meditate as to where he should search for her and how he should induce her to come back. Recently the one horse had been dispensed with because he found it cumbersome and beyond his needs. He took down his soft crush hat after he had dressed himself, a new glint of interest and determination in his eye, and taking his black crook cane from behind the door, where he had always placed it, started out briskly to look for her among the nearest neighbors. His old shoes clumped soundly in the dust as he walked, and his gray-black locks, now grown rather long, straggled out in a dramatic fringe or halo from under his hat. His short coat stirred busily as he walked, and his hands and face were peaked and pale.

"Why, hello, Henry! Where're yuh goin' this mornin'?" inquired Farmer Dodge, who, hauling a load of wheat to market, encountered him on the public road. He had not seen the aged farmer in months, not since his wife's death, and he wondered now, seeing him looking so spry.

"Yuh ain't seen Phœbe, have yuh?" inquired the old man, looking up quizzically.

"Phœbe who?" inquired Farmer Dodge, not for the moment connecting the name with Henry's dead wife.

"Why, my wife Phœbe, o' course. Who do yuh s'pose I mean?" He stared up with a pathetic sharpness of glance from under his shaggy, gray eyebrows.

"Wall, I'll swan, Henry, yuh ain't jokin', are

yuh?" said the solid Dodge, a pursy man, with a smooth, hard, red face. "It can't be your wife yuh're talkin' about. She's dead."

"Dead! Shucks!" retorted the demented Reifsneider. "She left me early this mornin', while I was sleepin'. She allus got up to build the fire, but she's gone now. We had a little spat last night, an' I guess that's the reason. But I guess I kin find her. She's gone over to Matilda Race's; that's where she's gone."

He started briskly up the road, leaving the amazed Dodge to stare in wonder after him.

"Well, I'll be switched!" he said aloud to himself. "He's clean out'n his head. That poor old feller's been livin' down there till he's gone outen his mind. I'll have to notify the authorities." And he flicked his whip with great enthusiasm. "Geddap!" he said, and was off.

Reifsneider met no one else in this poorly populated region until he reached the whitewashed fence of Matilda Race and her husband three miles away. He had passed several other houses en route, but these not being within the range of his illusion were not considered. His wife, who had known Matilda well, must be here. He opened the picket-gate which guarded the walk, and stamped briskly up to the door.

"Why, Mr. Reifsneider," exclaimed old Matilda herself, a stout woman, looking out of the door in answer to his knock, "what brings yuh here this mornin'?"

"Is Phœbe here?" he demanded eagerly.

"Phœbe who? What Phœbe?" replied Mrs. Race, curious as to this sudden development of energy on his part.

"Why, my Phœbe, o' course. My wife Phœbe. Who do yuh s'pose? Ain't she here now?"

"Lawsy me!" exclaimed Mrs. Race, opening her mouth. "Yuh pore man! So you're clean out'n your mind now. Yuh come right in and sit down. I'll git yuh a cup o' coffee. O' course your wife ain't here; but yuh come in an' sit down. I'll find her fer yuh after a while. I know where she is."

The old farmer's eyes softened, and he entered. He was so thin and pale a specimen, pantalooned and patriarchal, that he aroused Mrs. Race's extremest sympathy as he took off his hat and laid it on his knees quite softly and mildly.

"We had a quarrel last night, an' she left me," he volunteered.

"Laws! laws!" sighed Mrs. Race, there being no one present with whom to share her astonishment as she went to her kitchen. "The pore man! Now somebody's just got to look after him. He can't be allowed to run around the country this way lookin' for his dead wife. It's turrible."

She boiled him a pot of coffee and brought in some of her new-baked bread and fresh butter. She set out some of her best jam and put a couple of eggs to boil, lying whole-heartedly the while.

"Now yuh stay right there, Uncle Henry, till Jake comes in, an' I'll send him to look for Phœbe. I think it's more'n likely she's over to Swinnerton with some o' her friends. Anyhow, we'll find out. Now yuh just drink this coffee an' eat this bread. Yuh must be tired. Yuh've had a long walk this mornin'." Her idea was to take counsel with Jake, "her man," and perhaps have him notify the authorities.

She bustled about, meditating on the uncertainties of life, while old Reifsneider thrummed on the rim of his hat with his pale fingers and later ate abstractedly of what she offered. His mind was on his wife, however, and since she was not here, or did not appear, it wandered vaguely away to a family by the name of Murray, miles away in another direction. He decided after a time that he would not wait for Jake Race to hunt his wife but would seek her for himself. He must be on, and urge her to come back.

"Well, I'll be goin'," he said, getting up and looking strangely about him. "I guess she didn't come here after all. She went over to the Murrays', I guess. I'll not wait any longer, Mis' Race. There's a lot to do over to the house to-day." And out he marched in the face of her protests taking to the dusty road again in the warm spring sun, his cane striking the earth as he went.

It was two hours later that this pale figure of a man appeared in the Murrays' doorway, dusty, perspiring, eager. He had tramped all of five miles, and it was noon. An amazed husband and wife of sixty heard his strange query, and realized also that he was mad. They begged him to stay to dinner, intending to notify the authorities later and see what could be done; but though he stayed to partake of a little something, he did not stay long, and was off again to another distant farmhouse, his idea of many things to do and his need of Phœbe impelling him. So it went for that day and the next and the next, the circle of his inquiry ever widening.

The process by which a character assumes the significance of being peculiar, his antics weird, yet harmless, in such a community is often involute and pathetic. This day, as has been said, saw Reifsneider at other doors, eagerly asking his unnatural question, and leaving a trail of amazement, sympathy, and pity in his wake. Although the authorities were informed—the county sheriff, no less—it was not deemed advisable to take him into custody; for when those who knew old Henry, and had for so long, reflected on the condition of the county insane asylum, a place which, because of the poverty of the district, was of staggering aberration and sickening environment, it was decided to let him remain at large; for, strange to relate, it was found on investigation that at night he returned peaceably enough to his lonesome domicile there to discover whether his wife had returned, and to brood in loneliness until the morning. Who would lock up a thin, eager, seeking old man with iron-gray hair and an attitude of kindly, innocent inquiry, particularly when he was well known for a past of only kindly servitude and reliability? Those who had known him best rather agreed that he should be allowed to roam at large. He could do no harm. There were many who were willing to help him as to food, old clothes, the odds and ends of his daily life—at least at first. His figure after a time became not so much a common-place as an accepted curiosity, and the replies, "Why, no, Henry; I ain't see her," or "No, Henry; she ain't been here to-day," more customary.

For several years thereafter then he was an odd figure in the sun and rain, on dusty roads and muddy ones, encountered occasionally in strange and unexpected places, pursuing his endless search. Undernourishment, after a time, although the neighbors and those who knew his history gladly contributed from their store, affected his body; for he walked much and ate little. The longer he roamed the public highway in this manner, the deeper became his strange hallucination; and finding it harder and harder to return from his more and more distant pilgrimages, he finally began taking a few utensils with him from his home, making a small package of them, in order that he might not be compelled to return. In an old tin coffee-pot of large size he placed a small tin cup, a knife, fork, and spoon, some salt and pepper, and to the outside of it, by a string forced through a pierced hole, he fastened a plate, which could be released, and which was his woodland table. It was no trouble for him to secure the little food that he needed, and with a strange, almost religious dignity, he had no hesitation in asking for that much. By degrees his hair became longer and longer, his once black hat became an earthen brown, and his clothes threadbare and dusty.

For all of three years he walked, and none knew how wide were his perambulations, nor how he survived the storms and cold. They could not see him, with homely rural understanding and forethought, sheltering himself in hay-cocks, or by the sides of cattle, whose warm bodies protected him from the cold, and whose dull understandings were not opposed to his harmless presence. Overhanging rocks and trees kept him at times from the rain, and a friendly hay-loft or corn-crib was not above his humble consideration.

The involute progression of hallucination is strange. From asking at doors and being constantly rebuffed or denied, he finally came to the conclusion that although his Phœbe might not be in any of the houses at the doors of which he inquired, she might nevertheless be within the sound of his voice. And so, from patient inquiry, he began to call sad, occasional cries, that ever and anon waked the quiet landscapes and ragged hill regions, and set to echoing his thin "O-o-o Phœbe! O-o-o Phœbe!" It had a pathetic, albeit insane, ring, and many a farmer or plowboy came to know it even from afar and say, "There goes old Reifsneider."

Another thing that puzzled him greatly after a time and after many hundreds of inquiries was, when he no longer had any particular dooryard in view and no special inquiry to make, which way to go. These cross-roads, which occasionally led in four or even six directions, came after a time to puzzle him. But to solve this knotty problem, which became more and more of a puzzle, there came to his aid another hallucination. Phœbe's spirit or some power of the air or wind or nature would tell him. If he stood at the center of the parting of the ways, closed his eyes, turned thrice about, and called "O-o-o Phœbe!" twice, and then threw his cane straight before him, that would surely indicate which way to go for Phœbe, or one of these mystic powers would surely govern its direction and fall! In whichever direction it went, even though, as was not infrequently the case, it took him back along the path he had already come, or across fields, he was not so far gone in his mind but that he gave himself ample time to search before he called again. Also the hallucination seemed to persist that at some time he would surely find her. There were hours when his feet were sore, and his limbs weary, when he would stop in the heat to wipe his seamed brow, or in the cold to beat his arms. Sometimes, after throwing away his cane, and finding it indicating the direction from which he had just come, he would shake his head wearily and philosophically, as if contemplating the unbelievable or an untoward fate, and then start briskly off. His strange figure came finally to be known in the farthest reaches of three or four counties. Old Reifsneider was a pathetic character. His fame was wide.

Near a little town called Watersville, in Green County, perhaps four miles from that minor cen-

ter of human activity, there was a place or precipice locally known as the Red Cliff, a sheer wall of
red sandstone, perhaps a hundred feet high, which
raised its sharp face for half a mile or more above
the fruitful cornfields and orchards that lay beneath, and which was surmounted by a thick grove
of trees. The slope that slowly led up to it from the
opposite side was covered by a rank growth of
beech, hickory, and ash, through which threaded
a number of wagon-tracks crossing at various
angles. In fair weather it had become old Reifsneider's habit, so inured was he by now to the
open, to make his bed in some such patch of trees
as this to fry his bacon or boil his eggs at the foot
of some tree before laying himself down for the
night. Occasionally, so light and inconsequential
was his sleep, he would walk at night. More often,
the moonlight or some sudden wind stirring in the
trees or a reconnoitering animal arousing him, he
would sit up and think, or pursue his quest in the
moonlight or the dark, a strange, unnatural, half
wild, half savage-looking but utterly harmless creature, calling at lonely road crossings, staring at
dark and shuttered houses, and wondering where,
where Phœbe could really be.

That particular lull that comes in the systole-
diastole of this earthly ball at two o'clock in the
morning invariably aroused him, and though he
might not go any farther he would sit up and
contemplate the darkness or the stars, wondering. Sometimes in the strange processes of his
mind he would fancy that he saw moving among
the trees the figure of his lost wife, and then he
would get up to follow, taking his utensils, always
on a string, and his cane. If she seemed to evade
him too easily he would run, or plead, or, suddenly losing track of the fancied figure, stand
awed or disappointed, grieving for the moment
over the almost insurmountable difficulties of his
search.

It was in the seventh year of these hopeless
peregrinations, in the dawn of a similar spring-
time to that in which his wife had died, that he
came at last one night to the vicinity of this selfsame patch that crowned the rise to the Red Cliff.
His far-flung cane, used as a divining-rod at the
last cross-roads, had brought him hither. He had
walked many, many miles. It was after ten o'clock
at night, and he was very weary. Long wandering
and little eating had left him but a shadow of his
former self. It was a question now not so much of
physical strength but of spiritual endurance
which kept him up. He had scarcely eaten this
day, and now exhausted he set himself down in
the dark to rest and possibly to sleep.

Curiously on this occasion a strange suggestion

of the presence of his wife surrounded him. It
would not be long now, he counseled with himself, although the long months had brought him
nothing, until he should see her, talk to her. He
fell asleep after a time, his head on his knees. At
midnight the moon began to rise, and at two in the
morning, his wakeful hour, was a large silver disk
shining through the trees to the east. He opened
his eyes when the radiance became strong, making a silver pattern at his feet and lighting the
woods with strange lusters and silvery, shadowy
forms. As usual, his old notion that his wife must
be near occurred to him on this occasion, and he
looked about him with a speculative, anticipatory
eye. What was it that moved in the distant shadows along the path by which he had entered—a
pale, flickering will-o'-the-wisp that bobbed
gracefully among the trees and riveted his expectant gaze? Moonlight and shadows combined to
give it a strange form and a stranger reality, this
fluttering of bog fire or dancing of wandering fire-
flies. Was it truly his lost Phœbe? By a circuitous
route it passed about him, and in his fevered state
he fancied that he could see the very eyes of her,
not as she was when he last saw her in the black
dress and shawl but now a strangely younger
Phœbe, gayer, sweeter, the one whom he had
known years before as a girl. Old Reifsneider got
up. He had been expecting and dreaming of this
hour all these years, and now as he saw the feeble
light dancing lightly before him he peered at it
questioningly, one thin hand in his gray hair.

Of a sudden there came to him now for the
first time in many years the full charm of her
girlish figure as he had known it in boyhood, the
pleasing, sympathetic smile, the brown hair, the
blue sash she had once worn about her waist at a
picnic, her gay, graceful movements. He walked
around the base of the tree, straining with his
eyes, forgetting for once his cane and utensils, and
following eagerly after. On she moved before him,
a will-o'-the-wisp of the spring, a little flame above
her head, and it seemed as though among the
small saplings of ash and beech and the thick
trunks of hickory and elm that she signaled with a
young, a lightsome hand.

"O Phœbe! Phœbe!" he called. "Have yuh
really come? Have yuh really answered me?" And
hurrying faster, he fell once, scrambling lamely
to his feet, only to see the light in the distance
dancing illusively on. On and on he hurried until
he was fairly running, brushing his ragged arms
against the trees, striking his hands and face
against impeding twigs. His hat was gone, his
lungs were breathless, his reason quite astray,
when coming to the edge of the cliff he saw her

below among a silvery bed of apple-trees now blooming in the spring.

"O Phœbe!" he called. "O Phœbe! Oh, no, don't leave me!" And feeling the lure of a world where love was young and Phœbe as this vision presented her, a delightful epitome of their quondam youth, he gave a gay cry of "Oh, wait, Phœbe!" and leaped.

Some farmer-boys, reconnoitering this region of bounty and prospect some few days afterward, found first the tin utensils tied together under the tree where he had left them, and then later at the foot of the cliff, pale, broken, but elate, a molded smile of peace and delight upon his lips, his body. His old hat was discovered lying under some low-growing saplings the twigs of which had held it back. No one of all the simple population knew how eagerly and joyously he had found his lost mate.

MY BROTHER PAUL

❖

❰ FROM *Twelve Men* (1919).

❖

I LIKE best to think of him as he was at the height of his all-too-brief reputation and success, when, as the author and composer of various American popular successes ("On the Banks of the Wabash," "Just Tell Them That You Saw Me," and various others), as a third owner of one of the most successful popular music publishing houses in the city and as an actor and playwright of some small repute, he was wont to spin like a moth in the white light of Broadway. By reason of a little luck and some talent he had come so far, done so much for himself. In his day he had been by turn a novitiate in a Western seminary which trained aspirants for the Catholic priesthood; a singer and entertainer with a perambulating cure-all oil troupe or wagon ("Hamlin's Wizard Oil") traveling throughout Ohio, Indiana and Illinois; both end- and middle-man with one, two or three different minstrel companies of repute; the editor or originator and author of a "funny column" in a Western small city paper; the author of the songs mentioned and a hundred others; a black-face monologue artist; a white-face ditto,

at Tony Pastor's, Miner's and Niblo's of the old days; a comic lead; co-star and star in such melodramas and farces as "The Danger Signal," "The Two Johns," "A Tin Soldier," "The Midnight Bell," "A Green Goods Man" (a farce which he himself wrote, by the way), and others. The man had a genius for the kind of gayety, poetry and romance which may, and no doubt must be, looked upon as exceedingly middle-class but which nonetheless had as much charm as anything in this world can well have. He had at this time absolutely no cares or financial worries of any kind, and this plus his health, self-amusing disposition and talent for entertaining, made him a most fascinating figure to contemplate.

My first recollection of him is of myself as a boy of ten and he a man of twenty-five (my oldest brother). He had come back to the town in which we were then living solely to find his mother and help her. Six or seven years before he had left without any explanation as to where he was going, tired of or irritated by the routine of a home which for any genuine opportunity it offered him might as well never have existed. It was run dominantly by my father in the interest of religious and moral theories, with which this boy had little sympathy. He was probably not understood by any one save my mother, who understood or at least sympathized with us all. Placed in a school which was to turn him out a priest, he had decamped, and now seven years later was here in this small town, with fur coat and silk hat, a smart cane—a gentleman of the theatrical profession. He had joined a minstrel show somewhere and had become an "end-man." He had suspected that we were not as fortunate in this world's goods as might be and so had returned. His really great heart had called him.

But the thing which haunts me, and which was typical of him then as throughout life, was the spirit which he then possessed and conveyed. It was one of an agile geniality, unmarred by thought of a serious character but warm and genuinely tender and with a taste for simple beauty which was most impressive. He was already the author of a cheap song-book, *"The Paul Dresser Songster"* ("All the Songs Sung in the Show"), and some copies of this he had with him, one of which he gave me. But we having no musical instrument of any kind, he taught me some of the melodies "by ear." The home in which by force of poverty we were compelled to live was most unprepossessing and inconvenient, and the result of his coming could but be our request for, or at least the obvious need of, assistance. Still he was as much an enthusiastic part of it as though he belonged to it. He was happy in it, and the cause of his happiness was my mother, of whom he was intensely fond. I recall how he hung about her in the kitchen or wherever she happened to be, how enthusiastically he related all his plans for the future, his amusing difficulties in the past. He was very grand and youthfully self-important, or so we all thought, and still he patted her on the shoulder or put his arm about her and kissed her. Until she died years later she was truly his uppermost thought, crying with her at times over her troubles and his. He contributed regularly to her support and sent home all his cast-off clothing to be made over for the younger ones. (Bless her tired hands!)

As I look back now on my life, I realize quite clearly that of all the members of my family, subsequent to my mother's death, the only one who truly understood me, or, better yet, sympathized with my intellectual and artistic point of view, was, strange as it may seem, this same Paul, my dearest brother. Not that he was in any way fitted intellectually or otherwise to enjoy high forms of art and learning and so guide me, or that he understood, even in later years (long after I had written "Sister Carrie," for instance), what it was that I was attempting to do; he never did. His world was that of the popular song, the middle-class actor or comedian, the middle-class comedy, and such humorous æsthetes of the writing world as Bill Nye, Petroleum V. Nasby, the authors of the Spoopendyke Papers, and "Samantha at Saratoga." As far as I could make out—and I say this in no lofty, condescending spirit, by any means —he was entirely full of simple, middle-class romance, middle-class humor, middle-class tenderness and middle-class grossness, all of which I am very free to say early disarmed and won me completely and kept me so much his debtor that I should hesitate to try to acknowledge or explain all that he did for or meant to me.

Imagine, if you can, a man weighing all of three hundred pounds, not more than five feet ten-and-one-half inches in height and yet of so lithesome a build that he gave not the least sense of either undue weight or lethargy. His temperament, always ebullient and radiant, presented him as a clever, eager, cheerful, emotional and always highly illusioned person with so collie-like a warmth that one found him compelling interest and even admiration. Easily cast down at times by the most trivial matters, at others, and for the most part, he was so spirited and bubbly and emotional and sentimental that your fiercest or most gloomy intellectual rages or moods could scarcely withstand his smile. This tenderness or sympathy of his, a very human appreciation of the weaknesses and errors as well as the toils and tribulations of most of us, was by far his outstanding and most engaging quality, and gave him a very definite force and charm. Admitting, as I freely do, that he was very sensuous (gross, some people might have called him), that he had an intense, possibly an undue fondness for women, a frivolous, childish, horse-playish sense of humor at times, still he had other qualities which were absolutely adorable. Life seemed positively to spring up fountain-like in him. One felt in him a capacity to do (in his possibly limited field); an ability to achieve, whether he was doing so at the moment or not, and a supreme willingness to share and radiate his success—qualities exceedingly rare, I believe. Some people are so successful, and yet you know their success is purely selfish—exclusive, not inclusive; they never permit you to share in their lives. Not so my good brother. He was generous to the point of self-destruction, and that is literally true. He was the mark if not the prey of all those who desired much or little for nothing, those who previously might not have rendered him a service of any kind. He was all life and color, and thousands (I use the word with care) noted and commented on it.

When I first came to New York he was easily the foremost popular song-writer of the day and was the cause of my coming, so soon at least, having established himself in the publishing field and being so comfortably settled as to offer me a kind of anchorage in so troubled a commercial sea. I was very much afraid of New York, but with him here it seemed not so bad. The firm of which he was a part had a floor or two in an old residence turned office building, as so many are in New York, in Twentieth Street very close to Broadway, and here, during the summer months (1894–7) when the various theatrical road-companies, one of which he was always a part, had returned for the closed season, he was to be found aiding his concern in the reception and care of possible applicants for songs and attracting by his personality such virtuosi of the vaudeville and comedy stage as were likely to make the instrumental publications of his firm a success.

I may as well say here that he had no more business skill than a fly. At the same time, he was in no wise sycophantic where either wealth, power or fame was concerned. He considered himself a personage of sorts, and was. The minister, the moralist, the religionist, the narrow, dogmatic and self-centered in any field were likely to be the butt of his humor, and he could imitate so many phases of character so cleverly that he was the life of any idle pleasure-seeking party anywhere. To this day I recall his characterization of an old Irish washerwoman arguing; a stout, truculent German laying down the law; lean, gloomy, out-at-elbows actors of the Hamlet or classic school complaining of their fate; the stingy skinflint haggling over a dollar, and always with a skill for titillating the risibilities which is vivid to me, even to this day. Other butts of his humor were the actor, the Irish day-laborer, the negro and the Hebrew. And how he could imitate them! It is useless to try to indicate such things in writing, the facial expression, the intonation, the gestures; these are not things of words. Perhaps I can best indicate the direction of his mind, if not his manner, by the following:

One night as we were on our way to a theater there stood on a nearby corner in the cold a blind man singing and at the same time holding out a little tin cup into which the coins of the charitably inclined were supposed to be dropped. At once my brother noticed him, for he had an eye for this sort of thing, the pathos of poverty as opposed to so gay a scene, the street with its hurrying theater crowds. At the same time, so inherently mischievous was his nature that although his sympathy for the suffering or the ill-used of fate was overwhelming, he could not resist combining his intended charity with a touch of the ridiculous.

"Got any pennies?" he demanded.

"Three or four."

Going over to an outdoor candystand he exchanged a quarter for pennies, then came back and waited until the singer, who had ceased singing, should begin a new melody. A custom of the singer's, since the song was of no import save as a means of attracting attention to him, was to interpolate a "Thank you" after each coin dropped in his cup and between the words of the song, regardless. It was this little idiosyncrasy which evidently had attracted my brother's attention, although it had not mine. Standing quite close, his pennies in his hand, he waited until the singer had resumed, then began dropping pennies, waiting each time for the "Thank you," which caused the song to go about as follows:

"Da-a-'ling" (Clink!—"Thank you!") "I am—" (Clink!—"Thank you!") "growing o-o-o-ld" (Clink!—"Thank you!"), "Silve-e-r—" (Clink!—"Thank you!") "threads among the—" (Clink!—"Thank you!") "go-o-o-ld—" (Clink! "Thank you!"). "Shine upon my-y" (Clink!— "Thank you!") "bro-o-ow toda-a-y" (Clink!— "Thank you!"), "Life is—" (Clink!—"Thank you!") "fading fast a-a-wa-a-ay" (Clink!— "Thank you!")—and so on ad infinitum, until finally the beggar himself seemed to hesitate a little and waver, only so solemn was his rôle of want and despair that of course he dared not but had to go on until the last penny was in, and until he was saying more "Thank yous" than words of the song. A passerby noticing it had begun to "Hawhaw!", at which others joined in, myself included. The beggar himself, a rather sniveling specimen, finally realizing what a figure he was cutting with his song and thanks, emptied the coins into his hand and with an indescribably wry expression, half-uncertainty and half-smile, exclaimed, "I'll have to thank you as long as you keep putting pennies in, I suppose. God bless you!"

My brother came away smiling and content.

However, it is not as a humorist or song-writer or publisher that I wish to portray him, but as an odd, lovable personality, possessed of so many interesting and peculiar and almost indescribable traits. Of all characters in fiction he perhaps most suggests Jack Falstaff, with his love of women, his bravado and bluster and his innate good nature and sympathy. Sympathy was really his outstanding characteristic, even more than humor, although the latter was always present. One might recite a thousand incidents of his generosity and out-of-hand charity, which contained no least thought of return or reward. I recall that once there was a boy who had been reared in one of the towns in which we had once lived who had never had a chance in his youth, educationally or in any other way, and, having turned out "bad" and sunk to the level of a bank robber, had been detected in connection with three other men in the act of robbing a bank, the watchman of which was subsequently killed in the mêlée and escape. Of all four criminals only this one had been caught. Somewhere in prison he had heard sung one of my brother's sentimental ballads, "The Convict and the Bird," and recollecting that he had known Paul wrote him, setting forth his life history and that now he had no money or friends.

At once my good brother was alive to the pathos of it. He showed the letter to me and wanted to know what could be done. I suggested a lawyer, of course, one of those brilliant legal friends of his—always he had enthusiastic admirers in all walks—who might take the case for little or nothing. There was the leader of Tammany Hall, Richard Croker, who could be reached, he being a friend of Paul's. There was the Governor himself to whom a plain recitation of the boy's unfortunate life might be addressed, and with some hope of profit.

All of these things he did, and more. He went to the prison (Sing Sing), saw the warden and told him the story of the boy's life, then went to the boy, or man, himself and gave him some money.

He was introduced to the Governor through influential friends and permitted to tell the tale. There was much delay, a reprieve, a commutation of the death penalty to life imprisonment—the best that could be done. But he was so grateful for that, so pleased. You would have thought at the time that it was his own life that had been spared.

"Good heavens!" I jested. "You'd think you'd done the man an inestimable service, getting him in the penitentiary for life!"

"That's right," he grinned—an unbelievably provoking smile. "He'd better be dead, wouldn't he? Well, I'll write and ask him which he'd rather have."

I recall again taking him to task for going to the rescue of a "down and out" actor who had been highly successful and apparently not very sympathetic in his day, one of that more or less gaudy clan that wastes its substance, or so it seemed to me then, in riotous living. But now being old and entirely discarded and forgotten, he was in need of sympathy and aid. By some chance he knew Paul, or Paul had known him, and now because of the former's obvious prosperity—he was much in the papers at the time—he had appealed to him. The man lived with a sister in a wretched little town far out on Long Island. On receiving his appeal Paul seemed to wish to investigate for himself, possibly to indulge in a little lofty romance or sentiment. At any rate he wanted me to go along for the sake of companionship, so one dreary November afternoon we went, saw the pantaloon, who did not impress me very much even in his age and misery for he still had a few of his theatrical manners and insincerities, and as we were coming away I said, "Paul, why should you be the goat in every case?" for I had noted ever since I had been in New York, which was several years then, that he was a victim of many such importunities. If it was not the widow of a deceased friend who needed a ton of coal or a sack of flour, or the reckless, headstrong boy of parents too poor to save him from a term in jail or the reformatory and who asked for fine-money or an appeal to higher powers for clemency, or a wastrel actor or actress "down and out" and unable to "get back to New York" and requiring his or her railroad fare wired prepaid, it was the dead wastrel actor or actress who needed a coffin and a decent form of burial.

"Well, you know how it is, Thee" (he nearly always addressed me thus), "when you're old and sick. As long as you're up and around and have money, everybody's your friend. But once you're down and out no one wants to see you any more —see?" Almost amusingly he was always sad over

those who had once been prosperous but who were now old and forgotten. Some of his silliest tender songs conveyed as much.

"Quite so," I complained, rather brashly, I suppose, "but why didn't he save a little money when he had it? He made as much as you'll ever make." The man had been a star. "He had plenty of it, didn't he? Why should he come to you?"

"Well, you know how it is, Thee," he explained in the kindliest and most apologetic way. "When you're young and healthy like that you don't think. I know how it is; I'm that way myself. We all have a little of it in us. I have; you have. And anyhow youth's the time to spend money if you're to get any good of it, isn't it? Of course when you're old you can't expect much, but still I always feel as though I'd like to help some of these old people." His eyes at such times always seemed more like those of a mother contemplating a sick or injured child than those of a man contemplating life.

"But, Paul," I insisted on another occasion when he had just wired twenty-five dollars somewhere to help bury some one. (My spirit was not so niggardly as fearsome. I was constantly terrified in those days by the thought of a poverty-stricken old age for myself and him—why, I don't know. I was by no means incompetent.) "Why don't you save your money? Why should you give it to every Tom, Dick and Harry that asks you? You're not a charity organization, and you're not called upon to feed and clothe and bury all the wasters who happen to cross your path. If you were down and out how many do you suppose would help you?"

"Well, you know," and his voice and manner were largely those of mother, the same wonder, the same wistfulness and sweetness, the same bubbling charity and tenderness of heart, "I can't say I haven't got it, can I?" He was at the height of his success at the time. "And anyhow, what's the use being so hard on people? We're all likely to get that way. You don't know what pulls people down sometimes—not wasting always. It's thoughtlessness, or trying to be happy. Remember how poor we were and how mamma and papa used to worry." Often these references to mother or father or their difficulties would bring tears to his eyes. "I can't stand to see people suffer, that's all, not if I have anything," and his eyes glowed sweetly. "And, after all," he added apologetically, "the little I give isn't much. They don't get so much out of me. They don't come to me every day."

Another time—one Christmas Eve it was, when I was comparatively new to New York (my second or third year), I was a little uncertain what to do, having no connections outside of Paul and two sisters, one of whom was then out of the city. The other, owing to various difficulties of her own and a temporary estrangement from us—more our fault than hers—was therefore not available. The rather drab state into which she had allowed her marital affections to lead her was the main reason that kept us apart. At any rate I felt that I could not, or rather would not, go there. At the same time, owing to some difficulty or irritation with the publishing house of which my brother was then part owner (it was publishing the magazine which I was editing), we twain were also estranged, nothing very deep really—a temporary feeling of distance and indifference.

So I had no place to go except to my room, which was in a poor part of the town, or out to dine where best I might—some moderate-priced hotel, was my thought. I had not seen my brother in three or four days, but after I had strolled a block or two up Broadway I encountered him. I have always thought that he had kept an eye on me and had really followed me; was looking, in short, to see what I would do. As usual he was most smartly and comfortably dressed.

"Where you going, Thee?" he called cheerfully.

"Oh, no place in particular," I replied rather suavely, I presume. "Just going up the street."

"Now, see here, sport," he began—a favorite expression of his, "sport"—with his face abeam, "what's the use you and me quarreling? It's Christmas Eve, ain't it? It's a shame! Come on, let's have a drink and then go out to dinner."

"Well," I said, rather uncompromisingly, for at times his seemingly extreme success and well-being irritated me, "I'll have a drink, but as for dinner, I have another engagement."

"Aw, don't say that. What's the use being sore? You know I always feel the same even if we do quarrel at times. Cut it out. Come on. You know I'm your brother, and you're mine. It's all right with me, Thee. Let's make it up, will you? Put 'er there! Come on, now. We'll go and have a drink, see, something hot—it's Christmas Eve, sport. The old home stuff."

He smiled winsomely, coaxingly, really tenderly, as only he could smile. I "gave in." But now as we entered the nearest shining bar, a Christmas crowd buzzing within and without (it was the old Fifth Avenue Hotel), a new thought seemed to strike him.

"Seen E—— lately?" he inquired, mentioning the name of the troubled sister who was having a very hard time indeed. Her husband had left her and she was struggling over the care of two children.

"No," I replied, rather shamefacedly, "not in a week or two—maybe more."

He clicked his tongue. He himself had not been near her in a month or more. His face fell, and he looked very depressed.

"It's too bad—a shame really. We oughtn't to do this way, you know, sport. It ain't right. What do you say to our going around there," it was in the upper thirties, "and see how she's making out? —take her a few things, eh? Whaddya say?"

I hadn't a spare dollar myself, but I knew well enough what he meant by "take a few things" and who would pay for them.

"Well, we'll have to hurry if we want to get anything now," I urged, falling in with the idea since it promised peace, plenty and good will all around, and we rushed the drink and departed. Near at hand was a branch of one of the greatest grocery companies of the city, and near it, too, his then favorite hotel, the Continental. En route we meditated on the impossibility of delivery, the fact that we would have to carry the things ourselves, but he at last solved that by declaring that he could commandeer negro porters or bootblacks from the Continental. We entered, and by sheer smiles on his part and some blarney heaped upon a floor-manager, secured a turkey, sweet potatoes, peas, beans, a salad, a strip of bacon, a ham, plum pudding, a basket of luscious fruit and I know not what else—provender, I am sure, for a dozen meals. While it was being wrapped and packed in borrowed baskets, soon to be returned, he went across the way to the hotel and came back with three grinning darkies who for the tip they knew they would receive preceded us up Broadway, the nearest path to our destination. On the way a few additional things were picked up: holly wreaths, toys, candy, nuts—and then, really not knowing whether our plan might not miscarry, we made our way through the side street and to the particular apartment, or, rather, flat-house, door, a most amusing Christmas procession, I fancy, wondering and worrying now whether she would be there.

But the door clicked in answer to our ring, and up we marched, the three darkies first, instructed to inquire for her and then insist on leaving the goods, while we lagged behind to see how she would take it.

The stage arrangement worked as planned. My sister opened the door and from the steps below we could hear her protesting that she had ordered nothing, but the door being open the negroes walked in and a moment or two afterwards ourselves. The packages were being piled on table and floor, while my sister, unable quite to grasp this sudden visitation and change of heart, stared.

"Just thought we'd come around and have supper with you, E——, and maybe dinner tomorrow if you'll let us," my brother chortled. "Merry Christmas, you know. Christmas Eve. The good old home stuff—see? Old sport here and I thought we couldn't stay away—tonight, anyhow."

He beamed on her in his most affectionate way, but she, suffering regret over the recent estrangement as well as the difficulties of life itself and the joy of this reunion, burst into tears, while the two little ones danced about, and he and I put our arms about her.

"There, there! It's all over now," he declared, tears welling in his eyes. "It's all off. We'll can this scrapping stuff. Thee and I are a couple of bums and we know it, but you can forgive us, can't you? We ought to be ashamed of ourselves, all of us, and that's the truth. We've been quarreling, too, haven't spoken for a week. Ain't that so, sport? But it's all right now, eh?"

There were tears in my eyes, too. One couldn't resist him. He had the power of achieving the tenderest results in the simplest ways. We then had supper, and breakfast the next morning, all staying and helping, even to the washing and drying of the dishes, and thereafter for I don't know how long we were all on the most affectionate terms, and he eventually died in this sister's home, ministered to with absolutely restless devotion by her for weeks before the end finally came.

But, as I have said, I always prefer to think of him at this, the very apex or tower window of his life. For most of this period he was gay and carefree. The music company of which he was a third owner was at the very top of its success. Its songs, as well as his, were everywhere. He had in turn at this time a suite at the Gilsey House, the Marlborough, the Normandie—always on Broadway, you see. The limelight district was his home. He rose in the morning to the clang of the cars and the honk of the automobiles outside; he retired at night as a gang of repair men under flaring torches might be repairing a track, or the milk trucks were rumbling to and from the ferries. He was in his way a public restaurant and hotel favorite, a shining light in the theater managers' offices, hotel bars and lobbies and wherever those flies of the Tenderloin, those passing lords and celebrities of the sporting, theatrical, newspaper and other worlds, are wont to gather. One of his intimates, as I now recall, was "Bat" Masterson, the Western and now retired (to Broadway!) bad man; Muldoon, the famous wrestler; Tod Sloane, the jockey; "Battling" Nelson; James J. Corbett; Kid McCoy; Terry McGovern—prize-fighters all. Such Tammany district leaders as James Murphy, "The" McManus,

Chrystie and Timothy Sullivan, Richard Carroll, and even Richard Croker, the then reigning Tammany boss, were all on his visiting list. He went to their meetings, rallies and district doings generally to sing and play, and they came to his "office" occasionally. Various high and mighties of the Roman Church, "fathers" with fine parishes and good wine cellars, and judges of various municipal courts, were also of his peculiar world. He was always running to one or the other "to get somebody out," or they to him to get him to contribute something to something, or to sing and play or act, and betimes they were meeting each other in hotel grills or elsewhere and having a drink and telling "funny stories."

Apropos of this sense of humor of his, this love of horseplay almost, I remember that once he had a new story to tell—a vulgar one of course—and with it he had been making me and a dozen others laugh until the tears coursed down our cheeks. It seemed new to everybody and, true to his rather fantastic moods, he was determined to be the first to tell it along Broadway. For some reason he was anxious to have me go along with him, possibly because he found me at that time an unvarying fountain of approval and laughter, possibly because he liked to show me off as his rising brother, as he insisted that I was. At between six and seven of a spring or summer evening, therefore, we issued from his suite at the Gilsey House, whither he had returned to dress, and invading the bar below were at once centered among a group who knew him. A whiskey, a cigar, the story told to one, two, three, five, ten to roars of laughter, and we were off, over the way to Weber & Fields (the Musical Burlesque House Supreme of those days) in the same block, where to the ticket seller and house manager, both of whom he knew, it was told. More laughter, a cigar perhaps. Then we were off again, this time to the ticket seller of Palmer's Theater at Thirtieth Street, thence to the bar of the Grand Hotel at Thirty-first, the Imperial at Thirty-second, the Martinique at Thirty-third, a famous drugstore at the southwest corner of Thirty-fourth and Broadway, now gone of course, the manager of which was a friend of his. It was a warm, moony night, and he took a glass of vichy "for looks' sake," as he said.

Then to the quondam Hotel Aulic at Thirty-fifth and Broadway—the center and home of the then much-berated "Hotel Aulic or Actors' School of Philosophy," and a most impressive actors' rendezvous where might have been seen in the course of an evening all the "second leads" and "light comedians" and "heavies" of this, that and the other road company, all blazing with startling

clothes and all explaining how they "knocked
'em" here and there: in Peoria, Pasadena, Walla-
Walla and where not. My brother shone like a star
when only one is in the sky.

Over the way then to the Herald Building, its
owls' eyes glowing in the night, its presses thundering, the elevated thundering beside it. Here was a
business manager whom he knew. Then to the
Herald Square Theater on the opposite side of the
street, ablaze with a small electric sign—among
the newest in the city. In this, as in the business office of the *Herald* was another manager, and he
knew them all. Thence to the Marlborough bar
and lobby at Thirty-sixth, the manager's office of
the Knickerbocker Theater at Thirty-eighth, stopping at the bar and lobby of the Normandie, where
some blazing professional beauty of the stage
waylaid him and exchanged theatrical witticisms
with him—and what else? Thence to the manager's
office of the Casino at Thirty-ninth, some bar
which was across the street, another in Thirty-
ninth west of Broadway, an Italian restaurant on
the ground floor of the Metropolitan at Fortieth
and Broadway, and at last but by no means least
and by such slow stages to the very door of the
then Mecca of Meccas of all theater- and sport-
dom, the sanctum sanctorum of all those sportive-
ly au fait, "wise," the "real thing"—the Hotel
Metropole at Broadway and Forty-second Street,
the then extreme northern limit of the white-light
district. And what a realm! Rounders and what not
were here ensconced at round tables, their backs
against the leather-cushioned wall seats, the adjoining windows open to all Broadway and the
then all but somber Forty-second Street.

It was wonderful, the loud clothes, the bright
straw hats, the canes, the diamonds, the "hot"
socks, the air of security and well-being, so easily
assumed by those who gain an all too brief hour
in this pretty, petty world of make-believe and
pleasure and pseudo-fame. Among them my dearest brother was at his best. It was "Paul" here and
"Paul" there—"Why, hello, Dresser, you're just
in time! Come on in. What'll you have? Let me tell
you something, Paul, a good one——" More
drinks, cigars, tales—magnificent tales of successes
made, "great shows" given, fights, deaths, marvelous winnings at cards, trickeries in racing, prize-
fighting; the "dogs" that some people were, the
magnificent, magnanimous "God's own salt" that
others were. The oaths, stories of women, what
low, vice-besmeared, crime-soaked ghoulas certain reigning beauties of the town or stage were—
and so on and so on ad infinitum.

But his story?—ah, yes. I had all but forgotten.
It was told in every place, not once but seven,

eight, nine, ten times. We did not eat until we
reached the Metropole, and it was ten-thirty when
we reached it! The handshakes, the road stories—
"This is my brother Theodore. He writes; he's a
newspaper man." The roars of laughter, the
drinks! "Ah, my boy, that's good, but let me tell
you one—one that I heard out in Louisville the
other day." A seedy, shabby ne'er-do-well of a
song-writer maybe stopping the successful author
in the midst of a tale to borrow a dollar. Another
actor, shabby and distrait, reciting the sad tale of a
year's misfortunes. Everywhere my dear brother
was called to, slapped on the back, chuckled with.
He was successful. One of his best songs was the
rage, he had an interest in a going musical concern, he could confer benefits, favors.

Ah, me! Ah, me! That one could be so great,
and that it should not last for ever and for ever!

Another of his outstanding characteristics was
his love of women, a really amusing and at times
ridiculous quality. He was always sighing over the
beauty, innocence, sweetness, this and that, of
young maidenhood in his songs, but in real life he
seemed to desire and attract quite a different type
—the young and beautiful, it is true, but also the
old, the homely and the somewhat savage—a
catholicity of taste I could never quite stomach.
It was "Paul dearest" here and "Paul dearest"
there, especially in his work in connection with
the music-house and the stage. In the former,
popular ballad singers of both sexes, some of the
women most attractive and willful, were most numerous, coming in daily from all parts of the world
apparently to find songs which they could sing on
the American or even the English stage. And it
was a part of his duty, as a member of the firm and
the one who principally "handled" the so-called
professional inquirers, to meet them and see that
they were shown what the catalogue contained.
Occasionally there was an aspiring female song-
writer, often mere women visitors.

Regardless, however, of whether they were
young, old, attractive or repulsive, male or female,
I never knew any one whose manner was more
uniformly winsome or who seemed so easily to dis-
arm or relax an indifferent or irritated mood. He
was positive sunshine, the same in quality as that
of a bright spring morning. His blue eyes focused
mellowly, his lips were tendrilled with smiles. He
had a brisk, quick manner, always somehow suggestive of my mother, who was never brisk.

And how he fascinated them, the women!
Their quite shameless daring where he was concerned! Positively, in the face of it I used to wonder what had become of all the vaunted and so-
called "stabilizing morality" of the world. None of

it seemed to be in the possession of these women, especially the young and beautiful. They were distant and freezing enough to all who did not interest them, but let a personality such as his come into view and they were all wiles, bending and alluring graces. It was so obvious, this fascination he had for them and they for him, that at times it took on a comic look.

"Get onto the hit he's making," one would nudge another and remark.

"Say, some tenderness, that!" This in reference to a smile or a melting glance on the part of a female.

"Nothing like a way with the ladies. Some baby, eh, boys?"—this following the flick of a skirt and a backward-tossed glance perhaps, as some noticeable beauty passed out.

"No wonder he's cheerful," a sour and yet philosophic vaudevillian, who was mostly out of a job and hung about the place for what free meals he could obtain, once remarked to me in a heavy and morose undertone. "If I had that many women crazy about me I'd be too."

And the results of these encounters with beauty! Always he had something most important to attend to, morning, noon or night, and whenever I encountered him after some such statement "the important thing" was, of course, a woman. As time went on and he began to look upon me as something more than a thin, spindling, dyspeptic and disgruntled youth, he began to wish to introduce me to some of his marvelous followers, and then I could see how completely dependent upon beauty in the flesh he was, how it made his life and world.

One day as we were all sitting in the office, a large group of vaudevillians, song-writers, singers, a chance remark gave rise to a subsequent practical joke at Paul's expense. "I'll bet," observed some one, "that if a strange man were to rush in here with a revolver and say, 'Where's the man that seduced my wife?' Paul would be the first to duck. He wouldn't wait to find out whether he was the one meant or not."

Much laughter followed, and some thought. The subject of this banter was, of course, not present at the time. There was one actor who hung about there who was decidedly skillful in make-up. On more than one occasion he had disguised himself there in the office for our benefit. Coöperating with us, he disguised himself now as a very severe and even savage-looking person of about thirty-five—side-burns, mustachios and goatee. Then, with our aid, timing his arrival to an hour when Paul was certain to be at his desk, he entered briskly and vigorously and, looking about with a savage air, demanded, "Where is Paul Dresser?"

The latter turned almost apprehensively, I thought, and at once seemed by no means captivated by the man's looks.

"That's Mr. Dresser there," explained one of the confederates most willingly.

The stranger turned and glared at him. "So you're the scoundrel that's been running around with my wife, are you?" he demanded, approaching him and placing one hand on his right hip.

Paul made no effort to explain. It did not occur to him to deny the allegation, although he had never seen the man before. With a rising and backward movement he fell against the rail behind him, lifting both hands in fright and exclaiming, "Why—why—Don't shoot!" His expression was one of guilt, astonishment, perplexity. As some one afterwards said. "As puzzled as if he was trying to discover which injured husband it might be." The shout that went up—for it was agreed beforehand that the joke must not be carried far—convinced him that a hoax had been perpetrated, and the removal by the actor of his hat, sideburns and mustache revealed the true character of the injured husband. At first inclined to be angry and sulky, later on he saw the humor of his own indefinite position in the matter and laughed as heartily as any. But I fancy it developed a strain of uncertainty in him also in regard to injured husbands, for he was never afterwards inclined to interest himself in the much-married, and gave such wives a wide berth.

But his great forte was of course his song-writing, and of this, before I speak of anything else, I wish to have my say. It was a gift, quite a compelling one, out of which, before he died, he had made thousands, all spent in the manner described. Never having the least power to interpret anything in a fine musical way, still he was always full of music of a tender, sometimes sad, sometimes gay, kind—that of the ballad-maker of a nation. He was constantly attempting to work them out of himself, not quickly but slowly, brooding as it were over the piano wherever he might find one and could have a little solitude, at times on the organ (his favorite instrument), improvising various sad or wistful strains, some of which he jotted down, others of which, having mastered, he strove to fit words to. At such times he preferred to be alone or with some one whose temperament in no way clashed but rather harmonized with his own. Living with one of my sisters for a period of years, he had a room specially fitted up for his composing work, a very small room for so very large a man, within which he would shut himself and thrum a melody by the hour, especially toward evening or at night. He seemed to have a peculiar fondness for the twilight hour, and at this time might thrum over one strain and another until over some particular one, a new song usually, he would be in tears!

And what pale little things they were really, mere bits and scraps of sentiment and melodrama in story form, most asinine sighings over home and mother and lost sweethearts and dead heroes such as never were in real life, and yet with something about them, in the music at least, which always appealed to me intensely and must have appealed to others, since they attained so wide a circulation. They bespoke, as I always felt, a wistful, seeking, uncertain temperament, tender and illusioned, with no practical knowledge of any side of life, but full of a true poetic feeling for the mystery and pathos of life and death, the wonder of the waters, the stars, the flowers, accidents of life, success, failure. Beginning with a song called "Wide Wings" (published by a small retail music-house in Evansville, Indiana), and followed by such national successes as "The Letter That Never Came," "I Believe It, For My Mother Told Me So" (!), "The Convict and the Bird," "The Pardon Came Too Late," "Just Tell Them That You Saw Me," "The Blue and the Grey," "On the Bowery," "On the Banks of the Wabash," and a number of others, he was never content to rest and never really happy, I think, save when composing. During this time, however, he was at different periods all the things I have described—a black-face monologue artist, an end- and at times a middle-man, a publisher, and so on.

I recall being with him at the time he composed two of his most famous successes: "Just Tell Them That You Saw Me," and "On the Banks of the Wabash," and noting his peculiar mood, almost amounting to a deep depression which ended a little later in marked elation or satisfaction, once he had succeeded in evoking something which really pleased him.

The first of these songs must have followed an actual encounter with some woman or girl whose life had seemingly if not actually gone to wreck on the shore of love or passion. At any rate he came into the office of his publishing house one gray November Sunday afternoon—it was our custom to go there occasionally, a dozen or more congenial souls, about as one might go to a club— and going into a small room which was fitted up with a piano as a "try-out" room (professionals desiring a song were frequently taught it in the office), he began improvising, or rather repeating over and over, a certain strain which was evidently in his mind. A little while later he came out and said, "Listen to this, will you, Thee?"

He played and sang the first verse and chorus.

In the middle of the latter, so moved was he by the sentiment of it, his voice broke and he had to stop. Tears stood in his eyes and he wiped them away. A moment or two later he was able to go through it without wavering and I thought it charming for the type of thing it was intended to be. Later on (the following spring) I was literally astonished to see how, after those various efforts usually made by popular music publishers to make a song "go" —advertising it in the *Clipper* and *Mirror*, getting various vaudeville singers to sing it, and so forth— it suddenly began to sell, thousands upon thousands of copies being wrapped in great bundles under my very eyes and shipped express or freight to various parts of the country. Letters and telegrams, even, from all parts of the nation began to pour in —"Forward express today——copies of Dresser's 'Tell Them That You Saw Me.' " The firm was at once as busy as a bee-hive, on "easy street" again, as the expression went, "in clover." Just before this there had been a slight slump in its business and in my brother's finances, but now once more he was his most engaging self. Every one in that layer of life which understands or takes an interest in popular songs and their creators knew of him and his song, his latest success. He was, as it were, a revivified figure on Broadway. His barbers, barkeepers, hotel clerks, theatrical box-office clerks, hotel managers and the stars and singers of the street knew of it and him. Some enterprising button firm got out a button on which the phrase was printed. Comedians on the stage, newspaper paragraphers, his bank teller or his tailor, even staid business men wishing to appear "up-to-date," used it as a parting salute. The hand-organs, the bands and the theater orchestras everywhere were using it. One could scarcely turn a corner or go into a cheap music hall or variety house without hearing a parody of it. It was wonderful, the enormous furore that it seemed to create, and of course my dear brother was privileged to walk about smiling and secure, his bank account large, his friends numerous, in the pink of health, and gloating over the fact that he was a success, well known, a genuine creator of popular songs.

It was the same with "On the Banks of the Wabash," possibly an even greater success, for it came eventually to be adopted by his native State as its State song, and in that region streets and a town were named after him. In an almost unintentional and unthinking way I had a hand in that, and it has always cheered me to think that I had, although I have never had the least talent for musical composition or song versification. It was one of those delightful summer Sunday mornings (1896, I believe), when I was still connected with his firm as editor of the little monthly they were issuing, and he and myself, living with my sister E—— that we had gone over to this office to do a little work. I had a number of current magazines I wished to examine; he was always wishing to compose something, to express that ebullient and emotional soul of his in some way.

"What do you suppose would make a good song these days?" he asked in an idle, meditative mood, sitting at the piano and thrumming while I at a nearby table was looking over my papers. "Why don't you give me an idea for one once in a while, sport? You ought to be able to suggest something."

"Me?" I queried, almost contemptuously, I suppose. I could be very lofty at times in regard to his work, much as I admired him—vain and yet more or less dependent snip that I was. "I can't write those things. Why don't you write something about a State or a river? Look at 'My Old Kentucky Home,' 'Dixie,' 'Old Black Joe'—why don't you do something like that, something that suggests a part of America? People like that. Take Indiana—what's the matter with it—the Wabash River? It's as good as any other river, and you were 'raised' beside it."

I have to smile even now as I recall the apparent zest or feeling with which all at once he seized on this. It seemed to appeal to him immensely. "That's not a bad idea," he agreed, "but how would you go about it? Why don't you write the words and let me put the music to them? We'll do it together!"

"But I can't," I replied. "I don't know how to do those things. You write it. I'll help—maybe."

After a little urging—I think the fineness of the morning had as much to do with it as anything—I took a piece of paper and after meditating a while scribbled in the most tentative manner imaginable the first verse and chorus of that song almost as it was published. I think one or two lines were too long or didn't rhyme, but eventually either he or I hammered them into shape, but before that I rather shamefacedly turned them over to him, for somehow I was convinced that this work was not for me and that I was rather loftily and cynically attempting what my good brother would do in all faith and feeling.

He read it, insisted that it was fine and that I should do a second verse, something with a story in it, a girl perhaps—a task which I solemnly rejected.

"No, you put it in. It's yours. I'm through."

Some time later, disagreeing with the firm as to the conduct of the magazine, I left—really was forced out—which raised a little feeling on my part; not on his, I am sure, for I was very difficult to deal with.

Time passed and I heard nothing. I had been able to succeed in a somewhat different realm, that of the magazine contributor, and although I thought a great deal of my brother I paid very little attention to him or his affairs, being much more concerned with my own. One spring night, however, the following year, as I was lying in my bed trying to sleep, I heard a quartette of boys in the distance approaching along the street in which I had my room. I could not make out the words at first but the melody at once attracted my attention. It was plaintive and compelling. I listened, attracted, satisfied that it was some new popular success that had "caught on." As they drew near my window I heard the words "On the Banks of the Wabash" most mellifluously harmonized.

I jumped up. They were my words! It was Paul's song! He had another "hit" then—"On the Banks of the Wabash," and they were singing it in the streets already! I leaned out of the window and listened as they approached and passed on, their arms about each other's shoulders, the whole song being sung in the still street, as it were, for my benefit. The night was so warm, delicious. A full moon was overhead. I was young, lonely, wistful. It brought back so much of my already spent youth that I was ready to cry—for joy principally. In three more months it was everywhere, in the papers, on the stage, on the street-organs, played by orchestras, bands, whistled and sung in the streets. One day on Broadway near the Marlborough I met my brother, gold-headed cane, silk shirt, a smart summer suit, a gay straw hat.

"Ah," I said, rather sarcastically, for I still felt peeved that he had shown so little interest in my affairs at the time I was leaving. "On the banks, I see."

"On the banks," he replied cordially. "You turned the trick for me, Thee, that time. What are you doing now? Why don't you ever come and see me? I'm still your brother, you know. A part of that is really yours."

"Cut that!" I replied most savagely. "I couldn't write a song like that in a million years. You know I couldn't. The words are nothing."

"Oh, all right. It's true, though, you know. Where do you keep yourself? Why don't you come and see me? Why be down on me? I live here, you know." He looked up at the then brisk and successful hotel.

"Well, maybe I will some time," I said distantly, but with no particular desire to mend matters, and we parted.

There was, however, several years later, a sequel to all this and one so characteristic of him that it has always remained in my mind as one of the really beautiful things of life, and I might as well tell it here and now. About five years later I had become so disappointed in connection with my work and the unfriendly pressure of life that I had suffered what subsequently appeared to have been a purely psychic breakdown or relapse, not physical, but one which left me in no mood or condition to go on with my work, or any work indeed in any form. Hope had disappeared in a sad haze. I could apparently succeed in nothing, do nothing mentally that was worth while. At the same time I had all but retired from the world, living on less and less until finally I had descended into those depths where I was in the grip of actual want, with no place to which my pride would let me turn. I had always been too vain and self-centered. Apparently there was but one door, and I was very close to it. To match my purse I had retired to a still sorrier neighborhood in B——, one of the poorest. I desired most of all to be let alone, to be to myself. Still I could not be, for occasionally I met people, and certain prospects and necessities drove me to various publishing houses. One day as I was walking in some street near Broadway (not on it) in New York, I ran into my brother quite by accident, he as prosperous and comfortable as ever. I think I resented him more than ever. He was of course astonished, shocked, as I could plainly see, by my appearance and desire not to be seen. He demanded to know where I was living, wanted me to come then and there and stay with him, wanted me to tell him what the trouble was—all of which I rather stubbornly refused to do and finally got away—not however without giving him my address, though with the caution that I wanted nothing.

The next morning he was there bright and early in a cab. He was the most vehement, the most tender, the most disturbed creature I have ever seen. He was like a distrait mother with a sick child more than anything else.

"For God's sake," he commented when he saw me, "living in a place like this—and at this number, too!" (130 it was, and he was superstitious as to the thirteen.) "I knew there'd be a damned thirteen in it!" he ejaculated. "And me over in New York! Jesus Christ! And you sick and run down this way! I might have known. It's just like you. I haven't heard a thing about you in I don't know when. Well, I'm not going back without you, that's all. You've got to come with me now, see? Get your clothes, that's all. The cabby'll take your trunk. I know just the place for you, and you're going there tomorrow or next day or next week,

but you're coming with me now. My God, I should think you'd be ashamed of yourself, and me feeling the way I do about you!" His eyes all but brimmed.

I was so morose and despondent that, grateful as I felt, I could scarcely take his mood at its value. I resented it, resented myself, my state, my life.

"I can't," I said finally, or so I thought. "I won't. I don't need your help. You don't owe me anything. You've done enough already."

"Owe, hell!" he retorted. "Who's talking about 'owe'? And you my brother—my own flesh and blood! Why, Thee, for that matter, I owe you half of 'On the Banks,' and you know it. You can't go on living like this. You're sick and discouraged. You can't fool me. Why, Thee, you're a big man. You've just got to come out of this! Damn it—don't you see—don't make me"—and he took out his handkerchief and wiped his eyes. "You can't help yourself now, but you can later, don't you see? Come on. Get your things. I'd never forgive myself if I didn't. You've got to come, that's all. I won't go without you," and he began looking about for my bag and trunk.

I still protested weakly, but in vain. His affection was so overwhelming and tender that it made me weak. I allowed him to help me get my things together. Then he paid the bill, a small one, and on the way to the hotel insisted on forcing a roll of bills on me, all that he had with him. I was compelled at once, that same day or the next, to indulge in a suit, hat, shoes, underwear, all that I needed. A bedroom adjoining his suite at the hotel was taken, and for two days I lived there, later accompanying him in his car to a famous sanitarium in Westchester, one in charge of an old friend of his, a well-known ex-wrestler whose fame for this sort of work was great. Here I was booked for six weeks, all expenses paid, until I should "be on my feet again," as he expressed it. Then he left, only to visit and revisit me until I returned to the city, fairly well restored in nerves if not in health.

But could one ever forget the mingled sadness and fervor of his original appeal, the actual distress written in his face, the unlimited generosity of his mood and deed as well as his unmerited self-denunciation? One pictures such tenderness and concern as existing between parents and children, but rarely between brothers. Here he was evincing the same thing, as soft as love itself, and he a man of years and some affairs and I an irritable, distrait and peevish soul.

Take note, ye men of satire and spleen. All men are not selfish or hard.

The final phase of course related to his untimely end. He was not quite fifty-five when he died, and with a slightly more rugged quality of mind he might have lasted to seventy. It was due really to the failure of his firm (internal dissensions and rivalries, in no way due to him, however, as I have been told) and what he foolishly deemed to be the end of his financial and social glory. His was one of those simple, confiding, non-hardy dispositions, warm and colorful but intensely sensitive, easily and even fatally chilled by the icy blasts of human difficulty, however slight. You have no doubt seen some animals, cats, dogs, birds, of an especially affectionate nature, which when translated to a strange or unfriendly climate soon droop and die. They have no spiritual resources wherewith to contemplate what they do not understand or know. Now his *friends* would leave him. Now that bright world of which he had been a part would know him no more. It was pathetic, really. He emanated a kind of fear. Depression and even despair seemed to hang about him like a cloak. He could not shake it off. And yet, literally, in his case there was nothing to fear, if he had only known.

And yet two years before he did die, I knew he would. Fantastic as it may seem, to be shut out from that bright world of which he deemed himself an essential figure was all but unendurable. He had no ready money now—not the same amount anyhow. He could not greet his old-time friends so gayly, entertain so freely. Meeting him on Broadway shortly after the failure and asking after his affairs, he talked of going into business for himself as a publisher, but I realized that he could not. He had neither the ability nor the talent for that, nor the heart. He was not a business man but a song-writer and actor, had never been anything but that. He tried in this new situation to write songs, but he could not. They were too morbid. What he needed was some one to buoy him up, a manager, a strong confidant of some kind, some one who would have taken his affairs in hand and shown him what to do. As it was he had no one. His friends, like winter-frightened birds, had already departed. Personally, I was in no position to do anything at the time, being more or less depressed myself and but slowly emerging from difficulties which had held me for a number of years.

About a year or so after he failed my sister E—— announced that Paul had been there and that he was coming to live with her. He could not pay so much then, being involved with all sorts of examinations of one kind and another, but neither did he have to. Her memory was not short; she gave him the fullness of her home. A few months later he was ostensibly connected with another publishing house, but by then he was feeling so poorly physically and was finding consolation probably in some drinking and the caresses of those feminine friends who have, alas, only caresses to offer. A little later I met a doctor who said, "Paul cannot live. He has pernicious anæmia. He is breaking down inside and doesn't know it. He can't last long. He's too depressed." I knew it was so and what the remedy was—money and success once more, the petty pettings and flattery of that little world of which he had been a part but which now was no more for him. Of all those who had been so lavish in their greetings and companionship earlier in his life, scarcely one, so far as I could make out, found him in that retired world to which he was forced. One or two pegged-out actors sought him and borrowed a little of the little that he had; a few others came when he had nothing at all. His partners, quarreling among themselves and feeling that they had done him an injustice, remained religiously away. He found, as he often told my sister, broken horse-shoes (a "bad sign"), met cross-eyed women, another "bad sign," was pursued apparently by the inimical number thirteen—and all these little straws depressed him horribly. Finally, being no longer strong enough to be about, he took to his bed and remained there days at a time, feeling well while in bed but weak when up. For a little while he would go "downtown" to see this, that and the other person, but would soon return. One day on coming back home he found one of his hats lying on his bed, accidentally put there by one of the children, and according to my sister, who was present at the time, he was all but petrified by the sight of it. To him it was the death —sign. Some one had told him so not long before!!!

Then, not incuriously, seeing the affectional tie that had always held us, he wanted to see me every day. He had a desire to talk to me about his early life, the romance of it—maybe I could write a story some time, tell something about him! (Best of brothers, here it is, a thin little flower to lay at your feet!) To please him I made notes, although I knew most of it. On these occasions he was always his old self, full of ridiculous stories, quips and slight *mots*, all in his old and best vein. He would soon be himself, he now insisted.

Then one evening in late November, before I had time to call upon him (I lived about a mile away), a hurry-call came from E——. He had suddenly died at five in the afternoon; a blood-vessel had burst in the head. When I arrived he was already cold in death, his soft hands folded over his chest, his face turned to one side on the pillow, that indescribable sweetness of expression about the eyes and mouth—the empty shell of the beetle. There were tears, a band of reporters from the papers, the next day obituary news articles, and after that a host of friends and flowers, flowers, flowers. It is amazing what satisfaction the average mind takes in standardized floral forms—broken columns and gates ajar!

Being ostensibly a Catholic, a Catholic sister-in-law and other relatives insistently arranged for a solemn high requiem mass at the church of one of his favorite rectors. All Broadway was there, more flowers, his latest song read from the altar. Then there was a carriage procession to a distant Catholic graveyard somewhere, his friend, the rector of the church officiating at the grave. It was so cold and dreary there, horrible. Later on he was removed to Chicago.

But still I think of him as not there or anywhere in the realm of space, but on Broadway between Twenty-ninth and Forty-second Streets, the spring and summer time at hand, the doors of the grills and bars of the hotels open, the rout of actors and actresses ambling to and fro, his own delicious presence dressed in his best, his "funny" stories, his songs being ground out by the hand organs, his friends extending their hands, clapping him on the shoulder, cackling over the latest idle yarn.

Ah, Broadway! Broadway! And you, my good brother! Here is the story that you wanted me to write, this little testimony to your memory, a pale, pale symbol of all I think and feel. Where are the thousand yarns I have laughed over, the music, the lights, the song?

Peace, peace. So shall it soon be with all of us. It was a dream. It is. I am. You are. And shall we grieve over or hark back to dreams?

SANCTUARY

◊

〖 FROM *Chains—Lesser Novels and Stories* (1927).

◊

I

PRIMARILY, there were the conditions under which she was brought to fifteen years of age: the crowded, scummy tenements; the narrow green-painted halls with their dim gas-jets, making the entrance look more like that of a morgue than a dwelling-place; the dirty halls and rooms with their green or blue or brown walls painted to save the cost of paper; the bare wooden floors, long since saturated with every type of grease and filth from oleomargarine and suet leaked from cheap fats or meats, to beer and whiskey and tobacco-juice. A little occasional scrubbing by some would-be hygienic tenant was presumed to keep or make clean some of the chambers and halls.

And then the streets outside—any of the streets by which she had ever been surrounded—block upon block of other red, bare, commonplace tenements crowded to the doors with human life, the space before them sped over by noisy, gassy trucks and vehicles of all kinds. And stifling in summer, dusty and icy in winter; decorated on occasion by stray cats and dogs, pawing in ashcans, watched over by lordly policemen, and always running with people, people, people—who made their living heaven only knows how, existing in such a manner as their surroundings suggested.

In this atmosphere were always longshoremen, wagon-drivers, sweepers of floors, washers of dishes, waiters, janitors, workers in laundries, factories—mostly in indifferent or decadent or despairing conditions. And all of these people existed, in so far as she ever knew, upon that mysterious, evanescent and fluctuating something known as the weekly wage.

Always about her there had been drunkenness, fighting, complaining, sickness or death; the police coming in, and arresting one and another; the gas man, the rent man, the furniture man, hammering at doors for their due—and not getting it—in due time the undertaker also arriving amid a great clamor, as though lives were the most precious things imaginable.

It is entirely conceivable that in viewing or in meditating upon an atmosphere such as this, one might conclude that no good could come out of it. What! a dung-heap grow a flower? Exactly, and often, a flower—but not to grow to any glorious maturity probably. Nevertheless a flower of the spirit at least might have its beginnings there. And if it shrank or withered in the miasmatic atmosphere—well, conceivably, that might be normal, although in reality all flowers thus embedded in infancy do not so wither. There are flowers and flowers.

Viewing Madeleine Kinsella at the ages of five, seven, eleven and thirteen even, it might have been conceded that she was a flower of sorts—admittedly not a brave, lustrous one of the orchid or gardenia persuasion, but a flower nevertheless. Her charm was simpler, more retiring, less vivid than is usually accorded the compliment of beauty. She was never rosy, never colorful in the high sense, never daring or aggressive. Always, from her infancy on, she seemed to herself and others to be slipping about the corners and out-of-the-way places of life, avoiding it, staring at it with wide, lamblike eyes, wondering at things, often fearfully.

Her face, always delicately oval and pale, was not of the force which attracted. Her eyes, a milkish blue-gray with a suggestion of black in the iris, her hair black, her hands long-fingered and slim, were not of a type which would appeal to the raw youth of her world. Unconsciously, and ever, her slender, longish body sank into graceful poses. Beside the hard, garish, colorful, strident types of her neighborhoods—the girls whom the boys liked —she was not fascinating, and yet, contemplated at odd moments as she grew, she was appealing enough—at times beautiful.

What most affected her youth and her life was the internal condition of her family, the poverty and general worthlessness of her parents. They were as poor as their poorest neighbor and quarrelsome, unhappy and meanspirited into the bargain. Her father came dimly into her understanding at somewhere near her seventh or eighth year as an undersized, contentious and drunken and wordy man, always more or less out of a job, irritated with her mother and her sister and brother, and always, as her mother seemed to think, a little the worse for drink.

"You're a liar! You're a liar! You're a liar! You're a liar!"—how well she remembered this sing-song echoing reiteration of his, in whatever basement or hole they were living in at the time! "You're a liar! I never did it! You're a liar! I wasn't there!"

Her mother, often partially intoxicated or morose because of her own ills, was only too willing to rejoin in kind. Her elder sister and brother, much more agreeable in their way and as much put upon as herself, were always coming in or running out somewhere and staying while the storm lasted; while she, shy and always a little frightened, seemed to look upon it all as unavoidable, possibly even essential. The world was always so stern, so mysterious, so nonunderstandable to Madeleine.

Again it might be, and often was, "Here, you, you brat, go an' get me a can o' beer! Gwan, now!" which she did quickly and fearfully enough, running to the nearest wretched corner saloon with the "can" or "growler," her slim little fingers closed tightly over the five-cent piece or dime entrusted to her, her eyes taking in the wonders and joys of the street even as she ran. She was so small at the time that her little arms were unable to reach quite the level of the bar, and she had to accept the aid of the bartender or some drinker. Then she would patiently wait while one of them teased her as to her size or until the beer was handed down.

Once, and once only, three "bad boys," knowing what she was going for and how wretched and shabby was her father, not able to revenge himself on any one outside his family, had seized her en route, forced open her hand and run away with the dime, leaving her to return fearsomely to her father, rubbing her eyes, and to be struck and abused soundly and told to fight—"Blank-blank you, what the hell are you good for if you can't do that?"

Only the vile language and the defensive soberness of her mother at the time saved her from a worse fate. As for the boys who had stolen the money, they only received curses and awful imprecations, which harmed no one.

Wretched variations of this same existence were endured by the other two members of the family, her brother Frank and her sister Tina.

The former was a slim and nervous youth, given to fits of savage temper like his father and not to be ordered and controlled exactly as his father would have him. At times, as Madeleine recalled, he appeared terribly resentful of the conditions that surrounded him and cursed and swore and even threatened to leave; at other times he was placid enough, at least not inclined to share the dreadful scenes which no one could avoid where her father was.

At the age of twelve or thirteen he secured work in a box-factory somewhere and for a while brought his wages home. But often there was no breakfast or dinner for him, and when his father and mother were deep in their cups or quarreling things were so generally neglected that even where home ties were strong no one of any worldly experience could have endured them, and he ran away.

His mother was always complaining of "the lumbago" and of not being able to get up, even when he and Tina were working and bringing home a portion of their weekly wage or all of it. If she did, it was only to hover over the wretched cookstove and brew herself a little tea and complain as before.

Madeleine had early, in her ignorant and fearsome way, tried to help, but she did not always know how and her mother was either too ill or too disgruntled with life to permit her to assist, had she been able.

As it had been with Frank so it was with Tina, only it came sooner.

When Madeleine was only five Tina was a grown girl of ten, with yellow hair and a pretty, often smiling face, and was already working some-where—in a candy store—for a dollar and a half a week. Later, when Madeleine was eight and Tina thirteen, the latter had graduated to a button-works and was earning three.

There was something rather admirable and yet disturbing connected dimly with Tina in Made-leine's mind, an atmosphere of rebelliousness and courage which she had never possessed and which she could not have described, lacking as she did a mind that registered the facts of life clearly. She only saw Tina, pretty and strong, coming and go-ing from her ninth to her thirteenth year, refusing to go for beer at her father's order and being cursed for it, even struck at or thrown at by him, sometimes by her mother, and often standing at the foot of the stairs after work hours or on a Sun-day afternoon or evening, looking at the crowded street or walking up and down with other girls and boys, when her mother wanted her to be doing things in the house—sweeping, washing dishes, making beds—dreary, gray tasks all.

"Fixin' your hair again! Fixin' your hair again! Fixin' your hair again!" she could hear her father screaming whenever she paused before the one cracked mirror to arrange her hair. "Always in front of that blank-blank mirror fixin' her hair! If you don't get away from in front of it I'll throw you an' the mirror in the street! What the hell are you always fixin' your hair for? Say? What're you always fixin' your hair for? Say! What? What're you always fixin' your hair for?"

But Tina was never cast down apparently, only silent. At times she sang and walked with an air. She dressed herself as attractively as possible, as if with the few things she had she was attempting to cast off the burden of the life by which she was surrounded. Always she was hiding things away from the others, never wanting them to touch any-thing of hers. And how she had hated her father as she grew, in bitter moments calling him a "sot" and a "fool."

Tina had never been very obedient, refusing to go to church or to do much of anything about the house. Whenever her father and mother were drinking or fighting she would slip away and stay with some girl in the neighborhood that she knew. And in spite of all this squalor and misery and the fact that they moved often and the food was bad, Tina, once she was twelve or thirteen, always seemed able to achieve an agreeable appearance.

Madeleine often remembered her in a plaid skirt she had got somewhere, which looked beautiful on her, and a little gilt pin which she wore at her neck. And she had a way of doing her yellow hair high on her head, which had stuck in Madeleine's mind perhaps because of her father's rude comments on it.

II

IT IS not surprising that Madeleine came to her twelfth and thirteenth years without any real un-derstanding of the great world about her and with-out any definite knowledge or skill. Her drunken mother was now more or less dependent upon her, her father having died of pneumonia and her brother and sister having disappeared to do for themselves.

Aside from petty beginners' tasks in shops or stores, or assisting her mother at washing or clean-ing, there was little that she could do at first. Mrs. Kinsella, actually compelled by the need for rent or food or fuel after a time, would get occasional work in a laundry or kitchen or at scrubbing or window-cleaning, but not for long. The pleasure of drink would soon rob her of that.

At these tasks Madeleine helped until she se-cured work in a candy factory in her thirteenth year at the wage of three-thirty a week. But even with this little money paid in regularly there was no assurance that her mother would add sufficient to it to provide either food or warmth. Betimes, and when Madeleine was working, her mother cheered her all too obvious sorrows with the bot-tle, and at nights or week-ends rewarded Made-leine with a gabble which was all the more painful because no material comfort came with it.

The child actually went hungry at times. Usu-ally, after a few drinks, her mother would begin to weep and recite her past ills: a process which re-duced her timorous and very sympathetic daughter to complete misery. In sheer desperation the child sought for some new way in her own mind. A re-duction in the working-force of the candy factory, putting her back in the ranks of the work-seekers once more, and a neighbor perceiving her wretched state and suggesting that some extra helpers were wanted in a department store at Christmastime, she applied there, but so wretched were her clothes by now that she was not even considered.

Then a man who had a restaurant in a nearby street gave her mother and Madeleine positions as dishwashers, but he was compelled to discharge her mother, although he wished to retain Made-leine. From this last, however, because of the frightening attentions of the cook, she had to flee, and without obtaining a part of the small pittance which was due her. Again, and because in times past she had aided her mother to clean in one place and another, she was able to get a place as servant in a family.

Those who know anything of the life of a domestic know how thoroughly unsatisfactory it is—the leanness, the lack of hope. As a domestic, wherever she was—and she obtained no superior places for the time being—she had only the kitchen for her chief chamber or a cubby-hole under the roof. Here, unless she was working elsewhere in the house or chose to visit her mother occasionally, she was expected to remain. Pots and pans and scrubbing and cleaning and bed-making were her world. If any one aside from her mother ever wanted to see her (which was rare) he or she could only come into the kitchen, an ugly and by day inconvenient realm.

She had, as she soon came to see, no privileges whatsoever. In the morning she was expected to be up before any one else, possibly after working late the night before. Breakfast had to be served for others before she herself could eat—what was left. Then came the sweeping and cleaning. In one place which she obtained in her fifteenth year the husband annoyed her so, when his wife was not looking, that she had to leave; in another it was the son. By now she was becoming more attractive, although by no means beautiful or daring.

But wherever she was and whatever she was doing, she could not help thinking of her mother and Tina and Frank and her father, and of the grim necessities and errors and vices which had seemed to dominate them. Neither her brother nor her sister did she ever see again. Her mother, she felt (and this was due to a sensitiveness and a sympathy which she could not possibly overcome), she would have with her for the rest of her days unless, like the others, she chose to run away.

Daily her mother was growing more inadequate and less given to restraint or consideration. As "bad" as she was, Madeleine could not help thinking what a "hard" time she had had. From whatever places she obtained work in these days (and it was not often any more) she was soon discharged, and then she would come inquiring after Madeleine, asking to be permitted to see her. Naturally, her shabby dress and shawl and rag of a hat, as well as her wastrel appearance, were an affront to any well-ordered household. Once in her presence, whenever Madeleine was permitted to see her, she would begin either a cozening or a lachrymose account of her great needs.

"It's out o' oil I am, me dear," or "Wurra, I have no wood" or "bread" or "meat"—never drink. "Ye won't let yer pore old mother go cold or hungry, now, will ye? That's the good girl now. Fifty cents now, if ye have it, me darlin', or a quarter, an' I'll not be troublin' ye soon again. Even a dime, if ye can spare me no more. God'll

reward ye. I'll have work o' me own to-morra. That's the good girl now—ye won't let me go away without anything."

Oscillating between shame and sympathy, her daughter would take from the little she had and give it to her, tremulous for fear the disturbing figure would prove her undoing. Then the old woman would go out, lurching sometimes in her cups, and disappear, while an observant fellow servant was probably seeing and reporting to the mistress, who, of course, did not want her to come there and so told the girl, or, more practical still, discharged her.

Thus from her fourteenth to her sixteenth year she was shunted from house to house and from shop to shop, always in the vain hope that this time her mother might let her alone.

And at the very same time, life, sweetened by the harmonies of youth in the blood, was calling—that exterior life which promised everything because so far it had given nothing. The little simple things of existence, the very ordinary necessities of clothing and ornament, with which the heart of youth and the inherent pride of appearance are gratified, had a value entirely disproportionate to their worth. Yes, already she had turned the age wherein the chemic harmonies in youth begin to sing, thought to thought, color to color, dream to dream. She was being touched by the promise of life itself.

And then, as was natural, love in the guise of youth, a rather sophisticated gallant somewhat above the world in which she was moving, appeared and paid his all but worthless court to her. He was physically charming, the son of a grocer of some means in the vicinity in which she was working, a handsome youth with pink cheeks and light hair and blue eyes, and vanity enough for ten. Because she was shy and pretty he became passingly interested in her.

"Oh, I saw you cleaning the windows yesterday," this with a radiant, winning smile; or "You must live down toward Blake Street. I see you going down that way once in a while."

Madeleine acknowledged rather shamefacedly that it was true. That so dashing a boy should be interested in her was too marvelous.

In the evenings, or at any time, it was easy for a youth of his skill and *savoir-faire* to pick her out of the bobbing stream of humanity in which she occasionally did errands or visited her mother in her shabby room, and to suggest that he be permitted to call upon her. Or, failing that, because of her mother's shabby quarters and her mother herself, that the following Sunday would be ideal for an outing to one of those tawdry, noisy beaches to which he liked to go with other boys and girls in a car.

A single trip to Wonderland, a single visit to one of its halls where music sounded to the splash of the waves and where he did his best to teach her to dance, a single meal in one of its gaudy, noisy restaurants, a taste of its whirly pleasures, and a new color and fillip were given to hope, a new and seemingly realizable dream of happiness implanted in her young mind. The world was happier than she had thought, or could be made so; not all people fought and screamed at each other. There were such things as tenderness, soft words, sweet words.

But the way of so sophisticated a youth with a maid was brief and direct. His mind was of that order which finds in the freshness of womankind a mere passing delight, something to be deflowered and then put aside. He was a part of a group that secured its happiness in rifling youth, the youth of those whose lives were so dull and bleak that a few words of kindness, a little change of scene, the mere proximity of experience and force such as they had never known, were pay ample for anything which they might give or do.

And of these Madeleine was one.

Never having had anything in her own life, the mere thought of a man so vigorous and handsome, one with knowledge enough to show her more of life than she had ever dreamed of, to take her to places of color and light, to assure her that she was fitted for better things even though they were not immediately forthcoming, was sufficient to cause her to place faith where it was least worthy of being placed. To win his way there was even talk of marriage later on, that love should be generous and have faith—and then—

III

PLAIN-CLOTHESMAN Amundsen, patrolling hawklike the region of Fourteenth and K streets, not so far from Blake, where Madeleine had lived for a time, was becoming interested in and slightly suspicious of a new face.

For several days at odd hours, he had seen a girl half-slinking, half-brazening her way through a region the very atmosphere of which was blemishing to virtue. To be sure, he had not yet seen her speak to any one; nor was there that in her glance or manner which caused him to feel that she might.

Still—with the assurance of his authority and his past skill in trapping many he followed discreetly, seeing where she went, how she lingered for awhile nervously, then returned as she had come. She was very young, not more than seventeen.

He adjusted his tie and collar and decided to attempt his skill.

"Excuse me, Miss. Out for a little stroll? So am I. Mind my walking along with you a little way? Wouldn't like to come and have a drink, would you? I work in an automobile place over here in Grey Street, and I'm just off for the afternoon. Live here in the neighborhood?"

Madeleine surveyed this stranger with troubled eyes. Since the day her youthful lover had deserted her, and after facing every conceivable type of ill, but never being willing to confess or fall back upon her drunken, dreaming mother for aid, she had tested every device. The necessities and expenses incident to a prospective, and to her degrading state, as well as the continued care of her mother, had compelled her, as she had finally seen it, to come to this—for a time anyhow. A street girl, finding her wandering and crying, had taken her in hand and shown her, after aiding her for weeks, how to make her way.

Her burden that she feared so much was artificially if ruthlessly and criminally disposed of. Then she was shown the way of the streets until she could gain a new foothold in life; only, as she had since learned, it was difficult for her to accommodate herself to this fell traffic. She was not of it spiritually. She really did not intend to continue in it; it was just a temporary makeshift, born of fear and a dumb despair.

But neither Detective Amundsen nor the law was ready to believe that. To the former she seemed as worthless as any—one of those curious, uncared-for flowers never understood by the dull.

In a nearby café she had listened to his inquiries, the fact that he had a room in a nearby hotel, or could secure one. Contemning a fate which drove her to such favors, and fully resolved to leave it soon, to make something better of her life in the future, she went with him.

Then came the scarring realization that he was an officer of the law, a cynical, contemptuous hawk smirking over her tears and her explanations. It was absolutely nothing to him that she was so young and could scarcely have been as hardened as he pretended. She was compelled to walk through the streets with him to the nearest police station, while he nodded to or stopped to explain to passing brothers of the cloth the nature of his latest conquest.

There was the registering of her under the false name that she chose, rather than be exposed under her true one, before a brusque and staring sergeant in shirtsleeves; a cell with a wooden bench, the first she had ever known; a matron who searched her; then a ride somewhere in a closed vehicle, and the usual swift and confusing arraignment before a judge whose glance was seemingly so cold that it was frightening.

"Nellie Fitzpatrick; Officer Amundsen, Eighth Precinct."

The friend who had taught her the ways of the streets had warned her that if caught and arrested it might mean months of incarceration in some institution, the processes or corrective meaning of which she did not quite comprehend. All that she had grasped fully was that it meant a severance from her freedom, the few little things, pitiful as they were, that she could call her own. And now here she was, in the clutches of the law, and with no one to defend her.

The testimony of the officer was as it had been in hundreds of cases before this; he had been walking his beat and she had accosted him, as usual.

There being no legal alternative, the magistrate had held her for sentence, pending investigation, and the investigation proving, as it only could, that her life would be better were some corrective measures applied to it, she was sent away. She had never had any training worthy the name. Her mother was an irresponsible inebriate. A few months in some institution where she could be taught some trade or craft would be best.

And so it was that for a period of a year she was turned over to the care of the Sisterhood of the Good Shepherd.

IV

THE GRAY and bony walls of that institution starkly dominated one of the barest and most unprepossessing regions of the city. Its northern façade fronted a stone-yard, beyond which were the rocks of the racing Sound and a lighthouse. To the east, rocks and the river, a gray expanse in winter picked over by gulls, mourned over by the horns of endless craft. To the south, bare coal-yards, wagon-yards, tenements.

Twice weekly, sentenced delinquents of various ages—the "children," of whom Madeleine was one; the "girls," ranging from eighteen to thirty; the "women," ranging from thirty to fifty; and the old people, ranging from fifty until the last years of life—were brought here in an all but airtight cage, boxed like a great circus van, and with only small barred air-holes at the top. Inside the van were bare, hard benches, one against either wall. A representative of the probation and control system of the city, a gaunt female of many years, sat within; also an officer of such prodigious proportions that the mere sight of him might well raise the inquiry of why so much unnecessary luggage. For amusement in dull hours he smoothed his broad mouth with the back of his red, hairy hand, and dreamed of bygone days.

The institution itself was operated by a Mother Superior and thirty nuns, all of the order mentioned, all expert in their separate ways in cooking, housekeeping, laundering, buying, lace-making, teaching, and a half dozen other practical or applied arts.

Within the institution were separate wings or sections for each of the four groups before mentioned, sections in which each had its separate working, eating, sleeping and playing rooms. Only one thing was shared in common: the daily, and often twice or thrice daily, religious ceremonies in the great chapel, a lofty, magi-decorated and be-altared and be-candled chamber, whose tall, thin spire surmounted with a cross might easily be seen from many of the chambers in which the different groups worked. There were masses in the mornings, vespers and late prayers in the afternoons, often late prayers at night or on holidays, when additional services of one kind and another were held. To the religious-minded these were of course consoling. To the contrary-minded they became at times a strain.

Always, and over all the work and all the routine relaxations or pleasures of the institution, there hung the grim insistence of the law, its executive arm, upon order, seemliness, and, if not penance, at least a servility of mind which was the equivalent thereof. Let the voices of the nuns be never so soft, their footfalls light, their manners courteous, their ways gentle, persuasive, sympathetic, their mood tender; back of it all lay the shadow of the force which could forthwith return any or all to the rough hands of the police, the stern and not-to-be-evaded dictum of the courts.

This, much more than any look of disappointment or displeasure, if such were ever necessary, spoke to these delinquents or victims, whatever their mood, and quieted them in their most rebellious hours. Try as they would, they could not but remember that it was the law that had placed them here and now detained them. That there reigned here peace, order, sweetness and harmony, was well enough, comforting in cases, yet and always the life here had obviously a two-fold base: one the power of the law itself, the other the gentle, appealing, beautiful suasion of the nuns.

But to so inexperienced and as yet unreasoning a child as Madeleine all of this savored at this time of but one thing: the sharp, crude, inconsiderate and uninquiring forces of law or life, which seemed never to stop and inquire how or why, but only to order how, and that without mercy. Like some frightened animal faced by a terrifying enemy, she had thus far been able to think only of some darksome corner into which she might slip and hide, a secret place so inconspicuous and minute that the great savage world without would not trouble or care to follow.

And well enough the majority of the Sisterhood, especially those in immediate authority over her, understood the probable direction and ramifications of her present thoughts.

They knew her mood, for had they not during years past dealt with many such? And stern as was the law, they were not unmindful of her welfare. So long as she was willing and obedient there was but one thing more: that somehow her troubled or resentful or congealed and probably cruelly injured mind should be wooed from its blind belief in the essential injustice of life, to be made to feel, as they themselves were ready to believe, that all paths were not closed, all forces not essentially dark or evil.

For them there was hope of sorts for all, a way out, and many—even she—might find ways and means of facing life, better possibly than any she had ever known.

V

SISTER ST. AGNES, for instance, who controlled the spotlessly clean but barnlike and bleak room in which were a hundred machines for the sewing of shirtwaists, was a creature of none too fortunate a history herself.

Returning at the age of eighteen and at the death of her father from a convent in which she had been placed by him in order to escape the atmosphere of a home which he himself had found unsatisfactory, she had found a fashionable mother leading a life of which she could scarcely conceive, let alone accept. The taint, the subterfuge, the self-indulgent waste, had as soon sickened her as had the streets Madeleine.

Disappointed, she felt herself after a time incapable of enduring it and had fled, seeking first to make her way in a world which offered only meagre wages and a barren life to those incapable of enduring its rugged and often shameless devices; later, again wearied of her own trials, she had returned to the convent in which she had been trained and asked to be schooled for service there. Finding the life too simple for a nature grown more rugged, she had asked to be, and had been, transferred to the House of the Good Shepherd, finding there for the first time, in this institution, duties and opportunities which somehow matched her ideals.

And by the same token the Mother Superior of this same institution, Mother St. Bertha, who often came through and inquired into the story of each one, was of a history and of an order of mind which was not unlike that of Sister St. Agnes, only it had even more of genuine pathos and suffering in it. The daughter of a shoe manufacturer, she had seen her father fail, her mother die of consumption, a favorite brother drink and carouse until he finally fell under the blight of disease and died. The subsequent death of her father, to whom she had devoted her years, and the failing of her own dreams of a personal love, had saddened her, and she sought out and was admitted to this order in the hope that she, too, might still make especial use of a life that promised all too little in the world outside.

Her great comfort was in having some one or something to love, the satisfaction of feeling that lives which otherwise might have come to nothing had by some service of hers been lifted to a better state. And in that thought she worked here daily, going about among those incarcerated in different quarters, seeing to it that their tasks were not too severe, their comforts and hopes, where hope still remained, in nowise betrayed.

But to Madeleine at first the solemn habits of the nuns, as well as the gray gingham apron she had to don, the grayer woolen dress, the severe manner in which she had to dress her hair, her very plain shoes, the fact that she had to rise at six-thirty, attend mass and then breakfast at eight, work from eight-thirty to twelve-thirty, and again from one-thirty to four; lunch regularly at twelve-thirty and sup at six, attend a form of prayer service at four-thirty, play at simple games with her new companions between five and six and again between seven and nine, and then promptly retire to a huge sleeping-ward set with small white iron beds in long rows, and lit, after the retiring bell had sounded, by small oil cups or candles burning faintly before various images, all smacked of penance, the more disturbing because it was strange, a form of personal control which she had not sought and could not at once accept.

Nor could she help thinking that some severer form of punishment was yet to be meted out to her, or might ensue by reason of one unavoidable error or another. Life had always been so with her. But, once here a time, things proved not so bad.

The large workroom with its hundred machines and its tall windows, which afforded a stark view of the coal-pockets to the south, and the river with its boats and gulls, proved not unpleasing. The clean, bright windows, polished floors and walls— washed and cleaned by the inmates themselves, the nuns not disdaining to do their share—and the habits of the Sisters, their white-fringed hoods, black robes and clinking beads and their silent tread and low speech, impressed her greatly.

The fact that there was no severe reproof for any failure to comprehend at first, but only slow and patient explanations of simple things, not difficult in themselves to do; that aside from the routine duties, the marching in line with hands crossed over breast and head up, as well as genuflections at mass, prayers before and after meals, at rising and on retiring and at the peal of the Angelus, morning, noon and night, there was no real oppression, finally caused her to like it.

The girls who were here with her, shy or silent or cold or indifferent at first, and each with her world of past experiences, contacts and relationships locked in her heart, were still, placed as they were elbow to elbow at work, at meals, at prayer, at retiring, incapable of not achieving some kind of remote fellowship which eventually led to speech and confidences.

Thus the young girl who sat next at her right in the sewing-room—Viola Patters by name, a brave, blonde, cheerful little thing—although she had endured much that might be called ill-fortune, was still intensely interested in life.

By degrees and as they worked the two reached an understanding. Viola confessed that her father, who was a non-union painter by trade, had always worked well enough when he could get work, but that he managed badly and could not always get it. Her mother was sickly and they were very poor and there were many children.

Viola had first worked in a box-factory, where she had been able to earn only three dollars or less at piece work—"pasting corners," as she described it—and once she had been sworn at and even thrown away from a table at which she had been working because she didn't do it right, and then she quit. Then her father in turn swearing at her for her "uppishness," she had got work in a five-and-ten-cent store, where she had received three dollars a week and a commission of one per cent on her sales, which were not sufficient to yield more than a dollar more. Then she had secured a better place in a department store at five dollars a week, and there it was that she had come by the handsome boy who had caused her so much trouble.

He was a taxi-driver, who always had a car at his disposal when he worked, only it was very seldom that he cared to work. Although he married her swiftly enough and took her away from her family, still he had not supported her very well, and shortly after they were married he was arrested and accused with two others of stealing a machine and selling it, and after months and months of jail life he had been sentenced to three years in the penitentiary.

In the meantime he had called upon her to aid him, pressed her to raise sums of which she had never previously dreamed—and by ways of which she had never previously dreamed—was pleaded with, all but ordered—and still she loved him. And then in executing the "how" of it she had been picked up by the police and sent here, as had Madeleine, only she never told, not even to Madeleine, what the police had never discovered—that at the suggestion of her first love she had included robbery among her arts.

"But I don't care," she had whispered finally as they worked. "He was good to me, anyhow, when he had work. He was crazy about me, and he liked to go places and dance and eat and see shows when he had money, and he always took me. Gee, the times we've had! And if he wants me to stick to him when he gets out, I will. He ain't half as bad as some. Gee, you oughta hear some of the girls talk!"

And so it was finally that Madeleine was induced to tell her story.

There were other girls here who, once this bond of sympathy was struck, were keen enough to tell their tales—sad, unfortunate, harried lives all—and somehow the mere telling of them restored to Madeleine some of her earlier faint confidence or interest in life. It was "bad," but it was vivid. For in spite of their unfortunate beginnings, the slime in which primarily and without any willing of their own they had been embedded and from which nearly all were seeking to crawl upwards, and bravely enough, they had heart for and faith in life.

In all cases, apparently, love was their star as well as their bane. They thought chiefly of the joy that might be had in joining their lives with some man or being out in the free world, working again possibly, at least in touch in some feeble way with the beauty and gayety of life, as beauty and gayety manifested themselves to them.

And so by degrees, the crash of her own original hopes echoing less and less loudly in the distance, the pain of her great shame and rude awakening passed farther and farther from her. The smoothness and regularity of this austere life, indifferent as it seemed at times, consoled her by its very security and remoteness from the world. It was lean and spare, to be sure, but it offered safety and rest to the mind and heart. Now, rising in her dim, silent ward of a morning, repeating her instructed prayers, marching in silence to chapel, to breakfast, to work, hearing only the soft hum of the ma-

chines, marching again to chapel, playing each
day, but not too noisily, and finally retiring in the
same ordered and silent way to her tiny bed, she
was soothed and healed.

And yet, or perhaps because of this, she could
not help thinking of the clangor and crash of the
world without. It had been grim and painful to
her, but in its rude, brutal way it had been alive.
The lighted streets at night! The cars! That dancing pavilion in which once she had been taught to
dance by the great blue sea! The vanished touches
of her faithless lover's hands—his kisses—brief,
so soon over! Where was he now in the great
strange world outside? With whom? What was she
like? And would he tire of her as quickly? Treat
her as badly? Where was Tina? Frank? Her
mother? What had happened to her mother? Not a
word had she heard.

To Sister St. Agnes, after a time, sensing her
to be generous, faithful, patient, she had confided
all concerning herself and her mother, crying on
her shoulder, and the Sister had promised to learn
what she could. But the investigation proving that
her mother had been sent to the workhouse, she
deemed it best to say nothing for the present.
Madeleine would find her quickly enough on returning to the world. Why cloud the new budding
life with so shameful a memory?

VI

AND THEN once more, in due time, and with the
memory of these things clinging fast to her, she
was sent forth into the world, not quite as
poorly-armed as before, perhaps, but still with the
limited equipment which her own innate disposition and comprehension compelled.

After many serious and presumably wise injunctions as to the snares and pitfalls of this world, and
accompanied by a black-habited nun, who took her
direct to one of those moral and religious families
whose strict adherence to the tenets of this particular faith was held to provide an ideal example, she
was left to her own devices and the type of work
she had previously followed, the nuns themselves
being hard put to it to discover anything above the
most menial forms of employment for their various charges. Theirs was a type of schooling and
training which did not rise above a theory of
morality requiring not so much skill as faith and
blind obedience.

And again, here, as in the institution itself, the
idea of a faith, a religion, a benign power above
that of man and seeking his welfare, surrounded
her as the very air itself or as an aura, although she
personally was by no means ready to accept it,
never having given it serious thought.

Everywhere here, as in the institution itself,
were little images or colored pictures of saints,
their brows circled by stars or crowns, their hands
holding sceptres or lilies, their bodies arrayed in
graceful and soothing robes of white, blue, pink
and gold. Their faces were serene, their eyes be-
nignly contemplative, yet to Madeleine they were
still images only, pretty and graceful, even comforting, but at so great variance to life as she knew
it as to be little more than pretty pictures.

In the great church which they attended, and to
which they persuaded her to accompany them,
were more of these same candle-lit pictures of
saints, images and altars starred with candles,
many or few, at which she was wont to stare in
wonder and awe. The vestments of the priest and
the acolytes, the white-and-gold and red-and-
gold of the chasuble and the stole and the cope,
the gold and silver crosses, chalices and winecups,
overawed her inexperienced and somewhat impressionable mind without convincing it of the immanence of superior forces whose significance or
import she could in nowise guess. God, God, God
—she heard of Him and the passion and death of
the self-sacrificing Lord Jesus.

And here, as there, the silence, the order, the
cleanliness and regularity, as well as simplicity,
were the things which most invested her reason and
offered the greatest contrasts to her old life.

She had not known or sensed the significance of
these things before. Now, day by day, like the dripping of water, the ticking of time, they made an
impression, however slight. Routine, routine, routine, and the habit and order and color of a vast
and autocratic religion, made their lasting impression upon her.

And yet, in spite of an occasional supervisory
visit on the part of one or other of the nuns of the
probation department, she was not only permitted
but compelled to work out her life as best she
might, and upon such wages as she could command or devise. For all the prayers and the good-
will of the nuns, life was as insistent and driving
as ever. It did not appear to be so involved with
religion. In spite of the admonitions of the church,
the family for whom she was working saw little
more in its religious obligation than that she should
be housed and fed according to her material merits.
If she wished to better herself, as she soon very
clearly saw she must, she would have to develop
a skill which she did not now have and which, once
developed, would make her of small use here. At
the same time, if the months spent in the institution had conveyed to her the reasonableness of
making something better of her life than hitherto
she had been able to do, the world, pleasure,

hope, clanged as insistently and as wooingly as ever before.

But how? How? was the great problem. Hers was no resourceful, valiant soul, capable of making its own interesting way alone. Think as she would, and try, love, and love only, the admiration and ministering care of some capable and affectionate man was the only thing that seemed likely to solve for her the various earthly difficulties which beset her.

But even as to this, how, in what saving or perfect way, was love to come to her? She had made one mistake which in the development of any honest relationship with another would have to be confessed. And how would it be then? Would love, admiration, forgive? Love, love, love, and the peace and comfort of that happy routine home life which she imagined she saw operative in the lives of others—how it glimmered afar, like a star!

And again there was her mother.

It was not long after she had come from the institution that sheer loneliness, as well as a sense of daughterly responsibility and pity, had urged her to look up her mother, in order that she might restore to herself some little trace of a home, however wretched it might be. She had no one, as she proceeded to argue. At least in her own lonely life her mother provided, or would, an ear and a voice, sympathetic if begging, a place to go.

She had learned on returning to their last living-place on one of her afternoons off, that her mother had been sent away to the "Island," but had come back and since had been sent to the city poor-farm. This last inquiry led eventually to her mother's discovery of her and of her fixing herself upon her once more as a dependent, until her death somewhat over a year later.

But in the meantime, and after all, life continued to call and call and to drive her on, for she was still full of the hope and fever of youth.

Once, before leaving the institution in which they had worked together, Viola Patters had said to her in one of those bursts of confidence based on attraction:

"Once you're outa here an' I am, too, I'd like to see you again, only there ain't no use your writin' me here, for I don't believe they'd give it to me. I don't believe they'd want us to run together. I don't believe they like me as well as they do you. But you write me, wherever you are, care of——," and here she gave a definite address—"an' I'll get it when I get out."

She assured Madeleine that she would probably be able to get a good place, once she was free of the control of the Sisters, and then she might be able to do something for her.

Often during these dark new days she thought of this, and being hard-pressed for diverting interests in her life she finally wrote her, receiving in due time a request to come and see her.

But, as it proved, Viola was no avenue of improvement for her in her new mood. She was, as Madeleine soon discovered, part of a small group which was making its way along a path which she had promised herself henceforth to avoid. Viola was more comfortably placed in quarters of her own than Madeleine had ever been, but the method by which she was forwarding her life she could not as readily accept.

Yet her own life, move about as she might and did after a time from one small position to another, in store or factory, in the hope of bettering herself, held nothing either. Day by day as she worked she sensed all the more clearly that the meagre tasks at which she toiled could bring her nothing of permanent value. Her mother was dead now, and she more alone than ever. During a period of several years, in which she worked and dreamed, leading a thin, underpaid life, her mind was ever on love and what it might do for her—the pressure of a seeking hand, the sanctuary of an enveloping heart.

And then, for the second time in her brief life, love came, or seemed to—at least in her own heart if nowhere else.

She had by now, and through her own efforts, attained to a clerkship in one of the great stores at the salary of seven dollars a week, on which she was trying to live. And then, behold, one day among her customers one of those suave and artful masters of the art of living by one's wits, with a fortune of looks, to whom womanhood is a thing to be taken by an upward curl of a pair of mustachios, the vain placement of ringed locks, spotless and conspicuous linen, and clothes and shoes of a newness and lustre all but disturbing to a very work-a-day world. His manners and glances were of a winsomeness which only the feminine heart—and that unschooled in the valuelessness of veneer—fully appreciates.

Yes, the sheer grace of the seeking male, his shallow and heartless courtesy, the lustre of his eye and skin, a certain something of shabby-grand manner, such as she had never known in the particularly narrow world in which she moved, was sufficient to arrest and fix her interest.

He leaned over and examined the stationery and pencils which she sold, commenting on prices, the routine of her work, smiled archly and suggested by his manner entire that she was one in whom he could be deeply interested. At the same time a certain animal magnetism, of the workings of which she was no more conscious than might be any stick or stone, took her in its tow.

Here was one out of many, a handsome beau, who was interested in her and her little life. The oiled and curled hair became the crown of a god; the mustachios and the sharp, cruel nose harmonies of exquisite beauty. Even the muscular, prehensile hands were rhythmic, musical in their movements. She had time only to sense the wonder of his perfect self before he went away. But it was to return another day, with an even more familiar and insinuating grace.

He was interested in her, as he frankly said the next time, and she must be his friend. At lunchtime one day he was waiting to take her to a better restaurant than she would ever have dreamed of entering; on another day it was to dinner that she accompanied him.

According to him, she was beautiful, wonderful. Her flower-like life was being wasted on so rude a task. She should marry him, and then her difficulties would be solved. He was one who, when fortune was with him, so he said, made much, much money. He might even take her from the city at times to see strange places and interesting scenes.

As for her own stunted life, from most of the details of which she forbore, he seemed in nowise interested. It was not due to any lack on her part in the past that her life had been so ill. . . .

Love, love, love. . . . The old story. In a final burst of admiration and love for his generosity she told him of her one great error, which caused him a few moments of solemn cogitation and was then dismissed as nothing of importance, a pathetic, childish mistake. Then there followed one of those swift and seemingly unguarded unions, a commonplace of the tangled self-preserving underworld of poverty. A clergyman was found whose moral assurances seemed to make the union ideal. Then a room in a commonplace boarding-house, and the newer and better life which eventually was to realize all was begun.

VII

TO THOSE familiar with the brazen and relentless methods of a certain type of hawk of the underworld, which picks fledglings from the nest and springlings from the fields and finds life itself only a hunting-ground in which those mentally or physically weaker than itself may be enslaved, this description will seem neither strained nor inadequate. Fagins of sex, creatures who change their women as they would their coats, they make an easy if reprehensible bed of their lives, and such of their victims as have known them well testify that

for a while at least in their care or custody they were not unhappy.

So it was with Madeleine and her lover. With amused and laughing tolerance toward her natural if witless efforts to build up a home atmosphere about their presumably joint lives, to build for a future in which they should jointly share, he saw in them only something trivial or ridiculous, whereas to her it was as though the heavens had opened and she was surveying a new world. For in his love and care there was to be peace. Latterly, if not now—for already he complained of conditions which made it impossible for him to work—the results of their several labors were to be pooled in order to prepare for that something better which would soon be achieved—a home, an ideally happy state somewhere. Even children were in her mind.

The mere fact that he shortly complained of other temporary reverses which made it necessary for him and her to keep close watch over their resources, and that for the time being, until he "could arrange his affairs," she must find some employment which would pay much better than her old one, gave her no shock.

Indeed, it was an indescribable joy for her to do for her love, for love had come, that great solvent of all other earthly difficulties, that leveler of all but insurmountable barriers. Even now love was to make her life flower at last. There was an end to loneliness and the oppressive indifference of the great sea of life.

But, as in the first instance, so now the awakening was swift and disconcerting. Realizing the abject adoration in which she held his surface charms and that his thin, tricky soul was the beginning and the end of things for her, it was all the easier to assure her, and soon insist, that the easiest and swiftest way of making money, of which she was unfortunately aware, must be resorted to, for a great necessity had come upon him. The usual tale of a threatening disaster, a sudden loss at cards which might end in imprisonment for him and their enforced separation, was enough.

Swiftly he filled her ears with tales of rescues by women of many of his men friends similarly circumstanced, of the "fools" and "marks" that filled the thoroughfares to be captured and preyed upon by women. Why hesitate? Consider the meagre, beggarly wages she had previously earned, the nothingness of her life before. Why jeopardize their future now? Why be foolish, dull? Plainly it was nothing to love, as he saw it. Should it be so much to her? In this wise she was persuaded.

But now it was not the shame and the fear of arrest that troubled her, but the injury which love had done and was doing to her, that cut and burned and seared and scarred.

Love, as she now began dimly to realize once more, should not be so. More than anything else, if love was what she had always dreamed, should it not protect and save and keep her for itself? And now see. Love was sending her out again to loiter in doorways and before windows and to "make eyes."

It was this that turned like a wheel in her brain and heart. For in spite of the roughness of her emotional experiences thus far, she had faith to believe that love should not be so, should not do so.

Those features which to this hour, and long after, like those features of her first love, seemed so worship-worth, those eyes that had seemed to beam on her with love, the lips that had smiled so graciously and kissed hers, the hands and arms that had petted and held her, should not be part of the compulsion that sent her here.

No, love should be better than that. He himself had told her so at first—that she was worth more than all else to him—and now see!

And then one night, fully a year and a half later, the climax. Being particularly irritated by some money losses and the need of enduring her at all, even though she might still prove of some value as a slave, he turned on her with a savage fury.

"What, only . . . ! Get to hell outa here! What do you think I am—a sucker? And let go my arm. Don't come that stuff on me. I'm sick of it. Don't hang on my arm, I tell yah! I'm tired, damned tired! Get out! Go on—beat it, an' don't come back, see? I'm through—through—yuh hear me? I mean what I say. I'm through, once an' fer all. Beat it, an' fer good. Don't come back. I've said that before, but this time it *goes!* Go on, now quick— Scat!—an' don't ever let me see yah around here any more, yah hear?—yah damned piece o'mush, yah!"

He pushed her away, throwing open the door as he did so, and, finding her still pleading and clinging, threw her out with such force that she cut her left eye and the back of her left hand against the jamb of the door.

There was a cry of "Fred! Fred! Please! Please!" —and then the door was slammed and she was left leaning disconsolately and brokenly against the stair-rail outside.

And now, as before, the cruelty and inscrutability of life weighed on her, only now, less than before, had she hope wherewith to buoy herself. It was all so dark, so hopeless. Often in this hour she thought of the swift, icy waters of the river, glistening under a winter moon, and then again of the

peace and quiet of the House of the Good Shepherd, its shielding remoteness from life, the only true home or sanctuary she had ever known. And so, brooding and repressing occasional sobs, she made her way toward it, down the long streets, thinking of the pathetically debasing love-life that was now over—the dream of love that never, never could be again, for her.

VIII

THE STARK red walls of the institution stood as before, only dim and gray and cold under a frosty winter moon. It was three of a chill, cold morning. She had come a long way, drooping, brooding, half-freezing and crying. More than once on the way the hopelessness of her life and her dreams had given her pause, causing her to turn again with renewed determination toward the river—only the vivid and reassuring picture she had retained of this same grim and homely place, its restricted peace and quiet, the sympathy of Sister St. Agnes and Mother St. Bertha, had carried her on.

En route she speculated as to whether they would receive her now, so objectionable and grim was her tale. And yet she could not resist continuing toward it, so reassuring was its memory, only to find it silent, not a single light burning. But, after all, there was one, at a side door— not the great cold gate by which she had first been admitted but another to one side, to her an all but unknown entrance; and to it after some brooding hesitation she made her way, ringing a bell and being admitted by a drowsy nun, who ushered her into the warmth and quiet of the inner hallway. Once in she mechanically followed to the bronze grille which, as prison bars, obstructed the way, and here on one of the two plain chairs placed before a small aperture she now sank wearily and looked through.

Her cut eye was hurting her and her bruised hands. On the somewhat faded jacket and crumpled hat, pulled on indifferently because she was too hurt to think or care, there was some blown snow. And when the Sister Secretary in charge of the room after midnight, hearing footsteps, came to the grille, she looked up wanly, her little red, rough hands crossed on her lap.

"Mother," she said beseechingly, "may I come in?"

Then remembering that only Mother St. Bertha could admit her, added wearily:

"Is Mother St. Bertha here? I was here before. She will know me."

The Sister Secretary surveyed her curiously, sensing more of the endless misery that was ever here, but seeing that she was sick or in despair hastened to call her superior, whose rule it was that all such requests for admission should be referred to her. There was no stir in the room in her absence. Presently pattened feet were heard, and the face of Mother St. Bertha, wrinkled and a-weary, appeared at the square opening.

"What is it, my child?" she asked curiously if softly, wondering at the crumpled presence at this hour.

"Mother," began Madeleine tremulously, looking up and recognizing her, "don't you remember me? It is Madeleine. I was here four years ago. I was in the girls' ward. I worked in the sewing-room."

She was so beaten by life, the perpetual endings to her never more than tremulous hopes, that even now and here she expected little more than an indifference which would send her away again.

"Why, yes, of course I remember you, my child. But what is it that brings you now, dear? Your eye is cut, and your hand."

"Yes, mother, but please don't ask—just now. Oh, please let me come in! I am so tired! I've had such a hard time!"

"Of course, my child," said the Mother, moving to the door and opening it. "You may come in. But what has happened, child? How is it that your cheek is cut, and your hands?"

"Mother," pleaded Madeleine wearily, "must I answer now? I am so unhappy! Can't I just have my old dress and my bed for to-night—that little bed under the lamp?"

"Why, yes, dear, you may have them, of course," said the nun, tactfully sensing a great grief. "And you need not talk now. I think I know how it is. Come with me."

She led the way along bare, dimly lit corridors and up cold solid iron stairs, echoing to the feet, until once more, as in the old days, the severe but spotless room in which were the baths and the hampers for soiled clothes was reached.

"Now, my child," she said, "you may undress and bathe. I will get something for your eye."

And so here at last, once more, Madeleine put aside the pathetic if showy finery that for a time had adorned and shamed her: a twilled skirt she had only recently bought in the pale hope of interesting *him*, the commonplace little hat for which she had paid ten dollars, the striped shirtwaist, once a pleasure to her in the hope that it would please *him*.

In a kind of dumbness of despair she took off her shoes and stockings and, as the Mother left, entered the warm, clean bath which had been provided. She stifled a sob as she did so, and others as she bathed. Then she stepped out and dried her body and covered it with the clean, simple slip of white which had been laid on a chair, brushing her hair and touching her eye, until the Mother Sister returned with an unguent wherewith to dress it.

Then she was led along other silent passages, once dreary enough but now healing in their sense of peace and rest, and so into the great room set with row upon row of simple white iron beds, covered with their snowy linen and illuminated only by the minute red lamps or the small candles burning before their idealistic images here and there, beneath which so many like herself were sleeping. Over the bed which she had once occupied, and which by chance was then vacant, burned the one little lamp which she recognized as of old—her lamp, as she had always thought of it—a thin and flickering flame, before an image of the Virgin. At sight of it she repressed a sob.

"You see, my child," said the Mother Superior poetically, "it must have been waiting for you. Anyhow it is empty. Perhaps it may have known you were coming."

She spoke softly so that the long rows of sleepers might not be disturbed, then proceeded to turn down the coverlets.

"Oh, Mother," Madeleine suddenly whispered softly as she stood by the bed, "won't you let me stay always? I never want to go out any more. I have had such a hard time. I will work so hard for you if you will let me stay!"

The experienced Sister looked at her curiously. Never before had she heard such a plea.

"Why, yes, my child," she said. "If you wish to stay I'm sure it can be arranged. It is not as we usually do, but you are not the only one who has gone out in the past and come back to us. I am sure God and the Blessed Virgin will hear your prayer for whatever is right. But now go to bed and sleep. You need rest. I can see that. And to-morrow, or any time, or never, as you choose, you may tell me what has happened."

She urged her very gently to enter and then tucked the covers about her, laying finally a cool, wrinkled hand on her forehead. For answer Madeleine seized and put it to her lips, holding it so.

"Oh, Mother," she sobbed as the Sister bent over her, "don't ever make me go out in the world again, will you? You won't, will you? I'm so tired! I'm so tired!"

"No dear, no," soothed the Sister, "not unless you wish it. And now rest. You need never go out in the world again unless you wish."

And withdrawing the hand from the kissing lips, she tiptoed silently from the room.

FROM

AN AMERICAN TRAGEDY

◇

⟪ PUBLISHED in 1925 by Horace Liveright in New York, *An American Tragedy* is Dreiser's masterpiece. For comment on the chapters which follow as a perfect example of Dreiser's narrative method, see the editor's Introduction, pp. 469–71.

◇

FROM BOOK II

CHAPTER 38

THE FIRST effect of the doctor's decision was to shock and terrify them both—Roberta and Clyde—beyond measure. For apparently now here was illegitimacy and disgrace for Roberta. Exposure and destruction for Clyde. And this had been their one solution seemingly. Then, by degrees, for Clyde at least, there was a slight lifting of the heavy pall. Perhaps, after all, as the doctor had suggested—and once she had recovered her senses sufficiently to talk, she had told him—the end had not been reached. There was the bare possibility, as suggested by the druggist, Short and the doctor, that she might be mistaken. And this, while not producing a happy reaction in her, had the unsatisfactory result of inducing in Clyde a lethargy based more than anything else on the ever-haunting fear of inability to cope with this situation as well as the certainty of social exposure in case he did not which caused him, instead of struggling all the more desperately, to defer further immediate action. For, such was his nature that, although he realized clearly the probable tragic consequences if he did not act, still it was so hard to think to whom else to apply to without danger to himself. To think that the doctor had "turned her down," as he phrased it, and that Short's advice should have been worth as little as that!

But apart from nervous thoughts as to whom to turn to next, no particular individual occurred to him before the two weeks were gone, or after. It was so hard to just ask anywhere. One just couldn't do it. Besides, of whom could he ask now? Of whom? These things took time, didn't they? Yet in the meantime, the days going by, both he and Roberta had ample time to consider what, if any,

steps they must take—the one in regard to the other—in case no medical or surgical solution was found. For Roberta, while urging and urging, if not so much by words as by expression and mood at her work, was determined that she must not be left to fight this out alone—she could not be. On the other hand, as she could see, Clyde did nothing. For apart from what he had already attempted to do, he was absolutely at a loss how to proceed. He had no intimates and in consequence he could only think of presenting the problem as an imaginary one to one individual and another here or there in the hope of extracting some helpful information. At the same time, and as impractical and evasive as it may seem, there was the call of that diverting world of which Sondra was a part, evenings and Sundays, when, in spite of Roberta's wretched state and mood, he was called to go here and there, and did, because in so doing he was actually relieving his own mind of the dread specter of disaster that was almost constantly before it. If only he could get her out of this! If only he could. But how, without money, intimates, a more familiar understanding of the medical or if not that exactly, then the sub rosa world of sexual free-masonry which some at times—the bell-hops of the Green-Davidson, for instance, seemed to understand. He had written to Ratterer, of course, but there had been no answer, since Ratterer had removed to Florida and as yet Clyde's letter had not reached him. And locally all those he knew best were either connected with the factory or society—individuals on the one hand too inexperienced or dangerous, or on the other hand, too remote and dangerous, since he was not sufficiently intimate with any of them as yet to command their true confidence and secrecy.

At the same time he must do something—he could not just rest and drift. Assuredly Roberta could not long permit him to do that—faced as she was by exposure. And so from time to time he actually racked himself—seized upon straws and what would have been looked upon by most as forlorn chances. Thus, for instance, an associate foreman, chancing to reminisce one day concerning a certain girl in his department who had "gotten in trouble" and had been compelled to leave, he had been given the opportunity to inquire what he thought such a girl did in case she could not afford or did not want to have a child. But this particular foreman, being as uninformed as himself, merely observed that she probably had to see a doctor if she knew one or "go through with it"—which left Clyde exactly where he was. On another occasion, in connection with a conversation in a barber shop, relating to a local case reported in

The Star where a girl was suing a local ne'er-do-well for breach of promise, the remark was made that she would "never have sued that guy, you bet, unless she had to." Whereupon Clyde seized the opportunity to remark hopefully, "But wouldn't you think that she could find some way of getting out of trouble without marrying a fellow she didn't like?"

"Well, that's not so easy as you may think, particularly around here," elucidated the wiseacre who was trimming his hair. "In the first place it's agin' the law. And next it takes a lotta money. An' in case you ain't got it, well, money makes the mare go, you know." He snip-snipped with his scissors while Clyde, confronted by his own problem, meditated on how true it was. If he had a lot of money—even a few hundred dollars—he might take it now and possible persuade her—who could tell—to go somewhere by herself and have an operation performed.

Yet each day, as on the one before, he was saying to himself that he must find some one. And Roberta was saying to herself that she too must act—must not really depend on Clyde any longer if he were going to act so. One could not trifle or compromise with a terror of this kind. It was a cruel imposition on her. It must be that Clyde did not realize how terribly this affected her and even him. For certainly, if he were not going to help her out of it, as he had distinctly said he would do at first, then decidedly she could not be expected to weather the subsequent storm alone. Never, never, never! For, after all, as Roberta saw it, Clyde was a man—he had a good position—it was not he, but she, who was in this treacherous position and unable to extricate herself alone.

And beginning with the second day after the second period, when she discovered for once and all that her worst suspicions were true, she not only emphasized the fact in every way that she could that she was distressed beyond all words, but on the third day announced to him in a note that she was again going to see the doctor near Gloversville that evening, regardless of his previous refusal—so great was her need—and also asking Clyde whether he would accompany her—a request which, since he had not succeeded in doing anything, and although he had an engagement with Sondra, he instantly acceded to—feeling it to be of greater importance than anything else. He must excuse himself to Sondra on the ground of work.

And accordingly this second trip was made, a long and nervous conversation between himself and Roberta on the way resulting in nothing more than some explanations as to why thus far he had not been able to achieve anything, plus certain encomiums addressed to her concerning her courage in acting for herself in this way.

Yet the doctor again would not and did not act. After waiting nearly an hour for his return from somewhere, she was merely permitted to tell him of her unchanged state and her destroying fears in regard to herself, but with no hint from him that he could be induced to act as indeed he could act. It was against his prejudices and ethics.

And so once more Roberta returned, this time not crying, actually too sad to cry, choked with the weight of her impending danger and the anticipatory fears and miseries that attended it.

And Clyde, hearing of this defeat, was at last reduced to a nervous, gloomy silence, absolutely devoid of a helpful suggestion. He could not think what to say and was chiefly fearful lest Roberta now make some demand with which socially or economically he could not comply. However, in regard to this she said little on the way home. Instead she sat and stared out of the window—thinking of her defenseless predicament that was becoming more real and terrible to her hourly. By way of excuse she pleaded that she had a headache. She wanted to be alone—only to think more—to try to work out a solution. She must work out some way. That she knew. But what? How? What could she do? How could she possibly escape? She felt like a cornered animal fighting for its life with all odds against it, and she thought of a thousand remote and entirely impossible avenues of escape, only to return to the one and only safe and sound solution that she really felt should be possible—and that was marriage. And why not? Hadn't she given him all, and that against her better judgment? Hadn't he overpersuaded her? Who was he anyway to so cast her aside? For decidedly at times, and especially since this latest crisis had developed, his manner, because of Sondra and the Griffiths and what he felt to be the fatal effect of all this on his dreams here, was sufficient to make plain that love was decidedly dead, and that he was not thinking nearly so much of the meaning of her state to her, as he was of its import to him, the injury that was most certain to accrue to him. And when this did not completely terrify her, as mostly it did, it served to irritate and slowly develop the conclusion that in such a desperate state as this, she was justified in asking more than ordinarily she would have dreamed of asking, marriage itself, since there was no other door. And why not? Wasn't her life as good as his? And hadn't he joined his to hers, voluntarily? Then, why shouldn't he strive to help her now—or, failing that, make this final sacrifice which was the only one by which she could be rescued apparently. For who were all the society people with whom he was concerned anyhow? And why should he ask her in such a crisis to sacrifice herself, her future and good name, just because of his interest in them? They had never done anything very much for him, certainly not as much as had she. And, just because he was wearying now, after persuading her to do his bidding—was that any reason why now, in this crisis, he should be permitted to desert her? After all, wouldn't all of these society people in whom he was so much interested feel that whatever his relationship to them, she would be justified in taking the course which she might be compelled to take?

She brooded on this much, more especially on the return from this second attempt to induce Dr. Glenn to help her. In fact, at moments, her face took on a defiant, determined look which was seemingly new to her, but which only developed suddenly under such pressure. Her jaw became a trifle set. She had made a decision. He would have to marry her. She must make him if there were no other way out of this. She must—she must. Think of her home, her mother, Grace Marr, the Newtons, all who knew her in fact—the terror and pain and shame with which this would sear all those in any way identified with her—her father, brothers, sisters. Impossible! Impossible! It must not and could not be! Impossible. It might seem a little severe to her, even now, to have to insist on this, considering all the emphasis Clyde had hitherto laid upon his prospects here. But how, how else was she to do?

Accordingly the next day, and not a little to his surprise, since for so many hours the night before they had been together, Clyde received another note telling him that he must come again that night. She had something to say to him, and there was something in the tone of the note that seemed to indicate or suggest a kind of defiance of a refusal of any kind, hitherto absent in any of her communications to him. And at once the thought that this situation, unless cleared away, was certain to prove disastrous, so weighed upon him that he could not but put the best face possible on it and consent to go and hear what it was that she had to offer in the way of a solution—or—on the other hand, of what she had to complain.

Going to her room at a late hour, he found her in what seemed to him a more composed frame of mind than at any time since this difficulty had appeared, a state which surprised him a little, since he had expected to find her in tears. But now, if anything, she appeared more complacent, her nervous thoughts as to how to bring about a satis-factory conclusion for herself having called into play a native shrewdness which was now seeking to exercise itself.

And so directly before announcing what was in her mind, she began by asking: "You haven't found out about another doctor, have you, Clyde, or thought of anything?"

"No, I haven't, Bert," he replied most dismally and wearisomely, his own mental tether-length having been strained to the breaking point. "I've been trying to, as you know, but it's so darn hard to find any one who isn't afraid to monkey with a case like this. Honest, to tell the truth, Bert, I'm about stumped. I don't know what we are going to do unless you can think of something. You haven't thought or heard of any one else you could go to, have you?" For, during the conversation that had immediately followed her first visit to the doctor, he had hinted to her that by striking up a fairly intimate relationship with one of the foreign family girls, she might by degrees extract some information there which would be of use to both. But Roberta was not of a temperament that permitted of any such facile friendships, and nothing had come of it.

However, his stating that he was "stumped" now gave her the opportunity she was really desiring, to present the proposition which she felt to be unavoidable and not longer to be delayed. Yet being fearful of how Clyde would react, she hesitated as to the form in which she would present it, and, after shaking her head and manifesting a nervousness which was real enough, she finally said: "Well, I'll tell you, Clyde. I've been thinking about it and I don't see any way out of it unless—unless you, well, marry me. It's two months now, you know, and unless we get married right away, everybody'll know, won't they?"

Her manner as she said this was a mixture of outward courage born out of her conviction that she was in the right and an inward uncertainty about Clyde's attitude, which was all the more fused by a sudden look of surprise, resentment, uncertainty and fear that now transformation-wise played over his countenance; a variation and play which, if it indicated anything definite, indicated that she was seeking to inflict an unwarranted injury on him. For since he had been drawing closer and closer to Sondra, his hopes had heightened so intensely that, hearkening to this demand on the part of Roberta now, his brow wrinkled and his manner changed from one of comparatively affable, if nervous, consideration to that of mingled fear, opposition as well as determination to evade drastic consequence. For this would spell complete ruin for him, the loss of Sondra, his job, his social hopes and ambitions in connection with the Griffiths—all—a thought which sickened and at the same time caused him to hesitate about how to proceed. But he would not! he would not! He would not do this! Never! Never!! Never!!!

Yet after a moment he exclaimed equivocally: "Well, gee, that's all right, too, Bert, for you, because that fixes everything without any trouble at all. But what about me? You don't want to forget that that isn't going to be easy for me, the way things are now. You know I haven't any money. All I have is my job. And besides, the family don't know anything about you yet—not a thing. And if it should suddenly come out now that we've been going together all this time, and that this has happened, and that I was going to have to get married right away, well, gee, they'll know I've been fooling 'em and they're sure to get sore. And then what? They might even fire me."

He paused to see what effect this explanation would have, but noting the somewhat dubious expression which of late characterized Roberta's face whenever he began excusing himself, he added hopefully and evasively, seeking by any trick that he could to delay this sudden issue: "Besides, I'm not so sure that I can't find a doctor yet, either. I haven't had much luck so far, but that's not saying that I won't. And there's a little time yet, isn't there? Sure there is. It's all right up to three months anyway." (He had since had a letter from Ratterer who had commented on this fact.) "And I did hear something the other day of a doctor over in Albany who might do it. Anyway, I thought I'd go over and see before I said anything about him."

His manner, when he said this, was so equivocal that Roberta could tell he was merely lying to gain time. There was no doctor in Albany. Besides it was so plain that he resented her suggestion and was only thinking of some way of escaping it. And she knew well enough that at no time had he said directly that he would marry her. And while she might urge, in the last analysis she could not force him to do anything. He might just go away alone, as he had once said in connection with inadvertently losing his job because of her. And how much greater might not his impulse in that direction now be, if this world here in which he was so much interested were taken away from him, and he were to face the necessity of taking her and a child, too. It made her more cautious and caused her to modify her first impulse to speak out definitely and forcefully, however great her necessity might be. And so disturbed was he by the panorama of the bright world of which Sondra was the center and which was now at stake, that he could scarcely think clearly. Should he lose all this for such a world as he and Roberta could provide for themselves—a small home—a baby, such a routine work-a-day life as taking care of her and a baby on such a salary as he could earn, and from which most likely he would never again be freed! God! A sense of nausea seized him. He could not and would not do this. And yet, as he now saw, all his dreams could be so easily tumbled about his ears by her and because of one false step on his part. It made him cautious and for the first time in his life caused tact and cunning to visualize itself as a profound necessity.

And at the same time, Clyde was sensing inwardly and somewhat shamefacedly all of this profound change in himself.

But Roberta was saying: "Oh, I know, Clyde, but you yourself said just now that you were stumped, didn't you? And every day that goes by just makes it so much the worse for me, if we're not going to be able to get a doctor. You can't get married and have a child born within a few months—you know that. Every one in the world would know. Besides I have myself to consider as well as you, you know. And the baby, too." (At the mere mention of a coming child Clyde winced and recoiled as though he had been slapped. She noted it.) "I just must do one of two things right away, Clyde—get married or get out of this and you don't seem to be able to get me out of it, do you? If you're so afraid of what your uncle might think or do in case we get married," she added nervously and yet suavely, "why couldn't we get married right away and then keep it a secret for a while—as long as we could, or as long as you thought we ought to," she added shrewdly. "Meanwhile I could go home and tell my parents about it—that I am married, but that it must be kept a secret for a while. Then when the time came, when things got so bad that we couldn't stay here any longer without telling, why we could either go away somewhere, if we wanted to— that is, if you didn't want your uncle to know, or we could just announce that we were married some time ago. Lots of young couples do that nowadays. And as for getting along," she went on, noting a sudden dour shadow that passed over Clyde's face like a cloud, "why we could always find something to do—I know I could, anyhow, once the baby is born."

When first she began to speak, Clyde had seated himself on the edge of the bed, listening nervously and dubiously to all she had to offer. However, when she came to that part which related to marriage and going away, he got up—an irresistible impulse to move overcoming him. And when she concluded with the commonplace suggestion of going to work as soon as the baby was born, he looked at her with little less than panic in his eyes. To think of marrying and being in a position where it would be necessary to do that, when with a little luck and without interference from her, he might marry Sondra.

"Oh, yes, that's all right for you, Bert. That fixes everything up for you, but how about me? Why, gee whiz, I've only got started here now as it is, and if I have to pack up and get out, and I would have to, if ever they found out about this, why I don't know what I'd do. I haven't any business or trade that I could turn my hand to. It might go hard with both of us. Besides my uncle gave me this chance because I begged him to, and if I walked off now he never would do anything for me."

In his excitement he was forgetting that at one time and another in the past he had indicated to Roberta that the state of his own parents was not wholly unprosperous and that if things did not go just to his liking here, he could return west and perhaps find something to do out there. And it was some general recollection of this that now caused her to ask: "Couldn't we go out to Denver or something like that? Wouldn't your father be willing to help you get something for a time, anyhow?"

Her tone was very soft and pleading, an attempt to make Clyde feel that things could not be as bad as he was imagining. But the mere mention of his father in connection with all this—the assumption that he, of all people, might prove an escape from drudgery for them both, was a little too much. It showed how dreadfully incomplete was her understanding of his true position in this world. Worse, she was looking for help from that quarter. And, not finding it, later might possibly reproach him for that—who could tell—for his lies in connection with it. It made so very clear now the necessity for frustrating, if possible, and that at once, any tendency toward this idea of marriage. It could not be—ever.

And yet how was he to oppose this idea with safety, since she felt that she had this claim on him —how say to her openly and coldly that he could not and would not marry her? And unless he did so now she might think it would be fair and legitimate enough for her to compel him to do so. She might even feel privileged to go to his uncle—his cousin (he could see Gilbert's cold eyes) and expose him! And then destruction! Ruin! The end of all his dreams in connection with Sondra and everything else here. But all he could think of saying now was: "But I can't do this, Bert, not now, anyway," a remark which at once caused Roberta to assume that the idea of marriage, as she had interjected it here, was not one which, under the circumstances, he had the courage to oppose— his saying, "not now, anyway." Yet even as she was thinking this, he went swiftly on with: "Besides I don't want to get married so soon. It means too much to me at this time. In the first place I'm not old enough and I haven't got anything to get married on. And I can't leave here. I couldn't do half as well anywhere else. You don't realize what this chance means to me. My father's all right, but he couldn't do what my uncle could and he wouldn't. You don't know or you wouldn't ask me to do this."

He paused, his face a picture of puzzled fear and opposition. He was not unlike a harried animal, deftly pursued by hunter and hound. But Roberta, imagining that his total defection had been caused by the social side of Lycurgus as opposed to her own low state and not because of the superior lure of any particular girl, now retorted resentfully, although she desired not to appear so: "Oh, yes, I know well enough why you can't leave. It isn't your position here, though, half as much as it those society people you are always running around with. I know. You don't care for me any more, Clyde, that's it, and you don't want to give these other people up for me. I know that's it and nothing else. But just the same it wasn't so very long ago that you did, although you don't seem to remember it now." Her cheeks burned and her eyes flamed as she said this. She paused a moment while he gazed at her wondering about the outcome of all this. "But you can't leave me to make out any way I can, just the same, because I won't be left this way, Clyde. I can't! I can't! I tell you." She grew tense and staccato, "It means too much to me. I don't know how to do alone and I, besides, have no one to turn to but you and you must help me. I've got to get out of this, that's all, Clyde, I've got to. I'm not going to be left to face my people and everybody without any help or marriage or anything." As she said this, her eyes turned appealingly and yet savagely toward him and she emphasized it all with her hands, which she clinched and unclinched in a dramatic way. "And if you can't help me out in the way you thought," she went on most agonizedly as Clyde could see, "then you've got to help me out in this other, that's all. At least until I can do for myself I just won't be left. I don't ask you to marry me forever," she now added, the thought that if by presenting this demand in some modified form, she could induce Clyde to marry her, it might be possible afterwards that his feeling toward her would change to a much more kindly one. "You can leave me after a while if you want to. After I'm out of this. I can't prevent you from doing that and I wouldn't want to if I could. But you can't leave me now. You can't. You can't! Besides," she added, "I didn't want to get myself in this position and I wouldn't have, but for you. But you made me and made me let you come in here. And now you want to leave me to shift for myself, just because you think you won't be able to go in society any more, if they find out about me."

She paused, the strain of this contest proving almost too much for her tired nerves. At the same time she began to sob nervously and yet not violently—a marked effort at self-restraint and recovery marking her every gesture. And after a moment or two in which both stood there, he gazing dumbly and wondering what else he was to say in answer to all this, she struggling and finally managing to recover her poise, she added: "Oh, what is it about me that's so different to what I was a couple of months ago, Clyde? Will you tell me that? I'd like to know. What is it that has caused you to change so? Up to Christmas, almost, you were as nice to me as any human being could be. You were with me nearly all the time you had, and since then I've scarcely had an evening that I didn't beg for. Who is it? What is it? Some other girl, or what, I'd like to know—that Sondra Finchley or Bertine Cranston or who?"

Her eyes as she said this were a study. For even to this hour, as Clyde could now see to his satisfaction, since he feared the effect on Roberta of definite and absolute knowledge concerning Sondra, she had no specific suspicion, let alone positive knowledge concerning any girl. And coward-wise, in the face of her present predicament and her assumed and threatened claims on him, he was afraid to say what or who the real cause of this change was. Instead he merely replied and almost unmoved by her sorrow, since he no longer really cared for her: "Oh, you're all wrong, Bert. You don't see what the trouble is. It's my future here—if I leave here I certainly will never find such an opportunity. And if I have to marry in this way or leave here it will all go flooey. I want to wait and get some place first before I marry, see—save some money and if I do this I won't have a chance and you won't either," he added feebly, forgetting for the moment that up to this time he had been indicating rather clearly that he did not want to have anything more to do with her in any way.

"Besides," he continued, "if you could only find some one, or if you would go away by your-

self somewhere for a while, Bert, and go through with this alone, I could send you the money to do it on, I know. I could have it between now and the time you had to go."

His face, as he said this, and as Roberta clearly saw, mirrored the complete and resourceless collapse of all his recent plans in regard to her. And she, realizing that his indifference to her had reached the point where he could thus dispose of her and their prospective baby in this casual and really heartless manner, was not only angered in part, but at the same time frightened by the meaning of it all.

"Oh, Clyde," she now exclaimed boldly and with more courage and defiance than at any time since she had known him, "how you have changed! And how hard you can be. To want me to go off all by myself and just to save you—so you can stay here and get along and marry some one here when I am out of the way and you don't have to bother about me any more. Well, I won't do it. It's not fair. And I won't, that's all. I won't. And that's all there is to it. You can get some one to get me out of this or you can marry me and come away with me, at least long enough for me to have the baby and place myself right before my people and every one else that knows me. I don't care if you leave me afterwards, because I see now that you really don't care for me any more, and if that's the way you feel, I don't want you any more than you want me. But just the same, you must help me now—you must. But, oh, dear," she began whimpering again, and yet only slightly and bitterly. "To think that all our love for each other should have come to this—that I am asked to go away by myself—all alone—with no one—while you stay here, oh, dear! oh dear! And with a baby on my hands afterwards. And no husband."

She clinched her hands and shook her head bleakly. Clyde, realizing well enough that his proposition certainly was cold and indifferent but, in the face of his intense desire for Sondra, the best or at least safest that he could devise, now stood there unable for the moment to think of anything more to say.

And although there was some other discussion to the same effect, the conclusion of this very difficult hour was that Clyde had another week or two at best in which to see if he could find a physician or any one who would assist him. After that —well after that the implied, if not openly expressed, threat which lay at the bottom of this was, unless so extricated and speedily, that he would have to marry her, if not permanently, then at least temporarily, but legally just the same, until once again she was able to look after herself—a threat which was as crushing and humiliating to Roberta as it was torturing to him.

CHAPTER 39

OPPOSING views such as these, especially where no real skill to meet such a situation existed, could only spell greater difficulty and even eventual disaster unless chance in some form should aid. And chance did not aid. And the presence of Roberta in the factory was something that would not permit him to dismiss it from his mind. If only he could persuade her to leave and go somewhere else to live and work so that he should not always see her, he might then think more calmly. For with her asking continuously, by her presence if no more, what he intended to do, it was impossible for him to think. And the fact that he no longer cared for her as he had, tended to reduce his normal consideration of what was her due. He was too infatuated with, and hence disarranged by his thoughts of Sondra.

For in the very teeth of this grave dilemma he continued to pursue the enticing dream in connection with Sondra—the dark situation in connection with Roberta seeming no more at moments than a dark cloud which shadowed this other. And hence nightly, or as often as the exigencies of his still unbroken connection with Roberta would permit, he was availing himself of such opportunities as his flourishing connections now afforded. Now, and to his great pride and satisfaction, it was a dinner at the Harriets' or Taylors' to which he was invited; or a party at the Finchleys' or the Cranstons', to which he would either escort Sondra or be animated by the hope of encountering her. And now, also without so many of the former phases or attempts at subterfuge, which had previously characterized her curiosity in regard to him, she was at times openly seeking him out and making opportunities for social contact. And, of course, these contacts being identical with this typical kind of group gathering, they seemed to have no special significance with the more conservative elders.

For although Mrs. Finchley, who was of an especially shrewd and discerning turn socially, had at first been dubious over the attentions being showered upon Clyde by her daughter and others, still observing that Clyde was more and more being entertained, not only in her own home by the group of which her daughter was a part, but elsewhere, everywhere, was at last inclined to imagine that he must be more solidly placed in this world than she had heard, and later to ask her son and even Sondra concerning him. But receiving from Sondra only the equivocal information that, since he was Gil and Bella Griffiths' cousin, and was being taken up by everybody because he was so charming—even if he didn't have any money—she couldn't see why she and Stuart should not be allowed to entertain him also, her mother rested on that for the time being—only cautioning her daughter under no circumstances to become too friendly. And Sondra, realizing that in part her mother was right, yet being so drawn to Clyde was now determined to deceive her, at least to the extent of being as clandestinely free with Clyde as she could contrive. And was, so much so that every one who was privy to the intimate contacts between Clyde and Sondra might have reported that the actual understanding between them was assuming an intensity which most certainly would have shocked the elder Finchleys, could they have known. For apart from what Clyde had been, and still was dreaming in regard to her, Sondra was truly being taken with thoughts and moods in regard to him which were fast verging upon the most destroying aspects of the very profound chemistry of love. Indeed, in addition to handclasps, kisses and looks of intense admiration always bestowed when presumably no one was looking, there were those nebulous and yet strengthening and lengthening fantasies concerning a future which in some way or other, not clear to either as yet, was still always to include each other.

Summer days perhaps, and that soon, in which he and she would be in a canoe at Twelfth Lake, the long shadows of the trees on the bank lengthening over the silvery water, the wind rippling the surface while he paddled and she idled and tortured him with hints of the future; a certain forest path, grass-sodden and sun-mottled to the south and west of the Cranston and Phant estates, near theirs, through which they might canter in June and July to a wonderful view known as Inspiration Point some seven miles west; the country fair at Sharon, at which, in a gypsy costume, the essence of romance itself, she would superintend a booth, or, in her smartest riding habit, give an exhibition of her horsemanship—teas, dances in the afternoon and in the moonlight at which, languishing in his arms, their eyes would speak.

None of the compulsion of the practical. None of the inhibitions which the dominance and possible future opposition of her parents might imply. Just love and summer, and idyllic and happy progress toward an eventual secure and unopposed union which should give him to her forever.

And in the meantime, in so far as Roberta was concerned, two more long, dreary, terrifying months going by without that meditated action on her part which must result once it was taken in Clyde's undoing. For, as convinced as she was that apart from meditating and thinking of some way to escape his responsibility, Clyde had no real intention of marrying her, still, like Clyde, she drifted, fearing to act really. For in several conferences following that in which she had indicated that she expected him to marry her, he had reiterated, if vaguely, a veiled threat that in case she appealed to his uncle he would not be compelled to marry her, after all, for he could go elsewhere.

The way he put it was that unless left undisturbed in his present situation he would be in no position to marry her and furthermore could not possibly do anything to aid her at the coming time when most of all she would stand in need of aid —a hint which caused Roberta to reflect on a hitherto not fully developed vein of hardness in Clyde, although had she but sufficiently reflected, it had shown itself at the time that he compelled her to admit him to her room.

In addition and because she was doing nothing and yet he feared that at any moment she might, he shifted in part at least from the attitude of complete indifference, which had availed him up to the time that she had threatened him, to one of at least simulated interest and good-will and friendship. For the very precarious condition in which he found himself was sufficiently terrifying to evoke more diplomacy than ever before had characterized him. Besides he was foolish enough to hope, if not exactly believe, that by once more conducting himself as though he still entertained a lively sense of the problem that afflicted her and that he was willing, in case no other way was found, to eventually marry her (though he could never definitely be persuaded to commit himself as to this), he could reduce her determination to compel him to act soon at least to a minimum, and so leave him more time in which to exhaust every possibility of escape without marriage, and without being compelled to run away.

And although Roberta sensed the basis of this sudden shift, still she was so utterly alone and distrait that she was willing to give ear to Clyde's mock genial, if not exactly affectionate observations and suggestions. It caused her, at his behest, to wait a while longer, the while, as he now explained, he would not only have saved up some money, but devised some plan in connection with his work which would permit him to leave for a time anyhow, marry her somewhere and then establish her and the baby as a lawful married woman somewhere else, while, although he did not explain this just now, he returned to Lycurgus and

sent her such aid as he could. But on condition, of course, that never anywhere, unless he gave her permission, must she assert that he had married her, or point to him in any way as the father of her child. Also it was understood that she, as she herself had asserted over and over that she would, if only he would do this—marry her—take steps to free herself on the ground of desertion, or something, in some place sufficiently removed from Lycurgus for no one to hear. And that within a reasonable time after her marriage to him, although he was not at all satisfied that, assuming that he did marry her, she would.

But Clyde, of course, was insincere in regard to all his overtures at this time, and really not concerned as to her sincerity or insincerity. Nor did he have any intention of leaving Lycurgus even for the moderate length of time that her present extrication would require unless he had to. For that meant that he would be separated from Sondra, and such absence, for whatever period, would most definitely interfere with his plans. And so, on the contrary, he drifted—thinking most idly at times of some possible fake or mock marriage such as he had seen in some melodramatic movie —a fake minister and witnesses combining to deceive some simple country girl such as Roberta was not, but at such expense of time, resources, courage and subtlety as Clyde himself, after a little reflection, was wise enough to see was beyond him.

Again, knowing that, unless some hitherto unforeseen aid should eventuate, he was heading straight toward a disaster which could not much longer be obviated, he even allowed himself to dream that, once the fatal hour was at hand and Roberta, no longer to be put off by any form of subterfuge, was about to expose him, he might even flatly deny that he had ever held any such relationship with her as then she would be charging—rather that at all times his relationship with her had been that of a department manager to employee—no more. Terror—no less!

But at the same time, early in May, when Roberta, because of various gestative signs and ailments, was beginning to explain, as well as insist, to Clyde that by no stretch of the imagination or courage could she be expected to retain her position at the factory or work later than June first, because by then the likelihood of the girls there beginning to notice something, would be too great for her to endure, Sondra was beginning to explain that not so much later than the fourth or fifth of June she and her mother and Stuart, together with some servants, would be going to their new lodge at Twelfth Lake in order to supervise certain installations then being made before the regular season should begin. And after that, not later than the eighteenth, at which time the Cranstons, Harriets, and some others would have arrived, including very likely visits from Bella and Myra, he might expect a week-end invitation from the Cranstons, with whom, through Bertine, she would arrange as to this. And after that, the general circumstances proving fairly propitious, there would be, of course, other week-end invitations to the Harriets', Phants' and some others who dwelt there, as well as to the Griffiths' at Greenwood, to which place, on account of Bella, he could easily come. And during his two weeks' vacation in July, he could either stop at the Casino, which was at Pine Point, or perhaps the Cranstons or Harriets, at her suggestion, might choose to invite him. At any rate, as Clyde could see, and with no more than such expenditures as, with a little scrimping during his ordinary working days here, he could provide for, he might see not a little of that lake life of which he had read so much in the local papers, to say nothing of Sondra at one and another of the lodges, the masters of which were not so inimical to his presence and overtures as were Sondra's parents.

For now it was, and for the first time, as she proceeded to explain to him that her mother and father, because of his continued and reported attentions to her, were already beginning to talk of an extended European tour which might keep her and Stuart and her mother abroad for at least the next two years. But since, at news of this, Clyde's face as well as his spirits darkened, and she herself was sufficiently enmeshed to suffer because of this, she at once added that he must not feel so bad—he must not; things would work out well enough, she knew. For at the proper time, and unless between then and now, something— her own subtle attack if not her at present feverish interest in Clyde—should have worked to alter her mother's viewpoint in regard to him—she might be compelled to take some steps of her own in order to frustrate her mother. Just what, she was not willing to say at this time, although to Clyde's overheated imagination it took the form of an elopement and marriage, which could not then be gainsaid by her parents whatever they might think. And it was true that in a vague and as yet repressed way some such thought was beginning to form in Sondra's mind. For, as she now proceeded to explain to Clyde, it was so plain that her mother was attempting to steer her in the direction of a purely social match—the one with the youth who had been paying her such marked attention the year before. But because of her present passion for Clyde, as she now gayly declared, it was not easy to see how she was to be made to comply. "The only trouble with me is that I'm not of age yet," she here added briskly and slangily. "They've got me there, of course. But I will be by next October and they can't do very much with me after that, I want to let you know. I can marry the person I want, I guess. And if I can't do it here, well, there are more ways than one to kill a cat."

The thought was like some sweet, disarranging poison to Clyde. It fevered and all but betrayed him mentally. If only—if only—it were not for Roberta now. That terrifying and all but insoluble problem. But for that, and the opposition of Sondra's parents which she was thinking she would be able to overcome, did not heaven itself await him? Sondra, Twelfth Lake, society, wealth, her love and beauty. He grew not a little wild in thinking of it all. Once he and she were married, what could Sondra's relatives do? What, but acquiesce and take them into the glorious bosom of their resplendent home at Lycurgus or provide for them in some other way—he to no doubt eventually take some place in connection with the Finchley Electric Sweeper Company. And then would he not be the equal, if not the superior, of Gilbert Griffiths himself and all those others who originally had ignored him here—joint heir with Stuart to all the Finchley means. And with Sondra as the central or crowning jewel to so much sudden and such Aladdin-like splendor.

No thought as to how he was to overcome the time between now and October. No serious consideration of the fact that Roberta then and there was demanding that he marry her. He could put her off, he thought. And yet, at the same time, he was painfully and nervously conscious of the fact that at no period in his life before had he been so treacherously poised at the very brink of disaster. It might be his duty as the world would see it—his mother would say so—to at least extricate Roberta. But in the case of Esta, who had come to her rescue? Her lover? He had walked off from her without a qualm and she had not died. And why, when Roberta was no worse off than his sister had been, why should she seek to destroy him in this way? Force him to do something which would be little less than social, artistic, passional or emotional assassination? And when later, if she would but spare him for this, he could do so much more for her—with Sondra's money of course. He could not and would not let her do this to him. His life would be ruined!

CHAPTER 40

Two INCIDENTS which occurred at this time tended still more to sharpen the contrary points of view holding between Clyde and Roberta. One of these was no more than a glimpse which Roberta had one evening of Clyde pausing at the Central Avenue curb in front of the post-office to say a few words to Arabella Stark, who in a large and impressive-looking car, was waiting for her father who was still in the Stark Building opposite. And Miss Stark, fashionably outfitted according to the season, her world and her own pretentious taste, was affectedly posed at the wheel, not only for the benefit of Clyde but the public in general. And to Roberta, who by now was reduced to the verge of distraction between Clyde's delay and her determination to compel him to act in her behalf, she appeared to be little less than an epitome of all the security, luxury and freedom from responsibility which so enticed and hence caused Clyde to delay and be as indifferent as possible to the dire state which confronted her. For, alas, apart from this claim of her condition, what had she to offer him comparable to all he would be giving up in case he acceded to her request? Nothing—a thought which was far from encouraging.

Yet, at this moment contrasting her own wretched and neglected state with that of this Miss Stark, for example, she found herself a prey to an even more complaining and antagonistic mood than had hitherto characterized her. It was not right. It was not fair. For during the several weeks that had passed since last they had discussed this matter, Clyde had scarcely said a word to her at the factory or elsewhere, let alone called upon her at her room, fearing as he did the customary inquiry which he could not satisfy. And this caused her to feel that not only was he neglecting but resenting her most sharply.

And yet as she walked home from this trivial and fairly representative scene, her heart was not nearly so angry as it was sad and sore because of the love and comfort that had vanished and was not likely ever to come again . . . ever . . . ever . . . ever. Oh, how terrible, . . . how terrible!

On the other hand, Clyde, and at approximately this same time, was called upon to witness a scene identified with Roberta, which, as some might think, only an ironic and even malicious fate could have intended or permitted to come to pass. For motoring north the following Sunday to Arrow Lake to the lodge of the Trumbulls' to take advantage of an early spring week-end planned by Sondra, the party on nearing Biltz, which was in the direct line of the trip, was compelled to detour east in the direction of Roberta's home. And coming finally to a north and south road which ran directly from Trippettsville past the Alden farm, they turned north into that. And a few minutes later, came directly to the corner adjoining the Alden farm, where an east and west road led to Biltz. Here Tracy Trumbull, driving at the time, requested that some one should get out and inquire at the adjacent farmhouse as to whether this road did lead to Biltz. And Clyde, being nearest to one door, jumped out. And then, glancing at the name on the mail-box which stood at the junction and evidently belonged to the extremely dilapidated old farmhouse on the rise above, he was not a little astonished to note that the name was that of Titus Alden—Roberta's father. Also, as it instantly came to him, since she had described her parents as being near Biltz, this must be her home. It gave him pause, caused him for the moment to hesitate as to whether to go on or not, for once he had given Roberta a small picture of himself, and she might have shown it up here. Again the mere identification of this lorn, dilapidated realm with Roberta and hence himself, was sufficient to cause him to wish to turn and run.

But Sondra, who was sitting next him in the car and now noting his hesitation, called: "What's the matter, Clyde? Afraid of the bow-wow?" And he, realizing instantly that they would comment further on his actions if he did not proceed at once, started up the path. But the effect of this house, once he contemplated it thoroughly, was sufficient to arouse in his brain the most troubled and miserable of thoughts. For what a house, to be sure! So lonely and bare, even in this bright, spring weather! The decayed and sagging roof. The broken chimney to the north—rough lumps of cemented field stones lying at its base; the sagging and semi-toppling chimney to the south, sustained in place by a log chain. The unkempt path from the road below, which slowly he ascended! He was not a little dejected by the broken and displaced stones which served as steps before the front door. And the unpainted dilapidated outbuildings, all the more dreary because of these others.

"Gee!" To think that this was Roberta's home. And to think, in the face of all that he now aspired to in connection with Sondra and this social group at Lycurgus, she should be demanding that he marry her! And Sondra in the car with him here to see—if not know. The poverty! The reduced grimness of it all. How far he had traveled away from just such a beginning as this!

With a weakening and sickening sensation at the pit of his stomach, as of some blow administered there, he now approached the door. And then, as if to further distress him, if that were possible, the door was opened by Titus Alden, who, in an old, thread-bare and out-at-elbows coat, as well as baggy, worn, jean trousers and rough, shineless, ill-fitting country shoes, desired by his look to know what he wanted. And Clyde, being taken aback by the clothes, as well as a marked resemblance to Roberta about the eyes and mouth, now as swiftly as possible asked if the east and west road below ran through Biltz and joined the main highway north. And although he would have preferred a quick "yes" so that he might have turned and gone, Titus preferred to step down into the yard and then, with a gesture of the arm, indicate that if they wanted to strike a really good part of the road, they had better follow this Trippettsville north and south road for at least two more miles, and then turn west. Clyde thanked him briefly and turned almost before he had finished and hurried away.

For, as he now recalled, and with an enormous sense of depression, Roberta was thinking and at this very time, that soon now, and in the face of all Lycurgus had to offer him—Sondra—the coming spring and summer—the love and romance, gayety, position, power—he was going to give all that up and go away with and marry her. Sneak away to some out-of-the-way place! Oh, how horrible! And with a child at his age! Oh, why had he ever been so foolish and weak as to identify himself with her in this intimate way? Just because of a few lonely evenings! Oh, why, why couldn't he have waited and then this other world would have opened up to him just the same? If only he could have waited!

And now unquestionably, unless he could speedily and easily disengage himself from her, all this other splendid recognition would be destined to be withdrawn from him, and this other world from which he sprang might extend its gloomy, poverty-stricken arms to him and envelop him once more, just as the poverty of his family had enveloped and almost strangled him from the first. And it even occurred to him, in a vague way for the first time, how strange it was that this girl and he, whose origin had been strikingly similar, should have been so drawn to each other in the beginning. Why should it have been? How strange life was, anyway? But even more harrowing than this, was the problem of a way out that was before him. And his mind from now on, on this trip, was once more searching for some solution. A word of complaint from Roberta or her parents to his uncle or Gilbert, and assuredly he would be done for.

The thought so troubled him that once in the car, and although previously he had been chattering along with the others about what might be in store ahead in the way of divertissement, he now sat silent. And Sondra, who sat next to him and who previously had been whispering at intervals of her plans for the summer, now, instead of resuming the patter, whispered: "What come over de sweet phing?" (When Clyde appeared to be the least reduced in mind she most affected this patter with him, since it had an almost electric, if sweetly tormenting effect on him. "His baby-talking girl," he sometimes called her.) "Facey all dark now. Little while ago facey all smiles. Come make facey all nice again. Smile at Sondra. Squeeze Sondra's arm like good boy, Clyde."

She turned and looked up into his eyes to see what if any effect this baby-worded cajolery was having, and Clyde did his best to brighten, of course. But even so, and in the face of all this amazingly wonderful love on her part for him, the specter of Roberta and all that she represented now in connection with all this, was ever before him—her state, her very recent edict in regard to it, the obvious impossibility of doing anything now but go away with her.

Why—rather than let himself in for a thing like that—would it not be better, and even though he lost Sondra once and for all, for him to decamp as in the instance of the slain child in Kansas City—and be heard of nevermore here. But then he would lose Sondra, his connections here, and his uncle—this world! The loss! The loss! The misery of once more drifting about here and there; of being compelled to write his mother once more concerning certain things about his flight, which some one writing from here might explain to her afterwards—and so much more damagingly. And the thoughts concerning him on the part of his relatives! And of late he had been writing his mother that he was doing so well. What was it about his life that made things like this happen to him? Was this what his life was to be like? Running away from one situation and another just to start all over somewhere else—perhaps only to be compelled to flee from something worse. No, he could not run away again. He must face it and solve it in some way. He must!

God!

CHAPTER 41

THE FIFTH of June arriving, the Finchleys departed as Sondra had indicated, but not without a most urgent request from her that he be prepared to come to the Cranstons' either the second or third week-end following—she to advise him definitely later—a departure which so affected Clyde that he could scarcely think what to do with himself in her absence, depressed as he was by the tangle which Roberta's condition presented. And exactly at this time also, Roberta's fears and demands had become so urgent that it was really no longer possible for him to assure her that if she would but wait a little while longer, he would be prepared to act in her behalf. Plead as he might, her case, as she saw it, was at last critical and no longer to be trifled with in any way. Her figure, as she insisted (although this was largely imaginative on her part), had altered to such an extent that it would not be possible for her longer to conceal it, and all those who worked with her at the factory were soon bound to know. She could no longer work or sleep with any comfort—she must not stay here any more. She was having preliminary pains—purely imaginary ones in her case. He must marry her now, as he had indicated he would, and leave with her at once—for some place—any place, really—near or far—so long as she was extricated from this present terrible danger. And she would agree, as she now all but pleaded, to let him go his way again as soon as their child was born—truly—and would not ask any more of him ever—ever. But now, this very week—not later than the fifteenth at the latest—he must arrange to see her through with this as he had promised.

But this meant that he would be leaving with her before ever he should have visited Sondra at Twelfth Lake at all, and without ever seeing her any more really. And, besides, as he so well knew, he had not saved the sum necessary to make possible the new venture on which she was insisting. In vain it was that Roberta now explained that she had saved over a hundred, and they could make use of that once they were married or to help in connection with whatever expenses might be incurred in getting to wherever he should decide they were going. All that he would see or feel was that this meant the loss of everything to him, and that he would have to go away with her to some relatively near-by place and get work at anything he could, in order to support her as best he might. But the misery of such a change! The loss of all his splendid dreams. And yet, racking his brains, he could think of nothing better than that she should quit and go home for the time being, since as he now argued, and most shrewdly, as he thought, he needed a few more weeks to prepare for the change which was upon them both. For, in

spite of all his efforts, as he now falsely asserted, he had not been able to save as much as he had hoped. He needed at least three or four more weeks in which to complete the sum, which he had been looking upon as advisable in the face of this meditated change. Was not she herself guessing, as he knew, that it could not be less than a hundred and fifty or two hundred dollars—quite large sums in her eyes—whereas, above his current salary, Clyde had no more than forty dollars and was dreaming of using that and whatever else he might secure in the interim to meet such expenses as might be incurred in the anticipated visit to Twelfth Lake.

But to further support his evasive suggestion that she now return to her home for a short period, he added that she would want to fix herself up a little, wouldn't she? She couldn't go away on a trip like this, which involved marriage and a change of social contacts in every way, without some improvements in her wardrobe. Why not take her hundred dollars or a part of it anyhow and use it for that? So desperate was his state that he even suggested that. And Roberta, who, in the face of her own uncertainty up to this time as to what was to become of her had not ventured to prepare or purchase anything relating either to a trousseau or layette, now began to think that whatever the ulterior purpose of his suggestion, which like all the others was connected with delay, it might not be unwise even now if she did take a fortnight or three weeks, and with the assistance of an inexpensive and yet tolerable dressmaker, who had aided her sister at times, make at least one or two suitable dresses—a flowered gray taffeta afternoon dress, such as she had once seen in a movie, in which, should Clyde keep his word, she could be married. To match this pleasing little costume, she planned to add a chic little gray silk hat—poke-shaped, with pink or scarlet cherries nestled up under the rim, together with a neat little blue serge traveling suit, which, with brown shoes and a brown hat, would make her as smart as any bride. The fact that such preparations as these meant additional delay and expense, or that Clyde might not marry her after all, or that this proposed marriage from the point of view of both was the tarnished and discolored thing that it was, was still not sufficient to take from the thought of marriage as an event, or sacrament even, that proper color and romance with which it was invested in her eyes and from which, even under such an unsatisfactory set of circumstances as these, it could not be divorced. And, strangely enough, in spite of all the troubled and strained relations that had developed between them, she still saw Clyde in much the same light in which she had seen him at first. He was a Griffiths, a youth of geniune social, if not financial distinction, one whom all the girls in her position, as well as many of those far above her, would be delighted to be connected with in this way—that is, via marriage. He might be objecting to marrying her, but he was a person of consequence, just the same. And one with whom, if he would but trouble to care for her a little, she could be perfectly happy. And at any rate, once he had loved her. And it was said of men—some men, anyway (so she had heard her mother and others say) that once a child was presented to them, it made a great difference in their attitude toward the mother, sometimes. They came to like the mother, too. Anyhow for a little while—a very little while—if what she had agreed to were strictly observed, she would have him with her to assist her through this great crisis—to give his name to her child—to aid her until she could once more establish herself in some way.

For the time being, therefore, and with no more plan than this, although with great misgivings and nervous qualms, since, as she could see, Clyde was decidedly indifferent, she rested on this. And it was in this mood that five days later, and after Roberta had written to her parents that she was coming home for two weeks at least, to get a dress or two made and to rest a little, because she was not feeling very well, that Clyde saw her off for her home in Biltz, riding with her as far as Fonda. But in so far as he was concerned, and since he had really no definite or workable idea, it seemed important to him that only silence, *silence* was the great and all essential thing now, so that, even under the impending edge of the knife of disaster, he might be able to think more, and more, and more, without being compelled to do anything, and without momentarily being tortured by the thought that Roberta, in some nervous or moody or frantic state, would say or do something which, assuming that he should hit upon some helpful thought or plan in connection with Sondra, would prevent him from executing it.

And about the same time, Sondra was writing him gay notes from Twelfth Lake as to what he might expect upon his arrival a little later. Blue water—white sails—tennis—golf—horseback riding—driving. She had it all arranged with Bertine, as she said. And kisses—kisses—kisses!

CHAPTER 42

TWO LETTERS, which arrived at this time and simultaneously, but accentuated the difficulty of all this.

Pine Point Landing, June 10th.

CLYDE MYDIE:

How is my pheet phing? All whytie? It's just glorious up here. Lots of people already here and more coming every day. The Casino and golf course over at Pine Point are open and lots of people about. I can hear Stuart and Grant with their launches going up toward Gray's Inlet now. You must hurry and come up, dear. It's too nice for words. Green roads to gallop through, and swimming and dancing at the Casino every afternoon at four. Just back from a wonderful gallop on Dickey and going again after luncheon to mail these letters. Bertine says she'll write you a letter to-day or to-morrow good for any week-end or any old time, so when Sonda says come, you come, you hear, else Sonda whip hard. You baddie, good boy.

Is he working hard in the baddie old factory? Sonda wisses he was here wiss her instead. We'd ride and drive and swim and dance. Don't forget your tennis racquet and golf clubs. There's a dandy course on the Casino grounds.

This morning when I was riding a bird flew right up under Dickey's heels. It scared him so that he bolted and Sonda got all switched and scwatched. Isn't Clydie sorry for his Sonda?

She is writing lots of notes to-day. After lunch and the ride to catch the down mail, Sonda and Bertine and Nina going to the Casino. Don't you wish you were going to be there? We could dance to "Taudy." Sonda just loves that song. But she has to dress now. More to-morrow, baddie boy. And when Bertine writes, answer right away. See all 'ose dots? Kisses. Big and little ones. All for baddie boy. And wite Sonda every day and she'll write 'oo.

More kisses.

To which Clyde responded eagerly and in kind in the same hour. But almost the same mail, at least the same day, brought the following letter from Roberta.

Biltz, June 10th.

DEAR CLYDE:

I am nearly ready for bed, but I will write you a few lines. I had such a tiresome journey coming up that I was nearly sick. In the first place I didn't want to come much (alone) as you know. I feel too upset and uncertain about everything, although I try not to feel so now that we have our plan and you are going to come for me as you said.

(At this point, while nearly sickened by the thought of the wretched country world in which she lived, still, because of Roberta's unfortunate and unavoidable relation to it, he now experienced one of his old time twinges of remorse and pity in regard to her. For after all, this was not her fault. She had so little to look forward to—nothing but her work or a commonplace marriage. For the first time in many days, really, and in the absence of both, he was able to think clearly—and to sympathize deeply, if gloomily. For the remainder of the letter read:)

But it's very nice here now. The trees are so beautifully green and the flowers in bloom. I can hear the bees in the orchard whenever I go near the south windows. On the way up instead of coming straight home I decided to stop at Homer to see my sister and brother-in-law, since I am not so sure now when I shall see them again, if ever, for I am resolved that they shall see me respectable, or never at all any more. You mustn't think I mean anything hard or mean by this. I am just sad. They have such a cute little home there, Clyde—pretty furniture, a Victrola, and all, and Agnes is so very happy with Fred. I hope she always will be. I couldn't help thinking of what a dear place we might have had, if only my dreams had come true. And nearly all the time I was there Fred kept teasing me as to why I don't get married, until I said, "Oh, well, Fred, you mustn't be too sure that I won't one of these days. All good things come to him who waits, you know." "Yes, unless you just turn out to be a waiter," was the way he hit me back.

But I was truly glad to see mother again, Clyde. She's so loving and patient and helpful. The sweetest, dearest mother that ever, ever was. And I just hate to hurt her in any way. And Tom and Emily, too. They have had friends here every evening since I've been here—and they want me to join in, but I hardly feel well enough now to do all the things they want me to do—play cards and games—dance.

(At this point Clyde could not help emphasizing in his own mind the shabby home world of which she was a part and which so recently he had seen —that rickety house! those toppling chimneys! Her uncouth father. And that in contrast to such a letter as this other from Sondra.)

Father and mother and Tom and Emily just seem to hang around and try to do things for me. And I feel remorseful when I think how they would feel if they knew, for, of course, I have to pretend that it is work that makes me feel so tired and depressed as I am sometimes. Mother keeps saying that I must stay a long time or quit entirely and rest and get well again, but she just don't know of course—poor dear. If she did! I can't tell you how that makes me feel sometimes, Clyde. Oh, dear!

But there, I mustn't put my sad feelings over on you either. I don't want to, as I told you, if you will only come and get me as we've agreed. And I won't be like that either, Clyde. I'm not that way all the time now. I've started to get ready and do all the things it'll take to do in three weeks and that's enough to keep my mind off everything but work. But you will come for me, won't you, dear? You won't disappoint me any more and make me suffer this time like you have so far, for, oh, how long it has been now—ever since I was here before at Christmas time, really. But you were truly nice to me. I promise not to be a burden on you, for I know you don't really care for me any

more and so I don't care much what happens now, so long as I get out of this. But I truly promise not to be a burden on you.

Oh, dear, don't mind this blot. I just don't seem to be able to control myself these days like I once could.

But as for what I came for. The family think they are clothes for a party down in Lycurgus and that I must be having a wonderful time. Well, it's better that way than the other. I may have to come as far as Fonda to get some things, if I don't send Mrs. Anse, the dressmaker, and if so, and if you wanted to see me again before you come, although I don't suppose you do, you could. I'd like to see you and talk to you again if you care to, before we start. It all seems so funny to me, Clyde, having these clothes made and wishing to see you so much and yet knowing that you would rather not do this. And yet I hope you are satisfied now that you have succeeded in making me leave Lycurgus and come up here and are having what you call a good time. Are they so very much better than the ones we used to have last summer when we went about to the lakes and everywhere? But whatever they are, Clyde, surely you can afford to do this for me without feeling too bad. I know it seems hard to you now, but you don't want to forget either that if I was like some that I know, I might and would ask more. But as I told you I'm not like that and never could be. If you don't really want me after you have helped me out like I said, you can go.

Please write me, Clyde, a long, cheery letter, even though you don't want to, and tell me all about how you have not thought of me once since I've been away or missed me at all—you used to, you know, and how you don't want me to come back and you can't possibly come up before two weeks from Saturday if then.

Oh, dear, I don't mean the horrid things I write, but I'm so blue and tired and lonely that I can't help it at times. I need some one to talk to—not just any one here, because they don't understand, and I can't tell anybody.

But there, I said I wouldn't be blue or gloomy or cross and yet I haven't done so very well this time, have I? But I promise to do better next time—tomorrow or next day, because it relieves me to write to you, Clyde. And won't you please write me just a few words to cheer me up while I'm waiting, whether you mean it or not, I need it so. And you will come, of course. I'll be so happy and grateful and try not to bother you too much in any way.

Your lonely
BERT

And it was the contrast presented by these two scenes which finally determined for him the fact that he would never marry Roberta—never—nor even go to her at Biltz, or let her come back to him here, if he could avoid that. For would not his going, or her return, put a period to all the joys that so recently in connection with Sondra had come to him here—make it impossible for him to be with Sondra at Twelfth Lake this summer—make it impossible for him to run away with and marry her? In God's name was there no way? No outlet from this horrible difficulty which now confronted him?

And in a fit of despair, having found the letters in his room on his return from work one warm evening in June, he now threw himself upon his bed and fairly groaned. The misery of this! The horror of his almost insoluble problem! Was there no way by which she could be persuaded to go away—and stay—remain at home, maybe for a while longer, while he sent her ten dollars a week, or twelve, even—a full half of all his salary? Or could she go to some neighboring town—Fonda, Gloversville, Schenectady—she was not so far gone but what she could take care of herself well enough as yet, and rent a room and remain there quietly until the fatal time, when she could go to some doctor or nurse? He might help her to find some one like that when the time came, if only she would be willing not to mention his name.

But this business of making him come to Biltz, or meeting her somewhere, and that within two weeks or less. He would not, he would not. He would do something desperate if she tried to make him do that—run away—or—maybe go up to Twelfth Lake before it should be time for him to go to Biltz, or before she would think it was time, and then persuade Sondra if he could—but oh, what a wild, wild chance was that—to run away with and marry him, even if she wasn't quite eighteen—and then—and then—being married, and her family not being able to divorce them, and Roberta not being able to find him, either, but only to complain—well, couldn't he deny it—say that it was not so—that he had never had any relationship, other than that which any department head might have with any girl working for him. He had not been introduced to the Gilpins, nor had he gone with Roberta to see that Dr. Glenn near Gloversville, and she had told him at the time, she had not mentioned his name.

But the nerve of trying to deny it!

The courage it would take.

The courage to try to face Roberta when, as he knew, her steady, accusing, horrified, innocent blue eyes would be about as difficult to face as anything in all the world. And could he do that? Had he the courage? And would it all work out satisfactorily if he did? Would Sondra believe him—once she heard?

But just the same in pursuance of this idea, whether finally he executed it or not, even though he went to Twelfth Lake, he must write Sondra a letter saying that he was coming. And this he did at once, writing her passionately and yearn-ingly. At the same time he decided not to write Roberta at all. Maybe call her on long distance, since she had recently told him that there was a neighbor near-by who had a telephone, and if for any reason he needed to reach her, he could use that. For writing her in regard to all this, even in the most guarded way, would place in her hands, and at this time, exactly the type of evidence in regard to this relationship which she would most need, and especially when he was so determined not to marry her. The trickery of all this! It was low and shabby, no doubt. Yet if only Roberta had agreed to be a little reasonable with him, he would never have dreamed of indulging in any such low and tricky plan as this. But, oh, Sondra! Sondra! And the great estate that she had described, lying along the west shore of Twelfth Lake. How beautiful that must be! He could not help it! He must act and plan as he was doing! He must!

And forthwith he arose and went to mail the letter to Sondra. And then while out, having purchased an evening paper and hoping via the local news of all whom he knew, to divert his mind for the time being, there, upon the first page of the *Times-Union* of Albany, was an item which read:

ACCIDENTAL DOUBLE TRAGEDY AT PASS LAKE—UP-TURNED CANOE AND FLOATING HATS REVEAL PROB-ABLE LOSS OF TWO LIVES AT RESORT NEAR PITTS-FIELD—UNIDENTIFIED BODY OF GIRL RECOVERED —THAT OF COMPANION STILL MISSING

Because of his own great interest in canoeing, and indeed in any form of water life, as well as his own particular skill when it came to rowing, swimming, diving, he now read with interest:

Pancoast, Mass., June 7th. . . . What proved to be a fatal boat ride for two, apparently, was taken here day before yesterday by an unidentified man and girl who came presumably from Pittsfield to spend the day at Pass Lake, which is fourteen miles north of this place.

Tuesday morning a man and a girl, who said to Thomas Lucas, who conducts the Casino Lunch and Boat House there, that they were from Pittsfield, rented a small rowboat about ten o'clock in the morning and with a basket, presumably containing lunch, departed for the northern end of the lake. At seven o'clock last evening, when they did not return, Mr. Lucas, in company with his son Jeffrey, made a tour of the lake in his motor boat and discovered the row-boat upside down in the shallows near the north shore, but no trace of the occupants. Thinking at the time that it might be another instance of renters having decamped in order to avoid payment, he returned the boat to his own dock.

But this morning, doubtful as to whether or not an

accident had occurred, he and his assistant, Fred Walsh, together with his son, made a second tour of the north shore and finally came upon the hats of both the girl and the man floating among some rushes near the shore. At once a dredging party was organized, and by three o'clock to-day the body of the girl, concerning whom nothing is known here, other than that she came here with her companion, was brought up and turned over to the authorities. That of the man has not yet been found. The water in the immediate vicinity of the accident in some places being over thirty feet deep, it is not certain whether the trolling and dredging will yield the other body or not. In the case of a similar accident which took place here some fifteen years ago, neither body was ever recovered.

To the lining of the small jacket which the girl wore was sewed the tag of a Pittsfield dealer. Also in her shoe lining was stamped the name of Jacobs of this same city. But other than these there was no evidence as to her identity. It is assumed by the authorities here that if she carried a bag of any kind it lies at the bottom of the lake.

The man is recalled as being tall, dark, about thirty-five years of age, and wore a light green suit and straw hat with a white and blue band. The girl appears to be not more than twenty-five, five feet five inches tall, and weighs 130 pounds. She wore her hair, which was long and dark brown, in braids about her forehead. On her left middle finger is a small gold ring with an amethyst setting. The police of Pittsfield and other cities in this vicinity have been notified, but as yet no word as to her identity has been received.

This item, commonplace enough in the usual grist of summer accidents, interested Clyde only slightly. It seemed odd, of course, that a girl and a man should arrive at a small lake anywhere, and setting forth in a small boat in broad daylight thus lose their lives. Also it was odd that afterwards no one should be able to identify either of them. And yet here it was. The man had disappeared for good. He threw the paper down, little concerned at first, and turned to other things—the problem that was confronting him really—how he was to do. But later—and because of that, and as he was putting out the light before getting into bed, and still thinking of the complicated problem which his own life here presented, he was struck by the thought (what devil's whisper?—what evil hint of an evil spirit?)—supposing that he and Roberta—no, say he and Sondra—(no, Sondra could swim so well, and so could he)—he and Roberta were in a small boat somewhere and it should capsize at the very time, say, of this dreadful complication which was so harassing him? What an escape? What a relief from a gigantic and by now really destroying problem! On the other hand—hold—not so fast!—for could a man even think of such

a solution in connection with so difficult a problem as his without committing a crime in his heart, really—a horrible, terrible crime? He must not even think of such a thing. It was wrong—wrong —terribly wrong. And yet, supposing,—by accident, of course—such a thing as this did occur? That would be the end, then, wouldn't it, of all his troubles in connection with Roberta? No more terror as to her—no more fear and heartache even as to Sondra. A noiseless, pathless, quarrelless solution of all his present difficulties, and only joy before him forever. Just an accidental, unpremeditated drowning—and then the glorious future which would be his!

But the mere thinking of such a thing in connection with Roberta at this time—(why was it that his mind persisted in identifying her with it?) was terrible, and he must not, he must not, allow such a thought to enter his mind. Never, never, never! He must not. It was horrible! Terrible! A thought of murder, no less! Murder?!!! Yet so wrought up had he been, and still was, by the letter which Roberta had written him, as contrasted with the one from Sondra—so delightful and enticing was the picture of her life and his as she now described it, that he could not for the life of him quite expel that other and seemingly easy and so natural a solution of all his problem—if only such an accident could occur to him and Roberta. For after all he was not planning any crime, was he? Was he not merely thinking of an accident that, had it occurred or could it but occur in his case. . . . Ah—but that *"could it but occur."* There was the dark and evil thought about which he must not, *he must not think.* HE MUST NOT. And yet—and yet, . . . He was an excellent swimmer and could swim ashore, no doubt— whatever the distance. Whereas Roberta, as he knew from swimming with her at one beach and another the previous summer, could not swim. And then—and then—well and then, unless he chose to help her, of course. . . .

As he thought, and for the time, sitting in the lamplight of his own room between nine-thirty and ten at night, a strange and disturbing creepiness as to flesh and hair and finger-tips assailed him. The wonder and the horror of such a thought! And presented to him by this paper in this way. Wasn't that strange? Besides, up in that lake country to which he was now going to Sondra, were many, many lakes about everywhere—were there not? Scores up there where Sondra was. Or so she had said. And Roberta loved the out-of-doors and the water so—although she could not swim— could not swim—could not swim. And they or at least he was going where lakes were, or they might,

might they not—and if not, why not? since both had talked of some Fourth of July resort in their planning, their final departure—he and Roberta.

But, no! no! The mere thought of an accident such as that in connection with her, however much he might wish to be rid of her—was sinful, dark and terrible! He must not let his mind run on any such things for even a moment. It was too wrong—too vile—too terrible! Oh, dreadful thought! To think it should have come to him! And at this time of all times—when she was demanding that he go away with her!

Death!

Murder!

The murder of Roberta!

But to escape her of course—this unreasonable, unshakable, unchangeable demand of hers! Already he was quite cold, quite damp—with the mere thought of it. And now—when—when—! But he must not think of that! The death of that unborn child, too!!

But how could any one even think of doing any such thing with calculation—deliberately? And yet—many people were drowned like that—boys and girls—men and women—here and there—everywhere the world over in the summer time. To be sure, he would not want anything like that to happen to Roberta. And especially at this time. He was not that kind of a person, whatever else he was. He was not. He was not. He was not. The mere thought now caused a damp perspiration to form on his hands and face. He was not that kind of a person. Decent, sane people did not think of such things. And so he would not either—from this hour on.

In a tremulous state of dissatisfaction with himself—that any such grisly thought should have dared to obtrude itself upon him in this way—he got up and lit the lamp—re-read this disconcerting item in as cold and reprobative way as he could achieve, feeling that in so doing he was putting anything at which it hinted far from him once and for all. Then, having done so, he dressed and went out of the house for a walk—up Wykeagy Avenue, along Central Avenue, out Oak, and then back on Spruce and to Central again—feeling that he was walking away from the insinuating thought or suggestion that had so troubled him up to now. And after a time, feeling better, freer, more natural, more human, as he so much wished to feel—he returned to his room, once more to sleep, with the feeling that he had actually succeeded in eliminating completely a most insidious and horrible visitation. He must never think of it again! He must never think of it again. He must never, never, never think of it—never.

And then falling into a nervous, feverish doze soon thereafter, he found himself dreaming of a savage black dog that was trying to bite him. Having escaped from the fangs of the creature by waking in terror, he once more fell asleep. But now he was in some very strange and gloomy place, a wood or a cave or narrow canyon between deep hills, from which a path, fairly promising at first, seemed to lead. But soon the path, as he progressed along it, became narrower and narrower and darker, and finally disappeared entirely. And then, turning to see if he could not get back as he had come, there directly behind him were arrayed an entangled mass of snakes that at first looked more like a pile of brush. But above it waved the menacing heads of at least a score of reptiles, forked tongues and agate eyes. And in front now, as he turned swiftly, a horned and savage animal—huge, it was—its heavy tread crushing the brush—blocked the path in that direction. And then, horrified and crying out in hopeless desperation, once more he awoke—not to sleep again that night.

CHAPTER 43

YET A thought such as that of the lake, connected as it was with the predicament by which he was being faced, and shrink from it though he might, was not to be dismissed as easily as he desired. Born as it was of its accidental relation to this personal problem that was shaking and troubling and all but disarranging his own none-too-forceful mind, this smooth, seemingly blameless, if dreadful, blotting out of two lives at Pass Lake, had its weight. That girl's body—as some peculiar force in his own brain now still compelled him to think—being found, but the man's not. In that interesting fact—and this quite in spite of himself—lurked a suggestion that insisted upon obtruding itself on his mind—to wit, that it might be possible that the man's body was not in that lake at all. For, since evil-minded people, did occasionally desire to get rid of other people, might it not be possible that that man had gone there with that girl in order to get rid of her? A very smooth and devilish trick, of course, but one which, in this instance at least, seemed to have succeeded admirably.

But as for him accepting such an evil suggestion and acting upon it . . . never! Yet here was his own problem growing hourly more desperate, since every day, or at least every other day, brought him either letters from Roberta or a note from Sondra—their respective missives maintaining the same relative contrast between ease and misery, gayety of mood and the somberness of defeat and uncertainty.

To Roberta, since he would not write her, he was telephoning briefly and in as non-committal a manner as possible. How was she? He was so glad to hear from her and to know that she was out in the country and at home, where it must be much nicer than in the factory here in this weather. Everything was going smoothly, of course, and except for a sudden rush of orders which made it rather hard these last two days, all was as before. He was doing his best to save a certain amount of money for a certain project about which she knew, but otherwise he was not worrying about anything—and she must not. He had not written before because of the work, and could not write much—there were so many things to do—but he missed seeing her in her old place, and was looking forward to seeing her again soon. If she were coming down toward Lycurgus as she said, and really thought it important to see him, well, that could be arranged, maybe—but was it necessary right now? He was so very busy and expected to see her later, of course.

But at the same time he was writing Sondra that assuredly on the eighteenth, and the week-end following, if possible, he would be with her.

So, by virtue of such mental prestidigitation and tergiversation, inspired and animated as it was by his desire for Sondra, his inability to face the facts in connection with Roberta, he achieved the much-coveted privilege of again seeing her, over one week-end at least, and in such a setting as never before in his life had he been privileged to witness.

For as he came down to the public dock at Sharon, adjoining the veranda of the inn at the foot of Twelfth Lake, he was met by Bertine and her brother as well as Sondra, who, in Grant's launch, had motored down the Chain to pick him up. The bright blue waters of the Indian Chain. The tall, dark, spear pines that sentineled the shores on either side and gave to the waters at the west a band of black shadow where the trees were mirrored so clearly. The small and large, white and pink and green and brown lodges on every hand, with their boathouses. Pavilions by the shore. An occasional slender pier reaching out from some spacious and at times stately summer lodge, such as those now owned by the Cranstons, Finchleys and others. The green and blue canoes and launches. The gay hotel and pavilion at Pine Point already smartly attended by the early arrivals here! And then the pier and boathouse of the Cranston Lodge itself, with two Russian wolfhounds recently acquired by Bertine lying on the grass near the shore, apparently awaiting her return, and a servant John, one of a half dozen who attended the family here, waiting to take the single bag of Clyde, his tennis racquet and golf sticks. But most of all he was impressed by the large rambling and yet smartly-designed house, with its bright geranium-bordered walks, its wide, brown, wicker-studded veranda commanding a beautiful view of the lake; the cars and personalities of the various guests, who in golf, tennis or lounging clothes were to be seen idling here and there.

At Bertine's request, John at once showed him to a spacious room overlooking the lake, where it was his privilege now to bathe and change for tennis with Sondra, Bertine and Grant. After dinner, as explained by Sondra, who was over at Bertine's for the occasion, he was to come over with Bertine and Grant to the Casino, where he would be introduced to such as all here knew. There was to be dancing. To-morrow, in the morning early, before breakfast, if he chose—he should ride with her and Bertine and Stuart along a wonderful woodland trail through the forests to the west which led to Inspiration Point and a more distant view of the lake. And, as he now learned, except for a few such paths as this, the forest was trackless for forty miles. Without a compass or guide, as he was told, one might wander to one's death even—so evasive were directions to those who did not know. And after breakfast and a swim she and Bertine and Nina Temple would demonstrate their new skill with Sondra's aquaplane. After that, lunch, tennis, or golf, a trip to the Casino for tea. After dinner at the lodge of the Brookshaws of Utica across the lake, there was to be dancing.

Within an hour after his arrival, as Clyde could see, the program for the week-end was already full. But that he and Sondra would contrive not only moments but possibly hours together he well knew. And then he would see what new delight, in connection with her many-faceted temperament, the wonderful occasion would provide. To him, in spite of the dour burden of Roberta, which for this one week-end at least he could lay aside, it was as though he were in Paradise.

And on the tennis grounds of the Cranstons, it seemed as though never before had Sondra, attired in a short, severe white tennis skirt and blouse, with a yellow-and-green dotted handkerchief tied about her hair, seemed so gay, graceful and happy. The smile that was upon her lips! The gay, laughing light of promise that was in her eyes whenever she glanced at him! And now and then, in running to serve him, it was as though she were poised bird-like in flight—her racquet arm high, a single toe seeming barely to touch the ground, her head thrown back, her lips parted and smiling always. And in calling twenty love, thirty love, forty love, it was always with a laughing accent on the word love, which at once thrilled and saddened him, as he saw, and rejoiced in from one point of view, she was his to take, if only he were free to take her now. But this other black barrier which he himself had built!

And then this scene, where a bright sun poured a flood of crystal light upon a greensward that stretched from tall pines to the silver rippling waters of a lake. And off shore in a half dozen different directions the bright white sails of small boats —the white and green and yellow splashes of color, where canoes paddled by idling lovers were passing in the sun! Summertime—leisure— warmth—color—ease—beauty—love—all that he had dreamed of the summer before, when he was so very much alone.

At moments it seemed to Clyde that he would reel from very joy of the certain fulfillment of a great desire, that was all but immediately within his control; at other times (the thought of Roberta sweeping down upon him as an icy wind), as though nothing could be more sad, terrible, numbing to the dreams of beauty, love and happiness than this which now threatened him. That terrible item about the lake and those two people drowned! The probability that in spite of his wild plan within a week, or two or three at most, he would have to leave all this forever. And then of a sudden he would wake to realize that he was fumbling or playing badly—that Bertine or Sondra or Grant was calling: "Oh, Clyde, what are you thinking of, anyhow?" And from the darkest depths of his heart he would have answered, had he spoken, "Roberta."

At the Brookshaws', again that evening, a smart company of friends of Sondra's, Bertine's and others. On the dance floor a reëncounter with Sondra, all smiles, for she was pretending for the benefit of others here—her mother and father in particular—that she had not seen Clyde before— did not even know that he was here.

"You up here? That's great. Over at the Cranstons'? Oh, isn't that dandy? Right next door to us. Well, we'll see a lot of each other, what? How about a canter to-morrow before seven? Bertine and I go nearly every day. And we'll have a picnic to-morrow, if nothing interferes, canoeing and motoring. Don't worry about not riding well. I'll get Bertine to let you have Jerry—he's just a sheep. And you don't need to worry about togs, either. Grant has scads of things. I'll dance the next two dances with others, but you sit out the third one

with me, will you? I know a peach of a place outside on the balcony.

She was off with fingers extended but with a "we-understand-each-other" look in her eye. And outside in the shadow later she pulled his face to hers when no one was looking and kissed him eagerly, and, before the evening was over, they had managed, by strolling along a path which led away from the house along the lake shore, to embrace under the moon.

"Sondra so glad Clydie here. Misses him so much." She smoothed his hair as he kissed her, and Clyde, bethinking him of the shadow which lay so darkly between them, crushed her feverishly, desperately. "Oh, my darling baby girl," he exclaimed. "My beautiful, beautiful Sondra! If you only knew how much I love you! If you only knew! I wish I could tell you *all*. I wish I could."

But he could not now—or ever. He would never dare to speak to her of even so much as a phase of the black barrier that now lay between them. For, with her training, the standards of love and marriage that had been set for her, she would never understand, never be willing to make so great a sacrifice for love, as much as she loved him. And he would be left, abandoned on the instant, and with what horror in her eyes!

Yet looking into his eyes, his face white and tense, and the glow of the moon above making small white electric sparks in his eyes, she exclaimed as he gripped her tightly: "Does he love Sondra so much? Oh, sweetie boy! Sondra loves him, too." She seized his head between her hands and held it tight, kissing him swiftly and ardently a dozen times. "And Sondra won't give her Clydie up either. She won't. You just wait and see! It doesn't matter what happens now. It may not be so very easy, but she won't." Then as suddenly and practically, as so often was her way, she exclaimed: "But we must go now, right away. No, not another kiss now. No, no, Sondra says no, now. They'll be missing us." And straightening up and pulling him by the arm she hurried him back to the house in time to meet Palmer Thurston, who was looking for her.

The next morning, true to her promise, there was the canter to Inspiration Point, and that before seven—Bertine and Sondra in bright red riding coats and white breeches and black boots, their hair unbound and loose to the wind, and riding briskly on before for the most part, then racing back to where he was. Or Sondra halloing gaily for him to come on, or the two of them laughing and chatting a hundred yards ahead in some concealed chapel of the aisled trees where he could not see them. And because of the interest which Sondra was so obviously manifesting in him these days—an interest which Bertine herself had begun to feel might end in marriage, if no family complications arose to interfere—she, Bertine, was all smiles, the very soul of cordiality, winsomely insisting that he should come up and stay for the summer and she would chaperon them both so that no one would have a chance to complain. And Clyde thrilling, and yet brooding too—by turns—occasionally—and in spite of himself drifting back to the thought that the item in the paper had inspired—and yet fighting it—trying to shut it out entirely.

And then at one point, Sondra, turning down a steep path which led to a stony and moss-lipped spring between the dark trees, called to Clyde to "Come on down. Jerry knows the way. He won't slip. Come and get a drink. If you do, you'll come back again soon—so they say."

And once he was down and had dismounted to drink, she exclaimed: "I've been wanting to tell you something. You should have seen Mamma's face last night when she heard you were up here. She can't be sure that I had anything to do with it, of course, because she thinks that Bertine likes you, too. I made her think that. But just the same she suspects that I had a hand in it, I guess, and she doesn't quite like it. But she can't say anything more than she has before. And I had a talk with Bertine just now and she's agreed to stick by me and help me all she can. But we'll have to be even more careful than ever now, because I think if Mamma got too suspicious I don't know what she might do—want us to leave here, even now maybe, just so I couldn't see you. You know she feels that I shouldn't be interested in any one yet except some one she likes. You know how it is. She's that way with Stuart, too. But if you'll take care not to show that you care for me so much whenever we're around any one of our crowd, I don't think she'll do anything—not now, anyhow. Later on, in the fall, when we're back in Lycurgus, things will be different. I'll be of age then, and I'm going to see what I can do. I never loved any one before, but I do love you, and, well, I won't give you up, that's all. I won't. And they can't make me, either!"

She stamped her foot and struck her boot, the while the two horses looked idly and vacantly about. And Clyde, enthused and astonished by this second definite declaration in his behalf, as well as fired by the thought that now, if ever, he might suggest the elopement and marriage and so rid himself of the sword that hung so threateningly above him, now gazed at Sondra, his eyes filled with a nervous hope and a nervous fear. For she might refuse, and change, too, shocked by the suddenness of his suggestion. And he had no money and no place in mind where they might go either, in case she accepted his proposal. But she had, perhaps, or she might have. And having once consented, might she not help him? Of course. At any rate, he felt that he must speak, leaving luck or ill luck to the future.

And so he said: "Why couldn't you run away with me now, Sondra, darling? It's so long until fall and I want you so much. Why couldn't we? Your mother's not likely to want to let you marry me then, anyhow. But if we went away now, she couldn't help herself, could she? And afterwards, in a few months or so, you could write her and then she wouldn't mind. Why couldn't we, Sondra?" His voice was very pleading, his eyes full of a sad dread of refusal—and of the future that lay unprotected behind that.

And by now so caught was she by the tremor with which his mood invested him, that she paused—not really shocked by the suggestion at all—but decidedly moved, as well as flattered by the thought that she was able to evoke in Clyde so eager and headlong a passion. He was so impetuous—so blazing now with a flame of her own creating, as she felt, yet which she was incapable of feeling as much as he, as she knew—such a flame as she had never seen in him or any one else before. And would it not be wonderful if she could run away with him now—secretly—to Canada or New York or Boston, or anywhere? The excitement her elopement would create here and elsewhere—in Lycurgus, Albany, Utica! The talk and feeling in her own family as well as elsewhere! And Gilbert would be related to her in spite of him—and the Griffiths, too, whom her mother and father so much admired.

For a moment there was written in her eyes the desire and the determination almost, to do as he suggested—run away—make a great lark of this, her intense and true love. For, once married, what could her parents do? And was not Clyde worthy of her and them, too? Of course—even though nearly all in her set fancied that he was not quite all he should be, just because he didn't have as much money as they had. But he would have—would he not—after he was married to her—and get as good a place in her father's business as Gil Griffiths had in his father's?

Yet a moment later, thinking of her life here and what her going off in such a way would mean to her father and mother just then—in the very beginning of the summer season—as well as how it would disrupt her own plans and cause her mother to feel especially angry, and perhaps even to bring about the dissolution of the marriage on the ground that she was not of age, she paused—that gay light of adventure replaced by a marked trace of the practical and the material that so persistently characterized her. What difference would a few months make, anyhow? It might, and no doubt would, save Clyde from being separated from her forever, whereas their present course might insure their separation.

Accordingly she now shook her head in a certain, positive and yet affectionate way, which by now Clyde had come to know spelled defeat—the most painful and irremediable defeat that had yet come to him in connection with all this. She would not go! Then he was lost—lost—and she to him forever maybe. Oh, God! For while her face softened with a tenderness which was not usually there—even when she was most moved emotionally—she said: "I would, honey, if I did not think it best not to, now. It's too soon. Mamma isn't going to do anything right now. I know she isn't. Besides she has made all her plans to do a lot of entertaining here this summer, and for my particular benefit. She wants me to be nice to—well, you know who I mean. And I can be, without doing anything to interfere with us in any way, I'm sure —so long as I don't do anything to really frighten her." She paused to smile a reassuring smile. "But you can come up here as often as you choose, don't you see, and she and these others won't think anything of it, because you won't be our guest, don't you see? I've fixed all that with Bertine. And that means that we can see each other all summer long up here, just about as much as we want to, don't you see? Then in the fall, when I come back, and if I find that I can't make her be nice to you at all, or consider our being engaged, why, I will run away with you. Yes, I will, darling —really and truly."

Darling! The fall!

She stopped, her eyes showing a very shrewd conception of all the practical difficulties before them, while she took both of his hands in hers and looked up into his face. Then, impulsively and conclusively, she threw both arms about his neck and, pulling his head down, kissed him.

"Can't you see, dearie? Please don't look so sad, darling. Sondra loves her Clyde so much. And she'll do anything and everything to make things come out right. Yes, she will. And they will, too. Now you wait and see. She won't give him up ever—ever!"

And Clyde, realizing that he had not one moving argument wherewith to confront her, really— not one that might not cause her to think strangely and suspiciously of his intense anxiety, and that this, because of Roberta's demand, and unless— unless—well—, unless Roberta let him go it all spelled defeat for him, now looked gloomily and even desperately upon her face. The beauty of her! The completeness of this world! And yet not to be allowed to possess her or it, ever. And Roberta with her demand and his promise in the immediate background! And no way of escape save by flight! God!

At this point it was that a nervous and almost deranged look—never so definite or powerful at any time before in his life—the border-line look between reason and unreason, no less—so powerful that the quality of it was even noticeable to Sondra—came into his eyes. He looked sick, broken, unbelievably despairing. So much so that she exclaimed, "Why, what is it, Clyde, dearie—you look so—oh, I can't say just how—forlorn or— Does he love me so much? And can't he wait just three or four months? But, oh, yes he can, too. It isn't as bad as he thinks. He'll be with me most of the time—the lovekins will. And when he isn't, Sondra'll write him every day—every day."

"But, Sondra! Sondra! If I could just tell you. If you knew how much it were going to mean to me—"

He paused here, for as he could see at this point, into the expression of Sondra came a practical inquiry as to what it was that made it so urgent for her to leave with him at once. And immediately, on his part, Clyde sensing how enormous was the hold of this world on her—how integral a part of it she was—and how, by merely too much insistence here and now, he might so easily cause her to doubt the wisdom of her primary craze for him, was moved to desist, sure that if he spoke it would lead her to questioning him in such a way as might cause her to change—or at least to modify her enthusiasm to the point where even the dream of the fall might vanish.

And so, instead of explaining further why he needed a decision on her part, he merely desisted, saying: "It's because I need you so much now, dear—all of the time. That's it, just that. It seems at times as though I could never be away from you another minute any more. Oh, I'm so hungry for you all of the time."

And yet Sondra, flattered as she was by this hunger and reciprocating it in part at least, merely repeated the various things she had said before. They must wait. All would come out all right in the fall. And Clyde, quite numb because of his defeat, yet unable to forego or deny the delight of being with her now, did his best to recover his mood— and think, think, think that in some way—somehow—maybe via that plan of that boat or in some other way!

But what other way?

But no, no, no—not that. He was not a murderer and never could be. He was not a murderer—never—never—never.

And yet this loss.

This impending disaster.

This impending disaster.

How to avoid that and win to Sondra after all. How, how, how?

CHAPTER 44

AND THEN on his return to Lycurgus early Monday morning, the following letter from Roberta.

DEAR CLYDE:

My dear, I have often heard the saying, "it never rains but it pours," but I never knew what it meant until to-day. About the first person I saw this morning was Mr. Wilcox, a neighbor of ours, who came to say that Mrs. Anse would not be out to-day on account of some work she had to do for Mrs. Dinwiddie in Biltz, although when she left yesterday everything had been prepared for her so that I could help her a little with the sewing and so hurry things up a bit. And now she won't be here until to-morrow. Next word came that Mother's sister, Mrs. Nichols, is very ill and Mother had to go over to her house at Baker's Pond, which is about twelve miles east of here, Tom driving her, although he ought to be here to help father with all the work that there is to do about the farm. And I don't know if Mother will be able to get back before Sunday. If I were better and didn't have all this work of my own on my hands I would have to go too, I suppose, although Mother insists not.

Next, Emily and Tom, thinking all is going so well with me and that I might enjoy it, were having four girls and four boys come here to-night for a sort of June moon-party, with ice cream and cake to be made by Emily and Mother and myself. But now, poor dear, she has to do a lot of telephoning over Mr. Wilcox's phone, which we share, in order to put it off until some day next week, if possible. And she's just heartsick and gloomy, of course.

As for myself, I'm trying to keep a stiff upper lip, as the saying is. But it's pretty hard, dear, I'll tell you. For so far I have only had three small telephone talks with you, saying that you didn't think you would have the necessary money before July fifth. And to put the finishing touches on it, as I only learned to-day, Mamma and Papa have about decided to go to my Uncle Charlie's in Hamilton for over the fourth (from the fourth to the fifteenth) and take me with them, unless I decide to return to Lycurgus, while Tom and Emily visit with my sister at Homer. But, dear, I can't do that, as you know. I'm too sick and worried. Last night I vomited dreadful and have been half dead on my feet all day, and I am just about crazy to-night.

Dear, what can we do? Can't you come for me before July third, which will be the time they will be going? You will have to come for me before then, really, because I just can't go up there with them. It's fifty miles from here. I could say I would go up there with them if only you would be sure to come for me before they start. But I must be absolutely sure that you are coming—absolutely.

Clyde, I have done nothing but cry since I got here. If you were only here I wouldn't feel so badly. I do try to be brave, dear, but how can I help thinking at times that you will never come for me when you haven't written me one single note and have only talked to me three times since I've been up here. But then I say to myself you couldn't be so mean as that, and especially since you have promised. Oh, you will come, won't you? Everything worries me so now, Clyde, for some reason and I'm so frightened, dear. I think of last summer and then this one, and all my dreams. It won't make any real difference to you about your coming a few days sooner than you intended, will it, dear? Even if we have to get along on a little less. I know that we can. I can be very saving and economical. I will try to have my dresses made by then. If not, I will do with what I have and finish them later. And I will try and be brave, dear, and not annoy you much, if only you will come. You must, you know, Clyde. It can't be any other way, although for your sake now I wish it could.

Please, please, Clyde, write and tell me that you will be here at the end of the time that you said. I worry so and get so lonesome off here all by myself. I will come straight back to you if you don't come by the time you said. I know you will not like me to say this, but, Clyde, I can't stay here and that's all there is to it. And I can't go away with Mamma and Papa either, so there is only one way out. I don't believe I will sleep a wink to-night, so please write me and in your letter tell me over and over not to worry about your not coming for me. If you could only come to-day, dear, or this week-end, I wouldn't feel so blue. But nearly two weeks more! Every one is in bed and the house is still, so I will stop.

But please write me, dear, right away, or if you won't do that call me up sure to-morrow, because I just can't rest one single minute until I do hear from you.

Your miserable ROBERTA.

P.S.: This is a horrid letter, but I just can't write a better one. I'm so blue.

But the day this letter arrived in Lycurgus Clyde was not there to answer it at once. And because of that, Roberta being in the darkest and most hysterical mood and thought, sat down on Saturday afternoon and, half-convinced as she was that he might already have departed for some distant point without any word to her, almost shrieked or screamed, if one were to properly characterize the mood that animated the following:

Biltz, Saturday, June 14th.

MY DEAR CLYDE:

I am writing to tell you that I am coming back to Lycurgus. I simply can't stay here any longer. Mamma worries and wonders why I cry so much, and I am just about sick. I know I promised to stay until the 25th or 26th, but then you said you would write me, but you never have—only an occasional telephone message when I am almost crazy. I woke up this morning and couldn't help crying right away and this afternoon my headache is dreadful.

I'm so afraid you won't come and I'm so frightened, dear. Please come and take me away some place, anywhere, so I can get out of here and not worry like I do. I'm so afraid in the state that I'm in that Papa and Mamma may make me tell the whole affair or that they will find it out for themselves.

Oh, Clyde, you will never know. You have said you would come, and sometimes I just know you will. But at other times I get to thinking about other things and I'm just as certain you won't, especially when you don't write or telephone. I wish you would write and say that you will come just so I can stand to stay here. Just as soon as you get this, I wish you would write me and tell me the exact day you can come—not later than the first, really, because I know I cannot stand to stay here any longer than then. Clyde, there isn't a girl in the whole world as miserable as I am, and you have made me so. But I don't mean that, either, dear. You were good to me once, and you are now, offering to come for me. And if you will come right away I will be so grateful. And when you read this, if you think I am unreasonable, please do not mind it, Clyde, but just think I am crazy with grief and worry and that I just don't know what to do. Please write me, Clyde. If you only knew how I need a word.

ROBERTA.

This letter, coupled as it was with a threat to come to Lycurgus, was sufficient to induce in Clyde a state not unlike Roberta's. To think that he had no additional, let alone plausible, excuse to offer Roberta whereby she could be induced to delay her final and imperative demand. He racked his brains. He must not write her any long and self-incriminating letters. That would be foolish in the face of his determination not to marry her. Besides his mood at the moment, so fresh from the arms and kisses of Sondra, was not for anything like that. He could not, even if he would.

At the same time, something must be done at once, as he could see, in order to allay her apparently desperate mood. And ten minutes after he had finished reading the last of these two letters, he was attempting to reach Roberta over the telephone. And finally getting her after a troublesome and impatient half-hour, he heard her voice, thin and rather querulous as it seemed to him at first, but really only because of a poor connection, saying: "Hello, Clyde, hello. Oh, I'm so glad you called. I've been terribly nervous. Did you get my two letters? I was just about to leave here in the morning if I didn't hear from you by then. I just couldn't stand not to hear anything. Where have you been, dear? Did you read what I said about my parents going away? That's true. Why don't you write, Clyde, or call me up anyhow? What about what I said in my letter about the third? Will you be sure and come then? Or shall I meet you somewhere? I've been so nervous the last three or four days, but now that I hear you again, maybe I'll be able to quiet down some. But I do wish you would write me a note every few days anyhow. Why won't you, Clyde? You haven't even written me one since I've been here. I can't tell you what a state I'm in and how hard it is to keep calm now."

Plainly Roberta was very nervous and fearsome as she talked. As a matter of fact, except that the home in which she was telephoning was deserted at the moment she was talking very indiscreetly, it seemed to Clyde. And it aided but little in his judgment for her to explain that she was all alone and that no one could hear her. He did not want her to use his name or refer to letters written to him.

Without talking too plainly, he now tried to make it clear that he was very busy and that it was hard for him to write as much as she might think necessary. Had he not said that he was coming on the 28th or thereabouts if he could? Well, he would if he could, only it looked now as though it might be necessary for him to postpone it for another week or so, until the seventh or eighth of July—long enough for him to get together an extra fifty for which he had a plan, and which would be necessary for him to have. But really, which was the thought behind this other, long enough for him to pay one more visit to Sondra as he was yearning to do, over the next week-end. But this demand of hers, now! Couldn't she go with her parents for a week or so and then let him come for her there or she come to him? It would give him more needed time, and—

But at this Roberta, bursting forth in a storm of nervous disapproval—saying that most certainly if that were the case she was going back to her room at the Gilpins', if she could get it, and not waste her time up there getting ready and waiting for him when he was not coming—he suddenly decided that he might as well say that he was coming on the third, or that if he did not, that at least by then he would have arranged with her where to meet him. For even by now, he had not made up his mind as to how he was to do. He must have a little more time to think—more time to think.

And so now he altered his tone greatly and said:

"But listen, Bert. Please don't be angry with me. You talk as though I didn't have any troubles in connection with all this, either. You don't know what this may be going to cost me before I'm through with it, and you don't seem to care much. I know you're worried and all that, but what about me? I'm doing the very best I can now, Bert, with all I have to think about. And won't you just be patient now until the third, anyhow? Please do. I promise to write you and if I don't, I'll call you up every other day. Will that be all right? But I certainly don't want you to be using my name like you did a while ago. That will lead to trouble, sure. Please don't. And when I call again, I'll just say it's Mr. Baker asking, see, and you can say it's any one you like afterwards. And then, if by any chance anything should come up that would stop our starting exactly on the third, why you can come back here if you want to, see, or somewhere near here, and then we can start as soon as possible after that."

His tone was so pleading and soothing, infused as it was—but because of his present necessity only with a trace of that old tenderness and seeming helplessness which, at times, had quite captivated Roberta, that even now it served to win her to a bizarre and groundless gratitude. So much so that at once she had replied, warmly and emotionally, even: "Oh, no, dear. I don't want to do anything like that. You know I don't. It's just because things are so bad as they are with me and I can't help myself now. You know that, Clyde, don't you? I can't help loving you. I always will, I suppose. And I don't want to do anything to hurt you, dear, really I don't if I can help it."

And Clyde, hearing the ring of genuine affection, and sensing anew his old-time power over her, was disposed to reënact the rôle of lover again, if only in order to dissuade Roberta from being too harsh and driving with him now. For while he could not like her now, he told himself, and could not think of marrying her, still in view of this other dream he could at least be gracious to her—could he not?—Pretend! And so this conversation ended with a new peace based on this agreement.

The preceding day—a day of somewhat reduced activities on the lakes from which he had just returned—he and Sondra and Stuart and Bertine, together with Nina Temple and a youth named Harley Baggott, then visiting the Thurstons, had motored first from Twelfth Lake to Three Mile Bay, a small lakeside resort some twenty-five miles north, and from thence, between towering walls of pines, to Big Bittern and some other small-er lakes lost in the recesses of the tall pines of the region to the north of Trine Lake. And en route, Clyde, as he now recalled, had been most strangely impressed at moments and in spots by the desolate and for the most part lonely character of the region. The narrow and rain-washed and even rutted nature of the dirt roads that wound between tall, silent and darksome trees—forests in the largest sense of the word—that extended for miles and miles apparently on either hand. The decadent and weird nature of some of the bogs and tarns on either side of the only comparatively passable dirt roads which here and there were festooned with funereal or viperous vines, and strewn like deserted battlefields with soggy and decayed piles of fallen and criss-crossed logs—in places as many as four deep—one above the other—in the green slime that an undrained depression in the earth had accumulated. The eyes and backs of occasional frogs that, upon lichen or vine or moss-covered stumps and rotting logs in this warm June weather, there sunned themselves apparently undisturbed; the spirals of gnats, the solitary flick of a snake's tail as disturbed by the sudden approach of the machine, one made off into the muck and the poisonous grasses and water-plants which were thickly imbedded in it.

And in seeing one of these Clyde, for some reason, had thought of the accident at Pass Lake. He did not realize it, but at the moment his own subconscious need was contemplating the loneliness and the usefulness at times of such a lone spot as this. And at one point it was that a weir-weir, one of the solitary water-birds of this region, uttered its ouphe and barghest cry, flying from somewhere near into some darker recess within the woods. And at this sound it was that Clyde had stirred nervously and then sat up in the car. It was so very different to any bird-cry he had ever heard anywhere.

"What was that?" he asked of Harley Baggott, who sat next him.

"What?"

"Why, that bird or something that just flew away back there just now?"

"I didn't hear any bird."

"Gee! That was a queer sound. It makes me feel creepy."

As interesting and impressive as anything else to him in this almost tenantless region had been the fact that there were so many lonesome lakes, not one of which he had ever heard of before. The territory through which they were speeding as fast as the dirt roads would permit, was dotted with them in these deep forests of pine. And only occasionally in passing near one, were there any signs indicating a camp or lodge, and those to be reached only by some half-blazed trail or rutty or sandy road disappearing through darker trees. In the main, the shores of the more remote lakes passed, were all but untenanted, or so sparsely that a cabin or a distant lodge to be seen across the smooth waters of some pine-encircled gem was an object of interest to all.

Why must he think of that other lake in Massachusetts! That boat! The body of that girl found—but not that of the man who accompanied her! How terrible, really!

He recalled afterwards,—here in his room, after this last conversation with Roberta—that the car, after a few more miles, had finally swung into an open space at the north end of a long narrow lake —the south prospect of which appeared to be divided by a point or an island suggesting a greater length and further windings or curves than were visible from where the car had stopped. And except for the small lodge and boathouse at this upper end it had appeared so very lonesome—not a launch or canoe on it at the time their party arrived. And as in the case of all the other lakes seen this day, the banks to the very shore line were sentineled with those same green pines—tall, spear-shaped—their arms widespread like one outside his window here in Lycurgus. And beyond them in the distance, to the south and west, rose the humped and still smooth and green backs of the nearer Adirondacks. And the water before them, now ruffled by a light wind and glowing in the afternoon sun, was of an intense Prussian blue, almost black, which suggested, as was afterwards confirmed by a guide who was lounging upon the low veranda of the small inn—that it was very deep—"all of seventy feet not more than a hundred feet out from that boathouse."

And at this point Harley Baggott, who was interested to learn more about the fishing possibilities of this lake in behalf of his father, who contemplated coming to this region in a few days, had inquired of the guide who appeared not to look at the others in the car: "How long is this lake, anyhow?"

"Oh, about seven miles." "Any fish in it?" "Throw a line in and see. The best place for black bass and the like of that almost anywhere around here. Off the island down yonder, or just to the south of it round on the other side there, there's a little bay that's said to be one of the best fishin' holes in any of the lakes up this way. I've seen a coupla men bring back as many as seventy-five fish in two hours. That oughta satisfy anybody that ain't tryin' to ruin the place for the rest of us."

The guide, a thinnish, tall and wizened type,

with a long, narrow head and small, keen, bright blue eyes laughed a yokelish laugh as he studied the group. "Not thinkin' of tryin' your luck today?"

"No, just inquiring for my dad. He's coming up here next week, maybe. I want to see about accommodations."

"Well, they ain't what they are down to Racquette, of course, but then the fish down there ain't what they are up here, either." He visited all with a sly and wry and knowing smile.

Clyde had never seen the type before. He was interested by all the anomalies and contrarities of this lonesome world as contrasted with cities he had known almost exclusively, as well as the decidedly exotic and material life and equipment with which, at the Cranstons' and elsewhere, he was then surrounded. The strange and comparatively deserted nature of this region as contrasted with the brisk and vigorous life of Lycurgus, less than a hundred miles to the south.

"The country up here kills me," commented Stuart Finchley at this point. "It's so near the Chain and yet it's so different, scarcely any one living up here at all, it seems."

"Well, except for the camps in summer and the fellows that come up to hunt moose and deer in the fall, there ain't much of anybody or anything around here after September first," commented the guide. "I've been guidin' and trappin' for nigh onto seventeen years now around here and 'cept for more and more people around some of the lakes below here—the Chain principally in summer—I ain't see much change. You need to know this country purty well if yer goin't strike out anywhere away from the main roads, though o' course about five miles to the west o' here is the railroad. Gun Lodge is the station. We bring 'em by bus from there in the summer. And from the south end down there is a sorta road leadin' down to Greys Lake and Three Mile Bay. You musta come along a part of it, since it's the only road up into this country as yet. They're talkin' of cuttin' one through to Long Lake sometime, but so far it's mostly talk. But from most of these other lakes around here, there's no road at all, not that an automobile could make. Just trails and there's not even a decent camp on some o' 'em. You have to bring your own outfit. But Ellis and me was over to Gun Lake last summer—that's thirty miles west o' here and we had to walk every inch of the way and carry our packs. But, oh, say, the fishin' and moose and deer come right down to the shore in places to drink. See 'em as plain as that stump across the lake."

And Clyde remembered that, along with the

others, he had carried away the impression that for solitude and charm—or at least mystery—this region could scarcely be matched. And to think it was all so comparatively near Lycurgus—not more than a hundred miles by road; not more than seventy by rail, as he eventually came to know.

But now once more in Lycurgus and back in his room after just explaining to Roberta, as he had, he once more encountered on his writing desk, the identical paper containing the item concerning the tragedy at Pass Lake. And in spite of himself, his eye once more followed nervously and yet unwaveringly to the last word all the suggestive and provocative details. The uncomplicated and apparently easy way in which the lost couple had first arrived at the boathouse; the commonplace and entirely unsuspicious way in which they had hired a boat and set forth for a row; the manner in which they had disappeared to the north end; and then the upturned boat, the floating oars and hats near the shore. He stood reading in the still strong evening light. Outside the windows were the dark boughs of the fir tree of which he had thought the preceding day and which now suggested all those firs and pines about the shores of Big Bittern.

But, good God! What was he thinking of anyhow? He, Clyde Griffiths! The nephew of Samuel Griffiths! What was "getting into" him? Murder! That's what it was. This terrible item—this devil's accident or machination that was constantly putting it before him! A most horrible crime, and one for which they electrocuted people if they were caught. Besides, he could not murder anybody—not Roberta, anyhow. Oh, no! Surely not after all that had been between them. And yet—this other world!—Sondra—which he was certain to lose now unless he acted in some way—

His hands shook, his eyelids twitched—then his hair at the roots tingled and over his body ran chill nervous titillations in waves. Murder! Or upsetting a boat at any rate in deep water, which of course might happen anywhere, and by accident, as at Pass Lake. And Roberta could not swim. He knew that. But she might save herself at that—screaming—clinging to the boat—and then—if there were any to hear—and she told afterwards! An icy perspiration now sprang to his forehead; his lips trembled and suddenly his throat felt parched and dry. To prevent a thing like that he would have to—to—but no—he was not like that. He could not do a thing like that—hit any one—a girl—Roberta—and when drowning or struggling. Oh, no, no—no such thing as that! Impossible.

He took his straw hat and went out, almost before any one heard him *think,* as he would have

phrased it to himself, such horrible, terrible thoughts. He could not and would not think them from now on. He was no such person. And yet—and yet—these thoughts. The solution—if he wanted one. The way to stay here—not leave—marry Sondra—be rid of Roberta and all—all—for the price of a little courage or daring. But no!

He walked and walked—away from Lycurgus—out on a road to the southeast which passed through a poor and decidedly unfrequented rural section, and so left him alone to think—or, as he felt, not to be heard in his thinking.

Day was fading into dark. Lamps were beginning to glow in the cottages here and there. Trees in groups in fields or along the road were beginning to blur or smokily blend. And although it was warm—the air lifeless and lethargic—he walked fast, thinking, and perspiring as he did so, as though he were seeking to outwalk and outthink or divert some inner self that preferred to be still and think.

That gloomy, lonely lake up there!

That island to the south!

Who would see?

Who could hear?

That station at Gun Lodge with a bus running to it at this season of the year. (Ah, he remembered that, did he? The deuce!) A terrible thing, to remember a thing like that in connection with such a thought as this! But if he were going to think of such a thing as this at all, he had better think well—he could tell himself that—or stop thinking about it now—once and forever—forever. But Sondra! Roberta! If ever he were caught—electrocuted! And yet the actual misery of his present state. The difficulty! The danger of losing Sondra. And yet, murder—

He wiped his hot and wet face, and paused and gazed at a group of trees across a field which somehow reminded him of the trees of . . . well . . . he didn't like this road. It was getting too dark out here. He had better turn and go back. But that road at the south and leading to Three Mile Bay and Greys Lake—if one chose to go that way—to Sharon and the Cranston Lodge—whither he would be going afterwards if he did go that way. God! Big Bittern—the trees along there after dark would be like that—blurred and gloomy. It would have to be toward evening, of course. No one would think of trying to . . . well . . . in the morning, when there was so much light. Only a fool would do that. But at night, toward dusk, as it was now, or a little later. But, damn it, he would not listen to such thoughts. Yet no one would be likely to see him or Roberta either—would they—there? It would be so easy to go to a place like Big

Bittern—for an alleged wedding trip—would it not—over the Fourth, say—or after the fourth or fifth, when there would be fewer people. And to register as some one else—not himself—so that he could never be traced that way. And then, again, it would be so easy to get back to Sharon and the Cranstons' by midnight, or the morning of the next day, maybe, and then, once there he could pretend also that he had come north on that early morning train that arrived about ten o'clock. And then . . .

Confound it—why should his mind keep dwelling on this idea? Was he actually planning to do a thing like this? But he was not! He could not be! He, Clyde Griffiths, could not be serious about a thing like this. That was not possible. He could not be. Of course! It was all to impossible, too wicked, to imagine that he, Clyde Griffiths, could bring himself to execute a deed like that. And yet . . .

And forthwith an uncanny feeling of wretchedness and insufficiency for so dark a crime insisted on thrusting itself forward. He decided to retrace his steps toward Lycurgus, where at least he could be among people.

CHAPTER 45

THERE are moments when in connection with the sensitively imaginative or morbidly anachronistic—the mentality assailed and the same not of any great strength and the problem confronting it of sufficient force and complexity—the reason not actually toppling from its throne, still totters or is warped or shaken—the mind befuddled to the extent that for the time being, at least, unreason or disorder and mistaken or erroneous counsel would appear to hold against all else. In such instances the will and the courage confronted by some great difficulty which it can neither master nor endure, appears in some to recede in precipitate flight, leaving only panic and temporary unreason in its wake.

And in this instance, the mind of Clyde might well have been compared to a small and routed army in full flight before a major one, yet at various times in its precipitate departure, pausing for a moment to meditate on some way of escaping complete destruction and in the coincident panic of such a state, resorting to the weirdest and most haphazard of schemes of escaping from an impending and yet wholly unescapable fate. The strained and bedeviled look in his eyes at moments —the manner in which, from moment to moment and hour to hour, he went over and over his hitherto poorly balanced actions and thoughts but with

no smallest door of escape anywhere. And yet again at moments the solution suggested by the item in the *Times-Union* again thrusting itself forward, psychogenetically, born of his own turbulent, eager and disappointed seeking. And hence persisting.

Indeed, it was now as though from the depths of some lower or higher world never before guessed or plumbed by him . . . a region otherwhere than in life or death and peopled by creatures otherwise than himself . . . there had now suddenly appeared, as the genii at the accidental rubbing of Aladdin's lamp—as the Efrit emerging as smoke from the mystic jar in the net of the fisherman—the very substance of some leering and diabolic wish or wisdom concealed in his own nature, and that now abhorrent and yet compelling, leering and yet intriguing, friendly and yet cruel, offered him a choice between an evil which threatened to destroy him (and against his deepest opposition) and a second evil which, however it might disgust or sear or terrify, still provided for freedom and success and love.

Indeed the center or mentating section of his brain at this time might well have been compared to a sealed and silent hall in which alone and undisturbed, and that in spite terrifying desires or advice of some darker or primordial of himself, he now sat thinking on the mystic or evil and unregenerate nature of his own, and without the power to drive the same forth or himself to decamp, and yet also without the courage to act upon anything.

For now the genii of his darkest and weakest side was speaking. And it said: "And would you escape from the demands of Roberta that but now and unto this hour have appeared unescapable to you? Behold! I bring you a way. It is the way of the lake—Pass Lake. This item that you have read —do you think it was placed in your hands for nothing? Remember Big Bittern, the deep, blue-black water, the island to the south, the lone road to Three Mile Bay? How suitable to your needs! A rowboat or a canoe upset in such a lake and Roberta would pass forever from your life. She cannot swim! The lake—the lake—that you have seen —that I have shown you—is it not ideal for the purpose? So removed and so little frequented and yet comparatively near—but a hundred miles from here. And how easy for you and Roberta to go there—not directly but indirectly—on this purely imaginative marriage-trip that you have already agreed to. And all that you need do now is to change your name—and hers—or let her keep her own and you use yours. You have never permitted her to speak of you and this relationship, and she never has. You have written her but formal notes.

And now if you should meet her somewhere as you have already agreed to, and without any one seeing you, you might travel with her, as in the past to Fonda, to Big Bittern—or some point near there."

"But there is no hotel at Big Bittern," at once corrected Clyde. "A mere shack that entertains but few people and that not very well."

"All the better. The less people are likely to be there."

"But we might be seen on the train going up together. I would be identified as having been with her."

"Were you seen at Fonda, Gloversville, Little Falls? Have you not ridden in separate cars or seats before and could you not do so now? Is it not presumably to be a secret marriage? Then why not a secret honeymoon?"

"True enough—true enough."

"And once you have arranged for that and arrive at Big Bittern or some lake like it—there are so many there—how easy to row out on such a lake? No questions. No registry under your own name or hers. A boat rented for an hour or half-day or day. You saw the island far to the south on that lone lake. Is it not beautiful? It is well worth seeing. Why should you not go there on such a pleasure trip before marriage? Would she not be happy so to do—as weary and distressed as she is now—an outing—a rest before the ordeal of the new life? Is not that sensible—plausible? And neither of you will ever return presumably. You will both be drowned, will you not? Who is to see? A guide or two—the man who rents you the boat—the innkeeper once, as you go. But how are they to know who you are? Or who she is? And you heard the depth of the water."

"But I do not want to kill her. I do not want to kill her. I do not want to injure her in any way. If she will but let me go and she go her own way, I will be so glad and so happy never to see her more."

"But she will not let you go or go her way unless you accompany her. And if you go yours, it will be without Sondra and all that she represents, as well as all this pleasant life here—your standing with your uncle, his friends, their cars, the dances, visits to the lodges on the lakes. And what then? A small job! Small pay! Another such period of wandering as followed that accident at Kansas City. Never another chance like this anywhere. Do you prefer that?"

"But might there not be some accident here, destroying all my dreams—my future—as there was in Kansas City?"

"An accident, to be sure—but not the same. In this instance the plan is in your hands. You can arrange it all as you will. And how easy! So many boats upsetting every summer—the occupants of them drowning, because in most cases they cannot swim. And will it ever be known whether the man who was with Roberta Alden on Big Bittern could swim? And of all deaths, drowning is the easiest—no noise—no outcry—perhaps the accidental blow of an oar—the side of a boat. And then silence! Freedom—a body that no one may ever find. Or if found and identified, will it not be easy, if you but trouble to plan, to make it appear that you were elsewhere, visiting at one of the other lakes before you decided to go to Twelfth Lake. What is wrong with it? Where is the flaw?"

"But assuming that I should upset the boat and that she should not drown, then what? Should cling to it, cry out, be saved and relate afterward that . . . But no, I cannot do that—will not do it. I will not hit her. That would be too terrible . . . too vile."

"But a little blow—any little blow under such circumstances would be sufficient to confuse and complete her undoing. Sad, yes, but she has an opportunity to go her own way, has she not? And she will not, nor let you go yours. Well, then, is this so terribly unfair? And do not forget that afterwards there is Sondra—the beautiful—a home with her in Lycurgus—wealth, a high position such as elsewhere you may never obtain again—never—never. Love and happiness—the equal of any one here—superior even to your cousin Gilbert."

The voice ceased temporarily, trailing off into shadow,—silence, dreams.

And Clyde, contemplating all that had been said, was still unconvinced. Darker fears or better impulses supplanted the counsel of the voice in the great hall. But presently thinking of Sondra and all that she represented, and then of Roberta, the dark personality would as suddenly and swiftly return and with amplified suavity and subtlety.

"Ah, still thinking on the matter. And you have not found a way out and you will not. I have truly pointed out to you and in all helpfulness the only way—the only way—It is a long lake. And would it not be easy in rowing about to eventually find some secluded spot—some invisible nook near that south shore where the water is deep? And from there how easy to walk through the woods to Three Mile Bay and Upper Greys Lake? And from there to the Cranstons'? There is a boat from there, as you know. Pah—how cowardly—how lacking in courage to win the thing that above all things you desire—beauty—wealth—position—the solution of your every material and spiritual desire. And with poverty, commonplace, hard and poor work as the alternative to all this.

"But you must choose—choose! And then act. You must! You must! You must!"

Thus the voice in parting, echoing from some remote part of the enormous chamber.

And Clyde, listening at first with horror and in terror, later with a detached and philosophic calm as one who, entirely apart from what he may think or do, is still entitled to consider even the wildest and most desperate proposals for his release, at last, because of his own mental and material weakness before pleasures and dreams which he could not bring himself to forego, physically intrigued to the point where he was beginning to think that it might be possible. Why not? Was it not even as the voice said—a possible and plausible way—all his desires and dreams to be made real by this one evil thing? Yet in his case, because of flaws and weaknesses in his own unstable and highly variable will, the problem was not to be solved by thinking thus—then—nor for the next ten days for that matter.

He could not really act on such a matter for himself and would not. It remained as usual for him to be forced either to act or to abandon this most *wild* and terrible thought. Yet during this time a series of letters—seven from Roberta, five from Sondra—in which in somber tones in so far as Roberta was concerned—in gay and colorful ones in those which came from Sondra—was painted the now so sharply contrasting phases of the black rebus which lay before him. To Roberta's pleadings, argumentative and threatening as they were, Clyde did not trust himself to reply, not even by telephone. For now he reasoned that to answer would be only to lure Roberta to her doom —or to the attempted drastic conclusion of his difficulties as outlined by the tragedy at Pass Lake.

At the same time, in several notes addressed to Sondra, he gave vent to the most impassioned declarations of love—his darling—his wonder girl— how eager he was to be at Twelfth Lake by the morning of the Fourth, if he could, and so thrilled to see her there again. Yet, alas, as he also wrote now, so uncertain was he, even now, as to how he was to do, there were certain details in connection with his work here that might delay him a day or two or three—he could not tell as yet—but would write her by the second at the latest, when he would know positively. Yet saying to himself as he wrote this, if she but knew what those details were—if she but knew. Yet in penning this, and without having as yet answered the last importunate letter from Roberta, he was also saying to himself that this did not mean that he was planning to go to Roberta at all, or that if he did, it did not mean that he was going to attempt to kill her. Never once did he honestly, or to put it more accurately, forthrightly and courageously or coldly face the thought of committing so grim a crime. On the contrary, the nearer he approached a final resolution or the need for one in connection with all this, the more hideous and terrible seemed the idea—hideous and difficult, and hence the more improbable it seemed that he should ever commit it. It was true that from moment to moment—arguing with himself as he constantly was—sweating mental sweats and fleeing from moral and social terrors in connection with it all, he was thinking from time to time that he might go to Big Bittern in order to quiet her in connection with these present importunities and threats and hence (once more evasion—tergiversation with himself) give himself more time in which to conclude what his true course must be.

The way of the Lake.

The way of the Lake.

But once there—whether it would then be advisable so to do—or not—well who could tell. He might even yet be able to convert Roberta to some other point of view. For, say what you would, she was certainly acting very unfairly and captiously in all this. She was, as he saw it in connection with his very vital dream of Sondra, making a mountain—an immense terror—out of a state that when all was said and done, was not so different from Esta's. And Esta had not compelled any one to marry her. And how much better were the Aldens to his own parents—poor farmers as compared to poor preachers. And why should he be so concerned as to what they would think when Esta had not troubled to think what her parents would feel?

In spite of all that Roberta had said about blame, was she so entirely lacking in blame herself? To be sure, he had sought to entice or seduce her, as you will, but even so, could she be held entirely blameless? Could she not have refused, if she was so positive at the time that she was so very moral? But she had not. And as to all this, all that he had done, had he not done all he could to help her out of it? And he had so little money, too. And was placed in such a difficult position. She was just as much to blame as he was. And yet now she was so determined to drive him this way. To insist on his marrying her, whereas if she would only go her own way—as she could with his help—she might still save both of them all this trouble.

But no, she would not, and he would not marry her and that was all there was to it. She need not think that she could make him. No, no, no! At times, when in such moods, he felt that he could do anything—drown her easily enough, and she would only have herself to blame.

Then again his more cowering sense of what society would think and do, if it knew, what he himself would be compelled to think of himself afterwards, fairly well satisfied him that as much as he desired to stay, he was not the one to do anything at all and in consequence must flee.

And so it was that Tuesday, Wednesday and Thursday following Roberta's letter received on Monday, had passed. And then, on Thursday night, following a most torturesome mental day on his and Roberta's part for that matter, this is what he received:

Biltz, Wednesday, June 30th.

Dear Clyde:

This is to tell you that unless I hear from you either by telephone or letter before noon, Friday, I shall be in Lycurgus that same night, and the world will know how you have treated me. I cannot and will not wait and suffer one more hour. I regret to be compelled to take this step, but you have allowed all this time to go in silence really, and Saturday is the third, and without any plans of any kind. My whole life is ruined and so will yours be in a measure, but I cannot feel that I am entirely to blame. I have done all I possibly could to make this burden as easy for you as possible and I certainly regret all the misery it will cause my parents and friends and all whom you know and hold dear. But I will not wait and suffer one hour more.

Roberta.

And with this in his hands, he was finally all but numbed by the fact that now decidedly he must act. She was actually coming! Unless he could soothe or restrain her in some manner she would be here to-morrow—the second. And yet the second, or the third, or any time until after the Fourth, was no time to leave with her. The holiday crowds would be too great. There would be too many people to see—to encounter. There must be more secrecy. He must have at least a little more time in which to get ready. He must think now quickly and then act. Great God! Get ready. Could he not telephone her and say that he had been sick or so worried on account of the necessary money or something that he could not write—and that besides his uncle had sent for him to come to Greenwood Lake over the Fourth. His uncle! His uncle! No, that would not do. He had used his name too much. What difference should it make to him or her now, whether he saw his uncle once more or not? He was leaving once and for all, or so he had been telling her, on her account, was he not? And so he had better say that he was going to his uncle, in order to give a reason why he was going away so that, possibly, he might be able

to return in a year or so. She might believe that. At any rate he must tell her something that would quiet her until after the Fourth—make her stay up there until at least he could perfect some plan—bring himself to the place where he could do one thing or the other. One thing or the other.

Without pausing to plan anything more than just this at this time, he hurried to the nearest telephone where he was least likely to be overheard. And, getting her once more, began one of those long and evasive and, in this instance, ingratiating explanations which eventually, after he had insisted that he had actually been sick—confined to his room with a fever and hence not able to get to a telephone—and because, as he now said, he had finally decided that it would be best if he were to make some explanation to his uncle, so that he might return some time in the future, if necessary—he, by using the most pleading, if not actually affectionate, tones and asking her to consider what a state he had been in, too, was able not only to make her believe that there was some excuse for his delay and silence, but also to introduce the plan that he now had in mind; which was if only she could wait until the sixth, then assuredly, without fail as to any particular, he would meet her at any place she would choose to come—Homer, Fonda, Lycurgus, Little Falls—only since they were trying to keep everything so secret, he would suggest that she come to Fonda on the morning of the sixth in order to make the noon train for Utica. There they could spend the night since they could not very well discuss and decide on their plans over the telephone, now, and then they could act upon whatever they had decided. Besides he could tell her better then just how he thought they ought to do. He had an idea—a little trip maybe, somewhere before they got married or after, just as she wished, but—something nice anyhow—(his voice grew husky and his knees and hands shook slightly as he said this, only Roberta could not detect the sudden perturbation within him). But she must not ask him now. He could not tell her over the phone. But as sure as anything, at noon on the sixth, he would be on the station platform at Fonda. All she had to do after seeing him was to buy her ticket to Utica and get in one coach, and he would buy his separately and get in another—the one just ahead or behind hers. On the way down, if she didn't see him at the station beforehand, he would pass through her car for a drink so that she could see that he was there—no more than that—but she mustn't speak to him. Then once in Utica, she should check her bag and he would follow her out to the nearest quiet corner. After that he would go and get her bag, and then they could go to some little hotel and he would take care of all the rest.

But she must do this. Would she have that much faith in him? If so, he would call her up on the third—the very next day—and on the morning of the sixth—sure, so that both he and she would know that everything was all right—that she was starting and that he would be there. What was that? Her trunk? The little one? Sure. If she needed it, certainly bring it. Only, if he were she, he would not trouble to try to bring too much now, because once she was settled somewhere, it would be easy enough to send for anything else that she really needed.

As Clyde stood at the telephone in a small outlying drug store and talked—the lonely proprietor buried in a silly romance among his pots and phials at the back—it seemed as though the Giant Efrit that had previously materialized in the silent halls of his brain, was once more here at his elbow—that he himself, cold and numb and fearsome, was being talked through—not actually talking himself.

Go to the lake which you visited with Sondra!

Get travel folders of the region there from either the Lycurgus House here or the depot.

Go to the south end of it and from there walk south, afterwards.

Pick a boat that will upset easily—one with a round bottom, such as those you have seen here at Crum Lake and up there.

Buy a new and different hat and leave that on the water—one that cannot be traced to you. You might even tear the lining out of it so that it cannot be traced.

Pack all of your things in your trunk here, but leave it, so that swiftly, in the event that anything goes wrong, you can return here and get it and depart.

And take only such things with you as will make it seem as though you were going for an outing to Twelfth Lake—not away, so that should you be sought at Twelfth Lake, it will look as though you had gone only there, not elsewhere.

Tell her that you intend to marry her, but *after* you return from this outing, not before.

And if necessary strike a light blow, so as to stun her—no more—so that falling in the water, she will drown the more easily.

Do not fear!

Do not be weak!

Walk through the woods by night, not by day —so that when seen again you will be in Three Mile Bay or Sharon—and can say that you came from Racquette or Long Lake south, or from Lycurgus north.

Use a false name and alter your handwriting as much as possible.

Assume that you will be successful.

And whisper, whisper—let your language be soft, your tone tender, loving, even. It must be, if you are to win her to your will now.

So the Efrit of his own darker self.

CHAPTER 46

AND THEN at noon on Tuesday, July sixth, the station platform of the railroad running from Fonda to Utica, with Roberta stepping down from the train which came south from Biltz to await Clyde, for the train that was to take them to Utica was not due for another half hour. And fifteen minutes later Clyde himself coming from a side street and approaching the station from the south, from which position Roberta could not see him but from where, after turning the west corner of the depot and stationing himself behind a pile of crates, he could see her. How thin and pale indeed! By contrast with Sondra, how illy-dressed in the blue traveling suit and small brown hat with which she had equipped herself for this occasion—the promise of a restricted and difficult life as contrasted with that offered by Sondra. And she was thinking of compelling him to give up Sondra in order to marry her, and from which union he might never be able to extricate himself until such time as would make Sondra and all she represented a mere recollection. The difference between the attitudes of these two girls—Sondra with everything offering all—asking nothing of him; Roberta, with nothing, asking all.

A feeling of dark bitter resentment swept over him and he could not help but feel sympathetic toward that unknown man at Pass Lake and secretly wish that he had been successful. Perhaps he, too, had been confronted by a situation just like this. And perhaps he had done right, too, after all, and that was why it had not been found out. His nerves twitched. His eyes were somber, resentful and yet nervous. Could it not happen again successfully in this case?

But here he was now upon the same platform with her as the result of her persistent and illogical demands, and he must be thinking how, and boldly, he must carry out the plans which, for four days, or ever since he had telephoned her, and in a dimmer way for the ten preceding those, he had been planning. This settled course must not be interfered with now. He must act! He must not let fear influence him to anything less than he had now planned.

And so it was that he now stepped forth in order

that she might see him, at the same time giving her a wise and seemingly friendly and informative look as if to say, "You see I am here." But behind the look! If only she could have pierced beneath the surface and sensed that dark and tortured mood, how speedily she would have fled. But now seeing him actually present, a heavy shadow that was lurking in her eyes lifted, the somewhat down-turned corners of her mouth reversed themselves, and without appearing to recognize him, she nevertheless brightened and at once proceeded to the window to purchase her ticket to Utica, as he had instructed her to do.

And she was now thinking that at last, at last he had come. And he was going to take her away. And hence a kind of gratefulness for this welling up in her. For they were to be together for seven or eight months at the least. And while it might take tact and patience to adjust things, still it might and probably could be done. From now on she must be the very soul of caution—not do or say anything that would irritate him in any way, since naturally he would not be in the best mood because of this. But he must have changed some— perhaps he was seeing her in a more kindly light— sympathizing with her a little, since he now appeared at last to have most gracefully and genially succumbed to the unavoidable. And at the same time noting his light gray suit, his new straw hat, his brightly polished shoes and the dark tan suitcase and (strange, equivocal, frivolous erraticism of his in this instance) the tripod of a recently purchased camera together with his tennis racquet in its canvas case strapped to the side—more than anything to conceal the initials C. G.—she was seized with much of her old-time mood and desire in regard to his looks and temperament. He was still, and despite his present indifference to her, her Clyde.

Having seen her secure her ticket, he now went to get his own, and then, with another knowing look in her direction, which said that everything was now all right, he returned to the eastern end of the platform, while she returned to her position at the forward end.

(*Why was that old man in that old brown winter suit and hat and carrying that bird cage in a brown paper looking at him so? Could he sense anything? Did he know him? Had he ever worked in Lycurgus or seen him before?*)

He was going to buy a second straw hat in Utica to-day—he must remember that—a straw hat with a Utica label, which he would wear instead of his present one. Then, when she was not looking, he would put the old one in his bag with his other

things. That was why he would have to leave her for a little while after they reached Utica—at the depot or library or somewhere—perhaps as was his first plan, take her to some small hotel somewhere and register as Mr. and Mrs. Carl Graham or Clifford Golden or Gehring (there was a girl in the factory by that name) so if they were ever traced in any way, it would be assumed that she had gone away with some man of that name.

(*That whistle of a train afar off. It must be coming now. His watch said twelve-twenty-seven.*)

And again he must decide what his manner toward her in Utica must be—whether very cordial or the opposite. For over the telephone, of course, he had talked very soft and genial-like because he had to. Perhaps it would be best to keep that up, otherwise she might become angry or suspicious or stubborn and that would make it hard.

(*Would that train never get here?*)

At the same time it was going to be very hard on him to be so very pleasant when, after all, she was driving him as she was—expecting him to do all that she was asking him to do and yet be nice to her. Damn! And yet if he weren't?—Supposing she should sense something of his thoughts in connection with this—really refuse to go through with it this way and spoil his plans.

(*If only his knees and hands wouldn't tremble so at times.*)

But no, how was she to be able to detect anything of that kind, when he himself had not quite made up his mind as to whether he would be able to go through with it or not? He only knew he was not going away with her, and that was all there was to that. He might not upset the boat, as he had decided on the day before, but just the same he was not going away with her.

But here now was the train. And there was Roberta lifting her bag. Was it too heavy for her in her present state? It probably was. Well, too bad. It was very hot to-day, too. At any rate he would help her with it later, when they were where no one could see them. She was looking toward him to be sure he was getting on—so like her these days, in her suspicious, doubtful mood in regard to him. But here was a seat in the rear of the car on the shady side, too. That was not so bad. He would settle himself comfortably and look out. For just outside Fonda, a mile or two beyond, was that same Mohawk that ran through Lycurgus and past the factory, and along the banks of which the year before, he and Roberta had walked about this time. But the memory of that being far from pleasant now, he turned his eyes to a paper he had bought, and behind which he could shield himself as much as possible, while he once more began to observe the details of the more inward scene which now so much more concerned him—the nature of the lake country around Big Bittern, which ever since that final important conversation with Roberta over the telephone, had been interesting him more than any other geography of the world.

For on Friday, after the conversation, he had stopped in at the Lycurgus House and secured three different folders relating to hotels, lodges, inns and other camps in the more remote region beyond Big Bittern and Long Lake. (If only there were some way to get to one of those completely deserted lakes described by that guide at Big Bittern—only, perhaps, there might not be any rowboats on any of these lakes at all!) And again on Saturday, had he not secured four more circulars from the rack at the depot (they were in his pocket now)? Had they not proved how many small lakes and inns there were along this same railroad, which ran north to Big Bittern, to which he and Roberta might resort for a day or two if she would —a night, anyhow, before going to Big Bittern and Grass Lake—had he not noted that in particular— a beautiful lake it had said—near the station, and with at least three attractive lodges or country home inns where two could stay for as low as twenty dollars a week. That meant that two could stay for one night surely for as little as five dollars. It must be so surely—and so he was going to say to her, as he had already planned these several days, that she needed a little rest before going away to a strange place. That it would not cost very much—about fifteen dollars for fares and all, so the circulars said—if they went to Grass Lake for a night—this same night after reaching Utica —or on the morrow, anyhow. And he would have to picture it all to her as a sort of honeymoon journey—a little pleasant outing—before getting married. And it would not do to succumb to any plan of hers to get married before they did this—that would never do.

(*Those five birds winging toward that patch of trees over there—below that hill.*)

It certainly would not do to go direct to Big Bittern from Utica for a boat ride—just one day —seventy miles. That would not sound right to her, or to any one. It would make her suspicious, maybe. It might be better, since he would have to get away from her to buy a hat in Utica, to spend this first night there at some inexpensive, inconspicuous hotel, and once there, suggest going up to Grass Lake. And from there they would go to Big Bittern in the morning. He could say that Big Bittern was nicer—or that they would go down to Three Mile Bay—a hamlet really as he knew— where they could be married, but en route stop at Big Bittern as a sort of lark. He would say that he wanted to show her the lake—take some pictures of her and himself. He had brought his camera for that and for other pictures of Sondra later.

The blackness of this plot of his!

(*Those nine black and white cows on that green hillside.*)

But again, strapping that tripod along with his tennis racquet to the side of his suitcase, might not that cause people to imagine that they were passing tourists from some distant point, maybe, and if they both disappeared, well, then, they were not people from anywhere around here, were they? Didn't the guide say that the water in the lake was all of seventy-five feet deep—like that water at Pass Lake? And as for Roberta's grip—oh, yes, what about that? He hadn't even thought about that as yet, really.

(*Those three automobiles out there running almost as fast as this train.*)

Well, in coming down from Grass Lake after one night there (he could say that he was going to marry her at Three Mile Bay at the north end of Greys Lake, where a minister lived whom he had met), he would induce her to leave her bag at that Gun Lodge station, where they took the bus over to Big Bittern, while he took his with him. He could just say to some one—the boatman, maybe, or the driver, that he was taking his camera in his bag, and ask where the best views were. Or maybe a lunch. Was that not a better idea—to take a lunch and so deceive Roberta, too, perhaps? And that would tend to mislead the driver, also, would it not? People did carry cameras in bags when they went out on lakes, at times. At any rate it was most necessary for him to carry his bag in this instance. Else why the plan to go south to that island and from thence through the woods?

(*Oh, the grimness and the terror of this plan! Could he really execute it?*)

But that strange cry of that bird at Big Bittern. He had not liked that, or seeing that guide up there who might remember him now. He had not talked to him at all—had not even gotten out of the car, but had only looked out at him through the window; and in so far as he could recall the guide had not even once looked at him—had merely talked to Grant Cranston and Harley Baggott, who had gotten out and had done all the talking. But supposing this guide should be there and remember him? But how could that be when he really had not seen him? This guide would probably not remember him at all—might not even be there. But why should his hands and face be damp all the time now—wet almost, and cold—his knees shaky?

(*This train was following the exact curve of this stream—and last summer he and Roberta. But no—*)

As soon as they reached Utica now this was the way he would do—and must keep it well in mind and not get rattled in any way. He must not—he must not. He must let her walk up the street before him, say a hundred feet or so between them, so that no one would think he was following her, of course. And then when they were quite alone somewhere he would catch up with her and explain all about this—be very nice as though he cared for her as much as ever now—he would have to—if he were to get her to do as he wanted. And then—and then, oh, yes, have her wait while he went for that extra straw hat that he was going to—well, leave on the water, maybe. And the oars, too, of course. And her hat—and—well—

(*The long, sad sounding whistle of this train. Damn. He was getting nervous already.*)

But before going to the hotel, he must go back to the depot and put his new hat in the bag, or better yet, carry it while he looked for the sort of hotel he wanted, and then, before going to Roberta, take the hat and put it in his bag. Then he would go and find her and have her come to the entrance of the hotel he had found and wait for him, while he got the bags. And, of course, if there was no one around or very few, they would enter together, only she could wait in the ladies' parlor somewhere, while he went and registered as Charles Golden, maybe, this time. And then, well, in the morning, if she agreed, or to-night, for that matter, if there were any trains—he would have to find out about that—they could go up to Grass Lake in separate cars until they were past Twelfth Lake and Sharon, at any rate.

(*The beautiful Cranston Lodge there and Sondra.*)

And then—and then—

(*That big red barn and that small white house near it. And that wind-mill. So like those houses and barns that he had seen out there in Illinois and Missouri. And Chicago, too.*)

And at the same time Roberta in her car forward thinking that Clyde had not appeared so very unfriendly to her. To be sure, it was hard on him, making him leave Lycurgus in this way, and when he might be enjoying himself as he wished to. But on the other hand, here was she—and there was no other way for her to be. She must be very genial and yet not put herself forward too much or in his way. And yet she must not be too receding or weak, either, for, after all, Clyde was the one who had placed her in this position. And it was only fair, and little enough for him to do. She would have a baby to look after in the future, and all that trouble to go through with from now on. And later, she would have to explain to her parents this whole mysterious proceeding, which covered her present disappearance and marriage, if Clyde really did marry her now. But she must insist upon that—and soon—in Utica, perhaps—certainly at the very next place they went to—and get a copy of her marriage certificate, too, and keep it for her own as well as the baby's sake. He could get a divorce as he pleased after that. She would still be Mrs. Griffiths. And Clyde's baby and hers would be a Griffiths, too. That was something.

(*How beautiful the little river was. It reminded her of the Mohawk and the walks she and he had taken last summer when they first met. Oh, last summer! And now this!*)

And they would settle somewhere—in one or two rooms, no doubt. Where, she wondered—in what town or city? How far away from Lycurgus or Biltz—the farther from Biltz the better, although she would like to see her mother and father again, and soon—as soon as she safely could. But what matter, as long as they were going away together and she was to be married?

Had he noticed her blue suit and little brown hat? And had he thought she looked at all attractive compared to those rich girls with whom he was always running? She must be very tactful—not irritate him in any way. But—oh, the happy life they could have if only—if only he cared for her a little—just a little . . .

And then Utica, and on a quiet street Clyde catching up with Roberta, his expression a mixture of innocent geniality and good-will, tempered by worry and opposition, which was really a mask for the fear of the deed that he himself was contemplating—his power to execute it—the consequences in case he failed.

CHAPTER 47

AND THEN, as planned that night between them —a trip to Grass Lake the next morning in separate cars, but which, upon their arrival and to his surprise, proved to be so much more briskly tenanted than he anticipated. He was very much disturbed and frightened by the evidence of so much active life up here. For he had fancied this, as well as Big Bittern, would be all but deserted. Yet here now, as both could see, it was the summer seat and gathering place of some small religious organization or group—the Winebrennarians of Pennsylvania—as it proved, with a tabernacle and numerous cottages across the lake from the station. And Roberta at once exclaiming:

"Now, there, isn't that cute? Why couldn't we be married over there by the minister of that church?"

And Clyde, puzzled and shaken by this sudden and highly unsatisfactory development, at once announced: "Why, sure—I'll go over after a bit and see," yet his mind busy with schemes for circumventing her. He would take her out in a boat after registering and getting settled and remain too long. Or should a peculiarly remote and unobserved spot be found . . . but no, there were too many people here. The lake was not large enough, and probably not very deep. It was black or dark like tar, and sentineled to the east and north by tall, dark pines—the serried spears of armed and watchful giants, as they now seemed to him—ogres almost—so gloomy, suspicious and fantastically erratic was his own mood in regard to all this. But still there were too many people— as many as ten on the lake.

The weirdness of it.

The difficulty.

But whisper:—one could not walk from here through any woods to Three Mile Bay. Oh, no. That was all of thirty miles to the south now. And besides this lake was less lonely—probably continually observed by members of this religious group. Oh, no—he must say—he must say—but what—could he say? That he had inquired, and that no license could be procured here? Or that the minister was away, or that he required certain identifications which he did not have—or—or, well, well—anything that would serve to still Roberta until such hour to-morrow, as the train south from here left for Big Bittern and Sharon, where, of course, they would surely be married.

Why should she be so insistent? And why, anyhow, and except for her crass determination to force him in this way, should he be compelled to track here and there with her—every hour—every minute of which was torture—an unending mental crucifixion really, when, if he were but rid of her! Oh, Sondra, Sondra, if but now from your high estate, you might bend down and aid me. No more lies! No more suffering! No more misery of any kind!

But instead, more lies. A long and aimless and pestilential search for water-lilies, which because of his own restless mood, bored Roberta as much as it did him. For why, she was now thinking to herself as they rowed about, this indifference to this marriage possibility, which could have been arranged before now and given this outing the dream quality it would and should have had, if only—if only he had arranged for everything in Utica, even as she had wanted. But this waiting— evasion—and so like Clyde, his vacillating, indefinite, uncertain mood, always. She was beginning to wonder now as to his intentions again— whether really and truly he did intend to marry her as he had promised. To-morrow, or the next day at most, would show. So why worry now?

And then the next day at noon, Gun Lodge and Big Bittern itself and Clyde climbing down from the train at Gun Lodge and escorting Roberta to the waiting bus, the while he assured her that since they were coming back this way, it would be best if she were to leave her bag here, while he, because of his camera as well as the lunch done up at Grass Lake and crowded into his suitcase, would take his own with him, because they would lunch on the lake. But on reaching the bus, he was dismayed by the fact that the driver was the same guide whom he had heard talk at Big Bittern. What if it should prove now that this guide had seen and remembered him! Would he not at least recall the handsome Finchley car—Bertine and Stuart on the front seat—himself and Sondra at the back— Grant and that Harley Baggott talking to him outside?

At once that cold perspiration that had marked his more nervous and terrified moods for weeks past, now burst forth on his face and hands. Of what had he been thinking, anyhow? How planning? In God's name, how expect to carry a thing like this through, if he were going to think so poorly? It was like his failing to wear his cap from Lycurgus to Utica, or at least getting it out of his bag before he tried to buy that straw hat; it was like not buying the straw hat before he went to Utica at all.

Yet the guide did not remember him, thank God! On the contrary he inquired rather curiously, and as of a total stranger: "Goin' over to the lodge at Big Bittern? First time up here?" And Clyde, enormously relieved and yet really tremulous, replied: "Yes," and then in his nervous excitement asked: "Many people over there to-day?" a question which the moment he had propounded it, seemed almost insane. Why, why, of all questions, should he ask that? Oh, God, would his silly, self-destructive mistakes never cease?

So troubled was he indeed, now, that he scarcely heard the guide's reply, or, if at all, as a voice speaking from a long way off. "Not so many. About seven or eight, I guess. We did have about thirty over the Fourth, but most o' them went down yesterday."

The stillness of these pines lining this damp yellow road along which they were traveling; the cool and the silence; the dark shadows and purple and gray depths and nooks in them, even at high noon. If one were slipping away at night or by day, who would encounter one here? A blue-jay far in the depths somewhere uttered its metallic shriek; a field sparrow, tremulous upon some distant twig, filled the silver shadows with its perfect song. And Roberta, as this heavy, covered bus crossed rill and thin stream, and then rough wooden bridges here and there, commented on the clarity and sparkle of the water: "Isn't that wonderful in there? Do you hear the tinkling of that water, Clyde? Oh, the freshness of this air!"

And yet she was going to die so soon!

God!

But supposing now, at Big Bittern—the lodge and boathouse there—there were many people. Or that the lake, peradventure, was literally dotted with those that were there—all fishermen and all fishing here and there, each one separate and alone—no privacy or a deserted spot anywhere. And how strange he had not thought of that. This lake was probably not nearly as deserted as he had imagined, or would not be to-day, any more than Grass Lake had proved. And then what?

Well, flight then—flight—and let it go at that. This strain was too much—hell—he would die, thinking thoughts like these. How could he have dreamed to better his fortunes by any so wild and brutal a scheme as this anyhow—to kill and then run away—or rather to kill and pretend that he and she had drowned—while he—the real murderer—slipped away to life and happiness. What a horrible plan! And yet how else? How? Had he not come all this way to do this? And was he going to turn back now?

And all this time Roberta at his side was imagining that she was not going to anything but marriage—to-morrow morning sure; and now only to the passing pleasure of seeing this beautiful lake of which he had been talking—talking, as though it were something more important and delectable than any that had as yet been in her or his life for that matter.

But now the guide was speaking again, and to him: "You're not mindin' to stay over, I suppose.

I see you left the young lady's bag over there." He nodded in the direction of Gun Lodge.

"No, we're going on down to-night—on that 8:10. You take people over to that?"

"Oh, sure."

"They said you did—at Grass Lake."

But now why should he have added that reference to Grass Lake, for that showed that he and Roberta had been there before coming here. But this fool with his reference to "the young lady's bag!" And leaving it at Gun Lodge. The Devil! Why shouldn't he mind his own business? Or why should he have decided that he and Roberta were not married? Or had he so decided? At any rate, why such a question when they were carrying two bags and he had brought one? Strange! The effrontery! How should he know or guess or what? But what harm could it do—married or unmarried? If she were not found—"married or unmarried" would make no difference, would it? And if she were, and it was discovered that she was not married, would that not prove that she was off with some one else? Of course! So why worry over that now?

And Roberta asking: "Are there any hotels or boarding houses on the lake besides this one we're going to?"

"Not a one, miss, outside o' the inn that we're goin' to. There was a crowd of young fellers and girls campin' over on the east shore, yisterday, I believe, about a mile from the inn—but whether they're there now or not, I dunno. Ain't seen none of 'em to-day."

A crowd of young fellows and girls! For God's sake! And might not they now be out on the water —all of them—rowing—or sailing—or what? And he here with her! Maybe some of them from Twelfth Lake! Just as he and Sondra and Harriet and Stuart and Bertine had come up two weeks before—some of them friends of the Cranstons, Harriets, Finchleys or others who had come up here to play and who would remember him, of course. And again, then, there must be a road to the east of this lake. And all this knowledge and their presence there now might make this trip of his useless. Such silly plotting! Such pointless planning as this—when at least he might have taken more time—chosen a lake still farther away and should have—only so tortured had he been for these last many days, that he could scarcely think how to think. Well, all he could do now was to go and see. If there were many he must think of some way to row to some real lonely spot or may turn and return to Grass Lake—or where? Oh, what could or would he do—if there were many over here?

But just then a long aisle of green trees giving out at the far end as he now recalled upon a square of lawn, and the lake itself, the little inn with its pillared veranda, facing the dark blue waters of Big Bittern. And that low, small red-roofed boathouse to the right on the water that he had seen before when he was here. And Roberta exclaiming on sight, "Oh, it is pretty, isn't it—just beautiful." And Clyde surveying that dark, low island in the distance, to the south, and seeing but few people about—none on the lake itself—exclaiming nervously, "Yes, it is, you bet." But feeling half choked as he said it.

And now the host of the inn himself appearing and approaching—a medium-sized, red-faced, broad-shouldered man who was saying most intriguingly, "Staying over for a few days?"

But Clyde, irritated by this new development and after paying the guide a dollar, replying crustily and irritably, "No, no—just came over for the afternoon. We're going on down to-night."

"You'll be staying over for dinner then, I suppose? The train doesn't leave till eight-fifteen."

"Oh, yes—that's so. Sure. Yes, well, in that case, we will." . . . For, of course, Roberta on her honeymoon—the day before her wedding and on a trip like this, would be expecting her dinner. Damn this stocky, red-faced fool, anyway.

"Well, then, I'll just take your bag and you can register. Your wife'll probably be wanting to freshen up a bit anyway."

He led the way, bag in hand, although Clyde's greatest desire was to snatch it from him. For he had not expected to register here—nor leave his bag either. And would not. He would recapture it and hire a boat. But on top of that, being compelled "for the register's sake," as Boniface phrased it, to sign Clifford Golden and wife—before he could take his bag again.

And then to add to the nervousness and confusion engendered by all this, thoughts as to what additional developments or persons, even, he might encounter before leaving on his climacteric errand—Roberta announcing that because of the heat and the fact that they were coming back to dinner, she would leave her hat and coat—a hat in which he had already seen the label of Braunstein in Lycurgus—and which at the time caused him to meditate as to the wisdom of leaving or extracting it. But he had decided that perhaps afterwards—afterwards—if he should really do this—it might not make any difference whether it was there or not. Was she not likely to be identified anyhow, if found, and if not found, who was to know who she was?

In a confused and turbulent state mentally, scarcely realizing the clarity or import of any particular thought or movement or act now, he took up his bag and led the way to the boathouse platform. And then, after dropping the bag into the boat, asking of the boathouse keeper if he knew where the best views were, that he wanted to photograph them. And this done—the meaningless explanation over, assisting Roberta (an almost nebulous figure, she now seemed, stepping down into an insubstantial rowboat upon a purely ideational lake), he now stepped in after her, seating himself in the center and taking the oars.

The quiet, glassy, iridescent surface of this lake that now to both seemed, not so much like water as oil—like molten glass that, of enormous bulk and weight, resting upon the substantial earth so very far below. And the lightness and freshness and intoxication of the gentle air blowing here and there, yet scarcely rippling the surface of the lake. And the softness and furry thickness of the tall pines about the shore. Everywhere pines—tall and spearlike. And above them the humped backs of the dark and distant Adirondacks beyond. Not a rower to be seen. Not a house or cabin. He sought to distinguish the camp of which the guide had spoken. He could not. He sought to distinguish the voices of those who might be there—or any voices. Yet, except for the lock-lock of his own oars as he rowed and the voice of the boathouse keeper and the guide in converse two hundred, three hundred, five hundred, a thousand feet behind, there was no sound.

"Isn't it still and peaceful?" It was Roberta talking. "It seems to be so restful here. I think it's beautiful, truly, so much more beautiful than that other lake. These trees are so tall, aren't they? And those mountains. I was thinking all the way over how cool and silent that road was, even if it was a little rough."

"Did you talk to any one in the inn there just now?"

"Why, no; what makes you ask?"

"Oh, I thought you might have run into some one. There don't seem to be very many people up here to-day, though, does there?"

"No, I don't see any one on the lake. I saw two men in that billiard room at the back there, and there was a girl in the ladies' room, that was all. Isn't this water cold?" She had put her hand over the side and was trailing it in the blue-black ripples made by his oars.

"Is it? I haven't felt it yet."

He paused in his rowing and put out his hand, then resumed. He would not row directly to that island to the south. It was—too far—too early. She might think it odd. Better a little delay. A little time in which to think—a little while in which to reconnoiter. Roberta would be wanting to eat her lunch (her lunch!) and there was a charming looking point of land there to the west about a mile further on. They could go there and eat first—or she could—for he would not be eating to-day. And then—and then—

She was looking at the very same point of land that he was—a curved horn of land that bent to the south and yet reached quite far out into the water and combed with tall pines. And now she added: "Have you any spot in mind, dear, where we could stop and eat? I'm getting a little hungry, aren't you?" (If she would only not call him *dear,* here and now!)

The little inn and the boathouse to the north were growing momentarily smaller,—looking now, like that other boathouse and pavilion on Crum Lake the day he had first rowed there, and when he had been wishing that he might come to such a lake as this in the Adirondacks, dreaming of such a lake—and wishing to meet such a girl as Roberta —then—And overhead was one of those identical woolly clouds that had sailed above him at Crum Lake on that fateful day.

The horror of this effort!

They might look for water-lilies here to-day to kill time a little, before—to kill time . . . to kill, (God)—he must quit thinking of that, if he were going to do it at all. He needn't be thinking of it now, at any rate.

At the point of land favored by Roberta, into a minute protected bay with a small, curved, honey-colored beach, and safe from all prying eyes north or east. And then he and she stepping out normally enough. And Roberta, after Clyde had extracted the lunch most cautiously from his bag, spreading it on a newspaper on the shore, while he walked here and there, making strained and yet admiring comments on the beauty of the scene—the pines and the curve of this small bay, yet thinking— thinking, thinking of the island farther on and the bay below that again somewhere, where some-how, and in the face of a weakening courage for it, he must still execute this grim and terrible business before him—not allow this carefully planned opportunity to go for nothing—if—if—he were to not really run away and leave all that he most desired to keep.

And yet the horror of this business and the danger, now that it was so close at hand—the danger of making a mistake of some kind—if nothing more, of not upsetting the boat right—of not being able to—to—oh, God! And subsequently, maybe, to be proved to be what he would be— then—a murderer. Arrested! Tried. (He could not,

he would not, go through with it. No, no, no!)

And yet Roberta, sitting here with him now on the sand, feeling quite at peace with all the world as he could see. And she was beginning to hum a little, and then to make advisory and practical references to the nature of their coming adventure together—their material and financial state from now on—how and where they would go from here —Syracuse, most likely—since Clyde seemed to have no objection to that—and what, once there, they would do. For Roberta had heard from her brother-in-law, Fred Gabel, of a new collar and shirt factory that was just starting up in Syracuse. Might it not be possible for Clyde, for the time being at least, to get himself a position with that firm at once? And then later, when her own worst trouble was over, might not she connect herself with the same company, or some other? And temporarily, since they had so little money, could they not take a small room together, somewhere in some family home, or if he did not like that, since they were by no means so close temperamentally as they once had been, then two small adjoining rooms, maybe. She could still feel his unrelenting opposition under all this present show of courtesy and consideration.

And he thinking, Oh, well, what difference such talk now? And whether he agreed or whether he did not. What difference since he was not going— or she either—that way. Great God! But here he was talking as though to-morrow she would be here still. And she would not be.

If only his knees would not tremble so; his hands and face and body continue so damp.

And after that, farther on down the west shore of this small lake in this little boat, to that island, with Clyde looking nervously and wearily here and there to see that there was no one—no one—not anywhere in sight on land or water—no one. It was so still and deserted here, thank God. Here— or anywhere near here might do, really,—if only he had the courage so to do now, which he had not—yet. Roberta trailing her hand in the water, asking him if he thought they might find some water-lilies or wild flowers somewhere on shore. Water-lilies! Wild flowers! And he convincing himself as he went that there were no roads, cabins, tents, paths, anything in the form of a habitation among these tall, close, ranking pines—no trace of any little boat on the widespread surface of this beautiful lake on this beautiful day. Yet might there not be some lone, solitary hunter and trapper or guide or fisherman in these woods or along these banks? Might there not be? and supposing there were one here now somewhere? And watching?

Fate!

Destruction!

Death! Yet no sound and no smoke. Only—only —these tall, dark, green pines—spear-shaped and still, with here and there a dead one—ashen pale in the hard afternoon sun, its gaunt, sapless arms almost menacingly outstretched.

Death!

And the sharp metallic cry of a blue-jay speeding in the depths of these woods. Or the lone and ghostly tap-tap-tap of some solitary woodpecker, with now and then the red line of a flying tanager, the yellow and black of a yellow-shouldered blackbird.

"Oh, the sun shines bright in my old Kentucky home."

It was Roberta singing cheerfully, one hand in the deep blue water.

And then a little later—"I'll be there Sunday if you will," one of the popular dance pieces of the day.

And then at last, after fully an hour of rowing, brooding, singing, stopping to look at some charming point of land, reconnoitering some receding inlet which promised water-lilies, and with Roberta already saying that they must watch the time and not stay out too long,—the bay, south of the island itself—a beautiful and yet most funereally pine-encircled and land delimited bit of water— more like a smaller lake, connected by an inlet or passage to the larger one, and yet itself a respectable body of water of perhaps twenty acres of surface and almost circular in form. The manner in which to the east, the north, the south, the west, even, except for the passage by which the island to the north of it was separated from the mainland, this pool or tarn was encircled by trees! And cat-tails and water-lilies here and there—a few along its shores. And somehow suggesting an especially arranged pool or tarn to which one who was weary of life and cares—anxious to be away from the strife and contentions of the world, might most wisely and yet gloomily repair.

And as they glided into this, this still dark water seemed to grip Clyde as nothing here or anywhere before this ever had—to change his mood. For once here he seemed to be fairly pulled or lured along into it, and having encircled its quiet banks, to be drifting, drifting—in endless space where was no end of anything—no plots—no plans—no practical problems to be solved—nothing. The insidious beauty of this place! Truly, it seemed to mock him—this strangeness—this dark pool, surrounded on all sides by those wonderful, soft, fir trees. And the water itself looking like a huge, black pearl cast by some mighty hand, in anger possibly, in sport or phantasy maybe, into the bosom of this valley of dark, green plush—and which seemed bottomless as he gazed into it.

And yet, what did it all suggest so strongly? Death! Death! More definitely than anything he had ever seen before. Death! But also a still, quiet, unprotesting type of death into which one, by reason of choice or hypnosis or unutterable weariness might joyfully and gratefully sink. So quiet—so shaded—so serene. Even Roberta exclaimed over this. And he now felt for the first time the grip of some seemingly strong, and yet friendly sympathetic, hands laid firmly on his shoulders. The comfort of them! The warmth! The strength! For now they seemed to have a steadying effect on him and he liked them—their reassurance— their support. If only they would not be removed! If only they would remain always—the hands of this friend! For where had he ever known this comforting and almost tender sensation before in all his life? Not anywhere—and somehow this calmed him and he seemed to slip away from the reality of all things.

To be sure, there was Roberta over there, but by now she had faded to a shadow or thought really, a form of illusion more vaporous than real. And while there was something about her in color, form that suggested reality—still she was very insubstantial—so very—and once more now he felt strangely alone. For the hands of the friend of firm grip had vanished also. And Clyde was alone, so very much alone and forlorn, in this somber, beautiful realm to which apparently he had been led, and then deserted. Also he felt strangely cold—the spell of this strange beauty overwhelming him with a kind of chill.

He had come here for what?

And he must do what?

Kill Roberta? Oh, no!

And again he lowered his head and gazed into the fascinating and yet treacherous depths of that magnetic, bluish, purple pool, which, as he continued to gaze, seemed to change its form kaleidoscopically to a large, crystalline ball. But what was that moving about in this crystal? A form! It came nearer—clearer—and as it did so, he recognized Roberta struggling and waving her thin white arms out of the water and reaching toward him! God! How terrible! The expression on her face! What in God's name was he thinking of anyway? Death! Murder!

And suddenly becoming conscious that his courage, on which he had counted so much this long while to sustain him here, was leaving him, and he instantly and conspicuously plumbing the depths of his being in a vain search to recapture it.

Kit, kit, kit, Ca-a-a-ah!
Kit, kit, kit, Ca-a-a-ah!
Kit, kit, kit, Ca-a-a-ah!

(The weird, haunting cry of that unearthly bird again. So cold, so harsh! Here it was once more to startle him out of his soul flight into a realization of the real or unreal immediate problem with all of its torturesome angles that lay before him.)

He must face this thing! He must!

Kit, kit, kit, Ca-a-a-ah!
Kit, kit, kit, Ca-a-a-ah!

What was it sounding—a warning—a protest—condemnation? The same bird that had marked the very birth of this miserable plan. For there it was now upon that dead tree—that wretched bird. And now it was flying to another one—as dead—a little farther inland and crying as it did so. God!

And then to the shore again in spite of himself. For Clyde, in order to justify his having brought his bag, now must suggest that pictures of this be taken—and of Roberta—and of himself, possibly —on land and water. For that would bring her into the boat again, without his bag, which would be safe and dry on land. And once on shore, actually pretending to be seeking out various special views here and there, while he fixed in his mind the exact tree at the base of which he might leave his bag against his return—which must be soon now— must be soon. They would not come on shore again together. Never! Never! And that in spite of Roberta protesting that she was getting tired; and did he not think they ought to be starting back pretty soon? It must be after five, surely. And Clyde, assuring her that presently they would— after he had made one or two more pictures of her in the boat with those wonderful trees—that island and his dark water around and beneath her.

His wet, damp, nervous hands!

And his dark, liquid, nervous eyes, looking anywhere but at her.

And then once more on the water again—about five hundred feet from shore, the while he fumbled aimlessly with the hard and heavy and yet small camera that he now held, as the boat floated out nearer the center. And then, at this point and time looking fearfully about. For now—now—in spite of himself, the long evaded and yet commanding moment. And no voice or figure or sound on shore. No road or cabin or smoke! And the moment which he or something had planned for him, and which was now to decide his fate at hand! The moment of action—of crisis! All that he needed to

do now was to turn swiftly and savagely to one side or the other—leap up—upon the left wale or right and upset the boat; or, failing that, rock it swiftly, and if Roberta protested too much, strike her with the camera in his hand, or one of the oars at his right. It could be done—it could be done— swiftly and simply, were he now of the mind and heart, or lack of it—with him swimming swiftly away thereafter to freedom—to success—of course—to Sondra and happiness—a new and greater and sweeter life than any he had ever known.

Yet why was he waiting now?

What was the matter with him, anyhow?

Why was he waiting?

At this cataclysmic moment, and in the face of the utmost, the most urgent need of action, a sudden palsy of the will—of courage—of hate or rage sufficient; and with Roberta from her seat in the stern of the boat gazing at his troubled and then suddenly distorted and fulgurous, yet weak and even unbalanced face—a face of a sudden, instead of angry, ferocious, demoniac—confused and all but meaningless in its registration of a balanced combat between fear (a chemic revulsion against death or murderous brutality that would bring death) and a harried and restless and yet self-repressed desire to do—to do—to do—yet temporarily unbreakable here and now—a static between a powerful compulsion to do and yet not to do.

And in the meantime his eyes—the pupils of the same growing momentarily larger and more lurid; his face and body and hands tense and contracted—the stillness of his position, the balanced immobility of the mood more and more ominous, yet in truth not suggesting a brutal, courageous power to destroy, but the imminence of trance or spasm.

And Roberta, suddenly noticing the strangeness of it all—the something of eerie unreason or physical and mental indetermination so strangely and painfully contrasting with this scene, exclaiming: "Why, Clyde! Clyde! What is it? Whatever is the matter with you anyhow? You look so—so strange —so—so— Why, I never saw you look like this before. What is it?" And suddenly rising, or rather leaning forward, and by crawling along the even keel, attempting to approach him, since he looked as though he was about to fall forward into the boat—or to one side and out into the water. And Clyde, as instantly sensing the profoundness of his own failure, his own cowardice or inadequateness for such an occasion, as instantly yielding to a tide of submerged hate, not only for himself, but Roberta—her power—or that of life to restrain him in this way. And yet fearing to act in any way—being unwilling to—being willing only to say that never, never would he marry her—that never, even should she expose him, would he leave here with her to marry her—that he was in love with Sondra and would cling only to her—and yet not being able to say that even. But angry and confused and glowering. And then, as she drew near him, seeking to take his hand in hers and the camera from him in order to put it in the boat, he flinging out at her, but not even then with any intention to do other than free himself of her—her touch—her pleading—consoling sympathy—her presence forever—God!

Yet (the camera still unconsciously held tight) pushing at her with so much vehemence as not only to strike her lips and nose and chin with it, but to throw her back sidewise toward the left wale which caused the boat to careen to the very water's edge. And then he, stirred by her sharp scream, (as much due to the lurch of the boat, as the cut on her nose and lip), rising and reaching half to assist or recapture her and half to apologize for the unintended blow—yet in so doing completely capsizing the boat—himself and Roberta being as instantly thrown into the water. And the left wale of the boat as it turned, striking Roberta on the head as she sank and then rose for the first time, her frantic, contorted face turned to Clyde, who by now had righted himself. For she was stunned, horror-struck, unintelligible with pain and fear—her lifelong fear of water and drowning and the blow he had so accidentally and all but unconsciously administered.

"Help! Help!"

"Oh, my God, I'm drowning, I'm drowning. Help! Oh, my God!"

"Clyde, Clyde!"

And then the voice at his ear!

"But this—this—is not this that which you have been thinking and wishing for this while—you in your great need? And behold! For despite your fear, your cowardice, this—this—has been done for you. An accident—an accident—an unintentional blow on your part is now saving you the labor of what you sought, and yet did not have the courage to do! But will you now, and when you need not, since it is an accident, by going to her rescue, once more plunge yourself in the horror of that defeat and failure which has so tortured you and from which this now releases you? You might save her. But again you might

not! For see how she strikes about. She is stunned. She herself is unable to save herself and by her erratic terror, if you draw near her now, may bring about your own death also. But you desire to live! And her living will make your life not worth while from now on. Rest but a moment—a fraction of a minute! Wait—wait—ignore the pity of that appeal. And then—then—But there! Behold. It is over. She is sinking now. You will never, never see her alive any more—ever. And there is your own hat upon the water—as you wished. And upon the boat, clinging to that rowlock a veil belonging to her. Leave it. Will it not show that this was an accident?"

And apart from that, nothing—a few ripples—the peace and solemnity of this wondrous scene. And then once more the voice of that weird, contemptuous, mocking, lonely bird.

Kit, kit, kit, Ca-a-a-ah!
Kit, kit, kit, Ca-a-a-ah!
Kit, kit, kit, Ca-a-a-ah!

The cry of that devilish bird upon that dead limb—the weir-weir.

And then Clyde, with the sound of Roberta's cries still in his ears, that last frantic, white, appealing look in her eyes, swimming heavily, gloomily and darkly to shore. And the thought that, after all, he had not really killed her. No, no. Thank God for that. He had not. And yet (stepping up on the near-by bank and shaking the water from his clothes) had he? Or, had he not? For had he not refused to go to her rescue, and when he might have saved her, and when the fault for casting her in the water, however accidentally, was so truly his? And yet—and yet—

The dusk and silence of a closing day. A concealed spot in the depths of the same sheltering woods where alone and dripping, his dry bag near, Clyde stood, and by waiting, sought to dry himself. But in the interim, removing from the side of the bag the unused tripod of his camera and seeking an obscure, dead log farther in the woods, hiding it. Had any one seen? Was any one looking? Then returning and wondering as to the direction! He must go west and then south. He must not get turned about! But the repeated cry of that bird,—harsh, nerve shaking. And then the gloom, in spite of the summer stars. And a youth making his way through a dark, uninhabited wood, a dry straw hat upon his head, a bag in his hand, walking briskly and yet warily—south—south.

ERIC BENTLEY
Editor

Eugene O'Neill

1888-1953

The son of a famous romantic actor, his infancy and youth were spent in the atmosphere of the theatre while his father, James O'Neill, toured the country in *Monte Cristo* and Shakespearean repertoire. After a year at Princeton and a brief career as a reporter in New London, Connecticut, O'Neill went to sea on a Norwegian barque and at the end of two years earned his Able Seaman's certificate. In 1914, following a year in Professor Baker's famous English 47 class at Harvard, he devoted himself exclusively to playwriting. Since then no fewer than thirty plays have come from his pen, and the whole world has sought to do him honor. Awarded the gold medal for drama by the National Institute of Arts and Letters and the degree of Litt.D. by Yale University, three times winner of the Pulitzer Prize for drama, he achieved his highest accolade when he was given the Nobel Prize for Literature in 1936. Eugene O'Neill's plays have been translated into almost all languages and have been performed in every civilized country of the world. His plays, next to Shakespeare's, are read by more people than are the works of any other dramatist, living or dead.

THE FOREGOING is from an anonymous Note on the Author in *Nine Plays by Eugene O'Neill* (Modern Library). The tone is a little euphoric—even English 47 at Harvard is "famous"—and one wonders where the statistics come from that would prove O'Neill is read by more people than Bernard Shaw. My reasons for quoting the excerpt are, first, that it does give an outline of the facts up to 1941 (when

it was written) and, second, that it gives them in a distinctly typical way—typical of the O'Neill literature, typical of that American middlebrow culture which has been O'Neill's principal audience, typical of the world we live in and its Hollywoodian way of thinking about writers. The long and short of it is that O'Neill was a worldly success—in contrast, say, to E. E. Cummings of whom Mr. Gilbert Highet has written: ". . . he has never made a really solid impact on his world. Up to this time, for instance, he has not been awarded the Pulitzer Prize . . ."

The tone of a Note on the Author might be unimportant, only in this case the writer's assumptions are symptomatic enough to be significant. Not only, in his account, is the Harvard class a famous one. Harvard is famous too. Likewise the playwright's father. And the university at which he spent an undergraduate year. And when the playwright wrote plays, up rose "the whole world" and cried Hooray! "in almost all languages . . ."

All of which provides an excellent cue for the question: *What really happened?* By way of answer I shall rehearse a few well-established facts.

The author's father, James O'Neill, was indeed famous: he was a star actor. Eugene O'Neill was born into the theater—and, as it happened, literally on Broadway, New York

City. But Broadway is not much of a home to anyone and was not at all a home to Eugene O'Neill. "My first seven years," he has written, "were spent mainly in the larger towns all over the U.S. . . . I knew only actors and the stage. My mother nursed me in the wings and in dressing rooms."

It hardly even makes sense to say he was "sent away to boarding school"—away from where? (He went to school in Riverdale, Manhattan, and Stanford.) The only approximation to a home that his parents ever acquired was a summer place in New London, Connecticut, and which, therefore, was to play a role in their son's life.

The year at Princeton (1906–07) was a flop—otherwise it would have been *four* years at Princeton. O'Neill liked to make it out even more of a flop than it was, for he sometimes lent his authority to the myth that he had been expelled for throwing a bottle through President Woodrow Wilson's window. It turned out that the only person he had abused was the stationmaster. To top things off, he didn't take his exams.

At this point, the anonymous Note is seriously misleading. "After a year at Princeton and brief career as a reporter in New London, Connecticut, O'Neill went to sea on a Norwegian barque . . ." The word "barque" is very choice; but the rest is fudge. The period under review is 1909–12. There were three voyages (to Honduras, South America, and England respectively), not one, and each time O'Neill returned to his father—either to the New London summer place or a theater somewhere. He also got married, stayed with his wife long enough to get her pregnant, attempted suicide, and was divorced.

1912 was the most important adult year in O'Neill's whole formation. This was the year in which he not only worked as a reporter but also began to have his own work published. It was the year of his first divorce. It was the year of his romance with the girl whom he calls Muriel in *Ah, Wilderness!* And it was the year when he went to the hospital with tuberculosis.

I have no intention of putting down the facts of a whole lifetime—that has been done by others—but am setting the intellectual stage for interpretation. It is the early years—for any man—that are formative. No need, at this date, to stress the importance of childhood, but there is a critical age of which much less has been said: the first years of manhood. This is a particularly trying time for the children of the famous—enviable as Fame seems to anonymous annotators and the anonymous millions. Or, rather, just because Fame is so enviable, it is embarrassing, to say the least, if your own father has got it. The problem of rivaling and replacing the father—or at least establishing one's own place on his level—is compounded. The only complete solution is for the son to be a Goethe or a Mozart—and then it's Father who has his problems.

That solution was not open to Eugene O'Neill. He did say that his father would someday only be known as the father of Eugene O'Neill, and the prophecy has proved correct. But it was a disingenuous prophecy. For acting—or acting before the days of movies—is automatically forgotten, while even a second-rate writer can "live" for a generation or two. And actually O'Neill's rank among dramatists has turned out to be about what his father's was among actors: high but not quite among the highest.

O'Neill was unable to defeat his father and then love him. He remained forever in the original state of ambivalence with which he first rebelled.

And the mother? As a girl she had been taken to see James O'Neill play Sidney Carton in Cleveland and had fallen in love with him, though she was by no means of the theater herself, and had indeed thought of becoming a nun. Life proved less romantic than *A Tale of Two Cities*, and, as the world has learned from *A Long Day's Journey into Night*, Ella O'Neill took to drugs.

As the world knows from the same source, there was an elder brother, James, Jr. He was an alcoholic. He also kept company with prostitutes and made sure that his younger brother went along with him from time to time.

In the work of Eugene O'Neill, the ideas of "nun" and of "mother" very often go together. He was very much an Irishman, and the Virgin Mother composed an image he could not do without. He liked to use the phrase "God the

Mother." Otherwise, in the works of O'Neill, femininity is found largely in whores. The vices of James, Jr.—drink and whoring—are the standard recourse of any O'Neill character who has received a setback.

O'Neill married three times. From what has been published on the subject, it would seem clear that he looked less for a wife than for a mother—looked, indeed, for the image of the young Ella Quinlan whom he had never known—and that he thought sometimes, in his second and third marriages, that he had found her. It would seem, too, that he was greatly loved by his wives but experienced the utmost difficulty in accepting love. It may well be that he portrayed this aspect of himself in Hickey, the salesman who kills his wife because she keeps forgiving him.

And his playwriting? The art of an artist is often outrageously left out of account by his biographers, as if it were not as much a part of his life as his relations with men. Thoroughly wise to this error, a psychoanalyst has shown that the writing of drama came as the solution, or partial solution, to O'Neill's main problem in living. Dr. Philip Weissman points out that O'Neill's mode of living in the critical years 1909–12 constituted the "acting out" of the cruel ambivalence in his relation to his father. He would flee, and then return, time and again. But in 1912 that stopped: he had started writing. He wrote the story of his ambivalence again and again and again; devoted his life to doing so; was only able to live by doing so.

That isn't all Dr. Weissman says, but even this much helps us to understand the peculiarity of O'Neill's endeavor. He is no Broadway playwright writing to entertain, to make money, or to be one of the boys. Nor is he a man of letters with an interest in the whole give-and-take of literary, political, or scientific discussion. He lives, as it were, in a trance, writing and rewriting the story of the two Jameses, Ella, and Eugene. Or parts of the story. Or the story at a remove.

Whatever the isolation of writers from the average middle-class citizen, they at least belong to families, and as children were not so isolated after all. Yet in having the kind of family background most Americans think they want—namely a Famous one—O'Neill had a most hideous and painful upbringing. Some think talent thrives on that sort of thing. More probably, he was born strong and made his way through innate strength. The handicaps were enormous, and his writing is marked by them. What American writer has known so little of America—any part of the country or any class of its people? It is so taken for granted these days that the artist is isolated, is "alienated," that it is hard to realize that some artists are much more isolated than others. O'Neill was the outsider of outsiders. He did not "belong" in the beginning, and he did not try to belong later on. As a youth, he hankered after the *Lumpenproletariat* in waterfront dives or in Greenwich Village. When he made money, he used it to take himself away not only from the dives but from everyone. He chose the life of the luxury villa. Children embarrassed him, especially his own children, to whom, as to at least two of his three wives, he was extremely cruel. One son committed suicide, the other became a drug addict. Only his daughter made a go of things—on her own. Ever since he was in the sanatorium in 1913 he characterized himself as an invalid, and while occupied with his largest work—during World War II—he fell victim to Parkinson's disease. During the thirties, he had separated himself even from his audience by not releasing plays for publication or production. His last years were a living death: he was separated even from his work. His hands shook too much to allow him to write; and he could not compose orally.

If there is much success worship in America, there is also a widespread belief that successful people are unhappy. Like unsuccessful people, they are. What distinguishes them from other folk is that they must suffer the effects of success. In other words, Eugene O'Neill had to try to cope, eventually, not only with his father's success but with his own.

For he did have success, and not merely in the newspaper sense of the word. He had success in solving the particular problem to which he had addressed himself: rivaling and replacing his father. How better, in any case, can a man outdo an actor than by becoming a playwright? The actor is the playwright's mouthpiece and victim. At least he can be; and O'Neill, Jr., made sure that he would be. His father's theater—the Victorian theater of Booth and Irving—was an actor's theater. The modern theater would be a playwright's theater, and Eugene O'Neill was one of the principal playwrights who made it so.

The texts of the plays bear a relation to James O'Neill, Sr., not merely in frequently portraying men who are like him but in doing so in a style he could never have accepted. O'Neill, Sr., was, as the New York *Times*'s obituary put it in 1920, "the last of the old school . . . a lover of all that is true and good in dramatic art, always holding up with authority the best traditions of the American stage." Early that year he had sat in a box at the première of his son's first Pulitzer-prize-winning play, *Beyond the Horizon*. Afterwards he said to his son: "People come to the theatre to forget their troubles, not to be reminded of them. What are you trying to do—send them home to commit suicide?" Which certainly was to hit a bull's eye; for to send one particular person home to commit suicide was, in a symbolic sense, precisely the intention.

The public discussion of O'Neill has by this time gone beyond the above-mentioned anonymous Note and embraced the fact—announced so openly in *Long Day's Journey*—that he was his father's enemy. The anonymous annotator's success story has been undermined, and another school of interpretation has taken over the public mind: the school that finds fame interesting *as an ordeal*. At this point, books and articles on O'Neill come to resemble books and articles on, say, the late Diana Barrymore. In journalism, one stereotype follows hard on the heels of the next.

The newer school of thought will be willing enough to concede that the young O'Neill reacted against the elder O'Neill's type of theater. "James O'Neill," we read in Croswell Bowen's *The Curse of the Misbegotten* (1959),

. . . was seeing the passing of his kind of American theatre with its old-fashioned, flamboyant acting. Melodrama, pathos, blood and thunder, hearts and flowers were already a little passé. They were yielding to the neo-realism—to the interpretation of contemporary experience—that constitutes the serious aspect of Broadway today, and which his son was inaugurating.

And again: "Before O'Neill, the American theatre had been cheap, sentimental, and tawdry. It was 'afraid of its own emotions,' as Eugene said . . . It would not be too great an exaggeration to say that the emergence of an important American theatre is due . . ." etc.

Now it is true enough that Eugene O'Neill expressed contempt for *Monte Cristo*. As far as that goes, he even described his father, on one occasion, as the worst actor in America. The two statements may be equally personal and uncritical. Even if they are not, what does the younger O'Neill claim to be rejecting in the older theater? Only, it would seem, what was feeble about it—hearts and flowers, no doubt, but not "melodrama, pathos, blood and thunder" by any means. What does the same commentator say of one of O'Neill's early plays? *"The Web* is remarkable in that it includes many of O'Neill's characteristic elements: violent death, cruelty, and a good deal of theatrical action." Exactly—these are the characteristics of melodrama.

Ambivalence is ambivalence. If Eugene O'Neill hated his father and his father's great role of Edmond Dantès, he also loved them. The proposition that he rejected Victorian melodrama will be useless to criticism unless it is accompanied by its opposite: O'Neill undertook to free melodrama from what was cheap and tawdry and ineffective, and to write a melodrama that would be truly melodramatic —a *Monte Cristo* raised to the nth power. If the rebellious son wishes to destroy the father, in his ambivalence he wishes nothing so much as to validate him and, if necessary, to rehabilitate him.

Eugene O'Neill is generally at his best when he sticks to melodrama, but Mr. Bowen's words about a "serious" and "important" aspect call our attention to a problem. Even good melodrama does not have the reputation it might have. That much is clear even from Mr. Bowen's own tone. And what the son does to, with, and for the father must win recognition —must have a good reputation, must gain prestige. Hence the paradox that though the younger O'Neill succeeded in melodrama he was not thereby satisfied. He had to be serious too. And he had to be acknowledged as such by pundits, professors, and institutions that award prizes more august than Pulitzers—such as the Swedish Academy.

We have seen that he succeeded in his adventure into seriousness. The Swedish Academy and "the whole world" seriously approved. It remains a question, though, whether the seriousness was *artistically* successful, whether it even had any spontaneity, or any underlying purpose other than its author's private and neurotic one. Each reader, each spectator, must decide this for himself.

II

THE WRITING career of Eugene O'Neill falls into three parts:

I: 1912–24

The most notable premières were:
- 1920: *Beyond the Horizon*
  The Emperor Jones
- 1921: *Anna Christie*
- 1922: *The Hairy Ape*
- 1924: *Desire Under the Elms*

II: 1925–34

The most notable premières were:
- 1926: *The Great God Brown*
- 1928: *Strange Interlude*
  Lazarus Laughed (Pasadena, California)
- 1931: *Mourning Becomes Electra*

III: 1934–53

There were no O'Neill premières between 1934 and 1946. The last two named below were posthumous.
- 1946: *The Iceman Cometh*
- 1947: *A Moon for the Misbegotten* (Columbus, Ohio)
- 1956: *Long Day's Journey into Night*
- 1958: *A Touch of the Poet*

Eugene O'Neill's earliest efforts are somewhat ludicrous, not least because the form of the one-act simply would not carry the kind of weight he tried to put on it. Soon he was wise enough to reduce the load, and the result was a kind of one-act not quite like anything else that had yet been produced in the genre. The little plays of the sea, later gathered to-gether under the title *The Moon of the Caribees* (1919), are sketches of maritime life organized largely by a certain sense of romance, of "poetry." Brevity was an admirable discipline, preventing O'Neill from launching upon the *longueurs* that ruined many of his later works. Though people nowadays think of O'Neill as the author of very long plays, he was in fact one of the many modern playwrights who have difficulty filling up more than one act. A lot of his best work is in the one-act form, and some of his seemingly full-length works are but one-acts slightly extended —I don't necessarily mean padded. *The Emperor Jones* is one of O'Neill's most satisfactory creations. Essentially, it is a long one-act, and the culmination of all his work in the one-act form between 1912 and 1920.

Anna Christie is a play which proceeded splendidly for one full act but then went to pieces in the effort to become a full-length play. The tragedy of "old davil, sea" and its victory over Chris Christopherson was spoiled by the comedy of Anna and her Irish boy friend. Two one-acts do not make an integrated full-length play, and O'Neill confessed his own dissatisfaction with the result. Nonetheless *Anna Christie* remains a landmark. Such richly colloquial dialogue had not been heard in the American theater before. Here the genteel tradition—of Clyde Fitch and the rest—ended, and the rhythm of modern life—in a sense Whitman himself would have recognized—was heard on the New York stage.

O'Neill's dialogue has often been adversely criticized, and not without reason: it is often prosy and ponderous; his ear was not a fastidious one; nor was his knowledge of real dialects—as against stage dialects—particularly sure. Even so he was responsible, more than any other one man, for a change in the tone of stage dialogue in general, and people "talk O'Neill" on the American stage to this day. Such an author as Tennessee Williams may introduce local variations from New Orleans or St. Louis but the basic pattern is still, I think, the O'Neillian blend of vernacular with a kind of artifice that wavers between rhetoric and lyricism.

The best commentator on O'Neill's work as a whole, Edwin A. Engel, has shown that evolution is the idea behind both *The Emperor Jones* and *The Hairy Ape* and that, while in the latter we see a man vainly trying to evolve, in the former we see him looking back at the stage he has evolved from. I would add that the Darwinian philosophy is less important than the psychological implication, which is the same in both cases: namely, regression. To be sure, Yank does not regress. It is O'Neill who regresses; and we with him. People who talk lightly of O'Neill the able seaman forget that his visits to stokeholes and waterfront dives were the slumming of an ex-Princeton under-graduate and son of a Broadway celebrity. That *this* man chooses to identify himself with Yank and Brutus Jones is what is significant—a mal-adjusted young Bohemian who, in real life, goes slumming.

To go to sea can be itself the ultimate regres-sion—to go to sea as O'Neill went to sea, not for any practical reason, but in evident quest of certain purely psychic satisfactions, and par-ticularly, one would think, in quest of the mother he had never (sufficiently) had.

That it is not always desirable for an artist to become too conscious of what he is doing can be amply illustrated from the career of O'Neill's son-in-law, Charles Chaplin. When people explained to Charlie what was going on in his early films he unloaded their explanations into his later films, which consequently are weighed down with explanations. Though the artist, qua artist, does not explain himself, in our day explanatoriness has become the be-setting sin of the cultural climber: Charlie Chaplin thought by explanations—symbolism, message, philosophy—to come up in the world.

Up to a point, O'Neill's background was similar and his ambition identical. The parents in both cases belonged to the popular theater. The sons in both cases wanted all this and cul-ture too. Here "culture" means recognition from people who write about such things. Here "people who write about such things" means the critics of those newspapers and magazines who try to lay down the law. Even if these men were giants of disinterested thought it would not be wise for a Chaplin or an O'Neill to have them constantly in mind. Since by and large what they have is not brains but vested in-terests, to respect them in any way can only be a mistake.

The Hairy Ape has many of the merits of *The Emperor Jones* and the first act of *Anna Christie* but also marks the appearance on the scene of Eugene O'Neill the Intellectual. You only need to read it once through to gather that an explanation is expected of you. You only need to read it a second time to discover that the explanation has been supplied by the author in his dialogue. You only need to read it a third time to realize that this is precisely what is wrong with the dialogue. Perhaps for a brilliant reader three readings would not be needed, but for most, surely, the phonetic spelling will conceal for a while the far less uncouth mentality of the author. One can-not help thinking that the uncouth accents are only a device to cover intellectuality. Yank would not have talked about "belonging." The conception comes from the intelligentsia who have talked of nothing else for the past hun-dred years.

Desire Under the Elms is a better play be-cause it springs more directly from O'Neill's needs and preoccupations. So central is this play that Dr. Weissman has been able to take it as a sort of first draft of *Long Day's Jour-ney into Night*. In other words, it deals with O'Neill's relations with father and mother.

Directly incestuous relationships are avoided, in fiction as in other fantasy, by making the mother-figure only a stepmother. The device is at least as old as Euripides, and is familiar to many of us from Schiller's *Don Carlos*. A mod-ern touch is added by O'Neill, who brings the story nearer to overt incest by stressing that Eben Cabot has a "fixation" on his dead mother—as well as an affair with his live step-mother. That Eben loves both his mothers and hates his father is perhaps not so remarkable in modern writing as that the stepmother murders their child to prove she loves Eben. In the con-text, there is some logic in this act, because Eben has been told she only bore the child in order to get an inheritance. The murder does disprove the allegation. The question that arises is whether, even so, it is credible. In-fanticide is a crime that has often been com-mitted. Nonetheless, few women will kill their child just to prove a point. Each reader can decide for himself whether he finds O'Neill's story credible. What is beyond debate is that O'Neill's fantasy gave birth to a woman who commits an atrocity that is not only inhuman but quite rare because it is quite unfeminine. O'Neill's plays are full of items like this, which are chiefly of interest in relation to their author's life and make-up. Psychoanalysts to the contrary notwithstanding, this is a grave limitation.

Though it perhaps has a flaw near its center, *Desire Under the Elms* remains a superior play because most of the time O'Neill stays well within his emotional range, within the kind of world that is truly *his* world. The landscape is neither pretty nor varied. The father is an Old Testament tyrant—but recreated with something of the appropriate majesty. If in many later plays O'Neill tends toward the over-abstract, here the father is not derived from a bare idea. He seems to grow from the soil. The soil is given a reality, not, to be sure, through true local color, or sensitivity to the life around him, but by a curiously vivid sense of the bovine which O'Neill found, surely, in some marshy tract, not of New England, but of his soul. It is a nauseating play. But nausea is at least a thing of the senses, and one must grant that O'Neill at his best could communicate strong emotions, particularly negative ones. I am not even convinced that the negative emotions he most readily commanded are those he has been praised for commanding, such as terror. Are they not, rather, the mean and masochistic feelings? One may admire *Desire Under the Elms*, but one would look askance at anyone who positively relished it.

III

O'NEILL's more ardent admirers have been admirers above all of his second phase (1925–34). The less ardent of us feel compelled to regret that this phase ever happened, vain as it always is to scold artists or tell them, even beforehand, that they mustn't do whatever it is their hearts are set on doing.

I have stressed that playwriting was for O'Neill something much different from what it is for your Broadway entertainer. It may be well to elaborate at this stage a point of Dr. Weissman's. O'Neill was so disturbed in the period 1909–12 that he kept alternately fleeing from and returning to his father. That activity constitutes neurotic "acting out" and nearly went as far as suicide. Then it subsided considerably. Why? Presumably because O'Neill, in 1912, took up writing. At first he wrote precisely about the voyages and the returns, a theme, which, for that matter, he would revert to later. The career of O'Neill should interest those who see a connection between art and neurosis, and it would indicate that art is not so much a symptom as an attempt at cure. O'Neill was never cured—which of us is?—and he deserted wives—one in 1909, it is true, but one also in the middle twenties—as he had "deserted" parents. Yet it is quite tenable that only his writing kept O'Neill going at all. And why did it? Not, obviously, because it was art, but because it seemed a weapon in a personal battle. Everything we know about O'Neill suggests that he never emerged from the Oedipus conflict but remained in the immature and adolescent relation to both father and mother.

What O'Neill did was to take Victorian melodrama and add. When what he added was chiefly his own personal vehemence—as attached to his own complexes—the result could be impressive and even unpretentious. When he added more than this, the result was to many even more impressive—and very pretentious indeed. The New York *Times* was impressed. Which is to say that middlebrow culture was impressed, as well it might be, for what had O'Neill added to melodrama but the stock of ideas and attitudes which constitute middlebrow culture? O'Neill may have flunked out of Princeton but, down the years, he had been reading, reading, reading, and was now a rather formidable autodidact. He had a theory of theater which I for one am so far from taking issue with that, on the contrary, I would accept and applaud nearly all of it.

What was this theory? We have seen that O'Neill wanted to re-introduce the powerful emotions fearlessly. That perhaps was the main wish, and one that could not harm him unless he had it too much in his *head*. He also saw through the cult of character—the schoolteacher's idea that playwrights must portray "individuals, not types"—and realized that even better than "individuals" are archetypes.

He also realized that no kind of character— even an archetypal one—is enough, that the playwright should try to get at "the Force Beyond," at the part of the world that is *not* contained in the characters themselves, and at the problem which Goethe himself thought transcended all problems, that of belief.

In short, Eugene O'Neill saw through not only the tawdry, everyday commercial theater of his father's time but also through the drab, or homey, naturalistic theater of his own time and ours. His proposals for an alternative are admirable. Like most autodidacts, he had a nose, too, for the kind of reading that would mean most to him, and this nose led him unerringly to the philosopher who, of all philosophers, has entered most deeply into the spirit of tragedy, and who also happens to be the philosopher who laid the foundations of modern psychological understanding: Friedrich Nietzsche. One result of all this thinking of O'Neill's, and all this reading, was that he was able to re-invent Expressionism [1] on his own. For I believe we can take him at his word when he tells us he knew very little of the German Expressionists. There is ironic justice in the fact that one of them considered *Lazarus Laughed* the best of all Expressionist plays.

Unfortunately, all this proves no more than that Eugene O'Neill came to some good conclusions. No number of good conclusions will make a good play. And he also came to some bad conclusions. More precisely, he came to adopt an outlook which could affect actual playwriting—for the worse. There is no word for this outlook that I know of. I will call it psychologism. It proceeds by substituting notions about people's minds for actual observation of people's minds and contact with them.

Now an artist can often get by with very few formulations, provided he enjoys very lively contact with people. He need not *know* what people are like, but he certainly need *sense* what they are like, and he certainly must be

[1] Expressionism in the drama began with certain scenes in Wedekind's *Spring's Awakening* (1891) and developed through the dream plays of Strindberg into a school of playwriting whose most famous representatives were Georg Kaiser and Ernst Toller. The aim was to "express," or "bring out," the inner life— as against Impressionism, which aimed at rendering impressions of the external world.

able to communicate that sense. O'Neill came to maturity in the era of psychologism. Freud was then—as now, I suppose—chiefly a fad. One had to know his name. One had to bandy Freudian phraseology, actual or supposed. O'Neill had some canniness, it is true, and tried to avoid being a faddist. He denied having read much Freud. But in that atmosphere, non-reading was insufficient protection. Freud was "in the air." Worse: Jung was in the air. Then too, O'Neill said he *had* read Jung.

More important than the leading psychologists were the hundreds of non-leaders whose books and articles flooded the market. One of O'Neill's closest associates, Kenneth MacGowan, was co-author, with Dr. G. V. Hamilton, of a psychiatric treatise, *What Is Wrong with Marriage?* The heading for a chapter entitled "Oedipus Rex" reads: "Evidence that supports Freud's dictum of the part the mother-image plays in a man's choice of his wife . . . The happiest group of men have wives on the mother-pattern. Yet the fear of inbreeding makes men marry away from the mother." The next chapter is headed by the words: ". . . fear of incest, added to the fear of inbreeding, makes the women even less fortunate than the men in their marriage choices." This chapter is entitled: "The Tragedy of Electra."

Malcolm Cowley, who visited O'Neill in 1923, recorded:

[O'Neill] picks up a heavy green medical-looking book from the table beside us; it is one of Wilhelm Stekel's treatises on sexual aberrations—perhaps *The Disguises of Love*, which had recently been translated from the German. There are enough case histories in the book, Gene says, to furnish plots to all the playwrights who ever lived. He turns the pages and shows me the clinical record of a mother who seduced her only son and drove him insane.

The poet Meredith wrote: "passions spin the plot." It was left to O'Neill to imagine that case histories spin the plot. There could be no more clear-cut example of the kind of half-baked thinking that mars his work. *Strange Interlude* stands condemned right there: it is a gigantic appendix to Dr. Hamilton's *A Research in Marriage*. "My husband is unable to give me a healthy child. What shall I do?" In the spirit of the lady columnist running her readers' private lives, O'Neill writes out, not, to be sure, what we *should* do, but what Dr. Hamilton or Dr. Stekel says we *have* done.

I do not find *Strange Interlude* boring. Though not lowbrow, it is soap opera, and soap opera doesn't have to be boring, it only has to be foolish. Soap opera larded—or should one say lathered?—with would-be serious and up-to-date ideas is doubly foolish. The solemn farce got its deserved come-uppance when Groucho Marx—was it in *Animal Crackers?*—did an imitation of its manner.

Groucho used the comedian's privilege of attacking the weakest spot, which was the device of asides placed at the service of psychologism. The things that people think and don't say were written into the dialogue as long and numerous asides, delivered while everyone on stage stood petrified. The petrifaction would have been bearable had the monologues been bearable. But the principle behind the latter was simple-minded. It was that when a man is saying to a woman: "I love you!" he is murmuring to himself, "No I don't, I hate you, you bitch!" Of which the reverse form, even commoner in O'Neill, is: "I hate you, you bitch!" followed by: "Oh, what a cad I am, I don't hate her at all, I love her!" If, as one might certainly maintain, ambivalence is the main theme of O'Neill's writing, as of his life, this is no adequate way to present it.

What about the mask? It is the very prototype of theatrical artifices, and it was O'Neill's idea that it could be used to express ambivalence. For example, a mask may express innocence, while the face is haunted with guilt; a mask may exude confidence, while the face exudes timidity. This is one of a very few ideas by which *The Great God Brown* stands or falls. It proved more interesting in discussion than effective in the theater. So did the idea of having two actors play opposing sides of the same man in *Days Without End* (première 1934).

More of course was involved than technical devices. The plays of O'Neill's middle period were a very bold attempt to realize on the stage the vision of theater of O'Neill's generation. This was particularly the vision of three of his close associates, George Cram Cook, Robert Edmond Jones, and Kenneth Mac-Gowan. Jones was the most gifted American stage-designer of his day. He and MacGowan had toured the European theaters shortly after World War I and had returned to write and rhapsodize about "the theatre of tomorrow." Like all such dreams, this one had a good deal to do with yesterday. It had specifically to do with Wagner and Nietzsche, Adolphe Appia and Gordon Craig. The vision was of a release from realism, a release upwards, as it were, toward the sublime and downwards toward the instinctual. Cook's particular enthusiasm was Greece. It is Cook whom O'Neill is echoing when he speaks, in a letter, of the Greek dream being the noblest of them all. The word "dream" recurs a good deal, and the reference is less to Freud than to Apollo whom Nietzsche regarded as a symbol of the dream world in contrast to Dionysus, who stood for drunkenness.

The word "Dionysus" recurs even oftener. Bred a Catholic, and educated in popular Hellenism by Cook and others, O'Neill liked to see life as a conflict between the ascetic and the pagan spirit. Hence the name of the hero of *The Great God Brown*, Dion Anthony—Dionysus the drunken God and Anthony the ascetic saint. Closely related to Dionysus is "the great god Pan," with whom O'Neill contrasts the American businessman of the Babbitt era—the great god Brown.

One can only say of these antitheses what I have already said about O'Neill's whole theory of drama. In themselves they are splendid and full of possibilities. Very similar antitheses underlie tragic art of the greatest epochs. It was a contemporary of Shakespeare's who wrote:

O wearisome condition of humanity!
Born under one law, to another bound,
Vainly begot and yet forbidden vanity,
Created sick, commanded to be sound.
What meaneth nature by these diverse laws,
Passion and reason, self-division's cause?

And it was certainly permissible for O'Neill to champion passion against reason—instead of reason against passion as the Elizabethans had done. This he was inclined to do in the middle twenties when he took a Nietzschean position. Once, in the early thirties, he seemed, rather, to champion Anthony against Dionysus in a play that ends in reconciliation with the

Catholic Church, *Days Without End*. But this was a momentary point of rest, not a final conclusion.

The question was never of the permissibility of the ideas themselves but of O'Neill's ability to handle them—or, more exactly, of their suitability to the kind of work which he could do in art. In *Hamlet* the conflict between passion and reason is deeply sunk in an Action as well as in characters inwardly felt. Neither passion nor reason have to be mentioned by name, and, when they are, we do not have an embarrassing feeling of "There goes the main theme again." This embarrassing feeling is just what we do have in *Strange Interlude* when we hear:

a lot to account for, Herr Freud! . . . punishment to fit his crimes, be forced to listen eternally during breakfast while innumerable plain ones tell him dreams about snakes . . . pah, what an easy cure-all! . . . sex the philosopher's stone . . . "O Oedipus, O my king! The world is adopting you!". . .

and:

she has strange devious intuitions that tap the hidden currents of life . . . dark intermingling currents that become the one stream of desire . . .

and:

Perhaps he realizes subconsciously that I am his father, his rival in your love; but I'm not his father ostensibly, there are no taboos, so he can come right out and hate me . . .

and:

Yes, perhaps unconsciously Preston is a compensating substitute.

and:

I was only a body to you . . . I was never more to you than a substitute for your dead lover!

and:

I can remember that day seeing her kiss him . . . it did something to me I never got over.

These passages prompt the question: in what way should literature be psychological? It is good that great writers should be psychologically deep, and that Freud should say so, but is it good that an artist should read

Freud and reproduce him? Is it good that characters should sum themselves up, should spend their time diagnosing themselves—and everyone else? That, by consequence, human character should come to the audience in the form of summation and diagnosis? On the contrary, it is a disaster. The drama should provide an image of experience and character such as might be analyzed later. To begin with analysis is to put the cart before the horse—with the same result: immobility.

What is true of psychological ideas is true of all ideas in drama. The playwright Hebbel put it with witty overstatement: "In drama, no character should ever utter a thought: from the thought in a play come the speeches of *all* the characters." Now, if this principle applies to the relatively modest ideas of *Strange Interlude*, how much more is it called for when we confront *The Great God Brown* and *Lazarus Laughed!* So little are the ideas of these plays sunk in the action and the characters that neither action nor characters have any effective existence except to illustrate the ideas. And if there are obscurities, as in *The Great God Brown* there certainly are, they are cleared up, not by more work on action or character, but by a letter to the newspapers explaining the philosophy and the symbolism.

Lazarus Laughed is probably the most ambitious American play ever written by a gifted playwright. It cries out to be compared with the work which presumably prompted its writing, Nietzsche's *Thus Spake Zarathustra*. ("This book," writes O'Neill's second wife, Agnes Boulton, "had more influence on Gene than any other single book he ever read. It was a sort of Bible to him, and he kept it by his bedside . . .") Both works would ring out an old era, and ring in a new. Both authors would denounce the old era with the terrifying finality of a Jeremiah and, in hailing the new, reach the highest peaks of ecstasy. Nietzsche, however, was a master of ideas, and was not attempting drama. In *Lazarus* the ideas are too few and too grandiose ever to become active and interesting, while not enough is done by way of dialogue, action, and character to give us a real play. And if O'Neill had not had much success in depicting self-division, it was a false way out that he found in *Lazarus* when he picked a hero who was not divided.

O'Neill's Lazarus has little to do with the Biblical character and a great deal to do with the Greek god whom Nietzsche had already opposed to Christ: Dionysus. Following Nietzsche, O'Neill takes Christianity to be life-denial, the religion of Dionysus to be life-worship. One worships life and denies death. In that perhaps rather peculiar sense, one believes in immortality. "The fear of death," O'Neill wrote,

is the root of all evil, the cause of all man's blundering unhappiness. Lazarus knows there is no death, there is only change. He is reborn without that fear. Therefore he is the first and only man who is able to laugh affirmatively. His laughter is a triumphant Yes to life . . . And life itself is the self-affirmative joyous laughter of God.

Whatever we make of this as philosophy, we can hardly make much of it as theater or psychology. Theatrically, O'Neill asks laughter to do more than laughter *can* do. For an actor to be laughing so often and so loudly when he isn't even amused is to court confusion, even assuming he can keep it up. Laughter is not a pretty noise or a majestic one, a fact that is related to the psychic side. Laughter is not a suitable symbol of, or outlet for, affirmation because there is so much about it that is inherently and unmistakably negative. Laughter sounds aggressive for the good reason that it *is* aggressive. It is difficult to hear roars of laughter in which one is not personally involved without wishing to shut them up.

O'Neill was not always kind to his audience. *The Iceman Cometh* opens with a lot of men asleep on stage. In the theater, sleep is contagious, and some audiences have at once dozed off. Did O'Neill hate not only his family but his public? Lazarus' laughter would prove very annoying. Was that O'Neill's unconscious intention? If so, it is a pity that no conscious intention interfered. It is hard to resist the conclusion that O'Neill sometimes liked to flout his own theater sense because he identified it with his father. If the laughter of Lazarus stems from thought, it is an instance of the way in which a playwright should *not* be a thinker.

Though not more ambitious, *Mourning Becomes Electra* is a much longer play than *Lazarus Laughed* and is ambitious enough to invite the comparison with Aeschylus. Some of the most respected critics of the time, such as George Jean Nathan and Joseph Wood Krutch, thought it could sustain the comparison. For a time it was possible for many intelligent people to think of this play as at least one of the supreme American masterpieces like, say, *Moby-Dick* or *The Scarlet Letter*. Today there is no need to take issue with an opinion which is gone with the wind: it can serve only to educate us in the ways of the world. And there is an interesting human and historical problem: what was it about *Mourning Becomes Electra* that at first made a big impression and later did not?

The idea behind the play is that of an equivalent in terms of Freudian, or perhaps Jungian, psychology to the *Oresteia* of Aeschylus:[1] an equivalent and, following the reasoning of the man in street, an improvement. As O'Neill's latest biographer puts it: "*Electra* is based on sound modern concepts of psychological and biological cause and effect, not upon the inspiration of the Furies." It is certainly based on concepts. That may be the main trouble. Whether these concepts are so much sounder than Aeschylus is also open to debate. They are certainly more depressing. The *Oresteia* celebrates the establishment of community: it shows the rule of law take the place of the vendetta. *Mourning Becomes Electra* shows the vendetta going on and on and on and on. In place of the liberating, creative, and inspiring ideas of Aeschylus come ideas that at best are sobering.

The key terms reverse their meanings. Where Aeschylus describes a curse that can be lifted in the name of a justice that is real and that can be assured by a human nature not wholly lacking in wisdom, for O'Neill living is itself a curse, death is a release, and justice is not the opposite of revenge but the same thing.

The psychology of *Mourning Becomes Elec-*

[1] Students who wish to study the background of O'Neill's plays should read, first, his own notes on it in Barrett H. Clark's *European Theories of the Drama* (rev. ed. 1947) and, second, *The Oresteia* as translated by Richard Lattimore, available in paperback.

tra runs as thin as the philosophy. One thing leads to another in all too naïve and mechanical a way. It is as if a couple of psychoanalytic concepts, taken in ridiculously simple form, were held sufficient to demonstrate what tragic life is like. Daughters, for example, hate their mothers and love their fathers. This must have seemed a thrillingly novel idea in 1931, or how could anyone have thought O'Neill's presentation of it anything but monotonous? To do without the Furies is nothing but a loss if all you put in their place is the rhetoric of psychologism.

Orin grows to resemble his father, and Lavinia her mother. Such a development comes under the heading, in psychiatry, of "psychotic identification," and it seems that O'Neill has been "confirmed" by recent medical writers. Dr. Weissman congratulates him on his insight. But is it so remarkable? Isn't this particular "insight" in the logic of the whole argument? Isn't it also very much in the spirit of melodrama? And finally, do such "insights," however correct, constitute dramatic art?

Insofar as any big play can be summed up in a sentence, cannot *Mourning Becomes Electra* be summed up in this one: Eugene O'Neill feels that people wish to kill each other? O'Neill seems to have been imbued with hatred as St. Francis, say, or Gandhi was imbued with love; but how creative is mere hatred, even in art? Certainly, it is permissible for O'Neill to keep inventing people who kill each other or want to. But isn't it equally permissible for us to wonder that they don't have any other interests?

The question sounds like a jibe, and those who leap to O'Neill's defense might ask if one could not wonder the same about the frantic characters of Strindberg and Dostoevsky. I doubt it. The world of Dostoevsky's people, and even of Strindberg's, is a far larger one than that of O'Neill's. The Captain in Strindberg's *The Father* is a scientist and his intellectuality is made quite real to us. The Captain's fury attains to full dramatic force just because we have been made to feel his love of knowledge. Does not every author who presents the negative side have to make us feel the positive side even if he never shows it? Is an artist ever really a monomaniac? Must he

not always be able to *imagine* an alternative even if he does not propose one? Dostoevsky often did propose one. Not all his characters are possessed—unless one were to say that some are possessed by Christian love. O'Neill sometimes presents an alternative—but inadequately. The few characters not propelled downwards by the death wish are mere dummies. Peter and Hazel, in *Mourning Becomes Electra*, are examples.

For all his reading, O'Neill remained horrifyingly barbaric. Culture existed for him, it would seem, only as those books he lifted ideas from and in no degree as culture—the cultivation of the spirit and the tradition among men of such cultivation. In this respect, *Mourning Becomes Electra* stands at the opposite pole not only from the Greeks but from such characteristic attempts to revive Greek tragedy in modern times as Goethe's *Iphigenia in Tauris*. There, the poet's search was expressly for whatever in the myth might tend to the schooling of man and the taming of the beast in him —whatever might tend to the enhancement of life in possible sweetness and grace. Reading or seeing Goethe's play, we enter his mind and find it a spacious and truly edifying dwelling place. The paradox of *Mourning Becomes Electra* is that O'Neill took up a great testament of humane culture in order to spit in the face of humanity.

How is it no one said so? People bring such charges against authors much less guilty of them. Obviously, if O'Neill's points got across at all they did not carry a sting—which is to say they did not carry conviction. For when all is said against O'Neill's ideas, it must yet be admitted that such ideas might have gone to the making of very powerful drama. They did so when Wagner used them. (For is not the "tragic philosophy" of *Mourning Becomes Electra* much less that of Nietzsche than of Nietzsche's archenemy, the author of *Tristan and Isolde* and *The Nibelung's Ring*?) If initially one tends to reject this *Electra* because of the view of life it presents, one rejects it even more emphatically because it does not get this view across the footlights.

We are now perhaps in a position to answer the question as to what people were impressed by back in 1931: not by the nihilistic view of life, which did not come home to men's business and bosoms, but merely by the rhetoric of psychologism. One might not know exactly what the main intent was, but certainly much of the talk in scene after scene was close enough to the talk at the cocktail party before the show. Now even dead ideas can seem to come alive in a play when they happen to be alive in the current conversation of the public. And surely such ideas—though they may not be the main themes of the plays—come up in all the plays of O'Neill's middle period. They return to their graves as soon as they are no longer part of the current chatter, "the new small talk."

IV

BY 1930, the success story was written: Eugene O'Neill was far more prominent in the American theater than his father had ever been and a Nobel prize winner. Sinclair Lewis, was telling the Swedish Academy that:

had you chosen Mr. O'Neill who has done nothing much in American drama save to transform it utterly in ten or twelve years from a false world of neat and competent trickery to a world of splendor and fear and greatness, you would have been reminded that he has done something far worse than scoffing—he has seen life as not to be neatly arranged in the study of a scholar but as a terrifying, magnificent, and often quite horrible thing akin to the tornado, the earthquake, and the devastating fire.

How to survive such praise? After the success of *Mourning Becomes Electra*, what O'Neill attempted was to re-enter his past. In *Ah Wilderness!* (première 1933) he based a play upon that same New London summer of 1912 which later would yield *Long Day's Journey into Night*. After reading both plays, one comes to doubt that O'Neill meant even the latter to be pure autobiography. In any case, it is almost incredible that both plays present the same O'Neill in the same year. In neither play does he see himself as the actual twenty-three-year-old who was already a father and was in the process of being divorced. In *Ah Wilderness!* he sees himself as an adolescent and a virgin, dreams of belonging to a regular American home in a regular American town, and so relives the kind of childhood he had never lived

in the first place. In *Days Without End* he dreams himself back into the Church of his fathers. Incidentally, the priest he consulted on theological matters got no impression that O'Neill wanted more than to dream. The two plays belong to a moment of wistful pause, and perhaps of hesitation, before O'Neill embarked upon the most grandiose of his grandiose schemes: a cycle of plays in which he would write the spiritual history of his country. Six of these plays were undoubtedly completed, and five others planned. But in 1953 O'Neill sat down with his wife in the Hotel Shelton in Boston and tore up all the finished plays. "We tore them up bit by bit, together," says Mrs. O'Neill, "I helped him because his hands—he had this terrific tremor, he could tear just a few pages at a time. It was awful. It was like tearing up children."

Why Mrs. O'Neill cooperated in the tearing up of O'Neill's children shall remain, for the present at least, her business. A writer's life, on the other hand, belongs to the world, and the world has already speculated on Eugene O'Neill's reasons. All he said was: "I don't want anyone else finishing up a play of mine." But the plays, says Mrs. O'Neill, *were* finished —except for cutting. It is impossible not to connect this terrible act—which any fellow writer feels in the pit of his stomach—with O'Neill's many other destructive acts. He had killed himself as son, as father, and several times as husband—why not also as writer?

Everything that happened since the plays of the early thirties remains somewhat mysterious despite the labors of the biographers. O'Neill had lived the life of a wealthy man ever since he *became* a wealthy man in the early twenties. If he changed now, it was mainly to let it be known that he was going off—presumably forever—to work on the giant project. He seems to have worked on it regularly until 1939, and to have resumed it with less assiduity several years later. Shortly before the end of World War II O'Neill had a stroke. Afterwards a tremor of the hands which he had had for some time was much more marked, and he could not write. Echoing Mrs. O'Neill, I have already said that since he could not compose orally his writing days were over. This is an incomplete statement. Many men would have gradually learned to compose orally. Mrs. O'Neill says: "he died when he could no longer work— spiritually died and was dragging the poor diseased body along for a few more years until it too died." This does not explain why his will to work was insufficient to overcome his aversion to dictation. One must assume that this will was already dead or dying. Following such a clew, one might then move backwards into the mysterious years when the Cycle was being written. Did the plays of the Cycle, when finished, disappoint O'Neill? One, *A Touch of the Poet,* has survived and is certainly not among, say, his dozen best plays. Did the Cycle, in O'Neill's opinion, deserve to be destroyed? He seems never to have expressed the opinion that it was, as it was meant to be, the crown of his writing career. Could it be that most of the writing he did in California did not represent his further development as a playwright but a progressive withdrawal from the theater, a long day's journey into night? This is not a conclusion drawn by Dr. Weissman, but he provides evidence for it.

If O'Neill's "love affair with the world" was over, he sometimes longed for his old mistress, and we find him dropping the Cycle in 1939 and writing two of his best plays: *The Iceman Cometh* and *Long Day's Journey into Night*— as well as *A Moon for the Misbegotten* which is by no means one of his worst. To think of O'Neill's "final period" will always be to think of *The Iceman* and *Journey.*

Both are explorations of the year 1912. Neither is merely a memoir. *Long Day's Journey* does seem wholly a memoir the first time one reads it; at least it did when the facts of O'Neill's background were not yet public knowledge. One reads the play with amazement at what the O'Neills went through. Dr. Weissman soon pointed out that O'Neill had omitted facts of the utmost relevance, such as that Edmund is not represented as a father and divorcé. Dr. Weissman conjectures that these facts had been "repressed," and thinks that Barrett Clark also did a little "repressing" in his biography. This conjecture I find uncalled for. Clark said what he was allowed to say, and tried to give the impression he was supposed to give. O'Neill never stated that *Long Day's Journey* was pure history, and he was a good

enough playwright to know that history and drama must ever be distinct. O'Neill "played" with the facts of 1912 in no less than four dramas—*Hughie* is the only one not already mentioned here—and always in a different style, always with a different angle on the facts. In *Long Day's Journey* the camera is still at an angle to the subject, though admittedly a less oblique one.

If O'Neill was nihilistic in his views, and Bohemian in some of his conduct, he was not disorderly in his work. Indeed his work spelled order for him, just as it spelled somewhat better mental health. *The Iceman Cometh* and *Long Day's Journey*, prompted to some extent by the outbreak of World War II, were islands of order in the sea of a personal and more than personal chaos.

Long Day's Journey is a kind of classical quartet. Here O'Neill eschews the luxury of numerous minor characters, crowds, and a bustle of stage activity. He has a few people and they talk. This has given the public an impression of shapelessness. O'Neill's latest biographer says: "The play is essentially plotless . . . the deliberate formlessness of it all is enervating. Still, it is a dramatic achievement of the first order . . ." A biographer—in this case at least—is not a critic, or one might ask him how a piece of enervating formlessness can be a dramatic achievement of the first order. *Long Day's Journey* is a dramatic achievement which at first glance *seems* formless. Later, one discovers the form. The play has the outward calm and formality—not formlessness!—of French classical tradegies. Like them—and like *The Iceman*—it observes the unities. The form reveals itself in the interrelationship of people. The principal relationship here (dramaturgically speaking at least) is that between Edmund and his mother. The classical dramatist has to pull together on one day events which in actuality happened over a longer period. O'Neill found his action and his drama in the —presumably fictitious—coincidence of Mary's final relapse into drug addiction with the discovery of Edmund's tuberculosis. But a situation is only a premise of drama, not its realization. Before we have drama, the situation must move, and the dramatist must have discovered what makes it move. In *Long Day's Journey*,

Edmund has come to the point where he needs his mother very much. He is moving toward her. And only a short while ago he would have had a chance. But she has now relapsed, with an obvious finality, into drug addiction. She too is moving. She is moving away from Edmund, away from everyone. She is moving to the point—reached during the play as its culmination—where no one can reach her any more. That Mary moves away just when Edmund moves toward her is—in terms of dynamics—what makes possible the play and enables O'Neill to rescue it from "formlessness."

Admittedly, this is to speak only of two of the four main characters. Before the play is over we have got inside each of the four. As people, James, Sr., and James, Jr., may be just as salient: in the dramatic structure, as I see it, they are subordinated to Mary and Edmund because the action turns on the question, what is happening to the latter pair?

Sincerity has done far more for O'Neill in this drama than ambition could ever do for him in the "big" plays of the second period. In the handling of ambivalence, for example. Had it ever really been necessary to invent devices to show the phenomenon? The method O'Neill used in the later play was to work through to his feelings, and then let them speak. It is the hard kind of sincerity. And he must surely have been gratified to see how—under this dispensation—a character can turn from expressing his hate to expressing love without any kind of device at all. It "just happens."

The process called "working through" implies deliberately living through an experience a second time, to the end of understanding and liberation. If Aristotle's word catharsis implies a sort of thorough cleaning out of the emotional system, then it exaggerates what normally happens to us at the theater, even when there's a tragedy on. Perhaps it is not spectators but authors who experience catharsis. Mrs. O'Neill has given the following account of the composition of *Long Day's Journey*:

He came in and talked to me all night . . . He explained to me then that he had to write this play. He had to write it because it was a thing that haunted him . . . I think he felt freer when he got it out of his system. It was his way of making peace with his family and himself.

Catharsis, if I understand what Aristotle meant, is a matter of physical and mental health, but I cannot hold wholly mistaken the now discredited view that he may also have had moral considerations in mind. Whether or not Aristotle had them in mind, moral considerations do at once come up. Catharsis means purgation, and purgation is purgatorial. After it, if one is lucky, one is ready for heaven. It is the road on which a man learns to forgive.

The deeply human thing about this often inhuman artist, Eugene O'Neill, is his concern to be forgiven—and to be capable of forgiving. The absence of catharsis is a notable, and ugly, feature of the "big" plays. As Engel has put it, instead of catharsis, O'Neill proposes narcosis or necrosis. Not that even *Long Day's Journey* ends with anyone on stage actually forgiving anyone. Their journey is truly into night, not into love, but the dignity of the ending lies in what is *not* said. There throbs in the final speech that sense of an alternative, that sense of having lived and of having deserved to live, which I deplored the absence of in the "big" plays:

I had a talk with Mother Elizabeth [says Mary Tyrone] . . . I told her I wanted to be a nun. I explained how sure I was of my vocation, that I had prayed to the Blessed Virgin to make me sure and to find me worthy. I told Mother I had had a true vision when I was praying in the shrine of Our Lady of Lourdes on the little island in the lake. I said I knew as surely as I knew I was kneeling there that the Blessed Virgin had smiled and blessed me with her consent. But Mother Elizabeth told me I must be more sure than that, that I must prove it wasn't my imagination. She said, if I was so sure, then I wouldn't mind putting myself to a test by going home after I graduated and living as other girls lived, going out to parties and dances and enjoying myself, and then if after a year or two I still felt sure, I could come back to see her and we would talk it over again. I never dreamed Holy Mother would give me such advice! I was really shocked. I said of course I would do anything she suggested but I knew it was simply a waste of time. After I left her, I felt all mixed up, so I went to the shrine and prayed to the Blessed Virgin and found peace again because I knew she heard my prayer and would always love me and see no harm ever came to me as I never lost my faith in her. That was in the winter of senior year. Then in the spring something happened to me. Yes, I remember. I fell in love with James Tyrone and was so happy for a time.

V

The Iceman Cometh was almost as much of a new departure for O'Neill as *Long Day's Journey*, and it is equally the end of a long day's journey for the author. It marks the end of his voyagings after new forms and a "theatre of tomorrow." Here, finally, O'Neill settles for the theater of yesterday. The form of *The Iceman* is conservative and contains nothing that would have surprised his father. The Jones-MacGowan rejection of realism is itself rejected. We are back with the kind of theater of low life which Gorky envisaged for his *Lower Depths*. Gorky's naturalism was not, however, the dramaturgic model. There is nothing episodic about *The Iceman*. The structure is unified and, though large, almost symmetrical. It is possible that O'Neill was compulsive in this, and allowed himself too little freedom. Note the stage manager's pedantry with which he lays down in a lengthy stage direction just where everyone is to sit!

I have discussed the play at some length in my *In Search of Theatre* (1953), to which those interested are referred. This is how I summarized the main action of the play:

There is Hickey, and there is Parritt. Both are pouring out their false confessions and professions, and holding back their essential secret. Yet, inexorably, though against their conscious will, both are seeking punishment. Their two stories are brought together through Larry Slade whose destiny, in contrast to his intention, is to extract the secret of both protagonists. Hickey's secret explodes, and Larry at last gives Parritt what he wants: a death sentence. The upshot of the whole action is that Larry is brought from a posturing and oratorical pessimism to a real despair. . . . Larry is . . . the centre of the play, and the audience can watch the two stories being played out before him.

The summary is accurate enough, but what strikes me after a ten-year interval is that it betokens more interest in the intellectual than in the emotional dynamics of the play. I continued:

The main ideas are two: . . . that people may as well keep their illusions; second, that one

should not hate and punish but love and forgive . . . In a way the truth-illusion theme is a red herring, and . . . the author's real interest is in the love-hate theme . . . O'Neill is unclear . . . it is his play, and not life, that is unintelligible.

I now think that the play becomes more intelligible if we follow up this hint: "the author's real interest is in the love-hate theme." Hickey really hated his wife, as Parritt really hated his mother. These are the repressed truths which it is the function of the action to bring to the light of day. In Hickey's case:

I remember I heard myself speaking to her, as if it was something I'd always wanted to say: "Well, you know what you can do with your pipe dream now, you damned bitch!"

The implication could hardly be clearer, yet what follows can be confusing. "Good God," Hickey cries, "I couldn't have said that! If I did, I'd gone insane! Why, I loved Evelyn . . ." The idea appeals to Harry Hope. It gives him an "out." It gives all the men an "out." It enables them to discount all that has happened and return to their pipe dreams. Hickey is taken aback at this turn of events. After all, had he not embarked on his long, long narrative with exactly the opposite purpose in mind: finally to persuade them to abandon their dreams? He starts to object: "I see what you're driving at, but I can't let you get away with—" Then he thinks twice about it and, after a pause, gives in: "I *was* insane." He has decided to let them keep their dreams after all. Why? It is not a simple question. Ten years ago I would probably have answered: because he now sees the need which weak people have of illusions, for I thought of the play as a footnote to Ibsen's *The Wild Duck*. Today, I would find the clue in O'Neill's own stage direction: "Harry Hope's expression turns to resentful callousness again." It is to check this "resentful callousness" that Hickey agrees to be considered insane. Ten years ago, I wrote: Hickey "is a maniac," and there is a case for applying such a word to men who murder their wives under the illusion that they love them. Nonetheless, the dramatic point is different. Hickey regards himself as sane, but is willing to be regarded as insane by the others, so that

Harry Hope will stop being "resentfully callous" to him. We are back with the love-hate theme.

And there is a whole dimension of *The Iceman Cometh* about which I find nothing in my earlier account of the play: the drama of love and hate, merely recounted in the speeches of Hickey and Parritt, is re-enacted in the drama of this very recounting. One recounts *to* someone. This play presents what Theodore Reik calls the "compulsion to confess." The intent of Hickey's confession— whose weight and position make it the climax —as of his previous shorter declarations, is to bring "peace." The source of this peace is his supposed love for Evelyn. But where previously, before the men tried unsuccessfully to drop their dreams, Hickey's speech-making did elicit love—made this well-liked salesman even better liked—now they are all angry at him. They hate him. And Hickey, like many O'Neill characters, if not all, is a man completely at the mercy of other people's love and hate. As Evelyn's love drove him to hate and kill her, so the men's hate drives him to declare himself insane—and rush toward the electric chair.

Aristotle said that the chorus should be regarded as a character in the play. The men in Jimmy the Priest's are the chorus of this play, and a way of looking at the action perhaps just as valid as the one I have quoted from myself would be to take it as arising from the reciprocal relationship of Hickey and the chorus. Nowhere more than in the scene where the men rise up and try to make a new life do we feel the power of O'Neill's playwriting. We see, as various critics have noticed with approval, a pipe dream take shape before us. But is that just an incidental bit of virtuosity? Is not the chorus equally important—and dramatic—in the final scene?

An analogy can be drawn between *The Iceman Cometh* and *Lazarus Laughed*. If they are very different, it may well be because the pattern has been exactly, and perhaps deliberately, reversed. *Lazarus* was O'Neill's attempt to affirm life and love, and put down death and hate. Most of his life, as in *The Iceman Cometh*, death and hate dominated his thoughts and seemed to him to dominate the world: it is no bridegroom that cometh with love,[1] it is an iceman—bringing death. As for love, it is only lust—as is implied by popular sayings concerning housewives and their affairs with icemen. Now if we have in mind these two contrasting attitudes to life and death, we can take Lazarus and Hickey as corresponding figures. Both are salesmen to a clientele. Lazarus is selling love and everlasting life; Hickey is selling hate and everlasting death. But where Lazarus is candid, Hickey claims to be selling—precisely what Lazarus is selling! The earlier play is direct; the later, ironical. This is one factor, I believe, that makes *The Iceman* the superior play. And it would seem that O'Neill's natural bent was toward what is called realism, for what seems awkward and "arty" about the chorus in *Lazarus* falls into place in the everyday setting of *The Iceman*.

That the average spectator at *The Iceman* is not forced to think of a "chorus" at all but can just think of men shows something good about the play. At the same time, those who wish to explore O'Neill's mind cannot but be interested in the Nietzschean intention behind the "realistic" disguise. The Dionysian element is still large—even if it appears under the form of alcoholism or a birthday party or the euphoria of a drummer's "pitch" with its background of Midwestern revivalism. The chorus remains an integral part of the drama and has its own curve of action. As in *Lazarus Laughed*, the crowd is excited and inflamed by a Savior, only later to be disenchanted. They end in *Lazarus* shouting: "Hail to Death!" They end in *The Iceman*, first in complaints, and then in the noisy relief of a return to pipe dreams

In this way, *The Iceman Cometh* is seen to have its own peculiar emotional dynamics, and the ending effects a negative catharsis: the expenditure of emotion leads not to a new beginning but to the admission of exhaustion. There is something audacious and almost Quixotic about the application of so much histrionic ingenuity to such negative ends. "Life's a tragedy, hurrah!" the young O'Neill used to say in

---

[1] "Behold, the bridegroom cometh" (Matt. 25:6). In the Biblical context, the bridegroom himself symbolizes death, and the moral drawn is *memento mori*: "Watch therefore, for ye know neither the day nor the hour wherein the Son of man cometh."

humorous acknowledgment of a contradiction that vitiated all this thought. It is futile enough to profess pessimism in any art—but above all, perhaps, in the drama; for a play cannot but be playful.

If in *Long Day's Journey* O'Neill transcends his usual vision, *The Iceman Cometh* is the quintessence of O'Neillism. I have already tried to show how the word "justice" loses its meaning in O'Neill's world. Of necessity, the word "punishment" must also lose. If by justice, O'Neill only means revenge, by punishment he only means inflicted suffering—as when a boxer "takes a lot of punishment." Hence, in *The Iceman,* though there is a Dostoevskian sound to the word when we hear that Parritt seeks punishment, he actually is only seeking suffering and a conclusion. He is a masochist. He wants Larry to hurt him. And he has lost the wish to live, or will have as soon as he is hurt. He wishes his own death—the only alternative in O'Neill's bleak world to wishing other people's death. Life equals murder and suicide.

This conception deprives O'Neill of what would normally be the dramatic content of his material. Our story would normally be dramatic so long as we think of our men—Hickey and Parritt—as seeking punishment as we understand punishment, and, after all, one of them is heading for what we take as the very embodiment of punishment under its usual definition: the electric chair. But if life is not a blessing, death is not a punishment: in which case *The Iceman* has a happy ending!

We suffer some confusion of the feelings as to the direction, happy or unhappy, in which the main characters are traveling, but, in a very clever play, O'Neill does something very clever about this: Hickey's punishment is over before the cops arrive; Parritt's punishment is over before he kills himself. By that token, their punishment takes place before our eyes during our whole evening at the theater. Parritt is punished by Larry Slade, not at the end—which is a release—but all through. Hickey is punished by all the men—again, not at the end, but all through, except for one moment of vertigo when it seems they may be transformed.

This is where the pipe dreams of the three main characters come in. The illusions are what

stand between them and the punishment they seek. In what he thinks about illusions, O'Neill is systematic. Best is not to lose one's illusions and die as soon as possible. Second best is not to lose one's illusions and die later —like most of the men in *The Iceman.* Third best is to lose one's illusions and die as soon as one does so—like Hickey and Parritt. The worst fate of all is to lose your illusions and live on. This fate is reserved for Larry Slade —whom, on this interpretation as on others, we find to be the central figure in the composition. Now the spectator figure in literature is nearly always a portrait of the author. I imagine that Larry Slade represents a piece of self-criticism on O'Neill's part, that O'Neill puts into Larry his own tendency towards an empty and oratorical pessimism—the mere inversion of the official optimism of American society—and, since it is not in the cards that either Larry or O'Neill should turn optimist, the most that can be achieved is that his pessimism should turn from the spurious to the genuine. Larry learns sincerity: which was precisely what O'Neill was learning in the final phase of his writing career.

Larry learns sincerity, which is something— not love, which would be everything. However, O'Neill does try to cope with love in *The Iceman Cometh,* and the topic is a suitable one with which to close this discussion both of the play and the playwright. Taking my cue from O'Neill's own words and those of his biographers, I have spoken of ambivalence as a central fact, perhaps *the* central fact, of both the life and the work. If the word "ambivalence" implies an exact balancing of opposing attitudes, the formulation, finally, seems inexact. The relevant attitudes, in O'Neill's case, are indeed love and hate. But we do not find them balanced: we find the former utterly swamped by the latter.

This fact is not in itself surprising: the negative emotions are more prominent than the positive ones throughout the whole of literature. What is important, and disappointing, about O'Neill is that, while he does deal with love, it is always a very inadequate kind of love that he deals with—while the hate he feels would be adequate for blowing up the universe. I do not speak just quantitatively. It is the quality of the love that is insufficient—I mean of course for the purposes which O'Neill himself proposes. If we consider, for example, the relationship of Hickey and his wife Evelyn, we learn that she loves him, and we are given to understand that her love is simply wonderful because she keeps forgiving him. But to reread Hickey's long account is to realize that O'Neill, as his habit was, has equated true love with maternal warmth while leaving sex to prostitutes. Yet he does not use this fact to characterize Hickey with, because it is not a fact he can *see* as an artist—it is a fact that he is involved in as a man. The perfect marriage which Evelyn offered was the union of mother and child. What the play "ought" to have been about is Hickey's unresolved Oedipus complex. But it could not be about this because O'Neill's Oedipus complex was unresolved.

That at least is the interpretation which I submit for discussion. It would help to explain, I think, why Freudian critics, upon reading O'Neill, prick up their ears and reach for their pencils. He needs them to finish a job that he could not finish himself. Ibsen said, "to be a poet is chiefly to see." And I am assuming here that in literature the writer's complexes are not wallowed in, they are seen—and one can only see from a distance. The fantasies which derive from a writer's troubles must not merely exist; they must be transcended. They resemble the ordeal by fire and water: you have to pass through, yes; but you also have to emerge on the other side. Perhaps this is a matter of character, perhaps of talent, perhaps of both; or perhaps our terminology is inadequate and neither "talent" nor "character" tells the whole story. But anyone who uses psychoanalytic ideas at all must start out with at least a tentative answer to this question: why cannot any literate person with an Oedipus complex write an *Oedipus Rex?*

The Iceman Cometh is a typical O'Neill work in that, while it has very considerable merit, it does not achieve the transcendence I am speaking of, but substitutes the standard O'Neill pessimism—or rather a more sincere brand of it, as I have also tried to show. It is arguable, as I have indicated, that O'Neill did achieve transcendence in *Long Day's Journey into Night* and perhaps in some of the plays of his youth. An author's talent is often most abundantly at work in his least "serious efforts," and it may well be that such an item as *The Emperor Jones* will withstand time better than the big plays, just as *Charley's Aunt* withstands time better than *The Second Mrs. Tanqueray.* The reed withstands the hurricane better than the oak.

READING SUGGESTIONS

EDITIONS

The Plays of Eugene O'Neill, 3 vols. (Random House, rev. ed. 1951). This three-volume set contains all of O'Neill's published dramas except: the earliest plays, which are to be found in *Thirst* (1914) and *The Lost Plays of Eugene O'Neill* (1950); the posthumous plays, which have been published, one at a time, by the Yale University Press: *Long Day's Journey into Night* (1956), *A Touch of the Poet* (1957), and *Hughie* (1959); and *The Ancient Mariner,* which first appeared in its entirety in *Yale University Gazette,* XXXV (October, 1960), ed. by Donald Gallup.

Many letters and other utterances of O'Neill are quoted in Barrett Clark's book as cited below; also in Croswell Bowen's. Some of O'Neill's comments on drama are also reprinted in Toby Cole, editor, *Playwrights on Playwriting* (1960).

BIOGRAPHY AND CRITICISM

The student who wishes to go into the subject more deeply should use Miller, as listed here. Eric Bentley wishes to acknowledge the influence of all the writers listed below upon his Introduction to O'Neill. The kindness of Messrs. Chabrowe, Miller, and Lesser, in letting him see unpublished material, is particularly appreciated.

AGNES BOULTON, *Part of a Long Story* (1958). Memoirs of O'Neill's second wife.

CROSWELL BOWEN, *The Curse of the Misbegotten* (1959). By far the most informative account of O'Neill's life to date.

LEONARD CHABROWE, "The Classical Idea of Eugene O'Neill" (unpublished M.A. thesis, Columbia University, 1960). Works out very fully the analogy between *Lazarus* and *Iceman.* Shows how Jungian O'Neill was.

BARRETT H. CLARK, *Eugene O'Neill: The Man and His Plays* (rev. ed. 1947). The pioneer biography of O'Neill, the first version of which appeared in 1926. Clark also included O'Neill's notes on *Mourning Becomes Electra* in his *European Theories of the Drama* (rev. ed. 1947).

EDWIN A. ENGEL, *The Haunted Heroes of Eugene O'Neill* (1953). The finest study of the plays, particularly of their themes.

SIMON O. LESSER, "The Iceman Cometh: A Psychoanalytic Interpretation." An as yet (1961) unpublished paper by the author of *Fiction and the Unconscious*.

JORDAN YALE MILLER, "A Critical Bibliography of Eugene O'Neill" (unpublished Ph.D. thesis, Columbia University, 1957). Almost undoubtedly the most complete record of works by and about O'Neill. (747 pages. Available through University Microfilms, Ann Arbor, Michigan.)

PHILIP WEISSMAN, "Conscious and Unconscious Autobiographical Dramas of Eugene O'Neill," *Journal of the American Psycho-analytic Association* (July, 1957). A study of *Desire Under the Elms* and *Long Day's Journey* that breaks new ground.

MAX WYLIE, *Trouble in the Flesh* (1959, paperback reprint 1961).

The reviews of "first nights" are mostly confined to the files of newspapers and magazines, but some dramatic critics reprint their reviews in book form. Among the critics who have reprinted some or all of their comments on O'Neill are: James Agate, Eric Bentley, John Mason Brown, John Gassner, George Jean Nathan, and Stark Young.

After this essay was written, an important collection of O'Neill criticism appeared, which also contains excellent bibliographical material. This is *O'Neill and His Plays*, ed. by Oscar Cargill, N. Bryllion Fagin, and William J. Fisher (New York University Press, 1961).

THE ICEMAN COMETH

❖

⟨ *The Iceman Cometh*, according to Croswell Bowen, was written between September, 1939, and January, 1940. Those were, of course, the opening months of World War II. The play was produced on Broadway soon after the war was over, namely, on September 2, 1946. It was the first O'Neill opening since *Days Without End* (1934) in which O'Neill had seemed to come out for Roman Catholicism. Asked by Mr. Bowen if he had returned to the religion of his fathers, O'Neill answered: "Unfortunately, no. *The Iceman* is a denial of any other experience of faith in my plays. In writing it, I felt I had locked myself in with my memories." Mr. Bowen (*The Curse of the Misbegotten*, p. 319) thinks that the Hickey marriage is based on O'Neill's relations with his second wife, Agnes Boulton. Although O'Neill had earlier thought of *Lazarus Laughed* as his finest achievement, he finally took most satisfaction, it seems, in two of the late plays: *The Iceman Cometh* and *Long Day's Journey into Night*.

❖

CHARACTERS

HARRY HOPE, *proprietor of a saloon and rooming house* *

ED MOSHER, *Hope's brother-in-law, one-time circus man* *

PAT MCGLOIN, *one-time Police Lieutenant* *

WILLIE OBAN, *a Harvard Law School alumnus* *

JOE MOTT, *one-time proprietor of a Negro gambling house*

PIET WETJOEN ("THE GENERAL"), *one-time leader of a Boer commando* *

CECIL LEWIS ("THE CAPTAIN"), *one-time Captain of British infantry* *

JAMES CAMERON ("JIMMY TOMORROW"), *one-time Boer War correspondent* *

HUGO KALMAR, *one-time editor of Anarchist periodicals*

LARRY SLADE, *one-time Syndicalist-Anarchist* *

ROCKY PIOGGI, *night bartender* *

DON PARRITT *

PEARL * ⎫
MARGIE * ⎬ *street walkers*
CORA ⎭

CHUCK MORELLO, *day bartender* *

THEODORE HICKMAN (HICKEY), *a hardware salesman*

MORAN

LIEB

SCENES

ACT ONE

Scene—Back room and a section of the bar at Harry Hope's—early morning in summer, 1912.

ACT TWO

Scene—Back room, around midnight of the same day.

ACT THREE

Scene—Bar and a section of the back room—morning of the following day.

* Roomers at Harry Hope's.

ACT FOUR

Scene—Same as Act One. Back room and a section of the bar—around 1:30 A.M. of the next day.

Harry Hope's is a Raines-Law hotel of the period, a cheap ginmill of the five-cent whiskey, last-resort variety situated on the downtown West Side of New York. The building, owned by Hope, is a narrow five-story structure of the tenement type, the second floor a flat occupied by the proprietor. The renting of rooms on the upper floors, under the Raines-Law loopholes, makes the establishment legally a hotel and gives it the privilege of serving liquor in the back room of the bar after closing hours and on Sundays, provided a meal is served with the booze, thus making a back room legally a hotel restaurant. This food provision was generally circumvented by putting a property sandwich in the middle of each table, an old desiccated ruin of dust-laden bread and mummified ham or cheese which only the drunkest yokel from the sticks ever regarded as anything but a noisome table decoration. But at Harry Hope's, Hope being a former minor Tammanyite and still possessing friends, this food technicality is ignored as irrelevant, except during the fleeting alarms of reform agitation. Even Hope's back room is not a separate room, but simply the rear of the barroom divided from the bar by drawing a dirty black curtain across the room.

ACT ONE

SCENE: *The back room and a section of the bar of* HARRY HOPE'S *saloon on an early morning in summer, 1912. The right wall of the back room is a dirty black curtain which separates it from the bar. At rear, this curtain is drawn back from the wall so the bartender can get in and out. The back room is crammed with round tables and chairs placed so close together that it is a difficult squeeze to pass between them. In the middle of the rear wall is a door opening on a hallway. In the left corner, built out into the room, is the toilet with a sign "This is it" on the door. Against the middle of the left wall is a nickel-in-the-slot phonograph. Two windows, so glazed with grime one cannot see through them, are in the left wall, looking out on a backyard. The walls and ceiling once were white, but it was a long time ago, and they are now so splotched, peeled, stained and dusty that their color can best be described as* dirty. *The floor, with iron spittoons placed here and there, is covered with sawdust. Lighting comes from single wall brackets, two at left and two at rear.*

There are three rows of tables, from front to back. Three are in the front line. The one at left-front has four chairs; the one at center-front, four; the one at right-front, five. At rear of, and half between, front tables one and two is a table of the second row with five chairs. A table, similarly placed at rear of front tables two and three, also has five chairs. The third row of tables, four chairs to one and six to the other, is against the rear wall on either side of the door.

At right of this dividing curtain is a section of the barroom, with the end of the bar seen at rear, a door to the hall at left of it. At front is a table with four chairs. Light comes from the street windows off right, the gray subdued light of early morning in a narrow street. In the back room, LARRY SLADE *and* HUGO KALMAR *are at the table at left-front,* HUGO *in a chair facing right,* LARRY *at rear of table facing front, with an empty chair between them. A fourth chair is at right of table, facing left.* HUGO *is a small man in his late fifties. He has a head much too big for his body, a high forehead, crinkly long black hair streaked with gray, a square face with a pug nose, a walrus mustache, black eyes which peer near-sightedly from behind thick-lensed spectacles, tiny hands and feet. He is dressed in threadbare black clothes and his white shirt is frayed at collar and cuffs, but everything about him is fastidiously clean. Even his flowing Windsor tie is neatly tied. There is a foreign atmosphere about him, the stamp of an alien radical, a strong resemblance to the type Anarchist as portrayed, bomb in hand, in newspaper cartoons. He is asleep now, bent forward in his chair, his arms folded on the table, his head resting sideways on his arms.*

LARRY SLADE *is sixty. He is tall, raw-boned, with coarse straight white hair, worn long and raggedly cut. He has a gaunt Irish face with a big nose, high cheekbones, a lantern jaw with a week's stubble of beard, a mystic's meditative pale-blue eyes with a gleam of sharp sardonic humor in them. As slovenly as* HUGO *is neat, his clothes are dirty and much slept in. His gray flannel shirt, open at the neck, has the appearance of having never been washed. From the way he methodically scratches himself with his long-fingered, hairy hands, he is lousy and reconciled to being so. He is the only occupant of the room who is not asleep. He stares in front of him, an expression of tired tolerance giving his face the quality of a pitying but weary old priest's.*

All four chairs at the middle table, front, are occupied. JOE MOTT *sits at left-front of the table, facing front. Behind him, facing right-front, is* PIET WETJOEN *("The General"). At center of the table, rear,* JAMES CAMERON *("Jimmy Tomorrow") sits facing front. At right of table, opposite* JOE, *is* CECIL LEWIS *("The Captain").*

JOE MOTT *is a Negro, about fifty years old, brown-skinned, stocky, wearing a light suit that had once been flashily sporty but is now about to fall apart. His pointed tan buttoned shoes, faded pink shirt and bright tie belong to the same vintage. Still, he manages to preserve an atmosphere of nattiness and there is nothing dirty about his appearance. His face is only mildly negroid in type. The nose is thin and his lips are not noticeably thick. His hair is crinkly and he is beginning to get bald. A scar from a knife slash runs from his left cheekbone to jaw. His face would be hard and tough if it were not for its good nature and lazy humor. He is asleep, his nodding head supported by his left hand.*

PIET WETJOEN, *the Boer, is in his fifties, a huge man with a bald head and a long grizzled beard. He is slovenly dressed in a dirty shapeless patched suit, spotted by food. A Dutch farmer type, his once great muscular strength has been debauched into flaccid tallow. But despite his blubbery mouth and sodden bloodshot blue eyes, there is still a suggestion of old authority lurking in him like a memory of the drowned. He is hunched forward, both elbows on the table, his hand on each side of his head for support.*

JAMES CAMERON *("Jimmy Tomorrow") is about the same size and age as* HUGO, *a small man. Like* HUGO, *he wears threadbare black, and everything about him is clean. But the resemblance ceases there.* JIMMY *has a face like an old well-bred, gentle bloodhound's, with folds of flesh hanging from each side of his mouth, and big brown friendly guileless eyes, more bloodshot than any bloodhound's ever were. He has mouse-colored thinning hair, a little bulbous nose, buck teeth in a small rabbit mouth. But his forehead is fine, his eyes are intelligent and there once was a competent ability in him. His speech is educated, with the ghost of a Scotch rhythm in it. His manners are those of a gentleman. There is a quality about him of a prim, Victorian old maid, and at the same time of a likable, affectionate boy who has never grown up. He sleeps, chin on chest, hands folded in his lap.*

CECIL LEWIS *("The Captain") is as obviously English as Yorkshire pudding and just as obviously the former army officer. He is going on sixty. His hair and military mustache are white,* his eyes bright blue, his complexion that of a turkey. His lean figure is still erect and square-shouldered. He is stripped to the waist, his coat, shirt, undershirt, collar and tie crushed up into a pillow on the table in front of him, his head sideways on this pillow, facing front, his arms dangling toward the floor. On his lower left shoulder is the big ragged scar of an old wound.*

At the table at right, front, HARRY HOPE, *the proprietor, sits in the middle, facing front, with* PAT MCGLOIN *on his right and* ED MOSHER *on his left, the other two chairs being unoccupied.*

Both MCGLOIN *and* MOSHER *are big paunchy men.* MCGLOIN *has his old occupation of policeman stamped all over him. He is in his fifties, sandy-haired, bullet-headed, jowly, with protruding ears and little round eyes. His face must once have been brutal and greedy, but time and whiskey have melted it down into a good-humored, parasite's characterlessness. He wears old clothes and is slovenly. He is slumped sideways on his chair, his head drooping jerkily toward one shoulder.*

ED MOSHER *is going on sixty. He has a round kewpie's face—a kewpie who is an unshaven habitual drunkard. He looks like an enlarged, elderly, bald edition of the village fat boy—a sly fat boy, congenitally indolent, a practical joker, a born grafter and con merchant. But amusing and essentially harmless, even in his most enterprising days, because always too lazy to carry crookedness beyond petty swindling. The influence of his old circus career is apparent in his get-up. His worn clothes are flashy; he wears phony rings and a heavy brass watch-chain (not connected to a watch). Like* MCGLOIN, *he is slovenly. His head is thrown back, his big mouth open.*

HARRY HOPE *is sixty, white-haired, so thin the description "bag of bones" was made for him. He has the face of an old family horse, prone to tantrums, with balkiness always smoldering in its wall eyes, waiting for any excuse to shy and pretend to take the bit in its teeth. Hope is one of those men whom everyone likes on sight, a soft-hearted slob, without malice, feeling superior to no one, a sinner among sinners, a born easy mark for every appeal. He attempts to hide his defenselessness behind a testy truculent manner, but this has never fooled anyone. He is a little deaf, but not half as deaf as he sometimes pretends. His sight is failing but is not as bad as he complains it is. He wears five-and-ten-cent-store spectacles which are so out of alignment that one eye at times peers half over one glass while the other eye looks half under the other. He has badly fitting store teeth, which click like castanets when*

*he begins to fume. He is dressed in an old coat
from one suit and pants from another.*

In a chair facing right at the table in the second line, between the first two tables, front, sits
WILLIE OBAN, *his head on his left arm outstretched
along the table edge. He is in his late thirties, of
average height, thin. His haggard, dissipated face
has a small nose, a pointed chin, blue eyes with
colorless lashes and brows. His blond hair, badly
in need of a cut, clings in a limp part to his
skull. His eyelids flutter continually as if any light
were too strong for his eyes. The clothes he wears
belong on a scarecrow. They seem constructed of
an inferior grade of dirty blotting paper. His shoes
are even more disreputable, wrecks of imitation
leather, one laced with twine, the other with a bit
of wire. He has no socks, and his bare feet show
through holes in the soles, with his big toes sticking out of the uppers. He keeps muttering and
twitching in his sleep.*

As the curtain rises, ROCKY, *the night bartender,
comes from the bar through the curtain and
stands looking over the back room. He is a
Neapolitan-American in his late twenties, squat
and muscular, with a flat, swarthy face and beady
eyes. The sleeves of his collarless shirt are rolled
up on his thick, powerful arms and he wears a
soiled apron. A tough guy but sentimental, in his
way, and good-natured. He signals to* LARRY *with
a cautious "Sstt" and motions him to see if* HOPE
is asleep. LARRY *rises from his chair to look at*
HOPE *and nods to* ROCKY. ROCKY *goes back in
the bar but immediately returns with a bottle of
bar whiskey and a glass. He squeezes between the
tables to* LARRY.

ROCKY. (*In a low voice out of the side of his
mouth*) Make it fast. (LARRY *pours a drink and
gulps it down.* ROCKY *takes the bottle and puts it
on the table where* WILLIE OBAN *is*) Don't want
de Boss to get wise when he's got one of his tightwad buns on. (*He chuckles with an amused glance
at* HOPE) Jess, ain't de old bastard a riot when he
starts dat bull about turnin' over a new leaf?
"Not a damned drink on de house," he tells me,
"and all dese bums got to pay up deir room rent.
Beginnin' tomorrow," he says. Jees, yuh'd tink
he meant it! (*He sits down in the chair at* LARRY'S
left.)

LARRY. (*Grinning*) I'll be glad to pay up—
tomorrow. And I know my fellow inmates will
promise the same. They've all a touching credulity
concerning tomorrows. (*A half-drunken mockery
in his eyes*) It'll be a great day for them, tomorrow—the Feast of All Fools, with brass
bands playing! Their ships will come in, loaded

to the gunwales with cancelled regrets and promises fulfilled and clean slates and new leases!

ROCKY. (*Cynically*) Yeah, and a ton of hop!

LARRY. (*Leans toward him, a comical intensity
in his low voice*) Don't mock the faith! Have
you no respect for religion, you unregenerate
Wop? What's it matter if the truth is that their
favoring breeze has the stink of nickel whiskey on
its breath, and their sea is a growler of lager and
ale, and their ships are long since looted and
scuttled and sunk on the bottom? To hell with the
truth! As the history of the world proves, the
truth has no bearing on anything. It's irrelevant
and immaterial, as the lawyers say. The lie of a
pipe dream is what gives life to the whole misbegotten mad lot of us, drunk or sober. And
that's enough philosophic wisdom to give you for
one drink of rot-gut.

ROCKY. (*Grins kiddingly*) De old Foolosopher,
like Hickey calls yuh, ain't yuh? I s'pose you
don't fall for no pipe dream?

LARRY. (*A bit stiffly*) I don't, no. Mine are all
dead and buried behind me. What's before me is
the comforting fact that death is a fine long sleep,
and I'm damned tired, and it can't come too soon
for me.

ROCKY. Yeah, just hangin' around hopin' you'll
croak, ain't yuh? Well, I'm bettin' you'll have a
good long wait. Jees, somebody'll have to take an
axe to croak you!

LARRY. (*Grins*) Yes, it's my bad luck to be
cursed with an iron constitution that even Harry's
booze can't corrode.

ROCKY. De old anarchist wise guy dat knows all
de answers! Dat's you, huh?

LARRY. (*Frowns*) Forget the anarchist part of it.
I'm through with the Movement long since. I saw
men didn't want to be saved from themselves, for
that would mean they'd have to give up greed,
and they'll never pay that price for liberty. So I
said to the world, God bless all here, and may the
best man win and die of gluttony! And I took a
seat in the grandstand of philosophical detachment to fall asleep observing the cannibals do
their death dance. (*He chuckles at his own fancy
—reaches over and shakes Hugo's shoulder*) Ain't
I telling him the truth, Comrade Hugo?

ROCKY. Aw, fer Chris' sake, don't get dat bughouse bum started!

HUGO. (*Raises his head and peers at* ROCKY
*blearily through his thick spectacles—in a guttural
declamatory tone*) Capitalist swine! Bourgeois
stool pigeons! Have the slaves no right to sleep
even? (*Then he grins at* ROCKY *and his manner
changes to a giggling, wheedling playfulness, as
though he were talking to a child*) Hello, leedle

Rocky! Leedle monkey-face! Vere is your leedle slave girls? (*With an abrupt change to a bullying tone*) Don't be a fool! Loan me a dollar! Damned bourgeois Wop! The great Malatesta is my good friend! Buy me a drink! (*He seems to run down, and is overcome by drowsiness. His head sinks to the table again and he is at once fast asleep.*)

ROCKY. He's out again. (*More exasperated than angry*) He's lucky no one don't take his cracks serious or he'd wake up every mornin' in a hospital.

LARRY. (*Regarding* HUGO *with pity*) No. No one takes him seriously. That's his epitaph. Not even the comrades any more. If I've been through with the Movement long since, it's been through with him, and, thanks to whiskey, he's the only one doesn't know it.

ROCKY. I've let him get by wid too much. He's goin' to pull dat slave-girl stuff on me once too often. (*His manner changes to defensive argument*) Hell, yuh'd tink I wuz a pimp or somethin'. Everybody knows me knows I ain't. A pimp don't hold no job. I'm a bartender. Dem tarts, Margie and Poil, dey're just a side line to pick up some extra dough. Strictly business, like dey was fighters and I was deir manager, see? I fix the cops fer dem so's dey can hustle widout gettin' pinched. Hell, dey'd be on de Island most of de time if it wasn't fer me. And I don't beat dem up like a pimp would. I treat dem fine. Dey like me. We're pals, see? What if I do take deir dough? Dey'd on'y trow it away. Tarts can't hang on to dough. But I'm a bartender and I work hard for my livin' in dis dump. You know dat, Larry.

LARRY. (*With inner sardonic amusement—flatteringly*) A shrewd business man, who doesn't miss any opportunity to get on in the world. That's what I'd call you.

ROCKY. (*Pleased*) Sure ting. Dat's me. Grab another ball, Larry. (LARRY *pours a drink from the bottle on* WILLIE's *table and gulps it down.* ROCKY *glances around the room*) Yuh'd never tink all dese bums had a good bed upstairs to go to. Scared if dey hit the hay dey wouldn't be here when Hickey showed up, and dey'd miss a coupla drinks. Dat's what kept you up too, ain't it?

LARRY. It is. But not so much the hope of booze, if you can believe that. I've got the blues and Hickey's a great one to make a joke of everything and cheer you up.

ROCKY. Yeah, some kidder! Remember how he woiks up dat gag about his wife, when he's cockeyed, cryin' over her picture and den springin' it on yuh all of a sudden dat he left her in de hay wid de iceman? (*He laughs*) I wonder what's happened to him. Yuh could set your watch by his

periodicals before dis. Always got here a coupla days before Harry's birthday party, and now he's on'y got till tonight to make it. I hope he shows soon. Dis dump is like de morgue wid all dese bums passed out. (WILLIE OBAN *jerks and twitches in his sleep and begins to mumble. They watch him.*)

WILLIE. (*Blurts from his dream*) It's a lie! (*Miserably*) Papa! Papa!

LARRY. Poor devil. (*Then angry with himself*) But to hell with pity! It does no good. I'm through with it!

ROCKY. Dreamin' about his old man. From what de old-timers say, de old gent sure made a pile of dough in de bucket-shop game before de cops got him. (*He considers* WILLIE *frowningly*) Jees, I've seen him bad before but never dis bad. Look at dat get-up. Been playin' de old reliever game. Sold his suit and shoes at Solly's two days ago. Solly give him two bucks and a bum outfit. Yesterday he sells de bum one back to Solly for four bits and gets dese rags to put on. Now he's through. Dat's Solly's final edition he wouldn't take back for nuttin'. Willie sure is on de bottom. I ain't never seen no one so bad, except Hickey on de end of a coupla his bats.

LARRY. (*Sardonically*) It's a great game, the pursuit of happiness.

ROCKY. Harry don't know what to do about him. He called up his old lady's lawyer like he always does when Willie gets licked. Yuh remember dey used to send down a private dick to give him de rush to a cure, but de lawyer tells Harry nix, de old lady's off of Willie for keeps dis time and he can go to hell.

LARRY. (*Watches* WILLIE, *who is shaking in his sleep like an old dog*) There's the consolation that he hasn't far to go! (*As if replying to this,* WILLIE *comes to a crisis of jerks and moans.* LARRY *adds in a comically intense, crazy whisper*) Be God, he's knocking on the door right now!

WILLIE. (*Suddenly yells in his nightmare*) It's a God-damned lie! (*He begins to sob*) Oh, Papa! Jesus! (*All the occupants of the room stir on their chairs but none of them wakes up except* HOPE.)

ROCKY. (*Grabs his shoulder and shakes him*) Hey, you! Nix! Cut out de noise! (WILLIE *opens his eyes to stare around him with a bewildered horror.*)

HOPE. (*Opens one eye to peer over his spectacles—drowsily*) Who's that yelling?

ROCKY. Willie, Boss. De Brooklyn boys is after him.

HOPE. (*Querulously*) Well, why don't you give the poor feller a drink and keep him quiet? Bejees, can't I get a wink of sleep in my own back room?

ROCKY. (*Indignantly to* LARRY) Listen to that blind-eyed, deef old bastard, will yuh? He give me strict orders not to let Willie hang up no more drinks, no matter—

HOPE. (*Mechanically puts a hand to his ear in the gesture of deafness*) What's that? I can't hear you. (*Then drowsily irascible*) You're a cockeyed liar. Never refused a drink to anyone needed it bad in my life! Told you to use your judgment. Ought to know better. You're too busy thinking up ways to cheat me. Oh, I ain't as blind as you think. I can still see a cash register, bejees!

ROCKY. (*Grins at him affectionately now— flatteringly*) Sure, Boss. Swell chance of foolin' you!

HOPE. I'm wise to you and your sidekick, Chuck. Bejees, you're burglars, not barkeeps! Blind-eyed, deef old bastard, am I? Oh, I heard you! Heard you often when you didn't think. You and Chuck laughing behind my back, telling people you throw the money up in the air and whatever sticks to the ceiling is my share! A fine couple of crooks! You'd steal the pennies off your dead mother's eyes!

ROCKY. (*Winks at* LARRY) Aw, Harry, me and Chuck was on'y kiddin'.

HOPE. (*More drowsily*) I'll fire both of you. Bejees, if you think you can play me for an easy mark, you've come to the wrong house. No one ever played Harry Hope for a sucker!

ROCKY. (*To* LARRY) No one but everybody.

HOPE. (*His eyes shut again—mutters*) Least you could do—keep things quiet—(*He falls asleep.*)

WILLIE. (*Pleadingly*) Give me a drink, Rocky. Harry said it was all right. God, I need a drink.

ROCKY. Den grab it. It's right under your nose.

WILLIE. (*Avidly*) Thanks. (*He takes the bottle with both twitching hands and tilts it to his lips and gulps down the whiskey in big swallows.*)

ROCKY. (*Sharply*) When! When! (*He grabs the bottle*) I didn't say, take a bath! (*Showing the bottle to* LARRY—*indignantly*) Jees, look! He's killed a half pint or more! (*He turns on* WILLIE *angrily, but* WILLIE *has closed his eyes and is sitting quietly, shuddering, waiting for the effect.*)

LARRY. (*With a pitying glance*) Leave him be, the poor devil. A half pint of that dynamite in one swig will fix him for a while—if it doesn't kill him.

ROCKY. (*Shrugs his shoulders and sits down again*) Aw right by me. It ain't my booze. (*Behind him, in the chair at left of the middle table,* JOE MOTT, *the Negro, has been waking up.*)

JOE. (*His eyes blinking sleepily*) Whose booze?

Gimme some. I don't care whose. Where's Hickey? Ain't he come yet? What time's it, Rocky?

ROCKY. Gettin' near time to open up. Time you begun to sweep up in de bar.

JOE (*Lazily*) Never mind de time. If Hickey ain't come, it's time Joe goes to sleep again. I was dreamin' Hickey come in de door, crackin' one of dem drummer's jokes, wavin' a big bankroll and we was all goin' be drunk for two weeks. Wake up and no luck. (*Suddenly his eyes open wide*) Wait a minute, dough. I got idea. Say, Larry, how 'bout dat young guy, Parritt, came to look you up last night and rented a room? Where's he at?

LARRY. Up in his room, asleep. No hope in him, anyway, Joe. He's broke.

JOE. Dat what he told you? Me and Rocky knows different. Had a roll when he paid you his room rent, didn't he, Rocky? I seen it.

ROCKY. Yeah. He flashed it like he forgot and den tried to hide it quick.

LARRY. (*Surprised and resentful*) He did, did he?

ROCKY. Yeah, I figgered he don't belong, but he said he was a friend of yours.

LARRY. He's a liar. I wouldn't know him if he hadn't told me who he was. His mother and I were friends years ago on the Coast. (*He hesitates —then lowering his voice*) You've read in the papers about that bombing on the Coast when several people got killed? Well, the one woman they pinched, Rosa Parritt, is his mother. They'll be coming up for trial soon, and there's no chance for them. She'll get life, I think. I'm telling you this so you'll know why if Don acts a bit queer, and not jump on him. He must be hard hit. He's her only kid.

ROCKY. (*Nods—then thoughtfully*) Why ain't he out dere stickin' by her?

LARRY. (*Frowns*) Don't ask questions. Maybe there's a good reason.

ROCKY. (*Stares at him—understandingly*) Sure. I get it. (*Then wonderingly*) But den what kind of a sap is he to hang on to his right name?

LARRY. (*Irritably*) I'm telling you I don't know anything and I don't want to know. To hell with the Movement and all connected with it! I'm out of it, and everything else, and damned glad to be.

ROCKY. (*Shrugs his shoulders—indifferently*) Well, don't tink I'm interested in dis Parritt guy. He's nuttin' to me.

JOE. Me neider. If dere's one ting more'n anudder I cares nuttin' about, it's de sucker game you and Hugo call de Movement. (*He chuckles— reminiscently*) Reminds me of damn fool argument me and Mose Porter has de udder night. He's drunk and I'm drunker. He says, "Socialist and Anarchist, we ought to shoot dem dead. Dey's all no-good sons of bitches." I says, "Hold on, you talk 's if Anarchists and Socialists was de same." "Dey is," he says. "Dey's both no-good bastards." "No, dey ain't," I says. "I'll explain the difference. De Anarchist he never works. He drinks but he never buys, and if he do ever get a nickel, he blows it in on bombs, and he wouldn't give you nothin'. So go ahead and shoot him. But de Socialist, sometimes, he's got a job, and if he gets ten bucks, he's bound by his religion to split fifty-fifty wid you. You say—how about my cut, Comrade? And you gets de five. So you don't shoot no Socialists while I'm around. Dat is, not if dey got anything. Of course, if dey's broke, den dey's no-good bastards, too." (*He laughs, immensely tickled.*)

LARRY. (*Grins with sardonic appreciation*) Be God, Joe, you've got all the beauty of human nature and the practical wisdom of the world in that little parable.

ROCKY. (*Winks at* JOE) Sure, Larry ain't de on'y wise guy in dis dump, hey, Joe? (*At a sound from the hall he turns as* DON PARRITT *appears in the doorway.* ROCKY *speaks to* LARRY *out of the side of his mouth*) Here's your guy. (PARRITT *comes forward. He is eighteen, tall and broad-shouldered but thin, gangling and awkward. His face is good-looking, with blond curly hair and large regular features, but his personality is unpleasant. There is a shifting defiance and ingratiation in his light-blue eyes and an irritating aggressiveness in his manner. His clothes and shoes are new, comparatively expensive, sporty in style. He looks as though he belonged in a pool room patronized by would-be sports. He glances around defensively, sees* LARRY *and comes forward.*)

PARRITT. Hello, Larry. (*He nods to* ROCKY *and* JOE) Hello. (*They nod and size him up with expressionless eyes.*)

LARRY. (*Without cordiality*) What's up? I thought you'd be asleep.

PARRITT. Couldn't make it. I got sick of lying awake. Thought I might as well see if you were around.

LARRY. (*Indicates the chair on the right of table*) Sit down and join the bums then. (PARRITT *sits down.* LARRY *adds meaningfully*) The rules of the house are that drinks may be served at all hours.

PARRITT. (*Forcing a smile*) I get you. But, hell, I'm just about broke. (*He catches* ROCKY'S *and* JOE'S *contemptuous glances—quickly*) Oh, I know you guys saw—You think I've got a roll. Well, you're all wrong. I'll show you. (*He takes a small wad of dollar bills from his pocket*) It's all ones. And I've got to live on it till I get a job. (*Then*

with defensive truculence) You think I fixed up a phony, don't you? Why the hell would I? Where would I get a real roll? You don't get rich doing what I've been doing. Ask Larry. You're lucky in the Movement if you have enough to eat. (LARRY *regards him puzzledly.*)

ROCKY. (*Coldly*) What's de song and dance about? We ain't said nuttin'.

PARRITT. (*Lamely—placating them now*) Why, I was just putting you right. But I don't want you to think I'm a tightwad. I'll buy a drink if you want one.

JOE. (*Cheering up*) If? Man, when I don't want a drink, you call de morgue, tell dem come take Joe's body away, 'cause he's sure enuf dead. Gimme de bottle quick, Rocky, before he changes his mind! (ROCKY *passes him the bottle and glass. He pours a brimful drink and tosses it down his throat, and hands the bottle and glass to* LARRY.)

ROCKY. I'll take a cigar when I go in de bar. What're you havin'?

PARRITT. Nothing. I'm on the wagon. What's the damage? (*He holds out a dollar bill.*)

ROCKY. Fifteen cents. (*He makes change from his pocket.*)

PARRITT. Must be some booze!

LARRY. It's cyanide cut with carbolic acid to give it a mellow flavor. Here's luck! (*He drinks.*)

ROCKY. Guess I'll get back in de bar and catch a coupla winks before opening-up time. (*He squeezes through the tables and disappears, right-rear, behind the curtain. In the section of bar at right, he comes forward and sits at the table and slumps back, closing his eyes and yawning.*)

JOE. (*Stares calculatingly at* PARRITT *and then looks away—aloud to himself, philosophically*) One-drink guy. Dat well done run dry. No hope till Harry's birthday party. 'Less Hickey shows up. (*He turns to* LARRY) If Hickey comes, Larry, you wake me up if you has to bat me wid a chair. (*He settles himself and immediately falls asleep.*)

PARRITT. Who's Hickey?

LARRY. A hardware drummer. An old friend of Harry Hope's and all the gang. He's a grand guy. He comes here twice a year regularly on a periodical drunk and blows in all his money.

PARRITT. (*With a disparaging glance around*) Must be hard up for a place to hang out.

LARRY. It has its points for him. He never runs into anyone he knows in his business here.

PARRITT. (*Lowering his voice*) Yes, that's what I want, too. I've got to stay under cover, Larry, like I told you last night.

LARRY. You did a lot of hinting. You didn't tell me anything.

PARRITT. You can guess, can't you? (*He changes*

the subject abruptly) I've been in some dumps on the Coast, but this is the limit. What kind of joint is it, anyway?

LARRY. (*With a sardonic grin*) What is it? It's the No Chance Saloon. It's Bedrock Bar, The End of the Line Café, The Bottom of the Sea Rathskeller! Don't you notice the beautiful calm in the atmosphere? That's because it's the last harbor. No one here has to worry about where they're going next, because there is no farther they can go. It's a great comfort to them. Although even here they keep up the appearances of life with a few harmless pipe dreams about their yesterdays and tomorrows, as you'll see for yourself if you're here long.

PARRITT. (*Stares at him curiously*) What's your pipe dream, Larry?

LARRY. (*Hiding resentment*) Oh, I'm the exception. I haven't any left, thank God. (*Shortly*) Don't complain about this place. You couldn't find a better for lying low.

PARRITT. I'm glad of that, Larry. I don't feel any too damned good. I was knocked off my base by that business on the Coast, and since then it's been no fun dodging around the country, thinking every guy you see might be a dick.

LARRY. (*Sympathetically now*) No, it wouldn't be. But you're safe here. The cops ignore this dump. They think it's as harmless as a graveyard. (*He grins sardonically*) And, be God, they're right.

PARRITT. It's been lonely as hell. (*Impulsively*) Christ, Larry, I was glad to find you. I kept saying to myself, "If I can only find Larry. He's the one guy in the world who can understand—" (*He hesitates, staring at* LARRY *with a strange appeal.*)

LARRY. (*Watching him puzzledly*) Understand what?

PARRITT. (*Hastily*) Why, all I've been through. (*Looking away*) Oh, I know you're thinking, This guy has a hell of a nerve. I haven't seen him since he was a kid. I'd forgotten he was alive. But I've never forgotten you, Larry. You were the only friend of Mother's who ever paid attention to me, or knew I was alive. All the others were too busy with the Movement. Even Mother. And I had no Old Man. You used to take me on your knee and tell me stories and crack jokes and make me laugh. You'd ask me questions and take what I said seriously. I guess I got to feel in the years you lived with us that you'd taken the place of my Old Man. (*Embarrassedly*) But, hell, that sounds like a lot of mush. I suppose you don't remember a damned thing about it.

LARRY. (*Moved in spite of himself*) I remember well. You were a serious lonely little shaver. (*Then resenting being moved, changes the subject*) How is it they didn't pick you up when they got your mother and the rest?

PARRITT. (*In a lowered voice but eagerly, as if he wanted this chance to tell about it*) I wasn't around, and as soon as I heard the news I went under cover. You've noticed my glad rags. I was staked to them—as a disguise, sort of. I hung around pool rooms and gambling joints and hooker shops, where they'd never look for a Wobblie, pretending I was a sport. Anyway, they'd grabbed everyone important, so I suppose they didn't think of me until afterward.

LARRY. The papers say the cops got them all dead to rights, that the Burns dicks knew every move before it was made, and someone inside the Movement must have sold out and tipped them off.

PARRITT. (*Turns to look* LARRY *in the eyes—slowly*) Yes, I guess that must be true, Larry. It hasn't come out who it was. It may never come out. I suppose whoever it was made a bargin with the Burns men to keep him out of it. They won't need his evidence.

LARRY. (*Tensely*) By God, I hate to believe it of any of the crowd, if I am through long since with any connection with them. I know they're damned fools, most of them, as stupidly greedy for power as the worst capitalist they attack, but I'd swear there couldn't be a yellow stool pigeon among them.

PARRITT. Sure. I'd have sworn that, too, Larry.

LARRY. I hope his soul rots in hell, whoever it is!

PARRITT. Yes, so do I.

LARRY. (*After a pause—shortly*) How did you locate me? I hoped I'd found a place of retirement here where no one in the Movement would ever come to disturb my peace.

PARRITT. I found out through Mother.

LARRY. I asked her not to tell anyone.

PARRITT. She didn't tell me, but she'd kept all your letters and I found where she'd hidden them in the flat. I sneaked up there one night after she was arrested.

LARRY. I'd never have thought she was a woman who'd keep letters.

PARRITT. No, I wouldn't, either. There's nothing soft or sentimental about Mother.

LARRY. I never answered her last letters. I haven't written her in a couple of years—or anyone else. I've gotten beyond the desire to communicate with the world—or, what's more to the point, let it bother me any more with its greedy madness.

PARRITT. It's funny Mother kept in touch with

you so long. When she's finished with anyone, she's finished. She's always been proud of that. And you know how she feels about the Movement. Like a revivalist preacher about religion. Anyone who loses faith in it is more than dead to her; he's a Judas who ought to be boiled in oil. Yet she seemed to forgive you.

LARRY. (*Sardonically*) She didn't, don't worry. She wrote to denounce me and try to bring the sinner to repentance and a belief in the One True Faith again.

PARRITT. What made you leave the Movement, Larry? Was it on account of Mother?

LARRY. (*Starts*) Don't be a damned fool! What the hell put that in your head?

PARRITT. Why, nothing—except I remember what a fight you had with her before you left.

LARRY. (*Resentfully*) Well, if you do, I don't. That was eleven years ago. You were only seven. If we did quarrel, it was because I told her I'd become convinced the Movement was only a beautiful pipe dream.

PARRITT. (*With a strange smile*) I don't remember it that way.

LARRY. Then you can blame your imagination—and forget it. (*He changes the subject abruptly*) You asked me why I quit the Movement. I had a lot of good reasons. One was myself, and another was my comrades, and the last was the breed of swine called men in general. For myself, I was forced to admit, at the end of thirty years' devotion to the Cause, that I was never made for it. I was born condemned to be one of those who has to see all sides of a question. When you're damned like that, the questions multiply for you until in the end it's all question and no answer. As history proves, to be a worldly success at anything, especially revolution, you have to wear blinders like a horse and see only straight in front of you. You have to see, too, that this is all black, and that is all white. As for my comrades in the Great Cause, I felt as Horace Walpole did about England, that he could love it if it weren't for the people in it. The material the ideal free society must be constructed from is men themselves and you can't build a marble temple out of a mixture of mud and manure. When man's soul isn't a sow's ear, it will be time enough to dream of silk purses. (*He chuckles sardonically—then irritably as if suddenly provoked at himself for talking so much*) Well, that's why I quite the Movement, if it leaves you any wiser. At any rate, you see it had nothing to do with your mother.

PARRITT. (*Smiles almost mockingly*) Oh, sure, I see. But I'll bet Mother has always thought it was on her account. You know her, Larry. To hear her go on sometimes, you'd think she was the Movement.

LARRY. (*Stares at him, puzzled and repelled—sharply*) That's a hell of a way for you to talk, after what happened to her!

PARRITT. (*At once confused and guilty*) Don't get me wrong. I wasn't sneering, Larry. Only kidding. I've said the same thing to her lots of times to kid her. But you're right. I know I shouldn't now. I keep forgetting she's in jail. It doesn't seem real. I can't believe it about her. She's always been so free. I— But I don't want to think of it. (*LARRY is moved to a puzzled pity in spite of himself. PARRITT changes the subject*) What have you been doing all the years since you left—the Coast, Larry?

LARRY. (*Sardonically*) Nothing I could help doing. If I don't believe in the Movement, I don't believe in anything else either, especially not the State. I've refused to become a useful member of its society. I've been a philosophical drunken bum, and proud of it. (*Abruptly his tone sharpens with resentful warning*) Listen to me. I hope you've deduced that I've my own reason for answering the impertinent questions of a stranger, for that's all you are to me. I have a strong hunch you've come here expecting something of me. I'm warning you, at the start, so there'll be no misunderstanding, that I've nothing left to give, and I want to be left alone, and I'll thank you to keep your life to yourself. I feel you're looking for some answer to something. I have no answer to give anyone, not even myself. Unless you can call what Heine wrote in his poem to morphine an answer. (*He quotes a translation of the closing couplet sardonically*)

"Lo, sleep is good; better is death; in sooth,
The best of all were never to be born."

PARRITT. (*Shrinks a bit frightenedly*) That's the hell of an answer. (*Then with a forced grin of bravado*) Still, you never know when it might come in handy. (*He looks away. LARRY stares at him puzzledly, interested in spite of himself and at the same time vaguely uneasy.*)

LARRY. (*Forcing a casual tone*) I don't suppose you've had much chance to hear news of your mother since she's been in jail?

PARRITT. No. No chance. (*He hesitates—then blurts out*) Anyway, I don't think she wants to hear from me. We had a fight just before that business happened. She bawled me out because I was going around with tarts. That got my goat, coming from her. I told her, "You've always acted the free woman, you've never let anything stop you from—" (*He checks himself—goes on hurriedly*) That made her sore. She said she wouldn't give a damn what I did except she'd begun to suspect I was too interested in outside things and losing interest in the Movement.

LARRY. (*Stares at him*) And were you?

PARRITT. (*Hesitates—then with intensity*) Sure I was! I'm no damned fool! I couldn't go on believing forever that gang was going to change the world by shooting off their loud traps on soapboxes and sneaking around blowing up a lousy building or a bridge! I got wise it was all a crazy pipe dream! (*Appealingly*) The same as you did, Larry. That's why I came to you. I knew you'd understand. What finished me was this last business of someone selling out. How can you believe anything after a thing like that happens? It knocks you cold! You don't know what the hell is what! You're through! (*Appealingly*) You know how I feel, don't you, Larry? (LARRY *stares at him, moved by sympathy and pity in spite of himself, disturbed, and resentful at being disturbed, and puzzled by something he feels about* PARRITT *that isn't right. But before he can reply,* HUGO *suddenly raises his head from his arms in a half-awake alcoholic daze and speaks.*)

HUGO. (*Quotes aloud to himself in a guttural declamatory style*) "The days grow hot, O Babylon! 'Tis cool beneath thy villow trees!" (PARRITT *turns startledly as* HUGO *peers muzzily without recognition at him.* HUGO *exclaims automatically in his tone of denunciation*) Gottammed stool pigeon!

PARRITT. (*Shrinks away—stammers*) What? Who do you mean? (*Then furiously*) You lousy bum, you can't call me that! (*He draws back his fist.*)

HUGO. (*Ignores this—recognizing him now, bursts into his childish teasing giggle*) Hello, leedle Don! Leedle monkey-face! I did not recognize you. You have grown big boy. How is your mother? Where you come from? (*He breaks into his wheedling, bullying tone*) Don't be a fool! Loan me a dollar! Buy me a trink! (*As if this exhausted him, he abruptly forgets it and plumps his head down on his arms again and is asleep.*)

PARRITT. (*With eager relief*) Sure, I'll buy you a drink, Hugo. I'm broke, but I can afford one for you. I'm sorry I got sore. I ought to have remembered when you're soused you call everyone a stool pigeon. But it's no damned joke right at this time. (*He turns to* LARRY, *who is regarding him now fixedly with an uneasy expression as if he suddenly were afraid of his own thoughts—forcing a smile*) Gee, he's passed out again. (*He stiffens defensively*) What are you giving me the hard look for? Oh, I know. You thought I was go-

ing to hit him? What do you think I am? I've always had a lot of respect for Hugo. I've always stood up for him when people in the Movement panned him for an old drunken has-been. He had the guts to serve ten years in the can in his own country and get his eyes ruined in solitary. I'd like to see some of them here stick that. Well, they'll get a chance now to show— (*Hastily*) I don't mean— But let's forget that. Tell me some more about this dump. Who are all these tanks? Who's that guy trying to catch pneumonia? (*He indicates* LEWIS.)

LARRY. (*Stares at him almost frightenedly—then looks away and grasps eagerly this chance to change the subject. He begins to describe the sleepers with sardonic relish but at the same time showing his affection for them*) That's Captain Lewis, a one-time hero of the British Army. He strips to display that scar on his back he got from a native spear whenever he's completely plastered. The bewhiskered bloke opposite him is General Wetjoen, who led a commando in the War. The two of them met when they came here to work in the Boer War spectacle at the St. Louis Fair and they've been bosom pals ever since. They dream the hours away in happy dispute over the brave days in South Africa when they tried to murder each other. The little guy between them was in it, too, as correspondent for some English paper. His nickname here is Jimmy Tomorrow. He's the leader of our Tomorrow Movement.

PARRITT. What do they do for a living?

LARRY. As little as possible. Once in a while one of them makes a successful touch somewhere, and some of them get a few dollars a month from connections at home who pay it on condition they never come back. For the rest, they live on free lunch and their old friend, Harry Hope, who doesn't give a damn what anyone does or doesn't do, as long as he likes you.

PARRITT. It must be a tough life.

LARRY. It's not. Don't waste your pity. They wouldn't thank you for it. They manage to get drunk, by hook or crook, and keep their pipe dreams, and that's all they ask of life. I've never known more contented men. It isn't often that men attain the true goal of their heart's desire. The same applies to Harry himself and his two cronies at the far table. He's so satisfied with life he's never set foot out of this place since his wife died twenty years ago. He has no need of the outside world at all. This place has a fine trade from the Market people across the street and the waterfront workers, so in spite of Harry's thirst and his generous heart, he comes out even. He never worries in hard times because there's always old friends from the days when he was a jitney Tammany politician, and a friendly brewery to tide him over. Don't ask me what his two pals work at because they don't. Except at being his lifetime guests. The one facing this way is his brother-in-law, Ed Mosher, who once worked for a circus in the ticket wagon. Pat McGloin, the other one, was a police lieutenant back in the flush times of graft when everything went. But he got too greedy and when the usual reform investigation came he was caught red-handed and thrown off the Force. (*He nods at* JOE) Joe here has a yesterday in the same flush period. He ran a colored gambling house then and was a hell of a sport, so they say. Well, that's our whole family circle of inmates, except the two barkeeps and their girls, three ladies of the pavement that room on the third floor.

PARRITT. (*Bitterly*) To hell with them! I never want to see a whore again! (*As* LARRY *flashes him a puzzled glance, he adds confusedly*) I mean, they always get you in dutch. (*While he is speaking* WILLIE OBAN *has opened his eyes. He leans toward them, drunk now from the effect of the huge drink he took, and speaks with a mocking suavity.*)

WILLIE. Why omit me from your Who's Who in Dypsomania, Larry? An unpardonable slight, especially as I am the only inmate of royal blood. (*To* PARRITT—*ramblingly*) Educated at Harvard, too. You must have noticed the atmosphere of culture here. My humble contribution. Yes, Generous Stranger—I trust you're generous—I was born in the purple, the son, but unfortunately not the heir, of the late world-famous Bill Oban, King of the Bucket Shops. A revolution deposed him, conducted by the District Attorney. He was sent into exile. In fact, not to mince matters, they locked him in the can and threw away the key. Alas, his was an adventurous spirit that pined in confinement. And so he died. Forgive these reminiscences. Undoubtedly all this is well known to you. Everyone in the world knows.

PARRITT. (*Uncomfortably*) Tough luck. No, I never heard of him.

WILLIE. (*Blinks at him incredulously*) Never heard? I thought everyone in the world— Why, even at Harvard I discovered my father was well known by reputation, although that was some time before the District Attorney gave him so much unwelcome publicity. Yes, even as a freshman I was notorious. I was accepted socially with all the warm cordiality that Henry Wadsworth Longfellow would have shown a drunken Negress dancing the can can at high noon on Brattle Street. Harvard was my father's idea. He was an ambitious man. Dictatorial, too. Always knowing what was best for me. But I did make myself a brilliant student. A dirty trick on my classmates, inspired by revenge, I fear. (*He quotes*) "Dear college days, with pleasure rife! The grandest gladdest days of life!" But, of course, that is a Yale hymn, and they're given to rah-rah exaggeration at New Haven. I was a brilliant student at Law School, too. My father wanted a lawyer in the family. He was a calculating man. A thorough knowledge of the law close at hand in the house to help him find fresh ways to evade it. But I discovered the loophole of whiskey and escaped his jurisdiction. (*Abruptly to* PARRITT) Speaking of whiskey, sir, reminds me—and, I hope, reminds you—that when meeting a Prince the customary salutation is "What'll you have?"

PARRITT. (*With defensive resentment*) Nix! All you guys seem to think I'm made of dough. Where would I get the coin to blow everyone?

WILLIE. (*Sceptically*) Broke? You haven't the thirsty look of the impecunious. I'd judge you to be a plutocrat, your pockets stuffed with ill-gotten gains. Two or three dollars, at least. And don't think we will question how you got it. As Vespasian remarked, the smell of all whiskey is sweet.

PARRITT. What do you mean, how I got it? (*To* LARRY, *forcing a laugh*) It's a laugh, calling me a plutocrat, isn't it, Larry, when I've been in the Movement all my life. (*LARRY gives him an uneasy suspicious glance, then looks away, as if avoiding something he does not wish to see.*)

WILLIE. (*Disgustedly*) Ah, one of those, eh? I believe you now, all right! Go away and blow yourself up, that's a good lad. Hugo is the only licensed preacher of that gospel here. A dangerous terrorist, Hugo! He would as soon blow the collar off a schooner of beer as look at you! (*To* LARRY) Let us ignore this useless youth, Larry. Let us join in prayer that Hickey, the Great Salesman, will soon arrive bringing the blessed bourgeois long green! Would that Hickey or Death would come! Meanwhile, I will sing a song. A beautiful old New England folk ballad which I picked up at Harvard amid the debris of education. (*He sings in a boisterous baritone, rapping on the table with his knuckles at the indicated spots in the song:*)

"Jack, oh, Jack, was a sailor lad
And he came to a tavern for gin.
He rapped and he rapped with a (*Rap, rap, rap*)
But never a soul seemed in."

(*The drunks at the tables stir.* ROCKY *gets up from his chair in the bar and starts back for the entrance to the back room.* HOPE *cocks one irritable eye over his specs.* JOE MOTT *opens both of his and grins.* WILLIE *interposes some drunken whimsical exposition to* LARRY) The origin of this beautiful ditty is veiled in mystery, Larry. There was a legend bruited about in Cambridge lavatories that Waldo Emerson composed it during his uninformative period as a minister, while he was trying to write a sermon. But my own opinion is, it goes back much further, and Jonathan Edwards was the author of both words and music. (*He sings:*)

"He rapped and rapped, and tapped and tapped
Enough to wake the dead
Till he heard a damsel (*Rap, rap, rap*)
On a window right over his head."

(*The drunks are blinking their eyes now, grumbling and cursing.* ROCKY *appears from the bar at rear, right, yawning.*)

HOPE. (*With fuming irritation*) Rocky! Bejees, can't you keep that crazy bastard quiet? (ROCKY *starts for* WILLIE.)

WILLIE. And now the influence of a good woman enters our mariner's life. Well, perhaps "good" isn't the word. But very, very kind. (*He sings:*)

"Oh, come up," she cried, "my sailor lad,
And you and I'll agree,
And I'll show you the prettiest (*Rap, rap, rap*)
That ever you did see."

(*He speaks*) You see, Larry? The lewd Puritan touch, obviously, and it grows more marked as we go on. (*He sings:*)

"Oh, he put his arm around her waist,
He gazed in her bright blue eyes
And then he—"

(*But here* ROCKY *shakes him roughly by the shoulder.*)

ROCKY. Piano! What d'yuh tink dis dump is, a dump?

HOPE. Give him the bum's rush upstairs! Lock him in his room!

ROCKY. (*Yanks* WILLIE *by the arm*) Come on, Bum.

WILLIE. (*Dissolves into pitiable terror*) No! Please, Rocky! I'll go crazy up in that room alone! It's haunted! I— (*He calls to* HOPE) Please, Harry! Let me stay here! I'll be quiet!

HOPE. (*Immediately relents—indignantly*) What the hell you doing to him, Rocky? I didn't tell you to beat up the poor guy. Leave him alone, long as he's quiet. (ROCKY *lets go of* WILLIE *disgustedly and goes back to his chair in the bar.*)

WILLIE. (*Huskily*) Thanks, Harry. You're a good scout. (*He closes his eyes and sinks back in his chair exhaustedly, twitching and quivering again.*)

HOPE. (*Addressing* MCGLOIN *and* MOSHER, *who are sleepily awake—accusingly*) Always the way. Can't trust nobody. Leave it to that Dago to keep order and it's like bedlam in a cathouse, singing and everything. And you two big barflies are a hell of a help to me, ain't you? Eat and sleep and get drunk! All you're good for, bejees! Well, you can take that "I'll-have-the-same" look off your maps! There ain't going to be no more drinks on the house till hell freezes over! (*Neither of the two is impressed either by his insults or his threats. They grin hangover grins of tolerant affection at him and wink at each other.* HARRY *fumes*) Yeah, grin! Wink, bejees! Fine pair of sons of bitches to have glued on me for life! (*But he can't get a rise out of them and he subsides into a fuming mumble. Meanwhile, at the middle table,* CAPTAIN LEWIS *and* GENERAL WETJOEN *are as wide awake as heavy hangovers permit.* JIMMY TOMORROW *nods, his eyes blinking.* LEWIS *is gazing across the table at* JOE MOTT, *who is still chuckling to himself over* WILLIE'S *song. The expression on* LEWIS'S *face is that of one who can't believe his eyes.*)

LEWIS. (*Aloud to himself, with a muzzy wonder*) Good God! Have I been drinking at the same table with a bloody Kaffir?

JOE. (*Grinning*) Hello, Captain. You comin' up for air? Kaffir? Who's he?

WETJOEN. (*Blurrily*) Kaffir, dot's a nigger, Joe. (JOE *stiffens and his eyes narrow.* WETJOEN *goes on with heavy jocosity*) Dot's joke on him, Joe. He don't know you. He's still plind drunk, the ploody Limey chentleman! A great mistake I missed him at the pattle of Modder River. Vit mine rifle I shoot damn fool Limey officers py the dozen, but him I miss. De pity of it! (*He chuckles and slaps* LEWIS *on his bare shoulder*) Hey, wake up, Cecil, you ploody fool! Don't you know your old friend, Joe? He's no damned Kaffir! He's white, Joe is!

LEWIS. (*Light dawning—contritely*) My profound apologies, Joseph, old chum. Eyesight a trifle blurry, I'm afraid. Whitest colored man I ever knew. Proud to call you my friend. No hard feelings, what? (*He holds out his hand.*)

JOE. (*At once grins good-naturedly and shakes his hand*) No, Captain, I know it's mistake. Youse regular, if you is a Limey. (*Then his face hardening*) But I don't stand for "nigger" from nobody. Never did. In de old days, people calls me "nigger" wakes up in de hospital. I was de leader ob de Dirty Half-Dozen Gang. All six of us colored boys, we was tough and I was de toughest.

WETJOEN. (*Inspired to boastful reminiscence*) Me, in old days in Transvaal, I vas so tough and strong I grab axle of ox wagon mit full load and lift like feather.

LEWIS. (*Smiling amiably*) As for you, my balmy Boer that walks like a man, I say again it was a grave error in our foreign policy ever to set you free, once we nabbed you and your commando with Cronje. We should have taken you to the London zoo and incarcerated you in the baboons' cage. With a sign: "Spectators may distinguish the true baboon by his blue behind."

WETJOEN. (*Grins*) Gott! To dink, ten better Limey officers, at least, I shoot clean in the mittle of forehead at Spion Kopje, and you I miss! I neffer forgive myself! (JIMMY TOMORROW *blinks benignantly from one to the other with a gentle drunken smile.*)

JIMMY. (*Sentimentally*) Now, come, Cecil, Piet! We must forget the War. Boer and Briton, each fought fairly and played the game till the better man won and then we shook hands. We are all brothers within the Empire united beneath the flag on which the sun never sets. (*Tears come to his eyes. He quotes with great sentiment, if with slight application*) "Ship me somewhere east of Suez—"

LARRY. (*Breaks in sardonically*) Be God, you're there already, Jimmy. Worst is best here, and East is West, and tomorrow is yesterday. What more do you want?

JIMMY. (*With bleery benevolence, shaking his head in mild rebuke*) No, Larry, old friend, you can't deceive me. You pretend a bitter, cynic philosophy, but in your heart you are the kindest man among us.

LARRY. (*Disconcerted—irritably*) The hell you say!

PARRITT. (*Leans toward him—confidentially*) What a bunch of cuckoos!

JIMMY. (*As if reminded of something—with a pathetic attempt at a brisk, no-more-nonsense air*) Tomorrow, yes. It's high time I straightened out and got down to business again. (*He brushes his sleeve fastidiously*) I must have this suit cleaned and pressed. I can't look like a tramp when I—

JOE. (*Who has been brooding—interrupts*) Yes, suh, white folks always said I was white. In de days when I was flush, Joe Mott's de only colored man dey allows in de white gamblin' houses. "You're all right, Joe, you're white," dey says. (*He chuckles*) Wouldn't let me play craps, dough. Dey know I could make dem dice behave. "Any odder game and any limit you like, Joe," dey says. Man, de money I lost! (*He chuckles—then with an underlying defensiveness*) Look at de Big Chief in dem days. He knew I was white. I'd saved my dough so I could start my own gamblin' house. Folks in de know tells me, see de man at de top, den you never has trouble. You git Harry Hope give you a letter to de Chief. And Harry does. Don't you, Harry?

HOPE. (*Preoccupied with his own thoughts*) Eh? Sure. Big Bill was a good friend of mine. I had plenty of friends high up in those days. Still could have if I wanted to go out and see them. Sure, I gave you a letter. I said you was white. What the hell of it?

JOE. (*To* CAPTAIN LEWIS *who has relapsed into a sleepy daze and is listening to him with an absurd strained attention without comprehending a word*) Dere. You see, Captain. I went to see de Chief, shakin' in my boots, and dere he is sittin' behind a big desk, lookin' as big as a freight train. He don't look up. He keeps me waitin' and waitin', and after 'bout an hour, seems like to me, he says slow and quiet like dere wasn't no harm in him, "You want to open a gamblin' joint, does you, Joe?" But he don't give me no time to answer. He jumps up, lookin' as big as two freight trains, and he pounds his fist like a ham on de desk, and he shouts, "You black son of a bitch, Harry says you're white and you better be white or dere's a little iron room up de river waitin' for you!" Den he sits down and says quiet again, "All right. You can open. Git de hell outa here!" So I opens, and he finds out I'se white, sure 'nuff, 'cause I run wide open for years and pays my sugar on de dot, and de cops and I is friends. (*He chuckles with pride*) Dem old days! Many's de night I come in here. Dis was a first-class hangout for sports in dem days. Good whiskey, fifteen cents, two for two bits. I t'rows down a fifty-dollar bill like it was trash paper and says, "Drink it up, boys, I don't want no change." Ain't dat right, Harry?

HOPE. (*Caustically*) Yes, and bejees, if I ever seen you throw fifty cents on the bar now, I'd know I had delirium tremens! You've told that story ten million times and if I have to hear it again, that'll give me D.T.s anyway!

JOE. (*Chuckling*) Gittin' drunk every day for twenty years ain't give you de Brooklyn boys. You needn't be scared of me!

LEWIS. (*Suddenly turns and beams on* HOPE) Thank you, Harry, old chum. I will have a drink, now you mention it, seeing it's so near your birthday. (*The others laugh.*)

HOPE. (*Puts his hand to his ear—angrily*) What's that? I can't hear you.

LEWIS. (*Sadly*) No, I fancied you wouldn't.

HOPE. I don't have to hear, bejees! Booze is the only thing you ever talk about!

LEWIS. (*Sadly*) True. Yet there was a time when my conversation was more comprehensive. But as I became burdened with years, it seemed rather pointless to discuss my other subject.

HOPE. You can't joke with me! How much room rent do you owe me, tell me that?

LEWIS. Sorry. Adding has always baffled me. Subtraction is my forte.

HOPE. (*Snarling*) Arrh! Think you're funny! Captain, bejees! Showing off your wounds! Put on your clothes, for Christ's sake! This ain't no Turkish bath! Lousy Limey army! Took 'em years to lick a gang of Dutch hayseeds!

WETJOEN. Dot's right, Harry. Gif him hell!

HOPE. No lip out of you, neither, you Dutch spinach! General, hell! Salvation Army, that's what you'd ought t'been General in! Bragging what a shot you were, and, bejees, you missed him! And he missed you, that's just as bad! And now the two of you bum on me! (*Threateningly*) But you've broke the camel's back this time, bejees! You pay up tomorrow or out you go!

LEWIS. (*Earnestly*) My dear fellow, I give you my word of honor as an officer and a gentleman, you shall be paid tomorrow.

WETJOEN. Ve swear it, Harry! Tomorrow vidout fail!

MCGLOIN. (*A twinkle in his eye*) There you are, Harry. Sure, what could be fairer?

MOSHER. (*With a wink at* MCGLOIN) Yes, you can't ask more than that, Harry. A promise is a promise—as I've often discovered.

HOPE. (*Turns on them*) I mean the both of you, too! An old grafting flatfoot and a circus bunco steerer! Fine company for me, bejees! Couple of con men living in my flat since Christ knows when! Getting fat as hogs, too! And you ain't even got the decency to get me upstairs where I got a good bed! Let me sleep on a chair like a bum! Kept me down here waitin' for Hickey to show up, hoping I'd blow you to more drinks!

MCGLOIN. Ed and I did our damnedest to get you up, didn't we, Ed?

MOSHER. We did. But you said you couldn't bear the flat because it was one of those nights when memory brought poor old Bessie back to you.

HOPE. (*His face instantly becoming long and sad and sentimental—mournfully*) Yes, that's right, boys. I remember now. I could almost see her in every room just as she used to be—and it's twenty years since she— (*His throat and eyes fill up. A suitable sentimental hush falls on the room.*)

LARRY. (*In a sardonic whisper to* PARRITT) Isn't a pipe dream of yesterday a touching thing? By all accounts, Bessie nagged the hell out of him.

JIMMY. (*Who has been dreaming, a look of prim resolution on his face, speaks aloud to himself*) No more of this sitting around and loafing. Time I took hold of myself. I must have my shoes soled and heeled and shined first thing tomorrow morning. A general spruce-up. I want to have a well-groomed appearance when I— (*His voice fades out as he stares in front of him. No one pays any attention to him except* LARRY *and* PARRITT.)

LARRY. (*As before, in a sardonic aside to* PARRITT) The tomorrow movement is a sad and beautiful thing, too!

MCGLOIN. (*With a huge sentimental sigh—and a calculating look at* HOPE) Poor old Bessie! You don't find her like in these days. A sweeter woman never drew breath.

MOSHER. (*In a similar calculating mood*) Good old Bess. A man couldn't want a better sister than she was to me.

HOPE. (*Mournfully*) Twenty years, and I've never set foot out of this house since the day I buried her. Didn't have the heart. Once she'd gone, I didn't give a damn for anything. I lost all my ambition. Without her, nothing seemed worth the trouble. You remember, Ed, you, too, Mac— the boys was going to nominate me for Alderman. It was all fixed. Bessie wanted it and she was so proud. But when she was taken, I told them, "No, boys, I can't do it. I simply haven't the heart. I'm through." I would have won the election easy, too. (*He says this a bit defiantly*) Oh, I know there was jealous wise guys said the boys was giving me the nomination because they knew they couldn't win that year in this ward. But that's a damned lie! I knew every man, woman and child in the ward, almost. Bessie made me make friends with everyone, helped me remember all their names. I'd have been elected easy.

MCGLOIN. You would, Harry. It was a sure thing.

MOSHER. A dead cinch, Harry. Everyone knows that.

HOPE. Sure they do. But after Bessie died, I didn't have the heart. Still, I know while she'd appreciate my grief, she wouldn't want it to keep me cooped up in here all my life. So I've made up my mind I'll go out soon. Take a walk around the ward, see all the friends I used to know, get together with the boys and maybe tell 'em I'll let 'em deal me a hand in their game again. Yes, bejees, I'll do it. My birthday, tomorrow, that'd be the right time to turn over a new leaf. Sixty. That ain't too old.

MCGLOIN. (*Flatteringly*) It's the prime of life, Harry.

MOSHER. Wonderful thing about you, Harry, you keep young as you ever was.

JIMMY. (*Dreaming aloud again*) Get my things from the laundry. They must still have them. Clean collar and shirt. If I wash the ones I've got on any more, they'll fall apart. Socks, too. I want to make a good appearance. I met Dick Trumbull on the street a year or two ago. He said, "Jimmy, the publicity department's never been the same since you got—resigned. It's dead as hell." I said, "I know. I've heard rumors the management were at their wits' end and would be only too glad to have me run it for them again. I think all I'd have to do would be go and see them and they'd offer me the position. Don't you think so, Dick?" He said, "Sure, they would, Jimmy. Only take my advice and wait a while until business conditions are better. Then you can strike them for a bigger salary than you got before, do you see?" I said, "Yes, I do see, Dick, and many thanks for the tip." Well, conditions must be better by this time. All I have to do is get fixed up with a decent front tomorrow, and it's as good as done.

HOPE. (*Glances at* JIMMY *with a condescending affectionate pity—in a hushed voice*) Poor Jimmy's off on his pipe dream again. Bejees, he takes the cake! (*This is too much for* LARRY. *He cannot restrain a sardonic guffaw. But no one pays any attention to him.*)

LEWIS. (*Opens his eyes, which are drowsing again—dreamily to* WETJOEN) I'm sorry we had to postpone our trip again this April, Piet. I hoped the blasted old estate would be settled up by then. The damned lawyers can't hold up the settlement much longer. We'll make it next year, even if we have to work and earn our passage money, eh? You'll stay with me at the old place as long as you like, then you can take the *Union Castle* from Southampton to Cape Town. (*Sentimentally, with real yearning*) England in April. I want you to see that, Piet. The old veldt has its points, I'll admit, but it isn't home—especially home in April.

WETJOEN. (*Blinks drowsily at him—dreamily*) Ja, Cecil, I know how beautiful it must be, from all you tell me many times. I vill enjoy it. But I shall enjoy more ven I am home, too. The veldt, ja! You could put England on it, and it would look like a farmer's small garden. Py Gott, there is space to be free, the air like vine is, you don't need booze to be drunk! My relations vill so surprised be. They vill not know me, it is so many years. Dey vill be so glad I haf come home at last.

JOE. (*Dreamily*) I'll make my stake and get my new gamblin' house open before you boys leave. You got to come to de openin'. I'll treat you white. If you're broke, I'll stake you to buck any game you chooses. If you wins, dat's velvet for you. If you loses, it don't count. Can't treat you no whiter dan dat, can I?

HOPE. (*Again with condescending pity*) Bejees, Jimmy's started them off smoking the same hop. (*But the three are finished, their eyes closed again in sleep or a drowse.*)

LARRY. (*Aloud to himself—in his comically tense, crazy whisper*) Be God, this bughouse will drive me stark, raving loony yet!

HOPE. (*Turns on him with fuming suspicion*) What? What d'you say?

LARRY. (*Placatingly*) Nothing, Harry. I had a crazy thought in my head.

HOPE. (*Irascibly*) Crazy is right! Yah! The old wise guy! Wise, hell! A damned old fool Anarchist I-Won't-Worker! I'm sick of you and Hugo, too. Bejees, you'll pay up tomorrow, or I'll start a Harry Hope Revolution! I'll tie a dispossess bomb to your tails that'll blow you out in the street! Bejees, I'll make your Movement move! (*The witticism delights him and he bursts into a shrill cackle. At once* MCGLOIN *and* MOSHER *guffaw enthusiastically.*)

MOSHER. (*Flatteringly*) Harry, you sure say the funniest things! (*He reaches on the table as if he expected a glass to be there—then starts with well-acted surprise*) Hell, where's my drink? That Rocky is too damned fast cleaning tables. Why, I'd only taken one sip of it.

HOPE. (*His smiling face congealing*) No, you don't! (*Acidly*) Any time you only take one sip of a drink, you'll have lockjaw and paralysis! Think you can kid me with those old circus con games?—me, that's known you since you was knee-high, and, bejees, you was a crook even then!

MCGLOIN. (*Grinning*) It's not like you to be so hard-hearted, Harry. Sure, it's hot, parching work laughing at your jokes so early in the morning on an empty stomach!

HOPE. Yah! You, Mac! Another crook! Who asked you to laugh? We was talking about poor old Bessie, and you and her no-good brother start to laugh! A hell of a thing! Talking mush about her, too! "Good old Bess." Bejees, she'd never forgive me if she knew I had you two bums living in her flat, throwing ashes and cigar butts on her carpet. You know her opinion of you, Mac. "That Pat McGloin is the biggest drunken grafter that ever disgraced the police force," she used to say to me. "I hope they send him to Sing Sing for life."

MCGLOIN. (*Unperturbed*) She didn't mean it. She was angry at me because you used to get me drunk. But Bess had a heart of gold underneath her sharpness. She knew I was innocent of all the charges.

WILLIE. (*Jumps to his feet drunkenly and points a finger at* MCGLOIN—*imitating the manner of a cross-examiner—coldly*) One moment, please. Lieutenant McGloin! Are you aware you are under oath? Do you realize what the penalty for perjury is? (*Purringly*) Come now, Lieutenant, isn't it a fact that you're as guilty as hell? No, don't say, "How about your old man?" I am asking the questions. The fact that he was a crooked old bucket-shop bastard has no bearing on your case. (*With a change to maudlin joviality*) Gentlemen of the Jury, court will now recess while the D.A. sings out a little ditty he learned at Harvard. It was composed in a wanton moment by the Dean of the Divinity School on a moonlight night in July, 1776, while sobering up in a Turkish bath. (*He sings:*)

"Oh, come up," she cried, "my sailor lad,
And you and I'll agree.
And I'll show you the prettiest (*Rap, rap, rap on table*)
That ever you did see."

(*Suddenly he catches* HOPE'S *eyes fixed on him condemningly, and sees* ROCKY *appearing from the bar. He collapses back on his chair, pleading miserably*) Please, Harry! I'll be quiet! Don't make Rocky bounce me upstairs! I'll go crazy alone! (*To* MCGLOIN) I apologize, Mac. Don't get sore. I was only kidding you. (ROCKY, *at a relenting glance from* HOPE, *returns to the bar.*)

MCGLOIN. (*Good-naturedly*) Sure, kid all you like, Willie. I'm hardened to it. (*He pauses— seriously*) But I'm telling you some day before long I'm going to make them reopen my case. Everyone knows there was no real evidence against me, and I took the fall for the ones higher up. I'll be found innocent this time and reinstated. (*Wistfully*) I'd like to have my old job on the Force back. The boys tell me there's fine pickings these days, and I'm not getting rich here, sitting with a parched throat waiting for Harry Hope to buy a drink. (*He glances reproachfully at* HOPE.)

WILLIE. Of course, you'll be reinstated, Mac. All you need is a brilliant young attorney to handle your case. I'll be straightened out and on

the wagon in a day or two. I've never practiced but I was one of the most brilliant students in Law School, and your case is just the opportunity I need to start. (*Darkly*) Don't worry about my not forcing the D.A. to reopen your case. I went through my father's papers before the cops destroyed them, and I remember a lot of people, even if I can't prove— (*Coaxingly*) You will let me take your case, won't you, Mac?

MCGLOIN. (*Soothingly*) Sure I will and it'll make your reputation, Willie. (MOSHER *winks at* HOPE, *shaking his head, and* HOPE *answers with identical pantomime, as though to say, "Poor dopes, they're off again!"*)

LARRY. (*Aloud to himself more than to* PARRITT —*with irritable wonder*) Ah, be damned! Haven't I heard their visions a thousand times? Why should they get under my skin now? I've got the blues, I guess. I wish to hell Hickey'd turn up.

MOSHER. (*Calculatingly solicitous—whispering to* HOPE) Poor Willie needs a drink bad, Harry— and I think if we all joined him it'd make him feel he was among friends and cheer him up.

HOPE. More circus con tricks! (*Scathingly*) You talking of your dear sister! Bessie had you sized up. She used to tell me, "I don't know what you can see in that worthless, drunken, petty-larceny brother of mine. If I had my way," she'd say, "he'd get booted out in the gutter on his fat behind." Sometimes she didn't say behind, either.

MOSHER. (*Grins genially*) Yes, dear old Bess had a quick temper, but there was no real harm in her. (*He chuckles reminiscently*) Remember the time she sent me down to the bar to change a ten-dollar bill for her?

HOPE. (*Has to grin himself*) Bejees, do I! She coulda bit a piece out of a stove lid, after she found it out. (*He cackles appreciatively.*)

MOSHER. I was sure surprised when she gave me the ten spot. Bess usually had better sense, but she was in a hurry to go to church. I didn't really mean to do it, but you know how habit gets you. Besides, I still worked then, and the circus season was going to begin soon, and I needed a little practice to keep my hand in. Or, you never can tell, the first rube that came to my wagon for a ticket might have left with the right change and I'd be disgraced. (*He chuckles*) I said, "I'm sorry, Bess, but I had to take it all in dimes. Here, hold out your hands and I'll count it out for you, so you won't kick afterwards I short-changed you." (*He begins a count which grows more rapid as he goes on*) Ten, twenty, thirty, forty, fifty, sixty, seventy, eighty, ninety, a dollar. Ten, twenty, thirty, forty, fifty, sixty— You're counting with me, Bess, aren't you?—eighty, ninety, two dollars.

Ten, twenty— Those are pretty shoes you got on, Bess—forty, fifty, seventy, eighty, ninety, three dollars. Ten, twenty, thirty— What's on at the church tonight, Bess?—fifty, sixty, seventy, ninety, four dollars. Ten, twenty, thirty, fifty, seventy, eighty, ninety— That's a swell new hat, Bess, looks very becoming—six dollars. (*He chuckles.*) And so on. I'm bum at it now for lack of practice, but in those days I could have short-changed the Keeper of the Mint.

HOPE. (*Grinning*) Stung her for two dollars and a half, wasn't it, Ed?

MOSHER. Yes. A fine percentage, if I do say so, when you're dealing to someone who's sober and can count. I'm sorry to say she discovered my mistakes in arithmetic just after I beat it around the corner. She counted it over herself. Bess somehow never had the confidence in me a sister should. (*He sighs tenderly*) Dear old Bess.

HOPE. (*Indignant now*) You're a fine guy bragging how you short-changed your own sister! Bejees, if there was a war and you was in it, they'd have to padlock the pockets of the dead!

MOSHER. (*A bit hurt at this*) That's going pretty strong, Harry. I always gave a sucker some chance. There wouldn't be no fun robbing the dead. (*He becomes reminiscently melancholy*) Gosh, thinking of the old ticket wagon brings those days back. The greatest life on earth with the greatest show on earth! The grandest crowd of regular guys ever gathered under one tent! I'd sure like to shake their hands again!

HOPE. (*Acidly*) They'd have guns in theirs. They'd shoot you on sight. You've touched every damned one of them. Bejees, you've even borrowed fish from the trained seals and peanuts from every elephant that remembered you! (*This fancy tickles him and he gives a cackling laugh.*)

MOSHER. (*Overlooking this—dreamily*) You know, Harry, I've made up my mind I'll see the boss in a couple of days and ask for my old job. I can get back my magic touch with change easy, and I can throw him a line of bull that'll kid him I won't be so unreasonable about sharing the profits next time. (*With insinuating complaint*) There's no percentage in hanging around this dive, taking care of you and shooing away your snakes, when I don't even get an eye-opener for my trouble.

HOPE. (*Implacably*) No! (*MOSHER sighs and gives up and closes his eyes. The others, except LARRY and PARRITT, are all dozing again now. HOPE goes on grumbling*) Go to hell or the circus, for all I care. Good riddance, bejees! I'm sick of you! (*Then worriedly*) Say, Ed, what the hell you think's happened to Hickey? I hope he'll turn up. Always got a million funny stories. You and the other bums have begun to give me the graveyard fantods. I'd like a good laugh with old Hickey. (*He chuckles at a memory*) Remember that gag he always pulls about his wife and the iceman? He'd make a cat laugh! (*ROCKY appears from the bar. He comes front, behind MOSHER'S chair, and begins pushing the black curtain along the rod to the rear wall.*)

ROCKY. Openin' time, Boss. (*He presses a button at rear which switches off the lights. The back room becomes drabber and dingier than ever in the gray daylight that comes from the street windows, off right, and what light can penetrate the grime of the two backyard windows at left. ROCKY turns back to HOPE—grumpily*) Why don't you go up to bed, Boss? Hickey'd never turn up dis time of de mornin'!

HOPE. (*Starts and listens*) Someone's coming now.

ROCKY. (*Listens*) Aw, dat's on'y my two pigs. It's about time dey showed. (*He goes back toward the door at left of the bar.*)

HOPE. (*Sourly disappointed*) You keep them dumb broads quiet. I don't want to go to bed. I'm going to catch a couple more winks here and I don't want no damn-fool laughing and screeching. (*He settles himself in his chair, grumbling*) Never thought I'd see the day when Harry Hope's would have tarts rooming in it. What'd Bessie think? But I don't let 'em use my rooms for business. And they're good kids. Good as anyone else. They got to make a living. Pay their rent, too, which is more than I can say for— (*He cocks an eye over his specs at MOSHER and grins with satisfaction*) Bejees, Ed, I'll bet Bessie is doing somersaults in her grave! (*He chuckles. But MOSHER'S eyes are closed, his head nodding, and he doesn't reply, so HOPE closes his eyes. ROCKY has opened the barroom door at rear and is standing in the hall beyond it, facing right. A girl's laugh is heard.*)

ROCKY. (*Warningly*) Nix! Piano! (*He comes in, beckoning them to follow. He goes behind the bar and gets a whiskey bottle and glasses and chairs. MARGIE and PEARL follow him, casting a glance around. Everyone except LARRY and PARRITT is asleep or dozing. Even PARRITT has his eyes closed. The two girls, neither much over twenty, are typical dollar street walkers, dressed in the usual tawdry get-up. PEARL is obviously Italian with black hair and eyes. MARGIE has brown hair and hazel eyes, a slum New Yorker of mixed blood. Both are plump and have a certain prettiness that shows even through their blobby make-up. Each retains a vestige of youthful*) *freshness, although the game is beginning to get them and give them hard, worn expressions. Both are sentimental, feather-brained, giggly, lazy, good-natured and reasonably contented with life. Their attitude toward* ROCKY *is much that of two maternal, affectionate sisters toward a bullying brother whom they like to tease and spoil. His attitude toward them is that of the owner of two performing pets he has trained to do a profitable act under his management. He feels a proud proprietor's affection for them, and is tolerantly lax in his discipline.*)

MARGIE. (*Glancing around*) Jees, Poil, it's de Morgue wid all de stiffs on deck. (*She catches* LARRY'S *eye and smiles affectionately*) Hello, Old Wise Guy, ain't you died yet?

LARRY. (*Grinning*) Not yet, Margie. But I'm waiting impatiently for the end. (PARRITT *opens his eyes to look at the two girls, but as soon as they glance at him he closes them again and turns his head away.*)

MARGIE. (*As she and* PEARL *come to the table at right, front, followed by* ROCKY) Who's de new guy? Friend of yours, Larry? (*Automatically she smiles seductively at* PARRITT *and addresses him in a professional chant*) Wanta have a good time, kid?

PEARL. Aw, he's passed out. Hell wid him!

HOPE. (*Cocks an eye over his specs at them—with drowsy irritation*) You dumb broads cut the loud talk. (*He shuts his eye again.*)

ROCKY. (*Admonishing them good-naturedly*) Sit down before I knock yuh down. (MARGIE *and* PEARL *sit at left, and rear, of table,* ROCKY *at right of it. The girls pour drinks.* ROCKY *begins in a brisk, business-like manner but in a lowered voice with an eye on* HOPE) Well, how'd you tramps do?

MARGIE. Pretty good. Didn't we, Poil?

PEARL. Sure. We nailed a coupla all-night guys.

MARGIE. On Sixth Avenoo. Boobs from de sticks.

PEARL. Stinko, de bot' of 'em.

MARGIE. We thought we was in luck. We steered dem to a real hotel. We figgered dey was too stinko to bother us much and we could cop a good sleep in beds that ain't got cobble stones in de mattress like de ones in dis dump.

PEARL. But we was outa luck. Dey didn't bother us much dat way, but dey wouldn't go to sleep either, see? Jees, I never hoid such gabby guys.

MARGIE. Dey got onta politics, drinkin' outa de bottle. Dey forgot we was around. "De Bull Moosers is de on'y reg'lar guys," one guy says. And de other guy says, "You're a God-damned liar! And I'm a Republican!" Den dey'd laugh.

PEARL. Den dey'd get mad and make a bluff dey was goin' to scrap, and den dey'd make up and cry and sing "School Days." Jees, imagine tryin' to sleep wid dat on de phonograph!

MARGIE. Maybe you tink we wasn't glad when de house dick come up and told us all to git dressed and take de air!

PEARL. We told de guys we'd wait for dem 'round de corner.

MARGIE. So here we are.

ROCKY. (*Sententiously*) Yeah. I see you. But I don't see no dough yet.

PEARL. (*With a wink at* MARGIE—*teasingly*) Right on de job, ain't he, Margie?

MARGIE. Yeah, our little business man! Dat's him!

ROCKY. Come on! Dig! (*They both pull up their skirts to get the money from their stockings.* ROCKY *watches this move carefully.*)

PEARL. (*Amused*) Pipe him keepin' cases, Margie.

MARGIE. (*Amused*) Scared we're holdin' out on him.

PEARL. Way he grabs, yuh'd tink it was him done de woik. (*She holds out a little roll of bills to* ROCKY) Here y'are, Grafter!

MARGIE. (*Holding hers out*) We hope it chokes yuh. (ROCKY *counts the money quickly and shoves it in his pocket.*)

ROCKY. (*Genially*) You dumb baby dolls gimme a pain. What would you do wid money if I wasn't around? Give it all to some pimp.

PEARL. (*Teasingly*) Jees, what's the difference—? (*Hastily*) Aw, I don't mean dat, Rocky.

ROCKY. (*His eyes growing hard—slowly*) A lotta difference, get me?

PEARL. Don't get sore. Jees, can't yuh take a little kiddin'?

MARGIE. Sure, Rocky, Poil was on'y kiddin'. (*Soothingly*) We know yuh got a reg'lar job. Dat's why we like yuh, see? Yuh don't live offa us. Yuh're a bartender.

ROCKY. (*Genially again*) Sure, I'm a bartender. Everyone knows me knows dat. And I treat you goils right, don't I? Jees, I'm wise yuh hold out on me, but I know it ain't much, so what the hell, I let yuh get away wid it. I tink yuh're a coupla good kids. Yuh're aces wid me, see?

PEARL. You're aces wid us, too. Ain't he, Margie?

MARGIE. Sure, he's aces. (ROCKY *beams complacently and takes the glasses back to the bar.* MARGIE *whispers*) Yuh sap, don't yuh know enough not to kid him on dat? Serve yuh right if he beat yuh up!

PEARL. (*Admiringly*) Jees, I'll bet he'd give yuh

an awful beatin', too, once he started. Ginnies got awful tempers.

MARGIE. Anyway, we wouldn't keep no pimp, like we was reg'lar old whores. We ain't dat bad.

PEARL. No. We're tarts, but dat's all.

ROCKY. (*Rinsing glasses behind the bar*) Cora got back around three o'clock. She woke up Chuck and dragged him outa de hay to go to a chop suey joint. (*Disgustedly*) Imagine him standin' for dat stuff!

MARGIE. (*Disgustedly*) I'll bet dey been sittin' around kiddin' demselves wid dat old pipe dream about gettin' married and settlin' down on a farm. Jees, when Chuck's on de wagon, dey never lay off dat dope! Dey give yuh an earful every time yuh talk to 'em!

PEARL. Yeah. Chuck wid a silly grin on his ugly map, de big boob, and Cora gigglin' like she was in grammar school and some tough guy'd just told her babies wasn't brung down de chimney by a boid!

MARGIE. And her on de turf long before me and you was! And bot' of 'em arguin' all de time, Cora sayin' she's scared to marry him because he'll go on drunks again. Just as dough any drunk could scare Cora!

PEARL. And him swearin', de big liar, he'll never go on no more periodicals! An' den her pretendin'— But it gives me a pain to talk about it. We ought to phone de booby hatch to send round de wagon for 'em.

ROCKY. (*Comes back to the table—disgustedly*) Yeah, of all de pipe dreams in dis dump, dey got de nuttiest! And nuttin' stops dem. Dey been dreamin' it for years, every time Chuck goes on de wagon. I never could figger it. What would gettin' married get dem? But de farm stuff is de sappiest part. When bot' of 'em was dragged up in dis ward and ain't never been nearer a farm dan Coney Island! Jees, dey'd tink dey'd gone deef if dey didn't hear de El rattle! Dey'd get D.T.s if dey ever hoid a cricket choip! I hoid crickets once on my cousin's place in Joisey. I couldn't sleep a wink. Dey give me de heebie-jeebies. (*With deeper disgust*) Jees, can yuh picture a good barkeep like Chuck diggin' spuds? And imagine a whore hustlin' de cows home! For Christ sake! Ain't dat a sweet picture!

MARGIE. (*Rebukingly*) Yuh oughtn't to call Cora dat, Rocky. She's a good kid. She may be a tart, but—

ROCKY. (*Considerately*) Sure, dat's all I meant, a tart.

PEARL. (*Giggling*) But he's right about de damned cows, Margie. Jees, I bet Cora don't know which end of de cow has de horns! I'm

goin' to ask her. (*There is the noise of a door opening in the hall and the sound of a man's and woman's arguing voices.*)

ROCKY. Here's your chance. Dat's dem two nuts now. (CORA *and* CHUCK *look in from the hallway and then come in.* CORA *is a thin peroxide blonde, a few years older than* PEARL *and* MARGIE, *dressed in similar style, her round face showing more of the wear and tear of her trade than theirs, but still with traces of a doll-like prettiness.* CHUCK *is a tough, thick-necked, barrel-chested Italian-American, with a fat, amiable, swarthy face. He has on a straw hat with a vivid band, a loud suit, tie and shirt, and yellow shoes. His eyes are clear and he looks healthy and strong as an ox.*)

CORA. (*Gaily*) Hello, bums. (*She looks around*) Jees, de Morgue on a rainy Sunday night! (*She waves to* LARRY—*affectionately*) Hello, Old Wise Guy! Ain't you croaked yet?

LARRY. (*Grins*) Not yet, Cora. It's damned tiring, this waiting for the end.

CORA. Aw, gwan, you'll never die! Yuh'll have to hire someone to croak yuh wid an axe.

HOPE. (*Cocks one sleepy eye at her—irritably*) You dumb hookers, cut the loud noise! This ain't a cat-house!

CORA. (*Teasingly*) My, Harry! Such language!

HOPE. (*Closes his eyes—to himself with a gratified chuckle*) Bejees, I'll bet Bessie's turning over in her grave! (CORA *sits down between* MARGIE *and* PEARL. CHUCK *takes an empty chair from* HOPE'S *table and puts it by hers and sits down. At* LARRY'S *table,* PARRITT *is glaring resentfully toward the girls.*)

PARRITT. If I'd known this dump was a hooker hangout, I'd never have come here.

LARRY. (*Watching him*) You seem down on the ladies.

PARRITT. (*Vindictively*) I hate every bitch that ever lived! They're all alike! (*Catching himself guiltily*) You can understand how I feel, can't you, when it was getting mixed up with a tart that made me have that fight with Mother? (*Then with a resentful sneer*) But what the hell does it matter to you? You're in the grandstand. You're through with life.

LARRY. (*Sharply*) I'm glad you remember it. I don't want to know a damned thing about your business. (*He closes his eyes and settles on his chair as if preparing for sleep.* PARRITT *stares at him sneeringly. Then he looks away and his expression becomes furtive and frightened.*)

CORA. Who's de guy wid Larry?

ROCKY. A tightwad. To hell wid him.

PEARL. Say, Cora, wise me up. Which end of a cow is de horns on?

CORA. (*Embarrassed*) Aw, don't bring dat up. I'm sick of hearin' about dat farm.

ROCKY. You got nuttin' on us!

CORA. (*Ignoring this*) Me and dis overgrown tramp has been scrappin' about it. He says Joisey's de best place, and I says Long Island because we'll be near Coney. And I tells him, How do I know yuh're off of periodicals for life? I don't give a damn how drunk yuh get, the way we are, but I don't wanta be married to no soak.

CHUCK. And I tells her I'm off de stuff for life. Den she beefs we won't be married a month before I'll trow it in her face she was a tart. "Jees, Baby," I tells her. "Why should I? What de hell yuh tink I tink I'm marryin', a voigin? Why should I kick as long as yuh lay off it and don't do no cheatin' wid de iceman or nobody? (*He gives her a rough hug*) Dat's on de level, Baby. (*He kisses her.*)

CORA. (*Kissing him*) Aw, yuh big tramp!

ROCKY. (*Shakes his head with profound disgust*) Can yuh tie it? I'll buy a drink. I'll do anything. (*He gets up.*)

CORA. No, dis round's on me. I run into luck. Dat's why I dragged Chuck outa bed to celebrate. It was a sailor. I rolled him. (*She giggles*) Listen, it was a scream. I've run into some nutty souses, but dis guy was de nuttiest. De booze dey dish out around de Brooklyn Navy Yard must be as turrible bug-juice as Harry's. My dogs was givin' out when I seen dis guy holdin' up a lamppost, so I hurried to get him before a cop did. I says, "Hello, Handsome, wanta have a good time?" Jees, he was paralyzed! One of dem polite jags. He tries to bow to me, imagine, and I had to prop him up or he'd fell on his nose. And what d'yuh tink he said? "Lady," he says, "can yuh kindly tell me de nearest way to de Museum of Natural History?" (*They all laugh*) Can yuh imagine! At two A.M. As if I'd know where de dump was anyway. But I says, "Sure ting, Honey Boy, I'll be only too glad." So I steered him into a side street where it was dark and propped him against a wall and give him a frisk. (*She giggles*) And what d'yuh tink he does? Jees, I ain't lyin', he begins to laugh, de big sap! He says, "Quit ticklin' me." While I was friskin' him for his roll! I near died! Den I toined him 'round and give him a push to start him. "Just keep goin'," I told him. "It's a big white building on your right. You can't miss it." He must be swimmin' in de North River yet! (*They all laugh.*)

CHUCK. Ain't Uncle Sam de sap to trust guys like dat wid dough!

CORA. (*With a business-like air*) I picked twelve bucks offa him. Come on, Rocky. Set 'em up.

(ROCKY *goes back to the bar*. CORA *looks around the room*) Say, Chuck's kiddin' about de iceman a minute ago reminds me. Where de hell's Hickey?

ROCKY. Dat's what we're all wonderin'.

CORA. He oughta be here. Me and Chuck seen him.

ROCKY. (*Excited, comes back from the bar, forgetting the drinks*) You seen Hickey? (*He nudges* HOPE) Hey, Boss, come to! Cora's seen Hickey. (HOPE *is instantly wide awake and everyone in the place, except* HUGO *and* PARRITT, *begins to rouse up hopefully, as if a mysterious wireless message had gone round.*)

HOPE. Where'd you see him, Cora?

CORA. Right on de next corner. He was standin' dere. We said, "Welcome to our city. De gang is expectin' yuh wid deir tongues hangin' out a yard long." And I kidded him, "How's de iceman, Hickey? How's he doin' at your house?" He laughs and says, "Fine." And he says, "Tell de gang I'll be along in a minute. I'm just finishin' figurin' out de best way to save dem and bring dem peace."

HOPE. (*Chuckles*) Bejees, he's thought up a new gag! It's a wonder he didn't borry a Salvation Army uniform and show up in that! Go out and get him, Rocky. Tell him we're waitin' to be saved! (ROCKY *goes out, grinning.*)

CORA. Yeah, Harry, he was only kiddin'. But he was funny, too, somehow. He was different, or somethin'.

CHUCK. Sure, he was sober, Baby. Dat's what made him different. We ain't never seen him when he wasn't on a drunk, or had de willies gettin' over it.

CORA. Sure! Gee, ain't I dumb?

HOPE. (*With conviction*) The dumbest broad I ever seen! (*Then puzzledly*) Sober? That's funny. He's always lapped up a good starter on his way here. Well, bejees, he won't be sober long! He'll be good and ripe for my birthday party tonight at twelve. (*He chuckles with excited anticipation— addressing all of them*) Listen! He's fixed some new gag to pull on us. We'll pretend to let him kid us, see? And we'll kid the pants off him. (*They all say laughingly, "Sure, Harry," "Righto," "That's the stuff," "We'll fix him," etc., etc., their faces excited with the same eager anticipation.* ROCKY *appears in the doorway at the end of the bar with* HICKEY, *his arm around* HICKEY'S *shoulders.*)

ROCKY. (*With an affectionate grin*) Here's the old son of a bitch! (*They all stand up and greet him with affectionate acclaim, "Hello, Hickey!" etc. Even* HUGO *comes out of his coma to raise his head and blink through his thick spectacles with a welcoming giggle.*)

HICKEY. (*Jovially*) Hello, Gang! (*He stands a moment, beaming around at all of them affectionately. He is about fifty, a little under medium height, with a stout, roly-poly figure. His face is round and smooth and big-boyish with bright blue eyes, a button nose, a small, pursed mouth. His head is bald except for a fringe of hair around his temples and the back of his head. His expression is fixed in a salesman's winning smile of self-confident affability and hearty good fellowship. His eyes have the twinkle of a humor which delights in kidding others but can also enjoy equally a joke on himself. He exudes a friendly, generous personality that makes everyone like him on sight. You get the impression, too, that he must have real ability in his line. There is an efficient, business-like approach in his manner, and his eyes can take you in shrewdly at a glance. He has the salesman's mannerisms of speech, an easy flow of glib, persuasive convincingness. His clothes are those of a successful drummer whose territory consists of minor cities and small towns—not flashy but conspicuously spic and span. He immediately puts on an entrance act, places a hand affectedly on his chest, throws back his head, and sings in a falsetto tenor*) "It's always fair weather, when good fellows get together!" (*Changing to a comic bass and another tune*) "And another little drink won't do us any harm!" (*They all roar with laughter at this burlesque which his personality makes really funny. He waves his hand in a lordly manner to* ROCKY) Do your duty, Brother Rocky. Bring on the rat poison! (ROCKY *grins and goes behind the bar to get drinks amid an approving cheer from the crowd.* HICKEY *comes forward to shake hands with* HOPE—*with affectionate heartiness*) How goes it, Governor?

HOPE. (*Enthusiastically*) Bejees, Hickey, you old bastard, it's good to see you! (HICKEY *shakes hands with* MOSHER *and* MCGLOIN; *leans right to shake hands with* MARGIE *and* PEARL; *moves to the middle tables to shake hands with* LEWIS, JOE MOTT, WETJOEN *and* JIMMY; *waves to* WILLIE, LARRY *and* HUGO. *He greets each by name with the same affectionate heartiness and there is an interchange of* "How's the kid?" "How's the old scout?" "How's the boy?" "How's everything?" *etc., etc.* ROCKY *begins setting out drinks, whiskey glasses with chasers, and a bottle for each table, starting with* LARRY'S *table.* HOPE *says:*) Sit down, Hickey. Sit down. (HICKEY *takes the chair, facing front, at the front of the table in the second row which is half between* HOPE'S *table and the one where* JIMMY TOMORROW *is.* HOPE *goes on with excited pleasure*) Bejees, Hickey, it seems natural to see your ugly, grinning map. (*With a scornful nod to* CORA) This dumb broad was tryin' to tell us you'd changed, but you ain't a damned bit. Tell us about yourself. How've you been doin'? Bejees, you look like a million dollars.

ROCKY. (*Coming to* HICKEY'S *table, puts a bottle of whiskey, a glass and a chaser on it—then hands* HICKEY *a key*) Here's your key, Hickey. Same old room.

HICKEY. (*Shoves the key in his pocket*) Thanks, Rocky. I'm going up in a little while and grab a snooze. Haven't been able to sleep lately and I'm tired as hell. A couple of hours good kip will fix me.

HOPE. (*As* ROCKY *puts drinks on his table*) First time I ever heard you worry about sleep. Bejees, you never would go to bed. (*He raises his glass, and all the others except* PARRITT *do likewise*) Get a few slugs under your belt and you'll forget sleeping. Here's mud in your eye, Hickey. (*They all join in with the usual humorous toasts.*)

HICKEY. (*Heartily*) Drink hearty, boys and girls! (*They all drink, but* HICKEY *drinks only his chaser.*)

HOPE. Bejees, is that a new stunt, drinking your chaser first?

HICKEY. No, I forgot to tell Rocky— You'll have to excuse me, boys and girls, but I'm off the stuff. For keeps. (*They stare at him in amazed incredulity.*)

HOPE. What the hell— (*Then with a wink at the others, kiddingly*) Sure! Joined the Salvation Army, ain't you? Been elected President of the W.C.T.U.? Take that bottle away from him, Rocky. We don't want to tempt him into sin. (*He chuckles and the others laugh.*)

HICKEY. (*Earnestly*) No, honest, Harry. I know it's hard to believe but— (*He pauses—then adds simply*) Cora was right, Harry. I have changed. I mean, about booze. I don't need it any more. (*They all stare, hoping it's a gag, but impressed and disappointed and made vaguely uneasy by the change they now sense in him.*)

HOPE. (*His kidding a bit forced*) Yeah, go ahead, kid the pants off us! Bejees, Cora said you was coming to save us! Well, go on. Get this joke off your chest! Start the service! Sing a Goddamned hymn if you like. We'll all join in the chorus. "No drunkard can enter this beautiful home." That's a good one. (*He forces a cackle.*)

HICKEY. (*Grinning*) Oh, hell, Governor! You don't think I'd come around here peddling some brand of temperance bunk, do you? You know me better than that! Just because I'm through with the stuff don't mean I'm going Prohibition. Hell, I'm not that ungrateful! It's given me too many good times. I feel exactly the same as I always did. If anyone wants to get drunk, if that's the only way they can be happy, and feel at peace with themselves, why the hell shouldn't they? They have my full and entire sympathy. I know all about that game from soup to nuts. I'm the guy that wrote the book. The only reason I've quit is— Well, I finally had the guts to face myself and throw overboard the damned lying pipe dream that'd been making me miserable, and do what I had to do for the happiness of all concerned— and then all at once I found I was at peace with myself and I didn't need booze any more. That's all there was to it. (*He pauses. They are staring at him, uneasy and beginning to feel defensive.* HICKEY *looks round and grins affectionately— apologetically*) But what the hell! Don't let me be a wet blanket, making fool speeches about myself. Set 'em up again, Rocky. Here. (*He pulls a big roll from his pocket and peels off a ten-dollar bill. The faces of all brighten*) Keep the balls coming until this is killed. Then ask for more.

ROCKY. Jees, a roll dat'd choke a hippopotamus! Fill up, youse guys. (*They all pour out drinks.*)

HOPE. That sounds more like you, Hickey. That water-wagon bull— Cut out the act and have a drink, for Christ's sake.

HICKEY. It's no act, Governor. But don't get me wrong. That don't mean I'm a teetotal grouch and can't be in the party. Hell, why d'you suppose I'm here except to have a party, same as I've always done, and help celebrate your birthday tonight? You've all been good pals to me, the best friends I've ever had. I've been thinking about you ever since I left the house—all the time I was walking over here—

HOPE. Walking? Bejees, do you mean to say you walked?

HICKEY. I sure did. All the way from the wilds of darkest Astoria. Didn't mind it a bit, either. I seemed to get here before I knew it. I'm a bit tired and sleepy but otherwise I feel great. (*Kiddingly*) That ought to encourage you, Governor— show you a little walk around the ward is nothing to be so scared about. (*He winks at the others.* HOPE *stiffens resentfully for a second.* HICKEY *goes on*) I didn't make such bad time either for a fat guy, considering it's a hell of a ways, and I sat in the park a while thinking. It was going on twelve when I went in the bedroom to tell Evelyn I was leaving. Six hours, say. No, less than that. I'd been standing on the corner some time before Cora and Chuck came along, thinking about all of you. Of course, I was only kidding Cora with that stuff about saving you. (*Then seriously*) No, I wasn't either. But I didn't mean booze. I meant save you from pipe dreams. I know now, from my experience, they're the things that really poison and ruin a guy's life and keep him from finding any peace. If you knew how free and contented I feel now. I'm like a new man. And the cure for them is so damned simple, once you have the nerve. Just the old dope of honesty is the best policy—honesty with yourself, I mean. Just stop lying about yourself and kidding yourself about tomorrows. (*He is staring ahead of him now as if he were talking aloud to himself as much as to them. Their eyes are fixed on him with uneasy resentment. His manner becomes apologetic again*) Hell, this begins to sound like a damned sermon on the way to lead the good life. Forget that part of it. It's in my blood, I guess. My old man used to whale salvation into my heinie with a birch rod. He was a preacher in the sticks of Indiana, like I've told you. I got my knack of sales gab from him, too. He was the boy who could sell those Hoosier hayseeds building lots along the Golden Street! (*Taking on a salesman's persuasiveness*) Now listen, boys and girls, don't look at me as if I was trying to sell you a goldbrick. Nothing up my sleeve, honest. Let's take an example. Any one of you. Take you, Governor. That walk around the ward you never take—

HOPE. (*Defensively sharp*) What about it?

HICKEY. (*Grinning affectionately*) Why, you know as well as I do, Harry. Everything about it.

HOPE. (*Defiantly*) Bejees, I'm going to take it!

HICKEY. Sure, you're going to—this time. Because I'm going to help you. I know it's the thing you've got to do before you'll ever know what real peace means. (*He looks at* JIMMY TOMORROW) Same thing with you, Jimmy. You've got to try and get your old job back. And no tomorrow about it! (*As* JIMMY *stiffens with a pathetic attempt at dignity—placatingly*) No, don't tell me, Jimmy. I know all about tomorrow. I'm the guy that wrote the book.

JIMMY. I don't understand you. I admit I've foolishly delayed, but as it happens, I'd just made up my mind that as soon as I could get straightened out—

HICKEY. Fine! That's the spirit! And I'm going to help you. You've been damned kind to me, Jimmy, and I want to prove how grateful I am. When it's all over and you don't have to nag at yourself any more, you'll be grateful to me, too! (*He looks around at the others*) And all the rest of you, ladies included, are in the same boat, one way or another.

LARRY. (*Who has been listening with sardonic appreciation—in his comically intense, crazy whisper*) Be God, you've hit the nail on the head, Hickey! This dump is the Palace of Pipe Dreams!

HICKEY. (*Grins at him with affectionate kidding*) Well, well! The Old Grandstand Foolosopher speaks! You think you're the big exception, eh? Life doesn't mean a damn to you any more, does it? You're retired from the circus. You're just waiting impatiently for the end—the good old Long Sleep! (*He chuckles*) Well, I think a lot of you, Larry, you old bastard. I'll try and make an honest man of you, too!

LARRY. (*Stung*) What the devil are you hinting at, anyway?

HICKEY. You don't have to ask me, do you, a wise old guy like you? Just ask yourself. I'll bet you know.

PARRITT. (*Is watching* LARRY'S *face with a curious sneering satisfaction*) He's got your number all right, Larry! (*He turns to* HICKEY) That's the stuff, Hickey. Show the old faker up! He's got no right to sneak out of everything.

HICKEY. (*Regards him with surprise at first, then with a puzzled interest*) Hello. A stranger in our midst. I didn't notice you before, Brother.

PARRITT. (*Embarrassed, his eyes shifting away*) My name's Parritt. I'm an old friend of Larry's. (*His eyes come back to* HICKEY *to find him still sizing him up—defensively*) Well? What are you staring at?

HICKEY. (*Continuing to stare—puzzledly*) No offense, Brother. I was trying to figure— Haven't we met before some place?

PARRITT. (*Reassured*) No. First time I've ever been East.

HICKEY. No, you're right. I know that's not it. In my game, to be a shark at it, you teach yourself never to forget a name or a face. But still I know damned well I recognized something about you. We're members of the same lodge—in some way.

PARRITT. (*Uneasy again*) What are you talking about? You're nuts.

HICKEY. (*Dryly*) Don't try to kid me, Little Boy. I'm a good salesman—so damned good the firm was glad to take me back after every drunk—and what made me good was I could size up anyone. (*Frowningly puzzled again*) But I don't see— (*Suddenly breezily good-natured*) Never mind. I can tell you're having trouble with yourself and I'll be glad to do anything I can to help a friend of Larry's.

LARRY. Mind your own business, Hickey. He's nothing to you—or to me, either. (HICKEY *gives him a keen inquisitive glance.* LARRY *looks away and goes on sarcastically*) You're keeping us all in suspense. Tell us more about how you're going to save us.

HICKEY. (*Good-naturedly but seeming a little hurt*) Hell, don't get sore, Larry. Not at me. We've always been good pals, haven't we? I know I've always liked you a lot.

LARRY. (*A bit shamefaced*) Well, so have I liked you. Forget it, Hickey.

HICKEY. (*Beaming*) Fine! That's the spirit! (*Looking around at the others, who have forgotten their drinks*) What's the matter, everybody? What is this, a funeral? Come on and drink up! A little action! (*They all drink*) Have another. Hell, this is a celebration! Forget it, if anything I've said sounds too serious. I don't want to be a pain in the neck. Any time you think I'm talking out of turn, just tell me to go chase myself! (*He yawns with growing drowsiness and his voice grows a bit muffled*) No, boys and girls, I'm not trying to put anything over on you. It's just that I know now from experience what a lying pipe dream can do to you—and how damned relieved and contented with yourself you feel when you're rid of it. (*He yawns again*) God, I'm sleepy all of a sudden. That long walk is beginning to get me. I better go upstairs. Hell of a trick to go dead on you like this. (*He starts to get up but relaxes again. His eyes blink as he tries to keep them open*) No, boys and girls, I've never known what real peace was until now. It's a grand feeling, like when you're sick and suffering like hell and the Doc gives you a shot in the arm, and the pain goes, and you drift off. (*His eyes close*) You can let go of yourself at last. Let yourself sink down to the bottom of the sea. Rest in peace. There's no farther you have to go. Not a single damned hope or dream left to nag you. You'll all know what I mean after you— (*He pauses—mumbles*) Excuse—all in—got to grab forty winks— Drink up, everybody—on me— (*The sleep of complete exhaustion overpowers him. His chin sags to his chest. They stare at him with puzzled uneasy fascination.*)

HOPE. (*Forcing a tone of irritation*) Bejees, that's a fine stunt, to go to sleep on us! (*Then fumingly to the crowd*) Well, what the hell's the matter with you bums? Why don't you drink up? You're always crying for booze, and now you've got it under your nose, you sit like dummies! (*They start and gulp down their whiskies and pour another.* HOPE *stares at* HICKEY) Bejees, I can't figure Hickey. I still say he's kidding us. Kid his own grandmother, Hickey would. What d'you think, Jimmy?

JIMMY. (*Unconvincingly*) It must be another of his jokes, Harry, although— Well, he does appear changed. But he'll probably be his natural self again tomorrow— (*Hastily*) I mean, when he wakes up.

LARRY. (*Staring at* HICKEY *frowningly—more aloud to himself than to them*) You'll make a mistake if you think he's only kidding.

PARRITT. (*In a low confidential voice*) I don't like that guy, Larry. He's too damned nosy. I'm going to steer clear of him. (LARRY *gives him a suspicious glance, then looks hastily away.*)

JIMMY. (*With an attempt at open-minded reasonableness*) Still, Harry, I have to admit there was some sense in his nonsense. It is time I got my job back—although I hardly need him to remind me.

HOPE. (*With an air of frankness*) Yes, and I ought to take a walk around the ward. But I don't need no Hickey to tell me, seeing I got it all set for my birthday tomorrow.

LARRY. (*Sardonically*) Ha! (*Then in his comically intense, crazy whisper*) Be God, it looks like he's going to make two sales of his peace at least! But you'd better make sure first it's the real McCoy and not poison.

HOPE. (*Disturbed—angrily*) You bughouse I-Won't-Work harp, who asked you to shove in an oar? What the hell d'you mean, poison? Just because he has your number— (*He immediately feels ashamed of this taunt and adds apologetically*) Bejees, Larry, you're always croaking about something to do with death. It gets my nanny. Come on, fellers, let's drink up. (*They drink.* HOPE'S *eyes are fixed on* HICKEY *again*) Stone cold sober and dead to the world! Spilling that business about pipe dreams! Bejees, I don't get it. (*He bursts out again in angry complaint*) He ain't like the old Hickey! He'll be a fine wet blanket to have around at my birthday party! I wish to hell he'd never turned up!

MOSHER. (*Who has been the least impressed by* HICKEY'S *talk and is the first to recover and feel the effect of the drinks on top of his hangover—genially*) Give him time, Harry, and he'll come out of it. I've watched many cases of almost fatal teetotalism, but they all came out of it completely cured and as drunk as ever. My opinion is the poor sap is temporarily bughouse from overwork. (*Musingly*) You can't be too careful about work. It's the deadliest habit known to science, a great physician once told me. He practiced on street corners under a torchlight. He was positively the only doctor in the world who claimed that rattlesnake oil, rubbed on the prat, would cure heart failure in three days. I remember well his saying to me, "You are naturally delicate, Ed, but if you drink a pint of bad whiskey before breakfast every evening, and never work if you can help it, you may live to a ripe old age. It's staying sober and working that cuts men off in their

prime." (*While he is talking, they turn to him with eager grins. They are longing to laugh, and as he finishes they roar. Even* PARRITT *laughs.* HICKEY *sleeps on like a dead man, but* HUGO, *who had passed into his customary coma again, head on table, looks up through his thick spectacles and giggles foolishly.*)

HUGO. (*Blinking around at them. As the laughter dies he speaks in his giggling, wheedling manner, as if he were playfully teasing children*) Laugh, leedle bourgeois monkey-faces! Laugh like fools, leedle stupid peoples! (*His tone suddenly changes to one of guttural soapbox denunciation and he pounds on the table with a small fist*) I vill laugh, too! But I vill laugh last! I vill laugh at you! (*He declaims his favorite quotation*) "The days grow hot, O Babylon! 'Tis cool beneath thy villow trees!" (*They all hoot him down in a chorus of amused jeering.* HUGO *is not offended. This is evidently their customary reaction. He giggles good-naturedly.* HICKEY *sleeps on. They have all forgotten their uneasiness about him now and ignore him.*)

LEWIS. (*Tipsily*) Well, now that our little Robespierre has got the daily bit of guillotining off his chest, tell me more about your doctor friend, Ed. He strikes me as the only bloody sensible medico I ever heard of. I think we should appoint him house physician here without a moment's delay. (*They all laughingly assent.*)

MOSHER. (*Warming to his subject, shakes his head sadly*) Too late! The old Doc has passed on to his Maker. A victim of overwork, too. He didn't follow his own advice. Kept his nose to the grindstone and sold one bottle of snake oil too many. Only eighty years old when he was taken. The saddest part was that he knew he was doomed. The last time we got paralyzed together he told me: "This game will get me yet, Ed. You see before you a broken man, a martyr to medical science. If I had any nerves I'd have a nervous breakdown. You won't believe me, but this last year there was actually one night I had so many patients, I didn't even have time to get drunk. The shock to my system brought on a stroke which, as a doctor, I recognized was the beginning of the end." Poor old Doc! When he said this he started crying. "I hate to go before my task is completed, Ed," he sobbed. "I'd hoped I'd live to see the day when, thanks to my miraculous cure, there wouldn't be a single vacant cemetery lot left in this glorious country." (*There is a roar of laughter. He waits for it to die and then goes on sadly*) I miss Doc. He was a gentleman of the old school. I'll bet he's standing on a street corner in hell right now, making suckers of the damned, telling them there's nothing like snake oil for a bad burn. (*There is another roar of laughter. This time it penetrates* HICKEY'S *exhausted slumber. He stirs on his chair, trying to wake up, managing to raise his head a little and force his eyes half open. He speaks with a drowsy, affectionately encouraging smile. At once the laughter stops abruptly and they turn to him startledly.*)

HICKEY. That's the spirit—don't let me be a wet blanket—all I want is to see you happy— (*He slips back into heavy sleep again. They all stare at him, their faces again puzzled, resentful and uneasy.*)

CURTAIN

ACT TWO

SCENE: *The back room only. The black curtain dividing it from the bar is the right wall of the scene. It is getting on toward midnight of the same day.*

The back room has been prepared for a festivity. At center, front, four of the circular tables are pushed together to form one long table with an uneven line of chairs behind it, and chairs at each end. This improvised banquet table is covered with old table cloths, borrowed from a neighboring beanery, and is laid with glasses, plates and cutlery before each of the seventeen chairs. Bottles of bar whiskey are placed at intervals within reach of any sitter. An old upright piano and stool have been moved in and stand against the wall at left, front. At right, front, is a table without chairs. The other tables and chairs that had been in the room have been moved out, leaving a clear floor space at rear for dancing. The floor has been swept clean of sawdust and scrubbed. Even the walls show evidence of having been washed, although the result is only to heighten their splotchy leprous look. The electric light brackets are adorned with festoons of red ribbon. In the middle of the separate table at right, front, is a birthday cake with six candles. Several packages, tied with ribbon, are also on the table. There are two necktie boxes, two cigar boxes, a fifth containing a half dozen handkerchiefs, the sixth is a square jeweler's watch box.

As the curtain rises, CORA, CHUCK, HUGO, LARRY, MARGIE, PEARL *and* ROCKY *are discovered.* CHUCK, ROCKY *and the three girls have dressed up for the occasion.* CORA *is arranging a bouquet of flowers in a vase, the vase being a big schooner glass from the bar, on top of the piano.* CHUCK *sits in a chair at the foot* (*left*) *of the banquet table. He has turned it so he can watch her. Near the middle of the row of chairs behind the table,* LARRY *sits, facing front, a drink of whiskey before him. He is staring before him in frowning, disturbed meditation. Next to him, on his left,* HUGO *is in his habitual position, passed out, arms on table, head on arms, a full whiskey glass by his head. By the separate table at right, front,* MARGIE *and* PEARL *are arranging the cake and presents, and* ROCKY *stands by them. All of them, with the exception of* CHUCK *and* ROCKY, *have had plenty to drink and show it, but no one, except* HUGO, *seems to be drunk. They are trying to act up in the spirit of the occasion but there is something forced about their manner, an undercurrent of nervous irritation and preoccupation.*

CORA. (*Standing back from the piano to regard the flower effect*) How's dat, Kid?

CHUCK. (*Grumpily*) What de hell do I know about flowers?

CORA. Yuh can see dey're pretty, can't yuh, yuh big dummy?

CHUCK. (*Mollifyingly*) Yeah, Baby, sure. If yuh like 'em, dey're aw right wid me. (CORA *goes back to give the schooner of flowers a few more touches.*)

MARGIE. (*Admiring the cake*) Some cake, huh, Poil? Lookit! Six candles. Each for ten years.

PEARL. When do we light de candles, Rocky?

ROCKY. (*Grumpily*) Ask dat bughouse Hickey. He's elected himself boss of dis boithday racket. Just before Harry comes down, he says. Den Harry blows dem out wid one breath, for luck. Hickey was goin' to have sixty candles, but I says, Jees, if de old guy took dat big a breath, he'd croak himself.

MARGIE. (*Challengingly*) Well, anyways, it's some cake, ain't it?

ROCKY. (*Without enthusiasm*) Sure, it's aw right by me. But what de hell is Harry goin' to do wid a cake? If he ever et a hunk, it'd croak him.

PEARL. Jees, yuh're a dope! Ain't he, Margie?

MARGIE. A dope is right!

ROCKY. (*Stung*) You broads better watch your step or—

PEARL. (*Defiantly*) Or what?

MARGIE. Yeah! Or what? (*They glare at him truculently.*)

ROCKY. Say, what de hell's got into youse? It'll be twelve o'clock and Harry's boithday before long. I ain't lookin' for no trouble.

PEARL. (*Ashamed*) Aw, we ain't neider, Rocky. (*For the moment this argument subsides.*)

CORA. (*Over her shoulder to* CHUCK—*acidly*) A guy what can't see flowers is pretty must be some dumbbell.

CHUCK. Yeah? Well, if I was as dumb as you— (*Then mollifyingly*) Jees, yuh got your scrappin' pants on, ain't yuh? (*Grins good-naturedly*) Hell, Baby, what's eatin' yuh? All I'm tinkin' is, flowers is dat louse Hickey's stunt. We never had no flowers for Harry's boithday before. What de hell can Harry do wid flowers? He don't know a cauliflower from a geranium.

ROCKY. Yeah, Chuck, it's like I'm tellin' dese broads about de cake. Dat's Hickey's wrinkle, too. (*Bitterly*) Jees, ever since he woke up, yuh can't hold him. He's taken on de party like it was his boithday.

MARGIE. Well, he's payin' for everything, ain't he?

ROCKY. Aw, I don't mind de boithday stuff so much. What gets my goat is de way he's tryin' to run de whole dump and everyone in it. He's buttin' in all over de place, tellin' everybody where dey get off. On'y he don't really tell yuh. He just keeps hintin' around.

PEARL. Yeah. He was hintin' to me and Margie.

MARGIE. Yeah, de lousy drummer.

ROCKY. He just gives yuh an earful of dat line of bull about yuh got to be honest wid yourself and not kid yourself, and have de guts to be what yuh are. I got sore. I told him dat's aw right for de bums in dis dump. I hope he makes dem wake up. I'm sick of listenin' to dem hop demselves up. But it don't go wid me, see? I don't kid myself wid no pipe dream. (PEARL *and* MARGIE *exchange a derisive look. He catches it and his eyes narrow*) What are yuh grinnin' at?

PEARL. (*Her face hard—scornfully*) Nuttin'.

MARGIE. Nuttin'.

ROCKY. It better be nuttin'! Don't let Hickey put no ideas in your nuts if you wanta stay healthy! (*Then angrily*) I wish de louse never showed up! I hope he don't come back from de delicatessen. He's gettin' everyone nuts. He's ridin' someone every minute. He's got Harry and Jimmy Tomorrow run ragged, and de rest is hidin' in deir rooms so dey won't have to listen to him. Dey're all actin' cagey wid de booze, too, like dey was scared if dey get too drunk, dey might spill deir guts, or somethin'. And everybody's gettin' a prize grouch on.

CORA. Yeah, he's been hintin' round to me and Chuck, too. Yuh'd tink he suspected me and Chuck hadn't no real intention of gettin' married. Yuh'd tink he suspected Chuck wasn't goin' to lay off periodicals—or maybe even didn't want to.

CHUCK. He didn't say it right out or I'da socked him one. I told him, "I'm on de wagon for keeps and Cora knows it."

CORA. I told him, "Sure, I know it. And Chuck ain't never goin' to trow it in my face dat I was a tart, neider. And if yuh tink we're just kiddin' ourselves, we'll show yuh!"

CHUCK. We're goin' to show him!

CORA. We got it all fixed. We've decided Joisey is where we want de farm, and we'll get married dere, too, because yuh don't need no license. We're goin' to get married tomorrow. Ain't we, Honey?

CHUCK. You bet, Baby.

ROCKY. (*Disgusted*) Christ, Chuck, are yuh lettin' dat bughouse louse Hickey kid yuh into—

CORA. (*Turns on him angrily*) Nobody's kiddin' him into it, nor me neider! And Hickey's right. If dis big tramp's goin' to marry me, he ought to do it, and not just shoot off his old bazoo about it.

ROCKY. (*Ignoring her*) Yuh can't be dat dumb, Chuck.

CORA. You keep outa dis! And don't start beefin' about crickets on de farm drivin' us nuts. You and your crickets! Yuh'd tink dey was elephants!

MARGIE. (*Coming to* ROCKY'S *defense—sneeringly*) Don't notice dat broad, Rocky. Yuh heard her say "tomorrow," didn't yuh? It's de same old crap.

CORA. (*Glares at her*) Is dat so?

PEARL. (*Lines up with* MARGIE—*sneeringly*) Imagine Cora a bride! Dat's a hot one! Jees, Cora, if all de guys you've stayed wid was side by side, yuh could walk on 'em from here to Texas!

CORA. (*Starts moving toward her threateningly*) Yuh can't talk like dat to me, yuh fat Dago hooker! I may be a tart, but I ain't a cheap old whore like you!

PEARL. (*Furiously*) I'll show yuh who's a whore! (*They start to fly at each other, but* CHUCK *and* ROCKY *grab them from behind.*)

CHUCK. (*Forcing* CORA *onto a chair*) Sit down and cool off, Baby.

ROCKY. (*Doing the same to* PEARL) Nix on de rough stuff, Poil.

MARGIE. (*Glaring at* CORA) Why don't you leave Poil alone, Rocky? She'll fix dat blonde's clock! Or if she don't, I will!

ROCKY. Shut up, you! (*Disgustedly*) Jees, what dames! D'yuh wanta gum Harry's party?

PEARL. (*A bit shamefaced—sulkily*) Who wants to? But nobody can't call me a ——.

ROCKY. (*Exasperatedly*) Aw, bury it! What are you, a voigin? (PEARL *stares at him, her face growing hard and bitter. So does* MARGIE.)

PEARL. Yuh mean you tink I'm a whore, too, huh?

MARGIE. Yeah, and me?

ROCKY. Now don't start nuttin'!

PEARL. I suppose it'd tickle you if me and Margie did what dat louse, Hickey, was hintin' and come right out and admitted we was whores.

ROCKY. Aw right! What of it? It's de truth, ain't it?

CORA. (*Lining up with* PEARL *and* MARGIE—*indignantly*) Jees, Rocky, dat's a fine hell of a ting to say to two goils dat's been as good to yuh as Poil and Margie! (*To* PEARL) I didn't mean to call yuh dat, Poil. I was on'y mad.

PEARL. (*Accepts the apology gratefully*) Sure, I was mad, too, Cora. No hard feelin's.

ROCKY. (*Relieved*) Dere. Dat fixes everyting, don't it?

PEARL. (*Turns on him—hard and bitter*) Aw right, Rocky. We're whores. You know what dat makes you, don't you?

ROCKY. (*Angrily*) Look out, now!

MARGIE. A lousy little pimp, dat's what!

ROCKY. I'll loin yuh! (*He gives her a slap on the side of the face.*)

PEARL. A dirty little Ginny pimp, dat's what!

ROCKY. (*Gives her a slap, too*) And dat'll loin you! (*But they only stare at him with hard sneering eyes.*)

MARGIE. He's provin' it to us, Poil

PEARL. Yeah! Hickey's convoited him. He's give up his pipe dream!

ROCKY. (*Furious and at the same time bewildered by their defiance*) Lay off me or I'll beat de hell—

CHUCK. (*Growls*) Aw, lay off dem. Harry's party ain't no time to beat up your stable.

ROCKY. (*Turns to him*) Whose stable? Who d'yuh tink yuh're talkin' to? I ain't never beat dem up! What d'yuh tink I am? I just give dem a slap, like any guy would his wife, if she got too gabby. Why don't yuh tell dem to lay off me? I don't want no trouble on Harry's boithday party.

MARGIE. (*A victorious gleam in her eye—tauntingly*) Aw right, den, yuh poor little Ginny. I'll lay off yuh till de party's over if Poil will.

PEARL. (*Tauntingly*) Sure, I will. For Harry's sake, not yours, yuh little Wop!

ROCKY. (*Stung*) Say, listen, youse! Don't get no wrong idea— (*But an interruption comes from* LARRY *who bursts into a sardonic laugh. They all jump startledly and look at him with unanimous hostility.* ROCKY *transfers his anger to him*) Who de hell yuh laughin' at, yuh half-dead old stew bum?

CORA. (*Sneeringly*) At himself, he ought to be! Jees, Hickey's sure got his number!

LARRY. (*Ignoring them, turns to* HUGO *and shakes him by the shoulder—in his comically intense, crazy whisper*) Wake up, Comrade! Here's the Revolution starting on all sides of you and you're sleeping through it! Be God, it's not to Bakunin's ghost you ought to pray in your dreams, but to the great Nihilist, Hickey! He's started a movement that'll blow up the world!

HUGO. (*Blinks at him through his thick spectacles—with guttural denunciation*) You, Larry! Renegade! Traitor! I vill have you shot! (*He giggles*) Don't be a fool! Buy me a trink! (*He sees the drink in front of him, and gulps it down. He begins to sing the Carmagnole in a guttural basso, pounding on the table with his glass*) "Dansons la Carmagnole! Vive le son! Vive le son! Dansons la Carmagnole! Vive le son des canons!"

ROCKY. Can dat noise!

HUGO. (*Ignores this—to* LARRY, *in a low tone of hatred*) That bourgeois svine, Hickey! He laughs like good fellow, he makes jokes, he dares make hints to me so I see what he dares to think. He thinks I am finish, it is too late, and so I do not vish the Day come because it vill not be my Day. Oh, I see what he thinks! He thinks lies even vorse, dat I— (*He stops abruptly with a guilty look, as if afraid he was letting something slip—then revengefully*) I vill have him hanged the first one of all on de first lamppost! (*He changes his mood abruptly and peers around at* ROCKY *and the others—giggling again*) Vhy you so serious, leedle monkey-faces? It's all great joke, no? So ve get drunk, and ve laugh like hell, and den ve die, and de pipe dream vanish! (*A bitter mocking contempt creeps into his tone*) But be of good cheer, leedle stupid peoples! "The days grow hot, O Babylon!" Soon, leedle proletarians, ve vill have free picnic in the cool shade, ve vill eat hot dogs and trink free beer beneath the villow trees! Like hogs, yes! Like beautiful leedle hogs! (*He stops startledly, as if confused and amazed at what he has heard himself say. He mutters with hatred*) Dot Gottamned liar, Hickey. It is he who makes me sneer. I want to sleep. (*He lets his head fall forward on his folded arms again and closes his eyes.* LARRY *gives him a pitying look, then quickly drinks his drink.*)

CORA. (*Uneasily*) Hickey ain't overlookin' no bets, is he? He's even give Hugo de woiks.

LARRY. I warned you this morning he wasn't kidding.

MARGIE. (*Sneering*) De old wise guy!

PEARL. Yeah, still pretendin' he's de one exception, like Hickey told him. He don't do no pipe dreamin'! Oh, no!

LARRY. (*Sharply resentful*) I—! (*Then abruptly he is drunkenly good-natured, and you feel this drunken manner is an evasive exaggeration*) All right, take it out on me, if it makes you more content. Sure, I love every hair of your heads, my great big beautiful baby dolls, and there's nothing I wouldn't do for you!

PEARL. (*Stiffly*) De old Irish bunk, huh? We ain't big. And we ain't your baby dolls! (*Suddenly she is mollified and smiles*) But we admit we're beautiful. Huh, Margie?

MARGIE. (*Smiling*) Sure ting! But what would he do wid beautiful dolls, even if he had de price, de old goat? (*She laughs teasingly—then pats* LARRY *on the shoulder affectionately*) Aw, yuh're aw right at dat, Larry, if yuh are full of bull!

PEARL. Sure. Yuh're aces wid us. We're noivous, dat's all. Dat lousy drummer—why can't he be like he's always been? I never seen a guy change so. You pretend to be such a fox, Larry. What d'yuh tink's happened to him?

LARRY. I don't know. With all his gab I notice he's kept that to himself so far. Maybe he's saving the great revelation for Harry's party. (*Then irritably*) To hell with him! I don't want to know. Let him mind his own business and I'll mind mine.

CHUCK. Yeah, dat's what I say.

CORA. Say, Larry, where's dat young friend of yours disappeared to?

LARRY. I don't care where he is, except I wish it was a thousand miles away! (*Then, as he sees they are surprised at his vehemence, he adds hastily*) He's a pest.

ROCKY. (*Breaks in with his own preoccupation*) I don't give a damn what happened to Hickey, but I know what's gonna happen if he don't watch his step. I told him, "I'll take a lot from you, Hickey, like everyone else in dis dump, because yuh've always been a grand guy. But dere's tings I don't take from you nor nobody, see? Remember dat, or you'll wake up in a hospital— or maybe worse, wid your wife and de iceman walkin' slow behind yuh."

CORA. Aw, yuh shouldn't make dat iceman crack, Rocky. It's aw right for him to kid about it but—I notice Hickey ain't pulled dat old iceman gag dis time. (*Excitedly*) D'yuh suppose dat he did catch his wife cheatin'? I don't mean wid no iceman, but wid some guy.

ROCKY. Aw, dat's de bunk. He ain't pulled dat gag or showed her photo around because he ain't drunk. And if he'd caught her cheatin' he'd be drunk, wouldn't he? He'd have beat her up and den gone on de woist drunk he'd ever staged. Like any other guy'd do. (*The girls nod, convinced by this reasoning.*)

CHUCK. Sure! Rocky's got de right dope, Baby. He'd be paralyzed. (*While he is speaking, the Negro,* JOE, *comes in from the hallway. There is*

a noticeable change in him. He walks with a tough, truculent swagger and his good-natured face is set in sullen suspicion.)

JOE. (*To* ROCKY—*defiantly*) I's stood tellin' people dis dump is closed for de night all I's goin' to. Let Harry hire a doorman, pay him wages, if he wants one.

ROCKY. (*Scowling*) Yeah? Harry's pretty damned good to you.

JOE. (*Shamefaced*) Sure he is. I don't mean dat. Anyways, it's all right. I told Schwartz, de cop, we's closed for de party. He'll keep folks away. (*Aggressively again*) I want a big drink, dat's what!

CHUCK. Who's stoppin' yuh? Yuh can have all yuh want on Hickey.

JOE. (*Has taken a glass from the table and has his hand on a bottle when* HICKEY'S *names is mentioned. He draws his hand back as if he were going to refuse—then grabs it defiantly and pours a big drink*) All right, I's earned all de drinks on him I could drink in a year for listenin' to his crazy bull. And here's hopin' he gets de lockjaw! (*He drinks and pours out another*) I drinks on him but I don't drink wid him. No, suh, never no more!

ROCKY. Aw, bull! Hickey's aw right. What's he done to you?

JOE (*Sullenly*) Dat's my business. I ain't buttin' in yours, is I? (*Bitterly*) Sure, you think he's all right. He's a white man, ain't he? (*His tone becomes aggressive*) Listen to me, you white boys! Don't you get it in your heads I's pretendin' to be what I ain't, or dat I ain't proud to be what I is, get me? Or you and me's goin' to have trouble! (*He picks up his drink and walks left as far away from them as he can get and slumps down on the piano stool.*)

MARGIE (*In a low angry tone*) What a noive! Just because we act nice to him, he gets a swelled nut! If dat ain't a coon all over!

CHUCK. Talkin' fight talk, huh? I'll moider de nigger! (*He takes a threatening step toward* JOE, *who is staring before him guiltily now.*)

JOE. (*Speaks up shamefacedly*) Listen, boys, I's sorry. I didn't mean dat. You been good friends to me. I's nuts, I guess. Dat Hickey, he gets my head all mixed up wit' craziness. (*Their faces at once clear of resentment against him.*)

CORA. Aw, dat's aw right, Joe. De boys wasn't takin' yuh serious. (*Then to the others, forcing a laugh*) Jees, what'd I say, Hickey ain't overlookin' no bets. Even Joe. (*She pauses—then adds puzzledly*) De funny ting is, yuh can't stay sore at de bum when he's around. When he forgets de bughouse preachin', and quits tellin' yuh where yuh get off, he's de same old Hickey. Yuh can't help likin' de louse. And yuh got to admit he's got de right dope— (*She adds hastily*) I mean, on some of de bums here.

MARGIE. (*With a sneering look at* ROCKY) Yeah, he's coitinly got one guy I know sized up right! Huh, Poil?

PEARL. He coitinly has!

ROCKY. Cut it out, I told yuh!

LARRY. (*Is staring before him broodingly. He speaks more aloud to himself than to them*) It's nothing to me what happened to him. But I have a feeling he's dying to tell us, inside him, and yet he's afraid. He's like that damned kid. It's strange the queer way he seemed to recognize him. If he's afraid, it explains why he's off booze. Like that damned kid again. Afraid if he got drunk, he'd tell— (*While he is speaking,* HICKEY *comes in the doorway at rear. He looks the same as in the previous act, except that now his face beams with the excited expectation of a boy going to a party. His arms are piled with packages.*)

HICKEY. (*Booms in imitation of a familiar Polo Grounds bleacherite cry—with rising volume*) Well! Well!! Well!!! (*They all jump startledly. He comes forward, grinning*) Here I am in the nick of time. Give me a hand with these bundles, somebody. (MARGIE *and* PEARL *start taking them from his arms and putting them on the table. Now that he is present, all their attitudes show the reaction* CORA *has expressed. They can't help liking him and forgiving him.*)

MARGIE. Jees, Hickey, yuh scared me outa a year's growth, sneakin' in like dat.

HICKEY. Sneaking? Why, me and the taxi man made enough noise getting my big surprise in the hall to wake the dead. You were all so busy drinking in words of wisdom from the Old Wise Guy here, you couldn't hear anything else. (*He grins at* LARRY) From what I heard, Larry, you're not so good when you start playing Sherlock Holmes. You've got me all wrong. I'm not afraid of anything now—not even myself. You better stick to the part of Old Cemetery, the Barker for the Big Sleep—that is, if you can still let yourself get away with it! (*He chuckles and gives* LARRY *a friendly slap on the back.* LARRY *gives him a bitter angry look.*)

CORA. (*Giggles*) Old Cemetery! That's him, Hickey. We'll have to call him dat.

HICKEY. (*Watching* LARRY *quizzically*) Beginning to do a lot of puzzling about me, aren't you, Larry? But that won't help you. You've got to think of yourself. I couldn't give you my peace. You've got to find your own. All I can do is help you, and the rest of the gang, by showing you the way to find it. (*He has said this with a simple persuasive earnestness. He pauses, and for a second they stare at him with fascinated resentful uneasiness.*)

ROCKY. (*Breaks the spell*) Aw, hire a church!

HICKEY. (*Placatingly*) All right! All right! Don't get sore, boys and girls. I guess that did sound too much like a lousy preacher. Let's forget it and get busy on the party. (*They look relieved.*)

CHUCK. Is dose bundles grub, Hickey? You bought enough already to feed an army.

HICKEY. (*With boyish excitement again*) Can't be too much! I want this to be the biggest birthday Harry's ever had. You and Rocky go in the hall and get the big surprise. My arms are busted lugging it. (*They catch his excitement.* CHUCK *and* ROCKY *go out, grinning expectantly. The three girls gather around* HICKEY, *full of thrilled curiosity.*)

PEARL. Jees, yuh got us all het up! What is it, Hickey?

HICKEY. Wait and see. I got it as a treat for the three of you more than anyone. I thought to myself, I'll bet this is what will please those whores more than anything. (*They wince as if he had slapped them, but before they have a chance to be angry, he goes on affectionately*) I said to myself, I don't care how much it costs, they're worth it. They're the best little scouts in the world, and they've been damned kind to me when I was down and out! Nothing is too good for them. (*Earnestly*) I mean every word of that, too—and then some! (*Then, as if he noticed the expression on their faces for the first time*) What's the matter? You look sore. What—? (*Then he chuckles*) Oh, I see. But you know how I feel about that. You know I didn't say it to offend you. So don't be silly now.

MARGIE. (*Lets out a tense breath*) Aw right, Hickey. Let it slide.

HICKEY. (*Jubilantly, as* CHUCK *and* ROCKY *enter carrying a big wicker basket*) Look! There it comes! Unveil it, boys. (*They pull off a covering burlap bag. The basket is piled with quarts of champagne.*)

PEARL. (*With childish excitement*) It's champagne! Jees, Hickey, if you ain't a sport! (*She gives him a hug, forgetting all animosity, as do the other girls.*)

MARGIE. I never been soused on champagne. Let's get stinko, Poil.

PEARL. You betcha my life! De bot' of us! (*A holiday spirit of gay festivity has seized them all. Even* JOE MOTT *is standing up to look at the wine with an admiring grin, and* HUGO *raises his head to blink at it.*)

JOE. You sure is hittin' de high spots, Hickey. (*Boastfully*) Man, when I runs my gamblin' house, I drinks dat old bubbly water in steins! (*He stops guiltily and gives* HICKEY *a look of defiance*) I's goin' to drink it dat way again, too, soon's I make my stake! And dat ain't no pipe dream, neider! (*He sits down where he was, his back turned to them.*)

ROCKY. What'll we drink it outa, Hickey? Dere ain't no wine glasses.

HICKEY. (*Enthusiastically*) Joe has the right idea! Schooners! That's the spirit for Harry's birthday! (ROCKY *and* CHUCK *carry the basket of wine into the bar. The three girls go back and stand around the entrance to the bar, chatting excitedly among themselves and to* CHUCK *and* ROCKY *in the bar.*)

HUGO. (*With his silly giggle*) Ve vill trink vine beneath the villow trees!

HICKEY. (*Grins at him*) That's the spirit, Brother—and let the lousy slaves drink vinegar! (HUGO *blinks at him startledly, then looks away.*)

HUGO. (*Mutters*) Gottamned liar! (*He puts his head back on his arms and closes his eyes, but this time his habitual pass-out has a quality of hiding.*)

LARRY. (*Gives* HUGO *a pitying glance—in a low tone of anger*) Leave Hugo be! He rotted ten years in prison for his faith! He's earned his dream! Have you no decency or pity?

HICKEY. (*Quizzically*) Hello, what's this? I thought you were in the grandstand. (*Then with a simple earnestness, taking a chair by* LARRY, *and putting a hand on his shoulder*) Listen, Larry, you're getting me all wrong. Hell, you ought to know me better. I've always been the best-natured slob in the world. Of course, I have pity. But now I've seen the light, it isn't my old kind of pity— the kind yours is. It isn't the kind that lets itself off easy by encouraging some poor guy to go on kidding himself with a lie—the kind that leaves the poor slob worse off because it makes him feel guiltier than ever—the kind that makes his lying hopes nag at him and reproach him until he's a rotten skunk in his own eyes. I know all about that kind of pity. I've had a bellyful of it in my time, and it's all wrong! (*With a salesman's persuasiveness*) No, sir. The kind of pity I feel now is after final results that will really save the poor guy, and make him contented with what he is, and quit battling himself, and find peace for the rest of his life. Oh, I know how you resent the way I have to show you up to yourself. I don't blame you. I know from my own experience it's bitter medicine, facing yourself in the mirror with the old false whiskers off. But you forget that, once you're cured. You'll be grateful to me when all at once you find you're able to admit, without feeling ashamed, that all the grandstand foolosopher bunk and the waiting for the Big Sleep stuff is a pipe dream. You'll say to yourself, I'm just an old man who is scared of life, but even more scared of dying. So I'm keeping drunk and hanging on to life at any price, and what of it? Then you'll know what real peace means, Larry, because you won't be scared of either life or death any more. You simply won't give a damn! Any more than I do!

LARRY. (*Has been staring into his eyes with a fascinated wondering dread*) Be God, if I'm not beginning to think you've gone mad! (*With a rush of anger*) You're a liar!

HICKEY. (*Injuredly*) Now, listen, that's no way to talk to an old pal who's trying to help you. Hell, if you really wanted to die, you'd just take a hop off your fire escape, wouldn't you? And if you really were in the grandstand, you wouldn't be pitying everyone. Oh, I know the truth is tough at first. It was for me. All I ask is for you to suspend judgment and give it a chance. I'll absolutely guarantee— Hell, Larry, I'm no fool. Do you suppose I'd deliberately set out to get under everyone's skin and put myself in dutch with all my old pals, if I wasn't certain, from my own experience, that it means contentment in the end for all of you? (LARRY *again is staring at him fascinatedly.* HICKEY *grins*) As for my being bughouse, you can't crawl out of it that way. Hell, I'm too damned sane. I can size up guys, and turn 'em inside out, better than I ever could. Even where they're strangers like that Parritt kid. He's licked, Larry. I think there is only one possible way out you can help him to take. That is, if you have the right kind of pity for him.

LARRY. (*Uneasily*) What do you mean? (*Attempting indifference*) I'm not advising him, except to leave me out of his troubles. He's nothing to me.

HICKEY. (*Shakes his head*) You'll find he won't agree to that. He'll keep after you until he makes you help him. Because he has to be punished, so he can forgive himself. He's lost all his guts. He can't manage it alone, and you're the only one he can turn to.

LARRY. For the love of God, mind your own business! (*With forced scorn*) A lot you know about him! He's hardly spoken to you!

HICKEY. No, that's right. But I do know a lot about him just the same. I've had hell inside me. I can spot it in others. (*Frowning*) Maybe that's what gives me the feeling there's something familiar about him, something between us. (*He shakes his head*) No, it's more than that. I can't figure it. Tell me about him. For instance, I don't imagine he's married, is he?

LARRY. No.

HICKEY. Hasn't he been mixed up with some woman? I don't mean trollops. I mean the old real love stuff that crucifies you.

LARRY. (*With a calculating relieved look at him —encouraging him along this line*) Maybe you're right. I wouldn't be surprised.

HICKEY. (*Grins at him quizzically*) I see. You think I'm on the wrong track and you're glad I am. Because then I won't suspect whatever he did about the Great Cause. That's another lie you tell yourself, Larry, that the good old Cause means nothing to you any more. (LARRY *is about to burst out in denial but* HICKEY *goes on*) But you're all wrong about Parritt. That isn't what's got him stopped. It's what's behind that. And it's a woman. I recognize the symptoms.

LARRY. (*Sneeringly*) And you're the boy who's never wrong! Don't be a damned fool. His trouble is he was brought up a devout believer in the Movement and now he's lost his faith. It's a shock, but he's young and he'll soon find another dream just as good. (*He adds sardonically*) Or as bad.

HICKEY. All right. I'll let it go at that, Larry. He's nothing to me except I'm glad he's here because he'll help me make you wake up to yourself. I don't even like the guy, or the feeling there's anything between us. But you'll find I'm right just the same, when you get to the final showdown with him.

LARRY. There'll be no showdown! I don't give a tinker's damn—

HICKEY. Sticking to the old grandstand, eh? Well, I knew you'd be the toughest to convince of all the gang, Larry. And, along with Harry and Jimmy Tomorrow, you're the one I want most to help. (*He puts an arm around* LARRY's *shoulder and gives him an affectionate hug*) I've always liked you a lot, you old bastard! (*He gets up and his manner changes to his bustling party excitement—glancing at his watch*) Well, well, not much time before twelve. Let's get busy, boys and girls. (*He looks over the table where the cake is*) Cake all set. Good. And my presents, and yours, girls, and Chuck's, and Rocky's. Fine. Harry'll certainly be touched by your thought of him. (*He goes back to the girls*) You go in the bar, Pearl and Margie, and get the grub ready so it can be brought right in. There'll be some drinking and toasts first, of course. My idea is to use the wine for that, so get it all set. I'll go upstairs now and root everyone out. Harry the last. I'll

come back with him. Somebody light the candles on the cake when you hear us coming, and you start playing Harry's favorite tune, Cora. Hustle now, everybody. We want this to come off in style. (*He bustles into the hall.* MARGIE *and* PEARL *disappear in the bar.* CORA *goes to the piano.* JOE *gets off the stool sullenly to let her sit down.*)

CORA. I got to practice. I ain't laid my mits on a box in Gawd knows when. (*With the soft pedal down, she begins gropingly to pick out "The Sunshine of Paradise Alley"*) Is dat right, Joe? I've forgotten dat has-been tune. (*She picks out a few more notes*) Come on Joe, hum de tune so I can follow. (JOE *begins to hum and sing in a low voice and correct her. He forgets his sullenness and becomes his old self again.*)

LARRY. (*Suddenly gives a laugh—in his comically intense, crazy tone*) Be God, it's a second feast of Belshazzar, with Hickey to do the writing on the wall!

CORA. Aw, shut up, Old Cemetery! Always beefin'! (WILLIE *comes in from the hall. He is in a pitiable state, his face pasty, haggard with sleeplessness and nerves, his eyes sick and haunted. He is sober.* CORA *greets him over her shoulder kiddingly*) If it ain't Prince Willie! (*Then kindly*) Gee, kid, yuh look sick. Git a coupla shots in yuh.

WILLIE. (*Tensely*) No, thanks. Not now. I'm tapering off. (*He sits down weakly on* LARRY's *right.*)

CORA. (*Astonished*) What d'yuh know? He means it!

WILLIE. (*Leaning toward* LARRY *confidentially —in a low shaken voice*) It's been hell up in that damned room, Larry! The things I've imagined! (*He shudders*) I thought I'd go crazy. (*With pathetic boastful pride*) But I've got it beat now. By tomorrow morning I'll be on the wagon. I'll get back my clothes the first thing. Hickey's loaning me the money. I'm going to do what I've always said—go to the D.A.'s office. He was a good friend of my Old Man's. He was only assistant, then. He was in on the graft, but my Old Man never squealed on him. So he certainly owes it to me to give me a chance. And he knows that I really was a brilliant law student. (*Self-reassuringly*) Oh, I know I can make good, now I'm getting off the booze forever. (*Moved*) I owe a lot to Hickey. He's made me wake up to myself— see what a fool— It wasn't nice to face but— (*With bitter resentment*) It isn't what he says. It's what you feel behind—what he hints— Christ, you'd think all I really wanted to do with my life was sit here and stay drunk. (*With hatred*) I'll show him!

LARRY. (*Masking pity behind a sardonic tone*)

If you want my advice, you'll put the nearest bottle to your mouth until you don't give a damn for Hickey!

WILLIE. (*Stares at a bottle greedily, tempted for a moment—then bitterly*) That's fine advice! I thought you were my friend! (*He gets up with a hurt glance at* LARRY, *and moves away to take a chair in back of the left end of the table, where he sits in dejected, shaking misery, his chin on his chest.*)

JOE. (*To* CORA) No, like dis. (*He beats time with his finger and sings in a low voice*) "She is the sunshine of Paradise Alley." (*She plays*) Dat's more like it. Try it again. (*She begins to play through the chorus again.* DON PARRITT *enters from the hall. There is a frightened look on his face. He slinks in furtively, as if he were escaping from someone. He looks relieved when he sees* LARRY *and comes and slips into the chair on his right.* LARRY *pretends not to notice his coming, but he instinctively shrinks with repulsion.* PARRITT *leans toward him and speaks ingratiatingly in a low secretive tone.*)

PARRITT. Gee, I'm glad you're here, Larry. That damned fool, Hickey, knocked on my door. I opened up because I thought it must be you, and he came busting in and made me come downstairs. I don't know what for. I don't belong in this birthday celebration. I don't know this gang and I don't want to be mixed up with them. All I came here for was to find you.

LARRY. (*Tensely*) I've warned you—

PARRITT. (*Goes on as if he hadn't heard*) Can't you make Hickey mind his own business? I don't like that guy, Larry. The way he acts, you'd think he had something on me. Why, just now he pats me on the shoulder, like he was sympathizing with me, and says, "I know how it is, Son, but you can't hide from yourself, not even here on the bottom of the sea. You've got to face the truth and then do what must be done for your own peace and the happiness of all concerned." What did he mean by that, Larry?

LARRY. How the hell would I know?

PARRITT. Then he grins and says, "Never mind, Larry's getting wise to himself. I think you can rely on his help in the end. He'll have to choose between living and dying, and he'll never choose to die while there is a breath left in the old bastard!" And then he laughs like it was a joke on you (*He pauses.* LARRY *is rigid on his chair, staring before him.* PARRITT *asks him with a sudden taunt in his voice*) Well, what do you say to that, Larry?

LARRY. I've nothing to say. Except you're a bigger fool than he is to listen to him.

PARRITT. (*With a sneer*) Is that so? He's no fool where you're concerned. He's got your number, all right! (LARRY's *face tightens but he keeps silent.* PARRITT *changes to a contrite, appealing air*) I don't mean that. But you keep acting as if you were sore at me, and that gets my goat. You know what I want most is to be friends with you, Larry. I haven't a single friend left in the world. I hoped you— (*Bitterly*) And you could be, too, without it hurting you. You ought to, for Mother's sake. She really loved you. You loved her, too, didn't you?

LARRY. (*Tensely*) Leave what's dead in its grave.

PARRITT. I suppose, because I was only a kid, you didn't think I was wise about you and her. Well, I was. I've been wise, ever since I can remember, to all the guys she's had, although she'd tried to kid me along it wasn't so. That was a silly stunt for a free Anarchist woman, wasn't it, being ashamed of being free?

LARRY. Shut your damned trap!

PARRITT. (*Guiltily but with a strange undertone of satisfaction*) Yes, I know I shouldn't say that now. I keep forgetting she isn't free any more. (*He pauses*) Do you know, Larry, you're the one of them all she cared most about? Anyone else who left the Movement would have been dead to her, but she couldn't forget you. She'd always make excuses for you. I used to try and get her goat about you. I'd say, "Larry's got brains and yet he thinks the Movement is just a crazy pipe dream." She'd blame it on booze getting you. She'd kid herself that you'd give up booze and come back to the Movement—tomorrow! She'd say, "Larry can't kill in himself a faith he's given his life to, not without killing himself." (*He grins sneeringly*) How about it, Larry? Was she right? (LARRY *remains silent. He goes on insistently*) I suppose what she really meant was, come back to her. She was always getting the Movement mixed up with herself. But I'm sure she really must have loved you, Larry. As much as she could love anyone besides herself. But she wasn't faithful to you, even at that, was she? That's why you finally walked out on her, isn't it? I remember that last fight you had with her. I was listening. I was on your side, even if she was my mother, because I liked you so much; you'd been so good to me— like a father. I remember her putting on her high-and-mighty free-woman stuff, saying you were still a slave to bourgeois morality and jealousy and you thought a woman you loved was a piece of private property you owned. I remember that you got mad and you told her, "I don't like living with a whore, if that's what you mean!"

LARRY. (*Bursts out*) You lie! I never called her that!

PARRITT. (*Goes on as if* LARRY *hadn't spoken*) I think that's why she still respects you, because it was you who left her. You were the only one to beat her to it. She got sick of the others before they did of her. I don't think she ever cared much about them, anyway. She just had to keep on having lovers to prove to herself how free she was (*He pauses—then with a bitter repulsion*) It made home a lousy place. I felt like you did about it. I'd get feeling it was like living in a whore-house—only worse, because she didn't have to make her living—

LARRY. You bastard! She's your mother! Have you no shame?

PARRITT. (*Bitterly*) No! She brought me up to believe that family-respect stuff is all bourgeois, property-owning crap. Why should I be ashamed?

LARRY. (*Making a move to get up*) I've had enough!

PARRITT. (*Catches his arm—pleadingly*) No! Don't leave me! Please! I promise I won't mention her again! (LARRY *sinks back in his chair*) I only did it to make you understand better. I know this isn't the place to— Why didn't you come up to my room, like I asked you? I kept waiting. We could talk everything over there.

LARRY. There's nothing to talk over!

PARRITT. But I've got to talk to you. Or I'll talk to Hickey. He won't let me alone! I feel he knows, anyway! And I know he'd understand, all right—in his way. But I hate his guts! I don't want anything to do with him! I'm scared of him, honest. There's something not human behind his damned grinning and kidding.

LARRY. (*Starts*) Ah! You feel that, too?

PARRITT. (*Pleadingly*) But I can't go on like this. I've got to decide what I've got to do. I've got to tell you, Larry!

LARRY. (*Again starts up*) I won't listen!

PARRITT. (*Again holds him by the arm*) All right! I won't. Don't go! (LARRY *lets himself be pulled down on his chair.* PARRITT *examines his face and becomes insultingly scornful*) Who do you think you're kidding? I know damned well you've guessed—

LARRY. I've guessed nothing!

PARRITT. But I want you to guess now! I'm glad you have! I know now, since Hickey's been after me, that I meant you to guess right from the start. That's why I came to you. (*Hurrying on with an attempt at a plausible frank air that makes what he says seem doubly false*) I want you to understand the reason. You see, I began studying American history. I got admiring Wash-

ington and Jefferson and Jackson and Lincoln. I began to feel patriotic and love this country. I saw it was the best government in the world, where everybody was equal and had a chance. I saw that all the ideas behind the Movement came from a lot of Russians like Bakunin and Kropotkin and were meant for Europe, but we didn't need them here in a democracy where we were free already. I didn't want this country to be destroyed for a damned foreign pipe dream. After all, I'm from old American pioneer stock. I began to feel I was a traitor for helping a lot of cranks and bums and free women plot to overthrow our government. And then I saw it was my duty to my country—

LARRY. (*Nauseated—turns on him*) You stinking rotten liar! Do you think you can fool me with such hypocrite's cant! (*Then turning away*) I don't give a damn what you did! It's on your head—whatever it was! I don't want to know—and I won't know!

PARRITT. (*As if* LARRY *had never spoken—falteringly*) But I never thought Mother would be caught. Please believe that, Larry. You know I never would have—

LARRY. (*His face haggard, drawing a deep breath and closing his eyes—as if he were trying to hammer something into his own brain*) All I know is I'm sick of life! I'm through! I've forgotten myself! I'm drowned and contented on the bottom of a bottle. Honor or dishonor, faith or treachery are nothing to me but the opposites of the same stupidity which is ruler and king of life, and in the end they rot into dust in the same grave. All things are the same meaningless joke to me, for they grin at me from the one skull of death. So go away. You're wasting breath. I've forgotten your mother.

PARRITT. (*Jeers angrily*) The old foolosopher, eh? (*He spits out contemptuously*) You lousy old faker!

LARRY. (*So distracted he pleads weakly*) For the love of God, leave me in peace the little time that's left to me!

PARRITT. Aw, don't pull that pitiful old-man junk on me! You old bastard, you'll never die as long as there's a free drink of whiskey left!

LARRY. (*Stung—furiously*) Look out how you try to taunt me back into life, I warn you! I might remember the thing they call justice there, and the punishment for— (*He checks himself with an effort—then with a real indifference that comes from exhaustion*) I'm old and tired. To hell with you! You're as mad as Hickey, and as big a liar. I'd never let myself believe a word you told me.

PARRITT. (*Threateningly*) The hell you won't! Wait till Hickey gets through with you! (PEARL *and* MARGIE *come in from the bar. At the sight of them,* PARRITT *instantly subsides and becomes self-conscious and defensive, scowling at them and then quickly looking away.*)

MARGIE. (*Eyes him jeeringly*) Why, hello, Tight-wad Kid. Come to join de party? Gee, don't he act bashful, Poil?

PEARL. Yeah. Especially wid his dough. (PARRITT *slinks to a chair at the left end of the table, pretending he hasn't heard them. Suddenly there is a noise of angry, cursing voices and a scuffle from the hall.* PEARL *yells*) Hey, Rocky! Fight in de hall! (ROCKY *and* CHUCK *run from behind the bar curtain and rush into the hall.* ROCKY'S *voice is heard in irritated astonishment, "What de hell?" and then the scuffle stops and* ROCKY *appears holding* CAPTAIN LEWIS *by the arm, followed by* CHUCK *with a similar hold on* GENERAL WETJOEN. *Although these two have been drinking they are both sober, for them. Their faces are sullenly angry, their clothes disarranged from the tussle.*)

ROCKY. (*Leading* LEWIS *forward—astonished, amused and irritated*) Can yuh beat it? I've heard youse two call each odder every name yuh could think of but I never seen you— (*Indignantly*) A swell time to stage your first bout, on Harry's boithday party! What started de scrap?

LEWIS. (*Forcing a casual tone*) Nothing, old chap. Our business, you know. That bloody ass, Hickey, made some insinuation about me, and the boorish Boer had the impertinence to agree with him.

WETJOEN. Dot's a lie! Hickey made joke about me, and this Limey said yes, it was true!

ROCKY. Well, sit down, de bot' of yuh, and cut out de rough stuff. (*He and* CHUCK *dump them down in adjoining chairs toward the left end of the table, where, like two sulky boys, they turn their backs on each other as far as possible in chairs which both face front.*)

MARGIE. (*Laughs*) Jees, lookit de two bums! Like a coupla kids! Kiss and make up, for Gawd's sakes!

ROCKY. Yeah. Harry's party begins in a minute and we don't want no soreheads around.

LEWIS. (*Stiffly*) Very well. In deference to the occasion, I apoloigze, General Wetjoen—pro-vided that you do also.

WETJOEN. (*Sulkily*) I apologize, Captain Lewis—because Harry is my goot friend.

ROCKY. Aw, hell! If yuh can't do better'n dat—! (MOSHER *and* MCGLOIN *enter together from the hall. Both have been drinking but are not drunk.*)

PEARL. Here's de star boarders. (*They advance, their heads together, so interested in a discussion they are oblivious to everyone.*)

MCGLOIN. I'm telling you, Ed, it's serious this time. That bastard, Hickey, has got Harry on the hip. (*As he talks,* MARGIE, PEARL, ROCKY *and* CHUCK *prick up their ears and gather round.* CORA, *at the piano, keeps running through the tune, with soft pedal, and singing the chorus half under her breath, with* JOE *still correcting her mistakes. At the table,* LARRY, PARRITT, WILLIE, WETJOEN *and* LEWIS *sit motionless, staring in front of them.* HUGO *seems asleep in his habitual position*) And you know it isn't going to do us no good if he gets him to take that walk tomorrow.

MOSHER. You're damned right! Harry'll mosey around the ward, dropping in on everyone who knew him when. (*Indignantly*) And they'll all give him a phony glad hand and a ton of good advice about what a sucker he is to stand for us.

MCGLOIN. He's sure to call on Bessie's rela-tions to do a little cryin' over dear Bessie. And you know what that bitch and all her family thought of me.

MOSHER. (*With a flash of his usual humor—rebukingly*) Remember, Lieutenant, you are speaking of my sister! Dear Bessie wasn't a bitch. She was a God-damned bitch! But if you think my loving relatives will have time to discuss you, you don't know them. They'll be too busy telling Harry what a drunken crook I am and saying he ought to have me put in Sing Sing!

MCGLOIN. (*Dejectedly*) Yes, once Bessie's rela-tions get their hooks in him, it'll be as tough for us as if she wasn't gone.

MOSHER. (*Dejectedly*) Yes, Harry has always been weak and easily influenced, and now he's get-ting old he'll be an easy mark for those grafters. (*Then with forced reassurance*) Oh, hell, Mac, we're saps to worry. We've heard Harry pull that bluff about taking a walk every birthday he's had for twenty years.

MCGLOIN. (*Doubtfully*) But Hickey wasn't sick-ing him on those times. Just the opposite. He was asking Harry what he wanted to go out for when there was plenty of whiskey here.

MOSHER. (*With a change to forced carelessness*) Well, after all, I don't care whether he goes out or not. I'm clearing out tomorrow morning anyway. I'm just sorry for you, Mac.

MCGLOIN. (*Resentfully*) You needn't be, then. Ain't I going myself? I was only feeling sorry for you.

MOSHER. Yes, my mind is made up. Hickey may be a lousy, interfering pest, now he's gone teetotal on us, but there's a lot of truth in some of his bull. Hanging around here getting plastered with you, Mac, is pleasant, I won't deny, but the old booze gets you in the end, if you keep lapping it up. It's time I quit for a while. (*With forced enthusiasm*) Besides, I feel the call of the old carefree circus life in my blood again. I'll see the boss tomorrow. It's late in the season but he'll be glad to take me on. And won't all the old gang be tickled to death when I show up on the lot!

MCGLOIN. Maybe—if they've got a rope handy!

MOSHER. (*Turns on him—angrily*) Listen! I'm damned sick of that kidding!

MCGLOIN. You are, are you? Well, I'm sicker of your kidding me about getting reinstated on the Force. And whatever you'd like, I can't spend my life sitting here with you, ruining my stomach with rotgut. I'm tapering off, and in the morning I'll be fresh as a daisy. I'll go and have a private chin with the Commissioner. (*With forced enthusiasm*) Man alive, from what the boys tell me, there's sugar galore these days, and I'll soon be ridin' around in a big red automobile—

MOSHER. (*Derisively—beckoning an imaginary Chinese*) Here, One Lung Hop! Put fresh peanut oil in the lamp and cook the Lieutenant another dozen pills! It's his gowed-up night!

MCGLOIN. (*Stung—pulls back a fist threateningly*) One more crack like that and I'll—!

MOSHER. (*Putting up his fists*) Yes? Just start—! (CHUCK *and* ROCKY *jump between them.*)

ROCKY. Hey! Are you guys nuts? Jees, it's Harry's boithday party! (*They both look guilty*) Sit down and behave.

MOSHER. (*Grumpily*) All right. Only tell him to lay off me. (*He lets* ROCKY *push him in a chair, at the right end of the table, rear.*)

MCGLOIN. (*Grumpily*) Tell him to lay off me. (*He lets* CHUCK *push him into the chair on* MOSHER'S *left. At this moment* HICKEY *bursts in from the hall, bustling and excited.*)

HICKEY. Everything all set? Fine! (*He glances at his watch*) Half a minute to go. Harry's starting down with Jimmy. I had a hard time getting them to move! They'd rather stay hiding up there, kidding each other along. (*He chuckles*) Harry don't even want to remember its his birthday now! (*He hears a noise from the stairs*) Here they come! (*Urgently*) Light the candles! Get ready to play, Cora! Stand up, everybody! Get that wine ready, Chuck and Rocky! (MARGIE *and* PEARL *light the candles on the cake.* CORA *gets her hands set over the piano keys, watching over her shoulder.* ROCKY *and* CHUCK *go in the bar. Everybody at the table stands up mechanically.* HUGO *is the last, suddenly coming to and scrambling to his feet.* HARRY HOPE *and* JIMMY TOMORROW *appear in the hall outside the door.* HICKEY *looks up from his watch*) On the dot! It's twelve! (*Like a cheer leader*) Come on now, everybody, with a Happy Birthday, Harry! (*With his voice leading they all shout* "Happy Birthday, Harry!" *in a spiritless chorus.* HICKEY *signals to* CORA, *who starts playing and singing in a whiskey soprano* "She's the Sunshine of Paradise Alley." HOPE *and* JIMMY *stand in the doorway. Both have been drinking heavily. In* HOPE *the effect is apparent only in a bristling, touchy, pugnacious attitude. It is entirely different from the usual irascible beefing he delights in and which no one takes seriously. Now he really has a chip on his shoulder.* JIMMY, *on the other hand, is plainly drunk, but it has not had the desired effect, for beneath a pathetic assumption of gentlemanly poise, he is obviously frightened and shrinking back within himself.* HICKEY *grabs* HOPE'S *hand and pumps it up and down. For a moment* HOPE *appears unconscious of this hand-shake. Then he jerks his hand away angrily.*)

HOPE. Cut out the glad hand, Hickey. D'you think I'm a sucker? I know you, bejees, you sneaking, lying drummer! (*With rising anger, to the others*) And all you bums! What the hell you trying to do, yelling and raising the roof? Want the cops to close the joint and get my license taken away? (*He yells at* CORA *who has stopped singing but continues to play mechanically with many mistakes*) Hey, you dumb tart, quit banging that box! Bejees, the least you could do is learn the tune!

CORA. (*Stops—deeply hurt*) Aw, Harry! Jees, ain't I— (*Her eyes begin to fill.*)

HOPE. (*Glaring at the other girls*) And you two hookers, screaming at the top of your lungs! What d'you think this is, a dollar cathouse? Bejees, that's where you belong!

PEARL. (*Miserably*) Aw, Harry— (*She begins to cry.*)

MARGIE. Jees, Harry, I never thought you'd say that—like yuh meant it. (*She puts her arm around* PEARL—*on the verge of tears herself*) Aw, don't bawl, Poil. He don't mean it.

HICKEY. (*Reproachfully*) Now, Harry! Don't take it out on the gang because you're upset about yourself. Anyway, I've promised you you'll come through all right, haven't I? So quit worrying. (*He slaps* HOPE *on the back encouragingly.* HOPE *flashes him a glance of hate*) Be yourself, Governor. You don't want to bawl out the old gang just when they're congratulating you on your birthday, do you? Hell, that's no way!

HOPE. (*Looking guilty and shamefaced now—forcing an unconvincing attempt at his natural tone*) Bejees, they ain't as dumb as you. They know I was only kidding them. They know I appreciate their congratulations. Don't you, fellers? (*There is a listless chorus of "Sure, Harry," "Yes," "Of course we do," etc. He comes forward to the two girls, with* JIMMY *and* HICKEY *following him, and pats them clumsily*) Bejees, I like you broads. You know I was only kidding. (*Instantly they forgive him and smile affectionately.*)

MARGIE. Sure we know, Harry.

PEARL. Sure.

HICKEY. (*Grinning*) Sure. Harry's the greatest kidder in this dump and that's saying something! Look how he's kidded himself for twenty years! (*As* HOPE *gives him a bitter, angry glance, he digs him in the ribs with his elbow playfully*) Unless I'm wrong, Governor, and I'm betting I'm not. We'll soon know, eh? Tomorrow morning. No, by God, it's *this* morning now!

JIMMY. (*With a dazed dread*) *This* morning?

HICKEY. Yes, it's today at last, Jimmy. (*He pats him on the back*) Don't be so scared! I've promised I'll help you.

JIMMY. (*Trying to hide his dread behind an offended, drunken dignity*) I don't understand you. Kindly remember I'm fully capable of settling my own affairs!

HICKEY. (*Earnestly*) Well, isn't that exactly what I want you to do, settle with yourself once and for all? (*He speaks in his ear in confidential warning*) Only watch out on the booze, Jimmy. You know, not too much from now on. You've had a lot already, and you don't want to let yourself duck out of it by being too drunk to move— not this time! (JIMMY *gives him a guilty, stricken look and turns away and slumps into the chair on* MOSHER'S *right.*)

HOPE. (*To* MARGIE—*still guiltily*) Bejees, Margie, you know I didn't mean it. It's that lousy drummer riding me that's got my goat.

MARGIE. I know. (*She puts a protecting arm around* HOPE *and turns him to face the table with the cake and presents*) Come on. You ain't noticed your cake yet. Ain't it grand?

HOPE. (*Trying to brighten up*) Say, that's pretty. Ain't ever had a cake since Bessie—Six candles. Each for ten years, eh? Bejees, that's thoughtful of you.

PEARL. It was Hickey got it.

HOPE. (*His tone forced*) Well, it was thoughtful of him. He means well, I guess. (*His eyes, fixed on the cake, harden angrily*) To hell with his cake. (*He starts to turn away.* PEARL *grabs his arm.*)

PEARL. Wait, Harry. Yuh ain't seen de presents from Margie and me and Cora and Chuck and Rocky. And dere's a watch all engraved wid your name and de date from Hickey.

HOPE. To hell with it! Bejees, he can keep it! (*This time he does turn away.*)

PEARL. Jees, he ain't even goin' to look at our presents.

MARGIE. (*Bitterly*) Dis is all wrong. We gotta put some life in dis party or I'll go nuts! Hey, Cora, what's de matter wid dat box? Can't yuh play for Harry? Yuh don't have to stop just because he kidded yuh!

HOPE. (*Rouses himself—with forced heartiness*) Yes, come on, Cora. You was playing it fine. (CORA *begins to play half-heartedly.* HOPE *suddenly becomes almost tearfully sentimental*) It was Bessie's favorite tune. She was always singing it. It brings her back. I wish— (*He chokes up.*)

HICKEY. (*Grins at him—amusedly*) Yes, we've all heard you tell us you thought the world of her, Governor.

HOPE. (*Looks at him with frightened suspicion*) Well, so I did, bejees! Everyone knows I did! (*Threateningly*) Bejees, if you say I didn't—

HICKEY. (*Soothingly*) Now, Governor. I didn't say anything. You're the only one knows the truth about that. (HOPE *stares at him confusedly.* CORA *continues to play. For a moment there is a pause, broken by* JIMMY TOMORROW *who speaks with muzzy, self-pitying melancholy out of a sentimental dream.*)

JIMMY. Marjorie's favorite song was "Loch Lomond." She was beautiful and she played the piano beautifully and she had a beautiful voice. (*With gentle sorrow*) You were lucky, Harry. Bessie died. But there are more bitter sorrows than losing the woman one loves by the hand of death—

HICKEY. (*With an amused wink at* HOPE) Now, listen, Jimmy, you needn't go on. We've all heard that story about how you came back to Cape Town and found her in the hay with a staff officer. We know you like to believe that was what started you on the booze and ruined your life.

JIMMY. (*Stammers*) I—I'm talking to Harry. Will you kindly keep out of— (*With a pitiful defiance*) My life is not ruined!

HICKEY. (*Ignoring this—with a kidding grin*) But I'll bet when you admit the truth to yourself, you'll confess you were pretty sick of her hating you for getting drunk. I'll bet you were really damned relieved when she gave you such a good excuse. (JIMMY *stares at him strickenly.* HICKEY *pats him on the back again—with sincere sympathy*) I know how it is, Jimmy. I— (*He stops abruptly and for a second he seems to lose his self-assurance and become confused.*)

LARRY. (*Seizing on this with vindictive relish*) Ha! So that's what happened to you, is it? Your iceman joke finally came home to roost, did it? (*He grins tauntingly*) You should have remembered there's truth in the old superstition that you'd better look out what you call because in the end it comes to you!

HICKEY. (*Himself again—grins to* LARRY *kiddingly*) Is that a fact, Larry? Well, well! Then you'd better watch out how you keep calling for that old Big Sleep! (LARRY *starts and for a second looks superstitiously frightened. Abruptly* HICKEY *changes to his jovial, bustling, master-of-ceremonies manner*) But what are we waiting for, boys and girls? Let's start the party rolling! (*He shouts to the bar*) Hey, Chuck and Rocky! Bring on the big surprise! Governor, you sit at the head of the table here. (*He makes* HARRY *sit down on the chair at the end of the table, right. To* MARGIE *and* PEARL) Come on, girls, sit down. (*They sit side by side on* JIMMY'S *right.* HICKEY *bustles down to the left end of table*) I'll sit here at the foot. (*He sits, with* CORA *on his left and* JOE *on her left.* ROCKY *and* CHUCK *appear from the bar, each bearing a big tray laden with schooners of champagne which they start shoving in front of each member of the party.*)

ROCKY. (*With forced cheeriness*) Real Champagne, bums! Cheer up! What is dis, a funeral? Jees, mixin' champagne wid Harry's redeye will knock yuh paralyzed! Ain't yuh never satisfied? (*He and* CHUCK *finish serving out the schooners, grab the last two themselves and sit down in the two vacant chairs remaining near the middle of the table. As they do so,* HICKEY *rises, a schooner in his hand.*)

HICKEY. (*Rapping on the table for order when there is nothing but a dead silence*) Order! Order, Ladies and Gents! (*He catches* LARRY'S *eyes on the glass in his hand*) Yes, Larry, I'm going to drink with you this time. To prove I'm not teetotal because I'm afraid booze would make me spill my secrets, as you think. (LARRY *looks sheepish.* HICKEY *chuckles and goes on*) No, I gave you the simple truth about that. I don't need booze or anything else any more. But I want to be sociable and propose a toast in honor of our old friend, Harry, and drink it with you. (*His eyes fix on* HUGO, *who is out again, his head on his plate—To* CHUCK, *who is on* HUGO's *left*) Wake up our demon bombtosser, Chuck. We don't want corpses at this feast.

CHUCK. (*Gives* HUGO *a shake*) Hey, Hugo, come up for air! Don't yuh see de champagne? (HUGO *blinks around and giggles foolishly*)

HUGO. Ve vill eat birthday cake and trink champagne beneath the villow tree! (*He grabs his schooner and takes a greedy gulp—then sets it back on the table with a grimace of distaste—in a strange, arrogantly disdainful tone, as if he were rebuking a butler*) Dis vine is unfit to trink. It has not properly been iced.

HICKEY. (*Amusedly*) Always a high-toned swell at heart, eh, Hugo? God help us poor bums if you'd ever get to telling us where to get off! You'd have been drinking our blood beneath those willow trees! (*He chuckles.* HUGO *shrinks back in his chair, blinking at him, but* HICKEY *is now looking up the table at* HOPE. *He starts his toast, and as he goes on he becomes more moved and obviously sincere*) Here's the toast, Ladies and Gents! Here's to Harry Hope, who's been a friend in need to every one of us! Here's to the old Governor, the best sport and the kindest, biggest-hearted guy in the world! Here's wishing you all the luck there is, Harry, and long life and happiness! Come on, everybody! To Harry! Bottoms up! (*They have all caught his sincerity with eager relief. They raise their schooners with an enthusiastic chorus of "Here's how, Harry!" "Here's luck, Harry!" etc., and gulp half the wine down,* HICKEY *leading them in this.*)

HOPE. (*Deeply moved—his voice husky*) Bejees, thanks, all of you. Bejees, Hickey, you old son of a bitch, that's white of you! Bejees, I know you meant it, too.

HICKEY. (*Moved*) Of course I meant it, Harry, old friend! And I mean it when I say I hope today will be the biggest day in your life, and in the lives of everyone here, the beginning of a new life of peace and contentment where no pipe dreams can ever nag at you again. Here's to that, Harry! (*He drains the remainder of his drink, but this time he drinks alone. In an instant the attitude of everyone has reverted to uneasy, suspicious defensiveness.*)

ROCKY. (*Growls*) Aw, forget dat bughouse line of bull for a minute, can't yuh?

HICKEY. (*Sitting down—good-naturedly*) You're right, Rocky, I'm talking too much. It's Harry we want to hear from. Come on, Harry! (*He pounds his schooner on the table*) Speech! Speech! (*They try to recapture their momentary enthusiasm, rap their schooners on the table, call "Speech," but there is a hollow ring in it.* HOPE *gets to his feet reluctantly, with a forced smile, a smoldering resentment beginning to show in his manner.*)

HOPE. (*Lamely*) Bejees, I'm no good at speeches. All I can say is thanks to everybody again for remembering me on my birthday. (*Bitterness coming out*) Only don't think because I'm sixty I'll be a bigger damned fool easy mark than ever! No, bejees! Like Hickey says, it's going to be a new day! This dump has got to be run like other dumps, so I can make some money and not just split even. People has got to pay what they owe me! I'm not running a damned orphan asylum for bums and crooks! Nor a God-damned hooker shanty, either! Nor an Old Men's Home for lousy Anarchist tramps that ought to be in jail! I'm sick of being played for a sucker! (*They stare at him with stunned, bewildered hurt. He goes on in a sort of furious desperation, as if he hated himself for every word he said, and yet couldn't stop*) And don't think you're kidding me right now, either! I know damned well you're giving me the laugh behind my back, thinking to yourselves, The old, lying, pipe-dreaming faker, we've heard his bull about taking a walk around the ward for years, he'll never make it! He's yellow, he ain't got the guts, he's scared he'll find out— (*He glares around at them almost with hatred*) But I'll show you, bejees! (*He glares at* HICKEY) I'll show you, too, you son of a bitch of a frying-pan-peddling bastard!

HICKEY. (*Heartily encouraging*) That's the stuff, Harry! Of course you'll try to show me! That's what I want you to do! (HARRY *glances at him with helpless dread—then drops his eyes and looks furtively around the table. All at once he becomes miserably contrite.*)

HOPE. (*His voice catching*) Listen, all of you! Bejees, forgive me. I lost my temper! I ain't feeling well! I got a hell of a grouch on! Bejees, you know you're all as welcome here as the flowers in May! (*They look at him with eager forgiveness.* ROCKY *is the first one who can voice it.*)

ROCKY. Aw, sure, Boss, you're always aces wid us, see?

HICKEY. (*Rises to his feet again. He addresses them now with the simple, convincing sincerity of one making a confession of which he is genuinely ashamed*) Listen, everybody! I know you are sick of my gabbing, but I think this is the spot where I owe it to you to do a little explaining and apologize for some of the rough stuff I've had to pull on you. I know how it must look to you. As if I was a damned busybody who was not only interfering in your private business, but even sicking some of you on to nag at each other. Well, I have to admit that's true, and I'm damned sorry about it. But it simply had to be done! You must believe that! You know old Hickey. I was never one to start trouble. But this time I had to—for your own good! I had to make you help me with each other. I saw I couldn't do what I was after alone. Not in the time at my disposal. I knew when I came here I wouldn't be able to stay with you long. I'm slated to leave on a trip. I saw I'd have to hustle and use every means I could. (*With a joking boastfulness*) Why, if I had enough time, I'd get a lot of sport out of selling my line of salvation to each of you all by my lonesome. Like it was fun in the old days, when I traveled house to house, to convince some dame, who was sicking the dog on me, her house wouldn't be properly furnished unless she bought another wash boiler. And I could do it with you, all right. I know every one of you, inside and out, by heart. I may have been drunk when I've been here before, but old Hickey could never be so drunk he didn't have to see through people. I mean, everyone except himself. And, finally, he had to see through himself, too. (*He pauses. They stare at him, bitter, uneasy and fascinated. His manner changes to deep earnestness*) But here's the point to get. I swear I'd never act like I have if I wasn't absolutely sure it will be worth it to you in the end, after you're rid of the damned guilt that makes you lie to yourselves you're something you're not, and the remorse that nags at you and makes you hide behind lousy pipe dreams about tomorrow. You'll be in a today where there is no yesterday or tomorrow to worry you. You won't give a damn what you are any more. I wouldn't say this unless I knew, Brothers and Sisters. This peace is real! It's a fact! I know! Because I've got it! Here! Now! Right in front of you! You see the difference in me! You remember how I used to be! Even when I had two quarts of rotgut under my belt and joked and sang "Sweet Adeline," I still felt like a guilty skunk. But you can all see that I don't give a damn about anything now. And I promise you, by the time this day is over, I'll have every one of you feeling the same way! (*He pauses. They stare at him fascinatedly. He adds with a grin*) I guess that'll be about all from me, boys and girls—for the present. So let's get on with the party. (*He starts to sit down.*)

LARRY. (*Sharply*) Wait! (*Insistently—with a sneer*) I think it would help us poor pipe-dreaming sinners along the sawdust trail to salvation if you told us now what it was happened to you that converted you to this great peace you've found. (*More and more with a deliberate, provocative taunting*) I notice you didn't deny it when I asked you about the iceman. Did this great revelation of the evil habit of dreaming about tomorrow come to you after you found your wife was sick of you? (*While he is speaking the faces of the gang have lighted up vindictively, as if all at once they saw a chance to revenge themselves. As he finishes, a chorus of sneering taunts begins, punctuated by nasty, jeering laughter.*)

HOPE. Bejees, you've hit it, Larry! I've noticed he hasn't shown her picture around this time!

MOSHER. He hasn't got it! The iceman took it away from him!

MARGIE. Jees, look at him! Who could blame her?

PEARL. She must be hard up to fall for an iceman!

CORA. Imagine a sap like him advisin' me and Chuck to git married!

CHUCK. Yeah! He done so good wid it!

JIMMY. At least I can say Marjorie chose an officer and a gentleman.

LEWIS. Come to look at you, Hickey, old chap, you've sprouted horns like a bloody antelope!

WETJOEN. Pigger, py Gott! Like a water buffalo's!

WILLIE. (*Sings to his Sailor Lad tune*)

"Come up," she cried, "my iceman lad,
    And you and I'll agree—"

(*They all join in a jeering chorus, rapping with knuckles or glasses on the table at the indicated spot in the lyric*)

"And I'll show you the prettiest (*Rap, rap, rap*)
    That ever you did see!"

(*A roar of derisive, dirty laughter. But* HICKEY *has remained unmoved by all this taunting. He grins good-naturedly, as if he enjoyed the joke at his expense, and joins in the laughter.*)

HICKEY. Well, boys and girls, I'm glad to see you getting in good spirits for Harry's party, even if the joke is on me. I admit I asked for it by always pulling that iceman gag in the old days. So laugh all you like. (*He pauses. They do not laugh now. They are again staring at him with baffled uneasiness. He goes on thoughtfully*) Well, this forces my hand, I guess, your bringing up the subject of Evelyn. I didn't want to tell you yet. It's hardly an appropriate time. I meant to wait until the party was over. But you're getting the wrong idea about poor Evelyn, and I've got to stop that. (*He pauses again. There is a tense stillness in the room. He bows his head a little and says quietly*) I'm sorry to tell you my dearly beloved wife is dead. (*A gasp comes from the stunned company. They look away from him, shocked and miserably ashamed of themselves, except* LARRY *who continues to stare at him.*)

LARRY. (*Aloud to himself with a superstitious shrinking*) Be God, I felt he'd brought the touch of death on him! (*Then suddenly he is even more ashamed of himself than the others and stammers*) Forgive me, Hickey! I'd like to cut my dirty tongue out! (*This releases a chorus of shame-faced mumbles from the crowd. "Sorry,* HICKEY." "*I'm sorry,* HICKEY." "*We're sorry,* HICKEY."*)

HICKEY. (*Looking around at them—in a kindly, reassuring tone*) Now look here, everybody. You mustn't let this be a wet blanket on Harry's party. You're still getting me all wrong. There's no reason— You see, I don't feel any grief. (*They gaze at him startledly. He goes on with convincing sincerity*) I've got to feel glad, for her sake. Because she's at peace. She's rid of me at last. Hell, I don't have to tell you—you all know what I was like. You can imagine what she went through, married to a no-good cheater and drunk like I was. And there was no way out of it for her. Because she loved me. But now she is at peace like she always longed to be. So why should I feel sad? She wouldn't want me to feel sad. Why, all that Evelyn ever wanted out of life was to make me happy. (*He stops, looking around at them with a simple, gentle frankness. They stare at him in bewildered, incredulous confusion.*)

CURTAIN

ACT THREE

SCENE: *Barroom of* HARRY HOPE'S, *including a part of what had been the back room in Acts One and Two. In the right wall are two big windows, with the swinging doors to the street between them. The bar itself is at rear. Behind it is a mirror, covered with white mosquito netting to keep off the flies, and a shelf on which are barrels of cheap whiskey with spiggots and a small show case of bottled goods. At left of the bar is the doorway to the hall. There is a table at left, front, of barroom proper, with four chairs. At right, front, is a small free-lunch counter, facing left, with a space between it and the window for the dealer to stand when he dishes out soup at the noon hour. Over the mirror behind the bar are framed photographs of Richard Croker and Big Tim Sullivan, flanked by framed lithographs of John L. Sullivan and Gentleman Jim Corbett in ring costume.*

At left, in what had been the back room, with the dividing curtain drawn, the banquet table of Act Two has been broken up, and the tables are again in the crowded arrangement of Act One. Of these, we see one in the front row with five chairs at left of the barroom table, another with five chairs at left-rear of it, a third back by the rear wall with five chairs, and finally, at extreme left-front, one with four chairs, partly on and partly off stage, left.

It is around the middle of the morning of

HOPE's *birthday, a hot summer day. There is sunlight in the street outside, but it does not hit the windows and the light in the back-room section is dim.*

JOE MOTT *is moving around, a box of sawdust under his arm, strewing it over the floor. His manner is sullen, his face set in gloom. He ignores everyone. As the scene progresses, he finishes his sawdusting job, goes behind the lunch counter and cuts loaves of bread.* ROCKY *is behind the bar, wiping it, washing glasses, etc. He wears his working clothes, sleeves rolled up. He looks sleepy, irritable and worried. At the barroom table, front,* LARRY *sits in a chair, facing right-front. He has no drink in front of him. He stares ahead, deep in harried thought. On his right, in a chair facing right,* HUGO *sits sprawled forward, arms and head on the table as usual, a whiskey glass beside his limp hand. At rear of the front table at left of them, in a chair facing left,* PARRITT *is sitting. He is staring in front of him in a tense, strained immobility.*

As the curtain rises, ROCKY *finishes his work behind the bar. He comes forward and drops wearily in the chair at right of* LARRY's *table, facing left.*

ROCKY. Nuttin' now till de noon rush from de Market. I'm goin' to rest my fanny. (*Irritably*) If I ain't a sap to let Chuck kid me into workin' his time so's he can take de mornin' off. But I got sick of arguin' wid 'im. I says, "Aw right, git married! What's it to me?" Hickey's got de bot' of dem bugs. (*Bitterly*) Some party last night, huh? Jees, what a funeral! It was jinxed from de start, but his tellin' about his wife croakin' put de K.O. on it.

LARRY. Yes, it turned out it wasn't a birthday feast but a wake!

ROCKY. Him promisin' he'd cut out de bughouse bull about peace—and den he went on talkin' and talkin' like he couldn't stop! And all de gang sneakin' upstairs, leavin' free booze and eats like dey was poison! It didn't do dem no good if dey thought dey'd shake him. He's been hoppin' from room to room all night. Yuh can't stop him. He's got his Reform Wave goin' strong dis mornin'! Did yuh notice him drag Jimmy out de foist ting to get his laundry and his clothes pressed so he wouldn't have no excuse? And he give Willie de dough to buy his stuff back from Solly's. And all de rest been brushin' and shavin' demselves wid de shakes—

LARRY. (*Defiantly*) He didn't come to my room! He's afraid I might ask him a few questions.

ROCKY. (*Scornfully*) Yeah? It don't look to me

he's scared of yuh. I'd say you was scared of him.

LARRY. (*Stung*) You'd lie, then!

PARRITT. (*Jerks round to look at* LARRY—*sneeringly*) Don't let him kid you, Rocky. He had his door locked. I couldn't get in, either.

ROCKY. Yeah, who d'yuh tink yuh're kiddin', Larry? He's showed you up, aw right. Like he says, if yuh was so anxious to croak, why wouldn't yuh hop off your fire escape long ago?

LARRY. (*Defiantly*) Because it'd be a coward's quitting, that's why!

PARRITT. He's all quitter, Rocky. He's a yellow old faker!

LARRY. (*Turns on him*) You lying punk! Remember what I warned you—!

ROCKY. (*Scowls at* PARRITT) Yeah, keep outta dis, you! Where d'yuh get a license to butt in? Shall I give him de bum's rush, Larry? If you don't want him around, nobody else don't.

LARRY. (*Forcing an indifferent tone*) No. Let him stay. I don't mind him. He's nothing to me. (ROCKY *shrugs his shoulders and yawns sleepily.*)

PARRITT. You're right, I have nowhere to go now. You're the only one in the world I can turn to.

ROCKY. (*Drowsily*) Yuh're a soft old sap, Larry. He's a no-good louse like Hickey. He don't belong. (*He yawns*) I'm all in. Not a wink of sleep. Can't keep my peepers open. (*His eyes close and his head nods.* PARRITT *gives him a glance and then gets up and slinks over to slide into the chair on* LARRY's *left, between him and* ROCKY. LARRY *shrinks away, but determinedly ignores him.*)

PARRITT. (*Bending toward him—in a low, ingratiating, apologetic voice*) I'm sorry for riding you, Larry. But you get my goat when you act as if you didn't care a damn what happened to me, and keep your door locked so I can't talk to you. (*Then hopefully*) But that was to keep Hickey out, wasn't it? I don't blame you. I'm getting to hate him. I'm getting more and more scared of him. Especially since he told us his wife was dead. It's that queer feeling he gives me that I'm mixed up with him some way. I don't know why, but it started me thinking about Mother—as if she was dead. (*With a strange undercurrent of something like satisfaction in his pitying tone*) I suppose she might as well be. Inside herself, I mean. It must kill her when she thinks of me—I know she doesn't want to, but she can't help it. After all, I'm her only kid. She used to spoil me and made a pet of me. Once in a great while, I mean. When she remembered me. As if she wanted to make up for something. As if she felt guilty. So she must have loved me a little, even if she never let it interfere with her freedom. (*With a strange pa-*

thetic wistfulness) Do you know, Larry, I once had a sneaking suspicion that maybe, if the truth was known, you were my father.

LARRY. (*Violently*) You damned fool! Who put that insane idea in your head? You know it's a lie! Anyone in the Coast crowd could tell you I never laid eyes on your mother till after you were born.

PARRITT. Well, I'd hardly ask them, would I? I know you're right, though, because I asked her. She brought me up to be frank and ask her anything, and she'd always tell me the truth. (*Abruptly*) But I was talking about how she must feel now about me. My getting through with the Movement. She'll never forgive that. The Movement is her life. And it must be the final knockout for her if she knows I was the one who sold—

LARRY. Shut up, damn you!

PARRITT. It'll kill her. And I'm sure she knows it must have been me. (*Suddenly with desperate urgency*) But I never thought the cops would get her! You've got to believe that! You've got to see what my only reason was! I'll admit what I told you last night was a lie—that bunk about getting patriotic and my duty to my country. But here's the true reason, Larry—the only reason! It was just for money! I got stuck on a whore and wanted dough to blow in on her and have a good time! That's all I did it for! Just money! Honest! (*He has the terrible grotesque air, in confessing his sordid baseness, of one who gives an excuse which exonerates him from any real guilt.*)

LARRY. (*Grabs him by the shoulder and shakes him*) God damn you, shut up! What the hell is it to me? (ROCKY *starts awake.*)

ROCKY. What's comin' off here?

LARRY. (*Controlling himself*) Nothing. This gabby young punk was talking my ear off, that's all. He's a worse pest than Hickey.

ROCKY. (*Drowsily*) Yeah, Hickey— Say, listen, what d'yuh mean about him bein' scared you'd ask him questions? What questions?

LARRY. Well, I feel he's hiding something. You notice he didn't say what his wife died of.

ROCKY. (*Rebukingly*) Aw, lay off dat. De poor guy— What are yuh gettin' at, anyway? Yuh don't tink it's just a gag of his?

LARRY. I don't. I'm damned sure he's brought death here with him. I feel the cold touch of it on him.

ROCKY. Aw, bunk! You got croakin' on de brain, Old Cemetery. (*Suddenly* ROCKY'S *eyes widen*) Say! D'yuh mean yuh tink she committed suicide, 'count of his cheatin' or someting?

LARRY. (*Grimly*) It wouldn't surprise me. I'd be the last to blame her.

ROCKY. (*Scornfully*) But dat's crazy! Jees, if she'd done dat, he wouldn't tell us he was glad about it, would he? He ain't dat big a bastard.

PARRITT. (*Speaks up from his own preoccupation—strangely*) You know better than that, Larry. You know she'd never commit suicide. She's like you. She'll hang on to life even when there's nothing left but—

LARRY. (*Stung—turns on him viciously*) And how about you? Be God, if you had any guts or decency—! (*He stops guiltily.*)

PARRITT. (*Sneeringly*) I'd take that hop off your fire escape you're too yellow to take, I suppose?

LARRY. (*As if to himself*) No! Who am I to judge? I'm done with judging.

PARRITT. (*Tauntingly*) Yes, I suppose you'd like that, wouldn't you?

ROCKY. (*Irritably mystified*) What de hell's all dis about? (*To* PARRITT) What d'you know about Hickey's wife? How d'yuh know she didn't—?

LARRY. (*With forced belittling casualness*) He doesn't. Hickey's addled the little brains he's got. Shove him back to his own table, Rocky. I'm sick of him.

ROCKY. (*To* PARRITT, *threateningly*) Yuh heard Larry? I'd like an excuse to give yuh a good punch in de snoot. So move quick!

PARRITT. (*Gets up—to* LARRY) If you think moving to another table will get rid of me! (*He moves away—then adds with bitter reproach*) Gee, Larry, that's a hell of a way to treat me, when I've trusted you, and I need your help. (*He sits down in his old place and sinks into a wounded, self-pitying brooding.*)

ROCKY. (*Going back to his train of thought*) Jees, if she committed suicide, yuh got to feel sorry for Hickey, huh? Yuh can understand how he'd go bughouse and not be responsible for all de crazy stunts he's stagin' here. (*Then puzzledly*) But how can yuh be sorry for him when he says he's glad she croaked, and yuh can tell he means it? (*With weary exasperation*) Aw, nuts! I don't get nowhere tryin' to figger his game. (*His face hardening*) But I know dis. He better lay off me and my stable! (*He pauses—then sighs*) Jees, Larry, what a night dem two pigs give me! When de party went dead, dey pinched a coupla bottles and brung dem up deir room and got stinko. I don't get a wink of sleep, see? Just as I'd drop off on a chair here, dey'd come down lookin' for trouble. Or else dey'd raise hell upstairs, laughin' and singin', so I'd get scared dey'd get de joint pinched and go up to tell dem to can de noise. And every time dey'd crawl my frame wid de same old argument. Dey'd say, "So yuh agreed wid Hickey, do yuh, yuh dirty little Ginny? We're whores, are we? Well, we agree wid Hickey about you, see! Yuh're nuttin' but a lousy pimp!" Den I'd slap dem. Not beat 'em up, like a pimp would. Just slap dem. But it don't do no good. Dey'd keep at it over and over. Jees, I get de earache just thinkin' of it! "Listen," dey'd say, "if we're whores we gotta right to have a reg'lar pimp and not stand for no punk imitation! We're sick of wearin' out our dogs poundin' sidewalks for a double-crossin' bartender, when all de thanks we get is he looks down on us. We'll find a guy who really needs us to take care of him and ain't ashamed of it. Don't expect us to work tonight, 'cause we won't, see? Not if de streets was blocked wid sailors! We're goin' on strike and yuh can like it or lump it!" (*He shakes his head*) Whores goin' on strike! Can yuh tie dat? (*Going on with his story*) Dey says, "We're takin' a holiday. We're goin' to beat it down to Coney Island and shoot the chutes and maybe we'll come back and maybe we won't. And you can go to hell!" So dey put on deir lids and beat it, de bot' of dem stinko. (*He sighs dejectedly. He seems grotesquely like a harried family man, henpecked and brow-beaten by a nagging wife.* LARRY *is deep in his own bitter preoccupation and hasn't listened to him.* CHUCK *enters from the hall at rear. He has his straw hat with the gaudy band in his hand and wears a Sunday-best blue suit with a high stiff collar. He looks sleepy, hot, uncomfortable and grouchy.*)

CHUCK. (*Glumly*) Hey, Rocky. Cora wants a sherry flip. For her noives.

ROCKY. (*Turns indignantly*) Sherry flip! Christ, she don't need nuttin' for her noive! What's she tink dis is, de Waldorf?

CHUCK. Yeah, I told her, what would we use for sherry, and dere wasn't no egg unless she laid one. She says, "Is dere a law yuh can't go out and buy de makings, yuh big tramp?" (*Resentfully puts his straw hat on his head at a defiant tilt*) To hell wid her! She'll drink booze or nuttin'! (*He goes behind the bar to draw a glass of whiskey from a barrel.*)

ROCKY. (*Sarcastically*) Jees, a guy oughta give his bride anything she wants on de weddin' day, I should tink! (*As* CHUCK *comes from behind the bar,* ROCKY *surveys him derisively*) Pipe de bride-groom, Larry! All dolled up for de killin'! (LARRY *pays no attention.*)

CHUCK. Aw, shut up!

ROCKY. One week on dat farm in Joisey, dat's what I give yuh! Yuh'll come runnin' in here some night yellin' for a shot of booze 'cause de crickets is after yuh! (*Disgustedly*) Jees, Chuck, dat louse Hickey's coitinly made a prize coupla suckers outa youse.

CHUCK. (*Unguardedly*) Yeah. I'd like to give him one sock in de puss—just one! (*Then angrily*) Aw, can dat! What's he got to do wid it? Ain't we always said we was goin' to? So we're goin' to, see? And don't give me no argument! (*He stares at* ROCKY *truculently. But* ROCKY *only shrugs his shoulders with weary disgust and* CHUCK *subsides into complaining gloom*) If on'y Cora'd cut out de beefin'. She don't gimme a minute's rest all night. De same old stuff over and over! Do I really want to marry her? I says, "Sure, Baby, why not?" She says, "Yeah, but after a week yuh'll be tinkin' what a sap you was. Yuh'll make dat an excuse to go off on a periodical, and den I'll be tied for life to a no-good soak, and de foist ting I know yuh'll have me out hustlin' again, your own wife!" Den she'd bust out cryin', and I'd get sore. "Yuh're a liar," I'd say. "I ain't never taken your dough 'cept when I was drunk and not workin'!" "Yeah," she'd say, "and how long will yuh stay sober now? Don't tink yuh can kid me wid dat water-wagon bull! I've heard it too often." Dat'd make me sore and I'd say, "Don't call me a liar. But I wish I was drunk right now, because if I was, yuh wouldn't be keepin' me awake all night beefin'. If yuh opened your yap, I'd knock de stuffin' outa yuh!" Den she'd yell, "Dat's a sweet way to talk to de goil yuh're goin' to marry." (*He sighs explosively*) Jees, she's got me hangin' on de ropes! (*He glances with vengeful yearning at the drink of whiskey in his hand*) Jees, would I like to get a quart of dis redeye under my belt!

ROCKY. Well, why de hell don't yuh?

CHUCK. (*Instantly suspicious and angry*) Sure! You'd like dat, wouldn't yuh? I'm wise to you! Yuh don't wanta see me get married and settle down like a reg'lar guy! Yuh'd like me to stay paralyzed all de time, so's I'd be like you, a lousy pimp!

ROCKY. (*Springs to his feet, his face hardened viciously*) Listen! I don't take dat even from you, see!

CHUCK. (*Puts his drink on the bar and clenches his fists*) Yeah? Wanta make sometin' of it? (*Jeeringly*) Don't make me laugh! I can lick ten of youse wid one mit!

ROCKY. (*Reaching for his hip pocket*) Not wid lead in your belly, yuh won't!

JOE. (*Has stopped cutting when the quarrel started—expostulating*) Hey, you, Rocky and Chuck! Cut it out! You's ole friends! Don't let dat Hickey make you crazy!

CHUCK. (*Turns on him*) Keep outa our business, yuh black bastard!

ROCKY. (*Like* CHUCK, *turns on* JOE, *as if their own quarrel was forgotten and they became natu-*

618] *Eugene O'Neill*

ral allies against an alien) Stay where yuh belong, yuh doity nigger!

JOE. (*Snarling with rage, springs from behind the lunch counter with the bread knife in his hand*) You white sons of bitches! I'll rip your guts out! (CHUCK *snatches a whiskey bottle from the bar and raises it above his head to hurl at* JOE. ROCKY *jerks a short-barreled, nickel-plated revolver from his hip pocket. At this moment* LARRY *pounds on the table with his fist and bursts into a sardonic laugh.*)

LARRY. That's it! Murder each other, you damned loons, with Hickey's blessing! Didn't I tell you he'd brought death with him? (*His interruption startles them. They pause to stare at him, their fighting fury suddenly dies out and they appear deflated and sheepish.*)

ROCKY. (*To* JOE) Aw right, you. Leggo dat shiv and I'll put dis gat away. (JOE *sullenly goes back behind the counter and slaps the knife on top of it.* ROCKY *slips the revolver back in his pocket.* CHUCK *lowers the bottle to the bar.* HUGO, *who has awakened and raised his head when* LARRY *pounded on the table, now giggles foolishly.*)

HUGO. Hello, leedle peoples! Neffer mind! Soon you vill eat hot dogs beneath the villow trees and trink free vine— (*Abruptly in a haughty fastidious tone*) The champagne vas not properly iced. (*With guttural anger*) Gottamned liar, Hickey! Does that prove I vant to be aristocrat? I love only the proletariat! I vill lead them! I vill be like a Gott to them! They vill be my slaves! (*He stops in bewildered self-amazement—to* LARRY *appealingly*) I am very trunk, no, Larry? I talk foolishness. I am so trunk, Larry, old friend, am I not, I don't know vhat I say?

LARRY. (*Pityingly*) You're raving drunk, Hugo. I've never seen you so paralyzed. Lay your head down now and sleep it off.

HUGO. (*Gratefully*) Yes. I should sleep. I am too crazy trunk. (*He puts his head on his arms and closes his eyes.*)

JOE. (*Behind the lunch counter—brooding superstitiously*) You's right, Larry. Bad luck come in de door when Hickey come. I's an ole gamblin' man and I knows bad luck when I feels it! (*Then defiantly*) But it's white man's bad luck. He can't jinx me! (*He comes from behind the counter and goes to the bar—addressing* ROCKY *stiffly*) De bread's cut and I's finished my job. Do I get de drink I's earned? (ROCKY *gives him a hostile look but shoves a bottle and glass at him. Joe pours a brimful drink—sullenly*) I's finished wid dis dump for keeps. (*He takes a key from his pocket and slaps it on the bar*) Here's de key to my room. I ain't comin' back. I's goin' to my own folks where I belong. I don't stay where I's not wanted. I's sick and tired of messin' 'round wid white men. (*He gulps down his drink—then looking around defiantly he deliberately throws his whiskey glass on the floor and smashes it.*)

ROCKY. Hey! What de hell—!

JOE. (*With a sneering dignity*) I's on'y savin' you de trouble, White Boy. Now you don't have to break it, soon's my back's turned, so's no white man kick about drinkin' from de same glass. (*He walks stiffly to the street door—then turns for a parting shot—boastfully*) I's tired of loafin' 'round wid a lot of bums. I's a gamblin' man. I's gonna get in a big crap game and win me a big bankroll. Den I'll get de okay to open up my old gamblin' house for colored men. Den maybe I comes back here sometime to see de bums. Maybe I throw a twenty-dollar bill on de bar and say, "Drink it up," and listen when dey all pat me on de back and say, "Joe, you sure is white." But I'll say, "No, I'm black and my dough is black man's dough, and you's proud to drink wid me or you don't get no drink!" Or maybe I just says, "You can all go to hell. I don't lower myself drinkin' wid no white trash!" (*He opens the door to go out—then turns again*) And dat ain't no pipe dream! I'll git de money for my stake today, somehow, somewheres! If I has to borrow a gun and stick up some white man, I gets it! You wait and see! (*He swaggers out through the swinging doors.*)

CHUCK. (*Angrily*) Can yuh beat de noive of dat dinge! Jees, if I wasn't dressed up, I'd go out and mop up de street wid him!

ROCKY. Aw, let him go, de poor old dope! Him and his gamblin' house! He'll be back tonight askin' Harry for his room and bummin' me for a ball. (*Vengefully*) Den I'll be de one to smash de glass. I'll loan him his place! (*The swinging doors are pushed open and* WILLIE OBAN *enters from the street. He is shaved and wears an expensive, well-cut suit, good shoes and clean linen. He is absolutely sober, but his face is sick, and his nerves in a shocking state of shakes.*)

CHUCK. Another guy all dolled up! Got your clothes from Solly's, huh, Willie? (*Derisively*) Now yuh can sell dem back to him again tomorrow.

WILLIE. (*Stiffly*) No, I—I'm through with that stuff. Never again. (*He comes to the bar.*)

ROCKY. (*Sympathetically*) Yuh look sick, Willie. Take a ball to pick yuh up. (*He pushes a bottle toward him.*)

WILLIE. (*Eyes the bottle yearningly but shakes his head—determinedly*) No, thanks. The only way to stop is to stop. I'd have no chance if I went to the D.A.'s office smelling of booze.

CHUCK. Yuh're really goin' dere?

WILLIE. (*Stiffly*) I said I was, didn't I? I just came back here to rest a few minutes, not because I needed any booze. I'll show that cheap drummer I don't have to have any Dutch courage— (*Guiltily*) But he's been very kind and generous staking me. He can't help his insulting manner, I suppose. (*He turns away from the bar*) My legs are a bit shaky yet. I better sit down a while. (*He goes back and sits at the left of the second table, facing* PARRITT, *who gives him a scowling, suspicious glance and then ignores him.* ROCKY *looks at* CHUCK *and taps his head disgustedly.* CAPTAIN LEWIS *appears in the doorway from the hall.*)

CHUCK. (*Mutters*) Here's anudder one. (LEWIS *looks spruce and clean-shaven. His ancient tweed suit has been brushed and his frayed linen is clean. His manner is full of a forced, jaunty self-assurance. But he is sick and beset by katzenjammer.*)

LEWIS. Good morning, gentlemen all. (*He passes along the front of bar to look out in the street*) A jolly fine morning, too. (*He turns back to the bar*) An eye-opener? I think not. Not required, Rocky, old chum. Feel extremely fit, as a matter of fact. Though can't say I slept much, thanks to that interfering ass, Hickey, and that stupid bounder of a Boer. (*His face hardens*) I've had about all I can take from that fellow. It's my own fault, of course, for allowing a brute of a Dutch farmer to become familiar. Well, it's come to a parting of the ways now, and good riddance. Which reminds me, here's my key. (*He puts it on the bar*) I shan't be coming back. Sorry to be leaving good old Harry and the rest of you, of course, but I can't continue to live under the same roof with that fellow. (*He stops, stiffening into hostility as* WETJOEN *enters from the hall, and pointedly turns his back on him.* WETJOEN *glares at him sneeringly. He, too, has made an effort to spruce up his appearance, and his bearing has a forced swagger of conscious physical strength. Behind this, he is sick and feebly holding his booze-sodden body together.*)

ROCKY. (*To* LEWIS—*disgustedly putting the key on the shelf in back of the bar*) So Hickey's kidded the pants offa you, too? Yuh tink yuh're leavin' here, huh?

WETJOEN. (*Jeeringly*) Ja! Dot's vhat he kids himself.

LEWIS. (*Ignores him—airily*) Yes, I'm leaving, Rocky. But that ass, Hickey, has nothing to do with it. Been thinking things over. Time I turned over a new leaf, and all that.

WETJOEN. He's going to get a job! Dot's vhat he says!

ROCKY. What at, for Chris' sake?

LEWIS. (*Keeping his airy manner*) Oh, anything. I mean, not manual labor, naturally, but anything that calls for a bit of brains and education. However humble. Beggars can't be choosers. I'll see a pal of mine at the Consulate. He promised any time I felt an energetic fit he'd get me a post with the Cunard—clark in the office or something of the kind.

WETJOEN. Ja! At Limey Consulate they promise anything to get rid of him vhen he comes there tronk! They're scared to call the police and have him pinched because it vould scandal in the papers make about a Limey officer and chentleman!

LEWIS. As a matter of fact, Rocky, I only wish a post temporarily. Means to an end, you know. Save up enough for a first-class passage home, that's the bright idea.

WETJOEN. He's sailing back to home, sveet home! Dot's biggest pipe dream of all. What leetle brain the poor Limey has left, dot isn't in whiskey pickled, Hickey has made crazy! (LEWIS' *fists clench, but he manages to ignore this.*)

CHUCK. (*Feels sorry for* LEWIS *and turns on* WETJOEN—*sarcastically*) Hickey ain't made no sucker outa you, huh? You're too foxy, huh? But I'll bet you tink yuh're goin' out and land a job, too.

WETJOEN. (*Bristles*) I am, ja. For me, it is easy. Because I put on no airs of chentleman. I am not ashamed to vork vith my hands. I vas a farmer before the war ven ploody Limey thieves steal my country. (*Boastfully*) Anyone I ask for job can see vith one look I have the great strength to do work of ten ordinary mens.

LEWIS. (*Sneeringly*) Yes, Chuck, you remember he gave a demonstration of his extraordinary muscles last night when he helped to move the piano.

CHUCK. Yuh couldn't even hold up your corner. It was your fault de damned box almost fell down de stairs.

WETJOEN. My hands vas sweaty! Could I help dot my hands slip? I could de whole veight of it lift! In old days in Transvaal, I lift loaded oxcart by the axle! So vhy shouldn't I get job? Dot longshoreman boss, Dan, he tell me any time I like, he take me on. And Benny from de Market he promise me same.

LEWIS. You remember, Rocky, it was one of those rare occasions when the Boer that walks like a man—spelled with a double o, by the way—was buying drinks and Dan and Benny were stony. They'd bloody well have promised him the moon.

ROCKY. Yeah, yuh big boob, dem boids was on'y kiddin' yuh.

WETJOEN. (*Angrily*) Dot's lie! You vill see dis morning I get job! I'll show dot bloody Limey chentleman, and dot liar, Hickey! And I need vork only leetle vhile to save money for my passage home. I need not much money because I am not ashamed to travel steerage. I don't put on first-cabin airs! (*Tauntingly*) Und *I* can go home to my country! Vhen I get there, they vill let *me* come in!

LEWIS. (*Grows rigid—his voice trembling with repressed anger*) There was a rumor in South Africa, Rocky, that a certain Boer officer—if you call the leaders of a rabble of farmers officers—kept advising Cronje to retreat and not stand and fight—

WETJOEN. And I vas right! I vas right! He got surrounded at Poardeberg! He had to surrender!

LEWIS. (*Ignoring him*) Good strategy, no doubt, but a suspicion grew afterwards into a conviction among the Boers that the officer's caution was prompted by a desire to make his personal escape. His countrymen felt extremely savage about it, and his family disowned him. So I imagine there would be no welcoming committee waiting on the dock, nor delighted relatives making the veldt ring with their happy cries—

WETJOEN. (*With guilty rage*) All lies! You Gottamned Limey— (*Trying to control himself and copy* LEWIS' *manner*) I also haf heard rumors of a Limey officer who, after the war, lost all his money gambling vhen he vas tronk. But they found out it vas regiment money, too, he lost—

LEWIS. (*Loses his control and starts for him*) You bloody Dutch scum!

ROCKY. (*Leans over the bar and stops* LEWIS *with a straight-arm swipe on the chest*) Cut it out! (*At the same moment* CHUCK *grabs* WETJOEN *and yanks him back.*)

WETJOEN. (*Struggling*) Let him come! I saw them come before—at Modder River, Magersfontein, Spion Kopje—waving their silly swords, so afraid they couldn't show off how brave they vas!—and I kill them vith my rifle so easy! (*Vindictively*) Listen to me, you Cecil! Often vhen I am tronk and kidding you I say I am sorry I missed you, but now, py Gott, I am sober, and I don't joke, and I say it!

LARRY. (*Gives a sardonic guffaw—with his comically crazy, intense whisper*) Be God, you can't say Hickey hasn't the miraculous touch to raise the dead, when he can start the Boer War raging again! (*This interruption acts like a cold douche on* LEWIS *and* WETJOEN. *They subside, and* ROCKY *and* CHUCK *let go of them.* LEWIS *turns his back on the Boer.*)

LEWIS. (*Attempting a return of his jaunty manner, as if nothing had happened*) Well, time I was on my merry way to see my chap at the Consulate. The early bird catches the job, what? Good-bye and good luck, Rocky, and everyone. (*He starts for the street door.*)

WETJOEN. Py Gott, if dot Limey can go, I can go! (*He hurries after* LEWIS. *But* LEWIS, *his hand about to push the swinging doors open, hesitates, as though struck by a sudden paralysis of the will, and* WETJOEN *has to jerk back to avoid bumping into him. For a second they stand there, one behind the other, staring over the swinging doors into the street.*)

ROCKY. Well, why don't yuh beat it?

LEWIS. (*Guiltily casual*) Eh? Oh, just happened to think. Hardly the decent thing to pop off without saying good-bye to old Harry. One of the best, Harry. And good old Jimmy, too. They ought to be down any moment. (*He pretends to notice* WETJOEN *for the first time and steps away from the door—apologizing as to a stranger*) Sorry. I seem to be blocking your way out.

WETJOEN. (*Stiffly*) No. I vait to say good-bye to Harry and Jimmy, too. (*He goes to right of door behind the lunch counter and looks through the window, his back to the room.* LEWIS *takes up a similar stand at the window on the left of door.*)

CHUCK. Jees, can you beat dem simps! (*He picks up* CORA'S *drink at the end of the bar*) Hell, I'd forgot Cora. She'll be trowin' a fit. (*He goes into the hall with the drink.*)

ROCKY. (*Looks after him disgustedly*) Dat's right, wait on her and spoil her, yuh poor sap! (*He shakes his head and begins to wipe the bar mechanically.*)

WILLIE. (*Is regarding* PARRITT *across the table from him with an eager, calculating eye. He leans over and speaks in a low confidential tone*) Look here, Parritt. I'd like to have a talk with you.

PARRITT. (*Starts—scowling defensively*) What about?

WILLIE. (*His manner becoming his idea of a crafty criminal lawyer's*) About the trouble you're in. Oh, I know. You don't admit it. You're quite right. That's my advice. Deny everything. Keep your mouth shut. Make no statements whatever without first consulting your attorney.

PARRITT. Say! What the hell—?

WILLIE. But you can trust me. I'm a lawyer, and it's just occurred to me you and I ought to co-operate. Of course I'm going to see the D.A. this morning about a job on his staff. But that may take time. There may not be an immediate opening. Meanwhile it would be a good idea for me to take a case or two, on my own, and prove my brilliant record in law school was no flash in the pan. So why not retain me as your attorney?

PARRITT. You're crazy! What do I want with a lawyer?

WILLIE. That's right. Don't admit anything. But you can trust me, so let's not beat about the bush. You got in trouble out on the Coast, eh? And now you're hiding out. Any fool can spot that. (*Lowering his voice still more*) You feel safe here, and maybe you are, for a while. But remember, they get you in the end. I know from my father's experience. No one could have felt safer than he did. When anyone mentioned the law to him, he nearly died laughing. But—

PARRITT. You crazy mutt! (*Turning to* LARRY *with a strained laugh*) Did you get that, Larry? This damned fool thinks the cops are after me!

LARRY. (*Bursts out with his true reaction before he thinks to ignore him*) I wish to God they were! And so should you, if you had the honor of a louse! (PARRITT *stares into his eyes guiltily for a second. Then he smiles sneeringly.*)

PARRITT. And you're the guy who kids himself he's through with the Movement! You old lying faker, you're still in love with it! (LARRY *ignores him again now.*)

WILLIE. (*Disappointedly*) Then you're not in trouble, Parritt? I was hoping— But never mind. No offense meant. Forget it.

PARRITT. (*Condescendingly—his eyes on* LARRY) Sure. That's all right, Willie. I'm not sore at you. It's that damned old faker that gets my goat. (*He slips out of his chair and goes quietly over to sit in the chair beside* LARRY *he had occupied before —in a low, insinuating, intimate tone*) I think I understand, Larry. It's really Mother you still love—isn't it?—in spite of the dirty deal she gave you. But hell, what did you expect? She was never true to anyone but herself and the Movement. But I understand how you can't help still feeling— because I still love her, too. (*Pleading in a strained, desperate tone*) You know I do, don't you? You must! So you see I couldn't have expected they'd catch her! You've got to believe me that I sold them out just to get a few lousy dollars to blow in on a whore. No other reason, honest! There couldn't possibly be any other reason! (*Again he has a strange air of exonerating himself from guilt by this shameless confession.*)

LARRY. (*Trying not to listen, has listened with increasing tension*) For the love of Christ will you leave me in peace! I've told you you can't make me judge you! But if you don't keep still, you'll be saying something soon that will make you vomit your own soul like a drink of nickel rotgut that won't stay down! (*He pushes back his chair and springs to his feet*) To hell with you! (*He goes to the bar.*)

PARRITT. (*Jumps up and starts to follow him— desperately*) Don't go, Larry! You've got to help me! (*But* LARRY *is at the bar, back turned, and* ROCKY *is scowling at him. He stops, shrinking back into himself helplessly, and turns away. He goes to the table where he had been before, and this time he takes the chair at rear facing directly front. He puts his elbows on the table, holding his head in his hands as if he had a splitting headache.*)

LARRY. Set 'em up, Rocky. I swore I'd have no more drinks on Hickey, if I died of drought, but I've changed my mind! Be God, he owes it to me, and I'd get blind to the world now if it was the Iceman of Death himself treating! (*He stops, startledly, a superstitious awe coming into his face*) What made me say that, I wonder. (*With a sardonic laugh*) Well, be God, it fits, for Death was the Iceman Hickey called to his home!

ROCKY. Aw, forget dat iceman gag! De poor dame is dead. (*Pushing a bottle and glass at* LARRY) Gwan and get paralyzed! I'll be glad to see one bum in dis dump act natural. (LARRY *downs a drink and pours another.*)

(ED MOSHER *appears in the doorway from the hall. The same change which is apparent in the manner and appearance of the others shows in him. He is sick, his nerves are shattered, his eyes are apprehensive, but he, too, puts on an exaggeratedly self-confident bearing. He saunters to the bar between* LARRY *and the street entrance.*)

MOSHER. Morning, Rocky. Hello, Larry. Glad to see Brother Hickey hasn't corrupted you to temperance. I wouldn't mind a shot myself. (*As* ROCKY *shoves a bottle toward him he shakes his head*) But I remember the only breath-killer in this dump is coffee beans. The boss would never fall for that. No man can run a circus successfully who believes guys chew coffee beans because they like them. (*He pushes the bottle away*) No, much as I need one after the hell of a night I've had— (*He scowls*) That drummer son of a drummer! I had to lock him out. But I could hear him through the wall doing his spiel to someone all night long. Still at it with Jimmy and Harry when I came down just now. But the hardest to take was that flannel-mouth, flatfoot Mick trying to tell me where I got off! I had to lock him out, too. (*As he says this,* MCGLOIN *comes in the doorway from the hall. The change in his appearance and manner is identical with that of* MOSHER *and the others.*)

MCGLOIN. He's a liar, Rocky! It was me locked

him out! (MOSHER *starts to flare up—then ignores him. They turn their backs on each other.* MC-GLOIN *starts into the back-room section.*)

WILLIE. Come and sit here, Mac. You're just the man I want to see. If I'm to take your case, we ought to have a talk before we leave.

MCGLOIN. (*Contemptuously*) We'll have no talk. You damned fool, do you think I'd have your father's son for my lawyer? They'd take one look at you and bounce us both out on our necks! (WILLIE *winces and shrinks down in his chair.* MCGLOIN *goes to the first table beyond him and sits with his back to the bar*) I don't need a lawyer, anyway. To hell with the law! All I've got to do is see the right ones and get them to pass the word. They will, too. They know I was framed. And once they've passed the word, it's as good as done, law or no law.

MOSHER. God, I'm glad I'm leaving this madhouse! (*He pulls his key from his pocket and slaps it on the bar*) Here's my key, Rocky.

MCGLOIN. (*Pulls his from his pocket*) And here's mine. (*He tosses it to* ROCKY) I'd rather sleep in the gutter than pass another night under the same roof with that loon, Hickey, and a lying circus grifter! (*He adds darkly*) And if that hat fits anyone here, let him put it on! (MOSHER *turns toward him furiously but* ROCKY *leans over the bar and grabs his arm.*)

ROCKY. Nix! Take it easy! (MOSHER *subsides.* ROCKY *tosses the keys on the shelf—disgustedly*) You boids gimme a pain. It'd soive you right if I wouldn't give de keys back to yuh tonight. (*They both turn on him resentfully, but there is an interruption as* CORA *appears in the doorway from the hall with* CHUCK *behind her. She is drunk, dressed in her gaudy best, her face plastered with rouge and mascara, her hair a bit disheveled, her hat on anyhow.*)

CORA. (*Comes a few steps inside the bar—with a strained bright giggle*) Hello, everybody! Here we go! Hickey just tole us, ain't it time we beat it, if we're really goin'. So we're showin' de bastard, ain't we, Honey? He's comin' right down wid Harry and Jimmy. Jees, dem two look like dey was goin' to de electric chair! (*With frightened anger*) If I had to listen to any more of Hickey's bunk, I'd brain him. (*She puts her hand on* CHUCK'S *arm*) Come on, Honey. Let's get started before he comes down.

CHUCK. (*Sullenly*) Sure, anyting yuh say, Baby.

CORA. (*Turns on him truculently*) Yeah? Well, I say we stop at de foist reg'lar dump and yuh gotta blow me to a sherry flip—or four or five, if I want 'em!—or all bets is off!

CHUCK. Aw, yuh got a fine bun on now!

CORA. Cheap skate! I know what's eatin' you, Tightwad! Well, use my dough, den, if yuh're so stingy. Yuh'll grab it all, anyway, right after de ceremony. I know you! (*She hikes her skirt up and reaches inside the top of her stocking*) Here, yuh big tramp!

CHUCK. (*Knocks her hand away—angrily*) Keep your lousy dough! And don't show off your legs to dese bums when yuh're goin' to be married, if yuh don't want a sock in de puss!

CORA. (*Pleased—meekly*) Aw right, Honey. (*Looking around with a foolish laugh*) Say, why don't all you barflies come to de weddin'? (*But they are all sunk in their own apprehensions and ignore her. She hesitates, miserably uncertain*) Well, we're goin', guys. (*There is no comment. Her eyes fasten on* ROCKY—*desperately*) Say, Rocky, yuh gone deaf? I said me and Chuck was goin' now.

ROCKY. (*Wiping the bar—with elaborate indifference*) Well, good-bye. Give my love to Joisey.

CORA. (*Tearfully indignant*) Ain't yuh goin' to wish us happiness, yuh doity little Ginny?

ROCKY. Sure. Here's hopin' yuh don't moider each odder before next week.

CHUCK. (*Angrily*) Aw, Baby, what d'we care for dat pimp? (ROCKY *turns on him threateningly, but* CHUCK *hears someone upstairs in the hall and grabs* CORA'S *arm*) Here's Hickey comin'! Let's get outa here! (*They hurry into the hall. The street door is heard slamming behind them.*)

ROCKY. (*Gloomily pronounces an obituary*) One regular guy and one all-right tart gone to hell! (*Fiercely*) Dat louse Hickey oughta be croaked! (*There is a muttered growl of assent from most of the gathering. Then* HARRY HOPE *enters from the hall, followed by* JIMMY TOMORROW, *with* HICKEY *on his heels.* HOPE *and* JIMMY *are both putting up a front of self-assurance, but* CORA'S *description of them was apt. There is a desperate bluff in their manner as they walk in, which suggests the last march of the condemned.* HOPE *is dressed in an old black Sunday suit, black tie, shoes, socks, which give him the appearance of being in mourning.* JIMMY'S *clothes are pressed, his shoes shined, his white linen immaculate. He has a hangover and his gently appealing dog's eyes have a boiled look.* HICKEY'S *face is a bit drawn from lack of sleep and his voice is hoarse from continual talking, but his bustling energy appears nervously intensified, and his beaming expression is one of triumphant accomplishment.*)

HICKEY. Well, here we are! We've got this far, at least! (*He pats* JIMMY *on the back*) Good work, Jimmy. I told you you weren't half as sick as you pretended. No excuse whatever for postponing—

JIMMY. I'll thank you to keep your hands off me! I merely mentioned I would feel more fit tomorrow. But it might as well be today, I suppose.

HICKEY. Finish it now, so it'll be dead forever, and you can be free! (*He passes him to clap* HOPE *encouragingly on the shoulder*) Cheer up, Harry. You found your rheumatism didn't bother you coming downstairs, didn't you? I told you it wouldn't. (*He winks around at the others. With the exception of* HUGO *and* PARRITT, *all their eyes are fixed on him with bitter animosity. He gives* HOPE *a playful nudge in the ribs*) You're the damnedest one for alibis, Governor! As bad as Jimmy!

HOPE. (*Putting on his deaf manner*) Eh? I can't hear— (*Defiantly*) You're a liar! I've had rheumatism on and off for twenty years. Ever since Bessie died. Everybody knows that.

HICKEY. Yes, we know it's the kind of rheumatism you turn on and off! We're on to you, you old faker! (*He claps him on the shoulder again, chuckling.*)

HOPE. (*Looks humiliated and guilty—by way of escape he glares around at the others*) Bejees, what are all you bums hanging round staring at me for? Think you was watching a circus! Why don't you get the hell out of here and 'tend to your own business, like Hickey's told you? (*They look at him reproachfully, their eyes hurt. They fidget as if trying to move.*)

HICKEY. Yes, Harry, I certainly thought they'd have had the guts to be gone by this time. (*He grins*) Or maybe I did have my doubts. (*Abruptly he becomes sincerely sympathetic and earnest*) Because I know exactly what you're up against, boys. I know how damned yellow a man can be when it comes to making himself face the truth. I've been through the mill, and I had to face a worse bastard in myself than any of you will have to in yourselves. I know you become such a coward you'll grab at any lousy excuse to get out of killing your pipe dreams. And yet, as I've told you over and over, it's exactly those damned tomorrow dreams which keep you from making peace with yourself. So you've got to kill them like I did mine. (*He pauses. They glare at him with fear and hatred. They seem about to curse him, to spring at him. But they remain silent and motionless. His manner changes and he becomes kindly bullying*) Come on, boys! Get moving! Who'll start the ball rolling? You, Captain, and you, General. You're nearest the door. And besides, you're old war heroes! You ought to lead the forlorn hope! Come on, now, show us a little of that good old battle of Modder River spirit we've heard so much about! You can't hang around all day looking as if you were scared the street outside would bite you!

LEWIS. (*Turns with humiliated rage—with an attempt at jaunty casualness*) Right you are, Mister Bloody Nosey Parker! Time I pushed off. Was only waiting to say good-bye to you, Harry, old chum.

HOPE. (*Dejectedly*) Good-bye, Captain. Hope you have luck.

LEWIS. Oh, I'm bound to, Old Chap, and the same to you. (*He pushes the swinging doors open and makes a brave exit, turning to his right and marching off outside the window at right of door.*)

WETJOEN. Py Gott, if dot Limey can, I can! (*He pushes the door open and lumbers through it like a bull charging an obstacle. He turns left and disappears off rear, outside the farthest window.*)

HICKEY. (*Exhortingly*) Next? Come on, Ed. It's a fine summer's day and the call of the old circus lot must be in your blood! (MOSHER *glares at him, then goes to the door.* MCGLOIN *jumps up from his chair and starts moving toward the door.* HICKEY *claps him on the back as he passes*) That's the stuff, Mac.

MOSHER. Good-bye, Harry. (*He goes out, turning right outside.*)

MCGLOIN. (*Glowering after him*) If that crooked grifter has the guts— (*He goes out, turning left outside.* HICKEY *glances at* WILLIE *who, before he can speak, jumps from his chair.*)

WILLIE. Good-bye, Harry, and thanks for all your kindness.

HICKEY. (*Claps him on the back*) That's the way, Willie! The D.A.'s a busy man. He can't wait all day for you, you know. (WILLIE *hurries to the door.*)

HOPE. (*Dully*) Good luck, Willie. (WILLIE *goes out and turns right outside. While he is doing so,* JIMMY, *in a sick panic, sneaks to the bar and furtively reaches for* LARRY'S *glass of whiskey.*)

HICKEY. And now it's your turn, Jimmy, old pal. (*He sees what* JIMMY *is at and grabs his arm just as he is about to down the drink*) Now, now, Jimmy! You can't do that to yourself. One drink on top of your hangover and an empty stomach and you'll be oreyeyed. Then you'll tell yourself you wouldn't stand a chance if you went up soused to get your old job back.

JIMMY. (*Pleads abjectly*) Tomorrow! I will tomorrow! I'll be in good shape tomorrow! (*Abruptly getting control of himself—with shaken firmness*) All right. I'm going. Take your hands off me.

HICKEY. That's the ticket! You'll thank me when it's all over.

JIMMY. (*In a burst of futile fury*) You dirty swine! (*He tries to throw the drink in* HICKEY'S *face, but his aim is poor and it lands on* HICKEY'S *coat.* JIMMY *turns and dashes through the door, disappearing outside the window at right of door.*)

HICKEY. (*Brushing the whiskey off his coat—humorously*) All set for an alcohol rub! But no hard feelings. I know how he feels. I wrote the book. I've seen the day when if anyone forced me to face the truth about my pipe dreams, I'd have shot them dead. (*He turns to* HOPE—*encouragingly*) Well, Governor, Jimmy made the grade. It's up to you. If he's got the guts to go through with the test, then certainly you—

LARRY. (*Bursts out*) Leave Harry alone, damn you!

HICKEY. (*Grins at him*) I'd make up my mind about myself if I was you, Larry, and not bother over Harry. He'll come through all right. I've promised him that. He doesn't need anyone's bum pity. Do you, Governor?

HOPE. (*With a pathetic attempt at his old fuming assertiveness*) No, bejees! Keep your nose out of this, Larry. What's Hickey got to do with it? I've always been going to take this walk, ain't I? Bejees, you bums want to keep me locked up in here 's if I was in jail! I've stood it long enough! I'm free, white and twenty-one, and I'll do as I damned please, bejees! You keep your nose out, too, Hickey! You'd think you was boss of this dump, not me. Sure, I'm all right! Why shouldn't I be? What the hell's to be scared of, just taking a stroll around my own ward? (*As he talks he has been moving toward the door. Now he reaches it*) What's the weather like outside, Rocky?

ROCKY. Fine day, Boss.

HOPE. What's that? Can't hear you. Don't look fine to me. Looks 's if it'd pour down cats and dogs any minute. My rheumatism— (*He catches himself*) No, must be my eyes. Half blind, bejees. Makes things look black. I see now it's a fine day. Too damned hot for a walk, though, if you ask me. Well, do me good to sweat the booze out of me. But I'll have to watch out for the damned automobiles. Wasn't none of them around the last time, twenty years ago. From what I've seen of 'em through the window, they'd run over you as soon as look at you. Not that I'm scared of 'em. I can take care of myself. (*He puts a reluctant hand on the swinging door*) Well, so long— (*He stops and looks back—with frightened irascibility*) Bejees, where are you, Hickey? It's time we got started.

HICKEY. (*Grins and shakes his head*) No, Harry.

Can't be done. You've got to keep a date with yourself alone.

HOPE. (*With forced fuming*) Hell of a guy, you are! Thought you'd be willing to help me across the street, knowing I'm half blind. Half deaf, too. Can't bear those damned automobiles. Hell with you! Bejees, I've never needed no one's help and I don't now! (*Egging himself on*) I'll take a good long walk now I've started. See all my old friends. Bejees, they must have given me up for dead. Twenty years is a long time. But they know it was grief over Bessie's death that made me— (*He puts his hand on the door*) Well, the sooner I get started— (*Then he drops his hand—with sentimental melancholy*) You know, Hickey, that's what gets me. Can't help thinking the last time I went out was to Bessie's funeral. After she'd gone, I didn't feel life was worth living. Swore I'd never go out again. (*Pathetically*) Somehow, I can't feel it's right for me to go, Hickey, even now. It's like I was doing wrong to her memory.

HICKEY. Now, Governor, you can't let yourself get away with that one any more!

HOPE. (*Cupping his hand to his ear*) What's that? Can't hear you. (*Sentimentally again but with desperation*) I remember now clear as day the last time before she— It was a fine Sunday morning. We went out to church together. (*His voice breaks on a sob.*)

HICKEY. (*Amused*) It's a great act, Governor. But I know better, and so do you. You never did want to go to church or any place else with her. She was always on your neck, making you have ambition and go out and do things, when all you wanted was to get drunk in peace.

HOPE. (*Falteringly*) Can't hear a word you're saying. You're a God-damned liar, anyway! (*Then in a sudden fury, his voice trembling with hatred*) Bejees, you son of a bitch, if there was a mad dog outside I'd go and shake hands with it rather than stay here with you! (*The momentum of his fit of rage does it. He pushes the door open and strides blindly out into the street and as blindly past the window behind the free-lunch counter.*)

ROCKY. (*In amazement*) Jees, he made it! I'd a give yuh fifty to one he'd never— (*He goes to the end of the bar to look through the window—disgustedly*) Aw, he's stopped. I'll bet yuh he's comin' back.

HICKEY. Of course, he's coming back. So are all the others. By tonight they'll all be here again. You dumbbell, that's the whole point.

ROCKY. (*Excitedly*) No, he ain't neider! He's gone to de coib. He's lookin' up and down. Scared stiff of automobiles. Jees, dey ain't more'n two an hour comes down dis street, de old boob! (*He watches excitedly, as if it were a race he had a bet on, oblivious to what happens in the bar.*)

LARRY. (*Turns on* HICKEY *with bitter defiance*) And now it's my turn, I suppose? What is it I'm to do to achieve this blessed peace of yours?

HICKEY. (*Grins at him*) Why, we've discussed all that, Larry. Just stop lying to yourself—

LARRY. You think when I say I'm finished with life, and tired of watching the stupid greed of the human circus, and I'll welcome closing my eyes in the long sleep of death—you think that's a coward's lie?

HICKEY. (*Chuckling*) Well, what do you think, Larry?

LARRY. (*With increasing bitter intensity, more as if he were fighting with himself than with* HICKEY) I'm afraid to live, am I?—and even more afraid to die! So I sit here, with my pride drowned on the bottom of a bottle, keeping drunk so I won't see myself shaking in my britches with fright, or hear myself whining and praying: Beloved Christ, let me live a little longer at any price! If it's only for a few days more, or a few hours even, have mercy, Almighty God, and let me still clutch greedily to my yellow heart this sweet treasure, this jewel beyond price, the dirty, stinking bit of withered old flesh which is my beautiful little life! (*He laughs with a sneering, vindictive self-loathing, staring inward at himself with contempt and hatred. Then abruptly he makes* HICKEY *again the antagonist*) You think you'll make me admit that to myself?

HICKEY. (*Chuckling*) But you just did admit it, didn't you?

PARRITT. (*Lifts his head from his hands to glare at* LARRY—*jeeringly*) That's the stuff, Hickey! Show the old yellow faker up! He can't play dead on me like this! He's got to help me!

HICKEY. Yes, Larry, you've got to settle with him. I'm leaving you entirely in his hands. He'll do as good a job as I could at making you give up that old grandstand bluff.

LARRY. (*Angrily*) I'll see the two of you in hell first!

ROCKY. (*Calls excitedly from the end of the bar*) Jees, Harry's startin' across de street! He's goin' to fool yuh, Hickey, yuh bastard! (*He pauses, watching—then worriedly*) What de hell's he stoppin' for? Right in de middle of de street! Yuh'd tink he was paralyzed or somethin'! (*Disgustedly*) Aw, he's quittin'! He's turned back! Jees, look at de old bastard travel! Here he comes! (HOPE *passes the window outside the free-lunch counter in a shambling, panic-stricken run. He comes lurching blindly through the swinging doors and stumbles to the bar at* LARRY'S *right.*)

HOPE. Bejees, give me a drink quick! Scared me out of a year's growth! Bejees, that guy ought to be pinched! Bejees, it ain't safe to walk in the streets! Bejees, that ends me! Never again! Give me that bottle! (*He slops a glass full and drains it and pours another— To* ROCKY, *who is regarding him with scorn—appealingly*) You seen it, didn't you, Rocky?

ROCKY. Seen what?

HOPE. That automobile, you dumb Wop! Feller driving it must be drunk or crazy. He'd run right over me if I hadn't jumped. (*Ingratiatingly*) Come on, Larry, have a drink. Everybody have a drink. Have a cigar, Rocky. I know you hardly ever touch it.

ROCKY. (*Resentfully*) Well, dis is de time I do touch it! (*Pouring a drink*) I'm goin' to get stinko, see! And if yuh don't like it, yuh know what yuh can do! I gotta good mind to chuck my job, anyways. (*Disgustedly*) Jees, Harry, I thought yuh had some guts! I was bettin' yuh'd make it and show dat four-flusher up! (*He nods at* HICKEY— *then snorts*) Automobile, hell! Who d'yuh tink yuh're kiddin'? Dey wasn' no automobile! Yuh just quit cold!

HOPE. (*Feebly*) Guess I ought to know! Bejees, it almost killed me!

HICKEY. (*Comes to the bar between him and* LARRY, *and puts a hand on his shoulder—kindly*) Now, now, Governor. Don't be foolish. You've faced the test and come through. You're rid of all that nagging dream stuff now. You know you can't believe it any more.

HOPE. (*Appeals pleadingly to* LARRY) Larry, you saw it, didn't you? Drink up! Have another! Have all you want! Bejees, we'll go on a grand old souse together! You saw that automobile, didn't you?

LARRY. (*Compassionately, avoiding his eyes*) Sure, I saw it, Harry. You had a narrow escape. Be God, I thought you were a goner!

HICKEY. (*Turns on him with a flash of sincere indignation*) What the hell's the matter with you, Larry? You know what I told you about the wrong kind of pity. Leave Harry alone! You'd think I was trying to harm him, the fool way you act! My oldest friend! What kind of a louse do you think I am? There isn't anything I wouldn't do for Harry, and he knows it! All I've wanted to do is fix it so he'll be finally at peace with himself for the rest of his days! And if you'll only wait until the final returns are in, you'll find that's exactly what I've accomplished! (*He turns to* HOPE *and pats his shoulder—coaxingly*) Come now, Governor. What's the use of being stubborn, now when it's all over and dead? Give up that ghost automobile.

HOPE. (*Beginning to collapse within himself—dully*) Yes, what's the use—now? All a lie! No automobile. But, bejees, something ran over me! Must have been myself, I guess. (*He forces a feeble smile—then wearily*) Guess I'll sit down. Feel all in. Like a corpse, bejees. (*He picks a bottle and glass from the bar and walks to the first table and slumps down in the chair, facing left-front. His shaking hand misjudges the distance and he sets the bottle on the table with a jar that rouses* HUGO, *who lifts his head from his arms and blinks at him through his thick spectacles.* HOPE *speaks to him in a flat, dead voice*) Hello, Hugo. Coming up for air? Stay passed out, that's the right dope. There ain't any cool willow trees —except you grow your own in a bottle. (*He pours a drink and gulps it down.*)

HUGO. (*With his silly giggle*) Hello, Harry, stupid proletarian monkey-face! I vill trink champagne beneath the villow— (*With a change to aristocratic fastidiousness*) But the slaves must ice it properly! (*With guttural rage*) Gottamned Hickey! Peddler pimp for nouveau-riche capitalism! Vhen I lead the jackass mob to the sack of Babylon, I vill make them hang him to a lamp-post the first one!

HOPE. (*Spiritlessly*) Good work. I'll help pull on the rope. Have a drink, Hugo.

HUGO. (*Frightenedly*) No, thank you. I am too trunk now. I hear myself say crazy things. Do not listen, please. Larry vill tell you I haf never been so crazy trunk. I must sleep it off. (*He starts to put his head on his arms but stops and stares at* HOPE *with growing uneasiness*) Vhat's matter, Harry? You look funny. You look dead. Vhat's happened? I don't know you. Listen, I feel I am dying, too. Because I am so crazy trunk! It is very necessary I sleep. But I can't sleep here with you. You look dead. (*He scrambles to his feet in a confused panic, turns his back on* HOPE *and settles into the chair at the next table which faces left. He thrusts his head down on his arms like an ostrich hiding its head in the sand. He does not notice* PARRITT, *nor* PARRITT *him.*)

LARRY. (*To* HICKEY *with bitter condemnation*) Another one who's begun to enjoy your peace!

HICKEY. Oh, I know it's tough on him right now, the same as it is on Harry. But that's only the first shock. I promise you they'll both come through all right.

LARRY. And you believe that! I see you do! You mad fool!

HICKEY. Of course, I believe it! I tell you I know from my own experience!

HOPE. (*Spiritlessly*) Close that big clam of yours, Hickey. Bejees, you're a worse gabber than that nagging bitch, Bessie, was. (*He drinks his drink mechanically and pours another.*)

ROCKY. (*In amazement*) Jees, did yuh hear dat?

HOPE. (*Dully*) What's wrong with this booze? There's no kick in it.

ROCKY. (*Worriedly*) Jees, Larry, Hugo had it right. He does look like he'd croaked.

HICKEY. (*Annoyed*) Don't be a damned fool! Give him time. He's coming along all right. (*He calls to* HOPE *with a first trace of underlying uneasiness*) You're all right, aren't you, Harry?

HOPE. (*Dully*) I want to pass out like Hugo.

LARRY. (*Turns to* HICKEY—*with bitter anger*) It's the peace of death you've brought him.

HICKEY. (*For the first time loses his temper*) That's a lie! (*But he controls this instantly and grins*) Well, well, you did manage to get a rise out of me that time. I think such a hell of a lot of Harry— (*Impatiently*) You know that's damned foolishness. Look at me. I've been through it. Do I look dead? Just leave Harry alone and wait until the shock wears off and you'll see. He'll be a new man. Like I am. (*He calls to* HOPE *coaxingly*) How's it coming, Governor? Beginning to feel free, aren't you? Relieved and not guilty any more?

HOPE. (*Grumbles spiritlessly*) Bejees, you must have been monkeying with the booze, too, you interfering bastard! There's no life in it now. I want to get drunk and pass out. Let's all pass out. Who the hell cares?

HICKEY. (*Lowering his voice—worriedly to* LARRY) I admit I didn't think he'd be hit so hard. He's always been a happy-go-lucky slob. Like I was. Of course, it hit me hard, too. But only for a minute. Then I felt as if a ton of guilt had been lifted off my mind. I saw what had happened was the only possible way for the peace of all concerned.

LARRY. (*Sharply*) What was it happened? Tell us that! And don't try to get out of it! I want a straight answer! (*Vindictively*) I think it was something you drove someone else to do!

HICKEY. (*Puzzled*) Someone else?

LARRY. (*Accusingly*) What did your wife die of? You've kept that a deep secret, I notice—for some reason!

HICKEY. (*Reproachfully*) You're not very considerate, Larry. But, if you insist on knowing now, there's no reason you shouldn't. It was a bullet through the head that killed Evelyn. (*There is a second's tense silence.*)

HOPE. (*Dully*) Who the hell cares? To hell with her and that nagging old hag, Bessie.

ROCKY. Christ. You had de right dope, Larry.

LARRY. (*Revengefully*) You drove your poor

wife to suicide? I knew it! Be God, I don't blame her! I'd almost do as much myself to be rid of you! It's what you'd like to drive us all to— (*Abruptly he is ashamed of himself and pitying*) I'm sorry, Hickey. I'm a rotten louse to throw that in your face.

HICKEY. (*Quietly*) Oh, that's all right, Larry. But don't jump at conclusions. I didn't say poor Evelyn committed suicide. It's the last thing she'd ever have done, as long as I was alive for her to take care of and forgive. If you'd known her at all, you'd never get such a crazy suspicion. (*He pauses—then slowly*) No, I'm sorry to have to tell you my poor wife was killed. (LARRY *stares at him with growing horror and shrinks back along the bar away from him.* PARRITT *jerks his head up from his hands and looks around frightenedly, not at* HICKEY, *but at* LARRY. ROCKY'S *round eyes are popping.* HOPE *stares dully at the table top.* HUGO, *his head hidden in his arms, gives no sign of life.*)

LARRY. (*Shakenly*) Then she—was murdered.

PARRITT. (*Springs to his feet—stammers defensively*) You're a liar, Larry! You must be crazy to say that to me! You know she's still alive! (*But no one pays any attention to him.*)

ROCKY. (*Blurts out*) Moidered? Who done it?

LARRY. (*His eyes fixed with fascinated horror on* HICKEY—*frightenedly*) Don't ask questions, you dumb Wop! It's none of our damned business! Leave Hickey alone!

HICKEY. (*Smiles at him with affectionate amusement*) Still the old grandstand bluff, Larry? Or is it some more bum pity? (*He turns to* ROCKY—*matter-of-factly*) The police don't know who killed her yet, Rocky. But I expect they will before very long. (*As if that finished the subject, he comes forward to* HOPE *and sits beside him, with an arm around his shoulder—affectionately coaxing*) Coming along fine now, aren't you, Governor? Getting over the first shock? Beginning to feel free from guilt and lying hopes and at peace with yourself?

HOPE. (*With a dull callousness*) Somebody croaked your Evelyn, eh? Bejees, my bets are on the iceman! But who the hell cares? Let's get drunk and pass out. (*He tosses down his drink with a lifeless, automatic movement—complainingly*) Bejees, what did you do to the booze, Hickey? There's no damned life left in it.

PARRITT. (*Stammers, his eyes on* LARRY, *whose eyes in turn remain fixed on* HICKEY) Don't look like that, Larry! You've got to believe what I told you! It had nothing to do with her! It was just to get a few lousy dollars!

HUGO. (*Suddenly raises his head from his arms and, looking straight in front of him, pounds on the table frightenedly with his small fists*) Don't be a fool! Buy me a trink! But no more vine! It is not properly iced! (*With guttural rage*) Gottamned stupid proletarian slaves! Buy me a trink or I vill have you shot! (*He collapses into abject begging*) Please, for Gott's sake! I am not trunk enough! I cannot sleep! Life is a crazy monkeyface! Always there is blood beneath the villow trees! I hate it and I am afraid! (*He hides his face on his arms, sobbing muffledly*) Please, I am crazy trunk! I say crazy things! For Gott's sake, do not listen to me! (*But no one pays any attention to him.* LARRY *stands shrunk back against the bar.* ROCKY *is leaning over it. They stare at* HICKEY. PARRITT *stands looking pleadingly at* LARRY.)

HICKEY. (*Gazes with worried kindliness at* HOPE) You're beginning to worry me, Governor. Something's holding you up somewhere. I don't see why— You've faced the truth about yourself. You've done what you had to do to kill your nagging pipe dreams. Oh, I know it knocks you cold. But only for a minute. Then you see it was the only possible way to peace. And you feel happy. Like I did. That's what worries me about you, Governor. It's time you began to feel happy—

CURTAIN

ACT FOUR

SCENE: *Same as Act One—the back room with the curtain separating it from the section of the barroom with its single table at right of curtain, front. It is around half past one in the morning of the following day.*

The tables in the back room have a new arrangement. The one at left, front, before the window to the yard, is in the same position. So is the one at the right, rear, of it in the second row. But this table now has only one chair. This chair is at right of it, facing directly front. The two tables on either side of the door at rear are unchanged. But the table which was at center, front, has been pushed toward right so that it and the table at right, rear, of it in the second row, and the last table at right in the front row, are now jammed so closely together that they form one group.

LARRY, HUGO *and* PARRITT *are at the table at left, front.* LARRY *is at left of it, beside the window, facing front.* HUGO *sits at rear, facing front, his head on his arms in his habitual position, but he is not asleep. On* HUGO'S *left is* PARRITT, *his chair facing left, front. At right of table, an empty chair, facing left.* LARRY'S *chin is on his chest, his eyes fixed on the floor. He will not look at* PARRITT, *who keeps staring at him with a sneering, pleading challenge.*

Two bottles of whiskey are on each table, whiskey and chaser glasses, a pitcher of water.

The one chair by the table at right, rear, of them is vacant.

At the first table at right of center, CORA *sits at left, front, of it, facing front. Around the rear of this table are four empty chairs. Opposite* CORA, *in a sixth chair, is* CAPTAIN LEWIS, *also facing front. On his left,* MCGLOIN *is facing front in a chair before the middle table of his group. At right, rear, of him, also at this table,* GENERAL WETJOEN *sits facing front. In back of this table are three empty chairs.*

At right, rear, of WETJOEN, *but beside the last table of the group, sits* WILLIE. *On* WILLIE'S *left, at rear of table, is* HOPE. *On* HOPE'S *left, at right, rear, of table, is* MOSHER. *Finally, at right of table is* JIMMY TOMORROW. *All of the four sit facing front.*

There is an atmosphere of oppressive stagnation in the room, and a quality of insensibility about all the people in this group at right. They are like wax figures, set stiffly on their chairs, carrying out mechanically the motions of getting drunk but sunk in a numb stupor which is impervious to stimulation.

In the bar section, JOE *is sprawled in the chair at right of table, facing left. His head rolls forward in a sudden slumber.* ROCKY *is standing behind his chair, regarding him with dull hostility.* ROCKY'S *face is set in an expression of tired, callous toughness. He looks now like a minor Wop gangster.*

ROCKY. (*Shakes* JOE *by the shoulder*) Come on, yuh damned nigger! Beat it in de back room! It's after hours. (*But* JOE *remains inert.* ROCKY *gives up*) Aw, to hell wid it. Let de dump get pinched. I'm through wid dis lousy job, anyway! (*He hears someone at rear and calls*) Who's dat? (CHUCK *appears from rear. He has been drinking heavily, but there is no lift to his jag; his manner is grouchy and sullen. He has evidently been brawling. His knuckles are raw and there is a mouse under one eye. He has lost his straw hat, his tie is awry, and his blue suit is dirty.* ROCKY *eyes him indifferently*) Been scrappin', huh? Started off on your periodical, ain't yuh? (*For a second there is a gleam of satisfaction in his eyes.*)

CHUCK. Yeah, ain't yuh glad? (*Truculently*) What's it to yuh?

ROCKY. Not a damn ting. But dis is someting

to me. I'm out on my feet holdin' down your job. Yuh said if I'd take your day, yuh'd relieve me at six, and here it's half past one A.M. Well, yuh're takin' over now, get me, no matter how plastered yuh are!

CHUCK. Plastered, hell! I wisht I was. I've lapped up a gallon, but it don't hit me right. And to hell wid de job. I'm goin' to tell Harry I'm quittin'.

ROCKY. Yeah? Well, I'm quittin', too.

CHUCK. I've played sucker for dat crummy blonde long enough, lettin' her kid me into woikin'. From now on I take it easy.

ROCKY. I'm glad yuh're gettin' some sense.

CHUCK. And I hope yuh're gettin' some. What a prize sap you been, tendin' bar when yuh got two good hustlers in your stable!

ROCKY. Yeah, but I ain't no sap now. I'll loin dem, when dey get back from Coney. (*Sneeringly*) Jees, dat Cora sure played you for a dope, feedin' yuh dat marriage-on-de-farm hop!

CHUCK. (*Dully*) Yeah. Hickey got it right. A lousy pipe dream. It was her pulling sherry flips on me woke me up. All de way walkin' to de ferry, every ginmill we come to she'd drag me in to blow her. I got tinkin', Christ, what won't she want when she gets de ring on her finger and I'm hooked? So I tells her at de ferry, "Kiddo, yuh can go to Joisey, or to hell, but count me out."

ROCKY. She says it was her told you to go to hell, because yuh'd started hittin' de booze.

CHUCK. (*Ignoring this*) I got tinkin', too, Jees, won't I look sweet wid a wife dat if yuh put all de guys she's stayed wid side by side, dey'd reach to Chicago. (*He sighs gloomily*) Dat kind of dame, yuh can't trust 'em. De minute your back is toined, dey're cheatin' wid de iceman or someone. Hickey done me a favor, makin' me wake up. (*He pauses—then adds pathetically*) On'y it was fun, kinda, me and Cora kiddin' ourselves— (*Suddenly his face hardens with hatred*) Where is dat son of a bitch, Hickey? I want one good sock at dat guy— just one!—and de next buttin' in he'll do will be in de morgue! I'll take a chance on goin' to de Chair—!

ROCKY. (*Starts—in a low warning voice*) Piano! Keep away from him, Chuck! He ain't here now, anyway. He went out to phone, he said. He wouldn't call from here. I got a hunch he's beat it. But if he does come back, yuh don't know him, if anyone asks yuh, get me? (*As* CHUCK *looks at him with dull surprise he lowers his voice to a whisper*) De Chair, maybe dat's where he's goin'. I don't know nuttin', see, but it looks like he croaked his wife.

CHUCK. (*With a flash of interest*) Yuh mean

she really was cheatin' on him? Den I don't blame de guy—

ROCKY. Who's blamin' him? When a dame asks for it— But I don't know nuttin' about it, see?

CHUCK. Is any of de gang wise?

ROCKY. Larry is. And de boss ought to be. I tried to wise de rest of dem up to stay clear of him, but dey're all so licked, I don't know if dey got it. (*He pauses—vindictively*) I don't give a damn what he done to his wife, but if he gets de Hot Seat I won't go into no mournin'!

CHUCK. Me, neider!

ROCKY. Not after his trowin' it in my face I'm a pimp. What if I am? Why de hell not? And what he's done to Harry. Jees, de poor old slob is so licked he can't even get drunk. And all de gang. Dey're all licked. I couldn't help feelin' sorry for de poor bums when dey showed up tonight, one by one, lookin' like pooches wid deir tails between deir legs, dat everyone'd been kickin' till dey was too punch-drunk to feel it no more. Jimmy Tomorrow was de last. Schwartz, de copper, brung him in. Seen him sittin' on de dock on West Street, lookin' at de water and cryin'! Schwartz thought he was drunk and I let him tink it. But he was cold sober. He was tryin' to jump in and didn't have de noive, I figgered it. Noive! Jees, dere ain't enough guts left in de whole gang to battle a mosquito!

CHUCK. Aw, to hell wid 'em! Who cares? Gimme a drink. (ROCKY *pushes the bottle toward him apathetically*) I see you been hittin' de redeye, too.

ROCKY. Yeah. But it don't do no good. I can't get drunk right. (CHUCK *drinks.* JOE *mumbles in his sleep.* CHUCK *regards him resentfully*) Dis doity dinge was able to get his snootful and pass out. Jees, even Hickey can't faze a nigger! Yuh'd tink he was fazed if yuh'd seen him come in. Stinko, and he pulled a gat and said he'd plug Hickey for insultin' him. Den he dropped it and begun to cry and said he wasn't a gamblin' man or a tough guy no more; he was yellow. He'd borrowed de gat to stick up someone, and den didn't have de guts. He got drunk panhandlin' drinks in nigger joints, I s'pose. I guess dey felt sorry for him.

CHUCK. He ain't got no business in de bar after hours. Why don't yuh chuck him out?

ROCKY. (*Apathetically*) Aw, to hell wid it. Who cares?

CHUCK. (*Lapsing into the same mood*) Yeah. I don't.

JOE. (*Suddenly lunges to his feet dazedly—mumbles in humbled apology*) Scuse me, White Boys. Scuse me for livin'. I don't want to be where I's not wanted. (*He makes his way sway-ingly to the opening in the curtain at rear and tacks down to the middle table of the three at right, front. He feels his way around it to the table at its left and gets to the chair in back of* CAPTAIN LEWIS.)

CHUCK. (*Gets up—in a callous, brutal tone*) My pig's in de back room, ain't she? I wanna collect de dough I wouldn't take dis mornin', like a sucker, before she blows it. (*He goes rear.*)

ROCKY. (*Getting up*) I'm comin', too. I'm trough woikin'. I ain't no lousy bartender. (CHUCK *comes through the curtain and looks for* CORA *as* JOE *flops down in the chair in back of* CAPTAIN LEWIS.)

JOE. (*Taps* LEWIS *on the shoulder—servilely apologetic*) If you objects to my sittin' here, Captain, just tell me and I pulls my freight.

LEWIS. No apology required, old chap. Anybody could tell you I should feel honored a bloody Kaffir would lower himself to sit beside me. (JOE *stares at him with sodden perplexity—then closes his eyes.* CHUCK *comes forward to take the chair behind* CORA'S, *as* ROCKY *enters the back room and starts over toward* LARRY'S *table.*)

CHUCK. (*His voice hard*) I'm waitin', Baby. Dig!

CORA. (*With apathetic obedience*) Sure. I been expectin' yuh. I got it all ready. Here. (*She passes a small roll of bills she has in her hand over her shoulder, without looking at him. He takes it, glances at it suspiciously, then shoves it in his pocket without a word of acknowledgment.* CORA *speaks with a tired wonder at herself rather than resentment toward him*) Jees, imagine me kiddin' myself I wanted to marry a drunken pimp.

CHUCK. Dat's nuttin', Baby. Imagine de sap I'da been, when I can get your dough just as easy widout it!

ROCKY. (*Takes the chair on* PARRITT'S *left, facing* LARRY—*dully*) Hello, Old Cemetery. (LARRY *doesn't seem to hear. To* PARRITT) Hello, Tightwad. You still around?

PARRITT. (*Keeps his eyes on* LARRY—*in a jeeringly challenging tone*) Ask Larry! He knows I'm here, all right, although he's pretending not to! He'd like to forget I'm alive! He's trying to kid himself with that grandstand philosopher stuff! But he knows he can't get away with it now! He kept himself locked in his room until a while ago, alone with a bottle of booze, but he couldn't make it work! He couldn't even get drunk! He had to come out! There must have been something there he was even more scared to face than he is Hickey and me! I guess he got looking at the fire escape and thinking how handy it was, if he was really sick of life and only had the nerve to die! (*He pauses sneeringly.* LARRY'S *face has tautened, but he pretends he doesn't hear.* ROCKY *pays no attention. His head has sunk forward, and he stares at the table top, sunk in the same stupor as the other occupants of the room.* PARRITT *goes on, his tone becoming more insistent*) He's been thinking of me, too, Rocky. Trying to figure a way to get out of helping me! He doesn't want to be bothered understanding. But he does understand all right! He used to love her, too. So he thinks I ought to take a hop off the fire escape! (*He pauses.* LARRY'S *hands on the table have clinched into fists, as his nails dig into his palms, but he remains silent.* PARRITT *breaks and starts pleading*) For God's sake, Larry, can't you say something? Hickey's got me all balled up. Thinking of what he must have done has got me so I don't know any more what I did or why. I can't go on like this! I've got to know what I ought to do—

LARRY. (*In a stifled tone*) God damn you! Are you trying to make me your executioner?

PARRITT. (*Starts frightenedly*) Execution? Then you do think—?

LARRY. I don't think anything!

PARRITT. (*With forced jeering*) I suppose you think I ought to die because I sold out a lot of loud-mouthed fakers, who were cheating suckers with a phony pipe dream, and put them where they ought to be, in jail? (*He forces a laugh*) Don't make me laugh! I ought to get a medal! What a damned old sap you are! You must still believe in the Movement! (*He nudges* ROCKY *with his elbow*) Hickey's right about him, isn't he, Rocky? An old no-good drunken tramp, as dumb as he is, ought to take a hop off the fire escape!

ROCKY. (*Dully*) Sure. Why don't he? Or you? Or me? What de hell's de difference? Who cares? (*There is a faint stir from all the crowd, as if this sentiment struck a responsive chord in their numbed minds. They mumble almost in chorus as one voice, like sleepers talking out of a dully irritating dream,* "The hell with it!" "Who cares?" *Then the sodden silence descends again on the room.* ROCKY *looks from* PARRITT *to* LARRY *puzzledly. He mutters*) What am I doin' here wid youse two? I remember I had someting on my mind to tell yuh. What—? Oh, I got it now. (*He looks from one to the other of their oblivious faces with a strange, sly, calculating look—ingratiatingly*) I was tinking how you was bot' reg'lar guys. I tinks, ain't two guys like dem saps to be hangin' round like a coupla stew bums and wastin' demselves. Not dat I blame yuh for not woikin'. On'y suckers woik. But dere's no percentage in bein' broke when yuh can grab good jack for yourself and make someone else woik for

yuh, is dere? I mean, like I do. So I tinks, Dey're my pals and I ought to wise up two good guys like dem to play my system, and not be lousy barflies, no good to demselves or nobody else. (*He addresses* PARRITT *now—persuasively*) What yuh tink, Parritt? Ain't I right? Sure, I am. So don't be a sucker, see? Yuh ain't a bad-lookin' guy. Yuh could easy make some gal who's a good hustler, an' start a stable. I'd help yuh and wise yuh up to de inside dope on de game. (*He pauses inquiringly.* PARRITT *gives no sign of having heard him.* ROCKY *asks impatiently*) Well, what about it? What if dey do call yuh a pimp? What de hell do you care—any more'n I do.

PARRITT. (*Without looking at him—vindictively*) I'm through with whores. I wish they were all in jail—or dead!

ROCKY. (*Ignores this—disappointedly*) So yuh won't touch it, huh? Aw right, stay a bum! (*He turns to* LARRY) Jees, Larry, he's sure one dumb boob, ain't he? Dead from de neck up! He don't know a good ting when he sees it. (*Oily, even persuasive again*) But how about you, Larry? You ain't dumb. So why not, huh? Sure, yuh're old, but dat don't matter. All de hustlers tink yuh're aces. Dey fall for yuh like yuh was deir uncle or old man or someting. Dey'd like takin' care of yuh. And de cops 'round here, dey like yuh, too. It'd be a pipe for yuh, 'specially wid me to help yuh and wise yuh up. Yuh wouldn't have to worry where de next drink's comin' from, or wear doity clothes. (*Hopefully*) Well, don't it look good to yuh?

LARRY. (*Glances at him—for a moment he is stirred to sardonic pity*) No, it doesn't look good, Rocky. I mean, the peace Hickey's brought you. It isn't contented enough, if you have to make everyone else a pimp, too.

ROCKY. (*Stares at him stupidly—then pushes his chair back and gets up, grumbling*) I'm a sap to waste time on yuh. A stew bum is a stew bum and yuh can't change him. (*He turns away—then turns back for an afterthought*) Like I was sayin' to Chuck, yuh better keep away from Hickey. If anyone asks yuh, yuh don't know nuttin', get me? Yuh never even hoid he had a wife. (*His face hardens*) Jees, we all ought to git drunk and stage a celebration when dat bastard goes to de Chair.

LARRY. (*Vindictively*) Be God, I'll celebrate with you and drink long life to him in hell! (*Then guiltily and pityingly*) No! The poor mad devil— (*Then with angry self-contempt*) Ah, pity again! The wrong kind! He'll welcome the Chair!

PARRITT. (*Contemptuously*) Yes, what are you so damned scared of death for? I don't want your lousy pity.

ROCKY. Christ, I hope he don't come back, Larry. We don't know nuttin' now. We're on'y guessin', see? But if de bastard keeps on talkin'—

LARRY. (*Grimly*) He'll come back. He'll keep on talking. He's got to. He's lost his confidence that the peace he's sold us is the real McCoy, and it's made him uneasy about his own. He'll have to prove to us— (*As he is speaking* HICKEY *appears silently in the doorway at rear. He has lost his beaming salesman's grin. His manner is no longer self-assured. His expression is uneasy, baffled and resentful. It has the stubborn set of an obsessed determination. His eyes are on* LARRY *as he comes in. As he speaks, there is a start from all the crowd, a shrinking away from him.*)

HICKEY. (*Angrily*) That's a damned lie, Larry! I haven't lost confidence a damned bit! Why should I? (*Boastfully*) By God, whenever I made up my mind to sell someone something I knew they ought to want, I've sold 'em! (*He suddenly looks confused—haltingly*) I mean— It isn't kind of you, Larry, to make that kind of crack when I've been doing my best to help—

ROCKY. (*Moving away from him toward right —sharply*) Keep away from me! I don't know nuttin' about yuh, see? (*His tone is threatening but his manner as he turns his back and ducks quickly across to the bar entrance is that of one in flight. In the bar he comes forward and slumps in a chair at the table, facing front.*)

HICKEY. (*Comes to the table at right, rear, of* LARRY'S *table and sits in the one chair there, facing front. He looks over the crowd at right, hopefully and then disappointedly. He speaks with a strained attempt at his old affectionate jollying manner*) Well, well! How are you coming along, everybody? Sorry I had to leave you for a while, but there was something I had to get finally settled. It's all fixed now.

HOPE. (*In the voice of one reiterating mechanically a hopeless complaint*) When are you going to do something about this booze, Hickey? Bejees, we all know you did something to take the life out of it. It's like drinking dishwater! We can't pass out! And you promised us peace. (*His group all join in in a dull, complaining chorus, "We can't pass out! You promised us peace!"*)

HICKEY. (*Bursts into resentful exasperation*) For God's sake, Harry, are you still harping on that damned nonsense! You've kept it up all afternoon and night! And you've got everybody else singing the same crazy tune! I've had about all I can stand— That's why I phoned—(*He controls himself*) Excuse me, boys and girls. I don't mean that. I'm just worried about you, when you play dead on me like this. I was hoping by the time I got back you'd be like you ought to be! I thought you were deliberately holding back, while I was around, because you didn't want to give me the satisfaction of showing me I'd had the right dope. And I did have! I know from my own experience. (*Exasperatedly*) But I've explained that a million times! And you've all done what you needed to do! By rights you should be contented now, without a single damned hope or lying dream left to torment you! But here you are, acting like a lot of stiffs cheating the undertaker! (*He looks around accusingly*) I can't figure it—unless it's just your damned pigheaded stubbornness! (*He breaks— miserably*) Hell, you oughtn't to act this way with me! You're my old pals, the only friends I've got. You know the one thing I want is to see you all happy before I go— (*Rousing himself to his old brisk, master-of-ceremonies manner*) And there's damned little time left now. I've made a date for two o'clock. We've got to get busy right away and find out what's wrong. (*There is a sodden silence. He goes on exasperatedly*) Can't you appreciate what you've got, for God's sake? Don't you know you're free now to be yourselves, without having to feel remorse or guilt, or lie to yourselves about reforming tomorrow? Can't you see there is no tomorrow now? You're rid of it forever! You've killed it! You don't have to care a damn about anything any more! You've finally got the game of life licked, don't you see that? (*Angrily exhorting*) Then why the hell don't you get pie-eyed and celebrate? Why don't you laugh and sing "Sweet Adeline"? (*With bitterly hurt accusation*) The only reason I can think of is, you're putting on this rotten half-dead act just to get back at me! Because you hate my guts! (*He breaks again*) God, don't do that, gang! It makes me feel like hell to think you hate me. It makes me feel you suspect I must have hated you. But that's a lie! Oh, I know I used to hate everyone in the world who wasn't as rotten a bastard as I was! But that was when I was still living in hell—before I faced the truth and saw the one possible way to free poor Evelyn and give her the peace she'd always dreamed about. (*He pauses. Everyone in the group stirs with awakening dread and they all begin to grow tense on their chairs.*)

CHUCK. (*Without looking at* HICKEY—*with dull, resentful viciousness*) Aw, put a bag over it! To hell wid Evelyn! What if she was cheatin'? And who cares what yuh did to her? Dat's your funeral. We don't give a damn, see? (*There is a dull, resentful chorus of assent, "We don't give a damn."* CHUCK *adds dully*) All we want outa you is keep de hell away from us and give us a rest. (*A muttered chorus of assent.*)

HICKEY. (*As if he hadn't heard this—an obsessed look on his face*) The one possible way to make up to her for all I'd made her go through, and get her rid of me so I couldn't make her suffer any more, and she wouldn't have to forgive me again! I saw I couldn't do it by killing myself, like I wanted to for a long time. That would have been the last straw for her. She'd have died of a broken heart to think I could do that to her. She'd have blamed herself for it, too. Or I couldn't just run away from her. She'd have died of grief and humiliation if I'd done that to her. She'd have thought I'd stopped loving her. (*He adds with a strange impressive simplicity*) You see, Evelyn loved me. And I loved her. That was the trouble. It would have been easy to find a way out if she hadn't loved me so much. Or if I hadn't loved her. But as it was, there was only one possible way. (*He pauses—then adds simply*) I had to kill her. (*There is a second's dead silence as he finishes—then a tense indrawn breath like a gasp from the crowd, and a general shrinking movement.*)

LARRY. (*Bursts out*) You mad fool, can't you keep your mouth shut! We may hate you for what you've done here this time, but we remember the old times, too, when you brought kindness and laughter with you instead of death! We don't want to know things that will make us help send you to the Chair!

PARRITT. (*With angry scorn*) Ah, shut up, you yellow faker! Can't you face anything? Wouldn't I deserve the Chair, too, if I'd— It's worse if you kill someone and they have to go on living. I'd be glad of the Chair! It'd wipe it out! It'd square me with myself!

HICKEY. (*Disturbed—with a movement of repulsion*) I wish you'd get rid of that bastard, Larry. I can't have him pretending there's something in common between him and me. It's what's in your heart that counts. There was love in my heart, not hate.

PARRITT. (*Glares at him in angry terror*) You're a liar! I don't hate her! I couldn't! And it had nothing to do with her, anyway! You ask Larry!

LARRY. (*Grabs his shoulder and shakes him furiously*) God damn you, stop shoving your rotten soul in my lap! (PARRITT *subsides, hiding his face in his hands and shuddering.*)

HICKEY. (*Goes on quietly now*) Don't worry about the Chair, Larry. I know it's still hard for you not to be terrified by death, but when you've made peace with yourself, like I have, you won't give a damn. (*He addresses the group at right again—earnestly*) Listen, everybody. I've made up my mind the only way I can clear things up for you, so you'll realize how contented and carefree you ought to feel, now I've made you get rid of your pipe dreams, is to show you what a pipe dream did to me and Evelyn. I'm certain if I tell you about it from the beginning, you'll appreciate what I've done for you and why I did it, and how damned grateful you ought to be—instead of hating me. (*He begins eagerly in a strange running narrative manner*) You see, even when we were kids, Evelyn and me—

HOPE. (*Bursts out, pounding with his glass on the table*) No! Who the hell cares? We don't want to hear it. All we want is to pass out and get drunk and a little peace! (*They are all, except* LARRY *and* PARRITT, *seized by the same fit and pound with their glasses, even* HUGO, *and* ROCKY *in the bar, and shout in chorus, "Who the hell cares? We want to pass out!"*)

HICKEY. (*With an expression of wounded hurt*) All right, if that's the way you feel. I don't want to cram it down your throats. I don't need to tell anyone. I don't feel guilty. I'm only worried about you.

HOPE. What did you do to this booze? That's what we'd like to hear. Bejees, you done something. There's no life or kick in it now. (*He appeals mechanically to* JIMMY TOMORROW) Ain't that right, Jimmy?

JIMMY. (*More than any of them, his face has a wax-figure blankness that makes it look embalmed. He answers in a precise, completely lifeless voice, but his reply is not to* HARRY'S *question, and he does not look at him or anyone else*) Yes. Quite right. It was all a stupid lie—my nonsense about tomorrow. Naturally, they would never give me my position back. I would never dream of asking them. It would be hopeless. I didn't resign. I was fired for drunkenness. And that was years ago. I'm much worse now. And it was absurd of me to excuse my drunkenness by pretending it was my wife's adultery that ruined my life. As Hickey guessed, I was a drunkard before that. Long before. I discovered early in life that living frightened me when I was sober. I have forgotten why I married Marjorie. I can't even remember now if she was pretty. She was a blonde, I think, but I couldn't swear to it. I had some idea of wanting a home, perhaps. But, of course, I much preferred the nearest pub. Why Marjorie married me, God knows. It's impossible to believe she loved me. She soon found I much preferred drinking all night with my pals to being in bed with her. So, naturally, she was unfaithful. I didn't blame her. I really didn't care. I was glad to be free—even grateful to her, I think, for giving me such a good tragic excuse to drink as much as I damned well pleased. (*He stops like a mechanical doll that has run down. No one gives any sign of having heard him. There is a heavy silence. Then* ROCKY, *at the table in the bar, turns grouchily as he hears a noise behind him. Two men come quietly forward. One,* MORAN, *is middle-aged. The other,* LIEB, *is in his twenties. They look ordinary in every way, without anything distinctive to indicate what they do for a living.*)

ROCKY. (*Grumpily*) In de back room if yuh wanta drink. (MORAN *makes a peremptory sign to be quiet. All of a sudden* ROCKY *senses they are detectives and springs up to face them, his expression freezing into a wary blankness.* MORAN *pulls back his coat to show his badge.*)

MORAN. (*In a low voice*) Guy named Hickman in the back room?

ROCKY. Tink I know de names of all de guys—?

MORAN. Listen, you! This is murder. And don't be a sap. It was Hickman himself phoned in and said we'd find him here around two.

ROCKY. (*Dully*) So dat's who he phoned to. (*He shrugs his shoulders*) Aw right, if he asked for it. He's de fat guy sittin' alone. (*He slumps down in his chair again*) And if yuh want a confession all yuh got to do is listen. He'll be tellin' all about it soon. Yuh can't stop de bastard talkin'. (MORAN *gives him a curious look, then whispers to* LIEB, *who disappears rear and a moment later appears in the hall doorway of the back room. He spots* HICKEY *and slides into a chair at the left of the doorway, cutting off escape by the hall.* MORAN *goes back and stands in the opening in the curtain leading to the back room. He sees* HICKEY *and stands watching him and listening.*)

HICKEY. (*Suddenly bursts out*) I've got to tell you! Your being the way you are now gets my goat! It's all wrong! It puts things in my mind—about myself. It makes me think, if I got balled up about you, how do I know I wasn't balled up about myself? And that's plain damned foolishness. When you know the story of me and Evelyn, you'll see there wasn't any other possible way out of it, for her sake. Only I've got to start way back at the beginning or you won't understand. (*He starts his story, his tone again becoming musingly reminiscent*) You see, even as a kid I was always restless. I had to keep on the go. You've heard the old saying, "Ministers' sons are sons of guns." Well, that was me, and then some. Home was like a jail. I didn't fall for the religious bunk. Listening to my old man whooping up hell fire and scaring those Hoosier suckers into shelling out their dough only handed me a laugh, although I had to hand it to him, the way he sold them nothing for something. I guess I take after him, and that's what

made me a good salesman. Well, anyway, as I said, home was like jail, and so was school, and so was that damned hick town. The only place I liked was the pool rooms, where I could smoke Sweet Caporals, and mop up a couple of beers, thinking I was a hell-on-wheels sport. We had one hooker shop in town, and, of course, I liked that, too. Not that I hardly ever had entrance money. My old man was a tight old bastard. But I liked to sit around in the parlor and joke with the girls, and they liked me because I could kid 'em along and make 'em laugh. Well, you know what a small town is. Everyone got wise to me. They all said I was a no-good tramp. I didn't give a damn what they said. I hated everybody in the place. That is, except Evelyn. I loved Evelyn. Even as a kid. And Evelyn loved me. (*He pauses. No one moves or gives any sign except by the dread in their eyes that they have heard him. Except* PARRITT, *who takes his hands from his face to look at* LARRY *pleadingly.*)

PARRITT. I loved Mother, Larry! No matter what she did! I still do! Even though I know she wishes now I was dead! You believe that, don't you? Christ, why can't you say something?

HICKEY. (*Too absorbed in his story now to notice this—goes on in a tone of fond, sentimental reminiscence*) Yes, sir, as far back as I can remember, Evelyn and I loved each other. She always stuck up for me. She wouldn't believe the gossip—or she'd pretend she didn't. No one could convince her I was no good. Evelyn was stubborn as all hell once she'd made up her mind. Even when I'd admit things and ask her forgiveness, she'd make excuses for me and defend me against myself. She'd kiss me and say she knew I didn't mean it and I wouldn't do it again. So I'd promise I wouldn't. I'd have to promise, she was so sweet and good, though I knew darned well— (*A touch of strange bitterness comes into his voice for a moment*) No, sir, you couldn't stop Evelyn. Nothing on earth could shake her faith in me. Even I couldn't. She was a sucker for a pipe dream. (*Then quickly*) Well, naturally, her family forbid her seeing me. They were one of the town's best, rich for that hick burg, owned the trolley line and lumber company. Strict Methodists, too. They hated my guts. But they couldn't stop Evelyn. She'd sneak notes to me and meet me on the sly. I was getting more restless. The town was getting more like a jail. I made up my mind to beat it. I knew exactly what I wanted to be by that time. I'd met a lot of drummers around the hotel and liked 'em. They were always telling jokes. They were sports. They kept moving. I liked their life. And I knew I could kid people and sell things.

The hitch was how to get the railroad fare to the Big Town. I told Mollie Arlington my trouble. She was the madame of the cathouse. She liked me. She laughed and said, "Hell, I'll stake you, Kid! I'll bet on you. With that grin of yours and that line of bull, you ought to be able to sell skunks for good ratters!" (*He chuckles*) Mollie was all right. She gave me confidence in myself. I paid her back, the first money I earned. Wrote her a kidding letter, I remember, saying I was peddling baby carriages and she and the girls had better take advantage of our bargain offer. (*He chuckles*) But that's ahead of my story. The night before I left town, I had a date with Evelyn. I got all worked up, she was so pretty and sweet and good. I told her straight, "You better forget me, Evelyn, for your own sake. I'm no good and never will be. I'm not worthy to wipe your shoes." I broke down and cried. She just said, looking white and scared, "Why, Teddy? Don't you still love me?" I said, "Love you? God, Evelyn, I love you more than anything in the world. And I always will!" She said, "Then nothing else matters, Teddy, because nothing but death could stop my loving you. So I'll wait, and when you're ready you send for me and we'll be married. I know I can make you happy, Teddy, and once you're happy you won't want to do any of the bad things you've done any more." And I said, "Of course, I won't, Evelyn!" I meant it, too. I believed it. I loved her so much she could make me believe anything. (*He sighs. There is a suspended, waiting silence. Even the two detectives are drawn into it. Then* HOPE *breaks into dully exasperated, brutally callous protest.*)

HOPE. Get it over, you long-winded bastard! You married her, and you caught her cheating with the iceman, and you croaked her, and who the hell cares? What's she to us? All we want is to pass out in peace, bejees! (*A chorus of dull, resentful protest from all the group. They mumble, like sleepers who curse a person who keeps awakening them,* "What's it to us? We want to pass out in peace!" HOPE *drinks and they mechanically follow his example. He pours another and they do the same. He complains with a stupid, nagging insistence*) No life in the booze! No kick! Dishwater. Bejees, I'll never pass out!

HICKEY. (*Goes on as if there had been no interruption*) So I beat it to the Big Town. I got a job easy, and it was a cinch for me to make good. I had the knack. It was like a game, sizing people up quick, spotting what their pet pipe dreams were, and then kidding 'em along that line, pretending you believed what they wanted to believe about themselves. Then they liked you, they trusted you, they wanted to buy something to show their gratitude. It was fun. But still, all the while I felt guilty, as if I had no right to be having such a good time away from Evelyn. In each letter I'd tell her how I missed her, but I'd keep warning her, too. I'd tell her all my faults, how I liked my booze every once in a while, and so on. But there was no shaking Evelyn's belief in me, or her dreams about the future. After each letter of hers, I'd be as full of faith as she was. So as soon as I got enough saved to start us off, I sent for her and we got married. Christ, wasn't I happy for a while! And wasn't she happy! I don't care what anyone says, I'll bet there never was two people who loved each other more than me and Evelyn. Not only then but always after, in spite of everything I did— (*He pauses—then sadly*) Well, it's all there, at the start, everything that happened afterwards. I never could learn to handle temptation. I'd want to reform and mean it. I'd promise Evelyn, and I'd promise myself, and I'd believe it. I'd tell her, it's the last time. And she'd say, "I know it's the last time, Teddy. You'll never do it again." That's what made it so hard. That's what made me feel such a rotten skunk—her always forgiving me. My playing around with women, for instance. It was only a harmless good time to me. Didn't mean anything. But I'd know what it meant to Evelyn. So I'd say to myself, never again. But you know how it is, traveling around. The damned hotel rooms. I'd get seeing things in the wall paper. I'd get bored as hell. Lonely and homesick. But at the same time sick of home. I'd feel free and I'd want to celebrate a little. I never drank on the job, so it had to be dames. Any tart. What I'd want was some tramp I could be myself with without being ashamed—someone I could tell a dirty joke to and she'd laugh.

CORA. (*With a dull, weary bitterness*) Jees, all de lousy jokes I've had to listen to and pretend was funny!

HICKEY. (*Goes on obliviously*) Sometimes I'd try some joke I thought was a corker on Evelyn. She'd always make herself laugh. But I could tell she thought it was dirty, not funny. And Evelyn always knew about the tarts I'd been with when I came home from a trip. She'd kiss me and look in my eyes, and she'd know. I'd see in her eyes how she was trying not to know, and then telling herself even if it was true, he couldn't help it, they tempt him, and he's lonely, he hasn't got me, it's only his body, anyway, he doesn't love them, I'm the only one he loves. She was right, too. I never loved anyone else. Couldn't if I wanted to. (*He pauses*) She forgave me even when it all had to come out in the open. You know how it is when you keep taking chances. You may be lucky for a long time, but you get nicked in the end. I picked up a nail from some tart in Altoona.

CORA. (*Dully, without resentment*) Yeah. And she picked it up from some guy. It's all in de game. What de hell of it?

HICKEY. I had to do a lot of lying and stalling when I got home. It didn't do any good. The quack I went to got all my dough and then told me I was cured and I took his word. But I wasn't, and poor Evelyn— But she did her best to make me believe she fell for my lie about how traveling men get things from drinking cups on trains. Anyway, she forgave me. The same way she forgave me every time I'd turn up after a periodical drunk. You all know what I'd be like at the end of one. You've seen me. Like something lying in the gutter that no alley cat would lower itself to drag in—something they threw out of the D.T. ward in Bellevue along with the garbage, something that ought to be dead and isn't! (*His face is convulsed with self-loathing*) Evelyn wouldn't have heard from me in a month or more. She'd have been waiting there alone, with the neighbors shaking their heads and feeling sorry for her out loud. That was before she got me to move to the outskirts, where there weren't any next-door neighbors. And then the door would open and in I'd stumble—looking like what I've said—into her home, where she kept everything so spotless and clean. And I'd sworn it would never happen again, and now I'd have to start swearing again this was the last time. I could see disgust having a battle in her eyes with love. Love always won. She'd make herself kiss me, as if nothing had happened, as if I'd just come home from a business trip. She'd never complain or bawl me out. (*He bursts out in a tone of anguish that has anger and hatred beneath it*) Christ, can you imagine what a guilty skunk she made me feel! If she'd only admitted once she didn't believe any more in her pipe dream that some day I'd behave! But she never would. Evelyn was stubborn as hell. Once she'd set her heart on anything, you couldn't shake her faith that it had to come true—tomorrow! It was the same old story, over and over, for years and years. It kept piling up, inside her and inside me. God, can you picture all I made her suffer, and all the guilt she made me feel, and how I hated myself! If she only hadn't been so damned good— if she'd been the same kind of wife I was a husband. God, I used to pray sometimes she'd—I'd even say to her, "Go on, why don't you, Evelyn? It'd serve me right. I wouldn't mind. I'd forgive you." Of course, I'd pretend I was kidding—the

same way I used to joke here about her being in the hay with the iceman. She'd have been so hurt if I'd said it seriously. She'd have thought I'd stopped loving her. (*He pauses—then looking around at them*) I suppose you think I'm a liar, that no woman could have stood all she stood and still loved me so much—that it isn't human for any woman to be so pitying and forgiving. Well, I'm not lying, and if you'd ever seen her, you'd realize I wasn't. It was written all over her face, sweetness and love and pity and forgiveness. (*He reaches mechanically for the inside pocket of his coat*) Wait! I'll show you. I always carry her picture. (*Suddenly he looks startled. He stares before him, his hand falling back—quietly*) No, I'm forgetting I tore it up—afterwards. I didn't need it any more. (*He pauses. The silence is like that in the room of a dying man where people hold their breath, waiting for him to die.*)

CORA. (*With a muffled sob*) Jees, Hickey! Jees! (*She shivers and puts her hands over her face.*)

PARRITT. (*To* LARRY *in a low insistent tone*) I burnt up Mother's picture, Larry. Her eyes followed me all the time. They seemed to be wishing I was dead!

HICKEY. It kept piling up, like I've said. I got so I thought of it all the time. I hated myself more and more, thinking of all the wrong I'd done to the sweetest woman in the world who loved me so much. I got so I'd curse myself for a lousy bastard every time I saw myself in the mirror. I felt such pity for her it drove me crazy. You wouldn't believe a guy like me, that's knocked around so much, could feel such pity. It got so every night I'd wind up hiding my face in her lap, bawling and begging her forgiveness. And, of course, she'd always comfort me and say, "Never mind, Teddy, I know you won't ever again." Christ, I loved her so, but I began to hate that pipe dream! I began to be afraid I was going bughouse, because sometimes I couldn't forgive her for forgiving me. I even caught myself hating her for making me hate myself so much. There's a limit to the guilt you can feel and the forgiveness and the pity you can take! You have to begin blaming someone else, too. I got so sometimes when she'd kiss me it was like she did it on purpose to humiliate me, as if she'd spit in my face! But all the time I saw how crazy and rotten of me that was, and it made me hate myself all the more. You'd never believe I could hate so much, a good-natured, happy-go-lucky slob like me. And as the time got nearer to when I was due to come here for my drunk around Harry's birthday, I got nearly crazy. I kept swearing to her every night that this time I really wouldn't, until I'd made it a real final test to myself—and to her. And she kept encouraging me and saying, "I can see you really mean it now, Teddy. I know you'll conquer it this time, and we'll be so happy, dear." When she'd say that and kiss me, I'd believe it, too. Then she'd go to bed, and I'd stay up alone because I couldn't sleep and I didn't want to disturb her, tossing and rolling around. I'd get so damned lonely. I'd get thinking how peaceful it was here, sitting around with the old gang, getting drunk and forgetting love, joking and laughing and singing and swapping lies. And finally I knew I'd have to come. And I knew if I came this time, it was the finish. I'd never have the guts to go back and be forgiven again, and that would break Evelyn's heart because to her it would mean I didn't love her any more. (*He pauses*) That last night I'd driven myself crazy trying to figure some way out for her. I went in the bedroom. I was going to tell her it was the end. But I couldn't do that to her. She was sound asleep. I thought, God, if she'd only never wake up, she'd never know! And then it came to me—the only possible way out, for her sake. I remembered I'd given her a gun for protection while I was away and it was in the bureau drawer. She'd never feel any pain, never wake up from her dream. So I—

HOPE. (*Tries to ward this off by pounding with his glass on the table—with brutal, callous exasperation*) Give us a rest, for the love of Christ! Who the hell cares? We want to pass out in peace! (*They all, except* PARRITT *and* LARRY, *pound with their glasses and grumble in chorus: "Who the hell cares? We want to pass out in peace!"* MORAN, *the detective, moves quietly from the entrance in the curtain across the back of the room to the table where his companion,* LIEB, *is sitting.* ROCKY *notices his leaving and gets up from the table in the rear and goes back to stand and watch in the entrance.* MORAN *exchanges a glance with* LIEB, *motioning him to get up. The latter does so. No one notices them. The clamor of banging glasses dies out as abruptly as it started.* HICKEY *hasn't appeared to hear it.*)

HICKEY. (*Simply*) So I killed her. (*There is a moment of dead silence. Even the detectives are caught in it and stand motionless.*)

PARRITT. (*Suddenly gives up and relaxes limply in his chair—in a low voice in which there is a strange exhausted relief*) I may as well confess, Larry. There's no use lying any more. You know, anyway. I didn't give a damn about the money. It was because I hated her.

HICKEY. (*Obliviously*) And then I saw I'd always known that was the only possible way to give her peace and free her from the misery of loving me. I saw it meant peace for me, too, knowing she was at peace. I felt as though a ton of guilt was lifted off my mind. I remember I stood by the bed and suddenly I had to laugh. I couldn't help it, and I knew Evelyn would forgive me. I remember I heard myself speaking to her, as if it was something I'd always wanted to say: "Well, you know what you can do with your pipe dream now, you damned bitch!" (*He stops with a horrified start, as if shocked out of a nightmare, as if he couldn't believe he heard what he had just said. He stammers*) No! I never—!

PARRITT. (*To* LARRY—*sneeringly*) Yes, that's it! Her and the damned old Movement pipe dream! Eh, Larry?

HICKEY. (*Bursts into frantic denial*) No! That's a lie! I never said—! Good God, I couldn't have said that! If I did, I'd gone insane! Why, I loved Evelyn better than anything in life! (*He appeals brokenly to the crowd*) Boys, you're all my old pals! You've known old Hickey for years! You know I'd never— (*His eyes fix on* HOPE) You've known me longer than anyone, Harry. You know I must have been insane, don't you, Governor?

HOPE. (*At first with the same defensive callousness—without looking at him*) Who the hell cares? (*Then suddenly he looks at* HICKEY *and there is an extraordinary change in his expression. His face lights up, as if he were grasping at some dawning hope in his mind. He speaks with a groping eagerness*) Insane? You mean—you went really insane? (*At the tone of his voice, all the group at the tables by him start and stare at him as if they caught his thought. Then they all look at* HICKEY *eagerly, too.*)

HICKEY. Yes! Or I couldn't have laughed! I couldn't have said that to her! (MORAN *walks up behind him on one side, while the second detective,* LIEB, *closes in on him from the other.*)

MORAN. (*Taps* HICKEY *on the shoulder*) That's enough, Hickman. You know who we are. You're under arrest. (*He nods to* LIEB, *who slips a pair of handcuffs on* HICKEY'S *wrists.* HICKEY *stares at them with stupid incomprehension.* MORAN *takes his arm*) Come along and spill your guts where we can get it on paper.

HICKEY. No, wait, Officer! You owe me a break! I phoned and made it easy for you, didn't I? Just a few minutes! (*To* HOPE—*pleadingly*) You know I couldn't say that to Evelyn, don't you, Harry—unless—

HOPE. (*Eagerly*) And you've been crazy ever since? Everything you've said and done here—

HICKEY. (*For a moment forgets his own obsession and his face takes on its familiar expression of affectionate amusement and he chuckles*) Now,

Governor! Up to your old tricks, eh? I see what you're driving at, but I can't let you get away with— (*Then, as* HOPE's *expression turns to resentful callousness again and he looks away, he adds hastily with pleading desperation*) Yes, Harry, of course, I've been out of my mind ever since! All the time I've been here! You saw I was insane, didn't you?

MORAN. (*With cynical disgust*) Can it! I've had enough of your act. Save it for the jury. (*Addressing the crowd, sharply*) Listen, you guys. Don't fall for his lies. He's starting to get foxy now and thinks he'll plead insanity. But he can't get away with it. (*The crowd at the grouped tables are grasping at hope now. They glare at him resentfully.*)

HOPE. (*Begins to bristle in his old-time manner*) Bejees, you dumb dick, you've got a crust trying to tell us about Hickey! We've known him for years, and every one of us noticed he was nutty the minute he showed up here! Bejees, if you'd heard all the crazy bull he was pulling about bringing us peace—like a bughouse preacher escaped from an asylum! If you'd seen all the damned-fool things he made us do! We only did them because— (*He hesitates—then defiantly*) Because we hoped he'd come out of it if we kidded him along and humored him. (*He looks around at the others*) Ain't that right, fellers? (*They burst into a chorus of eager assent: "Yes, Harry!" "That's it, Harry!" "That's why!" "We knew he was crazy!" "Just to humor him!"*)

MORAN. A fine bunch of rats! Covering up for a dirty, cold-blooded murderer.

HOPE. (*Stung into recovering all his old fuming truculence*) Is that so? Bejees, you know the old story, when Saint Patrick drove the snakes out of Ireland they swam to New York and joined the police force! Ha! (*He cackles insultingly*) Bejees, we can believe it now when we look at you, can't we, fellers? (*They all growl assent, glowering defiantly at* MORAN. MORAN *glares at them, looking as if he'd like to forget his prisoner and start cleaning out the place.* HOPE *goes on pugnaciously*) You stand up for your rights, bejees, Hickey! Don't let this smart-aleck dick get funny with you. If he pulls any rubber-hose tricks, you let me know! I've still got friends at the Hall! Bejees, I'll have him back in uniform pounding a beat where the only graft he'll get will be stealing tin cans from the goats!

MORAN. (*Furiously*) Listen, you cockeyed old bum, for a plugged nickel I'd— (*Controlling himself, turns to* HICKEY, *who is oblivious to all this, and yanks his arm*) Come on, you!

HICKEY. (*With a strange mad earnestness*) Oh, I want to go, Officer. I can hardly wait now. I should have phoned you from the house right afterwards. It was a waste of time coming here. I've got to explain to Evelyn. But I know she's forgiven me. She knows I was insane. You've got me all wrong, Officer. I want to go to the Chair.

MORAN. Crap!

HICKEY. (*Exasperatedly*) God, you're a dumb dick! Do you suppose I give a damn about life now? Why, you bonehead, I haven't got a single damned lying hope or pipe dream left!

MORAN. (*Jerks him around to face the door to the hall*) Get a move on!

HICKEY. (*As they start walking toward rear—insistently*) All I want you to see is I was out of my mind afterwards, when I laughed at her! I was a raving rotten lunatic or I couldn't have said— Why, Evelyn was the only thing on God's earth I ever loved! I'd have killed myself before I'd ever have hurt her! (*They disappear in the hall.* HICKEY's *voice keeps on protesting.*)

HOPE. (*Calls after him*) Don't worry, Hickey! They can't give you the Chair! We'll testify you was crazy! Won't we, fellers? (*They all assent. Two or three echo* HOPE's *"Don't worry, Hickey." Then from the hall comes the slam of the street door.* HOPE's *face falls—with genuine sorrow*) He's gone. Poor crazy son of a bitch! (*All the group around him are sad and sympathetic, too.* HOPE *reaches for his drink*) Bejees, I need a drink. (*They grab their glasses.* HOPE *says hopefully*) Bejees, maybe it'll have the old kick, now he's gone. (*He drinks and they follow suit.*)

ROCKY. (*Comes forward from where he has stood in the bar entrance—hopefully*) Yeah, Boss, maybe we can get drunk now. (*He sits in the chair by* CHUCK *and pours a drink and tosses it down. Then they all sit still, waiting for the effect, as if this drink were a crucial test, so absorbed in hopeful expectancy that they remain oblivious to what happens at* LARRY's *table.*)

LARRY. (*His eyes full of pain and pity—in a whisper, aloud to himself*) May the Chair bring him peace at last, the poor tortured bastard!

PARRITT. (*Leans toward him—in a strange low insistent voice*) Yes, but he isn't the only one who needs peace, Larry. I can't feel sorry for him. He's lucky. He's through, now. It's all decided for him. I wish it was decided for me. I've never been any good at deciding things. Even about selling out, it was the tart the detective agency got after me who put it in my mind. You remember what Mother's like, Larry. She makes all the decisions. She's always decided what I must do. She doesn't like anyone to be free but herself. (*He pauses, as if waiting for comment, but* LARRY *ignores him*)

I suppose you think I ought to have made those dicks take me away with Hickey. But how could I prove it, Larry? They'd think I was nutty. Because she's still alive. You're the only one who can understand how guilty I am. Because you know her and what I've done to her. You know I'm really much guiltier than he is. You know what I did is a much worse murder. Because she is dead and yet she has to live. For a while. But she can't live long in jail. She loves freedom too much. And I can't kid myself like Hickey, that she's at peace. As long as she lives, she'll never be able to forget what I've done to her even in her sleep. She'll never have a second's peace. (*He pauses— then bursts out*) Jesus, Larry, can't you say something? (LARRY *is at the breaking point.* PARRITT *goes on*) And I'm not putting up any bluff, either, that I was crazy afterwards when I laughed to myself and thought, "You know what you can do with your freedom pipe dream now, don't you, you damned old bitch!"

LARRY. (*Snaps and turns on him, his face convulsed with detestation. His quivering voice has a condemning command in it*) Go! Get the hell out of life, God damn you, before I choke it out of you! Go up—!

PARRITT. (*His manner is at once transformed. He seems suddenly at peace with himself. He speaks simply and gratefully*) Thanks, Larry. I just wanted to be sure. I can see now it's the only possible way I can ever get free from her. I guess I've really known that all my life. (*He pauses—then with a derisive smile*) It ought to comfort Mother a little, too. It'll give her the chance to play the great incorruptible Mother of the Revolution, whose only child is the Proletariat. She'll be able to say: "Justice is done! So may all traitors die!" She'll be able to say: "I am glad he's dead! Long live the Revolution!" (*He adds with a final implacable jeer*) You know her, Larry! Always a ham!

LARRY. (*Pleads distractedly*) Go, for the love of Christ, you mad tortured bastard, for your own sake! (HUGO *is roused by this. He lifts his head and peers uncomprehendingly at* LARRY. *Neither* LARRY *nor* PARRITT *notices him.*)

PARRITT. (*Stares at* LARRY. *His face begins to crumble as if he were going to break down and sob. He turns his head away, but reaches out fumblingly and pats* LARRY'S *arm and stammers*) Jesus, Larry, thanks. That's kind. I knew you were the only one who could understand my side of it. (*He gets to his feet and turns toward the door.*)

HUGO. (*Looks at* PARRITT *and bursts into his silly giggle*) Hello, leedle Don, leedle monkey-face! Don't be a fool! Buy me a trink!

PARRITT. (*Puts on an act of dramatic bravado— forcing a grin*) Sure, I will, Hugo! Tomorrow! Beneath the willow trees! (*He walks to the door with a careless swagger and disappears in the hall. From now on,* LARRY *waits, listening for the sound he knows is coming from the backyard outside the window, but trying not to listen, in an agony of horror and cracking nerve.*)

HUGO. (*Stares after* PARRITT *stupidly*) Stupid fool! Hickey make you crazy, too. (*He turns to the oblivious* LARRY—*with a timid eagerness*) I'm glad, Larry, they take that crazy Hickey avay to asylum. He makes me have bad dreams. He makes me tell lies about myself. He makes me want to spit on all I have ever dreamed. Yes, I am glad they take him to asylum. I don't feel I am dying now. He vas selling death to me, that crazy salesman. I think I have a trink now, Larry. (*He pours a drink and gulps it down.*)

HOPE. (*Jubilantly*) Bejees, fellers, I'm feeling the old kick, or I'm a liar! It's putting life back in me! Bejees, if all I've lapped up begins to hit me, I'll be paralyzed before I know it! It was Hickey kept it from— Bejees, I know that sounds crazy, but he was crazy, and he'd got all of us as bughouse as he was. Bejees, it does queer things to you, having to listen day and night to a lunatic's pipe dreams—pretending you believe them, to kid him along and doing any crazy thing he wants to humor him. It's dangerous, too. Look at me pretending to start for a walk just to keep him quiet. I knew damned well it wasn't the right day for it. The sun was broiling and the streets full of automobiles. Bejees, I could feel myself getting sunstroke, and an automobile damn near ran over me. (*He appeals to* ROCKY, *afraid of the result, but daring it*) Ask Rocky. He was watching. Didn't it, Rocky?

ROCKY. (*A bit tipsily*) What's dat, Boss? Jees, all de booze I've mopped up is beginning to get to me. (*Earnestly*) De automobile, Boss? Sure, I seen it! Just missed yuh! I thought yuh was a goner. (*He pauses—then looks around at the others, and assumes the old kidding tone of the inmates, but hesitantly, as if still a little afraid*) On de woid of a honest bartender! (*He tries a wink at the others. They all respond with smiles that are still a little forced and uneasy.*)

HOPE. (*Flashes him a suspicious glance. Then he understands—with his natural testy manner*) You're a bartender, all right. No one can say different. (ROCKY *looks grateful*) But, bejees, don't pull that honest junk! You and Chuck ought to have cards in the Burglars' Union! (*This time there is an eager laugh from the group.* HOPE *is delighted*) Bejees, it's good to hear someone laugh again! All the time that bas—poor old Hickey was here, I didn't have the heart— Bejees, I'm getting drunk and glad of it! (*He cackles and reaches for the bottle*) Come on, fellers. It's on the house. (*They pour drinks. They begin rapidly to get drunk now.* HOPE *becomes sentimental*) Poor old Hickey! We mustn't hold him responsible for anything he's done. We'll forget that and only remember him the way we've always known him before —the kindest, biggest-hearted guy ever wore shoe leather. (*They all chorus hearty sentimental assent: "That's right, Harry!" "That's all!" "Finest fellow!" "Best scout!" etc.* HOPE *goes on*) Good luck to him in Matteawan! Come on, bottoms up! (*They all drink. At the table by the window* LARRY'S *hands grip the edge of the table. Unconsciously his head is inclined toward the window as he listens.*)

LARRY. (*Cannot hold back an anguished exclamation*) Christ! Why don't he—!

HUGO. (*Beginning to be drunk again—peers at him*) Vhy don't he what? Don't be a fool! Hickey's gone. He vas crazy. Have a trink. (*Then as he receives no reply—with vague uneasiness*) What's matter vith you, Larry? You look funny. What you listen to out in backyard, Larry? (CORA *begins to talk in the group at right.*)

CORA. (*Tipsily*) Well, I thank Gawd now me and Chuck did all we could to humor de poor nut. Jees, imagine us goin' off like we really meant to git married, when we ain't even picked out a farm yet!

CHUCK. (*Eagerly*) Sure ting, Baby. We kidded him we was serious.

JIMMY. (*Confidently—with a gentle, drunken unction*) I may as well say I detected his condition almost at once. All that talk of his about tomorrow, for example. He had the fixed idea of the insane. It only makes them worse to cross them.

WILLIE. (*Eagerly*) Same with me, Jimmy. Only I spent the day in the park. I wasn't such a damned fool as to—

LEWIS. (*Getting jauntily drunk*) Picture my predicament if I *had* gone to the Consulate. The pal of mine there is a humorous blighter. He would have got me a job out of pure spite. So I strolled about and finally came to roost in the park. (*He grins with affectionate kidding at* WETJOEN) And lo and behold, who was on the neighboring bench but my old battlefield companion, the Boer that walks like a man—who, if the British Government had taken my advice, would have been removed from his fetid kraal on the veldt straight to the baboon's cage at the London Zoo, and little children would now be asking their nurses: "Tell me, Nana, is that the Boer General, the one with the blue behind?" (*They all laugh uproariously.* LEWIS *leans over and slaps* WETJOEN *affectionately on the knee*) No offense meant, Piet, old chap.

WETJOEN. (*Beaming at him*) No offense taken, you tamned Limey! (WETJOEN *goes on—grinningly*) About a job, I felt the same as you, Cecil. (*At the table by the window* HUGO *speaks to* LARRY *again.*)

HUGO. (*With uneasy insistence*) What's matter, Larry? You look scared. What you listen for out there? (*But* LARRY *doesn't hear, and* JOE *begins talking in the group at right.*)

JOE. (*With drunken self-assurance*) No, suh, I wasn't fool enough to git in no crap game. Not while Hickey's around. Crazy people puts a jinx on you. (MCGLOIN *is now heard. He is leaning across in front of* WETJOEN *to talk to* ED MOSHER *on* HOPE'S *left.*)

MCGLOIN. (*With drunken earnestness*) I know you saw how it was, Ed. There was no good trying to explain to a crazy guy, but it ain't the right time. You know how getting reinstated is.

MOSHER. (*Decidedly*) Sure, Mac. The same way with the circus. The boys tell me the rubes are wasting all their money buying food and times never was so hard. And I never was one to cheat for chicken feed.

HOPE. (*Looks around him in an ecstasy of bleery sentimental content*) Bejees, I'm cockeyed! Bejees, you're all cockeyed! Bejees, we're all all right! Let's have another! (*They pour out drinks. At the table by the window* LARRY *has unconsciously shut his eyes as he listens.* HUGO *is peering at him frightenedly now.*)

HUGO. (*Reiterates stupidly*) What's matter, Larry? Why you keep eyes shut? You look dead. What you listen for in backyard? (*Then, as* LARRY *doesn't open his eyes or answer, he gets up hastily and moves away from the table, mumbling with frightened anger*) Crazy fool! You vas crazy like Hickey! You give me bad dreams, too. (*He shrinks quickly past the table where* HICKEY *had sat to the rear of the group at right.*)

ROCKY. (*Greets him with boisterous affection*) Hello, dere, Hugo! Welcome to de party!

HOPE. Yes, bejees, Hugo! Sit down! Have a drink! Have ten drinks, bejees!

HUGO. (*Forgetting* LARRY *and bad dreams, gives his familiar giggle*) Hello, leedle Harry! Hello, nice, leedle, funny monkey-faces! (*Warming up, changes abruptly to his usual declamatory denunciation*) Gottamned stupid bourgeois! Soon comes the Day of Judgment! (*They make derisive noises and tell him to sit down. He changes again, giggling good-naturedly, and sits at rear of the middle table*) Give me ten trinks, Harry. Don't be a fool. (*They laugh.* ROCKY *shoves a glass and bottle at him. The sound of* MARGIE'S *and* PEARL'S *voices is heard from the hall, drunkenly shrill. All of the group turn toward the door as the two appear. They are drunk and look blowsy and disheveled. Their manner as they enter hardens into a brazen defensive truculence.*)

MARGIE. (*Stridently*) Gangway for two good whores!

PEARL. Yeah! And we want a drink quick!

MARGIE. (*Glaring at* ROCKY) Shake de lead outa your pants, Pimp! A little soivice!

ROCKY. (*His black bullet eyes sentimental, his round Wop face grinning welcome*) Well, look who's here! (*He goes to them unsteadily, opening his arms*) Hello, dere, Sweethearts! Jees, I was beginnin' to worry about yuh, honest! (*He tries to embrace them. They push his arms away, regarding him with amazed suspicion.*)

PEARL. What kind of a gag is dis?

HOPE. (*Calls to them effusively*) Come on and join the party, you broads! Bejees, I'm glad to see you! (*The girls exchange a bewildered glance, taking in the party and the changed atmosphere.*)

MARGIE. Jees, what's come off here?

PEARL. Where's dat louse, Hickey?

ROCKY. De cops got him. He'd gone crazy and croaked his wife. (*The girls exclaim, "Jees!" But there is more relief than horror in it.* ROCKY *goes on*) He'll get Matteawan. He ain't responsible. What he's pulled don't mean nuttin'. So forget dat whore stuff. I'll knock de block off anyone calls you whores! I'll fill de bastard full of lead! Yuh're tarts, and what de hell of it? Yuh're as good as anyone! So forget it, see? (*They let him get his arms around them now. He gives them a hug. All the truculence leaves their faces. They smile and exchange maternally amused glances.*)

MARGIE. (*With a wink*) Our little bartender, ain't he, Poil?

PEARL. Yeah, and a cute little Ginny at dat! (*They laugh.*)

MARGIE. And is he stinko!

PEARL. Stinko is right. But he ain't got nuttin' on us. Jees, Rocky, did we have a big time at Coney!

HOPE. Bejees, sit down, you dumb broads! Welcome home! Have a drink! Have ten drinks, bejees! (*They take the empty chairs on* CHUCK'S *left, warmly welcomed by all.* ROCKY *stands in back of them, a hand on each of their shoulders, grinning with proud proprietorship.* HOPE *beams over and under his crooked spectacles with the air of a host whose party is a huge success, and rambles on happily*) Bejees, this is all right! We'll make this

my birthday party, and forget the other. We'll get paralyzed! But who's missing? Where's the Old Wise Guy? Where's Larry?

ROCKY. Over by de window Boss. Jees, he's got his eyes shut. De old bastard's asleep (*They turn to look.* ROCKY *dismisses him*) Aw, to hell wid him. Let's have a drink. (*They turn away and forget him.*)

LARRY. (*Torturedly arguing to himself in a shaken whisper*) It's the only way out for him! For the peace of all concerned, as Hickey said! (*Snapping*) God damn his yellow soul, if he doesn't soon, I'll go up and throw him off!—like a dog with its guts ripped out you'd put out of misery! (*He half rises from his chair just as from outside the window comes the sound of something hurtling down, followed by a muffled, crunching thud.* LARRY *gasps and drops back on his chair, shuddering, hiding his face in his hands. The group at right hear it but are too preoccupied with drinks to pay much attention.*)

HOPE. (*Wonderingly*) What the hell was that?

ROCKY. Aw, nuttin'. Someting fell off de fire escape. A mattress, I'll bet. Some of dese bums been sleepin' on de fire escapes.

HOPE. (*His interest diverted by this excuse to beef—testily*) They've got to cut it out! Bejees, this ain't a fresh-air cure. Mattresses cost money.

MOSHER. Now don't start crabbing at the party, Harry. Let's drink up. (HOPE *forgets it and grabs his glass, and they all drink.*)

LARRY. (*In a whisper of horrified pity*) Poor devil! (*A long-forgotten faith returns to him for a moment and he mumbles*) God rest his soul in peace. (*He opens his eyes—with a bitter self-derision*) Ah, the damned pity—the wrong kind, as Hickey said! Be God, there's no hope! I'll never be a success in the grandstand—or anywhere else! Life is too much for me! I'll be a weak fool looking with pity at the two sides of everything till the day I die! (*With an intense bitter sincerity*) May that day come soon! (*He pauses startledly, surprised at himself—then with a sardonic grin*) Be God, I'm the only real convert to death Hickey made here. From the bottom of my coward's heart I mean that now!

HOPE. (*Calls effusively*) Hey there, Larry! Come over and get paralyzed! What the hell you doing, sitting there? (*Then as* LARRY *doesn't reply he immediately forgets him and turns to the party. They are all very drunk now, just a few drinks ahead of the passing-out stage, and hilariously happy about it*) Bejees, let's sing! Let's celebrate! It's my birthday party! Bejees, I'm oreyeyed! I want to sing! (*He starts the chorus of "She's the Sunshine of Paradise Alley," and instantly they all burst into* song. But not the same song. Each starts the chorus of his or her choice. JIMMY TOMORROW'S is *"A Wee Dock and Doris"*; ED MOSHER'S, *"Break the News to Mother"*; WILLIE OBAN'S, *the Sailor Lad ditty he sang in Act One*; GENERAL WET-JOEN'S, *"Waiting at the Church"*; MCGLOIN'S, *"Tammany"*; CAPTAIN LEWIS'S, *"The Old Kent Road"*; JOE'S, *"All I Got Was Sympathy"*; PEARL'S and MARGIE'S, *"Everybody's Doing It"*; ROCKY'S, *"You Great Big Beautiful Doll"*; CHUCK'S, *"The Curse of an Aching Heart"*; CORA'S, *"The Oceana Roll"*; while HUGO jumps to his feet and, pounding on the table with his fist, bellows in his guttural basso the French Revolutionary "Carmagnole." A weird cacophony results from this mixture and they stop singing to roar with laughter. All but HUGO, who keeps on with drunken fervor.*)

HUGO.

Dansons la Carmagnole!
Vive le son! Vive le son!
Dansons la Carmagnole!
Vive le son des canons!

(*They all turn on him and howl him down with amused derision. He stops singing to denounce them in his most fiery style*) Capitalist svine! Stupid bourgeois monkeys! (*He declaims*) "The days grow hot, O Babylon!" (*They all take it up and shout in enthusiastic jeering chorus*) " 'Tis cool beneath thy willow trees!" (*They pound their glasses on the table, roaring with laughter, and* HUGO *giggles with them. In his chair by the window,* LARRY *stares in front of him, oblivious to their racket.*)

CURTAIN

LOUISE BOGAN
Editor

Robert Frost

1874-

THE CAREER of Robert [Lee] Frost, the American poet whose popularity, in his seventies and eighties, came to exceed that of any of his contemporaries, presents a number of paradoxes. For most of his life his reputation came to be based on the figure he presented to his audience: that of a New England poet who lived close to the land, and whose principal interests, apart from writing and teaching, were rural ones. Yet he spent his formative years—until the age of eleven—in San Francisco, where he was born in 1874, and his years of adolescence and young manhood in industrial New England towns and cities—chiefly Lawrence, Massachusetts. His direct forebears, moreover, on his father's side, were town-dwellers. His paternal grandfather was an overseer of a cotton mill in Lawrence, and his father, William Prescott Frost, Jr., after graduating from Harvard, moved west to become a newspaperman and politician in the growing city of San Francisco. His mother, Isabelle Moodie Frost, had come to America from Scotland as a girl of fifteen. She met Frost's father at Bucknell Academy in Lewistown, Pennsylvania, where the young Easterner on his way west had taken a teaching position, and where she herself taught mathematics. She, too, was city bred (in Edinburgh) and it is apparent that many of the poet's characteristics—his intuition and imagination, as well as his belief in

the importance of positive aims and values—were derived from her.

But there is no doubt that Frost's lifelong affection for the land was central and genuine. He possessed from the beginning the individualistic and independent nature which was, at one time, common not only in New England—where the Frost family had long been established—but in the rural areas of America as a whole. The elder Frost's streak of Yankee intransigence expressed itself in his youthful espousal of the theory of States' rights and the cause of the South; and he proved himself a member of the post-Civil War generation by his restless move toward the new opportunities lying westward. Frost's own temperament, as W. H. Auden—a knowledgeable admirer—has pointed out, was that of the "small-holder," of the farmer who owns and works his land. In Frost, the inheritance of the Yankee countryman and of the Scottish crofter met, and reinforced each other.

II

IN HIS later years, Frost has described to biographers the difficulties of his childhood in some detail. They were difficulties which contributed to many of the tensions of his adolescence and young manhood, as well as to his choice, at an early age, of a responsible pattern of behavior. His father's character, it would appear, had more of Yankee gregariousness than Yankee reserve, and as a newspaperman and a dabbler in politics, the elder Frost's free and untrammeled participation in San Francisco's ebullient frontier atmosphere was frequently shared by his son, who went along as his companion—missing school and catching glimpses of the growing city's rougher side. Frost's mother exhibited courage by keeping the family and the household together during the San Francisco years, and by persisting in her independent attitude toward Frost's rather grim and hard-fisted grandfather when, after Frost's father's death at thirty-four in 1885, she returned, with Robert and his younger sister, to Lawrence. Her Scottish inheritance included a respect for learning and an aptitude for teaching, and she soon took charge of a district school, in nearby Salem, New Hampshire. Here she put into practice her teaching methods—original for the time—seating her pupils according to their grades of excellence, giving them individual instruction, and getting them to commit to memory passages of poetry or prose which she read aloud. This harking back to an oral tradition—usual in a society where books are scarce—made a strong impression upon Frost, whose ear, as it turned out, was unusually true and accurate. Her dealings with her pupils were easy and natural; she was remembered singing children's ballads to the youngest, as she held them on her knee. Her religious interests were also marked; once a Unitarian, she later became interested in the mystical doctrines of Swedenborg.

Frost's devotion to his mother was complete; he willingly took on any small job that would "help out." He entered Lawrence High School—having been his mother's pupil up to that time—in the fall of 1888, at the age of fourteen. Here he acquired the rudiments of the old-fashioned classical education then prevalent in the New England public high schools. Latin, Greek, and ancient history were subjects in the curriculum, and he made good marks. It was now that he met Elinor Miriam White, the charming and talented daughter of a former Universalist minister, who was to share with young Frost the honor of being Valedictorian on their graduation in June of 1892. By this time Frost had published poems in the school paper, and had made plans to go to Dartmouth on funds contributed by his grandmother.

From this point on, the progress of young Frost toward what he began to sense as his true interests—the interests of a poet and perhaps, on his own terms, an instructor of the young—ran into a series of obstacles. His stay at Dartmouth was brief. His interest in poetry was becoming more definitely centered as his reading broadened, and he was writing verse. But his creative enthusiasm was baffled, rather than aided, by academic routine. Moreover, he felt that his mother—who had opened a small school in Methuen, Massachusetts—needed him. He left Dartmouth without giving official notice, and spent the winter of 1893 giving his mother the help she needed in managing her sometimes recalcitrant pupils. Mill work claimed him during the following summer and winter. It was at this period that he sold his first poem—"My Butterfly"—to the *Independent*, then a leading weekly, and attracted the attention not only of its editor, William Hayes Ward, but of the editor's sister, Miss Susan Ward. Part of the correspondence between the youthful poet of twenty and this learned spinster has been preserved at the Huntington Library, and Frost's positive belief in his talent comes through clearly (". . . I have but recently discovered my powers"). Frost now turned his back on the mills, for good.

Meanwhile, the relationship between himself and Elinor White was undergoing rapid changes, not always fortunate ones from Frost's point of view. Miss White had become a student at St. Lawrence, a Universalist college in upper New York State. She was therefore, except for summer visits home, out of direct communication with her young friend—whose devotion to her was constant. Moreover, Frost's inability to attach himself to any conventional way of making a living did not appeal to her family and her academic mentors. Frost, on a visit to St. Lawrence in the autumn of 1894, with a sheaf of privately printed poems in hand, felt himself to be severely rebuffed, and he reacted to this crucial disappointment by flight—to Maryland, Virginia, and North Carolina. His feeling of desperation at this time was to be recorded in a poem of his late maturity ("Kittyhawk 1894"), and he speaks of the "desperately absorbing experiences" of this journey in a letter to Miss Ward. This is the only break with a pattern of strict accountability to demands made upon him that the hard-pressed young poet allowed himself, in these transitional years.

Matters then took a better turn. The *Independent* gave "My Butterfly" a prominent place in its issue of November 8, 1894, and he became engaged to Elinor White at the Christmas season. Elinor returned to college for her final year, and Frost occupied himself with tutoring, teaching, and a short spell of reporting for the Lawrence *Sentinel*. The young couple, after their marriage in December, 1895, together took up teaching duties, again in Frost's mother's school, now situated in Lawrence.

The next five years were crowded ones. Frost's friendly relations with the Wards continued, and two other poems were published in the *Independent* in 1896 and 1897. The Frost's first child, Eliot, was born in September, 1896. And it was now that Frost made his second effort to enter college. The advantages of a college degree to a man whose talents and background seemed to fit him for a career as instructor to the young were evident; and Frost, after correspondence with Dean Briggs, entered Harvard in the fall of 1897. His grandfather paid his tuition, and Elinor Frost's mother took a house in Boston in order to make matters somewhat easier for the young family. As a freshman he "was too mature for [the required] English A and hated it." And, although he received high marks in the classics, in his sophomore year "nothing went well." In addition, his duties as a son, a husband, and a father, proved to be overwhelming. "Harvard," he later wrote, in the *Harvard Alumni Bulletin*, "had taken me away from the question whether I could write or not." He resigned from the sophomore class at the end of March, 1899. The next month, his daughter Lesley was born.

A way of life which was to prove over a long period of time a background for some of his most remarkable work was about to become possible, but a double tragedy was to intervene: Frost's mother was stricken with can-cer, and in July, 1900, his little son Eliot died. Elinor Frost, in spite of her grief, made the sensible request of Frost's grandfather that he buy them a farm, which the young husband and wife had "found for themselves" in West Derry, New Hampshire—"thirty acres, rather run down and poor, but with orchard, fields, pasture, woodland and spring." "Shall I give you a year? Will you settle down if I give you a year to try this out?" his grandfather asked. "Give me twenty!" Frost replied, and, as he said later, "that is just what it took. . . ."

Frost's mother died in November, 1900, soon after their move to the farm. She was fifty-six years old.

III

IN 1900, when Frost and his young family first settled in West Derry, it was not so difficult for a man to leave an industrial environment to seek out a subsistence living on a "one man, one horse" farm, as it would be today. But it was difficult enough, especially in New England, where the land was poor, and where the native Yankee stock had lost much of its vigor through the losses of the Civil War, the trek to the West, and the flight to the cities of many of its more adventuresome sons. For Frost, the step was drastic. He was going, it is true, toward a way of life he believed, instinctively, to be his: toward true, old-fashioned values, outside—and opposed to—the period's ethos of competition and "success." And he was saving that poet's part of himself which he had believed in from earliest adolescence. He and his wife were putting a touching trust in what they must have sensed was ultimately an impossible way of making a living. To persist in their desires for a world of their own, in which they could bring up children beyond the reach of mill-town blight and the interference of hard-fisted relations, took courage. This courage, and the idealism which existed at its center, proved to be the source of the most original, moving, and sincere poems of Frost's early work—very nearly all the poems in *A Boy's Will* and *North of Boston*, as well as much of *Mountain Interval*.

The farm, as it turned out, could not produce even a subsistence living for the Frosts. After six years, and the birth of four more children, one of whom died in earliest infancy, Frost turned once more to teaching, this time as a part-time teacher of English at the nearby Pinkerton Academy—"a good two-mile walk from the farm." His teaching methods were somewhat unorthodox, but his pupils remembered his genial informality, his "admirable" direction of certain Shakespeare plays, and his interest in botany and in baseball. The family now began to spend their summers in Bethlehem, in the White Mountains, for reasons of Frost's health—"a high, free mountain world." In 1910, they moved from the farm nearer to the academy, and in the fall of 1911, to Plymouth, where Frost began to teach psychology and education at the state normal school.

The lyric poems later to be collected in Frost's first volume, *A Boy's Will* (1913), continued to be written; and Frost has said that as early as 1905 he had discovered a new dramatic vein which was to result in the blank-verse poems in *North of Boston* (1914). Early in 1912, the impulse to break away from teaching —at which he was having a good deal of success—and to prove or disprove his faith in himself as a writer, took hold. The farm was now his to sell, and he sold it. With its price in hand, along with a small allowance from his grandfather's estate, he bought steamer passage for himself, his wife, and his four small children—destination, England—and sailed, in the early autumn of 1912, at the age of thirty-eight, from Boston to a country where he knew no one.

IV

FROST's departure for England roughly coincided with two major publishing ventures, which heralded the beginnings of a new serious attitude toward poetry written in English. In October, Harriet Monroe, in Chicago, published the first number of *Poetry: A Magazine of Verse*, and in England, in December, under the generous patronage of Edward Marsh, the first *Georgian Anthology* appeared. The Georgian group, whose admiration for the poetry of Thomas Hardy and of Robert Bridges was marked, included, at the time, Walter de la Mare, John Masefield, W. H. Davies, and Rupert Brooke. And in London, The Poetry Bookshop, which was to become a center for poetic activity, had recently been opened by Harold Monro. Frost knew nothing of any of these developments upon his arrival in England. His first preoccupation was to find a country place where he and his family could settle and farm. On the advice of a writer of a country column in a newspaper, he found a first home in Beaconsfield, Bucks. He then set about finding a publisher, and here good luck played into his hands.[1] Late in 1912, he was able to arrange for the publication of *A Boy's Will* with the firm of David Nutt.

A Boy's Will, published in his thirty-ninth year, made an immediate impression upon those critics to whom it was sent for review, and Frost began to meet, and to know, many members of the Georgian circle. Among these was Edward Thomas, who at the time was struggling with the pressures of a journalist's career. Thomas, like Frost, was a lover of the countryside and an amateur botanist. At the beginning of their close friendship Thomas had never written a line of verse. Frost advised him to begin, telling him that "he had been a poet all his life." Thomas, who had undergone periods of depression for many years, found in poetry a tremendous release, and he was a frequent visitor of the Frosts throughout their English stay.

Soon after *A Boy's Will* appeared, Frost met Ezra Pound. Pound's own career was beginning to expand into many areas. Already for some years established in London, with several books to his credit, the young Pound was beginning to take on his role of instigator and innovator, and in 1913 was actively engaged in formulating rules for the Imagists—a "school" with more experimental aims and interests than those of the Georgians, and he had already appointed himself foreign advisor to Harriet Monroe. Pound's review of *A Boy's Will* appeared in *Poetry* in May, 1913. Pound discovered, in Frost, a salutary attention paid to the truth, as well as compression and clarity of expression. "This man has the good sense to speak naturally and to paint the thing, the thing as he sees it." Another American poet

[1] Frost's publication in American magazines, through 1912, had been severely limited: several poems in the *Independent*, two in the *Youth's Companion*, and one in the *Forum*.

was helping to clear away the falsity and fustian of Victorian verse.

Pound's friendship with Frost was short-lived; the young enthusiast soon found that his older compatriot was intent on going his own way. But Pound expressed his admiration for Frost's rendering of "the natural speech of New England" in a review of *North of Boston*, published in *Poetry* late in 1914 under the title "Modern Georgics." "Mr. Frost's work is the work of a man who will make neither concessions or pretenses . . . His book is a contribution to American literature."

North of Boston, published by David Nutt in April, 1914, again impressed English reviewers. Edward Thomas, who was soon to die in the war, wrote of this collection of New England "eclogues":

This is one of the most exciting books of modern times, but one of the quietest and least aggressive . . . These poems are revolutionary because they lack the exaggeration of rhetoric . . . Many, if not most, of the separate lines and separate sentences are plain, and, in themselves, nothing. But they are bound together and made elements of beauty by a calm eagerness of emotion . . . [The best poems in the book] are masterpieces of deep and mysterious tenderness.[1]

V

IT IS interesting to come upon a portrait of this man of thirty-eight in the reminiscences of his English friends, just as he is emerging from his years of obscurity and isolation. Frost had evidently reached a point of spiritual equilibrium by the time of the English journey. Eleanor Farjeon, a close friend of the Thomases, speaks in Book I of her memoirs[2] of Frost and his family after they had settled near Little Iddens, in Herefordshire, in beautiful orchard country. Here

the Frosts were poor, and indifferent to the conditions of poverty. Frost had [evidently] always taken life as it came where he found it . . . Whatever he did he made worth doing . . . His manner was friendly and undemonstrative. He looked at you directly; his talk was shrewd and speculative, withholding nothing and derived

[1] The London *Daily News* and the *English Review* (August, 1914, unsigned review).

[2] Eleanor Farjeon, *Edward Thomas: The Last Years* (Oxford, 1958).

from nobody but himself. His New England speech came readily and leisurely, and of all the writers of worth I had met, he spoke with the least sophistication. [He was]unhurried in all he said and did. The Frosts did not live by the clock . . . their center was out of doors. Meals were taken at odd hours.

And when there were visitors, talk and the reading of poetry went on far into the night, by candlelight, in the home the poet and his wife had made of "a labourer's cottage standing in a rough plot of ground planted chiefly with potatoes."

The difficulties brought on by the outbreak of the war in August, 1914, proved insuperable, and the Frosts returned to America in February, 1915. An American publisher, Henry Holt & Company, had already brought out a small edition (150 copies) of *North of Boston* from imported English sheets; the first "strictly American" edition of it and of *A Boy's Will* appeared in March, 1915. Frost now experienced his first taste of success. At forty-one, he emerged from almost total obscurity into bestseller status, thus receiving from his new audience the kind of encouragement which proved, in his case, to be the source of fresh energy. The scars of his difficult youth and young manhood were still there, but, as it turned out, these were not irremediable. They became, in fact, important and available parts of his richly creative nature, which was to remain vigorous for many decades to come.

And Frost did not disappoint his audience. He began to publish regularly and at length. *Mountain Interval* appeared in 1916, and *New Hampshire* in 1923. Both volumes were filled with a variety of interesting and original work, although neither approached *North of Boston* in power of dramatic concept or depth of tragic implication. *New Hampshire* marked a revival, and even extension, of the poet's early lyricism. And the long title poem signaled the beginning of a new Frostian manner: the direct and open assumption of the role of shrewd Yankee sage; the translation of aphoristic Yankee wit and the charm of the born talker into poetic terms. This role, this manner, was to become, over the years, a perhaps too insistent one, but on its first appearance it was delightful.

Frost did not alter his way of living; he kept to the simple pattern of his early days. Having bought a farm near Franconia, he continued to live, if not as a farmer, at least as a thoroughly non-urban citizen. Soon he began to lecture and to teach; his connection with Amherst College dates back to 1917. He remained faithful to his native bent and worked, as far as possible, on his own terms. As the years drew him more and more into the circle of academic life, he continued to talk more than he wrote, and kept his published prose to a minimum. He left it to his listeners—some of whom were his warmest disciples—to take notes on his discourses, formal and informal; even the Charles Eliot Norton lectures which he delivered at Harvard in 1936 were never published. In this way, with an instinctive regard for both his gifts and his limitations, he recreated, in fairly unfavorable circumstances, the ancient oral tradition of the bard, as well as the refreshing legend of the "dry" Yankee sage.

VI

CLOSE critical examination of Frost's work has been slow to appear; it is only during the last decade that we find any sustained attempts at detached appraisal in appreciable quantity, as distinguished from the fulsome praise which certain colleagues and fellow poets have lavished on Frost, the man and the poet, since his work began to be known. Several factors explain this critical lag. In the first place, Frost, in a period of extreme experimentation with form, continued to write conventionally, and in a manner which presented to the reader no prosodic difficulty of any kind. Again, Frost's poetry, at a time when symbol and myth had become important carriers of meaning, was allusive only in a restricted way; it offered few leads into elaborate subtlety; it did not encourage "close" reading or fine-drawn explication. It stood outside those currents of avant-garde poetic theory which restlessly absorbed diverse ideas from many adjacent fields—those of anthropology, medical psychology, history, and religion. Finally, Frost's popularity with a large audience—a popularity, it is true, based on a very limited selection of his work—rendered the quality of his appeal suspect to those

who believed with Edwin Muir "that the imaginative writer today can be widely popular only by writing falsely."

Frost's diction has none of the "richness and virtuosity" characteristic of modern writing at large. But Frost's very limitation of means often leads the reader into the poet's most striking effects, and an inspection of his general poetic practice brings to light a very real power and control over language which is one basis of his incontestable originality. His mastery of formal poetics is remarkable from first to last; he is a trained and meticulous craftsman. His lyric style is flexible, musical, and completely natural. His form, moreover, is remarkably varied and never seems in any way to have been cut to fit the emotion. Each poem, from short lyric to longer dramatic blank verse, has its own "given" form, and the authenticity of the poet's gift is everywhere apparent.

Frost has put down, in "The Figure a Poem Makes," one of the most interesting and intelligible summations ever made by a poet of the genesis and progress of poetic composition. He describes the poet's ready passivity, open to the initial subconscious impulse, which must be undeviatingly followed and only lightly controlled, at the outset, by conscious ways and means. It is clear that Frost served a long technical apprenticeship. Actual influences, however, even in his early work, are difficult to trace. He had read, and admired, Edward Arlington Robinson's *The Town Down the River* (1908), and his Introduction to Robinson's *King Jasper* (1935) clearly shows his admiration for the work of the older man. Robinson, born in Maine in 1869, belonged to the cultivated New England town tradition (which had produced Emily Dickinson)—a tradition which had begun to dissolve and decay during his youth. His attitude toward this dissolution—of standards and manners as well as of material prosperity—was not entirely nostalgic. Robinson possessed an honest and unerring eye, and a talent for the "simple accuracy" that he admired in George Crabbe. He described his townsmen—particularly the failures, misfits, and outcasts produced by a society in transition—in sharp and tragic detail, and with insight, and he everywhere avoided the soft blur of outworn poetic terms. He turned toward the rhythm of the spoken idiom of his time and place—"Mr. Flood's Party," a favorite poem of Frost's, keeps closely to the turns of native speech.

But there is a great difference between Robinson's occasional approximation of the colloquial and Frost's final success in fitting the "cadences" of common speech to a regular verse pattern—perhaps his central contribution to modern poetic procedures. Poets contemporary with, or slightly older than Frost— among them Swinburne, Kipling, and Robert Bridges—had tried to vary the rhythms of English verse,[1] finding "the old, dull iambic Wordsworthian measures" tedious. Masefield, reviving the Chaucerian couplet with much success, had dealt boldly with the rough diction of the English working class.[2] Frost had evidently tried out one method after another (he has said that he tried to write "The Black Cottage" in rhymed couplets, while at Dartmouth). "We must write with the ear on the speaking voice," he later remarked. To that end he had worked in complete separation from the feeble and genteel American literary tendencies of his time, in the ten years from 1902 to 1912. His choice of blank verse proved to be exactly right for his special purposes. Through this unrhymed five-beat iambic line —which, since the sixteenth century, had been established as the most workable long carrying-line in English—the American poet was given a measure of freedom. The New England manner of speech—at once laconic and meandering —could be caught into this pattern without distortion, and with completely natural emphasis. Frost had, indeed, instinctively put into practice an Imagist tenet ("the natural words in the natural order") before that tenet was formulated (around 1913) by the Imagists themselves.

Certainly, at the time, a new, direct, and truth-telling attitude toward reality, as well as a complete refreshment of poetic diction and use of form, was in order, in poetry in English. The Romantic tradition—which had begun with Blake and ended with Keats—had become threadbare. The Romantic poets had made a conscious effort toward simplicity and clarity of espression; at the same time, their belief in the power of the imagination had enabled them successfully to describe strong and complex emotions. The Victorian era was one of uneasy compromise. The Victorian audience—largely unenlightened aesthetically and unsure of its moral values—began to demand from poets, and from artists in general, reassurance and consolation; and even Tennyson and Browning partially acceded to this demand. By the end of the nineteenth century, English poetry, in spite of isolated efforts, such as that of the Pre-Raphaelites, to bring life into a moribund situation, had become feeble and monotonously minor. The opening stanza of "By the Statue of King Charles at Charing Cross" by Lionel Johnson (1867–1902) illustrates one prevalent style:

> Sombre and rich, the skies,
> Great glooms, and starry plains;
> Gently the nightwind sighs;
> Else a vast silence reigns.

Here, the inflated emotion has drawn to itself language equally false. It was against such falsity that the best of the Georgians, together with the small but highly intelligent and articulate group of Imagists—with several Americans in their number—had begun their revolt. Frost, working in America in provincial isolation, with little but his instinct for sincerity and a sensitive eye and ear to guide him, had already succeeded in clarifying language and intensifying form.

It is difficult to speak of Frost's first two books with detachment. The harshness, bafflements, loneliness, and grief of his childhood and adolescence here have been made to surrender their meaning at the same time that the tragic aspects of a neglected countryside have been absorbed and recreated by an eager young sensibility. The tone, though often tender, is never romantic. C. Day Lewis speaks of Frost's preoccupation with "hard fact": "no working farmer is romantic—not about nature, at any rate."[3] And W. H. Auden has written:

---

[1] See Swinburne's "A Forsaken Garden," Kipling's "The Law of the Jungle," and Bridges' "London Snow."

[2] In *The Everlasting Mercy* (1911) and *The Widow in the Bye Street* (1912).

[3] C. Day Lewis, Introduction to *Selected Poems of Robert Frost* (Penguin, 1955).

"[Frost's] qualities of irony and understatement, his distrust of fine writing, are those of the practical man. His poems on natural objects . . . are always concerned with them not as *foci* for mystical meditation, but as things with which and on which man acts in the course of his daily gaining of a livelihood." [1] And both Day Lewis and Auden speak of the quality of "good gossip" which the blank-verse poems often take on. "[These] anecdotes" says Day Lewis, "are told in a discursive, racy, countryfied way, which may cause us to overlook their psychological penetration, the technical skill of their verse . . . and the economy of means behind their apparent ranginess." And he then singles out for special praise the poems "where Frost broods and comments on familiar country things, imperceptibly weaving a pattern, catching a truth in it almost absent-mindedly, like a conjurer reaching down a penny out of the air."

The dramatic monologue of Browning—which was to undergo a vigorous rehandling in the work of more than one of Frost's contemporaries, notably in Pound and T. S. Eliot—reappears in this most unpretentious of settings; and Frost's dialogues and monologues often resolve into talk so disarmingly natural that it seems to be overheard. This simplicity is by no means naïve; it involves a highly trained ear as well as the utmost probity of choice. "The Pasture," the lyric which served as an epigraph to *North of Boston*, written with a controlled and distilled simplicity, is a love song, among other things—surely one of the loveliest in the language.

As has been pointed out, Frost's power of close and accurate description, in which all the senses are involved, at times approaches clairvoyance. The early books, like many of the later ones, are scattered through with details from the natural scene: things seen, heard, caught in motion, breathed in, touched. "The slow wheel that pours the sand"; the blue berries of the woodbine and its "littered leaves"; the leaves of the hardwood grove that "fit the earth like a leather glove"; the brook's "slender tinkling fall"; the "tattered and swift" line-storm clouds; the "thawing wind" that invades

the house—these are things brought into focus by flashes of piercing vision.

In the West Derry years Frost came to take pleasure in—and derive courage from—the varied patterns of character in people whose circumscribed way of life was becoming increasingly difficult to maintain. This isolation was often burdensome, to a crippling degree, but they were on their own, and managing in some way to survive. Far from being "an isolated, brutish and taciturn peasantry" these New England farmers were, on the whole, gentle, high-minded and articulate. Frost presents a range of their emotions, often in first person narratives, from the normal, sympathetic and humane—"The Black Cottage," "The Death of the Hired Man"—through degrees of comedy—"A Hundred Collars," "Blueberries"—to hatred, terror and incipient madness—"The Housekeeper," "The Fear," "A Servant to Servants." Both "The Fear" and "Home Burial" describe extreme states (of panic guilt and obsessive grief, respectively) with clinical exactness.

Frost continued to explore, through several books, the possibilities of his blank verse, although the later short dramatic vignettes are less grim in subject and tone than those in *North of Boston*. Two narratives, "The Witch of Coös" and "The Pauper Witch of Grafton" (which appeared in *New Hampshire* (1923) under the covering title of "Two Witches") mark a high point in Frost's use of the form. In both, the mania of extreme old age is described, with the utmost insight into, and sympathy with, woman's nature and character beset by time. As Day Lewis points out, "The Witch of Coös," "all the more sinister for the homeliness and disturbing visual precision of its similes" (the skeleton mounts the stairs "like a pile of dishes"), is projected—in spite of its grisly detail—in a delicately established tone of high comedy. "The Pauper Witch of Grafton," a recreation of a love story in the most fantastic terms, ends upon a note of true pathos, with a passage which is one of the most memorable in Frost.

VII

FROST's early relations with the machine, and with man as a machine-tender, had left an indelible mark on his character, and understandably so. The relation of young people to the New England textile mills was a difficult and crucial one. Children went into the mills and, very often, remained in them throughout their lifetimes. Sarah Cleghorn's famous quatrain (1919)

> The golf links lie so near the mill
> That almost every day
> The laboring children can look out
> And see the men at play.

records a fact that Frost, who was later to write the Preface to Miss Cleghorn's *Threescore: An Autobiography* (1936), could verify in his own experience. The adult uneducated artisan, too, was trapped into long hours at a mechanical round, under the crudest of labor conditions. Not until the Lawrence strike of 1909 were these conditions brought into general notice.

Frost's experience implanted in him not only a dislike of supervised mechanical tasks, but a nightmare image of the machine as menace—an object to be viewed with fear and dread. The locomotive, the buzz saw, even the stones of the primitive grist mill, become, as it were, centers of evil force which override, kill and maim ("Out, Out—," "The Self-Seeker," "The Vanishing Red"). "The Lone Striker" is the single poem which brings a textile mill into sight (with certain of its processes meticulously described)—but then only as a trap which the young man in the poem must escape from at all costs. Frost is never concerned (as many poets and men of letters have shown themselves to be, since the beginning of the industrial revolution) with the blighting results of industry upon human beings in general. His is a personal feud, with the machine as adversary. "The Egg and the Machine," for example, which presents a singularly inept one-to-one encounter between a man and a locomotive headlight, occurs fairly late—in *West-Running Brook* (1928). And the long poem, "New Hampshire," while it lists many of that state's charming and diversified features, omits all mention of its mills and factories, which had flourished in numbers along its principal rivers for decades.

A central criticism brought to bear on Frost's middle and later work is pointed toward such omissions of ugly fact from the New England scene. Do these omissions constitute actual evasions; is Frost, at times, involved in the propagation of a kind of false pastoral? The scene to which he had become emotionally committed from youth on—the background of small town, village, and of isolated farms beyond the village—was, in fact, changing with great rapidity during his mature years. The railroads and the telegraph poles had already penetrated deeply into rural areas in the time of Thoreau, whose attitude toward both was not completely hostile. But with the appearance of the automobile and the telephone, the older concepts of speed and of communication were drastically altered. Certain features of the countryside and of local custom were gone for good; the tractor was soon to supersede the plow. And certain appurtenances and tools of the older way of living suddenly became completely obsolete. At the same time, a deeply felt nostalgia for a vanished way of rural existence began to manifest itself in a generation that had experienced the transition. It cannot truly be said of Frost that he catered to this nostalgia. His material was his by virtue of hard-won experience. His meticulous attention to his own craft was closely linked with the handcraftsman's love of method and material, so tellingly described in "The Axe-Helve." If a large proportion of his readers preferred to separate out from his work those poems which satisfied their yearning for some version of a lost American Golden Age, the fault was theirs.

It is true that Frost's conservatism—a natural trait in those who live on the land, "closely bound to the wheel of the seasons"—became more marked with the passage of the years. Although many of his admirers wished to think of him as "ordinary" to the core, Frost's nature, of course, was complicated in the extreme. As a poet, he was a man of strong feelings, and strong feelings are bound to include resentments. A relapse into small-mindedness is, however, a danger lying in wait for any artist of a conservative cast of mind. Statements come to be built not only on emotional conviction, but on hidden prejudice as well. Ill-tempered disputation is then in order, together with a wrong-headed pleasure in holding "notions." The detachment of the artist disappears; the work begins to be in favor of this or that small conception or opinion; the thought becomes whimsical; ideas are no longer large and centered. Emerson and Thoreau, local exemplars from whom Frost learned much, do not coerce the reader. They express themselves with deliberate casualness. This is the philosopher's, and the poet's, way—a way which rises above pettiness and irritability. Any other must lead toward constriction of vision and asperity of tone.

The fact that Frost's more sharply edged comments on national affairs and the state of the world began to appear in years of economic depression brought against him the charge of callousness. Many of the poems written in these crucial years are bitterly opposed to the main tenets of the liberal thought of the time—particularly to collective action, of which even the extreme individualist, Thoreau, approved. Frost's confidence that the terrors of his time could be adequately dealt with by processes of will and determination alone, his lack of flexibility toward the shifts and changes of modern life and society were certainly limiting, especially in view of the efforts made by many of his contemporaries —Yeats, Pound, Eliot and, later, Auden—not only to understand but to remedy, restore, and repair. The fact that Frost was able to hold to his convictions, in a period of great confusion of values, testifies to a central force of character that he was never in any danger of losing. But now for the first time in Frost's work, nature appears as a refuge to which man must retreat, rather than as a natural environment which man may freely choose as his own. Frost begins to repeat injunctions to stand fast, ward off, dig in, take care.

The three later books, A *Further Range* (1936), A *Witness Tree* (1942), and *Steeplebush* (1947), were not, however, consistently given over to preachments concerning the paths mankind should follow, or the policies the nation should adopt. Quick wit, apt comment and true lyricism are present in all three, together with a continuing insight into human motives. There are traces, too, of a new melancholy—"The Wind and the Rain" and "Come In"—as well as a new tenderness—"The Silken Tent." Frost had undergone tragedy and loss in these years (Mrs. Frost had died in 1938 and his son Carol in 1940); and they marked his passage into old age. His limitations and self-limitations were now fixed and, in all probability, were to remain unchanged: his tendency, when forced into a tight corner, to lapse into the ambiguous parable; his occasional narrowing of perspective; his inability to establish "a hierarchy of values." In Frost's late career, the evidence increasingly showed, there would be no shocking confrontations, as in the later Yeats, and no profound spiritual insights, as in the case of Eliot. On the other hand, with his own weapons, the old poet was still capable not only of standing his ground, but of dealing some wicked blows. His will remained indomitable. If he consistently clung to the middle regions of mild faith and to a middle tone—which ruled out the noble, "lofty," and transcendent manner—he did not slip back into any false romanticism of style or of attitude; and he continued to avoid the plaintive, the inflated, and the confused.

The tensions, dark conflicts, and passionate involvements which must inform poetry at any level—and had been evident in Frost's from the beginning—in the later Frost were by no means entirely suppressed. When allowed to come through, they pervade certain poems with almost nightmare intensity. The strangely projected pathos of "The Lovely Shall be Choosers" (a poem in memory of his mother); the suggestions of planned evil in "Design"; the thwarted and maimed human passions described, with the utmost compression and subtlety, in "The Subverted Flower" and "The Discovery of the Madeiras"; the strange timelessness and horror of "The Ingenuities of Debt"—these are unforgettable examples of the imagination working in deep psychic regions. Recurrent moments of anguish and of spiritual doubt and alienation in the later work, as in the earlier, are indicative, as one of Frost's more perceptive critics has pointed out, of "Frost's capacity for a kind of power frequently ignored or underestimated by his admirers." It is a power springing from the poet's close relation to the untouched, the wild and the primordial: to nature's pure but terrifying springs; to unobstructed height and depth; to snow, stars, darkness, and storm. And Frost has often been able to describe in unflinching terms the precarious balance in man, as in nature—the always imperfect resolution of conflicts in the human heart and mind. That this power and insight have persisted proves Frost extraordinary, in spite of his basic countryman's caution and his frequent shrewd assumption of the mask of "the ordinary man."

But, although Frost in age has maintained his creative energy past the crucial point where many poets decline into repetition or subside into silence, he has failed to achieve that last extension and renovation of thought and emotion—that masterful ordering of experience—which we constantly find in the later poems of Yeats, up to the time of his death in 1939, and in Eliot's *Four Quartets* (1935–43). Frost's *A Masque of Reason* (1945) and *A Masque of Mercy* (1947) seem extremely light in weight compared to these.

VIII

FROST's apotheosis in his middle eighties—his final emergence as an ideal manifestation of American character as well as of American poetic genius—has resulted, on the whole, in a happy and beneficent relation between the poet and the population at large. His honors —literary, academic, and, finally, national— were evidently a source of pleasurable satisfaction to the man who had experienced obscurity over a singularly extended period of time. The honorary degrees conferred by Oxford and Cambridge Universities in 1957 brought him back to England, where he had first met positive encouragement and warm literary friendships. Resolutions of the United States Senate on his seventy-fifth (1950) [1] and eighty-fifth (1959) birthdays, conferred on him a kind of unofficial poet-laureateship, and this standing was accented and reinforced by the invitation extended by John F. Kennedy when newly elected to the presidency in 1960, that Frost read one of his poems at the inaugural ceremony. Frost responded by writing "Dedi-

[1] The year 1874 was established as his correct birth date after this time.

cation: For John F. Kennedy His Inauguration," which, on the occasion itself, merciless winter sunlight prevented him from reading. He then, quite unperturbed, proceeded to recite "The Gift Outright" (from *A Witness Tree*)—"by heart."

A Witness Tree (1942) takes its title from trees "blazed" by early surveyors of the American wilderness to mark the corner of each square mile. As Edwin Way Teale explains, "When the bark that has grown over these scars is pried off, its inner side reveals, in a perfect negative, the scratches of the code-marks put there a century before." It is understandable why this symbol was chosen by an elder Frost —poet by gift, countryman by nature, and frequent explorer of the wilderness by choice.

READING SUGGESTIONS

Complete Poems of Robert Frost, 1949. The full texts of all Robert Frost's books of poetry through *A Masque of Mercy* (1947).
ROBERT FROST, *In the Clearing* (1962).
Interview with Robert Frost, *Saturday Evening Post* (November 19, 1960).
Interview with Robert Frost, *Paris Review* (Summer–Fall, 1960).
SIDNEY COX, *A Swinger of Birches: A Portrait of Robert Frost* (1957). Eulogy and interpretation of Frost as poet and man, by a friend who met Frost in New Hampshire, before the English stay.
ROBERT A. GREENBERG AND JAMES G. HEPBURN, *Robert Frost: An Introduction* (1961). This critical handbook for students collects in one place essays from many points of view and contains the record of the 1959 Lionel Trilling–J. Donald Adams exchanges.
GEORGE W. NITCHIE, *Human Values in the Poetry of Robert Frost* (1960). A serious and detailed critical appraisal.
LAWRANCE THOMPSON, *Fire and Ice: The Art and Thought of Robert Frost* (1942). A well-known interpretative appreciation.
RICHARD THORNTON, editor, *Recognition of Robert Frost* (1937). Appreciation and praise by various hands, British and American, in a series of essays published in celebration of the twenty-fifth aniversary of Frost's first book publication.
ELIZABETH SHEPLEY SERGEANT, *Robert Frost: The Trial by Existence* (1960). A work of affectionate impressionism, with much fresh information concerning Frost's childhood and youth, and many direct quotations from conversations and correspondence.

THE PASTURE

◇

(["The Pasture" first appeared as a kind of invitation, or foreword, to Frost's second book, *North of Boston* (London, 1914; New York, 1915). In *Collected Poems*, 1939, and in *Complete Poems of Robert Frost*, 1949, the poem assumes this function for all of Frost's verse.

◇

I'm going out to clean the pasture spring;
I'll only stop to rake the leaves away
(And wait to watch the water clear, I may):
I sha'n't be gone long.—You come too.

I'm going out to fetch the little calf
That's standing by the mother. It's so young
It totters when she licks it with her tongue.
I sha'n't be gone long.—You come too.

OCTOBER

O hushed October morning mild,
Thy leaves have ripened to the fall;
Tomorrow's wind, if it be wild,
Should waste them all.
The crows above the forest call;
Tomorrow they may form and go.
O hushed October morning mild,
Begin the hours of this day slow.
Make the day seem to us less brief.
Hearts not averse to being beguiled,   10
Beguile us in the way you know.
Release one leaf at break of day;
At noon release another leaf;
One from our trees, one far away.
Retard the sun with gentle mist;
Enchant the land with amethyst.
Slow, slow!
For the grapes' sake, if they were all,
Whose leaves already are burnt with frost,
Whose clustered fruit must else be lost—   20
For the grapes' sake along the wall.

FROM

A BOY'S WILL [1913]

IN HARDWOOD GROVES

The same leaves over and over again!
They fall from giving shade above
To make one texture of faded brown
And fit the earth like a leather glove.

Before the leaves can mount again
To fill the trees with another shade,
They must go down past things coming up,
They must go down into the dark decayed.

They *must* be pierced by flowers and put
Beneath the feet of dancing flowers.   10
However it is in some other world
I know that this is the way in ours.

FROM

NORTH OF BOSTON [1914]

THE BLACK COTTAGE

We chanced in passing by that afternoon
To catch it in a sort of special picture
Among tar-banded ancient cherry trees,
Set well back from the road in rank lodged grass,
The little cottage we were speaking of,
A front with just a door between two windows,
Fresh painted by the shower a velvet black.
We paused, the minister and I, to look.
He made as if to hold it at arm's length
Or put the leaves aside that framed it in.   10
'Pretty,' he said. 'Come in. No one will care.'
The path was a vague parting in the grass
That led us to a weathered window-sill.
We pressed our faces to the pane. 'You see,' he said,
'Everything's as she left it when she died.
Her sons won't sell the house or the things in it.

They say they mean to come and summer here
Where they were boys. They haven't come this
    year.
They live so far away—one is out west—
It will be hard for them to keep their word.   20
Anyway they won't have the place disturbed.'
A buttoned hair-cloth lounge spread scrolling
    arms
Under a crayon portrait on the wall,
Done sadly from an old daguerreotype.
'That was the father as he went to war.
She always, when she talked about the war,
Sooner or later came and leaned, half knelt
Against the lounge beside it, though I doubt
If such unlifelike lines kept power to stir
Anything in her after all the years.   30
He fell at Gettysburg or Fredericksburg,
I ought to know—it makes a difference which:
Fredericksburg wasn't Gettysburg, of course.
But what I'm getting to is how forsaken
A little cottage this has always seemed;
Since she went more than ever, but before—
I don't mean altogether by the lives
That had gone out of it, the father first,
Then the two sons, till she was left alone.
(Nothing could draw her after those two sons.   40
She valued the considerate neglect
She had at some cost taught them after years.)
I mean by the world's having passed it by—
As we almost got by this afternoon.
It always seems to me a sort of mark
To measure how far fifty years have brought us.
Why not sit down if you are in no haste?
These doorsteps seldom have a visitor.
The warping boards pull out their own old nails
With none to tread and put them in their
    place.   50
She had her own idea of things, the old lady.
And she liked talk. She had seen Garrison
And Whittier, and had her story of them.
One wasn't long in learning that she thought
Whatever else the Civil War was for,
It wasn't just to keep the States together,
Nor just to free the slaves, though it did both.
She wouldn't have believed those ends enough
To have given outright for them all she gave.
Her giving somehow touched the principle   60
That all men are created free and equal.
And to hear her quaint phrases—so removed
From the world's view today of all those things.
That's a hard mystery of Jefferson's.
What did he mean? Of course the easy way
Is to decide it simply isn't true.
It may not be. I heard a fellow say so.
But never mind, the Welshman got it planted
Where it will trouble us a thousand years.

Each age will have to reconsider it.   70
You couldn't tell her what the West was saying,
And what the South to her serene belief.
She had some art of hearing and yet not
Hearing the latter wisdom of the world.
White was the only race she ever knew.
Black she had scarcely seen, and yellow never.
But how could they be made so very unlike
By the same hand working in the same stuff?
She had supposed the war decided that.
What are you going to do with such a person?   80
Strange how such innocence gets its own way.
I shouldn't be surprised if in this world
It were the force that would at last prevail.
Do you know but for her there was a time
When to please younger members of the church,
Or rather say non-members in the church,
Whom we all have to think of nowadays,
I would have changed the Creed a very little?
Not that she ever had to ask me not to;
It never got so far as that; but the bare
    thought   90
Of her old tremulous bonnet in the pew,
And of her half asleep was too much for me.
Why, I might wake her up and startle her.
It was the words "descended into Hades"
That seemed too pagan to our liberal youth.
You know they suffered from a general onslaught.
And well, if they weren't true why keep right on
Saying them like the heathen? We could drop
    them.
Only—there was the bonnet in the pew.
Such a phrase couldn't have meant much to
    her.   100
But suppose she had missed it from the Creed
As a child misses the unsaid Good-night,
And falls asleep with heartache—how should *I*
    feel?
I'm just as glad she made me keep hands off,
For, dear me, why abandon a belief
Merely because it ceases to be true.
Cling to it long enough, and not a doubt
It will turn true again, for so it goes.
Most of the change we think we see in life
Is due to truths being in and out of favor.   110
As I sit here, and oftentimes, I wish
I could be monarch of a desert land
I could devote and dedicate forever
To the truths we keep coming back and back to.
So desert it would have to be, so walled
By mountain ranges half in summer snow,
No one would covet it or think it worth
The pains of conquering to force change on.
Scattered oases where men dwelt, but mostly
Sand dunes held loosely in tamarisk   120
Blown over and over themselves in idleness.

Sand grains should sugar in the natal dew
The babe born to the desert, the sand storm
Retard mid-waste my cowering caravans—
There are bees in this wall.' He struck the clap-
boards,
Fierce heads looked out; small bodies pivoted.
We rose to go. Sunset blazed on the windows.

AFTER APPLE-PICKING

My long two-pointed ladder's sticking through a
tree
Toward heaven still,
And there's a barrel that I didn't fill
Beside it, and there may be two or three
Apples I didn't pick upon some bough.
But I am done with apple-picking now.
Essence of winter sleep is on the night,
The scent of apples: I am drowsing off.
I cannot rub the strangeness from my sight
I got from looking through a pane of glass   10
I skimmed this morning from the drinking trough
And held against the world of hoary grass.
It melted, and I let it fall and break.
But I was well
Upon my way to sleep before it fell,
And I could tell
What form my dreaming was about to take.
Magnified apples appear and disappear,
Stem end and blossom end,
And every fleck of russet showing clear.   20
My instep arch not only keeps the ache,
It keeps the pressure of a ladder-round.
I feel the ladder sway as the boughs bend.
And I keep hearing from the cellar bin
The rumbling sound
Of load on load of apples coming in.
For I have had too much
Of apple-picking: I am overtired
Of the great harvest I myself desired.
There were ten thousand thousand fruit to
touch,   30
Cherish in hand, lift down, and not let fall.
For all
That struck the earth,
No matter if not bruised or spiked with stubble,
Went surely to the cider-apple heap
As of no worth.
One can see what will trouble
This sleep of mine, whatever sleep it is.
Were he not gone,
The woodchuck could say whether it's like his   40
Long sleep, as I describe its coming on,
Or just some human sleep.

F R O M

MOUNTAIN INTERVAL
[1916]

AN OLD MAN'S WINTER NIGHT

All out-of-doors looked darkly in at him
Through the thin frost, almost in separate stars,
That gathers on the pane in empty rooms.
What kept his eyes from giving back the gaze
Was the lamp tilted near them in his hand.
What kept him from remembering what it was
That brought him to that creaking room was age.
He stood with barrels round him—at a loss.
And having scared the cellar under him
In clomping here, he scared it once again   10
In clomping off;—and scared the outer night,
Which has its sounds, familiar, like the roar
Of trees and crack of branches, common things,
But nothing so like beating on a box.
A light he was to no one but himself
Where now he sat, concerned with he knew what,
A quiet light, and then not even that.
He consigned to the moon, such as she was,
So late-arising, to the broken moon
As better than the sun in any case   20
For such a charge, his snow upon the roof,
His icicles along the wall to keep;
And slept. The log that shifted with a jolt
Once in the stove, disturbed him and he shifted,
And eased his heavy breathing, but still slept.
One aged man—one man—can't keep a house,
A farm, a countryside, or if he can,
It's thus he does it of a winter night.

THE GUM-GATHERER

There overtook me and drew me in
To his down-hill, early-morning stride,
And set me five miles on my road
Better than if he had had me ride,
A man with a swinging bag for load
And half the bag wound round his hand.
We talked like barking above the din
Of water we walked along beside.
And for my telling him where I'd been
And where I lived in mountain land   10
To be coming home the way I was,
He told me a little about himself.
He came from higher up in the pass

Where the grist of the new-beginning brooks
Is blocks split off the mountain mass—
And hopeless grist enough it looks
Ever to grind to soil for grass.
(The way it is will do for moss.)
There he had built his stolen shack.
It had to be a stolen shack   20
Because of the fears of fire and loss
That trouble the sleep of lumber folk:
Visions of half the world burned black
And the sun shrunken yellow in smoke.
We know who when they come to town
Bring berries under the wagon seat,
Or a basket of eggs between their feet;
What this man brought in a cotton sack
Was gum, the gum of the mountain spruce.
He showed me lumps of the scented stuff   30
Like uncut jewels, dull and rough.
It comes to market golden brown;
But turns to pink between the teeth.

I told him this is a pleasant life
To set your breast to the bark of trees
That all your days are dim beneath,
And reaching up with a little knife,
To loose the resin and take it down
And bring it to market when you please.

THE SOUND OF TREES

I wonder about the trees.
Why do we wish to bear
Forever the noise of these
 More than another noise
So close to our dwelling place?
We suffer them by the day
Till we lose all measure of pace,
And fixity in our joys,
And acquire a listening air.
They are that that talks of going   10
 But never gets away;
And that talks no less for knowing,
As it grows wiser and older,
That now it means to stay.
My feet tug at the floor
And my head sways to my shoulder
Sometimes when I watch trees sway,
From the window or the door.
I shall set forth for somewhere,
I shall make the reckless choice   20
Some day when they are in voice
And tossing so as to scare
The white clouds over them on.
I shall have less to say,
But I shall be gone.

F R O M

NEW HAMPSHIRE [1923]

TWO WITCHES II

THE PAUPER WITCH OF GRAFTON

Now that they've got it settled whose I be,
I'm going to tell them something they won't like:
They've got it settled wrong, and I can prove it.
Flattered I must be to have two towns fighting
To make a present of me to each other.
They don't dispose me, either one of them,
To spare them any trouble. Double trouble's
Always the witch's motto anyway.
I'll double theirs for both of them—you watch me.
They'll find they've got the whole thing to do
        over,   10
That is, if facts is what they want to go by.
They set a lot (now don't they?) by a record
Of Arthur Amy's having once been up
For Hog Reeve in March Meeting here in Warren.
I could have told them any time this twelvemonth
The Arthur Amy I was married to
Couldn't have been the one they say was up
In Warren at March Meeting for the reason
He wa'n't but fifteen at the time they say.
The Arthur Amy I was married to   20
Voted the only times he ever voted,
Which wasn't many, in the town of Wentworth.
One of the times was when 'twas in the warrant
To see if the town wanted to take over
The tote road to our clearing where we lived.
I'll tell you who'd remember—Heman Lapish.
Their Arthur Amy was the father of mine.
So now they've dragged it through the law courts
        once
I guess they'd better drag it through again.
Wentworth and Warren's both good towns to
        live in,   30
Only I happen to prefer to live
In Wentworth from now on; and when all's said,
Right's right, and the temptation to do right
When I can hurt someone by doing it
Has always been too much for me, it has.
I know of some folks that'd be set up
At having in their town a noted witch:
But most would have to think of the expense
That even I would be. They ought to know
That as a witch I'd often milk a bat   40
And that'd be enough to last for days.
It'd make my position stronger, think,

If I was to consent to give some sign
To make it surer that I was a witch?
It wa'n't no sign, I s'pose, when Mallice Huse
Said that I took him out in his old age
And rode all over everything on him
Until I'd had him worn to skin and bones,
And if I'd left him hitched and unblanketed
In front of one Town Hall, I'd left him hitched 50
In front of every one in Grafton County.
Some cried shame on me not to blanket him,
The poor old man. It would have been all right
If someone hadn't said to gnaw the posts
He stood beside and leave his trade mark on them,
So they could recognize them. Not a post
That they could hear tell of was scarified.
They made him keep on gnawing till he whined.
Then that same smarty someone said to look—
He'd bet Huse was a cribber and had gnawed 60
The crib he slept in—and as sure's you're born
They found he'd gnawed the four posts of his bed,
All four of them to splinters. What did that prove?
Not that he hadn't gnawed the hitching posts
He said he had besides. Because a horse
Gnaws in the stable ain't no proof to me
He don't gnaw trees and posts and fences too.
But everybody took it for a proof.
I was a strapping girl of twenty then.
The smarty someone who spoiled everything 70
Was Arthur Amy. You know who he was.
That was the way he started courting me.
He never said much after we were married,
But I mistrusted he was none too proud
Of having interfered in the Huse business.
I guess he found he got more out of me
By having me a witch. Or something happened
To turn him round. He got to saying things
To undo what he'd done and make it right,
Like, 'No, she ain't come back from kiting yet. 80
Last night was one of her nights out. She's kiting.
She thinks when the wind makes a night of it
She might as well herself.' But he liked best
To let on he was plagued to death with me:
If anyone had seen me coming home
Over the ridgepole, 'stride of a broomstick,
As often as he had in the tail of the night,
He guessed they'd know what he had to put up
    with.
Well, I showed Arthur Amy signs enough
Off from the house as far as we could keep 90
And from barn smells you can't wash out of
    plowed ground
With all the rain and snow of seven years;
And I don't mean just skulls of Rogers' Rangers
On Moosilauke, but woman signs to man,
Only bewitched so I would last him longer.
Up where the trees grow short, the mosses tall,

I made him gather me wet snow berries
On slippery rocks beside a waterfall.
I made him do it for me in the dark.
And he liked everything I made him do. 100
I hope if he is where he sees me now
He's so far off he can't see what I've come to.
You *can* come down from everything to nothing.
All is, if I'd a-known when I was young
And full of it, that this would be the end,
It doesn't seem as if I'd had the courage
To make so free and kick up in folks' faces.
I might have, but it doesn't seem as if.

STOPPING BY WOODS ON A SNOWY EVENING

Whose woods these are I think I know.
His house is in the village though;
He will not see me stopping here
To watch his woods fill up with snow.

My little horse must think it queer
To stop without a farmhouse near
Between the woods and frozen lake
The darkest evening of the year.

He gives his harness bells a shake
To ask if there is some mistake. 10
The only other sound's the sweep
Of easy wind and downy flake.

The woods are lovely, dark and deep,
But I have promises to keep,
And miles to go before I sleep,
And miles to go before I sleep.

TO EARTHWARD

Love at the lips was touch
As sweet as I could bear;
And once that seemed too much;
I lived on air

That crossed me from sweet things
The flow of—was it musk
From hidden grapevine springs
Down hill at dusk?

I had the swirl and ache
From sprays of honeysuckle   10
That when they're gathered shake
Dew on the knuckle.

I craved strong sweets, but those
Seemed strong when I was young;
The petal of the rose
It was that stung.

Now no joy but lacks salt
That is not dashed with pain
And weariness and fault;
I crave the stain   20

Of tears, the aftermark
Of almost too much love,
The sweet of bitter bark
And burning clove.

When stiff and sore and scarred
I take away my hand
From leaning on it hard
In grass and sand,

The hurt is not enough:
I long for weight and strength   30
To feel the earth as rough
To all my length.

ON A TREE
FALLEN ACROSS THE ROAD

(TO HEAR US TALK)

The tree the tempest with a crash of wood
Throws down in front of us is not to bar
Our passage to our journey's end for good,
But just to ask us who we think we are

Insisting always on our own way so.
She likes to halt us in our runner tracks,
And make us get down in a foot of snow
Debating what to do without an ax.

And yet she knows obstruction is in vain:
We will not be put off the final goal   10
We have it hidden in us to attain,
Not though we have to seize earth by the pole

And, tired of aimless circling in one place,
Steer straight off after something into space.

FROM

WEST-RUNNING BROOK
[1928]

THE COCOON

As far as I can see this autumn haze
That spreading in the evening air both ways,
Makes the new moon look anything but new,
And pours the elm-tree meadow full of blue,
Is all the smoke from one poor house alone
With but one chimney it can call its own;
So close it will not light an early light,
Keeping its life so close and out of sight
No one for hours has set a foot outdoors
So much as to take care of evening chores.   10
The inmates may be lonely women-folk.
I want to tell them that with all this smoke
They prudently are spinning their cocoon
And anchoring it to an earth and moon
From which no winter gale can hope to blow it,—
Spinning their own cocoon did they but know it.

ACQUAINTED WITH THE NIGHT

I have been one acquainted with the night.
I have walked out in rain—and back in rain.
I have outwalked the furthest city light.

I have looked down the saddest city lane.
I have passed by the watchman on his beat
And dropped my eyes, unwilling to explain.

I have stood still and stopped the sound of feet
When far away an interrupted cry
Came over houses from another street,

But not to call me back or say good-by;   10
And further still at an unearthly height,
One luminary clock against the sky

Proclaimed the time was neither wrong nor right.
I have been one acquainted with the night.

THE EGG AND THE MACHINE

He gave the solid rail a hateful kick.
From far away there came an answering tick

And then another tick. He knew the code:
His hate had roused an engine up the road.
He wished when he had had the track alone
He had attacked it with a club or stone
And bent some rail wide open like a switch
So as to wreck the engine in the ditch.
Too late though, now, he had himself to thank.
Its click was rising to a nearer clank.   10
Here it came breasting like a horse in skirts.
(He stood well back for fear of scalding squirts.)
Then for a moment all there was was size
Confusion and a roar that drowned the cries
He raised against the gods in the machine.
Then once again the sandbank lay serene.
The traveler's eye picked up a turtle trail,
Between the dotted feet a streak of tail,
And followed it to where he made out vague
But certain signs of buried turtle's egg;   20
And probing with one finger not too rough,
He found suspicious sand, and sure enough,
The pocket of a little turtle mine.
If there was one egg in it there were nine,
Torpedo-like, with shell of gritty leather
All packed in sand to wait the trump together.
'You'd better not disturb me any more,'
He told the distance, 'I am armed for war.
The next machine that has the power to pass
Will get this plasm in its goggle glass.'   30

F R O M

A FURTHER RANGE [1936]

DESERT PLACES

Snow falling and night falling fast, oh, fast
In a field I looked into going past,
And the ground almost covered smooth in snow,
But a few weeds and stubble showing last.

The woods around it have it—it is theirs.
All animals are smothered in their lairs.
I am too absent-spirited to count;
The loneliness includes me unawares.

And lonely as it is that loneliness
Will be more lonely ere it will be less—   10
A blanker whiteness of benighted snow
With no expression, nothing to express.

They cannot scare me with their empty spaces
Between stars—on stars where no human race is.
I have it in me so much nearer home
To scare myself with my own desert places.

LEAVES COMPARED WITH FLOWERS

A tree's leaves may be ever so good,
So may its bark, so may its wood;
But unless you put the right thing to its root
It never will show much flower or fruit.

But I may be one who does not care
Ever to have tree bloom or bear.
Leaves for smooth and bark for rough,
Leaves and bark may be tree enough.

Some giant trees have bloom so small
They might as well have none at all.   10
Late in life I have come on fern.
Now lichens are due to have their turn.

I bade men tell me which in brief,
Which is fairer, flower or leaf.
They did not have the wit to say,
Leaves by night and flowers by day.

Leaves and bark, leaves and bark,
To lean against and hear in the dark.
Petals I may have once pursued.
Leaves are all my darker mood.   20

NEITHER OUT FAR NOR IN DEEP

The people along the sand
All turn and look one way.
They turn their back on the land.
They look at the sea all day.

As long as it takes to pass
A ship keeps raising its hull;
The wetter ground like glass
Reflects a standing gull.

The land may vary more;
But wherever the truth may be—   10
The water comes ashore,
And the people look at the sea.

They cannot look out far.
They cannot look in deep.
But when was that ever a bar
To any watch they keep?

PROVIDE, PROVIDE

The witch that came (the withered hag)
To wash the steps with pail and rag,
Was once the beauty Abishag,

The picture pride of Hollywood.
Too many fall from great and good
For you to doubt the likelihood.

Die early and avoid the fate.
Or if predestined to die late,
Make up your mind to die in state.

Make the whole stock exchange your own!   10
If need be occupy a throne,
Where nobody can call *you* crone.

Some have relied on what they knew;
Others on being simply true.
What worked for them might work for you.

No memory of having starred
Atones for later disregard,
Or keeps the end from being hard.

Better to go down dignified
With boughten friendship at your side   20
Than none at all. Provide, provide!

F R O M

A WITNESS TREE [1942]

THE SILKEN TENT

She is as in a field a silken tent
At midday when a sunny summer breeze
Has dried the dew and all its ropes relent,
So that in guys it gently sways at ease,
And its supporting central cedar pole,
That is its pinnacle to heavenward
And signifies the sureness of the soul,
Seems to owe naught to any single cord,
But strictly held by none, is loosely bound
By countless silken ties of love and thought   10
To everything on earth the compass round,
And only by one's going slightly taut
In the capriciousness of summer air
Is of the slightest bondage made aware.

THE WIND AND THE RAIN

I

That far-off day the leaves in flight
Were letting in the colder light.
A season-ending wind there blew
That as it did the forest strew
I leaned on with a singing trust
And let it drive me deathward too.
With breaking step I stabbed the dust,
Yet did not much to shorten stride,
I sang of death—but had I known
The many deaths one must have died   10
Before he came to meet his own!
Oh, should a child be left unwarned
That any song in which he mourned
Would be as if he prophesied?
It were unworthy of the tongue
To let the half of life alone
And play the good without the ill.
And yet 'twould seem that what is sung
In happy sadness by the young
Fate has no choice but to fulfill.   20

II

Flowers in the desert heat
Contrive to bloom
On melted mountain water led by flume
To wet their feet.
But something in it still in incomplete.
Before I thought the wilted to exalt
With water I would see them water-bowed.
I would pick up all ocean less its salt,
And though it were as much as cloud could bear
Would load it on to cloud,   30
And rolling it inland on roller air,
Would empty it unsparing on the flower
That past its prime lost petals in the flood,
(Who cares but for the future of the bud?)
And all the more the mightier the shower
Would run in under it to get my share.

'Tis not enough on roots and in the mouth,
But give me water heavy on the head
In all the passion of a broken drouth.

And there is always more than should be said.   40

As strong is rain without as wine within,
As magical as sunlight on the skin.

I have been one no dwelling could contain
When there was rain;
But I must forth at dusk, my time of day,
To see to the unburdening of skies.
Rain was the tears adopted by my eyes
That have none left to stay.

THE SUBVERTED FLOWER

She drew back; he was calm:
'It is this that had the power.'
And he lashed his open palm
With the tender-headed flower.
He smiled for her to smile,
But she was either blind
Or willfully unkind.
He eyed her for a while
For a woman and a puzzle.
He flicked and flung the flower,   10
And another sort of smile
Caught up like finger tips
The corners of his lips
And cracked his ragged muzzle.
She was standing to the waist
In goldenrod and brake,
Her shining hair displaced.
He stretched her either arm
As if she made it ache
To clasp her—not to harm;   20
As if he could not spare
To touch her neck and hair.
'If this has come to us
And not to me alone—'
So she thought she heard him say;
Though with every word he spoke
His lips were sucked and blown
And the effort made him choke
Like a tiger at a bone.
She had to lean away.   30
She dared not stir a foot,
Lest movement should provoke
The demon of pursuit
That slumbers in a brute.
It was then her mother's call
From inside the garden wall
Made her steal a look of fear
To see if he could hear
And would pounce to end it all
Before her mother came.   40
She looked and saw the shame:
A hand hung like a paw,
An arm worked like a saw
As if to be persuasive,
An ingratiating laugh
That cut the snout in half,
An eye become evasive.
A girl could only see
That a flower had marred a man,
But what she could not see   50
Was that the flower might be
Other than base and fetid:
That the flower had done but part,
And what the flower began

Her own too meager heart
Had terribly completed.
She looked and saw the worst.
And the dog or what it was,
Obeying bestial laws,
A coward save at night,   60
Turned from the place and ran.
She heard him stumble first
And use his hands in flight.
She heard him bark outright.
And oh, for one so young
The bitter words she spit
Like some tenacious bit
That will not leave the tongue.
She plucked her lips for it,
And still the horror clung.   70
Her mother wiped the foam
From her chin, picked up her comb
And drew her backward home.

THE GIFT OUTRIGHT

❲ THIS poem was read before the Phi Beta Kappa Society at William and Mary College, December 5, 1941, and recited from memory at President Kennedy's inauguration, January 20, 1961.

The land was ours before we were the land's.
She was our land more than a hundred years
Before we were her people. She was ours
In Massachusetts, in Virginia,
But we were England's, still colonials,
Possessing what we still were unpossessed by,
Possessed by what we now no more possessed.
Something we were withholding made us weak
Until we found out that it was ourselves
We were withholding from our land of living,   10
And forthwith found salvation in surrender.
Such as we were we gave ourselves outright
(The deed of gift was many deeds of war)
To the land vaguely realizing westward,
But still unstoried, artless, unenhanced,
Such as she was, such as she would become.

FROM

STEEPLE BUSH [1947]

ONE STEP BACKWARD TAKEN

Not only sands and gravels
Were once more on their travels,
But gulping muddy gallons
Great boulders off their balance
Bumped heads together dully
And started down the gully.
Whole capes caked off in slices.
I felt my standpoint shaken
In the universal crisis.
But with one step backward taken   10
I saved myself from going.
A world torn loose went by me.
Then the rain stopped and the blowing
And the sun came out to dry me.

DIRECTIVE

Back out of all this now too much for us,
Back in a time made simple by the loss
Of detail, burned, dissolved, and broken off
Like graveyard marble sculpture in the weather,
There is a house that is no more a house
Upon a farm that is no more a farm
And in a town that is no more a town.
The road there, if you'll let a guide direct you
Who only has at heart your getting lost,
May seem as if it should have been a quarry—   10
Great monolithic knees the former town
Long since gave up pretense of keeping covered.
And there's a story in a book about it:
Besides the wear of iron wagon wheels
The ledges show lines ruled southeast northwest,
The chisel work of an enormous Glacier
That braced his feet against the Arctic Pole.
You must not mind a certain coolness from him
Still said to haunt this side of Panther Mountain.
Nor need you mind the serial ordeal   20
Of being watched from forty cellar holes
As if by eye pairs out of forty firkins.
As for the woods' excitement over you
That sends light rustle rushes to their leaves,
Charge that to upstart inexperience.
Where were they all not twenty years ago?
They think too much of having shaded out
A few old pecker-fretted apple trees.

Make yourself up a cheering song of how
Someone's road home from work this once
    was,   30
Who may be just ahead of you on foot
Or creaking with a buggy load of grain.
The height of the adventure is the height
Of country where two village cultures faded
Into each other. Both of them are lost.
And if you're lost enough to find yourself
By now, pull in your ladder road behind you
And put a sign up CLOSED to all but me.
Then make yourself at home. The only field
Now left's no bigger than a harness gall.   40
First there's the children's house of make believe,
Some shattered dishes underneath a pine,
The playthings in the playhouse of the children.
Weep for what little things could make them glad.
Then for the house that is no more a house,
But only a belilaced cellar hole,
Now slowly closing like a dent in dough.
This was no playhouse but a house in earnest.
Your destination and your destiny's
A brook that was the water of the house,   50
Cold as a spring as yet so near its source,
Too lofty and original to rage.
(We know the valley streams that when aroused
Will leave their tatters hung on barb and thorn.)
I have kept hidden in the instep arch
Of an old cedar at the waterside
A broken drinking goblet like the Grail
Under a spell so the wrong ones can't find it,
So can't get saved, as Saint Mark says they
    mustn't.
(I stole the goblet from the children's play-
    house.)   60
Here are your waters and your watering place.
Drink and be whole again beyond confusion.

THE INGENUITIES OF DEBT

These I assume were words so deeply meant
They cut themselves in stone for permanent
Like trouble in the brow above the eyes:
'Take Care to Sell Your Horse before He Dies
The Art of Life Is Passing Losses on.'
The city saying it was Ctesiphon,
Which may a little while by war and trade
Have kept from being caught with the decayed,
Infirm, worn-out, and broken on its hands,
But judging by what little of it stands,   10
Not even the ingenuities of debt
Could save it from its losses being met.
Sand has been thrusting in the square of door
Across the tessellation of the floor,

And only rests, a serpent on its chin,
Content with contemplating, taking in,
Till it can muster breath inside a hall
To rear against the inscription on the wall.

PROSE

THE WATERSPOUT

❲ THESE few words were written by Frost as the Introduction to *The Arts Anthology: Dartmouth Verse 1925,* a collection of undergraduate verse.

NO ONE given to looking under-ground in spring can have failed to notice how a bean starts its growth from the seed. Now the manner of a poet's germination is less like that of a bean in the ground than of a waterspout at sea. He has to begin as a cloud of all the other poets he ever read. That can't be helped. And first the cloud reaches down toward the water from above and then the water reaches up toward the cloud from below and finally cloud and water join together to roll as one pillar between heaven and earth. The base of water he picks up from below is of course all the life he ever lived outside of books.

These, then, are the three figures of the waterspout and the first is about as far as the poet doomed to die young in everyone of us usually gets. He brings something down from Dowson, Yeats, Morris, Masefield, or the Imagists (often a long way down), but lifts little or nothing up. If he were absolutely certain to do as doomed and die young, he would hardly be worth getting excited over in college or elsewhere. But you can't be too careful about whom you will ignore in this world. Cases have been known of his refusing at the last minute to abdicate the breast in favor of the practical and living on to write lyric like Landor till ninety.

Right in this book he will be found surviving into the second figure of the waterspout, and, by several poems and many scattered lines, even into the third figure. [Certain poems], good as they are of their kind—accomplished and all that —are of the first figure and frankly derivative. They are meant to do credit to anyone's reading. But [certain others] . . . at least get up the salt water. Their realism represents an advance. They show acceptance of the fact that the way to better is often through worse. In [at least one poem] the pillar revolves pretty much unbroken.

We are here getting a long way with poetry, considering all there is against it in school and college. The poet, as everyone knows, must strike his individual note sometime between the ages of fifteen and twenty-five. He may hold it a long time, or a short time, but it is then he must strike it or never. School and college have been conducted with the almost express purpose of keeping him busy with something else till the danger of his ever creating anything is past. Their motto has been, the muses find some mischief still for idle hands to do. No one is asking to see poetry regularized in courses and directed by coaches like sociology and football. It must remain a theft to retain its savor. But it does seem as if it could be a little more connived at than it is. I for one should be in favor of the colleges setting the expectation of poetry forward a few years (the way the clocks are set forward in May), so as to get the young poets started earlier in the morning before the freshness dries off. Just setting the expectation of poetry forward might be all that was needed to give us our proportioned number of poets to Congressmen.

INTRODUCTION TO KING JASPER

[A POEM BY EDWIN ARLINGTON ROBINSON]

❲ FROST and Robinson are often compared merely because both are "Yankee" poets. The comparison does not get one very far in either poet and often serves as a way of avoiding both. This Preface to Robinson's first posthumous book—*King Jasper* (1935)—is the surviving poet's hail and farewell to the other.

IT MAY come to the notice of posterity (and then again it may not) that this, our age, ran wild in the quest of new ways to be new. The one old way to be new no longer served. Science put it into our heads that there must be new ways to be new. Those tried were largely by subtraction— elimination. Poetry, for example, was tried without punctuation. It was tried without capital letters. It was tried without metric frame on which to measure the rhythm. It was tried without any images but those to the eye; and a loud general intoning had to be kept up to cover the total loss of specific images to the ear, those dramatic tones of voice which had hitherto constituted the better half of poetry. It was tried without content under the trade name of poesie pure. It was tried without phrase, epigram, coherence, logic and consistency. It was tried without ability. I took the confession of one who had had deliberately to unlearn what he knew. He made a back-pedalling movement of his hands to illustrate the process. It was tried premature like the delicacy of unborn calf in Asia. It was tried without feeling or sentiment like murder for small pay in the underworld. These many things was it tried without, and what had we left? Still something. The limits of poetry had been sorely strained, but the hope was that the idea had been somewhat brought out.

Robinson stayed content with the old-fashioned way to be new. I remember bringing the subject up with him. How does a man come on his difference, and how does he feel about it when he first finds it out? At first it may well frighten him, as his difference with the Church frightened Martin Luther. There is such a thing as being too willing to be different. And what shall we say to people who are not only willing but anxious? What assurance have they that their difference is not insane, eccentric, abortive, unintelligible? Two fears should follow us through life. There is the fear that we shan't prove worthy in the eyes of someone who knows us at least as well as we know ourselves. That is the fear of God. And there is the fear of Man—the fear that men won't understand us and we shall be cut off from them.

We began in infancy by establishing correspondence of eyes with eyes. We recognized that they were the same feature and we could do the same things with them. We went on to the visible motion of the lips—smile answered smile; then cautiously, by trial and error, to compare the invisible muscles of the mouth and throat. They were the same and could make the same sounds. We were still together. So far, so good. From here on the wonder grows. It has been said that recognition in art is all. Better say correspondence is all. Mind must convince mind that it can uncurl and wave the same filaments of subtlety, soul convince soul that it can give off the same shimmers of eternity. At no point would anyone but a brute fool want to break off this correspondence. It is all there is to satisfaction; and it is salutary to live in the fear of its being broken off.

The latest proposed experiment of the experimentalists is to use poetry as a vehicle of grievances against the un-Utopian state. As I say, most of their experiments have been by subtraction. This would be by addition of an ingredient that latter-day poetry has lacked. A distinction must be made between griefs and grievances. Grievances are probably more useful than griefs. I read in a sort of Sunday-school leaflet from Moscow, that the grievances of Chekhov against the sordidness and dullness of his home-town society have done away with the sordidness and dullness of home-town society all over Russia. They were celebrating the event. The grievances of the great Russians of the last century have given Russia a revolution. The grievances of their great followers in America may well give us, if not a revolution, at least some palliative pensions. We must suffer them to put life at its ugliest and forbid them not, as we value our reputation for liberality.

I had it from one of the youngest lately: "Whereas we once thought literature should be without content, we now know it should be charged full of propaganda." Wrong twice, I told him. Wrong twice and of theory prepense. But he returned to his position after a moment out for reassembly: "Surely art can be considered good only as it prompts to action." How soon, I asked him. But there is danger of undue levity in teasing the young. The experiment is evidently started. Grievances are certainly a power and are going to be turned on. We must be very tender of our dreamers. They may seem like picketers or members of the committee on rules for the moment. We shan't mind what they seem, if only they produce real poems.

But for me, I don't like grievances. I find I gently let them alone wherever published. What I like is griefs and I like them Robinsonianly profound. I suppose there is no use in asking, but I should think we might be indulged to the extent of having grievances restricted to prose if prose will accept the imposition, and leaving poetry free to go its way in tears.

Robinson was a prince of heartachers amid countless achers of another part. The sincerity he wrought in was all sad. He asserted the sacred right of poetry to lean its breast to a thorn and sing its dolefullest. Let weasels suck eggs. I know better where to look for melancholy. A few superficial irritable grievances, perhaps, as was only human, but these are forgotten in the depth of griefs to which he plunged us.

Grievances are a form of impatience. Griefs are a form of patience. We may be required by law to throw away patience as we have been required to surrender gold; since by throwing away patience and joining the impatient in one last rush on the citadel of evil, the hope is we may end the need of patience. There will be nothing left to be patient about. The day of perfection waits on unanimous social action. Two or three more good national elections should do the business. It has been similarly urged on us to give up courage, make cowardice a virtue, and see if that won't end war, and the need of courage. Desert religion for science, clean out the holes and corners of the residual unknown, and there will be no more need of religion. (Religion is merely consolation for what we don't know.) But suppose there was some mistake, and the evil stood siege, the war didn't end, and something remained unknowable. Our having disarmed would make our case worse than it had ever been before. Nothing in the latest advices from Wall Street, the League of Nations, or the Vatican incline me to give up my holdings in patient grief.

There were Robinson and I, it was years ago, and the place (near Boston Common) was the Place, as we liked afterwards to call it, of Bitters, because it was with bitters, though without bitterness, we could sit there and look out on the welter of dissatisfaction and experiment in the world around us. It was too long ago to remember who said what, but the sense of the meeting was, we didn't care how arrant a reformer or experimentalist a man was if he gave us real poems. For ourselves, we should hate to be read for any theory upon which we might be supposed to write. We doubted any poem could persist for any theory upon which it might have been written. Take the theory that poetry in our language could be treated as quantitative, for example. Poems had been written in spite of it. And poems are all that matter. The utmost of ambition is to lodge a few poems where they will be hard to get rid of, to lodge a few irreducible bits where Robinson lodged more than his share.

For forty years it was phrase on phrase on phrase with Robinson, and every one the closest delineation of something that *is* something. Any poet, to resemble him in the least, would have to resemble him in that grazing closeness to the spiritual realities. If books of verse were to be indexed by lines first in importance instead of lines first in position, many of Robinson's poems would be represented several times over. This should be seen to. The only possible objection is that it could not be done by any mere hireling of the moment, but would have to be the work of someone who had taken his impressions freely before he had any notion of their use. A particular poem's being represented several times would only increase the chance of its being located.

The first poet I ever sat down with to talk about poetry was Ezra Pound. It was in London in 1913. The first poet we talked about, to the best of my recollection, was Edwin Arlington Robinson. I was fresh from America and from having read *The Town Down the River*. Beginning at that

book, I have slowly spread my reading of Robinson twenty years backward and forward, about equally in both directions.

I remember the pleasure with which Pound and I laughed over the fourth "thought" in

> Miniver thought, and thought, and thought,
> And thought about it.

Three "thoughts" would have been "adequate" as the critical praise-word then was. There would have been nothing to complain of, if it had been left at three. The fourth made the intolerable touch of poetry. With the fourth, the fun began. I was taken out on the strength of our community of opinion here, to be rewarded with an introduction to Miss May Sinclair, who had qualified as the patron authority on young and new poets by the sympathy she had shown them in *The Divine Fire*.

There is more to it than the number of "thoughts." There is the way the last one turns up by surprise round the corner, the way the shape of the stanza is played with, the easy way the obstacle of verse is turned to advantage. The mischief is in it.

> One pauses half afraid
> To say for certain that he played—

a man as sorrowful as Robinson. His death was sad to those who knew him, but nowhere near as sad as the lifetime of poetry to which he attuned our ears. Nevertheless, I say his much-admired restraint lies wholly in his never having let grief go further than it could in play. So far shall grief go, so far shall philosophy go, so far shall confidences go, and no further. Taste may set the limit. Humor is a surer dependence.

> And once a man was there all night,
> Expecting something every minute.

I know what the man wanted of Old King Cole. He wanted the heart out of his mystery. He was the friend who stands at the end of a poem ready in waiting to catch you by both hands with enthusiasm and drag you off your balance over the last punctuation mark into more than you meant to say. "I understand the poem all right, but please tell me what is behind it?" Such presumption needs to be twinkled at and baffled. The answer must be, "If I had wanted you to know, I should have told you in the poem."

We early have Robinson's word for it:

> The games we play
> To fill the frittered minutes of a day
> Good glasses are to read the spirit through.

He speaks somewhere of Crabbe's stubborn skill. His own was a happy skill. His theme was unhappiness itself, but his skill was as happy as it was playful. There is that comforting thought for those who suffered to see him suffer. Let it be said at the risk of offending the humorless in poetry's train (for there are a few such): his art was more than playful; it was humorous.

The style is the man. Rather say the style is the way the man takes himself; and to be at all charming or even bearable, the way is almost rigidly prescribed. If it is with outer seriousness, it must be with inner humor. If it is with outer humor, it must be with inner seriousness. Neither one alone without the other under it will do. Robinson was thinking as much in his sonnet on Tom Hood. One ordeal of Mark Twain was the constant fear that his occluded seriousness would be overlooked. That betrayed him into his two or three books of out-and-out seriousness.

Miniver Cheevy was long ago. The glint I mean has kept coming to the surface of the fabric all down the years. Yesterday in conversation, I was using "The Mill." Robinson could make lyric talk like drama. What imagination for speech in "John Gorham"! He is at his height between quotation marks.

> The miller's wife had waited long,
>   The tea was cold, the fire was dead;
> And there might yet be nothing wrong
>   In how he went and what he said:
> "There are no millers any more,"
>   Was all that she had heard him say.

"There are no millers any more." It might be an edict of some power against industrialism. But no, it is of wider application. It is a sinister jest at the expense of all investors of life or capital. The market shifts and leaves them with a car-barn full of dead trolley cars. At twenty I commit myself to a life of religion. Now, if religion should go out of fashion in twenty-five years, there would I be, forty-five years old, unfitted for anything else and too old to learn anything else. It seems immoral to have to bet on such high things as lives of art, business, or the church. But in effect, we have no alternative. None but an all-wise and all-powerful government could take the responsibility of keeping us out of the gamble or of insuring us against loss once we were in.

The guarded pathos of "Mr. Flood's Party" is what makes it merciless. We are to bear in mind the number of moons listening. Two, as on the planet Mars. No less. No more ("No more, sir; that will do"). One moon (albeit a moon, no sun) would have laid grief too bare. More than

two would have dissipated grief entirely and would have amounted to dissipation. The emotion had to be held at a point.

> He set the jug down slowly at his feet
> With trembling care, knowing that most things break;
> And only when assured that on firm earth
> It stood, as the uncertain lives of men
> Assuredly did not . . .

There twice it gleams. Nor is it lost even where it is perhaps lost sight of in the dazzle of all those golden girls at the end of "The Sheaves." Granted a few fair days in a world where not all days are fair.

> "Well, Mr. Flood, we have the harvest moon
> Again, and we may not have many more;
> The bird is on the wing, the poet says,
> And you and I have said it here before.
> Drink to the bird."

Poetry transcends itself in the playfulness of the toast.

Robinson has gone to his place in American literature and left his human place among us vacant. We mourn, but with the qualification that, after all, his life was a revel in the felicites of language. And not just to no purpose. None has deplored.

> The inscrutable profusion of the Lord
> Who shaped as one of us a thing

so sad and at the same time so happy in achievement. Not for me to search his sadness to its source. He knew how to forbid encroachment. And there is solid satisfaction in a sadness that is not just a fishing for ministration and consolation. Give us immedicable woes—woes that nothing can be done for—woes flat and final. And then to play. The play's the thing. Play's the thing. All virtue in "as if."

> As if the last of days
> Were fading and all wars were done.

As if they were. As if, as if!

THE FIGURE A POEM MAKES

¶ WRITTEN as a Preface to the 1939 *Collected Poems*, this celebrated statement was retained in the *Complete Poems* published ten years later.

ABSTRACTION is an old story with the philosophers, but it has been like a new toy in the hands of the artists of our day. Why can't we have any one quality of poetry we choose by itself? We can have in thought. Then it will go hard if we can't in practice. Our lives for it.

Granted no one but a humanist much cares how sound a poem is if it is only *a* sound. The sound is the gold in the ore. Then we will have the sound out alone and dispense with the inessential. We do till we make the discovery that the object in writing poetry is to make all poems sound as different as possible from each other, and the resources for that of vowels, consonants, punctuation, syntax, words, sentences, meter are not enough. We need the help of context—meaning—subject matter. That is the greatest help towards variety. All that can be done with words is soon told. So also with meters—particularly in our language where there are virtually but two, strict iambic and loose iambic. The ancients with many were still poor if they depended on meters for all tune. It is painful to watch our sprung-rhythmists straining at the point of omitting one short from a foot for relief from monotony. The possibilities for tune from the dramatic tones of meaning struck across the rigidity of a limited meter are endless. And we are back in poetry as merely one more art of having something to say, sound or unsound. Probably better if sound, because deeper and from wider experience.

Then there is this wildness whereof it is spoken. Granted again that it has an equal claim with sound to being a poem's better half. If it is a wild tune, it is a poem. Our problem then is, as modern abstractionists, to have the wildness pure; to be wild with nothing to be wild about. We bring up as aberrationists, giving way to undirected associations and kicking ourselves from one chance suggestion to another in all directions as of a hot afternoon in the life of a grasshopper. Theme alone can steady us down. Just as the first mystery was how a poem could have a tune in such a straightness as meter, so the second mystery is how a poem can have wildness and at the same time a subject that shall be fulfilled.

It should be of the pleasure of a poem itself to tell how it can. The figure a poem makes. It begins in delight and ends in wisdom. The figure is the same as for love. No one can really hold that the ecstasy should be static and stand still in one place. It begins in delight, it inclines to the impulse, it assumes direction with the first line laid down, it runs a course of lucky events, and ends in a clarification of life—not necessarily a great clarification, such as sects and cults are founded on, but in a momentary stay against confusion. It has denouement. It has an outcome that though unforeseen was predestined from the first image of the original mood—and indeed from the very mood. It is but a trick poem and no poem at all if the best of it was thought of first and saved for the last. It finds its own name as it goes and discovers the best waiting for it in some final phrase at once wise and sad—the happy-sad blend of the drinking song.

No tears in the writer, no tears in the reader. No surprise for the writer, no surprise for the reader. For me the initial delight is in the surprise of remembering something I didn't know I knew. I am in a place, in a situation, as if I had materialized from cloud or risen out of the ground. There is a glad recognition of the long lost and the rest follows. Step by step the wonder of unexpected supply keeps growing. The impressions most useful to my purpose seem always those I was unaware of and so made no note of at the time when taken, and the conclusion is come to that like giants we are always hurling experience ahead of us to pave the future with against the day when we may want to strike a line of purpose across it for somewhere. The line will have the more charm for not being mechanically straight. We enjoy the straight crookedness of a good walking stick. Modern instruments of precision are being used to make things crooked as if by eye and hand in the old days.

I tell how there may be a better wildness of logic than of inconsequence. But the logic is backward, in retrospect, after the act. It must be more felt than seen ahead like prophecy. It must be a revelation, or a series of revelations, as much for the poet as for the reader. For it to be that there must have been the greatest freedom of the material to move about in it and to establish relations in it regardless of time and space, previous relation, and everything but affinity. We prate of freedom. We call our schools free because we are not free to stay away from them till we are sixteen years of age. I have given up my democratic prejudices and now willingly set the lower classes free to be completely taken care of by the upper classes. Political freedom is nothing to me. I bestow it right and left. All I would keep for myself is the freedom of my material—the condition of body and mind now and then to summons aptly from the vast chaos of all I have lived through.

Scholars and artists thrown together are often annoyed at the puzzle of where they differ. Both work from knowledge; but I suspect they differ most importantly in the way their knowledge is come by. Scholars get theirs with conscientious thoroughness along projected lines of logic; poets theirs cavalierly and as it happens in and out of books. They stick to nothing deliberately, but let what will stick to them like burrs where they walk in the fields. No acquirement is on assignment, or even self-assignment. Knowledge of the second kind is much more available in the wild free ways of wit and art. A schoolboy may be defined as one who can tell you what he knows in the order in which he learned it. The artist must value himself as he snatches a thing from some previous order in time and space into a new order with not so much as a ligature clinging to it of the old place where it was organic.

More than once I should have lost my soul to radicalism if it had been the originality it was mistaken for by its young converts. Originality and initiative are what I ask for my country. For myself the originality need be no more than the freshness of a poem run in the way I have described: from delight to wisdom. The figure is the same as for love. Like a piece of ice on a hot stove the poem must ride on its own melting. A poem may be worked over once it is in being, but may not be worried into being. Its most precious quality will remain its having run itself and carried away the poet with it. Read it a hundred times: it will forever keep its freshness as a metal keeps its fragrance. It can never lose its sense of a meaning that once unfolded by surprise as it went.

MARK SCHORER
Editor

Sherwood Anderson

1876–1941

F. Scott Fitzgerald

1896–1940

Ernest Hemingway

1898–1961

OF HIS life Sherwood Anderson always wished to construct a parable, even a myth. It had various forms, but they all sprang from a central action. That action he recounted with varying details throughout his work, fiction and nonfiction, and that is why his fiction is never without autobiography just as his autobiographies are never without fiction. The central action is this: on November 27, 1912, a successful manufacturer in the town of Elyria, Ohio, dreaming sometimes of becoming a great benevolent tycoon, chafing more often at the stultifying routines of promotion and salesmanship, Sherwood Anderson, aged thirty-six, walked out of his office and away from his wife and family into the freedom of a wandering literary life, never to return to business. " 'For the rest of my life I will be a servant to [words] alone,' I whispered to myself as I went along a spur of railroad track, over a bridge, out of a town and out of that phase of my life."

It is a pretty fable that has considerable psychological relevance to the lives of many modern American writers even when its literal relevance is as slight as it was to the facts of Anderson's life.

Sherwood Anderson was born on September 13, 1876, the third child of a harness maker whose handicraft could not long compete with a rapidly developing mechanization throughout American enterprise. Forced out of business, he took to drink, spun endless tales for anyone who would listen, and became an itinerant sign and house painter. The family moved to Clyde, Ohio. Sherwood Anderson's education was always irregular and it ceased after one year of high school. His real education had come to him through the endless variety of odd jobs that filled his youth, through the wisdom of laborers and Negroes and livery stable hands and hangers-on, through race track touts and trainers, through tramps. When he was nineteen, his mother died, the father wandered off, the family broke up.

Sherwood Anderson went to Chicago to become a laborer in a cold-storage warehouse until, in desperation with that dogged work, he enlisted in the United States Army to fight in the Spanish-American War. His company did not reach Cuba until four months after the armistice had been signed, and he was released from the Army in less than a year after his enlistment. Back in Clyde, he worked on a farm, and in September of 1899, enrolled in the Wittenberg Academy in Springfield, Ohio, preparatory to enrolling in Wittenberg College when he would have been twenty-four years old. Before he reached that age, he gave up the brief academic dream and returned to Chicago.

In the opening year of the twentieth century, significantly enough, Sherwood Anderson became an advertising man, and soon he was writing copy in which, very much in keeping with the times, he glorified the adventure of business. Always attractive to women, he married a girl above him in social station, moved to Cleveland where he became the president of a mail-order firm, and from there to Elyria, Ohio —an enterprising family man who presently bought a paint factory that produced something called "Roof-Fix." Wanting to "ennoble" that business activity which he had chosen as his own, he was at the same time writing "lies" in his copy; a conflict developed between his wish to succeed in the ordinary commercial world and his wish to escape into the imaginative world and into real writing. More and more he brooded about the character of the artist and about his situation in an industrial society. In about 1910 he began to write short fiction, and by 1912 he had written drafts of what would become his first two novels. At the same time, torn by conflict, he had taken to drink, turned from his wife to the comforts of loose women, and was neglecting his business, which suffered accordingly. If, in his later recollections, he was to say that he let people think he was a little mad so that his creditors would forgive him when he deserted his busi-

ness, the fact is that he was a little mad. On November 27, that famous day of liberation, his nerves collapsed. Four days later, haggard, disheveled, and suffering from aphasia, he was found wandering around Cleveland in a daze and was hospitalized by the police. Late in December his wife brought him back to Elyria. In February he disposed of his business and left alone for Chicago, to return to the servitude of advertising. He was now thirty-six years old, his marriage would last another two years —when he would marry a sculptress named Tennessee Mitchell—but he would continue in advertising for another ten years.

When he was not in his office writing copy, still trying to make something good of a competitive life that he hated, he was working at his novels and at his queer, untutored short sketches. He began to meet writers. Through his brother, Karl, a painter, he met Floyd Dell, and chiefly through him, a whole circle of garrulous literary people including Ben Hecht, Burton Rascoe, Harry Hansen, Eunice Tietjens, Carl Sandburg, sometimes Theodore Dreiser, and, presently, Margaret Anderson, who was to found the *Little Review* in Chicago in 1914. When Floyd Dell read the manuscript of Anderson's first novel, *Windy McPherson's Son*, he was enthusiastic and took it upon himself to find a publisher. After many rejections, it found a publisher at last in the American branch of the English house of John Lane. It was published in 1916, and, having given Lane an option on his second novel, Anderson immediately produced the manuscript of that work, *Marching Men*, which was published in 1917.

These novels, although they caused considerable critical excitement as marking the appearance of an original genius, had small sales and were, in fact, poor novels. They are loose and sprawling works, without unity of theme or action, with comically unreal dialogue and with narrative and analytical passages written in long, straggling sentences that bear no relation to the style that Anderson presently would make his remarkable own. In the themes there are hints of what he was to become: the brooding boyhood in a drab Iowa town; the eccentric character of Windy, drawn, Anderson said, after his own father; and above all, the criticism of the myth of business idealism and the assertion at the end of the novel of his own myth —the break with manufacturing into freedom, to "find truth." In *Marching Men*, a curious story about a mindless and militant brotherhood formed by workers under the leadership of Beaut McGregor, intent on violence to free themselves from the routines of industrial slavery, both the inarticulate, somewhat Whitmanesque yearning for a bond between man and man and the aspiration to freedom, however ill-defined, suggest characteristic future themes. It is less easy to see the future Anderson at his best in the volume of inchoate poems called *Mid-American Chants*, published in 1918.

All the time, from 1913 on, Anderson was working toward something quite different from these books—his masterpiece, *Winesburg, Ohio*, published in 1919. A number of separate pieces from this work appeared in the *Little Review* and elsewhere between 1916 and the year of book publication, and these seemed to be autonomous if rather amorphous narrative entities. Only when the book as a whole was published was its over-all design and significance to appear.

The book comes directly out of the life of Anderson's boyhood in Clyde, and the central figure, who appears in most of the separate parts, George Willard, is drawn after Anderson in his late adolescence. Without explication of any sort, the book somehow evokes the dying end of an agrarian culture as it slips over into industrial culture. It evokes, too, the intellectual climate of that late nineteenth-century mid-America in which Anderson grew up: the world that fostered the heroic individualism of men like Abraham Lincoln and Mark Twain; the atmosphere that encouraged the atheism of a man like Robert Ingersol, the rhetoric of William Jennings Bryan, the "grass roots" stir of such a movement as the Populist party; the era that brought to an end gas-lit streets, wooden sidewalks and the cracker barrel, the flourishing village saloon, thriving village eccentrics.

All this is the inheritance of Sherwood Anderson, and within all this he had observed, and was still observing in Chicago, the character of individuals. How to use it? He was not happy with the more or less conventional novel form that he had already twice attempted. He was no more happy with the prevailing fashions in the short story, either in the formal sense—the slick machinery of O. Henry, for example—or in the conventional interpretation of village life—the sentimental romanticism of the Hoosier school. He had observed the pathos, the suffocation of hope and dream in small town characters, the cruelty no less than the comedy. And in form he wanted something loose and impressionistic and without the contrivances of "plot" that would permit him to get under the surface of manners and character, into the secret life, and into what he felt was the soft, warm flow that, taken together, all the secret lives made into life itself. "A man keeps thinking of his own life," he was later to write, in a note probably intended for his *Memoirs*, ". . . life itself is a loose, flowing thing. There are no plot stories in life."

What is wanted is a new looseness. Do we not live in a great, loose land, of many states and yet all of these states together do make something, a land, a country. I submit that the form of my Winesburg tales and all of the tales on which I am at work, even now, as I write . . . may offer a suggestion to other writers.

A new looseness, lives flowing past each other, the whole however to leave a definite impression, this as a form that fits one way of life. I submit it as something for our younger writers to be thinking about.

He had heard talk of Sigmund Freud in bohemian Chicago, and this helped him. He was reading, or was about to read, the fiction of D. H. Lawrence, and this would help him, too. Gertrude Stein's *Three Lives* (1909) had helped him to discover the language that he now knew he wanted to use—the colloquial language of Mark Twain, of everyday America, of country roads and village streets. Yet his problem was not solved until 1915, when he read Edgar Lee Masters' long poem, *The Spoon River Anthology*. As Masters had done in verse, so he could do in prose!

Like Masters, he would give a certain unification to the separate stories of his twenty-two characters through the background of a single community. As the stories progressed, characters would keep reappearing: someone who had been a minor figure in one story would presently emerge as the major figure in another, and so on, until a whole sense of the community would emerge. He would supplement Masters' unification with another means: in most of the stories George Willard would appear, and while the other characters would come to George in the dumb expectation that he could somehow tell their story, their stories would also be like gifts to him, gifts that would help him grow until, at the end, he was mature and made the characteristic gesture of flight into freedom. And he would have a third means of unification—a theory embodied in the opening section, a prelude called "The Book of the Grotesque."

A "grotesque" is formed, Anderson tells us, when an individual seizes on some single truth from the whole body of truths and tries to live by that alone. A single truth, a single wish, a single memory, a single obsessive ambition that distorts the self even as it compels it—these are the motivations of Sherwood Anderson's grotesques. But what is probably a further consequence of these motivations is perhaps more important than the grotesques themselves: in their single pursuits, the characters isolate themselves from one another, and in their isolation, they are at once lonely and mute. Everyone in this world seems to grope helplessly toward everyone else, but no one can communicate with anyone else—or only with the artist-reporter, George Willard. And that, as Anderson came to understand it, is the function of the artist: to absorb the lives of others into himself, and himself to become those others and their lives.

As a totality, as a book, that is, *Winesburg, Ohio* is the height of Anderson's achievement. Taken singly, however, none of its separate pieces is as good as any of a half-dozen or more truly separate short stories that he was to write then and later—stories like "The Egg" and "I Want to Know Why" from *The Triumph of the Egg* (1921), "I'm a Fool" and "The Man Who Became a Woman" from *Horses and Men* (1923), and "A Meeting South" and "Death in the Woods" from the volume called *Death in the Woods and Other Stories* (1933). Grotesques still appear in all of them; perhaps

Anderson's masterpiece of grotesquery is the father in "The Egg." Loneliness and isolation continue to be the condition of the characters, whether grotesques or adolescent boys such as the hero of "I Want to Know Why"—drawn again after Anderson himself. The style continues much the same—the slightly hesitant, slightly repetitious, and considerably rhythmical prose that bases itself so clearly on the spoken American language, sometimes, indeed, as in "I'm a Fool" and "I Want to Know Why," becoming the dialect itself, as it had been earlier used by Mark Twain in *Huckleberry Finn* and elsewhere.

Whatever similarities these later stories may bear to the slighter sketches of *Winesburg, Ohio*, it is nevertheless in their fuller embodiment that we can best see why Sherwood Anderson was nothing less than a revolutionary force in the American short story, and why the short story was the form most suited to the full expression of his talent. These stories, like the Winesburg pieces, seemed to contemporary readers to be a new victory for realism, and in a sense they were. They closed their eyes to nothing, glossed over nothing, neither the brutalities of men nor the beauty of animals. Their candid concern with the sexual relationship and with sexual motivations and repressions, their implied criticism of a society that frustrates individuality and of an individualism that creates a society of hermits, their accurate report of physical detail and of a certain range in the speaking voice—all this and more made Anderson seem to be the liberating champion of realism both in subject matter and in method. Yet when we put stories like "The Egg" or "I Want to Know Why" beside the work of such a realist as Stephen Crane or such a naturalist as Theodore Dreiser, we see readily enough that, with their impressionistic method, the first story is more nearly a fable and the second more nearly a poetic lamentation than either is a conventionally realistic or a naturalistic report, that Anderson's important observations are at once under the surface of manners and transcendant of the surface of society.

The short story was perfectly calculated to articulate those glimpses—James Joyce's word, "epiphany," is not inappropriate to Anderson's gift—into the secret, inarticulate life that was his special province. Yet over and over he would attempt the longer form of the novel where, over and over, he would lose his imaginative grip on his materials. Even before *Winesburg, Ohio* was published, Anderson began his next novel, *Poor White*. Finished and published in 1920, it is his best attempt in the form, but still much less satisfactory than the best of the stories. Bringing to it what he had learned about style in *Winesburg, Ohio* and hoping again to accommodate a certain "looseness" of structure by making the community itself the unifying center—the explicit theme now is the transformation of an agrarian to an industrial way of life—the narrative focus shifts so frequently and so drastically that the total is not "a new looseness" but a thematic confusion.

By the time that *Poor White* was published, Anderson had several times attempted to escape Chicago—and his second wife—by trips to New York and to various parts of the South; in the East he made new and important literary friends—Van Wyck Brooks, Waldo Frank, Paul Rosenfeld, Alfred Stieglitz—all of whom were enthusiastically responsive to his writing; but his books did not yet bring him an income adequate to free him from advertising once and for all, and in the winter of 1920–21, he was still writing copy in Chicago. In the summer of 1921, he escaped once more—but with his wife—when his friend, Paul Rosenfeld, invited them to come to Europe with him. Europe, and especially Paris—where he met Gertrude Stein, probably his most important contemporary literary "influence"—were to make Chicago forever impossible thereafter. Even those Chicago writers who were his friends and who were to have brought about that literary renaissance that had somehow fizzled, now seemed less than glamorous. In the summer of 1922, Anderson at last broke for good with advertising, with Chicago, and with his second wife. In the meantime, he had become acquainted with one younger Chicago writer, not of that older group nor of any group, who had impressed him more than any of his friends and who, in turn, had been impressed by the Anderson short stories. On December 3, 1921, Anderson wrote a letter of introduction to his new friend, Gertrude Stein,

for the unknown young writer on his way to Paris—Ernest Hemingway.

II

ERNEST HEMINGWAY, although a Midwesterner too, came, nevertheless, from a very different background. He was born into the respectable Chicago suburb of Oak Park on July 21, 1899, the son of a doctor who loved the out-of-doors, and of a gentle, rather pious mother. His father was more important to the boy than his mother, and the most important experiences of his boyhood were not to take place in genteel Oak Park but in the northern Michigan woods where the Hemingways spent their summers and where the father and son enjoyed hunting and fishing. The boy was an athlete, but in high school he also became interested in writing. He published stories in the high school literary magazine and imitated Ring Lardner in the school newspaper—Lardner was important to each of the three writers represented in these selections. He was graduated in 1917 and his ambition now was to enlist and get into the war in Europe, but his father forbade that, and Hemingway chafed through his last summer in Michigan. In the fall of 1917 he went to Kansas City to become a reporter on the Kansas City *Star*. He was eighteen and his formal education was over.

Many of the qualities of Hemingway's early prose style—among them, the short sentences, the sparse use of adjectives, the clarity of statement—were developed through his writing for the *Star* during the seven months of his employment. In April, 1918, he managed at last to get into the war as an honorary lieutenant in the Red Cross ambulance corps serving on the Italian front. His service was short: on July 8 he was severely wounded by the explosion of a mortar shell and the next three months he spent in a hospital in Milan. Nothing more important than this wounding was ever to happen to him. A wound was to become the central symbol of nearly everything he was to write, and the consequences of a wound his persistent thematic preoccupation.

He returned to Oak Park and to Chicago, spent the summer and autumn in northern Michigan trying to write, went to Canada to write for the Toronto *Star Weekly* for the first half of 1920, and then, back in Chicago, went to work for an advertising firm. His spare time he spent in loitering about gymnasiums, boxing and watching boxers, and in trying to write short stories and poems. Already familiar with the stories of Sherwood Anderson, some of whose material was drawn from the same areas of life as Hemingway's would be, he now met Anderson. The older man knew at once that he had met a young man who was going to become an important writer, and whether or not he influenced him profoundly—but surely Hemingway's early story, "My Old Man," is simply his version of Anderson's "I Want to Know Why"—the example of his success was a powerful incentive to the still unpublished but seriously struggling Hemingway. His style was to develop into something tighter, more concentrated, and more lucid than Anderson's and would achieve a character quite its own, but in diction and in rhythm it looks back to Anderson. Interestingly enough, both men thought of Mark Twain as the great model—in a moment of exaggeration Hemingway said (see p. 755) that *all* American literature came from *Huckleberry Finn*—and both men accepted the tutelage of the same contemporary, Gertrude Stein.

The famous remark that she would presently make to him—"You are all a lost generation" —marks the important difference between Hemingway and Anderson. In a long letter to his son, Robert (see p. 708), written in November, 1929, Anderson tried to explain the difference between their generations, the difference between men who were formed before the World War and men who were largely formed by it. The rebellion of the older generation, of men like Anderson, was against the repressive conventions of American life, but they still believed in American life and they still sought their values in its promises. The war ended those conventions at a blow, and the younger generation, men like Hemingway, had nothing to rebel against and found little in American life that they could believe in. Hemingway, Alfred Kazin has written, "had no basic relation to any prewar culture." In Chicago, he grew increasingly cynical about America and about his employment in particular—with reason, he soon discovered, for his employer was in fact committing an enormous fraud in his enterprise. In 1921 he married, obtained the promise of employment as roving correspondent for the Toronto *Star*, and left for Europe. The expatriation of Ernest Hemingway is as symbolic of his career as the hypothetical break with business is symbolic of Anderson's.

From Gertrude Stein, Hemingway learned his major lessons in style—learned about effective repetition of words, the most rigorous economy, and that degree of concentration on diction and rhythm that alone will evoke for the reader the essential physical quality of the object or experience that is under observation. In Paris, in the years before 1925, he was her attentive pupil. At the same time, as a newspaper correspondent, he was traveling all over Europe and the Near East, and thus broadening the scope of his subject matter. Nearly all of the brief vignettes that form the interchapters of his second book, *In Our Time*, are derived directly from his newspaper experience. These sketches were written in August, 1923, before his first published book, *Three Stories and Ten Poems*. The poems are negligible, but the stories—"My Old Man," "Out of Season," and "Up in Michigan"—announced the appearance of a brilliant and original talent. Two years later, with the publication of *In Our Time*, the future of that talent was assured.

It was Sherwood Anderson who urged the publication of this book on his publisher in New York, Horace Liveright. Like *Winesburg, Ohio*, it is a group of related short stories which must be read as a whole if the total impact of the book is to be felt. Like *Winesburg*, too, it has a central character, Nick Adams, modeled after the author in his youth and young manhood, who appears, if not in all the stories, at least throughout, and who, in the course of the book, like George Willard, comes into his maturity. The stories in which he does not actually appear are, one must assume, observations made by Nick Adams as he advances into his maturity. Unlike *Winesburg*, the stories in *In Our Time* are interspersed with brief vignettes about war, bullfighting, or journalism. Each of these recounts in the sparsest prose, without any commentary, events of brutal violence, and they include one which recounts the wounding of Nick Adams in the war. Brutal violence, they assert, is the characteristic of our time; and a mute, apparent indifference, grim and tight-lipped, they seem to assert, is the only possible attitude that one can take toward the brutal violence of our time. This is the Hemingway attitude, and the attitude of Hemingway's hero.

In the stories proper, we begin with Nick Adams as a small boy in Michigan, introduced to violence, to death, to sex, to the multiple pains and perplexities of his initiation into life. All this violence is brought to its climax in his battle wounds. At the end of the book, in "Big Two-Hearted River" (see pp. 744–52), he returns to Michigan, about twenty years old, and in this remarkable story that seems to be little more than an almost monotonously detailed report of two days in which Nick, alone, makes his camp on the river and fishes it for trout, we are given the man he has become.

He is not a well man. He is a man who has suffered not only physically but deeply in his spirit. He must occupy himself in physical acts so that his mind does not revert to the climax of his suffering or to the steps of lesser suffering that led to it. He must exhaust himself or he cannot sleep, and when he does sleep, he often has bad dreams. After he was wounded, "no patriot," he made "a separate peace" with the enemy and went a little insane. Now, symbolically, he makes his tent and gets into it. "He was there, in the good place" where he could keep his separate peace. And next day, again symbolically, he will not fish in the fearsome swamp into which the river flows, as he keeps his mind above that swamplike state into which it had fallen in his wartime trauma. Physically active, solitary, cut off from society, without either self-pity or hope, forever wounded, he will *endure* life, and only that.

This is the Hemingway hero and his famous "code," living by his "guts" alone, which is to say with "grace under pressure." He will appear in various guises throughout the rest of Hemingway's work except for his next book, *The Torrents of Spring* (1926), which is a sport, a parody of a successful book by his mentor, Sherwood Anderson.

III

IN 1922 Sherwood Anderson did at last flee business and Chicago, more or less on the heels of Hemingway. His major work was finished when finally he won his freedom. He left his second wife and presently married a third, Elizabeth Prall, and there was to be one more wife after her, Eleanor Copenhaver. Now, in 1922, he was quite appropriately working on a novel called *Many Marriages*. He wandered about in the South and in and out of literary New York. At the height of his fame, he was meeting many other writers, among them a phenomenal young success from Minnesota named F. Scott Fitzgerald. Fitzgerald thought Anderson's a "brilliant and almost inimitable prose style," but these two men, temperamentally so different, were never to have the kind of close association that, briefly, Anderson and Hemingway had enjoyed in Chicago, or that, later, Hemingway and Fitzgerald would enjoy in France.

Francis Scott Key Fitzgerald was born on September 24, 1896, in Saint Paul, Minnesota. His father was the somewhat shiftless descendant of an old American line; his mother was the daughter of an Irish immigrant. On one side was "breeding" and failure, on the other, money but not enough of it. To this situation Fitzgerald later attributed his inferiority complex, and to it he should have attributed his fascination with the very rich and with social success. Still, a good looking boy of charm and social grace, he got along well enough with the young people he admired, even though his family always lived on the periphery of the best neighborhoods, and in rather shabby circumstances. He began to write in the St. Paul Academy and continued to write at the Newman Academy, near New York City, where he finished his secondary school education, and was admitted to Princeton, with the dream of being a football player, in 1913. This ambition he was unable to realize, but he threw himself into other activities, literary and theatrical, and was elected to a top social club. A romantic young man, he found the social world of Princeton to be vastly glamorous and all-important. His academic work was undistinguished and it was not made better by his outside activities. In his junior year, when illness further retarded his already limping studies, he dropped out of Princeton for the rest of the year and was put on probation. When he returned, his interests were more serious and so were his friends— T. K. Whipple, John Peale Bishop, and Edmund Wilson were among them. All through that winter and spring, students were going off to war. Fitzgerald applied for a commission in the Army, received it, and left Princeton for Fort Leavenworth, Kansas in November of 1917. He did not get abroad but was transferred from training camp to training camp while he worked at a novel. Called *The Romantic Egotist*, it was declined by Charles Scribner's Sons in August of 1918. In the next month, at an officers' dance at Camp Sheridan, he met Zelda Sayre, a Montgomery, Alabama belle with whom he fell hopelessly in love.

Discharged from the Army early in 1919, he went to New York to earn enough money to persuade Zelda Sayre to marry him; the third of our trio, he entered an advertising agency at a miserable salary. When, by the summer of 1919, it was clear that this work could not make marriage possible, he left his job, returned to St. Paul, and rewrote *The Romantic Egotist*. It became his first novel, *This Side of Paradise*. Scribner's accepted it, and when it was published in March of 1920, it was a sensation. The "jazz age" had found its definition.

Before its publication, Fitzgerald, who, half the time, was behaving like one of his own characters in crazy, drunken carousing, was in the other half writing short stories, good and bad, with abandon, and selling them to magazines, chiefly the *Saturday Evening Post*, at about a thousand dollars each, often more. His success was sudden and spectacular. *This Side of Paradise*, a kind of autobiography, made him famous and gave Princeton a new reputation as a frenzied pleasure dome. Miss Sayre married him in April. A spectacular, champagne-drenched marriage and an extraordinary literary career were simultaneously launched, everything about both, for the moment, glittering and golden. Neither Anderson nor Hemingway had yet escaped from Chicago.

In New York, with money now, very popular, the dazzling young Fitzgeralds tried to realize their romantic dream of success and happiness through endless parties and debauchery, and for a time it was, indeed, fun. This life, with its night club glitter, its atmosphere of great, beautiful ballrooms, its irrepressible and irresponsible youthfulness, is evoked in story after story that Fitzgerald was writing in his sober hours and which he collected in two books—*Flappers and Philosophers* (1920) and *Tales of the Jazz Age* (1922). But where was it to lead them? The answer is contained in his next novel, the title of which in itself contains it; *The Beautiful and Damned* of 1922 is not so much an autobiographical novel as it is a prophecy of autobiography.

That work finished, they had a brief and frantic fling in Europe and then, disappointed and depressed, returned to the United States. They took a house in St. Paul and Fitzgerald wrote his publisher to say:

Loafing puts me in this particularly obnoxious and abominable gloom. My 3rd novel, if I ever write another, will I am sure be black as death with gloom. I should like to sit down with ½ a dozen chosen companions and drink myself to death but I am sick alike of life, liquor and literature. If it wasn't for Zelda I think I'd disappear out of sight . . .

Zelda presently gave birth to their only child, a girl named Frances. And Fitzgerald did, in fact, work very hard.

He wrote a play, *The Vegetable*, which, when it finally found a producer in 1923, was unsuccessful. And they moved East again, now to Long Island, and gave great parties and drove recklessly in and out of Manhattan even as Fitzgerald was writing that novel about great parties and reckless drives that would be *The Great Gatsby*. This work was interrupted by a burst of story writing, necessary to clear them of their debts, and that accomplished they went to Europe again with the partially completed novel. In November of 1924 he sent his first finished version of it to his publishers.

The Great Gatsby was published in 1925. Probably Fitzgerald's most flawless novel, it is certainly the point at which his talent was most fully consolidated and the point, too, at which all his themes and interests achieved their fullest synthesis. Here is the romantic dream of an impossibly glamorous existence, the frenetic, even orgiastic attempt to make it real, the corruption that underlies its approximation, the sense of disaster that pervades it, and the disaster in which it ends. Here, too, is that constant concern of Fitzgerald's with "the very rich," who "are different from you and me." When Fitzgerald made that observation to Hemingway, it is said, Hemingway replied, "Yes, they have more money." But for Fitzgerald, as for Jay Gatsby, the poor boy who has been made rich by bootlegging and crime but who has not been able to enter the world of those who were born to riches, there is a greater difference.

"She's got an indiscreet voice," I remarked. "It's full of —" I hesitated.

"Her voice is full of money," [Gatsby] said suddenly.

That was it. I'd never understood before. It was full of money—that was the inexhaustible charm that rose and fell in it, the jingle of it, the cymbals' song of it . . . High in a white palace the king's daughter, the golden girl . . ."

The romance of money! But there is also the reality of it:

I couldn't forgive him or like him, but I saw that what he had done was, to him, entirely justified. It was all very careless and confused. They were careless people, Tom and Daisy—they smashed up things and creatures and then retreated back into their money or their vast carelessness, or whatever it was that kept them together, and let other people clean up the mess they had made . . .

I shook hands with him; it seemed silly not to, for I felt suddenly as though I were talking to a child. Then he went into the jewelry store to buy a pearl necklace—or perhaps only a pair of cuff buttons—rid of my provincial squeamishness forever.

The narrator is a young man named Nick Carroway who has come from the Middle West to be an Easterner, and for him, finally, the Middle West comes to represent simplicity and innocence, and the East, complexity and corruption. Fitzgerald's use of Carroway is an act of technical brilliance, for it enables him to put a certain objective distance between himself and the subject matter that was in itself so fascinating for him. At his best—and certainly here in *The Great Gatsby*—Fitzgerald manages

to do two things simultaneously: to make us feel, along with him, the Circean charm and glamour and romance of the careless world of the very rich; and at the same time to judge it. When his stories fail, it is because the second element is missing, and when it is, the first is somehow shoddy and unreal. When they succeed, when these two elements are held in balance, he is among our greatest novelists of manners.

At just about the point at which *The Great Gatsby* was published, Fitzgerald began work on one of his finest short stories, "The Rich Boy" (see pp. 713–29), which occupied him for most of the summer of 1925. In this story he addressed himself directly to the matter of "the very rich," and the subtle revelation that the story makes through the character of Anson Hunter, and that a summary statement such as this can only debase, is that not only does their "carelessness" serve to be brutally destructive of others, but that their ease and pride and self-sufficiency prevent their own fulfillment in human relationships, numb the capacity for love, make personal commitment impossible. Once again, Fitzgerald managed—as he repeatedly would—the double imaginative act of making us feel, with his peculiar eloquence of style, the charged charm of a certain way of life, and demonstrating to us its rather terrible fatality. Many other fine stories in *All the Sad Young Men*, the volume in which "The Rich Boy" appeared in the next year, 1926, perform the same feat. This is all the more remarkable in that now, in the mid-twenties, Fitzgerald himself more and more succumbed to the gaudy pleasures of that world which would at last destoy him.

He was seeing a good deal of Ernest Hemingway in Paris, and Hemingway gives us a metaphorical glimpse of him:

It was at this point in the story, reader, that Mr. F. Scott Fitzgerald came to our home one afternoon, and after remaining for quite a while suddenly sat down in the fireplace and would not (or was it could not, reader?) get up and let the fire burn something else so as to keep the room warm.

IV

THE LAST quotation comes from Hemingway's book called *The Torrents of Spring*, published in 1926. Sherwood Anderson in 1925 had at last written a commercially successful novel in *Dark Laughter,* an unfortunate work that rests on a supposed contrast between the rich sensuality of Negroes and the anemic sterility of whites. At just this time, Fitzgerald was working to obtain a wider audience for Hemingway, and had urged his work upon his own publisher, Scribner's. Hemingway, however, was under option to Liveright, Anderson's publisher. *The Torrents of Spring,* which he said he wrote in ten days, was a professed and not very funny parody of *Dark Laughter.* When it was submitted to Liveright, that unhappy man could only decline to publish it since it treated his stellar author so outrageously. The refusal released Hemingway from his contract and Scribner's published the book. Anderson was hurt and bewildered, and his friendship with Hemingway came to an end. For Hemingway, the writing of that book was an act by which he exorcised an influence, and his next book would show that he was now nearly his own man.

Although Anderson had finally written a successful book, his work continued to decline. He became a country newspaper editor in Virginia and he turned his interest to the influence of machines on American life and to the situation of the American worker in the industrial South. Writing still an occasional good short story, his major efforts went into a number of works of semi-autobiography such as *A Story Teller's Story,* into impressionistic essays, and into two more novels, *Beyond Desire* and *Kit Brandon,* which reveal no significant extension of his thematic interests, even when labor became his subject matter. Like many another writer, he flirted with left-wing politics during the depression years in the 1930's, but Anderson was no man to commit himself to the disciplines of party politics. Even after he had his farm in Virginia, he continued to be a wanderer, yearning always for some freedom that his individuality was never quite satisfied that it had found. During the last twenty years of his life, when he was more or less free to serve words alone at last, he became in many ways his own legend. Yet that legend was suitable, somehow, only to an older, more expansive America. Symbolically

enough, his death, in 1941, occurred on a journey. No less symbolic was the cause of his death: peritonitis brought about by a fragment of colored toothpick that he had swallowed at a cocktail party.

V

IN THE mid-twenties, Anderson's lost friend, Ernest Hemingway, began to create his own legend. The devil-may-care, somehow bittersweet expatriate who fought bulls and studied the ritual of bullfighting, the athlete who boxed and sometimes brawled, the big game hunter and the deep-sea fisherman, the war-lover who turned up on every front in every war, the lover of women—he too had four wives—whose heroines are always the same submissive dream figure in different guises, the adventurer miraculously rescued from various physical catastrophes, and finally that "Papa" whose best friend was Marlene Dietrich. The legend is in large part true but it is partial, and, omitting Hemingway, the fine writer, it omits the most important fact about him and the fact that the legend tends to obscure.

If 1925 saw the appearance of one great American novel in *Gatsby,* 1926 saw another in *The Sun Also Rises.* This novel of the lost generation in Paris and Spain, with its wounded hero, Jake Barnes, and its bitterly gallant, unobtainable heroine, Brett Ashley, is not only Hemingway at his purest but perhaps the classic of postwar American fiction. Here Hemingway's prose has been distilled to its essence; here the code of endurance amidst fatality achieves its clearest definition; here the flicker of satire plays most effectively over the pathos; and here the style is the perfect expression of the subject, the attitude, the man himself.

Like Fitzgerald, Hemingway alternated his novels with books of short stories, and his short stories became more and more impressive, reaching their climax, perhaps, in those two of 1936, "The Short Happy Life of Francis Macomber" and "The Snows of Kilimanjaro," and in that extended short story of 1952, *The Old Man and the Sea,* which is said to be only a portion of a very big novel on which Hemingway had long been engaged. The short stories, with their technically brilliant finish and with their strangely reverberating depths, are all variations on the central pattern of Hemingway's fiction, which Philip Young has described as "the pattern of violence, psychological wounding, escape and death."

Farewell to Arms (1929), the novel that followed *The Sun Also Rises*, is a war novel that gives us the background of the earlier novel. Lieutenant Henry, disastrously wounded in the war, makes his "separate peace" and flees with his lovely nurse, Catharine Barkley, who dies in childbirth. He is left with nothing at all, like Jake Barnes, and can only, like the Hemingway hero always, enact the ritual of endurance as a kind of living demonstration of A. E. Housman's lines—

> Could man be drunk for ever
> With liquor, love, or fights,
> Lief should I rouse at morning
> And lief lie down of nights.
>
> But men at whiles are sober
> And think by fits and starts,
> And if they think, they fasten
> Their hands upon their hearts.

Physical activity, whether to keep from thinking or not, was as important to Hemingway as to his heroes, and in two works of nonfiction he gave extended treatment to two of the forms of physical activity that interested him most. *Death in the Afternoon* (1932) is about bullfighting and death; *The Green Hills of Africa* (1935) is about big game hunting, literary matters, and death. These are among Hemingway's lesser works, but, revealing as they do a man of bias and prejudice as well as of courage and daring, they are important to an understanding of a not entirely engaging literary personality. (Sherwood Anderson, who also in the end became a Scribner's author, felt as he read *Green Hills of Africa* that "it leaves a curious bad taste.")

Some of Hemingway's fiction leaves the same "curious bad taste." This is when his personality obtrudes upon his material, or when the material is not sufficiently objectified. In the 1930's, the Hemingways moved from France to Key West, Florida, and out of the Florida experience came the novel *To Have and Have Not* in 1937. Like Anderson, Hem-

ingway, observing the America of the depression years, was briefly pushed toward the left, and this novel is an attempt to vindicate the "outlaw" hero, Harry Morgan, for whom society makes an honest living impossible, and to denounce the decadent rich. Harry Morgan's chief virtue, however, seems to be his sexual prowess, which is hardly an adequate basis for a critique of the class system; but the novel is not really meant as serious criticism of capitalism; it seems rather to be the outlet for a large reservoir of personal spleen that had been aroused in Hemingway by a certain kind of visitor to Florida, and the spleen poisons the book, which is a fragmentary performance, unsatisfactory both in structure and in style.

The final wisdom of Harry Morgan, as he lies dying, is that no man can go it alone, that no man is an island. It is this wisdom—which may be taken as an ambiguous retraction of the code implicit in *The Sun Also Rises* and *A Farewell to Arms*—that provides the theme for Hemingway's next novel, *For Whom the Bell Tolls*, published in 1940. A novel about the Spanish Civil War, in which Hemingway was deeply involved both personally and professionally (it impelled him to write his single play, *The Fifth Column* of 1938), it is different from his other fiction in that his hero, although he must die for it, is committed to a cause. The novel attempts an epic scale unlike any other book that Hemingway published, and while it has many memorable scenes and some magnificently realized Spanish characters, the whole does not sustain the heroic intention. In the sexual encounters especially, one feels again that the personality of the author has been imposed upon the personality of Robert Jordan, the hero; and then Jordan becomes slightly absurd, and the great Hemingway style falters into bathos, and the tragic subject invites an uncomfortable smile.

The same problem plagues his first novel to be published after the Second World War, *Across the River and Into the Trees* of 1950. It is possible that the old pattern of the wounded hero who returns to the scene of his wounding for a kind of ritualistic exorcism is worn rather thin. It is possible that the lovely young heroine is too much an old man's fancy to be real. It is possible that Colonel Cantwell is too much like Hemingway himself, or too directly a transcription of his dream of himself, his legend. Yet there are those who argue that the true Hemingway *aficionado* can be tested by his response to this book, that if he does not think it great his entire judgment of Hemingway is suspect. In his review of this novel, John O'Hara—only one of the scores and scores of younger writers who have been influenced by Hemingway in style, in attitude, in the conception of fictional form—began by saying that Hemingway was "the most important, the outstanding author out of the millions of writers who have lived since 1616," since, that is, the death of William Shakespeare.

Many other readers, less certain in their judgment, were reassured by Hemingway's next book, the novelette called *The Old Man and the Sea*. It contained, for example, no women—only an old man, a small boy, and a large fish. And the athletic performance of the heroic old man was precisely as gratifying as the aesthetic performance of the heroically aging novelist. The point was the same as ever: winner take nothing.

VI

F. SCOTT FITZGERALD was no longer present, in these later years, to judge the performance of his friend, whom he had named once, together with Edmund Wilson, as his "conscience." But he felt, towards the end of his life, that he lived in Hemingway's shadow. "I don't write any more," he said to Thornton Wilder in the middle thirties. "Ernest has made all my writing unnecessary." In April of 1934 he had started—and he worked at this project off and on for the rest of his life—a fantastically ill-conceived novel to be called *The Count of Darkness*. Set in the ninth and tenth centuries, this novel was to have as its hero a daring young man named Phillipe who would play a part in the founding of France and in the consolidation of feudalism. "Fitzgerald's plan was that 'it shall be the story of Ernest' and his hope that 'just as Stendahl's portrait of a Byronic man made *Le Rouge et Noir* so couldn't *my* portrait of Ernest as Phillipe make the real modern man.'" It is not surprising that those portions of this work that he

finished are among the least satisfactory pieces of writing he ever did.

He managed, through a deteriorating life, still to achieve work that was equal to and perhaps greater than the old magnificence. The dizzy pace of the Fitzgeralds' life accelerated in the mid-twenties, in Paris and on the Riviera, until, with Zelda nervously ill and Fitzgerald himself nearly a physical ruin, they returned to the United States at the end of 1926 and went to Hollywood. There things were hardly quieter. They bought a large, serene house outside Wilmington, Delaware, and hoped for peace. He was working at a novel to be called *The World's Fair*, never to be finished. As their marriage had grown older, Zelda Fitzgerald had developed stronger and stronger competitive feelings about her husband, and now she decided that she must study ballet dancing, and chiefly for that purpose they returned to Paris in the summer of 1928. In 1929 he abandoned *The World's Fair*, and living much of the time on the Riviera, began to work on material that would lead to *Tender Is the Night*. In April of 1930, Mrs. Fitzgerald suffered a complete nervous collapse and spent nearly a year in a Swiss sanatarium. The diagnosis was schizophrenia, and the possibility of her recovery was slight. But there were brief recoveries. They returned to the United States. Hollywood again. Another breakdown. Another sanatarium. Another house, now near Baltimore, inappropriately called *La Paix*. Working on *Tender Is the Night*, Fitzgerald's life had nevertheless become a nightmare, with liquor necessary to work, and work necessary if he was to live. The novel was finished late in 1933 and published in the next April.

Much more complex than *The Great Gatsby*, the new novel, in spite of the circumstances of its composition, is probably Fitzgerald's greatest achievement. A story of "emotional bankruptcy," it depicts not only the dissolution of a life but of a way of life. It is the elegy of the 1920's, the allegory of the dream that Fitzgerald himself tried to make of reality and the dissipation of that dream. It is, quite simply, one of the most moving novels in all American fiction. And the reviews were lukewarm, obtuse, the sales trivial. It was Fitzgerald's greatest defeat.

His wife was now incurably insane, even though she managed to write a novel, *Save Me the Waltz* (1932), in one period of hospitalization. Fitzgerald managed one more collection of short stories (*Taps at Reveille*, 1935), but really, the remaining years of his life were all down-hill. Early in 1936 he published his extraordinary self-diagnosis in the three pieces that make "The Crack-Up" (see pp. 737–43), and was again in Hollywood, looking for work. Treated like a hack writer by producers, nearly forgotten by the public, a dim figure lost in the now legendary twenties, he was rescued by the columnist Sheilah Graham, and had, at the end of his life, at least his love for her, and hers. The story of his disastrous attempt to write a scenario with Budd Schulberg about Dartmouth College and its Winter Carnival is told in fictional form in Schulberg's novel, *The Disenchanted* (1950), and again in the play of that name, written by Schulberg and Harvey Breit. He managed to write a series of stories about a character named Pat Hobby ("he is what Fitzgerald in his worst moments saw himself becoming"),[1] and he began to make notes for and write fragments of another novel that, after his death, Edmund Wilson was to put together as *The Last Tycoon*. Had he lived to finish it, it would almost certainly have been the one great novel about Hollywood.

In November of 1940, he had a serious heart attack. He stopped drinking. But on December 21 he had a second attack, and that was fatal.

Sherwood Anderson, who had always brooded about the situation of the artist in America, felt sad, and in his *Memoirs*, which he at this time was straining to finish, he tried once more to define the problem for himself. What was it, in America, that destroyed its writers, or drove them to destroy themselves? "Did you ever hear of an artist who had an easy road to travel in life?" he exclaimed, rather than asked, in 1938. Ernest Hemingway, three years before, had given the world his speculations on the subject.

"We do not have great writers," I said. "Something happens to our good writers at a certain age.

[1] Arthur Mizener, *The Far Side of Paradise* (1951), p. 285.

I can explain but it is quite long and may bore you.". . .

"Please explain," he said. . . .

"We destroy them in many ways. First, economically. . . ."

"Tell me . . . what are the things, the actual, concrete things that harm a writer?"

I was tired of the conversation which was becoming an interview. So I would make it an interview and finish it. The necessity to put a thousand intangibles into a sentence, now, before lunch, was too bloody.

"Politics, women, drink, money, ambition. And the lack of politics, women, drink, money and ambition," I said profoundly. . . .

"But drink. I do not understand about that. That has always seemed silly to me. I understand it as a weakness."

"It is a way of ending a day. . . ."

What happened to Hemingway himself remains something of a mystery, but his violent death in 1961 reminds us that there are other and more final ways of ending a day.

While he was apparently sympathetic to the Castro regime, he nevertheless left Cuba in 1960 for his ranch in Idaho. He was ill, sick with who knows what besides depression, and he spent a long time under observation in the Mayo Clinic, where he twice underwent shock therapy that did not help him. Then early one morning the silence of the Idaho ranch house was shattered by the blast of a double-barreled shotgun. The entire world was shaken, and not alone by the death of the man but by the very force of the drama. With the end of this man, a legend had also been rounded out, brought to its end with a stunning symmetry.

READING SUGGESTIONS

SHERWOOD ANDERSON

Horace Gregory, Introduction to *The Portable Sherwood Anderson* (1949). A perceptive critical study that locates Anderson in his cultural milieu.

Irving Howe, *Sherwood Anderson*, in the American Men of Letters series (1951). An intelligent but by no means entirely sympathetic biocritical study.

Howard Mumford Jones and Walter B. Rideout, editors, *Letters of Sherwood Anderson* (1953). Anderson's letters reveal the degree of his self-knowledge (not always high) and the extent to which he could articulate his literary intentions.

Paul Rosenfeld, "Sherwood Anderson," *Port of New York* (1924; reissued in 1961 with an Introduction by Sherman Paul). Vividly invokes the literary atmosphere of the 1920's.

PAUL ROSENFELD, *The Sherwood Anderson Reader* (1947). The Introduction is a deeply sympathetic study by Anderson's good friend, and Rosenfeld's last work.

JAMES SCHEVILL, *Sherwood Anderson: His Life and Work* (1951). A rather stolid work, this is nevertheless the only extended biography of the subject.

Story: The Magazine of the Short Story, XIX, No. 91 (September–October, 1941). Especially useful are the essays by Waldo Frank, Henry Miller, Paul Rosenfeld, and Gertrude Stein.

F. SCOTT FITZGERALD

SHIELAH GRAHAM AND GEROLD FRANK, *Beloved Infidel: The Education of a Woman* (1958). A badly written book, it nevertheless contains in its second half important biographical material not to be found in Mizener (below).

F. SCOTT FITZGERALD, *The Crack-Up*, ed. by Edmund Wilson (1945; paperback 1956). Besides the Fitzgerald material, there are essays and comments by others, especially the essay by Paul Rosenfeld from *Men Seen* (1925).

WILLIAM BARRETT, "Fitzgerald and America," *Partisan Review*, XVIII (May–June, 1951). Brief, incisive speculation.

ALFRED KAZIN, editor, *F. Scott Fitzgerald: The Man and His Work* (1951). A collection of all the most important critical essays on Fitzgerald up to the date of its publication.

ARTHUR MIZENER, *The Far Side of Paradise* (1951). Until now, the standard biography. Sometimes rather elusive.

WRIGHT MORRIS, "The Function of Nostalgia— F. Scott Fitzgerald," *The Territory Ahead* (1958). An original and exciting interpretation.

JOHN H. RALEIGH, "Fitzgerald's *The Great Gatsby*,"

University of Kansas City Review, XXIII (June, 1957, and October, 1957). Fitzgerald in cultural history.

ANDREW TURNBULL, *Scott Fitzgerald* (1962). The most recent biography; contains much unique information.

ERNEST HEMINGWAY

CARLOS BAKER, *Hemingway: The Writer as Artist* (1952). The most serious critical study, this book is also perhaps unduly solemn about its subject. (Professor Baker has been authorized to write the official Hemingway biography.)

CHARLES A. FENTON, *The Apprenticeship of Ernest Hemingway: The Early Years* (1954). A detailed study of the formation of a talent and a style, with stress on Hemingway's debt to his newspaper experience.

JOHN K. McCAFFERY, editor, *Ernest Hemingway: The Man and His Work* (1951). A collection of all the most important critical essays on Hemingway up to the date of its publication.

DWIGHT MACDONALD, "Ernest Hemingway," *Encounter*, XVIII, No. 1 (January, 1962). Brief, brilliant, cruel, and possibly the judgment of history.

EDMUND WILSON, "Emergence of Ernest Hemingway," "The Sportsman's Tragedy," and "Letter to the Russians about Hemingway," in *The Shores of Light* (1952). Important reviews of Hemingway books by America's most substantial critic.

PHILIP YOUNG, *Ernest Hemingway*, Rinehart Critical Studies (1952). A bolder critical analysis than Carlos Baker's, based on persuasive psychological insights.

NOTE

As general background to the period in which these writers thrived, no book is more useful than Malcolm Cowley, *Exile's Return: A Literary Odyssey of the 1920's* (1951; paperback 1956). This is a revised edition of *Exile's Return: A Narrative of Ideas* (1934).

Sherwood Anderson

FROM

A STORY TELLER'S STORY

◊

❪ THIS book, the earliest of Sherwood Anderson's semi-autobiographical efforts, was written in 1923. Fictionalizing the facts of his life, he described it quite properly as a "tale of an American writer's journey through his own imaginative world and through the world of facts."

The characteristic departure from the facts is nowhere more evident than in the following selection, which is one of Anderson's literary accounts of the supposed climax in his life when, at thirty-seven years of age, he broke with business and strode into the freedom of the literary life.

◊

NOTE II

ON AN evening of the late summer I got off a train at a growing Ohio industrial town where I had once lived. I was rapidly becoming a middle-aged man. Two years before I had left the place in disgrace. There I had tried to be a manufacturer, a money-maker, and had failed, and I had been trying and failing ever since. In the town some thousands of dollars had been lost for others. An effort to conform to the standard dreams of the men of my times had failed and in the midst of my disgrace and generally hopeless outlook, as regards making a living, I had been filled with joy at coming to the end of it all. One morning I had left the place afoot, leaving my poor little factory, like an illegitimate child, on another man's doorstep. I had left, merely taking what money was in my pocket, some eight or ten dollars.

What a moment that leaving had been! To one of the European artists I afterward came to know the situation would have been unbelievably grotesque. Such a man could not have believed in my earnestness about it all and would have thought my feelings of the moment a worked-up thing. I can in fancy hear one of the Frenchmen, Italians or Russians I later knew laughing at me. "Well, but why get so worked up? A factory is a factory, is it not? Why may not one break it like an empty bottle? You have lost some money for others? See the light on that field over there. These others, for whom you lost money, were they compelled to beg in the streets, were their children torn by wolves? What is it you Americans get so excited about when a little money is lost?"

A European artist may not understand but an American will understand. The devil! It is not a question of money. No men are so careless and free with money as the Americans. There is another matter involved.

It strikes rather deeply at the roots of our beings. Childish as it all may have seemed to an older and more sophisticated world, we Americans, from the beginning, have been up to something, or we have wanted to think we were up to something. We came here, or our fathers or grandfathers came here, from a hundred diverse places—and you may be sure it was not the artists who came. Artists do not want to cut down trees, root stumps out of the ground, build towns and railroads. The artist wants to sit with a strip of canvas before him, face an open space on a wall, carve a bit of wood, make combinations of words and sentences, as I am doing now—trying to express to others some thought or feeling of his own. He wants to dream of color, to lay hold of form, free the sensual in himself, live more fully and freely in his contact with the materials before him than he can possibly live in life. He seeks a kind of controlled ecstasy and is a man

with a passion, a "nut," as we love to say in America. And very often, when he is not in actual contact with his materials, he is a much more vain and disagreeable ass than any man, not an artist, could possibly be. As a living man he is almost always a pest. It is only when dead he begins to have value.

The simple truth is that in a European country the artist is more freely accepted than he is among us, and only because he has been longer about. They know how harmless he really is—or rather do not know how subtly dangerous he can be—and accept him only as one might accept a hybrid cross between a dog and a cat that went growling mewing barking and spitting about the house. One might want to kill the first of such strange beasts one sees but after one has seen a dozen and has realized that, like the mule, they cannot breed their own kind one laughs and lets them live, paying no more attention to them than modern France for example pays to its artists.

But in America things are somewhat different. Here something went wrong in the beginning. We pretended to so much and were going to do such great things here. This vast land was to be a refuge for all the outlawed brave foolish folk of the world. The declaration of the rights of man was to have a new hearing in a new place. The devil! We did get ourselves into a bad hole. We were going to be superhuman and it turned out we were sons of men who were not such devilish fellows after all. You cannot blame us that we are somewhat reluctant about finding out the very human things concerning ourselves. One does so hate to come down off the perch.

We are now losing our former feeling of inherent virtue, are permitting ourselves occasionally to laugh at ourselves for our pretensions, but there was a time here when we were sincerely in earnest about all this American business, "the land of the free and the home of the brave." We actually meant it and no one will ever understand present-day America or Americans who does not concede that we meant it and that while we were building all of our big ugly hurriedly thrown-together towns, creating our great industrial system, growing always more huge and prosperous, we were as much in earnest about what we thought we were up to as were the French of the thirteenth century when they built the cathedral of Chartres to the glory of God.

They built the cathedral of Chartres to the glory of God and we really intended building here a land to the glory of Man, and thought we were doing it too. That was our intention and the affair only blew up in the process, or got perverted, be cause Man, even the brave and the free Man, is somewhat a less worthy object of glorification than God. This we might have found out long ago but that we did not know each other. We came from too many different places to know each other well, had been promised too much, wanted too much. We were afraid to know each other.

Oh, how Americans have wanted heroes, wanted brave simple fine men! And how sincerely and deeply we Americans have been afraid to understand and love one another, fearing to find ourselves at the end no more brave heroic and fine than the people of almost any other part of the world.

I however digress. What I am trying to do is to give the processes of my own mind at two distinct moments of my own life. First, the moment when after many years of effort to conform to an unstated and but dimly understood American dream by making myself a successful man in the material world I threw all overboard and then at another moment when, having come back to the same spot where I passed through the first moment, I attempted to confront myself with myself with a somewhat changed point of view.

As for the first of these moments, it was melodramatic and even silly enough. The struggle centered itself at the last within the walls of a particular moment and within the walls of a particular room.

I sat in the room with a woman who was my secretary. For several years I had been sitting there, dictating to her regarding the goods I had made in my factory and that I was attempting to sell. The attempt to sell the goods had become a sort of madness in me. There were certain thousands or perhaps hundreds of thousands of men living in towns or on farms in many states of my country who might possibly buy the goods I had made rather than the goods made in another factory by another man. How I had wheedled! How I had schemed! In some years I gave myself quite fully to the matter in hand and the dollars trickled in. Well, I was about to become rich. It was a possibility. After a good day or week, when many dollars had come, I went to walk and when I had got into a quiet place where I was unobserved I threw back my shoulders and strutted. During the year I had made for myself so many dollars. Next year I would make so many more, and the next year so many more. But my thoughts of the matter did not express themselves in the dollars. It never does to the American man. Who calls the American a dollar-lover is foolish. My factory was of a certain size—it was really a poor haphazardly enough run place—but after a

time I would build a great factory and after that a greater and greater. Like a true American, I thought in size.

My fancy played with the matter of factories as a child would play with a toy. There would be a great factory with walls going up and up and a little open place for a lawn at the front, shower baths for the workers with perhaps a fountain playing on a lawn, and up before the door of this place I would drive in a large automobile.

Oh, how I would be respected by all, how I would be looked up to by all! I walked in a little dark street, throwing back my shoulders. How grand and glorious I felt!

The houses along the street in which I walked were small and ugly and dirty-faced children played in the yards. I wondered. Having walked, dreaming my dream for a long time I returned to the neighborhood of my factory and opening my office went in to sit at my desk smoking a cigarette. The night watchman came in. He was an old man who had once been a school-teacher but, as he said, his eyes had gone back on him.

When I had walked alone I had been able to make myself feel somewhat as I fancied a prince might have felt but when anyone came near me something exploded inside. I was a deflated balloon. Well, in fancy, I had a thousand workmen under me. They were children and I was their father and would look out for them. Perhaps I would build them model houses to live in, a town of model houses built about my great factory, eh? The workmen would be my children and I would look out for my children. "Land of the free— home of the brave."

But I was back in my factory now and the night watchman sat smoking with me. Sometimes we talked far into the night. The devil! He was a fellow like myself, having the same problems as myself. How could I be his father? The thought was absurd. Once, when he was a younger man, he had dreamed of being a scholar but his eyes had gone back on him. What had he wanted to do? He spoke of it for a time. He had wanted to be a scholar and I had myself spent those earlier years eagerly reading books. "I would really like to have been a learned monk, one of those fellows such as appeared in the Middle Ages, one of the fellows who went off and lived by himself and gave himself up wholly to learning, one who believed in learning, who spent his life humbly seeking new truths—but I got married and my wife had kids, and then, you see, my eyes went back on me." He spoke of the matter philosophically. One did not let oneself get too much excited. After a time one got over any feeling of bitterness. The night watchman had a boy, a lad of fifteen, who also loved books. "He is pretty lucky, can get all the books he wants at the public library. In the afternoon after school is out and before I come down here to my job he reads aloud to me."

* * *

Men and women, many men and many women! There were men and women working in my factory, men and women walking in streets with me, many men and women scattered far and wide over the country to whom I wanted to sell my goods. I sent men, salesmen, to see them—I wrote letters; how many thousands of letters, all to the same purpose! "Will you buy my goods?" And again, "Will you buy my goods?"

What were the other men thinking about? What was I myself thinking about? Suppose it were possible to know something of the men and women, to know something of oneself, too. The devil! These were not thoughts that would help me to sell my goods to all the others. What were all the others like? What was I myself like? Did I want a large factory with a little lawn and a fountain in front and with a model town built about it?

Days of endlessly writing letters to men, nights of walking in strange quiet streets. What had happened to me? "I shall go get drunk," I said to myself and I did go and get drunk. Taking a train to a near-by city I drank until a kind of joy came to me and with some man I had found and who had joined in my carousal I walked in streets, shouting at other men, singing songs, going sometimes into strange houses to laugh with people, to talk with people I found there.

Here was something I liked and something the others liked too. When I had come to people in strange houses, half drunk, released, they were not afraid of me. "Well, he wants to talk," they seemed to be saying to themselves. "That's fine!" There was something broken down between us, a wall broken down. We talked of outlandish things for Anglo-Saxon trained people to speak of, of love between men and women, of what children's coming meant. Food was brought forth. Often in a single evening of this sort I got more from people than I could get from weeks of ordinary intercourse. The people were a little excited by the strangeness of two unknown men in their houses. With my companion I went boldly to the door and knocked. Laughter. "Hello, the house!" It might be the house of a laborer or that of a well-to-do merchant. I had hold of my new-found friend's arm and explained our presence as well as I could. "We are a little drunk and we are travelers.

We just want to sit and visit with you a while."

There was a kind of terror in people's eyes, and a kind of gladness too. An old workman showed us a relic he had brought home with him from the Civil War while his wife ran into a bedroom and changed her dress. Then a child awoke in a near-by room and began to cry and was permitted to come in in her nightgown and lie in my arms or in the arms of the new-found friend who had got drunk with me. The talk swept over strange intimate subjects. What were men up to? What were women up to? There was a kind of deep taking of breath, as though we had all been holding something back from one another and had suddenly decided to let go. Once or twice we stayed all night in the house to which we had gone.

And then back to the writing of letters—to sell my goods. In the city to which I had gone to carouse I had seen many women of the streets, standing at corners, looking furtively about. My thoughts got fixed upon prostitution. Was I a prostitute? Was I prostituting my life?

What thoughts in the mind! There was a note due and payable at the bank. "Now here, you man, attend to your affairs. You have induced others to put money into your enterprises. If you are to build a great enterprise here you must be up and at it."

How often in after years I have laughed at myself for the thoughts and emotions of that time. There is a thought I have had that is very delicious. It is this, and I dare say it will be an unwelcome thought to many, "I am the American man. I think there is no doubt of it. I am just the mixture, the cold, moral man of the North into whose body has come the warm pagan blood of the South. I love and am afraid to love. Behold in me the American man striving to become an artist, to become conscious of himself, filled with wonder concerning himself and others, trying to have a good time and not fake a good time. I am not English Italian Jew German Frenchman Russian. What am I? I am tremendously serious about it all but at the same time I laugh constantly at myself for my own seriousness. Like all real American men of our day I wander constantly from place to place striving to put down roots into the American soil and not quite doing it. If you say the real American man is not yet born, you lie. I am the type of the fellow."

This is somewhat of a joke on me but it is a greater joke on the reader. As respectable and conventional a man as Calvin Coolidge has me in him—and I have him in myself? Do not doubt it. I have him in me and Eugene Debs in me and the crazy political idealists of the Western States and

Mr. Gary of the Steel Trust and the whole crew. I accept them all as part of myself. Would to God they would thus accept me!

* * *

And being this thing I have tried to describe I return now to myself sitting between the walls of a certain room and between the walls of a certain moment too. Just why was that moment so pregnant? I will never quite know.

It came with a rush, the feeling that I must quit buying and selling, the overwhelming feeling of uncleanliness. I was in my whole nature a tale-teller. My father had been one and his not knowing had destroyed him. The tale-teller cannot bother with buying and selling. To do so will destroy him. No class of men I have ever known are so dull and cheerless as the writers of glad sentimental romances, the painters of glad pretty pictures. The corrupt unspeakable thing that had happened to tale-telling in America was all concerned with this matter of buying and selling. The horse cannot sing like a canary bird nor the canary bird pull a plow like a horse and either of them attempting it becomes something ridiculous.

NOTE III

THERE was a door leading out from my office to the street. How many steps to the door? I counted them, "five, six, seven." "Suppose," I asked myself, "I could take those five, six, seven steps to the door, pass out at the door, go along that railroad track out there, disappear into the far horizon beyond. Where was I to go? In the town where my factory was located I had still the reputation of being a bright young business man. In my first years there I had been filled with shrewd vast schemes. I had been admired, looked up to. Since that time I had gone down and down as a bright young man but no one yet knew how far I had gone. I was still respected in the town, my word was still good at the bank. I was a respectable man.

Did I want to do something not respectable, not decent? I am trying to give you the history of a moment and as a tale-teller I have come to think that the true history of life is but a history of moments. It is only at rare moments we live. I wanted to walk out at a door and go away into the distance. The American is still a wanderer, a migrating bird not yet ready to build a nest. All our cities are built temporarily as are the houses in which we live. We are on the way—toward what? There have been other times in the history of the world when many strange peoples came together in a new strange land. To assume that we

have made an America, even materially, seems to me now but telling ourselves fairy tales in the night. We have not even made it materially yet and the American man has only gone in for money-making on a large scale to quiet his own restlessness, as the monk of old days was given the Regula of Augustine to quiet him and still the lusts in himself. For the monk, kept occupied with the saying of prayers and the doing of many little sacred offices, there was no time for the lusts of the world to enter in and for the American to be perpetually busy with his affairs, with his automobiles, with his movies, there is no time for unquiet thoughts.

On that day in the office at my factory I looked at myself and laughed. The whole struggle I am trying to describe and that I am confident will be closer to the understanding of most Americans than anything else I have ever written was accompanied by a kind of mocking laughter at myself and my own seriousness about it all.

Very well, then, I wanted to go out of the door and never come back. How many Americans want to go—but where do they want to go? I wanted to accept for myself all the little restless thoughts of which myself and the others had been so afraid and you, who are Americans, will understand the necessity of my continually laughing at myself and at all things dear to me. I must laugh at the thing I love the more intensely because of my love. Any American will understand that.

It was a trying moment for me. There was the woman, my secretary, now looking at me. What did she represent? What did she not represent? Would I dare be honest with her? It was quite apparent to me I would not. I had got to my feet and we stood looking at each other. "It is now or never," I said to myself, and I remember that I kept smiling. I had stopped dictating to her in the midst of a sentence. "The goods about which you have inquired are the best of their kind made in the—"

I stood and she sat and we were looking at each other intently. "What's the matter?" she asked. She was an intelligent woman, more intelligent I am sure than myself, just because she was a woman and good, while I have never been good, do not know how to be good. Could I explain all to her? The words of a fancied explanation marched through my mind: "My dear young woman, it is all very silly but I have decided to no longer concern myself with this buying and selling. It may be all right for others but for me it is poison. There is this factory. You may have it if it please you. It is of little value I dare say.

Perhaps it is money ahead and then again it may well be it is money behind. I am uncertain about it all and now I am going away. Now, at this moment, with the letter I have been dictating, with the very sentence you have been writing left unfinished, I am going out that door and never come back. What am I going to do? Well now, that I don't know. I am going to wander about. I am going to sit with people, listen to words, tell tales of people, what they are thinking, what they are feeling. The devil! It may even be I am going forth in search of myself."

The woman was looking into my eyes the while I looked into hers. Perhaps I had grown a little pale and now she grew pale. "You're sick," she said and her words gave me an idea. There was wanted a justification of myself, not to myself but to the others. A crafty thought came. Was the thought crafty or was I, at the moment, a little insane, a "nut," as every American so loves to say of every man who does something a little out of the groove.

I had grown pale and it may be I was ill but nevertheless I was laughing—the American laugh. Had I suddenly become a little insane? What a comfort that thought would be, not to myself but to the others. My leaving the place I was then in would tear up roots that had gone down a little into the ground. The ground I did not think would support the tree that was myself and that I thought wanted to grow.

My mind dwelt on the matter of roots and I looked at my feet. The whole question with which I was at the moment concerned became a matter of feet. I had two feet that could take me out of the life I was then in and that, to do so, would need but take three or four steps to a door. When I had reached the door and had stepped out of my little factory office everything would be quite simplified, I was sure. I had to lift myself out. Others would have to tackle the job of getting me back, once I had stepped over that threshold.

Whether at the moment I merely became shrewd and crafty or whether I really became temporarily insane I shall never quite know. What I did was to step very close to the woman and looking directly into her eyes I laughed gayly. Others besides herself would, I knew, hear the words I was now speaking. I looked at my feet. "I have been wading in a long river and my feet are wet," I said.

Again I laughed as I walked lightly toward the door and out of a long and tangled phase of my life, out of the door of buying and selling, out of the door of affairs.

"They want me to be a 'nut,' will love to think of me as a 'nut,' and why not? It may just be that's what I am," I thought gayly and at the same time turned and said a final confusing sentence to the woman who now stared at me in speechless amazement. "My feet are cold wet and heavy from long wading in a river. Now I shall go walk on dry land," I said, and as I passed out at the door a delicious thought came. "Oh, you little tricky words, you are my brothers. It is you, not myself, have lifted me over this threshold. It is you who have dared give me a hand. For the rest of my life I will be a servant to you," I whispered to myself as I went along a spur of railroad track, over a bridge, out of a town and out of that phase of my life.

1924

THE BOOK OF THE GROTESQUE

◇

⟨ THIS strange little piece is the introduction—better called a prelude, perhaps—to *Winesburg, Ohio: A Group of Tales of Ohio Small-Town Life*. The stories were written over a number of years, and it is not clear whether this section was written before, during, or after the time in which the stories were written. It is known that Anderson first meant to give the title of this selection to the entire work. A "grotesque" is a creature obsessed with a single idea and, in his obsession, isolated from other human beings.

◇

THE WRITER, an old man with a white mustache, had some difficulty in getting into bed. The windows of the house in which he lived were high and he wanted to look at the trees when he awoke in the morning. A carpenter came to fix the bed so that it would be on a level with the window.

Quite a fuss was made about the matter. The carpenter, who had been a soldier in the Civil War, came into the writer's room and sat down to talk of building a platform for the purpose of raising the bed. The writer had cigars lying about and the carpenter smoked.

For a time the two men talked of the raising of the bed and then they talked of other things. The soldier got on the subject of the war. The writer, in fact, led him to that subject. The carpenter had once been a prisoner in Andersonville Prison and had lost a brother. The brother had died of starvation, and whenever the carpenter got upon that subject he cried. He, like the old writer, had a white mustache, and when he cried he puckered up his lips and the mustache bobbed up and down. The weeping old man with the cigar in his mouth was ludicrous. The plan the writer had for the raising of his bed was forgotten and later the carpenter did it in his own way, and the writer, who was past sixty, had to help himself with a chair when he went to bed at night.

In his bed the writer rolled over on his side and lay quite still. For years he had been beset with notions concerning his heart. He was a hard smoker and his heart fluttered. The idea had got into his mind that he would sometime die unexpectedly, and always when he got into bed he thought of that. It did not alarm him. The effect in fact was quite a special thing and not easily explained. It made him more alive, there in bed, than at any other time. Perfectly still he lay and his body was old and not of much use any more, but something inside him was altogether young. He was like a pregnant woman, only that the thing inside him was not a baby but a youth. No, it wasn't a youth, it was a woman, young, and wearing a coat of mail like a knight. It is absurd, you see, to try to tell what was inside the old writer as he lay on his high bed and listened to the fluttering of his heart. The thing to get at is what the writer, or the young thing within the writer, was thinking about.

The old writer, like all of the people in the world, had got, during his long life, a great many notions in his head. He had once been quite handsome and a number of women had been in love with him. And then, of course, he had known people, many people, known them in a peculiarly intimate way that was different from the way in which you and I know people. At least that is what the writer thought and the thought pleased him. Why quarrel with an old man concerning his thoughts?

In the bed the writer had a dream that was not a dream. As he grew somewhat sleepy, but was still conscious, figures began to appear before his eyes. He imagined the young indescribable thing within himself was driving a long procession of figures before his eyes.

You see, the interest in all this lies in the figures that went before the eyes of the writer. They were all grotesques. All of the men and women the writer had ever known had become grotesques.

The grotesques were not all horrible. Some were amusing, some almost beautiful, and one, a woman all drawn out of shape, hurt the old man by her grotesqueness. When she passed, he made a noise like a small dog whimpering. Had you come into the room you might have supposed the old man had unpleasant dreams or perhaps indigestion.

For an hour the procession of grotesques passed before the eyes of the old man, and then, although it was a painful thing to do, he crept out of bed and began to write. Some one of the grotesques had made a deep impression on his mind and he wanted to describe it.

At his desk the writer worked for an hour. In the end he wrote a book which he called 'The Book of the Grotesque.' It was never published, but I saw it once and it made an indelible impression on my mind. The book had one central thought that is very strange and has always remained with me. By remembering it I have been able to understand many people and things that I was never able to understand before. The thought was involved, but a simple statement of it would be something like this:

That in the beginning when the world was young there were a great many thoughts but no such thing as a truth. Man made the truths himself and each truth was a composite of a great many vague thoughts. All about in the world were the truths and they were all beautiful.

The old man had listed hundreds of the truths in his book. I will not try to tell you of all of them. There was the truth of virginity and the truth of passion, the truth of wealth and of poverty, of thrift and of profligacy, of carelessness and abandon. Hundreds and hundreds were the truths and they were all beautiful.

And then the people came along. Each as he appeared snatched up one of the truths, and some who were quite strong snatched up a dozen of them.

It was the truths that made the people grotesques. The old man had quite an elaborate theory concerning the matter. It was his notion that the moment one of the people took one of the truths to himself, called it his truth, and tried to live his life by it, he became a grotesque and the truth he embraced became a falsehood.

You can see for yourself how the old man, who had spent all of his life writing and was filled with words, would write hundreds of pages concerning this matter. The subject would become so big in his mind that he himself would be in danger of becoming a grotesque. He didn't, I suppose, for the same reason that he never published the book. It was the young thing inside him that saved the old man.

Concerning the old carpenter who fixed the bed

for the writer, I only mentioned him because he, like many of what are called very common people, became the nearest thing to what is understandable and lovable of all the grotesques in the writer's book.

1919

THE EGG

❖

⟨ THIS story, written in 1918, was first published in the *Dial* for March, 1919, under the title "The Triumph of the Egg." Anderson then took that title for a whole collection of short stories of which "The Egg" was to prove the keystone. His great success in the exploration of grotesques, a very funny story, it is also very sad. In a letter of October 10, 1932, to The Dramatic Publishing Company (see pp. 709–10), discussing a dramatized version of the story and his interest in maintaining a balance between comedy and pathos, he makes the intention of his story clear.

❖

MY FATHER was, I am sure, intended by nature to be a cheerful, kindly man. Until he was thirty-four years old he worked as a farm-hand for a man named Thomas Butterworth whose place lay near the town of Bidwell, Ohio. He had then a horse of his own and on Saturday evenings drove into town to spend a few hours in social intercourse with other farm-hands. In town he drank several glasses of beer and stood about in Ben Head's saloon—crowded on Saturday evenings with visiting farm-hands. Songs were sung and glasses thumped on the bar. At ten o'clock father drove home along a lonely country road, made his horse comfortable for the night and himself went to bed, quite happy in his position in life. He had at that time no notion of trying to rise in the world.

It was in the spring of his thirty-fifth year that father married my mother, then a country school-teacher, and in the following spring I came wriggling and crying into the world. Something happened to the two people. They became ambitious. The American passion for getting up in the world took possession of them.

It may have been that mother was responsible. Being a school-teacher she had no doubt read books and magazines. She had, I presume, read of how Garfield, Lincoln, and other Americans rose from poverty to fame and greatness and as I lay beside her—in the days of her lying-in—she may have dreamed that I would some day rule men and cities. At any rate she induced father to give up his place as a farm-hand, sell his horse and embark on an independent enterprise of his own. She was a tall silent woman with a long nose and troubled grey eyes. For herself she wanted nothing. For father and myself she was incurably ambitious.

The first venture into which the two people went turned out badly. They rented ten acres of poor stony land on Griggs's Road, eight miles from Bidwell, and launched into chicken raising. I grew into boyhood on the place and got my first impressions of life there. From the beginning they were impressions of disaster and if, in my turn, I am a gloomy man inclined to see the darker side of life, I attribute it to the fact that what should have been for me the happy joyous days of childhood were spent on a chicken farm.

One unversed in such matters can have no notion of the many and tragic things that can happen to a chicken. It is born out of an egg, lives for a few weeks as a tiny fluffy thing such as you will see pictured on Easter cards, then becomes hideously naked, eats quantities of corn and meal bought by the sweat of your father's brow, gets diseases called pip, cholera, and other names, stands looking with stupid eyes at the sun, becomes sick and dies. A few hens and now and then a rooster, intended to serve God's mysterious ends, struggle through to maturity. The hens lay eggs out of which come other chickens and the dreadful cycle is thus made complete. It is all unbelievably complex. Most philosophers must have been raised on chicken farms. One hopes for so much from a chicken and is so dreadfully disillusioned. Small chickens, just setting out on the journey of life, look so bright and alert and they are in fact so dreadfully stupid. They are so much like people they mix one up in one's judgments of life. If disease does not kill them they wait until your expectations are thoroughly aroused and then walk under the wheels of a wagon—to go squashed and dead back to their maker. Vermin infest their youth, and fortunes must be spent for curative powders. In later life I have seen how a literature has been built up on the subject of fortunes to be made out of the raising of chickens. It is intended to be read by the gods who have just eaten of the tree of the knowledge of good and evil. It is a hopeful literature and declares that much may be done by simple ambitious people who own a few hens. Do not be led astray by it. It was not written for you. Go hunt for gold on the frozen hills of Alaska, put your faith in the honesty of a politician, believe if you will that the world is daily growing better and that good will triumph over evil, but do not read and believe the literature that is written concerning the hen. It was not written for you.

I, however, digress. My tale does not primarily concern itself with the hen. If correctly told it will centre on the egg. For ten years my father and mother struggled to make our chicken farm pay and then they gave up that struggle and began another. They moved into the town of Bidwell, Ohio and embarked in the restaurant business. After ten years of worry with incubators that did not hatch, and with tiny—and in their own way lovely—balls of fluff that passed on into semi-naked pullethood and from that into dead henhood, we threw all aside and packing our belongings on a wagon drove down Griggs's Road toward Bidwell, a tiny caravan of hope looking for a new place from which to start on our upward journey through life.

We must have been a sad looking lot, not, I fancy, unlike refugees fleeing from a battlefield. Mother and I walked in the road. The wagon that contained our goods had been borrowed for the day from Mr. Albert Griggs, a neighbor. Out of its sides stuck the legs of cheap chairs and at the back of the pile of beds, tables, and boxes filled with kitchen utensils was a crate of live chickens, and on top of that the baby carriage in which I had been wheeled about in my infancy. Why we stuck to the baby carriage I don't know. It was unlikely other children would be born and the wheels were broken. People who have few possessions cling tightly to those they have. That is one of the facts that make life so discouraging.

Father rode on top of the wagon. He was then a bald-headed man of forty-five, a little fat and from long association with mother and the chickens he had become habitually silent and discouraged. All during our ten years on the chicken farm he had worked as a laborer on neighboring farms and most of the money he had earned had been spent for remedies to cure chicken diseases, on Wilmer's White Wonder Cholera Cure or Professor Bidlow's Egg Producer or some other preparations that mother found advertised in the poultry papers. There were two little patches of hair on father's head just above his ears. I remember that as a child I used to sit looking at him when he had gone to sleep in a chair before the stove on Sunday afternoons in the winter. I had at that time already begun to read books and have notions of my own and the bald path that led over the top of his

head was, I fancied, something like a broad road, such a road as Caesar might have made on which to lead his legions out of Rome and into the wonders of an unknown world. The tufts of hair that grew above father's ears were, I thought, like forests. I fell into a half-sleeping, half-waking state and dreamed I was a tiny thing going along the road into a far beautiful place where there were no chicken farms and where life was a happy eggless affair.

One might write a book concerning our flight from the chicken farm into town. Mother and I walked the entire eight miles—she to be sure that nothing fell from the wagon and I to see the wonders of the world. On the seat of the wagon beside father was his greatest treasure. I will tell you of that.

On a chicken farm where hundreds and even thousands of chickens come out of eggs surprising things sometimes happen. Grotesques are born out of eggs as out of people. The accident does not often occur—perhaps once in a thousand births. A chicken is, you see, born that has four legs, two pairs of wings, two heads or what not. The things do not live. They go quickly back to the hand of their maker that has for a moment trembled. The fact that the poor little things could not live was one of the tragedies of life to father. He had some sort of notion that if he could but bring into henhood or roosterhood a five-legged hen or a two-headed rooster his fortune would be made. He dreamed of taking the wonder about to county fairs and of growing rich by exhibiting it to other farm-hands.

At any rate he saved all the little monstrous things that had been born on our chicken farm. They were preserved in alcohol and put each in its own glass bottle. These he had carefully put into a box and on our journey into town it was carried on the wagon seat beside him. He drove the horses with one hand and with the other clung to the box. When we got to our destination the box was taken down at once and the bottles removed. All during our days as keepers of a restaurant in the town of Bidwell, Ohio, the grotesques in their little glass bottles sat on a shelf back of the counter. Mother sometimes protested but father was a rock on the subject of his treasure. The grotesques were, he declared, valuable. People, he said, liked to look at strange and wonderful things.

Did I say that we embarked in the restaurant business in the town of Bidwell, Ohio? I exaggerated a little. The town itself lay at the foot of a low hill and on the shore of a small river. The railroad did not run through the town and the station was a mile away to the north at a place called Pickleville. There had been a cider mill and pickle factory at the station, but before the time of our coming they had both gone out of business. In the morning and in the evening busses came down to the station along a road called Turner's Pike from the hotel on the main street of Bidwell. Our going to the out of the way place to embark in the restaurant business was mother's idea. She talked of it for a year and then one day went off and rented an empty store building opposite the railroad station. It was her idea that the restaurant would be profitable. Travelling men, she said, would be always waiting around to take trains out of town and town people would come to the station to await incoming trains. They would come to the restaurant to buy pieces of pie and drink coffee. Now that I am older I know that she had another motive in going. She was ambitious for me. She wanted me to rise in the world, to get into a town school and become a man of the towns.

At Pickleville father and mother worked hard as they always had done. At first there was the necessity of putting our place into shape to be a restaurant. That took a month. Father built a shelf on which he put tins of vegetables. He painted a sign on which he put his name in large red letters. Below his name was the sharp command—"EAT HERE"—that was so seldom obeyed. A show case was bought and filled with cigars and tobacco. Mother scrubbed the floor and the walls of the room. I went to school in the town and was glad to be away from the farm and from the presence of the discouraged, sad-looking chickens. Still I was not very joyous. In the evening I walked home from school along Turner's Pike and remembered the children I had seen playing in the town school yard. A troop of little girls had gone hopping about and singing. I tried that. Down along the frozen road I went hopping solemnly on one leg. "Hippity Hop To The Barber Shop," I sang shrilly. Then I stopped and looked doubtfully about. I was afraid of being seen in my gay mood. It must have seemed to me that I was doing a thing that should not be done by one who, like myself, had been raised on a chicken farm where death was a daily visitor.

Mother decided that our restaurant should remain open at night. At ten in the evening a passenger train went north past our door followed by a local freight. The freight crew had switching to do in Pickleville and when the work was done they came to our restaurant for hot coffee and food. Sometimes one of them ordered a fried egg. In the morning at four they returned north-bound and again visited us. A little trade began to grow up. Mother slept at night and during the day tend-

ed the restaurant and fed our boarders while father slept. He slept in the same bed mother had occupied during the night and I went off to the town of Bidwell and to school. During the long nights, while mother and I slept, father cooked meats that were to go into sandwiches for the lunch baskets of our boarders. Then an idea in regard to getting up in the world came into his head. The American spirit took hold of him. He also became ambitious.

In the long nights when there was little to do father had time to think. That was his undoing. He decided that he had in the past been an unsuccessful man because he had not been cheerful enough and that in the future he would adopt a cheerful outlook on life. In the early morning he came upstairs and got into bed with mother. She woke and the two talked. From my bed in the corner I listened.

It was father's idea that both he and mother should try to entertain the people who came to eat at our restaurant. I cannot now remember his words, but he gave the impression of one about to become in some obscure way a kind of public entertainer. When people, particularly young people from the town of Bidwell, came into our place, as on very rare occasions they did, bright entertaining conversation was to be made. From father's words I gathered that something of the jolly innkeeper effect was to be sought. Mother must have been doubtful from the first, but she said nothing discouraging. It was father's notion that a passion for the company of himself and mother would spring up in the breasts of the younger people of the town of Bidwell. In the evening bright happy groups would come singing down Turner's Pike. They would troop shouting with joy and laughter into our place. There would be song and festivity. I do not mean to give the impression that father spoke so elaborately of the matter. He was as I have said an uncommunicative man. "They want some place to go. I tell you they want some place to go," he said over and over. That was as far as he got. My own imagination has filled in the blanks.

For two or three weeks this notion of father's invaded our house. We did not talk much, but in our daily lives tried earnestly to make smiles take the place of glum looks. Mother smiled at the boarders and I, catching the infection, smiled at our cat. Father became a little feverish in his anxiety to please. There was no doubt, lurking somewhere in him, a touch of the spirit of the showman. He did not waste much of his ammunition on the railroad men he served at night but seemed to be waiting for a young man or woman from Bidwell to come in to show what he could do. On the counter in the restaurant there was a wire basket kept always filled with eggs, and it must have been before his eyes when the idea of being entertaining was born in his brain. There was something pre-natal about the way eggs kept themselves connected with the development of his idea. At any rate an egg ruined his new impulse in life. Late one night I was awakened by a roar of anger coming from father's throat. Both mother and I sat upright in our beds. With trembling hands she lighted a lamp that stood on a table by her head. Downstairs the front door of our restaurant went shut with a bang and in a few minutes father tramped up the stairs. He held an egg in his hand and his hand trembled as though he were having a chill. There was a half insane light in his eyes. As he stood glaring at us I was sure he intended throwing the egg at either mother or me. Then he laid it gently on the table beside the lamp and dropped on his knees beside mother's bed. He began to cry like a boy and I, carried away by his grief, cried with him. The two of us filled the little upstairs room with our wailing voices. It is ridiculous, but of the picture we made I can remember only the fact that mother's hand continually stroked the bald path that ran across the top of his head. I have forgotten what mother said to him and how she induced him to tell her of what had happened downstairs. His explanation also has gone out of my mind. I remember only my own grief and fright and the shiny path over father's head glowing in the lamp light as he knelt by the bed.

As to what happened downstairs. For some unexplainable reason I know the story as well as though I had been a witness to my father's discomfiture. One in time gets to know many unexplainable things. On that evening young Joe Kane, son of a merchant of Bidwell, came to Pickleville to meet his father, who was expected on the ten o'clock evening train from the South. The train was three hours late and Joe came into our place to loaf about and to wait for its arrival. The local freight train came in and the freight crew were fed. Joe was left alone in the restaurant with father.

From the moment he came into our place the Bidwell young man must have been puzzled by my father's actions. It was his notion that father was angry at him for hanging around. He noticed that the restaurant keeper was apparently disturbed by his presence and he thought of going out. However, it began to rain and he did not fancy the long walk to town and back. He bought a five-cent cigar and ordered a cup of coffee. He had a newspaper in his pocket and took it out and began to read. "I'm waiting for the evening train. It's late," he said apologetically.

For a long time father, whom Joe Kane had never seen before, remained silently gazing at his visitor. He was no doubt suffering from an attack of stage fright. As so often happens in life he had thought so much and so often of the situation that now confronted him that he was somewhat nervous in its presence.

For one thing, he did not know what to do with his hands. He thrust one of them nervously over the counter and shook hands with Joe Kane. "How-de-do," he said. Joe Kane put his newspaper down and stared at him. Father's eye lighted on the basket of eggs that sat on the counter and he began to talk. "Well," he began hesitatingly, "well, you have heard of Christopher Columbus, eh?" He seemed to be angry. "That Christopher Columbus was a cheat," he declared emphatically. "He talked of making an egg stand on its end. He talked, he did, and then he went and broke the end of the egg."

My father seemed to his visitor to be beside himself at the duplicity of Christopher Columbus. He muttered and swore. He declared it was wrong to teach children that Christopher Columbus was a great man when, after all, he cheated at the critical moment. He had declared he would make an egg stand on end and then when his bluff had been called he had done a trick. Still grumbling at Columbus, father took an egg from the basket on the counter and began to walk up and down. He rolled the egg between the palms of his hands. He smiled genially. He began to mumble words regarding the effect to be produced on an egg by the electricity that comes out of the human body. He declared that without breaking its shell and by virtue of rolling it back and forth in his hands he could stand the egg on its end. He explained that the warmth of his hands and the gentle rolling movement he gave the egg created a new centre of gravity, and Joe Kane was mildly interested. "I have handled thousands of eggs," father said. "No one knows more about eggs than I do."

He stood the egg on the counter and it fell on its side. He tried the trick again and again, each time rolling the egg between the palms of his hands and saying the words regarding the wonders of electricity and the laws of gravity. When after a half hour's effort he did succeed in making the egg stand for a moment he looked up to find that his visitor was no longer watching. By the time he had succeeded in calling Joe Kane's attention to the success of his effort the egg had again rolled over and lay on its side.

Afire with the showman's passion and at the same time a good deal disconcerted by the failure of his first effort, father now took the bottles containing the poultry monstrosities down from their place on the shelf and began to show them to his visitor. "How would you like to have seven legs and two heads like this fellow?" he asked, exhibiting the most remarkable of his treasures. A cheerful smile played over his face. He reached over the counter and tried to slap Joe Kane on the shoulder as he had seen men do in Ben Head's saloon when he was a young farm-hand and drove to town on Saturday evenings. His visitor was made a little ill by the sight of the body of the terribly deformed bird floating in the alcohol in the bottle and got up to go. Coming from behind the counter father took hold of the young man's arm and led him back to his seat. He grew a little angry and for a moment had to turn his face away and force himself to smile. Then he put the bottles back on the shelf. In an outburst of generosity he fairly compelled Joe Kane to have a fresh cup of coffee and another cigar at his expense. Then he took a pan and filling it with vinegar, taken from a jug that sat beneath the counter, he declared himself about to do a new trick. "I will heat this egg in this pan of vinegar," he said. "Then I will put it through the neck of a bottle without breaking the shell. When the egg is inside the bottle it will resume its normal shape and the shell will become hard again. Then I will give the bottle with the egg in it to you. You can take it about with you wherever you go. People will want to know how you got the egg in the bottle. Don't tell them. Keep them guessing. That is the way to have fun with this trick."

Father grinned and winked at his visitor. Joe Kane decided that the man who confronted him was mildly insane but harmless. He drank the cup of coffee that had been given him and began to read his paper again. When the egg had been heated in vinegar father carried it on a spoon to the counter and going into a back room got an empty bottle. He was angry because his visitor did not watch him as he began to do his trick, but nevertheless went cheerfully to work. For a long time he struggled, trying to get the egg to go through the neck of the bottle. He put the pan of vinegar back on the stove, intending to reheat the egg, then picked it up and burned his fingers. After a second bath in the hot vinegar the shell of the egg had been softened a little but not enough for his purpose. He worked and worked and a spirit of desperate determination took possession of him. When he thought that at last the trick was about to be consummated the delayed train came in at the

station and Joe Kane started to go nonchalantly out at the door. Father made a last desperate effort to conquer the egg and make it do the thing that would establish his reputation as one who knew how to entertain guests who came into his restaurant. He worried the egg. He attempted to be somewhat rough with it. He swore and the sweat stood out on his forehead. The egg broke under his hand. When the contents spurted over his clothes, Joe Kane, who had stopped at the door, turned and laughed.

A roar of anger rose from my father's throat. He danced and shouted a string of inarticulate words. Grabbing another egg from the basket on the counter, he threw it, just missing the head of the young man as he dodged through the door and escaped.

Father came upstairs to mother and me with an egg in his hand. I do not know what he intended to do. I imagine he had some idea of destroying it, of destroying all eggs, and that he intended to let mother and me see him begin. When, however, he got into the presence of mother something happened to him. He laid the egg gently on the table and dropped on his knees by the bed as I have already explained. He later decided to close the restaurant for the night and to come upstairs and get into bed. When he did so he blew out the light and after much muttered conversation both he and mother went to sleep. I suppose I went to sleep also, but my sleep was troubled. I awoke at dawn and for a long time looked at the egg that lay on the table. I wondered why eggs had to be and why from the egg came the hen who again laid the egg. The question got into my blood. It has stayed there, I imagine, because I am the son of my father. At any rate, the problem remains unsolved in my mind. And that, I conclude, is but another evidence of the complete and final triumph of the egg —at least as far as my family is concerned.

1919

I WANT TO KNOW WHY

◇

❰ WRITTEN in 1919, this story first appeared in *Smart Set*, edited by H. L. Mencken and George Jean Nathan, in November of that year. A reminiscence of the days when Anderson was known as "Jobby" around Clyde,

Ohio, the nickname deriving from the fact that he maintained himself and helped his family through a variety of odd jobs, this story is almost certainly the model of Hemingway's early story "My Old Man." It first appeared in book form in *The Triumph of the Egg* (1921).

❖

WE GOT up at four in the morning, that first day in the east. On the evening before we had climbed off a freight train at the edge of town, and with the true instinct of Kentucky boys had found our way across town and to the race track and the stables at once. Then we knew we were all right. Hanley Turner right away found a nigger we knew. It was Bildad Johnson who in the winter works at Ed Becker's livery barn in our home town, Beckersville. Bildad is a good cook as almost all our niggers are and of course he, like everyone in our part of Kentucky who is anyone at all, likes the horses. In the spring Bildad begins to scratch around. A nigger from our country can flatter and wheedle anyone into letting him do most anything he wants. Bildad wheedles the stable men and the trainers from the horse farms in our country around Lexington. The trainers come into town in the evening to stand around and talk and maybe get into a poker game. Bildad gets in with them. He is always doing little favors and telling about things to eat, chicken browned in a pan, and how is the best way to cook sweet potatoes and corn bread. It makes your mouth water to hear him.

When the racing season comes on and the horses go to the races and there is all the talk on the streets in the evenings about the new colts, and everyone says when they are going over to Lexington or to the spring meeting at Churchill Downs or to Latonia, and the horsemen that have been down to New Orleans or maybe at the winter meeting at Havana in Cuba come home to spend a week before they start out again, at such a time when everything talked about in Beckersville is just horses and nothing else and the outfits start out and horse racing is in every breath of air you breathe, Bildad shows up with a job as cook for some outfit. Often when I think about it, his always going all season to the races and working in the livery barn in the winter where horses are and where men like to come and talk about horses, I wish I was a nigger. It's a foolish thing to say, but that's the way I am about being around horses, just crazy. I can't help it.

Well, I must tell you about what we did and let you in on what I'm talking about. Four of us boys from Beckersville, all whites and sons of men who live in Beckersville regular, made up our minds we were going to the races, not just to Lexington or Louisville, I don't mean, but to the big eastern track we were always hearing our Beckersville men talk about, to Saratoga. We were all pretty young then. I was just turned fifteen and I was the oldest of the four. It was my scheme. I admit that and I talked the others into trying it. There was Hanley Turner and Henry Rieback and Tom Tumberton and myself. I had thirty-seven dollars I had earned during the winter working nights and Saturdays in Enoch Myer's grocery. Henry Rieback had eleven dollars and the others, Hanley and Tom had only a dollar or two each. We fixed it all up and laid low until the Kentucky spring meetings were over and some of our men, the sportiest ones, the ones we envied the most, had cut out— then we cut out too.

I won't tell you the trouble we had beating our way on freights and all. We went through Cleveland and Buffalo and other cities and saw Niagara Falls. We bought things there, souvenirs and spoons and cards and shells with pictures of the falls on them for our sisters and mothers, but thought we had better not send any of the things home. We didn't want to put the folks on our trail and maybe be nabbed.

We got into Saratoga as I said at night and went to the track. Bildad fed us up. He showed us a place to sleep in hay over a shed and promised to keep still. Niggers are all right about things like that. They won't squeal on you. Often a white man you might meet, when you had run away from home like that, might appear to be all right and give you a quarter or a half dollar or something, and then go right and give you away. White men will do that, but not a nigger. You can trust them. They are squarer with kids. I don't know why.

At the Saratoga meeting that year there were a lot of men from home. Dave Williams and Arthur Mulford and Jerry Myers and others. Then there was a lot from Louisville and Lexington Henry Rieback knew but I didn't. They were professional gamblers and Henry Rieback's father is one too. He is what is called a sheet writer and goes away most of the year to tracks. In the winter when he is home in Beckersville he don't stay there much but goes away to cities and deals faro. He is a nice man and generous, is always sending Henry presents, a bicycle and a gold watch and a boy scout suit of clothes and things like that.

My own father is a lawyer. He's all right, but don't make much money and can't buy me things and anyway I'm getting so old now I don't expect it. He never said nothing to me against Henry, but

Hanley Turner and Tom Tumburton's fathers did. They said to their boys that money so come by is no good and they didn't want their boys brought up to hear gamblers' talk and be thinking about such things and maybe embrace them.

That's all right and I guess the men know what they are talking about, but I don't see what it's got to do with Henry or with horses either. That's what I'm writing this story about. I'm puzzled. I'm getting to be a man and want to think straight and be O. K., and there's something I saw at the race meeting at the eastern track I can't figure out.

I can't help it, I'm crazy about thoroughbred horses. I've always been that way. When I was ten years old and saw I was growing to be big and couldn't be a rider I was so sorry I nearly died. Harry Hellinfinger in Beckersville, whose father is Postmaster, is grown up and too lazy to work, but likes to stand around in the street and get up jokes on boys like sending them to a hardware store for a gimlet to bore square holes and other jokes like that. He played one on me. He told me that if I would eat a half a cigar I would be stunted and not grow any more and maybe could be a rider. I did it. When father wasn't looking I took a cigar out of his pocket and gagged it down some way. It made me awful sick and the doctor had to be sent for, and then it did no good. I kept right on growing. It was a joke. When I told what I had done and why most fathers would have whipped me but mine didn't.

Well, I didn't get stunted and didn't die. It serves Harry Hellinfinger right. Then I made up my mind I would like to be a stable boy, but had to give that up too. Mostly niggers do that work and I knew father wouldn't let me go into it. No use to ask him.

If you've never been crazy about thoroughbreds it's because you've never been around where they are much and don't know any better. They're beautiful. There isn't anything so lovely and clean and full of spunk and honest and everything as some race horses. On the big horse farms that are all around our town Beckersville there are tracks and the horses run in the early morning. More than a thousand times I've got out of bed before daylight and walked two or three miles to the tracks. Mother wouldn't of let me go but father always says, "Let him alone." So I got some bread out of the bread box and some butter and jam, gobbled it and lit out.

At the tracks you sit on the fence with men, whites and niggers, and they chew tobacco and talk, and then the colts are brought out. It's early and the grass is covered with shiny dew and in another field a man is plowing and they are frying things in a shed where the track niggers sleep, and you know how a nigger can giggle and laugh and say things that make you laugh. A white man can't do it and some niggers can't but a track nigger can every time.

And so the colts are brought out and some are just galloped by stable boys, but almost every morning on a big track owned by a rich man who lives maybe in New York, there are always, nearly every morning, a few colts and some of the old race horses and geldings and mares that are cut loose.

It brings a lump up into my throat when a horse runs. I don't mean all horses but some. I can pick them nearly every time. It's in my blood like in the blood of race track niggers and trainers. Even when they just go slop-jogging along with a little nigger on their backs I can tell a winner. If my throat hurts and it's hard for me to swallow, that's him. He'll run like Sam Hill when you let him out. If he don't win every time it'll be a wonder and because they've got him in a pocket behind another or he was pulled or got off bad at the post or something. If I wanted to be a gambler like Henry Rieback's father I could get rich. I know I could and Henry says so too. All I would have to do is to wait 'til that hurt comes when I see a horse and then bet every cent. That's what I would do if I wanted to be a gambler, but I don't.

When you're at the tracks in the morning—not the race tracks but the training tracks around Beckersville—you don't see a horse, the kind I've been talking about, very often, but it's nice anyway. Any thoroughbred, that is sired right and out of a good mare and trained by a man that knows how, can run. If he couldn't what would he be there for and not pulling a plow?

Well, out of the stables they come and the boys are on their backs and it's lovely to be there. You hunch down on top of the fence and itch inside you. Over in the sheds the niggers giggle and sing. Bacon is being fried and coffee made. Everything smells lovely. Nothing smells better than coffee and manure and horses and niggers and bacon frying and pipes being smoked out of doors on a morning like that. It just gets you, that's what it does.

But about Saratoga. We was there six days and not a soul from home seen us and everything came off just as we wanted it to, fine weather and horses and races and all. We beat our way home and Bildad gave us a basket with fried chicken and bread and other eatables in, and I had eighteen dollars when we got back to Beckersville. Mother jawed and cried but Pop didn't say much. I told everything we done except one thing. I did and saw that alone. That's what I'm writing about. It got me upset. I think about it at night. Here it is.

At Saratoga we laid up nights in the hay in the shed Bildad had showed us and ate with the niggers early and at night when the race people had all gone away. The men from home stayed mostly in the grandstand and betting field, and didn't come out around the places where the horses are kept except to the paddocks just before a race when the horses are saddled. At Saratoga they don't have paddocks under an open shed as at Lexington and Churchill Downs and other tracks down in our country, but saddle the horses right out in an open place under trees on a lawn as smooth and nice as Banker Bohon's front yard here in Beckersville. It's lovely. The horses are sweaty and nervous and shine and the men come out and smoke cigars and look at them and the trainers are there and the owners, and your heart thumps so you can hardly breathe.

Then the bugle blows for post and the boys that ride come running out with their silk clothes on and you run to get a place by the fence with the niggers.

I always am wanting to be a trainer or owner, and at the risk of being seen and caught and sent home I went to the paddocks before every race. The other boys didn't but I did.

We got to Saratoga on a Friday and on Wednesday the next week the big Mullford Handicap was to be run. Middlestride was in it and Sunstreak. The weather was fine and the track fast. I couldn't sleep the night before.

What had happened was that both these horses are the kind it makes my throat hurt to see. Middlestride is long and looks awkward and is a gelding. He belongs to Joe Thompson, a little owner from home who only has a half dozen horses. The Mullford Handicap is for a mile and Middlestride can't untrack fast. He goes away slow and is always way back at the half, then he begins to run and if the race is a mile and a quarter he'll just eat up everything and get there.

Sunstreak is different. He is a stallion and nervous and belongs on the biggest farm we've got in our country, the Van Riddle place that belongs to Mr. Van Riddle of New York. Sunstreak is like a girl you think about sometimes but never see. He is hard all over and lovely too. When you look at his head you want to kiss him. He is trained by Jerry Tillford who knows me and has been good to me lots of times, lets me walk into a horse's stall to look at him close and other things. There isn't anything as sweet as that horse. He stands at the post quiet and not letting on, but he is just burning up inside. Then when the barrier goes up he is off like

his name, Sunstreak. It makes you ache to see him. It hurts you. He just lays down and runs like a bird dog. There can't anything I ever see run like him except Middlestride when he gets untracked and stretches himself.

Gee! I ached to see that race and those two horses run, ached and dreaded it too. I didn't want to see either of our horses beaten. We had never sent a pair like that to the races before. Old men in Beckersville said so and the niggers said so. It was a fact.

Before the race I went over to the paddocks to see. I looked a last look at Middlestride, who isn't such a much standing in a paddock that way, then I went to see Sunstreak.

It was his day. I knew when I see him. I forgot all about being seen myself and walked right up. All the men from Beckersville were there and no one noticed me except Jerry Tillford. He saw me and something happened. I'll tell you about that.

I was standing looking at that horse and aching. In some way, I can't tell how, I knew just how Sunstreak felt inside. He was quiet and letting the niggers rub his legs and Mr. Van Riddle himself put the saddle on, but he was just a raging torrent inside. He was like the water in the river at Niagara Falls just before it goes plunk down. That horse wasn't thinking about running. He don't have to think about that. He was just thinking about holding himself back 'til the time for the running came. I knew that. I could just in a way see right inside him. He was going to do some awful running and I knew it. He wasn't bragging or letting on much or prancing or making a fuss, but just waiting. I knew it and Jerry Tillford his trainer knew. I looked up and then that man and I looked into each other's eyes. Something happened to me. I guess I loved the man as much as I did the horse because he knew what I knew. Seemed to me there wasn't anything in the world but that man and the horse and me. I cried and Jerry Tillford had a shine in his eyes. Then I came away to the fence to wait for the race. The horse was better than me, more steadier, and now I know better than Jerry. He was the quietest and he had to do the running.

Sunstreak ran first of course and he busted the world's record for a mile. I've seen that if I never see anything more. Everything came out just as I expected. Middlestride got left at the post and was way back and closed up to be second, just as I knew he would. He'll get a world's record too some day. They can't skin the Beckersville country on horses.

I watched the race calm because I knew what would happen. I was sure. Hanley Turner and Henry Rieback and Tom Tumberton were all more excited than me.

A funny thing had happened to me. I was thinking about Jerry Tillford the trainer and how happy he was all through the race. I liked him that afternoon even more than I ever liked my own father. I almost forgot the horses thinking that way about him. It was because of what I had seen in his eyes as he stood in the paddocks beside Sunstreak before the race started. I knew he had been watching and working with Sunstreak since the horse was a baby colt, had taught him to run and be patient and when to let himself out and not to quit, never. I knew that for him it was like a mother seeing her child do something brave or wonderful. It was the first time I ever felt for a man like that.

After the race that night I cut out from Tom and Hanley and Henry. I wanted to be by myself and I wanted to be near Jerry Tillford if I could work it. Here is what happened.

The track in Saratoga is near the edge of town. It is all polished up and trees around, the evergreen kind, and grass and everything painted and nice. If you go past the track you get to a hard road made of asphalt for automobiles, and if you go along this for a few miles there is a road turns off to a little rummy-looking farm house set in a yard.

That night after the race I went along that road because I had seen Jerry and some other men go that way in an automobile. I didn't expect to find them. I walked for a ways and then sat down by a fence to think. It was the direction they went in. I wanted to be as near Jerry as I could. I felt close to him. Pretty soon I went up the side road—I don't know why—and came to the rummy farm house. I was just lonesome to see Jerry, like wanting to see your father at night when you are a young kid. Just then an automobile came along and turned in. Jerry was in it and Henry Rieback's father, and Arthur Bedford from home, and Dave Williams and two other men I didn't know. They got out of the car and went into the house, all but Henry Rieback's father who quarreled with them and said he wouldn't go. It was only about nine o'clock, but they were all drunk and the rummy looking farm house was a place for bad women to stay in. That's what it was. I crept up along a fence and looked through a window and saw.

It's what give me the fantods. I can't make it out. The women in the house were all ugly mean-looking women, not nice to look at or be near. They were homely too, except one who was tall and looked a little like the gelding Middlestride, but not clean like him, but with a hard ugly mouth. She had red hair. I saw everything plain. I

got up by an old rose bush by an open window and looked. The women had on loose dresses and sat around in chairs. The men came in and some sat on the women's laps. The place smelled rotten and there was rotten talk, the kind a kid hears around a livery stable in a town like Beckersville in the winter but don't ever expect to hear talked when there are women around. It was rotten. A nigger wouldn't go into such a place.

I looked at Jerry Tillford. I've told you how I had been feeling about him on account of his knowing what was going on inside of Sunstreak in the minute before he went to the post for the race in which he made a world's record.

Jerry bragged in that bad woman house as I know Sunstreak wouldn't never have bragged. He said that he made that horse, that it was him that won the race and made the record. He lied and bragged like a fool. I never heard such silly talk.

And then, what do you suppose he did! He looked at the woman in there, the one that was lean and hardmouthed and looked a little like the gelding Middlestride, but not clean like him, and his eyes began to shine just as they did when he looked at me and at Sunstreak in the paddocks at the track in the afternoon. I stood there by the window—gee!—but I wished I hadn't gone away from the tracks, but had stayed with the boys and the niggers and the horses. The tall rotten looking woman was between us just as Sunstreak was in the paddocks in the afternoon.

Then, all of a sudden, I began to hate that man. I wanted to scream and rush in the room and kill him. I never had such a feeling before. I was so mad clean through that I cried and my fists were doubled up so my finger nails cut my hands.

And Jerry's eyes kept shining and he waved back and forth, and then he went and kissed that woman and I crept away and went back to the tracks and to bed and didn't sleep hardly any, and then next day I got the other kids to start home with me and never told them anything I seen.

I been thinking about it ever since. I can't make it out. Spring has come again and I'm nearly sixteen and go to the tracks mornings same as always, and I see Sunstreak and Middlestride and a new colt named Strident I'll bet will lay them all out, but no one thinks so but me and two or three niggers.

But things are different. At the tracks the air don't taste as good or smell as good. It's because a man like Jerry Tillford, who knows what he does, could see a horse like Sunstreak run, and kiss a woman like that the same day. I can't make it out. Darn him, what did he want to do like that for? I keep thinking about it and it spoils looking at horses and smelling things and hearing niggers laugh and everything. Sometimes I'm so mad about it I want to fight someone. It gives me the fantods. What did he do it for? I want to know why.

1919

FOUR AMERICAN IMPRESSIONS:

Gertrude Stein, Paul Rosenfeld, Ring Lardner, Sinclair Lewis

❖

〖 LONG misdated, these four impressions first appeared in the *New Republic* for October 11, 1922, and were then reprinted in Sherwood Anderson's *Notebook* in 1926. The subjects of the first three impressions were his friends: Gertrude Stein, the expatriate American from whose *Three Lives* (1909) he learned a good deal; Paul Rosenfeld, critic of music and literature; Ring Lardner, the sardonic, finally very bitter newspaperman and short story writer. Sinclair Lewis, the first American to win the Nobel prize in literature, was not a friend. Although he pretended friendliness, Anderson was always offended by Lewis's great success. In his little book, *No Swank*, published in 1934, Anderson wrote:

. . . I talked of four Americans—Ring Lardner, Gertrude Stein, Sinclair Lewis and Paul Rosenfeld. I had, perhaps for some malicious reason, great delight in grouping them. I imagined the four together, say in a cabin on a mountain, in a snowstorm. All of this not in my article, which was quite dignified, but in fancy. I saw them in the room, staring at each other. A delicious thought came to me. It was that Paul and Ring would have quickly found a basis for understanding. I can imagine them withdrawing to a corner of the room to talk.

There is no fire in the room. A storm is raging outside. It is bitterly cold.

Gertrude Stein and Sinclair Lewis are left to talk together. It is bitterly cold. . . .

❖

ONE WHO thinks a great deal about people and what they are up to in the world comes inevitably in time to relate them to experiences connected with his own life. The round hard apples in this old orchard are the breasts of my beloved. The curved round hill in the distance is the body of my beloved, lying asleep. I cannot avoid practicing this trick of lifting people out of the spots on which in actual life they stand and transferring them to what seems at the moment some more fitting spot in the fanciful world.

And I get also a kind of aroma from people. They are green healthy growing things or they have begun to decay. There is something in this man, to whom I have just talked, that has sent me away from him smiling and in an odd way pleased with myself. Why has this other man, although his words were kindly and his deeds apparently good, spread a cloud over my sky?

In my own boyhood in an Ohio town I went about delivering newspapers at kitchen doors, and there were certain houses to which I went—old brick houses with immense old-fashioned kitchens—in which I loved to linger. On Saturday mornings I sometimes managed to collect a fragrant cooky at such a place but there was something else that held me. Something got into my mind connected with the great light kitchens and the women working in them that came sharply back when, last year, I went to visit an American woman, Miss Gertrude Stein, in her own large room in the house at 27 rue de Fleurus in Paris. In the great kitchen of my fanciful world in which, ever since that morning, I have seen Miss Stein standing there is a most sweet and gracious aroma. Along the walls are many shining pots and pans, and there are innumerable jars of fruits, jellies and preserves. Something is going on in the great room, for Miss Stein is a worker in words with the same loving touch in her strong fingers that was characteristic of the women of the kitchens of the brick houses in the town of my boyhood. She is an American woman of the old sort, one who cares for the handmade goodies and who scorns the factory-made foods, and in her own great kitchen she is making something with her materials, something sweet to the tongue and fragrant to the nostrils.

That her materials are the words of our English speech and that we do not, most of us, know or care too much what she is up to does not greatly matter to me. The impression I wish now to give you of her is of one very intent and earnest in a matter most of us have forgotten. She is laying word against word, relating sound to sound, feeling for the taste, the smell, the rhythm of the individual word. She is attempting to do something for the writers of our English speech that may be better understood after a time, and she is not in a hurry.

And I have always that picture of the woman in the great kitchen of words, standing there by a table, clean, strong, with red cheeks and sturdy legs, always quietly and smilingly at work. If her smile has in it something of the mystery, to the male at least, of the Mona Lisa, I remember that the women in the kitchens on the wintry mornings wore often that same smile.

She is making new, strange and to my ears sweet combinations of words. As an American writer I admire her because she, in her person, represents something sweet and healthy in our American life, and because I have a kind of undying faith that what she is up to in her word kitchen in Paris is of more importance to writers of English than the work of many of our more easily understood and more widely accepted word artists.

II

WHEN it comes to our Mr. Ring Lardner, here is something else again. Here is another word fellow, one who cares about the words of our American speech and who is perhaps doing more than any other American to give new force to the words of our everyday life.

There is something I think I understand about Mr. Ring Lardner. The truth is that I believe there is something the matter with him and I have a fancy I know what it is. He is afraid of the highbrows. They scare him to death. I wonder why. For it is true that there is often, in a paragraph of his, more understanding of life, more human sympathy, more salty wisdom than in hundreds of pages of, say Mr. Sinclair Lewis's dreary prose— and I am sure Mr. Lewis would not hesitate to outface any highbrow in his lair.

I said that I thought I knew what was the matter with Mr. Ring Lardner. He comes from out in my country, from just such another town as the one in which I spent my own boyhood, and I remember certain shy lads of my own town who always made it a point to consort mostly with the town toughs—and for a reason. There was in them something extremely sensitive that did not want to be hurt. Even to mention the fact that there was in such a one a real love of life, a quick sharp stinging hunger for beauty, would have sent a blush of shame to his cheeks. He was intent upon covering up, concealing from everyone, at any cost, the shy hungry child he was carrying about within himself.

And I always see our Mr. Ring Lardner as such a fellow. He is covering up, sticking to the gang, keeping out of sight. And that is all right too, if in secret and in his suburban home he is really using his talent for sympathetic understanding of life, if

in secret he is being another Mark Twain and working in secret on his own *Huckleberry Finn.* Mark Twain wrote and was proclaimed for writing his *Innocents Abroad, Following the Equator, Roughing It,* etc., etc., and was during his lifetime most widely recognized for such secondary work. And Mark Twain was just such another shy lad, bluffed by the highbrows—and even the glorious Mark had no more sensitive understanding of the fellow in the street, in the hooch joint, the ballpark and the city suburb than our Mr. Ring Lardner.

III

WHICH brings me to a man who, it seems to me, of all our American writers, is the one who is most unafraid, Mr. Paul Rosenfeld. Here is an American writer actually unashamed of being fine and sensitive in his work. To me it seems that he has really freed himself from both the high and the low brows and has made of himself a real aristocrat among writers of prose.

To be sure, to the man in the street, accustomed to the sloppiness of hurried newspaper writing, the Rosenfeld prose is sometimes difficult. His vocabulary is immense and he cares very, very much for just the shade of meaning he is striving to convey. Miss Jean Heap recently spoke of him as "our well-dressed writer of prose," and I should think Paul Rosenfeld would not too much resent the connotations of that. For, after all, Rosenfeld is our man of distinction, the American, it seems to me, who is unafraid and unashamed to live for the things of the spirit as expressed in the arts. I get him as the man walking cleanly and boldly and really accepting, daring to accept, the obligations of the civilized man. To my ears that acceptance has made his prose sound clearly and sweetly across many barren fields. To me it is often like soft bells heard ringing at evening across fields long let go to the weeds of carelessness and the general slam-it-through-ness of so much of our American writing.

IV

OF THE four American writers concerning whose handling of our speech I have had the temerity to express my own feeling there is left Mr. Sinclair Lewis.

The texture of the prose written by Mr. Lewis gives me but faint joy and I cannot escape the conviction that for some reason Lewis has himself found but little joy, either in life among us or in his own effort to channel his reactions to our life into prose. There can be no doubt that this man, with his sharp journalistic nose for news of the outer surface of our lives, has found out a lot of things about us and the way we live in our towns and cities, but I am very sure that in the life of every man woman and child in the country there are forces at work that seem to have escaped the notice of Mr. Lewis. Mr. Ring Lardner has seen them and in his writing there is sometimes real laughter, but one has the feeling that Lewis never laughs at all, that he is in an odd way too serious about something to laugh.

For after all, even in Gopher Prairie or in Indianapolis, Indiana, boys go swimming in the creeks on summer afternoons, shadows play at evening on factory walls, old men dig angleworms and go fishing together, love comes to at least a few men and women, and everything else failing, the baseball club comes from a neighboring town and Tom Robinson gets a home run. That's something. There is an outlook on life across which even the cry of a child, choked to death by its own mother, would be something. Life in our American towns and cities is barren enough and there are enough people saying that with the growth of industrialism it has become continually more and more ugly, but Mr. Paul Rosenfeld and Mr. Ring Lardner apparently do not find it altogether barren and ugly. For them and for a growing number of men and women in America there is something like a dawn that Mr. Lewis has apparently sensed but little, for there is so little sense of it in the texture of his prose. Reading Mr. Sinclair Lewis, one comes inevitably to the conclusion that here is a man writing who, wanting passionately to love the life about him, cannot bring himself to do so, and who, wanting perhaps to see beauty descend upon our lives like a rainstorm, has become blind to the minor beauties our lives hold.

And is it not just this sense of dreary spiritual death in the man's work that is making it so widely read? To one who is himself afraid to live there is, I am sure, a kind of joy in seeing other men as dead. In my own feeling for the man from whose pen has come all of this prose over which there are so few lights and shades, I have come at last to sense, most of all, the man fighting terrifically and ineffectually for a thing about which he really does care. There is a kind of fighter living inside Mr. Sinclair Lewis and there is, even in this dull, unlighted prose of his, a kind of dawn coming. In the dreary ocean of this prose, islands begin to appear. In *Babbitt* there are moments when the people of whom he writes, with such amazing attention to the outer details of lives, begin to think and feel a little, and with the coming of life into his people a kind of nervous, hurried beauty and life flits, like a lantern carried by a night watchman

past the window of a factory as one stands waiting and watching in a grim street on a night of December.

1922

FROM

LETTERS, 1918–1938

◇

❪ WE ARE fortunate in having the *Letters of Sherwood Anderson*, selected and edited by Howard Mumford Jones in association with Walter B. Rideout, published in 1953. Anderson was so much a "talking" writer that it is not surprising to find him at his greatest ease when he is "talking" to his friends through his nearly illegible pen. In his letters he could really be that spontaneous, uncalculating person that he pretended to be in his art. The selection here runs from 1918 to 1938.

◇

29: TO VAN WYCK BROOKS [1]

[Chicago, early April, 1918]

MY DEAR BROOKS:

Your letter has stirred up a world of thought in me. It isn't Twain I'm thinking of, but the profound truth of some of your own observations.

As far as Twain is concerned, we have to remember the influences about him. Remember how he came into literature—the crude buffoon of the early days in the mining camp, the terrible cheap and second-rate humor of much of *Innocents Abroad*. It seems to me that when he began he addressed an audience that gets a big laugh out of the braying of a jackass, and without a doubt Mark often brayed at them. He knew that later. There was tenderness and subtlety in Mark when he grew older.

You get the picture of him, Brooks—the river man who could write going East and getting in with that New England crowd, the fellows from barren hills and barren towns. The best he got out of the bunch was Howells, and Howells did Twain no good.

There's another point, Brooks. I can't help wishing Twain hadn't married such a good wom-

LETTERS. 1. **Van Wyck Brooks**: Brooks, the distinguished American critic (b. 1886) published *The Ordeal of Mark Twain* in 1920 [Ed.]. (Footnotes to the Anderson letters, save those followed by [Ed.], are from the *Letters of Sherwood Anderson*, ed. by Howard Mumford Jones and Walter Rideout.)

an. There was such a universal inclination to tame the man—to save his soul, as it were. Left alone, I fancy Mark might have been willing to throw his soul overboard and then—ye gods, what a fellow he might have been, what poetry might have come from him.

The big point is: it seems to me that this salvation of the soul business gets under everybody's skin. With artists it takes the form of being concerned with their reputation as writers. A struggle constantly goes on. Call the poet a poet and he is no longer the poet. You see what I mean.

There is a fellow like Waldo,[2] for example. He writes me long letters. His days are often made happy or miserable according to whether or not he is writing well.

Is it so important? What stardust we are. What does it matter?

The point is that I catch Waldo so often striving to say things in an unusual way. It makes me cringe. I want to beat him with my fists.

I pick on Waldo as an example because I love him and I know he feels deeply. He should write with a swing—weeping, praying, and crying to the gods on paper instead of making sentences as he so often does.

Well, now, you see I'm coming around. The cultural fellows got hold of Mark. They couldn't hold him. He was too big and too strong. He brushed their hands aside.

But their words got into his mind. In the effort to get out beyond that he became a pessimist.

Now, Brooks, you know a man cannot be a pessimist who lives near a brook or a cornfield. When the brook chatters or at night when the moon comes up and the wind plays in the corn, a man hears the whispering of the gods.

Mark got to that once—when he wrote *Huck Finn*. He forgot Howells and the good wife and everyone. Again he was the half-savage, tender, god-worshiping, believing boy. He had proud, conscious innocence.

I believe he wrote that book in a little hut on a hill on his farm. It poured out of him. I fancy that at night he came down from his hill stepping like a king, a splendid playboy playing with rivers and men, riding on the Mississippi, on the broad river that is the great artery flowing out of the heart of the land.

Well, Brooks, I'm alone in a boat on that stream sometimes. The rhythm and swing of it is in some of my songs that are to be published next month. It sometimes gets into some of the Winesburg

things. I'll ride it some more, perhaps. It depends on whether or not I can avoid taking myself serious[ly]. Whom the gods wish to destroy they first make drunk with the notion of being a writer.

Waldo is coming out to spend a month with me.

Wish I could see you sometime this summer. I'll be in the East for a month or more in June or July. Why couldn't you come to the mountains and have a few days' walk with me?

45: TO VAN WYCK BROOKS

[?Chicago, ?late December, 1919]

DEAR BROOKS:

I've been thinking about your letter of the other day and my answer that didn't say what I wanted it to say. Your not writing letters doesn't bother me. I have no special feeling about it at all.

I would in some way like you to know how I feel in another respect.

I dare say your book, when it comes, will not have the passionate flaming thing in it that Waldo's book[3] often has. But, Brooks, you must realize what an inciter to flame in others you are.

I have a hunch you are doomed to be a man whose voice will not be heard by many here for a long time, but you should realize what it means to those who do hear it.

When in speaking of *Winesburg* you use the word "adolescence," you struck more nearly than you know on the whole note of me. I am immature, will live and die immature. A quite terrible confession that would be if I did not represent so much.

I am conscious I do represent much, and often I feel like a very small boy in the presence of your mind and of Waldo's too.

What is true of me is true of Sandburg, but we are different. He is submerged in adolescence. I am in it and of it, but I look out. Give Sandburg a mind, and you perhaps destroy him. I don't know whether that would be true of me or not.

Be sure of this, Brooks. No matter how much you may seem to yourself to work in isolation, it is not true. Your voice always comes clear to me and will to some others. You have been the bearer of a lamp that has illuminated many a dark place for me.

Nothing that is going to happen next year will mean as much to me as getting my hand on your new book.[4]

You, Waldo, and me—could three men be more unlike? How truly I love you two men.

---

2. Waldo: Waldo Frank, novelist and editor of *The Seven Arts*, which published some early Anderson stories [Ed.]. **3. Waldo's book:** Waldo Frank, *Our America* (1919). **4. Your new book:** *The Ordeal of Mark Twain* (1920).

[P.S.] I think of my *Testament* [5] as a passionate attempt to get poetry into the thing you have expressed time and again and that you and Waldo have together made me a little conscious of. I want to have it be a distillation. God knows how far I shall succeed.

63: TO PAUL ROSENFELD

Palos Park, Illinois [after October 24, 1921]

DEAR PAUL:

It was good to hear from you. I have been in the country almost continuously since I got home, and whenever I have gone to town or whenever Tennessee has come out here, the greeting has been the same. "Have you heard from Paul?" It threatened to become one of those annoying family sayings that no one else understands, but that always makes the members of the family smile.

I'm glad you reminded me of *Windy*. I'll send it Monday from town. Also I'll have what there is of the *Testament* copied and send it at once. There should be more than the one copy anyway.

You understand, of course, Paul, that the *Testament* is a purely experimental thing with me. Many of the things you will now find in it will no doubt eventually be cast out altogether. However, I'm going to send it to you just as it is. In this book I am trying to get at something that I think was very beautifully done in some parts of the Old Testament by the Hebrew poets. That is to say, I want to achieve in it rhythm of words with rhythm of thought. Do I make myself clear? The thing if achieved will be felt rather tha[n] seen or heard, perhaps. You see, as the things are, many of them violate my own conception of what I am after. In making this book I have felt no call to responsibility to anything but my own inner sense of what is beautiful in the arrangement of words and ideas. It is in a way my own Bible. I think in a way you and Brooks and Waldo have always a little misunderstood something in me. Have you ever known well an old priest of the Catholic faith? He will make almost ribald remarks about Mother Church sometimes, but if you take that to mean he hasn't real love and devotion to her, you make a great mistake.

You see, after all I was raised in a different atmosphere than most of you fellows. Among workers, farmers, etc., here in the Middle West it used to be thought almost unwholesome to be outwardly serious about anything. After all, you see, I am a product of the same thing Brooks talks so much about in his Mark Twain.

There was, you see, an outward technique. If a man say anything seriously to another, he must immediately turn it about and make a kind of half joke of it. The serious, not the half-joking thing, was meant. The half-joking thing did, however, answer a purpose. "We must laugh or die" was at bottom the thing felt.

I emphasize this phase of myself to you, Paul, because you, Brooks, and Waldo were all brought up in a different atmosphere. I think your atmosphere was as difficult as my own to penetrate, but it was different. The New Englanders and the Jews have always at least had the privilege of being serious. You see, I put Brooks among the New Englanders. He may not have been born there, [6] but spiritually he belongs there and has in his make-up the beauty and the inner cold fright of the New Englander. That's what makes it so difficult for me to feel warm and close to him, as I so often do to you and Waldo, although I respect him sometimes more than any other living man. Is all this stupid? However, I will go on and try to get off my chest what I am trying to say. I have in my inner consciousness conceived of what we roughly speak of as the Middle West, and what I have so often called Mid-America, as an empire with its capital in Chicago. When I started writing, my conception wasn't so clear. Then I went only so far as to want health for myself. I was a money-getter, a schemer, a chronic liar. One day I found out that when I sat down to write, it was more difficult to lie. The lie lay before one on the paper. It haunted one at night.

Then, you see, I knew no writers, no artists. Everything was very much mixed up. When I began to know writers and painters, I couldn't abide the way most of them talked. They were also doing the American trick. They were putting it over.

You see, I had by this time got up out of the ranks of laborers and lived among businessmen, had them for my friends. I went to conferences, lunched with these men. They were always talking so earnestly and seriously about nothing. The nothingness back of the spirit of their lives led to sex-mussiness. Brooks, I believe, once called me "the phallic Chekhov." I really do not believe I have a sex-obsession, as has so often been said. I do not want to have, surely. When I want to flatter myself, at least, I tell myself that I want only not to lose the sense of life as it is, here, now, in the land and among the people among whom I live.

Please believe, Paul, that I am writing all this to

---

5. **Testament:** Anderson's *A New Testament*, published in 1927, a volume of loosely written poems, appeared serially in *Seven Arts* [Ed.].

6. Brooks was born in Plainfield, N.J.

you not having your article in mind, but rather in mind you as my friend, as a man I love.

Let me go on. You will see in *Windy* and in *Marching Men* the effects of a reaction from businessmen back to my former associates, the workers. I believe now it was a false reaction and carried with it something else. It is the thing Mencken calls "sentimental liberalism." For a time I did dream of a new world to come out of some revolutionary movement that would spring up out of the mass of people.

That went. A break came. You will see it in *Mid-American Chants*. What happened was something like this. A new conception came. Will you read now the first of the New Testaments. "In a purely subconscious way I am a patriot. I live in a wide valley of cornfields and men and towns and strange, jangling sounds, and in spite of the curious perversion of life here, I have a feeling that the great basin of the Mississippi River, where I have always lived and moved about, is one day to be the seat of the culture of the universe."

Now you understand, Paul, something in me. There is acceptance in that. I take these little, ugly factory towns, these big, sprawling cities into something. I wish it would not sound to[o] silly to say I pour a dream over it, consciously, intentionally, for a purpose. I want to write beautifully, create beautifully, not outside but in this thing in which I am born, in this place where, in the midst of ugly towns, cities, Fords, moving pictures, I have always lived, must always live. I do not want, Paul, even those old monks at Chartres, building their cathedral, to be at bottom any purer than myself.

There are infinite difficulties. You with your quick, warm nature will perhaps never quite understand my slowness or the slowness of men like Sandburg. I am stupid. You will never believe how stupid. There is something almost of the Negro in me there.

This leads to misunderstandings, too. There are men, like Jones [7] of the Chicago *Post,* who, having no doubt at some time heard me say something derogative to smart men and smartness, have got the idea fixed in their heads that I am without respect for old things, old beauty. Jones, for example, is always harping on the idea that I do not believe in reading the work of the old masters of my craft and that I am no respecter of words, am afraid of words. I do not blame Jones. If he has such a notion, it is because of something I have myself said.

I have had a great fear of phrase-making. Words, as you know, Paul, are very tricky things. Look, for example, how that man Mencken can rattle words like dice in a box. Our Ben Hecht, here in Chicago, has naturally the same talent, but I happen to know he isn't particularly proud of it, not at bottom.

Being, as I have said, slow in my nature, I do have to come to words slowly. I do not want to make them rattle. And well enough I know that you, Waldo, Brooks might do in a flash what I will never be able to do. You may get to heights I can never reach. That isn't quite the point. I'm not competitive. I want, if I can to save myself.

And now, you see, this brings me to the point of all this. Granted I am slow and stupid. Now, at this time, in America, culture is not a part of our lives out here in Mid-America. We are all, businessmen, workers, farmers, town, city and country dwellers, a little ashamed of trying for beauty. We are imprisoned. There is a wall about us. You will see, as you get into the spirit of the *New Testament,* how that wall has become a symbol of life to me. More men than you and I will ever know have become embittered and ugly in America, Paul. The flush-looking, hearty, go-with-a-slam-bang businessmen and others, what we have come to think of as the up-and-going American, are not so up-and-going. They are little children. Immaturity is the note of the age, and immaturity is a wall too.

And so in my inner self I have accepted my own Mid-America as a walled-in place. There are walls everywhere, about individuals, about groups. The houses are mussy. People die inside the walls without ever having seen the light. I want the houses cleaned, the doorsteps washed, the walls broken away. That can't happen in my time. Culture is a slow growth. How silly to think you won't understand all this, that you haven't understood from the first. Sometimes, however, you, Brooks, Waldo, all the men I love and respect seem so far away. I say stupid things, act stupidly. I grow afraid too.

You see, all I want is to have such men as you know at bottom that I love what you love—that is enough. Artists have to be strangers to the body of the people now in Chicago, in Ohio, in all this empire of Mid-America. I just don't want any of you fellows who are real, who love beauty and who understand more than I ever will, to be fooled by my crudeness or to be led to believe that I am not, in my own way, trying to live in the old tradition of artists. And that's all of that. "Thank God," you'll probably say. . . .

7. Jones: Llewellyn Jones (1884–   ), literary editor of the Chicago *Evening Post,* 1914–32.

65: TO MR. LEWIS GALANTIÈRE,[8] 33, RUE JEAN GOUJON, PARIS

[Chicago] November 28, 1921

MY DEAR LEWIS:

A friend of mine and a very delightful man, Ernest Hemingway, and his wife are leaving for Paris. They will sail December 8th and go to [the] Hotel Jacob, at least temporarily. Hemingway is a young fellow of extraordinary talent and, I believe, will get somewhere. He has been a quite wonderful newspaper man, but has practically given up newspaper work for the last year. Recently he got an assignment to do European letters for some Toronto newspaper[9] for whom he formerly worked, and this is giving him the opportunity he has wanted, to live in Europe for a time. I have talked to him a great deal about you and have given him your address. I trust you will be on the lookout for him at the Hotel Jacob along about the 20th or 21st of December. He is not like Stearns, and his wife is charming. They will settle down to live in Paris, and [I] am sure you will find them great playmates. As I understand it, they will not have much money, so that they will probably want to live over in the Latin Quarter. However, Hemingway can himself find quarters after he gets there, and the Hotel Jacob will do temporarily. . . .

67: TO MISS GERTRUDE STEIN,[10] 27, RUE DE FLEURUS, PARIS

Chicago, December 3, 1921

DEAR MISS STEIN:

I am writing this note to make you acquainted with my friend Ernest Hemingway, who with Mrs. Hemingway is going to Paris to live, and will ask him to drop it in the mails when he arrives there.

Mr. Hemingway is an American writer instinctively in touch with everything worth-while going on here, and I know you will find Mr. and Mrs. Hemingway delightful people to know.

They will be, temporarily, at the Hotel Jacob, rue Jacob.[11] Sincerely

[P.S.] Did you get my note about the introduction?[12] Love to Marsden Hartley.[13]

84: TO ALFRED STIEGLITZ [14]

[Reno, August 6, 1923]

DEAR ALFRED STIEGLITZ:

What a nut I am, not being more clear. The book I want to dedicate to you is not the *Horses and Men* book,[15] but the book on which I am now at work [16] and that belongs to you much more fully.

In this book I am trying to tell, as plainly and clearly as I can, the story of a man—myself—who found out just about what you have outlined in your letter today.

You see, dear man, I have been a long time finding out just that people are really innocent, and it may be that much more than you know of what I have found out has come to me because of a growing awareness of you. Since I have known you, your figure has been standing all the time a little more and more clear.

You see, the book in question (I may call it *A Modernist Notebook*) is an attempt at a man's story of his adventures with men. The man is puzzled. There is no definite leadership for him.

What he knows after a time is that, while a man may become aware of the innocence of people in general, he cannot quite love that innocence itself. It does not reach far enough. One wants comrades, grown men such as I have come to feel you, and Paul too.

We have together the love of horses. In my own boyhood I went to them, lived with them, was groom to running and trotting horses, now I know, because they were the most beautiful things about me.

But it did not suffice. Will not suffice. The horse is the horse, and we are men.

And it is just because I feel that way I waited for this book as being your book, most essentially. I should have made it clearer. You see, *Horses and Men* is the book of another year, put behind me now, but just coming toward others in the form of a book.

While this book is just forming now, and forming at a time when I am most aware of you.

I believe I have selected the right book to bear your name on the title page, because I believe it will have in it the most of you in me.

8. Lewis Galantière: Lewis Galantière (1895–   ), Chicago writer, attached to the International Chamber of Commerce in Paris, 1920–27.   **9.** The Toronto *Star.*   **10. Gertrude Stein:** Gertrude Stein (1874–1946), expatriate and influential experimental writer.   **11.** This has been changed, apparently by Hemingway, to read: "They will be at 74 Rue de Cardinal Lemoine."   **12.** Miss Stein had requested Anderson to write an introduction to her forthcoming book, *Geography and Plays* (1922).   **13. Marsden Hartley:** the American painter (1877–

1943).   **14. Alfred Stieglitz:** Alfred Stieglitz (1864–1946), founder and editor of *Camera Notes* (1907–03); editor and publisher of *Camera Work*. It was Stieglitz, more than anyone else in the United States, who was responsible for the development of photography as a fine art. He was married to the painter Georgia O'Keeffe in 1924 [Ed.].   **15. Horses and men book:** *Horses and Men* was dedicated to Theodore Dreiser.   **16.** *A Story Teller's Story.*

147: TO ROGER SERGEL [17]

[Troutdale, Virginia, ?October, 1927]

MY DEAR ROGER SERGEL:

Your letter of late August did me good. Like yourself, and I dare say all working artists, I get often the feeling that the bouquet has all gone off the wine. The smart men, it seems, rule. On all sides nothing but cleverness. I am in despair of ever doing anything myself and hear of others in the same state.

Then, as you suggest, something happens. God knows what it is. The rhythm (I hate that word, but know of no other to take its place) is picked up. We go along, sing a bit, dance a little in the moonlight.

In the country sometimes I go about looking at horses and cattle. They eat grass, make love, work when they have to, bear their young. I am sick with envy of them.

As for myself, I also have been in a bad state. Now look at the foolishness of us all. I dare say you mourn sometimes having to go to your foolish classes to make your living. You yearn for leisure. Be careful, man, you may sometime get it.

A little success. There you are. Some money comes in. I have had two years of comparative leisure and look back upon them aghast. "My God, what have I done with them?" The question frightens me.

When I was at work at something other than writing, I had at least the feeling that I was doing something out of necessity. Earning your living gives a certain sense of virtue. It is even good to feel wronged a bit. You know how it is.

And so here am I. No, the book is not done. I do not know when it will be done. I have thrown it aside.

Well, I have come to a resolution. I shall go to work at something other than writing. As you know, formerly I was in the position you are in. I made my living, not by teaching, but by advertising writing. My other writing was incidental. I had not tried to make a slave out of my pen. It could play over the paper.

Then corruption crept in. "Give me leisure," I cried, "and you will see what I shall do." The gods laughed. I got the leisure.

Long days nothing to do. "Write, man." But what shall I write?

I am sitting on a hill in the country or walking in the streets of a town. I am in despair, such despair as you know.

Well, I argue with myself. "But, man, you do not have to write. Live."

But I have come to live by writing. I want beauty and meaning always at my finger tips, and there is no beauty or meaning anywhere in me.

But I am only reviewing a state we are both often in. It is not new to you.

What I sat down to do was merely to give you news of myself. I have got a home now in the country. It is almost paid for. The country is very lovely. It does not cost much to live here.

Well, I am going to a nearby town and go to work. I am at present in negotiation for the purchase of a small town weekly paper.[18] If I secure it, and I hope I shall, I will become a country editor. The paper can make me a living. I shall live by it and not by my scribbling.

All of this to get something of my own weight off the back of my pen in order that, if the gods are good, it may run a bit more lightly over the paper.

Really, and what a curse to be an artist at all. It is the only way of life. It is at the same time the most terrible way of life. Sweet Jesus. Holy Mary, mother of God, why did you not make me a bricklayer, or a plumber?

I can imagine crawling under houses to fix drains. I look up through a crack in the floor. I see the slender legs of the woman of the house, wish to possess her. My days pass so. I get drunk and go home and beat my wife. On the whole a comparatively good life. At least when I lay my hands to a pipe, I can fix the pipe. You see what I mean. What offended me in your letter of the spring was, as you know, that you addressed me as a kind of great man, one removed from the things that sometimes almost drive you insane. I would not be so removed. O[h] my dear man, work accomplished means so little. It is in the past. What we all want is the glorious and living present.

But enough. If you are to have some leisure next year, why do you not think of coming down into these hills? A little house could be had for two or three dollars a month at least. If you were to come, we could arrange to have a garden planted for you in advance. There are mountain streams, woods, hills, green fields. Think of it during the winter. I know of no place where life can be lived more satisfactorily, if you are working, or where life costs less. Love to Ruth

---

17. **Roger Sergel:** Sergel, at this time a member of the English department of the University of Pittsburgh, was later to be the head of The Dramatic Publishing Company in Chicago and became a close friend of Anderson's [Ed.].

18. In Marion, Va.

162: TO ROBERT ANDERSON [19]

Richmond, Virginia [November, 1929]

DEAR BOB:

I am comfortably placed here at the Westmoreland Club, not at all expensive. They put me in a tiny room, but I am moving this afternoon to a large room on the second floor where there is a good-sized room in which to work.

It seems a bit silly of me sometimes, not to be there with you, but this whole thing has done me good.

I think what happened to me was rather strange and amusing.

I guess you do not know, and perhaps never will know, the underlying basic difference between your generation and mine. In my generation, as you know—you kids of mine had partly to pay for it—I was a rebel.

Could there be anything more strange than what has happened to me?

I wanted for people, quite frankly, many things my generation did not have. I fought for it in my life and in my work.

Then the War came. The War did more than anything I or my kind could have done to make people face life.

For example, the old battleground was sex. That led naturally to an emphasis on sex. We all saw, everyone saw, the effect of repressions.

I and my kind told the story of repressed life. I have never thought of myself as a profound thinker. I was the storyteller; I took my color from the life about me. You know that for a long time after I began writing I was condemned on all sides. That is pretty much forgotten now. My *Winesburg, Ohio,* was condemned as a sex-server. How strange that notion seems now.

And then came the Great War. Never mind what the War was. It was terrific in its physical aspects—bodies mangled, the young manhood of England, Germany and France blown away or bled white, a great nation like Germany humiliated in the end.

Never mind all that. That is past.

But something else got blown up in that war too: the repressions, the strange fear of sex, the resultant underestimate and overestimate of sex as a force on life got blown up too.

It may be that what happened in the Great War, because of it, was a truer estimate of life. The young men who went into it got, must have got, a profound sense of life's cheapness.

You, my son, did not get into the War. You

were too young. You just escaped it. Just the same you are are not at all the man you would have been but for the War.

Of course there came other forces at work—the flowering of the industrial age, speeded up, no doubt, by the War.

Thousand[s] of men, everywhere, jerked out of the old individualistic life—plenty of machinery to jerk them out fast, machinery to kill them in masses like cattle—hurled into a new mass life.

The old individualist—the man of the pre-War period, who was a young man then, who got his sharp impressions then (most of us continue all our lives to live in the impressions of youth; the men, the young men who got their sharp impressions of life in the War will probably continue to live in those impressions the rest of their lives)—the old individualist type of man—well, you see where he was.

Why talk of sex repressions now? Apparently there aren't any.

I remember, son, a certain woman who fought long and bitterly for woman's suffrage. The women got what they fought for.

But this particular woman couldn't quit fighting for woman suffrage. She kept right on. One day I was walking with a young woman, and we saw this older woman. As she knew me, she stopped. "What are you doing now?" I asked.

She began again on the rights of women. They had got some things but not enough. The words she was saying would have been glowing words twenty years ago. I shall never forget the puzzled look in the younger woman's eyes. She was a post-War kid. "Rights of women? What the devil is the old girl talking about?" she asked.

Well, you see where I am, son—or at least have been these last five years. I had a world, and it slipped away from me. The War blew up more than the bodies of men, as I have already suggested.

It blew ideas away—

Love
God
Romance.

I am working on a book. I call it *No God*.[20] I could just as well call it *No Love*. It is not without significance that Gauguin is your favorite modern painter while my favorite is Van Gogh. I remember what Gauguin said of love. "If I were to say the word, it would crack the teeth out of my mouth," he said.

---

19. Robert Anderson: Anderson's elder son, who took over his newspaper enterprise [Ed.].

20. *No God:* This title was abandoned after Horace Liveright protested in a telegram of November 11, 1929, that the phrase would be misinterpreted.

As regards this transition, this sweeping change that has come in the whole underlying conceptions of life, it is a profound one.

If I were a bit older, it would not make any difference to me. The old are old.

As a man, as a writer, I had to ask myself which road I wanted to take. I could simply have been old, not to have tried to understand you and your brother and sister.

I fought against you for a long time. Who has cried out more sharply than myself against the coming of industrialism, the death of individualism, the modern world?

Well, I had already told the story of the man crying in the wilderness. I have been going about for four or five years now saying to myself, "To hell with that."

I want to say to you now that I would very likely have lost this little private battle of mine, that concerns no one vitally but myself, but for you kids of mine.

It would have meant kindly tolerance on your part, "The old man's all right." You know, that sort of thing.

In *No God,* the novel on which I am now at work, I am telling the story of a man having his roots in the pre-War life, accepting the present day post-War life.

That is my man's story. He is a man who has had marriage in the old way—memories of it cling to him—and then he comes to accept a woman who is the product of the new world.

No God—No Love—in the old sense. That is what it means.

As for the woman, well, I see her every day on the street. I've a notion that she doesn't want and wouldn't take what men used to give women, calling it love. I hope I am right about her. She is the young female kid of today. She has had sex experience and will have more, when she wants it.

I look at her as my man in the book *No God* looks at her—glad of her, certainly all for her.

Writing about her and of my man's acceptance of her is fun. It is refreshing. It is good for me.

There is certainly plenty of the old pre-War thing in men, the fear of the new life that has constantly to be put down.

215: TO THE DRAMATIC PUBLISHING COMPANY, CHICAGO, ILLINOIS

[Marion, Virginia] October 10, 1932

DEAR SIRS:

The little play, *The Triumph of the Egg,* had its New York production with the Provincetown Players.[21] It was put on as a curtain-raiser for Eugene O'Neill's two-act play, *Different.* The play caught the fancy of the audience and was a success.

The Provincetown Players, however, did some things to the play that I rather liked. The scene of the mother and the child was done off stage, in a room opening off the restaurant, the father standing in the doorway and talking to the mother. The audience never did see the stage child and got the sense of him from the mother's talk and from the little voice of the child saying his prayers. One of the New York critics spoke of the child as the most satisfactory stage child ever in the New York theaters. You did not have to look at the child being an actor. Your own imagination—you being of the audience—made the child exist. You—being of the audience—recalled perhaps your own childhood. It was very effective and satisfactory.

At the last, by my friend Mr. Raymond O'Neil's [22] version of the story, you see the two people, the unsuccessful little restaurant keeper and his wife, they having thrown themselves sobbing on the bed. This ending did a little violate my own conception when I wrote the story. To me the whole point of the play should be that the audience stays balanced between laughter and tears. In the Provincetown Players' version and after the outburst of ineffectual anger on the part of the father—his throwing the eggs about the room, etc. —he goes behind the restaurant counter. For a moment he stands there, looking about, perplexed, his anger dying, hurt. He sits down on a stool, and his head falls into his hands. His elbows are on the counter.

The world, represented by the people passing along the road from the train, goes by the little restaurant. Joe Kane is telling his father about the queer people who run the restaurant. Joe Kane and his father stop a moment by the restaurant door. You hear the voices and the laughter, the talk of other people going up into Bidwell from the train. The poor, befuddled restaurant keeper does not raise his head.

The voices pass and silence comes. The voice of the woman, the mother, is heard—a voice full of sympathy now, all the weariness and irritation gone out of it.

"Father! Father!"

The father is sitting with his head in his hands, half raises his head. Curtain. I do not really know

21. Produced February 10, 1925, at the Provincetown Playhouse under the direction of James Light.   22. The Provincetown production was based on the dramatization made in 1922 by O'Neil and published in 1932 by The Dramatic Publishing Company with this letter as a foreword.

how much of this is from the Provincetown Players' version and how much my own imagination has built up since, but of this I am quite sure: to do the little play in this way will gain tremendous effectualness and will leave the audience, as it should be left, balanced between laughter and tears. Very truly yours

260: TO ROY JANSEN [23]

[Marion, Virginia, ?late April, 1935]

DEAR ROY JANSEN:

I think the most absorbingly interesting and exciting moment in any writer's life must come at the moment when he, for the first time, knows that he is a real writer. Any professional writer, any Hemingway, Wolfe, Faulkner, Stein, Dreiser, Lewis—I could name a dozen others, prosemen, I mean—will know what I mean. You begin, of course, being not yourself. We all do. There have been so many great ones. "If I could write as that man does." There is, more than likely, some one man you follow slavishly. How magnificently his sentences march. It is like a field being plowed. You are thinking of the man's style, his way of handling words and sentences.

You read everything the man has written, go from him to others. You read, read, read. You live in the world of books. It is only after a long time that you know that this is a special world, fed out of the world of reality, but not of the world of reality.

You have yourself not yet brought anything up out of the real world into this special world, to make it live there.

And then, if you are ever to be a real writer, your moment comes. I remember mine. I walked along a city street in the snow. I was working at work I hated. Already I had written several long novels. They were not really mine. I was ill, discouraged, broke. I was living in a cheap rooming house. I remember that I went upstairs and into the room. It was very shabby. I had no relatives in the city and few enough friends. I remember how cold the room was. On that afternoon I had heard that I was to lose my job.

I grew desperate, went and threw up a window. I sat by the open window. It began to snow. "I'll catch cold sitting here."

"What do I care?" There was some paper on a small kitchen table I had bought and had brought up into the room. I turned on a light and began to write. I wrote, without looking up—I never

changed a word of it afterwards—a story called "Hands." It was and is a very beautiful story.

I wrote the story and then got up from the table at which I had been sitting, I do not know how long, and went down into the city street. I thought that the snow had suddenly made the city very beautiful. There were people in the street, all sorts of people, shabby ones, brisk young ones, old discouraged ones. I went along wanting to hug people, to shout.

"I've done it. At last, after all these years I've done something." How did I know I had? I did know. I was drunk with a new drunkenness. I cannot remember all of the absurd, foolish things I did that evening. I had a little money in my pocket and went into saloons. I called men up to the bar. "Drink. Drink to me, men." I remember that a prostitute accosted me and that I threw some money toward her and ran away laughing. It must have been several hours before I got the courage to return to my room and read my own story.

It was all right. It was sound. It was real. I went to sit by my desk. A great many others have had such moments. I wonder what they did. I sat there and cried. For the moment I thought the world very wonderful, and I thought also that there was a great deal of wonder in me.

[P.S.] If you use this, will you see that I get copy?

284: TO RALPH CHURCH [24]

[Marion, Virginia, January 13, 1936]

DEAR RALPH:

I began reading Hemmy's *Green Hills of Africa* and thinking of him and a lot of things you said. It's really a lousy book, and the god awful thing is that he doesn't know it and never will.

I rather wonder, Ralph, if it isn't like this. You see, he's got this notion in his head, that you get there by chucking the imaginative world. He got it, of course, because it isn't his world. He can't feel his way around in it, can't get it; so he gets out of it by saying, "The hell with it."

And then you see what he does. He romanticizes what he calls the real world, gets ecstatic about shooting and killing, guts and dung.

There's the whole world of men he can't get at all; so he proclaims his own superiority to it and them.

And then, too, he's too concerned with writing, thinks of it too much like the eternal amateur he is and always will be, the small bad boy. "Kiss my ass," he crie[s] in ecstasy and then is heart-

---

23. **Roy Jansen:** author and proprietor of a bookstore in Pittsburgh.

24. **Ralph Church:** a professor of aesthetics at Cornell University [Ed.].

broken because we don't see any sense to it and won't.

I think it's rather like this, Ralph. Of course every man has a hell of a time. First he has to work to get someone else, usually some woman, out from between him and his canvas. That's a fight. Then he has to try to get himself out. That's the thing Hemmy can't do.

I wonder if I'm right.

342: TO GEORGE FREITAG [25]

[Troutdale, Virginia] August 27, 1938

DEAR GEORGE FREITAG:

It sometimes seems to me that I should prepare a book designed to be read by other and younger writers. This not because of accomplishment on my own part, but because of the experiences, the particular experiences, I have had.

It is so difficult for most of us to realize how fully and completely commercialism enters into the arts. For example, how are you to know that really the opinion of the publisher or the magazine editor in regard to your work, what is a story and what isn't, means nothing? Some of my own stories, for example, that have now become almost American classics, that are put before students in our schools and colleges as examples of good storytelling, were, when first written, when submitted to editors, and when seen by some of the so-called outstanding American critics, declared not stories at all.

It is true they were not nice little packages, wrapped and labeled in the O. Henry manner. They were obviously written by one who did not know the answers. They were simple little tales of happenings, things observed and felt. There were no cowboys or daring wild game hunters. None of the people in the tales got lost in burning deserts or went seeking the North Pole. In my stories I simply stayed at home, among my own people, wherever I happened to be, people in my own street. I think I must, very early, have realized that this was my milieu, that is to say, common everyday American lives. The ordinary beliefs of the people about me, that love lasted indefinitely, that success meant happiness, simply did not seem true to me.

Things were always happening. My eyes began to see, my ears to hear. Most of our American storytelling at that time had concerned only the rich and the well-to-do. I was a storyteller but not yet a writer of stories. As I came of a poor family,

25. **George Freitag:** George Freitag of Canton, Ohio, entered into correspondence with Anderson in the summer of 1938 on problems of the young writer. He published "The Transaction" in the *Atlantic* for August, 1938.

older men were always repeating to me the old saying.

"Get money. Money makes the mare go."

For a time I was a laborer. As I had a passion for fast trotting and pacing horses, I worked about race tracks. I became a soldier, I got into business.

I knew, often quite intensively, Negro swipes about race tracks, small gamblers, prize fighters, common laboring men and women. There was a violent, dangerous man, said to be a killer. One night he walked and talked to me and became suddenly tender. I was forced to realize that all sorts of emotions went on in all sorts of people. A young man who seemed outwardly a very clod suddenly began to run wildly in the moonlight. Once I was walking in a wood and heard the sound of a man weeping. I stopped, looked, and listened. There was a farmer who, because of ill luck, bad weather, and perhaps even poor management, had lost his farm. He had gone to work in a factory in town, but, having a day off, had returned secretly to the fields he loved. He was on his knees by a low fence, looking across the fields in which he had worked from boyhood. He and I were employed at the time in the same factory, and in the factory he was a quiet, smiling man, seemingly satisfied with his lot.

I began to gather these impressions. There was a thing called happiness toward which men were striving. They never got to it. All of life was amazingly accidental. Love, moments of tenderness and despair, came to the poor and the miserable as to the rich and successful.

It began to seem to me that what was most wanted by all people was love, understanding. Our writers, our storytellers, in wrapping life up into neat little packages were only betraying life. It began to seem to me that what I wanted for myself most of all, rather than so-called success, acclaim, to be praised by publishers and editors, was to try to develop, to the top of my bent, my own capacity to feel, see, taste, smell, hear. I wanted, as all men must want, to be a free man, proud of my own manhood, always more and more aware of earth, people, streets, houses, towns, cities. I wanted to take all into myself, digest what I could.

I could not give the answers, and so for a long time when my stories began to appear, at first only in little highbrow magazines, I was almost universally condemned by the critics. My stories, it seemed, had no definite ends. They were not conclusive and did not give the answers, and so I was called vague. "Groping" was a favorite term. It seems I could not get a formula and stick to it. I could not be smart about life. When I wrote my Winesburg stories—for the whole series I got eighty-five dollars—such critics as Mr. Floyd Dell and Henry Mencken, having read them, declared they were not stories. They were merely, it seemed, sketches. They were too vague, too groping. Some ten or fifteen years after Mr. Mencken told me they were not stories, he wrote, telling of how, when he first saw them, he realized their strength and beauty. An imagined conversation between us, that never took place, was spoken about.

And for this I did not blame Mr. Mencken. He thought he had said what he now thinks he said.

There was a time when Mr. Dell was, in a way, my literary father. He and Mr. Waldo Frank had been the first critics to praise some of my earlier work. He was generous and warm. He, with Mr. Theodore Dreiser, was instrumental in getting my first book published. When he saw the Winesburg stories, he, however, condemned them heartily. He was at that time, I believe, deeply under the influence of Maupassant. He advised me to throw the Winesburg stories away. They had no form. They were not stories. A story, he said, must be sharply definite. There must be a beginning and an end. I remember very clearly our conversation. "If you plan to go somewhere on a train and start for the station, but loiter along the way, so that the train comes into the station, stops to discharge and take on passengers, and then goes on its way, and you miss it, don't blame the locomotive engineer," I said. I daresay it was an arrogant saying, but arrogance is also needed.

And so I had written, let us say, the Winesburg stories. The publisher who had already published two of my early novels refused them, but at last I found a publisher. The stories were called unclean, dirty, filthy, but they did grow into the American consciousness, and presently the same critic who had condemned them began asking why I did not write more Winesburg stories.

I am telling you all of this, I assure you, not out of bitterness. I have had a good life, a full, rich life. I am still having a full, rich life. I tell it only to point out to you, a young writer, filled as I am made aware by your letter to me, of tenderness for life, I tell it simply to suggest to you plainly what you are up against. For ten or fifteen years after I had written and published the Winesburg stories, I was compelled to make my living outside of the field of writing. You will find none of my stories even yet in the great popular magazines that pay high prices to writers.

I do not blame the publishers or the editors. Once I was in the editorial rooms of a great magazine. They had asked me in for an editorial conference.

Would it not be possible for them to begin publishing my stories?

I advised against it. "If I were you, I would let Sherwood Anderson alone."

I had been for a long time an employee of a big advertising agency. I wrote the kind of advertisements on which great magazines live.

But I had no illusions about advertising, could have none. I was an advertising writer too long. The men employed with me, the businessmen, many of them successful and even rich, were like the laborers, gamblers, soldiers, race track swipes I had formerly known. Their guards down, often over drinks, they told me the same stories of tangled, thwarted lives.

How could I throw a glamour over such lives? I couldn't.

The Winesburg stories, when first published, were bitterly condemned. They were thrown out of libraries. In one New England town, where three copies of the book had been bought, they were publicly burned in the public square of the town. I remember a letter I once received from a woman. She had been seated beside me at the table of a friend. "Having sat beside you and having read your stories, I feel that I shall never be clean again," she wrote. I got many such letters.

Then a change came. The book found its way into schools and colleges. Critics who had ignored or condemned the book now praised it.

"It's Anderson's best work. It is the height of his genius. He will never again do such work."

People constantly came to me, all saying the same thing.

"But what else of mine have you read since?"

A blank look upon faces.

They had read nothing else of mine. For the most part they were simply repeating, over and over, an old phrase picked up.

Now, I do not think all of this matters. I am one of the fortunate ones. In years when I have been unable to make a living with my pen, there have always been friends ready and willing to help me. There was one man who came to me in a year when I felt, when I knew, that I had done some of my best and truest work, but when, no money coming in, I was trying to sell my house to get money to live.

He wanted, he said, one of my manuscripts. "I will lend you five thousand dollars." He did lend it, knowing I could never return his money, but he did not deceive me. He had an affection for me as I had for him. He wanted me to continue to live in freedom. I have found this sort of thing among the rich as well as the poor. My house where I live is filled with beautiful things, all given to me. I live well enough. I have no quarrel with life.

And I am only writing all of this to you to prepare you. In a world controlled by business why should we not expect businessmen to think first of business?

And do bear in mind that publishers of books, of magazines, of newspapers are, first of all, businessmen. They are compelled to be.

And do not blame them when they do not buy your stories. Do not be romantic. There is no golden key that unlocks all doors. There is only the joy of living as richly as you can, always feeling more, absorbing more, and, if you are by nature a teller of tales, the realization that by faking, trying to give people what they think they want, you are in danger of dulling and in the end quite destroying what may be your own road into life.

There will remain for you, to be sure, the matter of making a living, and I am sorry to say to say to you that in the solution of that problem, for you and other young writers, I am not interested. That, alas, is your own problem. I am interested only in what you may be able to contribute to the advancement of our mutual craft.

But why not call it an art? That is what it is.

Did you ever hear of an artist who had an easy road to travel in life?

F. Scott Fitzgerald

THE RICH BOY

◇

❲ WRITTEN shortly after *The Great Gatsby*, "The Rich Boy" was first published in *Red Book Magazine* in January and February of 1926. Later that year it proved to be one of the finest stories in the collection called *All The Sad Young Men*. The sad fate of Anson Hunter, who is so far "in" that he is in fact alone, should be contrasted with that of Jay Gatsby, the outsider, who cannot get "in" at all, and is in a way equally alone. "The Rich Boy" is Fitzgerald's classic statement of his lifelong concern with "the very rich."

◇

BEGIN with an individual, and before you know it you find that you have created a type; begin with a type, and you find that you have created—nothing. That is because we are all queer fish, queerer behind our faces and voices than we want any one to know or than we know ourselves. When I hear a man proclaiming himself an "average, honest, open fellow," I feel pretty sure that he has some definite and perhaps terrible abnormality which he has agreed to conceal—and his protestation of being average and honest and open is his way of reminding himself of his misprision.

There are no types, no plurals. There is a rich boy, and this is his and not his brothers' story. All my life I have lived among his brothers but this one has been my friend. Besides, if I wrote about his brothers I should have to begin by attacking all the lies that the poor have told about the rich and the rich have told about themselves—such a wild structure they have erected that when we pick up a book about the rich, some instinct prepares us for unreality. Even the intelligent and impassioned reporters of life have made the country of the rich as unreal as fairy-land.

Let me tell you about the very rich. They are different from you and me. They possess and enjoy early, and it does something to them, makes them soft where we are hard, and cynical where we are trustful, in a way that, unless you were born rich, it is very difficult to understand. They think, deep in their hearts, that they are better than we are because we had to discover the compensations and refuges of life for ourselves. Even when they enter deep into our world or sink below us, they still think that they are better than we are. They are different. The only way I can describe young Anson Hunter is to approach him as if he were a foreigner and cling stubbornly to my point of view. If I accept his for a moment I am lost—I have nothing to show but a preposterous movie.

II

ANSON was the eldest of six children who would some day divide a fortune of fifteen million dollars, and he reached the age of reason—is it seven? —at the beginning of the century when daring young women were already gliding along Fifth Avenue in electric "mobiles." In those days he and his brother had an English governess who spoke the language very clearly and crisply and well, so that the two boys grew to speak as she did—their words and sentences were all crisp and clear and not run together as ours are. They didn't talk exactly like English children but acquired an accent that is peculiar to fashionable people in the city of New York.

In the summer the six children were moved from the house on 71st Street to a big estate in northern Connecticut. It was not a fashionable locality—Anson's father wanted to delay as long as possible his children's knowledge of that side of life. He was a man somewhat superior to his class, which composed New York society, and to his period, which was the snobbish and formalized vulgarity of the Gilded Age, and he wanted his sons to learn habits of concentration and have sound constitutions and grow up into right-living and successful men. He and his wife kept an eye on them as well as they were able until the two older boys went away to school, but in huge establishments this is difficult—it was much simpler in the series of small and medium-sized houses in which my own youth was spent—I was never far out of the reach of my mother's voice, of the sense of her presence, her approval or disapproval.

Anson's first sense of his superiority came to him when he realized the half-grudging American deference that was paid to him in the Connecticut village. The parents of the boys he played with always inquired after his father and mother, and were vaguely excited when their own children were asked to the Hunters' house. He accepted this as the natural state of things, and a sort of impatience with all groups of which he was not the centre—in money, in position, in authority—remained with him for the rest of his life. He disdained to struggle with other boys for precedence—he expected it to be given him freely, and when it wasn't he withdrew into his family. His family was sufficient, for in the East money is still a somewhat feudal thing, a clan-forming thing. In the snobbish West, money separates families to form "sets."

At eighteen, when he went to New Haven, Anson was tall and thick-set, with a clear complexion and a healthy color from the ordered life he had led in school. His hair was yellow and grew in a funny way on his head, his nose was beaked— these two things kept him from being handsome— but he had a confident charm and a certain brusque style, and the upper-class men who passed him on the street knew without being told that he was a rich boy and had gone to one of the best schools. Nevertheless, his very superiority kept him from being a success in college—the independence was

mistaken for egotism, and the refusal to accept Yale standards with the proper awe seemed to belittle all those who had. So, long before he graduated, he began to shift the centre of his life to New York.

He was at home in New York—there was his own house with "the kind of servants you can't get any more"—and his own family, of which, because of his good humor and a certain ability to make things go, he was rapidly becoming the centre, and the débutante parties, and the correct manly world of the men's clubs, and the occasional wild spree with the gallant girls whom New Haven only knew from the fifth row. His aspirations were conventional enough—they included even the irreproachable shadow he would some day marry, but they differed from the aspirations of the majority of young men in that there was no mist over them, none of that quality which is variously known as "idealism" or "illusion." Anson accepted without reservation the world of high finance and high extravagance, of divorce and dissipation, of snobbery and of privilege. Most of our lives end as a compromise—it was as a compromise that his life began.

He and I first met in the late summer of 1917 when he was just out of Yale, and, like the rest of us, was swept up into the systematized hysteria of the war. In the blue-green uniform of the naval aviation he came down to Pensacola, where the hotel orchestras played "I'm sorry, dear," and we young officers danced with the girls. Every one liked him, and though he ran with the drinkers and wasn't an especially good pilot, even the instructors treated him with a certain respect. He was always having long talks with them in his confident, logical voice—talks which ended by his getting himself, or, more frequently, another officer, out of some impending trouble. He was convivial, bawdy, robustly avid for pleasure, and we were all surprised when he fell in love with a conservative and rather proper girl.

Her name was Paula Legendre, a dark, serious beauty from somewhere in California. Her family kept a winter residence just outside of town, and in spite of her primness she was enormously popular; there is a large class of men whose egotism can't endure humor in a woman. But Anson wasn't that sort, and I couldn't understand the attraction of her "sincerity"—that was the thing to say about her—for his keen and somewhat sardonic mind.

Nevertheless, they fell in love—and on her terms. He no longer joined the twilight gathering at the De Sota bar, and whenever they were seen together they were engaged in a long, serious dialogue, which must have gone on several weeks.

Long afterward he told me that it was not about anything in particular but was composed on both sides of immature and even meaningless statements—the emotional content that gradually came to fill it grew up not out of the words but out of its enormous seriousness. It was a sort of hypnosis. Often it was interrupted, giving way to that emasculated humor we call fun; when they were alone it was resumed again, solemn, low-keyed, and pitched so as to give each other a sense of unity in feeling and thought. They came to resent any interruptions of it, to be unresponsive to facetiousness about life, even to the mild cynicism of their contemporaries. They were only happy when the dialogue was going on, and its seriousness bathed them like the amber glow of an open fire. Toward the end there came an interruption they did not resent—it began to be interrupted by passion.

Oddly enough, Anson was as engrossed in the dialogue as she was and as profoundly affected by it, yet at the same time aware that on his side much was insincere, and on hers much were merely simple. At first, too, he despised her emotional simplicity as well, but with his love her nature deepened and blossomed, and he could despise it no longer. He felt that if he could enter into Paula's warm safe life he would be happy. The long preparation of the dialogue removed any constraint—he taught her some of what he had learned from more adventurous women, and she responded with a rapt holy intensity. One evening after a dance they agreed to marry, and he wrote a long letter about her to his mother. The next day Paula told him that she was rich, that she had a personal fortune of nearly a million dollars.

III

IT WAS exactly as if they could say "Neither of us has anything: we shall be poor together"—just as delightful that they should be rich instead. It gave them the same communion of adventure. Yet when Anson got leave in April, and Paula and her mother accompanied him North, she was impressed with the standing of his family in New York and with the scale on which they lived. Alone with Anson for the first time in the rooms where he had played as a boy, she was filled with a comfortable emotion, as though she were pre-eminently safe and taken care of. The pictures of Anson in a skull cap at his first school, of Anson on horseback with the sweetheart of a mysterious forgotten summer, of Anson in a gay group of ushers and bridesmaids at a wedding, made her jealous of his life apart from her in the past, and so completely did his authoritative person seem to sum up and typify these possessions of his that she was inspired with the idea of being married immediately and returning to Pensacola as his wife.

But an immediate marriage wasn't discussed—even the engagement was to be secret until after the war. When she realized that only two days of his leave remained, her dissatisfaction crystallized in the intention of making him as unwilling to wait as she was. They were driving to the country for dinner, and she determined to force the issue that night.

Now a cousin of Paula's was staying with them at the Ritz, a severe, bitter girl who loved Paula but was somewhat jealous of her impressive engagement, and as Paula was late in dressing, the cousin, who wasn't going to the party, received Anson in the parlor of the suite.

Anson had met friends at five o'clock and drunk freely and indiscreetly with them for an hour. He left the Yale Club at a proper time, and his mother's chauffeur drove him to the Ritz, but his usual capacity was not in evidence, and the impact of the steam-heated sitting-room made him suddenly dizzy. He knew it, and he was both amused and sorry.

Paula's cousin was twenty-five, but she was exceptionally naïve, and at first failed to realize what was up. She had never met Anson before, and she was surprised when he mumbled strange information and nearly fell off his chair, but until Paula appeared it didn't occur to her that what she had taken for the odor of a dry-cleaned uniform was really whiskey. But Paula understood as soon as she appeared; her only thought was to get Anson away before her mother saw him, and at the look in her eyes the cousin understood too.

When Paula and Anson descended to the limousine they found two men inside, both asleep; they were the men with whom he had been drinking at the Yale Club, and they were also going to the party. He had entirely forgotten their presence in the car. On the way to Hempstead they awoke and sang. Some of the songs were rough, and though Paula tried to reconcile herself to the fact that Anson had few verbal inhibitions, her lips tightened with shame and distaste.

Back at the hotel the cousin, confused and agitated, considered the incident, and then walked into Mrs. Legendre's bedroom, saying: "Isn't he funny?"

"Who is funny?"

"Why—Mr. Hunter. He seemed so funny."

Mrs. Legendre looked at her sharply.

"How is he funny?"

"Why, he said he was French. I didn't know he was French."

"That's absurd. You must have misunderstood." She smiled: "It was a joke."

The cousin shook her head stubbornly.

"No. He said he was brought up in France. He said he couldn't speak any English, and that's why he couldn't talk to me. And he couldn't!"

Mrs. Legendre looked away with impatience just as the cousin added thoughtfully, "Perhaps it was because he was so drunk," and walked out of the room.

This curious report was true. Anson, finding his voice thick and uncontrollable, had taken the unusual refuge of announcing that he spoke no English. Years afterward he used to tell that part of the story, and he invariably communicated the uproarious laughter which the memory aroused in him.

Five times in the next hour Mrs. Legendre tried to get Hempstead on the phone. When she succeeded, there was a ten-minute delay before she heard Paula's voice on the wire.

"Cousin Jo told me Anson was intoxicated."

"Oh, no. . . ."

"Oh, yes. Cousin Jo says he was intoxicated. He told her he was French, and fell off his chair and behaved as if he was very intoxicated. I don't want you to come home with him."

"Mother, he's all right! Please don't worry about——"

"But I do worry. I think it's dreadful. I want you to promise me not to come home with him."

"I'll take care of it, mother. . . ."

"I don't want you to come home with him."

"All right, mother. Good-by."

"Be sure now, Paula. Ask some one to bring you."

Deliberately Paula took the receiver from her ear and hung it up. Her face was flushed with helpless annoyance. Anson was stretched asleep out in a bedroom up-stairs, while the dinner-party below was proceeding lamely toward conclusion.

The hour's drive had sobered him somewhat—his arrival was merely hilarious—and Paula hoped that the evening was not spoiled, after all, but two imprudent cocktails before dinner completed the disaster. He talked boisterously and somewhat offensively to the party at large for fifteen minutes, and then slid silently under the table; like a man in an old print—but, unlike an old print, it was rather horrible without being at all quaint. None of the young girls present remarked upon the incident—it seemed to merit only silence. His uncle and two other men carried him up-stairs, and it was just after this that Paula was called to the phone.

An hour later Anson awoke in a fog of nervous agony, through which he perceived after a moment the figure of his uncle Robert standing by the door.

". . . I said are you better?"

"What?"

"Do you feel better, old man?"

"Terrible," said Anson.

"I'm going to try you on another bromo-seltzer. If you can hold it down, it'll do you good to sleep."

With an effort Anson slid his legs from the bed and stood up.

"I'm all right," he said dully.

"Take it easy."

"I thin' if you gave me a glassbrandy I could go down-stairs."

"Oh, no——"

"Yes, that's the only thin'. I'm all right now. . . . I suppose I'm in Dutch dow' there."

"They know you're a little under the weather," said his uncle deprecatingly. "But don't worry about it. Schuyler didn't even get here. He passed away in the locker-room over at the Links."

Indifferent to any opinion, except Paula's, Anson was nevertheless determined to save the débris of the evening, but when after a cold bath he made his appearance most of the party had already left. Paula got up immediately to go home.

In the limousine the old serious dialogue began. She had known that he drank, she admitted, but she had never expected anything like this—it seemed to her that perhaps they were not suited to each other, after all. Their ideas about life were too different, and so forth. When she finished speaking, Anson spoke in turn, very soberly. Then Paula said she'd have to think it over; she wouldn't decide to-night; she was not angry but she was terribly sorry. Nor would she let him come into the hotel with her, but just before she got out of the car she leaned and kissed him unhappily on the cheek.

The next afternoon Anson had a long talk with Mrs. Legendre while Paula sat listening in silence. It was agreed that Paula was to brood over the incident for a proper period and then, if mother and daughter thought it best, they would follow Anson to Pensacola. On his part he apologized with sincerity and dignity—that was all; with every card in her hand Mrs. Legendre was unable to establish any advantage over him. He made no promises, showed no humility, only delivered a few serious comments on life which brought him off with rather a moral superiority at the end. When they came South three weeks later, neither Anson in his satisfaction nor Paula in her relief at the reunion realized that the psychological moment had passed forever.

IV

HE DOMINATED and attracted her, and at the same time filled her with anxiety. Confused by his mixture of solidity and self-indulgence, of sentiment and cynicism—incongruities which her gentle mind was unable to resolve—Paula grew to think of him as two alternating personalities. When she saw him alone, or at a formal party, or with his casual inferiors, she felt a tremendous pride in his strong, attractive presence, the paternal, understanding stature of his mind. In other company she became uneasy when what had been a fine imperviousness to mere gentility showed its other face. The other face was gross, humorous, reckless of everything but pleasure. It startled her mind temporarily away from him, even led her into a short covert experiment with an old beau, but it was no use—after four months of Anson's enveloping vitality there was an anæmic pallor in all other men.

In July he was ordered abroad, and their tenderness and desire reached a crescendo. Paula considered a last-minute marriage—decided against it only because there were always cocktails on his breath now, but the parting itself made her physically ill with grief. After his departure she wrote him long letters of regret for the days of love they had missed by waiting. In August Anson's plane slipped down into the North Sea. He was pulled onto a destroyer after a night in the water and sent to hospital with pneumonia; the armistice was signed before he was finally sent home.

Then, with every opportunity given back to them, with no material obstacle to overcome, the secret weavings of their temperaments came between them, drying up their kisses and their tears, making their voices less loud to one another, muffling the intimate chatter of their hearts until the old communication was only possible by letters, from far away. One afternoon a society reporter waited for two hours in the Hunters' house for a confirmation of their engagement. Anson denied it; nevertheless an early issue carried the report as a leading paragraph—they were "constantly seen together at Southampton, Hot Springs, and Tuxedo Park." But the serious dialogue had turned a corner into a long-sustained quarrel, and the affair was almost played out. Anson got drunk flagrantly and missed an engagement with her, whereupon Paula made certain behavioristic demands. His despair was helpless before his pride and his knowledge of himself: the engagement was definitely broken.

"Dearest," said their letters now, "Dearest, Dearest, when I wake up in the middle of the night and realize that after all it was not to be, I feel that I want to die. I can't go on living any more. Perhaps when we meet this summer we may talk things over and decide differently—we were so excited and sad that day, and I don't feel I can live all my life without you. You speak of other people. Don't you know there are no other people for me, but only you. . . ."

But as Paula drifted here and there around the East she would sometimes mention her gaieties to make him wonder. Anson was too acute to wonder. When he saw a man's name in her letters he felt more sure of her and a little disdainful—he was always superior to such things. But he still hoped that they would some day marry.

Meanwhile he plunged vigorously into all the movement and glitter of post-bellum New York, entering a brokerage house, joining half a dozen clubs, dancing late, and moving in three worlds—his own world, the world of young Yale graduates, and that section of the half-world which rests one end on Broadway. But there was always a thorough and infractible eight hours devoted to his work in Wall Street, where the combination of his influential family connection, his sharp intelligence, and his abundance of sheer physical energy brought him almost immediately forward. He had one of those invaluable minds with partitions in it; sometimes he appeared at his office refreshed by less than an hour's sleep, but such occurrences were rare. So early as 1920 his income in salary and commissions exceeded twelve thousand dollars.

As the Yale tradition slipped into the past he became more and more of a popular figure among his classmates in New York, more popular than he had ever been in college. He lived in a great house, and had the means of introducing young men into other great houses. Moreover, his life already seemed secure, while theirs, for the most part, had arrived again at precarious beginnings. They commenced to turn to him for amusement and escape, and Anson responded readily, taking pleasure in helping people and arranging their affairs.

There were no men in Paula's letters now, but a note of tenderness ran through them that had not been there before. From several sources he heard that she had "a heavy beau," Lowell Thayer, a Bostonian of wealth and position, and though he was sure she still loved him, it made him uneasy to think that he might lose her, after all. Save for one unsatisfactory day she had not been in New York for almost five months, and as the rumors multiplied he became increasingly anxious to see her. In February he took his vacation and went down to Florida.

Palm Beach sprawled plump and opulent between the sparkling sapphire of Lake Worth, flawed here and there by house-boats at anchor, and the great turquoise bar of the Atlantic Ocean. The huge bulks of the Breakers and the Royal Poinciana rose as twin paunches from the bright level of the sand, and around them clustered the Dancing Glade, Bradley's House of Chance, and a dozen modistes and milliners with goods at triple prices from New York. Upon the trellised veranda of the Breakers two hundred women stepped right, stepped left, wheeled, and slid in that then celebrated calisthenic known as the double-shuffle, while in half-time to the music two thousand bracelets clicked up and down on two hundred arms.

At the Everglades Club after dark Paula and Lowell Thayer and Anson and a casual fourth played bridge with hot cards. It seemed to Anson that her kind, serious face was wan and tired—she had been around now for four, five, years. He had known her for three.

"Two spades."

"Cigarette? . . . Oh, I beg your pardon. By me."

"By."

"I'll double three spades."

There were a dozen tables of bridge in the room, which was filling up with smoke. Anson's eyes met Paula's, held them persistently even when Thayer's glance fell between them. . . .

"What was bid?" he asked abstractedly.

"Rose of Washington Square"

sang the young people in the corners:

> *"I'm withering there
> In basement air——"*

The smoke banked like fog, and the opening of a door filled the room with blown swirls of ectoplasm. Little Bright Eyes streaked past the tables seeking Mr. Conan Doyle among the Englishmen who were posing as Englishmen about the lobby.

"You could cut it with a knife."

". . . cut it with a knife."

". . . a knife."

At the end of the rubber Paula suddenly got up and spoke to Anson in a tense, low voice. With scarcely a glance at Lowell Thayer, they walked out the door and descended a long flight of stone steps—in a moment they were walking hand in hand along the moonlit beach.

"Darling, darling. . . ." They embraced recklessly, passionately, in a shadow. . . . Then Paula drew back her face to let his lips say what she wanted to hear—she could feel the words forming as they kissed again. . . . Again she broke away, listening, but as he pulled her close once more she realized that he had said nothing—only *"Darling! Darling!"* in that deep, sad whisper that always made her cry. Humbly, obediently, her emotions yielded to him and the tears streamed down her face, but her heart kept on crying: "Ask me—oh, Anson, dearest, ask me!"

"Paula. . . . *Paula!*"

The words wrung her heart like hands, and Anson, feeling her tremble, knew that emotion was enough. He need say no more, commit their destinies to no practical enigma. Why should he, when he might hold her so, biding his own time, for another year—forever? He was considering them both, her more than himself. For a moment, when she said suddenly that she must go back to her hotel, he hesitated, thinking, first, "This is the moment, after all," and then: "No, let it wait—she is mine. . . ."

He had forgotten that Paula too was worn away inside with the strain of three years. Her mood passed forever in the night.

He went back to New York next morning filled with a certain restless dissatisfaction. Late in April, without warning, he received a telegram from Bar Harbor in which Paula told him that she was engaged to Lowell Thayer, and that they would be married immediately in Boston. What he never really believed could happen had happened at last.

Anson filled himself with whiskey that morning, and going to the office, carried on his work without a break—rather with a fear of what would happen if he stopped. In the evening he went out as usual, saying nothing of what had occurred; he was cordial, humorous, unabstracted. But one thing he could not help—for three days, in any place, in any company, he would suddenly bend his head into his hands and cry like a child.

V

IN 1922 when Anson went abroad with the junior partner to investigate some London loans, the journey intimated that he was to be taken into the firm. He was twenty-seven now, a little heavy without being definitely stout, and with a manner older than his years. Old people and young people liked him and trusted him, and mothers felt safe when their daughters were in his charge, for he had a way, when he came into a room, of putting himself on a footing with the oldest and most conservative people there. "You and I," he seemed to say, "we're solid. We understand."

He had an instinctive and rather charitable knowledge of the weaknesses of men and women, and, like a priest, it made him the more concerned for the maintenance of outward forms. It was typical of him that every Sunday morning he taught in a fashionable Episcopal Sunday-school —even though a cold shower and a quick change into a cutaway coat were all that separated him from the wild night before.

After his father's death he was the practical head of his family, and, in effect, guided the destinies of the younger children. Through a complication his authority did not extend to his father's estate, which was administrated by his Uncle Robert, who was the horsey member of the family, a good-natured, hard-drinking member of that set which centres about Wheatley Hills.

Uncle Robert and his wife, Edna, had been great friends of Anson's youth, and the former was disappointed when his nephew's superiority failed to take a horsey form. He backed him for a city club which was the most difficult in America to enter—one could only join if one's family had "helped to build up New York" (or, in other words, were rich before 1880)—and when Anson, after his election, neglected it for the Yale Club, Uncle Robert gave him a little talk on the subject. But when on top of that Anson declined to enter Robert Hunter's own conservative and somewhat neglected brokerage house, his manner grew cooler. Like a primary teacher who has taught all he knew, he slipped out of Anson's life.

There were so many friends in Anson's life— scarcely one for whom he had not done some unusual kindness and scarcely one whom he did not occasionally embarrass by his bursts of rough conversation or his habit of getting drunk whenever and however he liked. It annoyed him when any one else blundered in that regard—about his own lapses he was always humorous. Odd things happened to him and he told them with infectious laughter.

I was working in New York that spring, and I used to lunch with him at the Yale Club, which my university was sharing until the completion of our own. I had read of Paula's marriage, and one afternoon, when I asked him about her, something moved him to tell me the story. After that he frequently invited me to family dinners at his house and behaved as though there was a special relation between us, as though with his confidence a little of that consuming memory had passed into me.

I found that despite the trusting mothers, his attitude toward girls was not indiscriminately pro-

tective. It was up to the girl—if she showed an inclination toward looseness, she must take care of herself, even with him.

"Life," he would explain sometimes, "has made a cynic of me."

By life he meant Paula. Sometimes, especially when he was drinking, it became a little twisted in his mind, and he thought that she had callously thrown him over.

This "cynicism," or rather his realization that naturally fast girls were not worth sparing, led to his affair with Dolly Karger. It wasn't his only affair in those years, but it came nearest to touching him deeply, and it had a profound effect upon his attitude toward life.

Dolly was the daughter of a notorious "publicist" who had married into society. She herself grew up into the Junior League, came out at the Plaza, and went to the Assembly; and only a few old families like the Hunters could question whether or not she "belonged," for her picture was often in the papers, and she had more enviable attention than many girls who undoubtedly did. She was dark-haired, with carmine lips and a high, lovely color, which she concealed under pinkish-gray powder all through the first year out, because high color was unfashionable—Victorian-pale was the thing to be. She wore black, severe suits and stood with her hands in her pockets leaning a little forward, with a humorous restraint on her face. She danced exquisitely—better than anything she liked to dance—better than anything except making love. Since she was ten she had always been in love, and, usually, with some boy who didn't respond to her. Those who did—and there were many—bored her after a brief encounter, but for her failures she reserved the warmest spot in her heart. When she met them she would always try once more—sometimes she succeeded, more often she failed.

It never occurred to this gypsy of the unattainable that there was a certain resemblance in those who refused to love her—they shared a hard intuition that saw through to her weakness, not a weakness of emotion but a weakness of rudder. Anson perceived this when he first met her, less than a month after Paula's marriage. He was drinking rather heavily, and he pretended for a week that he was falling in love with her. Then he dropped her abruptly and forgot—immediately he took up the commanding position in her heart.

Like so many girls of that day Dolly was slackly and indiscreetly wild. The unconventionality of a slightly older generation had been simply one facet of a post-war movement to discredit obsolete manners—Dolly's was both older and shabbier, and she saw in Anson the two extremes which the emotionally shiftless woman seeks, an abandon to indulgence alternating with a protective strength. In his character she felt both the sybarite and the solid rock, and these two satisfied every need of her nature.

She felt that it was going to be difficult, but she mistook the reason—she thought that Anson and his family expected a more spectacular marriage, but she guessed immediately that her advantage lay in his tendency to drink.

They met at the large débutante dances, but as her infatuation increased they managed to be more and more together. Like most mothers, Mrs. Karger believed that Anson was exceptionally reliable, so she allowed Dolly to go with him to distant country clubs and suburban houses without inquiring closely into their activities or questioning her explanations when they came in late. At first these explanations might have been accurate, but Dolly's worldly ideas of capturing Anson were soon engulfed in the rising sweep of her emotion. Kisses in the back of taxis and motor-cars were no longer enough; they did a curious thing:

They dropped out of their world for a while and made another world just beneath it where Anson's tippling and Dolly's irregular hours would be less noticed and commented on. It was composed, this world, of varying elements—several of Anson's Yale friends and their wives, two or three young brokers and bond salesmen and a handful of unattached men, fresh from college, with money and a propensity to dissipation. What this world lacked in spaciousness and scale it made up for by allowing them a liberty that it scarcely permitted itself. Moreover, it centred around them and permitted Dolly the pleasure of a faint condescension—a pleasure which Anson, whose whole life was a condescension from the certitudes of his childhood, was unable to share.

He was not in love with her, and in the long feverish winter of their affair he frequently told her so. In the spring he was weary—he wanted to renew his life at some other source—moreover, he saw that either he must break with her now or accept the responsibility of a definite seduction. Her family's encouraging attitude precipitated his decision—one evening when Mr. Karger knocked discreetly at the library door to announce that he had left a bottle of old brandy in the dining-room, Anson felt that life was hemming him in. That night he wrote her a short letter in which he told her that he was going on his vacation, and that in view of all the circumstances they had better meet no more.

It was June. His family had closed up the house and gone to the country, so he was living temporarily at the Yale Club. I had heard about his affair with Dolly as it developed—accounts salted with humor, for he despised unstable women, and granted them no place in the social edifice in which he believed—and when he told me that night that he was definitely breaking with her I was glad. I had seen Dolly here and there, and each time with a feeling of pity at the hopelessness of her struggle, and of shame at knowing so much about her that I had no right to know. She was what is known as "a pretty little thing," but there was a certain recklessness which rather fascinated me. Her dedication to the goddess of waste would have been less obvious had she been less spirited—she would most certainly throw herself away, but I was glad when I heard that the sacrifice would not be consummated in my sight.

Anson was going to leave the letter of farewell at her house next morning. It was one of the few houses left open in the Fifth Avenue district, and he knew that the Kargers, acting upon erroneous information from Dolly, had foregone a trip abroad to give their daughter her chance. As he stepped out the door of the Yale Club into Madison Avenue the postman passed him, and he followed back inside. The first letter that caught his eye was in Dolly's hand.

He knew what it would be—a lonely and tragic monologue, full of the reproaches he knew, the invoked memories, the "I wonder if's"—all the immemorial intimacies that he had communicated to Paula Legendre in what seemed another age. Thumbing over some bills, he brought it on top again and opened it. To his surprise it was a short, somewhat formal note, which said that Dolly would be unable to go the country with him for the week-end, because Perry Hull from Chicago had unexpectedly come to town. It added that Anson had brought this on himself: "—if I felt that you loved me as I love you I would go with you at any time, any place, but Perry is *so* nice, and he so much wants me to marry him———"

Anson smiled contemptuously—he had had experience with such decoy epistles. Moreover, he knew how Dolly had labored over this plan, probably sent for the faithful Perry and calculated the time of his arrival—even labored over the note so that it would make him jealous without driving him away. Like most compromises, it had neither force nor vitality but only a timorous despair.

Suddenly he was angry. He sat down in the lobby and read it again. Then he went to the phone, called Dolly and told her in his clear, compelling voice that he had received her note and would call for her at five o'clock as they had previously planned. Scarcely waiting for the pre-tended uncertainty of her "Perhaps I can see you for an hour," he hung up the receiver and went down to his office. On the way he tore his own letter into bits and dropped it in the street.

He was not jealous—she meant nothing to him —but at her pathetic ruse everything stubborn and self-indulgent in him came to the surface. It was a presumption from a mental inferior and it could not be overlooked. If she wanted to know to whom she belonged she would see.

He was on the door-step at quarter past five. Dolly was dressed for the street, and he listened in silence to the paragraph of "I can only see you for an hour," which she had begun on the phone.

"Put on your hat, Dolly," he said, "we'll take a walk."

They strolled up Madison Avenue and over to Fifth while Anson's shirt dampened upon his portly body in the deep heat. He talked little, scold-ing her, making no love to her, but before they had walked six blocks she was his again, apologizing for the note, offering not to see Perry at all as an atonement, offering anything. She thought that he had come because he was beginning to love her.

"I'm hot," he said when they reached 71st Street. "This is a winter suit. If I stop by the house and change, would you mind waiting for me down-stairs? I'll only be a minute."

She was happy; the intimacy of his being hot, of any physical fact about him, thrilled her. When they came to the iron-grated door and Anson took out his key she experienced a sort of delight.

Down-stairs it was dark, and after he ascended in the lift Dolly raised a curtain and looked out through opaque lace at the houses over the way. She heard the lift machinery stop, and with the notion of teasing him pressed the button that brought it down. Then on what was more than an impulse she got into it and sent it up to what she guessed was his floor.

"Anson," she called, laughing a little.

"Just a minute," he answered from his bed-room . . . then after a brief delay: "Now you can come in."

He had changed and was buttoning his vest. "This is my room," he said lightly. "How do you like it?"

She caught sight of Paula's picture on the wall and stared at it in fascination, just as Paula had stared at the pictures of Anson's childish sweet-hearts five years before. She knew something about Paula—sometimes she tortured herself with fragments of the story.

Suddenly she came close to Anson, raising her arms. They embraced. Outside the area window a soft artificial twilight already hovered, though the sun was still bright on a back roof across the way. In half an hour the room would be quite dark. The uncalculated opportunity overwhelmed them, made them both breathless, and they clung more closely. It was eminent, inevitable. Still holding one another, they raised their heads—their eyes fell together upon Paula's picture, staring down at them from the wall.

Suddenly Anson dropped his arms, and sitting down at his desk tried the drawer with a bunch of keys.

"Like a drink?" he asked in a gruff voice.

"No, Anson."

He poured himself half a tumbler of whiskey, swallowed it, and then opened the door into the hall.

"Come on," he said.

Dolly hesitated.

"Anson—I'm going to the country with you to-night, after all. You understand that, don't you?"

"Of course," he answered brusquely.

In Dolly's car they rode on to Long Island, closer in their emotions than they had ever been before. They knew what would happen—not with Paula's face to remind them that something was lacking, but when they were alone in the still, hot, Long Island night they did not care.

The estate in Port Washington where they were to spend the week-end belonged to a cousin of Anson's who had married a Montana copper op-erator. An interminable drive began at the lodge and twisted under imported poplar saplings toward a huge, pink, Spanish house. Anson had often visited there before.

After dinner they danced at the Linx Club. About midnight Anson assured himself that his cousins would not leave before two—then he ex-plained that Dolly was tired; he would take her home and return to the dance later. Trembling a little with excitement, they got into a borrowed car together and drove to Port Washington. As they reached the lodge he stopped and spoke to the night-watchman.

"When are you making a round, Carl?"

"Right away."

"Then you'll be here till everybody's in?"

"Yes, sir."

"All right. Listen: if any automobile, no matter whose it is, turns in at this gate, I want you to phone the house immediately." He put a five-dollar bill into Carl's hand. "Is that clear?"

"Yes, Mr. Anson." Being of the Old World, he neither winked nor smiled. Yet Dolly sat with her face turned slightly away.

Anson had a key. Once inside he poured a drink

for both of them—Dolly left hers untouched—then he ascertained definitely the location of the phone, and found that it was within easy hearing distance of their rooms, both of which were on the first floor.

Five minutes later he knocked at the door of Dolly's room.

"Anson?" He went in, closing the door behind him. She was in bed, leaning up anxiously with elbows on the pillow; sitting beside her he took her in his arms.

"Anson, darling."

He didn't answer.

"Anson. . . . Anson! I love you. . . . Say you love me. Say it now—can't you say it now? Even if you don't mean it?"

He did not listen. Over her head he perceived that the picture of Paula was hanging here upon this wall.

He got up and went close to it. The frame gleamed faintly with thrice-reflected moonlight—within was a blurred shadow of a face that he saw he did not know. Almost sobbing, he turned around and stared with abomination at the little figure on the bed.

"This is all foolishness," he said thickly. "I don't know what I was thinking about. I don't love you and you'd better wait for somebody that loves you. I don't love you a bit, can't you understand?"

His voice broke, and he went hurriedly out. Back in the salon he was pouring himself a drink with uneasy fingers, when the front door opened suddenly, and his cousin came in.

"Why, Anson, I hear Dolly's sick," she began solicitously. "I hear she's sick. . . ."

"It was nothing," he interrupted, raising his voice so that it would carry into Dolly's room. "She was a little tired. She went to bed."

For a long time afterward Anson believed that a protective God sometimes interfered in human affairs. But Dolly Karger, lying awake and staring at the ceiling, never again believed in anything at all.

VI

WHEN Dolly married during the following autumn, Anson was in London on business. Like Paula's marriage, it was sudden, but it affected him in a different way. At first he felt that it was funny, and had an inclination to laugh when he thought of it. Later it depressed him—it made him feel old.

There was something repetitive about it—why, Paula and Dolly had belonged to different generations. He had a foretaste of the sensation of a man of forty who hears that the daughter of an old

flame has married. He wired congratulations and, as was not the case with Paula, they were sincere—he had never really hoped that Paula would be happy.

When he returned to New York, he was made a partner in the firm, and, as his responsibilities increased, he had less time on his hands. The refusal of a life-insurance company to issue him a policy made such an impression on him that he stopped drinking for a year, and claimed that he felt better physically, though I think he missed the convivial recounting of those Celliniesque adventures which, in his early twenties, had played such a part of his life. But he never abandoned the Yale Club. He was a figure there, a personality, and the tendency of his class, who were now seven years out of college, to drift away to more sober haunts was checked by his presence.

His day was never too full nor his mind too weary to give any sort of aid to any one who asked it. What had been done at first through pride and superiority had become a habit and a passion. And there was always something—a younger brother in trouble at New Haven, a quarrel to be patched up between a friend and his wife, a position to be found for this man, an investment for that. But his specialty was the solving of problems for young married people. Young married people fascinated him and their apartments were almost sacred to him—he knew the story of their love-affair, advised them where to live and how, and remembered their babies' names. Toward young wives his attitude was circumspect: he never abused the trust which their husbands—strangely enough in view of his unconcealed irregularities—invariably reposed in him.

He came to take a vicarious pleasure in happy marriages, and to be inspired to an almost equally pleasant melancholy by those that went astray. Not a season passed that he did not witness the collapse of an affair that perhaps he himself had fathered. When Paula was divorced and almost immediately remarried to another Bostonian, he talked about her to me all one afternoon. He would never love any one as he had loved Paula, but he insisted that he no longer cared.

"I'll never marry," he came to say; "I've seen too much of it, and I know a happy marriage is a very rare thing. Besides, I'm too old."

But he did believe in marriage. Like all men who spring from a happy and successful marriage, he believed in it passionately—nothing he had seen would change his belief, his cynicism dissolved upon it like air. But he did really believe he was too old. At twenty-eight he began to accept with equanimity the prospect of marrying without romantic love; he resolutely chose a New York girl of his own class, pretty, intelligent, congenial, above reproach—and set about falling in love with her. The things he had said to Paula with sincerity, to other girls with grace, he could no longer say at all without smiling, or with the force necessary to convince.

"When I'm forty," he told his friends, "I'll be ripe. I'll fall for some chorus girl like the rest."

Nevertheless, he persisted in his attempt. His mother wanted to see him married, and he could now well afford it—he had a seat on the Stock Exchange, and his earned income came to twenty-five thousand a year. The idea was agreeable: when his friends—he spent most of his time with the set he and Dolly had evolved—closed themselves in behind domestic doors at night, he no longer rejoiced in his freedom. He even wondered if he should have married Dolly. Not even Paula had loved him more, and he was learning the rarity, in a single life, of encountering true emotion.

Just as this mood began to creep over him a disquieting story reached his ear. His aunt Edna, a woman just this side of forty, was carrying on an open intrigue with a dissolute, hard-drinking young man named Cary Sloane. Every one knew of it except Anson's Uncle Robert, who for fifteen years had talked long in clubs and taken his wife for granted.

Anson heard the story again and again with increasing annoyance. Something of his old feeling for his uncle came back to him, a feeling that was more than personal, a reversion toward that family solidarity on which he had based his pride. His intuition singled out the essential point of the affair, which was that his uncle shouldn't be hurt. It was his first experiment in unsolicited meddling, but with his knowledge of Edna's character he felt that he could handle the matter better than a district judge or his uncle.

His uncle was in Hot Springs. Anson traced down the sources of the scandal so that there should be no possibility of mistake and then he called Edna and asked her to lunch with him at the Plaza next day. Something in his tone must have frightened her, for she was reluctant, but he insisted, putting off the date until she had no excuse for refusing.

She met him at the appointed time in the Plaza lobby, a lovely, faded, gray-eyed blonde in a coat of Russian sable. Five great rings, cold with diamonds and emeralds, sparkled on her slender hands. It occurred to Anson that it was his father's intelligence and not his uncle's that had earned the fur and the stones, the rich brilliance that buoyed up her passing beauty.

Though Edna scented his hostility, she was unprepared for the directness of his approach.

"Edna, I'm astonished at the way you've been acting," he said in a strong, frank voice. "At first I couldn't believe it."

"Believe what?" she demanded sharply.

"You needn't pretend with me, Edna. I'm talking about Cary Sloane. Aside from any other consideration, I didn't think you could treat Uncle Robert——"

"Now look here, Anson——" she began angrily, but his peremptory voice broke through hers:

"—and your children in such a way. You've been married eighteen years, and you're old enough to know better."

"You can't talk to me like that! You——"

"Yes, I can. Uncle Robert has always been my best friend." He was tremendously moved. He felt a real distress about his uncle, about his three young cousins.

Edna stood up, leaving her crab-flake cocktail untasted.

"This is the silliest thing——"

"Very well, if you won't listen to me I'll go to Uncle Robert and tell him the whole story—he's bound to hear it sooner or later. And afterward I'll go to old Moses Sloane."

Edna faltered back into her chair.

"Don't talk so loud," she begged him. Her eyes blurred with tears. "You have no idea how your voice carries. You might have chosen a less public place to make all these crazy accusations."

He didn't answer.

"Oh, you never liked me, I know," she went on. "You're just taking advantage of some silly gossip to try and break up the only interesting friendship I've ever had. What did I ever do to make you hate me so?"

Still Anson waited. There would be the appeal to his chivalry, then to his pity, finally to his superior sophistication—when he had shouldered his way through all these there would be admissions, and he could come to grips with her. By being silent, by being impervious, by returning constantly to his main weapon, which was his own true emotion, he bullied her into frantic despair as the luncheon hour slipped away. At two o'clock she took out a mirror and a handkerchief, shined away the marks of her tears and powdered the slight hollows where they had lain. She had agreed to meet him at her own house at five.

When he arrived she was stretched on a *chaise-longue* which was covered with cretonne for the summer, and the tears he had called up at luncheon seemed still to be standing in her eyes. Then he was aware of Cary Sloane's dark anxious presence upon the cold hearth.

"What's this idea of yours?" broke out Sloane immediately. "I understand you invited Edna to lunch and then threatened her on the basis of some cheap scandal."

Anson sat down.

"I have no reason to think it's only scandal."

"I hear you're going to take it to Robert Hunter, and to my father."

Anson nodded.

"Either you break it off—or I will," he said.

"What God damned business is it of yours, Hunter?"

"Don't lose your temper, Cary," said Edna nervously. "It's only a question of showing him how absurd——"

"For one thing, it's my name that's being handed around," interrupted Anson. "That's all that concerns you, Cary."

"Edna isn't a member of your family."

"She most certainly is!" His anger mounted. "Why—she owes this house and the rings on her fingers to my father's brains. When Uncle Robert married her she didn't have a penny."

They all looked at the rings as if they had a significant bearing on the situation. Edna made a gesture to take them from her hand.

"I guess they're not the only rings in the world," said Sloane.

"Oh, this is absurd," cried Edna. "Anson, will you listen to me? I've found out how the silly story started. It was a maid I discharged who went right to the Chilicheffs—all these Russians pump things out of their servants and then put a false meaning on them." She brought down her fist angrily on the table: "And after Tom lent them the limousine for a whole month when we were South last winter——"

"Do you see?" demanded Sloane eagerly. "This maid got hold of the wrong end of the thing. She knew that Edna and I were friends, and she carried it to the Chilicheffs. In Russia they assume that if a man and a woman——"

He enlarged the theme to a disquisition upon social relations in the Caucasus.

"If that's the case it better be explained to Uncle Robert," said Anson dryly, "so that when the rumors do reach him he'll know they're not true."

Adopting the method he had followed with Edna at luncheon he let them explain it all away. He knew that they were guilty and that presently they would cross the line from explanation into justification and convict themselves more definitely than he could ever do. By seven they had taken the desperate step of telling him the truth—Robert

Hunter's neglect, Edna's empty life, the casual dalliance that had flamed up into passion—but like so many true stories it had the misfortune of being old, and its enfeebled body beat helplessly against the armor of Anson's will. The threat to go to Sloane's father sealed their helplessness, for the latter, a retired cotton broker out of Alabama, was a notorious fundamentalist who controlled his son by a rigid allowance and the promise that at his next vagary the allowance would stop forever.

They dined at a small French restaurant, and the discussion continued—at one time Sloane resorted to physical threats, a little later they were both imploring him to give them time. But Anson was obdurate. He saw that Edna was breaking up, and that her spirit must not be refreshed by any renewal of their passion.

At two o'clock in a small night-club on 53d Street, Edna's nerves suddenly collapsed, and she cried to go home. Sloane had been drinking heavily all evening, and he was faintly maudlin, leaning on the table and weeping a little with his face in his hands. Quickly Anson gave them his terms. Sloane was to leave town for six months, and he must be gone within forty-eight hours. When he returned there was to be no resumption of the affair, but at the end of a year Edna might, if she wished, tell Robert Hunter that she wanted a divorce and go about it in the usual way.

He paused, gaining confidence from their faces for his final word.

"Or there's another thing you can do," he said slowly, "if Edna wants to leave her children, there's nothing I can do to prevent your running off together."

"I want to go home!" cried Edna again. "Oh, haven't you done enough to us for one day?"

Outside it was dark, save for a blurred glow from Sixth Avenue down the street. In that light those two who had been lovers looked for the last time into each other's tragic faces, realizing that between them there was not enough youth and strength to avert their eternal parting. Sloane walked suddenly off down the street and Anson tapped a dozing taxi-driver on the arm.

It was almost four; there was a patient flow of cleaning water along the ghostly pavement of Fifth Avenue, and the shadows of two night women flitted over the dark façade of St. Thomas's church. Then the desolate shrubbery of Central Park where Anson had often played as a child, and the mounting numbers, significant as names, of the marching streets. This was his city, he thought, where his name had flourished through five generations. No change could alter the permanence of its place here, for change itself was the essential substratum by which he and those of his name identified themselves with the spirit of New York. Resourcefulness and a powerful will—for his threats in weaker hands would have been less than nothing—had beaten the gathering dust from his uncle's name, from the name of his family, from even this shivering figure that sat beside him in the car.

Cary Sloane's body was found next morning on the lower shelf of a pillar of Queensboro Bridge. In the darkness and in his excitement he had thought that it was the water flowing black beneath him, but in less than a second it made no possible difference—unless he had planned to think one last thought of Edna, and call out her name as he struggled feebly in the water.

VII

ANSON never blamed himself for his part in this affair—the situation which brought it about had not been of his making. But the just suffer with the unjust, and he found that his oldest and somehow his most precious friendship was over. He never knew what distorted story Edna told, but he was welcome in his uncle's house no longer.

Just before Christmas Mrs. Hunter retired to a select Episcopal heaven, and Anson became the responsible head of his family. An unmarried aunt who had lived with them for years ran the house, and attempted with helpless inefficiency to chaperone the younger girls. All the children were less self-reliant than Anson, more conventional both in their virtues and in their shortcomings. Mrs. Hunter's death had postponed the début of one daughter and the wedding of another. Also it had taken something deeply material from all of them, for with her passing the quiet, expensive superiority of the Hunters came to an end.

For one thing, the estate, considerably diminished by two inheritance taxes and soon to be divided among six children, was not a notable fortune any more. Anson saw a tendency in his youngest sisters to speak rather respectfully of families that hadn't "existed" twenty years ago. His own feeling of precedence was not echoed in them—sometimes they were conventionally snobbish, that was all. For another thing, this was the last summer they would spend on the Connecticut estate; the clamor against it was too loud: "Who wants to waste the best months of the year shut up in that dead old town?" Reluctantly he yielded—the house would go into the market in the fall, and next summer they would rent a smaller place in Westchester County. It was a step down from the expensive simplicity of his father's idea, and, while

he sympathized with the revolt, it also annoyed him; during his mother's lifetime he had gone up there at least every other week-end—even in the gayest summers.

Yet he himself was part of this change, and his strong instinct for life had turned him in his twenties from the hollow obsequies of that abortive leisure class. He did not see this clearly—he still felt that there was a norm, a standard of society. But there was no norm, it was doubtful if there had ever been a true norm in New York. The few who still paid and fought to enter a particular set succeeded only to find that as a society it scarcely functioned—or, what was more alarming, that the Bohemia from which they fled sat above them at table.

At twenty-nine Anson's chief concern was his own growing loneliness. He was sure now that he would never marry. The number of weddings at which he had officiated as best man or usher was past all counting—there was a drawer at home that bulged with the official neckties of this or that wedding-party, neckties standing for romances that had not endured a year, for couples who had passed completely from his life. Scarf-pins, gold pencils, cuff-buttons, presents from a generation of grooms had passed through his jewel-box and been lost—and with every ceremony he was less and less able to imagine himself in the groom's place. Under his hearty good-will toward all those marriages there was despair about his own.

And as he neared thirty he became not a little depressed at the inroads that marriage, especially lately, had made upon his friendships. Groups of people had a disconcerting tendency to dissolve and disappear. The men from his own college—and it was upon them he had expended the most time and affection—were the most elusive of all. Most of them were drawn deep into domesticity, two were dead, one lived abroad, one was in Hollywood writing continuities for pictures that Anson went faithfully to see.

Most of them, however, were permanent commuters with an intricate family life centring around some suburban country club, and it was from these that he felt his estrangement most keenly.

In the early days of their married life they had all needed him; he gave them advice about their slim finances, he exorcised their doubts about the advisability of bringing a baby into two rooms and a bath, especially he stood for the great world outside. But now their financial troubles were in the past and the fearfully expected child had evolved into an absorbing family. They were always glad to see old Anson, but they dressed up for him and tried to impress him with their present importance, and kept their troubles to themselves. They needed him no longer.

A few weeks before his thirtieth birthday the last of his early and intimate friends was married. Anson acted in his usual rôle of best man, gave his usual silver tea-service, and went down to the usual *Homeric* to say good-by. It was a hot Friday afternoon in May, and as he walked from the pier he realized that Saturday closing had begun and he was free until Monday morning.

"Go where?" he asked himself.

The Yale Club, of course; bridge until dinner, then four or five raw cocktails in somebody's room and a pleasant confused evening. He regretted that this afternoon's groom wouldn't be along—they had always been able to cram so much into such nights: they knew how to attach women and how to get rid of them, how much consideration any girl deserved from their intelligent hedonism. A party was an adjusted thing—you took certain girls to certain places and spent just so much on their amusement; you drank a little, not much, more than you ought to drink, and at a certain time in the morning you stood up and said you were going home. You avoided college boys, sponges, future engagements, fights, sentiment, and indiscretions. That was the way it was done. All the rest was dissipation.

In the morning you were never violently sorry—you made no resolutions, but if you had overdone it and your heart was slightly out of order, you went on the wagon for a few days without saying anything about it, and waited until an accumulation of nervous boredom projected you into another party.

The lobby of the Yale Club was unpopulated. In the bar three very young alumni looked up at him, momentarily and without curiosity.

"Hello there, Oscar," he said to the bartender. "Mr. Cahill been around this afternoon?"

"Mr. Cahill's gone to New Haven."

"Oh . . . that so?"

"Gone to the ball game. Lot of men gone up."

Anson looked once again into the lobby, considered for a moment, and then walked out and over to Fifth Avenue. From the broad window of one of his clubs—one that he had scarcely visited in five years—a gray man with watery eyes stared down at him. Anson looked quickly away—that figure sitting in vacant resignation, in supercilious solitude, depressed him. He stopped and, retracing his steps, started over 47th Street toward Teak Warden's apartment. Teak and his wife had once been his most familiar friends—it was a household where he and Dolly Karger had been

used to go in the days of their affair. But Teak had taken to drink, and his wife had remarked publicly that Anson was a bad influence on him. The remark reached Anson in an exaggerated form —when it was finally cleared up, the delicate spell of intimacy was broken, never to be renewed.

"Is Mr. Warden at home?" he inquired.

"They've gone to the country."

The fact unexpectedly cut at him. They were gone to the country and he hadn't known. Two years before he would have known the date, the hour, come up at the last moment for a final drink, and planned his first visit to them. Now they had gone without a word.

Anson looked at his watch and considered a weekend with his family, but the only train was a local that would jolt through the aggressive heat for three hours. And to-morrow in the country, and Sunday—he was in no mood for porch-bridge with polite undergraduates, and dancing after dinner at a rural roadhouse, a diminutive of gaiety which his father had estimated too well.

"Oh, no," he said to himself. . . . "No."

He was a dignified, impressive young man, rather stout now, but otherwise unmarked by dissipation. He could have been cast for a pillar of something—at times you were sure it was not society, at others nothing else—for the law, for the church. He stood for a few minutes motionless on the sidewalk in front of a 47th Street apartment-house; for almost the first time in his life he had nothing whatever to do.

Then he began to walk briskly up Fifth Avenue, as if he had just been reminded of an important engagement there. The necessity of dissimulation is one of the few characteristics that we share with dogs, and I think of Anson on that day as some well-bred specimen who had been disappointed at a familiar back door. He was going to see Nick, once a fashionable bartender in demand at all private dances, and now employed in cooling non-alcoholic champagne among the labyrinthine cellars of the Plaza Hotel.

"Nick," he said, "what's happened to everything?"

"Dead," Nick said.

"Make me a whiskey sour." Anson handed a pint bottle over the counter. "Nick, the girls are different; I had a little girl in Brooklyn and she got married last week without letting me know."

"That a fact? Ha-ha-ha," responded Nick diplomatically. "Slipped it over on you."

"Absolutely," said Anson. "And I was out with her the night before."

"Ha-ha-ha," said Nick, "ha-ha-ha!"

"Do you remember the wedding, Nick, in Hot

Springs where I had the waiters and the musicians singing 'God save the King'?"

"Now where was that, Mr. Hunter?" Nick concentrated doubtfully. "Seems to me that was——"

"Next time they were back for more, and I began to wonder how much I'd paid them," continued Anson.

"——seems to me that was at Mr. Trenholm's wedding."

"Don't know him," said Anson decisively. He was offended that a strange name should intrude upon his reminiscences; Nick perceived this.

"Naw—aw—" he admitted, "I ought to know that. It was one of *your* crowd—Brakins. . . . Baker——"

"Bicker Baker," said Anson responsively. "They put me in a hearse after it was over and covered me up with flowers and drove me away."

"Ha-ha-ha," said Nick. "Ha-ha-ha."

Nick's simulation of the old family servant paled presently and Anson went up-stairs to the lobby. He looked around—his eyes met the glance of an unfamiliar clerk at the desk, then fell upon a flower from the morning's marriage hesitating in the mouth of a brass cuspidor. He went out and walked slowly toward the blood-red sun over Columbus Circle. Suddenly he turned around and, retracing his steps to the Plaza, immured himself in a telephone-booth.

Later he said that he tried to get me three times that afternoon, that he tried every one who might be in New York—men and girls he had not seen for years, an artist's model of his college days whose faded number was still in his address book —Central told him that even the exchange existed no longer. At length his quest roved into the country, and he held brief disappointing conversations with emphatic butlers and maids. So-and-so was out, riding, swimming, playing golf, sailed to Europe last week. Who shall I say phoned?

It was intolerable that he should pass the evening alone—the private reckonings which one plans for a moment of leisure lose every charm when the solitude is enforced. There were always women of a sort, but the ones he knew had temporarily vanished, and to pass a New York evening in the hired company of a stranger never occurred to him—he would have considered that that was something shameful and secret, the diversion of a travelling salesman in a strange town.

Anson paid the telephone bill—the girl tried unsuccessfully to joke with him about its size—and for the second time that afternoon started to leave the Plaza and go he knew not where. Near the revolving door the figure of a woman, obviously with child, stood sideways to the light—a sheer beige cape fluttered at her shoulders when the door turned and, each time, she looked impatiently toward it as if she were weary of waiting. At the first sight of her a strong nervous thrill of familiarity went over him, but not until he was within five feet of her did he realize that it was Paula.

"Why, Anson Hunter!"

His heart turned over.

"Why, Paula——"

"Why, this is wonderful. I can't believe it, *Anson!*"

She took both his hands, and he saw in the freedom of the gesture that the memory of him had lost poignancy to her. But not to him—he felt that old mood that she evoked in him stealing over his brain, that gentleness with which he had always met her optimism as if afraid to mar its surface.

"We're at Rye for the summer. Pete had to come East on business—you know of course I'm Mrs. Peter Hagerty now—so we brought the children and took a house. You've got to come out and see us."

"Can I?" he asked directly. "When?"

"When you like. Here's Pete." The revolving door functioned, giving up a fine tall man of thirty with a tanned face and a trim mustache. His immaculate fitness made a sharp contrast with Anson's increasing bulk, which was obvious under the faintly tight cut-away coat.

"You oughtn't to be standing," said Hagerty to his wife. "Let's sit down here." He indicated lobby chairs, but Paula hesitated.

"I've got to go right home," she said. "Anson, why don't you—why don't you come out and have dinner with us to-night? We're just getting settled, but if you can stand that——"

Hagerty confirmed the invitation cordially.

"Come out for the night."

Their car waited in front of the hotel, and Paula with a tired gesture sank back against silk cushions in the corner.

"There's so much I want to talk to you about," she said, "it seems hopeless."

"I want to hear about you."

"Well"—she smiled at Hagerty—"that would take a long time too. I have three children—by my first marriage. The oldest is five, then four, then three." She smiled again. "I didn't waste much time having them, did I?"

"Boys?"

"A boy and two girls. Then—oh, a lot of things happened, and I got a divorce in Paris a year ago and married Pete. That's all—except that I'm awfully happy."

In Rye they drove up to a large house near the Beach Club, from which there issued presently three dark, slim children who broke from an English governess and approached them with an esoteric cry. Abstractedly and with difficulty Paula took each one into her arms, a caress which they accepted stiffly, as they had evidently been told not to bump into Mummy. Even against their fresh faces Paula's skin showed scarcely any weariness—for all her physical languor she seemed younger than when he had last seen her at Palm Beach seven years ago.

At dinner she was preoccupied, and afterward, during the homage to the radio, she lay with closed eyes on the sofa, until Anson wondered if his presence at this time were not an intrusion. But at nine o'clock, when Hagerty rose and said pleasantly that he was going to leave them by themselves for a while, she began to talk slowly about herself and the past.

"My first baby," she said—"the one we call Darling, the biggest little girl—I wanted to die when I knew I was going to have her, because Lowell was like a stranger to me. It didn't seem as though she could be my own. I wrote you a letter and tore it up. Oh, you were *so* bad to me, Anson."

It was the dialogue again, rising and falling. Anson felt a sudden quickening of memory.

"Weren't you engaged once?" she asked—"a girl named Dolly something?"

"I wasn't ever engaged. I tried to be engaged, but I never loved anybody but you, Paula."

"Oh," she said. Then after a moment: "This baby is the first one I ever really wanted. You see, I'm in love now—at last."

He didn't answer, shocked at the treachery of her remembrance. She must have seen that the "at last" bruised him, for she continued:

"I was infatuated with you, Anson—you could make me do anything you liked. But we wouldn't have been happy. I'm not smart enough for you. I don't like things to be complicated like you do." She paused. "You'll never settle down," she said.

The phrase struck at him from behind—it was an accusation that of all accusations he had never merited.

"I could settle down if women were different," he said. "If I didn't understand so much about them, if women didn't spoil you for other women, if they had only a little pride. If I could go to sleep for a while and wake up into a home that was really mine—why, that's what I'm made for, Paula, that's what women have seen in me and liked in me. It's only that I can't get through the preliminaries any more."

Hagerty came in a little before eleven; after a whiskey Paula stood up and announced that she was going to bed. She went over and stood by her husband.

"Where did you go, dearest?" she demanded.

"I had a drink with Ed Saunders."

"I was worried. I thought maybe you'd run away."

She rested her head against his coat.

"He's sweet, isn't he, Anson?" she demanded.

"Absolutely," said Anson, laughing.

She raised her face to her husband.

"Well, I'm ready," she said. She turned to Anson: "Do you want to see our family gymnastic stunt?"

"Yes," he said in an interested voice.

"All right. Here we go!"

Hagerty picked her up easily in his arms.

"This is called the family acrobatic stunt," said Paula. "He carries me up-stairs. Isn't it sweet of him?"

"Yes," said Anson.

Hagerty bent his head slightly until his face touched Paula's.

"And I love him," she said. "I've just been telling you, haven't I, Anson?"

"Yes," he said.

"He's the dearest thing that ever lived in this world; aren't you, darling? . . . Well, good night. Here we go. Isn't he strong?"

"Yes," Anson said.

"You'll find a pair of Pete's pajamas laid out for you. Sweet dreams—see you at breakfast."

"Yes," Anson said.

VIII

THE OLDER members of the firm insisted that Anson should go abroad for the summer. He had scarcely had a vacation in seven years, they said. He was stale and needed a change. Anson resisted.

"If I go," he declared, "I won't come back any more."

"That's absurd, old man. You'll be back in three months with all this depression gone. Fit as ever."

"No." He shook his head stubbornly. "If I stop, I won't go back to work. If I stop, that means I've given up—I'm through."

"We'll take a chance on that. Stay six months if you like—we're not afraid you'll leave us. Why, you'd be miserable if you didn't work."

They arranged his passage for him. They liked Anson—every one liked Anson—and the change that had been coming over him cast a sort of pall over the office. The enthusiasm that had invariably signalled up business, the consideration toward his equals and his inferiors, the lift of his vital presence—within the past four months his intense nervousness had melted down these qualities into the fussy pessimism of a man of forty. On every transaction in which he was involved he acted as a drag and a strain.

"If I go I'll never come back," he said.

Three days before he sailed Paula Legendre Hagerty died in childbirth. I was with him a great deal then, for we were crossing together, but for the first time in our friendship he told me not a word of how he felt, nor did I see the slightest sign of emotion. His chief preoccupation was with the fact that he was thirty years old—he would turn the conversation to the point where he could remind you of it and then fall silent, as if he assumed that the statement would start a chain of thought sufficient to itself. Like his partners, I was amazed at the change in him, and I was glad when the *Paris* moved off into the wet space between the worlds, leaving his principality behind.

"How about a drink?" he suggested.

We walked into the bar with that defiant feeling that characterizes the day of departure and ordered four Martinis. After one cocktail a change came over him—he suddenly reached across and slapped my knee with the first joviality I had seen him exhibit for months.

"Did you see that girl in the red tam?" he demanded, "the one with the high color who had the two police dogs down to bid her good-by."

"She's pretty," I agreed.

"I looked her up in the purser's office and found out that she's alone. I'm going down to see the steward in a few minutes. We'll have dinner with her to-night."

After a while he left me, and within an hour he was walking up and down the deck with her, talking to her in his strong, clear voice. Her red tam was a bright spot of color against the steel-green sea, and from time to time she looked up with a flashing bob of her head, and smiled with amusement and interest, and anticipation. At dinner we had champagne, and were very joyous—afterward Anson ran the pool with infectious gusto, and several people who had seen me with him asked me his name. He and the girl were talking and laughing together on a lounge in the bar when I went to bed.

I saw less of him on the trip than I had hoped. He wanted to arrange a foursome, but there was no one available, so I saw him only at meals. Sometimes, though, he would have a cocktail in the bar, and he told me about the girl in the red tam, and his adventures with her, making them all

bizarre and amusing, as he had a way of doing, and I was glad that he was himself again, or at least the self that I knew, and with which I felt at home. I don't think he was ever happy unless some one was in love with him, responding to him like filings to a magnet, helping him to explain himself, promising him something. What it was I do not know. Perhaps they promised that there would always be women in the world who would spend their brightest, freshest, rarest hours to nurse and protect that superiority he cherished in his heart.

1926

ECHOES OF
THE JAZZ AGE

◇

([FIRST published in *Scribner's Magazine* in November, 1931, this article was reprinted by Edmund Wilson in his New Directions volume, *The Crack-Up*, of 1945. The account evokes the atmosphere of Scott Fitzgerald's life in his most important decade; it also probably suggests that the 1920's provided free liquor for everyone and that everyone was mad, which was not, of course, quite the fact. But the piece is true for its author, and of especial interest are his remarks about Cap d'Antibes between 1926 and 1929, for this was the place and these were the years in which he gathered the impressions that he later translated into *Tender Is the Night*.

◇

November, 1931

IT IS too soon to write about the Jazz Age with perspective, and without being suspected of premature arteriosclerosis. Many people still succumb to violent retching when they happen upon any of its characteristic words—words which have since yielded in vividness to the coinages of the underworld. It is as dead as were the Yellow Nineties in 1902. Yet the present writer already looks back to it with nostalgia. It bore him up, flattered him and gave him more money than he had dreamed of, simply for telling people that he felt as they did, that something had to be done with all the nervous energy stored up and unexpended in the War.

The ten-year period that, as if reluctant to die outmoded in its bed, leaped to a spectacular death in October, 1929, began about the time of the May Day riots in 1919.[1] When the police rode down the demobilized country boys gaping at the orators in Madison Square, it was the sort of measure bound to alienate the more intelligent young men from the prevailing order. We didn't remember anything about the Bill of Rights until Mencken[2] began plugging it, but we did know such tyranny belonged in the jittery little countries of South Europe. If goose-livered business men had this effect on the government, then maybe we had gone to war for J. P. Morgan's loans after all.[3] But, because we were tired of Great Causes, there was no more than a short outbreak of moral indignation, typified by Dos Passos' *Three Soldiers*.[4] Presently we began to have slices of the national cake and our idealism only flared up when the newspapers made melodrama out of such stories as Harding and the Ohio Gang[5] or Sacco and Vanzetti.[6] The events of 1919 left us cynical rather than revolutionary, in spite of the fact that now we are all rummaging around in our trunks wondering where in hell we left the liberty cap—"I know I *had* it"—and the moujik blouse. It was characteristic of the Jazz Age that it had no interest in politics at all.

It was an age of miracles, it was an age of art, it was an age of excess, and it was an age of satire. A Stuffed Shirt, squirming to blackmail in a life-like way, sat upon the throne of the United States;[7] a stylish young man hurried over to represent to us the throne of England.[8] A world of girls yearned for the young Englishman; the old American groaned in his sleep as he waited to be

poisoned by his wife, upon the advice of the female Rasputin who then made the ultimate decision in our national affairs. But such matters apart, we had things our way at last. With Americans ordering suits by the gross in London, the Bond Street tailors perforce agreed to moderate their cut to the American long-waisted figure and loose-fitting taste, something subtle passed to America, the style of man. During the Renaissance, Francis the First looked to Florence to trim his leg. Seventeenth-century England aped the court of France, and fifty years ago the German Guards officer bought his civilian clothes in London. Gentlemen's clothes—symbol of "the power that man must hold and that passes from race to race."

We were the most powerful nation. Who could tell us any longer what was fashionable and what was fun? Isolated during the European War, we had begun combing the unknown South and West for folkways and pastimes, and there were more ready to hand.

The first social revelation created a sensation out of all proportion to its novelty. As far back as 1915 the unchaperoned young people of the smaller cities had discovered the mobile privacy of that automobile given to young Bill at sixteen to make him "self-reliant." At first petting was a desperate adventure even under such favorable conditions, but presently confidences were exchanged and the old commandment broke down. As early as 1917 there were references to such sweet and casual dalliance in any number of the *Yale Record* or the *Princeton Tiger*.

But petting in its more audacious manifestations was confined to the wealthier classes—among other young people the old standard prevailed until after the War, and a kiss meant that a proposal was expected, as young officers in strange cities sometimes discovered to their dismay. Only in 1920 did the veil finally fall—the Jazz Age was in flower.

Scarcely had the staider citizens of the republic caught their breaths when the wildest of all generations, the generation which had been adolescent during the confusion of the War, brusquely shouldered my contemporaries out of the way and danced into the limelight. This was the generation whose girls dramatized themselves as flappers, the generation that corrupted its elders and eventually overreached itself less through lack of morals than through lack of taste. May one offer in exhibit the year 1922! That was the peak of the younger generation, for though the Jazz Age continued, it became less and less an affair of youth.

The sequel was like a children's party taken over

ECHOES OF THE JAZZ AGE. 1. May 1 is a day set aside over much of the world for public demonstrations by trade unionists. In 1919 in New York, the year of an hysterical "red scare," the Manhattan police were particularly brutal. Fitzgerald later published a story called "May Day" (1920), which appears in his *Tales of the Jazz Age*. 2. **Mencken:** Henry Louis Mencken (1880–1956), American social critic, co-founder and editor of the influential *American Mercury*. 3. In "1919," the second part of John Dos Passos' trilogy *U S A* (1938), one reads: "By 1917 the Allies had borrowed one billion, nine-hundred million dollars through the House of Morgan: we went overseas for democracy and the flag; and by the end of the Peace Conference the phrase *J. P. Morgan suggests* had compulsion over a power of seventy-four billion dollars." 4. *Three Soldiers:* antiwar novel of 1921. 5. **Harding and the Ohio Gang:** Warren Gamaliel Harding (1865–1923), twenty-ninth President of the United States, "controlled" by Ohio politicians, known chiefly for the corruption of his administration. 6. **Sacco and Vanzetti:** Nicola Sacco (1891–1927) and Bartolomeo Vanzetti (1888–1927), the probably innocent victims of a notorious Massachusetts trial running from 1921 until their execution, the charge being the robbing and the murder of a shoe company paymaster. 7. A . . . United States: Warren Gamaliel Harding. 8. A . . . England: now Edward, Duke of Windsor; once King Edward VIII; then the Prince of Wales.

by the elders, leaving the children puzzled and rather neglected and rather taken aback. By 1923 their elders, tired of watching the carnival with ill-concealed envy, had discovered that young liquor will take the place of young blood, and with a whoop the orgy began. The younger generation was starred no longer.

A whole race going hedonistic, deciding on pleasure. The precocious intimacies of the younger generation would have come about with or without prohibition—they were implicit in the attempt to adapt English customs to American conditions. (Our South, for example, is tropical and early maturing—it has never been part of the wisdom of France and Spain to let young girls go unchaperoned at sixteen and seventeen.) But the general decision to be amused that began with the cocktail parties of 1921 had more complicated origins.

The word jazz in its progress toward respectability has meant first sex, then dancing, then music.[9] It is associated with a state of nervous stimulation, not unlike that of big cities behind the lines of a war. To many English the War still goes on because all the forces that menace them are still active—Wherefore eat, drink and be merry, for tomorrow we die. But different causes had now brought about a corresponding state in America—though there were entire classes (people over fifty, for example) who spent a whole decade denying its existence even when its puckish face peered into the family circle. Never did they dream that they had contributed to it. The honest citizens of every class, who believed in a strict public morality and were powerful enough to enforce the necessary legislation, did not know that they would necessarily be served by criminals and quacks, and do not really believe it to-day. Rich righteousness had always been able to buy honest and intelligent servants to free the slaves or the Cubans, so when this attempt collapsed our elders stood firm with all the stubbornness of people involved in a weak case, preserving their righteousness and losing their children. Silver-haired women and men with fine old faces, people who never did a consciously dishonest thing in their lives, still assure each other in the apartment hotels of New York and Boston and Washington that "there's a whole generation growing up that will never know the taste of liquor." Meanwhile their granddaughters pass the well-thumbed copy of *Lady Chatterley's Lover* [10] around the boarding-school and, if they get about at all, know the

taste of gin or corn at sixteen. But the generation who reached the maturity between 1875 and 1895 continue to believe what they want to believe.

Even the intervening generations were incredulous. In 1920 Heywood Broun [11] announced that all this hubbub was nonsense, that young men didn't kiss but told anyhow. But very shortly people over twenty-five came in for an intensive education. Let me trace some of the revelations vouchsafed them by reference to a dozen works written for various types of mentality during the decade. We begin with the suggestion that Don Juan leads an interesting life (*Jurgen*, 1919); [12] then we learn that there's a lot of sex around if we only knew it (*Winesburg, Ohio*, 1920), [13] that adolescents lead very amorous lives (*This Side of Paradise*, 1920), [14] that there are a lot of neglected Anglo-Saxon words (*Ulysses*, 1921), [15] that older people don't always resist sudden temptations (*Cytherea*, 1922), [16] that girls are sometimes seduced without being ruined (*Flaming Youth*, 1922), [17] that even rape often turns out well (*The Sheik*, 1922), [18] that glamorous English ladies are often promiscuous (*The Green Hat*, 1924), [19] that in fact they devote most of their time to it (*The Vortex*, 1926), [20] that it's a damn good thing too (*Lady Chatterley's Lover*, 1928), [21] and finally that there are abnormal variations (*The Well of Loneliness*, 1928, [22] and *Sodom and Gomorrah*, 1929).[23]

In my opinion the erotic element in these works, even *The Sheik* written for children in the key of *Peter Rabbit*, [24] did not one particle of harm. Everything they described, and much more, was familiar in our contemporary life. The majority of the theses were honest and elucidating—their effect was to restore some dignity to the male as opposed to the he-man in American life. ("And what is a 'He-man'?" demanded Gertrude Stein [25] one day. "Isn't it a large enough order to fill out to the dimensions of all that 'a man' has meant in the past? A 'He-man'!") The married woman

9. And then (now), *nonsense*, as in "all that jazz." 10. *Lady Chatterley's Lover:* controversial novel by D. H. Lawrence, not legally for sale in the United States until 1959.

11. **Heywood Broun:** Heywood Broun (1888–1939), American newspaperman. 12. *Jurgen,* 1919: by James Branch Cabell. 13. *Winesburg, Ohio,* 1920: by Sherwood Anderson. 14. *This Side of Paradise,* 1920: Fitzgerald's first novel. 15. *Ulysses,* 1921: by James Joyce. 16. *Cytherea,* 1922: by Joseph Hergesheimer. 17. *Flaming Youth,* 1922: by Warner Fabian. 18. *The Sheik,* 1922: by Edith M. Hull. 19. *The Green Hat,* 1924, by Michael Arlen. 20. *The Vortex,* 1926: a play by Noel Coward. 21. *Lady Chatterley's Lover,* 1928: by D. H. Lawrence. 22. *The Well of Loneliness,* 1928: by Radcliffe Hall. 23. *Sodom and Gomorrah,* 1929: Marcel Proust's *Sodome et Gomorrhe* was published in France in 1921–22; the English translation, *Cities of the Plain,* appeared in 1927. 24. *Peter Rabbit:* Peter is the hero of a series of famous children's books by Beatrix Potter. 25. **Gertrude Stein:** See "Letters," 10 n., p. 706.

can now discover whether she is being cheated, or whether sex is just something to be endured, and her compensation should be to establish a tyranny of the spirit, as her mother may have hinted. Perhaps many women found that love was meant to be fun. Anyhow the objectors lost their tawdry little case, which is one reason why our literature is now the most living in the world.

Contrary to popular opinion, the movies of the Jazz Age had no effect upon its morals. The social attitude of the producers was timid, behind the times and banal—for example, no picture mirrored even faintly the younger generation until 1923, when magazines had already been started to celebrate it and it had long ceased to be news. There were a few feeble splutters and then Clara Bow in *Flaming Youth;* promptly the Hollywood hacks ran the theme into its cinematographic grave. Throughout the Jazz Age the movies got no farther than Mrs. Jiggs,[26] keeping up with its most blatant superficialities. This was no doubt due to the censorship as well as to innate conditions in the industry. In any case, the Jazz Age now raced along under its own power, served by great filling stations full of money.

The people over thirty, the people all the way up to fifty, had joined the dance. We graybeards (to tread down F. P. A.)[27] remember the uproar when in 1912 grandmothers of forty tossed away their crutches and took lessons in the Tango and the Castle-Walk. A dozen years later a woman might pack the Green Hat with her other affairs as she set off for Europe or New York, but Savonarola was too busy flogging dead horses in Augean stables of his own creation to notice. Society, even in small cities, now dined in separate chambers, and the sober table learned about the gay table only from hearsay. There were very few people left at the sober table. One of its former glories, the less sought-after girls who had become resigned to sublimating a probable celibacy, came across Freud and Jung[28] in seeking their intellectual recompense and came tearing back into the fray.

By 1926 the universal preoccupation with sex had become a nuisance. (I remember a perfectly mated, contented young mother asking my wife's advice about "having an affair right away," though she had no one especially in mind, "because don't you think it's sort of undignified when you get

much over thirty?") For a while bootleg Negro records with their phallic euphemisms made everything suggestive, and simultaneously came a wave of erotic plays—young girls from finishing-schools packed the galleries to hear about the romance of being a Lesbian and George Jean Nathan[29] protested. Then one young producer lost his head entirely, drank a beauty's alcoholic bath-water and went to the penitentiary. Somehow his pathetic attempt at romance belongs to the Jazz Age, while his contemporary in prison, Ruth Snyder,[30] had to be hoisted into it by the tabloids—she was, as *The Daily News* hinted deliciously to gourmets, about "to cook, *and sizzle, AND FRY!"* in the electric chair.

The gay elements of society had divided into two main streams, one flowing toward Palm Beach and Deauville, and the other, much smaller, toward the summer Riviera. One could get away with more on the summer Riviera, and whatever happened seemed to have something to do with art. From 1926 to 1929, the great years of the Cap d'Antibes, this corner of France was dominated by a group quite distinct from that American society which is dominated by Europeans. Pretty much of anything went at Antibes—by 1929, at the most gorgeous paradise for swimmers on the Mediterranean no one swam any more, save for a short hang-over dip at noon. There was a picturesque graduation of steep rocks over the sea and somebody's valet and an occasional English girl used to dive from them, but the Americans were content to discuss each other in the bar. This was indicative of something that was taking place in the homeland—Americans were getting soft. There were signs everywhere: we still won the Olympic games but with champions whose names had few vowels in them—teams composed, like the fighting Irish combination of Notre Dame, of fresh overseas blood. Once the French became really interested, the Davis Cup gravitated automatically to their intensity in competition. The vacant lots of the Middle-Western cities were built up now—except for a short period in school, we were not turning out to be an athletic people like the British, after all. The hare and the tortoise. Of course if we wanted to we could be in a minute; we still had all those reserves of ancestral vitality, but one day in 1926 we looked down and found we had flabby arms and a fat pot and couldn't say boop-boop-a-doop to a Sicilian. Shades of Van Bibber!—no utopian ideal, God knows. Even golf, once considered an effeminate

26. **Mrs. Jiggs:** The "Maggie" in a famous cartoon strip, *Maggie and Jiggs.* 27. **F.P.A.:** Franklin Pierce Adams (1881–1960), newspaper columnist in whose column, "The Conning Tower," many famous writers made their literary debuts. 28. **Freud and Jung:** Sigmund Freud (1856–1939), founder of psychoanalysis; Carl Gustav Jung (1875–1961), Freud's pupil.

29. **George Jean Nathan:** George Jean Nathan (1882–1958), drama critic. 30. **Ruth Snyder:** Ruth Snyder, chief figure in a sensational murder trial.

game, had seemed very strenuous of late—an emasculated form appeared and proved just right.

By 1927 a wide-spread neurosis began to be evident, faintly signalled, like a nervous beating of the feet, by the popularity of cross-word puzzles. I remember a fellow expatriate opening a letter from a mutual friend of ours, urging him to come home and be revitalized by the hardy, bracing qualities of the native soil. It was a strong letter and it affected us both deeply, until we noticed that it was headed from a nerve sanitarium in Pennsylvania.

By this time contemporaries of mine had begun to disappear into the dark maw of violence. A classmate killed his wife and himself on Long Island, another tumbled "accidently" from a skyscraper in Philadelphia, another purposely from a skyscraper in New York. One was killed in a speakeasy in Chicago; another was beaten to death in a speak-easy in New York and crawled home to the Princeton Club to die; still another had his skull crushed by a maniac's axe in an insane asylum where he was confined. These are not catastrophes that I went out of my way to look for —these were my friends; moreover, these things happened not during the depression but during the boom.

In the spring of '27, something bright and alien flashed across the sky. A young Minnesotan [31] who seemed to have had nothing to do with his generation did a heroic thing, and for a moment people set down their glasses in country clubs and speak-easies and thought of their old best dreams. Maybe there was a way out by flying, maybe our restless blood could find frontiers in the illimitable air. But by that time we were all pretty well committed; and the Jazz Age continued; we would all have one more.

Nevertheless, Americans were wandering ever more widely—friends seemed eternally bound for Russia, Persia, Abyssinia and Central Africa. And by 1928 Paris had grown suffocating. With each new shipment of Americans spewed up by the boom the quality fell off, until toward the end there was something sinister about the crazy boatloads. They were no longer the simple pa and ma and son and daughter, infinitely superior in their qualities of kindness and curiosity to the corresponding class in Europe, but fantastic neanderthals who believed something, something vague, that you remembered from a very cheap novel. I remember an Italian on a steamer who promenaded the deck in an American Reserve Officer's uniform picking quarrels in broken English with Americans who criticised their own institutions in the bar. I remember a fat Jewess, inlaid with diamonds, who sat behind us at the Russian ballet and said as the curtain rose, "Thad's luffly, dey ought to baint a bicture of it." This was low comedy, but it was evident that money and power were falling into the hands of people in comparison with whom the leader of a village Soviet would be a gold-mine of judgment and culture. There were citizens travelling in luxury in 1928 and 1929 who, in the distortion of their new condition, had the human value of Pekinese, bivalves, cretins, goats. I remember the Judge from some New York district who had taken his daughter to see the Bayeux Tapestries and made a scene in the papers advocating their segregation because one scene was immoral. But in those days life was like the race in *Alice in Wonderland,* there was a prize for every one.

The Jazz Age had had a wild youth and a heady middle age. There was the phase of the necking parties, the Leopold-Loeb murder [32] (I remember the time my wife was arrested on Queensborough Bridge on the suspicion of being the "Bob-haired Bandit") and the John Held [33] Clothes. In the second phase such phenomena as sex and murder became more mature, if much more conventional. Middle age must be served and pajamas came to the beach to save fat thighs and flabby calves from competition with the one-piece bathing-suit. Finally skirts came down and everything was concealed. Everybody was at scratch now. Let's go—

But it was not to be. Somebody had blundered and the most expensive orgy in history was over.

It ended two years ago, because the utter confidence which was its essential prop received an enormous jolt, and it didn't take long for the flimsy structure to settle earthward. And after two years the Jazz Age seems as far away as the days before the War. It was borrowed time anyhow—the whole upper tenth of a nation living with the insouciance of grand ducs and the casualness of chorus girls. But moralizing is easy now and it was pleasant to be in one's twenties in such a certain and unworried time. Even when you were broke you didn't worry about money, because it was in such profusion around you. Toward

---

31. **A young Minnesotan:** Charles Augustus Lindbergh (b. 1902), made the first nonstop solo flight from New York to Paris in 1927, an event which made him the beau ideal of the American public.

32. **Leopold-Loeb murder:** Two young men in Chicago killed a small boy in a murder "experiment." 33. **John Held:** John Held, Jr., cartoonist of *College Humor,* a magazine popular in the 1920's.

the end one had a struggle to pay one's share; it was almost a favor to accept hospitality that required any travelling. Charm, notoriety, mere good manners, weighed more than money as a social asset. This was rather splendid, but things were getting thinner and thinner as the eternal necessary human values tried to spread over all that expansion. Writers were geniuses on the strength of one respectable book or play; just as during the War officers of four months' experience commanded hundreds of men, so there were now many little fish lording it over great big bowls. In the theatrical world extravagant productions were carried by a few second-rate stars, and so on up the scale into politics, where it was difficult to interest good men in positions of the highest importance and responsibility, importance and responsibility far exceeding that of business executives but which paid only five or six thousand a year.

Now once more the belt is tight and we summon the proper expression of horror as we look back at our wasted youth. Sometimes, though, there is a ghostly rumble among the drums, an asthmatic whisper in the trombones that swings me back into the early twenties when we drank wood alcohol and every day in every way grew better and better, and there was a first abortive shortening of the skirts, and girls all looked alike in sweater dresses, and people you didn't want to know said "Yes, we have no bananas," [34] and it seemed only a question of a few years before the older people would step aside and let the world be run by those who saw things as they were—and it all seems rosy and romantic to us who were young then, because we will never feel quite so intensely about our surroundings any more.

1931

RING

◊

❨ THIS memorial piece written about a dead friend was first published in the *New Republic* on October 11, 1933, and reprinted by Edmund Wilson in *The Crack-Up* in 1945. Ringgold Wilmer Lardner (1885–1933) was a sports writer and columnist in Chicago and New York before he became a well-known short story writer. The material of his stories, usually written in a racy

vernacular, was drawn largely from the worlds of Sports and Broadway. He grew increasingly bitter toward the end of his career and his characters became increasingly vicious. Fitzgerald, who sometimes almost persuaded himself that his own drinking habits existed only in Ernest Hemingway's mind, once said, "I am *his* alcoholic just like Ring is mine . . ."

◊

October, 1933

FOR A YEAR and a half, the writer of this appreciation was Ring Lardner's most familiar companion; after that, geography made separations and our contacts were rare. When my wife and I last saw him in 1931, he looked already like a man on his deathbed—it was terribly sad to see that six feet three inches of kindness stretched out ineffectual in the hospital room. His fingers trembled with a match, the tight skin on his handsome skull was marked as a mask of misery and nervous pain.

He gave a very different impression when we first saw him in 1921—he seemed to have an abundance of quiet vitality that would enable him to outlast anyone, to take himself for long spurts of work or play that would ruin any ordinary constitution. He had recently convulsed the country with the famous kitten-and-coat saga (it had to do with a world's series bet and with the impending conversion of some kittens into fur), and the evidence of the betting, a beautiful sable, was worn by his wife at the time. In those days he was interested in people, sports, bridge, music, the stage, the newspapers, the magazines, the books. But though I did not know it, the change in him had already begun—the impenetrable despair that dogged him for a dozen years to his death.

He had practically given up sleeping, save on short vacations deliberately consecrated to simple pleasures, most frequently golf with his friends, Grantland Rice or John Wheeler.[1] Many a night we talked over a case of Canadian ale until bright dawn, when Ring would rise and yawn: "Well, I guess the children have left for school by this time—I might as well go home."

The woes of many people haunted him—for example, the doctor's death sentence pronounced upon Tad, the cartoonist, (who, in fact, nearly outlived Ring)—it was as if he believed he could and ought to do something about such things. And as he struggled to fulfill his contracts, one of which, a comic strip based on the character of "the busher," was a terror, indeed, it was obvious that he felt his work to be directionless, merely "copy."

---

34. **"Yes, we have no bananas"**: This was the title of a popular song of the period.

RING.   1. Grantland Rice or John Wheeler: sports writers.

So he was inclined to turn his cosmic sense of responsibility into the channel of solving other people's problems—finding someone an introduction to a theatrical manager, placing a friend in a job, maneuvering a man into a golf club. The effort made was often out of proportion to the situation; the truth back of it was that Ring was getting off— he was a faithful and conscientious workman to the end, but he had stopped finding any fun in his work ten years before he died.

About that time (1922) a publisher undertook to reissue his old books and collect his recent stories and this gave him a sense of existing in the literary world as well as with the public, and he got some satisfaction from the reiterated statements of Mencken [2] and F. P. A.[3] as to his true stature as a writer. But I don't think he cared then—it is hard to understand but I don't think he really gave a damn about anything except his personal relations with a few people. A case in point was his attitude to those imitators who lifted everything except the shirt off his back—only Hemingway has been so thoroughly frisked—it worried the imitators more than it worried Ring. His attitude was that if they got stuck in the process he'd help them over any tough place.

Throughout this period of huge earnings and an increasingly solid reputation on top and beneath, there were two ambitions more important to Ring than the work by which he will be remembered; he wanted to be a musician—sometimes he dramatized himself ironically as a thwarted composer—and he wanted to write shows. His dealings with managers would make a whole story: they were always commissioning him to do work which they promptly forgot they had ordered, and accepting librettos that they never produced. (Ring left a short ironic record of Ziegfeld.) [4] Only with the aid of the practical George Kaufman [5] did he achieve his ambition, and by then he was too far gone in illness to get a proper satisfaction from it.

The point of these paragraphs is that, whatever Ring's achievement was, it fell short of the achievement he was capable of, and this because of a cynical attitude toward his work. How far back did that attitude go?—back to his youth in a Michigan village? Certainly back to his days with the Cubs.[6] During those years, when most men of promise achieve an adult education, if only in the school of war, Ring moved in the company of a few dozen illiterates playing a boy's game. A boy's game, with no more possibilities in it than a boy could master, a game bounded by walls which kept out novelty or danger, change or adventure. This material, the observation of it under such circumstances, was the text of Ring's schooling during the most formative period of the mind. A writer can spin on about his adventures after thirty, after forty, after fifty, but the criteria by which these adventures are weighed and valued are irrevocably settled at the age of twenty-five. However deeply Ring might cut into it, his cake had exactly the diameter of Frank Chance's diamond.[7]

Here was his artistic problem, and it promised future trouble. So long as he wrote within that enclosure the result was magnificent: within it he heard and recorded the voice of a continent. But when, inevitably, he outgrew his interest in it, what was Ring left with?

He was left with his fine linguistic technique— and he was left rather helpless in those few acres. He had been formed by the very world on which his hilarious irony had released itself. He had fought his way through to knowing what people's motives are and what means they are likely to resort to in order to attain their goals. But now he had a new problem—what to do about it. He went on seeing, and the sights traveled back to the optic nerve, but no longer to be thrown off in fiction, because they were no longer sights that could be weighed and valued by the old criteria. It was never that he was completely sold on athletic virtuosity as the be-all and end-all of problems; the trouble was that he could find nothing finer. Imagine life conceived as a business of beautiful muscular organization—an arising, an effort, a good break, a sweat, a bath, a meal, a love, a sleep—imagine it achieved; then imagine trying to apply that standard to the horribly complicated mess of living, where nothing, even the greatest conceptions and workings and achievements, is else but messy, spotty, tortuous—and then one can imagine the confusion that Ring faced on coming out of the ball park.

He kept on recording but he no longer projected, and this accumulation, which he has taken with him to the grave, crippled his spirit in the latter years. It was not the fear of Niles, Michigan, that hampered him—it was the habit of silence, formed in the presence of the "ivory" with which he lived and worked. Remember it was not humble ivory— Ring has demonstrated that—it was arrogant, im-

2. Mencken: See "Echoes," 2 n.   3. F.P.A.: See "Echoes," 27 n.   4. Ziegfeld: Florenz Ziegfeld (1869–1932), famous producer of musical reviews.   5. George Kaufman: George Simon Kaufman (1889–1961), American playwright and musical comedy librettist.   6. Cubs: the Chicago Cubs, major league baseball club.

7. Frank Chance's diamond: Frank LeRoy Chance (1877–1924) of the Chicago Cubs (National League), who from 1902 to 1912 played first base in the most famous double-play combination in baseball history—"Tinker to Evers to Chance."

perative, often megalomaniacal ivory. He got the habit of silence, then the habit of repression that finally took the form of his odd little crusade in the *New Yorker* against pornographic songs. He had agreed with himself to speak only a small portion of his mind.

The present writer once suggested to him that he organize some *cadre* [8] within which he could adequately display his talents, suggesting that it should be something deeply personal, and something on which Ring could take his time, but he dismissed the idea lightly; he was a disillusioned idealist but he had served his Fates well, and no other ones could be casually created for him—"This is something that can be printed," he reasoned; "this, however, belongs with that bunch of stuff that can never be written."

He covered himself in such cases with protests of his inability to bring off anything big, but this was specious, for he was a proud man and had no reason to rate his abilities cheaply. He refused to "tell all" because in a crucial period of his life he had formed the habit of not doing it—and this he had elevated gradually into a standard of taste. It never satisfied him by a damn sight.

So one is haunted not only by a sense of personal loss but by a conviction that Ring got less percentage of himself on paper than any other American of the first flight. There is *"You Know Me, Al,"* [9] and there are about a dozen wonderful short stories (my God, he hadn't even saved them —the material of *How to Write Short Stories* [10] was obtained by photographing old issues in the public library!), and there is some of the most uproarious and inspired nonsense since Lewis Carroll.[11] Most of the rest is mediocre stuff, with flashes, and I would do Ring a disservice to suggest it should be set upon an altar and worshipped, as have been the most casual relics of Mark Twain. Those three volumes should seem enough—to everyone who didn't know Ring. But I venture that no one who knew him but will agree that the personality of the man overlapped it. Proud, shy, solemn, shrewd, polite, brave, kind, merciful, honorable—with the affection these qualities aroused he created in addition a certain awe in people. His intentions, his will, once in motion, were formidable factors in dealing with him—he always did every single thing he said he would do. Frequently he was the melancholy Jaques, and sad company indeed, but under any conditions a noble dignity flowed from him, so that time in his presence always seemed well spent.

On my desk, at the moment, I have the letters Ring wrote to us; here is a letter one thousand words long, here is one of two thousand words— theatrical gossip, literary shop talk, flashes of wit but not much wit, for he was feeling thin and saving the best of that for his work, anecdotes of his activities. I reprint the most typical one I can find:

"The Dutch Treat show was a week ago Friday night. Grant Rice and I had reserved a table, and a table holds ten people and no more. Well, I had invited, as one guest, Jerry Kern,[12] but he telephoned at the last moment that he couldn't come. I then consulted with Grant Rice, who said he had no substitute in mind, but that it was a shame to waste our extra ticket when tickets were at a premium. So I called up Jones, and Jones said yes, and would it be all right for him to bring along a former Senator who was a pal of his and had been good to him in Washington. I said I was sorry, but our table was filled and, besides, we didn't have an extra ticket. "Maybe I could dig up another ticket somewhere," said Jones. "I don't believe so," I said, "but anyway the point is that we haven't room at our table." "Well," said Jones, "I could have the Senator eat somewhere else and join us in time for the show." "Yes," I said, "but we have no ticket for him." "Well, I'll think up something," he said. Well, what he thought up was to bring himself and the Senator and I had a hell of a time getting an extra ticket and shoving the Senator in at another table where he wasn't wanted, and later in the evening, the Senator thanked Jones and said he was the greatest fella in the world and all I got was goodnight.

"Well, I must close and nibble on a carrot. R.W.L."

Even in a telegram Ring could compress a lot of himself. Here is one: WHEN ARE YOU COMING BACK AND WHY PLEASE ANSWER   RING LARDNER

This is not the moment to recollect Ring's convivial aspects, especially as he had, long before his death, ceased to find amusement in dissipation, or indeed in the whole range of what is called entertainment—save for his perennial interest in songs. By grace of the radio and of the many musicians who, drawn by his enormous magnetism, made pilgrimages to his bedside, he had a consolation in the last days, and he made the most of it, hilariously rewriting Cole Porter's lyrics in the *New Yorker*. But it would be an evasion for the present writer not to say that when he was Ring's neighbor a decade ago, they tucked a lot under their belts in in many weathers, and spent many words on many men and things. At no time did I feel that I

---

8. *cadre*: a framework.   9. *"You Know Me, Al,"*: 1916.
10. *How to Write Short Stories*: 1924.   11. Lewis Carroll: author of *Alice in Wonderland*.

12. Jerry Kern: Jerome Kern (1885–1945), popular composer.

had known him enough, or that anyone knew him
—it was not the feeling that there was more stuff
in him and that it should come out, it was rather a
qualitative difference, it was rather as though, due
to some inadequacy in one's self, one had not
penetrated to something unsolved, new and unsaid. That is why one wishes that Ring had written
down a larger proportion of what was in his mind
and heart. It would have saved him longer for us,
and that in itself would be something. But I would
like to know what it was, and now I will go on
wishing—what did Ring want, how did he want
things to be, how did he think things were?

A great and good American is dead. Let us not
obscure him by the flowers, but walk up and look
at that fine medallion, all abraded by sorrows that
perhaps we are not equipped to understand. Ring
made no enemies, because he was kind, and to
many millions he gave release and delight.

1933

THE CRACK-UP

◊

⟦ THE THREE sketches that make up this autobiographical account of a psychic collapse were first published in
February, March, and April of 1936 in *Esquire,* which
then carried the subtitle "The Magazine for Young
Men." Fitzgerald was old beyond his years, and old
enough to write what is certainly one of the most extraordinarily candid pieces of self-examination in the
history of literature. The pieces were published more
permanently in Edmund Wilson's posthumous collection of Fitzgerald prose, called *The Crack-Up* (1945).
It is appropriate that Wilson, perhaps the best critic
in the United States, should have put together the
fugitive pieces of his old friend, for it is in the second
part of "The Crack-Up" that Fitzgerald named Wilson
as his "intellectual conscience."

◊

February, 1936

OF COURSE all life is a process of breaking down,
but the blows that do the dramatic side of the work
—the big sudden blows that come, or seem to
come, from outside—the ones you remember and
blame things on and, in moments of weakness, tell
your friends about, don't show their effect all at
once. There is another sort of blow that comes
from within—that you don't feel until it's too late
to do anything about it, until you realize with finali-

ty that in some regard you will never be as good a
man again. The first sort of breakage seems to happen quick—the second kind happens almost without your knowing it but is realized suddenly indeed.

Before I go on with this short history, let me
make a general observation—the test of a first-rate
intelligence is the ability to hold two opposed ideas
in the mind at the same time, and still retain the
ability to function. One should, for example, be
able to see that things are hopeless and yet be determined to make them otherwise. This philosophy
fitted on to my early adult life, when I saw the improbable, the implausible, often the "impossible,"
come true. Life was something you dominated if
you were any good. Life yielded easily to intelligence and effort, or to what proportion could be
mustered of both. It seemed a romantic business
to be a successful literary man—you were not ever
going to be as famous as a movie star but what
note you had was probably longer-lived—you were
never going to have the power of a man of strong
political or religious convictions but you were certainly more independent. Of course within the
practice of your trade you were forever unsatisfied
—but I, for one, would not have chosen any other.

As the twenties passed, with my own twenties
marching a little ahead of them, my two juvenile
regrets—at not being big enough (or good enough)
to play football in college, and at not getting overseas during the war—resolved themselves into
childish waking dreams of imaginary heroism
that were good enough to go to sleep on in restless
nights. The big problems of life seemed to solve
themselves, and if the business of fixing them was
difficult, it made one too tired to think of more
general problems.

Life, ten years ago, was largely a personal matter. I must hold in balance the sense of the futility
of effort and the sense of the necessity to struggle;
the conviction of the inevitability of failure and still
the determination to "succeed"—and, more than
these, the contradiction between the dead hand
of the past and the high intentions of the future. If
I could do this through the common ills—domestic, professional and personal—then the ego would
continue as an arrow shot from nothingness to
nothingness with such force that only gravity
would bring it to earth at last.

For seventeen years, with a year of deliberate
loafing and resting out in the center—things went
on like that, with a new chore only a nice prospect
for the next day. I was living hard, too, but: "Up
to forty-nine it'll be all right," I said. "I can count
on that. For a man who's lived as I have, that's all
you could ask."

—And then, ten years this side of forty-nine, I suddenly realized that I had prematurely cracked.

II

NOW a man can crack in many ways—can crack in the head—in which case the power of decision is taken from you by others! or in the body, when one can but submit to the white hospital world; or in the nerves. William Seabrook [1] in an unsympathetic book tells, with some pride and a movie ending, of how he became a public charge. What led to his alcoholism or was bound up with it, was a collapse of his nervous system. Though the present writer was not so entangled—having at the time not tasted so much as a glass of beer for six months—it was his nervous reflexes that were giving way—too much anger and too many tears.

Moreover, to go back to my thesis that life has a varying offensive, the realization of having cracked was not simultaneous with a blow, but with a reprieve.

Not long before, I had sat in the office of a great doctor and listened to a grave sentence. With what, in retrospect, seems some equanimity, I had gone on about my affairs in the city where I was then living, not caring much, not thinking how much had been left undone, or what would become of this and that responsibility, like people do in books; I was well insured and anyhow I had been only a mediocre caretaker of most of the things left in my hands, even of my talent.

But I had a strong sudden instinct that I must be alone. I didn't want to see any people at all. I had seen so many people all my life—I was an average mixer, but more than average in a tendency to identify myself, my ideas, my destiny, with those of all classes that I came in contact with. I was always saving or being saved—in a single morning I would go through the emotions ascribable to Wellington at Waterloo. I lived in a world of inscrutable hostiles and inalienable friends and supporters.

But now I wanted to be absolutely alone and so arranged a certain insulation from ordinary cares.

It was not an unhappy time. I went away and there were fewer people. I found I was good-and-tired. I could lie around and was glad to, sleeping or dozing sometimes twenty hours a day and in the intervals trying resolutely not to think—instead I made lists—made lists and tore them up, hundreds of lists: of cavalry leaders and football players and cities, and popular tunes and pitchers, and happy times, and hobbies and houses lived in and how many suits since I left the army and how many pairs of shoes (I didn't count the suit I

THE CRACK-UP.   1. William Seabrook: William Buehler Seabrook (1886–1945), American adventure and travel writer.

bought in Sorrento that shrunk, nor the pumps and dress shirt and collar that I carried around for years and never wore, because the pumps got damp and grainy and the shirt and collar got yellow and starch-rotted). And lists of women I'd liked, and of the times I had let myself be snubbed by people who had not been my betters in character or ability.

—And then suddenly, surprisingly, I got better.

—And cracked like an old plate as soon as I heard the news.

That is the real end of this story. What was to be done about it will have to rest in what used to be called the "womb of time." Suffice it to say that after about an hour of solitary pillow-hugging, I began to realize that for two years my life had been a drawing on resources that I did not possess, that I had been mortgaging myself physically and spiritually up to the hilt. What was the small gift of life given back in comparison to that?—when there had once been a pride of direction and a confidence in enduring independence.

I realized that in those two years, in order to preserve something—an inner hush maybe, maybe not—I had weaned myself from all the things I used to love—that every act of life from the morning tooth-brush to the friend at dinner had become an effort. I saw that for a long time I had not liked people and things, but only followed the rickety old pretense of liking. I saw that even my love for those closest to me was become only an attempt to love, that my casual relations—with an editor, a tobacco seller, the child of a friend, were only what I remembered I *should* do, from other days. All in the same month I became bitter about such things as the sound of the radio, the advertisements in the magazines, the screech of tracks, the dead silence of the country—contemptuous at human softness, immediately (if secretively) quarrelsome toward hardness—hating the night when I couldn't sleep and hating the day because it went toward night. I slept on the heart side now because I knew that the sooner I could tire that out, even a little, the sooner would come that blessed hour of nightmare which, like a catharsis, would enable me to better meet the new day.

There were certain spots, certain faces I could look at. Like most Middle Westerners, I have never had any but the vaguest race prejudices—I always had a secret yen for the lovely Scandinavian blondes who sat on porches in St. Paul but hadn't emerged enough economically to be part of what was then society. They were too nice to be "chickens" and too quickly off the farmlands to seize a place in the sun, but I remember going round blocks to catch a single glimpse of shining hair—the bright shock of a girl I'd never know. This is urban, unpopular talk. It strays afield from the fact that in these latter days I couldn't stand the sight of Celts, English, Politicians, Strangers, Virginians, Negroes (light or dark), Hunting People, or retail clerks, and middlemen in general, all writers (I avoided writers very carefully because they can perpetuate trouble as no one else can)—and all the classes as classes and most of them as members of their class . . .

Trying to cling to something, I liked doctors and girl children up to the age of about thirteen and well-brought-up boy children from about eight years old on. I could have peace and happiness with these few categories of people. I forgot to add that I liked old men—men over seventy, sometimes over sixty if their faces looked seasoned. I liked Katharine Hepburn's face on the screen, no matter what was said about her pretentiousness, and Miriam Hopkins' face, and old friends if I only saw them once a year and could remember their ghosts.

All rather inhuman and undernourished, isn't it? Well, that, children, is the true sign of cracking up.

It is not a pretty picture. Inevitably it was carted here and there within its frame and exposed to various critics. One of them can only be described as a person whose life makes other people's lives seem like death—even this time when she was cast in the usually unappealing role of Job's comforter. In spite of the fact that this story is over, let me append our conversation as a sort of postscript:

"Instead of being so sorry for yourself, listen—" she said. (She always says "Listen," because she thinks while she talks—*really* thinks.) So she said: "Listen. Suppose this wasn't a crack in you —suppose it was a crack in the Grand Canyon."

"The crack's in me," I said heroically.

"Listen! The world only exists in your eyes—your conception of it. You can make it as big or as small as you want to. And you're trying to be a little puny individual. By God, if I ever cracked, I'd try to make the world crack with me. Listen! The world only exists through your apprehension of it, and so it's much better to say that it's not you that's cracked—it's the Grand Canyon."

"Baby et up all her Spinoza?" [2]

"I don't know anything about Spinoza. I know—" She spoke, then, of old woes of her own, that seemed, in the telling, to have been more dolorous than mine, and how she had met them, over-ridden them, beaten them.

I felt a certain reaction to what she said, but I am a slow-thinking man, and it occurred to me simultaneously that of all natural forces, vitality is the incommunicable one. In days when juice came into one as an article without duty, one tried to distribute it—but always without success; to further mix metaphors, vitality never "takes." You have it or you haven't it, like health or brown eyes or honor or a baritone voice. I might have asked some of it from her, neatly wrapped and ready for home cooking and digestion, but I could never have got it—not if I'd waited around for a thousand hours with the tin cup of self-pity. I could walk from her door, holding myself very carefully like cracked crockery, and go away into the world of bitterness, where I was making a home with such materials as are found there—and quote to myself after I left her door:

"Ye are the salt of the earth. But if the salt hath lost its savour, wherewith shall it be salted?"
Matthew 5–13.

HANDLE WITH CARE

March, 1936

IN A previous article this writer told about his realization that what he had before him was not the dish that he had ordered for his forties. In fact—since he and the dish were one, he described himself as a cracked plate, the kind that one wonders whether it is worth preserving. Your editor thought that the article suggested too many aspects without regarding them closely, and probably many readers felt the same way—and there are always those to whom all self-revelation is contemptible, unless it ends with a noble thanks to the gods for the Unconquerable Soul.[3]

But I had been thanking the gods too long, and thanking them for nothing. I wanted to put a lament into my record, without even the background of the Euganean Hills [4] to give it color. There weren't any Euganean hills that I could see.

Sometimes, though, the cracked plate has to be retained in the pantry, has to be kept in service as a household necessity. It can never again be warmed on the stove nor shuffled with the other plates in the dishpan; it will not be brought out for company, but it will do to hold crackers late at night or to go into the ice box under leftovers . . .

Hence this sequel—a cracked plate's further history.

2. **Spinoza:** Benedictus de Spinoza (1632–77), Dutch philosopher.

3. **Unconquerable Soul:** a reference to "Invictus" by William Ernest Henley (1849–1903), British poet, self-avowed "master of my fate; . . . captain of my soul." 4. **Euganean Hills:** Shelley's poem, "Lines Written Among the Euganean Hills" (1818), attempts to transcend his deep despair.

Now the standard cure for one who is sunk is to consider those in actual destitution or physical suffering—this is an all-weather beatitude for gloom in general and fairly salutory day-time advice for everyone. But at three o'clock in the morning, a forgotten package has the same tragic importance as a death sentence, and the cure doesn't work—and in a real dark night of the soul it is always three o'clock in the morning, day after day. At that hour the tendency is to refuse to face things as long as possible by retiring into an infantile dream—but one is continually startled out of this by various contacts with the world. One meets these occasions as quickly and carelessly as possible and retires once more back into the dream, hoping that things will adjust themselves by some great material or spiritual bonanza. But as the withdrawal persists there is less and less chance of the bonanza—one is not waiting for the fade-out of a single sorrow, but rather being an unwilling witness of an execution, the disintegration of one's own personality . . .

Unless madness or drugs or drink come into it, this phase comes to a dead-end, eventually, and is succeeded by a vacuous quiet. In this you can try to estimate what has been sheared away and what is left. Only when this quiet came to me, did I realize that I had gone through two parallel experiences.

The first time was twenty years ago, when I left Princeton in junior year with a complaint diagnosed as malaria. It transpired, through an X-ray taken a dozen years later, that it had been tuberculosis—a mild case, and after a few months of rest I went back to college. But I had lost certain offices, the chief one was the presidency of the Triangle Club, a musical comedy idea, and also I dropped back a class. To me college would never be the same. There were to be no badges of pride, no medals, after all. It seemed on one March afternoon that I had lost every single thing I wanted—and that night was the first time that I hunted down the spectre of womanhood that, for a little while, makes everything else seem unimportant.

Years later I realized that my failure as a big shot in college was all right—instead of serving on committees, I took a beating on English poetry; when I got the idea of what it was all about, I set about learning how to write. On Shaw's principle that "If you don't get what you like, you better like what you get," it was a lucky break—at the moment it was a harsh and bitter business to know that my career as a leader of men was over.

Since that day I have not been able to fire a bad servant, and I am astonished and impressed by people who can. Some old desire for personal dominance was broken and gone. Life around me was a solemn dream, and I lived on the letters I wrote to a girl in another city. A man does not recover from such jolts—he becomes a different person and, eventually, the new person finds new things to care about.

The other episode parallel to my current situation took place after the war, when I had again over-extended my flank. It was one of those tragic loves doomed for lack of money, and one day the girl closed it out on the basis of common sense. During a long summer of despair I wrote a novel instead of letters, so it came out all right, but it came out all right for a different person. The man with the jingle of money in his pocket who married the girl a year later would always cherish an abiding distrust, an animosity, toward the leisure class—not the conviction of a revolutionist but the smouldering hatred of a peasant. In the years since then I have never been able to stop wondering where my friends' money came from, nor to stop thinking that at one time a sort of *droit de seigneur* [5] might have been exercised to give one of them my girl.

For sixteen years I lived pretty much as this latter person, distrusting the rich, yet working for money with which to share their mobility and the grace that some of them brought into their lives. During this time I had plenty of the usual horses shot from under me—I remember some of their names—*Punctured Pride, Thwarted Expectation, Faithless, Show-off, Hard Hit, Never Again.* And after awhile I wasn't twenty-five, then not even thirty-five, and nothing was quite as good. But in all these years I don't remember a moment of discouragement. I saw honest men through moods of suicidal gloom—some of them gave up and died; others adjusted themselves and went on to a larger success than mine; but my morale never sank below the level of self-disgust when I had put on some unsightly personal show. Trouble has no necessary connection with discouragement—discouragement has a germ of its own, as different from trouble as arthritis is different from a stiff joint.

When a new sky cut off the sun last spring, I didn't at first relate it to what had happened fifteen or twenty years ago. Only gradually did a certain family resemblance come through—an over-extension of the flank, a burning of the candle at both ends; a call upon physical resources that I did not command, like a man over-drawing at his bank. In its impact this blow was more violent

---

5. *droit de seigneur: droit du seigneur,* "master's right."

than the other two but it was the same in kind—a feeling that I was standing at twilight on a deserted range, with an empty rifle in my hands and the targets down. No problem set—simply a silence with only the sound of my own breathing.

In this silence there was a vast irresponsibility toward every obligation, a deflation of all my values. A passionate belief in order, a disregard of motives or consequences in favor of guess work and prophecy, a feeling that craft and industry would have a place in any world—one by one, these and other convictions were swept away. I saw that the novel, which at my maturity was the strongest and supplest medium for conveying thought and emotion from one human being to another, was becoming subordinated to a mechanical and communal art that, whether in the hands of Hollywood merchants or Russian idealists, was capable of reflecting only the tritest thought, the most obvious emotion. It was an art in which words were subordinate to images, where personality was worn down to the inevitable low gear of collaboration. As long past as 1930, I had a hunch that the talkies would make even the best selling novelist as archaic as silent pictures. People still read, if only Professor Canby's book of the month [6]—curious children nosed at the slime of Mr. Tiffany Thayer in the drugstore libraries—but there was a rankling indignity, that to me had become almost an obsession, in seeing the power of the written word subordinated to another power, a more glittering, a grosser power . . .

I set that down as an example of what haunted me during the long night—this was something I could neither accept nor struggle against, something which tended to make my efforts obsolescent, as the chain stores have crippled the small merchant, an exterior force, unbeatable—

(I have the sense of lecturing now, looking at a watch on the desk before me and seeing how many more minutes—).

Well, when I had reached this period of silence, I was forced into a measure that no one ever adopts voluntarily: I was impelled to think. God, was it difficult! The moving about of great secret trunks. In the first exhausted halt, I wondered whether I had ever thought. After a long time I came to these conclusions, just as I write them here:

(1) That I had done very little thinking, save within the problems of my craft. For twenty years a certain man had been my intellectual conscience. That was Edmund Wilson.

(2) That another man represented my sense of the "good life," though I saw him once in a decade, and since then he might have been hung. He is in the fur business in the Northwest and wouldn't like his name set down here. But in difficult situations I had tried to think what *he* would have thought, how *he* would have acted.

(3) That a third contemporary had been an artistic conscience to me—I had not imitated his infectious style, because my own style, such as it is, was formed before he published anything, but there was an awful pull toward him when I was on a spot.[7]

(4) That a fourth man [8] had come to dictate my relations with other people when these relations were successful: how to do, what to say. How to make people at least momentarily happy (in opposition to Mrs. Post's [9] theories of how to make everyone thoroughly uncomfortable with a sort of systematized vulgarity). This always confused me and made me want to go out and get drunk, but this man had seen the game, analyzed it and beaten it, and his word was good enough for me.

(5) That my political conscience had scarcely existed for ten years save as an element of irony in my stuff. When I became again concerned with the system I should function under, it was a man much younger than myself who brought it to me, with a mixture of passion and fresh air.[10]

So there was not an "I" any more—not a basis on which I could organize my self-respect—save my limitless capacity for toil that it seemed I possessed no more. It was strange to have no self—to be like a little boy left alone in a big house, who knew that now he could do anything he wanted to do, but found that there was nothing that he wanted to do—

(The watch is past the hour and I have barely reached my thesis. I have some doubts as to whether this is of general interest, but if anyone wants more, there is plenty left, and your editor will tell me. If you've had enough, say so—but not too loud, because I have the feeling that someone, I'm not sure who, is sound asleep—someone who could have helped me to keep my shop open. It wasn't Lenin, and it wasn't God.)

PASTING IT TOGETHER

April, 1936

I HAVE spoken in these pages of how an exceptionally optimistic young man experienced a crack-up

6. **Professor Canby's book of the month:** Henry Seidel Canby (1878–1961), once a professor at Yale, served for many years on the board of the Book of the Month Club.

7. The reference is to Ernest Hemingway.   8. **a fourth man:** Gerald Murphy, a wealthy American friend in France. 9. **Mrs. Post:** Emily Post, commercial authority on etiquette. 10. Probably Budd Schulberg, the American novelist (1914–   ).

of all values, a crack-up that he scarcely knew of until long after it occurred. I told of the succeeding period of desolation and of the necessity of going on, but without benefit of Henley's familiar heroics,[11] "my head is bloody but unbowed." For a check-up of my spiritual liabilities indicated that I had no particular head to be bowed or unbowed. Once I had had a heart but that was about all I was sure of.

This was at least a starting place out of the morass in which I floundered: "I felt—therefore I was." At one time or another there had been many people who had leaned on me, come to me in difficulties or written me from afar, believed implicitly in my advice and my attitude toward life. The dullest platitude monger or the most unscrupulous Rasputin who can influence the destinies of many people must have some individuality, so the question became one of finding why and where I had changed, where was the leak through which, unknown to myself, my enthusiasm and my vitality had been steadily and prematurely trickling away.

One harassed and despairing night I packed a brief case and went off a thousand miles to think it over. I took a dollar room in a drab little town where I knew no one and sunk all the money I had with me in a stock of potted meat, crackers and apples. But don't let me suggest that the change from a rather overstuffed world to a comparative asceticism was any Research Magnificent [12]—I only wanted absolute quiet to think out why I had developed a sad attitude toward sadness, a melancholy attitude toward melancholy and a tragic attitude toward tragedy—*why I had become identified with the objects of my horror or compassion.*

Does this seem a fine distinction? It isn't: identification such as this spells the death of accomplishment. It is something like this that keeps insane people from working. Lenin did not willingly endure the sufferings of his proletariat, nor Washington of his troops, nor Dickens of his London poor. And when Tolstoy tried some such merging of himself with the objects of his attention, it was a fake and a failure. I mention these because they are the men best known to us all.

It was dangerous mist. When Wordsworth decided that "there had passed away a glory from the earth," he felt no compulsion to pass away with it, and the Fiery Particle Keats never ceased his struggle against t. b. nor in his last moments relinquished his hope of being among the English poets.

My self-immolation was something sodden-dark. It was very distinctly not modern—yet I saw it in others, saw it in a dozen men of honor and industry since the war. (I heard you, but that's too easy—there were Marxians among these men.) I had stood by while one famous contemporary of mine played with the idea of the Big Out for half a year; I had watched when another, equally eminent, spent months in an asylum unable to endure any contact with his fellow men. And of those who had given up and passed on I could list a score.

This led me to the idea that the ones who had survived had made some sort of clean break. This is a big word and is no parallel to a jail-break when one is probably headed for a new jail or will be forced back to the old one. The famous "Escape" or "run away from it all" is an excursion in a trap even if the trap includes the south seas, which are only for those who want to paint them or sail them. A clean break is something you cannot come back from; that is irretrievable because it makes the past cease to exist. So, since I could no longer fulfill the obligations that life had set for me or that I had set for myself, why not slay the empty shell who had been posturing as it for four years? I must continue to be a writer because that was my only way of life, but I would cease any attempts to be a person—to be kind, just or generous. There were plenty of counterfeit coins around that would pass instead of these and I knew where I could get them at a nickel on the dollar. In thirty-nine years an observant eye has learned to detect where the milk is watered and the sugar is sanded, the rhinestone passed for diamond and the stucco for stone. There was to be no more giving of myself—all giving was to be outlawed henceforth under a new name, and that name was Waste.

The decision made me rather exuberant, like anything that is both real and new. As a sort of beginning there was a whole shaft of letters to be tipped into the waste basket when I went home, letters that wanted something for nothing—to read this man's manuscript, market this man's poem, speak free on the radio, indite notes of introduction, give this interview, help with the plot of this play, with this domestic situation, perform this act of thoughtfulness or charity.

The conjuror's hat was empty. To draw things out of it had long been a sort of sleight of hand, and now, to change the metaphor, I was off the dispensing end of the relief roll forever.

The heady villainous feeling continued.

I felt like the beady-eyed men I used to see on the commuting train from Great Neck fifteen years back—men who didn't care whether the

11. Henley's familiar heroics: See above, 3 n.   12. Research Magnificent: title of a novel by H. G. Wells, about a search for a fulfilling way of life.

world tumbled into chaos tomorrow if it spared their houses. I was one with them now, one with the smooth articles who said:

"I'm sorry but business is business." Or:

"You ought to have thought of that before you got into this trouble." Or:

"I'm not the person to see about that."

And a smile—ah, I would get me a smile. I'm still working on that smile. It is to combine the best qualities of a hotel manager, an experienced old social weasel, a headmaster on visitors' day, a colored elevator man, a pansy pulling a profile, a producer getting stuff at half its market value, a trained nurse coming on a new job, a body-vender in her first rotogravure, a hopeful extra swept near the camera, a ballet dancer with an infected toe, and of course the great beam of loving kindness common to all those from Washington to Beverly Hills who must exist by virtue of the contorted pan.

The voice too—I am working with a teacher on the voice. When I have perfected it the larynx will show no ring of conviction except the conviction of the person I am talking to. Since it will be largely called upon for the elicitation of the word "Yes," my teacher (a lawyer) and I are concentrating on that, but in extra hours. I am learning to bring into it that polite acerbity that makes people feel that far from being welcome they are not even tolerated and are under continual and scathing analysis at every moment. These times will of course not coincide with the smile. This will be reserved exclusively for those from whom I have nothing to gain, old worn-out people or young struggling people. They won't mind—what the hell, they get it most of the time anyhow.

But enough. It is not a matter of levity. If you are young and you should write asking to see me and learn how to be a sombre literary man writing pieces upon the state of emotional exhaustion that often overtakes writers in their prime—if you should be so young and so fatuous as to do this, I would not do so much as acknowledge your letter, unless you were related to someone very rich and important indeed. And if you were dying of starvation outside my window, I would go out quickly and give you the smile and the voice (if no longer the hand) and stick around till somebody raised a nickel to phone for the ambulance, that is if I thought there would be any copy in it for me.

I have now at last become a writer only. The man I had persistently tried to be became such a burden that I have "cut him loose" with as little compunction as a Negro lady cuts loose a rival on Saturday night. Let the good people function as such—let the overworked doctors die in harness, with one week's "vacation" a year that they can devote to straightening out their family affairs, and let the underworked doctors scramble for cases at one dollar a throw; let the soldiers be killed and enter immediately into the Valhalla of their profession. That is their contract with the gods. A writer need have no such ideals unless he makes them for himself, and this one has quit. The old dream of being an entire man in the Goethe-Byron-Shaw tradition, with an opulent American touch, a sort of combination of J. P. Morgan, Topham Beauclerk and St. Francis of Assisi, has been relegated to the junk heap of the shoulder pads worn for one day on the Princeton freshman football field and the overseas cap never worn overseas.

So what? This is what I think now: that the natural state of the sentient adult is a qualified unhappiness. I think also that in an adult the desire to be finer in grain than you are, "a constant striving" (as those people say who gain their bread by saying it) only adds to this unhappiness in the end—that end that comes to our youth and hope. My own happiness in the past often approached such an ecstasy that I could not share it even with the person dearest to me but had to walk it away in quiet streets and lanes with only fragments of it to distil into little lines in books—and I think that my happiness, or talent for self-delusion or what you will, was an exception. It was not the natural thing but the unnatural—unnatural as the Boom; and my recent experience parallels the wave of despair that swept the nation when the Boom was over.

I shall manage to live with the new dispensation, though it has taken some months to be certain of the fact. And just as the laughing stoicism which has enabled the American Negro to endure the intolerable conditions of his existence has cost him his sense of the truth—so in my case there is a price to pay. I do not any longer like the postman, nor the grocer, nor the editor, nor the cousin's husband, and he in turn will come to dislike me, so that life will never be very pleasant again, and the sign *Cave Canem* [13] is hung permanently just above my door. I will try to be a correct animal though, and if you throw me a bone with enough meat on it I may even lick your hand.

1936

13. *Cave Canem:* "Beware of the dog."

Ernest Hemingway

BIG TWO-HEARTED RIVER

❖

⟦ THIS story, which first appeared in the Parisian avant-garde review *This Quarter* in May of 1925, is also the climactic story in the volume *In Our Time*, which appeared in October of that year. This presentation of Nick Adams in his maturity may derive, in some ways, from a story by one of Hemingway's favorite authors —*Heart of Darkness* by Joseph Conrad. As that story rests on contrasts of light and darkness, so Hemingway's story opposes two stretches of the river—the river that Nick fishes, where all is bright, clear sunlight and pellucid water, and the swamp into which it flows, the threatening place of corruption, darkness, chaos, and disarray that, for the time being, Nick cannot contemplate. He has already been in the heart of darkness and for the present will remain in the better part of the two-hearted river.

❖

PART I

THE TRAIN went on up the track out of sight, around one of the hills of burnt timber. Nick sat down on the bundle of canvas and bedding the baggage man had pitched out of the door of the baggage car. There was no town, nothing but the rails and the burned-over country. The thirteen saloons that had lined the one street of Seney had not left a trace. The foundations of the Mansion House hotel stuck up above the ground. The stone was chipped and split by the fire. It was all that was left of the town of Seney. Even the surface had been burned off the ground.

Nick looked at the burned-over stretch of hill-side, where he had expected to find the scattered houses of the town and then walked down the railroad track to the bridge over the river. The river was there. It swirled against the log spiles of the bridge. Nick looked down into the clear, brown water, colored from the pebbly bottom, and watched the trout keeping themselves steady in the current with wavering fins. As he watched them they changed their positions by quick angles, only

to hold steady in the fast water again. Nick watched them a long time.

He watched them holding themselves with their noses into the current, many trout in deep, fast moving water, slightly distorted as he watched far down through the glassy convex surface of the pool, its surface pushing and swelling smooth against the resistance of the log-driven piles of the bridge. At the bottom of the pool were the big trout. Nick did not see them at first. Then he saw them at the bottom of the pool, big trout looking to hold themselves on the gravel bottom in a varying mist of gravel and sand, raised in spurts by the current.

Nick looked down into the pool from the bridge. It was a hot day. A kingfisher flew up the stream. It was a long time since Nick had looked into a stream and seen trout. They were very satisfactory. As the shadow of the kingfisher moved up the stream, a big trout shot upstream in a long angle, only his shadow marking the angle, then lost his shadow as he came through the surface of the water, caught the sun, and then, as he went back into the stream under the surface, his shadow seemed to float down the stream with the current, unresisting, to his post under the bridge where he tightened facing up into the current.

Nick's heart tightened as the trout moved. He felt all the old feeling.

He turned and looked down the stream. It stretched away, pebbly-bottomed with shallows and big boulders and a deep pool as it curved away around the foot of a bluff.

Nick walked back up the ties to where his pack lay in the cinders beside the railway track. He was happy. He adjusted the pack harness around the bundle, pulling straps tight, slung the pack on his back, got his arms through the shoulder straps and took some of the pull off his shoulders by leaning his forehead against the wide band of the tump-line. Still, it was too heavy. It was much too heavy. He had his leather rod-case in his hand and leaning forward to keep the weight of the pack high on his shoulders he walked along the road that paralleled the railway track, leaving the burned town behind in the heat, and then turned off around a hill with a high, fire-scarred hill on either side onto a road that went back into the country. He walked along the road feeling the ache from the pull of the heavy pack. The road climbed steadily. It was hard work walking up-hill. His muscles ached and the day was hot, but Nick felt happy. He felt he had left everything behind, the need for thinking, the need to write, other needs. It was all back of him.

From the time he had gotten down off the train and the baggage man had thrown his pack out of the open car door things had been different. Seney was burned, the country was burned over and changed, but it did not matter. It could not all be burned. He knew that. He hiked along the road, sweating in the sun, climbing to cross the range of hills that separated the railway from the pine plains.

The road ran on, dipping occasionally, but always climbing. Nick went on up. Finally the road after going parallel to the burnt hillside reached the top. Nick leaned back against a stump and slipped out of the pack harness. Ahead of him, as far as he could see, was the pine plain. The burned country stopped off at the left with the range of hills. On ahead islands of dark pine trees rose out of the plain. Far off to the left was the line of the river. Nick followed it with his eye and caught glints of the water in the sun.

There was nothing but the pine plain ahead of him, until the far blue hills that marked the Lake Superior height of land. He could hardly see them, faint and far away in the heat-light over the plain. If he looked too steadily they were gone. But if he only half-looked they were there, the far off hills of the height of land.

Nick sat down against the charred stump and smoked a cigarette. His pack balanced on the top of the stump, harness holding ready, a hollow molded in it from his back. Nick sat smoking, looking out over the country. He did not need to get his map out. He knew where he was from the position of the river.

As he smoked, his legs stretched out in front of him, he noticed a grasshopper walk along the ground and up onto his woolen sock. The grasshopper was black. As he had walked along the road, climbing, he had started many grasshoppers from the dust. They were all black. They were not the big grasshoppers with yellow and black or red and black wings whirring out from their black wing sheathing as they fly up. These were just ordinary hoppers, but all a sooty black in color. Nick had wondered about them as he walked, without really thinking about them. Now, as he watched the black hopper that was nibbling at the wool of his sock with its fourway lip, he realized that they had all turned black from living in the burned-over land. He realized that the fire must

have come the year before, but the grasshoppers were all black now. He wondered how long they would stay that way.

Carefully he reached his hand down and took hold of the hopper by the wings. He turned him up, all his legs walking in the air, and looked at his jointed belly. Yes, it was black too, iridescent where the back and head were dusty.

"Go on, hopper," Nick said, speaking out loud for the first time, "Fly away somewhere."

He tossed the grasshopper up into the air and watched him sail away to a charcoal stump across the road.

Nick stood up. He leaned his back against the weight of his pack where it rested upright on the stump and got his arms through the shoulder straps. He stood with the pack on his back on the brow of the hill looking out across the country, toward the distant river and then struck down the hillside away from the road. Underfoot the ground was good walking. Two hundred yards down the hillside the fire line stopped. Then it was sweet fern, growing ankle high, to walk through, and clumps of jack pines; a long undulating country with frequent rises ane descents, sandy underfoot and the country alive again.

Nick kept his direction by the sun. He knew where he wanted to strike the river and he kept on through the pine plain, mounting small rises to see other rises ahead of him and sometimes from the top of a rise a great solid island of pines off to his right or his left. He broke off some sprigs of the heathery sweet fern, and put them under his pack straps. The chafing crushed it and he smelled it as he walked.

He was tired and very hot, walking across the uneven, shadeless pine plain. At any time he knew he could strike the river by turning off to his left. It could not be more than a mile away. But he kept on toward the north to hit the river as far upstream as he could go in one day's walking.

For some time as he walked Nick had been in sight of one of the big islands of pine standing out above the rolling high ground he was crossing. He dipped down and then as he came slowly up to the crest of the ridge he turned and made toward the pine trees.

There was no underbrush in the island of pine trees. The trunks of the trees went straight up or slanted toward each other. The trunks were straight and brown without branches. The branches were high above. Some interlocked to make a solid shadow on the brown forest floor. Around the grove of trees was a bare space. It was brown and soft underfoot as Nick walked on it. This was the over-lapping of the pine needle floor, extending out beyond the width of the high branches. The trees had grown tall and the branches moved high, leaving in the sun this bare space they had once covered with shadow. Sharp at the edge of this extension of the forest floor commenced the sweet fern.

Nick slipped off his pack and lay down in the shade. He lay on his back and looked up into the pine trees. His neck and back and the small of his back rested as he stretched. The earth felt good against his back. He looked up at the sky, through the branches, and then shut his eyes. He opened them and looked up again. There was a wind high up in the branches. He shut his eyes again and went to sleep.

Nick woke stiff and cramped. The sun was nearly down. His pack was heavy and the straps painful as he lifted it on. He leaned over with the pack on and picked up the leather rod-case and started out from the pine trees across the sweet fern swale, toward the river. He knew it could not be more than a mile.

He came down a hillside covered with stumps into a meadow. At the edge of the meadow flowed the river. Nick was glad to get to the river. He walked upstream through the meadow. His trousers were soaked with the dew as he walked. After the hot day, the dew had come quickly and heavily. The river made no sound. It was too fast and smooth. At the edge of the meadow, before he mounted to a piece of high ground to make camp, Nick looked down the river at the trout rising. They were rising to insects come from the swamp on the other side of the stream when the sun went down. The trout jumped out of water to take them. While Nick walked through the little stretch of meadow alongside the stream, trout had jumped high out of water. Now as he looked down the river, the insects must be settling on the surface, for the trout were feeding steadily all down the stream. As far down the long stretch as he could see, the trout were rising, making circles all down the surface of the water, as though it were starting to rain.

The ground rose, wooded and sandy, to overlook the meadow, the stretch of river and the swamp. Nick dropped his pack and rod-case and looked for a level piece of ground. He was very hungry and he wanted to make his camp before he cooked. Between two jack pines, the ground was quite level. He took the ax out of the pack and chopped out two projecting roots. That leveled a piece of ground large enough to sleep on. He smoothed out the sandy soil with his hand and pulled all the sweet fern bushes by their roots. His hands smelled good from the sweet fern. He smoothed the uprooted earth. He did not want anything making lumps under the blankets. When he had the ground smooth, he spread his three blankets. One he folded double, next to the ground. The other two he spread on top.

With the ax he slit off a bright slab of pine from one of the stumps and split it into pegs for the tent. He wanted them long and solid to hold in the ground. With the tent unpacked and spread on the ground, the pack, leaning against a jackpine, looked much smaller. Nick tied the rope that served the tent for a ridge-pole to the trunk of one of the pine trees and pulled the tent up off the ground with the other end of the rope and tied it to the other pine. The tent hung on the rope like a canvas blanket on a clothes line. Nick poked a pole he had cut up under the back peak of the canvas and then made it a tent by pegging out the sides. He pegged the sides out taut and drove the pegs deep, hitting them down into the ground with the flat of the ax until the rope loops were buried and the canvas was drum tight.

Across the open mouth of the tent Nick fixed cheese cloth to keep out mosquitoes. He crawled inside under the mosquito bar with various things from the pack to put at the head of the bed under the slant of the canvas. Inside the tent the light came through the brown canvas. It smelled pleasantly of canvas. Already there was something mysterious and homelike. Nick was happy as he crawled inside the tent. He had not been unhappy all day. This was different though. Now things were done. There had been this to do. Now it was done. It had been a hard trip. He was very tired. That was done. He had made his camp. He was settled. Nothing could touch him. It was a good place to camp. He was there, in the good place. He was in his home where he had made it. Now he was hungry.

He came out, crawling under the cheese cloth. It was quite dark outside. It was lighter in the tent.

Nick went over to the pack and found, with his fingers, a long nail in a paper sack of nails, in the bottom of the pack. He drove it into the pine tree, holding it close and hitting it gently with the flat of the ax. He hung the pack up on the nail. All his supplies were in the pack. They were off the ground and sheltered now.

Nick was hungry. He did not believe he had ever been hungrier. He opened and emptied a can of pork and beans and a can of spaghetti into the frying pan.

"I've got a right to eat this kind of stuff, if I'm willing to carry it," Nick said. His voice sounded strange in the darkening woods. He did not speak again.

He started a fire with some chunks of pine he got with the ax from a stump. Over the fire he stuck a wire grill, pushing the four legs down into the ground with his boot. Nick put the frying pan on the grill over the flames. He was hungrier. The beans and spaghetti warmed. Nick stirred them and mixed them together. They began to bubble, making little bubbles that rose with difficulty to the surface. There was a good smell. Nick got out a bottle of tomato catchup and cut four slices of bread. The little bubbles were coming faster now. Nick sat down beside the fire and lifted the frying pan off. He poured about half the contents out into the tin plate. It spread slowly on the plate. Nick knew it was too hot. He poured on some tomato catchup. He knew the beans and spaghetti were still too hot. He looked at the fire, then at the tent, he was not going to spoil it all by burning his tongue. For years he had never enjoyed fried bananas because he had never been able to wait for them to cool. His tongue was very sensitive. He was very hungry. Across the river in the swamp, in the almost dark, he saw a mist rising. He looked at the tent once more. All right. He took a full spoonful from the plate.

"Chrise," Nick said, "Geezus Chrise," he said happily.

He ate the whole plateful before he remembered the bread. Nick finished the second plateful with the bread, mopping the plate shiny. He had not eaten since a cup of coffee and a ham sandwich in the station restaurant at St. Ignace. It had been a very fine experience. He had been that hungry before, but had not been able to satisfy it. He could have made camp hours before if he had wanted to. There were plenty of good places to camp on the river. But this was good.

Nick tucked two big chips of pine under the grill. The fire flared up. He had forgotten to get water for the coffee. Out of the pack he got a folding canvas bucket and walked down the hill, across the edge of the meadow, to the stream. The other bank was in the white mist. The grass was wet and cold as he knelt on the bank and dipped the canvas bucket into the stream. It bellied and pulled hard in the current. The water was ice cold. Nick rinsed the bucket and carried it full up to the camp. Up away from the stream it was not so cold.

Nick drove another big nail and hung up the bucket full of water. He dipped the coffee pot half full, put some more chips under the grill onto the fire and put the pot on. He could not remember which way he made coffee. He could remember an argument about it with Hopkins, but not which side he had taken. He decided to bring it to a boil.

He remembered now that was Hopkins's way. He had once argued about everything with Hopkins. While he waited for the coffee to boil, he opened a small can of apricots. He liked to open cans. He emptied the can of apricots out into a tin cup. While he watched the coffee on the fire, he drank the juice syrup of the apricots, carefully at first to keep from spilling, then meditatively, sucking the apricots down. They were better than fresh apricots.

The coffee boiled as he watched. The lid came up and coffee and grounds ran down the side of the pot. Nick took it off the grill. It was a triumph for Hopkins. He put sugar in the empty apricot cup and poured some of the coffee out to cool. It was too hot to pour and he used his hat to hold the handle of the coffee pot. He would not let it steep in the pot at all. Not the first cup. It should be straight Hopkins all the way. Hop deserved that. He was a very serious coffee maker. He was the most serious man Nick had ever known. Not heavy, serious. That was a long time ago. Hopkins spoke without moving his lips. He had played polo. He made millions of dollars in Texas. He had borrowed carfare to go to Chicago, when the wire came that his first big well had come in. He could have wired for money. That would have been too slow. They called Hop's girl the Blonde Venus. Hop did not mind because she was not his real girl. Hopkins said very confidently that none of them would make fun of his real girl. He was right. Hopkins went away when the telegram came. That was on the Black River. It took eight days for the telegram to reach him. Hopkins gave away his .22 caliber Colt automatic pistol to Nick. He gave his camera to Bill. It was to remember him always by. They were all going fishing again next summer. The Hop Head was rich. He would get a yacht and they would all cruise along the north shore of Lake Superior. He was excited but serious. They said good-bye and all felt bad. It broke up the trip. They never saw Hopkins again. That was a long time ago on the Black River.

Nick drank the coffee, the coffee according to Hopkins. The coffee was bitter. Nick laughed. It made a good ending to the story. His mind was starting to work. He knew he could choke it because he was tired enough. He spilled the coffee out of the pot and shook the grounds loose into the fire. He lit a cigarette and went inside the tent. He took off his shoes and trousers, sitting on the blankets, rolled the shoes up inside the trousers for a pillow and got in between the blankets.

Out through the front of the tent he watched the glow of the fire, when the night wind blew on it. It was a quiet night. The swamp was perfectly quiet. Nick stretched under the blanket comfortably. A mosquito hummed close to his ear. Nick sat up and lit a match. The mosquito was on the canvas, over his head. Nick moved the match quickly up to it. The mosquito made a satisfactory hiss in the flame. The match went out. Nick lay down again under the blankets. He turned on his side and shut his eyes. He was sleepy. He felt sleep coming. He curled up under the blanket and went to sleep.

PART II

IN THE morning the sun was up and the tent was starting to get hot. Nick crawled out under the mosquito netting stretched across the mouth of the tent, to look at the morning. The grass was wet on his hands as he came out. He held his trousers and his shoes in his hands. The sun was just up over the hill. There was the meadow, the river and the swamp. There were birch trees in the green of the swamp on the other side of the river.

The river was clear and smoothly fast in the early morning. Down about two hundred yards were three logs all the way across the stream. They made the water smooth and deep above them. As Nick watched, a mink crossed the river on the logs and went into the swamp. Nick was excited. He was excited by the early morning and the river. He was really too hurried to eat breakfast, but he knew he must. He built a little fire and put on the coffee pot. While the water was heating in the pot he took an empty bottle and went down over the edge of the high ground to the meadow. The meadow was wet with dew and Nick wanted to catch grasshoppers for bait before the sun dried the grass. He found plenty of good grasshoppers. They were at the base of the grass stems. Sometimes they clung to a grass stem. They were cold and wet with the dew, and could not jump until the sun warmed them. Nick picked them up, taking only the medium sized brown ones, and put them into the bottle. He turned over a log and just under the shelter of the edge were several hundred hoppers. It was a grasshopper lodging house. Nick put about fifty of the medium browns into the bottle. While he was picking up the hoppers the others warmed in the sun and commenced to hop away. They flew when they hopped. At first they made one flight and stayed stiff when they landed, as though they were dead.

Nick knew that by the time he was through with breakfast they would be as lively as ever. Without dew in the grass it would take him all day to catch a bottle full of good grasshoppers and he would have to crush many of them, slamming at them with his hat. He washed his hands at the stream. He was excited to be near it. Then he walked up to the tent. The hoppers were already jumping stiffly in the grass. In the bottle, warmed by the sun, they were jumping in a mass. Nick put in a pine stick as a cork. It plugged the mouth of the bottle enough, so the hoppers could not get out and left plenty of air passage.

He had rolled the log back and knew he could get grasshoppers there every morning.

Nick laid the bottle full of jumping grasshoppers against a pine trunk. Rapidly he mixed some buckwheat flour with water and stirred it smooth, one cup of flour, one cup of water. He put a handful of coffee in the pot and dipped a lump of grease out of a can and slid it sputtering across the hot skillet. On the smoking skillet he poured smoothly the buckwheat batter. It spread like lava, the grease spitting sharply. Around the edges the buckwheat cake began to firm, then brown, then crisp. The surface was bubbling slowly to porousness. Nick pushed under the browned under surface with a fresh pine chip. He shook the skillet sideways and the cake was loose on the surface. I won't try and flop it, he thought. He slid the chip of clean wood all the way under the cake, and flopped it over onto its face. It sputtered in the pan.

When it was cooked Nick regreased the skillet. He used all the batter. It made another big flapjack and one smaller one.

Nick ate a big flapjack and a smaller one, covered with apple butter. He put apple butter on the third cake, folded it over twice, wrapped it in oiled paper and put it in his shirt pocket. He put the apple butter jar back in the pack and cut bread for two sandwiches.

In the pack he found a big onion. He sliced it in two and peeled the silky outer skin. Then he cut one half into slices and made onion sandwiches. He wrapped them in oiled paper and buttoned them in the other pocket of his khaki shirt. He turned the skillet upside down on the grill, drank the coffee, sweetened and yellow brown with the condensed milk in it, and tidied up the camp. It was a nice little camp.

Nick took his fly rod out of the leather rod-case, jointed it, and shoved the rod-case back into the tent. He put on the reel and threaded the line through the guides. He had to hold it from hand to hand, as he threaded it, or it would slip back through its own weight. It was a heavy, double tapered fly line. Nick had paid eight dollars for it a long time ago. It was made heavy to lift back in the air and come forward flat and heavy and straight to make it possible to cast a fly which has no weight. Nick opened the aluminum leader box. The leaders were coiled between the damp flannel pads. Nick had wet the pads at the water cooler on the train up to St. Ignace. In the damp pads the gut leaders had softened and Nick unrolled one and tied it by a loop at the end to the heavy fly line. He fastened a hook on the end of the leader. It was a small hook; very thin and springy.

Nick took it from his hook book, sitting with the rod across his lap. He tested the knot and the spring of the rod by pulling the line taut. It was a good feeling. He was careful not to let the hook bite into his finger.

He started down to the stream, holding his rod, the bottle of grasshoppers hung from his neck by a thong tied in half hitches around the neck of the bottle. His landing net hung by a hook from his belt. Over his shoulder was a long flour sack tied at each corner into an ear. The cord went over his shoulder. The sack flapped against his legs.

Nick felt awkward and professionally happy with all his equipment hanging from him. The grasshopper bottle swung against his chest. In his shirt the breast pockets bulged against him with the lunch and his fly book.

He stepped into the stream. It was a shock. His trousers clung tight to his legs. His shoes felt the gravel. The water was a rising cold shock.

Rushing, the current sucked against his legs. Where he stepped in, the water was over his knees. He waded with the current. The gravel slid under his shoes. He looked down at the swirl of water below each leg and tipped up the bottle to get a grasshopper.

The first grasshopper gave a jump in the neck of the bottle and went out into the water. He was sucked under in the whirl by Nick's right leg and came to the surface a little way down stream. He floated rapidly, kicking. In a quick circle, breaking the smooth surface of the water, he disappeared. A trout had taken him.

Another hopper poked his head out of the bottle. His antennæ wavered. He was getting his front legs out of the bottle to jump. Nick took him by the head and held him while he threaded the slim hook under his chin, down through his thorax and into the last segments of his abdomen. The grasshopper took hold of the hook with his front feet, spitting tobacco juice on it. Nick dropped him into the water.

Holding the rod in his right hand he let out line against the pull of the grasshopper in the current. He stripped off line from the reel with his left hand and let it run free. He could see the hopper in the little waves of the current. It went out of sight.

There was a tug on the line. Nick pulled against the taut line. It was his first strike. Holding the now living rod across the current, he brought in the line with his left hand. The rod bent in jerks, the trout pumping against the current. Nick knew it was a small one. He lifted the rod straight up in the air. It bowed with the pull.

He saw the trout in the water jerking with his head and body against the shifting tangent of the line in the stream.

Nick took the line in his left hand and pulled the trout, thumping tiredly against the current, to the surface. His back was mottled the clear, water-over-gravel color, his side flashing in the sun. The rod under his right arm, Nick stooped, dipping his right hand into the current. He held the trout, never still, with his moist right hand, while he unhooked the barb from his mouth, then dropped him back into the stream.

He hung unsteadily in the current, then settled to the bottom beside a stone. Nick reached down his hand to touch him, his arm to the elbow under water. The trout was steady in the moving stream, resting on the gravel, beside a stone. As Nick's fingers touched him, touched his smooth, cool, underwater feeling he was gone, gone in a shadow across the bottom of the stream.

He's all right, Nick thought. He was only tired.

He had wet his hand before he touched the trout, so he would not disturb the delicate mucus that covered him. If a trout was touched with a dry hand, a white fungus attacked the unprotected spot. Years before when he had fished crowded streams, with fly fishermen ahead of him and behind him, Nick had again and again come on dead trout, furry with white fungus, drifted against a rock, or floating belly up in some pool. Nick did not like to fish with other men on the river. Unless they were of your party, they spoiled it.

He wallowed down the stream, above his knees in the current, through the fifty yards of shallow water above the pile of logs that crossed the stream. He did not rebait his hook and held it in his hand as he waded. He was certain he could catch small trout in the shallows, but he did not want them. There would be no big trout in the shallows this time of day.

Now the water deepened up his thighs sharply and coldly. Ahead was the smooth dammed-back flood of water above the logs. The water was smooth and dark; on the left, the lower edge of the meadow; on the right the swamp.

Nick leaned back against the current and took a hopper from the bottle. He threaded the hopper on the hook and spat on him for good luck. Then he pulled several yards of line from the reel and tossed the hopper out ahead onto the fast, dark water. It floated down towards the logs, then the weight of the line pulled the bait under the surface. Nick held the rod in his right hand, letting the line run out through his fingers.

There was a long tug. Nick struck and the rod came alive and dangerous, bent double, the line tightening, coming out of water, tightening, all in a heavy, dangerous, steady pull. Nick felt the moment when the leader would break if the strain increased and let the line go.

The reel ratcheted into a mechanical shriek as the line went out in a rush. Too fast. Nick could not check it, the line rushing out, the reel note rising as the line ran out.

With the core of the reel showing, his heart feeling stopped with the excitement, leaning back against the current that mounted icily his thighs, Nick thumbed the reel hard with his left hand. It was awkward getting his thumb inside the fly reel frame.

As he put on pressure the line tightened into sudden hardness and beyond the logs a huge trout went high out of water. As he jumped, Nick lowered the tip of the rod. But he felt, as he dropped the tip to ease the strain, the moment when the strain was too great; the hardness too tight. Of course, the leader had broken. There was no mistaking the feeling when all spring left the line and it became dry and hard. Then it went slack.

His mouth dry, his heart down, Nick reeled in. He had never seen so big a trout. There was a heaviness, a power not to be held, and then the bulk of him, as he jumped. He looked as broad as a salmon.

Nick's hand was shaky. He reeled in slowly. The thrill had been too much. He felt, vaguely, a little sick, as though it would be better to sit down.

The leader had broken where the hook was tied to it. Nick took it in his hand. He thought of the trout somewhere on the bottom, holding himself steady over the gravel, far down below the light, under the logs, with the hook in his jaw. Nick knew the trout's teeth would cut through the snell of the hook. The hook would imbed itself in his jaw. He'd bet the trout was angry. Anything that size would be angry. That was a trout. He had been solidly hooked. Solid as a rock. He felt like a rock, too, before he started off. By God, he was a big one. By God, he was the biggest one I ever heard of.

Nick climbed out onto the meadow and stood, water running down his trousers and out of his shoes, his shoes squelchy. He went over and sat on the logs. He did not want to rush his sensations any.

He wriggled his toes in the water, in his shoes, and got out a cigarette from his breast pocket. He lit it and tossed the match into the fast water below the logs. A tiny trout rose at the match, as it swung around in the fast current. Nick laughed. He would finish the cigarette.

He sat on the logs, smoking, drying in the sun, the sun warm on his back, the river shallow ahead entering the woods, curving into the woods, shallows, light glittering, big water-smooth rocks, cedars along the bank and white birches, the logs warm in the sun, smooth to sit on, without bark, gray to the touch; slowly the feeling of disappointment left him. It went away slowly, the feeling of disappointment that came sharply after the thrill that made his shoulders ache. It was all right now. His rod lying out on the logs, Nick tied a new hook on the leader, pulling the gut tight until it grimped into itself in a hard knot.

He baited up, then picked up the rod and walked to the far end of the logs to get into the water, where it was not too deep. Under and beyond the logs was a deep pool. Nick walked around the shallow shelf near the swamp shore until he came out on the shallow bed of the stream.

On the left, where the meadow ended and the woods began, a great elm tree was uprooted. Gone over in a storm, it lay back into the woods, its roots clotted with dirt, grass growing in them, rising a solid bank beside the stream. The river cut to the edge of the uprooted tree. From where Nick stood he could see deep channels, like ruts, cut in the shallow bed of the stream by the flow of the current. Pebbly where he stood and pebbly and full of boulders beyond; where it curved near the tree roots, the bed of the stream was marly and between the ruts of deep water green weed fronds swung in the current.

Nick swung the rod back over his shoulder and forward, and the line, curving forward, laid the grasshopper down on one of the deep channels in the weeds. A trout struck and Nick hooked him.

Holding the rod far out toward the uprooted tree and sloshing backward in the current, Nick worked the trout, plunging, the rod bending alive, out of the danger of the weeds into the open river. Holding the rod, pumping alive against the current, Nick brought the trout in. He rushed, but always came, the spring of the rod yielding to the rushes, sometimes jerking under water, but always bringing him in. Nick eased downstream with the rushes. The rod above his head he led the trout over the net, then lifted.

The trout hung heavy in the net, mottled trout back and silver sides in the meshes. Nick unhooked him; heavy sides, good to hold, big undershot jaw, and slipped him, heaving and big sliding, into the long sack that hung from his shoulders in the water.

Nick spread the mouth of the sack against the current and it filled, heavy with water. He held it up, the bottom in the stream, and the water poured out through the sides. Inside at the bottom was the big trout, alive in the water.

Nick moved downstream. The sack out ahead of him, sunk, heavy in the water, pulling from his shoulders.

It was getting hot, the sun hot on the back of his neck.

Nick had one good trout. He did not care about getting many trout. Now the stream was shallow and wide. There were trees along both banks. The trees of the left bank made short shadows on the current in the forenoon sun. Nick knew there were trout in each shadow. In the afternoon, after the sun had crossed toward the hills, the trout would be in the cool shadows on the other side of the stream.

The very biggest ones would lie up close to the bank. You could always pick them up there on the Black. When the sun was down they all moved out into the current. Just when the sun made the water blinding in the glare before it went down, you were liable to strike a big trout anywhere in the current. It was almost impossible to fish then, the surface of the water was blinding as a mirror in the sun. Of course, you could fish upstream, but in a stream like the Black, or this, you had to wallow against the current and in a deep place, the water piled up on you. It was no fun to fish upstream with this much current.

Nick moved along through the shallow stretch watching the banks for deep holes. A beech tree grew close beside the river, so that the branches hung down into the water. The stream went back in under the leaves. There were always trout in a place like that.

Nick did not care about fishing that hole. He was sure he would get hooked in the branches.

It looked deep though. He dropped the grasshopper so the current took it under water, back in under the overhanging branch. The line pulled hard and Nick struck. The trout threshed heavily, half out of water in the leaves and branches. The line was caught. Nick pulled hard and the trout was off. He reeled in and holding the hook in his hand, walked down the stream.

Ahead, close to the left bank, was a big log. Nick saw it was hollow; pointing up river the current entered it smoothly, only a little ripple spread each side of the log. The water was deepening. The top of the hollow log was gray and dry. It was partly in the shadow.

Nick took the cork out of the grasshopper bottle and a hopper clung to it. He picked him off, hooked him and tossed him out. He held the rod far out so that the hopper on the water moved into the current flowing into the hollow log. Nick lowered the rod and the hopper floated in. There was a heavy strike. Nick swung the rod against the pull. It felt as though he were hooked into the log itself, except for the live feeling.

He tried to force the fish out into the current. It came, heavily.

The line went slack and Nick thought the trout was gone. Then he saw him, very near, in the current, shaking his head, trying to get the hook out. His mouth was clamped shut. He was fighting the hook in the clear flowing current.

Looping in the line with his left hand, Nick swung the rod to make the line taut and tried to lead the trout toward the net, but he was gone, out of sight, the line pumping. Nick fought him against the current, letting him thump in the water against the spring of the rod. He shifted the rod to his left hand, worked the trout upstream, holding his weight, fighting on the rod, and then let him down into the net. He lifted him clear of the water, a heavy half circle in the net, the net dripping, unhooked him and slid him into the sack.

He spread the mouth of the sack and looked down in at the two big trout alive in the water.

Through the deepening water, Nick waded over to the hollow log. He took the sack off, over his head, the trout flopping as it came out of water, and hung it so the trout were deep in the water. Then he pulled himself up on the log and sat, the water from his trousers and boots running down into the stream. He laid his rod down, moved along to the shady end of the log and took the sandwiches out of his pocket. He dipped the sandwiches in the cold water. The current carried away the crumbs. He ate the sandwiches and dipped his hat full of water to drink, the water running out through his hat just ahead of his drinking.

It was cool in the shade, sitting on the log. He took a cigarette out and struck a match to light it. The match sunk into the gray wood, making a tiny furrow. Nick leaned over the side of the log, found a hard place and lit the match. He sat smoking and watching the river.

Ahead the river narrowed and went into a swamp. The river became smooth and deep and the swamp looked solid with cedar trees, their trunks close together, their branches solid. It would not be possible to walk through a swamp like that. The branches grew so low. You would have to keep almost level with the ground to move at all. You could not crash through the branches. That must be why the animals that lived in swamps were built the way they were, Nick thought.

He wished he had brought something to read. He felt like reading. He did not feel like going on into the swamp. He looked down the river. A big cedar slanted all the way across the stream. Beyond that the river went into the swamp.

Nick did not want to go in there now. He felt a reaction against deep wading with the water deepening up under his armpits, to hook big trout in places impossible to land them. In the swamp the banks were bare, the big cedars came together overhead, the sun did not come through, except in patches; in the fast deep water, in the half light, the fishing would be tragic. In the swamp fishing was a tragic adventure. Nick did not want it. He did not want to go down the stream any further today.

He took out his knife, opened it and stuck it in the log. Then he pulled up the sack, reached into it and brought out one of the trout. Holding him near the tail, hard to hold, alive, in his hand, he whacked him against the log. The trout quivered, rigid. Nick laid him on the log in the shade and broke the neck of the other fish the same way. He laid them side by side on the log. They were fine trout.

Nick cleaned them, slitting them from the vent to the tip of the jaw. All the insides and the gills and tongue came out in one piece. They were both males; long gray-white strips of milt, smooth and clean. All the insides clean and compact, coming out all together. Nick tossed the offal ashore for the minks to find.

He washed the trout in the stream. When he held them back up in the water they looked like live fish. Their color was not gone yet. He washed his hands and dried them on the log. Then he laid the trout on the sack spread out on the log, rolled them up in it, tied the bundle and put it in the landing net. His knife was still standing, blade stuck in the log. He cleaned it on the wood and put it in his pocket.

Nick stood up on the log, holding his rod, the landing net hanging heavy, then stepped into the water and splashed ashore. He climbed the bank and cut up into the woods, toward the high ground. He was going back to camp. He looked back. The river just showed through the trees. There were plenty of days coming when he could fish the swamp.

1925

F R O M

THE GREEN HILLS OF AFRICA

◇

⟨ THESE selections, taken from the opening pages of one of Hemingway's two books of nonfictional prose published in his lifetime, are interesting in that they provide the background in personal experience of such important short stories as "The Snows of Kilimanjaro," but more especially because they reveal some of Hemingway's literary attitudes and prejudices. Since he was not much given to talk about writing, these opinions about American literature and the situation of the American writer are all the more interesting.

◇

WE WERE sitting in the blind that Wanderobo hunters had built of twigs and branches at the edge of the salt-lick when we heard the truck coming. At first it was far away and no one could tell what the noise was. Then it was stopped and we hoped it had been nothing or perhaps only the wind. Then it moved slowly nearer, unmistakable now, louder and louder until, agonizing in a clank of loud irregular explosions, it passed close behind us to go on up the road. The theatrical one of the two trackers stood up.

"It is finished," he said.

I put my hand to my mouth and motioned him down.

"It is finished," he said again and spread his arms wide. I had never liked him and I liked him less now.

"After," I whispered. M'Cola shook his head. I looked at his bald black skull and he turned his face a little so that I saw the thin Chinese hairs at the corners of his mouth.

"No good," he said. *"Hapana m'uzuri."*

"Wait a little," I told him. He bent his head down again so that it would not show above the dead branches and we sat there in the dust of the hole until it was too dark to see the front sight on my rifle; but nothing more came. The theatrical tracker was impatient and restless. A little before the last of the light was gone he whispered to M'Cola that it was now too dark to shoot.

"Shut up, you," M'Cola told him. "The Bwana can shoot after you cannot see."

The other tracker, the educated one, gave another demonstration of his education by scratching his name, Abdullah, on the black skin of his leg with a sharp twig. I watched without admiration and M'Cola looked at the word without a shadow of expression on his face. After a while the tracker scratched it out.

Finally I made a last sight against what was left of the light and saw it was no use, even with the large aperture.

M'Cola was watching.

"No good," I said.

"Yes," he agreed, in Swahili. "Go to camp?"

"Yes."

We stood up and made our way out of the blind and out through the trees, walking on the sandy loam, feeling our way between trees and under branches, back to the road. A mile along the road was the car. As we came alongside, Kamau, the driver, put the lights on.

The truck had spoiled it. That afternoon we had left the car up the road and approached the salt-lick very carefully. There had been a little rain, the day before, though not enough to flood the lick, which was simply an opening in the trees with a patch of earth worn into deep circles and grooved at the edges with hollows where the animals had licked the dirt for salt, and we had seen long, heart-shaped, fresh tracks of four greater kudu bulls that had been on the salt the night before, as well as many newly pressed tracks of lesser kudu. There was also a rhino who, from the tracks and the kicked-up mound of strawy dung, came there each night. The blind had been built at close arrow-shot of the lick and sitting, leaning back, knees high, heads low, in a hollow half full of ashes and dust, watching through the dried leaves and thin branches I had seen a lesser kudu bull come out of the brush to the edge of the opening where the salt was and stand there, heavy-necked, gray, and handsome, the horns spiralled against the sun while I sighted on his chest and then refused the shot, wanting not to frighten the greater kudu that should surely come at dusk. But before we ever heard the truck the bull had heard it and run off into the trees and everything else that had been moving, in the bush on the flats, or coming down from the small hills through the trees, coming toward the salt, had halted at that exploding, clanking sound. They would come, later, in the dark; but then it would be too late.

So now, going along the sandy track of the road in the car, the lights picking out the eyes of night birds that squatted close on the sand until the bulk of the car was on them and they rose in soft panic; passing the fires of the travellers that all moved to the westward by day along this road, abandoning the famine country that was ahead of us; me sitting, the butt of my rifle on my foot, the barrel in the crook of my left arm, a flask of whiskey between my knees, pouring the whiskey into a tin cup and passing it over my shoulder in the dark for M'Cola to pour water into it from the canteen, drinking this, the first one of the day, the finest one there is, and looking at the thick bush we passed in the dark, feeling the cool wind of the night and smelling the good smell of Africa, I was altogether happy.

Then ahead we saw a big fire and as we came up and passed, I made out a truck beside the road. I told Kamau to stop and go back and as we backed into the firelight there was a short, bandy-legged man with a Tyroler hat, leather shorts, and an open shirt standing before an un-hooded engine in a crowd of natives.

"Can we help?" I asked him.

"No," he said. "Unless you are a mechanic. It has taken a dislike to me. All engines dislike me."

"Do you think it could be the timer? It sounded as though it might be a timing knock when you went past us."

"I think it is much worse than that. It sounds to be something very bad."

"If you can get to our camp we have a mechanic."

"How far is it?"

"About twenty miles."

"In the morning I will try it. Now I am afraid to make it go farther with that noise of death inside. It is trying to die because it dislikes me. Well, I dislike it too. But if I die it would not annoy it."

"Will you have a drink?" I held out the flask. "Hemingway is my name."

"Kandisky," he said and bowed. "Hemingway is a name I have heard. Where? Where have I heard it? Oh, yes. The *dichter*.[1] You know Hemingway the poet?"

"Where did you read him?"

"In the *Querschnitt*." [2]

"That is me," I said, very pleased. The *Querschnitt* was a German magazine I had written some rather obscene poems for, and published a long story in, years before I could sell anything in America.

"This is very strange," the man in the Tyroler hat said. "Tell me, what do you think of Ringelnatz?" [3]

GREEN HILLS OF AFRICA. **1.** *dichter:* poet. **2.** *Querschnitt:* a periodical published in Berlin by Propyläen-Verlag from 1921 to 1936. Typical of the literally scores of similar journals which flourished in German in the 1920's and thirties. **3.** Ringelnatz: Joachim Ringelnatz was the pseudonym of Hans Bötticher (1883–1934), a German writer rather well known for his slightly scurrilous satiric verse.

"He is splendid."

"So. You like Ringelnatz. Good. What do you think of Heinrich Mann?" [4]

"He is no good."

"You believe it?"

"All I know is that I cannot read him."

"He is no good at all. I see we have things in common. What are you doing here?"

"Shooting."

"Not ivory, I hope."

"No. For kudu."

"Why should any man shoot a kudu? You, an intelligent man, a poet, to shoot kudu."

"I haven't shot any yet," I said. "But we've been hunting them hard now for ten days. We would have got one tonight if it hadn't been for your lorry."

"That poor lorry. But you should hunt for a year. At the end of that time you have shot everything and you are sorry for it. To hunt for one special animal is nonsense. Why do you do it?"

"I like to do it."

"Of course, if you *like* to do it. Tell me, what do you really think of Rilke?" [5]

"I have read only the one thing."

"Which?"

"The Cornet." [6]

"You liked it?"

"Yes."

"I have no patience with it. It is snobbery. Valery,[7] yes. I see the point of Valery; although there is much snobbery too. Well at least you do not kill elephants."

"I'd kill a big enough one."

"How big?"

"A seventy pounder. Maybe smaller."

"I see there are things we do not agree on. But it is a pleasure to meet one of the great old *Querschnitt* group. Tell me what is Joyce like? I have not the money to buy it.[8] Sinclair Lewis [9] is nothing. I bought it. No. No. Tell me tomorrow. You do not mind if I am camped near? You are with friends? You have a white hunter?"

"With my wife. We would be delighted. Yes, a white hunter."

"Why is he not out with you?"

"He believes you should hunt kudu alone."

"It is better not to hunt them at all. What is he? English?"

"Yes."

"Bloody English?"

"No. Very nice. You will like him."

"You must go. I must not keep you. Perhaps I will see you tomorrow. It was very strange that we should meet."

"Yes," I said. "Have them look at the truck tomorrow. Anything we can do."

"Good night," he said. "Good trip."

"Good night," I said. . . .

. . . The people one would see if one saw whom one wished to see. You know all of those people? You must know them."

"Some of them," I said. "Some in Paris. Some in Berlin."

I did not wish to destroy anything this man had, and so I did not go into those brilliant people in detail.

"They're marvellous," I said, lying.

"I envy you to know them," he said. "And tell me who is the greatest writer in America?"

"My husband," said my wife.

"No. I do not mean for you to speak from family pride. I mean who really? Certainly not Upton Sinclair.[10] Certainly not Sinclair Lewis. Who is your Thomas Mann? [11] Who is your Valery?"

"We do not have great writers," I said. "Something happens to our good writers at a certain age. I can explain but it is quite long and may bore you."

"Please explain," he said. "This is what I enjoy. This is the best part of life. The life of the mind. This is not killing kudu."

"You haven't heard it yet," I said.

"Ah, but I can see it coming. You must take more beer to loosen your tongue."

"It's loose," I told him. "It's always too bloody loose. But *you* don't drink anything."

"No, I never drink. It is not good for the mind. It is unnecessary. But tell me. Please tell me."

"Well," I said, "we have had, in America, skillful writers. Poe is a skillful writer. It is skillful, marvellously constructed, and it is dead. We have had writers of rhetoric who had the good fortune to find a little, in a chronicle of another man and from voyaging, of how things, actual things, can be, whales for instance, and this knowledge is wrapped in the rhetoric like plums in a

4. **Heinrich Mann:** German writer (1871–1950), brother of Thomas. 5. **Rilke:** Rainer Maria Rilke (1875–1926), German poet. 6. **The Cornet:** *The Tale of the Love and Death of Cornet Christopher Rilke.* 7. **Valery:** Paul Valéry (1871–1945), influential French poet. 8. **it:** *Ulysses.* 9. **Sinclair Lewis:** Sinclair Lewis (1885–1951), first American novelist to win the Nobel prize in literature. The "it" may refer to any one of his many novels, but probably refers to *Babbitt*, his best-known novel in Europe.

10. **Upton Sinclair:** Upton Sinclair (1878–), American propagandistic novelist. Author of more than thirty-five novels, among them *The Jungle* (1906), *Oil* (1927), and the Lanny Budd series. 11. **Thomas Mann:** Thomas Mann (1875–1955), German novelist.

pudding. Occasionally it is there, alone, unwrapped in pudding, and it is good. This is Melville. But the people who praise it, praise it for the rhetoric which is not important. They put a mystery in which is not there."

"Yes," he said. "I see. But it is the mind working, its ability to work, which makes the rhetoric. Rhetoric is the blue sparks from the dynamo."

"Sometimes. And sometimes it is only blue sparks and what is the dynamo driving?"

"So. Go on."

"I've forgotten."

"No. Go on. Do not pretend to be stupid."

"Did you ever get up before daylight——"

"Every morning," he said. "Go on."

"All right. There were others who wrote like exiled English colonials from an England of which they were never a part to a newer England that they were making. Very good men with the small, dried, and excellent wisdom of Unitarians; men of letters; Quakers with a sense of humor."

"Who were these?"

"Emerson, Hawthorne, Whittier, and Company. All our early classics who did not know that a new classic does not bear any resemblance to the classics that have preceded it. It can steal from anything that it is better than, anything that is not a classic, all classics do that. Some writers are only born to help another writer to write one sentence. But it cannot derive from or resemble a previous classic. Also all these men were gentlemen, or wished to be. They were all very respectable. They did not use the words that people always have used in speech, the words that survive in language. Nor would you gather that they had bodies. They had minds, yes. Nice, dry, clean minds. This is all very dull, I would not state it except that you ask for it."

"Go on."

"There is one at that time that is supposed to be really good, Thoreau. I cannot tell you about it because I have not yet been able to read it. But that means nothing because I cannot read other naturalists unless they are being extremely accurate and not literary. Naturalists should all work alone and some one else should correlate their findings for them. Writers should work alone. They should see each other only after their work is done, and not too often then. Otherwise they become like writers in New York. All angleworms in a bottle, trying to derive knowledge and nourishment from their own contact and from the bottle. Sometimes the bottle is shaped art, sometimes economics, sometimes economic-religion. But once they are in the bottle they stay there. They are lonesome outside of the bottle. They do not

want to be lonesome. They are afraid to be alone in their beliefs and no woman would love any of them enough so that they could kill their lonesomeness in that woman, or pool it with hers, or make something with her that makes the rest unimportant."

"But what about Thoreau?"

"You'll have to read him. Maybe I'll be able to later. I can do nearly everything later."

"Better have some more beer, Papa."

"All right."

"What about the good writers?"

"The good writers are Henry James, Stephen Crane, and Mark Twain. That's not the order they're good in. There is no order for good writers."

"Mark Twain is a humorist. The others I do not know."

"All modern American literature comes from one book by Mark Twain called *Huckleberry Finn*. If you read it you must stop where the Nigger Jim is stolen from the boys. That is the real end. The rest is just cheating. But it's the best book we've had. All American writing comes from that. There was nothing before. There has been nothing as good since."

"What about the others?"

"Crane wrote two fine stories. *The Open Boat* and *The Blue Hotel*. The last one is the best."

"And what happened to him?"

"He died. That's simple. He was dying from the start."

"But the other two?"

"They both lived to be old men but they did not get any wiser as they got older. I don't know what they really wanted. You see we make our writers into something very strange."

"I do not understand."

"We destroy them in many ways. First, economically. They make money. It is only by hazard a writer makes money although good books always make money eventually. Then our writers when they have made some money increase their standard of living and they are caught. They have to write to keep up their establishments, their wives, and so on, and they write slop. It is slop not on purpose but because it is hurried. Because they write when there is nothing to say or no water in the well. Because they are ambitious. Then, once they have betrayed themselves, they justify it and you get more slop. Or else they read the critics. If they believe the critics when they say they are great then they must believe them when they say they are rotten and they lose confidence. At present we have two good writers who cannot write because they have lost confidence through reading critics. If they wrote, sometimes it would be good and sometimes not so good and sometimes it would be quite bad, but the good would get out. But they have read the critics and they must write masterpieces. The masterpieces the critics said they wrote. They weren't masterpieces, of course. They were just quite good books. So now they cannot write at all. The critics have made them impotent.

"Who are these writers?"

"Their names would mean nothing to you and by now they may have written, become frightened, and be impotent again."

"But what is it that happens to American writers? Be definite."

"I was not here in the old days so I cannot tell you about them, but now there are various things. At a certain age the men writers change into Old Mother Hubbard. The women writers become Joan of Arc without the fighting. They become leaders. It doesn't matter who they lead. If they do not have followers they invent them. It is useless for those selected as followers to protest. They are accused of disloyalty. Oh, hell. There are too many things happen to them. That is one thing. The others try to save their souls with what they write. That is an easy way out. Others are ruined by the first money, the first praise, the first attack, the first time they find they cannot write, or the first time they cannot do anything else, or else they get frightened and join organizations that do their thinking for them. Or they do not know what they want. Henry James wanted to make money. He never did, of course."

"And you?"

"I am interested in other things. I have a good life but I must write because if I do not write a certain amount I do not enjoy the rest of my life."

"And what do you want?"

"To write as well as I can and learn as I go along. At the same time I have my life which I enjoy and which is a damned good life."

"Hunting kudu?"

"Yes. Hunting kudu and many other things."

"What other things?"

"Plenty of other things."

"And you know what you want?"

"Yes."

"You really like to do this, what you do now, this silliness of kudu?"

"Just as much as I like to be in the Prado."

"One is not better than the other?"

"One is as necessary as the other. There are other things, too."

"Naturally. There must be. But this sort of thing means something to you, really?"

"Truly."

"And you know what you want?"

"Absolutely, and I get it all the time."

"But it takes money."

"I could always make money and besides I have been very lucky."

"Then you are happy?"

"Except when I think of other people."

"Then you think of other people?"

"Oh, yes."

"But you do nothing for them?"

"No."

"Nothing?"

"Maybe a little."

"Do you think your writing is worth doing—as an end in itself?"

"Oh, yes."

"You are sure?"

"Very sure."

"That must be very pleasant."

"It is," I said. "It is the one altogether pleasant thing about it."

"This is getting awfully serious," my wife said.

"It's a damned serious subject."

"You see, he is really serious about something," Kandisky said. "I knew he must be serious on something besides kudu."

"The reason every one now tries to avoid it, to deny that it is important, to make it seem vain to try to do it, is because it is so difficult. Too many factors must combine to make it possible."

"What is this now?"

"The kind of writing that can be done. How far prose can be carried if any one is serious enough and has luck. There is a fourth and fifth dimension that can be gotten."

"You believe it?"

"I know it."

"And if a writer can get this?"

"Then nothing else matters. It is more important than anything he can do. The chances are, of course, that he will fail. But there is a chance that he succeeds."

"But that is poetry you are talking about."

"No. It is much more difficult than poetry. It is a prose that has never been written. But it can be written, without tricks and without cheating. With nothing that will go bad afterwards."

"And why has it not been written?"

"Because there are too many factors. First, there must be talent, much talent. Talent such as Kipling had. Then there must be discipline. The discipline of Flaubert.[12] Then there must be the conception of what it can be and an absolute con-

---

12. **Flaubert**: Gustave Flaubert (1821–80), French novelist and master stylist, the author of *Madame Bovary*.

science as unchanging as the standard meter in Paris, to prevent faking. Then the writer must be intelligent and disinterested and above all he must survive. Try to get all these in one person and have him come through all the influences that press on a writer. The hardest thing, because time is so short, is for him to survive and get his work done. But I would like us to have such a writer and to read what he would write. What do you say? Should we talk about something else?"

"It is interesting what you say. Naturally I do not agree with everything."

"Naturally."

"What about a gimlet?" Pop asked. "Don't you think a gimlet might help?"

"Tell me first what are the things, the actual, concrete things that harm a writer?"

I was tired of the conversation which was becoming an interview. So I would make it an interview and finish it. The necessity to put a thousand intangibles into a sentence, now, before lunch, was too bloody.

"Politics, women, drink, money, ambition. And the lack of politics, women, drink, money and ambition," I said profoundly.

"He's getting much too easy now," Pop said.

"But drink. I do not understand about that. That has always seemed silly to me. I understand it as a weakness."

"It is a way of ending a day. . . ."

1935

R. P. BLACKMUR
Editor

T. S. Eliot

1 8 8 8 -

WHEN in 1880 Matthew Arnold wrote his "General Introduction" to Ward's *English Poets*—the fullest of all nineteenth-century anthologies—he found a good way of getting at the quality and variety of poetry in a set of brief quotations, ranging from Homer to Milton, which he called touchstones. It is something of this sort—and ranging quite outside poetry as well as within it—that I should like to find for T. S. Eliot; and it is appropriate that the suggestion should come from Arnold, for Arnold has been a touchstone for Eliot pretty much through his whole career as man of letters and public man. Indeed, Eliot has both fought with Arnold and used him since one of his earliest essays, "The Perfect Critic," which comes at the head of *The Sacred Wood* (1920). Eliot and Arnold are in the end, I think, more alike than unlike; but Eliot lived in a later age, with a different sensibility, different passions, and different hopes. Arnold had the war of 1870, the first downfall of Europe, behind him and saw an immense future for poetry ahead of him. Eliot did most of the work that confronts us when we think of his name from the beginning of the First World War in 1914 to the end of the Second in 1945 —"Prufrock" (1915) to *Notes Towards the Definition of Culture* (1948). I do not think Eliot would at any time have said that the future of poetry was "immense"; his vocabulary was different from Arnold's; he never had words for Arnold's hope that humanity alone could take care of its own needs by its own creation in art and poetry, or by substituting any one human faculty for any other. Poetry would never, as Arnold thought, do for religion. Eliot had another position, which I take to be a deep improvement of Arnold's, the more so since it begins much further back in human consciousness and sees further ahead. From "The Three Senses of 'Culture,'" the first chapter in his book *Notes Towards the Definition of Culture*, I take these sentences as one statement among many of Eliot's position:

Aesthetic sensibility must be extended into spiritual perception, and spiritual perception must be extended into aesthetic sensibility and disciplined taste before we are qualified to pass judgment upon decadence or diabolism or nihilism in art. To judge a work of art by artistic or by religious standards, to judge a religion by religious or artistic standards should come in the end to the same thing: though it is an end at which no individual can arrive.

To have sources that cannot be fathomed, to envisage ends that cannot be reached in any individual's experience, is to be in possession, I think, of the force that moves Eliot's mind and inhabits his poetry. It is one touchstone, but not the only one, for the use and assessment both of his poetry and of the prose that can be taken as accompanying it. It is perhaps a touchstone for other touchstones, and if so that is right, for it is a religious touchstone. There is a great deal both before and after the human that presses upon all our religion and into every monument—city, cathedral, poem —our imagination makes, and it is these pressures with which Eliot's poetry deals, and it is in this sense that his poetry is religious poetry. That the poetry should be so alive in a world as little religious as our own—at least the part of our world that makes and uses poetry—has been a puzzle to those who do not *live* very much of even what vestigial religion they have; but the puzzle is solved if we reflect that this poetry *lives* a good part of the religion we did not know we had missed: as if we failed to recognize someone unless he came incognito, so that we could call him whatever it was that moved us and for which we had no name. *Nomina, Numina*,[1] as Victor Hugo liked to repeat; in the name we find the greater power than ourselves that moves us. It is the name we give to the apparition of the stranger who pulls together the disparate in us into what is desperate hope.

These are difficult matters, which may be resolved only by the particular inclinations of readers; but luckily these matters are related to others more open to discussion. I refer to the matters of our culture and history without the presence of which in the reader—and without a particular urgency in that presence—no creditable reading or use of Eliot's poems can be made. Nothing could be more problematic than that culture and history, and nothing could raise the problem more sharply than Eliot's poems and the reactions to them. He writes with the weight, and, much more important, the momentum, of the Greek-Judaic-Roman-Christian tradition moving among his words. The reader who pursues every allusion is only making tracks on the water or playing parlor games for matches. The reader who explains or interprets more than a few samples of the poems avoids the force of the poem and

[1] *Nomina, Numina*: in the name, in the numinous power; name a thing and you touch its soul.

is very unlikely ever to come on what the poem made out of its materials by putting them together. Poems are above all idioms—fresh or vital twists of language—and idioms resist exact definition. Yet a dictionary is handy to see what the words were that got put together and changed in the idiom, but it is also good to remember that we do not have to know a word very well in order to understand it and often even use it. As Paul Valéry says in "Poetry and Abstract Thought,"

Each and every word that enables us to leap so rapidly across the chasm of thought, and to follow the prompting of an idea that constructs its own expression, appears to me like one of those light planks which one throws across a ditch or a mountain crevasse and which will bear a man crossing it rapidly. . . . Consult your own experience; and you will find that we understand each other, and ourselves, only thanks to our rapid passage over words. We must not lay stress upon them, or we shall see the clearest discourse dissolve into enigmas and more or less learned illusions.[2]

It is the last sentence perhaps that is most apt in thinking about the enormous mass of interpretive (but mainly not critical) writing about Eliot's poetry—a mass for which Eliot is partly responsible, since he began it all when he added his notes to "The Waste Land" in 1922. The naked poem as it first appeared in the *Criterion* (October, 1922) and the *Dial* (November, 1922) was much more exciting and promised an intimacy much deeper than any mere understanding, an intimacy that the notes obviated. In the poem Eliot had appropriated, and sometimes improved, the material he borrowed or alluded to, but the notes set it all loose again and ran into frightful bogs of learning. The trouble all comes about because we don't read the same books—if we did, Eliot once remarked, it wouldn't matter much which they were.

Yet, with Eliot, we ought to have read the same books. All the important ones have been part of humane education for a long time, and many of them are active forces in our own minds whether we have read them or not. In other words, to be intimate with the books that chiefly influenced Eliot's poetry would

[2] *The Art of Poetry* (New York, 1958), pp. 55–56.

constitute a good part of an excellent traditional education; but it is an education that
today one has largely to acquire for oneself;
this was always partly true, but in earlier days
it was expected and even taken for granted that
one would acquire it—which was a great help
in getting along with the job.

There is the Bible, which everyone knows
about and which is the best seller in our language, and for many there is also the Book of
Common Prayer or the Missal. From Shakespeare to our own day the language and intentions of these have penetrated the sensibility of
every child. I do not mean that they have been
read as literature, and I mean even less that
they have been used to improve morals or to
inflame bigotry, but I do mean that they have
been part of the way one learns to think and
feel and speak and to celebrate the passage of
life. It is in this way that they are present in
Eliot's work. For many persons today the Bible
seems, like Shakespeare, an enormous repository of confused and confusing quotations—
which is a very different thing. A repository and
a source of thought and feeling have as little as
possible in common. Perhaps the best the un-
penetrated reader can do is to read Eliot as if
he felt the presence of the Bible and the Prayer
Book; after all, this is no doubt how Eliot went
about it himself. Certainly the reader had
better depend on ancestral memories than
make any cursory matching of references.

No such simple advice unfolds itself about
the Greek and Latin classics, which are not
part of our speech except for solitary private
bursts, but which radically affect the shape and
limits of every other aspect of the mind which
is our inheritance if we choose to take it up;
they give much for us to put into our own
speech if we are poets or live readers of poetry.
I think, in Eliot's case, particularly of Homer
and Virgil, of Sophocles and Euripides; and
generally all round, of the *Metamorphoses* of
Ovid. I merely observe, moreover, that the
reader who is acquainted with these authors
will be more at home with what is most truly
alive, most exactly contemporary, in Eliot's
poems than the reader who is not. If we would
know what we are, we must find in us the impress of what others were. But there is a great
question as to the level of consciousness or

attention at which we should have this awareness. How far can we be content to be not the
masters but the subjects of our knowledge?

I do not think a clear statement can be made
as to the general question of the classics in their
effect on contemporary literature, and insist
only that the work of Eliot asks the general
question so that it grasps us close. But I should
like to reserve a special niche for the fragments
of Heraclitus. I have no idea whether Eliot
ever studied these fragments very seriously;
the mind casts about as much as it fastens; but
I am certain that they invaded him. There are
not many, only 138 if you include the dubious
or discarded ones, and ten or twelve pages in
an ordinary book would print them all. If you
read these ten or twelve pages as many times
you will perceive that they haunt the woods of
Eliot's poems, another tang in the air you
breathe. I quote only this fragment in Philip
Wheelwright's translation (where it is given
the number 2): "We should let ourselves be
guided by what is common to all. Yet, although
the Logos [the Word] is common to all, most
men live as if each of them had a private intelligence of his own." Eliot uses the second
sentence of this fragment in Greek as part of
the epigraph for "Burnt Norton," the first
of the *Four Quartets*. I have heard that he kept
the original Greek because he was not happy
with any translation he had seen, and indeed
if the Greek word which we transliterate as
phronesis is not permitted different equivalents
in different minds then its force is diminished.
Wheelwright's translation, "intelligence," is
certainly feasible, but it might be "insight," or
"sagacity," or even, as Reinhold Neibuhr prefers, "practical wisdom." However it may be, it
is to all the meanings in this dilemma that
"Burnt Norton," and indeed the three further
"Quartets," gives haunting voice. It is our dilemma.

If I ask a niche for Heraclitus, the apartment
reserved for Dante is much too big to open up
here. Eliot's own long essay is an excellent introduction to Dante; but it might not indicate
to the unwary that he had not only soaked him
up as he had Heraclitus, but that a considerable
part of Dante had become a considerable part
of Eliot. The essay is a kind of guided tour to
what Dante had already done and was yet to do

in Eliot's poems, and I think we can learn from it more about the *art* of Eliot's own poetry than from anything else he has written—but it is an intimate knowledge not to be precisely delineated. I merely make two small quotations, followed by a suggestion.

Dante and Shakespeare divide the modern world between them; there is no third. . . . Shakespeare gives the greatest *width* of human passion; Dante the greatest altitude and the greatest depth. They complement each other. It is futile to ask which undertook the more difficult job.

I suggest that it is a great advantage for a poet to be able to take so much from other poets, and that the fact that both the poem "Prufrock" and the book in which it first appeared should have epigraphs from Dante is no accident. It is no accident either, but a culmination, that in "Little Gidding," the last ambitious poem we have from Eliot, Dante's *terza rima* should find its most satisfactory English form in the great dawn colloquy on speech and the aftersight of age:

Since our concern was speech, and speech impelled us
  To purify the dialect of the tribe
  And urge the mind to aftersight and foresight,
Let me disclose the gifts reserved for age
  To set a crown upon your lifetime's effort.
  First, the cold friction of expiring sense
Without enchantment, offering no promise
  But bitter tastelessness of shadow fruit
  As body and soul begin to fall asunder.

It is our ancestors who exact our aspirations. I will say nothing about Shakespeare, since he seems to have exacted from any following poet nothing which he did not surpass in his gift, his mastery was in his departures from contemporary norms; Dante's mastery was in his power to subsume the human spirit of his time, and is therefore ever afterwards a model to build by, though without any practicable hope of equality. To make a departure, or to follow a model, is not so much a matter of choice as it is the recognition of a condition. We may be very much at the heart, or at the "reason," of human behavior, and indeed may come to much the same words, if we find talent taking one direction or the other. It is talent which it is death to hide. Depart, or follow. Eliot has

deeply followed, prompted by departures; the timbre of his voice is departure, but the burden of it is in following. Without the timbre, without the burden, there would be no voice. He found himself in the condition of Dante rather than the condition of Shakespeare, but only *rather than*. I like to think that this is the very distinction Eliot makes, in my quotations above, between the width of Shakespeare and the depth of Dante. It is often a question of what we hear best that prompts what voice we speak in.

We can recognize the "condition" of Eliot if we consider again the last part of the fragment from Heraclitus quoted above: "Although the Logos is common to all, most men live as if each of them had a private intelligence of his own." But considering the fragment this time, we must put it together with his addiction to Pascal and his admiration of Montaigne, and in saying this I think not half so much of the essay on Pascal—originally the Introduction to the Everyman edition of the *Pensées*—as I think of the apparition of Pascal in Eliot's poem, "Ash Wednesday." [1] The two seem to have been written not too far apart—the essay was dated 1931 and the poem a year earlier. Pascal he made polemics for in the essay, actual use of in the poem; but Montaigne he never confronted, either for polemics or use; yet he knew he ought to have done so—as witness (in the Pascal essay): "One cannot destroy Pascal, certainly; but of all authors Montaigne is one of the least destructible. You could as well dissipate a fog by flinging handgrenades into it. For Montaigne is a fog, a gas, a fluid, insidious element." That is fine as admiration; but this is better:

But what makes Montaigne a very great figure is that he succeeded, God knows how—for Montaigne very likely did not know that he had done it—it is not the sort of thing that men *can* observe about themselves, for it is essentially bigger than the individual's consciousness—he succeeded in giving expression to the scepticism of *every* human being. For every man who thinks and lives by thought must have his own scepticism, that which stops at the question, that which ends in denial, or that which leads to faith and which is somehow integrated into the faith which transcends it.

[1] Part I, 38–39, and Part VI, 27–28.

I said Eliot never confronted Montaigne, but the sentences I have quoted are a very fine tribute. (Eliot has superbly the gift of paying tribute, especially to those with a differently shaped soul from his own.) They are more than a tribute; they are another reminder of the promptings and the aspirations of Eliot's own mind, and of the perpetual dilemma between the two which his poems and all but his most polemical prose exhibit. One is reminded of the old intellectual catch-phrase: A man is known by the dilemmas he keeps. Eliot's mind has its skepticism in his own definition, "that which leads to faith and is somehow integrated into the faith which transcends it." We see this most clearly in "The Dry Salvages" (pp. 784–86).

There are, of course, many other "influences" at work in Eliot and there will no doubt someday be a set of studies which will assess all of them which are recoverable. There will surely be a chapter on Edward Lear, another on Remy de Gourmont, and still another on T. E. Hulme, and so on. But I hope the watermark left in him by Harvard College will be not overlooked because he has covered it over—not at all obliterating it—with so much of his own writing. I think of two figures, neither of them absolutely characteristic of Harvard, George Santayana and Irving Babbitt, as having deeply affected him. Of Babbitt, neo-Humanist and lover of Pascal, Eliot has written a number of times, but I do not seem to have noticed any words of his on Santayana. I like to think this is because Eliot has incorporated so much of him, perhaps as a part of his skepticism, perhaps as a part of his poetics. The interested reader might well take a look, *inter alia*, at Santayana's *Three Philosophical Poets* (1910) and then turn back to Eliot's "Dante."

II

TO SPEAK of Harvard carries us a little too near the personal life which can be no matter for our present concern beyond what may be found, for example, in F. O. Matthiessen's concise "Biographical Note," which precedes his excellent study *The Achievement of T. S. Eliot* (1935, 1947), and perhaps in the early poem (1917) "Mélange Adultère De Tout,"

where the first seven lines appear to be autobiographical:

> En Amérique, professeur;
> En Angleterre, journaliste;
> C'est à grands pas et en sueur
> Que vous suivrez à peine ma piste.
> En Yorkshire, conférencier;
> A Londres, un peu banquier,
> Vous me paierez bien la tête.

But perhaps we can mention St. Louis, Missouri, on the banks of the Mississippi River, where Eliot was born, and Boston, Massachusetts, on the sea's edge, which was profoundly familial ground, and do so because the river and the sea inhabit his work on an older chronology than that of either his American or English life. It may be true, as Eliot writes, that "it is often those writers whom we are lucky enough to know, whose books we can ignore; and the better we know them personally, the less need we may feel to read what they write"; but that is not the object we have in mind. Perhaps a summary of the imaginary life W. H. Auden made for Eliot when he reviewed *Notes Towards the Definition of Culture* will do us more service, especially because we can add phrases from Eliot's prose and verse. There were, said Auden, three inhabitants in Eliot's household: the violent old peasant grandmother who has seen everything, the prim archdeacon, and the boy who hands you the explosive cigar. For the old grandmother I think of the line "Humankind cannot bear very much reality" (Part I, "Burnt Norton"), and the line about the scarecrow—the live scarecrow—"Behaving as the wind behaves" (Part II, "The Hollow Men"). It is the prim archdeacon who says, at the end of "Thoughts After Lambeth" (1931): "The World is trying the experiment of attempting to form a civilized but non-Christian mentality. The experiment will fail; but we must be very patient in awaiting its collapse; meanwhile redeeming the time . . ." And again, only the archdeacon could have characterized the message heard by some of those who claim the Inner Voice as the eternal message of vanity, fear, and lust. The small boy with the explosive cigar is perhaps responsible for a good deal of both fragments of "Sweeney Agonistes," especially these lines spoken by Sweeney:

I knew a man once did a girl in
Any man might do a girl in
Any man has to, needs to, wants to
Once in a lifetime, do a girl in.
[Fragment of an Agon]

The lines echo on so anybody with the least gift for jingle could ad lib all night on them. But there is another echo in the line the small boy gives us at the end of *The Waste Land,* "Why then Ile fit you. Hieronymo's mad againe." You need only remember that Hieronymo bit off his tongue for the cigar to explode.

Against these lines let us put the following, where the several voices are together heard, not heard as one but heard together from three corners of a room where you are in the fourth. I print them as if one poem:

I gotta use words when I talk to you . . .
Looking into the heart of light, the silence. . . .
I should have been a pair of ragged claws
Scuttling across the floors of silent seas. . . .
My friend, blood shaking my heart
The awful daring of a moment's surrender
Which an age of prudence can never retract . . .
I that was near your heart was removed therefrom
To lose beauty in terror, terror in inquisition . . .
A man may sit at meat, and feel the cold in his
   groin.[1]

These lines set after each other make a poem that is more than plausible; or at any rate they turn out to be intimately related in much the same way the parts of an intended poem are. I say this because such is the mode of composition used in many of Eliot's poems. But that is not why the lines were quoted together at this juncture. They were put together to suggest the common nightmare of which Eliot is master and to suggest at the same time—in the same lines—that these nightmares may only be mastered by a man of civic virtue. The quality of Eliot's presence seems to me precisely that of nightmare and virtue, and I should like to call him the Master of Nightmare and Civic Virtue. There are many of course who pretend that it is civic nightmare and private virtue, and against that pretense all Eliot's conscious work is a series of blows. I speak of nightmares

[1] L. 1, "Fragment of an Agon"; l. 2, *The Waste Land;* ll. 3–4, "Prufrock"; ll. 5–7, *The Waste Land;* ll. 8–9, "Gerontion"; l. 10, *Murder in the Cathedral.*

that are only tolerable to a man of civic virtue—to a consenting member of society who is possessed by it and who in some sense possesses it, and who is a part of its behavior in himself and in the history of his society— though he may not be all these things simultaneously or continuously. There are gaps and chasms; one does not so much cross them as find oneself on the other side. The master of this nightmare is an individual with discontinuous connections and continuing aspiration. I hope now to illustrate what I mean by putting various things together mainly from Eliot but some from elsewhere. It is my hope that the reader will find other illustrations better for his way of taking my point.

I think first of the light shining in the darkness when Milton's *Lycidas* and Eliot's *The Waste Land* are set briefly side by side. Each poem is an acknowledgment and a kind of embodiment of a whole culture in a time of troubles. For Milton, at the moment of composition, the wars were just ahead, for Eliot just over; for each it was a time when the precious content of belief seemed in general either ignored or subject to malicious criticism —though for Milton there was also the exacerbation of belief which Eliot did not have to endure. But for both there was the whole of a culture demanding response. Milton's *Lycidas* is 193 lines in length, *The Waste Land* 434 lines. It is possible that this disparity in length may exist partly because Eliot had to put twice as much of his culture *into* his poem for the reader to know what was being acknowledged and embodied than Milton had to put into his poem. Of course, there is also the explanatory fact that Milton had in the Pastoral [1] a still—though barely—living convention which could hold together a many-voiced work, where Eliot had no convention with which to manage a similar work. Milton was wonderfully experimental with the conventional form he had—I mean both the Pastoral and the verse. Eliot

[1] Pastoral poetry runs back as far as the Idylls of Theocrites, where shepherds and nymphs sang to each other: simplicity of thought and action is the distinguishing feature. Shakespeare's *As You Like It* and Milton's *Comus* are both pastoral poetry. *Lycidas* is distinctive in that Milton fused with the classical pastoral tradition the far more powerful Christian pastoral tradition of the Good Shepherd and the sheep.

had to commit himself—without a conventional form and by the tact of his mind—to putting things together that *wanted* putting together, and to do so by the experiment of putting them side by side in deliberate analogy. Moreover, he had to do so even if such analogy were to appear disjunctive at first sight on the page and to persevere in it and so set side by side in one line—or several—references which do not disclose—or automatically gloss—each other. The peculiar rightness of this mode of composition to our time, where so many things jar upon rather than join each other, Eliot never doubted, nor is it doubtful now, even in the most difficult matters within poetry and beyond it.

How *The Waste Land* is put together is now rather like a convention—an agreement about how to take up serious matters—open to any talent that knows how to employ it, whereas the Pastoral convention Milton employed seems no longer immediately available, with or without talent, no matter how much at bottom the two conventions resemble each other as means combining disjunct material. I do not know that there is any gain involved in this change, though I do feel that there is an uncompensated loss. There is no way, in poetry, either of cutting your losses or cutting your gains. Let us put the difference between Milton and Eliot in this respect sharply. Both Milton and Eliot are poets who give clues to things which are inviting if you understand them, forbidding if you do not. Milton did not have to attend this matter—the tradition of a poetry heavily laden with thought was alive enough to use—but Eliot was compelled to be too much aware of it; there was the penalty upon him that he was expected to make clear what in earlier poets was taken for granted as inherently difficult. The difference is cultural, not substantial, and it is not only the culture of our society but the culture of our poets that makes the difference; but the difficulty infects our historians as well as our poets: in order to read most modern historians one has either to know the history ahead of time or look it up as one goes along. The poet's or the historian's signifying powers are in excellent condition, but their powers to indicate their reference seem negligible; there is a major modern disa-

bility to *say* what one is talking about, so that we have to find more in the unsaid than we have the skill for. As Arnold thought our romantic ancestors did not know enough to say what they thought, so their romantic descendants—and in our day a "classicist" is a romantic indeed—may be said to know too much.

But to get back to our immediate comparison, and to keep it concise, Milton and Eliot are both learned poets—not at all the same thing as to refer to a savant or a scholar who would be nothing without his learning; the poet has his learning partly in his bones, and for the rest, he picks it up where he needs it—but where learning was natural to Milton and a part of the "movement" of his times, for Eliot it is a job requiring almost an alien mastery before he can get it set into his verse sufficiently to move it forward. This is not because Eliot's learning is more difficult or more recondite than Milton's, but because we do not expect—and do not want—unified learning from our poets, and want even less specific reference. This is one of the mistakes of the human spirit in our time, and it can hardly be repaired in any one man's work, no matter how deeply, as in Eliot, he is aware of the mistake. The reader may reflect that there is far more work necessary to "understand" *Lycidas* than *The Waste Land*, if only because *The Waste Land* cannot help being in the stream of our time. *Our* April is the cruelest month; and this cruelty the movies and television and our politics show, since they quote it without reference.

But listen to Northrop Frye, in his *Anatomy of Criticism* (1957). When he gets to Milton's *Lycidas*, is he not also talking about Eliot's *The Waste Land*? There is only one emendation necessary, and the reader may accept it if he will. The first phrase should read: "A necessarily unconventional poem like *The Waste Land . . .*" I do not know that Frye would consent to the substitution, so I content myself with quoting what he wrote:

An avowedly conventional poem like "Lycidas" urgently demands the kind of criticism that will absorb it into the study of literature as a whole, and this activity is expected to begin at once, with the first cultivated reader. Here we have a situation in literature more like that of mathematics or science, where the work of genius is assimilated to the whole subject so quickly that one hardly notices the difference between creative and critical activity. [p. 100]

One never knows when a thing like this needs comment; one can say only that if *Lycidas* has been an argued subject for quite some time—over three hundred years—then *The Waste Land* is likely to be as strongly argued whenever it is rediscovered for quite some time to come. Frye's words about *Lycidas* are a way of describing *The Waste Land*. What he says of the one bears on the other—though the Muses give different laurels and Helicon is further off for Eliot than for Milton. Both the poems responded in *that way* to their society. Each found religion partly incarnated in culture and resurrected in the individual. The elements in their responses are different, and it may be are alien, but they are also commensurable.

There is a further reason for carrying Milton and Eliot at once in mind. In the place that is in common between them lies the best of what we may mean by the classic in literature—and I do not mean classic as opposed to romantic or to anything else, but a quality which inheres in a long line of literature and art, the very quality which makes the literature and art endure. It does not require the presence or absence of any other *particular* qualities, but it could hardly exist without the ambiance of *some* other qualities, and indeed could not be recognized apart from them. It is the central quality of many centers. It is the quality Coleridge had in mind when he argued that poetry "brings the whole soul of man into activity"; and this in turn had something to do with the concluding sentence of Eliot's *The Use of Poetry:* "The sad ghost of Coleridge beckons to me from among the shadows." But I do not wish to leave this to the poets. Here is a part of what Humphry House—in his book *Aristotle's Poetics* (London, 1956)—says about the Academy at fifth-century Athens. House was concerned with undergraduates at Oxford; we are interested in the poetry and prose of Eliot. There should be no trouble in passing from one to the other. Mr. House writes as follows:

The main business of the Academy was to teach men to be good men in the fullest sense, and good citizens. This fact underlies the attitude of both Plato and Aristotle towards poetry; it is the source of all the remarks . . . to the effect that the Greek attitude to poetry was more "ethical," more "moralistic," and less "aesthetic," than the typical modern attitude. . . . The reason is that poetry was never thought of in isolation; it was something in which all men shared, an activity of public importance, to be interpreted as part of the means by which the whole human personality was both educated and controlled.

[pp. 20–21]

It indicates something of importance about a society whether it takes such an attitude for granted, pushes it to a smothering extreme, ignores it, or denies and decries it altogether. It is of equal importance what attitude the poets take. Disinterestedness may be a deep sharing, revolt one deeper still; but any conservatism not a dead or suicidal conservatism—I think of such disparate figures as Aristophanes and Coleridge—may take a genuine share. Perhaps one of Eliot's own remarks in *The Uses of Poetry* (p. 107) will detach one aspect of how the poet may enjoy his secret share in the public importance of poetry. He is in the midst of his lifelong fight with Arnold about poetry and society. "Morals for the saint are only a preliminary matter; for the poet a secondary matter." One thinks of St. Francis of Assisi for the one and of Tolstoi for the other. But this is only one aspect and there should be put with it the single phrase, "The poetry does not matter," upon which I will leave Erich Heller in his book *The Hazard of Modern Poetry* (1953) to comment. Heller, as you will see, makes a powerful case for my own running theme.

"The poetry does not matter." These words from Mr. T. S. Eliot's *Four Quartets* acquire an all but revolutionary significance if we understand them not only in their particular context but also in the context of a period of poetry in which nothing mattered except poetry. Against this background the *Four Quartets* themselves appear, in all their complexity, as the poetry of simple civic virtue— the poetry of a poet trying to read the writing of the law that has become all but illegible. This, you may say, has nothing to do with poetry. On the contrary, it is one of the few truly hopeful signs that this civic virtue could once more be realized poetically. . . . Poetry is not only the human equivalent of the song of singing birds. It is also Virgil, Dante, and Hölderlin. It is also, in its own terms, the definition of the state of man. [pp. 38–39]

That is to say, the behavior of man, and in Eliot the behavior also of nature as it behaves on man from outside and in man from inside. The poems and plays make this clear enough to anyone whose intimacy with them is sensitive, as for example (in "The Dry Salvages," p. 785, ll. 52–53), "The silent withering of autumn flowers/Dropping their petals and remaining motionless." The examples are everywhere, from the last lines of "Prufrock" to the "stillness between two waves of the sea" at the end of "Little Gidding," the fourth Quartet. But there is a prose statement, grasping and generalizing so much, about the behavior of man, that I will let it stand for any number of instances in Eliot's verse.

The reflection that what we believe is not merely what we formulate and subscribe to, but that behavior is also belief, and that even the most conscious and developed of us live also at the level on which belief and behavior cannot be distinguished, is one that may, once we allow our imagination to play upon it, be very disconcerting. It gives an importance to our most trivial pursuits, to the occupation of our every minute, which we cannot contemplate long without the horror of nightmare. [*Notes Towards the Definition of Culture,* CHAP. 1]

I do not know that a man may gloss an experience or a thought before he has had it— though we are expected to do so whenever we take a vow or an oath; but it certainly may happen that a prolonged experience or a continuing thought may pass through phases which gradually reveal their identity and do so with the promise of still further revelation. We find suddenly that we have been thinking the same thought and experiencing the same experience for a long time. In the sameness is the illumination. It is like the compulsive discovery that there is only one emotion, which makes the same changes, permanent or transitory, in the body, no matter how different the object or source may seem to have been. Recognitions of this sort belong to the making of poetry and

to thinking about it whenever the poetry has any stake in life, and is not a mere plea or substitute for it. Perhaps this has something to do with the classic, with morality, with civic virtue, with how it may be that the poetry does not matter when it has touched in behavior "the horror of nightmare." It was the master of nightmare and civic virtue who wrote the sentences taken above from *Notes Towards the Definition of Culture.* Here is the same apprehension of experience, the same continuing thought, in what is only chronologically an earlier phase and had better be taken as an *intersecting* phase. It is again from the quarrel with Arnold, this time with his notion "that it is of advantage to a poet to deal with a beautiful world":

But for the poet is it so important? We mean all sorts of things, I know, by Beauty. But the essential advantage for a poet is not to have a beautiful world with which to deal: it is to be able to see beneath both beauty and ugliness; to see the boredom, and the horror, and the glory.
[*The Use of Poetry,* p. 98]

The ring in the last phrase is both of anathema and salutation. It may be commented that when Eliot says boredom he means not only the monkey's gesture or any other small talk; he means also the "restlessness" in George Herbert's poem "The Pulley" and the ennui in Pascal: that whole condition of life which is made buoyant by these two lines from the end of the first part—and repeated at the end of the last part—of "Ash Wednesday":

> Teach us to care and not to care
> Teach us to sit still

The ring in the passage about behavior and nightmare is very different. It is the ring of clairvoyance, and it is the same ring that is in the passage from *The Waste Land* beginning, "A woman drew her long black hair out tight" (l. 378).

III

THE QUALITY that these remarks have been circling about so long—the quality appropriate to the marriage of nightmare and civic virtue —is most vividly inherent in *The Family Reunion* (1939). As a play on the stage it has quite missed the success that belonged to it far more than to *Murder in the Cathedral* (1935) or *The Cocktail Party* (1950). Its only equal in my mind is the pair of playlets about Sweeney called "Sweeney Agonistes" (1932), unless it be the scene in *The Waste Land* beginning "When Lil's husband got de-mobbed." In all of these the language is itself a kind of action—an action of the psyche—which engorges, swallows, and feeds on the action of gesture and deed. The three plays through *The Elder Statesman* (1958) quite lack this quality; the relaxation of their language is prodigious; it serves mainly as accompaniment and mystification for the voices and actions of the players. *Murder in the Cathedral* has some of the earlier quality but in a kind of reductive transformation, it tends to slip off rather than engorge the action, sometimes into lyric cries, sometimes into prose that is nearly voiceless, short of a great actor. I know that I am much disagreed with in my high opinion of *The Family Reunion*; when I see it I know at once how it should have been directed, and when I reread it, I know even better: tirelessly attending to the language, leading every other action to support or to liberate the action in the language. For in a great part of *The Family Reunion* the genuine dramatic energy of the language of "Sweeney Agonistes" has been transformed to another level of attention, not in the least more difficult, but different from what Sweeney and Lil's husband demand: it makes another kind of play, feeling for itself another kind of form, than those we are used to. The rhythm of its action is unfamiliar to us, and the notation of it which Eliot gives us will seem inexact until we become familiar with it. The one mistake would be to look at it as a tragedy, either in form or in burden. Leaving the Greeks out of it, but thinking of Shakespeare, it has the kind of interest *Cymbeline* and *The Tempest* have, not that of *Othello* or *Antony and Cleopatra*. It may be another form of the same thing tragedy *was*, but it will only be the same thing if it does have another form. For example the language in this play leads to a cleansing that has nothing to do with katharsis as Aristotle discussed it but has a great deal to do with redemption or, if you like, an expurgation: it is still cleansing. For another thing the eminence of the hero is increased

rather than diminished, and the tragic fault or error is not made explicable in our sympathy but holds promise of a remote justification. What tragic hero of the past could speak the following words of Harry, which come here as a great promise?

Look, I do not know why,
I feel happy for a moment, as if I had come home.
It is quite irrational, but now
I feel quite happy, as if happiness
Did not consist in getting what one wanted
Or in getting rid of what can't be got rid of
But in a different vision. This is like an end.

To which Agatha responds, "And a beginning." But it is an end and a beginning out of this world; a way of giving, or finding, a meaning to the history we struggle through. It is not tragedy, it is a different vision; unless of course tragedy should come to have new and different burdens, and the individual—who sometimes seems a Christian product though often not a Christian himself—be broken another way than the older tragedy broke him. There is nothing here of Sophocles'—I use Yeats's version—"Never to have lived is best," and nothing here of Shakespeare's "Ripeness is all" or (Hamlet's) "the readiness is all"; and at the end of this play, or of any play like it, we cannot say, as Fortinbras says at the end of *Hamlet*: "This quarry cries on havoc." Greek tragedy and Christian insight have to do with the expiation of guilt, and Shakespeare—Racine, too, if you like—comes between. The Greeks had little care for the individual except to make him hero, the Christian vision had every care for the individual except to let him be; Shakespeare was tender and patient to the spirit of unaccommodated man. I do not say that there is a choice among these three, but a distinction to be remembered; we are haunted by all three, by the probably, the aspiring, the possibly hopeful. I do not say Eliot made a choice among these three, except as the accident of his sensibility led him. In lecturing on Goethe, for example, he pled off a little for the antipathy to him of "anyone like myself, who combines a Catholic cast of mind, a Calvinist heritage, and a puritan temperament." Indeed, one of the extraordinary things about Eliot is the magnanimity with which he does not make a final choice. He dines with the opposition, I am sure, not once but I imagine six times a week. One wishes the world did.

In *The Family Reunion* the example is plain in the conversion of the Eumenides into the Erinyes, which constitutes one of the deep motions of the play, and which corresponds, if you want to put it so, with the burden of these lines from Agatha which come just before Harry's declaration of the nature of happiness. At any rate, the lines ring.

It is possible that sin may strain and struggle
In its dark instinctive birth, to come to conscious-
ness
And so find expurgation. It is possible
You are the consciousness of your unhappy family,
Its bird sent flying through the purgatorial flame.

Had they been poets and playwrights, either Jung or Freud might have written this, Jung with the deepest sympathy, Freud with clinical aloofness; and both might have recognized the relation to the Eumenides and the Erinyes—a relation which is one of the deep organizing voices in this play, and, as I think, in all of Eliot's work. In the beginning of the play Harry is pursued by the Erinyes and in the end he pursues the Eumenides. This is one of the places where the mode of Greek tragedy is changed, but where its possibilities are employed in the larger service: Classical and Christian. The Erinyes, as any good classical dictionary and your own conscience will tell you, constituted the agents of the curse which disturbs things, and it depends on your family and your particular crimes how many they are —obviously always more than one. They are the ghosts of those slain within families, and their curse works automatically upon you once they are set going. They disturb the mind, as the earthquake in the nightmare. It is a little like the great cliché of Oscar Wilde, which strikes every one of us a glancing blow: that each man kills the thing he loves. Harry had, or had not, thrown his wife overboard in mid-ocean, one does not know whether in spreading blackness or in the bursting crash of invading, brilliant spray. One goes back to the first epigraph in a book of Eliot—to *Prufrock and Other Observations*—an epigraph from Dante, where in our love we treat shades as

solid things, clasping their knees—a euphuism for their hearts. The Erinyes were the agents of a curse, but at some point they could change to the kindlier form of the Eumenides, spirits of benison and fertility. There is a fragment of Heraclitus (Diels-Kranz, 94) which has a bearing. "The sun will not overstep his measures; if he were to do so, the Erinyes, handmaids of justice, would seek him out." Harry is sought out, is pursued, and finds, as they change—as he is converted, or "turned"—that he must pursue them. In Eliot, we always get back to Heraclitus: that overshadowing figure in our tradition of what we know that we do not know that we know: it is good that it comes to us in fragments, or we should be too presumptuous and think we might avoid the personal struggle. There is no such mistake in Eliot. He knows the hardship of saying:

This is what matters, but it is unspeakable,
Untranslateable: I shall talk in general terms
Because the particular has no language. One
    thinks to escape
By violence, but one is still alone
In an over-crowded desert, jostled by ghosts.
[*Collected Poems and Plays*, p. 235]

"The particular has no language." It is, rather, what we put into the language that we use which gives it the effect of particular force, and what we put in is the sense of things side by side. In *The Family Reunion* nightmare is put side by side with virtue, or should we say that out of nightmare is created virtue: the response to "the boredom and the horror and the glory."

Possibly there is a simpler way of stating it—this whole confrontation of nightmare and virtue—in three sentences taken from *After Strange Gods* (p. 30):

It would appear that while I maintain the most correct opinions in my criticism, I do nothing but violate them in my verse; and thus appear in a double, if not double-faced role. I feel no shame in this matter. . . . I should say that in one's prose reflexions one may be legitimately occupied with ideals, whereas in the writing of verse one can only deal with actuality.

Eliot makes a small mistake here, for in his verse he appears in both roles. Besides—and this is why I have not here treated them separately—the prose and the verse are two versions of the same history, two phases of the same thought and the same experience, which interpenetrate and interinanimate each other. "Tradition and the Individual Talent" (see pp. 787–91) and *The Waste Land* (see pp. 774–79) could not be more like each other without coalescing. Perhaps in time they will coalesce. At any rate, each spreads into the other in the mind that wills it. We have, in a phrase of Coleridge which Eliot did much to popularize, more than usual emotion with more than usual order trespassing one upon the other, like belief and disbelief, breeding lilacs out of the dead land. Thinking of Eliot and Coleridge together, and remembering the words at the end of *The Use of Poetry:* "The sad ghost of Coleridge beckons to me from the shadows," it may be that the epitaph Coleridge wrote for himself will do here.

Stop, Christian passer-by! Stop, child of God,
And read with gentle breast. Beneath this sod
A poet lies, or that which once seem'd he.
O, lift one thought in prayer for S. T. C.;
That he who many a year with toil of breath
Found death in life, may here find life in death!
Mercy for praise—to be forgiven for fame
He ask'd, and hoped, through Christ. Do thou the
    same.

THE LOVE SONG OF J. ALFRED PRUFROCK
[1915]

◆

⟦ THIS WAS first published in the June, 1915, issue of *Poetry* (Chicago). The epigraph is from Dante's *Inferno*, Canto XXVII, ll. 61–66, and is the response of one of the damned who has been asked to identify himself. In English it goes somewhat as follows: "If I believed that my answer were to anyone who could ever return to the world, this flame should shake no more, but since no one has ever returned alive from this

READING SUGGESTIONS

EDITIONS
The Complete Poems and Plays, 1909–1950 (1952). Includes *Four Quartets*.
Selected Essays, 1917–1932 (second American edition, 1950).
The Sacred Wood: Essays on Poetry and Criticism (1920).
After Strange Gods (1934).
The Idea of a Christian Society (1939).
Notes Towards the Definition of Culture (1948).
The Confidential Clerk (1954).
On Poetry and Poets (1957).
The Elder Statesman (1958).

BIBLIOGRAPHY
DONALD GALLUP, *T. S. Eliot: A Bibliography* (1947).

CRITICISM
ELIZABETH DREW, *T. S. Eliot: The Design of His Poetry* (1949). The emphasis is on interpretation.
HELEN GARDNER, *The Art of T. S. Eliot* (1949). The major part of the book discusses *Four Quartets*.
F. O. MATTHIESSEN (AND C. S. BARBER), *The Achievement of T. S. Eliot* (rev. ed. 1958). A thorough discussion, and citation, of Eliot's techniques.

COLLECTIONS OF ESSAYS
LEONARD UNGER, *T. S. Eliot: A Selected Critique* (1948). A liberal selection of essays and reviews dealing with Eliot—good to the date of publication. There is also a useful bibliography of critical work on Eliot.
T. S. Eliot: A Symposium. Compiled by Richard March and Tambimuttu (1948). A symposium for Eliot's sixtieth birthday, a portraitly collage.

depth, if what I hear be true, without fear of infamy I answer thee." It is an evil counselor who speaks, a man who played the fox rather than the lion; and to remember this may promote intimacy with the poem. The image of Hamlet, not so much the play by Shakespeare as the general symbolic image, runs through the poem in parallel to the symbolic force which Eliot expresses in the epigraph from Dante; they combine to make the tone of mind with which we look at the procession of images: the evening sky, the streets, the city fog, the tea-time ritual and the women's arms, the silent seas, and at the end the annihilating image of the sea-gods, "Till human voices wake us, and we drown." Other matters often annotated—sources hopefully named, symbolism greedily grasped—would seem better let alone; Eliot had digested and transformed them; it is for us to digest the poem.

◆

S'io credesse che mia risposta fosse
A persona che mai tornasse al mondo,
Questa fiamma staria senza piu scosse.
Ma perciocche giammai di questo fondo
Non torno vivo alcun, s'i'odo il vero,
Senza tema d'infamia ti rispondo.

Let us go then, you and I,
When the evening is spread out against the sky
Like a patient etherised upon a table;
Let us go, through certain half-deserted streets,
The muttering retreats
Of restless nights in one-night cheap hotels
And sawdust restaurants with oyster-shells:
Streets that follow like a tedious argument
Of insidious intent   9
To lead you to an overwhelming question . . .
Oh, do not ask, "What is it?"
Let us go and make our visit.

In the room the women come and go
Talking of Michelangelo.

The yellow fog that rubs its back upon the
     window-panes,
The yellow smoke that rubs its muzzle on the
     window-panes
Licked its tongue into the corners of the evening,
Lingered upon the pools that stand in drains,
Let fall upon its back the soot that falls from
     chimneys,
Slipped by the terrace, made a sudden leap,   20
And seeing that it was a soft October night,
Curled once about the house, and fell asleep.

And indeed there will be time
For the yellow smoke that slides along the street,
Rubbing its back upon the window-panes;
There will be time, there will be time
To prepare a face to meet the faces that you
     meet;
There will be time to murder and create,
And time for all the works and days of hands
That lift and drop a question on your plate;   30
Time for you and time for me,
And time yet for a hundred indecisions,
And for a hundred visions and revisions,
Before the taking of a toast and tea.

In the room the women come and go
Talking of Michelangelo.

And indeed there will be time
To wonder, "Do I dare?" and, "Do I dare?"
Time to turn back and descend the stair,
With a bald spot in the middle of my hair—   40
[They will say: "How his hair is growing thin!"]

My morning coat, my collar mounting firmly to
     the chin,
My necktie rich and modest, but asserted by a
     simple pin—
[They will say: "But how his arms and legs are
     thin!"]
Do I dare
Disturb the universe?
In a minute there is time
For decisions and revisions which a minute will
     reverse.

For I have known them all already, known
     them all:—
Have known the evenings, mornings, after-
     noons,   50
I have measured out my life with coffee spoons;
I know the voices dying with a dying fall
Beneath the music from a farther room.
     So how should I presume?

And I have known the eyes already, known
     them all—
The eyes that fix you in a formulated phrase,
And when I am formulated, sprawling on a pin,
When I am pinned and wriggling on the wall,
Then how should I begin
To spit out all the butt-ends of my days and
     ways?   60
     And how should I presume?

And I have known the arms already, known
     them all—
Arms that are braceleted and white and bare
[But in the lamplight, downed with light brown
     hair!]
Is it perfume from a dress
That makes me so digress?
Arms that lie along a table, or wrap about a
     shawl.
     And should I then presume?
     And how should I begin?

                    .   .   .   .   .

Shall I say, I have gone at dusk through narrow
     streets   70
And watched the smoke that rises from the pipes
Of lonely men in shirt-sleeves, leaning out of
     windows? . . .

I should have been a pair of ragged claws
Scuttling across the floors of silent seas.

And the afternoon, the evening, sleeps so peace-
     fully!
Smoothed by long fingers,

Asleep . . . tired . . . or it malingers,
Stretched on the floor, here beside you and me.
Should I, after tea and cakes and ices,
Have the strength to force the moment to its
    crisis?   80
But though I have wept and fasted, wept and
    prayed,
Though I have seen my head [grown slightly
    bald] brought in upon a platter,
I am no prophet—and here's no great matter;
I have seen the moment of my greatness flicker,
And I have seen the eternal Footman hold my
    coat, and snicker,
And in short, I was afraid.

And would it have been worth it, after all,
After the cups, the marmalade, the tea,
Among the porcelain, among some talk of you
    and me,
Would it have been worth while,   90
To have bitten off the matter with a smile,
To have squeezed the universe into a ball
To roll it toward some overwhelming question,
To say: "I am Lazarus, come from the dead,
Come back to tell you all, I shall tell you all"—
If one, settling a pillow by her head,
    Should say: "That is not what I meant at all.
    That is not it, at all."

And would it have been worth it, after all,
Would it have been worth while,   100
After the sunsets and the dooryards and the
    sprinkled streets,
After the novels, after the teacups, after the skirts
    that trail along the floor—
And this, and so much more?—
It is impossible to say just what I mean!
But as if a magic lantern threw the nerves in
    patterns on a screen:
Would it have been worth while
If one, settling a pillow or throwing off a shawl,
And turning toward the window, should say:
    "That is not it at all,
    That is not what I meant, at all."   110

. . . . .

No! I am not Prince Hamlet, nor was meant to be;
Am an attendant lord, one that will do
To swell a progress, start a scene or two,
Advise the prince; no doubt, an easy tool,
Deferential, glad to be of use,
Politic, cautious, and meticulous;
Full of high sentence, but a bit obtuse;
At times, indeed, almost ridiculous—
Almost, at times, the Fool.

I grow old . . . I grow old . . .   120
I shall wear the bottoms of my trousers rolled.

Shall I part my hair behind? Do I dare to eat a
    peach?
I shall wear white flannel trousers, and walk upon
    the beach.
I have heard the mermaids singing, each to each.

I do not think that they will sing to me.

I have seen them riding seaward on the waves
Combing the white hair of the waves blown back
When the wind blows the water white and black.

We have lingered in the chambers of the sea
By sea-girls wreathed with seaweed red and
    brown   130
Till human voices wake us, and we drown.

THE BOSTON EVENING TRANSCRIPT

[1915]

◆

⟨ THE NEWSPAPER of the title was the only literate
evening paper in Boston in its time and has not been
replaced since. It contained a genealogical page as well
as pages on the arts and letters. Its politics were conservative, its social news extensive, and its financial
pages complete. For its small subscription list it was a
narrow habit of life. It was read, some said, by the rich
and by their butlers, and more attentively by the butlers than by their masters. Nothing could be further
from the scene, and nothing more appropriate to Eliot's
tone toward the scene, than the apparition of Rochefoucauld in the seventh line. The *Maxims* of La Rochefoucauld (1613–80) are a masterpiece in summary
assessment of the psychology and behavior of a closed
society—whether at the court of Louis XIV or along
Beacon Street, Boston, in the early twentieth century.

◆

The readers of the *Boston Evening Transcript*
Sway in the wind like a field of ripe corn.

When evening quickens faintly in the street,
Wakening the appetites of life in some
And to others bringing the *Boston Evening Tran-
script,*

I mount the steps and ring the bell, turning
Wearily, as one would turn to nod good-bye to
    Rochefoucauld,
If the street were time and he at the end of the
    street,
And I say, "Cousin Harriet, here is the *Boston*
    Evening Transcript."

COUSIN NANCY [1915]

◊

⟨ THIS POEM was published together with "The *Boston
Evening Transcript*" and furnishes a different image of
the same society. Instead of La Rochefoucauld, the
poem invokes Matthew Arnold and Ralph Waldo
Emerson, whose works still stand in bookcases inaccessible because of glass doors, which so often seem to
keep the dust in rather than out. The last line—"The
army of unalterable law"—is also the last line of
George Meredith's "Lucifer in Starlight."

◊

Miss Nancy Ellicott
Strode across the hills and broke them,
Rode across the hills and broke them—
The barren New England hills—
Riding to hounds
Over the cow-pasture.

   Miss Nancy Ellicott smoked
And danced all the modern dances;
And her aunts were not quite sure how they felt
    about it,
But they knew that it was modern.   10

   Upon the glazen shelves kept watch
Matthew and Waldo, guardians of the faith,
The army of unalterable law.

LA FIGLIA CHE PIANGE [1917]

◊

⟨ THE TITLE may have a particular origin—a phrase in
a poem or the name of a picture—but I am glad I can
find no one who can tell me what that origin is. "The
girl who weeps," or "The weeping maiden," has an
authority derived from the poem, and directed a little
by the epigraph, which may be found in the *Aeneid*,
I.327: "By what name shall I call thee, o maiden," is
how the Loeb Library translation goes. It is Venus incognito, but Aeneas almost at once knows she may be
a goddess. Possibly Eliot's poem may pass for one of
the love songs which Prufrock never sang in the poem
under his name.

◊

O quam te memorem virgo . . .

Stand on the highest pavement of the stair—
Lean on a garden urn—
Weave, weave the sunlight in your hair—
Clasp your flowers to you with a pained surprise—
Fling them to the ground and turn
With a fugitive resentment in your eyes:
But weave, weave the sunlight in your hair.

   So I would have had him leave,
So I would have had her stand and grieve,
So he would have left   10
As the soul leaves the body torn and bruised,
As the mind deserts the body it has used.
I should find
Some way incomparably light and deft,
Some way we both should understand,
Simple and faithless as a smile and shake of the
    hand.

   She turned away, but with the autumn weather
Compelled my imagination many days,
Many days and many hours:
Her hair over her arms and her arms full of
    flowers.   20
And I wonder how they should have been to-
    gether!
I should have lost a gesture and a pose.
Sometimes these cogitations still amaze
The troubled midnight and the noon's repose.

WHISPERS OF IMMORTALITY [1918]

◊

⟨ JOHN WEBSTER (1580?–1625?), playwright and poet,
and John Donne (1571–1631), poet and divine, have
each been powerful attractive influences on modern

poetry; and one of the reasons for this fashion is that they inhabit the first four stanzas of this poem, where Eliot both makes them part of his poem and makes a literary criticism upon them. Grishkin, in the second half of the poem, does not make a literary criticism on anything, but when Eliot reminds us that she is always present, and sets her beside Webster and Donne, she makes a powerful poetic criticism. Nothing is so "expert beyond experience" as "Grishkin in a drawing-room."

◊

Webster was much possessed by death
And saw the skull beneath the skin;
And breastless creatures under ground
Leaned backward with a lipless grin.

    Daffodil bulbs instead of balls
Stared from the sockets of the eyes!
He knew that thought clings round dead limbs
Tightening its lusts and luxuries.

    Donne, I suppose, was such another
Who found no substitute for sense,   10
To seize and clutch and penetrate;
Expert beyond experience,

    He knew the anguish of the marrow
The ague of the skeleton;
No contact possible to flesh
Allayed the fever of the bone.

. . . . . .

Grishkin is nice: her Russian eye
Is underlined for emphasis;
Uncorseted, her friendly bust
Gives promise of pneumatic bliss.   20

    The couched Brazilian jaguar
Compels the scampering marmoset
With subtle effluence of cat;
Grishkin has a maisonette;

    The sleek Brazilian jaguar
Does not in its arboreal gloom
Distil so rank a feline smell
As Grishkin in a drawing-room.

    And even the Abstract Entities
Circumambulate her charm;   30
But our lot crawls between dry ribs
To keep our metaphysics warm.

THE WASTE LAND [1922]

◊

⟪ THE POEM was first published in the first issue of Eliot's magazine, the *Criterion*, in October, 1922, and in the *Dial* (New York) the following month. In December *The Waste Land*, augmented by Eliot's notes which now seem part of it, was published as a book. The epigraph is from the forty-eighth chapter of Petronius' *Satyricon* and in English runs somewhat as follows: "For with my own eyes I saw the sibyl of Cumae hanging in a basket, and when the boys cried to her, 'Sibyl, what do you wish?' she answered 'I wish to die.' " It should be remembered she was something like a thousand years old when the boys queried her, and death nowhere yet in sight. Eliot's notes seem sufficient to show the reader the sort of poem he is invited to become familiar with, and indeed Eliot may have made more than are necessary. The true echo or ring of the allusions and quotations Eliot makes is only blurred by mere factual knowledge of their sources; more is lost than gained by handbook understanding, and no other aid is possible except a commentary many times longer than the poem itself—a commentary that can properly be made only by each reader since it would necessarily differ with each reader's state of knowledge and sensibility. Eliot's own notes are printed as in the *Collected Poems*, with the exception that some of his citations from foreign languages are given in English as well as the original tongue.

◊

"Nam Sibyllam quidem Cumis ego ipse oculis meis vidi in ampulla pendere, et cum illi pueri dicerent: Σίβυλλα τί θέλεις; respondebat illa: ἀποθανεῖν θέλω."

FOR EZRA POUND
il miglior fabbro.

I. THE BURIAL OF THE DEAD

April is the cruellest month, breeding
Lilacs out of the dead land, mixing
Memory and desire, stirring
Dull roots with spring rain.
Winter kept us warm, covering
Earth in forgetful snow, feeding
A little life with dried tubers.
Summer surprised us, coming over the Starnbergersee
With a shower of rain; we stopped in the colonnade,
And went on in sunlight, into the Hofgarten,   10
And drank coffee, and talked for an hour.
Bin gar keine Russin, stamm' aus Litauen, echt deutsch.

And when we were children, staying at the arch-
duke's,
My cousin's, he took me out on a sled,
And I was frightened. He said, Marie,
Marie, hold on tight. And down we went.
In the mountains, there you feel free.
I read, much of the night, and go south in the
winter.

What are the roots that clutch, what branches
grow
Out of this stony rubbish? Son of man,   20
You cannot say, or guess, for you know only
A heap of broken images, where the sun beats,
And the dead tree gives no shelter, the cricket no
relief,
And the dry stone no sound of water. Only
There is shadow under this red rock,
(Come in under the shadow of this red rock),
And I will show you something different from
either
Your shadow at morning striding behind you
Or your shadow at evening rising to meet you;
I will show you fear in a handful of dust.   30
            Frisch weht der Wind
            Der Heimat zu
            Mein Irisch Kind,
            Wo weilest du?
"You gave me hyacinths first a year ago;
"They called me the hyacinth girl."
—Yet when we came back, late, from the Hya-
cinth garden,
Your arms full, and your hair wet, I could not
Speak, and my eyes failed. I was neither
Living nor dead, and I knew nothing,   40
Looking into the heart of light, the silence.
Oed' und leer das Meer.

Madame Sosostris, famous clairvoyante,
Had a bad cold, nevertheless
Is known to be the wisest woman in Europe,
With a wicked pack of cards. Here, said she,
Is your card, the drowned Phoenician Sailor,
(Those are pearls that were his eyes. Look!)
Here is Belladonna, the Lady of the Rocks,
The lady of situations.   50
Here is the man with three staves, and here the
Wheel,
And here is the one-eyed merchant, and this card,
Which is blank, is something he carries on his
back,
Which I am forbidden to see. I do not find
The Hanged Man. Fear death by water.

THE WASTE LAND.   *31-34. Frisch . . . du?:* "The wind blows
fresh towards home; my Irish child, where are you waiting?"
42. Oed' . . . Meer: "Wide and empty is the sea."

I see crowds of people, walking round in a ring.
Thank you. If you see dear Mrs. Equitone,
Tell her I bring the horoscope myself:
One must be so careful these days.

Unreal City,   60
Under the brown fog of a winter dawn,
A crowd flowed over London Bridge, so many,
I had not thought death had undone so many.
Sighs, short and infrequent, were exhaled,
And each man fixed his eyes before his feet.
Flowed up the hill and down King William Street,
To where Saint Mary Woolnoth kept the hours
With a dead sound on the final stroke of nine.
There I saw one I knew, and stopped him, crying:
"Stetson!
"You who were with me in the ships at Mylae! 70
"That corpse you planted last year in your garden,
"Has it begun to sprout? Will it bloom this year?
"Or has the sudden frost disturbed its bed?
"Oh keep the Dog far hence, that's friend to men,
"Or with his nails he'll dig it up again!
"You! hypocrite lecteur!—mon semblable,—mon
frère!"

II. A GAME OF CHESS

The Chair she sat in, like a burnished throne,
Glowed on the marble, where the glass
Held up by standards wrought with fruited vines
From which a golden Cupidon peeped out   80
(Another hid his eyes behind his wing)
Doubled the flames of sevenbranched candelabra
Reflecting light upon the table as
The glitter of her jewels rose to meet it,
From satin cases poured in rich profusion;
In vials of ivory and coloured glass
Unstoppered, lurked her strange synthetic per-
fumes,
Unguent, powdered, or liquid—troubled, con-
fused
And drowned the sense in odours; stirred by the
air
That freshened from the window, these ascended
In fattening the prolonged candle-flames,   91
Flung their smoke into the laquearia,
Stirring the pattern on the coffered ceiling.
Huge sea-wood fed with copper
Burned green and orange, framed by the coloured
stone,
In which sad light a carvèd dolphin swam.
Above the antique mantel was displayed
As though a window gave upon the sylvan scene
The change of Philomel, by the barbarous king
So rudely forced; yet there the nightingale   100
Filled all the desert with inviolable voice

And still she cried, and still the world pursues,
"Jug Jug" to dirty ears.
And other withered stumps of time
Were told upon the walls; staring forms
Leaned out, leaning, hushing the room enclosed.
Footsteps shuffled on the stair.
Under the firelight, under the brush, her hair
Spread out in fiery points   109
Glowed into words, then would be savagely still.

  "My nerves are bad to-night. Yes, bad. Stay
     with me.
"Speak to me. Why do you never speak. Speak.
  "What are you thinking of? What thinking?
     What?
"I never know what you are thinking. Think."

  I think we are in rats' alley
Where the dead men lost their bones.

  "What is that noise?"   117
                    The wind under the door.
"What is that noise now? What is the wind doing?"
                    Nothing again nothing.
                                          "Do
"You know nothing? Do you see nothing? Do you
     remember
"Nothing?"

     I remember
Those are pearls that were his eyes.
"Are you alive, or not? Is there nothing in your
     head?"
                                          But
O O O O that Shakespeherian Rag—
It's so elegant
So intelligent   130
"What shall I do now? What shall I do?"
"I shall rush out as I am, and walk the street
"With my hair down, so. What shall we do to-
     morrow?
"What shall we ever do?"
                    The hot water at ten.
And if it rains, a closed car at four.
And we shall play a game of chess,
Pressing lidless eyes and waiting for a knock upon
     the door.

  When Lil's husband got demobbed, I said—
I didn't mince my words, I said to her myself,
HURRY UP PLEASE ITS TIME   141
Now Albert's coming back, make yourself a bit
     smart.
He'll want to know what you done with that
     money he gave you
To get yourself some teeth. He did, I was there.

You have them all out, Lil, and get a nice set,
He said, I swear, I can't bear to look at you.
And no more can't I, I said, and think of poor
     Albert,
He's been in the army four years, he wants a good
     time,
And if you don't give it him, there's others will, I
     said.
Oh is there, she said. Something o' that, I said.
Then I'll know who to thank, she said, and give
     me a straight look.   151
HURRY UP PLEASE ITS TIME
If you don't like it you can get on with it, I said.
Others can pick and choose if you can't.
But if Albert makes off, it won't be for lack of
     telling.
You ought to be ashamed, I said, to look so an-
     tique.
(And her only thirty-one.)
I can't help it, she said, pulling a long face,
It's them pills I took, to bring it off, she said.
(She's had five already, and nearly died of young
     George.)   160
The chemist said it would be all right, but I've
     never been the same.
You are a proper fool, I said.
Well, if Albert won't leave you alone, there it is,
     I said,
What you get married for if you don't want chil-
     dren?
HURRY UP PLEASE ITS TIME
Well, that Sunday Albert was home, they had a
     hot gammon,
And they asked me in to dinner, to get the beauty
     of it hot—
HURRY UP PLEASE ITS TIME
HURRY UP PLEASE ITS TIME
Goonight Bill. Goonight Lou. Goonight May.
     Goonight.   170
Ta ta. Goonight. Goonight.
Good night, ladies, good night, sweet ladies, good
     night, good night.

III. THE FIRE SERMON

The river's tent is broken: the last fingers of leaf
Clutch and sink into the wet bank. The wind
Crosses the brown land, unheard. The nymphs are
     departed.
Sweet Thames, run softly, till I end my song.
The river bears no empty bottles, sandwich pa-
     pers,
Silk handkerchiefs, cardboard boxes, cigarette
     ends
Or other testimony of summer nights. The nymphs
     are departed.

And their friends, the loitering heirs of city di-
rectors;   180
Departed, have left no addresses.
By the waters of Leman I sat down and wept . . .
Sweet Thames, run softly till I end my song,
Sweet Thames, run softly, for I speak not loud or
long.
But at my back in a cold blast I hear
The rattle of the bones, and chuckle spread from
ear to ear.
A rat crept softly through the vegetation
Dragging its slimy belly on the bank
While I was fishing in the dull canal   189
On a winter evening round behind the gashouse.
Musing upon the king my brother's wreck
And on the king my father's death before him.
White bodies naked on the low damp ground
And bones cast in a little low dry garret,
Rattled by the rat's foot only, year to year.
But at my back from time to time I hear
The sound of horns and motors, which shall bring
Sweeney to Mrs. Porter in the spring.
O the moon shone bright on Mrs. Porter
And on her daughter   200
They wash their feet in soda water
*Et O ces voix d'enfants, chantant dans la cou-
pole!*

     Twit twit twit
Jug jug jug jug jug jug
So rudely forc'd.
Tereu

     Unreal City
Under the brown fog of a winter noon
Mr. Eugenides, the Smyrna merchant
Unshaven, with a pocket full of currants   210
C.i.f. London: documents at sight,
Asked me in demotic French
To luncheon at the Cannon Street Hotel
Followed by a weekend at the Metropole.

     At the violet hour, when the eyes and back
Turn upward from the desk, when the human en-
gine waits
Like a taxi throbbing waiting,
I Tiresias, though blind, throbbing between two
lives,
Old man with wrinkled female breasts, can see
At the violet hour, the evening hour that strives
Homeward, and brings the sailor home from sea,
The typist home at teatime, clears her breakfast,
lights   222
Her stove, and lays out food in tins.
Out of the window perilously spread

Her drying combinations touched by the sun's last
rays,
On the divan are piled (at night her bed)
Stockings, slippers, camisoles, and stays.
I Tiresias, old man with wrinkled dugs
Perceived the scene, and foretold the rest—
I too awaited the expected guest.   230
He, the young man carbuncular, arrives,
A small house agent's clerk, with one bold stare,
One of the low on whom assurance sits
As a silk hat on a Bradford millionaire.
The time is now propitious, as he guesses,
The meal is ended, she is bored and tired,
Endeavours to engage her in caresses
Which still are unreproved, if undesired.
Flushed and decided, he assaults at once;
Exploring hands encounter no defence;   240
His vanity requires no response,
And makes a welcome of indifference.
(And I Tiresias have foresuffered all
Enacted on this same divan or bed;
I who have sat by Thebes below the wall
And walked among the lowest of the dead.)
Bestows one final patronising kiss,
And gropes his way, finding the stairs unlit . . .

     She turns and looks a moment in the glass,
Hardly aware of her departed lover;   250
Her brain allows one half-formed thought to pass:
"Well now that's done: and I'm glad it's over."
When lovely woman stoops to folly and
Paces about her room again, alone,
She smoothes her hair with automatic hand,
And puts a record on the gramophone.

     "This music crept by me upon the waters"
And along the Strand, up Queen Victoria Street.
O City city, I can sometimes hear
Beside a public bar in Lower Thames Street,   260
The pleasant whining of a mandoline
And a clatter and a chatter from within
Where fishmen lounge at noon: where the walls
Of Magnus Martyr hold
Inexplicable splendour of Ionian white and gold.

               The river sweats
          Oil and tar
          The barges drift
          With the turning tide
          Red sails   270
          Wide
          To leeward, swing on the
               heavy spar.
          The barges wash
          Drifting logs
          Down Greenwich reach

Past the Isle of Dogs.
    Weialala leia
    Wallala leialala

Elizabeth and Leicester
Beating oars   280
The stern was formed
A gilded shell
Red and gold
The brisk swell
Rippled both shores
Southwest wind
Carried down stream
The peal of bells
White towers
    Weialala leia   290
    Wallala leialala

"Trams and dusty trees.
Highbury bore me. Richmond and Kew
Undid me. By Richmond I raised my knees
Supine on the floor of a narrow canoe."

"My feet are at Moorgate, and my heart
Under my feet. After the event
He wept. He promised 'a new start.'
I made no comment. What should I resent?"

"On Margate Sands.   300
I can connect
Nothing with nothing.
The broken fingernails of dirty hands.
My people humble people who expect
Nothing."

        la la

To Carthage then I came

Burning burning burning burning
O Lord Thou pluckest me out
O Lord Thou pluckest   310

burning

IV. DEATH BY WATER

Phlebas the Phoenician, a fortnight dead,
Forgot the cry of gulls, and the deep sea swell
And the profit and loss.
          A current under sea
Picked his bones in whispers. As he rose and fell
He passed the stages of his age and youth
Entering the whirlpool.
          Gentile or Jew
O you who turn the wheel and look to windward,
Consider Phlebas, who was once handsome and
    tall as you.   321

V. WHAT THE THUNDER SAID

After the torchlight red on sweaty faces
After the frosty silence in the gardens
After the agony in stony places
The shouting and the crying
Prison and palace and reverberation
Of thunder of spring over distant mountains
He who was living is now dead
We who were living are now dying
With a little patience   330

Here is no water but only rock
Rock and no water and the sandy road
The road winding above among the mountains
Which are mountains of rock without water
If there were water we should stop and drink
Amongst the rock one cannot stop or think
Sweat is dry and feet are in the sand
If there were only water amongst the rock
Dead mountain mouth of carious teeth that can-
    not spit
Here one can neither stand nor lie nor sit   340
There is not even silence in the mountains
But dry sterile thunder without rain
There is not even solitude in the mountains
But red sullen faces sneer and snarl
From doors of mudcracked houses
                  If there were water
    And no rock
    If there were rock
    And also water
    And water   350
    A spring
    A pool among the rock
    If there were the sound of water only
    Not the cicada
    And dry grass singing
    But sound of water over a rock
    Where the hermit-thrush sings in the pine trees
    Drip drop drip drop drop drop drop
    But there is no water

Who is the third who walks always beside you?
When I count, there are only you and I together
But when I look ahead up the white road   362
There is always another one walking beside you
Gliding wrapt in a brown mantle, hooded
I do not know whether a man or a woman
—But who is that on the other side of you?

What is that sound high in the air
Murmur of maternal lamentation
Who are those hooded hordes swarming
Over endless plains, stumbling in cracked earth
Ringed by the flat horizon only   371

What is the city over the mountains
Cracks and reforms and bursts in the violet air
Falling towers
Jerusalem Athens Alexandria
Vienna London
Unreal

A woman drew her long black hair out tight
And fiddled whisper music on those strings
And bats with baby faces in the violet light   380
Whistled, and beat their wings
And crawled head downward down a blackened
    wall
And upside down in air were towers
Tolling reminiscent bells, that kept the hours
And voices singing out of empty cisterns and ex-
    hausted wells.

In this decayed hole among the mountains
In the faint moonlight, the grass is singing
Over the tumbled graves, about the chapel
There is the empty chapel, only the wind's home.
It has no windows, and the door swings,   390
Dry bones can harm no one.
Only a cock stood on the rooftree
Co co rico co co rico
In a flash of lightning. Then a damp gust
Bringing rain

Ganga was sunken, and the limp leaves
Waited for rain, while the black clouds
Gathered far distant, over Himavant.
The jungle crouched, humped in silence.
Then spoke the thunder   400
DA
Datta: what have we given?
My friend, blood shaking my heart
The awful daring of a moment's surrender
Which an age of prudence can never retract
By this, and this only, we have existed
Which is not to be found in our obituaries
Or in memories draped by the beneficent spider
Or under seals broken by the lean solicitor
In our empty rooms   410
DA
Dayadhvam: I have heard the key
Turn in the door once and turn once only
We think of the key, each in his prison
Thinking of the key, each confirms a prison
Only at nightfall, aethereal rumours
Revive for a moment a broken Coriolanus
DA
Damyata: The boat responded
Gaily, to the hand expert with sail and oar   420
The sea was calm, your heart would have re-
    sponded

Gaily, when invited, beating obedient
To controlling hands

               I sat upon the shore
Fishing, with the arid plain behind me
Shall I at least set my lands in order?
London Bridge is falling down falling down fall-
    ing down
Poi s'ascose nel foco che gli affina
Quando fiam uti chelidon—O swallow swallow
Le Prince d'Aquitaine à la tour abolie   430
These fragments I have shored against my ruins
Why then Ile fit you. Hieronymo's mad againe.
Datta. Dayadhvam. Damyata.
    Shantih   shantih   shantih

NOTES ON "THE WASTE LAND"

NOT ONLY the title, but the plan and a good deal of the incidental symbolism of the poem were suggested by Miss Jessie L. Weston's book on the Grail legend: *From Ritual to Romance* (Cambridge). Indeed, so deeply am I indebted, Miss Weston's book will eluci- date the difficulties of the poem much better than my notes can do; and I recommend it (apart from the great interest of the book itself) to any who think such elucidation of the poem worth the trouble. To another work of anthropology I am indebted in gen- eral, one which has influenced our generation pro- foundly; I mean *The Golden Bough;* I have used especially the two volumes *Adonis, Attis, Osiris.* Any- one who is acquainted with these works will im- mediately recognise in the poem certain references to vegetation ceremonies.

I. THE BURIAL OF THE DEAD

LINE 20. Cf. Ezekiel II, i.
23. Cf. Ecclesiastes XII, v.
31. V. Tristan und Isolde, I, verses 5–8.
42. Id. III, verse 24.
46. I am not familiar with the exact constitution of the Tarot pack of cards, from which I have obviously departed to suit my own convenience. The Hanged Man, a member of the traditional pack, fits my pur- pose in two ways: because he is associated in my mind with the Hanged God of Frazer, and because I associate him with the hooded figure in the passage of the disciples to Emmaus in Part V. The Phoenician Sailor and the Merchant appear later; also the "crowds of people," and Death by Water is executed in Part IV. The Man with Three Staves (an authentic mem- ber of the Tarot pack) I associate, quite arbitrarily, with the Fisher King himself.
60. Cf. Baudelaire:
    "Fourmillante cité, cité pleine de rêves,
    "Où le spectre en plein jour raccroche le pas-
      sant." [1]

---

1. "Fourmillante . . . passant": "Swarming city, city full of dreams, Where the specter in full day accosts the passer-by."

63. Cf. Inferno III, 55–57:

> "si lunga tratta
> di gente, ch'io non avrei mai creduto
> che morte tanta n'avesse disfatta." [2]

64. Cf. Inferno IV, 25–27:

> "Quivi, secondo che per ascoltare,
> "non avea pianto, ma' che di sospiri,
> "che l'aura eterna facevan tremare." [3]

68. A phenomenon which I have often noticed.

74. Cf. the Dirge in Webster's *White Devil.*

76. V. Baudelaire, Preface to *Fleurs du Mal.*

II. A GAME OF CHESS

77. Cf. *Antony and Cleopatra,* II, ii, l. 190.

92. Laquearia. V. *Aeneid,* I, 726:

dependent lychni laquearibus aureis incensi, et noctem flammis funalia vincunt.[4]

98. Sylvan scene. V. Milton, *Paradise Lost,* IV, 140.

99. V. Ovid, *Metamorphoses,* VI, Philomela.

100. Cf. Part III, l. 204.

115. Cf. Part III, l. 195.

118. Cf. Webster: "Is the wind in that door still?"

126. Cf. Part I, l. 37, 48.

138. Cf. the game of chess in Middleton's *Women beware Women.*

III. THE FIRE SERMON

176. V. Spenser, *Prothalamion.*

192. Cf. *The Tempest,* I, ii.

196. Cf. Marvell, *To His Coy Mistress.*

197. Cf. Day, *Parliament of Bees:*

> "When of the sudden, listening, you shall hear,
> "A noise of horns and hunting, which shall bring
> "Actaeon to Diana in the spring,
> "Where all shall see her naked skin . . ."

199. I do not know the origin of the ballad from which these lines are taken: it was reported to me from Sydney, Australia.

202. V. Verlaine, *Parsifal.*

210. The currants were quoted at a price "carriage and insurance free to London"; and the Bill of Lading etc. were to be handed to the buyer upon payment of the sight draft.

218. Tiresias, although a mere spectator and not indeed a "character," is yet the most important personage in the poem, uniting all the rest. Just as the one-eyed merchant, seller of currants, melts into the Phoenician Sailor, and the latter is not wholly distinct from Ferdinand Prince of Naples, so all the women are one woman, and the two sexes meet in Tiresias. What Tiresias *sees,* in fact, is the substance of the

poem. The whole passage from Ovid is of great anthropological interest:

> '. . . Cum Iunone iocos et maior vestra profecto est
> Quam, quae contingit maribus,' dixisse, 'voluptas.'
> Illa negat; placuit quae sit sententia docti
> Quaerere Tiresiae: venus huic erat utraque nota.
> Nam duo magnorum viridi coeuntia silva
> Corpora serpentum baculi violaverat ictu
> Deque viro factus, mirabile, femina septem
> Egerat autumnos; octavo rursus eosdem
> Vidit et 'est vestrae si tanta potentia plagae,'
> Dixit 'ut auctoris sortem in contraria mutet,
> Nunc quoque vos feriam!' percussis anguibus isdem
> Forma prior rediit genetivaque venit imago.
> Arbiter hic igitur sumptus de lite iocosa
> Dicta Iovis firmat; gravius Saturnia iusto
> Nec pro materia fertur doluisse suique
> Iudicis aeterna damnavit lumina nocte,
> At pater omnipotens (neque enim licet inrita cuiquam
> Facta dei fecisse deo) pro lumine adempto
> Scire futura dedit poenamque levavit honore.[5]

221. This may not appear as exact as Sappho's lines, but I had in mind the "longshore" or "dory" fisherman, who returns at nightfall.

253. V. Goldsmith, the song in *The Vicar of Wakefield.*

257. V. *The Tempest,* as above.

264. The interior of St. Magnus Martyr is to my mind one of the finest among Wren's interiors. See *The Proposed Demolition of Nineteen City Churches:* (P. S. King & Son, Ltd.).

266. The Song of the (three) Thames-daughters begins here. From line 292 to 306 inclusive they speak in turn. V. *Götterdämmerung,* III, i: the Rhine-daughters.

279. V. Froude, *Elizabeth,* Vol. I, ch. iv, letter of De Quadra to Philip of Spain:

---

2. "si . . . disfatta":

> "so long a train
> of people, I had not ever believed
> that death had undone so many."

3. "Quivi . . . tremare": "Here there was no plaint that could be heard, except of sighs, which made the eternal air to tremble."

4. dependent . . . vincunt: "Lighted lamps hang down from the fretted roof of gold, and flaming torches drive out the night."

5. Cum . . . honore: (*Metamorphoses,* III.318–38) "It chanced that Jove (as the story goes), while warmed with wine, put care aside and bandied good-humored jests with Juno in an idle hour. 'I maintain,' said he, 'that your pleasure in love is greater than that which we [the male gods] enjoy.' She held the opposite view. And so they decided to ask the judgment of the wise Tiresias. He knew both sides of love. For once, with a blow of his staff, he had outraged two huge serpents mating in the green forest; and, wonderful to relate, from man he was changed into a woman, and in that form spent seven years. In the eighth year he saw the same serpents again and said: 'Since in striking you there is such magic power as to change the nature of the giver of the blow, now will I strike you once again.' So saying, he struck the serpents, and his former state was restored, and he became as he had been born. He, therefore, being asked to arbitrate the playful dispute of the gods, took sides with Jove. Saturnia [Juno], they said, grieved more deeply than she should and than the issue warranted, and condemned the arbitrator to perpetual blindness. But the Almighty Father (for no god may undo what another god has done) in return for his loss of sight gave Tiresias the power to know the future, lightening the penalty by the honor" (translation by Frank J. Miller in the Loeb Classical Library).

"In the afternoon we were in a barge, watching the games on the river. (The queen) was along with Lord Robert and myself on the poop, when they began to talk nonsense, and went so far that Lord Robert at last said, as I was on the spot there was no reason why they should not be married if the queen pleased."

293. Cf. *Purgatorio*, V, 133:

"Ricorditi di me, che son la Pia;
"Siena mi fe', disfecemi Maremma." 6

307. V. St. Augustine's *Confessions*: "to Carthage then I came, where a cauldron of unholy loves sang all about mine ears."

308. The complete text of the Buddha's Fire Sermon (which corresponds in importance to the Sermon on the Mount) from which these words are taken, will be found translated in the late Henry Clarke Warren's *Buddhism in Translation* (Harvard Oriental Series). Mr. Warren was one of the great pioneers of Buddhist studies in the Occident.

309. From St. Augustine's *Confessions* again. The collocation of these two representatives of eastern and western asceticism, as the culmination of this part of the poem, is not an accident.

V. WHAT THE THUNDER SAID

In the first part of Part V three themes are employed: the journey to Emmaus, the approach to the Chapel Perilous (see Miss Weston's book) and the present decay of eastern Europe.

357. This is *Turdus aonalaschkae pallasii,* the hermit-thrush which I have heard in Quebec Province. Chapman says (*Handbook of Birds of Eastern North America*) "it is most at home in secluded woodland and thickety retreats. . . . Its notes are not remarkable for variety or volume, but in purity and sweetness of tone and exquisite modulation they are unequalled." Its "water-dripping song" is justly celebrated.

360. The following lines were stimulated by the account of one of the Antarctic expeditions (I forget which, but I think one of Shackleton's): it was related that the party of explorers, at the extremity of their strength, had the constant delusion that there was *one more member* than could actually be counted.

367–77. Cf. Hermann Hesse, *Blick ins Chaos:* "Schon ist halb Europa, schon ist zumindest der halbe Osten Europas auf dem Wege zum Chaos, fährt betrunken im heiligem Wahn am Abgrund entlang und singt dazu, singt betrunken und hymnisch wie Dmitri Karamasoff sang. Ueber diese Lieder lacht der Bürger beleidigt, der Heilige und Seher hört sie mit Tränen." 7

402. "Datta, dayadhvam, damyata" (Give, sympathise, control). The fable of the meaning of the

Thunder is found in the *Brihadaranyaka—Upanishad,* 5, 1. A translation is found in Deussen's *Sechzig Upanishads des Veda,* p. 489.

408. Cf. Webster, *The White Devil*, V, vi:

". . . they'll remarry
Ere the worm pierce your winding-sheet, ere the spider
Make a thin curtain for your epitaphs."

412. Cf. *Inferno*, XXXIII, 46:

"ed io sentii chiavar l'uscio di sotto
all'orribile torre." 8

Also F. H. Bradley, *Appearance and Reality,* p. 346. "My external sensations are no less private to myself than are my thoughts or my feelings. In either case my experience falls within my own circle, a circle closed on the outside; and, with all its elements alike, every sphere is opaque to the others which surround it. . . . In brief, regarded as an existence which appears in a soul, the whole world for each is peculiar and private to that soul."

425. V. Weston: *From Ritual to Romance;* chapter on the Fisher King.

428. V. *Purgatorio*, XXVI, 148.

" 'Ara vos prec per aquella valor
'que vos guida al som de l'escalina,
'sovegna vos a temps de ma dolor.'
Poi s'ascose nel foco che gli affina." 9

429. V. *Pervigilium Veneris.* Cf. Philomela in Parts II and III.

430. V. Gerard de Nerval, Sonnet *El Desdichado*.

432. V. Kyd's *Spanish Tragedy*.

434. Shantih. Repeated as here, a formal ending to an Upanishad. "The Peace which passeth understanding" is our equivalent to this word.

JOURNEY OF THE MAGI
[1927]

◊

❲ THE FIRST lines of this poem are versified from a sermon by Bishop Lancelot Andrewes (1555–1626) on the Wise Men from the East. The readiest reference to the original is the essay on Andrewes in *Selected Essays,* p. 307, where Eliot quotes the passage as an example of "sentences in which, before extracting all the spiritual meaning of a text, Andrewes forces a concrete presence upon us." The concrete presence is what Eliot himself forces upon us, as it was concrete presence from which he drew. I should also call attention to this

---

6. "**Ricorditi . . . Maremma:** "Remember me, who am La Pia; Siena made me, Maremma unmade me." 7. "**Schon . . . Tränen**": "Already half Europe, at least half of Eastern Europe is on the way to chaos, driving drunken in sacred folly along the edge of the abyss and, drunken, singing hymn-like songs as Dimitri Karamazov sang. Offended by these songs the burgher laughs, while the saint and seer listen to them with tears" (translation by Agnes Eisenberger from *Blick ins Chaos* [*A Glimpse into Chaos*] by Hermann Hesse.

8. "**ed . . . torre**": "and below I heard the outlet of the horrible tower locked up." 9. "**Ara . . . affina**": "Now I pray you by that goodness that guides you to the top of the stairs, be mindful at times of my pain. Then he hid him in the fire that refines them."

list of images "which recur, charged with emotion."
Here is the list:

> The song of one bird, the leap of one fish, an old
> woman on a German mountain path, six ruffians
> seen through an open window playing cards at a
> small French railway junction where there was a
> water-mill: such memories may have symbolic value,
> but of what we cannot tell, for they come to repre-
> sent the depths of feeling into which we cannot peer.
> [*The Use of Poetry*, 1933, p. 141]

The second stanza of this poem is one reworking of
these images—there are others in other poems—in a
place or a context where they have a significance very
different from any that might have been expected of
them. The borrowing from reading and the borrowing
from personal memory are characteristic of Eliot's poetry. When set side by side, they are much the same
thing as the subject of the poem, which in the beginning had little to do with them.

❖

'A cold coming we had of it,
Just the worst time of the year
For a journey, and such a long journey:
The ways deep and the weather sharp,
The very dead of winter.'
And the camels galled, sore-footed, refractory,
Lying down in the melting snow.
There were times we regretted
The summer palaces on slopes, the terraces,
And the silken girls bringing sherbet.   10
Then the camel men cursing and grumbling
And running away, and wanting their liquor and
    women,
And the night-fires going out, and the lack of
    shelters,
And the cities hostile and the towns unfriendly
And the villages dirty and charging high prices:
A hard time we had of it.
At the end we preferred to travel all night,
Sleeping in snatches,
With the voices singing in our ears, saying
That this was all folly.   20

   Then at dawn we came down to a temperate
       valley,
Wet, below the snow line, smelling of vegetation;
With a running stream and a water-mill beating
    the darkness,
And three trees on the low sky,
And an old white horse galloped away in the
    meadow.
Then we came to a tavern with vine-leaves over
    the lintel,
Six hands at an open door dicing for pieces of
    silver,

And feet kicking the empty wine-skins.
But there was no information, and so we con-
    tinued
And arrived at evening, not a moment too soon
Finding the place; it was (you may say) satisfac-
    tory.   31

   All this was a long time ago, I remember,
And I would do it again, but set down
This set down
This: were we led all that way for
Birth or Death? There was a Birth, certainly,
We had evidence and no doubt. I had seen birth
    and death,
But had thought they were different; this Birth was
Hard and bitter agony for us, like Death, our
    death.
We returned to our places, these Kingdoms,   40
But no longer at ease here, in the old dispensation,
With an alien people clutching their gods.
I should be glad of another death.

LINES FOR AN OLD MAN
[1935]

❖

❨ THIS POEM is a part of the nightmare of behavior
(see Introduction, p. 767), and is another phase of the
recurrent theme of old age—or of the old man—which
runs through many poems, from "Prufrock" to "Little
Gidding." This poem, without location or involvement
and without role, is perhaps the bitterest of them all.
"Tell me if I am not glad!"

❖

The tiger in the tiger-pit   3
Is not more irritable than I.
The whipping tail is not more still
Than when I smell the enemy
Writhing in the essential blood
Or dangling from the friendly tree.
When I lay bare the tooth of wit
The hissing over the archèd tongue
Is more affectionate than hate,
More bitter than the love of youth,   10
And inaccessible by the young.
Reflected from my golden eye
The dullard knows that he is mad.
Tell me if I am not glad!

TWO CHORUSES

FROM *The Family Reunion*

[1939]

❖

⟨ THESE two choruses—the voices of our common knowledge—exemplify what Eliot meant by the quotation from *Notes Towards a Definition of Culture* (see Introduction p. 767) about the nightmare of our behavior. I call attention in the first chorus to lines 19–23 and in the second chorus to lines 22–30. The laws "in the nature of music" operate also "behind the smiling moon." There are also the last lines of each chorus which attach themselves at once to each other. "The international catastrophes" certainly come about because "we have lost our way in the dark." It is the nature of that dark which these choruses—like those in *Murder in the Cathedral*—specify in terms to which every one of us can give incident and which at the same time submit to laws "in the nature of music." This is why, in the Introduction, Eliot is called a master of nightmare and civic virtue.

❖

I

In an old house there is always listening, and more
    is heard than is spoken.
And what is spoken remains in the room, waiting
    for the future to hear it.
And whatever happens began in the past, and
    presses hard on the future.
The agony in the curtained bedroom, whether of
    birth or of dying,
Gathers in to itself all the voices of the past, and
    projects them into the future.
The treble voices on the lawn
The mowing of hay in summer
The dogs and the old pony
The stumble and the wail of little pain
The chopping of wood in autumn   10
And the singing in the kitchen
And the steps at night in the corridor
The moment of sudden loathing
And the season of stifled sorrow
The whisper, the transparent deception
The keeping up of appearances
The making the best of a bad job
All twined and tangled together, all are recorded.
There is no avoiding these things
And we know nothing of exorcism   20
And whether in Argos or England
There are certain inflexible laws

Unalterable, in the nature of music.
There is nothing at all to be done about it,
There is nothing to do about anything,
And now it is nearly time for the news
We must listen to the weather report
And the international catastrophes.

II

We do not like to look out of the same window,
    and see quite a different landscape.
We do not like to climb a stair, and find that it
    takes us down.
We do not like to walk out of a door, and find our-
    selves back in the same room.
We do not like the maze in the garden, because it
    too closely resembles the maze in the brain.
We do not like what happens when we are awake,
    because it too closely resembles what hap-
    pens when we are asleep.
We understand the ordinary business of living,
We know how to work the machine,
We can usually avoid accidents,
We are insured against fire,
Against larceny and illness,   10
Against defective plumbing,
But not against the act of God.
We know various spells and enchantments,
And minor forms of sorcery,
Divination and chiromancy,
Specifics against insomnia,
Lumbago, and the loss of money.
But the circle of our understanding
Is a very restricted area.
Except for a limited number   20
Of strictly practical purposes
We do not know what we are doing;
And even, when you think of it,
We do not know much about thinking.
What is happening outside of the circle?
And what is the meaning of happening?
What ambush lies beyond the heather
And behind the Standing Stones?
Beyond the Heaviside Layer
And behind the smiling moon?   30
And what is being done to us?
And what are we, and what are we doing?
To each and all of these questions
There is no conceivable answer.
We have suffered far more than a personal loss—
We have lost our way in the dark.

THE DRY SALVAGES
[1941]

❖

⟮ IT MAY be said that the *Four Quartets* are different versions, woven into one another, of a pilgrimage toward the emotion of reality. This notion is at least worth keeping in mind when reading "The Dry Salvages," the third of the Quartets. We have the river and the sea in apposition—"The river is within us, the sea is all about us"—as the two primitive forces of which we are most likely to be aware, each making its calamitous annunciation of disaster. Against and among these annunciations are set the Christian Annunciation and Incarnation, and perhaps the image—in Part III—of Krishna, the Hindu hero, who is worshiped as an incarnation of Vishnu, the preserver. In the first fifteen lines of Part V, Eliot sets out the other primitive forces which are of the fabric of what we call civilized life and which are an intimate part of our behavior—and which have been such from the furthest time of which we have record. It is possible that the "pre-conscious terrors" behind the "recurrent image" here referred to are at another level much the same as the forces of the river and the sea—the same ground swell running through them all, the heaving and give we feel under us at moments of special awareness. At any rate, if the reader will permit these images to interpenetrate each other he will see how the poem has unity and where it is going. As the poem says, "you are the music while the music lasts." But it should never be forgotten that in "The Dry Salvages" the river is the Mississippi near St. Louis, where Eliot lived as a boy, and the sea is the Atlantic Ocean off Gloucester, Massachusetts, where Eliot passed many of his summers. Nor should it be overlooked that the first thirty-six lines of Part II are a modified form of the sestina, a Provençal form which Dante brought to the highest perfection and complexity. It is right that Eliot should have made this tribute to Dante in his hymn to the masterless sea and "the ragged rock in the restless waters" which

> *". . . in the sombre season*
> *Or the sudden fury, is what it always was."*

❖

(The Dry Salvages—presumably *les trois sauvages*—is a small group of rocks, with a beacon, off the N.E. coast of Cape Ann, Massachusetts. *Salvages* is pronounced to rhyme with *assuages*. *Groaner:* a whistling buoy.)

I

I do not know much about gods; but I think that the river
Is a strong brown god—sullen, untamed and intractable,
Patient to some degree, at first recognised as a frontier;
Useful, untrustworthy, as a conveyor of commerce;
Then only a problem confronting the builder of bridges.
The problem once solved, the brown god is almost forgotten
By the dwellers in cities—ever, however, implacable,
Keeping his seasons and rages, destroyer, reminder
Of what men choose to forget. Unhonoured, unpropitiated
By worshippers of the machine, but waiting, watching and waiting.   10
His rhythm was present in the nursery bedroom,
In the rank ailanthus of the April dooryard,
In the smell of grapes on the autumn table,
And the evening circle in the winter gaslight.

The river is within us, the sea is all about us;
The sea is the land's edge also, the granite
Into which it reaches, the beaches where it tosses
Its hints of earlier and other creation:
The starfish, the hermit crab, the whale's backbone;
The pools where it offers to our curiosity   20
The more delicate algae and the sea anemone.
It tosses up our losses, the torn seine,
The shattered lobsterpot, the broken oar
And the gear of foreign dead men. The sea has many voices,
Many gods and many voices.
                    The salt is on the briar rose,
The fog is in the fir trees.
                    The sea howl
And the sea yelp, are different voices
Often together heard; the whine in the rigging,   30
The menace and caress of wave that breaks on water,
The distant rote in the granite teeth,
And the wailing warning from the approaching headland
Are all sea voices, and the heaving groaner
Rounded homewards, and the seagull:
Are under the oppression of the silent fog
The tolling bell
Measures time not our time, rung by the unhurried
Ground swell, a time
Older than the time of chronometers, older   40
Than time counted by anxious worried women
Lying awake, calculating the future,
Trying to unweave, unwind, unravel
And piece together the past and the future,

Between midnight and dawn, when the past is all
    deception,
The future futureless, before the morning watch
When time stops and time is never ending;
And the ground swell, that is and was from the
    beginning,
Clangs
The bell.   50

II

Where is there an end of it, the soundless wailing,
The silent withering of autumn flowers
Dropping their petals and remaining motionless;
Where is there an end to the drifting wreckage,
The prayer of the bone on the beach, the unpray-
    able
Prayer at the calamitous annunciation?

    There is no end, but addition: the trailing
Consequence of further days and hours,
While emotion takes to itself the emotionless
Years of living among the breakage   60
Of what was believed in as the most reliable—
And therefore the fittest for renunciation.

    There is the final addition, the failing
Pride or resentment at failing powers,
The unattached devotion which might pass for
    devotionless,
In a drifting boat with a slow leakage,
The silent listening to the undeniable
Clamour of the bell of the last annunciation.

    Where is the end of them, the fishermen sailing
Into the wind's tail, where the fog cowers?   70
We cannot think of a time that is oceanless
Or of an ocean not littered with wastage
Or of a future that is not liable
Like the past, to have no destination.

    We have to think of them as forever bailing,
Setting and hauling, while the North East lowers
Over shallow banks unchanging and erosionless
Or drawing their money, drying sails at dockage;
Not as making a trip that will be unpayable
For a haul that will not bear examination.   80

    There is no end of it, the voiceless wailing,
No end to the withering of withered flowers,
To the movement of pain that is painless and mo-
    tionless,
To the drift of the sea and the drifting wreckage,
The bone's prayer to Death its God. Only the
    hardly, barely prayable
Prayer of the one Annunciation.

It seems, as one becomes older,
That the past has another pattern, and ceases to
    be a mere sequence—
Or even development: the latter a partial fallacy,
Encouraged by superficial notions of evolution,
Which becomes, in the popular mind, a means of
    disowning the past.   91
The moments of happiness—not the sense of well-
    being,
Fruition, fulfilment, security or affection,
Or even a very good dinner, but the sudden illumi-
    nation—
We had the experience but missed the meaning,
And approach to the meaning restores the expe-
    rience
In a different form, beyond any meaning
We can assign to happiness. I have said before
That the past experience revived in the meaning
Is not the experience of one life only   100
But of many generations—not forgetting
Something that is probably quite ineffable:
The backward look behind the assurance
Of recorded history, the backward half-look
Over the shoulder, towards the primitive terror.
Now, we come to discover that the moments of
    agony
(Whether, or not, due to misunderstanding,
Having hoped for the wrong things or dreaded the
    wrong things,
Is not in question) are likewise permanent
With such permanence as time has. We appreciate
    this better   110
In the agony of others, nearly experienced,
Involving ourselves, than in our own.
For our own past is covered by the currents of
    action,
But the torment of others remains an experience
Unqualified, unworn by subsequent attrition.
People change, and smile: but the agony abides.
Time the destroyer is time the preserver,
Like the river with its cargo of dead Negroes,
    cows and chicken coops,
The bitter apple and the bite in the apple.
And the ragged rock in the restless waters,   120
Waves wash over it, fogs conceal it;
On a halcyon day it is merely a monument,
In navigable weather it is always a seamark
To lay a course by: but in the sombre season
Or the sudden fury, is what it always was.

III

I sometimes wonder if that is what Krishna
    meant—
Among other things—or one way of putting the
    same thing:

That the future is a faded song, a Royal Rose or a
    lavender spray
Of wistful regret for those who are not yet here to
    regret,
Pressed between yellow leaves of a book that has
    never been opened.   130
And the way up is the way down, the way forward
    is the way back.
You cannot face it steadily, but this thing is sure,
That time is no healer: the patient is no longer
    here.
When the train starts, and the passengers are set-
    tled
To fruit, periodicals and business letters
(And those who saw them off have left the plat-
    form)
Their faces relax from grief into relief,
To the sleepy rhythm of a hundred hours.
Fare forward, travellers! not escaping from the
    past
Into different lives, or into any future;   140
You are not the same people who left that station
Or who will arrive at any terminus,
While the narrowing rails slide together behind
    you;
And on the deck of the drumming liner
Watching the furrow that widens behind you,
You shall not think "the past is finished"
Or "the future is before us."
At nightfall, in the rigging and the aerial,
Is a voice descanting (though not to the ear,
The murmuring shell of time, and not in any lan-
    guage)   150
"Fare forward, you who think that you are voyag-
    ing;
You are not those who saw the harbour
Receding, or those who will disembark.
Here between the hither and the farther shore
While time is withdrawn, consider the future
And the past with an equal mind.
At the moment which is not of action or inaction
You can receive this: 'on whatever sphere of being
The mind of a man may be intent
At the time of death'—that is the one action
(And the time of death is every moment)   161
Which shall fructify in the lives of others:
And do not think of the fruit of action.
Fare forward.
             O voyagers, O seamen,
You who come to port, and you whose bodies
Will suffer the trial and judgement of the sea,
Or whatever event, this is your real destination."
So Krishna, as when he admonished Arjuna
On the field of battle.   170
                  Not fare well,
But fare forward, voyagers.

IV

Lady, whose shrine stands on the promontory,
Pray for all those who are in ships, those
Whose business has to do with fish, and
Those concerned with every lawful traffic
And those who conduct them.

    Repeat a prayer also on behalf of
Women who have seen their sons or husbands
Setting forth, and not returning: 180
Figlia del tuo figlio,
Queen of Heaven.
    Also pray for those who were in ships, and
Ended their voyage on the sand, in the sea's lips
Or in the dark throat which will not reject them
Or wherever cannot reach them the sound of the
    sea bell's
Perpetual angelus.

V

To communicate with Mars, converse with spirits,
To report the behaviour of the sea monster,
Describe the horoscope, haruspicate or scry,   190
Observe disease in singatures, evoke
Biography from the wrinkles of the palm
And tragedy from fingers; release omens
By sortilege, or tea leaves, riddle the inevitable
With playing cards, fiddle with pentagrams
Or barbituric acids, or dissect
The recurrent image into pre-conscious terrors—
To explore the womb, or tomb, or dreams; all
    these are usual
Pastimes and drugs, and features of the press:
And always will be, some of them especially   200
When there is distress of nations and perplexity
Whether on the shores of Asia, or in the Edgware
    Road.
Men's curiosity searches past and future
And clings to that dimension. But to apprehend
The point of intersection of the timeless
With time, is an occupation for the saint—
No occupation either, but something given
And taken, in a lifetime's death in love,
Ardour and selflessness and self-surrender.
For most of us, there is only the unattended   210
Moment, the moment in and out of time,
The distraction fit, lost in a shaft of sunlight,
The wild thyme unseen, or the winter lightning
Or the waterfall, or music heard so deeply
That it is not heard at all, but you are the music
While the music lasts. These are only hints and
    guesses,

THE DRY SALVAGES.   181. **Figlia . . . figlio:** "Daughter of thy
son," meaning the Virgin Mary. See Dante, *Paradiso*, XXXIII.1.

Hints followed by guesses; and the rest
Is prayer, observance, discipline, thought and
    action.
The hint half guessed, the gift half understood, is
    Incarnation.
Here the impossible union   220
Of spheres of existence is actual,
Here the past and future
Are conquered, and reconciled,
Where action were otherwise movement
Of that which is only moved
And has in it no source of movement—
Driven by daemonic, chthonic
Powers. And right action is freedom
From past and future also.
For most of us, this is the aim   230
Never here to be realised;
Who are only undefeated
Because we have gone on trying;
We, content at the last
If our temporal reversion nourish
(Not too far from the yew-tree)
The life of significant soil.

TRADITION AND THE INDIVIDUAL TALENT
[1919]

◊

⟪ IT IS in this essay, and in the essay "Hamlet and His Problems," that Eliot raised several of the chief critical ideas which come to mind when we think of Eliot as a critic. It is not, I think, that Eliot based his actual criticism on these ideas; rather, the ideas came out of the criticism, came out of the analysis, comparison, and elucidation that make up his critical practice. It is a question whether the ideas or the practice have more deeply penetrated the minds of subsequent readers. The practice has helped form many a taste and has repaired the judgment of previous critics to make them more accord with the needs of our own time. The ideas have become part of our critical mythology, and equally whether we accept them, or reject them, or deform them for the purposes of our private sensibility. In any case they have been detached from the places where they appeared, and have lost some of the precise suggestiveness which made them originally worth airing and useful. They have acquired, on the other hand, the kind of disengaged authority that goes with a maxim, or a proverb, or a line of verse. I refer, for example, to

the idea contained in the title of this essay: the idea that the whole of literature is a single order which is altered by any new work, and the idea that the individual writer is not concerned with expressing himself but with mastering and altering that order. There is a whole intellectual position involved here, and an ideal form is given to it that is a perfection of our possession of our tradition, which no individual can reach. Eliot's language in this essay is severe and authoritative, qualities which his later work mollifies. We may be sure of only one sense of tradition: it is the body of what is handed down, and Eliot wants the individual to have vital contact with it. We may be sure also that Eliot is one of our most individual poets, and we know from his prose works how deeply he loves individuals in the ordinary way—as for example in the memorial to Charles Whibley (*Selected Essays*, p. 439). These matters we must remember, but I do not think that the idea of the poet's mind as an untouched catalyst can be taken as more than an intriguing, and false, analogy.

◊

IN ENGLISH writing we seldom speak of tradition, though we occasionally apply its name in deploring its absence. We cannot refer to "the tradition" or to "a tradition"; at most, we employ the adjective in saying that the poetry of So-and-so is "traditional" or even "too traditional." Seldom, perhaps, does the word appear except in a phrase of censure. If otherwise, it is vaguely approbative, with the implication, as to the work approved, of some pleasing archaeological reconstruction. You can hardly make the word agreeable to English ears without this comfortable reference to the reassuring science of archaeology.

Certainly the word is not likely to appear in our appreciations of living or dead writers. Every nation, every race, has not only its own creative, but its own critical turn of mind; and is even more oblivious of the shortcomings and limitations of its critical habits than of those of its creative genius. We know, or think we know, from the enormous mass of critical writing that has appeared in the French language the critical method or habit of the French; we only conclude (we are such unconscious people) that the French are "more critical" than we, and sometimes even plume ourselves a little with the fact, as if the French were the less spontaneous. Perhaps they are; but we might remind ourselves that criticism is as inevitable as breathing, and that we should be none the worse for articulating what passes in our minds when we read a book and feel an emotion about it, for criticizing our own minds in their work of criticism. One of the facts that might come to light in this process is our tendency to insist, when we praise a poet, upon those aspects of his work in which he least resembles any one else. In these aspects or parts of his work we pretend to find what is individual, what is the peculiar essence of the man. We dwell with satisfaction upon the poet's difference from his predecessors, especially his immediate predecessors; we endeavour to find something that can be isolated in order to be enjoyed. Whereas if we approach a poet without this prejudice we shall often find that not only the best, but the most individual parts of his work may be those in which the dead poets, his ancestors, assert their immortality most vigorously. And I do not mean the impressionable period of adolescence, but the period of full maturity.

Yet if the only form of tradition, of handing down, consisted in following the ways of the immediate generation before us in a blind or timid adherence to its successes, "tradition" should positively be discouraged. We have seen many such simple currents soon lost in the sand; and novelty is better than repetition. Tradition is a matter of much wider significance. It cannot be inherited, and if you want it you must obtain it by great labour. It involves, in the first place, the historical sense, which we may call nearly indispensable to any one who would continue to be a poet beyond his twenty-fifth year; and the historical sense involves a perception, not only of the pastness of the past, but of its presence; the historical sense compels a man to write not merely with his own generation in his bones, but with a feeling that the whole of the literature of Europe from Homer and within it the whole of the literature of his own country has a simultaneous existence and composes a simultaneous order. This historical sense, which is a sense of the timeless as well as of the temporal and of the timeless and of the temporal together, is what makes a writer traditional. And it is at the same time what makes a writer most acutely conscious of his place in time, of his own contemporaneity.

No poet, no artist of any art, has his complete meaning alone. His significance, his appreciation is the appreciation of his relation to the dead poets and artists. You cannot value him alone; you must set him, for contrast and comparison, among the dead. I mean this as a principle of aesthetic, not merely historical, criticism. The necessity that he shall conform, that he shall cohere, is not one-sided; what happens when a new work of art is created is something that happens simultaneously to all the works of art which preceded it. The existing monuments form an ideal order among themselves, which is modified by the introduction of the new (the really new) work of art among them. The existing order is complete before the new work arrives; for order to persist after the supervention of novelty, the *whole* existing order must be, if ever so slightly, altered; and so the relations, proportions, values of each work of art toward the whole are readjusted; and this is conformity between the old and the new. Whoever has approved this idea of order, of the form of European, of English literature will not find it preposterous that the past should be altered by the present as much as the present is directed by the past. And the poet who is aware of this will be aware of great difficulties and responsibilities.

In a peculiar sense he will be aware also that he must inevitably be judged by the standards of the past. I say judged, not amputated, by them; not judged to be as good as, or worse or better than, the dead; and certainly not judged by the canons of dead critics. It is a judgment, a comparison, in which two things are measured by each other. To conform merely would be for the new work not really to conform at all; it would not be new, and would therefore not be a work of art. And we do not quite say that the new is more valuable because it fits in; but its fitting in is a test of its value—a test, it is true, which can only be slowly and cautiously applied, for we are none of us infallible judges of conformity. We say: it appears to conform, and is perhaps individual, or it appears individual, and many conform; but we are hardly likely to find that it is one and not the other.

To proceed to a more intelligible exposition of the relation of the poet to the past: he can neither take the past as a lump, an indiscriminate bolus, nor can he form himself wholly on one or two private admirations, nor can he form himself wholly upon one preferred period. The first course is inadmissible, the second is an important experience of youth, and the third is a pleasant and highly desirable supplement. The poet must be very conscious of the main current, which does not at all flow invariably through the most distinguished reputations. He must be quite aware of the obvious fact that art never improves, but that the material of art is never quite the same. He must be aware that the mind of Europe—the mind of his own country—a mind which he learns in time to be much more important than his own private mind—is a mind which changes, and that this change is a development which abandons nothing *en route,* which does not superannuate either Shakespeare, or Homer, or the rock drawing of the Magdalenian draughtsmen. That this development, refinement perhaps, complication certainly, is not, from the point of view of the artist, any improvement. Perhaps not even an improvement from the point of view of the psychologist or not to the extent which we imagine; perhaps only in the end based upon a complication in economics and machinery. But the difference between the present and the past is that the conscious present is an awareness of the past in a way and to an extent which the past's awareness of itself cannot show.

Some one said: "The dead writers are remote from us because we *know* so much more than they did." Precisely, and they are that which we know.

I am alive to a usual objection to what is clearly part of my programme for the *métier* of poetry. The objection is that the doctrine requires a ridiculous amount of erudition (pedantry), a claim which can be rejected by appeal to the lives of poets in any pantheon. It will even be affirmed that much learning deadens or perverts poetic sensibility. While, however, we persist in believing that a poet ought to know as much as will not encroach upon his necessary receptivity and necessary laziness, it is not desirable to confine knowledge to whatever can be put into a useful shape for examinations, drawing-rooms, or the still more pretentious modes of publicity. Some can absorb knowledge, the more tardy must sweat for it. Shakespeare acquired more essential history from Plutarch than most men could from the whole British Museum. What is to be insisted upon is that the poet must develop or procure the consciousness of the past and that he should continue to develop this consciousness throughout his career.

What happens is a continual surrender of himself as he is at the moment to something which is more valuable. The progress of an artist is a continual self-sacrifice, a continual extinction of personality.

There remains to define this process of depersonalization and its relation to the sense of tradition. It is in this depersonalization that art may be said to approach the condition of science. I, therefore, invite you to consider, as a suggestive analogy, the action which takes place when a bit of finely filiated platinum is introduced into a chamber containing oxygen and sulphur dioxide.

II

HONEST criticism and sensitive appreciation are directed not upon the poet but upon the poetry. If we attend to the confused cries of the newspaper critics and the *susurrus* of popular repetition that follows, we shall hear the names of poets in great numbers; if we seek not Blue-book knowledge but the enjoyment of poetry, and ask for a poem, we shall seldom find it. I have tried to point out the importance of the relation of the poem to other poems by other authors, and suggested the conception of poetry as a living whole of all the poetry that has ever been written. The other aspect of this Impersonal theory of poetry is the relation of the poem to its author. And I hinted, by an analogy, that the mind of the mature poet differs from that of the immature one not precisely in any valuation of "personality," not being necessarily more interesting, or having "more to say," but rather by being a more finely perfected medium in which special, or very varied, feelings are at liberty to enter into new combinations.

The analogy was that of the catalyst. When the two gases previously mentioned are mixed in the presence of a filament of platinum, they form sulphurous acid. This combination takes place only if the platinum is present; nevertheless the newly formed acid contains no trace of platinum, and the platinum itself is apparently unaffected; has remained inert, neutral, and unchanged. The mind of the poet is the shred of platinum. It may partly or exclusively operate upon the experience of the man himself; but, the more perfect the artist, the more completely separate in him will be the man who suffers and the mind which creates; the more perfectly will the mind digest and transmute the passions which are its material.

The experience, you will notice, the elements which enter the presence of the transforming catalyst, are of two kinds: emotions and feelings. The effect of a work of art upon the person who enjoys it is an experience different in kind from any experience not of art. It may be formed out of one emotion, or may be a combination of several; and various feelings, inhering for the writer in particular words or phrases or images, may be added to compose the final result. Or great poetry may be made without the direct use of any emotion whatever: composed out of feelings solely. Canto XV of the *Inferno* (Brunetto Latini) is a working up of the emotion evident in the situation; but the effect, though single as that of any work of art, is obtained by considerable complexity of detail. The last quatrain gives an image, a feeling attaching to an image, which "came," which did not develop simply out of what precedes, but which was probably in suspension in the poet's mind until the proper combination arrived for it to add itself to. The poet's mind is in fact a receptacle for seizing and storing up numberless feelings, phrases, images, which remain there until all the particles which can unite to form a new compound are present together.

If you compare several representative passages of the greatest poetry you see how great is the variety of types of combination, and also how completely any semi-ethical criterion of "sublimity" misses the mark. For it is not the "greatness," the intensity, of the emotions, the components, but the intensity of the artistic process, the pressure, so to speak, under which the fusion takes place, that counts. The episode of Paolo and Francesca employs a definite emotion, but the intensity of the poetry is something quite different from whatever intensity in the supposed experience it may give the impression of. It is no more intense, furthermore, than Canto XXVI, the voyage of Ulysses, which has not the direct dependence upon an emotion. Great variety is possible in the process of transmutation of emotion: the murder of Agamemnon, or the agony of Othello, gives an artistic effect apparently closer to a possible original than the scenes from Dante. In the *Agamemnon,* the artistic emotion approximates to the emotion of an actual spectator; in *Othello* to the emotion of the protagonist himself. But the difference between art and the event is always absolute; the combination which is the murder of Agamemnon is probably as complex as that which is the voyage of Ulysses. In either case there has been a fusion of elements. The ode of Keats contains a number of feelings which have nothing particular to do with the nightingale, but which the nightingale, partly, perhaps, because of its attractive name, and partly because of its reputation, served to bring together.

The point of view which I am struggling to attack is perhaps related to the metaphysical theory of the substantial unity of the soul: for my meaning is, that the poet has, not a "personality" to express, but a particular medium, which is only a medium and not a personality, in which impressions and experiences combine in peculiar and unexpected ways. Impressions and experiences which are important for the man may take no place in the poetry, and those which become important in the poetry may play quite a negligible part in the man, the personality.

I will quote a passage which is unfamiliar enough to be regarded with fresh attention in the light—or darkness—of these observations:

And now methinks I could e'en chide myself
For doating on her beauty, though her death
Shall be revenged after no common action.
Does the silkworm expand her yellow labours
For thee? For thee does she undo herself?
Are lordships sold to maintain ladyships
For the poor benefit of a bewildering minute?
Why does yon fellow falsify highways,
And put his life between the judge's lips,
To refine such a thing—keeps horse and men
To beat their valours for her? . . .

In this passage (as is evident if it is taken in its context) there is a combination of positive and negative emotions: an intensely strong attraction toward beauty and an equally intense fascination by the ugliness which is contrasted with it and which destroys it. This balance of contrasted emotion is in the dramatic situation to which the speech is pertinent, but that situation alone is inadequate to it. This is, so to speak, the structural emotion, provided by the drama. But the whole effect, the dominant tone, is due to the fact that a number of floating feelings, having an affinity to this emotion by no means superficially evident, have combined with it to give us a new art emotion.

It is not in his personal emotions, the emotions provoked by particular events in his life, that the poet is in any way remarkable or interesting. His particular emotions may be simple, or crude, or flat. The emotion in his poetry will be a very complex thing, but not with the complexity of the emotions of people who have very complex or unusual emotions in life. One error, in fact, of eccentricity in poetry is to seek for new human emotions to express; and in this search for novelty in the wrong place it discovers the perverse. The business of the poet is not to find new emotions, but to use the ordinary ones and, in working them up into poetry, to express feelings which are not in actual emotions at all. And emotions which he has never experienced will serve his turn as well as those familiar to him. Consequently, we must believe that "emotion recollected in tranquillity" is an inexact formula. For it is neither emotion, nor recollection, nor, without distortion of meaning, tranquillity. It is a concentration, and a new thing resulting from the concentration, of a very great number of experiences which to the practical and active person would not seem to be experiences at all; it is a concentration which does not happen consciously or of deliberation. These experiences are not "recollected," and they finally unite in an atmosphere which is "tranquil" only in that it is a passive attending upon the event. Of course this is not quite the whole story. There is a great deal, in the writing of poetry, which must be conscious and deliberate. In fact, the bad poet is usually unconscious where he ought to be conscious, and conscious where he ought to be unconscious. Both errors tend to make him "personal." Poetry is not a turning loose of emotion, but an escape from emotion; it is not the expression of personality, but an escape from personality. But, of course, only those who have personality and emotions know what it means to want to escape from these things.

III

ὁ δὲ νοῦς ἴσως θειότερόν τι χαὶ ἀπαθές ἐστιν.[1]

THIS essay proposes to halt at the frontier of metaphysics or mysticism, and confine itself to such practical conclusions as can be applied by the responsible person interested in poetry. To divert interest from the poet to the poetry is a laudable aim: for it would conduce to a juster estimation of actual poetry, good and bad. There are many people who appreciate the expression of sincere emotion in verse, and there is a smaller number of people who can appreciate technical excellence. But very few know when there is an expression of *significant* emotion, emotion which has its life in the poem and not in the history of the poet. The emotion of art is impersonal. And the poet cannot reach this impersonality without surrendering himself wholly to the work to be done. And he is not likely to know what is to be done unless he lives in what is not merely the present, but the present moment of the past, unless he is conscious, not of what is dead, but of what is already living.

HAMLET AND HIS PROBLEMS [1919]

[A Review of J. M. Robertson's *The Problem of Hamlet* (1919)]

◊

⟨ IN THIS essay Eliot sets up the idea of the "objective correlative." "The only way of expressing emotion in the form of art is by finding an 'objective correlative'; in other words, a set of objects, a situation, a chain of events that shall be the formula of that *particular* emotion." I would suppose that the great value of this famous notion would depend on how loosely it is applied; it is by applying it too tightly to *Hamlet* in this essay that Eliot prevents himself from experiencing much that the play manifests. But if the reader applies it loosely, there will be added apparent life to the play, and the material that had been thought intractable will become at least available. Eliot's own last paragraph suggests as much.

◊

FEW CRITICS have even admitted that *Hamlet* the play is the primary problem, and Hamlet the character only secondary. And Hamlet the character has had an especial temptation for that most dangerous type of critic: the critic with a mind which is naturally of the creative order, but which through some weakness in creative power exercises itself in criticism instead. These minds often find in Hamlet a vicarious existence for their own artistic realization. Such a mind had Goethe, who made of Hamlet a Werther; and such had Coleridge, who made of Hamlet a Coleridge; and probably neither of these men in writing about Hamlet remembered that his first business was to study a work of art. The kind of criticism that Goethe and Coleridge produced, in writing of Hamlet, is the most misleading kind possible. For they both possessed unquestionable critical insight, and both make their critical aberrations the more plausible by the substitution—of their own Hamlet for Shakespeare's—which their creative gift effects. We should be thankful that Walter Pater did not fix his attention on this play.

Two writers of our own time, Mr. J. M. Robertson and Professor Stoll of the University of Minnesota, have issued small books which can be praised for moving in the other direction. Mr. Stoll performs a service in recalling to our attention the labours of the critics of the seventeenth and eighteenth centuries,[1] observing that

"they knew less about psychology than more recent Hamlet critics, but they were nearer in spirit to Shakespeare's art; and as they insisted on the importance of the effect of the whole rather than on the importance of the leading character, they were nearer, in their old-fashioned way, to the secret of dramatic art in general."

Qua work of art, the work of art cannot be interpreted; there is nothing to interpret; we can only criticise it according to standards, in comparison to other works of art; and for "interpretation" the chief task is the presentation of relevant historical facts which the reader is not assumed to know. Mr. Robertson points out, very pertinently, how critics have failed in their "interpretation" of *Hamlet* by ignoring what ought to be very obvious; that *Hamlet* is a stratification, that it represents the efforts of a series of men, each making what he could out of the work of his predecessors. The *Hamlet* of Shakespeare will appear to us very differently if, instead of treating the whole action of the play as due to Shake-

---

TRADITION AND THE INDIVIDUAL TALENT. **1.** *ὁ . . . ἐστιν:* "The mind is probably more divine and is unaffected" (Aristotle, *De Anima* [*On the Soul*], I.iv.408b29).

HAMLET. **1.** "I have never, by the way, seen a cogent refutation of Thomas Rymer's objections to *Othello*" [Eliot's note].

speare's design, we perceive his *Hamlet* to be su-
perposed upon much cruder material which
persists even in the final form.

We know that there was an older play by
Thomas Kyd, that extraordinary dramatic (if not
poetic) genius who was in all probability the author of two plays so dissimilar as *The Spanish
Tragedy* and *Arden of Feversham;* and what this
play was like we can guess from three clues: from
The Spanish Tragedy itself, from the tale of Belle-
forest upon which Kyd's *Hamlet* must have been
based, and from a version acted in Germany in
Shakespeare's lifetime which bears strong evidence of having been adapted from the earlier,
not from the later, play. From these three sources
it is clear that in the earlier play the motive was
a revenge-motive simply; that the action or delay
is caused, as in *The Spanish Tragedy,* solely by
the difficulty of assassinating a monarch surrounded by guards; and that the "madness" of
Hamlet was feigned in order to escape suspicion,
and successfully. In the final play of Shakespeare,
on the other hand, there is a motive which is more
important than that of revenge, and which explicitly "blunts" the latter; the delay in revenge
is unexplained on grounds of necessity or expedi-
ency; and the effect of the "madness" is not to
lull but to arouse the king's suspicion. The alteration is not complete enough, however, to be convincing. Furthermore, there are verbal parallels
so close to *The Spanish Tragedy* as to leave no
doubt that in places Shakespeare was merely *revising* the text of Kyd. And finally there are unexplained scenes—the Polonius-Laertes and the
Polonius-Reynaldo scenes—for which there is little excuse; these scenes are not in the verse style of
Kyd, and not beyond doubt in the style of Shakespeare. These Mr. Robertson believes to be
scenes in the original play of Kyd reworked by
a third hand, perhaps Chapman, before Shakespeare touched the play. And he concludes, with
very strong show of reason, that the original play
of Kyd was, like certain other revenge plays, in
two parts of five acts each. The upshot of Mr.
Robertson's examination is, we believe, irrefra-
gable: that Shakespeare's *Hamlet,* so far as it is
Shakespeare's, is a play dealing with the effect of
a mother's guilt upon her son, and that Shakespeare was unable to impose this motive successfully upon the "intractable" material of the old
play.

Of the intractability there can be no doubt. So
far from being Shakespeare's masterpiece, the
play is most certainly an artistic failure. In several
ways the play is puzzling, and disquieting as is
none of the others. Of all the plays it is the longest

and is possibly the one on which Shakespeare
spent most pains; and yet he has left in it superfluous and inconsistent scenes which even hasty
revision should have noticed. The versification is
variable. Lines like

> Look, the morn, in russet mantle clad,
> Walks o'er the dew of yon high eastern hill,

are of the Shakespeare of *Romeo and Juliet.* The
lines in Act v, sc. ii,

> Sir, in my heart there was a kind of fighting
> That would not let me sleep . . .
> Up from my cabin,
> My sea-gown scarf'd about me, in the dark
> Grop'd I to find out them: had my desire;
> Finger'd their packet;

are of his quite mature. Both workmanship and
thought are in an unstable position. We are surely
justified in attributing the play, with that other
profoundly interesting play of "intractable" material and astonishing versification, *Measure for
Measure,* to a period of crisis, after which follow
the tragic successes which culminate in *Coriolanus. Coriolanus* may be not as "interesting" as
Hamlet, but it is, with *Antony and Cleopatra,*
Shakespeare's most assured artistic success. And
probably more people have thought *Hamlet* a
work of art because they found it interesting,
than have found it interesting because it is a work
of art. It is the "Mona Lisa" of literature.

The grounds of *Hamlet's* failure are not immediately obvious. Mr. Robertson is undoubtedly
correct in concluding that the essential emotion
of the play is the feeling of a son towards a guilty
mother:

"[Hamlet's] tone is that of one who has suffered
tortures on the score of his mother's degradation.
. . . The guilt of a mother is an almost intolerable motive for drama, but it had to be maintained
and emphasized to supply a psychological solution, or rather a hint of one."

This, however, is by no means the whole story.
It is not merely the "guilt of a mother" that cannot be handled as Shakespeare handled the suspicion of Othello, the infatuation of Antony, or the
pride of Coriolanus. The subject might conceivably have expanded into a tragedy like these, intelligible, self-complete, in the sunlight. *Hamlet,*
like the sonnets, is full of some stuff that the writer
could not drag to light, contemplate, or manipu-
late into art. And when we search for this feeling,
we find it, as in the sonnets, very difficult to lo-
calize. You cannot point to it in the speeches; indeed, if you examine the two famous soliloquies
you see the versification of Shakespeare, but a
content which might be claimed by another, per-

haps by the author of the *Revenge of Bussy d'Ambois,* Act v, sc. i. We find Shakespeare's Hamlet not in the action, not in any quotations that we might select, so much as in an unmistakable tone which is unmistakably not in the earlier play.

The only way of expressing emotion in the form of art is by finding an "objective correlative"; in other words, a set of objects, a situation, a chain of events which shall be the formula of that *particular* emotion; such that when the external facts, which must terminate in sensory experience, are given, the emotion is immediately evoked. If you examine any of Shakespeare's more successful tragedies, you will find this exact equivalence; you will find that the state of mind of Lady Macbeth walking in her sleep has been communicated to you by a skilful accumulation of imagined sensory impressions; the words of Macbeth on hearing of his wife's death strike us as if, given the sequence of events, these words were automatically released by the last event in the series. The artistic "inevitability" lies in this complete adequacy of the external to the emotion; and this is precisely what is deficient in *Hamlet.* Hamlet (the man) is dominated by an emotion which is inexpressible, because it is in *excess* of the facts as they appear. And the supposed identity of Hamlet with his author is genuine to this point: that Hamlet's bafflement at the absence of objective equivalent to his feelings is a prolongation of the bafflement of his creator in the face of his artistic problem. Hamlet is up against the difficulty that his disgust is occasioned by his mother, but that his mother is not an adequate equivalent for it; his disgust envelops and exceeds her. It is thus a feeling which he cannot understand; he cannot objectify it, and it therefore remains to poison life and obstruct action. None of the possible actions can satisfy it; and nothing that Shakespeare can do with the plot can express Hamlet for him. And it must be noticed that the very nature of the *données* of the problem precludes objective equivalence. To have heightened the criminality of Gertrude would have been to provide the formula for a totally different emotion in Hamlet; it is just *because* her character is so negative and insignificant that she arouses in Hamlet the feeling which she is incapable of representing.

The "madness" of Hamlet lay to Shakespeare's hand; in the earlier play a simple ruse, and to the end, we may presume, understood as a ruse by the audience. For Shakespeare it is less than madness and more than feigned. The levity of Hamlet, his repetition of phrase, his puns, are not part of a deliberate plan of dissimulation, but a form of emotional relief. In the character Hamlet it is

the buffoonery of an emotion which can find no outlet in action; in the dramatist it is the buffoonery of an emotion which he cannot express in art. The intense feeling, ecstatic or terrible, without an object or exceeding its object, is something which every person of sensibility has known; it is doubtless a subject of study for pathologists. It often occurs in adolescence: the ordinary person puts these feelings to sleep, or trims down his feelings to fit the business world; the artist keeps them alive by his ability to intensify the world to his emotions. The Hamlet of Laforgue is an adolescent; the Hamlet of Shakespeare is not, he has not that explanation and excuse. We must simply admit that here Shakespeare tackled a problem which proved too much for him. Why he attempted it at all is an insoluble puzzle; under compulsion of what experience he attempted to express the inexpressibly horrible, we cannot ever know. We need a great many facts in his biography; and we should like to know whether, and when, and after or at the same time as what personal experience, he read Montaigne, II. xii, *Apologie de Raimond Sebond.* We should have, finally, to know something which is by hypothesis unknowable, for we assume it to be an experience which, in the manner indicated, exceeded the facts. We should have to understand things which Shakespeare did not understand himself.

A SCEPTICAL PATRICIAN
A Review of *The Education of Henry Adams* [1919]

❖

❨ WHAT IS of interest here is the exhibition of the intimacy and the misunderstanding—amounting to a kind of patronage—which exists between one type of New Englander and another, or one type of Harvard man and another. Each would seem to have a secret superiority to the other, the nature of which he cannot confess but which he has no scruple to enforce. One says at least that Eliot was not at home either with the rhythm of Adams's prose or with his activities as a historian. What is most delightful is his assumption that Adams was not an educated man. This is how cousins call kin when they do not kiss.

❖

JOHN ADAMS, the second President of the United States, had, by his wife Abigail, John

Quincy Adams, the sixth President of the United States. John Quincy Adams begat Charles Francis Adams, Minister at the Court of St. James's under President Lincoln; and Charles Francis Adams had, by his wife Abigail, Henry Brooks Adams, the author of this autobiography.

Henry Adams was furthermore well connected; his grandfather Brooks was the richest man in Boston, and his uncle was President of Harvard College. The Unitarian pulpits of Boston were held by other relatives or connections. Henry Adams was born in 1838, and by 1905, when he wrote, he had known a surprising number of people in America and Europe and turned his mind to a surprising variety of studies. It is doubtful whether the book ought to be called an autobiography, for there is too little of the author in it; or whether it may be called Memoirs—for there is too much of the author in it; or a treatise on historical method, which in parts it is. For those who may be interested in different parts of the book the work may be separated as follows.

After the first few chapters, which deal with Adams's life as a boy in Boston, come his experiences and observations as an attaché of the Ministry in London during the Civil War: observations, often illuminating, of the British statesmen of the day, Palmerston, Russell, Bright, and others; some of the men of letters, like Monckton Milnes and Swinburne; and generally on London society of mid-Victoria. This part of the story will provide most entertainment for English readers. The personalities are thin, but not always formal:

The older daughter of the Milne Gaskells had married Francis Turner Palgrave . . . Old Sir Francis, the father, had been much the greatest of all the historians of England, the only one who was un-English; and the reason of his superiority lay in his name, which was Cohen, and his mind, which was Cohen also, or at least not English. He had changed his name to Palgrave in order to please his wife . . .

The comments of a young man, recollected in septuagenarian tranquillity, are honest, and, though not subtle, are pleasing:

Barring the atrocious insolence and brutality which Englishmen and especially Englishwomen showed to each other—very rarely, indeed, to foreigners—English society was much more easy and tolerant than American.
Balmoral was a startling revelation of royal taste. Nothing could be worse than the toilettes at Court unless it was the way they were worn . . . Fashion was not fashionable in London until the Americans and the Jews were let loose . . . There was not then—outside of a few bankers or foreigners—a good cook or a good table in London . . . If there was a well-

dressed woman at table, she was either an American or "Fast.". . . The result was mediæval, and amusing; sometimes coarse to a degree that might have startled a roustabout [*i.e.* navvy] and sometimes courteous and considerate to a degree that suggested King Arthur's Round Table . . .

These are revelations which are now household words, but it is pleasant to find that they were discovered, in 1862, by a serious young American of the best social position and an earnest desire to study the world and improve his mind and manners.

The second part of the book, concerned with the personalities in the quite sordid American politics from the reign of President Grant, is of even greater interest to those who are interested in the subject. This is as far as the book can be catalogued and indexed. The really impressive interest is in the mind of the author, and in the American mind, or that fragment of it, which he represents.

Henry Adams was an American patrician who had quite sufficient money, the best introductions, and no vocation forced upon him. An English analogy for Henry Adams would have been a George Wyndham; he would have found the straight road in politics, and he would have occupied his considerable leisure with writing on history, or archæology, or numismatics, or even metaphysics. The American was born to the governing-class tradition without the inherited power, and he was born to exercise governance, not to acquire it. He was much more refined than the equivalent Englishman, and had less vitality, though a remarkably restless curiosity, eager but unsensuous. And his very American curiosity was directed and misdirected by two New England characteristics: conscientiousness and scepticism.

Here is precisely what makes the book, as an "autobiography," wholly different from any European autobiography worth reading. Adams is perpetually busy with himself. Many of the best autobiographies have been by men who considered themselves more interesting than anybody else, even exclusively interesting; and their effrontery interests you in them. But Adams is superlatively modest, diffident. Conscience told him that one must be a learner all one's life, and as he had the financial means to gratify his conscience, he did so. This is conspicuously a Puritan inheritance: if some millionaires and philanthropists are occupied in doing good to others, and by force, in cheerful innocence of any need of cleansing or furnishing their own minds, still there are always others whose conscience lays upon them the heavy burden of self-improvement. They are usually sensitive people, and they want to do something great; dogged by the shadow of self-conscious incompetence, they are predestined failures.

The caricature which represents a nationality to foreigners is usually completed in its own country by an equally extreme antithesis. Against the naive, Adams represents the in some ways precociously and immaturely sophisticated American. Conscience made him aware that he had been imperfectly educated at Harvard and Berlin, and that there was a vague variety of things he ought to know about. He was also aware, as most Bostonians are, of the narrowness of the Boston horizon. But working with and against conscience was the Boston doubt: a scepticism which is difficult to explain to those who are not born to it. This scepticism is a product, or a cause, or a concomitant, of Unitarianism; it is not destructive, but it is dissolvent. When Emerson as a young man stood in his pulpit and made clear to his congregation that he could no longer administer the Communion, he impressed upon them that he had no prejudice and passed no judgment upon those who continued in the practice, but that he could take no part himself—because (in his own words) it did not interest him. That is an instance of the point of view of several thousands of well-bred people in a provincial American town; and, arrested at the point of ecclesiastical procedure, it is not without an austere grandeur. Henry Adams was of a later generation; a great many things interested him; but he could believe in nothing: neither in the sagacity of British statesmanship, nor in the perfection of the American form of government, nor in the New World, nor in the Old; not in Darwinism, or in Karl Pearson, or Ernst Mach, or in the wickedness of large issues of paper currency. He wrote a serious article for the *North American Review* in which he demolished the myths which had been erected around Pocahontas, the Indian Queen, and the pleasure of demolition turned to ashes in his mouth. As for Evolution,

Neither in the *Limulus* nor in the *Terebratula,* nor in the *Cestracion Philippi,* any more than the *Pteraspis,* could one conceive an ancestor, but, if one must, the choice mattered little.

Wherever this man stepped, the ground did not simply give way, it flew into particles; towards the end of his life he came across the speculations of Poincaré, and science disappeared, entirely. He was seeking for education, with the wings of a beautiful but ineffectual conscience beating vainly in a vacuum jar. He found, at best, two or three friends, notably the great John Hay, who had been engaged in settling the problems of China and Cuba and Manchuria. Adams yearned for unity, and found it, after a fashion, by writing a book on the thirteenth century.

The Erinyes which drove him madly through seventy years of search for education—the search for what, upon a lower plane, is called culture—left him much as he was born: well-bred, intelligent, and uneducated. He had attended to everything, respectfully, had accumulated masses of information and known nearly everybody; but he was unaware that education—the education of an individual—is a by-product of being interested, passionately absorbed. He had been too respectful of whatever was important, he laughed at nothing. It is not at all that he was an *amateur;* he would have liked to have been professional in everything; he abandoned lecturing at Harvard because of his doubts of the value of lecturing and the capacity of his pupils; but he had gone at the task in a thoroughly professional way. His extreme sensitiveness to all the suggestions which dampen enthusiasm or dispel conviction may be responsible for what one feels in him as immaturity, indeed as a lack of personality; an instability. The immaturity is marked: we are acutely, painfully aware of an elderly man approaching a new subject of study with "This will be good for me!" *That* is the type of egotism of Henry Adams; it is not a kind which we should expect to provide an agreeable autobiography; but Adams's is a remarkable confession of that peculiar mind.

For the immaturity there may be another reason. It is probable that men ripen best through experiences which are at once sensuous and intellectual; certainly many men will admit that their keenest ideas have come to them with the quality of a sense-perception; and that their keenest sensuous experience has been "as if the body thought." There is nothing to indicate that Adams's senses either flowered or fruited: he remains little Paul Dombey asking questions. Compare him with a man whom he now and then reminds us of: Henry Adams in 1858, and Henry James in 1870 (both at still receptive ages), land at Liverpool and descend at the same hotel.

The small hour was just that of my having landed at Liverpool in the gusty, cloudy, overwhelmingly English morning, and pursued, with immediate intensities of appreciation, . . . a course which had seated me at a late breakfast in the coffee-room of the old Adelphi Hotel ("Radley's" as I had to deplore its lately having ceased to be dubbed), and handed me over without a scruple to my fate. This doom of inordinate exposure to appearances, aspects, images, every protrusive item almost . . . I regard in other words as having settled upon me once for all while I observed for instance that in England the plate of buttered muffin and its cover . . .

So far James. And Adams:

The ocean, the *Persia,* Captain Judkins, and Mr. G. P. R. James, the most distinguished passenger, vanished one Sunday morning in a furious gale in the Mersey, to make place for the drearier picture of a Liverpool street as seen from the Adelphi coffee-room in November murk, followed instantly by the passionate delights of Chester and the romance of red-sandstone architecture.

The contrast could be carried further with James's memories of Tennyson and George Eliot against Adams on, say, Monckton Milnes. Henry James was not, by Adams's standards, "educated," but particularly limited; it is the sensuous contributor to the intelligence that makes the difference.

Henry James, however, was comparatively parvenu. He did not have the Presidents, the Minister, the Unitarian clergy in force behind him. . . .

WILLIAM BLAKE
[1920]

IF ONE follows Blake's mind through the several stages of his poetic development it is impossible to regard him as a naïf, a wild man, a wild pet for the supercultivated. The strangeness is evaporated, the peculiarity is seen to be the peculiarity of all great poetry: something which is found (not everywhere) in Homer and Aeschylus and Dante and Villon, and profound and concealed in the work of Shakespeare—and also in another form in Montaigne and in Spinoza. It is merely a peculiar honesty, which, in a world too frightened to be honest, is peculiarly terrifying. It is an honesty against which the whole world conspires because it is unpleasant. Blake's poetry has the unpleasantness of great poetry. Nothing that can be called morbid or abnormal or perverse, none of the things which exemplify the sickness of an epoch or a fashion, have this quality; only those things which, by some extraordinary labour of simplification, exhibit the essential sickness or strength of the human soul. And this honesty never exists without great technical accomplishment. The question about Blake the man is the

question of the circumstances that concurred to permit this honesty in his work, and what circumstances define its limitations. The favouring conditions probably include these two: that, being early apprenticed to a manual occupation, he was not compelled to acquire any other education in literature than he wanted, or to acquire it for any other reason than that he wanted it; and that, being a humble engraver, he had no journalistic-social career open to him.

There was, that is to say, nothing to distract him from his interests or to corrupt these interests: neither the ambitions of parents or wife, nor the standards of society, nor the temptations of success; nor was he exposed to imitation of himself or of any one else. These circumstances —not his supposed inspired and untaught spontaneity—are what make him innocent. His early poems show what the poems of a boy of genius ought to show, immense power of assimilation. Such early poems are not, as usually supposed, crude attempts to do something beyond the boy's capacity; they are, in the case of a boy of real promise, more likely to be quite mature and successful attempts to do something small. So with Blake, his early poems are technically admirable, and their originality is in an occasional rhythm. The verse of *Edward III* deserves study. But his affection for certain Elizabethans is not so surprising as his affinity with the very best work of his own century. He is very like Collins, he is very eighteenth century. The poem *Whether on Ida's Shady Brow* is eighteenth-century work; the movement, the weight of it, the syntax, the choice of words:

> The *languid* strings do scarcely move!
> The sound is *forc'd,* the notes are few!

this is contemporary with Gray and Collins, it is the poetry of a language which has undergone the discipline of prose. Blake up to twenty is decidedly a traditional.

Blake's beginnings as a poet, then, are as normal as the beginnings of Shakespeare. His method of composition, in his mature work, is exactly like that of other poets. He has an idea (a feeling, an image), he develops it by accretion or expansion, alters his verse often, and hesitates often over the final choice.[1] The idea, of course, simply

BLAKE. 1. "I do not know why M. Berger should say, without qualification, in his *William Blake: mysticisme et poésie,* that 'son respect pour l'esprit qui soufflait en lui et qui dictait ses paroles l'empêchait de les corriger jamais.' Dr. Simpson, in his Oxford edition of Blake, gives us to understand that Blake believed much of his writing to be automatic, but observes that Blake's 'meticulous care in composition is everywhere apparent comes, but upon arrival it is subjected to prolonged manipulation. In the first phase Blake is concerned with verbal beauty; in the second he becomes the apparent naïf, really the mature intelligence. It is only when the ideas become more automatic, come more freely and are less manipulated, that we begin to suspect their origin, to suspect that they spring from a shallower source.

The Songs of Innocence and of Experience, and the poems from the Rossetti manuscript, are the poems of a man with a profound interest in human emotions, and a profound knowledge of them. The emotions are presented in an extremely simplified, abstract form. This form is one illustration of the eternal struggle of art against education, of the literary artist against the continuous deterioration of language.

It is important that the artist should be highly educated in his own art; but his education is one that is hindered rather than helped by the ordinary processes of society which constitute education for the ordinary man. For these processes consist largely in the acquisition of impersonal ideas which obscure what we really are and feel, what we really want, and what really excites our interest. It is of course not the actual information acquired, but the conformity which the accumulation of knowledge is apt to impose, that is harmful. Tennyson is a very fair example of a poet almost wholly encrusted with opinion, almost wholly merged into his environment. Blake, on the other hand, knew what interested him, and he therefore presents only the essential, only, in fact, what can be presented, and need not be explained. And because he was not distracted, or frightened, or occupied in anything but exact statements, he understood. He was naked, and saw man naked, and from the centre of his own crystal. To him there was no more reason why Swedenborg should be absurd than Locke. He accepted Swedenborg, and eventually rejected him, for reasons of his own. He approached everything with a mind unclouded by current opinions. There was nothing of the superior person about him. This makes him terrifying.

II

BUT IF there was nothing to distract him from sincerity there were, on the other hand, the dangers to which the naked man is exposed. His philosophy, like his visions, like his insight, like his technique, was his own. And accordingly he was inclined to attach more importance to it than an artist should; this is what makes him eccentric, and makes him inclined to formlessness.

> But most through midnight streets I hear
> How the youthful harlot's curse
> Blasts the new-born infant's tear,
> And blights with plagues the marriage hearse,

is the naked vision;

> Love seeketh only self to please,
> To bind another to its delight,
> Joys in another's loss of ease,
> And builds a Hell in Heaven's despite,

is the naked observation; and *The Marriage of Heaven and Hell* is naked philosophy, presented. But Blake's occasional marriages of poetry and philosophy are not so felicitous.

> He who would do good to another must do it in
>   Minute Particulars.
> General Good is the plea of the scoundrel, hypo-
>   crite, and flatterer;
> For Art and Science cannot exist but in minutely
>   organized particulars. . . .

One feels that the form is not well chosen. The borrowed philosophy of Dante and Lucretius is perhaps not so interesting, but it injures their form less. Blake did not have that more Mediterranean gift of form which knows how to borrow as Dante borrowed his theory of the soul; he must needs create a philosophy as well as a poetry. A similar formlessness attacks his draughtsmanship. The fault is most evident, of course, in the longer poems—or rather, the poems in which structure is important. You cannot create a very large poem without introducing a more impersonal point of view, or splitting it up into various personalities. But the weakness of the long poems is certainly not that they are too visionary, too remote from the world. It is that Blake did not see enough, became too much occupied with ideas.

We have the same respect for Blake's philosophy (and perhaps for that of Samuel Butler) that we have for an ingenious piece of home-made furniture: we admire the man who has put it together out of the odds and ends about the house. England has produced a fair number of these resourceful Robinson Crusoes; but we are not really so remote from the Continent, or from our own past, as to be deprived of the advantages of culture if we wish them.

We may speculate, for amusement, whether it would not have been beneficial to the north of Europe generally, and to Britain in particular, to have had a more continuous religious history. The local divinities of Italy were not wholly exterminated by Christianity, and they were not reduced

in the poems preserved in rough draft . . . alteration on alteration, rearrangement after rearrangement, deletions, additions, and inversions . . .' " [E].

to the dwarfish fate which fell upon our trolls and pixies. The latter, with the major Saxon deities, were perhaps no great loss in themselves, but they left an empty place; and perhaps our mythology was further impoverished by the divorce from Rome. Milton's celestial and infernal regions are large but insufficiently furnished apartments filled by heavy conversation; and one remarks about the Puritan mythology its thinness. And about Blake's supernatural territories, as about the supposed ideas that dwell there, we cannot help commenting on a certain meanness of culture. They illustrate the crankiness, the eccentricity, which frequently affects writers outside of the Latin traditions, and which such a critic as Arnold should certainly have rebuked. And they are not essential to Blake's inspiration.

Blake was endowed with a capacity for considerable understanding of human nature, with a remarkable and original sense of language and the music of language, and a gift of hallucinated vision. Had these been controlled by a respect for impersonal reason, for common sense, for the objectivity of science, it would have been better for him. What his genius required, and what it sadly lacked, was a framework of accepted and traditional ideas which would have prevented him from indulging in a philosophy of his own, and concentrated his attention upon the problems of the poet. Confusion of thought, emotion, and vision is what we find in such a work as *Also Sprach Zarathustra;* it is eminently not a Latin virtue. The concentration resulting from a framework of mythology and theology and philosophy is one of the reasons why Dante is a classic, and Blake only a poet of genius. The fault is perhaps not with Blake himself, but with the environment which failed to provide what such a poet needed; perhaps the circumstances compelled him to fabricate, perhaps the poet required the philosopher and mythologist; although the conscious Blake may have been quite unconscious of the motives.

BEN JONSON [1919]

THE REPUTATION of Jonson has been of the most deadly kind that can be compelled upon the memory of a great poet. To be universally accepted; to be damned by the praise that quenches all desire to read the book; to be afflicted by the imputation of the virtues which excite the least pleasure; and to be read only by historians and antiquaries—this is the most perfect conspiracy of approval. For some generations the reputation of Jonson has been carried rather as a liability than as an asset in the balance-sheet of English literature. No critic has succeeded in making him appear pleasurable or even interesting. Swinburne's book on Jonson satisfies no curiosity and stimulates no thought. For the critical study in the "Men of Letters Series" by Mr. Gregory Smith there is a place; it satisfies curiosity, it supplies many just observations, it provides valuable matter on the neglected masques; it only fails to remodel the image of Jonson which is settled in our minds. Probably the fault lies with several generations of our poets. It is not that the value of poetry is only its value to living poets for their own work; but appreciation is akin to creation, and true enjoyment of poetry is related to the stirring of suggestion, the stimulus that a poet feels in his enjoyment of other poetry. Jonson has provided no creative stimulus for a very long time; consequently we must look back as far as Dryden—precisely, a poetic practitioner who learned from Jonson—before we find a living criticism of Jonson's work.

Yet there are possibilities for Jonson even now. We have no difficulty in seeing what brought him to this pass; how, in contrast, not with Shakespeare, but with Marlowe, Webster, Donne, Beaumont, and Fletcher, he has been paid out with reputation instead of enjoyment. He is no less a poet than these men, but his poetry is of the surface. Poetry of the surface cannot be understood without study; for to deal with the surface of life, as Jonson dealt with it, is to deal so deliberately that we too must be deliberate, in order to understand. Shakespeare, and smaller men also, are in the end more difficult, but they offer something at the start to encourage the student or to satisfy those who want nothing more; they are suggestive, evocative, a phrase, a voice; they offer poetry in detail as well as in design. So does Dante offer something, a phrase everywhere (*tu se' ombra ed ombra vedi*) [1] even to readers who have no Italian; and Dante and Shakespeare have poetry of design as well as of detail. But the polished veneer of Jonson reflects only the lazy reader's fatuity; unconscious does not respond to unconscious; no swarms of inarticulate feelings are aroused. The immediate appeal of Jonson is to the mind; his emotional tone is not in the single verse, but in the design of the whole. But not many people

BEN JONSON.   **1. tu . . . vedi:** "Thou art a shade and a shade thou seest" (Dante, *Purgatorio*, XXI.132).

are capable of discovering for themselves the beauty which is only found after labour; and Jonson's industrious readers have been those whose interest was historical and curious, and those who have thought that in discovering the historical and curious interest they had discovered the artistic value as well. When we say that Jonson requires study, we do not mean study of his classical scholarship or of seventeenth-century manners. We mean intelligent saturation in his work as a whole; we mean that in order to enjoy him at all, we must get to the centre of his work and his temperament, and that we must see him unbiased by time, as a contemporary. And to see him as a contemporary does not so much require the power of putting ourselves into seventeenth-century London as it requires the power of setting Jonson in our London.

It is generally conceded that Jonson failed as a tragic dramatist; and it is usually agreed that he failed because his genius was for satiric comedy and because of the weight of pedantic learning with which he burdened his two tragic failures. The second point marks an obvious error of detail; the first is too crude a statement to be accepted; to say that he failed because his genius was unsuited to tragedy is to tell us nothing at all. Jonson did not write a good tragedy, but we can see no reason why he should not have written one. If two plays so different as *The Tempest* and *The Silent Woman* are both comedies, surely the category of tragedy could be made wide enough to include something possible for Jonson to have done. But the classification of tragedy and comedy, while it may be sufficient to mark the distinction in a dramatic literature of more rigid form and treatment—it may distinguish Aristophanes from Euripides—is not adequate to a drama of such variations as the Elizabethans'. Tragedy is a crude classification for plays so different in their tone as *Macbeth, The Jew of Malta,* and *The Witch of Edmonton;* and it does not help us much to say that *The Merchant of Venice* and *The Alchemist* are comedies. Jonson had his own scale, his own instrument. The merit which *Catiline* possesses is the same merit that is exhibited more triumphantly in *Volpone; Catiline* fails, not because it is too laboured and conscious, but because it is not conscious enough; because Jonson in this play was not alert to his own idiom, not clear in his mind as to what his temperament wanted him to do. In *Catiline* Jonson conforms, or attempts to conform, to conventions; not to the conventions of antiquity, which he had exquisitely under control, but to the conventions of tragico-historical drama of his time. It is not

the Latin erudition that sinks *Catiline,* but the application of that erudition to a form which was not the proper vehicle for the mind which had amassed the erudition.

If you look at *Catiline*—that dreary Pyrrhic victory of tragedy—you find two passages to be successful: Act II, sc. i, the dialogue of the political ladies, and the Prologue of Sylla's ghost. These two passages are genial. The soliloquy of the ghost is a characteristic Jonson success in content and in versification—

Dost thou not feel me, Rome? not yet! is night
So heavy on thee, and my weight so light?
Can Sylla's ghost arise within thy walls,
Less threatening than an earthquake, the quick falls
Of thee and thine? Shake not the frighted heads
Of thy steep towers, or shrink to their first beds?
Or as their ruin the large Tyber fills,
Make that swell up, and drown thy seven proud
    hills? . . .

This is the learned, but also the creative, Jonson. Without concerning himself with the character of Sulla, and in lines of invective, Jonson makes Sylla's ghost, while the words are spoken, a living and terrible force. The words fall with as determined beat as if they were the will of the morose Dictator himself. You may say: merely invective; but mere invective, even if as superior to the clumsy fisticuffs of Marston and Hall as Jonson's verse is superior to theirs, would not create a living figure as Jonson has done in this long tirade. And you may say: rhetoric; but if we are to call it "rhetoric" we must subject that term to a closer dissection than any to which it is accustomed. What Jonson has done here is not merely a fine speech. It is the careful, precise filling in of a strong and simple outline, and at no point does it overflow the outline; it is far more careful and precise in its obedience to this outline than are many of the speeches in *Tamburlaine.* The outline is not Sulla, for Sulla has nothing to do with it, but "Sylla's ghost." The words may not be suitable to an historical Sulla, or to anybody in history, but they are a perfect expression for "Sylla's ghost." You cannot say they are rhetorical "because people do not talk like that," you cannot call them "verbiage"; they do not exhibit prolixity or redundancy or the other vices in the rhetoric books; there is a definite artistic emotion which demands expression at that length. The words themselves are mostly simple words, the syntax is natural, the language austere rather than adorned. Turning then to the induction of *The Poetaster,* we find another success of the same kind—

Light, I salute thee, but with wounded nerves . . .

Men may not talk in that way, but the Spirit of Envy does, and in the words of Jonson envy is a real and living person. It is not human life that informs envy and Sylla's ghost, but it is energy of which human life is only another variety.

Returning to *Catiline*, we find that the best scene in the body of the play is one which cannot be squeezed into a tragic frame, and which appears to belong to satiric comedy. The scene between Fulvia and Galla and Sempronia is a living scene in a wilderness of oratory. And as it recalls other scenes—there is a suggestion of the college of ladies in *The Silent Woman*—it looks like a comedy scene. And it appears to be satire.

They shall all give and pay well, that come here,
If they will have it; and that, jewels, pearl,
Plate, or round sums to buy these. I'm not taken
With a cob-swan or a high-mounting bull,
As foolish Leda and Europa were;
But the bright gold, with Danaë. For such price
I would endure a rough, harsh Jupiter,
Or ten such thundering gamesters, and refrain
To laugh at 'em, till they are gone, with my much
    suffering.

This scene is no more comedy than it is tragedy, and the "satire" is merely a medium for the essential emotion. Jonson's drama is only incidentally satire, because it is only incidentally a criticism upon the actual world. It is not satire in the way in which the work of Swift or the work of Molière may be called satire: that is, it does not find its source in any precise emotional attitude or precise intellectual criticism of the actual world. It is satire perhaps as the work of Rabelais is satire; certainly not more so. The important thing is that if fiction can be divided into creative fiction and critical fiction, Jonson's is creative. That he was a great critic, our first great critic, does not affect this assertion. Every creator is also a critic; Jonson was a conscious critic, but he was also conscious in his creations. Certainly, one sense in which the term "critical" may be applied to fiction is a sense in which the term might be used of a method antithetical to Jonson's. It is the method of *Education Sentimentale*. The characters of Jonson, of Shakespeare, perhaps of all the greatest drama, are drawn in positive and simple outlines. They may be filled in, and by Shakespeare they are filled in, by much detail or many shifting aspects; but a clear and sharp and simple form remains through these—though it would be hard to say in what the clarity and sharpness and simplicity of Hamlet consists. But Frédéric Moreau is not made in that way. He is constructed partly by negative definition, built up by a great number of observations. We cannot isolate him from the environment in which we find him; it may be an environment which is or can be universalized; nevertheless it and the figure in it consist of very many observed particular facts, the actual world. Without this world the figure dissolves. The ruling faculty is a critical perception, a commentary upon experienced feeling and sensation. If this is true of Flaubert, it is true in a higher degree of Molière than of Jonson. The broad farcical lines of Molière may seem to be the same drawing as Jonson's. But Molière—say in Alceste or Monsieur Jourdain—is criticizing the actual; the reference to the actual world is more direct. And having a more tenuous reference, the work of Jonson is much less directly satirical.

This leads us to the question of Humours. Largely on the evidence of the two Humour plays, it is sometimes assumed that Jonson is occupied with types; typical exaggerations, or exaggerations of type. The Humour definition, the expressed intention of Jonson, may be satisfactory for these two plays. *Every Man in his Humour* is the first mature work of Jonson, and the student of Jonson must study it; but it is not the play in which Jonson found his genius: it is the last of his plays to read first. If one reads *Volpone,* and after that re-reads *The Jew of Malta;* then returns to Jonson and reads *Bartholomew Fair, The Alchemist, Epicoene* and *The Devil is an Ass,* and finally *Catiline,* it is possible to arrive at a fair opinion of the poet and the dramatist.

The Humour, even at the beginning, is not a type, as in Marston's satire, but a simplified and somewhat distorted individual with a typical mania. In the later work, the Humour definition quite fails to account for the total effect produced. The characters of Shakespeare are such as might exist in different circumstances than those in which Shakespeare sets them. The latter appear to be those which extract from the characters the most intense and interesting realization; but that realization has not exhausted their possibilities. Volpone's life, on the other hand, is bounded by the scene in which it is played; in fact, the life is the life of the scene and is derivatively the life of Volpone; the life of the character is inseparable from the life of the drama. This is not dependence upon a background, or upon a substratum of fact. The emotional effect is single and simple. Whereas in Shakespeare the effect is due to the way in which the characters *act upon* one another, in Jonson it is given by the way in which the characters *fit in* with each other. The artistic result of *Volpone* is not due to any effect that Volpone, Mosca, Corvino, Corbaccio, Voltore have upon each other, but simply to their combination into a whole. And these figures are not personifications of passions; separately, they have not even that reality, they are constituents. It is a similar indication of Jonson's method that you can hardly pick out a line of Jonson's and say confidently that it is great poetry; but there are many extended passages to which you cannot deny that honour.

> I will have all my beds blown up, not stuft;
> Down is too hard; and then, mine oval room
> Fill'd with such pictures as Tiberius took
> From Elephantis, and dull Aretine
> But coldly imitated. Then, my glasses
> Cut in more subtle angles, to disperse
> And multiply the figures, as I walk. . . .

Jonson is the legitimate heir of Marlowe. The man who wrote, in *Volpone:*

>   for thy love,
> In varying figures, I would have contended
> With the blue Proteus, or the hornèd flood. . . .

and

>   See, a carbuncle
> May put out both the eyes of our Saint Mark;
> A diamond would have bought Lollia Paulina,
> When she came in like star-light, hid with jewels. . . .

is related to Marlowe as a poet; and if Marlowe is a poet, Jonson is also. And, if Jonson's comedy is a comedy of humours, then Marlowe's tragedy, a large part of it, is a tragedy of humours. But Jonson has too exclusively been considered as the typical representative of a point of view toward comedy. He has suffered from his great reputation as a critic and theorist, from the effects of his intelligence. We have been taught to think of him as the man, the dictator (confusedly in our minds with his later namesake), as the literary politician impressing his views upon a generation; we are offended by the constant reminder of his scholarship. We forget the comedy in the humours, and the serious artist in the scholar. Jonson has suffered in public opinion, as any one must suffer who is forced to talk about his art.

If you examine the first hundred lines or more of *Volpone* the verse appears to be in the manner of Marlowe, more deliberate, more mature, but without Marlowe's inspiration. It looks like mere "rhetoric," certainly not "deeds and language such as men do use." It appears to us, in fact, forced and flagitious bombast. That it is not "rhetoric," or at least not vicious rhetoric, we do not know until we are able to review the whole play. For the consistent maintenance of this manner conveys in the end an effect not of verbosity, but of bold, even shocking and terrifying directness. We have difficulty in saying exactly what produces this simple and single effect. It is not in any ordinary way due to management of intrigue. Jonson employs immense dramatic constructive skill: it is not so much skill in plot as skill in doing without a plot. He never manipulates as complicated a plot as that of *The Merchant of Venice;* he has in his best plays nothing like the intrigue of Restoration comedy. In *Bartholomew Fair* it is hardly a plot at all; the marvel of the play is the bewildering rapid chaotic action of the fair; it is the fair itself, not anything that happens in the fair. In *Volpone,* or *The Alchemist,* or *The Silent Woman,* the plot is enough to keep the players in motion; it is rather an "action" than a plot. The plot does not hold the play together; what holds the play together is a unity of inspiration that radiates into plot and personages alike.

We have attempted to make more precise the sense in which it was said that Jonson's work is "of the surface"; carefully avoiding the word "superficial." For there is work contemporary with Jonson's which is superficial in a pejorative sense in which the word cannot be applied to Jonson—the work of Beaumont and Fletcher. If we look at the work of Jonson's great contemporaries, Shakespeare, and also Donne and Webster and Tourneur (and sometimes Middleton), they have a depth, a third dimension, as Mr. Gregory Smith rightly calls it, which Jonson's work has not. Their words have often a network of tentacular roots reaching down to the deepest terrors and desires. Jonson's most certainly have not; but in Beaumont and Fletcher we may think that at times we find it. Looking closer, we discover that the blossoms of Beaumont and Fletcher's imagination draw no sustenance from the soil, but are cut and slightly withered flowers stuck into sand.

> Wilt thou, hereafter, when they talk of me,
> As thou shalt hear nothing but infamy,
> Remember some of these things? . . .
> I pray thee, do; for thou shalt never see me so again.
> Hair woven in many a curious warp,
> Able in endless error to enfold
> The wandering soul; . . .

Detached from its context, this looks like the verse of the greater poets; just as lines of Jonson, detached from their context, look like inflated or empty fustian. But the evocative quality of the verse of Beaumont and Fletcher depends upon a clever appeal to emotions and associations which they have not themselves grasped; it is hollow. It is superficial with a vacuum behind it; the superficies of Jonson is solid. It is what it is; it does not pretend to be another thing. But it is so very conscious and deliberate that we must look with eyes alert to the whole before we apprehend the significance of any part. We cannot call a man's work superficial when it is the creation of a world; a man cannot be accused of dealing superficially with the world which he himself has created; the superficies *is* the world. Jonson's characters conform to the logic of the emotions of their world. They are not fancy, because they have a logic of their own; and this logic illuminates the actual world, because it gives us a new point of view from which to inspect it.

A writer of power and intelligence, Jonson endeavoured to promulgate, as a formula and programme of reform, what he chose to do himself; and he not unnaturally laid down in abstract theory what is in reality a personal point of view. And it is in the end of no value to discuss Jonson's theory and practice unless we recognize and seize this point of view, which escapes the formulae, and which is what makes his plays worth reading. Jonson behaved as the great creative mind that he was: he created his own world, a world from which his followers, as well as the dramatists who were trying to do something wholly different, are excluded. Remembering this, we turn to Mr. Gregory Smith's objection—that Jonson's characters lack the third dimension, have no life out of the theatrical existence in which they appear— and demand an inquest. The objection implies that the characters are purely the work of intellect, or the result of superficial observation of a world which is faded or mildewed. It implies that the characters are lifeless. But if we dig beneath the theory, beneath the observation, beneath the deliberate drawing and the theatrical and dramatic elaboration, there is discovered a kind of power, animating Volpone, Busy, Fitzdottrel, the literary ladies of *Epicoene*, even Bobadil, which comes from below the intellect, and for which no theory of humours will account. And it is the same kind of power which vivifies Trimalchio, and Panurge, and some but not all of the "comic" characters of Dickens. The fictive life of this kind is not to be circumscribed by a reference to "comedy" or to "farce"; it is not exactly the kind of life which informs the characters of Molière or that which informs those of Marivaux—two writers who were, besides, doing something quite different the one from the other. But it is something which distinguishes Barabas from Shylock, Epicure Mammon from Falstaff, Faustus from— if you will—Macbeth; Marlowe and Jonson from Shakespeare and the Shakespeareans, Webster, and Tourneur. It is not merely Humours: for neither Volpone nor Mosca is a humour. No theory

of humours could account for Jonson's best plays or the best characters in them. We want to know at what point the comedy of humours passes into a work of art, and why Jonson is not Brome.

The creation of a work of art, we will say the creation of a character in a drama, consists in the process of transfusion of the personality, or, in a deeper sense, the life, of the author into the character. This is a very different matter from the orthodox creation in one's own image. The ways in which the passions and desires of the creator may be satisfied in the work of art are complex and devious. In a painter they may take the form of a predilection for certain colours, tones, or lightings; in a writer the original impulse may be even more strangely transmuted. Now, we may say with Mr. Gregory Smith that Falstaff or a score of Shakespeare's characters have a "third dimension" that Jonson's have not. This will mean, not that Shakespeare's spring from the feelings or imagination and Jonson's from the intellect or invention; they have equally an emotional source; but that Shakespeare's represent a more complex tissue of feelings and desires, as well as a more supple, a more susceptible temperament. Falstaff is not only the roast Manningtree ox with the pudding in his belly; he also "grows old," and, finally, his nose is as sharp as a pen. He was perhaps the *satisfaction* of more, and of more complicated feelings; and perhaps he was, as the great tragic characters must have been, the offspring of deeper, less apprehensible feelings: deeper, but not necessarily stronger or more intense, than those of Jonson. It is obvious that the spring of the difference is not the difference between feeling and thought, or superior insight, superior perception, on the part of Shakespeare, but his susceptibility to a greater range of emotion, and emotion deeper and more obscure. But his characters are no more "alive" than are the characters of Jonson.

The world they live in is a larger one. But small worlds—the worlds which artists create—do not differ only in magnitude; if they are complete worlds, drawn to scale in every part, they differ in kind also. And Jonson's world has this scale. His type of personality found its relief in something falling under the category of burlesque or farce—though when you are dealing with a *unique* world, like his, these terms fail to appease the desire for definition. It is not, at all events, the farce of Molière: the latter is more analytic, more an intellectual redistribution. It is not defined by the word "satire." Jonson poses as a satirist. But satire like Jonson's is great in the end not by hitting off its object, but by creating it; the satire is merely the means which leads to the aesthetic result, the impulse which projects a new world into a new orbit. In *Every Man in his Humour* there is a neat, a very neat, comedy of humours. In discovering and proclaiming in this play the new genre Jonson was simply recognizing, unconsciously, the route which opened out in the proper direction for his instincts. His characters are and remain, like Marlowe's, simplified characters; but the simplification does not consist in the dominance of a particular humour or monomania. That is a very superficial account of it. The simplification consists largely in reduction of detail, in the seizing of aspects relevant to the relief of an emotional impulse which remains the same for that character, in making the character conform to a particular setting. This stripping is essential to the art, to which is also essential a flat distortion in the drawing; it is an art of caricature, of great caricature, like Marlowe's. It is a great caricature, which is beautiful; and a great humour, which is serious. The "world" of Jonson is sufficiently large; it is a world of poetic imagination; it is sombre. He did not get the third dimension, but he was not trying to get it.

If we approach Jonson with less frozen awe of his learning, with a clearer understanding of his "rhetoric" and its applications, if we grasp the fact that the knowledge required of the reader is not archaeology but knowledge of Jonson, we can derive not only instruction in two-dimensional life —but enjoyment. We can even apply him, be aware of him as a part of our literary inheritance craving further expression. Of all the dramatists of his time, Jonson is probably the one whom the present age would find the most sympathetic, if it knew him. There is a brutality, a lack of sentiment, a polished surface, a handling of large bold designs in brilliant colours, which ought to attract about three thousand people in London and elsewhere. At least, if we had a contemporary Shakespeare and a contemporary Jonson, it might be the Jonson who would arouse the enthusiasm of the intelligentsia. Though he is saturated in literature, he never sacrifices the theatrical qualities— theatrical in the most favourable sense—to literature or to the study of character. His work is a titanic show. But Jonson's masques, an important part of his work, are neglected; our flaccid culture lets shows and literature fade, but prefers faded literature to faded shows. There are hundreds of people who have read *Comus* to ten who have read the *Masque of Blackness*. *Comus* contains fine poetry, and poetry exemplifying some merits to which Jonson's masque poetry cannot pretend. Nevertheless, *Comus* is the death

of the masque; it is the transition of a form of art—even of a form which existed for but a short generation—into "literature," literature cast in a form which has lost its application. Even though *Comus* was a masque at Ludlow Castle, Jonson had, what Milton came perhaps too late to have, a sense for the living art; his art was applied. The masques can still be read, and with pleasure, by any one who will take the trouble—a trouble which in this part of Jonson is, indeed, a study of antiquities—to imagine them in action, displayed with the music, costumes, dances, and the scenery of Inigo Jones. They are additional evidence that Jonson had a fine sense of form, of the purpose for which a particular form is intended; evidence that he was a literary artist even more than he was a man of letters.

THOMAS MIDDLETON
[1927]

THOMAS MIDDLETON, the dramatic writer, was not very highly thought of in his own time; the date of his death is not known; we know only that he was buried on July 4, 1627. He was one of the most voluminous, and one of the best, dramatic writers of his time. But it is easy to understand why he is not better known or more popular. It is difficult to imagine his "personality." Several new personalities have recently been fitted to the name of Shakespeare; Jonson is a real figure—our imagination plays about him discoursing at the Mermaid, or laying down the law to Drummond of Hawthornden; Chapman has become a breezy British character as firm as Nelson or Wellington; Webster and Donne are real people for the more intellectual; even Tourneur (Churton Collins having said the last word about him) is a "personality." But Middleton, who collaborated shamelessly, who is hardly separated from Rowley, Middleton who wrote plays so diverse as *Women Beware Women* and *A Game at Chesse* and *The Roaring Girle*, Middleton remains merely a collective name for a number of plays—some of which, like *The Spanish Gipsie*, are patently by other people.[1]

MIDDLETON.   1. "Mr. Dugdale Sykes has written authoritatively on this subject" [E].

If we write about Middleton's plays we must write about Middleton's plays, and not about Middleton's personality. Many of these plays are still in doubt. Of all the Elizabethan dramatists Middleton seems the most impersonal, the most indifferent to personal fame or perpetuity, the readiest, except Rowley, to accept collaboration. Also he is the most various. His greatest tragedies and his greatest comedies are as if written by two different men. Yet there seems no doubt that Middleton was both a great comic writer and a great tragic writer. There are a sufficient number of plays, both tragedies and comedies, in which his hand is so far unquestioned, to establish his greatness. His greatness is not that of a peculiar personality, but of a great artist or artisan of the Elizabethan epoch. We have among others *The Changeling, Women Beware Women,* and *A Game at Chesse;* and we have *The Roaring Girle* and *A Trick to Catch the Old One.* And that is enough. Between the tragedies and the comedies of Shakespeare, and certainly between the tragedies and the comedies of Jonson, we can establish a relation; we can see, for Shakespeare or Jonson, that each had in the end a personal point of view which can be called neither comic nor tragic. But with Middleton we can establish no such relation. He remains merely a name, a voice, the author of certain plays, which are all of them great plays. He has no point of view, is neither sentimental nor cynical; he is neither resigned, nor disillusioned, nor romantic, he has no message. He is merely the name which associates six or seven great plays.

For there is no doubt about *The Changeling.* Like all of the plays attributed to Middleton, it is long-winded and tiresome; the characters talk too much, and then suddenly stop talking and act; they are real and impelled irresistibly by the fundamental motions of humanity to good or evil. This mixture of tedious discourse and sudden reality is everywhere in the work of Middleton, in his comedy also. In *The Roaring Girle* we read with toil through a mass of cheap conventional intrigue, and suddenly realize that we are, and have been for some time without knowing it, observing a real and unique human being. In reading *The Changeling* we may think, till almost the end of the play, that we have been concerned merely with a fantastic Elizabethan morality, and then discover that we are looking on at a dispassionate exposure of fundamental passions of any time and any place. The usual opinion remains the just judgment: *The Changeling* is Middleton's greatest play. The morality of the convention seems to us absurd. To many intelligent readers this play has only an historical interest, and only serves to illustrate the moral taboos of the Elizabethans. The heroine is a young woman who, in order to dispose of a fiancé to whom she is indifferent, so that she may marry the man she loves, accepts the offer of an adventurer to murder the affianced, at the price (as she finds in due course) of becoming the murderer's mistress. Such a plot is, to a modern mind, absurd; and the consequent tragedy seems a fuss about nothing. But *The Changeling* is not merely contingent for its effect upon our acceptance of Elizabethan good form or convention; it is, in fact, no more dependent upon the convention of its epoch that a play like *A Doll's House.* Underneath the convention there is the stratum of truth permanent in human nature. The tragedy of *The Changeling* is an eternal tragedy, as permanent as *Oedipus* or *Antony and Cleopatra;* it is the tragedy of the not naturally bad but irresponsible and undeveloped nature, caught in the consequences of its own action. In every age and in every civilization there are instances of the same thing: the unmoral nature, suddenly trapped in the inexorable toils of morality—of morality not made by man but by Nature—and forced to take the consequences of an act which it had planned light-heartedly. Beatrice is not a moral creature; she becomes moral only by becoming damned. Our conventions are not the same as those which Middleton assumed for his play. But the possibility of that frightful discovery of morality remains permanent.

The words in which Middleton expresses his tragedy are as great as the tragedy. The process through which Beatrice, having decided that De Flores is the instrument for her purpose, passes from aversion to habituation, remains a permanent commentary on human nature. The directness and precision of De Flores are masterly, as is also the virtuousness of Beatrice on first realizing his motives—

> Why, 'tis impossible thou canst be so wicked,
> Or shelter such a cunning cruelty,
> To make his death the murderer of my honour!
> Thy language is so bold and vicious,
> I cannot see which way I can forgive it
> With any modesty

—a passage which ends with the really great lines of De Flores, lines of which Shakespeare or Sophocles might have been proud:

> Can you weep Fate from its determined purpose?
> So soon may you weep me.

But what constitutes the essence of the tragedy is something which has not been sufficiently remarked; it is the *habituation* of Beatrice to her sin; it becomes no longer sin but merely custom. Such is the essence of the tragedy of *Macbeth*— the habituation to crime. And in the end Beatrice, having been so long the enforced conspirator of De Flores, becomes (and this is permanently true to human nature) more *his* partner, *his* mate, than the mate and partner of the man for the love of whom she consented to the crime. Her lover disappears not only from the scene but from her own imagination. When she says of De Flores,

> A wondrous necessary man, my lord,

her praise is more than half sincere; and at the end she belongs far more to De Flores—towards whom, at the beginning, she felt strong physical repulsion—than to her lover Alsemero. It is De Flores, in the end, to whom she belongs as Francesca to Paolo:

> Beneath the stars, upon yon meteor
> Ever hung my fate, 'mongst things corruptible;
> I ne'er could pluck it from him; my loathing
> Was prophet to the rest, but ne'er believed.

And De Flores's cry is perfectly sincere and in character:

> I loved this woman in spite of her heart;
> Her love I earned out of Piracquo's murder . . .
> Yes, and her honour's prize
> Was my reward; I thank life for nothing
> But that pleasure; it was so sweet to me,
> That I have drunk up all, left none behind
> For any man to pledge me.

The tragedy of Beatrice is not that she has lost Alsemero, for whose possession she played; it is that she has won De Flores. Such tragedies are not limited to Elizabethan times: they happen every day and perpetually. The greatest tragedies are occupied with great and permanent moral conflicts: the great tragedies of Aeschylus, of Sophocles, of Corneille, of Racine, of Shakespeare, have the same burden. In poetry, in dramatic technique, *The Changeling* is inferior to the best plays of Webster. But in the moral essence of tragedy it is safe to say that in this play Middleton is surpassed by one Elizabethan alone, and that is Shakespeare. In some respects in which Elizabethan tragedy can be compared to French or to Greek tragedy *The Changeling* stands above every tragic play of its time, except those of Shakespeare.

The genius which blazed in *The Changeling* was fitful but not accidental. The best tragedy after *The Changeling* is *Women Beware Women*. The thesis of the play, as the title indicates, is more arbitrary and less fundamental. The play

itself, although less disfigured by ribaldry or clowning, is more tedious. Middleton sinks himself in conventional moralizing of the epoch; so that, if we are impatient, we decide that he gives merely a document of Elizabethan humbug—and then suddenly a personage will blaze out in genuine fire of vituperation. The wickedness of the personages in *Women Beware Women* is conventional wickedness of the stage of the time; yet slowly the exasperation of Bianca, the wife who married beneath her, beneath the ambitions to which she was entitled, emerges from the negative; slowly the real human passions emerge from the mesh of interest in which they begin. And here again Middleton, in writing what appears on the surface a conventional picture-palace Italian melodrama of the time, has caught permanent human feelings. And in this play Middleton shows his interest—more than any of his contemporaries —in innuendo and double meanings; and makes use of that game of chess, which he was to use more openly and directly for satire in that perfect piece of literary political art, *A Game at Chesse*. The irony could not be improved upon:

Did I not say my duke would fetch you o'er, Widow?
I think you spoke in earnest when you said it, madam.
And my black king makes all the haste he can too.
Well, madam, we may meet with him in time yet.
I've given thee blind mate twice.

There is hardly anything truer in Elizabethan drama than Bianca's gradual self-will and self-importance in consequence of her courtship by the Duke:

Troth, you speak wondrous well for your old house here;
'Twill shortly fall down at your feet to thank you,
Or stoop, when you go to bed, like a good child,
To ask you blessing.

In spite of all the long-winded speeches, in spite of all the conventional Italianate horrors, Bianca remains, like Beatrice in *The Changeling,* a real woman; as real, indeed, as any woman of Elizabethan tragedy. Bianca is a type of the woman who is purely moved by vanity.

But if Middleton understood women in tragedy better than any of the Elizabethans—better than the creator of the Duchess of Malfy, better than Marlowe, better than Tourneur, or Shirley, or Fletcher, better than any of them except Shakespeare alone—he was also able, in his comedy, to present a finer woman than any of them. *The Roaring Girle* has no apparent relation to Middleton's tragedies, yet it is agreed to be primarily the work of Middleton. It is typical of the comedies of Middleton, and it is the best. In his tragedies Middleton employs all the Italianate horrors of his time, and obviously for the purpose of pleasing the taste of his time; yet underneath we feel always a quiet and undisturbed vision of things as they are and not "another thing." So in his comedies. The comedies are long-winded; the fathers are heavy fathers, and rant as heavy fathers should; the sons are wild and wanton sons, and perform all the pranks to be expected of them; the machinery is the usual Elizabethan machinery; Middleton is solicitous to please his audience with what they expect; but there is underneath the same steady impersonal passionless observation of human nature. *The Roaring Girle* is as artificial as any comedy of the time; its plot creaks loudly; yet the Girl herself is always real. She may rant, she may behave preposterously, but she remains a type of the sort of woman who has renounced all happiness for herself and who lives only for a principle. Nowhere more than in *The Roaring Girle* can the hand of Middleton be distinguished more clearly from the hand of Dekker. Dekker is all sentiment; and, indeed, in the so admired passages of *A Fair Quarrel,* exploited by Lamb, the mood if not the hand of Dekker seems to the unexpert critic to be more present than Middleton's. *A Fair Quarrel* seems as much, if no more, Dekker's than Middleton's. Similarly with *The Spanish Gipsie,* which can with difficulty be attributed to Middleton. But the feeling about Moll Cut-Purse of *The Roaring Girle* is Middleton's rather than anybody's. In Middleton's tragedy there is a strain of realism underneath, which is one with the poetry; and in his comedy we find the same thing.

In her recent book on *The Social Mode of Restoration Comedy,* Miss Kathleen Lynch calls attention to the gradual transition from Elizabethan-Jacobean to Restoration comedy. She observes, what is certainly true, that Middleton is the greatest "realist" in Jacobean comedy. Miss Lynch's extremely suggestive thesis is that the transition from Elizabethan-Jacobean to later Caroline comedy is primarily economic: that the interest changes from the citizen aping gentry to the citizen become gentry and accepting that code of manners. In the comedy of Middleton certainly there is as yet no code of manners; but the merchant of Cheapside is *aiming* at becoming a member of the country gentry. Miss Lynch remarks: "Middleton's keen concentration on the spectacle of the interplay of different social classes marks an important development in realistic comedy." She calls attention to this aspect of Middleton's comedy, that it marks, better than the romantic comedy of Shakespeare, or the comedy of Jonson, occupied with what Jonson thought to be permanent and not transient aspects of human nature, the transition between the aristocratic world which preceded the Tudors and the plutocratic modern world which the Tudors initiated and encouraged. By the time of the return of Charles II, as Miss Lynch points out, society had been reorganized and formed, and social conventions had been created. In the Tudor times birth still counted (though nearly all the great families were extinct); by the time of Charles II only breeding counted. The comedy of Middleton, and the comedy of Brome, and the comedy of Shirley, is intermediate, as Miss Lynch remarks. Middleton, she observes, marks the transitional stage in which the London tradesman was anxious to cease to be a tradesman and to become a country gentleman. The words of his City Magnate in *Michaelmas Terme* have not yet lost their point:

"A fine journey in the Whitsun holydays, i'faith, to ride with a number of cittizens and their wives, some upon pillions, some upon side-saddles, I and little Thomasine i' the middle, our son and heir, Sim Quomodo, in a peach-colour taffeta jacket, some horse length, or a long yard before us—there will be a fine show on's I can tell you."

But Middleton's comedy is not, like the comedy of Congreve, the comedy of a set social behaviour; it is still, like the later comedy of Dickens, the comedy of individuals, in spite of the continual motions of city merchants towards county gentility. In the comedy of the Restoration a figure such as that of Moll Cut-Purse would have been impossible. As a social document the comedy of Middleton illustrates the transition from government by a landed aristocracy to government by a city aristocracy gradually engrossing the land. As such it is of the greatest interest. But as literature, as a dispassionate picture of human nature, Middleton's comedy deserves to be remembered chiefly by its real—perpetually real—and human figure of Moll the Roaring Girl. That Middleton's comedy was "photographic," that it introduces us to the low life of the time far better than anything in the comedy of Shakespeare or the comedy of Jonson, better than anything except the pamphlets of Dekker and Greene and Nashe, there is little doubt. But it produced one great play— *The Roaring Girle*—a great play in spite of the tedious long speeches of some of the principal characters, in spite of the clumsy machinery of the plot: for the reason that Middleton was a great observer of human nature, without fear, without sentiment, without prejudice.

And Middleton in the end—after criticism has subtracted all that Rowley, all that Dekker, all that others contributed—is a great example of great English drama. He has no message; he is merely a great recorder. Incidentally, in flashes and when the dramatic need comes, he is a great poet, a great master of versification:

I that am of your blood was taken from you
For your better health; look no more upon 't,
But cast it to the ground regardlessly,
Let the common sewer take it from distinction:
Beneath the stars, upon yon meteor
Ever hung my fate, 'mongst things corruptible;
I ne'er could pluck it from him; my loathing
Was prophet to the rest, but ne'er believed.

The man who wrote these lines remains inscrutable, solitary, unadmired; welcoming collaboration, indifferent to fame; dying no one knows when and no one knows how; attracting, in three hundred years, no personal admiration. Yet he wrote one tragedy which more than any play except those of Shakespeare has a profound and permanent moral value and horror; and one comedy which more than any Elizabethan comedy realizes a free and noble womanhood.

RELIGION AND LITERATURE
[1935]

WHAT I have to say is largely in support of the following propositions: Literary criticism should be completed by criticism from a definite ethical and theological standpoint. In so far as in any age there is common agreement on ethical and theological matters, so far can literary criticism be substantive. In ages like our own, in which there is no such common agreement, it is the more necessary for Christian readers to scrutinize their reading, especially of works of imagination, with explicit ethical and theological standards. The "greatness" of literature cannot be determined solely by literary standards; though we must remember that whether it is literature or not can be determined only by literary standards.[1]

RELIGION AND LITERATURE.   1. "As an example of literary criticism given greater significance by theological interests, I would call attention to Theodor Haecker: *Virgil* (Sheed and Ward)" [E].

We have tacitly assumed, for some centuries past, that there is *no* relation between literature and theology. This is not to deny that literature—I mean, again, primarily works of imagination—has been, is, and probably always will be judged by some moral standards. But moral judgements of literary works are made only according to the moral code accepted by each generation, whether it lives according to that code or not. In an age which accepts some precise Christian theology, the common code may be fairly orthodox: though even in such periods the common code may exalt such concepts as "honour," "glory" or "revenge" to a position quite intolerable to Christianity. The dramatic ethics of the Elizabethan Age offers an interesting study. But when the common code is detached from its theological background, and is consequently more and more merely a matter of habit, it is exposed both to prejudice and to change. At such times morals are open to being altered *by* literature; so that we find in practice that what is "objectionable" in literature is merely what the present generation is not used to. It is a commonplace that what shocks one generation is accepted quite calmly by the next. This adaptability to change of moral standards is sometimes greeted with satisfaction as an evidence of human perfectibility; whereas it is only evidence of what unsubstantial foundations people's moral judgements have.

I am not concerned here with religious literature but with the application of our religion to the criticism of any literature. It may be as well, however, to distinguish first what I consider to be the three senses in which we can speak of "religious literature." The first is that of which we say that it is "religious literature" in the same way that we speak of "historical literature" or of "scientific literature." I mean that we can treat the Authorized translation of the Bible, or the works of Jeremy Taylor, as literature, in the same way that we treat the historical writing of Clarendon or of Gibbon—our two great English historians —as literature; or Bradley's *Logic,* or Buffon's *Natural History.* All of these writers were men who, incidentally to their religious, or historical, or philosophic purpose, had a gift of language which makes them delightful to read to all those who can enjoy language well written, even if they are unconcerned with the objects which the writers had in view. And I would add that though a scientific, or historical, or theological, or philosophic work which is also "literature," may become superannuated as anything but literature, yet it is not likely to be "literature" unless it had its scientific or other value for its own time. While

I acknowledge the legitimacy of this enjoyment, I am more acutely aware of its abuse. The persons who enjoy these writings *solely* because of their literary merit are essentially parasites; and we know that parasites, when they become too numerous, are pests. I could fulminate against the men of letters who have gone into ecstasies over "the Bible as literature," the Bible as "the noblest monument of English prose." Those who talk of the Bible as a "monument of English prose" are merely admiring it as a monument over the grave of Christianity. I must try to avoid the by-paths of my discourse: it is enough to suggest that just as the work of Clarendon, or Gibbon, or Buffon, or Bradley would be of inferior literary value if it were insignificant as history, science and philosophy respectively, so the Bible has had a *literary* influence upon English literature *not* because it has been considered as literature, but because it has been considered as the report of the Word of God. And the fact that men of letters now discuss it as "literature" probably indicates the *end* of its "literary" influence.

The second kind of relation of religion to literature is that which is found in what is called "religious" or "devotional" poetry. Now what is the usual attitude of the lover of poetry—and I mean the person who is a genuine and first-hand enjoyer and appreciator of poetry, not the person who follows the admirations of others—towards this department of poetry? I believe, all that may be implied in his calling it a *department*. He believes, not always explicitly, that when you qualify poetry as "religious" you are indicating very clear limitations. For the great majority of people who love poetry, *"religious* poetry" is a variety of *minor* poetry: the religious poet is not a poet who is treating the whole subject matter of poetry in a religious spirit, but a poet who is dealing with a confined part of this subject matter: who is leaving out what men consider their major passions, and thereby confessing his ignorance of them. I think that this is the real attitude of most poetry lovers towards such poets as Vaughan, or Southwell, or Crashaw, or George Herbert, or Gerard Hopkins.

But what is more, I am ready to admit that up to a point these critics are right. For there is a kind of poetry, such as most of the work of the authors I have mentioned, which is the product of a special religious awareness, which may exist without the general awareness which we expect of the major poet. In some poets, or in some of their works, this general awareness may have existed; but the preliminary steps which represent it may have been suppressed, and only the end-product presented. Between these, and those in which the religious or devotional genius represents the *special* and limited awareness, it may be very difficult to discriminate. I do not pretend to offer Vaughan, or Southwell, or George Herbert, or Hopkins as major poets: [2] I feel sure that the first three, at least, are poets of this limited awareness. They are not great religious poets in the sense in which Dante, or Corneille, or Racine, even in those of their plays which do not touch upon Christian themes, are great Christian religious poets. Or even in the sense in which Villon and Baudelaire, with all their imperfections and delinquencies, are Christian poets. Since the time of Chaucer, Christian poetry (in the sense in which I shall mean it) has been limited in England almost exclusively to minor poetry.

I repeat that when I am considering Religion and Literature, I speak of these things only to make clear that I am not concerned primarily with Religious Literature. I am concerned with what should be the relation between Religion and all Literature. Therefore the third type of "religious literature" may be more quickly passed over. I mean the literary works of men who are sincerely desirous of forwarding the cause of religion: that which may come under the heading of Propaganda. I am thinking, of course, of such delightful fiction as Mr. Chesterton's *Man Who Was Thursday,* or his *Father Brown.* No one admires and enjoys these things more than I do; I would only remark that when the same effect is aimed at by zealous persons of less talent than Mr. Chesterton the effect is negative. But my point is that such writings do not enter into any serious consideration of the relation of Religion and Literature: because they are conscious operations in a world in which it is assumed that Religion and Literature are not related. It is a conscious and limited relating. What I want is a literature which should be *un*consciously, rather than deliberately and defiantly, Christian: because the work of Mr. Chesterton has its point from appearing in a world which is definitely not Christian.

I am convinced that we fail to realize how completely, and yet how irrationally, we separate our literary from our religious judgements. If there could be a complete separation, perhaps it might not matter: but the separation is not, and never can be, complete. If we exemplify literature by the novel—for the novel is the form in which literature affects the greatest number—we may re-

2. "I note that in an address delivered in Swansea some years later (subsequently published in *The Welsh Review* under the title of "What Is Minor Poetry?") I stated with some emphasis my opinion that Herbert is a major, not a minor poet. I agree with my later opinion [1949]" [E].

mark this gradual secularization of literature during at least the last three hundred years. Bunyan, and to some extent Defoe, had moral purposes: the former is beyond suspicion, the latter may be suspect. But since Defoe the secularization of the novel has been continuous. There have been three chief phases. In the first, the novel took the Faith, in its contemporary version, for granted, and omitted it from its picture of life. Fielding, Dickens and Thackeray belong to this phase. In the second, it doubted, worried about, or contested the Faith. To this phase belong George Eliot, George Meredith and Thomas Hardy. To the third phase, in which we are living, belong nearly all contemporary novelists except Mr. James Joyce. It is the phase of those who have never heard the Christian Faith spoken of as anything but an anachronism.

Now, do people in general hold a definite opinion, that is to say religious or anti-religious; and do they read novels, or poetry for that matter, with a separate compartment of their minds? The common ground between religion and fiction is behaviour. Our religion imposes our ethics, our judgement and criticism of ourselves, and our behaviour toward our fellow men. The fiction that we read affects our behaviour towards our fellow men, affects our patterns of ourselves. When we read of human beings behaving in certain ways, with the approval of the author, who gives his benediction to this behaviour by his attitude toward the result of the behaviour arranged by himself, we can be influenced towards behaving in the same way.[3] When the contemporary novelist is an individual thinking for himself in isolation, he may have something important to offer to those who are able to receive it. He who is alone may speak to the individual. But the majority of novelists are persons drifting in the stream, only a little faster. They have some sensitiveness, but little intellect.

We are expected to be broadminded about literature, to put aside prejudice or conviction, and to look at fiction as fiction and at drama as drama. With what is inaccurately called "censorship" in this country—with what is much more difficult to cope with than an official censorship, because it represents the opinions of individuals in an irresponsible democracy, I have very little sympathy; partly because it so often suppresses the wrong books, and partly because it is little more effective than Prohibition of Liquor; partly because it is one manifestation of the desire that state control should take the place of decent domestic influence; and wholly because it acts only from custom and habit, not from decided theological and moral principles. Incidentally, it gives people a false sense of security in leading them to believe that books which are *not* suppressed are harmless. Whether there *is* such a thing as a harmless book I am not sure: but there very likely are books so utterly unreadable as to be incapable of injuring anybody. But it is certain that a book is not harmless merely because no one is consciously offended by it. And if we, as readers, keep our religious and moral convictions in one compartment, and take our reading merely for entertainment, or on a higher plane, for aesthetic pleasure, I would point out that the author, whatever his conscious intentions in writing, in practice recognizes no such distinctions. The author of a work of imagination is trying to affect us wholly, as human beings, whether he knows it or not; and we are affected by it, as human beings, whether we intend to be or not. I suppose that everything we eat has some other effect upon us than merely the pleasure of taste and mastication; it affects us during the process of assimilation and digestion; and I believe that exactly the same is true of anything we read.

The fact that what we read does not concern merely something called our *literary taste,* but that it affects directly, though only amongst many other influences, the whole of what we are, is best elicited, I think, by a conscientious examination of the history of our individual literary education. Consider the adolescent reading of any person with some literary sensibility. Everyone, I believe, who is at all sensible to the seductions of poetry, can remember some moment in youth when he or she was completely carried away by the work of one poet. Very likely he was carried away by several poets, one after the other. The reason for this passing infatuation is not merely that our sensibility to poetry is keener in adolescence than in maturity. What happens is a kind of inundation, of invasion of the undeveloped personality by the stronger personality of the poet. The same thing may happen at a later age to persons who have not done much reading. One author takes complete possession of us for a time; then another; and finally they begin to affect each other in our mind. We weigh one against another; we see that each has qualities absent from others, and qualities incompatible with the qualities of others: we begin to be, in fact, critical; and it is our growing critical power which protects us from excessive possession by any one literary personality. The good critic—and we should all try to be critics, and not leave criticism to the fellows who write reviews in the papers—is the man who, to

3. "Here and later I am indebted to Montgomery Belgion. *The Human Parrot* (chapter on The Irresponsible Propagandist)" [E].

a keen and abiding sensibility, joins wide and increasingly discriminating reading. Wide reading is not valuable as a kind of hoarding, an accumulation of knowledge, or what sometimes is meant by the term "a well-stocked mind." It is valuable because in the process of being affected by one powerful personality after another, we cease to be dominated by any one, or by any small number. The very different views of life, cohabiting in our minds, affect each other, and our own personality asserts itself and gives each a place in some arrangement peculiar to ourself.

It is simply not true that works of fiction, prose or verse, that is to say works depicting the actions, thoughts and words and passions of imaginary human beings, *directly* extend our knowledge of life. Direct knowledge of life is knowledge directly in relation to ourselves, it is our knowledge of *how* people behave in general, of *what* they are like in general, in so far as that part of life in which we ourselves have participated gives us material for generalization. Knowledge of life obtained through fiction is only possible by another stage of self-consciousness. That is to say, it can only be a knowledge of other people's knowledge of life, not of life itself. So far as we are taken up with the happenings in any novel in the same way in which we are taken up with what happens under our eyes, we are acquiring at least as much falsehood as truth. But when we are developed enough to say: "This is the view of life of a person who was a good observer within his limits, Dickens, or Thackeray, or George Eliot, or Balzac; but he looked at it in a different way from me, because he was a different man; he even selected rather different things to look at, or the same things in a different order of importance, because he was a different man; so what I am looking at is the world as seen by a particular mind"—then we are in a position to gain something from reading fiction. We are learning *something* about life from these authors direct, just as we learn something from the reading of history direct; but these authors are only really helping us when we can see, and allow for, their differences from ourselves.

Now what we get, as we gradually grow up and read more and more, and read a greater diversity of authors, is a variety of views of life. But what people commonly assume, I suspect, is that we gain this experience of other men's views of life only by "improving reading." This, it is supposed, is a reward we get by applying ourselves to Shakespeare, and Dante, and Goethe, and Emerson, and Carlyle, and dozens of other respectable writers.

The rest of our reading for amusement is merely killing time. But I incline to come to the alarming conclusion that it is just the literature that we read for "amusement," or "purely for pleasure" that may have the greatest and least suspected influence upon us. It is the literature which we read with the least effort that can have the easiest and most insidious influence upon us. Hence it is that the influence of popular novelists, and of popular plays of contemporary life, requires to be scrutinized most closely. And it is chiefly *contemporary* literature that the majority of people ever read in this attitude of "purely for pleasure," of pure passivity.

The relation to my subject of what I have been saying should now be a little more apparent. Though we may read literature merely for pleasure, of "entertainment" or of "aesthetic enjoyment," this reading never affects simply a sort of special sense: it affects us as entire human beings; it affects our moral and religious existence. And I say that while individual modern writers of eminence can be improving, contemporary literature as a whole tends to be degrading. And that even the effect of the better writers, in an age like ours, may be degrading to some readers; for we must remember that what a writer does to people is not necessarily what he intends to do. It may be only what people are capable of having done to them. People exercise an unconscious selection in being influenced. A writer like D. H. Lawrence may be in his effect either beneficial or pernicious. I am not sure that I have not had some pernicious influence myself.

At this point I anticipate a rejoinder from the liberal-minded, from all those who are convinced that if everybody says what he thinks, and does what he likes, things will somehow, by some automatic compensation and adjustment, come right in the end. "Let everything be tried," they say, "and if it is a mistake, then we shall learn by experience." This argument might have some value, if we were always the same generation upon earth; or if, as we know to be not the case, people ever learned much from the experience of their elders. These liberals are convinced that only by what is called unrestrained individualism will truth ever emerge. Ideas, views of life, they think, issue distinct from independent heads, and in consequence of their knocking violently against each other, the fittest survive, and truth rises triumphant. Anyone who dissents from this view must be either a mediaevalist, wishful only to set back the clock, or else a fascist, and probably both.

If the mass of contemporary authors were

really individualists, every one of them inspired Blakes, each with his separate vision, and if the mass of the contemporary public were really a mass of *individuals* there might be something to be said for this attitude. But this is not, and never has been, and never will be. It is not only that the reading individual today (or at any day) is not enough an individual to be able to absorb all the "views of life" of all the authors pressed upon us by the publishers' advertisements and the reviewers, and to be able to arrive at wisdom by considering one against another. It is that the contemporary authors are not individuals enough either. It is not that the world of separate individuals of the liberal democrat is undesirable; it is simply that this world does not exist. For the reader of contemporary literature is not, like the reader of the established great literature of all time, exposing himself to the influence of divers and contradictory personalities; he is exposing himself to a mass movement of writers who, each of them, think that they have something individually to offer, but are really all working together in the same direction. And there never was a time, I believe, when the reading public was so large, or so helplessly exposed to the influences of its own time. There never was a time, I believe, when those who read at all, read so many more books by living authors than books by dead authors; there never was a time so completely parochial, so shut off from the past. There may be too many publishers; there are certainly too many books published; and the journals ever incite the reader to "keep up" with what is being published. Individualistic democracy has come to high tide: and it is more difficult today to be an individual than it ever was before.

Within itself, modern literature has perfectly valid distinctions of good and bad, better and worse: and I do not wish to suggest that I confound Mr. Bernard Shaw with Mr. Noel Coward, Mrs. Woolf with Miss Mannin. On the other hand, I should like it to be clear that I am not defending a "high"-brow against a "low"-brow literature. What I do wish to affirm is that the whole of modern literature is corrupted by what I call Secularism, that it is simply unaware of, simply cannot understand the meaning of, the primacy of the supernatural over the natural life: of something which I assume to be our primary concern.

I do not want to give the impression that I have delivered a mere fretful jeremiad against contemporary literature. Assuming a common attitude between my readers, or some of my readers, and myself, the question is not so much, what is to be done about it? as, how should we behave towards it?

I have suggested that the liberal attitude towards literature will not work. Even if the writers who make their attempt to impose their "view of life" upon us were really distinct individuals, even if we as readers were distinct individuals, what would be the result? It would be, surely, that each reader would be impressed, in his reading, merely by what he was previously prepared to be impressed by; he would follow the "line of least resistance," and there would be no assurance that he would be made a better man. For literary judgement we need to be acutely aware of two things at once: of "what we like," and of "what we *ought* to like." Few people are honest enough to know either. The first means knowing what we really feel: very few know that. The second involves understanding our shortcomings; for we do not really know what we ought to like unless we also know why we ought to like it, which involves knowing why we don't yet like it. It is not enough to understand what we ought to be, unless we know what we are; and we do not understand what we are, unless we know what we ought to be. The two forms of self-consciousness, knowing what we are and what we ought to be, must go together.

It is our business, as readers of literature, to know what we like. It is our business, as Christians, *as well as* readers of literature, to know what we ought to like. It is our business as honest men not to assume that whatever we like is what we ought to like; and it is our business as honest Christians not to assume that we do like what we ought to like. And the last thing I would wish for would be the existence of two literatures, one for Christian consumption and the other for the pagan world. What I believe to be incumbent upon all Christians is the duty of maintaining consciously certain standards and criteria of criticism over and above those applied by the rest of the world; and that by these criteria and standards everything that we read must be tested. We must remember that the greater part of our current reading matter is written for us by people who have no real belief in a supernatural order, though some of it may be written by people with individual notions of a supernatural order which are not ours. And the greater part of our reading matter is coming to be written by people who not only have no such belief, but are even ignorant of the fact that there are still people in the world so "backward" or so "eccentric" as to continue to believe. So long as we are conscious of the gulf fixed between ourselves and the greater part of contemporary literature, we are more or less protected from being harmed by it, and are in a position to extract from it what good it has to offer us.

There are a very large number of people in the world today who believe that all ills are fundamentally economic. Some believe that various specific economic changes alone would be enough to set the world right; others demand more or less drastic changes in the social as well, changes chiefly of two opposed types. These changes demanded, and in some places carried out, are alike in one respect, that they hold the assumptions of what I call Secularism: they concern themselves only with changes of a temporal, material, and external nature; they concern themselves with morals only of a collective nature. In an exposition of one such new faith I read the following words:

"In our morality the one single test of any moral question is whether it impedes or destroys in any way the power of the individual to serve the State. [The individual] must answer the questions: 'Does this action injure the nation? Does it injure other members of the nation? Does it injure my ability to serve the nation?' And if the answer is clear on all those questions, the individual has absolute liberty to do as he will."

Now I do not deny that this is a kind of morality, and that it is capable of great good within limits; but I think that we should all repudiate a morality which had no higher ideal to set before us than that. It represents, of course, one of the violent reactions we are witnessing, against the view that the community is solely for the benefit of the individual; but it is equally a gospel of this world, and of this world alone. My complaint against modern literature is of the same kind. It is not that modern literature is in the ordinary sense "immoral" or even "amoral"; and in any case to prefer that charge would not be enough. It is simply that it repudiates, or is wholly ignorant of, our most fundamental and important beliefs; and that in consequence its tendency is to encourage its readers to get what they can out of life while it lasts, to miss no "experience" that presents itself, and to sacrifice themselves, if they make any sacrifice at all, only for the sake of tangible benefits to others in this world either now or in the future. We shall certainly continue to read the best of its kind, of what our time provides; but we must tirelessly criticize it according to our own principles, and not merely according to the principles admitted by the writers and by the critics who discuss it in the public press.

MILTON
I and II [1936, 1947]

◇

⟨ WHEN the second of these two essays appeared, there was something of an academic and a little of a critical storm because to many it seemed a repudiation of the heretical position taken in the first essay. There were some who rejoiced to welcome back the lost sheep, and some who were dismayed at an assumption of conformity. The reader who examines both these essays will see that the second develops out of the first, and that if there is any change it is the change of amelioration and strengthening. Eliot's whole subject was the poet's care and cure of the language. The reader has only to compare the last sentences of each essay. I would suppose that the two essays taken together afford us an excellent example of Eliot's idea of tradition and the individual talent.

◇

MILTON I [1]

WHILE it must be admitted that Milton is a very great poet indeed, it is something of a puzzle to decide in what his greatness consists. On analysis, the marks against him appear both more numerous and more significant than the marks to his credit. As a man, he is antipathetic. Either from the moralist's point of view, or from the theologian's point of view, or from the psychologist's point of view, or from that of the political philosopher, or judging by the ordinary standards of likeableness in human beings, Milton is unsatisfactory. The doubts which I have to express about him are more serious than these. His greatness as a poet has been sufficiently celebrated, though I think largely for the wrong reasons, and without the proper reservations. His misdeeds as a poet have been called attention to, as by Mr. Ezra Pound, but usually in passing. What seems to me necessary is to assert at the same time his greatness—in that what he could do well he did better than anyone else has ever done—and the serious charges to be made against him, in respect of the deterioration—the peculiar kind of deterioration—to which he subjected the language.

Many people will agree that a man may be a great artist, and yet have a bad influence. There is

MILTON I.   1. Contributed to *Essays and Studies* of The English Association, Oxford University Press, 1936.

more of Milton's influence in the badness of the bad verse of the eighteenth century than of anybody's else: he certainly did more harm than Dryden and Pope, and perhaps a good deal of the obloquy which has fallen on these two poets, especially the latter, because of their influence, ought to be transferred to Milton. But to put the matter simply in terms of 'bad influence' is not necessarily to bring a serious charge: because a good deal of the responsibility, when we state the problem in these terms, may devolve on the eighteenth-century poets themselves for being such bad poets that they were incapable of being influenced except for ill. There is a good deal more to the charge against Milton than this; and it appears a good deal more serious if we affirm that Milton's poetry could *only* be an influence for the worse, upon any poet whatever. It is more serious, also, if we affirm that Milton's bad influence may be traced much farther than the eighteenth century, and much farther than upon bad poets: if we say that it was an influence against which we still have to struggle.

There is a large class of persons, including some who appear in print as critics, who regard any censure upon a 'great' poet as a breach of the peace, as an act of wanton iconoclasm, or even hoodlumism. The kind of derogatory criticism that I have to make upon Milton is not intended for such persons, who cannot understand that it is more important, in some vital respects, to be a *good* poet than to be a *great* poet; and of what I have to say I consider that the only jury of judgment is that of the ablest poetical practitioners of my own time.

The most important fact about Milton, for my purpose, is his blindness. I do not mean that to go blind in middle life is itself enough to determine the whole nature of a man's poetry. Blindness must be considered in conjunction with Milton's personality and character, and the peculiar education which he received. It must also be considered in connexion with his devotion to, and expertness in, the art of music. Had Milton been a man of very keen senses—I mean of *all* the five senses—his blindness would not have mattered so much. But for a man whose sensuousness, such as it was, had been withered early by book-learning, and whose gifts were naturally aural, it mattered a great deal. It would seem, indeed, to have helped him to concentrate on what he could do best.

At no period is the visual imagination conspicuous in Milton's poetry. It would be as well to have a few illustrations of what I mean by visual imagination. From *Macbeth:*

> This guest of summer,
> The temple-haunting martlet, does approve
> By his loved mansionry that the heaven's breath
> Smells wooingly here: no jutty, frieze,
> Buttress, nor coign of vantage, but this bird
> Hath made his pendent bed and procreant cradle:
> Where they most breed and haunt, I have observed
> The air is delicate.

It may be observed that such an image, as well as another familiar quotation from a little later in the same play,

> Light thickens, and the crow
> Makes wing to the rooky wood

not only offer something to the eye, but, so to speak, to the common sense. I mean that they convey the feeling of being in a particular place at a particular time. The comparison with Shakespeare offers another indication of the peculiarity of Milton. With Shakespeare, far more than with any other poet in English, the combinations of words offer perpetual novelty; they enlarge the meaning of the individual words joined: thus 'procreant cradle,' 'rooky wood.' In comparison, Milton's images do not give this sense of particularity, nor are the separate words developed in significance. His language is, if one may use the term without disparagement, *artificial* and *conventional*.

> O'er the smooth enamel'd green . . .

> . . . paths of this drear wood
> The nodding horror of whose shady brows
> Threats the forlorn and wandering passenger.

['Shady brow' here is a diminution of the value of the two words from their use in the line from *Dr. Faustus*

> Shadowing more beauty in their airy brows.]

The imagery in *L'Allegro* and *Il Penseroso* is all general:

> While the ploughman near at hand,
> Whistles o'er the furrowed land,
> And the milkmaid singeth blithe,
> And the mower whets his scythe,
> And every shepherd tells his tale,
> Under the hawthorn in the dale.

It is not a particular ploughman, milkmaid, and shepherd that Milton sees [as Wordsworth might see them]; the sensuous effect of these verses is entirely on the ear, and is joined to the concepts of ploughman, milkmaid, and shepherd. Even in his most mature work, Milton does not infuse new life into the word, as Shakespeare does.

The sun to me is dark
And silent as the moon,
When she deserts the night
Hid in her vacant interlunar cave.

Here *interlunar* is certainly a stroke of genius, but is merely combined with 'vacant' and 'cave,' rather than giving and receiving life from them. Thus it is not so unfair, as it might at first appear, to say that Milton writes English like a dead language. The criticism has been made with regard to his involved syntax. But a tortuous style, when its peculiarity is aimed at precision [as with Henry James], is not necessarily a dead one; only when the complication is dictated by a demand of verbal music, instead of by any demand of sense.

Thrones, dominations, princedoms, virtues, powers,
If these magnific titles yet remain
Not merely titular, since by decree
Another now hath to himself engrossed
All power, and us eclipsed under the name
Of King anointed, for whom all this haste
Of midnight march, and hurried meeting here,
This only to consult how we may best
With what may be devised of honours new
Receive him coming to receive from us
Knee-tribute yet unpaid, prostration vile,
Too much to one, but double how endured,
To one and to his image now proclaimed?

With which compare:

'However, he didn't mind thinking that if Cissy should prove all that was likely enough their having a subject in common couldn't but practically conduce; though the moral of it all amounted rather to a portent, the one that Haughty, by the same token, had done least to reassure him against, of the extent to which the native jungle harboured the female specimen and to which its ostensible cover, the vast level of mixed growths stirred wavingly in whatever breeze, was apt to be identifiable but as an agitation of the latest redundant thing in ladies' hats.'

This quotation, taken almost at random from *The Ivory Tower,* is not intended to represent Henry James at any hypothetical 'best,' any more than the noble passage from *Paradise Lost* is meant to be Milton's hypothetical worst. The question is the difference of intention, in the elaboration of styles both of which depart so far from lucid simplicity. The sound, of course, is never irrelevant, and the style of James certainly depends for its effect a good deal on the sound of a voice, James's own, painfully explaining. But the complication, with James, is due to a determination not to simplify, and in that simplification lose any of the real intricacies and by-paths of mental movement; whereas the complication of a Miltonic sentence is an active complication, a complication deliberately introduced into what was a previously simplified and abstract thought. The dark angel here is not *thinking* or conversing, but making a speech carefully prepared for him; and the arrangement is for the sake of musical value, not for significance. A straightforward utterance, as of a Homeric or Dantesque character, would make the speaker very much more real to us; but reality is no part of the intention. We have in fact to read such a passage not analytically, to get the poetic impression. I am not suggesting that Milton has no idea to convey which he regards as important: only that the syntax is determined by the musical significance, by the auditory imagination, rather than by the attempt to follow actual speech or thought. It is at least more nearly possible to distinguish the pleasure which arises from the *noise,* from the pleasure due to other elements, than with the verse of Shakespeare, in which the auditory imagination and the imagination of the other senses are more nearly fused, and fused together with the thought. The result with Milton is, in one sense of the word, *rhetoric.* That term is not intended to be derogatory. This kind of 'rhetoric' is not necessarily bad in its influence; but it may be considered bad in relation to the historical life of a language as a whole. I have said elsewhere that the living English which was Shakespeare's became split up into two components one of which was exploited by Milton and the other by Dryden. Of the two, I still think Dryden's development the healthier, because it was Dryden who preserved, so far as it was preserved at all, the tradition of conversational language in poetry: and I might add that it seems to me easier to get back to healthy language from Dryden that it is to get back to it from Milton. For what such a generalization is worth, Milton's influence on the eighteenth century was much more deplorable than Dryden's.

If several very important reservations and exceptions are made, I think that it is not unprofitable to compare Milton's development with that of James Joyce. The initial similarities are musical taste and abilities, followed by musical training, wide and curious knowledge, gift for acquiring languages, and remarkable powers of memory perhaps fortified by defective vision. The important difference is that Joyce's imagination is not naturally of so purely auditory a type as Milton's. In his early work, and at least in part of *Ulysses,* there is visual and other imagination of the highest kind; and I may be mistaken in thinking that the later part of *Ulysses* shows a turning from the visible world to draw rather on the resources of phantasmagoria. In any case, one may suppose that the replenishment of visual imagery during later years has been insufficient; so that what I find in *Work in Progress* is an auditory imagination abnormally sharpened at the expense of the visual. There is still a little to be seen, and what there is to see is worth looking at. And I would repeat that with Joyce this development seems to me largely due to circumstances: whereas Milton may be said never to have seen anything. For Milton, therefore, the concentration on sound was wholly a benefit. Indeed, I find, in reading *Paradise Lost,* that I am happiest where there is least to visualize. The eye is not shocked in his twilit Hell as it is in the Garden of Eden, where I for one can get pleasure from the verse only by the deliberate effort not to visualize Adam and Eve and their surroundings.

I am not suggesting any close parallel between the 'rhetoric' of Milton and the later style of Joyce. It is a different music; and Joyce always maintains some contact with the conversational tone. But it may prove to be equally a blind alley for the future development of the language.

A disadvantage of the rhetorical style appears to be, that a dislocation takes place, through the hypertrophy of the auditory imagination at the expense of the visual and tactile, so that the inner meaning is separated from the surface, and tends to become something occult, or at least without effect upon the reader until fully understood. To extract everything possible from *Paradise Lost,* it would seem necessary to read it in two different ways, first solely for the sound, and second for the sense. The full beauty of his long periods can hardly be enjoyed while we are wrestling with the meaning as well; and for the pleasure of the ear the meaning is hardly necessary, except in so far as certain key-words indicate the emotional tone of the passage. Now Shakespeare, or Dante, will bear innumerable readings, but at each reading all the elements of appreciation can be present. There is no interruption between the surface that these poets present to you and the core. While therefore, I cannot pretend to have penetrated to any 'secret' of these poets, I feel that such appreciation of their work as I am capable of points in the right direction; whereas I cannot feel that my appreciation of Milton leads anywhere outside of the mazes of sound. That, I feel, would be the matter for a separate study, like that of Blake's prophetic books; it might be well worth the trouble, but would have little to do with my interest in the poetry. So far as I perceive anything, it is a glimpse of a theology that I find in large part repellent, expressed through a my-

thology which would have better been left in the Book of *Genesis,* upon which Milton has not improved. There seems to me to be a division, in Milton, between the philosopher or theologian and the poet; and, for the latter, I suspect also that this concentration upon the auditory imagination leads to at least an occasional levity. I can enjoy the roll of

> . . . Cambula, seat of Cathaian Can
> And Samarchand by Oxus, Temir's throne,
> To Paquin of Sinaean kings, and thence
> To Agra and Lahor of great Mogul
> Down to the golden Chersonese, or where
> The Persian in Ecbatan sate, or since
> In Hispahan, or where the Russian Ksar
> On Mosco, or the Sultan in Bizance,
> Turchestan-born . . . ,

and the rest of it, but I feel that this is not serious poetry, not poetry fully occupied about its business, but rather a solemn game. More often, admittedly, Milton uses proper names in moderation, to obtain the same effect of magnificence with them as does Marlowe—nowhere perhaps better than in the passage from *Lycidas:*

> Whether beyond the stormy Hebrides,
> Where thou perhaps under the whelming tide
> Visit'st the bottom of the monstrous world;
> Or whether thou to our moist vows deny'd
> Sleep'st by the fable of Bellerus old,
> Where the great vision of the guarded Mount
> Looks toward Namancos and Bayona's hold . . .

than which for the single effect of grandeur of sound, there is nothing finer in poetry.

I make no attempt to appraise the 'greatness' of Milton in relation to poets who seem to me more comprehensive and better balanced; it has seemed to me more fruitful for the present to press the parallel between *Paradise Lost* and *Work in Progress;* and both Milton and Joyce are so exalted in their own kinds, in the whole of literature, that the only writers with whom to compare them are writers who have attempted something very different. Our views about Joyce, in any case, must remain at the present time tentative. But there are two attitudes both of which are necessary and right to adopt in considering the work of any poet. One is when we isolate him, when we try to understand the rules of his own game, adopt his own point of view: the other, perhaps less usual, is when we measure him by outside standards, most pertinently by the standards of language and of something called Poetry, in our own language and in the whole history of European literature. It is from the second point of view that my objections to Milton are made: it is from this point of view that we can go so far as to say that, although his work realizes superbly one important element in poetry, he may still be considered as having done damage to the English language from which it has not wholly recovered.

1936

MILTON II [1]

SAMUEL JOHNSON, addressing himself to examine Milton's versification, in the *Rambler* of Saturday, January 12, 1751, thought it necessary to excuse his temerity in writing upon a subject already so fully discussed. In justification of his essay this great critic and poet remarked: 'There are, in every age, new errors to be rectified, and new prejudices to be opposed.' I am obliged to phrase my own apology rather differently. The errors of our own times have been rectified by vigorous hands, and the prejudices opposed by commanding voices. Some of the errors and prejudices have been associated with my own name, and of these in particular I shall find myself impelled to speak; it will, I hope, be attributed to me for modesty rather than for conceit if I maintain that no one can correct an error with better authority than the person who has been held responsible for it. And there is, I think, another justification for my speaking about Milton, besides the singular one which I have just given. The champions of Milton in our time, with one notable exception, have been scholars and teachers. I have no claim to be either: I am aware that my only claim upon your attention, in speaking of Milton or of any other great poet, is by appeal to your curiosity, in the hope that you may care to know what a contemporary writer of verse thinks of one of his predecessors.

I believe that the scholar and the practitioner in the field of literary criticism should supplement each other's work. The criticism of the practitioner will be all the better, certainly, if he is not wholly destitute of scholarship; and the criticism of the scholar will be all the better if he has some experience of the difficulties of writing verse. But the orientation of the two critics is different. The scholar is more concerned with the understanding of the masterpiece in the environment of its author: with the world in which that author lived, the temper of his age, his intellectual formation, the books which he had read, and the influences which had moulded him. The practitioner is concerned less with the author than with the poem;

MILTON II.   1. The Henrietta Hertz Lecture, delivered to the British Academy, 1947, and subsequently at the Frick Museum, New York.

and with the poem in relation to his own age. He asks: Of what *use* is the poetry of this poet to poets writing to-day? Is it, or can it become, a living force in English poetry still unwritten? So we may say that the scholar's interest is in the permanent, the practitioner's in the immediate. The scholar can teach us where we should bestow our *admiration* and *respect:* the practitioner should be able, when he is the right poet talking about the right poet, to make an old masterpiece actual, give it contemporary importance, and persuade his audience that it is interesting, exciting, enjoyable, and *active.* I can give only one example of contemporary criticism of Milton, by a critic of the type to which I belong if I have any critical pretensions at all: that is the Introduction to Milton's *English Poems* in the 'World Classics' series, by the late Charles Williams. It is not a comprehensive essay; it is notable primarily because it provides the best prolegomenon to *Comus* which any modern reader could have; but what distinguishes it throughout [and the same is true of most of Williams's critical writing] is the author's warmth of feeling and his success in communicating it to the reader. In this, so far as I am aware, the essay of Williams is a solitary example.

I think it is useful, in such an examination as I propose to make, to keep in mind some critic of the past, of one's own type, by whom to measure one's opinions: a critic sufficiently remote in time, for his local errors and prejudices to be not identical with one's own. That is why I began by quoting Samuel Johnson. It will hardly be contested that as a critic of poetry Johnson wrote as a practitioner and not as a scholar. Because he was a poet himself, and a good poet, what he wrote about poetry must be read with respect. And unless we know and appreciate Johnson's poetry we cannot judge either the merits or the limitations of his criticism. It is a pity that what the common reader to-day has read, or has remembered, or has seen quoted, are mostly those few statements of Johnson's from which later critics have vehemently dissented. But when Johnson held an opinion which seems to us wrong, we are never safe in dismissing it without inquiring why he was wrong; he had his own 'errors and prejudices,' certainly, but for lack of examining them sympathetically we are always in danger of merely countering error with error and prejudice with prejudice. Now Johnson was, in his day, very much a modern: he was concerned with how poetry should be written in his own time. The fact that he came towards the end, rather than the beginning of a style, the fact that his time was rapidly passing away, and that the canons of taste which he observed were about to fall into desuetude, does not diminish the interest of his criticism. Nor does the likelihood that the development of poetry in the next fifty years will take quite different directions from those which to me seem desirable to explore, deter me from asking the questions that Johnson implied: How should poetry be written now? and what place does the answer to this question give to Milton? And I think that the answers to these questions may be different now from the answers that were correct twenty-five years ago.

There is one prejudice against Milton, apparent on almost every page of Johnson's *Life of Milton,* which I imagine is still general: we, however, with a longer historical perspective, are in a better position than was Johnson to recognize it and to make allowance for it. This is a prejudice which I share myself: an antipathy towards Milton the man. Of this in itself I have nothing further to say: all that is necessary is to record one's awareness of it. But this prejudice is often involved with another, more obscure: and I do not think that Johnson had disengaged the two in his own mind. The fact is simply that the Civil War of the seventeenth century, in which Milton is a symbolic figure, has never been concluded. The Civil War is not ended: I question whether any serious civil war ever does end. Throughout that period English society was so convulsed and divided that the effects are still felt. Reading Johnson's essay one is always aware that Johnson was obstinately and passionately of another party. No other English poet, not Wordsworth, or Shelley, lived through or took sides in such momentous events as did Milton; of no other poet is it so difficult to consider the poetry simply as poetry, without our theological and political dispositions, conscious and unconscious, inherited or acquired, making an unlawful entry. And the danger is all the greater because these emotions now take different vestures. It is now considered grotesque, on political grounds, to be of the party of King Charles; it is now, I believe, considered equally grotesque, on moral grounds, to be of the party of the Puritans; and to most persons to-day the religious views of both parties may seem equally remote. Nevertheless, the passions are unquenched, and if we are not very wide awake their smoke will obscure the glass through which we examine Milton's poetry. Something has been done, certainly, to persuade us that Milton was never really of any party, but disagreed with everyone. Mr. Wilson Knight, in *Chariot of Wrath,* has argued that Milton was more a monarchist than a republican, and not in any modern sense a 'democrat,' and Professor Saurat has produced evidence to show that Mil-

ton's theology was highly eccentric, and as scandalous to Protestants as to Catholics—that he was, in fact, a sort of Christadelphian, and perhaps not a very orthodox Christadelphian at that; while on the other hand Mr. C. S. Lewis has opposed Professor Saurat by skilfully arguing that Milton, at least in *Paradise Lost,* can be acquitted of heresy even from a point of view so orthodox as that of Mr. Lewis himself. On these questions I hold no opinion: it is probably beneficial to question the assumption that Milton was a sound Free Churchman and member of the Liberal Party; but I think that we still have to be on guard against an unconscious partisanship if we aim to attend to the poetry for the poetry's sake.

So much for our prejudices. I come next to the positive objection to Milton which has been raised in our own time, that is to say, the charge that he is an unwholesome influence. And from this I shall proceed to the permanent strictures of reproof [to employ a phrase of Johnson's] and, finally, to the grounds on which I consider him a great poet and one whom poets to-day might study with profit.

For a statement of the *generalized* belief in the unwholesomeness of Milton's influence I turn to Mr. Middleton Murry's critique of Milton in his *Heaven and Earth*—a book which contains chapters of profound insight, interrupted by passages which seem to me intemperate. Mr. Murry approaches Milton after his long and patient study of Keats; and it is through the eyes of Keats that he sees Milton.

'Keats [*Mr. Murry writes*] as a poetic artist, second to none since Shakespeare, and Blake, as a prophet of spiritual values unique in our history, both passed substantially the same judgement on Milton: "Life to him would be death to me." And whatever may be our verdict on the development of English poetry since Milton, we must admit the justice of Keats's opinion that Milton's magnificence led nowhere. "English must be kept up," said Keats. To be influenced beyond a certain point by Milton's art, he felt, dammed the creative flow of the English genius in and through itself. In saying this, I think, Keats voiced the very inmost of the English genius. To pass under the spell of Milton is to be condemned to imitate him. It is quite different with Shakespeare. Shakespeare baffles and liberates; Milton is perspicuous and constricts.'

This is a very confident affirmation, and I criticize it with some diffidence because I cannot pretend to have devoted as much study to Keats, or to have as intimate an understanding of his difficulties, as Mr. Murry. But Mr. Murry seems to me here to be trying to transform the predicament of a particular poet with a particular aim at a particular moment in time into a censure of timeless validity. He appears to assert that the liberative function of Shakespeare and the constrictive menace of Milton are permanent characteristics of these two poets. 'To be influenced beyond a certain point' by any one master is bad for any poet; and it does not matter whether that influence is Milton's or another's; and as we cannot anticipate where that point will come, we might be better advised to call it an *un*certain point. If it is not good to remain under the spell of Milton, is it good to remain under the spell of Shakespeare? It depends partly upon what *genre* of poetry you are trying to develop. Keats wanted to write an epic, and he found, as might be expected, that the time had not arrived at which another English epic, comparable in grandeur to *Paradise Lost,* could be written. He also tried his hand at writing plays: and one might argue that *King Stephen* was more blighted by Shakespeare than *Hyperion* by Milton. Certainly, *Hyperion* remains a magnificent fragment which one rereads; and *King Stephen* is a play which we may have read once, but to which we never return for enjoyment. Milton made a great epic impossible for succeeding generations; Shakespeare made a great poetic drama impossible; such a situation is inevitable; and it persists until the language has so altered that there is no danger, because no possibility, of imitation. Anyone who tries to write poetic drama, even to-day, should know that half of his energy must be exhausted in the effort to escape from the constricting toils of Shakespeare: the moment his attention is relaxed, or his mind fatigued, he will lapse into bad Shakespearian verse. For a long time after an epic poet like Milton, or a dramatic poet like Shakespeare, nothing can be done. Yet the effort must be repeatedly made; for we can never know in advance when the moment is approaching at which a new epic, or a new drama, will be possible; and when the moment does draw near it may be that the genius of an individual poet will perform the last mutation of idiom and versification which will bring that new poetry into being.

I have referred to Mr. Murry's view of the bad influence of Milton as generalized, because it is implicitly the whole personality of Milton that is in question: not specifically his beliefs, or his language or versification, but the beliefs as realized in that particular personality, and his poetry as the expression of it. By the *particular* view of Milton's influence as bad, I mean that view which attends to the language, the syntax, the versification, the imagery. I do not suggest that there is here a complete difference of subject matter: it is the difference of approach, the difference of the focus of interest, between the philosophical critic and the literary critic. An incapacity for the abstruse, and an interest in poetry which is primarily a technical interest, dispose my mind towards the more limited and perhaps more superficial task. Let us proceed to look at Milton's influence from this point of view, that of the writer of poetry in our own time.

The reproach against Milton, that his technical influence has been bad, appears to have been made by no one more positively than by myself. I find myself saying, as recently as 1936, that this charge against Milton 'appears a good deal more serious if we affirm that Milton's poetry could *only* be an influence for the worse, upon any poet whatever. It is more serious, also, if we affirm that Milton's bad influence may be traced much farther than the eighteenth century, and much farther than upon bad poets: if we say that it was an influence against which we still have to struggle.'

In writing these sentences I failed to draw a threefold distinction, which now seems to me of some importance. There are three separate assertions implied. The first is, that an influence has been bad in the past: this is to assert that good poets, in the eighteenth or nineteenth century, would have written better if they had not submitted themselves to the influence of Milton. The second assertion is, that the contemporary situation is such that Milton is a master whom we should avoid. The third is, that the influence of Milton, or of any particular poet, can be *always* bad, and that we can predict that wherever it is found at any time in the future, however remote, it will be a bad influence. Now, the first and third of these assertions I am no longer prepared to make, because, detached from the second, they do not appear to me to have any meaning.

For the first, when we consider one great poet of the past, and one or more other poets, upon whom we say he has exerted a bad influence, we must admit that the responsibility, if there be any, is rather with the poets who were influenced than with the poet whose work exerted the influence. We can, of course, show that certain tricks or mannerisms which the imitators display are due to conscious or unconscious imitation and emulation, but that is a reproach against their injudicious choice of a model and not against their model itself. And we can never prove that any particular poet would have written better poetry if he had escaped that influence. Even if we assert, what can only be a matter of faith, that Keats would have written a very great epic poem if Milton had not preceded him, is it sensible to pine for an unwritten masterpiece, in exchange for one which we possess and acknowledge? And as for the remote future, what can we affirm about the poetry that will be written then, except that we should probably be unable to understand or to enjoy it, and that therefore we can hold no opinion as to what 'good' and 'bad' influences will *mean* in that future? The only relation in which the question of influence, good and bad, is significant, is the relation to the immediate future. With that question I shall engage at the end. I wish first to mention another reproach against Milton, that represented by the phrase 'dissociation of sensibility.'

I remarked many years ago, in an essay on Dryden, that:

'In the seventeenth century a dissociation of sensibility set in, from which we have never recovered; and this dissociation, as is natural, was due to the influence of the two most powerful poets of the century, Milton and Dryden.'

The longer passage from which this sentence is taken is quoted by Dr. Tillyard in his *Milton.* Dr. Tillyard makes the following comment:

'Speaking only of what in this passage concerns Milton, I would say that there is here a mixture of truth and falsehood. Some sort of dissociation of sensibility in Milton, not necessarily undesirable, has to be admitted; but that he was responsible for any such dissociation in others [at least till this general dissociation had inevitably set in] is untrue.'

I believe that the general affirmation represented by the phrase 'dissociation of sensibility' [one of the two or three phrases of my coinage— like 'objective correlative'—which have had a success in the world astonishing to their author] retains some validity; but I now incline to agree with Dr. Tillyard that to lay the burden on the shoulders of Milton and Dryden was a mistake. If such a dissociation did take place, I suspect that the causes are too complex and too profound to justify our accounting for the change in terms of literary criticism. All we can say is, that something like this did happen; that it had something to do with the Civil War; that it would even be unwise to say it was caused by the Civil War, but that it is a consequence of the same causes which brought about the Civil War; that we must seek the causes in Europe, not in England alone; and for what these causes were, we may dig and dig until we get to a depth at which words and concepts fail us.

Before proceeding to take up the case against Milton, as it stood for poets twenty-five years ago —the second, and only significant meaning of 'bad influence'—I think it would be best to consider what permanent strictures of reproof may be drawn: those censures which, when we make them, we must assume to be made by enduring laws of taste. The essence of the permanent censure of Milton is, I believe, to be found in Johnson's essay. This is not the place in which to examine certain particular and erroneous judgments of Johnson; to explain his condemnation of *Comus* and *Samson* as the application of dramatic canons which to us seem inapplicable; or to condone his dismissal of the versification of *Lycidas* by the specialization, rather than the absence, of his sense of rhythm. Johnson's most important censure of Milton is contained in three paragraphs, which I must ask leave to quote in full.

'Throughout all his greater works [*says Johnson*] there prevails an uniform peculiarity of *diction,* a mode and cast of expression which bears little resemblance to that of any former writer; and which is so far removed from common use, that an unlearned reader, when he first opens the book, finds himself surprised by a new language.

'This novelty has been, by those who can find nothing wrong with Milton, imputed to his laborious endeavours after words suited to the grandeur of his ideas. *Our language,* says Addison, *sunk under him.* But the truth is, that both in prose and in verse, he had formed his style by a perverse and pedantic principle. He was desirous to use English words with a foreign idiom. This in all his prose is discovered and condemned; for there judgment operates freely, neither softened by the beauty, nor awed by the dignity of his thoughts; but such is the power of his poetry, that his call is obeyed without resistance, the reader feels himself in captivity to a higher and nobler mind, and criticism sinks in admiration.

'Milton's style was not modified by his subject; what is shown with greater extent in *Paradise Lost* may be found in *Comus.* One source of his peculiarity was his familiarity with the Tuscan poets; the disposition of his words is, I think, frequently Italian; perhaps sometimes combined with other tongues. Of him at last, may be said what Jonson said of Spenser, that he *wrote no language,* but has formed what Butler called a *Babylonish dialect,* in itself harsh and barbarous, but made by exalted genius and extensive learning the vehicle of so much instruction and so much pleasure, that, like other lovers, we find grace in its deformity.'

This criticism seems to me substantially true: indeed, unless we accept it, I do not think we are in the way to appreciate the peculiar greatness of Milton. His style is not a *classic* style, in that it is not the elevation of a *common* style, by the final touch of genius, to greatness. It is, from the foundation, and in every particular, a personal style, not based upon common speech, or common prose, or direct communication of meaning. Of some great poetry one has difficulty in pronouncing just what it is, what infinitesimal touch, that has made all the difference from a plain statement which anyone could make; the slight transformation which, while it leaves a plain statement a plain statement, has always the maximal, never the minimal, alteration of ordinary language. Every distortion of construction, the foreign idiom, the use of a word in a foreign way or with the meaning of the foreign word from which it is derived rather than the accepted meaning in English, every idiosyncrasy is a particular act of violence which Milton has been the first to commit. There is no cliché, no poetic diction in the derogatory sense, but a perpetual sequence of original acts of lawlessness. Of all modern writers of verse, the nearest analogy seems to me to be Mallarmé, a much smaller poet, though still a great one. The personalities, the poetic theories of the two men could not have been more different; but in respect of the violence which they could do to language, and justify, there is a remote similarity. Milton's poetry is poetry at the farthest possible remove from prose; his prose seems to me too near to half-formed poetry to be a good prose.

To say that the work of a poet is at the farthest possible remove from prose would once have struck me as condemnatory: it now seems to me simply, when we have to do with a Milton, the precision of its peculiar greatness. As a poet, Milton seems to me probably the greatest of all eccentrics. His work illustrates no general principles of good writing; the only principles of writing that it illustrates are such as are valid only for Milton himself to observe. There are two kinds of poet who can ordinarily be of use to other poets. There are those who suggest, to one or another of their successors, something which they have not done themselves, or who provoke a different way of doing the same thing: these are likely to be not the greatest, but smaller, imperfect poets with whom later poets discover an affinity. And there are the great poets from whom we can learn negative rules: no poet can teach another to write well, but some great poets can teach others some of the things to avoid. They teach us what to avoid, by showing us what great poetry can do without— how *bare* it can be. Of these are Dante and Racine. But if we are ever to make use of Milton we

must do so in quite a different way. Even a small poet can learn something from the study of Dante, or from the study of Chaucer: we must perhaps wait for a great poet before we find one who can profit from the study of Milton.

I repeat that the remoteness of Milton's verse from ordinary speech, his invention of his own poetic language, seems to me one of the marks of his greatness. Other marks are his sense of structure, both in the general design of *Paradise Lost* and *Samson,* and in his syntax; and finally, and not least, his inerrancy, conscious or unconscious, in writing so as to make the best display of his talents, and the best concealment of his weaknesses.

The appropriateness of the subject of *Samson* is too obvious to expatiate upon: it was probably the one dramatic story out of which Milton could have made a masterpiece. But the complete suitability of *Paradise Lost* has not, I think, been so often remarked. It was surely an intuitive perception of what he could not do, that arrested Milton's project of an epic on King Arthur. For one thing, he had little interest in, or understanding of, individual human beings. In *Paradise Lost* he was not called upon for any of that understanding which comes from an affectionate observation of men and women. But such an interest in human beings was not required—indeed its *absence* was a necessary condition—for the creation of his figures of Adam and Eve. These are not a man and woman such as any we know: if they were, they would not be Adam and Eve. They are the original *Man* and *Woman,* not types, but prototypes. They have the general characteristics of men and women, such that we can recognize, in the temptation and the fall, the first motions of the faults and virtues, the abjection and the nobility, of all their descendants. They have ordinary humanity to the right degree, and yet are not, and should not be, ordinary mortals. Were they more particularized they would be false, and if Milton had been more interested in humanity, he could not have created them. Other critics have remarked upon the exactness, without defect or exaggeration, with which Moloch, Belial, and Mammon, in the second book, speak according to the particular sin which each represents. It would not be suitable that the infernal powers should have, in the human sense, characters, for a character is always mixed; but in the hands of an inferior manipulator, they might easily have been reduced to *humours.*

The appropriateness of the material of *Paradise Lost* to the genius and the limitations of Milton is still more evident when we consider the visual imagery. I have already remarked, in a paper written some years ago, on Milton's weakness of visual observation, a weakness which I think was always present—the effect of his blindness may have been rather to strengthen the compensatory qualities than to increase a fault which was already present. Mr. Wilson Knight, who has devoted close study to recurrent imagery in poetry, has called attention to Milton's propensity towards images of engineering and mechanics; to me it seems that Milton is at his best in imagery suggestive of vast size, limitless space, abysmal depth, and light and darkness. No theme and no setting, other than that which he chose in *Paradise Lost,* could have given him such scope for the kind of imagery in which he excelled, or made less demand upon those powers of visual imagination which were in him defective.

Most of the absurdities and inconsistencies to which Johnson calls attention, and which, so far as they can justly be isolated in this way, he properly condemns, will I think appear in a more correct proportion if we consider them in relation to this general judgment. I do not think that we should attempt to *see* very clearly any scene that Milton depicts: it should be accepted as a shifting phantasmagory. To complain, because we first find the arch-fiend 'chain'd on the burning lake,' and in a minute or two see him making his way to the shore, is to expect a kind of consistency which the world to which Milton has introduced us does not require.

This limitation of visual power, like Milton's limited interest in human beings, turns out to be not merely a negligible defect, but a positive virtue, when we visit Adam and Eve in Eden. Just as a higher degree of characterization of Adam and Eve would have been unsuitable, so a more vivid picture of the earthly Paradise would have been less paradisiacal. For a greater definiteness, a more detailed account of flora and fauna, could only have assimilated Eden to the landscapes of earth with which we are familiar. As it is, the impression of Eden which we retain, is the most suitable, and is that which Milton was most qualified to give: the impression of *light*—a daylight and a starlight, a light of dawn and of dusk, the light which, remembered by a man in his blindness, has a supernatural glory unexperienced by men of normal vision.

We must, then, in reading *Paradise Lost,* not expect to see clearly; our sense of sight must be blurred, so that our *hearing* may become more acute. *Paradise Lost,* like *Finnegans Wake* [for I can think of no work which provides a more interesting parallel: two books by great blind musicians, each writing a language of his own based

upon English] makes this peculiar demand for a readjustment of the reader's mode of apprehension. The emphasis is on the sound, not the vision, upon the word, not the idea; and in the end it is the unique versification that is the most certain sign of Milton's intellectual mastership.

On the subject of Milton's versification, so far as I am aware, little enough has been written. We have Johnson's essay in the *Rambler,* which deserves more study than it has received, and we have a short treatise by Robert Bridges on *Milton's Prosody.* I speak of Bridges with respect, for no poet of our time has given such close attention to prosody as he. Bridges catalogues the systematic irregularities which give perpetual variety to Milton's verse, and I can find no fault with his analysis. But however interesting these analyses are, I do not think that it is by such means that we gain an appreciation of the peculiar rhythm of a poet. It seems to me also that Milton's verse is especially refractory to yielding up its secrets to examination of the single line. For his verse is not formed in this way. It is the period, the sentence and still more the paragraph, that is the unit of Milton's verse; and emphasis on the line structure is the minimum necessary to provide a counter-pattern to the period structure. It is only in the period that the wave-length of Milton's verse is to be found: it is his ability to give a perfect and unique pattern to every paragraph, such that the full beauty of the line is found in its context, and his ability to work in larger musical units than any other poet—that is to me the most conclusive evidence of Milton's supreme mastery. The peculiar feeling, almost a physical sensation of a breathless leap, communicated by Milton's long periods, and by his alone, is impossible to procure from rhymed verse. Indeed, this mastery is more conclusive evidence of his intellectual power, than is his grasp of any *ideas* that he borrowed or invented. To be able to control so many words at once is the token of a mind of most exceptional energy.

It is interesting at this point to recall the general observations upon blank verse, which a consideration of *Paradise Lost* prompted Johnson to make towards the end of his essay.

'The music of the English heroic lines strikes the ear so faintly, that it is easily lost, unless all the syllables of every line co-operate together; this co-operation can only be obtained by the preservation of every verse unmingled with another as a distinct system of sounds; and this distinctness is obtained and preserved by the artifice of rhyme. The variety of pauses, so much boasted by the lovers of blank verse, changes the measures of an English poet to the periods of a declaimer; and there are only a few skilful and happy readers of Milton, who enable their audience to perceive where the lines end or begin. *Blank verse,* said an ingenious critic, *seems to be verse only to the eye.'*

Some of my audience may recall that this last remark, in almost the same words, was often made, a literary generation ago, about the 'free verse' of the period: and even without this encouragement from Johnson it would have occurred to my mind to declare Milton to be the greatest master of free verse in our language. What is interesting about Johnson's paragraph, however, is that it represents the judgment of a man who had by no means a deaf ear, but simply a *specialized* ear, for verbal music. Within the limits of the poetry of his own period, Johnson is a very good judge of the relative merits of several poets as writers of blank verse. But on the whole, the blank verse of his age might more properly be called unrhymed verse; and nowhere is this difference more evident than in the verse of his own tragedy *Irene:* the phrasing is admirable, the style elevated and correct, but each line cries out for a companion to rhyme with it. Indeed, it is only with labour, or by occasional inspiration, or by submission to the influence of the older dramatists, that the blank verse of the nineteenth century succeeds in making the absence of rhyme inevitable and right, with the rightness of Milton. Even Johnson admitted that he could not wish that Milton had been a rhymer. Nor did the nineteenth century succeed in giving to blank verse the flexibility which it needs if the tone of common speech, talking of the topics of common intercourse, is to be employed; so that when our more modern practitioners of blank verse do not touch the sublime, they frequently sink to the ridiculous. Milton perfected nondramatic blank verse and at the same time imposed limitations, very hard to break, upon the use to which it may be put if its greatest musical possibilities are to be exploited.

I come at last to compare my own attitude, as that of a poetical practitioner perhaps typical of a generation twenty-five years ago, with my attitude to-day. I have thought it well to take matters in the order in which I have taken them to discuss first the censures and detractions which I believe to have permanent validity, and which were best made by Johnson, in order to make clearer the causes, and the justification, for hostility to Milton on the part of poets at a particular juncture. And I wished to make clear those excellences of Milton which particularly impress me, before explaining why I think that the study of his verse might at last be of benefit to poets.

I have on several occasions suggested, that the important changes in the idiom of English verse which are represented by the names of Dryden and Wordsworth, may be characterized as successful attempts to escape from a poetic idiom which had ceased to have a relation to contemporary speech. This is the sense of Wordsworth's Prefaces. By the beginning of the present century another revolution in idiom—and such revolutions bring with them an alteration of metric, a new appeal to the ear—was due. It inevitably happens that the young poets engaged in such a revolution will exalt the merits of those poets of the past who offer them example and stimulation, and cry down the merits of poets who do not stand for the qualities which they are zealous to realize. This is not only inevitable, it is right. It is even right, and certainly inevitable, that their practice, still more influential than their critical pronouncements, should attract their own readers to the poets by whose work they have been influenced. Such influence has certainly contributed to the taste [if we can distinguish the *taste* from the *fashion*] for Donne. I do not think that any modern poet, unless in a fit of irresponsible peevishness, has ever denied Milton's consummate powers. And it must be said that Milton's diction is not a poetic diction in the sense of being a debased currency: when he violates the English language he is imitating nobody, and he is inimitable. But Milton does, as I have said, represent poetry at the extreme limit from prose; and it was one of our tenets that verse should have the virtues of prose, that diction should become assimilated to cultivated contemporary speech, before aspiring to the elevation of poetry. Another tenet was that the subject-matter and the imagery of poetry should be extended to topics and objects related to the life of a modern man or woman; that we were to seek the nonpoetic, to seek even material refractory to transmutation into poetry, and words and phrases which had not been used in poetry before. And the study of Milton could be of no help here: it was only a hindrance.

We cannot, in literature, any more than in the rest of life, live in a perpetual state of revolution. If every generation of poets made it their task to bring poetic diction up to date with the spoken language, poetry would fail in one of its most important obligations. For poetry should help, not only to refine the language of the time, but to prevent it from changing too rapidly: a development of language at too great a speed would be a development in the sense of a progressive deterioration, and that is our danger to-day. If the poetry of the rest of this century takes the line of development which seems to me, reviewing the progress of poetry through the last three centuries, the right course, it will discover new and more elaborate patterns of a diction now established. In this search it might have much to learn from Milton's extended verse structure; it might also avoid the danger of a *servitude* to colloquial speech and to current jargon. It might also learn that the music of verse is strongest in poetry which has a definite meaning expressed in the properest words. Poets might be led to admit that a knowledge of the literature of their own language, with a knowledge of the literature and the grammatical construction of other languages, is a very valuable part of the poet's equipment. And they might, as I have already hinted, devote some study to Milton as, outside the theatre, the greatest master in our language of freedom within form. A study of *Samson* should sharpen anyone's appreciation of the justified irregularity, and put him on guard against the pointless irregularity. In studying *Paradise Lost* we come to perceive that the verse is continuously animated by the departure from, and return to, the regular measure; and that, in comparison with Milton, hardly any subsequent writer of blank verse appears to exercise any freedom at all. We can also be led to the reflection that a monotony of unscannable verse fatigues the attention even more quickly than a monotony of exact feet. In short, it now seems to me that poets are sufficiently liberated from Milton's reputation, to approach the study of his work without danger, and with profit to their poetry and to the English language.

1947

IRVING HOWE

Editor

William Faulkner

1 8 9 7 –

No TWENTIETH-CENTURY American novelist, with the possible exception of Hemingway, has been so greatly admired, discussed, and emulated as William Faulkner. During the thirties, when he was publishing one remarkable book after another, he suffered shameful neglect from the literary public; as late as 1945 all of his books were out of print; then, in the years since the Second World War, there occurred a major shift of critical opinion, and Faulkner has become the most celebrated living American novelist. We have learned to see that his series of novels centered on Yoknapatawpha County—his imaginary locale in northern Mississippi—not only provides a brilliant portrait of life in the deep South but also dramatizes some of the most insistent problems of human consciousness in our time.

Faulkner's work can be difficult: it abounds in jumbled time sequences, involuted narrative structures, mangled syntax, and torturous diction. It demands from the reader that he take psychic and intellectual risks. One must bring to his novels a capacity for concentration, a readiness to abandon set notions about life and literature, and above all, a willingness to expose oneself to a gamut of feelings. At a time when men in a mass society often believe that their possibilities for significant experience are shrinking, Faulkner insists upon the largeness of human possibility. He returns to traditional dramatic gestures, he reasserts the claims of uncompromising tragedy, extreme melodrama, wild comedy. The force of human desire breaks through in his novels with a grandeur and terror that are almost unequaled in our time. Indeed, it is this readiness for confronting the largest ranges of experience which helps explain the hold Faulkner has won upon modern readers, both those who admire his work and even some who do not.

Faulkner is a prodigious talent, sweeping and erratic, inventive and wasteful, utterly caught up in the demands of his imaginative vision. He follows in the American tradition of the "natural genius"—the untutored or self-tutored writer whose impulse is to strive for relaxed and open forms rather than for tidiness of presentation, the writer who appropriates myths and legends from the collective memory of his homeland rather than inventing neatly compressed plots, the writer who offers encompassing statements and images of the human condition rather than resting content with self-sufficient dramatizations.

I

THE WORLD in which William Faulkner grew up was laden with memories of the regional past—and to the South, it should be remembered, the region was actually a nation, a *lost* nation. At the center of these memories stood a figure who, with time, had acquired a legendary stature. William C. Falkner,[1] the novelist's great-grandfather, had come to Mississippi in 1839 as a poor fourteen-year-old boy. Energetic, wilful, and hot-tempered, he had worked his way up to economic and political prominence, so much so that by the time of the Civil War he took command as colonel of the Second Mississippi Regiment. But as the novelist indicates in his fictional portrait of the great-grandfather—who appears as Colonel Bayard Sartoris in the novel *Sartoris*—Colonel Falkner was not quite a conventional Southerner. By temperament and conviction somewhat apart from the plantation aristocracy, he also showed recurrent signs of impatience with the grandiose self-delusion and moral falseness of "the Southern way of life." Colonel Falkner was one of those rising "new men," strong and independent figures who by the force of circumstance became defenders of a society they did not entirely accept. And it may not be too farfetched to suppose that this mixture of attitudes toward the South was partly inherited by the novelist William Faulkner, in whose work ambivalent feelings toward the homeland would become a major element.

The Second Mississippi Regiment saw a good deal of action in the Civil War, but when it replaced Falkner as its colonel, he simply packed up, went home, and formed a guerilla band which harassed the Northern armies that were slicing into Mississippi. Once the war was over, Falkner refused to sink into lethargy or compensating daydreams; instead, he became an active figure in Mississippi politics, built a local railroad, and wrote a best-selling novel called *The White Rose of Memphis*. His life came to an end, characteristically, through a stroke of violence: he was murdered on the street by a business associate in 1889. Colonel Falkner's son, who also appears as a character in *Sartoris*, was a colorful man, and his grandson, the father of the novelist, a decent one; but they clearly represent a decline in personal forcefulness, a decline that parallels the fate of the homeland itself.

During his childhood William Faulkner—he

[1] The novelist himself would add the *u* to the family name.

was born in 1897—heard an endless number of stories about his great-grandfather and other heroes of the South, stories about gallantry, courage, and honor, told with all the greater emphasis as the past seemed less and less retrievable. As a boy Faulkner did not need to study the history of the South, he lived in its shadow and suffered its decay. It was inevitable that the figure of the great-grandfather—a figure, one supposes, who became inseparable from the archetypal Southern hero—should come to seem splendid in his mind and that, like other Southern boys, he should saturate himself in legends of a past which if not more virtuous certainly seemed more vigorous than the present.

Most of Faulkner's childhood and youth were spent in Oxford, Mississippi, a university town which figures in his novels as Jefferson. His education was erratic. He did not formally complete high school, but in his late teens he read widely, especially in Romantic poetry which, as he would remember, "completely satisfied me and filled my inner life." He formed a lasting friendship with Phil Stone, a young Mississippian studying to be a lawyer (and later to serve as a model for Gavin Stevens, the spokesman-character who appears in several Faulkner novels). Caught up in a passion for literature, Stone helped introduce the young Faulkner to the world of culture and to a somewhat more critical, or at least ironic, view of the South than was common at the time.

Back in Mississippi, after having served for a time in the Canadian Air Force during the First World War, Faulkner took some courses at the state university—it is amusing, perhaps encouraging, that he did poorly in English—but remained a student for only a year. He then became something of a town "character," affecting eccentricities and supporting himself by doing odd jobs. He held a brief appointment as university postmaster, but a disinclination to distribute the mail regularly cut short his career.

Like many young men home from the war and uncertain as to what to make of themselves, Faulkner was now badly adrift. It can even be said that he had entered a period of crisis which would serve as a necessary prelude to his career as a writer. He had no skill, no training, no visible prospects; he showed a marked distaste for regular employment, and he shared some of the vague discontents that were afflicting young men in the postwar years. The usual kinds of release which the more sensitive members of Faulkner's generation found for their restlessness—the Left Bank in Paris, the New York literary world, political radicalism—did not interest him. Mississippi itself—sluggish, poor, bigoted—was not an entirely satisfying place for a young man with literary tastes, even though it contained the only stretch of earth he knew well and loved entirely. At times, the land to which he returned was like an old battlefield, and its people seemed to be living in a dream world of the past, lost to a willed and romantic nostalgia. The evidence of his early novels—*Soldiers' Pay* (1926) and *Mosquitoes* (1927), both unsuccessful apprentice work—suggests that to Faulkner the two wars, the 1914 one in Europe and the old war of his homeland, had a way of melting into one desolation. And at least as disturbing was the fact that slowly the South *was* beginning to change. The traditional society was starting to break up; new and unattractive figures—later to be immortalized in Faulkner's Snopes clan—were coming to the forefront.

In 1924 Faulkner published a little book of verse called *The Marble Faun*, most of which showed little more than an indulgence in provincial romanticism. That Faulkner commands a major gift for poetic evocation, his fiction makes clear; but it is not a gift that can be contained within the strict limits of verse. The book won neither attention nor sales, and perhaps in order to find a more sympathetic environment, perhaps simply out of boredom, Faulkner left Oxford in 1924 and settled for a time in New Orleans. There he fell in with a group of literary intellectuals who were publishing a little magazine, *The Double Dealer*, and more importantly, met Sherwood Anderson, the author of *Winesburg, Ohio*, who was then at the peak of his success. The two men became friends, meeting in the afternoons to talk, drink, and tell each other tall tales. Years later Faulkner would recall that when he saw how attractive Anderson's life as a writer was, he decided to become one too. He then—so

Faulkner's story continues—sat down to write a novel and six weeks later brought *Soldiers' Pay* to Anderson, who agreed to recommend it to his publisher on the condition that he would not have to read it first. Faulkner's is a story which satisfies the need of so many American writers to feel that their writing is something casually undertaken—years later, at the climax of a productive career, Faulkner would describe himself as "a farmer!"—and that they do not share the veneration for the "creative" which is to be found among some literary people. Such stories may be taken with grains of salt. Faulkner, from this time on, would devote himself with a ferocious energy to writing novels and stories; indeed, for our present purposes, his biography becomes almost indistinguishable from the record of his literary production.

Faulkner's first two novels were of minor consequence. *Soldiers' Pay*, the story of a mangled war veteran, is a book that quivers with intense emotions; it records Faulkner's feeling, so similar to that of many other writers in the 1920's, that the war generation was "lost"; but in the book itself he did not succeed in sufficiently dramatizing the problem. *Mosquitoes* was an effort to write a satiric comedy in the manner of Aldous Huxley, a genre for which Faulkner had no particular gifts. Still, both novels offer plenty of evidence that their young author had a considerable flair for language—indeed, the writing tends to go soft and purple —but that he had not yet found his true subject.

Faulkner never felt entirely at ease in the cosmopolitan environment of New Orleans, and soon he returned to Oxford, where he was to make his permanent home. Outwardly his life has been quiet. He has had little to do with other novelists or literary intellectuals; he has preserved a manner of taciturn solitariness; and until the 1950's, when he suddenly began to make public pronouncements on everything from segregation to the future of man, he has steadily kept himself apart from cultural and intellectual disputes. Except for brief engagements as a Hollywood script-writer, undertaken to support his family, Faulkner has spent most of his mature life in the place he knows with an intimacy deeper than love or hate; and there he has written the books that made him an international figure and for which in 1950 he won the Nobel prize.

The early Faulkner, as he moves beyond his apprentice novels, is a writer in quest, both of some organizing principle in experience and a subject by which to release it in his writing. Once he discovers this subject, he will stay with it in almost all his books, for the truth is that the subject really discovers him, grips and controls him with the power of an intolerable but inescapable memory. As André Gide has remarked, a writer needs "a special world of which he alone has the key."

II

FAULKNER'S "special world," his great subject, is the South: the Southern memory, the Southern reality, the Southern myth.

Perhaps because it had so little else to give its people, the post-Civil War South nurtured in them a generous and often obsessive sense of the past. The rest of the country might be committed to commercial expansion or addicted to the notion of progressive optimism, but the South was unable to accept these dominant American values. It had been left behind, broken in defeat; it was living on the margin of history, a position that often provides the keenest perspective on history itself. During the later years of the nineteenth and earlier years of the twentieth century, the writers of the South could maintain a relation to American life comparable, in miniature, to the relation between Russian writers and West European life in the nineteenth century. Czarist Russia was essentially a backward country, yet its writers managed to use that situation as a vantage point from which to observe West European life and to arrive at a profound criticism of bourgeois morality. It was this advantage of distance, this perspective from the social rear, that was the major dispensation the South could offer its writers.

The Southern writer did not have to cast about for his materials; he hardly enjoyed a spontaneous choice in his use of them, for they welled within him like a recurrent dream. Faulkner has given a vivid if somewhat idealized description of this subject in *Intruder in the Dust:*

For every Southern boy fourteen years old, not once but whenever he wants it, there is the instance when it's still not two o'clock on that July afternoon in 1863, the brigades are in position behind the rail fence, the guns are laid and ready in the woods and the furled flags are already loosened to break out and Pickett himself with his long oiled ringlets and his hat in one hand probably and his sword in the other looking up the hill waiting for Longstreet to give the word and it's all in the balance, it hasn't happened yet, it hasn't even begun . . .

But of course it has happened, it must begin. The basic Southern subject is the defeat of the homeland, though its presentation in Faulkner's work can vary from the romancing in parts of *Sartoris* to the despairing portrait of social loss in *The Sound and the Fury.* Nor, for the moment, does it much matter whether one defines this subject as the humiliation of the homeland through superior force and its later degradation by carpetbaggers and scalawags, or as the defeat of a decadent slave-owning class followed by its partial recapture of power through corrupt and unscrupulous means. Regardless of which interpretation one accepts, the important point is that for a writer like Faulkner the subject is implacably *there.* Not long before the Civil War Nathaniel Hawthorne had remarked on "the difficulty of writing a romance about a country where there is no shadow, no antiquity, no picturesque and gloomy wrong, nor anything but a commonplace prosperity." But now the war and Reconstruction gave the Southern writers all that Hawthorne had found lacking—all but antiquity. And there were ruins to take its place.

It was not until the First World War, however, that most serious Southern writing began to appear; that is, not until Southern regional consciousness had begun to break down. For it was the reality of twentieth-century life, in all its provocation, which drove so many Southern writers to a regional past that in happier circumstances they might have learned peaceably to forget.

Before the Southern writers could make imaginative statements about their own past, they had to be exposed to intellectual drafts from beyond their regional horizon. Southern literature at its best—the work of Faulkner, the early Caldwell, Allen Tate—was conceived in an explosive mixture of provincialism and cosmopolitanism, tradition and modernity. To measure the stature of their ancestor Poe, the Southern writers had first to understand what he meant to Baudelaire, and for that they had to gain a sophisticated awareness of the European literary past. For the Southern imagination to burst into high flame it had to be stimulated, or irritated, by the pressures of European and Northern ideas and literary modes. Left to itself, a regional consciousness is seldom likely to result in anything but a tiresome romanticizing of the past. Once, however, the South reached the point at which it still remained a distinct region but was already cracking under alien influences, it could begin to yield serious works of art.

It is therefore insufficient to say, as some critics do, that Faulkner is a Southern traditionalist or conservative moralist drawing his creative strength from his attachment to the past of the homeland. The truth is that he writes in opposition to his received pieties as well as in acceptance, that he struggles against the conventional vision of the South even as he continues to acknowledge its power and charm. As he moves from book to book, turning a more critical and mature eye upon his material, the rejection of an inherited tradition takes on a much greater intellectual and emotional force than its defense. At no point, neither in his early romanticizing nor his later moral realism, is Faulkner's attitude toward the Southern tradition a simple or fixed one. His relation to his own beliefs is characteristically "modern," full of instability, self-consciousness, and ambivalence. He is working with the decayed fragments of a myth, the soured pieties of regional memory—which is one reason his language is so often tortured, forced and even incoherent—but the mind he brings to bear upon this subject is a mind deeply committed to the idea of life as *problematic*. He offers queries not certainties, anxieties not assurances. One reads him, to borrow a phrase from the novelist Franz Kafka, "in order to ask questions."

We have been using the word "myth," a tricky word which in popular terms often sig-

nifies little more than a lie and in literary discussion takes on an astonishing range of meanings. But as we use it here, the Southern myth refers to a story or cluster of stories that expresses the deepest attitudes and reflects the most fundamental experiences of a people. The homeland—so the story goes—had proudly insisted that it alone should determine its destiny; provoked into a war impossible to win, it had nevertheless fought to its last strength, and had fought this war with a reckless gallantry and superb heroism. Yet the homeland fell, and from this fall came misery and squalor: the ravaging by the conquerors, the loss of faith among the descendants of the defeated, and the rise of a new breed of faceless men who would batten on their neighbors' troubles. From such stories there follows that pride in ancestral glory and that mourning over the decline of the homeland which constitute the psychology of "the lost cause"—a sentiment often expressed in Faulkner's earlier novels.

The Southern myth, like any other, is less an attempt at historical description than a voicing of the collective imagination, perhaps of the collective will. The Old South over which it chants in threnody is an ideal image—a buried city, as Allen Tate has called it. And perhaps, also, a buried city that can never be found.

Such myths form the raw material of literature. The writer often comes to a myth eager to acquiesce, but after absorbing its assumptions into his work he may begin to wonder about its meaning, its value. In his novels and stories Faulkner has set his pride in the past against his despair over the present, and from this counterpoint has come much of the tension in his work. He has investigated the myth itself insofar as it pretends to historical description; wondered about the relation between the Southern tradition he partly admires and that memory of Southern slavery to which he is compelled to return; tested not only the present by the past but also the past by the myth, and finally the myth by that morality which has slowly emerged from this entire process of exploration. This testing of the myth, though by no means the only important activity in Faulkner's work, is basic to the Yoknapatawpha novels and stories.

III

YOKNAPATAWPHA COUNTY—Faulkner has slyly remarked that he is its sole owner and proprietor—bears some rough similarities to Lafayette County, Mississippi. It is 2400 square miles in area, bounded by the Talahatchie and Yoknapatawpha rivers, and comprises mainly farm lands and pine hills. After a private census which by now may be somewhat dated, Faulkner announced that of 15,611 people living in Yoknapatawpha County 6298 are white and 9313 Negro. The preciseness of these figures is whimsy, the proportion not. For they indicate how closely the imaginary world of Yoknapatawpha County is related to the patch of the deep South in which Faulkner has spent his life. If we are able to feel that in some sense the implications of Faulkner's work are "universal," that is because he is so thoroughly a master at describing a particular time and place —he knows exactly how a farm girl sits in a wagon when she goes to town, or how the members of a decaying aristocratic family talk to one another, or how Negroes will set up social masks in order to get by in a hostile world. One of Faulkner's major subjects is human rootlessness, but it is a subject made possible by the rootedness of his own experience.

Like Mississippi itself, Yoknapatawpha is a land blighted by poverty, and while it does have social classes, they are either remnants of the Old South or embryos of the New South. Most of Yoknapatawpha is kept from splitting into distinct social classes by the flattening pressures of poverty and the scarcity of industrialization—indeed, it is important to bear in mind that the bulk of Faulkner's work, and the best part of it too, is set roughly between the 1890's and the late 1930's, that is, at a time when social change was beginning to break the crust of traditional Southern customs. This was a time when the ideology of regional separateness and its attendant Confederate rhetoric were being threatened by new ideas and new commerce, but when there was still some reason for saying that the deep South possessed a style of life notably different from that of the rest of the country. It is Faulkner's particular strength as a writer to have been the most faithful—which is to say, most loving and

critical—recorder of that style of life, while still managing to "transcend" mere local idiosyncracies. In his best work, as in all serious literature, universal implications are entirely imbedded in and inseparable from the depiction of particular human events.

Clan rather than class forms the basic social unit in the world of Yoknapatawpha. Pride in family and reverence for ancestors are central motives in behavior—which is to be expected in a society where the past clings to the present like a habitual lover neither relinquished nor enjoyed. Each of the major families in Faulkner's world comes to signify a distinct mode of conduct based upon a moral code, and the breakup of traditional Southern patterns of life is depicted through the breakup of the clans. Such families as the Compsons, Sartorises, and McCaslins not only provide the narrative matter of Faulkner's chronicle— they respond to the invasion of modernity in Yoknapatawpha with a range of styles that reveals a spectrum of moral valuations. Thus, the Sartorises come to stand for chivalric recklessness and self-destruction, the Compsons for a more extreme and tragic disintegration, and the McCaslins for a profound expiation of the evil of the past. The Snopes clan, on a lower social level, represents the amoralism of the "sourceless" flotsam (the adjective is Faulkner's) which takes over once a society starts falling apart.

Now there is always a danger of exaggerating the degree of coherence and conscious planning in the Yoknapatawpha books. The events of Faulkner's world are hardly meant to illustrate social tendencies, nor do they stem from a methodical scheme for the representation of Southern history. They may be reduced to such a scheme by the critic and perhaps they have to be, but in doing so he risks overestimating the extent to which they have been explicitly designed and underestimating the extent to which they have been imaginatively summoned. Despite the virtuosity that goes into much of Faulkner's work, his fundamental source is less the artificer's plan than the chronicler's vision, less a conscious worked-out scheme than a sudden "seeing" of the past of the homeland.

Though neither social photography nor historical record, the Yoknapatawpha chronicle is intimately related to the milieu from which it derives; it is an appropriation from a communal memory, some great store of half-forgotten legends of which Faulkner is the last grieving recorder. It is as if the whole thing, no longer available to public experience, lived fresh and imperious in his mind: a tragic charade of the past. And as Faulkner tells these stories, there is always a desperate search for order, not merely as a strategy in narrative but also as a motive for composition. Incidents reappear from book to book, their meanings changed and tone modified; characters trivial in one book reach major dimension in another; narrative bits left fallow for years are suddenly worked over with great energy.

Faulkner's vision of life is hardly to be formulated in simple terms, nor is it at all the same as the resolution or sum of his attitudes toward the South. But for the moment let us agree to consider mainly the latter. Malcolm Cowley has described Faulkner's social view as that of an "anti-slavery Southern nationalist," while George Marion O'Donnell finds him a "traditional moralist" defending the "Southern socio-economic-ethical tradition." Perhaps if Faulkner's responses to the South were kneaded into a tight ideological ball it would resemble antislavery nationalism, but actually his work contains a wide range of attitudes toward the South, from sentimentality to denunciation, from identification to rejection. While in his earlier books he may be seen as a "traditional moralist" defending—though even then, only in part—the Old South, his work shows a gradual recognition that his values can now be realized only in new and untested social groups. The Southern myth appears in its simplest version in Faulkner's collection of Civil War stories called *The Unvanquished,* a few of which are barely distinguishable from the romancing of popular fiction. The Southern myth appears in its most torturous version in *Absalom, Absalom!,* a novel written out of sheer pain, in which Faulkner has forced himself to see how the will to domination had corrupted the white community. Between these two extremes lies the bulk of his major fiction.

Faulkner did his best work during a span of twelve or thirteen years, from 1929 to 1942. And during those years there was a shorter period of truly astonishing creativity, between 1928 and 1932, when he wrote *The Sound and the Fury, As I Lay Dying, Sanctuary,* and *Light in August.* Fine things have come from his pen during the 1940's and 1950's, usually bits and sections of novels, but nothing to compare with the outpouring of these inspired early years.

The novels written between 1929 and 1932 form a profound criticism of Southern society —but far more important, a profound criticism of modern life. Many of the dominant and recurrent themes of contemporary literature— the disintegration of moral values under the pressures of commercialism, the loss of the capacity for making close human connections, the costs and terrors of isolation in an impersonal world, the bewilderment of sensitive men and the powerlessness of good ones before the onslaughts of rapacity and vulgarity—all these are dramatized in Faulkner's earlier novels with a marvelous concreteness of detail and pictorial imagery. It is hard to think of another twentieth-century novelist who has given us so many living characters: the idiot Benjy Compson and his money-chasing brother Jason in *The Sound and the Fury;* the whole Bundren clan in *As I Lay Dying;* the criminal Popeye and the flapper Temple Drake in *Sanctuary;* the crucified mulatto Joe Christmas and the bovine madonna Lena Grove in *Light in August;* and many more, companions of our imagination who survive in memory long after one has put away the books in which they appear.

Surely the greatest of these novels is *The Sound and the Fury,* a book recording the fall of a family and the death of a world. As it penetrates the life of the Compsons—the neurasthenic mother who evades reality with her claims to gentility; Benjy, the idiot son, whose chaotic burden of memory holds the family's past in a purity of suspension; Jason, the superbly comic son, who has made his peace with and embodies the amorality of commercialism —*The Sound and the Fury* exudes the smell of death, the death of the traditional South but of much more as well. The plot line is rigidly confined to a single family, moving from the consciousness of one member to another, and seeming almost claustrophobic in its concentration on a narrow sequence of events; yet its effect is to suggest a full awareness of human trouble, for we see that the moral death of the Compsons, and behind them of Yoknapatawpha, is an acting-out of the disorder of our time.

A contrast and companion-piece to *The Sound and the Fury* is *As I Lay Dying*, a tragicomic story, at once both grotesque and tender, about the blundering efforts of the poor-white Bundrens to bring the body of their dead mother back to Jefferson for burial. The book explores in subtle detail the inner workings and relationships of the family, and as such—but this is true of all Faulkner's books—it has values and implications that cannot be apprehended merely by placing it in the context of the Yoknapatawpha saga. To the extent, however, that it may be so limited, *As I Lay Dying* seems to be saying that even the Bundrens can come together for a brief act of humanity in a way the once proud and aristocratic Compsons no longer can.

Still further explorations into the life of contemporary Yoknapatawpha—contemporary here signifies the 1930's—are two of Faulkner's most powerful novels, *Sanctuary* and *Light in August*. The first of these is a sensationalistic picture of human ugliness, a book both marred and memorable; the second, a masterpiece in the genre of naturalistic realism. The two novels have similarities of theme: both examine the failure of a serious man to oppose injustice with the vigor his conscience requires, both can be read as fables of Southern (as also modern) life in which innocent men are ground between a decadent past and an inhuman present, and in both violence of tone serves as a barometer of the moral atmosphere. *Sanctuary* is primarily a tour of society's criminal recesses, the underworld of Popeye, a Memphis tough who is one of Faulkner's most terrifying figures. Full of violence, hatred, and nausea, but nevertheless an extremely serious work, *Sanctuary* is also the story of an invasion. Into the social gap left by the collapse of the Compsons and Sartorises, there creep the Snopes clan from the backwoods and Popeye from the city, two embodiments of evil, with Flem Snopes bent on aping the respectability of the Yokna-

patawpha middle class and Popeye unregenerately criminal.

Light in August, a novel which shows some signs of the social concerns of the 1930's, plunges directly into the life of modern Yoknapatawpha, as this life is shaped by hatred, alienation, martyrdom, isolation, and social division. Full of brilliant scenes and sharply evoked characters, *Light in August* renders not only Faulkner's immediate sense of the injustice so often at the heart of twentieth-century life, but also, and more "timelessly," his sense of the crushing weight of all human experience. The book is organized about three major figures: Joe Christmas, who believes he has mixed blood, cannot bear the guilt or pain that being categorized as white or Negro would cause him, and after vainly seeking some mode of personal independence climaxes his life as a martyr to both the vindictiveness of society and his own buried striving toward human dignity; the Reverend Hightower, a sensitive man lost to delusional memories of the past and therefore unable to help, even as he sympathizes with, Joe Christmas; and Lena Grove, pregnant and serene, who breezes through the turmoil of the book as if she represented the very principle of life survival. Between the fate of Joe Christmas and the fate of Lena Grove—he all anxious striving, she benign passivity—there is a discrepancy so radical that nothing can justify it; as Faulkner would say, this discrepancy reflects the very outrage of existence. The arrangement of the book thus comes to resemble an early Renaissance painting: in the foreground a bleeding martyr, far to the rear a scene of bucolic peacefulness, with women working quietly in the fields. *Light in August* is a book which touches on a theme profoundly significant for the American imagination: the theme of human lostness and loneliness.

In the three major works that follow—*Absalom, Absalom!*, *The Hamlet* and *Go Down, Moses*—Faulkner turns again to the Southern past, as if to re-examine the historical sources of the human debacle he has portrayed in his novels of the present. *Absalom, Absalom!*, written in a highly rhetorical style that sometimes approaches grandeur and sometimes hysteria, focuses on Thomas Sutpen, a plantation owner in the mid-nineteenth century whose amoral willfulness summarizes a whole side of Southern experience. In *The Hamlet*, a racy comic extravaganza which borrows from the American tradition of the tall tale, Faulkner concentrates on the Snopeses, that vermin-like clan which spreads its corruption and nihilism over the entire surface of Yoknapataw-pha. And in *Go Down, Moses* he returns to one of his major themes: the relations between Negro and white. The central figure of this book is also the moral hero of the Yoknapatawpha saga: Isaac McCaslin emerges as a saintly man who decides that his heritage has been fouled by the sins of the past—slavery, above all—and who therefore refuses that heritage in order to live as a poor and simple carpenter. The centerpiece of *Go Down, Moses* —as, in some ways, the centerpiece of Faulkner's entire work—is a novelette called "The Bear" (see pp. 866–913), both a beautiful account of a hunt and a symbolic fable concerning the moral growth of Isaac McCaslin.

Like many of Faulkner's stories, "The Bear" turns to the past. It turns to a vision of American life not yet soiled by greed or commerce, nor tainted by the anxieties of social existence and the sordidness of urban life. When the men of Yoknapatawpha, taking with them young Isaac McCaslin, go off on their annual visit to the forest, "not to hunt bear and deer but to keep the yearly rendezvous with the bear which they did not even intend to kill," their expedition soon takes on the tone of a religious retreat: away from money, away from the town, away from women, away from social distinctions. This yearly hunting trip becomes, as Faulkner says, "a pageant-rite"—and not only for the adult figures who lead it but still more so for sixteen-year-old Isaac and for Sam Fathers, the "taintless and incorruptible" old man of mixed Negro and Indian blood who is the boy's mentor in the hunt and the acknowledged priest of the ceremony that can be held only in the forest.

This "pageant-rite" stirs a rich association of memories for anyone acquainted with American literature. For the idea of a pastoral retreat to the Eden of the wilderness where men can again find the rhythmic harmonies of the natural world, in contrast to the frenzy and corruption of social life, is a recurrent and pro-foundly-embraced theme in American fiction. It can be found in the Leatherstocking tales of Cooper, the picaresque narratives of Mark Twain, the novels of Melville—where the sea replaces the forest—and some of Hemingway's stories. All of these American writers posit a radical disjunction between man and nature. The wilderness is primal, the source and scene of mobility, of freedom, of innocence; society, soon after it appears in the New World, begins to suffocate these values. In "The Bear" this myth is dramatized through a series of contrasts between the hunt sections, marvelous for their aura of composure, and Section 4, in which all the rasping discords of Southern history seem to be compressed.

The myth of a natural return is a myth of space, possible only to a people for whom the land once seemed to stretch out endlessly, as an invitation for men to accept with love and a temptation for men to violate with greed. It is a myth of space, recalling a time when men could measure their independence by their distance from each other, and when, as Faulkner writes, "personal liberty and freedom were almost physical conditions like fire and flood." In magnified volume but steady pitch, it records the secret voice of a society yearning for its innocent past and regretting its very existence.

Meanwhile, however, it knows there is no choice—indeed, the power and poignancy of the myth reside largely in the sense that the past cannot be recaptured. Each year, as the forest line recedes, the men of Yoknapatawpha go back for two weeks, to find rest and pleasure, forgiveness and cleansing, but above all, those energies of renewal that only the natural world can yield them and with which they may find it possible to survive until their next return.

In "The Bear" the hunt becomes a ceremony of initiation and maturing, a test of proper conduct through which Isaac McCaslin ceases to be a boy; yet truly to become a man he must retain something of that awe before truth characteristic of boyhood. When he meets the great bear Ben, it is only after having stripped himself of such material objects— and social possessions—as his watch and compass. Seeing the bear, the boy experiences an ecstacy of communion which results in his refusal to kill the animal. For to destroy the bear would mean to violate the mute bond with nature that the "pageant-rite" is intended to establish, and thereby to disrupt the fraternity of the men in the hunting camp; yet as they all know, such a violation is sooner or later inevitable, a part of the historic transformation of their lives. At the end it will be given to Isaac—even as the Biblical Isaac, the son blessed by the father—to lead in the killing of the bear, the destruction of the totem. He alone will keep true the memory of the totem and the tribe, not so much the rites themselves or the men who performed them but the meaning of the rites and the value of the men. And he will do this by the mode of life he will adopt in the town, where his refusal to accept his heritage and his decision to live in simple poverty will perhaps break the chain of guilt binding him to the communal past.

Faulkner's more recent books, both those set in Yoknapatawpha—like *Intruder in the Dust, Requiem for a Nun, The Town,* and *The Mansion*—and those set elsewhere—like *The Fable,* a grandiose story about a Second Coming during the First World War—represent a decline in creative energy and achievement. These books were all written during the 1940's and 1950's, years that brought Faulkner many honors but also a slowly mounting crisis in his work. Despite some excellent parts, these novels are forced, anxious and often shrill, the work of a man, no longer driven, who must now drive himself. *Intruder in the Dust* is marred by stretches of dead Southern oratory, *The Fable* by intellectual pretentiousness and a mechanically whipped-up style, *The Town* and *The Mansion* by efforts to deal with subject matter for which Faulkner is not entirely equipped.

What went wrong in these last years? It is too early to say and at most we can only speculate, but a few symptoms of the trouble can be noted. In all these works there is a reliance on a high-powered rhetoric which bears the outer marks of Faulkner's earlier style, but is really a kind of willful self-imitation. The very abandon with which Faulkner now uses language seems itself calculated, a device in the repertoire of a writer who senses the dangers of relaxation even as he approaches the dangers of exhaustion.

There is also in these later novels a tendency to fall back upon high jinks of plot, a flaunting arbitrariness of invention—as if Faulkner, having examined and brooded upon human life for so long and with such pain, now felt that *anything* is possible to man and that our desire for realism in fiction is little more than a reluctance to confront the strangeness of reality; or as if Faulkner, wearied of telling stories and creating characters, were now ready to betray his impatience with his own skill. In the ripeness of his honor, he is in many ways as baffled and perplexed as when he first published his melancholy poems. But perhaps that is in the nature of the human journey.

Still, Faulkner remains one of the most brilliant writers America has ever produced, and as long as he is capable of putting pen to paper, so long can we expect that he will again surprise and delight us.

IV

THROUGHOUT Faulkner's novels one can detect a steady though uneven and painful growth of moral vision, and perhaps the most dramatic evidence of this growth lies in his changing attitudes toward the Negroes. For all Southern writers the Negroes form a particularly difficult challenge: in moral terms, for here they must try to grapple with and overcome inherited pieties, and in literary terms, for here they must try to break past the stereotypes of conventional perception.

Faulkner's early treatment of Negro characters is indulgent, mild and occasionally condescending. When one of them, like Caspey in *Sartoris,* is shown as rebellious, it is not with any acute sense of either the power of feeling behind that rebelliousness or the power of resistance among the whites. What is damaging in these early portraits is not so much Faulkner's laziness of treatment as the assumption, which he then shared with so many Southerners, that Negroes are *easily knowable:* an assumption that is, of course, at the heart of benevolent paternalism. But even in the early books overtones of doubt creep in. And in *The Sound and the Fury* the Negro cook, though conceived within the boundaries of benevolent paternalism, is a figure remarkable for her poise, her dignity, and her hard realism. Dilsey is the last of Faulkner's Negroes who can still believe that the South is a "natural" community to which they totally belong. After Dilsey, there is only estrangement and oblique rebellion; and after her, Faulkner breaks away from the received notions of the South.

The Faulkner to whom Negro characters had seemed so accessible now begins to stress that for the whites the Negro often exists not as a distinct person but as a specter or phantasm. In *Light in August* he writes brilliantly of what might be called the fetishism of false perception, the kind of false perception that has become systematic and acquired a pseudoreligious sanction. Joanna Burden, daughter of abolitionists but raised in the South, confesses:

I had seen and known Negroes since I could remember. I just looked at them as I did at rain, or furniture, or food or sleep. But after that I seemed to see them for the first time not as people, but as a thing, a shadow in which I lived, we lived, all white people, all other people . . . And I seemed to see the black shadow in the shape of a cross.

What is so remarkable about this passage is that here the false perception comes from a mixture of fright and humaneness, the two no longer separable, but bound together in an apocalyptic image of martyrdom and violation.

In Faulkner's treatment of Negroes there is, then, a quick and steep ascent: from benevolence to recognition of injustice, from amusement over idiosyncracies to a principled concern with human status, from cozy familiarity to a discovery of the profound estrangement of the races. And as Faulkner discovers the difficulties of approaching Negroes, he also develops an admirable sense of reserve, a blend of shyness and respect.

Faulkner now begins to see the Negro as victim and to write a good deal about mulattoes. Trapped between the demarcated races, the mulatto is an unavoidable candidate for the role of victim. Velery Bon in *Absalom, Absalom!* is a man adrift. The Negroes "thought he was a white man and believed it only the more strongly when he denied it," while the whites, "when he said he was a Negro, believed that he lied in order to save his skin." Joe

Christmas in *Light in August* is cursed by "that stain on his white blood or his black blood, whichever you will." Surely the most affecting of Faulkner's Negro characters, Christmas becomes a summation of the predicament of Yoknapatawpha, his existence torn by the conflict of color as violently and wastefully as the land itself. He is one of the most extreme instances in all modern literature of man as victim, man estranged from awareness and friendship—a figure in whom neither good nor evil counts nearly so much as the sheer fact of his suffering. He is entirely vulnerable, and if he were able to articulate a creed, he might say that the condition of his humanity is that he remain vulnerable.

Not only are the mulattoes important in Faulkner's novels because they underscore the inhumanity and irrationality of the racial scheme; they also figure as living agents of the "threat" of miscegenation, a threat which seems most to disturb Faulkner whenever he is most sympathetic to the Negro. All rationalizations for prejudice having crumbled, there remains only a fierce emotional resistance to an idea that is both immediately frightening and distantly attractive. For even as the thought of blood mixture triggers the fears of the white unconscious, it also suggests, as Faulkner hints in the story "Delta Autumn" (a self-sufficient part of *Go Down, Moses,* 1942), a vision of a distant time when barriers of caste and color will be removed.

The last major Negro figure in Faulkner's world is Lucas Beauchamp, neither at home in the South, like Dilsey, nor homeless, like Joe Christmas. Lucas is well enough aware of white society and he knows exactly what it is. But as he strides into full sight in *Intruder in the Dust,* a man powerful and complete, he is entirely on his own: he has put society behind him. Too proud to acquiesce in submission, too self-contained to be either outcast or rebel, Lucas has transformed the stigma of alienation into a mark of assurance. Apparently meant by Faulkner as a tribute to the strength and endurance of the Negroes, Lucas is something better still: a member of an oppressed group who appears not as a catalogue of disabilities or even virtues, but as a human being in his own right.

Ultimately Faulkner's greatest tribute to the Negroes is a novelist's tribute: a body of dramatic actions, a group of realized characters. No other American novelist has watched them so carefully and patiently; none other has listened with such fidelity to the nuances of their speech; none other has exposed his imagination so freely to discover their meaning for American life.

And in doing this Faulkner returns again and again to a sort of primal vision: a buried memory of boyhood friendship, unaffected by social grade and resting on that intuitive sense of scruple, that belief in *fairness* available to boys. It is a vision, a memory that runs through much of American literature, though seldom with such persistence and poignancy as in Faulkner. In "The Fire and the Hearth," for example, Roth Edmonds, the white boy, and Henry Beauchamp, the Negro boy, feel that their homes have "become interchangeable . . . sleeping on the same pallet in the white man's house or in the same bed in the Negro's . . ." And then comes the moment of pride, when the white boy refuses to share his bed with the Negro and lies alone "in a rigid fury of the grief he could not explain, the shame he would not admit." Later he knew "it was grief and was ready to admit it was shame also, wanted to admit it only it was too late then, forever and forever."

Forever and forever—the terribleness of this estrangement recurs in Faulkner's work as a cry of bafflement and loss. It is as if his novels keep saying that ultimately the whole apparatus of separation must seem too wearisome in its call to alertness, too costly in its tax on the emotions, and simply tedious as a brake on spontaneous life.

V

WHAT finally concerns Faulkner most, as it concerns every significant writer, is to release a vision of human life that will be serious and mature: a vision that can include both moral criticism and pleasure in sensuous experience, a vision that will accept both the power of fate, all that binds and breaks us, and the possibility of freedom, all that permits us to shape our being.

When Faulkner steps forth to "talk philoso-phy," he is somewhat less than impressive. In explicit statement he shows an alarming fondness for platitude, a fondness that lures him into portentous abstractions. But at his best Faulkner is a writer deeply concerned with the moral qualities of—as distinct from mere moral formulas about—human existence.

As might be expected from a writer bred in the South, Faulkner is much occupied with the notion of honor. Frequently invoked in his books, particularly the earlier ones, it is a notion that proves strangely elusive—more a cry than a substance—and increasingly cut off from moral issues. It allows some of Faulkner's characters a gamut of theatrical display, as also, at times, a release of more substantial values, such as their readiness to stake everything on a personal act defined not so much through its intrinsic value as through the fullness of passion that is brought to it. But the concept of honor remains hard to define, and the code of honor hard to embody and justify in actual conduct.

As Faulkner's work develops there is a gradual shift in emphasis from honor to integrity, a shift that reveals his deepening humaneness and thoughtfulness. Honor points to what one is in the world, integrity to what one is in oneself. Honor involves a standard of pride and dignity, a level of status and reputation; integrity an ease of being and a security of conscience. Honor depends upon an assertion of one's worth, integrity upon a readiness to face the full burden of one's existence. Many of the whites in Faulkner's novels are eager to preserve their honor; the more impressive among the Negroes, though not they alone, exemplify the life of integrity. As Faulkner develops and deepens his sense of human life and human trouble, he places a greater and greater stress upon the way a man turns inward, living out a dialogue with his own needs and conscience, confronting his own defeats and acknowledging his own value.

Some attempts have been made to see Faulkner as a Christian traditionalist. There can be no doubt that one of the more important sources of his moral outlook is an imperiled version of Christianity. The South in which Faulkner grew up was perhaps more concerned with Christian belief than most other sections of the country, but the quality of that concern was hardly such as to win the adherence of a sensitive young writer. Faulkner encountered Christianity more closely than most other American novelists of his generation, but encountered it mainly in a state of decay. For him the idea of Christianity can survive only when wrenched from its institutional and perhaps historical context: it survives, that is, as an extreme possibility of personal saintliness.

Like the Southern past, Christianity is felt mainly and most poignantly through its absence. Easter week forms a backdrop for the Compson tragedy in *The Sound and the Fury*; the crucifixion of Christ, for the murder of Joe Christmas in *Light in August*. Christianity appears as an occasional standard of judgment, a force to resist, a memory that troubles, a principle of contrast; but not as a secure inheritance. Faulkner struggles to define his moral outlook against the background of a dissolution of traditional beliefs, and usually the struggle matters more than the background.

His work, to be sure, is full of symbols, references, and echoes drawn from Christian drama, theology, and tradition. The recurrent figures of simple virtue—Dilsey, Byron Bunch, Isaac McCaslin—may be seen as embodiments of primitive Christian virtues, and Faulkner's commitment to these virtues as rooted in a sympathy for the uncontaminated Christianity which has sometimes flourished among rural Negroes in the South. At the other extreme in Faulkner's imagination there are figures and emblems of crucifixion which show how deeply the story of Jesus and the stern doctrines of Protestantism have left their mark. None of these, however, is enough to warrant our speaking of Faulkner as a traditional Christian writer, for they constitute fragments of belief and memory rather than an integrated outlook. In moral outlook Faulkner is a writer who moves between the far extremes of simplicity and sophistication, and he does this as a man thoroughly caught up in the "modern".— that is, an uncertain and problematic—view of life.

Given the fact that he shares at least part of the "modern" outlook, it becomes understandable why Faulkner, like other contemporary writers, should place so heavy a stress upon integrity, the virtue which flows from within and does not depend upon the presence of a set belief. As Faulkner sees it, integrity is accessible to people of every social grade and is to be found in a wide variety of situations— though in his novels he favors the use of extreme situations because he wishes to submit all that is "intractable" and "indomitable" in human character to the most urgent pressures. Dramatically, this test occurs in the clash of antithetical forces of freedom and necessity in the Yoknapatawpha world. Cursed by the tragic need to compromise their freedom, men can still redeem themselves through a gesture which, if it does not mitigate their defeat, can at least declare their humanity in defeat.

A curse hangs over all those Faulkner characters who reach into the depths of experience or struggle to extend the range of their consciousness. It is the curse of whatever in life cannot be escaped, whatever is *conditioned*: Joe Christmas battling his whiteness and his blackness; the Reverend Hightower unable to mediate between dream and reality; Bayard Sartoris wondering whether his existence has any purpose; Thomas Sutpen compelled to die in a squalor of exploitation; Quentin Compson driven to suicide by the sheer pain of consciousness. Whatever is burden in life—be it the consequence of society or character, economics or sin, injustice or evil—constitutes the curse. A key word in most of Faulkner's books is *outrage*, a word which for him signifies both the workings of this curse and the violence with which men act it out.

But there also remains available to each man the gesture, striking or subdued, by which he can declare himself. This gesture can be one of rebellion or submission; it can signify adherence to ritual or the need to accept defeat in total loneliness; it can be, as with Ab Snopes in the short story "Barn Burning," an arbitrary sign of selfhood or, as with Popeye's request that his hair be fixed just before he is to be executed, a final assertion of indifference. But always it is the mark of distinct being, the way a man defines himself.

The opposition between curse and gesture forms the dramatic and moral pattern of Faulkner's work, and within that opposition he declares the items of his bias: his respect before suffering, his contempt for deceit, his belief in the rightness of self-trust, his enlarging compassion for the defeated. At its greatest, the gesture shows that for Faulkner heroism signifies exposure, the taking and enduring and resisting of everything that comes to man between birth and death. And thereby it brings a kind of freedom.

VI

FAULKNER is a constant and restless experimenter in his use of the novel. He is quite capable of putting together a well-made piece of fiction in which every incident and (almost) every word is "functionally" justified, in which there is a neat pattern of events moving from a precise beginning to a precise end, and in which the language serves as a clear glass enabling the reader to get immediately to the matter of the story. But only seldom does he choose to abide with the familiar conventions of the novel. He prefers, instead, to break up and jumble his time sequences; to divide his narrative into fragments told by a variety of participants and observers; to weight his prose with lyric intensities, baroque displays, and philosophic speculations; to lure the reader from difficulty to difficulty, so that the very effort to read a Faulkner novel forces one into an act of esthetic and moral discovery, parallel to those discoveries his narrators make in the course of telling their stories. In *Absalom, Absalom!*, for example, the main action of the novel is not a line of events traced by the author and followed by the reader, but the struggle of the narrator, Quentin Compson, to piece together the facts concerning the life of Thomas Sutpen, a ruthless figure in the Southern past, and to make out what these facts really meant. The story is unfolded not in the orderly sequence of the traditional novel, which assumes that an omniscient author has everything under control, but rather in a— temporarily bewildering—series of intuitions, false starts, gasps, and corrections.

There are, to be sure, times when some of Faulkner's technical experiments seem wanton or trivial; but whenever he is at or near his best, they always have a serious purpose. That purpose is usually to draw the reader into a more direct and perilous relation to the happenings of the story; to saturate him in the atmospheres of an imagined world; to force him to abandon the posture of a passive listener and become an active participant struggling, like some of Faulkner's characters themselves, to discover meaning in the represented events. Faulkner wants the reader to share with his characters the full weight of human experience, so that, in a sense, the reader becomes "part of" the novel. All of Faulkner's devices— such as his use of stream of consciousness, multiple narrators, interior monologues and a convoluted style—are put to the service of making us active collaborators in the working out of the Yoknapatawpha saga.

From book to book Faulkner employs different methods. In *The Sound and the Fury* he penetrates the private consciousness of several members of the Compson family: with the idiot Benjy, through a flow of language resembling what psychoanalysts call "free association," and with the villainous Jason, through an interior monologue which bears outer signs of rational structure. The effect Faulkner creates is like a spiraling back and forth over the same stretch of human history, but each time in terms of radically different moral perceptions and each time with a further dissolution of the boundary between past and present, so that the past becomes part of the present, a memory imprisoned in consciousness.

In most of his other novels Faulkner continues to experiment. *As I Lay Dying*, his most astonishing piece of virtuosity, is composed somewhat like a cantata in which a theme is pursued through a succession of voices: fifteen characters speak through sixty narrative and reflective fragments. Nothing being explained, everything must be shown. The danger is that the frequent breaks in point of view will impede the flow of narrative—a danger Faulkner overcomes with great skill. In *Light in August* Faulkner moves closer to the naturalistic novel, with its accumulation of social detail, its sense of human fatality, and its readiness to face the grimness of modern existence. In *Sanctuary* he turns to grotesquerie, sometimes comic and sometimes appalling, so that in its blurred intensity the book comes to resemble an expressionist nightmare. *Absalom, Absa-*

lom! employs some of the mildewed properties of the Gothic romance—Faulknerian versions of the haunted house, the demon lover, the passively suffering heroine—but endows these with a seriousness that lifts the book far above the mechanical diabolism and shrillness one usually associates with the Gothic. Structurally, there is a relaxation in both *The Hamlet* and *Go Down, Moses*, both books being organized through a succession of loosely connected and rather sprawling tales. In *The Hamlet* Faulkner borrows from the tradition of the American tall tale, with its slyness of understatement and extravagance of action. In *The Wild Palms* Faulkner weaves together alternating sections of two distinct narratives, so that the meaning of one becomes involved with the meaning of the other. And in *Requiem for a Nun* he shuttles between the acts of a play and elegiac prose rhapsodies about the Yoknapatawpha past.

Faulkner is especially gifted at a certain kind of narrative which we may call the tale, and which is somewhere between the short story and the novel in length and approach. "The Bear," "Spotted Horses" and parts of some of his novels can be read as long tales, which by their nature forgo the strict requirements of the short story and the somewhat less strict requirements of the novel. "That Evening Sun" shows that, when he cares to be, Faulkner is a master of the short story: it is a work all compact, economical, and terse. In the tale, by contrast, there is no inescapable need for either that economy of effect which is essential to the short story or those complications of social behavior which are often depicted in the novel. Sharing some of the qualities of fable and myth, the tale inclines toward simplicity of action, spaciousness and freedom of invention, and the elaboration of folk materials. It can spin or wander off on its own, in a flexible style that allows for a wide variety of effects, ranging (in parts of "The Bear") from bardic eloquence to (in "Spotted Horses") native humor.

As Faulkner's work develops, there occurs an interesting, though sometimes troublesome, shift in his strategy of narration. The earlier books employ one of two methods: either the objective, impersonal narration that is found in *Sanctuary* and *Light in August* or the subjective revelation of character through inner voices and reflections, as in *The Sound and the Fury* and *As I Lay Dying*. But beginning with *Light in August*, and becoming increasingly evident in many of the later novels, there is a new voice, not really that of any of the characters and finally not that of Faulkner himself. It is, so to say, an "over-voice" speaking for the memories and conscience of a people: a voice which carries some of the impassioned rhetoric of traditional Southern oratory, as well as some of its unfortunate fondness for pasteboard flashiness and grandiloquent rhythms. In *Intruder in the Dust* this oratory is "official," groaning with echoes of addresses to Southern state legislatures and Fourth of July orations; but in *Absalom, Absalom!* it is private—private to Faulkner's vision of the South—in both source and quality. The voice we now hear, in the best of the later novels, speaks for an afflicted imagination, a grieved mind familiar with the springs of evil; it evokes an image of a man rasping from the heart, perhaps to no one but himself: a man who cries out with the burden of human history. Its effect is somewhat like that which Morris Croll, in a fine study, "The Baroque Style," attributes to sixteenth-century rhetoricians: "Their purpose was to portray, not a thought, but a mind thinking, or in Pascal's words, *la peinture de la pensée*. They knew that an idea separated from the act of experiencing it is not the idea that was experienced."

This description holds for most of Faulkner's writing, no matter what pitch he strikes in his prose or what shape he gives it at a particular moment: it is true for his writing no matter which of his several styles he employs. His mimetic capacities—his gift for rendering the precise nuances of speech, for differentiating among a variety of accents and stresses—are granted even by his most hostile critics. But Faulkner is also capable of writing the sort of clean, simple, efficient prose which is so much favored in our time: the prose of unadorned evocation, of the pure picture. The following passage from *The Sound and the Fury*, for example, in which the Negro cook Dilsey is seen working in the kitchen while Mrs. Compson keeps whimpering after her, is a strong and exact rendering of person and place:

Dilsey prepared to make biscuit. As she ground the sifter steadily above the bread board, she sang, to herself at first, something without particular tune or words, repetitive, mournful and plaintive, austere, as she ground a faint, steady snowing of flour onto the breadboard. The stove had begun to heat the room and to fill it with murmurous minors of the fire, and presently she was singing louder, as if her voice too had been thawed out by the growing warmth, and then Mrs. Compson called her name again from within the house. Dilsey raised her face as if her eyes could and did penetrate the walls and ceiling and saw the old woman in her quilted dressing gown at the head of the stairs, calling her name with machine-like regularity.

"Oh Lawd," Dilsey said . . .

Faulkner's novels and stories are full of realistic evocations done in strong outline and primary colors. But if Faulkner can, upon need, write a severely disciplined prose—as in "That Evening Sun," where every word is bent to the purpose of a harshly sensous evocation—he is also quite capable of moving toward other styles. In parts of "The Bear" he achieves a ruminative bardic style of quiet gravity; in *Absalom, Absalom!* a fierce grinding rhetoric which makes that book so difficult and memorable to read; and in *The Hamlet* a wildly exuberant prose, full of juice and bounce.

It would be pointless to deny, of course, that in some of Faulkner's books, especially the later ones, the language tends to cascade wildly, noun upon noun, adjective upon adjective, breathless phrase upon phrase. The syntax can become hopelessly entangled in its own convolutions: a thickly matted jungle of clauses and phrases defying, by clear intention, the schoolbook rules of grammar. Such prose is clearly vulnerable to criticism and even sneering; it involves greater risks than the taut style of a Hemingway, but at least on occasion it also brings greater rewards. In fiction there is no single "good" or "accepted" style. The clumsy, leaden prose of a Dreiser can be remarkably moving and powerful. The artful simplicities of Sherwood Anderson's style can help evoke moods of loneliness and sadness. The tough restraints of Hemingway's prose can give one the exact "feel" of an object.

There are many possibilities in the use of language in fiction, and none can be prejudged, all depend upon the specific context in which they appear and the particular skill with which they are employed. When Faulkner seems to be torturing some of his sentences and wrenching some of his words, crowding into a unit of language more than seems possible for it to bear, this is not because he is indifferent to the need for clarity or the value of communication. His more rhetorical style is the result of his desire not merely to pack into a sentence or paragraph a description of a present state of being or a continuing action, but also to communicate something of its half-buried causes, its complicating consequences, its ironic contraries, its continuous muddle and possible magnificence. It is as if he were trying to pack into a sentence or a paragraph the sense of simultaneity which is so characteristic of human consciousness, the sense of the palpitating complexity of felt experience. This means that he sometimes strains, sometimes drives too hard, sometimes falls into obscurity. But when he succeeds—and that is often enough—the result is marvelously rich, a full impression of the way an experience feels, the way a relationship moves, the way a human being responds at one and the same time to the pressures of his outer life and the needs of his inner life.

These remarks are the merest beginning of a discussion of Faulkner's style, but then the two selections that follow are the merest beginning of a display of his gifts. The reader who enjoys them should turn both to Faulkner's stories and, more important, to that sequence of remarkable novels which forms the achievement of his great period in the 1930's. It is not, to be sure, an easy journey and no one can take it who would read while he runs. Faulkner demands attention and offers difficulties, but in literature, as elsewhere, the confrontation of difficulties can bring large and unexpected rewards.

READING SUGGESTIONS

EDITIONS

All of Faulkner's novels are now available either in their original printings or in inexpensive reprints, many of the latter in paperback. Several of the novels appear in the Modern Library reprint series.

CRITICISM AND BIOGRAPHY

No full-scale biography is yet available, but biographical information appears in several of the critical studies listed below.

RICHARD CHASE, *The American Novel and Its Tradition* (1957). Contains an interesting chapter on Faulkner.

MALCOLM COWLEY, editor, *The Portable Faulkner* (1946). A pioneer anthology of Faulkner's work, compiled at a time when Faulkner was not yet in critical favor and most of his books were out of print. Cowley's Introduction is first-rate.

FREDERICK HOFFMAN AND OLGA VICKERY, *Three*

Decades of Faulkner Criticism (1960). A collection of articles. Especially important in the history of Faulkner criticism are those by George Marion O'Donnell and Robert Penn Warren.

IRVING HOWE, *William Faulkner: A Critical Study* (1952). A general introduction, with special stress on the social significance of Faulkner's work. Reissued and brought up to date as a paperback in 1961.

H. H. WAGGONER, *William Faulkner: From Jefferson to the World* (1959). A study of the novels, with particular emphasis on their relation to Christian thought.

WILLIAM VAN O'CONNOR, *The Tangled Fires of William Faulkner* (1954). A general introduction.

OLGA VICKERY, *The Novels of William Faulkner* (1959). A close study of literary techniques.

SPOTTED HORSES

◇

❲ "SPOTTED HORSES" is one of the loosely connected tales which constitute *The Hamlet* (1940), a racy comic extravaganza which blends some extremely amusing tall tales with an account of how the Snopes family, led by the sinister but unforgettable Flem Snopes, gradually takes over Frenchman's Bend, a hamlet in Yoknapatawpha County. "Spotted Horses" is notable for the ease and skill with which Faulkner employs a folk idiom; for the pathos with which he portrays the plight of the Armstids when they are trapped with one of the wild ponies; for the introduction of Ratliff, the country salesman, who is Faulkner's most sympathetic and intelligent observer; and for a hundred other things —but above all, for the spring and raciness which make it one of the great specimens of American humor.

◇

I

A LITTLE while before sundown the men lounging about the gallery of the store saw, coming up the road from the south, a covered wagon drawn by mules and followed by a considerable string of obviously alive objects which in the levelling sun resembled vari-sized and -colored tatters torn at random from large billboards—circus posters, say—attached to the rear of the wagon and inherent with its own separate and collective motion, like the tail of a kite.

"What in the hell is that?" one said.

"It's a circus," Quick said. They began to rise, watching the wagon. Now they could see that the animals behind the wagon were horses. Two men rode in the wagon.

"Hell fire," the first man—his name was Freeman—said. "It's Flem Snopes." They were all standing when the wagon came up and stopped and Snopes got down and approached the steps. He might have departed only this morning. He wore the same cloth cap, the minute bow tie against the white shirt, the same gray trousers. He mounted the steps.

"Howdy, Flem," Quick said. The other looked briefly at all of them and none of them, mounting the steps. "Starting you a circus?"

"Gentlemen," he said. He crossed the gallery; they made way for him. Then they descended the steps and approached the wagon, at the tail of which the horses stood in a restive clump, larger than rabbits and gaudy as parrots and shackled to one another and to the wagon itself with sections of barbed wire. Calico-coated, small-bodied, with delicate legs and pink faces in which their mismatched eyes rolled wild and subdued, they huddled, gaudy, motionless, and alert, wild as deer, deadly as rattlesnakes, quiet as doves. The men stood at a respectful distance, looking at them. At that moment Jody Varner came through the group, shouldering himself to the front of it.

"Watch yourself, doc," a voice said from the rear. But it was already too late. The nearest animal rose on its hind legs with lightning rapidity and struck twice with its forefeet at Varner's face, faster than a boxer, the movement of its surge against the wire which held it travelling backward among the rest of the band in a wave of thuds and lunges. "Hup, you broom-tailed, hay-burning sidewinders," the same voice said. This was the second man who had arrived in the wagon. He was a stranger. He wore a heavy, densely black moustache, a wide pale hat. When he thrust himself through and turned to herd them back from the horses they saw, thrust into the hip pockets of his tight jeans pants, the butt of a heavy pearl-handled pistol and a florid carton such as small cakes come in. "Keep away from them, boys," he said. "They've got kind of skittish, they ain't been rode in so long."

"Since when have they been rode?" Quick said. The stranger looked at Quick. He had a broad, quite cold, wind-gnawed face and bleak, cold eyes. His belly fitted neat and smooth as a peg into the tight trousers.

"I reckon that was when they were rode on the ferry to get across the Mississippi River," Varner said. The stranger looked at him. "My name's Varner," Jody said.

"Hipps," the other said. "Call me Buck." Across the left side of his head, obliterating the tip of that ear, was a savage and recent gash gummed over with a blackish substance like axle-grease. They looked at the scar. Then they watched him remove the carton from his pocket and tilt a gingersnap into his hand and put the gingersnap into his mouth, beneath the moustache.

"You and Flem have some trouble back yonder?" Quick said. The stranger ceased chewing. When he looked directly at anyone, his eyes became like two pieces of flint turned suddenly up in dug earth.

"Back where?" he said.

"Your nigh ear," Quick said.

"Oh," the other said. "That." He touched his ear. "That was my mistake. I was absent-minded one night when I was staking them out. Studying about something else and forgot how long the wire was." He chewed. They looked at his ear. "Happen to any man careless around a horse. Put a little axle-dope on it and you won't notice it tomorrow though. They're pretty lively now, lazing along all day doing nothing. It'll work out of them in a couple of days." He put another gingersnap into his mouth, chewing, "Don't you believe they'll gentle?" No one answered. They looked at the ponies, grave and noncommittal. Jody turned and went back into the store. "Them's good, gentle ponies," the stranger said. "Watch now." He put the carton back into his pocket and approached the horses, his hand extended. The nearest one was standing on three legs now. It

appeared to be asleep. Its eyelid drooped over the cerulean eye; its head was shaped like an ironing-board. Without even raising the eyelid it flicked its head, the yellow teeth cropped. For an instant it and the man appeared to be inextricable in one violence. Then they became motionless, the stranger's high heels dug into the earth, one hand gripping the animal's nostrils, holding the horse's head wrenched half around while it breathed in hoarse, smothered groans. "See?" the stranger said in a panting voice, the veins standing white and rigid in his neck and along his jaw. "See? All you got to do is handle them a little and work hell out of them for a couple of days. Now look out. Give me room back there." They gave back a little. The stranger gathered himself then sprang away. As he did so, a second horse slashed at his back, severing his vest from collar to hem down the back exactly as the trick swordsman severs a floating veil with one stroke.

"Sho now," Quick said. "But suppose a man don't happen to own a vest."

At that moment Jody Varner, followed by the blacksmith, thrust through them again. "All right, Buck," he said. "Better get them on into the lot. Eck here will help you." The stranger, the severed halves of the vest swinging from either shoulder, mounted to the wagon seat, the blacksmith following.

"Get up, you transmogrified hallucinations of Job and Jezebel," the stranger said. The wagon moved on, the tethered ponies coming gaudily into motion behind it, behind which in turn the men followed at a respectful distance, on up the road and into the lane and so to the lot gate behind Mrs. Littlejohn's. Eck got down and opened the gate. The wagon passed through but when the ponies saw the fence the herd surged backward against the wire which attached it to the wagon, standing on its collective hind legs and then trying to turn within itself, so that the wagon moved backward for a few feet until the Texan, cursing, managed to saw the mules about and so lock the wheels. The men following had already fallen rapidly back. "Here, Eck," the Texan said. "Get up here and take the reins." The blacksmith got back in the wagon and took the reins. Then they watched the Texan descend, carrying a looped-up blacksnake whip, and go around to the rear of the herd and drive it through the gate, the whip snaking about the harlequin rumps in methodical and pistol-like reports. Then the watchers hurried across Mrs. Littlejohn's yard and mounted to the veranda, one end of which overlooked the lot.

"How you reckon he ever got them tied together?" Freeman said.

"I'd a heap rather watch how he aims to turn them loose," Quick said. The Texan had climbed back into the halted wagon. Presently he and Eck both appeared at the rear end of the open hood. The Texan grasped the wire and began to draw the first horse up to the wagon, the animal plunging and surging back against the wire as though trying to hang itself, the contagion passing back through the herd from animal to animal until they were rearing and plunging again against the wire.

"Come on, grab a holt," the Texan said. Eck grasped the wire also. The horses laid back against it, the pink faces tossing above the back-surging mass. "Pull him up, pull him up," the Texan said sharply. "They couldn't get up here in the wagon even if they wanted to." The wagon moved gradually backward until the head of the first horse was snubbed up to the tail-gate. The Texan took a turn of the wire quickly about one of the wagon stakes. "Keep the slack out of it," he said. He vanished and reappeared, almost in the same second, with a pair of heavy wire-cutters. "Hold them like that," he said, and leaped. He vanished, broad hat, flapping vest, wire-cutters and all, into a kaleidoscopic maelstrom of long teeth and wild eyes and slashing feet, from which presently the horses began to burst one by one like partridges flushing, each wearing a necklace of barbed wire. The first one crossed the lot at top speed, on a straight line. It galloped into the fence without any diminution whatever. The wire gave, recovered, and slammed the horse to earth where it lay for a moment, glaring, its legs still galloping in air. It scrambled up without having ceased to gallop and crossed the lot and galloped into the opposite fence and was slammed again to earth. The others were now freed. They whipped and whirled about the lot like dizzy fish in a bowl. It had seemed like a big lot until now, but now the very idea that all that fury and motion should be transpiring inside any one fence was something to be repudiated with contempt, like a mirror trick. From the ultimate dust the stranger, carrying the wire-cutters and his vest completely gone now, emerged. He was not running, he merely moved with a light-poised and watchful celerity, weaving among the calico rushes of the animals, feinting and dodging like a boxer until he reached the gate and crossed the yard and mounted to the veranda. One sleeve of his shirt hung only at one point from his shoulder. He ripped it off and wiped his face with it and threw it away and took out the paper carton and shook a gingersnap into his hand. He was breathing only a little heavily. "Pretty lively now," he said. "But it'll work out of them in a couple of days." The ponies still

streaked back and forth through the growing dusk like hysterical fish, but not so violently now.

"What'll you give a man to reduce them odds a little for you?" Quick said. The Texan looked at him, the eyes bleak, pleasant and hard above the chewing jaw, the heavy moustache. "To take one of them off your hands?" Quick said.

At that moment the little periwinkle-eyed boy came along the veranda, saying, "Papa, papa; where's papa?"

"Who you looking for, sonny?" one said.

"It's Eck's boy," Quick said. "He's still out yonder in the wagon. Helping Mr. Buck here." The boy went on to the end of the veranda, in diminutive overalls—a miniature replica of the men themselves.

"Papa," he said. "Papa." The blacksmith was still leaning from the rear of the wagon, still holding the end of the severed wire. The ponies, bunched for the moment, now slid past the wagon, flowing, stringing out again so that they appeared to have doubled in number, rushing on; the hard, rapid, light patter of unshod hooves came out of the dust. "Mamma says to come on to supper," the boy said.

The moon was almost full then. When supper was over and they had gathered again along the veranda, the alteration was hardly one of visibility even. It was merely a translation from the lapidary-dimensional of day to the treacherous and silver receptivity in which the horses huddled in mazy camouflage, or singly or in pairs rushed, fluid, phantom, and unceasing, to huddle again in mirage-like clumps from which came high, abrupt squeals and the vicious thudding of hooves.

Ratliff was among them now. He had returned just before supper. He had not dared to take his team into the lot at all. They were now in Bookwright's stable a half mile from the store. "So Flem has come home again," he said. "Well, well, well. Will Varner paid to get him to Texas, so I reckon it ain't nor more than fair for you fellows to pay the freight on him back." From the lot there came a high, thin squeal. One of the animals emerged. It seemed not to gallop but to flow, bodiless, without dimension. Yet there was the rapid light beat of hard hooves on the packed earth.

"He ain't said they was his yet," Quick said.

"He ain't said they ain't neither," Freeman said.

"I see," Ratliff said. "That's what you are holding back on. Until he tells you whether they are his or not. Or maybe you can wait until the auction's over and split up and some can follow Flem and some can follow that Texas fellow and watch to see which one spends the money. But then, when a man's done got trimmed, I don't reckon he cares who's got the money."

"Maybe if Ratliff would leave here tonight, they wouldn't make him buy one of them ponies tomorrow," a third said.

"That's fact," Ratliff said. "A fellow can dodge a Snopes if he just starts lively enough. In fact, I don't believe he would have to pass more than two folks before he would have another victim intervened betwixt them. You folks ain't going to buy them things sho enough, are you?" Nobody answered. They sat on the steps, their backs against the veranda posts, or on the railing itself. Only Ratliff and Quick sat in chairs, so that to them the others were black silhouettes against the dreaming lambence of the moonlight beyond the veranda. The pear tree across the road opposite was now in full and frosty bloom, the twigs and branches springing not outward from the limbs but standing motionless and perpendicular above the horizontal boughs like the separate and up-streaming hair of a drowned woman sleeping upon the uttermost floor of the windless and tideless sea.

"Anse McCallum brought two of them horses back from Texas once," one of the men on the steps said. He did not move to speak. He was not speaking to anyone. "It was a good team. A little light. He worked it for ten years. Light work, it was."

"I mind it," another said. "Anse claimed he traded fourteen rifle cartridges for both of them, didn't he?"

"It was the rifle too, I heard," a third said.

"No, it was just the shells," the first said. "The fellow wanted to swap him four more for the rifle too, but Anse said he never needed them. Cost too much to get six of them back to Mississippi."

"Sho," the second said. "When a man don't have to invest so much into a horse or a team, he don't need to expect so much from it." The three of them were not talking any louder, they were merely talking among themselves, to one another, as if they sat there alone. Ratliff, invisible in the shadow against the wall, made a sound, harsh, sardonic, not loud.

"Ratliff's laughing," a fourth said.

"Don't mind me," Ratliff said. The three speakers had not moved. They did not move now, yet there seemed to gather about the three silhouettes something stubborn, convinced, and passive, like children who have been chidden. A bird, a shadow, fleet and dark and swift, curved across the moonlight, upward into the pear tree and began to sing; a mockingbird.

First one I've noticed this year," Freeman said.

"You can hear them along Whiteleaf every night," the first man said. "I heard one in February. In that snow. Singing in a gum."

"Gum is the first tree to put out," the third said. "That was why. It made it feel like singing, fixing to put out that way. That was why it taken a gum."

"Gum first to put out?" Quick said. "What about willow?"

"Willow ain't a tree," Freeman said. "It's a weed."

"Well, I don't know what it is," the fourth said. "But it ain't no weed. Because you can grub up a weed and you are done with it. I been grubbing up a clump of willows outen my spring pasture for fifteen years. They are the same size every year. Only difference is, it's just two or three more trees every time."

"And if I was you," Ratliff said, "that's just exactly where I would be come sunup tomorrow. Which of course you ain't going to do. I reckon there ain't nothing under the sun or in French-man's Bend neither that can keep you folks from giving Flem Snopes and that Texas man your money. But I'd sholy like to know just exactly who I was giving my money to. Seems like Eck here would tell you. Seems like he'd do that for his neighbors, don't it? Besides being Flem's cousin, him and that boy of his, Wallstreet, helped that Texas man tote water for them to-night and Eck's going to help him feed them in the morning too. Why, maybe Eck will be the one that will catch them and lead them up one at a time for your folks to bid on them. Ain't that right, Eck?"

The other man sitting on the steps with his back against the post was the blacksmith. "I don't know," he said.

"Boys," Ratliff said, "Eck knows all about them horses. Flem's told him, how much they cost and how much him and that Texas man aim to get for them, make off of them. Come on, Eck. Tell us." The other did not move, sitting on the top step, not quite facing them, sitting there beneath the successive layers of their quiet and intent concentrated listening and waiting.

"I don't know," he said. Ratliff began to laugh. He sat in the chair, laughing while the others sat or lounged upon the steps and the railing, sitting beneath his laughing as Eck had sat beneath their listening and waiting. Ratliff ceased laughing. He rose. He yawned, quite loud.

"All right. You folks can buy them critters if you want to. But me, I'd just as soon buy a tiger or a rattlesnake. And if Flem Snopes offered me either one of them, I would be afraid to touch it for fear it would turn out to be a painted dog or a piece of garden hose when I went up to take possession of it. I bid you one and all goodnight." He entered the house. They did not look after him, though after a while they all shifted a little and looked down into the lot, upon the splotchy, sporadic surge and flow of the horses, from among which from time to time came an abrupt squeal, a thudding blow. In the pear tree the mockingbird's idiot reiteration pulsed and purled.

"Anse McCallum made a good team outen them two of hisn," the first man said. "They was a little light. That was all."

When the sun rose the next morning a wagon and three saddled mules stood in Mrs. Littlejohn's lane and six men and Eck Snopes' son were already leaning on the fence, looking at the horses which huddled in a quiet clump before the barn door, watching the men in their turn. A second wagon came up the road and into the lane and stopped, and then there were eight men beside the boy standing at the fence, beyond which the horses stood, their blue-and-brown eyeballs rolling alertly in their gaudy faces. "So this here is the Snopes circus, is it?" one of the newcomers said. He glanced at the faces, then he went to the end of the row and stood beside the blacksmith and the little boy. "Are them Flem's horses?" he said to the blacksmith.

"Eck don't know who them horses belong to any more than we do," one of the others said. "He knows that Flem come here on the same wagon with them, because he saw him. But that's all."

"And all he will know," a second said. "His own kin will be the last man in the world to find out anything about Flem Snopes' business."

"No," the first said. "He wouldn't even be that. The first man Flem would tell his business to would be the man that was left after the last man died. Flem Snopes don't even tell himself what he is up to. Not if he was laying in bed with himself in a empty house in the dark of the moon."

"That's a fact," a third said. "Flem would trim Eck or any other of his kin quick as he would us. Ain't that right, Eck?"

"I don't know," Eck said. They were watching the horses, which at that moment broke into a high-eared, stiff-kneed swirl and flowed in a patchwork wave across the lot and brought up again, facing the men along the fence, so they did not hear the Texan until he was among them. He wore a new shirt and another vest a little too small for him and he was just putting the paper carton back into his hip pocket.

"Morning, morning," he said. "Come to get an early pick, have you? Want to make me an offer for one or two before the bidding starts and runs the prices up?" They had not looked at the stranger long. They were not looking at him now, but at the horses in the lot, which had lowered their heads, snuffing into the dust.

"I reckon we'll look a while first," one said.

"You are in time to look at them eating breakfast, anyhow," the Texan said. "Which is more than they done without they staid up all night." He opened the gate and entered it. At once the horses jerked their heads up, watching him. "Here, Eck," the Texan said over his shoulder, "two or three of you boys help me drive them into the barn." After a moment Eck and two others approached the gate, the little boy at his father's heels, though the other did not see him until he turned to shut the gate.

"You stay out of here," Eck said. "One of them things will snap your head off same as a acorn before you even know it." He shut the gate and went on after the others, whom the Texan had now waved fanwise outward as he approached the horses which now drew into a restive huddle, beginning to mill slightly, watching the men. Mrs. Littlejohn came out of the kitchen and crossed the yard to the woodpile, watching the lot. She picked up two or three sticks of wood and paused, watching the lot again. Now there were two more men standing at the fence.

"Come on, come on," the Texan said. "They won't hurt you. They just ain't never been in under a roof before."

"I just as lief let them stay out here, if that's what they want to do," Eck said.

"Get yourself a stick—there's a bunch of wagon stakes against the fence yonder—and when one of them tries to rush you, bust him over the head so he will understand what you mean." One of the men went to the fence and got three of the stakes and returned and distributed them. Mrs. Littlejohn, her armful of wood complete now, paused again halfway back to the house, looking into the lot. The little boy was directly behind his father again, though this time the father had not discovered him yet. The men advanced toward the horses, the huddle of which began to break into gaudy units turning inward upon themselves. The Texan was cursing them in a loud steady cheerful voice. "Get in there, you banjo-faced jack rabbits. Don't hurry them, now. Let them take their time. Hi! Get in there. What do you think that barn is— a law court maybe? Or maybe a church and somebody is going to take up a collection on you?" The animals fell slowly back. Now and then one feinted to break from the huddle, the Texan driving it back each time with skillfully thrown bits of dirt. Then one at the rear saw the barn door just behind it but before the herd could break the Texan snatched the wagon stake from Eck and, followed by one of the other men, rushed at the horses and began to lay about the heads and shoulders, choosing by unerring instinct the point animal and striking it first square in the face then on the withers as it turned and then on the rump as it turned further, so that when the break came it was reversed and the entire herd rushed into the long open hallway and brought up against the further wall with a hollow, thunderous sound like that of a collapsing mineshaft. "Seems to have held all right," the Texan said. He and the other man slammed the half-length doors and looked over them into the tunnel of the barn, at the far end of which the ponies were now a splotchy, phantom moiling punctuated by crackings of wooden partitions and the dry reports of hooves which gradually died away. "Yep, it held all right," the Texan said. The other two came to the doors and looked over them. The little boy came up beside his father now, trying to see through a crack, and Eck saw him.

"Didn't I tell you to stay out of here?" Eck said. "Don't you know them things will kill you quicker than you can say scat? You go and get outside of that fence and stay there."

"Why don't you get your paw to buy you one of them, Wall?" one of the men said.

"Me buy one of them things?" Eck said. "When I can go to the river anytime and catch me a snapping turtle or a moccasin for nothing? You go on, now. Get out of here and stay out." The Texan had entered the barn. One of the men closed the doors after him and put the bar up again and over the top of the doors they watched the Texan go on down the hallway, toward the ponies which now huddled like gaudy phantoms in the gloom, quiet now and already beginning to snuff experimentally into the long lipworn trough fastened against the rear wall. The little boy had merely gone around behind his father, to the other side, where he stood peering now through a knot-hole in a plank. The Texan opened a smaller door in the wall and entered it, though almost immediately he reappeared.

"I don't see nothing but shelled corn in here," he said. "Snopes said he would send some hay up here last night."

"Won't they eat corn either?" one of the men said.

"I don't know," the Texan said. "They ain't

never seen any that I know of. We'll find out in a minute though." He disappeared, though they could still hear him in the crib. Then he emerged once more, carrying a big double-ended feed-basket, and retreated into the gloom where the parti-colored rumps of the horses were now ranged quietly along the feeding-trough. Mrs. Littlejohn appeared once more, on the veranda this time, carrying a big brass dinner bell. She raised it to make the first stroke. A small commotion set up among the ponies as the Texan approached but he began to speak to them at once, in a brisk loud unemphatic mixture of cursing and cajolery, disappearing among them. The men at the door heard the dry rattling of the corn-pellets into the trough, a sound broken by a single snort of amazed horror. A plank cracked with a loud report; before their eyes the depths of the hallway dissolved in loud fury, and while they stared over the doors, unable yet to begin to move, the entire interior exploded into mad tossing shapes like a downrush of flames.

"Hell fire," one of them said. "Jump!" he shouted. The three turned and ran frantically for the wagon, Eck last. Several voices from the fence were now shouting something but Eck did not even hear them until, in the act of scrambling madly at the tail-gate, he looked behind him and saw the little boy still leaning to the knot-hole in the door which in the next instant vanished into matchwood, the knot-hole itself exploding from his eye and leaving him, motionless in the diminutive overalls and still leaning forward a little until he vanished utterly beneath the towering parti-colored wave full of feet and glaring eyes and wild teeth which, overtopping, burst into scattering units, revealing at last the gaping orifice and the little boy still standing in it, unscratched, his eye still leaned to the vanished knot-hole.

"Wall!" Eck roared. The little boy turned and ran for the wagon. The horses were whipping back and forth across the lot, as if while in the barn they had once more doubled their number; two of them rushed up quattering and galloped all over the boy again without touching him as he ran, earnest and diminutive and seemingly without progress, though he reached the wagon at last, from which Eck, his sunburned skin now a sickly white, reached down and snatched the boy into the wagon by the straps of his overalls and slammed him face down across his knees and caught up a coiled hitching-rope from the bed of the wagon.

"Didn't I tell you to get out of here?" Eck said in a shaking voice. "Didn't I tell you?"

"If you're going to whip him, you better whip

the rest of us too and then one of us can frail hell out of you," one of the others said.

"Or better still, take the rope and hang that durn fellow yonder," the second said. The Texan was now standing in the wrecked door of the barn, taking the gingersnap carton from his hip pocket. "Before he kills the rest of Frenchman's Bend too."

"You mean Flem Snopes," the first said. The Texan tilted the carton above his other open palm. The horses still rushed and swirled back and forth but they were beginning to slow now, trotting on high, stiff legs, although their eyes were still rolling whitely and various.

"I misdoubted that damn shell corn all along," the Texan said. "But at least they have seen what it looks like. They can't claim they ain't got nothing out of this trip." He shook the carton over his open hand. Nothing came out of it. Mrs. Littlejohn on the veranda made the first stroke with the dinner bell; at the sound the horses rushed again, the earth of the lot becoming vibrant with the light dry clatter of hooves. The Texan crumpled the carton and threw it aside. "Chuck wagon," he said. There were three more wagons in the lane now and there were twenty or more men at the fence when the Texan, followed by his three assistants and the little boy, passed through the gate. The bright cloudless early sun gleamed upon the pearl butt of the pistol in his hip pocket and upon the bell which Mrs. Littlejohn still rang, peremptory, strong, and loud.

When the Texan, picking his teeth with a splintered kitchen match, emerged from the house twenty minutes later, the tethered wagons and riding horses and mules extended from the lot gate to Varner's store, and there were more than fifty men now standing along the fence beside the gate, watching him quietly, a little covertly, as he approached, rolling a little, slightly bowlegged, the high heels of his carved boots printing neatly into the dust. "Morning, gents," he said. "Here Bud," he said to the little boy, who stood slightly behind him, looking at the protruding butt of the pistol. He took a coin from his pocket and gave it to the boy. "Run to the store and get me a box of gingersnaps." He looked about at the quiet faces, protuberant, sucking his teeth. He rolled the match from one side of his mouth to the other without touching it. "You boys done made your picks, have you? Ready to start her off, hah?" They did not answer. They were not looking at him now. That is, he began to have the feeling that each face had stopped looking at him the second before his gaze reached it. After a moment Freeman said:

"Ain't you going to wait for Flem?"

"Why?" the Texan said. Then Freeman stopped looking at him too. There was nothing in Freeman's face either. There was nothing, no alteration, in the Texan's voice. "Eck, you done already picked out yours. So we can start her off when you are ready."

"I reckon not," Eck said. "I wouldn't buy nothing I was afraid to walk up and touch."

"Them little ponies?" the Texan said. "You helped water and feed them. I bet that boy of yours could walk up to any one of them."

"He better not let me catch him," Eck said. The Texan looked about at the quiet faces, his gaze at once abstract and alert, with an impenetrable surface quality like flint, as though the surface were impervious or perhaps there was nothing behind it.

"Them ponies is gentle as a dove, boys. The man that buys them will get the best piece of horseflesh he ever forked or druv for the money. Naturally they got spirit; I ain't selling crowbait. Besides, who'd want Texas crowbait anyway, with Mississippi full of it?" His stare was still absent and unwinking; there was no mirth or humor in his voice and there was neither mirth nor humor in the single guffaw which came from the rear of the group. Two wagons were now drawing out of the road at the same time, up to the fence. The men got down from them and tied them to the fence and approached. "Come up, boys," the Texan said. "You're just in time to buy a good gentle horse cheap."

"How about that one that cut your vest off last night?" a voice said. This time three or four guffawed. The Texan looked toward the sound, bleak and unwinking.

"What about it?" he said. The laughter, if it had been laughter, ceased. The Texan turned to the nearest gatepost and climbed to the top of it, his alternate thighs deliberate and bulging in the tight trousers, the butt of the pistol catching and losing the sun in pearly gleams. Sitting on the post, he looked down at the faces along the fence which were attentive, grave, reserved and not looking at him. "All right," he said. "Who's going to start her off with a bid? Step right up; take your pick and make your bid, and when the last one is sold, walk in that lot and put your rope on the best piece of horseflesh you ever forked or druv for the money. There ain't a pony there that ain't worth fifteen dollars. Young, sound, good for saddle or work stock, guaranteed to outlast four ordinary horses; you couldn't kill one of them with a axle-tree—" There was a small violent commotion at the rear of the group. The little boy appeared, burrowing among the motionless overalls. He approached the post, the new and unbroken paper carton lifted. The Texan leaned down and took it and tore the end from it and shook three or four of the cakes into the boy's hand, a hand as small and almost as black as that of a coon. He held the carton in his hand while he talked, pointing out the horses with it as he indicated them. "Look at that one with the three stocking-feet and the frost-bit ear; watch him now when they pass again. Look at that shoulder-action; that horse is worth twenty dollars of any man's money. Who'll make me a bid on him to start her off?" His voice was harsh, ready, forensic. Along the fence below him the men stood with, buttoned close in their overalls, the tobacco-sacks and worn purses the sparse silver and frayed bills hoarded a coin at a time in the cracks of chimneys or chinked into the logs of walls. From time to time the horses broke and rushed with purposeless violence and huddled again, watching the faces along the fence with wild mismatched eyes. The lane was full of wagons now. As the others arrived they would have to stop in the road beyond it and the occupants came up the lane on foot. Mrs. Littlejohn came out of her kitchen. She crossed the yard, looking toward the lot gate. There was a blackened wash pot set on four bricks in the corner of the yard. She built a fire beneath the pot and came to the fence and stood there for a time, her hands on her hips and the smoke from the fire drifting blue and slow behind her. Then she turned and went back into the house. "Come on, boys," the Texan said. "Who'll make me a bid?"

"Four bits," a voice said. The Texan did not even glance toward it.

"Or, if he don't suit you, how about that fiddle-head horse without no mane to speak of? For a saddle pony, I'd rather have him than that stocking-foot. I heard somebody say fifty cents just now. I reckon he meant five dollars, didn't he? Do I hear five dollars?"

"Four bits for the lot," the same voice said. This time there were no guffaws. It was the Texan who laughed, harshly, with only his lower face, as if he were reciting a multiplication table.

"Fifty cents for the dried mud offen them, he means," he said. "Who'll give a dollar more for the genuine Texas cockle-burrs?" Mrs. Littlejohn came out of the kitchen, carrying the sawn half of a wooden hogshead which she set on a stump beside the smoking pot, and stood with her hands on her hips, looking into the lot for a while without coming to the fence this time. Then she went back into the house. "What's the matter with you boys?" the Texan said. "Here, Eck, you been help-ing me and you know them horses. How about making me a bid on that wall-eyed one you picked out last night? Here. Wait a minute." He thrust the paper carton into his other hip pocket and swung his feet inward and dropped, cat-light, into the lot. The ponies, huddled, watched him. Then they broke before him and slid stiffly along the fence. He turned them and they whirled and rushed back across the lot; whereupon, as though he had been waiting his chance when they should have turned their backs on him, the Texan began to run too, so that when they reached the opposite side of the lot and turned, slowing to huddle again, he was almost upon them. The earth became thunderous; dust arose, out of which the animals began to burst like flushed quail and into which, with that apparently unflagging faith in his own invulnerability, the Texan rushed. For an instant the watchers could see them in the dust—the pony backed into the angle of the fence and the stable, the man facing it, reaching toward his hip. Then the beast rushed at him in a sort of fatal and hopeless desperation and he struck it between the eyes with the pistol-butt and felled it and leaped onto its prone head. The pony recovered almost at once and pawed itself to its knees and heaved at its prisoned head and fought itself up, dragging the man with it; for an instant in the dust the watchers saw the man free of the earth and in violent lateral motion like a rag attached to the horse's head. Then the Texan's feet came back to earth and the dust blew aside and revealed them, motionless, the Texan's sharp heels braced into the ground, one hand gripping the pony's forelock and the other its nostrils, the long evil muzzle wrung backward over its scarred shoulder while it breathed in labored and hollow groans. Mrs. Littlejohn was in the yard again. No one had seen her emerge this time. She carried an armful of clothing and a metal-ridged washboard and she was standing motionless at the kitchen steps, looking into the lot. Then she moved across the yard, still looking into the lot, and dumped the garments into the tub, still looking into the lot. "Look him over, boys," the Texan panted, turning his own suffused face and the protuberant glare of his eyes toward the fence. "Look him over quick. Them shoulders and—" He had relaxed for an instant apparently. The animal exploded again; again for an instant the Texan was free of the earth, though he was still talking: "—and legs you whoa I'll tear your face right look him over quick boys worth fifteen dollars of let me get a holt of who'll make me a bid whoa you blare-eyed jack rabbit, whoa!" They were moving now—a kaleido-scope of inextricable and incredible violence on the periphery of which the metal clasps of the Texan's suspenders sun-glinted in ceaseless orbit, with terrific slowness across the lot. Then the broad clay-colored hat soared deliberately outward; an instant later the Texan followed it, though still on his feet, and the pony shot free in mad, staglike bounds. The Texan picked up the hat and struck the dust from it against his leg, and returned to the fence and mounted the post again. He was breathing heavily. Still the faces did not look at him as he took the carton from his hip and shook a cake from it and put the cake into his mouth, chewing, breathing harshly. Mrs. Littlejohn turned away and began to bail water from the pot into the tub, though after each bucketful she turned her head and looked into the lot again. "Now, boys," the Texan said. "Who says that pony ain't worth fifteen dollars? You couldn't buy that much dynamite for just fifteen dollars. There ain't one of them can't do a mile in three minutes; turn them into pasture and they will board themselves; work them like hell all day and every time you think about it, lay them over the head with a single-tree and after a couple of days every jack rabbit one of them will be so tame you will have to put them out of the house at night like a cat." He shook another cake from the carton and ate it. "Come on, Eck," he said. "Start her off. How about ten dollars for that horse, Eck?"

"What need I got for a horse I would need a bear-trap to catch?" Eck said.

"Didn't you just see me catch him?"

"I seen you," Eck said. "And I don't want nothing as big as a horse if I got to wrastle with it every time it finds me on the same side of a fence it's on."

"All right," the Texan said. He was still breathing harshly, but now there was nothing of fatigue or breathlessness in it. He shook another cake into his palm and inserted it beneath his moustache. "All right. I want to get this auction started. I ain't come here to live, no matter how good a country you folks claim you got. I'm going to give you that horse." For a moment there was no sound, not even that of breathing except the Texan's.

"You going to give it to me?" Eck said.

"Yes. Provided you will start the bidding on the next one." Again there was no sound save the Texan's breathing, and then the clash of Mrs. Littlejohn's pail against the rim of the pot.

"I just start the bidding," Eck said. "I don't have to buy it lessen I ain't over-topped." Another wagon had come up the lane. It was battered and paintless. One wheel had been repaired by crossed planks bound to the spokes with baling wire and

the two underfed mules wore a battered harness patched with bits of cotton rope; the reins were ordinary cotton plowlines, not new. It contained a woman in a shapeless gray garment and a faded sunbonnet, and a man in faded and patched though clean overalls. There was not room for the wagon to draw out of the lane so the man left it standing where it was and got down and came forward—a thin man, not large, with something about his eyes, something strained and washed-out, at once vague and intense, who shoved into the crowd at the rear, saying,

"What? What's that? Did he give him that horse?"

"All right," the Texan said. "That wall-eyed horse with the scarred neck belongs to you. Now. That one that looks like he's had his head in a flour barrel. What do you say? Ten dollars?"

"Did he give him that horse?" the newcomer said.

"A dollar," Eck said. The Texan's mouth was still open for speech; for an instant his face died so behind the hard eyes.

"A dollar?" he said. "One dollar? Did I actually hear that?"

"Durn it," Eck said. "Two dollars then. But I ain't——"

"Wait," the newcomer said. "You, up there on the post." The Texan looked at him. When the others turned, they saw that the woman had left the wagon too, though they had not known she was there since they had not seen the wagon drive up. She came among them behind the man, gaunt in the gray shapeless garment and the sunbonnet, wearing stained canvas gymnasium shoes. She overtook the man but she did not touch him, standing just behind him, her hands rolled before her into the gray dress.

"Henry," she said in a flat voice. The man looked over his shoulder.

"Get back to that wagon," he said.

"Here, missus," the Texan said. "Henry's going to get the bargain of his life in about a minute. Here, boys, let the missus come up close where she can see. Henry's going to pick out that saddle-horse the missus has been wanting. Who says ten——"

"Henry," the woman said. She did not raise her voice. She had not once looked at the Texan. She touched the man's arm. He turned and struck her hand down.

"Get back to that wagon like I told you." The woman stood behind him, her hands rolled again into her dress. She was not looking at anything, speaking to anyone.

"He ain't no more despair than to buy one of

them things," she said. "And us not but five dollars away from the poorhouse, he ain't no more despair." The man turned upon her with that curious air of leashed, of dreamlike fury. The others lounged along the fence in attitudes gravely inattentive, almost oblivious. Mrs. Littlejohn had been washing for some time now, pumping rhythmically up and down above the washboard in the sud-foamed tub. She now stood erect again, her soap-raw hands on her hips, looking into the lot.

"Shut your mouth and get back in that wagon," the man said. "Do you want me to take a wagon stake to you?" He turned and looked up at the Texan. "Did you give him that horse?" he said. The Texan was looking at the woman. Then he looked at the man; still watching him, he tilted the paper carton over his open palm. A single cake came out of it.

"Yes," he said.

"Is the fellow that bids in this next horse going to get that first one too?"

"No," the Texan said.

"All right," the other said. "Are you going to give a horse to the man that makes the first bid on the next one?"

"No," the Texan said.

"Then if you were just starting the auction off by giving away a horse, why didn't you wait till we were all here?" The Texan stopped looking at the other. He raised the empty carton and squinted carefully into it, as if it might contain a precious jewel or perhaps a deadly insect. Then he crumpled it and dropped it carefully beside the post on which he sat.

"Eck bids two dollars," he said. "I believe he still thinks he's bidding on them scraps of bob-wire they come here in instead of on one of the horses. But I got to accept it. But are you boys——"

"So Eck's going to get two horses at a dollar a head," the newcomer said. "Three dollars." The woman touched him again. He flung her hand off without turning and she stood again, her hands rolled into her dress across her flat stomach, not looking at anything.

"Misters," she said, "we got chaps in the house that never had shoes last winter. We ain't got corn to feed the stock. We got five dollars I earned weaving by firelight after dark. And he ain't no more despair."

"Henry bids three dollars," the Texan said. "Raise him a dollar, Eck, and the horse is yours." Beyond the fence the horses rushed suddenly and for no reason and as suddenly stopped, staring at the faces along the fence.

"Henry," the woman said. The man was watching Eck. His stained and broken teeth showed a little beneath his lip. His wrists dangled into fists below the faded sleeves of his shirt too short from many washings.

"Four dollars," Eck said.

"Five dollars!" the husband said, raising one clenched hand. He shouldered himself forward toward the gatepost. The woman did not follow him. She now looked at the Texan for the first time. Her eyes were a washed gray also, as though they had faded too like the dress and the sunbonnet.

"Mister," she said, "if you take that five dollars I earned my chaps a-weaving for one of them things, it'll be a curse on you and yours during all the time of man."

"Five dollars!" the husband shouted. He thrust himself up to the post, his clenched hand on a level with the Texan's knees. He opened it upon a wad of frayed banknotes and silver. "Five dollars! And the man that raises it will have to beat my head off or I'll beat hisn."

"All right," the Texan said. "Five dollars is bid. But don't you shake your hand at me."

At five o'clock that afternoon the Texan crumpled the third paper carton and dropped it to the earth beneath him. In the copper slant of the levelling sun which fell also upon the line of limp garments in Mrs. Littlejohn's backyard and which cast his shadow and that of the post on which he sat long across the lot where now and then the ponies still rushed in purposeless and tireless surges, the Texan straightened his leg and thrust his hand into his pocket and took out a coin and leaned down to the little boy. His voice was now hoarse, spent. "Here, bud," he said. "Run to the store and get me a box of gingersnaps." The men still stood along the fence, tireless, in their overalls and faded shirts. Flem Snopes was there now, appeared suddenly from nowhere, standing beside the fence with a space the width of three or four men on either side of him, standing there in his small yet definite isolation, chewing tobacco, in the same gray trousers and minute bow tie in which he had departed last summer but in a new cap, gray too like the other, but new, and overlaid with a bright golfer's plaid, looking also at the horses in the lot. All of them save two had been sold for sums ranging from three dollars and a half to eleven and twelve dollars. The purchasers, as they had bid them in, had gathered as though by instinct into a separate group on the other side of the gate, where they stood with their hands lying upon the top strand of the fence, watching with a still more sober intensity the animals which some of them had owned for seven and eight hours now but had not yet laid hands upon. The husband, Henry, stood beside the post on which the Texan sat. The wife had gone back to the wagon, where she sat gray in the gray garment, motionless, looking at nothing, still, she might have been something inanimate which he had loaded into the wagon to move it somewhere, waiting now in the wagon until he should be ready to go on again, patient, insensate, timeless.

"I bought a horse and I paid cash for it," he said. His voice was harsh and spent too, the mad look in his eyes had a quality glazed now and even sightless. "And yet you expect me to stand around here till they are all sold before I can get my horse. Well, you can do all the expecting you want. I'm going to take my horse out of there and go home." The Texan looked down at him. The Texan's shirt was blotched with sweat. His big face was cold and still, his voice level.

"Take your horse then." After a moment Henry looked away. He stood with his head bent a little, swallowing from time to time.

"Ain't you going to catch him for me?"

"It ain't my horse," the Texan said in that flat still voice. After a while Henry raised his head. He did not look at the Texan.

"Who'll help me catch my horse?" he said. Nobody answered. They stood along the fence, looking quietly into the lot where the ponies huddled, already beginning to fade a little where the long shadow of the house lay upon them, deepening. From Mrs. Littlejohn's kitchen the smell of frying ham came. A noisy cloud of sparrows swept across the lot and into a chinaberry tree beside the house, and in the high soft vague blue swallows swooped and whirled in erratic indecision, their cries like strings plucked at random. Without looking back, Henry raised his voice: "Bring that ere plow-line." After a time the wife moved. She got down from the wagon and took a coil of new cotton rope from it and approached. The husband took the rope from her and moved toward the gate. The Texan began to descend from the post, stiffly, as Henry put his hand on the latch. "Come on here," he said. The wife had stopped when he took the rope from her. She moved again, obediently, her hands rolled into the dress across her stomach, passing the Texan without looking at him.

"Don't go in there, missus," he said. She stopped, not looking at him, not looking at anything. The husband opened the gate and entered the lot and turned, holding the gate open but without raising his eyes.

"Come on here," he said.

"Don't you go in there, missus," the Texan said. The wife stood motionless between them, her face almost concealed by the sunbonnet, her hands folded across her stomach.

"I reckon I better," she said. The other men did not look at her at all, at her or Henry either. They stood along the fence, grave and quiet and inattentive, almost bemused. Then the wife passed through the gate; the husband shut it behind them and turned and began to move toward the huddled ponies, the wife following in the gray and shapeless garment within which she moved without inference of locomotion, like something on a moving platform, a float. The horses were watching them. They clotted and blended and shifted among themselves, on the point of breaking though not breaking yet. The husband shouted at them. He began to curse them, advancing, the wife following. Then the huddle broke, the animals moving with high, stiff knees, circling the two people who turned and followed again as the herd flowed and huddled again at the opposite side of the lot.

"There he is," the husband said. "Get him into that corner." The herd divided; the horse which the husband had bought jolted on stiff legs. The wife shouted at it; it spun and poised, plunging, then the husband struck it across the face with the coiled rope and it whirled and slammed into the corner of the fence. "Keep him there now," the husband said. He shook out the rope, advancing. The horse watched him with wild, glaring eyes; it rushed again, straight toward the wife. She shouted at it and waved her arms but it soared past her in a long bound and rushed again into the huddle of its fellows. They followed and hemmed it again into another corner; again the wife failed to stop its rush for freedom and the husband turned and struck her with the coiled rope. "Why didn't you head him?" he said. "Why didn't you?" He struck her again; she did not move, not even to fend the rope with a raised arm. The men along the fence stood quietly, their faces lowered as though brooding upon the earth at their feet. Only Flem Snopes was still watching—if he ever had been looking into the lot at all, standing in his little island of isolation, chewing with his characteristic faint sidewise thrust beneath the new plaid cap.

The Texan said something, not loud, harsh and short. He entered the lot and went to the husband and jerked the uplifted rope from his hand. The husband whirled as though he were about to spring at the Texan, crouched slightly, his knees bent and his arms held slightly away from his sides, though his gaze never mounted higher than the Texan's carved and dusty boots. Then the Texan took the husband by the arm and led him back toward the gate, the wife following, and through the gate which he held open for the woman and then closed. He took a wad of banknotes from his trousers and removed a bill from it and put it into the woman's hand. "Get him into the wagon and get him on home," he said.

"What's that for?" Flem Snopes said. He had approached. He now stood beside the post on which the Texan had been sitting. The Texan did not look at him.

"Thinks he bought one of them ponies," the Texan said. He spoke in a flat still voice, like that of a man after a sharp run. "Get him on away, missus."

"Give him back that money," the husband said, in his lifeless, spent tone. "I bought that horse and I aim to have him if I got to shoot him before I can put a rope on him." The Texan did not even look at him.

"Get him on away from here, missus," he said.

"You take your money and I take my horse," the husband said. He was shaking slowly and steadily now, as though he were cold. His hands open and shut below the frayed cuffs of his shirt. "Give it back to him," he said.

"You don't own no horse of mine," the Texan said. "Get him on home, missus." The husband raised his spent face, his mad glazed eyes. He reached out his hand. The woman held the banknote in her folded hands across her stomach. For a while the husband's shaking hand merely fumbled at it. Then he drew the banknote free.

"It's my horse," he said. "I bought it. These fellows saw me. I paid for it. It's my horse. Here." He turned and extended the banknote toward Snopes. "You got something to do with these horses. I bought one. Here's the money for it. I bought one. Ask him." Snopes took the banknote. The others stood, gravely inattentive, in relaxed attitudes along the fence. The sun had gone now; there was nothing save violet shadow upon them and upon the lot where once more and for no reason the ponies rushed and flowed. At that moment the little boy came up, tireless and indefatigable still, with the new paper carton. The Texan took it, though he did not open it at once. He had dropped the rope and now the husband stooped for it, fumbling at it for some time before he lifted it from the ground. Then he stood with his head bent, his knuckles whitening on the rope. The woman had not moved. Twilight was coming fast now; there was a last mazy swirl of swallows against the high and changing azure. Then the Texan tore the end from the carton and tilted one of the cakes into his hand; he seemed to be watch-

ing the hand as it shut slowly upon the cake until a fine powder of snuff-colored dust began to rain from his fingers. He rubbed the hand carefully on his thigh and raised his head and glanced about until he saw the little boy and handed the carton back to him.

"Here, Bud," he said. Then he looked at the woman, his voice flat, quiet again. "Mr. Snopes will have your money for you tomorrow. Better get him in the wagon and get him on home. He don't own no horse. You can get your money tomorrow from Mr. Snopes." The wife turned and went back to the wagon and got into it. No one watched her, nor the husband who still stood, his head bent, passing the rope from one hand to the other. They leaned along the fence, grave and quiet, as though the fence were in another land, another time.

"How many you got left?" Snopes said. The Texan roused; they all seemed to rouse then, returning, listening again.

"Got three now," the Texan said. "Swap all three of them for a buggy or a——"

"It's out in the road," Snopes said, a little shortly, a little quickly, turning away. "Get your mules." He went on up the lane. They watched the Texan enter the lot and cross it, the horses flowing before him but without the old irrational violence, as if they too were spent, vitiated with the long day, and enter the barn and then emerge, leading the two harnessed mules. The wagon had been backed under the shed beside the barn. The Texan entered this and came out a moment later, carrying a bedding-roll and his coat, and led the mules back toward the gate, the ponies huddled again and watching him with their various unmatching eyes, quietly now, as if they too realized there was not only an armistice between them at last but that they would never look upon each other again in both their lives. Someone opened the gate. The Texan led the mules through it and they followed in a body, leaving the husband standing beside the closed gate, his head still bent and the coiled rope in his hand. They passed the wagon in which the wife sat, her gray garment fading into the dusk, almost the same color and as still, looking at nothing; they passed the clothesline with its limp and unwinded drying garments, walking through the hot vivid smell of ham from Mrs. Littlejohn's kitchen. When they reached the end of the lane they could see the moon, almost full, tremendous and pale and still lightness in the sky from which day had not quite gone. Snopes was standing at the end of the lane beside an empty buggy. It was the one with the glittering wheels and the fringed parasol top in which he and Will Varner had used to drive. The Texan was motionless too, looking at it.

"Well well well," he said. "So this is it."

"If it don't suit you, you can ride one of the mules back to Texas," Snopes said.

"You bet," the Texan said. "Only I ought to have a powder puff or at least a mandolin to ride it with." He backed the mules onto the tongue and lifted the breast-yoke. Two of them came forward and fastened the traces for him. Then they watched him get into the buggy and raise the reins.

"Where you heading for?" one said. "Back to Texas?"

"In this?" the Texan said. "I wouldn't get past the first Texas saloon without starting the vigilance committee. Besides, I ain't going to waste all this here lace-trimmed top and these spindle wheels just on Texas. Long as I am this far, I reckon I'll go on a day or two and look-see them Northern towns. Washington and New York and Baltimore. What's the short way to New York from here?" They didn't know. But they told him how to reach Jefferson.

"You're already headed right," Freeman said. "Just keep right on up the road past the schoolhouse."

"All right," the Texan said. "Well, remember about busting them ponies over the head now and then until they get used to you. You won't have any trouble with them then." He lifted the reins again. As he did so Snopes stepped forward and got into the buggy.

"I'll ride as far as Varner's with you," he said.

"I didn't know I was going past Varner's," the Texan said.

"You can go to town that way," Snopes said. "Drive on." The Texan shook the reins. Then he said,

"Whoa." He straightened his leg and put his hand into his pocket. "Here, Bud," he said to the little boy, "run to the store and— Never mind. I'll stop and get it myself, long as I am going back that way. Well, boys," he said. "Take care of yourselves." He swung the team around. The buggy went on. They looked after it.

"I reckon he aims to kind of come up on Jefferson from behind," Quick said.

"He'll be lighter when he gets there," Freeman said. "He can come up to it easy from any side he wants."

"Yes," Bookwright said. "His pockets won't rattle." They went back to the lot; they passed on through the narrow way between the two lines of patient and motionless wagons, which at the end was completely closed by the one in which the woman sat. The husband was still standing beside the gate with his coiled rope, and now night had completely come. The light itself had not changed so much; if anything, it was brighter but with that other-worldly quality of moonlight, so that when they stood once more looking into the lot, the splotchy bodies of the ponies had a distinctness, almost a brilliance, but without individual shape and without depth—no longer horses, no longer flesh and bone directed by a principle capable of calculated violence, no longer inherent with the capacity to hurt and harm.

"Well, what are we waiting for?" Freeman said. "For them to go to roost?"

"We better all get our ropes first," Quick said. "Get your ropes everybody." Some of them did not have ropes. When they left home that morning, they had not heard about the horses, the auction. They had merely happened through the village by chance and learned of it and stopped.

"Go to the store and get some then," Freeman said.

"The store will be closed now," Quick said.

"No it won't," Freeman said. "If it was closed, Lump Snopes would a been up here." So while the ones who had come prepared got their ropes from the wagons, the others went down to the store. The clerk was just closing it.

"You all ain't started catching them yet, have you?" he said. "Good; I was afraid I wouldn't get there in time." He opened the door again and amid the old strong sunless smells of cheese and leather and molasses he measured and cut off sections of plow-line for them and in a body and the clerk in the center and still talking, voluble and unlistened to, they returned up the road. The pear tree before Mrs. Littlejohn's was like drowned silver now in the moon. The mockingbird of last night, or another one, was already singing in it, and they now saw, tied to the fence, Ratliff's buckboard and team.

"I thought something was wrong all day," one said. "Ratliff wasn't there to give nobody advice." When they passed down the lane, Mrs. Littlejohn was in her backyard, gathering the garments from the clothesline; they could still smell the ham. The others were waiting at the gate, beyond which the ponies, huddled again, were like phantom fish, suspended apparently without legs now in the brilliant treachery of the moon.

"I reckon the best way will be for us all to take and catch them one at a time," Freeman said.

"One at a time," the husband, Henry, said. Apparently he had not moved since the Texan had led his mules through the gate, save to lift his hands to the top of the gate, one of them still clutching the coiled rope. "One at a time," he said. He began to curse in a harsh, spent monotone. "After I've stood around here all day, waiting for that—" He cursed. He began to jerk at the gate, shaking it with spent violence until one of the other slid the latch back and it swung open and Henry entered it, the others following, the little boy pressing close behind his father until Eck became aware of him and turned.

"Here," he said. "Give me that rope. You stay out of here."

"Aw, paw," the boy said.

"No sir. Them things will kill you. They almost done it this morning. You stay out of here."

"But we got two to catch." For a moment Eck stood looking down at the boy.

"That's right," he said. "We got two. But you stay close to me now. And when I holler run, you run. You hear me?"

"Spread out, boys," Freeman said. "Keep them in front of us." They began to advance across the lot in a ragged crescent-shaped line, each one with his rope. The ponies were now at the far side of the lot. One of them snorted; the mass shifted within itself but without breaking. Freeman, glancing back, saw the little boy. "Get that boy out of here," he said.

"I reckon you better," Eck said to the boy. "You go and get in the wagon yonder. You can see us catch them from there." The little boy turned and trotted toward the shed beneath which the wagon stood. The line of men advanced, Henry a little in front.

"Watch them close now," Freeman said. "Maybe we better try to get them into the barn first—" At that moment the huddle broke. It parted and flowed in both directions along the fence. The men at the ends of the line began to run, waving their arms and shouting. "Head them," Freeman said tensely. "Turn them back." They turned them, driving them back upon themselves again; the animals merged and spun in short, huddling rushes, phantom and inextricable. "Hold them now," Freeman said. "Don't let them get by us." The line advanced again. Eck turned; he did not know why—whether a sound, what. The little boy was just behind him again.

"Didn't I tell you to get in that wagon and stay there?" Eck said.

"Watch out, paw!" the boy said. "There he is! There's ourn!" It was the one the Texan had given Eck. "Catch him, paw!"

"Get out of my way," Eck said. "Get back to that wagon." The line was still advancing. The ponies milled, clotting, forced gradually backward toward the open door of the barn. Henry was still slightly in front, crouched slightly, his thin figure, even in the mazy moonlight, emanating something of that spent fury. The splotchy huddle of animals seemed to be moving before the advancing line of men like a snowball which they might have been pushing before them by some invisible means, gradually nearer and nearer to the black yawn of the barn door. Later it was obvious that the ponies were so intent upon the men that they did not realize the barn was even behind them until they backed into the shadow of it. Then an indescribable sound, a movement desperate and despairing, arose among them; for an instant of static horror men and animals faced one another, then the men whirled and ran before a gaudy vomit of long wild faces and splotched chests which overtook and scattered them and flung them sprawling aside and completely obliterated from sight Henry and the little boy, neither of whom had moved though Henry had flung up both arms, still holding his coiled rope, the herd sweeping on across the lot, to crash through the gate which the last man through it had neglected to close, leaving it slightly ajar, carrying all of the gate save the upright to which the hinges were nailed with them, and so among the teams and wagons which choked the lane, the teams springing and lunging too, snapping hitch-reins and tongues. Then the whole inextricable mass crashed among the wagons and eddied and divided about the one in which the woman sat, and rushed on down the lane and into the road, dividing, one half going one way and one half the other.

The men in the lot, except Henry, got to their feet and ran toward the gate. The little boy once more had not been touched, not even thrown off his feet; for a while his father held him clear of the ground in one hand, shaking him like a rag doll. "Didn't I tell you to stay in that wagon?" Eck cried. "Didn't I tell you?"

"Look out, paw!" the boy chattered out of the violent shaking, "there's ourn! There he goes!" It was the horse the Texan had given them again. It was if they owned no other, the other one did not exist; as if by some absolute and instantaneous rapport of blood they had relegated to oblivion the one for which they had paid money. They ran to the gate and down the lane where the other men had disappeared. They saw the horse the Texan had given them whirl and dash back and rush through the gate into Mrs. Littlejohn's yard and run up the front steps and crash once on the wooden veranda and vanish through the front door. Eck and the boy ran up onto the veranda. A lamp sat on a table just inside the door. In its mellow light they saw the horse fill the long hallway like a pinwheel, gaudy, furious and thunderous. A little further down the hall there was a varnished yellow melodeon. The horse crashed into it; it produced a single note, almost a chord, in bass, resonant and grave, of deep and sober astonishment; the horse with its monstrous and antic shadow whirled again and vanished through another door. It was a bedroom; Ratliff, in his underclothes and one sock and with the other sock in his hand and his back to the door, was leaning out the open window facing the lane, the lot. He looked back over his shoulder. For an instant he and the horse glared at one another. Then he sprang through the window as the horse backed out of the room and into the hall again and whirled and saw Eck and the little boy just entering the front door, Eck still carrying his rope. It whirled again and rushed on down the hall and onto the back porch just as Mrs. Littlejohn, carrying an armful of clothes from the line and the washboard, mounted the steps.

"Get out of here, you son of a bitch," she said. She struck with the washboard; it divided neatly on the long mad face and the horse whirled and rushed back up the hall, where Eck and the boy now stood.

"Get to hell out of here, Wall!" Eck roared. He dropped to the floor, covering his head with his arms. The boy did not move, and for the third time the horse soared above the unwinking eyes and the unbowed and untouched head and onto the front veranda again just as Ratliff, still carrying the sock, ran around the corner of the house and up the steps. The horse whirled without breaking or pausing. It galloped to the end of the veranda and took the railing and soared outward, hobgoblin and floating, in the moon. It landed in the lot still running and crossed the lot and galloped through the wrecked gate and among the overturned wagons and the still intact one in which Henry's wife still sat, and on down the lane and into the road.

A quarter of a mile further on, the road gashed pallid and moony between the moony shadows of the bordering trees, the horse still galloping, galloping its shadow into the dust, the road descending now toward the creek and the bridge. It was of wood, just wide enough for a single vehicle. When the horse reached it, it was occupied by a wagon coming from the opposite direction and drawn by two mules already asleep in the harness and the soporific motion. On the seat was Tull and his wife, in splint chairs in the wagon behind them sat their four daughters, all returning belated from an all-day visit with some of Mrs. Tull's kin. The horse neither checked nor swerved. It crashed once on

the wooden bridge and rushed between the two mules which waked lunging in opposite directions in the traces, the horse now apparently scrambling along the wagon-tongue itself like a mad squirrel and scrabbling at the end-gate of the wagon with its forefeet as if it intended to climb into the wagon while Tull shouted at it and struck at its face with his whip. The mules were now trying to turn the wagon around in the middle of the bridge. It slewed and tilted, the bridge-rail cracked with a sharp report above the shrieks of the women; the horse scrambled at last across the back of one of the mules and Tull stood up in the wagon and kicked at its face. Then the front end of the wagon rose, flinging Tull, the reins now wrapped several times about his wrist, backward into the wagon bed among the overturned chairs and the exposed stockings and undergarments of his women. The pony scrambled free and crashed again on the wooden planking, galloping again. The wagon lurched again; the mules had finally turned it on the bridge where there was not room for it to turn and were now kicking themselves free of the traces. When they came free, they snatched Tull bodily out of the wagon. He struck the bridge on his face and was dragged for several feet before the wrist-wrapped reins broke. Far up the road now, distancing the frantic mules, the pony faded on. While the five women still shrieked above Tull's unconscious body, Eck and the little boy came up, trotting, Eck still carrying his rope. He was panting. "Which way'd he go?" he said.

In the now empty and moon-drenched lot, his wife and Mrs. Littlejohn and Ratliff and Lump Snopes, the clerk, and three other men raised Henry out of the trampled dust and carried him into Mrs. Littlejohn's back yard. His face was blanched and stony, his eyes were closed, the weight of his head tautened his throat across the protruding larynx; his teeth glinted dully beneath his lifted lip. They carried him on toward the house, through the dappled shade of the chinaberry trees. Across the dreaming and silver night a faint sound like remote thunder came and ceased. "There's one of them on the creek bridge," one of the men said.

"It's that one of Eck Snopes'," another said. "The one that was in the house." Mrs. Littlejohn had preceded them into the hall. When they entered with Henry, she had already taken the lamp from the table and she stood beside an open door, holding the lamp high.

"Bring him in here," she said. She entered the room first and set the lamp on the dresser. They followed with clumsy scufflings and pantings and laid Henry on the bed and Mrs. Littlejohn came to the bed and stood looking down at Henry's peaceful and bloodless face. "I'll declare," she said. "You men." They had drawn back a little, clumped, shifting from one foot to another, not looking at her nor at his wife either, who stood at the foot of the bed, motionless, her hands folded into her dress. "You all get out of here, V. K.," she said to Ratliff. "Go outside. See if you can't find something else to play with that will kill some more of you."

"All right," Ratliff said. "Come on, boys. Ain't no more horses to catch in here." They followed him toward the door, on tiptoe, their shoes scuffling, their shadows monstrous on the wall.

"Go get Will Varner," Mrs. Littlejohn said. "I reckon you can tell him it's still a mule." They went out; they didn't look back. They tiptoed up the hall and crossed the veranda and descended into the moonlight. Now that they could pay attention to it, the silver air seemed to be filled with faint and sourceless sounds—shouts, thin and distant, again a brief thunder of hooves on a wooden bridge, more shouts faint and thin and earnest and clear as bells; once they even distinguished the words: "Whooey. Head him."

"He went through that house quick," Ratliff said. "He must have found another woman at home." Then Henry screamed in the house behind them. They looked back into the dark hall where a square of light fell through the bedroom door, listening while the scream sank into a harsh respiration: "Ah. Ah. Ah" on a rising note about to become screaming again. "Come on," Ratliff said. "We better get Varner." They went up the road in a body, treading the moon-blanched dust in the tremulous April night murmurous with the moving of sap and the wet bursting of burgeoning leaf and bud and constant with the thin and urgent cries and the brief and fading bursts of galloping hooves. Varner's house was dark, blank and without depth in the moonlight. They stood, clumped darkly in the silver yard and called up at the blank windows until suddenly someone was standing in one of them. It was Flem Snopes' wife. She was in a white garment; the heavy braided club of her hair looked almost black against it. She did not lean out, she merely stood there, full in the moon, apparently blank-eyed or certainly not looking downward at them—the heavy gold hair, the mask not tragic and perhaps not even doomed: just damned, the strong faint lift of breasts beneath marblelike fall of the garment; to those below what Brunhilde, what Rhinemaiden on what spurious river-rock of papiermache, what Helen returned to what topless and shoddy Argos, waiting for no one. "Evening,

Mrs. Snopes," Ratliff said. "We want Uncle Will. Henry Armstid is hurt at Mrs. Littlejohn's." She vanished from the window. They waited in the moonlight, listening to the faint remote shouts and cries, until Varner emerged, sooner than they had actually expected, hunching into his coat and buttoning his trousers over the tail of his nightshirt, his suspenders still dangling in twin loops below the coat. He was carrying the battered bag which contained the plumber-like tools with which he drenched and wormed and blistered and floated or drew the teeth of horses and mules; he came down the steps, lean and loosejointed, his shrewd ruthless head cocked a little as he listened also to the faint bell-like cries and shouts with which the silver air was full.

"Are they still trying to catch them rabbits?" he said.

"All of them except Henry Armstid," Ratliff said. "He caught his."

"Hah," Varner said. "That you, V. K.? How many did you buy?"

"I was too late," Ratliff said. "I never got back in time."

"Hah," Varner said. They moved on to the gate and into the road again. "Well, it's a good bright cool night for running them." The moon was now high overhead, a pearled and mazy yawn in the soft sky, the ultimate ends of which rolled onward, whorl on whorl, beyond the pale stars and by pale stars surrounded. They walked in a close clump, tramping their shadows into the road's mild dust, blotting the shadows of the burgeoning trees which soared, trunk branch and twig against the pale sky, delicate and finely thinned. They passed the dark store. Then the pear tree came in sight. It rose in mazed and silver immobility like exploding snow; the mockingbird still sang in it. "Look at that tree," Varner said. "It ought to make this year, sho."

"Corn'll make this year too," one said.

"A moon like this is good for every growing thing outen earth," Varner said. "I mind when me and Mrs. Varner was expecting Eula. Already had a mess of children and maybe we ought to quit then. But I wanted some more gals. Others had done married and moved away, and a passel of boys, soon as they get big enough to be worth anything, they ain't got time to work. Got to set around the store and talk. But a gal will stay home and work until she does get married. So there was a old woman told my mammy once that if a woman showed her belly to the full moon after she had done caught, it would be a gal. So Mrs. Varner taken and laid every night with the moon on her nekid belly, until it fulled and after. I could lay my ear to her belly and hear Eula kicking and scrouging like all get-out, feeling the moon."

"You mean it actually worked sho enough, Uncle Will?" the other said.

"Hah," Varner said. "You might try it. You get enough women showing their nekid bellies to the moon or the sun either or even just to your hand fumbling around often enough and more than likely after a while there will be something in it you can lay your ear and listen to, provided something come up and you ain't got away by that time. Hah, V. K.?" Someone guffawed.

"Don't ask me," Ratliff said. "I can't even get nowhere in time to buy a cheap horse." Two or three guffawed this time. Then they began to hear Henry's respirations from the house: "Ah. Ah. Ah" and they ceased abruptly, as if they had not been aware of their closeness to it. Varner walked on in front, lean, shambling, yet moving quite rapidly, though his head was still slanted with listening as the faint, urgent, indomitable cries murmured in the silver lambence, sourceless, at times almost musical, like fading bell-notes; again there was a brief rapid thunder of hooves on wooden planking.

"There's another one on the creek bridge," one said.

"They are going to come out even on them things, after all," Varner said. "They'll get the money back in exercise and relaxation. You take a man that ain't got no other relaxation all year long except dodging mule-dung up and down a field furrow. And a night like this one, when a man ain't old enough yet to lay still and sleep, and yet he ain't young enough anymore to be tomcatting in and out of other folks' back windows, something like this is good for him. It'll make him sleep tomorrow night anyhow, provided he gets back home by then. If we had just knowed about this in time, we could have trained up a pack of horse-dogs. Then we could have held one of these field trials."

"That's one way to look at it, I reckon," Ratliff said. "In fact, it might be a considerable comfort to Bookwright and Quick and Freeman and Eck Snopes and them other new horse-owners if that side of it could be brought to their attention, because the chances are ain't none of them thought to look at it in that light yet. Probably there ain't a one of them that believes now there's any cure a tall for that Texas disease Flem Snopes and that Dead-eye Dick brought here."

"Hah," Varner said. He opened Mrs. Littlejohn's gate. The dim light still fell outward across the hall from the bedroom door; beyond it, Armstid was saying "Ah. Ah. Ah" steadily. "There's a pill for every ill but the last one."

"Even if there was always time to take it," Ratliff said.

"Hah," Varner said again. He glanced back at Ratliff for an instant, pausing. But the little hard bright eyes were invisible now; it was only the bushy overhang of the brows which seemed to concentrate downward toward him in writhen immobility, not frowning but with a sort of fierce risibility. "Even if there was time to take it. Breathing is a sight-draft dated yesterday."

II

AT NINE o'clock on the second morning after that, five men were sitting or squatting along the gallery of the store. The sixth was Ratliff. He was standing up, and talking: "Maybe there wasn't but one of them things in Mrs. Littlejohn's house that night, like Eck says. But it was the biggest drove of just one horse I ever seen. It was in my room and it was on the front porch and I could hear Mrs. Littlejohn hitting it over the head with that washboard in the back yard all at the same time. And still it was missing everybody everytime. I reckon that's what that Texas man meant by calling them bargains: that a man would need to be powerful unlucky to ever get close enough to one of them to get hurt." They laughed, all except Eck himself. He and the little boy were eating. When they mounted the steps, Eck had gone on into the store and emerged with a paper sack, from which he took a segment of cheese and with his pocket knife divided it carefully into two exact halves and gave one to the boy and took a handful of crackers from the sack and gave them to the boy, and now they squatted against the wall, side by side and, save for the difference in size, identical, eating.

"I wonder what that horse thought Ratliff was," one said. He held a spray of peach bloom between his teeth. It bore four blossoms like miniature ballet skirts of pink tulle. "Jumping out windows and running indoors in his shirt-tail? I wonder how many Ratliffs that horse thought he saw."

"I don't know," Ratliff said. "But if he saw just half as many of me as I saw of him, he was sholy surrounded. Everytime I turned my head, that thing was just running over me or just swirling to run back over that boy again. And that boy there, he stayed right under it one time to my certain knowledge for a full one-and-one-half minutes without ducking his head or even batting his eyes. Yes sir, when I looked around and seen that varmint in the door behind me blaring its eyes at me, I'd a made sho Flem Snopes had brought a tiger back from Texas except I knowed that couldn't no just one tiger completely fill a entire room."

They laughed again, quietly. Lump Snopes, the clerk, sitting in the only chair tilted back against the door-facing and partly blocking the entrance, cackled suddenly.

"If Flem had knowed how quick you fellows was going to snap them horses up, he'd a probably brought some tigers," he said. "Monkeys too."

"So they was Flem's horses," Ratliff said. The laughter stopped. The other three had open knives in their hands, with which they had been trimming idly at chips and slivers of wood. Now they sat apparently absorbed in the delicate and almost tedious movements of the knife-blades. The clerk had looked quickly up and found Ratliff watching him. His constant expression of incorrigible and mirthful disbelief had left him now; only the empty wrinkles of it remained about his mouth and eyes.

"Has Flem ever said they was?" he said. "But you town fellows are smarter than us country folks. Likely you done already read Flem's mind." But Ratliff was not looking at him now.

"And I reckon we'd a bought them," he said. He stood above them again, easy, intelligent, perhaps a little sombre but still perfectly impenetrable. "Eck here, for instance. With a wife and family to support. He owns two of them, though to be sho he never had to pay money for but one. I heard folks chasing them things up until midnight last night, but Eck and that boy ain't been home at all in two days." They laughed again, except Eck. He pared off a bit of cheese and speared it on the knife-point and put it into his mouth.

"Eck caught one of hisn," the second man said.

"That so?" Ratliff said. "Which one was it, Eck? The one he give you or the one you bought?"

"The one he give me," Eck said, chewing.

"Well, well," Ratliff said. "I hadn't heard about that. But Eck's still one horse short. And the one he had to pay money for. Which is pure proof enough that them horses wasn't Flem's because wouldn't no man even give his own blood kin something he couldn't even catch." They laughed again, but they stopped when the clerk spoke. There was no mirth in his voice at all.

"Listen," he said. "All right. We done all admitted you are too smart for anybody to get ahead of. You never bought no horse from Flem or nobody else, so maybe it ain't none of your business and maybe you better just leave it at that."

"Sholy," Ratliff said. "It's done already been left at that two nights ago. The fellow that forgot to shut that lot gate done that. With the exception of Eck's horse. And we know that wasn't Flem's, because that horse was give to Eck for nothing."

"There's others besides Eck that ain't got back home yet," the man with the peach spray said. "Bookwright and Quick are still chasing theirs. They was reported three miles west of Burtsboro Old Town at eight o'clock last night. They ain't got close enough to it yet to tell which one it belongs to."

"Sholy," Ratliff said. "The only new horse-owner in this country that could a been found without bloodhounds since whoever it was left the gate open two nights ago, is Henry Armstid. He's laying right there in Mrs. Littlejohn's bedroom where he can watch the lot so that any time the one he bought happens to run back into it, all he's got to do is to holler at his wife to run out with the rope and catch it——" He ceased, though he said, "Morning, Flem," so immediately afterward and with no change whatever in tone, that the pause was not even discernible. With the exception of the clerk, who sprang up, vacated the chair with a sort of servile alacrity, and Eck and the little boy who continued to eat, they watched above their stilled hands as Snopes in the gray trousers and the minute tie and the new cap with its bright overplaid mounted the steps. He was chewing; he already carried a piece of white pine board; he jerked his head at them, looking at nobody, and took the vacated chair and opened his knife and began to whittle. The clerk now leaned in the opposite side of the door, rubbing his back against the facing. The expression of merry and invincible disbelief had returned to his face, with a quality watchful and secret.

"You're just in time," he said. "Ratliff here seems to be in a considerable sweat about who actually owned them horses." Snopes drew his knife-blade neatly along the board, the neat, surgeon-like sliver curling before it. The others were whittling again, looking carefully at nothing, except Eck and the boy, who were still eating, and the clerk rubbing his back against the door-facing and watching Snopes with that secret and alert intensity. "Maybe you could put his mind at rest." Snopes turned his head slightly and spat, across the gallery and the steps and into the dust beyond them. He drew the knife back and began another curling sliver.

"He was there too," Snopes said. "He knows as much as anybody else." This time the clerk guffawed, chortling, his features gathering toward the center of his face as though plucked there by a hand. He slapped his leg, cackling.

"You might as well to quit," he said. "You can't beat him."

"I reckon not," Ratliff said. He stood above them, not looking at any of them, his gaze fixed apparently on the empty road beyond Mrs. Littlejohn's house, impenetrable, brooding even. A hulking, half-grown boy in overalls too small for him, appeared suddenly from nowhere in particular. He stood for a while in the road, just beyond spitting-range of the gallery, with the air of having come from nowhere in particular and of not knowing where he would go next when he should move again and of not being troubled by that fact. He was looking at nothing, certainly not toward the gallery, and no one on the gallery so much as looked at him except the little boy, who now watched the boy in the road, his periwinkle eyes grave and steady above the bitten cracker in his halted hand. The boy in the road moved on, thickly undulant in the tight overalls, and vanished beyond the corner of the store, the round head and the unwinking eyes of the little boy on the gallery turning steadily to watch him out of sight. Then the little boy bit the cracker again, chewing. "Of course there's Mrs. Tull," Ratliff said. "But that's Eck she's going to sue for damaging Tull against that bridge. And as for Henry Armstid——"

"If a man ain't got gumption enough to protect himself, it's his own look-out," the clerk said.

"Sholy," Ratliff said, still in that dreamy, abstracted tone, actually speaking over his shoulder even. "And Henry Armstid, that's all right because from what I hear of the conversation that taken place, Henry had already stopped owning that horse he thought was his before that Texas man left. And as for that broke leg, that won't put him out none because his wife can make his crop." The clerk had ceased to rub his back against the door. He watched the back of Ratliff's head, unwinking too, sober and intent; he glanced at Snopes who, chewing, was watching another sliver curl away from the advancing knife-blade, then he watched the back of Ratliff's head again.

"It won't be the first time she has made their crop," the man with the peach spray said. Ratliff glanced at him.

"You ought to know. This won't be the first time I ever saw you in their field, doing plowing Henry never got around to. How many days have you already given them this year?" The man with the peach spray removed it and spat carefully and put the spray back between his teeth.

"She can run a furrow straight as I can," the second said.

"They're unlucky," the third said. "When you are unlucky, it don't matter much what you do."

"Sholy," Ratliff said. "I've heard laziness called bad luck so much that maybe it is."

"He ain't lazy," the third said. "When their mule died three or four years ago, him and her broke their land working time about in the traces with the other mule. They ain't lazy."

"So that's all right," Ratliff said, gazing up the empty road again. "Likely she will begin right away to finish the plowing; that oldest gal is pretty near big enough to work with a mule, ain't she? or at least to hold the plow steady while Mrs. Armstid helps the mule?" He glanced again toward the man with the peach spray as though for an answer, but he was not looking at the other and he went on talking without any pause. The clerk stood with his rump and back pressed against the door-facing as if he had paused in the act of scratching, watching Ratliff quite hard now, unwinking. If Ratliff had looked at Flem Snopes, he would have seen nothing below the down-slanted peak of the cap save the steady motion of his jaws. Another sliver was curling with neat deliberation before the moving knife. "Plenty of time now because all she's got to do after she finishes washing Mrs. Littlejohn's dishes and sweeping out the house to pay hers and Henry's board, is to go out home and milk and cook up enough vittles to last the children until tomorrow and feed them and get the littlest ones to sleep and wait outside the door until that biggest gal gets the bar up and gets into bed herself with the axe——"

"The axe?" the man with the peach spray said.

"She takes it to bed with her. She's just twelve, and what with this country still more or less full of them uncaught horses that never belonged to Flem Snopes, likely she feels maybe she can't swing a mere washboard like Mrs. Littlejohn can —and then come back and wash up the supper dishes. And after that, not nothing to do until morning except to stay close enough where Henry can call her until it's light enough to chop the wood to cook breakfast and then help Mrs. Littlejohn wash the dishes and makes the beds and sweep while watching the road. Because likely any time now Flem Snopes will get back from wherever he has been since the auction, which of course is to town naturally to see about his cousin that's got into a little legal trouble, and so get that five dollars. 'Only maybe he won't give it back to me,' she says, and maybe that's what Mrs. Littlejohn thought too, because she never said nothing. I could hear her——"

And where did you happen to be during all this?" the clerk said.

"Listening," Ratliff said. He glanced back at the clerk, then he was looking away again, almost standing with his back to them. "—could hear her dumping the dishes into the pan like she was throwing them at it. 'Do you reckon he will give it back to me?' Mrs. Armstid says. 'That Texas man give it to him and said he would. All the folks there saw him give Mr. Snopes the money and heard him say I could get it from Mr. Snopes tomorrow.' Mrs. Littlejohn was washing the dishes now, washing them like a man would, like they was made out of iron. 'No,' she says. 'But asking him won't do no hurt.'—'If he wouldn't give it back, it ain't no use to ask,' Mrs. Armstid says. —'Suit yourself,' Mrs. Littlejohn says. 'It's your money.' Then I couldn't hear nothing but the dishes for a while. 'Do you reckon he might give it back to me?' Mrs. Armstid says. 'That Texas man said he would. They all heard him say it.'— 'Then go and ask him for it,' Mrs. Littlejohn says. Then I couldn't hear nothing but the dishes again. 'He won't give it back to me,' Mrs. Armstid says. —'All right,' Mrs. Littlejohn says. 'Don't ask him, then.' Then I just heard the dishes. They would have two pans, both washing. 'You don't reckon he would, do you?' Mrs. Armstid says. Mrs. Littlejohn never said nothing. It sounded like she was throwing the dishes at one another. 'Maybe I better go and talk to Henry,' Mrs. Armstid says.—'I would,' Mrs. Littlejohn says. And I be dog if it didn't sound exactly like she had two plates in her hands, beating them together like these here brass bucket-lids in a band. 'Then Henry can buy another five-dollar horse with it. Maybe he'll buy one next time that will out and out kill him. If I just thought he would, I'd give him back that money, myself.'—'I reckon I better talk to him first,' Mrs. Armstid says. And then it sounded just like Mrs. Littlejohn taken up the dishes and pans and all and throwed the whole business at the cookstove—" Ratliff ceased. Behind him the clerk was hissing "Psst! Psst! Flem. Flem!" Then he stopped, and all of them watched Mrs. Armstid approach and mount the steps, gaunt in the shapeless gray garment, the stained tennis shoes hissing faintly on the boards. She came among them and stood, facing Snopes but not looking at anyone, her hands rolled into her apron.

"He said that day he wouldn't sell Henry that horse," she said in a flat toneless voice. "He said you had the money and I could get it from you." Snopes raised his head and turned it slightly again and spat neatly past the woman, across the gallery and into the road.

"He took all the money with him when he left," he said. Motionless, the gray garment hanging in rigid, almost formal folds like drapery in bronze, Mrs. Armstid appeared to be watching something near Snopes' feet, as though she had not heard him, or as if she had quitted her body as soon as she finished speaking and although her

body, hearing, had received the words, they would have no life nor meaning until she returned. The clerk was rubbing his back steadily against the door-facing again, watching her. The little boy was watching her too with his unwinking ineffable gaze, but nobody else was. The man with the peach spray removed it and spat and put the twig back into his mouth.

"He said Henry hadn't bought no horse," she said. "He said I could get the money from you."

"I reckon he forgot it," Snopes said. "He took all the money away with him when he left." He watched her a moment longer, then he trimmed again at the stick. The clerk rubbed his back gently against the door, watching her. After a time Mrs. Armstid raised her head and looked up the road where it went on, mild with spring dust, past Mrs. Littlejohn's, beginning to rise, on past the not-yet-bloomed (that would be in June) locust grove across the way, on past the schoolhouse, the weathered roof of which, rising beyond an orchard of peach and pear trees, resembled a hive swarmed about by a cloud of pink-and-white bees, ascending, mounting toward the crest of the hill where the church stood among its sparse gleam of marble headstones in the sombre cedar grove where during the long afternoons of summer the constant mourning doves called back and forth. She moved; once more the rubber soles hissed on the gnawed boards.

"I reckon it's about time to get dinner started," she said.

"How's Henry this morning, Mrs. Armstid?" Ratliff said. She looked at him, pausing, the blank eyes waking for an instant.

"He's resting, I thank you kindly," she said. Then the eyes died again and she moved again. Snopes rose from the chair, closing his knife with his thumb and brushing a litter of minute shavings from his lap.

"Wait a minute," he said. Mrs. Armstid paused again, half-turning, though still not looking at Snopes nor at any of them. Because she can't possibly actually believe it, Ratliff told himself, any more than I do. Snopes entered the store, the clerk, motionless again, his back and rump pressed against the door-facing as though waiting to start rubbing again, watched him enter, his head turning as the other passed him like the head of an owl, the little eyes blinking rapidly now. Jody Varner came up the road on his horse. He did not pass but instead turned in beside the store, toward the mulberry tree behind it where he was in the habit of hitching his horse. A wagon came up the road, creaking past. The man driving it lifted his hand; one or two of the men on the gallery lifted theirs in response. The wagon went on. Mrs. Armstid looked after it. Snopes came out of the door, carrying a small striped paper bag and approached Mrs. Armstid. "Here," he said. Her hand turned just enough to receive it. "A little sweetening for the chaps," he said. His other hand was already in his pocket, and as he turned back to the chair, he drew something from his pocket and handed it to the clerk, who took it. It was a five-cent piece. He sat down in the chair and tilted it back against the door again. He now had the knife in his hand again, already open. He turned his head slightly and spat again, neatly past the gray garment, into the road. The little boy was watching the sack in Mrs. Armstid's hand. Then she seemed to discover it also, rousing.

"You're right kind," she said. She rolled the sack into the apron, the little boy's unwinking gaze fixed upon the lump her hands made beneath the cloth. She moved again. "I reckon I better get on and help with dinner," she said. She descended the steps, though as soon as she reached the level earth and began to retreat, the gray folds of the garment once more lost all inference and intimation of locomotion, so that she seemed to progress without motion like a figure on a retreating and diminishing float; a gray and blasted tree-trunk moving, somehow intact and upright, upon an unhurried flood. The clerk in the doorway cackled suddenly, explosively, chortling. He slapped his thigh.

"By God," he said, "You can't beat him."

Jody Varner, entering the store from the rear, paused in midstride like a pointing bird-dog. Then, on tiptoe, in complete silence and with astonishing speed, he darted behind the counter and sped up the gloomy tunnel, at the end of which a hulking, bear-shaped figure stooped, its entire head and shoulders wedged into the glass case, which contained the needles and thread and snuff and tobacco and the stale gaudy candy. He snatched the boy savagely and viciously out; the boy gave a choked cry and struggled flabbily, cramming a final handful of something into his mouth, chewing. But he ceased to struggle almost at once and became slack and inert save for his jaws. Varner dragged him around the counter as the clerk entered, seemed to bounce suddenly into the store with a sort of alert concern. "You, Saint Elmo!" he said.

"Ain't I told you and told you to keep him out of here?" Varner demanded, shaking the boy. "He's damn near eaten that candy-case clean. Stand up!" The boy hung like a half-filled sack from Varner's hand, chewing with a kind of fatalistic desperation, the eyes shut tight in the vast flaccid colorless face, the ears moving steadily and faintly to the chewing. Save for the jaw and the ears, he appeared to have gone to sleep chewing.

"You, Saint Elmo!" the clerk said. "Stand up!" The boy assumed his own weight, though he did not open his eyes yet nor cease to chew. Varner released him. "Git on home," the clerk said. The boy turned obediently to re-enter the store. Varner jerked him about again.

"Not that way," he said. The boy crossed the gallery and descended the steps, the tight overalls undulant and reluctant across his flabby thighs. Before he reached the ground, his hand rose from his pocket to his mouth; again his ears moved faintly to the motion of chewing.

"He's worse than a rat, ain't he?" the clerk said.

"Rat, hell," Varner said, breathing harshly. "He's worse than a goat. First thing I know, he'll graze on back and work through that lace leather and them hame-strings and lap-links and ring-bolts and eat me and you and him all three clean out the back door. And then be damned if I wouldn't be afraid to turn my back for fear he would cross the road and start in on the gin and the blacksmith shop. Now you mind what I say. If I catch him hanging around here one more time, I'm going to set a bear-trap for him."

He went out onto the gallery, the clerk following. "Well, Eck," he said, "I hear you caught one of your horses."

"That's right," Eck said. He and the little boy had finished the crackers and cheese and he had sat for some time now, holding the empty bag.

"It was the one he give you, wasn't it?" Varner said.

"That's right," Eck said.

"Give the other one to me, paw," the little boy said.

"What happened?" Varner said.

"He broke his neck," Eck said.

"I know," Varner said. "But how?" Eck did not move. Watching him, they could almost see him visibly gathering and arranging words, speech. Varner, looking down at him, began to laugh steadily and harshly, sucking his teeth. "I'll tell you what happened. Eck and that boy finally run it into that blind lane of Freeman's, after a chase of about twenty-four hours. They figured it couldn't possibly climb them eight-foot fences of Freeman's so him and the boy tied their rope across the end of the lane, about three feet off the ground. And sho enough, soon as the horse come to the end of the lane and seen Freeman's barn, it whirled just like Eck figured it would and come helling back up that lane like a scared hen-hawk. It probably never even seen the rope at all. Mrs. Freeman was watching from where she had run up onto the porch. She said that when it hit that rope, it looked just like one of these here great big Christmas pinwheels. But the one you bought got clean away, didn't it?"

"That's right," Eck said. "I never had time to see which way the other one went."

"Give him to me, paw," the little boy said.

"You wait till we catch him," Eck said. "We'll see about it then."

III

THE TWO actions of Armstid pl. vs. Snopes, and Tull pl. vs. Eckrum Snopes (and anyone else named Snopes or Varner either which Tull's irate wife could contrive to involve, as the village well knew) were accorded a change of venue by mutual agreement and arrangement among the litigants. Three of the parties did, that is, because Flem Snopes flatly refused to recognize the existence of the suit against himself, stating once and without heat and first turning his head slightly aside to spit, "They wasn't none of my horses," then fell to whittling again while the baffled and helpless bailiff stood before the tilted chair with the papers he was trying to serve.

So the Varner surrey was not among the wagons, the buggies, and the saddled horses and mules which moved out of the village on that May Saturday morning, to converge upon Whiteleaf store eight miles away, coming not only from Frenchman's Bend but from other directions too, since by that time what Ratliff had called 'that Texas sickness,' that spotted corruption of frantic and uncatchable horses, had spread as far as twenty and thirty miles. By the time the Frenchman's Bend people began to arrive, there were two dozen wagons, the teams reversed and eased of harness and tied to the rear wheels in order to pass the day, and twice that many saddled animals already standing about the locust grove beside the store and the site of the hearing had already been transferred from the store to an adjacent shed where in the fall cotton would be stored. But by nine o'clock it was seen that even the shed would not hold them all, so the palladium was moved again, from the shed to the grove itself. The horses and mules and wagons were cleared from it; the single chair, the gnawed table bearing a thick Bible which had the appearance of loving and constant use of a piece of old and perfectly-kept machinery and an almanac and a copy of *Mississippi Reports* dated 1881 and bearing along its opening edge a single thread-thin line of soilure, as if during all the time of his possession its owner (or user) had opened it at only one

page though that quite often, were fetched from the shed to the grove; a wagon and four men were dispatched and returned presently from the church a mile away with four wooden pews for the litigants and their clansmen and witnesses; behind these in turn the spectators stood—the men, the women, the children, sober, attentive, and neat, not in their Sunday clothes to be sure, but in the clean working garments donned that morning for the Saturday's diversion of sitting about the country stores or trips into the county seat, and in which they would return to the field on Monday morning and would wear all that week until Friday night came round again.

The Justice of the Peace was a neat, small, plump old man resembling a tender caricature of all grandfathers who ever breathed, in a beautifully laundered though collarless white shirt with immaculate starch-gleaming cuffs and bosom, and steel-framed spectacles and neat, faintly curling white hair. He sat behind the table and looked at them—at the gray woman in the gray sunbonnet and dress, her clasped and motionless hands on her lap resembling a gnarl of pallid and drowned roots from a drained swamp; at Tull in his faded but absolutely clean shirt and the overalls which his womenfolks not only kept immaculately washed but starched and ironed also, and not creased through the legs but flat across them from seam to seam, so that on each Saturday morning they resembled the short pants of a small boy, and the sedate and innocent blue of his eyes above the month-old corn-silk beard which concealed most of his abraded face and which gave him an air of incredible and paradoxical dissoluteness, not as though at last and without warning he had appeared in the sight of his fellowmen in his true character, but as if an old Italian portrait of a child saint had been defaced by a vicious and idle boy; at Mrs. Tull, a strong, full-bosomed though slightly dumpy woman with an expression of grim and seething outrage which the elapsed four weeks had apparently neither increased nor diminished but had merely set, an outrage which curiously and almost at once began to give the impression of being directed not at any Snopes or at any other man in particular but at all men, all males, and of which Tull himself was not at all the victim but the subject, who sat on one side of her husband while the biggest of the four daughters sat on the other as if they (or Mrs. Tull at least) were not so much convinced that Tull might leap up and flee, as determined that he would not; and at Eck and the little boy, identical save for size, and Lump, the clerk, in a gray cap which someone actually recognized as being the one which Flem Snopes had worn when he went to Texas last year, who between spells of rapid blinking would sit staring at the Justice with the lidless intensity of a rat—and into the lens-distorted and irisless old-man's eyes of the Justice there grew an expression not only of amazement and bewilderment but, as in Ratliff's eyes while he stood on the store gallery four weeks ago, something very like terror.

"This—" he said. "I didn't expect—I didn't look to see—. I'm going to pray," he said. "I ain't going to pray aloud. But I hope—" He looked at them. "I wish. . . . Maybe some of you all anyway had better do the same." He bowed his head. They watched him, quiet and grave, while he sat motionless behind the table, the light morning wind moving faintly in his thin hair and the shadow-stipple of windy leaves gliding and flowing across the starched bulge of bosom and the gleaming bone-buttoned cuffs, as rigid and almost as large as sections of six-inch stovepipe, at his joined hands. He raised his head. "Armstid against Snopes," he said. Mrs. Armstid spoke. She did not move, she looked at nothing, her hands clasped in her lap, speaking in that flat, toneless and hopeless voice:

"That Texan man said——"

"Wait," the Justice said. He looked about at the faces, the blurred eyes fleeing behind the thick lenses. "Where is the defendant? I don't see him."

"He wouldn't come," the bailiff said.

"Wouldn't come?" the Justice said. "Didn't you serve the papers on him?"

"He wouldn't take them," the bailiff said. "He said——"

"Then he is in contempt!" the Justice cried.

"What for?" Lump Snopes said. "Ain't nobody proved yet they was his horses." The Justice looked at him.

"Are you representing the defendant?" he said. Snopes blinked at him for a moment.

"What's that mean?" he said. "That you aim for me to pay whatever fine you think you can clap onto him?"

"So he refuses to defend himself," the Justice said. "Don't he know that I can find against him for that reason, even if pure justice and decency ain't enough?"

"It'll be pure something," Snopes said. "It don't take no mind-reader to see how you mind is——"

"Shut up, Snopes," the bailiff said. "If you ain't in this case, you keep out of it." He turned back to the Justice. "What you want me to do: go over to the Bend and fetch Snopes here anyway? I reckon I can do it."

"No," the Justice said. "Wait." He looked about at the sober faces again with that bafflement, that dread. "Does anybody here know for sho who them horses belonged to? Anybody?" They looked back at him, sober, attentive—at the neat immaculate old man sitting with his hands locked together on the table before him to still the trembling. "All right, Mrs. Armstid," he said. "Tell the court what happened." She told it, unmoving, in the flat, inflectionless voice, looking at nothing, while they listened quietly, coming to the end and ceasing without even any fall of voice, as though the tale mattered nothing and came to nothing. The Justice was looking down at his hands. When she ceased, he looked up at her. "But you haven't showed yet that Snopes owned the horses. The one you want to sue is that Texas man. And he's gone. If you got a judgment against him, you couldn't collect the money. Don't you see?"

"Mr. Snopes brought him here," Mrs. Armstid said. "Likely that Texas man wouldn't have knowed where Frenchman's Bend was if Mr. Snopes hadn't showed him."

"But it was the Texas man that sold the horses and collected the money for them." The Justice looked about again at the faces. "Is that right? You, Bookwright, is that what happened?"

"Yes," Bookwright said. The Justice looked at Mrs. Armstid again, with that pity and grief. As the morning increased the wind had risen, so that from time to time gusts of it ran through the branches overhead, bringing a faint snow of petals, prematurely bloomed as the spring itself had condensed with spendthrift speed after the hard winter, and the heavy and drowsing scent of them, about the motionless heads.

"He give Mr. Snopes Henry's money. He said Henry hadn't bought no horse. He said I could get the money from Mr. Snopes tomorrow."

"And you have witnesses that saw and heard him?"

"Yes, sir. The other men that was there saw him give Mr. Snopes the money and say that I could get it——"

"And you asked Snopes for the money?"

"Yes, sir. He said that Texas man taken it away with him when he left. But I would. . . ." She ceased again, perhaps looking down at her hands also. Certainly she was not looking at anyone.

"Yes?" the Justice said. "You would what?"

"I would know them five dollars. I earned them myself, weaving at night after Henry and the chaps was asleep. Some of the ladies in Jefferson would save up string and such and give it to me and I would weave things and sell them. I earned that money a little at a time and I would know it when I saw it because I would take the can outen the chimney and count it now and then while it was making up to enough to buy my chaps some shoes for next winter. I would know it if I was to see it again. If Mr. Snopes would just let——"

"Suppose there was somebody seen Flem give that money back to that Texas fellow," Lump Snopes said suddenly.

"Did anybody here see that?" the Justice said.

"Yes," Snopes said, harshly and violently. "Eck here did." He looked at Eck. "Go on. Tell him." The Justice looked at Eck; the four Tull girls turned their heads as one head and looked at him, and Mrs. Tull leaned forward to look past her husband, her face cold, furious, and contemptuous, and those standing shifted to look past one another's heads at Eck sitting motionless on the bench.

"Did you see Snopes give Armstid's money back to the Texas man, Eck?" the Justice said. Still Eck did not answer nor move, Lump Snopes made a gross violent sound through the side of his mouth.

"By God, I ain't afraid to say it if Eck is. I seen him do it."

"Will you swear that as testimony?" Snopes looked at the Justice. He did not blink now.

"So you won't take my word," he said.

"I want the truth," the Justice said. "If I can't find that, I got to have sworn evidence of what I will have to accept as truth." He lifted the Bible from the two other books.

"All right," the bailiff said. "Step up here." Snopes rose from the bench and approached. They watched him, though now there was no shifting nor craning, no movement at all among the faces, the still eyes. Snopes at the table looked back at them once, his gaze traversing swiftly the crescent-shaped rank; he looked at the Justice again. The bailiff grasped the Bible; though the Justice did not release it yet.

"You are ready to swear you saw Snopes give that Texas man back the money he took from Henry Armstid for that horse?" he said.

"I said I was, didn't I?" Snopes said. The Justice released the Bible.

"Swear him," he said.

"Put your left hand on the Book raise your right hand you solemnly swear and affirm——" the bailiff said rapidly. But Snopes had already done so, his left hand clapped onto the extended Bible and the other hand raised and his head turned away as once more his gaze went rapidly along the circle of expressionless and intent faces, saying in that harsh and snarling voice:

"Yes. I saw Flem Snopes give back to that Texas man whatever money Henry Armstid or anybody else thinks Henry Armstid or anybody else paid Flem for any of them horses. Does that suit you?"

"Yes," the Justice said. Then there was no movement, no sound anywhere among them. The bailiff placed the Bible quietly on the table beside the Justice's locked hands, and there was no movement save the flow and recover of the windy shadows and the drift of the locust petals. Then Mrs. Armstid rose; she stood once more (or still) looking at nothing, her hands clasped across her middle.

"I reckon I can go now, can't I?" she said.

"Yes," the Justice said, rousing. "Unless you would like——"

"I better get started," she said. "It's a right far piece." She had not come in the wagon, but on one of the gaunt and underfed mules. One of the men followed her across the grove and untied the mule for her and led it up to a wagon, from one hub of which she mounted. Then they looked at the Justice again. He sat behind the table, his hands still joined before him, though his head was not bowed now. Yet he did not move until the bailiff leaned and spoke to him, when he roused, came suddenly awake without starting, as an old man wakes from an old man's light sleep. He removed his hands from the table and, looking down, he spoke exactly as if he were reading from a paper:

"Tull against Snopes. Assault and——"

"Yes!" Mrs. Tull said. "I'm going to say a word before you start." She leaned, looking past Tull at Lump Snopes again. "If you think you are going to lie and perjure Flem and Eck Snopes out of——"

"Now, mamma," Tull said. Now she spoke to Tull, without changing her position or her tone or even any break or pause in her speech:

"Don't you say hush to me! You'll let Eck Snopes or Flem Snopes or that whole Varner tribe snatch you out of the wagon and beat you half to death against a wooden bridge. But when it comes to suing them for your just rights and a punishment, oh no. Because that wouldn't be neighborly. What's neighborly got to do with you lying flat on your back in the middle of planting time while we pick splinters out of your face?" By this time the bailiff was shouting,

"Order! Order! This here's a law court!" Mrs. Tull ceased. She sat back, breathing hard, staring at the Justice, who sat and spoke again as if he were reading aloud:

"—assault and battery on the person of Vernon Tull, through the agency and instrument of one horse, unnamed, belonging to Eckrum Snopes. Evidence of physical detriment and suffering, defendant himself. Witnesses, Mrs. Tull and daughters——"

"Eck Snopes saw it too," Mrs. Tull said, though with less violence now. "He was there. He got there in plenty of time to see it. Let him deny it. Let him look me in the face and deny it if he——"

"If you please, ma'am," the Justice said. He said it so quietly that Mrs. Tull hushed and became quite calm, almost a rational and composed being. "The injury to your husband ain't disputed. And the agency of the horse ain't disputed. The law says that when a man owns a creature which he knows to be dangerous and if that creature is restrained and restricted from the public commons by a pen or enclosure capable of restraining and restricting it, if a man enter that pen or enclosure, whether he knows the creature in it is dangerous or not dangerous, then that man has committed trespass and the owner of that creature is not liable. But if that creature known to him to be dangerous ceases to be restrained by that suitable pen or enclosure, either by accident or design and either with or without the owner's knowledge, then that owner is liable. That's the law. All necessary now is to establish first, the ownership of the horse, and second, that the horse was a dangerous creature within the definition of the law as provided."

"Hah," Mrs. Tull said. She said it exactly as Bookwright would have. "Dangerous. Ask Vernon Tull. Ask Henry Armstid if them things was pets."

"If you please, ma'am," the Justice said. He was looking at Eck. "What is the defendant's position? Denial of ownership?"

"What?" Eck said.

"Was that your horse that ran over Mr. Tull?"

"Yes," Eck said. "It was mine. How much do I have to p——"

"Hah," Mrs. Tull said again. "Denial of ownership. When there were at least forty men—fools too, or they wouldn't have been there. But even a fool's word is good about what he saw and heard —at least forty men heard that Texas murderer give that horse to Eck Snopes. Not sell it to him, mind; give it to him."

"What?" the Justice said. "Gave it to him?"

"Yes," Eck said. "He give it to me. I'm sorry Tull happened to be using that bridge too at the same time. How much do I——"

"Wait," the Justice said. "What did you give him? a note? a swap of some kind?"

"No," Eck said. "He just pointed to it in the lot and told me it belonged to me."

"And he didn't give you a bill of sale or a deed or anything in writing?"

"I reckon he never had time," Eck said. "And after Lon Quick forgot and left that gate open, never nobody had time to do no writing even if we had a thought of it."

"What's all this?" Mrs. Tull said. "Eck Snopes has just told you he owned that horse. And if you won't take his word, there were forty men standing at that gate all day long doing nothing, that heard that murdering card-playing whiskey-drinking anti-christ——" This time the Justice raised one hand, in its enormous pristine cuff, toward her. He did not look at her.

"Wait," he said. "Then what did he do?" he said to Eck. "Just lead the horse up and put the rope in your hand?"

"No," Eck said. "Him nor nobody else never got no ropes on none of them. He just pointed to the horse in the lot and said it was mine and auctioned off the rest of them and got into the buggy and said good-bye and druv off. And we got our ropes and went into the lot, only Lon Quick forgot to shut the gate. I'm sorry it made Tull's mules snatch him outen the wagon. How much do I owe him?" Then he stopped, because the Justice was no longer looking at him and, as he realized a moment later, no longer listening either. Instead, he was sitting back in the chair, actually leaning back in it for the first time, his head bent slightly and his hands resting on the table before him, the fingers lightly overlapped. They watched him quietly for almost a half-minute before anyone realized that he was looking quietly and steadily at Mrs. Tull.

"Well, Mrs. Tull," he said, "by your own testimony, Eck never owned that horse."

"What?" Mrs. Tull said. It was not loud at all. "What did you say?"

"In the law, ownership can't be conferred or invested by word-of-mouth. It must be established either by recorded or authentic document, or by possession or occupation. By your testimony and his both, he never gave that Texan anything in exchange for that horse, and by his testimony the Texas man never gave him any paper to prove he owned it, and by his testimony and by what I know myself from these last four weeks, nobody yet has ever laid hand or rope either on any one of them. So that horse never came into Eck's possession at all. That Texas man could have given that same horse to a dozen other men standing around that gate that day, without even needing to tell Eck he had done it; and Eck himself could have transferred all his title and equity in it to Mr. Tull right there while Mr. Tull was lying unconscious on that bridge just by thinking it to himself, and Mr. Tull's title would be just as legal as Eck's."

"So I get nothing," Mrs. Tull said. Her voice was still calm, quiet, though probably no one but Tull realized that it was too calm and quiet. "My team is made to run away by a wild spotted mad dog, my wagon is wrecked; my husband is jerked out of it and knocked unconscious and unable to work for a whole week with less than half of our seed in the ground, and I get nothing."

"Wait," the Justice said. "The law——"

"The law," Mrs. Tull said. She stood suddenly up—a short, broad, strong woman, balanced on the balls of her planted feet.

"Now, mamma," Tull said.

"Yes, ma'am," the Justice said. "Your damages are fixed by statute. The law says that when a suit for damages is brought against the owner of an animal which has committed damage or injury, if the owner of the animal either can't or won't assume liability, the injured or damaged party shall find recompense in the body of the animal. And since Eck Snopes never owned that horse at all, and since you just heard a case here this morning that failed to prove that Flem Snopes had any equity in any of them, that horse still belongs to that Texas man. Or did belong. Because now that horse that made your team run away and snatch your husband out of the wagon, belongs to you and Mr. Tull."

"Now, mamma!" Tull said. He rose quickly. But Mrs. Tull was still quiet, only quite rigid and breathing hard, until Tull spoke. Then she turned on him, not screaming: shouting; presently the bailiff was banging the table-top with his hand-polished hickory cane and roaring "Order! Order!" while the neat old man, thrust backward in his chair as though about to dodge and trembling with an old man's palsy, looked on with amazed unbelief.

"The horse!" Mrs. Tull shouted. "We see it for five seconds, while it is climbing into the wagon with us and then out again. Then it's gone, God don't know where and thank the Lord He don't! And the mules gone with it and the wagon wrecked and you laying there on the bridge with your face full of kindling-wood and bleeding like a hog and dead for all we knew. And he gives us the horse! Don't hush me! Get on to that wagon, fool that would sit there behind a pair of young mules with the reins tied around his wrist! Get on to that wagon, all of you!"

"I can't stand no more!" the old Justice cried. "I won't! This court's adjourned! Adjourned!"

THE BEAR

◇

⟪ "THE BEAR" is a self-contained short novel which appears as a major part of Faulkner's volume *Go Down, Moses* (1942). Earlier versions of parts of "The Bear" were printed in *Harper's* (1935) and the *Saturday Evening Post* (1942); these consisted mainly of the hunt sections. The difficult Section 4 was included only in *Go Down, Moses*, and it is this complete version which follows. There can be no justification for reprinting "The Bear" without Section 4, as is sometimes done, for that section must be judged an integral part of the story. Unquestionably, Section 4, with its dredging up of old records and its convoluted dialogue between Isaac McCaslin and his cousin, makes "The Bear" harder to read than it would be if only the hunt sections were included. But Section 4 also enriches the work: it helps explain the nature of the historic guilt which troubles Isaac and which prompts him to undertake the act of expiation and cleansing that is embodied in the ritual hunt of the bear.

◇

I

THERE was a man and a dog too this time. Two beasts, counting Old Ben, the bear, and two men, counting Boon Hogganbeck, in whom some of the same blood ran which ran in Sam Fathers, even though Boon's was a plebeian strain of it and only Sam and Old Ben and the mongrel Lion were taintless and incorruptible.

He was sixteen. For six years now he had been a man's hunter. For six years now he had heard the best of all talking. It was of the wilderness, the big woods, bigger and older than any recorded document:—of white man fatuous enough to believe he had bought any fragment of it, of Indian ruthless enough to pretend that any fragment of it had been his to convey; bigger than Major de Spain and the scrap he pretended to, knowing better; older than old Thomas Sutpen of whom Major de Spain had had it and who knew better; older even than old Ikkemotubbe, the Chickasaw chief, of whom old Sutpen had had it and who knew better in his turn. It was of the men, not white nor black nor red but men, hunters, with the will and hardihood to endure and the humility and skill to survive, and the dogs and the bear and deer juxtaposed and reliefed against it, ordered and compelled by and within the wilderness in the ancient and unremitting contest according to the ancient and immitigable rules which voided all re-grets and brooked no quarter;—the best game of all, the best of all breathing and forever the best of all listening, the voices quiet and weighty and deliberate for retrospection and recollection and exactitude among the concrete trophies—the racked guns and the heads and skins—in the libraries of town houses or the offices of planta-tion houses or (and best of all) in the camps themselves where the intact and still-warm meat yet hung, the men who had slain it sitting before the burning logs on hearths when there were houses and hearths or about the smoky blazing of piled wood in front of stretched tarpaulins when there were not. There was always a bottle present, so that it would seem to him that those fine fierce instants of heart and brain and courage and wili-ness and speed were concentrated and distilled into that brown liquor which not women, not boys and children, but only hunters drank, drinking not of the blood they spilled but some condensation of the wild immortal spirit, drinking it moderately, humbly even, not with the pagan's base and base-less hope of acquiring thereby the virtues of cun-ning and strength and speed but in salute to them. Thus it seemed to him on this December morning not only natural but actually fitting that this should have begun with whisky.

He realised later that it had begun long before that. It had already begun on that day when he first wrote his age in two ciphers and his cousin Mc-Caslin brought him for the first time to the camp, the big woods, to earn for himself from the wilder-ness the name and state of hunter provided he in his turn were humble and enduring enough. He had already inherited them, without ever having seen it, the big old bear with one trap-ruined foot that in an area almost a hundred miles square had earned for himself a name, a definite designation like a living man:—the long legend of corn-cribs broken down and rifled, of shoats and grown pigs and even calves carried bodily into the woods and devoured and traps and deadfalls overthrown and dogs mangled and slain and shotgun and even rifle shots delivered at point-blank range yet with no more effect than so many peas blown through a tube by a child—a corridor of wreckage and destruction beginning back before the boy was born, through which sped, not fast but rather with the ruthless and irresistible deliberation of a locomotive, the shaggy tremendous shape. It ran in his knowledge before he ever saw it. It loomed and towered in his dreams before he even saw the unaxed woods where it left its crooked print, shaggy, tremendous, red-eyed, not malevolent but just big, too big for the dogs which tried to bay it,

for the horses which tried to ride it down, for the men and the bullets they fired into it; too big for the very country which was its constricting scope. It was as if the boy had already divined what his senses and intellect had not encompassed yet: that doomed wilderness whose edges were being con-stantly and punily gnawed at by men with plows and axes who feared it because it was wilderness, men myriad and nameless even to one another in the land where the old bear had earned a name, and through which ran not even a mortal beast but an anachronism indomitable and invincible out of an old dead time, a phantom, epitome and apotheosis of the old wild life which the little puny humans swarmed and hacked at in a fury of ab-horrence and fear like pygmies about the ankles of a drowsing elephant;—the old bear, solitary, indomitable, and alone; widowered childless and absolved of mortality—old Priam reft of his old wife and outlived all his sons.

Still a child, with three years then two years then one year yet before he too could make one of them, each November he would watch the wagon containing the dogs and the bedding and food and guns and his cousin McCaslin and Ten-nie's Jim and Sam Fathers too until Sam moved to the camp to live, depart for the Big Bottom, the big woods. To him, they were going not to hunt bear and deer but to keep yearly rendezvous with the bear which they did not even intend to kill. Two weeks later they would return, with no trophy, no skin. He had not expected it. He had not even feared that it might be in the wagon this time with the other skins and heads. He did not even tell himself that in three years or two years or one year more he would be present and that it might even be his gun. He believed that only after he had served his apprenticeship in the woods which would prove him worthy to be a hunter, would he even be permitted to distinguish the crooked print, and that even then for two No-vember weeks he would merely make another mi-nor one, along with his cousin and Major de Spain and General Compson and Walter Ewell and Boon and the dogs which feared to bay it and the shotguns and rifles which failed even to bleed it, in the yearly pageant-rite of the old bear's furious immortality.

His day came at last. In the surrey with his cousin and Major de Spain and General Comp-son he saw the wilderness through a slow drizzle of November rain just above the ice point as it seemed to him later he always saw it or at least always remembered it—the tall and endless wall of dense November woods under the dissolving afternoon and the year's death, sombre, impenetrable (he could not even discern yet how, at what point they could possibly hope to enter it even though he knew that Sam Fathers was waiting there with the wagon), the surrey moving through the skeleton stalks of cotton and corn in the last of open country, the last trace of man's puny gnawing at the immemorial flank, until, dwarfed by that perspective into an almost ridiculous diminishment, the surrey itself seemed to have ceased to move (this too to be completed later, years later, after he had grown to a man and had seen the sea) as a solitary small boat hangs in lonely immobility, merely tossing up and down, in the infinite waste of the ocean while the water and then the apparently impenetrable land which it nears without appreciable progress, swings slowly and opens the widening inlet which is the anchorage. He entered it. Sam was waiting, wrapped in a quilt on the wagon seat behind the patient and steaming mules. He entered his novitiate to the true wilderness with Sam beside him as he had begun his apprenticeship in miniature to manhood after the rabbits and such with Sam beside him, the two of them wrapped in the damp, warm, negro-rank quilt while the wilderness closed behind his entrance as it had opened momentarily to accept him, opening before his advancement as it closed behind his progress, no fixed path the wagon followed but a channel nonexistent ten yards ahead of it and ceasing to exist ten yards after it had passed, the wagon progressing not by its own volition but by attrition of their intact yet fluid circumambience, drowsing, earless, almost lightless.

It seemed to him that at the age of ten he was witnessing his own birth. It was not even strange to him. He had experienced it all before, and not merely in dreams. He saw the camp—a paintless six-room bungalow set on piles above the spring high-water—and he knew already how it was going to look. He helped in the rapid orderly disorder of their establishment in it and even his motions were familiar to him, foreknown. Then for two weeks he ate the coarse, rapid food—the shapeless sour bread, the wild strange meat, venison and bear and turkey and coon which he had never tasted before—which men ate, cooked by men who were hunters first and cooks afterward; he slept in harsh sheetless blankets as hunters slept. Each morning the gray of dawn found him and Sam Fathers on the stand, the crossing, which had been allotted him. It was the poorest one, the most barren. He had expected that; he had not dared yet to hope even to himself that he would even hear the running dogs this first time. But he did hear them. It was on the third morning—a murmur, sourceless, almost indistinguishable, yet he knew what it was although he had never before heard that many dogs running at once, the murmur swelling into separate and distinct voices until he could call the five dogs which his cousin owned from among the others. "Now," Sam said, "slant your gun up a little and draw back the hammers and then stand still."

But it was not for him, not yet. The humility was there; he had learned that. And he could learn the patience. He was only ten, only one week. The instant had passed. It seemed to him that he could actually see the deer, the buck, smoke-colored, elongated with speed, vanished, the woods, the gray solitude still ringing even when the voices of the dogs had died away; from far away across the sombre woods and the gray half-liquid morning there came two shots. "Now let your hammers down," Sam said.

He did so. "You knew it too," he said.

"Yes," Sam said. "I want you to learn how to do when you didn't shoot. It's after the chance for the bear or the deer has done already come and gone that men and dogs get killed."

"Anyway, it wasn't him," the boy said. "It wasn't even a bear. It was just a deer."

"Yes," Sam said, "it was just a deer."

Then one morning, it was in the second week, he heard the dogs again. This time before Sam even spoke he readied the too-long, too-heavy, man-size gun as Sam had taught him, even though this time he knew the dogs and the deer were coming less close than ever, hardly within hearing even. They didn't sound like any running dogs he had ever heard before even. Then he found that Sam, who had taught him first of all to cock the gun and take position where he could see best in all directions and then never to move again, had himself moved up beside him. "There," he said. "Listen." The boy listened, to no ringing chorus strong and fast on a free scent but a moiling yapping an octave too high and with something more than indecision and even abjectness in it which he could not yet recognise, reluctant, not even moving very fast, taking a long time to pass out of hearing, leaving even then in the air that echo of thin and almost human hysteria, abject, almost humanly grieving, with this time nothing ahead of it, no sense of a fleeing unseen smoke-colored shape. He could hear Sam breathing at his shoulder. He saw the arched curve of the old man's inhaling nostrils.

"It's Old Ben!" he cried, whispering.

Sam didn't move save for the slow gradual turning of his head as the voices faded on and the faint steady rapid arch and collapse of his nostrils.

"Hah," he said. "Not even running. Walking."

"But up here!" the boy cried. "Way up here!"

"He do it every year," Sam said. "Once. Ash and Boon say he comes up here to run the other little bears away. Tell them to get to hell out of here and stay out until the hunters are gone. Maybe." The boy no longer heard anything at all, yet still Sam's head continued to turn gradually and steadily until the back of it was toward him. Then it turned back and looked down at him—the same face, grave, familiar, expressionless until it smiled, the same old man's eyes from which as he watched there faded slowly a quality darkly and fiercely lambent, passionate and proud. "He dont care no more for bears than he does for dogs or men neither. He come to see who's here, who's new in camp this year, whether he can shoot or not, can stay or not. Whether we got the dog yet that can bay and hold him until a man gets there with a gun. Because he's the head bear. He's the man." It faded, was gone; again they were the eyes as he had known them all his life. "He'll let them follow him to the river. Then he'll send them home. We might as well go too; see how they look when they get back to camp."

The dogs were there first, ten of them huddled back under the kitchen, himself and Sam squatting to peer back into the obscurity where they crouched, quiet, the eyes rolling and luminous, vanishing, and no sound, only that effluvium which the boy could not quite place yet, of something more than dog, stronger than dog and not just animal, just beast even. Because there had been nothing in front of the abject and painful yapping except the solitude, the wilderness, so that when the eleventh hound got back about mid-afternoon and he and Tennie's Jim held the passive and still trembling bitch while Sam daubed her tattered ear and raked shoulder with turpentine and axle-grease, it was still no living creature but only the wilderness which, leaning for a moment, had patted lightly once her temerity. "Just like a man," Sam said. "Just like folks. Put off as long as she could having to be brave, knowing all the time that sooner or later she would have to be brave once so she could keep on calling herself a dog, and knowing beforehand what was going to happen when she done it."

He did not know just when Sam left. He only knew that he was gone. For the next three mornings he rose and ate breakfast and Sam was not waiting for him. He went to his stand alone; he found it withoug help now and stood on it as Sam had taught him. On the third morning he heard the dogs again, running strong and free on a true scent again, and he readied the gun as he had

learned to do and heard the hunt sweep past on since he was not ready yet, had not deserved other yet in just one short period of two weeks as compared to all the long life which he had already dedicated to the wilderness with patience and humility; he heard the shot again, one shot, the single clapping report of Walter Ewell's rifle. By now he could not only find his stand and then return to camp without guidance, by using the compass his cousin had given him he reached Walter waiting beside the buck and the moiling of dogs over the cast entrails before any of the others except Major de Spain and Tennie's Jim on the horses, even before Uncle Ash arrived with the one-eyed wagon-mule which did not mind the smell of blood or even, so they said, of bear.

It was not Uncle Ash on the mule. It was Sam, returned. And Sam was waiting when he finished his dinner and, himself on the one-eyed mule and Sam on the other one of the wagon team, they rode for more than three hours through the rapid shortening sunless afternoon, following no path, no trail even that he could discern, into a section of country he had never seen before. Then he understood why Sam had made him ride the one-eyed mule which would not spook at the smell of blood, of wild animals. The other one, the sound one, stopped short and tried to whirl and bolt even as Sam got down, jerking and wrenching at the rein while Sam held it, coaxing it forward with his voice since he did not dare risk hitching it, drawing it forward while the boy dismounted from the marred one which would stand. Then, standing beside Sam in the thick great gloom of ancient woods and the winter's dying afternoon, he looked quietly down at the rotted log scored and gutted with claw-marks and, in the wet earth beside it, the print of the enormous warped two-toed foot. Now he knew what he had heard in the hounds' voices in the woods that morning and what he had smelled when he peered under the kitchen where they huddled. It was in him too, a little different because they were brute beasts and he was not, but only a little different—an eagerness, passive; an abjectness, a sense of his own fragility and impotence against the timeless woods, yet without doubt or dread; a flavor like brass in the sudden run of saliva in his mouth, a hard sharp constriction either in his brain or his stomach, he could not tell which and it did not matter; he knew only that for the first time he realised that the bear which had run in his listening and loomed in his dreams since before he could remember and which therefore must have existed in the listening and the dreams of his cousin and Major de Spain and even old General Compson before they began to remember in their turn, was a mortal animal and that they had departed for the camp each November with no actual intention of slaying it, not because it could not be slain but because so far they had no actual hope of being able to. "It will be tomorrow," he said.

"You mean we will try tomorrow," Sam said. "We aint got the dog yet."

"We've got eleven," he said. "They ran him Monday."

"And you heard them," Sam said. "Saw them too. We aint got the dog yet. It wont take but one. But he aint there. Maybe he aint nowhere. The only other way will be for him to run by accident over somebody that had a gun and knowed how to shoot it."

"That wouldn't be me," the boy said. "It would be Walter or Major or——"

"It might," Sam said. "You watch close tomorrow. Because he's smart. That's how come he has lived this long. If he gets hemmed up and has got to pick out somebody to run over, he will pick out you."

"How?" he said. "How will he know. . . ." He ceased. "You mean he already knows me, that I aint never been to the big bottom before, aint had time to find out yet whether I . . ." He ceased again, staring at Sam; he said humbly, not even amazed: "It was me he was watching. I dont reckon he did need to come but once."

"You watch tomorrow," Sam said. "I reckon we better start back. It'll be long after dark now before we get to camp."

The next morning they started three hours earlier than they had ever done. Even Uncle Ash went, the cook, who called himself by profession a camp cook and who did little else save cook for Major de Spain's hunting and camping parties, yet who had been marked by the wilderness from simple juxtaposition to it until he responded as they all did, even the boy who until two weeks ago had never even seen the wilderness, to a hound's ripped ear and shoulder and the print of a crooked foot in a patch of wet earth. They rode. It was too far to walk: the boy and Sam and Uncle Ash in the wagon with the dogs, his cousin and Major de Spain and General Compson and Boon and Walter and Tennie's Jim riding double on the horses; again the first gray light found him, as on that first morning two weeks ago, on the stand where Sam had placed and left him. With the gun which was too big for him, the breech-loader which did not even belong to him but to Major de Spain and which he had fired only once, at a stump on the first day to learn the recoil and how to reload it with the paper shells, he

stood against a big gum tree beside a little bayou whose black still water crept without motion out of a cane-brake, across a small clearing and into the cane again, where, invisible, a bird, the big woodpecker called Lord-to-God by negroes, clattered at a dead trunk. It was a stand like any other stand, dissimilar only in incidentals to the one where he had stood each morning for two weeks; a territory new to him yet no less familiar than that other one which after two weeks he had come to believe he knew a little—the same solitude, the same loneliness through which frail and timorous man had merely passed without altering it, leaving no mark nor scar, which looked exactly as it must have looked when the first ancestor of Sam Fathers' Chickasaw predecessors crept into it and looked about him, club or stone axe or bone arrow drawn and ready, different only because, squatting at the edge of the kitchen, he had smelled the dogs huddled and cringing beneath it and saw the raked ear and side of the bitch that, as Sam had said, had to be brave once in order to keep on calling herself a dog, and saw yesterday in the earth beside the gutted log, the print of the living foot. He heard no dogs at all. He never did certainly hear them. He only heard the drumming of the woodpecker stop short off, and knew that the bear was looking at him. He never saw it. He did not know whether it was facing him from the cane or behind him. He did not move, holding the useless gun which he knew now he would never fire at it, now or ever, tasting in his saliva that taint of brass which he had smelled in the huddled dogs when he peered under the kitchen.

Then it was gone. As abruptly as it had stopped, the woodpecker's dry hammering set up again, and after a while he believed he even heard the dogs —a murmur, scarce a sound even, which he had probably been hearing for a time, perhaps a minute or two, before he remarked it, drifting into hearing and then out again, dying away. They came nowhere near him. If it was dogs he heard, he could not have sworn to it; if it was a bear they ran, it was another bear. It was Sam himself who emerged from the cane and crossed the bayou, the injured bitch following at heel as a bird dog is taught to walk. She came and crouched against his leg, trembling. "I didn't see him," he said. "I didn't, Sam."

"I know it," Sam said. "He done the looking. You didn't hear him neither, did you?"

"No," the boy said. "I——"

"He's smart," Sam said. "Too smart." Again the boy saw in his eyes that quality of dark and brooding lambence as Sam looked down at the bitch trembling faintly and steadily against the boy's leg. From her raked shoulder a few drops of fresh blood clung like bright berries. "Too big. We aint got the dog yet. But maybe some day."

Because there would be a next time, after and after. He was only ten. It seemed to him that he could see them, the two of them, shadowy in the limbo from which time emerged and became time: the old bear absolved of mortality and himself who shared a little of it. Because he recognised now what he had smelled in the huddled dogs and tasted in his own saliva, recognised fear as a boy, a youth, recognises the existence of love and passion and experience which is his heritage but not yet his patrimony, from entering by chance the presence or perhaps even merely the bedroom of a woman who has loved and been loved by many men. *So I will have to see him,* he thought, without dread or even hope. *I will have to look at him.* So it was in June of the next summer. They were at the camp again, celebrating Major de Spain's and General Compson's birthdays. Although the one had been born in September and the other in the depth of winter and almost thirty years earlier, each June the two of them and McCaslin and Boon and Walter Ewell (and the boy too from now on) spent two weeks at the camp, fishing and shooting squirrels and turkey and running coons and wildcats with the dogs at night. That is, Boon and the negroes (and the boy too now) fished and shot squirrels and ran the coons and cats, because the proven hunters, not only Major de Spain and old General Compson (who spent those two weeks sitting in a rocking chair before a tremendous iron pot of Brunswick stew, stirring and tasting, with Uncle Ash to quarrel with about how he was making it and Tennie's Jim to pour whisky into the tin dipper from which he drank it) but even McCaslin and Walter Ewell who were still young enough, scorned such other than shooting the wild gobblers with pistols for wagers or to test their marksmanship.

That is, his cousin McCaslin and the others thought he was hunting squirrels. Until the third evening he believed that Sam Fathers thought so too. Each morning he would leave the camp right after breakfast. He had his own gun now, a new breech-loader, a Christmas gift; he would own and shoot it for almost seventy years, through two new pairs of barrels and locks and one new stock, until all that remained of the original gun was the silver-inlaid trigger-guard with his and McCaslin's engraved names and the date in 1878. He found the tree beside the little bayou where he had stood that morning. Using the compass he ranged from that point; he was teaching himself to be better than a fair woodsman without even knowing he

was doing it. On the third day he even found the gutted log where he had first seen the print. It was almost completely crumbled now, healing with unbelievable speed, a passionate and almost visible relinquishment, back into the earth from which the tree had grown. He ranged the summer woods now, green with gloom, if anything actually dimmer than they had been in November's gray dissolution, where even at noon the sun fell only in windless dappling upon the earth which never completely dried and which crawled with snakes —moccasins and watersnakes and rattlers, themselves the color of the dappled gloom so that he would not always see them until they moved; returning to camp later and later and later, first day, second day, passing in the twilight of the third evening the little log pen enclosing the log barn where Sam was putting up the stock for the night. "You aint looked right yet," Sam said.

He stopped. For a moment he didn't answer. Then he said peacefully, in a peaceful rushing burst, as when a boy's miniature dam in a little brook gives way: "All right. Yes. But how? I went to the bayou. I even found that log again. I——"

"I reckon that was all right. Likely he's been watching you. You never saw his foot?"

"I . . ." the boy said. "I didn't . . . I never thought . . ."

"It's the gun," Sam said. He stood beside the fence, motionless, the old man, son of a negro slave and a Chickasaw chief, in the battered and faded overalls and the frayed five-cent straw hat which had been the badge of the negro's slavery and was now the regalia of his freedom. The camp—the clearing, the house, the barn and its tiny lot with which Major de Spain in his turn had scratched punily and evanescently at the wilderness—faded in the dusk, back into the immemorial darkness of the woods. *The gun,* the boy thought. *The gun.* "You will have to choose," Sam said.

He left the next norning before light, without breakfast, long before Uncle Ash would wake in his quilts on the kitchen floor and start the fire. He had only the compass and a stick for the snakes. He could go almost a mile before he would need to see the compass. He sat on a log, the invisible compass in his hand, while the secret night-sounds which had ceased at his movements, scurried again and then fell still for good and the owls ceased and gave over to the waking day birds and there was light in the gray wet woods and he could see the compass. He went fast yet still quietly, becoming steadily better and better as a woodsman without yet having time to realise it; he jumped a doe and a fawn, walked them out of the bed, close enough to see them—the crash of undergrowth, the white scut, the fawn scudding along behind her, faster than he had known it could have run. He was hunting right, upwind, as Sam had taught him, but that didn't matter now. He had left the gun; by his own will and relinquishment he had accepted not a gambit, not a choice, but a condition in which not only the bear's heretofore inviolable anonymity but all the ancient rules and balances of hunter and hunted had been abrogated. He would not even be afraid, not even in the moment when the fear would take him completely: blood, skin, bowels, bones, memory from the long time before it even became his memory—all save that thin clear quenchless lucidity which alone differed him from this bear and from all the other bears and bucks he would follow during almost seventy years, to which Sam had said: "Be scared. You cant help that. But dont be afraid. Aint nothing in the woods going to hurt you if you dont corner it or it dont smell that you are afraid. A bear or a deer has got to be scared of a coward the same as a brave man has got to be."

By noon he was far beyond the crossing on the little bayou, farther into the new and alien country than he had ever been, travelling now not only by the compass but by the old, heavy, biscuit-thick silver watch which had been his father's. He had left the camp nine hours ago; nine hours from now, dark would already have been an hour old. He stopped, for the first time since he had risen from the log when he could see the compass face at last, and looked about, mopping his sweating face on his sleeve. He had already relinquished, of his will, because of his need, in humility and peace and without regret, yet apparently that had not been enough, the leaving of the gun was not enough. He stood for a moment—a child, alien and lost in the green and soaring gloom of the markless wilderness. Then he relinquished completely to it. It was the watch and the compass. He was still tainted. He removed the linked chain of the one and the looped thong of the other from his overalls and hung them on a bush and leaned the stick beside them and entered it.

When he realised he was lost, he did as Sam had coached and drilled him: made a cast to cross his backtrack. He had not been going very fast for the last two or three hours, and he had gone even less fast since he left the compass and watch on the bush. So he went slower still now, since the tree could not be very far; in fact, he found it before he really expected to and turned and went to it. But there was no bush beneath it, no compass nor watch, so he did next as Sam had coached and drilled him: made this next circle

in the opposite direction and much larger, so that the pattern of the two of them would bisect his track somewhere, but crossing no trace nor mark anywhere of his feet or any feet, and now he was going faster though still not panicked, his heart beating a little more rapidly but strong and steady enough, and this time it was not even the tree because there was a down log beside it which he had never seen before and beyond the log a little swamp, a seepage of moisture somewhere between earth and water, and he did what Sam had coached and drilled him as the next and the last, seeing as he sat down on the log the crooked print, the warped indentation in the wet ground which while he looked at it continued to fill with water until it was level full and the water began to overflow and the sides of the print began to dissolve away. Even as he looked up he saw the next one, and, moving, the one beyond it; moving, not hurrying, running, but merely keeping pace with them as they appeared before him as though they were being shaped out of thin air just one constant pace short of where he would lose them forever and be lost forever himself, tireless, eager, without doubt or dread, panting a little above the strong rapid little hammer of his heart, emerging suddenly into a little glade and the wilderness coalesced. It rushed, soundless, and solidified—the tree, the bush, the compass and the watch glinting where a ray of sunlight touched them. Then he saw the bear. It did not emerge, appear: it was just there, immobile, fixed in the green and windless noon's hot dappling, not as big as he had dreamed it but as big as he had expected, bigger, dimensionless against the dappled obscurity, looking at him. Then it moved. It crossed the glade without haste, walking for an instant into the sun's full glare and out of it, and stopped again and looked back at him across one shoulder. Then it was gone. It didn't walk into the woods. It faded, sank back into the wilderness without motion as he had watched a fish, a huge old bass, sink back into the dark depths of its pool and vanish without even any movement of its fins.

2

SO HE should have hated and feared Lion. He was thirteen then. He had killed his buck and Sam Fathers had marked his face with the hot blood, and in the next November he killed a bear. But before that accolade he had become as competent in the woods as many grown men with the same experience. By now he was a better woodsman than most grown men with more. There was no territory within twenty-five miles of the camp that he did not know—bayou, ridge, landmark trees and path; he could have led anyone direct to any spot in it and brought him back. He knew game trails that even Sam Fathers had never seen; in the third fall he found a buck's bedding-place by himself and unbeknown to his cousin he borrowed Walter Ewell's rifle and lay in wait for the buck at dawn and killed it when it walked back to the bed as Sam had told him how the old Chickasaw fathers did.

By now he knew the old bear's footprint better than he did his own, and not only the crooked one. He could see any one of the three sound prints and distinguish it at once from any other, and not only because of its size. There were other bears within that fifty miles which left tracks almost as large, or at least so near that the one would have appeared larger only by juxtaposition. It was more than that. If Sam Fathers had been his mentor and the backyard rabbits and squirrels his kindergarten, then the wilderness the old bear ran was his college and the old male bear itself, so long unwifed and childless as to have become its own ungendered progenitor, was his alma mater.

He could find the crooked print now whenever he wished, ten miles or five miles or sometimes closer than that, to the camp. Twice while on stand during the next three years he heard the dogs strike its trail and once even jump it by chance, the voices high, abject, almost human in their hysteria. Once, still-hunting with Walter Ewell's rifle, he saw it cross a long corridor of down timber where a tornado had passed. It rushed through rather than across the tangle of trunks and branches as a locomotive would, faster than he had ever believed it could have moved, almost as fast as a deer even because the deer would have spent most of that distance in the air; he realised then why it would take a dog not only of abnormal courage but size and speed too ever to bring it to bay. He had a little dog at home, a mongrel, of the sort called fyce by negroes, a ratter, itself not much bigger than a rat and possessing that sort of courage which had long since stopped being bravery and had become foolhardiness. He brought it with him one June and, timing them as if they were meeting an appointment with another human being, himself carrying the fyce with a sack over its head and Sam Fathers with a brace of the hounds on a rope leash, they lay downwind of the trail and actually ambushed the bear. They were so close that it turned at bay although he realised later this might have been from surprise and amazement at the shrill and frantic uproar of the fyce. It turned at bay against the trunk of a big cypress, on its hind feet; it seemed to the boy that

it would never stop rising, taller and taller, and even the two hounds seemed to have taken a kind of desperate and despairing courage from the fyce. Then he realised that the fyce was actually not going to stop. He flung the gun down and ran. When he overtook and grasped the shrill, frantically pinwheeling little dog, it seemed to him that he was directly under the bear. He could smell it, strong and hot and rank. Sprawling, he looked up where it loomed and towered over him like a thunderclap. It was quite familiar, until he remembered: this was the way he had used to dream about it.

Then it was gone. He didn't see it go. He knelt, holding the frantic fyce with both hands, hearing the abased wailing of the two hounds drawing further and further away, until Sam came up, carrying the gun. He laid it quietly down beside the boy and stood looking down at him. "You've done seed him twice now, with a gun in your hands," he said. "This time you couldn't have missed him."

The boy rose. He still held the fyce. Even in his arms it continued to yap frantically, surging and straining toward the fading sound of the hounds like a collection of live-wire springs. The boy was panting a little. "Neither could you," he said. "You had the gun. Why didn't you shoot him?"

Sam didn't seem to have heard. He put out his hand and touched the little dog in the boy's arms which still yapped and strained even though the two hounds were out of hearing now. "He's done gone," Sam said. "You can slack off and rest now, until next time." He stroked the little dog until it began to grow quiet under his hand. "You's almost the one we wants," he said. "You just aint big enough. We aint got that one yet. He will need to be just a little bigger than smart, and a little braver than either." He withdrew his hand from the fyce's head and stood looking into the woods where the bear and the hounds had vanished. "Somebody is going to, some day."

"I know it," the boy said. "That's why it must be one of us. So it wont be until the last day. When even he dont want it to last any longer."

So he should have hated and feared Lion. It was in the fourth summer, the fourth time he had made one in the celebration of Major de Spain's and General Compson's birthday. In the early spring Major de Spain's mare had foaled a horse colt. One evening when Sam brought the horses and mules up to stable them for the night, the colt was missing and it was all he could do to get the frantic mare into the lot. He had thought at first to let the mare lead him back to where she had become separated from the foal. But she would not do it. She would not even feint toward any particular part of the woods or even in any particular direction. She merely ran, as if she couldn't see, still frantic with terror. She whirled and ran at Sam once, as if to attack him in some ultimate desperation, as if she could not for the moment realise that he was a man and a long-familiar one. He got her into the lot at last. It was too dark by that time to back-track her, to unravel the erratic course she had doubtless pursued.

He came to the house and told Major de Spain. It was an animal, of course, a big one, and the colt was dead now, wherever it was. They all knew that. "It's a panther," General Compson said at once. "The same one. That doe and fawn last March." Sam had sent Major de Spain word of it when Boon Hogganbeck came to the camp on a routine visit to see how the stock had wintered —the doe's throat torn out, and the beast had run down the helpless fawn and killed it too.

"Sam never did say that was a panther," Major de Spain said. Sam said nothing now, standing behind Major de Spain where they sat at supper, inscrutable, as if he were just waiting for them to stop talking so he could go home. He didn't even seem to be looking at anything. "A panther might jump a doe, and he wouldn't have much trouble catching the fawn afterward. But no panther would have jumped that colt with the dam right there with it. It was Old Ben," Major de Spain said. "I'm disappointed in him. He has broken the rules. I didn't think he would have done that. He has killed mine and McCaslin's dogs, but that was all right. We gambled the dogs against him; we gave each other warning. But now he has come into my house and destroyed my property, out of season too. He broke the rules. It was Old Ben, Sam." Still Sam said nothing, standing there until Major de Spain should stop talking. "We'll back-track her tomorrow and see," Major de Spain said.

Sam departed. He would not live in the camp; he had built himself a little hut something like Joe Baker's, only stouter, tighter, on the bayou a quarter-mile away, and a stout log crib where he stored a little corn for the shoat he raised each year. The next morning he was waiting when they waked. He had already found the colt. They did not even wait for breakfast. It was not far, not five hundred yards from the stable—the three-months' colt lying on its side, its throat torn out and the entrails and one ham partly eaten. It lay not as if it had been dropped but as if it had been struck and hurled, and no cat-mark, no claw-mark where a panther would have gripped it while finding its throat. They read the tracks where the frantic mare had circled and at last rushed in with that same ultimate desperation with which she had whirled on Sam Fathers yesterday evening, and the long tracks of dead and terrified running and those of the beast which had not even rushed at her when she advanced but had merely walked three or four paces toward her until she broke, and General Compson said, "Good God, what a wolf!"

Still Sam said nothing. The boy watched him while the men knelt, measuring the tracks. There was something in Sam's face now. It was neither exultation nor joy nor hope. Later, a man, the boy realised what it had been, and that Sam had known all the time what had made the tracks and what had torn the throat out of the doe in the spring and killed the fawn. It had been foreknowledge in Sam's face that morning. *And he was glad,* he told himself. *He was old. He had no children, no people, none of his blood anywhere above earth that he would ever meet again. And even if he were to, he could not have touched it, spoken to it, because for seventy years now he had had to be a negro. It was almost over now and he was glad.*

They returned to camp and had breakfast and came back with guns and the hounds. Afterward the boy realised that they also should have known then what killed the colt as well as Sam Fathers did. But that was neither the first nor the last time he had seen men rationalise from and even act upon their misconceptions. After Boon, standing astride the colt, had whipped the dogs away from it with his belt, they snuffed at the tracks. One of them, a young dog hound without judgment yet, bayed once, and they ran for a few feet on what seemed to be a trail. Then they stopped, looking back at the men, eager enough, not baffled, merely questioning, as if they were asking "Now what?" Then they rushed back to the colt, where Boon, still astride it, slashed at them with the belt.

"I never knew a trail to get cold that quick," General Compson said.

"Maybe a single wolf big enough to kill a colt with the dam right there beside it dont leave scent," Major de Spain said.

"Maybe it was a hant," Walter Ewell said. He looked at Tennie's Jim. "Hah, Jim?"

Because the hounds would not run it, Major de Spain had Sam hunt out and find the tracks a hundred yards farther on and they put the dogs on it again and again the young one bayed and not one of them realised then that the hound was not baying like a dog striking game but was merely bellowing like a country dog whose yard has been invaded. General Compson spoke to the boy and Boon and Tennie's Jim: to the squirrel hunters. "You boys keep the dogs with you this morning. He's probably hanging around somewhere, waiting to get his breakfast off the colt. You might strike him."

But they did not. The boy remembered how Sam stood watching them as they went into the woods with the leashed hounds—the Indian face in which he had never seen anything until it smiled, except that faint arching of the nostrils on that first morning when the hounds had found Old Ben. They took the hounds with them on the next day, though when they reached the place where they hoped to strike a fresh trail, the carcass of the colt was gone. Then on the third morning Sam was waiting again, this time until they had finished breakfast. He said, "Come." He led them to his house, his little hut, to the corn-crib beyond it. He had removed the corn and had made a dead-fall of the door, baiting it with the colt's carcass; peering between the logs, they saw an animal almost the color of a gun or pistol barrel, what little time they had to examine its color or shape. It was not crouched nor even standing. It was in motion, in the air, coming toward them—a heavy body crashing with tremendous force against the door so that the thick door jumped and clattered in its frame, the animal, whatever it was, hurling itself against the door again seemingly before it could have touched the floor and got a new purchase to spring from. "Come away," Sam said, "fore he break his neck." Even when they retreated the heavy and measured crashes continued, the stout door jumping and clattering each time, and still no sound from the beast itself—no snarl, no cry.

"What in hell's name is it?" Major de Spain said.

"It's a dog," Sam said, his nostrils arching and collapsing faintly and steadily and that faint, fierce milkiness in his eyes again as on that first morning when the hounds had struck the old bear. "It's the dog."

"*The* dog?" Major de Spain said.

"That's gonter hold Old Ben."

"Dog the devil," Major de Spain said. "I'd rather have Old Ben himself in my pack than that brute. Shoot him."

"No," Sam said.

"You'll never tame him. How do you ever expect to make an animal like that afraid of you?"

"I dont want him tame," Sam said; again the boy watched his nostrils and the fierce milky light in his eyes. "But I almost rather he be tame than scared, of me or any man or any thing. But he wont be neither, of nothing."

"Then what are you going to do with it?"

"You can watch," Sam said.

Each morning through the second week they would go to Sam's crib. He had removed a few shingles from the roof and had put a rope on the colt's carcass and had drawn it out when the trap fell. Each morning they would watch him lower a pail of water into the crib while the dog hurled itself tirelessly against the door and dropped back and leaped again. It never made any sound and there was nothing frenzied in the act but only a cold and grim indomitable determination. Toward the end of the week it stopped jumping at the door. Yet it had not weakened appreciably and it was not as if it had rationalised the fact that the door was not going to give. It was as if for that time it simply disdained to jump any longer. It was not down. None of them had ever seen it down. It stood, and they could see it now— part mastiff, something of Airedale and something of a dozen other strains probably, better than thirty inches at the shoulders and weighing as they guessed almost ninety pounds, with cold yellow eyes and a tremendous chest and over all that strange color like a blued gun-barrel.

Then the two weeks were up. They prepared to break camp. The boy begged to remain and his cousin let him. He moved into the little hut with Sam Fathers. Each morning he watched Sam lower the pail of water into the crib. By the end of that week the dog was down. It would rise and half stagger, half crawl to the water and drink and collapse again. One morning it could not even reach the water, could not raise its forequarters even from the floor. Sam took a short stick and prepared to enter the crib. "Wait," the boy said. "Let me get the gun———"

"No," Sam said. "He cant move now." Nor could it. It lay on its side while Sam touched it, its head and the gaunted body, the dog lying motionless, the yellow eyes open. They were not fierce and there was nothing of petty malevolence in them, but a cold and almost impersonal malignance like some natural force. It was not even looking at Sam nor at the boy peering at it between the logs.

Sam began to feed it again. The first time he had to raise its head so it could lap the broth. That night he left a bowl of broth containing lumps of meat where the dog could reach it. The next morning the bowl was empty and the dog was lying on its belly, its head up, the cold yellow eyes watching the door as Sam entered, no change whatever in the cold yellow eyes and still no sound from it even when it sprang, its aim and coordination still bad from weakness so that Sam had time to strike it down with the stick and leap from the crib and slam the door as the dog, still without having had time to get its feet under it to jump again seemingly, hurled itself against the door as if the two weeks of starving had never been.

At noon that day someone came whooping through the woods from the direction of the camp. It was Boon. He came and looked for a while between the logs, at the tremendous dog lying again on its belly, its head up, the yellow eyes blinking sleepily at nothing: the indomitable and unbroken spirit. "What we better do," Boon said, "is to let that son of a bitch go and catch Old Ben and run him on the dog." He turned to the boy his weather-reddened and beetling face. "Get your traps together. Cass says for you to come on home. You been in here fooling with that horse-eating varmint long enough."

Boon had a borrowed mule at the camp; the buggy was waiting at the edge of the bottom. He was at home that night. He told McCaslin about it. "Sam's going to starve him again until he can go in and touch him. Then he will feed him again. Then he will starve him again, if he has to."

"But why?" McCaslin said. "What for? Even Sam will never tame that brute."

"We dont want him tame. We want him like he is. We just want him to find out at last that the only way he can get out of that crib and stay out of it is to do what Sam or somebody tells him to do. He's the dog that's going to stop Old Ben and hold him. We've already named him. His name is Lion."

Then November came at last. They returned to the camp. With General Compson and Major de Spain and his cousin and Walter and Boon he stood in the yard among the guns and bedding and boxes of food and watched Sam Fathers and Lion come up the lane from the lot—the Indian, the old man in battered overalls and rubber boots and a worn sheepskin coat and a hat which had belonged to the boy's father; the tremendous dog pacing gravely beside him. The hounds rushed out to meet them and stopped, except the young one which still had but little of judgment. It ran up to Lion, fawning. Lion didn't snap at it. He didn't even pause. He struck it rolling and yelping for five or six feet with a blow of one paw as a bear would have done and came on into the yard and stood, blinking sleepily at nothing, looking at no one, while Boon said, "Jesus. Jesus.—Will he let me touch him?"

"You can touch him," Sam said. "He dont care. He dont care about nothing or nobody."

The boy watched that too. He watched it for the next two years from that moment when Boon touched Lion's head and then knelt beside him, feeling the bones and muscles, the power. It was as if Lion were a woman—or perhaps Boon was the woman. That was more like it—the big, grave, sleepy-seeming dog which, as Sam Fathers said, cared about no man and no thing; and the violent, insensitive, hard-faced man with his touch of remote Indian blood and the mind almost of a child. He watched Boon take over Lion's feeding from Sam and Uncle Ash both. He would see Boon squatting in the cold rain beside the kitchen while Lion ate. Because Lion neither slept nor ate with the other dogs though none of them knew where he did sleep until in the second November, thinking until then that Lion slept in his kennel beside Sam Fathers' hut, when the boy's cousin McCaslin said something about it to Sam by sheer chance and Sam told him. And that night the boy and Major de Spain and McCaslin with a lamp entered the back room where Boon slept— the little, tight, airless room rank with the smell of Boon's unwashed body and his wet hunting-clothes—where Boon, snoring on his back, choked and waked and Lion raised his head beside him and looked back at them from his cold, slumbrous yellow eyes.

"Damn it, Boon," McCaslin said. "Get that dog out of here. He's got to run Old Ben tomorrow morning. How in hell do you expect him to smell anything fainter than a skunk after breathing you all night?"

"The way I smell aint hurt my nose none that I ever noticed," Boon said.

"It wouldn't matter if it had," Major de Spain said. "We're not depending on you to trail a bear. Put him outside. Put him under the house with the other dogs."

Boon began to get up. "He'll kill the first one that happens to yawn or sneeze in his face or touches him."

"I reckon not," Major de Spain said. "None of them are going to risk yawning in his face or touching him either, even asleep. Put him outside. I want his nose right tomorrow. Old Ben fooled him last year. I dont think he will do it again."

Boon put on his shoes without lacing them; in his long soiled underwear, his hair still tousled from sleep, he and Lion went out. The others returned to the front room and the poker game where McCaslin's and Major de Spain's hands waited for them on the table. After a while McCaslin said, "Do you want me to go back and look again?"

"No," Major de Spain said. "I call," he said to Walter Ewell. He spoke to McCaslin again. "If you do, dont tell me. I am beginning to see the first sign of my increasing age: I dont like to know that my orders have been disobeyed, even when I knew when I gave them that they would be.—A small pair," he said to Walter Ewell.

"How small?" Walter said.

"Very small," Major de Spain said.

And the boy, lying beneath his piled quilts and blankets waiting for sleep, knew likewise that Lion was already back in Boon's bed, for the rest of that night and the next one and during all the nights of the next November and the next one. He thought then: *I wonder what Sam thinks. He could have Lion with him, even if Boon is a white man. He could ask Major or McCaslin either. And more than that. It was Sam's hand that touched Lion first and Lion knows it.* Then he became a man and he knew that too. It had been all right. That was the way it should have been. Sam was the chief, the prince; Boon, the plebeian, was his huntsman. Boon should have nursed the dogs.

On the first morning that Lion led the pack after Old Ben, seven strangers appeared in the camp. They were swampers: gaunt, malaria-ridden men appearing from nowhere, who ran trap-lines for coons or perhaps farmed little patches of cotton and corn along the edge of the bottom, in clothes but little better than Sam Fathers' and nowhere near as good as Tennie's Jim's, with worn shotguns and rifles, already squatting patiently in the cold drizzle in the side yard when day broke. They had a spokesman; afterward Sam Fathers told Major de Spain how all during the past summer and fall they had drifted into the camp singly or in pairs and threes, to look quietly at Lion for a while and then go away: "Mawnin, Major. We heerd you was aimin to put that ere blue dawg on that old two-toed bear this mawnin. We figgered we'd come up and watch, if you dont mind. We wont do no shooting, lessen he runs over us."

"You are welcome," Major de Spain said. "You are welcome to shoot. He's more your bear than ours."

"I reckon that aint no lie. I done fed him enough cawn to have a sheer in him. Not to mention a shoat three years ago."

"I reckon I got a sheer too," another said. "Only it aint in the bear." Major de Spain looked at him. He was chewing tobacco. He spat. "Hit was a heifer calf. Nice un too. Last year. When I finally found her, I reckon she looked about like that colt of yourn looked last June."

"Oh," Major de Spain said. "Be welcome. If you see game in front of my dogs, shoot it."

Nobody shot Old Ben that day. No man saw him. The dogs jumped him within a hundred yards of the glade where the boy had seen him that day in the summer of his eleventh year. The boy was less than a quarter-mile away. He heard the jump but he could distinguish no voice among the dogs that he did not know and therefore would be Lion's, and he thought, believed, that Lion was not among them. Even the fact that they were going much faster than he had ever heard them run behind Old Ben before and that the high thin note of hysteria was missing now from their voices was not enough to disabuse him. He didn't comprehend until that night, when Sam told him that Lion would never cry on a trail. "He gonter growl when he catches Old Ben's throat," Sam said. "But he aint gonter never holler, no more than he ever done when he was jumping at that two-inch door. It's that blue dog in him. What you call it?"

"Airedale," the boy said.

Lion was there; the jump was just too close to the river. When Boon returned with Lion about eleven that night, he swore that Lion had stopped Old Ben once but that the hounds would not go in and Old Ben broke away and took to the river and swam for miles down it and he and Lion went down one bank for about ten miles and crossed and came up the other but it had begun to get dark before they struck any trail where Old Ben had come up out of the water, unless he was still in the water when he passed the ford where they crossed. Then he fell to cursing the hounds and ate the supper Uncle Ash had saved for him and went off to bed and after a while the boy opened the door of the little stale room thunderous with snoring and the great grave dog raised its head from Boon's pillow and blinked at him for a moment and lowered its head again.

When the next November came and the last day, the day on which it was now becoming traditional to save for Old Ben, there were more than a dozen strangers waiting. They were not all swampers this time. Some of them were townsmen, from other county seats like Jefferson, who had heard about Lion and Old Ben and had come to watch the great blue dog keep his yearly rendezvous with the old two-toed bear. Some of them didn't even have guns and the hunting-clothes and boots they wore had been on a store shelf yesterday.

This time Lion jumped Old Ben more than five miles from the river and bayed and held him and this time the hounds went in, in a sort of desperate emulation. The boy heard them; he was that near. He heard Boon whooping; he heard the two shots when General Compson delivered both barrels, one containing five buckshot, the other a single ball, into the bear from as close as he could force his almost unmanageable horse. He heard the dogs when the bear broke free again. He was running now; panting, stumbling, his lungs bursting, he reached the place where General Compson had fired and where Old Ben had killed two of the hounds. He saw the blood from General Compson's shots, but he could go no further. He stopped, leaning against a tree for his breathing to ease and his heart to slow, hearing the sound of the dogs as it faded on and died away.

In camp that night—they had as guests five of the still terrified strangers in new hunting coats and boots who had been lost all day until Sam Fathers went out and got them—he heard the rest of it: how Lion had stopped and held the bear again but only the one-eyed mule which did not mind the smell of wild blood would approach and Boon was riding the mule and Boon had never been known to hit anything. He shot at the bear five times with his pump gun, touching nothing, and Old Ben killed another hound and broke free once more and reached the river and was gone. Again Boon and Lion hunted as far down one bank as they dared. Too far; they crossed in the first of dusk and dark overtook them within a mile. And this time Lion found the broken trail, the blood perhaps, in the darkness where Old Ben had come up out of the water, but Boon had him on a rope, luckily, and he got down from the mule and fought Lion hand-to-hand until he got him back to camp. This time Boon didn't even curse. He stood in the door, muddy, spent, his huge gargoyle's face tragic and still amazed. "I missed him," he said. "I was in twenty-five feet of him and I missed him five times."

"But we have drawn blood," Major de Spain said. "General Compson drew blood. We have never done that before."

"But I missed him," Boon said. "I missed him five times. With Lion looking right at me."

"Never mind," Major de Spain said. "It was a damned fine race. And we drew blood. Next year we'll let General Compson or Walter ride Katie, and we'll get him."

Then McCaslin said, "Where is Lion, Boon?"

"I left him at Sam's," Boon said. He was already turning away. "I aint fit to sleep with him."

So he should have hated and feared Lion. Yet he did not. It seemed to him that there was a fatality in it. It seemed to him that something, he didn't know what, was beginning; had already begun. It was like the last act on a set stage. It was the beginning of the end of something, he didn't know what except that he would not grieve. He would be humble and proud that he had been found worthy to be a part of it too or even just to see it too.

3

IT WAS December. It was the coldest December he had ever remembered. They had been in camp four days over two weeks, waiting for the weather to soften so that Lion and Old Ben could run their yearly race. Then they would break camp and go home. Because of these unforeseen additional days which they had had to pass waiting on the weather, with nothing to do but play poker, the whisky had given out and he and Boon were being sent to Memphis with a suitcase and a note from Major de Spain to Mr Semmes, the distiller, to get more. That is, Major de Spain and McCaslin were sending Boon to get the whisky and sending him to see that Boon got back with it or most of it or at least some of it.

Tennie's Jim waked him at three. He dressed rapidly, shivering, not so much from the cold because a fresh fire already boomed and roared on the hearth, but in that dead winter hour when the blood and the heart are slow and sleep is incomplete. He crossed the gap between house and kitchen, the gap of iron earth beneath the brilliant and rigid night where dawn would not begin for three hours yet, tasting, tongue palate and to the very bottom of his lungs the searing dark, and entered the kitchen, the lamplit warmth where the stove glowed, fogging the windows, and where Boon already sat at the table at breakfast, hunched over his plate, almost in his plate, his working jaws blue with stubble and his face innocent of water and his coarse, horse-mane hair innocent of comb—the quarter Indian, grandson of a Chickasaw squaw, who on occasion resented with his hard and furious fists the intimation of one single drop of alien blood and on others, usually after whisky, affirmed with the same fists and the same fury that his father had been the full-blood Chickasaw and even a chief and that even his mother had been only half white. He was four inches over six feet; he had the mind of a child, the heart of a horse, and little hard shoe-button eyes without depth or meanness or generosity or viciousness or gentleness or anything else, in the ugliest face the boy had ever seen. It looked like somebody had found a walnut a little larger than a football and with a machinist's hammer had shaped features into it and then painted it, mostly red; not Indian red but a fine bright ruddy color which whisky might have had something to do with but which was mostly just happy and violent out-of-doors, the wrinkles in it not the residue of the forty years it had survived but from squinting into the sun or into the gloom of cane-brakes where game had run, baked into it by the camp fires before which he had lain trying to sleep on the cold November or December ground while waiting for daylight so he could rise and hunt again, as though time were merely something he walked through as he did through air, aging him no more than air did. He was brave, faithful, improvident and unreliable; he had neither profession job nor trade and owned one vice and one virtue: whisky, and that absolute and unquestioning fidelity to Major de Spain and the boy's cousin McCaslin. "Sometimes I'd call them both virtues," Major de Spain said once. "Or both vices," McCaslin said.

He ate his breakfast, hearing the dogs under the kitchen, wakened by the smell of frying meat or perhaps by the feet overhead. He heard Lion once, short and peremptory, as the best hunter in any camp has only to speak once to all save the fools, and none other of Major de Spain's and McCaslin's dogs were Lion's equal in size and strength and perhaps even in courage, but they were not fools; Old Ben had killed the last fool among them last year.

Tennie's Jim came in as they finished. The wagon was outside. Ash decided he would drive them over to the log-line where they would flag the outbound log-train and let Tennie's Jim wash the dishes. The boy knew why. It would not be the first time he had listened to old Ash badgering Boon.

It was cold. The wagon wheels banged and clattered on the frozen ground; the sky was fixed and brilliant. He was not shivering, he was shaking, slow and steady and hard, the food he had just eaten still warm and solid inside him while his outside shook slow and steady around it as though his stomach floated loose. "They wont run this morning," he said. "No dog will have any nose today."

"Cep Lion," Ash said. "Lion dont need no nose. All he need is a bear." He had wrapped his feet in towsacks and he had a quilt from his pallet bed on the kitchen floor drawn over his head and wrapped around him until in the thin brilliant starlight he looked like nothing at all that the boy had ever seen before. "He run a bear through a thousand-acre ice-house. Catch him too. Them other dogs dont matter because they aint going to keep up with Lion nohow, long as he got a bear in front of him."

"What's wrong with the other dogs?" Boon said. "What the hell do you know about it anyway? This is the first time you've had your tail out of that kitchen since we got here except to chop a little wood."

"Aint nothing wrong with them," Ash said. "And long as it's left up to them, aint nothing going to be. I just wish I had knowed all my life how to take care of my health good as them hounds knows."

"Well, they aint going to run this morning," Boon said. His voice was harsh and positive. "Major promised they wouldn't until me and Ike get back."

"Weather gonter break today. Gonter soft up. Rain by night." Then Ash laughed, chuckled, somewhere inside the quilt which concealed even his face. "Hum up here, mules!" he said, jerking the reins so that the mules leaped forward and snatched the lurching and banging wagon for several feet before they slowed again into their quick, short-paced, rapid plodding. "Sides, I like to know why Major need to wait on you. It's Lion he aiming to use. I aint never heard tell of you bringing no bear nor no other kind of meat into this camp."

Now Boon's going to curse Ash or maybe even hit him, the boy thought. But Boon never did, never had; the boy knew he never would even though four years ago Boon had shot five times with a borrowed pistol at a negro on the street in Jefferson, with the same result as when he had shot five times at Old Ben last fall. "By God," Boon said, "he aint going to put Lion or no other dog on nothing until I get back tonight. Because he promised me. Whip up them mules and keep them whipped up. Do you want me to freeze to death?"

They reached the log-line and built a fire. After a while the log-train came up out of the woods under the paling east and Boon flagged it. Then in the warm caboose the boy slept again while Boon and the conductor and brakeman talked about Lion and Old Ben as people later would talk about Sullivan and Kilrain and, later still, about Dempsey and Tunney. Dozing, swaying as the springless caboose lurched and clattered, he would hear them still talking, about the shoats and calves Old Ben had killed and the cribs he had rifled and the traps and deadfalls he had wrecked and the lead he probably carried under his hide—Old Ben, the two-toed bear in a land where bears with trap-ruined feet had been called Two-Toe or Three-Toe or Cripple-Foot for fifty years, only Old Ben was an extra bear (the head bear, General Compson called him) and so had earned a name such as a human man could have worn and not been sorry.

They reached Hoke's at sunup. They emerged from the warm caboose in their hunting clothes, the muddy boots and stained khaki and Boon's blue unshaven jowls. But that was all right. Hoke's was a sawmill and commissary and two stores and a loading-chute on a sidetrack from the main line, and all the men in it wore boots and khaki too. Presently the Memphis train came. Boon bought three packages of popcorn-and-molasses and a bottle of beer from the news butch and the boy went to sleep again to the sound of his chewing.

But in Memphis it was not all right. It was as if the high buildings and the hard pavements, the fine carriages and the horse cars and the men in starched collars and neckties made their boots and khaki look a little rougher and a little muddier and made Boon's beard look worse and more unshaven and his face look more and more like he should never have brought it out of the woods at all or at least out of reach of Major de Spain or McCaslin or someone who knew it and could have said, "Dont be afraid. He wont hurt you." He walked through the station, on the slick floor, his face moving as he worked the popcorn out of his teeth with his tongue, his legs spraddled and stiff in the hips as if he were walking on buttered glass, and that blue stubble on his face like the filings from a new gun-barrel. They passed the first saloon. Even through the closed doors the boy could seem to smell the sawdust and the reek of old drink. Boon began to cough. He coughed for something less than a minute. "Damn this cold," he said. "I'd sure like to know where I got it."

"Back there in the station," the boy said.

Boon had started to cough again. He stopped. He looked at the boy. "What?" he said.

"You never had it when we left camp nor on the train either." Boon looked at him, blinking. Then he stopped blinking. He didn't cough again. He said quietly:

"Lend me a dollar. Come on. You've got it. If you ever had one, you've still got it. I dont mean you are tight with your money because you aint. You just dont never seem to ever think of nothing you want. When I was sixteen a dollar bill melted off of me before I even had time to read the name of the bank that issued it." He said quietly: "Let me have a dollar, Ike."

"You promised Major. You promised McCaslin. Not till we get back to camp."

"All right," Boon said in that quiet and patient voice. "What can I do on just one dollar? You aint going to lend me another."

"You're damn right I aint," the boy said, his voice quiet too, cold with rage which was not at Boon, remembering: Boon snoring in a hard chair in the kitchen so he could watch the clock and wake him and McCaslin and drive them the seventeen miles in to Jefferson to catch the train to Memphis; the wild, never-bridled Texas paint pony which he had persuaded McCaslin to let him buy and which he and Boon had bought at auction for four dollars and seventy-five cents and fetched home wired between two gentle old mares with pieces of barbed wire and which had never even seen shelled corn before and didn't even know what it was unless the grains were bugs maybe and at last (he was ten and Boon had been ten all his life) Boon said the pony was gentled and with a towsack over its head and four negroes to hold it they backed it into an old two-wheeled cart and hooked up the gear and he and Boon got up and Boon said, "All right, boys. Let him go" and one of the negroes—it was Tennie's Jim—snatched the towsack off and leaped for his life and they lost the first wheel against a post of the open gate only at that moment Boon caught him by the scruff of the neck and flung him into the roadside ditch so he only saw the rest of it in fragments: the other wheel as it slammed through the side gate and crossed the back yard and leaped up onto the gallery and scraps of the cart here and there along the road and Boon vanishing rapidly on his stomach in the leaping and spurting dust and still holding the reins until they broke too and two days later they finally caught the pony seven miles away still wearing the hames and the headstall of the bridle around its neck like a duchess with two necklaces at one time. He gave Boon the dollar.

"All right," Boon said. "Come on in out of the cold."

"I aint cold," he said.

"You can have some lemonade."

"I dont want any lemonade."

The door closed behind him. The sun was well up now. It was a brilliant day, though Ash had said it would rain before night. Already it was warmer; they could run tomorrow. He felt the old lift of the heart, as pristine as ever, as on the first day; he would never lose it, no matter how old in hunting and pursuit: the best, the best of all breathing, the humility and the pride. He must stop thinking about it. Already it seemed to him that he was running, back to the station, to the tracks themselves: the first train going south; he must stop thinking about it. The street was busy. He watched the big Norman draft horses, the Percherons; the trim carriages from which the men in the fine overcoats and the ladies rosy in furs descended and entered the station. (They were still next door to it but one.) Twenty years ago his father had ridden into Memphis as a member of Colonel Sartoris' horse in Forrest's command, up Main street and (the tale told) into the lobby of the Gayoso Hotel where the Yankee officers sat in the leather chairs spitting into the tall bright cuspidors and then out again, scot-free——

The door opened behind him. Boon was wiping his mouth on the back of his hand. "All right," he said. "Let's go tend to it and get the hell out of here."

They went and had the suitcase packed. He never knew where or when Boon got the other bottle. Doubtless Mr Semmes gave it to him. When they reached Hoke's again at sundown, it was empty. They could get a return train to Hoke's in two hours; they went straight back to the station as Major de Spain and then McCaslin had told Boon to do and then ordered him to do and had sent the boy along to see that he did. Boon took the first drink from his bottle in the wash room. A man in a uniform cap came to tell him he couldn't drink there and looked at Boon's face once and said nothing. The next time he was pouring into his water glass beneath the edge of a table in the restaurant when the manager (she was a woman) did tell him he couldn't drink there and he went back to the wash room. He had been telling the negro waiter and all the other people in the restaurant who couldn't help but hear him and who had never heard of Lion and didn't want to, about Lion and Old Ben. Then he happened to think of the zoo. He had found out that there was another train to Hoke's at three oclock and so they would spend the time at the zoo and take the three oclock train until he came back from the wash room for the third time. Then they would take the first train back to camp, get Lion and come back to the zoo where, he said, the bears were fed on ice cream and lady fingers and he would match Lion against them all.

So they missed the first train, the one they were supposed to take, but he got Boon onto the three oclock train and they were all right again, with Boon not even going to the wash room now but drinking in the aisle and talking about Lion and the men he buttonholed no more daring to tell Boon he couldn't drink there than the man in the station had dared.

When they reached Hoke's at sundown, Boon was asleep. The boy waked him at last and got him and the suitcase off the train and he even persuaded him to eat some supper at the sawmill commissary. So he was all right when they got in the caboose of the log-train to go back into the woods, with the sun going down red and the sky already overcast and the ground would not freeze tonight. It was the boy who slept now, sitting behind the ruby stove while the springless caboose jumped and clattered and Boon and the brakeman and the conductor talked about Lion and Old Ben because they knew what Boon was talking about because this was home. "Overcast and already thawing," Boon said. "Lion will get him tomorrow."

It would have to be Lion, or somebody. It would not be Boon. He had never hit anything bigger than a squirrel that anybody ever knew, except the negro woman that day when he was shooting at the negro man. He was a big negro and not ten feet away but Boon shot five times with the pistol he had borrowed from Major de Spain's negro coachman and the negro he was shooting at outed with a dollar-and-a-half mail-order pistol and would have burned Boon down with it only it never went off, it just went snick-snicksnicksnicksnick five times and Boon still blasting away and he broke a plate-glass window that cost McCaslin forty-five dollars and hit a negro woman who happened to be passing in the leg only Major de Spain paid for that; he and McCaslin cut cards, the plate-glass window against the negro woman's leg. And the first day on stand this year, the first morning in camp, the buck ran right over Boon; he heard Boon's old pump gun go whow. whow. whow. whow. whow. and then his voice: "God damn, here he comes! Head him! Head him!" and when he got there the buck's tracks and the five exploded shells were not twenty paces apart.

There were five guests in camp that night, from Jefferson: Mr Bayard Sartoris and his son and General Compson's son and two others. And the next morning he looked out the window, into the gray thin drizzle of daybreak which Ash had predicted, and there they were, standing and squatting beneath the thin rain, almost two dozen of them who had fed Old Ben corn and shoats and even calves for ten years, in their worn hats and hunting coats and overalls which any town negro would have thrown away or burned and only the rubber boots strong and sound, and the worn and blueless guns and some even without guns. While they ate breakfast a dozen more arrived, mounted and on foot: loggers from the camp thirteen miles below and sawmill men from Hoke's and the only gun among them that one which the log-train conductor carried: so that when they went into the woods this morning Major de Spain led a party almost as strong, excepting that some of them were not armed, as some he had led in the last darkening days of '64 and '65. The little yard would not hold them. They overflowed it, into the lane where Major de Spain sat his mare while Ash in his dirty apron thrust the greasy cartridges into his carbine and passed it up to him and the great grave blue dog stood at his stirrup not as a dog stands but as a horse stands, blinking his sleepy topaz eyes at nothing, deaf even to the yelling of the hounds which Boon and Tennie's Jim held on leash.

"We'll put General Compson on Katie this

morning," Major de Spain said. "He drew blood last year; if he'd had a mule then that would have stood, he would have——"

"No," General Compson said. "I'm too old to go helling through the woods on a mule or a horse or anything else any more. Besides, I had my chance last year and missed it. I'm going on a stand this morning. I'm going to let that boy ride Katie."

"No, wait," McCaslin said. "Ike's got the rest of his life to hunt bears in. Let somebody else——"

"No," General Compson said. "I want Ike to ride Katie. He's already a better woodsman than you or me either and in another ten years he'll be as good as Walter."

At first he couldn't believe it, not until Major de Spain spoke to him. Then he was up, on the one-eyed mule which would not spook at wild blood, looking down at the dog motionless at Major de Spain's stirrup, looking in the gray streaming light bigger than a calf, bigger than he knew it actually was—the big head, the chest almost as big as his own, the blue hide beneath which the muscles flinched or quivered to no touch since the heart which drove blood to them loved no man and no thing, standing as a horse stands yet different from a horse which infers only weight and speed while Lion inferred not only courage and all else that went to make up the will and desire to pursue and kill, but endurance, the will and desire to endure beyond all imaginable limits of flesh in order to overtake and slay. Then the dog looked at him. It moved its head and looked at him across the trivial uproar of the hounds, out of the yellow eyes as depthless as Boon's, as free as Boon's of meanness or generosity or gentleness or viciousness. They were just cold and sleepy. Then it blinked, and he knew it was not looking at him and never had been, without even bothering to turn its head away.

That morning he heard the first cry. Lion had already vanished while Sam and Tennie's Jim were putting saddles on the mule and horse which had drawn the wagon and he watched the hounds as they crossed and cast, snuffing and whimpering, until they too disappeared. Then he and Major de Spain and Sam and Tennie's Jim rode after them and heard the first cry out of the wet and thawing woods not two hundred yards ahead, high, with that abject, almost human quality he had come to know, and the other hounds joining in until the gloomed woods rang and clamored. They rode then. It seemed to him that he could actually see the big blue dog boring on, silent, and the bear too: the thick, locomotive-like shape which he had seen that day four years ago crossing the blow-down, crashing on ahead of the dogs faster than he had believed it could have moved, drawing away even from the running mules. He heard a shotgun, once. The woods had opened, they were going fast, the clamor faint and fading on ahead; they passed the man who had fired—a swamper, a pointing arm, a gaunt face, the small black orifice of his yelling studded with rotten teeth.

He heard the changed note in the hounds' uproar and two hundred yards ahead he saw them. The bear had turned. He saw Lion drive in without pausing and saw the bear strike him aside and lunge into the yelling hounds and kill one of them almost in its tracks and whirl and run again. Then they were in a streaming tide of dogs. He heard Major de Spain and Tennie's Jim shouting and the pistol sound of Tennie's Jim's leather thong as he tried to turn them. Then he and Sam Fathers were riding alone. One of the hounds had kept on with Lion though. He recognised its voice. It was the young hound which even a year ago had had no judgment and which, by the lights of the other hounds anyway, still had none. *Maybe that's what courage is,* he thought. "Right," Sam said behind him. "Right. We got to turn him from the river if we can."

Now they were in cane: a brake. He knew the path through it as well as Sam did. They came out of the undergrowth and struck the entrance almost exactly. It would traverse the brake and come out onto a high open ridge above the river. He heard the flat clap of Walter Ewell's rifle, then two more. "No," Sam said. "I can hear the hound. Go on."

They emerged from the narrow roofless tunnel of snapping and hissing cane, still galloping, onto the open ridge below which the thick yellow river, reflectionless in the gray and streaming light, seemed not to move. Now he could hear the hound too. It was not running. The cry was a high frantic yapping and Boon was running along the edge of the bluff, his old gun leaping and jouncing against his back on its sling made of a piece of cotton plowline. He whirled and ran up to them, wild-faced, and flung himself onto the mule behind the boy. "That damn boat!" he cried. "It's on the other side! He went straight across! Lion was too close to him! That little hound too! Lion was so close I couldn't shoot! Go on!" he cried, beating his heels into the mule's flanks. "Go on!"

They plunged down the bank, slipping and sliding in the thawed earth, crashing through the willows and into the water. He felt no shock, no cold, he on one side of the swimming mule, grasping the pommel with one hand and holding his gun above the water with the other, Boon opposite him. Sam was behind them somewhere, and then the river, the water about them, was full of dogs. They swam faster than the mules; they were scrabbling up the bank before the mules touched bottom. Major de Spain was whooping from the bank they had just left and, looking back, he saw Tennie's Jim and the horse as they went into the water.

Now the woods ahead of them and the rain-heavy air were one uproar. It rang and clamored; it echoed and broke against the bank behind them and reformed and clamored and rang until it seemed to the boy that all the hounds which had ever bayed game in this land were yelling down at him. He got his leg over the mule as it came up out of the water. Boon didn't try to mount again. He grasped one stirrup as they went up the bank and crashed through the undergrowth which fringed the bluff and saw the bear, on its hind feet, its back against a tree while the bellowing hounds swirled around it and once more Lion drove in, leaping clear of the ground.

This time the bear didn't strike him down. It caught the dog in both arms, almost loverlike, and they both went down. He was off the mule now. He drew back both hammers of the gun but he could see nothing but moiling spotted hound-bodies until the bear surged up again. Boon was yelling something, he could not tell what; he could see Lion still clinging to the bear's throat and he saw the bear, half erect, strike one of the hounds with one paw and hurl it five or six feet and then, rising and rising as though it would never stop, stand erect again and begin to rake at Lion's belly with its forepaws. Then Boon was running. The boy saw the gleam of the blade in his hand and watched him leap among the hounds, hurdling them, kicking them aside as he ran, and fling himself astride the bear as he had hurled himself onto the mule, his legs locked around the bear's belly, his left arm under the bear's throat where Lion clung, and the glint of the knife as it rose and fell.

It fell just once. For an instant they almost resembled a piece of statuary: the clinging dog, the bear, the man stride its back, working and probing the buried blade. Then they went down, pulled over backward by Boon's weight, Boon underneath. It was the bear's back which reappeared first but at once Boon was astride it again. He had never released the knife and again the boy saw the almost infinitesimal movement of his arm and shoulder as he probed and sought; then the bear surged erect, raising with it the man and the dog too, and turned and still carrying the man and the dog it took two or three steps toward the woods on its hind feet as a man would have walked and crashed down. It didn't collapse, crumple. It fell all of a piece, as a tree falls, so that all three of

them, man dog and bear, seemed to bounce once.

He and Tennie's Jim ran forward. Boon was kneeling at the bear's head. His left ear was shredded, his left coat sleeve was completely gone, his right boot had been ripped from knee to instep; the bright blood thinned in the thin rain down his leg and hand and arm and down the side of his face which was no longer wild but was quite calm. Together they prized Lion's jaws from the bear's throat. "Easy, goddamn it," Boon said. "Cant you see his guts are all out of him?" He began to remove his coat. He spoke to Tennie's Jim in that calm voice: "Bring the boat up. It's about a hundred yards down the bank there. I saw it." Tennie's Jim rose and went away. Then, and he could not remember if it had been a call or an exclamation from Tennie's Jim or if he had glanced up by chance, he saw Tennie's Jim stooping and saw Sam Fathers lying motionless on his face in the trampled mud.

The mule had not thrown him. He remembered that Sam was down too even before Boon began to run. There was no mark on him whatever and when he and Boon turned him over, his eyes were open and he said something in that tongue which he and Joe Baker had used to speak together. But he couldn't move. Tennie's Jim brought the skiff up; they could hear him shouting to Major de Spain across the river. Boon wrapped Lion in his hunting coat and carried him down to the skiff and they carried Sam down and returned and hitched the bear to the one-eyed mule's saddle-bow with Tennie's Jim's leash-thong and dragged him down to the skiff and got him into it and left Tennie's Jim to swim the horse and the two mules back across. Major de Spain caught the bow of the skiff as Boon jumped out and past him before it touched the bank. He looked at Old Ben and said quietly: "Well." Then he walked into the water and leaned down and touched Sam and Sam looked up at him and said something in that old tongue he and Joe Baker spoke. "You dont know what happened?" Major de Spain said.

"No, sir," the boy said. "It wasn't the mule. It wasn't anything. He was off the mule when Boon ran in on the bear. Then we looked up and he was lying on the ground." Boon was shouting at Tennie's Jim, still in the middle of the river.

"Come on, goddamn it!" he said. "Bring me that mule!"

"What do you want with a mule?" Major de Spain said.

Boon didn't even look at him. "I'm going to Hoke's to get the doctor," he said in that calm voice, his face quite calm beneath the steady thinning of the bright blood.

"You need a doctor yourself," Major de Spain said. "Tennie's Jim——"

"Damn that," Boon said. He turned on Major de Spain. His face was still calm, only his voice was a pitch higher. "Cant you see his goddamn guts are all out of him?"

"Boon!" Major de Spain said. They looked at one another. Boon was a good head taller than Major de Spain; even the boy was taller now than Major de Spain.

"I've got to get the doctor," Boon said. "His goddamn guts——"

"All right," Major de Spain said. Tennie's Jim came up out of the water. The horse and the sound mule had already scented Old Ben; they surged and plunged all the way up to the top of the bluff, dragging Tennie's Jim with them, before he could stop them and tie them and come back. Major de Spain unlooped the leather thong of his compass from his buttonhole and gave it to Tennie's Jim. "Go straight to Hoke's," he said. "Bring Doctor Crawford back with you. Tell him there are two men to be looked at. Take my mare. Can you find the road from here?"

"Yes, sir," Tennie's Jim said.

"All right," Major de Spain said. "Go on." He turned to the boy. "Take the mules and the horse and go back and get the wagon. We'll go on down the river in the boat to Coon bridge. Meet us there. Can you find it again?"

"Yes, sir," the boy said.

"All right. Get started."

He went back to the wagon. He realised then how far they had run. It was already afternoon when he put the mules into the traces and tied the horse's lead-rope to the tail-gate. He reached Coon bridge at dusk. The skiff was already there. Before he could see it and almost before he could see the water he had to leap from the tilting wagon, still holding the reins, and work around to where he could grasp the bit and then the ear of the plunging sound mule and dig his heels and hold it until Boon came up the bank. The rope of the led horse had already snapped and it had already disappeared up the road toward camp. They turned the wagon around and took the mules out and he led the sound mule a hundred yards up the road and tied it. Boon had already brought Lion up to the wagon and Sam was sitting up in the skiff now and when they raised him he tried to walk, up the bank and to the wagon and he tried to climb into the wagon but Boon did not wait; he picked Sam up bodily and set him on the seat. Then they hitched Old Ben to the one-eyed mule's saddle again and dragged him up the bank and set two skid-poles into the open tail-gate and got him into

the wagon and he went and got the sound mule and Boon fought it into the traces, striking it across its hard hollow-sounding face until it came into position and stood trembling. Then the rain came down, as though it had held off all day waiting on them.

They returned to camp through it, through the streaming and sightless dark, hearing long before they saw any light the horn and the spaced shots to guide them. When they came to Sam's dark little hut he tried to stand up. He spoke again in the tongue of the old fathers; then he said clearly: "Let me out. Let me out."

"He hasn't got any fire," Major said. "Go on!" he said sharply.

But Sam was struggling now, trying to stand up. "Let me out, master," he said. "Let me go home."

So he stopped the wagon and Boon got down and lifted Sam out. He did not wait to let Sam try to walk this time. He carried him into the hut and Major de Spain got light on a paper spill from the buried embers on the hearth and lit the lamp and Boon put Sam on his bunk and drew off his boots and Major de Spain covered him and the boy was not there, he was holding the mules, the sound one which was trying again to bolt since when the wagon stopped Old Ben's scent drifted forward again along the streaming blackness of air, but Sam's eyes were probably open again on that profound look which saw further than them or the hut, further than the death of a bear and the dying of a dog. Then they went on, toward the long wailing of the horn and the shots which seemed each to linger intact somewhere in the thick streaming air until the next spaced report joined and blended with it, to the lighted house, the bright streaming windows, the quiet faces as Boon entered, bloody and quite calm, carrying the bundled coat. He laid Lion, blood coat and all, on his stale sheetless pallet bed which not even Ash, as deft in the house as a woman, could ever make smooth.

The sawmill doctor from Hoke's was already there. Boon would not let the doctor touch him until he had seen to Lion. He wouldn't risk giving Lion chloroform. He put the entrails back and sewed him up without it while Major de Spain held his head and Boon his feet. But he never tried to move. He lay there, the yellow eyes open upon nothing while the quiet men in the new hunting clothes and in the old ones crowded into the little airless room rank with the smell of Boon's body and garments, and watched. Then the doctor cleaned and disinfected Boon's face and arm and leg and bandaged them and, the boy in front with a lantern and the doctor and McCaslin and Major de Spain and General Compson following, they went to Sam Fathers' hut. Tennie's Jim had built up the fire; he squatted before it, dozing. Sam had not moved since Boon had put him in the bunk and Major de Spain had covered him with the blankets, yet he opened his eyes and looked from one to another of the faces and when McCaslin touched his shoulder and said, "Sam. The doctor wants to look at you," he even drew his hands out of the blanket and began to fumble at his shirt buttons until McCaslin said, "Wait. We'll do it." They undressed him. He lay there—the copper-brown, almost hairless body, the old man's body, the old man, the wild man not even one generation from the woods, childless, kinless, peopleless —motionless, his eyes open but no longer looking at any of them, while the doctor examined him and drew the blankets up and put the stethoscope back into his bag and snapped the bag and only the boy knew that Sam too was going to die.

"Exhaustion," the doctor said. "Shock maybe. A man his age swimming rivers in December. He'll be all right. Just make him stay in bed for a day or two. Will there be somebody here with him?"

"There will be somebody here," Major de Spain said.

They went back to the house, to the rank little room where Boon still sat on the pallet bed with Lion's head under his hand while the men, the ones who had hunted behind Lion and the ones who had never seen him before today, came quietly in to look at him and went away. Then it was dawn and they all went out into the yard to look at Old Ben, with his eyes open too and his lips snarled back from his worn teeth and his mutilated foot and the little hard lumps under his skin which were the old bullets (there were fifty-two of them, buckshot rifle and ball) and the single almost invisible slit under his left shoulder where Boon's blade had finally found his life. Then Ash began to beat on the bottom of the dishpan with a heavy spoon to call them to breakfast and it was the first time he could remember hearing no sound from the dogs under the kitchen while they were eating. It was as if the old bear, even dead there in the yard, was a more potent terror still than they could face without Lion between them.

The rain had stopped during the night. By midmorning the thin sun appeared, rapidly burning away mist and cloud, warming the air and the earth; it would be one of those windless Mississippi December days which are a sort of Indian summer's Indian summer. They moved Lion out to the front gallery, into the sun. It was Boon's idea. "Goddamn it," he said, "he never did want to stay in the house until I made him. You know that." He took a crowbar and loosened the floor boards under his pallet bed so it could be raised, mattress and all, without disturbing Lion's position, and they carried him out to the gallery and put him down facing the woods.

Then he and the doctor and McCaslin and Major de Spain went to Sam's hut. This time Sam didn't open his eyes and his breathing was so quiet, so peaceful that they could hardly see that he breathed. The doctor didn't even take out his stethoscope nor even touch him. "He's all right," the doctor said. "He didn't even catch cold. He just quit."

"Quit?" McCaslin said.

"Yes. Old people do that sometimes. Then they get a good night's sleep or maybe it's just a drink of whisky, and they change their minds."

They returned to the house. And then they began to arrive—the swamp-dwellers, the gaunt men who ran trap-lines and lived on quinine and coons and river water, the farmers of little corn-and cotton-patches along the bottom's edge whose fields and cribs and pig-pens the old bear had rifled, the loggers from the camp and the sawmill men from Hoke's and the town men from further away than that, whose hounds the old bear had slain and traps and deadfalls he had wrecked and whose lead he carried. They came up mounted and on foot and in wagons, to enter the yard and look at him and then go on to the front where Lion lay, filling the little yard and overflowing it until there were almost a hundred of them squatting and standing in the warm and drowsing sunlight, talking quietly of hunting, of the game and the dogs which ran it, of hounds and bear and deer and men of yesterday vanished from the earth, while from time to time the great blue dog would open his eyes, not as if he were listening to them but as though to look at the woods for a moment before closing his eyes again, to remember the woods or to see that they were still there. He died at sundown.

Major de Spain broke camp that night. They carried Lion into the woods, or Boon carried him that is, wrapped in a quilt from his bed, just as he had refused to let anyone else touch Lion yesterday until the doctor got there; Boon carrying Lion, and the boy and General Compson and Walter and still almost fifty of them following with lanterns and lighted pine-knots—men from Hoke's and even further, who would have to ride out of the bottom in the dark, and swampers and trappers who would have to walk even, scattering toward the little hidden huts where they lived. And Boon would let nobody else dig the grave either and lay Lion in it and cover him and then General Compson stood at the head of it while the blaze and smoke of the pine-knots streamed away among the winter branches and spoke as he would have spoken over a man. Then they returned to camp. Major de Spain and McCaslin and Ash had rolled and tied all the bedding. The mules were hitched to the wagon and pointed out of the bottom and the wagon was already loaded and the stove in the kitchen was cold and the table was set with scraps of cold food and bread and only the coffee was hot when the boy ran into the kitchen where Major de Spain and McCaslin had already eaten. "What?" he cried. "What? I'm not going."

"Yes," McCaslin said, "we're going out tonight. Major wants to get on back home."

"No!" he said. "I'm going to stay."

"You've got to be back in school Monday. You've already missed a week more than I intended. It will take you from now until Monday to catch up. Sam's all right. You heard Doctor Crawford. I'm going to leave Boon and Tennie's Jim both to stay with him until he feels like getting up."

He was panting. The others had come in. He looked rapidly and almost frantically around at the other faces. Boon had a fresh bottle. He upended it and started the cork by striking the bottom of the bottle with the heel of his hand and drew the cork with his teeth and spat it out and drank. "You're damn right you're going back to school," Boon said. "Or I'll burn the tail off of you myself if Cass dont, whether you are sixteen or sixty. Where in hell do you expect to get without education? Where would Cass be? Where in hell would I be if I hadn't never went to school?"

He looked at McCaslin again. He could feel his breath coming shorter and shorter and shallower and shallower, as if there were not enough air in the kitchen for that many to breathe. "This is just Thursday. I'll come home Sunday night on one of the horses. I'll come home Sunday, then. I'll make up the time I lost studying Sunday night, McCaslin," he said, without even despair.

"No, I tell you," McCaslin said. "Sit down here and eat your supper. We're going out to——"

"Hold up, Cass," General Compson said. The boy did not know General Compson had moved until he put his hand on his shoulder. "What is it, bud?" he said.

"I've got to stay," he said. "I've got to."

"All right," General Compson said. "You can stay. If missing an extra week of school is going to throw you so far behind you'll have to sweat to find out what some hired pedagogue put between the covers of a book, you better quit altogether.—

And you shut up, Cass," he said, though McCaslin had not spoken. "You've got one foot straddled into a farm and the other foot straddled into a bank; you aint even got a good hand-hold where this boy was already an old man long before you damned Sartorises and Edmondses invented farms and banks to keep yourselves from having to find out what this boy was born knowing and fearing too maybe but without being afraid, that could go ten miles on a compass because he wanted to look at a bear none of us had ever got near enough to put a bullet in and looked at the bear and came the ten miles back on the compass in the dark; maybe by God that's the why and the wherefore of farms and banks.—I reckon you still aint going to tell what it is?"

But still he could not. "I've got to stay," he said.

"All right," General Compson said. "There's plenty of grub left. And you'll come home Sunday, like you promised McCaslin? Not Sunday night: Sunday."

"Yes, sir," he said.

"All right," General Compson said. "Sit down and eat, boys," he said. "Let's get started. It's going to be cold before we get home."

They ate. The wagon was already loaded and ready to depart; all they had to do was to get into it. Boon would drive them out to the road, to the farmer's stable where the surrey had been left. He stood beside the wagon, in silhouette on the sky, turbaned like a Paythan and taller than any there, the bottle tilted. Then he flung the bottle from his lips without even lowering it, spinning and glinting in the faint starlight, empty. "Them that's going," he said, "get in the goddamn wagon. Them that aint, get out of the goddamn way." The others got in. Boon mounted to the seat beside General Compson and the wagon moved, on into the obscurity until the boy could no longer see it, even the moving density of it amid the greater night. But he could still hear it, for a long while: the slow, deliberate banging of the wooden frame as it lurched from rut to rut. And he could hear Boon even when he could no longer hear the wagon. He was singing, harsh, tuneless, loud.

That was Thursday. On Saturday morning Tennie's Jim left on McCaslin's woods-horse which had not been out of the bottom one time now in six years, and late that afternoon rode through the gate on the spent horse and on to the commissary where McCaslin was rationing the tenants and the wage-hands for the coming week, and this time McCaslin forestalled any necessity or risk of having to wait while Major de Spain's surrey was being horsed and harnessed. He took their own, and with Tennie's Jim already asleep in the back seat he drove in to Jefferson and waited while Major de Spain changed to boots and put on his overcoat, and they drove the thirty miles in the dark of that night and at daybreak on Sunday morning they swapped to the waiting mare and mule and as the sun rose they rode out of the jungle and onto the low ridge where they had buried Lion: the low mound of unannealed earth where Boon's spade-marks still showed and beyond the grave the platform of freshly cut saplings bound between four posts and the blanket-wrapped bundle upon the platform and Boon and the boy squatting between the platform and the grave until Boon, the bandage removed, ripped, from his head so that the long scoriations of Old Ben's claws resembled crusted tar in the sunlight, sprang up and threw down upon them with the old gun with which he had never been known to hit anything although McCaslin was already off the mule, kicked both feet free of the irons and vaulted down before the mule had stopped, walking toward Boon.

"Stand back," Boon said. "By God, you wont touch him. Stand back, McCaslin." Still McCaslin came on, fast yet without haste.

"Cass!" Major de Spain said. Then he said "Boon! You, Boon!" and he was down too and the boy rose too, quickly, and still McCaslin came on not fast but steady and walked up to the grave and reached his hand steadily out, quickly yet still not fast, and took hold the gun by the middle so that he and Boon faced one another across Lion's grave, both holding the gun, Boon's spent indomitable amazed and frantic face almost a head higher than McCaslin's beneath the black scoriations of beast's claws and then Boon's chest began to heave as though there were not enough air in all the woods, in all the wilderness, for all of them, for him and anyone else, even for him alone.

"Turn it loose, Boon," McCaslin said.

"You damn little spindling—" Boon said. "Dont you know I can take it away from you? Dont you know I can tie it around your neck like a damn cravat?"

"Yes," McCaslin said. "Turn it loose, Boon."

"This is the way he wanted it. He told us. He told us exactly how to do it. And by God you aint going to move him. So we did it like he said, and I been sitting here ever since to keep the damn wildcats and varmints away from him and by God—" Then McCaslin had the gun, downslanted while he pumped the slide, the five shells snicking out of it so fast that the last one was almost out before the first one touched the ground and McCaslin dropped the gun behind him without once having taken his eyes from Boon's.

"Did you kill him, Boon?" he said. Then Boon moved. He turned, he moved like he was still drunk and then for a moment blind too, one hand out as he blundered toward the big tree and seemed to stop walking before he reached the tree so that he plunged, fell toward it, flinging up both hands and catching himself against the tree and turning until his back was against it, backing with the tree's trunk his wild spent scoriated face and the tremendous heave and collapse of his chest, McCaslin following, facing him again, never once having moved his eyes from Boon's eyes. "Did you kill him, Boon?"

"No!" Boon said. "No!"

"Tell the truth," McCaslin said. "I would have done it if he had asked me to." Then the boy moved. He was between them, facing McCaslin; the water felt as if it had burst and sprung not from his eyes alone but from his whole face, like sweat.

"Leave him alone!" he cried. "Goddamn it! Leave him alone!"

4

then he was twenty-one. He could say it, himself and his cousin juxtaposed not against the wilderness but against the tamed land which was to have been his heritage, the land which old Carothers McCaslin his grandfather had bought with white man's money from the wild men whose grandfathers without guns hunted it, and tamed and ordered or believed he had tamed and ordered it for the reason that the human beings he held in bondage and in the power of life and death had removed the forest from it and in their sweat scratched the surface of it to a depth of perhaps fourteen inches in order to grow something out of it which had not been there before and which could be translated back into the money he who believed he had bought it had had to pay to get it and hold it and a reasonable profit too: and for which reason old Carothers McCaslin, knowing better, could raise his children, his descendants and heirs, to believe the land was his to hold and bequeath since the strong and ruthless man has a cynical foreknowledge of his own vanity and pride and strength and a contempt for all his get: just as, knowing better, Major de Spain and his fragment of that wilderness which was bigger and older than any recorded deed: just as, knowing better, old Thomas Sutpen, from whom Major de Spain had had his fragment for money: just as Ikkemotubbe, the Chickasaw chief, from whom Thomas Sutpen had had the fragment for money or rum or whatever it was, knew in his turn

that not even a fragment of it had been his to relinquish or sell

not against the wilderness but against the land,
not in pursuit and lust but in relinquishment, and
in the commissary as it should have been, not the
heart perhaps but certainly the solar-plexus of the
repudiated and relinquished: the square, galleried,
wooden building squatting like a portent above the
fields whose laborers it still held in thrall '65 or no
and placarded over with advertisements for snuff
and cures for chills and salves and potions manufactured and sold by white men to bleach the pigment and straighten the hair of negroes that they
might resemble the very race which for two hundred years had held them in bondage and from
which for another hundred years not even a
bloody civil war would have set them completely
free

himself and his cousin amid the old smells of
cheese and salt meat and kerosene and harness,
the ranked shelves of tobacco and overalls and
bottled medicine and thread and plow-bolts, the
barrels and kegs of flour and meal and molasses
and nails, the wall pegs dependant with plowlines
and plow-collars and hames and trace-chains, and
the desk and the shelf above it on which rested the
ledgers in which McCaslin recorded the slow outward trickle of food and supplies and equipment
which returned each fall as cotton made and
ginned and sold (two threads frail as truth and impalpable as equators yet cable-strong to bind for
life them who made the cotton to the land their
sweat fell on), and the older ledgers clumsy and
archaic in size and shape, on the yellowed pages of
which were recorded in the faded hand of his
father Theophilus and his uncle Amodeus during
the two decades before the Civil War, the manu-
mission in title at least of Carothers McCaslin's
slaves:

'Relinquish,' McCaslin said. 'Relinquish. You,
the direct male descendant of him who saw the
opportunity and took it, bought the land, took the
land, got the land no matter how, held it to bequeath, no matter how, out of the old grant, the
first patent, when it was a wilderness of wild beasts
and wilder men, and cleared it, translated it into
something to bequeath to his children, worthy of
bequeathment for his descendants' ease and security and pride and to perpetuate his name and accomplishments. Not only the male descendant but
the only and last descendant in the male line and in
the third generation, while I am not only four generations from old Carothers, I derived through a
woman and the very McCaslin in my name is mine
only by sufferance and courtesy and my grandmother's pride in what that man accomplished

whose legacy and monument you think you can
repudiate.' and he

'I cant repudiate it. It was never mine to repudiate. It was never Father's and Uncle Buddy's to
bequeath me to repudiate because it was never
Grandfather's to bequeath them to bequeath me to
repudiate because it was never old Ikkemotubbe's
to sell to Grandfather for bequeathment and repudiation. Because it was never Ikkemotubbe's
fathers' fathers' to bequeath Ikkemotubbe to sell to
Grandfather or any man because on the instant
when Ikkemotubbe discovered, realised, that he
could sell it for money, on that instant it ceased
ever to have been his forever, father to father to
father, and the man who bought it bought nothing.'

'Bought nothing?' and he

'Bought nothing. Because He told in the Book
how He created the earth, made it and looked at it
and said it was all right, and then He made man.
He made the earth first and peopled it with dumb
creatures, and then He created man to be His
overseer on the earth and to hold suzerainty
over the earth and the animals on it in His name,
not to hold for himself and his descendants inviolable title forever, generation after generation, to
the oblongs and squares of the earth, but to
hold the earth mutual and intact in the communal
anonymity of brotherhood, and all the fee He
asked was pity and humility and sufferance and endurance and the sweat of his face for bread. And
I know what you are going to say,' he said: 'That
nevertheless Grandfather—' and McCaslin

'—did own it. And not the first. Not alone and
not the first since, as your Authority states, man
was dispossessed of Eden. Nor yet the second and
still not alone, on down through the tedious and
shabby chronicle of His chosen sprung from
Abraham, and of the sons of them who dispossessed Abraham, and of the five hundred years during which half the known world and all it contained was chattel to one city as this plantation
and all the life it contained was chattel and revoke-
less thrall to this commissary store and those
ledgers yonder during your grandfather's life, and
the next thousand years while men fought over
the fragments of that collapse until at last even the
fragments were exhausted and men snarled over
the gnawed bones of the old world's worthless
evening until an accidental egg discovered to them
a new hemisphere. So let me say it: That nevertheless and notwithstanding old Carothers did own
it. Bought it, got it, no matter; kept it, held it, no
matter; bequeathed it: else why do you stand here
relinquishing and repudiating? Held it, kept it for
fifty years until you could repudiate it, while He

—this Arbiter, this Architect, this Umpire—condoned—or did He? looked down and saw—or did He? Or at least did nothing: saw, and could not, or did not see; saw, and would not, or perhaps He would not see—perverse, impotent, or blind: which?' and he

'Dispossessed.' and McCaslin

'What?' and he

'Dispossessed. Not impotent: He didn't condone; not blind, because He watched it. And let me say it. Dispossessed of Eden. Dispossessed of Canaan, and those who dispossessed him dispossessed him dispossessed, and the five hundred years of absentee landlords in the Roman bagnios, and the thousand years of wild men from the northern woods who dispossessed them and devoured their ravished substance ravished in turn again and then snarled in what you call the old world's worthless twilight over the old world's gnawed bones, blasphemous in His name until He used a simple egg to discover to them a new world where a nation of people could be founded in humility and pity and sufferance and pride of one to another. And Grandfather did own the land nevertheless and notwithstanding because He permitted it, not impotent and not condoning and not blind because He ordered and watched it. He saw the land already accursed even as Ikkemotubbe and Ikkemotubbe's father old Issetibbeha and old Issetibbeha's fathers too held it, already tainted even before any white man owned it by what Grandfather and his kind, his fathers, had brought into the new land which He had vouchsafed them out of pity and sufferance, on condition of pity and humility and sufferance and endurance, from that old world's corrupt and worthless twilight as though in the sailfuls of the old world's tainted wind which drove the ships—' and McCaslin

'Ah.'

'—and no hope for the land anywhere so long as Ikkemotubbe and Ikkemotubbe's descendants held it in unbroken succession. Maybe He saw that only by voiding the land for a time of Ikkemotubbe's blood and substituting for it another blood, could He accomplish His purpose. Maybe He knew already what that other blood would be, maybe it was more than justice that only the white man's blood was available and capable to raise the white man's curse, more than vengeance when—' and McCaslin

'Ah.'

'—when He used the blood which had brought in the evil to destroy the evil as doctors use fever to burn up fever, poison to slay poison. Maybe He chose Grandfather out of all of them He might have picked. Maybe He knew that Grandfather himself would not serve His purpose because Grandfather was born too soon too, but that Grandfather would have descendants, the right descendants; maybe He had foreseen already the descendants Grandfather would have, maybe He saw already in Grandfather the seed progenitive of the three generations He saw it would take to set at least some of His lowly people free—' and McCaslin

'The sons of Ham. You who quote the Book: the sons of Ham.' and he

'There are some things He said in the Book, and some things reported of Him that He did not say. And I know what you will say now: That if truth is one thing to me and another thing to you, how will we choose which is truth? You dont need to choose. The heart already knows. He didn't have His Book written to be read by what must elect and choose, but by the heart, not by the wise of the earth because maybe they dont need it or maybe the wise no longer have any heart, but by the doomed and lowly of the earth who have nothing else to read with but the heart. Because the men who wrote his Book for Him were writing about truth and there is only one truth and it covers all things that touch the heart.' and McCaslin

'So these men who transcribed His Book for Him were sometime liars.' and he

'Yes. Because they were human men. They were trying to write down the heart's truth out of the heart's driving complexity, for all the complex and troubled hearts which would beat after them. What they were trying to tell, what He wanted said, was too simple. Those for whom they transcribed His words could not have believed them. It had to be expounded in the everyday terms which they were familiar with and could comprehend, not only those who listened but those who told it too, because if they who were that near to Him as to have been elected from among all who breathed and spoke language to transcribe and relay His words, could comprehend truth only through the complexity of passion and lust and hate and fear which drives the heart, what distance back to truth must they traverse whom truth could only reach by word-of-mouth?' and McCaslin

'I might answer that, since you have taken to proving your points and disproving mine by the same text, I dont know. But I dont say that, because you have answered yourself: No time at all if, as you say, the heart knows truth, the infallible and unerring heart. And perhaps you are right, since although you admitted three generations from old Carothers to you, there were not three.

There were not even completely two. Uncle Buck and Uncle Buddy. And they not the first and not alone. A thousand other Bucks and Buddies in less than two generations and sometimes less than one in this land which so you claim God created and man himself cursed and tainted. Not to mention 1865.' and he

'Yes. More men that Father and Uncle Buddy,' not even glancing toward the shelf above the desk, nor did McCaslin. They did not need to. To him it was as though the ledgers in their scarred cracked leather bindings were being lifted down one by one in their fading sequence and spread open on the desk or perhaps upon some apocryphal Bench or even Altar or perhaps before the Throne Itself for a last perusal and contemplation and refreshment of the Allknowledgeable before the yellowed pages and the brown thin ink in which was recorded the injustice and a little at least of its amelioration and restitution faded back forever into the anonymous communal original dust

the yellowed pages scrawled in fading ink by the hand first of his grandfather and then of his father and uncle, bachelors up to and past fifty and then sixty, the one who ran the plantation and the farming of it and the other who did the housework and the cooking and continued to do it even after his twin married and the boy himself was born

the two brothers who as soon as their father was buried moved out of the tremendously-conceived, the almost barn-like edifice which he had not even completed, into a one-room log cabin which the two of them built themselves and added other rooms to while they lived in it, refusing to allow any slave to touch any timber of it other than the actual raising into place the logs which two men alone could not handle, and domiciled all the slaves in the big house some of the windows of which were still merely boarded up with odds and ends of plank or with the skins of bear and deer nailed over the empty frames: each sundown the brother who superintended the farming would parade the negroes as a first sergeant dismisses a company, and herd them willynilly, man woman and child, without question protest or recourse, into the tremendous abortive edifice scarcely yet out of embryo, as if even old Carothers McCaslin had paused aghast at the concrete indication of his own vanity's boundless conceiving: he would call his mental roll and herd them in and with a hand-wrought nail as long as a flenching-knife and suspended from a short deer-hide thong attached to the door-jamb for that purpose, he would nail to the door of that house which lacked half its windows and had no hinged back door at all, so that presently and for fifty years afterward, when the boy himself was big to hear and remember it, there was in the land a sort of folk-tale: of the countryside all night long full of skulking McCaslin slaves dodging the moonlit roads and the Patrol-riders to visit other plantations, and of the unspoken gentlemen's agreement between the two white men and the two dozen black ones that, after the white man had counted them and driven the home-made nail into the front door at sundown, neither of the white men would go around behind the house and look at the back door, provided that all the negroes were behind the front one when the brother who drove it drew out the nail again at daybreak

the twins who were identical even in their hand-writing, unless you had specimens side by side to compare, and even when both hands appeared on the same page (as often happened, as if, long since past any oral intercourse, they had used the diurnally advancing pages to conduct the unavoidable business of the compulsion which had traversed all the waste wilderness of North Mississippi in 1830 and '40 and singled them out to drive) they both looked as though they had been written by the same perfectly normal ten-year-old boy, even to the spelling, except that the spelling did not improve as one by one the slaves which Carothers McCaslin had inherited and purchased— Roscius and Phoebe and Thucydides and Eunice and their descendants, and Sam Fathers and his mother for both of whom he had swapped an underbred trotting gelding to old Ikkemotubbe, the Chickasaw chief from whom he had likewise bought the land, and Tennie Beauchamp whom the twin Amodeus had won from a neighbor in a poker-game, and the anomaly calling itself Percival Brownlee which the twin Theophilus had purchased, neither he nor his brother ever knew why apparently, from Bedford Forrest while he was still only a slave-dealer and not yet a general (It was a single page, not long and covering less than a year, not seven months in fact, begun in the hand which the boy had learned to distinguish as that of his father:

Percavil Brownly 26yr Old. cleark @ Book-epper. bought from N.B.Forest at Cold Water 3 Mar 1856 $265. dolars

and beneath that, in the same hand:

5 mar 1856 No bookepper any way Cant read. Can write his Name but I already put that down My self Says he can Plough but dont look like it to Me. sent to Feild to day Mar 5 1856 and the same hand:

> *6 Mar 1856 Cant plough either Says he aims
> to be a Precher so may be he can lead live
> stock to Crick to Drink*

and this time it was the other, the hand which he now recognised as his uncle's when he could see them both on the same page:

> *Mar 23th 1856 Cant do that either Except
> one at a Time Get shut of him*

then the first again:

> *24 Mar 1856 Who in hell would buy him*

then the second:

> *19th of Apr 1856 Nobody You put yourself
> out of Market at Cold Water two months
> ago I never said sell him Free him*

the first:

> *22 Apr 1856 Ill get it out of him*

the second:

> *Jun 13th 1856 How $1 per yr 265$ 265 yrs
> Wholl sign his Free paper*

then the first again:

> *1 Oct 1856 Mule josephine Broke Leg @ shot
> Wrong stall wrong niger wrong everything
> $100. dolars*

and the same:

> *2 Oct 1856 Freed Debit McCaslin @ McCas-
> lin $265. dolars*

then the second again:

> *Oct 3th Debit Theophilus McCaslin Niger
> 265$ Mule 100$ 365$ He hasnt gone yet
> Father should be here*

then the first:

> *3 Oct 1856 Son of a bitch wont leave What
> would father done*

the second:

> *29th of Oct 1856 Renamed him*

the first:

> *31 Oct 1856 Renamed him what*

the second:

> *Chrstms 1856 Spintrius*

) took substance and even a sort of shadowy life with their passions and complexities too as page followed page and year year; all there, not only the general and condoned injustice and its slow amortization but the specific tragedy which had not been condoned and could never be amortized, the new page and the new ledger, the hand which he could now recognise at first glance as his father's:

> *Father dide Lucius Quintus Carothers Mc-
> Caslin, Callina 1772 Missippy 1837. Dide
> and burid 27 June 1837*
> *Roskus. rased by Granfather in Callina Dont
> know how old. Freed 27 June 1837 Dont
> want to leave. Dide and Burid 12 Jan 1841
> Fibby Roskus Wife. bought by granfather in
> Callina says Fifty Freed 27 June 1837 Dont
> want to leave. Dide and burd 1 Aug 1849
> Thucydus Roskus @ Fibby Son born in Cal-
> lina 1779. Refused 10acre peace fathers Will
> 28 Jun 1837 Refused Cash offer $200. dolars
> from A.@ T. McCaslin 28 Jun 1837 Wants
> to stay and work it out*

and beneath this and covering the next five pages and almost that many years, the slow, day-by-day accrument of the wages allowed him and the food and clothing—the molasses and meat and meal, the cheap durable shirts and jeans and shoes and now and then a coat against rain and cold—charged against the slowly yet steadily mounting sum of balance (and it would seem to the boy that he could actually see the black man, the slave whom his white owner had forever manumitted by the very act from which the black man could never be free so long as memory lasted, entering the commissary, asking permission perhaps of the white man's son to see the ledger-page which he could not even read, not even asking for the white man's word, which he would have had to accept for the reason that there was absolutely no way under the sun for him to test it, as to how the account stood, how much longer before he could go and never return, even if only as far as Jefferson seventeen miles away) on to the double pen-stroke closing the final entry:

> *3 Nov 1841 By Cash to Thucydus McCaslin
> $200. dolars Set Up blaksmith in J. Dec
> 1841 Dide and burid in J. 17 feb 1854*
> *Eunice Bought by Father in New Orleans
> 1807 $650. dolars. Marrid to Thucydus
> 1809 Drownd in Crick Cristmas Day 1832*

and then the other hand appeared, the first time he had seen it in the ledger to distinguish it as his uncle's, the cook and housekeeper whom even McCaslin, who had known him and the boy's father for sixteen years before the boy was born, remembered as sitting all day long in the rocking chair from which he cooked the food, before the kitchen fire on which he cooked it:

June 21th 1833 Drownd herself

and the first:

23 Jun 1833 Who in hell ever heard of a niger drownding him self

and the second, unhurried, with a complete finality; the two identical entries might have been made with a rubber stamp save for the date:

Aug 13th 1833 Drownd herself

and he thought *But why? But why?* He was sixteen then. It was neither the first time he had been alone in the commissary nor the first time he had taken down the old ledgers familiar on their shelf above the desk ever since he could remember. As a child and even after nine and ten and eleven, when he had learned to read, he would look up at the scarred and cracked backs and ends but with no particular desire to open them, and though he intended to examine them someday because he realised that they probably contained a chronological and much more comprehensive though doubtless tedious record than he would ever get from any other source, not alone of his own flesh and blood but of all his people, not only the whites but the black one too, who were as much a part of his ancestry as his white progenitors, and of the land which they had all held and used in common and fed from and on and would continue to use in common without regard to color or titular ownership, it would only be on some idle day when he was old and perhaps even bored a little since what the old books contained would be after all these years fixed immutably, finished, unalterable, harmless. Then he was sixteen. He knew what he was going to find before he found it. He got the commissary key from McCaslin's room after midnight while McCaslin was asleep and with the commissary door shut and locked behind him and the forgotten lantern stinking anew the rank dead icy air, he leaned above the yellowed page and thought not Why drowned herself, but thinking what he believed his father had thought when he found his brother's first comment: Why did Uncle Buddy think she had drowned herself? finding, beginning to find on the next succeeding page what he knew he would find, only this was still not it because he already knew this:

Tomasina called Tomy Daughter of Thucydus @ Eunice Born 1810 dide in Child bed June 1833 and Burd. Yr stars fell

nor the next:

Turl Son of Thucydus @ Eunice Tomy born Jun 1833 yr stars fell Fathers will

and nothing more, no tedious recording filling this page of wages day by day and food and clothing charged against them, no entry of his death and burial because he had outlived his white half-brothers and the books which McCaslin kept did not include obituaries: just *Fathers will* and he had seen that too: old Carothers' bold cramped hand far less legible than his sons' even and not much better in spelling, who while capitalising almost every noun and verb, made no effort to punctuate or construct whatever, just as he made no effort either to explain or obfuscate the thousand-dollar legacy to the son of an unmarried slave-girl, to be paid only at the child's coming-of-age, bearing the consequence of the act of which there was still no definite incontrovertible proof that he acknowledged, not out of his own substance but penalising his sons with it, charging them a cash forfeit on the accident of their own paternity; not even a bribe for silence toward his own fame since his fame would suffer only after he was no longer present to defend it, flinging almost contemptuously, as he might a cast-off hat or pair of shoes, the thousand dollars which could have had no more reality to him under those conditions than it would have to the negro, the slave who would not even see it until he came of age, twenty-one years too late to begin to learn what money was. *So I reckon that was cheaper than saying My son to a nigger* he thought. *Even if My son wasn't but just two words. But there must have been love* he thought. *Some sort of love. Even what he would have called love: not just an afternoon's or a night's spittoon.* There was the old man, old, within five years of his life's end, long a widower and, since his sons were not only bachelors but were approaching middleage, lonely in the house and doubtless even bored since his plantation was established now and functioning and there was enough money now, too much of it probably for a man whose vices even apparently remained below his means; there was the girl, husbandless and young, only twenty-three when the child was born: perhaps he had sent for her at first out of loneliness, to have a young voice and movement in the house, summoned her, bade her mother send her each morning to sweep the floors and make the beds and the mother acquiescing since that was probably already understood, already planned: the only child of a couple who were not field hands and who held themselves something above the other slaves not alone for that reason but because the husband and his fa- ther and mother too had been inherited by the white man from his father, and the white man himself had travelled three hundred miles and bet- ter to New Orleans in a day when men travelled by horseback or steamboat, and bought the girl's mother as a wife for

and that was all. The old frail pages seemed to turn of their own accord even while he thought *His own daughter His own daughter. No No Not even him* back to that one where the white man (not even a widower then) who never went any- where any more than his sons in their time ever did and who did not need another slave, had gone all the way to New Orleans and bought one. And Tomey's Terrel was still alive when the boy was ten years old and he knew from his own observa- tion and memory that there had already been some white in Tomey's Terrel's blood before his father gave him the rest of it; and looking down at the yellowed page spread beneath the yellow glow of the lantern smoking and stinking in that rank chill midnight room fifty years later, he seemed to see her actually walking into the icy creek on that Christmas day six months before her daughter's and her lover's (*Her first lover's* he thought. *Her first*) child was born, solitary, in- flexible, griefless, ceremonial, in formal and suc- cinct repudiation of grief and despair who had already had to repudiate belief and hope

that was all. He would never need look at the ledgers again nor did he; the yellowed pages in their fading and implacable succession were as much a part of his consciousness and would re- main so forever, as the fact of his own nativity:

Tennie Beauchamp 21yrs Won by Amodeus McCaslin from Hubert Beauchamp Esqre Possible Strait against three Treys in sigt Not called 1859 Marrid to Tomys Turl 1859

and no date of freedom because her freedom, as well as that of her first surviving child, derived not from Buck and Buddy McCaslin in the commis- sary but from a stranger in Washington and no date of death and burial, not only because McCas- lin kept no obituaries in his books, but because in this year 1883 she was still alive and would remain so to see a grandson by her last surviving child:

Amodeus McCaslin Beauchamp Son of tomys Turl @ Tennie Beauchamp 1859 dide 1859

then his uncle's hand entire, because his father was now a member of the cavalry command of that man whose name as a slave-dealer he could

not even spell: and not even a page and not even a full line:

Dauter Tomes Turl and tenny 1862

and not even a line and not even a sex and no cause given though the boy could guess it because McCaslin was thirteen then and he remembered how there was not always enough to eat in more places than Vicksburg:

Child of tomes Turl and Tenny 1863

and the same hand again and this one lived, as though Tennie's perseverance and the fading and diluted ghost of old Carothers' ruthlessness had at last conquered even starvation: and clearer, fuller, more carefully written and spelled than the boy had yet seen it, as if the old man, who should have been a woman to begin with, trying to run what was left of the plantation in his brother's absence in the intervals of cooking and caring for himself and the fourteen-year-old orphan, had taken as an omen for renewed hope the fact that this nameless inheritor of slaves was at least re- maining alive long enough to receive a name:

James Thucydus Beauchamp Son of Tomes Turl and Tenny Beauchamp Born 29th december 1864 and both Well Wanted to call him Theophilus but Tride Amodeus McCaslin and Callina McCaslin and both dide so Disswaded Them Born at Two clock A,m, both Well

but no more, nothing; it would be another two years yet before the boy, almost a man now, would return from the abortive trip into Tennessee with the still-intact third of old Carothers' legacy to his Negro son and his descendants, which as the three surviving children established at last one by one their apparent intention of surviving, their white half-uncles had increased to a thousand dol- lars each, conditions permitting, as they came of age, and completed the page himself as far as it would even be completed when that day was long passed beyond which a man born in 1864 (or 1867 either, when he himself saw light) could have expected or himself hoped or even wanted to be still alive; his own hand now, queerly enough resembling neither his father's nor his uncle's nor even McCaslin's, but like that of his grandfather's save for the spelling:

Vanished sometime on night of his twenty- first birthday Dec 29 1885. Traced by Isaac McCaslin to Jackson Tenn. and there lost. His third of legacy $1000.00 returned to McCaslin Edmonds Trustee this day Jan 12 1886 but not yet: that would be two years yet, and now his father's again, whose old commander was now quit of soldiering and slave-trading both; once more in the ledger and then not again and more illegible than ever, almost indecipherable at all from the rheumatism which now crippled him and almost completely innocent now even of any sort of spelling as well as punctuation, as if the four years during which he had followed the sword of the only man ever breathing who ever sold him a negro, let alone beat him in a trade, had convinced him not only of the vanity of faith and hope but of orthography too:

Miss sophonsiba b dtr t t @ t 1869

but not of belief and will because it was there, written, as McCaslin had told him, with the left hand, but there in the ledger one time more and then not again, for the boy himself was a year old, and when Lucas was born six years later, his father and uncle had been dead inside the same twelve-months almost five years; his own hand again, who was there and saw it, 1886, she was just seventeen, two years younger than himself, and he was in the commissary when McCaslin entered out of the first of dusk and said, 'He wants to marry Fonsiba,' like that: and he looked past McCaslin and saw the man, the stranger, taller than McCaslin and wearing better clothes than McCaslin and most of the other white men the boy knew habitually wore, who entered the room like a white man and stood in it like a white man, as though he had let McCaslin precede him into it not because McCaslin's skin was white but simply because McCaslin lived there and knew the way, and who talked like a white man too, looking at him past McCaslin's shoulder rapidly and keenly once and then no more, without further interest, as a mature and contained white man not impatient but just pressed for time might have looked. 'Marry Fonsiba?' he cried. 'Marry Fonsiba?' and then no more either, just watching and listening while McCaslin and the Negro talked:

'To live in Arkansas, I believe you said.'

'Yes. I have property there. A farm.'

'Property? A farm? You own it?'

'Yes.'

'You dont say Sir, do you?'

'To my elders, yes.'

'I see. You are from the North.'

'Yes. Since a child.'

'Then your father was a slave.'

'Yes. Once.'

'Then how do you own a farm in Arkansas?'

'I have a grant. It was my father's. From the United States. For military service.'

'I see,' McCaslin said. 'The Yankee army.'

'The United States army,' the stranger said; and then himself again, crying it at McCaslin's back:

'Call aunt Tennie! I'll go get her! I'll——' But McCaslin was not even including him; the stranger did not even glance back toward his voice, the two of them speaking to one another again as if he were not even there:

'Since you seem to have it all settled,' McCaslin said, 'why have you bothered to consult my authority at all?'

'I dont,' the stranger said. 'I acknowledge your authority only so far as you admit your responsibility toward her as a female member of the family of which you are the head. I dont ask your permission. I——'

'That will do!' McCaslin said. But the stranger did not falter. It was neither as if he were ignoring McCaslin nor as if he had failed to hear him. It was as though he were making, not at all an excuse and not exactly a justification, but simply a statement which the situation absolutely required and demanded should be made in McCaslin's hearing whether McCaslin listened to it or not. It was as if he were talking to himself, for himself to hear the words spoken aloud. They faced one another, not close yet at slightly less than foils' distance, erect, their voices not raised, not impactive, just succinct:

'—I inform you, notify you in advance as chief of her family. No man of honor could do less. Besides, you have, in your way, according to your lights and upbringing——'

'That's enough, I said,' McCaslin said. 'Be off this place by full dark. Go.' But for another moment the other did not move, contemplating McCaslin with that detached and heatless look, as if he were watching reflected in McCaslin's pupils the tiny image of the figure he was sustaining.

'Yes,' he said. 'After all, this is your house. And in your fashion you have. . . . But no matter. You are right. This is enough.' He turned back toward the door; he paused again but only for a second, already moving while he spoke: 'Be easy. I will be good to her.' Then he was gone.

'But how did she ever know him?' the boy cried. 'I never even heard of him before! And Fonsiba, that's never been off this place except to go to church since she was born——'

'Ha,' McCaslin said. 'Even their parents dont know until too late how seventeen-year-old girls ever met the men who marry them too, if they are lucky.' And the next morning they were both gone, Fonsiba too. McCaslin never saw her again, nor did he, because the woman he found at last five months later was no one he had ever known.

He carried a third of the three-thousand-dollar fund in gold in a money-belt, as when he had vainly traced Tennie's Jim into Tennessee a year ago. They—the man—had left an address of some sort with Tennie, and three months later a letter came, written by the man although McCaslin's wife Alice had taught Fonsiba to read and write too a little. But it bore a different postmark from the address the man had left with Tennie, and he travelled by rail as far as he could and then by contracted stage and then by a hired livery rig and then by rail again for a distance: an experienced traveller by now and an experienced bloodhound too and a successful one this time because he would have to be; as the slow interminable empty muddy December miles crawled and crawled and night followed night in hotels, in roadside taverns of rough logs and containing little else but a bar, and in the cabins of strangers and the hay of lonely barns, in none of which he dared undress because of his secret golden girdle like that of a disguised one of the Magi travelling incognito and not even hope to draw him but only determination and desperation, he would tell himself: *I will have to find her. I will have to. We have already lost one of them. I will have to find her this time.* He did. Hunched in the slow and icy rain, on a spent hired horse splashed to the chest and higher, he saw it—a single log edifice with a clay chimney which seemed in process of being flattened by the rain to a nameless and valueless rubble of dissolution in that roadless and even pathless waste of unfenced fallow and wilderness jungle—no barn, no stable, not so much as a hen-coop: just a log cabin built by hand and no clever hand either, a meagre pile of clumsily-cut firewood sufficient for about one day and not even a gaunt hound to come bellowing out from under the house when he rode up— a farm only in embryo, perhaps a good farm, maybe even a plantation someday, but not now, not for years yet and only then with labor, hard and enduring and unflagging work and sacrifice; he shoved open the crazy kitchen door in its awry frame and entered an icy gloom where not even a fire for cooking burned and after another moment saw, crouched into the wall's angle behind a crude table, the coffee-colored face which he had known all his life but knew no more, the body which had been born within a hundred yards of the room that he was born in and in which some of his own blood ran but which was now completely inheritor of generation after generation to whom an unannounced white man on a horse was a white man's hired Patroller wearing a pistol sometimes and a blacksnake whip always; he entered the next room, the only other room the

cabin owned, and found, sitting in a rocking chair before the hearth, the man himself, reading—sitting there in the only chair in the house, before that miserable fire for which there was not wood sufficient to last twenty-four hours, in the same ministerial clothing in which he had entered the commissary five months ago and a pair of gold-framed spectacles which, when he looked up and then rose to his feet, the boy saw did not even contain lenses, reading a book in the midst of that desolation, that muddy waste fenceless and even pathless and without even a walled shed for stock to stand beneath: and over all, permeant, clinging to the man's very clothing and exuding from his skin itself, that rank stink of baseless and imbecile delusion, that boundless rapacity and folly, of the carpet-bagger followers of victorious armies.

'Dont you see?' he cried. 'Dont you see? This whole land, the whole South, is cursed, and all of us who derive from it, whom it ever suckled, white and black both, lie under the curse? Granted that my people brought the curse onto the land: maybe for that reason their descendants alone can—not resist it, not combat it—maybe just endure and outlast it until the curse is lifted. Then your peoples' turn will come because we have forfeited ours. But not now. Not yet. Dont you see?'

The other stood now, the unfrayed garments still ministerial even if not quite so fine, the book closed upon one finger to keep the place, the lense-less spectacles held like a music master's wand in the other workless hand while the owner of it spoke his measured and sonorous imbecility of the boundless folly and the baseless hope: 'You're wrong. The curse you whites brought into this land has been lifted. It has been voided and discharged. We are seeing a new era, an era dedicated, as our founders intended it, to freedom, liberty and equality for all, to which this country will be the new Canaan——'

'Freedom from what? From work? Canaan?' He jerked his arm, comprehensive, almost violent: whereupon it all seemed to stand there about them, intact and complete and visible in the drafty, damp, heatless, negro-stale negro-rank sorry room—the empty fields without plow or seed to work them, fenceless against the stock which did not exist within or without the walled stable which likewise was not there. 'What corner of Canaan is this?'

'You are seeing it at a bad time. This is winter. No man farms this time of year.'

'I see. And of course her need for food and clothing will stand still while the land lies fallow.'

'I have a pension,' the other said. He said it as a

man might say *I have grace* or *I own a gold mine.* 'I have my father's pension too. It will arrive on the first of the month. What day is this?'

'The eleventh,' he said. 'Twenty days more. And until then?'

'I have a few groceries in the house from my credit account with the merchant in Midnight who banks my pension check for me. I have executed to him a power of attorney to handle it for me as a matter of mutual——'

'I see. And if the groceries dont last the twenty days?'

'I still have one more hog.'

'Where?'

'Outside,' the other said. 'It is customary in this country to allow stock to range free during the winter for food. It comes up from time to time. But no matter if it doesn't; I can probably trace its footprints when the need——'

'Yes!' he cried. 'Because no matter: you still have the pension check. And the man in Midnight will cash it and pay himself out of it for what you have already eaten and if there is any left over, it is yours. And the hog will be eaten by then or you still cant catch it, and then what will you do?'

'It will be almost spring then,' the other said. 'I am planning in the spring——'

'It will be January,' he said. 'And then February. And then more than half of March—' and when he stopped again in the kitchen she had not moved, she did not even seem to breathe or to be alive except her eyes watching him; when he took a step toward her it was still not movement because she could have retreated no further: only the tremendous fathomless ink-colored eyes in the narrow, thin, too thin coffee-colored face watching him without alarm, without recognition, without hope. 'Fonsiba,' he said. 'Fonsiba. Are you all right?'

'I'm free,' she said. Midnight was a tavern, a livery stable, a big store (that would be where the pension check banked itself as a matter of mutual elimination of bother and fret, he thought) and a little one, a saloon and a blacksmith shop. But there was a bank there too. The president (the owner, for all practical purposes) of it was a translated Mississippian who had been one of Forrest's men too: and his body lightened of the golden belt for the first time since he left home eight days ago, with pencil and paper he multiplied three dollars by twelve months and divided it into one thousand dollars; it would stretch that way over almost twenty-eight years and for twenty-eight years at least she would not starve, the banker promising to send the three dollars himself by a trusty messenger on the fifteenth of each month and put it

into her actual hand, and he returned home and that was all because in 1874 his father and his uncle were both dead and the old ledgers never again came down from the shelf above the desk to which his father had returned them for the last time that day in 1869. But he could have completed it:

Lucas Quintus Carothers McCaslin Beauchamp. Last surviving son and child of Tomey's Terrel and Tennie Beauchamp, March 17, 1874

except that there was no need: not *Lucius Quintus @c @c @c*, but *Lucas Quintus*, not refusing to be called Lucius, because he simply eliminated that word from the name; not denying, declining the name itself, because he used three quarters of it; but simply taking the name and changing, altering it, making it no longer the white man's but his own, by himself composed, himself selfprogenitive and nominate, by himself ancestored, as, for all the old ledgers recorded to the contrary, old Carothers himself was

and that was all: 1874 the boy; 1888 the man, repudiated denied and free; 1895 and husband but no father, unwidowed but without a wife, and found long since that no man is ever free and probably could not bear it if he were; married then and living in Jefferson in the little new jerrybuilt bungalow which his wife's father had given them: and one morning Lucas stood suddenly in the doorway of the room where he was reading the Memphis paper and he looked at the paper's dateline and thought *It's his birthday. He's twenty-one today* and Lucas said: 'Whar's the rest of that money old Carothers left? I wants it. All of it.'

that was all: and McCaslin

'More men than that one Buck and Buddy to fumble-heed that truth so mazed for them that spoke it and so confused for them that heard yet still there was 1865:' and he

'But not enough. Not enough of even Father and Uncle Buddy to fumble-heed in even three generations not even three generations fathered by Grandfather not even if there had been nowhere beneath His sight any but Grandfather and so He would not even have needed to elect and choose. But He tried and I know what you will say. That having Himself created them He could have known no more of hope than He could have pride and grief but He didn't hope He just waited because He had made them: not just because He had set them alive and in motion but because He had already worried with them so long: worried with them so long because He had seen how in individual cases they were capable of anything any height or depth remembered in mazed incomprehension out of heaven where hell was created too and so He must admit them or else admit His equal somewhere and so be no longer God and therefore must accept responsibility for what He Himself had done in order to live with Himself in His lonely and paramount heaven. And He probably knew it was vain but He had created them and knew them capable of all things because He had shaped them out of the primal Absolute which contained all and had watched them since in their individual exaltation and baseness and they themselves not knowing why nor how nor even when: until at last He saw that they were all Grandfather all of them and that even from them the elected and chosen the best the very best He could expect (not hope mind: not hope) would be Bucks and Buddies and not even enough of them and in the third generation not even Bucks and Buddies but—' and McCaslin

'Ah:' and he

'Yes. If He could see Father and Uncle Buddy in Grandfather He must have seen me too. —an Isaac born into a later life than Abraham's and repudiating immolation: fatherless and therefore safe declining the altar because maybe this time the exasperated Hand might not supply the kid—' and McCaslin

'Escape:' and he

'All right. Escape.—Until one day He said what you told Fonsiba's husband that afternoon here in this room: *This will do. This is enough:* not in exasperation or rage or even just sick to death as you were sick that day: just *This is enough* and looked about for one last time, for one time more since He had created them, upon this land this South for which He had done so much with woods for game and streams for fish and deep rich soil for seed and lush springs to sprout it and long summers to mature it and serene falls to harvest it and short mild winters for men and animals and saw no hope anywhere and looked beyond it where hope should have been, where to East North and West lay illimitable that whole hopeful continent dedicated as a refuge and sanctuary of liberty and freedom from what you called the old world's worthless evening and saw the rich descendants of slavers, females of both sexes, to whom the black they shrieked of was another specimen another example like the Brazilian macaw brought home in a cage by a traveller, passing resolutions about horror and outrage in warm and air-proof halls: and the thundering cannonade of politicians earning votes and the medicine-shows of pulpiteers earning Chatauqua fees, to whom the outrage and the injustice were as much

abstractions as Tariff or Silver or Immortality and who employed the very shackles of its servitude and the sorry rags of its regalia as they did the other beer and banners and mottoes redfire and brimstone and sleight-of-hand and musical hand-saws: and the whirling wheels which manufactured for a profit the pristine replacements of the shackles and shoddy garments as they wore out and spun the cotton and made the gins which ginned it and the cars and ships which hauled it, and the men who ran the wheels for that profit and established and collected the taxes it was taxed with and the rates for hauling it and the commissions for selling it: and He could have repudiated them since they were his creation now and forever more throughout all their generations until not only that old world from which He had rescued them but this new one too which He had revealed and led them to as a sanctuary and refuge were become the same worthless tideless rock cooling in the last crimson evening except that out of all that empty sound and bootless fury one silence, among that loud and moiling all of them just one simple enough to believe that horror and outrage were first and last simply horror and outrage and was crude enough to act upon that, illiterate and had no words for talking or perhaps was just busy and had no time to, one out of them all who did not bother Him with cajolery and adjuration then pleading then threat and had not even bothered to inform Him in advance what he was about so that a lesser than He might have even missed the simple act of lifting the long ancestral musket down from the deerhorns above the door, whereupon He said *My name is Brown too* and the other *So is mine* and He *Then mine or yours cant be because I am against it* and the other *So am I* and He triumphantly *Then where are you going with that gun?* and the other told him in one sentence one word and He: amazed: Who knew neither hope nor pride nor grief *But your Association, your Committee, your Officers. Where are your Minutes, your Motions, your Parliamentary Procedures?* and the other *I aint against them. They are all right I reckon for them that have the time. I am just against the weak because they are niggers being held in bondage by the strong just because they are white.* So He turned once more to this land which He still intended to save because He had done so much for it—' and McCaslin

'What?' and he

'—to these people He was still committed to because they were his creations—' and McCaslin

'Turned back to us? His face to us?' and he

'—whose wives and daughters at least made

soups and jellies for them when they were sick and carried the trays through the mud and the winter too into the stinking cabins and sat in the stinking cabins and kept fires going until crises came and passed but that was not enough: and when they were very sick had them carried into the big house itself into the company room itself maybe and nursed them there which the white man would have done too for any other of his cattle that was sick but at least the man who hired one from a livery wouldn't have and still that was not enough: so that He said and not in grief either Who had made them and so could know no more of grief than He could of pride or hope: *Apparently they can learn nothing save through suffering, remember nothing save when underlined in blood*—' and McCaslin

'Ashby on an afternoon's ride, to call on some remote maiden cousins of his mother or maybe just acquaintances of hers, comes by chance upon a minor engagement of outposts and dismounts and with his crimson-lined cloak for target leads a handful of troops he never saw before against an entrenched position of backwoods-trained riflemen. Lee's battle-order, wrapped maybe about a handful of cigars and doubtless thrown away when the last cigar was smoked, found by a Yankee Intelligence officer on the floor of a saloon behind the Yankee lines after Lee had already divided his forces before Sharpsburg. Jackson on the Plank Road, already rolled up the flank which Hooker believed could not be turned and, waiting only for night to pass to continue the brutal and incessant slogging which would fling that whole wing back into Hooker's lap where he sat on a front gallery in Chancellorsville drinking rum toddies and telegraphing Lincoln that he had defeated Lee, is shot from among a whole covey of minor officers and in the blind night by one of his own patrols, leaving as next by seniority Stuart that gallant man born apparently already horsed and sabred and already knowing all there was to know about war except the slogging and brutal stupidity of it: and that same Stuart off raiding Pennsylvania hen-roosts when Lee should have known of all of Meade just where Hancock was on Cemetery Ridge: and Longstreet too at Gettysburg and that same Longstreet shot out of saddle by his own men in the dark by mistake just as Jackson was. His face to us? His face to us?' and he

'How else have made them fight? Who else but Jacksons and Stuarts and Ashbys and Morgans and Forrests?—the farmers of the central and middle-west, holding land by the acre instead of the tens or maybe even the hundreds, farming it themselves and to no single crop of cotton or tobacco or cane, owning no slaves and needing and wanting none and already looking toward the Pacific coast, not always as long as two generations there and having stopped where they did stop only through the fortuitous mischance that an ox died or a wagon-axle broke. And the New England mechanics who didn't even own land and measured all things by the weight of water and the cost of turning wheels and the narrow fringe of traders and ship-owners still looking backward across the Atlantic and attached to the continent only by their counting-houses. And those who should have had the alertness to see: the wildcat manipulators of mythical wilderness townsites; and the astuteness to rationalise: the bankers who held the mortgages on the land which the first were only waiting to abandon and on the railroads and steamboats to carry them still further west, and on the factories and the wheels and the rented tenements those who ran them lived in; and the leisure and scope to comprehend and fear in time and even anticipate: the Boston-bred (even when not born in Boston) spinster descendants of long lines of similarly-bred and likewise spinster aunts and uncles whose hands knew no callus except that of the indicting pen, to whom the wilderness itself began at the top of tide and who looked, if at anything other than Beacon Hill, only toward heaven—not to mention all the loud rabble of the camp-followers of pioneers: the bellowing of politicians, the mellifluous choiring of self-styled men of God, the—' and McCaslin

'Here, here. Wait a minute:' and he

'Let me talk now. I'm trying to explain to the head of my family something which I have got to do which I dont quite understand myself, not in justification of it but to explain it if I can. I could say I dont know why I must do it but that I do know I have got to because I have got myself to have to live with for the rest of my life and all I want is peace to do it in. But you are the head of my family. More. I knew a long time ago that I would never have to miss my father, even if you are just finding out that you have missed your son. —the drawers of bills and the shavers of notes and the schoolmasters and the self-ordained to teach and lead and all that horde of the semiliterate with a white shirt but no change for it, with one eye on themselves and watching each other with the other one. Who else could have made them fight: could have struck them so aghast with fear and dread as to turn shoulder to shoulder and face one way and even stop talking for a while and even after two years of it keep them still so wrung with terror that some among them would seriously propose moving their very capital into a foreign country lest it be ravaged and pillaged by a people whose entire white male population would have little more than filled any one of their larger cities: except Jackson in the Valley and three separate armies trying to catch him and none of them ever knowing whether they were just retreating from a battle or just running into one and Stuart riding his whole command entirely around the biggest single armed force this continent ever saw in order to see what it looked like from behind and Morgan leading a cavalry charge against a stranded man-of-war. Who else could have declared a war against a power with ten times the area and a hundred times the men and a thousand times the resources, except men who could believe that all necessary to conduct a successful war was not acumen nor shrewdness nor politics nor diplomacy nor money nor even integrity and simple arithmetic but just love of land and courage——'

'And an unblemished and gallant ancestry and the ability to ride a horse,' McCaslin said. 'Dont leave that out.' It was evening now, the tranquil sunset of October mazy with windless woodsmoke. The cotton was long since picked and ginned, and all day now the wagons loaded with gathered corn moved between field and crib, processional across the enduring land. 'Well, maybe that's what He wanted. At least, that's what He got.' This time there was no yellowed procession of fading and harmless ledger-pages. This was chronicled in a harsher book and McCaslin, fourteen and fifteen and sixteen, had seen it and the boy himself had inherited it as Noah's grandchildren had inherited the Flood although they had not been there to see the deluge: that dark corrupt and bloody time while three separate peoples had tried to adjust not only to one another but to the new land which they had created and inherited too and must live in for the reason that those who had lost it were no less free to quit it than those who had gained it were:—those upon whom freedom and equality had been dumped overnight and without warning or perparation or any training in how to employ it or even just endure it and who misused it not as children would nor yet because they had been so long in bondage and then so suddenly freed, but misused it as human beings always misuse freedom, so that he thought *Apparently there is a wisdom beyond even that learned through suffering necessary for a man to distinguish between liberty and license;* those who had fought for four years and lost to preserve a condition under which that franchisement was anomaly and paradox, not because they were opposed to freedom as freedom but for the old reasons for which man (not the generals and politicians but man) has always fought and died in wars: to preserve a status quo or to establish a better future one to endure for his children; and lastly, as if that were not enough for bitterness and hatred and fear, that third race even more alien to the people whom they resembled in pigment and in whom even the same blood ran, than to the people whom they did not,—that race threefold in one and alien even among themselves save for a single fierce will for rapine and pillage, composed of the sons of middleaged Quartermaster lieutenants and Army sutlers and contractors in military blankets and shoes and transport mules, who followed the battles they themselves had not fought and inherited the conquest they themselves had not helped to gain, sanctioned and protected even if not blessed, and left their bones and in another generation would be engaged in a fierce economic competition of small sloven farms with the black men they were supposed to have freed and the white descendants of fathers who had owned no slaves anyway whom they were supposed to have disinherited and in the third generation would be back once more in the little lost county seats as barbers and garage mechanics and deputy sheriffs and mill- and gin-hands and power-plant firemen, leading, first in mufti then later in an actual formalised regalia of hooded sheets and pass-words and fiery christian symbols, lynching mobs against the race their ancestors had come to save: and of all that other nameless horde of speculators in human misery, manipulators of money and politics and land, who follow catastrophe and are their own protection as grasshoppers are and need no blessing and sweat no plow or axe-helve and batten and vanish and leave no bones, just as they derived apparently from no ancestry, no mortal flesh, no act even of passion or even of lust: and the Jew who came without protection too since after two thousand years he had got out of the habit of being or needing it, and solitary, without even the solidarity of the locusts and in this a sort of courage since he had come thinking not in terms of simple pillage but in terms of his great-grandchildren, seeking yet some place to establish them to endure even though forever alien: and unblessed: a pariah about the face of the Western earth which twenty centuries later was still taking revenge on him for the fairy tale with which he had conquered it. McCaslin had actually seen it, and the boy even at almost eighty would never be able to distinguish certainly between what he had seen and what had been told him: a lightless and gutted and empty land where women crouched with the huddled children behind locked doors and men armed in sheets and masks rode the silent roads and the bodies of white and black both, victims not so much of hate as of desperation and despair, swung from lonely limbs: and men shot dead in polling-booths with the still wet pen in one hand and the unblotted ballot in the other: and a United States marshal in Jefferson who signed his official papers with a crude cross, an ex-slave called Sickymo, not at all because his ex-owner was a doctor and apothecary but because, still a slave, he would steal his master's grain alcohol and dilute it with water and peddle it in pint bottles from a cache beneath the roots of a big sycamore tree behind the drug store, who had attained his high office because his half-white sister was the concubine of the Federal A.P.M.: and this time McCaslin did not even say Look but merely lifted one hand, not even pointing, not even specifically toward the shelf of ledgers but toward the desk, toward the corner where it sat beside the scuffed patch on the floor where two decades of heavy shoes had stood while the white man at the desk added and multiplied and subtracted. And again he did not need to look because he had seen this himself and, twenty-three years after the Surrender and twenty-four after the Proclamation, was still watching it: the ledgers, new ones now and filled rapidly, succeeding one another rapidly and containing more names than old Carothers or even his father and Uncle Buddy had ever dreamed of; new names and new faces to go with them, among which the old names and faces that even his father and uncle would have recognised, were lost, vanished—Tomey's Terrel dead, and even the tragic and miscast Percival Brownlee, who couldn't keep books and couldn't farm either, found his true niche at last, reappeared in 1862 during the boy's father's absence and had apparently been living on the plantation for at least a month before his uncle found out about it, conducting impromptu revival meetings among negroes, preaching and leading the singing also in his high sweet true soprano voice and disappeared again on foot and at top speed, not behind but ahead of a body of raiding Federal horse and reappeared for the third and last time in the entourage of a travelling Army paymaster, the two of them passing through Jefferson in a surrey at the exact moment when the boy's father (it was 1866) also happened to be crossing the Square, the surrey and its occupants traversing rapidly that quiet and bucolic scene and even in that fleeting moment and to others beside the boy's father giving an illusion of flight and illicit holiday like a man on an excursion during his wife's absence with his wife's personal maid, until Brownlee glanced up and saw his late co-master and gave him one defiant female glance and then broke again, leaped from the surrey and disappeared this time for good and it was only by chance that McCaslin, twenty years later, heard of him again, an old man now and quite fat, as the well-to-do proprietor of a select New Orleans brothel; and Tennie's Jim gone, nobody knew where, and Fonsiba in Arkansas with her three dollars each month and the scholar-husband with his lenseless spectacles and frock coat and his plans for the spring; and only Lucas was left, the baby, the last save himself of old Carothers' doomed and fatal blood which in the male derivation seemed to destroy all it touched, and even he was repudiating and at least hoping to escape it;—Lucas, the boy of fourteen whose name would not even appear for six years yet among those rapid pages in the bindings new and dustless too since McCaslin lifted them down daily now to write into them the continuation of that record which two hundred years had not been enough to complete and another hundred would not be enough to discharge; that chronicle which was a whole land in miniature, which multiplied and compounded was the entire South, twenty-three years after surrender and twenty-four from emancipation—that slow trickle of molasses and meal and meat, of shoes and straw hats and overalls, of plowlines and collars and heel-bolts and buckheads and clevises, which returned each fall as cotton—the two threads frail as truth and impalpable as equators yet cable-strong to bind for life them who made the cotton to the land their sweat fell on: and he

'Yes. Binding them for a while yet, a little while yet. Through and beyond that life and maybe through and beyond the life of that life's sons and maybe even through and beyond that of the sons of those sons. But not always, because they will endure. They will outlast us because they are—' it was not a pause, barely a falter even, possibly appreciable only to himself, as if he couldn't speak even to McCaslin, even to explain his repudiation, that which to him too, even in the act of escaping (and maybe this was the reality and the truth of his need to escape) was heresy: so that even in escaping he was taking with him more of that evil and unregenerate old man who could summon because she was his property, a human being because she was old enough and female, to his widower's house and get a child on her and then dismiss her because she was of an inferior race, and then bequeath a thousand dollars to the infant because he would be dead then and wouldn't have to pay it, than even he had feared. 'Yes. He didn't want to. He had to. Because they will endure. They are better than we are. Stronger than we are. Their vices are vices aped from white men or that white men and bondage have taught them: improvidence and intemperance and evasion—not laziness: evasion: of what white men had set them to, not for their aggrandisement or even comfort but his own—' and McCaslin

'All right. Go on: Promiscuity. Violence. Instability and lack of control. Inability to distinguish between mine and thine—' and he

'How distinguish, when for two hundred years mine did not even exist for them?' and McCaslin

'All right. Go on. And their virtues—' and he

'Yes. Their own. Endurance—' and McCaslin

'So have mules:' and he

'—and pity and tolerance and forbearance and fidelity and love of children—' and McCaslin

'So have dogs:' and he

'—whether their own or not or black or not. And more: what they got not only not from white people but not even despite white people because they had it already from the old free fathers a longer time free than us because we have never been free—' and it was in McCaslin's eyes too, he had only to look at McCaslin's eyes and it was there, that summer twilight seven years ago, almost a week after they had returned from the camp before he discovered that Sam Fathers had told McCaslin: an old bear, fierce and ruthless not just to stay alive but ruthless with the fierce pride of liberty and freedom, jealous and proud enough of liberty and freedom to see it threatened not with fear nor even alarm but almost with joy, seeming deliberately to put it into jeopardy in order to savor it and keep his old strong bones and flesh supple and quick to defend and preserve it; an old man, son of a Negro slave and an Indian king, inheritor on the one hand of the long chronicle of a people who had learned humility through suffering and learned pride through the endurance which survived the suffering, and on the other side the chronicle of a people even longer in the land than the first, yet who now existed there only in the solitary brotherhood of an old and childless Negro's alien blood and the wild and invincible spirit of an old bear; a boy who wished to learn humility and pride in order to become skillful and worthy in the woods but found himself becoming so skillful so fast that he feared he would never become worthy because he had not learned humility and pride though he had tried, until one day an old man who could not have defined either led him as though by the hand to where an old bear and a little mongrel dog showed him that, by possessing one thing other, he would possess them both; and a little dog, nameless and mongrel and many-fathered, grown yet weighing less than six pounds, who couldn't be dangerous because there was nothing anywhere much smaller, not fierce because that would have been called just noise, not humble because it was already too near the ground to genuflect, and not proud because it would not have been close enough for anyone to discern what was casting that shadow and which didn't even know it was not going to heaven since they had already decided it had no immortal soul, so that all it could be was brave even though they would probably call that too just noise. *'And you didn't shoot,' McCaslin said. 'How close were you?'*

'I dont know,' he said. 'There was a big wood tick just inside his off hind leg. I saw that. But I didn't have the gun then.'

'But you didn't shoot when you had the gun,' McCaslin said. 'Why?' But McCaslin didn't wait, rising and crossing the room, across the pelt of the bear he had killed two years ago and the bigger one McCaslin had killed before he was born, to the bookcase beneath the mounted head of his first buck, and returned with the book and sat down again and opened it. 'Listen,' he said. He read the five stanzas aloud and closed the book on his finger and looked up. 'All right,' he said. 'Listen,' and read again, but only one stanza this time and closed the book and laid it on the table. 'She cannot fade, though thou hast not thy bliss,' McCaslin said: 'Forever wilt thou love, and she be fair.'

'He's talking about a girl,' he said.

'He had to talk about something,' McCaslin said. Then he said, 'He was talking about truth. Truth is one. It doesn't change. It covers all things which touch the heart—honor and pride and pity and justice and courage and love. Do you see now? He didn't know. Somehow it had seemed simpler than that, simpler than somebody talking in a book about a young man and a girl he would never need to grieve over because he could never approach any nearer and would never have to get any further away. He had heard about an old bear and finally got big enough to hunt it and he hunted it four years and at last met it with a gun in his hands and he didn't shoot. Because a little dog— But he could have shot long before the fyce covered the twenty yards to where the bear waited, and Sam Fathers could have shot at any time during the interminable minute while Old Ben stood on his hind legs over them. . . . He ceased. McCaslin watched him, still speaking, the voice, the words as quiet as the twilight itself was: 'Courage and honor and pride, and pity and love of justice and of liberty. They all touch the heart, and

what the heart holds to becomes truth, as far as we know truth. Do you see now?' and he could still hear them, intact in this twilight as in that one seven years ago, no louder still because they did not need to be because they would endure: and he had only to look at McCaslin's eyes beyond the thin and bitter smiling, the faint lip-lift which would have had to be called smiling;—his kins-man, his father almost, who had been born too late into the old time and too soon for the new, the two of them juxtaposed and alien now to each other against their ravaged patrimony, the dark and ravaged fatherland still prone and panting from its etherless operation:

'*Habet* then.—So this land is, indubitably, of and by itself cursed:' and he

'Cursed:' and again McCaslin merely lifted one hand, not even speaking and not even toward the ledgers: so that, as the stereopticon condenses into one instantaneous field the myriad minutia of its scope, so did that slight and rapid gesture establish in the small cramped and cluttered twilit room not only the ledgers but the whole plantation in its mazed and intricate entirety—the land, the fields and what they represented in terms of cotton ginned and sold, the men and women whom they fed and clothed and even paid a little cash money at Christmas-time in return for the labor which planted and raised and picked and ginned the cot-ton, the machinery and mules and gear with which they raised it and their cost and upkeep and re-placement—that whole edifice intricate and com-plex and founded upon injustice and erected by ruthless rapacity and carried on even yet with at times downright savagery not only to the human beings but the valuable animals too, yet solvent and efficient and, more than that: not only still in-tact but enlarged, increased; brought still intact by McCaslin, himself little more than a child then, through and out of the debacle and chaos of twen-ty years ago where hardly one in ten survived, and enlarged and increased and would continue so, sol-vent and efficient and intact and still increasing so long as McCaslin and his McCaslin successors lasted, even though their surnames might not even be Edmonds then: and he: '*Habet* too. Because that's it: not the land, but us. Not only the blood, but the name too; not only its color but its desig-nation: Edmonds, white, but, a female line, could have no other but the name his father bore; Beauchamp, the elder line and the male one, but, black, could have had any name he liked and no man would have cared, except the name his father bore who had no name—' and McCaslin

'And since I know too what you know I will say now, once more let me say it: And one other,

and in the third generation too, and the male, the eldest, the direct and sole and white and still McCaslin even, father to son to son—' and he

'I am free:' and this time McCaslin did not even gesture, no inference of fading pages, no postulation of the stereoptic whole, but the frail and iron thread strong as truth and impervious as evil and longer than life itself and reaching beyond record and patrimony both to join him with the lusts and passions, the hopes and dreams and griefs, of bones whose names while still fleshed and capable even old Carothers' grandfather had never heard: and he: 'And of that too:' and McCaslin

'Chosen, I suppose (I will concede it) out of all your time by Him as you say Buck and Buddy were from theirs. And it took Him a bear and an old man and four years just for you. And it took your fourteen years to reach that point and about that many, maybe more, for Old Ben, and more than seventy for Sam Fathers. And you are just one. How long then? How long?' and he

'It will be long. I have never said otherwise. But it will be all right because they will endure—' and McCaslin

'And anyway, you will be free.—No, not now nor ever, we from them nor they from us. So I repudiate too. I would deny even if I knew it were true. I would have to. Even you can see that I could do no else. I am what I am; I will be always what I was born and have always been. And more than me. More than me, just as there were more than Buck and Buddy in what you called His first plan which failed:' and he

'And more than me:' and McCaslin

'No. Not even you. Because mark. You said how on that instant when Ikkemotubbe realised that he could sell the land to Grandfather, it ceased forever to have been his. All right; go on: Then it belonged to Sam Fathers, old Ikkemotub-be's son. And who inherited from Sam Fathers, if not you? co-heir perhaps with Boon, if not of his life maybe, at least of his quitting it?' and he

'Yes. Sam Fathers set me free.' And Isaac Mc-Caslin, not yet Uncle Ike, a long time yet before he would be uncle to half a county and still father to none, living in one small cramped fireless rented room in a Jefferson boardinghouse where petit juries were domiciled during court terms and iten-erant horse- and mule-traders stayed, with his kit of brand-new carpenter's tools and the shotgun McCaslin had given him with his name engraved in silver and old General Compson's compass (and, when the General died, his silver-mounted horn too) and the iron cot and mattress and the blankets which he would take each fall into the woods for more than sixty years and the bright tin coffeepot

there had been a legacy, from his Uncle Hubert Beauchamp, his godfather, that bluff burly roaring childlike man from whom Uncle Buddy had won Tomey's Terrel's wife Tennie in the poker-game in 1859—'posible strait against three Treys in sigt Not called'—; no pale sentence or paragraph scrawled in cringing fear of death by a weak and trembling hand as a last desperate sop flung backward at retribution, but a Legacy, a Thing, possessing weight to the hand and bulk to the eye and even audible: a silver cup filled with gold pieces and wrapped in burlap and sealed with his godfather's ring in the hot wax, which (intact still) even before his Uncle Hubert's death and long before his own majority, when it would be his, had become not only a legend but one of the family lares. After his father's and his Uncle Hubert's sister's marriage they moved back into the big house, the tremendous cavern which old Carothers had started and never finished, cleared the remaining negroes out of it and with his mother's dowry completed it, at least the rest of the windows and doors and moved into it, all of them save Uncle Buddy who declined to leave the cabin he and his twin had built, the move being the bride's notion and more than just a notion and none ever to know if she really wanted to live in the big house or if she knew before hand that Uncle Buddy would refuse to move: and two weeks after his birth in 1867, the first time he and his mother came down stairs, one night and the silver cup sitting on the cleared dining-room table beneath the bright lamp and while his mother and his father and McCaslin and Tennie (his nurse: carrying him)—all of them again but Uncle Buddy—watched, his Uncle Hubert rang one by one into the cup the bright and glinting mintage and wrapped it into the burlap envelope and heated the wax and sealed it and carried it back home with him where he lived alone now without even his sister either to hold him down as McCaslin said or to try to raise him up as Uncle Buddy said, and (dark times then in Mississippi) Uncle Buddy said most of the niggers gone and the ones that didn't go even Hub Beauchamp could not have wanted: but the dogs remained and Uncle Buddy said Beauchamp fiddled while Nero fox-hunted.

they would go and see it there; at last his mother would prevail and they would depart in the surrey, once more all save Uncle Buddy and McCaslin to keep Uncle Buddy company until one winter Uncle Buddy began to fail and from then on it was himself, beginning to remember now,

and his mother and Tennie and Tomey's Terrel to drive: the twenty-two miles into the next county, the twin gateposts on one of which McCaslin could remember the half-grown boy blowing a fox-horn at breakfast dinner and supper-time and jumping down to open to any passer who happened to hear it but where there were no gates at all now, the shabby and overgrown entrance to what his mother still insisted that people call Warwick because her brother was if truth but triumphed and justice but prevailed the rightful earl of it, the paintless house which outwardly did not change but which on the inside seemed each time larger because he was too little to realise then that there was less and less in it of the fine furnishings, the rosewood and mahogany and walnut which for him had never existed anywhere anyway save in his mother's tearful lamentations and the occasional piece small enough to be roped somehow onto the rear or the top of the carriage on their return (And he remembered this, he had seen it: an instant, a flash, his mother's soprano 'Even my dress! Even my dress!' loud and outraged in the barren unswept hall; a face young and female and even lighter in color than Tomey's Terrel's for an instant in a closing door; a swirl, a glimpse of the silk gown and the flick and glint of an ear-ring: an apparition rapid and tawdry and illicit yet somehow even to the child, the infant still almost, breathless and exciting and evocative: as though, like two limpid and pellucid streams meeting, the child which he still was had made serene and absolute and perfect rapport and contact through that glimpsed nameless illicit hybrid female flesh with the boy which had existed in that stage of inviolable and immortal adolescence in his uncle for almost sixty years; the dress, the face, the ear-rings gone in that same aghast flash and his uncle's voice: 'She's my cook! She's my new cook! I had to have a cook, didn't I?' then the uncle himself, the face alarmed and aghast too yet still innocently and somehow even indomitably of a boy, they retreating in their turn now, back to the front gallery, and his uncle again, pained and still amazed, in a sort of desperate resurgence if not of courage at least of self-assertion: 'They're free now! They're folks too just like we are!' and his mother: 'That's why! That's why! My mother's house! Defiled! Defiled!' and his uncle: 'Damn it, Sibbey, at least give her time to pack her grip:' then over, finished, the loud uproar and all, himself and Tennie and he remembered Tennie's inscrutable face at the broken shutterless window of the bare room which had once been the parlor while they watched, hurrying down the lane at a stumbling trot, the routed compounder of his uncle's uxory:

the back, the nameless face which he had seen only for a moment, the once-hooped dress ballooning and flapping below a man's overcoat, the worn heavy carpet-bag jouncing and banging against her knee, routed and in retreat true enough and in the empty lane solitary young-looking and forlorn yet withal still exciting and evocative and wearing still the silken banner captured inside the very citadel of respectability, and unforgettable.)

the cup, the sealed inscrutable burlap, sitting on the shelf in the locked closet, Uncle Hubert unlocking the door and lifting it down and passing it from hand to hand: his mother, his father, McCaslin and even Tennie, insisting that each take it in turn and heft it for weight and shake it again to prove the sound, Uncle Hubert himself standing spraddled before the cold unswept hearth in which the very bricks themselves were crumbling into a litter of soot and dust and mortar and the droppings of chimney-sweeps, still roaring and still innocent and still indomitable: and for a long time he believed nobody but himself had noticed that his uncle now put the cup only into his hands, unlocked the door and lifted it down and put it into his hands and stood over him until he had shaken it obediently until it sounded then took it from him and locked it back into the closet before anyone else could have offered to touch it, and even later, when competent not only to remember but to rationalise, he could not say what it was or even if it had been anything because the parcel was still heavy and still rattled, not even when, Uncle Buddy dead and his father, at last and after almost seventy-five years in bed after the sun rose, said: 'Go get that damn cup. Bring that damn Hub Beauchamp too if you have to:' because it still rattled though his uncle no longer put it even into his hands now but carried it himself from one to the other, his mother, McCaslin, Tennie, shaking it before each in turn, saying: 'Hear it? Hear it?' his face still innocent, not quite baffled but only amazed and not very amazed and still indomitable: and, his father and Uncle Buddy both gone now, one day without reason or any warning the almost completely empty house in which his uncle and Tennie's ancient and quarrelsome great-grandfather (who claimed to have seen Lafayette and McCaslin said in another ten years would be remembering God) lived, cooked and slept in one single room, burst into peaceful conflagration, a tranquil instantaneous sourceless unanimity of combustion, walls floors and roof: at sunup it stood where his uncle's father had built it sixty years ago, at sundown the four blackened and smokeless chimneys rose from a light white powder of ashes and a few charred ends of planks which did not even appear to have been very hot: and out of the last of evening, the last one of the twenty-two miles, on the old white mare which was the last of that stable which McCaslin remembered, the two old men riding double up to the sister's door, the one wearing his fox-horn on its braided deerhide thong and the other carrying the burlap parcel wrapped in a shirt, the tawny wax-daubed shapeless lump sitting again and on an almost identical shelf and his uncle holding the half-opened door now, his hand not only on the knob but one foot against it and the key waiting in the other hand, the face urgent and still not baffled but still and even indomitably not very amazed and himself standing in the half-opened door looking quietly up at the burlap shape become almost three times its original height and a good half less than its original thickness and turning away and he would remember not his mother's look this time nor yet Tennie's inscrutable expression but McCaslin's dark and aquiline face grave insufferable and bemused: then one night they waked him and fetched him still half-asleep into the lamp light, the smell of medicine which was familiar by now in that room and the smell of something else which he had not smelled before and knew at once and would never forget, the pillow, the worn and ravaged face from which looked out still the boy innocent and immortal and amazed and urgent, looking at him and trying to tell him until McCaslin moved and leaned over the bed and drew from the top of the night shirt the big iron key on the greasy cord which suspended it, the eyes saying Yes Yes Yes now, and cut the cord and unlocked the closet and brought the parcel to the bed, the eyes still trying to tell him even when he took the parcel so that was still not it, the hands still clinging to the parcel even while relinquishing it, the eyes more urgent than ever trying to tell him but they never did; and he was ten and his mother was dead too and McCaslin said, 'You are almost halfway now. You might as well open it:' and he: 'No. He said twenty-one:' and he was twenty-one and McCaslin shifted the bright lamp to the center of the cleared dining-room table and set the parcel beside it and laid his open knife beside the parcel and stood back with that expression of old grave intolerant and repudiating and he lifted it, the burlap lump which fifteen years ago had changed its shape completely overnight, which shaken gave forth a thin weightless not-quite-musical curiously muffled clatter, the bright knife-blade hunting amid the mazed intricacy of string, the knobby gouts of wax bearing his uncle's Beauchamp seal rattling onto the table's polished top and, standing amid the collapse of burlap folds, the unstained tin coffeepot still brand new, the handful of copper coins and now he knew what had given them the muffled sound: a collection of minutely-folded scraps of paper sufficient almost for a rat's nest, of good linen bond, of the crude ruled paper such as negroes use, of raggedly-torn ledger-pages and the margins of newspapers and once the paper label from a new pair of overalls, all dated and all signed, beginning with the first one not six months after they had watched him seal the silver cup into the burlap on this same table in this same room by the light even of this same lamp almost twenty-one years ago:

I owe my Nephew Isaac Beauchamp Mc-Caslin five (5) pieces Gold which I,O.U constitutes My note of hand with Interest at 5 percent.
Hubert Fitz-Hubert Beauchamp
at Warwick 27 Nov 1867

and he: 'Anyway he called it Warwick:' once at least, even if no more. But there was more:

Isaac 24 Dec 1867 I.O.U. 2 pieces Gold H.Fh.B. I.O.U. Isaac 1 piece Gold 1 Jan 1868 H.Fh.B.

then five again then three then one then one then a long time and what dream, what dreamed splendid recoup, out of any injury or betrayal of trust because it had been merely a loan: nay, a partnership:

I.O.U. Beauchamp McCaslin or his heirs twenty-five (25) pieces Gold This & All preceeding constituting My notes of hand at twenty (20) percentum compounded annually. This date of 19th January 1873
Beauchamp

no location save that in time and signed by the single not name but word as the old proud earl himself might have scrawled Nevile: and that made forty-three and he could not remember himself of course but the legend had it at fifty, which balanced: one: then one: then one: then one and then the last three and then the last chit, dated after he came to live in the house with them and written in the shaky hand not of a beaten old man because he had never been beaten to know it but of a tired old man maybe and even at that tired only on the outside and still indomitable, the simplicity of the last one the simplicity not of resignation but merely of amazement, like a sim-

ple comment or remark, and not very much of that:

One silver cup. Hubert Beauchamp

and McCaslin: 'So you have plenty of coppers anyway. But they are still not old enough yet to be either rarities or heirlooms. So you will have to take the money:' except that he didn't hear McCaslin, standing quietly beside the table and looking peacefully at the coffee-pot and the pot sitting one night later on the mantel above what was not even a fireplace in the little cramped icelike room in Jefferson as McCaslin tossed the folded banknotes onto the bed and, still standing (there was nowhere to sit save on the bed) did not even remove his hat and overcoat: and he

'As a loan. From you. This one:' and McCaslin

'You cant. I have no money that I can lend to you. And you will have to go to the bank and get it next month because I wont bring it to you:' and he could not hear McCaslin now either, looking peacefully at McCaslin, his kinsman, his father almost yet no kin now as, at the last, even fathers and sons are no kin: and he

'It's seventeen miles, horseback and in the cold. We could both sleep here:' and McCaslin

'Why should I sleep here in my house when you wont sleep yonder in yours?' and gone, and he looking at the bright rustless unstained tin and thinking and not for the first time how much it takes to compound a man (Isaac McCaslin for instance) and of the devious intricate choosing yet unerring path that man's (Isaac McCaslin's for instance) spirit takes among all that mass to make him at last what he is to be, not only to the astonishment of them (the ones who sired the McCaslin who sired his father and Uncle Buddy and their sister, and the ones who sired the Beauchamp who sired his Uncle Hubert and his Uncle Hubert's sister) who believed they had shaped him, but to Isaac McCaslin too

as a loan and used it though he would not have had to: Major de Spain offered him a room in his house as long as he wanted it and asked nor would ever ask any question, and old General Compson more than that, to take him into his own room, to sleep in half of his own bed and more than Major de Spain because he told him baldly why: 'You sleep with me and before this winter is out, I'll know the reason. You'll tell me. Because I dont believe you just quit. It looks like you just quit but I have watched you in the woods too much and I dont believe you just quit even if it does look damn like it:' using it as a loan, paid his board and rent for a month and bought the tools, not simply because he was good with his hands because he had intended to use his hands and it could have been with horses, and not in mere static and hopeful emulation of the Nazarene as the young gambler buys a spotted shirt because the old gambler won in one yesterday, but (without the arrogance of false humility and without the false humbleness of pride, who intended to earn his bread, didn't especially want to earn it but had to earn it and for more than just bread) because if the Nazarene had found carpentering good for the life and ends He had assumed and elected to serve, it would be all right too for Isaac McCaslin even though Isaac McCaslin's ends, although simple enough in their apparent motivation, were and would be always incomprehensible to him, and his life, invincible enough in its needs, if he could have helped himself, not being the Nazarene, he would not have chosen it: and paid it back. He had forgotten the thirty dollars which McCaslin would put into the bank in his name each month, fetched it in to him and flung it onto the bed that first one time but no more; he had a partner now or rather he was the partner: a blasphemous profane clever old dipsomaniac who had built blockade-runners in Charleston in '62 and '3 and had been a ship's carpenter since and appeared in Jefferson two years ago nobody knew from where nor why and spent a good part of his time since recovering from delirium tremens in the jail; they had put a new roof on the stable of the bank's president and (the old man in jail again still celebrating that job) he went to the bank to collect for it and the president said, 'I should borrow from you instead of paying you:' and it had been seven months now and he remembered for the first time, two-hundred-and-ten dollars, and this was the first job of any size and when he left the bank the account stood at two-twenty, two-forty to balance, only twenty dollars more to go, then it did balance though by then the total had increased to three hundred and thirty and he said, "I will transfer it now:' and the president said, 'I cant do that. McCaslin told me not to. Haven't you got another initial you could use and open another account?' but that was all right, the coins the silver and the bills as they accumulated knotted into a handkerchief and the coffee-pot wrapped in an old shirt as when Tennie's great-grandfather had fetched it from Warwick eighteen years ago, in the bottom of the iron-bound trunk which old Carothers had brought from Carolina and his landlady said, 'Not even a lock! And you dont even lock your door, not even when you leave!' and himself looking at her as peacefully as he had looked at McCaslin that first night in this same room, no kin to him at all yet more than kin as those who serve you even for pay are your kin and those who injure you are more than brother or wife

and had the wife now, got the old man out of jail and fetched him to the rented room and sobered him by superior strength, did not even remove his own shoes for twenty-four hours, got him up and got food into him and they built the barn this time from the ground up and he married her: an only child, a small girl yet curiously bigger than she seemed at first, solider perhaps, with dark eyes and a passionate heart-shaped face, who had time even on that farm to watch most of the day while he sawed timbers to the old man's measurements: and she: 'Papa told me about you. That farm is really yours, isn't it?' and he

'And McCaslin's:' and she

'Was there a will leaving half of it to him?' and he

'There didn't need to be a will. His grandmother was my father's sister. We were the same as brothers:' and she

'You are the same as second cousins and that's all you ever will be. But I dont suppose it matters:' and they were married, they were married and it was the new country, his heritage too as it was the heritage of all, out of the earth, beyond the earth yet of the earth because his too was of the earth's long chronicle, his too because each must share with another in order to come into it and in the sharing they become one: for that while, one: for that little while at least, one: indivisible, that while at least irrevocable and unrecoverable, living in a rented room still but for just a little while and that room wall-less and top-less and floorless in glory for him to leave each morning and return to at night; her father already owned the lot in town and furnished the material and he and his partner would build it, her dowry from one: her wedding-present from three, she not to know it until the bungalow was finished and ready to be moved into and he never know who told her, not her father and not his partner and not even in drink though for a while he believed that, himself coming home from work and just time to wash and rest a moment before going down to supper, entering no rented cubicle since it would still partake of glory even after they would have grown old and lost it: and he saw her face then, just before she spoke: 'Sit down:' the two of them sitting on the bed's edge, not even touching yet, her face strained and terrible, her voice a passionate and expiring whisper of immeasurable promise: 'I love you. You know I love you. When are we going to move?' and he

'I didn't—I didn't know—Who told you—' the

hot fierce palm clapped over his mouth, crushing his lips into his teeth, the fierce curve of fingers digging into his cheek and only the palm slacked off enough for him to answer:

'The farm. Our farm. Your farm:' and he

'I—' then the hand again, finger and palm, the whole enveloping weight of her although she still was not touching him save the hand, the voice: 'No! No!' and the fingers themselves seeming to follow through the cheek the impulse to speech as it died in his mouth, then the whisper, the breath again, of love and of incredible promise, the palm slackening again to let him answer:

'When?' and he

'I—' then she was gone, the hand too, standing, her back to him and her head bent, the voice so calm now that for an instant it seemed no voice of hers that he ever remembered: 'Stand up and turn your back and shut your eyes:' and repeated before he understood and stood himself with his eyes shut and heard the bell ring for supper below stairs and the calm voice again: 'Lock the door:' and he did so and leaned his forehead against the cold wood, his eyes closed, hearing his heart and the sound he had begun to hear before he moved until it ceased and the bell rang again below stairs and he knew it was for them this time and he heard the bed and turned and he had never seen her naked before, he had asked her to once, and why: that he wanted to see her naked because he loved her and he wanted to see her looking at him naked because he loved her but after that he never mentioned it again, even turning his face when she put the nightgown on over her dress to undress at night and putting the dress on over the gown to remove it in the morning and she would not let him get into bed beside her until the lamp was out and even in the heat of summer she would draw the sheet up over them both before she would let him turn to her: and the landlady came up the stairs up the hall and rapped on the door and then called their names but she didn't move, lying still on the bed outside the covers, her face turned away on the pillow, listening to nothing, thinking of nothing, not of him anyway he thought then the landlady went away and she said, 'Take off your clothes:' her head still turned away, looking at nothing, thinking of nothing, waiting for nothing, not even him, her hand moving as though with volition and vision of its own, catching his wrist at the exact moment when he paused beside the bed so that he never paused but merely changed the direction of moving, downward now, the hand drawing him and she moved at last, shifted, a movement one single complete inherent not practiced and one time older than man, looking at

him now, drawing him still downward with the one hand down and down and he neither saw nor felt it shift, palm flat against his chest now and holding him away with the same apparent lack of any effort or any need for strength, and not looking at him now, she didn't need to, the chaste woman, the wife, already looked upon all the men who ever rutted and now her whole body had changed, altered, he had never seen it but once and now it was not even the one he had seen but composite of all woman-flesh since man that ever of its own will reclined on its back and opened, and out of it somewhere, without any movement of lips even, the dying and invincible whisper: 'Promise:' and he

'Promise?'

'The farm.' He moved. He had moved, the hand shifting from his chest once more to his wrist, grasping it, the arm still lax and only the light increasing pressure of the fingers as though arm and hand were a piece of wire cable with one looped end, only the hand tightening as he pulled against it. 'No,' he said. 'No:' and she was not looking at him still but not like the other but still the hand: 'No, I tell you. I wont. I cant. Never:' and still the hand and he said, for the last time, he tried to speak clearly and he knew it was still gently and he thought, *She already knows more than I with all the man-listening in camps where there was nothing to read ever even heard of. They are born already bored with what a boy approaches only at fourteen and fifteen with blundering and aghast trembling:* 'I cant. Not ever. Remember:' and still the steady and invincible hand and he said Yes and he thought, *She is lost. She was born lost. We were all born lost* then he stopped thinking and even saying Yes, it was like nothing he had ever dreamed, let alone heard in mere man-talking until after a no-time he returned and lay spent on the insatiate immemorial beach and again with a movement one time more older than man she turned and freed herself and on their wedding night she had cried and he thought she was crying now at first, into the tossed and wadded pillow, the voice coming from somewhere between the pillow and the cachinnation: 'And that's all. That's all from me. If this dont get you that son you talk about, it wont be mine:' lying on her side, her back to the empty rented room, laughing and laughing

5

HE WENT back to the camp one more time before the lumber company moved in and began to cut the timber. Major de Spain himself never saw it again. But he made them welcome to use the house and hunt the land whenever they liked, and in the winter following the last hunt when Sam Fathers and Lion died, General Compson and Walter Ewell invented a plan to corporate themselves, the old group, into a club and lease the camp and the hunting privileges of the woods—an invention doubtless of the somewhat childish old General but actually worthy of Boon Hogganbeck himself. Even the boy, listening, recognized it for the subterfuge it was: to change the leopard's spots when they could not alter the leopard, a baseless and illusory hope to which even McCaslin seemed to subscribe for a while, that once they had persuaded Major de Spain to return to the camp he might revoke himself, which even the boy knew he would not do. And he did not. The boy never knew what occurred when Major de Spain declined. He was not present when the subject was broached and McCaslin never told him. But when June came and the time for the double birthday celebration there was no mention of it and when November came no one spoke of using Major de Spain's house and he never knew whether or not Major de Spain knew they were going on the hunt though without doubt old Ash probably told him: he and McCaslin and General Compson (and that one was the General's last hunt too) and Walter and Boon and Tennie's Jim and old Ash loaded two wagons and drove two days and almost forty miles beyond any country the boy had ever seen before and lived in tents for the two weeks. And the next spring they heard (not from Major de Spain) that he had sold the timber-rights to a Memphis lumber company and in June the boy came to town with McCaslin one Saturday and went to Major de Spain's office—the big, airy, book-lined second-storey room with windows at one end opening upon the shabby hinder purlieus of stores and at the other a door giving onto the railed balcony above the Square, with its curtained alcove where sat a cedar water-bucket and a sugar-bowl and spoon and tumbler and a wicker-covered demijohn of whiskey, and the bamboo-and-paper punkah swinging back and forth above the desk while old Ash in a tilted chair beside the entrance pulled the cord.

"Of course," Major de Spain said. "Ash will probably like to get off in the woods himself for a while, where he wont have to eat Daisy's cooking. Complain about it, anyway. Are you going to take anybody with you?"

"No sir," he said. "I thought that maybe Boon—" For six months now Boon had been town-marshall at Hoke's; Major de Spain had compounded with the lumber company—or per-

haps compromised was closer, since it was the lumber company who had decided that Boon might be better as a town-marshall than head of a logging gang.

"Yes," Major de Spain said. "I'll wire him today. He can meet you at Hoke's. I'll send Ash on by the train and they can take some food in and all you will have to do will be to mount your horse and ride over."

"Yes sir," he said. "Thank you." And he heard his voice again. He didn't know he was going to say it yet he did know, he had known it all the time: "Maybe if you . . ." His voice died. It was stopped, he never knew how because Major de Spain did not speak and it was not until his voice ceased that Major de Spain moved, turned back to the desk and the papers spread on it and even that without moving because he was sitting at the desk with a paper in his hand when the boy entered, the boy standing there looking down at the short plumpish grey-haired man in sober fine broadcloth and an immaculate glazed shirt whom he was used to seeing in boots and muddy corduroy, unshaven, sitting the shaggy powerful long-hocked mare with the worn Winchester carbine across the saddlebow and the great blue dog standing motionless as bronze at the stirrup, the two of them in that last year and to the boy anyway coming to resemble one another somehow as two people competent for love or for business who have been in love or in business together for a long time sometimes do. Major de Spain did not look up again.

"No. I will be too busy. But good luck to you. If you have it, you might bring me a young squirrel."

"Yes sir," he said. "I will."

He rode his mare, the three-year-old filly he had bred and raised and broken himself. He left home a little after midnight and six hours later, without even having sweated her, he rode into Hoke's, the tiny log-line junction which he had always thought of as Major de Spain's property too although Major de Spain had merely sold the company (and that many years ago) the land on which the sidetracks and loading-platforms and the commissary store stood, and looked about in shocked and grieved amazement even though he had had forewarning and had believed himself prepared: a new planing-mill already half completed which would cover two or three acres and what looked like miles and miles of stacked steel rails red with the light bright rust of newness and of piled crossties sharp with creosote, and wire corrals and feeding-troughs for two hundred mules at least and the tents for the men who drove them;

so that he arranged for the care and stabling of his mare as rapidly as he could and did not look any more, mounted into the log-train caboose with his gun and climbed into the cupola and looked no more save toward the wall of wilderness ahead within which he would be able to hide himself from it once more anyway.

Then the little locomotive shrieked and began to move: a rapid churning of exhaust, a lethargic deliberate clashing of slack couplings traveling backward along the train, the exhaust changing to the deep slow clapping bites of power as the caboose too began to move and from the cupola he watched the train's head complete the first and only curve in the entire line's length and vanish into the wilderness, dragging its length of train behind it so that it resembled a small dingy harmless snake vanishing into weeds, drawing him with it too until soon it ran once more at its maximum clattering speed between the twin walls of unaxed wilderness as of old. It had been harmless once. Not five years ago Walter Ewell had shot a six-point buck from this same moving caboose, and there was the story of the half-grown bear: the train's first trip in to the cutting thirty miles away, the bear between the rails, its rear end elevated like that of a playing puppy while it dug to see what sort of ants or bugs they might contain or perhaps just to examine the curious symmetrical squared barkless logs which had appeared apparently from nowhere in one endless mathematical line overnight, still digging until the driver on the braked engine not fifty feet away blew the whistle at it, whereupon it broke frantically and took the first tree it came to: an ash sapling not much bigger than a man's thigh and climbed as high as it could and clung there, its head ducked between its arms as a man (a woman perhaps) might have done while the brakeman threw chunks of ballast at it, and when the engine returned three hours later with the first load of outbound logs the bear was halfway down the tree and once more scrambled back up as high as it could and clung again while the train passed and was still there when the engine went in again in the afternoon and still there when it came back out at dusk; and Boon had been in Hoke's with the wagon after a barrel of flour that noon when the train-crew told about it and Boon and Ash, both twenty years younger then, sat under the tree all that night to keep anybody from shooting it and the next morning Major de Spain had the log-train held at Hoke's and just before sundown on the second day, with not only Boon and Ash but Major de Spain and General Compson and Walter and McCaslin, twelve then, watching, it came down

the tree after almost thirty-six hours without even water and McCaslin told him how for a minute they thought it was going to stop right there at the barrow-pit where they were standing and drink, how it looked at the water and paused and looked at them and at the water again, but did not, gone, running, as bears run, the two sets of feet, front and back, tracking two separate though parallel courses.

It had been harmless then. They would hear the passing log-train sometimes from the camp; sometimes, because nobody bothered to listen for it or not. They would hear it going in, running light and fast, the light clatter of the trucks, the exhaust of the diminutive locomotive and its shrill peanut-parcher whistle flung for one petty moment and absorbed by the brooding and inattentive wilderness without even an echo. They would hear it going out, loaded, not quite so fast now yet giving its frantic and toylike illusion of crawling speed, not whistling now to conserve steam, flinging its bitten laboring miniature puffing into the immemorial woodsface with frantic and bootless vainglory, empty and noisy and puerile, carrying to no destination or purpose sticks which left nowhere any scar or stump as the child's toy loads and transports and unloads its dead sand and rushes back for more, tireless and unceasing and rapid yet never quite so fast as the Hand which plays with it moves the toy burden back to load the toy again. But it was different now. It was the same train, engine cars and caboose, even the same enginemen brakeman and conductor to whom Boon, drunk then sober then drunk again then fairly sober once more all in the space of fourteen hours, had bragged that day two years ago about what they were going to do to Old Ben tomorrow, running with its same illusion of frantic rapidity between the same twin walls of impenetrable and impervious woods, passing the old landmarks, the old game crossings over which he had trailed bucks wounded and not wounded and more than once seen them, anything but wounded, bolt out of the woods and up and across the embankment which bore the rails and ties then down and into the woods again as the earth-bound supposedly move but crossing as arrows travel, groundless, elongated, three times its actual length and even paler, different in color, as if there were a point between immobility and absolute motion where even mass chemically altered, changing without pain or agony not only in bulk and shape but in color too, approaching the color of wind, yet this time it was as though the train (and not only the train but himself, not only his vision which had seen it and his memory which remembered it but his clothes too, as garments carry back into the clean edgeless blowing of air the lingering effluvium of a sick-room or of death) had brought with it into the doomed wilderness even before the actual axe the shadow and portent of the new mill not even finished yet and the rails and ties which were not even laid; and he knew now what he had known as soon as he saw Hoke's this morning but had not yet thought into words: why Major de Spain had not come back, and that after this time he himself, who had had to see it one time other, would return no more.

Now they were near. He knew it before the engine-driver whistled to warn him. Then he saw Ash and the wagon, the reins without doubt wrapped once more about the brake-lever as within the boy's own memory Major de Spain had been forbidding him for eight years to do, the train slowing, the slackened couplings jolting and clashing again from car to car, the caboose slowing past the wagon as he swung down with his gun, the conductor leaning out above him to signal the engine, the caboose still slowing, creep-ing, although the engine's exhaust was already slatting in mounting tempo against the unecho-ing wilderness, the crashing of draw-bars once more travelling backward along the train, the ca-boose picking up speed at last. Then it was gone. It had not been. He could no longer hear it. The wilderness soared, musing, inattentive, myriad, eternal, green; older than any mill-shed, longer than any spur-line. "Mr Boon here yet?" he said.

"He beat me in," Ash said. "Had the wagon loaded and ready for me at Hoke's yistiddy when I got there and setting on the front steps at camp last night when I got in. He already been in the woods since fo daylight this morning. Said he gwine up to the Gum Tree and for you to hunt up that way and meet him." He knew where that was: a single big sweet-gum just outside the woods, in an old clearing; if you crept up to it very quietly this time of year and then ran suddenly into the clear-ing, sometimes you caught as many as a dozen squirrels in it, trapped, since there was no other tree near they could jump to. So he didn't get into the wagon at all.

"I will," he said.

"I figured you would," Ash said, "I fotch you a box of shells." He passed the shells down and be-gan to unwrap the lines from the brake-pole.

"How many times up to now do you reckon Major has told you not to do that?" the boy said.

"Do which?" Ash said. Then he said: "And tell Boon Hogganbeck dinner gonter be on the table in a hour and if yawl want any to come on and eat it."

"In an hour?" he said. "It aint nine oclock yet." He drew out his watch and extended it face-toward Ash. "Look." Ash didn't even look at the watch.

"That's town time. You aint in town now. You in the woods."

"Look at the sun then."

"Nemmine the sun too," Ash said. "If you and Boon Hogganbeck want any dinner, you better come on in and get it when I tole you. I aim to get done in that kitchen because I got my wood to chop. And watch your feet. They're crawling."

"I will," he said.

Then he was in the woods, not alone but soli-tary; the solitude closed about him, green with summer. They did not change, and, timeless, would not, anymore than would the green of sum-mer and the fire and rain of fall and the iron cold and sometimes even snow

the day, the morning when he killed the buck and Sam marked his face with its hot blood, they returned to camp and he remembered old Ash's blinking and disgruntled and even outraged dis-belief until at last McCaslin had had to affirm the fact that he had really killed it: and that night Ash sat snarling and unapproachable behind the stove so that Tennie's Jim had to serve the supper and waked them with breakfast already on the table the next morning and it was only half-past one oclock and at last out of Major de Spain's angry cursing and Ash's snarling and sullen re-joinders the fact emerged that Ash not only wanted to go into the woods and shoot a deer also but he intended to and Major de Spain said, 'By God, if we dont let him we will probably have to do the cooking from now on:' and Walter Ewell said, 'Or get up at midnight to eat what Ash cooks:' and since he had already killed his buck for this hunt and was not to shoot again unless they needed meat, he offered his gun to Ash un-til Major de Spain took command and allotted that gun to Boon for the day and gave Boon's un-predictable pump gun to Ash, with two buckshot shells but Ash said, 'I got shells:' and showed them, four: one buck, one of number three shot for rabbits, two of birdshot and told one by one their history and their origin and he remembered not Ash's face alone but Major de Spain's and Walter's and General Compson's too, and Ash's voice: 'Shoot? In course they'll shoot! Genl Cawmpson guv me this un'—the buckshot—'right outen the same gun he kilt that big buck with eight years ago. And this un'—it was the rabbit shell: triumphantly—'is oldern thisyer boy!' And that morning he loaded the gun him-self, reversing the order: the bird-shot, the rabbit, then the buck so that the buckshot would feed first into the chamber, and himself without a gun, he and Ash walked beside Major de Spain's and Tennie's Jim's horses and the dogs (that was the snow) until they cast and struck, the sweet strong cries ringing away into the muffled falling air and gone almost immediately, as if the constant and unmurmuring flakes had already buried even the unformed echoes beneath their myriad and weightless falling, Major de Spain and Tennie's Jim gone too, whooping on into the woods; and then it was all right, he knew as plainly as if Ash had told him that Ash had now hunted his deer and that even his tender years had been forgiven for having killed one, and they turned back to-ward home through the falling snow—that is, Ash said, 'Now whut?' and he said, 'This way'—him-self in front because, although they were less than a mile from camp, he knew that Ash, who had spent two weeks of his life in the camp each year for the last twenty, had no idea whatever where they were, until quite soon the manner in which Ash carried Boon's gun was making him a good deal more than just nervous and he made Ash walk in front, striding on, talking now, an old man's garrulous monologue beginning with where he was at the moment then of the woods and of camping in the woods and of eating in camps then of eating then of cooking it and of his wife's cook-ing then briefly of his old wife and almost at once and at length of a new light-colored woman who nursed next door to Major de Spain's and if she didn't watch out who she was switching her tail at he would show her how old was an old man or not if his wife just didn't watch him all the time, the two of them in a game trail through a dense brake of cane and brier which would bring them out within a quarter-mile of camp, approaching a big fallen tree-trunk lying athwart the path and just as Ash, still talking, was about to step over it the bear, the yearling, rose suddenly beyond the log, sitting up, its forearms against its chest and its wrists limply arrested as if it had been surprised in the act of covering its face to pray: and after a certain time Ash's gun yawed jerkily up and he said, 'You haven't got a shell in the barrel yet. Pump it:' but the gun already snicked and he said, 'Pump it. You haven't got a shell in the bar-rel yet:' and Ash pumped the action and in a certain time the gun steadied again and snicked and he said, 'Pump it:' and watched the buckshot shell jerk, spinning heavily, into the cane. This is the rabbit shot: he thought and the gun snicked and he thought: The next is bird-shot: and he

didn't have to say Pump it; he cried, 'Dont shoot! Dont shoot!' but that was already too late too, the light dry vicious snick! before he could speak and the bear turned and dropped to all-fours and then was gone and there was only the log, the cane, the velvet and constant snow and Ash said, 'Now whut?' and he said, 'This way. Come on:' and began to back away down the path and Ash said, 'I got to find my shells:' and he said, 'Goddamn it, goddamn it, come on:' but Ash leaned the gun against the log and returned and stooped and fumbled among the cane roots until he came back and stooped and found the shells and they rose and at that moment the gun, untouched, leaning against the log six feet away and for that while even forgotten by both of them, roared, bellowed and flamed, and ceased: and he carried it now, pumped out the last mummified shell and gave that one also to Ash and, the action still open, himself carried the gun until he stood it in the corner behind Boon's bed at the camp

—; summer, and fall, and snow, and wet and saprife spring in their ordered immortal sequence, the deathless and immemorial phases of the mother who had shaped him if any had toward the man he almost was, mother and father both to the old man born of a Negro slave and a Chicka-saw chief who had been his spirit's father if any had, whom he had revered and harkened to and loved and lost and grieved: and he would marry someday and they too would own for their brief while that brief unsubstanced glory which inher-ently of itself cannot last and hence why glory: and they would, might, carry even the remem-brance of it into the time when flesh no longer talks to flesh because memory at least does last: but still the woods would be his mistress and his wife.

He was not going toward the Gum Tree. Ac-tually he was getting farther from it. Time was and not so long ago either when he would not have been allowed here without someone with him, and a little later, when he had begun to learn how much he did not know, he would not have dared be here without someone with him, and later still, be-ginning to ascertain, even if only dimly, the limits of what he did not know, he could have attempted and carried it through with a compass, not be-cause of any increased belief in himself but be-cause McCaslin and Major de Spain and Walter and General Compson too had taught him at last to believe the compass regardless of what it seemed to state. Now he did not even use the compass but merely the sun and that only subconsciously, yet he could have taken a scaled map and plotted at any time to within a hundred feet of where he actually was; and sure enough, at almost the exact moment when he expected it, the earth began to rise faintly, he passed one of the four concrete markers set down by the lumber company's surveyor to establish the four corners of the plot which Major de Spain had reserved out of the sale, then he stood on the crest of the knoll itself, the four corner-markers all visible now, blanched still even beneath the winter's weathering, lifeless and shockingly alien in that place where dissolution itself was a seething turmoil of ejaculation tumescence conception and birth, and death did not even exist. After two winters' blanketings of leaves and the flood-waters of two springs, there was no trace of the two graves anymore at all. But those who would have come this far to find them would not need headstones but would have found them as Sam Fathers himself had taught him to find such: by bearings on trees: and did, almost the first thrust of the hunting knife finding (but only to see if it was still there) the round tin box manufactured for axel-grease and containing now Old Ben's dried mutilated paw, resting above Lion's bones.

He didn't disturb it. He didn't even look for the other grave where he and McCaslin and Major de Spain and Boon had lain Sam's body, along with his hunting horn and his knife and his tobacco-pipe, that Sunday morning two years ago; he didn't have to. He had stepped over it, perhaps on it. But that was all right. *He probably knew I was in the woods this morning long before I got here,* he thought, going on to the tree which had supported one end of the platform where Sam lay when McCaslin and Major de Spain found them— the tree, the other axel-grease tin nailed to the trunk, but weathered, rusted, alien too yet healed already into the wilderness' concordant generality, raising no tuneless note, and empty, long since empty of the food and tobacco he had put into it that day, as empty of that as it would presently be of this which he drew from his pocket—the twist of tobacco, the new bandanna handkerchief, the small paper sack of the peppermint candy which Sam had used to love; that gone too, almost before he had turned his back, not vanished but merely translated into the myriad life which printed the dark mold of these secret and sunless places with delicate fairy tracks, which, breathing and biding and immobile, watched him from beyond every twig and leaf until he moved, moving again, walking on; he had not stopped, he had only paused, quitting the knoll which was no abode of the dead because there was no death, not Lion and not Sam: not held fast in earth but free in earth and not in earth but of earth, myriad yet undiffused

of every myriad part, leaf and twig and particle, air and sun and rain and dew and night, acorn oak and leaf and acorn again, dark and dawn and dark and dawn again in their immutable progression and, being myriad, one: and Old Ben too, Old Ben too; they would give him his paw back even, certainly they would give him his paw back: then the long challenge and the long chase, no heart to be driven and outraged, no flesh to be mauled and bled— Even as he froze himself, he seemed to hear Ash's parting admonition. He could even hear the voice as he froze, immobile, one foot just taking his weight, the toe of the other just lifted behind him, not breathing, feeling again and as always the sharp shocking inrush from when Isaac McCaslin long yet was not, and so it was fear all right but not fright as he looked down at it. It had not coiled yet and the buzzer had not sounded either, only one thick rapid contraction, one loop cast sideways as though merely for purchase from which the raised head might start slightly backward, not in fright either, not in threat quite yet, more than six feet of it, the head raised higher than his knee and less than his knee's length away, and old, the once-bright markings of its youth dulled now to a monotone concordant too with the wilderness it crawled and lurked: the old one, the ancient and accursed about the earth, fatal and solitary and he could smell it now: the thin sick smell of rotting cucumbers and something else which had no name, evocative of all knowledge and an old weariness and of pariah-hood and of death. At last it moved. Not the head. The elevation of the head did not change as it began to glide away from him, moving erect yet off the perpendicular as if the head and that elevated third were complete and all: an entity walking on two feet and free of all laws of mass and balance and should have been because even now he could not quite believe that all that shift and flow of shadow behind that walking head could have been one snake: going and then gone; he put the other foot down at last and didn't know it, standing with one hand raised as Sam had stood that afternoon six years ago when Sam led him into the wilderness and showed him and he ceased to be a child, speaking the old tongue which Sam had spoken that day without premeditation either: "Chief," he said: "Grandfather."

He couldn't tell when he first began to hear the sound, because when he became aware of it, it seemed to him that he had been already hearing it for several seconds—a sound as though someone were hammering a gun-barrel against a piece of railroad iron, a sound loud and heavy and not rapid yet with something frenzied about it, as the hammerer were not only a strong man and an earnest one but a little hysterical too. Yet it couldn't be on the log-line because, although the track lay in that direction, it was at least two miles from him and this sound was not three hundred yards away. But even as he thought that, he realised where the sound must be coming from: whoever the man was and whatever he was doing, he was somewhere near the edge of the clearing where the Gum Tree was and where he was to meet Boon. So far, he had been hunting as he advanced, moving slowly and quietly and watching the ground and the trees both. Now he went on, his gun unloaded and the barrel slanted up and back to facilitate its passage through brier and undergrowth, approaching as it grew louder and louder that steady savage somehow queerly hysterical beating of metal on metal, emerging from the woods, into the old clearing, with the solitary gum tree directly before him. At first glance the tree seemed to be alive with frantic squirrels. There appeared to be forty or fifty of them leaping and darting from branch to branch until the whole tree had become one green maelstrom of mad leaves, while from time to time, singly or in twos and threes, squirrels would dart down the trunk then whirl without stopping and rush back up again as though sucked violently back by the vacuum of their fellows' frenzied vortex. Then he saw Boon, sitting, his back against the trunk, his head bent, hammering furiously at something on his lap. What he hammered with was the barrel of his dismembered gun, what he hammered at was the breech of it. The rest of the gun lay scattered about him in a half-dozen pieces while he bent over the piece on his lap his scarlet and streaming walnut face, hammering the disjointed barrel against the gun-breech with the frantic abandon of a madman. He didn't even look up to see who it was. Still hammering, he merely shouted back at the boy in a hoarse strangled voice:

"Get out of here! Dont touch them! Dont touch a one of them! They're mine!"

AUTHOR-TITLE INDEX

THIS is a combined index for both volumes of *Major Writers of America*. The appropriate volume number is indicated by a roman numeral after each entry. Authors' names are in **boldface type,** and the page numbers of the introductions to their writings are in *italics*.

Abraham to kill him, II, 34
Acquainted with the Night, II, 659
Adams, Henry, II, *269–82*; 283–382
Adrift! A little boat adrift! II, 17
Adventure of the German Student, I, 262–65
Advocate with the Father, An, I, 70
Aeolian Harp, The, I, 927
After Apple-Picking, II, 656
After great pain, a formal feeling comes– II, 23
After the Burial, I, 833–34
After the Pleasure Party, I, 930–31
Alhambra, The, I, 270–77
Almighty, The, I, 73
Alone, I, 384
American and English Notebooks, The (HAWTHORNE), I, 764–69
American Democrat, The, I, *350–61*
American Scholar, The, I, 501–09
American Tragedy, An, II, *516–56*
Anderson, Sherwood, II, *671–84*; 684–713
Angels, in the early morning, II, 18
Annabel Lee, I, 397–98
Apology for Printers, I, 115–18
Apparition, The, I, 926
Arsenal at Springfield, The, I, 808–09
Art, I, 931–32
Art of Fiction, The, II, 252–62
Artist of the Beautiful, The, I, 746–57
As I Ebb'd with the Ocean of Life, I, 1046–48
As the Starved Maelstrom laps the Navies, II, 29
At Half past Three, a single Bird, II, 32
Attic Landscape, The, I, 932
Autobiography (FRANKLIN), I, 98–103, 106–14

Back from the cordial Grave I drag thee, II, 36
Bartleby the Scrivener, I, 904–20
Battle-Pieces and Aspects of the War, I, 920–27

Bear, The, II, 864–911
Beast in the Jungle, The, II, 214–34
Beauty of the World, The, I, 176–77
Because I could not stop for Death– II, 27
Because my Brook is fluent, II, 33
Bee his burnished Carriage, A, II, 34
Bees are Black, with Gilt Surcingles– II, 35
Beleaguered City, The, I, 803
Ben Jonson (ELIOT), II, 798–803
Berg, The, I, 927–28
Big Two-Hearted River, II, 744–52
Billy Budd, Foretopman, I, *932–68*
Billy in the Darbies, I, 968
Birthmark, The, I, 730–38
Bivouac on a Mountain Side, I, 1053
Black Cottage, The, II, 654–56
Bliss is the plaything of the child– II, 36
Blue-Bird, The, I, 932
Body grows without–, The, II, 26
Book of the Grotesque, The, II, 689–91
Boston Evening Transcript, The, II, 772–73
Boston Hymn, I, 585–86
Boy's Ambition, The, II, 62–63
Bracebridge Hall, I, 258–62
Bradford, William, I, *3–11*; 11–49
Brahma, I, 584–85
Bride Comes to Yellow Sky, The, II, 444–49
Bright and Morning Star, The, I, 78–79
Bring me the sunset in a cup, II, 18–19
Bryant, William Cullen, I, *279–94*; 361–67
By Chivalries as tiny, II, 18

Cape Cod, I, 641–48
Captain Montgomery, II, 66–67
Case of Hyde vs. Morgan, The, II, 70–72

Cathedral, The, I, 868–76
Cavalry Crossing a Ford, I, 1053
Cayote, The, II, 83–84
Celebrated Jumping Frog of Calaveras County, The, II, 80–83
Celestial Railroad, The, I, 738–46
Chartres, II, 313–42
Chaucer (LONGFELLOW), I, 823
City in the Sea, The, I, 386–87
City of Orgies, I, 1042
Civil Disobedience, I, 612–22
Clock stopped–, A, II, 21
Clover's simple Fame, The, II, 33
Cocoon, The, II, 659
Coliseum, The, I, 388–89
College Colonel, The, I, 924
Colonel Sellers, II, 74–79
Color–Caste–Denomination– II, 30
"Coming Storm, The," I, 924–25
Concord Hymn, I, 584
Conflict of Convictions, The, I, 921–22
Conqueror Worm, The, I, 390–91
Cooper, James Fenimore, I, *279–94*; 294–361
Cousin Nancy, II, 773
Crack-Up, The, II, 737–43
Crane, Stephen, II, *383–97*; 397–460
Crisis is a Hair, II, 29
Cross of Snow, The, I, 827
Crossing Brooklyn Ferry, I, 1036–39
Cruelty to Animals: The Histrionic Pig, II, 79–80
Custom House, The, I, 781–88

Daisy Miller, II, 149–74
Dalliance of the Eagles, The, I, 1066–67
Days, I, 586–87
Death and the Child, II, 449–58
Dedication from *The Seaside and the Fireside,* I, 813
Dedication from *Michael Angelo: A Fragment,* I, 828
Deerslayer, The, I, 294–339
Democracy: An American Novel, II, 283–89

Desert Places, II, 660

Devil and Tom Walker, The, I, 265–70

Dialogue Between Franklin and the Gout, I, 131–33

Dickinson, Emily, II, 3–17; 17–46

Did life's penurious length, II, 37

Did We abolish Frost, II, 31

Did you ever stand in a Cavern's Mouth– II, 26

Difference between Despair, The, II, 22

Directive, II, 663

Dissertation Concerning the End for Which God Created the World, I, 168–75

Ditch is dear to the Drunken Man, The, II, 36

Divina Commedia, I, 822–23

Divine and Supernatural Light, A, I, 147–51

Do not weep, maiden, for war is kind, II, 459

Dogood Papers, I, 104–06

Domain of Arnheim, The, I, 453–60

Dream, A, I, 383

Dream-Land, I, 391–92

Dreiser, Theodore, II, 461–72; 472–556

Drunkard cannot meet a Cork, A, II, 36

Dry Salvages, The, II, 784–87

Dupont's Round Fight, I, 923

Each and All, I, 570–71

Echoes of the Jazz Age, II, 729–34

Edict by the King of Prussia, An, I, 125–27

Education of Henry Adams, The, II, 345–71

Edwards, Jonathan, I, 83–98; 136–78

Egg, The, II, 691–95

Egg and the Machine, The, II, 659–60

Eldorado, I, 396

Elements and Mottoes, I, 588–90

Eliot, T. S., II, 759–70; 770–823

Emblem of Human Life, An, I, 129

Emerson, Ralph Waldo, I, 477–89; 490–591

Emerson the Lecturer, I, 834–38

Ephemera, The, I, 128–29

Esther, II, 289–97

Estranged from Beauty–none can be– II, 35

Ethan Brand, I, 757–64

Eureka, I, 474–75

'Europe,' II, 206–14

Evening Star, I, 382

Except the smaller size, II, 32

Exordium, I, 462–65

Experiment in Misery, An, II, 399–404

Fable for Critics, A, I, 828–33

Fairy-Land, I, 384–85

Fall of the House of Usher, The, I, 410–19

Fame is the one that does not stay– II, 35

Family Reunion, The, II, 783

Far from Love the Heavenly Father, II, 31

Farewell Sermon, I, 175–76

Fate, I, 552–65

Faulkner, William, II, 823–39; 839–911

Fenimore Cooper's Further Literary Offenses, II, 99–102

Figlia Che Piange, La, II, 773

Figure a Poem Makes, The, II, 667–69

Finding is the first Act, II, 29

Fingers of the Light, The, II, 31

Fire of Drift-Wood, The, I, 811

First Day's Night had come–, The, II, 24

Fitz Adam's Story, I, 861–68

Fitzgerald, F. Scott, II, 671–84; 713–43

For Annie, I, 396–97

Forbidden Fruit a flavor has, II, 34

Forest Hymn, A, I, 365–67

Four American Impressions: Gertrude Stein, Paul Rosenfeld, Ring Lardner, Sinclair Lewis, II, 700–02

Fragments of a Lost Gnostic Poem of the 12th Century, I, 929

Franklin, Benjamin, I, 83–98; 98–135

Frost, Robert, II, 643–53; 654–69

Further in Summer than the Birds, II, 32

Future Punishment of the Wicked Unavoidable and Intolerable, The, I, 151–55

Gift Outright, The, II, 662

Give All to Love, I, 580

Given in Marriage unto Thee, II, 28

Gladiatorial Spectacles in the Coliseum, II, 92–94

Glee–The great storm is over– II, 26

Glimpse, A, I, 1042–43

Go not too near a House of Rose– II, 35

Goblet of Life, The, I, 806

Gods Determinations Touching His Elect, I, 63–66

God's-Acre, I, 805

Good to hide, and hear 'em hunt! II, 28–29

Good-Bye My Fancy! I, 1067

Grace, I, 590–91

Greek Architecture, I, 932

Green Hills of Africa, The, II, 752–57

Grief is a Mouse– II, 28

Gum-Gatherer, The, II, 656–57

Guy de Maupassant (JAMES), II, 239–52

Hamatreya, I, 576–77

Hamlet and His Problems, II, 791–93

Hand-Mirror, A, I, 1041

Haunted Palace, The, I, 389–90

Hawthorne, Nathaniel, I, 683–94; 694–792

Hawthorne (JAMES), II, 234–39

Hawthorne and His Mosses, I, 891–99

He Is a New Creature, I, 68–69

He Is the Propitiation for Our Sin, I, 71–72

He Sent a Man Before Them, Even Joseph, Who Was Sold, I, 72–73

Hemingway, Ernest, II, 671–84; 744–84

History of New York from the Beginning of the World to the End of the Dutch Dynasty by Diedrich Knickerbocker, A, I, 197–225

History of the United States During the Administrations of Jefferson and Madison, The, II, 297–313

Histrionic Pig, The, II, 79–80

Hours Continuing Long, Sore and Heavy-Hearted, I, 1041–42

House-Top, The, I, 925–26

How happy is the little Stone, II, 36

How many times these low feet staggered– II, 19

How to Tell a Story, II, 96–99

Huswifery, I, 66

I am afraid to own a Body– II, 32

I Am the Root and Offspring of David, I, 78

I Am the Rose of Sharon, I, 66–67

I breathed enough to take the Trick– II, 20

I felt a Funeral in my Brain, II, 21

I Give unto Them Eternal Life, I, 75–76

I had not minded–Walls– II, 23

I Have Eate My Hony Comb with My Hony. I Have Drunk My Wine with My Milk, I, 74–75

I have heard the sunset song of the birches, II, 459

I heard a Fly buzz–when I died– II, 24

I heard as if I had no Ear, II, 31
I like a look of Agony, II, 20
I like to see it lap the Miles– II, 26
I never lost as much but twice, II, 18
I never saw a Moor– II, 31
I Saw in Louisiana a Live-Oak Growing, I, 1042
I saw no Way–The Heavens were stitched– II, 23
I should not dare to be so sad, II, 33
I taste a liquor never brewed– II, 19
I thought that nature was enough, II, 33
I took my Power in my Hand– II, 25–26
I Want to Know Why, II, 695–700
I would not paint–a picture– II, 25
Iceman Cometh, The, II, 576–641
Ideals are the Fairy Oil, II, 30
If any sink, assure that this, now standing– II, 23
If your Nerve, deny you– II, 21–22
Illusions, I, 565–70
Images or Shadows of Divine Things, I, 177–78
In a Bye-Canal, I, 929
In a Garret, I, 931
In Harwood Groves, II, 654
In the Churchyard at Cambridge, I, 813–14
In the night, II, 459–60
In the Prison Pen, I, 924
Indian at the Burial-Place of His Father, An, I, 365
Indian Crow, The, II, 88–89
Ingenuities of Debt, The, II, 663–64
Inscription for the Entrance to a Wood, I, 364
Inspiration, I, 680–81
Introduction to *King Jasper,* II, 664–67
Introduction to *The Biglow Papers,* Second Series, I, 842–61
Inward Morning, The, I, 678–79
Irving, Washington, I, 179–93; 193–277
Israfel, I, 385–86
It sifts from Leaden Sieves– II, 22
I've dropped my Brain–My Soul is numb– II, 31

James, Henry, II, 137–48; 149–268
Jewish Cemetery at Newport, The, I, 814
Jim Baker's Bluejay Yarn, II, 86–88
John Bull, I, 240–44
John Marr and Other Sailors, I, 927–29
Journey of the Magi, II, 781–82
Jugurtha, I, 828

Just lost, when I was saved! II, 19

King Witlaf's Drinking-Horn, I, 812–13
Knickerbocker's History of New York, I, 197–225

Lake: To —, The, I, 383
Lay this Laurel on the One, II, 34
Leatherstocking Tales, The, I, 294–350
Leaves Compared with Flowers, II, 660
Legend of Sleepy Hollow, The, I, 244–58
Lenore, I, 387–88
Let Him Kiss Me with the Kisses of His Mouth, I, 76–77
Letters (ADAMS), II, 371–82: to Charles Francis Adams, Jr., 372–74, 374–75; to his wife, Marian Hooper Adams, 376; to Elizabeth Cameron, 377–79; to Charles Milnes Gaskell, 381; to John Hay, 379–81; to Henry James, 381–82; to William James, 375–76
Letters (ANDERSON), II, 702–13: to Robert Anderson, 708–09; to Van Wyck Brooks, 702–03, 703–04; to Ralph Church, 710–711; to the Dramatic Publishing Company, Chicago, Illinois, 709–10; to George Freitag, 711–13; to Mr. Lewis Galantière, 706; to Roy Jansen, 710; to Paul Rosenfeld, 704–05; to Roger Sergel, 707; to Miss Gertrude Stein, 706; to Alfred Stieglitz, 706
Letters (DICKINSON), II, 38–46: to Samuel Bowles, 38–39, 44; to Mrs. Samuel Bowles, 45; to Samuel Bowles the younger, 45; to Edward (Ned) Dickinson, 45; to Martha Dickinson, 45; to Susan Gilbert Dickinson, 45, 45–46, 46; to T. W. Higginson, 39, 39–40, 40, 40–41, 41, 42, 43, 44, 45; to Dr. and Mrs. J. G. Holland, 41, 41–42; to Mrs. J. G. Holland, 43–44, 44–45; to Louise and Frances Norcross, 42–43
Letters (JAMES), II, 264–68: to Henry Adams, 267–68; to Henry James, Sr., 265–66; to William James, 265; to Charles Eliot Norton, 266–67; to Miss Grace Norton, 267
Letters to Hawthorne (MELVILLE), I, 899–904
Life Without Principle, I, 669–77
Ligeia, I, 403–10

Limits, I, 591
Lines for an Old Man, II, 782
Lives he in any other world, II, 36
Loneliness One dare not sound–, The, II, 28
Longfellow, Henry Wadsworth, I, 793–803; 803–28
Loss of something ever felt I–, A, II, 30
Lost in a Snowstorm, II, 67–70
Lost Phoebe, The, II, 484–91
Love can do all but raise the Dead, II, 37
Love Song of J. Alfred Prufrock, The, II, 770–72
Lowell, James Russell, I, 793–803; 828–76

Maldive Shark, The, I, 928
Malvern Hill, I, 923–24
Man adrift on a slim spar, A, II, 460
Man feared that he might find an assassin, A, II, 459
Man of the Crowd, The, I, 429–33
Man That Corrupted Hadleyburg, The, II, 113–34
Manhood, I, 681
March into Virginia, The, I, 922–23
Marginalia, I, 471–74
Masque of the Red Death, The, I, 435–38
May-Day and Other Pieces, I, 584–90
Maypole of Merry Mount, The, I, 712–17
Me prove it now–Whoever doubt, II, 25
Melville, Herman, I, 877–91; 891–968
Merops, I, 580–81
Milton (LONGFELLOW), I, 824
Milton I and II (ELIOT), II, 812–23
Minister's Black Veil, The, I, 718–24
Misgivings, I, 921
Mist, I, 680
Mob within the heart, The, II, 38
Monody, I, 929
Monster, The, II, 419–44
Montaigne: or The Skeptic, I, 540–50
Mont-Saint-Michel and Chartres, II, 313–42
Morituri Salutamus, I, 824–27
Ms. Found in a Bottle, I, 398–403
Mushroom is the Elf of Plants–, The, II, 34
My Brother Paul, II, 491–503
My Dove Is the Only One of Her Mother the Choice One of Her That Bare Her, I, 79–80

My Father, and Your Father, To My God, and Your God, I, 67–68

My Kinsman, Major Molineux, I, 694–702

My life closed twice before its close, II, 37

My Lost Youth, I, 815–16

Mysterious Chambers, The, I, 270–77

Mystery of Heroism, A, II, 404–08

Nahant, I, 590

Nature, I, 490–501

Nature and God–I neither knew, II, 28

Nature of True Virtue, The, I, 163–67

Narrow Fellow in the Grass, A, II, 30

Neither Out Far Nor in Deep, II, 660

New England Reformers, I, 521–30

Nigger Jeff, II, 472–84

No Rack can torture me– II, 23

Noiseless Patient Spider, A, I, 1060–61

Not probable–The barest Chance– II, 23

Notebooks of Henry James, The, II, 262–64

Notes on the Mind, I, 143–47

Nuremberg, I, 807–08

Ocean said to me once, The, II, 459

October, II, 654

Ode Inscribed to W. H. Channing, I, 577–79

Ode to Beauty, I, 579–80

Of all the Souls that stand create– II, 27

Of Plymouth Plantation, I, 11–49: The First Book, 11–22; The Second Book, 22–49

Oh Fairest of the Rural Maids, I, 364

Oh Future! thou secreted peace, II, 36

Old Man's Winter Night, An, II, 656

Old Manse, The, I, 769–80

Old Marlborough Road, The, I, 625

On a Tree Fallen Across the Road, II, 659

On the New Jersey Coast, II, 397–99

On the Photograph of a Corps Commander, I, 926

On the Slain Collegians, I, 925

Once there came a man, II, 458

One Blessing had I than the rest, II, 27

One Step Backward Taken, II, 663

O'Neill, Eugene, II, 557–76; 576–641

Only Ghost I ever saw, The, II, 20–21

Open Boat, The, II, 408–19

Our lives are Swiss– II, 18

Out of the Cradle Endlessly Rocking, I, 1048–52

Oval Portrait, The, I, 433–35

Over the Mountains, II, 89–91

Passage to India, I, 1061–66

Pasture, The, II, 654

Pathfinder, The, I, 339–45

Pauper Witch of Grafton, The, II, 657–58

Personal Narrative (Edwards), I, 136–42

Pilgrim Bird, The, II, 83

Pioneers, The, I, 346–50

Pit and the Pendulum, The, I, 438–45

Pit–but Heaven over it–, A, II, 37

Platform Readings, II, 106–11

Plea for Captain John Brown, A, I, 648–58

Poe, Edgar Allan, I, 369–82; 382–475

Poems (Emerson), I, 570–84

Poet, The, I, 530–40

Poetic Principle, The, I, 469–71

Poet's Tale, The, I, 819–20

Popular Heart is a Cannon first–, The, II, 33

Portent, The, I, 921

Prayer to the Virgin of Chartres, II, 342–44

Preface to *Leaves of Grass*, 1855 edition, I, 1067–1112

Preface to *Mosses from an Old Manse*, I, 769–81

Preface to *The House of the Seven Gables*, I, 790–91

Preface to *The Marble Faun*, I, 791–92

Preface to *The Raven and Other Poems*, I, 469

Preface to *The Scarlet Letter*, I, 781–88

Preface to *Twice-Told Tales*, 1851 edition, I, 788–90

Prelude to *Evangeline*, I, 812

Prison gets to be a friend–, A, II, 26–27

Problem, The, I, 571–72

Prometheus, I, 815

Prophetic Pictures, The, I, 724–30

Props assist the House, The, II, 33

Proud of my broken heart, since thou didst break it, II, 37–38

Provide, Provide, II, 661

Pupil, The, II, 174–94

Purloined Letter, The, I, 445–53

Quarles Farm, The, II, 59–62

Quatrains (Emerson), I, 590

Rank and Dignity of Piloting, II, 63–66

Rather arid delight, II, 37

Ravaged Villa, The, I, 932

Raven, The, I, 392–94

Real Thing, The, II, 194–206

Reconciliation, I, 1055

Religion and Literature (Eliot), II, 807–12

Return, Oh Shulamite, Return Return, I, 81–82

Review of Nathaniel Hawthorne's *Twice-Told Tales*, I, 465–68

Review of Thomas Moore's *Alciphron*, I, 460–62

Revolution is the Pod, II, 32

Rhodora, The, I, 577

Rich Boy, The, II, 713–29

Ring, II, 734–37

Rip Van Winkle, I, 227–35

Road was lit with Moon and Star–, The, II, 35

Robin is a Gabriel, The, II, 35–36

Romance, I, 384

Route of Evanescence, A, II, 35

Sacramental Meditations, I, 66–82

Saddest noise, the sweetest noise, The, II, 38

Safe in their Alabaster Chambers– II, 19–20

Sale of the Hessians, The, I, 127–28

Salmagundi: or, The Whim-Whams and Opinions of Launcelot Langstaff, Esq., and Others, I, 193–97

Sanctuary, II, 503–16

Sarah Pierrepont, I, 143

Savior must have been, The, II, 36

Scented Herbage of My Breast, I, 1045–46

Seaweed, I, 809

Self-Reliance, I, 510–21

Shakespeare (Longfellow), I, 823–24

Shall I take thee, the Poet said, II, 32

She sights a Bird–she chuckles– II, 25

Shiloh, I, 927

Sic Vita, I, 678

Sicilian's Tale, The, I, 816–19

Silken Tent, The, II, 661

Skeleton in Armor, The, I, 803–05

Skeptical Patrician, A, II, 793–96

Sketch Book, The, I, 226–27

Slave in the Dismal Swamp, The, I, 806–07

Sleeper, The (POE), I, 387

Sleepers, The (WHITMAN), I, 1027–32

Smoke, I, 680

Snow-Storm, The, I, 577

So Long! I, 1044–45

Solemn thing within the Soul, A, II, 24–25

Some, too fragile for winter winds, II, 19

Song of Myself, I, 988–1023

Sonnet—to Science, I, 383

Sonnet—Silence, I, 390

Soul selects her own Society–, The, II, 22

Soul unto itself, The, II, 27

Soul's Superior instants, The, II, 22

Sound of Trees, The, II, 657

Spanish Jew's Tale, The, I, 819

Sparkles from the Wheel, I, 1060

Specimen Days, I, 1112–19

Speech of Polly Baker, The, I, 118–19

Speech on Affairs in Kansas, I, 550–52

Sphinx, The, I, 574–76

Split the Lark–and you'll find the Music– II, 29

Spontaneous Me, I, 1033–34

Spotted Horses, II, 839–64

Spurn the temerity, II, 35

Stopping by Woods on a Snowy Evening, II, 658

Story of the Old Ram, The, II, 72–74

Story Teller's Story, A, II, 684–89

Stout Gentleman, The, I, 258–62

Student's Tale, The, I, 820–22

Subverted Flower, The, II, 662

Success is counted sweetest, II, 18

Sun and Moon must make their haste–, The, II, 29

Sunthin' in the Pastoral Line, I, 838–42

Sweet–safe–Houses– II, 24

Sympathy, I, 677–78

Tales of a Traveller, I, 262–70

Talk with prudence to a Beggar, II, 18

Taylor, Edward, I, 51–62; 62–82

Tell all the Truth but tell it slant– II, 32–33

Tell me not in joyous numbers, II, 458

Terminus, I, 588

Thanatopsis, I, 363–64

That it will never come again, II, 38

There came a Day at Summer's full, II, 22–23

There is a morn by men unseen– II, 17

There is a solitude of space, II, 37

There Was a Child Went Forth, I, 1032–33

There's a certain Slant of light, II, 20

They talk as slow as Legends grow, II, 37

This Compost, I, 1035–36

This Consciousness that is aware, II, 28

This is a Blossom of the Brain– II, 29–30

This is my letter to the World, II, 24

This–is the land–the Sunset washes– II, 20

This was a Poet–It is That, II, 24

Thomas Middleton (ELIOT), II, 803–07

Thoreau, Henry David, I, 593–605; 605–81

Though the great Waters sleep, II, 36

Thoughts on the Revival of Religion in New England, I, 155–57

Threnody, I, 581–84

Through lane it lay–thro' bramble– II, 17

Tide Rises, the Tide Falls, The, I, 824

Timoleon, I, 929–32

'Tis so appalling–it exhilirates– II, 21

To ———, I, 395–96

To a Waterfowl, I, 362–63

To Cole, the Painter Departing for Europe, I, 367

To die–without the Dying, II, 31

To Earthward, II, 658–59

To Ezra Stiles, I, 134–35

To Helen, I, 385

To Jared Ingersoll, I, 123–24

To Ned, I, 928–29

To One in Paradise, I, 389

To pile like Thunder to it's close, II, 33

To Samuel Mather, I, 133–34

To the Driving Cloud, I, 809–10

To the Editor of a Newspaper, I, 124–25

To the Maiden in the East, I, 679–80

To Think of Time, I, 1023–26

To You, I, 1039–41

Tom Quartz, the Cat, II, 84–86

Tradition and the Individual Talent, II, 787–91

Transition, I, 590

Treatise Concerning Religious Affections, A, I, 157–63

True Story Repeated Word for Word as I Heard It, A, II, 111–13

Tuft of Kelp, The, I, 928

Twain, Mark, II, 47–59; 59–135

Two Rivers, I, 587

Two Witches II, II, 657–58

Ulalume—A Ballad, I, 394–95

Unable are the Loved to die, II, 28

Unwind my riddle, II, 460

Uriel, I, 572–73

Utilitarian View of the Monitor's Fight, A, I, 923

Valley of Unrest, The, I, 388

Voluntaries, I, 586

Wakefield, I, 709–12

Waldeinsamkeit, I, 587–88

Walden, I, 635–41

Walking, I, 622–35

Walter von der Vogelweid, I, 810–11

War Prayer, The, II, 134–35

Waste Land, The, II, 774–81

Water makes many Beds, II, 35

Waters chased him as he fled, The, II, 38

Waterspout, The, II, 664

Way to Wealth, The, I, 119–23

We dream–it is good we are dreaming– II, 25

We knew not that we were to live– II, 35

We should not mind so small a flower– II, 18

Weeds and Wildings, I, 932

Wellfleet Oysterman, The, I, 641–48

Westminster Abbey, I, 235–39

What mystery pervades a well! II, 34

What shall I do when the Summer troubles– II, 30

When I hoped I feared– II, 33

When Lilacs Last in the Dooryard Bloom'd, I, 1055–60

When They Had Sung an Hymn, I, 77

Where I Lived and What I Lived for, I, 635–41

Whether Paul or Apollos, or Cephas, I, 69–70

While the King Sitteth at His Table, My Spicknard Sendeth Forth the Smell Thereof, I, 73–74

Whispers of Immortality, II, 773–74

Whistle, The, I, 130–31

Whitman, Walt, I, 969–87; 988–1119

Whittier Birthday Dinner Speech, II, 94–96
Who Is She That Looks Forth as the Morning. Fair as the Moon Clear as the Sun. Terrible as an Army with Banners, I, 80–81
Whoever You Are Holding Me Now in Hand, I, 1043–44
Wild Apples, I, 658–68
Wild Nights–Wild Nights! II, 20

William Blake (ELIOT), II, 796–98
William Dean Howells (TWAIN), II, 102–06
William Wilson (POE), I, 419–29
Wind and the Rain, The, II, 661
Winter Memories, I, 679
Winter Walk, A, I, 605–12
Witch Trial at Mount-Holly, A, I, 114–15

Word made Flesh is seldom, A, II, 36–37
World-Soul, The, I, 573–74
Wound-Dresser, The, I, 1053–54

Xenophanes, I, 581

Yellow Violet, The, I, 361–62
Young Goodman Brown, I, 702–08

INDEX OF FIRST LINES BY VOLUME

VOLUME I

A call in the midst of the crowd, 1015

A child said *What is the grass?* fetching it to me with full hands, 991

A glimpse through an interstice caught, 1042

A line in long array where they wind betwixt green islands, 1053

A moody child and wildly wise, 530

'A new commandment,' said the smiling Muse, 590

A noiseless patient spider, 1060

A reminiscence of the vulgar fate, 1024

A Star, Bright Morning Star, the shining Sun, 78

A swoon of noon, a trance of tide, 929

A vision as of crowded city streets, 823

About the Shark, phlegmatical one, 928

Ah, broken is the golden bowl!—the spirit flown forever! 387

All day the waves assailed the rock, 590

All dripping in tangles green, 928

All Dull, my Lord, my Spirits flat, and dead, 72

All feeling hearts must feel for him, 924

All truths wait in all things, 1005

Alone for in the wilds and mountains I hurt, 993

An old man bending I come among new faces, 1053

An old man in a lodge within a park; 823

An old song, made by an aged old pate, 240

And as to you Death, and you bitter hug of mortality, it is idle to try to alarm me. 1021

And ye shall succor men; 550

Announced by all the trumpets of the sky, 577

As I ebb'd with the ocean of life, 1046

As one who, walking in the twilight gloom, 813

At midnight in the month of June, 387

Ay, man is manly. Here you see, 926

Behind the house the upland falls, 930

Beneath you Larkspur's azure bells, 932

Blind loving wrestling touch, sheath'd hooded sharp-tooth'd touch! 1005

Bulkeley, Hunt, Willard, Hosmer, Meriam, Flint, 576

By a route obscure and lonely, 391

By fate, not option, frugal Nature gave, 581

By the rude bridge that arched the flood, 584

City of orgies, walks and joys, 1042

Convulsions came; and, where the field, 926

Daughters of Time, the hypocritic Days, 586

Dazzling and tremendous how quick the sun-rise would kill me, 1003

Delicate omens traced in air, 553

Did all the lets and bars appear, 922

Dim vales—and shadowy floods— 384

Endless unfolding of works of ages! 1001

Enough! enough! enough! 1013

Eternal Life! What Life is this, I pray? 75

Far through the memory shines a happy day, 869

Filled is Life's goblet to the brim; 806

Flaunt of the sunshine I need not your bask—lie over! 1013

Flood-tide below me! I see you face to face! 1036

Flow, flow the waves hated, 565

Found a family, build a state, 929

From childhood's hour I have not been, 384

From my years young in days of youth, 8

Gaily bedight, 396

Gems and jewels let them heap— 931

Give all to love; 580

Gloomy and dark art thou, O chief of the mighty Omahas; 809

Gold and iron are good, 588

Good of the Chaplain to enter Lone Bay, 968

Good-bye my Fancy! 1067

Hanging from the beam, 921

Has any one supposed it lucky to be born? 992

He rides at their head; 924

Helen, thy beauty is to me, 385

Help, oh! my Lord, anoint mine Eyes to see, 78

Hold it up sternly—see this it sends back, (who is it? is it you?), 1041

Hours continuing long, sore and heavy-hearted, 1041

Houses and rooms are full of perfumes, the shelves are crowded with perfumes, 988

How cold are thy baths, Apollo! 828

How much, preventing God, how much I owe, 591

How strange it seems! These Hebrews in their graves, 814

I am a parcel of vain strivings tied, 678

I am he bringing help for the sick as they pant on their backs, 1014

I am not wiser for my age, 590

I am of old and young, of the foolish as much as the wise, 997

I am the poet of the Body and I am the poet of the Soul, 999

I am the teacher of athletes, 1020

I believe a leaf of grass is no less than the journey-work of the stars, 1005

I believe in you my soul, the other I am must not abase itself to you, 990

I celebrate myself, and sing myself, 988

I do not count the hours I spend, 587

I do not despise you priests, all time, the world over, 1016

I have heard what the talkers were talking, the talk of the beginning and the end, 989

I have read, in some old, marvellous tale, 803

I have said that the soul is not more than the body, 1021

I know I have the best of time and space, and was never measured and never will be measured. 1019

I like a church; I like a cowl; 571

I like that ancient Saxon phrase, which calls, 805

I love to see the man, a long-lived child, 681

I pace the sounding sea-beach and behold, 824

I saw a ship of martial build, 927

I saw in Louisiana a live-oak growing, 1042

I see before me now a traveling army halting, 1053

I swear I think now that every thing without exception has an eternal soul! 1026

I think I could turn and live with animals, they are so placid and self-contained, 1006

I wander all night in my vision, 1027

If the red slayer think he slays, 585

In an age of fops and toys, 586

In dark fens of the Dismal Swamp, 806

In Heaven a spirit doth dwell, 385

In Heaven soaring up, I dropt an Eare, 65

In hoc est hoax, cum quiz et jokesez, 193

In May, when sea-winds pierced our solitudes, 577

In placid hours well pleased we dream, 931

In shards the sylvan vases lie, 932

In spring of youth it was my lot, 383

In the greenest of our valleys, 390, 415

In the long, sleepless watches of the night, 827

In the suburb, in the town, 521

In the valley of the Pegnitz, where across broad meadow-lands, 807

In the village churchyard she lies, 813

In time and measure perfect moves, 923

In two years' time 't had thus, 663

In visions of the dark night, 383

Infinity, when all things it beheld, 63

Is this then a touch? quivering me to a new identity, 1004

It fell in the ancient periods, 572

It is not to diffuse you that you were born of your mother and father, it is to identify you, 1025

It is the spot I came to seek— 365

It is time to be old, 588

It is time to explain myself—let us stand up. 1017

It was many and many a year ago, 397

King Solomon, before his palace gate, 819

Lately, alas, I knew a gentle boy, 677

Light-winged Smoke, Icarian bird, 680

List the harp in window wailing, 927

Listless he eyes the palisades, 924

Little thinks, in the field, you red-cloaked clown, 570

Lo! Death has reared himself a throne, 386

Lo! 't is a gala night, 390, 406

Lord, art thou at the Table Head above, 66

Low-anchored cloud, 680

Low in the eastern sky, 679

Make me, O Lord, thy Spining Wheele complete. 66

My Deare Deare Lord, I know not what to say: 81

My onely Lord, when with no muddy Sight, 76

My shattred Phancy stole away from mee, 67

No sleep. The sultriness pervades the air, 925

Not a day passes, not a minute or second without an accouchement, 1023

Not long ago, the writer of these lines, 395

Not magnitude, not lavishness, 932

Nothing that is shall perish utterly, 828

Now I tell what I know in Texas in my early youth, 1010

Now I will do nothing but listen, 1003

"O Cæsar, we who are about to die, 824

O span of youth! ever-push'd elasticity. 1018

O! What a thing is Might right mannag'd? 'Twill, 73

Of Prometheus, how undaunted, 815

Oft have I seen at some cathedral door, 822

Often I think of the beautiful town, 815

Oh! Angells, stand agastard at my Song; 74

Oh fairest of the rural maids! 364

Oh! thou, my Lord, thou king of Saints, here mak'st, 73

Oh! What a thing is Man? Lord, Who am I? 70

Olger the Dane and Desiderio, 819

On starry heights, 921

Once git a smell o' muck into a draw, 838

Once it smiled a silent dell, 388

Once upon a midnight dreary, while I pondered, weak and weary, 392

Out of the cradle endlessly rocking, 1048

Packed in my mind lie all the clothes, 679

Peace, Peace, my Hony, do not Cry, 64

Plain be the phrase, yet apt the verse, 923

Robert of Sicily, brother of Pope Urbane, 817

Romance, who loves to nod and sing, 384

Scented herbage of my breast, 1045

Science! true daughter of Old Time thou art! 383

See yonder leafless trees against the sky, 590

Singing my days, 1061

Skimming lightly, wheeling still, 927

Skirting the river road, (my forenoon walk, my rest,), 1066

Slow moving and black lines go ceaselessly over the earth, 1026

Something startles me where I thought I was safest, 1035

Space and Time! now I see it is true, what I guess'd at, 1006

"Speak! speak! thou fearful guest! 804

Spontaneous me, Nature, 1033

Still I complain; I am complaining still. 71

Stranger, if thou has learned a truth which needs, 364

Stretch'd and still lies the midnight, 1012

Thank Heaven! the crisis, 396

Thanks to the morning light, 573

The Angells sung a Carole at thy Birth, 77

The big doors of the country barn stand open and ready, 993

The butcher-boy puts off his killing-clothes, or sharpens his knife at the stall in the market, 994

The Daintiest Draught thy Pensill ever Drew: 68

The fire is burning clear and blithely, 868

The friendly and flowing savage, who is he? 1013

The full ethereal round, 612

The groves were God's first temples. Ere man learned, 365

The little one sleeps in its cradle, 992

The markets, the government, the working-man's wages, to think what account they are through our nights and days, 1025

The negro holds firmly the reins of his four horses, the block swags underneath on its tied-over chain, 994

The next whose fortune 't was a tale to tell, 862

The past and present wilt—I have fill'd them emptied them, 1022

The pure contralto sings in the organ loft, 995

The rounded world is fair to see, 589

The skies they were ashen and sober; 394

The sluggish smoke curls up from some deep dell, 606

The South-wind brings, 581

The Sphinx is drowsy, 574

The spotted hawk swoops by and accuses me, he complains of my gab and my loitering. 1022

The tide rises, the tide falls, 824

The wild gander leads his flock through the cool night, 995

The wings of Time are black and white, 588

The word of the Lord by night, 585

There are some qualities—some incorporate things, 390

"There comes Emerson first, whose rich words, every one, 829

There is that in me—I do not know what it is—but I know it is in me. 1022

There was a child went forth every day, 1032

These are really the thoughts of all men in all ages and lands, they are not original with me, 997

They talk of short-lived pleasure—be it so— 291

Thine eyes shall see the light of distant skies; 367

This is he, who, felled by foes, 589

This is the Arsenal. From floor to ceiling, 808

This is the forest primeval. The murmuring pines and the hemlocks, 812

This is the meal equally set, this the meat for natural hunger, 998

Thou wast that all to me, love, 389

Though loath to grieve, 577

Thy Grace, Dear Lord's my golden Wrack, I finde, 69

Thy summer voice, Musketaquit, 587

To be in any form, what is that? 1004

To conclude, I announce what comes after me. 1044

To have known him, to have loved him, 929

To him who in the love of Nature holds, 363

To think of time—of all that retrospection, 1023

To think the thought of death merged in the thought of materials, 1024

Tourist, spare the avid glance, 932

Trippers and askers surround me, 990

True Brahmin, in the morning meadows wet, 590

'T was noontide of summer, 382

Twenty-eight young men bathe by the shore, 993

Type of the antique Rome! Rich reliquary, 388

Vogelweid the Minnesinger, 810

Walt Whitman, a kosmos, of Manhattan the son, 1001

Was never form and never face, 589

We sat within the farm-house old, 811

What care I, so they stand the same,— 580

What shall I say, my Deare Deare Lord? most Deare, 79

What will be will be well, for what is is well, 1025

Whate'er we leave to God, God does, 680

When Alcuin taught the sons of Charlemagne, 820

When beechen buds begin to swell, 362

When descends on the Atlantic, 809

When lilacs last in the dooryard bloom'd, 1055

When ocean-clouds over inland hills, 921

When Winter fringes every bough, 609

Where is the world we roved, Ned Bunn? 928

Where the city's ceaseless crowd moves on the livelong day, 1060

Where they once dug for money, 625

Whither, midst falling dew, 362

Who gave thee, O Beauty, 579

Who goes there? hankering, gross, mystical, nude; 998

Who knows this or that? 591

Who shall tell what did befall, 589

Whoever you are holding me now in hand; 1043

Whoever you are, I fear you are walking the walks of dreams, 1039

With music strong I come, with my cornets and my drums, 998

Within the circuit of this plodding life, 679

Witlaf, a king of the Saxons, 812

Wonders amazed! Am I espousd to thee? 80

Word over all, beautiful as the sky, 1055

Would you hear of an old-time sea-fight? 1011

Ye elms that wave on Malvern Hill, 923

Yes, faith is a goodly anchor; 833

You laggards there on guard! look to your arms! 1012

You sea! I resign myself to you also—I guess what you mean, 1000

Youth is the time when hearts are large, 925

VOLUME II

A bee his burnished Carriage, 34

A clock stopped— 21

'A cold coming we had of it, 782

A Drunkard cannot meet a Cork, 36

A loss of something ever felt I— 30

A man adrift on a slim spar, 460

A man feared that he might find an assassin; 459

A narrow Fellow in the Grass, 30

A Pit—but Heaven over it— 37

A Prison gets to be a friend— 26

A Route of Evanescence, 35

A soldier of the Legion lay dying in Algiers; 384

A Solemn thing within the Soul, 24

A tree's leaves may be ever so good, 660

A Word made Flesh is seldom, 36

A youth in apparel that glittered, 404

Abraham to kill him, 34

Adrift! A little boat adrift! 17

After great pain, a formal feeling comes— 23

All out-of-doors looked darkly at him, 656

Angels, in the early morning, 18
April is the cruelest month, breeding, 774
As far as I can see this autumn haze, 659
As if I asked a common Alms, 40
As the Starved Maelstrom laps the Navies, 29
At Half past Three, a single Bird, 32
Back from the cordial Grave I drag thee, 36
Back out of all this now too much for us, 663
Because I could not stop for Death– 27
Because my Brook is fluent, 33
Bees are Black, with Gilt Surcingles– 35
Bliss is the plaything of the child– 36
Blustering God, 392
Bring me the sunset in a cup, 18
By chivalries as tiny, 18
Color–Caste–Denomination– 30
Count not that for that can be had, 42
Crisis is a Hair, 29
Did life's penurious length, 37
Did We abolish Frost, 31
Did you ever stand in a Cavern's Mouth– 26
Do not weep, maiden, for war is kind. 459
En Amérique, professeur; 763
Estranged from Beauty–none can be– 35
Except the smaller size, 32
Fame is the one that does not stay– 35
Far from Love the Heavenly Father, 31
Finding is the first Act, 29
Forbidden Fruit a flavor has, 34
Further in Summer than the Birds, 32
Given in Marriage unto Thee, 28
Glee–The great storm is over– 26
Go not too near a House of Rose– 35
Good to hide, and hear 'em hunt! 28
Great Streets of Silence led away, 43
Grief is a Mouse– 28
He gave the solid rail a hateful kick, 659
How happy is the little Stone, 36
How many times these low feet staggered– 19
I am afraid to own a Body– 32
I breathed enough to take the Trick– 20
I do not know much about gods; but I think that the river, 784
I felt a Funeral in my Brain, 21
I had not minded–Walls– 23
I have been one acquainted with the night, 659
"I have heard the sunset song of the birches, 459
I heard a Fly buzz–when I died– 24
I heard as if I had no Ear, 31
I like a look of Agony, 20
I like to see it lap the Miles– 26
I never lost as much but twice, 18
I never saw a Moor– 31
I saw no Way–The Heavens were stitched– 23
I should not dare to be so sad, 33
I taste a liquor never brewed– 19
I thought that nature was enough, 33
I took my Power in my Hand– 25
I wonder about the trees. 657
I would not paint–a picture– 25
Ideals are the Fairy Oil, 30
If any sink, assure that this, now standing– 23

If your Nerve, deny you– 21
I'm going out to clean the pasture spring; 654
In an old house there is always listening, and more is heard than is spoken, 783
In the night, 459
It sifts from Leaden Sieves– 22
I've dropped my Brain–My Soul is numb– 31
Just lost, when I was saved! 19
Lay this Laurel on the One, 34
Let us go then, you and I, 771
Lives he in any other world, 36
Love at the lips was touch, 658
Love can do all but raise the Dead, 37
Me prove it now–Whoever doubt, 25
Miss Nancy Ellicott, 773
Morning is due to all– 45
My life closed twice before its close; 37
My long two-pointed ladder's sticking through a tree, 656
Mysterious Power! Gentle Friend! 343
Nature and God–I neither knew, 28
No Rack can torture me– 23
Not only sands and gravels, 663
Not probable–The barest Chance– 23
Now that they've got it settled whose I be, 657
O hushed October morning mild, 654
Of all the Souls that stand create– 27
Oh Future! thou secreted peace, 36
Once there came a man, 458
One Blessing had I than the rest, 27
Our lives are Swiss– 18
Pass to thy Rendezvous of Light, 46
Proud of my broken heart, since thou didst break it, 37
Rather arid delight, 37
Revolution is the Pod, 32
Safe in their Alabaster Chambers– 19
Shall I take thee, the Poet said, 32
She drew back; he was calm: 662
She is as in a field a silken tent, 661
She sights a Bird–she chuckles– 25
Simple as when I asked your aid before; 342
Snow falling and night falling fast, oh, fast, 660
Some, too fragile for winter winds, 19
Split the Lark–and you'll find the Music– 29
Spurn the temerity, 35
Stand on the highest pavement of the stair— 773
Success is counted sweetest, 18
Sweet–safe–Houses– 24
Talk with prudence to a Beggar, 18
Tell all the Truth but tell it slant– 32
Tell me not in joyous numbers, 458
That far-off day the leaves in flight, 661
That it will never come again, 38
The body grows without– 26
The Clover's simple Fame, 33
The difference between Despair, 22
The Ditch is dear to the Drunken Man, 36
The Fingers of the Light, 31
The first Day's Night had come– 24
The land was ours before we were the land's. 662
The Life we have is very great. 44

The Loneliness One dare not sound– 28
The mob within the heart, 38
The Mushroom is the Elf of Plants– 34
The ocean said to me once, 459
The only Ghost I ever saw, 20
The people along the sand, 660
The Popular Heart is a Cannon first– 33
The Props assist the House, 33
The readers of the *Boston Evening Transcript,* 772
The Riddle that we guess, 43
The Road was lit with Moon and Star– 35
The Robin is a Gabriel, 35
The saddest noise, the sweetest noise, 38
The same leaves over and over again! 654
The Savior must have been, 36
The Soul selects her own Society– 22
The Soul unto itself, 27
The Soul's Superior instants, 22
The Sun and Moon must make their haste– 29
The tiger in the tiger-pit, 782
The tree the tempest with a crash of wood, 659
The waters chased him as he fled, 38
The witch that came (the withered hag), 661
There came a Day at Summer's full, 22
There is a morn by men unseen– 17
There is a solitude of space, 37
There overtook me and drew me in, 656
There's a certain Slant of light, 20

These I assume were words so deeply meant, 663
They talk as slow as Legends grow, 37
This Consciousness that is aware, 28
This is a Blossom of the Brain– 29
This is my letter to the World, 24
This–is the land–the Sunset washed– 20
This was a Poet–It is That, 24
Though the great Waters sleep, 36
Through lane it lay–thro' bramble– 17
'Tis so appalling–it exhilirates– 21
To die–without the Dying, 31
To pile like Thunder to it's close, 33
To the maiden, 408
Unable are the Loved to die, 28
Unwind my riddle. 460
Water makes many Beds, 35
We chanced in passing by that afternoon, 654
We do not like to look out of the same window, and
    see quite a different landscape. 783
We dream–it is good we are dreaming– 25
We knew not that we were to live– 35
We should not mind so small a flower– 18
Webster was much possessed by death, 774
What mystery pervades a well! 34
What shall I do when the Summer troubles– 30
When I hoped I feared– 33
Whose woods these are I think I know. 658
Wild Nights– Wild Nights! 20